ENCYCLOPEDIA OF RELIGION

SECOND EDITION

ENCYCLOPEDIA OF RELIGION

15

SECOND EDITION

APPENDIX
•
SYNOPTIC OUTLINE
•
INDEX

LINDSAY JONES
EDITOR IN CHIEF

MACMILLAN REFERENCE USA
An imprint of Thomson Gale, a part of The Thomson Corporation

THOMSON
GALE

Detroit • New York • San Francisco • San Diego • New Haven, Conn. • Waterville, Maine • London • Munich

THOMSON
GALE

Encyclopedia of Religion, Second Edition

Lindsay Jones, Editor in Chief

For more information, contact
Macmillan Reference USA
An imprint of Thomson Gale
27500 Drake Rd.
Farmington, Hills, MI 48331-3535
Or you can visit our Internet site at
http://www.gale.com

LIBRARY OF CONGRESS CATALOGING-IN-PUBLICATION DATA

Encyclopedia of religion / Lindsay Jones, editor in chief.— 2nd ed.
p. cm.
Includes bibliographical references and index.
ISBN 0-02-865733-0 (SET HARDCOVER : ALK. PAPER) — ISBN 0-02-865734-9 (V. 1) — ISBN 0-02-865735-7 (v. 2) — ISBN 0-02-865736-5 (v. 3) — ISBN 0-02-865737-3 (v. 4) — ISBN 0-02-865738-1 (v. 5) — ISBN 0-02-865739-X (v. 6) — ISBN 0-02-865740-3 (v. 7) — ISBN 0-02-865741-1 (v. 8) — ISBN 0-02-865742-X (v. 9) — ISBN 0-02-865743-8 (v. 10) — ISBN 0-02-865980-5 (v. 11) — ISBN 0-02-865981-3 (v. 12) — ISBN 0-02-865982-1 (v. 13) — ISBN 0-02-865983-X (v. 14) — ISBN 0-02-865984-8 (v. 15)
1. RELIGION—ENCYCLOPEDIAS. I. JONES, LINDSAY, 1954-
BL31.E46 2005
200'.3—dc22 2004017052

This title is also available as an e-book.
ISBN 0-02-865997-X
Contact your Thomson Gale representative for ordering information.

Printed in the United States of America
10 9 8 7 6 5 4 3 2

EDITORS AND CONSULTANTS

Harvard Forum on Religion and Ecology
Ecology and Religion

JOSEPH HARRIS
Francis Lee Higginson Professor of English Literature and Professor of Folklore, Harvard University
Germanic Religions

URSULA KING
Professor Emerita, Senior Research Fellow and Associate Member of the Institute for Advanced Studies, University of Bristol, England, and Professorial Research Associate, Centre for Gender and Religions Research, School of Oriental and African Studies, University of London
Gender and Religion

DAVID MORGAN
Duesenberg Professor of Christianity and the Arts, and Professor of Humanities and Art History, Valparaiso University
Color Inserts and Essays

JOSEPH F. NAGY
Professor, Department of English, University of California, Los Angeles
Celtic Religion

MATTHEW OJO
Obafemi Awolowo University
African Religions

JUHA PENTIKÄINEN
Professor of Comparative Religion, The University of Helsinki, Member of Academia Scientiarum Fennica, Finland
Arctic Religions and Uralic Religions

TED PETERS
Professor of Systematic Theology, Pacific Lutheran Theological Seminary and the Center for Theology and the Natural Sciences at the Graduate Theological Union, Berkeley, California
Science and Religion

FRANK E. REYNOLDS
Professor of the History of Religions and Buddhist Studies in the Divinity School and the Department of South Asian Languages and Civilizations, Emeritus, University of Chicago
History of Religions

GONZALO RUBIO
Assistant Professor, Department of Classics and Ancient Mediterranean Studies and Department of History and Religious Studies, Pennsylvania State University
Ancient Near Eastern Religions

SUSAN SERED
Director of Research, Religion, Health and Healing Initiative, Center for the Study of World Religions, Harvard University, and Senior Research Associate, Center for Women's Health and Human Rights, Suffolk University
Healing, Medicine, and Religion

LAWRENCE E. SULLIVAN
Professor, Department of Theology, University of Notre Dame
History of Religions

WINNIFRED FALLERS SULLIVAN
Dean of Students and Senior Lecturer in the Anthropology and Sociology of Religion, University of Chicago
Law and Religion

TOD SWANSON
Associate Professor of Religious Studies, and Director, Center for Latin American Studies, Arizona State University
South American Religions

MARY EVELYN TUCKER
Professor of Religion, Bucknell University, Founder and Coordinator, Harvard Forum on Religion and Ecology, Research Fellow, Harvard Yenching Institute, Research Associate, Harvard Reischauer Institute of Japanese Studies
Ecology and Religion

HUGH B. URBAN
Associate Professor, Department of Comparative Studies, Ohio State University
Politics and Religion

CATHERINE WESSINGER
Professor of the History of Religions and Women's Studies, Loyola University New Orleans
New Religious Movements

ROBERT A. YELLE
Mellon Postdoctoral Fellow, University of Toronto
Law and Religion

ERIC ZIOLKOWSKI
Charles A. Dana Professor of Religious Studies, Lafayette College
Literature and Religion

TABLE OF CONTENTS

ABBREVIATIONS AND SYMBOLS USED IN THIS WORK

abbr. abbreviated; abbreviation
abr. abridged; abridgment
AD *anno Domini,* in the year of the (our) Lord
Afrik. Afrikaans
AH *anno Hegirae,* in the year of the Hijrah
Akk. Akkadian
Ala. Alabama
Alb. Albanian
Am. *Amos*
AM *ante meridiem,* before noon
amend. amended; amendment
annot. annotated; annotation
Ap. *Apocalypse*
Apn. *Apocryphon*
app. appendix
Arab. Arabic
ʿArakh. *ʿArakhin*
Aram. Aramaic
Ariz. Arizona
Ark. Arkansas
Arm. Armenian
art. article (pl., arts.)
AS Anglo-Saxon
Asm. Mos. *Assumption of Moses*
Assyr. Assyrian
A.S.S.R. Autonomous Soviet Socialist Republic
Av. Avestan
ʿA.Z. *ʿAvodah zarah*
b. born
Bab. Babylonian
Ban. Bantu
1 Bar. *1 Baruch*
2 Bar. *2 Baruch*
3 Bar. *3 Baruch*
4 Bar. *4 Baruch*
B.B. *Bavaʾ batraʾ*
BBC British Broadcasting Corporation
BC before Christ
BCE before the common era
B.D. Bachelor of Divinity
Beits. *Beitsah*
Bekh. *Bekhorot*
Beng. Bengali
Ber. *Berakhot*
Berb. Berber
Bik. *Bikkurim*
bk. book (pl., bks.)
B.M. *Bavaʾ metsiʿaʾ*
BP before the present
B.Q. *Bavaʾ qammaʾ*
Brāh. *Brāhmaṇa*
Bret. Breton
B.T. Babylonian Talmud
Bulg. Bulgarian
Burm. Burmese
c. *circa,* about, approximately
Calif. California
Can. Canaanite
Catal. Catalan
CE of the common era
Celt. Celtic
cf. *confer,* compare
Chald. Chaldean
chap. chapter (pl., chaps.)
Chin. Chinese
C.H.M. Community of the Holy Myrrhbearers
1 Chr. *1 Chronicles*
2 Chr. *2 Chronicles*
Ch. Slav. Church Slavic
cm centimeters
col. column (pl., cols.)
Col. *Colossians*
Colo. Colorado
comp. compiler (pl., comps.)
Conn. Connecticut
cont. continued
Copt. Coptic
1 Cor. *1 Corinthians*
2 Cor. *2 Corinthians*
corr. corrected
C.S.P. Congregatio Sancti Pauli, Congregation of Saint Paul (Paulists)
d. died
D Deuteronomic (source of the Pentateuch)
Dan. Danish
D.B. Divinitatis Baccalaureus, Bachelor of Divinity
D.C. District of Columbia
D.D. Divinitatis Doctor, Doctor of Divinity
Del. Delaware
Dem. *Demaʾi*
dim. diminutive
diss. dissertation
Dn. *Daniel*
D.Phil. Doctor of Philosophy
Dt. *Deuteronomy*
Du. Dutch
E Elohist (source of the Pentateuch)
Eccl. *Ecclesiastes*
ed. editor (pl., eds.); edition; edited by

'Eduy. *'Eduyyot*
e.g. *exempli gratia,* for example
Egyp. Egyptian
1 En. *1 Enoch*
2 En. *2 Enoch*
3 En. *3 Enoch*
Eng. English
enl. enlarged
Eph. *Ephesians*
'Eruv. *'Eruvin*
1 Esd. *1 Esdras*
2 Esd. *2 Esdras*
3 Esd. *3 Esdras*
4 Esd. *4 Esdras*
esp. especially
Est. Estonian
Est. *Esther*
et al. *et alii,* and others
etc. *et cetera,* and so forth
Eth. Ethiopic
EV English version
Ex. *Exodus*
exp. expanded
Ez. *Ezekiel*
Ezr. *Ezra*
2 Ezr. *2 Ezra*
4 Ezr. *4 Ezra*
f. feminine; and following (pl., ff.)
fasc. fascicle (pl., fascs.)
fig. figure (pl., figs.)
Finn. Finnish
fl. *floruit,* flourished
Fla. Florida
Fr. French
frag. fragment
ft. feet
Ga. Georgia
Gal. *Galatians*
Gaul. Gaulish
Ger. German
Giṭ. *Giṭṭin*
Gn. *Genesis*
Gr. Greek
Ḥag. *Ḥagigah*
Ḥal. *Ḥallah*
Hau. Hausa
Hb. *Habakkuk*
Heb. Hebrew
Heb. *Hebrews*
Hg. *Haggai*
Hitt. Hittite
Hor. *Horayot*
Hos. *Hosea*
Ḥul. *Ḥullin*
Hung. Hungarian
ibid. *ibidem,* in the same place (as the one immediately preceding)
Icel. Icelandic
i.e. *id est,* that is
IE Indo-European
Ill. Illinois
Ind. Indiana
intro. introduction
Ir. Gael. Irish Gaelic
Iran. Iranian
Is. *Isaiah*
Ital. Italian
J Yahvist (source of the Pentateuch)
Jas. *James*
Jav. Javanese
Jb. *Job*
Jdt. *Judith*
Jer. *Jeremiah*
Jgs. *Judges*
Jl. *Joel*
Jn. *John*
1 Jn. *1 John*
2 Jn. *2 John*
3 Jn. *3 John*
Jon. *Jonah*
Jos. *Joshua*
Jpn. Japanese
JPS Jewish Publication Society translation (1985) of the Hebrew Bible
J.T. Jerusalem Talmud
Jub. *Jubilees*
Kans. Kansas
Kel. *Kelim*
Ker. *Keritot*
Ket. *Ketubbot*
1 Kgs. *1 Kings*
2 Kgs. *2 Kings*
Khois. Khoisan
Kil. *Kil'ayim*
km kilometers
Kor. Korean
Ky. Kentucky
l. line (pl., ll.)
La. Louisiana
Lam. *Lamentations*
Lat. Latin
Latv. Latvian
L. en Th. Licencié en Théologie, Licentiate in Theology
L. ès L. Licencié ès Lettres, Licentiate in Literature
Let. Jer. *Letter of Jeremiah*
lit. literally
Lith. Lithuanian
Lk. *Luke*
LL Late Latin
LL.D. Legum Doctor, Doctor of Laws
Lv. *Leviticus*
m meters
m. masculine
M.A. Master of Arts
Ma 'as. *Ma'aserot*
Ma 'as. Sh. *Ma' aser sheni*
Mak. *Makkot*
Makh. *Makhshirin*
Mal. *Malachi*
Mar. Marathi
Mass. Massachusetts
1 Mc. *1 Maccabees*
2 Mc. *2 Maccabees*
3 Mc. *3 Maccabees*
4 Mc. *4 Maccabees*
Md. Maryland
M.D. Medicinae Doctor, Doctor of Medicine
ME Middle English
Meg. *Megillah*
Me 'il. *Me'ilah*
Men. *Menaḥot*
MHG Middle High German
mi. miles
Mi. *Micah*
Mich. Michigan
Mid. *Middot*
Minn. Minnesota
Miq. *Miqva'ot*
MIran. Middle Iranian
Miss. Mississippi
Mk. *Mark*
Mo. Missouri
Mo'ed Q. *Mo'ed qaṭan*
Mont. Montana
MPers. Middle Persian
MS. *manuscriptum,* manuscript (pl., MSS)
Mt. *Matthew*
MT Masoretic text
n. note
Na. *Nahum*
Nah. Nahuatl
Naz. *Nazir*
N.B. *nota bene,* take careful note
N.C. North Carolina
n.d. no date
N.Dak. North Dakota
NEB New English Bible
Nebr. Nebraska

Ned. *Nedarim*
Neg. *Nega'im*
Neh. *Nehemiah*
Nev. Nevada
N.H. New Hampshire
Nid. *Niddah*
N.J. New Jersey
Nm. *Numbers*
N.Mex. New Mexico
no. number (pl., nos.)
Nor. Norwegian
n.p. no place
n.s. new series
N.Y. New York
Ob. *Obadiah*
O.Cist. Ordo Cisterciencium, Order of Cîteaux (Cistercians)
OCS Old Church Slavonic
OE Old English
O.F.M. Ordo Fratrum Minorum, Order of Friars Minor (Franciscans)
OFr. Old French
Ohal. *Ohalot*
OHG Old High German
OIr. Old Irish
OIran. Old Iranian
Okla. Oklahoma
ON Old Norse
O.P. Ordo Praedicatorum, Order of Preachers (Dominicans)
OPers. Old Persian
op. cit. *opere citato,* in the work cited
OPrus. Old Prussian
Oreg. Oregon
'Orl. *'Orlah*
O.S.B. Ordo Sancti Benedicti, Order of Saint Benedict (Benedictines)
p. page (pl., pp.)
P Priestly (source of the Pentateuch)
Pa. Pennsylvania
Pahl. Pahlavi
Par. *Parah*
para. paragraph (pl., paras.)
Pers. Persian
Pes. *Pesahim*
Ph.D. Philosophiae Doctor, Doctor of Philosophy
Phil. *Philippians*
Phlm. *Philemon*
Phoen. Phoenician
pl. plural; plate (pl., pls.)
PM *post meridiem,* after noon
Pol. Polish
pop. population
Port. Portuguese
Prv. *Proverbs*
Ps. *Psalms*
Ps. 151 *Psalm 151*
Ps. Sol. *Psalms of Solomon*
pt. part (pl., pts.)
1Pt. *1 Peter*
2 Pt. *2 Peter*
Pth. Parthian
Q hypothetical source of the synoptic Gospels
Qid. *Qiddushin*
Qin. *Qinnim*
r. reigned; ruled
Rab. *Rabbah*
rev. revised
R. ha-Sh. *Ro'sh ha-shanah*
R.I. Rhode Island
Rom. Romanian
Rom. *Romans*
R.S.C.J. Societas Sacratissimi Cordis Jesu, Religious of the Sacred Heart
RSV Revised Standard Version of the Bible
Ru. *Ruth*
Rus. Russian
Rv. *Revelation*
Rv. Ezr. *Revelation of Ezra*
San. *Sanhedrin*
S.C. South Carolina
Scot. Gael. Scottish Gaelic
S.Dak. South Dakota
sec. section (pl., secs.)
Sem. Semitic
ser. series
sg. singular
Sg. *Song of Songs*
Sg. of 3 *Prayer of Azariah and the Song of the Three Young Men*
Shab. *Shabbat*
Shav. *Shavu'ot*
Sheq. *Sheqalim*
Sib. Or. *Sibylline Oracles*
Sind. Sindhi
Sinh. Sinhala
Sir. *Ben Sira*
S.J. Societas Jesu, Society of Jesus (Jesuits)
Skt. Sanskrit
1 Sm. *1 Samuel*
2 Sm. *2 Samuel*
Sogd. Sogdian
Soṭ. *Soṭah*
sp. species (pl., spp.)
Span. Spanish
sq. square
S.S.R. Soviet Socialist Republic
st. stanza (pl., ss.)
S.T.M. Sacrae Theologiae Magister, Master of Sacred Theology
Suk. *Sukkah*
Sum. Sumerian
supp. supplement; supplementary
Sus. *Susanna*
s.v. *sub verbo,* under the word (pl., s.v.v.)
Swed. Swedish
Syr. Syriac
Syr. Men. *Syriac Menander*
Ta' an. *Ta'anit*
Tam. Tamil
Tam. *Tamid*
Tb. *Tobit*
T.D. *Taishō shinshū daizōkyō,* edited by Takakusu Junjirō et al. (Tokyo,1922–1934)
Tem. *Temurah*
Tenn. Tennessee
Ter. Terumot
Ṭev. Y. *Ṭevul yom*
Tex. Texas
Th.D. Theologicae Doctor, Doctor of Theology
1 Thes. *1 Thessalonians*
2 Thes. *2 Thessalonians*
Thrac. Thracian
Ti. *Titus*
Tib. Tibetan
1 Tm. *1 Timothy*
2 Tm. *2 Timothy*
T. of 12 *Testaments of the Twelve Patriarchs*
Ṭoh. *ṭohorot*
Tong. Tongan
trans. translator, translators; translated by; translation
Turk. Turkish
Ukr. Ukrainian
Upan. *Upaniṣad*
U.S. United States
U.S.S.R. Union of Soviet Socialist Republics
Uqts. *Uqtsin*
v. verse (pl., vv.)
Va. Virginia
var. variant; variation
Viet. Vietnamese

viz. *videlicet,* namely
vol. volume (pl., vols.)
Vt. Vermont
Wash. Washington
Wel. Welsh
Wis. Wisconsin
Wis. *Wisdom of Solomon*
W.Va. West Virginia
Wyo. Wyoming

Yad. *Yadayim*
Yev. *Yevamot*
Yi. Yiddish
Yor. Yoruba
Zav. *Zavim*
Zec. *Zechariah*
Zep. *Zephaniah*
Zev. *Zevaḥim*

* hypothetical
? uncertain; possibly; perhaps
° degrees
+ plus
– minus
= equals; is equivalent to
× by; multiplied by
→ yields

APPENDIX

The following articles were not included in the main body of the Encyclopedia due to time constraints. The titles of these articles do not appear in the List of Articles or the List of Contributors (in volume 1), but these articles are referenced in the Synoptic Outline of Contents and in the Index (in volume 15).

BUDDHIST BOOKS AND TEXTS: CANON AND CANONIZATION-ABHIDHARMA
Rupert Gethin (2005)
University of Bristol

CARIBBEAN RELIGIONS: HISTORY OF STUDY
Stephen D. Glazier (2005)
University of Nebraska-Lincoln

CHING, JULIA
Vincent Shen (2005)
University of Toronto

DIVINATION: IFA DIVINATION
Jacob Olupona (2005)
University of California, Davis

FICTION: SOUTH ASIAN FICTION AND RELIGION
Christoph Emmrich (2005)
South Asia Institute, University of Heidelberg

GENDER AND RELIGION: GENDER AND AFRICAN AMERICAN RELIGIONS
Cheryl Townsend Gilkes (2005)
Colby College

HISTORY OF RELIGIONS [FURTHER CONSIDERATIONS]
Giovanni Casadio (2005)
Università degli Studi di Salerno

MATERIALITY
Philip P. Arnold (2005)
Syracuse University

MERKAVAH MYSTICISM
Michael Swartz (2005)
Ohio State University

NATIVE AMERICAN CHURCH
Kenneth Littlefish (2005)
Port Angeles, Washington

OXTOBY, WILLARD G.
Alan F. Segal (2005)
Barnard College, Columbia University

PERIODICAL LITERATURE
Gustavo Benavides (2005)
Villanova University

POLITICS AND RELIGION: POLITICS AND JUDAISM
Menachem Lorberbaum (2005)
Tel Aviv University

PRIMITIVISM
Philip P. Arnold (2005)
Syracuse University

RAMAKRISHNA [FURTHER CONSIDERATIONS]
Narasingha P. Sil (2005)
Western Oregon University

RITES OF PASSAGE: NORTH AMERICAN INDIAN RITES
Inés Talamantez (2005)
University of California, Santa Barbara
Zelda Yazzie (2005)
Mescalero, New Mexico

STUDY OF RELIGION: THE ACADEMIC STUDY OF RELIGION IN CHINA
Chi-tim Lai (2005)
The Chinese University of Hong Kong

STUDY OF RELIGION: THE ACADEMIC STUDY OF RELIGION IN WESTERN EUROPE
Gustavo Benavides (2005)
Villanova University

TRANSCULTURATION AND RELIGION: RELIGION IN THE FORMATION OF THE MODERN UNITED STATES
Philip P. Arnold (2005)
Syracuse University

VAIṢṆAVISM: AN OVERVIEW [FURTHER CONSIDERATIONS]
Srilata Raman (2005)
University of Heidelberg

VIVEKANANDA [FURTHER CONSIDERATIONS]
Narasingha P. Sil (2005)
Western Oregon University

BUDDHIST BOOKS AND TEXTS: CANON AND CANONIZATION—ABHIDHARMA

The Sanskrit term *abhidharma* (Pali, *abhidhamma)* typically refers to the texts that constitute the third of the "three baskets" *(tripiṭaka)* of the Buddhist canon. Yet most of the early accounts of the first "collective recitation" *(saṃgīti)* of Buddhist texts, which took place in Rājagṛha shortly after the Buddha's death (c. 400 BCE), envisage the texts as falling into just two main categories: (1) the "teaching" *(dharma)*, consisting of the various "sayings" *(sutta/sūtra)* delivered by the Buddha on specific occasions, and (2) the "discipline" (vinaya) governing individual and communal monastic life. Some accounts, however, mention "lists" *(mātṛkā)* as a third category. This seems to refer to lists extracted from the discipline and sayings of the Buddha that functioned partly as summaries and partly as maps of the teaching; a number of early Abhidharma texts are built around such lists, and their use and elaboration seems at least in part to be associated with the development of the Abhidharma literature.

The term *abhidharma* itself seems to derive from the expression *abhi dhamme*, which is found in several texts of the Pali Sutta and Vinaya *piṭakas* in the sense of "concerning the teaching(s)." As the name of the third division of Buddhist canonical texts, however, *abhidharma* has usually been interpreted by the Buddhist exegetical tradition as meaning "higher," "special," or "further" teaching.

Commentators usually contrast the method and style of this special teaching with the method and style of the discourses of the Buddha (Pali, *suttanta;* Skt., *sūtrānta).* Thus the texts of the Sūtra Piṭaka are regarded as characteristically addressed to particular individuals in particular circumstances; their language is conventional *(vohāra/ vyavahāra),* and terms must be understood relative to context *(pariyāyena).* The texts of the Abhidharma Piṭaka, on the other hand, present the Buddha's teaching without any concession to individual circumstances; their language is absolute *(paramattha/paramārtha)* and terms must be understood as having fixed, final meanings *(nippariyāyena).* In fact this kind of distinction between relative and absolute statements of the teaching is already clearly present in some contexts in the discourses of the Sūtra Piṭaka, indicative of the manner in which the Abhidharma method develops preexisting tendencies in early Buddhist literature.

THE CANONICAL ABHIDHARMA OF THE SARVĀSTIVĀDINS AND THERAVĀDINS. It is generally assumed that just as various ancient Indian schools preserved their own versions of the Sūtra and Vinaya texts, so they also preserved their own canonical Abhidharma collections, yet definite knowledge of the Abhidharma Piṭaka is restricted to the texts of two schools: the Sarvāstivādins, who flourished particularly in northern India, and the Theravādins, who flourished especially on the island of Lanka and represent a southern branch of the Sthaviras.

Of the canonical Abhidharma collections recognized by other schools nothing is known for certain. It may be that they represented different recensions of the Sarvāstivādin or Theravādin materials. Certainly it seems that in some cases they consisted of texts that are now lost; the Pudgalavādins, for example, are said to have possessed an Abhidharma in nine parts, which has not survived. Nevertheless, there is evidence suggestive of the widespread interest in Abhidharma literature: The vast corpus of translated works that constitutes the Chinese Tripiṭaka preserves at least one or two Abhidharma treatises that might belong to schools other than the Sarvāstivāda and Theravāda; new Sanskrit and Middle Indic textual fragments that have to do with Abhidharma continue to come to light. Moreover, there can be little doubt that the kinds of ideas found articulated in Abhidharma texts were crucial to the development of Indian Buddhist thought. It therefore seems clear that the schools of ancient Indian Buddhism generally recognized some form of the Abhidharma.

The developed exegetical traditions of both the Sarvāstivādins and Theravādins understand the canonical Abhidharma to consist of a definite set of seven texts. The two schools, however, each specify a quite different set of texts.

The Sarvāstivādin Abhidharma comprises the *Saṃgītiparyāya* (Discourse on the collective recitation), the *Dharmaskandha* (Compendium of *dharmas*), the *Prajñaptiśstra* (Manual of instruction), the *Vijñānakāya* (Compendium of consciousness), *Dhātukāya* (Compendium of elements), the *Prakaraṇa* (Treatise), and the *Jñānaprasthāna* (Foundation of knowledge). These seven texts survive in full only in their ancient Chinese translations and have yet to be translated into a modern European language.

The Theravādin Abhidhamma comprises the *Dhammasaṅgaṇi* (Enumeration of *dhammas)*, the *Vibhaṅga* (Analysis), the *Dhātukathā* (Discourse on elements), the *Puggalapaññatti* (Designation of types of person), the *Kathāvatthu* (Points of discussion), the *Yamaka* (Pairs), and the *Paṭṭhāna* (Conditions). The seven texts of the Theravādins are preserved in the hybrid Middle Indian dialect known today as Pali, and all but the *Yamaka* have been translated into English, though in the case of the *Paṭṭhāna* not completely.

THE ABHIDHARMA AS "THE WORD OF THE BUDDHA." The Buddhist tradition's own general lack of consensus about the content of the Abhidharma Piṭaka contrasts with the relative consensus concerning the core contents of the Vinaya and Sūtra *piṭakas*, and suggests again that the third *piṭaka* came into existence somewhat later than the other two.

Later Buddhist exegetical literature contains indications of discussion and disagreements over the texts to be included in the Abhidharma Piṭaka. Nevertheless, like the Sūtra and Vinaya, the Abhidharma was generally regarded as "the word of the Buddha" *(buddhavacana),* and just as the Sūtra in fact contained some texts explicitly attributed to the Buddha's

chief disciples rather than the Buddha himself (though sometimes endorsed by him at the close), so some early Abhidharma works—especially according to Sarvāstivādin tradition—are associated with the names of the Buddha's disciples. Thus the *Saṃgītiparyāya* of the Sarvāstivādin Abhidharma takes the form of a commentary on a sūtra *(sutta)* attributed to Śāriputra that is preserved in the collection of long sayings *(Dīrghāgama/Dīgha Nikāya)* of the Sūtra Piṭaka. Other Abhidharma texts are associated with the names of other immediate disciples, such as Maudgalyāyana and Kātyāyana, while some texts, for example the Sarvāstivādin *Vijñānakāya* and the Theravādin *Kathāvatthu,* are attributed to disciples—Devaśarman and Moggaliputtatissa, respectively—who according to tradition lived some time after the death of the Buddha. Significantly the attribution of texts to specific disciples is inconsistent: Chinese tradition, for example, attributes the *Dharmaskandha* to Śāriputra, while Tibetan and Sanskrit tradition attributes it to Maudgalyāyana. There is also a more general tendency to associate the Abhidharma with the name of Śāriputra, the disciple of the Buddha who in the sūtras is said to be chief in wisdom. A text whose affiliation is uncertain is styled "the treatise on the Abhidharma of Śāriputra" *(Śāriputrābhidharma Śāstra).* Moreover, according to Theravādin tradition, while the Buddha worked out the content of the Abhidhamma in the fourth week after his awakening, he did not make it known until much later, when he spent the three months of the rainy season in the Heaven of the Thirty-Three teaching his mother and the assembled gods. The story goes that each day he would retire to a grove of sandal trees on the shores of the mythical Lake Anotatta, where he would impart to Sāriputta what he had taught earlier; Sāriputta in turn passed it on to his five hundred disciples. The fact that the Abhidharma was associated with disciples of the Buddha who in some cases were acknowledged to have lived some time after him, meant that it was open to the challenge that it was not, either as a whole or in part, the "word of the Buddha." The introduction to the fifth century CE *Atthasālinī,* a commentary on the *Dhammasaṅgaṇī,* refers to some who accepted only an Abhidhamma consisting of six books, since they rejected the *Kathāvatthu* on the grounds that it was not the word of the Buddha, but the work of Moggaliputtatissa (third century BCE). Such challenges were generally countered, however, by the insistence that the Abhidharma's real author was indeed the Buddha: While his disciples may have elaborated certain details, they had done so on the basis of a structure and framework that the Buddha himself had established for each text.

THE DEVELOPMENT OF THE EARLY ABHIDHARMA LITERATURE. All this suggests that the early Abhidharma texts should perhaps be seen as the work of the first generations of the Buddha's disciples, rather than of the Buddha himself; the Buddhist tradition itself seems to acknowledge this, while at the same time wishing to emphasize that the profundity of these texts is proof that they are ultimately the products of the perfect wisdom of a buddha.

It seems likely that what came to be regarded as canonical Abhidharma treatises were not works composed at a particular time by single authors, but evolved over decades, if not centuries, out of materials and in accordance with certain literary and philosophical tendencies already present in the Sūtra and Vinaya portions of the canon.

That the lines between Sūtra and Abhidharma are on occasion somewhat blurred is apparent from the fact that certain texts of the fifth collection *(Khuddaka Nikāya)* of the Theravādin Sutta Piṭaka—texts such as the *Niddesa* and *Paṭisambhidāmagga*—would seem to belong in form and spirit to the Abhidhamma Piṭaka.

The Abhidharma use of lists has already been referred to. The prevalence of lists in early Buddhist literature is partly a consequence of its being composed and for some centuries preserved orally: Lists were clearly useful mnemonic devices. Already in the Sūtra Piṭaka certain texts take the form of collections of lists, providing bare definitions of items that are treated more discursively elsewhere. Once such text is the *Saṃgīti Sūtra,* which survives in several versions and which, as mentioned above, formed the basis of one of the canonical works of the Sarvāstivādin Abhidharma. One of the four primary divisions (Āgama/Nikāya) of the Sūtra Piṭaka is the collection of "grouped" *(saṃyukta/saṃyutta)* sayings, which groups the sayings of the Buddha connected with specific topics. The topics highlighted in the grouped collection include the twelve links of dependent origination, the five aggregates, the six senses, the four ways of establishing mindfulness, the four right efforts, the four bases of success, the five faculties, the five powers, the seven constituents of awakening, the eightfold path, the four noble truths, the four stages of meditation, and the four divine abidings. Essentially the same list of items provides the table of contents for two Abhidharma works, the Theravādin *Vibhaṅga* and Sarvāstivādin *Dharmaskandha.* The characteristic literary style of the Abhidharma in this context is to take a list derived from the sūtras and provide a succinct statement and definition of terms.

Another literary style developed from the Sūtra Piṭaka (again, particularly the *Saṃyuktāgama/Saṃyutta Nikāya*), is the application of formulaic treatments to a number of different items without setting out the text in full: The variables are indicated in summary fashion and the text is set out in a radically abbreviated form, leaving it somewhat open ended. In fact it is said in the exegetical tradition that if the seven texts of the Theravādin Abhidhamma were elaborated in full, each would be infinite in extent.

Another feature of the Abhidharma use of lists reflects certain intellectual developments in Buddhist thought. Lists of terms that in the discourses of the Buddha are apparently presented as sequential descriptions of a process are reinterpreted in the Abhidharma as applying to momentary events. The well known list of twelve links of "dependent origination" *(pratītya-samutpāda/paṭicca-samuppāda)*—ignorance, formations, consciousness, name and form, six senses,

contact, feeling, craving, attachment, becoming, birth, old age and death—appears in the discourses to describe a process that involves a succession of events arising over some period of time, possibly more than a single life. In an Abhidhamma text like the *Vibhaṅga* of the Theravādins, the time scale of this process of dependent origination is reduced, and the process is now seen as operating from moment to moment. This reflects the fundamental Abhidharma vision of the processes of causality that lie at the heart of reality and involve the interaction of nothing more than *dharmas* (Pali, *dhamma*), momentary mental and physical "qualities."

LATER EXEGETICAL ABHIDHARMA LITERATURE. The development of systematic Buddhist thought is to be associated with the Abhidharma literature in general, yet the canonical texts—at least as presented in the Theravādin and Sarvāstivādin collections—still represent somewhat loose and unsystematic expositions of certain aspects of Buddhist thought; there is no attempt at a systematic exposition of the whole. This lack seems to have been felt by the tradition, which from perhaps the first century CE began to produce commentaries and summary manuals offering definitive interpretations of the canonical material and filling in certain gaps. With the production of these exegetical texts the term *Abhidharma* comes to denote not so much a set of texts, but the more general systematic exposition of Buddhist thought in accordance with the traditions of the earlier Abhidharma texts and their commentaries.

For the Sarvāstivādins the crucial text is a *vibhāṣā* or "commentary" on the *Jñānaprasthāna* of the Abhidharma Piṭaka, which was composed in northwest India in perhaps the first or second century and circulated in at least three different recensions. The commentary gives its name to a school of Abhidharma interpretation, the Vaibhāṣikas or "followers of the views and opinions found in the *vibhāṣā*." The Vaibhāṣika tradition of Abhidharma also finds expression in a series of shorter summary manuals, such as the "Heart of Abhidharma" *(abhidharmahṛdaya)* works of Upaśānta and Dharmatrāta (third and fourth centuries). The Vaibhāṣika-Sarvāstivādin interpretation of Abhidharma was not the only one current in northern India. For the Buddhist traditions of China and Tibet down to the present day, the term *Abhidharma* has come to be equated with one text in particular, the *Abhidharmakośa* or "Treasury of Abhidharma" of Vasubandhu (fourth or fifth century), a set of verses with an auto prose commentary *(bhāṣya)*, which sets out a critique of certain key Vaibhāṣika doctrines, such as their theory of existence in relation to past, present, and future time. Works such as Saṅghabhadra's *Abhidharma-samaya-pradīpika* (Illumination of Abhidharma) and the anonymous *Abhidharmadīpa* (The lamp of Abhidharma) are attempts on the part of Vaibhāṣika masters to address Vasubandhu's criticisms.

In making his critique, Vasubandhu often refers to the views of the Sautrāntikas or "those who follow the sūtras," a loosely affiliated group that questioned certain aspects of the Vaibhāṣika Abhidharma vision that they argued were not supported by the sūtras. Although the Sautrāntikas did not acknowledge the Abhidharma as the "word of the Buddha," their position did not amount to a wholehearted rejection of the value of the Abhidharma tradition. In works such as Asaṅga's (fourth century) *Abhidharmasamuccaya* (Compendium of Abhidharma), the traditions of the Sautrāntika-Sarvāstivādin Abhidharma were reworked by the Mahāyāna philosophical school known as Yogācāra, exponents of a form of philosophical idealism *(vijñaptimātra)*. Indeed, the author of the *Abhidharmakośa* is possibly identical with the Yogācārin Vasubandhu (fourth century).

In the south the Theravādins also produced summary manuals of their Abhidhamma system. The earliest surviving texts appear to be two works of Buddhadatta (fourth or fifth century): the *Rūpārūpavibhāga* (Analysis of the material and immaterial) and *Abhidhammāvatāra* (Introduction to Abhidhamma). In more recent centuries Theravādin Abhidhamma studies has flourished particularly in Burma (present-day Myanmar), where tradition has focused on a set of seven relatively concise "little finger" *(let than)* manuals of diverse date (tenth to fifteenth centuries) and origin (Lanka, southern India, Burma): *Abhidhammatthasaṅgaha*, *Paramatthavinicchaya*, *Nāmarūpapariccheda*, *Saccasaṅkhepa*, *Nāmarūpasamāsa*, *Nāmacāradīpika*, and *Mohavicchedanī;* sometimes the little finger manuals are counted as nine, by including Buddhadatta's manuals. Of these seven or nine manuals, it is the first, Anuruddha's "Summary of the Topics of Abhidhamma," composed in Lanka in perhaps the tenth century, that has long been the standard textbook of Abhidhamma in the lands of Theravāda Buddhism. This summary of some fifty pages is often supplemented by its various commentaries, especially Sumaṅgala's *Abhidhammatthavibhāvinīṭīkā* (Exposition of the topics of Abhidhamma) composed in Lanka in the twelfth century.

BIBLIOGRAPHY

Bodhi, Bhikkhu, ed. *A Comprehensive Manual of Abhidhamma: The Abhidhammattha Sangaha of Ācariya Anuruddha.* Kandy, Sri Lanka, 1993. A substantial revision of Nārada Thera's *Manual of Abhdhamma* (4th ed., Kandy, 1980). Contains the Pali text and English translation of the most widely used Theravādin Abhidhamma primer (dating perhaps from the tenth century), with a full modern explanatory commentary by Bodhi and U Rewata Dhamma that draws on material from traditional commentaries. See also the item by Wijeratne and Gethin below.

Bronkhorst, Johannes. "Dharma and Abhidharma." *Bulletin of the School of Oriental and African Studies* 48 (1985): 305–320. A consideration of the possible evolution of the lists *(mātṛkā)* that underlie the early Abhidharma texts.

Cousins, L. S. "The Paṭṭhāna and the Development of the Theravādin Abhidhamma." *Journal of the Pali Text Society* 9 (1981): 22–46. Shows that the basic principles of the later consciousness process *(citta-vīthi)*, which is well known from the Pali commentaries, are already embedded in the system of causal relations set out in the *Paṭṭhāna*, an important find-

ing for the dating of the development of Abhidhamma thought.

Cox, Collett. *Disputed Dharmas: Early Buddhist Theories on Existence: An Annotated Translation of the Section on Factors Dissociated from Thought from Saṅghabhadra's Nyānusāra.* Tokyo, 1995. As well as providing an annotated translation of sections of Saṅghabahdra's response to criticisms leveled by Vasubandhu in his *Abhidharmakośabhāṣya,* the book contains an excellent introduction, which outlines the state of scholarship with regard to the history of the Sarvāstivādin Abhidharma, drawing not only on European and American scholarship, but also on Japanese scholarship.

Frauwallner, Erich. *Studies in Abhidharma Literature and the Origins of Buddhist Philosophical Systems.* Albany, N.Y., 1995. An English translation of an influential series of papers originally published in German in *Wiener Zeitschrift für die Kunde Süd- und Ostasiens* between 1963 and 1973. Frauwallner's work represents the only sustained attempt to sketch the evolution of early Abhidharma literature, taking into account the Theravādin and Sarvāstivādin materials. His conclusions remain tentative, however.

Gethin, Rupert. "The Mātikās: Memorization, Mindfulness, and the List." *In the Mirror of Memory: Reflections on Mindfulness and Remembrance in Indian and Tibetan Buddhism,* edited by Janet Gyatso, pp. 149–172. Albany, N.Y., 1992. A consideration of how lists found in the *suttas* operate as a map for the structure of Buddhist thought, and provide a framework for the development of Abhidhamma texts.

Hinüber, Oskar von. *A Handbook of Pāli Literature.* Berlin, 1996. An essential reference work for Pali literature, setting out the basic factual information (as far as it is known) concerning date, authorship, and the provenance of individual texts; for the Abhidhamma see especially pages 64–75 and 160–165.

Norman, K. R. *Pāli Literature: Including the Canonical Literature in Prakrit and Sanskrit of All the Hīnayāna Schools of Buddhism.* Wiesbaden, Germany, 1983. A more discursive history of Pali literature focusing on the issues of authorship and the relative chronology of the texts; for the Abhidhamma see especially pages 96–107 and 151–153.

Nyanaponika, Thera. *Abhidhamma Studies: Buddhist Explorations of Consciousness and Time.* Boston, 1998. A fourth, revised (by Bhikkhu Bodhi) edition of a book originally published in 1949. The book is particularly important as one of the only studies that considers the significance of portions of the *Dhammasaṅgaṇi,* the first book of the canonical Theravādin Abhidhamma.

Nyanatiloka, Mahāthera. *Guide through the Abhidhamma-Piṭaka,* 4th ed. Kandy, Sri Lanka, 1983. Originally published in 1938 and enlarged and revised in 1957 by Nyanaponika, this is an extremely useful outline of the basic content, structure, and method of each of the seven works of the Theravādin Abhidhamma Piṭaka.

Potter, Karl H., ed. *Abhidharma Buddhism to 150 A.D.* Vol. 7: *Encyclopedia of Indian Philosophies.* Delhi, 1996. Contains summaries of twenty-three Abhidharma texts, many of which are otherwise untranslated, including six works of the Sarvāstivādin Abhidharma Piṭaka, the Sarvāstivādin Abhidharma commentary, the *Mahāvibhāṣā,* and one of the few early Abhidharma works to survive from outside Theravādin and Sarvāstivādin circles, the *Śāriputrābhidharma Śāstra.* The volume also contains a useful essay on the development of Abhidharma literature by Robert Buswell and Padmanabh Jaini.

Pruden, Leo M., trans. *Abhidharmakośabhāṣyam* by Louis de La Vallée Poussin. 4 vols. Berkeley, 1988–1990. An English translation of La Vallée Poussin's *L'Abhidharmakośa de Vasubandhu* (6 vols., Paris, 1923–1931; reprint, Brussels, 1971). La Vallée Poussin translated Xuan Zang's Chinese translation (seventh century) of Vasubandhu's *Abhidharmakośa-ṣya* before the original Sanskrit text was rediscovered, but this still remains a great work of scholarship with, in addition to the annotated translation, important introductory essays on the history and philosophy of the Sarvāstivādin Abhidharma.

Wijeratne, R. P., and Rupert Gethin, trans. *Summary of the Topics of Abhidhamma and Exposition of the Topics of Abhidhamma.* Oxford, 2002. A translation of the most widely used Theravādin Abhidhamma handbook, the tenth-century *Abhidhammatthasṅgaha,* along with its most influential commentary, the twelfth-century *Abhidhammatthavibhāvinīṭīkā.* See also the item by Bodhi above.

Willemen, Charles, Bart Dessein, and Collett Cox. *Sarvāstivāda Buddhist Scholasticism.* Leiden, 1998. An up-to-date survey concentrating on the evolution of Sarvāstivādin Abhidharma literature, with a particularly useful extended essay by Collett Cox (pp. 138–254) on the canonical Sarvāstivādin literature and its commentarial compendia *(vibhāṣā),* as well as Dessein's discussion of the "Heart of Abhidharma" *(abhidharmahṛdaya)* manuals.

RUPERT GETHIN (2005)

CARIBBEAN RELIGIONS: HISTORY OF STUDY

This essay attempts to address the study of Caribbean religion from the time of initial European contact to the beginning of the twenty-first century. As such, it encompasses both aboriginal Caribbean religions and African-derived religions. While the study of Caribbean religions could be seen as a gradual progression from a focus on the exotic to more objective, tolerant, or sympathetic portrayals, such is not always the case. At every stage in the study of Caribbean religions, highly sensationalized accounts—whether of alleged cannibalism among the island-Caribs or the bizarre acts attributed to vodou practitioners in Haiti—continue to exist alongside more objective and sympathetic accounts. Even today, sensationalism abounds in media portrayals of Haitian vodou. For example, Wes Craven's 1988 movie version of Wade Davis's *Serpent and the Rainbow* (1985) still commands greater attention than Davis's scholarly work. Joseph M. Murphy states: "One of the highest hurdles to be overcome in interpreting diasporan traditions to outsiders is the deep-seated popular image of them as 'voodoo' malign 'black magic.' Hundreds of books and scores of films have portrayed the spirituality of millions of people of African descent as crazed, depraved, or demonic manipulations of gullible and irrational people" (1994, p. x).

EARLY MISSIONARY AND TRAVELERS' REPORTS. As Dale Bisnauth correctly points out in his *History of Religions in the*

Caribbean (1989), the study of Caribbean religions begins with Catholic missionary activities among aboriginal peoples. Initial reports concerning Caribbean religions were largely written by Europeans who had two agendas: (1) the conversion of native populations to Catholicism, and (2) the subjugation of aboriginal populations. In the later part of the twentieth century, new translations of the early chroniclers became available (e.g., Dunn and Kelley, 1988). These new translations provide greater insight into European perceptions of aboriginal Caribbean religions.

Christopher Columbus's initial statements concerning aboriginal religions indicate that he did not think the natives to be religious at all. In his diary of the first voyage, he mentioned native religions three times. In the first instance, he suggested that the natives of San Salvador would become Christians easily because "it would seem to me that they had no religion at all." On the island of Hispaniola, he again asserts that it should be easy to convert them to Christianity since they "have no religion of their own and are not idolaters."

Columbus's statements concerning the lack of religion among Amerindians are echoed in writings from the sixteenth and seventeenth centuries. But most contemporary scholars contend to the contrary that the aboriginal people of the Caribbean were among the most religious people on earth. A measure of their religious intensity is the relatively low rate of conversion to Christianity noted by the early chroniclers. Spanish and later French missionaries experienced little immediate success with Caribbean natives and complained that the natives rapidly reverted to pagan ways whenever the opportunity presented itself. Conversion to Christianity was rarely complete, even into the seventeenth century.

From a religious standpoint, the most intense and protracted contact between Europeans and Amerindians took place on the island of Hispaniola. On his third voyage in 1495, Columbus commissioned a poorly educated Hieronymite priest, Raymond Pane, to live among the Taino for two years and compile a description of their religious beliefs and practices. Very little is known concerning Pane and the fate of his report to Columbus, which he completed around 1496 or 1497. Pane's original report has been lost, but was reconstructed in 1968 by José Arrom from a 1571 Italian translation. Father Pane holds two important distinctions. He was the first Caribbean ethnographer, and he baptized Guaticabantu, the first Caribbean native to become a Christian.

With the notable exception of Gonzalo Fernández de Oviedo y Valdés (1535), early Spanish accounts are of limited value to historians. During the seventeenth and eighteenth centuries French missionaries wrote more detailed descriptions of aboriginal religion, including the astute and careful observations of Mathias du Puis, Jean Baptiste du Tertre, and Jean Baptiste Labat, as well as the comprehensive Carib-French/French-Carib dictionary composed by Raymond Breton.

Twentieth-century interpreters of island-Carib religion emphasize that the religious life was greatly influenced by the harsh physical environment. As Bisnauth concluded, "hostile environments bred hostile spirits" (1989, p. 10).

With respect to aboriginal religions, few new sources have emerged, but there have been major advances in archaeological research (Rouse, 1992; Wilson, 1990). The most noteworthy advances have occurred as a result of the introduction of new techniques in underwater archaeology. The exploration of flooded caves (see Becker et al., 2002) has yielded numerous religious objects fashioned from wood and cloth. Raymond Pane's account emphasized the importance of wooden objects for Taino religion, but few examples had been found. Now, thanks to advances in underwater archaeology researchers have access to examples of wooden stools, *zemis,* and other decorated objects that are of finer workmanship and much more detailed than their stone counterparts.

In the eighteenth and nineteenth centuries, the aboriginal population declined and attention increasingly focused on the religions of African slaves. Perhaps the best-known account is Méredec Louis-Elie Moreau de Saint-Méry's *Description topographique, physique, civile, politique, et historique de la partie française de l'isle Saint-Dominque* (1797). Moreau (vol. 1, p. 55) has the distinction of providing one of the first descriptions of an early vodou ceremony. Another excellent eighteenth-century source is Bryan Edwards's *The History, Civil and Commercial, of the British Colonies in the West Indies* (1794). Edwards's history contains important data on religious practices of the Black Caribs.

Accounts of travelers and socialites like Mrs. A. C. Carmichael's *Domestic Manners and Social Conditions of the White, Colored, and Negro Population of the West Indies* (1833) provide insights into the religions of both planters and slaves. Plantation owners—especially the French Creoles of Martinique, Guadeloupe, and Trinidad—made a surprising number of astute observations concerning slave religion. Yvonne Chireau (2003) makes excellent use of these materials. Although Chireau's book focuses on the United States, it also includes considerable information on Caribbean religious beliefs and practices.

By the middle of the nineteenth century, Protestant missionaries replaced Catholic missionaries as the primary observers of Afro-Caribbean religions. Missionary writings, of course, always reflect a great deal about the missionaries themselves as well as their prospective converts. Arthur Charles Dayfoot (1999) points out that nineteenth-century Protestant missionaries took ample note of native religious practices.

The late nineteenth and early twentieth centuries mark the beginning of anthropological interest in Caribbean religions—both aboriginal and African American, and a great deal of Caribbean research (notably the works of Daniel Brinton and Jesse Walter Fewkes) was conducted under the auspices of the Bureau of American Ethnology and

the Smithsonian Institution. Martha Beckwith undertook important studies of Caribbean folklore. In 1929, Beckwith published *Black Roadways: A Study of Jamaican Folk Life*, which includes an insightful analysis of Jamaican religions, as well as a sampling of Jamaican proverbs, children's games, and Christmas mumming. Harold Courlander is by far the most influential Caribbean folklorist. Courlander conducted fieldwork both in Haiti and the Dominican Republic. His best-known work is *The Drum and the Hoe: Life and Lore of the Haitian People* (1960).

Twentieth-century ethnographic accounts examined local practices and isolated communities (e.g., the Herskovitses' fieldwork in the remote village of Toco, Trinidad). A number of highly sensationalized accounts of Haitian vodou and "black magic" were published (notably Seabrook, 1929), as well as numerous accounts of witchcraft and Obeah in the West Indies (Williams, 1932). Scholarly expositions on Haitian religions include the works of Alfred Métraux, Melville J. Herskovits, Maya Deren, and James Leyburn.

The juxtaposition of sensationalized and scholarly accounts continued in the work of Wade Davis, whose best-selling book *The Serpent and the Rainbow* served as the basis for a sensationalized movie, but who also published a number of first-rate ethnographic analyses of Haitian vodou. Davis's major contribution was in pointing out possible ethnobotanical and neurophysiological bases for widespread Haitian beliefs concerning zombies.

MELVILLE J. HERSKOVITS, E. FRANKLIN FRAZIER, AND THE QUEST FOR "AFRICANISMS" IN THE NEW WORLD. In the mid-twentieth century, scholars began to seek connections between African and New World religions. A lively debate ensued between Melville J. Herskovits, who believed that African elements had survived the rigors of slavery and could easily be discerned in the New World, and E. Franklin Frazier (1964), who contended that slavery had been so disruptive of African cultural patterns that few African retentions could be identified in the New World. It is significant that Herskovits and his students (notably William Bascom) began their ethnographic fieldwork in Africa and ended up researching the Americas. George Eaton Simpson was one of Herskovits's most loyal disciples. Elsewhere in the United States, advocates of "Pan-Africanism" like W. E. B. Du Bois did not consider Caribbean religion to be an appropriate focus (Zuckerman, 2000). Du Bois seems to have paid little attention to African-derived religions outside of the United States.

European approaches to African-derived religions evidence a slightly different focus than that of Herskovits. Europeans charted the influence of African religions on New World religions as part of an abstract, global process—what Roger Bastide termed "the interpenetration of civilizations."

The twentieth century also saw a number of locally-based ethnographies dealing with specific religions on specific islands: Santería in Cuba (Lydia Cabrera, Fernando Ortiz, George Brandon, Joseph M. Murphy), Rastafarianism in Jamaica (Rex Nettleford, Leonard Barrett, Barry Chevannes), and the Spiritual Baptists in Trinidad and Grenada (George Eaton Simpson, Stephen D. Glazier, Kenneth Lum, and Wallace Zane). These accounts include much information about religious organization, rituals, beliefs, and music. Of special note is the attempt by Sidney Mintz and Richard Price (1992) to come to terms with processes of syncretism with reference to African-American religious history.

While the bulk of these locally-based studies dealt with African-derived religions, a small number of twentieth-century ethnographies addressed the growing presence of Asian religions in the Caribbean. Most notable among these are Steven Vertovec's *Hindu Trinidad* (1992), Morton Klass's *Singing with Sai Baba* (1996), and Aisha Khan's *Callaloo Nation* (2004). There is still need for more studies of local variants of world religions like Islam, Buddhism, Bahāʾī, Mormonism, the Unification Church, and so on, as well as the impact of these religions on particular Caribbean islands.

The complex relationships between religions in Africa and African religions in the New World are replete with examples of what Pierre Verger termed "flux and reflux" (1968, p. 31). Building on a lifetime of fieldwork and archival research, Verger documented extensive and continuous contact between religious specialists in Africa and religious organizations in the New World. He painstakingly demonstrated that the slave trade was not only *of* Africans (i.e., the trade itself), but *by* Africans as well. Africans and African Americans were producers and traders as well as laborers in the plantation system, and they played an active role—not just a passive one—in the ongoing drama of slavery. The quest for Africa in the New World continues, but with new and refined sensibilities. The question is no longer *whether*, but how much?

As Stuart Hall—commenting on the *Présence Africaine* in his native Jamaica—noted:

> Africa was, in fact, present everywhere, in the everyday life and customs of the slave quarters, in the language and patois of the plantations, in names and words; often disconnected from their taxonomies, in the secret syntactical structure through which other languages were spoken, in the stories and tales told to children, in religious practices and belief in the spiritual life, the arts, crafts, music and rhythms of slave and post-emancipation society. . . . Africa remained and remains the unspoken, unspeakable "presence" in Caribbean culture. It is "hiding" behind every verbal inflection, every narrative twist of Caribbean cultural life. (1990, p. 228)

SYNCRETISM. In the 1950s and 1960s, much research on Caribbean religions addressed the concept of syncretism first introduced to anthropology by Melville Herskovits in 1938. Syncretism is defined as an attempt to merge religious traditions and establish analogies between originally discrete reli-

gious and mythological traditions. At various times and places, religions have embraced syncretism, while at other times, these same religions have rejected the practice as lacking in "authenticity" (Glazier, 1996). Syncretism has sometimes been seen as a devaluation of real, salient religious distinctions.

A number of conceptual shortcomings have been identified in Herskovits's original formulation (Greenfield and Droogers, 2002). Nevertheless, most contemporary anthropologists agree that it may be more valid to look at syncretism in terms of power relations. With respect to Caribbean religions, it may be more useful to examine syncretism from the perspectives of those who do the "syncretizing." When seen from the perspectives of "syncretizers," syncretism appears as a series of individual acts rather than as an abstract and impersonal process.

Central to this discussion is the perceived relationship between African-derived religions and Roman Catholicism. Earlier, it was suggested that Catholic elements within African-derived religions like *orişa* and vodun were brought in to mask or hide African forms of worship under the "cloak" of Christianity. This explanation is not altogether satisfactory. As David Trotman (1976) astutely observed, if early followers of the *orişa* wanted to "disguise" their religion by incorporating elements of Roman Catholicism, it would not have been a very good disguise because no one could have confused African and Catholic rituals. Trotman also correctly contended that if devotees identified Catholic saints and Yorùbá deities attempting to "disguise" the latter, any saint would have provided an equally good "disguise." But such was never the case. Only *some* saints became identified with a limited number of *orişas*, and many Catholic saints were neglected altogether. Ultimately, Trotman concluded that it is most likely that African-derived religions and the veneration of the Catholic saints evolved together.

No one suggests that syncretism does not exist in Caribbean religions. Obviously, cultures that come into contact influence one another. But the term *syncretism*—as it has been applied to Afro-Caribbean religions—assumes too much passivity on the part of slave populations. As Morton Klass opined, "in a universe where gods can do anything, theological studies are manifestly more important and interesting than the study of history, biology, geology, and astronomy put together. It follows that if a god is alleged to create the entire universe in the blink of an eye and knows all that has happened, is happening, and will happen—any inkling of that god's plans, whims, or preferences are of the utmost concern to humans" (1991, p. 32). Caribbean slaves had more than a passing interest in the religion of their masters. They had an urgent need to incorporate European gods (and the powers of those gods) into their own lives. This urgent need, too, is perhaps at the root of perceived correspondences between African deities and Catholic saints.

VODOU: A HISTORY OF STUDY. Few Caribbean religions have captured the scholarly and media attention that has been devoted to Haitian vodou. From the sixteenth century onward, almost every visitor to Haiti has commented on the religion. It became the focus of both popular and scholarly attention and the subject of countless books and articles.

As noted previously, Moreau de Saint-Méry (1797) was among the first to provide a description of vodou ceremonies. He was also the first person to use of the term *vaudoux* with reference to Haitian religion. Moreau writes of a dance led by a group of slaves from the West African town of Arada. According to Moreau, *vaudoux* is a kind of "serpent" possessing oracular powers, who communicates through the medium of a priest or priestess. Moreau correctly interpreted the ceremony as both a deity and a dance, and noted that it is only through the movement of the dance that the spirits *(lwa)* were able to be fully present to the congregation.

Of mid-twentieth-century researchers, Maya Deren (1953) was perhaps the most sensitive to the workings of the spirit. In the eighteenth century, Moreau had recognized *vaudoux*'s political potential, a theme that has dominated twentieth-century studies of vodou (Laguerre, 1989). The later part of the twentieth century saw greater attention paid to community studies (Herskovits, 1937; Métraux, 1959), to vodou as a belief system (Hurbon, 1995; McAlister, 2002), historical-literary studies (Dayan, 1995), and the complex relationship between vodou and the Roman Catholic Church (Desmangles, 1993). Leslie Desmangles's work identifying patterns of symbiosis and juxtaposition in Haitian vodou contrasts markedly with the earlier scholarship of Roger Bastide, George Eaton Simpson, and Melville Herskovits. What makes Desmangles's research unique is his careful attention to the tremendous variety of religious forms and influences within African and African-American religions. Drawing on firsthand research in Haiti and the Republic of Benin, he underscores vodou's continuities and discontinuities with its African past.

RASTAFARI: A HISTORY OF STUDY. As religions change, research methodologies also change. Since the 1980s Rastafarianism has experienced the most dramatic changes of any Caribbean religion. Many people throughout the world became familiar with Rastafari when reggae performers, most notably Bob Marley, started to bring its message to an international audience in the 1970s. Rastafari is an example of a religious movement that has spread globally through the medium of popular culture (Yawney and Homiak, 2001, p. 266). While remaining true to its central tenants (as outlined over forty years ago by George Eaton Simpson), Rastafari claims adherents from all over the world. Following the approach of Kamari Clarke (2004), it may be useful to begin thinking of Rastafari as a vast "network" stretching from "Trench Town" in Jamaica to Africa to Europe to North America to Japan to the Pacific Islands to New Zealand.

When Roy Augier, M. G. Smith, and Rex Nettleford began researching Rastafarianism in the 1960s the movement was little more than a loosely organized federation of homeless men hanging out in the slums of Kingston. There

were few established norms and Rasta theology was—as it still is—in the process of being "worked out." Augier, Smith, and Nettleford conducted their inquiry in response to police concerns about vagrant men who, it was feared, might be involved in criminal activities. Later researchers like Simpson and Barrett also adopted a local (Kingston-based) perspective. Rastafarianism was thus examined first as a local problem, later as a local religion, then as a regional religious movement, but not until the end of the twentieth century was it recognized as a worldwide religious and political movement.

Twenty-first-century researchers have had to adopt what Carole Yawney and John P. Homiak call a "reticulate research model" that allows for both multiple centers and diverse channels of diffusion. Yawney's research, for example, has followed the religion from Jamaica to South Africa to Canada and back again.

SEX ROLES AND ALTERED STATES OF CONSCIOUSNESS. In 1963, Vittorio Lanternari published a seminal study relating spirit possession, so-called ecstatic religion, and social structure. While not dealing exclusively with the Caribbean, Lanternari's *Religions of the Oppressed* inspired further studies, most notably I. M. Lewis's *Ecstatic Religion* (1971) and a large-scale cross-cultural study of spirit possession and trance states directed by Erika Bourguignon, an anthropologist who did her dissertation fieldwork in Haiti under Melville Herskovits. Bourguignon was able to secure funding to send a number of graduate students to the Caribbean and Mexico to study spirit possession and altered states of consciousness.

A major focus of late twentieth-century research has been the changing roles of women in Afro-Caribbean religions. This is especially true with respect to the Trinidad *oriṣa* movement. Female leaders (*iya*) have always existed within the movement. Earlier researchers—who were predominantly male—did not seek them out. Today, a majority of the Trinidadian leadership is female. Rawle Gibbons (1999, p. 196) estimates that women own over 50 percent of *oriṣa* shrines.

The status of women in Afro-Caribbean religions is changing rapidly. In exploring gender roles, it is important to keep in mind the contributions of John K. Thornton, J. Lorand Matory, and Ruth Landes. Thornton, in *The Kingdom of Kongo: Civil War and Transition, 1641–1718* (1983), underscores the changing nature of African politics and religion at the height of the slave trade. It has been common for scholars to focus on syncretism in the formation of New World societies but to lose sight of the fact that such syncretisms and a great deal of religious change was going on in Africa at the same time. Many of the same forces that led to the formation and expansion of vodou in Haiti were also at work in the Kongo. In *Sex and the Empire that Is No More* (1994), Matory takes this argument one step further. Matory not only underscores syncretic and innovative aspects of Ọ̀yọ́ religion, he also emphasizes the general malleability of sex roles and religious leadership in African society and religion.

Ruth Landes's *The City of Women* (1947)—based on fieldwork conducted in northern Brazil during the late 1930s—challenged prevailing notions of Afro-Brazilian religious leadership, as well as shedding light on the roles of women in these organizations. Her work was first published in 1947. Both the work and its author were largely ignored and never entered into the mainstream of Afro-Brazilian studies then dominated by Herskovits, Verger, and Bastide. Some critiques of Landes's book took the form of personal attack. She was accused of going to Bahia primarily to have sex with the natives. The charges against her were unfounded since the focus of her research was on celibate, female religious orders. Treatment of Landes's work has been redressed, at least in part, by the 1994 reissue of *The City of Women* by the University of New Mexico Press, with a new introduction that gives a history of the anthropological reception to the work. In 1947, Landes established once and for all the malleability of sex roles and leadership in Afro-Brazilian religious organizations, and, by implication, in Caribbean religions as well. But it has taken scholars fifty years to recognize her role.

Malleability of sex roles is apparent in New World religions like Ṣango. In Cuba, and now in Trinidad, Ṣango has become increasingly identified with Santa Barbara. In attempting to account for Ṣango's identification with Santa Barbara, Ṣango leaders (both male and female) emphasize that *oriṣas* are not limited by human categories and attributes. All *oriṣas* have the potential to be male and female, black and white, and young and old. In Trinidad, for example, Ṣango is often depicted as a mulatto. Trinidadian followers of Ṣango—like Ṣango devotees in Cuba (Bascom, 1972, p. 14)—argue that Ṣango may wear the clothes of a woman, but he is the epitome of maleness because of his many wives and love affairs. It is emphasized that Ṣango has many names because he used different names as he went from town to town seeking out amorous adventures. Bourguignon suggests that Herskovits did not foreground transvestitism and homosexuality in his depictions of African and African-American rituals because he believed it would be detrimental to the cause of blacks in the United States.

Landes concluded *The City of Women* by noting that women occupy dominant positions within supposedly patriarchal structures. Her findings for Bahia indicate that surface male authority hid real female authority. But it is not an either/or situation. Males and females have different conceptions of power and authority. A real question is whether or not scholars have grasped the true nature of female religious authority in the Caribbean. Women constitute the overwhelming majority of adherents in all of these faiths. The anthropological literature characterizes these religions—following Lanternari and Lewis—as "peripheral" cults. But what is meant by "peripheral"? Are these religions considered "peripheral" because they are predominantly composed of females (which is Lanternari's assertion), or are females attracted to these religions because women see them as "peripheral"

(which is Lewis's argument)? The relationship between gender, power, and authority is always complex. Lewis's original research on spirit possession and gender wars in Somalia concluded that spirit possession provides a mechanism by which the weak can appropriate symbols of power. But as Bourguignon has pointed out, Lewis's theory is predicated on a shared understanding and acceptance of how the world works.

Unlike many issues in the academic study of religion, debates about gender and authority can be resolved empirically, with attention to denominational structures and the place of women within these structures. For over twenty years, Stephen D. Glazier has examined the position of women among Trinidad's Ṣango Baptists. The results are clear. Women constitute the overwhelming majority of participants in all Ṣango Baptist rituals, and women own the vast majority of Ṣango Baptist religious structures (Baptist churches, *palais,* and *chapelles*). How could this not affect the status of Ṣango Baptist women? It should be emphasized that while women may own the buildings outright, they do not always own the land upon which these structures rest. But even if we do not count cases where men actually own the land, women still own over 58 percent of the buildings (twenty-eight out of forty-six in Glazier's 1999 sample of Ṣango structures in Trinidad), and they sponsor over half the feasts.

Previous generations of researchers looked for male dominance within Ṣango Baptist organizations, and they found it. The trappings are there. Almost all paramount leaders and bishops are male. Only males are allowed to perform the sacraments; only males are allowed to preach from a raised pulpit in the front of the church; only males are allowed to "line-out" hymns and direct readings from the Bible; and only males can initiate prayer. In a number of Ṣango Baptist churches, participants are segregated according to sex (males sit on the right, females sit on the left). On the other hand, males are usually *invited* (by females) to officiate at religious ceremonies. The do not own the churches. They are guests. And if the predominantly female congregation is not pleased, they will not be invited back—suggesting that power relations between males and females are not always as they at first appear.

ORAL TRADITION AND THE INTERNET. Throughout the twentieth century, African languages constituted a major barrier for some researchers and some informants. Many of the difficulties that George Eaton Simpson encountered while compiling a list of *oriṣa* in Trinidad were a result of his lack of familiarity with the Yorùbá language. In reproducing a list of *oriṣas,* for example, Simpson names Adoweh, Ahmeeoh, Aireeahsan, and Aireelay (1980, p. 17). He cautions the reader that he is unsure if these names represent a single *oriṣa* or four separate *oriṣas.* Only recently (Warner-Lewis, 1996) have scholars begun to utilize linguistic analyses to document the religious significance of Yorùbá retentions in the Caribbean.

There are also issues surrounding oral transmission. At the time Herskovits, Bascom, Simpson, and Frances Henry conducted their research, most religious knowledge was transmitted orally. Past generations of *oriṣa* leaders in Trinidad (e.g., Fitzroy Small and King Ford) knew little Yorùbá aside from the opening songs they had learned by rote. This contrasts with contemporary *oriṣa* leaders—like Rawle Gibbons and Patricia McLeod (Iya Ṣango Wumi)—who have formally studied Yorùbá.

As Manfred Kremser (2001, pp. 111–114) points out in his discussion of African-derived religions in cyberspace, new technologies have transformed Caribbean worldviews and ritual systems into new forms of world culture. This, too, raises issues of authority and legitimacy as greater numbers of non-black, non-Caribbean people are identifying with African-derived religions like Santería, vodun, or the *oriṣa* movement. Aboriginal religions have also secured a presence on the web. The Santa Rosa Carib community of Trinidad, for example, maintains an elaborate website with New Zealand anthropologist Maximilian Forte as their webmaster. What happens when religious traditions that have been transmitted orally from person-to-person become instantly accessible via the internet?

CENTRALIZATION AND "AUTHORITY" IN THE TRINIDAD *ORIṢA* MOVEMENT. Some contemporary followers of the *oriṣa* have expressed a desire to "liberate" the *oriṣa* from Catholicism and to reassert what they see as its fundamental Yorùbá elements. They seek to emphasize Yorùbá elements at shrines and expunge Catholic ones. Such attempts on the part of African-American religious leaders have met with varying degrees of success elsewhere in the New World.

Funso Aiyejina and Rawle Gibbons underscore a major difference between *oriṣa* ceremonies held in Africa and *oriṣa* ceremonies held in the New World: "Among the Yoruba of Nigeria, each individual/family/community is associated with a particular *oriṣa.* In Trinidad, all or as many of the *oriṣa* as possible are represented in the yard" (1999, p. 195). Aiyejina and Gibbons interpret this as the "unification of Orisa under one roof." This may be an oversimplification, but it is nonetheless an important distinction. *Oriṣa* feasts in the Caribbean tend to be inclusive rather than exclusive. One of the more dramatic expressions of inclusiveness is to be found in the Nation Dance—one of the most studied of Caribbean rituals (see McDaniel, 1998).

Frances Henry, who has conducted research on Ṣango for nearly fifty years, concluded her entry to *The Encyclopedia of African and African American Religions* (2001, pp. 256–258) by noting that contemporary leaders in the *oriṣa* movement are attempting to create centralized structures along denominational lines (e.g., to establish an "Oriṣa Council of Elders"). Adherents want the *oriṣa* movement to be recognized as a "legitimate" religion by the Trinidadian government so that their *iya* and *mongba* can officiate at weddings and funerals.

Henry (2003, pp. 108–136) also documented a concerted effort to "Africanize" *orișa* rituals. While scholarly debates surrounding the origins and authenticity of New World African ritual are far from new (Glazier, 1996, pp. 420–421), current debates are more significant because the major participants are themselves members of the religions in question. This establishes a different tone to the debate, and there is greater perceived urgency. A major change is that the forum of debate has shifted. Debate is no longer carried out exclusively within the domain of books, conferences, and paper presentations. It occurs in heated arguments taking place within the context of worship itself.

BIBLIOGRAPHY

Aiyejina, Funso, and Rawle Gibbons. "Orișa (Orisha) Tradition in Trinidad." Paper presented at the Ninth International Orișa Congress, Port of Spain, Trinidad, 1999.

Barnes, Sandra T. *Africa's Ogun: Old World and New.* Bloomington, Ind., 1989; 2d ed., 1997.

Barrett, Leonard. *The Rastafarians: Sounds of Cultural Dissonance.* Boston, 1977; 2d ed., 1988.

Bascom, William. *Shango in the New World.* Austin, Tex., 1972.

Becker, Charles D., Geoffrey W. Conrad, and John W. Foster. "Taino Use of Flooded Caverns in the East National Park Region, Dominican Republic." *Journal of Caribbean Archaeology* 3 (2002): 1–26.

Beckwith, Martha Warren. *Black Roadways: A Study of Jamaican Folk Life.* New Haven, 1929.

Bisnauth, Dale. *History of Religions in the Caribbean.* Kingston, Jamaica, 1989.

Bourguignon, Erika. *Possession.* San Francisco, 1976.

Bourguignon, Erika. "Relativism and Ambivalence in the Work of M. J. Herskovits." *Ethnos* 28, no. 1 (2000): 103–114.

Carmichael, Mrs. A. C. *Domestic Manners and Social Conditions of the White, Colored, and Negro Population of the West Indies.* London, 1833.

Castor, Nicole. "Virtual Community: The Orișa Tradition in the New World and Cyberspace." Paper presented at the Ninth International Orișa Congress, Port of Spain, Trinidad, 1999.

Chevannes, Barry. *Rastafari: Roots and Ideology.* Syracuse, N.Y., 1994.

Chireau, Yvonne. *Black Magic: Religion and the African American Conjuring Tradition.* Berkeley, 2003.

Clarke, Kamari Maxine. *Mapping Yorùbá Networks: Power and Agency in the Making of Transnational Communities.* Durham, N.C., 2004.

Conner, Randy P., with David Hatfield Sparks. *Queering Creole Spiritual Traditions: Lesbian, Gay, Bisexual, and Transgender Participation in African-Inspired Traditions in the Americas.* Binghamton, N.Y., 2004.

Davis, Wade. *The Serpent and the Rainbow.* New York, 1985.

Dayan, Joan. *Haiti, History, and the Gods.* Berkeley, 1995.

Dayfoot, Arthur Charles. *The Shaping of the West Indian Church.* Mona, Jamaica, 1999.

Deren, Maya. *Divine Horseman: The Living Gods of Haiti.* New York, 1953.

Desmangles, Leslie G. *The Faces of the Gods: Vodou and Roman Catholicism in Haiti.* Chapel Hill, N.C., 1993.

Du Bois, W. E. B. *The Souls of Black Folk.* Chicago, 1903.

Dunn, Oliver, and James A. Kelley Jr., trans. and eds. *The Diario of Christopher Columbus's First Voyage to America, 1492–1493.* Norman, Okla., 1988.

Frazier, E. Franklin. *The Negro Church in America.* New York, 1964.

Gibbons, Rawle. "Introduction and Welcome." Paper presented at the Ninth International Orișa Congress, Port of Spain, Trinidad, 1999.

Glazier, Stephen D. "The Religious Mosaic: Playful Celebration in Trindadian Shango." *Play and Culture* 1 (1988): 216–235.

Glazier, Stephen D. *Marchin' the Pilgrims Home: A Study of the Spiritual Baptists of Trinidad.* Salem, Wis., 1991.

Glazier, Stephen D. "New World African Ritual: Genuine and Spurious." *Journal for the Scientific Study of Religion* 35, no. 4 (1996): 420–431.

Glazier, Stephen D., ed. *The Encyclopedia of African and African American Religions.* New York, 2001.

Greenfield, Sidney M., and André Droogers. *Reinventing Religions: Syncretism and Transformation in Africa and the Americas.* New York, 2002.

Hall, Stuart. "Cultural Identity and Diaspora Identity." In *Identity: Community, Culture, Difference,* edited by Jonathan Rutherford, pp. 222–237. London, 1990.

Henry, Frances. "The Orisha (Shango) Movement in Trinidad." In *The Encyclopedia of African and African American Religions,* edited by Stephen D. Glazier, pp. 256–258. New York, 2001.

Henry, Frances. *Reclaiming African Religions in Trinidad: The Socio-Political Legitimization of the Orisha and Spiritual Baptist Faiths.* Mona, Jamaica, 2003.

Herskovits, Melville J. *Life in a Haitian Valley.* New York, 1937.

Herskovits, Melville J. *Acculturation: the Study of Culture Contact.* New York, 1938.

Herskovits, Melville J., and Frances Herskovits. *Trinidad Village.* New York, 1947.

Houk, James T. *Spirits, Blood, and Drums: The Orisha Religion in Trinidad.* Philadelphia, 1995.

Hucks, Tracey E. "Trinidad, Africa-Derived Religions in." In *The Encyclopedia of African and African American Religions,* edited by Stephen D. Glazier, pp. 338–343. New York, 2001.

Hurbon, Laënnec. *Voodoo: Search for the Spirit.* Translated by Lori Frankel. New York, 1995.

Khan, Aisha. *Callaloo Nation: Metaphors of Race and Religious Identity among South Asians in Trinidad.* Durham, N.C., 2004.

Klass, Morton. "When God Can Do Anything: Belief Systems in Collision." *Anthropology of Consciousness* 2 (1991): 3–34.

Klass, Morton. *Singing with Sai Baba: Politics of Revitalization in Trinidad.* Boulder, Colo., 1996.

Kremser, Manfred. "Cyberspace, African and African-Derived Religions in." In *The Encyclopedia of African and African American Religions,* edited by Stephen D. Glazier, pp. 111–114. New York, 2001.

Laguerre, Michel. *Voodoo and Politics in Haiti.* New York, 1989.

Landes, Ruth. *The City of Women.* New York, 1947; reprint, Albuquerque, N.Mex., 1994.

Lanternari, Vittorio. *The Religions of the Oppressed: A Study of Modern Messianic Cults.* Translated by Lisa Sergio. New York, 1963.

Lewis, I. M. *Ecstatic Religion.* Middlesex, U.K., 1971; 3d ed., London and New York, 2003.

Leyburn, James. *The Haitian People.* New Haven, 1941; rev. ed., 1966.

Lum, Kenneth A. *Praising His Name in the Dance: Spirit Possession in the Spiritual Baptist Faith and Orisha Work in Trinidad, West Indies.* Amsterdam, 2000.

Matory, J. Lorand. *Sex and the Empire that Is No More: Gender and the Politics of Metaphor in Oyo Yoruba Religion.* Minneapolis, 1994.

McAlister, Elizabeth. *Rara!: Vodou, Power, and Performance in Haiti and Its Diaspora.* Berkeley, 2002.

McDaniel, Lorna. *The Big Drum Ritual of Carriacou: Praisesongs in Memory of Flight.* Gainesville, Fla., 1998.

McLeod, Patricia (Iya Ṣango Wumi). "World Congress—Caribbean Report." Paper presented at the Ninth International Oriṣa Congress, Port of Spain, Trinidad, 1999.

Métraux, Alfred. *Voodoo in Haiti.* Translated by Hugo Charteris. New York, 1959.

Mintz, Sidney, and Richard Price. *An Anthropological Approach to the Afro-American Past: The Birth of African American Culture—An Anthropological Perspective.* Boston, 1992.

Mischel (Henry), Frances. "African Powers in Trinidad: The Shango Cult." *Anthropological Quarterly* 30 (1958): 45–59.

Murphy, Joseph M. *Working the Spirit: Ceremonies of the African Diaspora.* Boston, 1994.

Rouse, Irving. *The Tainos: Rise and Decline of the People Who Greeted Columbus.* New Haven, 1992.

Seabrook, William B. *The Magic Island.* New York, 1929.

Simpson, George Eaton. *Religious Cults of the Caribbean: Trinidad, Jamaica, and Haiti.* 3d ed. Rio Piedras, Puerto Rico, 1980.

Thornton, John K. *The Kingdom of Kongo: Civil War and Transition, 1641–1718.* Madison, Wis., 1983.

Trotman, David. "The Yoruba and Orisha Worship in Trinidad and British Guiana, 1938–1970." *African Studies Review* 19, no. 2 (1976): 1–17.

Verger, Pierre. *Flux et reflux de la traite des nègres entre le Golfe de Bénin et Bahia de Todos los Santos, du XVIIe au XIXe siècle.* The Hague, 1968.

Vertovec, Steven. *Hindu Trinidad: Religion, Ethnicity, and Socio-Economic Change.* London, 1992.

Warner-Lewis, Maureen. *Trinidad Yoruba: From Mother Tongue to Memory.* Tuscaloosa, Ala., 1996.

Williams, Joseph J. *Voodoos and Obeahs: Phases of West Indian Witchcraft.* New York, 1932.

Wilson, Samuel M. *Hispaniola: Caribbean Chiefdoms in the Age of Columbus.* Tuscaloosa, Ala., 1990.

Yawney, Carole, and John P. Homiak. "Rastafari in Global Context." In *The Encyclopedia of African and African American Religions*, edited by Stephen D. Glazier, pp. 266–268. New York, 2001.

Zuckerman, Philip. *Du Bois on Religion.* Lanham, Md., 2000.

STEPHEN D. GLAZIER (2005)

CHING, JULIA (1934–2001), a scholar of comparative religion, was one of the major contributors in the last three decades of the twentieth century to the Western world's understanding of Chinese religions, especially Confucianism, and their dialogue with Christianity.

Julia Ching was born on October 15, 1934, in Shanghai, and completed her high school education in Hong Kong before she studied at the College of New Rochelle in New York, majoring in history, philosophy, and theology. She completed a master's degree in European History at the Catholic University of America in Washington, D.C. Ching's intellectual curiosity and spiritual openness led her to a progressively deeper knowledge of Western culture and Christianity, culminating in her service as an Ursuline nun for two decades.

In 1971, Ching obtained her Ph.D. degree in Asian studies at the Australian National University in Canberra with a thesis later published in 1976 as *To Acquire Wisdom: The Way of Wang Yang-ming.* She started her academic career first as a lecturer at Australian National University (1969–1974), then as visiting associate professor at Columbia University (1974–1975), and later as associate professor of philosophy at Yale University (1975–1979). Finally she moved to the University of Toronto (1978–2000), first as visiting associate professor in 1978. Ching was tenured in 1979 and promoted to a professorship in 1981 in the Department of Religion; she was cross-appointed to the Department of East Asian Studies in 1979 and the Department of Philosophy in 1990. For her eminent scholarly achievement, she was elected a fellow of the Royal Society of Canada in 1990, named University Professor of the University of Toronto in 1994, selected to be the inaugural holder of the R. C. and E. Y. Lee Chair of Chinese Thought and Culture at the University of Toronto in 1998, and finally named a member of the Order of Canada in July 2000. She died on October 26, 2001, in Toronto, after a long battle with cancer.

Through her intellectual work Ching attempted to bridge China and the West on the level of philosophy and religion by her unceasing quest of wisdom. For her, when interpreting Wang Yangming, wisdom is,

> the harmony and purity of the mind-and-heart, perfect in its spontaneity, true to its pristine nature. Wisdom is also the proven ability of dealing with a variety of human situations according to an inborn moral intuition, developed and realized to its fullest by earnest self-cultivation, unchanging in its constant attachment to goodness and virtue, and yet flexible in its judgment of variables and in its freedom of decision. (1976, p. 73)

More effort was made by Ching to launch scholarly religious dialogue between representatives of Chinese religions and

Christianity. Her *Confucianism and Christianity: A Comparative Study* (1977) is a great contribution to the dialogue between Confucianism and Christianity. *Christianity and Chinese Religion* (1989), a major work she coauthored with Hans Küng, provided some fundamental perspectives for the dialogue of the three major Chinese religions—Confucianism, Daoism, and Buddhism—with Christianity. For her, these traditions challenge all of us to redefine "religion," not only as something related to God, but also and especially "as a striving for self-transcendence that remains open to Heaven, to the Great Ultimate, to the True Self and to the Pure Land" (1989, p. 229).

Apart from these scholarly works in religious dialogue, Ching was an expert in Confucianism, especially neo-Confucianism. She began by studying Wang Yangming (1472–1529), a neo-Confucian of idealist orientation in the Ming dynasty. She edited with her own major contribution the English translation of the *Records of Ming Scholars* by Huang Zongxi (1610–1695). In 2000, she published *The Religious Thought of Chu Hsi*, focusing on the great neo-Confucian of realist orientation in the Song dynasty, Zhu Xi (1130–1200). This book was her last major work, and it gave an excellent interpretation and reconstruction of the religious thought of Zhu Xi, focusing on issues such as the Great Ultimate, spiritual beings, rituals, personal cultivation, and Zhu Xi's relation with Daoism and Buddhism.

Instead of clinging to either the idealist or the realist neo-Confucianists, Ching made an effort to draw out the best of their wisdom. She paid special attention to the religious dimension of human experience, though she always equilibrated it with humanistic philosophical reflections. She had a humanist concern for religion, with a hope that the human person could transcend himself or herself up to a better world by self-cultivation, a holistic world vision, and good governance.

The "sage" was one of her focuses in studying Chinese religions. In *Mysticism and Kingship in China* (1997), she mediated religion, philosophy, and politics by working on the myth of the sage and its relation to kingship in China. She examined shamanic kingship and kingship as cosmic paradigm, and the sage both as moral teacher and as metaphysician. The idea of the sage-king had deeply influenced not only Chinese political philosophy but also self-cultivation and family life. She explored all these with a sense of critique, showing that the idea of the sage had, like benevolent despotism in the West, hindered the development of democracy in China, which was also one of her major concerns. Nevertheless, the "sage" is, more essential for her, an invitation to find our own identity "in a continuous effort of self-transcendence."

Approaching the end of her life, Ching showed in her autobiography *The Butterfly Healing* (1998) a comprehensive and altruistic understanding of wisdom, in saying that, "Meaning is also called wisdom, even compassion—loving others as we do ourselves, or at least trying to do so. Call it Buddhism, Taoism, or Christianity. The labels don't matter. Meaning is found in living and loving, in giving and receiving, and hopefully, also in dying when the time comes" (p. 218).

See Also Chinese Religion, overview article; Confucianism, article on History of Study; Zhu Xi.

Bibliography

Ching, Julia, trans. and ed. *The Philosophical Letters of Wang Yang-ming*. Canberra, 1972. An excellent English translation of selected letters of Wang Yangming, which are indispensable sources for understanding his philosophy.

Ching, Julia. *To Acquire Wisdom: The Way of Wang Yang-ming*. New York, 1976. The first full-length study of the philosophical and religious thoughts of Wang Yangming, developed from the author's Ph.D. thesis completed in 1971.

Ching, Julia. *Confucianism and Christianity: A Comparative Study*. Tokyo, 1977. Lays the historical and philosophical foundations of dialogue between Confucianism and Christianity, focusing especially on problems of Man, God and self-transcendence.

Ching, Julia, trans. and ed. *The Records of Ming Scholars*. By Huang Zongxi; a selected translation, edited with the collaboration of Chaoying Fang. Honolulu, 1987. A selective translation of historical documentation and some essential works of famous Confucians in the Ming dynasty, edited by Huang Zongxi.

Ching, Julia. *Probing China's Soul: Religion, Politics, and Protest in the People's Republic*. San Francisco, 1990. Deals with problems of politics, culture, and religion related to the student movement and Tiananmen massacre of June 1989.

Ching, Julia. *Chinese Religions*. Maryknoll, N.Y., 1993. A general survey of major religious traditions in China.

Ching, Julia. *Mysticism and Kingship in China: The Heart of Chinese Wisdom*. Cambridge, U.K., 1997. Examines the sage-king myth and ideal and their historical transformation in China.

Ching, Julia. *The Butterfly Healing: A Life between East and West*. Maryknoll, N.Y., 1998. An intellectual autobiography focusing on Ching's life experiences between East and West.

Ching, Julia. *The Religious Thought of Chu Hsi*. New York, 2000. Gives the most updated interpretation and reconstruction of the religious thought of Zhu Xi, focusing on issues such as the Great Ultimate, spiritual beings, rituals, personal cultivation, and Zhu Xi's relation with Daoism and Buddhism.

Küng, Hans, and Julia Ching. *Christentum und Chinesische Religion*. Munich, 1988. Translated into English as *Christianity and Chinese Religion* (New York, 1989). An excellent survey and analysis of problems involved in the potential dialogue of Christianity with the three major Chinese religious traditions.

Shen, Vincent, and Willard Oxtoby, eds. *Wisdom in China and the West*. Washington, D.C., 2004. Contains twenty papers presented for the international conference held at the University of Toronto on November 21–22, 2002, in memory of Julia Ching. Includes contributions from authors such as Hans Küng, Robert Neville, Alan Segal, John Berthrong, and Livia Kohn, some specifically on Julia Ching's thought.

Vincent Shen (2005)

DIVINATION: IFA DIVINATION

The Yorùbá people of southwestern Nigeria possess a highly complex divination system called *Ifa.* Ifa is a central feature of Yorùbá religion, culture, and society, and it constitutes a main source for their knowledge, cosmology, and belief system. Ifa refers to both the divination practice and the Yorùbá god of divination, also called Ọrunmila. Ifa divination is also practiced among other West African peoples, especially the Fon people of the Republic of Benin. Divination is a ritual performance in which the priest-diviner, the clients, and the social and cosmological order of the Yorùbá people interact to produce meaningful results to a client's quest and purpose for consultation. Consultation takes place when a client inquires of the supernatural order concerning problems or issues that are not quite clear to the client. Typically, clients inquire about illness, auspicious marriages, a planned journey, or choice of the succeeding king. No dilemma or issue is too small or complex in traditional Yorùbá society to lend itself to consulting Ifa. The rationale for such depth of trust and promise is based in Yorùbá cosmology and moral order, which entrusted the Ifa deity with the knowledge of all that exists in the universe. Ifa is personified as the all-knowing historian, storyteller, and intermediary between the gods and the people. Ifa represents the people's intellectual deity and the public relations officer of the Yorùbá pantheon.

Furthermore, Ifa's role and function as an omnipotent healer in Yorùbá society is highly esteemed. Through the agency of Ifa, healing takes place when a diviner successfully diagnoses the source of a client's illness, and prescribes and carries out the appropriate sacrifice. The Ifa divination process begins when a client consults a diviner, and the diviner casts the divining chain (*opele*) on the divining mat or uses a set of sixteen palm nuts to arrive at a solution. The result of divination is referred to as the Signature or Signs of Ifa, which in principle may be one of 256 possible signs, forming a double tetragram produced by manipulating the sixteen palm nuts of the divining chain. With his finger, the diviner traces the Signs of Ifa, now discernible in the yellow divining powder (*iyerosun*) sprinkled over the surface of the divining tray (*opon Ifá*). Thus, the diviner pronounces the results, and chanting, he recites the message of the Signature of the Ifa deity who appears in the process. The diviner explains the message to the client, prescribing appropriate sacrifices to be carried out. During long and intensive periods of apprenticeship, which may take from fifteen to thirty years or more, the priest-diviners memorize a comprehensive repertoire of complex Ifa verses.

Scholarly study of Ifa divination began with William Bascom when he carried out his fieldwork on Yorùbá social organization in Ile-Ifẹ, Nigeria, and other parts of Yorùbáland between 1936 and 1938. He began publishing his research, with his major works *Ifa Divination: Communication between Gods and Men in West Africa* (1969) and *Sixteen Cowries: Yorùbá Divination from Africa to the New World* (1980). Other scholarly works also appeared, such as Wande Abimbola's *Ifá: An Exposition of Ifá Literary Corpus* (1976) and *Ifá Divination Poetry* (1977). Abimbola, more than anyone else, gave Ifa divination the prestige it enjoys in the academic world today.

Today a large body of timeless Ifa poetry—safeguarded remarkably only in the memory of individual oral historians—has been collected, transcribed, and translated into English and French. Stored in these principal oral texts, the verses are now used as sources for exploring the moral order and ritual practices of the Yorùbá people. Representing a significant genre of oral traditions as far back as ancient times, Ifa verses represent compilations of myths, legends, proverbs, songs, and praise poetry. They signify numerous themes, events, occasions, and places in Yorùbá culture and history, such as mythic and historical characters, migration stories, and biographies of cultural heroes, ancestors, animals, and such natural phenomena as trees, groves, and rivers. They also refer to ethical and aesthetic ideas, philosophy, and metaphors, and to sacred journeys carried out by famous ancient diviners. The Yorùbá themselves regard the Ifa verses as their primary source of instructions for daily life. The verses constitute the Yorùbá encyclopedia of knowledge through the interpretation of these texts, and scholars are now examining many deep-seated values and concerns in Yorùbá culture and society.

A number of interpretive works have emerged reflecting on various aspects of Ifa indigenous knowledge and Yorùbá theory of knowledge in the Ifa divination texts. Among them are Philip Peek's edited volume, *African Divination Systems* (1991), and J. O. Sodipe and Barry Hallen's *Knowledge, Belief, and Witchcraft* (1986). As comprehensive collections and interpretations of Ifa verses, these works enable us to have a better understanding of Yorùbá systems of thought and culture. We are able to interpret Yorùbá-derived religions in the Americas, called Santería (Afro-Cuban), Candomblé (Afro-Brazilian), and Vodou (Afro-Haitian)—all of which are making significant inroads in the United States.

In the United States, there is a remarkable renaissance of Yorùbá religion, especially in major urban centers. Though often classified and labeled as a popular religion, American adherents often refer to the Yorùbá tradition as *Orisa* tradition, as it is becoming an alternative religious and devotional system for African Americans, Latinos, and some European Americans. The Ifa divination system is the central focus of these traditions. *Orisa* devotees are eager to acquire Ifa divination texts for devotional practices and religious education.

A case in point was Jacob Olupona's encounter with devotees of the *Orisa* Yorùbá tradition. In April 1994, at the invitation of the Phoebe Hearst Museum of Anthropology at the University of California, Berkeley, he gave a seminar titled "Ifa: Owner of the Day and Regulator of the Universe." After this presentation, he was besieged by many *Orisa* devotees who had come from as far as Oakland, San Francisco, and Los Angeles. They wanted to know where

they could obtain access to Ifa divination texts. His response then was that he was mainly interested in the scholarly study of Ifa divination analysis.

Early in the twenty-first century, increasing numbers of *Orișa* devotees in the United States express great demands for Ifa divination texts. Popular demand for Ifa materials is indicated by the very large number of internet websites appearing on Ifa. Yorùbá religion is in the process of achieving the status of a global religion, undergoing similar transformations that the scriptural traditions of Hinduism and Buddhism went through before they reached their present "canonical" status. That is, they existed first primarily as oral texts, and subsequently were written down to assist the Yorùbá in the diaspora who are cut off from the home and source of the tradition.

The iconography of Ifa divination is the subject of investigation by art historians Rowland Abiodun, John Pemberton, and Henry Drewal—to mention just a few. Not only are Ifa divination objects used as instruments of divination, but they also are regarded as objects of aesthetic and metaphysical value. In Ifa oral poetry, the fly-whisk, the divination tray, and the diviner's satchel are also interpreted as ornamental objects, bestowing honor and prestige on Ifa and on Ifa diviners, who are members of an elite class in traditional Yorùbá societies.

Rowland Abiodun (1975) and others have elaborated on the artistic use of Ifa paraphernalia and divining objects. The most important are the *opon Ifá* (divination tray), the *iroke* (fly-whisk), the *opa Osun* (the diviner's iron working stick), and the *apo Ifá* (diviner's bag), without which proper divination cannot take place. A cursory look at these religious and art objects reveals that most of them are expressed in the female form, described as the "wives" of Ifa. Numerous Yorùbá oral traditions show the symbolic and cultural contexts in which Ifa objects are portrayed as female, rather than male, clearly indicating the significance of gendered meaning of Ifa objects in Ifa divination theory and practice.

Bibliography

Abimbola, Wande. *Ifá: An Exposition of Ifá Literary Corpus.* New York and Ibadan, Nigeria, 1976.

Abimbola, Wande, trans. and ed. *Ifá Divination Poetry.* New York, 1977.

Abiodun, Rowland. "Ifa Art Objects: An Interpretation Based on Oral Tradition." In *Yorùbá Oral Tradition: Selections from the Papers Presented at the Seminar on Yorùbá Oral Tradition, Poetry in Music, Dance, and Drama,* edited by Wande Abimbola, pp. 421–469. Ile-Ifẹ, Nigeria, 1975.

Adeoye, C. L. *Ìgbàgbọ́ àti Ẹ̀sìn Yorùba.* Ibadan, Nigeria, 1985.

Bascom, William. *Ifa Divination: Communication between Gods and Men in West Africa.* Bloomington, Ind., 1969; reprint, 1991.

Bascom, William. *Sixteen Cowries: Yorùbá Divination from Africa to the New World.* Bloomington, Ind., 1980.

Du Bois, John. "Meaning without Intension: Lessons from Divination." In *Responsibility and Evidence in Oral Discourse,* edited by Jane H. Hall and Judith Irvine, pp. 48–71. Cambridge, U.K., 1994.

Hallen, Barry, and J. O. Sodipe. *Knowledge, Belief, and Witchcraft: Analytic Experiments in African Philosophy.* London, 1986; reprint, Stanford, Calif., 1997.

Olupona, Jacob K. "Owner of the Day and Regulator of the Universe: Ifa Divination and Healing among the Yorùbá of Southwestern Nigeria." In *Divination and Healing: Potent Vision,* edited by Michael Winkelman and Philip M. Peek, pp. 103–117. Tucson, Ariz., 2004.

Peek, Philip M., ed. *African Divination Systems: Ways of Knowing.* Bloomington, Ind., 1991.

Pemberton, John, ed. *Insight and Artistry in African Divination.* Washington, D.C., 2000.

Jacob Olupona (2005)

FICTION: SOUTH ASIAN FICTION AND RELIGION

The various literary forms in which narrative, plot-centered literature is found pose challenges to any attempt to delineate the domain of what could be called South Asian "fiction" (see Preminger and Brogan, 1993). Whereas dramatic texts in South Asian literature are easily distinguishable from narrative ones through the orchestration of direct speech and their performance, the boundaries between texts such as sermons and narrative literature on the one hand, and poetry and narrative literature on the other, are much more difficult to draw. In fact, storytelling from the Vedic hymns to the epic *Mahābhārata* and *Rāmāyaṇa,* the mainly theistic and proto-historical Purāṇas and chronicles *(vaṃśa),* and the hagiographies of medieval devotional literature have been generally recorded in metric poetry. Early South Asian prose is primarily used in doctrinal contexts, such as the Upaniṣads, the Brāhmaṇas, the commentarial literature, and the Jaina and Buddhist sermons and birth stories *(jātaka),* as well as in the collections of didactic fables, *Pañcatantra* and *Hitopadeśa.*

The spread of birth stories and didactic literature in South Asia around the beginning of the Common Era was an important step in creating new literary forms and in canonizing so-called folk narrative material, which had not found its way into the epics or the Purāṇas. All these forms of narrative, both in meter and in prose, betray their oral roots not so much because they are older than writing in South Asia, but because the constitution and the tradition of the texts can largely be explained by their continued oral performance. The single work with possibly the greatest influence on South Asian fictional literature is Guṇāḍhya's third-century Śaivite collection of stories, the monumental *Bṛhatkathā* (Great tale), said to have been composed in a Prakrit called Paiśācī, probably in Eastern India, and lost but partly translated and conserved in Sanskrit and several other regional languages. Its extant successors are Somadeva's tenth-century Kaśmīri work *Kathāsaritsāgara*

(The ocean of story), as well as Śivadāsa's tenth-century *Vetālapañcaviṃsatikā* (The twenty-five tales of the demon), both collections of mainly satirical stories with a Śaivite-Tantric background and a strong anti-ascetic, particularly anti-Jaina, tendency.

The development of a court-centered written *kāvya* literature starting from the turn of the sixth to seventh centuries CE included the introduction of a new narrative literature in prose, termed *Kunstroman* by German-speaking Indologists (Winternitz, 1909–1920), which consists mostly of collections of picaresque tales framed by a meta-narrative. Examples of this again mainly Śaivite and anti-ascetic fiction are Daṇḍin's *Daśakumāracarita* (The deeds of the ten princes), Subandhu's *Vāsavadatta*, and Bāṇa's *Harṣacarita* (The deeds of Harṣa) and *Kādambarī*, all from the seventh century. The extensive Jaina narrative literature in both Middle Indic (Prakrit, Apabhrāṃśa) and Modern Indic languages, covering *Kunstroman*, didactic, and hagiographical literature intimately connected to the practice of preaching, constitutes the oldest unbroken tradition of prose storytelling in South Asia. However, it is hagiography that became the most widespread and influential narrative literary form between the twelfth and the eighteenth centuries, spanning confessional and regional boundaries.

Fiction in the modern sense of the word, which includes the forms of the novel, the novella, the short story, and the travelogue, to name the most important ones, is a modern addition to South Asian literatures. It was first formulated in the fully developed modern South Asian languages, such as Hindi, Urdu, Bengali, and Tamil, toward the middle of the nineteenth century. Those forms would open a new perception of history, sharpen the eye for social conditions, and help constitute bourgeois subjectivity. Regarding the novel *(nāvil),* attempts have been made to connect this form with the Sanskritic *Kunstroman* named *kādaṃbarī* after that very work; or with the term *upanyāsa* (literally, "laying down"), the mostly religious *kathā* (instructive tale); or generally with the expression *purāṇa* (literally, "old"; viz., "tale"). On the other hand, Perso-Arabic influence, especially from the corpus of tales of romance and adventure known to the West as the "Tales From One Thousand Nights and One Night" can be traced already in medieval Jaina literature. However, the influence of literature brought to South Asia through the colonial encounter and the associated ruptures and discontinuities are at least as momentous as the indigenous literature is basic to the development of modern South Asian fiction. It appears that traditional modes of narrating were crucial where European models, like the realist or the gothic novel, did not entirely fit the South Asia context.

HINDI FICTION. In prose, Hindi fiction has its immediate precursors in seventeenth-century sectarian, mainly Vallabhan, hagiographies and literary tales in the tradition of the *Hitopadeśa* in Brajbhāṣā, as well as Sikh chronicles in Khaṛī bolī, before which there is little use of prose at all. Interestingly, the first text apparently free of colonial influences and still classifiable as a novel in this literary tradition is *Rānī Ketakī kī Kahānī* (The story of Queen Ketakī, 1801) by Inshā'allāh Khān, a princely love story written in Khaṛī bolī, in which all conflicts are eventually solved by the appearance of the king of gods, Indra. At the beginning of Hindi fiction toward the end of the nineteenth century stands the conflict between traditionalists *(sanātanists)* and reformers (Ārya Samājīs). The first novel claimed for Hindi literature, Lāl Śrīnivās Dās's *Parīkṣāguru* (Training as a teacher, 1882), thematizes education and status within a colonial setting as a process of mirroring, assimilation, and transformation, thus subverting the identity of the *gurū* as the traditional institution for learning and spiritual development.

An important focus for translations from Sanskrit and Bengali, among others, as well as for experimental fiction, was the Benares-based literary circle of the publicist and playwright Bhāratendu Hariścandra, the so-called Father of Modern Hindi, whose pleas for Vaiṣṇavism as the unifying religion for all Hindus had a strong impact on the ways early Hindi fiction would deal with religion. Yet, while Devakīnandan Khatrī's early best-sellers, *Candrakāntā* (1891) and *Candrakāntā santati* (1905), which present Hindu Rajput heroes in tales of adventure similar to the Persian *dāstān,* owe their success to a very low ideological profile, Premcand's early stories, partly written in Urdu around 1907, stress the moral superiority of Hindu, particularly Rajput women, along the lines of Vivekananda's arguments about the religious mission of Indian spirituality. The instrumentalization of religious virtues for nationalism inaugurated an equivocation that had repercussions on the treatment of religion in fiction for generations to come.

Mohandas Gandhi's influence on Hindi fiction, starting from his return from South Africa, cannot be underestimated. The utopian community with strong traits of the Hindu ascetic community *(āśrama)* became a topos in Hindi fiction, as in Premcand's *Sevādadan* (The house of service, 1918), where the context of joint-family and caste remain paramount and non-Hindus are regarded as a danger to moral standards. In contrast, Jayśankar Prasād's strongly contested *Kankāl* (The skeleton, 1929) starkly describes the moral degradation of Hindu society as part of a cosmic process understood within a Śaivite theological framework. As the Gandhian model lost its political weight, the religious and social foundations of family and society were critically revisited. Premcand's famous *Godān* (The gift of the cow, 1936), the story of the ruin of a dutiful Indian peasant, is in part a criticism aimed at the unscrupulous *brahman* to whom the dying farmer gifts his cow without ever having owned it.

Kedārnāth Pāṇḍey (also known as Rāhul Sānkṛtāyan), who would later convert to Buddhism, presented a Marxist interpretation of history in his novels *Sinha Senāpati* and *Jay Yaudheya* (both 1946), in which "capitalist" Hindu kingdoms defeat the "communist" Buddhist societies and religion becomes a mere marker for conflicting economic ideol-

ogies. Postindependence fiction saw a decline in religious themes as the lines set out by Premcand's *Godān* were followed and Hindu writers claimed to write out of a secular commitment. However, the Muslim Rāhi Masūm Razā's *Ādhā gāv* (Half a village, 1966), an account of the decline of Muslim supremacy, partition, and land reform divided into ten chapters after the ten assemblies of mourning *(muḥarram)* for the Shī'ī ancestor Ḥusayn in remembrance of his martyrdom at Karbala, is a powerful historical novel that thematizes Muslim self-perception within a supposedly secular nation. Influenced by the cycle of novels by Upendranāth Aśk about the protagonist Centan, which range from the late 1940s to the early 1970s, the late 1960s and 1970s saw a focus on the difficulties of the individual in coming to terms with religion within disintegrating familial and social structures, as in Nareś Methā's *Nadī zaśasvī* (The river is famous, 1967) or Sureś Sinhā's novel set in Delhi, *Patthāro kā śahar* (City of stones, 1971). However, this period also produced a revival of religious biographies, of which Tulsīdās's *Mānas kā hans* (The swan of the holy lake, 1972) by Nāgārjun is only one example.

URDU FICTION. The nineteenth century sees the start of Urdu fiction with anecdotal literature *(nakl* or *latifeh)* that tells stories of Ṣūfī saints and other semilegendary figures for didactic purposes, a genre that remained dominant until the early twentieth century. The late nineteenth century saw the rise of a modernist Urdu fiction and the first novels, its main representative being Nazīr Ahmad's *Ibn-ul-Vaqt* (The son of the moment, 1888), which advocates the free practice of religion and criticizes "superstitions" and traditional expressions of irrationalism. The nineteenth century also saw the rise of a genre of historical novels created by 'Abdul Halīm Sharar (*Malik-ul-'Azīz Varjana*, 1888) under the influence of Sir Walter Scott; these novels depicted historical heroes of the Islamic past. Religion acquired a new meaning in the context of the "two-nation theory," where Islam came to mark national identity. Qurratulain Hyder's pathbreaking novel *Āg ka Darya* (River of fire, 1959) is an example of how much of South Asian history can be absorbed into a predominantly Muslim narrative.

Postindependence Urdu fiction in India has focused increasingly on the problems and opportunities of multiple identities, as in Abdussamad's *A Strip of Land, Two Yards Long* (1997). However, it becomes more and more clear that it is not religiosity that lies at the heart of these texts, but political, economic, and social status, whereas religion becomes the setting within which stories of conflict and closure are narrated. Urdu fiction in Pakistan since independence has been dominated by the so-called Islamic novel *(islami nāvil)* in the tradition of Sharar, both immensely popular and patriotic, thus often associated with the official literary scene. On the other hand there are younger authors of fiction writing from within a Ṣūfī tradition who criticize forms of religion that quell dissent and foster passivity and complacency in matters of faith and society.

BENGALI FICTION. Bengali fiction dates back to the sixteenth-century *maṅgal kāvyas* with metrical narratives concerning local deities, including the triad of Candī, Manasa, and Dharma, as well as hagiographies of the Vaiṣṇava *bhakti* saint Caitanya. The beginnings of Bengali Islamic hagiographical fiction can be traced back to the same period with the *rasul carit* literature ("Deeds of the Prophet"), of which Syed Sultan's *Nābi Vaṃśa* is one important example. Modern Bengali prose narrative literature is to be understood within the context of the nineteenth-century Bengal Renaissance and its attempt to redefine religion as a major force in constituting Indian nationalism both as an agent of social reform and as directed against the colonizer. In Bankim Chattopadhyaya's novel *Ānanda maṭh* (Monastery of bliss, 1882) the revolt of a community of ascetics devoted to Kālī against the rule of the British is a barely disguised call for the retrieval of the empowering faith in the mother goddess *(vande mātaram)* lost in times of religious decadence and enslavement. In contrast, Rabindranath Tagore's depiction of religion in his fiction, *Gorā* (Horse, 1889) and *Ghare Bhine* (Home and world, 1892), mirrors the diverse and conflicting religious positions of his time, ranging from conservative Bengali Vaiṣṇavism to modernist utilitarian tendencies, rather than his own, which he saw represented in the universalist religiosity of the *bāuls*.

After Tagore, Bengali fiction witnessed the breakup of unifying religious visions and ambitions. In East Pakistan, Syed Walliullah's *Lāl salu* (Red shal tree, 1948) criticized the postindependence moves to exercise political control at the village level through the establishment of new religious shrines. Tasleema Nasreen's docu-novel *Lajjā* (Shame, 1993), a description of how Hindu identity is forced upon a non-Muslim middle-class family in Bangladesh as a consequence of the 1992 Indian anti-Muslim riots in Ayodhyā, is an example of the politicization of literature in a language that transcends the Hindu–Muslim divide. In contrast, besides developing a strong Marxist fiction with an antireligious bias, West Bengal literature produced Samares Baru's (Kalkut) *Amrit Kumbh* (Pot of nectar, 1960), an empathetic ethnographic novel in experimental prose on the forces of asceticism and community underlying the Kumbha Melā.

MODERN TAMIL FICTION. This form of South Asian fiction is said to begin with Veetanāyakam Piḷḷai's *Piratāpa Mutaliyār Carittiram* (The story of Piratāpa Mutaliyār, 1876), which is structured along the lines of the Sanskritic collection of stories within stories and deals with themes of socioreform, the importance of the mother, and the dangerous consequences of superstitious behavior within a plot dominated by romance. In his introduction Veetanāyakam Piḷḷai refers to paper in contrast to palm leaves as an opportunity for writing narratives that are long and in prose, qualities that he attributes to modern fiction. P. R. Rājam Aiyar's novel *Āpattukkiṭamāṉa apavātam, allatu Kamalāmpāl carittiram* (Kamalambal, or the fatal rumor, 1893–1895) introduces Balzacian realism in dealing with religious themes, avoiding the fantastic and accurately portraying South Indi-

an *brahman* home life while the main intention of the story is the popularizing of neo-Vedāntic ideas. The main source for conflict is slander and the transfer of social responsibilities to supernatural forces. Whereas both Piḷḷai's and Rājam Aiyar's works focus more on the problematic consequences of wrong religious practice, A. Māravaiyā's pathbreaking *Muttu Mīnākṣī* (1903), in which a *brahman* girl endures hardship, including widowhood, until her childhood friend shows her that there is scriptural sanction for remarrying, argues in favor of taking into account alternative voices of tradition within a modernizing setup.

Communism plays a major role in the assessment of religion in modern Tamil fiction and has influenced the work of the most influential Tamil prose writer, Taṇṭapāṇi Jeyakāntan. His psychoanalytically informed shorter prose deals repeatedly with the creation of sacrality by the interplay of social circumstances and the human need for deification, as in "Turkkai" (Durga, 1962), where a irresponsible husband projects the image of the fierce goddess onto his reproachful wife, accusing her of a death that occurred close to the deity's village shrine, or in "Apayam" (Danger, 1965), where a boy, believed to have drowned, is turned into a god, and again in "Kurupiṭam" (The guru's seat, 1971), where a beggar turns into a holy man identified with Murukan through a young man's worship. One of his later novels, *Jaya jaya cankara. . .* (Hail, hail Śankara. . . , 1977), presents a social utopia based on the life of the Śankarācārya of Kānci Kāmakoṭipīṭam, who tells the story of Ādiśankara to inspire devotion among a group of protagonists said to be suffering from rationalism and atheism; this novel promotes Gandhian ideas of equality by using narrative structures taken from classical hagiography. The urban fiction of Putumaipittan (also known as Viruttācalam) from the 1960s, consisting mainly of short stories collected in *Kācumalai* (Coinnecklace, 1971), continues the tradition of depicting a modernizing religion, stressing the tension between woman and man, the rural and the urban. A feminist stance toward religion is taken by Ambai in her collection of short stories from the 1960s, *Viṭṭin mūlayil oral camaiyalaṟai* (The shop at the corner of the house, 1967). The loss of traditional religious life among lower middle-class *brahmans* is depicted in Ashokamittiran's novel *Padinattavadu atchakodu* (The eighteenth parallel, 1977). The 1990s saw the emergence of a Tamil *dalit* fiction that is not confined by the early anti-brahmanical thrust, but broadens its scope, one representative being Perumāl Murugan's *Koolla Madari* (Seasons of the palm, 1990).

SOUTH ASIAN FICTION IN ENGLISH. Finally, since the second half of the twentieth century, South Asian fiction in English has grown to become an important literature for the South Asian middle class, as well as for a global English-speaking public. R. K. Narayan's *The Guide* (1958), where a young man is granted the status of sainthood, is a gentle satire on the inescapable burden of "gurudom." Salman Rushdie's interlinked tales of the Prophet and two South Asian aliens in the United Kingdom, *The Satanic Verses* (1988), is a complex arrangement of picaresque, hagiographical, and satirical narratives, though more along the lines of a rereading of certain traditions of European fiction and their reception of Asian religion than a continuation of either traditional or modern South Asian fiction. Amitav Ghosh's *In an Antique Land* (1992) explores North African and West Asian religiosity from an anthropological perspective, applying a fractured postcolonial gaze to Islam and the Judeo–Arabic tradition as the "other." Gita Hariharan's *In a State of Siege* (2003), finally, is an example of engaged literature dealing with the pressures that a liberal historian faces when writing on religious history in a political atmosphere dominated by Hindu revisionism.

BIBLIOGRAPHY

Aruṇācalam, Mn. *Tamil Ilakkiya Varalāru.* Tiruchitrambalam, India, 1973.

Gaeffke, Peter. *Hindi Literature in the Twentieth Century.* Wiesbaden, Germany, 1978.

McGregor, Ronald Stuart. *Hindi Literature from Its Beginnings to the Nineteenth Century.* Wiesbaden, Germany, 1984.

Pollock, Sheldon, ed. *Literary Cultures in History: Reconstructions from South Asia.* Oxford and New York, 2003.

Preminger, Alex, and T. V. F. Brogan. *The New Princeton Encyclopedia of Poetry and Poetics.* Princeton, 1993.

Sadiq, Muhammad. *A History of Urdu Literature.* 2d ed. Oxford and New York, 1984.

Sen, Sukumar. *Bāṃlār Sāhitya Itihās.* Delhi, 1965.

Winternitz, Moritz. *Geschichte der indischen Literatur.* 2 vols. Leipzig, 1909–1920.

Zvelebil, Kamil. *Tamil Literature.* Wiesbaden, Germany, 1974.

CHRISTOPH EMMRICH (2005)

GENDER AND RELIGION: GENDER AND AFRICAN AMERICAN RELIGIONS

Religion, spirituality, the church, faith, holiness, the spirit—all of these have been invoked to explain the roles of African American women in the survival of their communities in the United States, their emergence as prominent leaders in every organized response to racial oppression, and their aggregate ability to thrive in spite of the appalling evidence of deprivations experienced by a substantial proportion of the population in the late twentieth and early twenty-first centuries. Furthermore, African American women, especially Christians, have invented traditions of leadership and engendered practices that empower women in contexts that presume and prescribe male leadership.

African American women's religious experience is as old and as varied as their existence in the Americas. We do not know the name of the first African woman to come to the Americas, but we do know that a woman named Isabella arrived in Jamestown, Virginia, with a group of Africans in 1619. Between 1619 and 1865, Africans and their descen-

dants developed a religious life in the context of an imposed English Protestantism and remembered African traditional religions. Although it is estimated that 10 to 18 percent of Africans coming to North America were Muslims, it has been difficult to assess fully their impact and role in the development of African American Christianity. Margaret Creel has found that the daughters of at least one Muslim slave were responsible for organizing a Baptist church in the South Carolina sea islands, the area that served as the Ellis Island for North American slavery.

The majority of African Americans in the United States are Christians—Protestant Christians, Baptist, Methodist, and Pentecostal. The seven largest denominations are the National Baptist Convention, USA; the National Baptist Convention of America; the Progressive National Baptist Convention; the African Methodist Episcopal (A.M.E.) Church; the African Methodist Episcopal Zion Church; the Christian Methodist Episcopal Church; and the Church of God in Christ. These seven top the list of over one hundred distinct Christian bodies—denominations and congregational networks—that serve African American spiritual needs in some way. Alongside and in interaction with Christianity, one of the fastest growing traditions is Islam. Historically associated with the Nation of Islam in the twentieth century, African American Muslims are also part of the Sunnī, Ṣūfī, and other traditions.

Religion is a gendered experience filled with distinctive experiences for women alongside tensions and conflicts over options and limits surrounding women's leadership. African American women are predominantly but not exclusively Christian. W. E. B. Du Bois, Kelly Miller, and Mary Church Terrell in 1903 pointed out: "Upon the women of no race have the truths of the gospel taken a firmer and deeper hold than upon the colored women of the United States." Women are central to the life of their churches and mosques. Women are not only the majority of African Americans, but they make up the overwhelming majorities of churchgoers, between 75 and 90 percent in attendance on Sundays. Although Islam was often presented during the period of the Civil Rights movement as "the religion of the black man," Minister Louis Farrakhan, addressing the Million Man March in 1995, admitted that women were also the backbone of the mosque. By placing gender in the foreground of our perspective, it is possible to examine the importance of religious women and the variety of their roles in the United States and to see "the black church" and other expressions of faith and spirituality in a more nuanced and multifaceted light.

Enslaved African American women played multiple roles in slave communities, through the family, the "invisible church," and the slave women's network. All three roles had spiritual implications. As the primary caretakers of enslaved children, these women are cited throughout slave narratives as the principal sources of children's religious socialization. Children heard and observed women's prayers for freedom, learning that the spirit world was important and that there was a difference between what Thomas Webber called "slaveholding priestcraft" and the true religion of the folk. Webber also observed that women served as prayer leaders, preachers, and worship leaders for the entire community. During the slavery era a few black women evangelists were given safe conduct into the South to conduct revivals and to speak at camp meetings—meetings that slaves also attended. As members of a somewhat self-contained network within slave communities, women supported one another in their childrearing responsibilities, and they also served the entire slave community as healers and midwives. Within this women's network, according to Deborah Gray White, women convened their own prayer meetings and developed autonomous women leaders, some of whom were able to influence the entire community through their preaching and prayers. In this there was a certain degree of continuity with women's spiritual leadership in West and Central African societies as priestesses, healers, and diviners. The roles of religious leaders in enslaved Christian communities also paralleled those of women in African-derived religions in other parts of the New World, such as vodun in Haiti, Candomblé in Brazil, and Santería in Cuba and Puerto Rico. Women became a central motor force in the spiritual history of slave communities, a role that was at odds with the presumptions of subservience and silence that governed women's roles in white churches.

Sojourner Truth and Harriet Tubman, two of the most famous women of the slavery period, were both embodiments of African American women's faith and spirituality. Truth grounded her antislavery narrative in her understanding of the Bible, using a banner on which she quoted *Leviticus* 25—"Proclaim liberty across the land"—to advertise her lectures. In addition to Truth's antislavery preaching, Nell Painter describes her as a well-respected Adventist preacher who traveled throughout the northeastern United States. After slavery was abolished Truth conducted a campaign to obtain land for freed people in the western United States. Tubman, popularly known as a *conductor* but more correctly understood as an *abductor* of slaves on the Underground Railroad, was deeply spiritual and a member of the A.M.E. Zion Church, where she exhibited the ecstatic spirituality associated with African American Christianity that W. E. B. Du Bois called "the frenzy."

Not only did black women form their own antislavery, mutual-aid, and burial societies, they were among the groups of African Americans north and south who founded and established churches before the Civil War. Women like Jarena Lee and Julia Foote sought preaching licenses in Methodist churches. Other women emerged as leaders in such movements as Shakerism. Black women were present and active in every single expression of religion in which black people could be found during the slavery era. Toward the end of slavery, during the Civil War, they were also among the missionaries who carried the gospel to freed people gathered in

and near Union Army camps. In doing so, women linked their leadership roles within black churches to education.

Black women were among the missionaries, white and black, who went to the South to establish schools for freedmen and women. Sponsored by church groups, these women became part of the emerging leadership class of "educators." Men in that class were often preachers as well as teachers in the local schools. Women ran schools that were funded by church groups, in some cases seeing their vocation as educators as their Christian mission. Mary McLeod Bethune, for instance, was educated at Moody Bible Institute, and she prepared for life in the mission fields of Africa. When told by the Presbyterian Church that there were no posts for Negroes in Africa, she taught in the South, founding her own school in Daytona, Florida. Newly established black colleges routinely sent their students as "missionaries" to teach in the rural South during the summers.

Freedom from slavery brought dilemmas in religious life. African Americans sought education for their children, but not at the expense of community, traditions, and religious folkways. Some northern missionaries, for instance Daniel Payne of the A.M.E. Church, encouraged slaves to abandon their ecstatic worship practices in favor of the more restrained styles of Anglo Americans. African American Christians were distinctly committed to the person of the Holy Ghost or Holy Spirit and insisted upon worship that celebrated this. Women as well as men articulated the folk theologies defending these practices. Furthermore, African American women are far more numerous and prominent in religious traditions emphasizing the Holy Spirit.

During and after Reconstruction, the A.M.E. and A.M.E. Zion churches grew, the Colored Methodist Episcopal Church was formed, and the National Baptist Convention became the largest religious body among African Americans. Black churches, as Evelyn Brooks Higginbotham points out with specific reference to the Baptists, became the primary public square for African Americans. Beyond the local congregations, national meetings provided the spaces where a national community became a reality. In addition to worship, the most pressing social issues were discussed and women participated in almost all of these deliberations.

The resistance to women in ministry prompted women to oppose their marginalization through the formation of missionary societies and auxiliary conventions. Within these organizations they discussed the business of their churches and theological issues surrounding their roles. Although Baptist men rejected women as preachers, women created platforms for their own voices. Women in all traditions utilized their economic power to advance their points of view. As Tera Hunter reveals, black women were at least half the urban working class, so their cash money was responsible for building the churches that men insisted upon pastoring. Although in conflict over the role of women clergy, black churches enthusiastically welcomed women as "educators" within their congregations and denominations and as leaders in church-related and church-sponsored schools. Women used their importance as educators as a wedge to expand their opportunities for religious leadership as evangelists, missionaries, and, sometimes successfully, as clergy.

The conflicts over women's leadership in churches led to two parallel developments by the turn of the twentieth century. Women joined the newly organized Holiness churches, where they were welcome to preach (or "teach"), and churchwomen formed a secular organized movement to address social change and to offer leadership. As was to become typical of black women's organizing around gender, the leaders of this new movement stressed that they were not becoming separatists or withdrawing from the community but that they were simply coming forward as *leaders* and inviting men to join with them. By 1896, these women had formed the Nation Association of Colored Women as a federation of at least four hundred clubs, and they proceeded to send "organizers" into states that were unrepresented in the Association.

By 1895, the Church of God in Christ, the first of a series of new churches that carried forward worship emphasizing the Holy Spirit, was organized as a Holiness church. Women joined this church in large numbers. In spite of this church's restriction on their ordination, women in this denomination carved out what was to become typical of Holiness and later Pentecostal churches, the semiautonomous "women's department." Holiness and Pentecostal churches came to be called collectively the "Sanctified Church," a term indigenous to the African American experience. Where women are 75 percent of the black church overall, they are often more than 90 percent of some Holiness and Pentecostal congregations. These churches, in addition to offering a doctrine that affirmed the traditional worship emphasis on the Holy Spirit, addressed a range of problems confronting black people in the early twentieth century: education, standards of beauty, economic security, race relations, physical safety, urban migration, and, most importantly, women's religious roles.

The case of the Church of God in Christ is instructive. Although it began as a Holiness church, the Church of God in Christ became the first legally organized Pentecostal church in the United States. The founder, Bishop Charles Harrison Mason, was unmarried at the time, so he chose Mother Lizzie Woods Roberson to set up and lead the women's department. This established a tradition that separated women's leadership from the role of bishop's wife, a departure from the practices of the A.M.E. and other denominations. This separation reinforced a degree of autonomy for women in the denomination. Mother Roberson, a Baptist educator, also served to educate the clergy of the church. While the Church of God in Christ did not ordain women to be elders, pastors, or bishops or to "preach," the church allowed the women to "teach" the gospel and to lead churches when the pastors were "absent." The women's teaching expanded to a form of religious discourse that is not

only indistinguishable from preaching, but has become one of the strongest preaching traditions in African American Christianity.

Among most African American Christian churches, the leadership of pastors' and bishops' wives is assumed. These women are expected to be leaders of the women, excellent public speakers, and, often but not always, consummate musicians. They serve prominently in the church-as-public-square and occasionally lead within the traditions of worship (prayer, preaching, testimony, and song). In many congregations, these wives are experienced fundraisers, Sunday school superintendents, choir directors, and deaconesses, and they fill other vital roles. The tendency to look only at the pulpit in order to interpret and understand the church not only places too large an emphasis on male leaders but also masks and obscures the centrality of these clearly subordinate women's roles to the survival and advancement of churches. Interestingly, in all of the churches, women without restriction perform religious tasks that are sometimes associated with priestly ministry: praying, anointing with oil, and the laying on of hands for healing.

Women in the twentieth century also became prominent church founders. One in particular, Bishop Ida Robinson of the Mount Sinai Holy Church, founded a new denomination when the denomination in which she had been ordained made it clear that although she could serve as a pastor and vote for bishops, she could not herself become a bishop. Among other settings in the Sanctified Church it was standard practice for women to travel to new locations, preach on street corners until they had developed a following, and then "dig out" the new church.

Women persisted in finding creative ways to affirm and develop their leadership in the church. One particularly important strategy was to call for a "Women's Day." After observing such practices in a few congregations and regional conventions, Nannie Helen Burroughs introduced the idea of a national Women's Day to the National Baptist Convention in 1901. The idea was to develop women from the local congregations as public speakers, and Women's Day caught on and spread to every African American denomination and to nearly every congregation. Although Burroughs later complained that the day focused too heavily on fundraising, women used the day not only to foster solidarity within their congregations but to promote women's preaching and speaking. While some African American women clergy see Women's Day as tokenism, many churches have expanded the day to a cluster of activities involving revivals, retreats, and programs that empower laywomen and affirm preaching women.

Women's creativity is also apparent in the traditions of sacred music. Not only are women's voices prominent in descriptions of oral traditions, but women are also often the chief musicians of denominations, becoming the arbiters for what is acceptable within large networks of churches. Two such women, Lucie Campbell, who directed music in the National Baptist Convention, and Dr. Mattie Moss Clark, minister of music in the Church of God in Christ, not only guided the musical tastes of the denomination, but shaped their hymnbooks and composed music that contributed to a gospel music tradition that reached beyond the boundaries of churches. Some women, including Shirley Caesar, Dorothy Norwood, and Mother Willie Mae Ford Smith, combined the role of gospel singer and evangelist in order to circumvent the discrimination against women who preached.

The prominence of black male preachers was underscored during the Civil Rights movement when these men emerged as leaders and spokespersons for massive campaigns of civil disobedience. Subsequent research on the Civil Rights movement has revealed the roles of women throughout the period. These women were members and leaders of churches and on occasion, as in the case of Rosa Parks in the 1955 Montgomery, Alabama, bus boycott, their moral authority as leaders derived from the communitywide respect they garnered in religious and political leadership. Fannie Lou Hamer, a Mississippian and participant in the Mississippi Freedom Democratic Party, attained her prominence and leadership partly through her connections with the church and her role as a prominent song leader. The Civil Rights movement also advanced a concern for black men that was particularly addressed by the rise of the Nation of Islam. C. Eric Lincoln and Larry Mamiya point out that the Nation of Islam represented one of the most serious challenges to the unquestioned dominance of the black church. Often espoused as "the religion of the black man," it offered an alternative to Christianity and its racism that is particularly appealing to men.

In spite of Islam's masculine appeal, women are an integral part of African American Islam. During his speech at the 1995 Million Man March, Minister Louis Farrakhan admitted that women were the backbone of the mosque in ways similar to the role of women in the churches. Research in this area is very new and very limited. However, Carolyn Rouse, in her book *Engaged Surrender: African American Women and Islam,* points out that Islam's appeal to African American women is centered in visions of a just community and society and in hopes for family stability. Additionally, like Christian women, African American Muslim women are seeking a spiritual life in relation with the divine. Beverly Aminah McLeod also emphasizes the importance of social justice for African American women along with a sense of membership in a world community. Anecdotal evidence suggests that women who were formerly Christian are less likely to remain Muslim than are men. While Islam's emphases on prayer, fasting, and modesty parallel similar emphases among Pentecostal and Holiness women, the primary motivation for a "return" to Christianity is the women's attachment to elements of the Afro-Christian tradition such as gospel music and other aspects of tradition. Former Muslims in Christian churches are often catalysts for a more Afrocentric and political activist focus. Other anecdotes suggest that the traditional roles of

women in African American churches have had an effect on the way that African American Muslim men engage South Asian Muslim immigrants in America. African American Muslims may be more accommodating to women than their immigrant counterparts, although for the most part African American and South Asian Muslims attend separate mosques.

In addition to the rise of Islam, the Civil Rights movement evolved into the Black Power movement. That movement prompted the development of "Black Theology." Theologians such as James Cone advanced a liberation theology that depicted God as on the side of the poor and the oppressed. In response to the masculinism of Black Theology, a number of African American women scholars advanced a set of ideas that have come to be called *womanist.* Drawing on author Alice Walker's introduction of the term *womanist* with a dictionary-style definition, black women religious scholars have developed a conversation that explores black women's experiences in church and society with reference to every area of religious and theological studies. Social ethicist Katie Cannon emphasizes that the womanist idea represents "a critique of all human domination in light of Black Women's experience . . . that unmasks whatever threatens the well-being of the poorest women of color."

Toward the end of the twentieth century, women's leadership as ordained clergy faced less resistance. The growth and development of exceptionally large congregations called megachurches coincided with the development of prominent pastoral partnerships between married couples, providing visible role models for women. In 2000, the A.M.E. Church ordained its first woman bishop, Vashti Murphy McKenzie; her husband accepted the role of Episcopal supervisor, a role previously filled by bishops' wives. Bishop McKenzie was not only a prominent and nationally recognized preacher, she also served as chaplain to one of the largest secular organizations of black women, the Delta Sigma Theta Sorority. The synergistic relationship she established between leadership in an autonomous women's organization and leadership in an organization controlled by men was paralleled in the earlier roles of Mary McLeod Bethune and Dorothy Height.

At the end of the twentieth century, many scholars and clergy in African American churches were asking about the absence of men, while taking for granted the presence of women. Although exploring gender in African American religions should not be reduced to examining the roles of women, the gender question forces one to look beyond the prominence of the black male preacher to recognize that the most dominant tradition, African American Christianity, consists largely of women.

SEE ALSO African American Religions, overview article; Feminist Theology, article on Christian Feminist Theology; Women's Studies in Religion.

BIBLIOGRAPHY

Andrews, William L., ed. *Sisters of the Spirit: Three Black Women's Autobiographies of the Nineteenth Century.* Bloomington, Ind., 1986. The narratives of three women preachers illustrate the importance of the Holy Spirit in the religious beliefs of African Americans early in their Christian history in the United States.

Clinton, Catherine. *Harriet Tubman: The Road to Freedom.* New York, 2004. Scholarly biography illuminating the religious experience of Tubman along with her heroic exploits as an "abductor" for the Underground Railroad.

Collier-Thomas, Bettye. *Daughters of Thunder: Black Women Preachers and their Sermons, 1850–1979.* San Francisco, 1998. A collection of sermons establishing the importance of women's voices in the most masculine of black religious activities.

Creel, Margaret Washington. *A Peculiar People: Slave Religion and Community Culture among the Gullahs.* New York, 1988. Important study of slavery's Ellis Island detailing the African origins of religious practices that reach beyond the South Carolina sea islands.

Dodson, Jualynne E. *Engendering Church: Women, Power, and the AME Church.* Lanham, Md., 2002. Offers a connected history of twentieth-century churchwomen and clubwomen.

Dodson, Jualynne E., and Cheryl Townsend Gilkes. "Something Within: Social Change and Collective Endurance in the Sacred World of Black Christian Women." In *Women and Religion in America,* Vol. 3: *1900–1968,* edited by Rosemary Radford Ruether and Rosemary Skinner Keller, pp. 80–128. San Francisco, 1986.

Du Bois, W. E. B., ed. *The Negro Church: Report of a Social Study.* Atlanta, 1903. Significant study and compilation of conference papers that underscores the centrality of the black church and provides an early comment on the importance of women.

Gilkes, Cheryl Townsend. "Roundtable Discussion: Christian Ethics and Theology in Womanist Perspective." *Journal of Feminist Studies in Religion* 5, no. 2 (1989): 105–109. Alice Walker's concept "womanist" is evaluated in terms of its usefulness for African American Christian women.

Gilkes, Cheryl Townsend. *If It Wasn't for the Women: Black Women's Experience and Womanist Culture in Church and Community.* Maryknoll, N.Y., 2001. Presents a variety of Gilkes's essays on women in the Sanctified Church, on community activists, and on cultural pressures confronting black women.

Hanson, Joyce A. *Mary McLeod Bethune and Black Women's Political Activism.* Columbia, Mo., 2003. Hanson's pathbreaking biography explores every aspect of Bethune's national leadership and provides the most detailed descriptions of her religious education and seminary training.

Higginbotham, Evelyn Brooks. *Righteous Discontent: The Women's Movement in the Black Baptist Church, 1880–1920.* Cambridge, Mass., 1993. Higginbotham underscores the central importance of the national convocation in shaping women's opportunities for leadership and establishing a national community.

Hunter, Tera. *To 'Joy My Freedom: Southern Black Women's Lives and Labors after the Civil War.* Cambridge, Mass., 1997. In

telling the story of women in the nineteenth-century urban South, Hunter provides an important portrait of black women's roles in building religious and fraternal communities.

Lincoln, C. Eric, and Lawrence H. Mamiya. *The Black Church in the African American Experience.* Durham, N.C., 1990. Explores the seven largest denominations and includes a chapter on women.

Murphy, Joseph M. *Working the Spirit: Ceremonies of the African Diaspora.* Boston, 1994. Murphy places the practices of the Sanctified Church in the context of the practices of other African-derived religions in the New World.

Painter, Nell Irvin. *Sojourner Truth: A Life, A Symbol.* New York, 1996. Details not only Truth's antislavery activism but also her prominence as an Adventist preacher.

Raboteau, Albert J. *Slave Religion: The "Invisible Institution" in the Antebellum South.* New York, 1978. Raboteau details the religious practices of slaves in the hush harbor of plantations and in towns, and also mediates the debate between Frazier and Herskovitz.

Ross, Rosetta. *Witnessing and Testifying: Black Women, Religion, and Civil Rights.* Minneapolis, 2003. Provides an important set of case studies that reveal the role of women and their faith in the success of the Civil Rights movement.

Rouse, Carolyn Moxley. *Engaged Surrender: African American Women and Islam.* Berkeley, 2004. Anthropological study of African American women in Los Angeles that demonstrates the diversity among African American women Muslims while detailing their strategies for being good Muslims.

Walker, Alice. "Womanist." *In Search of Our Mothers' Gardens: Womanist Prose,* pp. xi–xii. San Diego, Calif., 1983. This definition of *womanist* and the volume of essays it introduces provides biographical insights into Walker's writing and philosophy.

Webber, Thomas L. *Deep Like the Rivers: Education in the Slave Quarter Community, 1831–1865.* New York, 1978. While describing the fundamental cultural themes slaves shared, Webber details the centrality of women as leaders and agents of tradition.

White, Deborah Gray. *Ar'n't I a Woman: Female Slaves in the Plantation South.* New York, 1985; rev. ed., 1999. White's study points to the paramount importance of the African American slave women's network, a probable cultural foundation for the effectiveness of African American women's organizations in later periods.

Wiggins, Daphne C. "'Where Somebody Knows My Name': A Social and Cultural Analysis of Church Attendance among African American Women." Ph.D. diss., Emory University, Atlanta, 1997.

Williams, Dolores S. *Sisters in the Wilderness: The Challenge of Womanish God-Talk.* Maryknoll, N.Y., 1993.

CHERYL TOWNSEND GILKES (2005)

HISTORY OF RELIGIONS [FURTHER CONSIDERATIONS].

The historical study of religions as it was theorized and practiced in the second half of the twentieth century by scholars like Geo Widengren, Angelo Brelich, Ugo Bianchi, Kurt Rudolph, and Carsten Colpe in Europe, or Mircea Eliade and Joseph Kitagawa in the United States, has since the 1970s been seriously challenged by macro-historical events—most notably, the emancipation of women and decolonization—that have dramatically shaken our vision of past and present history, and by the emergence of new scientific paradigms that have deeply affected the customary practice of writing history. Even the most strict practitioner of the historicist methodology cannot avoid reckoning with these novel perspectives, which are not antithetical, but rather complementary to the traditional historiography based on comparative historical and social scientific approaches. Consequently, it is impossible to write about the theory and practice of the history of religions without taking into consideration primarily the two approaches—feminist and postcolonial—that convert the role of women and decolonized peoples from objects to subjects (actors) in the religious history of humankind.

FEMINIST APPROACHES. In traditional historiography much of what claims to be objective scholarship about human experience is actually a depiction of prevalently male experience from an exclusively male point of view. If we accept this well-founded assumption, wholly new routes must be searched to recover the lives of women commonly overlooked by historians. Thus, historical work done according to feminist guidelines moves beyond traditional horizons and sources to look for women's actual experience and practices, causing a shift in the scholarly vantage point that fundamentally alters conventional contours of historical religious processes. This procedure develops frameworks for interpreting women's experiences that shatter the norms of canonical historiography, which usually takes the male outlook as the measure of human experience, and entails a radically new approach to the treatment of historical texts written by men about women and the far fewer yet increasing numbers of historical texts written by women.

A series of examples, taken from various religious traditions but tested in a cross-cultural perspective with a comparative mirror, can serve to emphasize the gains resulting from this approach. Original work done by feminist scholars of religion provides a more complete and accurate account of non-Western religious observance. For example, in conflict with traditional views canonized by androcentric scholarship, it has been demonstrated that women of Australia and India have a rich, elaborate set of religious practices that involve no male participation or control. Commonplaces of Christian and Islamic apologetics (occasionally shared by secular scholarship) concerning an allegedly improved status for women can also be seriously questioned if subjected to a feminist historical critique.

In the field of mythology the use of a feminist method can contribute to a reformulation of the controversial issue of the role of goddesses in both the Hindu and the ancient

Mediterranean pantheons. Fundamental religious typologies like monotheism, polytheism, and dualism can be reconfigured by emphasizing correlations with, respectively, patriarchy (involving a female subordination), female priesthood (related to divine feminine), and gender asymmetry (masculinity and femininity as the most fundamental structural opposition). On the other hand, utterly new typologies can be formulated based on the criterion of gender power balance correlated with the distinction between socially oriented and individually oriented religions. With regard to values and mores (e.g., African genital operations and Islamic segregation of women) espoused in religious systems against which an engaged historian of religions must take a critical stance, feminist scholarship can offer an original and important contribution if equipped with serious training in the cross-cultural study of religion combined with the intent to understand otherness with empathy free from cultural imperialism.

Postcolonial Approaches. The postcolonial approach emerged in the 1970s as an intellectual and political project prompted by literary theorists and cultural critics. They based their work on postphilosophical premises, mainly the post-Marxism of Antonio Gramsci (the concept of "subaltern" transferred into a colonial dimension), the post-Freudianism of Jacques Lacan (the notion of "other" as an image in the mirror serving to construct one's own self-image), the post-structuralism of Michel Foucault (the ambivalent relationship between knowledge and power), the deconstructionism of Jacques Derrida (the critique of binary opposition and consequent subversion of categories), the combat sociology of Pierre Bourdieu (the theory of practice, habitus, and field), and the postmodernism of Jean-Louis Lyotard (relativism of truth and values). Preeminent advocates of this approach include Edward W. Said (1935–2003), a Christian Arab from Palestine; Gayatri Chakravorty Spivak (b. 1942), a Hindu woman from Calcutta; and Homy K. Bhabha (b. 1949), a Parsi Indian from Bombay. They are all of Asiatic origin but were all educated at prominent Anglo-Saxon academic institutions and they teach (or have taught) in top North American universities. For a series of reasons (scarce familiarity with historical realities and methodology, political bias, jargon-heavy and convoluted style, and irritating narcissism), their works, more than valuable additions to the field of postcolonial studies, are rather conspicuous specimens of neocolonialist attitudes by elite intellectuals whose ideas have been molded in the most bourgeois Western think tanks and remain impenetrable to the colonized subaltern peoples they claim to represent. In spite of this fundamental flaw, the work of these gurus has been very influential on practiced scholars of religion who have tried to identify biases of various kinds in traditional scholarship and to introduce into the field a more self-reflexive attitude with an epistemological consciousness of cultural diversity.

After the initial critique of European colonial representations of "others" joined to an overtly political agenda, as in the case of the Martinique prophet of Third World uprising, Frantz Fanon (1925–1961), postcolonial theory has developed mainly in two directions: (1) the recovery of the genuine indigenous tradition of the colonized from colonial distortions; and (2) the analysis of the intercultural space resulting from the contacts, relations, and exchanges between the colonized and the colonizer (situations of hybridity or syncretism). Some case studies that can be investigated proficiently from the standpoint of the history of religions will be examined briefly.

The risk of a shift from reflexive historiography to specious, fictional constructionism involved in the conflation of Western academic (post)-isms with the political claims of the subaltern perspective becomes evident in the debate about the emergence of Hinduism as a concept and as a historical reality. Since Hinduism is the dominant religion in South Asia and also one of the major world religions (spreading into South East Asia and Central America) its definition is of paramount importance for history of religions generally. Drawing on heretofore overlooked sources, many researchers have explored the ways in which colonial administrators, with the support of Orientalist scholars, constructed knowledge about the society and culture of India and the processes through which that cumulated experience has shaped past and present reality. At the same time, focusing on indigenous accounts, memories, and interpretations, it has been possible to decenter the historical discourse and to present an alternative history of many local realities. Parallel to this process of indigenization of religious histories, the project has been carried on of placing the European colonizer and the colonized Asian into a shared historical space by stressing the mutual impact of Britain's colonization on Indian and British culture—from gastronomic mores to continuously recast religious identities. On the other hand, on the basis of manipulated evidence and postmodern fashionable theory, the idea has been formulated that Hinduism as a category was invented or constructed by European (mostly British) colonizers sometime after 1800. In other words, for the supporters (mostly British) of this theory, Hinduism is arguably a construct of Western scholars who, upon encountering Indian culture, created a religion along the lines of their own Christian conception of what a religion ought to be. And, to put it into political terms, this construction of a world religion abetted the colonial exploitation through a cultural alienation of Indians. This claim, with its political corollaries, is patently false, since Hinduism as a mark of shared religious identity—not just an ethno-geographical denomination—grew in the insiders' collective consciousness starting from post-Vedic times and was first recognized as such by an outsider approximately in 1030 CE—an outsider who was not British but Persian, the Muslim cultural historian and comparative religionist al-Bīrūnī.

This case is paradigmatic insofar as it has been argued that, on the basis of the alleged deconstruction of Hinduism as a coherent phenomenon, the concept of religion itself should be abandoned, because its ethnocentrism distorts so-

ciocultural realities of non-Western peoples. This argument, apart from being denied by historical analysis, is no less Western-centered than the traditional view of religion as a *sui generis* component of culture, and it can (from an axiological point of view) foster latent communalist tendencies. The postcolonial discourse has been applied to construct, deconstruct, and reconstruct religious realities in Asia (mainly Buddhism and Japan), Africa (mainly southern Africa and the British commonwealth), Oceania (Hawai'i), Latin America (Mexico), and North America (African America and Native America) with similar results, which can be either compelling and innovative or truistic or completely unfounded.

SOCIOBIOLOGICAL APPROACHES. Sociobiological approaches, which represent in a sense a naturalistic counterpoise to the culture-centered approaches of feminist and postcolonial studies, present yet another challenge to previous versions of the history of religions. The study of religion as a phylogenetic type arises in the 1970s and can hardly be conceived outside of a general neo-Darwinian frame of reference and the establishment of ethology as a science that included the study of *Homo sapiens sapiens* as a zoological species. To Konrad Lorenz (1903–1989) we owe the discovery of *imprinting*, an especially rapid and relatively irreversible learning process that occurs early in the individual's life, and the correlate innate release mechanism, whereby organisms are genetically predisposed to be especially responsive to certain stimuli. On the basis of ethology and the theory of genetic cultural transmission as exposed by the geneticist Luigi Luca Cavalli-Sforza (b. 1922) it can be held that the evolution of human culture (embracing language, art, and religion) is bound to the same mechanism as biological evolution.

However, the father of sociobiology as a science arguing that social animals, including humans, behave largely according to rules written in their very genes is the entomologist Edward O. Wilson (b. 1929). No less than such basic instincts as aggression and greed (with their nasty consequences, such as warfare and sex role imbalance), the religious tendency is deeply ingrained in our genetic baggage. To put it bluntly, genes tether culture, including religion and morality; consequently, the developments of religions can be envisaged as adaptive modifications based on a survival strategy following the same evolutionary rules of biology. Through a systematic sociobiological study all the highest forms of religious practice can be demonstrated to confer biological advantage (congealing identities is one of its characteristic goals). In the words of one of its main critics, "sociobiology challenges the integrity of culture as a distinctive and symbolic human creation. In place of a social constitution of meanings, it offers a biological determination of human interactions with a source primarily in the general evolutionary propensity of individual genotypes to maximize their reproductive success" (Sahlins, 1976, p. x). In spite of this and other (ideologically biased) accusations of "social Darwinism," if history of religions is meant to avoid metaphysical musings, on the one hand, and the excess of cultural relativism, on the other, it might best proceed on the theoretical presupposition of "human universals" located at the confluence between biologically based constraints and their sociohistorical constructions.

The sociobiological approach had precursors also among scholars of humanities, including the leading art historian Aby Warburg (1866–1929), who situated the origin and development of religious art against the background of the natural environment interfering with basic human emotions such as fear, and the classical philologist and folklorist Karl Meuli (1891–1968), who detected the origins of sacrifice in prehistoric hunters' rituals. The sociobiological approach has also found valid support in (evolutionary) psychology of religion (as represented by the ethnopsychoanalyst Georges Devereux [1908–1986] and the anthropologist with psychoanalytical background Weston la Barre [1911–1996] with his theory of "neoteny," or biological infantilization at the basis of human culture) and in (behavioral) ecology of religion (advocated by postfunctionalist anthropologists like Marvin Harris [1927–2001] and Roy A. Rappaport [1926–1997]). A biological perspective is avowedly present in the seminal work of the German historian of ancient religions Walter Burkert (b. 1931) and, *mutatis mutandis*, in that of the Dutch Indologist and comparatist Frits Staal (b. 1930), which similarly touches upon ethological analogies.

COGNITIVE APPROACHES. The basic premise of cognitive approaches to the study of religion is that religion is rooted in evolved cognitive capacities common to all humans, which can explain recurrent patterns in religious realities. Given that these capacities are not specific to the religious domain but comply with the working of human mind, the main corollary is that religion is not *sui generis:* It is defined, instead, by the ways that these universal cognitive capacities assume by participating in sociocultural processes. The basic procedure is to draw on experimental work in cognitive psychology in order to explain patterns in religious representations. The cognitive approach was first applied to the explanation (1990) of religious ritual systems by a philosopher of science, Robert N. McCauley, and a comparative religionist, E. Thomas Lawson. It privileges exclusively the communicative—linguistic and symbolic—aspects of religions. As such it is not based on any empirical investigation of cultural data but on the linguistic theory of Noam Chomsky (b. 1928), the founder of a cognitive, evolutionary approach to linguistics, and the "epidemiology of representations," a naturalistic approach to culture devised by the French social and cognitive scientist Dan Sperber. Starting from Chomsky's contention that grammars of natural languages are biologically based, these scholars maintain, contrary to Chomsky, that cognitive naturalistic methods can also prove relevant to the study of sociocultural phenomena, including religion. And, following Sperber's claim that humans have an innate symbolic mechanism genetically guided, but countering his stark distinction between linguistic and symbolic phenomena, they make a strong plea for connecting cognition and culture

and, at the same time, for the combination of interpretation and explanation in the study of religion.

The idea that religious materials are mental representations is obviously a truism, since George Berkeley (1685–1753) a shared notion that should be well known to every humanist scholar without recourse to neuroscience. We learn, further, that many apparently specific features of religious behavior result from activating cognitive resources for thinking about (superhuman) agents and that religion is characterized by counterintuitive representation. (In a more sophisticated version of the theory, religious notions result from a delicate balance between intuitive and counterintuitive ontologies.) The presence itself of counterintuitive mental images is a necessary but not sufficient criterion for religiousness. The fallacy of this criterion is self-evident: the counterintuitiveness of any mental product is to be assessed only in the frame of a specific historical context and is conditioned by cultural and individual factors.

Critics of the cognitive approach have argued that it does not say anything about the meaning of religion, that it is scientistic, reductionist, and detrimental from the point of view of humanistic values and that it is of no use for understanding the human condition. In spite of these and other evident defects this approach can be instrumental to the progress of the history of religions, if cognitive scholars renounce meta-theoretical ruminations and try to measure themselves against empirical (ethnographic or historical) evidence. Although this is still an emerging field limited to a narrow circle of scholars roaming between North America and Scandinavia, some good work has already been produced on specific issues, for example, on the origin of religions, a very controversial issue indeed, or on Melanesian religion, studied according to the theory of divergent modes of religiosity.

UN-CONCLUSION. After the examination of all these new approaches, which are in a way entrenched in contrasting views on the relationship between science and society, a few words must be said against any monolithic tyranny of whatever methodology. Historians of religions who are inclined to inflexible rationalism or to staunch support of a given method should be made acquainted with some epistemological novelties that revolutionized the sociology of scientific knowledge and are also bound to exert a profound influence on the practice and conceptualization of all the humanities disciplines. In 1973 the American historian Hayden White (b. 1928) published a book offering an ambitious schema of the "poetics of history." He asserted that the vision of a given historian derives not from the evidence, since his vision selects in advance what will constitute the relevant evidence, but rather from conscious or unconscious choices made among a series of possibilities. Thus the version of the past chosen by the historian depends on moral and aesthetic values shared by him and his ideal audience, rather than depending on presumptive raw data. In his own words, "histories . . . contain a deep structural content which is generally poetic, and specifically linguistic, in nature, and which serves as the precritically accepted paradigm of what a distinctively 'historical' explanation should be" (1973, p. ix). Given the presence of this "metahistorical" element in all historical works, every pretense of objectivity is unrealistic. Ultimately, this book is the demystification of histories and historians who claim to present things "as they are," while providing some methods for determining in what ways a given account can be envisaged as ideologically biased.

Within a broader theoretical framework, in 1975 the anarchistic message of rejection of the existence of universal methodological rules by the Austrian philosopher of science Paul Feyerabend (1924–1994) exploded as a bombshell in the scientific quarters. Parting company from the strong empiricism of his own school (Karl Popper [1902–1994]), he maintained that new (supposedly correct) theories have only an aesthetic advantage vis-à-vis the old (supposedly falsified) theories. Feyerabend objected to any single prescriptive scientific method on the grounds that in most cases new successful theories came to be accepted not because of their scientific exactness, but because their supporters made use of any trick—rational, rhetorical, or ribald—in order to advance their cause. (This argument is also applicable to modern and postmodern developments in the field of religious studies.) In a hyperbolical way, he held that negative views about astrology and the effectiveness of rain dances were not justified by scientific investigation, and, more generally, he thought that there is no justification for valuing scientific claims over claims by other ideologies like religions. This caveat, and any other warning against excessive trust into the explanatory power of science, should give us a stimulus for keeping aloof from the pitfalls of dogmatism.

SEE ALSO Colonialism and Postcolonialism; Gender and Religion, article on History of Study; Historiography, article on Western Studies; Sociobiology and Evolutionary Psychology, overview article; Subaltern Studies.

BIBLIOGRAPHY

Feminist Approaches

The best introduction by a scholar commanding both women's studies and the comparative study of religions is Rita M. Gross, *Feminism and Religion: An Introduction* (Boston, 1996), which offers an invaluable reconstruction of the historical growth of the field and a rich bibliography. Among many collections of articles dealing with theoretical issues, see "Gender and the Study of Religion," edited by Randi R. Warne, a special issue of *Method and Theory in the Study of Religion* 13, no. 2 (2001), with contributions by Susan Starr Sered, Morni Joy, Dawne McCance, Virginia Lieson Brereton, Margaret Lamberts Bendroth, and Rita M. Gross. Among countless excellent collectanea including a wide range of perspectives from diverse cultures of the present or the past and different disciplinary approaches with regional and/or thematic focus are *Beyond Androcentrism: New Essays on Women and Religion,* edited by Rita M. Gross (Missoula, Mont., 1977); *Women in the World's Religions: Past and Present,* edited by Ursula King (New York, 1987); *Women in*

World Religions, edited by Arvind Sharma (Albany, N.Y., 1987); *Unspoken Worlds: Women's Religious Lives*, edited by Nancy Auer Falk and Rita M. Gross (Belmont, Calif., 1989; 3d ed., 2000); *Today's Woman in World Religions*, edited by Arvind Sharma (Albany, N.Y., 1994); *Religion and Women*, edited by Arvind Sharma (Albany, N.Y., 1994); *Religion and Gender*, edited by Ursula King (Oxford, 1995); *Women and Goddess Traditions: In Antiquity and Today*, edited by Karen L. King with an introduction by Karen Jo Torjesen (Minneapolis, 1997); *Gender/Bodies/Religions*, edited by Sylvia Marcos (Cuernavaca, Mexico, 2000); *Christian and Islamic Gender Models*, edited by Karl Elisabeth Börresen (Rome, 2004); and *Gender, Religion, and Diversity: Cross-Cultural Perspectives*, edited by Ursula King and Tina Beattie (London, 2004), which offers a more inclusive perspective as it includes work on men's studies in religion. There are also collections of primary texts providing a firsthand resource. Especially noteworthy is *Women's Religions in the Greco-Roman World: A Sourcebook*, edited by Ross Shepard Kraemer (Oxford, 2004), which contains a cornucopia of eloquent evidence (in English translations) with excellent introductions and bibliographies.

Postcolonial Approaches

Edward Said, *Orientalism* (New York, 1978; 2d ed. with a postface London, 1995: see pertinent criticism by Giovanni Casadio, "Studying Religious Traditions between the Orient and the Occident: Modernism vs Post-modernism," in *New Paths in the Study of Religion: FS in Honour of Michael Pye* [Munich, 2004], pp. 119–135; and Philip A. Mellor, "Orientalism, Representation and Religion: The Reality behind the Myth," *Religion* 34, No. 2 [2004]: 99–12); Homi K. Bhabha, *The Location of Culture* (London, 1994); and Gayatri Spivak, *A Critique of Postcolonial Reason: Toward a History of the Vanishing Present* (Cambridge, Mass., 1999), are the gospels of the postcolonial approach in postmodern style. *Europe and the People without History* (Berkeley, 1982) is instead a robust historical book written by Eric Wolf, a Marxist anthropologist who endeavors to show that European expansion not only transformed the lifestyles of non-European societies but also reconstituted the account of their past history. Robert J. C. Young, *Postcolonialism: An Historical Introduction* (Oxford, 2001), is perhaps the best general reader on the subject, albeit not focused on religion. David Chidester, "Colonialism," in *Guide to the Study of Religions*, edited by Willi Braun and Russell T. McCutcheon (London and New York, 2000), pp. 423–437, provides a well-informed if not unprejudiced introduction to the postcolonial study of religion.

The deconstruction and reconstruction of Hinduism in terms that make it interesting for consumption by Western intelligentsia is at the center of several influential books: *Hinduism Reconsidered*, edited by Gunther-Dietz Sontheimer and Hermann Kulke (New Delhi, 1989; 2d ed., 1997); *Orientalism and the Postcolonial Predicament*, edited by Carol Appadurai Breckenridge and Peter van der Veer (Philadelphia, 1993); and Peter van der Veer, *Imperial Encounters: Religion and Modernity in India and Britain* (Princeton, 2001), stressing hybridism more than cultural alienation. For the Indian periphery, see Margaret J. Wiener, *Visible and Invisible Realms: Power, Magic, and Colonial Conquest in Bali* (Chicago, 1995), criticizing colonial accounts and recounting Balinese memories; and Ananda Abeysekara, *Colors of the Robe: Religion, Identity, and Difference* (Columbia, S.C., 2002), dealing with Sri Lankan Buddhism in a blatantly postmodern style (see the review by Jonathan S. Walters, *History of Religions* 43, no. 4 [2004]: 336–339). About Buddhism in general, *Curators of the Buddha: The Study of Buddhism under Colonialism*, edited by Donald S. Lopez Jr. (Chicago, 1995), is the founding text. See the review by Kay Koppedrayer in *Method and Theory in the Study of Religion* 11, no. 4 (1999): 427–432. Richard King, *Orientalism and Religion: Postcolonial Theory, India, and the "Mystic East"* (London, 1999), is a synthesis of this approach applied to Hinduism, Buddhism, mysticism, and religion, including some good analysis but flawed by unabashed homage to the most reckless post-ism. See the "Review Symposium" in *Method and Theory in the Study of Religion* 14, no. 2 (2002): 231–292 (especially the intervention of Donald Wiebe, which is also relevant for Chidester's below-mentioned book). Even wilder is Timothy Fitzgerald, *The Ideology of Religious Studies* (Oxford, 2000), which, combining incongruously Marx with Derrida, and India with Japan, argues that the concept of religion itself should be abandoned and the discipline of religious studies expelled from the academic agenda as a dangerous instrument of neocolonialism. (See the insightful comments by Gustavo Benavides in *Religious Studies Review* 27, no. 2 [2001]: 105–108.) For a sound criticism of this fashionable trend see David N. Lorenzen, "Who Invented Hinduism?" *Comparative Studies in Society and History* 41 (1999): 630–659, reprinted in *Defining Hinduism: A Reader*, edited by J. E. Llewellyn (London and New York, 2005), a multifarious volume giving the word to all the protagonists of this hot debate, which is highly significant for religious studies generally.

With regard to Islam the leading figure is Talal Asad, an anthropologist, or rather an intellectual historian, working on the concept of secularity vis-à-vis modernity in the effort to demystify its tendentious universality. His approach is much refined and less generalizing than that of Said but at times no less biased by his own preconceptions: See especially *Formations of the Secular: Christianity, Islam, Modernity* (San Francisco, 2003). On Africa the most comprehensive contributions are *Postcolonial Identities in Africa*, edited by Richard Werbner and Terence Ranger (Cape Town, 1996) and David Chidester, *Savage Systems: Colonialism and Comparative Religion in Southern Africa* (Charlottesville, Va., 1996). Both present stimulating new perspectives about the emergence of concepts such as witchcraft or religion on colonial frontiers but also denounce the insidious action of methodological triumphalism. See the reviews of Chidester by Jeffrey C. Ruff in *Method and Theory in the Study of Religion* 11, no. 2 (1999): 163–169, and Eric Bain-Selbo in *Journal of Religion & Society* 5 (2003), who speaks of "an unproductive (even if fairly interesting) self-loathing."

With regard to Oceania, Gananath Obeyesekere produced *The Apotheosis of Captain Cook: European Mythmaking in the Pacific* (Princeton, 1992), one of the most provocative—and most controversial—items in the pantheon of postcolonial literature, which should be, of course, utilized with due attention to the opposite views of the Hawai'i specialist Marshall Sahlins. Norman J. Girardot's *The Victorian Translation of China: James Legge's Oriental Pilgrimage* (Berkeley and Los

Angeles, 2002) reinterprets a fundamental moment in the prehistory of Sinology without paying homage to any post-ism.

For North America, especially relevant is the work of Charles H. Long, who in *Significations: Signs, Symbols, and Images in the Interpretation of Religion* (Philadelphia, 1986) shows inter alia how the experience of God for black Americans has been molded by their West African heritage. The mélange that resulted from Latin America colonization is studied by Serge Gruzinski, *The Mestizo Mind: The Intellectual Dynamics of Colonization and Globalization* (London, 2002), in a typically Parisian style. A more genuine approach is the work of a Mexican pioneer of postcolonial gender studies, Sylvia Marcos: See the interview "Latin American Scholarship," *Religious Studies News* 19, no. 4 (2004): 7 and 18–19 (with reference to *Dialogue and Difference: Feminisms Challenge Globalization* [New York, 2005]), advocating a decolonization of the meanings imposed on indigenous discourses (on gender distinction) by Spanish colonizers.

The debate on ancient Mediterranean religions (especially Egypt and Greece) has been revitalized by a series of volumes (and the relevant critiques in journals and books) written by Martin Bernal. The most influential (and most controversial) is *Black Athena: The Afroasiatic Roots of Classical Civilization* (London, 1987). Although Bernal's attempt to decolonize the historiography of ancient classical civilization is highly stimulating, his appreciation of primary and secondary literature is at times unsound.

Sociobiological Approaches

The groundbreaking books by scientists (mainly zoologists) to which reference is made are the following: Konrad Lorenz, *Das sogenannte Böse: Zur Naturgeschichte der Aggression* (Vienna, 1963), Engl. trans. *On Aggression* (New York, 1963); Luigi Luca Cavalli-Sforza and M. W. Feldman, *Cultural Transmission and Evolution: A Quantitative Approach* (Princeton, 1981); and Edward O. Wilson, *Sociobiology: The Modern Synthesis* (Cambridge, Mass., 1975), *On Human Nature* (Cambridge, Mass., 1978), and *Consilience: The Unity of Knowledge* (New York, 1998). Noteworthy among countless critiques is that of a preeminent anthropologist, Marshall Sahlins, *The Use and Abuse of Biology: An Anthropological Critique of Sociobiology* (Ann Arbor, Mich., 1976). The following works pioneering sociobiological research are to be mentioned: Aby Warburg, *Schlangenritual: Ein Reisebericht* (London, 1939; Berlin, 1988); Karl Meuli, *Gesammelte Schriften* (Basel and Stuttgart, 1975); and Raoul Weston la Barre, *The Human Animal* (Chicago, 1954), *The Ghost Dance: Origins of Religion* (New York, 1970: See the telling review by the ecological ethnologist Åke Hultkrantz, *Temenos* 7 [1971]: 137–144), and *Shadow of Childhood: Neoteny and the Biology of Religion* (Norman, Okla., 1991). The two seminal works by Walter Burkert are *Homo Necans* (Berlin and New York, 1972; Berkeley, 1983) and *Creation of the Sacred: Tracks of Biology in Early Religions* (Cambridge, Mass., 1996). Based on historical exploration of ancient Mediterranean religions, Burkert suggests natural foundations for sacrifices and rituals of escape, for the concept of guilt and punishment, for the practice of gift exchange and the notion of a cosmic hierarchy, and for the development of a system of signs for negotiating with an uncertain environment. His basic assumption of an innateness of some phenomena common to all human civilizations (*universalia*), "inasmuch as everywhere people eat, drink, and defecate, work and sleep, enjoy sex and procreate, get sick and die," has encountered serious criticism: See, for example, Benson Saler, "Biology and Religion," *Method and Theory in the Study of Religion* 11, no. 3 (1999): 386–394.

An effort to relate religion and biology is to be found also in the groundbreaking studies of ritual and mysticism by Frits Staal, *Exploring Mysticism* (Harmondsworth, U.K., 1975) and *Rules without Meaning: Ritual, Mantras, and the Human Sciences* (Toronto, 1989), where he takes up a firm stance against cultural relativism and any artificial distinction between "East" and "West" or the sciences and humanities. In *Why Gods Persist: A Scientific Approach to Religion* (London and New York, 1999) the foremost biologist (ethologist and psychologist) Robert A. Hinde argues that religious aspects of human life arise from natural tendencies. A general, balanced survey of theoretical and idiographic research is given by Joel Sweek, "Biology of Religion," *Method and Theory in the Study of Religion* 14, no. 2 (2002): 196–218. Notable case studies are the following: Hans-Peter Hasenfratz, *Das Christentum: Eine kleine Problemgeschichte* (Zurich, 1992); Luther Martin, "Comparativism and Sociobiological Theory," *Numen* 48, no. 3 (2001): 290–308 (the kinship–kingship model of socioreligious organization of China and Greece in its biological roots); Johannes Bronkhorst, "Asceticism, Religion, and Biological Evolution," *Numen* 13, no. 4 (2001): 374–418 (asceticism as a universal shared, innate human predisposition studied in classical India and early Christianity); Hans-Peter Müller, "Religion als Teil der Natur der Menschen," *Archiv für Religionsgeschichte* 5, no. 1 (2003): 227–242 (derivations in terms of human ethology are attempted on magic, myth, ritual, and god worship with examples from the Old Testament); and Ina Wunn, "The Evolution of Religions," *Numen* 50, no. 4 (2003): 387–415 (an ambitious attempt to contribute a theory that explains the distribution and development of religions from a genetic and historical point of view, based on the Darwinian theory of evolution).

Cognitive Approaches

E. Thomas Lawson, "Cognition," in *Guide to the Study of Religions*, edited by Willi Braun and Russell T. McCutcheon (London and New York, 2000), pp. 75–84, provides a succinct account by one of the two pioneers of this approach (after the theoretical foundations by Dan Sperber, *Rethinking Symbolism* [Cambridge, U.K., 1975] and the anthropological prelude by Stewart Guthrie in 1980). The lines of this cognitive explanatory project were first exposed in E. Thomas Lawson and Robert N. McCauley, *Rethinking Religion: Connecting Cognition and Culture* (Cambridge, U.K., 1990). More refined and substantial are the books by the French psychologist Pascal Boyer, *Tradition as Truth and Communication: A Cognitive Description of Traditional Discourse* (Cambridge, U.K., 1990), *The Naturalness of Religious Ideas: A Cognitive Theory of Religion* (Berkeley, 1994), and *Religion Explained: The Evolutionary Origins of Religious Thought* (New York, 2001). See the brilliant review essay of Gustavo Benavides, "Postmodern Disseminations and Cognitive Constraints," *Religion* 27 (1997): 129–138. Another work, very ambitious but fallacious in its own theoretical foundations, is *How Religion Works: Towards a New Cognitive Sci-*

ence of Religion (Leiden, 2001) by Ilkka Pyysiäinen, a Finnish scholar who has some idiographic experience (Indian Buddhism). From the standpoint of the history of religions only a few works are relevant, such as Harvey Whitehouse, *Arguments and Icons: Divergent Modes of Religiosity* (Oxford, 2000), and *Current Approaches in the Cognitive Science of Religion*, edited by Ilkka Pyysiäinen and Veikko Anttonen (London and New York, 2002), containing little more than theoretical rumination (for a balanced criticism see the review by Steven Engler, *Numen* 51, no. 3 [2004]: 354–358). After two conferences on Whitehouse's theory of "modes of religiosity," with the participation of prominent anthropologists and historians respectively, and further theoretical volumes by Lawson, McCauley and Pyysiäinen, a well-argued and informed introduction to the cognitive approach which can be useful also for historians is Harvey Whitehouse, *A Cognitive Theory of Religious Transmission*, Walnut Creek, Calif., 2004. Despite all its merits, it is apparent that this fast-increasing cumulated theory will hardly convince scholars working with a historical, idiographic methodology.

Un-conclusion

The books referred to are Hayden White, *Metahistory: The Historical Imagination in Nineteenth-Century Europe* (Baltimore and London, 1973); and Paul K. Feyerabend, *Against Method* (London, 1975; 3d ed., 1993). Despite its ambition, Cristiano Grottanelli and Bruce Lincoln's "A Brief Note on (Future) Research in the History of Religions," *Method and Theory in the Study of Religion* 10, no. 3 (1998): 311–325, offers nothing substantially new except a professed dissatisfaction with the current state of the art.

GIOVANNI CASADIO (2005)

MATERIALITY. The concept of *materiality of religion* has largely been developed within the discipline of the history of religions and follows the work of Charles H. Long (b. 1926) and Mircea Eliade (1907–1986). Both of these scholars have been concerned with the origin of religion. In the case of Eliade the origin of religion is associated with the human connection to the material world. For Long the origin of religion emerges through *intercultural contact*, a term that refers not just to interhuman contact but to contact between distinctive orientations to material life, or a cosmology of relationships. Of dramatic significance for the origins of religion has been *modernity*, which followed the "Age of Discovery."

One of the defining features of modernity has been the often catastrophic encounters between Western expansionism and empirical "others" (i.e., people locally and indigenously organized). In this world of cultural contact religion has played an important, yet ambiguous role. The expansionist powers of Europe held together their empires by intellectualist means: the use of books and military hardware were combined with religious, scholarly, economic, and political institutions to forge a sense of the superiority of the West. Ironically, however, the West (as we have come to know it) has been, and continues to be, radically transformed in its encounters with others. In large part the way the West defines itself is due to the influences of its dominated peoples from throughout the world. These influences have been rigorously and fastidiously denied and ignored by academics, even though the material and bodily aspects of our "global culture" are propped up by a staggering degree of cultural diversity.

Disjunction between ideological and material constructions of the West reveals a profound ambiguity embedded within modern understandings of religion. It is the task of the history of religions to work through the diverse meanings embedded within these occasions of cultural contact. The history of religions is involved with a self-conscious interrogation of religion with respect to other cultures and their perceived understandings of the world.

Through the history of religions, contact with empirical others, however, must be situated in a context of the sacred. While not a necessary condition for the historian of religions, an understanding of the various interpretations of the sacred has profoundly influenced the discipline. Contact with the sacred Other has been conceived as awe-inspiring and an engagement with absolute power, or a manifestation of the sacred (i.e., hierophany). For Rudolf Otto, Gerardus van der Leeuw, and Eliade, archaic people (i.e., people who are primarily concerned with archetypal meanings embedded in material life) meaningfully evaluate their world with reference to negotiating various manifestations of a powerful Other—the hierophany. Ultimate and absolute power, the sacred, is opaque to direct human interpretations because human life is understood as being *wholly* contingent on the sacred Other. The hierophany, a presentation of absolute and therefore sacred power, is the experience that organizes or founds the world. A meaningful orientation to the material world is only understood with reference to this wholly significant Other.

Contact with empirical others during the modern period is the anthropological analog of a history of religions formulation of contact with the sacred Other. It is the fiction of transparency of empirical others that determines the character of the modern world. For while they are rendered variously as noble savages or wild men, empirical others are rarely understood to be intimately involved in cultural exchanges with civilization. Empirical others are discussed, examined, sympathized with, and so on, but rarely are they understood to be actively engaged in the formation of modernity. Empirical others have been seen as religious but have not gained the same status as the sacred Other—an opaque reality that constitutes our modern phenomenal existence. Instead, according to Long, empirical others have been "signified" as transparent and peripheral to modernity. Many of the issues that have traditionally emerged in the history of religions with reference to the Other have tremendous potential in the current, postmodern climate for the critical evaluation of the otherness embedded in modernity.

MATERIALITY AND THE PLACE OF RELIGION. Another defining feature of modernity has been mobility—the freedom of movement. But this freedom from the European perspective deprived other cultures of their own freedom when they butted against conquistadors, merchants, and explorers. The consequence of European movement into territories not traditionally their own was the radical disruption, and often extermination, of indigenous people's traditions and practices—or what has been called *cultural genocide.* Simultaneous with the development of the freedom of movement for European people was the loss of freedom for indigenous people to remain in their place. This is reflective of colliding materialities.

The consequences of contact between once disparate people have been enormous. The Age of Discovery pushed cultures into situations of negotiation in intimate proximity with other cultures that were once seen as remote and radically "other." Europeans developed elaborate interpretive strategies in order to camouflage deep and abiding relationships with others. These strategies constituted an important mythic corpus that included ultimate authority of the book, objectivity or omniscience, a "primitive/civilized" classificatory schema (as well as other schemas), and religious justifications for colonialism, warfare, enslavement, consumerism, and so on. These mythic themes have all manner of tragedies attached to them, and it is their materialization that defines the modern age.

It is the disruption of meaningful places that makes the history of religions possible and necessary. Although the devastation of places has had a long history in the European and Mediterranean worlds, it becomes particularly endemic and reified during the modern era. Central to the imperial projects of European kingdoms was the development of strategies for occupying what were seen as "new" worlds. Conceptual tools were required in order to leave home and occupy other people's homes. The inevitable consequence was a contentious intimacy with indigenous peoples upon whose lives the survival of colonial people depended. With the loss of home the essential nature of one's cultural self-definition is forever transformed. The prevailing emotion of the Age of Discovery and the Enlightenment was the headiness and lightness of disorientation that arises from a peripatetic philosophy embracing the virtues of freedom in movement. (For an examination of the consequences of colonialism, see works by Todorov and Dussel in the bibliography.)

From various perspectives the modern era epitomizes a shift in the human material orientation from *locative* to *utopian* (i.e., "no place"). This shift is not new in human history but was rigorously endorsed and promoted by modernity. Europeans had to justify far-flung imperial projects by emphasizing the ultimate significance of "placelessness." Indigenous people underwent extermination from discoverers, colonists, and merchants; to survive they likewise had to radically transform their traditional practices in order to maintain their locative orientations. The structure of modernity is generated by the fictive (utopian, placeless) status of formulations of meaning. The ultimate meanings of people's lives are determined by others—books, institutions, intellectuals—or on the whole modalities removed from an immediate living reality and context. Material referents for the creative impulses of the modern era are rigorously signified by abstract symbols like the Bible or heaven. Abstraction of material existence swept a larger universe (or empire) under its influence and obscured the nature of power.

The consequences of modernity for colonized people has been catastrophic. Without minimizing the "American holocaust," however, it is also the task of the history of religions to reflect on the consequences of modernity on the culture of the colonizer, which in various ways is articulated as the modern university. This move completes the hermeneutical circle—a return to the self in light of the approximation of the other. But it is also an attempt to regain a critical interpretive location in the context of an experience of modernity.

HISTORY OF RELIGIONS AND MATERIALITY. The history of religions has hit upon a way of short-circuiting the dangers of articulating others within the academy. In its recent past the discipline was dominated by the quest for understanding the "sacred" in all of its manifestations. This was an encyclopedic enterprise inspired by assumptions about the possibility of such knowledge. While such an enterprise is not probable now because of an almost universal affirmation of the cultural embeddedness of our understandings, an important feature of this work was its grammatical thrust—expressed as a morphology of the sacred. Apart from the essentialist nature of the discipline, a morphology can move toward articulating the other as a radical critique of the self.

Material elements such as water, stones, mountains, and trees are the referents for religious activity throughout the world. More importantly they also serve as referents for interhuman contact. The key feature of this, however, is that the meanings of these material referents (say, a plot of land in Jerusalem) are opposed to one another. The history of religions has the faculties to discuss a morphology of contact rooted in a phenomenology in which ultimate meanings of the world are at stake. Various understandings of the world are mediated by material life. Taking seriously the development of the history of religions as a search for the meanings of the sacred Other, recent disciplinary emphasis has been on the embeddedness of the academic examination of empirical others, which is negotiated through the materiality of human existence. The religious meanings of material life has always been a feature of indigenous religions all over the world. Historians of religions, intrigued by its origins, have explored the rituals of a wide variety of indigenous religions. They have recorded insights on how material life is a constant source of reflection and revelation into the reality of the sacred Other. It is though the ritual process that the meaning of material life is actively engaged. The materiality of religion, therefore, is both the point of origin for religion as well as the discipline of the History of Religions.

Nearly from its inception the history of religions has been populated by those who have been deemed "other" by the Western university. To the standard list of atheist, Jewish, Christian, Muslim, Hindu, and Buddhist are also added Africans, African Americans, Europeans, European Americans, Asians, Asian Americans, Chicanos, Latin Americans, Native Americans, and ongoing permutations of these categorical distinctions. This is not an exhaustive list of groups from which historians of religions originate, but simply an illustration of the diversity of interpretive locations that have constituted the discipline. Methodologies of the history of religions have been constructed in such a way as to give as authentic a voice as possible to others who have moved into the academy. Others proximate to, yet excluded from, the creation of modernity can actively participate in the vitality of the discipline by engaging in methodological discussions through their orientations to their material worlds. It is no longer simply the case that scholars of religions pass judgment about "other" religions, but rather they are actively engaged in a more subtle and risky venture of exploring how the "other" has been materially involved with the "self." From the start and up until the recent past, therefore, methodological discussions have been seen as critical in the formation of the discipline.

In the late twentieth century there was often perceived to be a struggle for the heart and soul of the university. Various strategies were adopted to include underrepresented groups in university organization. Some scholars have lamented that these struggles amount to a loss of the central organizing principle of the Western intellectual tradition. Others maintain that a politics of domination has been justified and instigated by the university, and thus the inclusion of those seen as peripheral to its development is an important corrective measure. To these debates regarding the future of the university, the history of religions could add something important. First, the West was never constructed out of whole cloth, but arose from the ambiguous material situations that grew out of world subjugating enterprises. Empirical others have always been proximate, and therefore there is no Western self-sufficient self-definition. Intellectual moves to reify an authentic "self" within the university were always implemented with reference to what was perceived as a dangerous "other" either in its midst or just outside its walls. The more proximate the "other," the more dangerous it is. It is the universities' esteemed push toward clarity that obfuscates a morphology of contact.

Second, and more importantly, if there is to be a future for the university it must find modalities for discussion across all sorts of cultural, gendered, racial, and ethnic lines—however arbitrary the history of the development of those lines may be. This strategy of organization is in contrast to the move toward entrenchment of area studies programs that see the survival of themselves, as "others" within the university (women, African Americans, Native Americans, etc.), as necessarily adopting the citadel mentality of the West. In contrast, the history of religions has developed, and continues to develop, interpretive strategies for interrogating the meanings of the modern world by engaging human creativity at its deepest level. Seriously navigating the worlds of marginalized people is the future of the university. Moving these worlds into theoretical and methodological reflection is the means by which conversation can occur. This is the future of the university and will require that it reframe its intellectual activity away from the citadel to an exploration of radical material diversity. This is a risky business in which living by one's wits takes on a new energy because everything—competing cosmologies—is at stake. At the very least, if intense interaction of peoples characterizes the modern world, that interaction must be adequately reflected in the university. It seems also to be the case that others can offer powerful criticisms of, interpretations of, and alternatives to modernity.

The pressure exerted by an approximation of other meaningful orientations to material life (or other *materialities*) generates a critical faculty within the history of religions. It is not simply an authentic reduplication of another's voice, but rather a rigorous amplification and directing of that voice. The other cannot, in the final analysis, be completely relegated to an interpreter's grammar. It is not a self-appointed other whose existence is simply an extension of the writer's imaginative labors. Rather, the other operates on the historian of religions and exerts sometimes enormous pressure to be known, and in doing so transforms. While this may happen in large measure within the imaginative and creative confines of the scholar's work, it nonetheless unmasks the intimate other—a critical voice—and thus unleashes new possibilities for understanding the world. The materiality of the present situation is a mythic construction of the past. This past was constituted out of sustained cultural contact between a wide variety of "others" who, together, have worked to create the present world. From a history of religion perspective, the material world is not so much a factual reality as a mythic reality, one that requires constant creative engagement of concern.

See Also Economics and Religion; Gardens, article on Gardens in Indigenous Traditions; Sacrament, overview article.

Bibliography

For an understanding of a history of religions approach to materiality read: Davíd Carrasco, ed. *The Imagination of Matter: Religion and Ecology in Mesoamerican Traditions* (Oxford, 1989); Enrique Dussel, *The Invention of the Americas: Eclipse of "The Other" and the Myth of Modernity,* translated by Michael D. Barber (New York, 1995); Charles H. Long, *Significations: Signs, Symbols, and Images in the Interpretation of Religion* (Philadelphia, 1986); Mircea Eliade, *Myth of the Eternal Return, or, Cosmos and History,* translated by Willard R. Trask (New York, 1954; rev. ed., 1965), and *Patterns in Comparative Religion,* translated by Rosemary Sheed (New York, 1958); Rudolf Otto, *The Idea of the Holy: An Inquiry into the Non-rational Factor in the Idea of the Divine and Its*

Relation to the Rational, translated by John W. Harvey (London, 1923; 2d ed., 1950); Jonathan Z. Smith, *Map Is Not Territory: Studies in the History of Religions* (Leiden, 1978); Tzvetan Todorov, *La conquête de l'Amérique: la question de l'autre,* translation by Richard Howard published as *The Conquest of America: The Question of the Other* (New York, 1984); and Gerardus van der Leeuw, *Religion in Essence and Manifestation: A Study in Phenomenology,* translated by J. E. Turner (London, 1938).

PHILIP P. ARNOLD (2005)

MERKAVAH MYSTICISM is a term used in modern scholarship for the phenomenon behind the Jewish visionary literature of late antiquity. This literature, composed in Hebrew and Aramaic between the third century and the eighth century CE, is known as *heikhalot* literature and is preserved in manuscripts written mostly in medieval Germany and the Mediterranean. This literature describes journeys to heaven undertaken by rabbis such as ʿAqivaʾ and Yishmaʿeʾl through the seven "palaces" *(heikhalot)* to the divine throne-room, where God is seated on his chariot-throne *(merkavah).* Some of these texts also describe the conjuration of an angel who imparts to the conjurer a prodigious memory and profound wisdom. This literature is often considered to be the first stage in the history of Jewish mysticism.

Merkavah is the Hebrew word for chariot. The word appears in *1 Chronicles* 28:18 to describe the superstructure of the Ark of the Covenant in the ancient Temple, which constituted a kind of earthly throne for God. In this structure, two angelic creatures called *cherubs* framed the ark with their outstretched wings. However, the term was later used to identify the traveling throne of God seen by Ezekiel in his vision in *Ezekiel* 1–3. *Merkavah* is used in this way in the book of *Ben Sira (Ecclesiasticus)* 49:8. In the Angelic Liturgy in the Dead Sea Scrolls the term is used in the context of the heavenly temple. In the *heikhalot* literature, the *merkavah* is the grand throne in the highest layer of heaven on which God is seated, surrounded by angelic hosts, as in *Ezekiel* 1–3 and *Isaiah* 6.

Gershom Scholem, who brought this literature to the attention of scholars in his monumental studies of Jewish mysticism (*Major Trends in Jewish Mysticism,* 1941, chap. 2 and *Jewish Gnosticism, Merkavah Mysticism, and Talmudic Tradition,* 1965), argued that these texts reflected a practice of cultivating ecstatic visions of an anthropomorphic God. In recent decades, students of this literature have questioned this thesis, asking whether these texts constituted stories to be read and recited, liturgical texts, or magical texts for achieving specific practical goals.

ANTECEDENTS AND PARALLELS. *Merkavah* mysticism has precedents in apocalyptic literature, which abounds in stories of ancient heroes who took guided tours to heaven. However, in apocalyptic texts such as the books of *Enoch* these ascents are undertaken at God's initiation, whereas the ascents in *merkavah* mysticism are taken by the traveler himself. The Dead Sea Scrolls include an intriguing Angelic Liturgy known as the *Songs of the Sabbath Sacrifice,* in which the liturgist depicts a heavenly temple where angels officiate. This liturgy has many affinities with *heikhalot* texts, especially *Maʿaseh Merkavah,* but here too the worshiper does not ascend but simply describes the workings of the heavenly temple.

The *merkavah* is mentioned in several places in rabbinic literature. One of the most prominent texts is based on the law given in *Mishnah Ḥagigah* 2:2 that "The *merkavah* may not be expounded before one person unless he is a sage and understands of his own knowledge." Given the context, the Mishnah would seem to be speaking of exegetical traditions about *Ezekiel* chapter 1. But the Tosefta, a supplementary collection of extra-Mishnaic traditions, adds several curious details. The most striking of these is a cryptic story about four sages who entered the orchard (Heb., *pardes).* Of these, Ben ʿAzzʾai glimpsed and died; Ben Zoma glimpsed and went mad; (the heretical Rabbi) Elishaʿ ben Avuyah "cut the shoots"; and ʿAqivaʾ ascended and descended safely (t. *Ḥagigah* 2:3). This enigmatic tradition is given no further explanation, but *merkavah* tradition took it to mean that there were dangers inherent in visiting the divine precinct. An equally puzzling statement in the Babylonian Talmud (b. *Ḥagigah* 14b) relates this to a warning given by Rabbi ʿAqivaʾ not to cry "water, water" when one sees marble palaces. A similar text in *Heikhalot Zutarti,* one of the texts of merkavah mysticism, relates this warning to the ascent to the *merkavah.* Based on these parallels, Scholem and others have suggested that *merkavah* mysticism, that is, cultivation of visions of ascent to heaven, stemmed from the central circles of early rabbinic leadership. David Halperin's study of these traditions, however, shows that the earliest stages of rabbinic literature do not yield evidence for such a practice.

THE ASCENT TEXTS. The *heikhalot* texts appear in their most complete form in manuscripts transmitted from the fourteenth century to the sixteenth century by scribes associated with the German Jewish pietists known as the Ashkenazic Ḥasidim. Fragments of the texts also appear in the *Cairo Genizah,* a collection of discarded manuscripts from medieval Egypt. Traces of the literature and the phenomena they represent can be found in Jewish magical literature, Talmud and midrash, and the Jewish controversial literature of the early Middle Ages. The major works have been published in two pioneering synoptic editions by Peter Schäfer. The texts can be divided into two types: *ascent texts* that describe how a rabbi traveled to the divine throne-room, and *adjuration texts* that provide instructions for conjuring an angel known as the Prince of the Torah (*Sar ha-Torah*) or Prince of Wisdom (*Sar ha-Ḥokhmah*), who will grant the practitioner wisdom and skill in learning the Torah. Related to the ascent texts are the *Shiʿur Qomah* texts, which describe in graphic detail the measurements of God's body. Although they are attributed to rabbis who lived in the second century CE, they were almost certainly not written by those rabbis.

The paradigmatic ascent text is *Heikhalot Rabbati* (The greater [book of the] palaces). In the core narrative of this text Rabbi Yishmaʿeʾl relates how he, with a company of colleagues, including his teacher Rabbi Naḥunyaʿ ben ha-Qanah, learned the secrets of ascending (a process that is paradoxically described sometimes as "descending") to "see the King in his beauty." The text proceeds to describe the wonders, dangers, and rewards of this journey. The cosmology underlying the narration is that of a celestial abode of God surrounded by seven palaces (*heikhalot*). At the gate to each palace stand fearsome angelic guards who are waiting to attack anyone who is not properly qualified to enter. The traveler succeeds in entering each palace by having in his possession elaborate divine names (sometimes known as "seals"), which he presents to the angelic guard, and by having esoteric knowledge of the heavenly topography and the names and characteristics of specific angels. One prevailing motif of the ascent narrative is the awe and terror that grips the traveler as he confronts the angels or witnesses the rivers of fire or vast chambers of the divine realm. At the same time, the adept is rewarded and assured if he does manage to gain admission to the next *hekhal.* A passage from *Heikhalot Rabbati* illustrates this dynamic. The passage depicts the moment when a man who wishes to descend to the *merkavah* arrives at the gate of the seventh *hekhal.* He is met by the angel Anafiel, who opens the gate for him. However, when the *ḥayot,* the holy creatures described in *Ezekiel* 1:5–12, cast their five hundred and twelve eyes on him, "he trembles, quakes, recoils, panics, and falls back fainting. But the angel Anafiel and the sixty-three guards of the seventh palace assist him and say, 'Do not fear, son of the beloved seed! Enter and see the King in his beauty. Your eyes will see, you will not be slaughtered, and you will not be burned!'" (Schäfer, 1981, sec. 248).

Another important component of the ascent texts is hymnology. The major ascent texts are embellished by hymns praising God or, in the case of a set of poems in *Heikhalot Rabbati,* singing of the dangers and rewards of the vision. One *heikhalot* text, *Maʿaseh Merkavah* (The work of the chariot), consists largely of esoteric prayers framed by narrative of the vision of the heavens and the cultivation of the *Sar-Torah. Heikhalot Rabbati* contains two distinctive types of hymns. One type consists of hymns of praise in an elaborate style, replete with profusions of synonyms for praise. When the traveler reaches the seventh *hekhal,* the divine throne-room, the text breaks into a long list of adjectives describing God as king: "He is a righteous king, a faithful king, a gentle king, a humble king, a just king, a loving king, a holy king, a pure king," and so on (Schäfer, 1981, sec. 249). This passage may have been placed at this strategic point in the narrative of *Heikhalot Rabbati* to illustrate the angelic liturgy in which the traveler participates. Another style follows a more complex pattern and contains allusions to the journey itself. These also culminate in the recitation of the liturgical *qedushah,* the doxology sung by the angels in *Isaiah* 6:3. One such hymn addresses the angels directly (Schäfer, 1981, sec. 158):

> You who annul the decree, who dissolve the oath, who repel wrath, who turn back jealousy. . . why is it that you sing praises, and at times you rejoice, and you are fearful, and at times you recoil?. . . They said, "When the wheels of the divine glory of the *Merkavah* darken, we stand in great dread, but when the radiance of the *Merkavah* gives light, we are very happy," as it is said, "Holy, Holy, Holy is the Lord of Hosts, the fullness of the earth is his glory." (*Is.* 6:3)

A third style, found in other texts, especially *Maʿaseh Merkavah,* draws from the earliest stage of post-biblical Hebrew liturgical poetry, called *piyyut.* This style uses parallelism (the prevailing characteristic of biblical poetry), as well as a steady rhythm, usually of four feet, to convey the praise of God and the participation of both angels and humans in this praise. One hymn in *Maʿaseh Merkavah* expresses it this way:

> Angels stand in heaven, and the righteous are sure in their remembrance of You, and Your name hovers over them all. (Schäfer, 1981, sec. 587)

This hymn emphasizes that God (especially the divine name, which plays an important role in the text) transcends both the angelic community in heaven and the human worshipers (the "righteous"). This reinforces the idea prominent in the text that humans have the right to praise God in correspondence with the angelic liturgy. In the texts themselves, prayer and hymnology have several functions. For *Heikhalot Rabbati,* which emphasizes the ascent through the seven palaces, extravagant praise of God is the duty and privilege of the traveler when he reaches the divine chambers. For the ascent texts in *Maʿaseh Merkavah,* prayer actually causes the divine vision. Rabbi ʿAqivaʾ declares, "When I recited this prayer I saw 6,400,000,000 angels of glory facing the throne of glory" (Schäfer, 1981, sec. 551).

While the culmination of the ascent texts is clearly the vision of God, the end result of this vision is not always made clear. For *Heikhalot Rabbati,* "seeing the king in his beauty" may be sufficient. But there are hints that according to some of these texts, the human traveler is to be transformed into an angelic being himself. This is what happens to the biblical Enoch in *Sefer Heikhalot* (The book of the palaces), also known as *3 Enoch.* In this late fusion of *heikhalot* and apocalyptic narrative traditions, Enoch relates to Rabbi Yishmaʿeʾl how he ascended to heaven, and, having resisted the challenge of angelic guards of the divine presence, was transformed into Metatron, the archangel who stands at God's right hand. In a fragment from the *Cairo Genizah,* each person who qualifies to enter the seventh *hekhal* is seated "on a seat that has been reserved before the Throne of Glory." If the traveler does not actually become an angelic being, he is at least allowed to participate in the angelic divine service of God's praise.

THE *SAR-TORAH* TEXTS. Another important sector of this literature is found alongside the ascent texts but concerns

quite a different subject: the conjuration of an angel, the Prince of the Torah (*Sar ha-Torah*) or Prince of Wisdom (*Sar ha-Ḥokhmah*), who will grant the individual prodigious powers of memory, intelligence, and skill in the study of Torah, thus transforming any simpleton into a great rabbi. Like the ascent texts in the *heikhalot* corpus, these texts are attributed to rabbinic heroes such as Rabbi Yishma'e'l and his teacher Naḥunya' ben ha-Qanah. But unlike them, these texts do not concern an ascent to heaven but the process of bringing an angel down to earth. These texts are an indication of the centrality of memory in the scholastic society formed by rabbinic Judaism. At the same time, they draw on the extensive Jewish magical tradition, which preserves other rituals and incantations for the improvement of memory.

The texts, like the ascent texts, are cast as narratives. However, the narrative serves to introduce ritual instructions and to attest to the effectiveness of the ritual. These instructions usually involve extensive rituals of preparation. The practitioner is instructed, sometimes by an informing angel, to purge himself of all traces of ritual impurity by elaborate rituals of seclusion, fasting, ablution, and avoidance of infinitesimal traces of menstrual impurity (*niddah*). These rituals go well beyond those prescribed in rabbinic law for ritual purity. The object of these rituals of purification is to prepare the individual for the encounter with the angel, who will tolerate no contamination in his presence. Another important feature is the recitation of prayers and incantations that include elaborate magical names. These, like the "seals" of the ascent texts, provide the assurance to the intermediaries that the practitioner's request carries with it divine authority.

When the angel does arrive and grant the practitioner the skill in learning that he desires, the narrative relates the miraculous transformation of the ordinary student into a great scholar. In a *Sar-Torah* text appended to *Heikhalot Rabbati*, Rabbi Yishma'e'l attests that "I did not believe [in the effectiveness of the incantation] until I brought a certain fool and he became equal to me" in learning (Schäfer, 1981, sec. 305). In addition to these abilities, the practitioner acquires cosmic secrets and the specific esoteric knowledge transmitted by the magical tradition.

THE *SHI'UR QOMAH*. Another distinctive genre within *heikhalot* literature is the *Shi'ur Qomah*, or "Measurement of the Body." The *Shi'ur Qomah* consists of enumerations of the dimensions of the body of God. Each part of the divine body is given a specific measurement, given in *parsangs* (Persian miles), as well as an esoteric name: "The left ankle of the Creator is named 'TRQM,' may he be blessed. It is 190,000,000 *parsangs* tall . . . from his ankles to the knee of the Creator is called GMGY, may he be blessed, and has a height of 600,000,080 *parsangs*" (Cohen, 1985, pp. 30–31). It is explained that one of the divine *parsangs* equals 1,640,000,025,000 terrestrial *parsangs*. The text seems to have been written for the purpose of liturgical recitation and also contains several hymns. This text represents an extreme example of anthropomorphic tendencies prevalent in *heikhalot* literature, as well as its tendency to ascribe gargantuan dimensions to heaven and its inhabitants.

However, in *heikhalot* ascent texts God rarely speaks directly to humans, even if they visit in his throne room. He is portrayed anthropomorphically but not anthropopathically, distinguishing this genre from apocalyptic literature, in which God initiates the encounter with the human who is snatched up to heaven, and delivers a message (by himself or through an angelic informant) concerning the secrets of history and the destiny of Israel. In *heikhalot* literature, God simply radiates splendor from his throne. He is there to be adored by angels and humans.

***MERKAVAH* MYSTICISM AS A RELIGIOUS PHENOMENON.** Exactly what gave rise to *merkavah* literature and what is its purpose is a matter of debate. The term *mysticism* was first used to describe this phenomenon in the nineteenth century by scholars such as Heinrich Graetz and Phillip Bloch but was developed most fully by Gershom Scholem. In describing the phenomenon as *merkavah* mysticism Scholem argued that these stories of ascent derived from a practice of cultivating ecstatic visions of God through the chanting of numinous hymns and the rituals of preparation, which include social isolation, fasting, and ritual immersion. The rabbis of the narratives, by this account, were pseudepigraphic stand-ins for the authors, whose visions of God and the heavenly array were then recorded as the journeys undertaken by Rabbi 'Aqiva' and Rabbi Yishma'e'l. Scholem further argued that the repetitious style, the rhythm, the profusion of synonyms, and the numinous descriptions of God and the angels in the hymns were meant to induce a state of trance in the mystic who chanted the hymns and thus were instrumental in producing the vision recorded in the texts. Scholem also argued that this phenomenon arose in the central circles of early rabbinic Judaism in the first few centuries CE.

Since the latter decades of the twentieth century, Scholem's thesis has come under question. While some scholars, such as Ithamar Gruenwald, maintain that *heikhalot* literature reflects a practice of ecstatic vision of the heavens, Martha Himmelfarb, in her study of ascent to heaven in ancient Judaism, asked whether this literature constitutes stories to be recited rather than rituals to be practiced. David Halperin, in his book *The Faces of the Chariot* (1988), argued that the ascent traditions in *heikhalot* literature were ancillary to the *Sar-Torah* traditions and that they were based on the midrashic motif of Moses' ascent. Michael Swartz has focused on the liturgical and ritual aspects of the literature and found that rituals of preparation accompany the *Sar-Torah* texts and not the ascent texts. Schäfer's synoptic edition of the major manuscripts shows that the texts take a wide variety of forms in various recensions, which argues against seeing each text as a unified account of an individual's experience. It has also been pointed out, by Himmelfarb and others, that there are distinct echoes of priestly piety in the literature. Scholem's thesis about the social location of the literature has also been questioned. Halperin argues that

the authors were members of the lower classes (corresponding to what the Rabbis called *ʿAm ha-ʾareṣ*), while Swartz is inclined to locate them in circles of a secondary elite. Whether or not the *heikhalot* literature yields direct evidence for an ancient mystical practice, it deserves attention as a rich source of myths, rituals, and conceptions of the divine and human that vary in significant ways from the classical literature of rabbinic Judaism.

SEE ALSO Apocalypse, articles on Jewish Apocalypticism to the Rabbinic Period and Medieval Jewish Apocalyptic Literature; ʿAqivaʾ ben Yosef; Ashkenazic Hasidism; Elishaʿ ben Avuyah; Gnosticism; Rabbinic Judaism in Late Antiquity; Yishmaʿeʾl ben Elishaʿ.

BIBLIOGRAPHY

The major *heikhalot* texts are edited in Peter Schäfer, *Synopse zur Hekhalot-Literatur* (Tübingen, Germany, 1981) and *Genizah-Fragmente zur Hekhalot-Literatur* (Tübingen, Germany, 1984). Schäfer has translated most of the *heikhalot* corpus into German: *Übersetzung der Hekhalot-Literatur,* 4 vols. (Tübingen, Germany, 1987–1995). Not all of the texts have been translated into English. Reliable translations include Philip Alexander, "3 (Hebrew Apocalypse of) Enoch," in *The Old Testament Pseudepigrapha,* edited by J. H. Charlesworth, vol. 1, pp. 223–315 (Garden City, N.Y., 1983); *Maʿaseh Merkavah,* in Michael D. Swartz, *Mystical Prayer in Ancient Judaism,* pp. 224–251 (Tübingen, Germany, 1992); Martin S. Cohen, *The Shiʿur Qomah: Texts and Recensions* (Tübingen, Germany, 1985); and Michael D. Swartz, "The Seal of the Merkavah," in *Religions of Late Antiquity in Practice,* edited by Richard Valentasis, pp. 322–329 (Princeton, 2000). There are also many translations of individual units in the studies cited below.

Gershom Scholem's foundational accounts of *merkavah* mysticism are chapter 2 of *Major Trends in Jewish Mysticism,* pp. 40–79 (New York, 1941), and his *Jewish Gnosticism, Merkavah Mysticism, and Talmudic Tradition,* 2d ed. (New York, 1965). The study of *merkavah* mysticism has flourished since the early 1980s. A very good up-to-date introduction to *heikhalot* literature is Peter Schäfer, *The Hidden and Manifest God: Some Major Themes in Early Jewish Mysticism* (Albany, N.Y., 1992). Ithamar Gruenwald, *Apocalyptic and Merkavah Mysticism* (Leiden, 1980), analyzes the main texts and seeks to show relationships with apocalyptic literature. An interesting survey of the idea of ascent in late antiquity is Martha Himmelfarb, *Ascent to Heaven in Jewish and Christian Apocalypses* (Oxford, 1993). David J. Halperin's study of rabbinic sources on the *merkavah, The Merkabah in Rabbinic Literature* (New Haven, 1983), paved the way for a reexamination of the historical context of the phenomenon. In his *Faces of the Chariot* (Tübingen, Germany, 1988), he argues for the centrality of the *Sar-Torah* practices to the purpose of the whole literature. Michael D. Swartz, *Scholastic Magic: Ritual and Revelation in Early Jewish Mysticism* (Princeton, 1996), studies the *Sar-Torah* literature and its rituals and traditions as a distinct phenomenon. Another sophisticated study of ritual and magic in *heikhalot* literature is Rebecca Macy Lesses, *Ritual Practices to Gain Power: Angels, Incantations, and Revelation in Early Jewish Mysticism* (Harrisburg, Pa., 1998).

MICHAEL SWARTZ (2005)

NATIVE AMERICAN CHURCH.

The "peyote way," which is over 15,000 years old, and the Native American Church, which is about 100 years old, are flourishing. The use of peyote started in what is now southern Texas and northern Mexico, the only region in the world where the peyote cactus, classified as *Lophophora Williamsii* (Anderson, 1980, chap 8), is found in its natural habitat. The Native American Church (NAC), which uses peyote in its rituals, is alive and growing despite many efforts to eradicate this powerful way of worshiping. The existence of the NAC is in large part due to the many individuals who have sacrificed and struggled on behalf of peyote use as a religious sacrament. One such individual is Spotted Tail of the Oglala Sioux, who was arrested along with other members of his band in 1868 while using peyote as part of a tepee ceremony. At that time, only "pipe carriers" were allowed in tipis that were being used in conjunction with peyote.

While Spotted Tail awaited adjudication in a stockade, a Bureau of Indian Affairs (BIA) official advised him that if he told the court that he was conducting a church service, the court might allow him to continue the use of peyote in ceremonies. Spotted Tail did so, and the court granted the continued use of peyote in the context of a bona fide church service. There was one stipulation, however, made at that time by the BIA and the court: The participants could not use pipes in the ceremony. The newly formed United States government requested the removal of the sacred pipes from the peyote ceremony because government officials did not understand the role of the pipes, and they feared the use of the pipes in conjunction with the medicine (peyote). With the absence of sacred pipes, the participants began to use tobacco rolled in a cornhusk; by the beginning of the twenty-first century, however, tobacco is no longer always used in peyote ceremonies.

The Big Moon Ceremony, founded after 1800 by John Wilson, a Caddo roadman (Fikes, 1996), makes use of a large horseshoe-shaped, earthen altar. The altar is meant to represent the hoof print of the donkey that Jesus rode on Palm Sunday. A similar ceremony, called the Half-Moon Ceremony, derives its name from a crescent-shaped altar formed from earth inside the tepee. The Big Moon and Half-Moon ceremonies both include peyote use, and both reflect the influence of Native American culture and Christianity. Both ceremonial "ways" oppose the use of alcohol and drugs. The NAC does not view peyote as a drug. From the understanding of many indigenous peoples of North and South America, God did not create drugs; God created medicinal plants and herbs, but humans made drugs and alcohol.

Participants in both ceremonies use similar sacred instruments, and the ceremonies both perform the same functions for the people: baptisms, marriages, healing services, and other celebrations of life's milestones. Both ceremonies are all-night prayer services. The Big Moon Ceremony includes use of the Bible, which is placed at the top of the altar, and this ceremony does not incorporate tobacco use. In the

Half-Moon Ceremony, on the other hand, a peyote button or "Chief" is placed on the altar, and the service includes the use of tobacco.

The first recognized Native American church, called the First Born Church of Christ, was formed in Oklahoma in 1914 by Johnathan Kashiway, a Sac and Fox "Roadman" (a person who conducts an all-night prayer service). Tobacco was prohibited from church services, and it was not mentioned in the articles of incorporation (Hirschfelder and Molin, 1992, p. 193). In 1921 the Winnebago of Nebraska established the first charter outside of Oklahoma. Called the Peyote Church of Christ, the charter was amended in 1922, and the church name was changed to the Native Church of Winnebago, Nebraska. Other Native American churches were soon organized and chartered in South Dakota, Montana, Idaho, Wisconsin, Iowa, Utah, and New Mexico.

In 1944, the Native American Church of Oklahoma changed its charter and name to the Native American Church of the United States, becoming the first national peyote organization (Smith and Snake, 1998). In 1955 the organization changed its name to the Native American Church of North America so that Canadian peyotists could attend services. Canadian Cree, Assiniboine, Ojibwa, and Blood Indians formed the Native American Church of Canada in 1954 in Red Pheasant, Saskatchewan.

The Native American Church of California and Nevada was established in 1954. In 1966 the Native American Church of Navaholand was formed; this church is independent of the Native American Church of North America. In 1970 and 1971 the NAC of Navaholand sought incorporation from the state of Arizona and was refused because of state opposition to the use of peyote. New Mexico agreed to incorporate the church in 1973. The NAC of Navaholand encompasses the country's largest group of peyotists.

Many independent peyote groups exist in the United States. The exact number of American peyotists is difficult to determine, but estimates are more than 250,000 and growing, as of 2004.

For many years, the NAC and its ritual use of peyote has suffered from the misconceptions of those outside the church who have tried to suppress it. Peyote is a small spineless cactus, and its ingestion is neither habit forming nor addictive, although it may produce nausea in some people. Within the NAC it is used only in sacred ceremonies.

It is said "sacred medicine" came to the people from a Grandmother. Her people were starving so she went into the desert to pray to the creator to have pity on them. While in the desert, a voice led her to peyote, who told her to partake of it. After eating it, this Grandmother was shown how to use peyote in ceremonies. She was instructed to take the "medicine" back to her people and to share it with them, so that they would live.

Opposition to peyote use dates back to at least 1620, when the Spanish Inquisition and the Catholic Church condemned it. Similar opposition by other European-based individuals and governments continued over the next four centuries. The Carrizo, Lipan, and Mescalero Apaches were probably the first to ingest peyote. The Tonkawa and Caddo Indians first experienced opposition to its use during the nineteenth century. Christians viewed the use of peyote as heathenism and began a campaign to wipe it out. They threatened to withhold food and imprison Native people who continued to use it.

In 1899, A. E. Woodson, a federal agent of the Cheyenne and Arapaho Agency in Darlington, Oklahoma, implemented the first statute banning the use of peyote in Indian territory (Stewart, 1993, p. 131). A number of Native ceremonies had been forbidden in earlier decades, but non-Native authorities often confused peyote with mescal bean (Anderson, 1980), and early decrees were made against the mescal bean, rather than peyote. For example, an 1890 directive from Bureau of Indian Affairs Commissioner Thomas Jay Morgan stated: "The Court of Indian Offenses at your agency shall consider the Use, Sale, Exchange gift or introduction of the Mescal Bean as a misdemeanor punishable under Section 9 [on intoxicants] of the rules governing the Court of Indian offenses" (Hirschfelder and Molin, 1992, p. 216).

During the 1900s anti-peyote laws were passed by fifteen states: Kansas (1919); Utah, Colorado, and Nevada (1917); Arizona, Montana, North Dakota, and South Dakota (1923); Iowa (1925); New Mexico and Wyoming (1929); Idaho (1933); California (1959); New York (1965); and Texas (1967). Utah, Idaho, and North Dakota later amended their anti-peyote laws to permit peyote use as part of NAC religious ceremonies. Texas too amended its anti-peyote law in 1969. The new law, called the Texas Narcotics Law of 1969, addresses the possession and distribution of peyote by the NAC in ceremony. Anti-peyote laws in California and New York were aimed at non-Indian drug users. However, in 1996 Paul Skyhorse and Buzz Berry, both Native American members of the NAC, were arrested in Ventura County, California, for the transportation of peyote. Both men were incarcerated and their peyote confiscated, although they were later released, and the peyote was returned to them.

At the beginning of the twenty-first century, the legality of peyote-use varies from state to state. In 1994 the United States federal government amended the 1978 American Indian Religious Freedom Act to legalize peyote use as a religious sacrament throughout the country. The Supreme Court later voided the 1978 act and the 1994 amendments. Peyote use within the Native American Church is no longer protected by the federal government, and the church must rely on state protection (Anderson, 1996, p. 223).

To be a legally recognized chapter of the NAC, a charter has to be written and accepted by the state in which the chapter exists. In Texas, for example, this charter must be filed with the Texas Department of Safety and Transportation and the state of Texas Drug Enforcement Agency. After re-

ceiving verification from the state, the NAC chapter is free to purchase peyote from certified peyote distributors, who will ask to see a permit and an Indian identification card before the sale.

The leadership of the NAC is chosen every four years from the existing chapters represented by the various tribes and nations. Many states have more than one reservation, or even several Indian nations, within their boundaries, and thus more than one NAC chapter. For example, the Kiowa, Comanche, and Cherokee nations all exist on different reservations within the state of Oklahoma. These three nations have different charters and various NAC chapters within the boundaries of their Oklahoma reservations.

Annual national NAC conferences are held throughout the United States with representatives from the various chapters. Participants discuss issues faced by the NAC, such as proposed changes by the federal Drug Enforcement Administration regarding the harvesting of peyote, which affects its pricing and availability. Non-Indian participation in NAC ceremonies is also an issue, personally, socially, spiritually, and legally.

SEE ALSO Apache Religious Traditions; Native American Christianities.

BIBLIOGRAPHY

Anderson, Edward F. *Peyote: The Divine Cactus.* Tucson, Ariz., 1980; 2d ed., 1996.

Fikes, Jay. "A Brief History of the Native American Church." In *One Nation under God: The Triumph of the Native American Church,* edited by Huston Smith and Reuben Snake. Santa Fe, N.Mex., 1996.

Hirschfelder, Arlene, and Paulette Molin. *The Encyclopedia of Native American Religions.* New York, 1992; updated ed., 2000.

Maroukis, Thomas Constantine. *Peyote and the Yankton Sioux: The Life and Times of Sam Necklace.* Norman, Okla., 2004.

Smith, Huston, and Reuben Snake, eds. *One Nation under God: The Triumph of the Native American Church.* Santa Fe, N.Mex., 1996.

Stewart, Omer C. *Peyote Religion: A History.* Norman, Okla., 1987; reprint, 1993.

KENNETH LITTLEFISH (2005)

OXTOBY, WILLARD G. Willard Gurdon Oxtoby (1933–2003), one of the twentieth century's foremost scholars of comparative religion, was born on July 29, 1933, in Kentfield, California, across the bay from San Francisco. He died on March 6, 2003, in Toronto, Ontario, of colon cancer at the age of sixty-nine. Oxtoby was for twenty-eight years a professor of religious studies at the University of Toronto, where he became the founding director of the Centre for Religious Studies, the one center or institute, among the dozens devoted to religious study in this large international university, dedicated exclusively to the history and comparison of religions. The founding of this center completed the University of Toronto's credentials as one of the foremost resources for the study of religion in North America.

Oxtoby began his Bible studies at age five when his father, a professor of the Bible at a Presbyterian seminary, taught him the Twenty-third Psalm in Hebrew to encourage the elder Oxtoby's graduate Hebrew class. Initially, Oxtoby followed his father into biblical studies, training at Princeton (Ph.D. 1962) after his undergraduate major in philosophy at Stanford (B.A. 1955, Phi Beta Kappa). He spent two years in Jerusalem helping to prepare the Dead Sea Scrolls for publication, with his new wife Layla Jurji, the daughter of a Princeton Theological Seminary professor of comparative religion. With Layla, he began a family of two children, David (b.1960) and Susan (b. 1963). Oxtoby's dissertation was a critical edition of the inscriptions of pre-Islamic Arabia. His first teaching assignment was at McGill University in Montreal. But he soon realized the importance of Persian religion for Judaism and Christianity, so he entered Harvard University in Cambridge, Massachusetts, on a postdoctoral fellowship to study Zoroastrianism and ancient Persian at the Center for World Religions under the stewardship of Wilfred Cantwell Smith.

After this fellowship, Oxtoby took up a position in Zoroastrianism and comparative religion at Yale University in New Haven, Connecticut, in 1966. He taught at Yale for five years and then accepted a full professorship in 1971 at the prestigious Trinity College of the University of Toronto, where he remained until his retirement in 1999. His first assignment was to establish the internationally renowned Centre for Religious Studies, which he directed from 1976 to 1981.

In June 1980 Oxtoby's wife Layla died of cancer. The following year he began to study the Chinese language with his colleague Julia Ching, a collaboration that developed into his second marriage and a long-standing publishing partnership specializing in the comparison of Abrahamic faiths and Asian faiths. Julia predeceased him in 2001 after a long bout with cancer. Although his life contained more than its share of grief, much of it from disparate cancers among his loved ones, Oxtoby was able to conquer that sorrow with the solace that his own religion gave him.

In the course of his life Oxtoby was a member of countless professional organizations, including the Canadian Society for the Study of Religion, the Canadian Asian Studies Association, the American Academy of Religion, the American Oriental Society, and the Society for Values in Higher Education (formerly the Society for Religion in Higher Education). Of all his responsibilities, perhaps most satisfying to Oxtoby was his membership in and service to the American Society for the Study of Religion, an honorary society devoted to the comparison of religion. First elected in 1964, he served as secretary (1969), executive councilor (1984–1985), vice president (1985–1988), and president (1990–1993) of that organization.

Oxtoby's detailed knowledge of the languages, cultures, and history of world religions was unmatched. In the course of his career he authored, coauthored, and edited over a dozen books on disparate topics, ranging from pre-Islamic inscriptions; to *Experiencing India: European Descriptions and Impressions, 1498–1898*, a catalog for the 1998 exhibit of four hundred years of Indian publishing at the Thomas Fisher Rare Book Library of the University of Toronto; to *Sikh History and Religion in the Twentieth Century* (1988); to *Moral Enlightenment: Leibniz and Wolff on China* (1992). He is perhaps best known for editing the massive two-volume textbook *World Religions: Eastern Traditions* and *World Religions: Western Traditions* (1996/2002). As well as serving as the general editor of this work, he authored the sections on Sikhism, Zoroastrianism, Christianity, primitive religions, and modern developments. He used common terms for these religions as a matter of convenience (e.g., Eastern and Western religions) but argued strongly throughout the books against essentializing any religion, or seeing any religion in isolation from its social and historical setting, or ignoring the other religions with which it came into contact. When he died Oxtoby was actively engaged in a series of lectures as the American Academy of Religion Distinguished Lecturer in Comparative Religion for 2003 to 2004, showing how differently Islam developed as it encountered Persia, India, Africa, Europe, and North America. The lectures, had they been finished, were contracted for publication at Columbia University Press. Oxtoby's sudden and unexpected death also interrupted several other ambitious retirement projects, including a massive collection of Near Eastern texts spanning from the ancient beginning of civilization in that part of the world to modern Islam and the Israeli–Palestinian problem.

Oxtoby was a practicing Presbyterian and a minister of that denomination. He never thought of himself as anything other than a Christian, but he pioneered a comparativist Christianity rather than an exclusivist one. Oxtoby concluded in his 1983 book, *The Meaning of Other Faiths*, that "My Christianity, including my sense of Christian ministry, has commanded that I be open to learn from the faith of others."

SEE ALSO Ching, Julia.

BIBLIOGRAPHY

Ching, Julia, and Willard G. Oxtoby, eds. *Discovering China: European Interpretations in the Enlightenment.* Rochester, N.Y., 1992.

Ching, Julia, and Willard G. Oxtoby. *Moral Enlightenment: Leibniz and Wolff on China.* Nettetal, Germany, 1992.

O'Connell, Joseph T., Milton Israel, and Willard G. Oxtoby, eds. *Sikh History and Religion in the Twentieth Century.* Toronto, 1988.

Oxtoby, Willard G. *Ancient Iran and Zoroastrianism in Festschriften: An Index.* Waterloo, Ontario, 1973.

Oxtoby, Willard G. *The Meaning of Other Faiths.* Philadelphia, 1983.

Oxtoby, Willard G., ed. *World Religions: Eastern Traditions.* Toronto, 1996; 2d ed., 2002.

Oxtoby, Willard G., ed. *World Religions: Western Traditions.* Toronto, 1996; 2d ed., 2002.

ALAN F. SEGAL (2005)

PERIODICAL LITERATURE. The appearance of periodical publications devoted to the study of religion, rather than to theology, missionary, or pastoral concerns, is inseparable from the institutionalization of the study of religion, which resulted in the establishment of the first chairs in the history of religions, beginning in 1873. An example of this is the *Revue de l'histoire des religions*, founded in 1880, shortly after Albert Réville became the first professor of history of religions at the Collège de France, a process of institutionalization that would be solidified six years later with the creation of the Fifth Section, Sciences religieuses, of the École Pratique des Hautes Études. A similar development took place almost half century later in Italy when Raffaele Pettazzoni, appointed to the first Italian chair of history of religions in 1924, founded the journal *Studi e materiali di storia delle religioni* in 1925. Given the role played by the study of Asian religions in the development of the discipline, attention must be paid to the fact that the *Journal asiatique*, the oldest journal devoted to Asian studies, was founded in 1822, not long after the discoveries of Abraham-Hyacinthe Anquetil-Duperron, Jean-François Champollion and William Jones, to mention just a few of the pioneers in the deciphering of ancient languages. The *Journal of the Royal Asiatic Society* followed suit in 1834, the *Journal of the American Oriental Society* in 1843, the *Zeitschrift der Deutschen Morgenländischen Gesellschaft* in 1847, the *Wiener Zeitschrift für die Kunde des Morgenlandes* in 1877 and *Le Muséon: Revue d'études orientales* in 1882. What one encounters since the nineteenth century in terms of periodical publications on religion, then, is a situation that mirrors the debates that take place to this day: On the one hand, the assumption that insofar as one can determine the boundaries of "religion" as a phenomenon, one can also have periodical publications devoted exclusively to its study, journals that generally have words such as *religion* or *religione* as part of their titles. On the other hand, there is the realization that insofar as religion pervades the life of ancient and nonmodern contemporary cultures, its study must be carried out in publications such as the *Journal asiatique*, devoted to the history, philology and archaeology of those cultures, as well as in publications such as *American Anthropologist* or *Anthropos*, founded in 1888 and 1906, respectively.

If one examines the journals devoted specifically to the study of religion one finds that most of the early ones, besides publishing studies in the history of various religions, were concerned with theoretical issues such as the origins of religion, a topic that is only recently being studied again. One also realizes the precariousness of the academic conceptual apparatus, for now-abandoned terms such as *mana*, *tabu* and *totem*, were as current in the late nineteenth and early twenti-

eth centuries as *discourse, social construction* and *transgression* are in the late twentieth and early twenty-first centuries. We find also that these journals, although open to foreign scholars, tended to publish work produced in a specific language—French in the case of the *Revue de l'histoire des religions,* German in that of the *Archiv für Religionswissenschaft* (1898–1942), and Italian in that of the *Studi e materiali di storia delle religioni.* This is a trend that continues in the case of periodicals established later in the twentieth century, such as the *Zeitschrift für Religions- und Geistesgeschichte* (1948); *Kairos: Zeitschrift für Religionswissenschaft und Theologie* (1959); *History of Religions* (1961); *Religion* (1971); *Religious Studies Review* (1975); the *Zeitschrift für Religionswissenschaft* (1993); and *Ilu, Revista de ciencias de las religiones* (1995), some of which are the publications of national associations. Exceptions to this trend are *History of Religions* (1961) and *Religion* (1971), two English-language journals that were conceived as international publications, rather than as the organs of a national association. Another exception, although in the opposite direction, is *Archæus: Études d'histoire des religions/Studies in the History of Religions* (1997), a Romanian journal that publishes studies in English, French and Italian. Scandinavian, rather than national or, strictly speaking, international, is *Temenos: Studies in Comparative Religion Presented by Scholars in Denmark, Finland, Norway and Sweden* (1965). A special case is *Studies in Religion/Sciences religieuses* (1971), published in the two official languages of Canada—English and French. Of the journals devoted to the history of religions, the only one that is both multilingual and international is the journal of the International Association for the History of Religions, *Numen: International Review for the History of Religions,* founded in 1954 by Pettazzoni.

The journals listed above tend to publish philological, historical and anthropological studies of religion, in some cases from a comparative perspective. Methodological, theoretical and meta-theoretical concerns are present, explicitly or implicitly, but they are not generally the focus of the articles. Specifically devoted to theoretical issues is *Method and Theory in the Study of Religion* (*MTSR,* 1989), the official journal of the North American Association for the Study of Religion, a group of scholars concerned precisely with the theory of religion. The North American Association for the Study of Religion and *MTSR* constitute the theoretical, nonconfessional, counterpart to the American Academy of Religion, an organization that represents scholars of religion as well as theologians working in the United States. Its official publication began in 1933 as the *Journal of the National Association of Biblical Instructors*; in 1937 it changed its name to the *Journal of Bible and Religion,* becoming the *Journal of the American Academy of Religion* (*JAAR*) in 1966. Unlike *MTSR* and the journals mentioned earlier, a typical issue of *JAAR* is likely to contain articles that deal with history of religions and theoretical issues, but also with philosophy of religion and "theological reflection." Among journals that deal with religion mainly from history of ideas, philosophical, and theological angles we may mention the *Journal of Religion* (1921) and *Religious Studies* (1965)—the latter, despite its name, being devoted almost exclusively to philosophy of religion and philosophical theology. On the other hand, the *Harvard Theological Review* (1908) publishes, despite its title, studies that deal with religion from theological and nontheological perspectives.

The tension between scholarly and theological approaches that has characterized the study of religion is present not only in the existence of journals such as *MTSR* and *JAAR,* or in the coexistence of historical, theoretical, philosophical, and theological articles in the pages of *JAAR,* but also in the trajectories of journals now devoted to the sociology of religion, some of which began as theological publications or as the publishing outlets of Catholic sociologists. A case in point is *Social Compass: Revue Internationale de Sociologie de la Religion/International Review of Sociology of Religion,* now the respected journal of the International Society for the Sociology of Religion/Société Internationale de Sociologie des Religions, which began in 1953 as a Catholic pastoral publication of a Thomist orientation. Similarly, *Sociology of Religion* began in 1940 as the *American Catholic Sociological Review*; the title was changed to *Sociological Analysis* in 1963, acquiring its current name in 1993. To be sure, not all sociology of religion periodicals have a theological background; it should be enough to mention the *Année sociologique,* the journal founded by Émile Durkheim in 1898, whose pages saw the publication of some of the most influential studies in the sociology of religion—studies by Durkheim, Marcel Mauss and Henri Hubert on the nature of religion, magic, and sacrifice. Three other important journals must be mentioned: *Archives de sciences sociales des religions,* founded in 1956 as *Archives de sociologie des religions,* where one finds articles that approach religion from sociological and anthropological perspectives; the *Journal for the Scientific Study of Religion* (1961), where one finds mainly quantitative studies of sociology and to a lesser extent psychology of religion; and the *Internationales Jahrbuch für Wissens- und Religionssoziologie,* published from 1965 to 1973 as the *Internationales Jahrbuch für Religionssoziologie.* An overview of research trends can be found in the *Annual Review of the Social Sciences of Religion* (1977). Changes in the religious landscape give rise to new journals; thus contemporary developments, such as New Age and, in general, noninstitutional forms of religion, are studied in *Nova Religio: The Journal of Alternative and Emergent Religions* (1997) and in *Implicit Religion* (1998). Occasionally one finds valuable contributions to the sociology of religion in general sociology journals, such as the *Kölner Zeitschrift für Soziologie und Sozialpsychologie* (1949), the *British Journal of Sociology* (1950), and *Sociologus: Zeitschrift für Völkerpsychologue und Soziologie/Sociologus: A Journal of Sociology and Social Psychology* (1951).

Turning to anthropology, in addition to *American Anthropologist* and *Anthropos,* scholars of religion can find a wealth of material on the religions of small-scale societies, as

well as on topics such as mythology, ritual, and the theory of religion, in the *Journal of the Royal Anthropological Institute* (1995), previously published as *Man* (1901–1994); in *Comparative Studies in Society and History* (1948); *Ethnohistory* (1954); *L'Homme: Revue française d'anthropologie* (1961); *American Ethnologist* (1974); *L'uomo: Società, tradizione, sviluppo* (1977); and *History and Anthropology* (1986). One of the aspects of religion to which anthropologists have paid a great deal of attention has been that of ritual, a component of religion discussed in many of the journals mentioned already, there being, in addition, a *Journal of Ritual Studies* (1987). Ritual constitutes a link among sociological, political, anthropological and psychological approaches to religion. To these disciplines one must now add cognitive and ethological approaches to ritual and to religion in general; contributions informed by these approaches can be found in history of religions and anthropology journals such as *Numen* and *Man*, and in the *Journal of Cognition and Culture* (2001). Specifically devoted to the psychology of religion are the *Archiv für Religionspsychologie/Archive for the Psychology of Religion* (1914) and the *International Journal for the Psychology of Religion* (1991).

The religious practices of contemporary large-scale societies are sometimes examined in the periodicals mentioned above; more often, however, contemporary developments are studied in articles that, along with those devoted to historical and philological research, are published in journals devoted to Asian societies. In addition to the *Journal asiatique*, the *Journal of the Royal Asiatic Society*, the *Journal of the American Oriental Society*, the *Zeitschrift der Deutschen Morgenländischen Gesellschaft*, the *Wiener Zeitschrift für die Kunde des Morgenlandes*, and *Le Muséon*, mention should be made of *T'ung Pao* (established as *T'oung Pao* in 1890); the *Bulletin de l'École française d'Extrême-Orient* (1901); the *Rivista degli studi orientali* (1907); the *Rocznik orientalistyczny* (1914); the *Bulletin of the School of Oriental and African Studies* (1917); the *Archív orientální* (1929); the *Journal of Asian Studies* (1941, known until 1956 as the *Far Eastern Quarterly*); *Asiatische Studien/Études asiatiques* (1947); the *Wiener Zeitschrift für die Kunde Südasiens und Archiv für indische Philosophie* (1957); *A.I.O.N.: Annali dell'Istituto Universitario Orientale di Napoli* (1979); and the *Cahiers d'Extrême-Asie* (1985)—all of which contain a wealth of articles dealing with all aspects of religion, from the ancient Near East to West, South, Southeast, Central, and East Asia. Most of these journals publish studies that deal from various perspectives with the religious traditions of India, as do all the history of religions journals mentioned earlier. In addition to those publications, mention should be made of *Indologica Taurinensia* (1973), which has published the proceedings of many of the World Sanskrit Conferences. The *Journal of Indian Philosophy* (1970), which because of its title one would expect to deal exclusively with the philosophical aspects of the Indian tradition, narrowly understood, contains valuable studies on the history of religions, including Buddhism. Articles dealing with the history, philosophy, archaeology, mythology and ritual practices of Buddhism can be found in most of the journals listed above. In addition, there are specialized publications, such as the *Journal of the Pali Text Society* (1882); the *Mélanges chinois et bouddhiques* (1932), where one finds Louis de La Vallée Poussin's still indispensable contributions; the *Indo-Iranian Journal* (1957), most of whose reviews were written by one of its two editors, the boundlessly erudite Jan Willem de Jong; the *Eastern Buddhist* (1966); the *Journal of the International Association of Buddhist Studies* (1978); the *Journal of Buddhist Ethics* (1994); and the *Journal of Global Buddhism* (2000).

The religions of East Asia are also dealt with in the publications already mentioned, as well as in specialized periodicals such as the *Journal of Chinese Religions* (1982). As in the case of the study of Indian religions, articles dealing with Chinese religion can be found in periodicals whose titles do not contain the term *religion*, such as the *Journal of Chinese Philosophy* (1973), *Early China* (1975), *Modern China* (1975), and *Early Medieval China* (1994). The issue of boundaries is not, however, confined to approaches or disciplines: It also involves sensitive political considerations regarding the status of a cultural/linguistic area; a case in point is Tibet, whose religion is more likely to be studied in the history of religions, Asian, and Buddhist studies journals mentioned above or in such periodicals as the *Central Asiatic Journal* (1955) or *Studies in Central and East Asian Religions* (1988) than in those devoted exclusively to Chinese religions. Work on the religious traditions of Japan can be found in *Japanese Religions* (1959) and the *Japanese Journal of Religious Studies* (1974, first published in 1960 as *Contemporary Religions in Japan*). Contributions to the study of African religions, on the other hand, are published in *Journal of African Religion/Religion en Afrique* (1967) as well as in the anthropology journals mentioned above. It is also in anthropology journals that one finds studies of Latin American religion; other valuable studies can be found in specialized publications such as the *Journal de la Société des américanistes* (1896) and the *Journal of Latin American Lore* (1975).

A mere list of the journals that deal with Christianity and, because of their role in the emergence of this religion, with Israelite and other Near Eastern religions, would exceed the length allotted to this entry. The same applies to periodicals devoted to the Greco-Roman world, a world whose philosophical, religious, and cultic vocabulary lives on in the languages of the West. Among the periodicals that publish studies of the religions of the Ancient Orient, along with those that deal with the writings canonized by Christians as the Old Testament, one may mention the *Zeitschrift für die alttestamentalische Wissenschaft* (1881), *Orientalia* (1920), *Analecta orientalia* (1931), *Orientalia christiana periodica* (1935), *Zeitschrift für Assyriologie und vorderasiatsiche Archäologie* (1886, published until 1938 as *Zeitschrift für Assyriologie und verwandte Gebiete*), *Vetus Testamentum* (1951), *Orientalia suecana* (1952), *Oriens antiquus* (1962), *Altorientalische Forschungen* (1974) and the *Journal of Ancient Near*

Eastern Religions (2001). Studies of Greek and Roman religion are found in *Rheinisches Museum für Philologie* (1883); the *Journal for Hellenic Studies* (1880); *Gnomon: Kritische Zeitschrift für die gesamte klassische Altertumswissenschaft* (1925); *Greek, Roman and Byzantine Studies* (1958); *Arethusa* (1968); *Helios* (1974); *Classical Antiquity* (1982); *Metis: Revue d'anthropologie du monde grec ancien* (1988); and *Kernos: Revue internationale et pluridisciplinaire de religion grecque antique* (1988). Studies of the early Christian world, in most cases in the context of the religions of late antiquity, can be found in the *Zeitschrift für die neutestamentalische Wissenschaft und die Kunde der ältere Kirche* (published from 1900 to 1920 as the *Zeitschrift für die neutestamentalische Wissenschaft und die Kunde des Urchristentums*); the *Jahrbuch für Antike und Christentum* (1958, published as *Antike und Christentum, Kultur- und religionsgeschichtliche Studien* from 1929 to 1950); *Vigiliæ Christianæ: A Revue of Early Christian Life and Languages* (1947); *Novum Testamentum* (1956); the *Journal of Early Christian Studies* (published as *Second Century* from 1981 to 1992); *Zeitschrift für Antikes Christentum/Journal of Ancient Christianity* (1997); and the *Journal of Greco-Roman Christianity and Judaism* (2000).

The world of medieval Christendom is the subject of a multitude of periodicals; some of them, such as the *Archives d'histoire doctrinale et littéraire du Moyen Âge* (1926), are dedicated to the study, exegesis and, in some cases, promotion of Christian theological speculation, while others, such as *Le Moyen âge: Revue d'histoire et de philologie* (1888); the *Frühmittelalterliche Studien* (1967); *Viator: Medieval and Renaissance Studies* (1970); and *Mediaevistk: Internationale Zeitschrift für interdisziplinäre Mittelalterforschung* (1988), approach medieval and early modern Christianity from historical and other perspectives. Among the journals that encompass the entire history of Christianity mention should be made of the *Zeitschrift für Kirchengeschichte* (1877), the *Revue d'histoire ecclésiastique* (1900), *Church History* (1932), and the *Journal of Ecclesiastical History* (1950). It goes without saying that given the role of Christianity in the history of the world, general history journals such as the *American Historical Review* (1895); the *Annales: Histoire, sciences sociales* (founded in 1929 as *Annales d'histoire économique et sociale*, later known as *Économies, sociétés, civilisations*); *Sæculum* (1950); and *Past and Present* (1952), regularly publish articles on the history of this religion.

Of the religions that emerged after Christianity, none is more important than Islam, a fact that is reflected in the number of publications devoted to its study. Among the journals dedicated to the study of the Islamic world, we may mention *Der Islam: Zeitschrift für Geschichte und Kultur des islamischen Orients* (1910); *Die Welt des Islams: International Journal for the Study of Modern Islam* (1913); *Arabica: Journal of Arabic and Islamic Studies/Revue d'études arabs et islamiques* (1954); *Annales islamologiques* (1954); *Al-Masaq: Islam and the Medieval Mediterranean* (1988); the *Journal of Islamic Studies* (1990); and the *Journal of Arabic and Islamic Studies* (1996). More specialized periodicals include the *Journal of Qur'anic Studies* (1999); the *Journal of the History of Sufism/Journal d'histoire du soufisme* (2000); and the *Journal of Islamic Philosophy* (2003).

If one approaches the world of journals from the point of view of a given religious tradition, one realizes soon enough that, given the fluid boundaries of what constitutes "religion," in order to do justice to that tradition one must make use of journals in several disciplines—religion, anthropology, sociology, philosophy, and history, among others. But given the fact that religious traditions are not self-contained entities, one must also consult periodicals that deal with traditions and with geographical areas that border the cultures with which one is concerned. Thus, a scholar primarily interested in Indian Buddhism is likely to find relevant research in the *Mélanges chinois et bouddhiques*, the *Journal of the International Association of Buddhist Studies*, the *Journal of Indian Philosophy*, the *Indo-Iranian Journal*, the *Wiener Zeitschrift für die Kunde Süd-Asiens*, and the *Journal asiatique*, as well as in the *Revue de l'histoire des religions*, *Numen*, *History of Religions*, *Religion*, and *Man*, not to mention periodicals that deal with Southeast and Central Asian cultures. Likewise, if one is interested in religions that predate the written record one needs to consult periodicals such as the *Journal of Indo-European Studies* (1973) and the *Journal of Prehistoric Religion* (1987), along with publications that deal with archaeology. On the other hand, if one pursues research in comparative religion or in theoretical issues from a comparative perspective, then the range of publications that are likely to contain material relevant to one's research is virtually unlimited. For example, research on religion from an ethological perspective would require consulting psychology and also biology and animal behavior periodicals.

Two issues must be mentioned when dealing with periodical literature. One of them involves the language of the contributions. Unlike periodicals devoted primarily to ancient religions and philologies, most of the religious studies journals published in the English-speaking world, France, Germany, or Italy have traditionally published articles in the languages of the country in question, *Numen* being one of the few journals that as a matter of policy publishes contributions in the main Western European languages—a fact not unrelated to the role of Dutch publishing houses since the time of the Reformation. The situation is now changing. Some of those changes would seem to be positive—as when, for example, one finds English articles in French and German journals, as this would seem to indicate an openness towards international scholarship. The truth is, however, that some of those articles have been written, for example, by French or German speakers who are forced to publish in English, for otherwise their work will not be read beyond the French- or German-speaking world. Even *Numen* now receives few submissions in languages other than English; the same being true of the *Archiv für Religionspsychologie/International Archive for the Psychology of Religion*, which de-

scribes itself as trilingual, but which also acknowledges that most of its articles are in English. It is true that Eastern European journals such as the *Rocznik orientalistyczny* have traditionally published articles in languages other than Polish, including some by Poles, such as the Buddhist scholar Stanislaw Schayer. This, however, did not involve a virtual linguistic monopoly such as the one we are witnessing today. Among the many dangers of this linguistic monopoly is that the research of authors who publish in languages other than English will be ignored, as articles are not generally translated after they have appeared in a journal. In addition, even if everything were to appear in English and everyone were able to read that language, the vast amount of work published in a variety of languages since the first scholarly periodicals saw the light of day would become as inaccessible as if they had been inscribed in cuneiform script. The situation regarding reviews is even more grave, as some English-language journals do not review books published in languages other than English. An example of this systematic ignoring of scholarship is the *Journal of the American Academy of Religion*, where one would look in vain for reviews of important theoretical and historical works published in languages such as French, German, and Italian. Such scandalous neglect both reflects and perpetuates the provincialism of the North American discussion in various fields of scholarship in religion, especially in the area of theory of religion, a field in which, with the exception of research on religion and cognition, the most interesting work is not being done in English.

Even more urgent is the issue of price. Periodicals usually have different rates for individual and for institutional subscribers, the cost for individuals being substantially lower. In either case, however, the prices are increasing. As a result of the concentration of ownership, the situation is more dire in the case of the sciences, but even journals in the humanities and social sciences are being priced beyond the reach of many institutions, even in rich countries, not to mention individual scholars. This is a problem beyond the control of the contributors and also of the editors of existing journals. The situation is complicated by the growth in the number of academics, the increase in specialized research, and, not least, the need to publish in order to maintain one's academic position and, increasingly, even to obtain an entry-level one. Fortunately, the situation is being ameliorated by the electronic availability of periodicals; but it must be noted that such availability presupposes an institution's electronic subscription to a periodical as well as the availability of computers.

SEE ALSO Festschriften; Reference Works.

BIBLIOGRAPHY

Because of the constant appearance of new journals, surveys of periodical publications become outdated as soon as they are published. Keeping that in mind, as well as the fact that encyclopedia articles dealing with journals tend to focus on those that deal with theological, biblical and Christian themes, one can consult the entries "Zeitschriften: I. Evangelische, II. Katholische," in the third edition (1962) of *Die Religion in Geschichte und Gegenwart*, vol. 6, col. 1885–1881 (the entry in the fourth edition, scheduled for completion in 2005, will include references to humanities, social sciences, and religious studies journals); "Zeitschriften, Theologische" in the *Theologische Realenziklopädie* vol. 36, 2004, pp. 615–625, as well as "Periodical Literature" in the first edition of the *Encyclopedia of Religion*, vol. 11, pp. 243–246. See also the *Bulletin signalétique 519: Philosophie, sciences religieuses* and the *Bulletin signalétique 527: Histoire et Sciences des Religions* (Paris), as well as the *Zeitschriften Verzeichnis Theologie* (Universität Tübingen, 1977). Other sources include *Guide to Social Science and Religion in Periodical Literature* (Flint, Mich., 1965); John Regazzi, *A Guide to Indexed Periodicals in Religion* (Metuchen, N.J., 1975); David Westerfer, *Les revues en sciences religieuses: éléments pour un programme international de recherches, liste de base des revues* (Strasbourg, 1976); Otto Lankhorst, *Les revues de sciences religieuses: approache bibliographique internationale*, Strasbourg, Cerdic, 1979; Michael J. Walsh, *Religious Bibliographies in Serial Literature: A Guide* (Westport, Conn., 1981); J. P. Cornish, *Religious Periodicals Directory* (Santa Barbara, Calif., 1986); Eugene C. Fieg, *Religion Journals and Serials: An Analytical Guide* (New York, 1988); James Dawsey, *A Scholar's Guide to Academic Journals in Religion* [ATLA Bibliography Series 23] (Metuchen, N.J., and London, 1988); and Willem Audenaert, *Clavis foliorum periodicorum theologicorum* (Louvain, Belgium, 1994).

GUSTAVO BENAVIDES (2005)

POLITICS AND RELIGION: POLITICS AND JUDAISM

The Jewish religion is foundationally political. God is imagined by means of a religious language replete with political roles (king, warrior, judge) and political relations (ruling, lawgiving, providing). Central to the Jewish religion is a law that mediates revelation addressed to an elected people. And history is marked by the polar extremes of exile and messianic redemption. These themes are succinctly encapsulated in the preamble to the Sinaitic covenant in which God addresses the newly redeemed people of Israel that have exited Egypt with the following calling: "Now then, if you will obey Me faithfully and keep My covenant, you shall be My treasured possession among all the peoples. Indeed, all the earth is Mine, but you shall be to Me a kingdom of priests and a Holy nation" (*Ex.* 19:5–6, New JPS). Israel is envisaged as a kingdom and a nation.

From the moment this religion is conceived of as a religion of a people, as a religion in which individuals approach God from within a congregation, Judaism is conceived of as a political project. Election, covenant, law, prophecy, priesthood, monarchy, and redemption all emanate from this religio-political core. Furthermore, over its continuing history, the Jewish religion and the Jewish people have created various religious and political institutions and regimes (monarchies, communities, and a nation-state). These in turn have

generated a variety of claims to authority, divine and human, Jewish and Gentile, sacred and worldly. These positions have received articulation in texts that have undergone the painstaking process of continuous redaction and canonization over millennia. The basic Judaic narrative structure of election in terms of exile and redemption has been reiterated time and again in Western history by national movements and liberation movements, as indeed has been the role of the prophet as a divinely inspired social critic.

It should be noted that the foundational texts of Judaism predate the sharp distinction between *politics* and *religion.* The term *politics* is Greek in origin. In medieval Hebrew it is translated *medini* from *medinah,* city, and is used in modern Hebrew for "state." The closest word to politics as a domain of activity in biblical Hebrew is probably *melukhah* or *malkhut,* both meaning kingship, or *memshalah,* governance (cf. the distinction in *2 Chron.* 19:11 between "matters of the Lord" and "matters of the king"). The former two may signify the general activity of governance but are distinctively monarchic. The medieval and modern Hebrew equivalent of the Latinate *religion* is *dat,* law. Prior to medieval theological reconstructions of Judaism such terms were not used as organizing concepts. Our present use of them is for analytic purposes but the cultural relativity of these concepts should be kept in mind.

Rather than claim a unified political theory of Judaism the present discussion limits itself to an examination of a set of tensions characterizing this core itself as expressed in the canonical presentation of foundational texts. It will not address all manners of power relations and domination but rather focus on the institutional organization of polity and nation and then turn to the core value of justice echoing throughout Judaic canonical texts.

Theocratic and Secularizing Conceptions of Politics. The political nature of theology in Jewish religious discourse generates a set of tensions and problems regarding the legitimacy of human politics that permeate most layers of historical Judaism. The politicization of theology that claims political agency for God affects the very possibility of human political agency. Human initiative in political action, the founding of human institutions, and the possibility of rational comprehension of political events is thus constantly problematized in this religious tradition: "For My plans are not your plans, nor are My ways your ways—declares the Lord. But as the heavens are high above the earth, so are My ways high above yours and My plans above your plans" (*Is.* 56:8–9).

This voice, however, is only a partial representation of the political complexity of the Jewish political tradition. Thematically speaking, we may distinguish between two fundamental trends regarding politics in the canonical texts of the Jewish religion. The first trend, which may indeed be termed *theocratic,* views politics and political agency as a divine prerogative. Josephus coined the term *theocracy*:

> There is endless variety in the details of the customs and laws, which prevail in the world at large. To give but a summary enumeration: some peoples have entrusted the supreme political power to monarchies, others to oligarchies, yet others to the masses. Our lawgiver, however, was attracted by none of these forms of polity, but gave to his constitution the form of what—if a forced expression be permitted—may be termed a "theocracy," placing all sovereignty and authority in the hands of God. (*Contra Apion,* 164–167)

In contradistinction to the Mishnaic notion of *malkhut shamayim,* the kingdom of heaven (*Berakhot* 2:2), which denotes a normative space whose authority and yoke a person accepts in the daily recitation of the *shema,* Josephus's theocracy is an institution: It is not a regimen, it is a regime. Josephus's theocratic conceptualization of the Sinaitic regime is developed again in the pre-Enlightenment political philosophy of early modernity by such thinkers as Thomas Hobbes (*Leviathan,* chap. 35), Barukh Spinoza (*Theological-Political Treatise,* chap. 17), and John Locke (*Letter Concerning Toleration,* p. 73). These thinkers reexamined the biblical conception of politics in their efforts to articulate a theory of legitimacy for the modern republic. The theocratic conception of Judaism was developed again in the twentieth century. Martin Buber developed Spinoza's favorable description of the pure theocracy of ancient Israel, arguing in his *Kingship of God* for an anarchistic conception of a holy community. Buber argues his point historically, but his position provides a utopian articulation to his own dialogical religious philosophy. On the other hand, and following Hobbes's and Spinoza's critique of religion, Gershon Weiler's *Jewish Theocracy* critically equates theocracy with clerical power and portrays it as inimical to democratic civil society.

Human attempts to assume political agency are viewed on the theocratic account as an act of hubris and as idolatrous insofar as they express the usurpation of a divine attribute. Theocratic positions assume that there are select human beings who have some form of direct access to God's will and often maintain that divine rule is not exercised directly by God but by human intermediaries. This latter point is emphasized by critics of theocracy, among them Spinoza, who argue that theocracy in effect, means not the reign of God but the rule of his human representatives.

The second trend, no less authentic to the Jewish religious tradition, may be termed a "secularizing" trend; it views politics as a worldly activity and as a legitimate human endeavor. Rather than serve as a radical alternative, theology on this account variously sets boundaries, guides and affirms the human exercise of power; it may either curtail human power or legitimate it.

Politics, on the secularizing account, is a human and worldly affair. Ensuring the king does not become a god does not necessitate turning God into a king. Theocracy, argue its worldly critics, leads either to anarchy or to a clerical despotism. The biblical critique of theocracy finds its expression both in the Pentateuch and in the Prophets. The overall nar-

rative structure of the book of *Numbers* can be construed as an antitheocratic argument according to which even Moses, the first and foremost of prophetic leaders, was incapable of generating stable political leadership. Similarly, the book of *Judges* can be read to argue that the loose tribal federation of premonarchic Israel led to an anarchy typified by the three cardinal sins: idolatry, bloodshed, and sexual license. "In those days there was no king in Israel, everyone did as he pleased" (*Jgs.* 21:25).

The founding moment of worldly politics is the description of the creation of the monarchy in *1 Samuel* 8. Human political agency is asserted in the initiative to constitute a regime. And although God in this chapter expresses reservations concerning the very enterprise, Samuel the prophet is directed to heed the people all that they ask. This worldly conception of politics is echoed in classic future discussions. The Mishnah places the king beyond the reach of the human representative of divine law: "The king neither judges, nor is he subject to judgment" (*Sanhedrin* 2:3). Kings are necessary for social existence, and in what can be read as a rebuke of prophetic political subversion, the Mishnah seems to maintain the position that bad kings are better than no kings. This form of realism was followed by the mainstream of rabbinic decisors in the Middle Ages. It finds its fullest theoretical expression in Moses Maimonides, who codifies this ruling in his *Mishneh Torah* and in the *Guide of the Perplexed.* Maimonides begins his discussion of *halakhic* regimentation in the latter, citing Aristotle's maxim "man is political by nature" (II: 40). Human political association is ultimately grounded in our worldly, rational character as a species.

The secularizing conception of politics ultimately carries the day in biblical political history the moment a monarchy was constituted in ancient Israel. Moreover, the founding of the Davidic monarchy radically altered the Jewish religion. It created Jerusalem as its capital city with a permanent Temple, and implanted the messianic idea that would ultimately form the horizon of Jewish historical self-understanding.

Yet given the deep roots of both these conflicting tendencies in the Jewish religion a general characterization is in place. Jewish politics has traditionally a worldly base that must always negotiate the holy—especially when it finds expression in the form of a theocratic impulse—as part of its politics. The question whether the sacred will curb human violence or sanction it ought to be a central standard for judging political theologies. The long history of Jewish communal existence has indeed given rise to various such political theologies for legitimizing authority by means of the adequate channeling of the sacred. Some predate the exile, such as the Davidic political theology, and some serve to justify the renunciation of power of an exilic community. The great medieval theolgians such as Judah Halevi, Maimonides and Moses Nahmanides all provided theological-political paradigms as an integral element of their work. Among the basic strategies for negotiating the theocratic impulse that can be discerned in Jewish political history three are especially pertinent. One is biblical and monarchic and the other two are modern and relate to the modern project of the secularization of culture. The two latter models are especially important in understanding the major forms of Jewish political life in modernity. First is the diasporic Jewish community that lacks political autonomy and whose members are citizens of the non-Jewish hosting republican civil society. Second is the Jewish secular nation-state of Israel.

The Davidic recasting of theology. The foremost monarchic dynasty of ancient Israel deeply affected the entire theological structure of the Jewish religion. Central to the theory of legitimacy of the house of David is a political theology whose purpose is to recast the role of the sacred in Jewish theology. This new theology receives its clearest biblical articulation in the "royal" psalms (e.g., *Ps.* 2, 89). Although the king is not conceived as a deity as in the Mesopotamian or Egyptian models, he is a pivotal figure politically and religiously. The king is God's anointed one (Heb., *mashiah*; "messiah" in its anglicized form), his inheritance, and his son. The covenant with the people of Israel now passes through him. Whereas in earlier texts the covenant is conditional upon its performance, in its Davidic form it is eternal. The Temple of Jerusalem is founded by this dynasty in its capital city and operates under its auspices. Theology here provides the legitimating basis of monarchy and dynasty.

Spinozistic sovereign supremacy. Spinoza views the sovereign to have supreme authority over all public expressions of religion. The sovereign himself is not a religious figure, but no sovereign can afford to remain indifferent to religion. Therefore it is the role of political theology to provide religious support for the democratic secular republic as the best means to further peace and security. His biblical criticism aside, Spinoza believed the Bible is well equipped to provide such support to the republic because the political history it includes depicts the original covenant of God and Israel as a democratic social contract.

Zionist appropriation of national history and destiny. The Zionist movement of the late nineteenth and twentieth centuries argued that there was no place for Jews in a Europe made up of nation-states and called for the creation of a Jewish nation-state in the land of Israel (Palestine) as the only viable solution to the plight of Jews in Europe. It was primarily a movement of secular Jews that called for a repudiation of traditional Jewish exilic historical passivity. Zionism provides a classic model of the modern appropriation of traditional theological models by secular states and political movements. Although it was primarily a secular movement, its appropriation of responsibility for the national destiny of Jews and its discourse of redemption enabled it to change the political forms of Jewish life. The movement succeeded in creating the State of Israel and was imagined by many Jews in the twentieth century to be a carrier of national historical identity. Zionism is thus a unique model of secular political theology that appropriates the salient political features of a

theological tradition without (so it hoped) its sacral and theistic components.

JUSTICE AS A CORE VALUE. The commitment to justice as a core value is derivative of the very political character of the Jewish religion, for justice is the criteria for evaluating the basic institutions of society and the exercise of power and its distribution. The Abrahamic theology of the tetragrammaton is presented in the book of *Genesis* in terms of a moral commitment. God singles out Abraham as one who will "instruct his children and his posterity to keep the way of the Lord [= tetragrammaton] by doing what is just and what is right" (18:19). God's way is the way of justice and of righteousness and this is repeated throughout the Bible and the rabbinic tradition.

Two main avenues are developed in the Judaic tradition to ensure justice. The first is law. The centrality of law in the Jewish religion reflects the reasoned organization of divine authority and social structure. The rulelike character of law ensures generality and equality before the law (cf. *Nm.* 15:16–17) and minimizes arbitrariness. The foundation of the law is the covenant that ensures the inclusivity of society and the grounds of acceptance (cf. *Dt.* 29:9–28).

The second is the prophet who gives voice to the suffering of injustice in society and rebukes the violence of unbridled power. Many prophets are often characterized by their noninstitutional role and at times subversive stance with regard to the reigning powers. Indeed the prophetic posture and its attendant divinely charged rhetoric have been reiterated throughout history (consider such diverse twentieth-century figures as Martin Luther King Jr. or Abraham Joshua Heschel). Caution, however, is due in identifying prophecy with social criticism. For although prophets often did fulfill such a role they also engaged in promoting the divinely sanctioned foreign policy as they understood it to be over and against the realpolitik of human monarchs (see, e.g., *Is.* 10:5–20, chaps. 36–39).

Perhaps it is the tension between institutionalized law and charismatic prophecy that leads the Bible to construct the image of Moses as a prophetic lawgiver spanning both these roles in his person. A different form of this combination may be seen in the traditional portrayal of David as an inspired king. The vitality of these synthetic combinations can be seen echoed again in such leadership roles as that of the Hasidic *tsaddiq* millennia later in early modernity. They also reflect the need to combine divine claims, justice, and legitimacy in a viable worldly politics.

BIBLIOGRAPHY

Biale, David. *Power and Powerlessness in Jewish History.* New York, 1987. The most important study relating Jewish political history to political self-understanding.

Blidstein, Gerald J. *Political Concepts in Maimonidean Halakha* (Hebrew). Ramat Gan, Israel, 1983. Indispensable for students of Maimonides but unfortunately available only in Hebrew.

Bright, John. *Covenant and Promise: The Prophetic Understanding of the Future in Pre-Exilic Israel.* London, 1977.

Buber, Martin. *Kingship of God.* Translated by Richard Scheimann. London, 1990. A classic work articulating an anarchistic conception of theocracy.

Cohen, Stuart A. *The Three Crowns.* Cambridge, U.K., 1990.

Elazar, Daniel J., ed. *Kinship and Consent* (KC). Ramat Gan, Israel, 1987. Elazar is the pioneer of Jewish political thought and this collection of essays remains an ongoing valuable source.

Frankfort, Henri. *Kingship and the Gods: A Study of Ancient Near Eastern Religion as the Integration of Society and Nature.* Chicago, 1949.

Funkenstein, Amos. *Perceptions of Jewish History.* Berkeley, 1993.

Halbertal, Moshe, and Avishai Margalit. *Idolatry.* Translated by Naomi Goldblum. Cambridge, Mass., 1992.

Hobbes, Thomas. *Leviathan.* Edited by C. B. Macpherson. London, 1968.

Josephus Flavius. *Against Apion.* Translated by H. St. J. Thackeray. Cambridge, Mass., 1961.

Kreisel, Howard. *Maimonides' Political Thought: Studies in Ethics, Law, and the Human Ideal.* Albany, N.Y., 1999.

Locke, John. *A Letter Concerning Toleration.* Latin and English texts revised and edited by Mario Montouri. The Hague, 1963.

Lorberbaum, Menachem. *Politics and the Limits of Law: Secularizing the Political in Medieval Jewish Thought.* Stanford, Calif., 2001.

Maimonides, Moses. *The Code of Maimonides: Book IV, The Book of Judges.* Translated by A. M. Hershman. New Haven and London, 1963.

Maimonides, Moses. *The Guide of the Perplexed.* Translated with introduction and notes by Shlomo Pines. Chicago, 1963.

Melamed, Abraham. *The Philosopher-King in Medieval and Renaissance Jewish Thought.* Albany, N.Y., 2002.

Mowinckel, Sigmund. *He That Cometh.* Translated by G. W. Anderson. New York, 1959.

Ravitzky, Aviezer. *Messianism, Zionism, and Jewish Religious Radicalism.* Translated by Michael Swirsky and Jonathan Chipman. Chicago, 1996.

Scholem, Gershom G. *The Messianic Idea in Judaism.* New York, 1971.

Schorsch, Ismar. "On the History of the Political Judgment of the Jew." In *From Text to Context: The Turn to History in Modern Judaism.* Hanover, N.H., and London, 1994.

Spinoza, Barukh. *A Theologico-Political Treatise.* In *The Chief Works of Benedict de Spinoza,* vol. 1. Translated by R. H. M. Elwes. New York, 1951.

Walzer, Michael. *Exodus and Revolution.* New York, 1985.

Walzer, Michael, Menachem Lorberbaum, and Noam J. Zohar, eds.; Yair Lorberbaum, co-editor. *The Jewish Political Tradition* (JPT), vol. 1: *Authority.* New Haven, 2000.

Walzer, Michael, Menachem Lorberbaum, and Noam J. Zohar, eds.; Ari Ackerman, co-editor. *The Jewish Political Tradition,* vol. 2: *Membership.* New Haven, 2003. These two volumes (out of a projected four) are the most thorough mapping out of the discourse of the Jewish political tradition and its primary sources.

Weiler, Gershon. *Jewish Theocracy*. Leiden, 1988. A most forceful critical presentation of Jewish political thinking and its theocratic commitments.

MENACHEM LORBERBAUM (2005)

PRIMITIVISM is an ideological position that developed in Western civilization in order to characterize subjugated people as "other." Even though the term *primitive* has been used for an extensive period, it has been particularly important since the beginning of modernity and the Age of Discovery. During this time its influence has been pervasive, with dramatic and often traumatic consequences on the cultural developments of both "civilized" and "primitive" peoples.

From the beginning of cultural contact with Europeans, other people of the world were characterized as "primitive." Since 1492, however, the term has expressed an ambiguity. On one hand, the idea of *primitivism* was initially utilized as a way to justify conquest and colonial exploitation of a variety of human beings. On the other hand, *primitivism* referred to a way of forming a Protestant Christian response to the authority of the Catholic Church.

The most prevalent uses of the term *primitive* in the fifteenth century relate to the early Christian church. The "primitive church" has been a positive conceptualization in the West of a communal organization of like-minded Christians whose society was untarnished by the corruptive influences of civilization. Primitive Christianity has been a dominant mythological formulation of European groups who were oppressed in their cultural situations. This mythology fueled a push toward establishing new communal, or utopian, experimental communities in various parts of the world around a more directly inspired form of Christian devotion.

The development of Protestant Christianity corresponded with the Age of Discovery. In response to perceived abuses in Rome, Protestants, primarily in Northern Europe, formed a different understanding of a Christian community. Ironically it has only been in the context of large colonial enterprises, and particularly in the British Empire, that such groups could materially achieve their dream of establishing a primitive Christian community. Such is the case with the Puritans in North America, for example. Conceptually, the notion of primitivism underscores a cultural feature in the development of Christianity in Europe, where there is an emphasis on, and yearning for, the origins of the church. While initially this might be seen as a contradictory use of *primitivism,* there is actually a unity between a yearning for the pristine state of the "primitive" Christian community and colonial exploitation of people who have been characterized as primitive.

Primitivism, therefore, in its first more positive meaning, is directly associated with what is "primary" for proper life. Locating where to promote this sort of Christianity proved more of a dilemma. The utopian character of the primitive develops from an ongoing search for God in Europe. For Europeans the conceptual dilemma with Christianity as the basis of authority was displacement. From the time of the conversion of Europe, beginning in the eleventh century, through the Crusades and into the Renaissance and the early modern period, European kingdoms based their hierarchical authority on the God-Man, Jesus Christ, whose people, language, and culture were in a foreign land. Christ's miraculous appearance in the world had taken place in a now foreign place that was controlled by non-Christian people. The origins of Christianity, and therefore its power to authorize Europeans to extend its message around the world, were in some other place under the control of "primitives." The irony of the ideology of primitivism is a foundational feature in the development of Western Christianity. On one hand primitivism is associated with a utopian vision of the original church. On the other hand primitivism is associated with those non-Christians who have dominion over the lands and resources necessary for the "correct" propagation of the faith.

Primitivism has been valued positively as that which is primary or fundamental to meaningful human community. It has also been used as an oppositional structure upon which "civilization" has been built. A double-edged understanding of the primitive has been extended by academics interested in conceptualizing the origins of religion. In general, academics in this area have valued the primitive to such an extent that their theories have been seen as disparaging of civilization, or the very cultural formulation that makes scholarly reflection possible. In anthropology, E. B. Tylor, Bronislaw Malinowski, Lucien Lévy-Bruhl, and Arthur Lovejoy are examples of major theorists of religion who have appealed to seemingly primary appearance in what were regarded as the most basic religious formulations in primitive people. Scholars credited with having founded entire academic disciplines have utilized the idea of the primitive to understand the general phenomenon of religion in areas of philosophy (William James), psychology (Sigmund Freud, C. G. Jung), religious studies (Mircea Eliade), sociology (Émile Durkheim), political science (Max Weber), and economics (Karl Marx).

There is, therefore, a gap between the Western conception of primitive religions (articulated here as *primitivism*) and the experience of empirical others that have undergone Western imperialism. There have been ongoing attempts by scholars, activists, and members of indigenous communities to more accurately account for their conceptualization as "primitive" as a strategy to devalue and discount a tremendously rich and varied array of traditional knowledge. Acknowledging the cultural limits of knowing about other religions, and particularly in the Western academy, would include considering the dilemma of writing about others who do not write. Writing, a scholarly activity with direct association to the "Great religions" of the West, has often had dramatically negative consequences for indigenous traditions, or those people that have not organized their religious practices around sacred books.

How then do *indigenous* people (the preferred term for people who were once characterized as *primitive*) understand the role of religion in their traditions? Often they point out that there is no clearly decipherable element of their society that could be called "religion." Rather, a sacred reality permeates all aspects of their lives. The category of "religion" therefore does violence to the integrity of their traditions. Religion did not rise from a "worship of nature" but from the sacred reality embedded in the material world. The hierophany (i.e., manifestation of the sacred) in the natural world refers to the manner in which animals, plants, the sky, and the landscape reveal modalities of reality to human beings. Even though these phenomena also have utilitarian value, this does not explain why "religious" veneration is an important component of dealing with them.

The oldest deities in most cultures are sky-gods. The sky expresses eternity, infinity, and transcendence. Wilhelm Schmidt refers to this as "primitive monotheism." Even though sky-gods form an important component of ancient religious practice, they nevertheless are *dei otiosi,* seen as being removed from direct contact with the material world. As a result, veneration of sky-gods is often regarded as less urgent than veneration of those deities that populate an immediate environment.

Animals, which were venerated at prehistoric sites from Paleolithic through Neolithic times, are another venue for hierophany. The use of animal bones for divination ceremonies, and cave paintings of animals in all parts of the world, including Europe, has been understood as magico-religious. The pursuit of game animals not only required great skill, training, and courage, but also that the hunter negotiate with the animal through ceremonial means. "Bear magic" among the Ainu of Japan and the early Paleolithic people of Western Europe, for example, referred to strategies to connect human beings with the spiritual beings of animals. Not only would bear magic ensure a successful hunt, but it would also ensure that the bear would continue to make itself available as food. Carvings and cave paintings from all over the world represent animals and are bound up with hunting culture. Various levels of exchange ranging from the material/pragmatic to the magico/spiritual developed between humans and animals. For indigenous people there is no essential break between the two, yet for more "civilized" people these levels of exchange form the basis of the distinct character of "religion."

In Western scholarship much attention has been paid to "primitive totemism." From Freud to Durkheim to Eliade, the totem has been seen as a dominant mythic/symbolic force in the organization of "primitive" society. Two features have been most pronounced about the totem. First, the existence and identity of a human group is inextricably linked with a particular animal in a clan or ceremonial complex. Second, there are various rules of behavior (taboos) that surround the totem animal. For the history of religions, however, it is enough to acknowledge that around the totem animal there is understood to be a sacred power, and the continued existence of the human community materially and spiritually is linked to this animal.

Plants have also been an important element in the religious understanding of the natural world. The transition from the Paleolithic to Neolithic ages is defined, to a great extent, by the creation of new understandings of the relationships between human and plant life. Agriculture brought into being a structure of the sacred. The emphasis was on dying and resurrecting gods (such as Adonis, Attis, and Osiris, according to James Frazer). When the structure of the sacred is seen as representative of the life of plants, then the manifestations of that sacred power, as with all living beings, must also undergo death and resurrection.

Lunar symbolism is also associated with the periodicity of life in all of its forms, including human. But these innovations should not be seen as a natural consequence of the development of agriculture. Rather, these religious discoveries, or new hierophanies, were the result of the "new world" that was created with the domestication of plants and animals. In addition, the fertility cycle of the earth (including the agricultural and seasonal cycles) was directly connected to the periodicity of human life. Birth and new birth ceremonies mark the beginning of the agricultural cycle, while death and ancestor veneration are generally connected with the harvest and the end of the agricultural cycle. The earth as mother is a truly ancient understanding. Much Western scholarship on primitivism emphasizes how the nurturing quality of the earth as mother is a "primary" or "archaic" religious formulation.

In discussions of primitivism specific categories are advanced as universal among "primitive people." These often include the understanding of the leadership of ancient empires as "theocracies" in which the power of the priest is combined with the power of the warrior. The kingly lineages of Europeans are often fused with the chief of "tribal societies." The other office among "primitives" was understood to be the *shaman,* a term that originated from Siberian peoples but has been applied to indigenous people all over the world. In general, Western scholarship has designated the offices of king, chief, shaman, and medicine man (as well as more pejorative terms like *witch-doctor*) to "primitive" societies. The reality, however, is much more complex. Indigenous terms for leadership positions reflect a tremendous variety of relationships. For example, the Haudenosaunee term for chief is *royaner* (in Mohawk), which means "good mind" and refers to a person whose principal responsibility is to speak well enough so that people will overcome their conflicts. This is a far cry from the popular understanding of the chief who rules by brutish physical power. Simply adopting categories that have been universalized to suit all indigenous people tends to diminish what is unique and important about each group. Rather than looking to construct the universal of "primitivism," the tendency now is to utilize the local insights of various groups as social critiques of Western assumptions and to appreciate the cultural insights of indigenous people.

But Western scholars have been largely correct in emphasizing the importance of a leader's relationship with the sacred. In general the leader of local, indigenous communities can be seen as an intermediary of some kind, often an intermediary between several different communities of beings. In this sense the sacred for indigenous people has been a consistent example of the efficacy and power of religion. Several authors throughout the nineteenth and twentieth centuries have emphasized the unadulterated influence that the sacred has had on "primitive societies." The sacred is seen as a powerful reality, as with *mana* among Melanesians, *orenda* for the Haudenosaunee (Iroquois), and *wakanda* for the Lakota (Sioux). All of these concepts are similar and yet distinct from one another. Power in material forms is just one aspect of these indigenous understandings.

The conceptualization of primitivism has played a vital role in the organization and characterization of civilization. This has had dramatic consequences for the development of modernity and often traumatic consequences for those deemed "primitive." On the one hand the "primitive" are often seen as wholly in touch with their surroundings, and as a result they are imagined to be more "religious" than modern human beings. This is in spite of the fact that it is often understood that "primitive societies" have no notion of "religion" per se. Because modernity has to cope with both the fictive status of the "primitive" of its own fabrication and with the empirical other of indigenous peoples with whom it has come into contact, one often gets mixed messages about these groups. The solution for gaining a more reliable knowledge of indigenous or local cultures and people, however, is not simply to go into the field (as anthropologists do). The fictive status of the "primitive" is too strongly entrenched in the modern imagination for it to be shaken loose by coming face-to-face, so to speak, with the "primitive." Rather, one has to incorporate the cultural dimensions of the interreligious contact and negotiation that has occurred over the last five hundred plus years for an adequate picture of indigenous religions to emerge.

SEE ALSO Colonialism and Postcolonialism; Materiality; Orientalism; Shamanism, overview article, and article on Neoshamanism.

BIBLIOGRAPHY

Durkheim, Émile. *The Elementary Forms of the Religious Life: A Study in Religious Sociology* (1912). Translated by J. W. Swain. New York, 1915.

Eliade, Mircea. *Myth of the Eternal Return, or, Cosmos and History.* Translated by Willard Trask. Princeton, 1954; rev. ed., 1965.

Eliade, Mircea. *Patterns in Comparative Religion.* Translated by Rosemary Sheed. New York, 1958.

Frazer, Sir James George. *The Golden Bough: A Study in Magic and Religion.* New York and London, 1890–1915.

Freud, Sigmund. *Totem and Taboo: Resemblances between the Psychic Lives of Savages and Neurotics* (1913). Translated by A. A. Bill. London, 1918.

Long, Charles H. "Primitive and Civilized: The Locus of a Problem." *History of Religions* 20 (1980): 43–61.

Long, Charles H. *Significations: Signs, Symbols, and Images in the Interpretation of Religion.* Philadelphia, 1986.

Malinowski, Bronislaw. *Coral Gardens and Their Magic*; Vol. 2: *The Language of Magic and Gardening.* Bloomington, Ind., 1965.

Mauss, Marcel. *The Gift: Forms and Functions of Exchange in Archaic Societies.* Translated by Ian Cunnison. Glencoe, Ill., 1954; New York, 1967.

Otto, Rudolf. *The Idea of the Holy: An Inquiry into the Nonrational Factor in the Idea of the Divine and Its Relation to the Rational.* Translated by John W. Harvey. London, 1923; 2d ed., 1950.

Schmidt, Wilhelm. *The Origin and Growth of Religion: Facts and Theories.* Translated by H. J. Rose. New York and London, 1931.

Smith, Jonathan Z. *Map Is Not Territory: Studies in the History of Religions.* Leiden, 1978.

Smith, Jonathan Z. *Imagining Religion: From Babylon to Jonestown.* Chicago, 1982.

van der Leeuw, Gerardus. *Religion in Essence and Manifestation: A Study in Phenomenology.* Translated by J. E. Turner. London, 1938.

PHILIP P. ARNOLD (2005)

RAMAKRISHNA [FURTHER CONSIDERATIONS].

Gadādhar (or Gadai) Chattopadhyay was born into a poor *brahman* priest family of Kamarpukur, an obscure village some sixty miles northwest of Calcutta in the state of West Bengal. He studied in his village school from the age of five till his seventeenth year, and later, at the *ṭol* (traditional elementary school for Sanskrit learning) of his elder brother in Rāmkumār in Calcutta. Though not totally illiterate he was practically uneducated; he never read any scriptures, though he was fond of reading stories about the holy men and *bhaktas* (devotees) of Viṣṇu and copied out four religious dramas as well as a portion of the Bengali *Rāmāyaṇa,* in Krittivas Ojha's translation. Possessed of prodigious memory, the boy also memorized a number of devotional songs *(kīrtanas)* and recitations of sacred poems *(kathās)* by the itinerant troubadours of Bengal.

Gadādhar earned a reputation in his village as an ecstatic when, at the age of seven, he reportedly fell into a trance at the sight of flying cranes in a cloudy sky. Later, in an open-air theater, he fell into a trance while enacting the part of Lord Śiva. His reputation for momentarily losing consciousness made people regard him as a divinely endowed child. A few years later, when the adolescent Gadādhar was appointed as the priest of the Kālī temple at Dakshineshwar, some five miles north of Calcutta, his ecstasies were accompanied by crazy behavior. His mother and his village neighbors, as well his employers, Rani Rasmani, owner of the Dakshineshwar temple, and her son-in-law Mathuranath Biswas, the temple

manager, attributed this behavior to his celibacy and counseled marriage. The twenty-three-year-old Gadādhar was married to a six-year-old girl named Sāradāmaṇi from the village of Jairambati. When his symptoms persisted, he was treated by some native naturopaths *(vaidyas or kavirājas)* and by a roving *bhairavī* (female practitioner of rituals in Tantric circles or *chakras*) named Yogeśvarī, whose diagnosis was that he was afflicted with divine madness *(divyonmattata)*. The acme of this state was reached during his training under a Vedāntic monk named Ishwara Totāpurī from the Punjab, when he underwent an undifferentiated state of enstasis in which all diversities disappeared into an undifferentiated oneness *(nirvikalpa samādhi)*. Gadādhar now graduated from his training and assumed, probably at the behest of his mentor, the new name Ramakrishna, as well as the honorific title of *thakur* (master).

RAMAKRISHNA'S ECLECTICISM. Ramakrishna proclaimed that anyone who could become dependent on God, like a little child on its parents, could realize God as personal (*sākāra* or "with form") or impersonal (*nirākāra* or "formless"). In Ramakrishna's terms, one should try to realize God not by reading the scriptures to acquire divine knowledge (as a *jñānī)* but by becoming able to see, touch, and converse with God through pure devotion (as a *vijñānī)*. His favorite deities from the Hindu pantheon were Kṛṣṇa, the great lover, and Kālī, the terrible but tenderhearted black Mother Goddess. He had been so desperately eager to see the Goddess Kālī (sometime during the 1856 to 1867 period) that he attempted to kill himself. During the period of his sweet or erotic devotional state *(madhurabhava)*, around 1867 to 1871, he felt a deep longing for Kṛṣṇa as if he were Rādhā, Kṛṣṇa's principal consort.

Ramakrishna's religious eclecticism was expressed in his saying "*yato mat tato path*" ("as many views, so many venues"). This sentiment, already known from the *Mahimna Stotra* and from the *Bhagavadgītā's* statements about unity in diversity, distanced Hinduism simultaneously from Brāhmoism within Indian society and Christian evangelicalism outside it. It was a statement of his conviction that the various Hindu sectarian practices and beliefs were valid pathways to realize the *Advaita Brāhmaṇ* or *Chinmayi Srisrijagadamba* (the Twice-Blessed Mother of the Universe Consciousness) (Mrigananda, 1994, pp. 17, 19).

Ramakrishna's syncretic devotionalism was such that he could become in turn a Śākta, a Vaiṣṇava, an Advaitin, or a follower of yoga, *bhakti,* and *jñāna.* Going beyond Hinduism, he set aside Hindu ways while he prayed to Allah after the manner of the Muslims. Moreover, after he beheld a polychrome reproduction of Raphael's *Madonna and the Child* at the garden retreat of Yadunath Mullick, he "felt disinclined even to see Hindu deities, not to speak of saluting them, inasmuch as the Hindu mode of thought vanished altogether from [his] mind"; his "love and devotion to the Devas and Devis vanished, and in their stead, a great faith in, and reverence for Jesus and his religion occupied his mind." He even claimed that his *sādhana* in Christian faith was facilitated by the Twice-Blessed Mother of the Universe (Saradananda, vol. 1, 1983–1984, pp. 299, 338–339). For him, then, God was really not the same for all. One could not possibly realize Allah or Jesus through the Hindu way.

WOMEN AND GOLD. Ramakrishna's *dicta* against *kāminī-kañcan* ("woman and wealth" or "lust and lucre") saw women as the root of all evils and any gainful employment as degrading slavery. He thus urged most of his devotees and disciples never to trust women nor to get married or employed, but to devote their life to contemplation. He ruled that men might marry, raise a family, and earn a living to maintain them, though they must at all times remain disciplined and virtuous. But for those whom he considered possessed of spiritual potential, he counseled a life of austerity and celibacy. Despite his verbal adoration of women as Śakti or mother, and despite the fact that he owed his upbringing and his success as a public figure to women, such as his mother Chandramani, his employer Rasmani, his putative Tantric mentor Yogeśvarī, and his wife Sāradāmaṇi (who devoted her entire married life to her husband and his followers), he remained suspicious of women and, as a celibate husband, even expressed a measure of apprehension about his wife's chastity. He was fearful of prostitutes (or unchaste women) as much as he was of low-caste people.

Ramakrishna was equally ambivalent about gold. Though he derided material wealth, he personally enjoyed an epicurean life and even showed a good deal of interest in *kañcan* (gold). He never gave up the world but always lived at home like a householder, luxuriating in physical comforts without doing any work. He maintained a diary listing every kind of expense, such as defraying the cost of a horoscope for himself, paying the physicians he often consulted for ailments, buying ornaments for his wife and even for her maidservant, and above all, investing in landed property at his native village, Kamarpukur, and the neighboring village, Sihore. He himself admitted having felt alarmed after he had flung some coins into the river water because he feared this action might infuriate Lakṣmī, the goddess of wealth and welfare, and cause her to stop his daily food supply. Thus he prayed to the goddess to "stay in [his] heart." Yet the tradition continues to regard him as a renunciant. The image of Ramakrishna constructed by Swami Vivekananda was perpetuated by the Ramakrishna Order that Vivekananda founded. The most elaborate theological interpretation of Ramakrishna's life and teachings based on Vivekananda's interpretation was provided by Ramakrishna's monastic biographer Swami Saradananda.

RAMAKRISHNA'S TANTRIC CONNECTION. One of Ramakrishna's early biographers, Satyacharan Mitra, regarded Ramakrishna as a "*ghora* (consummate) *tāntrika,*" though he never really explained or described Ramakrishna's Tantric training under Yogeśvarī Bhairavī, an episode shrouded in obscurity. Ramakrishna's training in Tantra under her guidance reads in vernacular sources like a venture by a naive and

inquisitive initiate. As a *tāntrika* initiate, Ramakrishna came to a very Vaiṣṇava realization that the world is full of Viṣṇu *(sarvam Viṣṇumayam jagat)*. Ramakrishna's Tantric connection is supported by his association with the Dakshineshwar Kālī temple and his Tantric practices under Yogeśvarī. In the early 1940s Heinrich Zimmer and, following him, Walter Neevel in 1975, argued that Ramakrishna was essentially Tantric. The Danish scholar Anders Blichfeldt stated that Ramakrishna's "commitment to right-handed Tantra . . . seems to have been a permanent influence" (1982, p. 46). Jeffrey Kripal concluded that "it was the Kali of the Sakta tradition that was the focus of Ramakrishna's life," and thus "Ramakrishna's world . . . was a Tantric world" (1995, pp. 25, 27). Kripal utilized Ramakrishna's Tantric orientation to harness Ramakrishna's mystic image to his unconscious or unacknowledged homosexuality. Christopher Isherwood also commented on Ramakrishna's homosexual impulses, and Jeffrey Masson as well as Narasingha Sil speculated on sexual trauma in Ramakrishna's boyhood and adolescence that might have caused his gynephobia and virility anxiety. Kripal sees "latent or hidden themes that structured much of Ramakrishna's own experience" and that were concealed as much by Ramakrishna's own awareness as by the deliberate design of his biographer, Mahendranath Gupta.

Hagiographers and theologians look upon Ramakrishna as a divine incarnation *(avatāra)* who descended to earth to proclaim the efficacy of Hindu devotionalism. Sociohistorical and psychohistorical scholarship sees Ramakrishna as a human being with human sexuality, ailments, and caste and gender bias, who preached a traditional Hindu piety that is asocial and apolitical.

BIBLIOGRAPHY

A select list of monographs in English and only two in Bengali are appended below. See Narasingha P. Sil's *Ramakrishna Revisited* for a comprehensive bibliography of vernacular and English sources.

Advaita Ashrama. *Life of Ramakrishna Compiled from Various Authentic Sources.* Calcutta, 1964. Standard biography by the scholars of the Ramakrishna Order.

Blichfeldt, Anders. "Tantra in the Ramakrishna Math and Mission." *Update* 6 (1982): 30–47. An interesting and provocative interpretation.

Chatterjee, Partha. "A Religion of Urban Domesticity: Sri Ramakrishna and the Calcutta Middle Class." *Subaltern Studies VIII: Writings on South Asian History and Society,* edited by Partha Chatterjee and Gyanendra Pandey, pp. 40–68. New Delhi, 1992. A seminal sociological analysis of the Ramakrishna phenomenon by a noted political scientist.

Isherwood, Christopher. *My Guru and His Disciple.* London and New York, 1980. Reprint, Harmondsworth, 1981. Reference to Ramakrishna's homosexuality occurs on p. 247 of this biography of the author's spiritual mentor Swami Prabhavananda.

Kripal, Jeffrey J. *Kālī's Child: The Mystical and the Erotic in the Life and Teachings of Ramakrishna.* Chicago, 1995; 2d rev. ed., 1998. A *tour de force* arguing for Ramakrishna's sacred homosexuality.

Masson, Jeffrey M. *The Oceanic Feeling: The Origins of Religious Sentiment in Ancient India.* Dordrecht, 1980. An influential Freudian analysis of Hindu spirituality and mysticism.

Matchett, Freda. "The Teaching of Ramakrishna in Relation to the Hindu Tradition and as Interpreted by Vivekananda." *Religion* 11, no. 1 (1982): 171–184. A seminal study.

Mrigananda, Swami. *Yata Mat Tata Path: Hindu Aikyer Bhitti.* Jadavpur, India, 1994. A searching critique of Ramakrishna's most popular sermon by a scholar monk.

Müller, Friedrich Max. *Rāmakrishna: His Life and Sayings.* London, 1898; 5th Indian ed., Calcutta, 1995. One of the earliest scholarly and reliable biographies, though the author had no access to the vernacular sources.

Neevel, Walter G. "The Transformation of Śrī Rāmakrishna." In *Hinduism: New Essays in the History of Religions,* edited by Bardwell L. Smith, pp. 53–97. Leiden, 1976. A forceful interpretation of Ramakrishna's spiritual crisis and its resolution.

Parsons, William B. "Psychoanalysis and Mysticism: The Case of Ramakrishna." *Religious Studies Review* 23, no. 4 (1999): 355–361. Lengthy reviews of Sil and Kripal's works published in 1991 and 1995 respectively.

Prabhananda, Swami. *Amritarup Ramakrishna.* Calcutta, 1991. An anthology of interesting articles by a distinguished scholar monk.

Saradananda, Swami. *Sri Ramakrishna, the Great Master.* Translated by Swami Jagadananda. 2 vols. 6th rev. ed. Mylapore, India, 1983–1984. A monumental hagiography by one of Ramakrishna's intimate disciples.

Sarkar, Sumit. *An Exploration of the Ramakrishna Vivekananda Tradition.* Shimla, India, 1993. A powerful analysis of the socio-cultural factors behind the tradition by a distinguished historian.

Schneiderman, Leo. "Ramakrishna: Personality and Social Factors in the Growth of a Religious Movement." *Journal of the Scientific Study of Religion* (Spring 1969): 60–71. An elegant psychological study of Ramakrishna's spirituality.

Sil, Narasingha P. *Ramakrishna Paramahamsa: A Psychological Profile.* Leiden, 1991. The first book-length psychological interpretation of Ramakrishna's sexuality and spirituality.

Sil, Narasingha P. *Ramakrishna Revisited: A New Biography.* Lanham, Md. 1998. A revisionist biography that attempts a psychological and historical analysis of Ramakrishna humanity and spirituality.

Tyagananda, Swami, and Pravrajika Vrajaprana. *Kali's Child Revisited: Questions of Language, Cultural Understanding, and Documentation.* New Delhi, 2004. A magisterial critique.

Vivekananda, Swami. *Inspired Talks: My Master and Other Writings.* Rev. ed. New York, 1987.

NARASINGHA P. SIL (2005)

RITES OF PASSAGE: NORTH AMERICAN INDIAN RITES

When Arnold van Gennep wrote about rites of passage, he commented that rarely do physical and social puberty con-

verge. However, this rare convergence may occur as it is ritually performed by the Mescalero Apache in 'Isánáklésh Gotal. In this example the physiological changes in a girl as she reaches menarche are marked and accompanied by a change in social status. The meaning of this ceremony is embedded in the ritual transformation of the pubescent girl as she moves through the door of adolescence from one state of mind or spiritual being into the transformative state in which she incorporates the deity into herself and becomes 'Isánáklésh. If the ceremony is successful, she leaves behind the ways of childhood, and emerges as a responsible young Apache woman, able to carry on the Apache traditions and to bestow the gift of life.

In this ritual sequence, the tripartite schema of separation, transition, and incorporation that van Gennep identified as features of rites of passage collapses into one ceremony. Initially, the young girl is *separated* from her family and her usual daily activities to live in her own private tipi at the ceremonial site specifically constructed for her ceremony. In the preliminal rites of this stage of separation, she is without social status, no longer a child but not yet a woman.

During the process of ritual transformation she is in *transition*. In this state of liminality, the rites are designed to inscribe in her the traditional Apache knowledge and wisdom as she changes from girl to deity and then into a transformed female. After this stage, she is *incorporated* back into the community with a new social status. The postliminal rites involve using her new power by blessing those in the community who so request it. She is also allowed time to reflect back on the ceremony and the powerful changes she has just undergone.

Each of these stages is accompanied by sacred songs, which generate *diye*, power. They are used to distort the present time and return the participants to mythological time, when the deities were present on earth. They then bring time forward to the present by reenacting the myth, which becomes ceremony with its designated sacred rituals. Through song, the young girl is transformed into the deity and finally into a new Apache woman. This complex system is nourished through the rituals that are composed of symbols as the smallest component of the ceremony. The sacred meaning of ceremonies that have persisted over time is transferred to the Apache through these sacred symbols of power, which are used to distinguish ritual reality from everyday life. Without such symbols, the primary participants could not enter into the state of ritual, and thus be properly prepared for ceremonial transformation.

In Mescalero Apache cosmology, 'Isánáklésh is described as one of the five divine deities present at the time of creation. In those first days, she appeared with the lower half of her face painted with white earth clay and her body completely covered with yellow cattail pollen; she wore a necklace of abalone shell as she watched over all things growing on earth. Using her sacred power, *diye*, she ripened trees, plants, the flowers of the fields, fruits, and medicinal herbs. Her compassion and creative wisdom as healer provided information from the beginning of time about the animals, plants, and people in order to aid those who suffered from disease, injury, or distress. Before this time, healing knowledge did not exist. This myth or sacred narrative is critical for understanding the young woman's initiation ceremony and the religious values of Mescalero Apache, since 'Isánáklésh was the first young woman to receive this ceremony. The myth was given to the Apache people by 'Isánáklésh herself, and it is important because it provides the framework for the ceremony that is practiced today. In addition, if one reflects upon the myth, one begins to see the religious, intellectual, and aesthetic climate in which the ceremony takes its beginning and how these beginnings continue to influence the community today.

'Isánáklésh, the Apache female deity as a young pubescent girl, was given the first ceremony of initiation into womanhood by her parents, First Man and First Woman. She ran vigorously, danced vigorously, and thought deeply about how beautiful the ceremony was. She commented that it should be given as a gift to all Apache girls. This is the same female initiation ceremony that is celebrated today on the Mescalero Apache reservation. The ceremony serves to acknowledge the power of women, to teach young girls what they need to know to be good Apaches, and to restore 'Isánáklésh to her youth. When she begins to feel old, she has only to walk toward the young initiate as she runs to the east during her ceremony, and 'Isánáklésh will again be renewed in one of the religious transformations that occur during the ceremony.

The decision to have a ceremony for a young pubescent girl requires that she begin spiritual, physical and psychological preparations well in advance of her menarche. Inquiries are made about the past illnesses of the young girl, and the parents are asked about any traumas that have taken place that might affect the state of mind or the body of the girl. During the first morning, the medicine people pray so that the young girl can live without the past affecting her future. The teachings and symbols that are used in the young girl's instruction vary to some degree for each initiate, but the overall purpose of such instruction, as well as the ceremonial structure itself, is to convince the adolescent that she will undergo good and positive changes and live a good long life if she participates fully in the ceremony.

Today some of the girls require more convincing than others. Those who have been instructed from a very young age about the importance of the ceremony for a good healthy life and have been influenced continually by female kin, begin to anticipate their ceremony. Female kin begin to discuss the importance of the ceremony as they prepare for the feast at the time of a girl's first menstruation. Long before this, many prepubescent girls have observed and quietly listened as older girls are prepared for their ceremonies.

Whenever a ceremony is held, prepubescent girls will gather at the tipi to observe the initiate. It is clear that some

of these girls gather around because they are interested to know what to expect when their feast occurs. Many times mothers or other women say to these little girls, "Go on up toward the front where you can see and hear everything better." And then the girls begin slowly to make their way through the crowd of people to the front of the ceremonial tipi. Young girls observing an initiate dancing in the sacred tipi will often remark: "I can hardly wait for my feast. My mother is preparing many special things for my ceremony. But I am a little scared."

At this young age, the initiates are considered to be soft and moldable; they are still capable of being conditioned and influenced by female kin. Some girls, it is said, are easier to convince about the importance of participating than are others. Some need to be awakened to their female identity; others, on the other hand, need to be calmed down and taught to be more feminine within the ritual design of the ceremony. Two concepts are at work here: One is awakening the initiate to the world around her and to her abilities, and the other is carefully calming down the unrestrained nature of adolescence. Both concepts, as well as the teachings that strengthen the concept of self, which is central to the transformative process, are nurtured and encouraged in the everyday activities of young Apache girls. Through the many life cycle ceremonies that mark the main transition periods of Apache life, these same rituals and symbols are engaged again and again.

Many women who experienced the ceremony themselves strongly urge their daughters and granddaughters to continue the tradition. Because of the elevated status of older women, a grandmother's wishes are taken seriously. Great efforts are made to share expenses and labor so that a family's final decision whether or not to hold a ceremony will be based primarily on family and kin support rather than on economic criteria. A ceremony represents an opportunity to demonstrate reciprocity with relatives. The family may also receive support from nonrelatives, usually friends who are concerned with the well-being of the young girl and her family.

In some families, preparations for the ceremony begin very early in a young girl's life. She is slowly and carefully guided away from her special childhood of minimal responsibilities. In a family where female kin have watched over her from the time of her birth, in adolescence she is suddenly placed in a demanding learning environment. Menarche signals a psychological as well as a physiological marker that the young girl is taught to recognize. Suddenly her life changes dramatically.

Today a girl's first menstruation is sometimes celebrated in the old way with a private feast, *dahindah,* which is usually attended only by family and close friends. The small ceremony includes pollen blessings for the young girls, songs, and a dinner for select relatives and friends. According to tradition, it is at this smaller rite that the family selects a *gutaal* chanter, singer, and a *nade 'kleshn* female sponsor. It is here also that they announce and set the time for the girl's feast, when she will symbolically run out of childhood and into womanhood. Although it is not the central ceremony, this rite is sacred, and for its duration the girl is referred to as *'Isánáklésh.* She is sung over by a singer who emphasizes to her the importance of this intimate religious celebration, the gift of long life from 'Isánáklésh to a young changing woman.

This family gathering encourages the girl to begin her preparations for the rigorous physical, mental, and spiritual challenges that she will face during the more elaborate celebration. Young girls sometimes are reluctant to agree to participate in the ceremony. Whether it is shyness or fear of being the center of attention, girls may be hesitant to comply with their family's wishes. But in a traditional family, a girl's participation is expected and she is prepared carefully for this event long in advance. Once she accepts her role as an initiate, the demanding preparations begin. Her female relatives view the ceremony as a joyous religious occasion and put forth every effort to make the feast a special and solemn ceremony.

Nearly all girls had this ceremony in earlier times. The women must have recognized how difficult it was for young girls to live to a wise old age. Life was hard for women who were always on the move, gathering food resources, preparing and storing them, raising children, and attending to the ill and the elderly.

Today *dahindah* is usually given in families that are most traditional. Families that do not celebrate *dahindah* will announce the girl's feast in another away. The announcement itself enters the family into an obligation to hold the ceremony. In announcing the feast they are acknowledging 'Isánáklésh Gotal, and therefore they must adhere to the ceremony as it is set out in the myth and by tradition. To not follow through after making the announcement is to misuse sacred power and to risk danger.

As soon as possible after a girl's first menstruation, if she did not have a *dahindah,* her family should choose a *gutaal.* They approach the *gutaal* and ask: "We are here requesting your help to sing for our daughter." If he decides they are the "right family," meaning they are people who follow or respect the Apache traditional ways, he usually agrees. The family then offers the *gutaal* feathers, cigarettes, shells, and pollen as gifts in confirmation of the agreement. Then, in the family's presence, the *gutaal* prays that he will be in a good frame of mind for the ceremony, so that it will go well for all concerned. He prays for a clear mind and the strength to perform the rituals according to sacred tradition. The *gutaal* is responsible for assuring that everyone involved carries out his or her specific ritual roles in a sacred manner and according to tradition.

The family and relatives then begin to gather the ceremonial objects that will be placed in the special ceremonial basket. Expeditions are planned to the countryside in order

to collect the pollen. One must wade in the river's edges for the white and red earth clays, and galena is usually gathered. The initiate is expected to participate in the gathering. She accompanies the older women and is instructed in the method of selecting and gathering the needed materials. Trips to collect yucca usually take longer, and other materials are gathered yearly when the season is right.

Extended kin and friends are asked to assist in the detailed preparation. Thus the preparations engender female bonds of solidarity and spirituality as all unite to give support to the initiate and her immediate family in planning for a successful ceremony. The family must also select a *nade 'kleshn,* a female sponsor, who will assume the responsibility of preparing their daughter for the ceremony. This woman will play an important role in the immediate preparation and in the actual ceremonial process. She will be like a mother and mentor to the initiate. Once selected, the family engages in appropriate gift giving to the *nade 'kleshn* just like for the initiate's singer. In this way, the ritual relationship is established and affirmed. This mother–daughter relationship will endure through the lifetime of the initiate.

Usually the *nade 'kleshn* is a woman who is well versed in the traditional ways and is respected in the community because she has lived her life in an exemplary manner. In one case, when the initiate's family arrived at the house of the woman whom they had chosen, the morning star was still bright in the sky. Timing here is important, as the morning star is to be the guide for the initiate's future. The family brings pollen to the woman and makes the request of her to be *nade 'kleshn* for their daughter. A woman must never refuse such a request; to do so would be considered a refusal of 'Isánáklésh. In this way, the ritual familial relationship is established and affirmed.

The *nade 'kleshn* begins to instruct the young girl as soon as the family has selected and engaged her. The instruction centers on this basic message to the initiate: "So far your life has been simple and easy. You have had very little responsibility. Now I need to prepare you for what to expect as a woman." The basic instruction includes how the girl is to deal with her first menstruation and her subsequent monthly periods. The *nade 'kleshn* teaches her about hygiene, as well as about pregnancy and childbirth.

Much is expected from a young woman who has a feast. Her preparation focuses on her future responsibilities to her people, to her self, and to her country. Self-worth is emphasized; the girl learns to understand that her life has a greater purpose. Her people need her in order that their culture can continue, because now she is a carrier of those traditions. This religious, cultural, and historical training instills in the adolescent a strong conviction of self and cultural esteem. It empowers her to comprehend and value the uniqueness of her Apache heritage, and thereby alleviate many problems of identity that most teenagers experience. The *nade 'kleshn* teaches and differentiates among the girl's future roles: her roles as wife, as mother, as a member of the Apache culture, and as an Apache woman. She deals with the problems and advantages of living in two cultures, the American and the Apache, and learns how to respect both. In addition, the *nade 'kleshn* emphasizes the girl's responsibilities as a member of both cultures. She relates all her instruction to the actual upcoming ceremony. It is through the experience of being cared for by the *nade 'kleshn* and her female relatives that the initiate will learn the value of caring for others.

In having the sensation of being cared for by others, she learns and experiences the good feelings such care generates. She then will extend such caring to others in the future. The *nade 'kleshn* emphasizes the importance of education, in the ways of the Apache culture as well as the dominant society's educational system. Both types are important in order to be a successful woman and member of the tribe. Great attention is paid to the structural details of the ritual activity, symbols, Apache philosophy, aesthetics, and their corresponding meanings. The *nade 'kleshn* explains to the initiate how to understand and incorporate the important cultural elements that she will now be charged to maintain and live by. After her ceremony she will be in a position to one day guide another young girl in her own feast preparations and ceremony.

The instruction also includes certain restrictions. The young girl learns a series of taboos, some related to food, water, and rain. She must avoid looking at a rainbow because of the power that this natural phenomenon generates. During the ceremony, she is also instructed on other specific restrictions: She must not smile or act in a lazy or tired manner, or display a negative attitude. She must not scratch herself with her fingernails but must use the designated scratching stick created for such purposes. During the ceremony she cannot drink water directly but must use a special drinking tube when she wants water. She is told to be careful with her words, how she speaks, and how she acts among the people. If she follows this advice, she will never be put in a position of shame, and she will always be respected.

The *nade 'kleshn* reviews the entire ceremony with the initiate so that the girl will be well prepared and know what is happening and what it means. She explains how she will be washed, bathed, and fed, about the songs, and how she must run towards the east and dance vigorously. She will be blessed in the manner in which she must bless others. She will be taught her part in starting the ceremonial fire, and she will be given knowledge of the symbolism that is used throughout the ceremony.

The girl learns the importance of generosity through the example of her family, who must provide large quantities of food and other materials for the guests for four days. In the early 1990s a single private feast cost nearly $10,000. Some families begin saving for their daughter's feast at her birth. The fact that families continue to hold ceremonies for their daughters illustrates how much they value and depend on women to carry the culture and people into the next generations. By reenacting the origins of Mescalero culture, the cer-

emony continually ensures cultural continuity into the future.

BIBLIOGRAPHY

Ariès, Philippe. *Centuries of Childhood: A Social History of Family Life.* Translated by Robert Baldick. New York, 1962.

Basso, Keith. *The Gift of Changing Woman.* Washington, D.C., 1966.

Breuninger, Evelyn, Elbys Hugar, and Ellen Ann Lathan, comps. *Mescalero Apache Dictionary.* Mescalero, N.Mex., 1982.

Driver, Harold E. "Girls' Puberty Rites in Western North America." *University of California Anthropological Records* 6, no. 2 (1941): 21–90.

Frisbie, Charlotte J. *Kinaalda: A Study of the Navajo Girls' Puberty Ceremony.* Middletown, Conn., 1967; reprint, Salt Lake City, 1993.

Gifford, E. W. "Culture Element Distributions: XII Apache-Pueblo." *University of California Anthropological Records* 4, no. 1 (1940): 1–208.

Goodwin, Greville. *Social Organization of the Western Apache.* Chicago, 1942; reprint, Tucson, Ariz., 1969.

Gunnerson, Delores. "The Southern Athabascans: Their Arrival in the Southwest." *El Palacio* 63, nos. 11–12 (1956): 346–365.

Hall, G. Stanley. *Adolescence.* New York, 1904.

Hoijer, Harry. *Chiricahua and Mescalero Apache Texts.* Chicago, 1938.

Lincoln, Bruce. *Emerging from the Chrysalis: Studies in Rituals of Women's Initiation.* Cambridge, Mass., 1981. Reprinted with the title *Emerging from the Chrysalis: Rituals of Women's Initiation.* New York, 1991.

McLucas, Anne Dhu, and Inés Talamantez, "The Mescalero Girls' Puberty Ceremony: The Role of Music in Structuring Ritual Time." *Yearbook of the International Council for Traditional Music* 18 (1986).

Talamantez, Inés M. "Ethnopoetics Theory and Method: A Study of *'Isánáklésh Gotal.*" Ph.D. diss., University of California, San Diego, 1977.

Tedlock, Barbara. "Songs of the Zuni Kachina Society: Composition, Rehearsal, and Performance." In *Southwestern Indian Ritual Drama,* edited by Charlotte J. Frisbie, pp. 7–35. Albuquerque, N.Mex., 1980.

van Gennep, Arnold. *The Rites of Passage.* Translated by Monika B. Vizedom and Gabrielle L. Caffee. Chicago, 1960.

Warner, W. Lloyd. *The Living and the Dead: A Study of the Symbolic Life of Americans.* New Haven, 1959; reprint, Westport, Conn., 1975.

Whitaker, Kathleen. "NA IH ES at San Carlos." *Masterkey* 43, no. 4 (1969): 151.

Whitaker, Kathleen. "NA IH ES: An Apache Puberty Ceremony." *Masterkey* 45, no. 1 (1971): 4–12.

Wyman, Leland C., and Flora L. Bailey. "Navaho Girl's Puberty Rite." *New Mexico Anthropologist* 6 (1943): 3–12.

INÉS TALAMANTEZ (2005)
ZELDA YAZZIE (2005)

STUDY OF RELIGION: THE ACADEMIC STUDY OF RELIGION IN CHINA

In post-Mao China, the Communist government's policy on religion has marked a departure from the repressive policies of the Maoist period. The official "Document No. 19" issued by the Chinese Communist Party in 1982 states that the party's basic policy on religion is one of respect for and protection of the freedom of religious belief, pending such future time when religion itself will disappear. This more tolerant policy on religion brought about a revival of religious traditions, including their activities and organizations, in many parts of China. Temples, churches, and mosques, most of which were destroyed by the Red Guards or occupied by nonreligious organizations during the Cultural Revolution (1966–1976), have been restored and rebuilt. This revival is an aspect of a greater social and academic freedom in China. The reform policy also led to a gradual loosening and opening of the conditions for academic research on religion. As a result, academic religious studies in mainland China have prospered, despite some problems with the country's education system, standards of publication, and methods of research. The most significant changes are in the following three areas: the development of academic religious studies, including the basic conception of religion and its study; religious studies in educational institutions and scholarly publications; and the relationships of academic religious studies to the academic, religious, and general communities in China.

THOUGHT: THE DEVELOPMENT OF ACADEMIC RELIGIOUS STUDIES IN CHINA. The development of academic religious studies in China since the 1910s began with the problem of the modern concept of "religion." There is no equivalent indigenous term in Chinese for the generic term *religion.* Neither had there been any systematic, comparative, and critical studies of religions in premodern China, but only apologetic learning within a particular school of *jiao,* a term that means both instruction and teaching. In traditional China, there were the "three teachings" *(sanjiao)* of Confucius *(rujiao),* Laozi *(daojiao),* and Buddha *(fojiao).* As a result of contact with Japanese scholars of religion in the late nineteenth century, Chinese intellectuals brought the Japanese translation of the Western term *religion* (i.e., *shūkyō*) into China and began to refer to the three schools of teaching as three Chinese religions (*zongjiao*). Without clearly taking into account the critical difference between the Western term *religion* and the native characters *zong* and *jiao,* the translation of *zongjiao* into Western languages as "religion" gave rise to serious misunderstandings and confusion among Chinese intellectuals whenever they discussed the religious nature of Chinese traditional *jiao* in the beginning of the twentieth century and even today.

The traditional Chinese characters of *zong* and *jiao* were not used to discern theism in the Western European sense nor were they used to designate an isolatable aspect of human life. *Zong* means to honor, revere, and obey; *jiao* means teaching and learning. The very difficulty of defining, or

even finding, "religious" qualities within *rujiao, daojiao,* or *fojiao* reflects the problems encountered when uncritically using the Western concept of "religion" to correspond to non-Western traditional cultures. In spite of these differences, almost all Chinese scholars today are used to defining Daoism, Buddhism, Christianity, Islam, and folk belief and ritual as "religion." Few are aware of the origin of the concept of religion, let alone the changes in meaning the term has undergone in the West.

While the Western term *religion* does not correspond to the native Chinese term *zongjiao,* the difference does not mean that the scholarly study of religion has not occurred in modern China. Beginning in the early twentieth century, skeptical and rational studies of religion by Chinese scholars began to appear. The spread of Western learning brought Chinese scholars some entirely new ideas, theories, and methodologies. Distancing themselves from traditional and apologetic attitudes, Chinese scholars in this period, including Liang Qichao, Hu Shi, Chen Yinque, Tang Yongtong, Chen Yuan, Xu Dishan, and Zhen Hanzhang, were able to study Buddhism, Daoism, and Islam on a scholarly and objective level by applying modern historical, linguistic, and literary-critical approaches to their studies. Throughout the first half of the twentieth century, owing to these scholars' strength and interest in history, literature, and philosophy, the major achievement of academic religious studies in China was largely concentrated on the history and philosophy of particular religious traditions. Consideration of common assumptions and methodological principles of religious studies as a scientific and autonomous discipline was not evident in the religious studies field during this period. This was due in part to the antireligious attitude generally adopted by Chinese intellectuals who were calling for a critical overhaul of Chinese traditional culture, including all of its religious, superstitious, and feudal elements, during the May Fourth/New Cultural movement of 1920s China. At that time, therefore, religious studies was not generally seen as a scientific discipline, and with the exception of the School of Religious Studies *(zongjiao xueyuan)* of Yanching University, founded by an American missionary in Beijing in 1926, there were no known major programs of religious studies established in universities in China.

When the Communist Party took over China in 1949, all academic activities, like all other cultural and social activities, became subject to Marxism, Leninism, and Maoism, and all academic institutions were placed under the control of the Communist Party. Like every branch of the study of literature, the arts, and culture, serious religious studies became nonexistent, and neither were there any research and teaching institutions in the field of religious studies. Religion was severely attacked and dismissed as superstitious and counterrevolutionary, and academic religious studies was considered something of a "bourgeois pseudoscience." That era saw few new articles and publications on the subject of religion. What little was produced was used as an instrument of the party's policy on political campaigns and became part of its atheist propaganda. For example, from the late 1950s on, Hou Wailu and Ren Jiyu criticized Buddhist thought and analyzed its social basis in terms of Marxist historical materialism.

The most dramatic change in religious studies in China occurred when Deng Xiaoping's new policy of "reform and opening" was adopted and implemented at the end of 1978, two years after the death of Mao Zedong in 1976. The more tolerant policy on religion led to the lifting of the prohibition on religious activities and academic research on religion. Beginning in the early 1980s, Buddhist and Daoist temples, Muslim mosques, and Christian churches were rebuilt one by one and opened to the public. The speed of restoration and reconstruction of religious centers accelerated in the following two decades. The rapid revival of religions in the 1980s was not unrelated to the "spiritual crisis" of the Chinese people, who were disillusioned with Communist values. An enthusiastic turn to studying religious traditions and culture also occurred within scholarly groups. First, the former extremely "leftist" attitude toward religion, which considered religion to be "the opium of the people," was no longer trusted by scholars in China. Second, facing a serious chaos in values in post-Mao China, many Chinese intellectuals chose to return to studying traditional Chinese culture, including religion, in an attempt to search for some new cultural value system that might help Chinese people disentangle themselves from the past decades of political and cultural disturbance.

This cultural tendency is referred to as a "fever" for religious culture. On the one hand, it liberates scholars from the dogmatic Marxist theory of religion by repositioning religion as a form of human culture. On the other hand, this new tendency shapes studies of religions in a way that treats religion as one cultural phenomenon among others. Such journals as *Jidujiao wenhua pinglun* (Christian cultural review), *Fojiao wenhua* (Buddhist culture), *Zongjiao yu wenhua* (Religion and culture), and *Daojia wenhua* (Daoist culture) have begun to appear. In addition, numerous books and articles on religion's relationship to art, morality, literature, culture, philosophy, science, economy, and law are published for general consumption.

Aside from popular interest in religious culture, since the early 1990s academic religious studies in China have advanced enormously. This is due in part to the fact that many research institutions focused on religious studies and many religious studies programs came to be established in universities as a result of the expansion of higher education in China. In particular, many graduate theses on diverse religious traditions brought a new direction to religious studies scholarship in China. Among the subject areas included are Buddhism, Chinese Christianity, Daoism, Tibetan Buddhism, Islam, Zoroastrianism, folk religion, and the religions of ethnic nationalities in many parts of China. In contrast to the scholarship of the previous decade, which focused only on the gen-

eral history of a particular religion, more religious studies are devoted to rituals, village lineages, social changes, sectarian developments, and cross-cultural and local interactions within diverse religious traditions.

In the area of theories and methods of religious studies, Lu Daji, He Guanghu, and Zhuo Xinping are leading scholars introducing Western theories of religion to Chinese students. Many of the works available in translation, however, are more concentrated on the subject areas of philosophy of religion, theology, sociology of religion, and anthropology of religion. As examples, works by James Frazer, Émile Durkheim, Max Weber, Peter Berger, John Hick, John Macquarrie, and Paul Tillich are widely translated and well known to Chinese scholars and have had a definite impact on academic work. Nevertheless, a broader introduction to the variety of theories of religion in the West would help Chinese students to be able to scrutinize critically the Western category of "religion" and the changes in meaning that it has undergone since the late twentieth century. As of 2005, there were few if any university courses that discussed the nature of religion and religions or the methods of religious studies in Chinese cultural contexts.

Chinese students of religious studies also need to be introduced to the field of religious studies with an emphasis upon the search for the transdisciplinary nature of religious experience and for the perennial patterns underlying the myths, rites, and symbols of diverse religious traditions. Indeed, some Chinese scholars of religion often compare the actual practice of religious tradition with the most idealized or outmoded theories of the West, theories that were the product of the Enlightenment. Recently, some Chinese scholars have voiced the opinion that it is of paramount importance for students of religious studies in China to pay more attention to the well-established scholarly tradition of *Religionswissenschaft* in the West and to recognize this field as a scholarly effort to study religious values that can account for not just why people do certain religious things in this or that historical context, but why they do them in the first place.

INSTITUTIONALIZATION: RELIGIOUS STUDIES IN EDUCATIONAL INSTITUTIONS AND SCHOLARLY PUBLICATIONS. Before the early 1980s, one could not find any religious studies programs established as part of the undergraduate study of humanities in universities in China, nor were there academic research institutions for serious religious studies. In 1963, because of Mao Zedong's words to the effect that "One cannot write well on histories of philosophy, of literature, and of the world without criticism of theology," the first state-founded institution for studying religion was set up in Beijing—the Institute of World Religions. But during the 1960s and 1970s political campaigns and dogmatic Marxist theories of religion undermined the development within the institute of serious religious studies. In 1978, with the restoration of schools, universities, and research institutions, the Institute of World Religions regained its academic status and started research activities anew, marking the first time in the educational history of religious studies in mainland China that more than twenty graduate students were admitted into the institute for academic religious studies. Their major subject areas included Protestant Christianity, Buddhism, Islam, Daoism, Confucianism, and atheism. In 1979, the first national Chinese Association of Religious Studies was established. In addition, three journals or magazines of religious studies began to be published in Beijing and Nanjing, namely, *Shijie Zongjiao Yanjiu*, *Shijie Zongjiao Ziliao*, and *Zongjiao.* These three developments are usually regarded as milestones for the revival of academic religious studies in post-Mao China.

Despite these advances, institutionally-based academic religious studies saw little growth during the early 1980s. This was due in part to the ongoing influence of Marxist ideology upon scholars and educational institutions in China. Evidence of this during the early 1980s may be found in an influential scholarly debate on Marxist theory of religion that occurred among scholars from Beijing and Shanghai. The second problem that prevented more rapid development of academic religious studies in the 1980s was the dominant cultural agenda that shaped religious studies. In retrospect, some Chinese scholars today admit that studying religions as culture is too subjective and pragmatic, and, as a result, ignores complex religious phenomena as an autonomous subject for serious study.

From the late 1980s to the 1990s, a new pattern of change in academic religious studies occurred in universities in China. Institutional education on religious studies ceased to be the preserve of the stated-founded Institute of World Religions, which, in 1978, was put under the Chinese Academy of Social Sciences, with ten regional institutes in various provinces. Between 1978 and 1998, twenty-seven doctoral students completed their research theses at the Institute of World Religions. In the mid-1980s, Beijing University and Wuhan University became the first to set up religious studies programs for undergraduates in their own departments of philosophy. Subsequently, Sichuan University, Nanjing University, Renmin University, Fudan University, and Shandong University founded institutes or centers for academic religious studies. Thus the number of professional researchers increased greatly. Among the major characteristics shared by these university-based religious studies programs, the goal of fostering understanding of religious traditions supplanted the traditional ideological criticism of religion. However, the location of religious studies programs within departments of philosophy obviously prevented students from broadening their approaches to studying religious traditions within both disciplinary and multidisciplinary contexts. Apart from the philosophical and historical aspects of religion, the field of *Religionswissenschaft* and different methods of comparative, linguistic, anthropological, archaeological, sociological, and literary approaches to the complex phenomena of religious belief and practice would appear to be

neglected in religious studies programs in China today; as a result, a comprehensive curriculum of religious studies programs has yet to emerge. In the early 2000s, some Chinese universities received official approval from the state to set up undergraduate programs of religious studies, despite the unchanged practice of locating such departments within the department of philosophy. However, it remains to be seen whether there will be more faculty members with full-time appointments in religious studies and whether greater contributions of faculty from a variety of humanities and social science disciplines will be permitted in the future.

Besides offering religious studies programs, these universities are also expanding their graduate enrollments and research activities by establishing research institutes for religious studies. Among these research institutes, Sichuan University is the best for Daoist studies, and Nanjing University and Renmin University are the leading institutions for Buddhist studies. By the turn of the century, Sichuan University and Renmin University had further developed as the state-supported humanities research bases for academic religious studies because of the excellence of their academic programs.

Besides the Chinese Academy of Social Sciences and university-based institutions, religious studies are conducted in the State Bureau for Religious Affairs. The High Party School of the Central Committee of the Chinese Community Party has also set up institutes for the study of religions under its direct supervision. In addition, some government sanctioned religious associations (e.g., national associations of Buddhism, Daoism, Islam, and Roman Catholic and Protestant Christianity) have established their own colleges for recruitment and education of their young professionals.

CONTEXTUALIZATION: RELATIONSHIPS OF ACADEMIC RELIGIOUS STUDIES TO THE ACADEMIC, RELIGIOUS, AND GENERAL COMMUNITIES IN CHINA. It is difficult to deny that the Communist state retains political control and enforces legal restrictions on religion and religious studies in China. According to the Chinese constitution, people have the freedom to believe or not believe in religion, but this refers to government-approved forms of the five major traditions—Daoism, Buddhism, Islam, and Roman Catholic and Protestant Christianity. For Chinese scholars of religions, the problem with this limited definition of approved religions is that it prevents them from studying beliefs and practices of other religious traditions. As examples, Chinese popular religious sects are labeled as "feudal superstition" unworthy of recognition as religion. In addition, academic studies of China's fifty-six ethnic minority groups may put scholars in jeopardy of being accused of dividing the country if their publications contravene state policy over the governance of minority communities. Furthermore, since the relationship between the Chinese government and the Vatican remains conflictual, China's underground Catholic churches, with six to eight million adherents, are subject to repression. Circumscribed by the official stance on underground churches, Chinese scholars are unwilling to take up this subject of study. These are but a few examples among many that show how the party's policy on religion continues to determine the scope and character of academic religious studies in China. In the late 1990s, party authorities reiterated the call for the adaptation of religion to socialism. Required to respond to this call, some Chinese religious studies scholars immediately proposed research projects aimed at promoting such adaptation.

Despite this, there is no doubt that academic religious studies have had a remarkable influence on Chinese society by giving the public more accurate and objective information about the growing reality of religious activities and faith among the Chinese people today. According to Communist Party law, normal religious activities must be confined within registered religious buildings and organizations. Because of this kind of control over religious organizations and their activities, academic studies of religions are an alternative means by which nonbelievers in the society can relate to religion. The public effect of serious religious studies may be to help the larger community build a more sympathetic and sensible understanding of religion. The influence of the flourishing publications of religious studies can be traced in such public media as newspapers, television, films, and broadcasting, all of which reflect an increased interest in religion.

The effect of academic religious studies upon China's religious communities is twofold. First, because religious organizations have very limited resources for developing systematic studies of their own traditions, religious studies scholars, through invitations to lecture, publications, and good relationships, can increase and deepen believers' understanding of their own faith. Some religious leaders highly appreciate the work of scholars for their contribution to improving the quality of believers. Second, some religious studies scholars are named by the public as "Cultural Christians," "Cultural Buddhists," or "Cultural Daoists," because of the influence of their publications in increasing the public's knowledge of Christianity, Buddhism, or Daoism. In this regard, religious studies scholars sometimes play a more influential role in spreading religions in society than such insiders as clergy, *saṃgha* members, or Daoist masters.

The future of religious studies in China is linked to the fate of the government's policy on religious and academic freedom. The success of academic studies, including religious studies, in China is dependent on the extent of the Communist regime's open, tolerant, and pluralistic policy. Along with this political factor, religious studies programs have not yet taken root in higher education in China. It will require substantial effort on the part of scholars to warrant the state's recognition that religious studies should constitute a separate discipline with its own methods and curriculum in Chinese universities.

Bibliography

Cao Zhongjian, ed. *Zhongguo zongjiao yanjiu nianjian* (Annual of religious studies in China). Beijing, 1996–1997, 1997–1998, 1999–2000, 2001–2002.

Chinese Association of Religious Studies, ed. *Zhongkuo zongjiaoxue*, vol. 1. Beijing, 2003.

Overmyer, Daniel L. "From 'Feudal Superstition' to 'Popular Beliefs': New Directions in Mainland Chinese Studies of Chinese Popular Religion." *Cahiers d'Extrême-Asia* 12 (2001): 103–126.

Overmyer, Daniel L., ed. *Religion in China Today.* Cambridge, U.K., 2003.

Chi-tim Lai (2005)

STUDY OF RELIGION: THE ACADEMIC STUDY OF RELIGION IN WESTERN EUROPE

While avoiding an approach to religion and discourses about it in a manner that presupposes their existence as self-evident objects, one should also avoid a purely constructionist approach, for the contours assumed by religion and by its scholarship, rather than being merely the result of scholarly arbitrariness, take shape within certain constraints. In terms of the study of religion, the most pervasive pattern involves the tension that results from a position according to which religious phenomena, being the reflection of supernatural realities, must be approached in a reverential manner, and one that seeks to discern—or, more radically, to unmask—the connections between religions beliefs/practices and mundane realities, especially those that have to do with power relations. In this regard, as a sacralizing or as a critical enterprise, the study of religion is part and parcel of the struggle surrounding a society's mechanisms of legitimization.

In the area with which we are concerned, the study of religion can be traced back to Herodotos's interest in the beliefs and practices of non-Greeks, to the demythologizing efforts of Xenophanes, and to the reflexivity implied in the changing attitudes towards supernatural power found in terms such as *gōes/gōeteia* and *mágos/mageia.* The emergence of Christianity forced a confrontation between Christian *religio* and Roman *ritus,* Christian apologists becoming engaged in the delimitation of true religion and the condemnation of heresy and superstition. That apologetic approach continued during the medieval period, interspersed by ecumenical efforts such as Nicholas of Cusa's (1401–1464) *Cribatio Alkorani* (1461). Closer to the academic study of religion as such is the critique-of-ideology approach employed by the theorists associated with the Enlightenment. Most of them, especially the *philosophes,* do not usually appear in histories of the study of religion. But an eighteenth-century thinker, David Hume (1711–1776), must be mentioned among the early scholars of religion; indeed, one must agree with J. Samuel Preus, who regards Hume as the founder of the scientific study of religion. Hume's works, especially *The Natural History of Religion* (1757) and *Dialogues concerning Natural Religion* (posthumously published in 1779), contain insights that are yet to be fully assimilated about the role played by "the ordinary affections of human life" in the generation of religion. No less important is Ludwig Feuerbach (1804–1872), whose ideas about projection in *Das Wesen des Christentums* (1841) were anchored in political realities by Karl Marx (1818–1883), and then elaborated upon by Ernst Topitsch (1919–1993). It could be said, in fact, that Feuerbach's discoveries are present, however implicitly, at the heart of the cognitive approach.

Between Philology and Experience. While a critique-of-ideology approach to religion was taking place in the eighteenth and nineteenth centuries, there also occurred a linguistic deciphering that, having been made possible by European hegemony, has been itself subject to ideological analysis. The best-known cases involve the access to ancient Iranian, Egyptian and Mesopotamian texts, made possible in the eighteenth century by Abraham-Hyacinthe Anquetil-Duperron (1731–1805) and in the nineteenth century by Jean-François Champollion (1790–1832), Georg Friedrich Grotefend (1775–1853), and Henry Rawlinson (1810–1895). In India, on the other hand, Sanskrit, learned by Europeans toward the end of the eighteenth century, did not have to be deciphered, inasmuch as its transmission within *brahman* circles had survived political and cultural upheavals. It could be said, nevertheless, that a translation of sorts took place, insofar as William Jones (1746–1794) and Gaston-Laurent Coeurdoux (1691–1779), and then Franz Bopp (1791–1867) and Rasmus Kristian Rask (1787–1832) recognized the kinship between Sanskrit and languages later to be known as Indo-European or *Indogermanisch.* Unlike the Enlightenment critique-of-ideology approach, the early study of Sanskrit texts by European intellectuals such as the Schlegel brothers tended to be carried out in a reverential manner, a reverence that was consonant with the political reaction against the desacralizing impetus of the Enlightenment and the French Revolution. The Romantics distrusted the deleterious effects of reason, stressing the power of the irrational and the immediacy of experience—an attitude we will encounter once again in the early decades of the twentieth century. Still influential regarding the role of experience in religion is Friedrich Schleiermacher's (1768–1834) *Reden über die Religion* (1799), addressed to religion's "cultured despisers," a work that in bypassing traditional theological concern with doctrine is centered around religious experience. Experience also plays a role in F. Max Müller (1823–1900), one of the pioneers of the comparative study of religion, for whom "Religion is a mental faculty or disposition which, independent of, nay, in spite of sense and reason, enables man to apprehend the Infinite under different names and under various disguises." Müller, once a celebrated scholar and essayist, is now remembered for his work as editor of the *Ṛgveda* and as general editor of the fifty-volume series "The Sacred Books of the East," as well as for emphasizing the role of language in the generation of mythology in ways that re-

semble Francis Bacon's (1561–1626) theory of the idols of the mind.

Origins and Evolution. Müller's was but one of many nineteenth-century attempts to explain the origins and function of religion. Another influential suggestion was Edward Burnett Tylor's (1832–1917) theory of animism, according to which "a minimum definition of Religion" involves "the belief in Spiritual Beings." In Tylor's evolutionary perspective, "animism characterizes tribes very low in the scale of humanity, and thence ascends, deeply modified in its transmission, but from first to last preserving unbroken continuity, into the midst of high modern culture." This approach was carried one step further by Robert Ranulph Marett (1866–1943), whose theory of "animatism" proposed an earlier stage of impersonal forces, related to concepts such as "*tabu*" and "*mana*" that had been recently popularized by ethnographers. Moving in the opposite direction, Andrew Lang (1844–1912) rejected the idea that gods originated in ghosts, maintaining the primacy of the belief in high gods, a thesis that would find its culmination in Wilhelm Schmidt's (1868–1954) primordial monotheism (*Urmonotheismus*). Schmidt's theologically based theory reverses evolutionary assumptions, postulating a degeneration in conceptions of the divine. Working within an evolutionary framework, James George Frazer (1854–1941) wrote several massive works, the most popular of which was *The Golden Bough*, whose third edition in twelve volumes was published between 1913 and 1924. Trained in classics but writing from a comparative religion perspective, Frazer postulated a sequence from magic to religion to science, the section about "contagious" and "sympathetic" magic having become part of the vocabulary of the study of religion. Unlike today's scholarly debates, which have no repercussion among the public at large, the theories of Müller, Tylor, Marett, Lang, and Frazer were presented in widely sold books, in public lectures, and in encyclopedia articles, being debated in the press, not least because of the general interest in evolution.

In addition to their speculative character, their concern with the origins of religion, and the interest they awakened among the cultivated public, some of the theories mentioned above also shared the fact of their being based on reports by travelers and explorers, who in addition to collecting myths described ritual behavior. When the interest in ritual behavior was combined with philological rigor, and when this was done in a manner willing to disregard confessional prejudices, the results could be productive, albeit distressing to those who wanted to defend the uniqueness of Christianity. Just as the placing of Indian religious texts in the context of Indo-European mythology opened up new areas of research along with ideological controversies that last to this day, the discoveries of Mesopotamian and, later, Ugaritic materials allowed scholars to place the practices and beliefs of the ancient Israelites in the context of ancient Near Eastern religions. However, given the absorption of Israelite texts into the Christian Bible as the "Old Testament," the postulation of commonalities between Israelite and other Near Eastern religions has been regarded in certain circles as an attack on the uniqueness of the Christian message. A notorious example of this reaction occurred in 1881, when William Robertson Smith (1846–1894) lost his position at the University of Aberdeen after he wrote about the commonalities between ancient Israelite and Arabic sacrificial practices. As Julius Wellhausen (1844–1918) had already done, Smith focused on the ritual aspects of Israelite religion, paying special attention to sacrificial practices. No less controversial were the attempts by the scholars associated with the *Religionsgeschichtliche Schule* to understand early Christianity in the context of the religions of late antiquity. The approach to Israelite, Jewish and Christian religions from a comparative perspective, inaugurated by Hermann Gunkel (1862–1932), Wilhelm Bousset (1865–1920), Ernst Troeltsch (1865–1923), and Hugo Gressmann (1877–1927), among others, laid the foundations of the scholarly approaches on Old and New Testament studies prevalent today.

Around the time these controversies were taking place, sacrifice, ritual and in general the role of society in the genesis of religion were studied systematically by Émile Durkheim (1858–1917) and his collaborators, Marcel Mauss (1872–1950), Henri Hubert (1872-1927), and Robert Hertz (1881–1915), in articles published in the *Année Sociologique*. In France, as elsewhere in Europe, the period around 1900 was pivotal in the study of religion. It saw the publication of important works such as Durkheim's "De la définition des phénomènes religieux" (1898), Hubert and Mauss's "Essai sur la nature et la fonction du sacrifice" (1899) and "Esquisse d'une théorie générale de la magie" (1903). The seminal character of that period becomes even more evident when we recall that in 1904 and 1905 Max Weber (1864–1920) published his study on the spirit of capitalism and the Protestant ethic, which continues to be debated a century later. The culmination of this approach to religion is found in Durkheim's *Les formes élémentaires de la vie religieuse* (1912) and in Weber's *Gesammelte Aufsätze zur Religionssoziologie*, as well as his "Religionssoziologie," published between 1920 and 1922.

The Institutionalization of the Study of Religion. Already several decades before these developments, chairs in history of religions were created in Geneva (1873), the Netherlands (1876–1877) and Paris (1879). The creation of the chairs occupied in Leiden by Cornelis Petrus Tiele (1830–1902), in Amsterdam by Pierre Daniel Chantepie de la Saussaye (1848–1920) and at the Collège de France by Albert Réville (1826–1906), involving as they did decisions at the governmental level, constituted the institutionalization of the study of religion as well as the transfer of resources from the field of theology to that of history of religions. The process was carried a step further in laic France, when the Protestant Réville became in 1886 president of the newly established Fifth Section, Sciences religieuses, of the École Pratique des Hautes Études, which to this day assembles the largest concentration in Europe of scholars devoted to nonconfessional research on religion. As important as the cre-

ation of chairs were the scholarly exchanges that took place during the extended period of peace that preceded World War I. We have already encountered Max Müller, a German who, after studying in Leipzig and Berlin, moved to Oxford to work on a critical edition of the *Ṛgveda*, partly as a result of the encouragement he received in Paris from Eugène Burnouf (1801–1852). Similarly, Robertson Smith was inspired by Wellhausen in Leipzig. Réville, in turn, studied in Holland. The exchanges among the Scandinavian countries, the Netherlands, and Germany were even more intense. It is sufficient to recall the Swede Nathan Söderblom (1866–1931), who after studying Iranian philology in Paris under Antoine Meillet (1866–1936), held a chair in Leipzig from 1912 to 1914. Another student of Meillet, the Dane Edvard Lehmann (1862–1930), was appointed to a chair in Berlin in 1910, after holding from 1900 to 1910 the first Danish chair in history of religions. He was succeeded by Vilhelm Grønbech (1873–1948). Likewise, the Norwegian William Brede Kristensen (1867–1953) taught in Leiden from 1901 to 1937, as successor of Tiele, one of his students being Gerardus van der Leeuw (1890–1950). These academic lineages and appointments are mentioned in order to call attention to the intellectual cross-fertilization that occurred in large portions of Europe during the period of peace that would come to an abrupt end in August 1914.

PHENOMENOLOGY AND THE REVOLT AGAINST REASON. Several of the scholars named above have been identified with the phenomenology of religion, a term used for the first time by Chantepie de la Saussaye in 1887. Because of its vagueness this method or approach has been understood in a number of ways—the vagueness having also resulted in uncertainty as to who qualifies as a phenomenologist of religion. In general, phenomenologists attempted to discover the essence of religious phenomena, thus contributing to the postulation of the distinctive and indeed *sui generis* nature of a cluster of phenomena; they also sought to describe and classify the manifestations of religion, using categories such as "myth," "ritual," and "magic," still employed today. How the bracketing that allows the identification of the "religious" is achieved was generally left unexplained, for terms such as *epoché* and *essence* were used almost as incantations. Similarly, the procedure used to determine the "religious" character of certain practices and representations tended to involve circular reasoning. In some cases without using the term *phenomenology* in the title, Tiele, Chantepie de la Saussaye, Kristensen, and van der Leeuw authored widely read phenomenologies of religion—van der Leeuw's *Phänomenologie der Religion* (1933) being available still in several languages.

Besides the authors already mentioned, many of the early twentieth-century scholars identified with the history of religions in general, rather than with research in one religious tradition, were concerned with identifying and defending religiousness. This attitude can be seen among the theorists who worked in Germany during the first decades of the twentieth century: Rudolf Otto (1869–1937), Walter F. Otto (1874–1958), Jakob Wilhelm Hauer (1881–1962), Friedrich Heiler (1892–1967), and Joachim Wach (1898–1955), among others. Renowned as they once were, some of them are now known only to specialists in the history of the study of religions. An exception is Rudolf Otto, whose book *Das Heilige* (1917) is a phenomenology of a "holy" that transcends morality and reason. For Otto and many of his contemporaries, the precondition for the study of religion is having experienced religion's *sui generis* reality. Much like the theories of the jurist of the Third Reich, Carl Schmitt (1888–1985), about the foundations of sovereignty, Otto's conception of the "holy" is to be understood in the context of the revolt against the disintegrating effects of reason prevalent in European intellectual circles during the first decades of the twentieth century—a revolt that in many ways resembles the situation during the Romantic period. Even more popular than Otto, Mircea Eliade (1907–1986) continues to epitomize for many the proper, nonreductionist, approach to the world of religion. But as it happened with Otto, Eliade's conceptual apparatus—the sacred, hierophany, myth, *homo religiosus*, total hermeneutics—has been subject to conceptual and ideological critiques. The latter have been particularly forceful, having explored the links between Eliade's scholarly work and his right-wing political sympathies before and during the second world war, which he spent in Antonio de Oliveira Salazar's Portugal as cultural attaché of the Romanian regime. The same ideological analysis has been applied to the work of historians of religion associated with the Eranos meetings held in Ascona since 1933, some of whom advocated an esoteric, mystical approach to religion.

Whatever the phenomenologists' failings, even from a resolutely nontheological position it would be unwise to reject a priori the existence of the human proclivities that, perhaps because of the peculiarities of our cognitive apparatus, generate the building blocks of religion—conceptions of superhuman agency, mechanisms of legitimization and boundary creation involving sacredness, repetitious patterned behavior, narratives about origins, and the like. It may be observed at this point that despite the generalized distrust of evolutionary approaches among scholars in the humanities, many of the same scholars assume that current theories are by definition superior to those held fifty or a hundred years ago. Yet if one looks at several of the theories mentioned above, one can see that their demise is far from certain. One can refer, for example, to Carsten Colpe's (b. 1929) attempt to reground the phenomenological approach; to Kurt Rudolph's (b. 1929) use of a critique-of-ideology approach indebted to Marx, Weber, and Durkheim; to Robin Horton's rehabilitation of some of the positions advanced by Tylor and Frazer; to Walter Burkert's (b. 1931) ethological approach to the role played by emotion in religion; to Fritz Stolz's (1942–2001) use of functionalist approaches; to neurological research that seems to validate some of the aims of a hermeneutic based on empathy; to ecological and ethologi-

cal validation of Hume's theories; to cognitive science views of projection that validate Feuerbach.

Reflexivity. A survey of the many areas of European research in religion since the early twentieth century would require discussing large bodies of scholarship on specific traditions or, more generally, cultural areas; to subdisciplines such as anthropology, sociology, and psychology of religion; as well as to comparative research on, among other topics, "magic," "mysticism," "ritual," "myth," and "religion" itself. Regarding the very concept of "religion," it can be said that after attempts in the nineteenth and early twentieth centuries to provide a definition of religion, as well as an account of its origin, efforts in that direction have diminished considerably, being replaced by an examination of the conditions within which the discourses that constitute religion emerge. Indeed, concern with the political dimensions of one's scholarly activities and the questioning of received categories have characterized the study of religion, especially at the turn of the millennium. In terms of the political aspects of the study of religion, reference may be made to Indo-European studies, perhaps the field that has aroused the most ideologically charged controversies in recent times. Much of this has to do with the ideological manipulation of archaeological and linguistic evidence by the Nazis; some is related to the political sympathies of scholars identified with Indo-European studies, the best-known of whom is Georges Dumézil (1898–1986). But despite the abuses at the hands of fascists and political reactionaries, it must be remembered that Dumézil's postulation of a parallel between the tripartite organization of society and an equally tripartite structure of the Indo-European pantheon is an application of Durkheim's social theory of religion. In any event, when confronting these issues it is necessary to keep in mind not just the work of Nazi sympathizers such as Stig Wikander (1908–1983) and Jan de Vries (1890–1964), but also the labor of scholars such as Émile Benveniste (1902–1976) and Bernard Sergent (b. 1946), who rightly protests that one can be an "indo-européaniste" without being a Nazi.

The current practice of seeking to establish a correlation between scholarly activities and the political and religious background of scholars constitutes a sharp departure from the academic practices prevalent just a few decades ago. One may remember in this regard the angry reaction of Henrik Samuel Nyberg (1889–1974) over attempts to link his approach to Iranian religions to his Lutheran background. In his response to the critiques by W. B. Henning (1908–1967), R. C. Zaehner (1913–1967) and others, Nyberg referred, among other things, to the "gentleman's agreement," according to which the religious background of a scholar is not to be mentioned in scholarly debates. In later times, on the contrary, it is not uncommon to focus on the religious or ethnic background of scholars or on their political sympathies when trying to understand or, more frequently, to refute their theories. In the field of Iranian studies the clearest example is offered by the rejection of Wikander's theories about the *Männerbünde*—bands of Indo-Iranian warriors—because this theory was proposed by an author with national-socialist sympathies in a book published in 1938. Similarly, when dealing with religious allegiances, nobody would be surprised if in trying to assess Zaehner's theological approach to mysticism or E. E. Evans-Pritchard's (1902–1973) account of Zande theistic beliefs one were to take into account the fact that both converted to Catholicism. Similarly, nobody has objected to Gregory Schopen's (b. 1947) referring to "Protestant presuppositions" in his critique of purely doctrinal approaches to Indian Buddhism, an approach he detects even in Catholic scholars such as Louis de La Vallée Poussin (1869–1938) and his disciple Monsignor Étienne Lamotte (1903–1983), two of the great scholars of Buddhism in the twentieth century.

Reflexivity concerning the concept of religion has resulted in Michel Despland's (b. 1936) studies of the changing meanings of this term in the West; in Hans Kippenberg's (b. 1939) having placed the history of the study of religions within the social transformation that gave rise to modernity; as well as in Hans-Michael Haussig's comparative studies of the concept of "religion" in various cultures. Taking a radical position, scholars such as Dario Sabbatucci (1923–2002), Timothy Fitzgerald (b. 1947), and Daniel Dubuisson (b. 1950) have sought to show that religion is a Western construct suffused by ideological presuppositions. Besides this radical position, there has been a concerted effort to study nonofficial forms of religion, variously labeled as "popular," "folk," or "local," scholars having become aware of the need to avoid accepting official or clerical versions of what constitutes "magic," "superstition," "heresy," or "syncretism." It is instructive in this regard to compare Ulrich von Wilamowitz-Moellendorff's (1848–1931) negative attitude toward Greek magic to that of Samson Eitrem (1872–1966), not to mention that of Fritz Graf (b. 1944) or Jan Bremmer (b. 1944), scholars who have made substantial contributions to the elucidation of magical practices in the Greco-Roman world. There is now an increased awareness of the fact that religious traditions are not to be understood as self-contained units, or as being coterminous with a geographical area. This realization has led to research projects dealing on the one hand with a "European religious history" that is more than just the history of Christianity and, on the other, with the forms assumed by diaspora religions in various parts of the world.

Beyond Official Religion. Rejection of a purely doctrinal/textual approach to religion has led to a revalorization of ritual activities and of nonofficial forms of religion in general. Lack of space allows for little more than mentioning the work of almost forgotten pioneers such as Peter Browe (1876–1949) and of influential scholars such as Marc Bloch (1886–1944), Georges Duby (1919–1996), Aaron Gurevich (b. 1924), Jacques Le Goff (b. 1924), Arnold Angenendt (b. 1934), Jean-Claude Schmitt (b. 1946), and Peter Dinzelbacher (b. 1948) on medieval Christianity; Julio Caro Baroja (1914–1995), Jean Delumeau (b. 1923), Keith Thomas (b. 1933), Richard van Dülmen (b. 1937), and

Robert Muchembled (b. 1944) on early modern European religion; Kristofer Schipper (b. 1934) on Daoism; Axel Michaels (b. 1949) on Hinduism; and Michael Stausberg (b. 1966) on Zoroastrianism. The work of the scholars working on Asian traditions has the added significance of combining historico-philological approaches, involvement with contemporary practitioners—including Schipper's ordination as a Daoist master in Taiwan—along with interest in the theoretical implications of their research, especially regarding the issue of ritual. It is true that European scholars' acquaintance with lived Asian religions is not new—one need only think of Johann Jakob Maria de Groot (1854–1921), Marcel Granet (1884–1940), Henri Maspero (1883–1945), Giuseppe Tucci (1894–1984), Paul Mus (1902–1969), and Rolf Stein (1911–1999) in the fields of Chinese, Southeast Asian and Tibetan religion—but it would not be unfair to say that there is now among some scholars a heightened recognition of the need to combine history, philology, and anthropology, as well as of the need to be aware of one's frequently unstated theoretical presuppositions.

In order to achieve something more than the ritualized bemoaning of the mixing of history of religions and theology, reflexivity and meta-theoretical research require a high level of abstraction along with a knowledge of materials from many traditions. Some of the most rigorous work in this regard has been carried out by Fritz Stolz—whose premature death was a great loss to the field—and by Burkhard Gladigow (b. 1939), whose many contributions to the study of religion, unfortunately still not collected in book form, include his service as one of the editors of the *Handbuch religionswissenschaftlicher Grundbegriffe* (1988–2001), a work devoted to the study of the conceptual apparatus of *Religionswissenschaft.* The *Handbuch* is just one of the reference works currently being published in the field of religion; indeed, despite the pervasive talk about the questioning of "master narratives" and the like, ours seems to be the age of compendia, encyclopedias, dictionaries, guides, and introductions to the study of religion. *Die Religion in Geschichte und Gegenwart* is now appearing in its fourth edition. The *Metzler Lexikon Religion* (1999–2002), edited by Christopher Auffarth, Jutta Bernard, and Hubert Mohr, emphasizes the role of lived, everyday religion, in full awareness of the authors' European perspective.

Among collections designed to provide a comprehensive overview of the religious history of humanity none is more ambitious than *Die Religionen der Menschheit,* whose first two volumes were published in 1960. Several less ambitious collective works appeared around 1970: the *Illustreret religionshistorie,* edited by Jes P. Asmussen and Jørgen Læssøe (1968; revised German edition, *Handbuch der Religionsgeschichte,* 1971–1972); the fourth edition of *La storia delle religioni,* edited by Giuseppe Castellani (1970); and the *Histoire des religions* (1970–1972) edited by Henri-Charles Puech. The most recent attempt to present a multivolume panorama of the religions of humanity is the *Storia delle religioni* edited by Giovanni Filoramo (1995–1999). Among publications that deal with the phenomenon of religion we may mention Mircea Eliade, *Traité d'histoire des religions* (1949, translated into several languages); Kurt Goldammer, *Die Formenwelt des Religiösen* (1960); Friedrich Heiler, *Erscheinungsformen und Wesen der Religion* (1961); Geo Widengren, *Religionsphänomenologie* (1969); Fritz Stolz, *Grundzüge der Religionswissenschaft* (1988) and *Weltbild der Religionen* (2001); Francisco Diez de Velasco, *Introducción a la Historia de las Religiones* (1995); and Giovanni Filoramo, *Che cos'è religione* (2004).

NATIONAL TRADITIONS. As already indicated, a survey of the study of religion in twentieth-century Europe would require much more space than is available here. Regarding French-speaking countries, in addition to the authors mentioned elsewhere in this essay, reference must be made to the contributions of Jacques Duchesne-Guillemin (b. 1910), Philippe Gignoux (b. 1931), and Jean Kellens (b. 1944) on Iranian religions; to Jean-Pierre Vernant (b. 1914), Pierre Vidal-Naquet (b. 1930), and Marcel Detienne (b. 1935), whose approach to Greek mythology and ritual, particularly sacrifice, has influenced scholarship far beyond the domain of classical studies. As influential as French work on Greek religion is that produced by scholars associated with the École Française d'Extrême-Orient (established in 1900), especially the research on Daoism by Schipper and Anna Seidel (1938–1991). On the other hand, the absence of chairs devoted to the comparative study or the theory of religion at the Fifth Section of the École Pratique des Hautes Études and at the Collège de France has resulted in the neglect of theory as well as in the sparse participation of French scholars in the most recent international gatherings devoted to the study of religions. It may be pointed out in this context that the theoretical introductory chapter in the *Histoire des religions* edited by Puech was written by an Italian scholar, Angelo Brelich (1913–1977). That Brelich was invited to write that chapter, and that Dario Sabbatucci contributed the essay on "Kultur und Religion" for the *Handbuch religionswissenschaftlicher Grundbegriffe,* is an indication of the esteem in which Italian scholarship on religion is held. This prestige is inextricably related to the work of Raffaele Pettazzoni (1883–1959), holder of the first Italian chair of history of religions at the University of Rome (1924). The author of books on the ancient mysteries, Iranian religions, and, above all, conceptions of supreme beings, as well as the founder of *Numen, International Review for the History of Religions* (1954–) and president of the International Association for the History of Religions (1950–1959), Pettazzoni was a proponent of the comparative method, which he pursued with rigor. Pettazzoni was also the teacher of several scholars—Brelich, Sabbatucci, Ernesto de Martino (1908–1965) and Ugo Bianchi (1922–1995)—who in turn trained most of the current holders of chairs in religion in Italy. On the other hand, the study of Indian, Tibetan, and Iranian religions was promoted by Giuseppe Tucci, among whose disciples we may mention the Indologist Raniero Gnoli (b. 1931) and the specialist in

Iranian religions Gherardo Gnoli (b. 1937). Among German-speaking scholars who have pursued historico-philological approaches while also being concerned with theoretical issues we may refer again to Colpe and Rudolph, and to Burkert, whose research on ritual, sacrifice and violence, is as influential as his work on ancient Greek religion. We find the same combination of historico-philological expertise and theoretical concerns in the next generation: the already mentioned Gladigow, Stolz, and Kippenberg, along with Hubert Seiwert (b. 1949), Seiwert being the only one among those named here to have occupied himself with religion in East Asia. In addition to the British anthropologists and historians of religion mentioned throughout this essay—Tylor, Lang, Smith, Frazer, Marett, Evans-Pritchard, Zaehner, Horton—mention must be made of the substantial contributions to the study of Iranian religions made by Mary Boyce (b. 1920) and to David Martin's (b. 1929) work on the sociology of religion.

The Scandinavian scene was dominated for many years by Geo Widengren (1907–1996), a scholar of ancient Near Eastern, especially Iranian, religions (Iranian studies having flourished in Scandinavia since the days of Rask and N. L. Westergaard [1815–1878] to those of Nyberg, Wikander and, more recently, Jes P. Asmussen [1928–2002] and Anders Hultgård [b. 1936]). Widengren was also concerned with methodological and theoretical issues, to which he devoted numerous articles as well as a work of synthesis, the *Religionsphänomenologie*, which despite its title has little in common with the approaches found in van der Leeuw's or Heiler's phenomenologies. Widengren's achievements should not prevent us from remembering Haralds Biezais (1909–1995), who in addition to studies of Latvian religion made important theoretical contributions. The same applies to the Finnish folklorist Lauri Honko (1932–2002), author of works on Finnish mythology and comparative religion. The study of religion continues to be pursued with distinction in Scandinavia, where large departments of religious studies are found in the capital cities as well as in Uppsala, Turku, Århus, and Bergen. In the Netherlands, the country that saw the creation of some of the first chairs of history of religions, the study of religion has continued to be carried out on several areas; it is sufficient to consider the significance of Schipper and Erik Zürcher (b. 1928) in Sinology and of Jan Gonda (1905–1991) and J. C. Heesterman (b. 1925) in Indology. Among scholars who have made contributions to the study of the historiography and theory of religion, myth, ritual and magic beyond their primary areas of expertise we may mention Jacques Waardenburg (b. 1930), Henk S. Versnel (b. 1936), and Jan Bremmer. In assessing the significance of the Netherlands for the study of religion one must not forget the role played by E. J. Brill, the publishing house active in Leiden for more than three centuries.

In Switzerland, the country in which a chair in history of religions was created as early as 1873, the study of religion is pursued in a way that exemplifies the various approaches mentioned in this article. Thus while Philippe Borgeaud (b. 1946) has made substantial contributions to the study of Greek religion as well as to theoretical and historiographic issues, Martin Baumann (b. 1961) studies diaspora Hinduism. In Spain, the post-Franco period has seen a resurgence of scholarship in religion, whose most important practitioner was for decades Julio Caro Baroja, author of works on witchcraft and popular religion, including one on "the complex forms of religious life" in sixteenth- and seventeenth-century Spain. In Portugal as well, important work on heterodox forms of religion has been carried out by Francisco Bethencourt and José Pedro Paiva.

We may conclude this survey by mentioning the establishment in 2000 of a European Association for the Study of Religions (EASR), to which most European national associations are affiliated. As of 2004 the EASR had held four international conferences: Cambridge (2001), Paris (2002), Bergen (2003), and Santander (2004).

BIBLIOGRAPHY

Bianchi, Ugo. *La storia delle religioni.* Turin, Italy, 1970.

Bianchi, Ugo, ed. *The Notion of "Religion" in Comparative Research.* Rome, 1994.

Bianchi, Ugo, Claas Bleeker, and Alessandro Bausani, eds. *Problems and Methods of the History of Religions.* Leiden, 1972.

Cancik, Hubert, Burkhard Gladigow, Matthias Laubscher, and Karl-Heinz Kohl, eds. *Handbuch Religionswissenschaftlicher Grundbegriffe.* 5 vols. Stuttgart, Germany, 1988–2001.

Casadio, Giovanni, ed. *Ugo Bianchi: Una vita per la Storia delle Religioni.* Rome, 2002.

Despland, Michel. *La Religion en Occident: Évolution des idées et du vécu.* Montreal, 1979.

Dubuisson, Daniel. *Mythologies du XXe siècle: Dumézil, Lévi-Strauss, Eliade.* Lille, France, 1993.

Dubuisson, Daniel. *L'Occident et la religion: Mythes, science et idéologie.* Brussels, 1998.

Elsas, Christoph, ed. *Religion: Ein Jahrhundert theologischer, philosophischer, soziologischer und psychologischer Interpretationsansätze.* Munich, 1975.

Evans-Pritchard, E. E. *Theories of Primitive Religion.* Oxford, 1965.

Filoramo, Giovanni, and Carlo Prandi. *Le scienze delle religioni.* Brescia, Italy, 1987; 3d ed., 1997.

Fitzgerald, Timothy. *The Ideology of Religious Studies.* New York and Oxford, 2000.

Gisel, Pierre, and Jean-Marc Tétaz, eds. *Théories de la religion: Diversité des pratiques de recherche, changements des contextes socio-culturel, requêtes réflexives.* Geneva, 2002.

Gladigow, Burkhard, and Hans G. Kippenberg, eds. *Neue Ansätze in der Religionswissenschaft.* Munich, 1983.

Hakl, Hans Thomas. *Der verborgene Geist von Eranos: Unbekannte begegnungen von Wissenschaft und Esoterik.* Bretten, Germany, 2001.

Hjelde, Sigurd, ed. *Man, Meaning, and Mystery: 100 Years of History of Religions in Norway.* Leiden, 2000.

Honko, Lauri, ed. *Science of Religion.* The Hague, 1979.

Jong, J. W. de. *A Brief History of Buddhist Studies in Europe and America.* Tokyo, 1997.

Kippenberg, Hans G. *Die Entdeckung der Religionsgeschichte: Religionswissenschaft und Moderne.* Munich, 1997. Translated by Barbara Harshaw as *Discovering Religious History in the Modern Age.* Princeton, 2002.

Kippenberg, Hans G., and Brigitte Luchesi, eds. *Religionswissenschaft und Kulturkritik.* Marburg, Germany, 1991.

Lopez, Donald S., Jr., ed. *Curators of the Buddha: The Study of Buddhism under Colonialism.* Chicago, 1995.

Michaels, Axel, ed. *Klassiker der Religionswissenschaft. Von Friedrich Schleiermacher bis Mircea Eliade.* Munich, 1997.

Michaels, Axel, Daria Pezzoli-Olgiati, and Fritz Stolz, eds. *Noch eine Chance für die Religionsphänomenologie?* Bern, Switzerland, 2001.

Morris, Brian. *Anthropological Studies of Religion.* Cambridge, U.K., 1987.

Müller, Max. *The Essential Max Müller: On Language, Mythology, and Religion.* Edited by Jon R. Stone. New York, 2002.

Papoušek, Dalibor, Luther H. Martin, and Iva Doļealová, eds. *The Academic Study of Religion during the Cold War: East and West.* New York, 2001.

Preus, J. Samuel. *Explaining Religion: Criticism and Theory from Bodin to Freud.* New Haven, 1987.

Rudolph, Kurt. *Die Religionsgeschichte an der Leipziger Universität und die Entwicklung der Religionswissenschaft.* Berlin, 1962.

Rudolph, Kurt. *Geschichte und Probleme der Religionswissenschaft.* Leiden, 1992.

Sharpe, Eric J. *Comparative Religion: A History.* La Salle, Ill., 1975; 2d ed., 1986.

Sharpe, Eric J. *Nathan Söderblom and the Study of Religion.* Chapel Hill, N.C., 1990.

Strenski, Ivan. *Contesting Sacrifice: Religion, Nationalism, and Social Thought in France.* Chicago, 2002.

Vries, Jan de. *Godsdienstgeschiedenis in Vogelvlucht.* Utrecht, 1961. Translated by Kees W. Bolle as *Perspectives in the History of Religions.* Berkeley, 1977.

Waardenburg, Jacques. *Classical Approaches to the Study of Religion.* The Hague, 1973; New York and Berlin, 1999.

Wasserstrom, Steven. M. *Religion after Religion: Gershom Scholem, Mircea Eliade, and Henry Corbin at Eranos.* Princeton, 1999.

Zinser, Hartmut, ed. *Religionswissenschaft: eine Einführung.* Berlin, 1988.

GUSTAVO BENAVIDES (2005)

TRANSCULTURATION AND RELIGION: RELIGION IN THE FORMATION OF THE MODERN UNITED STATES

While it has usually been conceived as a Christian nation, founded by Protestant idealists, the United States was actually formed by a series of cultural interactions and exchanges between indigenous and immigrant communities involving a tremendous variety of people from Africa, Asia, Polynesia, South America, and North America, as well as Europe, with a wide array of religious orientations that include traditions on both global and local scales. The narrative that Christianity is the religion of the United States is not the whole story, as it turns out, and not even half the story. As a result of these realizations, those involved in the academic study of "American religion" have made strenuous efforts since the 1980s to include in their scope religious traditions other than the "great" textual traditions of Christianity, Buddhism, Islam, Judaism, and so on. Native American, African, and African-American traditions, as well as issues concerning ethnic and gender studies, have pressured scholarly academic models for understanding "American religion" to such an extent that new and revised methods are needed to analyze the phenomenon of religion in America. "American religion" is generally understood as the spread of denominational Christianity across the continent. A struggle for inclusion of traditions other than Christianity into the religious narrative of the United States is not just a struggle to include distinctive types of religious institutions. Nor should it be seen as a constant conflict about religious truth and certainty between the different groups of people who populate the United States. Inclusion of a religious dynamic in the formation of the United States requires a shift in our understanding of what constitutes *religion.* Understanding how exchanges between groups created a unique American identity requires us to characterize *religion* in ways that include the innovations of indigenous people who did not form religious institutions nor utilize or create written texts, but nevertheless had a tremendous influence on the unique cultural development and character of the United States.

The history of cultural contact in the United States is one between immigrant and indigenous groups and between immigrant and indigenous religious orientations. This way of organizing the place of religion in the formation of the United States requires that we look at religion as *habitation* and as *exchange.* Defining *religion* as habitation and exchange, rather than as an ideological position, shifts *religion* away from what groups believe to what they do, from what they think to how they act. For example, on one hand religion was a pivotal element in the justification of colonial occupation of the lands of Native Americans and was utilized in the justification of slavery and thus the removal of millions of Africans from their native land in what was called the *Middle Passage.* Religion was used to justify violence against women and other indentured servants until the implementation of cultural reforms beginning in the mid-nineteenth century. Religion and religious language have been used to exclude Latin Americans from decent working conditions and to justify the forced internment of Japanese people during World War II. Racialized views of entire populations were imagined and then codified by law using the moral language of religion. On the other hand, religion helped these oppressed groups of people overcome their difficult situa-

tions and, in the case of African Americans, inhabit the New World in ways that differed from the slave owners. Distinctive styles of *inhabiting* the world, therefore, are primarily religious in nature.

Native American groups offer the clearest contrast to the immigrant styles of colonizers. Native American religious styles of habitation and exchange highlight aspects of religious practice among other groups of people that might be called *indigenous religion* among these groups. Investigating the "religion" of Native Americans in light of cultural contact with immigrant people is fundamental to forming a more complete picture of the cultural formation of the United States, because Native American priorities involving community formation and sustainability are radically different from those that have dominated American culture. The religious concerns and priorities of Native American traditions can be fruitfully applied to other groups, making *indigenous religions* a category with wide application that reveals unsung and unnoticed religious elements of all human communities, particularly those that have not been part of the religious narrative of the United States. Even though "indigenous religion" should be seen as a theme running through all religious activity, here we will emphasize Native American religious traditions in contact with colonizing and dominating forces in the United States as the clearest expression of an indigenous perspective.

Situating Native American traditions in the development of American religion has proven to be particularly vexing. Texts (sacred or otherwise) in the conventional sense of a phonetically inscribed folio have not traditionally held the same privileged place in Native traditions. Consequently, a reliance on texts by ethno-historians and scholars of Native American religions has tended to marginalize indigenous interpretations of sacred realities in favor of what has been written down by colonial people. As a result, Native American traditions have had less influence in considerations of what constitutes authentic American religious life. Through the development of new ways of thinking about religion and new approaches to Native American "religions," a greater understanding of women, African-American, and Latino/a traditions, and what those traditions say about the meaning of America, can be appreciated.

Part of the difficulty of including indigenous traditions in American religions is that we have lacked methods of interpretation. The disciplines of history of religions, comparative religions, and anthropology of religions, among others, have commonly been associated with the study of various native, or indigenous, traditions and have formed new and important methodologies, strategies, and insights into the religious dimensions of American life beyond textual evidences. While the study of "American religion" has tended to stress the historical development of Christian denominations as revealed in historical texts, aspects of the history of religions, for example, have emphasized a comparative framework that seeks to situate scholarly interpretations within the distinctive meanings of material existence.

The primary focus of the study of American religions has been on the immigrant people and cultures that followed the "discovery" of America. The stories of the "discovery of America" are powerful cosmogonic myths, or founding myths, that communicate the meaning of inhabiting the Americas for immigrant people. Notable explorers (in order and tied to European kingdoms) like Christopher Columbus, Hernando Cortés, Juan Ponce de León, Hernando de Soto, Jacques Cartier, Samuel de Champlain, Sir Walter Raleigh, Giovanni da Verrazano, Commodore Matthew Perry, Daniel Boone, Robert Peary, and General George Armstrong Custer as well as countless others, are regarded as culture heroes of what came to be known as the United States. They articulate the immigrant mythology of American culture. They outline a religious dynamic of inhabiting the land as immigrants in opposition to those who are indigenous. Most often the heroic deeds of discoverers and explorers came at the price of devaluing and exterminating the native inhabitants. More importantly, however, these founding mythologies of discovery have devalued an indigenous religious awareness in United States culture. More highly prized is the conquering spirit of the rugged individual rather than the warrior who is fighting in defense of family and community. In general, a religious appreciation of the environment as a sacred reality has suffered the most, as has regard for the dead and for the living spiritual beings of the earth.

The religious styles of colonizing people have usually been organized, and therefore studied, by means of sacred and secular texts, making them mobile ideologies. Native American traditions have been neglected because their religious styles are indigenous (tied to styles in which people *inhabit* their homes). The reconstruction of early encounters between indigenous and immigrant people has relied almost entirely on those rare inclusions of indigenous peoples in the writing of the colonists. Any attempt to include Native American religions into the field of American religion must therefore: (1) shift the definition of *religion* from a structure of belief or ideology to *religion* as an orientation to material life, in particular an orientation to the meaning of land, and thus (2) use a comparative method that can bring together both the indigenous (oral/performative) and textual spheres of the religions of the Americas, while (3) leaving room for a process of self-conscious, self-critical reflection in such a way as to (4) reveal the deep and abundant cultural exchanges that have occurred throughout American history between the distinctive communities that led to the culture of the United States.

Many Native Americans who still practice their ceremonial traditions and who are asked about their religion are quick to point out that they have none. Instead, they practice a *spirituality*. This is not to say they are atheistic, nor are they materialistic. On the contrary, they understand their ceremonial and spiritual practices as completely integral to the rest of their lives. The objection to *religion*, therefore, is that their practices cannot be distinguished from the political, eco-

nomic, sexual, familial, social, cultural, and other dimensions of their lives. In fact, it is a violent misrepresentation to reduce these traditions to the category of *religion* because they are not practices that are easily isolatable from other aspects of human existence. Native American ceremonies are pragmatic strategies for interacting with a living world. Ceremonies address living beings who are responsible for food, healing, knowledge, and prosperity. *Habitation*, for indigenous people, is about forming relationships with a variety of beings, human and otherwise, who populate the world, so that they may live a happy life. These beings include water, rocks, trees, animals, birds, ancestors, stars, sun, moon, and the Creator or Great Spirit. Maintaining relationships with a host of living beings requires being constantly aware of continuous exchanges between themselves and other-than-human beings. It is often said that indigenous people are never alone. This is also an important point for communities of immigrant people, including minority communities, as well as zealous Christian, Jewish, and Muslim communities, who cannot and will not separate the "religious" from the "material" dimensions of their lives. Indeed, throughout the world an understanding of the world as saturated with spiritual beings is one of the defining characteristics of the origins of religious perception.

To the consternation of culture leaders, there persists a constant element of what might be called *superstition* among modern and civilized people. Active beliefs in spirits and the possibility of communicating with them, divination (or gaining knowledge from spiritual resources through tarot cards or séances, for example), and healing with hands, faith, snakes, and other spiritual means have not only persisted but seem to be thriving in some quarters. These can be seen as examples of the persistence of indigenous religious practices. Some of these practices are well organized among Haitians in New York City, or Cubans in Miami, for example, within the practice of vodou or Lukumi. Seventh-day Adventists who actively practice Mary Baker Eddy's injunction of "healing by faith alone"; Spiritualists, Pagans, and Neopagans who consult the spirits of the dead (many of those traditions that are regarded as "New Age" religions); fundamentalist and evangelical Christians, Jews, and Muslims who are actively battling the forces of the devil in their community and their country; and even Catholics and other members of mainline churches who are active in petitioning saints and other spiritual beings for healing, special consideration of their problems, and the suffering of their loved ones, and who are witness to apparitions of the Virgin Mary—in this context, are all continuing *indigenous* religious practices. When considering religion as an active force in the development of American culture it is not helpful, therefore, to think of religion as an item of personal belief, as is made explicitly clear in American constitutional understandings and interpretations. Rather it is more useful to understand religion as a feature of material life; what Charles Long has called the "materiality of religion." To understand the transcultural expressions of religion in the United States it is vital to first understand the materiality of religion, in contrast to more conventional constructions of religion as an ideology, because only then can one appreciate how material exchanges between indigenous and immigrant communities, economic networks, and relationships with animals, landscapes, food, and so on can reveal larger "religious" realities in the formation of the United States.

A fertile ground for these methodological considerations is a reflection on distinctive meanings of inhabiting the American landscape. The meaning of land has long been considered a primary consideration for understanding Native American religions. Sacred spaces and ritual topographies have been important starting points for reflecting on the manifold meanings of these traditions. By utilizing indigenous meanings of land we can reflect on the significance of land in other forms of American religious life. In contrast to indigenous modes of occupying the Americas there have been colonial, modern, and postmodern options. Until fairly recently discussions of "sacred space" have generally been neglected in American religion. The reason for this is that immigrant religions, like Christianity for example, did not originate in the Americas. Sacred places for the religions of the globe are now foreign places in Israel, Saudi Arabia, Italy, and so on. This means that the United States has never been *founded* (Eliade) or revealed to immigrant populations due to their having neglected the revelations of indigenous people. Because of an immigrant emphasis on conquest, extermination of Native Americans, theories of moral and cultural superiority, enslavement of workers, and an understanding of land as private property, the meaning of inhabiting the United States remains a strange and disturbing question for most Americans.

The contentiousness of various meaningful landscapes in American religious life can be highlighted by utilizing categories of *locative* religions, descriptive of Native American and indigenous traditions, in contrast with *utopian* (from the Greek "no place") religions, descriptive of the great textual and global traditions since 1492. These modes of meaningfully occupying the Americas interact with each other, often with catastrophic results, and can be organized around issues of colonialism, industrialism, and consumerism. Although these are expressions of a modern material worldview that were initiated with the "Age of Discovery," they are also mythic ideologies that are essentially religious in nature. Thus the meanings of the material and economic valuations of the American landscape necessarily come into play, resulting in a shift of our definitions of religion away from belief—interior to human consciousness and faith communities (or an anthropocentric understanding of religion), to religion as a set of material practices (i.e., materiality)—specifically, a practice of occupying or residing on land. This follows Long's definition of religion as "orientation in the ultimate sense, that is, how one comes to terms with the ultimate significance of one's place in the world" (1986, p. 7).

A key organizing principle for a coherent and useful history of American religions is *contact*. Religious contact is de-

fined by the interaction of human groups in a material context but involving a collision of cosmologies, or worldviews. Initially, cultural contact between immigrant and indigenous peoples was organized on the periphery of what is now the United States. In the Southeast, contact between Spanish *conquistadores* and native populations was initiated in Florida, Louisiana, and along the Mississippi River where Spaniards came into contact with densely settled areas that were reminiscent of the urban populations of central Mexico. In the Southwest, Spaniards from Florida met an enormous diversity of native cultural groups speaking a host of distinctive languages in what are now New Mexico, Arizona, and California. In the Northeast and along the eastern seaboard, Dutch, French, and English explorers came into long-term contact with various indigenous confederations of smaller tribal groups. Trading with these groups over a period of close to two hundred years led to incredible wealth among Europeans and an ongoing exchange of ideas. From these areas of contact the United States took on its unique cultural characteristics. African slaves were forced to relocate to North America to grow new kinds of plants introduced to Europeans by Native Americans. Latin Americans have the oldest communities in the United States, having come to North America with the early Spanish explorers. Over the centuries they learned to live with local native populations in areas of the Southwest. In addition, Nordic communities in Minnesota have a long history of residing in the Americas, making this a unique place in the cultural formation of the northern Midwest. French communities like New Orleans were originally colonial outposts that evolved with a unique blend of Caribbean, African, and French-Canadian influences.

The most notable arenas of cultural contact between immigrant and indigenous people have taken place in the heart of the country. Contact between the Lakota (i.e., Sioux) and the United States military in the post–Civil War era, for example, resulted in the famed "Indian Wars" of the Great Plains. Colonists, gold prospectors, soldiers, and other immigrants started the westward migration across the North American continent. Standing in the way of this massive resettlement were indigenous people of a wide variety of linguistic and cultural orientations. Immigrants understood that land was to be possessed by human beings and that it was evaluated only in monetary terms. This stands in stark contrast to indigenous sensibilities, which understand that earth is a living "Mother" to human beings and other types of beings. Therefore, mining and farming (particularly with the deep-plow techniques brought by Europeans) were inconceivably violent activities for indigenous people. The collision between immigrant and indigenous communities largely involved their differing views of the land and thus its ultimate value. These conflicts had catastrophic results at Little Big Horn (called Greasy Grass by the Lakota), Wounded Knee, Sand Creek, and many other places. Such conflicts reveal that these opposing perspectives are fundamentally about religious orientations to the land, as well as political, economic, and social orientations.

But contact implies more than "cultural contact," or the interaction between humans. Of critical importance for the survival of all communities is also contact between human beings and the material world they inhabit. To explore this dimension of contact requires an assessment of both the interaction between the indigenous and immigrant groups that inhabit the Americas, and the construction and organization of their respective landscapes. One question might be: What are the material conditions of the land—riverine, oceanic, forested, desert, and so on—that organize religiousness in America? Because Native American traditions are not organized by texts, sacred landscapes and ritual life are the primary data by which to understand these traditions. Immigrant religious traditions, however, have largely been studied from historical and textual perspectives. A focused phenomenological perspective could reflect on larger issues surrounding the development of religion in the United States. For example, as we have discussed, indigenous people have an understanding of their landscape as a living being that is "peopled" with a host of living beings. In contrast to that view are the built landscapes of the expansive cities in the United States—New York, Boston, Washington, D.C., Chicago, Saint Louis, New Orleans, San Francisco, Los Angeles. They each reflect a distinctive character that orients them to their history of migrations and to their landscapes (i.e., human and "natural" contexts). The urban environments were made possible by ideological worldviews of colonialism, mercantilism, and consumerism (to name a few). There were, however, large-scale indigenous cities on this continent well before the formation of the United States. These are most often associated with the Mississippian cultures. Remnants of their cities are found near Saint Louis and along the Mississippi, Missouri, and Ohio rivers. The difference between indigenous and immigrant understandings of the built landscape can be characterized as locative and utopian. As in Mesoamerica, with which indigenous cities north of the Rio Grande have great affinity, Mississippian cities are oriented around a founding hierophany, or "manifestation of the sacred" (Eliade). These cities function fundamentally as ceremonial centers and, as a consequence, they exert enormous political and economic control over the surrounding landscape. They are locative in the sense that the city exists only with respect to the sacred realities that preexist the structures built by human beings. They are built to honor and celebrate the spiritual beings of the material world. In stark contrast the modern American city is a utopian construction. It is built as a celebration of the human spirit. Most often cities are attempts to express a perfect world that lives in the human imagination. Very little attention is paid to the living beings that preexist its current formulation. Indeed the modern American city is conceived and built at odds with the environment.

Immigrant and indigenous communities also have distinctive understandings of the medium of exchange.

Throughout the history of the United States, fundamental to immigrant and utopian worldviews is a confidence in money and its power. Currency is a reflection of the United States, of its power and prestige all over the world, in valuing and evaluating all material life. Whatever other names of worldviews can be utilized to characterize a given era of the United States, money is always the common denominator that unifies the nation. But it is important to recall that money has no intrinsic value ("not worth the paper it's printed on"); its value is derived only from the symbols it holds. Yet, at the same time, money is a "total fact" of modern life. Its ability to empower and peripheralize individuals and communities is awe-inspiring. So money is *the* religion of the United States. It is the medium of exchange between human beings, and it undergirds a utopian vision that has been with Americans since the Pilgrims sailed to New England with the financial assistance of venture capitalists in London. Money is symbolic, "faith-based," and the basis of ideologies.

Likewise indigenous people have their own mediums of exchange. An important case of an indigenous system interacting with money is the *wampum* of the Haudenosaunee (better known as the Iroquois). Wampum is a worked shell bead that was manufactured along the eastern seaboard. Its colors of purple (black) and white had, and still have, cosmological significance for the Haudenosaunee. Purple is associated with the earth, the night, and the mischievous forces of creation, and white is associated with the sky, the day, and the benign forces of creation. The story of creation includes stories of the creator twins who embody these opposing forces. Wampum is also featured in the story of the founding of the Great Law of Peace that marks the beginning of the League of the Iroquois, or the Haudenosaunee, which is composed of the Seneca, Tuscarora, Cayuga, Onondaga, Oneida, and Mohawk. Wampum has been used continuously among the Haudenosaunee in ceremonies for the harvest, for beings of the sky and earth, for the installation of chiefs and clan mothers, and for a host of other activities.

Throughout U.S. history, however, the Dutch, French, English, and Americans had a different view of wampum. It was seen as a monetary item that was used to gain access to beaver pelts. Its exchange value was directly related to the transatlantic trade in beaver pelts. This was one of the linchpins in the development of the North American continent. New York City, which was founded as New Amsterdam, could not have developed into its present form without the trade between European and Native American people in beaver pelts. For colonists, therefore, wampum was money. As money it was involved in a radically different cosmology of relations than for the Haudenosaunee. Both Europeans and Native Americans acknowledged wampum as a viable system of exchange, but for opposing reasons. For Europeans wampum was money and could be utilized to expand their colonial kingdoms. It was seen as functioning in the service of the utopian ideal of expanding a Christian empire of God. For the Haudenosaunee, wampum was a medium of exchange because it embodied the workings of cosmological understandings. It expanded the Great Law of Peace to other human communities.

An important example of a religious *contact zone*, a physical context that forms the basis for the generation of new religions, is the Erie Canal. Most Americans view water in marked contrast to the Haudenosaunee. Since the end of the eighteenth century there has been an aggressively dominant meaning of water. The Erie Canal, the most important major hydrological project of the early nineteenth century, was part of a canal building phase initiated in the 1820s and 1830s. The Erie Canal connected the Hudson and Mohawk rivers to Lake Erie, and was used to move remote agricultural, mining, and forestry products through New York City to the rest of the world. As envisioned by powerful bankers and merchants, the Erie Canal was an ambitious enterprise, predating the railroad, that connected New York City to the interior of the continent.

The Erie Canal's heyday corresponds directly to the era of the "Burned over District," a site of intense evangelical fervor and religious experimentation in the early nineteenth century that was said to have swept through this landscape like a brushfire. Historians of American religion cannot understand key phenomena like the Second Great Awakening and westward migration without an adequate understanding of the Burned over District. Along the banks of the canal important religious groups emerged, including the Mormons, Spiritualists, and Millerites. In contrast to the locative character of Haudenosaunee tradition, various self-conscious utopian experimental communities sprang up, including the Oneida and Shaker communities. The evangelical fervor in such New York cities as Utica, Syracuse, and Rochester likewise follows the canal. We can ask, then, what were the consequences of canals—or the industrialization of water—for the development of American religions? In the canal zone people of various ethnic and linguistic communities from all over the world were pushed into direct contact with one another and, more importantly, into contact with a new kind of proto-industrial landscape. Russians, Irish, Poles, Africans, Italians, and others who had recently immigrated to America were dislocated, placeless people, and therefore, for reasons of survival, strained toward the realization of a utopian vision. Is a utopian religious option a consequence of an industrialization of land and water? How are American religions tied to interpretations of the landscape? Utopianism, or the formation of a perfect place, is emphasized in American religious life, but contrasts starkly with the locative emphasis of Native American traditions. This may also help explain the importance of strong millenarian elements in these religious traditions, as religious utopianism usually looks toward a transcendent vision of salvation or the perfection of human society. It likewise offers insights into the symbolic and mythic structures that have been assumed by America's economic and political institutions.

The example of religion along the Erie Canal illustrates how the landscape is fashioned to resemble a sacred world

by human imagination and labor. The assumption, however, is that the landscape does not necessarily reflect a sacred reality previous to human intervention. In both indigenous and utopian contexts the landscape is understood as sacred. But these worldviews differ dramatically in how human beings understand their relation to the land. An interesting and important dimension of this comparison is transcendentalism. The transcendentalists can be seen as utopian in their emphasis on the radical disjunction of the human and "natural" worlds. While they were less concerned with "scaping" the land, a preservationist perspective is more concerned with shifting the terms of a meaningful existence from human beings to nature (devoid of humans).

As Long writes, the "myth of the New World obscured the reality of the contact . . . [w]e know, for example, that Europeans in North America were absolutely dependent on Indian culture for several generations after their arrival. We know that North America was not a 'virgin land.' What is more important, the early European settlers knew it!" (1986, pp. 114–115). More is being learned about the importance of cultural contact between indigenous and immigrant traditions in the formation of American culture. Musical styles like the blues, jazz, rock, folk, Motown, rhythm and blues, and hip-hop are all the result of cultural exchanges. Knowledge of foods in the New World transformed the Old World. Perhaps the most profound exchange, however, was the inspiration of Haudenosaunee structures of government on the development of democracy in the United States. Chiefs of the Iroquois would often sit in council with colonial leaders discussing the way to form a sensible, representative government. In 1987, the United States Congress officially thanked the Haudenosaunee for their role in forming the United States.

The legacy of cultural contact between indigenous and immigrant orientations in the development of the United States has not been a happy one, but neither has it been all bad. The Americas have been a place well suited for religious innovation and tremendous religious creativity. This is not likely to change. Many of the leading intellectuals of the nineteenth century were certain that as human beings progressed they would no longer need religion. None would have predicted, at that time, that religion would play as vital a role in American life as it does today. Material conditions of the past, including cultural contact, geography, and economics, have crafted the unique religious character of the United States.

Bibliography

For an understanding of a history of religions approach to this topic read: Davíd Carrasco, *Religions of Mesoamerica: Cosmovision and Ceremonial Centers* (San Francisco, 1990); Charles H. Long, *Significations: Signs, Symbols, and Images in the Interpretation of Religion* (Philadelphia, 1986); Mircea Eliade, *Myth of the Eternal Return, or, Cosmos and History,* translated by Willard R. Trask (New York, 1954; rev. ed., 1965), and *Patterns in Comparative Religion,* translated by Rosemary Sheed (New York, 1958); Rudolf Otto, *The Idea of the Holy: An Inquiry into the Non-rational Factor in the Idea of the Divine and Its Relation to the Rational,* translated by John W. Harvey (London, 1923; 2d ed., 1950); and Jonathan Z. Smith, *Map Is Not Territory: Studies in the History of Religions* (Leiden, 1978).

For works on Native American religions read: William Cronon, *Changes in the Land: Indians, Colonists, and the Ecology of New England* (New York, 1983); Alfred Crosby, *Ecological Imperialism: The Biological Expansion of Europe, 900–1900* (Cambridge, U.K., 1986; 2d ed., 2004); Vine Deloria Jr., *God Is Red: A Native View of Religion* (New York, 1973; 3d ed., Golden, Colo., 2003); Raymond DeMallie, ed., *The Sixth Grandfather: Black Elk's Teachings Given to John G. Neihardt* (Lincoln, Neb., 1984); G. Peter Jemison and Anna Schein, eds., *The Treaty of Canandaigua, 1794: Two Hundred Years of Treaty Relations between the Iroquois Confederacy and the United States* (Santa Fe, N.Mex., 2000); Donald Grinde Jr. and Bruce Johansen, *Ecocide of Native America: Environmental Destruction of Indian Lands and Peoples* (Santa Fe, N.Mex., 1995); Francis Jennings, *The Invasion of America: Indians, Colonialism, and the Cant of Conquest* (Chapel Hill, N.C., 1975); Oren Lyons et al., *Exiled in the Land of the Free: Democracy, Indian Nations, and the U.S. Constitution* (Santa Fe, N.Mex., 1992); John Neihardt, *Black Elk Speaks: Being the Life Story of a Holy Man of the Oglala Sioux* (New York, 1932); Tzvetan Todorov, *The Conquest of America: The Question of the Other,* translated by Richard Howard (New York, 1984); Paul A. W. Wallace, *White Roots of Peace: The Iroquois Book of Life* (Philadelphia, 1946); and Jace Weaver, ed., *Defending Mother Earth: Native American Perspectives on Environmental Justice* (Maryknoll, N.Y., 1996).

For works on religion and nature and the Burned over District read: Catherine Albanese, *Nature Religion in America: From the Algonkian Indians to the New Age* (Chicago, 1990); Michael Barkun, *Crucible of the Millennium: The Burned-over District of New York in the 1840s* (Syracuse, N.Y., 1986); David Chidester and Edward T. Linenthal, eds., *American Sacred Space* (Bloomington, Ind., 1995); Whitney Cross, *The Burned-over District: The Social and Intellectual History of Enthusiastic Religion in Western New York, 1800–1850* (New York, 1950); and Neal Salisbury, *Manitou and Providence: Indians, Europeans, and the Making of New England, 1500–1643* (New York, 1982).

For works on religion and American economics read: William Leach, *Land of Desire: Merchants, Power, and the Rise of a New American Culture* (New York, 1993); Wolfgang Schivelbusch, *Tastes of Paradise: A Social History of Spices, Stimulants, and Intoxicants,* translated by David Jacobson (New York, 1992), and *The Railway Journey: The Industrialization of Time and Space in the 19th Century* (Berkeley, 1986); and Leigh Eric Schmidt, *Consumer Rites: The Buying and Selling of American Holidays* (Princeton, 1995).

PHILIP P. ARNOLD (2005)

VAIṢṆAVISM: AN OVERVIEW [FURTHER CONSIDERATIONS]

Scholarship on Vaiṣṇavism increasingly acknowledges that the term *Vaiṣṇavism* can only be used as a broad heuristic de-

vice to refer to various religious texts and practices that center around the figures of Viṣṇu, Vāsudeva, Kṛṣṇa, Nārāyaṇa, and Rāma. Thus, recent scholarship has moved away from attempts to establish a linear chronology for the emergence of religious movements associated with each of these figures and the subsequent amalgamation of their cults because of the difficulty of retrieving the social and political background of these traditions prior to the sixth century CE. As a result, there is now an increasing emphasis on the specificity and diversity of regional traditions that emerged after this period, accompanied by a new historiographical sensitivity seeking to dismantle monolithic and essentialist views of Vaiṣṇavism and *bhakti.* Important strands of this scholarship include work on the Pāñcarātra textual tradition, on Śrī Vaiṣṇavism and the Vaikhānasas, on the *nirguṇī bhakti* traditions of North India, and, finally, on a new devotion to Rāma and his devotee Hanumān that is closely associated with the rise of Hindu religious nationalism.

PĀÑCARĀTRA STUDIES. Recent research on the development of the Vaiṣṇava Tantric tradition of Pāñcarātra has yielded rich if tentative results. It is now being suggested that the earliest strata of important texts, the *Jayākhya, Sattvata,* and *Pauṣkara saṃhitās,* are likely to have been compiled in Kashmir around the eighth to ninth centuries CE, reflecting a ritual system emphasizing private worship, much influenced by earlier Śaiva Siddhānta models already in existence in Kashmir. A chronologically later layer of South Indian texts, such as the *Lakṣmī Tantra* and the *Ahirbudhnya Saṃhitā,* reflect eleventh-century Kashmiri influence, with the former text reproducing a goddess-centered theology that owes much to Śākta Śaivism. After the eleventh century the major influence on South Indian Pāñcarātra was Śrī Vaiṣṇavism and its philosophical base, Viśiṣṭādvaita Vedānta, an influence seen in the increasing use of the terminology of the latter, a stress on the soteriological doctrine of self-surrender *(śaraṇāgati, prapatti)* instead of yogic and meditative practice, a substitution of the mention of older Tantric forms of initiation *(dīkṣā)* with the Śrī Vaiṣṇava initiation of *pañcasaṃskāra,* and an emphasis on public temple worship rather than private worship. The exact contours of this general transition, as well as the sheer heterogeneity of the texts (for it is now accepted that there is no uniform Pāñcarātra doctrine), remain to be mapped out through the painstaking study of individual texts.

ŚRĪ VAIṢṆAVISM. Research on this religious tradition of a South Indian community of Viṣṇu devotees whose ultimate god is Viṣṇu-Nārāyaṇa, together with his consort Śrī-Lakṣmī, focused in the 1970s on epigraphy and temple records. This evidence, detailing the interaction between kings, local chieftains, and religious heads, has led to the mapping of the temple as a sociocultural institution and a site of disputed power. The rise of sectarianism within the religious community, which gained strength after the sixteenth century, resulting in its split into the two subgroups—"Northerners" (Vaṭakalai) and "Southerners" (Teṅkalai)—is now linked to the control of important temples. Further, such fissiparous tendencies within the community also strengthened with colonialism, which intervened in the intricate balance of power forged in local communities between various groups. The result was the fragmentation of the idea of worship as a cooperative enterprise.

Substantial work has also emerged on a long neglected area of Śrī Vaiṣṇava studies: Tamil devotional poetry, the *Divyaprabandham,* and the commentaries on it. The religion of the authors of this poetry, the Āḻvārs, is now seen as a composite arising out of the mingling of Northern sources of Kṛṣṇa myth and poetry and the Tamil Caṅkam literature, eventually reaching a pan-Indian audience through the *Bhāgavata Purāṇa.* The schismatic period of the tradition, starting from the thirteenth century, has also been subjected to unprecedented scrutiny with an understanding of how the mingling of Sanskrit and Tamil, the hermeneutical strategies, and the development of new genres such as hagiography influenced and changed theological doctrines.

VAIKHĀNASAS. Vaikhānasa is, along with Pāñcarātra, one of the two ritual traditions followed in the Vaiṣṇavite temple worship of South India. Less well-known than the Pāñcarātra, the tradition has come into prominence in some recent scholarship. We learn that the Vaikhānasas were originally a renunciate Vedic tradition, with the self-perception that they were a Vedic *śākhā,* who evolved into a community of professional priests practicing temple rituals. Epigraphy from the eleventh century depicts this transition, showing that the Vaikhānasas competed with the Pāñcarātrins to be priests at Vaiṣṇava temples, gradually experiencing an erosion of their powers in the competition with Śrī Vaiṣṇavas. Their medieval corpus, composed largely between the ninth and the thirteenth to fourteenth centuries, stresses their congenital Vaiṣṇava identity; unlike a Pāñcarātrin, a Vaikhānasa did not need special initiation to become a Vaiṣṇava. The theology of these texts was a kind of theistic Sāṃkhya, with a theogonical conception of the five manifestations *(pañcamūrti)* of Viṣṇu as Viṣṇu Puruṣa, Satya, Acyuta, and Aniruddha. A substantial portion of these texts is dedicated to various kinds of prescriptions relating to temple worship, as well as forms of initiation for various categories of aspirants to Vaikhānasa worship. The later literature of the Vaikhānasas shows a doctrinal dependence on Śrī Vaiṣṇavism, which must be viewed as part of an acculturative process that accelerated after the fourteenth century.

NORTH INDIAN *NIRGUṆĪ BHAKTI.* The recent study of North Indian *bhakti* traditions emphasizes the difference between the *saguṇī* and *nirguṇī bhakti* traditions of North India. Here, the shift is away from obvious similarities of theology—stemming from the same historical roots—to the scrutiny of the differences of social ideology and praxis. *Saguṇī bhakti,* even while it admits subaltern groups such as the *dalits* and women into its fold, remains anchored in the caste and *varṇa* model of society, a fact that is also mirrored in the caste status of the founders of *saguṇī* movements and their followers. In contrast, the exploration of the *nirguṇī*

traditions of the devotional movements of Kabir, Raidās, Gurū Nānak, Dādū, and others stemming from the fifteenth century onward shows that both the founders and the followers have tended to be from subaltern groups. Further, *nirguṇī bhakti* emerged as a direct challenge to the social ideology of *saguṇī bhakti* in its radical critique of caste, even while it incorporated much of the latter's beliefs and practices. This, in turn, has led to the current exploration of it as a movement of protest against the hegemonic ideology of *saguṇī bhakti* and of modern Hindu society.

Rāma Bhakti. Devotion to the god-king Rāma has, since the mid-1980s, come to be tied to a militant Hindu nationalism and to a specific Hindu struggle to reoccupy his mythic birth site in the town of Ayodhyā. This struggle led to the destruction of the mosque that had long stood on the disputed site, the Babri Masjid, in 1992, an act carried out by Hindu nationalists, which threatened the secular fabric of India. The scholarship on what is uniformly seen as a new form of militant devotionalism to Rāma has thus come to acquire a historical urgency. It is the commonly held view that the convergence of *bhakti* toward Rāma and Hindu political power is not new. Thus, there was a rise in the importance of the Rāma cult from the twelfth century onward in north and central India at a historical juncture when there was a repeated threat from Afghan and Turkic invaders.

Nevertheless, the image of Rāma until recently in the pan-Indian tradition was that of the spiritualized king as well as suffering hero—the emphasis is on someone who bears adversity with fortitude, even while he takes up arms in a just cause against the demon-king, Rāvaṇa. This conception of Rāma is also reflected in the traditional iconography, which depicts a handsome, even androgynous youthful god who carries his bow and yet does not bear arms, who is always escorted by his wife Sītā, his brother Lakṣmana, and his devotee, the monkey Hanumān, and who exudes quietude, *śānta rasa.* In militant Hinduism there is a redrawing of these traditional paradigms reflected literally in the iconography. Here, Rāma comes to be identified with a Hinduism that has inclusivistic and monolithic claims, which refuses to acknowledge the heterogeneity of Hindu traditions, a Hinduism that is coeval with the territory of Bhārat. In this Hinduism, the "other" is the Muslim, now identified as the invading Mughal. The battle between Rāma and Rāvaṇa is now transposed into a battle between Rāma and the Mughal king Babar as the symbol of all Muslims. Through such a transposition religious antagonism is dignified as a heroic mythologically sanctioned conflict. The new valorization of Rāma is sanctioned by a new iconography that depicts him in a twofold way: either as poised to strike with his arrows, aggressively masculine and militaristic, or as Rāmlalā, the helpless child who is in need of protection from the enemy, who is the Muslim. In either case, the changed iconography of Rāma is but a graphic depiction of a new religious movement that lays claim to traditional structures but departs from them in radical ways.

Bibliography

Appadurai, Arjun. *Worship and Conflict under Colonial Rule: A South Indian Case.* Cambridge, U.K., 1981.

Bakker, Hans. *Ayodhyā.* Gröningen, Netherlands, 1986.

Burghart, Richard. "The Founding of the Ramanandi Sect." *Ethnohistory* 25 (1978): 121–139.

Clooney, Francis X. *Seeing through Texts: Doing Theology among the Śrīvaiṣṇavas of South India.* Albany, N.Y., 1996.

Colas, Gérard. "History of Vaiṣṇava Traditions." In *The Blackwell Companion to Hinduism,* edited by Gavin Flood, pp. 229–270. Malden, Mass., 2003.

Datta, Pradip Kumar. "VHP's Ram: The Hindutva Movement in Ayodhyā." In *Hindus and Others: The Question of Identity in India Today,* edited by Gyanendra Pandey, pp. 46–73. New York, 1993.

Hardy, Friedhelm. *Viraha-Bhakti: The Early History of Kṛṣṇa Devotion in South India.* Delhi, 1983.

Kapur, Anuradha. "Deity to Crusader: The Changing Iconography of Ram." In *Hindus and Others: The Question of Identity in India Today,* edited by Gyanendra Pandey, pp. 74–109. New York, 1993.

Lorenzen, David N., ed. *Bhakti Religion in North India: Community Identity and Political Action.* Albany, N.Y., 1996.

Matsubara, Mitsunori. *Pāñcarātra Saṃhitās and Early Vaiṣṇava Theology.* Delhi, 1994.

Mumme, Patricia. *The Śrīvaiṣṇava Theological Dispute: Maṇavāḷamāmuni and Vedānta Deśika.* Madras, India, 1988.

Raman Mueller, Srilata. "Soteriology in the Writings of Rāmānuja: *Bhakti* and/or *Prapatti*?" In *Zeitschrift der Deutschen Morgenländischen Gesellschaft* 154, no. 1 (2004): 85–130.

Schomer, Karine, and W. H. McLeod, eds. *The Sants: Studies in a Devotional Tradition of India.* Delhi and Berkeley, 1987.

Srilata Raman (2005)

VIVEKANANDA [FURTHER CONSIDERATIONS].

Narendranath Datta was born into a middle-class family of north Calcutta. He met Ramakrishna in November 1881, and, after obtaining a B.A. degree from the Scottish Church College, he became Ramakrishna's devotee in 1884. He tried to train as a lawyer, but his legal studies were interrupted after Ramakrishna's death in 1886, and he became a renunciant. Narendranath's ascetic wanderings in northern and southern India from 1887 to 1893 brought him into contact with a number of scholars, such as Pramadadas Mitra of Vārāṇasī, Paṇḍits Narayan Das and Sunderlal Ojha of Khetri, and Shankar Pandurang of Porbandar, with whom he studied Sanskrit and read Hindu texts. Raja Ajit Singh of Khetri and Alasinga Perumal of Madras provided financial backing for him to participate in the World's Parliament of Religions in September 1893 in Chicago. He traveled to the United States as Swami Vivekananda, the monastic name suggested most probably by the *raja* of Khetri.

Vivekananda in the West. Vivekananda had not come to the Parliament as an invited speaker, but, at the recommen-

dations of John Henry Wright of Harvard and of a fellow Indian in the selection committee at Chicago, the Brāhmo scholar Protap Chunder Mozoomdar, he was admitted to the Parliament of Religions as a representative of the Hindu monastic order, and he spoke there on September 11, 1893.

In 1894 Vivekananda began to give lectures in which he proclaimed the anteriority and superiority of Hinduism over all other religions of the world and claimed that Christ's teachings were based on the Buddha's sermons, which were, in turn, derived from the Hindu Vedānta. He identified the Hindus with the Aryans and declared that Aryan civilization consisted of the Greek (aesthetic and immoral), Roman (imperial and organizational), and Hindu (metaphysical and spiritual).

VIVEKANANDA ON THE CASTE SYSTEM. Vivekananda justified the Hindu caste *(jāti)* system by arguing that it was conducive to individuality and diversity, as well as essential for Sanskrit learning, the foundation of the Hindu civilization. He harbored all the prejudices of the caste-conscious Bengali elite *(bhadralok),* proudly claiming his descent from the *kṣatriyas,* the warrior class, ranked second among the four classes (or *varṇas*), though in fact he belonged to the *kāyastha* caste, generally subsumed under the third class, of merchants and professionals, the *vaiśyas*. And, while lamenting the degraded state of the lowest class, the *śūdras,* he stated that "Brahminhood is the ideal of humanity in India" and insisted that the "solution is not by bringing down the higher, but by raising the lower up to the level of the higher"—a task he assigned to a select band of young *saṃnyāsins* recruited from "the highest classes, not the lowest" (*Complete Works,* 1990, vol. 7, p. 406).

VIVEKANANDA'S PRACTICAL VEDĀNTA. Vivekananda's endorsement of the caste system undercut his claims for the inclusivity and catholicity of the Hindu philosophy called Vedānta, which he regarded as the practical religion of the Hindus and which he began to preach from the fall of 1894, hoping to render "the dry, abstract Advaita" something "living" and "poetic" (*Complete Works,* 1990, vol. 4, pp. 104–105). He delivered four lectures on Practical Vedānta in London on November 10–18, 1896. In various sermons delivered in the United States and England, Vivekananda preached that "the different sectarian systems of India all radiate from one central idea of unity in dualism. . . . This, which we see as many, is God"(*Complete Works,* 1990, vol. 8, p. 250).

Much of what Vivekananda said about the history and culture of India was derivative of the teachings of his contemporaries and predecessors in Bengal (Keshub Chandra Sen, Rajnarain Basu, Bankim Chandra Chattopadhyay, and Rabindranath Tagore) and in the West (such as the German scholar of the Upaniṣads, Paul Deussen). Ramakrishna had utter contempt for Vedāntic knowledge, which he considered "the wisdom of a householder," deserving to be spat and urinated on, as he once quipped (Sil, 1998, pp. 162, 227). As Freda Matchett has demonstrated, Vivekananda distorted the mystico-spiritual visions and sermons of his teacher in order to align them with Śaṅkarācārya's Advaita (Monist) Vedānta. Vivekananda emphasized the efficacy of personal experience (*anubhava*) over scripture (*śruti,* the Vedas) as the source of the knowledge of Brahman. He equated *mokṣa* with the superconscious state, *nirvikalpa samādhi.* In this, Vivekananda's version of the Advaita Vedānta accommodated the anti-intellectual teachings of Ramakrishna, who had claimed that the pinnacle of his Vedāntic training was reached with his *nirvikalpa samādhi* under the mentorship of Totāpurī, a naked Vedāntist from the Punjab, and who also believed in the direct experience of the divine through *bhakti.* Vivekananda thus reformulated Advaita by devaluing scripture and privileging firsthand experience over intellection. This is what Vivekananda called *Practical Vedānta.*

VIVEKANANDA AND SOCIAL SERVICE. Vivekananda's humanitarian concern for the *gaṇa nārāyaṇa* or *daridra nārāyaṇa* (God as the poor multitude) was expressed in such statements as "Let her [India] arise—out of the peasants' cottage, grasping the plough; out of the huts of the fishermen, the cobbler, and the sweeper" (*Complete Works,* 1990, vol. 7, p. 27). Yet he does not seem to have been conscious of the efficacy of *jīvasevā* (service to humanity) prior to his Western travels; he began to proclaim the virtues of social service in India only upon his return in 1897. Moreover, he preached *jīvasevā* only to the upper classes, whom he advised to go out in the world and teach the poor, inter alia, religion, Sanskrit, astronomy, and geography. In a letter to Alasinga Perumal, he denied having ever supported social reform, for he regarded social and political improvements as secondary to religious regeneration. Throughout his life the Swami remained steadfast in his apolitical quiescence, without any understanding of the dynamics of social change. His final admonition was: "India is immortal if she persists in her search for God. But if she goes in for politics and social conflict, she will die" (Rolland, 1965, p. 168). Yet he founded the Ramakrishna Mission in Calcutta in the face of severe criticism by some of Ramakrishna's monastic and householder disciples, for Ramakrishna had contemptuously rejected philanthropy as a mark of arrogance and social service as an impediment to the spiritual goal of God-realization.

VIVEKANANDA ON WOMEN. Vivekananda inherited much of his gender consciousness from Ramakrishna's admonitions against women and wealth (*kāminī-kañcan*). He often confused femininity with effeminacy, identifying cowardice, lethargy, lust, and lure as characteristics of women. He claimed that Hindu women were the most spiritual in the world, but that contemporary Indian women were degenerate, lacking in spirituality, like American women, "the grandest women in the world," who were lustful and immoral. But, he argued, the Hindu scriptures were the only religious books in the whole world to praise women, and he proposed to educate Indian women so that they would be "fearless . . . and fit to be mothers of heroes," since the ideal for an Indian woman was either to be a wife and mother or to be a *saṃnyāsinī* (nun) dedicated to the welfare of humanity.

Though he made an impassioned plea for uplifting the standard and status of women, he defended the Hindu practice of widow-burning *(satī)*, claiming, first, that the Hindus never believed in widow-burning even though they permitted the custom, and, second, that those widows who immolated themselves on the funeral pyres of their husbands were either "fanatics" or considered *satī* a holy and happy occasion and went to their death agony merrily "believing for the most part that such an act meant the glories of Paradise" for themselves and their families (Burke, 1983–1984, vol. 1, p. 447).

VIVEKANANDA'S SELF-ASSESSMENT. Within a year of his instructions from the United States, Vivekananda wrote to his devotee Alasinga Perumal: "I have given up at present my plan for the education of the masses. It will come by degrees" (*Complete Works*, 1990, vol. 5, p. 67). His enthusiasm during his first visit to the United States and the United Kingdom (1893–1896) declined appreciably during his second visit (1899–1900). All available evidence suggests that from around 1897 he became despondent. A number of factors may have contributed to this feeling, including his failing health. His chronic diabetic condition, his weak heart and generally fragile health, his obesity, and his bouts of asthma, exacerbated by his unrestrained eating and smoking habits, had begun to take their toll. He was gradually overcome by a gnawing sense of nothingness and extinction. The Vedāntic eclecticism of his earlier years gave way to a parochial conviction in the merits of traditional Hinduism. He wrote in 1899 that "India's gods and goddesses are my God." In March 1901 he admitted in a public lecture in Dhaka (Bangladesh) that he belonged to the ancient sect that believed in the soteriological merits of the Ganges water. On June 17, 1900, he wrote from Calcutta to his American devotee Mary Hale: "This is the world, a hideous, beastly corpse. Who thinks of helping it is a fool!" Vivekananda died on July 4, 1902, at Belur, a few miles north of Calcutta, where a grand mausoleum dedicated to his memory stands today.

BIBLIOGRAPHY

Basu, Shankariprasad. *Vivekananda O Samakalin Bharavarsa.* 7 vols. Calcutta, 1975–1982. Extremely helpful for a comprehensive history of India during Vivekananda's lifetime.

Basu, Shankariprasad. *Swami Vivekananda in Contemporary Indian News (1893–1902): With Sri Ramakrishna and the Mission.* Vol. 1. Calcutta, 1997. Invaluable source on the media campaign for and against Vivekananda's activities in India and in the West.

Beckerlegge, Gwilym. *The Ramakrishna Mission: The Making of a Modern Hindu Movement.* New Delhi, 2000. A judicious analysis of the Ramakrishna–Vivekananda historiography and Vivekananda's spiritual and social thought.

Bryson, Thomas L. "The Hermeneutic of Religious Syncretism: Swami Vivekananda's Practical Vedanta." Ph.D. diss., University of Chicago, 1992. Detailed study and competent bibliography.

Burke, Marie Louis. *Swami Vivekananda in the West: New Discoveries.* 6 vols. 3d ed. Calcutta, 1983–1987. Vols. 1–2: *His Prophetic Mission* (1983–1984); Vols. 3–4: *The World Teacher* (1985–1986); Vols. 5–6: *A New Gospel* (1987). Monumental study; indispensable for researchers and scholars.

Dasgupta, Rabindra Kumar, ed. *Swami Vivekananda, a Hundred Years since Chicago: A Commemorative Volume.* Belur, India, 1994. A number of important, though adulatory, studies on Vivekananda in commemoration of his debut at the World's Parliament of Religions in 1893.

Dhar, Niranjan. *Vivekananda Anya Chokhe.* 3d ed. Calcutta, 1995. Pioneering critical examination of the odyssey and achievements of Vivekananda.

Dhar, Sailendra Nath. *A Comprehensive Biography of Swami Vivekananda.* 2 vols. Chennai, India, 1990. A massive biography, though uncritical.

Gambhirananda, Swami. *Yuganayak Vivekananda.* 3 vols. 6th ed. Calcutta, 1993–1996. Standard hagiographical account of the life and teachings of Vivekananda.

Matchett, Freda. "The Teaching of Ramakrishna in Relation to the Hindu Tradition as Interpreted by Vivekananda." *Religion* 11, no. 1 (1982): 171–184.

Radice, William, ed. *Swami Vivekananda and the Modernization of Hinduism.* Delhi, 1998. A helpful anthology containing articles on Vivekananda's achievements. The articles by Dermot Killingley, Gwilym Beckerlegge, Kenneth Jones, and Indira Chowdhury-Sengupta are especially noteworthy.

Rambachan, Anantanand. *The Limits of Scripture: Vivekananda's Reinterpretation of the Vedas.* Honolulu, 1994. A brilliant analysis of Vivekananda's understanding of the Vedas and the Vedānta.

Rolland, Romain. *The Life of Vivekananda and the Universal Gospel.* 6th ed. Calcutta, 1965.

Sil, Narasingha P. *Prophet Disarmed: Vivekananda and Nivedita.* Clayton, Australia, 1997. A probe into Vivekananda's experience with his foremost female disciple, Margaret Noble, and an attempt to fathom the nature of their relationship.

Sil, Narasingha P. *Swami Vivekananda: A Reassessment.* Selinsgrove, Pa., 1997. A revisionist biography that seeks to rescue the historical Vivekananda from the maze and haze of hagiographical tradition.

Sil, Narasingha P. *Ramakrishna Revisited: A New Biography.* Lanham, Md., 1998. A revisionist biography that attempts a psychological and historical analysis of Ramakrishna's humanity and spirituality.

Sil, Narasingha P. "Ramakrishna–Vivekananda Research: Hagiography versus Hermeneutics." *Religious Studies Review* 27, no. 4 (2001): 355–362. Review article.

Vivekananda, Swami. *Letters of Swami Vivekananda.* 6th ed. Calcutta, 1986.

Vivekananda, Swami. *Inspired Talks: My Master and Other Writings.* Rev. ed. New York, 1987.

Vivekananda, Swami. *Vedanta: Voice of Freedom.* Edited by Swami Chetanananda. Saint Louis, Mo., 1990.

Vivekananda, Swami. *The Complete Works of Swami Vivekananda.* 8 vols. Mayavati Memorial edition. Calcutta, 1990.

NARASINGHA P. SIL (2005)

SYNOPTIC OUTLINE OF CONTENTS

The outline presented here is intended to provide a general view of the conceptual scheme of this encyclopedia. It is divided into two parts: I. *The Religions* and II. *Religious Studies*. To show the conceptual components of the Encyclopedia's coverage, each of these general parts is subdivided into a variety of sections and sub-sections. The categories used in this outline are intended to be heuristic and thereby serviceable in guiding users through the Encyclopedia. Because the rubrics used as section headings are not necessarily mutually exclusive, certain entries in the Encyclopedia are listed in more than one section. Entries marked with an asterisk(*) are among those appearing in the Appendix in this volume.

I. THE RELIGIONS

Part I of this outline presents the Encyclopedia's coverage of the diversity of religious traditions organized according to historical, geographical, and ethnographic continuities. It is arranged in forty-four broad sections:

African Religions
African American Religions
Altaic Religions
Ancient Near Eastern Religions
Arctic Religions
Australian Indigenous Religions
Baltic Religion
Buddhism
Caribbean Religions
Celtic Religion
Chinese Religion
Christianity
Egyptian Religion
European Traditions
Germanic Religion
Greek Religion
Hellenistic Religions
Hinduism
Indian Religions
Indo-European Religions
Inner Asian Religions
Iranian Religions
Islam
Israelite Religion
Jainism
Japanese Religions
Judaism
Korean Religion
Mandaean Religion
Mesoamerican Religions
Mesopotamian Religions
New Religious Movements
North American Indian Religions
Oceanic Religions
Prehistoric Religions
Roman Religion
Sikhism
Slavic Religion
South American Indian Religions
Southeast Asian Religions
Thracian Religion
Tibetan Religions
Uralic Religions
Zoroastrianism

In addition to the lists of entries that appear under these forty-four broad headings, cross-references are given under the names of religious traditions outlined under other headings.

African Religions

PRINCIPAL ARTICLES

African Religions
- An Overview
- Mythic Themes
- New Religious Movements
- History of Study

Central Bantu Religions
East African Religions
- An Overview
- Ethiopian Religions
- Northeastern Bantu Religions

Southern African Religions
- An Overview
- Southern Bantu Religions

West African Religions

SUPPORTING ARTICLES

Affliction
- African Cults of Affliction

African American Religions
- An Overview

Afterlife
- African Concepts

Akan Religions
Aksumite Religion
Bambara Religion
Bemba Religion
Berber Religion
Christianity
- Christianity in Sub-Saharan Africa [First Edition]
- Christianity in Sub-Saharan Africa [Further Considerations]

Cosmology
- African Cosmologies

Diola Religion
Divination
- Ifa Divination*

Dogon Religion

Drama
  African Religious Drama
Edo Religion
Fiction
  African Fiction and Religion
Fon and Ewe Religion
Fulbe Religion
Gardens
  Gardens in Indigenous Traditions
Gender and Religion
  Gender and African Religious Traditions
God
  African Supreme Beings
Healing and Medicine
  Healing and Medicine in Africa
  Healing and Medicine in the African Diaspora
Iconography
  Traditional African Iconography
Igbo Religion
Interlacustrine Bantu Religions
Islam
  Islam in North Africa
  Islam in Sub-Saharan Africa
Khoi and San Religion
Kingship
  Kingship in Sub-Saharan Africa
Kongo Religion
Kushite Religion
Law and Religion
  Law and Religion in Indigenous Cultures
Luba Religion
Lugbara Religion
Mami Wata
Masks
Mawu-Lisa
Mbona
Music
  Music and Religion in Sub-Saharan Africa
Ndembu Religion
Nuer and Dinka Religion
Nyakyusa Religion
Politics and Religion
  Politics and African Religious Traditions
Prophecy
  African Prophetism
Pygmy Religions
Rites of Passage
  African Rites
Shona Religion
Soul
  Concepts in Indigenous Religions
Study of Religion
  The Academic Study of Religion in Sub-Saharan Africa
Swazi Religion
Tiv Religion
Tricksters
  African Tricksters
Tswana Religion
uNkulunkulu
Witchcraft
  African Witchcraft
Yoruba Religion
Zulu Religion

BIOGRAPHIES
  Alinesitoue
  Dan Fodio, Usuman
  Harris, William Wade
  Kimbangu, Simon
  Kinjikitile
  Lenshina, Alice
  Maranke, John
  Muḥammad Aḥmad
  Shembe, Isaiah
  ʿUmar Tāl

African American Religions

PRINCIPAL ARTICLE
  African American Religions
    An Overview
    History of Study

SUPPORTING ARTICLES
  African American Religions
    Muslim Movements
  Afro-Brazilian Religions
  Afro-Surinamese Religions
  Black Theology
  Caribbean Religions
    Afro-Caribbean Religions
  Christianity
    Christianity in Latin America
    Christianity in the Caribbean Region
    Christianity in North America
  Divination
    Ifa Divination*
  Gender and Religion
    Gender and African American Religions*
  Healing and Medicine
    Healing and Medicine in the African Diaspora
  Islam
    Islam in the Americas
  Jonestown and Peoples Temple
  Kardecism
  Nation of Islam
  Nuwaubians
  Political Theology
  Santería
  Vodou
  Yoruba Religion

BIOGRAPHIES
  Allen, Richard
  Crummell, Alexander
  Elijah Muḥammad
  Father Divine
  Garvey, Marcus
  Jones, Absalom
  Liele, George
  Malcolm X
  Seymour, William
  Turner, Henry McNeal

Altaic Religions

PRINCIPAL ARTICLES
  Mongol Religions
  Tunguz Religion
  Turkic Religions

SUPPORTING ARTICLES
  Buriat Religion
  Chinggis Khan
  Chuvash Religion
  Dolgan Religion
  Erlik
  Gesar
  Inner Asian Religions
  Ongon
  Southern Siberian Religions
  Tengri
  Ülgen
  Umai
  Yakut Religion

Amerindian Religions

See in this outline under North American Indian Religions; South American Indian Religions; Caribbean Religions.
See also Mesoamerican Religions.

Ancient Near Eastern Religions

PRINCIPAL ARTICLES

- Aramean Religion
- Canaanite Religion
  - An Overview
  - The Literature
- Eblaite Religion
- Egyptian Religion
  - An Overview
  - The Literature
  - History of Study
- Hittite Religion
- Hurrian Religion
- Israelite Religion
- Mandaean Religion
- Mesopotamian Religions
  - An Overview [First Edition]
  - An Overview [Further Considerations]
  - History of Study
- Moabite Religion
- Nabatean Religion
- Philistine Religion
- Phoenician Religion [First Edition]
- Phoenician Religion [Further Considerations]

SUPPORTING ARTICLES

- Anat
- Astarte
- Athirat
- Baal
- Dagan
- Drama
  - Ancient Near Eastern Ritual Drama [First Edition]
  - Ancient Near Eastern Ritual Drama [Further Considerations]
- El
- Eshmun
- Gender and Religion
  - Gender and Ancient Near Eastern Religions
- Goddess Worship
  - Goddess Worship in the Ancient Near East
- Healing and Medicine
  - Healing and Medicine in the Ancient Near East
- Kingship
  - Kingship in the Ancient Mediterranean World
- Melqart
- Politics and Religion
  - Politics and Ancient Mediterranean Religions
- Reshef
- Soul
  - Ancient Near Eastern Concepts
- Temple
  - Ancient Near Eastern and Mediterranean Temples
- Teshub
- Tithes

Arctic Religions

PRINCIPAL ARTICLES

- Arctic Religions
  - An Overview
  - History of Study

SUPPORTING ARTICLES

- Inuit Religious Traditions
- Khanty and Mansi Religion
- Num
- Sami Religion
- Samoyed Religion
- Sedna
- Shamanism
  - Siberian and Inner Asian Shamanism
  - North American Shamanism
- Soul
  - Concepts in Indigenous Religions
- Southern Siberian Religions
- Tunguz Religion
- Yakut Religion

Australian Indigenous Religions

PRINCIPAL ARTICLES

- Australian Indigenous Religions
  - An Overview
  - Mythic Themes [First Edition]
  - Mythic Themes [Further Considerations]
  - New Religious Movements
  - Aboriginal Christianity
  - History of Study [First Edition]
  - History of Study [Further Considerations]

SUPPORTING ARTICLES

- Afterlife
  - Australian Indigenous Concepts
- All-Father
- Cosmology
  - Australian Indigenous Cosmology
- Djan'kawu
- Dreaming, The
- Fiction
  - Australian Fiction and Religion
- Gadjeri
- Gender and Religion
  - Gender and Australian Indigenous Religions
- Healing and Medicine
  - Healing and Medicine In Indigenous Australia
- Iconography
  - Australian Aboriginal Iconography
- Law and Religion
  - Law and Religion in Indigenous Cultures
- Music
  - Music and Religion in Indigenous Australia
  - Music and Religion in Oceania
- Ngukurr Religion
- Rainbow Snake
- Soul
  - Concepts in Indigenous Religions
- Study of Religion
  - The Academic Study of Religion in Australia and Oceania
- Tjurungas
- Ungarinyin Religion
- Wandjina
- Wawalag
- Yulunggul Snake

Baltic Religion

PRINCIPAL ARTICLES

- Baltic Religion
  - An Overview
  - New Religious Movements
  - History of Study

SUPPORTING ARTICLES

- Ancestors
  - Baltic Cult of Ancestors
- Baltic Sanctuaries
- Māra (and Great Mothers)
- Dainas
- Laima
- Perkons
- Saule

Twins
Baltic Twin Deities
Zeme
RELATED ARTICLES
Indo-European Religions
An Overview
History of Study

Buddhism

PRINCIPAL ARTICLES
Buddhism
An Overview
Buddhism in India
Buddhism in Southeast Asia
Buddhism in Central Asia
Buddhism in Mongolia
Buddhism in Tibet
Buddhism in China
Buddhism in Korea
Buddhism in Japan
Buddhism in the West
Buddhist Studies

SCHOOLS OF THOUGHT
Buddhism, Schools of
Early Doctrinal Schools of Buddhism
Mahāyāna Philosophical Schools of Buddhism
Tantric Ritual Schools of Buddhism [First Edition]
Tantric Ritual Schools of Buddhism [Further Considerations]
Tibetan and Mongolian Buddhism
Himalayan Buddhism
Chinese Buddhism
Japanese Buddhism
East Asian Buddhism
Chan
Dge lugs pa
Huayan
Jingtu
Jōdo Shinshū
Jōdoshū
Mādhyamika
Mahāsāṃghika
Nichirenshū
Reiyūkai Kyōdan
Risshō Kōseikai
Sarvāstivāda
Sautrāntika
Shingonshū
Sōka Gakkai
Tendaishū
Theravāda
Tiantai
Yogācāra
Zen
Zhenyan

SUPPORTING ARTICLES
Ālaya-vijñāna
Arhat
Bodhisattva Path
Buddhas and Bodhisattvas
Celestial Buddhas and Bodhisattvas
Ethical Practices Associated with Buddhas and Bodhisattvas
Buddhist Books and Texts
Canon and Canonization
Canon and Canonization—Vinaya
Canon and Canonization—Abhidharma*
Ritual Uses of Books
Translation
Exegesis and Hermeneutics
Buddhist Ethics
Buddhist Meditation
Tibetan Buddhist Meditation
East Asian Buddhist Meditation
Buddhist Philosophy
Buddhist Religious Year
Cakrasamvara
Cakravartin
Ciji
Cosmology
Buddhist Cosmology
Councils
Buddhist Councils
Dalai Lama
Dhammakāya Movement
Dharma
Buddhist Dharma and Dharmas
Dzogchen
Ecology and Religion
Ecology and Buddhism
Eightfold Path
Engaged Buddhism
Enlightenment
Foguangshan
Folk Religion
Folk Buddhism
Four Noble Truths
Fudō
Gender and Religion
Gender and Buddhism
Gozan Zen
Guhyasamāja
Hevajra
Iconography
Buddhist Iconography
Indra
Kālacakra
Karma pas
Karman
Buddhist Concepts
Karuṇā
Language
Buddhist Views of Language
Law and Religion
Law and Religion in Buddhism
Mahāmudrā
Mahāsiddhas
Maṇḍalas
Buddhist Maṇḍalas
Mappō
Meditation
Merit
Buddhist Concepts
Missions
Buddhist Missions
Monasticism
Buddhist Monasticism
Music
Music and Religion in China, Korea, and Tibet
Nāgas and Yakṣas
Nianfo
Nichirenshū
Nirvāṇa
Nuns
Buddhist Nuns
Orgy
Orgy in Asia
Pali Text Society
Pāramitās
Pilgrimage
Buddhist Pilgrimage in South and Southeast Asia
Buddhist Pilgrimage in East Asia
Politics and Religion
Politics and Buddhism
Prajñā
Pratītya-samutpāda
Priesthood
Buddhist Priesthood

Pūjā
Buddhist Pūjā
Pure and Impure Lands
Rnying ma pa (Nyingmapa) School
Saṃgha
An Overview
Saṃgha and Society in South and Southeast Asia
Saṃgha and Society in Tibet
Sarasvati
Shugs ldan (Shugden)
Soteriology
Soul
Buddhist Concepts
Stupa Worship
Śūnyam and Śūnyatā
Tathāgata
Tathāgata-garbha
Tathatā
Temple
Buddhist Temple Compounds in South Asia
Buddhist Temple Compounds in East Asia
Buddhist Temple Compounds in Tibet
Buddhist Temple Compounds in Southeast Asia
Treasure Tradition
Upāya
Vajradhara
Vajrapāṇi
Vajrasattva
Worship and Devotional Life
Buddhist Devotional Life in Southeast Asia
Buddhist Devotional Life in East Asia
Buddhist Devotional Life in Tibet
Yama

BUDDHAS AND BODHISATTVAS
Amitābha
Avalokiteśvara
Bhaiṣajyaguru
Buddha
Kṣitigarbha
Mahāvairocana
Maitreya
Mañjuśrī
Māra
Tārā

BIOGRAPHIES[1]
Ambedkar, B. R.
Amoghavajra
Ani Lochen
Āryadeva
Asanga
Aśoka
Atīśa
Benchō
Bhāvaviveka
Bodhidharma
Bu ston
Buddhadāsa
Buddhaghosa
Buddhapālita
Candrakīrti
Dao'an
Daochuo
Daosheng
Devānaṃpiyatissa
Dharmakīrti
Dharmapāla
Dignāga
Dōgen
Dushun
Duṭṭhagāmaṇī
Eisai
Enchin
Ennin
Faxian
Fazang
Ganjin
Genshin
Gyōgi
Hakuin
Hōnen
Huineng
Huiyuan
Ikkyū Sōjun
Ippen
Jien
Jizang
Kamalaśīla
Keizan
Klong chen rab 'byams pa (Longchenpa)
Kōben
Kong sprul Blo gros Mtha' yas (Kongtrul Lodro Taye)
Kumārajīva
Liang Wudi
Linji
Ma gcig Lab sgron (Machig Labdron)
Malalasekera, G. P.
Mar pa
Mi la ras pa (Milarepa)
Moggaliputtatissa
Mongkut
Musō Sōseki
Nā ro pa
Nāgārjuna
Nanjō Bunyū
Nichiren
Nikkō
Padmasambhava
Paramārtha
Rennyo
Saichō
Sakya Paṇḍita (Sa skya Paṇḍita)
Śāntarakṣita
Śāntideva
Sengzhao
Sgam po pa (Gampopa)
Shandao
Shinran
Shotoku Taishi
Śīlabhadra
Sthiramati
Śubhākarasṃha
Suzuki Shōsan
Suzuki, D. T.
Taixu
Tang Yongtong
Tanluan
Tanyao
Tsong kha pa
U Nu
Vajrabodhi
Vasubandhu
Xinxing
Xuanzang
Ye shes Mtsho rgyal (Yeshe Tsogyal)
Yijing
Zhiyan
Zhiyi
Zhuhong
Zongmi

[1] *For additional relevant biographies, see also in part II of this outline under* The Study of Religion, *sub-section on* Scholars of Religion.

Caribbean Religions

PRINCIPAL ARTICLES

Caribbean Religions
- Pre-Columbian Religions
- Afro-Caribbean Religions
- History of Study*

SUPPORTING ARTICLES

Afro-Surinamese Religions
Cuna Religion
Divination
- Ifa Divination*

Fiction
- Latin American Fiction and Religion

Garifuna Religion
Healing and Medicine
- Healing and Medicine in the African Diaspora

Inquisition, The
- The Inquistion in the New World

Santería
Transculturation and Religion
- Religion in the Formation of the Modern Caribbean

Voudou
Yoruba Religion

Celtic Religion

PRINCIPAL ARTICLES

Celtic Religion
- An Overview
- History of Study

SUPPORTING ARTICLES

Annwn
Arthur
Brighid
Conall Cernach
Druids
Epona
Ferghus mac Roich
Fomhoire
Gender and Religion
- Gender and Celtic Religions

Head
- The Celtic Head Cult

Lugh
Mabinogion
Maponos
Matres
Merlin
Patrick
Sídh
Taliesin
Tuatha Dé Danann

RELATED ARTICLES

Indo-European Religions
- An Overview
- History of Study

Chinese Religion

PRINCIPAL ARTICLES

Chinese Religion
- An Overview
- Popular Religion
- Mythic Themes
- History of Study

Confucianism
- An Overview
- The Classical Canon
- The Imperial Cult
- History of Study

Daoism
- An Overview
- The Daoist Religious Community
- Daoist Literature
- History of Study

SUPPORTING ARTICLES

Afterlife
- Chinese Concepts

Alchemy
- Chinese Alchemy

Buddhism
- Buddhism in China

Buddhism, Schools of
- Chinese Buddhism
- East Asian Buddhism

Buddhist Meditation
- East Asian Buddhist Meditation

Calligraphy
- Chinese and Japanese Calligraphy

Chinese Philosophy
Chinese Religious Year
Dao and De
Domestic Observances
- Chinese Practices

Drama
- East Asian Dance and Theater

Ecology and Religion
- Ecology and Confucianism
- Ecology and Daoism

Falun Gong
Fangshi
Fiction
- Chinese Fiction and Religion

Foguangshan
Gender and Religion
- Gender and Chinese Religions

Gozan Zen
Healing and Medicine
- Healing and Medicine in China

Huangdi
Humor and Religion
- Humor and Religion in East Asian Contexts

Iconography
- Daoist Iconography
- Confucian Iconography

Islam
- Islam in China

Jiao
Kingship
- Kingship in East Asia

Law and Religion
- Law and Religion in Chinese Religions

Legalism
Li
Magic
- Magic in East Asia

Millenarianism
- Chinese Millenarian Movements

Monism
Music
- Music and Religion in China, Korea, and Tibet

Orgy
- Orgy in Asia

Poetry
- Chinese Religious Poetry

Politics and Religion
- Politics and Chinese Religion

Priesthood
- Daoist Priesthood

Qi
Ren and Yi
Shangdi
Soul
- Chinese Concepts

Study of Religion
- The Academic Study of Religion in China*

Taiji
Taiping
Taiwanese Religions

Temple
Buddhist Temple Compounds in East Asia
Daoist Temple Compounds
Confucian Temple Compounds
Tian
Worship and Devotional Life
Buddhist Devotional Life in East Asia
Daoist Devotional Life
Xian
Xiao
Yao and Shun
Yinyang Wuxing
Yu
Yuhuang
Zhenren

BIOGRAPHIES
Amoghavajra
Bodhidharma
Cheng Hao
Cheng Yi
Confucius
Dai Zhen
Dao'an
Daochuo
Daosheng
Dong Zhongshu
Du Guangting
Dushun
Faxian
Fazang
Ge Hong
Gu Yanwu
Guo Xiang
Han Fei Zi
Huineng
Huiyuan
Jizang
Kang Yuwei
Kou Qianzhi
Kuiji
Kumārajīva
Laozi
Li Shaojun
Liang Wudi
Linji
Liu An
Liu Deren
Lu Xiangshan
Lu Xiujing
Mengzi
Mozi
Paramārtha
Sengzhao
Shandao
Sima Chengzhen
Subhakarasimha
Taixu
Tang Yongtong
Tanluan
Tanyao
Tao Hongjing
Vajrabodhi
Wang Bi
Wang Chong
Wang Fuzhi
Wang Yangming
Wang Zhe
Xi Wang Mu
Xiao Baozhen
Xinxing
Xuanzang
Xunzi
Yijing
Zhang Daoling
Zhang Jue
Zhang Lu
Zhang Xuecheng
Zhang Zai
Zhiyan
Zhiyi
Zhou Dunyi
Zhu Xi
Zhuangzi
Zhuhong
Zongmi
Zouyan

Christianity

PRINCIPAL ARTICLES
Christianity
An Overview
Christianity in the Middle East
Christianity in North Africa
Christianity in Eastern Europe
Christianity in Western Europe
Christianity in Latin America
Christianity in the Caribbean Region
Christianity in North America
Christianity in Sub-Saharan Africa [First Edition]
Christianity in Sub-Saharan Africa [Further Considerations]
Christianity in Asia
Christianity in Australia and New Zealand
Christianity in the Pacific Islands [First Edition]
Christianity in the Pacific Islands [Further Considerations]
Eastern Christianity
Protestantism
Roman Catholicism [First Edition]
Roman Catholicism [Further Considerations]

COMMUNITIES
Anabaptism
Anglicanism
Armenian Church
Baptist Churches
Benedictines
Branch Davidians
Christian Identity Movement
Christian Science
Churches of Christ
Cistercians
Congregationalism
Coptic Church
Denominationalism
Disciples of Christ
Dominicans
Ethiopian Church
Family, The
Franciscans
Grail Movement
Greek Orthodox Church
Holy Order of MANS
Hutterian Brethren
Jehovah's Witnesses
Jesuits
Jesus Movement
Lutheranism
Mennonites
Methodist Churches
Moravians
Mormonism
Movement for the Restoration of the Ten Commandments of God
Nestorian Church
Pietism
Presbyterianism, Reformed
Puritanism
Quakers
Quietism

Religious Communities
  Christian Religious Orders
Russian Orthodox Church
Salvation Army
Seventh-day Adventism
Shakers
Syrian Orthodox Church of Antioch
Twelve Tribes
Uniate Churches
Unitarian Universalist Association
Unity

SUPPORTING ARTICLES
Afterlife
  Christian Concepts
Antichrist
Apostles
Arianism
Ashram
Atonement
  Christian Concepts
Attributes of God
  Christian Concepts
Australian Indigenous Religions
  Aborginal Christianity
Baptism
Bardaisan
Basilica, Cathedral, and Church
Biblical Exegesis
  Christian Views
Biblical Literature
  Hebrew Scriptures
  Apocrypha and Pseudepigrapha
  New Testament
Black Theology
Blasphemy
  Christian Concept
Carnival
Cathari
Christian Ethics
Christian Liturgical Year
Christian Social Movements
Christmas
Church
  Church Polity
  Ecclesiology
  Church Membership
Constantinianism
Councils
  Christian Councils
Creeds
  Christian Creeds
Crusades
  Christian Perspective
Cult of Saints
Day of the Dead
Deism
Discipleship
Docetism
Dogma
Domestic Observances
  Christian Practices
Donatism
Drama
  European Religious Drama [First Edition]
  European Religious Drama [Further Considerations]
  Modern Western Theater
Easter
Ebionites
Ecology and Religion
  Ecology and Christianity
Ecumenical Movement
Enlightenment, The
Epiphany
Eucharist
Evangelical and Fundamental Christianity
Excommunication
Existentialism
Feminist Theology
  Christian Feminist Theology
Free Will and Predestination
  Christian Concepts
Gallicanism
Gender and Religion
  Gender and Christianity
Gnosticism
  Gnosticism as a Christian Heresy
God
  God in the Hebrew Scriptures
  God in the New Testament
  God in Postbiblical Christianity
Gospel
Grace
Halloween
Healing and Medicine
  Healing and Medicine in Christianity
Heresy
  Christian Concepts
History
  Christian Views
Humanism
Hypostasis
Iconoclasm
  Iconoclasm in the Byzantine Tradition
Iconography
  Christian Iconography
Icons
Inquisition, The
  The Inquisition in the Old World
  The Inquistion in the New World
Jerusalem
  An Overview
  Jerusalem in Judaism, Christianity, and Islam
Justification
Kingdom of God
Law and Religion
  Law and Religion in Medieval Europe
Liberation Theology
Literature
  Religious Dimensions of Modern Western Literature [First Edition]
  Religious Dimensions of Modern Western Literature [Further Considerations]
Logos
Lord's Prayer
Manichaeism
  Manichaeism and Christianity
Marcionism
Merit
  Christian Concepts
Ministry
Missions
  Christian Missions
Modernism
  Christian Modernism
Monastery
Monasticism
  Christian Monasticism
Monophysitism
Montanism
Music
  Music and Religion in Greece, Rome, and Byzantium
  Religious Music in the West
Mystical Union in Judaism, Christianity, and Islam
Nag Hammadi
Native American Christianities
Neoorthodoxy

Neoplatonism
Nestorianism
Nominalism
Nuns
  Christian Nuns and Sisters
Orgy
  Orgy in Medieval and Modern Europe
Papacy
Pelagianism
Pentecostal and Charismatic Christianity
Persecution
  Christian Experience
Pilgrimage
  Roman Catholic Pilgrimage in Europe
  Roman Catholic Pilgrimage in the New World
  Eastern Christian Pilgrimage
Poetry
  Christian Poetry
Polemics
  Jewish-Christian Polemics
  Christian-Muslim Polemics
Political Theology
Politics and Religion
  Politics and Christianity
Priesthood
  Christian Priesthood
Proofs for the Existence of God
Prophecy
  Biblical Prophecy
Reformation
Sacrament
  Christian Sacraments
Schism
  Christian Schism
Scholasticism
Soul
  Christian Concepts
Theology
  Christian Theology
Trent, Council of
Trinity
Two Books, The
Ultramontanism
Vatican Councils
  Vatican I
  Vatican II [First Edition]
  Vatican II [Further Considerations]
Waldensians
Worship and Devotional Life
  Christian Worship

BIOGRAPHIES[2]
Abelard, Peter
Aksakov, Ivan
Albertus Magnus
Alcuin
Allen, Richard
Ambrose
Anselm
Anthony of Padua
Apollinaris of Laodicea
Arminius, Jacobus
Asbury, Francis
Athanasius
Athenagoras
Augustine of Canterbury
Augustine of Hippo
Avvakum
Bacon, Francis
Bacon, Roger
Barlaam of Calabria
Barth, Karl
Basil of Caesarea
Bauer, Bruno
Bede
Bellarmino, Roberto
Benedict of Nursia
Berdiaev, Nikolai
Berengar of Tours
Bergson, Henri
Bernard of Clairvaux
Beza, Theodore
Blondel, Maurice
Boehme, Jakob
Boethius
Bonaventure
Bonhoeffer, Dietrich
Boniface
Boniface VIII
Booth, William
Borromeo, Carlo
Browne, Robert
Brunner, Emil
Bruno, Giordano
Bucer, Martin
Bulgakov, Sergei
Bultmann, Rudolf
Bunyan, John
Bushnell, Horace
Butler, Joseph
Cabasilas, Nicholas
Calvert, George
Calvin, John
Campbell, Alexander
Canisius, Peter
Carroll, John
Cassian, John
Catherine of Siena
Cerularios, Michael
Channing, William Ellery
Charlemagne
Chrysostom
Clement of Alexandria
Clement of Rome
Clotilda
Coke, Thomas
Coleridge, Samuel Taylor
Comenius, Johannes Amos
Constantine
Contarini, Gasparo
Copernicus, Nicolaus
Cranmer, Thomas
Crummell, Alexander
Cyprian
Cyril and Methodius
Cyril I
Cyril of Alexandria
Cyril of Jerusalem
Daddy Grace
Damian, Peter
Dante Alighieri
Day, Dorothy
Descartes, René
Dionysius the Areopagite
Döllinger, Johann
Dominic
Dostoevsky, Fyodor
Duns Scotus, John
Dwight, Timothy
Eck, Johann
Eckhart, Johannes
Eddy, Mary Baker
Edwards, Jonathan
Emerson, Ralph Waldo
Ephraem of Syria
Erasmus, Desiderius
Eriugena, John Scottus
Eusebius
Eutyches
Evagrios of Pontus

[2]*For Old Testament figures, see in this outline under* Israelite Religion. *For additional relevant biographies, see also in part II of this outline under* The Study of Religion, *sub-section on* Scholars of Religion.

Farel, Guillaume
Fénelon, François
Feuerbach, Ludwig
Fichte, Johann Gottlieb
Ficino, Marsilio
Filaret of Moscow
Fillmore, Charles and Myrtle
Flacius, Matthias
Florenskii, Pavel
Fox, George
Francis of Assisi
Francke, August Hermann
Gage, Matilda Joslyn
Galileo Galilei
Garvey, Marcus
Gibbons, James
Gilson, Étienne
Gregory I
Gregory of Cyprus
Gregory of Datev
Gregory of Narek
Gregory of Nazianzus
Gregory of Nyssa
Gregory of Sinai
Gregory Palamas
Gregory the Illuminator
Gregory VII
Grotius, Hugo
Grundtvig, Nikolai Frederik Severin
Hegel, G. W. F.
Heidegger, Martin
Hildegard of Bingen
Hincmar
Hocking, William Ernest
Hooker, Richard
Hooker, Thomas
Hrotsvit
Hugh of Saint-Victor
Hume, David
Hus, Jan
Hutchinson, Anne
Ignatius Loyola
Ignatius of Antioch
Innocent I
Innocent III
Innokentii Veniaminov
Ioann of Kronstadt
Irenaeus
Irving, Edward
Isaac the Syrian
Isidore of Seville
Jaspers, Karl
Jeremias II
Jerome
Jesus
Joachim of Fiore
Joan of Arc
John of Damascus
John of the Cross
John the Baptist
John the Evangelist
John XXIII
Jones, Absalom
Joseph of Volokolamsk
Julian of Halicarnassus
Julian of Norwich
Justin Martyr
Justinian I
Kagawa Toyohiko
Kant, Immanuel
Kempe, Margery
Kepler, Johannes
Khomiakov, Aleksei
Kierkegaard, Søren
King, Martin Luther, Jr.
Kireevskii, Ivan
Knox, John
Koresh, David
Kosmas Aitolos
Las Casas, Bartolomé de
Law, William
Lee, Ann
Leibniz, Gottfried Wilhelm
Leo I
Leo XIII
Leontius of Byzantium
Lessing, G. E.
Lewis, C. S.
Liele, George
Locke, John
Lonergan, Bernard
Luke the Evangelist
Lull, Ramón
Luther, Martin
Makarios of Egypt
Marcion
Marie de l'Incarnation
Maritain, Jacques
Mark of Ephesus
Mark the Evangelist
Marsilius of Padua
Martineau, James
Mary
  An Overview
  Feminist Perspectives
Mary Magdalene
Mashtots', Mesrop
Mather Family
Matthew the Evangelist
Maurice, Frederick Denison
Maximos the Confessor
McPherson, Aimee Semple
Melanchthon, Philipp
Mercier, Désiré Joseph
Merezhkovskii, Dmitrii
Merton, Thomas
Möhler, Johann Adam
Montanus
Moody, Dwight L.
Morrison, Robert
Müntzer, Thomas
Nersēs of Cla
Nersēs the Great
Nestorius
Newman, John Henry
Newton, Isaac
Nicholas of Cusa
Niebuhr, Reinhold
Nietzsche, Friedrich
Nightingale, Florence
Nikephoros
Nikephoros Kallistos
Nikodimos of the Holy Mountain
Nikon
Noyes, John Humphrey
Olaf the Holy
Origen
Pachomius
Paracelsus
Pascal, Blaise
Patrick
Paul the Apostle
Paul VI
Pecham, John
Pelagius
Penn, William
Peter Lombard
Peter the Apostle
Petr Moghila
Petre, Maude Dominica
Photios
Pico della Mirandola, Giovanni
Pius IX
Pobedonostsev, Konstantin
Prokopovich, Feofan
Psellus, Michael
Pusey, Edward Bouverie
Rahner, Karl
Ramabai, Pandita
Rauschenbusch, Walter
Reimarus, Hermann Samuel

Ricci, Matteo
Ritschl, Albrecht
Rousseau, Jean-Jacques
Ruusbroec, Jan van
Sahak Parthev
Savonarola, Girolamo
Sayers, Dorothy L.
Scheler, Max
Schelling, Friedrich
Schleiermacher, Friedrich
Scholarios, Gennadios
Serafim of Sarov
Sergii
Sergii of Radonezh
Serra, Junipero
Servetus, Michael
Seton, Elizabeth
Severus of Antioch
Seymour, William
Shenoute
Simons, Menno
Skobtsova, Maria
Smith, Hannah Whitall
Smith, Joseph
Sölle, Dorothee
Solov'ev, Vladimir
Sorskii, Nil
Sozzini, Fausto Pavolo
Spener, Philipp Jakob
Spurgeon, Charles Haddon
Stanton, Elizabeth Cady
Strauss, David Friedrich
Suárez, Francisco
Swedenborg, Emanuel
Symeon the New Theologian
Tarasios
Tauler, Johannes
Teilhard de Chardin, Pierre
Tekakwitha, Kateri
Teresa of Ávila
Tertullian
Theodore of Mopsuestia
Theodore of Studios
Theodoret of Cyrrhus
Theodosius
Thérèse of Lisieux
Thomas à Kempis
Thomas Aquinas
Tikhon
Tikhon of Zadonsk
Tillich, Paul Johannes
Timothy Ailuros
Tolstoy, Leo
Torquemada, Tomás de
Troeltsch, Ernst
Trubetskoi, Evgenii
Trubetskoi, Sergei
Turner, Henry McNeal
Tyndale, William
Tyrrell, George
Uchimura Kanzō
Vico, Giovanni Battista
Vladimir I
Ward, Mary
Weil, Simone
Wesley Brothers
White, Ellen Gould
Whitefield, George
Whitehead, Alfred North
William of Ockham
Williams, Roger
Willibrord
Wise, John
Wittgenstein, Ludwig
Wolff, Christian
Wyclif, John
Xavier, Francis
Young, Brigham
Zinzendorf, Nikolaus
Zwingli, Huldrych

Confucianism

See in this outline under Chinese Religion.

Daoism

See in this outline under Chinese Religion.

East Asian Religions

See in this outline under Chinese Religion, Japanese Religions, and Korean Religion.
See also Tibetan Religions.

Egyptian Religion

PRINCIPAL ARTICLES
Egyptian Religion
An Overview
The Literature
History of Study

SUPPORTING ARTICLES
Akhenaton
Amun
Anubis
Atum
Drama
Ancient Near Eastern Ritual Drama [First Edition]
Ancient Near Eastern Ritual Drama [Further Considerations]
Gender and Religion
Gender and Ancient Mediterranean Religions
Goddess Worship
Goddess Worship in the Ancient Near East
Goddess Worship in the Hellenistic World
Hathor
Healing and Medicine
Healing and Medicine in the Ancient Near East
Horus
Iconography
Egyptian Iconography
Isis
Kingship
Kingship in the Ancient Mediterranean World
Melqart
Mystery Religions
Osiris
Ptah
Ptolemy
Pyramids
Egyptian Pyramids
Re
Seth
Temple
Ancient Near Eastern and Mediterranean Temples
Thoth

European Traditions

Alchemy
Hellenistic and Medieval Alchemy
Renaissance Alchemy
All Fools' Day
Anthroposophy
Baltic Religion
An Overview
Carnival
Celtic Religion
An Overview
Christianity
Christianity in Eastern Europe
Christianity in Western Europe

Copernicus, Nicolaus
Crusades
  Christian Perspective
Cult of Saints
Dance
  Popular and Folk Dance [First Edition]
  Popular and Folk Dance [Further Considerations]
  Theatrical and Liturgical Dance [First Edition]
  Theatrical and Liturgical Dance [Further Considerations]
Dante Alighieri
Drama
  European Religious Drama [First Edition]
  European Religious Drama [Further Considerations]
  Modern Western Theater
Einstein, Albert
Enlightenment, The
Esotericism
Etruscan Religion
Existentialism
Faust
Fiction
  The Western Novel and Religion
Finno-Ugric Religions
  An Overview
Folklore
Freemasons
Galileo Galilei
Germanic Religion
  An Overview
Gnosticism
  Gnosticism from Its Origins to the Middle Ages [First Edition]
  Gnosticism from Its Origins to the Middle Ages [Further Considerations]
  Gnosticism from the Middle Ages to the Present
Grail, The
Greek Religion [First Edition]
Greek Religion [Further Considerations]
Hellenistic Religions
Hermetism
Hobbes, Thomas
Iberian Religion
Indo-European Religions
  An Overview
Islam
  Islam in Modern Europe
Judaism
  Judaism in Northern and Eastern Europe to 1500
  Judaism in Northern and Eastern Europe since 1500
Kepler, Johannes
Law and Religion
  Law and Religion in Medieval Europe
Literature
  Religious Dimensions of Modern Western Literature [First Edition]
  Religious Dimensions of Modern Western Literature [Further Considerations]
Magic
  Magic in Medieval and Renaissance Europe
  Magic in Eastern Europe
Marx, Karl
Masks
Music
  Religious Music in the West
Nature
  Religious and Philosophical Speculations
New Religious Movements
  New Religious Movements in Europe
Newton, Isaac
Occultism
Orgy
  Orgy in Medieval and Modern Europe
Paganism, Anglo-Saxon
Paracelsus
Philosophy
  An Overview
Pilgrimage
  Roman Catholic Pilgrimage in Europe
Poetry
  Poetry and Religion
Prehistoric Religions
  Old Europe
Roman Religion
  The Early Period
  The Imperial Period
Rosicrucians
Sartre, Jean-Paul
Sexuality
  Sexual Rites in Europe
Slavic Religion
Study of Religion
  The Academic Study of Religion in Eastern Europe and Russia
  The Academic Study of Religion in Western Europe*
Theosophical Society
Thracian Religion
Utopia
Winter Solstice Songs
Witchcraft
  Concepts of Witchcraft

Finno-Ugric Religions

See in this outline under Uralic Religions.

Germanic Religion

PRINCIPAL ARTICLES

Germanic Religion
  An Overview
  History of Study

SUPPORTING ARTICLES

Álfar
Baldr
Berserkers
Dvergar
Eddas
Freyja
Freyr
Fylgjur
Heimdallr
Jötnar
Landvættir
Loki
Njǫrðr
Óðinn
Olaf the Holy
Paganism, Anglo-Saxon
Runes [First Edition]
Runes [Further Considerations]
Sagas
Saxo Grammaticus
Snorri Sturluson
Thor
Týr
Valhǫll
Valkyries

RELATED ARTICLES

Indo-European Religions
  An Overview
  History of Study

Geto-Dacian Religion
See in this outline under
Thracian Religion.

Greek Religion
PRINCIPAL ARTICLES
Greek Religion [First Edition]
Greek Religion [Further Considerations]
SUPPORTING ARTICLES
Adonis
Aegean Religions
Afterlife
Greek and Roman Concepts
Agōgē
Anthesteria
Aphrodite
Apocatastasis
Apollo
Apotheosis
Aristotelianism
Aristotle
Artemis
Asklepios
Athena
Baubo
Catharsis
Delphi
Demeter and Persephone
Demiurge
Dionysos
Divination
Greek and Roman Divination
Eleusinian Mysteries
Eros
Euclid
Euhemerus and Euhemerism
Galen
Gender and Religion
Gender and Ancient Mediterranean Religions
Good, The
Hades
Hekate
Healing and Medicine
Healing and Medicine in Greece and Rome
Hellenistic Religions
Hera
Herakles
Hermes
Hesiod
Hestia
Hippocrates
Homer
Hypostasis
Iconography
Greco-Roman Iconography
Logos
Magic
Magic in Greco-Roman Antiquity
Muses
Music
Music and Religion in Greece, Rome, and Byzantium
Mystery Religions
Orgy
Orgy in the Ancient Mediterranean World
Orpheus
Orphic Gold Tablets
Pan
Panathenaia
Parmenides
Plato
Platonism
Plotinus
Plutarch
Politics and Religion
Politics and Ancient Mediterranean Religions
Poseidon
Prometheus
Ptolemy
Pythagoras
Skeptics and Skepticism
Socrates
Sophia
Soul
Greek and Hellenistic Concepts
Temple
Ancient Near Eastern and Mediterranean Temples
Thesmophoria
Theurgy
Thiasoi
Virgin Goddess
Xenophanes
Zeus
RELATED ARTICLES
Indo-European Religions
An Overview
History of Study

Hellenistic Religions
PRINCIPAL ARTICLE
Hellenistic Religions
SUPPORTING ARTICLES
Agnōstos Theos
Aion
Alchemy
Hellenistic and Medieval Alchemy
Anamnesis
Apocalypse
Jewish Apocalypticism to the Rabbinic Period
Apocatastasis
Apostles
Apotheosis
Bardaisan
Biblical Literature
Apocrypha and Pseudepigrapha
New Testament
Cybele
Dead Sea Scrolls
Demiurge
Egyptian Religion
An Overview
The Literature
Essenes
Euhemerus and Euhemerism
Gender and Religion
Gender and Ancient Mediterranean Religions
Gnosticism
Gnosticism from Its Origins to the Middle Ages [First Edition]
Gnosticism from Its Origins to the Middle Ages [Further Considerations]
Goddess Worship
Goddess Worship in the Hellenistic World
Greek Religion [First Edition]
Greek Religion [Further Considerations]
Healing and Medicine
Healing and Medicine in Greece and Rome
Hermes Trismegistos
Hermetism
Hypostasis
Iconography
Greco-Roman Iconography
Iupiter Dolichenus
Jesus

Kingship
Kingship in the Ancient Mediterranean World
Law and Religion
Law and Religion in the Ancient Mediterranean World
Logos
Magic
Magic in Greco-Roman Antiquity
Manichaeism
An Overview
Manichaeism and Christianity
Mishnah and Tosefta
Mithra
Mithraism
Music
Music and Religion in Greece, Rome, and Byzantium
Mystery Religions
Neoplatonism
Orgy
Orgy in the Ancient Mediterranean World
Paul the Apostle
Philo Judaeus
Plutarch
Rabbinic Judaism in Late Antiquity
Roman Religion
The Imperial Period
Sadducees
Skeptics and Skepticism
Sophia
Soul
Greek and Hellenistic Concepts
Stoicism
Tannaim
Theurgy
Wisdom Literature
Theoretical Perspectives

Hinduism

PRINCIPAL ARTICLE[3]
Hinduism

SECTARIAN SCHOOLS AND COMMUNITIES
Durgā Hinduism
Gāṇapatyas
Kṛṣṇaism
Śaivism
An Overview
Śaiva Siddhānta
Vīraśaivas
Nāyāṉārs
Krama Śaivism
Trika Śaivism
Śaivism in Kashmir
Pratyabhijñā
Pāśupatas
Kāpālikas
Saura Hinduism
Sri Vaisnavas
Tantrism
An Overview
Hindu Tantrism
Vaikhanasas
Vaiṣṇavism
An Overview [First Edition]
An Overview [Further Considerations]
Bhāgavatas
Pāñcarātras
Vedism and Brahmanism

SUPPORTING ARTICLES
Ahiṃsā
Alchemy
Indian Alchemy
Āḻvārs
Ārya Samāj
Ashram
Avatāra
Avidyā
Āyurveda
Banaras
Bengali Religions
Bhagavadgītā
Bhakti
Brahman
Brāhmaṇas and Āraṇyakas
Brāhmo Sāmaj
Cakras
Chanting
Cosmology
Hindu Cosmology
Dharma
Hindu Dharma
Dīvālī
Domestic Observances
Hindu Practices
Drama
Indian Dance and Dance Drama
Balinese Dance and Dance Drama
Javanese Wayang
Ecology and Religion
Ecology and Hinduism
Fiction
South Asian Fiction and Religion*
Ganges River
Gender and Religion
Gender and Hinduism
Goddess Worship
The Hindu Goddess
Guṇas
Haṭhayoga
Healing and Medicine
Healing and Medicine in Ayurveda and South Asia
Hindi Religious Traditions
Hinduism in Southeast Asia
Hindu Religious Year
Hindu Tantric Literature
Holī
Iconography
Hindu Iconography
Indian Philosophies
Indus Valley Religion
International Society for Krishna Consciousness
Īśvara
Jīvanmukti
Jñāna
Karman
Hindu and Jain Concepts
Khmer Religion
Kumbha Melā
Kuṇḍalinī
Kurukṣetra
Law and Religion
Law and Religion in Hinduism
Līlā
Lotus
Magic
Magic in South Asia
Mahābhārata
Maṇḍalas
Hindu Maṇḍalas
Mantra
Marathi Religions

[3] *For additional relevant entries, see also in this outline under* Indian Religions.

Māyā
Mīmāṃsā
Mokṣa
Mudrā
Mūrti
Music
 Music and Religion in India
Navarātri
Nyāya
Oṃ
Orgy
 Orgy in Asia
Pilgrimage
 Hindu Pilgrimage
Poetry
 Indian Religious Poetry
Prakṛti
Pralaya
Prāṇa
Priesthood
 Hindu Priesthood
Pūjā
 Hindu Pūjā
Purāṇas
Puruṣa
Rāmāyaṇa
Rites of Passage
 Hindu Rites
Ṛta
Sādhus and Sādhvīs
Samādhi
Sāṃkhya
Saṃnyāsa
Saṃsāra
Śāstra Literature
Sati
Soma
Soul
 Indian Concepts
Study of Religion
 The Academic Study of Religion in South Asia
Sūtra Literature
Swaminarayan Movement
Tapas
Tamil Religions
Temple
 Hindu Temples
Transcendental Meditation
Transculturation and Religion
 Religion in the Formation of Modern India
Untouchables, Religions of
Upaniṣads
Vaiśeṣika
Varṇa and Jāti
Vedāṅgas
Vedānta
Vedas
Vṛndāvana
Worship and Devotional Life
 Hindu Devotional Life
Yantra
Yoga

THEOGRAPHIES
Agni
Arjuna
Balarāma
Brahmā
Gaṇeśa
Hanumān
Indra
Kṛṣṇa
Manu
Murukaṉ
Prajāpati
Rādhā
Rāma
Rudra
Sarasvatī
Śiva [First Edition]
Śiva [Further Considerations]
Varuṇa
Viṣṇu
Vṛtra
Yama

BIOGRAPHIES
Abhinavagupta
Ānandamayī Mā
Aurobindo Ghose
Bādarāyaṇa
Caitanya
Gauḍapāda
Gorākhnāth
Jayadeva
Kabīr
Madhva
Māṇikkavācakar
Meykaṇṭār
Mirabai
Nimbārka
Patañjali
Patañjali the Grammarian
Piḷḷai Lokācārya
Prabhupada, A. C. Bhaktivedanta
Ramabai, Pandita
Ramakrishna
Ramakrishna [Further Considerations]*
Rāmānuja
Śaṅkara
Śārāda, Devī
Sūrdās
Tulsīdās
Umāpati Śivācārya
Vallabha
Vālmīki
Vijñānabhikṣu
Vivekananda
Vivekananda [Further Considerations]*
Yāmuna
Yogananda

Indian Religions

PRINCIPAL ARTICLES
Indian Religions
 An Overview
 Rural Traditions
 Mythic Themes
 History of Study

RELIGIONS AND SECTS
Ājīvikas
Buddhism
 Buddhism in India
Cārvāka
Hinduism
Jainism
Sikhism

SUPPORTING ARTICLES
Ahiṃsā
Alchemy
 Indian Alchemy
Āḻvārs
Ārya Samāj
Ashram
Avatāra
Avidyā
Banaras
Bengali Religions
Bhakti
Brahman
Brāhmo Sāmaj
Cakras
Cakrasamvara
Chanting
Cosmology
 Hindu Cosmology
 Jain Cosmology

Drama
Indian Dance and Dance Drama
Fiction
South Asian Fiction and Religion*
Ganges River
Guṇas
Haṭhayoga
Healing and Medicine
Healing and Medicine in Ayurveda and South Asia
Hindi Religious Traditions
Indian Philosophies
Indus Valley Religion
International Society for Krishna Consciousness
Islam
Islam in South Asia
Jīvanmukti
Jñāna
Kuṇḍalinī
Kurukṣetra
Lotus
Magic
Magic in South Asia
Mantra
Marathi Religions
Māyā
Mokṣa
Mudrā
Mūrti
Music
Music and Religion in India
Oṃ
Orgy
Orgy in Asia
Pañcatantra
Poetry
Indian Religious Poetry
Prakṛti
Pralaya
Prāṇa
Puruṣa
Ṛta
Sādhus and Sādhvīs
Sai Baba Movement
Samādhi
Saṃgha
Saṃgha and Society in South and Southeast Asia
Saṃnyāsa
Saṃsāra
Śāstra Literature
Sinhala Religion
Soma
Soul
Indian Concepts
Study of Religion
The Academic Study of Religion in South Asia
Sūtra Literature
Swaminarayan Movement
Tapas
Tamil Religions
Tantrism
An Overview
Temple
Buddhist Temple Compounds in South Asia
Transcendental Meditation
Transculturation and Religion
Religion in the Formation of Modern India
Untouchables, Religions of
Varṇa and Jāti
Vedāṅgas
Vedānta
Vṛndāvana
Yantra
Yoga

BIOGRAPHIES[4]
Abhinavagupta
Akbar
Ānandamayī Mā
Aurobindo Ghose
Bādarāyaṇa
Bhave, Vinoba
Caitanya
Dayananda Sarasvati
Gandhi, Mohandas
Gauḍapāda
Gorākhnāth
Gośāla
Jayadeva
Kabīr
Madhva
Mirabai
Panini
Patañjali
Patañjali the Grammarian
Prabhupada, A. C. Bhaktivedanta
Radhakrishnan, Sarvepalli
Rajneesh
Ramabai, Pandita
Ramakrishna
Ramakrishna [Further Considerations]*
Roy, Ram Mohan
Śaṅkara
Śārāda, Devī
Sen, Keshab Chandra
Sūrdās
Tagore, Rabindranath
Tilak, Bal Gangadhar
Tulsīdās
Vālmīki
Vivekananda
Vivekananda [Further Considerations]*

RELATED ARTICLE
Indo-European Religions
An Overview

Indo-European Religions

PRINCIPAL ARTICLES
Indo-European Religions
An Overview
History of Study

SUPPORTING ARTICLES
Armenian Religion
Baltic Religion
An Overview
Celtic Religion
An Overview
Etruscan Religion
Germanic Religion
An Overview
Greek Religion [First Edition]
Greek Religion [Further Considerations]
Hittite Religion
Indian Religions
An Overview
Iranian Religions
Manichaeism
Manichaeism in Iran
Manichaeism in the Roman Empire
Roman Religion
The Early Period
The Imperial Period
Scythian Religion

[4] *For additional relevant biographies, see also in part II of this outline under* The Study of Religion, *sub-section on* Scholars of Religion.

Slavic Religion
Thracian Religion

RELATED ARTICLES
War and Warriors
Indo-European Beliefs and Practices
Winter Solstice Songs

Indonesian Religions
See in this outline under Southeast Asian Religions.

Inner Asian Religions
PRINCIPAL ARTICLE[5]
Inner Asian Religions

SUPPORTING ARTICLES
Buddhism
Buddhism in Central Asia
Buddhism in Mongolia
Buddhism in Tibet
Buriat Religion
Dolgan Religion
Finno-Ugric Religions
An Overview
Hun Religion
Iranian Religions
Islam
Islam in the Caucasus and the Middle Volga
Islam in Central Asia
Khanty and Mansi Religion
Manichaeism
An Overview
Manichaeism in Central Asia and China
Mongol Religions
Orgy
Orgy in Asia
Prehistoric Religions
The Eurasian Steppes and Inner Asia
Samoyed Religion
Sarmatian Religion
Scythian Religion
Shamanism
Siberian and Inner Asian Shamanism
Slavic Religion
Soul
Concepts in Indigenous Religions
Southern Siberian Religions
Tibetan Religions
An Overview
Turkic Religions
Tunguz Religion

Iranian Religions
PRINCIPAL ARTICLE
Iranian Religions

SUPPORTING ARTICLES
Mani
Manichaeism
An Overview
Manichaeism in Iran
Mazdakism
Mithra
Mithraism
Mystery Religions
Zoroastrianism
Zurvanism

RELATED ARTICLE
Indo-European Religions
An Overview

Islam
PRINCIPAL ARTICLES
Islam
An Overview [First Edition]
An Overview [Further Considerations]
Islam in North Africa
Islam in Andalusia
Islam in Sub-Saharan Africa
Islam in the Caucasus and the Middle Volga
Islam in Central Asia
Islam in China
Islam in South Asia
Islam in Southeast Asia
Islam in Modern Europe
Islam in the Americas
Islamic Studies [First Edition]
Islamic Studies [Further Considerations]
Shiism
An Overview

SCHOOLS, GROUPS, AND COMMUNITIES
Aḥmadiyah
ʿAlawīyūn
Ashʿarīyah
Druzeḥanābilah
Ibāḍiyyah
Ishrāqīyah
Khārijīs
Muʿtazilah
Qarāmiṭah
Shaykhīyah
Shiism
Ismāʿīlīyah
Ithnā ʿAshariyah
Wahhābīyah

SUPPORTING ARTICLES
African American Religions
Muslim Movements
Afterlife
Islamic Concepts
Aga Khan
Ahl Al-Bayt
Al-Azhar
Alchemy
Islamic Alchemy
Arabian Religions
Aristotelianism
ʿĀshūrāʾ
Assassins
Attributes of God
Islamic Concepts
Bābīs
Bahāʾīs
Blasphemy
Islamic Concept
Caliphate
Calligraphy
Islamic Calligraphy
Creeds
Islamic Creeds
Crusades
Muslim Perspective
Darwīsh
Daʿwah
Dhikr
Drama
Middle Eastern Narrative Traditions
Domestic Observances
Muslim Practices
Ecology and Religion
Ecology and Islam
Eschatology
Islamic Eschatology

[5] *For additional relevant entries, see also in this outline under* Uralic Religions *and* Altaic Religions.

Falsafah
Folk Religion
  Folk Islam
Free Will and Predestination
  Islamic Concepts
Gardens
  Islamic Gardens
Gender and Religion
  Gender and Islam
Ghaybah
Ginān
God
  God in Islam
Hadīth
Ḥaram and Ḥawṭah
Hawzah
Healing and Medicine
  Healing and Medicine in Islamic Texts and Traditions
  Popular Healing Practices in Middle Eastern Cultures
Humor and Religion
  Humor and Islam
Iconography
  Islamic Iconography
Iʿjāz
Ijmāʿ
Ijtihād
Ikhwān al-Ṣafāʾ
Imamate
Īmān and Islām
Islamic Law
  Sharīʿah
  Personal Law
Islamic Religious Year
ʿIṣmah
Jamāʿat-i Islāmī
Jerusalem
  Jerusalem in Judaism, Christianity, and Islam
Jihād
Kaʿbah
Kalām
Karbala
Khānagāh
Madhhab
Madrasah
Magic
  Magic in Islam
Maṣlaḥah
Mawlid
Messianism
  Messianism in the Muslim Tradition
Miʿrāj
Modernism
  Islamic Modernism
Mosque
  History and Tradition
  Architectural Aspects
Music
  Music and Religion in the Middle East
Muslim Brotherhood
Mystical Union in Judaism, Christianity, and Islam
Nation of Islam
Nubūwah
Nūr Muḥammad
Occasionalism
Pilgrimage
  Muslim Pilgrimage
Poetry
  Islamic Poetry
Polemics
  Muslim-Jewish Polemics
  Christian-Muslim Polemics
Politics and Religion
  Politics and Islam
Qāḍī
Qarāmiṭah
Qiyās
Qurʾān
  Tradition of Scholarship and Interpretation
  Its Role in Muslim Practice and Life
Rāwẓah-khvānī
Rites of Passage
  Muslim Rites
Ṣalāt
Samāʿ
Ṣawm
Shahādah
Shaykh al-Islām
Soul
  Islamic Concepts
Study of Religion
  The Academic Study of Religion in North Africa and the Middle East
Sufism
Ṣuḥbah
Sunnah
Tafsīr
Taqīyah
Ṭarīqah
Taʿziyah
Tilāwah
ʿUlamāʾ
Ummah
Uṣūl al-Fiqh
Walāyah
Waqf
Worship and Devotional Life
  Muslim Worship
Zakāt

BIOGRAPHIES[6]

ʿAbd al-Jabbār
ʿAbd al-Rāziq, ʿAlī
ʿAbduh, Muḥammad
Abū al-Hudhayl al-ʿAllāf
Abū Bakr
Abū Ḥanīfah
Abū Yūsuf
Afghānī, Jamāl al-Dīn al-
Ahmad Khan, Sayyid
ʿĀʾishah bint Abī Bakr
ʿAlī ibn Abī Ṭālib
ʿAlī Shīr Navāʾī
Ameer Ali, Syed
Ashʿarī, al-
ʿAṭṭār, Farīd al-Dīn
Bayḍāwī, al-
Bīrūnī, al-
Bisṭāmī, Abū Yazīd al-
Bukhārī, al-
Dārā Shikōh
Elijah Muhammad
Fārābī, al-
Fāṭimah bint Muḥammad
Ghazāli, Abū Ḥāmid al-
Gökalp, Zīyam
Ḥāfiẓ Shīrāzī
Ḥallāj, al-
Ḥasan al-Baṣrī
Ḥillī, al-
Hujwīrī, al-
Ḥusayn ibn ʿAlī, al-
Ibn ʿAbd al-Wahhāb, Muḥammad
Ibn al-ʿArabī
Ibn al-Fāriḍ
Ibn ʿAṭāʾAllāh

[6] *For additional relevant biographies, see also in part II of this outline under* The Study of Religion, *sub-section on* Scholars of Religion.

Ibn Bābawayhi
Ibn Bājjah
Ibn Ḥazm
Ibn Khaldūn
Ibn Rushd
Ibn Sīnā
Ibn Taymīyah
Ījī, ʿAḍud al-Dīn al-
Iqbal, Muhammad
Jaʿfar al-Ṣādiq
Junayd, al-
Kalābādhī, al-
Khusraw, Amīr
Kubrā, Najm al-Dīn
Lāhorī, Muḥammad ʿAlī
Majlisī, al-
Malcolm X
Mālik ibn Anas
Māturīdī, al-
Māwardī, al-
Mawdūdī, Sayyid Abū al-Aʿlā
Muḥammad
Mullā Ṣadrā
Nāṣir-i Khusraw
Naẓẓām, al-
Niẓām al-Dīn Awliyāʾ
Niẓām al-Mulk
Qāḍī al Nuʿmān
Qurrat al-ʿAyn Ṭāhirah
Qutb, Sayyid
Rābiʿah al-ʿAdawīyah
Rashīd Riḍā, Muḥammad
Rāzī, Fakhr al-Dīn al-
Rūmī, Jalāl al-Dīn
Saʿdī
Shabistarī, al-
Shāfiʿī, al-
Shahrastānī, al-
Sirhindī, Aḥmad
Suhrawardī, Shihāb al-Dīn Yaḥyā
Ṭabarī, al-
Ṭabāṭabāʾī, ʿAllāma
Taftāzānī, al-
Ṭūsī, Naṣīr al-Dīn
ʿUmar ibn al-Khaṭṭāb
Walī Allāh, Shāh
Yunus Emre
Zamakhsharī, al-
Zaynab bint ʿAlī

Israelite Religion

PRINCIPAL ARTICLE
Israelite Religion

SUPPORTING ARTICLES
Biblical Literature
Hebrew Scriptures
Biblical Temple
Ecclesiastes
God
God in the Hebrew Scriptures
Ḥokhmah
Israelite Law
An Overview
Personal Status and Family Law
Property Law
Criminal Law
State and Judiciary Law
Levites
Prophecy
Biblical Prophecy
Prophecy in Post-Biblical Judaism
Psalms
Ten Commandments
Wisdom Literature
Biblical Books [First Edition]
Biblical Books [Further Considerations]

BIBLICAL FIGURES
Aaron
Abraham
Adam
Amos
Cain and Abel
Cyrus II
Daniel
David [First Edition]
David [Further Considerations]
Elijah
Elisha
Enoch
Esther
Eve
Ezekiel
Ezra
Hosea
Isaac
Isaiah
Ishmael
Jacob
Jeremiah
Job
Jonah
Joseph
Joshua
Josiah
Micah
Miriam
Moses
Nathan
Nehemiah
Noah
Rachel and Leah
Rebecca
Ruth and Naomi
Samson
Samuel
Sarah
Saul
Solomon

Jainism

PRINCIPAL ARTICLE
Jainism

SUPPORTING ARTICLES
Ahiṃsā
Cosmology
Jain Cosmology
Ecology and Religion
Ecology and Jainism
Gender and Religion
Gender and Jainism
Jīvanmukti
Jñāna
Karman
Hindu and Jain Concepts
Mahāvīra
Tīrthaṃkaras

Japanese Religions

PRINCIPAL ARTICLES
Japanese Religions
An Overview
Popular Religion
The Study of Myths
Religious Documents

SUPPORTING ARTICLES
Ainu Religion
Amaterasu Ōmikami
Ame no Koyane
Aum Shinrikyō
Buddhism
Buddhism in Japan
Buddhism, Schools of
Japanese Buddhism
East Asian Buddhism
Buddhist Meditation
East Asian Buddhist Meditation

Bushidō
Calligraphy
  Chinese and Japanese Calligraphy
Confucianism in Japan
Domestic Observances
  Japanese Practices
Drama
  East Asian Dance and Theater
Ecology and Religion
  Ecology and Confucianism
  Ecology and Shintō
Fiction
  Japanese Fiction and Religion
Fudō
Gender and Religion
  Gender and Japanese Religions
Gozan Zen
Healing and Medicine
  Healing and Medicine in Japan
Hijiri
Honjisuijaku
Humor and Religion
  Humor and Religion in East Asian Contexts
Izanagi and Izanami
Jōdo Shinshū
Jōdoshū
Kami
Kingship
  Kingship in East Asia
Kokugaku
Konkōkyō
Kurozumikyō
Magic
  Magic in East Asia
Music
  Music and Religion in Japan
New Religious Movements
  New Religious Movements in Japan
Nichirenshū
Norito
Okinawan Religion
Ōkuninushi no Mikoto
Ōmotokyō
Onmyōdō
Orgy
  Orgy in Asia
Poetry
  Japanese Religious Poetry
Politics and Religion
  Politics and Japanese Religions
Priesthood
  Shintō Priesthood
Shingonshū
Shintō
Shugendō
Study of Religion
  The Academic Study of Religion in Japan
Susano-o no Mikoto
Temple
  Buddhist Temple Compounds in East Asia
Tendaishū
Tenrikyō
Transculturation and Religion
  Religion in the Formation of Modern Japan
Worship and Devotional Life
  Buddhist Devotional Life in East Asia
Zen

BIOGRAPHIES [7]
Anesaki Masaharu
Benchō
Dōgen
Eisai
Enchin
Ennin
En no Gyōja
Fujiwara Seika
Ganjin
Genshin
Gyōgi
Hakuin
Hayashi Razan
Hirata Atsutane
Hōnen
Ikkyū Sōjun
Ippen
Ishida Baigan
Itō Jinsai
Jien
Jimmu
Jingō
Kaibara Ekken
Kamo no Mabuchi
Keizan
Kōben
Kumazawa Banzan
Kūya
Motoori Norinaga
Musō Sōseki
Nakae Tōju
Nakayama Miki
Nanjō Bunyū
Nichiren
Nikkō
Nishida Kitarō
Ogyū Sorai
Rennyo
Saichō
Shinran
Shoku
Shotoku Taishi
Suzuki, D. T.
Yamaga Sokō
Yamato Takeru
Yamazaki Ansai

Judaism

PRINCIPAL ARTICLES[8]
Judaism
  An Overview
  Judaism in the Middle East and North Africa to 1492
  Judaism in the Middle East and North Africa since 1492
  Judaism in Northeast Africa
  Judaism in Asia
  Judaism in Northern and Eastern Europe to 1500
  Judaism in Northern and Eastern Europe since 1500
Jewish People
Jewish Studies
  Jewish Studies from 1818 to 1919
  Jewish Studies since 1919

MODERN FORMS
Conservative Judaism
Orthodox Judaism [First Edition]
Orthodox Judaism [Further Considerations]
Reconstructionist Judaism
Reform Judaism
Jewish Renewal Movement

SUPPORTING ARTICLES
Afterlife
  Jewish Concepts

[7] *For additional relevant biographies, see also in part II of this outline under* The Study of Religion, *sub-section on* Scholars of Religion.
[8] *For additional relevant entries, see also in this outline under* Israelite Religion.

Agudat Yisra'el
Amoraim
Anti-Semitism
Apocalypse
  Jewish Apocalypticism to the Rabbinic Period
  Medieval Jewish Apocalyptic Literature
Ashkenazic Hasidism
Atonement
  Jewish Concepts
Attributes of God
  Jewish Concepts
Beit Hillel and Beit Shammai
Biblical Exegesis
  Jewish Views
Biblical Literature
  Hebrew Scriptures
  Apocrypha and Pseudepigrapha
Blasphemy
  Jewish Concept
Calligraphy
  Hebrew Micrography
Chanting
Dead Sea Scrolls
Domestic Observances
  Jewish Practices
Dönmeh
Dybbuk
Ecology and Religion
  Ecology and Judaism
Essenes
Folk Religion
  Folk Judaism
Gender and Religion
  Gender and Judaism
God
  God in the Hebrew Scriptures
  God in Postbiblical Judaism
Halakhah
  History of Halakhah
  Structure of Halakhah
Hanukkah
Hasidism
  An Overview
  Habad Hasidism
  Satmar Hasidism
Healing and Medicine
  Healing and Medicine in Judaism
History
  Jewish Views
Holocaust, The
  History
  Jewish Theological Responses
Iconography
  Jewish Iconography [First Edition]
  Jewish Iconography [Further Considerations]
Jerusalem
  Jerusalem in Judaism, Christianity, and Islam
Jewish Religious Year
Jewish Thought and Philosophy
  Premodern Philosophy
  Modern Thought
  Jewish Ethical Literature
Karaites
Kashrut
Kingdom of God
Lilith
Magen David
Marranos
Merkavah Mysticism*
Messianism
  Jewish Messianism
Midrash and Aggadah [First Edition]
Midrash and Aggadah [Further Considerations]
Miqveh
Mishnah and Tosefta
Musar Movement
Music
  Music and Religion in the Middle East
  Religious Music in the West
Mystical Union in Judaism, Christianity, and Islam
Oral Torah
Orgy
  Orgy in Medieval and Modern Europe
Passover
Patriarchate
Persecution
  Jewish Experience
Pesher
Pilgrimage
  Contemporary Jewish Pilgrimage
Polemics
  Jewish-Christian Polemics
  Muslim-Jewish Polemics
Politics and Religion
  Politics and Judaism*
Priesthood
  Jewish Priesthood
Prophecy
  Biblical Prophecy
  Prophecy in Post-Biblical Judaism
Purification
  Purification in Judaism
Purim
Purim Plays
Qabbalah
Rabbinate
  The Rabbinate in Pre-Modern Judaism
  The Rabbinate in Modern Judaism
Rabbinic Judaism in Late Antiquity
Rites of Passage
  Jewish Rites
Ro'sh ha-Shanah and Yom Kippur
Sadducees
Samaritans
Sanhedrin
Sefer Yetsirah
Shabbat
Shavu'ot
Shekhinah
Siddur and Maḥzor
Soul
  Jewish Concept
Sukkot
Synagogue
Talmud
Tannaim
Tekhines
Torah
Tosafot [First Edition]
Tosafot [Further Considerations]
Tsaddiq
Wisdom Literature
  Biblical Books [First Edition]
  Biblical Books [Further Considerations]
Worship and Devotional Life
  Jewish Worship
Yeshivah
Zealots
Zekhut Avot
Zionism
Zohar

BIOGRAPHIES[9]
- Abbahu
- Abbaye
- Abravanel, Isaac
- Abulafia, Me'ir
- Adler, Felix
- Adret, Shelomoh ben Avraham
- Agnon, Shemu'el Yosef
- Albo, Yosef
- Alfasi, Yitsḥaq ben Ya'aqov
- Alkalai, Yehudah ben Shelomoh
- 'Anan ben David
- 'Aqiva' ben Yosef
- Asher ben Yeḥi'el
- Ashi
- Avraham ben David of Posquières
- Ba'al Shem Tov
- Baeck, Leo
- Baḥye ibn Paquda
- Bar-Ilan, Me''ir
- Beruryah
- Buber, Martin
- Cohen, Arthur A.
- Cohen, Hermann
- Cordovero, Mosheh
- Crescas, Ḥasdai
- Dov Ber of Mezhirich
- El'azar ben 'Azaryah
- El'azar ben Pedat
- Eli'ezer ben Hyrcanus
- Elimelekh of Lizhensk
- Elisha' ben Avuyah
- Eliyyahu ben Shelomoh Zalman
- Fackenheim, Emil
- Feinstein, Moshe
- Frank, Jacob
- Frankel, Zacharias
- Gamli'el of Yavneh
- Gamli'el the Elder
- Geiger, Abraham
- Gershom ben Yehudah
- Gersonides
- Ginzberg, Asher
- H'ai Gaon
- Heschel, Abraham Joshua
- Hildesheimer, Esriel
- Hillel
- Hirsch, Samson Raphael
- Hoffmann, David
- Holdheim, Samuel
- Huna'
- Ibn Daud, Avraham
- Ibn 'Ezra', Avraham
- Ibn Gabirol, Shelomoh
- Isserles, Mosheh
- Josephus Flavius
- Kagan, Yisra'el Me'ir
- Kalischer, Tsevi Hirsch
- Kaplan, Mordecai
- Karo, Yosef
- Kaufmann, Yeḥezkel
- Kimḥi, David
- Kohler, Kaufmann
- Kook, Avraham Yitsḥaq
- Kotler, Aharon
- Krochmal, Naḥman
- Leeser, Isaac
- Levi Yitsḥaq of Berdichev
- Luria, Isaac
- Luria, Shelomoh
- Maid of Ludmir
- Maimonides, Abraham
- Maimonides, Moses
- Malbim
- Me'ir
- Me'ir ben Barukh of Rothenburg
- Mendelssohn, Moses
- Mohilever, Shemu'el
- Montagu, Lily
- Nahmanides, Moses
- Naḥman of Bratslav
- Philo Judaeus
- Rabbah bar Nahmani
- Rashi
- Rav
- Rava'
- Reines, Yitsḥaq Ya'aqov
- Revel, Bernard
- Rosenzweig, Franz
- Sa'adyah Gaon
- Salanter, Yisra'el
- Schechter, Solomon
- Schenirer, Sarah
- Schneerson, Menachem M.
- Scholem, Gershom
- Shabbetai Tsevi [First Edition]
- Shabbetai Tsevi [Further Considerations]
- Shemu'el the Amora
- Sherira' Gaon
- Shim'on bar Yoḥ'ai
- Shim'on ben Gamli'el II
- Shim'on ben Laqish
- Shne'ur Zalman of Lyady
- Sofer, Mosheh
- Soloveitchik, Joseph Baer
- Spektor, Yitsḥaq Elḥanan
- Spinoza, Barukh
- Szold, Henrietta
- Tam, Ya'aqov ben Me'ir
- Ṭarfon
- Vital, Ḥayyim
- Wise, Isaac M.
- Wise, Stephen S.
- Wittgenstein, Ludwig
- Ya'aqov ben Asher
- Yehoshu'a ben Ḥananyah
- Yehoshu'a ben Levi
- Yehudah bar Il'ai
- Yehudah bar Yeḥezqe'l
- Yehudah ha-Levi
- Yehudah ha-Nasi'
- Yishma'e'l ben Elisha'
- Yoḥanan bar Nappaḥa'
- Yoḥanan ben Zakk'ai
- Yose ben Ḥalafta'

Korean Religion

PRINCIPAL ARTICLE
- Korean Religion

SUPPORTING ARTICLES
- Buddhism
  - Buddhism in Korea
- Buddhism, Schools of
  - East Asian Buddhism
- Ch'ŏndogyo
- Confucianism in Korea
- Drama
  - East Asian Dance and Theater
- Humor and Religion
  - Humor and Religion in East Asian Contexts
- Kingship
  - Kingship in East Asia
- Magic
  - Magic in East Asia
- Music
  - Music and Religion in China, Korea, and Tibet
- Temple
  - Buddhist Temple Compounds in East Asia
- Unification Church

[9] *For biblical figures, see in this outline under* Israelite Religion. *For additional relevant biographies, see also in part II of this outline under* The Study of Religion, *sub-section on* Scholars of Religion.

BIOGRAPHIES
Chinul
Chŏng Yagyong
Sŏ Kyŏngdŏk
Ŭich'ŏn
Ŭisang
Wŏnhyo
Yi T'oegye
Yi Yulgok

Mandaean Religion

PRINCIPAL ARTICLES
Mandaean Religion
Ginza
Manda d'Hiia

Melanesian Religions
See in this outline under Oceanic Religions.

Mesoamerican Religions

PRINCIPAL ARTICLES
Mesoamerican Religions
Pre-Columbian Religions
Formative Cultures
Classic Cultures
Postclassic Cultures
Colonial Cultures
Contemporary Cultures
Mythic Themes
History of Study

SUPPORTING ARTICLES
Aztec Religion
Ballgames
Mesoamerican Ballgames
Calendars
Mesoamerican Calendars
Coatlicue
Cosmology
Indigenous North and Mesoamerican Cosmologies
Day of the Dead
Drama
Mesoamerican Dance and Drama
Fiction
Latin American Fiction and Religion
Funeral Rites
Mesoamerican Funeral Rites
Gender and Religion
Gender and Mesoamerican Religions
Huichol Religion
Huitzilopochtli
Human Sacrifice
Aztec Rites
Iconography
Mesoamerican Iconography
Inquisition, The
The Inquistion in the New World
Kingship
Kingship in Mesoamerica and South America
Law and Religion
Law and Religion in Indigenous Cultures
Maximón
Maya Religion
Music
Music and Religion in Mesoamerica
Nahuatl Religion
New Religious Movements
New Religious Movements in Latin America
Olmec Religion
Otomí Religion
Quetzalcoatl
Rites of Passage
Mesoamerican Rites
Tarascan Religion
Temple
Mesoamerican Temples
Tezcatlipoca
Tlaloc
Tlaxcalan Religion
Toltec Religion
Totonac Religion
Tricksters
Mesoamerican and South American Tricksters
Zapatismo and Indigenous Resistance

Mesopotamian Religions

PRINCIPAL ARTICLES
Mesopotamian Religions
An Overview [First Edition]
An Overview [Further Considerations]
History of Study

SUPPORTING ARTICLES
Adad
Akitu
An
Ashur
Atrahasis
Drama
Ancient Near Eastern Ritual Drama [First Edition]
Ancient Near Eastern Ritual Drama [Further Considerations]
Dumuzi
Enki
Enlil
Enuma Elish
Gender and Religion
Gender and Ancient Near Eastern Religions
Gilgamesh
Goddess Worship
Goddess Worship in the Ancient Near East
Healing and Medicine
Healing and Medicine in the Ancient Near East
Iconography
Mesopotamian Iconography
Inanna
Kingship
Kingship in the Ancient Mediterranean World
Marduk
Nabu
Nanna
Nergal
Ninhursaga
Ninurta
Soul
Ancient Near Eastern Concepts
Temple
Ancient Near Eastern and Mediterranean Temples
Utu

Micronesian Religions
See in this outline under Oceanic Religions.

Mongol Religions
See in this outline under Altaic Religions.

Native American Religions
See in this outline under North American Indian Religions, Mesoamerican Religions, and South American Indian Religions.
See also Caribbean Religions.

New Religious Movements

PRINCIPAL ARTICLES

New Religious Movements
- An Overview
- History of Study
- Scriptures of New Religious Movements
- New Religious Movements and Women
- New Religious Movements and Children
- New Religious Movements and Millennialism
- New Religious Movements and Violence
- New Religious Movements in the United States
- New Religious Movements in Europe
- New Religious Movements in Japan
- New Religious Movements in Latin America

SUPPORTING ARTICLES

African Religions
- New Religious Movements

African American Religions
- Muslim Movements

Anthroposophy
Anticult Movements
Association for Research and Enlightenment
Ārya Samāj
Aum Shinrikyō
Australian Indigenous Religions
- New Religious Movements

Bahā'īs
Baltic Religion
- New Religious Movements

Brāhmo Samāj
Brainwashing (Debate)
Branch Davidians
Buddhism
- Buddhism in the West

Cao Dai
Cargo Cults [First Edition]
Cargo Cults [Further Considerations]
Charisma
Ch'ŏndogyo
Christian Identity Movement
Christian Science
Church Universal and Triumphant
Ciji
Civil Religion
Cults and Sects
Deprogramming
Dhammakāya Movement
Earth First!
Eckankar
Esotericism
Ethical Culture
Falun Gong
Family, The
Foguangshan
Freemasons
Ghost Dance
Grail Movement
Healing and Medicine
- Alternative Medicine in the New Age

Healthy, Happy, Holy Organization (3HO)
Heaven's Gate
Hermetism
Holy Order of MANS
I Am
International Society for Krishna Consciousness
Jamā'at-i Islāmī
Jehovah's Witnesses
Jesus Movement
Jonestown and Peoples Temple
Law and Religion
- Law and New Religious Movements

Maximón
Mesoamerican Religions
- Contemporary Cultures

Mormonism
Movement for the Restoration of the Ten Commandments of God
Muslim Brotherhood
Nation of Islam
Native American Church*
Neopaganism
New Age Movement
New Thought Movement
North American Indian Religions
- New Religious Movements

Nuwaubians
Oceanic Religions
- Missionary Movements
- New Religious Movements

Occultism
Point Loma Theosophical Community
Raëlians
Rastafarianism
Reiyūkai Kyōdan
Risshō Kōseikai
Rites of Passage
- Neopagan Rites

Sai Baba Movement
Satanism
Scientology
Seventh-day Adventism
Shakers
Shamanism
- Neoshamanism

Sōka Gakkai
Southeast Asian Religions
- New Religious Movements in Insular Cultures

Spiritualism
Swaminarayan Movement
Swedenborgianism
Temple Solaire
Theosophical Society
Transcendental Meditation
Twelve Tribes
UFO Religions
Unarius Academy of Science
Unification Church
Unity
Wicca
World's Parliament of Religions

BIOGRAPHIES[10]

Ambedkar, B. R.
Aurobindo Ghose
Bennett, John G.
Besant, Annie
Bhave, Vinoba
Blavatsky, H. P.
Cayce, Edgar
Crowley, Aleister
Daddy Grace
Dan Fodio, Usuman
Dayananda Sarasvati
Eddy, Mary Baker

[10]*For additional relevant biographies, see also in part II of this outline under* The Study of Religion, *sub-section on* Scholars of Religion.

Elijah Muḥammad
Father Divine
Fillmore, Charles and Myrtle
Gage, Matilda Joslyn
Gandhi, Mohandas
Gurdjieff, G. I.
Harris, William Wade
Hopkins, Emma Curtis
Hubbard, L. Ron
Jones, Jim
Judge, William Q.
Kimbangu, Simon
King, Martin Luther, Jr.
Koresh, David
Krishnamurti, Jiddu
Lee, Ann
Lenshina, Alice
Malalasekera, G. P.
Malcolm X
Maranke, John
Mawdūdī, Sayyid Abū al-Aʿlā
Meher Baba
Muḥammad Aḥmad
Nakayama Miki
Neolin
Olcott, Henry Steel
Ouspensky, P. D.
Prabhupada, A. C. Bhaktivedanta
Prophet, Mark and Elizabeth Clare
Radhakrishnan, Sarvepalli
Rajneesh
Ramakrishna
Ramakrishna [Further Considerations]*
Roy, Ram Mohan
Sen, Keshab Chandra
Shembe, Isaiah
Smith, Joseph
Steiner, Rudolf
Swedenborg, Emanuel
Tagore, Rabindranath
Tilak, Bal Gangadhar
Tingley, Katherine
ʿUmar Tāl
Vivekananda
Vivekananda [Further Considerations]*
White, Ellen Gould
Wovoka
Yogananda

Norse Religion
See in this outline under Germanic Religion.

North American Indian Religions

PRINCIPAL ARTICLES
North American Indian Religions
An Overview
Mythic Themes
New Religious Movements
History of Study
North American Indians
Indians of the Far North
Indians of the Northeast Woodlands
Indians of the Southeast Woodlands
Indians of the Plains
Indians of the Northwest Coast [First Edition]
Indians of the Northwest Coast [Further Considerations]
Indians of California and the Intermountain Region
Indians of the Southwest

SUPPORTING ARTICLES
Anishinaabe Religious Traditions
Apache Religious Traditions
Athapaskan Religious Traditions
An Overview
Athapaskan Concepts of Wind and Power
Ballgames
North American Indian Ballgames
Black Elk
Blackfeet Religious Traditions
Cherokee Religious Traditions
Cosmology
Indigenous North and Mesoamerican Cosmologies
Deloria, Ella Cara
Drama
North American Indian Dance and Drama
Ecology and Religion
Ecology and Indigenous Traditions
Fiction
Native American Fiction and Religion
Gardens
Gardens in Indigenous Traditions
Gender and Religion
Gender and North American Indian Religious Traditions
Ghost Dance
Haida Religious Traditions
Handsome Lake
Iconography
Native North American Iconography
Inuit Religious Traditions
Iroquois Religious Traditions
Lakota Religious Traditions
Law and Religion
Law and Religion in Indigenous Cultures
Manitou
Masks
Native American Christianities
Native American Church*
Native American Science
Navajo Religious Traditions
Neolin
Nez Perce (Niimíipuu) Religious Traditions
Osage Religious Traditions
Poetry
Native American Poetry and Religion
Politics and Religion
Politics and Native American Religious Traditions
Potlatch
Rites of Passage
North American Indian Rites*
Shamanism
North American Shamanism
Soul
Concepts in Indigenous Religions
Sun Dance [First Edition]
Sun Dance [Further Considerations]
Tecumseh
Tomol
Tricksters
North American Tricksters [First Edition]
North American Tricksters [Further Considerations]
Vision Quest
White Buffalo Calf Woman
Wovoka

Oceanic Religions

PRINCIPAL ARTICLES

Oceanic Religions
An Overview
Missionary Movements
New Religious Movements
History of Study [First Edition]
History of Study [Further Considerations]
Melanesian Religions
An Overview
Mythic Themes
Micronesian Religions
An Overview
Mythic Themes
Polynesian Religions
An Overview
Mythic Themes

SUPPORTING ARTICLES

Afterlife
Oceanic Concepts
Atua
Cargo Cults [First Edition]
Cargo Cults [Further Considerations]
Christianity
Christianity in the Pacific Islands [First Edition]
Christianity in the Pacific Islands [Further Considerations]
Cosmology
Oceanic Cosmologies
Ecology and Religion
Ecology and Indigenous Traditions
Fiction
Oceanic Fiction and Religion
Gardens
Gardens in Indigenous Traditions
Gender and Religion
Gender and Oceanic Religions
Hawaiian Religion
Law and Religion
Law and Religion in Indigenous Cultures
Mana
Maori Religion [First Edition]
Maori Religion [Further Considerations]
Masks
Māui
Music
Music and Religion in Oceania
New Caledonia Religion
New Guinea Religions [First Edition]
New Guinea Religions [Further Considerations]
Politics and Religion
Politics and Oceanic Religions
Rites of Passage
Oceanic Rites
Solomon Islands Religions
Soul
Concepts in Indigenous Religions
Southeast Asian Religions
Insular Cultures
Study of Religion
The Academic Study of Religion in Australia and Oceania
Taboo
Tangaroa
Tikopia Religion
Transculturation and Religion
Religion and the Formation of Modern Oceania
Vanuatu Religions

Polynesian Religions

See in this outline under
Oceanic Religions.

Prehistoric Religions

PRINCIPAL ARTICLES

Prehistoric Religions
An Overview
Old Europe
The Eurasian Steppes and Inner Asia

SUPPORTING ARTICLES

Megalithic Religion
Prehistoric Evidence
Neolithic Religion
Paleolithic Religion

Roman Religion

PRINCIPAL ARTICLES

Roman Religion
The Early Period
The Imperial Period

SUPPORTING ARTICLES

Afterlife
Greek and Roman Concepts
Apotheosis
Arval Brothers
Augustus
Cicero
Dea Dia
Diana
Divination
Greek and Roman Divination
Emperor's Cult
Fasti
Fides
Flamen
Fortuna
Gender and Religion
Gender and Ancient Mediterranean Religions
Goddess Worship
Goddess Worship in the Hellenistic World
Healing and Religion
Healing and Medicine in Greece and Rome
Hellenistic Religions
Herakles
Iconography
Greco-Roman Iconography
Iupiter Dolichenus
Janus
Juno
Jupiter
Lares
Law and Religion
Law and Religion in the Ancient Mediterranean World
Ludi Saeculares
Lupercalia
Lustratio
Magic
Magic in Greco-Roman Antiquity
Manichaeism
Manichaeism in the Roman Empire
Mars
Minerva
Music
Music and Religion in Greece, Rome, and Byzantium
Mystery Religions
Numen

Orgy
Orgy in the Ancient Mediterranean World
Orphic Gold Tablets
Parentalia
Penates
Politics and Religion
Politics and Ancient Mediterranean Religions
Pontifex
Priapus
Quirinus
Sibylline Oracles
Sol Invictus
Temple
Ancient Near Eastern and Mediterranean Temples
Venus
Vergil
Vesta

RELATED ARTICLES
Indo-European Religions
An Overview
History of Study

Śaivism
See in this outline under Hinduism.

Scandinavian Religion
See in this outline under Germanic Religion.

Shintō
See in this outline under Japanese Religions.

Siberian Religions
See in this outline under Arctic Religions and Inner Asian Religions.

Sikhism

PRINCIPAL ARTICLE
Sikhism

SUPPORTNG ARTICLES
Ādi Granth
Dasam Granth
Gender and Religion
Gender and Sikhism
Gurū Granth Sāhib
Healthy, Happy, Holy Organization (3HO)
Hindi Religious Traditions
Nānak
Poetry
Indian Religious Poetry
Singh, Gobind

Slavic Religion

PRINCIPAL ARTICLE
Slavic Religion

SUPPORTING ARTICLES
Baba Yaga
Dazhbog
Mokosh
Perun
Sventovit
Triglav
Veles-Volos

RELATED ARTICLES
Indo-European Religions
An Overview
History of Study

South American Indian Religions

PRINCIPAL ARTICLES
South American Indian Religions
An Overview
Mythic Themes
History of Study
South American Indians
Indians of the Andes in the Pre-Inca Period
Indians of the Colonial Andes
Indians of the Modern Andes
Indians of the Northwest Amazon
Indians of the Central and Eastern Amazon
Indians of the Gran Chaco

SUPPORTING ARTICLES
Afro-Brazilian Religions
Atahuallpa
Bochica
Calendars
South American Calendars
Cosmology
South American Cosmologies
Ethnoastronomy
Fiction
Latin American Fiction and Religion
Ge Mythology
Gender and Religion
Gender and South American Religions
Inca Religion
Inquisition, The
The Inquistion in the New World
Inti
Kingship
Kingship in Mesoamerica and South America
Manco Capac and Mama Ocllo
Mapuche Religion
Masks
Messianism
South American Messianism
Muisca Religion
Music
Music and Religion in South America
New Religious Movements
New Religious Movements in Latin America
Selk'nam Religion
Shamanism
South American Shamanism
Tehuelche Religion
Viracocha
Warao Religion
Yurupary

Southeast Asian Religions

PRINCIPAL ARTICLES
Southeast Asian Religions
History of Study
Mainland Cultures
Insular Cultures
New Religious Movements in Insular Cultures

SUPPORTING ARTICLES
Acehnese Religion
Balinese Religion
Batak Religion
Bornean Religions
Buddhadāsa
Buddhism
Buddhism in Southeast Asia
Bugis Religion
Burmese Religion
Cao Dai
Dhammakāya Movement

Drama
  Balinese Dance and Dance Drama
  Javanese Wayang
Fiction
  Southeast Asian Fiction and Religion
Hinduism in Southeast Asia
Islam
  Islam in Southeast Asia
Javanese Religion
Khmer Religion
Lao Religion
Music
  Music and Religion in Southeast Asia
Nats
Negrito Religions
  An Overview
  Negritos of the Philippine Islands
  Negritos of the Andaman Islands
  Negritos of the Malay Peninsula
Orgy
  Orgy in Asia
Saṃgha
  Saṃgha and Society in South and Southeast Asia
Sundanese Religion
Temple
  Buddhist Temple Compounds in Southeast Asia
Thai Religion
Toraja Religion
U Nu
Vietnamese Religion
Worship and Devotional Life
  Buddhist Devotional Life in Southeast Asia

Thracian Religion

PRINCIPAL ARTICLES
Thracian Religion
Geto-Dacian Religion

SUPPORTING ARTICLES
Bendis
Dacian Riders
Sabazios
Thracian Rider
Zalmoxis

RELATED ARTICLES
Indo-European Religions
  An Overview
  History of Study

Tibetan Religions

PRINCIPAL ARTICLES
Tibetan Religions
  An Overview
  History of Study
Bon

SUPPORTING ARTICLES
Avalokiteśvara
Buddhism
  Buddhism in Tibet
Buddhism, Schools of
  Tantric Ritual Schools of Buddhism [First Edition]
  Tantric Ritual Schools of Buddhism [Further Considerations]
  Tibetan and Mongolian Buddhism
  Himalayan Buddhism
Buddhist Meditation
  Tibetan Buddhist Meditation
Cakrasamvara
Chanting
Dalai Lama
Dzogchen
Gesar
Healing and Medicine
  Healing and Medicine in Tibet
Kālacakra
Karma pas
Kingship
  Kingship in East Asia
Magic
  Magic in East Asia
Mahāmudrā
Merit
  Buddhist Concepts
Music
  Music and Religion in China, Korea and Tibet
Orgy
  Orgy in Asia
Pilgrimage
  Tibetan Pilgrimage
Rnying ma pa (Nyingmapa) School
Saṃgha
  Saṃgha and Society in Tibet
Shugs ldan (Shugden)
Tantrism
  An Overview
Temple
  Buddhist Temple Compounds in Tibet
Treasure Tradition
Worship and Devotional Life
  Buddhist Devotional Life in Tibet

BIOGRAPHIES
Ani Lochen
Atīśa
Bu ston
Klong chen rab 'byams pa (Longchenpa)
Kong sprul blo gros mtha' yas (Kongtrul Lodro Taye)
Ma gcig lab sgron (Machig Labdron)
Mar pa
Mi la ras pa (Milarepa)
Nā ro pa
Padmasambhava
Sakya Paṇḍita (Sa skya Paṇḍita)
Sgam po pa (Gampopa)
Tsong kha pa
Ye shes Mtsho rgyal (Yeshe Tsogyal)

Turkic Religions

See in this outline under Altaic Religions.

Uralic Religions

PRINCIPAL ARTICLES
Finno-Ugric Religions
  An Overview
  History of Study
Samoyed Religion

SUPPORTING ARTICLES
Finnish Religions
Hungarian Religion
Ilmarinen
Karelian Religion
Khanty and Mansi Religion
Komi Religion
Lemminkäinen
Lönnrot, Elias
Mari and Mordvin Religion
Num-Tūrem
Sami Religion
Tuonela
Ukko
Väinämöinen

Vaiṣṇavism
See in this outline under Hinduism.

Vedism and Brahamanism
See in this outline under Hinduism.

Zoroastrianism

PRINCIPAL ARTICLE
Zoroastrianism

SUPPORTING ARTICLES
Ahura Mazdā and Angra Mainyu
Ahuras
Airyana Vaējah
Amesha Spentas
Anāhitā
Ateshgah
Avesta
Chinvat Bridge
Daivas
Dakhma
Frashōkereti
Fravashis
Gender and Religion
Gender and Zoroastrianism
Haoma
Khvarenah
Magi
Parsis
Saoshyant
Yazatas
Zarathushtra

RELATED ARTICLES
Indo-European Religions
An Overview
History of Study
Iranian Religions

II. RELIGIOUS STUDIES

Part II of this outline presents the Encyclopedia's coverage of thematic topics in religion and the study of religion. It is organized according to the following scheme:

Religious Phenomena

Art, Science, and Society
Art and Religion
Science and Religion
Society and Religion

The Study of Religion
History of Study
Methods of Study
Philosophy and Religion
Scholarly Terms
Scholars of Religion

In the first two sections, Religious Phenomena *and* Art, Science, and Society, *are listed entries that present results from the scholarly study of religion. In the third section,* The Study of Religion, *are listed entries that focus attention on the history and techniques of religious studies themselves.*

Religious Phenomena

Here are listed thematic entries that concern objects, practices, beliefs, and motifs that are observable in numerous religious traditions.

Ablutions
Affliction
An Overview
Afterlife
An Overview
Geographies of Death
Ages of the World
Agriculture
Alchemy
An Overview
Almsgiving
Alphabets
Altar
Amulets and Talismans
Anamnesis
Ancestors
Ancestor Worship
Mythic Ancestors
Anchor
Androgynes
Angels
Animals
Apocalypse
An Overview
Apologetics
Apostasy
Ascension
Ashes
Astrology
Attention
Baptism
Baths
Bears
Beauty
Beverages
Binding
Birds
Birth
Blades
Blessing
Blood
Boats
Bodily Marks
Bones
Bread
Breath and Breathing
Bridges
Bull-Roarers
Calendars
An Overview
Cannibalism
Canon
Cards
Carnival
Castration
Casuistry
Cats
Cattle
Caves
Celibacy
Chance
Chaos
Charity
Chastity
Child
Chronology
Circle
Circumambulation
Circumcision
Cities
Clitoridectomy
Clothing
Clothing and Religion in the East
Clothing and Religion in the West
Clowns
Cocks
Codes and Codification
Colors
Confession of Sins
Conscience
Consciousness, States of
Consecration
Covenant
Creeds
An Overview
Crossroads
Crown

Cursing
Death
Demons
  An Overview
  Psychological Perspectives
Descent into the Underworld
Deserts
Desire
Devils
Devotion
Diamond
Dismemberment
Divination
  An Overview
Doctrine
Dogs
Doubleness
Dragons
Dreams
Drums
Eagles and Hawks
Earth
Ecstasy
Egg
Election
Elephants
Elixir
Enlightenment
Eremitism
Eternity
Evil
Exile
Exorcism
Expulsion
Eye
Fairies
Faith
Fall, The
Family
Fasting
Fate
Feet
Fire
Fish
Flight
Flood, The
Flowers
Food
Fountain
Foxes
Frogs and Toads
Funeral Rites
  An Overview
Gambling
Games
Gardens
  An Overview
Genealogy
Geography
Geomancy
Geometry
Ghosts
Gift Giving
Glossolalia
Goddess Worship
  An Overview
Gods and Goddesses
Gold and Silver
Golden Age
Golden Rule
Good, The
Gurū
Hair
Hands
Head
  Symbolism and Ritual Use
Healing and Medicine
  An Overview
Heart
Heaven and Hell
Hedgehogs
Heroes
Hierodouleia
Historiography
  An Overview
Home
Homosexuality
Hope
Horns
Horses
Hospitality
Human Body
  Myths and Symbolism
  Human Bodies, Religion, and Gender
  Human Bodies, Religion, and Art
Human Sacrifice
  An Overview
Humor and Religion
  An Overview
Idolatry
Images
  Veneration of Images
  Images, Icons, and Idols
Incantation
Incarnation
Incense
Initiation
  An Overview
  Men's Initiation
  Women's Initiation
Insects
Inspiration
Jade
Jaguars
Judgment of the Dead
Keys
Kingdom of God
Kingship
  An Overview
Kinship
Knees
Knots
Knowledge and Ignorance
Labyrinth
Lakes
Laity
Language
  Sacred Language
Leaven
Lesbianism
Left and Right
Libation
Liberation
Life
Light and Darkness
Liminality
Lions
Lotus
Marriage
Martial Arts
  An Overview
Martyrdom
Masks
Meditation
  An Overview
Memorization
Mendicancy
Menstruation
Merit
  An Overview
Metals and Metallurgy
Miracles
  An Overview
Mirrors
Missions
  Missionary Activity
Monasticism
  An Overview
Money
Monkeys

Monsters
Moon
Mortification
Mountains
Mystical Union in Judaism, Christianity, and Islam
Names and Naming
Necromancy
New Year Festivals
Nimbus
Nonviolence
Nudity
Numbers
  An Overview
  Binary Symbolism
Nuns
  An Overview
Obedience
Oceans
Omophagia
Oracles
Ordeal
Ordination
Orgy
  An Overview
Otherworld
Owls
Pain
Parables and Proverbs
Paradise
Paradox and Riddles
Patriarchy and Matriarchy
Peace
Pearl
Performance and Ritual
Phallus and Vagina
Pigs
Pilgrimage
  An Overview
Portals
Portents and Prodigies
Postures and Gestures
Prayer
Priesthood
  An Overview
Procession
Prophecy
  An Overview
Psychedelic Drugs
Purification
  An Overview
Quaternity
Quests
Rabbits
Rain
Redemption
Reincarnation
Rejuvenation
Relics
Religious Communities
  Religion, Community, and Society
Religious Education
Repentance
Resurrection
Retreat
Revelation
Revenge and Retribution
Rivers
Sacrifice [First Edition]
Sacrifice [Further Considerations]
Sainthood
Salt
Salutations
Sanctuary
Satan
Sati
Scapegoat
Scripture
Sexuality
  An Overview [First Edition]
  An Overview [Further Considerations]
Shamanism
  An Overview [First Edition]
  An Overview [Further Considerations]
Shape Shifting
Sheep and Goats
Shrines
Sin and Guilt
Sky
  The Heavens as Hierophany
  Myths and Symbolism
Sleep
Smoking
Snakes
Spells
Spirit Possession
  An Overview
  Women and Possession
Spiritual Discipline
Spirituality
Spittle and Spitting
Stars
Stones
Suffering
Suicide
Sun
Swans
Tears
Temptation
Tobacco
Touching
Transmigration
Trees
Triads
Truth
Turtles and Tortoises
Twins
  An Overview
Underworld
Vegetation
Violence
Virginity
Visions
Vocation
Vows and Oaths
War and Warriors
  An Overview
Water
Webs and Nets
Wisdom
Wolves
Work
Yoni

Art, Science, and Society
The next three sub-sections of this outline list entries that address religion in relation to, respectively, art, science, and society.

Art and Religion
PRINCIPAL ARTICLE
Art and Religion
SUPPORTING ARTICLES
Aesthetics
  Philosophical Aesthetics
  Visual Aesthetics
Architecture
Autobiography
Basilica, Cathedral, and Church
Beauty
Biography
Bodily Marks
Calligraphy
  An Overview
  Chinese and Japanese Calligraphy

- Hebrew Micrography
- Islamic Calligraphy

Caves
Chanting
Clothing
- Clothing and Religion in the East
- Clothing and Religion in the West
- Dress and Religion in America's Sectarian Communities

Colors
Dance
- Dance and Religion
- Popular and Folk Dance [First Edition]
- Popular and Folk Dance [Further Considerations]
- Theatrical and Liturgical Dance [First Edition]
- Theatrical and Liturgical Dance [Further Considerations]

Drama
- Drama and Religion
- Ancient Near Eastern Ritual Drama [First Edition]
- Ancient Near Eastern Ritual Drama [Further Considerations]
- Middle Eastern Narrative Traditions
- Indian Dance and Dance Drama
- Balinese Dance and Dance Drama
- Javanese Wayang
- East Asian Dance and Theater
- African Religious Drama
- North American Indian Dance and Drama
- Mesoamerican Dance and Drama
- European Religious Drama [First Edition]
- European Religious Drama [Further Considerations]
- Modern Western Theater

Drums
Epics
Fiction
- History of the Novel
- The Western Novel and Religion
- Latin American Fiction and Religion
- Chinese Fiction and Religion
- Japanese Fiction and Religion
- South Asian Fiction and Religion*
- Southeast Asian Fiction and Religion
- Australian Fiction and Religion
- Oceanic Fiction and Religion
- African Fiction and Religion
- Native American Fiction and Religion

Film and Religion
Gardens
- An Overview
- Gardens in Indigenous Traditions
- Islamic Gardens

Human Body
- Myths and Symbolism
- Human Bodies, Religion, and Art

Iconoclasm
- An Overview
- Iconoclasm in the Byzantine Tradition

Iconography
- Iconography as Visible Religion [First Edition]
- Iconography as Visible Religion [Further Considerations]
- Traditional African Iconography
- Australian Aboriginal Iconography
- Native North American Iconography
- Mesoamerican Iconography
- Mesopotamian Iconography
- Egyptian Iconography
- Greco-Roman Iconography
- Hindu Iconography
- Buddhist Iconography
- Daoist Iconography
- Confucian Iconography
- Jewish Iconography [First Edition]
- Jewish Iconography [Further Considerations]
- Christian Iconography
- Islamic Iconography

Icons
Idolatry
Images
- Veneration of Images
- Images, Icons, and Idols

Law and Religion
- Law, Religion, and Literature

Literature[11]
- Literature and Religion
- Religious Dimensions of Modern Western Literature [First Edition]
- Religious Dimensions of Modern Western Literature [Further Considerations]
- Critical Theory and Religious Studies

Masks
Monastery
Mosque
- Architectural Aspects

Museums and Religion
Music
- Music and Religion
- Music and Religion in Sub-Saharan Africa
- Music and Religion in Indigenous Australia
- Music and Religion in Oceania
- Music and Religion in Mesoamerica
- Music and Religion in South America
- Music and Religion in the Middle East
- Music and Religion in India
- Music and Religion in Southeast Asia
- Music and Religion in China, Korea, and Tibet
- Music and Religion in Japan
- Music and Religion in Greece, Rome, and Byzantium
- Religious Music in the West

Percussion and Noise
Performance and Ritual
Play

[11] *For the religious literatures of various traditions, see in part I of this outline under the names of specific religious traditions.*

Poetry
- Poetry and Religion
- Indian Religious Poetry
- Chinese Religious Poetry
- Japanese Religious Poetry
- Christian Poetry
- Islamic Poetry
- Native American Poetry and Religion

Portals
Postures and Gestures
Purim Plays
Pyramids
- An Overview
- Egyptian Pyramids

Sacred Space
Sacred Time
Shrines
Synagogue
Ta'ziyah
Temple
- Hindu Temples
- Buddhist Temple Compounds in South Asia
- Buddhist Temple Compounds in East Asia
- Buddhist Temple Compounds in Tibet
- Buddhist Temple Compounds in Southeast Asia
- Daoist Temple Compounds
- Confucian Temple Compounds
- Ancient Near Eastern and Mediterranean Temples
- Mesoamerican Temples

Textiles
Tombs
Towers
Visual Culture and Religion
- An Overview
- Outsider Art

Science and Religion

PRINCIPAL ARTICLE

Science and Religion

SUPPORTING ARTICLES

Anthropology, Ethnology, and Religion
Archaeology and Religion
Artificial Intelligence
Bioethics
Chaos Theory
Copernicus, Nicolaus
Cosmology
- Scientific Cosmologies

Cybernetics
Ecology and Religion
- Science, Religion, and Ecology

Einstein, Albert
Ethnoastronomy
Euclid
Eugenics
Evolution
- The Controversy with Creationism
- Evolutionism
- Evolutionary Ethics

Gaia
Galen
Galileo Galilei
Genetics and Religion
Geometry
Healing and Medicine
- An Overview
- Healing and Medicine in Africa
- Healing and Medicine in the African Diaspora
- Healing and Medicine in the Ancient Near East
- Healing and Medicine in Judaism
- Healing and Medicine in Islamic Texts and Traditions
- Popular Healing Practices in Middle Eastern Cultures
- Healing and Medicine in Greece and Rome
- Healing and Medicine in Christianity
- Alternative Medicine in the New Age
- Healing and Medicine in Ayurveda and South Asia
- Healing and Medicine in China
- Healing and Medicine in Tibet
- Healing and Medicine in Japan
- Healing and Medicine in Indigenous Australia

Health and Religion
Hippocrates
Intelligent Design
Kepler, Johannes
Magic
- Theories of Magic

Medical Ethics
Native American Science
Neuroscience and Religion
- An Overview
- Neuroepistemology
- Neurotheology

Newton, Isaac
Numbers
- An Overview
- Binary Symbolism

Paracelsus
Physics and Religion
Psychology
- Psychology of Religion
- Psychotherapy and Religion
- Schizoanalysis and Religion

Ptolemy
Sociobiology and Evolutionary Psychology
- An Overview
- Darwinism and Religion

Sociology
- Sociology and Religion [First Edition]
- Sociology and Religion [Further Considerations]
- Sociology of Religion [First Edition]
- Sociology of Religion [Further Considerations]

Two Books, The

Society and Religion

PRINCIPAL ARTICLES

Society and Religion [First Edition]
Society and Religion [Further Considerations]

SUPPORTING ARTICLES

Authority
Ceremony
Charisma
Cities
Civil Religion
Community
Conversion
Cults and Sects
Ecology and Religion
- An Overview
- Ecology and Indigenous Traditions
- Ecology and Hinduism
- Ecology and Jainism
- Ecology and Buddhism
- Ecology and Confucianism
- Ecology and Daoism

Ecology and Shintō
Ecology and Judaism
Ecology and Christianity
Ecology and Islam
Environmental Ethics, World Religions, and Ecology
Science, Religion, and Ecology
Ecology and Nature Religions
Economics and Religion
Engaged Buddhism
Folk Religion
An Overview
Functionalism
Gender Roles
Gender and Religion
An Overview
History of Study
Gender and Hinduism
Gender and Jainism
Gender and Buddhism
Gender and Sikhism
Gender and Chinese Religions
Gender and Japanese Religions
Gender and Judaism
Gender and Christianity
Gender and Islam
Gender and Zoroastrianism
Gender and Ancient Near Eastern Religions
Gender and Ancient Mediterranean Religions
Gender and Celtic Religions
Gender and Australian Indigenous Religions
Gender and Oceanic Religions
Gender and African Religious Traditions
Gender and African American Religions*
Gender and North American Indian Religious Traditions
Gender and Mesoamerican Religions
Gender and South American Religions
Globalization and Religion
Health and Religion
Human Rights and Religion
Humor and Religion
An Overview
Humor and Religion in East Asian Contexts
Humor and Religion in Islam
Humor, Irony, and the Comic in Western Theology and Philosophy
Implicit Religion
Intellectuals
Invisible Religion
Journalism and Religion
Law and Religion
An Overview
Law and Religion in the Ancient Mediterranean World
Law and Religion in Medieval Europe
Law and Religion in Indigenous Cultures
Law and Religion in Hinduism
Law and Religion in Buddhism
Law and Religion in Chinese Religions
Law, Religion, and Literature
Law, Religion, and Critical Theory
Law, Religion, and Human Rights
Law, Religion, and Morality
Law, Religion, and Punishment
Law and New Religious Movements
Leadership
Legitimation
Media and Religion
Modernity
Migration and Religion
Morality and Religion
Museums and Religion
New Religious Movements
An Overview
History of Study
Scriptures of New Religious Movements
New Religious Movements and Women
New Religious Movements and Children
New Religious Movements and Millenialism
New Religious Movements and Violence
New Religious Movements in the United States
New Religious Movements in Europe
New Religious Movements in Japan
New Religious Movements in Latin America
Politics and Religion
An Overview
Politics and Buddhism
Politics and Chinese Religion
Politics and Japanese Religions
Politics and Ancient Mediterranean Religions
Politics and Judaism*
Politics and Christianity
Politics and Islam
Politics and African Religious Traditions
Politics and Oceanic Religions
Politics and Native American Religious Traditions
Popular Culture
Popular Religion
Religious Broadcasting
Religious Communities
Religion, Community, and Society
Religious Diversity
Revival and Renewal
Revolution
Rites of Passage
An Overview [First Edition]
An Overview [Further Considerations]
African Rites
Oceanic Rites
North American Indian Rites*
Mesoamerican Rites
Hindu Rites
Jewish Rites
Muslim Rites
Neopagan Rites
Ritual [First Edition]
Ritual [Further Considerations]
Secret Societies
Secularization
Sociology
Sociology and Religion [First Edition]
Sociology and Religion [Further Considerations]
Sociology of Religion [First Edition]
Sociology of Religion [Further Considerations]
Sports and Religion
Tourism and Religion

Tradition
Transculturation and Religion
An Overview
Religion in the Formation of the Modern United States*
Religion in the Formation of Modern Canada
Religion in the Formation of the Modern Caribbean
Religion in the Formation of Modern Japan
Religion in the Formation of Modern India
Religion and the Formation of Modern Oceania
Utopia
Visual Culture and Religion
An Overview
Outsider Art
Wealth

The Study of Religion

The final five sub-sections of this outline list entries that examine disciplinary, methodological, speculative, and theoretical issues in the study of religion as well as entries that report on the people who have formed that study.

History of Study

PRINCIPAL ARTICLES

Study of Religion
An Overview
The Academic Study of Religion in Australia and Oceania
The Academic Study of Religion in China*
The Academic Study of Relgion in Eastern Europe and Russia
The Academic Study of Religion in Japan
The Academic Study of Religion in North Africa and the Middle East
The Academic Study of Religion in North America
The Academic Study of Religion in South Asia
The Academic Study of Religion in Sub-Saharan Africa
The Academic Study of Religion in Western Europe*

SUPPORTING ARTICLES

African Religions
History of Study
African American Religions
History of Study
Arctic Religions
History of Study
Australian Indigenous Religions
History of Study [First Edition]
History of Study [Further Considerations]
Baltic Religion
History of Study
Buddhist Studies
Caribbean Religions
History of Study*
Chinese Religion
History of Study
Confucianism
History of Study
Daoism
History of Study
Egyptian Religion
History of Study
Finno-Ugric Religions
History of Study
Gender and Religion
History of Study
Germanic Religion
History of Study
Gnosticism
History of Study
Indian Religions
History of Study
Indo-European Religions
History of Study
Islamic Studies [First Edition]
Islamic Studies [Further Considerations]
Japanese Religions
The Study of Myths
Jewish Studies
Jewish Studies from 1818 to 1919
Jewish Studies since 1919
Mesoamerican Religions
History of Study
Mesopotamian Religions
History of Study
New Religious Movements
History of Study
North American Indian Religions
History of Study
Oceanic Religions
History of Study [First Edition]
History of Study [Further Considerations]
South American Indian Religions
History of Study
Southeast Asian Religions
History of Study
Tibetan Religions
History of Study

Methods of Study

Anthropology, Ethnology, and Religion
Archaeology and Religion
Classification of Religions
Comparative-Historical Method [First Edition]
Comparative-Historical Method [Further Considerations]
Comparative Mythology
Comparative Religion
Deconstruction
Ecology and Religion
An Overview
Encyclopedias
Ethnoastronomy
Ethology of Religion
Evolution
Evolutionism
Feminism
Feminism, Gender Studies, and Religion
French Feminists on Religion
Feminist Theology
An Overview
Christian Feminist Theology
Festschriften
Hermeneutics
Historiography
An Overview
Western Studies [First Edition]
Western Studies [Further Considerations]
History of Religions [First Edition]
History of Religions [Further Considerations]*
Kulturkreiselehre
Literature
Critical Theory and Religious Studies
Men's Studies in Religion
Myth and Ritual School

Pali Text Society
Periodical Literature*
Phenomenology of Religion
Philosophy
  Philosophy of Religion
Psychology
  Psychology of Religion
  Schizoanalysis and Religion
Reference Works
Religionsgeschichtliche Schule
Ritual Studies
Sociobiology and Evolutionary Psychology
  An Overview
  Darwinism and Religion
Sociology
  Sociology of Religion [First Edition]
  Sociology of Religion [Further Considerations]
Structuralism [First Edition]
Structuralism [Further Considerations]
Study of Religion
  An Overview
Subaltern Studies
Theology
  Comparative Theology
Women's Studies in Religion

Philosophy and Religion

PRINCIPAL ARTICLES

Philosophy
  An Overview
  Philosophy and Religion
  Philosophy of Religion

SUPPORTING ARTICLES[12]

Aesthetics
  Philosophical Aesthetics
  Visual Aesthetics
Analytic Philosophy
Apologetics
Aristotelianism
Atheism
Bioethics
Buddhist Ethics
Buddhist Philosophy
Chaos Theory
Chinese Philosophy
Christian Ethics
Dao and De
Deism
Deity
Doubt and Belief
Dualism
Ecology and Religion
  Ecology and Nature Religions
Empiricism
Enlightenment, The
Epistemology
Esotericism
Eternity
Evil
Evolution
  Evolutionary Ethics
Existentialism
Falsafah
Free Will and Determinism
Free Will and Predestination
  An Overview
  Christian Concepts
  Islamic Concepts
Gnosticism
  Gnosticism from Its Origins to the Middle Ages [First Edition]
  Gnosticism from Its Origins to the Middle Ages [Further Considerations]
  Gnosticism from the Middle Ages to the Present
  Gnosticism as a Christian Heresy
  History of Study
God
  God in the Hebrew Scriptures
  God in the New Testament
  God in Postbiblical Judaism
  God in Postbiblical Christianity
  God in Islam
  African Supreme Beings
Golden Rule
Good, The
Henotheism
Hermeneutics
Hermetism
Humanism
Human Rights and Religion
Humor and Religion
  Humor, Irony, and the Comic in Western Theology and Philosophy
Idealism
Indian Philosophies
Intuition
Jewish Thought and Philosophy
  Premodern Philosophy
  Modern Thought
  Jewish Ethical Literature
Knowledge and Ignorance
Language
  Sacred Language
  Buddhist Views of Language
Law and Religion
  Law, Religion, and Human Rights
  Law, Religion, and Morality
  Law, Religion, and Punishment
Liberation Theology
Logic
Logical Positivism
Materialism
Medical Ethics
Metaphysics
Monism
Monotheism
Morality and Religion
Mysticism [First Edition]
Mysticism [Further Considerations]
Naturalism
Nature
  Religious and Philosophical Speculations
Neoplatonism
Nominalism
Occultism
Ontology
Pantheism and Panentheism
Phenomenology of Religion
Platonism
Positivism
Proofs for the Existence of God
Reflexivity
Relativism
Religion [First Edition]
Religion [Further Considerations]
Religious Experience
Scholasticism
Semantics
Skeptics and Skepticism

[12] *For additional relevant entries, see also in this outline under* The Study of Religion, *sub-section on* Scholars of Religion. *For biographies of specific philosophers, see in part I of this outline under the names of specific religious traditions.*

Soul
- Concepts in Indigenous Religions
- Ancient Near Eastern Concepts
- Greek and Hellenistic Concepts
- Indian Concepts
- Buddhist Concepts
- Chinese Concepts
- Jewish Concept
- Christian Concepts
- Islamic Concepts

Stoicism
Structuralism [First Edition]
Structuralism [Further Considerations]
Supernatural, The
Thealogy
Theism
Theodicy
Theurgy
Transcendence and Immanence
Truth
Utopia
Via Negativa
Wisdom

Scholarly Terms

Androcentrism
Animism and Animatism
Anthropomorphism
Archetypes
Asceticism
Atheism
Atua
Authority
Axis Mundi
Center of the World
Ceremony
Charisma
Colonialism and Postcolonialism
Community
Conversion
Cosmogony
Cosmology
- An Overview

Couvade
Creolization
Cults and Sects
Culture
Culture Heroes
Deconstruction
Deification
Deity
Deus Otiosus
Dialogue of Religions
Dualism
Dying and Rising Gods
Dynamism
Ecology and Religion
- An Overview

Enthusiasm
Eschatology
- An Overview

Esotericism
Euhemerus and Euhemerism
Evolution
- The Controversy with Creationism
- Evolutionism

Feminine Sacrality
Feminism
- Feminism, Gender Studies, and Religion
- French Feminists on Religion

Fetishism
Flow Experience
Folklore
Folk Religion
- An Overview

Free Will and Predestination
- An Overview

Frenzy
Gaia
Gender and Religion
- An Overview

Gender Roles
Globalization and Religion
Goddess Worship
- Theoretical Perspectives

Gynocentrism
Henotheism
Heresy
- An Overview

Hierophany
Hieros Gamos
Holy, Idea of the
Homo Religiosus
Iconoclasm
- An Overview

Implicit Religion
Invisible Religion
Kinship
Lady of the Animals
Leadership
Legitimation
Lesbianism
Liberation
Liminality
Liturgy
Lord of the Animals
Magic
- Theories of Magic

Mana
Manism
Masculine Sacrality
Materiality*
Megalithic Religion
- Prehistoric Evidence
- Historical Cultures

Messianism
- An Overview

Meteorological Beings
Millenarianism
- An Overview

Miracles
- Modern Perspectives

Modernity
Monism
Monotheism
Mysticism [First Edition]
Mysticism [Further Considerations]
Myth
- An Overview
- Myth and History

Nature
- Religious and Philosophical Speculations
- Worship of Nature

Neolithic Religion
Occultism
Oral Tradition
Orientalism
Orientation
Orthodoxy and Heterodoxy
Orthopraxy
Paleolithic Religion
Pantheism and Panentheism
Patriarchy and Matriarchy
Perfectibility
Performance and Ritual
Play
Polytheism
Popular Religion
Power
Preanimism
Primitivism*
Reflexivity
Reform
Religion [First Edition]
Religion [Further Considerations]
Religious Diversity

Religious Experience
Revival and Renewal
Rites of Passage
  An Overview [First Edition]
  An Overview [Further Considerations]
Ritual [First Edition]
Ritual [Further Considerations]
Sacrament
  An Overview
Sacred and the Profane, The
Sacred Space
Sacred Time
Sacrifice
Sacrilege
Schism
  An Overview
Seasonal Ceremonies
Secret Societies
Secularization
Shamanism
  An Overview [First Edition]
  An Overview [Further Considerations]
Soteriology
Spirit Possession
  An Overview
  Women and Possession
Spiritual Guide
Spirituality
Supernatural, The
Superstition
Supreme Beings
Symbolic Time
Symbol and Symbolism
Syncretism [First Edition]
Syncretism [Further Considerations]
Taboo
Thealogy
Theism
Theocracy
Theodicy
Therianthropism
Totemism
Tradition
Transcendence and Immanence
Transculturation and Religion
  An Overview
Tricksters
  An Overview
Utopia
Via Negativa
Wisdom Literature
  Theoretical Perspectives
Witchcraft
  Concepts of Witchcraft
World Religions

Scholars of Religion[13]

Adams, Hannah
Andrae, Tor
Anesaki Masaharu
Baal, Jan van
Bachofen, J. J.
Bakhtin, M. M.
Baur, F. C.
Benedict, Ruth
Berndt, Catherine H.
Berndt, Ronald
Bertholet, Alfred
Beth, Karl
Bianchi, Ugo
Bleeker, C. Jouco
Boas, Franz
Brandon, S. G. F.
Brelich, Angelo
Breuil, Henri
Burckhardt, Titus
Burnouf, Eugène
Campbell, Joseph
Capps, Walter
Cassirer, Ernst
Castrén, Matthias Alexander
Chantepie de la Saussaye, P. D.
Child, Lydia Maria
Ching, Julia*
Christensen, Arthur
Clemen, Carl
Codrington, R. H.
Comte, Auguste
Coomaraswamy, Ananda
Corbin, Henry
Creuzer, G. F.
Culianu, Ioan Petru
Cumont, Franz
Delitzsch, Friedrich
Deloria, Ella Cara
de Martino, Ernesto
Demiéville, Paul
Dieterich, Albrecht
Dieterlen, Germaine
Dilthey, Wilhelm
Dömötör, Tekla
Donner, Kai
Dumézil, Georges
Durkheim, Émile
Eliade, Mircea [First Edition]
Eliade, Mircea [Further Considerations]
Evans, Arthur
Evans-Pritchard, E. E.
Evola, Julius
Firth, Raymond
Foucher, Alfred
Frankfort, Henri
Frazer, James G.
Freud, Sigmund
Frick, Heinrich
Frobenius, Leo
Frye, Northrop
Fustel de Coulanges, N. D.
Gaster, Theodor H.
Gennep, Arnold van
Gillen, Francis James, and Baldwin Spencer
Gimbutas, Marija
Glasenapp, Helmuth von
Goblet d'Alviella, Eugène
Goldenweiser, Alexander A.
Goldziher, Ignácz
Goodenough, Erwin R.
Görres, Joseph von
Graebner, Fritz
Granet, Marcel
Griaule, Marcel
Grimm Brothers
Groot, J. J. M. de
Guénon, René
Haavio, Martti
Hall, G. Stanley
Harnack, Adolf von
Harrison, Jane E.
Hartland, E. Sidney
Harva, Uno
Hastings, James
Haydon, A. Eustace
Heiler, Friedrich
Herder, Johann Gottfried
Hobbes, Thomas
Honko, Lauri
Horner, I. B.
Howitt, A. W.

[13] *For other scholars of religion, modern and premodern, who are closely associated with particular religions, see also in part I of this outline the biographies listed under the names of specific religious traditions.*

Hügel, Friedrich von
Husserl, Edmund
James, E. O.
James, William
Jensen, Adolf E.
Jevons, F. B.
Jonas, Hans
Jung, C. G.
Kaberry, Phyllis M.
Kenyon, Kathleen
Kerényi, Károly
Kitagawa, Joseph M.
Klimkeit, Hans-Joachim
Kraemer, Hendrik
Kramrisch, Stella
Kristensen, W. Brede
Laestadius, Lars Levi
Lamotte, Étienne
Lang, Andrew
Langer, Susanne
La Vallée Poussin, Louis de
Lawrence, Peter
Leach, Edmund
Leenhardt, Maurice
Leeuw, Gerardus van der
Lehmann, Edvard
Leuba, James H.
Lévi, Sylvain
Lévy-Bruhl, Lucien
Loisy, Alfred
Lönnrot, Elias
Lowie, Robert H.
Malinowski, Bronislaw
Mannhardt, Wilhelm
Marett, R. R.
Marie de l'Incarnation
Marx, Karl
Maspero, Henri
Massignon, Louis
Mauss, Marcel
Mead, Margaret
Moore, George Foot
Müller, F. Max
Müller, Karl O.
Myerhoff, Barbara G.
Neumann, Erich
Nilsson, Martin P.
Nock, Arthur Darby
Nyberg, H. S.
Oldenberg, Hermann
Otto, Rudolf
Otto, Walter F.
Oxtoby, Willard G.*
Pauck, Wilhelm
Pettazzoni, Raffaele
Pinard de la Boullaye, Henri
Pratt, James B.
Preuss, Konrad T.
Przyluski, Jean
Radcliffe-Brown, A. R.
Radin, Paul
Rappaport, Roy A.
Reguly, Antal
Reinach, Salomon
Renan, Ernest
Renou, Louis
Richardson, Cyril C.
Rohde, Erwin
Róheim, Géza
Said, Edward W.
Scheler, Max
Schimmel, Annemarie
Schlegel, Friedrich
Schleiermacher, Friedrich
Schmidt, Wilhelm
Schweitzer, Albert
Seidel, Anna Katharina
Shahrastānī, al-
Sharpe, Eric J.
Smart, Ninian
Smith, Morton
Smith, Wilfred Cantwell
Smith, W. Robertson
Snouck Hurgronje, Christiaan
Söderblom, Nathan
Sohm, Rudolf
Ṣorokin, Pitirim Aleksandrovich
Spencer, Herbert
Stanner, W. E. H.
Starbuck, E. D.
Stcherbatsky, Theodore
Sundén, Hjalmar
Taubes, Jakob
Tiele, C. P.
Tönnies, Ferdinand
Troeltsch, Ernst
Tucci, Giuseppe
Turner, Victor
Tylor, E. B.
Underhill, Evelyn
Usener, Hermann
Vierkandt, Alfred
Vries, Jan de
Wach, Joachim [First Edition]
Wach, Joachim [Further Considerations]
Waldman, Marilyn Robinson
Walker, James R.
Warburg, Aby
Weber, Max
Wellhausen, Julius
Wensinck, A. J.
Wheatley, Paul
Widengren, Geo
Wikander, Stig
Wissowa, Georg
Wundt, Wilhelm
Yates, Frances Amelia
Zaehner, R. C.
Zimmer, Heinrich Robert
Zolla, Elémire

INDEX

Page numbers in **bold** indicate main entries. Page numbers in *italic* indicate illustrations. Color inserts are identified by volume number.

A

Aachen (Germany)
  Charlemagne at, 1557
  Grannus cult at, 1483
A-ak (music), 6296–6297
Aalto, Alvar, 801
Aamskaapipiikani, 958
Aapatohsipiikani, 958
AAPC. *See* American Association of Pastoral Counseling
AAR. *See* American Academy of Religion
Aarnes, Antti, 770
Aaron (biblical figure), **1–2**
  genealogy of, 5423
  Miriam and, 6062
  in priesthood, 1–2, 5423, 6852
  as prophet, 1
  scapegoat ritual by, 8144
Aaron ben Elijah, writings of, 5085, 5086
Aaron ben Joseph, writings of, 5085
Aaronites (priests), 7399
Abaasys (spirits), 9865–9866
Abaj Takalik site (Guatemala), Stele 2 at, 5882
Abakan Tartars, 9577
Abandonment, of Jesus, by God, 4845
Abangan. *See* Agami Jawi
Abangans (nominal Muslims), 4563
Abarbanel, Isaac. *See* Abravanel, Isaac
Abaris (shaman), 6050
Abba (father), God as, 3544, 6407
Abba' bar Ayyvu. *See* Rav
Abba' bar Yudan, on suffering, 8805
Abbahu (amora), **2**
  on God's unity, 3548
Abbas Hamdani, 4375
Abbasid caliphate
  Abbasid revolution, Shiism, role of, 8321
  Abū Ḥanīfah and, 21
  'Āshūrā' under, 550
  under Buyid control, 4572
  Crusades and, 2078
  festivals under, 6731
  imperial tradition, 1366
  Jews in, 4979, 4988
  Karbala and, 5088
  Mumluks of Egypt and, 1367
  Mu'tazilah in, 6319
  Nestorians under, 6480
  origin of, 1365
  political and social changes in, 4562
  predestinarian views under, 3210
  qāḍī under, 7540, 7541
  Qarāmiṭah and, 7543
  scientific history and, 8181
  al-Shāfi'ī and, 8263
  sunnah and, 8853
  Sunnī jurists on, 4394
  Syriac Orthodox Church and, 8939
  translation movement under, 2970–2971
  and Umayyad caliphate, 4591, 4594, 4695
  walāyah in, 9658
Abbassi, Abdulaziz, on circumcision, 4212
Abbaye (amora), **2–3**
  on Mishnah, 3
  Rava' and, 3, 7631
Abbey, Edward, 2563–2564
  nature writing of, as spiritual autobiography, 703
Abbey of the Holy Ancestor (Zungsheng Guan), 2196
Abbey of Thelema. *See* Thelema, Abbey of
"Abbeys of Fools," Carnival and, 1441
Abbington, James, 77
Abbott, John, 2542
Abbott, Nabia
  on authenticity of *ḥadīths,* 3727–3728
  on *tafsīr,* 8951
'Abd al-Bahā', 738–739
'Abd al-Jabbār, **3–5**
  on attributes of God, 6323
  as chief judge, 3–4
  in Mu'tazilah, 3–4, 6320
  on *'iṣmah,* 4725
  on Qur'ān, 4371
  writings of, 3, 4, 6320
'Abd al-Jalīl al-Qazvīnī, 6641
'Abd al-Karīm al-Jīlī, 6767
'Abd Allāh al-Afṭaḥ, Imami succession and, 8322
'Abd Allāh Efendī, 5623
'Abd Allāh ibn 'Abbās, 8951
'Abd Allāh ibn Maymūn al-Qaddāḥ, emergence of Ismāīlīyah and, 8327
'Abd Allāh ibn Muḥammad Ādam, 6228
'Abdallāh ibn Saba' al-Hamdānī, 3523
'Abd Allāh ibn Sayf, 4254–4255
'Abd Allāh ibn Yāsīn, 4585
'Abd al-Malik (caliph)
  and Dome of the Rock (Jerusalem), 6736
  Ḥasan al-Baṣrī and, 3785
'Abd al-Mu'min, 4586
'Abd al-Nāṣir, Jamāl
  al-Azhar university under, 231
  Muslim Brotherhood under, 7575
'Abd al-Qādir al-Jīlānī
  anniversary of, 4713
  madrasah of, 3766
  al-Mukharrimī and, 3767
  shrines of, 4649
  Ṣūfī order of, 3767, 4571, 8824, 9006, 9008
Abd al-Raḥmān
  as son of Abū Bakr, 19
  conversion to Islam, 19
  in battles against Muḥammad, 19
'Abd al-Raḥmān, Sayyid, as son of Muḥammad Aḥmad, 6229
'Abd al-Raḥmān I (Umayyad ruler), 4591, 4592
'Abd al-Raḥmān III (Umayyad ruler), 4591, 4593
'Abd al-Ra'ūf (Muslim writer), 4663
'Abd al-Ra'ūf al-Sinkilī, 25
'Abd al-Rāzīq, 'Alī, **5**
  al-Azhar's condemnation of, 231
  writings of, 5
'Abd al-Ṣabūr, Ṣalāḥ, on al-Ḥallāj, 3758
'Abd al-Wahhāb. *See* Ibn 'Abd al-Wahhāb, Muḥammad
Abdisa (metropolitan of Nisibis), 6483
'Abduh, Muḥammad, **5–6**
  Afghānī and, 5, 64, 4589
  on free will and predestination, 3213
  influence in Southeast Asia, 4665–4666
  in *'Urwah al-wuthqaā,* 5, 6098
  kalām (theology) of, 5059, 5067–5068
  modernism of, 6097–6098
  on *sharī'ah,* 4700
  Rashīd Riḍā influenced by, 7621
  tafsīr (Qur'anic exegesis) of, 7567, 8955
  on women, 3365, 3369
  writings of, 5, 6, 5067–5068
'Abdul Laṭīf, Shāh, 4644
Abdussamad (South Asian writer), 10035
Abe, Masao, 9130

Abe Kōbō, 3074
Abel, Cain and, 986, **1344–1345**
Abelard, Peter, **6–8**
on atonement, 597, 4844
autobiography of, 698, 4038
Bernard's critique of, 839
on knowledge, 5204
on merit, 5876
on problem of universals, 6644
Scholasticism of, 8174
students of, 7–8
on theology, 9134
writings of, 7
Abendländische Eschatologie (Taubes), 9021
Aberle, David F., 6671, 6672
Abeyta, Bernardo, El Santuario de Chimayó and, 8377
Abhavya, 4768
Abhayagiri monastery (Sri Lanka), 1194, 9147
Abhayākaragupta, on *maṇḍalas,* 5643
Abhāya mudrā (gesture), 4330
Abhidhamma Piṭaka (Buddhist text), 1198–1199
Buddhaghosa's commentary on, 1074
Abhidhammatthasangaba (Buddhist text), 1199
Abhidhammāvatāra (Buddhadatta), 10022
Abhidharma, 1206, 1269
Candrakīrti's treatise on, 1401
canon of, 1108, 1252, **10020–10023**
commentators on, 10020
content of, 9146, 10020
dependent arising in, 7365
development of, 10021–10022
Dharmaguptaka school and, 8120
dharma in, 2029, 2333, 5308
as exegesis, 1270, 10022
as hermeneutics, 1270, 1273, 1275
instructions to monastic order in, 1091
Jñānaprasthāna text in, 2037
karman in, 5099–5100
lists in, 10021
as moral psychology, 1278
nirvāṇa and *dharma* in, Sarvāstivādin texts *vs.,* 2029
nirvāṇa in, 6628–6629, 6630
origin of term, 10020
Pāṭaliputra council in, 2037
philosophy of, 1112, 1297–1298
Prajñāpāramitā Sūtras on masters of, 8856
Sarvāstivādin, 8118, 8120, 10020, 10021, 10022
Sautrāntika view of, 8119, 8136
Stcherbatsky (Theodore) on, 8737
tathāgata in, 9015
Theravādin, 10020, 10021, 10022
vs. Sūtra literature, 10021
as word of Buddha, 10020–10021
Abhidharmadīpa (Buddhist text), 10022
Abhidharmakośa (Vasubandhu), 9526, 9527
as Sarvāstivādin treaty, 1199, 1201
Chinese translation of, 1202, 1313
cosmology in, 2026–2030
in Dge lugs pa curriculum, 2322
personalist doctrine in, 1297
prajñā in, 7357–7358
as standard textbook, 8120
Vaibhāṣika school criticized in, 10022
Abhidharmakośa-marma-dīpa (Dignāga), 2351
Abhidharma-nyāyānusāra (Buddhist text), 1199
Abhidharma-samaya-pradīpika (Buddhist text), 10022
Abhidharmasamuccaya (Buddhist text), 10022
Abhijñā/abhiññā (extraordinary knowledge), 2793
Abhinavabhāratī (Abhinavagupta), 9
Abhinavagupta (Indian philosopher), **8–9**
in Trika Śaivism, 8046–8047
on *mantras,* 5678
on *Bhagavadgītā,* 854
on Kashmir Śaiva school Pratyabhijñā Saivism in, 8048
and *rasas* (tastes), 4006
on Matsyendranāth, 3637–3638
philosophy of, 8417
on poetry, 7208
Śaṅkara and, 8105
Abhiniṣkramaṇa Sūtra (Buddhist text), 1064
Abhiprāya (contextual meaning), 1274
Ābhīra clan, 5249
Abhisamayālamkāṃra (Buddhist text), 2322
Abhisaṃdhi (hidden intention), 1274
Abhiṣeka (empowerment), 1157, 1218, 1221
Abhūta-parikalpa (unreal imagination), 9899
Abiās, 123
Abiathar (biblical figure), 5421
'Ābid (man of God), 4584
Ability to Mourn, The (Homans), 7480
Abimbola, 'Wande, 80, 117, 10032
Abimelech the Ethiopian, sleep in legend of, 8440
Abiodun, Rowland, 10033
Abisha Scroll, in Samaritan tradition, 8070
Ablutions, **9–13,** 780
in Christianity, 10 (*See also* Baptism)
definition of, 9
in Hinduism, 2403–2404
in Islam, 10, 11, 2401, 7157
for *ṣalāt* (prayer), 8057
in Judaism, 10, 11, 780
occasions for, 9–12
syncretism and, 8931
Abolitionism, 66, 68, 69
Child (Lydia Maria), role of, 1569
Enlightenment values and, 1816
in evangelicalism, 2888
Holiness movement and, 4083
social movements and, 1451
Stanton (Elizabeth Cady), role of, 8730, 8731
women in, 10037–10038
Abominable Snowman, 6166
Aboreh ritual, 7806
Aboriginal and Torres Strait Islander Heritage Protection Act (1984, Australia), 641, 650, 2479, 6244
Aboriginal Christianity, **675–680**
God in, 676
leadership of, 675–680
political activism in, 676–677
theology of, 678, 680
Aboriginal Evangelical Fellowship, 677
Aboriginal Evangelical Fellowship of Australia (AEF), 677–678
Aboriginal Land Rights (Northern Territory) Act (1976, Australia), 641, 688, 690, 2479, 3390–3391
Aboriginal languages
contemporary survival of, 637
number of, 636, 637
Aboriginal people (Australia)
ancestors of, 3083
Central Desert, 644
kinship of, 5185
New Year ceremonies of, 6590
number of groups of, 635, 636
population of, 635–636
decline of, 685
religions of (*See* Australian Indigenous religions)
societies of, 636, 5704
use of term, 635
Western Desert, 644, 5704
women, 840–841
Aboriginal religions. *See* Australian Indigenous religions
Aboriginal Theology movement. *See* Aboriginal Christianity
Aboriginal Women (Kaberry), 3390
Aborigines Inland Mission (AIM), 676, 677
Abortion, 941
excommunication for, 2921
in Islam, 5813
in Japanese religion
Mizuko Jizo (buddha for aborted fetuses), 3869
pacification rites and, 2241
Jewish bioethicists on, 8191
in Judaism, 5812–5813
medical ethics regarding, 5810, 5812–5813
in Protestantism, 5812
in Roman Catholicism, 5812
in Sikhism, 3337
social consequences of, 2882
U.S. Supreme Court on, 5810
in Zoroastrianism, 3374
Abosom (Akan deities), 215
About the Structure of Man (Gregory of Datev), 3693
Abracadabra, as word of power, 8676
Abraham (biblical figure), **13–17**
ancestors of, 13
Canaanite parallels, 1396
in Christianity, 16
circumcision and, 7818
construction of the Ka'bah by, 5050, 7155, 7156
covenant of God with, 2048
Freemasons on, 3195
God's covenant with, 15
hospitality of, 4139
Isaac offered by, 15, 16, 4544
altar in, 277
Ishmael as son of, 4551, 4552
in Islam, 16, 3561, 6224, 6734, 6736
and *ḥājj,* 7155–7156, 7159
and monotheism, 4362–4363
Muslim (term) given by, 4561
in *James,* 916
in Judaism, 14–16, 10063
and merit, concept of, 5871
and monotheism, 6157
morality in stories of, 6183
Muḥammad on, 16, 6224
obedience to God by, 15
Paul the Apostle on, 7017, 7019
Philo Judaeus on, 7107
pilgrimage begun by, 5050
temptation of, 9071
Abraham, Apocalypse of, 410, 902
Abraham, Book of, in Mormonism, 8447
Abraham ibn Ezra. *See* Ibn 'Ezra,' Avraham
Abram, name changed to Abraham, 15
Abravanel, Isaac, **17–18**
apocalypses and, 420
biblical exegesis of, 866, 867, 868
in Jewish thought and philosophy, 4897
on prophecy, 7440
Abraxas (Dieterich), 2348
Abraxas, as word of power, 8676
Abrek (bandits of honor), 4615

Absalom (biblical figure), Canaanite religion and, 1399
Absolute
Hegel on, 3893, 3894, 6148
Christianity as, 1819, 3894
in Hinduism, *brahman* as (*See also* Brahman)
historiography and, 4025
in Upaniṣads, 3993
Scheler (Max) on, 8147
Absolute certainty, 2428
Absolute Mind, Hocking (William Ernest) on, 4076
Absolute self, 2905
Absolutheit des Christentums und die Religionsgeschichte, Die (Troeltsch), 9365
Absolution
casuistry and, 1455
confession and, 1889
Abstinence. *See* Celibacy; Chastity; Spiritual discipline
Abstract art
human body in, 4172
reality in, 55
subject matter of, 55
Suzuki Daisetz and, 500
Abstraction, of time, 7991
Abū ʿAbd Allāh al-Baṣrī, ʿAbd al-Jabbār under, 3, 4
Abū al-ʿAbbās al-Mursī, 4261
Abū al-Fath, on Samaritans, 8068, 8070
Abū al-Faẓl ʿAllami, Akbar's image created by, 216
Abū al-Ḥakam, in opposition to Muḥammad, 6222
Abū al-Ḥasan. *See* Ashʿarī, (Abū al-Ḥasan) al-
Abū al-Ḥasan ʿAbd al-Jabbār ibn Aḥmad al-Hamadhānī. *See* ʿAbd al-Jabbār
Abū al-Ḥasan al-Māwardī, on caliphate, 1366
Abū al-Ḥasan al-Shādhilī, 9009
Abū al-Hudhayl al-ʿAllāf, **18–19**
on atomism, 19, 6323
on human beings, 6323–6324
in Muʿtazilah, 18–19, 6319
five principles of, 6321–6322
al-Naẓẓām and, 6444, 6445
worldview of, 6323–6324, 6325
Abū al-Ḥusayn al-Baṣri
ʿAbd al-Jabbār and, 4
in Muʿtazilah, 6320
Abū ʿAlī al-Jubbāʾī. *See* Jubbāʾī, Abū ʿAlī al-
Abū ʿAlī al-Sindī, 955
Abū al-Maʿālī Muḥammad bin ʿUbayd Allāh, *al-Milal wa al-Nihal* work of, 8781
Abū ʿAmr al-Shaʿbī, Abū Ḥanīfah and, 21
Abū Bakr (caliph), **19–21**
ʿAlī ibn Abī Ṭālib and, 257
family of, 19
ʿĀʾishah bint Abī Bakr in, 19, 211
Fāṭimah's disagreement with, 257
interest in Fāṭimah, 3008
migration to Medina, 6223
Muḥammad's relationship with, 19–20
persecution in Mecca, 6222
Qurʾān collected by, 20
selection as caliph, 257, 1365
Abū Bishr Mattā ibn Yūnus, 2971, 2973, 2991
Abū Dāʾūd al-Sijistānī, Ḥanābilah and, 3763
Abū Dāwūd, *Sunan* compilation of, 3730
Abū Ḥanīfah, **21–23**. *See also* Ḥanafīyah
ʿAnan ben David advised by, 317
on blasphemy, 976
governmental patronage refused by, 21
ḥadīth rejected by, 4566
in Ḥanafīyah, development of, 22–23, 24–25, 5547
legal contributions of, 22–23, 4695
on *īmān* and *islām,* 4400
al-Shāfiʿī's disagreement with, 8264
theological doctrines of, 21–22
Abū Hāshim al-Jubbāʾī. *See* Jubbāʾī, Abū Hāshim al-
Abū Ḥātim al-Rāzī
Ḥanābilah and, 3763
on mahdī, 8328–8329
Abū ʿImrān al-Fāsī, 4585
Abū ʿĪsā al-Isfahānī, 4991
ʿAbū Iṣāq ibn ʿAyyāsh, ʿAbd al-Jabbār under, 3
Abū Isḥāq Injü, 4372
Abū Jaʿfar, Sharīf, Ḥanābilah and, 3765, 3766
Abū Jahl, in opposition to Muḥammad, 6222
Abuk (mythic figure), 3573
Abulafia, Abraham
Adret (Shelomoh ben Avraham) opposing, 36
meditation technique of, 5817, 6353
on methods of prayer, 604
and mystical Qabbalah, 7537
on mystical union, 6340
prophetic works of, 7441
Sefer yetsirah and, 8221
Abulafia, Meʾir, **23–24**
Abū Lahab, 975
Abullu (feast), 187
Abu-Lughod, Lila, on culture, 2088
media and, 5807
Abū Madyan, 4257
on God, 3564–3565
Abū Manṣūr ʿAbd al-Qāhir al-Baghdādī, on caliphate, 1366
Abū Maʿshar, astrological translations by, 563–564
Abū Muḥammad al-Ḥusayn ibn Aḥmad ibn Mattawayh, ʿAbd al-Jabbār and, 4
a-bu-mul (Eblaite priest), 2598
Abū Mūsā, in ʿAlī's arbitration, 258–259
Abun (rabbi), 5011
Abundance, deities of, in Hawaiian religion, 3797–3798
Abū Rashīd al-Nisābūrī, ʿAbd al-Jabbār and, 4
Abū Saʿīd, 894
and anamnesis, 312
on spiritual guides, 8710–8711
Abu Sayyaf movement (Philippines), 4672
Abusch, Tzvi, on counter-witchcraft rituals, 2102
Abuse. *See* Child abuse; Violence
Abu Simel, temple at, 1472
Abusir Papyrus, 2725
Abū Sufyān
conversion to Islam, 6226
Hubal invoked by, 444
in opposition to Muḥammad, 6222, 6225
Abū Ṭāhir, 7542–7543
Abū Ṭālib, 256
death of, 6222
Muḥammad raised by, 6220
Abū ʿUbayd, 8952
Abū ʿUbaydah, 8952
Abū ʿUthmān Sa ʿīd al-Dimashqī, 2971
Abū Yaʿlā, Qāḍī, Ḥanābilah and, 3764–3765
Abu Yaʿqūb (Almohad ruler), 2976
Abū Yaʿqūb Yūsuf (Almohad ruler), 4270
Abū Yūsuf, **24–25**
as chief judge, 24, 25
in Ḥanafīyah, 22, 24–25, 4695, 5547
Mālik ibn Anas and, 5627
on *waqf,* 9677
Abū Zakarīyāʾ, 4583
Abū Zayd, Nasr Hamid, as apostate, 434
Abyaṅs (chant), 6298–6299
Abydos (Egypt), 6920
Abyss, Sumerian god of, 2791
Abyssinia
Arabia invaded by, 442, 443
Ethiopianism and, 1438
Abyssinian Church. *See* Ethiopian Church
Āb-zōhr (libations), 4535
Acacia, 3198
Acacian Schism (484–519), 6154
Acacius (patriarch of Constantinople)
Cyril of Jerusalem's break with, 2118
and Monophysitism, 6154
Acacius of Melitene, Sahak Parthev, correspondence with, 8026
Academia
esotericism in, 2843–2845
Orientalism in, 6882
religion and ecology in, in Western tradition, 2606–2608
women's studies in religion in, 9793
Academic skepticism, arguments of, 8420
Académie des Inscriptions et Belles-Lettres, 1631
Academy Movement, in Swedenborgianism, 8904, 8905
Academy of Geneva, 851
Academy of Social Sciences (Australia), 841
Acadia (Canada)
Catholicism in, 9299, 9302
Miʾkmaq Indians in, 9299, 9300, 9302
Acamapichtli (king), as first legitimate Aztec king, 5173
Ācān Man Phūrithattha (Buddhist monk), 9096
Ācān Nāēp (Buddhist master), 9096
Ācarāṅga Sūtra
nature in, 2624
on trees, 2625
Ācārya Hṛdayam (Nammāḻvār), 7172
Ācāryas (teachers), 7494, 8974
central concern of, 8976
in Śrī Vaiṣṇavas Sampradāya, 8727, 8728
in Swaminarayan movement, 8890
ACBC. *See* All-Ceylon Buddhist Congress
Accacius (catholicos), 6480
Acca Larentia (deity), 5321
Accents and chanting, 1533, 1534–1535
Accommodationism, of Jesuits in China, 1918, 1919, 1920
Accommodative, revival and renewal activities described by, 7784
Accountability, conscience and, 1945
Account of the English Colony in New South Wales, An (Collins), 685
Acculturation, 9305. *See also* Transculturation
masculine sacrality in, 5762
syncretism and, 8928
Acculturative, revival and renewal activities described by, 7784
Accusation, confession and, 7755
Acehnese language, 25

Acehnese religion (Indonesia), **25–27**
Islam, 25–27, 4660, 4661, 4664, 4669
mysticism in, 25, 27
reform movement in, 26–27, 4665
rituals in, 25–26
Snouck Hurgronje (Christiaan) in, 25, 26, 8460
Acehnese War (1873–1914?), 26
Achachilas (mountain spirits), in Andean religion, in modern era, 8615–8616
Achaemenian Empire, Zoroastrianism and, 10001–10002
Achaemenid Aramaic script, 6385
Achaemenid calendar, Magi and, 1354
Achaemenid kings, 5165
Achaemenid period (Persia), magi in, 5560
Achaemenid relief sculptures, *khvarenah* in, 5140
Achard, Jean-Luc, 9190
Achard of Saint-Victor, Abbot, in Victorine tradition, 4151
Aché (Paraguay), birth rites of, 2559
Achebe, Chinua, 3087, 3088
Achieropaeic (not made by hands) images, 497, 4286, 4352, 4392
Achilles
initiation of, 184
invulnerability of, river Styx and, 7863
Achilpa religion, sacred pillar in, 1502
Acholi group, in Lord's Resistance Army, 106
Achterberg, Jeanne, on soul loss, 8279
Achuar religion, 281–284. *See also* Amazonian religions, Quechua
Acllas (chaste girls), 3417
ACLU. *See* American Civil Liberties Union
ACMs. *See* Anticult movements
Acoma tribe (North America)
ballgame played by, 752
poetry of, 7225, 7226
Acorn Feast, 574
Acosta, José de
on Andean calendar, 1360–1361
on *huacas* and the Trinity, 8608
Acrobats of God (Graham), 2159
Acronyms, in letter mysticism, 273–274
Acrostics, 274
Act, in Vedic ritual, 9561–9562
Acta Archelai, Mani in, 5647, 5651, 5664
"Act and Being" (Bonhoeffer), 1017
Act in Restraint of Appeals to Rome (1533), 7662
Action
in Buddhism, in eightfold path, 2738
consequences of, in wisdom, 9748–9749
in Judaism, 4986
thought and, in environmental ethics, 2654
Wang Yangming on, 9674
Zhu Xi on, 9974
Action, l' (Blondel), 985
Action Catholique (Canada), 9301
Active way *(praktikē),* 1447–1448
Activism. *See* Environmental activism; Social activism
Act of Supremacy (England, 1534), king as head of church in, 2051
Act of Supremacy (England, 1559), 349
Act of Uniformity of 1662 (England), Congregationalism suppressed by, 1937
Acton, John, 9530
Acts of John, Round Dance of the Cross from, 2153
Acts of Paul and Thecle, 9101, 9102
Acts of Peter, 7069
Acts of Peter and the Twelve Apostles, 7069
Acts of the Apostles, 873, 908–910
apocatastasis in, 422
apostleship in, 435
audience of, 909
author of, 908–909
Luke as, 5529
canon of, 920
placement in, 1410
church history genre and, 4038
condemnation of idolatry in, 4385
council of apostles in, 2039
criticism of, 7013
dating of, 7017
dogma in, 2387
enthusiasm in, 2807
Europe in, 1688
exorcism in, 2928–2929
Gamli'el the Elder in, 3270
gifts of the Holy Spirit in, 1549–1550
glossolalia in, 3504
God in, 3545
"gospel" in, 3641
and history, Christian views of, 4052
John in, 910
John Mark of Jerusalem in, 5714
knowledge in, 5203
Mary in, 5751, 5752
miracles in, 6054, 6056
outline of, 908
parallelism in, 909–910
Paul in, 911, 7014, 7020, 9274
Pentecost in, 7028–7029
Peter the Apostle in, 7068
Psalms interpreted in, 7465
purpose of, 909
spread of Christianity documented in, 2580
Acts of Thomas
ouroboros serpent in, 1793
virginity in, 9608
Actual sins, 1888–1889
Acupuncture, modern medicine and, 3863–3864
AD *(anno Domini),* origin of concept, 173
Adab (Arabic corpus of belles lettres)
humor in, 4214–4215
tricksters in, 4214
Ādāb al-murīdīn (al-Suhrawardī), 9006, 9008
Adad (deity), **27–29**. *See also* Hadad
Ashur combined with, 548
Baal as, 27, 28, 723, 2536
in Eblaite religion, 2597, 2598
iconography of, 4317
in triad, 9349
in Ugaritc prayer, 1383
as vegetation god, 28–29
Adadnirari II (Assyrian king), 448
Adair, James, 6670
Adal (Muslim state), 4606
'Adala (uprightness), in *ḥadīth* authenticity, 3731
Adam, **29–30**
in ages of world, 175
as androgyne, 338, 339–340, 2896
androgyny of, 29
in ballet, 2163
in Catharism, 1457
in Christianity, 30, 3358
creation of, 29
diet of, 29–30, 6982
as divine man, 3508, 3509
Druze manuscripts on, 2502–2503
Eve and, 2896
expulsion of, 2938
Freemasons on, 3194
as gardener, 3277
in Garden of Eden, 2967, 6982
and gender in Christianity, 3358
in Gnosticism, 5202
in Islam, 2837, 2968, 2969, 4564, 6736
in *mi'rāj,* 6060
Satan's refusal to prostrate himself before, 8406
sin and, 8407
in Jehovah's Witnesses theology, 4822
Jesus as new, 30, 3358
in Judaism, 30
Lillith and, 5459
in Mandaean religion, 5635–5636
Ginza of, 3494, 5634
in Manichaeism, 2967, 5654, 5667
marriage of, 5724, 5727
as mythic ancestor, 325
Noah linked to, 6642
nudity of, 6741
Nuwaubians on, 6769
Satan and, 8125, 8406
sin/fall of (*See also* Fall, the)
evil resulting from, 626
explanations for, 30
Irenaeus on, 8406
in Islam, 8407
Pelagius on, 7025
punishment for, 6982
Puritans on, 7519
results for humanity, 30
sleep as, 339, 340
temptation and, 9069, 9071
in Sistine Chapel, 8755
skull of, in legend, 3805
tail of, 6151
temptation of, Satan and, 8125
Adam, Alfred, 3533
Adam, Apocalypse of, 902
Adam, Apocryphon of, 6396
Adam cult, 6870
Adamma (deity)
Eblaite festival of, 2597
as Reshef's consort, 7761–7762
Adam of Bremen, 767
on cosmic tree, 3449
on Freyr, statue of, 3220
historiography of, 4038
on Óðinn, 3454
on Thor, 9165
Adam of Purity, in Druze movement, 8330
Adam of Saint-Victor, in Victorine tradition, 4151
Adamovičs, Ludvigs, 327, 770, 5691
on Latvian Saule (sun) myth, 8134
Adams, Brooks, 9109
Adams, Don, 4822
Adams, Hannah, **30–32**
Adams, John, 974
Adams, John (composer), 6313
Adams, John (president), Adams (Hannah) and, 31
Adams, Robert M., 454
Adamski, George, 9433
Adapa (drum), 2498
Adapa (mythic figure), 2792, 5953
Adaptationism, 6904, 6905
Adaptive, revival and renewal activities described by, 7784
Adat (village custom), 800
Adath Jeshurun (synagogue), 7668
'Adawīyah, Rābi'ah al-, 3369, 7207–7208, 9007
Adda. *See* Adad
Addadian religion. *See* Adad
Addams, Charles, 6243
Adderet Eliyahi (Bashyatchi), 5086
Addis Ababa (Ethiopia), urban nature of, 2566
Addison, Joseph, 5356

Address to the Roman Catholics, An (Carroll), 1445
Adedeji, Joel, 2435
Adelaide (Australia), as center of Aboriginal studies, 686
Adelard of Bath, on magic, 5578
Adena culture, circular architecture in, 1794
Adeodatus (Augustine's son), 624, 625
Ādhā gāv (Rāhi), 10035
Adhān (call to prayer), 9816
overview of, 8056–8057
Adholoka (Lower World), in Jain cosmology, 2024
Adhvaryu priests, 7405
Yajurveda as province of, 3991
Adhyāśayasaṃcodana Sūtra (Buddhist text), 1271, 1274, 1276
Adhyātma Rāmāyaṇa, 7609
Ādi Buddha, 1068, 1214
Ādi Granth (Gurū Granth Sāhib) (Sikh text), **32–33,** 2220, **3715–3718**
as Gurū, 3716–3717
compilation of, 8394
gender in, 3336
guruship and, 8394
Kabīr's words in, 5052
languages in, 32
message of, 32–33, 6413
Nānak and, 32, 6413
recensions of, 32, 3717
ritual veneration of, 8199
scholarship on, 3717
Sikh Darma movement and, 3878
Sikh worship focused on, 3986
Singh (Gobind) and, 8407–8408
translations of, 3717
use in worship, 3716, 8396
in weddings, 8397
Ādi Śakti (primordial power), 4433
Ādisura (Bengali king), 825
Aditi (deity), 9556, 9559
Ādityas (suns), 779, 4440
as *deva,* 8135
Ādityas (Vedic gods), 9555–9556
Adivasi (India), 2616
Ādivasis (tribal communities), cosmologies of, 2019
Adjá (double bell), 7037
Adja (spirit), in Caribbean neo-African cults, 1433
Adjurations, medical, 5578
Adjustive, revival and renewal activities described by, 7784
Adjustment Movement in Arnhem Land, An (Berndt), 841
ʿAdl (God's justice), ʿAbd al-Jabbār on, 4
Adler, Alfred, Freud and, 3215
Adler, Felix, **33–34,** 2857–2858
Adler, Gerhard, 6484
Adler, Margot, 7830
Adler, Mortimer, 9285
Adler, Natan, Sofer (Mosheh) and, 8507
Adler, Rachel, 3430
Adler, Samuel, 33, 6312
Administrative texts, Egyptian, 2725
Administrator (deity), in Khoi and San religion, 5135, 5136, 5137
Admirable, the. *See* Ruusbroec, Jan van
Admirable History (Michaëlis), 2315
Admiralty Islands
Manus people of
ghosts and, 5833, 5834
healing herbs, origin myths on, 3811
water in cosmogony of, 9698
Admor (teacher), 9377
Adnjamathana people (Australia), rituals of, 7842–7843
Adobe (sun-dried brick), 9065
Adolescence
initiation rites for, as sacraments, 7956
psychological concept of, 3755, 7796
rites of passage in (*See* Puberty rites)
saṃskāras of, 7814–7815
Adonai (Lord), in Qabbalah, 8676
Adonijah (biblical figure), 5421
Adonis (deity), **34–36**
Baal compared with, 7767
castration, hypothetical, 1451
cult of, 34, 35
women in, 3383
death of, 3968
dove as symbol of, 948
Dumuzi compared with, 2521, 7767
as fecundator, 2985
festivals of, 35, 2536, 7131–7132
gardens of *(kepoi),* 2536
and gender roles, 3383
killing and revival of, 35, 2535–2536
mystery religion of, ecstasy in, 2678
myths regarding, 34–35
in Phoenician religion, 7130, 7131–7132
pig sacrifice to, 7144
sacrifices to, 7131–7132
temple of, 34
Adoption
kinship relations and, 5184
in Langkawi culture, 5184
Adoptionism
Alcuin on, 254
Council of Frankfurt (794) condemning, 4286
Adoptive Rite, 3198
Adora (deity), 5526
Adorno, Theodor
Gnosticism and, 3527
on popular culture, 7321
Adosada pyramid, 5899
Adret, Shelomoh ben Avraham, **36–37**
ban on Greek philosophy promulgated by, 36
Asher ben Yeḥi'el on, 539
on capital punishment, 3753
opposition to Abulafia (Avraham), 36, 7537
refuting Ibn Ḥazm, 7239
responsa of, 36
Adrian (saint), relics of, 7689
Adrian I (pope), 4290
Adrian II (pope), and Cyril and Methodius in Moravia, 2116–2117
Adrian VI (pope), 6967, 6972
Adroa (deity), in Lugbara religion, 2567
Adso (monk), on Antichrist, 395
Adulis (Ethiopia), Christianity in, 2859
Adultery
in Christianity, in *John,* 921–922
confession of, 1884
in Islam
false accusations of, 4566
laws on, 4566
witnesses required in charges of, 211
in Israelite religion, laws on, 4733–4734, 4737, 4738, 4740
judgment of, 6848
Adulthood
baptism in, 782, 783
in Orthodox Church, 2592
in Protestantism, 7455
evolutionism and, 2915, 2916
initiation into (*See also* Rites of passage)
African rituals for, 88–89
Greek rituals for, 183–184
Mardu rituals for, 5705
Oceanic rituals for, 7807–7808
psychic, evolutionism and, 2915, 2916
Ādurbād ī Māraspandān, 5660, 5661
Advaita (nondualism), 828, 6144
Abhinavagupta on, 8417
qualified (*See Viśiṣṭādvaita*)
Advaita Ācārya, Vaiṣṇavism and, 1347
Advaita Vedānta. *See also* Daśanāmī sect
afterlife in, 130
deep ecology influenced by, 2608
gurūs in, 3714
jīvanmuka and, 4926
jñāna in, 4928
līlā in, 5456
māyā in, 5795
mokṣa (liberation) in, 4003–4004
monastic centers founded by Śaṅkara, 8105
monism in, 6964
Ramakrishna influenced by, 7612, 7613
Rāmānuja, repudiation by, 4005
saint-singer traditions, impact on, 4005
Śaṅkara, role of, **8014–8016**
and *smārta* orthodoxy, revival of, 4003–4004
Śaṅkara *vs.,* 8105
self in, 8546
in Transcendental Meditation, 9289
unity and plurality in, 4422
vs. Dvaita Vedānta, 5551
vs. Vaiṣṇava Vedānta, 6623
Advancement of Learning, The (Bacon), 733
Advayavajra, writings of, 5555
Advent, domestic observances of, 2400
Advent Church (Swedenborgian), Bendade (William) and, 8904
Adventism. *See also* Seventh-day Adventism
in Caribbean, 1437
revival and renewal activities in, 7785
in United States and Canada, 1713–1714
Adventist Christian Church, Millerite movement and, 8235
Adventures of a Black Girl in Search of God (Sears), 2477
Adventures of Huckleberry Finn (Twain), 7370–7371
Adversary, the, in *Job,* 4931
Advertisements, vol. 7 color insert
Advisory Discourse (Barlaam of Calabria), 788
Adytum (special room), 9063
Aeacus (mythic figure), 165
Aedesius (priest), 2859
AEF. *See* Aboriginal Evangelical Fellowship of Australia
Aegean religions, **37–44.** *See also* Minoan religion; Mycenaean religion
temples in, 9062
Aegis, of Athena, 586
Ælbert, Alcuin influenced by, 254
Ælfric of Eynsham, 6943, 9165
Aelia Capitolina, 4836
Aelianos (Greek writer), on moon, 6175
Aelius Aristides
on Asklepios, 6051
on Athena, 587
on incubation, 8441
Aeneid (Vergil), 9583
Charon in, 989
fate in, 3000–3001

Aeneid (Vergil) ***continued***
fertility in, 7602
magic in, 5575
mythology in, 2814
pius used in, 2955
sculpture based on, vol. 2 color insert
serpent in, 5277
underworld in, 166, 3015
Aeneolithic cultures, 7382
Aenesidemus (philosopher), skepticism and, 8420
Aenigma (enigma), 6986
A-e-oina Kamuy (deity), 9337
Aerophones, 6251
Aeschylus
on Africans, 111
on Aphrodite, 407
on Artemis, 508
on divine malevolence, 5469
on magic, 5575
on memory, 5852
on retribution, 7783
on sacrifice, 3682
Aesculapius (deity). *See also* Asklepios
in Roman religion, 3841
Aēshma (deity), 2128
Æsir (Germanic deities), 3449–3450
álfar and, 254
body parts sacrificed by, 3452
in creation of man, 3454
Freyja and, 3218
Freyr and, 3219
giants and, 4960
Loki enumerated among, 5508, 5509
marriage among, 3460
Óðinn, 6808–6810
origin of, 3449
in origin of mead myth, 849
Thor as strongest of, 9165–9167
in war with Vanir, 3449–3450, 9685, 9686
Aesthetic existence, Kierkegaard on, 5142
Aesthetics, **44–56**. *See also* Art; *Rasa*
Abhinavagupta on, 9, 4006
in Capps's system of religious study, 1413
etymology of term, 494
feeling and, 46, 48, 494
history of, 9621
of human body, 4170
interactive (creative) discipline and, 8701–8702
Lincoln (Bruce) on, 8471
Maritain (Jacques) on, 5713
of millenarianism, 6029–6030
Nānak on, 6413
philosophical, **44–53**
classical, 44–46
development of, 7110
Eastern, 50–52
Enlightenment, 46–48, 811
Western, 810–811
religious experience and, 48–50, 56, 810, 811, 812–813, 7695–7696
of sacred spaces, vol. 5 color insert
science and religion and, 2660
symbol theory and, 8908
theological, of Balthasar (Hans Urs von), 5482
visual, **53–56**
Aeterni Patris encyclical (Leo XIII), 5411, 9164
Thomis in, 8176
Aetherius Society, 6567, 9433, 9434–9435
Aetios, Arianism of, 478
Aetius (Roman general), 4490–4491
Afanasieva, Veronika, on the Flood, 600
Afendopolo, Caleb, writings of, 5085
Affectional Alchemy, 6874
Affirmations
"decreeing," in New Thought, 1782
religious, Hegel (G. W. F.) on, 3894
Affirmative theology, 2355
Affliction, **56–64**. *See also* Exorcism; Spirit possession
African cults of, 57, **60–64**
central Bantu, 1509–1510, 1511
emergence of, 84
Ndembu, 62, 6446, 7838
in Southern Africa, 8659
agents of, 56–57
Christian views of, healing and, 3848
healing of, 57–59, 60–63
overview of, **56–59**
signs of, 56, 57
victims of, 56, 57, 58
Afghānī, Jamāl al-Dīn al-, **64–65**
ʿAbduh (Muḥammad) and, 5, 64, 4589
and Salafīyah, 4589
influence in Southeast Asia, 4665–4666
modernism of, 6097–6098
Afghanistan and Afghani religions
archaeology of, Foucher (Alfred) and, 3176
Buddhism, 1145, 1146, 1195, 1201
diversity of practice in, folk stories reflecting, 3162
Taliban in
destruction of art and, vol. 11 color insert
globalization and, 3501, 3502
and law, 4703
women in, 3366
women's clothing in, 1833
Afiqoman (dessert), 7004
Africa (journal), 118
Africa and African religions, **83–119**. *See also specific countries, regions, and religions*
academic study of religion in (*See* Study of religion, in Africa)
affliction in, cults of, 57, **60–64**
ancestors in, 60–61, 63
central Bantu, 1509–1510
emergence of, 84
Ndembu, 62, 6446
in southern Africa, 8659
African American religions influenced by, 65–67, 73–74
afterlife in, **139–144**
ancestors in, 89, 141, 142–143
commonalities among, 139
external influences on, 141–143
judgment in, 139, 142
mortuary rituals and, 140–141
nature of humans in, 89, 140–141
amulets and talismans in, 300
ancestors in
and afterlife, views of, 89, 141, 142–143
carved images of, 89
Christian influence on, 142–143
in cults of affliction, 60–61, 63
qualifications for becoming, 89, 141, 322
role of, 85, 89, 141
shrines to, 85, 89, 215
status of, 141
androgynes in, 338
anthropomorphism in, 3569
art of
androgynes in, 338
carved figures, 89, 90
history of study of, 117
ironworking and, 83–84
Asian religions in, 108–109
in Brazil (*See* Afro-Brazilian religions)
Buddhism, 108–109
calendars, 1353
charisma in, 1547
Christianity
adapted forms of, 87
as African *vs.* foreign tradition, 3400
afterlife and, 141–143
Anglicanism, 353, 1721–1722, 1723
beginnings of, 1717–1718
among central Bantu, 1510
Charismatic, 106–107
Churches of Christ in, 1781
in colonial period, 1718–1719
denominations in, 1721–1722
and education, 7292
European leadership of, 104, 7293
growth and expansion of, 1717, 1723, 7290–7291
Harris (William Wade), role of, 3779–3780
independent churches in (*See* African Independent Churches)
indigenous theology of, 2689–2690
among interlacustrine Bantu, 4520–4521
Islam, relations with, 1724, 7292
music in, 6258–6259
new movements in, 102–107
nuns and sisters, 6765
and Nyakyusa religion, 6771, 6772
Pentecostalism, 1724, 7030, 7031, 7032
politics and, 1723–1724, 7292–7295
reforms of, 7293–7294
Roman Catholicism, 1718–1719, 1722, 1723, 6765
in Shona country, 8373–8374
sub-Saharan Africa, **1717–1725**
and supreme beings, 3576, 3577
theology in, 1722
traditional culture merged with, 1721
women in, 3402
among Zulu, 10011
circumcision in, 1798, 1799
clitoridectomy in, 1824, 1825
colonialism in
and African Independent Churches, 104, 105
in Belgian Congo, 2001
Christianity and, 1717–1719, 4520–4521
and cults of affliction, 60, 62
"discovery" and construction of indigenous religions, 1856–1857
fiction exploring, 3087–3088
kingship affected by, 5171–5172
life and, 5449
Maasai, effect on, 2000
mythic interpretation of, 1854–1855
and new religious movements, 102
postcolonial indigeneity, 1858
and prophets, 7443–7444
and religious studies, 115, 8793
Ṣūfī orders, resistance from, 8824

commerce of images in, vol. 7 color insert
commonalities among, 84–85, 139
cosmologies, **1998–2002**
human acts, centrality of, 1992
creation stories of (*See* Creation, in African religions)
cultural diversity in, 1998
culture/ethnicity tied to religions, 66, 83
dance in, 2456–2358
in African Independent Churches, 103
and cultural identity, 2164
study of, 76
trance induced by, 83
deities of, lesser
in daily life, 85
gender of, 3401
heroes as, 86
history of study of, 111, 112
Melqart, 5848
personal encounters with, 86
shrines to, 85
destiny in, 89
diaspora of
Garvey (Marcus) and, 7624
gender in, 3404
healing and medicine in, **3821–3824**
disease and illness in, 60, 62
healing of, 87, 118
as sacred calling, 87
divination in (*See* Divination, in African religions)
dogs in, 2393, 2394
drums in, 2494, 2495–2496, 2500, 7035, 7036–7037
dynamism of, 139
Eckankar in, 2602
Egypt in context of, 2731
elephants in, 2750
ethnic diversity in, 139
ethnological research on, Frobenius (Leo) and, 3222
in evolutionary theory, 113–115
father gods in, 2984, 2985
fetish worship in, 3044, 3045
fiction of, 3085–3089
films from, 3098
frog in, 3223
funeral rites in (*See* Funeral rites, in African religions)
gardens in, 3281
and Garifuna religion, 3283, 3284
gender in, **3400–3406**
fluidity of, 3402, 3403
Mami Wata and, 5630
gender studies in, 3400–3404
geomancy in, 3437
ghosts in, 89, 3476–3477
glossolalia in, 3506
healing in (*See* Healing and medicine, in Africa)
Hinduism, 108
historical background of, 83–84
history of, African *vs.* European focus in, 117–118
history of study of, 73, 75–76, **111–119**
bias and stereotype in, 1998
stasis, assumption of, 1999–2000
supreme beings in, 114, 3576–3577
household shrines in, 4106
human nature in, 84, 85, 89
evil and, 90
imperfection of, 84
iconography of (*See* Iconography, African)
Islam
as African *vs.* foreign tradition, 3400
and afterlife, 141–142
architecture of mosques in, 6209
childbirth practices in, 3819
colonialism and, 4608–4609
and Fulbe religion, 3228, 3229
music in, 6258
in North Africa, **4579–4591**
spread of, 4563, 4601, 4603, 4604, 4607, 4608–4609, 7290–7291
as state religion, 7295
in sub-Saharan Africa, **4600–4612**
Ṣūfī saints and healing, 1547
and supreme beings, 3577
trade and, 4601, 4603, 4604, 4607
women in, 3402–3403, 4609–4610
journals devoted to, 10058
Kimbangu (Simon) in, 5143–5144
kingship in, **5169–5172**
Benin, 5170, 7805–7806
death of king, 7845
divinity of, 84
Edo, 7805–7806
Frazer (James G.) on, 5169, 5170
functions of, 5155
iconography of, 4301–4302
interlacustrine Bantu, 4520
myths about, 95–96, 97, 5171
role of, 84
Lady of the Animals in, 5280
in Latin American fiction, 3064–3065
left and right symbolism in, 5394
lesbianism in, 5414
liberation theology in, 5442
life in, 5445
living dead in, 141, 577
Mami Wata in, **5629–5631**
masks in, 90, 116
distribution of, 5766
as sacred objects, vol. 4 color insert
in secret societies, vol. 6 color insert
mediums in, 87, 89
in southern Africa, 8659
metallurgy in, 94–95, 98–99, 5988
microcosm and macrocosm in, conversion and, 1971
money in, 6137
monotheism in, 85, 86
pantheon of intermediaries and, 3816–3817
Moon and Sun in, 3017, 3018
music in, **6256–6260**
organization of, 6256–6258
time in, 6255
myths of, **91–102**
binary oppositions in, 96–99
blacksmiths in, 94–95, 98–99, 4301, 5988
about creation (*See* Creation, in African religions)
the Fall in, 2960–2961
gender in, 3401–3402
heroes in, 86, 97
mediators between order and disorder in, 91, 93–96
origin of death in, 1875
personal encounters with God in, 91, 92–93, 100
prevalence of, 91
supreme being in, 3567–3568
themes of, 85–86, 91–92
theosophical, 99
tricksters in (*See* Tricksters, in African religions)
Neolithic religions in, 6460, 6465
new movements in, **102–111**
Asian-derived, 108–109
among central Bantu, 1511
Christian, 102–107
classification systems for, 102–103
and disease and cure, interpretations of, 3815
Harrist Church, 3780–3781
Islam-derived, 107–108
native, 6568
neotraditionalist, 109–110
political independence and, 105–106
New Year ceremonies in, 6590
ocean and, 6807
oral traditions of, 3086
ordination in, 6852
overview of, **83–91**
politics and, **7290–7295**
polytheistic aspects of, 85, 86
prophets in (*See* Prophecy and prophets, in African religions)
proverbs of, 91, 6977
purification in (*See* Purification, in African religions)
Rastafari and African identity, 1438, 7622, 7627
redemption in, 7641
reincarnation in, 106, 7677, 9326
religious broadcasting in, 7714
repatriation of, by Rastas, 7622, 7627
rites of passage in (*See* Rites of passage, in African religions)
rituals in, 87–89
animal sacrifice in, 88
conscious component of, 7836
history of study of, 118
human renewal through, 84–85
iconography in, 4303–4304
initiatory (*See* Initiation, in African religions)
for rites of passage, 85, 87–89
without myth, wisdom of, 91
rivers in, 7862
Roman Catholicism, in new religious movements, 105
Roman conquests in, 7911
scarification and cicatrization in, 1003
secret societies in, 7719
secularization in, 8219
shamanism in
origins of, 83
in Sudanese religion, 8849–8850
shrines in, 90
to ancestors, 85, 89, 215
to Mami Wata, 5629, 5630
soul in
origin of, 8533

soul in ***continued***
types of, 8532
spirit possession in, 84, 86, 89, 107, 3402
dance and, 2139
supreme being (God) in, **3567–3579**
anthropomorphism of, 3569
attributes of, 3568
conversion and, 3576, 3577
creation by, 3567–3568, 3621
gender created by, 3401
history of study of, 114, 3576–3577
humans' relationship to, 3568–3569
increasing emphasis on, 84, 85
in Luba religion, 5524
names of, 3568, 6409
near-universal belief in, 85, 86, 92, 3567
notable, 3569–3574, *3575–3576*
personal encounters with, 91, 92–93, 100
in southern African religions, 8655–8656
spiritual beings' relationship to, 3568–3569
as ultimate principle, 85, 86
Western doubts about existence of, 3576–3577
worship of, 3574–3576
temples in, 85, 90, 3576
temptation in, 9069
theism, 1721
tobacco in, 9216–9217
trade and, 66
and spread of Islam, 4601, 4603, 4604, 4607
Vodou and, 2150, 9635
witchcraft in (*See* Witches, in African religions)
women in, **3400–3406**
feminine sacrality of, 3021
secret societies of, vol. 6 color insert
African American religions, **65–83**
African influences on, 65–67, 73–74
Bahā'ī faith, 739
Baptist churches, 784
Liele (George) and, 5442–5443
biblical studies in, 80
black theology's influence on, 77–79
Christianity, 66–70 (*See also* Black theology)
Churches of Christ, 1780–1781
conversion, 1709
evangelicalism in, 2891
missions to South after emancipation, 1751
Pentecostalism, 69, 70, 7029, 10038
percussive breathing in, 7037
segregation in, 4950–4951
Seventh-day Adventism and, 8237
women in, 10037–10039
Crummell (Alexander), role of, 2073, 2074
dance in, 2135, 2150
and cultural identity, 2164
definition of, 65
diversification of, 69–70
drama in, 2476–2477
drums in, 2495–2496, 2500
Du Bois (W. E. B.) on, 66–67, 73–74, 77
gender in, 3361, **10036–10041**
gospel music in, 2477, 6313
history of study of, 66–67, **73–83**
Holiness movement in, 4083, 4084, 10038
hoodoo in, 3142
institutionalization of, 68–69
Islam, 4563, 4686, 4687–4690, 6563 (*See also* Moorish Science; Nation of Islam)
Aḥmadiyah movement, 4687, 4688, 4689
in early America, 6418
Islamic Brotherhood, 4687–4688
Muslim movements, **71–73,** 81
Nuwaubians, 6516, 6768–6770
Qur'ān in, 4687, 4688
spread of, 4687, 4689
studies of, 81
Universal Islamic Society, 4687
women in, 10037, 10039–10040
Judaism, 6563
studies of, 81
kingdom of God in, 5153
liberation theology in, 77–78, 5440–5441, 10040
Masonic lodges, 3198
missions targeting, 71, 72
music in, 77, 6313
gospel, 2477, 6313
women in, 10039
new religious movements, 6563
overview of, **65–71**
Peoples Temple cult and, 4954
prayer in, women leading, 10037
preacher's performance in, 3145
during slavery, 65–66, 68–69
United House of Prayer, 2124–2125
women in, 966
in abolitionism, 10037–10038
Christian, 10037–10039
churches established by, 10037, 10039
in civil rights movement, 10039–10040
as educators, 10038
as leaders, 10036, 10037–10040
as missionaries, 10037–10038
in music, 10039
Muslim, 10037, 10039–10040
roles of, 67, 70, 10036, 10037
and slave religion, 10037
studies by, 76, 80–81, 10040
studies on, 10036–10037
African American Religious Studies (Wilmore), 79
African Americans
American civil religion and, 1815–1816
"black church," emergence of, 1775
in feminism, 3311
Great Migration of, 6418
outsider art of, 9626
in Peace Mission movement, 3007
in Peoples Temple cult, 4954
womanist theology of the body and, 4167
African Americans and the Bible (Wimbush), 80
African Association for the Study of Religions (AASR), role of, 8795
African Baptist Church, establishment of, 104
African Church (U.S.), 4951
African Colonization Society, 9404
African Concepts of God (Mbiti), 117
African Divination Systems (Peek), 117, 10032
African Ideas of God (Smith), 96, 115–116, 3577
African Independent Churches (AICs), 103–105, 2571
amaNazaretha church
establishment of, 103, 1720–1721
Shembe (Isaiah) and, 8316–8317
charismatic Christianity compared with, 106
Ethiopian *vs.* Zionist, 8316
Lumpa church controversy with, 5408–5409
messianic, 8316
mission Christianity criticized by, 103–104
mission Christianity in origins of, 6086
music in, 103, 6259
Nigerian sociopolitical context and, 1723
opposition to, 103, 104
origins of, 6513, 6514
Pentecostalism critique of, 1724
in southern Africa and Congo, 103
in Shona country, 8374
syncretism in, 8933
as synthetist movement, 102
in West Africa, 103–105
African Independent Pentecostal Church, 103
African Initiated Churches. *See* African Independent Churches
African languages
Christian music in, 6259
in Dogon myth, 100–101
Islamization of, 4611
and names of supreme beings, 3568
African Methodist Episcopal (AME) Church, 68
Allen (Richard) as founder of, 68, 264
establishment of, 5998
growth of, 10038
portraits of clergy, vol. 10 color insert
Turner (Henry McNeal) in, 9404
woman bishop of, 10040
African Methodist Episcopal Zion (AMEZ) Church
establishment of, 68, 5998
growth of, 10038
Tubman (Harriet) in, 10037
women as priests in, 68
"African Musical Rhythm and Concepts of Time-Reckoning" (Merriam), 2496
African Orthodox Church, establishment of, 3287
African Religions and Philosophy (Mbiti), 117
African Religions in Western Scholarship (P'Bitek), 117
African Religions of Brazil, The (Bastide), 76
African Systems of Thought (Fortes and Dieterlen), 116, 2350
African Traditional Religion (Idowu), 117
African Union Society, 68
Afrikaner heute und morgen, der (Westermann), 116
Āfrīnagān ritual, 9998
Afro-American Religious History (Sernett), 79
Afro Athlican Constructive Church, 6531
Afro-Brazilian religions, **119–125**. *See also* Candomblé; Umbanda
African religions influencing, 120
commonalities among, 120
geographic distribution of, 120–121
history of study of, 76, 121
Islam, mosques of, 6209
music in, 6272

number of devotees, 121
origins of, 120
persecution of, 124
popular culture influenced by, 124–125
race of devotees, 121
rituals in, 123
Roman Catholicism influencing, 120–121, 124
samba schools hidden in, 1444
slaves and, 120
South American Indian religions influencing, 120
spiritism in, 5091
transculturation of, 9308–9309
women in, 122–123, 10027
Afro-Caribbean religions, **1432–1440**
ancestral cults in, 1435–1436
ashe (vital energy) in, 3823
creolization in, 2066
healing in, **3821–3824**
neo-African cults in, 1433–1435
religio-political cults in, 1437–1438
revivalist cults in, 1436–1437
Shango cult of Trinidad in, 1434–1435
studies of, 10024, 10025–10026
wanga charms in, 3823
Afro-Surinamese religions, **125–127**
Christianity distinct from, 126
origins of, 126
rituals in, 126–127
slaves in, 126
Afterlife, **127–173**. *See also* Ghosts; Heaven; Hell; Immortality; Otherworld; Salvation; Underworld
in African religions, 89, **139–144**
in Kushite religion, 5270
in Shona religion, 8372
ancestors in (*See* Ancestors and ancestor worship)
in Arabian religions, 445
in Aramean religion, 450
in Arctic religions, 472
in Australian Indigenous religions, **144–145,** 147
in Baltic religions, Latvian Saule (sun) cult and, 8132
in Buddhism, 128, 129, 131, 133, 134 (*See also* Saṃsāra)
Chinese, 3136
Pure Land, 1600, 3887–3888
in Bugis religion, 1317–1318
in Caribbean religions, 1428
in Celtic religion, Lucan on, 8392
centrality of beliefs about, 136
in Chinese religion, **169–172** (*See also* Tian)
Buddhism, 3136
Pudu ritual, 1643
purgatory in, 1606
in Christianity, **156–159,** 6926, 7684
Africans influenced by, 142–143
biblical, 156–157
community in, 132
heaven and hell in, 3884–3885
intercession in, 129
medieval, 157–158
Mesoamericans influenced by, 151
nature of humans in, 130
resurrection of body in, 131
Roman Catholicism, 7885–7886
time in, 132, 133
community and, 131–132
differentiation of destinies in, 137–138
distinction from life, 5449
duration of, 136
in Egyptian religion, 9452
in *Book of Going Forth by Day,* 2719
in burial customs, 2703
cosmology of, 2705
divinity in, 2711–2712
geography of, 136, 138
heterodox views of, 2721
importance of, 2716
judgment in, 128–129, 139, 5871
justice in, 128–129
nature of humans in, 130
Osiris and, 7763, 7767
resurrection of body in, 131, 2237, 7763, 7767
shawabtis and, vol. 9 color insert
study of, 2731
time in, 132
eternity and, 2853, 2855
in Etruscan religion, 2874
flowers associated with, 3136
genetic research and, 3428
geographies of, **136–139,** 150
in Germanic religion, **167–169,** 3448, 3456
in sagas, 8025
Greek concepts of, **163–166,** 3678
in Greek religion, 7697, 8542–8543
in Hades, **3724–3726**
in Hawaiian religion, *ʿaumakua* (guardian gods) and, 3799
in Hellenistic religions, 8543–8544
in Hinduism, 128, 129
community in, 131
human nature in, 140
nature of humans in, 130
time in, 132
in Hittite religion, 4069, 4072–4073
hope and, 4126
in Inca religion, 4412
Indian concepts of, 128
intercession and, 129–130
intermediate state in, 134
in Iranian religions, 4537
in Islam, **159–163**
in classical period, 161–162
community in, 131–132, 160–161
falsafah, 2971, 2977
in formative period, 160–161
Heaven and Hell in, 3885
in Qurʾān, 159–162
intercession in, 129, 161
justice in, 129
modern, 162
nature of humans in, 130
rebirth in, 133
resurrection in, 131, 133, 162, 7766–7767
savior concept in, 133
time in, 132
vision of God in, 128
in Japanese religion, heaven and hell in, 3888
in Judaism, **152–156** (*See also* Gehenna; Sheʾol)
in apocalyptic literature, 4975
biblical, 152
genetic research and, 3428
heaven and hell in, 3884
Hellenistic, 152
human nature in, 130
justice in, 129
medieval, 153–155
modern, 155
rabbinic, 152–153, 3548
resurrection of body in, 131, 152, 153, 154
time in, 132
judgment in (*See* Judgment of the dead)
in Khanty religion, 5123
in Kushite religion, 5270
literal *vs.* symbolic interpretations of, 134–135, 162
in Mandaean religion, 3511
Ginza of, 3494–3495
in Mansi religion, 5123
merit in concepts of, 5871–5872
in Mesoamerican religions, **148–152**
Aztec, 3243, 5892
Christian influence on, 151
geography of, 150
human body and, 149–151
notions of death and, 148–149
in Mesopotamian religions
justice in, 128
vision of gods in, 128
in Moabite religion, 6095
in Nabatean religion, 6388
nature of divinity and, 128–130
nature of humankind and, 130–131
in North American Indian religions
cosmology and, 2008
Delaware, 6681
Plains nations, 6703
Pueblo, 6729
in Oceanic religions, **145–148,** 2006–2007, 6784–6785
in Micronesian religions, 6007
in Solomon Islands religions, 8514–8515
overview of, **128–135**
in Phoenician religion, 7132
Plutarch on, 7200
prevalence of belief in, 135, 136
punishment in, 5371
reality in, structure of, 133–135
resurrection of body in, 131–132
reward and punishment in, 134, 136
in Roman religion, **163–166**
Cumont (Franz) on, 2094
in Sami religion, 8087–8088
in Samoyed religion, 8096
scientific proof of, 135
selection for entry into, 136
in South American Indian religions
in Juruna religions, 8629
in Lengua religion, 8634–8635
in Selkʾnam religion, 8225
in Tukanoan religions, 8622–8623
time and history in, 132–133
vision of divine in, 128
war legitimized by, 9680
in Zoroastrianism, 130–131, 9936, 9996
Chinvat Bridge, **1647**
heaven and hell in, 3884
women in, 3373
Afterlife in Roman Paganism (Cumont), soul and immortality in, 2094
Against Apion (Josephus), 427, 925, 4957–4958
Against Celcus (Origen), 6888
Against Eunomius (Basil of Caesarea), 798
Against Heresies (Irenaeus), 3529, 3530, 4538–4539, 6966

Against Hermogenes (Tertullian), 9086
Against Marcion (Justin), 4539
Against Marcion (Tertullian), 9086
Against Praxeas (Tertullian), 9086
Against the Christians (Porphyry), 7191
Against the Errors of the Greeks (Aquinas), 9161, 9162
Against the Heathen (Athanasius), 572
Against the Jews (Tertullian), 9085
Against the Manichaeans (Photios), 7136
Against the Nestorians and Eutychians (Leontius of Byzantium), 5412
Against the Pagans (Arnobius), 4361
Against the Valentinians (Tertullian), 9086
Aga Khan, **172–173**
  creation of title, 172
  ghaybah (concealment) and, 3469
  Ismāʿīlī Shiism under, 4572, 4698–4699, 8333
Aga Khan Development Network, 4646
Aga Khan Foundation, 173
Aga Khan I, 172–173, 4646
Aga Khan II, 173
Aga Khan III, 173, 558, 4646
Aga Khanis. *See* Nizārī Ismāʿīlīyah
Aga Khan IV, 173, 199, 558, 4646
Aga Khan University (Karachi), 173
Agallamh na Senórach, 1495
Agalmata (statues of gods), 4357–4358
Āgamas (Hindu texts), 1198, 4766
  Śaiva Tantras, 4019, 4020
Āgama Śāstra (Indian text), Gauḍapāda as author of, 3289, 3290
Āgama Tīrtha, 746. *See also* Bali and Balinese religion
Agamemnon (mythic king), Hegel (G. W. F.) on, 4220
Agami Islam Santri (Santri Islam religion), 4816, 4817–4818
Agami Jawi (Javanese religion), 4816–4817
Agape. *See* Charity; Eucharist
Agape Europe (Christian mission), 7713–7714
Agarkar, G. G., 9198
Agatai. *See* Kamo no Mabuchi
Agatha (saint), relics of, 7689
Agathangelos, on Gregory the Illuminator, 3700
Agatha Tyche, 1526
Agathoi (good), 7184
Agathon, 2824
Agave (mythic figure), 3383
Agaw religion (Ethiopia), 2573
Agbebi, Mojola, on mission Christianity, 104
Agẹmọ festival, 9910
Agency
  spirit possession and, 8694
  superhuman, in rituals, 7851
Age of Aquarius, 4872, 6495. *See also* New Age movement
Age of Fable, The (Bulfinch), 4459
Age of Reason (Paine), 974
Age of Spiritual Machines, The (Kurzweil), 513
Age-set system, of Agikuyu people, 7805
Ages of the world, **173–177**
  in Aztec religion, 177, 716–717, 5907
  by binary periodization, 173–174
  in Buddhism, 5685–5687
  in Christian historiography, 4028
  gold and silver in, 3626
  in Maya religion, 177, 5934
  in millenarianism, 6029–6030
  by serial periodization, 174–177
Aggadah (Jewish writings), 888, **6013–6023**
  Abraham in, 16
  chosenness of Israel in, 4860
  definition of, 6015
  feminism and, 6021
  as folklore, 6020
  vs. halakhah, 6015
  halakhah and, 3751
  as history *vs.* literature, 6020
  Maimonides (Moses) on, 5615
  midrash, 6014–6017
  Moses in, 6203
  orality of, 6020
  Rashi on, 866
  of Shimʿon ben Laqish, 8348
  Solomon in, 8513
  translations of, 6019–6020
  Yehoshuʿa ben Levi as master of, 9876
Aggañña Sutta (Buddhist text)
  cosmology in, 1134
  politics in, 1090, 7261
Aggeloi (messengers), 2277
Aghlabid dynasty, 4582, 4583
Aghorins (Śaiva ascetics), ritual cannibalism of, 3805
Agikuyu people (Kenya), initiation rites of, 7805
Āg ka Darya (Hyder), 10035
Agla *(Atah Gibbor Le-ʿolam Adonai),* 2932
Aglabem (monster), Malecite myth of, 2091
Aglaia (brilliance), 7174
Aglibol (deity), 449
Aglipay, Gregorio, Philippine Independent Church and, 1727
Aglipay Church. *See* Iglesia Filipina Independiente
Aglona Cathedral, 775
Agni (deity), **178–179**
  on altars, 276
  angels and, 345
  birth of, 4440
  development of, 178
  as fire god, 178–179, 2404, 3116, 3117, 7507, 9557
  inspiration given by, 4509
  in *mantras,* 5677
  mythology of, 178–179
  personality of, 178–179
  Prajāpati identified with, 7356
  as priest, 7405
  as ram, 8311
  redemption and, 7641
  ritual context of, 178
  Rudra associated with, 7934
  in sacrifice, 9821
  tapas of, 8997
  in Vedism, 3990, 9557
Agni-Bora religion (Ivory Coast), funeral rites in, 3236
Agnicayana sacrifice
  altars in, 276
    maṇḍalas in, 5640
  in devotional life, 9821
  human sacrifice in, 4184
Agnīdh (priest), 7405
Agnihotra sacrifice, 9562
  in Brahmanism, 9569
  in devotional life, 9821
  place for, 9564
Agni Purāṇa (Hindu text), 9456
Agniṣṭoma sacrifice, 9562–9563
Agnon, Esther Marx, 179
Agnon, Shemuʾel Yosef, **179–181**
  Nobel prize for, 179
Agnosticism. *See also* Belief; Doubt
  Cārvāka and, 1447
  in evolution of religion, 2914
  knowledge in, 5208
  of Sophists, 3909–3910
  Spencer (Herbert) and, 8678
Agnōstos theos (unknown gods), **181–183**
Agobard of Lyons, on Satan, 8125
Agōgē (Spartan youth training), **183–185**
Agonshū
  in Europe, 6568
  growth of, 6574
  Shingon Buddhism and, 8352
  Shōkō (Asahara) in, 631
  teachings of, 631
Agora of Athens, shrines to Meter in, 2109
Agora sect (India), preparation for death in, 2244
Agrai, Lesser Mysteries at, 6329
Agrat (demon), 5458, 5459
Agricola, Michael, 3110, 4378, 5093
Agricola, Rodolphus. *See* Huysman, Roelof
Agriculture, **185–194**. *See also* Gardens
  in African religions
    Bambara, 776, 777
    central Bantu, 1507
    Diola, 261–262
    Dogon, 2390
    East African, 2566
    impact of, 83
    myths regarding, 93
  ashes in, 541
  in Australian Indigenous religion, 636
  in Aztec religion, 718–719
  in Baltic religion, 757–758
    and Finno-Ugric religions, 3108
    Laima and, 5286
  biodynamic, in anthroposophy, 393
  in Bornean religion, ceremonies of, 1021–1022
  Cain as ancestor of, 1344
  cash cropping, 3280
  cattle and, 1464
  cultures based on
    New Year festivals in, 6590, 6591–6592
    types of, 6591
  dainas (folk songs) dealing with, 2127
  death in, 8402–8403
  deities and spirits of, 188–190, 3622
    in Confucianism, 1913
    examples of, 3622
    in Haitian Vodou, 1433
    in Japanese religion, 5072–5073
    Mars as, 5728
    morphology of, 3617
    in New Caledonia religion, 6501
    nimbus in depictions of, 6624
    Shen Nong (Chinese), 1627
  development and spread of, 186
    and monotheism, 2301–2302
  discovery of, 9578–9579
  divination in, 2371
  emergence of
    economic change from, 3975
    great goddess and, 3975–3976
  and fate, concept of, 2999
  and folk religion, 3150–3151
  geographic distribution of, 185
  given to humankind, 2751
  horn symbolism and, 4130–4131
  humor in, 4197
  in Inca religion, 4524
  in India, rural, 4432
  invention by women, 5281
  in Jainism, 2625
  in Japanese religion, *kami* in, 5072–5073
  in Judaism, Mishnah of, 6066, 6067
  in Komi religion, 5218
  in Korean religion, 5229
  magic in, 5562
  in Maya religion, 5796
    myths of, 191, 192

in Mesoamerica, emergence of, 5880
in Mesopotamia, 5946, 5947
moon and, 6170
mystery religions and, 193, 6328–6329
Neolithic Revolution, 1464
in North American Indian religions, 6654–6655
Iroquois, 6682
in Oceanic religions, gender roles in, 3396
origins of, 185–186
Iroquois myth about, 6682
myths about, 191–192
and prehistoric religions, 7376
rain deities and, 7602
redistribution of produce, 192–193
as ritual, 9578
rituals of, 186–190
creation reenacted in, 2556
earth mother and, 2558–2559
Finnish, 9438
humor in, 4197
Japanese, 2640–2641
in northeast Bantu religion, 2576
orgy at, 6863–6864
origins of, 7835
plant harvest and, 9575–9576
vaginal fluids in, 9907–9908
in Roman religion, festivals of, 7897
sacrifice in
blood and fertility in, 7998
cultic functionaries in, 7997
as homage, 8002
as magic, 8003
as primordial reenactment, 8004
Schmidt (Wilhelm) on, 8168
seasonal ceremonies in, 8208
sexuality in, 8239
sexual symbolism and *hieros gamos* (sacred marriage) in, 3975–3976
in South American Indian religions
Andean ritual calendar and, 8618
origin myths of, 8590
in Southeast Asia, prehistoric, 8641
stability of, protection of nature for, 2632–2633
subsistence, 3278, 3279–3281
as symbolic ritual, 2606
syncretism and, 8928
values associated with, 192–193
violence implicit in, 3015
virgin sacrifice and, 5277
visions of, 9616
in winter carols, 9744
in Zionism, 4906, 9980
zones by crop, 185
Agrippa, Henricus Cornelius
on angels, 348
Hermetism and, 3947, 3948
on magic, 5579
Agrippinilla, Pompeia, 7920
Agta religion, 6455
Agudat Yisra'el (Orthodox movement), **194–197**
anti-Zionism of, 9982
Baiš Ya'akov movement in, 8149
in Eastern Europe, 6902–6903
electoral success of, 195–196
establishment of, 194–195
goals of, 194
Great Assemblies of, 195, 196
ideology of, 194, 195, 196
in Israel, 6903
organization of, 196
Aguilar, Faustino, 3079
Aguna (anchored women), 7822
Agung (sultan of Mataram), 4660, 4661
Agus, Irving, on Me'ir ben Barukh of Rothenburg, 5831
Agushaya (deity), 4405
Agwé, in Haitian Vodou, 1433
Agwu (spirit), 4366
Ägyptische Religion, Die (Erman), 2730
Aha, Rabbi, 9236
Ahab (biblical figure)
fasting by, 2997
Melqart and, 5847
Ahad Ha'am. *See* Ginzberg, Asher
Ahaṃkāra ("I-making"), self and, 8553
Aharon Horwitz of Starosielce, Shne'ur Zalman of Lyady and, 8371
Aharoni, Yohanan, 13
Aḥaronim ("later ones"), *halakhah* and, 3743–3744
Aharon of Lincoln, 5013
Ahasuerus (Perisan king), in *Esther,* 2848
Ahauob (lords or rulers), 5886–5887
Ahaz (king of Judah), 926, 4546, 4547, 4548
Ahaziah (king of Israel), 7103
'Ahd (injunction), election and, 2748
Ahenakew, Alice, on women's curses, 2100
Ahern, Emily, 7268
on Chinese rituals, 7839
Ahijah (prophet), 7436
Ahimelech (biblical figure), 5421
Ahiṃsā (nonviolence), **197–198,** 6645
in Brahmanism, 9571
in Buddhism, 197, 6646
emergence of doctrine, 197, 1467
Gandhi (Mohandas) on, 197, 3272, 4425, 5399, 7023, 7257
in Hindu ethics, 4428
in Indian religions, 6646
in Jainism, 197, 2624–2625, 4429, 5096, 6646, 7023
sacred cow and, 1467
shalom compared with, 6647
and vegetarianism, 197, 7505
verses on, 1105
Ahiqar, 904
Ahirs (India), 4434
Ahithophel (biblical figure), death of, 8829
Aḥkām al-sulṭānīyah, al- (al-Māwardī), 4393, 5787
Ah Kin, calendar and, 1355–1356, 1359
Ahl al-bayt (family of the Prophet), **198–199,** 3008
'Alī ibn Abī Ṭālib as, 198, 199, 256
Sunnī *vs.* Shī'ī belief on, 198–199, 257, 6737
Ahl al-ḥadīth (traditionalism)
ahl al-kalām (rationalism) *vs.*
Ḥanābilah and, 3760–3762, 3765
in historiography, 4029
origins of, 5547
Ahl al-kalām (rationalism). *See also* Mu'tazilah
in Ḥanābilah, 3765
traditionalism *(ahl al-ḥadīth) vs.*
Ḥanābilah and, 3760–3761, 3765
in historiography, 4029
Ahl al-kitāb (people of scripture)
in Qur'ān, 8197
al-Shahrastānī's expansion of concept of, 8267, 8781
Ahl al-Tawḥīd. See Druze
Ahl-i Ḥadīth (Islamic reformist group), 4645, 4653
Ahl-i Ḥaqq movement
as *ghulāt* (extremist), 8324
dualism in, 2514
Ahl-i Qur'ān (Islamic reformist group), 4653
Ahmad, Imtiaz, 3161
Ahmad, Khurshid, 4719
Aḥmad, Masrūr, 200
Aḥmad, Muḥammad. *See* Muḥammad Aḥmad
Aḥmad, Naẓīr, 4652, 10035
Aḥmad Abū Hāshim al-Ḥusaynī, 'Abd al-Jabbār and, 4
Aḥmad al-'Alawī, lineage of, 8711
Ahmad Baba (scholar), 4603
Aḥmad Gangohī, Rashīd, 4652
Ahmad Gran (Ahmad ibn Ibrāhīm al-Ghāzī), 2860, 4606
Aḥmad ibn Ḥanbal
followers of, 3763–3768 (*See also* Ḥanābilah)
on God, attributes of, 617–618, 619, 3563, 3565
Ibn Taymīyah influenced by, 4277–4278
Inquisition *(miḥnah)* and, 3760
life of, 3762–3763
Niẓām al-Mulk on, 6641
on Qur'ān, 3563
traditionalism of, 5548
works of, 3763
Ahmad ibn Ibrāhīm al-Ghāzī (Ahmad Gran), 2860, 4606
Aḥmadī Mosque (Ṭanṭa), 'Abduh (Muḥammad) at, 5
Aḥmadiyah (Islamic movement), **200–201**
in Africa, 108
African Americans in, 72, 4687, 4688, 4689
eschatology of, 2839
Ghulām Aḥmad (Mirza) leading, 72, 108, 200, 4573, 5284
in India, 200
Lāhōrī branch of, 5284–5285
on *jihād,* 200
origins of, 200
pacifism of, 6648
in Pakistan, 200, 4654, 6738
agitation against, 4773
propagation of Islam by, 200–201
on prophecy, 200, 4573, 6738
in South Asia, 4650
split in, 200
Ahmad Khan, Sayyid, **201–203**
and Aligarh movement, 4651–4652
education of, 201
jihād doctrine interpreted by, 4919
on political rights for Muslims, 4654
tafsīr (Qur'anic exegesis) of, 7567, 8955
writings of, 201–202
Aḥmad Riḍā Khān, 4653
Ahmad Shah (sultan of Malacca), 4662
Aḥmad Yasawī (Yasavi), 4616, 4621
Ahmed, Leila, 3314, 3365
Ahmose Nefertari (Egyptian queen), cult of, 2712
Ahmu. dan (servants), 1330
'Aho'eitu (demigod), 7314
Ahreman. *See* Ahriman
Ahriman (Ahreman) (deity), 203–204, 2276, 2985, 10014. *See also* Ahura Mazda; Angra Mainyu
as demiurge-trickster, 2510
evil and sickness caused by, 3809

Ahriman (Ahreman) (deity) ***continued***
in Manichaeism, 5652
opposition to Ohrmazd, 5165
twin of, 9412, 9416
world-periods based on, 174
Aḥruf (letters), 9200
Ahsā'ī, Shaykh Aḥmad al-, 728. *See also* Shaykhīyah movement
excommunication of, 8324
life and thought of, 8307–8308
Ahui, John, Harrist Church and, 3780
Ahura Mazdā (deity), **203–204**
Amesha Spentas and, 290
angels assisting, 344
in Armenian religion, 491, 492
in cosmogony, 9995
creation by, 203, 204
divine kingship of, 5147
in eschatology, 9997
fire in worship of, 570
fravashis as combatants for, 3190
gender of, 3372
and golden age of humanity, 2964, 3629
image of, 4536, vol. 8 color insert
justice of, 129, 4727
as leader of *ahuras*, 2276
light associated with, 5451
Mithra and, 6087
in Mongol religions, 6140
and monotheism, 6157
morality and, 7651
origins of, 4536
prophet of, 2128
qualities of, 3118
rain associated with, 7602
represented in rock tomb, 1472
resurrection of bodies by, 131, 7764
as Spenta Mainyu's father, 9412
Varuṇa identified with, 9524
world-periods based on, 174
Zarathushtra and, 9934
in Zoroastrianism, 9989, 9994–9995
Zurvan and, 10012
Ahuras (lords), **204–205,** 2276, 2314
AI. *See* Artificial intelligence
Ai-apaec (deity), iconography of, 8602
AICs. *See* African Independent Churches
Aided Aenfhir Aífe, Cú Chulainn in, 1494
Aidi (emperor), homosexuality and, 4114
AIFRA. *See* American Indian Religious Freedom Act
Ailey, Alvin, 2159, 2164
Aillén mac Midgna (deity)
death of, 1494
at Samhain, 1492
Ailly, Pierre d', 6645
AIM. *See* Aborigines Inland Mission; American Indian Movement
Ainigma (enigma), 6986
Ainu religion (East Asia), **205–207**
bear ceremony in, 205, 206, 2237, 5514, 10065
deities of, 205–207
family spirits *(inaw)* in, 4106
frenzied behavior among women in, 3214
in Japan, 4780
ocean in, 6806
Old Goddess of the Hearth in, 3018
soul in, 205
time in calendar of, 7990
trees in, 9334, 9336, 9337
Aion, **207–210**
as cosmic god, 208–209
and deification, 2249, 2250
in Gnosticism, 209
meaning of, 207–209, 2855–2856
Osiris identified with, 6921
as sacred time, 7992
Air. *See also* Breath and breathing
in West African religions, worship sites and, 9720
Airāvata (mythic region), 2750
in Jain cosmology, 2023
Air for the G String (Bach), 2158–2159
Airmedh (deity), 9391
Air Primitive (dance style), 2158
Airs, Waters, and Places (Hippocrates), 2606
Airyana Vaējah, **210–211**
geographic location of, 210
"Aischylos" (Dieterich), 2348
'Ā'isha al-Mannūbīyah, 9007
'Ā'ishah bint Abī Bakr, **211**
Abū Bakr as father of, 19, 211
'Alī in conflict with, 211, 258
as Muḥammad's wife, 211, 6224
at Muḥammad's death, 6227
on *mi'rāj,* 6060
political activism of, 211
tafsīr of, 8956
'A'isha Qandisha (spirit), possession by, 8692
Aissaoua (religious society), 6823
'A'isyiyah (reform movement), 3365, 4667
Aitāllāh (martyr), 5660
Aitareya Brāhmaṇa, 824
Aitawe (deity), as "high god," 2006
Aithiopika (Heliodorus of Emesa), 3052, 3054, 3055
Ai Tian, 1609
Aiwel Longar (mythic figure), 96
Aiyanar (deity), 4444
Aiyejina, Funso, 10028
Aiyyappan (deity), 8979
Aĭyys (spirits), 9865
Aĭyy Toĭon (deity), 9081
Aizen'en, 6825
Ajal (term of life), Qur'ān on, 3209
Ajami spirits, in Nanay shamanism, 8284
Ajantā caves, 1076, 1471–1472, 9042, 9043
Ajāwīd (initiated Druze), 2502
Ajax (mythic figure), 4321
Ajikan
meditation, 1294
visualization, in Shingon Buddhism, 8351
Ajita. *See* Maitreya
Ājīvikas (Indian sect), **211–214**
asceticism of, 212–213, 3639
Buddhists criticizing, 1102
determinism of, 213, 3639–3640
doctrines of, 213, 3639–3640
establishment of, 211–212, 3639
Gośāla in, 211–212, 3639–3640
sources on, 3639
temples of, 9040
Ajñā (perfect knowledge), 7357
Ājñā cakra, location of, 1348
Ajnadayn, Battle of (634), 20
Ājñāta Kauṇḍinya (disciple of Buddha), Rājagṛha council and, 2035
Ājurrī, Abū Bakr al-, Ḥanābilah and, 3764
Ajwibah al-fākhirah, al- (al-Qarāfī), 7239–7240
Akaanga (deity), 938
Akademie für die Wissenschaft des Judentums (Berlin), 4882
Akaiṣṭha Heaven, Mahāvairocana and, 5607
Akalogolu (spirits), 4365
Akāl Ustat (hymn from *Dasam Granth*), 2221
Akamboüe (deity), in Island Carib religion, 1427
Akan Doctrine of God (Danquah), 115, 3570
Akan religion (West Africa), **214–216**. *See also* Ashanti religion
ancestors in, 215
Christianity and, 215–216
deities of, 215
diviner-diagnosticians in, 3818
external influences on, 214, 215–216
festivals of, 215
healing rituals in, 118, 215
psychiatric disturbance and, 3821
health and disease in, 3817
bonesetters as healers in, 3820
myths of, 214
creation, 214, 3570
trickster, 86
shrines in, 214, 215
studies of, 115, 118
supreme being of (Nyame), 214, 3570, 5445
transmigration in, 9326
Aka Pygmy religion (Central Africa), 7523–7524
Ākāśagarbha *(bodhisattva),* 1079
"Akashic Record," 392
Akayuš (king of Eqron), 7103
Akazawa Bunji. *See* Konkō Daijin
Akbar (emperor of India), **216–217**
and Chishtīyah, 9009
attitudes toward Islam, 216–217, 4647, 4648–4650
attitudes toward Parsis, 6998
expansion of empire under, 216
gardens and, 3277
Jaina protections under, 2626
Mirabai and, 6048
religious policies of, 216–217, 8414
and Sikh women, 3336
syncretism of, 4007
Akçura, Yusuf, 3624
Akete drums, Rastafarianism and, 1438
Akh (spirit), 2711
Akhādā (military orders), ascestics in, 8021
Akhbār al-Ḥallāj (al-Ḥallāj), anecdotes in, 3757
Akhbārīyah movement, 4697
Ijtihād in, 8343
Shaykh Aḥmad and, 8307
Akhenaton (pharaoh), **217–221**
and Amun, 217, 219, 301, 4320
death of, 219
family of, 217
iconoclasm under, 4285, 4386
portrait of, vol. 10 color insert
religion of, 217–221, 2707, 2711, 4285, 7277, 8837
as monolatry, 3540
monotheism of, 6157, 6159, 8837
tattoos of, 1002
Akhetaton (city in Egypt), 218, 2707
Akhlāq-i Muḥtashimī (Ṭūsī), 9408
Akhlāq-i Nāṣirī (Ṭūsī), 9408
Ākhyānatantra (explanation), 1275
Akihito (Japanese emperor), 4810
Akindynos, Gregory, Gregory Palamas and, 3698
Akitu festival (Mesopotamia), **221–224,** 2959, 6592
Ashur in, 549
in Assyria, 223, 549
Marduk in, 222–223, 6390
Nabu in, 222, 223, 6390
procession in, 7418
rituals in, 2444, 2537–2538
Zimmern (Heinrich) on, 2522
Akitu temple, 221
Akiva ben Joseph. *See* 'Aqiva' ben Yosef

Akkad (Mesopotamia), 5946–5947
- cities of, 5946
- economic activity in, 5947
- Euphrates River in, 5946–5947
- rulers of, 5948

Akkadian language
- dialects of, 5946
- gender in, 3375
- problems with translation of, 5967, 5971
- *vs.* Sumerian language, 5963
- Sumerian language replaced by, 3375

Akkadian religion. *See also* Canaanite religion; Hurrian religion
- cities in, 1802–1803
- cult functionaries, 1386–1387
- deities of, 1382, 1383, 1384 (*See also* An (Anu); Enki; Inanna)
- *hieros gamos* (sacred marriage) in, 3976
- iconography of, 4316, 4317
- literature of, 5967
- myths of, *vs.* Sumerian myths, 5963–5964
- repentance in, 7756–7757
- syncretism and, 8930
- underworld in, 9452
- wisdom of, 9748–9749

Akkadians, ethnic relation to Sumerians, 5963–5964

Akombo (symbol), 9211

'Akraba,' Battle of al-, 20

Aksakov, Ivan, **224**

Akṣarabrahman (god-realized saint), in BAPS movement, 8891

Akṣaradhāma (Hindu concept), in Swaminarayan movement, 8891

Akṣobhya (buddha), 1068, 4329, 9513
- as *tathāgata,* 9016
- Vajrasattva identified with, 9514

Aksum (Ethiopia)
- before Christianity, 224–225
- Christianity in, 2859
- origins of kingdom, 224

Aksumite religion (Ethiopia), **224–225**
- deities of, 224
- temples of, 224–225

Ak'ta (dance), 2466

Aktsini' (deity), 9255

Akutagawa Ryūnosuke, 9315

Ala (deity), 3572

'Ala' al-Dīn Khaljī, 6639

'Alā' al-Dīn Uṣūlī, 6638

Al-Aaraf, bridge of, Judgment and, 3885

Alabês, 123

Alacaluf religion (South America)
- deluge myth in, 8589
- geography of, 8576
- supreme being in, 8579

Al'adam (nonexistence), Mu'tazilah *vs.* Ash'ariyah on, 8568

Aladura movement (Nigeria), 104–105
- common characteristics of, 103
- development of, 104
- as independent churches, 1719–1720
- prayer in, 104
- prophets of, 104, 1720
- worship in, 104–105

Alagaddūpama Sutta (Buddhist text), 1269

'Alah curse, 4740
- in Hebrew scriptures, 2103

Alalu (deity), 302, 2311
- kingship of, 4070
- in Kumarbi cycle, 4231

Alamagest (Ptolemy), astronomy in, 1976

'Ālam al-mithāl (world of symbolic images), 4552

Ālambana-parīkṣā (Dignāga), 2351

Alani religion, Ammianus Marcellinus on, 8114

Alan of Lille, on *Corpus Hermeticum,* 3945

Alans (Caucasus), 4614

Alaric, 628

Alas dialect, 25

Alaska. *See also* Aleut Indians; Inuit religious traditions
- Northern Athapaskan religious traditions in, 572–573
- Russian Orthodoxy in, 1713
  - missions of, 2588, 4497, 7942

Alaskan brown bear, 807

Alastor (spirit), 2277

'Alawī. *See* 'Alawīyūn

'Alawīyūn (Shiism), **225–228**
- as *ghulāt* (extremist), 8323–8324
- Christian influences on, 226–227
- contemporary importance of, 227
- development of, 226
- origins of, 225–226
- reincarnation in, 9330
- rites of passage of, 7825
- Shiism's relation to, 226–227
- size of, 227

Ālaya-vijñāna (storehouse consciousness), **228–229**
- Asaṅga on, 228, 517
- Dharmapāla on, 2338
- Dignāga on, 2351
- in *Laṅkāvatāra Sūtra,* 9018
- in Mahāyāna Buddhism, 1211–1212
- in Yogācāra Buddhism, 9898, 9900–9901
  - emptiness and, 8858
- karmic stream and, 8552
- and perfect enlightenment, 9020
- principles of, 9019

Al-Azhar university (Cairo), **229–231**
- 'Abd al-Rāzīq ('Alī) at, 5
- 'Abduh (Muḥammad) at, 5
- books condemned by, 231
- curriculum at, 229–230, 231
- development of, 229–230
- establishment of, 229
- reforms at, 230–231
- women at, 230

Alba Longa (Italy), 7898

Alban. *See* Monte Albán (Mexico)

Albanese, Catherine, 2661–2662, 2663
- on civil religion, 1814–1815
- on subtle energy in New Age spirituality, 3850

Alban Hills (Italy), 7898–7899

Albania
- Christianity in, 1686
- Islam in, 1686, 4674, 4677

Albanian language, alphabet of, 5764

Albanian Orthodox Church
- autocephalous status of, 2588
- in Orthodox structure, 2589

Alber, Patricia, 3410

Alberic of Brittany, convicted of sacrilege, 8013

Albert (bishop), 767

Alberti, Leon Battista, on Italian Renaissance humanism, 4175

Albert of Hohenzollern (archbishop), Luther (Martin) and, 5535, 7657

Albert the Great. *See* Albertus Magnus

Albertus Magnus, **232–233**
- on Aristotle, 232, 233
- on comets, 8735
- Eckhart (Johannes) under, 2603
- on Hermetism, 3945
- Ibn Rushd opposed by, 4272, 4273
- influence of, 232–233
- on knowledge, 5204
- on magic, 5578
- on nature, 6432
- students of, 232
- Thomas Aquinas and, 232, 9160
- writings of, 232–233

Albigensian crusade, 1458, 4496, 4498, 4499, 7061

Albigensians. *See* Cathari

Albinos
- as monsters, 6165
- sacrifice of, in Africa, 99

Albinus
- on Demiurge, 7189
- writings of, 7189

Albo, Yosef, **233–234**
- Abravanel (Isaac) opposing, 18
- on afterlife, 154
- biblical exegesis of, 866
- Crescas (Ḥasdai) and, 233, 234, 2069
- on God, omnipotence of, 3550
- on prophecy, 7440
- writings of, 233–234

Albornoz, Cristóbal de, 5984

Albrecht, Paul, 2610

Albright, William F., on Israelite monotheism, 3539

Albright, William Foxwell, on Hebrew law, 2098

Alcaeus (Greek poet), 992

Alcala, Jerónimo de, 3244

Alchemist, The (Jonson), 5987

Alchemy, **234–254**
- angels in, 348
- beliefs about metals underlying, 236, 3626
- Boehme (Jakob) and, 1006
- child as symbol in, 1567
- Chinese, **237–241**
  - beliefs underlying, 236, 240
  - elixirs in, 2771
  - external *vs.* internal, 239, 240, 1603
  - Ge Hong on, 3290–3291
  - goals of, 237–238, 240–241
  - history of, 239–240
  - Huangdi (Yellow Emperor deity) in, 4144
  - immorality in, 235, 237–238, 1589, 1597, 3625
  - metallurgy in, 236
  - origin of, 2990
  - *qi* cultivation and, 3862
  - and reversal of time, 7683
  - secrecy in, 235
  - techniques of, 238–239
- Christian dogma in, 252
- color in, 251, 1862
- as completion of nature, 236, 5987
- Daoist, 237, 238, 241, 2184–2185, 2636–2637, 5318, 8996, 9845
- definitions of, 237
- elixir in, 2770, 2771
- in esotericism, Faivre paradigm of, 2844
- esoteric traditions associated with, 235
- Eucharist as, in Holy Order of MANS, 4102
- goals of, 234–235, 3626
- Hellenistic and medieval, **244–248**
- Hermetism and
  - German writers on, 3951
  - medicine and, 3949
  - texts on, 3940
- in Hungary, 4226
- and immortality, 2237
- Indian, **241–244**
  - goals of, 242, 243
  - history of, 243–244

Indian ***continued***
principles of, 242
Tantric Buddhism and, 3866
techniques of, 242
inner, 2185, 2187, 2188
in China, Liu An and, 5494–5495
in Korea, 2189
writings on, 2211
internal, *Arcana Arcanorum* as, 8252
Islamic, **248–250**
language of, 246–247
massa confusa, 1540
mortification of kings in, 6198
and nature, philosophy of, 6433
Newton and, 6589
origins of, 235, 239, 247, 248
overview of, **234–237**
Renaissance, **250–254**
and reversal of time, 7683
Rosicrucian, 253, 7930
salt used in, 8059
science based on, 250, 252–253
scientific interest in, 234
secrecy in, 235, 246
as spiritual discipline, 234–235, 252
time mastered through, 236–237, 7683
in Western esotericism, 2843
writings on, obscurity of, 252
in yoga, 7641
Alcheringa (spirit being), reincarnation and, 7677
Alchi (Buddhist temple), 9051
Alcibiades, 971
on Socrates, 8709
Alciphron (Berkeley), 2779
Alciphron (Greek rhetorician), 991
Alcis (divine twins), 3450, 3451
Alcmaeon of Croton, on catasterism, 8424
Alcman (Greek poet), on Africans, 111
Alcmene (Queen of Thebes), Zeus and, 3916
Alcohol, Tobacco, and Firearms, Bureau of, and Branch Davidians, 5237
Alcoholic beverages, 848–850. *See also* Beer; *Haoma; Soma;* Temperance movement; Wine
abstinence from
in Buddhism, 3168
in Hinduism, 3168
in Islam, 3168, 4683
in Baltic religion, 757
in Bambari religion, 776–777
in Hinduism
abstinence from, 3168
Balarāma's addiction to, 743
in Huastec religion, 5910
in Indo-European religions, 4455
and inspiration, 4509
in North American Indian culture, colonialism and, 6664
as sacrifice, 849
in South American Indian religions, 848
Alcoholics Anonymous (AA), as holistic health system, 3851
Alcott, Louisa May, 7323
Alcuin (scholar), **254,** 7280
Alder tree, 9336
Aldhelm of Sherborne (bishop), 6943
Ale, 848
ʿAleinu (prayer), in *siddur* liturgy, 8389
Aleksandr Nevskiy (prince), 7941
Alekseev, N. A., 475
Aleksei (tsar of Russia), 6621, 6622
Alembert, Jean le Rond d', 2783–2784
in French Enlightenment, 2796
ʿAlenu (Jewish prayer), 5148
ALEPH (Alliance for Jewish Renewal), 4869
Aleph, Aum Shinrikyō as, 631, 632
Aleppo (Syria)
Adad in, 27–28
Dagan in, 2126
Melqart in, 5846–5847
Aletophilus, *Corpus Hermeticum* and, 3950–3951
Aleutian language, 4497
Aleut Indians
calendar, 1353
Russian Orthodox missions to, 4497
Alevis. *See* ʿAlawīyūn
Alexander, Bobby C., 7859
Alexander, Lindsay, 499
Alexander, Samuel, atheism and, 584
Alexander II (pope), Gregory VII under, 3690
Alexander II (Russian tsar), anti-Muslim campaigns of, 4617
Alexander III. *See* Alexander the Great
Alexander III (pope)
on papal elections, 6971
Waldensians and, 9662
Alexander III (Russian tsar), anti-Muslim campaigns of, 4617
Alexander V (pope)
election of, 6971
Great Western Schism and, 8157
Hus (Jan), recognition by, 4233
Alexander VI (pope)
and Torquemada (Tomás de), 9242
election of, 9341
notoriety of, 6972
as Paul III's mentor, 9341, 9342
on Pico della Mirandola, 7141
Alexander VII (pope)
Jansenism condemned by, 7001
laxism rejected by, 6973
Alexander VIII (pope), rigorism rejected by, 6973
Alexander Jannaeus (Hasmonean king), 7064
Alexander Lysimachus (brother of Philo Judaeus), 7105
Alexander of Alexandria
Arianism opposed by, 478
Athanasius and, 571
Alexander of Aphrodisas
on Aristotle, 479, 481
influence on *falsafah,* 2971
Maimonides (Moses) influenced by, 5617
Alexander of Hales, 7067
Alexander Polyhistor, 901
on the Flood, 599–600
Alexander the Great
and anti-Semitism, 398
apotheosis of, 437–438
Aristotle as tutor of, 483
and culture, 4322
death of, division of empire following, 5167
and decline of Delphi, 2266
as divine, 3902, 3903
dragon as father of, 2433
Egyptian religion under, 2709
Hellenism and, 3900, 3901
in Hellenistic period, 3599
kneeling before, 5196
Melqart and, 5847
Phoenicians ruled by, 7129
temples built by, 9063
Zoroastrianism and, magi denouncement of, 9990
Alexandra (anchoress), 2825
Alexandre, Charles, on *Sibylline Oracles,* 8384
Alexandria (Egypt)
catechetical school of, 1979
Christian persecution in, 7059
as cultural capital, Hellenistic, 3901
Cyrenaica and Christianity in, 1677–1678
in early Christian structure, 2581
in early Christian theology, 2583, 2584, 2884–2885
ecumenical councils and, 1979
Gnosticism in, 3511–3512, 3516
Greek Orthodox patriarchate of, 3658
as intellectual center, 2710
Jews of, and Septuagint, 890
parabalani (medical corps) in, 3844
theological diversity in, 1823
Alexandria, school of, biblical interpretation at, 5486
Alexandria, Synod of (362), three hypostases doctrine at, 4241
Alexandrian Wicca, 9729
Alexandrinus Codex, 891
Alexarchus, utopian Ouranopolis founded by, 3906
Alexie, Sherman, 3093, 7226
Alexikakos ("He Who Protects from Evil"), Herakles as, 3917
Álfa dróttinn, 2693
Álfar (elves), **254–255**
Alfarabi (Islamic philosopher), on prophecy, 7439
Alfardas (flat ramps), 9066
Alfasi, Yitsḥaq ben Yaʿaqov, **255–256,** 4990
writings of, 255
Alföldi, Andreas, Brelich (Angelo) studying under, 1047
Alfonsine Tables (Alfonso X of Castile), 7492
Alfonso V (king of Aragon), government of, Abravanel (Isaac) in, 17
Alfonso VI (king of Castile), 4591
Alfonso X the Wise (king of Castile), 4597, 7492
Algebra
geometrical, *3439,* 3440
in Islam, 3566
Algeria
immigrants from, 4675, 4676, 4677, 4678, 4679
Islam in
Islamic law, 4701
as state religion, 4590
waqf in, 9678
Khārijīs in, 5127
literature of, 3088
Sephardic Jews in, 4996
Algonquian (Algonkian) religion (North America)
burial practices in, 6684
cosmology of, 6680
creation myth of, rabbit in, 7590
frenzied behavior in, 3214
Lady of the Animals in, 5280
lord of the animals in, 5515
manitou in, 5673, 6650, 6680
Michabo, miraculous birth of, 1568
in Northeast Woodlands region, 6679
in Plains region, 6656, 6696
puberty rites of, 6683
revelatory retreats of, 7769
sacred lodge in, 1504
in sub-Arctic region, 6655, 6674
mythology, 6675
supreme being in, 8870–8871
tobacco in, 9218
tricksters in, 9355
turtles in, 9407
Windigo monster in, 1403
Ali, Kecia, 3367
Ali, Noble Drew. *See* Drew, Timothy
ʿAlī al-Riḍā (caliph)
Imami succession and, 8322
and Muʿtazilah, 6319
Alianza Islamica, 4690

'Alids (progeny of 'Alī)
  caliphate and, 1366
  and dominance of Shiism in North Africa, 4583
Alienation
  Marx (Karl) on, 5745
  vs. membership, in sociology, 8482
Aliens. *See* UFO religions
Alif (letter), calligraphy and, 1373
Aligarh movement (India), 4651–4652
'Alī ibn Abī Ṭālib, **256–261**
  as *ahl al-bayt,* 198, 199, 256
  'Ā'ishah bint Abī Bakr in conflict with, 211, 258
  alchemy and, 248
  and origin of Khārijīs, 5126
  in arbitration, 258–259
  as Fāṭimah's husband, 256, 3008
  as first *imām,* 259
  as *kāfir,* 4567
  as Muḥammad's companion, 256–257
  as Muḥammad's successor, 257
  assassination of, 259, 7285
  caliphate and, 1366
  caliphate of, 257–259, 4693
    challenges to, 258–259
    legitimacy of, 259
  caliphs opposed by, 257
  devotional allegiance to, 9819
  family of, 256
  followers of (*See* 'Alawīyūn)
  frenzy in battle, 3213
  ghaybah (concealment) of, 3468
  Kufic calligraphy and, 1372
  legacy of, 259–260
  mawlid of, 5788
  on *mahdī,* 5981
  on *taqīyah,* 8999
  in Shiism, 257, 259, 4693
    devotion to, 9658–9659
    founding of, 8320
  shrine of, 260
  in Sufism, 260
  Sunnī *vs.* Shī'ī belief regarding, 257, 259
  walāyah and, 9658
  as warrior, 256
'Alī ibn 'Uthmān ibn 'Alī al-Jullābī al-Ghaznawī al-Hujwīrī. *See* Hujwīrī, al-
'Ali ibn Waḥshīyā', on alchemy, 249
'Alīm (religious scholar), 4648
'Alī Muḥammad, Sayyid. *See* Bāb, the
Alinesitoue Diatta, **261–262**
  prophecy of, 261–262, 2355, 7444
'Alī Shāh. *See* Aga Khan II
'Alī Shīr Navā'ī, Mīr Niẓām al-Dīn, **262–263**
'Ali Turshīzī, Mullā Shaykh, 728
Aliyan Baal, 2536
  in Canaanite religion, 1383
'Aliyyah le-regel (pilgrimage), 7161
'Aliyyat neshamah, 726
'Alī Zayn al-'Ābidīn, 550
Alkabets, Shelomoh ha-Levi
  and Qabbalah, 7534
  relationship with Karo (Yosef), 5104
Alkabetz, Shelomoh, automatic speech from, 1985
Alkalai, Yehudah ben Shelomoh, **263–264**
  nationalism of, 263
  Zionism of, 9979
Alkas (hill), 774
Alkinoos, 7189
Allāh. *See also* Islam, God in
  in Agami Jawa, 4816
  Bugis name of, 1317
  derivation of name, 2252
  in eschatology, 2837
  exclusive divinity of, 4385
  as god of rain, 2301
  in Shahāda, 8014, 8266
  meaning of term, 2063
  origins of term, 3560–3561, 6407
  power of name, 6406
  translations of term, 3561, 6407
  verbal mentioning of, 2339
  water and, 7602
Allama Prabhu (poet), 7210
All-American Council (Orthodox), 1766
Allani (deity), 3595
Allāt (deity), 2984
  in Arabian religions, 444
  in Aramean religion, 449–450
  Muḥammad's ban on, 6222
  in Nabatean religion, 6386, 6389, 6390
All Beings, Council of, in Earth First!, 2563
All-Ceylon Buddhist Congress (ACBC), 5625
Allegorical interpretation
  in Christianity, Hugh of Saint-Victor on, 4151
  Figurist movement and, 1631
  in Islamic eschatology, 2839
  of myths, 6365
  Philo Judaeus influenced by, 7106
  in Stoicism, 3912
    historiography and, 4036
    on Homeric scenes, 4108
Allegory of the Jewish Law (Philo Judaeus), 16, 4359
Allelophagia, 2357
Allen, Douglas, 7097
  on study of religion, 7746
Allen, Grant, 114
  on manism, 5671, 5673
Allen, Horace, 5234
Allen, N. J., 4465
Allen, Paula Gunn, 3093
  on female concepts of sacredness, 3406–3407
Allen, Richard, **264–265,** 4950–4951
  AME Church founded by, 68, 264
Allen, Roland, 677
All-Europe Pentecostal Conference, 7033
All-Father (spirit), **265–266**
  divinity of, 265
  Howitt (A. W.) on, 265, 4142
  names for, 265
  studies on, 265
All Fools' Day, **266**
All Hallows Eve. *See also* Halloween
  Samhain and, 3759
Alliance for Jewish Renewal. *See* ALEPH
Alliance Israélite Universelle, 5000
  Alkalai (Yehudah ben Shelomoh) and, 263
Alliance of Religion and Conservation (ARC), 2613
Alliance of the Orthodox One with the Powers, 9844
Alliances, marriage for creating, 5725
Alligator Jump dance, in Arawak religion, 8583
All-India Kashiraj Trust, 7497
All-India Women's Conference, 845
Allione, Tsultrim, 9190
All-Mother, Sophia as, 8523
Allogenes (Gnostic text), *hypostasis* in, 4242
Allotactic initiation, 9721
Allport, Gordon, 7476, 7477
All-Russian Church Council, 7942
All Saints, Feast of, Samhain and, 3759
All Saints Church (England), 7029
All Saints Day, 2227
  in Balto-Finnic areas, 3108
  beliefs and practices of, 2229–2230
  observances of, 2228
  in Tarascan religion, 9002
All Souls Day, 2227
  belief in ghosts and, 3475
  beliefs and practices of, 2229, 2230
  liturgical status of, 2229
  observances of, 2228–2229
  in Tarascan religion, 9002
All Souls Festival
  ancestor worship in, 323
  domestic observances of, 2399
Almagest (Ptolemy), 7491, 7492
Almagro-Gorbea, Martin, 4251
'Almah (virgin), 7233
Almanacs
  Chinese
    calendar as, 1641
    magic in, 5593
  pre-Columbian, 1359
Almas (Bulgar king), 4616
Almazan, Pascual, 4684
Almodóvar, Pedro, 3099
Almohad dynasty, 4585–4587
  in Andalusia, 4592, 4593, 4595, 4596
  faqīh challenged by, 4585–4586
  reform movements in, 835
Almond, Philip, and Australian theory of religion, 8769
Almoravid dynasty, 4585
  in Andalusia, 4592, 4593
  faqīh in, 4585
  reform movements in, 835
  and spread of Islam, 4601
Almsgiving, **266–269**. *See also* Charity
  in Buddhism, 267, 268, 3483, 5099
  in Christianity, 267, 268
  definition of, 266
  in Islam, 267, 268
  in Judaism, 267–268
  to mendicants, 5855–5856
Aloni, N., on *Sefer yetsirah,* 8221
Ālp Arsalān, 6639, 6640
Alphabetic encyclopedias, 2783
Alphabet of Ben Sira (Hebrew text), Lilith in, 5459
Alphabets, **269–275**. *See also* Calligraphy; Writing
  Albanian, 5764
  Alif, meaning of, 1373
  in amulets and talismans, 298
  Armenian, 492
    Mashtots' (Mesrop) and, 5763–5764
    Sahak Parthev and, 8026
  Avestan, invention of, 5561
  calendars and, 1353
  Cuneiform, 1382
  Cyrillic, 2116
  definition of, 269
  Georgian, 5764
  Hebrew
    meditation based on, 5817
    mystical speculation on, 271–272, *273,* 544
  Maya, 5886
  mystical speculation on, 270–274
    in Qabbalah, in *Sefer yetsirah,* 8221
  in *New England Primer,* vol. 14 color insert
  origin of, 269–270
  runic, 7938–7941
alpha Centauri (constellation), in ethnoastronomy, 2866
Alp Ilteber (Hun prince), conversion of, 4229

Alps, attitudes toward, 6212
Alroy, David, messianism of, 5977
Alshekh, Mosheh, 867
Alsop, George, 6985
Alster, Bent, 2522
Alston, William, religion defined by, 7703–7704
Altaic language family, 4488
Altaic religion. *See also* Siberia and Siberian religions
  Castrén (Matthias) on, 1453
  creation story of, 3223
  migration to Japan, 4780
  ocean in, 6807
  Tengri as sky god of, 9081
  Umai in, 9443
  white shamans in, 8272
Altai-Sayan religion, Erlik in, 2831–2832
Altan Khan, 1149, 1154, 1228
  Buddhism and, 6142
  and Dalai Lama designation, 2131
"Altar, The" (Herbert), 7204
Altars, **275–279**
  African
    skull in family altars in, 3806
    for supreme beings, 3576
    West African, 9719
  Armenian, 491
  Brahmanic, 7837
  Chinese, 2408
  Christian, 277–278
    focus on, 793, 796
    multiplication of, 793
    relics in, 7688
  circular, 1792
  Etruscan, 9064
  functions of, 275
  Greek sacrificial, 4381
  Hindu, 275–276, 9038, 9039–9040
    maṇḍalas in, 5640
  Israelite, in Temple, 925, 932
  Japanese, 2410–2411
  Jewish, 276–277
  Mesoamerican, in colonial period, 5920
  Roman, 9064–9065
  Sarmatian, zoomorphic images on, 8115
  Scythian, 8205
  Tibetan, in museum, 6244
  Vedic, *maṇḍalas* and, 5645
  Vietnamese, 9594
  in Vodou, 9634–9635
Altekar, A. S., on women, 3320–3321
Altepetl, 9214
  in Aztec Mexico, 5172
Alter, Robert, 5474, 5488, 6377, 6378
Altered states of consciousness. *See* Consciousness, states of
Alternative medicine. *See* Healing and medicine
Alternative religions. *See* New religious movements
Altertumswissenschaft (science of antiquity), ancient Jews excluded from, 4875
Älteste Urkunde des Menschengeschlechts (Herder), Biblical hermeneutics in, 3919
Althaus, Paul, on kingdom of God, 5151
Althusser, Louis, 3028
Altizer, Thomas J. J., 4283
  on death of God, 585, 5489
Altruism
  evolution and, 2660
  in sociobiology, 8474
  Sorokin (Pitirim Aleksandrovich) on, 8524
Altynsaryn, Ibrai, 4622, 4623
Aluelap (deity), 6010
Aluk To Dolo. *See* Toraja religion
Alusi (spirits), 4365
Alvaro I (king of Congo), 112
Āḻvārs (Hindu poets), **279–280,** 4430, 9503
  in Śrī Vaiṣṇavas Sampradāya, 8727, 8728
  Kṛṣṇa and, 5252
  poetry of, 7210, 8974, 10088
  saint-singer tradition and, 4005–4006
  Viṣṇu and, 5252
Alvarus (Andalusian martyr), 4593
Alvíss (dwarf), 2532, 2693
Alvíssmál (eddic poem), 2532, 2693
"Always Is He Criticized" (Young Bear), 7225
Alypius, 624, 625
AMA. *See* American Medical Association
Āma, in Āyurveda, 3855
Amadlozi (ancestors), 10008, 10009–10010
Amado, Jorge, 3064, 3065
Amaethon (deity), 1489
  in *Mabinogion,* 5546
Amaicuva (cave), in Caribbean religions, 1429
Amaka (bear), 9394
Amal (burdensome toil), in *Ecclesiastes,* 2600
Amalarius of Metz, 2468
Amalek (biblical figure)
  Haman and, 2848
  Joshua and, 4958
Amalgation, syncretism and, 8932
Ama-mul (Eblaite priest), 2598
Amānah (trust or stewardship), 4761
  nature in, 2604
Amana Society, 6558
AmaNazaretha (Nazareth Baptist Church)
  establishment of, 103, 1720–1721
  ideology of, 103
  liturgy of, 103
  Shembe (Isaiah) as founder of, **8316–8317**
Amangkurat I (sultan of Aceh), 4665
Amanita muscaria, 849
AMA-ra (deity), Eblaite festival of, 2597
Amaranth, 3137
Amaraśakti (king of Mahilaropya), 6959
Amar Dās
  and *Ādi Granth,* 32
  conversion to Sikhism, 3335
  women and, 3335–3336
Amarna (Egypt)
  Akhenaton in, 218–219
  archaeology at, 456
Amarna letters, Canaanite religion and, 1381
Amaro, Bibi, 3335
Amaro of Hira (Arab king), 5660
Amaru (serpent), 4411
  Inca calendar and, 1364
Amasanga (spirit master), 281–282, 284
Amasank. *See* Amasanga
Amata-dundubhiḥ (drum), 2496
Amaterasu Ōmikami (deity), **280–281,** 2984, 3018, 4416, 4755
  and Ame no Koyane, 289–290
  canonization of, 4783
  in creation, 4801
  and domestic observances, 2410
  in drama, 2454
  emperor descended from, 5157, 8367
    canonization of, 4783
    Shintō and, 2639
  enthronement ceremony and, 1514–1515
  Fudō identified with, 3226
  Gyōgi and, 3721
  humor in myth of, 4206
  in Kurozumikyō, 5267
  in *Kojiki,* 4810
  as Lady of the Animals, 5280
  Māra and, 5691
  mirrors and, 280–281, 6063
  in new religious movements, 6572, 6573
  in *Nihonshoki,* 4810
  Ninigi and, 5180
  pilgrimages for, 4798
  relationship with brother, 2985
  as sun goddess, 8841
  Tenshō kōtai jingū kyō movement and, 8369
  during Tokugawa shogunate, 6572
  Yamato clan and, 8358
  at Yoshida shrine (Kyoto), 8364
Amaunet (deity), 301
  in Egyptian pantheon, 2704
Amaushumgalana (deity), 5949
  Dumuzi as, 5957
  marriage of, 5951
Amāvsāsyā (new moon), in Hindu calendar, 4015
Amawolo/Amarawi (deity), 5445
Ama-Ziyoni, 103
Amazonian religions
  afterlife in, in Tukanoan religion, 8622–8623
  animal dances in, 8581
  Arawak (*See* Arawak Indians)
  Araweté, 8628
  Baniwa and Kuripako
    disease, myth of origin of, 3809
    overview of, 8624–8625
  Carib (*See* Carib Indians)
  central and eastern Amazon, **8626–8632**
    caboclo religion in, 8631–8632
    contact history of, 8627
    contemporary religions in, 8627–8631
    prehistoric cultures and religious manifestations in, 8627
  Christianity in
    caboclos and, 8632
    Evangelical Protestantism, 8625
    missionary penetration in, 8623–8624
    Palikur Indians and, 8627–8628
  cosmology in
    Baniwa, 8624–8625
    Juruna, 8628–8629
    Kulina, 2012
    Maku, 8625
    Palikur, 8628
    Tukanoan, 8622
    Yanomami, 8625
  creation myths in
    Baniwa, 8624
    Makiritare, 8626
    Palikur, 8627–8628
    Tukanoan, 8622
  geography of, 8575
    central and eastern region, 8626–8627
    northwest region, 8621
  Ge-Timbira, 8629–8631
    Canela in, 8629
    Kayapó in, 8630
    Krahó in, 8629–8630
    Xikrin in, 8630–8631
  initiation in, 4486
  jaguar imagery in, 4763
  Kulina, transformation and metamorphosis in, 2012
  Lévi-Strauss (Claude) on, 8596
  Makiratare, 8626
  Maku, 8625
  in Mundurucú
    ancestor worship in, 8584
    deities of, 8577
    mother spirit in, 8580–8581
  music in, 6272
  nativistic movements in, 6576
  in Northwest Amazon, **8621–8626**
    contemporary religions in, 8622–8626
    early history of, 8621

psychedelic drugs in, 7470, 7472
Quechua, **281–285**
creation myths of, 3130
dreams in, 2484
flood myth in, 3130, 3131, 3132
history of study of, 281
spirit masters in, 281–282
shamanism in, Tukanoan, 8623
transformation in, 2011–2012
Tukanoan, 8622–8624
Tupian
Juruna religion in, 8628–8629
myth of Korupira, 2091
Witóto, deities of, 8576–8577
Yanomami
overview of, 8625–8626
plant hallucinogens in, 8292
Yurupary in, 9917–9920
Zapiteri Mashco, World Fire myth in, 8589
Amazonians (mythic figures), and gender roles, 3383
Amazonism, 731
Amba people (East Africa), ablutions in, 11
Ambedkar, B. R., **285–287,** 1126, 1282, 2689, 2785, 5400
conversion to Buddhism, 286–287, 5699, 9477
Ambidj (Rainbow Snake), 7606
Ambikā (deity), 2526
Ambrim religions. *See* Vanuatu and Vanuatu religions
Ambrose of Milan, **287–288**
on asceticism, 7723
Augustine and, 288, 624, 625
on chastity, 1558
ethics of, 287
on morality, 1651
poetry of, 7218
and Theodosius, 9124
theological issues addressed by, 2581
writings of, 287–288
Ambundu people, kingship of, 5157
A mchi medicine (Tibetan)
overview of, 3865–3866
specialists in, 3864
Amduat (Egyptian text), 2708, 4318, 4319
AME. *See* African Methodist Episcopal
Ame (heaven), in Japanese religion, 3888
Ameer Ali, Syed, **288–289**
apologetics of, 429
education of, 288
writings of, 288–289, 4652
Ameimar (amora), on *shekhinah,* 8314
Ameipsias, on Socrates, 8501
Amelineau, M. A., 3532
Amelius, 6474
Amen, in Qabbalah, 8676
Amenemhet I (Egyptian king), 2706
Amenhotep I (Egyptian king), cult of, 2712
Amenhotep II (Egyptian king), cult of Reshef and, 7760
Amenhotep III (Egyptian king), 2707
Amenhotep IV. *See* Akhenaton
Amenhotep Son of Hapu (architect), cult of, 2712
Amenirdis I (Divine Adoratress of Amun), 2709
Ame no Koyane (deity), **289–290**
Amenophis II, Rashap as patron god of, 1384
Amenophis III and IV, Canaanite religion and, 1381
Ame no Uzume (deity)
Amaterasu Ōmikami and, 280
in drama, 2454
humor and, 4206
Amenta Club (Temple Solaire), 6554, 9067
Ameretāt (spirit), 290
in Armenian religion, 492
gender of, 3372
America. *See* United States
American Academy of Jewish Research, 4883–4884
American Academy of Religion (AAR)
journal of, 10057
men's studies in, 5862
role of, 8788
study of new religions in, 6565
subaltern studies and, 8802
women's studies in, 3313
American Adam, The (Lewis), 6985
American Anthropological Association, 3614
American Anthropologist (journal), 10056
American Association of Pastoral Counseling (AAPC), 7487
American Baptist Association, 786
American Baptist Churches, 784
American Baptist Convention, Consolidated, 69
American black bear, 807
American Catholic church, Carroll's plan for, 1445
American Catholic Missionary Society, in Latin America, 1702
American Christian Missionary Society, Campbell (Alexander) and, 1377
American Civil Liberties Union (ACLU), opposing deprogramming, 2292
American civil religion. *See* Civil religion
American Civil War
African American religions after, 69
civil religion and, 1814
denominational splits and, 1712
Disciples of Christ during, 2365
Turner (Henry McNeal) as chaplain in, 9404
American colonies. *See* United States, colonial
American Council of Christian Churches, 2890
American Ethical Union, 2857
American Family Foundation, 396, 397, 4522
American Genesis (Taylor), 2163
American Indian Autobiography (Brumble), 702
American Indian Movement (AIM), 6667–6668
American Indian religions. *See* North American Indian religions
American Indian Religious Freedom Act (AIFRA) of 1978, 6668, 6711, 10054
American Indian Religious Freedom Resolution (1978), 7303
American Indians. *See* North American Indian religions
American Indian Stories (Zitkala-Sa), 3090
American Islamic Mission, 4563
American Islamic Propaganda Movement, 4686
American Jewish Congress, Gaster (Theodor H.) in, 3288
American Jewish Historical Society, 4879
American Jewish Orthodoxy, 7773
American Lutheran Church, 5540
American Lutheranism, 5539
American Medical Association (AMA), *Code of Ethics* of, 5810
American Medical Missionary College, founding of, 8236–8237
American Museum of Natural History (New York), Mead (Margaret) at, 5803
American Muslim Mission, 72, 6419
American Negro Academy, Crummell (Alexander) and, 2074
American Oriental Society, 1315
American Psychological Association (APA), on cultic brainwashing, 1033
American Revolution
anti-Semitism and, 401
civil religion and, 1814, 1815
religious elements in, 7257
religious toleration and, 1711, 7283
American Rhythm, The: Studies and Reëxpressions of Amerindian Songs (Austin), 7224
American Scientific Affiliation, and field of science and religion, 8184
American Shakers, 5389
American Society for the Study of Religion (ASSR)
Eliade in, 2756
Oxtoby (Willard) in, 10055
American Society of Bioethics and Humanities, 940
American Theosophical Society. *See also* Point Loma Theosophical Community
Gage (Matilda Joslyn) in, 3252
American Unitarian Association, 9469–9470. *See also* Unitarian Universalist Association
Channing's leadership in, 1530
emergence of, 1712
Ames, William (Amesius), 7142
Âmes de Dogon, les (Dieterlen), 116
Amesha Spentas (spirits), **290–291**
as angels, 344
gender of, 3372
in opposition to archdemons, 2128
origins of, 4537
AMEZ. *See* African Methodist Episcopal Zion
Amhairghin (mythic figure), 1488, 1489
Amhara-Tigriña people (Ethiopia), 2573
Amharic language, 3085
Amichai, Yehuda, 6021
ʿAmida (prayer), 983
Amida Buddha. *See* Amitābha
Amida Buddhism. *See* Pure Land Buddhism
ʿAmidah (Jewish prayer), 9806
resurrection in, 7765
Amida *mantra,* 3155–3156
Amidism. *See* Pure Land Buddhism; *See* Amitābha
Amīn, Qāsim, 3365
Amine, Abdul Rahman C., 5812
Amīr al-Muʾminīn (counselor of the believers), 9444
Amīr Khusraw. *See* Khusraw, Amīr
Amish
dress code and social control among, 1835–1836
schools of, 7734
split from other Mennonites, 5861
Amitābha (buddha), **291–293,** 1067–1068, 1078. *See also* Pure Land Buddhism
as *tathāgata,* 9016
Avalokiteśvara and, 291, 705, 706

Amitābha (buddha), **291–293,** 1067–1068 ***continued***
in Chinese Buddhism, 1162, 1167, 1238–1239
images of, 1596
cult of, 1083, 1147
Daichuo on, 2176
development of, 291
Dharmākara and, 1079, 6632
great compassion of, 5105
Huiyuan and, 1576, 1596
iconography of, 292, 1596, 4329, 5454
in Jōdo Shinshū school, 4933–4935, 7753
in Jōdoshū, 4937
invocation of, of Kūya, 5270
in Japanese Buddhism, 1179, 4119, 8350
Shinran on, 8354–8355
in Jingtu, 4921–4925
lotus associated with, 5519
Mahāsthāmaprāpta and, 291
meditation on, 1291, 1293–1294
name of, 6408
origins of, 291, 1067
paradise of, 6984
popularization of, 3155
in Pure Land Buddhism, 1600–1601, 8981, 8982
Pure Land of, 7502
recitation of name, 5310
nianfo, 8298–8299
salvation and, 7641
saving power of, 3887
Shandao on, 8298, 8299
as subject of *nianfo,* 6601
temple to, 9047, 9049, 9050
thinking of, at moment of death, 2029
vow of, 1086
Amitāyur-dhyāna sūtra (Buddhist text), 1293
Avalokiteśvara in, 705
in Jōdoshū, 4937
nianfo in, 6601–6602
Amitāyus. *See* Amitābha
ʿAmm (deity), Athirat and, 589
Amma (deity), 3569–3570
altars for, 3576
contact with, 9717
in creation myths, 100, 325, 2390, 2392, 3569–3570
creation of human beings, 3569
creation of nature, 3569
trickster created by, 9353
twins as sons of, 9415, 9416
water and, 9700
Amma (mother), 7495
Amman (Jordan), excavation outside, goddess worship in, 3585
Ammārah souls, in Islam, 8567
ʿAmmār ibn Yasīr, 8999
Amma Seru (Dogon ancestor), 2391
Ammasilik people (Greenland)
and bears, 808
shamanistic initiation in, 8271
Ammerman, Nancy T., 75
Ammianus Marcellinus
on Adonis, 35
on Alani religion, 8114
on druids, 2492
on Hun religion, 4228, 4490
Ammit (deity), souls eaten by, 138
Ammonius, 6474
Plotinus studying under, 7198
Plutarch studying under, 7189
Ammonius Saccas, 432, 6346
Ammons, Archie Randolph, 5483–5484
Ammu (deity), in Canaanite religion, 1387
Amoghasiddhi (buddha), 1068, 1078, 4329
Amoghavajra (Buddhist monk), **293–294,** 1133, 1214, 1240
Kūkai studying under, 1243
on *Guhyasamāja Tantra,* 3708
translations by, 1164–1165
Vajrabodhi and, 9510
in Zhenyan Buddhism, 9961
Amó:hi atsvʔ:sdi (ritual bathing), 754–755
Amok, 3214
Amon (king of Judah), 4828
Amon, Hans, Hutterian Brethren and, 4239
Amora/amoraim, **294–295**
Abbahu as, **2**
Abbaye as, **2–3**
Ashi as, 294, **541**
definition of, 294
Elʿazar ben Pedat as, 2743
rabbinic law and, 3748–3750
Rava' as, 7631
on resurrection, 8557
Shemu'el the Amora, **8318**
Yehudah bar Yeḥezqe'l, 9877
yeshivot under, 9883
Yoḥanan bar Nappaḥa', 9903–9904
on *zekhut avot,* 9941
AMORC. *See* Ancient and Mystical Order Rosae Crucis
Amorite Mari, Canaanite religion in, 1381
Amos (biblical book), 295–297, 879
music in worship in, 7463
pesher of, 7064
ritual efforts in, 6182
Solomon's Temple in, 923–924
Amos (prophet), **295–297**
apocalypse and, 415
authority of, 7434
background of, 296
literary style of, 296–297
message of, 296
on morality, 7652
on mountains, 6214
Amphiaraos (deity), 551
Amphiaraus (Greek diviner), 2376
Amphilochia (Photios), 7136
Amphitheatre of External Wisdom, The (Khunrath), 252
Amphithyron (curtain), 9091
Amr (commandment), heteronomous discipline and, 8700
AM radio, religious broadcasting on, 7711
Amram (father of Aaron), 1
Amram Gaon, 4989
prayer book of, 8387
Amran ben Ishaq, 1534
ʿAmr ibn al-ʿĀṣ
ʿAlī challenged by, 258–259
Egypt conquered by, 2710
ʿAmr ibn ʿUbayd, 3211
in Muʿtazilah, 6318
Amrit, 3336
in Sikhism, 8395, 8397
Amritsar, India. *See* Golden Temple at Amritsar, India
Amrta (beverage)
cosmic tree and, 3449, 9338
Viṣṇu and, 9619
Amrullah, Haji Abdul Malik Karim, 3078
Amsterdam (Netherlands), Jews in, 5016
Amsterdam Declaration on Global Change (2001), 3253
Amulets and talismans, **297–301**
bibliomancy and, 8200
in Buddhism, 4532
in Caribbean religion, *wanga* charms, 3823
in Chinese religion, written, 8677
in Daoism, 5593
definition of, 297–298
in Egyptian religion, 2713–2714, 4508
hand of Faṭimah
in Middle Eastern popular tradition, 3837
symbolism of, 3769
in Hellenistic religions, medical charms in, 3904
in Shintō, 2410
in Inuit religion, 4527
in Islam
African, 4609
disease warded off by, 3831
in Israelite religion, 4742
in Japanese religion, from temples and shrines, 3869
in Judaism
folk, 3158, 3159
Lilith and, 5459
paper, vol. 14 color insert
Magen David on, 5558
in magic
early Christian, 5576
East Asian, 5593
Greco-Roman, 5573
Islamic, 5585–5586
materials used as, 298
in Middle Eastern popular practice, 3837
in North American Indian religions, Huron power charms, 6684
ouroboros and cosmic circles in, 1793
protection from, against witchcraft, 9777
rings as, 3770
in Samoyed religion, 8096
in Thailand, and spiritual power of saints, 8080
written words in, 6844
Amun (deity), **301**
Akhenaton and, 217, 219, 301, 4320
as Amun-Re, 217, 301, 5451, 7277, 7634
cult of
growth of, 2706
interpretations of, 2730
in Egyptian pantheon, 2704
in Kushite religion, 5269
Medinet Habu and, 2706–2707
Queen Olympias and, 3903
temple of, 9061
Amunhotep IV. *See* Akhenaton
Amun of Nitria, 2824
Amun-Ra. *See* Amun-Re
Amun-Re (deity), 7277
in dynastic politics, 2706
feasts of, 2715
in North Africa, 834
Amurru (deity), 4317
Amyara people, armadillo myth of, 5198
ʿAm yhwh (people of Yahweh), 4745
ʿAm Yisra'el (people of Israel). *See* Jewish people
An (Anu) (deity), **301–303,** 5951–5952
Alalu overpowered by, 2311
calendar and, 5952
in Canaanite religion, 1387, 1398
castrated by Kumarbi, 1450, 4070
death of, 2811
and Dumuzi, 2520
family of, 302–303
in general assembly of gods, 5951
and Inanna, 4403, 4404
equal status of, 3586
Ishtar and, 1398
and kingship, 5162
in Kumarbi cycle, 4231
names for, 301, 303
sky's relationship to, 301, 302, 5952
in Sumerian pantheon, 5964
Teshub as son of, 9087
in triad, 9349
in Uruk, 5952
veneration of image of, 4381
An (nunnery), 9056
"Anā al-ḥaqq" ("I am the Creative Truth"), al-Ḥallāj on, 3756, 3757, 8812
Anabaptism, **304–305**
adult baptism in, 782, 783, 1669–1670, 9810
beliefs of, 304–305
and biblical exegesis, 874

blasphemy prosecution of, 973
Dutch, Simons (Menno), role in, 8400–8401
ecclesiology of, 1774
enthusiasm of, 2805
on ethics, 1655
Hutter (Jacob) and, 4239
leadership of, 304–305
Mennonites and, 5861
Müntzer (Thomas) and, 304, 305, 6239
origins of, 304, 7660
and pacifism, 6648
plain dress in, 1836
on predestination, 3204
Reformation and, 1663, 7660–7661
on separation of church and state, 1968, 7453
shunning in, as excommunication, 2105
Zwingli and, 10015–10016
Anacletus II (pope), 839
Anacondas, in Amazonian Quechua religions, 282, 284
Anafiel (angel), 10051
Anāgatawaṃsa (Buddhist text), 1199
Anāhata cakra, location of, 1348
Anahit (deity), 491, 492
Anāhitā (deity), **305–306**
in Armenian religion, 491, 492, 10002
Artemis identified with, 506
characteristics of, 305
in Iranian religion, 10002
Mithra and, 4536, 6087
origins of, 305
Anahuac, or Mexico and the Mexicans, Ancient and Modern (Tylor), 9424
A-na-kui (Ruanruan leader), 4491
Analects (lunyu) of Confucius, 946
biographical data in, 1934
canonization of, 1900
derivation of, 1893–1894
dialogs in, 1908
ethics in, 1908–1909
Golden Rule in, 3631, 3632
Huang Kan on, 1899
in Japan, 1926
Jesuits and, 1918
noble ideal in, 1894
sage-kings in, 8037
Zhixu influenced by, 9180
Zhou institutions taken as model in, 1892
Anales de Quauhtitlan, Maya calendar and, 1360
Analogy
in history of religions approach to concept of religion, 4062
in Islamic law *(qiyās),* al-Shāfiʿī on, 8265
principle of, Newman (John Henry) on, 6510
in science and magic, links between, 5567–5568, 5572
theology of, *vs.* anthropomorphism, 391
Analogy of Religion (Butler), 1339
Analyst and the Mystic, The (Kakar), 7478
Analytical psychology, 5031–5036, 7476, 7484–7485. *See also* Archetypes
of goddess worship, 7485
of illusion, 7484
Jung as founder of, 7474–7475, 7476, 7484
of polytheism, 7485
vs. psychoanalysis, 7475, 7484
Analytic philosophy, **306–309**
definition of, 306
of Abū al-Hudhayl al-ʿAllāf, 18–19
origins of, 306
Analytic school of Judaism, Talmudic commentary in, 3745–3746
Anamnesis (recollection), **309–317,** 7182, 7185
in Australian Indigenous religions, 314–316
eternity and, 2854
in Eucharist, 9810–9811
in Gnosticism, 311–312
in Manichaeism, 312, 5653
Plato on, 309–311, 315–316, 5990
in Qabbalah, 313–314
in Sufism, 312–313
Anan, Kofi, on global stewardship, 2613
ʿAnan ben David, **317–318**
code of law of, 5084
as founder of Karaites, 5083
Karaites consolidated under, 4991
Ānanda (Buddha's disciple), 1105
Buddha cremated by, 7163
on Buddhist nuns, 6759
in Sautrāntika, 8136
Rājagṛha council and, 2035
tested by *arhats,* 4483
on worship, 7496
Ānanda (bliss), 5447–5448, 7082–7083
Ananda Ashram, 6568
Ananda Marga
children in, 6543
in Europe, 6568
Ānanda Maṭh (Bankimcandra), 829
Ānanda maṭh (Chattopadhyaya), 10035
"Ānandamayī" (Islam), 830
Ānandamayī Mā, **318–319**
disciples of, 318
fame of, 3715
teachings of, 318–319
Ānanda Temple (stupa), 1135
Anandatīrtha. *See* Madhva
Ānandavana (Banaras), 778
Anand Karaj (wedding), in Sikhism, 8397
Ananites, 317. *See also* ʿAnan ben David
Anankē, 3002
vs. Mesopotamian notion of fate, 3003
Anansesem (spider stories), 9352
Ananse the Spider, 86, 9352
Anantaboga (deity), 746
Anantaśeṣa (serpent), 7500
Ānapānasati (breathing), 1045
Anaphora (Eucharistic prayer), of Syriac Orthodox Church, 8941
Anarchist spirituality, neoshamanism and, 8296
Anarchy
Earth First! and, 2562
religious, 7666
Anasazi culture (North America), 6721
descendents of, 6657
Mesoamerican influences on, 6654
Anastasius (assistant to Nestorius), 6483
Anastasius I (emperor), Severus of Antioch and, 8238
Anastasius I (pope), 4495
Anastasius III (pope), schism and, 8156
Anat (deity), **319–320**
as Adad's consort, 28
aggression of, 319–320
in Aqhat cycle, 320, 1397, 1398, 1399
Astarte and, 561, 562
and Baal, 319–320, 3596, 7767
in Baal cycle, 724, 1392–1393, 1394, 2536
in Canaanite literature, 319–320
in Egyptian religion, 320, 3596
envy aroused in, 1388
Ishtar, fusion with, 1383, 1398
origins of, 3596
in personal names, 1387
prominence of, 3596
vs. other goddesses, 3376
in ritual drama, 2442
worship of, 3596
Anath. *See* Anat
Anāthapiṇḍika, political support for, 6128
Anathema (votive offering), 4381. *See also* Cursing and curses
formal procedures for, in early church, 2105
Anātman (no-self), 6486
Buddha on, 8547
in Buddhist ethics, 1279
ecological ethic in, 2630
hope and, 4126
in Mahāyāna Buddhism, 1206, 1207
in Sautrāntika, 8137
in priesthood, 7407
reality of, 9017
sacrilege and, 8015
saṃghas and, 8076
śūnyatā as, 7365
Anatolia and Anatolian religions. *See also* Hittite religion; Hurrian religion
Armenian religion in, 490–491
Artemis in, 506
deities of (*See* Cybele; Hebat; Irshappa; Sabazios; Sharruma)
goddess worship in, 3595
Hattians in, 4068
Islam in, ʿAlawi extremist movements in, 8324
Kubaba as Great Mother in, 1451, 2109
Lady of the Animals in, 5280
Mawlawi and Bektāshi Sufism in, 8822–8823
medical practices, 3825
moon in, 6172
Neolithic settlements in, 6461–6462
Rūmī (Jalāl al-Dīn) in, 7935
sacrifice in, 8005
scapegoat in, 2598, 8143, 8144
soul in, 8538–8540
syncretism in, 8932
ṭarīqah in, 9007
written records from, 5161
Anatomy
Āyurvedic view of, 3854–3855
heart, **3881–3884**
knowledge of, in Africa, 3819–3820
mystical, in *Haṭhayoga,* 3794–3795
in New Age, energy anatomy of Myss (Caroline), 3851
Servetus (Michael) on, 8232
Anatomy of Criticism (Frye), 3223
Anatta (no-self), 9146
Áña Túmpa (mythic figure), in Chiriguano religion (South America), 8634
Anau religion (prehistoric), 7383
Āṇava (action), salvation through, in Trika Śáivism, 8047
Anawati, Georges C., 533, 4717
Anawrata of Bamar (king), Buddhism under, 5349
Anawratha (king of Myanmar), *nats* (spirits) and, 6427
Anaxagoras (Greek philosopher), 971
atheism and, 581
on nature, 6431
religion questioned by, 3909
Anaximander (Greek philosopher), 5452, 6374
on evil, 8405
Anaximenes, on *pneuma,* 8542

Ancestors and ancestor worship, **320–332**
in African religions, 89, 322
and afterlife, views of, 89, 141, 142–143
Akan, 215
carved images of, 89
central Bantu, 1508
Christian ban on, 142–143, 1721
Christian influence on, 142–143
vs. cult of dead, 322
cults of affliction, 60–61, 63
Dogon, 2390–2391, 3569, 4301
drums identified with, 2494, 2496
East African, 2568–2569
Edo, 2697
houses and villages, protection of, 4106
iconography of, 4301–4303
Igbo, 4365–4366
interlacustrine Bantu, 4519
kingship and, 5171
kinship and, 5185
Limba, 7806
Ndembu, 6447
neotraditional, 109
northeast Bantu, 2575
psychedelic drugs in, 7469–7470
qualifications for becoming, 89, 141, 322
reincarnation and, 7677
role of, 85, 89, 141
as shades, 3817
shades in southern African religions, 8656
Shona, 8372, 8696
shrines to, 85, 89, 215
status of, 141
studies of, 321–322
Sudanese, 8849
Swazi, 8896
Tiv, 9210
Tswana, 9388–9389
Yoruba, 4302, 9910
Zulu, 10008, 10009–10010
in Afro-Caribbean religions
creolization and, 2066
cults of, 1435–1436
in Agami Jawi, 4817
in ancient religions, 2662
animals as, 5185
in Anishinaabe religion, 370
in Asian religions, kinship and, 5185
in Australian Indigenous religions, 2002–2004
animals as, 2003–2004
reincarnation and, 7677
skulls of, 3806
in Warlpiri religion, 9693–9694
in Babylonian mythology, 2982
Baltic cult of, **327–332**
in Bambara religion, 776–777
in Bemba religion, 817
in Buddhism, 323–324
merit transference and, 5874
in Buriat religion, 1325–1326, 1327
and cannibalism, among Wari', 1403
in Caribbean religions, 1427, 1435–1436
in Celtic religion, skulls of, 3806
characteristics of, 320–321
in Chinese religion, 322, 323–324, 326, 2408–2409, 2982, 9857–9858
ancestors as category, 1618
beginnings of, 1582
Cheng Yi on, 1563
clans and, 1616
cult of imperial ancestors, 1912–1913
entertainment of the dead, 4206
food offerings, 3170
ghosts and, 1605
gods, difference from, 1605
illness and, 3860
imperial, 7266
king's power and, 5178
law and, 5352
Mengzi on, 1587
offerings by emperor, 8005
Qingming Jie festival, 1642
in Shang dynasty, 1582
in Zhou dynasty, 1583, 1892
in Christianity, All Souls Day, 2228–2229
as city founders, 326
in Confucianism, 323–324, 5233
in creation stories, 325–326
definition of "worship," 89, 320
dragons as, 2433–2434
in Egyptian religion, 2719–2720
of pharaohs, 5164
in evolution of religion, 2914
as family founders, 326
fear of vengeance and, 7781
in Finno-Ugric religions, 3109
in Fon and Ewe religion, 3165–3166
functions of, 320, 321
in Garifuna religion, 3284, 3285–3286
gender-based bifurcation in, 324
in Greek religion, 321, 326
heroes as, 3665–3666
in Hawaiian religion, deification and transfiguration of, 3799
in Hinduism, 322–323
in devotional life, 9821
and pilgrimage, 7169, 7170
rural traditions, 4435–4436
transfer of *karman* in, 5096
as household spirits, 4106
immortality associated with, 2982
in Inca religion, 4412, 5176–5177
in India, 322–323, 2982
in Indonesian religions, 3235
in Reiyūkai Kyōdan, 7861–7862
in Shintō, 324
Hirata Atsutane on, 5215
in Vädda religion (Sri Lanka), 8409–8410
in Israelite religion, 4743
in Japanese religions, 324, 2240, 2410–2411, 4797
health and, 3867
memorial rites by Hijiri ascetics in, 3979
secularization and, 8219
Shintō, 2639, 4795
at jubilation rites, 8210
in Judaism, 9940–9941
kinship and, 5184–5185
in Komi religion, 5218–5219
in Korean religions, 324
Confucianism, 5233
shamanism, 5229, 5233, 5235
in Madagascar, stone cult and, 8745
in Mari and Mordvin religion, 5710
in Maya religion, 5175
in Mesoamerican religions
in Huichol religion, 4152, 4153
in Maya religion, 5798
in Mixtec religion, 5911
mythic, **325–327**
names and, 5185
necromancy associated with, 6451
in Neolithic religions
European, 6465
Natufian, 6460–6461
in New Guinea religions, 6504, vol. 6 color insert
in North American Indian religions
in Haida tradition, 3736
kinship and, 5185
in North American religions, 2982
in Oceanic religions
in Melanesian religions, 322, 5833, 5834, 5839, 5844, 6265, 7144–7145, vol. 10 color insert
in Micronesian religions, 6003, 6005, 6007, 6010–6011
music in, 6265, 6266
in Papua New Guinea, 2005, 6266
in Okinawan religion, 6813
in Paleolithic religion, 3806
in Polynesian religions, 7306, 8980
possession by, 1436
problems with term "worship," 89, 321, 322
reincarnation and, 7677
rites of, 320
and ritual, soteriological function of, 8527
in Roman religion
honoring, 6994–6995, vol. 10 color insert
lares, 5320–5322
sacrifice and, 8009
serpents associated with, 8457
in shamanism
ascent to upperworld and, 8272
in initiation, 8284
in Korea, 5229, 5233, 5235
sin of, 2590
skulls of, 3806
in Slavic religion, *domovoi* (family founder spirits), 4106
social effects of, 320
in South American Indian religions, 8584
Andean Feast with the Dead, 8618
in Southeast Asian religions, traditional, 8651
studies of, 320, 321–323
Fustel de Coulanges and, 3245
in Syria, 5164
in Tanganyika, 5181
in Toraja religion, 9241
trees as, 9336–9337
in Trobriand Islanders religion, 5184
in Turkic religions, 9402
in Vanuatu religions, 9520
in Vedism, 9559, 9566
fire of, 9557
karman transfer in, 5096
in Vietnamese religion, 9593
in Vodou, 1434, 9637
in West African religions, 9718–9719
worship, **320–325**
in Yap culture, 5183
in Yurupary cult, 9919
Ancestor Worship in Contemporary Japan (Smith), 324
Ancestral Connections (Morphy), 647, 4306
Ancestral sin, 2590. *See also* Original sin
Anchorites and anchoritism, 2822–2823, 2824–2825
Cassian on, 1447
hair symbolism and, 3739
of Julian of Norwich, 5029
meditation in, 5817–5818
Anchors, **332**

Ancient and Mystical Order Rosae Crucis (AMORC), 7710, 7930, 9067. *See also* Rosicrucians
Ancient Arabic Order of the Nobles of the Mystic Shrine (Shriners), 3198
Ancient Church of the East. *See* Nestorian (Assyrian) Church
Ancient City, The (Fustel de Coulanges), 326
Ancient Egyptian Religion (Frankfort), 2730
Ancient Goddesses (Goodison and Morris), 3617
Ancient Gods Speak: a Guide to Egyptian Religion, The, 2732
Ancient Jewish Art and Archaeology in the Land of Israel (Hachlili), 4342
Ancient Learning (Kogaku)
  proponents of, 1928
  Shintō, 5215
  in Tokugawa period, 9311
Ancient Magic and Ritual Power (Meyer and Mirecki), 7858
Ancient Mystic Order of Melchizedek, 6769
Ancient Teachings of the Masters, The (ATOM), 2602, 2603
Andalusia. *See also* Iberian Peninsula
  Christian rule in, 4596
  Christians (Mozarabs) in, 4593, 4596–4597, 7282
  Islam in, **4591–4600**
    Almohad dynasty, 4592, 4593, 4595, 4596
    Almoravid dynasty, 4592, 4593
    culture, 4592–4593
    legacy of, 4596–4598
    literature, 4595–4596, 4597
    Mālikī school of law, 4593, 4594–4595
    religious doctrines and practices, 4595–4596
    Shāfiʿī school of law, 4594–4595
    Umayyad caliphate, 4591–4593, 4594
  Jews in, 4593, 4596–4597
  Karaite sect in, 5084, 5085
  Muslim-Christian relations in
    Arabization, 4593
    Christianization, 4596, 4597
    military conflict, 4591, 4592
Andaman Islanders, Radcliffe-Brown's (A. R.) study of, 7592
Andaman Islanders, The (Radcliffe-Brown), 5566, 9025
Andaman Islands
  Negrito religions of, 6455–6456
  New Year ceremonies of, 6590
  Schmidt (Wilhelm) *vs.* Radcliffe-Brown (A. R.) on, 8169–8170
Andean religions. *See also* Inca religion; South American Indian religions
  agrarian rites of, Pachamama in, 2558
  Araucanian
    geography of, 8576
    supreme being in, 8580
  Christianity in
    cofradías (confraternities) in, 8609
    Evangelical Protestantism in, 8620
    huacas and cult of saints, convergence of, 8605–8606, 8609–8612
    in modern period, 8619–8620
  chronicles of, 1361–1362
  in colonial period, **8605–8614**
    perceptions in, 8606–8609
  cosmologies in, 6576
  creation myths in, 8600
  dancing diseases in, 3815
  deities of, 8600–8602 (*See also* Illapa; Inti; Pachamama; *See also* Pachacámac; Viracocha)
    gods of sustenance, 8600–8602
    high gods in, 8590
    iconography of, 8602
  dynastic legends, 1363–1364
  and earth, sacredness of, 3971
  earth shrines in, 8616
  gender in, 3415–3417
    parallelism and complementarity of, 3415, 3416
  geography of, 8575, 8599
  healing in, 3811
    mesa divination in, 3810
  huacas in (*See Huacas*)
  human origin myths in, 8619
  human sacrifice, 1364
  image veneration in, 4384–4385, 4386
  mesas (ritual meals) in, 8616
  messianism in, 5983–5984
  Milky Way in, 8871
  modern, **8614–8621**
    ayllus in, 8617–8618
    Christianity in, 8619–8620
    cosmology in, 8618–8619
    cultural ecology in, 8615
    demographics of, 8614–8615
    diviners in, 8616
    huacas (earth shrines) in, 8616
    Pachamama and Achachilas in, 8615–8616
    ritual calendar in, 8618
    sickness and health in, 8619
    sorcerers in, 8616–8617
  music in, 6272
  naturalization of images and institutions in, 8609–8611
  nature in, 5291
  in pre-Inca period, **8599–8605**
    gods of sustenance in, 8600–8602
    iconography in, 8602
    medicine and magic in, 8603–8604
    messianism in, 8604
    prehistory of, 8599
    sources of documentation on, 8599–8600
    subsistence and religion in, 8600
    worship in, 8602–8603
  quipus, 1360–1361
  social and political divisions, 1362–1363
  structuralist studies of, 8596
  Tacana Indian religion, supreme beings in, 8576
  water in, Lake Titicaca, 5291
  women in, 3415–3417, 8601
Andersen, Hans Christian, 3016
Anderson, Arthur J. O., 5939
Anderson, Barbara, 2611
Anderson, Christopher, 689
Anderson, David, 117–118
Anderson, H. George, 5754
Anderson, Herbert, 7858–7859
Anderson, James, 3194, 3195, 3196
Anderson, Mother Leafy, 6536
Anderson, Nancy Fix, 845
Anderson, Pamela Sue, 3314
Anderson, Victor, 79, 9730
Andersson, Roy, 3099
Andes mountains, in the Flood, 6213
"And God Saw That It Was Good," 2613
Andhaka school of Buddhism
  doctrines of, 1197
  origin of, 1194
Andi tribe (Caucasus), 4614
Andler, Charles, Mauss (Marcel) and, 5785
Andō Shōeki, 9311
Andrae, Tor, **333–334,** 945, 4717
  education of, 333
  and Nyberg (H. S.), 6774
  writings of, 333
Andrarchy, 7007
Andrea, Johann Valentin, 253, 564, 7929
Andree, Richard, 3222
  on masks, 5765
Andrew (apostle), missions to Scythia, 1682
Andrew of Saint-Victor, Hugh of Saint-Victor and, 4151
Andrews, Charles F.
  in ashram movement, 546
  Gandhi (Mohandas) and, 3272
Androcentrism, **334–337**
  definition of, 334, 3298
  feminist critique of, 3298–3299, 3313
    in gynocentrism, 3719
  Judeo-Christian, 334–336
  in Mariology, 5754
  Melanesian, 4115
  vs. misogyny, 3299
  pervasiveness of, 334
  receptivity from perspective of, 8695
  in *Religionswissenschaft* school, 9789
  in study of religion, 3313, 9785–9786
Androgynes, **337–342**
  definition of, 337
  distribution of concept, 337
  fusing, 337, 339
  Śiva as, 8417
  splitting, 337–338
  types of, 337–338
Androgyny
  vs. androgyne, 337, 339
  in Australian Indigenous religions, 8239
  in Aztec deities, 3411
  in creation myths, 1987, 2555
  of deities, 3975
  in Gnosticism, 8247
  of God, in Qabbalah, 8315
  in Heaven's Gate movement, 3890
  idealization of, 8243
  of Jesus, 341
  in Mesoamerican deities, 3411, 3413
  Sophia and, 8523
Andronicus III Palaeologus (Byzantine emperor), 788
  Gregory Palamas and, 3698
Andronicus II Palaeologus (Byzantine emperor)
  Gregory Palamas and, 3698
  Nikephoros Kallistos and, 6620
Andronicus of Rhodes, Aristotle's writings edited by, 479
Andronikos. *See* Andronicus
Andros, Sir Edmund, 5779
Anecdotes, in Chan Buddhism, 1521, 1522, 1524
Aneirin (Welsh poet), 1480
Anekāntavāda (Many-pointed Doctrine), 4768
Anesaki Masaharu, **342–343**
  on Shingon, 5608
  and study of religion in Japan, 8777
Anetso (ballgame), 754
Aṅga (genre), 1270–1271
  in Jain scriptures, 4766–4767

Angad (Sikh leader), 6412
wife of, 3335
Angaité people (Paraguay), 8634
Angakkoq (shaman), 4528
Aṅgas (yogic exercises), 9894
Angas, George French, 5680
Ang Duong (king), 5130
Angel Cave, 1471
Angels, **343–349**. *See also* Satan
in African religions, Christian missions and, 142
Aristotle and, 480, 481
Cathari doctrine on, 1457
in Christianity, 346, 2275, 2356, vol. 8 color insert
of death
in Chuvash religion, 1785
in Islam, 1785
definitions of, 343
in Gnosticism, 344, 347, 3525
guardian, vol. 8 color insert
in Hellenistic religions, dualism with devils, 3904
images of, vol. 8 color insert
in Raëlian religion, 7598–7599
in Islam, 346, 1785
Ibn Sīnā on, 4554
iconography of, 4350, vol. 8 color insert
magic and, 5583
al-Suhrawardī on, 4554–4555
in Israelite religion, 4742
in Judaism, 345–346, 2275
apocalypses of, 414–415
explaining God's favoritism, 3548
images of, vol. 8 color insert
tsaddiq as, 9378
latitudinal order of, 4554–4555
longitudinal order of, 4554–4555
in Manichaeism, 347, 5655
in Mesopotamia, 345
as messengers, 9616, vol. 8 color insert
Suhrawardī and Corbin on, 1984
in Zoroastrianism, 344–345
Angelus Silesius, 1006
Angelus Temple (Santa Monica), religious broadcasting and, 7710
Anger
in African religions, Hyakyusa, 6772
in goddess worship, 3590
Anger, Kenneth, 3102
Anggor (New Guinea), violence among, 9681
Angim (Mesopotamian myth), Ningirsu in, 5953
Angina (Inner Winds), illness and, 3810
Ăngki (deity). *See* Kalteś
Angkola people (Indonesia), 799, 800
Angkor period, Khmer religion in, 5128, 5129
Angkor Wat, 5129
architecture, Indian connections in, 4011, 4012, 4013
building of, 4013
Anglican Church Missionary Society, in Buganda, 2578
Anglican Communion. *See* Anglicanism
Anglican Consultative Council, 352
Anglicanism, **349–354**. *See also* Church of England; Episcopalianism; *specific countries*
Anglo-Catholicism, ecclesiology and, 1774
Arminianism in, Calvinist Puritanism opposed by, 493
atonement in, 597
Calvinism and, 1692
casuistry in, 1455
Catholic *vs.* Protestant elements of, 349
church architecture of, 795
confessional statement of (*See* Thirty-nine Articles)
conflicts within, 352–353
deism in, 7449
early history of, 349–350
Eastern Orthodox Church and, 2588
on ethics, 1656
eucharistic theology in, sacrifice and, 8007
evangelical, 352
on free will and predestination, 3208
government of churches in, 350
homosexuality in, 353, 5808, 7404
media coverage of gay ordination, 5808
identity in, 2056
in interfaith dialogue, 352–353
liberalism of, 6105
liturgical year in, 1744
liturgy in, 5490
Mary in, 5754
menstruation in, 5867
ministry in, 6045
missions
in Australia and New Zealand, 1731–1732
in Korea, 1727
Melanesian Brotherhood, 1739
Melanesian Mission, 1738, 1847, 9197
modernism of, 6105
music in, 6310
number of denominations in, 7448
Oriental Orthodoxy, ecumenical agreement with, 8940
origin of, 349
Oxford movement in, 352, 6510, 6765, 7523
polity of, 1766, 7452
prayer book of (*See Book of Common Prayer*)
schools sponsored by, in Australia and New Zealand, 1733
Society of Saint Francis in, 3183
theology of, 350, 9138
Vatican I and, 9528
women in, ordination of, 353, 1735–1736
in World Council of Churches, 2685
Anglo-Americans, religious experience and, 7737–7738
Anglo-Israelism, 1657–1658
Anglo-Saxon Chronicle, 6943
Anglo-Saxon Federation of America, 1658, 1659
Anglo-Saxons
Catholic missions to, Augustine of Canterbury in, 623
converting to Christianity, 6942–6943
paganism of, **6942–6944**
poetry of, 7218
Angola. *See also* Central Bantu religions; Kongo religion
Apostolic Church of John Maranke in, 5695
Chokwe religion in, masks in, 2141
Khoi religion in, 5135
San religion in, 5135
slave trade in, 1510
Angra Mainyu (spirit), **203–204,** 2315, 9412
in cosmogony, 9995
gender of, 3372
morality and, 7651
pollution created by, 9997
in Zoroastrianism, 9989, 9995
Aṅgulimāla (Buddhist student), 1086
Aṅgulimālīya Sūtra (Buddhist text), 9018
Angus, Samuel, in Australia, 8768
Aṅguttara Nikāya (Buddhist text), 2332
cosmology in, 2027
//angwa (deity), 5135–5136, *5136*
An Hyang, Confucianism and, 1930
ANI. *See* Association of National Investigators
Anicca (momentariness), 9146
Aniconic (abstract) images, 4389
Aniconism
definition of, 6389
in Nabatean religion, 6389–6390
Aniga (Nepalese artist), 1149
Ani Lochen, **354–355**
Animal Apocalypse, 415
Animal deities, 3620. *See also* Therianthropism
in Ainu religion, 205–206
examples of, 3620
functions of, 3620
in Hinduism, 359
in Inuit religion, 8220–8221
in Tupian religion, 2091
Animal liberation, as environmental ethic, religion and, 2655
Animal magnetism, Mesmer on, 1947, 3849
Animal Mother, in Yakut shamanism, 8284
Animal rescue, Jaina, 2625–2626
Animal rights, as environmental ethic, religion and, 2655
Animals, **355–362**. *See also* Hunting; Totemism; *specific animals*
in African religions
art of, 90, 117
Khoi religion, 5135
Kushite religion, 5269
myths of, 92, 3570–3571
San religion, 5135
Swazi religion, 5169, 5170
in witchcraft, 9777–9778
Anat as protector of, 319
ancestry extended to, 5185
ancient views of, 356–357, 358
in Anishinaabe religion, 369
in Apache religion, 405
in Aramean religion, 450
in Arctic religions
ceremonialism for, 469, 471, 9394
history of study of, 474
masters of, 470
myths of, 472
spirits portrayed as, 469–470
in Athapaskan religion, sacred stories of, 573
in Australian Indigenous religions
ancestral beings as, 2003–2004
as kin, 2004
myths of, 655
behavior of, as source of ritual, 2868–2869
in Berber religion, 834
biological study of, 357, 358
bones of, in rituals, 1013, 1015
brains of, 6488
in Buddhism, 356, 359–360, 1259
stories of, 6959–6960
in cave art, 1471
in Celtic religion, 1487, 1494–1495
in Christianity, 356, 361
human rule over, 2648
communication with, 361
complexity of, 357, 358
as constellations, in ethnoastronomy, 2863

cruelty to, desensitization based on, 358
culture heroes as, 2092
deification of, 2250
deities (*See* Animal deities)
depictions of, nimbus in, 6624
divination with viscera of, 1387
domestication of, 1464
in Egyptian religion, 2712
iconography of, 4318
ethical concerns regarding, 357–358
in ethnoastronomy, 2864
classification and symbolism of, 2864–2866
extrasensory perception in, 6057
in Garden of Eden, 6982
glossolalia and, 3507
hair symbolism and, 3739
in Hinduism, 359
mythic themes, 4437–4439
Rudra associated with, 7934
horns of, **4130–4131**
humans as distinct from
culture hero myths and, 2091
myths of, 5198
religion in, 2913
in indigenous traditions, in balance of life, 2618
in Indus Valley religion, 3989, 4473–4474
inherited preconceptions about, 357
in Inuit religion, 4527
in Islam, 361
abuse of, 2651
Islamic law on, 2652
Muḥammad on, 2651
speech of, 2651
in Judaism, 360
as food, 5106–5108
as models for conduct, 2643
protection of, 2644
slaughter of, 5106
kinship extended to, 5185
Lady of the (*See* Lady of the Animals)
liberation of, as environmental ethic, 2655
Lord of the (*See* Lord of the animals)
in Mesoamerican religions
myths of, 5938
smoking by, 8455
in Mesopotamian iconography, 4315–4316
as meteorological beings, 5995–5996
in Micronesian myths, 6010–6011
as monsters, 6164
moon and, 6170
naming of, 6406
in Neolithic religions, funerary practices, 6460
in North American Indian religions
creation stories, 6661, 6692
of Far North, 6676
iconography of, 4309
of Northwest Coast, 6707
in poetry, 7225–7226
prohibition against killing, 7299–7300
ritual burial of, 6652
of Southeast Woodlands, 6692
in Olmec iconography, 5881
oppression of, 358
in Paleolithic religion, 6952–6953, 7375
Plutarch on, 7200
in Polynesian religions, 7307
postures and gestures of, 7341
power of, 7351
in prehistoric religions, 7376–7378, 7382–7385, 7387
in primitive religions, 10065
in proverbs, 6977
rebirth of, rituals with bones and, 1014
rescue of, Jaina, 2625–2626
rights of, as environmental ethic, 2655
rituals of, and human rituals, 7049
in Roman Catholicism, 356
in Roman religions, 7641
sacred space and, 7979
sacrifice of (*See* Animal sacrifice)
in Sami religion, 8087
in Samoyed religion, 8096
in Sarmatian religion, 8115
in Scandinavian religions, spirits in form of, 3246
in Scythian art, 8206
sexual organs of, human consumption/ transplantation of, for rejuvenation, 7684
in shamanism, religious ecology of, 2619
shelters for, Jaina, 2625–2626
social, moral evolution of, 2918
in South American Indian religions, 1364
in Andean religions, pre-Incan, 8602
dances and, 8581
master of the animals in, 8580
spirit possession by, 9155
storms associated with, 5995–5996
in Sufism, 2653
sun associated with, 8835
as symbols, 357
touching, to transfer evil to, 9256
transmission of views on, 357, 358
treatment of, 358
as tricksters (*See* Tricksters)
wild, as evil, 360
in winter carols, 9743–9744
worship of, 6440
Animals, Lady of. *See* Lady of the Animals
Animal sacrifice, 1364. *See also* Extispicy; Sacrifice; Scapegoat; *specific animals*
in African religions, 88
at childbirth, 3819
Dinka religion, 5305
functions of, 88
in Limba funeral rituals, 7806
myths of, 99
northeast Bantu, 2575, 2576
Nuer and Dinka religion, 6744
occasions for, 88
Qemant, 2573
West African, 9719
in Arabian religions, 445
in Arctic religions, 474
ashes from, 541
in Babylonian religion, of goats, 8311
bloodless consecration, 7998
in Brahmanism, 9571
by Muḥammad, 445
in Caribbean religions, 1433–1434, 1435, 1436
in Santería, 8108
of cats, 1463
in Celtic religion, 1493
in Chinese religion, 1582, 1590, 1620, 6293
feast at sacrifice to Heaven, 1914
in Christianity, religious reform and, 7655
distribution of meat, 1466
domesticated animals in, 7998
in Etruscan religion, 2873
expiatory purpose of, Smith (W. Robertson) on, 4183
in Garifuna religion, 3285, 3286
in goddess worship, 3590
in Greek religion, 3667–3670, 3682–3683
to Asklepios, 551
libations in, 5433
in Hawaiian religion, pig sacrifice, 3798
in Hinduism, 359
in *Śrauta* (solemn) rites, 3992
in popular Hinduism, 4007
history of, 8006
in Hittite religion, 4072
in Iberian religion, 4253
in Igbo religion, 4366
in Indus Valley religion, 3989
in Islam, 9818
for naming ceremonies, 7826
in Israelite religion, 926, 927, 986, 4746, 4972
in Judaism
human atonement through, 360, 8144
kashrut laws on, 5106
religious reform and, 7655
in Khanty religion, 5124–5125
in Komi religion, 5217
in Madagascar religion, 8746
in Mansi religion, 5124–5125
martyrdom compared to, 5738
in Minoan religion, 39–40
in Muisca religion, 6230
in oath-taking, 9642
in Phoenician religion, 7132, 7134
for purification, 1459, 7509
for rain, 7603
for rejuvenation, 7684
in Roman religion, 1452
for *Feriae Latinae,* 7898
for *lectisternia* ritual, 7905
for lustratio, 5534
to Mars, 5728
taurobolium, 7917, 7922
in Scandinavian religions, 3220
in Scythian religion, 4489
in Siberian religions, 6755
skulls in, 3804
in Southeast Asian religions, traditional, 8650
as substitution for human sacrifice, 7999
in Turkic religion, 2831
in United States, media coverage of, 4964–4965
in Vanuatu religions, 9519–9520
in Vedism, 9562, 9564
horse sacrifice, 1350, 1493, 9563–9564
place for, 9564–9565
Prajāpati identified with, 7356
violence of, 9598–9599
in Vodou, 9638
Animal shelters, Jaina, 2625–2626
Animatism. *See* Preanimism
Anime (animation), and Japanese Buddhism, 1184
Animism, **362–368**. *See also* Preanimism; Tylor, Edward Burnett
African religions in, 114
Benedict (Ruth) on, 820
in Bon, 1007, 1008

Animism *continued*
in Buddhism, 1131, 1133
folk, 3154
in Chinese religion, *qi* and,
8554–8555
as classification of religion,
1818–1819
critique of, 2543, 7372
definition of, 362, 363, 7347
deity in, 2258
dynamism and, 2540
in East Asia, and dance and
theater, 2453–2455
influence of, 363–365
in Shintō, 2639
in Komi religion, 5217–5218
literacy and, 2896
vs. manism, 5673
in Mesopotamian religions,
5968
in Middle Volga, 4616
in nature religions, 2662,
2883
in Negrito religions,
Philippine, 6454
power in, 7347, 7348
problems with, 364–365, 367
search for origins and, 365–
367, 7347, 7372
shamanism and, 8277
in Southeast Asia, insular,
8649–8650
supreme beings and, 8876
in Turkic religions, 9398
in Zapotec religion, 5903
Anin, Shahid, subaltern studies
and, 8800
Aningaaq (deity), 4528
Aniruddha (king of Pagan), 1135,
1136, 9148, 9149
Ānisaṃsa (blessings), 9094,
9832–9833
Anishinaabe religious traditions,
368–371
Anisimov, A. F., 475
on shamanic inheritance,
8283
on Sun Dance, 8844
Anisimov, Arkadii, 2619
Anjanā, as mother of Hanumān,
3775
Anjin (faith), 2320
Aṇkālaparamēcuvari (deity), 3608
Ankermann, Bernhard, on
kulturkreis, 5260
Ankh, 2713
in amulets and talismans, 299
relationship to keys, 5116
Ankhesenamun, 219
Ankulomeitas (wily), 7419
Anloji (Daochuo), 2176
An Lushan, 1598
Anna (Russian empress), anti-
Muslim campaigns of, 4617
Annadāmaṅgal (Bhāratcandra
Rāy), 825, 829
An-Naʾim, Abdullahi, 5364
Anna Karenina (Tolstoy), 9220,
9221
Annales School, historical method
and, 1873

Annals (Tacitus), Germanic
religion in, 3450
Annals of the gods (Egypt), 2724
Anna of Friesland, on
Mennonites, 5860
Anna Perenna (deity), 7902
Annaud, Jean-Jacques, 3098
Anne (saint)
and motherhood, 3360
spirits identified with in
Caribbean religions, 1433,
1434
Année sociologique (journal),
10057
Année sociologique, l' (periodical),
2527–2528
Mauss (Marcel) in, 5785,
5786
Annen (Buddhist monk), 9077,
9078
Anne of Savoy, 3698
Annihilation, in mystical union,
6335, 6338, 6339, 6340. *See
also* Fanāʾ
Annihilationist views in Cārvāka,
1446
Annis, Sheldon, 5929
Anno, Hideaki, 3097
Annual Conferences, in United
Methodist Church, 1767
Annunciation, Feast of the, in
Christian liturgical calendar,
1743
Annwn (Celtic otherworld), **371–
372**
apple trees and, 1491
in Fionn cycle, 1495
head of Bendigeidvran in,
3807
Lord of, 1490
Pwyll as lord of, 1490
Samhain and, 3758
Anointed class, in Jehovah's
Witnesses theology, 4821, 4822
Anointing. *See also* Chrismation
baptism and, 9809
of king, in Ebla, 5164
in Protestantism, in
charismatic and Pentecostal
movements, 7963
of the sick
in Eastern Orthodox
Church, 7960
medieval practices, 7961
Anomoeans, baptism of, 782
Anorexia, in Buriat religion, 1326
Anquetil-Duperron, A.-H., 4446
Ansaar Pure Sufi, 6768
Ansaaru Allah Community, 6769
Anṣāb (raised stones), 4361, 4362
Anṣār (helpers), of Muḥammad,
6223, 6224–6225
Anṣari, ʿAbd Allāh
epigrams and theology of,
8816–8817
on free will and
predestination, 8816
on good and evil, and ethics,
8817
Anṣārī, Murtaḍā, 4700
Ansari, Zafar Isḥāq, 4719

Anṣārī al-Harawī, ʿAbd Allāh,
Hanābilah and, 3765
Ansarullah Nubian Islamic
Hebrews, 4689
Anselm of Canterbury, **372–373**
on atonement, 596, 4843–
4844
Barth (Karl) studying, 791
criticism of, 7123
death of, 372
doctrine of, 372–373
Duns Scotus (John) and,
2524–2525
early Western Christianity
influenced by, 2582
epistemology of, 2819
in exile, 372
on existence of God, 582,
7123, 7421, 7422, 9103
on free will and
predestination, 3207
on God's compassion, 9282–
9283
on iconography, 4345
on knowledge, 5204
on passion of Christ, 3882–
3883
on perfection of God, 7039
pictured Jesus as mother hen,
953
realism of, 6644
on reconciliation, 1667
theology of, 9136
on Trinity, 9361
writings of, 372–373
Anselm of Laon, Abelard (Peter)
studying under, 7
Anshar, in *Enuma elish*, 2810
An-shar (deity), Ashur identified
with, 548–549
Anshe Emet (synagogue), 7637
An Shigao (Buddhist translator),
1146, 1163, 1266, 1290, 1576,
1594, 2171
Ansky, S., 2534
Anšlavs (deity), 769
ʿAṇṣrah (summer solstice), 835
Ansud (deity), 5949, 5952
Answer to Christians (al-Ṭabarī),
7242
Antarābhava (intermediate
existence), 1197
Antarakalpas (intermediate
kalpas), in Hinayana Buddhist
cosmology, 2028
Anteater, in ethnoastronomy,
2864
Antelope, in African art, 90, 117
Anthesteria festival, **374–376**
Diasia festival and, 9953
and gender roles, 3383
Anthimus (patriarch of
Constantinople), 6154
Severus of Antioch and, 8238
Anthologies
on African American
religions, 79–80
on African religions, 115–116
of *bhakti* poetry, 3984
as gardens, 3279
of Jewish texts, by Agnon
(Shemuʾel Yosef), 180

*Anthology of Sacred Texts By and
About Women, An* (Young),
3300
Anthology of the Patriarchal Hall,
1523
Anthon transcript, vol. 14 color
insert
Anthony, conversion of, 6740
Anthony, Dick, 1033, 6515,
6522, 6523
Anthony, Susan B.
Gage (Matilda Joslyn) and,
3251–3252
Stanton (Elizabeth Cady) and,
8731
Anthony (Antony) of Egypt (saint
and desert father)
eremitism of, 1980, 2824,
2825, 2826, 2828
Makarios of Egypt and, 5624
monasteries established by,
2582
monasticism and, 6131
religious experience of, 7722
seduction of, 4165
Anthony of Kiev, 7941
monachism of, 2826
Anthony of Padua (saint), **376–
378**
Anthony the Hermit, Legba
identified with in Vodou, 1433
Anthropic principle, 2659–2660
and science and religion,
questions raised in, 8189
scientific cosmology and,
2033
Anthropinon (human), 7182
Anthropocentrism, 357–358
in Abrahamic traditions, 360–
361
of Buddhist ethics, 2628
of Christianity, in creation,
2648
of Confucianism, 2631–2632
Earth First! and, 2561
Gaia hypothesis and, 3253
in historiography, 4030–4035
in *Job*, 9758–9759
Anthropocosmism
in Confucianism, 2632
definition of, 2605
Anthropogenesis, 9033
Anthropogony (myths of human
origins), 5443–5444
in Australian religions, 5444
in Chinese myth, 1625
earth in, 2556–2557
in Edo religion, 2697
in Egyptian religion, 2710
hands of God in, 3769
in Hinduism, 4439–4440
in Indonesian religions,
5444–5445
knot symbolism in, 5198
in Komi religion, 5217
in Lugbara religion, 5526
in Maasai religion, elephants
in, 2750
macrocosm-microcosm in,
4159
in Manichaeism, 5653–5654,
5666–5667

in Melanesian religions, 5843
in Mesoamerican Indian religions, 1468, 1469
in Cuna religion, 2095
in Mesoamerican religions, 5934–5935
in Mesopotamian religion, 8535–8538
Babylonian, 2810
and kingship, 5162
Sumerian, 2800
in North American Indian religions, 1469
in Orphism, 6893
resurrection as repetition of, 4159–4160
in Roman Catholicism, 7883
in science, 2658
in South American Indian religions, 8589
Andean, 8619
Lengua, 8634
in UFO religions, 9433
of untouchables, 9475
water in, 9700
in Zulu religion, 9474
Anthropological atheism, 7422
Anthropologie der Naturvölker (Waitz), 114
Anthropology, **378–388**. *See also* Archaeology; Ethnographies; Ethology; Evolution
on African religions, 113, 115, 118
on Arctic religions, 473
on Australian Indigenous religions
history of study, 683–685
new movements in, 670–671
biases of, study of sacred time and, 7992–7993
British school of, 2350, 2420–2421, 9424
on cargo cults, 1416, 1421–1425
categories of Geertz (Clifford) in, 8500
Christian theology as, Feuerbach (Ludwig) on, 3047–3048
Codrington on, 1848
comparative religion and, 1878
contemporary, 378
cultural, **2086–2090**
liturgy and, 5491–5492
Southeast Asian religion and, 8639–8640
culture-and-personality school of, 5804
on cursing, 2098–2099
definitions of religion in, 378
dualism in, 2505–2506, 2507, 2509, 2511
ecological studies in, 2611, 2664
of ecstasy, 2678
of Empedocles, 2776
Evans-Pritchard (E. E.) in, 2895–2896
exorcism studied in, 2935
field research in, 2915
on food customs, 3173
French school of, 2350
Freud's influence on, 2916
functionalism in, 4043, 5381, 7840
future of, 385–386
goals of, 378
on goddess worship, 3613, 3614
historical revaluations of, 380–381
historiography and
in Britain, 4043, 4048
in North America, 4044, 4049
in Scandinavia, 4047
humanistic and relativistic, 820
humor and, 4203
on Indian religions, 4448–4449
in Indo-European religious studies, 4460
on initiation, 4480
in Qur'ān, 5060
intellectualist approach to, 2914
James (E. O.) in, 4774–4775
journals devoted to, 10057–10058
legal, 5339
Malinowski in, 6801
"markers" for concepts in, 5631
Marxist, rituals in, 7838, 7845
methodology of
accommodations in, 383–385
foundations of, 378–379
problems with, 379–380
social anthropology *vs.* ethnology, 7592
of Native American culture, desecration and, 8011
nature religions and, 2664–2665
neutrality in, 378–379
North American study of religion and, 8785
on Oceanic religions, 6800
operational, Stanner (W. E. H.) on, 8729
on popular religion, 7325, 7326
and positivism, 7340
on potlatch, 7345
on primitive religion, 379–380, 3141
on primitivism, 10064
on psychedelic drugs, 7467
psychoanalytic, Róheim (Géza) and, 7872
on purification, 7504
Rappaport's (Roy A.) methods of, 7618
relativism in, 2867
religion defined by, 7693
in religious studies, 2608
on ritual, 7833
sacredness defined by, 7693
Schmidt (Wilhelm), role of, 8168, 8169
sorcery concepts in, 9768–9770
on sorcery *vs.* witchcraft, 57
South American Indian religions, studies of, 8594–8595
of Southeast Asia, religious studies *vs.*, 8639–8640
structuralist (*See* Structuralism)
study of dreams in, 2486
symbolic theory and, 8910–8911
syncretism as concept in, 8936
on taboo, 8948
on transmigration, 9326
trends in, 381–383, 385–386
Vierkandt (Alfred) in, 9590
in visual culture, 9620
wisdom concepts in, 9748
witchcraft concepts in, 9768–9770
in women's studies, 9790
Zolla (Elémire) in, 9984–9986
Anthropology (Tylor), 9424
Anthropomorphism, **388–392**
in African religions, 3569
in art, 4171–4172
definition of, 388
in Greek religion, 389, 3679, 5201, 5468
in Islam, 618, 620, 6322
in Judaism, 389, 390, 3543
in Ashkenazic Hasidism, Yehudah ben Shemu'el on, 544
postbiblical, 3547–3548
Kant (Immanuel) on, 5078
in Khanty religion, 5119, 5122
in Mansi religion, 5119, 5122
of matter, in alchemy, 245
in Mesopotamian religions, 5950–5951
mysticism as response to, 390–391
in North American Indian religions, and manitous, 5673–5674
in Paleolithic religion, 6952–6953
physical *vs.* mental, 389, 390
primary *vs.* secondary, 389
purging of, 390–391
Spinoza (Baruch) on, 8681
transcendence and immanence of God in, 9283
Xenophanes on, 4108
Anthropopathism, 389, 390
Anthropos (journal), 10056
Anthropos (periodical), 5260
Anthropos Institute
Bornemann (Fritz) and, 8170
Schmidt (Wilhelm) and, 8168
Anthroposophical Leading Thoughts (Steiner), 392
Anthroposophical Society, establishment of, 392, 393
Anthroposophy, **392–394**
French government report on, 6570
reincarnation in, 9330
Steiner (Rudolf) in, 392–393, 2160, **8738–8739**
teachings of, 392–393
Antichrist, **394–395**
Bacon (Roger) on warfare with, 735
in millenarianism, 6029, 6032
origins of, 394
pope as, 395
Servetus (Michael) on, 8232
Solov'ev (Vladimir) on, 8520
Anticlericalism, 2474
Spiritualism and, 8715
superstition charges and, 8866
Anticosmic dualism, 2508–2510, 2512
Anticult movements (ACMs), **395–397,** 6551, 6561
brainwashing theory and, 1032, 2085–2086
children as new weapon for, 6539
in Europe, 6569
Holy Order of MANS as target of, 4102–4103
against International Society for Krishna Consciousness, 4522
legislation, 1033–1034, 1038
and mass suicide at Peoples Temple, 7255
vs. new religious movements, 395–397, 5375
Satanism scare, 8127–8128
scholars of new religions and, 6566
Scientology and, 8194
against Temple Solaire, 9067–9068
against Twelve Tribes, 9410–9411
Antigonish Movement (Canada), 9301
Antihylic dualism, 2509
Antilas (bathing ceremony), 802
Antilope du soleil (Zahan), 117
Anti-martyrs, 5741
Antimension (cloth with relics sewn in), 7688
Antimimon pneuma, 521

Antinomianism
  Hutchinson (Anne) and, **4238**
  of Shabbetai Tsevi, 8259, 8260
  in Sufism, 4214
    ʿAbd Allāh Anṣarī and, 8817
Antinous (Hadrian's lover), 440
  miracles performed by, 7915
Antioch
  in early Christian structure, 2581
  in early Christian theology, 2583, 2584, 2884–2885
  hermits of, 2826
  rival patriarchs and bishops of, 2586
  schism in, 2586
Antioch, school of, 873, 5486, 9121–9122
  Cyril of Alexandria, opposition from, 2117
  on justification, 1651
Antioch, Syrian Church in. *See* Syriac Orthodox Church of Antioch
Antiochus (king), in *2 Maccabees,* 7765
Antiochus I of Commagene, syncretism of, 3909
Antiochus III (Seleucid king), and anti-Semitism, 398
Antiochus IV Epiphanes (Seleucid king)
  as Antichrist, 394
  Hellenization of Jerusalem under, 4835
  against idolatrous cults, 4359
  Jewish persecution by, 925, 7055
    apocalypses based on, 410, 415, 417
    apostasy and, 430
    Temple of Jerusalem defiled by, 7144
  in *1 Maccabees,* 900
Antiochus of Ascalon, 7188
Antiochus of Athens, 245
Anti-Oedipus (Deleuze and Guattari), 7488
Antipater of Tarsus, Stoicism and, 8740
Antiphon (Athenian orator), on repentance, 7756
Antiquity, of scriptures, 8202
Antireductionism, in phenomenology, 7088, 7091, 7092, 7094, 7097
Anti-Semitism, **397–403**. *See also* Holocaust; Persecution, of Jews
  alleged Jewish crimes and, 399–400
  vs. anti-Jewish behavior, 397
  anti-modernist movements and, 4085
  Campbell accused of, 1380
  Christian Identity movement, **1657–1660**
  in Christianity, 398–403
  coining of term, 397, 7056
  definition of, 397
  Eliade and, 2758–2760
  of Evola (Julius), 2906
  Gnosticism and, 3526
  Hoffmann (David), defense by, 4077
  in Japan, 5008
  in Jewish identity, 4863
  Jewish studies and, 4879
  modern Judaism and, 4984
  Orientalism and, 6883
  responses to, 5020–5021
  in Soviet Union, 5021
  two-seed theory, 1658
  use of term, 7056
  Zionism and, 9979
Antisthenes
  on knowledge, 5201
  theism of, 3910
Antistites (priests), 4559
Antitheses (Marcion), 5701, 5702
Antitrinitarianism. *See also* Unitarianism
  blasphemy prosecution of, 973
  in Reformation, 7661
  Servetus (Michael) and, 8233
  Sozzini (Fausto Pavolo) on, 8673
Anti-Zionism, 9982–9983
Antlers. *See also* Horns
  in Mesoamerican religions, in Huichol peyote cult, 4153
Antonelli, Giacomo, 5411
Antoni, Klaus, 7273
Antonine movement (Africa), 1511, 5221
Antony, Mark
  and Anthesteria, 375
  as Dionysus, 426
Antonyms, in alchemy, 246–247
Antony of Egypt. *See* Anthony of Egypt
Antrimps (deity), 769
Ants, 4508
  in Mesoamerican myths, 5936
Anu (deity). *See* An
Anubis (deity), **403–404,** 2393
  and gender roles, 3384
  Hermanubis as Hermes and Anubis fused, 3938
  in Kushite religion, 5269
Anugītā (epic), *Bhagavadgītā* compared to, 852
Anuket (deity), 7861
Anulap (deity), 6009
Anuloma marriages, in Indian caste system, 3996
Anum. *See* An
Anumāna (inference), 1301
Anu nyayuga (cosmic creative power), in Sudanese religion, 8849
Anuruddha (Buddhist monk), 1199
Anuttarayoga Tantras, 1215–1216, 1218
Anuvrata (Small Vows), of Jain laity, 4770
Anuyoga (Subsequent Yoga), 7870
Anwār al-tanzīl wa-asrār al-taʾwīl (al-Bayḍāwī), 806, 4662, 8953
Anwar Ibrahim, 4668
Anxiety
  cosmology and, 1992
  in existentialism, 2926
  "playing God" problem and, 8187
  Puritanism and, Weber (Max) on, 8494
  rites of passage and, 7797, 7802
  sacrifice and, 8004
Anyanwu (deity), 3572
Anyāpoha (exclusion of the other), 1301
Anz, Wilhelm, 3532
Anzac Day, 1734
Anzu (deity)
  death of, 2811
  and Ninurta, 6627
Aobi feast, 187
Aoko, Gaudencia, 105
Ao-Naga people (India), ritual calendar of, agriculture and, 187
Aondo (deity), 9210
Aónikenk religion. *See* Tehuelche religion
Aoyama, Shutai, Shingon Buddhism and, 8352
Aoyama San'u, on calligraphy, 1371
Aoyama Sensei, 6761
APA. *See* American Psychological Association
Apabraṃśa dialect, songs in, in *Hevajra Tantra,* 3965
Apache religion and society (North America), **404–407**
  as Athapaskan nation, 573, 574
  bears in, 809
  buffalo hunting in, 404
  cosmology of, 10069
  culture hero myth in, 2091
  deities of, 404, 405, 574
  drama in, 2461, 2462
  initiation rites in, 10069–10071
  life in, 5444
  Navajo traditions compared with, 6443
  peyote in, 404, 406
  place-names in, significance of, 2611
  in Plains region, 6656
  in Southwest region, 6657, 6720
  spiders in, 4507
  wind and power in, concepts of, 576
Āpaddharma (rules for emergency), 2330
Āpaḥ (deities), 9558–9559
Apąm Napāt (deity)
  Agni as, 179
  as *ahura,* 205
Apāna (breath), 1043, 7362, 7363
Apaosha (deity), 2128
Aparā (deity), in Trika Śaivism, 8046
Aparagodānīya. *See* Godānīya (mythic island)
Aparaśaila sect, origin of, 1194
Āpas (deity), 4535
Apaśabda (incorrect speech), 7005
Āpastamba Dharmasūtra, salutations in, 8060
Apatheia (indifference), 2360, 2825
Apaturia festival, 587
Apauruṣeya doctrine, 4423, 9549–9550
  Vedas and, 3994, 3995, 9549–9550
Apedemak (deity), in Kushite religion, 5269
Apelles (Marcionite), 5702
Apes. *See* Monkeys
Apess, William, 702
Aphorisms
  in alchemy, 246–247
  in Biblical wisdom, 9755
  of ʿAlī ibn Abī Ṭālib, 260
  in *Proverbs,* 9757–9758
  wisdom in, 9748
Aphrodite (deity), **407–409**
  Adonis and, 34, 35, 1451, 2536, 7767
  Astarte identified with, 7130
  birth of, 407, 408, 1450
  cults of, 407–409
  dove as symbol of, 948
  Eros and, 2832–2833
  and fish symbolism, 3122
  functions of, 3680
  hare associated with, 7590
  in Hellenistic religions, 3601–3602
  iconography of, 4322
  as Lady of the Animals, 5279, 5282
  origin of, 408–409
  Pandora fashioned by, 7419
  sacrifices to, 1467
  shape shifting and, 8302
  son of, 7392, 7393
  specialization of, 2984
  statues of, representing social position of women, 4298–4299
  as virgin, 9604
  worship of, 3601–3602
Aphroditism, 731
Aphthartodocitae, 5028
Api (deity), 7386
  in Scythian cosmology, 8205
Apilum (Aplum, Apiltum) (answering), in Eblaite religion, 2599
Apinagé religion (Brazil)
  origin of agriculture in, 8590
  plants used by, 9575
  solar god in, 8578
  Sun and moon in, 2862
Apion, Josephus Flavius's response to, 427
Apis bull (Egypt), 2710, 2712, 6921
Apladda (deity), 28
Apo (Akan festival), 215

Apocacuva Guaraní Indians. *See* Guaraní-Apapocuvá religion
Apocalypse, **409–420**. *See also* Millenarianism
Antichrist in, 395
apostasy in, 431, 432, 433
ascension in, 410–411, 416, 518, 522–523
Branch Davidians and, 5238, 6545, 6546, 6554
Christian, 411–413 (*See also* Revelation)
early, 409, 411–412
interpretation of, 874
Church Universal and Triumphant on, 1783, 7446
definitions of, 409, 410, 413
environmental, 2562, 2564
Ezra's visions of, 2947
in Germanic religion, 3456–3457
and Gnosticism, 5202
of Heaven's Gate, 6555
Islamic, 413
Qur'ān on, 159–160, 413
Israelite, 4748–4749
wisdom and, 9750
Jewish, 4975
ascension in, 522–523
historical, 409–410, 414–416, 417–418
medieval, **419–420**
Moses in, 6203
otherworldly journey in, 410, 416, 418
in Pseudepigrapha, 901, 902–903
to rabbinic period, **414–419**
and time and history, view of, 4058
in Jones's (Jim) theology, 4953
as narrative of violence, 9599
new religions on, 6531
origins of, 410–411
overview of, **409–414**
Qumran sect and, 2234
Raëlians and, 7597
Solov'ev (Vladimir) on, 8520
in Temple Solaire, 6554, 9067
in UFO groups, 6495
in Ugandan religions, 6216–6217
United House of Prayer and, 2124–2125
in Zoroastrianism, 9936, 9996–9997, 10002
Apocalypse of Abraham, 410, 902
Apocalypse of Adam, 902
Apocalypse of Baruch, 7765
Apocalypse of Daniel, 902
Apocalypse of Enoch. See Enoch, Apocalypse of
Apocalypse of Ezra, 2947
Apocalypse of Moses, 3126–3127
Apocalypse of Paul, 919
Apocalypse of Peter, 917, 919, 7068–7069
laughter of Jesus in, 4197
Apocalypse of Weeks, 174–175, 431
Apocalyptic, 410, 413
Apocalypticism, 6545–6546. *See also* Apocalypse; Millenarianism
vs. apocalypse, 410
avertive, 6547–6548
definition of, 410
Apocatastasis, **420–423**
Apochryphon of John (Gnostic text), 5202
Apocrypha, **878–896**. *See also* Biblical literature
Confucian *(chenwei),* 1908
cursing in, 2104
demons in, 2277
evil, inclination toward, in, 8404
heavens, multiple, in, 3884
Hermetism and, 3940, 3941
historical books in, 900–901
ḥokhmah in, 4079
importance of, 896
Jewish election in, 2745
legends and romantic stories in, 897–899
to New Testament, 919
number of books of, 896
origin of word, 896
Protestant position toward, 881, 896
Satan in, 8123–8124
scripture, terms for, in, 8196
Spiritualism and, 8716
wisdom and philosophical literature in, 899–900
women in, 3359
Apocrypha and Pseudepigrapha of the Old Testament, The (Charles), 901
Apocryphon of Adam, 6396
Apocryphon of James, 3513, 6396
Apocryphon of John, 521, 3510, 3511, 3517
hypostasis in, 4242
Irenaeus of Lyons and, 6397
Sophia in, 8523
Apocryphon of Joshua, 7063, 7065
Apodictic laws, Israelite, 4728
Apodictic Treatises (Gregory Palamas), 3698, 3699
Apoha (theory of concepts), 2336–2337
language as exclusion in, 5308
Apo Ifá (diviner's bag), 10033
Apokatastasis, 9072
Apokryphen und Pseudepigraphen des Alten Testaments, Die (Kautzsch), 901
Apoliticism, of Eliade, 2758–2759
Apollinaire, Guillaume, calligrams of, 1369
Apollinarianism, 424
Athanasian Creed against, 2057
doctrine of, 7876
Nestorius *vs.,* 2117
Apollinaris of Laodicea, **423–424**
Christology of, 4242
Gregory of Nazianzus and, 423, 424, 3695
heresy of, 424
Monophysitism of, 6153
Theodore of Mopsuestia against, 9121
writings of, 423
Apollo (Balanchine), 2161–2162
Apollo (deity), **424–426**
apocatastasis and, 421
as Apollo Medicus (Apollo the Physician), 3841
archery of, 424, 425
Artemis and, 506
Asklepios and, 551
Augustus and, 7913
birth of, 425
cattle stolen from, 1465
Celtic parallels, 1483–1484
cults of, 425–426
and Dionysos, in partnership, 2357, 2358
divination and chance and, 1528
Eshmun and, 2840, 2842
in Etruscan pantheon, 2871
etymology of name, 424, 3679
festivals of, 425
functions of, 3679–3680
Hermes and, 3936
iconography of, 4321, 4322
in initiation rites, 184, 3679–3680
inspiration given by, 4510
Maponos identified with, 5685
Muses and, 6242
music and, 6304
in Orphism, 6895
paradox of, 3905
Pindar on, 7174
as prophet of Zeus, 3664
Pythagoras and, 7528, 7529
retribution and, 7783
in Rome, 7904–7905
sanctuaries of, 425
serpent killed by, 2431
sibyls and, 8383
Socrates and, 8503
stones dedicated to, 8745
as sun, 8839–8840, 8841
temple of (Delphi), 2265–2266
taken from Mother Earth, 5282
temple of (Dreros), 9063
trees as symbols of, 9337
Apollo Aiguieus (sacred column), 8745
Apollo and Daphne (Bernini), vol. 13 color insert
Apollodorus (scholar)
on Adonis, 34
on Athena, 586
on Hermes, 3937
on Prometheus, 7420
Apollo Karneios (deity), 5275
Apollonius of Tyana
biography of, 4038
Gauḍapāda and, 3290
magic and miracles of, 3905, 6051
Apologetics, **426–430**
Ash'arīyah, 531
audience targeted by, 426–427
and Buddhist hermeneutics, 1277
Christian, 427–430
of Athenagoras, 589
early, 1660–1661
of Justin Martyr, 5043–5045
of Leibniz, 5406
for monotheism, 3545
of Otto (Rudolf), 6929
of Tertullian, 9085
on idolatry, 4360–4361
Islamic, 428–429
in *kalām,* 5059
Jewish, 427, 4899–4900 (*See also* Kuzari)
Schmidt (Wilhelm) on, 8170
and study of Jewish iconography, 4341–4343
Apologia pro vita sua (Newman), 2426
Apologie oder Schutzschrift für die vernünftigen Gottes (Reimarus), 7675
Apologue of Menenius Agrippa, corporate imagery in, 4161
1 Apology (Justin Martyr), 5043
2 Apology (Justin Martyr), 5044
Apology (Abelard), 7
Apology (Aristides), 4360
Apology (al-Hāshimī), 7242
Apology (Barclay), 7547
Apology (Justin Martyr), 4360
Apology (Plato), 427
Apology (Tertullian), 9085
Apology for the Augsburg Confession, 5831
Apophatic meditation, 5816, 5817
Apophatic theology, 9139
Apophatism, 7190
Apophis (deity), 2712
Re and, 8456
Apophthegmata Patrum, 2824–2825
Apopis (dragon), 2431
Aporphine (opiate), 7470
Apostasy, **430–434**
in Christianity, 430, 431–433
definition of, 430
of Elisha' ben Avuyah, 2769
Ezekiel on, 2944

Apostasy ***continued***
in Islam, 433–434, 4575
as transgression against the Shahādah, 8014
in Judaism, 430–431
meanings of, in confessional religions, 3921
sin as, 8404
A posteriori knowledge, Kant (Immanuel) on, 5077
Apostles, **434–437,** 920
disciples as, 435
Mani as, 436, 5647, 5665, 5666
Mary Magdalene as, 5757
miracles of, 6054, 6056
revelation to, 7777–7778
Ritschl (Albrecht) on, 7832
Apostles' Creed, 2958
affirmation of, 4417
in Anglican *Book of Common Prayer,* 2052
history of, 2056
"holy catholic church" added to, 1771
as "symbol," 2054
Apostolic Armenian Church. *See* Armenian church
Apostolic Church of John Maranke (Africa), 1511
doctrines of, 5695
leadership structure of, 5695
Maranke (John) in, **5694–5696**
Passover in, 5694–5695
schisms in, 5695
spread of, 5695–5696
Apostolic Church of John Masowe (Africa), 1511
Apostolic Constitutions, 904
Apostolic faith, heresy and, 3926
Apostolic Faith Mission Church of God, Seymour (William J.) and, 8254
Apostolic Faith movement (Pentecostal), 7029
Apostolic orders. *See also* Jesuits
decline of, 6135
for women, 6135
Apostolic succession
heresy and, 3927
and history, ecclesiastical view of, 4055
Apostolic Tradition (Hippolytus)
on baptism, 9809–9810
on Eucharist, 9810–9811
Apotheosis, **437–441**
Campbell on myth as, 1379
vs. deification, 2248
descent into the underworld and, 2298–2299
honjisuijaku theory and, 4121–4122
in Roman religion, 7915
self-apotheosis, in Hindu Tantras, 4019
Apotropaism (warding off evil)
hand gestures for, 3770
yoni in, 9908
Apoyan Táchu, in Zuni creation myth, hierogamy of, 2555–2556
Appalachian Spring (Graham), 2159
Appar (Śaiva saint)
as Nāyaṉār, 8044
on Śaiva Siddhanta, 8042
poetry by, 8417
Apparitions. *See* Ghosts; Mary, apparitions of; Visions
Apparitions of the Self (Gyatso), 701
Appeal in Favor of That Class of Americans Called Africans (Child), 1569
Appiah, Joseph William Egyanka, as sorcerer, 104
Appiah-Kubi, Kofi, 118
on diviner-diagnosticians, 3818
Applewhite, Marshall Herff (Do), Heaven's Gate and, 3889–3891, 6555, 6561
Applied Eugenics (Popenoe and Johnson), 2881
Applied philosophy, 940
Apprenticeship
of Caribbean shamans, 1431
of North American Indian healers, 7300
Approaches to God (Maritain), 5713
Approaching Elegance (Erya), 1909
Approaching the African God (Hucks), 79
Approaching the Qur'ān (Sells), 7222
Appu, Tales of
in Hittite myth, 4070
in Hurrian myth, 4232
April Fools' Day. *See* All Fools' Day
A priori knowledge, Kant (Immanuel) on, 5077
A priori theory
opposed by history of religions approach, 4061, 4062
sacred *vs.* profane and, 7975–7976
Spinoza (Baruch) on, 8684
Apsaras (nymphs), 4467
Apse, 792–793
Apsu (deity), 952, 2962
in *Enuma elish,* 2809, 3377
and Tiamat as pair, 1994, 7861
Apsu (waters), 932, 3178, 9699, 9700
ablutions with, 10
Apte, Mahadev L., on ritual humor, 4198
Apuleius, 3053, 7189. *See also* Metamorphoses (Apuleius)
Asinus aureus, 3051, 3052
and the Grail, 3651
on Isis, 3384, 3604–3605, 4558, 4559, 6156, 6331, 7189, 7921
on magic, 3905, 5573, 5575, 7914
orations of, 7189
syncretism and, 3908, 3909
Apulu (deity), 2871
'Aqā'id. See 'Aqidah/'aqā'id
'Aqd (contract), election and, 2748
'Aqedah. *See* Isaac
'Aqedah (binding), as Holocaust paradigm, 4088
Aqhat, Epic of
Anat in, 320, 1383
in Canaanite religion, 1396–1398
Danil in, 1382, 1388
Kirta cycle in, 1390
kotharat in, 1384
marzih feast in, 1386
Aqhat (deity), as dying and rising god, 1874–1875
'Aqīdah al-ḥamawīyah, al- (Ibn Taymīyah), 4277
'Aqīdah al-rafīyah, Al- (Ibn Daud), 4264–4265, 4267
'Aqidah/'aqā'id (articles of belief), 8944
as creeds, 2053, 2062
fiqh founded on, 4587
'Aqīdah wāsiṭīyah (Ibn Taymīyah), 4277
Aqīmū al-ṣalāt (perform the prayer), 4374
'Aqiva' ben Yosef, **441–442**
biblical exegesis of, 441–442
on capital punishment, 3751
constructive exegesis and, 3748
on free will and predestination, 3203
influence of, 441–442, 888
martyrdom of, 442, 3548, 5739, 7056, 8806
Me'ir studying with, 5830
'Omer period and, 4867
on thrones in heaven, 3509
torture of, 9116
'Aql (reason), 4374, 4761
Aqṣā. *See Masjid al-aqṣā, al-*
Aquarian Conspiracy, 6496
Aquarius, Age of, 6495. *See also* New Age movement
Church Universal and Triumphant and, 1782
Aquila (Jewish proselyte), Greek Bible revised by, 891, 892, 893
Aquinas, Thomas. *See* Thomas Aquinas
Aquino, Michael, Temple of Set and, 8127
Aquino, Pilar, 5440
Āqūlī, Ṭalḥah al-, Ḥanābilah and, 3766
Arabia and Arabian religions, **442–446**
afterlife in, 445
astral worship in, 443
Christianity, 442
and biblical translations into Arabic, 894
deities of (*See also* Athirat; *specific deities*)
astral, 443–445
in Hejaz, 444–445
ghūl (desert demons), 1463
homosexuality in, 4113, 4114
Islam
establishment of, 6223
Imāmī (Twelvers) Shiism, 4698
Judaism, 442
Nabatean religion and, 6389–6390
political history of, 443
pre-Islamic
history of, 442–445
predestination in, 3209
spring and autumn festivals in, 6593
rituals in, 445
sacrifice in, 8006
Smith (W. Robertson) on, 8452
stones in, 8744
temples in, 444
trade and, 443
Arabia Felix, 443
Arabic language
alphabet of
and Dogon script, 101
mystical speculation on, *273*
in Andalusia, 4593, 4596
Aristotle's works translated into, 479
astrological books translated into, 563–564
and attributes of God, 616–617, 6322
autobiographies in, 700
biblical exegesis in, 865
biblical translations into, 894–895, 922
calligraphy, 1368
Coptic texts in, 1981
in East Africa, 2566
essentiality to Qur'ān, 5060, 7561
essentiality to *sharī'ah,* 4698
Galen's works translated into, 3256
gender in, 3364
grammar in, 616
"holy" in, 7968
magical instructions in, 5578–5579
Malay language influenced by, 4657
music in, in Southeast Asia, 6290
Pañcatantra translated into, 6959–6960
Pentateuch translated into, 894, 8950
poetry in, 7221–7222
Smith (W. Robertson) on, 8452
study of, 7563
Arab–Israeli conflict
Buber (Martin) on, 1058
Christian emigration and, 1676
Ginzberg (Asher) predicting, 3496
Ḥamās and, 7257
Arabs
in Andalusia, 4591, 4592–4593

Crusades and commerce with Europe, 2078
naming tradition of, 19, 3562, 6410
nationalism and *nahḍa* movement, 1674–1675, 7287, 7621 (*See also* Fundamentalism, Islamic)
on nature, 6432
North Africa, emigration to, 1680, 4581–4582
proverbs of, 6977
sacred enclaves of (*ḥaram* and *ḥawṭah*), **3776–3778**
tribalism and the caliphate, 1366
Arab Women's Solidarity Association, 3366
A'rāf. See Druze
Arafat, Mount, 6213
Arafat (Saudi Arabia), as station of *ḥājj*, 7157, 7159
Aragon, Judaism in
Adret (Shelomoh ben Avraham) and, 36
Crescas (Ḥasdai), role of, 2069
rabbis in, 7579
Arahant. See Arhats
Arai Hakuseki, Confucianism and, 1928
Aram (region), 446
Arama, Yitsḥaq, 866
Aramaic language
Apocrypha in, 897, 898
Aramean dialects of, 446
in Aramean religion, 446–450
Athirat (Asherah) in, 591
biblical translations into, 887–889, 894, 922
cantillation by Yemenite Jews, 1533
earliest text found in, 447
importance of, 887
incantations in, 4407
Jesus speaking, 887, 906
Nabatean version of, 6385
as official language of Persia, 887
Shavu'ot hymn in, 8305–8306
Syriac language as cognate of, 447
used in Septuagint, 890
Ara Maxima (Very Large Altar) in Rome, Hercules worshipped at, 3917
Aramazd (deity), 491, 492
Aramean religion (Near East), **446–451**
afterlife in, 450
deities of, 447–450 (*See also* Hadad; Sin)
associations of, 448
kingship in, 5164
late, 448–450
supernatural in, 450
and Tel Dan inscription, 2224
Āramgāh (cemetery), 6998
Aranda religion (Australia)
binding in, 938
bull-roarers used in, 1320–1321, **9211–9213**
deus otiosus in, 2312
iconography of, 4305
kadaitcha sorcerers in, 3871
miracles in, 6049
myths in, 662
Emianga, 655–656
moon in, 6174
rebirth in, 315, 7677
sacred pillar in, 1502
sexuality in, 8239
souls in, 4415
totem ancestors in, 2961
transmigration in, 9326–9327
Arandic kinship system, 9694
Aran islanders, 1490
Araññavāsm (forest dwellers), *saṃgha* and, 8074, 8080–8081
Āraññikas (Buddhist monks), 1096, 9148, 9149
Aranrhod (deity), 1489, 1490
in *Mabinogion,* 5546
Āraṇyakas (Sanskrit text), **1026–1028**
as transition between Brāhmaṇas and Upaniṣads, 3992–3993
eremitism of, 2823
Upaniṣads and, 9481
in Vedas, 9553
Vedism, relation to, 3989
Arapaho religion (North America)
creation story of, 6704
sacred bundle of, 6652
Sun Dance in, 8846, 8848
Arapesh people (New Guinea)
celibacy, temporary, 1475
initiation rites of, 7807
ritual calendar of, agriculture and, 187
supernaturalism of, 5804
Arara religion (Amazon), 8631. *See also* Carib Indians
Ararat, Mount, 6212
Ararbanel, Isaac. *See* Abravanel, Isaac
Ararma (Mesopotamia), Utu in, 5949, 5956
Aratus, on Golden Age, 3627
Aratus of Soli, on pantheism, 3909
Araucanian religion (Andes). *See also* Mapuche religion
geography of, 8576
shamanism in, 8584
supreme being in, 8580
Araújo, Maria de, 6577
Aravnah (Canaanite ruler), 933
Arawak Indians, Garifuna people descended from, 3283
Arawak religions (South America). *See also* Island Arawak
Baniwa and Kuripako, 8624–8625
disease, myth of origin of, 3809
Chané, 8637
Enawenê Nawê, cosmology of, 2012–2013
fertility rites of, 8582, 8583
Island Arawak separate from, 1426
Mojo, jaguar cult in, 8582
music in, 8582–8583
Palikur, 8627–8628
Arawa tribe (New Zealand), on primeval parents, 3015
Araweté religion (Amazon), overview of, 8628
Arawn (king of Annwn), 371, 372, 1490
Arba'ah ṭurim (Asher), 5104, 9864
'Arb'a Turim (Jacob ben Asher), 9236
Arberry, A. J., 4718
Arbman, Ernst
on ecstasy, 2681
on soul, Greek conception of, 8541
Arbre cosmique, l' (Pâques), 99
ARC. *See* Alliance of Religion and Conservation; Association for Cultural Research
Arcadia (Sidney), 3051
Arcadia Club (Temple Solaire), 6554, 9067
Arcana Arcanorum, as sexual magic, 8252
Arcana Caelestia (Swedenborg), theology in, 8899
Arcane School, women in, 6536
Arcesilas (philosopher), skepticism and, 8420
Arcesilaus, 7188
Arch, Roman, 794
religious associations in, in middle republic, 7909
Archaeoastronomy, 453
Archaeology, **451–457**
on Arctic religions, 474
biblical, 451–452, 455
Buddhist, Foucher (Alfred) and, 3176
Canaanite sites, 455, 1381
definition of, 451
direct-historical approach to, 452
Druid studies and, 1499
eternal time in, biases about, 7992–7993
excavation methods of
Wheeler-Kenyon method, 5111
Wheeler method, 5111
Finno-Ugric, 3114
of grave goods, 9225–9226
history of, 451–454
Hittite sites, 4068, 4070–4071
in Israel, tenth-century, 2224
in Jerusalem, tenth-century, 2224
of Jewish synagogues, 8923–8924
limitations on, 451
Mesoamerican, 9066
methodology of, 452–453
Nabatean, 6386–6388, *6387*
Near Eastern
Frankfort (Henri) and, 3188
Kenyon's (Kathleen) work in, 5110–5111
Neolithic, 6459
"new," 453
Olmec, 6817
pre-Columbian, 452, 456–457
prehistoric, 452–453, 456, 7375, 7376, 7384
protohistoric, 451–452
recent contributions by, 454–457
of Rome, 7893, 7895
South American Indian religions, studies of, 8595
in Southeast Asia, Hindu traditions, evidence of, 4010, 4011
of textiles, 9088
Archaeomythology, of Gimbutas (Marija), 3493
Archagathus (physician), in Rome, 3841
Archaic culture theory. *See Urkultur* (oldest culture)
Archaic mentality, 2282–2283
Archangels
possession by, in Revival Zion, 1437
al-Suhrawardī on, 4554–4555
Archbishops
of Baltimore
Carroll (John) and, 1445
Gibbons (James) as, 3478–3479
of Canterbury (*See* Canterbury)
in church polity
Greek Orthodox, 1765
Roman Catholicism, 1764
in Roman Empire, 1763
in early Christian structure, 2581
Archdiocese of America (Greek Orthodox), 1765
Archery
of Apollo, 424, 425
of Artemis, 506
in *Upaniṣads,* 8724
in Zen Buddhism, 8724
Arches, Roman, 794
religious associations in, in middle republic, 7909

Archetypes, **457–460**
conversion, archetypal theories on, 1970
Eliade on, 458–459, 460
etymology of term, 457–458
of Great Mother, Neumann (Erich) on, 3612
Ibn al-ʿArabī on, 8820
Jung on, 458, 459–460, 5114
in collective unconscious, 7485
goddess worship in, 3611–3612
power in, 7350
Kant (Immanuel) on, 5079
Kérenyi (Károly) on, 5114
myth and, 1379
in hero myths, 3958
and mythopoetics, 5862
in ritual, 7834
symbol theory and, 8913
Archilochus, on chance, 1527
Archimedes, on geometry, 3443–3444
Architecture, **460–468**. *See also specific types*
Aksumite, 224–225
appropriation of styles, vol. 8 color insert
archaeology and, 453
Christian
in early Eastern Christianity, 2582
numerical symbolism in, 6746
church (*See* Church architecture)
circle symbolism in, 1791–1792, 1794
classification of, 460–467
Egyptian (*See also* Pyramids)
under Akhenaton, 218–219
geometry in, 3439
grace in, 3647
Greek, 4322
heaven and earth connected in, 7980
Hindu
Kramrisch (Stella) on, 5242–5243
of temples, 7837
Iranian, fire in, 569–570
Islamic
calligraphy in, 6207, 6208
geometry in, 6208
of *madrasahs,* 5556
in Southeast Asia, 4672
studies on, 4718
in sub-Saharan Africa, 4608
Kushite, 5269
of law, 5360
macrocosm and microcosm in, 7983
maṇḍalas in, 5640
Maya, 1359, 5796, 5799, 5882, 5886
Mesoamerican
in Teotihuaćan, 149, 5888, 5900
in Toltec religion, 5906–5907
Mesopotamian, 5960
of monasteries, **6117–6121**
of mosques, **6207–6210**
classification of, 461, 467, 6208–6210
in first Medina mosque, 6205–6206
Nabatean, 6386–6387
negation of sacred space in, 7980
orientation of, to center of sacred universe, 7694
of sacred spaces, 7694
sky hierophany and, 8428–8429
of synagogues, 8921–8926
temple urbanism in India, 1805–1806
Archives de sciences sociales de religions (journal), 10057
Arcona (Bournonville), 2156
Arctic Home of the Vedas, The (Tilak), 9199
Arctic religions, **468–476**. *See also specific religions*
afterlife in, 472
animals in
ceremonialism for, 469, 471
history of study of, 474
masters of, 470
myths of, 472
souls of, 4527
spirits portrayed as, 469–470
bears in
ceremonies for, 471, 474, 9394
myths of, 472, 9394–9395
cultic practices of, 470–472
culture and, 468–469, 472
deities of, 469–470 (*See also specific deities*)
mother-goddess, 470
supreme, 469
development of, 472, 474
history of study of, **473–476**
hunting culture in, 468, 472, 4527
myths of, 472
bears in, 472, 9394–9395
history of study of, 473–474
overview of, **468–473**
rituals in, 470–471
shamanism in
history of study of, 474, 475
Inuit, 4528
prevalence of, 469
in sacrificial ceremonies, 470
soul beliefs in, 471
spirits' relationships with, 469
trances and, 471
spirits in, 469–470, 4528
Ardashīr II (Sasanid king), 6479
Arda Viraf, Book of, 411
Ardā Wirāz Nāmag, 519–520, 9993
Ardhamāgadhī language, 4766
Ardhanarisvara (deity), 4324
Ardhaphālaka (partially clothed), 4765
ʿArḍīi (angels), 4554–4555
Ardirri (spirit), 144
Ardvi Sura Anahita (deity), 3595
ARE. *See* Association for Research and Enlightenment
Arecuná religion (South America), hunting dances of, 8581
Areimanius (deity)
in Mithraism, 6092
obliteration of, 3907
Areitos (dances), in Caribbean religions, 1429
Arenda (leaseholding), 5015
Arendt, Hannah
on American civil religion, 1815
on decline of authority, 5397
on politics and Protestantism, 7453
Arensnuphis (deity), in Kushite religion, 5269
ARE Press, 560
Ares (deity)
Aphrodite and, 408
functions of, 3680
Kemosh identified with, 6094
sword as symbol of, 9686
in Thracian religion, 9169
violence of, 9597
Aretas IV (Nabatean king), 4943, 6386
Aretē (warlike prowess), homosexuality and, 4112
Arethas, on Athenagoras, 589
Argall, Samuel, 9302
Argei, feast of, 7896–7897
Argentina. *See also* Gran Chaco region; Mapuche religion; *See also* Mataco-Makká religion; Tehuelche religion; Tierra del Fuego
Islam in, 4685
Roman Catholicism in, pilgrimage in, 7149
Arginy movement, 9067
Argonautika (Orpheus), 2271
Argonauts of the Western Pacific (Malinowski), 5628, 5629
Argos (Greece), Hera cult in, 3915
Argos (mythic figure), murder of, by Hermes, 3936–3937
Arguing about Aborigines (Hiatt), 3392
Argument from Marginal Cases, in animal rights, 2655
Argumentum (Ficino)
"genealogy of wisdom" in, 3946
Hermetism in, 3945
*Arhat*s (worthy ones), **476–478**. *See also* Bodhisattvas
Ānanda tested by, 4483
as saints in Theravāda, 8036
becoming, 996, 999, 1088, 7357
bodhisattvas renouncing, 6994
Buddhist schools disputing over, 1110, 1193, 1195–1196, 1197
canonical literature on, 1112
cult of, 1080
enlightenment of, 2793
iconography of, 4330, vol. 1 color insert
in Hīnayāna Buddhism, 1080, 1085, 1192
in Mahāsāṃghika Buddhism, 5601–5602
in Mahāyāna Buddhism, 1080, 1085, 1114, 1192
Sarvāstivāda Buddhism, 8119
in Theravāda Buddhism, 476–477, 8036, 9146, 9152
in Jainism, 476
morality of, 1280
nirvāṇa of the buddha *vs.,* 2029
path from *Śrāvaka* toward, 2028
Sinhala Buddha created by, vol. 12 color insert
Sumedha as, 998
in Vedism, 476
Ariadne (Greek mythic figure), 5274
Arianhdit (prophet), 2570, 6745
Arianism, **478–479**
Apollinaris of Laodicea against, 423
Athanasius against, 478, 571–572, 972
on baptism, 782
Basil of Caesarea against, 798
blasphemy prosecution of, 973
in Channing's Unitarian Christology, 1530
Constantine the Great and, 479
Council of Nicaea and, 571, 1966–1967, 2039–2040, 3927, 7279
in Cyrenaica, 1678
Cyril of Jerusalem and, 2118
doctrine of, 7876
in early Christian theological issues, 2581
Eusebius and, 2884, 2885
filioque and, 2585
of Goths, 1689
Gregory of Nazianzus against, 3695
Gregory of Nyssa against, 3696–3697
Nestorius *vs.,* 2117
Nicene creed exclusion of, 2056
of Vandals, 1679
Aricia (Italy), 7898
Ariès, Philippe
on death, 2239–2240, 2244
on rites of passage, 7796
Ariki (chiefs), 9195, 9196
Ariki Fangarere (Tikopia chief), 9196

Ariki Kafika (Tikopia chief), 9196
Ariki Tafua (Tikopia chief), 9196, 9197
Ariki Taumako (Tikopia chief), 9196, 9197, 9198
Arimaspeans (legendary people), 6165
Ariosophy, 3526
Arische Männerbund, Der (Wikander), 9735
Arishima Takeo, 3072, 3073
Aristeas of Proconnesus
ascension by, 520
miracles of, 6050
wandering soul of, 8541
Aristide, Jean-Bertrand, 9636
Aristides
on Asklepios, 552
on dreams, 2376
on "gospel," 3641
on idolatry, 4360
Aristobulus, Philo Judaeus influenced by, 7106
Aristocracy, genealogy and, 3424–3425
Aristonicus of Pergamum, utopian Heliopolis founded by, 3906
Aristophanes
on Adonis, 35
and androgynes, 338
on auspices, 7335
on catasterism, 8424
on Hera, 3679, 3914
on heroes, 3681
on initiation, 4487
on magic, 5575
on moon, 6171
obscenity in works of, 7079
ritual patterns used by, 2443
on Socrates, 8501
Aristotelianism, **479–483**
Bible, attempts to reconcile with, 8181, 8182
in Christianity, 480, 482
and God, 3555
Copernicanism *vs.*, 8183
creation from nothing and, 8182
in *falsafah* (Islamic philosophy), 479
soul in, 8569, 8570
Hobbes (Thomas) on, 4074
influence of, 480–482
of Islamic scholars, 8181–8182
Italian Renaissance humanism and, 4176
in Judaism, 479, 4993
and afterlife, 154
assault by Crescas (Ḥasdai) on, 2069
creation in, 2642
Gersonides and, 480, 481, 3462
Ibn Daud and, 4264
opposition to, 17, 18, 481
soul in, 8558, 8559
of Origen, 6890
in Roman Catholicism
in astronomy, 1978
Descartes, breakdown caused by, 1996
in Scholasticism, 8175, 8176
in science, steady state theory as return to, 2032
witchcraft and, 9772
Aristotle, **483–486**
Abelard (Peter) displaced by, 7
aesthetics of, 45
agnōstos theos and, 181, 182
on *aion,* 207
Albertus Magnus on, 232, 233
Alexander of Aphrodisas's commentaries on, 479, 481
Andronicus of Rhodes editing works of, 479
on apocatastasis, 420, 421
on apotheosis, 437
on asceticism, 6946
astronomy of, 1976, 1977
on comets, 8735
Augustine influenced by, 624
and Bacon's (Roger) philosophy, 734
Boethius translating works of, 480, 1007, 7192
and Bonaventure, 1012
Bruno (Giordano) rejecting concepts of, 1055
casuistry of, 1454
on chance, 1526
on change, 3056
on charity, 1554
on choice, 3055
on demons, 2280
on dreams, 2376, 2378, 2485
Duns Scotus (John) modifying system of, 2524–2525
Eck's (Johann) works on, 2601
on economy, 2668
education of, 483
on Eleusinian mysteries, 3671
on ethics, 485–486, 7109
al-Fārābī's commentaries on, 2992
on fault and sin, 8405
on free will, 3200
on friendship, 3911
Galen influenced by, 3255
Galileo Galilei and, 480, 482, 3257
on geometry, 3439, 3441, 3442
Gersonides on, 480, 481, 3462
on God, 7114
gods, references to, 4036
on Golden Rule, 3632
on heart, 3882
on history, 4027
human being defined by, 7111
on human perfectibility, 7038
on humor and laughter, 4199, 4218, 4221
Ibn Rushd on, 4270–4271, 4272, 8421
Ibn Sīnā on, 4274, 4275, 4553
on intuition, 4525
Islamic philosophy *(falsafah)* influenced by, 2971
and soul, definition of, 8569, 8570
Isserles (Mosheh) on, 4750
on knowledge, 5201
definition of, 2818–2819
divine, 6960, 6961, 6962
on laws of Solon, 1846
on literature, 5486
Lyceum of, 479, 483
on magic, 5573
Maimonides (Moses) influenced by, 479, 481, 5617
on matter, 485, 4355, 5775–5776, 7119–7120
metaphysics of, 484–485, 5990
Middle Platonists on, 7189
monotheism and, 6156
Moses defended against, 4893–4894
on naturalism, 6428
Neoplatonic texts attributed to, 6475
on numbers, 6752
on *psuchē,* 8542
ontology of, 6830
Pecham (John) opposing, 7025
and physics, 7136
at Plato's Academy, 7187
on Plato's World Soul, 6963
and Plotinus, 7198
on poetry, 5160, 9652
on politics, 7109
Pomponazzi (Pietro) on, 4273
on Priapus, 7393
on primates, 6151
and problem of universals, 6644
on Pythagoras, 7529–7530, 8709
on reflexivity, 7648
on revelation, 7775
on sacred time, *vs.* Augustine, 7989
ship symbolism of, 992
on Socratic *elenchus,* 8503
on soul, 8182, 8564
transmigration of, 7186, 9328
on substance, concept of, 484, 485
on suicide, 8829
ten categories of, 6749
Themistius's commentaries on, 479
theology of, 480, 483–484, 2383, 9134, 9137
Thomas Aquinas on, 46, 480, 481–482, 4273, 9162–9163
and existence of God, 582
metaphysics of, 5990
on tragedy, 45
catharsis and, 1459, 5469
music in, 6304
translations of, 479–480
Arabic, 479
Latin, 480
on truth, 9374
writings of, 483–486
Aristoxenus, musical theory of, 6304
Arithmology, 6746
Arius. *See also* Arianism
Arianism promulgated by, 478
on Jesus as incarnation, 3553
ARiY. *See* Luria, Isaac
Ariyaratna, A. T., 1283
Gandhi (Mohandas) influencing, 3273
Ariyoshi Sawako, 3073
Arjan Dev, 32
and *Ādi Granth,* 3717
Sikhism, role in, 8394–8395
women and, 3336
writings of, 3878
Arjuna (epic hero), **486–487**
at Kurukṣetra, 5268
compassion of, 7023
cult of, 9499
dharma of, 853
free from desire, 2305
in *Bhagavadgītā,* 487, 852, 4001
Indra as father of, 486–487
in *Mahābhārata,* 486, 5595
Karṇa and, 486–487
Kṛṣṇa and, 487, 852–853, 854, 2317, 2321, 5249, 5251, 5268, 8303
morality in, 6188
in puppet theater, 2453
quest of, 7552, 7553
Ark of the Covenant
cult of, David and, 923
iconography of, 4340
Philistines and, 7103
temple of
David and, 2222, 2223
music of, 2223
as throne of Yahveh, 7981
Arkoun, Mohammed, 4719
Arles, Council (614), Donatus and, 1966
Arm (command), spirit and, 8567
Armadillo, 2490
myths of, 5198
Ārmaiti, 2128
Armenia. *See also* Armenian church; Armenian religion; Caucasus
division between Rome and Persia, 488
Armenian Catholic Church, 488, 1673

Armenian church (Armenian Apostolic Church), **487–490,** 2585
canons of, 490
catholicos of, 488, 489, 6478
creeds of, 490
and Days of the Dead, 2230
development of, 487–489
divisions within, 488, 489
doctrine of, 490
establishment of, 487–488
Gregory the Illuminator in, 488, 492, 3700
independence for, 488
jurisdiction of, 489
Latinizing movement in, 488
liturgy of, 489–490
in Middle East, 1673
modern, 489–490
mysticism in, Gregory of Narek and, 3694
under Ottoman Empire, 488–489
pilgrimage in, 7154
postures and gestures in, 7343
Sahak Parthev as bishop of, **8026**
saints of, 6478, 6479
in Turkey, 1675
Armenian language
alphabet of, 492, 8026
invention of, 5763–5764
biblical translations into, 492, 922
council canons translated into, 8026
Persian influence on, 491
Armenian religion, **490–492**
Armenian massacres (1915) and, 492
chanting in, 1534–1535
Christianity (*See also* Armenian church)
Armenian Catholic Church, 488, 1673
Chalcedon statement rejected by, 2584
introduction of, 487–488, 492
as state religion, 488
deities of, 490–492
Gnosticism, 3523
Iranian influence on, 491–492
Zoroastrianism, 491–492
Arminianism
in Adventist theology, 8235
Anglican *vs.* non-Anglican, 493
of Arminius (Jacobus), 492–493
free will *vs.* predistination in, 492
human achievements in, 7454
Arminius, Jacobus, **492–493**
on predestination, 492, 493, 3204, 3208
Armour, Ellen, on body theology, 4167
Armstrong, A. H., 2509
Arnauld, Antoine, 7001
Arndt, Johann, 3185
Spener (Philipp Jakob), influence on, 8678
Arnheim, Rudolf, 501, 4300
Arnhelm Land (Australia)
Galka (sorcerers) in, 3871–3872
life in, 5444
Marrnggitj healers of, 3873
moieties of, 5185
Rainbow Snake in, 7606, 7607
sexuality as sacred in, 8239
Arnim, Achim von, 3639
Arnobius (Christian writer), 1679
on ascension, 522
on Baubo, 804
on idolatry, 4361
on lack of temples and altars, 792
Arnold, Edwin, 1187
Campbell (Joseph) and, 1378
Arnold, Gottfried, 340
on Gnosticism, 3514, 3531
Pietism of, 7143
on truth and heresy, 3920, 3928
Arnold, Sir Joseph, on Aga Khan I, 173
Arnold, Kenneth, 9432
Arnold, Matthew, 1497, 7206, 7321, 9283
on Emerson (Ralph Waldo), 6105
Arnold, Thomas, 6105
Arnott, John, 7031
'Aron haqodesh (holy ark), 9240
Aronilth, Wilson, Jr., 6441
Aro religion, Ibo influenced by, 66
Arousa cult, 109
Árpád (Magyar chief), 948
Arpino, Gerald, 2162
'Arr (curse), in Hebrew scriptures, 2103–2104
Arrernte religion (Australia)
biblical translation and, 686
Gillen and Spencer on, 3489, 3490–3491
Arrogance, Gurū Nānak on, 8395
Arrom, José, 10024
Arrowroot Man (mythic figure), 653
Arrows. *See* Archery
Arsacius, Chrysostom and, 1762
Arsay (deity), in Canaanite religion, 1384
Arsenius, 2824
Arshak II (king of Armenia), 6479
Arshtāt, Chinvat Bridge and, 1647
Arson, employed by environmental activists, 2562
Arsūf (Palestine), cult of Reshef in, 7761
Ars wa-Shamem, in Canaanite religion, 1383
Art, **493–506**. *See also* Aesthetics; Calligraphy; Colors; Iconography; Sculpture; Visual culture
abstract, 55–56
human body in, 4172
Zen and, 500
Adam portrayed in, 30
African
androgynes in, 338
animals in, 90, 117
carved figures, 89, 90
history of study of, 117
ironworking and, 83–84
rock paintings, 83, 5137
shamanism in, 83
Arctic, wooden figures, 471
attitudes toward, 496
Australian Indigenous, 2480, 4304–4307
based on Dreaming, 639–640, 666, 667, 668, vol. 1 color insert
history of study of, 668
international audience for, 639–640
belief of artists and, 54–55
Buddhist (*See* Buddhist art)
categories for, 497–498
cave art, 1470–1472
in Paleolithic Age, 1470–1471, 5280–5281, 6952–6953, 8279
sheep and goats in, 8309–8310
Celto-Roman, 1481
Christian
Anthony of Padua in, 377
Augustine on, 46
body in, 4168
early Eastern, 2582
history of salvation depicted in churches, 7984
history of study of, 499–500
nimbus in, 6624
Protestant, 7459
sacred geography in, 3436
Zwingli (Huldrych) on, 7659–7660
Christ portrayed in, feet, 3013
in Cistercian monasteries, 6119
communication through, 498
of Dacian Riders, 2123, 2124
deities of, 3623
destruction of (*See* Iconoclasm)
devotion expressed in, 2319
Djan'kawu, 2379–2380
Egyptian, under Akhenaton, 219
Eros in, 2832
Etruscan, 2870
Freud (Sigmund) on, 7111
functions of, 498
goddesses in (*See* Goddess worship)
grace in, 3647
Greek
Asklepios in, 552
as expression of religion, 3662, 3679
Muses presiding over, 6242
Hindu
attitudes toward, 496
Bengali, 824
earth symbolism in, 3014–3015
history of
definitions of, 9621
visual culture and, 9620–9621
Warburg (Aby) in, 9689–9690
history of study of, 494–496, 499–502
methodologies for, 495–496, 500–502
human body and, **4168–4174**
humor in, in East Asia, 4209
imagery in, 53–56 (*See also* Images)
Indian
bas reliefs in Southeast Asia, 4013
Coomaraswamy on, 1975
Hevajra (image of) in, 3965
Kramrisch's (Stella) study of, 5242–5243
interactive (creative) discipline and, 8701–8702
Islamic
studies on, 4718
in sub-Saharan Africa, 4608
Japanese, in Ashikaga period, 4787
Jewish, in Palestinian synagogues, 8923
in Jewish studies, 4880–4881, 4883
kingdom of God portrayed in, 5152
labyrinths in, 5276, 5278
Maya, 5799
Melanesian, 5838–5839, vol. 6 color insert
Mesoamerican
afterlife in, 149
drama in, 2465–2466
earliest, 5880
in Formative (Preclassic) period, 5880, 5895–5897
in Teotihuaćan, 5899–5900
Mesopotamian, gender in, 3379
Minoan, *37, 38,* 38–40, *39*
monkeys in, 6151
museums of, 6244
music as, 6249
Mycenaean, 41, *42*
nature mysticism in, 6342
Neolithic
geometry in, 3438, *3438*
goddess worship in, 3584–3585

neoshamanism and mythic imagination, 8296
Nietzsche on, 6615, 6616
North American Indian, Haid identity and, 3736–3737
Olmec, 6819
outsider, 9624–9627
Paleolithic, 1048
cave art, 1470–1471, 5280–5281, 6952–6953, 8279
goddess worship in, 3583–3584, 3593, 3613
ornaments, 6951–6952
Venus figures, 6953, 7079
patronage of, 498, vol. 6 color insert
placement/site of, 498, 502
popular, 7321, 7322, 7323
power in relationship between religion and, 496
prehistoric, hand prints in, 3770
primitivism in, 9625
Rastafari, 7628
reality status of, 53–54, 55
religious belief and, Frye (Northrop) on, 3223
responses to, 498–499
theories of, 500–501, 502
rock (*See* Rock art)
Roman, funerary art, 2094
sacred gaze in, vol. 11 color insert
sacred/secular dichotomy, 4168
Sarmatian animal iconography, 8115
scripture and, 8198, 8204
Scythian, 8206
South Asian, Kramrisch's (Stella) study of, 5242–5243
subject matter of, 54–56
Swedenborgianism, influence of, 8899–8900, 8903–8904
symbolism of, Langer (Susanne) on, 5301
theory and aesthetics, history of, 9621
time in, 3005
Ungarinyin, 9458–9459
veneration of, 497
visual narratives, vol. 2 color insert
visual theology of, 497
Wach's (Joachim) interest in, 9650–9651
Art and Judaism During the Greco-Roman Period (Fine), 4343
Art and Religion in Africa (Hackett), 117
Art as Experience (Dewey), 49
Artaud, Antonin, 2438, 2475
Artavahisht (deity), 6731
Artaxerxes II (king of Persia), 305
Ezra and, 2946
Art Brut, 9625–9626
Artemidorus
on moon, 6175
on mummy case, vol. 13 color insert
Artemidorus Daldianus, on mirrors, 6064
Artemis (deity), **506–508**
Apollo and, 506
Bendis identified with, 819
birth of, 506
castrated priests of, 1451
deities identified with, 506
Diana identified with, 2347, 5514
in Ephesus, 7912
etymology of name, 506
functions of, 3680
and gender roles, 3383
in Hellenistic religions, 3602
hunting by, 506–507
iconography of, 4321–4322
as Lady of the Animals, 5279, 5282, 5513–5514
roles of, 506–508
specialization of, 2984
temple of, 9063
in Thracian religion, 9169, 9170
as virgin, 9603–9604
worship of, 3601, 3602
and young men and women, 507–508
Zeus as father of, 506
Artemis Agrotera (deity), 507
Artemis Laphria (deity), 507
Artemis Tauropolos (deity), 507
Artha, 1274, 2305
Arthaśāstra (Kauṭilya)
dharma in, 2329
economy in, 9708
as handbook for governance, 5345
overview of, 8122
pilgrimage in, 7169
priesthood in, 7406
Puruṣārthas (four goals of humankind) in, 3996
sexuality in, 5415
study of, 8123
Arthaśāstra (science of polity), 6959
Arthur (legendary king), **508–509**
in the Grail stories, 3651
historical existence of, 508
Maponos/Mabon and, 5685
Merlin and, 5878
origins of, 508
Articles of faith. *See* Confessions of faith; Creeds
Artificial (imaginative) dialogue, 2342
Artificial intelligence (AI), **509–513**. *See also* Cybernetics
coining of term, 510
functional or weak, 510–511
relational approach to, 511–512
religious and ethical implications of, 512–513
in science fiction, 512
symbolic or classical, 510
Artio (deity), 5514
Artistry of the Mentally Ill, The (Prinzhorn), 9625
Artists
in ancient times, 4296
beliefs of, 54–55, 498
cultural meaning of word, 4283
inventing rituals, 7051
Artless Jew, The: Medieval and Modern Affirmations and Denials of the Visual (Bland), 4342
Arukh, 889
Aruṇakirinātar (poet), 8977
Aruṇanti Śivācariyar (poet), 8976
Arundale, George, 9143
Arunta, The (Spencer and Gillen), 3489
Arunta people. *See* Aranda religion
Arūpaloka (world of form), heavens in, 3887
Arval Brothers *(fratres arvales),* **513–514**
Acca Larentia and, 2232
Dea Dia and, 2232
duties of, 7908
on Mars, 5728
Arwidsson, A. I., Reguly (Antal) influenced by, 7673
Āryabhaṭa (astronomer-sage), treatises of, 2019
Āryadeva (Buddhist thinker), **514–515**
on *bodhisattvas,* 1119
Candrakīrti's commentaries on, 1401
in Mādhyamika Buddhism, 5552
on *Guhyasamāja Tantra,* 3708
Aryans. *See also* Vedism
in Bengal, 824–825
caste system of, 3990
Ganges River and, 3274
in Indus Valley, 4468
arrival in, cultural contrast and, 3989–3990
racist myth of, 3526
in rural India, 4433–4434
Vedic, 9550
Vivekananda on, 10090
Āryas (Vedic elites), *soma* rite and, 8521
Ārya Samāj, **515–516**
alliance with Theosophical Society, 9142
Dayananda Sarasvati in, 515–516, 2226–2227
doctrinal principles of, 515
establishment of, 515
founding of, 2227, 4431
in Hindu reform movement, 1028, 4431
iconoclasm in, 4282, 4285, 4392
monotheism in, 4008
ʿAṣabah (agnatic heirs), 4709, 4710
ʿAṣabīyah (group feeling), 4269–4270
"As above, so below." *See* Macrocosm and microcosm
Asad, Muhammad, autobiography of, 700
Asad, Talal, 378
American study of religion, role in, 8787
on penance, 5372
religion defined by, 7702, 7705
structuralism and, 8759
Asahara Shōkō, 6575
charismatic leadership of, 6515
crimes of, 631–632, 6575
in Aum Shinrikyō, **631–633,** 4800
inner circle of, 6547
as messiah, 6547
readings of *Revelation,* 6531
Asalluhe (deity), 5955
family of, 5951, 5955
Asaṃkhyeya cosmology
buddhakṣetras (buddha fields) in, 2026
overview of, 2030
Aṣamm, al-, in Muʿtazilah, 6318
Asaṃskṛta (unconditioned *dharma*), 2333–2335, 7357
in Sautrāntika Buddhism, 8138
nirvāṇa described as, 6628
Āsanas (body postures), 9894–9895
aṣṭāṅgayoga (eight-limbed discipline), 8704
Asaṅga (Buddhist philosopher), **516–518,** 1210–1212
as founder of Yogācāra, 1119–1120, 1210–1212, 1300
on consciousness, 8858
conversion of, 517
on interpreting scriptures, 1274
in Yogācāra Buddhism, 516–517, 9899
on knowledge, 5200
on mirrors, 6064
on *ālaya-vijñāna,* 228, 517, 1211–1212
on ātman, 1210
on Nāgārjuna, 5552
on *nirvāṇa,* 6629
on *śūnyatā,* 1211
on *trisvabhāva,* 1211
treatises of, 517
Vasubandhu and, 9526, 9527
Yogācārabhūmi attributed to, 9898

Asante religion (West Africa), mediums in, diagnosis of illness by, 3818
Asaph, as author of *Psalms,* 7461
ʿAsarah be-Ṭevet (Fast of the Tenth of Ṭevet), in Jewish calendar, 4867
Asarhaddon (king), 5163
Asarluhi (deity), Marduk identified with, 5702–5703
Asase Afwa (mythic figure), 98
Asase Yaa (mythic figure), 98, 214, 9717
Āsatha. *See* Phra Phimonlatham
Āsavas, ending of, 2737
Asbury, Francis, **518**
and African Methodist Episcopal Zion Church, 68
in American Methodism, 5997–5998
Coke (Thomas) and, 1852
Holiness movement and, 4082
Ascended masters
in Holy Order of MANS, 4102
Summit Lighthouse/Church Universal and Triumphant and, 1781–1783
Ascended Master University, 1783
Ascensio Isaiae, 523
Ascension, **518–526,** 3129. *See also* Flight
in apocalypses, 410–411, 416, 518, 522–523
in Christianity, 523, 524
ecstasy and, 518–519
of Elijah, 2765
in Greek religion, 520–521
in Hellenistic religions, 521–522
in Iranian religion, 519–520
in Islam, 523–524
of Jesus, 523
in Judaism, 522–523
ladders in, 518, 522
of Mani, 5649
in New Thought teachings, Summit Lighthouse and, 1782
of Muḥammad (*See Miʿrāj*)
origins of concept, 518
in shamanism, 519
of *tsaddiq,* 2768
Ascent of Mount Carmel (John of the Cross), 9374
Asceticism, **526–530**. *See also* Celibacy; Deprivation; Fasting; Monasticism; Spiritual discipline
Buddhist, 1104, 4428–4429
Buddha as example for, 1061, 1103–1104
forest dwellers and, 8080
in Japan, 8379
castration and, 1452
in Catharism, 1457
Christian
androcentrism of, 336
of Basil of Caesarea, 797, 7723
capitalism rooted in, 2674
of Cassian, 1447–1448
of Clement of Alexandria, 7723
devotion in, 2320
dualism and, 528
eremitism and, 2824
healing and, 3844
humor rejected in, 4200
of John the Baptist, 4848, 7722
at Lent, 9814–9815
in monasticism, 6135
vs. normal behavior, 529
objectives of, 528
of Origen, 7723
pain in, 6946
of Paul the Apostle, 7722
religious orders and, 7721–7725
of widows, 7722–7723
definition of, 526
devotional aspect of, 2320
dualism and, 528–529
ecstatic discipline and, 8703
Essene, 2847
fasting in, 2996, 2997, 3171–3172
female body and, 4165
forms of, 527–528
of Gandhi (Mohandas), 3272
Gnostic, sexual rites and, 8247
hair symbolism and, 3739
Hindu, 9822–9823, vol. 13 color insert (*See also* Saṃnyāsa)
and *bhakti,* 857, 858
initiation rites of, 7816
in Pratyabhijñā Saivism, 8049
in Śaiva Tantras, 4019
in pilgrimage, 7169
in Ājīvikas, 212–213, 3639
Indian
Agni in, 179
meditation and, 5819
sadhus/sadhvis as, 8020, 8021
Islamic
of Ḥasan al-Baṣrī, 8810–8811
of Ibrāhīm ibn Adham, 8811
of Rābiʿah al-ʿAdawīyah, 7591, 8811
pain in, 6946
Jain, 527, 528, 4769, 5288
of Mahāvīra, 5609
in Japan, 3156
in Shugendō, 8352, 8379, 8380
of Jerome, 4832
of Jesus, 4848
Jewish
in Ashkenazic Hasidism, 542, 543
Baḥye on, 741
of Essenes, 7722
in Hasidism, 4993
in Therapeutae, 7722
in Khlysty sect, 8248
as minor martyrdom, 5738
in monasticism, 6123, 6125, 6135
mortification as part of, 6197
mystical union through, 527, 528
in Nag Hammadi codices, 3530–3531
and nudity, 6740–6741
objectives of, 527–528
of En no Gyōja, 2802
origins of, 526–527
as penance, 528
in primitive religions, 526–527
psychology of, 529
of Pythagoras, 7722
of Ramakrishna, 7611–7614
in religious law, 5371–5372
renunciation of world in, 2237
sacred *vs.* profane and, 7973
sainthood and, 2081
path to, 8037
Śaiva, ritual cannibalism and, 3805
salvation through, 527–528
sexual self-control and, 8239–8240
sleep interruption in, 8441
spiritual/inner, 527 (*See also* Spiritual discipline)
in Sufism, 527, 6351, 9004
development of, 8810–8812
women and, 6757 (*See also* Nuns)
work in, 9798
Yoga and, 9893–9897
Asceticism and Eroticism in the Mythology of Śiva (O'Flaherty), 2305
Asceticon (Basil of Caesarea), 798
Ascher, Saul, 7667
Asclepius (deity). *See* Asklepios
Asclepius (text). *See also* Logos Teleios (text)
extant form of, 3944
German translation of, 3947
in Hermetic corpus, 3939, 3940
Nag Hammadi compared to, 3941
prayer in, 3939
responses to
in 4th and 5th centuries, 3944
in late Middle Ages, 3945
in Renaissance, 3945–3946
Ascriptive communities, Chinese, 1615–1616
'Asdzáá Náleehé. *See* Changing Woman
Àṣẹ (power/authority), 4304, 9912
dance and, 2141
Asein-thei (death), 1330
Ásgarðr (dwelling of gods)
creation of, 3447
giants and, 4960
Ash (deity), Seth associated with, 8233
Asha (deity), 2128, 5451
Asha (Zoroastrian concept), 9989
gender of term, 3372
Mithra as guardian of, 6087
possession of, 4537
as truth, 9371, 9372
Asham (offering), 927
laws on, 4741, 4742
Ashaninka people (South America), messianism of, 5984–5985
Ashanti (Rattray), 115
Ashanti people (Ghana), in Akan group, 214
Ashanti religion (Ghana). *See also* Akan religion
creation stories of, 3015
ghosts in, 3476
handshaking in, 9259
myths of, 92, 98
rites of passage of, 88
shrines of, 90, 214
studies of, 115
supreme being of (Nyame), 214, 3576
temples in, 3576
tricksters in, 9352
weaving in, 938
witchcraft in, 7755
Ashʿarī, (Abū al-Ḥasan) al-, **530–533**
and *kalām, 5065,* 5067
development of, 3212, 5059, 5064, 5204
on attributes of God, 619, 4568
al-Bayḍāwī as follower of, 806
break from Muʿtazilah of, 5064
disciples of, 533–534
Ḥanābilah and, 3761
influence of, 532–533
in Shāfiʿī school, 4568
al-Māturidī and, 5781
methods of, 532, 619
in Muʿtazilah, 530, 531, 619, 4568
on *īmān* and *islām,* 4399
on Qādarī ideas, 3212
school of (*See* Ashʿarīyah)
teachings of, 531–532, 4568
theodicy of, 9118
writings of, 530–531
Ashʿarī school. *See* Ashʿarīyah
Ashʿarīyah (school of Islamic theology), **533–539**
on afterlife, 162
on *Alʿadam* (nonexistence), 8568
apologists for, 531
atomism of, 3564, 4568
classical period of, 533, 534–537, 538
doctrine of, 531–532, 533, 534–535
falsafah in, 533
on free will, 2064
predestination and, 3212, 8816

Ghazālī (Abū Ḥāmid al-) in, 534, 537–538, 3469, 3470, 4569
God in
attributes of, 532, 534–535, 536, 538, 619–621, 2063, 4568
determinism and, 535, 3563–3565
ḥadīth and, 8855
Ibn Taymīyah opposed to, 4277–4278, 4568–4569
later developments in, 537–538
Māturīdī school and, 5781
methods of, 532, 536
Mu'tazilah opposed by, 531–532
occasionalism of, 3564
philosophical problems in, 536–537
principal figures in, 533–534, 537
Qur'ān in, 531–532, 535
rationalism in, 3765 (*See also* Ahl al-kalām)
Rāzī (Fakhr al-Dīn al-) on, 7633
resurrection in, 8568
Shāfi'ī *madhhab* and, 3761–3762
al-Shahrastānī and, 8267
success of, 4568
vs. Ḥanābilah, 531
Asha Vahishta, 290
Asha-van (followers of truth), 1647
Ashbery, John, 5483
Ashbury, Frances, 264
Ashdod (Philistine city), 7102, 7104
Ashe (vital energy), in Caribbean religions, healing with, 3823
Ashella of Hapalla, on scapegoat ritual, 8143
Asher, Yitsḥaq ben. *See* Riva'
Asherah (deity). *See* Athirat
Asherah (holy site), 590–591
Asher ben Yeḥi'el, **539–540**
responsa by, 540
tosafot of, 9244, 9246
Asher Loeb (rabbi), 7580–7581
Ashertu (deity), in Hittite myth, 4070
Ashes, **540–541**
in Caribbean religions, 1428
in Inca religion, 1364
in Indian religions, in renunciate sects, 8019–8020
purification by, 540–541
Ashes, Ashes (drama), 2439
Ashi (amora), **541**
as last amora, 294
Ashikaga Gakkō (Zen academy), 1181
Ashikaga (Muromachi) period (Japan)
pilgrimage in, 7166
religion in, 4787
temples in, 9049
Ashipu (exorcist), in Mesopotamian religion, 3824–3825
Ashiratum. *See* Athirat
Ashkenazic Hasidism, **542–545**
asceticism of, 542, 543
cultural unity in, 5017
development of, 542
Gershom ben Yehudah in, 3461
and ecstatic Qabbalah, 7538
ethics of, 4913–4914
folk traditions of, Holocaust destroying, 7517–7518
halakhah and, 3743, 3744
humanism's influence on, 5016
in Hungary, 4224
initiation into, 543
medieval, 4981–4982, 4982
merkavah mysticism in, 10050–10051
mourning in, 7823
music in, 6308
mysticism in, 544–545
naming of girls in, 7819
non-Pietist Jews's view of, 543
in Ottoman Empire, 4997
polygyny, ban on, 3749–3750
rabbis in, 7579–7580
Sefer yetsirah and, 8221
siddur and *maḥzor* (prayer books) in, 8387, 8388, 8390
socioreligious program of, 543–544
spirit possession in, 2533–2534
will of God in, 542
in *Wissenschaft des Judentums,* 4877
yeshivot of, 9884
Ashmed'ai (demon), 3158
Ashmole, Elias, 3193, 7930
Ashoka. *See* Aśoka
Ashokamittiran (South Asian writer), 10036
Ashrāf (caste), 829, 4643
Ashrams (retreats), **545–548**
Christian, 546–547
in Healthy, Happy, Holy Organization (3HO), 3877
Hindu, 545–547
Gandhi (Mohandas) and, 545, 546, 547, 3272
gurūs in, 3713
influence of, 546–547
in Maharashtra, 5699
monasticism of, 6122
revival of, 545–546
of Rajneesh (Bhagwan Shree), 7608
of *sadhus/sadhvis* (renunciates), 8019, 8020
Ashratum. *See* Athirat
Ashtabi (deity), in Canaanite religion, 1384
Ashtapi, Eblaite festival of, 2597
Ashtar (deity)
Astarte and, 561
in Eblaite religion, 2598
Kemosh and, 6094
Ashtart. *See* Astarte
Ashton, Frederick, 2162, 2163
Ashtoret (deity). *See also* Ishtar
as Lady of the Animals, 5280
Ashukhshaykhah (tin can rattles), 7035
Ashur (deity), **548–549,** 5960
Enlil and, 2800
as national god of Assyria, 548, 7276–7277
origins of, 548
in Sargonid dynasty, 548–549
transformation of, 548–549
'Āshūrā' (Muslim holy day), **549–550**
development of celebration, 550
observance of, 4562, 4712, 7285
origins of, 549–550
political ideology and, 1517
Ashurbanipal (Assyrian king), 447–448
Ashurnasirpal II, vol. 8 color insert
Ashurnirari V (king of Assyria), Melqart and, 5847
Ash Wednesday. *See also* Carnival; Lent
in Christian liturgical calendar, 1743
Pantagruelian feast in Rome, 1442
Asia and Asian religions. *See also specific countries, regions, and religions*
African movements derived from, new, 108–109
attention in, 603
Buddhism, engaged, 2785–2787
Christianity, **1725–1731**
Anglicanism, 353
Batak people, 799, 800
indigenous theology of, 2689–2690
Jesuits in, 4842
liberation theology in, 5442
nuns and sisters, 6765
Pentecostalism, 7030, 7031, 7032
clothing in, **1826–1830**
dance in
and cultural identity, 2164
dance-dramas, 2152
definition of religion in, 7693
economies of, 2671
epic tradition of, 2815
eschatology in, 2834
eternity in, 2854
Evola (Julius) and, 2904–2906
journals dedicated to, 10056, 10058
Judaism, **5004–5011**
liberation theology in, 5442
magic in, **5587–5594**
monism in, 6144–6146
Neolithic religions in, 6460
and North American Indian religions, influence on, 6653–6654
orgy in, 6877–6881
religious broadcasting and, 7713, 7714
religious communities in, 7700
religious experience in, 7694, 7695
scientific history in, 8180
in United States, 6559
and Western Esotericism, 6497–6498
Asia Minor. *See* Anatolia; Turkey
Asiatic black bear, 807
Asiatic Society of Bengal. *See* Royal Asiatic Society of Bengal
'Āṣim (reciter of Qur'ān), 9200
Asimov, Isaac, 512
Asinus aureus (Apuleius), 3051, 3052
Askew, A., 3508
Askew (Askewianus) Codex (Gnostic text), discovery of, 3508, 3515
Askiya dynasty (West Africa), 4602–4603
Asklepios (Asclepius) (deity), 425, **550–553**
Christianity and, 552
cult of
healing and, 3840, 3842
in Hellenism, 3904
origins of, 550–551
Eshmun as, 2840, 2841, 2842, 7130
as healer, 550–552
incubation oracles and, 6833
miracles of, 6051
as patron of physicians, 4022
in Rome, 3841, 3842, 7904
shrines to, 552
Askr (first man), 3454
Aslama (surrendering to God), 4397
Asmakhta' (indirect scriptural exegesis), in rabbinic law, 3748
Asmat people (Irian Jaya), masks of, 5769
Asmimāna (ego conceit), enlightenment and, 8552–8553
Asmodeus (demon), 2277
Asningái (mythic figure), myth cycle of, 8633
Asobi (dancers), 7216
Asobime (singers), 6301
Asohsná bird, myth cycle of, 8633
Aśoka (Indian emperor), **553–557**
Ājīvikas sect under, 212

Aśoka (Indian emperor)
continued
authority of, 696
Buddha's birth in relation to, 1061
Buddha's relics and, 7690
Buddhism under, 553–556, 1089, 1090–1091, 1145, 1161, 6077
as Buddhist, 5348
as *cakravartin*, 1351
daughter of, 9146
Devānaṃpiyatissa as ally of, 2313
devotional programs of, 1086, 1090
dharma of, 553–554, 555
as ideal king, 1135, 7261
imperialism of, 554
inscriptions of, 553–555
legends of, 554–556, 1091
and missions, Buddhist, 6077, 9145–9146
as model Buddhist, 2630
Moggaliputtatissa and, 6112
and monasticism, Buddhist, 1091, 3154, 3331, 6077, 6112, 6128, 7720
and nonviolence, 6646
Pāṭaliputra council and, 2037
peace efforts by, 7023
saṃgha and, 8074, 8079
stupas erected by, 1066, 1107, 4383, 7163, 7495, 9041
stupa worship and, 8797
successors of, 554–555
Aśokāvadāna, 1091
ASOPA. *See* Australian School of Pacific Administration
Aspectual comparativism, 1880
Aspersions, 1458
Aspirations of the World (Child), 1570
Āśramas (religious communities), 3713, 3714, 7816–7817. *See also* Ashrams
Āśramas (stages of life), 2329, 2330, 4421, 4441, 9276–9277. *See also* Saṃnyāsa
in Brahmanism, 9570–9571
castes and, 3995–3996
celibacy and, 1476–1477
hospitality and, 4140
relational discipline and, 8707
Śaṅkara on, 4004
As-rār-i khudī (Iqbāl), 4534
Āśrava/āsava (projection), 2794
Āśraya-parāvṛtti (transformation of basis), 9900–9901
Ass, Feast of the, inversion in, 1441
Assagioli, Roberto, on personality, 1949
Assassins (Islamic group), **557–559**
martyrdom and, 8831
origins of, 226, 8324
Assayer, The (Galileo), 3257
Assemani, Joseph Simeon, 5637
Assemblies of God, 7029
in Australia and New Zealand, 1735
in Pacific islands, 1741
Assembly, divine, Near Eastern notion of, 1384
Assembly of Jewish Notables (1806), 7666
Assimilation, of Jews, Schneerson (Menachem) on, 8171–8172
Assists, in icons, 1861
Assmann, Jan, 2730–2731
Associate Reformed Presbyterian Church, 7391
Association de Défense de la Famille et de l'Individu (ADFI), 6569
Association for Clinical Pastoral Education, 7486
Association for Cultural Research (ARC), 9068
Association for Lithuanian Ethnic Culture, 764
Association for Research and Enlightenment (ARE), **559–561**
Cayce and, 559–561, 1474
study groups of, 559–560
Association for the Advancement of Buddhism, 8967
Association for the Study of Local Culture, 764
Association of Adventist Forums (AAF), formation of, 8237
Association of Friends of the Spirits. *See* Reiyukai Kyodan
Association of Indian Muslims in America, 830
Association of Jewish Studies, 4884
Association of National Investigators (ANI), 559
Association of Reform Zionists of America (ARZA), 7672
Association of Sananda and Sanat Kumara, 9433
Association of Unity Churches, 9472
Association of Vineyard Churches, 7031
Association psychology, Harva (Uno) and, 3784
ASSR. *See* American Society for the Study of Religion
Assumption, Virgin Mary of the, Sistine Chapel and, 8755
Assumption of Moses, 6203
Assur (deity), 7603
Assurance, in Pure Land Buddhism, Shinran on, 8355
Assyria. *See also* Assyrian religion
Akitu festival in, 223, 549
Arameans defeated by, 446
Ashur as national god of, 548
Babylonian rivalry with, 5948
cities of, 5946
contracts and loyalty oaths in, 2047, 2048
fall of, 5948
geographic boundaries of, 5946
homosexuality in, 4113
Isaiah on, 4545, 4546, 4547, 4548
Judah under, 4828
kingship in, 5162–5163
laws in, 1844
Phoenicians ruled by, 7128, 7129
rise of, 5946
Sumerian city-states taken over by, 1802–1803
use of term, 5946
Assyrian Church. *See* Nestorian Church
Assyrian language, 5946
Assyrian religion. *See also* Mesopotamia and Mesopotamian religions
chant-remedy in, 3811
creation myth in, 3811
deities of (*See specific deities*)
fish symbolism in, 3122
iconography of, 4315, 4316, 4317, vol. 8 color insert
and Israelite religion, 4359
judgment of the dead in, 5025
libations in, 5433
Mars in, 8428
moon in, 6172
politics and, 7276–7277
ritual drama in, 2441–2442, 2444–2445
spell of healing in, 8676
sun in, 8838
underworld in, 9452
Assyriology, 2263
definition of, 3375
gender in, 3375
Aṣṭabhuja (deity), 4433
Aṣṭadaśa Rahasyam (Piḷḷai), 7172
Aṣṭādhyāyī (Pāṇini), commentary on, 7005
Aṣṭamahapratiharya (scenes), 4329
Aṣṭāṅgahṛdaya Saṃhitā (Vāgbhaṭa)
as Āyurvedic text, 3853
Āyurvedic principles in, 3854–3855
in Tibet, 3865
Aṣṭāṅgayoga (eight-limbed discipline), stages of, 8704–8705
Astarte (Ashtart) (deity), **561–563,** 2984
Anat and, 561, 562
joined in Atargatis, 562–563
Aphrodite identified with, 34, 7130
in Baal cycle, 1392
ballet about, 2162
in Canaanite religion, 1399
Cybele identified with, 7130
in Egyptian religion, 561, 562, 3596
Eshmun and, 2841
and fish symbolism, 3122
in Hebrew scriptures, 561, 562–563, 3541, 7103
Hera identified with, 7130
Inanna identified with, 3586
as Lady of the Animals, 5280
Melqart and, 562, 5846, 5847, 5848
origins of, 3596
in Philistine religion, 7103
in Phoenician religion, 561–562, 3596, 7129, 7130, 7131
popular worship in Israel, 3157
prominence of, 3596
vs. other goddesses, 3376
son-consort of, 2983
in Syrian religion, 561–562
as virgin, 9604
worship of, 3586, 3596
Astarte (Joffrey), 2162
Aṣṭasāhasrikā (Buddhist text), 1114
Aṣṭasāhrikāprajñāpāramitā (Buddhist text), 1114, 7502
Astat (Eustathius), 2971
Astghik (deity), 491
As through a Veil (Schimmel), 7223
Astley, Thea, 3081–3082, 3084
Astōvīdhātu (deity), 2128
Astral conjunctions, Hindu holidays and, 4015, 4016
Astral mythology. *See* Sky; Stars
Astroarchaeology, 8734
Astrology, **563–566.** *See also* Ethnoastronomy
in alchemy, 251
apocatastasis in, 421
"as above, so below" and, 8426
Babylonian, 3901
in Caribbean religions, 1429
Chinese, 2372
healing and, 3865
in magic, 5592
confutations of, 564
and deification, 2249
development of, 563
diffusion of, 563–564, 2999–3000
goat in, 8312
in Greek and Roman religion, 563–566
Cumont on, 2093–2094
healing and, 3841
philosophical reactions to, 8840
heavenly book concept and, 8425
Hellenistic, individual and, 3901–3902
in Hinduism, 2372, 3000, 3002
in Hindu calendar, 4015
Kumbha Melā and, 5265
in *onmyōdō,* 6828–6829
in Jewish Renewal, 4872
lions in, 5464
Mesoamerican
Maya calendar and, 1356
in Texcoco religion, 8426
methods of, 564–566
moon in, 6175
origins of, 563
political aspects of, 2372

predictions based on
in Renaissance, 564
types of, 566
of Ptolemy, 7492
Reformation rejection of, 8182
in Renaissance art, 9690
in Roman Empire, 2373, 2378
Tibetan
healing and, 3865
travel and, vol. 3 color insert
translations of works on, 563–564
in Turkic religions, 9399
in Western esotericism, 2843
women interested in, 2372
after World War II, 2999
Astrology and Religion among the Greeks and Romans (Cumont), astrological determinism in, 2093–2094
Astrology of the Four Horsemen, The (Prophet), 7446
Astronomia nova (Kepler), 5112
Astronomy. *See also* Calendars; Ethnoastronomy; Stars
in ancient cultures, 1994
archaeology and, 453
Aristotelian, 1976, 1977
at Tenochtitlán, 8734
Aztec, 8734
Buddhist cosmology and, 2028
calendar and, 1353
Copernicus and, **1976–1979**
cosmology, scientific, **2031–2034**
in early antiquity, 2999
Egyptian, temple alignment, 8733
of Galileo Galilei, 1978, 3256–3257
geometry in, 3442
Gersonides on, 3462
Hindu, calendrical system and, 4015–4016
Inca, 1361–1363
in *onmyōdō,* 6828–6829
in Japanese culture, creation myth interpreted in accordance with, 4022–4023
Kepler's work in, 1978, 5111–5112
Maya calendar and, 1356, 1358–1359, 8842
stelae at Copán linked to, 2009–2010
megalithic, 5825
in North American Indian religions, 8734
Zuni calendar and cosmology linked to, 2008–2009
of Parmenides, 6996
Ptolomaic, 1976–1977, 7491–7493
religion and, 2660
Scholasticism and, 8176
in Southeast Asia, Hindu temples and, 4013
at Stonehenge, 8734
temples, stellar alignment of, 8733–8734
in Vedism, 2014
Western history of, 8181–8183
Astrov, Margot, 7224
Astruc, Jean, 883
Asturias, Miguel Ángel, 2439
Astvatereta ("he who embodies truth"), as Saoshyant (redeemer), 8110
Astydamia (mythological figure), 9685
Asuman (Akan deities), 215
Asuras (gods or demons), 2314
Ādityas and, 9556
vs. ahuras, 204–205
Dāsas (slaves) identified with, 4467
devas and, in Vedism, 3990
devas conflict with, 1027, 1197, 2276, 9560
gods in conflict with, 4442
Skanda as slayer of, 4017
Viṣṇu and, 9619
vs. rākṣasas, 2315
Aśvaghoṣa (Indian poet)
on Buddha, miracles of, 6053
Buddha biography by, 1064, 1092, 1111, 7211
on Buddha's bodily marks, 1004
Chinese translation of works of, 1200
on *puruṣa,* 7521
Aśvamedha (sacrifice), 1025, 1350, 1493, 2393, 9563–9564
in devotional life, 9821
Asvattha (fig tree), 9335, 9337
Aśvins (mythic figures), 4467, 4509, 7683, 9416
in Vedism, 9556–9557, 9564
Asylum, sanctuary as place of, 8101
Asymmetrical binary oppositions, 5393
Ataecina (deity), 4253
Ata-Emit. *See* Emitai
Ataentsic (deity), moon created by, 6173–6174
Atahuallpa (Inca ruler), **566–568**
anticipated resurrection of, 567–568
conversion of, 567, 5177
mummification of, 5177
Spanish capture of, 5177
Atahuallpa, Juan Santos, 5984
ʿAṭāʾ ibn Abī Rabāḥ, Abū Ḥanīfah and, 21
Ātakhsh-zōhr (libations), 4535
Ātar (deity), 4535
Atargatis (deity)
as Adad's consort, 28
in Aramean religion, 449
Astarte and Anat joined in, 562–563
and fish symbolism, 3122
fusion with Hellenic goddesses, 3908
in Hellenistic religions, 3602
in Phoenician religion, 7130
priests of, description by Apuleius, 3909
in Ugaritic incantation texts, 1383
Ātash bahrām (victory fire), 6997
Ātashparast (fire worshipper), 10003, 10004
Atatürk, Mustafa Kemal, 1518, 4945
sharīʿah abandoned by, 4703
Ṣūfī orders suppressed by, 4571
Sufism, suppression of, 8824
Atcholi religion (Uganda), confession of adultery in, 1884
Atē, in Homeric religion, 5469
Atē (deity), 3001
Atea (deity), 8980
ʿAteret zeqenim (Abravanel), 17
Ateshgah (place of fire), **568–571**
Atete (deity), in Macha Oromo religion, 2573
Athabascan religious traditions. *See* Athapaskan religious traditions
Athaliah (queen of Judah), 3541
Athanasian Creed
faith in, 1666
overview of, 2057
Athanasius (bishop of Alexandria), **571–572**
on Anthony of Egypt, 6131
Arianism opposed by, 478, 571–572, 972
Athanasian Creed attributed falsely to, 2057
"canon" used as term by, 1406
Christology and, 2581
doctrine of incarnation under, 3553
Europe, connections to, 1688
in exile, 571, 572, 7060
Frumentius consecrated by, 2859
isolation of, 2829
legitimacy as bishop, 571–572
monastery founded by, 2826
on monastic initiation, 7769–7770
monasticism founded by, 7875
and Nag Hammadi codices, 6396
on religious orders, 7722
on Thecla, 9102
theology of, 572
and Trinity doctrine, 9361
on "two books," 9421
writings of, 572
Athapascan religious traditions. *See* Athapaskan religious traditions
Athapaskan religious traditions (North America), **572–576**. *See also* Apache religion; Navajo religious traditions
Christianity's influence on, 573, 574
history of study of, 574–575
iconography of, 4309
Northern, 572–573
overview of, **572–575**
of Pacific Northwest, 572, 574–575
in Plains region, 6656, 6696
sacred stories of, 572–574
Southern, 572, 573–574
in Southwest region, 6657, 6720
in sub-Arctic region, 6655, 6674–6675
mythology, 6675–6676
wind and power in, concepts of, **575–576**
Āthār al-bāqiyah ʿan al-qurūn al-khāliyah, al- (al-Bīrūnī), 954
Atharvaveda (Vedic text), 9551, 9554
Āyurveda and, 714, 3853
Brāhmaṇas of, 1026
Brahmans and, 3991
chanting of, 1535
cure for baldness in, 4159
funeral rite in, 2559
īśvara in, 4751
Kumbha Melā in, 5265
magic in, 5590
Māra in, 5690
priesthood in, 7405
riddles in, 6987
rites in, 1121, 4426
Rudra-Śiva in, 8040
spells in, 8677
tapas in, 8998
water in, 9698
Atheism, **576–586**. *See also* Doubt
in Africa, studies on, 114
anthropological, 7422
attacking proofs for existence of God, 7422
of Besant (Annie), 844
definition of, 576
Durkheimians as, 2528
environmentalist religion and, 2564
ethical, 7422
evolutionary psychology and, 8479
existentialism and, 2925, 7111
of Galicians, 4253
in Greek society
absence of, 3677
of Diagoras, 3910
inside *vs.* outside religious perspective and, 3926

Atheism ***continued***
mysticism and, convergence of, 391
of Raëlians, 7596
in Protestantism, 7449
psychological, 7422
Sartre (Jean-Paul) on, 8116
socioeconomic, 7422
of unconscious, 7489–7490
"Atheistic Theology" (Rosenzweig), 4904–4905
Athena (deity), **586–588**
Anat equated with, 320
Athens linked to, 586, 587
birth of, 586–587
functions of, 3679
iconography of, 586, 4321, 4322, 4381
as Lady of the Animals, 5279, 5282
Minerva and, 6043
in Mycenaean religion, 42, 586
Neopagans worshipping, 6471
owl as symbol of, 6936
Panathenaia festival of, **6958–6959**
temple of, 9063
as virgin, 9603–9604
as war goddess, 586
worship of, 3601
Zeus and, 586–587, 3679
Athenagoras, **589**
on idolatry, 4360
on inspiration, 4510
on *Logos,* 5504
Paul VI and, 7012
Athenian Popular Religion (Mikalson), 7327
Athenian school, on ethics, 1653
Athens (Greece)
Agora of, shrines to Meter in, 2109
Athena linked to, 586, 587
cattle sacrifice in, 1466–1467
Demetrius Poliorcetes honored as divine in, 3902
in Eleusinian mysteries, 2751–2752
festivals in
Anthesteria, 374–375
Panathenaia, **6958–6959**
Herakles cult in, 3917
human sacrifice in, 1459
kingship of, 5166
oracles received by, 2375, 2376, 7278
Parthenon in, 4322, 9063
politics and religion in, 7277
Zeus in, 3663–3664
Athi (servants), 1330
Athirat (Asherah) (deity), **589–592**
and Baal, 589
in Baal cycle, 724, 1392, 1393, 1395
in Canaanite literature, 1383–1384
in Hebrew scriptures, 3541, 4742, 4743
Ḥokhmah as parallel to, 4079
holy sites of, 590–591
in *ilma naimima,* 1386
Israelite worship of, 4972
in Kirta cycle, 1388, 1399
in Phoenician religion, 7134
popular worship in Israel, 3157
prominence of, 3595–3596
vs. other goddesses, 3376
as sun goddess, 589
worship of, 3595–3596
Yahveh identified with, 8523
Athos, Mount, monasteries of, 2582, 2826–2827
Athram, al-, Ḥanābilah and, 3763
Athtar (deity), 443, 2442
Athirat and, 589
in Canaanite religion, 1384, 1387
Athtart (deity). *See also* Astarte; Ishtar
in Canaanite religion, 1385, 1392
Atimārga (higher path), in Śaiva canon, 4019
Atīśa (Buddhist monk), **592–593**
Buddhist school established by, 1096, 1153, 1215, 1224
on chain of instruction, 8713
emigrating to Tibet, 1126, 1152, 1230
iconography of, 4330
in Mādhyamika Buddhism, 5555
on meditation, 1285–1286
nature of, 1153
and revival of Buddhism, 1300
synthesis of Mahāyāna and Tantrism by, 8083
Tārā cult introduced by, 9000
Atiyoga. *See* Dzogchen
Atjeh (Sumatra)
childbirth in, 7825, 7827–7828
marriage in, 7825
Atkinson, Clarissa, 3312, 3313
Atkinson, Gail, in Eckankar, 2602
Atlanta Club (Temple Solaire), 9067
Atlantic University, 1474
closure of, 559
reopening of, 561
Atlantic World
African American religions in context of, 65
definition of, 65
Atlas, Mount, 6214
Atlases, as reference works, 7642, 7643
Atlas mountain range, 6212
Ātman (soul or self), 6486
aesthetics and, 50–51
Asaṅga on, 1210
brahman identified with, 9569
denying existence of, 2333, 9328
in Buddhism, 8551
dualism and, 2508
in heart, 3881
identity of, 4422, 4423, 4427
in *Bhagavadgītā,* 7677–7678
in Śaivism
in Trika Śáivism, 8047
Śiva as *ātman* in, 4006
in *Śākta* Tantrism, 8547
in Upaniṣadic cosmology, 2015, 8546
in Upaniṣads, 9480, 9482
Madhva on, 8547
in magical idealism (Evola), 2905
misperception of, 9017
mysticism and, 6343
mythic themes of, 4440
Nāgārjuna on, 6391
Rāmānuja on, 7615–7616
Śaṅkara on, 8105
in Swaminarayan movement, 8891
via negativa and, 6990
Western concepts *vs.,* 8545
ATOM (The Ancient Teachings of the Masters), 2602, 2603
Atomism
concept of culture in, 5260
in Ājīvikas, 213
in Islam
Abū al-Hudhayl al-ʿAllāf on, 19, 6323
Ashʿarīyah on, 3564, 4568
Muʿtazilah on, 6323
soul doctrine and, 8568
materialism and, 5776
Vaiśeṣika theory of, 3997
Aton (deity), 218, 219, *219,* 4285, 7634. *See also* Re
Akhenaton's devotion to, 2707, 2711, 6157, 7277
monolatry dedicated to, 3540
monotheistic worship of, 8837
Atonement, **593–598**. *See also* Expiation
Christian concepts of, **594–598,** 4843–4844
in Adventist theology, 8237
early Western, 2582
scapegoat and, 8145
sin and, 8405
suffering servant doctrine and, 8807
in Islam (*See Kaffārah*)
Jewish concepts of, **593–594** (*See also* Yom Kippur)
Cohen (Hermann) on, 4903
Holocaust and, 4090
scapegoat and, 8144–8145
Smith (W. Robertson) on, 8453
Atonement and Personality (Moberly), 597
Atrahasis (myth), **598–600**
An in, 302
anthropogonic story in, 8535–8538
Enki/Ea in, 5954
Enlil in, 2800, 5954
history of text of, 599
in other documents, 599–600
structure of story, 599
subdivision of pantheon in, 5965
Atrahasis (Utanapishtim) (mythic hero)
and Enki-Ea, 3131, 3132
Enoch identified with, 2803
and Gilgamesh, 4477
myth of the Fall, 2962, 2963
in myth of the Flood, 598–600
Atran, Scott, on religiosity, 8478
Ātrap (caste), 829
Atrigupta, 8
Atropos (deity), 968, 3001, 9088. *See also* Moirai
ʿAtseret. *See* Shavuʿot (Pentecost)
Atsugewi religion (North America), bears in, 809
Atsutane, Hirata. *See* Hirata Atsutane
Attabeira (deity), in Island Arawak religion, 1427
Attachment, in Jungian analysis of hero myths, 3959
Attachment theory, 7478
of conversion, 1970
ʿAṭṭār, Farīd al-Dīn, **600–603,** 949
mathnavī poetry of, 8817–8818
mirrors and, 6063
on al-Ḥallāj, 3756, 3757
on light of Muḥammad, 6767
on Rābiʿah al-ʿAdawīyah, 7591
Ṣūfī master of, 601
wish to fly, 3128
writings of, 601–602, 7222
ʿAṭṭārīn (herbalists), in Egypt, as class of healer, 3836
Attawanadi (deity), 2312
as trickster, in Makiritare religion (Amazon), 8626
Attempt at a Critique of All Revelation (Fichte), 3049
Attem re'item (Agnon), 180
Attenborough, David, 3273
Attention, **603–610**. *See also* Meditation; Spiritual discipline
contemplative
nature of, 605–606
vs. ordinary attention, 605
significance of exercises for, 606–609
in *rājayoga* tradition, 8704–8705
interactive discipline and, 8702
as religious *vs.* psychological phenomenon, 603, 605
Aṭṭhakavagga (Buddhist text), 1104
Atthasālinī (Buddhist text), 10021
At the Foot of the Mountain (theater group), 2439
Atthitā (existence), 7364

Atticus
 Aristotle interpreted by, 7189
 Chrysostom and, 1762
 on Demiurge, 7188–7189
 Mashtotsʿ (Mesrop) and, 5764
Attila the Hun, 4490–4491
 death and burial of, 4228–4229
 sword narrative about, 4229
Attis (deity). *See also* Cybele
 castration of, 986, 1451–1452, 2536
 cult of, 2110
 as dying and rising god, 2536–2537
 in Greek tradition, 2109–2110
 in Hellenistic religions, 3603–3604
 Magna Mater associated with, 3385
 mystery religion of, 6330
  ecstasy in, 2678
 phallus of, 7080
 pig sacrifice to, 7144
 Roman celebration of, 987
 Roman story of Cybele and, 1451, 7917
 veneration of, 6866
Attjie (deity), sacrifices to, 8088
Attributes of God, **613–622**. *See also* God; *specific attributes*
 in African religions, 3568
 and afterlife, 128–130
 anthropomorphism of, 390
 Christian concepts of, **615–616**
  Anselm on, 373
  biblical, 615–616
  Calvin on, 1376
  fecundity or fertility of, Hildegard of Bingen on, 3980
  postbiblical, 3553
 Islamic concepts of, **616–622**
  Bāqillānī (Abū Bakr al-) on, 619–620
  vs. essence of God, 621
  extremist, 617–618
  in *falsafah,* 621
  Ghazālī (Abū Ḥāmid al-) on, 620–621
  in Ashʿarīyah, 532, 534–535, 536, 538, 619–621
  in Ḥanafī creed, 2063
  Juwaynī (Abū al-Maʿālī al-) on, 617, 619, 620
  in Muʿtazilah, 618–619
 Jewish concepts of, **613–615**
  Baḥye on, 4890–4891
  biblical, 613, 614
  Crescas on, 4896–4897
  vs. essence of God, 613, 614
  Gersonides on, 4895
  justice *vs.* mercy in, 613–614
  other gods blended into, 3541
  postbiblical, 3549
  Saʿadyah Gaon on, 4888, 7952
 justice as, and afterlife, 128–129
 Spinoza (Baruch) on, 8683, 8684
Attribution deities, planets as, 8426–8428
Attribution theory of conversion, 1970
Atua (deity or spirit), 7306, 9195
Atua Fafine (deity), 9195
Atua i Fangarere (deity), 9195
Atua i Kafika (deity), 9195
Atua i Tafua (deity), 9195
Atua i Taumako (deity), 9195
Atua Lasi (deity), 9195
Atuas (deities or spirits), **622–623**
 in Maori religion, 5679–5682
Atum (deity), **623**
 deities produced by, 3596, 7491
 in Egyptian pantheon, 2704
 in Egyptian pharoahs' funerals, 5164
 Osiris identified with, 6921
 Re and, 7634
Atumpan (drum), 2495
Atunis (deity), 35
Atwood, Mary Anne, on Hermetism, 3952
Ātyantika pralaya (spiritual liberation), in Purāṇic cosmology, 2018
Aubrey, John, 2493
Audacht Morainn, 1492
Audience
 in visual culture, 9620
 for winter carols, 9745
Audience cults, Stark and Bainbridge on, 2085
Auditing, in Scientology, 8192, 8193
Auðumla (mythic figure), creation of, 3446, 3447
Auerbach, Erich, 5471, 5472, 5485
Aufklärung. See Enlightenment, The
Aufrecht, Theodor, 4446
Aufrère, Syndey, 2730
Augier, Roy, 10026–10027
Augsburg, Peace of (1555)
 Lutheranism recognized by, 2057, 5539, 7659
 Protestantism recognized by, 7659
Augsburg (Germany), Protestant disputation at, Eck (Johann) in, 2601
Augsburg Confession (1530)
 Formula of Concord and, 2055
 goals of, 2057–2058
 Lutheranism, role in, 2057, 5536, 5539
 Melanchthon (Philipp) as author of, 5831
 Reformation and, 7658–7659
 Roman Catholic criticism of, 2058
 sola gratia, sola fide, sola Scriptura (only grace, only faith, only Scripture) principles, 1691
Augsburg Interim, 7659
Augsburg-Leipzig Interim (1548–1549), 5832
Augures (diviners), 2377
Augurium maximum, 7907–7908
Augury, 2370–2371
 in Roman religion, 7903, 7907–7908
Augusta, Jan, 6190
August Earth God. *See* Huangdi chi
Auguste Comte and Positivism (Mill), 7339
August Heaven. *See* Shangdi
Augustine of Canterbury, **623–624,** 821
 Gregory I and, 623, 3688
Augustine of Hippo, **624–630**. *See also* City of God; *Confessions, The*
 Abelard (Peter) opposing, 8
 and abortion, 5812
 aesthetics of, 45–46, 55
 as African, 624
 in African councils, 626
 on afterlife, 157
 on ages of world, 175, 4053
 Ambrose and, 288, 624, 625
 androcentrism of, 334–335
 on angels, 347
 on animals, 358, 361
 and animism, 365, 366
 Anselm and, 372–373
 Anthony of Padua influenced by, 377
 on anthropomorphism, 388
 on apocalypse, 412
 autobiographies influenced by, 698, 699
 autobiography of (*See Confessions*)
 biblical exegesis of, 871, 874, 5486
 on bishops, 7402
 on blasphemy, 972
 and Bonaventure, 1011, 1012
 bridge symbolism used by, 1051
 on Cain and Abel, 1345
 Calvin influenced by, 630, 1375
 Cassian's opposition to, 1448
 casuistry of, 1455
 on chance, 1527
 on charity, 1554
 on church and state relationship, 5150
 on conscience, 1940
 conversion of, 625, 698, 2377, 7192
 cosmology and, 2606
 on creation, 3555, 5663–5664
 Cyprian's influence on, 2114
 death of, 629
 on desire, 2304, 2307–2308
 on devotion, 2321
 on doctrine, 2382, 2384
 against Donatists, 626, 2417, 7061
 on doubt, 2424
 on Easter, 2579
 ecclesiology of, 1771–1772, 1773, 1777
 education of, 624–625
 epistemology of, 2819
 on eremitism, 2825–2826, 2827
 eschatology, 1652
 on eternity
  God's existence in, 3205
  of world, 2855
 ethics of, 628
 on eucharist, 837
 on Euhemerus, 2883
 Europe, connections to, 1688
 on evil, 626, 3205–3206, 3645
 experience at Ostia, 3127
 on the fall, 3645
 on fish symbolism, 3123
 on free will, 626–627, 1667, 3200, 3201, 3645, 8742
 al- Ghazālī compared with, 3221
 on God, 3555
  divine providence of, 7791
  existence of, 582, 7421
  nature of, 55, 5663
 on Gospels, inconcinnities in, 4845–4846
 on grace, 627, 1667, 3645, 8406
 on Greek knowledge, 8181
 on heart, 3882
 on Hell, 9454
 on Hermes Trismegistos, 3938
 on Hermetism, 3944
 on history, 4053, 4054
 on human nature, 627, 7025, 7026, 7027, 7353
 on human perfectibility, 7039
 on idolatry, 834, 4358, 4361, 4363–4364, 4385
 on images, 4285, 6347
 influence of, 629, 7192
 on intuition, 4525
 Jansenism and, 7877
 on Jews
  and anti-Semitism, 399
  toleration of, 399
 on *John,* 922
 on justification, 5040–5041
 on knowledge, 5203
 and language of fire, 3120
 on life, 5446, 5449
 on literature, 5470

Augustine of Hippo
continued
literature of, 5471
on *Logos,* 5504
on magic, 5333, 5577
Manichaeism of, 624, 5653, 5663, 5665, 5667
Manichaeism opposed by, 626, 5652, 5663–5664, 5667, 9325–9326
on Mary Magdalene, 5757
on mathematics, 2878
on merit, 5876
on miraculous cures, 3843
monasticism and, 7724
on Montanism, 6167, 6168
on morality, 1651–1652
mother of (Monica), 624–625
on music, 46, 6305, 6308, 6309, 7204
mysticism of, 5990, 6347
Neoplatonism and, 6475, 7192
on numbers, 6745, 6748
on obedience and virtues, 1670
overview of life and work, 1679
on pain, 6946
on peace, 7022
Pecham (John) influenced by, 7025
Pelagius and, 626–627, 7025, 7026, 7027, 7353, 8406
Platonism of, 625
Possidius's biography of, 628–629
on predestination, 3203, 3207
double, 8406
in priesthood, 625–626
on relics, 7688
on resurrection of body, 131
on revelation, 7776
on Roman Empire and kingdom of God, 1661, 1679
sacramental theology of, 7961
on sacraments, 626, 627
on salvation, 7876
Vatican II and, 9538
on semantics, 8227
on Septuagint, 881
on sexual activity, 3513–3514
on sexual desire, 8247–8248
rejection of, 2308
ship symbolism of, 992
on sin, 1667
original sin theory, 8406
on sleep as enlightenment, 8441–8442
Stoicism and, 8742
on suicide, 8830
on superstition, 8865
on symmetry, 6361
as teacher, 624
on temporal *vs.* eternal order, 8464
on temptation, 9070
Teresa of Ávila influenced by, 9084
against theater, 7044
theodicy of, 9117
theological issues addressed by, 2581
on theology, 2383
theology of, 9134, 9136
on time, 3555
vs. Aristotle, 7989
on Trinity, 627–628, 2585, 9361
on truth, 3555
on "two books," 9421–9422
on virginity, 4164
Vulgate Bible opposed by, 893
writings of, 624, 625
Augustinian Canons, 7724
Augustinians
mendicancy of, 5856
missions of
in colonial Mesoamerica, 5915
Latin American, 1696, 1697
monasteries of, architecture of, 6119
Augustinus (Jansen), 7001
Augustus (Roman emperor), **630–631**
Apollo and, 426
apotheosis of, 439
and Arval Brothers, 513, 2232
Caesar's relationship with, 630
and cult of Fides, 3094
and Dea Dia, 2232
and Diana cult, 2347
divination controlled by, 2372, 2378
divinization of, 7913
dragon as father of, 2433
Druids persecuted by, 7921
in golden age of Rome, 630
imperial cults and, 7915
ludi saeculares and, 5525
magic practices prohibited by, 6452
Mausoleum Augusti, circularity of, 1792
paganism *vs.* Christianity under, 4038
as *pontifex maximus,* 7319, 7913
recreating Roman religious values, 4323
on religion, 7912
Roman religion under, 630, 7279
temples built by, 9064
temples to, 7915–7916
in Vesta cult, 3385
Aukhé (mythic hero), 5985
Aulén, Gustaf
on atonement, 596
and neoorthodoxy, 6466, 6469
Auliyā, Nizāmuddīn, music and, 6284
Aulos (musical instrument), 6304
Aulus Postumius (Roman dictator), 7902
Aum. *See Oṃ*
ʿAumakua (guardian gods)
in Hawaiian pantheon, 3796
illness and, 3799
images of, vol. 9 color insert
Aumism, 6568
Aum Shinrikyō, **631–633**
brainwashing in, 6515
Buddhist traditions and, 6551
establishment of, 631
as fragile movement, 6517, 6549
members of, 6575
origins of, 6574, 6575
popularity of, 4799–4800
practices of, 632–633
reaction to, 4793
readings of *Revelation,* 6531
religious studies and, 8778
secondary leaders of, 6547
terrorist activities of, 631–632, 6531, 7274–7275
and violence, conditions leading to, 6553
worldview of, 632–633
Aung San Suu Kyi, 1283
Aung Thwin, Michael, 7261–7262
Auniņš, Roberts Kārlis, 769
Aurangzeb (emperor), 4645
calligraphy and, 1369
Aurelian (emperor), Sol worship and, 8510, 8840–8841
Aurelius (bishop), 2417
Aurgelmir. *See* Ymir
Auriaria (mythic figure), 6010
Aurobindo Ashram, 546
Aurobindo Ghose, **633–634**
in ashram revival, 545, 546
charisma of, 1549
didactic play written by, 829
education of, 633
on evolution of consciousness, 633–634
Integral Yoga of, 634
on *māyā,* 5795
Tantric symbols used by, 8988
Western following of, 4008
Aurohuaca Indians (Columbian Sierra Nevada), 7759
Aurora (Boehme), 1006
Aurora Consurgens, 252
Auschwitz (Poland). *See also* Holocaust, the
as pilgrimage site, 8377
Auseinandersetzung (coming to terms), 2285
Auseklis (deity), 9420
Auseklis, Miķelis Krogzemis-, 762–763
Auspices, 2377. *See also* Portents
in Greek religion, 7335–7336
in Roman religion, 7335–7336, 7903
Auster, Paul, 703
Austerity, of Cistercians, 6132
Austin, Alfredo López, 7811
Austin, Allan, 81
Austin, J. L., 307, 5306, 7858
on liturgy, 5492
Austin, John
on knowledge, 2427
on law and religion, 5326, 5369
on performative language, 2099
Austin, John Langshaw, on ritual language, 5328
Austin, Mary, 7224
Australia and Australian religions. *See also* Australian Indigenous religions
academic study of religion in, **8767–8771**
academic programs in, 8768–8771
biblical scholarship in, 8771
early intellectuals in, 8768
pioneer missionaries, reports of, 8767–8768
anticolonial movements in, 671
British penal settlements, 1731, 1732
Buddhism, 1189, 1190
engaged, 2786
cargo cults and, 1417, 1418, 1424
Christianity, **1731–1737**
in 1960s, 1735–1736
Anglicanism, 1732, 1735–1736
beginnings of, 3083
Catholicism, 1732, 1734–1735
church development in, 1732
church-state relations in, 1733–1734, 1737
indigenous cultures, contacts with, 1731, 1735
lack of continuous intellectual tradition, 3080
Orthodox, 2589
Pentecostalism in, 1735
Presbyterianism, 7391
Warlpiri and, 9696–9697
women in, 1735–1736
World War II and Depression and, 1734–1735
church and state in, 1733–1734, 1737
climate of, 635
colonialism in, 636
and new religious movements, 670–671
and studies of Indigenous religions, 680–681, 685
cyclones in, 7605
education in, 1733, 1735
external influences, 1736
fiction of, 3079–3083
films from, 3097–3098
funeral rites in, 7808
geography of, 635
Indigenous (*See* Australian Indigenous religions)
International Society for Krishna Consciousness in, 4522

life in, 5444
moon in, 6174
new religious movements in
colonialism and, 670–671
government policy on, 6570
New Year ceremonies in, 6590
Perth, Aboriginal claims in, 1810
reincarnation in, 7677
religious broadcasting in, 7714
settlers in, 3083
Uniting Church, 1735
women in, 1734, 1735–1736
in World Wars I and II, 1734
Zoroastrianism, fire in, 570
Australian Aboriginal Evangelical Fellowship, 677
Australian Aborigines (Maddock), 3390
Australian Indigenous religions, **634–692**. *See also specific religions*
afterlife in, **144–145,** 147
All-Father in, **265–266**
anamnesis in, 314–316
ancestors in
country created by, 638
in the Dreaming, 638, 3434
as family founders, 326
role of, 670
skulls of, 3806
androgyny in, 8239
art of, 2480, 4304–4307
the Dreaming in, 639–640, 666, 667, 668, vol. 1 color insert
international audience for, 639–640
assimilative policies and, 1734
birth in, 951
blood in, 987
blood vengeance in, 7780
bull-roarers used in, 1320–1321, 7035, 9211–9213
ceremonies of, women's *vs.* men's, 3390–3391, 3392
charisma in, 1547
Christianity, 1731–1737
Aboriginal, **675–680**
in new movements, 671
prevalence of, 640
in traditional rituals, 645–646
Christian missions and, 671, 672, 676
studies conducted by, 685–686
circumcision in, 4476, 4477
cosmology, **2002–2004,** 9697
"country" in, concept of, 636, 638
creation in, 2986
language in, 5302
supreme beings in, 8869, 8870
culture heroes in, disappearance of, 2091
death in, 5051
by sorcery, 2099
desert in rituals of, 2302
Djan'kawu in, **2378–2380**
the Dreaming in (*See* Dreaming)
dreams in, 2483, 2487
evil spirits in, health and, 3872–3873
existence of, scholarly debate over, 681, 685
fasting in, 2996, 2997
father gods in, 2984
and fiction, 3083–3084
funeral rites in, 5051
gender in, **3389–3395**
Gill (Sam D.) on, 8786
healing in, **3870–3875**
history of study of, **680–692,** 2478–2479
advances in, 683
Berndts (Catherine and Ronald) in, 840–842
colonialism and, 680–681, 685
Durkheim (Émile) in, 2478–2479, 2528–2529, 4461
Gillen and Spencer in, 3489–3491
Kaberry (Phyllis M.) in, 5050–5051
land rights in, 688–690
by missionaries, 685–686
myths in, 667–668
new movements in, 670–671, 681–683
outside academia, 687–688
phases of, 683–684
women in, 682, 686–687, 690, 3389–3390
iconography of, **4304–4307**
tjurungas, 9212–9213
initiation rituals in
for boys, 4476, 4477, 4480, 4481, 5051
circumcision in, 1799
for girls, 4478
history of study of, 681, 682
for medicine men, 4477
mimicking of maternal role, 2985
ordeals of, 4477
sacrifice in, 7845
tjurungas in, 9212
intichiuma ceremonies in, totemism and, 8003
kinship in, 5185
knowledge in, 639, 648, 650, 689–690
of music, 6261, 6262
restricted *vs.* unrestricted, 6260–6261
land in
history of study of, 688–690
myths of, 662
new movements of, 673–674
political struggle for, 640–641, 648, 649–651, 690
sacrality of, 3972
secrecy and, 649–651, 689
women and, 689, 3390–3391
languages and worldviews, diversity in, 2002
law in, dreamtime derivation of, 2002, 2003–2004
life in, 5444
masculine sacrality in, 5759, 5760
medicine men, initiation rites of, 1470
meteorological beings in, 5993
miracles in, 6049
music in, **6260–6263**
categories of, 6261
knowledge of, 6261, 6262
myths as songs, 655–656, 660–661
sequence of songs, 5705–5706, 5707
terms for, 6261
myths of, **652–670** (*See also* Dreaming, the)
for children, 656, 3392
cosmological, 5051
everyday life in, 653–654
the Fall in, 2961
fate and destiny in, 656–658
the Flood in, 3131, 3132, 3223
Gadjari in, **3249–3251**
history of study of, 667–668
information provided by, 654
interconnecting themes in, 659–662
in legal system, 649–651, 666–667
oral transmission of, 652
paths/tracks in, 658–659
precedents for behavior in, 662–664
Rainbow Snake in, 7605
regional patterns in, 654–662
rituals linked with, 652
self-representation of, 667
social relations in, 654, 663–664
Wawalag, 9704–9706
women in, 663–664, 3392
names in, 6408–6409, 6411
new movements in, **670–675**
Christianity in, 671
classification of, 670–671
colonialism and, 670–671
history of study of, 670–671, 681–683
sexual abuse in, 5377
New Year ceremonies in, 6590
Ngarrangkarni (Time Long Past) in, 5050–5051
Ngukurr religion, 6597–6601
ordination in, 6853
overview of, **634–652**
politics of, 640–641
power in, 7346
psychedelic drugs in, 7468–7469
rainmaking in, 7603
rebirth in, 314–316
reincarnation in, 7677
revelation in, 639, 689–690
rituals in, 7835
sacred geography of, 3433–3434
sacred pillar in, 1502
Schmidt (Wilhelm) on, 8168
seasons in, 661
sedentarization of, 9693, 9695
Seven Sisters story in, 642–644
sexuality in, 8239
social issues, 1735
sorcery in
counter-sorcery of healers, 3873–3874
death and illness from, 3871–3872
soul in, 8532
Southeastern region, Howitt (A. W.) on, 4142
spirits in, 5051
terms for, 6260
Stanner (W. E. H.) on, 8729–8730
supreme beings of, as creators, 8869, 8870
Swain (Tony) on, 8770
taboo in, 7842–7843, 8948
time in
eternity and, 314
ideal, 132
tjurunga (sacred stone) in, vol. 4 color insert
totemism in (*See* Totemism, in Australian Indigenous religions)
trade and, 637
transmigration in, 9326–9327
trees in, 9336, 9337
twins in, 9414
urban spaces, claims to, 1810
wandjina in, 9668–9670
women in, 638–639, **3389–3395**
ceremonies of, 3390–3391, 3392
feminine sacrality of, 3021

women in ***continued***
history of study of, 682, 686–687, 690, 3389–3393
Kaberry (Phyllis M.) on, 5050–5051
land claims by, 689, 3390–3391, 3392
myths of, 663–664, 3392
problems with sources on, 3389–3390
secret business of, 639, 649–651, 3392
Australian Labour Party, Catholicism and, 1734
Australian School of Pacific Administration (ASOPA), 5380
Australian Totemism (Róheim), 7872
Austria
Islam in, 4677–4678, 4680
Judaism in
rabbis in, 7579–7580
Reform Judaism, 7669
Austroasiatic languages, Schmidt (Wilhelm) on, 8168
Austro-Hungarian Empire
church and state in, 1685–1686
Islam in, 4674
Judaism in, *tsaddiq* in, 9380
Uniate church under, 9463–9464
Austronesian languages
in insular Southeast Asia, 8647
in mainland Southeast Asia, 8641
mana in, 8515
Schmidt (Wilhelm) on, 8168
Authenticity
of conversion, using process theory, 1972
Heidegger (Martin) on, 3896
of *sahīh ḥadīths,* 3731
of saints, 2082–2083
Sohm (Rudolf) on fall from, 8507
Authoritative Teaching (Gnostic text), 5202
Authority, **692–697**
in archaic religions, 692–693
of biblical literature, 694–695
in Buddhism, 693–694, 696
Rājagṛha council and, 2035
Cārvāka view on, 1446
charisma and, 1544
in Christianity, 694–695, 696–697
of bishops, Council of Nicaea and, 2040
Calvinist churches and, 1376
early, 1661
Vatican II and, 9540
church authority, Roman Catholic hierarchical model, 1668, 1681
colonialism and, Spanish *Requirement* formula, 1854
in Confucianism, vol. 6 color insert
consecration and, 1956
of creeds, 2053, 2055–2056
decline of, legitimation and, 5397–5398
dharma and, 2328
of discipleship, 2361
of epics, 6362
Hus (Jan) on, 4234
intellectuals confronting, 4513
in *walāyah,* 9657–9658
in Islam, 695–696
modernism in struggle over, 6097
in Japanese culture, emperor *vs.* noble families, in historiography, 4026
in Judaism, rabbinical, 3749, 4059
of kings (*See* Kings)
legitimacy of, 692, 5385–5386
lineage and, 3424
of martyrs, 5738, 5739
of myths, 692, 6359–6360, 6362
through ordination, 6852, 6858–6859
in politics and religion, 7249
portraiture establishing, vol. 10 color insert
power *vs.*, in sociology, 8481
in primitive religions, 692
prophetic, biblical, 7433–7434
in Protestantism, on scripture along *(sola scriptura),* medicine and, 3846
reestablishing, through epic, 2816
Reformation and, 1663, 8158
in religious communities, 1864
religious *vs.* secular, 3690–3691
law and, 5327
Marsilius of Padua on, 5729–5730
tension between, 696–697
schism and, 8153
of scripture, 8201
and source and antiquity of, 8202
of shamans *vs.* political leaders, in South American and Caribbean religions, 1430–1431
social, 8483
sources of, 692
in spiritual discipline, heteronomous, 8700
types of, 692
Weber (Max) on, charismatic, traditional and rational-bureaucratic, 8483
Authors, intention of, in hermeneutics, 3931–3932
Autobiography, **697–704**. *See also* Biography; *specific works*
Buddhist, 701
Chinese, 701–702
Christian, 698–699
definitions of, 698, 703
Hindu, 700–701
Islamic, 699–700
Japanese, 702
Jewish, 703
medieval, 4038
in men's studies, 5863
North American Indian, 702
as religious act, 703
Russian, 712
spiritual, 702–703
Autobiography (Müller), 6235
Autobiography (Teresa of Ávila), 5818
Autobiography and Life of George Tyrrell (Petre), 7070
Autobiography of a Winnebago Indian (Blowsnake), 7596
Autobiography of a Yogi (Yogananda), 700
Autocephalies, in Eastern Orthodox Church, 1765, 1772
Autocephalous status, for Russian Orthodox Church, 2588
Automatic writing, in UFO religions, 9434
Automatism, psychic, attention and, 607–609
Automaton (fortuitousness), 1526
Automessianism, 5978
Automobiles, purification of, in Japan, 3869–3870
Autonomous discipline, 8700–8701
Autonomous Republic of Karelia, 5092
Autopsy, 2244
Autosacrifice. *See* Bloodletting
Autumnal equinox, in Japan, 2411
Avadana literature, Sarvāstivādin canon, 8118, 8119
Avadhi dialect, literary tradition of, 3984
Avalambana. *See* All Souls Festival
Avalokiteśvara *(bodhisattva),* **704–707**. *See also* Kannon
Ajantā painting of, 1076
Amitābha and, 291, 705, 706
artistic transformation of gender of, 1827
as Lokeśvara, 1079
blessing on Rang byung rdo rje by, 5102
in Chinese Buddhism, 705, 1162, 3343
Zhenyan, 9963
in Chinese religion (as Guanyin)
birthday of, 1644
sacrifices to, 1643
cult of, 1082, 1157, 1217, 1224, 1231
Dalai Lama as incarnation of, 705, 706, 1082, 2131, 4416, 9184
dharma taught by, 7408
epithets of, 704
etymology of name, 704, 705
feminine counterpart of, 1079, 1082
gender of, 3343
Gesar as emanation of, 3463
handmaidens of, 1079
iconography of, 705–706, 4329, vol. 8 color insert
as leading *bodhisattva,* 1082, 1117
litany of, 1118
Longchenpa on, 5193
Mahāsthāmaprāpta and, 705, 706
mantra of, 1079, 1157, 1217, 5310, 5678, 9184
origins of, 704–705
Padmapāṇi identified with, 1076, 9512–9513
in Paradise, 705
pāramitās practiced by, 6993
as protector of Tibet, 9184
Pure Land of, 7503
scriptural sources on, 704–705
as subject of *nianfo,* 6601
Tārā associated with, 4330
temple to, 9047
in Tibetan Buddhism, 9841
under Vajrapāṇi's command, 1077
writings of, 5553–5554
Avalon, Arthur. *See* Woodroffe, John
Avam Samoyed religion, shaman account in, 8271
Āvarṇas (sheaths), 4424–4425
Avars, 1556
in Byzantine Empire, 4491–4492
Islam of, 4614
and Ruanruan, 4491
sources on, 4491
Avataṃsaka Sūtra (Buddhist text), 1217, 1302, 7503, 9018, 9177. *See also* Huayan jing
earliest surviving version of, 4146
Huayan Buddhism, role in, 1600
Mahāvairocana in, 5607
Mañjuśrī in, 5675
Avatāra (descents) doctrine
bhakti synthesis and, 4000–4001
caste system and four *puruṣārthas* upheld by, 4001
time and, 2017
Avatāras (incarnations of deity), **707–708**. *See also* Viṣṇu
in Pāñcarātra, 9508
Kṛṣṇa as, 5249, 5251
Avdimi of Haifa, on *shekhinah,* 8314
Ave Maria prayer, 5753
Avempace. *See* Ibn Bājjah
Avenarius, Richard, 7341
Avencebrol. *See* Ibn Gabirol, Shelomoh
Aventine Hill (Rome), 7897
Avenue of the Dead, in Teotihuacán, 5898–5899
Averroës. *See* Ibn Rushd

Averroists, 481
Avesta (Zoroastrian text), **708–710,** 9992–9993
Ahura Mazdā in, 203–204
Amesha Spentas in, 290
Anāhitā in, 305
angels in, 344
author of, 9933–9934
Burnouf (Eugène) on, 1333–1334
Christensen on, 1650
as competition for Manichaean books, 5661
confessions of faith in, 2052
cows in, 1467
Dēnkard text of, evil and sickness, origins of, in, 3809
dualism in, 2506, 2507
exegetical translations of, 5560–5561
fate in, 3004
fire in, 569
Frashōkereti in, 3189
fravashis in, 3190
gender in, 3372
Golden Age in, 2964, 3629–3630
Haoma in, 3776
horses in, 7385
in Indo-European language study, 4458
khvarenah in, 5139–5140
language of, 709
"magi" in, 5559
memorizing texts of, 7396
Mithra in, 6087
Nyberg (H. S.) and study of, 6774
in oral tradition, 708, 5561
priests' role in transmitting, 5560–5561
publication of, 709
resurrection in, 7763
sections of, 709
sun in, 7384, 8838
surviving portions of, 708–709
translations of, 5560–5561
written form of, 8199
yasatas in, 9874–9875
Zarathushtra in, 9934–9935
Avestan language, 709
alphabet of, invention of, 5561
gender in, 3372
and "holy," concept of, 7968–7969
Avicebron. *See* Ibn Gabirol, Shelomoh
Avicembron. *See* Ibn Gabirol, Shelomoh
Avicenna. *See* Ibn Sīnā
Avidyā (ignorance), **710–711,** 1205, 1207, 5200–5201, 9017, 9020, 9546, 9547
māyā and, 5795
Nāgārjuna on, 6391, 6392
Avigad, Nahman, 924
Avignon papacy, 6971, 7280
Catherine of Sienna and, 1461
and centralization of authority, 2042, 6971
duration of, 6971
factors of, 6971
Avinu malkenu (liturgical poem), at Ro'sh ha-Shanah and Yom Kippur, 8390
'Avodah (poetic saga), in Yom Kippur liturgy, 8390–8391
Avot. See Mishnah
Avraam, Renos, 1038
Avraham bar Hiyya', ethics of, 4912
Avraham ben David of Posquières, **711–712,** 970, 4264
on Christianity, 7234
on God's corporeality, 3549
writings of, 711
Avraham ben Yitsḥaq of Narbonne, 4264
Avraham ibn Daud, on God's foreknowledge, 3549
Avraham "the Angel," Shne'ur Zalman of Lyady and, 8371
Avvakum (Russian archpriest), **712**
Awake! (Jehovah's Witnesses publication), 4823
Awakening
in Korean Sŏn Buddhism, 1646
in Raëlian religion, 7598
in Japanese Shingon Buddhism, 8350–8351
and sleep and ignorance, 8441
Awakening of Faith, The (Suzuki), 1183
Awakenings, The (film), 646–647, 651
Awaliyā. See Walī/awaliyā (saints)
Awareness, interactive discipline and, 8702
'Awārif al-ma'ārif (al-Suhrawardī), 9008
Awatelin Tsita, in Zuni creation myth, hierogamy of, 2555–2556
Awe, Jonas (Hans) on the sacred and, 7976
Awemba. *See* Bemba people
Awen'hai'i (deity), 9218
Awilum (higher class), 4730
Awitelin Tsita, prayer to, 2554
'Awl (proportionate reduction), 4710
Awlad Nā'il religion (North Africa), hierodouleia (sacred prostitution) in, 3969–3970
Awliyā' (Ṣūfī saints), 4647, 9819–9820
Awn rites, 5689
Awonawilona, in Zuni creation myth, hierogamy of, 2555–2556
Awzā'ī, al-, Abū Ḥanīfah compared with, 22
Axé (power), 9308
Axes
double
in Minoan religion, 40, *41,* 4320
in Mycenaean religion, 41, 4320, 5275
images on heads of, in Olmec religion, vol. 3 color insert
stone, in Caribbean Kele cult, 1436
Axial Age, civilizations in, 7726
center-periphery relations in, 7727, 7729
collectivities of, 7727
construction of, 7726–7730
differences between, 7728–7729
dynamics of, 7727–7728
elites of, 7726, 7729
heterodoxies *vs.* sects, 7730
monolithic *vs.* heterogenous elites in, 7730
otherworldy *vs.* this-worldy orientation of, 7729–7730
religious dynamics in, 7730
ruling classes of, 7730
social centers in, 7727
social dynamics in, 7730
symbols in, 7729–7730
Axis mundi (axis of universe), **712–713**. *See also* Center of the world
cave as, 1468
as center of the world, 1501, 1502, 1503
Chinese court attire and, 1830
dasiri as, 777
Eliade on, 1879
functions of, 713
images of, 712–713
through king, in Saka religion, 7386–7387
masculine sacrality and, 5761
mountain as, 712, 1502, 1625, 6212
in Olmec religion, vol. 3 color insert
pillar as, 713
in North American Indian religions, 6651, 6681
Smith (Jonathan Z.), critique of, 1879
soma as, 4439
in South American Indian religions
cosmic levels and, 8587
in shamanism, 8291
in Southeast Asian religions, *maṇḍalas* and, 8644
Sun Tree as, in Baltic religion, 8132
tower as, 9266
tree as, 712, 9576–9577
in Germanic religion, 3449
ultimate orientation and, 1581
Axogún, 123
Ayahuasca (plant), 6274
Ayahusca (hallucinogen), 7468, 7470
Ayala, Francisco, 4516
Ayana (divine agents), in Macha Oromo religion, 2573
Ayatollahs (Muslim religious leaders), as charismatic leaders, 1546
Āyatullāh (sign of God), as title, 3801
Āyatullāh *al-uzma* (biggest sign of God), as title, 3801
Aycock, D. Alan, structuralism and, 8755
Ayer, A. J., 2780, 7118, 7127
Ayer, Alfred Jules
on knowledge, 5210
on logical empiricism, 5499
Āyi Vaḍil (deified ancestor), 4436
Ayllus
in Andean religion, in modern era, 8617–8618
organization of, 5176
Aymara religion (Andes). *See also* Andean religions, modern
demographics of, 8614–8615
fertility rites in, 8583
'Ayn, Qurrat al-, 728, 737
'Ayn al-Quḍāt, mystical theology of, 8813–8814
Ayodhya, India, mosque destroyed in, 8011
Ayoré religion (Paraguay)
cultural origin myths in, 8590
death, myths of origin of, 8590–8591
religion of, 8633
Āyurveda (Hindu system of medicine), **713–715**
healing and medicine in, **3852–3858**
karman in, 5096
magic and, 5589, 5591
origins of, 714
politics of, 3856–3857
principles of, 3854–3856
texts of, 714, 5591
textual tradition of, 3852–3854
theory of disease in, 714
in Tibet, 3865
treatment in, 714
Vedism and, 3853
Ayutthayā (Siamese kingdom), 9095
Ayyūbid dynasty
al-Azhar under, 230
Crusades and, 2075
Ayyūb Khān, Muḥammad, 4773
Azād, Abū al-Kalām, 8955
Azag (mythic figure), 5952–5953
Azaletch, Mama, 8691
Azalīs (Iran), 729, 737

A'zami, Muḥammad Muṣṭafā, on authenticity and documentation of *ḥadīths*, 3728
Azande religion (East Africa)
Evans-Pritchard (E. E.) and, 2895
healing in, herbalists, 3819
high deity in, 2567
homosexuality in, 4114
magic in, 5567, 5571
myths of, 94
ordination in, 6853
sorcery beliefs in, 2569–2570
tricksters in, 9352
witchcraft beliefs in, 2569–2570, 9769, 9778, 9779
Azāriqah sect, 5126
Azazel (demon), 2277
Azcapotzalco (Mexico)
rise of, 5907
Tepanec kingdom centered in, 5173
Azerbaijan. *See* Caucasus
Azhar, al-. *See* Al-Azhar university
Azharot (Ibn Gabirol), 4266
Azhi Dahaka (monster), 2431–2432
Āzi (spirit), gender of, 3372
Azimua (deity), 5959
Azitawadda (king of Adana), 7130
Azjal (poetry), 4597
A-Z of African Proverbs, The (Knappert), 6977
Azra, Azyumardi, 4665
Azraqī, al-, 4362
on Arabian religion, 444
Aztec religion and society (Mexico), **715–720**. *See also* Mesoamerica and Mesoamerican religions; *See also* Tenochtitlán
afterlife in, 149–150, 5892
ages of world in, 177, 716–717, 5907
ballgames played in, 749
birth rites in, 7862
bread in, 1041
calendar of, 719, 1353, 1354, 1355, 1357–1358, 5908, vol. 3 color insert
cannibalism in, 1403
as ecological adaptation, 2868
ceremonies in, 719, 4190, 5908
charisma in, 1548
codices, 1360
comets in, 8736
converting to Christianity, 4501
cosmic rites of passage in, 7813
cosmogony of, 716–717, 5907, 6269
cosmology of, 716–717, 5907
human sacrifice and, 4186–4187
societal implications of, 5173
creation-destruction cycles, 1357–1358
creation myth, 1468
cult of war and human sacrifice, female deities associated with, 3020
death in, 2242, 7863
deities of, 717–719, 1469 (*See also* Coatlicue; Huitzilopochtli; Quetzalcoatl; Tezcatlipoca; Tlaloc)
creator, 718, 5907
duality of, 5891
of earth, 1841
fertility, 718–719
gender of, 3411
iconography of, 5891
nature, 5293
origins of, 5890, 5906
patron, 718
prince of flowers, 3135
of rain, 1469
self-sacrifice of, 4187
storm, ambivalence of, 5993–5994
of sun, 8842
themes/complexes of, 5907–5908
Tonatiuh, 1357, 8842
of war, 3020
Xipe Totec, 1469
divine destiny in, 5890–5891
drama in, 2464, 2465, 2466
drums in, 2499, 6269, 7036
origins of, 6270
fasting in, 2996
fertility and regeneration in, 718–719, 5293
floods in, 3130
funeral rites in, 3238, 3243–3244, 7813
games in, cosmic significance of, 3260
gender in, 3411–3412
grotto of Balankanché, 1468
history of study of, 5942
Huastec religion and, 5910
human sacrifice in (*See* Human sacrifice, in Aztec religion)
iconography of, 4313–4314, 5891
jade in, 4759–4760
jaguar in, 4763
kingship in, 5172–5174
acquisition of Toltec royal lineage in, 5173
legitimacy of, 5173–5174
vulnerability of, 5173–5174
light and darkness symbolism in, 5451
medical specialties in, 3813
metallurgy in, 5987
migration in, 718, 5890, 5937
military power of, 5173
moon in, 6174
mountains in, 6214
music in, 6269–6270
nature in, 5293
Olmec and, 6817–6818
origins of, 715, 5890
Otomí and, 6926–6927
paradise in, 3136
Pleiades in, 8735
pre-Columbian, 5890–5893
in Postclassic period, 5907–5909
priesthood in, 5908
pyramids of, 5293
quarters in structure of, 715–716, 717–718, 5907
redemption in, 7641
rejuvenation myths in, 7684
rites of passage in, 7811
birth rites, 7811–7812
cosmic rites, 7813
funeral rites, 7813
marriage rites, 7812–7813
rituals in, 5908–5909
rivers in, 7863
sacrifice in, 717, 2556, 5891–5893
by gods, 717
shamanism in, 5908–5909
Spanish colonialism and, 716, 719
Spanish conquest of, 1695
star patterns in, 8428–8429
sun stone in, vol. 3 color insert
tears in, 9026
Templo Mayor in, 718, 719, 1359, 5892–5893
time in, 3064
tobacco and smoking in, 8455–8456, 9218
vs. Totonac people, 9254
towers in, 9266
trees in, 9335
tricksters in, 9357
warfare in, 5891, 9680
water in, 9213–9214
Lake Texcoco, 5292–5294
Valley of Mexico, 5292–5294
women in, 3411–3412
writing system in, 5851
Xochiyaoyotl (Flowery Wars), 4186–4187
Aztec Sun Stone, cyclic cosmology on, 1357
Azu (doctor), in Mesopotamian religion, 3824–3825
Azu (Syria), Dagan in, 2126
Azure Ox Palace (Chengdu), 9058
Azusa Street Apostolic Faith Mission (Pentecostal), 7029
Azusa Street Apostolic Faith Mission, Seymour (William J.) and, 8254
Azyme Controversy, 5388

B

Ba (soul)
in Egyptian religion, 2711, 7763
in Kushite religion, 5270
Baader, Franz von, 340
on androgyny, 8523
on Hermetism, 3951
mystics reformed by, 2603
on nature, 6435
Baal (deity), **723–725**
Adad as, 27, 28, 723, 2536
Adonis as, 34
Aliyan, 1383, 2536
Anat and, 319–320, 724, 2536, 3596, 8539
Astarte and, 561–562
Athirat (Asherah) and, 589
in Canaanite literature, 1382–1383, 1384, 1385, 1387, 1388, 1391–1395
cow of, 319
death (Mot), battle with, 723, 724, 2431, 2442, 2536
death of
Anat's response to, 319–320
challenge to, 1384, 1388, 1393–1395
derivation of name, 1383
divine dwelling of, 6213
divine kingship of, 5146
as dying and rising god, 1874, 7767
El and, 723, 724, 2742, 7129
Eshmun and, 2840–2841, 2842
as god of fertility, 723, 724, 7602
as god of storm, 723–724
as healer, 2840
Hephaestus identified with, 7129
in Hittite myth, 4070
house of, 1392–1393
humor and, 4196
iconography of, 723
as king of gods, 723–724
in Moabite religion, 6094
in personal names, 1387
in Phoenician religion, 7129, 7130, 7131, 7134
popular worship in Israel, 3157
resurrection of, 724, 2536
Sabazios identified with, 7953
sea (Yamm), battle with, 723, 724, 1383, 1384, 1387, 1391–1392, 1393, 1875, 2431, 2442
symbolic aspect, 1388
water and, 9700
as Yahveh, 724, 6407
vs. Yahveh, 2765
Zeus identified with, 7129
Baal (king of Tyre)
Melqart and, 5847
treaty between king Esarhaddon and, 7129–7130, 7134
Baal, Jan van, **725–726**
on illusions, 6368
on sacrifice and offering, 725, 7997, 8000
on symbols, 725
Baalat (deity), 7130
Baal Cycle, 724, 2536
Ba'ale shem (masters of the name), 4982
Baal-Hammon (deity), 834, 7130
Baal-*krntrysh* (deity), 7130
Baal-Malage (deity), 7129, 7134

Baal-Safon (deity), 7129
Baal-Shamem (deity), 7129, 7131, 7134
Baalshamin (deity), 448
in Nabatean religion, 6389
Ba'al Shem Tov (BeSHT), **726–727,** 4982, 7583
and amulets, use of, 3160
circle of, 3786–3787
and Dov Ber of Mezhirich, 2429
and fire, 3119
followers of, 7427
as founder of Hasidism, 726, 3785, 5017
on Frankist movement and Shabbetai Tsevi, 3786
legends about, 3791
messianism of, 8173
and music, 6310
mysticism of, 6354
Naḥman of Bratslav and, 6401
on nature, divine in, 2606–2607
teachings of, 726–727
as *tsaddiq,* 9378, 9379, 9381
tsaddiqim and, 8035–8036
Ba'al Teshuva movement
in contemporary Judaism, 4985
Jewish Renewal and, 4872
Baal Zebub (deity), 3158
in Philistine religion, 7103
Bāb ("gate"), 728
Bāb, the, 727–728
disciples of, 4572
execution of, 4572, 6549
on Qurrat al-'Ayn Ṭāhirah, 7575
shrine of, 738, 740
tafsīr of, 8954
writings of, 728
Baba (funerary statues), 9403
Baba, Sathya Sai, 2623
Baba (deity), family of, 5951, 5958
Bābā Farīd al-Dīn Ganj-i Shakar, 6638
Babai the Great (theologian), 6483
Babajan, Hazrat, 3369
Babakilo (Bemba councilor), 817
Bābā Lāl Dās (Hindu yogi), discussions with Dārā, 2219
Babalawos (priests), Ifa divination by, 8108
Bāb al-ḥādī 'ashar, al- (al-Ḥillī), importance of, 3982
Babaluaiye, in Santería, 1434
Baba Rabba, Samaritan reform and, 8069
Baba Yaga (deity), **727,** 8437
Babb, Lawrence, 7508
on Sai Baba movement, 8027
Babbage, Charles, 9423
Babel-Bible controversy, 2263
Babenya (ritual object), 817
Bābī-Azalīs (Iran), 729, 737
Babiri brothers, and Dacian Riders, 2123
Bābīs, **727–729**
as followers of the Bāb, 727–728
Bahā'īs and, 728–729, 737
calendar of, 729
on Cyprus, 729, 737
doctrines of, 729
in Iran, 729
jihād of, 728, 729
martyrs of, Qurrat al-'Ayn Ṭāhirah as, 7574–7575
in Ottoman Empire, 728, 737
persecution of, 728, 737, 4573
Shaykhīyah and, 8307, 8308–8309
Ṣubḥ-i Azal as leader of, 728–729, 737
Babi Yar (Yevtushenko), 7205
Baboon, 9168
Baboons, 6151
Babri Majid Mosque, desecration of, 8011
Bābur, 6638
Babylon
Akitu festival in (*See* Akitu festival)
cattle sacrifice in, 1466
divine kingship in, 5146, 5147
Eridu supplanted by, 2810–2811
as first city, 2810–2811
geometry in, 3440–3441, 3443
Israelite religion in
destruction of Solomon's Temple, 923, 935, 4549, 4746
Isaiah on, 4548–4549
Marduk as god of, 5702, 5955
moon in, 6172
Phoenician invasion of, 7128
Rastafarian symbolism of, 1438
rise of, 5946
social justice in, 1553
Sumerian city-states taken over by, 1802–1803
Babylon and Infidelity Foredoomed of God (Irving), 4544
Babylonia. *See also* Babylonian religion
Aramaic incantation bowls from, 5458–5459
Assyrian rivalry with, 5948
astronomy in, 2999
end of independence in, 5948
geographic boundaries of, 5946
Jewish exile to, 2922
collective obligations and, 4857
elect status and, 2744–2745
and the Fall, 2900
Jeremiah on, 4830
return from, 2946
yeshivot in, 9883
Jewish submission to, 4827
as Judaic center, 4988–4989
Judaism in (*See also* Gaonate)
amoraim of, 294
rabbinical authority in, 3749
rabbinic Judaism, 7583
kings in, mortification of, 6198
knot symbolism in, 5197, 5198
number system in, 6752
origins of settlement of, 5947
Rava' in, 7631
Rav in, 7630
rulers and dynasties of, 5948
use of term, 5946
Babyloniaka (Iamblichos), 3053
Babylonian Captivity (papacy), 6971
Babylonian language
Canaanites and, 1381
sacred and profane in, 7969
Babylonian periods
Middle, Dagan in, 2126
Old
Dagan in, 2126
Nabu in, 6390
Babylonian religion. *See also* Mesopotamia and Mesopotamian religions
ablutions in, 10
afterlife in, 137
ages of world in, 175–176
Akitu festival in (*See* Akitu festival)
amulets and talismans in, 298
ancestor worship in, 2982
astronomy in, 3901
Atrahasis myth in, **598–600**
blades in, 967
cantillation and accents, 1533
chaos in, 1539
confession in, 1887–1888
cosmogony of, water in, 9699
creation myth of (*See Enuma elish*)
crossing Waters of Death in, 988–989
Cyrus the Great and, 2119
deities of (*See specific deities*)
divination, 1387, 2371
divine triad in, 6746–6747
dragons in, 2431, 2441–2442
fasting in, 2996
fish symbolism in, 3122, 3123
goats in, 8311
haruspices in, 7336
hierodouleia (sacred prostitution) in, 3966
iconography of, 4316–4317, 4380, 4389
immortality in, 989
judgment of the dead in, 5025
keys in myths of, 5116
kingship in
divine role in, 5965
divinity of, 7276–7277
Dumuzi and, 2522, 2523
libations in, 5433
literature of, revolutionary nature of, 5965–5967
music in, 6275–6276
number symbolism in, 6746–6747, 6749, 6750
planetary gods in, 8424, 8428
politics and, 7276–7277
postures and gestures in, 7343
priesthood in, 7398
procession in, 7418
riddles in, 6986
ritual drama in, 2441–2442, 2444–2445
sacred marriage *(hieros gamos)* in, 2445, 3976
sacrifice in, redemption and, 7641
Sumerian religion influencing, 5964–5965
sun in, 8838
temple in, 1502
tree symbolism in, 1502, 3449, 9335
triads in, 9349
underworld in, 9452
water in, 779
wisdom in, 9748–9749
Babylonian Talmud. *See* Talmud, Babylonian
Babylonian Theodicy, 4931–4932
Bacchae (Euripides), 375
facets of Dionysos in, 2357, 3673, 6865
frenzied behavior described in, 3214
gender and, 3383–3384
omophagia in, 6822
ritual drama in, 2443
thiasoi in, 9158
Bacchanalia
enthusiasm in, 2807
Italian, persecution of, 7909
repression of, 6866
Bacchants, 2357, 2358
Orphic, and deification, 2249
Bacchic Gold Tablets. *See* Orphic Gold Tablets
Bacchic mystery religion
catharsis in, 1459, 1460
civic religion and, 3672–3673
Dionysian orgies, 1459
Bacchus. *See* Dionysos
Bach, Johann Sebastian
cantatas and passion music of, 6311–6312, 6313
modern dance set to music of, 2158–2159
organ music of, 6311
as Protestant composer, 7459
Bach, Marcus, 560
on new religions, 6521, 6565

Bachelard, Gaston, on childhood, 1568–1569
Bachofen, J. J., **730–733**
on cultural stratum, 5259
Gimbutas (Marija) and, 3493
on goddess worship and matriarchy, 731, 3611, 3612–3613, 3616, 7008–7009, 7079, 9601
life of, 730
on mother right, 2983, 3612–3613
Neumann's (Erich) critique of, 3612
reception and influence of, 731–732
as Roman law scholar, 730
on symbols, 731
symbol theory and, 8909
writings of, 730–731
Bachue (deity), 6230
Bacik, James J., on spirituality *vs.* religion, 8720
Bäckman, Louise, 474
Backslider, in Christianity, Cyprian on, 2112, 2113
Back to Godhead (magazine), 4521, 4522, 7355
Backus, Isaac, 784
Bacon, Francis, **733–734**
epistemology of, 2819
as forerunner of the Enlightenment, 734
on history, 4030
on nature, 2607
as predecessor of positivism, 7340
Rosicrucianism and, 253, 7930
on "two books," 9422
writings of, 733–734
Bacon, Roger, **734–735**
on Albertus Magnus, 232
Aristotle's influence on, 734
on conversion, 735
as harbinger of modern science, 734–735
on Hermetism, 3945
Ibn Sīnā's influence on, 4275
on magic, 735
on nature, 6432–6433
as predecessor of positivism, 7340
writings of, 734
Bacot, Jacques, 9189
Bactrian language, Buddhist writings in, 1145, 1146–1147
Bada' (mutability), 3212–3213
Badaliya sodality, 5774
Bādarāyaṇa (Hindu author), **735–736,** 5455, 9544–9545
Badari culture, 6465
Badā'ūnī, on Akbar, 216
Bade (spirit), in Haitian Vodou, 1433
Baden (Germany), Protestant disputations held in, 2601
Bader, Françoise, 4454
Badger, George P., 6481
Badhbh (deity), 2984
Badimo (spirits), 9388–9389
Bado-Fralick, Nikki, 3148
on rites of passage, 7859
Badr, Battle of (624), 6225
Abd al-Raḥmān in, 19
Badran, Margot, 3366
Badrināth (India), pilgrimage to, 7170
Badt, Kurt, 56
Baḍu Caṇḍīdāsa, 827
Baeck, Leo, **736–737**
fighting Nazism, 736–737
and Reform Judaism, 7670
writings of, 736–737
Baer, Gerhard, on bird and shamanism, 8291–8292
Baer, Hans, 75
Baer, Seligman, on *siddur* and *maḥzor* (prayer books), 8387
Baetke, Walter, 3459
preanimism criticized by, 7373–7374
Baetyls, 444, 445
Baez, Joan, Gandhi influencing, 3273
Baez Jorge, Félix, 5945
Baffin Island Inuit religion, Sedna myths in, 8220, 8221
Bagai, Council of (394), 2416
Baganda people (Africa), redemption and, 7641
Bagasin cult (New Guinea), repentance in, 7756
Bagga'adowe (ballgame), 755
Baghdad (Iraq)
caliphate of (*See* Abbasid caliphate)
madrasahs in, 5557
Ḥanbālī, 3766
ribāṭs in, 5117
Baghdadi (Middle Eastern Jews), in India, 5006
Bagre myth, 91, 95, 99
Bagrot (Snoy), 9613
Bagshaw, Geoffrey, 689
Bagyidaw (Burmese ruler), 1139
Bahā' al-Dīn al-'Āmilī, 6231
Bahā' al-Dīn al-Sāmmūqī, 2503
Bahā' al-Dīn-i Walad, 9008
Bahā' al-Dīn Naqshband, 4614, 4621, 9009–9010
Bahā' al-Dīn Walad, 7935
Bahā' Allāh, 728–729, 737–738, 4572
grave of, 738
as messenger figure, 6733, 6738
writings of, 737–738
Bahā'ī House of Worship (Illinois), vol. 8 color insert
Bahā'īs, **737–740**
'Abd al-Bahā' as leader of, 738
in Africa, 108
architecture appropriated by, vol. 8 color insert
Bābīs and, 728–729, 737
Bahā' Allāh as leader of, 728–729, 737–738, 4572
beliefs and practices of, 739–740, 4572–4573
in Canada, 739
in Iran, 739
number of, 739
in Ottoman Empire, 737
in Palestine, 737
persecution of, 739, 4573, 6549
sacred number of, 6750
Shoghi Effendi as leader of, 738–739
tafsīr of, 8954
in United States, 738, 739
Bahá'u'lláh (prophet), imprisonment of, 6549
Bahia (Brazil), Afro-Brazilian religions in, 120, 121
Bāhilī, al-, in Ash'arīyah, 534
Bahktin, M., 7329
Bahmān (angel), 4554
Bahman Yasht, 411
Baḥr al-fawā'id (al-Kalābādhī), 5055
Bahrām I (king of Persia), Mani and, 5655, 5665
Bahrein, Qarāmiṭah of, 7542–7544
Bahu, Josephine, cargo cults and, 1414, 1415, 1419
Bāhubali (Indian prince), 4765, vol. 10 color insert
Bahuchara Mata (deity), *Hijra* transvestites and, 3968
Bahuguna, Sunderlal, 2622
Bahuśrutīya school of Buddhism
geographic distribution of, 1195
literature of, 1200
Mahāsāṃghika Buddhism and, 5602
origin of, 1194
Baḥya ben Asher ibn Halawa, ethics of, 4913
Baḥye ben Asher, 867
Baḥye ibn Paquda, **740–741**
asceticism of, 527
on duties, 313
ethics of, 4911–4912
in Jewish thought and philosophy, 4890–4891
philosophy of, 741
poems of, 740
writings of, 740–741
Baiame (deity), 671, 2984
creation by, 5993
name of, 6409
as sky god, 5993, 6438
as supreme being, 5993
waganna for, 671
Baĭanaĭ (helpers of hunters), 2395
Baidrama (deity), in Island Arawak religion, 1427
Baiga (priest), 4435
Baigent, Michael, 3196
Baigona movement, cargo cults and, 1414
Baijang (Chan master), 1308
Bai Juyi (poet), 7216
Baile Chuind, 1492
Baile in Scáil (Irish tale), 1483, 1492, 5529
Bailey, Alice, 844
and Arcane School, 6536
and New Age movement, 6495, 6496
in Theosophical Society, 6535
Bailey, Edward, 4401
Bailey, F. Lee, 6522
Bailey, Randall, 80
Baillie, Donald M., 6466, 6469
Baillie, John, 6466, 6469
Bailou (entrance), 7333
Bainbridge, William Sims, 6527
on churches, sects, and cults, 2084–2085
Bainton, Roland, on Servetus (Michael), 8231
Baird, Robert D., historiography of, 4049
Bais Ya'akov movement, Schenirer (Sarah) and, 8149
Baituloi (animated stones), in Greek religion, 8745
Bai Ülgen (deity), 9081
in Altaic shamanism, 8272
Baiwen pian (Daoist text), 2211
Baiyun guan (White Cloud Abbey), 9056
Baizhang, Master, 3139
Baizhang Huaihai, 1522, 1524, 1604
Baja California, cave art in, 1471
Bajiao (eight teachings), 9177
Bajjan (deity), sacrifices to, 8088
Bāj ritual, 9998
Bājūrī, Ibrāhīm al-, *kalām* of, 5059–5060, 5067
Bakabilo, 817, 818
Baka Pygmy religion (Central Africa), 7524
Bakchis oracles, 6834–6835
Baker, Augustine, 822
Baker, George, 6522
Baker, Samuel, on African religions, supreme beings of, 3576
Bakheng temple (Cambodia), tower of, 4012
Bakhtin, Mikhail M., **741–743**
on Carnival, 1440, 4202, 8242
and Finno-Ugric religions, studies of, 3114
on humor, 4218, 4219
on moral *vs.* grotesque, 3396
on the novel, 3058
Bakhtiyār-nāmah (Malay book), 4665
Bakhtyār, Muḥammad, 827
Baking, feminine sacrality and, 3019
Bakongo religion
history of study of, 113
spirit containers in, vol. 9 color insert
supreme being (Nzambi) in, 113, 3573
Bakrī, al-, 835
on African religions, 111
Bakufu (military government) school, Confucianism and, 1928
Bakunin, Mikhail, nihilism of, 2427

Bakwa Luntu (central Africa), 5522
Bakweri people (Cameroon), glossolalia of, 3506
Bal, Mieke, 5488
Bala. *See* Balarāma
Balaam (biblical figure), 2942
Balabhadra. *See* Balarāma
Baladeva. *See* Balarāma
Balag (drum), 2498
Balaji temple, exorcisms at, 2934
Balam (jaguar priest), throne of, 1469
Balams (deities), smoking by, 8455
Balance
in African protection rituals, 3820
conservation and, in indigenous traditions, 2618
Doctrine of the Mean on, 2634
in Āyurveda, 3855
in Islam, Qurʾān on, 2651
in Japanese religion, health and, 3867, 3868
Balanchine, George, 2161–2162
Balankanché, grotto of, 1469
Balar, Lugh's defeat of, 1494, 5528–5529
Balarāma (deity), **743**
birth of, 743
Viṣṇu paired with, 743
weapons of, 743
wife of, 743
Balbal (stone pillars), 4491
Balche (drink), 9338
Baldachin (dome), 794
Balderus (deity), 744
Baldick, Julian, 4465
Baldness, alloformic cure for, 4159
Baldr (deity), **743–745**
death of, 744, 1875, 3452, 3455–3456, 4461, 5509
in *Poetic Edda,* 2692
resurrection of, 744, 3456
Baldrian-Hussein, Farzeen, 239
Baldridge, William, 6424
Baldrs draumar (Eddic poetry), 744, 2693
Baldus, Herbert, on Eschetewuarha (mother of the universe), 8579
Baldwin, James, 3060
Baldwin, Lewis, 80
Balewa, Saddiq, 3098
Balfour, A. J. Earl, on knowledge, 5208
Balfour Declaration (1917), 3495, 5021
Bali (demon king), 2368, 7501
Bali (offering), 778
Balian (curers), 2451
Bali and Balinese religion, **745–749**
castes in, 746, 747, 748
complementary dualism in, 8649
cremation in, 748, 3239, 3240
dance drama in, **2450–2452**
funeral rites in, 3239, 3240, 9226
gambling in, 3260
healing waters in, 7862
Hindu-Buddhist kingdoms in, 745
indianization of, 745–746
libraries in, 746–747
living traditions of, 746–747
location of, 745
megalithic religion, 5828
Metal Age in, 745
Neo-Hinduism in, 8653
political ceremony in, 1513–1514, 1517
reincarnation in, 748
rites of passage in, 7796
rituals in, 747–748
sources of, 745–746
Tantric element in, 748
textiles in, 9088, 9089, 9090
trance in, 5804, 7048–7049
Bali Hindu, as name of official Balinese religion, 746
Bāl-i Jibrīl (Iqbāl), 4534
Balik Bayat (deity), 9081
Balinese Icaka calendar, 748
Balinese language, 745
Balinese religion. *See* Bali and Balinese religion
Balkans. *See also* Bogomils; *specific countries*
independence revolutions, 1685
Thracian religion in (*See* Thracian religion)
Balkhī. *See* Rūmī, Jalāl al-Dīn
"Ballad of Ancient Heroes, The," 600
"Ballad of the Abandoned Princess"(Korean *muga*), 5233
Ballad of True Thomas, The, 2953
Ballanche, Pierre-Simon, 340
Ballard, Donald, 4245–4247
Ballard, Edna, 4245–4247
on ascended masters, 1781–1782
Ballard, Guy, 2772, 4245–4246, 4247
on ascended masters, 1781–1782
Ballard, William L., 6672
Ballet
in Baroque and pre-Romantic periods, 2154–2155
biblical themes in, 2163
in Britain, 2162
classical, 2156
in Denmark, 2156
in France, 2154–2155
Jesuit-sponsored, 2136
opera and, 2154
on *pointe,* 2163
in Romantic period, 2155–2156
in Russia, 2156, 2161–2162
twentieth-century, 2161–2163
Ballet comique de la reine, le, 2154
Ballet d'action, 2155
Ballet of the Pope, The (Le Fevre), 2155
Ballets Russes, 2161–2162
Ballgames, **749–756**
gambling on, 3260
Mesoamerican, **749–752**
ballcourts for, 750–751
balls for, 750
in Classic period, 5904
cosmic time and, 7988
equipment for, 749–750
rules of, 751
sacrifice and, 8723
social, political, and religious significance of, 751
temporal and regional diversity of, 749
North American Indian, **752–756**
ball racing, 752–753
ball throwing, 752
racket games, 753–755
shinny, 752
and war, 754–755
Olmec, 6819
Ballou, Hosea, 9470
Ballowe, Camille, 2602
Ball racing, 752–753
Balls, masquerade, at Carnival, 1441, 1443
Ball throwing, 752
Balodis, Francis, on Baltic rites, 756
Baltais Aplis, 766
Bal tashchit ("do not destroy"), 2644
Balthasar, Hans Urs von
on beauty, 812–813, 7206
postmodern literature and, 5482
Rahner (Karl) criticized by, 7601
Balthi (deity), Adonis and, 34, 35
Balth'u (spiritual power), of Dime chief, 5170
Baltic cultures, significance of religion in, 2128
Baltic languages, 756, 768
words for "dead" in, 329
Baltic religion, **756–773**
ancestors in, cult of, **327–332**
burial in, 327, 328
in Canada, 765
Christianity in, and ancestor worship, 328, 329
dainas (folk songs) in, 2127–2128
death in, Laima and, 5286
deities of (*See also specific deities*)
prosperity and welfare, 760–761, 769
sky, 757–760
destiny in, Laima and, 5285–5286
doubleness in, 2423
fatalism in, 5286
fertility in, Laima and, 5285, 5286
hills in, 775
history of study of, **767–773**
ancestors in, 327–328
archaeological evidence used in, 756
folklore used in, 756–757, 768, 769–771
historical documents used in, 767–769
sources for, 327
during Soviet era, 771
lakes and rivers in, 774–775
marriage in, 5285–5286
moon in, 6173
new religious movements of, **762–767**
construction of Baltic paganism as, 762–763, 769–770
Dievturi as, 763–764, 765–766
Romuva as, 763, 764–765, 774
during Soviet and Nazi era, 764
Saule (sun) cult in, **8131–8135**
Slavic religion, influence on, 8432
trees in, 759, 768, 773, 774, 1502
twins in, **9419–9421**
in United States, 764, 765
Baltic sanctuaries, **773–776**
Catholic, 773, 775
pagan, 773–775
study of, 770
Baltimore, archbishop of
Carroll (John) and, 1445
Gibbons (James) as, 3478–3479
Baltimore, Lord (George Calvert), **1373–1374**
Baltrusaitis, Jurgis, 5277
Baltų religijos ir mitologijos šaltiniai (Vėlius), 771
Balún Canan (Castellanos), 9930–9931
Baly, Denis, 2302
Balys, Jonas, 328, 330, 771
on Latvian folk songs, 8134
Balzac, Honoré de
androgyne of, 340–341
sins depicted by, 3059
Bamah (high place), 932, 934
Bamana. *See* Bambara religion
Bamba, Aḥmad/Ahmadu/Amadou, 107
pilgrimage to Touba and, 1808–1809, 4609
as prophet, 7443
Bamba, Amadou (saint), vol. 7 color insert

Bambara, in Umarian *jihād,* 9445
Bambara religion (Mali), **776–778**
ancestor worship in, 776–777
art in, 90
creation in, 776
Dasiri cult in, 777
flood in, 3130
history of study of, 116
iconography in, 4303
initiatory societies and spiritual life in, 777
Islam and, 4603
masquerade dances of, 2141
mirrors in, 6064
myths of, 98
soul in, 8533
supreme being in, 776
weaving in, 938
witchcraft in, women's role in, 2100
Bamberger, Seligmann Ber, 6900
Bamboo, 808
Bambuti Pygmäen vom Ituri, Die (Schebesta), 114
Bamidele, Abdul Salami, 107
Bamidele movement, 107
Bamileke religion (Cameroon)
funeral rites in, 3235
skull in family altars in, 3806
Bán, Aladár, 3112
Bana (musical instrument), 4434
Bāṇaliṅga (stone), 4326
Banaras (India), **778–779**
as city of Śiva, 778–779, 7170
as maṇḍala, 779
as city of light, 5454
death in, 779
Ganges and, 3987
heavenly prototype of, 7983
in Purāṇas, 778
pilgrimage to, 778, 779, 3274, 7169
Banbha (deity), 1488, 1490
Bancroft, H. H., 3628
Baṇḍāra cult, in Sinhala religion, 8410–8412
Banda religion, myths of, 93
Bandelier, Adolph, 5291, 5292
"Bande Mātaram," 830
Bandhas (postures), 1044
Bandis. *See* Bandua
Bandjalang people, Pentecostalism of, 671
Bandltanze (dance), 5277
Bandua (deity), 4253
Banerjee, Sumanta, 829
Bañez, Domingo, on predestination, 3204
Bangalore (India), Karaga festival and sacred space in, 1807
Bangalore Consultation (1967), study of religion in Indian universities and, 8789–8790
Bangarra Dance Theatre, 639, 642, 651
Bang Klang Hao (king of Sukhōthai), 1136
Bangkok (Thailand)
Buddhism in, 5130, 5131
Judaism in, 5010
Bangladesh and Bangladeshi religions
Buddhism, 824
Christianity, 828, 1730
creation of, 830, 4654
films from, 3097
Hinduism, caste in, 825
immigrants from, 4675
Islam, as state religion, 830, 4654
religious studies in, 8791
Banishment, 2938–2939. *See also* Utksepaniya-karma
in Anabaptism (*See* Shunning)
Banisteriopsis caapi (hallucinogen), 7470
Baniwa religion (Amazon). *See also* Arawak Indians
disease, myth of origin of, 3809
overview of, 8624–8625
tricksters of, 9358
Banka (funerary poem), 7215
Bankei Yōtaku (Buddhist monk), 9949
Bankimcandra Chatterjee, 827, 829
Banks Islands religion, supreme being in, 8871
Banners, 9092, 9403
Banno, 32, 3717
Banpo Neolithic cemetery (China), 169
Banqueting, in Minoan religion, 39
Banshee, 2952
Bantu languages, in East Africa, 2566
Bantu religions (Africa). *See also* Shona religion; Southern African religions; Swazi religion
Central Bantu, **1505–1512**
Christianity, prevalence of, 1717
circumcision in, 1799
cosmogonies of, 2960
python in, 8663
cults of affliction in, 60, 62, 84
father gods of, 2984
funeral rites in, 3235
history of study of, 113, 116
illness in, 3817
interlacustrine, **4518–4521**
Islam, 4607
kingship in, 5157
myths of
binary oppositions in, 97
creation, 85–86, 92
trickster, 94
northeast Bantu, **2574–2579**
southern Bantu, **8662–8668**
circumcision in, 8665–8668
cosmology and sacred kingship in, 8664–8665
python cult in, 8663–8664
thermodynamic conception in, 8662–8663
supreme being (Mulungu) in, 3572–3573
truth in, 9370
Bantu-speaking societies, 4518
Banū Maʿrūf. See Druze
Banyan tree, 9336
Banzarov, Dorzi, 6142
Banzhou sanmei ritual, 4923
Baojuan (morality books), 2187–2188
Maitreya in, 5620
Baopuzi (Ge Hong), 2181, 3290, 3291, 5319
miracles in, 6052
Baotang school of Buddhism (Korea), 1172
BAPS movement. *See* Bochasanwasi Shri Akshar Purushottam Swaminarayan
Baptai (baptized ones), 780
Baptandier, Brigitte, 3340
Baptism, **779–783**
as ablution, 10
in Afro-Caribbean religion, 1437
androcentrism in, 335
in architecture, 466
by blood
in Cybele cult, 780
in Roman bull sacrifice, 2110
in cargo cults, 1418
Christian, 781–782
of adults, 782, 783, 7455, 9810
in Anabaptism, 304, 782, 783, 7660
in Anglicanism, 350
of Anomoeans, 782
Arians on, 782
in Armenian church, 489
believer's baptism, 7962
catecheses before and after, Cyril of Jerusalem and, 2118
Catholic, 782
of children, 782
of Christ, 1743–1744
Christ-*kerygma* as baptismal confession, 2056
confession with, 1888
confirmation and, 7956
conversion and, 7758
Dionysius on, 2356
Donatist rebaptism, 782
in early church, 781–782, 7959
at Easter, 2579–2580, 9815
Eastern Orthodox, 7960
and enlightenment, 782
at Epiphany, 2818
exorcism at, 2929
grace and, 3645
of heretics, 2113
in Holy Spirit (*See* Spirit Baptism)
of infants, 782, 7455, 7956, 9810
infant *vs.* adult, 1669–1670
as initiation, 9809–9810
Irenaeus on, 4540
in Jehovah's Witnesses, 4823
of Jesus, 4848
Jewish roots of, 7958–7959
by John the Baptist, 780, 781
John the Baptist and, 4942–4943
Justin Martyr on, 782, 5045
in Latin America, 1696
Lent and, 9815
in Lumpa church, 5409
Lutheran, 5538
membership in the church and, 1777, 1778
methods of, 7962
naming in, 6406
in New Testament, 1669
nudity in, 781, 782, 6740
ordo of, 2468
Orthodox, 2591, 2592
at Paschal vigil, 1742
Pelagius on, 7025
Protestant, 7455, 7962
as purification, 7507
as rejuvenation, 781
repentance and, 7758
ritual of, 781–782
Servetus (Michael) on, 8232
significance of, 781
Simons (Menno) on, 8401
soteriology and, 8527
symbolism of, 781
Thomas Aquinas on, 9163
transferability of, 7963
virginity in, 9607
cognates of, in comparative studies, 7955–7956
Cyril of Jerusalem on, 2118
of dead, 779–780
of drums, 7037
in Egypt, 779, 780
in Gnosticism, 780, 3515
in Greek religion, 780
group, in United House of Prayer, 2125
in Holy Order of MANS, 4102
and immortality, 780
in Judaism, 780–781
in Mandaean religion, 780, 781, 5636
origin of word, 779
Raëlian, 7597, 7598
rebaptism, Cyprian on, 2113
as rebirth, 953
spiritual, in Catharism, 1457
syncretism and, 8931
in Tarascan religion, 9001
water in, 7862
Baptismal regeneration, Spurgeon (Charles Haddon) on, 8727
Baptist Bible Fellowship, 2891

Baptist denominations (churches), **783–786**
in Africa, 1722
African American, 68, 69, 784, 1709
Liele (George) and, 5443
in Australia and New Zealand, 1733
baptism in, 9810
believers', 1669–1670
Black Baptists of Jamaica (Myalists), 1437
Calvinism and, 783, 784
in Canada, Black churches, 1709
in Caribbean, creolization and, 2067
Cherokee, 1565
congregational polity of, 1768
conventions in, 1768
in England, 783–784, 785
Spurgeon (Charles Haddon), role of, 8727
features of, 785–786
on free will and predestination, 3208
in Germany, 785
in Latin America, 6579
missions
to American slaves, 1709
in Burma, 1728
in West Indies, 1706, 1707
origin of name, 783
origins of, 783–784
in Russia, 785
sectarianism in, 1713
on separation of church and state, 1968
Shouters (Spiritual Baptists), 1435
in United States, 783, 784–785
development and growth, 1712
Baptistic (Finished Work) Pentecostalism, 7029, 7033
Baptist Missionary Society, in Jamaica, 1706
Baptist Union, Spurgeon (Charles Haddon) and, 8727
Baptist World Alliance, 785
Baqā' (remaining), 4259, 4569, 5030
in mystical union, 6338
Bāqillānī, Abū Bakr al-, 4371, 4399, 4585
on attributes of God, 619–620
in Ash'arīyah, 534, 537
on *tamhīd,* 619, 5064–5066
writings of, 534
Bāqir, Muḥammad al-
imamate and, 8321
in Shī'ism, 4760
Baqlī, Rūzbihān, on mystical union, 6338
Baqshi (Buddhist monks), 1149
Baraca (blessing), 983
Baradai, Jacob, on Monophysitism, 6154, 6155
Baraita de-Niddah (Jewish legal literature), 7515
Baraitot
Abbaye on, 3
Rabbah bar Nahmani on, 7577
Barakah (benign force or blessing)
as charisma, 1546
of dead saints, 3835, 8035
of Egyptian spiritist healers, 3836
and healing, 4609
vs. mana, 7348, 8947
of *awliyā,* 8821
of Nāṣir al-Dīn, 4604
Barama (deity), 2597
Baranī, al- (historian), on Indian Muslims, 4643
Barasana religion (South America)
house as center of the world, 1503
Milky Way in, 2863
ritual and myth in, 8591
Barashnūm ī nō shab (purification ritual), 9997–9998
Barat, Madeleine Sophie, 6764
Barazofsky, Shalom Noah, 9382
Barbara (saint), Shango identified with in Santeria, 1434
Barbara branch, 2400
Barbarhārī, al-, Ḥanābilah and, 3764
Barbarianos sect, 5764
Barbarians
Christianity among, 1682, 1683
invasions (fifth century), 7876
migration and, 6025
Roman Empire, attacks on, 1682
Barbaro, G., on Mordvin religion, 5709
Barbary apes, 6151
Barbé, Dominique, on kingdom of God, 5153
Barbēlō (deity), 3517
Barbelo Gnostics, sexual rites of, 8247
"Barber paradox," 6988
Barbin, Herculine, 339
Barbo, Luigi, 822
Barbour, Ian, 2658
on evolution *vs.* creationism, 2907
and field of science and religion, 8184
Barbour, John D., 699
Barcelona (Spain), Judaism in, 36
Barclay, Robert, 3181
Quaker writings of, 7547
Bardaisan, **786–787**
Mani influenced by, 5648, 5665
Bardesanes. *See* Bardaisan
Bardesanites, 786–787
Bar do'i sems can (intermediate stage), ecstatic discipline and, 8703
Bar do thos grol. See Book of the Dead (Tibet)
Bards
Celtic, 1479, 1497
Gesar epic transmitted by, 3464
Bardtke, Hans, 898
Bardunjarijanu rituals, 5706
Bareau, André, 1063, 1312
Pāṭaliputra council, 2036
Barēlī, Aḥmad, 4650, 4651
Barelwī school (Islam), 4645, 4653
Bareshnūm (Great Purification), 4535
Bare Willows and Distant Mountains (Ma Yuan), vol. 11 color insert
Bargen, Doris, on spirit possession, 8696
Barghawāṭah religion (Morocco), 835
Bārhaspatya sūtras, 1446
Bariba religion (Benin), healing in, 3818
midwives, 3819
Bar-Ilan, Me'ir, **787–788**
Bar-Ilan University, 788
Baringin tree, 799
Barjatya, Sooraj R., 3098
Barker, Eileen, 6521, 6522, 6523, 6524, 6527
Bark of tree, 9336
paintings on, in Australian Indigenous religions, vol. 1 color insert
Bar Kokhba
'Aqiva' ben Yosef on, 442
charismatic leadership of, 1545
rebellion led by, 6647
Bar Kokhba Revolt
'Aqiva' ben Yosef in, 441, 442
and messianism, 5974–5975
Mishnah and, 6067
persecution after, 7055
social control of martyrs and, 5742
Barkow, Jerome, on complex psychology, 8475
Barkun, Michael, 413
Barlaam and Joasaph (John of Damascus), 4941
Barlaam of Calabria, **788–789,** 2587
Gregory Palamas and, 3698
Barlach, Ernst, 2475
Barlas, Asma, Qur'anic exegesis of, 7568
Barlow, Connie, 2666
Barmakids, and Mu'tazilah, 6319
Barmen Declaration (1934), 791, 2685
purpose of, 2061
Bar mitzvah, 4482, 7818, 7820–7821
Hebrew School and, 1962
in Reform Judaism, 7672
Barnabas, Epistle of, 873, 920
Barnabas, Gospel of, 7243
Barnard, Alan, on diffusion theory, 8169
Barnard College
Gaster (Theodor H.) at, 3288
Mead (Margaret) at, 5803
Barnenez (Brittany), megalithic religion in, 5823
Barnes, Albert, on denominationalism, 2286
Barnes, E. W., 6105
Barnett, Homer, 6671
Barnmarn (healer and composer), 9461
Barok people (New Ireland)
afterlife of, 147
totemism of, 9252
Baron, Salo, 7056
Baronius, Cesare, 7136
on Copernican revolution, 8183
on evidence analysis, 4039
Galileo Galilei on, 3257
Baroque period
aesthetics of, the supernatural and, 8861
architecture in
church, 794–795
monastery, 6120
dance in, 2154–2155
iconography in, 4346, 4347
music in, 6311–6312
Barr, James, 6378
Barrakib (king), 447
Barratt, Thomas Ball, 7029
Barreiros, António, 4505
Barrel drums, 2497
"Barren," 7078, 7080
Barreto, Paulo. *See* João do Rio
Barrett, Anthony, 4558
Barrett, David, on African independent churches, 8152
Barrett, David B., 6085, 7033, 7447
Barrett, John, 6484
Barrett, Leonard, on Rastafari, 7623
Barrett, William, on Suzuki (D. T.), 8887
Barrios (quasi-socioreligious units), 9215
Barrios, Justo Rufino, 5928
Barrow, Isaac, 6588
Barry, Herbert, on rites of passage, 7798
Bar Sauma (bishop), 6480
Barth, Frederick, on ritual symbolism, 7839
Barth, Jakob, 869
Barth, Karl, **789–792**
atheism and, 584
on atonement, 597
and Barmen Declaration, 791, 2061

Barth, Karl ***continued***
biblical exegesis of, 875, 5486–5487
Bonhoeffer influenced by, 1016
Bultmann (Rudolf) and, 791, 1322
Christian Socialism and, 790
damnation, rejection of, 3885
Epistle to the Romans, 6466, 6467
fighting Nazism, 789, 791
Gnosticism and, 3527
on God, 790–791, 3558, 9283
and Gogarten, split with, 6468
on Heidegger, 3896
on historiography, 4034
Kierkegaard's influence on, 5142
on kingdom of God, 5151
Kirchliche Dogmatik, 6468–6469
on knowledge, 5208–5209
against liberalism, 6104, 6107
Maurice (Frederick Denison) compared to, 5784
and neoorthodoxy, 6466, 6468
and philosophy and religion, 7117–7118
philosophy of, 789–790
on predestination, 3204, 3208
on resurrection of Jesus, 790
on revelation, 7118, 7774
on Ritschl (Albrecht), 7832
on salvation, 790
on Sohm (Rudolf) and Brunner (Emil), 8508
studies of, 789–790
theology of, 9130, 9137, 9138
on Trinity, 791
writings of, 789, 790, 791
Barthes, Roland, 3028, 5488
semiotics of, 8751
Bartholomeusz, Tessa, 7264
Bartholomew (Greek Orthodox patriarch)
in Armenia, 487
ecological leadership of, 2649–2650
on environmental degradation, 2613
Bartholomew the Englishman, on nature, 6433
Barton, Benjamin, 6670
Barton, George A., on Satan, 8123
Barton cylinder, 6624–6625
Baru (priest), 7336
Baruch, 4079
1 Baruch, 899
2 Baruch, 418, 902
3 Baruch, 418, 902
Baruch (biblical figure), 4827, 4830
Baruch, Apocalypse of, 7765
Baruffald, Libushka, Smart (Ninian) and, 8442
Barwick, Diane, 3391
Barwick, Linda, 3390
Bar-Yosef, Ofer, on masks, 5767
Barzabīnī, Ya'qūb al-, Ḥanābilah and, 3766
Barzakh (state between life and death), 7767
in Qur'ān, 2838
Barzanjī, al-, on *mi'rāj,* 6061
Basanavičius, Jonas, 328
Basava (Hindu reformer), 4424, 7210
Basavaṇṇa. *See* Basava
Basaveśwara. *See* Basava
Bascom, William R.
on Ifa divination, 10032
on oral tradition, 10028
on Yoruba religion, 75
Ifa divination in, 117
Baseball, 8725–8726
Base communities
in liberation theology, 1775–1776, 5439
political activism of, 6580
Basedow, Ludwig von, 6234
Basel, council at (1430–1439), reunion with Greek church attempted at, 2043
Bases of the Social Concept of the Russian Orthodox Church, The, 7944–7945
Basham, A. L., 7261
Bashir, Omar Hassan al-, 3365–3366
Bashō (poet), 9949
autobiographical writings of, 702
haiku of, 8702
poetry of, 7207, 7217
Bashyatchi, Elijah, writings of, 5085, 5086
Bashyatchi, Moses, writings of, 5085
Basil
on pain, 6946
Trinity and, 2582
Basil I (Byzantine emperor), 7135
Basilica, **792–797**
architecture of
classification of, 461, 467
development of, 9265
nature of, 792–793
origin of word, 792
Roman, 792–793
synagogues, basilica-type, 8923
Basilides (Christian scholar)
apocatastasis and, 421–422
apophatism of, 7190
on ascension, 521
on cosmic seeds, 7190
Gnosticism of, 3511, 3512, 3518
Basilio di San Francesco, 5637
Basiliscus (Roman emperor), 6153–6154, 9205
Basil of Caesarea, **797–799**
Apollinaris of Laodicea and, 423
asceticism of, 797
on Athanasius, 572
baptism of, 797
as bishop of Caesarea, 797
charitable works under, 6117
charity taught by, 2582
on eremitism, 2825
on evil, 8406
on God, 3554
Gregory of Nazianzus and, 3695
Gregory of Nyssa and, 3696
on Holy Spirit, 3554
on images, 4290
life of, 797
liturgy of, 2592
in Armenian church, 489
monasticism and, 7723
Neoplatonic traditions and, 6475
pilgrimage of, 7153
rule of, 798
on salvation, 798
Theodore of Studios following rules of, 9122
on Trinity, 798, 4241
writings of, 798
Basil the Great. *See* Basil of Caesarea
Basin of Mexico
in Formative (Preclassic) period, 5895–5896
in Postclassic period, 5907
Basket weaving
in Warao religion, 9575
in Yurupary cult, 9919
Baskin, Judith, 6021
Basmalah (Islamic phrase)
calligraphy and, 1369
in Qur'ān, 3561
uses for, 3561
BASR. *See* British Association for the Study of Religion
Basra (Iraq)
Khārijīs in, 5126, 5127
Mu'tazilah in, 6317–6318
school of law in, 5547
Bas reliefs, in Southeast Asia, of Hindu mythology, 4013
Baṣrī, Ḥasan al-. *See* Ḥasan al-Baṣrī
Basso, Keith, 2611
Bast (deity), as cat, 1462
Bastardization rituals, 7809
Bastein, Joseph, 3021
Bastian, Adolf, on masks, 5765
Bastide, Roger
on Afro-Brazilian religions, 76, 121
on Afro-Caribbean religions, 10025
on ritual regicide, 5159
structuralism and, 8748
on syncretic cults, 75
Bastien, Joseph W., 3418
Bastos, Augusto Roa, 3063
Bat (mythic figure), 663
Batá (drum), 7037
Bataille, Georges, 5483, 6740, 7854
on sexuality, 8242, 8252
Batak religion (Indonesia), **799–800**
Christianity in, 1729
creation in, 799
fertility in, 799
kinship system and, 799
marriage in, 799
rituals of, 799–800
soul in, 799
textiles in, 9089
ragidup, 1828
yearly cycle of rice cultivation and, 799
Baṭalyawsī, Ibn al-Sīd al-, on *mi'rāj,* 6061
Batara Guru (Bugis mythical figure), 1317
Batel Ok'ot (war dance), 2466
Bates, Daisy, 687–688, 3390
Bates, Joseph, 1036
Bateson, Bernard, 5488
Bateson, Gregory, 385, 6801
on gender in Pacific, 6508
Mead (Margaret) and, 5804
on oral tradition, 6845
on play, 3265, 7194
Bateson, Mary Catherine, 4964
Bath, shrine of, 1484
Bathhouse spirit, in Komi religion, 5218
Bathonga people (Fiji Islands), ablutions of, 10, 11
Baths, **800–803**. *See also* Sauna; Sweat bath/lodge
Celtic, 801
Hindu, 2403–2404, 7815
during pilgrimage, 7168–7169
Indus Valley, 4472
Japanese, 801
Jewish, 2398, 7928
miqveh, **6046–6048**
Native American, 801, 7300
Oceanic, 7807
in purification, 7507, 7511
Roman, 801
Turkish, 801
Bathsheba
ballet based on story of, 2163
Nathan and, 6417
Bāṭil marriage (void marriage), 4706
Bāṭin (esoteric), as aspect of religion, Qarmaṭī on, 7543
Bat mitzvah, 7820–7821
Hebrew School and, 1962
Kaplan (Mordecai) and, 7636
in Reform Judaism, 7672
Battista, Cícero Romão, 6577
Battle. *See* War and warriors; *specific battles by location*
Battle-Axe culture, 1479
Battle Creek Sanitarium, Seventh-day Adventism and, 8236, 8237
Battle Drama (Mesopotamia), 5961
Batu (grandson of Chinggis Khan), 4493
Batuque, distribution of, 120
Bau (deity)
cosmic tree and, 3449
sacred tree and, 1502
Baubo (Greek mythical figure), **803–804**
Bauckham, Richard, 360
Baudelaire, Charles
and spiritualizing of art, 499

symbolism and, 8909–8910
Baudet, Henri, 9294
Bauer, Bruno, **804**
on Jewish people, 5745
Marx (Karl) and, 5745
Bauer, Christian, on orthodoxy, 3928
Bauer, Walter, on heresy and orthodoxy, 3921, 3922, 3928
Baule religion
carved figures in, 90
iconography of, 4303
Baum, L. Frank, 7323
Baum, Robert, 118
on subjectivity in prophets, 8695
Bauman, Richard, 3145, 3146
Baumann, Hermann, 115
on egg symbolism, 1987
on primordial paradise, 6983
Baumgarten, Albert I., 7131
Baumgarten, Alexander Gottlieb, 46, 7110
Bäumler, Alfred, 732
Baur, F. C., **805,** 875
on Gnosticism, 3514, 3532
Möhler (Johann Adam) and, 6114
Ritschl (Albrecht) and, 6104
Bauro (culture hero), source of illness and, 3809
Bausani, Alessandro, 863
historiography of, 4050
Bawon Samidi (first male buried in cemetery), 9637
Baxter, Richard
devotional writings of, 7521
on kingdom of God, 5152
on Puritan morality, 7520
on "two books," 9423
Bayʿah (acclamation), caliph selection, 1365
Bayān (the Bāb), 728, 729
Bayān iʿjāz al-Qurʾān (al-Khaṭṭābī), 4371
Bayan Khangay, 6826
Bāyazīd al-Bisṭāmī. *See* Bisṭāmī, Abū Yazīd al-
Bāyazīd Anṣārī, 4649, 7223
Bāyazīdian school, 956
Bayḍāwī, al-, **805–806**
tafsīr of, 8953
writings of, 806, 4662
Bayhaqī, al-, 4662
Ba yin (eight sounds), 2499
Bayle, Pierre, 2505, 7283
the Enlightenment influenced by, 2795
on relativism, 7685
on skepticism, 8421
Bayley, James R., 3478
Bayon temple, 5129
Bayt al-māl (public treasury), 4709
Bazaar of Heracleides (Nestorius), 6483
Ba Zha festival, as hospitality, 4140–4141
Bazin, André, 3097, 3101
Bazin-Foucher, Eugéne, 3176
BC (before Christ), origin of concept, 173
BCE (before common era), origin of concept, 173
Bcud len (extraction of essences), 1288
Bdud 'joms Rin po che 'Jigs bral ye shes rdo rje, 7869
BE. *See Bēluml baʿ alum* (lord)
Beads, glass, as money, 6137
Beagle (ship), 2908
Beaker culture, 1479
Beal, Samuel, 1314
Bear, Feast of the, in Southern Siberian religions, 8670, 8671
Bear, The (Faulkner), 5480
Beard, Mary
on Roman gender roles, 3381
on Vestal Virgins, 3385
Bear people (North America), 807
Bears, **806–810**
in Ainu religion, 205, 206, 2237, 5514, 10065
in Arctic religions
ceremonies for, 471, 474, 9394
myths of, 472
in Chinese medicine, 807
in Dolgan religion, 2395
in European religions, 5514
in Finno-Ugric religions, 3107
in Gaulish religion, 5514
in Greek religion, Artemis cult of, 507, 5514
in Khanty and Mansi religion, 807, 5120–5121, 5125
in Komi religion, 5217, 5218
in Korean religion, 5229
in North American Indian religions, 806, 807–809, 4309
Arctic influence and, 6653
Koyukon, 6676
medicine men and, 6652
Menomini, 6680
ritual around slaying of, 6652, 6653
in Paleolithic religion, 6952–6953
religious significance of
common themes of, 809
habitat diversity and, 808–809
species diversity and, 807–808
in Roman religion, 5514
in Sami religion, 8087
in Samoyed religion, 8096
in Scandinavian religions, 3246
in shamanism, 808, 809
in South American Indian religions, 808
in Southern Siberian religions, 8670
as symbol of rebirth, 807, 809
in Tunguz religion, 9394–9395
Beasts, in Maya religion, 5798
Beatifications, Egyptian, 2718, 2723
Beat poets, Zen Buddhism and, 9950
Béatrice, Dona, 1511, 5221
Beatrice, in Dante's *Commedia,* 524, 2170
Beatson, Peter, 3081
Beattie, J. H. M., on sacrifice, 7845
Beattie, Tina, 812
on Mary, 5756
on non-Western gender studies, 3315
Beatty, Chester, 5662
Beaumont, Winifred, 832
Beautiful writing, definition of, 1369
Beauty, **810–814**. *See also* Aesthetics
artistic, 7206
contemporary, 812–813
cultivation of, 810, 812
deities and spirits of, in Haitian Vodou, 1433
female, 810, 811, 812–813
and love, 810, 811, 812, 813
male, 811, 812–813
perfect form of, 810
Plato on, 7775
race and, 812
and sublime, 811
theology of, 812–813
writing about, 810–811
Beauvoir, Simone de, 4484
Bebali (sacred cloth), 9089
Beccaria, Cesare, on retribution, 5373
Beccus, John, deposed, 2042
Becher, Hans, on South American supreme beings, 8577
Bechert, Heinz, 1061, 1312, 7263
Beck, Charlotte Joko, 6536
Becker, Carl Heinrich, 4716
Becker, Judith, 6255
Becker, Peter, 7143
Becket, Thomas
in Anselm's canonization, 373
shrine of, revenue from, 7689
Beckett, Jeremy, 668
Beckett, Samuel, 2475, 7111
on women and death, 4165
Beckford, James, 6521, 6526
Beckmann, Max, 4348
Beckwith, Martha, 10025
Becoming, in Chinese tradition, *dahua,* 8554
"Becoming a Sangoma" (Binsbergen), 118
Bede, the Venerable, **814,** 821, 6942–6943
Bédier, Joseph, 7218
Bednarowski, Mary Farrell, 6516
Bedouin religion (Middle East)
bride-price in, 7780
healing in, 3832–3833
hospitality in, 4139, 4140
and Islam, 4561
vengeance in, 7781
Bedu spirits, masks of, 2141
Beecher, Lyman, 2532
Beef, taboo on, 3167
Beelshamen (deity), 448, 449
Beelzebub's Tales to His Grandson (Gurdjieff), 3711
Beelzebul (Baʿal Zebub), 3158
Beer
in Baltic religion, 757
in Bambari religion, 776–777
in Chaco religion, 9575
in Indo-European religions, 4455
in northeast Bantu religious rites, 2575, 2576
in Viking religions, 5434
Beeri Chettiar merchants, Komata Chettiars, competition with, 1806–1807
Beersheba (Israel), tradition as cult place, 13
Bees, 4508, 7377
Beethoven, Ludwig van, 6312
Beetles, in Lengua religion (Gran Chaco), 8634
Begay, Meredith, 404, 405–406
Begay, Victor, vol. 3 color insert
Beggars. *See also* Almsgiving
Baltic ancestors' food given to, 331
in Greek religion, avenging spirits of, 2100–2101
mendicant, 5855–5856
Saṃnyāsin as, 8093
Beginnings. *See* Anthropogony; Cosmogony; Cosmology; Creation
Begochiddy (creator figure), in Navajo religion, 6659
"Beg pardon" dance, in Big Drum Dance, 1436
Beguines movement, 3359, 6763
Behaviorism, 2867
on psychology of religion, 7477, 7478–7479
Behe, Michael, 2911, 4517
Beheading. *See* Decapitation; Head(s)
Behemoth, in Canaanite religion, 1392
BEIC. *See* British East India Company
Beidelman, T. O., 9352
on kingship in Africa, 5169–5170
Beijing (China), archbishop of, 6083
Being. *See also* Existence; Ontology
in Buddhism (See also Śūnyam and *śūnyatā*)

Being ***continued***
in Chinese tradition, continuity of being in, 8554–8555
God and, Thomas Aquinas on, 3555
Greek notion of divine as, Heschel (Abraham Joshua), opposition of, 3962
Heidegger (Martin) on, 3896, 3934
interactive awareness and, 8702
orgy and, 6861–6862
ultimate, soteriology and, 8526
unity of (*See Waḥdat al-wujūd*)
Being and Nothingness (Sartre), atheistic existentialism in, 8116
Being and Time (Heidegger), 50
Dasein in, 3896
fall in, 8402
hermeneutics in, 3933–3934
Beishung (Book of Odes), 808
Beit, Hedwig von, 1051
Beit din/batei din (courts), Sanhedrin and, 8102
Beit-Hallahmi, Benjamin, 7475
Beit Hillel, **815–816**
Beit Midrash Gevohah (New Jersey), 5239
Beit Shammai, **815–816**
Beit Yaʿakov schools, 195
Beit Yisraʾel. See Jewish people
Beit Yosef (Karo), 4751, 5104
Beivie (sun), in Sami religion, 8088
Beiya (Chinese text), 7023
Béjart, Maurice, 2163, 2164
Béji (deity), in Caribbean religions, 1434
Bek (mythic figure), 657, 658
Bekoff, Marc, 361
Bektāsh, Ḥajjī, Bektāshīyah and, 8823
Bektashī Sufism
calendar of, 4714
characteristics of, 8823
establishment of, 9009
in Europe, 4681
al-Ḥallāj and, 3758
samāʿ khānahs (music halls) in, 8065
"Whirling Dervishes" and, 8823
Bel (deity). *See also* Marduk
in Akitu festival, 222, 223
in Aramean religion, 449
Bel (tree), 9339
Bel and the Dragon, 898, 899
Belau (Micronesia), myths of, 6011
Belavin, Tikhon, election of, as patriarch of Moscow, 2588
Belbog (deity), in Slavic religion, 8434
Belenus (deity), 1483, 1484
Belgic Confession (1561), on free will and predestination, 3208
Belgium
Islam in, 4675, 4676, 4678, 4680
new religious movements in, discrimination against, 6518, 6526, 6541, 6570
Beliar, 394
Belief. *See also* Doubt; Faith; Knowledge
of artists, 54–55, 498
biological roots of, 2869
culture and, 2089
doubt as component of, 2424–2425, 2427, 2428
vs. faith, 2425–2427
and knowledge, 2427, 5199
in orthopraxy, 6916
statements of, analysis of, 307
Believers
artist as, 54–55, 498
definition of, 54
priesthood of all, in ecumenism, 2689
Belize, Black Carib ancestral cult in, 1436
Bell, Betty Louise, 3093
Bell, Catherine, 386, 1513, 1514–1516
on ritual, 7852–7853, 7857, 7859
Bell, Charles, 9189
Bell, Clive, 7206
Bell, Diane, 644–645, 650, 664, 2481
on Australian Indigenous women, 682, 686–687, 690, 3390, 3391, 3392, 3393
on Walpiri women as healers, 3874
Bellah, Robert, 379
on civil religion, 7327
ceremony and, 1516–1517
as good or bad, 1815
on Kennedy (John F.) and, 1813
obligation under, 8498
as systematic and organic, 8468
on cultural analysis of religion, 8470, 8471
Durkheim (Émile) compared to, 8498
evolutionary classification of religions, 1821, 6181
on Japanese religious ethics, 8778
on modernism, 7264
on modernization and religion, 8489
on reflexivity, 7649
on ritual, 7845–7846, 7855
and study of new religions, 6522
on symbolic realism, 8496, 8498
on Tokugawa religion, 8489
on truth of religion, 8498–8499
Bellamy, Joseph, Edwards' (Jonathan) influence on, 2700
Bellarmino, Roberto, **816**
canonization of, 816
Galileo Galilei warned by, 3257
on membership in the church, 1777
at Roman College, 816
writings of, 816
Bellaton, Dominique, 9068
Bell Curve, The (Herrnstein and Murray), 2882
Bello, Muhammadu, 3229
Belloc, Hilaire, on European Christianity, 1687
Bellow, Saul, 2758
Bellows, Henry Whitney, 9470
Bells, 7036, 7037
in Mesoamerican music, 6268–6269
in Middle Eastern music, 6276
Bellum iustum (just war), 9596
Bellwood, Peter, 5827
Belly of the Whale motif, Campbell (Joseph) on, 1379
Belobog (deity), in Slavic religion, 8434
Beloved, The (Horton), 2159
Belsham, Thomas, 1530
Beltene (Beltane) (festival), 7829, 7830
Amhairghin at, 1488
in Celtic calendar, 1491, 3758
Beltrame, Giovanni, 113
Beltrán, Aguirre, 5942
Bēluml baʿ alum (lord), 2125–2126
Belun (deity), in Slavic religion, 8434–8435
Beman, Amos, 68
Bemba (deity), 776, 4486
Bemba people (Zambia)
chief of, 817–818
matrilineal clan structure of, 817
origins of, 816–817
Bemba religion (Zambia), **816–818**. *See also* Central Bantu religions; Southern African religions
ancestors in, 817
childbirth in, 817
female initiation ceremony in, 818, 8659
funeral rites in, 817–818
Lesa in, 817
Lumbo church movement, 5408
Bembe (deity), in Pygmy religions, 7523
Be-midbar. See Numbers
Ben'a. *See* Benchō
Benade, William H., General Church of the New Jerusalem and, 8904–8905
Benade, William Henry, 6246
Ben-Ali diary (Muslim manuscript), 4683
Benandanti cult, Ginzburg (Carlo) on, 8250
Benares Hindu University, 845
Bencao jing jizhu (Tao), 8996
Benchō (Buddhist monk), **818–819,** 4938
Bender, Harold S., 5861
Bender, Wilhelm, Anesaki Masaharu influenced by, 342
Bendideia (ceremony), 819
Bendigeidvran (or Bran the Blessed, deity), 3123
head of, 3807
in family of Llŷr, 1489
Bendis (deity), **819,** 9170
Benedict XII (pope), 788
and Benedictines, 821–822
on souls and judgment, 8565
Benedict XIII (pope), 6971
Benedict XIV (pope)
on Chinese converts to Christianity, 7793
on Jesuits, 6973
on Virgin of Guadalupe, 5922
Benedict XV (pope)
impartiality of, during World War I, 6974
Maximum Illus encyclical of, 8169
Benedict, Ruth, **819–821,** 2264
vs. Malinowski, 5629
revaluation of, 380
and study of North American Indian religions, 6671
on vision quest, 9609
Benedict XI (pope), and Duns Scotus (John), 2524
Benedictine Abbey of Saint John (Minnesota), 6120
Benedictine College of Sant'Anselmo, 822
Benedictines, **821–822**. *See also specific figures*
19th-century revival of, 6134
architecture of monasteries, 6117–6119
Benedict XII and, 821–822
Clamor and Humiliation of the Saints rituals, 2105
Cluniac monasticism in restoration of, 6132
decline of, 821, 822
discipline of, 2309
foundation of, 821
gardens of, 3278
Gregory I and, 821, 3687
Leo XIII and, 822
Louis I and, 821
monasticism of, 7724
new edition of Vulgate Bible by, 893
reform of, 821–822
Thomas Aquinas in, 9160
traditional life of, 822
women as, 822
Benedictio Latina (votive gesture), in cult of Sabazios, 7954
Benediction, prayer of, 7369
Benedict of Aniane, 821
monastic reforms of, 7724
Benedict of Nursia, **822–824**
on care of the sick, 3845
Cassian's influence spread through, 1448

desires renounced by, 2309
Eastern influence on, 2582
Gregory I on, 823, 3688
monasteries founded by, 821, 823, 6117, 7724
Obatala identified with in Shango, 1434
as patron saint of Europe, 823
relics of, 823
Rule of, 1689 (*See also* Benedictines)
body discipline in, 8704
celibacy and, 1477
Cistercians and, **1800–1801**
dominance of, 6132
eremitism and, 2827
Francis of Assisi, modifications by, 8704
guidelines of, 6131–6132
spiritual values affirmed by, 823–824
Bene 'el (Sons of God), 4742
Bene ha'elohim (Sons of God), 4742
Benei Elim (deities), 5147
Benei Elohim, story of, 2968
Benei ha-nevi'im (sons of the prophets), 7431–7432
Bene Israel (Indian Jews), 5006–5007
Benei Yisra'el. See Jewish people
Bene Luluwa (central Africa), 5522
Benevolence
in Confucianism (*See Ren*)
of God *vs.* nature, 2908
Ben Ezra synagogue (Cairo), Bairo Genizah in, 2233
Bengal and Bengali religions, **824–832**
Akbar's defeat of, 216
ashrams in, 546
British rule in, 1029
Buddhism, 824, 1126
Vajrayāna (Tantric) Buddhism, 827
Caitanya's influence on, 826, 1346–1347
castes in, 825, 826, 829, 1029
Christianity, 828, 1029
goddess worship, 826
Hinduism
art, 824
Brāhmo Samāj, 828, **1028–1030**
Buddha as Viṣṇu in, 824
cats in, 1462
Holī festival in, 4017
humanism and domestication of deities in, 827
and Islam, 829–830
Kṛṣṇa devotion, 826
līlā in, 5456, 5457
Navarātri festival of, 6443–6444
pantheism, 6964–6965
Rādhā devotion, 826
rural traditions of, 4435, 4436
saint-singer tradition in, 4005
Tantrism, 825, 827, 4430
in United States, 830–831
Vaiṣṇavism, 4430
Holī in, 4081
idolatry, debates on, 828–829
Islam, 825, 829–830
cats in, 1463
conversion to, 825, 4642
Hinduism and, 829–830
literature, 4649
madrasahs, 4645
reform movements in, 4651
Sufism, 4647
in United States, 830–831
Jainism, 828
Judaism, 828
mystical folk poetry, 6767
pride in regional identity in, 827–828, 829
Sikhism, 828
Vedism, 824–825
Bengali language
erotic poetry in, 829
fiction in, 10035
Hindu texts in, 825
on idolatry, 828–829
Islam texts in, 825
rise of, 825–826
study of, 4458
Tantric literature in, 825
Bengali Women (Roy), 3321
Bengal Renaissance, 828, 9316, 9319, 10035
Bengal Satī Regulation (1829), 2330
Bengel, Johann Albrecht, 7142
Benin religion, 2696–2697. *See also* Edo religion; Fon and Ewe religion
blood-pact rite in, 3806
funeral rites in, 3236, 7805–7806
healing in, 3818
kingship in, 5170, 7805–7806
Benitez, Paz Marquez, 3079
Benjamin, Walter
on angels, 348
on fetishism, 3046
and film studies, 3101
political theology of, 7245
on popular culture, 7321
Benjamin (patriarch), Arab conquest of Egypt and, 1981
Benjamin of Tudela
historiography of, 4038
on Samaritans, 8069
Benjamin tribe, 7592
Benji jing (Daoist text), 2197, 2211
Benjō-gami (deity), 2410
Ben Meir, Matthias, 9037
Bennett, Dennis, 7030
Bennett, John G., **832–833**
Bennett, Lynn, 3321
Benoist, Alain de, on monotheism, 6161
Benoit, Hubert, 609
Ben Sira, 899–900, 5423. *See also* Ecclesiastes
artisans in, 4296
blasphemy in, 972
content of, 900
date of, 900
health and healing in, 3829
ḥokhmah in, 4079
Israelite religion in, 4974
merkavah in, 10050
midrash in, 6014
psalm in, 7461
Second Temple in, 926
Sophia in, 8522
tradition in, 9757
in various canons, 879, 880
wisdom in, 9755, 9759
personified, 9757
Torah as, 9762–9763
Benson, Herbert
on faith factor, 6057
on meditative state, 1951
Benson, Richard M., 7724
Bentham, Jeremy
on asceticism, 5372
on deep play, 3261
on law and morality, 5368
on law and religion, 5326, 5329–5330
on punishment, 5371, 5374
on retribution, 5373
Bento, Saint, healing of skin by, 3812
Bentzen, Aage, in Myth and Ritual school, 6381
Benveniste, Émile, 4462
on Indo-European religions, 1499
on superstition, 8864
Benz, Ernst, parapsychology, use of, 4043
Beowulf
boat in, 991
Christian influence on, 7218
Christianity in, 2814
Berab, Jacob (rabbi), 7580
Berab, Ya'aqov
mysticism of, 4998
on rabbinical ordination, 5104
Berakhah/berakhot (blessing), 982, 983, 5307
in rabbinic Judaism, 4976–4977
Bera Pennu. *See* Tari Pennu
Berber, origin of word, 833
Berbers and Berber religions (Morocco), **833–836,** 4579, 4580–4581
ancient, 834, 4580
in Andalusia, 4591, 4592–4593
Arab conquest of, 4581
Barghawāṭah religion, 835
Christianity, 834, 1678
in Cyrenaica, 1678
ghosts in, 3476
Ḥā-Mīm's religion, 835
Islam, 834–835
acceptance of, 1679–1680
dynasties of, 4584–4588
Mu'tazilah in, 6321
spread of, 4583, 4600, 4601
Khārijīs and, 835, 4600, 4601
literature of, 4583
revolt against Umayyad caliphate, 4583, 4592
rituals in, 835
witchcraft in, women's curses in, 2100
Berdache (multiple-gendered person), 3410, 3422, 4116
Berdiaev, Nikolai, **836–837,** 6964
on androgynes, 341
communitarian personalism, 1653
in exile, 836
on Florenskii (Pavel) theology, 3134
Berdichev, Levi Yitsḥaq of, **5428**
Berdichevsky, M. Y., on Zionism, 9980
Berengar of Tours, **837**
eucharistic views of, Gregory VII and, 3689
Bere'shit. See Genesis
Beresnevičius, Gintaras, 328, 771
Berg, C. C., 4661–4662
Berg, David Brandt, 2987, 4853, 6560
Berg, Virginia Brandt, 2987
Bergaigne, Abel Henri Joseph, on Vedic mythology, 9559
Bergelmir (mythic figure), in creation myth, 3446–3447
Berger, David, on Habad messianism as heresy, 3793
Berger, Iris, 118
Berger, Peter L., 7702
modern social theory, contributions to, 8495
phenomenology and, 8495
on propriety of religion and "bad faith," 8497–8498
on society and religion, 8468, 8472, 8488
on truth of religion, 8498
Bergman, Ingmar, 2472, 3100, 9736
Bergman, Jan, 4557
Bergmann, Gustav, on liturgy, 5492
Bergson, Henri, **838**
atheism and, 584
and Bakhtin (M. M.), 742
Durkheim (Émile) and, 2527
influence of, 838, 6636
on intuition, 4525
on knowledge, 5207, 5209

Bergson, Henri ***continued***
on laughter, 4222
Maritain (Jacques) and, 5712
metaphysics of, 5991
on morality, 838
Neoplatonism and, 6475–6476
on philosophy of nature, 6431
rule of, and animism, 365
Sundén (Hjalmar) on, 8851
writings of, 838
Berguer, Georges, 7474
Berit. See B'rît (covenant)
Berke (grandson of Chinggis Khan), 4493, 4613
Berkeley, George, 4355
on idea of God, origin of, 2779
metaphysics of, 5991
Berkouwer, G. C., on free will and predestination, 3208
Berkovits, Eliezer, Holocaust, response to
on free will and, 4091
on Suffering Servant doctrine and, 4089
Berlandier, Jean, 406
Berlin, Adele, 6377
Berlin, Ira, 77
Berlin, Isaiah, 3288
Berlin, Me'ir. *See* Bar-Ilan, Me'ir
Berlin, Naftali, 788
biblical exegesis of, 868
Berlin Academy, Manichaean texts at, 5662
Berliner, Abraham, 888
Berlin Institutum Judaicum, 4883
Berlioz, Hector, 6312
Berman, Harold, 5325, 5329
on Roman law, 5332
Bern, John, 3391–3392
Bernal, Ignacio, 5903
Bernardin, Susan, 3090
Bernardino of Siena, 3183
Bernard of Clairvaux, **838–839**
Abelard (Peter) opposed by, 7, 839
on art, 4286
as child of *incubus,* 2278
Cistercians and, 1800–1801
on Holy spirit, 839
on love, 6349, 8706
love of God expressed in erotic terms, 8037
on Mary, 5753
monasteries founded by, 838, 839
and monastery architecture, 6119
on mystical union, 6337
mysticism of, 6349
on nature, divine in, 2606–2607
on nonviolence, 839
theology of, 9136
on wounded heart, 3883
writings of, 838–839
Bernard of Saisset, 1019
Berndt, Catherine H., **839–841,** 3080
on Australian Indigenous religions
myths of, 666, 668
women in, 681–682, 3389–3390, 3391, 3392, 3393
on Ngarrindjeri people, 649
role in studies, 686
Berndt, Ronald, 840, **841–842,** 951, 3080
on Australian Indigenous religions
men in, 3391
myths of, 666, 668
new movements in, 681, 682
on the Dreaming, 2478
on Ngarrindjeri people, 649
role in studies, 686
Berndt Museum of Anthropology, 842
Berner, Ulrich, on syncretism, 8935–8936
Bernier, François, 4446
Bernini, Gian Lorenzo, vol. 11 color insert, vol. 13 color insert
Bernstein, Ellen, 2646
Bernstein, Leonard, 2470, 6312
Berossus
on ages of world, 176
on Babylon
cosmology of, 2811
as first city, 2810, 2811
Berque, Augustin, on Shintō, 2639
Berque, Jacques, 4718
Berrigan, Daniel, Sölle (Dorothee) and, 8512
Berry, Buzz, 10054
Berry, Thomas
on animals, 362
cosmology and, rethinking of, 2610
Earth First! influenced by, 2564
on nature as sacred, in science, 2665–2666
Bers, Sof'ia Andreevna, 9220
Berserkers (warriors), **842–843,** 4478
Berserksgangr (going berserk), 842
Berthier, Jacques, 6313
Berthoff, Warner, 5482
Bertholet, Alfred, **843**
Beruryah, **843–844,** 3354
Beruryah Incident, 844
Berytos (Beruit), Eshmun in, 2841
Beržanskis-Klausutis, Jonas Gediminas, 763
Bes (deity)
clay figures representing, 4296
Yahveh as, 4296
Besançon, Alain, 4380
Besant, Annie, **844–846**
atheism and socialism of, 844
in India, 845
Judge (William Q.) and, 5024
Krishnamurti (Jiddu) and, 5244
messiah of, 6547
as president of Indian National Congress, 9143
as prophet, 6546
Steiner (Rudolf) breaking with, 392
in Tamil, 8978
in Theosophical Society, 844–845, 6535, 9142–9143
theosophy of, 844–845
Beschi, Constantine, 8978
BeSHT. *See* Ba'al Shem Tov
Beshtian Hasidism. *See* Hasidism
Bessi tribe (Thracian), 9168
Best, Elsdon, on Maori religion, 8768
Best, Joel, 6524
Best, Wallace, 74
b Centauri (constellation)ïβ Centauri (constellation), in ethnoastronomy, 2866
Bēta Esra'ēl, **5002–5004,** 9982
Betanzos, Domingo de, 4504
Betanzos, Juan de, 5292
on Inca calendar, 1361
Bete religion (Africa)
funeral rites in, 3236
myth of the Fall in, 2960
witchcraft in, 7755
Beth, Karl, **846–847**
Beth Alpha, synagogue art at, 8923–8924
Bethany Ashram, 547
Bethany College, Campbell (Alexander) and, 1377
Beth-Dagon (Philistine city), 7102
Bethel (deity)
Anat as consort of, 320
in Aramean religion, 448
Bethel (God's house), 4757
Bethel (Palestinian city), 923–924, 933
altar of, destruction of, 4828
naming of, 4838
Bethel Church, 68, 264
Bethlehem, pilgrimage to, 7161
Beth Medrash Govoha (New Jersey), 7582
Bethune, Mary McLeod, 10038
Beti, Mongo, 3087
Beti religion (Africa), revenge in, 7780
Betrothal, in Jewish law, 3752
Bettelheim, Bruno, 4481
Betti, Emilio
on Gadamer (Hans Georg), 3934
hermeneutics and, 3932
Bettignies, Marie Ragon de, on Hermetism, 3951
Between Theater and Anthropology (Schechner), 2436
Between Two Worlds: The Dybbuk (Ansky), 2534
"Betwixt and Between: The Liminal Period in *Rites de Passage*" (Turner), 9405–9405
Betyls (cult-stones), Nabatean, 6388, 6389
Betz, Hans Dieter, 7017
Beureu'eh, Daud, 26–27
Beverages, **847–850**. *See also* Alcoholic beverages
milk, 847
in New Year festivals, 6590
tea, 847–848
Beyer, Hermann, 5941
Beyer, Peter, on European differentiation of religion, 8472
Beyerland, Abraham Willemsz van, on Hermetism, 3949
Beyond Belief (Bellah), 6181
Beyond God the Father (Daly), 3312, 7008
Beyond Phenomenology: Rethinking the Study of Religion (Flood), 7098
Beyond Power: On Women, Men, and Morals (French), 7008
Beyond the Kubea (Hides), 146
Beza, Theodore, **850–851**
Arminius (Jacobus) as student of, 493
on divine providence, 7791
on predestination, 3204
as Presbyterian, 7390
as successor of Calvin, 850–851
writings of, 851
Bhabha, Homi, 3046, 6998
Bhadrakāḷi (deity), 3608
Bhadralok (caste), in Bengal, 825, 829
Bhadrayānīya school of Buddhism, 1194
Bhagavadgītā (Hindu text), **851–855**. *See also* Mahābhārata
Arjuna in, 487, 852
as *kāvya* (great poem), 7205
ātman in, 7677–7678
avatāra theory in, 4000–4001
bhakti as pathway to liberation in, 3886, 4751
bhakti synthesis and, 4001–4002
bhaktiyoga in, 853, 857, 5097
Caitanya on, 854
castes in, 4001
context of, 852
cosmology in, 5447
daily reading of, 851
desire in, 2304–2305
devotion described in, 2317, 2321
dharma in, 853, 2621, 4442
divine love in, 8706
English translation of, 4446
eye in, 2941
ghosts in, 3477
God in, 5456
in Vaiṣṇavism, 851, 854, 4428
in Vedānta, 852, 853, 9543
īśvara in, 4751–4752
Jñāneśvar on, 5696
karman in, 853, 5096–5097
Kṛṣṇa in, 5249
and Kṛṣṇaism, 5251
and Arjuna, 852–853, 854, 2317, 2321

as Supreme Being, 853, 854
Kurukṣetra in, 5268
lion symbolism in, 5465
mokṣa in, 2621, 6115, 6116
morality in, 6188
mysticism of, 6344
new religious movements and reinterpretation of, 6529
pantheism in, 6964
peace in, 7023
power in, 7347
as prototype for devotional literature, 854
Ramakrishna on, 852
Rāmānuja on, 852, 853, 854, 7615
samādhi (meditative absorption) in, 8066
Sāṃkhya in, 852, 853
saṃsāra in, 7677–7678
Śaṅkara on, 852, 853, 854
self-realization in, 853
shape shifting in, 8303
studies of, 4446
three (number) in, 9346
Tilak (Bal Gangadhar) on, 854, 9199
Trimūrti in, 9346
Viṣṇu in, as *avatāra,* 707, 7501
wisdom in, 9752
Bhagavad-Gita As It Is (Prabhupada), 6529–6530
Bhagavan (lord or God)
in Brahmanism, 9572
the Buddha as, 1060, 1063
in Jainism, 4770
Bhagavān (ultimate conscious reality)
in Caitanya's theology, 1346
in Vaiṣṇavism, 9501–9502
Bhagavat. See Bhagavan
Bhāgavata (Hindu sect). *See also* Bhakti
earliest, 9502–9503
Vaiṣṇavism and, 9499–9500, **9501–9506**
Vedism and, 9501
Bhāgavata Purāṇa (Hindu text)
avatāras of Viṣṇu in, 7500
Balarāma mentioned in, 743
Burnouf (Eugène) on, 1334, 4446
Caitanyan commentaries on, 1346
dance drama inspired by, 2449
devotion in, 2317
in Vaiṣṇavism, 4430, 9503
Kṛṣṇa in, 5249, 5252, 5254, 5456
in Madhva movement, 9503
milkmaid lovers of Kṛṣṇa in, 854, 5249
narrative in, 7498
Prabhupada's commentaries on, 7355
Sūrdās's poetry retelling of, 8881
Trimūrti in, 9346
yugas in, 7499
Bhāgavata-sandarbha. See Saṭ-sandarbha
Bhagavatī Sūtra, Gośāla in, 211–212
Bhagīratha (mythic figure), 3274–3275
Bhago, Mai, 3336
Bhahba, Homi, on colonial hybridity, 1858–1859
Bhāī Gurdās
and *Ādi Granth,* 32
on Nānak, 6413
Bhairava (deity), 4324, 8985
Bhairavas (terrible ones), 779
Bhairava Tantras, classification of, 4020
Bhaiṣajyaguru (buddha), **855–856,** 1068, 1084
bodhisattva assistants of, 856
in Chinese Buddhism, 1162
depiction of, 856
as subject of *nianfo,* 6601
sūtras of, 1086
Bhaiṣajyaraja *(bodhisattva),* 1079
Bhajan, Yogi (Harbhajan Singh Puri)
Healthy, Happy, Holy Organization (3HO) and, **3877–3880**
White Tantric Yoga of, 3878
Bhajans (songs), 6281, 6282
bhakti poetry and, 3985
in Sai Baba movement, 8028, 8029
Bhaktamāla (hagiographies), 858
Bhaktāmara Stotra (Mānatuṅga), 7212
Bhakti (devotion), **856–860**. *See also* Bhāgavata
adoration in, 3886
as aim of life, 5448
and *jñāna* and *karma,* 4421, 4423
asceticism and, 857, 858
and ashrams, 547
as Brahmanic orthodoxy, 4004
in Brahmanism, 9572
Caitanya and, 1345, 1346
dance and, 2135
in dance drama, 2450
elixir in, 2771
emergence of, 3998
in epic cosmology, 2016
forms of, 857
guru as saint in, 8036
and Hinduism, consolidation of, 3998–4002
in *Bhagavadgītā,* 853, 857, 4751, 5097
in Holī and Kamā festivals, 4081, 4082
in Pāñcarātras, 9507
in Śaivism, 857, 858, 8417, 8976
in Śaiva Siddhanta, 8043, 8418
as inspiration, 4509
in Vaiṣṇavism, 857, 858, 859, 4430, 8976, 9500, 10088–10089
Śaṅkara on Iśvara as identical with *brahman,* 4004
love in, 8706
meaning of word, 856, 858
mokṣa and, 6116
movements of, 858
mythology of, 4441
origins of, 857
Pañcāyatanapūjā (five-shrine worship) and *iṣṭadevatā* (deity of choice) in, 4004
as path to perfection, 7041
as poetry, 7207, 7208, 7209, 7210, 7211
in Hindi tradition, 3983–3987
in Sikh Panth, 3986
redemption and, 7641
renunciation in, 8093
revivalism in, sectarian traditions and, 4004
rituals of, 858
saguṇa ("with qualities") *vs. nirguṇa* ("without qualities") tradition, 3984–3986, 4004
Sāṃkhya rejection of, 3997
Sankara on, 4004
sectarian and saint-singer movements as alternatives to, 4004–4005
as state of *rasa* (aesthetic appreciation), 4006
Sufism combined with, 4007
Tamil, 857, 858, 859, 8974–8975, 8976, 8977
temple worship and universalization of, 4006
time for, 857–858
Tulsīdās and, 9393
understanding, 859
use of word, 856–857
yoga of
desire and, 2305
in *Bhagavadgītā,* 853, 857, 4928, 5097
Bhakti cults (India), 3002, 9498. *See also* Bhāgavata
Rāmā in, 7609, 10089
Vaisnava, 9500
Vāsudeva, 9498–9499
Bhaktikāla (time for devotion), 858
Bhaktimārga (path of devotion), 856–857
Bhaktirasāmṛtasindhu, Gōsvamins and, 1346
Bhakti-rasa-śāstra, Gōsvamins and, 1346
Bhaktisiddhanta Sarasvati Thakura, 7355
Bhanakas, 1252
Bhandarkar, R. G., 4446–4447
Bhangra (Punjabi folk dance), in Sikhism, 8397
Bhani, Bibi, 3336
Bharata (brother of Rāmā), 7617
Bhārata (mythic region)
in Purāṇic cosmology, 2017
in Jain cosmology, 2023
Bhārata Muni, 2136
on art, 494
Bharata Samaj, Krishnamurti (Jiddu) as priest of, 5244
Bhāratcandra Rāy, 825, 826, 829
Bhardwaj, Surinder M., 3590
Bhartṛhari, 9547
Bhāskara, 9548
Bhāṣya (commentary), 1271
Bhatriya Janata Party (BJP) (India), 7256
Bhaṭṭa, Gopāla, works of, 1346
Bhatta, Jayanta, 6774
Bhattacharya, V., 3289
Bhaṭṭāraka clerics, 4765
Bhāṭṭa school of Indian philosophy, 6042–6043
Bhāva (emotion), 857
Bhāvamiśra, on Āyurveda, 3853
Bhāvana (meditation), 5820. *See also* Buddhist meditation
Bhāvanākramas (Kamalaśīla), 998–999, 5070
mārga in, 5436
Bhāvaviveka (Indian philosopher), **860–861,** 1119, 1212
and Nāgārjuna, 860, 1212–1213, 1299, 5552, 5553
on *bodhisattva* path, 1300
Buddhapālita criticized by, 1075, 5553
on Buddhist schools, 1204, 1310
Candrakīrti and, 860, 1213, 1401
on philosophy, 1295
writings of, 5553
Bhave, Vinoba, **861–862**
in ashram revival, 546
in Sarvodaya movement, Gandhi and, 3273
Bhavya. *See* Bhāvaviveka
Bhawani Mandir (Ghose), 829
Bhedābheda. *See* Dvaitādvaita
Bhela Saṃhitā, as Āyurvedic text, 3853
Bherī (drum), 2496
Bherighoṣa (drum), 2496
Bhikkhus (monks), 7407, 7409
Bhikṣu (mendicant), 1105, 1107, 1156, 4421, 4766
Bhikṣuṇī. See Nuns, Buddhist
Bhiksuvage Urumaya (Walpola Rahula), 7264
Bhils (India), 4434–4435, 4436
Bhīma (Hindu figure), 743
Bhīṣmaparvan (Hindu text), Durgā in, 2526
Bhog ceremony, in Sikhism, 8396, 8397

Bhoodān movement, 861
Bhopās (musicians), 4434–4435
Bhṛgu (sage), 9346
Bhrukuṭi (Buddhist figure), 1079
Bhūmis (*bodhisattva* stages), progression through, in Mahāyāna Buddhism, 2217
Bhūmisparśa mudrā (gesture), 4328, 4329
Māra and, 5690
Bhutan
Klong chen Rab 'byams pa (Longchenpa) in, 5194
Tibetan Buddhism in
clothing in, 1828
kingship in, 7262–7263, 8985
as official religion, 9182
temples in, 9052
Bhūtas (phantoms of the dead), 2315, 3477
Bhutto, Ẕulfiqār 'Alī, 4773
Bi (jade disk), 4759
Bialik, Hayyim Nahman, Ginzberg (Asher) influencing, 3496
Bianchi, Ugo, **862–865**
dualism of, 2506
on Dumuzi, 2522
on dynamism, 2543
on Gnosticism, 3534
historiography of, 4050
on Jensen (Adolf E.), 4825
Biandrata, Giorgio, in Unitarianism, 9468–9469
Bianhua (transformation), 2636
Bian Shao, 5316
Bianzong lun (Xie Lingyun), 2217
Biardeau, Madeleine, 5594, 7362, 8991
Bibile (image), 5768
Bible. *See also* Biblical literature; Hebrew scriptures (Old Testament); Hermeneutics; New Testament; *specific books*
African American studies of, 80
afterlife in, 152, 156–157
animals in, 360
archaeological studies of, 451–452, 455
attributes of God in, 613, 614
authority of (*See* Biblical literature, authority of)
ballets based on themes from, 2163
in Christian worship, 9811–9813
Copernican revolution and, 8183
dietary laws in, 5106
divinatory techniques mentioned in, 6452
Enuma elish and, 2811–2812
in eremitism, 2825
essence of Christianity in, 1665
Ethiopian, 2859
exegesis of (*See* Biblical exegesis)
exile in, 2816
femininity in, Rachel and Leah as examples of, 7591
feminist approaches to, 3036–3037
and fiction, influence on, 3058
free will and predestination in, 3206–3207
gardens in, 3278
gender in, 3358–3359
as historical source, in Medieval historiography, 4038
historiography of, 4028
on David, 2224
text criticism applied to, 4032
Hobbes on "abuses of the scripture," 4074–4075
Hooker (Richard) on, as not self-authenticating, 4124
Ibn Hazm (Ahmad) on, 8781
illustration of, 8198, 8204
inerrancy of, 2889, 2910
in Adventist theology, 8236
justification in, 5039–5040
kingship in, 5164
kissing in, 7344
kneeling in, 5196
as literature, 5488
literature influenced by, 8203
meaning and origin of word, 878
in Mennonites' faith, 5860
as mirror, 6063
morality based on, 6182
in Mormonism, 6192–6193
names taken from, 6409
as natural revelation, 7774–7775
new religious movements and reinterpretation of, 6529
numerical allegory in, 6746
oaths in, 9642–9643
oral history and, 6843–6844
ordeal in, 6847
Protestantism and, liberal *vs.* fundamentalist interpretation, 1655
in Rastafari, 7627
readings from, at Easter, 2579
Reformation emphasis on, ethics and, 1655
retribution in, 7784
as structure of authority, 1661
terms referring to, 8197
term used in general sense, 8197
text criticism applied to, historiography and, 4032
translation of
African, 1718
early, 2581
"holy" and "sacred" in, 4098
Hungarian, 4226
by Jehovah's Witnesses, 4821
Korean, 5234
Russian, 3095
Septuagint (*See* Septuagint)
unity of, 2049
violent images of divinity in, 6647
vows in, 9640–9641
Vulgate version of (*See* Vulgate Bible)
as wisdom literature, 9754–9762
in women's movement, 3297
writing's origins in, 269
Bible Christians (Methodist branch), 5998
Bible movement, liberation theology and, 5440
Bible Presbyterian Church, 7391
Bible societies, in Latin America, 1700
Bibliander, Theodor, on predestination, 3204
Biblical exegesis, **865–878,** 5473–5474. *See also* Hermeneutics; *specific scholars*
Australasian scholarship, 8771
Christian views, **865–870**
allegorical, 870, 872–873, 873–875
in Australasia, 8771
Bultmann (Rudolf) on, 3934
contemporary trends, 876–877
contextual, 870–871, 876–877
deconstruction and, 5488
Eastern Christianity, 874
Eusebius, 2884, 2885
feminist, 877, 8731
foundations of, 872–877
historical, 871, 876–877
history of, 5473
Hobbes on, 4075
Hugh of Saint-Victor on, 4151
Jerome, 4833
and Jewish Bible, 871–872
liberationist, 876–877
and life of faith, 871
literal, 870, 873
Marxism and, 876
moral, 873
Origen, 6888, 6889
Protestant, 874, 876
Rashi's influence on, 7620
in Scholasticism, 8175
Schweitzer (Albert) on, 8179
significance of, 871
Strauss (David Friedrich) on, 8747–8748
Swedenborg (Emanuel) on, 8899, 8900
traditional, 871
typological, 872
Gnostic, 3525
hermeneutics distinguished from, 865
Jewish views, **870–878** (*See also* Midrash; *Pesher/Pesharim*)
Ashkenazic, 4981
Beit Hillel *vs.* Beit Shammai, 815
contemporary trends, 869
direct *vs.* indirect, 3748
Enlightenment and, 869
Franco-German, 865–866
halakhah and, 3748
Hillel on, 3981
medieval, 866–867
modern, 867–869
of Kaufmann (Yeḥezkel), 5108
of Rashi, 7619–7620
Spinoza (Baruch) on, 8683
in *Wissenschaft des Judentums,* 4877
of Yishma'e'l ben Elisha', 9891
Locke (John) and, 5496–5497
of Uchimura Kanzō, 9432
Qumran sect and, 2234
Smith (W. Robertson) on, 8451
Söderblom (Nathan) on, 8506
structuralist, 8753, 8754
Biblical Judaism, 4971–4973
definition of, 4970
Biblical literature, **878–923**. *See also* Hebrew scriptures (Old Testament); New Testament; *specific books*
and ancient Near East, 884–885
anti-Semitism in, 397–398
Apocrypha (*See* Apocrypha)
authority of, 694–695, 882
Protestant position on, 881
questioned, during Enlightenment, 875
Sozzini (Fausto Pavolo) on, 8673–8674
Bauer's (Bruno) critique of, 804
birth in, 953
blades in, 967, 968
as blessing, 981
blood in, 986
breath and breathing in, 1042
codices of, 890, 891, 921
demons in, 2277–2278, 2284, 2314
dragons in, 2431
dreams in, 2489
faith in, 2425, 2426
healing touch in, 9255–9256
Hebrew scriptures (*See* Hebrew scriptures)
higher criticism of
Hertz's (Joseph) attack on, 869
Spinoza (Barukh) on, 865, 8683
Spiritualism and, 8716
idolatry in, 4358–4360, 4385

Masoretic text of, 885, 886–887
moral teachings *vs.* ethics, 1650–1651
New Testament (*See* New Testament)
noncanonical, 919–920
Bēta Esra'ēl, 5003
Old Testament (*See* Hebrew scriptures)
pain in, 6944, 6946
paradise in, 6981–6982, 6984
peace in, 7021–7022
perfection of God in, 7039
pilgrimage in, 7152–7153
printing of, Gutenberg and, 893
proverbs and parables in, 6978, 6979
Pseudepigrapha (*See* Pseudepigrapha)
Satan in, 2314
Schopenhauer (Arthur) on, 4447
scrolls of, 879, 890
temptation in, 9069–9072, 9073
textual diversity in, 885–886
theodicy in, 9115–9117
translations of, 922
Aboriginal, 686
ancient, 885
Arabic, 894–895, 922
Aramaic, 887–889, 894, 922
Armenian, 492, 922
Chinese, 1632–1633
Coptic, 922
English, 9425
German, 1056, 7926
Gothic, 922
Greek (*See* Greek language, Biblical literature in; Septuagint)
Syriac, 893–894, 922
Vulgate (*See* Vulgate Bible)
wisdom in, 884–885
Biblical movement, in Catholic Church, 9533
Biblical paradigm, Schmidt (Wilhelm) and, 8169
Biblical Temple (Jerusalem), **923–937**
archaeological excavations of, 923, 924, 925, 931
in Christianity, 4841
cult of, 926–928
heterodoxy and centralization of, 934–936
purification in, 927, 934, 7511, 7512, 7515
sacrifices in, 926–928
songs and prayers in, 927–928, 935
structure of, 926
design of, 923–925, 931–932, 933–934, 4746
first (*See* Solomon's Temple)
function and phenomenology of, 931–934, 4746
funding and administration of, 928–931
history of, 923–925
king maintaining, 4745
Levites' functions in, 5426
maintenance of, 5426–5427
in Mishnah, 4977
offerings made at, 4972
origin of word, 923
pilgrimage to, 7161
priests in, 5424, 7400
prophecies on, 7434
purification of, 927, 934, 4747
in rabbinical Judaism, 4977
sanctity of, 933–934, 4840
second (*See* Second Temple)
in *Temple Scroll,* 2234
women excluded from, 934–935
Biblical theology movement, neoorthodoxy and, 6466
Bibliographie bouddhique (periodical), 7460
Bibliographies, as reference works, 7642, 7643
Bibliolatry
as magic or superstition, 8200
and power of written word, 8201
Bibliomancy
chance and, 1528
as divination, 8200
Bibliotheca Philosophica Hermetica library, Hermetic materials in, 3953
Bibliotheke (Photios), 3053
Bicitra Nātak (hymn from *Dasam Granth*), 2221
autobiographical material in, 8408
Bickerman, Elias, 928, 930
Bid'ah (innovation), *sunnah vs.,* 8853
Bidāyat al-ḥikma (Ṭabāṭabā'ī), 8946
Biddick, Kathleen, 9295
Biddle, Jennifer, 3390
Biddle, John, 973, 9469
Biel, Gabriel, 6645
on justification by works, 5040–5041
Reformation and, 7657
Bielenstein, August, on Baltic religion, 759, 9421
Bierhorst, John, 7224
Biersack, Aletta, 3396
Biezais, Haralds, 327–328, 771, 10081
on Latvian Saule (sun) myth, 8134
on Māra, 5691
Bifrost (tremulous way), 7604
Bigamy. *See also* Polygamy
Council of Trent on, 4505
Bigandet, Bishop, 1728
Big Bang
cosmology of, 2032–2033, 8184
in creation, 7138
development of theory of, 7138
Pius XII on, 7138
science and religion, questions raised in, 8189
Big Bow, Nelson, 406
Big Drum Dance, in Grenada and Carriacou, 1436
Bigfoot, 6166
Big Foot Memorial Horseback Ride, 5295
Big Head cult (North America), 6718
Big Horn Medicine Wheel, 1794
Bigi-man (spirit), in Kromanti dance, 1436
Bigmanship, 6784
Big men, in New Guinea religions, 6506
Big Moon Ceremony, 10053
Big Nambas religion and society (Vanuatu), homosexuality in, 4115
Big Raven (mythic figure), 472
Biguan (wall contemplation), 1292
Bigyny. *See also* Polygyny
in Israelite religion, 4733
Bihar, 824
Biḥār al-anwār (al-Majlisī), 5623
Bīja (sacred syllable), 5310
Bījak, 5052
Bilah songs, in Kumina, 1435
Bilāl the Abyssinian, freed by Abū Bakr, 19
Bile. *See* Humors of the body
Bile (trees), 1486–1487
Bilge Kaghan (Türk ruler), 4491
Billingsley, Andrew, 74
Billy Graham Evangelistic Association, 7712
Billy Sunday (Page), 2163
Bimaadiziwin, in Anishinaabe religion, 369
Bimba (image), 4323
Bimin-Kuskusmin people, cannibalism among, 1404
Binary classification of religions, 1818–1819
Binary oppositions. *See also* Duality
in African myths, 96–99
coincidentia oppositorum (conjunction of opposites), Dhū al-Nūn al-Miṣrī on, 8812
in Hindu conception of time, 4015–4016
in Sāṃkhya Hinduism, 8089, 8091
male-female polarity, in sex magic, 8251
in metaphysics, 5990
in philosophy of Heschel (Abraham Joshua), 3962–3963
of sex and gender, 3296–3297, 3299
structuralism and, 8752
Binary periodization, 173–174
Binary symbolism, **6751–6753**
Binash, Eblaite religion in, 2598
Binder, Louis R., 6521
Binding, **937–939,** 9089. *See also* Knots
in cosmology, 5197–5198
of Sun, myths of, 5198
and transposition, 5197
"Binding complex," 937–938
Binding of the Years ceremony (Aztec), human sacrifice in, 4190
Binet, Alfred, on fetishism, 3045–3046
Binford, Lewis R., 453
Binford, Sally R., on goddess worship, 3613
Bing, Gertrud, 9690–9691
Bingdi, He, 456
Bingemer, María Clara, on Mary, 5755
Bingham, Kate (Mrs. Frank), 6584
Bini. *See* Benin
Bin Lādin, Usāmah
as disciple of Quṭb (Sayyid), 6227
fatwa of, 6099–6100
jihād of, 7290
message of, 7288–7289
terrorist network of, 7258, 7288–7289
Binomial gods, in Canaanite religion, 1383
Binsheng. *See* Du Guangting
Binu Seru (ancestor), 2391
Binyamin al-Nahāwandī, 4992
Binyamin of Tudela, 6165
Biocentrism
of Earth First!, 2561
environmental ethics *vs.,* 2655–2656
Biodiversity
in environmental movements, 2562
in India, conservation of, 2623
Bioethics, **939–943**. *See also* Medical ethics
casuistry and, 1455–1456
in Europe, 942
genetics and, 8187–8188, 8190–8191
Jewish, on abortion, 8191
origins of, 939
philosophers on, 940
"playing God" problem and, 8190
Protestant view of, nonmalificence *vs.* beneficence in, 8191

Bioethics *continued*
religious perspectives on, 941–943
Roman Catholic position on
on beneficence *vs.* nonmalificence, 8191
on genetic research and engineering, 8190–8191
shifts in context of, 940–941
in United States, 940–942
Bioethics centers, 940
Biogenetic structuralism, in ritual studies, 7857
Biographia Literaria (Coleridge), 47
Biographical Process, The: Studies in the History and Psychology of Religion (Reynolds and Capps), 944, 947
Biographical reconstruction, conversion and, 1971
Biography. *See also* Autobiography
Roman, paganism *vs.* Christianity and, 4038
sacred, **943–947**
and founders, 944–946
history of designation of, 943–944
recent directions in, 946–947
vs. secular biography, 943
Biography in Late Antiquity: A Quest for the Holy Man (Cox), 947
Biological design, 4516, 4517–4518
Biology. *See also* Sociobiology and evolutionary psychology
of animals, implications of, 357, 358
anthropology and, 385
culture and, 2088, 2869, 5261, 8474
Darwinism in, 2908–2909
evolutionary, and field of science and religion, 8189–8190
as historical science, 2869
millenarian-type activities interpreted through, 7788
religion and, 2660, 2869, 7850–7851
taxonomic classification in, 2909
Bion, W. R., 6034
Biondo, Flavio, Italian Renaissance humanism and, 4175
Biopiracy, 2623
Bio-politics, 7252
Bioregionalism, 2563
Bipartate or binary classification of religions, 1818–1819
Bipradāsa (Bengali poet), 825
Biran, Maine de, on knowledge, 5206
Birch, Charles, 2610
Birch trees, in Buriat shaman initiation, 8271–8272
Bird-David, Nurit, on kinship, 5185
Bird mask, 947
Birds, **947–949**. *See also* Auspices; *specific types of birds*
in Australian Indigenous myths, 654, 656–657
in Celtic religion, 1487
deities as, in Maya religion, 5798
as epiphanies of gods, 948, 949
as food, *kashrut* laws on, 5106
in Hinduism, 4437, 4438, 7387
horses associated with, 4134, 4135
in megalithic religion, 5825
in Mesoamerican iconography, 4312
in Minoan-Mycenaean iconography, 4320
in Muisca religion, 6230
in New Caledonia religion, 6501
in New Guinea music, 6265
in North American Indian religions, 6698–6699, 6717, 6724, 6726
in prehistoric religions, 947, 7376, 7377, 7378, 7387
sacrifice of, in Hurrian religion, 4072
in Saka religion, 7387
in shamanism, 947–948
South American, 8291–8292
as souls of the dead, 948–949
in Southern Siberian religions, 8670
spirits as, 947–948
storms associated with, 5995–5996
Sun and moon as, 2863
sun associated with, 8835
swan-maiden myth, 4134–4135
symbolism of, 948, 3127
masculine sacrality in, 5760
in Turkic religions, 9400, 9402
Birds (Aristophanes), 7335
Birkeland, Harris, 8951
Birket-Smith, Kai, 473, 474, 475
Birket-Smith, Kaj, 6671
Birkhot ha-Shaḥar (Morning Benedictions), in *siddur* liturgy, 8389
Birlia, Ovidiu, 3143
Birlma (song), 2379
Birrinydji (creational being), 647–648
Birt, Theodor, 6754
Birth, **949–954**
ablutions during and after, 10–11, 12
in African religions
in Bemba religion, 817
in Dogon religion, 2390, 2391, 2392
healing practices in, 3819
Ndebele birth ritual, 7804–7805
in Sudanese religion, 8849
in Tsonga religion, 8662
in Australian Indigenous religions
myths of, 3250
taboos and, 3873
in Baltic religions, Laima and, 5285
blood sacrifice in opposition to, 8009
blood taboo and, 1459–1460
Caribbean *couvade* ritual, 1430
celibacy surrounding, 1475
clitoridectomy and, 1826
confession of adultery and, 1884
couvade and, 950, **2046–2047**
creation as, 1988
of culture heroes, 2091
dainas (folk songs) dealing with, 2127
deities and spirits of
Artemis, 507–508
flowers and, 3135
in Haitian Vodou, 1433
Hekate as, 3900
Isis as, 4557
Juno, 5036
Māra, 5693
divine, of Hanumān, 3775
from earth, belief in, 2557
father-gods and, 2985
female body and, 4164
funeral rites evoking, 3236
in Guayaki religion, sacred time and, 7986
of heroes, 1568
in hospitals, ritualization of, in modern society, 7803
in Indian religions, 951–952
in Inuit religion, 4527–4528
in Islam, 7825–7826
in Japanese religion
Nakayama-dera Temple and, 3869
Tenrikyō, 6405–6406
in Judaism, knees and, 5195
lotus symbolism and, 5519
magic and, 5588
in Maori religion, 5679, 5681
in Mesoamerican religions, 7811–7812
death during, 7812
in Mesopotamian religion, 8536–8537
midwives for, African, 3819
in monotheistic religions, 952–953
moon linked to, 3017
motif of, 949–950
natality *vs.* mortality, in feminist theology, 4166
in Neopaganism, 7829–7830
in North American Indian religions, 6682
in Lakota religion, 5297
in Oceanic religions, 7807
in Melanesian religions, 5836, 5837
in Polynesian religions, 7311
onto earth, 2559
pains of, 953, 2896
and pollution, 2405, 2407, 4732, 7504, 7505, 7511
in prehistoric religions, 950–951, 7383
in primal religions, 950–951
as reenactment of emergence, 2557
rituals associated with, 2983
in Roman religion, 3841
lustratio and, 5534
sacred power of, 3020
in saunas, 802
second (*See* Rebirth)
transitional sacraments associated with, 7956
transition rituals of, 950, 952
in Tukanoan religion, 8623
virgin, 9608
in Zoroastrianism, 9999
Birth control
Besant's (Annie) pamphlet on, 844
in Manichaeism, 5664
Paul VI on, 6975, 7012–7013
Birthdays
of Chinese deities, 1643–1644
mawlids, **5788–5790**
Birth-givers, 951, 952
Birth-giving goddess (prehistoric), 7377
Birth of the Gods (Hesiod), Helios in, 8839
Birth of the Living God, The (Rizzuto), 7478, 7483
Birth of Tragedy, The (Nietzsche), 3053, 6614
Birth order, in Oceanic religions, 7807
Bīrūnī, al-, **954–955**
historiography of, 4038
on Indian religions, 4445
life of, 954
on Mani, 5651
on Purāṇic cosmology, 2019
writings of, 954–955, 8780
Biṣaharī (deity), Bengali worship of, 826
Bisa religion. *See* Central Bantu religions
Bisarjan (Tagore), 829
Biscop, Benedict, 814
Bisexuality
age-structured homosexuality and, 4112–4115
castration and, 1452
Eliade on "divine bisexuality," 4116
in Melanesian societies, 4114
Bishnoi tradition (India), 2622
Bishops
Anglican, 1766–1767
apostolic succession, heresy and, 3927

in Armenian church, 490
authority of
Council of Nicaea and, 2040
political, 7279–7280
Boy Bishop, in Carnival, 1441
Cathari, 1458
in Counter-Reformation, 6972–6973
Cyprian on unity of, 2113–2114
in early Christian church, 1763, 2581, 7401–7402
ecclesiology and, 1771
in Episcopal form of church government, 1763–1767
episcopal residence of, 9344
Lutheran, 7452
in orders of ministry, 6044, 6045
in Orthodox Church, ordination of, 2593
in Protestantism, 7452, 7453
Roman Catholic
American independence and, 1445–1446
appointment of, 1764
Augustine on role of, 626
in church polity, 7886
collegiality of, and ecumenism, 2686, 7886
collegial responsibility under Vatican II, 1668, 2044–2045, 6975, 7011, 9535
disciplining heretics, 4498
in episcopal form of government, 1763–1765
in Latin America, 1695, 1699
political power of, 7279–7280
pyramidal model of authority, 1668
subordination of, to pope, 4496
synods of, 7886
of Rome (*See* Papacy; Pope)
Scottish Presbyterian anti-episcopal sentiments, 1774
synods in second and third centuries, 2039
Bishops' Council, of Russian Orthodox Church, 7945
Bishr al-Marīsī, 6319
Bishr ibn al-Muʿtamir, 6318, 6319
Bismillāh (in the name of God), 4351
Bisnauth, Dale, 10023–10024
Bison
in cave art, 1471
in North American Indian religions, 6662
Bissu (transvestite priests), 1316, 1317
Bisṭāmī, Abū Yazīd al-, **955–957**
blasphemies of, 4569, 7427
ecstasy of, 8812
followers of, 956, 8820, 8821
and language of fire, 3120
miʿrāj and, 6061
mystical theology of, 956, 8812
on mystical union, 6338, 6339
sayings of, 955, 976
B'itol (creator being), 5797
Bit rimki (washing house), 10
Bitruji, al-, Gersonides and, 3462
Bitsanip, 146
Biwahōshi (priests), 7216
Bka' brgyud pa (Kagyu) order (Tibetan Buddhism), 5101, 5103, 5223
branches of, 1226
Btsun pa Chos legs in, 1233
dominance of, 1228
formation of, 1215
Hevajra Tantra and, 3966
lamas in, 8713
mahāmudrā in, 5596, 5597–5598, 5599
masters of, 1225–1226
Mi la ras pa in, 6026
monasticism and, 8082
Nā ro pa in, 6415
Sgam po pa (Gampopa), role of, **8254–8256**
Stag tshang ras pa in, 1230
Tantrism in, 8083
teachings of, 1157, 1225
Bka' gdams pa order (Buddhism), 1153, 1224, 1228, 1230
lamas in, 8713
redevelopment of monasticism, role in, 8082
Sgam po pa and, 8255
teachings of, 5223
Bka' 'gyur (Buddhist text), 1008, 1009, 1215, 1256, 1310
Bla (vitality or soul), Tibetan medicine and, 3865
Bla chen Dgongs pa rab gsal (lama), 1152
Blachernae, Synod of (1285), 3692
Black (color)
in human perception, 1860
in Native American tradition, 1862
Black, Galen, 7303–7304
Black, Jeremy, 9261
Black Americans. *See* African Americans
Black art, use of term, 6451
Black bears
American, 807
Asiatic, 807
"Black Book of Carmarthen," 1480
Black Brazilians, in Afro-Brazilian religions, 120, 121, 124
Blackburn, Gideon, 1566
Black Caribs. *See also* Garifuna religion
ancestral cult of, 1436
couvade among, 2046
origin of name, 3283
Black Church. *See also* African American religions; Black Theology; *specific denominations*
Aboriginal, 676, 679
in civil rights movement, 5402
history of study of, 74–75
Black Civilization, A (Warner), 683, 684
Black consciousness
Garvey (Marcus) and, 3287
Peoples Temple cult and, 4954
Black Cross (Malevich), vol. 11 color insert
Black Death, 2138
Jews and, 5013
mass suicide and, 8829
Black Demeter of Phigalia (deity), syncretism and, 3908
Black Drink, 1564
Black Eagle, Chief, 6769
Black Elk, **957–958,** 2484
autobiography of, 361, 702
on circles, 1794
colors in visions of, 1862
on crossroads, 2071
and quaternity, 7550
research on, 6672
on spirit keeping, 5296
on Sun Dance, 8846
on sweat lodge and cosmology, 7981
Black Elk Speaks (Neihardt), 361, 702, 957, 958
circles in, 1794
translation in, 9609
Blacker, Carmen, 3347
Blackfeet religious traditions (North America), **958–963**
bears in, 809
ceremonial bundles in, 960
challenges of, 962
cosmogony in, 958–959
dreams and visions in, 960
poetry in, 7226
practices in, 961–962
stories and oral tradition in, 959–960
Sun Dance in, 6700, 8846
universe in, 959, 960–961
Black Fields, in Jainism. *See* Kṛṣṇarājī
Blackfoot Confederacy, 958
Blackfoot language, 959, 960, 962
Blackfoot tribe
origin of name, 958
present population of, 958
Black Friars. *See* Dominicans
Black Gods of the Metropolis (Fauset), 74
Black Hat Karma pa, of Tibetan Buddhism, 2131
Black Heung Jin Nim, 9467
Black Hills (He Sapa), 5295
Black liberation theology. *See* Black Theology
Black magic. *See also* Necromancy
depiction in novels, 3062
in Islam, 5583–5585
Black Mass
in Khlysty sect, 8248
sexuality and, 8250
Black Metropolis (Drake and Cayton), 74
Black Muslims. *See* Nation of Islam
Black Muslims in America (Lincoln), 77
Black nationalism, 78–79, 9435
Garvey (Marcus) and, 3287
in Nation of Islam, 2767
Rastafari and, 7622
Black Power movement, 5402
black theology and, 78
in the Caribbean, 7625
Black religion. *See* African American religions; Black Theology
Black Religion (Washington), 77, 964
Black Religion and Black Radicalism (Wilmore), 69, 78
Black Road, 957
Black Roadway: A Study of Jamaican Folk Life (Beckwith), 10025
Blacksmiths
in Africa
myths of, 94–95, 98–99, 4301, 5988
social status of, 5988
products for gods made by, 5988
rituals of, 5988–5989
Black Spiritualist churches, founder of, 6536
Black Star Line, 3287
Black Stone, of the Kaʿbah, 5049, 5050, 7158, 7344, 9258
Blackstone, William, on law and religion, 5326, 5368
Black Theology, **963–967,** 5440
African American religions and, 77–79, 5440–5441
Christianity critiqued in, 78
Christology in, 5441
critique of, 965
God in, color of, 3559, 5441
history of study of, 77–78
Jesus in, color of, 5441
liberation in, 5441
major themes of, 77–78
message of, 964–965
origins of, 963, 964
rise of, 77
sources of, 963
theologians in, 963–964
white theology compared to, 78
womanist theology and, 5441, 10040
Black Theology: A Documentary History (Cone and Wilmore), 79

Black Theology and Black Power (Cone), 77, 965
Black Theology II: Essays on the Formation and Outreach of Contemporary Black Theology (Bruce and Jones), 966
Black Theology of Liberation, A (Cone), 77, 965
Bladder festival, 471, 4528
Blades, **967–968**. *See also* Swords
Blaeser, Kimberly, 3090, 3092, 7224
Blahoslav, Jan, 6190
Blaisdell, Kekuni, on Hawaiian sovereignty, 5341–5342
Blake, William
  on angels, 348
  apocalypse and, 413
  on conscience, 1943
  on druids, 1497
  on fairies, 2953
  on friendship, 3911
  Frye (Northrop) on, 3224
  Gnosticism of, 3514, 3526
  Görres (Joseph von) and, 3639
  Neoplatonism and, 6475
  on Newton, 6588
  on poetic imagination, 7206
  on sexuality, 7080
  subject matter of, 4347
  Swedenborgianism and, 8902
Bla ma. See Lama
Bla ma Dbu ma pa (Buddhist monk), 9386
Blanchot, Maurice, 5482, 5483
Bland, Kalman, 4342
Blanquerna (Lull), 5530
Blanshard, Brand, 6962
Blanton, Richard, 5902, 5903
Blasius (saint), in Slavic religion, 8435
Blasphemy, **968–977**
  Christian concept, **971–974**
    origin of, 971–972
    Protestant, 973
    punishment for, 971
    Roman Catholic, 972, 973 (*See also* Inquisition)
  in Greek religion, 971
  Islamic concept, **974–977**
    in early Islam, 975
    in Islamic law, 975–976
    in Islamic theology and philosophy, 976
    overlapping with infidelity, 975, 976
    punishment for, 975
    in Sufism, 976, 4569, 7427
  Jewish concept, **968–971**
    in Hebrew scriptures, 969–970, 971–972
    Jewish Law on, 968, 969
    punishment for, 969
  origin of word, 971
Blasphemy Act (1698) (England), 973
Blassingame, John, 77
Blatty, William Peter, 2931
Blaurock, Georg, in Anabaptism, 304
Blavatsky, H. P., **977–978**
  Besant (Annie) and, 844–845
  and concept of *karma,* 6498
  eclectic worldview of, 6535
  in engaged Buddhism, 2787–2788
  Judge (William Q.) and, 5023–5024
  and modern Buddhist philosophy, 1302
  Olcott (Henry Steel) and, 6815
  Randolph (Pascal) and, 8251
  on religious experience, 7738
  Steiner (Rudolf) compared with, 392, 8738
  teachings of, 977–978, 9330
  in Theosophical Society, 977, 978, 1187, 6516, 6535, 6559, 6563, 7228, 9142, 9205
  writings of, 977, 7228
Blavatsky, Nikifor, 977
Blazer, Yitsḥaq, 6241
Bleak House (Dickens), 5356
Bleda (Hun leader), 4490
Bleeker, C. Jouco, **978–979**
  on Egyptian religion, 978
  on goddesses, 3589
  historiography of, 4042
  as initiator of Amsterdam congress, 843
  Pettazzoni (Raffaele) and, 7074
  on phenomenology of religion, 978–979, 7086–7087, 7092
Blessing, **979–985**
  in Buddhism, 981, 982, 984
  Chinese traditions of, 981, 984
  in Christianity, 983
  components of, 980–981
  by El, 1396–1397, 1399
  forms and contents of, 981–982
  hands and, 3770
  in Hinduism, 980, 983–984
  in Islam, 982, 983 (*See also* Barakah)
  in Jainism, 980
  in Judaism, 982–983
    in worship, 9806
  meanings of, 979
  origin of word, 979
  process of, 979, 980
  symbolism of, 980
  in Vedism, 981, 983
  of waters, at Epiphany, 2818
"Blessing the Waters" (Bruchac), 7225
Blessingway (Navajo chant), 5444
BLIA. *See* Buddha's Light International Association
Blighton, Earl W., Holy Order of MANS and, 4101–4102
Blighton, Helen Ruth, Holy Order of MANS and, 4101–4102
Blinding, 2941
Blindness, owl as symbol of, 6936
Blind Watchmaker, The (Dawkins), 4518
Bliss, in Buddhism. *See Sukha*
Blo bzang chos kyi rgyal mtshan (Lobsang Chokyi Gyaltsen), on *mahāmudrā,* 5598
Blo bzang grags pa. *See* Tsong kha pa
Bloch, Ernst, 5701, 6312, 9072
Bloch, Maurice, 1015
  on ritual, 1514, 7845
Bloch, Phillip, 10052
Blodeuwedd (deity), 1489
Blondeau, Anne-Marie, 9189
Blondel, Maurice, **985**
  on knowledge, 5209
Blood, **985–987**. *See also* Menstruation
  in African religions, gender and, 3403
  of animal sacrifice
    in African religions, 88
    and altars, 277
  assimilation to water, as rainmaking offering, 7603
  in Australian Indigenous religions, 987
  in Bambara religion, 777
  baptism of
    in Cybele cult, 780
    in Roman bull sacrifice, 2110
  covenant through, 987
  in goddess worship, 3590
  in Greek religion, 986
  in Hinduism, 986, 7083
  in initiation rituals, 4481
  in Islam, prohibition on consuming, 986
  in Judaism, 985, 987
    prohibition on consuming, 986, 3167
    sacrificial, 926, 927, 7845
    in Temple, 926, 927
  as kinship substance
    in Langkawi society, 5184
    in Trobriand Islanders religion, 5184
  menstrual (*See* Menstruation)
  natural *vs.* ritual, 9706
  in North American Indian religions, in Sun Dance, 8848
  in primitive religions, 985
  red symbolism and, 1860
  in Roman religion, 985, 987, 2110
  as sacrifice, 986–987, 7998, 7999 (*See also* Sacrifice)
    in Israelite religion, 5434
    in Khanty religion, 5124
    libations and, 5433
    in Mansi religion, 5124
    in Semang religion, 6457
  soul located in, 8532
  spilling of, ban on, 985–986
  in Sumerian anthropogonic myths, 2800
  as symbol of the soul, 7781, 7782
  taboo of, 1459–1460
  transfusion of, Jehovah's Witnesses and, 4823
  vengeance and, 7780, 7781–7782
  in Wawalag myth, 9705–9706
Blood and Soil: Walter Darré and Hitler's Green Party (Bramwell), 2663
Bloodletting
  Aztec autosacrifice, 1403, 4189
  and confession, in Mexico, 1885–1886
  Maya, 1358, 1804, 5799, 5884, 5886
  in Melanesian religions, 5837
Blood libel, 5000
Blood-price, 7780, 7782
Bloom, Harold, 5487
Bloomfield, Maurice, on magic, 5588
Blows, Johanna M., 668
Bloy, Léon, Maritain (Jacques) and, 5712
Blue (color)
  in Christian symbolism, 1861
  Klee (Paul) on, 1860
Blue Annals ('Gos Lo tsa ba Gzon nu dpal)
  Karma pas in, 5103
  Shamar pas in, 5103
Blue Cloud, Peter, 7226
Blue Hill Marta, 775
Blue laws, 2154
  Seventh-day Adventists and, 8236
Blue Sūtra, in Reiyūkai Kyōdan, 7682
Bluḳa (log), 768
Blum, Mark, 1246, 1249
Blumenberg, Hans, Gnosticism and, 3527
Blumenthal, Edwin, Cayce (Edgar) and, 559
Blumenthal, Morton Harry, 1474
  Cayce (Edgar) and, 559
Blumhardt, Christoph, 6468
Bly, Robert, 5862, 7831
Blyden, Edward Wilmot
  on Christian *vs.* Muslim missions, 71, 104
  on Ethiopianism, 75
  on Islam in black religious thought, 81
B'nai B'rith, 3198
B'nai Ephraim, 5007
Bnei Moshe (Jewish group), 3496
Bn'il (Children of El), 4742
Bnoš Youth Organization, Schenirer (Sarah) and, 8149
Boal, Augusto, 2477
Boaliri (mythological figure), 9704–9705
Boann (deity), 1484, 1486
Boar
  Adonis killed by, 35
  in Celtic religion, 1487
  Prajāpati as, 7356
  sacrifice of, 7144

in Scandinavian religion, god associated with, 3218
Viṣṇu in form of, 707, 4438, 7144, 7501
Board games, gambling on, 3260
Boas, Franz, **987–988**
American study of religion, role in, 8785
on Arctic religions, 473, 475, 4528
Benedict (Ruth) studying under, 819
Campbell, influence on, 1378
on culture, 5261
and Deloria (Ella Cara), 2264
dynamism of, 2542
on food customs, 3173
Goldenweiser (Alexander A.) studying under, 3633
Hurston (Zora Neale) supported by, 76
on magic, 576
methodological critiques by, 379
on miracles, 6050
North American Indian religions studied by, 576, 988, 6671
on Sedna (Sea Woman), 8220
symbol theory and, 8910
Boats, **988–993**. *See also specific types*
burials in, 989–991
in Anglo-Saxon paganism, 6943
burning, 168
in Germanic religion, 989–990, 3457
Neolithic Southeast Asian, 8642
in North American Indian religions, 991
in Polynesian religions, 991
crossing waters of death, 988–989
and fertility cults, 3219
in megalithic religion, 5825
in Southern Siberian religions, 8671
symbolism of, 991–992
tales of, 991
Boaz (biblical figure), 7947, 7948
Bo'az (column), 924
Bobancu, Serban, 3467
Bob Jones University, 2892
Bobo Dreads, 7623, 7627
Boccaccio, Giovanni
Italian Renaissance humanism and, 4175
on wombs, 4165–4166
Bochart, Samuel, on paganism and Judaism, 4039
Bochasanwasi Shri Akshar Purushottam Swaminarayan (BAPS)
formation of, 8890
practice and spread of, 8892
teachings of, 8891
Bochica (deity), **993,** 6230
Bock, Kenneth, on evolutionary psychology, 8475
Böckh, August, 730
Müller (Karl Otfried) and, 6237
Bocock, Robert, on ritual, 7846
Bodawpaya (king of Burma), 9151
Boddy, Alexander A., 7029
Boddy, Janice, 107
on spirit possession, 8694
Bodha. See Jñāna
Bodhbh (deity), 1490
Bodh Gayā, shrine at, sacred space and, 7982
Bodhi (awakening). *See also* Enlightenment (spiritual state)
achievement of
Asanga on, 5200
debate at Bsam yas on, 5069–5070
stages of, 5070
as enlightenment, 2793
Huineng on, 4154
in Zhenyan Buddhism, 9962
Bodhibhadra, writings of, 5555
Bodhicaryāvatāra (Śāntideva)
bodhisattva path in, 999, 1084
in Dge lugs pa curriculum, 2322
Four Noble Truths in, 3179
Mahāyāna philosophy in, 8109
pūjā in, 7497
rituals and practices of monks in, 1119
Bodhicitta (enlightenment-spirit), 9017, 9020, 9178
Śāntideva on, 8109, 8110
Bodhidharma, **993–996**
celebration of, 1307
as founder of Chan Buddhism, 994–995, 1239, 1521, 5822
iconography of, 4330
life of, 993–994
martial arts of, 5731
on meditation, 1292
teachings of, 994
Bodhipathapradīpa (Buddhist text), 1300
Bodhiruci (Buddhist monk), 8982
Bodhisattva mahāsattva, 996
Bodhisattva of Compassion, Dalai Lama as incarnation of, 2131
Bodhisattvaprātimokṣa (Buddhist text), 1118
Bodhisattvas (buddhas-to-be), **1075–1087**. *See also* Maitreya; *See also* Avalokiteśvara; *See also* Mañjuśrī; *See also* Vajrapāṇi; Vajrasattva
aesthetics and, 51
and *tathāgata,* 9016
arhats renounced by, 6994
as Bhaiṣajyaguru's assistants, 855, 856
in Bayon temple, 5129
birds as epiphanies of, 949
born in evil existences, 1197
buddhas distinguished from, 1082
cave art of, 1471–1472
celebration of, 1307
in Central Asian Buddhism, 1145
in Chinese Buddhism, 1162
cult of, 1079–1080, 1081–1082, 1116
definition of term, 1076
in early Buddhism, 1116
ethical practices of, **1083–1087,** 1118, 1280–1282
etymology of term, 996
festivals dedicated to, 1097
halos of, 6624
handmaidens of, 1079–1080, 1081
as hosts, 4140
images of, 1111, 4327, 4329, vol. 8 color insert
in Indian Buddhism, 1082
in Hīnayāna Buddhism, 1068, 1076, 1085, 1116
in Lokottaravāda school, 1196
in Mahāsāṃghika Buddhism, 5602
in Mahāyāna Buddhism, 1083, 1192, 6630
bodhisattva path, 996–997, 998–999, 1116
celebration of, 1307
development of, 1076
doctrine of, 1076, 1077, 1115–1117
ideal of, 1298–1299
king as *bodhisattva,* 1068
names of, 1079
roles of, 1113
sūtras on, 1093
traveling between buddha fields, 1077
intercession of, 129, 1086–1087
in Theravāda Buddhism, 997, 1085, 1329
in Vajrayāna (Tantric) Buddhism, 1123, 1125, 1221
in Japanese Buddhism, 1175, 1176, 1177, 1179, 1244, 3721
karman of, 5100
kings as, 1068
merit making and transference by, 5874–5875
monastic and lay types of, 8798
as moral heroes, 1083–1085
mountains associated with, 6213–6214
multiple, belief in, 1116
names of, 1079
Northern school Chan explanation of, 1521
pāramitās developed by, 6993–6994
path of, **996–1000,** 3180
heroic actions on, 1084
in Hinayana Buddhism, 2028–2029
in Huayan Buddhism, 4145–4146
in Mādhyamika Buddhism, 1300
in Mahāyāna Buddhism, 996–997, 998–999, 1116
in Sarvāstivāda Buddhism, 999, 8119, 8120
in Theravāda, 997, 1085
and meditation, 1285–1286
merit in, 5874–5875
Sakya Paṇḍita on, 8052
Śāntideva on, 8109–8110
soteriology and, 8528
sources of, 997, 998–999
stages of, 997, 999–1000, 1085, 1116, 7358
śūnyatā (emptiness) and, 8856–8857
in Tibetan Buddhism, 1156, 1224
Zhengyan's Compassion Relief (Ciji) mission and, 1789
in Zhenyan Buddhism, 9962
poetry of, 7211
prajñā attained by, 7358
in Pure Land Buddhism, 1114, 8982
qualities of, 997–998, 999, 1082
exchanged with other religions, 8932
rebirth of, 998, 2131
refusing to enter *nirvāṇa,* 1083, 1116
as role models, 1085
saving power of, 3887
as spiritual guides, 8712
stupas and, 8797–8798
in Tibetan Buddhism, 1082, 1152, 1156, 1224
upāya used by, 9485–9486
Vasubandhu as, 9527
vows of (*See* Vows and oaths, Buddhist)
wisdom and compassion of, 2630
women as, 3333, 8038
worship of, 7495
Bodhissatvabhūmi (Buddhist text), 5436
Bodhi trees, in Southeast Asian Buddhism, 9830
Bodhivaṃsa (Buddhist text), 1199
Bödiger, Ute, on jaguars in shamanism, 8291

Bodily marks, **1000–1005**. *See also specific marks*
in African religious drama, 2456, 2457–2458
forbidden in Islam, 1001
forbidden in Judaism, 1001, 1002
forbidden in Roman Catholicism, 1001
permanent, 1001
in South American Indian religions, in Pilagá religion (Gran Chaco), 8636
of supernatural election, 1004–1005
temporary, 1001
Bodman, Whitney S., on Satan, 8125–8126
Bodnath stupa, 7166–7167
Bo dong Paṇ chen Phyogs las rnam rgyal, 1233
Bo dong pa order (Buddhism), 1233
Bǫðvarr Bjarki (hero), 9166
Body
divine
and disease, origin of, 3809
in feminist theology, 4166
of God, descriptions of, 6741
human (*See* Human body)
of Jesus
church in correspondence with, 7983
female embodiment and, 3037
Thomas Aquinas on, 3170
"Body, Brain and Culture" (Turner), 9407
Body in Pain, The (Scarry), 6947
Body *maṇḍala* practice, 5642
in Cakrasamvara tradition, 1350
Body of Faith: Judaism as Corporeal Election, The (Wyschogrod), 2746
Body painting, 1001, 1004
in African religious drama, 2456, 2457–2458
in Australian Indigenous religions, 4305, 4306
in Caribbean religions, 1427
Djan'kawu, 2379, 2380
masks and, 5765, 5766
in North American Indian drama, 2462
Body-soul *(thumos),* in Greek religion, 8541
Boeckh, August, 9650
Boehme, Jakob, **1006**
on androgynes, 339–340
on angels, 348
disciples of, 1006
on knowledge, 5206
and language of fire, 3120
modern gnosis launched by, 3514
and nature, 6434
Schelling (Friedrich), influence on, 8148
on Sophia, 8523
on theodicy, 1006
on *Ungrund,* 1540
writings of, 1006
Boekine (shrine), 7444
Boethius, **1007**
Aristotle's works translated by, 480, 1007, 7192
on eternity, 2855, 3200
execution of, 1007, 7192
metaphysics of, 5990
on music, 6305
Neoplatonism and, 6475
on numbers, 6746
and problem of universals, 6644
on shape shifting, 8302
theism of, 9104
on Trinity, 9361
writings of, 1007, 7192
Boethusians
calendar of, 8018–8019
Sadducees, alliance with, 8018
Boff, Clodovis, 877
Boff, Leonardo, liberation theology of
charisma in, 5439
Christology and, 5439
ecology and, 2610
in progressive Islam, 6098, 6099
Bofu (musical instrument), 6293, 6294
Bogatyrev, Pierre, 5580
Bogazköy (Hittite text), 2431
Bogazköy (Turkey), Hittite archaeological site at, 4068, 4070–4071
Boggart (spirit), 2952
Bogomil (priest), 3523
Bogomils (Balkan sect)
angels and, 347–348, 3523
decline of, 3524
dualistic doctrine of, 1456, 2505, 2508, 2509, 2511, 2513–2514, 3523–3524, 9415
election in, 2747
Gnostic elements of, 3523–3524
Manichaeism and, 5657, 5668
Bogoras, W. G., 1015
Bogoraz, Waldemar, 473, 474–475
Bögüči (sorcerer), 1785
Bohannan, Laura, 5850
Bohemia
Christianity in, women's monasteries, 6763
Moravians in, 6190–6191
Bohl, Franz Marius Theodor, on *Epic of Gilgamesh,* 3487
Böhlig, Alexander, 3533
Bohm, David
chaos theory and, 1542
influence on Frye (Northrop), 3224
on nature, 6437
Böhme, Jakob, biblical exegesis of, 3525
Bohoras. *See* Musta'lī Ismā'īlīyah
Bohoras (India), Ṭayyibīyah and, 8335
Bohr, Niels, 7138, 7139
Bohu imperial conference, 1575
Boileau, Nicolas, 3051
Boime, Albert, 4282
Boisen, Anton T., 7477, 7486
Boisselier, Brigitte, 7598, 7599
Bo Jui (poet), 7214
Bokero (deity), 5181
Boldogasszony (Holy Virgin Mary), meanings of, 4225
Bole-Maru cult (North America), 6718
Bolívar, Simón, spirit cult invoking, 6579
Bolivia
Chiriguano people of, 8634
Guarasu religion in, lord of animals in, 8580
Qolla-huaya people of
ayllu of, 8617
herbal healers among, 3811
Siriono people of, Yasi (moon) and, 6439
Bollandists, historiography of, 4030
Boloi (magic), 9389
Boloi ba bosigo (night sorcery), 9389
Boloi ba motshegare (day sorcery), 9389
Bolsheviks, Merezhkovskii (Dmitrii) opposing, 5869
Boman, Thorleif, 6374
Bombardment techniques, trances induced by, 8688
Bomberg Rabbinic Bible, 888
Bon. *See* Bon religion
Bon (Swami), on knowledge, 5199
Bona Dea (deity), women in cult of, 3385–3386
Bonald, Louis de, on religion as social phenomena, 8492
Bonardel, Françoise, on Hermetism, 3953–3954
Bonato, Guido, 564
Bonaventure, **1010–1013,** 3183
on angels, 347
on demons, 2278
on existence of God, 7421
Francis of Assisi and, 3185
as friar, 7724
on heart of Jesus, 3883
influence of, 1013
on knowledge, 5204
life of, 1010–1011
on meditation, 5818
mysticism of, 6349
on nature, 6432
theology of, 1011–1013, 9136
on Trinity, 9361
on "two books," 9422
Victorine tradition and, 4151
writings of, 1011
Bond, George, 9015
Bondi, Hermann, steady state theory and, 2032
Bonds. *See* Binding
Bondye (deity), in Vodou, 9636
Bone, Gavin, 9730
Bones, **1013–1016**. *See also* Burial
animal
in Arctic religions, 471, 474
lord of the animals and, 5513
in rituals, 1013, 1015
in Caribbean religions, 1427
divination by, in prehistoric China, 1582, 1583, 1628, 1891
in Hawaiian religion, royal bones, encasement of, 3799
in Indonesian religions, 3235
in Melanesian religions, ghosts and, 5833, 5838
in Mesoamerican religions
creation myths of, 5934–5935
musical instruments made from, 6267, 6268
in mortuary practices, 1014–1015
Neanderthal use of, 6950, 6951
in Paleolithic religion, 1014, 6953
as relics (*See* Relics)
in shamanistic initiations, 8271
skulls, symbolism and ritual of, 3804–3805
in South American Indian religions, bone souls and, 8583–8584
Bonfire, at Easter, 2579
Bong, Sharon, 3304
Bongaka (therapy), 9389
Bongo, Peter, 6746
Bongo ghosts, in Caribbean religions, 1435
Bongosan (chanting), 6301
Bonhoeffer, Dietrich, **1016–1017**
on atonement, 597
autobiography of, 699
on deputyship, 5479
execution of, 1016–1017
fighting Nazism, 1016–1017
on God, 3558–3559
on imitation of Christ, 1670
on implicit religion, 4401
on kingdom of God, 5151
legacy of, 1017
on temptation, 9071
theology of, 9138
writings of, 1017, 5478
Boniface (English missionary), **1017–1018**
as archbishop of Mainz, 1018
in Germany, 821, 1018
paganism, efforts against, 1689
sacred oak destroyed by, 6083
and Lioba, 6763
nuns assisting, 822, 1018
riddles of, 6987
Boniface VIII (pope), **1018–1020**
achievements of, 1019

in conflict with Philip IV, 2524, 7280
and Duns Scotus (John), 2524
extravagances of, 9340
Great Western Schism and, 8157
Böning, Ewald, on Mapuche religion, 8580
Boni religion (Guyana), funeral rites in, 3236
Bonnell, Victoria E., on social categories, 8470
Bonney, Charles C., 9804
Bonn University, 804
Bonpos. *See* Bon religion
Bon religion (Tibet), **1007–1010,** 1150–1151, 7868, 9186. *See also* Dzogchen
beliefs and practices in, 1008–1009
and Buddhism, 3154, 9182, 9186, 9841–9842
struggle between, 5222, 5223
diffusion of, 1009–1010
drums in, 2497–2498
literature, 2549, 2550
music in, 6298
origins of, 1008, 9186
Rnying ma pa school of Buddhism distinct from, 7868
shamanism in, 8273
study of, 9188, 9190
Treasure tradition in, 9331, 9333
Bonsai (tree), 9334
Bonuman, 126–127
Bonus, Petrus, 252
on nature, 6433
Bonvecchio, Claudio, on kingship, 5160
Böö (shaman), 1326
Boodin, J. E., 6964
Booger Dance, 1565, 7197
Book banning. *See also* Censorship
in Tibetan Buddhism, 5224
Book burning
in classical China, 1574, 1590
of Talmud manuscripts, 8971
Book Concern Department, 68
Book of Abraham, in Mormonism, 8447
Book of Adversity (ʿAṭṭār), 601
Book of Aḥiqar, ḥokhmah in, 4079
Book of Beliefs and Opinions, The (Saʿadyah), 154, 4887, 7438
Book of Caverns (Egyptian text), 4319
Book of Changes. See Yijing
Book of Commandments, A (Mormon text), 6193
Book of Common Order (document of Scottish Reformation), 5212
Book of Common Prayer (Anglican)
Apostles' Creed in, 2052
Cranmer (Thomas) and, 2051, 5328, 7281, 7662
under Elizabeth I, 349, 7663
Hooker (Richard), defense by, 4124
identity and, 2056
liturgy in, 350, 5328
Paschal vigil, 1742
on prayer, 9812
revised for American Methodists, 5998
revision of (1552), 2051–2052
Book of Concord (Lutheran, 1580), 5538
creeds in, 2057
doctrine in, 2055
Book of Confessions (Presbyterian)
purpose of, 2061
role of, 2058
Book of Daniel, and messianism, 5975
Book of Discipline, in African American churches, 68
Book of Durrow (Burckhardt), 1324
Book of Family Ritual, ancestor worship in, 323
Book of Gates (Egypt), 2708, 4319
Book of Giants (Mani), 347
Book of Going Forth by Day (Egypt), 138, 779, 1553, 2708, 2719
boats in, 989
bread in, 1041
eye in, 2940
the Fall in, 2962
as funerary offering, 4318, 4319, 7634
innocence in, 7757
judgment in, 139, 5026
merit and, 5871
pigs in, 7144
publications of, 2729
Re in, 7634
Thoth in, 9168
translations of, 2729
Book of Invasions, 1480, 1488
Book of John (Mandaean text), 5635
Manda d'Hiia in, 5634
Book of Justifying a Man in the Realm of the Dead (Egypt), 2718
Book of Kells (Burckhardt), 1324
Book of Khusraw (ʿAṭṭār), 601
Book of Lamentation (Gregory of Narek), 3694
Book of Leinster, 1480
Book of Malachi, 933
Book of Martyrs (Foxe), 7662–7663
Book of Master Zhuang. See Zhuangzi
Book of Mercy, 249
Book of Mormon, 6516, 6529
Bible's relation to, 6192–6193
mystery of, vol. 14 color insert
Smith (Joseph) and, 6192, 8447
translation of, 8203
Book of Mysteries (ʿAṭṭār), 601
Book of Mysteries, The (Mani), 787
Book of Odes
afterlife in, 169
giant panda in, 808
Maspero (Henri) and, 5773
Book of Opinions and Beliefs, The (Saʿadia ben Joseph), 9236
Book of Questions, The (Jabès, 5483
Book of Religion and Empire (al-Ṭabarī), 7242
Book of Revelation. See Revelation, Book of
Book of Rites (Liji), 1561, 1562–1563
Book of Rules (Tyconius), 874
Book of Ruth. See Ruth
Book of Sects and Creeds, The (al-Sharashtānī), 9128
Book of Selections (ʿAṭṭār), 601
Book of Sentences (Peter Lombard), 8, 7066, 7067, 9136
Book of Taliesin (Welsh text), 8968, 8969
Book of the Balances, 249
Book of the Cave Treasures, 1502
Book of the Commandments (Maimonides), 5615
Book of the Courtier (Castiglione), 4367
Book of the Covenant, as law code, 1845
Book of the Dead (Egypt). *See Book of Going Forth by Day*
Book of the Dead (Tibet), 1151, 1153, 1313, 7868
deities as reflections of humans in, 131, 134–135
geographical instructions in, 136
instructions to departed souls in, 8703
shamanistic elements in, 3156
Book of the Goddess (Olson), 3612
Book of the Law (Liber AL vel Legis) (Crowley), third age in, 2072
Book of the Laws of the Countries, The (Bardesanite doctrine), 786, 787
Book of Tobit, bread in, 1041
Book of Tradition, The (Ibn Daud). *See Sefer ha-qabbalah* (Ibn Daud)
Book of Two Ways (Egypt), 2705, 4318
Book religions. *See* Scriptural religions
Books of Enoch, The: Aramaic Fragments of Qumran Cave 4 (Milik), 902
Books of Jeu (Gnostic text), 3508, 3515
Boorstin, Daniel, 7321
Booth, Catherine
Palmer (Phoebe), inspiration from, 4083
Salvation Army, role in, 8063
Booth, Evangeline, Salvation Army, role in, 8063
Booth, William, **1020–1021**
Salvation Army, role in, 8063, 8064
Booths, Festival of. *See* Sukkot
Bopp, Franz, 4458, 6234
Bora ceremonies
history of study of, 681, 682
Rainbow Snake in, 7605
Boran Oromo religion (Ethiopia), 2573
Bordaş, Liviu, on Eliade, 2760
Bordreuil, Pierre, 5846
Borg, Sonia, 3391
Borgia Codex, 5275–5276
Maya calendar and, 1360
Boris I of Bulgaria, Byzantine *vs.* Western Christianity and, 1683
Bormana (deity), 1484
Bormo (deity), 1483
Born, Max, on chance, 1527
"Born again." *See* Evangelical Christianity
Born-again experiences, soteriology and, 8528
Bornemann, Fritz, on culture, 8170
Bornemisza, Péter, humanism and, 4226
Borneo and Bornean religions, **1021–1022.** *See also* Dayak religion; Ngaju Dayak religion
agricultural rites in, 1021–1022
ethnic diversity of, 1021
funeral rites in, 1021, 3235, 3237, 9227
head hunting in, 1022, 3805
hierodouleia (sacred prostitution) in, 3969
Islam, spread of, 4658
tattooing in, 1003
women in, 1022
Bornkamm, Günther, on merit, 5875
Borobudur (stupa), 1134, 1135, 9052–9053
Boróro religion (Brazil)
death cults and ancestor worship in, 8584
hunting rituals in, 8582
jaguar in, 8581
myths of, 3292
Golden Age in, 3628
knot symbolism of, 5198
society of, 3292
villages and cosmology in, 7984

Borowitz, Eugene, 7672
Borr (mythic figure)
birth of, 3446
sons of, 3446, 3454
Borrichius, Olaus (Olaf Borch), Hermetism and alchemy, apology for, 3949
Borromeo, Carlo, **1022–1023**
Borromeo Codex (Savonarola), development of author's thought in, 8139
Borthwick, Meredith, 3321
Bortnyansky, Dimitry, 6310
Boru Meda, Council of, 2861
Borvo (deity), 1483
Bosch, David J., evangelical Dutch Reformed tradition and, 1724
Bose, Netaji Subhascandra, 827, 829
Boshier, Adrian, 9613
Bosman, Willem, 3044, 9326
Bosnia-Herzogovina
in Austro-Hungarian Empire, 4674
independence of, 1686
Islam in, 4674, 4677
Boss, Sarah Jane, on Mary, 5756
Bosses, Bartholomew de, Leibniz's correspondence with, 5407
Bossuet, Jacques-Bénigne, 173
and Gallicanism, 3258–3259
Leibniz's (Gottfried) correspondence with, 5406
Boston, John S., on masks, 5768
Boston (Massachusetts), Museum of Fine Arts in, 500
Boston Church of Christ, International Churches of Christ and, 1781
Boston Movement, 6561
Boswell, John, 5413, 5414, 5862
on sexual orientation, 8244
Bōt (hall), 9054, 9055
Botkin, B. A., 77
Botocudo religion (South America), supreme being in, 8578
Botswana
Khoi religion in, 5135
San religion in, 5135
Tswana religion in, 7805
Bottéro, Jean, 5969
Böttiger, Karl, 3045
Boturini Codex, Huitzilopochtli in, 4155
Boucher, Daniel, 1262
Boucher, Sandy, 3330, 6536
Boudicca (British queen), 3387
Bouglé, Célestin, 5785
Boullaye, Henri Pinard de la, cultural-historical method of, 5260
Bounama, Bilali, 3086
Boundaries
clowns and, 1838–1840
sacred places and
division of space and, 7982
in Maori religion, 7982
sacrilege and, 8010–8011
Boundary stones
in *ḥaram* and *ḥawṭah,* 3777
Kudurru (inscriptions), oath/curse formula and, 2102
Bouphonia (ox-slaying), 1466–1467
Bourbon family, in Reformation, 7662
Bourdieu, Pierre, 379
"habitus" and "practice" rather than "culture," 2088
on myth, 1986
and postcolonial theory, 10042
structuralism and, 8759
Bourgeois, Louis, 6310
Bourguignon, Erika, 76
on sex roles, 10027, 10028
on spirit possession, 8687, 10027
Bourke, J. G., 6670
Bournonville, Auguste, 2156
Bous (mythical figure), 744
Bousset, Wilhelm
on Antichrist, 394
on Gnosticism, 3514, 3532
and liberal Protestantism, 6104
on mystery religions, 6327
on origins of Christianity, 7707
in Religionsgeschichtliche Schule, 7707
Boutroux, Émile
Durkheim (Émile) influenced by, 2527
on science and religion, 7341
Bouvet, Joachim, Hermetism and, 3950
Bouzid, Nouri, 3098
Bowen, Harold, 4718
Bowen, John, 379
Bower Manuscripts, as Āyurvedic text, 3853
Bowing (posture), in Muslim worship, 7342
Bowlby, John, attachment theory of, 1970
Bows and arrows. *See* Archery
Bowser, G. P., in Churches of Christ, 1781
Box, G. H., 900
Boxer Rebellion, 1610
Christian missions and, 1725–1726
Boxing, *shaolin,* 5731, 5736
Boyarin, Daniel
on gender, 3297
in Judaism, 3351
on midrash, 6020, 6021
Boy Bishop, Carnival and, 1441
Boyce, Mary, 204, 2964
Boyd, Martin, 3081, 3084
Boyd, R. H., 69
Boyd, Robert, on dual inheritance system, 8475
Boyd, Stephen, in men's studies, 5862, 5863
Boyd, Stephen B., 3314
Boyer, Carl B., 3438, 3444
Boyer, Pascal, 385
on religious beliefs, 2089, 8479
Boyés (Carib leaders)
in Caribbean religions, 1430
politics and, 1431
Boyle, Kevin, on human rights, 5363
Boyle, Robert, 253
on God, 3556
mechanistic model and, 8183
Boyne (deity), 1484, 1486
Bo You, resurrection of, 7763
Boy Scouts, in India, 845
Boys' Day (Japan), 2411
Bo Yuan (Buddhist monk), 5317
Božä (deity), 2574
Bozhang (Buddhist monk), on teaching methods, 8714
Brace, Charles Loring, 7487
Bracketing
in phenomenology, 7088
in sociology, 8495
Bracteates (Germanic medallions), 3459
runic inscriptions on, 7940
Braden, Charles S., 6565, 6583
Bradlaugh, Charles, 844
Bradley, David, 75
Bradley, F. H.
and analytic philosophy, 306
monistic philosophy of, 6146
pantheism of, 6962
Bradney, Anthony, 6542
Bradwardine, Thomas, 3203
on Hermetism, 3945
against Pelagianism, 7026
Brady, Don, 675–677, 678, 679
Brady, Veronica, 3080, 3082
Bragi (deity), 849
role in Germanic pantheon, 3453
Brahe, Tycho
geo-heliocentric model of, 1977
relationship with Kepler (Johannes), 5112
Brahmā (deity), **1023–1024**
and Ādi Śakti, 4433
bird of, 4438
as creator of drama, 2436
day of/year of, 2018 (*See also* Pralaya)
death of
bhakti synthesis and, 3999–4000
and Goddess, reintegration of, 3999
in Śiva-Kapālin myth, 8050
penance of Śiva for, 8040
in Puranas, 8415
egg symbolism and, 2701
heads of, 7550
iconography of, 1025
in conflict with Śiva, 1024
in Purāṇas, 7500
in *trimūrti,* 4000
methods of creation used by, 1023–1024
origin of name, 1024
Prajāpati as prototype of, 3992
Sarasvatī as consort of, 4326
self-reproduction of, 1024
Śiva revealing himself to, 4324
status of, 1023, 1024–1025
swans and, 8894
tapas produced by, 8998
temples to, in Southeast Asia, 4012
in Trinity, 4422, 4423, 4443, 9346
Brahmacārin (student), 2330, 4522, 9566. *See also* Āśramas
celibacy and, 1476, 1477
Brahmachārya (novice), 4421
Brahma Kumaris
celibacy among, 6516
in Europe, 6568
Brahmaloka, in Hinayana Buddhist cosmology, 2027
Brahmamudi (Brahma knot), 5275
Brahman (Hindu concept), **1024–1026**
achievement of, as end of reincarnation, 7678
and *īśvara,* 4751
as Goddess, in *Śākta* Tantrism, 8547
ātman identified with, 9569
attainment of, 8546
Bādarāyaṇa on, 736
brahman-ātman equation
in Upaniṣads, 3993
swan as symbol of, 8894
Brāhmo Samāj worship of, 7932
in Caitanya's theology, 1346
as cosmic principle, 1024, 1026, 7405
as cosmic riddle, 1025–1026, 6987
delight in, 3881
description of, 9481
etymology of word, 1024
and *flamen,* common etymology of, 3125
as foundational essence, 8546
Hegel on, 4447
historiography and, 4025
human connection to, 8546
in *Atharvaveda Saṃhitā,* 9551
in Purāṇas, 7501
in Upaniṣadic cosmology, 2015, 2016
in Upaniṣads, 9480
in Vedānta, 9546–9549
knowledge of, 5200–5201
light associated with, 5452
māyā and, 5794, 5795
meanings of, 1024, 2254, 4427–4428, 6408
monism and, 6144, 6149
mysticism and, 6343
mythology of, 1024–1025
Nimbārka on, 6623
personal *vs.* impersonal, 853, 6623
place for, in Hindu temple, 9039

Radhakrishnan (Sarvepalli) on, 6145
Rāmānuja on, 710–711, 4422
as sacred formula, 1025
Śaṅkara on, 4003–4004, 4422, 6144, 8105–8106, 8546
search for, 4427
semantic development of, 1025–1026
as space or abode, 2015
in Swaminarayan movement, 8891
and universe, 4422–4423
Brāhamaṇas (expositions of the *brahman*), 1024, **1026–1028**. *See also* Śatapatha Brāhmaṇa
Agni in, 179
breath in, 1043
cognitive element of, 5199
cosmology in, 2014–2015, 5447
death in, 4440
development of, 1026
in development of Hinduism, 3991–3992
heaven in, 3886
Indra in, 4467
īśvara in, 4751
Kurukṣetra in, 5268
mantras in, 5677
music in, 6281
mythology in, 9555
origin and meaning of word, 1026
origins of, 1026–1027
Prajāpati in, 1023, 7356
priests, four classes of, and, 3991
ritual in, 3991–3992, 9566–9567
Rudra in, 7934, 7935
sacrificial rituals in, 1026–1027, 7356
Saṃhitās and, 9551
sectarian attitudes toward, 4004
as source of Vedas, 1026, 4426
suicide in, 8831
supplements to, 4427
tapas in, 8998
triads in, 9345
Upaniṣads and, 9481
in Vedas, 9553
karman in, 5094
Vedism, relation to, 3989
brahmāṇḍa, ("egg of Brahmā"), *bhakti and,* 3999–4000
Brahmanism (Indian religion), **9568–9574**
Ahiṃsā in, 197
animal sacrifice in, 9571
Bhagavatism in, 9503
bhakti development as orthodoxy in, 4004
Buddhism and, 1133, 1138
confession in, 1886
deities in, 9571
fountain of youth in, 3177
karman in, 5094, 5095
vs. in Buddhism, 1887
monasticism in, 8093
philosophy in, 5200
renunciation and, 8093 (*See also* Saṃnyāsa)
rituals of, 9568–9569
ṛta in, 3001
sacred hearth fire in, 4106
sacrifice in, as cosmic process, 8003
Śaivism and, 8048
in Kashmir, 8047
sectarian and saint-singer movements as alternatives to, 4004–4005
Tantrism *vs.,* 4002–4003
texts of, 9568–9569
varṇa and *jāti* in, 9570
vs. Vedism, 9552–9553
Vietnamese religion influenced by, 9591
Brahmans (caste of priests), 1024, 9522–9523
aesthetics and, 50–51
in Bengal, 824, 825
creation of, 9522–9523
in dance drama, 2451
dances taught by, 2136
development as class, 3990
dharma of, 5346
eligibility for, 7395
functions of, 7405
goddess worship of, 826
hospitality code of, 4140
initiation of, 7815
in *varṇāśramadharma* theory of castes, 3995–3996
Kṛṣṇa and, 5251, 5252, 5253–5254
memorization of Vedas by, 5852
music in, 6280, 6281
mythology of, 4441
ordination of, 6853–6854
patronage of, 4429
power of, 7352
privileges of, 1102
pūjā performed by, 9265
purity of, 9570
retirement as *saṃnyāsin,* 8020–8021
as ritual overseers, 3991
sacred responsibility of, 7405
in Sikhism, *Ādi Granth* on, 33
Smārtas brahmans, 9503
social duties of, 2329–2330
supremacy of, 4428, 7254
in Tamil, 8974, 8975, 8976
vs. Śramaṇas, 1102
as winner of Brahmodya, 1025, 1026
Brahmasambandha mantra, 9517
Brahma Sūtra. See Vedānta Sūtra
Brahmavaivarta Purāṇa, 5457
Brahmaveda. See Atharvaveda
Brahmā Vidyā Mandir Ashram, 546
Brahmodya (Vedic ritual), 1025–1026, 6987
Brāhmo Samāj, **1028–1030**
goal of, 1028, 1029, 4431
iconoclasm of, 4283, 4285
leadership of, 1029
membership of, 1028
Muslim and Christian influences in, 4007
Roy (Ram Mohan) as founder of, 828, 1028, 1029, 4007, 4431, 7932, 9317
Sen (Keshab Chandra) and, 8227
Unitarianism influencing, 828, 1029, 9317
Vivekananda in, 9629, 9630
on women, 3320
Brahms, Johannes, 6312
Braide, Garrick, prophetic movement, 1720
Brain
aesthetics and, 50
comparison with computer, 6486
evolution of, 2917
imaging of, in psychology of religion, 7479
left *vs.* right hemisphere dominance, 5393
oral tradition and, 6425–6426
research on (*See* Neuroscience)
sacred time through neural patterning in, 7987–7988
structuralism and, 8750
structure of, shamanism and, 8279
in trance, 7049
visualization in, 6425–6427
Brain, Robert, 1002
Brain death, in Islam, 5812
Brainwashing, **1030–1036**
anticult movements on, 396, 1032, 2085–2086
Chinese ideology of, 2085–2086
communist, 1030–1031
cultic, 1031–1034
legal claims based on, 5376–5377
legislation on, 1033–1034
in new religious movements
allegations regarding, 6561–6562
debate on, 6515–6516, 6522–6523, 6525
origin of term, 1030
process of, 1031, 1032
reversing, 1032, 1033, 2291–2293
studies on, 1032, 1033, 1034–1035
Braithwaite, R. B., 307
Braj (city), Kṛṣṇa and, 5249, 5250
Braj Bhāṣā dialect, literary tradition of, 3984
Brakhage, Stan, 3101, 3102
Bralgu spirits, 661
Bramfield, Harry, 643–644
Bramwell, Anna, 2663
Bran (deity), 1489
Branch Davidians, **1036–1039,** 6553–6554
apocalypse and, 413, 5238
catastrophic millennialism (apocalypticism) of, 6545, 6546, 6554
child abuse allegations against, 6541
core beliefs of, 5237–5238
FBI siege of, 1036, 1037–1038, 5237, 7255
federal raid on (1993), 6516–6517, 6518, 6548, 6554, 6561
Cult Awareness Network's role in, 6525
fire in, 6564
gender roles in, 6516
history of, 6561
under Koresh (David), 1036, 1037, 1038, 5237–5239, 6553–6554, 6561
messiah of, 6547
origins of, 1036–1037, 5237, 6513
Seventh-day Adventism and, 6551
after siege, 1038–1039
tensions with society, 6548
and violence, conditions leading to, 6553
Brancusi, Constantin, 949
Brandeis University
Goodenough (Erwin R.) at, 3637
Jewish Renewal movement and, 4869
Jewish studies at, 4884
Brandenstein, C.-G. von, 9252
Brandewie, Ernest, Schmidt (Wilhelm), defense of, 8170
Brandon, George, 80
Brandon, S. G. F., 501, **1039–1040**
on Myth and Ritual school, 6381
Sharpe (Eric) and, 8304
Brandt, John Lincoln, 2987
Branham, William, 7030
Bran son of Febhal (deity), 1491
Bran the Blessed. *See* Bendigeidvran
Branwen (deity), 1489
Branwen Daughter of Llŷr (deity), 1486, 1490
in *Mabinogion,* 5546
'Bras pung monastery, 2131
institutional structure of, 8085
Brass, Paul, on politics of Āyurveda, 3856
Brasseur, Charles, 2435–2436

Brastiņš, Arvīds, 764
on Māra, 5691
Brastiņš, Ernests, 763–764
on Māra, 5691
Bratslav Hasidism, Naḥman in, 6401–6402
as *tsaddiq ha-emet* ("true *tsaddiq*"), 3790, 6401
Braude, Ann, on spirit possession, 8696
Braulio (bishop), 4556
Bravmann, René, on masks, 5766
Bray, Anna Eliza, 2952
Bray, Thomas, 350
Brazil and Brazilian religions. *See also* Amazonian religions; Ge religion; *See also* Boróro religion; Umbanda
African religions in (*See* Afro-Brazilian religions)
Buddhism, 1188, 1190
Carnival in, 1443–1444
Cinta Larga religion, creation myth in, 2013
Enawenê Nawê people, cosmology of, 2012–2013
films from, 3099
Inquisition in, 4503, 4505, 4506
Islam, 4682, 4683, 4684
Kardecism in, 5090–5091
literature of, 3063, 3064
African influences on, 3064–3065
Macumba, 120
spirit possession in, 2139
missions and colonialism in
French, 1698
Portuguese, 1695, 1697
missions to Africa from, 107
music in, 6272, 6273–6274
new religious movements in
with Japanese origins, 6574
nativistic, 6576, 6577
Protestant-related, 6579
spiritist cults, 6578
noise in, 7037
nonviolent resistance in, 5153
Pentecostalism, 6579, 7029
popular culture of, Afro-Brazilian religions in, 124–125
psychedelic drugs in, 7470
Roman Catholicism
campaign against spiritism by, 5091
ecclesiastical districts, 1701
pilgrimage in, 7149, 7150
Samba schools, 1444
syncretism in, 8933
Tapirape healers in, 3812
transculturation of, 9308–9309
trees in, 9337
tricksters in, 9358
Upper Xingu peoples, 2011, 6273
variety of religions in, 119
Bread, **1040–1041**
in Aztec religion, 1041
in Christianity, 3171
in Eucharist, 848, 987, 1040, 1041, 3171
in Lord's Prayer, 5517
in Egyptian religion, 1041
in Greek religion, 1040–1041
in Islam, 2401
in Israelite religion, 1040, 1041
in Judaism, 2398, 7003
Marrano, 5719
in Poland, 2400
in rituals, 1040, 1041
as symbol, 1041
unleavened, 1040, 2400, 5388
Bread for the World, 3174
Breadfruit, in Micronesian religions, 6006
Breasted, James, 2730
"Breast" goddesses, 3607–3608
Breast milk
in goddess worship, 3588
as kinship substance, 5184
Breath and breathing, **1041–1047**
in Amazonian Quechua religions, 284
in Bible, 1042
in Buddhism, 1045
in Chinese religion, 1043, 1045–1046
qi cultivation and, 3862
in Christianity, 1042, 1046
prayer of the heart and, 3883
in Daoism, 9845
French feminists on, 3030
in Gnosticism, 3510
in Greek religion, 1041–1042
in Hinduism, 1043–1045, 7362–7363
aṣṭāṅgayoga (eight-limbed discipline), 8704
in *Haṭhayoga*, 3795
in Islam, 1042–1043, 1046
in Judaism, 1042
in meditation, 5820
miracles and, 6052
percussive, 7037–7038
and prayer, 1046
of shamans, 9218
as sign of life, 5443
soul and, 8532
in Transcendental Meditation, 9290
in vision inducement, 9613
in Yoga, 1043–1046, 5819, 7038, 9895
Breath spirits
in Khanty religion, 5122
in Mansi religion, 5122
Breault, Marc, 1037
Brébeuf, Jean de, 753–754
Brecht, Bertolt, 2474, 2476
Bregžis-Marovskis, Karlis, 763–764
Brelich, Angelo, 863, **1047–1048,** 2905, 4486–4487
historiography of, 4046
on religious behavior, origin of, 4825
Bremen, Adam von, 3103
Bremmer, Jan, 5469
Bremond, Henri, and Marie de l'Incarnation, 5712
Brent, Charles Henry, 352
Philippine missions, 1727–1728
Brentano, Clemens, Görres (Joseph von) and, 3639
Brentano, Franz, 7088
Bres (mythic figure), 1488, 5528, 9390, 9391
Breslau (Germany), *Wissenschaft des Judentums* at, 4878
Bresson, Robert, 3100, 3101
Brest, Council of (Synod of Brest-Litovsk, 1596)
Cyril and, 2114–2115
Uniatism and, 1685
Brethren, Hutterian. *See* Hutterian Brethren
Brethren, Swiss, 304
Brethren of Purity. *See* Ikhwān al-Ṣafāʾ
Brethren of the Common Life, 1685
Brethren of the Free Spirit, 6869–6870
Breton folklore, keys in, 5116
Breton language, 1478
Breuer, Isaac, 196, 6902–6903
Breuer, Josef, 3215
Breuer, Marcel, 6120
Breuer, Mordecai, 869
Breuil, Henri, **1048**
Breyer, Jacques, 9067
Breysig, Kurt, on *Heilbringer,* 2090
Brezhnev, Leonid, Russian Orthodox Church under, 7944
Brgyud pa (Buddhist lineage), 1222
Bṛhadāraṇyaka Upaniṣad
breath as life in, 5443
guṇas in, 8090
heart in, 3881
karman in, 5095
liberation in, 8546
mind in, 2016
monism in, 6144
puruṣa in, 7522
Bṛhad-bhāgavatāmṛ ta, devotion in, 1346
Bṛhaddevatā (Vedic text), goddess worship in, 2525
Bṛhaspati (mythic figure)
Cārvāka and, 1446
in *Ṛgveda,* 4326
Bṛhatkathā (Guṇāḍhya), 10033
Bṛhat Saṃhitā (Hindu text), 9038, *9039,* 9040
Bribes, sacrificial gifts as, 8002
Briçonnet, Bishop, 2992
Bridal chamber rite *(thalamos nymphon),* in Gnosticism, 8247
Bride-price, 5725, 7780, 7782
in Tswana marriage ritual, 7805
Brides. *See also* Weddings
spirit possession of, 2934
virginity of, 9607
Brideshead Revisited (Waugh), 3061
Bridewealth, cattle as, 1464
"Bridge at Arta, The" (folk song), 1051
Bridge of Pain, 1051
Bridges, **1048–1052**
in Buddhism, 1050–1051
in Christianity, 1050, 1051
in Indo-Iranian religions, 1049
in Islam, 1049–1050, 1051
al-Aaraf bridge, after judgment, 3885
in Judaism, 1049
in ritual sacrifices, 1051
symbolism of, 1051–1052
Warao snake-bridge, 1503–1504
in Zoroastrian tradition, Chinvat Bridge, 1052, **1647**
Bridge to Freedom, 1781, 1782
Bridge to Spiritual Freedom, 4247
Bridgman, P. W., 5499
Briefe Declaraccion of the Chiefe Poyntes of the Christian Religion, Set Forth in a Table of Predestination, A (Beza), 851
Brief Outline on the Study of Theology (Schleiermacher), 429
Briffault, Robert Stephen, 2983
on matriarchy, 3611, 3612
Brigham Young University, 6195
Brighid (Brigit) (deity), 1053
in Celtic religion, 9390–9391
Roman parallels, 1484
Brighid of Kildare (Brigit of Kildare), **1052–1054,** 1484, 3388, 6763, 9391
Brighter Society Movement, 7795
Brightman, E. S., 6962
Brightman, Robert, on culture, 2088
Brighton Convention, Smith (Hannah Whitall) at, 8445–8446
Brigit. *See* Brighid
ʾBri gung ʾJig rten gsum mgon (Drikung Jikten Sumgon), on *mahāmudrā,* 5598
ʾBri gung pa order (Buddhist), 1230
ʾBri gung Skyob pa ʾJig rten gsum mgon (Drigung Kyopa), 1226
Brikmanis, Jānis, 765
Bringing Ritual to Mind: Psychological Foundations of Cultural Forms (Lawson and McCauley), 7851, 7858
Brink, André, 3088
Brinnin, J. M., 3279
Brinton, Daniel G., 4459–4460, 5941
Bʿrît (covenant), 4745
in Hosea, 4137
meaning of term, 2047
naming rituals and, 7819
in rabbinic Judaism, 2050
in Septuagint, 2049

Britain and British religions. *See also* Anglicanism; England; Ireland; Scotland; Wales
affliction in, 58
Afghānī (Jamāl al-Dīn al-) on, 64
Aga Khan I as ally of, 173
All Souls Day in, 2230
Arthur in, 508–509
ballet in, 2162
broadcasting in, religious, 7714
Buddhism, 1187, 1188–1189, 1190, 1191
cats in, 1463
Celtic settlement, 1478
China, study of, 1635
colonialism of
African religions, interpretation of, 1856–1857
in Canada, 9299, 9300–9301
in India (*See* India, British rule in)
missions in, 6084
in North America, 1708, 7301
in Southeast Asia, 4660
dance influenced by, 2135
drama in, 2477
Earth Liberation Front in, 2562
ecclesiology in, 1774
education in, religious, 7734
the Enlightenment in, 2797
evangelicalism in, 2887–2888, 2890, 2892
feminism in
first-wave, 3320
and Hindu women, 3320
second-wave, 3310–3311
folklore of
elves in, 2952
goblins in, 2952
yarthkins in, 2952
fundamentalism in, 2890
games in, 3267
Graham (Billy) in, 2890
Hinduism, Swaminarayan movement in, 8892
historiography in, 4043, 4048–4049
India under (*See* India, British rule in)
International Society for Krishna Consciousness in, 4522
Islam, 4674, 4675, 4676, 4679–4680
Israelism in, British, 1657–1658
Jainism, 4770
Judaism
liberal, 6166–6167
women in, 3354–3355
megalithic religion, 5823, 5824
Melqart in, 5848–5849
Moravians in, 6191
museums in, 6243, 6245, 6246
Myth and Ritual school of, 6380–6381
new religious movements in, 6568–6569
observatories (ancient) in, 8835–8836 (*See also* Stonehenge)
Pentecostalism, 7029
philosophy in, on conscience, 1943
Rastafari in, 7624
religious studies in, 1872
runic inscriptions in, 7940
spiritism in, 5090
ʿUrābī revolt against (1881–1882), 5
Wicca movement in, 3021–3022, 9728
British and Foreign Bible Society
on Apocrypha, 881
in Latin America, 1699–1700
British Association for the Study of Religion (BASR), women's studies in, 3313
British Conference of the New Church (Swedenborgian), history of, 8902–8903
British Council of Churches, 2684
British East India Company (BEIC), and missionaries, 6196
British empiricism, Hume (David), role of, 4192
British Ethical Union, 2857
British Guiana, population in, 1698
British Isles. *See* Anglicanism; Britain; Ireland
British-Israelism, 1657–1658, 1659
British Museum (London), 6243
British North America Act (1867), 9300–9301
Brittany. *See also* Celtic religion
Celts in, 1478
megalithic religion in, 5823, 5824
Britten, Benjamin, 6313
Bṛndāvan (India), Kṛṣṇaism in, 5253–5254
Broadcasting, religious, **7709–7716**
Broad Church movement
Coleridge, role of, 1853
and liberal Protestantism, 6105
Broadlands estate, camp meetings at, 8445
Broca, Paul, 6485
Brockopp, Jonathan, 5627
Brod, Harry, 3314
Broda, Johanna, 5943
on Aztec human sacrifice, 4187
Brodie, Veronica, 648–649, 650
Brody, Hugh, 6678
'Brog mi (Drokmi), 1153, 1224
Hevajra Tantra and, 3966
Mar pa and, 5715
Bromley, David G., 2292, 6523, 6524, 6525, 6526, 6527, 6553
'Brom ston Rgyal ba'i 'byung gnas (Dromtön), 1153, 1224
Bromwich, Rachel, 5878
Bronze
drums made of, 2494
inscriptions on, in Zhou dynasty, 5352
mining of, 5987
smelting of, 5987
in Southeast Asian musical instruments, 6288
Bronze Age
graves, 989
circle symbolism in, 1791
temples, 9062
Brook, Peter, 2476, 3711
Brooklyn Museum of Art, 4282
Brooks, Alethea, 6585
Brooks, Cleanth, 5474
Brooks, Douglas, 8988
Brooks, Nona, 6584, 6585
Brooks, Phillips, 2289
Brooks, Rodney, 511
Brooten, Bernadette, 3352, 5413, 5414
Brorson, Hans Adolf, 3705
Brosses, Charles de, 113
and animism, 365–366
comparative mythology of, 6366
Cult of the Fetish Gods, 3043, 3044, 3045
on fetishism, 366, 4040, 4363
Brossier, Marthe, 2931
Brother. *See* Siblings
Brotherhood, sworn, in Icelandic literature, 5509
Brotherhood of Eulis, sexual magic and, 8251
Brotherhood of the Cross and Star
in Europe, 6568
reincarnation in, 106
"Brotherly Union" statement, 305, 5860
Brothers and Sisters of Penance, 3182, 3183
Brothers Karamazov, The (Dostoevsky), 2422, 3059, 3062
Jesus in, 4845
Broughton, Thomas, reference book by, 30, 31
Broughton, William Grant, as bishop of Australia, 1732
Brouwer, Hendrik H. J., 3386
Brown, Antoinette, 3310
Brown, C. Mackenzie, 3590
Brown, Joseph Epes, 957, 3090
Brown, Judith, 5413
Brown, Karen McCarthy, 81
Brown, Margaret, Campbell (Alexander) and, 1377
Brown, Marilyn, 5414
Brown, Michael, 3085, 6576
Brown, Peter, 946–947, 4380
on relics, 7688
Brown, Raymond E., on Lord's Prayer, 5517
Brown, Robert, 4459
Brown, Terry, on Christianity in Solomon Islands, 8517
Brown, Truesdell S., 2883
Brown, William, 68
on knowledge, 5207
Brown, William Adams, liberal Protestantism of, 6103, 6105–6106
Brown bear, 807–809
Brown Brothers of Holy Light, Holy Order of MANS and, 4102
Brown Bull of Cuailnge, 1485, 1487, 1493
Browne, E. Martin, 2476
Browne, Robert, **1054**
on Puritanism, 7663
Browne, Thomas, Hermetism and, 3950
Brownies (spirits), 2952
Browning, Don, 7479
Brownists (England), 1054
Brownson, Orestes, 2289
Broyda, Simḥa Zisl, 6241
Brten 'gyur (Bon text), 1008, 1009
Bruce, Calvin E., 966
Bruce, James, 3508
Bruce (Brucianus) Codex (Gnostic text), discovery of, 3508, 3515
Bruchac, Joseph, 7225
Brucker, Jacob, on Hermetism, 3951
Bruckner, Anton, 6312
Bruderhofs, of Hutterian Brethren, 4239
Bruder Klaus, eremitism of, 2827
'Brug chen Padma dkar po (Drukchen Pema Karpo), 1232
on *mahāmudrā,* 5598
'Brug pa order (Buddhism), 1230, 1232, 1233
Bruigh na Bóinne. *See also* Newgrange
Mac ind Óg and, 1484
Brull, Jacob, on ʿAqivaʾ ben Yosef, 441
Brumble, H. David, 702
Brundage, Burr C., on Aztec human sacrifice, 4185
Bruņenieks, Mārtiņš, 327, 770
on Māra, 5691
Brunner, Emil, **1054–1055**
on divine-human encounter, 7118
and neoorthodoxy, 6466, 6467, 6468, 6469
on predestination, 3204
on Ritschl (Albrecht), 7832
Sohm (Rudolf) and, 8508
theology of, 9137

Bruno, Giordano, **1055**
on angels, 348
Aristotelianism and, 480
and art of memory, 3196
belief in reincarnation, 9330
convicted of blasphemy, 973, 4501
on Copernican astronomy, 1978
on erotic magic, 8248
expelled from Dominican order, 1055
as heretic, 1055
Hermetism and, 3947
Italian Renaissance humanism, role of, 4176
on magic, 5580
Neoplatonism and, 6475
Nicholas of Cusa's influence on, 6610
on progress, 7340
in search for origins, 367
writings of, 1055
Bruno of Toul. *See* Leo IX
Bruns, Gerald, 5485
Brunschweig, Léon, on knowledge, 5207
Bryan, Andrew, 5443
Bryan, Gerald B., 4246
Bryan, William Jennings, 2889–2890
Scopes Monkey Trial and, 4200–4201
Brythonic languages, 1478
Bsam yas monastery (Tibet), 1152, 6940–6941, 9050
debate at, Kamalaśīla at, 5069–5070
establishment of, 8082
Klong chen Rab 'byams pa (Longchenpa) at, 5192
Śāntarakṣita and, 8106
Sarvāstivādin lineage at, 2038
Bskal bzaṅ rgya mtsho (Dalai Lama), 2132
Bskyed rim (generation phase), 1286–1287
Bsod nams rgya mtsho (Dalai Lama), 1230–1231, 2131
Bsod nams rtse mo (Sönam Tsemo), 1225
Bstan 'dzin rab rgyas, 1232
Bstan 'dzin rgya mtsho (Dalai Lama), 2132–2133. *See also* Dalai Lama
Bstan 'gyur (Buddhist text), 1256
Btsun pa Chos legs (Buddhist teacher), 1233
Bua' (ceremony), 9242
Buana agung (outer world of self), 748
Buana alit (inner world of self), 748
Buanann (deity), 1490
Buber, Martin, **1055–1059**
Agnon (Shemu'el Yosef) and, 179
on automessianism, 5978
biblical exegesis of, 869, 1056
on Daoism, 1057
on "eclipse of God," 4090
Fackenheim (Emil) study of, 2949
on faith, 1057–1058
Ginzberg (Asher) and, 3496
on God, 3551
existence of, 7422
Hasidic tale collection of, 9383
on Hasidism, 1055–1056
Hebrew Bible translated into German by, 1056, 7926
on human relation with nature, 2645–2646
influence of, 1058
on I–Thou relationship, 1057, 1058, 2343, 4905, 7118
on Jesus, 4845
on Jewish community, 1058
in Jewish studies, 4883
on Job, 4089
Kierkegaard's influence on, 5142
in modern Jewish thought, 4905–4906
and neoorthodoxy, 6468
philosophy of, 1056–1057, 7118
Reform Judaism and, 7671–7672
on religious experience, 7739
Rosenzweig (Franz) and, 7826
Scholem (Gershom), criticism from, 8177
on Spinoza (Baruch), 8685
on theocracy, 10061
on Torah as law, 9238
writings of, 1056, 2343
in Zionism, 1055
Buberian dialogue, 2344
Bubonic plague, 2138
Bucareli y Ursúla, Antonio María, Serra (Junipero) and, 8231
Buccellati, Giorgio, on *Epic of Gilgamesh,* 3487–3488
Bucer, Martin, **1059**
and Anabaptism, 304
Luther (Martin) and, 5832
on predestination, 3204
in Sacramentarian Controversy, 1059
on theocracy, 9110
Buchanan, Constance H., 3313
Buchanan, Francis, 1311
Buchanan, James, and Mormonism, 6194
Bücheler, Franz, Dieterich (Albrecht) studying under, 2348
Buchu (spirit), 2297
Buck, Adriaan de, 2729
Buck, Carrie, 2880
Bucke, R. C., on psychology of religion, 7475
Bucke, Richard Maurice
consciousness, evolutionary model of, 1949
on "Cosmic Consciousness," 6489
Buckelew, Frederick, 406
Buckland, Ray, 9730
Buckland, Raymond, 6471
Buckley, Thomas, 5866
Buckley, William F., Jr., on Goodenough (Erwin R.), 3637
Budai (Laughing Buddha)
humor and, 4208–4209
as Maitreya, 4209
Budapest, Zsuzsanna, 9730
Buddha
Chinese pronunciation of, 1160
meanings of word, 1059–1060, 1070
Buddha, the (Gautama Buddha), **1059–1071**
Abhidharma as word of, 10020–10021
aesthetics and, 51
on animals, 356, 359
appropriation and, vol. 8 color insert
as ascetic, 1061, 1103–1104
as exaple of *karuṇā,* 5105
as Viṣṇu, 708, 824, 1312, 4442
attempted murder of, 8015
authority of, 693–694, 1089–1090, 1273, 1274
as *bhagavan,* 1060, 1063
biographies of, 1061–1065
early, 1063, 1111
Foucher's, 3177
Hīnayāna, 1092
studies of, 945, 1061, 1063–1065, 1103, 1312
birth of, 952, 1061, 1076, 1568
celebration of, 1304–1305
elephant in, 2750
purity of, 7084
as *bodhisattva,* 997, 1076, 1077, 1082, 1113, 1116, 2737
bodies of
dharmakāya (body of truth), 1064, 1065, 1069–1070, 1077, 1117, 1217, 1261, 4416, 9347
nirmāṇakāya (physical body), 1069, 1077, 1117, 4416, 9347
rūpakāya (physical body), 1064, 1217, 9015
saṃbhogakāya (enjoyment body), 1063, 1069, 1077, 1117, 9347, 9510–9511, 9962
textual, 1261–1262
trikāya (three bodies), 1063, 1069
body marks of, 1004
as *cakravala cakravartin,* 1350, 1351
canonization of sermons, 1409
caste system opposed by, 1105
in cave paintings, 1471–1472
celebration of, 1304–1306, 4328
Chan Buddhism and, 1520
charisma of, 1061, 1062, 1549
in China, washing of, 1642
commission of, great, 6077
concentrations of, in Mahāyāna, 2030
as cosmic person, 1063, 1065
death of, 1061, 1064
account of, 1063
anniversary of, 1061
celebration of, 1304–1305
compassion toward host during, 4140
cremation of, 7163
funeral rites, 1065
symbol of, 1065
as symbol of peace, 1104
decision making by, 5347–5348
depictions of, 6624
as *dharmacakrapravartatayati,* 1350
disciples of, 1063, 1104–1105, 10020–10021
emperors as incarnations of, 4416
enlightenment of, 1075–1076, 2793, 5098
autonomous discipline and, 8701
and Buddha's authority, 1089
celebration of, 1158, 1304–1305
description of, 2793–2794
as intuitive peak, 4525
pilgrimage to site of, 7163
preparation for, 1060
stages of mental concentration in, 7357
as symbol, 1104
teachings during, 9177
temples marking place of, 9043
texts on, 1064, 1065
Vinaya literature on, 1260
epithets of, 1062–1063
eremitism of, 2823
as exemplary prophet, 5384
fatigue and illness of, 1064
feet of, replicas of, 9830
and food taboos, 3168
Four Noble Truths proclaimed by, 1104, 2957, **3178–3180**
on gambling, 3263
and ghost festival, 5231
gold in representations of, 3625–3626
gold symbolism in immaterial body of, 1861
greeting of, 8061
as hero figure, 7552, 7553
Hinduism, renunciation of, 8483
on human condition, 8547
on human existence, 5448
on human personality, 7364, 7365
on ignorant persons, 8551

images of, 1076, 1091, 4327–4329
in biographies, 1063–1065
Central Asian, 1145
in China, 1596, 1642
colossal, 4328
destruction of, 4284
development of, 1111
devotions to, 9827
early images, 4328, 4382
epithets, 1062–1063
mudrās (gestures) in, 3769
nine great events of life, vol. 2 color insert
offerings to, 4330
prohibition of, 4328
for reflection and meditation, 4327
and rituals, 4330–4331
sacred time and, vol. 1 color insert
scenes in, 4328, 4329
in stupas, 9042
veneration of, 4382–4383
visual symbols of, 1065–1066, 4327–4328
in *Mahāvagga,* 3154
in *Mahāvastu,* 5601
intercession of, 1087
invocation of name, with meditation, in Chan Buddhism, 1604
Jesus identified with, 1570
kami as manifestations of, 4785
language of, 1108
Laozi as, 2194, 2199, 5317
on laughter, 4199–4200
law and, 5347–5348, 5350
lineage of, 1062, 1063
lotus symbolism of, 5519
Mahāvīra, 4764
manifestations of, 1078–1079
Māra challenging, 1078, 5690
Māra defeated by, vol. 2 color insert
marks left by, 7163
on miracles, 6053
miraculous powers of, 6053
in Theravāda traditions, 3155
and missions, 6077
monasticism modeled on, 6126–6127
mortification by, 6197
mother of, 7084
mudrā of (hand posture), 4328, 9257
nāgas and *yakṣas* converted by, 6394–6395
name of, 1060, 1063, 6408
nirvāṇa of, 6628
and number eighteen, 6750
on nuns, 6759–6760
objects used by, 7163
as part of monastic community, 1196
perfection attained by, 1063, 1064
as personification of *dharma,* 2332
poetry of, 7211
and previous buddhas, 1066, 1067
previous lives of, 997, 1064, 1065, 1111, 1113, 1116
as prince, 5347
quest of, 7552
rebirths of, 5098
on reincarnation, 7678
relics of, 1107
in China, 7691
commemoration of, 1305
consecration of space and, 1955
images of, vol. 14 color insert
in India, 7690
as objects of devotion, 2317, 4383, 7495, 7690–7691, vol. 4 color insert
in Southeast Asia, 8644
in Sri Lanka, 7690–7691, 9148
in stupas, 7163, 8796, 9041, 9227, vol. 4 color insert (*See also* Stupas and stupa worship)
transportation of, 7164
veneration of, 8376
as renunciant, 1061, 4441
saṃgha established by, 8071, 8073
scholars on, 1061
on self-causation, 7363
in Sinhala religion, 8412
social upheaval during lifetime of, 1102
on society, 5347
son of, 7084
statues of, 1066, 1151
as subject of *nianfo,* 6601
successor, lack of, 2034
on suffering, 9119
suicide or self-sacrifice of, 8832
as supreme "good friend," 1279
as "supreme physician," 855
tathāgata applied to, 1063, 1106, 9015
as teacher, 1060, 1062–1063, 1067, 1104
teachers of, 1103–1104
teachings of
apolitical nature of, 7260
and Buddhist philosophy, 1296
divisions of, 1275–1276
during enlightenment, 9177
honoring, 1305–1306
oral transmission of, 1193, 1252
organization of, 2218
sermons, 1104
social dimension of, 7260–7261
studies on, 1310
texts of, 1192, 1261–1262
transmission of, 1265, 5213
titles for, 9015
trees and, 2629
upāya used by, 9484–9485
Vajrapāṇi and, 9512
visions of, 9612
on women, 3330, 3331, 4165
on worship, 7495–7496
in Zhenyan Buddhism, 9962–9963
Buddha and His Dhamma, The (Ambedkar), 286
Buddha anusmṛti (recollection of the Buddha), 4331
Buddhabhadra (scholar), *Huayan jing,* translation of, 4146
Buddhabhūmi Śāstra (Buddhist text), 1271
Buddhacarita (Aśvaghoṣa), 1004, 1064, 1092, 1111, 1200, 7211
miracles of Buddha in, 6053
Buddhadāsa (Thai monk), **1071–1073,** 1142–1143, 1283
Buddhadatta (Buddhist monk), 997, 1199, 1200, 9148, 10022
Buddhadhamma, 1072
Buddhadhamma Association, 1072
Buddha fields. *See Buddhakṣetras*
Buddhaghosa (Buddhist commentator), **1073–1074,** 1200
on *arahant,* 477
in Burma, 9148
on Four Noble Truths, 3179
life of, 1073–1074
on morality, 1280
on Cārvāka, 1446
on *prajñā,* 7357
in Sri Lanka, 9148
writings of, 1074, 1093, 1199, 9148
Buddhaghosuppatti (Pali text), 1073
Buddhaguhya (Buddhist scholar), 1214, 1217
on *maṇḍalas,* 5643
Buddhahood, 1060, **1068–1070**
aspiration for (*See Bodhicitta*)
attainment of, 1207
Chinul on, in Korean Sŏn, 1646
dharmakāya and, 1069–1070
dimensions of, 1069
in Huayan Buddhism, 4147
manifestations of, 1125
path to (*See Bodhisattvas,* path of)
Saichō on, 8030
Śīlabhadra on, 8399
states of, 1077–1079
Sthiramati on, 8739, 8740
stupa worship and, 8798
virtues of, 1120
vyākaraṇa as condition of, 1085
Buddha Jayanti, 2132
Buddhakāya (buddha-nature), 2628–2629
Buddhakṣetras (buddha fields). *See also* Pure Lands
in Hinayana Buddhist cosmology, 2027
in *asaṃkhyeya* cosmology, 2026
in Mahāyāna *asaṃkhyeya* cosmology, 2030
in Mahāyāna Buddhism, 1077, 1079, 1114, 1117, 1207
Buddha mind
in Huayan Buddhism, 4147
in Zen, as "no-mind," 8859
Buddha nature. *See also* Tathāgata-garbha
in Caodong school, 1239–1240
in Chan Buddhism, 1521, 1522–1523
Daosheng on, 1576
Dōgen on, 1245
and enlightenment, 1070
experiencing true reality of, 2306
in Lokottaravāda school, 1196, 5602
Mādhyamika teaching on, 1156
manifestation of, 1125
as nonempty, 8858
universal mind and, 1577
in Zen Buddhism, 1183
Buddhānusmṛti (meditation), 1063, 1085, 1111, 1291
Chinese term for, 6601
Buddhapālita (Buddhist commentator), **1075,** 1119
Candrakīrti's defense of, 1299, 1401
on Nāgārjuna, 1299, 5552
prasaṅga arguments of, 5552–5553
Buddha pūjā (honoring the Buddha), 4330
Buddharāja (incarnate buddhas), 1135, 1138
Buddhas, 1066–1068, **1075–1087**
aesthetics and, 51
appearance linked to time, in Hinayana belief, 2029
birds as epiphanies of, 949
bodhisattvas distinguished from, 1082
bodies of, three, 8349
celestial, 1067–1068, **1075–1083** (*See also* Amitābha; *See also* Bhaiṣajyaguru)
heroic actions of, 1084
of horrific appearance, 1081

celestial ***continued***
iconography of, 4329
incarnation of, 4417
in Mahāyāna Buddhism, 1067, 1081, 1117
living buddhas as incarnations of, 1068
number of, 1067
vows of, 1086
characteristics of, 1069
in Chinese Buddhism, 1162
cosmic, 1068, 1077–1078 (*See also* Mahāvairocana)
enlightenment of, 1060
ethical practices of, **1083–1087**
future (*See* Maitreya)
horrific, 1081
in Mahāsāṃghika Buddhism, 5602
intercession of, 1086–1087
in Vajrayāna (Tantric) Buddhism, 1080, 1214
in Japanese Buddhism, 1175, 1176
goriyaku (benevolent functions) of, 3870
jizō (guardian buddha of children), 3869
living, 1068
in Esoteric Buddhism, 1068
as incarnations of celestial buddhas, 1068
kings as, 1068
mission of, 2332
as moral heroes, 1083–1085
previous, 1066–1067, 1078, 1107
as role models, 1085
universality of, 1350
worship of, 7495
Buddhasadana (periodical), 1071
Buddha's Day, 1304–1305
Buddha Shakyamuni and Scenes from the Life of Buddha, vol. 2 color insert
Buddha's Light International Association (BLIA), 1168, 3139, 3140
Buddha's Light Mountain. *See* Foguangshan
Buddhas of the ten regions. *See Daśadigbuddhas*
Buddhavacana (word of the Buddha), 10020–10021
Buddhavaṃsa (Pali text)
bodhisattva path in, 997
encounter between buddha and *bodhisattva* in, 1085
lives of twenty-four buddhas in, 1066–1067
pāramitās in, 6993
Buddhāvaṃsaka Sūtra (Buddhist text), 1276
Buddhica (series), 7460
Buddhism, **1087–1192**. *See also* Buddha, the; *specific countries, doctrines, and types of Buddhism*
Abhidarma (*See* Abhidharma)
aesthetics in, 51–52
afterlife in
intercession in, 129
justice and judgment in, 129
nature of humankind in, 131
rebirth in, 133
reward and punishment in, 134
vision of divine in, 128
ahiṃsā in, 197, 6646
alchemy in, 241, 243–244
almsgiving in, 267, 268, 3483
Ambedkar's (B. R.)
conversion to, 286–287, 5699, 9477
ancestor worship in, 323–324
and Ājīvikas, 1102
animals in, 356, 359–360, 1259
animism in, 1131, 1133
anthropomorphism in, 389, 391
arhat in (*See Arhat*)
art of (*See* Buddhist art)
asceticism in (*See* Asceticism, Buddhist)
Aśoka's impact on, 1089, 1090–1091, 1145, 1161
atheism in, 578, 579
attention in, 603
authority in, 693–694, 696
autobiography in, 701
binary periodization in, 173
birds in, 949
blessing in, 981, 982, 984
bodhisattvas in (*See Bodhisattvas*)
books and texts (*See* Buddhist books and texts)
Brahmanism and, 1133, 1138
breath and breathing in, 1045
bridge in, 1050–1051
buddhas in (*See* Buddhas)
cakras and, 1348
calendar of (*See* Buddhist religious year)
Campbell and, 1379–1380
capitalism and, 1098
castes criticized by, 4421
cause and effects in, 5200
caves and cave art, 1471–1472
Chan (*See* Chan Buddhism)
charisma in, 1549
charity in, 1107, 1555
Chengs, criticism by, 1560, 1563
Chinese (*See* Chinese Buddhism)
Christianity and
and Buddhist studies, 1310–1311, 1313
comparison of, 9801
missions, 1098–1099, 1167, 1186
resistance to evangelism, 1728
Western Buddhism and, 1187
as civilizational religion, 1090–1094, 1095, 1099
clothing, cross-gender, 1827
colonialism and, 1098, 1099, 1138–1139, 1311–1312
communism and (*See* Communism, and Buddhism)
community in, eremitism and, 2828
concept of, 1087–1088
Confucianism and
and bushidō, 1336
common goal of, 1167, 1172
criticism of, 1150
philosophical influence of, 1165
reconciliation between, 1173
consecration in, 1956–1957
conversion to, missionary ceremonies for, 6081
cosmology in (*See* Cosmology, Buddhist)
councils of (*See* Buddhist councils)
critical, 1250, 1277, 2386
as cultural religion, 1089, 1094–1098, 1098–1099
dalit, 9477
dances of, 2138, 4533
Daoism and, 1161, 1595
adaptations of Buddhism into Daoism, 2179, 2194, 2196
Bodhidharma in, 995
Chan Buddhism, 995, 1293
common goal of, 1167, 1172
conflicts between, 2183–2184, 2186, 2194, 2199
and philosophy, 1301
reconciliation between, 1173
research on, 2213
Sengzhao and, 8228
demons in, 2276, 7197
dependent arising in, 5098, 7364, 7365
dependent co-origination doctrine (*See pratītya-samutpāda*)
desire in, 2306
devils in, 2315
devotion in (*See* Devotion, in Buddhism)
dharma in (*See Dharma,* Buddhist)
diamond symbolism in, 2345
diffusion of, 5348–5349
under Aśoka, 1351
discursive thought in, 5308
diversity within, 2605
as doctrinal system, 1103, 1104, 1106–1107, 1109–1110, 2382, 2383
dogs in, 2393
dreams in, 2488
drums in, 2496–2497, 7036
Dumje ceremony in, 2138
Earth First! influenced by, 2563
ecology and, **2627–2631**
four dimensions of, 2627–2628
economics and, 2674, 9708
ecstasy in, 2678
and *nirvāṇa,* 2682
education in
in Dge lugs pa order, 2322–2323
Dharmapāla and, 1126
religious, 7734
at universities, 1118–1121, 1125, 1156, 2322–2323
eightfold path of (*See* Eightfold Path)
emptiness in (See Śūnyam and *śūnyatā*)
engaged, 1283
environmentalism in, 2788
eremitism of, 2822
and human solidarity, 2829
eschatology in, 2834, 9859
eternity in, 2856
ethics of (*See* Ethics, Buddhist)
European "discovery" of, 9801
evil in, origin of concept, 2902–2903
Evola (Julius) and, 2905
and Falun Gong, 2979
fasting in, 2996, 2997
feminist analysis of, 3032, 3033
and fiction
Chinese, 3066, 3067, 3068, 3069
Japanese, 3071, 3074
Thai, 3076
Vietnamese, 3078
and film, 3097, 3098
fish symbolism in, 3123
and flower arrangement (ikebana), 3135
folk traditions in, **3153–3158**
food offerings in, 3170
food taboos in, 3168
violations as spiritual practices in, 3170
as founded religion, 4067, 7718
Four Noble Truths of (*See* Four Noble Truths)
funeral rites in, 3155
burial mounds, 1065
in China, 1098
gambling in, 3263
gardens in, 3277, 3278
Gauḍapāda influenced by, 3290, 9545
gender in, **3330–3335**
Chinese, 3343–3344
Japanese, 3346, 3348
geographical expansion of, 1091–1092, 1093–1094
Gesar linked with, 3463, 3464
ghosts in, 3477
Ghost Festival, 9835

gift giving in, 3482–3483
    merit making through,
    5873
goddess worship in, 1079–
    1080, 1081, 1082, 3587,
    4330, 9000
Golden Rule in, 3632
gold in, 1861, 7386
grace in, 3647
healing in, in China, 3863
heavens in, soteriology and,
    8529–8530
as heterodoxy, 6909–6910
heterodoxy in, 6910–6911
Hinduism and, 4429
    and Theravāda Buddhism,
    9148, 9150
    appropriation of ideas
    from, vol. 8 color insert
    comparison of doctrines,
    6344
    and decline of Buddhism,
    1095, 1121, 1125–
    1126, 6072
    and rituals, 1113–1114,
    1115
    siddha teachers and
    Cakrasamvara, 1349–
    1350
    in Southeast Asia, 1133,
    1135, 1138, 5346
historiography in, 4025–4026
hope, reintegration as, 4126
human flourishing in, ecology
    of, 2629
Humanistic, Foguangshan
    and, 3139–3140
human nature in, 5448
human perfectibility in,
    7040–7041
human personality in, 7364–
    7365, 7366
humor in, 4199–4200, 4202,
    4207
iconoclasm in, 4284
iconography of (*See*
    Iconography, Buddhist)
imperial (*See* Kings, in
    Buddhism)
imperial-way, violence of,
    2787
in Aum Shinrikyō, 631, 633
incantation in, 4407–4408,
    5309
incarnation in, 2131, 4416–
    4417
and indigenous religions,
    synthesis of, 3154
initiation in, 4483
    of novitiate, 7770
    rites of, 7816
inspiration in, 4509
international movement of,
    samgha communities and,
    8075
intuition in, 4525
Islam and
    and decline of Buddhism,
    1095

relations with, 4575
    in Southeast Asia, 4657
Jainism and, 1102, 1125–
    1126, vol. 8 color insert
Jevons (F. B.) on, 4854
jñāna in, 4927
journals devoted to, 10058
Kālacakra tradition in, 5056–
    5058
karman in (*See Karma/
    karman,* in Buddhism)
karuṇā in, 5105
kingship in (*See* Kings, in
    Buddhism)
kneeling in, 5196
knowledge in, 5200, 5554–
    5555
    mirror, 6064
Ko-yi, 5485
lamas in, medicine and, 3864
language in, **5308–5313**
    doctrinal background of,
    5308–5309
    interpretive frameworks
    of, 5311
    in religious practice,
    5309–5311
    sacred, 5307
    sectarian manifestations
    of, 5310–5311
law in, **5347–5351**
    the Buddha and, 5347–
    5348
    legal pluralism and, 5349
    transmission of, 5348–
    5349
Law of Causation in, 7678
legitimation in, 5400–5401
libations in, discontinuation
    of, 5288
life in, 5448
light and darkness symbolism
    in, 5453
lightning bolt in, 7603–7604
li in, 5431
lion symbolism in, 5465
literary theory and
    interpretation in, 5484–
    5485
literature of (*See* Buddhist
    books and texts)
logic in, 1120, 1301
lotus symbolism in, 5518,
    5519, 5520
Mādhyamika (*See*
    Mādhyamika Buddhism)
magic in, 5592–5594, 5605
mahāmudrā in, **5596–5601**
Mahāsāṃghika (*See*
    Mahāsāṃghika Buddhism)
Mahāyāna (*See* Mahāyāna
    Buddhism)
maṇḍalas in (*See Maṇḍalas*)
Manichaeism and, 5660,
    5668, 5669
Mani influenced by, 5646,
    5648
mantras in, 5676–5678
in Marathi religions, 5699

in martial arts, 5736
māyā in, 5794
media in, 5805
meditation in (*See* Buddhist
    meditation)
meditative perfection, states
    of consciousness and, 1951
mendicancy in, 5855
menstruation in, 5866
merit in, **5872–5875**
    development of concept,
    5870, 5872
    karman and, 5099, 5870,
    5872–5874
    making of, 5870, 5872–
    5875
    transference of, 1113,
    5874–5875
metaphysics of, 51
migration in, 6024
millenarianism in, 1100,
    1331–1332, 6030, 6039,
    6040, 6545, 9152
on mind-body relation, 6486
miracles in, 6053
mirrors in, 6064
missions (*See* Missions,
    Buddhist)
modern, 1098–1100, 1126–
    1127, 7264–7265
monasteries in (*See*
    Monasteries, Buddhist)
monism in, 6145
monkeys in, 6152
monotheism in, 6157
moral ideals of, 2630
morality in, 6182–6188,
    7651
moral precepts in, violation
    of, 8015
mortification in, 6197
mountains in, 4796, 6212–
    6214
    as cosmic centers, 6212
    as divine dwellings, 6213–
    6214
    revelation on, 6213
    symbolism of, 1501
mudrās in, 6219
murder in, 1259
music in
    Chinese, 6294–6295
    Japanese, 6300–6302
    Korean, 6297–6298
    settings of, 6255
    Southeast Asian, 6282–
    6283, 6288–6289
    Tibetan, 6283, 6298–
    6299
as mystery religion, 6327
mysticism in, 6244–6245
    ecstasy of, 2680
as new religion in U.S., 6536
New Year celebrations in,
    6594
Nichiren school of (*See*
    Nichirenshū)
non-self in, 5097–5098

nontheism of, 7316, 7318–
    7319
number symbolism in, 6747,
    6750
nuns in (*See* Nuns, Buddhist)
obedience in, 6777
offerings in
    to *arhat,* 477
    to Buddha image, 4330
    incense, 4419
Okinawan religion influenced
    by, 6813
opposing Gandhi
    (Mohandas), 286, 5400
ordination in, 6854–6855
    temporary, 6879
orthodoxy in, 6910–6911
otherworld in, 6924
pantheism in, 6965
paradise in (*See* Paradise, in
    Buddhism)
paradox in, 6988, 6989, 6990
peace in, 7023
persecution, 2194
    in China, 5240, 7213,
    7255, 7268
    in Japan, 9075–9076
    in Tibet, 9186
petitions in, vol. 9 color
    insert
phallus in, 7083, 7084
philosophy of (*See* Buddhist
    philosophy)
pilgrimage in (*See* Pilgrimage,
    Buddhist)
political theology, Kublai
    Khan and, 1645
politics and (*See* Politics, and
    Buddhism)
pollution in (*See* Pollution, in
    Buddhism)
popularity of, 2197
portraits in, vol. 10 color
    insert
postures and gestures in, 7343
power in, 7350, 7353–7354
Prāsaṅgika-Mādhyamaka
    school of, 5070
pratimoksa (recitation of
    transgressions) in, 1886–
    1887
prayer in, 7369–7370
predicted decline of, 2176
priesthood in (*See* Priesthood,
    in Buddhism)
psychophysical realms, 1350
Pure Land (*See* Pure Land
    Buddhism)
purification in, 7509
quaternity in, 7550, 7551
rainbow symbolism in, 7604
rainmaking in, 7603
rebirth in, 952, 998
    Buddhadāsa on, 1072
    in Chinese Buddhism,
    1161, 1162
    emptiness and, 1117
    gender and, 3330–3331

Vol. 1: 1–610, Vol. 2: 611–1340, Vol. 3: 1341–2120, Vol. 4: 2121–2850, Vol. 5: 2851–3580, Vol. 6: 3581–4292, Vol. 7: 4293–5046, Vol. 8:
5047–5748, Vol. 9: 5749–6448, Vol. 10: 6449–7176, Vol. 11: 7177–7864, Vol. 12: 7865–8572, Vol. 13: 8573–9286, Vol. 14: 9287–10018,
Appendix: 10019–10091

ENCYCLOPEDIA OF RELIGION, SECOND EDITION

rebirth in ***continued***
in Theravāda Buddhism, 1067, 1197
reference works on, 7645
reincarnation in, 2131, 7676, 7678–7679 (*See also* Saṃsāra)
relics in, 7690–7691
as religion, 7692
religious communities in, 7699, 7700, 7716
religious experience in, 7694, 7695, 7700, 7737, 7740–7741
rituals in, 1097–1098, 1107–1108, 1111–1112
books and texts and, **1261–1265**
in East Asia, 9834, 9838
iconography of, 4330–4331
Shingon, 8350–8351
Tibetan, 9840, 9841
Zhenyan, 9962
rivers in, 7863
sacred objects in, 7698
sacred time in, vol. 1 color insert
sacrifice in, 8006
sacrilege in, 8015–8016
salutations in, 8061
salvation in (*See* Salvation, in Buddhism)
Sarasvatī in, 8113
schools of, **1192–1251,** 1204–1205, 1235 (*See also specific schools*)
appearance of, 1091, 1109–1110, 1112–1115, 1204, 9145
in China, 1575–1577, 1596, 3012
conflicts between, 7752–7753
doctrinal differences of, 1195–1197, 1297
early doctrinal, **1192–1203**
"Eighteen Schools," 1109–1110, 1115, 1223, 1253, 9145
expansion of, 1201–1202
geographical distribution of, 1194–1195
in Japan, 4784
literature of, 1197–1200, 1252
modern, 1099–1100
notable personabilities in, 1200–1201
origins of, 1089–1090, 1193–1194, 8073–8074, 9145
on salvation, 1088–1089
studies on, 1193, 1246–1251
stupas, formation around, 8797–8798
scientific history and, 8180
secret societies in, misinterpretation of, 7719
sectarianism in
beginnings of, 2036
in *saṃgha* and, 8079–8080
in Sri Lanka, 8077
sects in, 7730
Self in, Śākyamuni Buddha on, 7678
sexuality in, 2138, 5415
Shintō and (*See* Shintō, Buddhism, relationship with)
shrines in
portable, vol. 4 color insert
sacredness of, 7698
silence in, 5308–5309
Sinhala religion and, 8409, 8411, 8412
social classes in, 4421
social reform in, 7652–7653
society, relations with, 8463
soul in, 8547–8548, **8550–8554**
spiritual discipline in, autonomous, 8701
spiritual guides in, 8712–8714
spread of, 3154
and temples, 9042–9045
Stcherbatsky (Theodore) on, 8737
studies of (*See* Buddhist studies)
stupas in
architecture of, 7837
ascension of, 1502
circling of, 1796
as sacred objects, vol. 4 color insert
as sacred spaces, vol. 5 color insert
suicide, attitudes toward, 8831–8832
symbols in, 7697
syncretism in, 2605
talismans in, 4532
Tantrism in (*See* Vajrayāna (Tantric) Buddhism)
tathāgata in, 1063, 1106, 1117
temples of (*See* Temples, Buddhist)
textiles in, 9089, 9090
theodicy in, 9112, 9119–9120
Theravāda (*See* Theravāda Buddhism)
Three Jewels of, 1103–1105, 2332, 7496, 7497
Three Turnings in, 1275–1276
thunderbolt in, 7603–7604
tian in, 9172
Tiantai school (*See* Tiantai school)
touch of reverence in, 9257
tradition in, 9277
transmission of, 5348–5349
transnationalism of, 3500
Treasure tradition in (*See* Treasure tradition)
trees in, 9335, 9337
triads in, 9346–9347
Triple Refuge as profession of faith in, 2053
Ülgen in, 9441
universalism in, 1878, 4067
upāya in, 9484–9486
vagina in, 7084
Vajrayāna (*See* Vajrayāna (Tantric) Buddhism)
Vedic tradition criticized by, 4421
vegetarianism in, 360, 3483
vestments in, 1829
via negativa in, 9588
vows in (*See* Vows and oaths, Buddhist)
wealth and, 9708
Western (*See* Western Buddhism)
wisdom in, 9752–9753, 9764
women in, 1595, 3033, **3330–3335,** 6536
advances for, 6757
ascetics, 6759
Chinese, 3343–3344
international association of, 6762
Japanese, 3346, 3348
myths of, 3333
pilgrimage of, 7168
salvation of, 7084
in Tendai school, 9076
in Thailand, 9095
Theravāda Buddhism, 9146, 9147, 9152
World Fellowship of Buddhists, establishment of, 2038
as world religion, 9801–9802
at World's Parliament of Religions, 9805
worship and devotional life in
in East Asia, **9834–9839**
in Southeast Asia, **9826–9834**
in Tibet, **9839–9842**
Yogācāra school of (*See* Yogācāra school)
Zhenyan (*See* Zhenyan Buddhism)
Buddhism after Patriarchy (Gross), 3330
Buddhism in Chinese History (Wright), 1250
Buddhismus und seine Geschichte in Indien, der (Kern), 945
Buddhist art
attitudes toward, 496
Avalokiteśvara in, 705–706
in Central Asia, 1145
in China, 1165
color symbolism in, 1861, 1862
development of, 1065–1066, 1091, 1111
earth symbolism in, 3015
gold in, 3625–3626
Himalayan, 1232–1233
in Ajantā caves, 1076
in India, 5242
in Japan, 4782
Maitreya in, 5620
maṇḍalas in, 5643
in Mongolia, 1149
Wheel of Existence, vol. 3 color insert
Buddhist Association of the Republic of China, 8963
Buddhist Bible, A (Goddard), 1313
Buddhist books and texts, **1251–1278**
Ājīvikas in, 3639
animals in, 6959–6960
archaeological finds, 1634
ascetic morality in, 1104
authority of, 694
bianwen (transformation texts), 3067
Buddhaghosa's commentaries on, 1073–1074
Buddha image in, 1066
as Buddha's body, 1261–1262
Buddhist councils compiling and redacting, 1108, 1110, 1252–1253, 1269
Burmese, 1253
Cakrasamvara Tantra, **1349–1350**
Cambodian, 1253
canon and canonization, 1092, 1108, 1109, 1110, **1251–1258,** 1407, 1409
Abhidharma, **10020–10023**
authority of, 694
Chinese, 1252, 1253–1258, 1266–1268, 7269
distribution of, 1254–1255
early recitation of the Dharma and Vinaya and, 2035
exegesis of, 1269
formation, overview of, 1409
function of, 1252
future of, 1257
Japanese, 1256
modern, 1256–1257
preservation of, 1255–1256, 1267
sermons in larger collection, 1407
Theravāda Tipiṭaka canon established, 2037
Tibetan, 1256, 1338
"Transmission of the lamp" texts in, 1524
Vinaya, **1258–1261**
Central Asian, 1146, 1147
Chinese, 1162–1163, 1164–1165, 1198–1200, 1236–1237, 1523, 1596, 1604, 7207, 7212–7214, 10021, 10022
chuanqi tales, 3067
dharma in, 2333
doxographies, 1204, 1213
early Buddhist literature, 1104
engaged Buddhism in, 2786–2787

exegesis and hermeneutics of (*See* Exegesis, Buddhist; Hermeneutics, Buddhist)
exoteric, Klong chen Rab 'byams pa (Longchenpa) on, 5191
Fang Shan stones as, 1254
genres of, 1252
Hevajra Tantra, siddha movement in, 3965
Himalayan, 1253
Hīnayāna, 1092, 1093
Indian, 1198, 1199, 1200, 1260, 1271
Japanese, 1175, 1176, 1177, 1178, 1181
Korean, 1254–1255
La Vallée Poussin (Louis de) and, 5323
Mongolian, 1148–1149
pāramitās in, 6993
poetry, 1111, 1199, 7207, 7211–7212, 7215–7216
production of, 1262–1263
recitation of, 1263
ritual uses of, **1261–1265**
sacred, 5309
sacred biographies, 944, 945
of schools, 1197–1200, 1252
Southeast Asian, 1134, 1136, 1137
Sri Lankan, 1096–1097, 1199, 1260, 9146–9147
sūtras and calligraphy, 1370
Tantric, 1124, 1214, 1215–1216
Thai, 1253, 1262
Theravāda, 1199, 1252, 1262, 1263, 1265, 1266
Tiantai, 9175–9176, 9177–9178
Tibetan, 1152, 1155, 1198, 1199, 1266, 7167, 10021, 10022
transformative agency of, 1263–1264
translations of, 1253–1254, **1265–1268** (*See also* Chinese language)
and acculturation, 1267–1268
into English, 1256, 6955–6956
language choice in, 1266–1267
La Vallée Poussin's (Louis de), 5323
modern, 1256–1257
techniques of, 1265–1266
Western, 1187, 1189
zhiguai anthologies, 3066
Buddhist Catechism (Olcott), 1187, 6816
Buddhist Churches of America, 1188
Buddhist Compassion Relief (Ciji) Foundation, 1610
Buddhist councils, 1108, **2034–2039**
and *saṃgha,* history of, 8073
Buddhist texts compiled and redacted by, 1108, 1110, 1252–1253, 1269
Indian councils, 2035–2037
Jālandhara, 1110
Lhasa, 1095, 2037–2038
literature on, 2034–2035
orthodoxy and heterodoxy and, 6910–6911
Rājagṛha, 1108, 1269, 4483
and monasticism, 6127–6128
Rangoon, 1253
Sasana, 1140
Therāvadin councils, 2037, 2038
Third, Moggaliputtatissa in, 6112
Vaiśālī, 1090, 1109, 1193, 2035–2036, 5601
World Fellowship of Buddhists and, 2038
Buddhist Dragon Flower Association, 8964–8965
Buddhist epistemology, 1120, 1212–1213, 1301, 2336, 2351
Buddhist House (Berlin), 1188
Buddhist Institute, 5132
Buddhist Lodge of the Theosophical Society, 1188
Buddhist meditation, **1284–1295,** 5820–5821
adversary of, 2903
attention in, 603, 5820
breathing in, 5820
buddhānusmṛti, 1063, 1085, 1111, 1291
in Chan Buddhism, 1096, 1167, 1179, 1292–1293, 1520–1523, 1524, 1577, 1601, 5821–5822
chanting in, 6283
in Chinese Buddhism, 1096, 1290–1294, 5821–5822
Chinul's techniques, 1646
development of, 1096, 1111–1112
as devotion, 2319, 2320
early practices of, 1105
in East Asian Buddhism, **1290–1295,** 9834
emptiness *(śūnyatā)* and, 8856
in enlightenment, 2793, 2794
Four Immeasurable Attitudes cultivated in, 5105
goal of, 1278–1279, 5820
Hakuin on, 3742, 8714
Hinayana cosmology and salvation and, 2028–2029
Humanistic, 3139
imagery in, vol. 11 color insert
in Mahāyāna Buddhism, 1117–1118, 1290
in Theravāda Buddhism, 9152, 9373
in Vajrayāna (Tantric) Buddhism, 1123, 1124, 1286–1288, 5821
generation phase practices of, 1286–1287
imagery in, vol. 11 color insert
perfection phase practices of, 1286, 1287–1288
preliminary practices of, 1286
Shingon practice of, 1294
in Japanese Buddhism, 1096, 1290–1294, 9076
Kamalaśīla on, 5070
kinhin (walking meditation), 7417
merit making through, 5873
mindfulness in, 5820
modern, 1294
music and sound in, 6282–6283
nembutsu zammai (meditational trance) in Japanese Tendai Buddhism, 4119
nianfo, **6601–6603**
in Pure Land Buddhism, 1293–1294, 5821
as devotion, 2320
riddles in, 6987–6988
samādhi (meditative absorption) in, **8066–8067**
Śāntideva on, 8110
sitting posture in, 7343 (*See also* Zazen)
in Southeast Asia, 1142
states of consciousness and, 1951, 1952–1953
in Tendai school, 1291–1292, 9076
in Thai Buddhism, 9096–9097, 9152
in Tiantai school, 1291–1292, 9178
in Tibetan Buddhism, 1157, **1284–1290,** 5070
analytical and stabilizing meditation, 1284
and *bodhisattva* path, 1285–1286
calm abiding and insight meditation, 1284
meditation on compassion, 1285
meditation on emptiness, 1284–1285
post-Tantra, 1288–1289
and states of consciousness, 1951, 1952–1953
Tsong kha pa on, 1279, 1286
in Western Buddhism, 1189
in Zen Buddhism, 1292–1293, 5311, 9946
as devotion, 2319
as epitome of meditation, 9834
object of, 1276
sitting meditation as, 1179, 1180, 1244–1245, 2306, 2386
Buddhist Mission to North America, 1188
Buddhist philosophy, 1204–1205, **1295–1303**. *See also* Metaphysics, in Buddhism
of abhidharma, 1112, 1297–1298
Bhāvaviveka on, 1295
Buddha's teachings and, 1296
in Chinese Buddhism, 1301–1302
darśana, 1295
early, 1296–1297
in Mādhyamika Buddhism, 1299–1300
in Mahāyāna Buddhism, 1204, 1205, 1298–1299
Sarvāstivāda, 8118–8120
in Śāstras, 8122
in Sautrāntika, 8137–8138
in Yogācāra Buddhism, 1300–1301
Japanese, 1302
logic in, 1120, 1301, 2336, 2351
metaphor of, 1295–1296
Middle Way principle in, 1073, 1119, 1296
modern, 1302
on *duḥkha* (suffering), 1296–1297
"Personalist Controversy," 1297
philosophical division, 1088, 1089
in Tibetan Buddhism, 1301
understanding, 1296
Buddhist religious year, **1303–1309**
Burmese, 1304, 1306, 1307
Cambodian, 1307
celebrating Buddha, 1158, 1304–1306
celebrating Buddhism, 1306–1308
Chinese, 1304, 1306, 1307, 1308
Indian, 1304, 1305
Japanese, 1304, 1308
Korean, 1306, 1308
Lao, 1307
New Year festivals, 1304, 1308, 9387
seasonal celebrations, 1308
Southeast Asian, 1304, 1306, 9831–9832
Sri Lankan, 1304, 1305, 1307, 1308
Thai, 1304, 1306, 1307, 1308
Tibetan, 1304, 1308
Buddhist Sangha Act (1962) (Thailand), 1141

Buddhist socialism, 1140–1141, 1283, 9152, 9153
Buddhist Society, 1127
Buddhist Society of Great Britain and Ireland, 1187
Buddhist studies, **1309–1316**
on Buddha's biographies, 945, 1061, 1063–1065, 1103, 1312
on Buddha's language, 1108
on Buddhist scriptures, 1110
on Burmese Buddhism, 1311
on Chinese Buddhism, 1311, 1314–1315, 8981
Christian missions and, 1310–1311, 1313
"classical paradigm" of, 1247–1248
cultural division of Buddhism in, 1088–1089
on Dge lugs pa education, 2322
on early Buddhist teachings, 1090
"encounter paradigm" of, 1250–1251
European, 1310–1314, 7460
expeditions to Asia and, 1313–1314
on Himalayan Buddhism, 1311, 1313
on Japanese Buddhism, 1235, 1311, 1313–1314
Nanjō Bunyū in, 6414
on Mongolian Buddhism, 1311, 1312
Oldenberg (Hermann) in, 6816–6817
on Mahāyāna Buddhism, 1313
origins of, 1112–1113
on Theravāda Buddhism, 1313, 6955–6956
on Vajrayāna (Tantric) Buddhism, 1221
philosophical division of Buddhism in, 1088, 1089
on role of colonialism, 1311–1312
on schools, 1193, 1246–1251
on Sri Lankan Buddhism, 1311, 1312
on Thai Buddhism, 1311, 1313
on Tibetan Buddhism, 1223, 1311, 1312, 1314, 1315
traditional, 1310
in United States, 1315–1316
Buddhist universities, 1118–1121, 1125, 1156, 2322–2323
Buddhist women's movement, 3033
Budé, Guillaume, French humanism and, 4176
Budge, E. A. Wallis, 2729
Budin, Stephanie Lynn, 408
Budi Utomo movement, Hindu-Buddhist-Javanist revival and, 8652
Budkiewicz, Konstantin, 9193
Budō (martial ways), 5732
Buffalo
Hindu sacrifice of, in popular Hinduism, 4007
hunting of
by Cheyennes, 7299–7300
by Lipan Apaches, 404
in Indus Valley religion, 4473–4474
Mashṣāsura (buffalo demon) in Indus Valley religion, 3989
in megalithic religion, 5827–5828
rain associated with, 7603
in Toraja religion, 9241
Buffalo Bill, 957
Buffon, Georges-Louis de
Diderot (Denis) and, 5776
naturalism of, 6434–6435
Bugaku (dance), 2455
Buganda (East Africa)
hero gods of, 2576
Islam spread in, 2578
rituals of, 2577
Bugge, Sophus, 3459
Bugha (world), 9393–9394
Bughadi oron (reindeer), 9394
Bugha sangarin (sky hole), 9394
Bugis religion (Indonesia), **1316–1318**
afterlife in, 1317–1318
creation in, 1316–1317
origin of term, 1316
political myths in, 1317
rituals of, 1317
Buhl, Frants, 4717
Bühler, Georg, 4447
Bühlmann, Walter, 2748
Builder (creator being), 5797
Buisson, Paul, 5711
Bujutsu (martial arts), 5732
Bukhara (Uzbekistan), Jews in, 5009
Bukhārī, al- (Muslim scholar), **1318–1319**
ḥadīth collection of, 3729–3730, 4663
life of, 1318
on touch of Muḥammad, 9256, 9257
writings of, 1318–1319
Bukkyo daijiten (Mochizuki Shinkō), 1314
Bukong. *See* Amoghavajra
Bulfinch, Thomas, 4459
Bulgakov, Sergei, **1319–1320**
communitarian personalism, 1653
and Florenskii (Pavel), 3134
as Marxist, 1319
in Russian Orthodox Church, 1320, 7943
writings of, 1320
Bulgaria and Bulgarian religions. *See also* Slavic religion
agricultural rituals of, 189
Bogomils in, 3523–3524
Christianity, Eastern *vs.* Western form of, 1683
Gnosticism, 3523–3524
icon painting in, 4353
Islam, 4616, 4674, 4677, 4678
John XXIII (pope) in, 4944–4945
magic in, 5581
Manichaeism and, 5657
Mongol invasion of, 4613, 4616
Neolithic religion in, 6464
new religious movement originating from, 6568
Pentecostalism, 7029
prehistoric culture in, 7379, 7380–7381
Roman Catholic missionaries in, objections to, 2585
winter solstice songs in, 9741–9746
Bulgarian Orthodox Church
autocephalous status of, 2588
communism and, restrictions imposed on, 2588
in Orthodox structure, 2589
political involvement of, 2588–2589
Bulgar people (Eastern Europe), magic of, 5581
Bulgars, 4492
Bullinger, Heinrich
on covenant theology, 2049
on predestination, 3204
Bull-roarers, **1320–1321,** 7035
in African religions, 6257
in Australian Indigenous religions, 1320–1321, 7035
Gadjeri as, 3249
tjurunga as, 1320–1321, **9211–9213**
in Greek religion, 1320
in New Guinea religions, 1321, 6265
in North American Indian religions, 7035, 7603
in South American religions, 1320
Bulls
Adad's sacred animal as, 28
in Andean religions, in pre-Inca magic, 8604
Bull of Heaven in *Epic of Gilgamesh,* 1465–1466
in Celtic religion, 1485, 1487
in Dinka religion, sacrifice of, 2366
in Egyptian religion, 2710, 2712
in Hinduism
mythic themes of, 4438
Rudra's association with, 7934
Il/El as, 1382, 1391
in Indus Valley religion, 4473
in Israelite religion, sacrifice of, 926, 927
masculine sacrality of, 5762
in Mesopotamian iconography, 4315
in Mithraism, 6088, 6089, 6090, 6091
in Neolithic religion, 6462, 6464
in prehistoric religions, 7378, 7383
in Roman religion, sacrifice of, 2366
in Cybele cult, 1452, 2249, 7917
in Feriae Latinae ceremony, 1466, 7898
in *taurobolium,* 7917, 7922
storm deities and, 5992, 5993, 5996
Yahveh as, 3542
Bultmann, Rudolf, **1321–1322**
and Kérenyi (Károly), 5115
on anthropomorphism, 391
atheism and, 584
and Barth (Karl), 791, 1322
on Bible, existential interpretation of, 2649
biblical exegesis of, 875, 1321–1322, 5487
comparative theology of, 9130
on death and resurrection of Christ, 8807–8808
on Gnosticism, 3508, 3514, 3532
on Gospels, 4847
on Heidegger (Martin), 3934
Heidegger (Martin) on, 3896
on hermeneutics, 3934, 5487
on historiography, 4030
on history as foundation of religion, 7117
Jonas (Hans) and, 4948
Jung and, 5034
Kierkegaard's influence on, 5142
on kingdom of God, 5151
on knowledge, 5209
and liberal Protestantism, 6104
miracles and, 6056
and neoorthodoxy, 6466, 6467, 6468, 6469
in Religionsgeschichtliche Schule, 7707
Sölle (Dorothee), influence on, 8511
symbol theory and, 8912
writings of, 1321, 1322
Bumba (deity), and gender, 3401
Bumin (Türk leader), 4491
Bun (merit), in Lao religion, 5314
Bun Bang Fai (rocket festival), in Lao religion, 5314
Bundahishn (Zoroastrian cosmological text), 411
resurrection in, 7763–7764
Bunjil (deity), 2310, 2984
Angel Cave and, 1471
Bunjirō, Kawate, 6573
Bunraku (theater), 2455
Buñuel, Luis, 3099
Bunyan, John, **1322–1323**
autobiography of, 698–699, 1323
life of, 1322–1323

Pilgrim's Progress, 1322–1323, 2952
novels inspired by, 3085, 3086
as Protestant writer, 7459, 7521
writings of, 1323
Bunyip (snake-like character), 7605
Bunyoro (East Africa)
kingship in, 5170, 5171
rituals of, 2577
Bunzel, Ruth L., 6671
Buonaiuti, Ernesto, Modernism of, 6106
Burāq (legendary steed), 6060
Burbung (spirit), 265
Burchard, John, 6540
Burckhardt, Jakob, on games, 3265
Burckhardt, Titus, **1323–1325**
comparative study of art by, 501
Hermetism and, 3953
Burda (Ka'b), 7222
Burdach, Karl Friedrich, 6435
Burdens, in Judaism, suffering and, 8805
Bureaucracy
divine
of Daoism, 2178
Mesopotamian deities in, 5951, 5994
and martyrdom, 5743
in religious institutions, modernity and, 6110
Bureau of American Ethnology, 10024–10025
Bureau of Indian Affairs (United States), 7302, 7303, 10053
Burgess, Anthony, Roman Catholic thought behind work of, 3060
Burgess, Joseph A., 5754
Burghley, Lord, 1054
Burgon, Thomas, 6138
Burgos, Paulus, Servetus (Michael) and, 8231
Burgoyne, Thomas H., Hermetic Brotherhood of Luxor and, 8251
Burhān al-Dīn Gharīb, 6639
Burhān I (Deccan shāh), 4646
Búri (mythic figure), 3446
Burial, 3238–3239. *See also* Cremation; Funeral rites; Tombs
ablutions and, 11
in African religions, 140–141
in Bemba religion, 817–818
in Edo religion, 2697
in Limba religion, 7806
in Swazi religion, 8896
in Amazonian religions
Arara, 8631
Tukanoan, 8622–8623
in Andean religions, pre-Incan, 8603
in Australian Indigenous religions, 5051
history of study of, 688
in Baltic religion, ancestors and, 327, 328
in boats (*See* Boats, burials in)
in Celtic religion, of women, 3388
cemeteries as sacred space, 2082
in Central Asia, of goats and rams, 8311
in Chinese religion, 169, 171–172
in Christianity, 9226
Orthodox, 2593
circle symbolism in, 1792
of criminals at crossroads, 2071
in Egyptian religion, 2703
in Europe, of suicides, 8830
in fetal position, 2559, 5196, 7344
flowers used in, 3136
in Garifuna religion, 3284
in Germanic religion, 168, 3457
in Greek religion, 164, 9227
in Hawaiian religion, 3799
in Hittite religion, 4072–4073
in Hun religion, 4228–4229
in Bēta Esra'ēl, 5003
in Islam, 7827, 9226
alive of infant daughters, 445
in Japanese religion, of Yamato rulers, 8358
in Judaism, 4868
Reform Judaism, 7667, 7668
religious *vs.* secular norms, 7823
live, in Nuer and Dinka religion, 6744
in Mesoamerican religions
dogs as companions in, 148, 151, 5896
in Teotihuacán, 5900
musical instruments in, 6267, 6268
in Micronesian religions, 6005
Neolithic
at Çatal Hüyük site (Turkey), 1802
at Jericho, 1802
in Near East, 6460–6461
in Southeast Asia, 8641–8642
in Southeastern Europe, 6463, 6464
in Western Europe, 6465
in North American Indian religions
of Great Plains, 6697
of Northeast Woodlands, 6684
protection of burial sites, 8011
repatriation of Haida remains, 3737
in Oceanic religions, 6784–6785
in Tonga, 2005
in Paleolithic age, absence of, 6951
in paleolithic religions, 454
in Roman religions, 166, 9227
saints, translation (moving the remains) of, 2082
in Samoyed religion, 8096
in Sarmatian religion, 8114–8115
in Scythian religion, 8206
in Selk'nam religion, 8225
in Southeast Asian religions, 2239
traditional, 8650–8651
substitute sacrifices in, 7999
in Ungarinyin religion, 9460–9461
in Zoroastrianism, gender and, 3373
Burial Mound cultures (North America), 6654
Burial of Count Orgaz (El Greco), vol. 11 color insert
Burial texts, Egyptian. *See also* Coffin Texts
in Ramessid period, 2707–2709
Buriat religion (Mongolia), **1325–1328**. *See also* Shamanism; Southern Siberian religions
birds in, 948
Buddhism, 9182
deities of, 2831, 9441
fox in, 3182
hedgehogs in, 3892
home in, 4104
ordination in, 6852
shamanism in, 1325–1327, 4477
female shamans in, 1326
healing in, 8273
initiation in, 8271–8272
miracles and, 6050
vs. Mongol shamanism, 6140
sky creators in, 1326–1327
trees in, 1326
turtles in, 9407
Burke, David G., 899
Burke, Edmund, 6612
Burke, Kenneth, 3145
on reflexivity, 7648
Burke, Peter, 7324
Burkert, Walter, 7850
on astral religion, 8424–8425
on biological perspective of religion, 10043
on bones in rituals, 1014
historiography of, 4048
on mystery religions, 6328
on Prometheus, 7420
on sacrifice, 8008–8009
on women's initiation, 4487
Burkett, Randall, 75
Burkett, Walter, 2868
Burkhart, Louise, 5915
Burkhert, Walther, on pain, 6947
Burkina Faso (Upper Volta)
films from, 3098
funeral rites in, 3234, 3235, 3236
myth of the Fall in, 2960
Burkut-baba (saint), 4622
Burlingame, Eugene W., 1315
Burma/Myanmar and Burmese religions. *See also* Southeast Asia
Buddhism (Burmese religion), **1328–1333**
arhat in, 477
Aśoka and, 556
celebrations in, 1304, 1306, 1307
in colonial era, 1098, 1139, 7263
death in, 1330
devils in, 2315
dreams in, 2488
festivals in, 6427–6428
ghosts in, 3477
incantation in, 4407–4408
kingship in, 1328–1330, 7261–7262
literature of, 1253
Mahāyāna Buddhism, 1132, 1332
marriage in, 5726
meditation in, 1142, 9152
messianic groups in, 3155
millenarian movements in, 1100, 1331–1332
modern, 1140, 1142
monasteries, 1096
Mon Buddhism (*See* Mon Buddhism)
as national religion, 1728
nats (spirits) in, 1328–1331, 2315, **6427–6428**
nikayas (schools), division into, 8074
nuns in, 6760
pilgrimages in, 9832
political role of, 1140–1141
politics and, 7260, 9153
in postcolonial era, 7264
priesthood in, 7408, 7409
reforms in, 9149, 9151
revival of, 9149
Shwe Dagon shrine and, 7982
spread of, 9147
studies on, 1311
syncretism in, 1328
synthesis of indigenous religions and, 3154
temples of, 9044, 9053–9054, 9055

Buddhism (Burmese religion) ***continued***
Theravāda Buddhism, 1135–1136, 1195, 1202, 1328, 1329, 1332
transmission of, 5349
U Nu in, 9479
women in, 1331
Christianity, 1728
Anglicanism, 1728
missions, 6085
Roman Catholicism, 1728
eingsaung nat spirits in, 4106
fiction of, 3076, 3077
funeral rites in, 3155
Judaism, 5010
maṇḍalas of kings in, 8644
music in, 6290
nat cultus in, parallels in Sri Lanka, 8410, 8411
ordination in, 6853
rebellion against British, 6547
shamanism in, 8273
in World War II, 5380–5381
Burmans, *vs.* Burmese people, 1328
Burmese language, 1328
Burmese people, *vs.* Burmans, 1328
Burmese religion. *See* Burma, Buddhism
Burnet, Edward, on mountains, 6212
Burnet, George, on nature, inherent design of, 2607
Burnier, Radha, 9143
Burning, capital punishment by, 4742
Burning bush, Moses and, 6200
Burnouf, Eugène, 1187, 1312, 1313, **1333–1334,** 4446
Müller (F. Max) and, 6234
Burns, Kathryn, 3416, 3417
Burnt offering
in Greek religion, 3667–3669
in Vajrayāna (Tantric) Buddhism, 1220
in Israelite religion, 925, 926, 927, 931–932, 4746–4747
Burong (spirits), in Acehnese religion, 26
Burrell, David, 7125
Burridge, Kenelm
on beliefs, 2089
on cargo cults, 1416, 6801–6802
on study of religion, advances in, 683
on Tangu religion, 6802
Burris, Virginia, 6742
Burroughes, Jeremiah, 2287, 2288
Burroughs, Nannie Helen, 10039
Burrows, Herbert, 844
Burrus, Virginia, 3359
Bursa pavonis (Eck), 2601
Burt, Ben
on *mana,* 8515
on taboo, 8516
Burton, Robert, Hermetism and, 3950
Burzūye (physician), 6959
Bush, George W. H., Native American policy of, 7303
Bush, George W., on bioethics, 941
Bushi (warriors), *Nihonshoki* and, 4804
Bushidō (warrior code), 1247, **1334–1337,** 2815
Confucianism and, 1928
in Meiji period, 1336
modern, 1336
origin and development of, 1334–1335, 5732
in Tokugawa period, 1335–1336
Zen Buddhism and, 9946
Bushmen. *See* Khoi and San religion
Bushnell, Horace, **1337–1338**
on atonement, 597
Dwight's (Timothy) influence on, 2532
liberalism of, 6105
Bushnell, O. A., 3085
Bushrūyah, Mullā Ḥusayn, 728
Būshyąstā (deity), 2128
Busia, K. A., 116
Būṣīrī, al-, 6738
Būstān (Saʿdi)
dating of, 8022
material in, 8023
Bustan al-Salatin (al-Rānīrī), 4664
Bust of Saint Margaret of Antioch (Gerhaert), vol. 13 color insert
Bu ston Rin chen grub (Butön Rinchendrub), 1215, 1227, 1310, **1338–1339,** 9017–9018
Buswell, Robert, 1248–1249
Būta yajña (demon), 748
Butler, John, 2162
Butler, Joseph, **1339**
Butler, Josephine, 3361
Butler, Judith, 386
on gender, 3296, 3314, 3420–3421
and queer theory, 3314
Butoh (Japanese dance form), 2164
But She Said (Fiorenza), 7008
Butsudan (altar), 2410
Butte, Wilhelm, 6435
Butter, in Agni myths, 178, 179
Butterfly, 4507, 4508, 7377
Butterfly effect, chaos theory and, 1541
Butterfly Healing, The (Ching), 10031
Buxu ci (Daoist text), 2209
Buyid dynasty
ʿĀshūrāʾ under, 550
caliphate and, 1366, 4572
political power of, 4562
Buyl, Bernardo, 4503
Buzhou, Mount, 1625
Buzzeti, Vincenzo, Thomism and, 8176
Bwalya Chabala, 817
Bwami (spiritual power), of Lega king, 5170
Bwiti religion
psychedelic drugs in, 7469–7470
studies of, 383
Byang chub brtson 'grus, 1232
Byang chub lam gyi sgron ma (Atīśa), 1224, 1285
Byang chub 'od (Changcup-ö), 1224
Byblos, Adonis in, 34, 35
Byhan, Artur, 473
By Light Light (Goodenough), 3637
Bynum, Caroline Walker, 3037, 3172, 3313, 3314, 3360
on rites of passage, 7802
Byron, Gay, 80
Byron, Lord, Gnosticism and, 3526
By These Hands (Pinn), 79
Byzantine Christianity. *See* Eastern Christianity
Byzantine Empire
Arab conquest of, 4581
authority in, religious *vs.* secular, 696
Avars in, 4491–4492
charity in, 1554
Christian culture of, 1661–1662
Crusades and, 2074, 2077
fall of, Italian Renaissance humanism, influence on, 4175
Galen's influence in, 3256
Gnosticism in, 3523–3524
Greek Orthodox Church in, 3656–3657
iconoclasm in (*See* Iconoclasm, Byzantine)
iconography of, 4345, 4352–4354
Islamic conquest of, 20, 1684
and Greek Orthodox Church, 3657
Judaism in, Patriarchiate in, 7006–7007
medicine in, 3844
music in, 1534, **6302–6306,** 6309
politics and religion in, 7279, 7280
Türks in conflict with, 4491–4492
Byzantium. *See* Constantinople

C

Cabasilas, Nicholas, **1343–1344,** 2587
Cabasilas, Nilos, nephew taught by, 1343
Cabezón, José, 9190
Cabildos, 66
Caboclo (mixed race) religion (Amazon)
emergence of population, 8627
master of the animals in, 8580
overview of, 8631–8632
Caboclo spirits
in Candomblé, 122
in Umbanda, 124
Cabora, Saint of (Teresa Urrea), 6578
Cabredo, Rodrigo de, on veneration of images, 8611
Cabrera, Lydia, 3065
Cabtillation. *See* Chanting
Caches, in Olmec ritual, 6819
Cadastral cults, in prehistoric Southeast Asia, 8642
Caddoan language, 6696
Caddo people (North America), 6696
calendar, 1353
Caddy, Peter, 561
Cadoux, C. J., liberal Protestantism of, 6103, 6105
Caduveo people (South America), religion of, 8636–8637
Cady, H. Emilie, 6584, 6586, 9472–9473
Caecilian (bishop), 2416, 7060
Cædmon (poet), 7218
Caelestis (deity), 7920
Caesar, Julius
apotheosis of, 438–439
Augustus's relationship with, 630
calendar under, 6171
on Celtic religion, 1479, 1481–1482, 1491, 9329
deification of, 2777
divinization of, 7913
on druids, 2492
memorization by, 5851
on Germanic religion, 3450
haruspex of, 2874
nomination for *flamen,* 3126
as *pontifex maximus,* 7278, 7319, 7912
on private associations, 5334
Caesarea (Palestine)
Abbahu in, 2
Armenian church's connection to, 488
Eusebius at, 2884
Origen at, 6888
Caesarius of Arles
on charity, 1554
on nuns, 6763
Caesarius of Heisterbach, 2279
Caesaropapism, 1661. *See also* Constantinianism
Čagadai (son of Chinggis Khan), 4493, 6142
Cage, John, 500
Čaghan Ebügen (deity), 6142
Cagni, Luigi, 222–223
Cahen, Claude, 4716, 4722
Cahiers d'Extrême-Asie, Seidel (Anna) and, 8223
Cahill, Lisa Sowle, 3429
Cahill, Suzanne, 3342
Cahokia (Illinois archaeological site)
ceremonial center at, 1805
earth mounds at, 9226
Cahuilla tribe (North America)
bears and, 806
dreams of, 2488
Cailleacha (old women), 1486
Caillois, Roger, on games, 3267

Cain (biblical figure)
and Abel, 986, **1344–1345**
Freemasons on, 3194
Satan as father of, in two-seed theory and, 1658
temptation of, 9069
Cairns. *See also* Stones
conditional curses in, 2101
ḥawṭah marked by, 3777
Hermes and, 3936
in Madagascar stone cult, 8745
in megalithic religion, 5823
Cairo (Egypt)
al-Azhar in (*See* Al-Azhar university)
Mansuri Hospital in, 3832
mawlids in, 5789
Cairo Codex of the Prophets
Bible with *masorah* in, 1372
Hebrew micrography in, 1371
Cairo Genizah, 10050, 10051
Cairo University, Massignon (Louis) at, 5774
Cai state, Confucius in, 1935
Caitanya (Hindu mystic), **1345–1348**. *See also* Sadhus/Sadhvis (renunciates)
absorbed into image of Jagannātha, 859
as devotee, 2317, 2318
ecstatic dancing and singing of, 4006
Gauḍīya Sampradāya (order) and, 3985–3986
on *gurus,* 8712
influence of, 1346–1347
in Bengal, 826
in Vaiṣṇavism, 9505–9506
life of, 1345–1346
on meditation, 8704
on *Bhagavadgītā,* 854
poetry of, 7211
preaching devotion to Kṛṣṇa, 7354
theology of, 1346
Vaiṣṇava *bhakti* cult and, 9500
Vṛndāvana and, 9645
worship of divine child by, 2983
Caitika school of Buddhism
geographical distribution of, 1195
origin of, 1194
Caityas (chapels), 1107
at Ajantā caves, 1471
Chinese versions of, 9046
evolution of, 9042
on large platforms, 9043
nāgas and *yakṣas* in, 6394
stupas *vs.,* 8796–8797
Cakkavattin (king), 1134, 1135, 1139, 1305, 1329
Cakkavattisihanada-sutta (Buddhist text), 7261
Cakkrī (Siamese general), 9095
Cakrābja Maṇḍala, 5641
Cakra pūjā, in Tantrism, 1348
Cakras, **1348–1349**
breathing and, 1044, 7038
in *Haṭhayoga,* 3795
interior *maṇḍalas* and, 1503
Kuṇḍalinī and, 5266
in meditation, 5820
serpent as first *cakra,* 5277
and sexuality, 1045
in Tantrism, 8992–8993
in therapeutic touch healing, 3851
therapies involving crystals and, vol. 4 color insert
Cakrasamvara, **1349–1350**
Cakravāla (single-world system), cosmology of, 2026–2027
Cakravala cakravartin
Buddha as, 1350
as paramount ruler, 1350
Cakravartin (universal king), 1063, 1329, **1350–1352,** 4415, 7267
history of ideal, 1350–1351
in *Arthaśāstra,* 8122
religious dimensions of, 1351
saṃgha and, 8078
Calancha, Antonio de la, on Mary images in the Andes, 8611
Caland, Willem, 4446
on magic, 5588
Calatinus, A. Atilius, 3094
Calcination, in alchemy, 251
Calculus, Leibniz *vs.* Newton as founder of, 5406
Calcutta Unitarian Society, 9317
Calder, Norman, 5627
Calderón de la Barca, Pedro, 2474
Calendae (festival days), 7906
Calendars, **1352–1365**. *See also* Chronology; Sacred time; Time; *specific events*
agricultural, 186–188
Ainu, 7990
Akan, 215
almsgiving in, 268
alphabet and, 1353
animals in, ethnoastronomy and, 2864
Aztec, 719, 1354, 1355, 5908, 8842, vol. 3 color insert
Bābī, 729
Balinese, 748
Baltic, 764
ancestors in, 329
Buddhist (*See* Buddhist religious year)
Celtic, 1491
Chinese, 1621, 1640–1644
calendar house, time represented in, 7984
Christian
"AD" and "BC" in, 4054
and history, view of, 4053–4054
liturgical year (*See* Liturgical year, Christian)
Protestant, 7456–7457
chronology and, 1758
days of the week, pagan gods in names of, 1689, 1873
Dolgan, 2394–2395
Egyptian, 1354, 8836
star clock and, 8733
Geto-Dacian, 3467
Greek, 1355
festivals of Dionysos in, 375
moon and, 6171
Gregorian, 1355, 1357, 1361
hierophany (manifestation of the sacred) and, 3973
Hindu
cosmology and, 2018, 2019
in devotional life, 9825
in Marathi religions, 5698
pilgrimage in, 7171
religious year in, **4014–4019**
solar and lunar systems combined in, 4015–4016
Inca, 4410
in *onmyōdō,* 6828–6829
Islamic
in Cambodia, 1353–1354
ḥājj in, 7155, 7157
in Java, 4661
lunar year, 1354, 6171
tilāwah in, 9202
Jain, 4771
Jewish, **4865–4868**
Boethusians *vs.* Pharisees on, 8018–8019
development of, 4865–4866
of Karaites, 5086
of Rabbanites, 5086
unity of Israel and, 4858
Komi, 5216
Korean, 5230
lunar and lunisolar, 1354, 1361, 6170–6171
in China, 1640
Maya, 1355–1360, 1473, 2009–2010, 5796–5797, 5884–5886, 8842
memorials of dead on, 2244
Mesoamerican, 1353, **1355–1360**
basic calendrical units in, 1356–1357
creation and, 1357–1358
deep structure of time in, 1357
divinitory, 7811
Mixtec, 5887, 5911
modernity and, 6110
moon and, 6170–6171
mythic qualities of time in, 1358–1360
North American Indian, 1353
Zuni astronomy and, 2008–2009
of Bēta Esra'ēl, 5002–5003
Olmec, 5881–5882
origination, 1352
overview, **1352–1355**
Raëlian, 7598
Roman
fasti, **2993–2995**
history of Roman religion and, 7893
holidays in, 7906
moon and, 6170–6171
profane and sacred days in, 7906
solar calendar, 7894
Slavic, 8434
South American, 1353, **1360–1365**
in Amazonian religion, Tukanoan, 8623
in Andean religion, modern, 8618
archaeoastronomy at Coricancha and, 1362
Ceque calendar system, 1362–1363
chronicler accounts of, 1361
chronicler interpretations of, 1361–1362
myths and legends and, 1363–1364
ritual and, 1364
social divisions, calendrical, 1362
Southeast Asian, Hindu temples and, 4013
and time, concepts of, 7992
Tlaxcalan, 9215
Ugaritic (Canaanite), 1385
ritual time and, 7988
vacant period in, mortification rites and, 8208
Zoroastrian, 9991
of Parsis, 6998
Calendar temple, at Sarmizegetusa Regia, in Geto-Dacian religion, 3467
Calf, of Jeroboam I, 2. *See also* Golden calf
California
Point Loma Theosophical community in, 6546
Spanish mission in, Serra (Junipero) and, 8231
California Indians, 6657, **6712–6719**
creation stories of, 6713
first-fruit rites of, 6714–6715
fox in mythology of, 3181–3182
girls' puberty rites in, 6715
Kuksu cult of, 6717
mourning anniversaries of, 6717

California Indians ***continued***
Roman Catholic missionization of, 6718
shamanism of, 6714
spirits and personal power of, 6713–6714
sweat baths of, 6715
toloache use by, 6716–6717
World Renewal cult of, 6717–6718
world renewal rituals of, 6651
Caligula (Camus), 2475
Caliphate, **1365–1368,** 7285. *See also* Abbasid caliphate; *See also* Fāṭimid dynasty; Umayyad caliphate; *specific caliphs*
ʿAbd al-Rāzīq (ʿAlī) on, 5
ʿAlī's objections to, 257
Ameer Ali (Syed) supporting, 289
authority of, 695–696
character of ruler in, 7285
classical theories of, 1365–1366
Crusades and, 2078
Ḥanābilah and, 3764
historical influences on, 1366–1367
historiography and, 4029
imamate identical with, 4393
invention of, 4577–4578
al-Māwardī on, 5787
revival and end of, 1367
ummah and, 9447
Calixtines, Hus (Jan), influence of, 4234
Calixtus, Georg
humanism and, 4177
systematic ethics, 1655
Callahan, Allen, 80
Callahan, S. Alice, *Wynema: A Child of the Forest,* 3090–3091
Callaway, Henry, 113
on Zulu religion, 1857
"Called to Common Mission," 1769
Callicott, J. Baird, 2656
Calligrams, of Apollinaire (Guillaume), 1369
Calligraphy, **1368–1373**. *See also* Alphabets; Writing
"beautiful writing," 1369
Chinese and Japanese, 1368–1369, **1370–1371**
Confucian, 4338
contemporary, 1369
Hebrew micrography, 1369, **1371–1372**
emergence of art of, 1371–1372
later developments in, 1372
Islamic, 1368, 1369, **1372–1373,** 4350, 4351, vol. 14 color insert
cultural influence of, 8204
in mosques, 6207, 6208
overview, **1368–1370**
scripture and, 8198, 8204
society and religion, position of calligrapher in, 1368–1369
tools and materials, 1368, 1373
Western, 1368
Callimachus (Greek writer)
versions of myths by, 3662
on Zeus, 3663, 3664
Callisto (nymph), 507
Calm abiding, for achievement of *bodhi,* 5070
Calmecac (priestly houses), 9215
Calpulli (Aztec social unit), organization of, 5173
Calsari (European secret society), 7719
Căluş ritual, in Romania, 2147
Calvary Chapel, 2893
Jesus Movement and, 4852
Calvert, George, **1373–1374**
Calvin, John, **1374–1377,** 2308. *See also* Calvinism
on astrology, 8182
on atonement, 596
Augustine's influence on, 629
on authority, 695
Beza (Theodore) as successor to, 850–851
biblical exegesis of, 874
on conscience, 1942
Copernican revolution and, 8182
on disciplined church, 7390
ecclesiology of, 1773–1774
on election, 2748
on ethics, 1655
and execution of Servetus, 7061, 7282
on faith, 1376, 2426
Farel (Guillaume) and, 2993, 7281
and Genevan Reformation, 7281
on gifts, 267
on God, 3556, 7661
on Gospels, literalness of, 4846
on grace, 3646
on heresy, 3928
on hierarchy of church, 5288
on Holy Spirit, 7454
on human perfectibility, 7040
on idolatry, 7449
on knowledge of God, 1375–1376, 5205
on liturgy, 7389
on Mary, 5753
mediatory role of saints, rejection of, 2083
and merit, 5877
on ministry, 6045
on miracles, 6056
on music, 6310
on nature, character of, 2607
on pain, 6946
on polity, 7389–7390
on predestination, 1375, 3002, 3204, 3208
Arminius (Jacobus) criticizing, 492, 493
on priesthood, 7403
on redemption, 1376
in Reformation, 7661
on relics, 7686–7687, 7689
on religious art, 4286
on salvation, 7661
on superstition, 8866
as theatergoer, 2474
theology of, 9137
on "two books," 9422
Calvinism
Antitrinitarianism in, 7661
Arminianism opposing, 493
Arminius (Jacobus) opposing, 492–493
and Baptist churches, 783, 784
Spurgeon (Charles Haddon), role of, 8727
Bunyan (John) on, 1323
and capitalism, 7251, 7458
capitalism and, 2669, 2672–2673
Christian Science and, 1745
church architecture of, 795
Confession of 1629 (Cyril I) influenced by, 2588
Congregationalism and, 1938
covenant theology in, 2049–2050
and dance, 2154
Eastern Orthodox Church and
Confession of Dosítheos against, 2059
Cyril and, 2115
election in, 2748
French (Gallican) Confession (1559) in, 2058
God in, 3556
Holiness movement and, 4083, 4084
missions, 1375
in China, 1632
New School of, Holiness movement and, 4083
predestination doctrine (*See* Predestination)
and Puritanism, 7519
Reformation principles, 1691–1692, 7661
sacramental theology in, Lutheran perspective *vs.,* 7963
skepticism and, 8421
Spinoza (Baruch) *vs.,* 8682
Spiritualism *vs.,* 8716
spread and success of, 1376
Stanton (Elizabeth Cady) on, 8730
theocracy in, 9110
theodicy in, 9117
theology, 1375
Weber (Max) on, 8494
work ethic and, 8481
Camaldoli, monastic congregation of, 2827
Câmara, Helder, on kingdom of God, 5153
Camaxtli (deity), 5935
Camay Quilla, Inca calendar and, 1361–1362
Camayura religion (Brazil), ancestor worship in, 8584
Cambodia and Cambodian religions. *See also* Khmer religion; Southeast Asia
Buddhism
celebrations in, 1307
colonial influences and, 1139
communism and, 1100, 1143
future of, 1131
imperial, 1134–1135
literature of, 1253
Mahāyāna Buddhism, 1137–1138, 1202
mediation in, 9152
modern, 1140, 1142
monasteries, 1096, 1142
Mon Buddhism, 1137–1138
nikayas (schools), division into, 8074
origins of, 1133
politics and, 1141, 9153
reforms in, 9151
revival of, 9149–9150
temples of, 9044, 9055
Theravāda Buddhism, 1137–1138, 1195, 1202
Cham calendar, 1353–1354
Christianity, 1728
deities of, 4012
fiction of, 3076, 3077
Hinduism, lineages and, 4010
history of, 3075
Khmer religion in, 5127–5135
lineage in, 4013
music in, 6287, 6289, 6290
origin stories, 4010
rivers in, 4012
Śaivism in, 1135
temples in (*See also* Angkor Wat)
architecture of, 4012–4013
at Bakheng, 4012
women rulers in, 4011
Cambridge Camden Society, 795
Cambridge Platform (1648)
Congregationalism and, 1938
Mather (Richard) and, 5778
Puritans and, 7520
Cambridge University
Jewish studies at, 4883
Merton (Thomas) at, 5879
Cambyses, Egypt conquered by, 2709
Camel, Battle of the. *See* Jamal, Battle of al-
Camerarius, Joachim, humanism and, 4177
Cameron, William, Christian Identity movement and, 1658
Cameroon
Bakweri people of, glossolalia of, 3506
Bamileke people of
funeral rites in, 3235
skull in family altars in, 3806

Fali people of, myths of, 95, 98–99
funeral rites in, 3235
literature of, 3087–3088
Maitatsine movement in, 107
myth of the Fall in, 2960
prophetic movements in, sickness, role of, 3815
Camillus (Roman emperor), 3175, 7894, 7899
Camitic people (Africa), 1451
Camlan, Battle of (539), 508, 509
Camma (priestess), 3387
Cammann, Schuyler, 5645
Camões, Luis de, 7219
Campantar (Śaiva saint), on *bhakti,* 8043
Campany, Robert, 2637
Campas people (Peru), 2312–2313
ethnoastronomy of, 2865
Campbell, Alexander, **1377,** 2289, 2364–2365. *See also* Disciples of Christ
educational model of, 1780
Rigdon (Sidney) and, 6193
Campbell, Colin, 6527, 6568
Campbell, J. McLeod, on atonement, 597
Campbell, Jan, on phallus, 7077
Campbell, Joseph, **1377–1380**
on birth of heroes, 1568
on card suits, 1414
criticisms of, 1379–1380
early years of, 1378
and Germanic religion, studies of, 3460
on goddess worship, 3612–3613
on hunter-gatherers, 3173
Jungianism in work of, 3958
on matriarchy, 3612–3613
myth concepts of, 1378–1379
on psychology of religion, 7476
scholarly work of, 1378
Zimmer (Heinrich) and, 9975
Campbell, June, Tibetan Buddhism, feminist analysis of, 8243–8244
Campbell, Leroy A., 6088
Campbell, Lucie, 10039
Campbell, R. J., 6105
Campbell, Richard, 3080
Campbell, Thomas, 1377, 2289, 2364
Campbell, William, 8964
Camphill movement, 393
Campion, Jane, 3097
Camp meetings. *See also* Revivalism
of Holiness movement, 4083
Smith (Hannah Whitall) and, 8445
Spiritualist, 8717
Camp Ramah, 1962
Camps, Gabriel, 834
Campus Martius (Field of Mars)
functions of, 7897
lustratio in, 5534
sanctuary of Isis on, 7914
Camus, Albert, 2475
atheism of, 7422
on individualism, 4127
on inequality, 4181
CAN. *See* Cult Awareness Network
Canaan
anti-Semitism in, 397–398
defined, 1390
gift to Abraham of, 15
Israelite conquest of, 4958
Nuwaubians on, 6769
ownership of, Yavheh in, 4857
Canaanite movement (Young Hebrew movement), 9980
Canaanite religion, **1380–1401**
amulets and talismans in, 299
archaeology of, 455
body and soul in, 8538–8539
calendar in, 7988
comparative theology of, 9127
deities of, 1382–1384 (*See also* Anat; Astarte; Athirat; Baal; Dagan; El; Il)
Egyptian religion influenced by, 2716
homosexuality in, 4113
and Israelite religion, 4742
Jerusalem in, 4839
literature of, 1381–1384, 1387–1388, **1390–1401**
Aqhat epic in, 1396–1398
Baal cycle in, 1391–1395
"Birth of the beautiful and gracious gods" in, 1395
characteristics of the texts, 1390–1391
"El's banquet" in, 1395–1396
Kirta cycle in, 1398–1400
"Marriage of Nikkal and the moon god" in, 1395
Rephaim texts in, 1398
merit in, 5871
moon in, 6172
ocean in, 6806
overview, **1380–1390**
and Philistine religion, 7104
and Phoenician religion, 7129, 7130–7131
pillars in, 8744
popular religion in, 1387–1388
resurrection in, 724, 7764
ritual and cultic personnel in, 1384–1387
ritual drama in, 2442
sacrifice in, 8005
survivals of, 1388–1389
Canada and Canadian religions
Bahā'īs in, 739
Baltic religion in, 765
Buddhism, 1190
Christianity
Black churches, 1709
Church of England, 9300
denominationalism, 1711, 1712–1713, 1715
Eastern Orthodoxy, 1713
evangelicalism and moral crusades, 1710
Hutterian Brethren in, 4239
missions and evangelism, 1708, 1709, 9299–9300
nature of, 1714–1716
Presbyterianism, 7391
regionalism, 1715
revivalism, 1710
church attendance declining in, 9301
colonies in
English, 9299, 9300–9301
French, 9299–9300
French-English conflict in, 9299–9300, 9301, 9302, 9303
contemporary, 9303–9304
drama in, 2477
Eskimo religions in (*See* Inuit religious traditions)
films from, 3099
formation of, 9300–9301
Islam, 4685–4686
Islamic studies in, 4723
Micmac people of Nova Scotia, 1353
Native American Church, 10054
new religious movements, 1714
Temple Solaire, 9067–9068
Northern Athapaskan religious traditions in, 572–573
North-West Rebellion of 1885 in, 9302–9303
political theology in, 7246
popular culture criticism in, 7321
psychology of religion in, 7475
religious studies in, 8788
Roman Catholicism
history of, 1711, 9299–9300
influence in politics, 9301
Jesuits, 9302
missions, 9299
pilgrimage in, 7150, 7151
Protestant
denominationalism and, 1712–1713
sectarian movements, 1713
secularization in, 9301–9302
transculturation in, **9299–9304**
United Church of Canada, formation of, 1713, 7391, 9301
Canadian Corporation for Studies in Religion (CCSR), role of, 8788
Canadian Council of Churches, 1713
Can a Rich Man Be Saved? (Clement of Alexandria), 1455
Cana wedding feast, Epiphany and, 9814
Canciani, Frank, 5942
Cancuc, rebellion of (Mexico), 6576
Cancuc, Tzeltal Revolt in, 5921
Caṇḍālas ("untouchables"), mixed marriage and, 3996
Caṇḍamahāroṣaṇa (buddha), 1081, 3227
Candelaria, María de, 3412–3413
Caṇḍī (deity), Bengali worship of, 826
Caṇḍīdāsa (poet), 826, 5253, 7211
Caṇḍīmaṅgal (Mukundarāma Cakrabartī), 825
Candles, at Easter, 2579
Candomblé (Brazil), 121–124. *See also* Afro-Brazilian religions
in Africa, 109
Caboclo, 122
Catholicism and, 121
creolization and, 2066–2067
ethnic nations of, 121–122
food symbolism and ritual in, 3171
history of study of, 121
influences on, 120
initiation rites of, 122, 123
music in, 6274
origins of, 120, 121
possession and transcendence in, 7987
ritual communities of (*terreiros*), 121, 122–123
transculturation of, 9308
and Umbanda movement, 6578
women in, 122–123
Yoruba religion and, 120, 121–122
Candragomin, 1338, 9000
Candragupta (king), 1351
Candragupta Maurya, 554
Candrakālā Devī (artist), 4432
Candrakāntā (Khatrī), 10034
Candrakāntā santati (Khatrī), 10034
Candrakīrti (Indian Buddhist dialectician), **1401.** *See also* Mādhyamika Buddhism
and Bhāvaviveka, 860, 1213, 5553
and Prāsaṅgika school, 1119
on *bodhisattva* path, 1300
on *bodhisattvas,* 8712
Buddhapālita defended by, 1299

Candrakīrti (Indian Buddhist dialectician) ***continued***
commentary on *Guhyasamāja Tantra,* 1216, 1275
on meditation, 1285
on *Guhyasamāja Tantra,* 3708
on Nāgārjuna, 5552, 5553
writings of, 1285, 1300, 2322, 5553
Candrāvatī (poet), 827
Canela religion (Amazon). *See also* Ge religions
origin myths of, 8629
Canella religion (Brazil)
death cult in, 8584–8585
solar and lunar gods in, 8578
Canelos Quechua religion (South America), 281–284
agrarian rites of, women in, 2558
plants and, 9575
Quilla (moon) in, 6439
Cang Jian, calligraphy and, 1370
Caniengas Mohawk religion, creation myth of, emergence in, 2557
Can I Get a Witness? (Riggs), 80
Canis familiaris. See Dogs
Canisius, Peter, **1401–1402**
Cannadine, David, on ritual, 1514
Cannibal Hymn (Egypt), 2713
Cannibalism, **1402–1405**. *See also* Human sacrifice
in African religions, 1404
in Lugbara religion, 5526
by Aghorins, 3805
as agricultural rite, 9578
in Aztec religion, 1403, 7957
as ecological adaptation, 2868
in Batak religion, 799
in Caribbean, reports of, 1429–1430
complexity of form in, 1402–1403
in funeral rites, 3169, 3238, 3239
head hunting and, 3805
in Lower Paleolithic Period, 6951
monsters and, 6165
in New Guinea religions, 3169
in North American Indian religions, 1403, 6652
in Pacific Islands, 1403–1404
to prevent rotting of corpse, 1403, 1404
Sanday (Peggy Reeves) on, 8009
in secret societies, 1404, 8212
in South American Indian religions
bone souls and, 8584
Catholic Communion compared to, 8593
endocannibalism and exocannibalism in, 1403
in symbolism and myth, 1403
totemism and, 4183
in witchcraft, diabolical, 9771
witchcraft and sorcery associated with, 1404
of Yurupary, 9918
Cannon, Katie, 79, 10040
Cannupa Wakan (sacred pipe), 5295–5296
Canoes, 991. *See also* Tomol
in Maori religion, 5680, 5682
in Micronesian myths, 6012
Canon, **1405–1411**. *See also* Scripture
in Armenian church, 490
in Buddhism (*See* Buddhist books and texts)
in Catharism, 1456
in Christianity
ecclesiology and, 1771
extrabibilical materials as, 1408
Gospels in, 1410
Hebrew scriptures in, 880–881, 891, 896
Hellenistic influence on, 1406
law and, 5355
Marcion's influence on, 5701
Nag Hammadi codices and, 6398
in Confucianism, 1407, 1900, **1905–1910**
imperial cult rituals and, 1913
Zhu Xi and, 1917
contemporary usage of, 1407
in Daoism, 1597
definition of, 882, 920, 5328
etymology and earliest historical usages of term, 1406–1407
of Hebrew scriptures (*See* Hebrew scriptures, canon of)
heresy and, 3921
canon as tool against, 3926
hermeneutical implications of, 1407–1410
in Hinduism, 1407
in Śaivism, 5999
higher path *vs. mantra* path in, 4019
Nāyaṉmār poems in, 4005
in Islam, 1407, 1409
ḥadīth, 9274–9275
tilāwah and, 9200–9201
in Judaism, 1406–1407, 1408, 1409–1410
wisdom literature and, 9761
law (*See* Canon law)
in Manichaeism, 1408, 1409
of New Testament (*See* New Testament, canon of)
prophecy under influence of, 7426–7427
prophets' words becoming, 7425
scriptural religions and, in history of religions approach, 4066
scripture and, 1410
structuralist view of, 8753
and unicity, affirmation of, 8201, 8202
Canon (Shenoute), monasticism in, 8319
Canon Actionis/Canon Missae, 9811
Canonical Prayerbook (Mandaean text), 5635
Canonization
as regimentation of tradition, 9274–9275
of saints, 2082–2083
Canon law, 5328–5329
casuistry in, 1455
Christian
origins of, 1406, 5336–5338
Sohm (Rudolf) on, 8507
on Crusades, 2076
Islamic, 1407 (*See also* Qur'ān)
Orthodox, Quinisext Synod and, 2041
religious canon related to, 5355, 5358
Roman Catholicism, 7876, 7886
Canons of Dordt (1619), on free will and predestination, 3208
Canon of Prémontré, 7724
Canons regular, 7724
Canopic jars, 4319
Canstein Bible Institute, 3185
Cantabrian, Spain, 1471
Cantar de mio Cid (Spanish poem), 7218–7219
Cantares Mexicanos (song), 2466
Cantatas, 6311–6312, 6313
Canterbury, archbishops of
Anselm as, 372
Augustine of Canterbury as, 623
church polity and, 1766
under Elizabeth I, 349
jurisdiction of, 350
list of, *351*
Canterbury Cathedral, monastery in, 6119
Canterbury Tales, The (Chaucer), 7218, 7554
relics in, 7689
Canticle of Brother Sun (Francis of Assisi), 6349
Cantillation, 1532–1534
Cantona (Mexico), in Classic period, 5902
Cantors, 6308, 6312
in Sephardic Judaism, 7582
Cão, Diogo, 5220
Cao Cao (Chinese general)
and Way of the Heavenly Masters, 2192
Xiongnu people defeated by, 4491
Cao Dai movement, **1411–1412**
Caodaism, 6568
Caodong lineage
Huineng and, 4155
origination of, 1522
overshadowed by Linji, 1523
silent illumination in, 1524
zuochan approach to meditation, 1604
Caodong school of Buddhism, 1293
buddha nature in, 1239–1240
Dōgen in, 1244–1245, 2385
origins of, 1172
Caoilte mac Rónáin (mythic figure), 1495
Cao Pi (Chinese emperor), 7267
Cao Xueqin, *Dream of the Red Chamber,* or *Story of the Stone,* 3057, 3068
Cao Zhi (poet), 7213
Capaccocha (tribute), human sacrifice as, 8603
Capacocha (festival), 4411
Capell, A., 2543
Capella, Martianus
on ascension, 522
on knowability of God, 182
on numbers, 6746
Capital (Marx), 5746–5747
Capitalism
Calvinist ethics and, 7251, 7458
Confucianism and, 1921–1922
criticized by Latin American bishops, 1704
development of, 2669, 9707
gender and, 3361
German critiques of, 2669–2670
globalization and, 3498, 9931–9932
government role in, 2670
Islamic conduciveness to, 2677
Marx on, 5746–5747
in modern ethos, 2672
in modern world system, 2675–2677
origins of, 2671, 9711
Protestantism and, Weber (Max) on, 8464, 8494
religion in, 2669
Roman Catholic Church on, 2670
social movements and, 1754
spirit of, 2672–2674
Tillich (Paul) on, 9203
Zapatismo and, 9932–9933
Capitalism and Slavery (Williams), 67
Capital punishment. *See* Death penalty
Capital sins, 1888
Capito, Wolfgang, and Anabaptism, 304
Capitolia (Rome), 7893
Capitoline temple (Rome), 7895, 7901
Capitoline triad, 7900, 7901
Mars in, 5727–5728
Minerva in, 6043
Cappadocia (Turkey), early Christianity in, 2581
Cappadocians, on Trinity, 2582, 4241
Capps, Donald, 944, 947

Capps, Walter, **1412–1413**
on society and religion, 8470
Capra, Fritjof, 6437, 6496
Capreolus, John, 9164
"Captivity" (Erdrich), 7226
Capua Tile, 2870
Capuchins, 3183
Caquiahuaca (deity), in Tacana religion, 8576
Caracalla (Roman emperor), 7914
imperial cult of, 7916
Cara Cognatio (feast), 7909
Carajá people (South America), masks of, 5767
Caraka Saṃhitā
Āyurveda in, 714, 3853, 3854
branches of medicine *(aṣṭaṅga)* in, 3853
karman in, 5096
magic in, 5591
Caraṇa (liturgical observances), of Vedic texts, 9554
Carbon, anthropic principle and, 2033
Carbon-14 dating, of megaliths, 5822
Cardeña, Etzel, on religious experience, 7747
Cardenal, Ernesto, 3063, 7246
Cárdenas, Nabor, 6577
Cardinal, Roger, 9625
Cardinals, in Roman Catholic Church
in church polity, 1764, 7886
in papal elections, 6970, 6971
Cards, **1413–1414**
CARE, 1555, 3174
Carey, Hilary M., 671
Carey, Peter, 3084
Cargo, 6927
in Mesoamerican religions, 5925
gender and, 3413
Cargo Cult (Lindstrom), 1421, 1423–1424
Cargo cults, **1414–1425**
in colonial imagination, 1422–1423
composite approach to, 1416–1417
on death, 2237
decolonization and globalization and, 1424
dema myth complex and, 4825–4826
effects of, 1418–1420
Ghost Dance compared with, 6666
history-making context of, 1422
Lawrence (Peter) on, 5380, 7788
Melanesian, 5380, 7789
cosmologies reflected in, 2007
messianism of, 5973
millenarianism in, 6034
motivation for, 1417–1418
nation-states and, 1424–1425
in New Guinea religions, 6506, 6509
as new religious movements, 1739–1740
origins of term, 5380, 9296
overt cargo phenomena, 1414–1416
problematization of the analytic concept, 1421–1422
repentance in, 7756
as revival and renewal movements, 7785
in Solomon Islands, 8516–8517
study of, 6801–6802, 6803–6804
symbolic activities in, 7789
syncretism in, 8933
transculturation and, 9296, 9321–9322, 9323, 9324
Vailala Madness, 6797
visions of, 9613
Western analyses of, 1416
Western discourse about, 1423–1424
women in, 3398
Cargueros (load bearers), 9002
Cariacou, Big Drum Dance in, 1436
Caribbean Discourses (Dash), 9297
Caribbean region
colonialism in
antisuperstition laws and, 3823
Christianity and, 1706–1707
cultural transmission in, 1426
identity and cultural hybridity, 1859
Inquisition in, 4503
literature of, African influences on, 3064–3065
slavery in, 9305, 9306
Spanish conquest of, 1695, 9305
Caribbean religions, **1426–1440**. *See also* Garifuna religion; Rastafari; *See also* Santería; Vodou; *specific countries and religions*
Afro-Caribbean, **1432–1440**
ancestral cults in, 1435–1436
ashe (vital energy) in, 3823
creolization in, 2066
healing in, **3821–3824**
neo-African cults in, 1433–1435
religio-political cults in, 1437–1438
revivalist cults in, 1436–1437
Shango cult of Trinidad in, 1434–1435
studies of, 10024, 10025–10026
wanga charms in, 3823
altered states of consciousness in, 10026
Christianity, **1706–1708**
conversion to, 10024
demographics of, 1707
early history of, 1706
Evangelical Pentecostal, and Charismatic, 2067–2068
Protestantism, 1707, 2067, 10024
Roman Catholicism, 1706–1707, 2067, 10024, 10026
social structure and, 1706–1707
creolization in, **2065–2068**
ethnographies of, 10024–10025
Hinduism, creolization and, 2068
history of study of, **10023–10030**
centralization and authority in, 10028–10029
on Internet, 10028
missionary and travelers' reports, 10023–10025
quest for "Africanisms" in, 10025
syncretism in, 10025–10026, 10027
Islam, 4682, 4683–4685
oral tradition in, 10028
pre-Columbian, **1426–1432**
deities of, 1426–1428
origin myths in, 1428–1429
rites and ceremonies in, 1429–1430
shamanism in, 1430–1431
Rastafari influence in, 7624
spirit possession in, 10027
tobacco in, 9217
transculturation in (*See* Transculturation, in Caribbean)
twins in, 9415, 9418
women in, 10027–10028
Carib Indians. *See also* Island Carib
Arara religion, 8631
cannibalism reported among, 1429–1430
hunting dances of, 8581
Makiratare (Orinoko), 8626
Marikitari, cosmology of, 8587
star lore of, 8588
Waiwai (Guyana), human origin myth of, 8589
Warikyana (Guianas), Pura as supreme being in, 8577
World Fire myth of, 8589
Carisi people (Brazil), origin myths of, 5198
Carismáticos, 5930
Caristia (feast), 7909
Caritas (love), 2308
Cariyāpiṭaka (Buddhist text), 6993, 6994
Carlebach, Shlomo, 4869–4874, 9383
Carlitz, Katherine, 3341
Carlos of Texcoco, 5917–5918
Carlota Joaquiná, Princess, marriage of, 1443
Carlsen, Robert, 5796, 5945
Carlyle, Thomas
on heroes, 3956–3957
Swedenborgianism and, 8903
Carman, John, Bangalore Consultation presentation, 8790
Carmathians. *See* Qarāmiṭah
Carmelite order
Carroll's sponsorship of, 1446
Discalced, 6764
founded by Teresa of Ávila, 9084
mendicancy of, 5856
origin of, 2827
reform of, John of the Cross in, 4941–4942
Thérèse of Lisieux in, 9154–9155
Carmen (Catullus), 2346
Carmenta (deity), priest of, 3126
Carmichael, A. C., 10024
Carmina burana (Butler), 2162
Carmody, Denise Lardner, 3313
Carmun, 1483
Carnac (Brittany, France), 6465
Carnap, Rudolf, 7118
on knowledge, 5210
Carneades (philosopher), 7188
skepticism and, 8420
Stoicism *vs.*, 8740
Carnegie, Andrew, 6585
Carneiro, Edison, 121
Carnival, **1440–1445**. *See also* Holī
as antireligious religious performance, 7045
in Brazil, 1443–1444
characteristics of, 7045–7046
domestic observances of, 2399
in Europe, 1441–1443
humor in, 4198, 4218
as inversion of social norms, 1440, 1444, 7196
in Italy, 2147–2148
as ritual, 1444
roots of, 7046
scholarly interpretations of, 5765
as setting for revolutionary activities, 7329–7330
sexuality in, 8242
in Trinidad, 7045, 7046
Carnival in Romans (Ladurie), 7330
Carnivores, omophagia and, 6821–6824
Carnoy, Albert, 4461

Caro, Joseph. *See* Karo, Yosef
Caroling. *See* Winter solstice, songs of
Carolingians
decline of, 6132
Judaism and, 5011
schism and, 8155
Carpatho-Russia, Uniate church of, 2588, 9463–9464
Carpenter, Edward, 5864
Carpenter, Lant, 9317
Carpentier, Alejo, 3063, 3064
Carpets, 9091, 9092
felt
in Central Asian king initiation rites, 5179
in shamanic initiation rites, 5179
Carpocrates (Gnostic leader), 3516
on transmigration, 9329
Carrasco, Davíd, 5944, 5945
on sacrifice, 8009
Carrasco, Pedro, 5942
Carrera, Carlos, 3099
Carrera, Magali, 9296
Carrier, Joseph, on homosexuality in Latin America, 4117
Carriers of the Dream Wheel (Native American poetry anthology), 7225
Carrizo Nation, peyote used by, 406
Carroll, Charles, 1445
Carroll, John, **1445–1446**
Adams (Hannah) and, 31
Carroll, Michael, 7480
Cars. *See* Automobiles
Carson, Anne, 5484
Carson, James T., 6694
Carson, Rachel, 2609
Carsten, Janet, on kinship, 5184
Carta Atenagórica, La (Sor Juana), 4967
Cartailhac, Émile, 1048
Cartesian method, 2293, 2294
knowledge in, 5205–5206
and metaphysics, 5990–5991
Carthage
Christianity in, 1677, 1678–1679
persecution of, 7059
Eshmun in, 2841–2842
Melqart in, 5848
as Phoenician colony, 7128
Carthage, Council of (412), condemnation of Celestius at, 7025–7026
Carthage, Council of (416), condemnation of Pelagius at, 7027
Carthage, Council of (418), condemnation of Pelagius at, 7027
Carthage, First Council of, exorcist ordination prescribed by, 2929
Carthusians, monasteries of, architecture of, 6119
Cartier, Jacques, 9299
Cartomancy, 2373
Cartonnage, in Nag Hammadi codices, 6396
Cartwright, Thomas, 7519
Carus, Carl Gustav, 6435
on dreams, 8909
Carus, Paul, 1313, 7740
popular writings of, 1635
Suzuki (D. T.), influence on, 8885
Cārvāka school (Indian philosophy), **1446–1447**. *See also* Materialism
atheism of, 578, 579
castes criticized by, 4421
mokṣa rejected by, 4421
soul in, 4421
Vedic tradition criticized by, 4421
Carved figures
African, 89, 90
Arctic, 471
Oceanic, 6789
Caryā (conduct), 9507
Caryāpadas (Bengali text), 825
Caryā Tantras, 1215–1216, 1217
Casablanca (Morocco), Hassan II Mosque in, 6210
Casadio, Giovanni
on Gnosticism, 3534
on Jonas (Hans), 3533
on Plutarch, 7201
Casanova, Jose, on relevance of religion, 4179
Casaubon, Isaac, 3703
Case, Clarence Marsh, 6648
"Cases of conscience," 1455
Cash cropping, 3280
Caso, Alfonso, 5903, 5942–5943
Cass, Lewis, 6670
Cassian, John, **1447–1448**
aesthetics and, 46
cenobitism and, 2827
on ecstasy, 2680
on spiritual guidance, 8710
Cassinese Congregation, 822
Cassiodorus (monk), on care of the sick, 3845
Cassirer, Ernst, **1448–1449**
on iconography, 4297
Langer (Susanne) and, 7837
on Nicholas of Cusa, 6610
on rituals, 7837
symbolism of, 7839
on symbols, 4298
symbol theory and, 8912–8913
Cassuto, Umberto, 869
Castaneda, Carlos, 2680
neoshamanism and, 8294
Castelli, Elizabeth, 6742
Castellio, Sebastian, 7282
Castelnau, Peter, 1458
Castes
in Bali, 746, 747, 748
in Bengal, 825, 826, 829, 1029
in India, 5289 (*See also* Dalits; *Khatri* caste; *See also* Varṇāśramadharma theory of caste)
Ambedkar (B. R.) in reform of, 285–286
and authority of Hinduism, 8483
British colonialism, effect of, 1858
Buddha opposed to, 1105
Buddhism criticizing, 4421
Cārvāka criticizing, 4421
Christianity and, 1729–1730
creation of, 2367, 4440
development of, 3990
dharma and, 5289, 5343, 5346
Dumézil (Georges) on, 4462
duties of, 2329–2330
in epics, 4001
hospitality and, 4140
impure gods and, 4006
in *Ādi Granth,* 32
in Ārya Samāj, 516
inequality of, 5289
in Vīraśaivism, 8043
Jainism criticizing, 4421
jātis (categories) in, 3996
Kabīr on, 3986
karman and, 5289
local worship, implications for, 4006–4007
merit and, 8061
mixing of, 3996
music and, 6280, 6281
of outsiders, 4465
Parsis as, 6998, 7000
and pollution, 7506
potlatch system compared with, 3480
Ravidās on, 3986
religious power above political power in, 7254
and response to desire, 2305
ritualized greetings and, 8060–8061
Sarvodaya movement and, 862
sectarian movements and, 4004
Sen (Keshab Chandra) on, 8227
of *siddhas,* 5604
Sikh rejection of, 8393, 8395
society-religion relations and, 8463
studies on, 4448–4449
subaltern studies and, 8800
taboos and, 7843
untouchables *(dalits)* (*See* Untouchables)
varṇa and *jāti* in, 9522–9524
Vivekananda on, 10090
origins of, *Vāyu Purāṇa,* 2963
in Southeast Asia
ceremonial orders, limited to, 4013
modification from Indian model, 8644
Castiglione, Baldassare, 4367
Casting of lots, in Israelite religion, 5425
Castitas (chastity), 1558
Castor (deity), 7902
Castor, bishop of Apt, 1447
Castration, **1450–1453**. *See also* Androgynes; Clitoridectomy; Dying and rising gods
of Attis, 986, 1451–1452, 2109–2110, 2536
in Christianity, as explicit sexual phenomenon, 7077
in Cybele cult, 1451–1453, 2109–2110
Freud on, 7974
in Greek myth, 1450, 1451
in Heaven's Gate movement, 3890–3891, 6555
hierodouleia (sacred prostitution) and, 3968–3969
in Hittite myth, 1450–1451, 4070, 4231
of Indra, 4467
in myths, 1450–1451
of Śiva, 7083
origins of, 1452–1453
of Osiris, 4557
of Ouranos, 986
ritual practices of, 1451–1452
sexual repression through, 8248
Skoptsy and, 1452, 8248
Castrén, Matthias Alexander, 474, **1453–1454,** 2421, 3104, 3112
Castro, Daniel Romero, III, 405
Castro, Fidel, Afro-Cuban cults and, 1434
Castro, Santos Peralez, 406
Castro, Viveiros de, perspectivist theory of, 2012
Casubon, Isaac, on Hermetism, 3949
Casuistic laws, Israelite, 4728
Casuistry, **1454–1455**
in Christian era, 1455–1456
conscience and, 1942
in law codes, 1845
methodology of, 1456
in non-Christian contexts, 1454–1455
Catacombs (Rome), 1472, 3637, vol. 4 color insert
Catalepsy, ascension and, 520
Çatal Hüyük (Turkey), 5281–5282
archaeological finds at, 6461–6462
excavation at, 1801–1802
goddess worship at, 3585, 3589, 3593, 6462, 7376
life column motif at, 7380
ram symbolism at, 8310
Catalina of Cardona, eremitism of, 2827
Catalog of the Three Caverns, 2183, 2195
Catalog of Women, authorship of, 3963
"Catalogue" (Edwards), 2699

Cataphatic meditation and contemplation, 5817
Catasterism (transfer of humans to the heavens), 8424–8425
heroes and, 8733
Twain (Mark) on, 8735
Catawba people (North America), 6689
Catecheses (Cyril of Jerusalem), aim of, 2118
Catechesis (confessional) approach, to religious education, 7731
Catéchisme positiviste (Comte), 7339
Catechism of the Catholic Church, The, 9540
Catechisms
obedience and, 1670
in Pure Land Buddhism, 4923
Zoroastrian, 9994
Catechists, African, 1719
Catechumenate, restoration of, after Vatican II, 7961–7962
Categorical imperative, 7652
Categories (Aristotle), 6644
Categories of religion. *See* Classification of religions
Catequil (deity), Augustinian friars *vs.*, 8608
Caterwauling, 1463
Cathari sect (Christian), **1456–1458,** 7719
adherents of
classes of, 3524
persecution of, 3524, 4498, 6567, 6971
angels in, 347–348
Dominic preaching in, 2412
dualism of, 2508, 2509, 2513–2514, 9771
election of, 2747–2748
enthusiasm of, 2805
Gnosticism in, 3524
and the Grail myth, 3650, 3652
as heresy, 3928
Manichaeism and, 5657, 5668
orgies of, 6870
transmigration in, 9330
Catharsis, **1458–1461,** 5469, 7509. *See also* Purification
Cathartic deification, 2248–2249
Cathedral of Tomorrow (television ministry program), 7711
Cathedrals, **792–797**
architecture of
classification of, 461
development of, 9265
sacred geography in, 3436
in Middle Ages, 793, 9265
as museums, 6245
origin of word, 792
Catherine (saint), in Shango cult, 1434
Catherine II (empress of Russia)
anti-Muslim campaigns halted by, 4617
Hook (Sidney) on, as hero, 3956
Catherine of Aragon, marriage to Henry VIII, annulment of, 7662
Catherine of Genoa, and language of fire, 3120
Catherine of Siena, **1461–1462,** 2414
fasting by, 3172
Catholic, definition of, 7880
Catholic Action movement, 1701, 9533
in Mesoamerica, 5930, 5932
Catholic Apostolic Church, 4543, 4544
Catholic Bishops' Conference for the Pacific, 1739
Catholic Colonialism (van Oss), 5924
Catholic Demonstrations, The (Leibniz), 5406
Catholic Eastern Churches (non-Roman), autonomy of, 1765
"Catholic epistles," 916
Catholic Hour, The (radio program), 7712
Catholicism
Christianity and, 7880
Constantinian, 7875
definition of, 7874, 7880
Eastern-rite (*See* Eastern Catholic churches)
East-West schism (*See* Great East-West Schism)
history of, Petrine ministry and, 7874–7875
post-Tridentine, 7877–7878
Roman (*See* Roman Catholicism)
sectarianism in opposition to, 7874
social doctrine of, 7874, 7878
spirituality and ethos of, 7887
Uniate (*See* Uniate Churches)
values of, 7880–7882
Catholicism and Independence: Being Studies in Spiritual Liberty (Petre), 7070
Catholic Reformation. *See* Counter-Reformation
Catholic schools, 7734, 7889
Catholic Sociological Society, American sociology and, 8496
Catholic Synod of African Bishops, on ancestors, 142
Catholic University of Nijmegen, Grail movement at, 3653
Catholic Worker, 2226
Catholic Worker movement, 3173
Catholic Youth Movement, 796
Cathubodua (deity), 1490
Catimbó, 120
Catoptromancy, 6064
Cato the Elder
as folk physician, 3841
on Mars, 5728
Cats, **1462–1464**
deities associated with, 1462–1463
flying or winged, in Andean religions, 8602
in folklore, 1463–1464
goddess associated with, in Scandinavian religion, 3218
sacrifice of, 1463
Cattell, James, 3505
Cattle and cows, **1464–1468**. *See also* Golden calf
of Baal, 319
bones of, 1015
in Brahmanism, 9571
Buriat shamanism associated with breeding of, 1325–1327
domestication of, 1464
dung of, in purification, 7508
in Finno-Ugric religions, 3108
in Germanic religion, 3446, 3447
in Greek and Roman religion
Herakles associated with, 3917
Hermes and, 3936, 3937
sacrifice of, 3682
Hathor as god of, 3795
in Hinduism
mythic themes of, 4438
veneration of, as symbol of nonviolence, 6646
in Kushite religion, 5269
Māra as protector of, 5692
in Nuer and Dinka religion, 6743
in pastoral societies, 1464–1465
in prehistoric religions, 7384
raiding and, 1465–1466
sacred, in India, 1467
sacrifice of, 1466–1467
in Indo-European religions, 4454
in Scythian religion, 4489
in Zoroastrianism, 6997–6998
in Southern Siberian religions, 8671
taboos on eating of, 3167
Tiamat in form of, 1466
urine of, 4535
in Vedism, 9560
in domestic ritual, 9565–9566
in *soma* sacrifice, 9563
in Zoroastrianism, 9997
Cattle-raiding myth
Indo-European, 2431–2432
Irish, 8960
Cattle shed, spirit of, in Komi religion, 5218
Catuḥśatakaṭīkā (Candrakīrti), commentary in, 1401
Catullus, Gaius Valerius, on Diana, 2346
Caturānanda (four joys), in *Hevajra Tantra,* 3965–3966
Cāturmāsya (retreat), 9824
Caturvarga (duties), in Āyurveda, 3854
Caturviṃśatistava (praise to the twenty-four Jinas), 4769
Caturyāma-dharma (law of four restraints), 9208
Caucasus
Christianity in, 4612–4613, 4614
Islam in, **4612–4620**
jihād, 4614–4615
Sufism, 4613, 4614–4615
Sunnī, 4614
ṭarīqah in, 4615, 9007
Judaism in, 4612–4613
Mongol invasion of, 4613–4614
Zoroastrianism in, 4613
Caughey, James, 1020
Cauim festival, in Tupian religion (Amazon), 8628
Caulibus, John de, 7772
Causation. *See also* Free will; Occasionalism
in Buddhism
causal interdependence, 2627, 2628–2629, 2630
dependent co-origination doctrine, 1527, 5200
in eightfold path, 2738
karman and, 5098
quantum theory and, 8188
science and, 8180
wheel of life, 5448
chaos theory and, 1542–1543
in Chinese philosophy, resonant causality concept, 1572
determination *vs.* causality, and chance, 1527
divine causality, Schleiermacher (Friedrich) on, 8166
hermeneutics and, 8499
in Sāṃkhya Hinduism, 8089–8090
in Islam
falsafah ideas on, 2975
kalām ideas on, 2974–2975
scientific history and, 8181
in mythology, 6362–6363
parallel causalities, in African diaspora medicine, 3822–3823
in primitive *vs.* civilized society, Lévy-Bruhl (Lucien) on, 5429
in science and religion, 2659
Cautery, as medical practice, in Middle East, 3836–3837
Cauvin, Gérard, 1374

Cauvin, Jean. *See* Calvin, John
Cavalli-Sforza, L. L.
on evolution of human culture, 10043
on fertility rates, 8475
Cavazzi, Giovanni Antonio, 112
Cavendish, William, Hobbes (Thomas) and, 4073
Caves, **1468–1473**. *See also* Labyrinth
artificial, 1471–1472
art in, 1470–1471
Paleolithic, 1470–1471, 5280–5281, 6952–6953, 8279
shamanic elements in, 8279
in Australian Indigenous religions, 1470
as *axis mundi,* 1468
Buddhist images in, 9829
as Buddhist temples, 9042, 9046, 9048
in Caribbean origin myths, 1429
in China, 1471
Maitreya figures in, 5620
as earth womb, 3015–3016
as emergence place, 1469
in Europe, 1470–1471
in Greek religion, of Hermes, as passageway to Hades, 3937
Grotto at Lourdes, France, 1470
as Hindu shrines, 9039
in India, 1470–1471
masks found in, 5767
in Maya religion, 5796
sacred geography of, 3434
in Mende myths, 3570–3571
in Mesoamerican religions
afterlife and, 149
cenotes as tombs in, 1471–1473
in creation myths, 1468
gods and rites of, 1469–1470
in Huichol religion, 4152
in Teotihuacán, 5898
in Zapotec religion, 5912
in North American Indian religions, 1469, 1470
in Oceanic religions
as doors to underworld, 2007
as shrines, 2006
in Olmec cosmology, 6818–6819
prehistoric, 7381
rites of passage and, 1470
rock temples and tombs, 1472–1473
sacred *vs.* profane and, 7974
significance in religious belief and practice, 3015
in Ungarinyin religion, 9458–9461
as *yoni,* 9906
Zalmoxis and, 9927–9928
Caves, Monastery of the (Kiev), Serafim of Sarov and, 8229
Caw cam (master of ritual), 5313, 5314
Cawek (Mayan warrior), 2435, 2466
Caws, Peter, on structuralism, 8757, 8759
Caxaa (Mixtec priest), 5918
Caxton, William, 3475
Hermetic texts and, 3946
Cayce, Charles Thomas, in Association for Research and Enlightenment, 561
Cayce, Edgar, **1473–1474**
in Association for Research and Enlightenment, 559–561, 1474
psychic readings of, development of, 559
Cayce, Hugh Lynn, 1474
in Association for Research and Enlightenment, 559–560
initiatives after father's death, 559–560
Cayton, Horton, 74
Cayuga tribe (North America). *See also* Iroquois religion
ballgame played by, 754
Cazeneuve, Jean, on taboos, 7842
CBN. *See* Christian Broadcasting Network
CCAR. *See* Central Conference of American Rabbis
CCSR. *See* Canadian Corporation for Studies in Religion
Ceata Fetelor (female folk society), 9743
CE–BCE system, 173
Cebes (philosopher), on repentance, 7756
Cecil, Robert, Calvert (George) and, 1373
Cecilian Society, music in, 6312–6313
Cédshamhain, 1491
CELAM. *See* Latin American Council of Bishops
Celan, Paul, 5483, 7207
Cel ati (deity), 2871
Celestial buddhas. *See* Buddhas, celestial
Celestial Hierarchy (Dionysius), 2355–2356, 7402
Celestiality, of supreme beings, 8868–8869
Celestial Masters/Heavenly Masters (Tianshi dao), 1593, 1597, 1602, 2180–2181, 2192–2194, 2199, 2635, 2636, 9843–9845
children initiated into, 7414
Correct and Orthodox Covenant with the Powers of, 2180–2181, 2193
Dao de jing/Laozi teachings in, 2180, 2193
decline of, 2181, 2200–2201
deities of, 2181
disease and illness in, 2181
disregard for, 2195
founding of, 7710
Ge Hong and, 2181–2182
hierarchy of, 7413
Kou Qianzhi and, 2183, 2194, 5240–5241
Laozi (Lord Lao) in, 5317
legends of, 2180
libationers in, 2180, 2181, 2192, 7413
literature of, 2204, 2206
Lu Xiujing and, 5542–5543
and marriage, 2181
marriage rituals of, 2181, 2182, 2193
millenarianism of, 6038
official recognition of, 1597
reforms of, 2181–2183
registers of generals in, 2193, 2200
rituals of, 1593
utopian nature of, 2192–2193
Xu Mi and, 2195
Yang Xi and, 2182
Zhang Daoling and, 2180, 2192, 9954
Zhang Lu and, 2181, 2192, 9955–9956
Zhengyi sect and, 1602, 1608
Celestial portents, 7336–7337
Celestial prodigies, 7337
Celestial Road (Milky Way), and stars as land of the dead, 8733
Celestial Worthy of Primordial Commencement, 2183
Celestine (pope), 6483
Celestine V (pope), 1019
Celestine Prophecy, The (Redfield), 6496
Celestius (disciple of Pelagius), condemnation of, 7025–7026
Celibacy, **1474–1478**. *See also* Asceticism; Chastity; Virginity
in Buddhism, 1475, 1477
castration and, 1452
in Christianity, 1452, 1475, 1476, 1477, 2647, 7081, 9607–9608
Augustine and, 2308
of Catholic priesthood, 9541
medieval, 7403
Orthodox, 2593, 4833
Paul VI on, 7013
in Daoism, 1475
and decline of priesthood, 7398
Essene, 2847
in Hinduism, 1475, 1476–1477, 7083
Islamic rejection of, 7082
in Judaism, 1476
as sin, 7586
permanence of, 9607
place in society of, 1476–1477
as purification, 7509
rationales for, 7397
in Roman religion, of Vestal Virgins, 3385
of Shakers, 1475, 1477, 5389, 6516, 8268
traditional perceptions of, 1475–1476
in vocational priesthood, 7395
Cella (space containing cult statue), 9062, 9063, 9064–9065
Cellarius, Christopher, on ancient medieval, and modern periods, 4030
Cells, in monastery architecture, 6118, 6119
Celsus
anti-Christian treaty by, 6474
on apostasy, 432
on ascension, 522
on Christian persecution, 7059
on gnosticism, 5202
on images, 4352
on Mithraism, 6091, 6092
Celtes, Conrad, Hrotsvit and, 4143
Celtic bath, 801
Celtic cross, runic inscriptions on, 7941
Celtic languages, 1478, 1495, 1497
Celtic religion, **1478–1501**. *See also* Druids; Iberian religion; *See also* Tuatha Dé Danann
All Saints Day in, 2229–2230
aquatic monsters in, 4134
Augustine of Canterbury and, 623
boat burials in, 990
calendar, 1355
Christianity and, women and, 3388–3389
Conall Cernach in, **1883**
deities of (*See also* Brighid; Maponos; *specific deities*)
of British Celts, 1489–1491
Caesar's interpretation of, 1481–1482
classification of, 1482–1483
divine consorts, 1485–1486
female, 3388
Gaulish deities and insular equivalents, 1481–1487
goddesses, 1485–1486, 1490–1491
matres, 1490–1491, 5779
nature associations in, 1486–1487
Roman parallels, 1481–1486
three-headed god in, 3804
zoomorphic, 1487
divination in, 2374
Dumézil (Georges) on, 4453, 4462, 4463, 4464
eyes in, 2941
Ferghus mac Roich in, **3040**
Fomhoire in, 1488, **3164–3165,** 9686
gender in, **3387–3389**
the Grail in, 3651
Hartland (E. Sidney) on, 3782

head cult in, 3805, 3806, **3807**
head hunting in, 3805, 3807
heroic ideal in, 1493–1494
history of study of, **1497–1501**
horse sacrifice in Ireland, 4132
mythical intercourse and, 8239
iconography in, 1481–1487
Invasions in, 1487–1489
kingship in, 1491–1495
learned classes (druids, *fildh,* and bards), 1479
literature of (*See also* Mabinogion; *See also* Táin Bó Cuailnge (saga))
Fionn Cycle, 1494–1495
formlessness of corpus, 1495–1496
Leabhar Gabhála Éireann, 1480, 1485, 1488
manuscripts, 1479–1481
Ulster Cycle, 1493–1494, 1499–1500
memorization in, 5851
mythic space and time in, 1491
ocean in, 6806
oral tradition, 1479
laws and, 1842
otherworld in (*See* Annwn)
overview, **1478–1497**
paradise in, 6985
rainmaking in, 7603
rejuvenation myths in, 7603
seasonal festivals (*See* Beltene; Imbolg; Lughnasadh; Samhain)
sídh/sídhe in, 1489, **8392–8393**
social structure in, 4453
sources on, 1479–1481
sun in, 8836
tales of sea journeys in, 991
transmigration in, 9329
Tuatha Dé Danann in, 2951, 3164–3165
Wicca influenced by, 9731
women in, **3387–3389**
yoni in, 9908
Celts (stone axe heads), in Olmec religion, vol. 3 color insert
Cemeteries, 9228. *See also* Tombs
as sacred space, 2082
in Vodou ritual, 9637
Cempoallan. *See* Zempoala
Cena de le ceneri, la (Bruno), 7340
Cenobitic monasticism. *See also* Monasticism
in Buddhism, sectarianism and, 8080
characteristics of, 6939–6940
as eremitic preparation, 2826
hospitals and, 3844
origins of, 7723
Pachomius and, 7723
Cenotaph (ship burial), 6943, 9227
Cenotes, 1469, 1472–1473
Censorship
of books, in Tibetan Buddhism, 5224
of Celtic literature, by Christian monks, 1495
and iconoclasm, 4281–4282, 4287, 4348
modern, 7085
in United States, 4282
of Gage (Matilda Joslyn), 3252
Centaurs, 6164–6165
"Centenary Perspective, A" (Borowitz), 7672–7673
Centeotl (deity), 1468, 5911
Center. *See also* Circumambulation
in Celtic religion, 1491
cities as ceremonial centers, 1803–1805
sacrifice and ceremonial centers, 8009
Smith (Jonathan Z.), critique of, 1879
of world (*See* Center of the world)
Center for Theology and the Natural Sciences (CTNS), 2661, 8184
Center for the Studies on New Religions, 6524
Center for the Study of World Religions
ecology conferences at, 2613
Shintō conference at, 2638
Center of the world, **1501–1505,** 6886. *See also* Axis mundi; Cities; Consecration; Home; Mountains; Orientation; Trees
in Amazonian religions, 8630
in Central Asian religions, Iurak disanimation myth, 8532
cosmic tree and, 9576–9577
in Greek religion, Delphi as, 8745
in North American Indian religions
in Lakota sweat lodges, 7981–7982
in Sun Dance lodges, 8845–8846
rituals and attitudes on, 1504
Roman cities and, 7983
in shamanism, 8272, 8283–8284
symbolic forms of, 1501–1504
water at, 9701
"Center Out There, The: Pilgrims' Goal" (Turner), 9406
Central African Republic. *See* Banda religion
Central America. *See* Mesoamerica; *specific countries*
Central Asia and Central Asian religions. *See also specific countries and religions*
Arab invasion of, 4620, 4621
Buddhism, **1144–1148**
art, 1145
bodhisattvas in, 1145
drums in, 2497
forms of, 1146
instability of, 1094, 1095
and Korean Buddhism, 1170, 1171
under Kushan empire, 1092, 1109, 1132, 1145–1146
languages of, 1145, 1146–1147
literature of, 1146, 1147
Mahāyāna Buddhism, 1093, 1145, 1146
monasteries, 1095, 1146, 1147
spread of, 1091–1092, 1093, 1145, 1147, 1201, 4490
Chinese displaced by Arabs, 1599
as geographical concept, 4620
vs. Inner Asia, 4488
Iruak religion, disanimation myth in, 8532
Islam, **4620–4630**
cult of saints in, 4622
literature, 4629–4630
marriage in, 4625
post-September 2001, 4630
post-Soviet, 4626–4630
revival of, 4625–4626
under Soviet rule, 4623–4626
spread of, 4620–4621
Sufism, 4621–4622, 4625, 4629
Sunnī, 4620, 4621, 4627
ṭarīqah in, 4621, 9007, 9010
under tsarist rule, 4622–4623
Twelver Shiism, 4620
Wahhabiyah, 4626, 4627, 4628
Judaism, 5008–5010
kingship in, 5179
Manichaeism, **5668–5670**
Mongolian invasion of, 4493, 4620, 4621
orgy in, 6879
sheep and goats in, 8311, 8312
Central Bantu religions (Africa), **1505–1512**. *See also* Bemba religion; Kimbangu, Simon; Kongo religion; Lenshina, Alice; Maranke, John; Ndembu religion
affliction cults in, 1509–1510
ancestral spirits and domestic cults in, 1508
common base in, 1506–1507
creator cult, absence of, 1507
initiation in secret cults in, 1507
interlacustrine, **4518–4521**
professional cults in, 1509
religious transformation in, 1510–1511
social setting of, 1507
territorial cults, heroes, and nature spirits in, 1508–1509
Central Conference of American Rabbis (CCAR), 7665, 7666, 7670, 7671
"A Centenary Perspective" of, 7672
Central Council for Research in Indian Medicine and Homeopathy (CCRIM&H), politics of, 3856
Central domed mosques, 6209
Central Europe, Jewish migration to, 5016
Central Hindu College, 845
Central Hindu Girls' School, 845
Central Intelligence Agency (CIA), on brainwashing, 1030–1031
Central Inuit. *See* Inuit religious traditions
Centre National de la Recherche Scientifique (CNRS), 2350
Cepheid variables, standard candle measure and, 2031
Ceque system, Inca calendar and, 1362
Ceramese religion (Indonesia)
agricultural myth in, 191, 4824, 4825–4826
Hainuwele story in, 2091–2092, 3015, 3018, 9578–9579
pig sacrifice in, 7145
Ceramics
in Amazonian Quechua religions, 283
Mayan, 4312
musical instruments made from, 6268
Cerberus. *See* Kerberos
Cereal
cultivation of
mythology from, 9579
origins of, 185–186
Demeter's gift of, 2751
Ceremonial dance, definition of, 2146
Ceremonial magicians, 6471
Ceremonies, **1512–1519**. *See also* Ritual; *specific ceremonies and religious traditions*
in Amazonian Quechua religions, 284
in Arctic religions, for animals, 471
in Australian religion, Howitt (A. W.) on, 4142
in Aztec religion, 719, 5908

Ceremonies ***continued***
in Blackfoot religion, 960
definitions of, 1512–1513
Djan'kawu, 2380
Erasmus (Desiderius) on, 8866
in Candomblé, 123
in Minoan religion, 39–40
in North American Indian religions
in Native American Church, 10053–10054
Navajo, 6442, 6443
Osage, 6917
vision quest, 9609
political power and, 1513–1516
and sacred *vs.* secular or profane, 1516–1518
in Scythian religion, 4489
as symbolic ritual, 2606
in Toltec religion, 9222
in Toraja religion, 9241–9242
in Vedism, 4426
in Vietnamese religion, 9592–9593
in Vodou, 9637–9638
in Warlpiri religion, 9694, 9695
Ceremonies and Rituals (Yili), 1907–1908
Ceremony (Silko), 1515–1516, 3091–3092
Ceres (deity)
deities assisting, 7899
feast of, 7899
priest of, 3126
relationship to Dea Dia, 2232
Cerialia (festival), 7897, 7899
Cerlarios, Michael, **1519–1520**
Cernunnos (deity)
animals associated with, 1487
Roman parallels, 1485
torques around neck of, 1481
Cernythian hind, caught by Herakles, 3916
Ceroklis (deity), 761
Cerros (Maya center), 5886
Certainty, 2428
absolute, 2428
conscience and, 1942
epistemological, 2428
logical (mathematical), 2428
psychological, 2428
Certeau, Michel de, 2930, 2936
Cerularios, Michael. *See* Michael Cerularios
Cervantes, Fernando, 5919, 9297
Cervantes, Miguel de
Don Quixote
in history of the novel, 3050, 3051
religious motifs in, 3058–3059
humanism and, 4176
proverb defined by, 6976
Cesair, 1488
Cetiya (stupa), 1134, 1305
in Southeast Asia, 9829–9830
Ceucy (Pleiades), as mother of Yurupary, 9918
Ceylon. *See* Sri Lanka
Ceylonese religion. *See* Sinhala religion
Chaak (deity), 5798
Chabad Hasidism. *See* Habad (Lubavitcher) Hasidism
Chabad Houses, Schneerson (Menachem) and, 8173
Chabrol, Claude, structuralism and, 8752, 8755
Chac (deity)
as fertility god, 9213
offerings to, 1469
as rain god, 7602
Ch'a ching (Lu Yü), 847
Chacmools (sculptures), 9222
Chaco Indian religion, 9575
Chad (Africa), kingship in, death of king in, 5170
Chadavarkar, Rajnarayan, on subaltern studies, 8800
Chadbourne, Paul, 9423
Chadō (tea ceremony), 847
hospitality and, 4141
Chagall, Marc, 4348
Adam in works of, 30
Bible illustrations of, 53
Chagga people (Tanzania)
African Independent Churches among, 2571
mortuary rituals of, 140
Chahine, Youssef, 3098
Chai (ritual fasting), 2996
Chaikin, Joseph, 2438
Chaireas and Kallirhoe (Chariton of Aphrodisias), 3051, 3052
theme of resistance in, 3055
Chaitanya. *See* Caitanya
Chakralavī, ʿAbdullāh, 4653
Chakyars (acting families), 2448
Chalcedon, Council of (451)
Armenian church rejecting, 490
Coptic Church and, 1979–1981
division of Christianity and, 2583, 2584–2585
Ethiopian Church and, rejection of, 2859
Eutyches and, 2885–2886
hypostasis and Christology at, 4241, 4242
on incarnation, 3553
on Jesus as God incarnate, 4417
Jesus Christ defined by, 7876
Leo, declaration on, 1688, 5410, 6966–6967
Leontius of Byzantium on, 5412
and Mark the Evangelist, line of succession to, 1979
on Mary as *theotokos* (Mother of God), 5753
Melkite Catholics and, 9463
on Monophysitism, 4354, 6153
Nestorianism vindicated at, 6483
Niceno-Constantinopolitan Creed and, 2040
Oriental Orthodox dissent from, 1673
overview of, 2040
Syriac Orthodox Church dissent from, 8938–8939
Timothy Ailuros rejecting, 9205
Chalcedonian Orthodoxy. *See* Eastern Orthodox Church
Chalchiuhtlicue (deity), 2984
fertility and, 719
mountains and, 1468
ritual impersonations of, 5293–5294
Chalcidius, 6475
Chaldaean Oracles, 7191, 7921, 9156–9157
Chaldean Catholic Church, 1673
origins of, 6480
Chalk, in Sarmatian burial practices, 8115
Challis, W., 113
Chalma, sacred cave at, 1469
Chalmers, David, 6487
'Cham (ritual drama), 2140, 6299
Chamacoco religion (Paraguay)
mother goddess in, 8578–8579
overview of, 8633–8634
Chambers, John D., on Hermetism, 3952
Cham dances, 1827–1828
Chameleons, in African myths, 92
Champaigne, Philippe de, vol. 12 color insert
Cham people, 9591
calendar of, 1353–1354
Champier, Symphorien, Hermetism and, 3946
Champrenaud, Léon, 3706
Chamula, rebellion of (Mexico), 6576
Chamula language, 5303
Chan, Wing-tsit, Neo-Confucianism of, 1922–1923
Chan Bahlum (Maya ruler), 5887
Chan Buddhism, 1165–1166, 1239–1240, **1520–1526**. *See also* Zen Buddhism
aesthetics and, 51
Bodhidharma as founder of, 994–995, 1239
Confucianism and, 1901
Daoism and, 994, 1293
desire in, 2306
emergence of, 1601
emptiness *(śūnyatā)* in, 8859
ethics of, 1281
gender in, 3343
Gozan Zen and, 3643
historical development of
early Chan, 1521–1522
late imperial, 1524
middle Chan, 1522–1523
modern, 1524
proto-Chan, 1521
in Song dynasty, 1523–1524
Huayan Buddhism and, 4147
Huineng, role of, **4153–4155**
humor in, 4202, 4207
iconography of, 4330
international growth of, 1610
invocation with meditation, 1604
in Korea, 1172
kung fu in, 8724
language of, 5310–5311
Linju sect of, 5463–5464
literature, 1524
"mad Chanists," 1578
in martial arts, 5731, 5732
masters, 1523
meditation in, 1096, 1167, 1179, 1292–1293, 5821
monasticism in, 1240, 1524, 1604
mysticism in, 6345
nirvāṇa in, 6631–6632
Northern school of, 1521–1522, 6631
oral tradition of instruction in, 8713–8714
origination of, 1577
Oxhead school of, 1522
paradox in, 6989
patriarchs of, 1577
succession of, 1163, 1239
philosophy of, 1302
Pure Land Buddhism and, 292, 4923–4925
Pure Lands in, 7503
in Qing dynasty, 1609
revelation and sacred time in, 7988
Sakya Paṇḍita on, 8052
in Song dynasty, 1604
Southern school of, 1522, 6631
temples of, 9047, 9048
Tiantai school and, 1238
and Tibetan Buddhism, 9184
Western study of, 1638
women in, 3343
Wuzhun in, vol. 10 color insert
Zen Buddhism and, 9943–9944
Zhuhong in, 9972
Zongmi in, 9987
Chance, **1526–1529**. *See also* Divination; Fate; Gambling
Buddhist radical contingency and, 1527
in Christianity and Rationalist philosophy, 1527
in deep play, 3261
definition of, 1526
divination and, 1528
Greek views of, 1526–1527
Jung on, 1528
miracles and, 1528
Roman view of, 1527
as serendipity, 1527
unknowability and, 1528–1529
Chancellor, James, 6541
Chan Chan (Peru), burials at, 4183
Chānd, Shaykh, 6767
Chaṇḍa (mythic figure), 4434
Chāndogya Upaniṣad, 7363, 9347
brahman-ātman in (*See Brahman*)
guṇas in, 8090

monism in, 6144
nonviolence in, 6645
spiritual guides in, 8711
Chandra Khonnokyoong (Čhan Khonnokyūng), 2324
Chané people (Argentina), 8637
Chang (constant), 9372
Chang'an (China), 9963
Islam in, 4631
Changbu (spirit), humor and, 4208
Chang Chüeg. *See* Zhang Jue
Changchun Abbey (Abbey of Eternal Spring), 2199
Changchunzi Panxii ji (Daoist text), 2210
Change
comparative-historical method and, 1870
dancing to effect, 2138–2139
process of, 7123
sociological concept of, 8485
tradition and, 9278–9180
Chang E (deity), gender studies on, 3339
Changelings, 2953
Chang Hsüeh-Ch'eng. *See* Zhang Xuecheng
Changing of the Gods (Goldenberg), 9098
Changing Woman (mythic figure), 3019
in Apache religious traditions, 574
impregnation of, 9907–9908
in Navajo religious traditions, 573, 3408, 4485–4486, 6441–6442, 6659–6660, 7682, 7684
rejuvenation of, 7682, 7684
Chang Lu. *See* Zhang Lu
Chang Naizhou, on martial arts, 5735
Ch'ang-o (deity), 3018
Changó el gran Putas (Zapata Olivella), 3065
Chang Tao-Ling. *See* Zhang Daoling
Chang Tsa. *See* Zhang Zai
Chan Htoon, U, 1140
Chania (Crete), religious art in, 38, *38*
Channing, William Ellery, **1529–1530,** 9317, 9469
liberalism of, 6105
Martineau (James) and, 5737
Chanoyu (tea ceremony), 847
as hospitality, 4141
Chanson de Roland (French poem), 7218
Chantepie de la Saussaye, Pierre Daniël, **1530–1531**
Lehmann (Edvard) influenced by, 5405
on phenomenology of religion, 7086, 7089
Tylor's animism criticized by, 363
Chanter, Tina, on body theology, 4167
Chanting, **1532–1536**. *See also* Incantation; *Mantras;* Music; Recitation; Tilawah
Armenian, 1534–1535
as blessing, 981, 982
in Bornean religion, 1022
Buddhist
Japanese, 1177, 1179, 6300–6302
Korean, 6297–6298
in meditation, 1291, 6283
Southeast Asian, 9828
Tibetan, 6298
in Tibetan Buddhism, 1535–1536
Byzantine, 6305–6306
Christian
early, 6305
medieval, 6309
in Orthodox worship, 2591
definition of, 6251
Gregorian, 1534
Gregory I and, 3688, 6309
origins of, 3688, 6309
revival of, 6313
in healing, 3811
Hebrew, 1532–1534
Hindu
and *bhakti,* 857, 858
great prayer, 1347
inŚrī Vaiṣṇavas Sampradāya, 8728
in Ch'ŏndogyo, 1648
in Indian religions, of Vedas, 1535
in International Society for Krishna Consciousness, 4522
in Islam
in *ṣalāt* (prayer), 8057
of Qur'ān, 1535
in Sunnism *vs.* Twelver Shiism, 8345
Jewish, 6307
in Micronesian medicine, 6005
in Navajo religious traditions, 6442
in Neopaganism, in seidr ritual, 8295
of poetry, 7204
quasi-magical use of, 8200
in Roman religion, 6304
of scripture, 8200
secular, 1536
in shamanism, 8278
in Sufism, *samāʿ* (listening parties), **8064–8066,** 8822
Chantry chapels, 793
Chanul soul, 5798
Chanyuan qinggui (Buddhist text), 9945–9946
Chaos, **1537–1541**. *See also* Cosmic eggs; Order and disorder
in Babylonian religion, 1538–1539
in Chinese myth
combat mythology and, 1626
Gonggong as chaos monster, 1625
hundun, 1540, 1624–1625
sacred time and, 7987
in Christianity, 1540
in creation myths
androgynes and, 337–338
creation from chaos, 1537–1538, 1986–1987
embryonic condition of, 1538
paradigm of evil in, 2898–2899
primordiality and, 1989
as symbolic pattern, 1986–1987
in Daoism, 2175
dragons associated with, 6163
in Germanic religion, 1537
Hesiod on, 1537, 1538
humor as, 4215
images of, 1537
in Indian religions, 1539–1540
meaning of term, 1537
negative and positive evaluations of, 1538–1540
orgy as, 6864
perfected, 2175
time and space models of, 1986–1987
Chaos, King of, Carnival and, 1440
Chaos theory, **1541–1543**
metaphysics of, 1542–1543
quantum chaology in, 1543
religion and, 2660, 7139
unpredictabilities in, 1541–1542
Chapaṭa (Mon monk), 1136, 9149
Chapayekam (masked figures), 7045, 7050
Chapels
chantry, 793
classification of architecture, 461
Chapman, Audrey, 3428
Chappaz-Wirthner, Suzanne, on Carnival, 5765
Chapter houses, in monasteries, 6118
Charavilh tax, Carnival and, 1441
Charcot, Jean Martin, 7474
Chardin, Pierre Teilhard de. *See* Teilhard de Chardin, Pierre
Charībi, Driss, 3088
Chari-Nile languages, in East Africa, 2566
Chariots
in Greek mythology, 6995–6996
horses and, 4132
sun and, 8835, 8838
Charis (grace), 3644–3645, 7174
Charisma, **1543–1553**. *See also* Charismatic leadership
in African religions, 1547
in Australian and Pacific religions, 1547
in Aztec religion, 1548
and brainwashing, 1034
in Buddhism, 1549
of Gautama Buddha, 1061, 1062
sectarianism and, 8080
in Chinese religion, 1549, 1606, 1618, 7353
in Christianity, 1545, 1546, 1549–1550
definition of, 7352–7353
heresy and, 3923
in Hinduism, 1548–1549
in Islam, 1546–1547
in Japan religion, 5267
of Jesus, 9271
in Judaism, 1545–1546
Hasidic *tsaddiq* and, 3789
of King (Martin Luther, Jr.), 5402
in Korean and Japanese shamanism, 1548
of leaders, 5385, 5387
Lewis (I. M.) on, 1547–1548
in liberation theology, 5439
mana as, 1547, 7353
in millenarianism, 6034
in North American Indian religions, 1547
and power, 7352–7353
of Prophet (Elizabeth Clare), 1784
revival and renewal activities and, 7785
schism and, 8153
as sociological concept, 1544–1545
Sohm (Rudolf) on, 8507
in Sufism, 9660
Weber (Max) on charismatic authority, 8483
Charisma and Sacred Biography (William), 947
Charismatic Christianity, **7028–7034**. *See also* Pentecostalism
in Africa
contemporary forms of, 106–107
in Zionist churches, 8316
belief and practice in, 7031–7032
in Caribbean, creolization and, 2067
Catholic, in Oceania, 6793
exorcism in, 2931
faith healing in (*See* Miracles)
glossolalia in, 7031

Charismatic Christianity *continued*
gospel of health and wealth in, 7030–7031
in Mesoamerica, 5930
origin of term, 7028
origins of, 7028–7029, 7718
in Philippines, 1728
as renewal movement, 1550
revival of, 7030
social character of, 7032
in United States, evangelicalism influenced by, 2893
worship in, 7031
Charismatic leadership
in millennial movements, 6546
and movement volatility, 6552
move to collective administration, 6564–6565
in new religious movements, 6515, 6523, 6546, 6562
development stages of, 6564–6565
in Japan, 6573
and violence, 6552, 6553
and violence, speculations about, 6552, 6553
Charitable institutions, in early Eastern Christianity, 2582
Charites, the, 1554
Chariton of Aphrodisias, 3051, 3052, 3055
Charity, **1553–1556**. *See also* Almsgiving; Hospitality; *See also* Zakāt (tax)
as act of devotion, 2320–2321
in Buddhism, 1107
Compassion Relief (Ciji) movement, **1787–1790**
in Chinese religion, 1616
in Christianity, 2320–2321
care of the sick, 3843–3845
institutions of charity, founding of, 1750
Swedenborg (Emanuel) on, 8899
Duns Scotus (John) on, 2524–2525
in Islam (*See Waqf*)
in monasticism, 6124
moral principles regarding, 6183–6184
Sharpe (Eric) on, 8305
wealth and, 9709
Charity and Its Fruits (Edwards), 2699
Charlemagne, **1556–1557**
Alcuin and, 254, 7280
authority of, 696
Byzantine church under, 2586
Christianity under, 7280
Constantinianism of, 1968
crowning of, 1662, 1689
filioque doctrine and, 8155
Leo III and, 696, 6967, 7280
Savonarola (Girolamo) on, 8139
Charles II (king of England), theaters allowed to reopen under, 2474
Charles V (Holy Roman emperor)
Herakles as symbol of royalty for, 3917
and Inquisition, 4503
Lutheranism and, 5536, 5539
and Paul III, 9342
in Reformation, 7658, 7659
Charles VII (king of France)
and Gallicanism, 3258
Joan of Arc and, 4929–4930
Charles, R. H., 899, 900, 901
on Antichrist, 394
Charles Martel (Frankish ruler), 1018
Charles the Bald, Eriugena (John Scottus) and, 2830
Charles the Hammer (Frank ruler), 7280
Charlesworth, James H., 901
on dualism, 2509
Charlesworth, Max, 636
at Deakin University, 8770
Charm for the Unfruitful Land, 6943
Charmides (Plato), 2273
Zalmoxis in, 3466
Charms. *See* Amulets and Talismans
Charon (mythic figure), 165, 166, 989, 992, 2296, 2871
Charon, Jean, 6437
Charpentier, Jarl, 7493
Charrière, G., 3467
Charter myths, in Micronesian religions, 6002–6003
Chartres, school of, nature in, 6432
Charun (demon), 2277
Chase, Richard, 4458
Chastisement, in Judaism, suffering and, 8805
Chastity, **1557–1560**. *See also* Asceticism; Celibacy; Virgin goddess; Virginity
in African religions, sacred kingship and, 8665
Ambrose on, 287
Christian view of, 1558
clitoridectomy and, 1825
Greek and Roman notions of, 1558
Hindu view of, 1559
Islamic view of, 1559
Jewish view of, 1558–1559
meaning of term, 1557
of Mahāyāna *bodhisattvas*, 8038
as religious prerequisite, 9607
sacrifices, as sacrificial gifts, 7998–7999
sainthood, path to, 8037
Chatā (fate), 9094
Chateaubriand, Edict of (1551), 7662
Chateaubriand, François René de, on religion as social phenomena, 8492
Chateillon, Sébastien, on religious tolerance, 8233
Chatterjee, Partha, on peasant consciousness, 8800
Chatterton, Percy, 9324
Chattopadhyaya, Bankim, 10035
Chattopadhyaya, Debiprasad, on Vedic *vs.* Āyurvedic medicine, 3853
Chaucer, Geoffrey, 6086, 7218, 7554
on relics, 7689
Chauncy, Charles, Great Awakening opposed by, 2698
Chau Ta Kuan (Buddhist monk), 1138
Chavannes, Édouard, 1634, 3655
Groot (J. J. M. de) and, 3702, 3703
Maspero (Henri) and, 5773
Chavero, Alfredo, 5940
Chaves, Jonathan, 3341
Chavín art (Andean), iconography of, 8602
Chavín de Huántar (cult center), jaguar images at, 4762
Chechens, Islam of, 4613, 4614, 4615
Cheda Sūtras, in Jain scriptures, 4767
Cheese and the Worms, The (Ginzburg), 7327
Ch'egwan (Buddhist scholar), 1172
Cheironomy, 1533
Cheju Island (Korea), Maitreya in, 5621
Chekhov, Anton, 2474–2475
Chela (student), in Eckankar, 2601
Chelčický, Petr, 6190
Chelhod, Joseph, on left and right symbolism, 5393–5394
Chemical ecstasy, 2679–2680
Chemosh. *See* Kemosh
Ch'en, Kenneth, 6072
Chen Chun, 4337–4338
Cheng (authenticity), 2634
Chenggong Xing, Kou Qianzhi as student of, 5240
Chengguan (Buddhist monk), Huayan and Chan schools of Buddhism, role in, 4147
Cheng Hao, **1560–1561**, 4337
cosmology of, 1560–1561
historical context of, 1560
moral psychology of, 1578
Neo-Confucianism and, 1603
on *ren*, 7752
Chenghuang (deity), 1616
Chengshi school of Buddhism, 1201–1202
Chen Guofu, 2214
Cheng Yan, 1610
Cheng Yen. *See* Zhengyan
Cheng Yi, **1562–1563**, 4337. *See also* Cheng-Zhu school of Confucianism
Buddhism criticized by, 1563
cosmology of, 1562–1563
on ghosts and spirits, 1563
historical context of, 1562
influences on, 1562
metaphysics of, 1578
Neo-Confucianism and, 1603
on *ren*, 7752
on sagehood, 1562
Zhu Xi and, 1900–1901
Cheng-Zhu school of Confucianism
designation of, 1901
development of, 1603
Mengzi and, 5858–5859
metaphysics in, 1577
promoted by Qing emperors, 1579
self-cultivation in, 5858
Chengzu (Ming dynasty ruler)
and Daoism, 2187
and legend of Zhang Sanfeng, 2187
Chen-Jen. *See* Zhenren
Chen Jinggu, 3340
Chen Kaige, 3097
Chen Mengjia, 3339
Chennai. *See* Madras, India
Chen Tao (God's Salvation Church), 6552, 9435
syncretism of, 9433
Chen Wentong, 3070
Chen Xianzheng, on cosmic principle, 1902
Chen-Yen. *See* Zhenyan
Chenzong (emperor), role in promoting Daoism, 1602
Cheops (Egyptian king), 7527
Cheremis. *See* Mari and Mordvin religion
Cherkess people (Caucasus), 4613, 4614
Chernoglav (deity), 9359
Cherokee Nation v. Georgia, 7301–7302
Cherokee religion and society (North America), **1563–1566**
ancestors of, 6688
ballgame played in, 753, 754–755
bears in, 807
Booger Dance, 1565, 7197
contemporary landscape of, 6690
Corn Woman narrative in, 6692
cosmology of, 6691–6692
creation story of, 6692
ethics in, 1564–1565
fasting in, 2997
forced migration and, 6690, 6696
Green Corn ceremony in, 1564, 1566
incantation in, 4407, 4408, 4409
insects in, 4508
land of, 7301–7302
Mississippian culture and, 6655
poetry in, 7224
Prophet movement in, 6666
Protestantism in, 1566

religious resistance movements in, 1565
rituals in, 6693–6694
shamanism in, 6693
Snake movement in, 6666, 6667
social history and geography of, 1563–1564
stomp dance in, 1565–1566
supreme being of, 6691
Chertkov, Vladimir, 9221
Cherubim and Seraphim (movement), 6568
Chery-heb (lector priest), 2714
Chesler, Phyllis, 3420
Chess, artificial intelligence playing, 510, 511
Chesterton, G. K., 3062
on civil religion, 7256
on paradox, 6990
on Thomas Aquinas, 9162
Chettiar merchants, competition among, 1806–1807
Chevannes, Barry, on Rastafari, 7623, 7624
Chevet, 793
Chewa religion. *See also* Central Bantu religions
masquerade dances of, 2140
vimbusa healing dance of, 2140
witchcraft in, 9777
Cheyenne religion and society (North America)
circle symbolism in, 1794
creation story of, 6704
culture hero and origin of maize in, 2092
earth in, 2554, 2555
food taboos in, 7299–7300
gender in, 3407, 3409
historical roots of, 6656
iconography of, 4310
"intercourse with the buffalo" ceremony, 8239
Sacred Arrow Renewal ceremony of, 6704
study of, 6672
Sun Dance in, 8846
Chézy, Leonard de, 1333
Ch'i. *See Qi*
Chi (human spirits), 4365
Chiao. *See* Jiao
Chiapa de Corzo (Mexico), Stele 2 of, 5882
Chiapanec Mayan cults, 6576
Chiapas (Mexico)
Maya stelae in, 5882
Roman Catholicism in, 3413
Zapatista Army of National Liberation in, 3414, 9930, 9932
uprising of (1994), 5931–5932
Chibchacum (deity), 6229, 6230
Chibcha religion. *See* Muisca religion
Chicago "history of religions" approach
Eliade and, 4047
Kitagawa (Joseph) and, 4044
Chicago World's Fair (1893), World's Parliament of Religions at, 6559
Chicano movement, Virgin of Guadalupe in, 3064
Chichén Itzá
cenote at, 1472–1473
sky hierophany and, 8428–8429
Chichimec people, 716, 718
settlement patterns of, 5173
Chichiní (deity), 5910, 9254
Chickasaw tribe (North America)
ballgame played by, 753
forced migration of, 6690
poetry of, 7225
supernatural being of, 6691
Chickens and hens
in Micronesian myths, 6012
in Yoruba creation myth, 3571
Chicomecoatl (deity), 5280, 9578
Chicomoztoc (seven caves), 1468
Chicueyozumatli (deity), 9255
Chidester, David, 3044
Chiefs. *See also* Kings and kingship
in North American Indian religions, 7300
Chumash, 9228
in potlatch, 7345
in Oceanic religions, 7295–7296, 7297
in Polynesian religion, 7296, 7307, 7309
in Tikopia religion, 9195, 9196, 9197
Chigaku, Tanaka, 6608
Chiga religion (Uganda), 2961
Chihamba, the White Spirit (Turner), 9405
Chihamba cult (Zambia), initiation rite of, 4197–4198
Chih-i. *See* Zhiyi
Chih-yen. *See* Zhiyan
Chikafusa, Kitabatake, 4812
Chikamatsu Monzaemon, 2455
Chikō (Buddhist figure), 2299
Chikri people (Brazil), 1004
Child, Lydia Maria, **1569–1570**
Child abuse
new religious movements and, 5377
sexual, 5377, 7889–7890
in Roman Catholicism, scandal, 7889–7890
Childbirth. *See* Birth
Childe, V. Gordon, 185
Childhood (Tolstoy), 9220
Child of Water, 405
Children, **1566–1569,** 2982–2983
abuse of (*See* Child abuse)
affliction in, 57
African, as ghosts, 3476
in afterlife, 136
ambivalent treatment of, 2982
in Ashkenazic Hasidism, 542
Australian Indigenous myths for, 656, 3392
baptism of, 782
in Blackfoot religion, as participants, 961
as Buddhist monks, 1156
burials of
in Iberian religion, 4251–4252
Neanderthal, 6950
changelings, 2953
Chisungu, dances of, 2138
in Christianity, mass or services for, 4199
corporal punishment of, 5377
custody of, new religious movements and, 5377
deities of
in Chinese religion, 1643
in Japanese Buddhism, 3869
developmental stages of, in Mesoamerican religions, 7812
disciplining of, controversy over, 6540
dreams of, 2484
evil eye and, 3837
funeral rites for, in Zoroastrianism, 2130
games, cosmological significance of, 1503
Halloween and, 3759
health care of, in new religious movements, 5377
home schooling of, 5377
humor and, 4199, 4211–4212
incorporation into family, 2983
in International Society for Krishna Consciousness, 4523
in Inuit religion, 4528
in Islam
ḥājj of, 7156
inheritance to, 4709
paternity of, 4710–4711
in Israelite religion, laws on, 4731–4732
in Japanese religion, Nakayama-dera Temple and, 3869
in Jesus Movement, 4853
kinship relations of, in Langkawi culture, 5184
in Latvian Saule (sun) cult, 8133
Maitreya's relationship with, 5620, 5621
in Melanesian religions, 5836, 5837
in Mesoamerican religions, developmental stages of, 7812
in mythology, 1567–1568
naming ceremonies for, in North American Indian religions, 6683
newborns, and blood taboo, 1460
in new religious movements, 6516–6517, 6526, **6538–6544,** 6564
child abuse charges, 6516, 6526, 6539–6541
legal concerns and, 5377
in North American Indian religions
Hako ceremony for, 6704
naming ceremonies for, 6683
Nuwaubians and abuse of, 6770
in Orthodox Church, 2592
at Point Loma Theosophical Community, 7229, 9206
psychological interpretation of motif of, 1568–1569
psychology of, Hall (G. Stanley) and "child study" movement, 3755
rites of transition for, 7956
sacrifice of
in Aztec religion, 1469
in Inca religion, 4411
in Maya religion, 1472–1473
in Moabite religion, 6095
in Phoenician religion, 4580, 7132, 7134
saṃskāras for, 7814
Satanism scare and, 8127
Sikh, gender of, 3337
souls of, 9443
as symbol of deity, 2983
transitional objects used by, 7483–7484
treatment of, changes in over time, 7796
in Twelve Tribes, 9410–9411
in Ungarinyin religion, 9461
Children for Krishna, 4523
Children of El (Israelite deities), 4742
Children of God (new religious movement). *See* Family, the
Children's Crusade (1212), 2075
Children's Day, 2411
Child study movement, Hall (G. Stanley) and, 3755
Chile. *See also* Mapuche religion
Islam in, 4684
papal delegation to, Pius IX in, 7179
Pentecostalism in, 7029
Roman Catholicism in, pilgrimage in, 7149, 7150
Chiluba, Frederick, 106
evangelical Christians and, 1723–1724
Chimayó (Mexico), El Sanctuario de (pilgrimage site), 8377
Chimera (monster), 6165

Chimes, in Southeast Asian music, 6287–6288
Chiminigagua (deity), 6229–6230
Chimu empire (Peru), human sacrifice in, 4183
Ch'in (musical instrument), 6300
China and Chinese religions, **1580–1640**. *See also specific religions*
  ablutions in, 10, 11
  aesthetics in, 51
  afterlife in, **169–172** (*See also* Ancestors; Ghosts)
    Heaven in (*See Tian*)
    hell in, 5352
    netherworld and, 1614
    Pudu ritual, 1643
    purgatory, in popular religion, 1606
    Xi Wang Mu in, 9860
  agricultural rituals in, 190
  alchemy in (*See* Alchemy, Chinese)
  ancestors in (*See* Ancestors, in Chinese religion)
  anticult legislation in, 1033–1034
  archaeology in, 455–456
  astrology in, 2372
    in magic, 5592
  atheism in, 577, 578
  authority in, 692
  autobiography in, 701–702
  birth rituals of, lying on soil in, 2559
  blessing in, 981, 984
  Boxer Rebellion, 1610, 1725–1726
  breath and breathing in, 1043, 1045–1046
  Buddhism (*See* Chinese Buddhism)
  burial in, secondary, 1014–1015
  calendar and religious year, 1621, **1640–1644**
    domestic observances in, 2408–2409
    pan-Chinese observances, 1641–1643
    popular cults and deity birthdays, 1643–1644
    state rituals in, 1644
  capitalism in, Confucianism and, 1924
  cards, history of, 1413
  cats in, 1463
  centralization of power in, 2184
  chai (ritual fasting) in, 2996
  chaos *(hundun)* in, 1540
  charisma in, 1549, 7353
  Christianity
    calendar, 1355
    under Communist rule, 1611, 6085
    Jesuits in, 4842
    during Ming dynasty, 1608
    missions and, 1098, 1099, 1167, 1186
    music in, 6292
    Nestorian, 1598–1599, 6480
    overview, 1725–1726
    Pentecostalism, 7030
    Russian Orthodox Church in, 7946
    Russian Orthodox missions to, 2588
  city as ceremonial center in, 1803, 6886, 7984, 8428
  civil service examinations (*See* Civil service examinations)
  classification of, 9888–9889
    problems with, 3339
  clothing and hairstyle in, 1827
  Communist Party
    and Buddhism, 1098, 1167–1168, 7268
    Confucianism and, 1924
    exerting political power over religious institutions, 7255, 7268
    and Islam, 4636–4637, 4640
    religious freedom and, 5353–5354, 10072
    study of religion and, 10073
  Confucianism (*See* Confucianism)
  constitution of, 7266
  contemplation in, 5821–5822
  cosmology (*See* Cosmology, Chinese)
  court attire in, 1830
  creation myth in, sky in, 8428
  Cultural Revolution, 1610
  dance in, 6293
  Daoism (*See* Daoism)
  death in
    as journey, 1628
    souls and, 8554
  deities of (*See also specific deities*)
    vs. ancestors, 1605
    birthdays of, 1643–1644
    of creation, 1600
    development of pantheon, 1910
    di gods, 8299
    earth gods, 1615–1616, 1911–1912, 1913
    gender of, 3343
    goddess worship, 3587
    high god (*See* Shangdi)
    of immortality, 1592–1593
    names of, 6408
    nature gods, 1584
    at New Years, 1641–1642
    overlapping pantheon, 1619
    personified, 1593, 1594, 1605
    in popular tradition, 1605, 1606, 1619, 1643–1644
    star god, 1591
    stove god, 4106–4107
    territorial, 1615–1616
  divination in (*See* Divination, in Chinese religion)
  domestic observances in, **2406–2409**
  dragons in, 2433, 5996
  drama in, 2453, 2454, 2455
  dreams in, 2484
  drums in, 2499, 7036
  dualism in, 2508, 6746, 9888
  dynasties of (*See also specific dynasties*)
    founding of, *de* and, 2173
  early empire (Qin and Han), 1574–1575, 1589–1594
  early historical period, 1570–1574, 1582–1589
  economic expansion of, Confucianism and, 1924
  egg symbolism in, 2701
  Eisia's pilgrimage to, 2741
  emperor (*See also specific emperors*)
    jade used by, 4759
    rituals of, 1590
    yinyang wuxing ideology for, 9889
  Enchin in, 2781
  encyclopedias in, 2783
  Ennin in, 2801
  environmental culture in, 2614
  epic tradition and, 2815
  eschatology in, 2834
  eternity in, 2856
  Falun Gong in, 1611, **2978–2981**
  fangshi in, **2989–2991,** 5494
  fate and fatalism in, 3004
  films from, 3097
  fish symbolism in, 3123
  folklore of, fox in, 3182
  food customs in, 3170, 3172
  food taboos in, 3169
  Forbidden City, sacrifice to Shangdi and, 1914–1915
  funeral rites in, 3234, 3236
    domestic rituals of, 2408
    royal tombs, 9225
    studies of, 3703
    Xi Wang Mu in, 9860
  games in, cosmic symbolism in, 3260
  gardens in, cosmic, 3277–3278
  gender in, **3338–3345**
  gender studies in, 3338–3339
  geomancy in, 3437–3438
  geometry in, tonal, 3441–3442
  ghost festival in, 5231
  ghosts and demons in, 1584, 1605, 1606, 1614, 1641, 1642–1643, 3477
  gift giving in, 3483–3484
  goddess worship in, 3587
  gold in, 3625
  governance of, *de* and, 2173
  government authorization of religion, 1605, 1611, 1615
  Gozan Zen monasteries in, 3642–3644
  healing in, **3859–3864** (*See also* Chinese medicine)
  heaven, concept of (*See* Tian)
  hell in, 5352
  heterodoxy in, 6911
  historical development of (*See also specific dynasties*)
    Confucius (Kongzi) in, 1585–1586
    disunion period (post-Han) in, 1594–1598
    early historical period, 1582–1589
    empire consolidation period, 1598–1607
    in Han dynasty, 1590–1594
    Mengzi in, 1587
    in Ming dynasty, 1607–1609
    Mozi in, 1586–1587
    postimperial period, 1610–1611
    in Qin dynasty, 1589–1590
    in Qing dynasty, 1609–1610
    in Shang dynasty, 1582
    in Song and Yuan dynasties, 1602–1603, 1604–1605
    spirit mediums in, 1589
    in Tang dynasty, 1599–1602
    Xunzi in, 1587–1588
    in Yuan (Mongol) dynasty, 1606–1607
    in Zhou dynasty, 1582–1585
  historiography
    modern, 4032
    traditional, 4026, 4030
  history of study, **1629–1640**
    Granet (Marcel) in, 3655–3656
    Groot (J. J. M. de) in, 3702–3703
    historical methodology in, 4032
    nineteenth century, 1631–1634
    Seidel (Anna), role of, 8222–8223
    seventeenth and eighteenth centuries, 1630–1631
    trends in, 1637–1639
    twentieth century, 1634–1637
  homosexuality in, 4114, 4117, 5415
  hope in, 4127
  humor in, 4199
  immorality, quest for, 1588–1589, 1590, 1592, 1603
  insects in, 4508
  Islam, 1599, **4630–4640** (*See also* Hui Muslims; Xinjiang, Islam in)
    architecture of mosques in, 6209–6210

Communist Party and, 4636–4637, 4640
Confucianism influencing, 4632
contemporary, 4633–4639
domestic observances in, 2401
education, 4633–4634
food prohibitions in, 2401
funeral rites, 4635–4636
Gedimu, 4633, 4635
ḥājj in, 4633, 4637
in Han dynasty, 4631
imāms, 4633, 4634, 4635, 4637
literature, 4639
in Ming dynasty, 4632
music in, 6292
number of converts, 4563, 4638
in Qing dynasty, 4632–4633
Shiism, 4634–4635
spread of, 4631–4632
Sufism, 4633, 4635–4636, 4640
Sunnī, 4633, 4639
suppression of, 5354
in Tang dynasty, 4631
terms for, 4631
jade in, 4758–4759
Japan influenced by, 4782, 4795–4796, 4809
journals devoted to, 10058, 10073
Judaism, 1599, 1608–1609, 1610, 5005–5006, 5007–5008
judgment of the dead in, 5026
kingship in, 5178
authority of, 693
establishment of, 5178
functions of, 5179
in Han dynasty, 5178
law and, 5352–5353
in Qin dynasty, 5178
in Shang dynasty, 5178
in Zhou dynasty, 5178
Korea and, 5228–5236
Lady of the Animals in, 5280
Lantern festival in, 6594
law in, **5351–5355**
lay societies and voluntary sects, 1604–1605, 1606, 1615–1617
left and right symbolism in, 5394
libations in, 5434
life and death in, 9671–9672
light and darkness symbolism in, 5453
lightning symbolism in, 7604
literature of (*See* Chinese literature)
Longmen Grottoes, 1472
lotus symbolism in, 5519
magic in, 5592–5594
Manichaeism, 1598, 5656, **5668–5670**
early history of, 5668–5669
laws concerning, 5353
as secret religion, 5669–5670
marriage in, 2407
martial arts in, 5731–5732, **5733–5736**
May Fourth Movement, 1922
medicine (*See* Chinese medicine)
meditation in, 5821–5822
merit in, 5870
migration in, 6025
millenarianism in, **6038–6042**
early, 6038–6039
Golden Age in, 6030
late imperial, 6040–6041
medieval, 6039–6040
modern, 6041
minority groups, Christianity and, 1726
miracles in, 6052, 6053
mirrors in, 5645, 6063, 6064
missionaries in
in colonial period, 6084
Confucianism and, 1918–1920
Jesuit, 1355, 1608, 1609, 1633–1634, 1918–1921, 6084
from London Missionary Society, 6196
Manichaean and Nestorian, 1598–1599
Mongolian empire and, 1606
Protestant, 1608, 1632–1633, 1921
money in, 6137–6138
Mongolian invasion of, 4494, 4632, 7165
Mongol shamanism in, 6141–6142
monism in, 6146
monkeys in, 6152
morality in, 6182–6188
mountains in, as divine dwelling, 6213–6214
music in, 6289, **6292–6299**
mystery societies/communities in, 7719
mythic themes in, **1622–1629**
beginnings and return in, 1623–1628
broken stories and thematic function, 1622–1623
divination of structure, myth as, 1628
problem of, 1622
names in, 6408, 6409, 6410–6411
nature in, 2631
Neolithic religion, 6465
burial sites in, 8642
Nestorian Church, Manichaeism and, 5669, 5670
"New Culture" intellectuals, 1922
new religious movements in, 5377
suppression of, 7270
New Year festival in, 6594
number symbolism in, 6747, 6749, 6750
oaths in, 5352
occult sciences in, *vs.* magic, 5592
ocean in, 6806
operas in, 1620
Opium War (1839-1842) in, 4633
oracles in, 6833, 6835
orgy in, 6879
orthodoxy in, 6911
orthopraxy in, 6915
overview, **1580–1613**
People's Republic, 1610–1611, 1726
brainwashing, ideology of, 2085–2086
Period of the Hundred Philosophers, 1583, 1595
philosophy of, **1570–1580**
pilgrims from, Aśoka and, 555
politics in (*See* Politics, in China)
polytheism of, 7317–7318
popular (folk) religion, 1605–1606, **1613–1621** (*See also* Divination, in Chinese religion)
concept of "religion" and, 1580–1581, 1614
vs. Daoism, 9842
Daoism and, 3342
gender in, 3339–3340
historical constructions in, 1614–1615
imperial ancestor cult and, 1912–1913
law and, 5352
liturgy and ritual in, 1619–1620
music in, 6292
in postimperial era, 1610, 1611
in Qing dynasty, 1609
religious specialists in, 1617–1618
scholarship and historiography on, 1620–1621
seasonal celebrations in, 1643–1644
social structures in, 1615–1617
soul in, 8556
state, relations with, 1618
study of, 10075
temples in, 1617
theology of, 1618–1619
trickster fox in, 8303
postimperial, 1610–1611
prayers, 1619–1620
pregnancy in, 2407
prehistoric, 1581–1582
purification in
cleaning graves as, 7509
Confucian ritual purity, 1914
Shangdi sacrifice, preparation for, 1915
qigong movement in, 2978–2979
rabbit symbols in, 7590
rain symbolism in, 7604
rejuvenation myths in, 7603
"religion" as problematic category in, 1580–1582, 1614, 10072–10073
religious freedom in, 5353–5354, 10072
revolutions in, 7790
political, 1615
rituals in
jade in, 4759
law and, 5353
rivers in, female deities associated with, 3016
Roman Catholicism, 2228, 7269
under communists, 1611, 1726
Jesuit missions, 1355, 1608, 1609, 1630–1631, 1633–1634, 1725, 6084
saints in, 2228
suppression of, 5354
sacred and profane in, 7969–7970
sacred geography of, 3434, 3435
sacrifices
Confucian imperial cult, **1910–1916**
divination and, 1582
emperor offerings, 8005
Han rituals, 1591, 7267
human (*See* Human sacrifice, in Chinese religion)
official state rituals, 1644
Qin rituals, 1590, 7267
at seasonal festivals, 1641, 1642
to Shangdi, 1914
temple festival and, 1620
Zhou rituals, 1584
salutations in, 8060
salvation in
by becoming ancestors or gods, 1619
Daoist *vs.* Confucian methods of, 1626
messianic hope, 1594, 1597

salvation in *continued*
in Pure Land Buddhism, 1600
three ages theory of history and, 1576
in Way of Celestial Masters, 1593
scapulimancy in, 1015
scholarship in, on Daoism, 2213–2214
scientific history in, 8180
scripture in (*See* Chinese literature)
secondary burial in, 1014–1015
secret societies in, 7719, 8213
shamanism in (*See* Shamanism, in Chinese religion)
Six Dynasties period, 1576, 1594–1598
societal development, 1581–1582
souls (*po* and *hun)* in, 1589, 1605, 3860, **8554–8556**
Southeast Asia, influence in, 8643–8644
spells in, 8677
spirit mediums in, 1589, 1614, 1617
spirit writing, 1608, 1615, 1616
study of religion in, **10072–10076**
development of, 10072–10074
educational institutions for, 10074–10075
influence of, 10075
Sufism in, 1599
Suiko (empress) and, 5180
syncretism in, 1578
Taiping Rebellion (184 CE), 8961
Taiping Rebellion (1850-1865) in, 4633, 7022, 7257, 7268, 8961
Taiping Tianguo movement, 1609–1610
tea drinking in, 847
temples, 1605, 1616, 1620
textiles in, 9088, 9089, 9091
"three teachings," 1580, 1608, 1898–1899
Tibet invaded by, 1100, 1158–1159, 1168, 1315, 2132, 7269, 9188
tradition in, 9273
trees in, 9334
truth in, 9372
turtles in, 9407–9408
Venus in (*See* Hokuloa)
Vietnam, cultural influence in, 1411
Vietnam under, 9590–9592
visionary journeys in, 2182
Warring States period, 1583, 1585
wisdom in, 9753
women in, **3338–3345**
in domestic observances, 2407
written talismans in, 8677
xian in, 9856–9857
xiao in, 9857–9858
Xi Wang Mu in mythology of, 9859–9860
Yamato (Japan) kingdom under, 4780–4782
Yao and Shun in, 9872–9873
yin and yang concept in, 3021
yinyang wuxing in, 9887–9890
Yuhuang in, 9915
Yu in, 9914–9915
Zoroastrianism, 1598, 1599, 10003
China Inland Mission, 1725
Chinchaycama (deity), Spanish perceptions of, 8607
Chine antique, la (Maspero), 5773
Chineke. *See* Chukwu
Chinese Academy of Social Sciences, 10074, 10075
Chinese Association of Religious Studies, 10074
Chinese Autonomous Orthodox Church, 7946
Chinese Buddhism, **1160–1169**. *See also* China and Chinese religions
afterlife in, 3136
ālaya-vijñāna in, 229
almsgiving in, 268
Amitābha in, 291–292, 1162, 1167, 1238–1239
art, 1165
Āryadeva in, 514–515
Avalokiteśvara in, 705, 3343
Bodhidharma and, 994–995
bodhisattvas in, 1162, 5255
buddhas in, 1162
canon, 1252, 1253–1258, 1266–1268
celebrations in, 1304, 1306, 1307, 1308
Chan school (*See* Chan Buddhism)
Christian missionaries and, 1098, 1099, 1167
communism and, 1098, 1167–1168
Confucianism and, 1898–1899, 1901, 1909
cosmology in, 1161, 1162
Dao'an and, 2170–2172
Daochuo and, 2175–2176
Daoism and, 1595, 1603
Daosheng and, 2216–2218
development of, 1575–1577, 1594–1596, 1899
eschatology in, 2834
Esoteric Buddhism, 1240
ethics of, 1161, 1167, 1280
folk, 5352
foreign and native elements in, 1160
funerary rites, 1098
future of, 1168
Ghost Festival of, 9835
ghosts in, 3477
Gyōnen on, 1246, 1247
healing in, 3863
Hevajra Tantra in, 3966
historiography adjusted to traditionalism, 4026
history of study of, 1629–1638
Huayan school (*See* Huayan school of Buddhism)
iconography of, 4329, 4330
images carved into caves and cliffs, 1596
independent spirit of, 1094
and Indian Buddhism, 1094–1095, 1160
instability of, 1094, 1095
and Japanese Buddhism, 1176, 1179–1180, 1242, 1244, 9075, 9076, 9077
Japan influenced by, 4783–4784
kingship in, 1161, 1164, 1166, 7267, 8994–8995
knowledge in, 5200
and Korean Buddhism, 1170, 1171, 1172
Kṣitigarbha in, 5255
law in, 5352, 5353
of lay people, 1096, 1161, 1162, 1168
literature of, 1162–1163, 1164–1165, 1236–1237, 7207, 7212–7214, 10021, 10022
local cults, attempts to control, 1615
Mādhyamika Buddhism, 1164, 1202, 5555–5556
Mahāvairocana in, 5607
Mahāyāna Buddhism, 1093, 1202 (*See also* Tiantai school)
Maitreya in, 1162, 1166, 5620–5621, 7503
Manichaean texts in, 1598
mappō in, 5685–5687
meditation in, 1096, 1290–1294, 5821–5822
in Ming dynasty, 1578, 1607
missions and, 1093, 1163, 6072
modern, 1167–1168
monasteries, 1095, 1162, 1163, 1164, 1165, 1167–1168, 1238, 1240
monastic, 1595
Monkey and Buddha narrative, 4209
music in, 6294–6295
nianfo in, 6601–6602
nirvāṇa in, 1161, 6630–6631
nonviolence in, 6646
nuns in, 6760–6761
ordination in, 6855
origins of, 1160, 1163
persecution of, 5240, 7213, 7255, 7268
philosophy of, 1301–1302
pilgrimage in, 1097, 7164–7165
pilgrims to India, 3010–3011
political role of, 1160–1161, 1164
politics and, 7260
popularization of, 3155
priesthood in, 7407–7408
Pure Land Buddhism, 1096, 1162, 1166, 1236, 1238–1239, 2175–2176, 3019, 4921–4925
Pure Lands in, 7502, 7503
rebellion of, 7257, 7268
reforms in, 8967, 8968
relics in, 7691
revival of, 8994, 8995
ritual calendar of, 1097
rituals of, 1162, 1165, 1166, 1167
Sarvāstivāda school in, 8117–8118, 8120
schools of, **1235–1241** (*See also specific schools*)
defining, 1246–1247
encounter paradigm of, 1250–1251
exegetical lineages of, 1236–1237
formation of, 1165–1166, 1194–1195
systematic, 1237–1238
terminology of, 1235–1236
sectarian groups in, 3155, 3156
influence on, 1607
Sengzhao, role of, **8228**
services of, 6294
sinicization of, 6072
in Song dynasty, 1604–1605
soul and, 8556
spread of, 1092, 1093, 1160, 1163–1165, 4490
as state religion, 1166, 9836
studies on, 1246–1247, 1248, 1250–1251, 1311, 1314–1315, 8981
śūnyatā (emptiness) in, 8858–8859
suppression of, 1602
and Taiwanese Buddhism, 8963
in Tang dynasty (*See* Tang dynasty, Buddhism in)
temple managers *(zhuchi)*, 1617
temples of, 9045–9048
and Tibetan Buddhism, 1151, 1152, 1154, 1155, 1158–1159, 1166, 9184
transmission of, 5349
trends in, 1161–1163
in United States, 1187–1188
Vajrayāna (Tantric) Buddhism, 1121, 1214, 1215, 1221, 8985
Vinaya, translation of, 8072
Vinaya school of, 3275
visions of descent into the underworld in, 2299
women in, 3343–3344
xiao in, 9857–9858
Yijing in, 9886–9887
Yogācāra Buddhism, 1202, 1238, 6992, 9901

Zhenyan Buddhism, 9960–9964
Chinese Buddhist Association, 1158, 1168, 1254, 8967, 8968
Chinese Catholic Patriotic Association, 7269
Chinese Daoist Association, 2189, 2215, 2637
Chinese Exclusion Act (1882) (United States), 1188
Chinese Islamic Association, 4636, 4637
Chinese language. *See also* Chinese literature
Bible translation and, 1632–1633
Buddhist chanting in, 6301
Buddhist scriptures translated into, 1162, 1198–1202, 1253–1254
and acculturation, 1267–1268
by Amoghavajra, 1164–1165
by An Shigao, 1146, 1163, 1266, 1290
by Dharmarakṣa, 1147, 1163
by Gītamitra, 1146
by Kumārajīva, 1147, 1236, 1246, 1266, 1291
by Lokakṣema, 1291
by Mokṣala, 1146
by Paramārtha, 1202, 1250
in Dharmaguptaka school, 1146
Dōgen organizing, 2385
grammatical complexity of, 1253
importance of, 1160, 1253
language of, 1266–1267
of Hīnayāna texts, 1576
of Mahāyāna texts, 1594
regularization of, 1266
Sarvāstivāda canon, 1110
Vinaya Piṭaka, 1202, 5601
volume of, 1093
by Xuanzang, 855, 1164, 1202, 1250
by Yijing, 1164
calligraphy, 1368, **1370–1371**
Manichaean texts in, 5669
Qur'ān in, 4632
as sacred Buddhist language, 1093
study of, 1635
Chinese literature
Buddhist, 1162–1163, 1164–1165, 1236–1237, 1521–1522, 1523, 1524, 1596, 1604
Confucian (*See* Confucianism, literature and canon of)
Daoist (*See* Daoist literature)
fiction, 3056–3057, 3066–3071
Ge Hong and, 2181–2182
Granet's (Marcel) analysis of, 3655
panda in, 808
poetry (*See* Poetry, Chinese)
sectarian and vernacular scriptures, 1607, 1608, 1609
Yang Xi and, 2182
Chinese medicine, **3859–3864**
alchemy in, 239
bears in, 807
diagnostic scheme of, 2636
folk healers in, 1617
modern biomedical, 3863–3864
qi in, 7544
Chinese Patriotic Catholic Association, 1611
Chinese philosophy, **1570–1580**
Ching, Julia, **10030–10031,** 10055
Chin'gak Hyesim (Buddhist scholar), 1172
Chinggis Khan, **1644–1645,** 2771, 4493
and Buddhism, 1148
in China, 4632
deification of, 1645
eagle symbol of, 948
initiation rites of, 5179
Judaism and, 5009
myth of origin of, 2394
and Quanzhen Daoism, 2186, 2199
shamanism and, 6141
sons of, 4493
Chingichngish (deity), 6718, 6719
Ch'ing-mu, on Nāgārjuna, 5552
Ching-T'u. *See* Jingtu
Chinhŭng (Silla king), 1171
Chinul (National Master Puril Pojo), 1172, **1646,** 6631
Chinvat Bridge, 1052, **1647**
Chiodi, Eilvia M., 222
Chiodi, Silvia, 4403
on myth of Nergal and Ereshkigal, 6477
Chione, 3053
Chion of Heraklea, 3052
theme of resistance in, 3055
Chiowotmahki (deity), 4507
Chipko movement (India), 2622, 2623
Chippewa religion (North America), **368–371**
Chips from a German Workshop (Müller), 6235
Chirāgh 'Alī, 4652
Chirassi, Ileana, on Jensen (Adolf E.), 4825, 4826
Chireau, Yvonne, 80, 81, 10024
Chiriguano people (Bolivia), 8634
Chiripá religion (Paraguay), music in, 1504
Chiron
Achilles initiated by, 184
Asklepios and, 551
Chiropractic, vital energy and, 3850
Chishin. *See* Ippen
Chisho Daishi. *See* Enchin
Chishtīyah (Ṣūfī order)
devotional poetry of, 4644, 9009
establishment of, 9009
khānagāhs of, 5118, 5139
music in, 6284
saints of, 6638–6639
samā' khānahs (music halls) in, 8065
in South Asia, 4644, 4647, 4648–4649
'nder Alwiyā', Shayk Niẓām al-Dīn, 5139
vs. Naqshbandīyah, 9010
Chissori (chant), 6297–6298
Chisungu (ceremony), 818, 4486
Chisungu, dances of, 2138
Chi-Tsang. *See* Jizang
Chivalry
'Alī ibn Abī Ṭālib and, 260
in poems, 7218, 7219
Rosicrucian, 7930
Chi Wara (deity), 90
masquerade dances for, 2141
Chizuo, Matsumoto. *See* Asahara Shōkō
Cho, Francisca, 3101
Choctaw tribe (North America)
ballgame played by, 753, 755
Christian missions to, 6423
Corn Woman narrative of, 6692
forced migration of, 6690
Mississippi reservation of, 6690
shamanism practiced by, 6693
Snake movement of, 6666, 6667
supernatural being of, 6691
Chodkiewicz, Michel, 4256
Ch'oe Ch'iwŏn, Confucianism and, 1929
Ch'oe Ch'ung, National Academy and, 1929
Ch'oe Ikhyŏn, Confucian orthodoxy and, 1933
Chōgen (Japanese holy man), 1179
Chogye-chong school of Buddhism (Korea), 1172, 1173
Chogye school of Buddhism
Chinul and, 1646
Maitreya in, 5621
Chōgyū, Takayama, 6608
Chogyur Lingpa, 5222
Choice
in biblical story of the Fall, 2968
Crescas (Ḥasdai) on, 2069
divine, 3202, 3205
free will as freedom of, 3202
in novels, ancient, 3055
Choirs, 6312
Choksy, Kairshasp, 6999
Chokwe religion. *See also* Central Bantu religions
masks in, 2141, 2457–2458
Cholula (Mexico)
in Classic period, 5902
deities of, 5902
Chomsky, Noam, 7851
linguistic theory of, 10043
secular humanism of, in progressive Islam, 6098
Ch'ŏndogyo, **1647–1648,** 5234
beliefs in, 1648
five practices in, 1648
God in, 1648
Chŏng Chedu, Wang Yangming and, 1932
Chŏng Chiun, on Four Beginnings and Seven Emotions, 1931
Ch'ŏngsu (pure water), 1648
Chŏng Tojŏn, Buddhism, challenge of, 1930
Chŏng Yagyong (Tasan), **1648–1649**
Practical Learning movement and, 1933
Chongyang fenli shihua ji (Daoist text), 2209
Chongyang jiaohua ji (Daoist text), 2209
Chongyang lijiao shiwu lun (Daoist text), 2209–2210
Chongyang shou Danyang erhshisi (Daoist text), 2209
Ch'ŏnju (deity), 1648
Ch'ŏnt'ae school of Buddhism (Korea), 1172, 1173, 9436. *See also* Tiantai school
Chopan-ata (saint), 4622
Chopp, Rebecca, liberation theology of, in progressive Islam, 6098
Chora (matter), 7190
Chōra (receptacle), 2273
Chordophones, 6251
Choreographers, Jewish, 2154
Choron, Jacques, on suicide, 8828
Choroti people (Argentina), religion of, 8635–8636
Chos 'byung (Bu ston), 1338
Chos dbang (Chöwang), 6941
Chos dbang rgyal mtshan, 1233
Chos dbyings rdo rje (Chöying Dorje), 1155
Chosen People. *See* Election
Chosen Vessel, 1038
Chos kyi sgron me, 1233
Chosŏn Buddhism, 1172–1173, 5232
Chosŏn dynasty (Korea), 5232–5233
Daoism in, 2189
development of, 5228–5229
musok in, 5228
origin myth of, 5179, 5229–5230

Chos rgyal 'Phags pa (Chögyal Phakpa), 1225
Chos rje don grub rin chen (Buddhist monk), 9386
Chotolok (caste), in Bengal, 825
Chousor (deity), 7129
Chou Tun-i. *See* Zhou Dunyi
Chrétien de Troyes
on Grail, 3649–3653
Mabinogion and, 5546
poetry of, 7219
Chrismation (anointing), in Orthodox Church, 2592
baptism and, 7960
Christ. *See* Jesus (Christ)
Christ, Carol P., 3312–3313
ancient Mediterranean religions and, 3386
on female divine, 4166
on gender of deities, 3613–3614
as thealogian, 9100
Christ, eternal or cosmic
in Christian Science, 1746
in Holy Order of MANS, 4102
Christ consciousness, in human soul, in New Thought teachings, 1782
Christening, during baptism, 6406
Christensen, Arthur, **1649–1650**
Christensen, Laird, 3091
Christian, William, on Andean Christian interculture, 8611
Christian, William A., Jr., 3142
Christian and Oriental Philosophy of Art (Coomaraswamy), 50
Christian Association of Nigeria (CAN), sociopolitical context and, 1723
Christian Baptist (periodical), 2365
Campbell (Alexander) and, 1377
Christian Broadcasting Network (CBN), 7712–7713
international reach of, 7713
Christian Brotherhood of Battle, 3133
Christian Catholic Apostolic Church in Zion, 103
Christian Century (journal), 2366
Christian Church (denomination). *See* Disciples of Christ
Christian Coalition, 2892–2893
Christian Community (church), 393
Steiner (Rudolf), role of, 8738
Christian Democratic parties
in Europe, 1693
in Latin America, 1701
Christian Dogmatics (Barth), 791
Christian ethics. *See* Ethics, Christian
Christian Ethics for Black Theology (Jones), 965
Christian-Evangelist (journal), 2365
Christian Faith, The (Schleiermacher), 48, 6103
Christian Fellowship Church (Solomon Islands), 6796
Christian Gnosis (Baur), 3514
Christian Holiness Partnership, Holiness movement and, 4084
Christian humanism, 2821
Christiani, Pablo, 7233
Christian Identity movement, **1657–1660,** 6514
catastrophic millennialism of, 6546, 6564
conduct, patterns of, 1658–1659
government and law, relations with, 1659
history of, 1657–1658
organization and authority in, 1659
origins of, 6546
worldview and doctrines of, 1658
Christianisme césarien, Le (Alta), 6781
Christianismi Restitutio (Servetus), themes in, 8232–8233
Christianity, **1660–1741**. *See also specific countries, denominations, doctrines, and regions*
ablutions in, 10
Aboriginal, **675–680**
Abraham in, 16
as absolute religion, Hegel (G. W. F.) on, 1819, 3894
adultery in, in *John*, 921–922
afterlife in (*See* Afterlife, in Christianity)
ages of world in
binary periodization for, 173
serial periodization for, 175
Akan religion influenced by, 215–216
Albo's (Yosef) critique of, 234
All Saints Day in, 2227–2228
All Souls Day in, 2227–2228
almsgiving in, 267, 268
altars in, 277–278
amulets and talismans in, 300
ancestral cult as complementary to, 1436
anchor symbolism in, 332
androcentrism in, 334–336
androgynes in, 341
angels in, 346, 2275, 2356, vol. 8 color insert
animals in, 356, 361
in Anishinaabe religion, 370
anointing of the sick in, 3236, 3241
anthropocentrism in, 2649
anthropomorphism in, 389–391
Antichrist in, 394–395
anti-Semitism in, 398–403
apocalypse in, 409, 411–412
apocatastasis in, 422
apologetics in, 427–430
by Athenagoras, 589
for monotheism, 3545
in Western Europe, 10076
apostasy in, 430, 431–433
apostles in, 434–436
architecture of, classification of, 462, 464
Aristotelianism in, 480, 482
artistic expression in, 2141
art of (*See* Art, Christian)
ascension in, 523, 524, 3129
asceticism in
androcentrism of, 336
dualism and, 528
monastic, 6135
vs. normal behavior, 529
objectives of, 528
ashram movement in, 546–547
and Athapaskan religious traditions, 573, 574
atheism in, 582–585
atonement in, **594–598**
attention in, 604
attractiveness of, 1973
authority in, 694–695
religious *vs.* secular, 696–697
autobiography in, 698–699
in Baltic religion, and ancestor worship, 328, 329
baptism in (*See* Baptism, Christian)
Bauer's (Bruno) critique of, 804
belief patterns, 1666–1668 (*See also specific doctrines*)
biblical exegesis in (*See* Biblical exegesis, Christian views)
biocentrism opposed to, in deep ecology, 2561–2562
biographies in, sacred, 944
bioregional center of, 2605
birds in, 949
birth in, 953
blasphemy in (*See* Blasphemy, Christian concept)
blessing in, 983
breath and breathing in, 1042, 1046
bridge in, 1050, 1051
Buddhism and
and Buddhist studies, 1310–1311, 1313
comparison of, 9801
missions, 1098–1099, 1167, 1186
Western Buddhism and, 1187
cargo cults based on, 1415–1416, 1418, 1419, 1425
Catholicism and, 7880
celibacy in, 1452, 1475, 1476, 1477, 7081
chance in, 1527
chanting in, 1534–1535
charismatic leadership in, 1546
charity in, 1554, 2320–2321
chastity in, 1558
child motif, 1567
Child (Lydia Maria) on, 1569–1570
Christ in (*See* Christology; Jesus)
church architecture in (*See* Church architecture)
church in, feminine imagery for, 3019
circumambulation in, 1796–1797
circumcision in, Paul the Apostle on, 7016–7017
clothing and modesty in, 1831
cocks in, 1842
color symbolism in, 1861
communism and, relation to, 2688
community in, eremitism and, 2828–2829
confession in (*See* Confession of sins)
and Confucianism, 10030–10031
Confucianism and, Jesuit comparisons of, 1918–1919
conscience in, 1940–1942, 1944
contemplation in, 5817–5818
conversion to
Anglo-Saxons, 6942–6943
of Augustine of Hippo, 7192
Bacon (Roger) on, 735
Black Elk's, 957, 958
in Caribbean region, 10024
of Constantine the Great, 792, 891
Dolgans, 2394
from Hinduism, 828
from Islam, 4596, 4614, 4616–4617 (*See also* Moriscos)
from Judaism, 3186 (*See also* Conversos)
by Marranos, **5716–5724**
in Oceania, 9320, 9322
Tertullian's, 9085
of Visigoths, 4556
covenant in, elect status from, 2746
creation in
divine order of, 2606–2607
language in, 5302
creeds in (*See* Creeds, in Christianity)
dance in, 2135, 2144, 2152–2153
in Middle Ages, 2136, 2153
rejection by church, 2145, 2153
in Renaissance, 2136, 2153–2154
in Romantic period, 2155–2156
for worship and honor, 2136
darkness in, 5454
David in, 2223

Days of the Dead in, 2227–2228
Dead Sea Scrolls and, 2235
defined by Schleiermacher, 1660
deification in, 2250
deism in, 2251
demons in, 2275, 2278–2279, 2280–2281, 2314, 2373, 4359, 4360–4361
denominations of (*See also specific denominations*)
  mergers between, 2687
desire in, 2307–2309
Devil in, 2276, 2314, 2315 (*See also* Satan)
devotion in (*See* Devotion, in Christianity)
in dialogue of religions, 2342, 2343, 2344–2345
and Diola religion, 2354
divination in, 2373
divine providence in, 7791
doctrine of, 2382 (*See also specific doctrines*)
  in ecumenical movement, 2684, 2685
dogs in, 2393
domestic observances in, **2399–2401**
dragons in, 2431, 2432–2433
drama in (*See* Drama, Christian)
dreams in, 2489
drums in, 2498, 2499
dualism in, 2512–2514
early
  anti-Semitism in, 398–399
  apostles in, 434–436
  atheism in, 582
  baptism in, 781–782
  cursing in, 2105
  desire in, 2307–2308
  development of, 1660–1661
  in Eastern Europe, 1682
  ecclesiology in, 1771
  eremitism of, 2824–2826
  Etruscan religion and, 2874
  gender in, 3358–3359
  Greek church in, 3656
  healing and illness in, 3843–3844
  heresy and orthodoxy in, 3921, 3926
  hierarchical structure, 1763
  iconoclasm in, 4285–4286
  iconography of, 4297, 4344
  Jewish criticism of, 7230–7231
  languages in, 2581
  magic in, 5576
  martyrdom in, 6647
  music in, 6305, 6307–6308
  Neoplatonism and, 6475, 6476
  papacy in, 6966–6967
  pilgrimage in, 7153
  politics in, 7279–7280
  priesthood in, 7401–7402
  reconstructions of (19th and 20th centuries), 3928
  reincarnation doctrine opposed in, 9329
  spread of, 2580, 6479
  structural development of, 2581
  theological perspectives in, 2581–2582
  theology in, 9135–9136
Eastern (*See* Eastern Christianity)
ecology and, **2647–2650**
economics and, 9709
ecstasy in, and eternal life, 2682
egg symbolism in, 2702
Egyptian influence on, 2716
election in, 2746–2748
  Judaism challenged by, 2745, 2746–2747
elixir in, 2771
emotion in, legitimacy of, 2700
engaged Buddhism and, 2787–2788
the Enlightenment and, movements to combat, 1664
Enoch in, 2803
enthusiasm in, 2805–2806, 2807–2808
environmental and social challenges addressed by, 2612
environmental crisis blamed on, 2608, 2627, 2649
eremitism of, 2822, 2829
eschatology of, 2835
essence of, 1665–1671
  community of worship in, 1668–1670
  faith, hope, and love in, 1671
  key beliefs in, 1666–1668
  way of life in, 1670–1671
Essenes' influence on, 2847–2848
ethics (*See* Ethics, Christian)
European history of, 6567
evil eye and, 2942
evil in, 2903
  good and, 3636
and evolutionary theory, Teilhard de Chardin on, 9032, 9033
excommunication in, 2920–2921
exile in, 2923
exorcism in
  necromancy and, 2279
  Vatican II on, 2280
Ezra in, 2947
fasting in, 2996, 2997, 3171
  as purification, 7508
fate in, 3002
feminism on
  history of, 3301, 3311–3312
  influence of, 3356
  on patriarchy, 7008
  potential for reform, 3301, 3312
and fiction
  African, 3087–3088
  ancient, 3052, 3056
  Australian, 3079–3082, 3083, 3084
  Chinese, 3070
  Japanese, 3072–3073
  Native American, 3090–3091
  Philippine, 3079
and film, 3097
fire in, 3119–3120
fish symbolism in, 3123
flower symbolism in, 3135, 3136
food customs in, 3170, 3171
food taboos in, 3168
as founded religious community, 7718
free will and determinism in, 3201
free will and predestination in, 3203–3204, **3206–3209**
fundamentalist (*See* Fundamentalism, Christian)
Gaia hypothesis and, 3253–3254
Galen on, 3255–3256
gambling in, 3262, 3263
games in, 3267
Gandhi (Mohandas) influenced by, 3272
gardens in, 3276–3277, 3280
gender in, **3356–3364**
genealogy in, 3425–3426
genetics and, 3428–3429
geometry in, 3441
in Germanic religion, 3457, 3460
ghosts in, 3475–3476
gift giving in, 3484–3485
and globalization, 3499–3500
glossolalia in, 3504–3505, 3506
Gnosticism in, 3511–3513, 3516–3520
goddess in, lack of, 7082
God in, **3543–3547, 3553–3560**
  Arianism on, 478
  attributes of, **615–616**
  Barth (Karl) on, 790–791
  Bonaventure on, 1011, 1012
  Catherine of Sienna on, 1462
  compassion of, 4844
  cursing, 972
  desires directed toward, 2307, 2308
  in *Ecclesiastes,* 2600
  Eddy (Mary Baker) on, 2695
  emergence of conception of, 582
  as Father, 3544
  feminist critique of, 3028, 3036
  Feuerbach (Ludwig) on, 3047
  Ficino (Marsilio) on, 3049–3050
  gender of, 3559
  goodness of, 1344, 3635–3636
  heart of, in mysticism, 3882–3883
  Herder (Johann Gottfried) on, 3919
  and history, view of, 4054
  history as revelation of, 2829
  homoerotic relationship with, 7082
  humanity's relationship with, 864
  Irenaeus on, 4539
  Jesus abandoned by, 4845
  Jesus as, 3546, 4417
  Jesus as face of, 4844–4845
  kingdom of, 5148, 5149–5153
  knowability of, 182–183
  knowledge of, 1375–1376
  life of, 5446
  in Lord's Prayer, 5517
  love of, 3636
  love of, and morality, 1652
  monk's relationship with, 823
  as mother, 2695
  names of, 6407
  neoorthodoxy on, 6467, 6468
  in New Testament, **3543–3547**
  perfection of, 615, 3560, 7039
  postbiblical, **3553–3560**
  proofs for existence of (*See* Proofs for the existence of God)
  redemption through, 2700
  Ruusbroec (Jan van) on, 7948–7949
  seeing, 2942
  Thomas Aquinas on, 9163
  Trinity of, 3546 (*See also* Trinity)
  Troeltsch (Ernst) on, 9364, 9366
  as white, 3559
  will of, 1655

God in *continued*
wisdom of, 3545–3546
Golden Age in, 3627–3629
Golden Rule in, 3630, 3632
gold in, 3626
"gospel" in, 3640–3642
grace in, 3644–3647
Arminius (Jacobus) on, 492
Augustine on, 627, 3645
Protestant *vs.* Catholic, 158, 3646
the Grail in, 3649–3651, 3652
Grail movement in, **3653–3654**
Greek, 3656–3657
Greek religion and, Asklepios in, 552
healing and medicine in (*See* Healing and medicine)
heart in, 3882–3883
Hebrew scriptures in, 4858–4859
Hellenism and, 6474
hellenization of
Harnack (Adolf von) on, 3778
heart symbolism and, 3882
hermeneutics in, 5485, 5486
Alexandrian *vs.* Antioch school of, 5486
Hermetism and, 2843, 3952
heterodoxy in, 6912
Hinduism and, Sen (Keshab Chandra) on, 8227, 8228
historical development of, 1660–1665
Byzantium, Christian culture of, 1661–1662
early, 1660–1661
East-West contacts, 1664
in Middle Ages, 1662–1663
post-Reformation, 1664–1665
Reformation and, 1663–1664
historiography
anthropocentric, 4030–4035
traditional, 4028–4029
holy family of, 2982
homosexuality in, 4113
human perfectibility in, 7039–7040
humor in (*See* Humor, in Christianity)
iconoclasm in (*See* Iconoclasm, in Christianity)
iconography of (*See* Iconography, Christian)
as idolatrous, Jewish trade and, 5016
idolatry condemned in, 4358, 4359–4361, 4380, 4385, 7014
immortality in, Lateran Council of 1513 on, 2280–2281
incarnation in, 4414, 4417
Jewish polemics on, 7232
inculturation/contextualization of, 1730
and indigenous religions
African, 6771, 6772
Finno-Ugric, 3106
New Guinea, 6507, 6508–6509
North American, 6666, 6667, 6672, 6690–6691, 6698, 6718–6719, 6721
initiation in, 4479, 4482–4483
inspiration in, 4510
Islam and
in Andalusia, 4591, 4592
Christian-Muslim polemics, **7242–7244**
messengers in, 6736
relations with, 4575
spread of Islam, impact of, 1662
Islamic eschatology and, 2836
jaguar imagery in, 4763
Jerusalem in, **4838–4841**
sanctity of, 4840–4841
symbolism of, 4836
Jevons (F. B.) on, 4854
on Jewish history, 9295
Job in, 4932–4933
journals devoted to, 10058–10059
Judaism and
affinities between, 1660
Baeck (Leo) on, 737
censorship of Hebrew literature, 968
challenge of, 2747
Christian missionary efforts, 7235
Christian persecution, 7058
communal bond of, 4855
Jewish-Christian polemics, **7230–7236**
Jewish persecution, 7055–7056
Marcion on, 5701
status of, 4979
judgment of the dead in, 5027
Jung on mythology of, 5034
justification in, **5039–5042**
kalām based in, 5061
key symbolism in, 5117
Kierkegaard on, 5140–5143
kingship in
Constantine and, 5167–5168
models of, 5157
kinship in, extension of, 5185
kneeling in, 5195, 5196
knowledge in, 5202
Lady of the Animals in, 5280
laity in, 5287–5288
language of
analytic philosophy on, 307
sacred, 5305, 5306, 5307
last sacraments in, 3236
in Latin America, **1694–1705**
law, canonical (*See* Canon law)
law of talion in, 7783
lesbianism in, 5414
libations in, discontinuation of, 5288
liberation theology in (*See* Liberation theology)
life in, 5445–5446
light and darkness symbolism in, 5453
liturgical year in (*See* Liturgical year, Christian)
liturgy in (*See* Liturgy, Christian)
Logos in, 5502–5506
Lucian on, 3910
magic in
early, 5576
medieval and Renaissance, 5577–5580
magi in, 5561–5562
Mandaean religion and, 5635, 5638, 5639
Manichaeism and, **5665–5668**
in Maori religion, 5682, 5683
in Marathi religions, 5700
in Mardu religion, 5705
in Mari and Mordvin religion, 5709, 5710–5711
martyrdom in
apologetics and, 428
in crescive societies, 5739–5740
nonviolence and, 6647
preparation for, 5741–5742
Marxism and, relation to, 2688
materialism and, 5777–5778
in Maya religion, 5799
media and, 5805, 5807
medieval (*See* Middle Ages, Christianity in)
meditation in, 5817–5818
memorization in, 5852
mendicancy in, 5855–5856
men's studies in, 5862–5864
menstruation in, 5866–5867
merit in, **5875–5878**
medieval view of, 5876–5877
patristic view of, 5876
Reformation and, 5877
rise of concept, 5870, 5871, 5872, 5875–5876
message of, eschatology as, 2835
messianism in, 5972–5973
migration in, 6023–6024
millennialism in, 6545, 6546
ministry in, **6044–6046**
miracles in, 6053–6054, 6056
Aquinas on, 1528
mi'rāj in, 6061
mirrors in, 6063, 6064
misogyny in, 9773–9774
missions of (*See* Christian missions)
models of, Vergil as, 9583–9584
modern
heterodoxy in, 6912
orthodoxy in, 6912
modernism in, **6102–6108**
Mokosh in, 6115
monasticism (*See* Monasticism, Christian; *specific orders*)
monism in, 6146–6149
monkeys in, 6151
monolatry in, 2228
monotheism of, 2228
historical ethical, 6160–6161
Roman ruler cult as problem for, 3902
moon in, 6171
morality in, 6181–6188, 7651–7652
Kant (Immanuel) on, 5078–5079
mortification in, 6196–6197, 6198, vol. 13 color insert
mountain symbolism, 1502
music in, **6307–6314**
in Africa, 6258–6259
Augustine on, 46, 6305, 6308, 6309
baroque, 6311–6312
in China, 6292
early, 6305, 6307–6308
in India, 6285
in Korea, 6296
medieval, 6308–6309
modern, 5808, 6312–6313
in Polynesia, 6264
Renaissance, 6309–6311
women's participation in, 6308
in Muslim countries, 1673–1674
mystery religions and, 6327, 6332
mystical union in, **6334–6341**
mysticism in (*See* Mysticism, Christian)
names of power in, 8676
Native American, **6421–6425**
natural religion and, Hocking (William Ernest) on, 4076
nature in, ambivalence about, 2607
in Nazism, 2663
in Ndembu religion, 6447
New Year observances in, 6593–6594
Noah in, 6643
nonviolence in, 6647–6648
number symbolism in, 6746, 6749
obedience in, 1670, 6777
offerings in, 4420
oral tradition and, 6842–6843
ordination in, 6857–6858
orgy and, 6867–6868, 6869–6870, 6877

origins of
Religionsgeschichtliche Schule on, 7707, 10077
Renan (Ernest) on, 7750
Orpheus in, 6895
orthodoxy in, 1661, 6912, 7730
orthopraxy in, 6914, 6915
otherworld in, 6924, 6925
overview, **1660–1672**
owl symbol in, 6936–6937
pacifist movements in, 6648
paganism and
Christian holidays associated with, 1743, 9487
conflict with pagan philosophers, 6474
conversion from, 4859
Frazer on, 3192
superstition charges and, 8864–8865
pain in, 6946
paradise in (*See* Paradise, in Christianity)
peace in, 7021–7022
phallus in, 7081–7082
demonization of, 7080
pilgrimages in (*See* Pilgrimage, Christian)
Plutarch on, 7201
poetry of (*See* Poetry, Christian)
political theology of (*See* Political theology, Christian)
politics and (*See* Politics, and Christianity)
postures and gestures in, 7342, 7343, 7344
prayer in (*See* Prayer, in Christianity)
priesthood in (*See* Priesthood, in Christianity)
primal religions influenced by, 2835
primitive, 10064
procession in, 7417, 7418
proverbs and parables in, 6979
punishment in, 5372
quaternity in, 7550
quietism in, 7558
rainbow symbolism in, 7604
redemption in, 7640
reference works on, 7645–7646
Reformation, Protestant (*See* Reformation)
reform in
religious, 7654
social, 7652–7653
relativism in, 7685
relics in
early Christian, 7687–7688
opposition to, 7686–7687
Religionsgeschichtliche Schule on, 7706–7708
religious broadcasting and, 7709, 7714
religious communities in, 7700, 7716
religious education in, 7735
Sunday schools, 7733
religious experience in, 7700
pre-Reformation, 7737–7738
religious orders in, **7721–7725**
repentance in, 7756, 7758
resurrection in, 7765–7766
retreats in
for monastic initiation, 7770
for spiritual renewal, 7770–7773
retribution in, 5373, 7783
revelation in, 7777–7778
revival and renewal activities in, 7787
revivalism, in North America, 1710
revolution in, 7791
riddles in, 6987
Ritschl (Albrecht) on, 7116
rituals in, 7698–7699
and history, view of, 4053
humor or laughter in, 4197
rivers in, 7863
Roman Catholicism within, 7874
runic inscriptions referencing, 7939, 7940, 7941
sacred geography of, 3435–3436
sacred matter in, vol. 4 color insert
sacrifice in, 986–987, 8006–8007, 8009
sacrilege in, 8013–8014
Samaritans, view of, 8071
Schleiermacher (Friedrich) on, 8161–8163
servitude as positive attribute in, 2986
sexuality in, 2135
demonization of, 7080
ship symbolism in, 992
sin in (*See* Sin)
Smith (W. Robertson) on, 8453
social movements in, **1748–1756**
social transformation and, 1671
society, relations with, 8464
sociology, traditional, in, 8490
soul in, Origen on, 873
as speculative knowledge, Hegel (G. W. F.) on, 4220
spiritual guides in, 8709–8710
sport metaphors in, 8723–8724
spread of, medieval, 4860
study of, in Asia, 1730
suicide, attitudes toward, 8830
superiority argument, in classification of religions, 1818, 1819, 1820–1821
the supernatural in, 8860
temptation in, 9069–9073
textiles in, 9090, 9091, 9092
theater forbidden in, 2437, 2438, 2467–2468, 2474, 7044–7048
theocracy in (*See* Theocracy, Christian)
theodicy in, 9116–9118
theology of (*See* Theology, Christian)
tithes in, 9209, 9210
transnationalism of, 3499–3500
trees in, 9337–9338, 9339
true images in, vol. 12 color insert
true *vs.* false religion in, 365, 6366
truth in (*See* Truth, in Christianity)
underworld in, 9454–9455
uniqueness of, defense of, 10077
unity in
and human unity, 2689
imposed by Constantine, 1967
universal vision of, 1671
utopianism of, 9492
vagina in, 7081–7082
via negativa in, 9587
violence and, 9598
virginity in, 7081, 9605, 9606–9607
visionary journeys in, 9616
vows in, 9641
warfare and, 9597
way of life as system of love, 1670–1671
wealth and, 9709
winter solstice and, 9741, 9744–9745, 9745
wisdom in, 5502, 9751–9753
wolf symbolism in, 9785
women in, **3356–3364**
African American, 966
androcentrism and, 334–336
Benedictine, 822, 1018
literacy among, 1369
in music, 6308
ordination of, 6857
Ramabai (Pandita) on, 7610
subordination of, 3252
world religions and, 9800–9803
relation to, 2684, 2688
as universal religion, 9802
worship in, 1668–1670, **9809–9815**
on writing, origin of, 270
Zoroastrianism and, 10002
Christianity, Islam, and the Negro Race (Blyden), 71
Christianity and Chinese Religion (Ching), 10031
Christianity at the Cross-Roads (Tyrrell), 9427
Christianization theory, conversion in, 1972–1973
Christian liberalism. *See* Liberalism, Christian
Christian literature, 5469–5472
in modern Western society, 5477
Christian liturgical year. *See* Liturgical year, Christian
Christian Message in a Non-Christian World, The (Kraemer), 9130
Christian Mission, Salvation Army and, 8063
Christian missions, **6082–6087**
achievements of, 6085
Adventist, 8236
in Africa, 1717–1719
and afterlife, 142
contemporary, 106–107
decline in, 1722
and decline of interlacustrine Bantu religions, 4520–4521
dress, influence on, 1833
to East Africans, 2572
to Edo, 2697
Harris (William Wade) and, 3780
Igbo religion influenced by, 4365
Kongo religion, effects on, 2001, 5221
Lenshina (Alice) influenced by, 5408
music in, 6259
and new religious movements, 103–105
religions studied by, 112–113
Shona and, 8373–8374
study of religion, contribution to, 8793
in Swaziland, 8897
and Tswana religion, 9389
African American, 69
Anglican, 352
apostles in, 435
Arabic Bibles for, 895
to Armenians, 487–489
in Asia, 1730
in Australia, 1731–1733, 1734
and Aboriginal Christianity, 676
history of studies by, 685–686
and new religious movements, 671, 672
in Bengal, 828, 1029
from Britain, 6084

Christian missions ***continued***
vs. Buddhist missions, 6078
and Buddhist studies, 1310–1311, 1313
Calvinist, 1375
cargo cults and, 1414–1415, 1416, 1418, 1423
in Caribbean, 1706–1707, 10023–10025
creolization and, 2067
Charlemagne and, 1556
in China (*See* China and Chinese religions, missionaries in)
in colonial period, 6083–6085
Congregationalism and, 1938
conversion by, nature of, 6084–6085
Coptic (Egyptian), 1980
definition of, new, 6086
and dialogue of religions, 2342, 2343
divisions imposed by, 2683–2684
Dominican, 2414
early, 6082–6083
in early Eastern Christianity, 2582, 2585
Eastern, 6083
in Eastern Europe, 1682, 1683
in ecumenical movement, 2683
evangelical, 2888, 2893
Franciscan, 3183
in Germany, 821, 1018
Gothic Bibles for, 922
government associations with, 6084
Greek Orthodox, 3657
"high" *vs.* "low" religions, 1920
to Huns, 4229
independent churches developed from, 6086
in India, 1729, 6084, 6086
and Indological studies, 4447
Sikhism and, 8395
internationalization of, 6084
vs. Islamic missions, 6083
in Jamaica, 1436
in Japan, 1098, 1186, 4791, 7273, 9310 (*See also* Kirishitan)
Jesuit (*See* Jesuits)
to Jews, 7235
in Korea, 1727, 5233–5234
language, vernacular *vs.* Latin, 1662
in Latin America, 1695–1703
in Andes, 8605–8612
Lutheran, 6084
in Melanesia, 5832
in Mesoamerica, Huichol resistance to, 4152
Methodist, 5998
modern, 6085–6086
in Mongolia, 1150, 1186
Moravian, 6191
Mormon, 6195
motives of, 6085
in Nestorian Church, 1598–1599, 2583
to New Guinea, 9321
in New Zealand, 1731–1733, 1734
nineteenth-century, 1665
in North America, 1708–1711
Roman Catholic, 6422, 6423
to North American Indians, 1565, 1566, 1708–1709, 6421–6424 (*See also* Franciscans)
and Ghost Dance movement, 3474
Native American perspective on, 3092
in Oceania, 6790–6794, 6804, 7297, 9321–9324
study of religion, contribution to, 8767–8768
between older and younger churches, 2689
in Pacific islands, 1738–1739, 1740–1741, 1847
persecution and, 6082
in Polynesia, 3122
music and, 6264
postdenominationalism and, 1775
Reformation and, 1664
resistance to, 6072
restrictions on, 6085
Roman Catholic, 7879
in Canada, 9299
colonial, 6083–6084
in England, Augustine of Canterbury in, 623
in Japan, 9310
to Japan (*See* Kirishitan)
monopoly of, 6083–6084
in North America, 6422, 6423
to Oceania, 6791
under Pius IX, 7180
of Xavier (Francis), 9853–9854
in Russia, disputed by Russian Orthodox Church, 2588–2589
Russian Orthodox, 7942–7943
in Alaska, 4497, 9193
to slaves, 66
social movements and, 1751–1752
Söderblom (Nathan) on, 8506
in South Asia, 4650
in Sri Lanka, 1098, 1099
in Taiwan, 1726, 8963–8964
in Tamil, 8978
in Tibet, 1186
as two-way street, 6086
in unity, 2684
variety of activities of, 6084
Western thought in, 6071
of Willibrord, 9740
Christian names, 6409
Christian Natural Theology, A (Cobb), 2610
Christianopolis (Andrea), 253
Christian Qabbalah, 7535–7536
development of, 6527
in Western esotericism, 2843
Christian Realism. *See also* Neoorthodoxy
proponents of, 6466
social justice and, 1753
Christian Research Institute. *See* Anticult movements
Christian Right. *See* Religious Right
Christians, names of, 6409
Christian Science, **1745–1748**. *See also* Eddy, Mary Baker; New Thought Movement
children in, concern about, 6541
Fillmore (Charles and Myrtle) and, 3096
founding of, 2695, 6516, 6535, 6563
on *Genesis*, 6530
God in, 1746
healing in
as cognitive restructuring, 3813
mesmerism and, 3850
health care and, 5377
Hopkins (Emma Curtis), role of, 4127–4128
leadership of, 6564
as new religious movement, 1714, 6513
and New Thought movement, 6582, 6583, 6584
in North America, 1714
response to modernity by, 6110
St. Denis (Ruth) and, 2157
women in, 6535
Christian Science Monitor, 2695
purpose of, 1747
Christian Science Theological Seminary, Hopkins (Emma Curtis), role of, 4128
Christians for Socialism, 5399
Christian socialism
and Barth (Karl), 790
on capitalism, 2670
of Maurice (Frederick Denison), 5784
and neoorthodoxy, 6468
revolutionary Europe and, 1693
Christian social movements. *See* Social movements, Christian
Christian Spiritualists, 8716
Christian spirituality, Bonaventure on, 1012
Christian's Secret of a Happy Life, The (Smith), popularity of, 8445
Christian Standard (journal), 2365
Christian Theology (Abelard), 7
Christian Thought: Its History and Application (Troeltsch), 9366
Christianus Arabicus. *See* Lull, Raymond
Christie, Agatha, 3062
Christ-*kerygma* (deeds of God in Jesus Christ)
in Athanasian Creed, 2057
recital of, as creed, 2054, 2056
Christliche Glaube, Der (*Christian Faith,* Schleiermacher), dogmatics in, 8161, 8165–8166
Christliche Mystik, Die (Görres), 3638
Christmas, **1756–1757**
carnivalization of, in Brazil, 1443–1444
carols, winter solstice songs and, 9741
dancing at, 2153, 2156
date of, 1743, 1756
Sol Invictus Mithra and, 8511, 8841
gift giving in, 3484–3485
in liturgical calendar, 9814
and history, view of, 4054
origin of, 1756, 7327, 7654
pilgrimage during, 7154
Pueblo celebration of, 6729
religious reform and, 7654
trees, 2400
Christmas Carol, A (Dickens), 363
Christo (artist), 7047
Christogenesis, 9033
Christology. *See also* Arianism; Jesus; Trinity
apostleship in, 436
in Athanasian Creed, 2057
Augustine on, 627–628
Balthasar's (Hans Urs von), 812–813
in black liberation theology, 5441
Bonaventure's, 1011–1012
in Catharism, 1457
in Channing's Unitarianism, 1530
in Christian Science, 1746
communicatio idiomatum doctrine, Cyril of Alexandria on, 2117
Council of Chalcedon and, 1979–1981, 2040
Council of Constantinople (553) and, 2040
Council of Ephesus and, 2040
Council of Nicaea and, 1967–1968
doctrinal disputes of 5th century, papacy and, 1763
in early theological issues, 2581
in Eastern Christianity
in early theological issues, 2583–2585
Justinian I and, 5042
in Ethiopian Church, 2860–2861
of Eusebius, 2884
of Eutyches, 2885

Harnack (Adolf von) on dogma of, 3778
of heavenly flesh, Simons (Menno) on, 8401
heresy based on, 3927
history of doctrine, 1666
Homoousios ("of the same substance") doctrine
Athanasius as champion of, 1979
Cyril of Jerusalem's avoidance of term, 2118
hypostasis in, 4241–4242
of *John,* 911, 918, 3546
of Leontius of Byzantium, 5412, 5413
of liberation theology, 5439
of *Mark,* 906
Mary in, 5753
of *Matthew,* 906
Maximos', 5793
in Niceno-Constantinopolitan Creed, 2056
of Sölle (Dorothee), 8511
Old Testament references to *(Glaphura),* Cyril of Alexandria on, 2117
of Orthodox Church, 2590
Schleiermacher (Friedrich) on, 8166
Servetus (Michael) on, 8232, 8233
sole lordship of Christ, in Reformed confessions, 2058
Sozzini (Fausto Pavolo) on, 8673, 8674
Spinoza (Baruch) on, 8683
spirit *(pneuma)* and, 8562–8563
two natures (diophysite) doctrine, 1666
hupostasi vs. phusis and, 4241–4242
vs. one nature (monophysite), 1979–1981, 2040
of Unitarianism, 9468–9469
wisdom-Christology, 9751
Christos paschon (drama), 2467
Christotokos (Birthgiver of Christ), 2583
Christ Suffering and Christ Triumphant (Paolo), vol. 13 color insert
Christ the Conqueror (Leivestad), 596
Christ the Saviour Brotherhood, Holy Order of MANS and, 4103
Christus Dominus (Decree on the Pastoral Office of the Church), 9540
Christus Victor (Aulén), 596
Christy, Henry, 9424
Christy sect. *See* Khlysty sect
Chrodegang of Metz, monasticism reformed by, 7724
Chronica Shlavorum (Helmold), 7062
Chronicle (Jerome), 4834
Chronicles
Aaron in, 5423
David in, 2222–2223
Levites in, 5421, 5423
Temple procedures in, 928, 930, 933
on "Torah of Moses," 883
1 Chronicles
Asaph in, 7461
Astarte in, 7103
chanting psalms in, 7463
David in, 2222–2223, 7461
Ezekiel and, 2945
Koraḥ in, 7461
merkavah in, 10050
temptation in, 9070
2 Chronicles
David in, 2222–2223
Elijah in, 2764–2765
2 Ezra as rewriting of, 898
Isaiah in, 4546
Joash in, 931
Levites in, 5426
Sabbath laws in, 4740
Chronicles, Egyptian, 2724
Chronicon terrae Prussiae (Petrus de Dusburg), 767, 774
Chronikoi kanones (Eusebius), 4834
Chronological Chart of the Visions of Daniel and John, A, vol. 1 color insert
Chronology, **1757–1761**. *See also* Calendars; Time
archaeological, 456
Christian historiography and, 4028
hierarchy of, in science, 2659
materialization of, 1353–1354
Chronos (Greek concept), sacred time and, 7992
Chrysanthemum and the Sword, The (Benedict), 820
Chrysanthos Aitolos, 6621
Chrysaphius (eunuch), 2885
Chrysippus (Stoic philosopher), 992. *See also* Stoicism
on fate, 8742
on heart, 3882
on proof of God, 3912
on reality, 8741
on religion, 8742
role in Stoicism, 8740
on world citizenship, 3906
Chrysopassus (Eck), 2601
Chrysostom (John Chrysostom), **1761–1763**
on baptism, 781
Cassian and, 1447, 1448
charity taught by, 2582
commentaries of, 4940
Innocent I and, 4495
on knowledge, 5203
on laughter, 4200, 4218
liturgy of, 2592
on Mary Magdalene, 5757
on music, 6308
on priesthood, 7402
on synagogue customs, 8924
and Theodore of Mopsuestia, 9121
on "two books," 9421
Chrystal, William G., 6612
Chthonic creativity, as cosmological theme, 1993
Chthonic deities. *See also* Underworld, deities of
darkness associated with, 7934
Rudra as, 7934
vengeance wrought by, 7782, 7783
Chuan fabao ji (Buddhist text), 994, 995
Chuangmu (deity), 1641, 2407
Chuang-Tzu. *See Zhuangzi*
Chuan-hin (Chinese emperor), as dragon slayer, 2433
Chuchhardt, Carl, on Slavic religion, 8433
Chuchi anthology, 1622, 1628
Chuci (Qu Yuan), 169–170, 7213
Chugu (feeding of the dead) rituals, 3285
Chu His. *See* Zhu Xi
Chu-Hung. *See* Zhuhong
Chukchi religion (Siberia), 468, 1015. *See also* Shamanism; Siberia and Siberian religions
New Year ceremonies of, 6591
shamans in
homosexuality and, 4116, 4117
occupational rites in, 8281
séances in, 8286
whale feasts of, 6655
Chukwu (deity), 97–98, 3572, 4365, 4366, 5445
Chulalongkorn (king of Siam), 1139–1140, 1141, 1253, 9095–9096
Ch'ulel soul, 5798
Chulupí people (Argentina), 8635
Chumash religion and society (North America)
bears in, 809
creation story in, 6661
elite socioreligious guild in, 6716
language of, 9228
population growth of, 9229
ritual art, 1471
sacred history of, 6662
social structure of, 9228
tomol in (*See Tomol*)
trade and travel of, 9228, 9229
Chumun (incantation), 1648
Chungichnish (deity), 808
Chung Pyung Lake (Korea), 9467
Chungsan (Korean prophet), 5621
Chungsan-gyo (Korea), Maitreya in, 5621
Chunqiu. See Spring and Autumn
Chunqiu fanlu (CQFL), Dong Zhongshu as assumed author of, 2418–2419
Chunyang (Korean folk figure), 5233
Chunyang zhenren huncheng ji (Daoist text), 2209
Chuon Nath, 3077
Churalin (demoness), 2315
Church(es), **1763–1779**. *See also* Ecclesiology; Sanctuaries
apostolic foundations and authority, 1661
architecture of (*See* Church architecture)
attendance at
health, relationship with, 3876
secularization and, 8217
Augustine on role of, 626, 627
authority of, 694–695
pyramidal model, 1668
Byzantine, as intersection of realms, 7980
Calvin on role of, 1376
as category, 1866
Cathari view of, 1457
consecration of, 1955
dedication of, feasts commemorating, 1744
definition of, 2084, 2085
in Ethiopian religions, 2573
feminine imagery for, 3019
globalization and urban growth of, 1810
histories of
historiography and, 4029, 4034
Richardson's (Cyril C.) study of, 7793–7794
Roman, 4038
theologians and historians of, set apart, 4056
historiography and, 4034
as "holy catholic church," 1668
infallibility of, in ecumenism, 2689
inside *vs.* outside and meaning of, 3925–3926
labyrinths in, 5275
membership in (*See* Membership in the church)
in monasteries, 6118
origin of word, 792
in Orthodox Christianity, 2590
orthodoxy *vs.* heresy and, 3922
polity of (*See* Church polity)
in Protestantism, 1668
authority of, 7451–7452
in Roman Catholicism, 7885
Vatican II concept of, 9535–9536
sacredness of, 7698
salvation history depicted in, 7984

Church(es) *continued*
Schelling (Friedrich) on, 8148
Schleiermacher (Friedrich) on, 8163, 8165
sects and cults *vs.*, 2084–2085, 8467
Simons (Menno) on, 8401
Sohm (Rudolf) on, 8507
Sölle (Dorothee) on, 8512
Spener (Philipp Jakob) on, 8680
and state (*See* Church and state)
storefront, vol. 5 color insert
structure of, Reformation and, 1663
term, meaning of, 1770
Uchimura Kanzō on, 9432
Zwingli on, 10016
Church and Society in Latin America movement (ISAL), theology and, 1704
Church and state, 5150. *See also* Secularization; Society and religion
Anabaptists on, 7453
in Australia and New Zealand, 1733–1734, 1737
in Calvin's Geneva, 1375
ecclesiology and, 1773–1774
Carroll on separation of, 1445
in China, Huiyuan on, 4156
Constantinianism, **1967–1968**
differentiated state religions, 8472–8473
in Donatism, 1968
in free churches of the Reformation, 1968
Gage (Matilda Joslyn) for separation of, 3252
Gallicanism on, 3258–3259
heresy and, 3927
in Islam, 8462
in Japan
Shintō and World War II, 8368–8369
Sōka Gakkai and, 8509
in Latin America, 1700–1701
rupture of, 1699
law and, 5360
Mendelssohn (Moses) on, 5854
in modern Europe, 1693–1694
papacy and, 1772
secularization and, 8217
Smart (Ninian) on, 8444
social differentiation and, 8472–8473
in Southeast Asia, 8654
in United States, 5330
in Western Christianity
early, 2582
vs. Eastern Christianity, 1690
Church and the Second Sex, The (Daly), 3311–3312, 9787
Church architecture, **792–797**
ambulatories in, 1796–1797
classification of, 462–465
contemporary, 796–797
Counter-Reformation and, 794–795
development of, 9265
Eastern Orthodoxy and, 794
Gothic revival in, 795–796
meanings of, 9266
in Middle Ages, 793–794
origins of, 792, 793
Protestantism and, 795, 7456, vol. 5 color insert
Protestant "plain style," negation of sacred space in, 7980
Reformation and, 794, 795
Roman Catholicism and, 794–795, 796–797
symbolism of quests in, 7553–7554
Church Dogmatics (Barth), 789, 791
Churches of Christ, **1779–1781**. *See also* Disciples of Christ
and Boston Movement, 6561
Churches of North and South India, at Methodist Conferences, 5999
Churches Uniting in Christ (CUIC), formation of, 1769
Church government. *See* Church polity
Church History (Eusebius)
Montanism in, 6167, 6168
Origen in, 6887
as prototype of the genre, 4038
Churchill, Mary, 3430, 6695
Church in Island Pond; 9410
Church Is One, The (Khomiakov), 5138
Churchland, Paul, on time and the brain, 7988
Churchman, John, Hooker (Richard) and, 4124
Church meetings, in Congregationalism, 1939
Church militant, the, Hus (Jan) on, 4234
Church Missionary Society
and African Independent Churches, 104
establishment of, 352
an Maori, missions to, 1731–1732
Church of Albania. *See* Albanian Orthodox church
Church of All Worlds, 6472, 6473
Church of Christ. *See* Disciples of Christ
Church of Christ, Scientist. *See* Christian Science
Church of Constantinople. *See also* Eastern Christianity
missionary activity of, 2585
Church of Cyprus, 3658–3659
Church of England. *See also* Anglicanism
Arminianism in, 493
Bunyan (John) challenging, 1322–1323
in Canada, 1712–1713, 9300
Congregationalism and, 1937
ecclesiology in, 1774
Elizabeth I and, 7663
eremitism in, 2828
evangelicalism in, 2890
on free will and predestination, 3204
Hare's (David) play criticizing, 2477
Hooker (Richard), defense by, 4124
in Jamaica, 1707
knowledge in, 5210
liturgy in, 5490
missions
in Caribbean, 1706, 1707, 2067
Latin America, 1699–1700
among Nestorians, 6481
in North America, 1706
Society for the Propagation of the Gospel in Foreign Part, 350–352, 1706
music in, 6313
polity of, 1766
pre-Reformation practices of, 7448–7449
proposed covenant with United Reformed Church (1980–1982), 1939
Puritan concerns about, 783, 7518–7519
Reformation in, 1692
Cranmer, role of, **2051–2052**
on religious art, 4286
religious education and, 7735
Thirty-nine Articles of, 2059
touch in, 9257
Wesley (John) on, 5997
Westminster Confession of, 2044
Church of Eritrea, 2585
Church of Ethiopia, 2585
Church of God (Anderson, Indiana). *See* Holiness movement
Church of God and Saints of Christ, 6563
Church of God in Christ (Pentecostal), 7029, 10038, 10039
Church of Greece, 3657–3658. *See also* Greek Orthodox Church
Church of Jesus Christ of Latter-day Saints, 6192–6195. *See also* Mormonism
headquarters of, 6192
membership of, 6192
Church of Jesus Christ of Latter Day Saints (Strangite), 6192
Church of Jesus Christ on Earth through the Prophet Simon Kimbangu. *See* Kimbangu, Simon; Kimbanguist Church
Church of Malankara, 2585. *See also* Malankara Syrian Orthodox Church
Church of Rome. *See* Roman Catholicism
Church of Russia. *See* Russian Orthodox Church
Church of Saint Foy (France), vol. 1 color insert
Church of San Vitale (Italy), vol. 5 color insert
Church of Satan
influence of, 8128
Satanism and, 8126–8127
sexual magic in, 8251
Church of Scientology. *See* Scientology
Church of Scotland
anti-episcopal sentiments, 1774
ecclesiology, Presbyterian, 1774
English protection of, 7281
Knox (John) and, 5212
missions
in Africa, 5408
in Jamaica, 1706
Westminster Confession in, 2044, 2055
Church of South India, reunification of, 2687
Church of the Brethren, 785
Church of the East. *See* Nestorian Church
Church of the Holy Sepulchre (Jerusalem), 4837
Church of the Lamb of God, violence by, 6551
Church of the Nazarene. *See also* Holiness movement
in Africa, 1722
Holiness movement in, 1714
Church of the New Jerusalem. *See* Swedenborgianism
Church of World Messianity. *See* Sekai Kyusei Kyō
Church polity (form of government), **1763–1770**
Anglican, 7452
Calvinist, 1376
in colonial New England, 1938
conciliarism, church councils on, 2042–2043
congregational form of, 1768, 1938, 1939
contingent forms of, 1768–1769
Eastern Catholic churches, 7887
ecumenism and, 1769
episcopal form of, 1763–1767
individualism and, 1939
Lutheran, 7452
presbyterial form of, 1767–1768
Presbyterian, 7389–7390, 7453
Protestant, 7452–7453
Reformed Churches, 7452–7453
Roman Catholicism, 7886–7887
in Swedenborgianism, 8902, 8903, 8904

Church Slavonic, 7943
Church Universal and Triumphant (CUT), **1781–1784,** 4247, 7445, 7446
children in, 6539
homeschooling of, 6542
in Europe, 6568
scriptural text of, 6529
secondary leaders of, 6547
Churchyard (Taylor), 2161
Churinga. *See Tjurunga*
Chute d'un ange, la (Lamartine), 3525
Chuuk Islands (Micronesia)
dance in, 6007
the dead in, 6007
fertility rituals in, 6006
myths in, 6009
creation, 6009
fire in, 6012
religious practitioners in, 6007–6008
spirit possession in, 6005
Chuvash religion, **1784–1786**
Chuxi (New Year's eve), 1641
Chymical, Medicinal, and Churgical Addresses, 253
Chymische Hochzeit Christiani Rosencreutz (Rosicrucian text), 7929, 7930
Ci (shrine), 9056
CIA. *See* Central Intelligence Agency
CIAI. *See* Council of the International African Institute
Cian (deity), shape shifting of, 8301
Ciboney Indians
burial customs of, 1428
records of, 1426
Ciborium, 794
Cicada, 4508
jade carvings of, 4758
Cicatrization, 1001, 1003
Cicero, **1786–1787**
Academic skepticism and, 8420
Ambrose influenced by, 287, 288
on apocatastasis, 421
on apotheosis, 437, 438
on ascension, 521
on atheism, 577, 582
Augustine influenced by, 624
on Bona Dea, 3386
casuistry of, 1454–1455
comparative theology of, 9128
on *conscientia* (conscience), 1940
on conversion, 7756
on dance, 2154
on Demeter, 2270
on Diana, 2346
on divination, 2378
on druids, 2492
on Fortuna of Praeneste, 3175
on haruspices, 2872
on intercalation, 6171
on laughter and humor, 4199
on Melqart, 5847
on myths, rational explanations of, 6365
on oracle *vs.* divination, 6832
on origins of Roman religion, 7895
on primitive religions, 577
on religion, 7894
ship symbolism of, 992
on superstition, 8864, 8865
on theologies of poets, philosophers, and statesmen, 4038
Cicibagiagua (cave), in Caribbean religions, 1429
Cidwanga dance, 2137
Ci'en (Buddhist monk), 1238
Ci'en Dashi. *See* Kuiji
Cieplak, Ioann, 9193
Cieza de Léon, Pedro, 5292
on *huacas,* 8606, 8607
Cigars. *See* Smoking; Tobacco
Cihuacoatl (Aztec government office), 5172
Cihuacoatl (deity), 3020
childbirth assisted by, 7812
French feminists on, 3030
tricksters and, 9357
Cihuateteo (sculptures), 9254
Ciji (Compassion Relief), **1787–1790,** 6761
development of, 1788–1789
founding of, 1787–1788
Ciji Hui (Chinese Buddhist organization), 3141
Cincalco (house of maize), 1468
Cincvad (India), Gaṇeśa in, 3271
Cinema. *See* Film
Činggis Khan. *See* Chinggis Khan
Ci nian ritual, 1641
Cinnabar
in alchemy
Chinese, 237, 238, 239, 2771
Indian, 243
in Daoism, 2178
Cinta Larga people (Brazil), creation myth of, 2013
Činvatō Peretu. *See* Chinvat Bridge
Cioran, Émile Michel, 3527–3528
Cipactonal (mythic figure), 5935
Circe (mythic figure), as magician, 3904
Circle Dances, of Hay (Deborah), 2161
Circles, **1790–1795**
altars and temples, round, 1792
in ancient Greece and Rome, 1791–1792
in ancient Israel and early Judaism, 1793–1794
Buddhist *maṇḍalas* as, 5641–5642, 5643
cakras as, 1348
culture (*See Kulturkreiselehre*)
and magic, ancient Mediterranean, 1792–1793 (*See also* Ouroboros)
in Native American cultures, 1794–1795
in Navajo religious traditions, 7550
in Neolithic and Bronze ages, 1791
in Neopagan rituals, 7828–7829
in *Ringwallbilder* labyrinth, 5276
as symbol and ritual patter, 1790–1791
Circle Sanctuary (Wisconsin), 6472, 6473
Circulation, Servetus (Michael) on, 8232
Circumambulation, **1795–1798**. *See also* Maṇḍalas
in Buddhism, 1796
in burial, 1797
in meditation, 1291, 9076, 9078, 9840
in pilgrimage, 7167
in stupa worship, 8798
in Christianity, 1796–1797
in Hebrew scriptures and Judaism, 1793, 1796
in burial rites, 1797
in Hellenic sacrifice, 1792
in Hinduism, 1795–1796, 1797
during marriage rites, 7814
in Islam, 1797
in *ḥājj,* 7158, 7160
at tombs of saints, 7687
in marriage rites, 1797, 7814, 8397
in Native American traditions, 1796
of Muḥammad, in the Ka'bah, 5049
vs. procession, 7416–7417
in Sikh weddings, 8397
in stupa worship, 1107, 8798
in Tibetan popular religion, 9184
Circumcellions (Donatist extremists), 2417
Circumcision, **1798–1800**. *See also* Castration; Clitoridectomy; Subincision; Superincision
in African religions
Agikuyu, 7805
Bambara, 777
Dogon, 1470, 2391, 2392
ethnic differences, 1798
in initiation rites, 1799, 7805
Ndembu, 6446, 7505
northeast Bantu, 2577
Pygmy, 7525
southern African, 8658, 8659
southern Bantu, 8665–8668
in Australian Indigenous religions, 1799
myths of, 657
Ngukurr, 6598
in Australian religions, 4476, 4477
Bettelheim (Bruno) on, 4481
as castration, symbolic, 7974
in Christianity, 5864
Jerusalem Council on, 7081
Paul the Apostle on, 7016–7017, 7081
death symbolism of, 4481
debate on meaning of, 2957
for eliminating femininity, 987
ethnicity and, 1798
Freud (Sigmund) on, 4481
geographic distribution of, 1798
in Bēta Esra'ēl, 5003
initiation rites and, 1798–1799
in Islam, 1798, 1825, 7082, 7825, 7826
Abbassi (Abdulaziz) on, 4212
as explicit sexual phenomenon, 7077
function of, 987
local variations in, 7828
mass rites, 6740
not recognized as rebirth, 953
slave traditions of, 4683
of women, 7828
in Israelite religion
in Abraham's covenant, 15, 16
of Isaac, 4544
of Ishmael, 4552
in Judaism, 1798, 5864, 7818–7819
baptism after, 780
Elijah and, 2766
as explicit sexual phenomenon, 7077
function of, 987
not recognized as rebirth, 953
nudity in, 6740
origins of, 7080
stages of, 7818–7819
symbolism of, 7080
in Mardu religion, 5705
in Oceanic religions, 7809
ordeals of, 4481
Paul on, 912, 913
as purification rite, 7505, 7508
in Samaritan practice, 8070
Semitic, 1798
in Totonac religion, 9255
in Ungarinyin religion, 9461
in Vanuatu religions, 9520

Circumpolar religions. *See* Arctic religions
Circuses
clowns in, 1839
Roman, time and, 1353
Cisneros, Jiménez de, humanism and, 4176
Cistercians, **1800–1801,** 6132–6133. *See also* Bernard of Clairvaux
19th-century revival of, 6134
austerity of, 6132
decline of, 6133
economic activities of, 6132
female, 6763
land acquisition by, 6132–6133
on love, 8706
Merton (Thomas) in, 5879
monasteries of
architecture of, 6119
expansion of, 6132
in reform of monasticism, 821, 7724
spirituality of, 6132
women in, 6135
work in, 6132, 6135
Cité antique, la (Fustel de Coulanges), 321
Cîteaux, Abbey of, Cistercians and, 1800, 6119
Cities, **1801–1812**
ancestors as founders of, 326
ceremonial centers, 1803–1805, 7984
deities of, 3622
Artemis as, 506, 508
Athena as, 587
in Chinese religion, 1616
in Greek religion, 3665
Herakles as, 3917
in Mesopotamian religions, 3593, 5949–5950
in Near Eastern religions, 3376, 3593
development of, in Uruk, 5161
in Greek religion, 3665–3667
heavenly prototypes of, 7983
Mesopotamian, 1802–1803, 7984
modern imaginaries and urban religiosity, 1809–1810
myths in, functions of, 6362
Nabatean rock city, 1472
orientation of, 6886
pilgrimages and religious movement in, 1808–1809
as sacred places, 1502–1503, 7984
as sanctuaries, 8101
in South Asia
courts, markets, and performance in, 1806–1807
temple urbanism in, 1805–1806
study of, 9722–9723
in *Sumerian King List,* 5162
violence and, 1807–1808
wealth and religion in, 9708
Wicca in, 9731
Citimukulu (chief), 817–818
Citizens, Quirinus as god of, 7560
Citizens Freedom Foundation, 396, 2292, 4522, 9410
Citizenship
genetics and, 3429
world, in Hellenistic thought, 3906
Cittamātra (mind-only) teaching, in Buddhism, 8739, 8740
Cittars (poets), 8977
City of David, archaeological excavation of, 5111
City of God (Augustine), 628
ages of world in, 175, 4053
chapters of, 6750
charity in, 1554
church and state relationship in, 5150
City of God concept, 1661
desire in, 2307, 2308
ecclesiology in, 1772
ethics in, 628
Hermetism in, 3944
history, view of, in, 4054
idolatry in, 4361
literary value of, 5471
magic in, 5333, 5577
morality in, 628, 1651–1652
peace in, 7022
resurrection of body in, 131
Roman Empire's fall and, 628
suicide in, 8830
summary of, 1679
superstition in, 8865
temporal *vs.* eternal order in, 8464
writing of, 628
City of Women, The (Landes), 10027–10028
City-states
Greek (*See Polis*)
Mesoamerican, in Postclassic period, 5906
Ciudadela compound, 5899
sacrifice in, 149
Civaṉāṉapōtam (Meykaṇṭār), 5999–6000
Civic humanism, republicanism and, 4175
Civil disobedience, by Earth First!, 2562, 2563
"Civil Disobedience" (Thoreau), King (Martin Luther, Jr.) influenced by, 5145
Civilizational approach, to Reconstructionist Judaism, 7635–7636
Civilization and Its Discontents (Freud)
mystical experience in, 1949
pain in, 6947
Civilizations
British approach to religion and, 1872
Daoism as enemy of, 5201
development of
in Chinese myth, 1627
goddess worship in, 3585–3587
evolution of, archaeology on religion in, 453–454
myths in, functions of, 6362
origins of, death and, 2238–2239
primitive societies and, 10066
time and, 1760
Civilized societies, organization of, kinship and, 5182
Civil law. *See also* Law(s)
definition of, 4737
Jewish, 3752, 4978
Kant (Immanuel) on, 5368
Civil religion, **1812–1817,** 7256
Bellah (Robert) on, 7327
ceremony and, 1516–1517
as good or bad, 1815
on Kennedy (John F.) and, 1813
obligation under, 8498
as systematic and organic, 8468
definition of, 4401
Durkheim (Émile) on, 8493, 8498
nationalism and, 5398
popular religion as, 7327
Rousseau on, 1812–1813, 3230, 7256
top-down *vs.* bottom-up, 8472–8473
in United States, 1715, 7256, 7327
in academy, 1813
as bottom-up, 8473
critical interpretations of, 1815–1816
historical background and manifestations of, 1814
and "Novus Ordo Seclorum," founding of, 1814–1815
symbols of, 9266–9267
Civil rights movement
and Black Theology, 964
King (Martin Luther, Jr.) in, 5145–5146, 5401–5402, 7257
and legitimation, 5401–5402
Malcolm X in, 72
Nation of Islam opposing, 4688–4689
religious leaders in, 2614
women in, 10039–10040
Civil service examinations
in China
Kaifeng Jews and, 1608–1609
Neo-Confucianism and, 1603
in Song dynasty, 1602
in Tang dynasty, 1909
in Yuan dynasty, 1917
in Korea, 1930
Civil Society International, 1555
Civil War, American. *See* American Civil War
Civitate Dei, de. See City of God (Augustine)
Cixous, Hélène, 2439, 3027, 3029–3030, 3314
gynocentrism of, 3719–3720
CLAI. *See* Latin American Church Council
Clairvoyance
in anthroposophy, 393
of Apollonius of Tyana, 3905
of Cayce (Edgar), 559
of Cuna shamans, 2095
definition of, 6057
of ecstatic healers, 3813
of Norman (Ernest), 9448
of Swedenborg (Emanuel), 8899
Clamor ritual
in Benedictine monasteries, 2105
exorcism liturgy as, 2929
Clans. *See also* Kinship
in Australian Indigenous religions, children and, 7677
in Chinese folk religion, 1616
in Confucianism, 5233
images used by, vol. 6 color insert
kinship in, 5185
in North American Indian cultures, in Zuni social structure, 2008
in Siberian shamanism, 8281, 8285
in West African religions, 9717
Clar, Lynn Schofield, 3101
Clare, Monica, 3080
Clarence 13x, 4689, 6420
Clare of Asissi, 3182, 3183, 3184
Claret, Anthony M., 7770
Clark, Elmer T., 6521, 6565
Clark, James Freeman, American study of religion, role in, 8784
Clark, John, 6522
Clark, Kenneth, on nudity, 4171
Clark, Mattie Moss, 10039
Clarke, David, 453
Clarke, Graham, 452
Clarke, J. J., 7479
Clarke, James Freeman, 9125
Clarke, John, 784
Clarke, John Henrick, 75
Clarke, Kamari, 81, 10026
Clarke, Marcus, 3080, 3082, 3084
Clarke, Peter, 6523, 6524
Clarke, Philip, 2481
Clarke, Samuel, 7124
Clarke, Sathianathan, on subaltern theology, 8802
Claros, oracle of Apollo at, on afterlife, 8543
Clart, Philip, 1638
Class, socioeconomic
in American sects and denominations, 1866
Hoge (Dean) on schism and, 8152
in Aztec society, gender and, 3411–3412
in Buddhism, 4421

conflict among, economics in Germany and, 2669–2670
Marx and, 2669
dance to distinguish among, 2144, 2145, 2146
freedom from, during pilgrimage, 7146
Gurū Nānak on, 8395
hakham (wise) *as,* 9761
Hindu, *dharma* and, 2622
in Israelite religion, lack of, 4730–4731
in Jainism, 4421
of Jews, medieval, 4860–4861
in Mesopotamian religion, 4730
ordination and, 6853
in Roman society, 7902–7903
Smith (Wilfred Cantwell) on, 8450
in social theory, 8484
status *vs.,* in sociology, 8481–8482
and tomb elaboration, 9226
vision quest and, 9611
warriors as, 9683–9684
Classical Approaches to the Study of Religion (Waardenburg), 7091
Classical Indian Philosophy (Mohanty), 4420
Classical Judaism. *See* Rabbinic Judaism
Classical music, 6312, 6313
Classical Reform Judaism. *See* Reform Judaism, Classical
Classical Yoga. *See* Yoga, classical
Classic of Changes. *See Yijing*
Classic of Documents. *See Shujing*
Classic of Filial Piety. See Xiaojing
Classic of Odes. *See* Odes, Classic of/Scripture of
Classification of religions, **1817–1822,** 7703. *See also* Comparative religion; Phenomenology of religion; Study of religion
Brelich (Angelo) on, 4046
British approach to religion and, 1872
British colonialism and "Hinduism" as classification, 1855
Chinese religion, problems with, 3339
comparative-historical method and, 1870
cosmology, geographic classification of, 1992–1993
dynamic phenomenology, 1870
early modern, 1818
ethnic *vs.* founded, 4064–4067
geographical, 1819
history of religions approach to, 4063–4067
imperialist bias in, 1855–1857
linguistic issues in, 8762
Mensching (Gustav) on, 4043
normative, 1818–1819
Pertold (Otakar) on, 8774
in phenomenology of religion, 1820
philosophical, 1819–1820
recent attempts as, 1820–1821
religious communities, categories of, 1866–1867
religious phenomena, classes of, 1878
Saler (Benson) on, 7704
Troeltsch (Ernst) and, 8493
"Classroom" in Heaven's Gate movement, 3890
Clastres, Pierre, on Guayaki time, 7986
Claudel, Paul, 2470–2471, 5477
Claudius (Roman emperor)
apotheosis of, 439
Etruscan religion under, 2874
Clausen, Henrik Nikolai, 3704
Clavigero, Francisco Javier, 5940
Clavus annalis, Roman calendar and, 1353
Clawed Old Man (deity). *See* Holy City Old Man
Clay drums, 7036
Clay tablets, Canaanite, 1390
Clean, Well-Lighted Place, A (Hemingway), 5481
Clean Government Party (Japan), 7264
Cleanliness. *See* Purification
Cleanthes (Stoic philosopher)
on divine kingship, 5148
on existence of God, 7124
Hymn to Zeus of, 3912
on Law of Zeus, 8743
on proof of God, 3912
Stoicism, role in, 8740
on Zeus (God), 8742
Clear Light Mantra. *See* Kōmyō Shingon (Clear Light Mantra)
Cleaving. *See also* Devequt
mystical union and, 6339–6340
Clefts, as *yoni,* 9907
Cleirbault, Gilbert, 7446
Cleland, John, 3059
Clemen, Carl, **1822**
Clemens, Titus Flavius. *See* Clement of Alexandria
Clement I (pope), 6966
Clement II (pope), 3052
Clement III (antipope), installation of, 3691
Clement IV (pope), 734
Clement V (pope)
at Council of Vienne, 2042
Great Western Schism and, 8157
moving papal residence to Avignon, 6971
Clement VII (pope)
as antipope, 1461
election of, 6971
Great Western Schism and, 8157
in Reformation, 7663
reforms avoided by, 9341
Clement VIII (pope), 816
and Clementine Bible, 893
on debate between Dominicans and Jesuits, 6973
Hermetism and, 3948
Clement XI (pope)
and Anselm, 373
on Chinese converts to Christianity, 7793
Clement XII (pope), Freemasonry prohibited by, 3197, 6973
Clement XIV (pope)
Jesuits disbanded by, 6134
Jesuits suppressed by, 1445, 1921, 4842, 6973
1 Clement, 920
authorship and themes of, 1824
Christian persecution in, 7058
citations from *Hebrews* in, 916
priesthood in, 7401
2 Clement, 920
authorship of, 1824
blasphemy in, 972
Clément, Catherine, 3027, 3029
consideration of non-Western traditions by, 3030
Le Voyage de Théo, 3061
Clementine Bible, 893
Clementine Homiliae
on *aion,* 208
on knowability of God, 182
Clement of Alexandria, **1822–1824**
on apocatastasis, 422
on asceticism, 7723
on baptism, 782
on Baubo, 803
biblical interpretation of, 5486
on Buddhism, 1310
Can a Rich Man Be Saved?, 1455
ethics of, 7191
on "gospels," 3642
on idols, 4357–4358, 4360
on images, 4285
on knowability of God, 182, 3554
on knowledge, 5203
on *Logos,* 1823, 5505
on *Mark,* 908
on Mark, secret gospel of, 8448–8449
on Mark the Evangelist, 5714
on martyrdom *vs.* suicide, 8830
on meditation, 5817
on music, 6305, 6308
on mystery religions, 6330
on predestination, 3207
and religion and philosophy, 7113
on *Sibylline Oracles,* 8384
theology of, 1823
Clement of Rome, **1824**
anchor identified with, 332
Clements, William, 3144
Cleomedes of Astypalaia (Greek hero), 3666–3667
Clergy. *See also* Bishops; Priesthood; Seminaries
in Christianity
Ambrose on, 287, 288
apostolica authority and, heresy and, 3927
in Armenian church, 490
distinction from laity, 5287
in Eucharist, 2877
medicine and, 3845–3847
origins of, 1763
Protestant, 3846–3847, 7452
Reformation and, 7657
clothing for (*See* Vestments)
depiction in novels, 3060
in Hittite religion, 4071
humor targeting, 3162
in Islam, education in hawzah of, 3800–3802
in Manichaeism, classes of, 5656, 5665
necromancy practiced by, accusations of, 6453
pastoral counseling by, 939, 7477, 7479, 7486–7487
performance approach to, 3145
pollution rules for, 7506–7507
religious reform and, 7653–7654
rule by, 9109
women, folklorist study of, 3147–3148
Clermont, Council of (1095), Crusades intiated at, 2075
Client-centered psychotherapy, 7485
Client cults, Stark and Bainbridge on, 2085
"Cliff Hanger, The" (Twitchell), 2601
Clifford, James, 3701
Climacus, Johannes. *See* Kierkegaard, Søren
Clinical pastoral education (CPE), 7486
Cliodhna (deity), 1487
Clitoridectomy, **1824–1826**
in Agikuyu religion, 7805
in Dogon religion, 2392
in northeast Bantu religion, 2577
Cloacina (deity), 7317
Clockmaker, Cosmic
chaos theory and, 1541
Newtonia worldview and, 8183

Clocks, stopped at death, 7986
Clodius, 7913
Cloisters, in monastery architecture, 6118, 6119
Clonaid (Raëlian cloning company), 7599
Cloning, 942, 9435
ethics of, 5814
Raëlians and, 7597, 7599
Closed confessionalism, definition of, 2056
Clothing, 1000, **1826–1837**. *See also* Masks; Textiles; Vestments
absence of (*See* Nudity)
in African religions
and political resistance in Swahili, 1515
in religious drama, 2457–2458
of Swazi kings, 8897
in American sectarian (ethno-religious) groups, **1834–1837**
of Amish and Mennonites, 1836
of Hasidic Jews, 1836–1837
modesty and female sexuality in, 1835
plain dress, 1836
religious ideologies and, 1834–1835
social change and, 1837
and social control in, 1835–1836
in art, 4171
body symbolism and, 4160
in Buddhism, 1829
cross-gender attire and, 1827
for nuns, 6760
Tibetan *khamar,* 1828
in Chinese religion, functions of, 1827
in Christianity, 1831, 1832, 1833
cross-gender, 1827
for dance and performance, 1827–1828
in Daoism, 1828–1829
in Eastern religions and cultures, **1826–1830**
identity and, 1826–1828
in private worship, 1829–1830
ritual clothing, 1828
secular, 1830
vestments, 1828–1829
in Hinduism, 1829–1830
in Santería, vol. 4 color insert
in Shintō, 1828
in Islam
Chinese, 4631
during *ḥājj,* 7158
gender and, 1827
modesty and, 1559, 1833
pilgrimage to Mecca in, 1832–1833
in private worship, 1829
ṣalāt (prayer) requirements, 8055
in worship, 1831
in Judaism, 1831–1832
maṇḍalas on, 5643
in Mesoamerican religions, rites of passage and, 7812
monastic, 6123
in New Year ceremonies, 6590, 6593, 6594
in North American dance drama, 2460, 2461, 2462
of Parsis, 6997
in Samaritan religion, 8070
of Samoyed shamans, 8097, 8272, 8285
shamanism and, 1827
in Sikh Dharma, 3879
social change and class differences and, 1833
in Western religions and cultures, **1831–1834**
hierarchy and group membership and, 1831–1832
religious traditions and, 1832
sacred dress in, 1831
and social control and morality, 1832–1833
in Zoroastrian initiation, 9999–10000
Clotho (deity), 3001, 9088. *See also* Moirai
Clotilda (queen), **1837–1838**
Cloud of Unknowing, The, on ecstasy, 2680
Clouds
in Australian Indigenous myths, 661
in Navajo creation myth, 6659
in Pueblo religion, 6723, 6729
in Zapotec religion, 5903
Clouds, The (Aristophanes), moon in, 6171
Clovis (king)
Clotilda (consort of), **1837–1838**
converting to Christianity, 7280
Visigoths and, 1689
Clowes, John, Swedenborgianism, role in, 8901, 8902
Clowns, **1838–1841**. *See also* Masks; Tricksters
at Carnival, 1442
in North American Indian religions, 6686
as ritual humorists, 4198
in Zuni religion, 1838, 1839, 8016–8017
Cluniac monasticism, 6132
women in, 6135
Cluny
Benedictine monastery founded at, 821
Cistercian reform at, 1800
and Cluniac monasticism, 6132
recluses of, 2827
Clytemnestra (Greek mythical figure), 986, 7783
CNRS. *See* Centre National de la Recherche Scientifique
Coabai (death), in Caribbean religions, 1428
Coakley, Sarah, 3037
Coalition on Environment and Jewish Life (COEJL), 2613, 2643
Coarelli, Filippo, 4558
Coatlicue (deity), 719, **1841,** 3020
Coyolxauhqui and, 4188
gender of, 3411
Huitzilopochtli and, 4155, 5890
in Templo Mayor, 5892
Coatrischio (deity), in Island Arawak religion, 1427
Coats, George W., 6376
Coats, John, 9143
Cobb, John
comparative theology of, 9130
ecotheology of, 2610
Cobo, Bernabé, on Inca calendar, 1361, 1362
Coca
divination with, 8616, 8619
as divine plant in Andean religion, 8615
Coccejus, Johannes, covenant theology of, 2049–2050
Cochinim Jews, 5005, 5006
Cochin Synagogue, 5005
Cochiti Pueblo people, agriculture in myths of, 191
Cocijo (deity), 5887, 5903, 5912, 9213
Cockfighting
deep play in, 3260, 3261
and evolutionary theory, 3267
gambling on, 3260, 3261, 3264
and social life, 3268
Cock Lane and Common Sense (Lang), 7372
Cocks, **1841–1842**. *See also* Cockfighting
Cocktail Party, The (Eliot), 2476
Coconut trees, in Micronesian myths, 6011
Coded language. *See* *Sandhyā-bhāṣā*
Code Noir, and Christianity in French Caribbean, 1706
Code of Canon Law, 6764
in Roman Catholicism, 7886
Code of Hammurabi. *See* Hammurabi, Code of
Codes and codification, **1842–1847,** 5328–5329. *See also* *specific codes*
and custom *vs.* law, 1842
Greek and Roman, 1845–1846
Jewish, 1845
Mesopotamian, 1844–1845
and restitution *vs.* punishment, 1842–1844
on stelae, scrolls, and codices, 1842–1843
Codex/codices. *See also* Nag Hammadi; *specific codices*
definition of, 1842
of Hebrew scripture, 890, 891
Mesoamerican calendars and, 1356, 1359–1360
Mixtec, 5887
of New Testament, 921
in Roman law, 5334–5335
Codex Gómez de Orozco, 5887
Codex Iustinianus/Justinianus, 5333, 5334–5335
Codex Regius. See Eddas
Codex Reuchlinianus, 889
Codex Selden, 5887
Codex Sinaiticus, 891, 921
Codex Theodosianus, 5333, 5334
Codex Vaticanus, 891, 921
Codex Vindobonensis, 5887
Codice Vaticano Latino 3738, 150
CODIMUJ. *See* Diocesan Coordination of Women
Codreanu, Corneliu Zelea, 2759, 2760
Codrington, R. H., **1847–1848,** 2915
and animatism, 364, 365, 2540, 7372
on ghosts and spirits, 8514
on *mana,* 1847–1848, 2540, 5835, 6754, 7347–7348, 7372
on New Caledonia deities, 6500
Oceanic religions and, 6800
Coe, George Albert, on prayer, 7841–7842
Coe, Michael D., on Olmec iconography, 5881
Coedes, George, on "Indianization" in Southeast Asia, 4009
COEJL. *See* Coalition on Environment and Jewish Life
Coercive persuasion. *See* Brainwashing
Coercive Persuasion (Schein), 1031
Coffey, Essie, 3391
Coffin, Henry Sloane, 6611
Coffin Texts (Egypt), 2705, 2706, 2718–2719, 4318
Book of Going Forth by Day from, 2719
judgment of the dead in, 5026
publication of, 2729
translations of, 2729
Cofradías (confraternity), 9215
in colonial Andes, 8609
in colonial Mesoamerica, 5918–5919, 5925
in contemporary Mesoamerica, 5925–5926
Cog (machine), 511
Co-ge-wea (Mourning Dove), 3090
"Cogito ergo sum" (Descartes), 2293–2294, 2424, 7110
Cogitosus, 1053

Cognition theory
hermeneutics of the sacred and, 7977
Nyāya's, 6773
of ritual, 7839, 7851, 7858
of Steiner (Rudolf), 8738
Cognitive dissonance theory, 7798–7799
Cognitive Man, Soloveitchik (Joseph Baer) on, 8518
Cognitive modules/operators, 6492–6493
Cognitive restructuring, healing through, 3813
Cognitive science
critical theory *vs.*, in study of religion, 8766
and history of religions, 10043–10044
religion and, 6930–6931
sacred time through neural patterning in, 7987–7988
Cohen, Arthur A., **1848–1850**
early theology of, 1848–1849
fiction and literary essays of, 1849–1850
Holocaust, response to, 1489, 4091, 4093–4094
post-Holocaust theology of, 1849
Cohen, David, 4464
on Kook (Avraham Yitsḥaq), 5226
Cohen, Hermann, **1850–1852**
and Bakhtin (M. M.), 742
Gersonides's cosmology and, 3462–3463
influence of, 1851–1852
on Jewish ethics, 4903–4904
Jewish philosophy of, 1851
Kant, exegetical readings of, 1850–1851
philosophy system of, 1851
on revelation, 7441
Rosenzweig (Franz) and, 7826
as scholar, 1850
on Spinoza (Baruch), 8685
Cohen, Michael, 646–647
Cohen, Morris Raphael, Spinoza (Baruch), influence of, 8686
Cohn, Norman, 6985
on millennialism, 6544
Cohn, Norman R. C.
on defamation in Roman Empire, 8013
on millenarism, 7788
on sexual allegations, 8249
Cohon, Samuel, 7671
Coifi (high priest of Deira), 6943
Coincidence, in Yoga philosophy. *See Samāpatti*
Coincidentia oppositorum (conjunction of opposites)
'Ayn al-Quḍāt on, 8813–8814
Dhū al-Nūn al-Miṣrī on, 8812
Coincidentia oppositorum (paradoxical logic), 6989
Coins, 6138. *See also* Money
Cóir Anmann, 1480
Coirbre, 1488
Coke, Edward, 5359
Coke, Thomas, **1852–1853**
in American Methodism, 5998
Asbury (Francis) and, 518
Coker, Daniel, 68, 264
Cōḷa period (Tamil), 8975–8976, 9148, 9265
Colaxis (mythic king), in Scythian festival, 8205
Colberg, Ehregott Daniel, on Hermetism, 3949
Cold War, end of, human rights and, 4178–4179
Cole, Johnnetta, 75
Colebrooke, Henry Thomas, 4446
Coleridge, Samuel Taylor, **1853**
aesthetics of, 47
on conscience, 1944
on fetishism, 3045
Maurice (Frederick Denison) influenced by, 5783
Neoplatonism and, 6475
on poetic imagination, 7206
on Spinoza (Baruch), 8685
symbol theory and, 8908
Colet, John, humanism and, 4176
Colette of Corbie, 3183
Coligny, 1491
"La Collana Viola" (de Martino and Pavese), 2267
Collationes oxoniense et parisienses (Duns Scotus), 2524
Collations on the Six Days of Creation (Bonaventure), 1011
Collected Poems ('Aṭṭār), 601
Collected Writings (Blavatsky), 9142
Collective, interdependence with individual, 7796–7797
Collective psychology, 7349
Collective suicide. *See* Suicide
Collective unconsciousness
Eliade on, 7476
Hopkins (Emma Curtis) and concept of, 4128
Jung on, 1950, 5114, 7475, 7485
Collège de France
Maspero (Henri) at, 5773
Massignon (Louis) at, 5774
Mauss (Marcel) at, 5786
College of Bishops, in Roman Catholic polity, 1764
College of Medical Evangelists, Seventh-day Adventism and, 8237
College of Saint Bonaventure, 1013
Colleges and universities. *See also specific schools*
Christian ethics in, 1656
Churches of Christ founding of, 1780
in Eastern Europe, 8774–8775
in Latin America (Jesuit), 1697
of Mennonites, 5861
religious founding of, 1750
Scholasticism in, 8174–8175
and study of religion
in Australia, 8768, 8769, 8770
emergence of, 8761–8762
in Japan, 8777, 8779
in Middle East and North Africa, 8782–8784
in New Zealand, 8768, 8770–8771
in North America, 8785, 8787–8788
in South Asia, 8789–8792
Collegia (funeral cooperatives), 9227
Collegiality of bishops, Vatican II on, 9535
Collegia sacerdotum, 7907
Collegium (association), in Roman religion
early period, 7909
imperial period, 7914
Colleyn, Jean-Paul, 107
Collier, George, 5931–5932
Collier, Jeremy, 2438
Collier, John, 7302
Collier, Robert, 3007
Collinder, Björn, 474
Collins, David, 685
Collins, J. J., 518
Collinson, Patrick, 4280
Collison, Ernie, on Haida art, 3736
Colloquy, Smith (Wilfred Cantwell) on, 8450
Colloquy of Worms (1539), 7659
Collur Riti festival, in Andean religion, 8603
Cologne (Germany), Eckhart in, 2603
Cologne Mani Codex, 5665, 5666
Colombia. *See also* Desana religion; Macuna religion; Tucano religion
ballgames played in, 749, 750, 751
Cuiba religion in, origin of night in, 8588
Goajira people of, 2302
Muisca creation myth in, 8587
Colonia, Simone da, 236
Colonial Encounters: Europe and the Native Caribbean, 1492-1797 (Hulme), 9295
Colonial Habits (Burns), 3416
Colonialism, **1853–1860**. *See also* Missions; Postcolonialism; *specific colonies, countries, and regions*
archaeology and, 452
assimilation as goal of, 670
and Aztec religion, 716, 719
biblical exegesis and, 5488
and Buddhism, 1098, 1099, 1138–1139, 1312–1313
and caliphate, revival of, 1367
cargo cults and, **1414–1425,** 2007
Code Noir (French), 1706
comparative study of religion and, 1855–1857
and comparative theology, 9128–9129
comparativism and, 1879
conscience and, 1943
creolization in, **2065–2068**
definition of, 1853–1854
and fetishism, invention of, 3044
forced conversions, external forces in, 1973
gardens in, 3280
and Hinduism, 10042
history making, 1422
and iconoclasm, 4386
iconography influenced by, 7322
indigenous religions influenced by, 10047
Islam, effect on, humor and, 4213
and mobility, 10048
in Muslim world
Afghānī (Jamāl al-Dīn al-) on, 64
and *tafsīr,* 8955
and Islamic law, 4701
and nativist millennial movements, 6547
and new religious movements, 6514
political economy of, 1854
and politics and religion, 7248, 7282, 7286, 7291–7292, 7296–7297, 7301–7302
and postcolonialism, economic gap created by, 2675–2676
and study of religion, emergence of, 8761, 8763–8764
Ṣūfī lodges and, 1547
and transculturation, 9292, 9294, 9295–9297
Colonna, Sciarra, 1019
Colorado River, 7862
Colored Methodist Episcopal Church, 5998, 10038
Colors, **1860–1862**. *See also specific colors*
in alchemy, 251, 1862
of amulets and talismans, 298, 300
Christian symbolism of, 1861–1862
of fairies, 2954
in herbalism, in African religions, 3819
in Hinduism, 4326
in I Am movement, 4246

Colors *continued*
in Islam, 4350
in Jainism, in cosmology and karmic theory, 2024–2025
in Judaism, on Yom Kippur, 7929
liturgical, in Christianity, 1744
Mesoamerican use of, 1860–1861
in Native American traditions, 1862
in Tehuelche religion, 9029–9030
in visions, 9612
in winter carols, 9745
Colossians, 914, 920
angels in, 346
author of, 911, 914, 915
content of, 914
Ephesians compared to, 914
Luke in, 908
Mark in, 5714
pain in, 6946
Colpe, Carsten, 3041
on Gnosticism, 3532, 3534–3535
historiography of, 4048
on vegetation theory, 6328
Colporteur on his Rounds, vol. 7 color insert
Coltrane, John, 6313
Columbia University
American Indian language studies at, 2264
Benedict (Ruth) at, 819, 820
Gaster (Theodor H.) at, 3288
Goldenweiser (Alexander A.) at, 3633
Mead (Margaret) at, 5803
Merton (Thomas) at, 5879
"Columbia Watershed: Caring for Creation and the Common Good, The," 2613
Columbus, Christopher
on Caribbean religions, 1428, 1429–1430, 10024
on entrance to Paradise, 3063
prayers of, 7838
Columbus Platform (1937), 7671
Columns. *See* Pillars
Colville people (North America), 6714
Comarius, 245
Co-Masonic Order, 5244
Combat myth, 1539
in Chinese tradition, 1626
Combs-Schilling, Elaine, on rites of passage, 7803
Comedy. *See* Humor
Comenius, Johannes Amos, **1862–1863**
and Moravians, 6191
on nature, 6434
Comets, 8735–8736
as prodigy, 7337
Coming of Age in Samoa (Mead), 5804
Comitatus (war band), 4462
as *männerbund,* 9684
Comitium (place of assembly), circle symbolism in, 1791
Commandments
in Islam *(amr),* heteronomous discipline and, 8700
in Judaism (*See also* Mitsvot)
in Torah, 9074, 9235, 9237
Ten (*See* Ten Commandments)
Commands and Admonitions for the Families of the Great Dao (Daoist text), 2181
Commedia (Dante). *See Divine Comedy* (Dante)
Commedia dell'arte, Carnival and, 1441–1442
Commentariolus (Copernicus), moving earth in, 1977
Commentarius in psalmos Davidicos (Peter Lombard), 7066
Commentary on the Mishnah (Maimonides), 153, 5615
aggadah in, 5615
health in, 3831
oral law in, 5615
translation into Hebrew, 5615
Commentary on the Pauline Epistles (Peter Lombard), 7067
Commentary on the Timaeus (Proclus), 7191
Comment on the Commentaries, A (Bentham), 5368
Commerce
Crusades, effect of, 2078
of images, vol. 7 color insert
Jewish law and, 3752
in Oceania, mission involvement in, 6792
shrines as centers of service and commerce, 8378
Commercial litigation, in rabbinic Judaism, 7589
Commercial terminology, in *Ecclesiastes,* 2599
Commission for Intellectual Cooperation of the League of Nations, 838
Commission of European Bishops' Conferences, 942
Commission on Faith and Order. *See* World Council of Churches
Commission on Life and Work, in ecumenical movement, 2684
Commitment stage of conversion, 1972
Committee on Ethnographic Film, 2350
Committee on the Status of Women in India, 3321
Commodification, media and, 5805–5806, 5808
Commodus (Roman emperor), Galen and, 3255
Common Faith, A (Dewey), 49
Campbell (Joseph) and, 1378
Common-law. *See* Law(s), common-law
Common Lutheran Conference, 5539
Common-origin associations, in Chinese religion, 1616
Common property, nature as, in Islam, 2651
Common religion, 4401
Common-sense philosophy, Scottish, Channing (William Ellery), influence on, 1530
Common service, as ecumenical concern, 2684, 2685, 2690
Communal meals, of Essenes, 2847
Communes, 6986
utopianism of, 9492
Communicants and noncummunicants, membership in the church and, 1778
Communicatio idiomatum doctrine, Cyril of Alexandria on, 2117
Communication
through art, 498
culture and, 2087
Cybernetics, **2111–2112**
prayer as, 7367–7368
ritual as form of, 7849–7851
sacred places as means of, 7980–7981
Schleiermacher (Friedrich) on, 8163
Communications Act of 1934, 7710
Communion. *See also* Eucharist
in Anglicanism, 352–353
in Armenian church, 489
in early church, 7959
with God (*See Devequt;* Mystical union)
in Lutheranism, 5538
Luther (Martin) on, 5536, 5537
in mystical ecstasy, 2680
Nikodimos of the Holy Mountain on, 6621
sacramental, forbidden for Catholics with Orthodox, 2588
sacrificial rites and, 7999–8000, 8002–8003
Communion and Liberation (movement), 6568
Communion of the Christian with God, The (Herrmann), 6104
Communion theodicy, 9115
Communism
in Baltic states, 764, 770–771, 775, 1686
and brainwashing, 1030–1031
and Buddhism
in Cambodia, 1100, 1143
in China, 1098, 1167–1168, 7268
in Korea, 1098, 1100
in Laos, 1143
in Mongolia, 1098, 1100, 1148, 1150, 1189
in Tibet, 1098, 1100, 1158–1159
in Vietnam, 1100
in Cambodia, 5132–5133
and Buddhism, 1100, 1143
in China, 1579
and Buddhism, 1098, 1167–1168, 7268
exerting political power over religious institutions, 7255, 7268
and Islam, 4636–4637, 4640
religious freedom and, 5353–5354, 10072
study of religion and, 10073
Christianity and, in ecumenical movement, 2688
and Confucianism, 4339, 7268
Eliade and, denunciation of, 2759
iconography of, 4348
of Jones (Jim), 4952, 4953
in Korea, 5235
and Mazdakism, 5800
missionary activity of, 6070, 6071
Muslim, in Middle Volga, 4619
religious broadcasting and, 7713–7714
in Romania, 2754
in Soviet bloc, 1686
as utopianism, 9492
in Vietnam, 7264
Communitarianism, 5398
Christian (*See also* Utopianism)
Shakers and, 8268
Communitarian personalism, 1653
Communitas (sense of bonding), in pilgrimage, 7146, 7147
Islamic, 7158
Community, **1863–1868**. *See also* Religious communities
in afterlife, 131–132
characteristics of, 1864–1865
Christian, worship and, 1668–1670
consensus of, in Islam, 5060
creeds, role of, 2053
deities of, 3622
eclipse of, in mortification rites, 8208–8209
eremitism and, 2828–2829
excommunication from, 2920–2921
of faith, 2957
in healing rituals, 3814–3815
images of, vol. 6 color insert
interests of, individualism superseded by, vol. 6 color insert
Jewish, Rubenstein (Richard) on, 4094
in Judaism, 4907
Orthodox, 6899, 6900, 6901
Reconstructionist, 7639
natural (undifferentiated) religious groups, 1865–1866
Osage, 6918

sacred, 7716 (*See also* Religious communities)
Schleiermacher (Friedrich) on, 8163, 8165
vs. society, 7716, 8481
Durkheim (Émile) on, 7716
Marx on, 7716
Tönnies (Ferdinand Julius) on, 7716
specific (voluntary) religious groups, 1866–1867
subgroups, 1867–1868
in visionary experiences, 9614–9615
in vision quest, 9610
in West African religions, 9719
Community in Island Pond, Vermont, 6540
Community of Baltic Faith Romuva, 764–765
Community of Christ (Reorganized Church of Jesus Christ of Latter Day Saints), 6192, 6193–6194, 6195
Community-oriented socialism, 9230
Comoro Islands, religious systems in, 3137
Companies of Kings festival, 6272
Companionship, in Mesoamerican funeral rites, 148–149
Company of Mystic Animals (Iroquois), 4542
Company of St. Ursula. *See* Ursuline order
Comparative ecclesiology, in ecumenical movement, 2684
Comparative-historical method, **1868–1873**. *See also* Historiography; History of religions
aims of, 1869–1870
on confession, 1883–1884
dialectic nature of, 4063
and diffusion *vs.* parallelism, 4063
general considerations on, 1868–1869
high cultures and, 4065
ideographic research *vs.*, 4063
intra- and extrareligious explanations in, 1870
of Lanternari (Vittorio), 4046
Pettazzoni (Raffaele) developing, 7073
problems in, 1869, 1871–1873
theology and, 1871
"Comparative Method in Sociological Anthropology, The" (Radcliffe-Brown), 7592–7593
Comparative mythology, **1873–1877**
death and immortality theme, 1875
Dumézil (Georges) and, 2518–2519, 4461–4464
dying and reviving god theme, 1874–1875
earth diver theme, 1875–1876
flood theme, 1876
of Indo-European religions, 1874, 4458–4465
killing of the dragon theme, 1875
naturistic school of, 4459–4460
of Near Eastern mythologies, 1874–1875
of Müller, 4459, 6234
origin of death theme, 1875
"Comparative Mythology" (Müller), 4459
Comparative religion (comparativism), **1877–1881**. *See also* History of religions approach; Science, of religion; Study of religion
African religions ignored in, 113
art in, 501, 502
aspectual, limited comparative focus in, 1880
Bertholet (Alfred) on, 843
binding in, 938–939
Ching (Julia) on, 10030–10031
classification of religions, **1817–1822**
colonialist and imperialist bias in, 1855–1857
commonalities, 2089 (*See also* Universal)
differences, affirmation of, 1880–1881
doctrines in, 2382–2383
Evola (Julius) in, 2906
goddess worship in, 3614–3615
Harva (Uno), comparative-typological method of, 3783
history of field of
criticisms of, 1879–1880
Eliade (Mircea), role of, 1878–1879
rearticulations of, 1880–1881
religious versions of, 1877–1878
rise of academic field of, 1877–1878
"holiness" in, 4098–4099, 4100
ideal-types in, 5436
in India, 8790–8791
Islamic
centers and university departments for, 8782–8784
Milal wa Nihal studies ("Sects and Heresies"), 8780–8781
Jesuit studies of Confucianism and, 1919–1921
Jevons (F. B.) in, 4854
Jews, role of, in 19th century, 4041
masks in, 5764–5765
in Myth and Ritual school, 6382
Orientalism and, 1631–1632
Oxtoby (Willard) on, 10055–10056
in phenomenology of religion, 7093
Pinard de la Boullaye on, 7173
Pratt (James) on, 7367
prophecy in, 7428
psychology in, 7479
Radhakrishnan (Sarvepalli) on, 7595
Reinach (Salomon) on, 7675–7676
religious studies preceded by, 2608
ritual studies and, 7857
Schleiermacher (Friedrich) on, 8162
Sharpe (Eric) on, 8304–8305
Smith (W. Robertson), role of, 8451
sociology and, 8496
in South Asia, 8790–8791
syncretism and, 2089
Comparative Religion (Jevons), 4854
Comparative Religion (Sharpe), 7091
impact of, 8769
Comparative theology. *See* Theology, comparative
Comparet, Bertrand, Christian Identity movement and, 1658, 1659
Comparetti, Domenico, 3104
Compassion
in Buddhism, 1555, 2627 (*See also* Karuṇā)
Bodhisattva of, 2131
engaged Buddhism, 2788
Mahāyāna, 6630
missions and, 6079
Nāgārjuna on, 6393
wisdom and, 2630
female personification of, 3019
of God, 9282–9283
of Jesus, 4844
in morality, 6185–6186
for possessing spirits, 2932
Compassion Relief Tzu Chi Association (Ciji), **1787–1790**
Compendium of the Teachings of Mani the Buddha of Light, 5669
Compendiums, of Egyptian mythology, 2724
Compensation, in penitential rites, 7755
Compitalia (festival), 5320–5321
Compleat Body of Divinity (Willard), 2287
Complementarity, 7139
unequal, in Christianity and Confucianism, Jesuit interpretation of, 1920
Complete Account of the Settlement at Port Jackson, A (Tench), 685
Completed Testament Age (CTA), 9467
Complete good *(summum bonum),* Kant (Immanuel) on, 5077–5078
Complete Guide to Buddhist America (Morreale), 1190
Complexity
irreducible, 4517
specified, 4516–4517
Complexity theory, 2660
Compulsion, free will as absence of, 3202
Computers
analogy between brains and, 6486
and art, study of, 502
artificial intelligence in, **509–513**
binary numbers and, 6751
Computer simulation, of religious and cultural systems, 2660
Comstock, Anthony, 3252
Comte, Auguste, **1882–1883**
on African religions, 113
and animism, 366
on concept of science, 7340
on fetishism, 3045
and functionalism, 3230, 3231
on historiography, 4033
on Indian religions, 4447
on knowledge, 5206
on natural philosophy, 6431
positivism of, 7339–7341
reconstruction of religion by, 6430
on secularization, 8214
on society and religion, 8465
on sociology, 8480, 8492
Con (deity), as high god, 8590
Conaire Mór (deity), 1491–1492
Conall Cernach, **1883**
Concealment. *See Ghaybah*
Concentration. *See also* Attention; Meditation
in eightfold path, 2738–2739
in vision inducement, 9613
Concentration camps. *See also* Holocaust, the
Christian prisoners of, unity among, 2685
history of, 4086
Conception
in Australian Indigenous religions, 9668
myths of, 658, 9669
in Warlpiri religion, 9693

Conception *continued*
immaculate, in Roman Catholicism, 5754
life beginning at, in Roman Catholicism, 5811, 5812
in Trobriand Islanders religion, 5184
in Ungarinyin religion, 9461
Conception dreams, 2489
Conception of Buddhist Nirvāṇa (Stcherbatsky), 1089
Concept of Anxiety, The (Kierkegaard), 5142
Concept of God after Auschwitz, The (Jonas), 4949
Concept of Irony, with Constant Reference to Socrates (Kierkegaard), 5141
Conceptual analysis, in Buddhism, of Kamalaśīla, 5070
Concerned African women's theology, 3035
Concerned Christians, 6552
Concerning Divination (Cicero), 2378
Concerning the Spiritual in Art (Kandinsky), 4348, 9144
Conches
as Viṣṇu symbol, 4325
in Melanesian music, 6265
Conchobhar mac Nessa (king), 1493, 3040
Conciliar decrees, of Vatican I, 9528–9532
Conciliarism
church councils on, 2042–2043, 2044, 6971
ecumenism and, 2044
Eugenius IV and, 8157
Febronianism as, 6973
Gallicanism as, 6973
Josephism as, 6973
Concise Account of the London Society for Promoting Christianity amongst the Jews (Adams), 30
Conclave, law of, 6971
Concluding Unscientific Postscript (Kierkegaard, pseud. Climacus), humor and irony in, 4220–4221
Conclusiones (Pico), 7141
Concordance, in esotericism, Faivre paradigm of, 2844
Concord of Discordant Canons (Gratian). *See Decretum* (Gratian)
Concubines, 9907
Concupiscence, 9070
Condillac, Étienne Bonnot, abbé de, in French Enlightenment, 2796
Condorcanqui, José Gabriel, 5984, 6576
Condorcet, on scientific progress, 7340
Cone, Cecil, 77–79, 965, 5441
Cone, James, 77, 79, 80, 963, 964, 965
on God as white, 3559, 5441
on kingdom of God, 5153
liberation theology of, 5441, 10040
CONELA. *See* Evangelical Confraternity of Latin America
Conference of Church Workers among Colored People, Crummell (Alexander) and, 2074
Conference of the Birds (ʿAṭṭār), 601
Conferences. *See specific types*
Conferences of the Fathers (Cassian), 1447
Conferencia Evangélica Latinoamericana (CELA), 1702
Confessing Church (Germany), Barmen Declaration of, 2685
Confession
of faith (*See* Confessions of faith)
in men's studies, 5863
of sins (*See* Confession of sins)
Confession (Patrick), 7009, 7010
Confession (Turner), 70
Confession, A (Tolstoy), 9220
Confessional religions, heresy as concept in, 3921, 3922
Confession of 1629 (Cyril I), Calvinist perspectives in, 2588
Confession of Dosítheos, as opposition to Calvinism, 2059
Confession of Faith (Abelard), 7
Confession of Faith (Cyril), Calvinism in, 2115
Confession of Faith (Dositheos), Roman Catholic perspectives in, 2588
Confession of Faith (document of Scottish Reformation), 5212
Confession of Jerusalem (1673), on free will and predestination, 3208
Confession of sins, **1883–1890**. *See also* Purification; Repentance
in African religions, healing through, 3821
in Babylonian religion, 1887–1888
in Buddhism, 1886–1887
in meditation, 1291
casuistry and, 1455
Celestial Masters and, 2181
in Christianity, 1888–1889
communal form of, in Roman Catholicism, 7962
in Eastern Christianity, 1889, 7960
medieval practices, 7961
in Orthodox Church, 2592–2593
in Protestantism, 7452, 7963
as sacrament, 1889, 7956
as tribunal of conscience, 1941
in Daoism, 1886, 9844–9845
definition of, 7755
expulsion in, 2939
in Greek and Roman religion, 1887
healing through, 3812
in Hittite religion, 4072
in Huichol religion, 7759
in Inca religion, 1886
in Indian religions, 1886
of Indian Shakers, 7759
in Inuit religions, 7505, 7509, 7759
in Islam, 7757–7758
in Jainism, 1886
in Judaism, 1888, 7757
for atonement, 593
on Yom Kippur, 7757, 8390
knots and, 5197
in Mandaean religion, 1889
in Maya religion, 7759
in Mesoamerican religion, 1885–1886
in nonliterate cultures, 1884–1885
in North American Indian religions, 7759
in Nuer religion, 7758–7759
in penitential rites, 7755
Pettazzoni (Raffaele) on, 7075, 8402
prayer of, 7369
public *vs.* private, 7755, 7756
reflexive character of, 7649–7650
in repentance, 7755
as sacrament, 1670
as self-accusation, 7755
in Shinto, 1886
in Totonac religion, 9254
in Zoroastrianism and Manichaeism, 1889
Confession of the Christian Faith (Beza), 851
Confessions, The (Augustine), 626
autobiographical nature of, 698
autobiographies influenced by, 698, 699
conscience in, 1940
desire in, 2304, 2307
heart symbolism in, 3882
Islamic autobiography compared to, 700
literary value of, 5471
in men's studies, 5863
morality in, 1651–1652
music in, 6308
nature of God in, 55
revelation through narrative of, 46
Teresa of Ávila influenced by, 9084
writing of, 626
Confessions, The (Rousseau), 699, 7931
Confessions of faith. *See also* Creeds
antidogmatism and, 2060–2061
apostasy and, 3921
closed, open, and descriptive confessionalism, 2056
creeds *vs.*, 2053, 2054
and history, Christian views of, 4053
in Islam (*See ʿAqidah/ʿaqāʾid; See* Shahādah)
in Protestantism, 2053, 2057–2061
authority of, 2055–2056
in Zoroastrianism, 2052
Confessors
of the church, as saints, 8034
Jesuits as, 4842
Confirmation
in Christianity
baptism and, 9810
in early church, 7959
in Protestantism, 7455
as sacrament, 1670, 7956
in Judaism (*See* Bar mitzvah; Bat mitzvah)
Orthodox (*See* Chrismation)
rituals of, 7841–7843
Conflation, in visual narratives, vol. 2 color insert
Conflict
religious (*See also* Violence)
in Australia, Catholics *vs.* Protestants, 1733–1734
desecration and, 8011–8012
in India, Muslims *vs.* Hindus, desecration and, 8011
in media coverage, 4962–4963
representation in film, 3097
in science and religion typology, 2658
in Vedism, 9560–9561, 9567
Conflict and peace studies, 9596
Conflict-dualism, 2509
Conflict resolution, Gandhi's method of, 6646
Confucianism, **1890–1932**
ablutions in, 10
aesthetics in, 51
afterlife in, 172
ancestor worship in, 323–324
anthropocosmism of, 2632
autobiography in, 701
biographies in, sacred, 945, 946
books burned in Qin dynasty, 1590
Buddhism and
and bushidō, 1336
common goal of, 1167, 1172
criticism of, 1150
in Japan, 4787
laws concerning, 5353
philosophical influence of, 1165
reconciliation between, 1173
in Six Dynasties period, 1898–1899
in Song dynasty, 1901
vision of enlightenment in, 6630
Zen, 9948
chaos in, 1540, 1624

charisma in, 7353
Cheng Hao in, 1561
Cheng-Zhu school, 1577, 1579
China identified with, 1920–1921
Christianity and, 10030–10031
clans and, 1616
clerics *(lisheng),* 1617
communism and, 4339, 7268
community in, vol. 6 color insert
cosmological basis for in Dong, 1591
dao in, 2172
Daoism and, Seidel (Anna) on, 8223
de in, 2173, 2174
deities of, Shangdi in, 8300
doctrine in, 2382
dragons in, 2433
drama in, 2455
drums in, 2499
dynastic cycle in, 1627
ecology and, **2631–2635**
economics and, 9708
education in, 9674–9675
enlightenment in, 2218
eschatology and, 2834
essential cultural self-definition and, 1924
ethics combined with Buddhist *karma,* 1604
faith and works in, 2955–2956
fasting in, 2996
fate in, 3004
feminist analysis of, 3033–3034
and film, 3097
gender in, 3340–3341, 3346
gift giving in, 3483
golden age in, 1628
Golden Rule in, 3631, 3632, 3633
Guo Xiang on, 3710
Gu Yanwu on, 3718
in Han dynasty, 7267
Han Fei Zi and, 3773
Han philosophy and, 1590–1591, 1897–1898
harmony in, 3888
Heaven in, 3888 (*See also* Tian)
historical development of
classics study in Qing period, 1903–1904
daotong (transmission of the Way) in Tang and Song periods, 1899–1901
early sages, legacies of, 1891–1892
Kongzi and disciples, early traditions around, 1892–1895
medieval encounter with Buddhism, 1898–1899
practice and politics in Ming and Yuan periods, 1901–1903
in Qin and Han periods, 1897–1898
self-transformation and rulership (4th and 3rd centuries BCE), 1895–1897
historiography and, 4026
history of study of, 1629–1638, **1916–1926**
agnostic relation of *ru* and the imperium, 1917–1918
Ching (Julia) in, 10030–10031
comparative theology and the *Confucius Sinarum Philosophus* in, 1919–1921
indigenous values and, 1922–1923
invention and intercultural communication in, 1918–1919
nativism and new Confucianism, 1923–1924
ru concept and, 1916–1917
twentieth-century repudiation and recovery in, 1921–1922
willful divergence of China and the West on, 1921–1922
hospitality in, 4140–4141
humans in, 2631–2633
humor and, 4199, 4206
iconography of (*See* Iconography, Confucian)
immortality in, 8555
debate over, 1576
imperial cult in, **1910–1916**
formation of, 1910–1914
political legitimation and, 1914
ritual purity and, 1914
sacrifice to Shangdi in, 1914–1915
institutionalization of, 1166
Islam in China influenced by, 4632
in Japan (*See* Japan and Japanese religions, Confucianism)
Jesuit study and construction of, 1918–1921
Judaism and, 5005–5006
Kaibara Ekken in, 5055
Kang Yuwei on, 5075–5076
kingship in, 1161
knowledge in, 5201
in Korea (*See* Korea and Korean religions, Confucianism)
laity in, 5288–5289
Legalism condemned by, 1574
li in, 5431
literature and canon of, **1905–1910** (*See also* Yijing)
apocrypha, 1908
burning of, 1574
Five Scriptures *(wujing),* 1585, 1905–1909
in Han dynasty, 1590–1591, 1897
imperial cult and, 1913
models of canon formation in, 1909
New Text *vs.* Old Text, 1574–1575
poetry, 7212–7214
the Thirteen Classics and the Four Books in, 1407, 1900, 1909
translations of, 1633
Zhongyong, 1587
local cults, attempts to control, 1615
in Meiji restoration, 4791
of Mengzi, 1587, 5857–5859
merging with Daoism and Buddhism, 2187
merit in, 5870
in Ming dynasty, 1578, 1608, 1901–1903
missionaries and, 1630–1631
in modern China, 1611, 1904, 1922–1924
morality in, 6182–6188, 7651
moral thought in, will of Heaven and, 1584
Mozi and, 1586–1587, 6217–6218
music in, 6293–6294, 6296–6297
Japanese, 6300
names in, 6408
Nativism and, 1923–1924
nature in, 2631–2632
New Confucianism, 1923–1924 (*See also* Neo-Confucianism)
New Text school *vs.* Old Text school, 1574–1575, 1592
noise in, 7037
obedience in, 6778
Ōgyu Sorai in, 6810–6811
Okinawan religion influenced by, 6813
orthodoxy and heterodoxy and, 6911
orthopraxy in, 6914–6915
overview, **1890–1905**
proverbs in, 6978
purity in, 7510
qi in, 7544, 7545
in Qing dynasty, 1578–1579, 1903–1904, 2187
rainmaking in, 7603
rebellion ideologies from, 2834
as religion, 1579, 1581, 7692
ren in, 5075–5076, 7751–7752
revitalization of, Kang Yuwei in, 5075–5076
ritual in, 1894–1895
Xunzi on, 9863
salvation in, 1626
schools in classical period, 1572
self-realization in, 2633
Shidian ritual for, 5434
Shintō and, 3802, 9870
society, relations with, 8462
in Song dynasty (*See* Song dynasty, Confucianism in)
suicide, attitudes toward, 8832
syncretism in, 2605
in Tang dynasty (*See* Tang dynasty, Confucianism in)
temples in (*See* Temples, Confucian)
term, meaning of, 1916
textiles in, 9089, 9090
tian in, 9172–9173
triad of, 2631, 2633
truth in, 9372
Wang Yangming in, 9673–9675
wealth and, 9708
Weber on, 1921–1922
wisdom in, 9753
women in, 1591, 3340–3341, 3346
xiao in, 9857–9858
Xunzi in, 1573, 1586–1587, 9862–9863
Yamazaki Ansai in, 9869–9870
yi in, 5075–5076, 7751–7752
yinyang thought in, 1591
Zhang Xuecheng on, 9956
in Zheng sect of Daoism, 5495
Confucianism and Christianity: A Comparative Study (Ching), 10031
Confucian's Progress, The (Wu), 701
Confucius (Kongzi), **1933–1937**. *See also* Analects of Confucius
on afterlife, 172
Ancient Learning school in Japan and, 1928
atheism and, 578
biographies of, 945, 946
birth of, 2180
canon of books of, 1407
as deity, cult of, 1913
denying novelty of message of, 9272
disciples of, 1935
temple built by, 9058–9060
ethics of, 1908–1909
given name of, 5315
on golden age, 6038
on government service, 1586
iconography of, 4337, 4338

Confucius (Kongzi) ***continued***
  Jesuit interest in, 1918, 1920
  jokes by, 4206
  Kitagawa (Joseph M.) on, 5187–5188
  Lao Dan/Laozi as teacher of, 5315–5316
  Lunyu (Analects), 1585
  on moral character, 8462
  narratives and lore on, 1892–1895
  New Text schools on, 1575
  on the odes, 1905
  overview, 1585–1586
  philosophy, overview of, 1571, 1935–1936
  proverbs of, 6978
  Qing view of, 1903–1904
  on quaternity, 7550
  on religious rites, 5431
  on ritual, 6182
  on sage-kings, 8037
  on sages, 1549
  as semidivine, 1592
  on society and religion, 8462
  Zhou institutions taken as model by, 1892
Confucius: The Man and the Myth (Creel), 946
Confucius and the Chinese Way (Creel), 946
Confucius-Mencius Society, 8965
Confucius Sinarum philosophus, 1919–1920
Congar, Yves, 2686
Conger, Arthur L., 7230
Congo. *See also* Central Bantu religions; Kongo religion; Luba religion
  African Independent Churches in, 103
  Mouvement Croix-Koma in, 105
  Pentecostalism in, 7030
  religious studies in, 112
Congo (Carnival festivity), 1443
Congolese people
  kingship of, 5157, 5159
  spirit containers of, vol. 9 color insert
Congregation
  in Chinese religion, 1616
  at Eucharist, in Orthodox Christianity, 2592
  in Orthodox Judaism, 6900
  Weber's (Max) definition of, 5384
  in Western religions, 7693
Congregational form of church government, 1768–1769
  in colonial New England, 1938
  individualism and, 1939
Congregationalism, **1937–1939**. *See also* United Church of Christ
  African American, 69
  beliefs and practices of, 1938–1939
  in Canada, 1712
  church architecture of, 796
  ecclesiology of, 1774
  Eddy (Mary Baker) in, 2694
  historical survey of, 1937–1938
  Morse attack on liberalism in, 1530
  in New Guinea, 1738–1739
  Plan of Union with Presbyterians (1801), 1938
  Puritanism as roots of, 1712
  Savoy Declaration (1658), authority of, 2055
  in Swedenborgianism, 8902, 8903
  Unitarianism and, 1938
  in United Reformed Church (England), 1938
  in World Alliance of Reformed Churches, 2055
Congregational worship, and architecture, 466
Congregation for the Doctrine of Faith. *See* Congregation of the Holy Office; Roman Inquisition
Congregation of Latvian Dievturi, 763, 765
Congregation of the Holy Office. *See also* Roman Inquisition heresy, and Index of Forbidden Books, 3928
Congregation of the Index, suspension of Copernicus's work by, 1978
Congregation of the Propagation of the Faith, 7877
  Carroll (John) and, 1445
Congregation of the Sisters of Our Lady of the Cenacle, 7772
Conjecture, Nicholas of Cusa on, 6610
Conjunctions, theories of, in astrology, 564
Conjuration. *See also* Hoodoo
  Jewish, in exorcism liturgy, 2930
  magical
    of demons, 5579
    in Islam, 5584
Conla son of Conn (deity), 1491
Conlon, James, on spirituality, 8720
Conn Cétchathach, 1492
Connecticut, colonial, Hooker (Richard) and Puritanism in, 4125
Connubial gods, in Andean iconography, 8602
Conquerors
  migration and, 6024–6025
  millenarianism and, 6031
Conquest, kingship established via, 5156–5157
Conquista de Jerusalén, La (drama), 2438
Conrad, Geoffrey W., 454
Conrad, Joseph
  on conscience, 1944
  Said (Edward) on, 8032
Conrad III of Germany (king), Crusades and, 2075
Conring, Hermann, on Hermetism, 3949
Consanguinity
  kinship based on, 5182
  and marriage laws, in Karaite sect, 5086–5087
Conscience, **1939–1946**
  anthropological and theological considerations on, 1944–1945
  application to study of religion and ethics, 1944
  Augustine on, 1940–1941
  in Christianity, 1940–1942
    Newman (John Henry) on, 6510
    Paul the Apostle on, 7018–7019
    in Protestantism, medical ethics and, 3847
  Cicero on, 1940
  collective, Durkheim (Émile) on, 8493
  Descartes on, 1942–1943
  in Hebrew scriptures, 1939–1940
  in Hinduism, as source of *dharma,* 5343
  historical development of, 1940–1943
  inner light theory of, 1943
  Kant on, 1943, 1944
  latihan, 833
  modern conflict with consciousness, 1943–1944
  Montaigne on, 1942
  origin of notion, 1939–1940
  Paul on, 1940, 1945
  Reformation view of, 1941–1942
  Thomas Aquinas on, 1941
Conscience and Its Problems (Church of England), 1455
Conscience collective, Durkheim (Émile) on, 8493
Conscientiae, van der Leeuw (Gerardus) on *homo religiosus* and, 4110
Conscientização, 7791
Consciousness. *See also* Consciousness, states of
  African American, 67
  ālaya-vijñāna, **228–229,** 517, 1211–1212
  attentional exercises and, 606–607
  Berger (Peter L.) on cosmos and, 8468
  in Buddhism
    bhavaṅga form of, 8548
    in Mahāyāna, 8552
    in Yogācāra, 8858, 9897, 9900–9901
    Sthiramati on, 8740
    types of, 2338
  cakras and, 1349
  Cassirer on, 1448
  Chantepie de la Saussaye on, 1531
  comic, Hegel on, 4220
  conscience, conflict with, 1943–1944
  cosmic, 7475
  cybernetics and, 2111
  of deity, 2258–2261
  development of, 2282–2285
  doubling of, in spirit possession, 8689
  evolution of
    Aurobindo Ghose on, 633–634
    Steiner (Rudolf) on, 8738
  Gurdjieff (G. I.) on, 3711
  Hegel on religious consciousness, 3893, 4220
  hermeneutics and, 3930
  in Hinduism (*See also* Puruṣa)
    in Pratyabhijñā Saivism, 8048
    in Trika Śáivism, 8047
    subtle thought *(sūkṣmacitta)* as, 8138
  integrative mode of, in shamanism, 8277
  in Jungian psychology, hero myths and, 3959
  Lessing (G. E.) on, 5417
  Neumann (Erich) on, 6484
  neuroscientists on, 6487
  New Thought movement on, 6583
  orientation and, 6887
  peasant consciousness, in subaltern studies, 8800–8801
  phenomenological analysis of, in existentialism, 2926
  in Rastafari, 7622
  religious
    Hegel on, 3893, 4220
    Schleiermacher (Friedrich) on, 8165, 8166
    and science, dialogue with, 8191
    theology of, anthropomorphism and, 391
  in religious experience, 7695
  ritualization of, 7841–7842
  sacred as element of structure of, 7975
  Scheler (Max) on, 8147
  Schelling (Friedrich) on, 8148
  self- (*See* Self-consciousness)
  in Sikhism, 8549
  of sin, in Hebrew scriptures, 8403
  Socrates on, 8503
  states of (*See* Consciousness, states of)
  transcendent, expression of truth through, 9372–9374
  transcendental, Husserl (Edmund) on, 4237
  in Transcendental Meditation, 9291
  transference of (yogic practice), 1288
  Trubetskoi (Sergei) on, 9368
  in Yoga, 9895

Consciousness, states of, **1946–1954**. *See also* Dreams; Ecstasy; Enthusiasm; Frenzy; Inspiration; Sleep; Visions
altered, 1951–1952
in Caribbean religions, 10026
counterculture movement and, 8294
definition of, 8688
for healing, 3813
hypersuggestibility in, 7468, 7469
laws on, 7468
Mandell (Arnold) on, 8276
as means to access knowledge of afterlife, 2237
in Pentecostal Christianity, 2237
in popular Sufism, 8822
psychedelic drugs and, 1951–1952, 7467–7468, 7471, 7477
scientific study of, 1951–1952
in shamanism, 8275–8277, 8294
spirit possession and, 1433–1434, 8687, 8688–8689
trauma theory and, 8245
in Vodou, 1433–1434
Asian concepts of, 1950–1951
Assagioli (Roberto) on, 1949
brain and mental states, correlation between, 1952–1953
Bucke (Richard) on, 1949
in existential-humanistic and transpersonal psychologies, 1950
Fechner (Gustav Theodor) on, 1947
Flournoy (Théodore) on, 1949
Freud on, 1949
in Yoga *samādhi,* 8066–8067
James (William) on, 1947–1948
Janet (Pierre) on, 1948–1949
Jung (C. G.) on, 1949–1950
Maslow (Abraham) on, 1950
Mesmer (Franz Anton) on, 1947
Myers (F. W. H.) on, 1949
mystical, 6355, 6356 (*See also* Mysticism)
in neuroscience, neurophilosophy, and neurotheology, 1952
positivist view of, 1946
psychodynamic view of, 1946
symbolic view of, 1946–1947
in Western mystical tradition, 1951
Consciousness-raising, feminist research and, 9790
Consecration, **1954–1957**
of animals, in bloodless sacrifice, 7998
of art, 497
in Christianity, circumambulation in, 1797
divine authority, bestowal of, 1956
as hierophany (manifestation of the sacred), 3972
in Hinduism (*See Dīkṣā*)
of homes, 4105
horns of, in Minoan religion, 40, *40*
of images, 1955–1956
in Judaism, of harvest, 2644
in Korean religion, in *mudang* shamanism, 4105
personal consecrations and renewal, 1956–1957
and relics, deposition of, 7979
"sacred" and, 4098
of sacred space, 1504, 1954–1955
sacrum as, 7966
of time or moments, 3973
Consecration possession, 2140
Conselheiro, Antonio, 6577
Consequences, in wisdom, 9748–9749
Consequences stages of conversion, 1972
Conservation
balance and, in indigenous traditions, 2618
in ecology, 2608
Conservation biology, development of, 2609
Conservation movement, development of, 2609
Conservative Judaism, **1957–1966**. *See also* Reconstructionist Judaism
bat mitzvah in, 1962, 7821
centrism and suburbanization in, 1964–1965
divides, ideological and theological, in, 1960
divorce in, 3754
"early Seminary" movement in, 1958
education and youth in, 1961–1962, 1963
in Great Depression and World War II, 1959–1960
halakhah in, 4983
havurah movement in, 1963
historiography in, 4059–4060
ideological and institutional origins of, 1957–1958
in Israel, modern, 9982
Jewish Law and, 1960–1961
kashrut laws of, 5107
modernity and, 4983
national identity and, 1961
organizational growth in, 1959
prayer books of, 8388
Reconstructionist schism in, 1962
relationship with Reconstructionist Judaism, 5082, 7636
Schechter (Solomon) and, 1958–1959, 8146–8147
seminary of, in Germany, 7581
Shabbat laws in, 8257
Suffering Servant doctrine in, 4089
synagogues in
emergence of, 1959
as temples, 8925
women in, 3354–3355, 7582
ordination of, 1963–1964
Conservatorships, new religious movements and, 5375–5376
Consilience (Wilson), 2916
Consolamentum (baptism rite), in Catharism, 1457
Consolation of Philosophy (Boethius), 7192
Consonance, hypothetical consonance model of science and religion, 8186
Consonants, mystical speculation on, 271
Consorts, in goddess worship, 3588–3589
Constance, Council of (1414–1418), 6971, 7280, 9340–9341
Hus (Jan) judged at, 4234
overview of, 2042–2043
Constans I (Roman emperor), Athanasius and, 571–572
Constant, Benjamin, 3045
Constantine (apostle to the Slavs). *See* Cyril and Methodius
Constantine I (Constantine the Great) (Roman emperor), **1966–1967**
Adonis shrine destroyed by, 34
apotheosis and, 439, 440
Arianism and, 479
Athanasius exiled by, 571
basilicas established by, 792
and Christian iconography, 4344, 4385
Christianity made official by, 1660, 1661, 7060
ecclesiology and, 1771
Edict of Milan and, 7723
heresy suppression and, 3927, 7060
missions after, 6082
Christian persecution and, 2580
conversion of, 792, 891, 1688–1689, 1966
and Constantinian Catholicism, 7875
impact on monarchy of Rome, 5167–5168
Council of Nicaea and, 2039, 7279
divination controlled by, 2372
and Donatism, 2416
funeral for, 440
imperial cults and, 7916
Jerusalem under, 4836
Judaism under, conversion to, 4859
and papacy, 6966
political power of, 7279
and priesthood, 7402
and production of Greek Bibles, 891
Sol worship and, 8511
Constantine IX (emperor), *filioque* doctrine and, 8156
Constantine V (Byzantine emperor)
iconoclasm of, 2041
icon veneration forbidden by, 2585
on images, 4290
persecution initiated by, 6619
Constantine VI (Byzantine emperor), on images, 4290
Constantine of Mananalis, 3523
Constantine the Great. *See* Constantine I
Constantinian Catholicism, 7875
Constantinianism, **1967–1968**
Constantinople. *See also* Istanbul
Armenian patriarchate of, 489
capture of, 1664
Constantine I building, 7279
in Crusades, 2075
in early Christian structure, 2581
fall of, 2587
in Fourth Crusade, 2586
Greek Orthodox patriarchate of, 3657–3659
Gregory I in, 3687
Karaites in, 5084
literature of, 5085
Leo I in, 5410
music in, 6309
as "New Rome," 1661, 7280
schism in, 2586, 7877
Constantinople, Council of (381)
on Apollinaris of Laodicea, 424, 6153
Evagrios of Pontus at, 2886
overview of, 2040
and Theodosius, 9124
on Trinity, 9361
Constantinople, Council of (553)
on apocatastasis, 422
Monophysitism at, 6154–6155
overview of, 2040
Sahak Parthev's letter read in, 8026
Severus of Antioch condemned at, 8238
Constantinople, Council of (680–681)
Maximos the Confessor in, 5794
overview of, 2040

Constantinople, Council of, Christology at, 2583
Constantinople, Council of (1869–1870), Photios *vs.* Ignatius and, 2041
Constantinopolitan school, on ethics, 1653
Constantius I Chlorus (Roman emperor), Christian persecution by, 7060
Constantius II (Roman emperor)
 Arianism of, 479, 572
 Athanasius and, 571–572
 on magic, 5333
 against paganism, 7061
Constellations. *See also* Astrology
 catasterism (transfer of humans to the heavens), 8424–8425, 8733
 in ethnoastronomy, 2865
 as heavenly book, 8424
 star organization and, 8732
 in technomorphic cosmologies, 8423
 in Yurupary myth, 9920
Constitution, U.S.
 First Amendment of, 5330
 religious tolerance in, 7283
Constitution of Medina, *ḥaram* in, 3777
Constitution on the Church *(Lumen gentium). See* Dogmatic Constitution on the Church
Constitution on the Church in the Modern World *(Gaudium et spes)*, 9536
 ecumenism in, 2045
Construction sacrifices
 consecration function of, 1504
 supplication in, 8001
Constructive discipline, 8703–8704
Constructivism, on mysticism, 6356–6357
Consualia (festival), 7899
Consultation on Church Union (COCU), 2687
 on baptism, 1778
 formation of, 1769
 ministry in, orders of, 6045
Consultative Assembly of Indonesian Muslims (Masyumi), 4669, 9012
Consumerism, 2674
 commerce of images and, vol. 7 color insert
 and New Age movement, 6498, 6499
Consus (deity), 7899
Contact (Sagan), 4516
Contagious magic, 5571
 healing and, 3811–3812
 relics and, 7686
Contarini, Gasparo, **1968–1969**
Conte del Graal (Chrétien), 3649–3653
Contemplation. *See also* Attention; Meditation; Prayer
 apophatic, 5816
 attention in, 605–606
 in Buddhism, music and, 6282–6283
 cataphatic, 5817
 in Christianity, 5817–5818
 in Daoism, 5821
 definition of, 5816
 etymology of term, 5816
 experience of
  in Christian theology, 2856
  in eternity, 2853, 2854
  in Muslim theology, 2856
 in Hinduism, mysticism and, 6343
 in Judaism, 5817
 vs. meditation, 5816
 in mysticism, 6357
 passive, 7558–7559
 in Quietism, 7558–7559
 reflexive character of, 7649–7650
 in seclusion, objectives of, 528
 Spinoza (Baruch) on, 8684
Contemplative way *(theoretikē)*, 1447–1448
Contextualism
 on mysticism, 6357
 Tafsīr (Qur'anic exegesis) of, 7569
Contextuality, in women's studies in religion, 9791–9792
Contextualization of Christian theology. *See also* Inculturation theology
 in Asia, 1730
Con-Ticsi-Viracocha (deity), 4412, 5292
Continence. *See also* Celibacy; Chastity
 in Christianity, 1452
 spiritual power and, 1475
Contingency. *See also* Pratītya-samutpāda
 in ancient Israel, scientific history and, 8181
 chance and, 1527
 in God, *6961,* 6961–6962, 7124
 quantum theory and, 8188
 radical, in Buddhism, 1527
Continuity of being (Chinese concept), soul and, 8554–8555
Contraception. *See* Birth control
Contracts. *See also* Covenant
 Israelite laws on, 4734–4735
Contradictions, in *Ecclesiastes,* 2600
Contra impugnantes Dei cultum et religionem (Aquinas), 9161
Contributions to the Science of Mythology (Müller), 6235
Contribution to the Critique of Political Economy (Marx), 5746
Contrition. *See* Confession of sins; Penitence; Repentance
Control, religion and, in sociology, 8491–8492
Controller of the Waters, 1643
Controversial (didactic) dialogue, 2342
Conventicle of God's Real Servants, 1006
Convention on the Elimination of All Forms of Discrimination against Women, adoption of, 4181
Convergence models of conversion, 1972–1973
Convergence theory, Ratzel (Friedrich) on, 5259
Conversations with Ogotemmêli (Griaule), 100, 116, 3701
Conversation with N. Motovilov (Serafim of Sarov), personal testimony in, 8229
Conversion, **1969–1974**. *See also* Missions
 adolescence and, 3755
 in African religions, 118
 of Anthony (saint), 6740
 of Augustine, 625, 698, 7192
 in autobiography
  Christian, 698, 699
  Islamic, 700
 Bacon (Roger) on, 735
 to Buddhism, missionary ceremonies for, 6081
 catastrophic millennialism and, 6545
 to Catholicism
  Nestorian, 6480
  of Newman (John Henry), 6510
 to Christianity
  fundamentalist, study of, 3144
  from Judaism, 3186
  missions in, 6084–6085
  of Muslims in Crusades, 1461
 of Constantine, 792, 891, 1688–1689, 1966
 convergence models of, 1972–1973
 in Earth First! road shows, 2563
 exorcism at, 2929
 forced, 1973
  by Charlemagne, 1556
  of Jews (*See* Marranos)
  in missionary activity, 6071
 illustrations of, 1973–1974
 images and, 4391
 to Islam
  in Bengal, 825, 4642
  of Berbers, 834–835
  in Caucasus, 4613
  from Judaism, 2419, 2420
  nonviolent approach to, 6648
  of Parsis, 6997
  personal laws on, 4706, 4708
  profession of faith in, 5062
  in South Asia, 4642
  in Southeast Asia, 4661–4662
  in sub-Saharan Africa, 4601
  Sufism and increase in, 4563
 Islamic law on, 1674
 to Judaism, 4971, 7757, 7823–7824
  baptism of proselytes, 780
  debate over, 3754
  Khazars, 4492
  nudity in, 6740
  postbiblical, 4858
  Reform Judaism, 7666
 of Justin Martyr, 5043
 Leuba (James H.) on, 8785
 meaning of term, 1969
 in Mesoamerica
  colonial, sincerity of, 5919–5920
  economics of, 5929–5930
  as social backlash, 5929–5930
 migration and, 6023
 neuroepistemology on, 6489
 news and, 4963
 in Norway, 6814–6815
 personalistic theories of, 1970
 and relics of saints replacing pagan gods, 2082
 religious/spiritual theories of, 1971–1972
 repentance and, 7756
 Simons (Menno) on, 8401
 social/cultural theories of, 1970–1971
 soteriology and, 8528
 Starbuck (E. D.) on, 8732
 superstition and, 8865
 to theosophy, 7228
 war legitimized by, 9680
 of Waugh (Evelyn), 3170
 to Zoroastrianism, 7000
Conversionist movements, in Africa, 102
Conversion of the Harlot Thaïs, The (Hrotsvit), 4143
Conversion to Islam (Levtzion), 4662
Conversos (converted Jews), 4860, 4996, 5716–5717. *See also* Marranos; Sephardic Judaism
 emigration of, to Brazil, 4503, 4505
 Portuguese Inquisition directed against, 4498, 4501, 4505
 Shabbateanism and, 8260–8261
 Spanish Inquisition directed against, 4498, 4500, 4501, 4502, 4505
Convince ritual, in Caribbean, 1435
Convulsionaries, 2805
Conze, Edward, 1098
Coocoochee (Mohawk prophetess), 9027
Cook, David, 6546
Cook, James
 in Australian Indigenous religions, new movements of, 674
 death of, 1403, 9320

greeted as god/chief, 3797–3798, 9320
Maoris and, 5679
on *tapu,* 8947
Cook, Michael, 4719
Cooke, G. A., 444
Cooking, feminine sacrality and, 3019
Cook Islands Christian Church, split in, 1740
Cook Islands religions. *See also* Oceania and Oceanic religions
cosmology in, 2005
creation myths in, 7313, 7314
Tangaroa in, 8980
Cookworthy, William, Swedenborgianism and, 8901
Cooley, Charles H., on "looking-glass self," 8482
Coolidge, Calvin, Garvey (Marcus) pardoned by, 3287
Coomaraswamy, Ananda, **1974–1976**
aesthetics of, 50
on angels, 344
on art and religion, 499–500
and Burckhardt (Titus), 1324
Guénon (René) and, 3706, 3707
on swords, 967
on temples, 9040
Coonen Cross revolt, Syriac Orthodox Church and, 8939
Cooper, Anna Julia, 80
Cooper, Anthony Ashley, on humor, 4201
Cooper, Eugene, 3484
Cooper, John, 6672
Cooper, John M., on Araucanian religion, 8580
Cooper, Wesley, on James (William), 4776–4777
Cooper-Lewter, Nicholas C., 6977
Coorgs (South India), 4448
Co-origination, dependent. *See Pratītya-samutpāda*
Cop, Nicholas, Calvin (John) and, 1374
Copacabana, Virgin of, spread of images of, 8610
Copacabana Peninsula, 5292
Copán (Honduras)
Stela D monument of, 1358
Temple 22 at, 1359
Copan kingdom (Maya), 5798
Copeland, Kenneth, 7030, 7714
Copeland, M. Shawn, 79
Copernicus, Nicolaus, **1976–1979**
astronomy and, 1976–1978
Bruno (Giordano) on, 367
Galileo Galilei and, 3257, 7136
reactions to theory of, 1978
revolution of, role in scientific history, 8182–8183
Coping theory, 7478
Copper, smelting of, 5987
Coptic Church, **1979–1983**
amulets and talismans in, 300
Arab conquest and Muslim rule, 1981–1982
and catechetical school of Alexandria, 1979
circumcision in, 1798
Coptic Catholic church, 1673
Coptic Orthodox Church, 2585
in Oriental Orthodox family, 1673
drums in, 2495
ecumenical councils and, 1979–1981
Egyptian, 1675
Egyptian influence on, 2716
eremitism in, 2826
Ethiopian Church as, 2859
literature of, *ouroboros* and magic circles in, 1793
missionary endeavors of, 1980
in modern period, 1982
monasticism in, 1980
Monophysitism in, 6155
postures and gestures in, 7343
Severus of Antioch and, 8238
Shenoute as saint in, 8319
Synesius of Cyrene made bishop, 1678
tattooing in, 1002
textiles in, 9091
Timothy Ailuros as patriarch of, 9205
Uniate, 9465
Coptic language. *See also* Nag Hammadi
biblical translations into, 922
dialects of, in Nag Hammadi codices, 6396
Gnostic texts in, 3515
Coptic Museum, 6395
Copway, George, 702, 7224
Coquixee (deity), 5912
Coral Gardens and Their Magic (Malinowski), 3280
Coral Tree. *See Paradise of the Ceiba*
Corbin, Henry, **1983–1984**
Islamic studies of, 4718
on Ismāʿīlīyah, 558, 8335
on religious experience, 7740
Ṭabāṭabāʾī's debates with, 8946
Cordero, Julie, 9229
Córdoba, Pedro de, 4503
Córdoba (Spain), Great Mosque of, 6208
Córdova, Juan de, 5903, 5912
Cordova (Spain), hermits of, 2828
Cordoverian Qabbalah, *sefirot* in, 7536
Cordovero, Mosheh (Moses ben Jacob Cordovero), **1984–1985,** 4914, 7534, 7535, 9378
on mystical union, 6340
on sacred time, 7989
Coriancha (Temple of the Sun), 4384, 4411, 4524
Inca calendar and, 1362, 1363
Corinth (Greece), Paul's missionary journey to, 7015–7016, 7018, 7019
Corinthian church, factions in, 2683
Corinthian columns, 9063, 9064, 9065
1 Corinthians, 912–913, 920
allegorical exegesis of, 872
apostles in, 435
asceticism in, 7722
Canaanite parallels, 1394
charity in, 1554
condemnation of idolatry in, 4359
content of, 912–913, 7015–7016
criticism of, 7013
dating of, 7017
"gospel" in, 3641
hymn to love in, 1550
illness caused by poor ritual in, 3810
as ongoing application, 871
Peter the Apostle in, 7067, 7068
resurrection in, 7766
spiritual gifts in, 1550
2 Corinthians, 912–913, 920
ascension in, 523
content of, 913, 7015–7016
criticism of, 7013
as letter of tears, 7019
on literal exegesis, 870
paradise in, 6984
suffering in, 8807, 8808
Coriolanus, legend of, 3175
Corippus, Flavius Cresconius, 111
Cormac mac Airt (deity), 1491
Corn (maize)
Aztec goddesses of, sacrifice of, 2556
in Maya religion and society, 5796, 5798
in Mesoamerican religions
caves and, 1468, 1470
in Inca worship, 4524
myths of, 5936
Tlaloc and, 9214
in North American Indian religions
Corn Mother narrative, 3017
Corn Woman narrative, 6692
Green Corn Ceremony, 6694
iconography of, 4309
Navajo, 6660
Pueblo, 6726
religious innovation associated with, 6654
Osiris associated with, 6921
Cornaro Chapel (Rome), vol. 11 color insert
Corneille, Thomas, 2474
Cornelius, Janet, 74
Cornell, Rkia Elaroui, 3369
Cornell University
Adler (Felix) at, 33
Turner (Victor) at, 9405
Cornford, Francis
on Greek drama, 2443
on theater, 7050
on World Soul, 6963
Cornides, Daniel, 3111
Cornish, Samuel, 68
Corn Is Our Blood (Sandstrom), 5925
Corn Mother
in Finno-Ugric religions, 3108
in Greek religion (*See* Demeter)
in North American Indian religions, 3017
rainmaking and, 7603
in Slavic religion, 8437
Cornu, Philippe, 9191
Cornucopia, in Celto-Roman art, 1481
Cornutus
on Apollo as sun, 8840
on *hypostasis,* 4240
on Stoic allegory, 4036
Corn Woman, 1564, 6692
Coronado, Francisco Vasquez de, 6729
Coronis, 551
Corporal punishment
of children, 5377
in Jewish law, 3752
Corporate world, United House of Prayer and, 2125
Corporeality of God
and afterlife, views of, 128
in Judaism, 3549
Sa'adyah Gaon on, 7438
Corpses, 2241–2242
absence of, 2241–2242
bending of knees of, in prehistoric burial practices, 5196
exposure of, 2130, 2240, 10001
impurity of
in ancient Israel, 7687
in Hinduism, 7687
in Limba funeral rites, 7806
liminal status of, 2240
in Oceanic religions, 7808
reanimation of, exorcism of, 2929
of saints, 2244
"Corpse worms" (demonic agents), in Chinese medicine, 3862
Corpus Christi, Feast of
establishment of, 2437
Franciscans performing pageant during, 2438

Corpus Christi Church (Aachen, Germany), 796
Corpus Christi festivals
dancing at, 2153
procession at, 7418
Corpus codicum astrologorum graecorum (Cumont), astrology in, 2094
Corpus Cristi, Monastario of (Mexico City), 3412
Corpus Hermeticum. See also Hermetism
Aion in, 208
"as above, so below" in, 3948
commentaries on, 3949, 3950
dating controversy over, 3949
deification in, 2249–2250
divine man in, 3509
gnosis in, 3508, 3515
as gnostic document, 3515, 3519
and the Grail, 3652–3653
Hermetic communities described in, 3942
in Hermetic philosophy, 3939, 3940–3941, 3942
magic in, 5579
mystery religions in, 6332
in Nag Hammadi codices, 6397
occultist texts on, 3951–3952
philosophy, influence on, 3953–3954
Platonism influencing, 7190
prayers in, 3939–3940
in Renaissance, 3945
repentance in, 7756
theosophy and, 3952
translations of, 3949
in Dutch, 3954
in English, 3949, 3952
in French, 3952
in German, 3947, 3950–3952
in Latin, 5579
transmigration in, 9329
treatises of, 3944
Corpus juris civilis (Justinian I), 5042, 5333, 5358–5359
Correggio, Giovanni da, Hermetism and, 3946
Correlative cosmology, 4332
Correspondence, systems of
in Chinese *Yinyang wuxing* philosophy, 3861
in Confucianism, 2632
divination of illness and, 3810–3811
in esotericism, Faivre paradigm of, 2844
in Japanese religion, *kampō* healing system and, 3868
in metaphysical movements, healing and, 3849, 3850
Swedenborg (Emanuel) on, 8899, 8900
Corrigan, Michael A., 3479
Corruption, of human nature, in Judeo-Christian tradition, 8404
Corsair, Kierkegaard's criticism of, 5140–5141
Corso parades, in Carnival, 1442
Cortés, Hernando, in Mesoamerica, 1695
Moctezuma II and, 5174
Moctezuma's meeting with, 5914
priests traveling with, 5914, 5915
and Totonac religion, 5910
Cortius Rufus, Quintus, on Saka religion, 7384
Corvinus, Matthias (king), humanism and, 4226
Coryllus (Dacian king), 3466
Cosmas and Damian (twin saints), spirits in Caribbean religions identified with, 1433, 1434
Cosmic ages, 176–177
Cosmic background radiation, Big Bang and, 2032–2033
Cosmic buddhas. *See* Buddhas, cosmic
Cosmic center. *See* Center of the world
Cosmic consciousness, 7475
Cosmic Consciousness (Bucke), 7475
Cosmic deities, 3618–3620
Aion as, 208–209
Cosmic (procosmic) dualism, 2508–2509, 2509–2510, 2512
Cosmic eggs
in African myths, 98–99, 100, 325
Dogon creation myth, 1987, 1988
chaos and, 1538
in Chinese alchemy, 239
creation from, 1987
in Greek and Hellenistic religions, 3903
independent origination of myths on, 1994
in Hinduism (*brahmāṇḍa,* "egg of Brahmā"), *bhakti and,* 3999–4000
moon created from, 6173
ocean and, 6805–6806
in rural Indian myths, 4433
water and, 9699
"Cosmic epochs" hypothesis, 9281
Cosmic eschatology, 2834
Cosmic isotropy, inflation of the universe and, 2033–2034
Cosmic man
archaic mentality of, 2282–2283
classes born of, 9522
sacrifice of, 2283–2284
Cosmic mountains, 6212–6213
Cosmic religion, peasant cultures and, 2753–2754
Cosmic religious orientation, Eliade on, 1821
Cosmic seeds
Basilides on, 7190
Plato on, 7190
Cosmic tree. *See* Trees, cosmic
Cosmic waters, 9700–9701
Cosmides, Leda, on evolutionary psychology, 8475
Cosmogenesis, 9033
Cosmogony. *See also* Creation and cosmogonic myths; *specific religious traditions*
African, 139–140
in afterlife, beliefs about, 133–134, 139–140
ancestors in, 325–326
archetypes in, 458
Aztec, 716–717, 5907
Blackfoot, 958–959
eschatology tied to, 6362
Manichaean, 5653–5654, 5666–5667
Melanesian, 5842–5843
significance of, 6361–6362
Cosmograms
cities as ceremonial centers, 1805
as space-related time system, 1356
Cosmographia (Münster), 768
Cosmology, **1991–2034**. *See also* Astronomy; Metaphysics
African, **1998–2002,** 3065
of Bantu-speaking peoples, 2960, 8664–8665
Deity in, 2566–2567
gender in, 3401
history of study of, 118
Khoi, 5135
Kongo, 2001–2002, 5221–5222
Maasai, 2000–2001
Swazi, 8895
Yoruba, 1998–2000
ages of world in, periodization systems for, 173–177
Amazonian
Baniwa, 8624–8625
Juruna, 8628–8629
Kulina, 2012
Maku, 8625
Palikur, 8628
transformation theme in, 2011–2012
Tukanoan, 8622
Yanomami, 8625
Andean, modern, 8618–8619
of Aristotle, 480–481
Australian Indigenous, **2002–2004,** 5051
Yanyuwa, 6260
Aztec, 5173
Babylonian, 2811
in *Enuma elish,* 2809, 2811
Baltic, Saule (sun) worship and, 8132
Berger (Peter L.) on consciousness and, 8468
Buddhist, **2026–2031** (*See also* Pure and Impure Lands)
Chinese Buddhism, 1161, 1162
Daoism and, 1595
Dhammakāya movement, 2325
early, 1077
Hīnayāna Buddhism, 1092, 2027–2030
in Huayan school, 4147
Mahāyāna Buddhism, 1077, 1078, 1092, 1117, 2030
moral issues in, 2628
single-world system in, 2026–2027
in temple architecture, 7983
Theravāda Buddhism, 1134
Triple World *(trailokya),* 1350
calendar and, 1353
Cārvāka, 1446
Celtic, 1487
center, ceremonial, and, 1804–1805
center of the world, **1501–1505**
children's games and, 1503
Chinese, 1624–1628, 2178 (*See also* Yinyang Wuxing philosophy)
of Cheng Hao, 1560–1561
of Cheng Yi, 1562–1563
Confucian rituals and, 1902, 1908
court attire symbolism and, 1830
Daoist vestments, symbols on, 1828–1829
imperial cult sacrifices and, 1911–1912
in martial arts, 5735–5736
Shangdi in, 8300
shared in common, 1618
in Song dynasty, 1578
Yiching and, 1583
Christian
Aristotelian, 1978
in Christian Science, 1745–1746
pre-Copernican, 1976–1977
of Swedenborg (Emanuel), 8898
Chuvash, 1785
classification of, 7846
common characteristics, 1994–1995
correlative, 4332, 9887–9888
correspondence systems and, 3810–3811
Cosmic Clockmaker and chaos theory, 1541
cross-cultural variation in, 7846
cultural themes and classification of, 1993–1994
Cuna (Panama), 2096
Daoist, 2177, 2178, 9843
environment and, 2635–2636
in *Zhuangzi,* 9970
defined, 1991
diversity of, 2605
of Dong, 1591

ecology and, 2605
rethinking, 2610
Egyptian, sky in, 8426
Enawenê Nawê, 2012–2013
environmental ethics and, 2604
Evenk, shaman's tent configured on, 2619
Finnish (Finno-Ugrian), 3104, 3109
in games, 3260
Ge, 3293
gender blurring in, 4115–4116
geographic classification of, 1992–1993
geometry in, 2879
Germanic, 3447–3448
in Gran Chaco
Angaité, 8634
Toba, 8636
Greek, circle symbolism in, 1791
heaven and hell and, 8530
Hebrew, circles in, 1793
hierophanies (sacred manifestations) and, 3971
Hindu, **2014–2022,** 7195–7196, 7500
bhakti synthesis and, 3999–4001
epic, 2016–2017
in *haituka* schools of philosophy, 3997
in Sāṃkhya school, 3997, 3998, 8089–8090
Purāṇic, 2017–2019
science and, 2019–2020
in sectarian movements, 4004
Śiva in, 8415
in South India, 2019
and time, conception of, 4015
time in, 3999
in tribal communities, 2019
Upaniṣadic, 2015–2016
Vedic, 2014–2015
water in, 9699
Hittite, 4073
Iatmul, 7195, 7196
Inca, 4410–4411
Indian, of Ājīvikas sect, 213
of indigenous cultures, cultural absorption and, 2617
Indochinese, 2960
Indo-European, 4454, 4464
Iranian, 4536
Iroquois, 4541
Islamic
falsafah concepts, 2973, 2974
in Ismāʿīlīyah, 8326
in *Rasāʾil Ikhwān al-Ṣafāʾ*, 4376
Qarāmiṭah, 8328
underworld in, 9455
Jain, 579, **2022–2026,** 2625
early development of, 2022
ethical system from, 2624
liberation and, 8548
Lower World in, 2024
Middle World in, 2023–2024
realm of the liberated in, 2025
structure of the *loka* (universe) in, 2023
Upper World in, 2024–2025
Japanese, 4781
Confucian, 1927
Jewish, 2641–2642
Abravanel (Isaac) on, 18
firmament, in Hebrew scriptures, 8426
Gersonides on, 3462–3463, 4895–4896
in Habad Hasidism, 3792
Khanty, 5119–5121
knot symbolism of, 5197–5198
Kulina cosmography, 2012
Mansi, 5119–5121
Melanesian, 5843
mesa divination and, 3810
Mesoamerican, **2008–2010,** 5923–5924
in Aztec religion, 716–717, 5907
city structure and, 1804–1805
commonalities in, 148
in Maya religion, 5796–5797
Micronesian, 6002–6004
mountains in, 1501–1502, 6212–6213
Muisca, 6229–6230
mythic themes and
abandoned child motif and beginnings, 1568
divine male fashioner motif, 1993
generating earth motif, 1993
independent origins *vs.* diffusion of, 1994
world parents motif, 1993–1994
Negrito
Andamanese, 6456
Semang, 6456–6457
Neolithic, 6464
New Guinea, 6503, 6507
North American Indian, **2008–2010**
Anishinaabe, 368
Apache, 10069
cave myth, 1469
circle symbolism in, 1794
iconography of, 4307
Navajo, 6441–6442, 6443
Nez Perce, 6595
of Northeast Woodlands, 6680–6682
Pueblo, 6722–6723
of Southeast Woodlands, 6691–6692
Zuni, 6660
Oceanic, **2004–2007,** 6788–6789
Olmec, 6818–6819
Osage, 6917–6918, 6919
overview, **1991–1998**
Paleolithic, 1470
play and, 7194–7196
Polynesian, 7305–7306
in proofs for existence of God, 7422, 9103–9105
Ptolomaic astronomy and, 1976
in sacred space, 7981–7982, 7983
Śaivist, in Kashmir Saíva school, 4006
Sami, 8088
science and, 1991, 1995–1996, **2031–2034**
anthropic principle in, 2033
Big Bang theory and, 2032–2033, 8184, 8189
cosmic destiny and, 2034
in Hinduism, 2019–2020
inflation of the universe in, 2033–2034
relativity theory and, 2031–2032
science and religion, questions raised in, 8189
scientific imperialism and, 8185
steady-state cosmology, 2020
scientific, religion and, 2660
in Scythian religion, 8205
serpents in, 8458
Shintō, 2639
Siberian, 2999, 6754, 8283–8284
sky, technomorphic representations of, 8423–8424
South American Indian, **2010–2014,** 8587–8588
Southeast Asian
in insular traditional religion, 8648–8649
prehistoric, 8642–8643
Spencer (Herbert) on, 8679
structuralist view of, 8752
in Tehuelche religion, 9029
Tibetan, pre-Buddhist, 9183
Tlaxcalan, 9215
Toraja, 9241
transcendental, Kant (Immanuel) on, 5077
transformation theme in, 2011–2013
tree of life in, 9577
Tunguz, 9394
Turkic, 9398–9399
violent universe theme in, 2013
Warao, 9688
Warlpiri, 9693
of Whitehead (Alfred North), 9727–9728
worldview and, 1992
Yakut, 9865
Cosmopolitanism. *See also* Universalism
in Hellenism and Stoicism, 3906–3907
linguistic, 4098
universalism *vs.*, 4067
Cosmos
center of, as sacred place, 6885–6886
chaos and, 1537
dualistic images of, economics in, 2671–2672
Etruscan model of, 2873
expansion of, 2740
Hellenistic model of, in Islam, 2652
human body as model of, 7837
mystical union with, 6342
wisdom as insight to, 9748–9749, 9749
Cosmos and History (Eliade), 458
Cossack uprising, in Ukraine, 5016
Cost of Discipleship, The (Bonhoeffer), 1017
Costumbre (custom), in Mesoamerican religions, 5924–5925
Costume. *See* Clothing; Masks
Cosus (deity), 4253
Cotaa (deity), 9335
Cotton, John, 2288
Congregationalism and, 1938
Hutchinson (Anne) and, 4238
Cottonwood trees, in Sun Dance, 8845–8846
Cotys (deity), 9170
Coualina (spirit), in Island Carib religion, 1428
Coues, Elliot, Blavatsky (Helena Petrovna) libeled by, 5024
Coughenour, John C., 2292
Coulianu, Ioan, 2509
Council of Four (governing body), in Aztec Mexico, 5172
Council of Liberal Churches. *See* Unitarian Universalist Association
Council of the Churches of the Middle East (CCME), 1673
Council of the International African Institute (CIAI), 2350
Council of Torah Sages. *See* Moʿetset Gedolei ha-Torah
Councils, **2034–2046**. *See also specific locations*
Buddhist (*See* Buddhist councils)

Councils *continued*
Christian, **2039–2046** (*See also specific locations*)
Alexandria and the Coptic Church in, 1979–1980
Christology in, 1666
Cyril and, 2114–2115
in early church, 2039
early ecumenical councils, 2039–2041
and Eastern churches, structure of, 1765, 1773
ecumenical status of, 2057
European influence in, 1688
heresy, tool against, 3927
Latin American Council of Bishops (CELAM), 1703–1704
medieval councils, 2041–2043
modern, 2044–2045
provincial, in Latin America, 1695–1696
in Reformation period, 2043–2044
reform movements and, 1691
schism and, 8155
Counseling
pastoral, 939, 7477, 7479, 7486–7487
in Scientology, 8192, 8193
Counsels, wisdom in, 9749
Countercult movement, 6551, 6561
Counterculture movement (1960s), neoshamanism and, 8294
Counterhegemony, definition of, 2088
Counterincantation, 4408
Counterpossession, 2934
Counter-Reformation (Catholic Reformation), 7663–7664, 7877–7878. *See also* Trent, Council of
Bellarmino's (Roberto) positive theology of, 816
Borromeo (Carlo) in, 1023
Capuchins during, 3183
church architecture of, 794–795
Copernicus and, 1978
drama in, 2474
in Hungary, 4226
iconography used in, 4346
Jesuits in, 4842
Mass during, 795
Orthodox Church involvement in, 2587
poetry in, 7219–7220
as Roman Catholic Reformation, 1663, 1692
skepticism and, 8421
Talmud manuscripts burned in, 8971
Couplet, Philippe, Hermetism and, 3950
Courage to Be, The (Tillich), 7477
Courlander, Harold, 10025
Cours de philosophie positive (Comte), 1882, 7339
Course in Miracles, A (Shucman), 6531
Court attire in South and East Asia, 1830
Court cairns, 5823
Courtenay, William, 9848–9849
Courthouse, architecture of, 5360
Court Jews, 5017
Court scholarship under Charlemagne, 1556–1557
Courtship, in Greek novels, 3055–3056
Court tombs, 5823
Cousins, Ewart, on spirituality, 8719
Cousins, Norman, on cosmic healing energies, 3851
Couturier, M. A., 4348
Couturier, Paul, 2686
Couvade, 950, **2046–2047**
Island Carib rite, 1430
Couvreur, Séraphin, 1633
Covelluzzo, Giovanni di, on cards, 1413–1414
Covenantal Man, Soloveitchik (Joseph Baer) on, 8519
Covenant and covenant theology, **2047–2051**. *See also* Vows and oaths
Assyrian, 2047
through blood, 987
in Christianity, 2049–2050
American civil religion and, 1813
collective identity and, 8464
elect status from, 2746, 2748
good conscience and, 1942
Justin Martyr on, 5044
Pilgrims and Puritans, and social reform, 1750–1751
rainbow symbolism in, 7604
Westminster Confession and, 2044
curse formulae in, 2102–2104
in Islam, primordial covenant, in Sufism, 8810
in Israelite religion, 4745–4746
in Judaism, 2047–2049, 4971–4972
Abraham's, 15, 2048
b'rît notion, 2047
contemporary, 4986
covenant theology, 2047–2048
curses and, 2102–2103
elect status from, 2744–2745
Greenberg (Irving) on Holocaust and new covenantal age, 4092–4093
historiography and, 4027
in Hosea, 4137
Jeremiah and, 4828–4831
of Joshua and Jeremiah, 2048–2049
law and, 5357–5358
monotheism in, 3540
Moses', 3540
in rabbinic period, 2050
redemption through, 4856–4857
renewal of, 4831
sacred national community of Jews and, 7717
and sacrilege, view of, 8012
and sin, theology of, 8403–8404
social impact of, 8463–8464
Teitelbaum (Yo'el) on Zionism as breaking of, 4091
as vassalage, 4830–4831
Covenant of the Goddess, 6473
Covenant of 'Umar, 9444
Cover, Robert, 5328
on law and literature, 5357
Covering Islam (Said), Arab-Western relations in, 8032
Cow. *See* Cattle and cows
Cow and the Fisherman, in Hittite religion, 4070
Coward, Noël, on Balinese rituals, 747
Cowart, Donald "Dax," 5810
Cowdery, Oliver, 6193
Cowgill, George L., 5899
Cowley, Joy, 3085
Cowley Fathers. *See* Society of Saint John the Evangelist
Cowrie shells
in Candomblé, 122
as money, 6137
symbolism of, 6137
as *yoni,* 9909
Cows. *See* Cattle and cows
Cox, George W., 4459
Cox, Patricia, 947
Coyolxauhqui (deity)
Huitzilopochtli and, 4188
in Templo Mayor, 5892
Coyote, 4308
in Apache religion, 405
in California religions, 6713
in Chumash religion, 6661
as creator, 9355
death introduced by, 9418
helpers of, 9355
in Karuk religion, 6661–6662
moon and, 6174
in poems, 7225, 7226
in Pueblo religion, 6722
tobacco given by, 9218
tree bark used by, 9336
wives of, 9355
in Yokuts religion, 6661
"Coyotes' Desert Lament" (TallMountain), 7226
CPE. *See* Clinical pastoral education
Cracow (Poland), Talmudic academy of, 5014
Craftmen
Minerva as deity of, 6043
time and, 1760
Cragg, Kenneth, 9118
Craho religion (Brazil), origin of agriculture in, 8590
Cramer, Malinda, 6584, 6585
Cranach, Lucas, the Elder, 4346, 7459
Cranach, Lucas, the Younger, vol. 14 color insert
Cranko, John, 2163
Cranmer, George, Hooker (Richard) and, 4123, 4124
Cranmer, Thomas, **2051–2052,** 7281
introduction to *Book of Common Prayer,* 7662
marriage of, 7662
Crashaw, Richard, 7220
Crater Hermetis (Lazzarelli), Hermetic-Christian syncretism in, 3946
Cratylus (Plato), 6957
Craven, Wes, 10023
Crawford, James R., 9779
Crawford, O. G. S., 5824
Crawford, S. Cromwell, 5810
Crawley, A. E.
on magic, 5564
revaluation of, 380
Crawley, Ernest
on cursing, 2098
on sacred and profane dress, 1831
"Creation, According to Coyote, The" (Ortiz), 7225
Creation and cosmogonic myths, **1985–1991**. *See also* Anthropogony; Cosmogony; Cosmology; *specific religious traditions*
of Adam, 29–30
in African religions, 85–86, 92–93, 3019
and afterlife, 139–140
Akan, 214, 3570
binary oppositions in, 96–99
death in, 85–86, 92–93
deus otiosus in, 2309–2310
Dinka, 3573
Dogon, 97, 100, 325, 2390–2391, 3569–3570, 4301
East African, 2567
Edo, 2697, 3572
Fon, 3166
gender in, 3401
human condition in, 84, 85–86, 92
Igbo, 3572
Luba, 5524
Lubgbara, 5526
Mende, 3570–3571
northeast Bantu, 2574–2575
Nuer, 5445
personal encounters with God in, 92, 100
supreme beings in, 214, 3567–3568, 3569, 8869

Venda python myth, 8663
West, 9717–9718
women in, 85
Yoruba, 3571
ages of world in, 174–177
Akkadian, Enki in, 2792
in Amazonian religions
Baniwa, 8624
Ge-Timbira, 8629
Makiritare, 8626
Palikur, 8627–8628
Tukanoan, 8622
ancestors in, 325–326
androgyny in, 2555
archetypes in, 458
Aristotle on, 480–481
ashes in, 540
Assyrian, chant-remedy and, 3811
in Australian religions, 2986
language in, 5302
Rainbow Snake in, 7606
supreme beings in, 8869
in Aztec religion
cycles of creation and destruction, 1357–1358
human sacrifice and, 4187
in Babylonian myth, 2810, 5146, 6806 (*See also* Enuma elish)
in Baltic religion, 758
in Bambara religion, 776
in Batak religion, 799
biblical stories of, 2967
androcentrism of, 334
Big Bang as, 2032
birds in, 948
in Blackfoot religion, 960–961
in Bugis religion, 1316–1317
Caribbean origin myths, 1428–1429
on Hispaniola, 1468
in Catharism, Satan as creator, 1456
center rituals and, 1504
chaos and, 1537–1538, 1986–1987
androgynes and, 337–338
in Chinese novels, 3068
in Chinese tradition, 1624–1625, 1626
in myths, 1624, 1628
qi in, 8554
in Christianity, 5445–5446
binary system proving, 6751–6752
Bonaventure on, 1012
compared to other creation myths, 876
Enuma elish compared to, 2811
evolution and, 1665
of gender, 3358
God's love for, 2606–2607
and history, view of, 4052, 4053
in image and likeness of God, 1652
language in, 5302
literal interpretation of, 2910
local and universal in, 2606
on natural world, 2648
in Roman Catholicism, 7883
Schleiermacher on, 8165–8166
in Sistine Chapel, 8755
in winter solstice songs, 9743
through consecration of sacred space, 1504
cosmic egg and, 1987
cosmic trees in, 9336
creatio continua, in Chinese myth, 1628
culture heroes and, 2090
as source of sickness, 3809
and cure, origins of, 3811
Daoist, in *Dao de jing,* 2636
death as repetition of, 4159–4160
decapitation in, 3804–3805
dei otiosus in, 757, 2309–2310, 2311, 2312
dismemberment as repetition of, 2366, 2367
dogs in, 2394
dragons in, 2431, 2441–2442
dualism in, 2505
earth divers in (*See* Earth diver myths)
earth in, 2555–2557, 3015
earth mother deities in, 1993
egg as symbol of, 2701–2702, 2702
in Egyptian religion, 2710, 2720, 2961
lotus and, 5518
sexuality in, 8239
spitting in, 8721
emergence in, 1988, 2556–2557
Eriugena's theology of, 2830–2831
in eternity, 2853
ethics and, 1989–1990
in Etruscan religion, 2874–2875
evil and, 8403
ex nihilo or *de novo* (from nothing), 1986
in Islam, 2063
in Finno-Ugric religions, 3108–3109
Kalevala epic, 3016
floods associated with, 2960, 3130–3131
fountains in, 3177
as fundamental myths, 6363
as genealogy, 9698
genetics and, 3429–3430
in Germanic religion, 1451, 3446–3447, 3454–3455
in Gnosticism, 5202
sexuality and, 8239
God in
hands, use of, 3769
power of, 1986
and Satan in earth diver myths, 1988
as good, 1344, 3636
in Greek religion, 1450
Eros in, 2832
Okeanos in, 6805
purification and, 1460
in Hermetism, 3944
hierogamy in, 2555–2556
in Hinduism, 3016, 4439–4440, 5447, 7254
bhakti synthesis and, 3999–4000
Brahmā's role in, 1023–1024
corporate symbolism in, 4161
humor of, 6364
language in, 5302
in *Laws of Manu,* 5328
Prajāpati and, 1023, 5302, 5447, 5518, 7640
Rudra in, 8414
rural myths, 4433
Viṣṇu and, 5518
yantras and, 9871
Hittite myth of, 1450–1451
human responsibility for, 2654
humans as part of cosmos in, 5443–5444
in Inca religion, 5292
in Indo-European religions, 4439–4440, 4453, 4454
in Raëlian religion, 7597
insects in, 4507, 4508
in Shintō, 4754, 4799
in Iranian religion, 4536
kings and, 5165
in Islam, 2968–2969, 5446
vs. Creator, 2652
falsafah ideas on, 2972
garden in, 3282
God in, 4563–4564
hands of God in, 3769
Ḥasan al-Baṣrī on, 8810
Ibn al-ʿArabī on, 8819, 8820
in Ashʿarīyah, 532, 537
in Ḥanafī creed, 2063
in Ismāʿīlīyah, 8326
in *kalām,* 5060
natural law and harmony in, 3831
nūr Muḥammad in, 6766–6767
in Japanese religion, 4801–4802
Amaterasu as sun goddess in, 8841
Hirata Atsutane on, 4022
sacred space and, 7978–7979
in Judaism, 5445 (*See also* Qabbalah)
Crescas on, 4897
Delmedigo on, 4898
Gersonides on, 4895–4896
God's role in, 3549
in Habad Hasidism, 3792
Ibn Rushd on, 4895
in image of God, consciousness of sin and, 8403
Mainmonides on, 4893–4894
Philo Judaeus on, 7107
Saʿadyah Gaon on, 4888
and sacrilege, views of, 8012
sin and guilt and, 8403
Torah in, 7584
wisdom and, 9756
in Khoi religion, 5135
knot symbolism in, 5198
in Komi religion, 5217
in Korean religion, 5229–5230
language in, 5302, 6363
light and darkness in, 5450–5454
Logos in, 5504–5505
in Lutheran theology, ethics and, 1655
macrocosm-microcosm in, 4159
in Mandaean religion, in *Ginza,* 3494, 3495
in Manichaeism, 5653–5654, 5666–5667
in Maori religion, 1450, 5683
in Mari and Mordvin religion, 5710
marriage in, 5727
masculine sacrality in, 5759
in Melanesian religions, 5842–5843
in Mesoamerican religions, 1468, 5934–5935
in Aztec religion, 716–717, 5907
in Cuna religion, 2095
Inti in (Inca), 4524
in Maya religion, 5797, 5934, 5935
in Mixtec religion, 5911
Quetzalcoatl in, 7557
in Mesopotamian religions (*See Enuma elish*)
in Micronesian religions, 6004, 6009–6010
moon in, 6173–6174
motive for, Duns Scotus (John) on, 2524
music in, 6252
nature absent from, 2649
in New Age teachings, Summit Lighthouse, 1782

Creation and cosmogonic myths ***continued***
in New Caledonia religion, 6501
in new religious movements, 6530–6531
in North American Indian religions, 2984, 3015, 3016, 6659–6661
Algonquin, 7590
Apache, 404, 405
California, 6713
Cherokee, 6692
Chumash, 6661
Delaware, 6681
earth diver in, 6653, 6660, 6661, 6692, 6713
gambling in, 3260
games in, 3266
gender in, 3407
Haida, 3735
Hopi, 1469, 6660
imitation in annual rites, 6653
Lakota, 5296, 6662
Menomini, 6680
Mother Earth in, 2984, 3015
Mvskoke, 6692
Navajo, 1450, 3015, 6441–6442, 6659–6660, 8426
Nez Perce, 6595
of Northwest Coast, 6709
Oglala, 3015
Ojibwa, 6660–6661
Plains peoples, 6703–6704
Pueblo, 1469, 3015, 6660, 6722
Seminole, 6692
Seneca, 6680
supreme beings in, 8869
tricksters in, 6651
water in, 3016
Zuni, 1469, 2555–2557, 3015, 6660
nothing, creation from, 1987
Aristotle and, 8182
in Oceanic religions, 6786, 6788
supreme beings in, 8869
ocean in, 6805–6807
Orphic, 6894–6895
Pāñcarātra, 9507–9508
parthenogenesis in, 2555
in Phoenician religion, 7131
in Polynesian religions, 7305–7306, 7312–7314
power of, 7350
primordial parents in, 1450–1451, 1987–1988
in Romanian myth, hedgehogs, assistance of, 3892, 4508
sacred space in, 7983
sacrifice in, 2556
in San religion, 5135
in Scientology, 8193
in Selk'nam religion, 8224
serpents in, 8456–8457
sexuality in, 8239
sexual symbolism in
androgyny in, 1987
castration theme in, 1450–1451
cosmic egg and, 1987
in Siberian mythology, 3016
and sickness, origins of, 3808–3809
sky in, 8428
in South American Indian religions
Inca, 5633
as mythic struggle, 2013
overview of, 8586–8587
Pachacámac and, 8600
self-transformation theme in, 2011–2012
supreme beings in, 8869, 8870
upper Xingu myths, 2011
in Southeast Asian religions
animism and, 8649
complementary duality in, 8648–8649
spitting in, 8721–8722
in Sumerian religion, 5964
Enki in, 2791
language in, 5302
sun in, 8835
supreme beings, cosmogonic power of, 8867, 8869–8870, 8872
swan dive in, 8894
in Tehuelche religion, 9030
in Tunguz religion, 9394
Turkic, 9441
types of myths on, 1986–1989
in Vedism, 9559–9560
solar deities in, 3990
violence in, 9597–9598
Warao, 9687–9688
water in, 3016, 9697–9700
wisdom in, Gnosticism and, 9760
words, creative power in, 8200
work in, 9797
in Zoroastrianism
multiple versions of, 5561
origins of, 4536
Creation and Fall (Bonhoeffer), 9071
Creationism. *See also* Intelligent Design
Big Bang and, 2032
vs. evolution, **2907–2913**
fundamentalism and, 8185
intelligent design compatible with, 4516, 4517–4518
religious intention overlooked in, 1995
Roman Catholic, bioethics and, 8190
science in, 2910–2911
scientific creationism, 8185, 8189
soul theory of, 8563
in Turkish Islam, 8186
young earth creationists in, 8189
Creation of Adam (Michelangelo), 30
Creative altruism, Sorokin (Pitirim Aleksandrovich) on, 8524
Creativity
and female body, in art, 4170
historical, 1047
interactive discipline and, 8701–8702
myth and, 8471
neoshamanism and, 8296
Nishida Kitarō's emphasis on, 6637
and play, 7194
in Sayers (Dorothy), trinitarian theology of, 8142
Whitehead (Alfred North) on, 49
of women, 10039
Creator deities
in central Bantu religion, 1507
chaos theory and, 1543
in Chinese religion, 1600
Laozi, 1593
Cosmic Clockmaker as, 1541
destruction by, disease and, 3808–3809
as *deus otiosus* (god withdrawn), 1993
in Inca religion, 9600–9601
in Oceanic religions, 2006
as sky deities, 1986
in South American Indian religions, 8576
in West African religions, 9717–9718
Crech ríg (royal foray), 1493
Creeds, **2052–2065**. *See also* Confessions of faith
authority, sources of, 2053
in Christianity, **2054–2062** (*See also specific creeds*)
anticreedalism, 2055–2056, 2060–2061
authority of, 2055–2056
defined, 2054
ecclesiology and, 1771
ecumenical creeds and councils, 2056–2057
heresy, tool against, 3927
and history, view of, 4053
modern, 2060–2061
in Protestantism, 7452
in Reformation, 2054, 2057–2060
as stabilizing force, 1661
types of, 2054–2055
definitions of, 2052, 2053, 2054
functions of, 2053
in Islam, **2062–2065** (*See also* 'Aqidah/'aqā'id)
Al-bāb al-ḥādī ʿashar (al-Ḥillī), 3982
attributes of God in, 617
authority of, 2053
development of, 2062–2063
Ḥanābilah and, 3761
Shīʿī, 2064–2065
Sunni, 2062–2064
Tajrīd al-Iʿtiqād, al-Ḥillī, commentary by, 3982
overview, **2052–2054**
Smith (W. Robertson) on, 8452
Creek Confederacy, 6665, 6689
Creek religion and society (North America), 6655–6656. *See also* Muskogee tribe
maternal clan system of, 6655
poetry of, 7224
in Red Stick War, 6666, 6667
relations with other Native nations, 6665
Snake movement of, 6666, 6667
Creel, H. G., 946
Creel, Margaret Washington, 76, 10037
Cree religion (North America), 6674
bears in, 809
funerary rites in, 6697
study of, 6671
woman's curse, story of, 2100
Creidhne the Metalworker (deity), 1485
Cremation, 9228. *See also* Funeral rites
in African religions, 141
in Balinese religion, 748, 3239, 3240, 9226
in Caribbean religions, 1428
in Germanic religion, 168
in Hinduism, 7687, 7815, 9821
in Iberian religion, 4251
in Indian religion, 3240
in Judaism, 7823
in Mesoamerican religions, 3242, 3244
in Phoenician religion, 7132
in Roman religions, 166, 7895, 9226–9227
in Sikhism, 8397
in Thai religion, 3240
in Thracian religion, 9170
in Vedism, 9566
Cremation grounds, in *maṇḍalas*, 5643
Creole language, in Vodou, 9634
Creoles
definition of, 66, 9297
in Latin America, 1698
in Surinam, 126
religion of (*See* Winti religion)
Creolization, **2065–2068**
and African American religions, 66
definition of, 66, 9297
in diaspora, 2068
of language, 2065
of religion, 2065–2066
as religious acculturation, 2066–2067
in Surinam, 126
Crescas, Ḥasdai, **2069–2070**
Abravanel (Isaac) opposing, 18

on afterlife, 154
Albo (Yosef) and, 233, 234, 866
Aristotelianism critiqued by, 481
on God
attributes of, 614
knowledge of, 3549
in Jewish thought and philosophy, 4896–4897
on prophecy, 7440
soul, theory of, 8560
on Torah, 9237
Crescens, 5043–5044
Crescent, 4350–4351
as symbol of Nanna, 6415
Crescive societies, martyrdom in, 5739–5740
Cressman, Luther, 5804
Cresson, Hilborne T., 6266
Cretans, The (Euripides), 6823
Crete and Cretan religions, 37–43. *See also* Minoan religion
baptism in, 780
kingship in, 5165–5166
Lady of the Animals in, 5280, 5282
lion symbolism in, 5464
national epic of, 3053–3054
ritual homosexuality in, 4112
temples in, 9062, 9063
Zeus in, 3664, 9953–9954
Creuzer, Georg Friedrich, **2070**
Bachofen (J. J.) inspired by, 731
on comparative method, 4458
on myth, 6367
symbol theory and, 8909
Cribbage, gambling on, 3260
Cricket, in North American Indian mythology, 6661
Crime. *See also* Law(s); *specific crimes*
Christian Identity movement and, 1659
in hero myths, 3958
Girard (René) on, 3960
punishment for (*See* Punishment; Retribution; Revenge)
Crimea, Karaite sect in, 5084
Criminal law
Christian, witch hunts and, 8013–8014
definition of, 4737
in Israelite religion (*See* Israelite law, criminal law)
Jewish, 3752–3753
Crisis
in millenarianism, 6033
rituals of, in Marathi religions, 5698–5699
as stage in conversion, 1972
Crisis cults
eschatology and, 2835
in Kongo society, 5220
in Mexico, 2139
Criterion group, Eliade in, 2754, 2758
Critias, atheism and, 582
Critical Buddhism, 1250, 1277, 2386, 9950
"Critical Buddhism and Returning to the Sources" (Lusthaus), 1250
Critical Examination of the Life and Teachings of Mohammad (Ameer Ali), 288–289
"Critical phrase" *(huatou)* contemplation, 1524
Critical Terms for Religious Studies (Taylor), 3297
Critical theory
law and religion and, **5358–5361**
popular culture criticism in, 7321
Criticism. *See also* Literary criticism
of religion
anthropomorphism and, 389–390
meaning of, 389–390
Schleiermacher (Friedrich) on, 8164
Criticism of Dogmatic Theology, A (Tolstoy), 9220
Critique of Judgment, The (Kant), 46
hope in, 7109
transition between worlds of phenomena and noumena in, 5080
Critique of Practical Reason (Kant), 46, 583
morality in, 5077–5078
question of ethics in, 7109
Critique of Pure Reason (Kant), 46, 583, 4517
empiricism *vs.* rationalism in, 5076–5077
existence of God in, 7422
question of knowledge in, 7109
and theological liberalism, 6102
transcendental dialectic in, 5077
Croatia
Christianity in, history of, 1683–1684, 1686
museums in, 6245
Croce, Benedetto, 2266, 7073
on knowledge, 5207
Croce, Ricoldo da Monte, 7243
Crocker, William, 5985
Crocodiles
in Australian Indigenous myths, 654
in Bantu rites of passage, 8667
Croesus (king of Lydia), 508
Croll, Oswald, 6434
Cromer, Lord, 6096
Cromwell, Oliver, Fox (George) and, 3180, 3181
Crone, Patricia, 4719, 5801
Cronenberg, David, 3099
Croning rituals (Neopagan rites), 7830
Cronyn, George W., 7224
Crosby, Fanny, 6313
Cross
anchor as form of, 332
axis mundi as, 713
from crucifixion of Jesus, relics from, 7688
desecration of, in diabolical witchcraft, 9771
making sign of, 7342
in Maya religion, sacred geography of, 3434
pecked crosses in Teotihuaćan, 5898
reverence for, in Ethiopian Church, 2860
salvation and, 4845
sign of, hands and, 3770
symbol of, 9338–9339
Cross, Frank Leslie, in Myth and Ritual school, 6381
Cross, Frank Moore, 5422
Cross, James, 9303
Crossan, John Dominic, on Jesus, 4847
Cross-cultural studies. *See also* Comparative-historical method; Comparative religion
of ecstasy, 2681
of Lévi (Sylvain), 5418–5419
Cross labyrinth, 5277–5278
Crossroads, **2070–2071**
Hekate shrines or statuettes as, 3899–3900
Croton (Italy), Pythagoras in, 7528, 7529, 7530
Crouch, Paul and Jan, 7713
Crow, 948
Crowdy, William S., 6563
Crowell, Stephen, on socialist movement, 5398
Crowley, Aleister, **2071–2072**
on angels, 348
and ceremonial magicians, 6471
esoteric orders associated with, 6568
occultism and, 6783
in Order of the Golden Dawn, 7930
Ordo Templi Orientis (OTO) and, 8251
"sexual magic" of, 3527, 6874
Wicca and, 9729
Crowley, Daniel, 75
Crowley, Vivianne, 9729–9730
Crown of Royalty, The (Ibn Gabirol), 4890
Crown Pith. *See Spyi ti*
Crowns, **2072–2073**
as symbol of royalty, 5155
Crow people (North America)
area populated by, 6656
Sun Dance of, 8844, 8845, 8846
tobacco in culture of, 6698
Crowther, Patricia, 9729
Crowther, Samuel Ajayi
Krio Christianity and, 1718
removal of, and African Independent Churches, 104
Croxton Play of the Sacrament, The (medieval drama), 2437
Crucifixion of Jesus
and anti-Semitism, 398–399
atonement and, 595, 8405
suffering servant doctrine and, 8807
Bultmann (Rudolf) on, 8807–8808
and history, Christian views of, 4052
Holocaust as parallel to, 4089–4090
images of, 4345, 4346, 4845
Jewish role in, 398–399
lamb symbolism in, 8310
literary interpretations of, 5479–5480
pierced heart symbolism in, 3882–3883
Pontius Pilate ordering, 7058
redemption and, 7640
relics from, 7688, 7689–7690
in Roman Catholicism, 7884
sanctity of Jerusalem and, 4840
as self-giving, 8006
Smith (W. Robertson) on, 8453
in worship, 9809
Cruise, Richard, 7307
Crumlin, Rosemary, 502
Crummell, Alexander, 75, **2073–2074**
in abolitionist movement, 68
Crusades, **2074–2078**
Bacon (Roger) disapproving, 735
campaigns of, 2074–2076
Catherine of Sienna's support for, 1461
Children's Crusade (1212), 2075
Christian perspective, **2074–2077**
Eastern Church affected by, 2586
East-West schism, effect on, 8156–8157
the Grail and, 3650
Hasidism and, 4913
heresy and, 3927–3928
historiography and, 4038
Hungary and, 4225
Innocent III and, 4496, 4499
Jerusalem in, 4837
Jewish suicide and martyrdom in, 542–543, 5012, 7055, 7056–7057
Jews killed in, memory books for, 7823
justification for, 6971
migration in, 6023
Muslim perspective, **2077–2078**

Crusades ***continued***
outcome of, 2076–2077
roots and causes of, 2074
and transculturation, 9293
uniting and dividing forces in, 1690
"Cry from an Indian Wife, A" (Johnson), 7225
Crying. *See* Tears
Crylatus, on change, 8420
Crystals
in New Age religion, healing through, 3851
as sacred objects, vol. 4 color insert
transmutation of, Indian references to, 2557
CTA. *See* Completed Testament Age
Ctesias (deity), 7103
Cua, Paulus, 3077
Cuba
Christianity in, 1707
drums in, 7037
films from, 3099
Islam in, 4683, 4684
Santería in, 1434
Theosophical Society in, 7228
transculturation in, 9292, 9305–9306
Cuban missile crisis, John XXIII in, 4946
Cubeo religion (South America)
ancestor cult in, 8584
fertility rites in, 8583
genealogy and, 3424
Cuchama, Mount, 6214
Cú Chulainn (hero), 4479, 8960. *See also* Táin Bó Cuailnge
furor of, 3213–3214
as hero, 1493–1494
Cucuteni culture (prehistoric), 7379, 7380, 7381, 7382–7383
Cudworth, Ralph
on Hermetism, 3950
Neoplatonism and, 6475
Cuecuechcuicatl (dance), 2464
Cuerauaperi (deity), 5909
Cuevas, Mariano, 5922
Cuiba religion (Colombia), origin of night in, 8588
Cuicacalli (house of flowers), 2464, 2465
Cui Hao, 1598, 8994, 8995
Kuo Qianzhi and, 5240
Cuius regio eius religio, Calvert (Lord Baltimore) and, 1373
Cui Wen Zi, 9843
Cūlavaṃsa (Buddhist text), 1199
Culesius, Petrus, 331
Culhuacan (city), Toltec royal lineage of, 5173
Culianu, Ioan Petru, **2079–2081**
on Gnosticism, 3534
historiography of, 4050–4051
on Jonas (Hans), 3533
on Zolla (Elémire), 9986
Culin, Stewart, 752
on gambling, 3260
on games, 3266
Cullaniddesa (Buddhist text), 1270
Cullavagga (Buddhist text), 1260
Culler, Jonathan, 5474, 9262
Culsu (deity), 2871
Cult awareness movement, 6522. *See also* Anticult movements; Countercult movement
dissolution of, 6523
Cult Awareness Network (CAN), 396, 397, 2292, 6566
deprogramming and, 2085
against International Society for Krishna Consciousness, 4522
and raid on Branch Davidians, 6525
Cult-based communities, 7719
Cultic Milieu, The (Kaplan and Lööw), 2663
Cultivation. *See* Agriculture; Self-cultivation
Cult of Earth (Confucian), 1911–1912
Cult of Heaven/Shangdi, 1911
Cult of Saints, **2081–2084**. *See also* Saint(s)
Cult of the Fetish Gods (Brosse), 3043, 3044, 3045
Cult of the Hand, 4302
Cult of the Mother Goddess, The (James), 3616
Cult of the Virgin Mary, The (Carroll), 7480
Cults and sects, **2084–2086**. *See also* Anticult movements; New religious movements; Sectarianism; *specific cults and sects*
in African religions
agricultural development and, 83
of dead, *vs.* ancestor worship, 322
early history of, 83–84
interlacustrine Bantu, 4519, 4520, 4521
kings in, 84, 5171
Kongo religion, 5220–5221
analysis of concept of "cult," 1422
in Baltic religion, of ancestors, **327–332**
Barker (Eileen) on, 2085
in Brahmanism, 9571–9572
brainwashing in, 1031–1034
as categories, 1866
civil suits against, 1033, 1034
in Daoism, 9843
definition of, 6557
dismantling of, 6523
Emperor's, **2776–2778**
eschatological, 2836
of Eshmun, 2841
Gnosticism as sect, 3923
"heresy," sects as
in Greek philosophy, 3922
in New Testament, 3920
history of study of, 75, 76, 77
in Inca religion, of ancestors, 5176–5177
in Khanty religion, 5119–5122
in Komi religion, 5218
in Kongo religion, 5220–5221
in Mansi religion, 5119–5122
movements against (*See* Anticult movements)
negative connotation of terms, 6513, 6518, 6522, 6557
new religious movements distinguished from, 6513
opposition to, 1032, 1033, 1034, 1038
Peoples Temple (*See* Jones, Jim; Jonestown and Peoples Temple)
recruits of, 1031–1032, 1033
relics and (*See* Relics)
reversing programming by, 1032, 1033
sacred languages of, 5303
Stark (Rodney) and Bainbridge (William Sims) on, 2084–2085
studies on, 1032–1033, 1034
syncretism in, 75, 76
Troeltsch (Ernst) on, 2084
UFO-centered, 9433
violence in, 1034–1035
of warrior heroes, 2815, 2817
Wilson (Bryan) on, 2084
vs. worship, 466
Yinger (J. Milton) on, 2084
in Zoroastrianism, 9989–9992
Cultural analysis of religion, in society-and-religion studies, 8470–8472
Cultural area, 5259, 5261
Cultural determinants, in news, 4962
Cultural diffusion. *See* Diffusion
Cultural-historical method. *See* *Kulturkreiselehre*
Cultural history
Schmidt (Wilhelm) on, 8168
supreme beings from perspective of, 8876–8878
Cultural hybridity, 1859
Cultural imperialism, missions and, 6071
Cultural relativism. *See* Relativism, cultural
Cultural Revolution (China), 1610
exerting political power over religious institutions, 7255, 7268
persecution of Muslims under, 4636–4637
persecution of Tibetan Buddhists under, 9186
Cultural sciences *(Geisteswissenschaften),* Dilthey's vision of hermeneutics and, 3930, 3932–3933
Cultural stratum, 5259, 5260
Cultural studies
ecological studies in, 2611–2612
subaltern studies and, 8801
Cultural systems, Geertz (Clifford) on, 8467–8468
Cultural transmission
and concept of culture, 2088
consequences of transmissability, 2087
of religions, 2089
sea as barrier to, 1426
social reform and, 7653
Cultural violence, 9596
Culture, **2086–2090**. *See also* Popular Culture; Tradition
atomistic concept of, 5260
in binary oppositions, 2086–2087
biology and, 5261
Bornemann (Fritz) on, 8170
Carnivalesque, 1440
Cassirer on, 1448
changes in, modernity and, 6109
characteristics of, 7468, *7469*
combat myth and cultural order (China), 1626
comparative study and, 2089
contact between, in millenarianism, 6033–6034
continuities between, in history of religions approach, 4065
contradictory character of, 8468
conversion theories and, 1970–1971
deities of, 3623
in early Eastern Christianity, 2582
evolution of, religion shaped by, 2869
fundamentalism and, 2887, 2889
heresy and, 3923
heteronomy of, 5482–5483
high-context, American sectarian groups as, 1834
history of concept, 2087–2088
homosexuality and, 4112
and human rights, 5364
inculturation/contextualization of Christian theology, 1730
in Japan, Zen influence on, 9946–9947
knowledge of, in Amazonian Quechua religions, 283, *283*
Lévi-Strauss (Claude) on, 8750, 8751
male-centered (*See* Androcentrism)
meaning of, Geertz (Clifford) on, 8500
monotheism and, 1993
nature and, 7796, 7803
gender in, 3421
nature of, and popular religion, 7328–7329
New Age religion and, 3852
oral *vs.* literate, 5305

Parsons (Talcott) on, 3232, 8495
popular (*See* Popular culture)
relationship with religion, 2089
religion as resource for, in globalization, 3500–3501
ritual and, 1513
Schmidt (Wilhelm) on, 8170, 8876
scriptures, impact of, 8203–8204
shame *vs.* guilt, 7755–7756
social sciences and humanities, current use and contestation in, 2088–2089
sociobiology and, 8474, 8475
Sorokin (Pitirim) on ideational *vs.* sensate cultures, 8524
studies of, psychology of religion and, 7479–7480
Swidler (Ann) on, 8470
Tillich (Paul) on, 9203, 9204
time, cultural, 1354
time and, 1760, 5260
Urkultur and primary cultures, Schmidt (Wilhelm) on, 8168
use of term, 7320
visual (*See* Visual culture)
Wach (Joachim) and, 9650–9651
Culture and Anarchy (Arnold), 7321
Culture and Imperialism (Said), 6881–6884
Culture areas theory
criticism of, 8170
Schmidt (Wilhelm) on, 8168
Culture bringers. *See* Culture heroes
Culture circles. *See also* Kulturkreiselehre
of Graebner (Fritz), 3648
masks and, 5770–5771
Culture ecology, 452–453
Culture heroes, **2090–2093**. *See also* Tricksters; *specific figures*
in African religions
in Luba religion, 5524
in Lugbara religion, 3739, 5526–5527
animals as, 2092
in Arctic religions, 472, 4528
Arthur as, 509
birth of, 2091
characteristic activities of, 2091
in Chinese religion, Huangdi as, 4144
cities founded by, 326
in creation stories, 325
as source of sickness, 3809
deities as, 3623
disappearance and transmutation of, 2091–2092
hedgehogs as, 3892
history of study of, 2090–2091
insects as, 4507, 4508
masculine sacrality in, 5761
in Melanesian religions, 5834, 5843–5844
in Mesoamerican religions, 5936–5937
in Mixtec religion, 5911
in North American Indian religions, 325
of Anishinaabe, 369
in earth diver myths, 1988
iconography of, 4307
in Oceanic religions
creativity of, 2006
gender of, 3397
in Solomon Islands religions, 8515
in South American religions
Kuai as source of disease in Baniwa religion, 3809
as supreme beings, 8576–8577
tricksters as, 2092
as twins, 2092
Culture-historical method
of Graebner (Fritz), 3648
Schmidt (Wilhelm) and, 8169, 8170
Cultures of the Jews, 4884
Cultus externus, in Kant's (Immanuel) philosophy, 5078
Culwch and Olwen, 1484
Cumae, Orphic community at, 6894
Cumaen Sibyl, *Sibylline Oracles* and, 8383, 8384
Cumberland Presbyterian Church, 7391
Cumiechúcuaro (underworld), 151
Cumming, Alfred, 6194
Cummings, Thomas B. F., 502
Cummins, Thomas, on Andean Christian interculture, 8611
Cumont, Franz, **2093–2095**
and Aion, 208
on Mithraism, 6088, 6089, 6090
on myth, 6367
on Pythagorean astral thesis, 8425
on Roman religion, Oriental influences on, 7916
on Sabazios, 7953
Cun (preserve), 2634
Cuna religion (Panama), **2095–2097**
cosmogony and mythic themes in, 2095–2096
cult organization in, 2095
cultural origin myth in, 2096
God and morality in, 2096
mythology and cultural survival of, 2096–2097
Cunda the smith, death of the Buddha and, 4140
Cuneiform alphabet
in Canaanite religion, 1382
in Hurrian religion, 4229
urbanization and, 1802
Cuneiform script
adapted for Akkadian language, 3375
difference from Egyptian hieroglyphics, 5161
invention of, 3375
music in, 6275
Cuneiform tablets, 3375
goddess worship in, 3586
Cunha, Euclides da, 3063
Cunningham, Merce, 500, 2161
Cuntara (Śaiva saint), on *bhakti,* 8043
Cuntaramūrtti (Saiva saint), 8974
as Nāyāṉār, 8044
Cupid, 811, 812, 813
Cupiditas (lust), 2308
Cupitt, Don, 5489, 7082
Cupping (medical practice), in Middle East, 3836
Curanderos (healers), 3418
in Andean religion, 8603–8604, 8619
Curators of the Buddha (Gomez), 7479
Cur deus homo (Anselm), 596
Curia, Romulus and, 5167
Curia Romana
Luther (Martin) and, 5535–5536
modernism and, 7879
reform of, 6972, 7012
in Roman Catholic polity, 1764, 7886–7887
Curicaueri (deity), 5909
Curing. *See* Healing and medicine
Curio maximus, 7908
Curiosity and Pilgrimage (Zacher), 9293
Currency. *See* Money
Currier, Nathaniel, vol. 11 color insert
Cursillos de Cristiandad movement, 7772
Cursing and curses, **2097–2108**. *See also* Spells
in Bible, 2104–2105
definition and types of, 2097
Greco-Roman, 2097–2098
curse figurines, 5574
curse tablets, 5573–5574
history of study, 2098–2099
in Islam, 4213
in Israelite religion, laws on, 4732, 4737
in Judaism, 968–969
Kudurru (boundary stone inscriptions) and covenants, 2102–2104
modern, 2105–2106
personal curses, 2097, 2099–2100
professional curses, 2100
protective, 2101–2102
in Roman religion, 7914
sin and, in Hebrew scriptures, 8404
social justice, 2100–2101
women and, 2100
Curtains, 9091
Curtis, John, 3083
Curtius, E. R., 5469–5470, 5472
Curtius, Ernst, 6138
Curzil (deity), 111
Cusanus. *See* Nicholas of Cusa
Cuscat, Pedro Díaz, 6514, 6576
Cuscat's War (Mexico), 6514, 6576
Cushing, Frank Hamilton, 6670
Cushite religion. *See* Kushite religion
Cushitic languages. *See also* Hamitic languages
in Ethiopia, 2572
Cusi Yupanqui (king), visions of, 5176
Custody battles, over children, in new religious movements, 5377
Custom
in Buddhist devotion, 9830
Hindu, as source of *dharma,* 5343, 5344
in Jewish law (*See Minhag*)
juridical law of, Suárez (Francisco) on, 8799
and *kashrut* laws, 5107
law *vs.,* 1843
Custom and Myth (Lang), Marett (R. R.) influenced by, 5708
CUT. *See* Church Universal and Triumphant
Cuthbert, 814
body of, in Durham Cathedral, 8376
Cuthwin (monk), 814
Cutten, George B., 6521
Cutting, divine power of, 967–968
Cuzco (Peru)
attacks on, 5176
calendar and, 1361, 1363–1364
as capital of Inca empire, 5176
Catholic convents in, 3416, 3417
expansion of, 4410–4411
foundation of, 4524
gender in, 3416
human sacrifice at, 3417
royal mummy cult of, 5176–5177
as sacred city, 1503, 4411
Temple of Sun in, 4384, 4411, 4524, 8842–8843
Cwezi (heroic figures), 4519
in Nyoro and Nkore religions, 2575–2576
Cwezi cult, 63

Cybele (deity), **2108–2111,** 2984. *See also* Attis
  Anatolian background of, 2108–2109
  Artemis identified with, 506
  Astarte identified with, 7130
  Attis and, 1451, 2109
  cult of
    baptism of blood in, 780
    castration in, 1451–1452, 2109–2110
    deification in, 2249
    eunuch priests of, 3968
    initiation into, 2249
  drums of, 2498
  festival of, 2537
  in Greek religion, 2109–2110
  in Hellenistic religions, 3603–3604
  as keeper of keys, 5116
  as Lady of the Animals, 5280
  as Magna Mater, 1451
  meteorite of, 8736
  moved from Rome to Anatolia, 3017
  mystery religion of, 6330
  in Roman religion, 2110
  in Rome, 7905–7906, 7917
  son-consort of, 2983
  veneration of, 6866
  worship of, 3587, 3603–3604
Cybernetic immortality, 513
Cybernetics, **2111–2112**. *See also* Artificial intelligence
  applications of, 2111
  philosophical and theological implications of, 2111–2112
Cycladic religion, lack of information about, 37
Cycle of life, religious integration with, 2604
Cycle plays, 2437, 7046–7047
Cycles
  Aztec creation-destruction, 1357–1358
  historiography, cyclical organic model of, 4031
  Maya zero and, 1357
  Mesoamerican calendar and, 1356, 1357–1358
  in *yingyang wuxing,* 9888–9889
Cyclical time, *vs.* linear time, 6373, 6374
Cyclones, in Australia, 7605
Cyc project, 510
Cylinder drums, 7036
Cymbals, 7036
Cynics
  on casuistry, 1454
  diatribē rhetoric of, 3910
  on knowledge, 5201
  on naturalism, 6428
  religion, criticism of, 3910
  on world citizenship, 3906
Cynocephalus (dog-head), 6151
Cypress tree, 9337
Cyprian (bishop of Carthage), **2112–2114**
  on apostasy, 432
  on bishops, 1668, 1771, 7402
  on election of Israel, 2747
  in exile, 7059
  on merit, 5876
  overview of life and work, 1679
  on Roman church, 6966
  Tertullian's influence on, 9085
  theological issues addressed by, 2581
Cypriano, Tania, 3099
Cyprus
  Bābīs on, 729, 737
  Bronze-Age necropolis and circle symbolism, 1791
  cult of Reshef in, 7761
  Greek Orthodox Church in, 3658–3659
  Melqart in, 5847–5848
  Nestorian community on, 6480
Cyprus, Church of, 3658–3659
Cyprus Orthodox Church, in Orthodox structure, 2589
Cyrenaica, Christianity in, 1677–1678
Cyril I (Kyrillos Loukaris) (patriarch of Constantinople), **2114–2116**
  Confession of 1629 by, 2588
  Confession of Dosítheos against, 2059
  Eutyches and, 2885
Cyril IV (pope), Coptic Church and, 1982
Cyril and Methodius, **2116–2117**
  missionary activity of, 2585
  missions to Moravia, 1683, 2116–2117
Cyrillic alphabet, creation of, 2585
Cyrillic script, 274
  formation of, 2116
Cyril of Alexandria, **2117–2118**
  on Adonis festivals, 2536
  Christology and, 2581, 2583, 2584, 5042
  Council of Chalcedon and, 1980
  Council of Ephesus and, 2040, 6483
  on hypostatic union, 4242
  on Jesus, 6482
  on Mary, 6483
  on Monophysitism, 6153, 6155
  Theodoret criticizing, 9123
Cyril of Jerusalem, **2118–2119**
  on baptism, 2468
Cyrus (patriarch of Alexandria), 5792
Cyrus I (king of Persia), victories of, 4549
Cyrus II (Cyrus the Great) (king of Persia), **2119**
  Armenians conquered by, 491
  in Babylon, 5948
  edict of, 924, 928
  Egyptian religion under, 2709
  Isaiah on, 4549
  messianism and, 5974
  raised by dog, myth of, 2393
Czaczkes, Shemu'el Yosef. *See* Agnon, Shemu'el Yosef
Czaplicka, M. A., 473, 475
Czech and Slovakian Orthodox Church, in Orthodox structure, 2589
Czechoslovak Hussite Church (Czechoslovak National Church), Hussite tradition and, 4234
Czechoslovakia. *See also* Slavic religion
  Hus (Jan) and, 4234
  pacifist movements in, 6648
  Protestantism in, 1685, 1686
  Roman Catholicism in, 1686
  study of religion in, 8772, 8773, 8774

D

Da'ā'im al-Islām (Qāḍī al-Nu'mān), 7541
Da'at miqra', 869
Da'at Torah doctrine, 196
Daba/Dabo (devil), 2231
Dabir (deity), 2597
Dabog (deity), 2231
Dabra Libanos (monastery), 2860
Dabus (rebel leader), 7756
Dachangding Monastery (Buddhist temple), 9047
Dachengyue (music), 6293
Da chidu lun (Buddhist text), Kumārajīva's translation of, 5263
Dacia. *See* Geto-Dacian religion
Dacian people (Thrace). *See* Geto-Dacian religion
Dacian Riders, **2123–2124**
  artwork of, 2123, 2124
  iconography of, 2123, 2124
  initiation rites of, 2124
  Mithraism and, 2123–2124
  myth of, 2124
Daco-Getic religion. *See* Geto-Dacian religion
Dacula, Georgia, 1810
Dad. *See* Adad
Dadaism, of Evola (Julius), 2904
Dadao sect, 1602
Daddy Grace, **2124–2125,** 6563
  religious movement started by, 69–70
Dādgāh (fire), 6997, 6999
Dadhyañc (mythic figure), 4467
Dadism, Cohen (Arthur A.) on, 1849–1850
Dādistān ī Mēnōg i Khrad, 9752
Dādū (saint), 7211
  in *bhakti* poetry tradition, 3985
Daedalus (Greek mythic figure)
  dance and, 5276
  escape from labyrinth, 5274, 5275
Daēnā (heavenly counterpart of soul), in Zoroastrianism, 7763
Daevas. See Daivas
Dafa (Daoist ritual), 2186
Da fangguang fo Huayan jing. See Huayan jing
Daff (drum), 2498
Dafora, Asadata, 2164
Dagan (deity), **2125–2127**
  cult of, 7102–7103
  in Eblaite pantheon, 2596, 2597
  etymology of name, 2126, 7102
  in Philistine religion, 7102–7103
  son of, 28, 724
  temples of, 7102, 7103
  texts on, 1382–1383
Dagar, Faiyazuddin, 6286
Dagar, Zahiruddin, 6286
Dagestan (Caucasus)
  Christianity in, 4612–4613, 4614
  Islam in, 4612–4614
  Judaism in, 4612–4613
  Timurid rule in, 4614
  Zoroastrianism in, 4613
Daghdha (deity), 9390
  cauldron of, 1488
  children of, 1484
  Roman parallels, 1485
Dagoda, 9048
Dagon. *See* Dagan
DaGraca, Marceline Manuel. *See* Daddy Grace
Dagu (musical instrument), 6294
Dahindah (Apache celebration), 10070
Dahlan, K. H. Achmad, 4818
Dahlan, Kiai H. A., 4667
Dahlgren, Barbro, 5942, 5944
Dahlke, Paul, 1188
Dahomean religion. *See* Fon and Ewe religion
Dahomey (West Africa), prostitution by *koi* priestesses in, 3969
Dahr (time), Qur'ān on, 3209
Dahriyya (Zoroastrian sect), 10014
Dahua (great transformation or becoming), soul and, 8554
Dahui Zonggao, 1165, 1292–1293, 1524, 1604, 1646
Dai, Mount (China), pilgrimage to, 7165
Daibutsuji (Buddhist monastery), 2385
Daicoviciu, Constantin, 3467
Daicoviciu, Hadrian, 3467
Dai De, ritual writings, 1908
Da'if (weak) *ḥadīth*
  in Shī'ī collections, 3733
  in Sunni collections, 3729
Daigu (Great Fool) (Buddhist monk), 9949
Daigūji (chief priest), 7410
Daijōji monastery, 5109
Daikoku (deity), 2410
  humorous myth of, 4208
Daikoku bashira (post), 2410
Daily Hallel, in *siddur* and *maḥzor,* 8389
Daily Word (periodical), 6585
Dā'im, Muḥammad Sharīf Nūr al-, 6228
Daimoku, chanting of, in Sōka Gakkai, 8508

Daimoku *maṇḍalas,* in Risshō Kōseikai, 7795
Daimon (spirit), 9770
Daimonia (divinities or daemons), Socrates and, 8504
Daimuryōjukyō (Larger Pure Land Sutra), Shinran on, 8354
Dainas (folk songs), **2127–2128**
ancestors in, 327
and dance, 2127–2128
dealing with childbirth, 2127
dealing with death, 2127
dealing with festival cycle, 2127
dealing with life cycle, 2127
dealing with love, 2127
dealing with nature, 2128
etymology of term, 2127
religious dimensions of, 2127–2128
Saule (sun) worship in, 8131–8132, 8133–8135
Dainihonshi (History of great Japan), 4789
Dainihon Shūsaikai, 6825
Dainos (folk songs), 2127
Dainzú (Mexico), 5903–5904
Daiō (tea master), 847
Da'irah. See Khānagāh
Dairi Batak people (Indonesia), 799
Dā'īs (Ismāʿīlīyah Shīʿī leaders), 2225
Dai Sheng, ritual writings, 1908
Dai shi (Daoist text), 2208
Daitō (Zen master), 6988
Daityas (demons), 4440. *See also* Asuras
Daivas (daevas), **2128–2129,** 2276, 2284, 9995
etymology of word, 2128
gender of, 3372
yazatas and, 9875
in Zoroastrianism, 9936
Daiyi (Grand Unity), 9347
Dai Zhen, **2129–2130**. *See also* Mengzi
Han Studies *(Hanxue)* movement and, 1903
on Mengzi, 5858–5859
Zhang Xuecheng and, 1579
Daizong (emperor of China), Amoghavajra and, 293
Dajboi (demon), 2231
Da Jin xuandu boazang (Daoist text), 2203
Daji yuezang jing (Buddhist text), *mappō* in, 5685, 5686
Dajjāl, al-
as Antichrist, 395
in Islamic eschatology, Sunnī, 2838
Dakhma (tower of silence), **2130,** 3238
consecration of, 2130
etymology of word, 2130
Ḍākinīs (spirits), 9332
Dakota tribe (North America)
ballgame played by, 753
power in, concepts of, 576
proverbs of, 6977
souls in, 8534
wakan charisma in, 1547
Dakṣiṇāūmurti (deity), 4324
Daladāsirita (Buddhist text), 1305
Dalā'il al-khayrāt (Ibn Sulayman), 4588
Dalai Lama, **2131–2133**. *See also* Dge lugs pa
Altan Khan as, 1154
altar presented to museum by, 6244
as Avalokiteśvara's incarnation, 705, 706
as incarnation of Avalokiteśvara, 1082, 4416, 9184
celebration of, 1304
collaborating with scholars, 1283
ecological ethic of, 2630
emergence of leadership of, 8083
engaged Buddhism of, 2786, 2787
on environmental protection, 2613
etymology of term, 2131
in exile, 1100, 1158–1159, 1315, 2323, 2924, 7269, 9186
images of, 1159
as incarnation of Bodhisattva of Compassion, 2131
initiations into Kālacakra tradition offered by, 5058
Jewish exile and, 2924
and monasticism, 1156
Nobel Peace Prize to, 1283, 9186
nongenealogical succession of, 3426
Panchen Lama recognized by, 1159, 7269
Panchen Lamas rivaling, 1155
Potala Palace of, 9051–9052, 9184
and progressive Islam, 6100
rebirth of, procedure for discovering, 2131
as religio-political symbol, 7254, 7262
religious power of, 2131
ritual basis of, 8382
on Shugs ldan (Shugden), 8382
succession of, 8037
supporters of, 1158
and Tibetan Buddhist schools, 1223, 1224
as treasure discoverers, 9333
veneration of, 9841
Dalang (puppeteer), 2452, 6288, 7044
Dale, Andrew, 115
Dali, 1642
Dali, Salvador, 4348
Dali flana (second creation), 776
Dali folo (creation of beginning), 776
Dalit Buddhism, 9477
Dalits (formerly "Untouchables")
Christianity and, 1729–1730
Gauḍīya and Vallbha orders, exclusion from, 3986
Dalit Sahitya movement, 286
Dalit women's theology, 3035, 5442
Dall, Charles, 9317, 9318
Daly, Herman, environmental economics and, 2610
Daly, Mary, 3035
on Catholic antifeminism, 9787
on God, 3559
on Goddess, 9099
gynocentrism of, 3720
on lesbian studies, 5413
on patriarchy, 7008
on politics and religion, 7252
on reform of Christianity, 3311–3312
Daly River region (Australia), Stanner (W. E. H.) on, 8729
Damaḥkhiṃ (drum), 2497
Damanhur
child socialization and education in, 6542, 6543
origins of, 6568
Ḍamaru (drum), 2499, 7036
Damascene, John. *See* John of Damascus
Damascius (Greek philosopher)
on Attis, 2537
Dionysian writings relying on, 2356
on the good, 3635
as head of Plato's Academy, 6474
on knowability of God, 181–182
Damascus (Syria)
Adad in, 28
in Crusades, 2075
Ḥanābilah in, 3768
Orthodox Church in, in communion with Rome, 2588
Damascus Affair (1840), 263, 5000
Damascus Document (Hebrew text), 2233, 2234, 7063, 7065
Damasio, Antonio, 6486, 6488, 6493
on Spinoza (Baruch), 8685
Damasus I (pope), 6966
on Apollinaris of Laodicea, 424
on Roman bishop, 6966
and Vulgate Bible, 892, 922, 6966
Da Matta, Roberto, 5985
Dambala (*lwa* spirit), in Haitian Vodou, 1433, 9636
Dambala-wédo (*lwa* spirit), description of, 8690
Dam-dingir (Eblaite priest), 2598
Dames, Michael, 5824
Dames de la Retraite, 7772
Damgalnunna (deity), 5953
Damian, Peter, **2133–2134**
on hermits, 2829
Da Ming Daozang jing (Daoist text), 2203
Damm, Hans, on masks, 5769
Damnation
Barth (Karl), rejection of doctrine by, 3885
development of concept, 8564–8565
female body as model of, 4165
sacred *vs.* profane and, 7966
West African religions and, 9718
Damo. *See* Bodhidharma
Damona (deity), 1484
Dam pa Bde gshegs (Buddhist monk), 7868
Damu (deity), 2522, 5949
Dämwamit (deity), in Gurage religion, 2574
Dan, Joseph, 544
Dāna (gift giving), 1280, 1332, 4770, 6994, 7407, 7408
merit making through, 5873
Danaids (Aeschylus), 407
Dance, **2134–2167**. *See also* Drama
in affliction, healing of, 60, 61–62
in African American religions, 2135, 2150
and cultural identity, 2164
in African religions, 2456–2358
in African Independent Churches, 103
and cultural identity, 2164
in Dogon religion, 2391
history of study of, 76
in initiation rituals, 4483, 4485
in Khoi religion, 5136
in Pgymy religions, 7524
in San religion, 5136
trance state induced by, 83
in Asian religions, and cultural identity, 2164
in Australian Indigenous religions, 639, 640, 642, 646–647
Ngukurr, 6599
in Bambara religion, 777
for blessing, 980
blue laws against, 2154
British influences on, 2135
in Buddhism, 2138, 4533
Calvinism and, 2154
in Caribbean religions, 1429, 1436, 1437
at Carnival, 1441, 1443–1444

Dance *continued*
ceremonial, definition of, 2146
in Chinese religion, 6293
Yangge dances, 4208
in Christianity, 2135, 2144
gnosticism, 2153
in Middle Ages, 2136, 2153
rejection by church, 2145, 2153
in Renaissance, 2136, 2153–2154
in Romantic period, 2155–2156
Shakers, 2138
in churches, 1441
communicating with spirits through, 2453–2455
costumes for, 1827–1828
couple forms
condemnation of, 2154
Hasidism, 2147
in Renaissance, 2154
at a *veglia* (Italian social event), 2148
criticism of, 2151
in Daoism, 6295
Pace of Yu, 6749
definitions of, 2134
Delsarte, François and, 2156
devotion expressed in, 2319
Djan'kawu, 2380
in Dogon religion, 2134
in Dolgan religion, 2396
in Eastern Orthodox Church, 2135
as element of *dainas* (Baltic folk songs), 2127–2128
in England, in Baroque period, 2155
as entertainment, 2151
in Europe and European religions, 2135, 2138–2139
in Baroque period, 2154–2155
in Middle Ages, 2153
popular and folk dance, 2144
in Pre-Romantic period, 2154–2155
religious and ceremonial, 2146–2148
in Renaissance, 2153–2154
in Romantic period, 2155–2156
evolution of, 2134–2135
fasting accompanying or preceding, 2997
fertility, 2135
of Ganda people, 2137
of Sandawe people, 2137
folk dance, 2141
Franciscans and, 2136
in Garifuna religion, 3284, 3285
Ghost (*See* Ghost Dance)
as gift from gods, 2143
in Greek religion, 2135
group forms, Hasidism, 2147
Hindu, 2134, 2135–2136, 2319
and *bhakti,* 858, 2135
of Kṛṣṇa, 5250
of Kṛṣṇa, 5249, 5456
of Śiva, 4324, 4428, 4444, 5455, 7043, 7170
Śiva as lord of, 8415–8416
historical accounting of, 2145, 2151, 2166
human body and, 4172
Inca, 567
Indian, ecological concerns raised through, 2623
intoxication and purification, 1459
in Islam, 2135, 2136
for initiations, 2136
in Israel, 2164
in Japanese religions
and cultural identity, 2164
music with, 6299–6300
Jesuits and, 2136
in Baroque period, 2155
in Judaism, 2135, 2136, 2143–2144, 2319
cultural identity of Jews and, 2163–2164
Hasidism, 2146–2147
on Simḥat Torah, 2149
sacred, 2165
Tanzhausen and, 2154
Kumina (Jamaica), 1435
labyrinths and, 5276, 5277
in Lakota religion, 5297
liturgical, 2152, 2164–2165, **2166–2167**
masks in, 5767, 5768
Mayan, 2435–2436, 2439, 2465–2466
meanings of, 2134
medicinal, 3814–3815
in Melanesian religions, 6265, vol. 9 color insert
in Mexico, 2139
in Micronesian religions, 6007
in Middle East, 2148–2149
modern
Central European, 2159–2160
cultural identity in, 2163–2164
first generation of, 2157–2160
second generation of, 2160–2161
in New World, 2149–2150
in New Year festivals, 6590, 6591, 6592
nonsacred theatrical and recreational, 2141–2142
in North American Indian religions, 2136, 6651, 6653 (*See also* Ghost Dance; Sun Dance)
of Northwest Coast, 6710
purpose of, 7343
of Southeast Woodlands, 6694
of Southwest, 6725
Stomp dance, 1565–1566
in Oceanic religions, 6788–6789
origin myths of, 2134
in Polynesian religions, 6264
popular and folk, **2143–2152**
definitions of, 2144–2146
postmodern, 2161
vs. procession, 7417
Protestantism and, 2154
Puritanism and, 2154
purposes of, 2134
rain, 7603
recreational, 2141–2142, 2146
religious, **2134–2143**
acceptance of, 2135–2136
definition of, 2146
typology of, 2136–2142
in Western cultures, 2152–2153
of Salome, 2135
Samba schools in Brazil, 1444
scholarly neglect of, 2145
and sexuality, 2135
of Shakers, 2138, 2149
in Sikhism, 8397
social, definition of, 2146
solo forms, Hasidism, 2147
in South American Indian religions
animal dances, 8581
in Tupi-Guarani religion, 8533
of spirit possession, 2139–2140, 2150
in Sufism, 2319, 7936
ecstasy induced by, 5818–5819
sustenance, 2135
technology and, 2142
theatrical, **2152–2167**
religious content in, 2152–2153
Tibetan Cham dances, 1827
in Tikopia religion, 9196
as transformative ritual, 7051
typology of, 2136–2142
conducting supernatural beneficence, 2137–2138
creating and re-creating social roles, 2136–2137
effecting change, 2138–2139
embodying the supernatural, 2139–2141
explaining religion, 2136
merging with supernatural toward enlightenment or self-detachment, 2140
nonsacred theatrical and recreational, 2141–2142
personal possession, 2139–2140
revelation of divinity, 2141
self-help, 2141
technology and religious practice, 2142
worship or honor, 2137
vernacular, 2146–2148, 2151
definition of, 2146
in Vodou ceremonies, 2139, 2150
in Western religions, for explanation of religion, 2136
in Yoruba religion, 2435, 9911
Dance Collection, of New York Library for the Performing Arts, 2151
Dance Gazing at the Sun. *See* Sun Dance
Dance of Death, 2138, 2153
Dance of Flowers, 2464
Dance of the Cross, in Amazonian religion, 8621
"Dance the goddess," 2934
Dancing the gods, in Kalabari religion, 2139
Dandekar, R. N., on Vedism, 8039
Danel (mythic figure), in Canaanite religion, 1391, 1396–1398
Dan Fodio, Usuman, **2167–2168,** 3229
jihād declared by, 4606
as prophet, 7443
as teacher, 4605–4606
Dangbi (deity), priestesses of, 3969
Dangdut music, 6291
D'Angelo, Mary, 5414
Dangji (possession intermediaries), 6834
Danhak pai (alchemy schools), in Korea, 2189
Danhom religion (West Africa), possession and transcendence in, 7987
Daniel (biblical book), **2168–2169**
additions to, 898–899
afterlife in, 152
Antichrist in, 394
anti-Semitism in, 398
as apocalypse, 412, 414–415
apostasy in, 431
authorship of, 2168
blasphemy in, 971
chronology of, 2168–2169
in Dead Sea Scrolls, 417
description of Yahveh in, 4296
Enoch influenced by, 418
Jewish persecution in, 7055, 7056
judgment in, 5027
messianism in, 5972, 5975
Miller (William) on, 8235
periodization in, 174
pesher of, 7063, 7065–7066
rabbinic discussion on, 9235
resurrection in, 152, 7764, 8557
Sibylline Oracles and, 8384, 8385
theodicy in, 9116

Daniel (biblical figure), **2168–2169**
as fictitious character, 415
Timur Shah and, 5009
Daniel, Apocalypse of, 902
Daniélou, Jean, 3533
Daniels, David D., III, 70
Daniepan jing shu (Guanding), 9179
Daniepan jing xuanyi (Guanding), 9179
Danil (mythic figure), in Canaanite religion, 1382, 1386, 1388
Danish church, Kierkegaard's criticism of, 5140–5141
Dānish-nāmah-i 'Alā'ī (Ibn Sīnā), 4274
Danites, Levites and, 5420
Daniyye'l. *See* Daniel
Dan people (Liberia), masks of, 5766, 5767
Danquah, Joseph B.
on Akan religion, 115, 3570
on Ashanti religion, 115
Danses et légendes (Granet), 3655
Dan-speaking peoples, carved images of, 90
Dante Alighieri, **2169–2170**
apocalypse and, 412
on ascension, 524
Egyptian influences and, 3054
epistemology of, 2819
on Fedeli d'Amore, 8248
on hell, 157–158, 3885
on historical *vs.* universal truth, 54
Ibn Rushd's influence on, 4272–4273
Ibn Sīnā's influence on, 4275
Inferno of, 3015–3016
Islamic sources used by, 524, 6061
literary accomplishments of, 5471–5472
literary style of, 5373
mi'rāj and, 6061
number symbolism and, 6748
poetic style of, 7204, 7205, 7219
Ptolemy's influence on, 7492
Sayers (Dorothy) on, 8142–8143
on suicide, 8830
on "two books," 9422
on underworld, 9455
Danu (deity), 9390
Danubian Riders. *See* Dacian Riders
Danzi (musical instrument), 6294
Danzin Rabjai (incarnate lama), 1149
Dao (Way)
alienation of humankind from, 1626
atheism and, 577
basic concepts, 1597
charisma and, 7353
Confucius' goal of restoring, 1585
contemplation on, 5821
in *Dao de jing,* 1574, 1588
and *de* (virtue), **2172–2175**
definitions of, 2172–2173, 2177, 5198
disturbance of, confession and, 1886
ecology and, 2635
energies in, 9844
eternal, 2173
ethical teachings of Confucius and, 1586
knowledge of, 2175
Laozi as embodiment of, 5318
in Legalism, 5395
Lu Xiangshan on, 5541
meditation on, 5821
monism and, 6146
name of, 6408
vs. popular religion, 9842
rhythms of order and, 1590
as water, 9842–9843
as Way of all nature in *Zhuangzi,* 1573
Yang Zhu on, 1572
of Yu the Great, 1626
in *Zhuangzi,* 9968–9970
Dao'an (Buddhist scholar), 1271, **2170–2172**
disciples of, 1576
Huiyuan and, 4156
Maitreya and, 5620
and popularization of Buddhism, 3155
skills of, 1596
Daochuo (Buddhist scholar), 1239, 1276, **2175–2176**
on *mofa,* 5686
Pure Land Buddhism founded by, 1601, 4922
and recitative *nianfo,* 6602
Shandao and, 8298
Dao-de (morality), 2172
Dao de jing/Laozi (Daoist text)
atheism and, 577
attribution to Laozi, 5315, 5316
Buber (Martin) on, 1057
Celestial Masters teachings of, 2180, 2193
dao-de in, 2174
Dao in, 2172, 2173, 2174, 5821
dao in, 2172, 2173, 2174
de in, 2173–2174
desire in, 2304, 2306
equivalence of saint and sage ruler in, 4332
meditation in, 5821
nature and, 2636
overview of, 1574, 1588
peace in, 7022
practices and, 9843
priests reciting, 7413
as revelation, 2204
in Tang Dynasty, 2184
teaching of, 5318
translations of, 1632, 1633
via negativa used in, 6990
visual form in, 4333
Xiang'er commentary to, 2180–2181, 2193, 2204
in *Zhuangzi,* 9969
Daofa huiyuan (Daoist text), 2206
Daoism, **2176–2216**. *See also* Qi; *Yinyang Wuxing* philosophy
aesthetics in, 51
afterlife in, 172
immortality, quest for, 3887
immortality debate, 1576
alchemy in, 237, 238, 241, 2184–2185, 2187, 9845
internal *vs.* external, 1603
and reversal of time, 7683
writings on, 2211
amulets and talismans in, 5593
art of, vol. 3 color insert, vol. 11 color insert
attention in, 603
basic concepts, 1597
bird in, 948
Buber (Martin) on, 1057
Buddhism and, 1161, 3154
absolute principle in, 6630
at beginnings of Buddhism in China, 1595
Bodhidharma in, 995
Chan Buddhism, 995, 1293
common goal of, 1167, 1172
conflicts between, 2183–2184, 2186, 2194, 2199
convergence with, in Han dynasty, 1576
doctrine and practice adapted from, 2179, 2194, 2196
immortality debate, 1606
and philosophy, 1301
reconciliation between, 1173
research on, 2213
bureaucratic pantheons of, 2178
Celestial Masters, 2180–2181, 2192–2193, 5240–5241
celibacy and, 1475
chaos in, 2175
chaotic *hundun* theme in, 1624
charisma in, 7353
Cheng's criticism of, 1563
cinnabar fields of, 2178
confession in, 1886
Confucianism and, Seidel (Anna) on, 8223
contemplation in, 5821
contemporary issues in, 2637–2638
cosmology of, 2177, 2178
cult of chaos *(hundun),* 1540
cults in, 9843
current history of, 2189–2190
Dai Zhen on, 2129
dance in, 6295
Pace of Yu, 6749
dao and *de* in, **2172–2175,** 2177
Daoist religious community, **2192–2202**
daoyin gymnastics in, 5734
definitions of, 2176–2177
deities in, 1588 (*See also specific deities*)
changeable nature of, 2178
female, 3342
iconography of, 4334–4335
qi and, 2177
seasonal festivals and, 1642
Shangdi in, 8300
zhenren (perfected ones), 1597
desire in, 2304, 2306
disease and illness in, 2177, 2179
on disease and madness, origins of, 3809
doctrine in, 2382
flexibility of, 2178, 2179
dreams in, 2489–2490
early development, 1588–1589
ecology and, **2635–2638**
economics and, 9708
elixir of immortality and, 2771
as enemy of civilization, 5201
eschatology of, 2178–2179, 2834
eternity in, 2856
fangshi and, 2989, 2990, 5494
fasting in, 2996
feminist analysis of, 3033–3034
and fiction, Chinese, 3066, 3067, 3068–3069
and film, 3097
food taboos in, 3169
funeral rites in, 3234
music in, 6295
Ge Hong and, 2181–2182, 3290, 3291
gender in, 3341–3342
gift giving in, 3483
golden age in, 1628
governing body of, 2189
government involvement in, 2177, 2183–2184, 2186–2187, 2189, 2196, 2202
Guo Xiang on, 3710
in Han dynasty, 4332, 7165, 7257, 7268, 9670–9671
Han political philosophy and, 1590–1591

Daoism *continued*
history of study of, 1629–1638, **2212–2216**
early, 5773
Seidel (Anna) in, 8222–8223
hospitality in, 4141
humor in, 4206–4207
iconography of (*See* Iconography, Daoist)
immortality in, 4332, 8556
incantation in, 4407
initiation into, 2195, 7683
intuition in, 4526
Jade Emperor in, 1606, 9915
jade symbolism in, 4759
in Japan, 4782
in popular religion, 4795, 4797
Shugendō movement and, 8379
kingship in, 1161, 7267
knowledge in, 5201
kōshin practices in, 2188
Kou Qianzhi and, 5240–5241
Kunlun as cosmic mountain, 1501
liberation in, by shape shifting, 8302
literature of (*See* Daoist literature)
local cults, attempts to control, 1615
Lu Xiujing and, 5542–5543
macrocosm-microcosm in, 2177–2178
Shangqing scriptures and, 2182
magic in, 5592–5593
Mandate of Heaven concept in, 2178–2179
Manichaean texts in, 1598
Manichaeism and, 5669, 5670
in martial arts, 5731–5732, 5735
Maspero (Henri) on, 8222
mediation in, 2177, 2178
meditation in, 5821
merit in, 5870
meritocracy system of, 2193
messianism of, 2195–2196
millenarianism in, 6030, 6039
in Ming dynasty, 1607–1608
miracles in, 6052
mirrors in, 6064
monasteries in, 1162, 1603
monasticism of, 2196–2197, 2201, 9845
during Tang dynasty, 2184
monkeys in, 6152
morality in, 2179, 2183, 2193, 6183–6185
mountains in, 2178, 2197, 2199, 2207, 2208, 4796, 6214
music in, 6295–6296
mystery societies/communities in, 7719
mysticism in, women in, 3342
nature in, 2631, 2636
in *Neijing tu*, 2635
as sacred space, 2637
offerings in, 2198, 4419
ordination in, 6855–6856
posthumous, 9846
orgy and, 6879
Orthodox Unity Daoism, 2192, 2193, 2200
orthodoxy and heterodoxy and, 6911
paradox of life in, 6991
peace in, 7022
phallus in, 7084–7085
pilgrimage in, 7165
popularity of, 2197
popular (folk) religion in, 3342
portraits in, vol. 10 color insert
precepts of, 2637
precursors to, 1572
priests in (*See* Priesthood, in Daoism)
principles of, 9970
and Pure Land Buddhism, 292
immortality and, 3887
purposive, 1574
qi in, 2177, 7544
in Qing dynasty, 1609
Quanzhen (*See* Quanzhen Daoism)
rebellion ideologies from, 2834
rebirth in, 2183
recreation of the world theme, 1626
and Rectifying Rites of Tianxin, 2180
relations with other religions, 2179, 2183–2184
as religion, 7692
religious experience in, 7700
religious *vs.* philosophical, 1575
resurrection in, 7762–7763
rise and development of, 1596–1598
rituals of, 2178, 2185, 2186, 2193, 2196
in literature, 2204–2206
sacred biographies in, 946
sacred time in, 7987
sacrifice in, 4915–4916
salvation in, 1593, 1594, 1597, 1626, 2204
scriptures, 1597
seclusion in, objectives of, 528
sectarian scriptures and, 1607
sexual control in, 8240
Shangqing (Highest Clarity) scriptures of, 2182, 2194–2195
Sima Chengzhen and, 2174
Sima Chengzhen, role of, 8399–8400
in Six Dynasties Period, 2192–2195
society, relations with, 8463
in Song and Yuan dynasties, 1602–1603
in Song dynasty (*See* Song dynasty, Daoism in)
space and time in, 2178
spirits in, 2178
suppression of, in Tang dynasty, 1599
syncretism in, 2605
in Taiwan, 1610, 2189
in Tang dynasty (*See* Tang dynasty, Daoism in)
temple managers *(zhuchi)*, 1617
temples in (*See* Temples, Daoist)
textiles in, 9090
tian in, 9172
time and space in, 2178
trees in, 9334
triads in, 9347–9348
universalism of, 2194
vagina in, 7084–7085
via negativa in, 9587–9588
visualization in, 9845
Way of Filial Piety, 2197–2198
Way of the Celestial Masters, 1593, 1597, 1602
Way of the Great Peace, 1593
wealth and, 9708
women in, 3341–3342
nuns, 6758
worship and devotional life in, **9842–9846**
wuwei (nonaction) in (*See Wuwei*)
xian in, 9857
xiao in, 9857–9858
Yang Xi and, 2182
yoga in, 1045–1046
in Yuan dynasty, ban on, 1166
Zhang Daoling and, 2180
Zhang Jue and, 2180
Zhenda school of, 5495–5496
Zhengyi (*See* Zhengyi Daoism)
zhenren in, 1597, 9959–9960
Zhuangzi in, 9968–9971
Daoist Assembly of the Republic of China, 8963
Daoist Association of the Province of Taiwan, 8963
"Daoist Ecology: The Inner Transformation" (Schipper), 2636
Daoist literature, 1588, 1593, **2202–2212,** 2517–2518. *See also* Dao de jing; *Zhuangzi*
Benji jing, 2197, 2211
canon/catalog of, 2183, 2202
chuanqi tales, 3067
civil service examinations and, 1909
Daofa huiyuan, 2206
Daozang, 2202–2209
contents of, 2204–2209
encyclopedic anthologies, 2210–2211
hagiography, 2206–2207
history of compilation, 2202–2203
literary collections and dialogic treatises, 2209–2211
Lu Xiujing and, 5542
organizational divisions of, 2203
research of, 2204
revelation and ritual, 2204–2206
topography, epigraphy, and historiography, 2207–2209, 2211
use in research, 2213
Daozang jiyao, 2211
Duren jing, 2205, 2206
Ge Hong and, 3290, 3291
Huainanzi, 5494–5495
Huangting jing, 2181, 2205
on iconography, 4333
Lingbao scriptures, 2183, 2186, 2194, 2196, 2203, 2205
poetry, 7207, 7212–7214
publication of, 5773
Sanhuang scriptures, 2195, 2203
Shangqing scriptures, 2182, 2194–2195, 2203, 2205
Taiping jing, 2192, 2204
Taiqing manuals, 2205
Three Caverns of, 2183, 2195, 2203, 7414
Four Supplements to, 2203
translations of, 1633
women in, 3342
Wushang biyao, 2184, 2195
Wushang huanglu dazhai licheng yi, 2205
Zhengao, 2182–2183, 2205
zhiguai anthologies, 3066
Daojiao, 2176, 2177
Daojiao linghan ji (Records of Daoist miracles), 2198
Daoren tong (director of monks), 8995
Daosheng (Buddhist philosopher), **2216–2218**
on Buddha nature and enlightenment, 1576
influence of, 1596
Daoshi. See Fangshi
Dao shu (Daoist text), 2211
Daoti lun, dao and *de* in, 2174–2175
Daoxin (Buddhist teacher), 1521, 1601
Daoxuan (Buddhist writer), 994
Daoxue (learning of the path)
as Neo-Confucianism, 1923
Zhu Xi and, 1917
Daoyin. *See* Sima Chengzhen
Daoyin gymnastics, 5734, 5735

Daozang (Daoist canon), 2202–2209
- contents of, 2204–2209
  - encyclopedic anthologies, 2210–2211
  - hagiography, 2206–2207
  - literary collections and dialogic treatises, 2209–2211
  - revelation and ritual, 2204–2206
  - topography, epigraphy, and historiography, 2207–2209
- history of compilation, 2202–2203
- Lu Xiujing and, 5542
- organizational divisions of, 2203
- research of, 2204
- use in research, 2213

Daozang jiyao (Daoist text), 2211
Daphne (deity)
- images of, vol. 13 color insert
- shape shifting and, 8301

Daphnis and Chloe (Longus), 3052
Daqing (musical instrument), 6294, 6295
D'Aquili, Eugene
- on meditation, 6487, 6490
- and neurotheology, 6492
- neurotheology and, 1952, 7850, 7857
- on psychedelic drugs, 7467

Dar (drum), 7036
Dār al-Imāra (residence of the commander), 6206
Daramulun (deity), 2310
- as supreme being, 5993

Ḍarar (injurious treatment), 4708
Dārā Shikōh, Muḥammad, **2218–2220**
- artistic endeavors of, 2219
- interest in Hinduism, 2219
- military defeats of, 2219
- philosophy of, 4421

Daratista, Inul, 6291
Darazī, Muḥammad ibn Ismāʿīl al-, 2502, 2503
Darby, Henry Clifford, 9722
Darby, John Nelson, 412, 6032
Dar es-Salaam, urban nature of, 2566
Dargāh, 4648, 4649, 9005. *See also* Khānagāh
Darger, Henry, 9626
Dargyay, Eva, 9189
Dar'i, Moses, writings of, 5085
Daribi people (Papua New Guinea)
- afterlife of, 146
- study of, 6802
- taboos of, 8949

Darijing shu (Buddhist text), 9078
Darijing yishi (Buddhist text), 9078
Darika (demon), 2449
Darius (king of Persia), magi and, 5559
Darius I (king of Persia), 4489
Dark Ages, Christianity in, 2229
Dark City, 169–170
Dark clouds, in Milky Way, in ethnoastronomy, 2864
Dark Dance. *See* Little People Society
Dark energy, anthropic principle and, 2033
Darkhei ha-Mishnah (Frankel), "law of Moses from Sinai" in, 3748
Darkhei Mosheh (Isserles), 4751
Dark Meadow (Graham), 2159
Darkness, **5450–5455**
- abolition of, 5450
- in Buddhism, 5453
- in Chinese religion, 5453
- in Christianity, 5454
- chthonic deities associated with, 7934
- complementary to *vs.* opposition to light, 5450–5451
- in esotericism, 5454
- in Gnosticism, 5452
- in Greek philosophy, 5452
- in Hermeticism, 5452
- in Ishrāqīyah, 4554
- in Mandaean religion, 5452–5453
- in Manichaeism, 5452–5453, 5648, 5652, 5666
  - millenarianism of, 6040
- in Mazdakism, 5800
- in Mesoamerican religions, 5451
- in mysticism, 5454
- in South American cosmologies, 2013, 8588
  - in Maku religion (Amazon), 8625
  - in Muisca religion, 6229–6230
- supreme beings and, 8871
- of warrior, 9684

Dark night of the soul, chaos and, 1539
Darmapāla (Yoga master), Śīlabhadra and, 8398–8399
Darmesteter, James, 6088
Darna (harmony), 765
Darnton, Robert, on media, 4961–4962
Darodaro (megaliths), 5827
Darrow, Clarence, 2890
- Scopes Monkey Trial and, 4200–4201

Darśan ("sight")
- *bhakti* poetry and, 3985
- in Hinduism, vol. 11 color insert

Darśana (auspicious seeing), 1295, 4383, 4384, 4420
- *smārta* and *haituka* schools in, 3997–3998
- in worship, 9823
- in Yoga, 9893–9894

Dars-e kharij (stage of learning), hawzah and, 3801
Dārṣṭāntika school of Buddhism, 1196
- on mental series, 8138
- Sarvāstivāda and, 8119

Darul Islam, 4689
Dār ul-ʿUlūm *(madrasah)*, 4645
Daruma. *See* Bodhidharma
Daruma sanchōden, 995
Daruma school of Zen Buddhism, 9944
Ḍarūrah (necessity), 4394
Darwin, Charles Robert
- on ethics, 2656
- eugenics and, 2879
- evolutionary theory of (*See also* Evolution)
  - and animism, 362
  - battle over, 8185–8186
  - Creationism and, 1665
  - ethics and, 2917–2918
  - in ethology of religion, 2867
  - Gurdjieff (G. I.) on, 3711
  - Müller (F. Max) on, 6235–6236
  - theism challenged by, 3558
- on gardens, 3279
- on knowledge, 5208
- on natural philosophy, 6431
- nature religions influenced by, 2662
- times of, 2907–2908

Darwinism, **8477–8480**. *See also* Evolution; Sociobiology and evolutionary psychology
- anthropocentrism in, 2608
- applied to psychology, 4776
- *vs.* evangelicalism, 2888
- intelligent design challenging, 4516, 4518
- social (*See* Social Darwinism)

Darwin's Black Box (Behe), 2911, 4517
Darwīsh, **2220**
- etymology of, 2220
- negative connotations of, 2220

Das, C. R., 827
Das, Veena, 3161
Daśabhūmika Sūtra, 998, 6993
Daśadigbuddhas (Buddhas of the ten regions), in Mahāyāna *asaṃkhyeya* cosmology, 2030
Daśahrā festival, *rāma līlā* dramas at, 3985
Dasam Granth (Sikh text), 32, **2220–2221**
- *Akāl Ustat* from, 2221
- *Bicitra Nāṭak* hymn from, 2221
- Durgā-Caṇḍī poems in, 2221
- *Jaapu* hymn from, 2221
- *Khālsā Mahima* hymn from, 2221
- Singh (Gobind) and, 8408

Daśanāmī sect. *See also* Advaita Vedānta
- *akhāḍā* military units in, 8021
- network of, 8105
- *sadhus/sadhvis* (renunciates) in, 8020

Daśaratha (king), in *Rāmāyaṇa*, 7617
Dāśaratha Jātaka (Buddhist text), 7609
Dāsas (slaves), 4467
Dasein, 50
- being and, Heidegger (Martin) on, 3896

Dasgupta, S. N., 4420, 6773
Dasgupta, Surendranath, 2760, 6623
Dash, J. Michael, 9297
Dash, Julie, 3098
Dasheng daji dizang shilun jing (Buddhist text), 5255
Dasheng Ji. *See* Kuiji
Dasheng pusa benyuan jing (Buddhist text), 5255
Dasheng qixin lun (Treatise on awakening of faith), 1576, 9019, 9077
Dashwood, Francis, sexual magic and, 8250–8251
Dasiri cult, 777
Daskhuranci, Moses, on Hun religion, 4228, 4229
Dasuttara Sutta (Buddhist text), *dharma* in, 2333
Dasyus (slaves), 4467
Datagaliwabe (deity), 6505
Dates, 2401
- Inanna and, 5956

Dates, Dawn, 677
Dāṭhāvaṃsa (Buddhist text), 1199
Datong (great unity), 1628
Datta, Bimalprasad (Bhaktisiddanta Sarasvati), Gauḍīya Math and, 1347
Datta, Kedardnath (Bhaktivinode Thakur), Vaiṣṇavism and, 1347
Datta, Michael Madhusudan, 827
Datta, Narendranath. *See* Vivekananda
Datta (deity), in Marathi religions, 5697
Dattātreya (deity), 5253
- in Sai Baba movement, 8026–8027

Datu (Batak sorcerer), 799
Datu Patoto (Datu Palanro) (Bugis mythical figure), 1317
Datura, 9218
- in Amazonian Quechua religions, 282

Datwún rite, 5689
Daube, David, on Hillel (Jewish sage), 3982
Dā'ūd al-Ẓāhirī, 4373, 4374
Daud Beureu'eh, 4669
Daudi Boharas, 108
Daughter of Israel (Kahana), 7515

Daughters of Charity, 6764
founding, 1446
Daughters of the Dreaming (Bell), 644, 645, 687, 2481, 3390
Dau Katau (deity), 6004
Daumal, René, 3711
Daumal, Vera, 3711
Davenport, Charles, 2879–2881
David (Armenian catholicos), 488
David (biblical figure), **2221–2225**
Absolom's revolt against, 1400
as author of *Psalms,* 2223, 7461–7462
and Bathsheba, 2223
charisma of, 1545
in Christianity, 2223
court history of, 2222
dance of, before Ark of Covenant, 2153
dynastic promise of, 2222, 2223
Freemasons on, 3195
in Hebrew scriptures, narrative forms of, 6375, 6376
in Qur'ān, 2223
in Islam, 2223
and Jerusalem, 923, 4834–4835
judicial decisions by, 4739
as king of Israel, historical accuracy of, 2224
Koresh (David) as heir to, claims regarding, 6553
in messianism, 5972, 5974, 5975
on murder, 986
Nathan in court of, 6417
in New Testament, 2223
political theology and, 10062
priests employed by, 5421
in prophecy, 2223
in *Psalms,* 2223
in rabbinic Judaism, 2223
redeemer from, 2835
rise to power of, 2222
Saul and, 2222, 7436
in succession story, 6417
tears of, 9026
Temple in honor of, 932
temptation of, 9070
as *tsaddiq,* 9378
Dávid, Ferenc
convicted of blasphemy, 973
Sozzini (Fausto Pavolo) and, 8673
in Transylvanian Unitarianism, 9469
David, Star of. *See* Magen David
David ha-Kohen (rabbi), 7580
David ha-Tsaddiq, 5009
Davidian Adventists, 1036, 5237, 6561. *See also* Branch Davidians
Davidic Psalter, 902, 904
Davidman, Lyn, 3354
David-Neel, Alexandra, 6052
Davids, Caroline Rhys, Horner (I. B.) and, 4129
Davidson, Peter, Hermetic Brotherhood of Luxor and, 8251
Davidson, Ronald M., 5645, 8984
David the Invincible, 6478
Davies, Sir John, on dance, 2154
Davies, W. D., on merit, 5871
Davis, Adelle, 560
Davis, Andrew Jackson, Spiritualism, role in, 8715
Davis, Charles, on ecstasy, reductionist explanations of, 2682
Davis, Cyprian, 75
Davis, Edith. *See* Turner, Edith
Davis, Gerald, 3145
Davis, Kortright, 80
Davis, Natalie Zemon
on almsgiving, 267
on Reformation violence, 1808
on violence, 9597
Davis, Tenney L., 1635
Davis, Wade, 10023, 10025
Davis-Floyd, Robbie, on rites of passage, 7803, 7859
Davy, Sir Humphrey, 6435
Da'wah, **2225–2226**
as curse, 2097
meanings of, 2225
Dawkins, Richard, 2658, 4518
on "selfish gene," 8474
Dawn
and dusk
in Canaanite literature, 1395
in Slavic religion, 8435
in Vedism, 9559
Muḥammad compared with, 6768
in Pueblo religion, 6724
Dawson, Lorne, 6527
Dawula (drum), 2497
Daxing Mountain Monastery (Buddhist temple), 9047
Daxue. See Great Learning
Day(s)
Jewish concept of, 4865–4866
of the week
Maya names for, 5885
pagan gods in names of, 1689, 1873
Day, Dorothy, **2226**
autobiography of, 699
Day, Peggy, 319
Dayak religion (Borneo). *See also* Ngaju Dayak religion
funeral rites in, 3237
head hunting in, 3805
shields in warfare, 9682–9683
Dayananda Sarasvati, **2226–2227**
in Calcutta, 2227
in Ārya Samāj, 515–516, 4431
monotheism and, 4008
Sen's (Keshab Chandra) influence on, 9318
Dayan Khan, 1149
Dāyāt (midwives), in Egypt, as class of healer, 3836
Dayfoot, Arthur Charles, 10024
Day of *Alast,* in Sufism, 8810
Day of Atonement. *See* Yom Kippur
Day of Remembrance (Yom ha-Zikkaron), 6593
Day of Sounding the Shofar (Yom Teruah), 6593
Day of the Dead, **2227–2231**
beliefs and practices of, 2229–2230
development of observances of, 2228–2229
in Korea, 5231
in Mexico, 3238
Day of the Three Kings, 2400
Dayong (ritual therapist), 1003
Days of Awe. *See* Ro'sh ha-Shanah; Yom Kippur
Dazai Jun, Hirata Atsutane, criticism by, 4022
Dazhbog (deity), **2231–2232**
Da zhidu lun (Buddhist text), 9174
Dazhong (musical instrument), 6294
Da zhuan calligraphy, in Zhou dynasty, 1370
Dbyaṇ chants, 1536
De (virtue)
charisma and, 7353
Confucius on, 1571, 1585–1586, 1894, 1936
and *dao,* **2172–2175**
in *Dao de jing,* 1574
definitions of, 2173–2174
as principle of creativity, 1627
virtue ethics in, 1894–1895
in *Zhuangzi,* 9968
Dea Arduinna (deity), 1487
Dea Artio (deity), 1487
Deacons
in Armenian church, 490
charitable work of, care of the sick, 3844
in church polity, in early church, 1763, 7401
in ministry, orders of, 6044, 6045
in Orthodox Church, ordination of, 2593
Dead, Feast of the
in Cree and Ojibwa religions, 6697
in Huron religion, 6684
Dead, Feast with the, in Andean religion, 8618
Dead, Festival of the, in Japan, 2411
Dead, the. *See also* Afterlife; Ancestors; Death; Ghosts; Spirit(s); Underworld
African cults of
vs. ancestor worship, 322
in Lugbara religion, 5527
in African religions
Luba religion, 5523–5524
West, 9718–9719
in agricultural rituals, 190
in Apache religion, 406
in Aztec religion, 5892
in Buddhism, Korean, 5231–5232
in Buriat religion, 1326
catharsis, posthumous, 1460
Catholic masses for, in Africa, 142
Chinese cult of (prehistoric), 1581–1582
in Chinese geomancy, grave location, 1594
in Christianity
masses for, 2241
prayer for, 8565
communication with, 2240–2241 (*See also* Necromancy)
in Inca religion, 5176
communion with, 6925
contact with, and purification, 1459
crowning of, 2073
Days of the Dead, **2227–2231**
in Egyptian religion
Anubis and, 403–404
communication with, 2719–2720
in Germanic religion, in sagas, 8025
gold decorating, 3625
in Greek religion, 3666, 8542–8543
hair used in relationships with, 3740
illness from breach with, in central Bantu religion, 1508
in Japanese religion, 4797
judgment of (*See* Judgment of the dead)
in Komi religion, 5219
libations for, 5433
liminal status of, 2240
living (*See* Living dead)
in manism, 5671–5673
in Mari and Mordvin religion, 5709–5710
masks and, 5769–5770
in Melanesian religions, 5833, 5838
mementos of, 2241
memories of, 2243
in Micronesian religions, 6007
mountains associated with, 6214
in New Year ceremonies, 6591
in North American Indian religions, 6651
in Oceanic religions, 6784–6785, 6789
in mythology, 6788
in Roku, 2006
pacification of, 2241
photographs of, vol. 9 color insert
in Pueblo religions, 6723
realm of (*See also* Underworld)
in Kongo cosmology, 2001
in otherworld, 6923

remembrance of
All Souls Day, 2227–2230
Roman, 6994–6995
sacrifice, receipt of, 8001
in shamanism, escorted to underworld in, 8272–8273
in South American Indian religions, cults of the dead in, 8584–8585
in Southeast Asian religions, in insular traditional religion, 8650
in Southern Siberian religions, 8671
spirits of (*See* Ghosts; *Lares*)
thirst of, 9703
in Turkic religions, 2831–2832
vengeance of, 7781
in Vodou, 9637
fear of power of, 1434
water and, 9703
in Yakkut religion, 9866
Dea Dia (deity), **2232–2233**
assimilations of, 2232
Dead Sea Scrolls, **2233–2235**. *See also* Pesher/Pesharim; Qumran sect
apocalypses in, 410, 417
biblical canon of, 880
biblical textual diversity in, 885–886
categories of, 2233–2234
Christian exegesis of, 872
contents of, 2233–2234
dating of, 2233
day of atonement in, 8144
discovery of, 2233
dualism in, 2509, 2512
Essenes and, 2847
exorcism in, 2931–2932
fire symbolism in, 3119
Gaster's (Theodor H.) translation of, 3288
God as master of time in, 7990
and history of religions, 2234–2235
Isaiah, 4545, 4550
on Israelite religion, 4974
Jeremiah in, 4827
and Karaite sect, 5087
knowledge in, 5202
merkavah in, 10050
predestination in, 3203
Psalms, 880, 7461, 7463–7464, 7465
purity in, 7514
resurrection in, 7765
revelation in, 7777
Sadducees in, 8018
Ten Commandments in, 9074
Torah, 9231, 9234
wisdom in, 9761, 9763
Dead Sea Scrolls in English, The (Vermès), 2745
Dead Sea sect (Jewish), 2234–2235, 2362
Dead Souls Remembrance Day (Baltics), 328, 331
Deakin University (Australia), program development at, 8770
Dean, Kenneth, on Daoism, 3342
Dea Syria, 6866–6867
Death, **2235–2245**. *See also* Cannibalism; Funeral rites; Martyrdom; Murder; Suicide
ablutions and, 10, 11, 12
in African religions
creation myths of, 85–86, 92–93
Dogon, 2392
dogs associated with, 2393
as journey, 140
as paradox, 141
rites of passage of, 88
rituals for, 89, 140–141
West, 9718–9719
and agriculture
myths of, 191
rituals of, 189–190
arbitrary nature of, 2244
in Australian Indigenous religions, 5051
myths of, 661–662, 663
Baal's conflict with, 723, 724, 1384, 1388, 1393–1395, 2431, 2442, 2536
in Baltic religion, 5286
baptism after, 779–780
in Buddhism, as cyclical transition, 3887 (*See also* Saṃsāra)
in Burmese religion, 1330
Campbell on mortality, 1379
in Canaanite religion, 1383, 1386
cats associated with, 1463
causes of, 2236–2237
caves associated with, 3015–3016
center of the world and, 1503
in Central Asian religions, dogs associated with, 2393
ceremonies after (*See* Funeral rites)
in Chinese religion, 1628
Wang Chong on, 9671–9672
in Christianity (*See also* Extreme unction)
anniversaries of, 2399
Paul rejecting, 156
as sleep, 8565
confrontation with
in quests, 7553, 7555
in rituals, 7836–7837
continued presence in life, 2243–2244
as cosmogonic repetition, 4159–4160
dainas (folk songs) dealing with, 2127
dances dealing with, 2138–2139
in Daoism, 2179
"death without weeping," 2243
deities of, 3622–3623
Celto-Roman, 1485
Chuvash, 1785
Edo, 2697
female, 2984, 3016, 3020
in Islam, 1785
in Mexico, modern, 8677–8678
in Samoyed religion, 8095
in Slavic religion, 8437
supreme beings as, 8870
depicted on Greek vases, 4296, 4298
dogs associated with, 2392–2393
eagle and hawk associated with, 2553
earth and, 2559–2560
Elijah and, 2765–2766
in epics, 2816–2817
Epicurus on, 3911
in existentialism, 2926
explanation of, need for, 2244
as fact of life, 2235
the Fall and, concept of, 2960
female power over, 9907
feminist perspective on, female body and, 4166
ferry across waters of, 988–989
fertility symbols associated with, 2239
and food, myths associating, 3169
frog associated with, 3223
in Garifuna religion, 3284–3286
genetic research and, 3428
in Greek religion, 3725
sleep as brother of, 8439, 8441
in Group of Ur, 8252
in Hawaiian religion, *ʿaumakua* (guardian gods) and, 3799
in Hinduism, 4440–4441
in Banaras, 779
karman and, 5095
in Vedic cosmology, 2014
in Hittite religion, 4072–4073
home and, 4104, 4105–4106
as horse, 4135
in Indo-European religions, 4456
in Indonesian religions, 5444
inevitability of, myths on, 7684
in initiation rituals, 4476, 4477–4478, 4480–4481
in Inuit religion, 4528
in Iranian religions, 4537
in Islam, 7827
barzakh and, 2837
diagnosis of, 5812
rituals for, 162
in Jainism, 4769
Jaspers (Karl) on, 4815
as journey, in Chinese tradition, 1628, 1643
in Judaism, 5445, 7822–7823
as returning to dust, 4158
soul and, 8558
in Khanty religion, 5122–5123
in Khoi religion, 5135
of king, 5155–5156
in Egypt, 5164
in Hittite religion, 5165
in Ugarit, 5164
in Komi religion, 5219
in Lakota religion, 5296–5297
life after (*See* Afterlife)
in Mansi religion, 5122–5123
in Mari and Mordvin religion, 5709–5710
in Mesoamerican religions, 148–149
during childbirth, 7812
Christian influences on, 151
life associated with, 148, 150
motion of, 148–149
in Micronesian religions, 6007, 6011
modern views of, "playing God" problem and, 8187
in monasticism, 6124–6125
moon and, 6170, 6174–6175
in mortification, 6198
in oath-taking, 9640
in Oceanic religions, 7808
origins of, 2236–2237
in African myths, 1875, 2091
mythic ancestors in, 326
in Orphic Gold Tablets, 6897
in Orphism, 6892
Osiris and, 6919–6920
overcoming, 2237
owls as symbols of, 6936
pain and, 6944–6945
and pollution, 2405, 2408, 7505, 7506, 7511, 7513
in Polynesian religions, 7311
prediction of own, 2244
in prehistoric religions, 7377
preparation for facing, 2241, 2244
as punishment for sin, 8404
purification after contact with, 1459
in homes, 4105
questions raised by, 2236
and rebirth of Mesoamerican healers, 1470
rites of
vs. ancestor worship, 320, 321

rites of ***continued***
and kinship, 5184
rivers of, 7862–7863
in Roman religions, 166
Feriae Denecales and, 7909
lustratio and, 5534
sacrificial, 2242–2243
in Samoyed religion, 8096
in San religion, 5135
serpents associated with, 8458
sexual activity as metaphor for, 2238
in shamanism
in initiation rites, 8270–8271
knowledge of, from soul flight, 8273
in Slavic religion, 8435
deities of, 727
sleep as metaphor for, 8441
by sorcery, 2099
so that others may live, 2243
in South American Indian religions
death cults in, 8584–8585
myths of origin of, 8590–8591
in Southeast Asian religions, traditional, 8650–8651
study of, 2236, 2239–2240
comparative perspective on, 2240–2244
taboos surrounding, Freud on, 2239
in Tarascan religion, 9001
theories on, and origins of religion, 2236, 2237–2240
in Tibetan religion, 3866
instructions to dead in, 8703
time and, clocks stopped at, 7986
timing of, control over, 2241, 2244
Tolstoy (Leo) obsessed with, 9220, 9221
as transitional state, 2240
trees as symbols of, 9339
in Tunguz religion, 9395
ubiquitous presence of, and immunity to significance of, 2243
Ugaritic cult of the dead, 1386
in Ungarinyin religion, 9460–9461
universal nature of, 2244
in Vedism, 8545–8546
violent
and afterlife in Ocean religions, 145–146
and ghosts, 3477–3478
Vodou spirit of (Haiti), 1433
in Warlpiri religion, 9696
women associated with, 4165
in Yurupary myth, 9920
in Zoroastrianism, 7763, 10001
Death, Property, and the Ancestors (Goody), 321–322
Death and Resurrection of Bel-Marduk, The (Assyrian text), 2537
Death and the King's Horseman (Soyinka), 2439
Death camps, Nazi, history of, 4086. *See also* Holocaust, the
Death Drama (Mesopotamia), 5961
Death of Atahuallpa, The (dance drama), 567
Death of Ivan Il'ich, The (Tolstoy), 9221
Death penalty
for blasphemy, 969, 973, 975–976
in Chinese law, 5395
for heresy, 973
in Inquisition, 8014
in Israelite religion
for crimes against king, parents, and authorities, 4737
for cursing, 4732, 4737
for homicide and manslaughter, 4737, 4738
for idolatry, 4737, 4738
methods of, 4741
for sexual offenses, 4737
in Jewish law, 3752–3753
'Aqiva' ben Yosef on, 3751
for Manichaeism, in Roman Empire, 5664
Death Sentence (Jabès), 5483
De augmentis scientarum (Bacon), 733
Deautomatization, 608–609
Deavoavai (deity), in Tacana religion, 8576
de Bary, William Theodore, Neo-Confucianism of, 1922–1923
Debate between Bird and Fish (Sumerian myth), 2791
Debate between Sheep and Grain (Sumerian myth), 2800
De Berry, W. N., 69
De Boer, T. J., 4717–4718
Deborah (biblical figure), as prophetess, 7435
Debt
at Chinese New Year, 1642
Greek laws on, 1846
Israelite laws on, 4731, 4734
Jewish law on, 3749
Hillel's *prozbul* enactment on, 3981
pain as, 6945–6946
Deb ther sngon po ('Gos lo tsā ba Gzhon nu dpal), 1223
Debt slavery, law codes on, 1844–1845, 1846
Decadence, of Roman, ancient historians on, 4027
Décadents, 341
Decaeneus (Getae priest), 3466, 9927
Decalogue. *See* Ten Commandments
Decapitation. *See also* Head(s)
in Andean human sacrifice, 8603
in Aztec human sacrifice, 4190
in myth and ritual, 3804–3805
Decebalus (Daco-Getae king), 3466
Decentius (bishop), 4495
Deception
shape shifting and, 8301
truth as corrective to, 9369
Deceptive and Indirect Methods of Persuasion and Control (DIM-PAC), 1033
De Certeau, Michael, on spirit possession, 8695
De Chardin, Pierre Teilhard. *See* Teilhard de Chardin, Pierre
Dechristianization, secularization *vs.,* 8215
Decius (emperor)
Christian persecution by, 7059
persecution under, 2112, 6888
De civitate Dei (Augustine). *See City of God* (Augustine)
Declaration and Address (Campbell), 2364
Declaration of Independence, U.S., religious rhetotic in, 7257
"Declaration of the Religions for a Global Ethic" (Kung), 2657
Declaration on the Elimination of All Forms of Intolerance and Discrimination Based on Religion or Belief, 5363
Decoherence, 1543
Decolonization. *See* Colonialism; Postcolonialism
De conceptu virginali (Anselm), 373
De concordia gratiae Dei cum libero arbitrio (Anselm), 373
Deconstruction, **2245–2248**
biblical exegesis and, 5488
definition of, 2246
for literary study, 5475–5476
Deconversion, in autobiography, 699
Decorations, for rituals/celebrations, vol. 7 color insert
Decreeing (practice), in New Thought, 1782
Decree on the Pastoral Office of the Church *(Christus Dominus),* 9540
Decretum (Gratian), as foundation for canon law, 1406, 5336, 5338, 5359
De dea Syria (Lucianus), 35
Dede cult (Africa), 5528
De divortio Lotharii et Teutbergae (Hincmar), Lothair II criticized in, 3983
De doctrina christiana (Augustine). *See On Christian Doctrine* (Augustine)
De două mii de ani (Sebastian), 2759
Dedrick, Cora, 3096
Deductive logic, 5497
Dee, John
on angels, 348
Hermetism and, 3948
Deep Blue program, 511
Deep ecology, 2608
Earth First! and, 2561–2562
Deeply into the Bone (Grimes), 7801, 7802, 7803, 7859
Deep play, 3260, 3261
Deep time, in Maya religion, 5796–5797
Deer
Artemis associated with, 5513, 5514
in Ge mythology, 3294
in Huichol peyote cult, 4153
Deer Dance, 2463
De falsis diis (Ælfric of Eynsham), 6943, 9165
Defamation
Christianity and, 8013
against new religious movements, 5378
Defensiones (Capreolus), 9164
Defensor pacis (Marsilius of Padua), 5729
Defert, Daniel, 9294
Defilement. *See also* Purification; Sacrilege
catharsis and, 1459
evil caused by, 8403
"Defiling the hands," as criterion for Hebrew scripture, 1406, 1408
Definitions of Hermes Trismegistos for Asclepius, in Hermetic corpus, 3939, 3940, 3942
Defoe, Daniel, 3051
Deforestation, in Japan, 2638–2639, 2640
De Ganay, Solange, 116
Degarrod, Lydia, 2484, 2487
Degenerationism, 5260
De George, Fernande M., structuralism and, 8748
De George, Richard T., structuralism and, 8748
Deggwā, in Ethiopian liturgy, 2860
De grammatico (Anselm), 373
Deguchi Onisaburo, 5622
de Guignes, Joseph, 1631, 1632
De harmonice mundi (Kepler), 5112
Dehumanization
by expulsion, 2939
in warfare, 9681, 9683
Dehuntshigwa'es (ballgame), 754
Deification, **2248–2251**
of animals, 2250
vs. apotheosis, 2248
cathartic, 2248–2249
in Eastern Orthodoxy, ethics and, 1652
funerary, 2250
gnostic, 2249–2250
in Hawaiian religion, of ancestors, 3799
hermits and, 2249–2250
in Hinduism, of *gurus,* 8712

iconographic, 2250
initiatory, 2249
magical, 2250
in manism, 5672
in mystery religions, 2249
in Orthodox theology, 2590–2591
Pythagoreanism and, 2248–2249
of Roman emperors, 2777, 7913
in Roman religion, by apotheosis, 7915
theurgic, 2250
Dei filius constitution, approved in Vatican Council I, 2044
De initio poenitentiae (Eck), 2601
Deir al-Bahri, 1472
Deism, **2251–2252**
in Anglicanism, 7449
definition of, 2251
deity in, 2253, 2258
in England, 2251
in the Enlightenment, 2797
Indian religious studies in, 4446
Kant (Immanuel) misrepresented as Deist, 5079
Locke (John) as Deist, 5497
nature in, 2607
in Protestantism, 7449
as response to classical physics, 7137
Deissman, Gustav Adolf, in Australia, 8768
Dé Istar, Zohl, 3390
Deity, **2252–2263**. *See also* Divinity; Gods and goddesses; *specific deities*
ambiguity of, 2252–2253
distinction from God, 2254
between God and sacred, 2261
hands as symbol of, 3769
historical background of, 2255
history of idea of, 9487
horizons of, 2255–2257
human consciousness of, 2258–2261
linguistic background of, 2254–2255
Logos as, 5501
meta-anthropological horizon of, 2256
metacosmological horizon of, 2255–2256
meta-ontological horizon of, 2256–2257
methods for understanding, 2257–2258
phenomenological method, 2257–2258
philosophical method, 2258
theological method, 2257
names of, 2259–2260
polemical usage of, 2253
polysemy of, 2252–2253
relativity of, 2253
Scheler (Max) on, 8147
structure of, 2255–2258
in Vedism, 5094
Deity yoga, 1286–1287, 2323
Dēkla (deity), 769
Delacroix, Henri, on subconscious, 7474
de la Cruz, José Francisco, 5986
de la Fuente, Julio, 5629
de la Garza, Mercedes, 5943
De Laguna, Frederica, 6708
Delatte, A., on astral representations, 8425
de la Vega, Luis Laso, 5921, 5922
Delaware religion (North America)
Big House ceremony of, 6651, 6666, 6681–6682
creation myth of, emergence in, 2557
iconography of, 4307, 4310
lord of the animals in, 5515
naming ceremony of, 6683
origin myth of, 6681
prophet of, 6458, 6666
puberty rites of, 6683
revelatory retreats of, 7769
supreme being of, 6651
Delay of the Divine Vengeance, The (Plutarch). *See Divine Vengeance, The* (Plutarch)
De l'esprit géométrique (Pascal), 7002
Deleuze, Gilles, and schizoanalysis, 7488–7491
Delhi (India)
courts and sacred space in, 1806
IAHR Conference in (2003), 8791, 8792
De Liagre Böhl, Mario Theodoro, 222
De libero arbitrio (Anselm), 373
De libero arbitrio (Augustine), 626
De libero arbitrio (Erasmus), 2821
De libero arbitrio (Pelagius), 7027
Delitzsch, Franz, 2263, 4877
Delitzsch, Friedrich, **2263–2264**
Deliverance. *See also* Exorcism
in Daoism, Sima Chengzhen on, 8400
distinction from liberation, 5435
giving thanks for, vol. 7 color insert
Deliverance de Renaud, le, 2154
Della Scala, Can Grande, 54
Delluc, Louis, 3100
Delmedigo, Yosef Shelomoh, 4897–4898, 7107
Deloria, Ella Cara, **2264–2265,** 3090
on Lakota religion, 5296
Deloria, Philip, 2264
Deloria, Vine, Jr., 702, 2617, 3090, 6672
Deloria, Vine V., 2264
Delorme, Hermann, 9067
Delos
geranos dance of, 5277
purification of, 1459, 1460
Delphi (Greece), **2265–2266**
Apollo in, 425, 426
temple of, 2265–2266, 5282
as center of the world, 8745
decline of, 2266
Dionysos in, 2357
musical relics in, 6304
omphalos (navel) at, 3017, 8745
oracle of, 2265–2266, 6831–6835
Athenians interpreting, 2375, 2376, 7278
authority of, 7278
divination at, 6832
fame of, 2265
ritual of consulting, 2265–2266
role of, 2265
on Socrates, 8503
sun and, 8839
oreibasia at, 6865
Phythian games at, 8723
politics and religion in, 7277–7278
Delphy, Christine, on gender, 3305
Delsarte, François, 2156–2157
Deluge. *See* Flood, the
Deluge (Cossack uprising), 5016
Delusion, Campbell on, 1379
Del Vasto, Lanza, Gandhi (Mohandas) influencing, 3273
Dema (Baal), 725
Dema deity
Jensen (Adolf E.) on, 4464
as mythic ancestor, 325–326, 4824, 4825–4826
De magistro (Augustine), 2382
de Maistre, Joseph, on religion, 7790
DeMallie, Raymond, 958, 6672
Demarest, Andrew, on Inca religion, 5176
De Martino, Ernesto, 863, **2266–2268,** 5261
historiography of, 4046
Dembski, William, 2911, 4517
Demerath, N. J., on civil religion, 8473
Demeter (deity), **2268–2272**
and agriculture, 2270
origins of, 191, 192
Bachofen (J. J.) on, 731
Baubo's spectacle to, 803–804
as bread goddess, 1040–1041, 2268
as bride of Zeus, 2268
chariot of the sun and, 8839
cults of, 2269–2271
festivals of, 2269, 2270
rituals in, 2269
in Sicily, 2269–2270
spread of, 2269, 2270
and Demophoon, 3118
in Eleusinian mysteries, 3382–3383, 3671, 6329
as fertility goddess, 2270
festivals for, 3684, 7144, 9156
forms of, 3908
French feminists on, 3028
functions of, 3680
and gender roles, 3382–3383
in Hellenistic religions, 3602
Homer on, 803, 2268, 2443
Isis identified with, 3908, 4557
justice and, 7783
as mare, 4133
as mother of Persephone, 2268, 2269, 3382
Pindar on, 7173
polarization with Persephone, 2984
shape shifting of, 8301
in triad, 9348–9349
Demeter Eleusinia, cult of, 2751–2752
Demetrius (biblical figure), 918, 7064
Demetrius III Eukerus (Seleucid king), 7064
Demetrius Poliorcetes, as divine, 3902
Demian (Hesse), 949
Demiéville, Paul, 1314, **2272**
positions of, 2272
writings of, 2272
DeMille, Cecil B., 3097, 3100
Demiourgoi (physicians), in *Odyssey* (Homer), 3839
Demiurge *(Dēmiourgos),* **2272–2275**. *See also* Culture heroes
as artisan, 2272, 2273
as creator, 2272, 2273, 6963
in Gnosticism, 3511
of Gnostics, 2274
inferiority of, 2274
as magistrate, 2272
Middle Platonists on, 7188–7189
philosophers using term of, 2272–2274
Plato on, 2273–2274, 6963, 7183–7184
Plutarch on, 7188–7189, 7200–7201
role of, 2273–2274
writers using term of, 2272, 2273
Democracy
in Africa, 7293
American civil religion and, 1812–1814
and Christianity in Europe, 1693
and Cold War, end of, human rights and, 4178–4179

Democracy ***continued***
Derrida (Jacques) on, 2247
in Earth Charter, 2657
journalism and, 4960–4961
in Muslim world, debate on, 7290
primitive
Fustel de Coulanges on, 3245
in Mesopotamia, 5947
religion and, Tocqueville on, 3230, 7328
in Romania, 2754
sociology and, 8481
in Zapatismo, 9932
Democracy in America (Tocqueville), 4960
Democratic Kampuchea, Khmer Rouge as leaders of, 5132–5133
Democratic Republic of the Congo. *See* Central Bantu religions; Congo; Kongo religion
Democritus
atheism and, 581
on chance, 1526
on cosmopolitanism, 3906
magic and, 5575
materialism and, 5776
monism of, 6146
naturalism of, 6428, 6429
De Monarchia (Dante), 4272–4273
Demonic language, in exorcism, 2930
Demonic magic, necromancy as, 6452
Demonolatry, 4359
Demonology, 4359, 4360–4361, 4361
magic and, 5580
Demons, **2275–2286**. *See also* Angels; Devils; Ghosts; Monsters; Spirit(s)
in Ainu religion, 206
in Balinese religion, 748
in Buddhism, 2276, 7197
cats as, 1463
chaos and, 1538
characteristics of, 2275
in Chinese religion
definition of, 1618–1619
disease caused by, 3860
exorcism of, 1606
possession by, 1614
"three corpse worms," 3862
in Christianity, 2275, 2278–2279, 2280–2281, 2314, 2373, 4359, 4360–4361
in witchcraft, 9770
clerks, in Daoism, 2193
denial of existence of, 2280–2281, 2284–2285
dogs associated with, 2393
in Egyptian religion, 7144
elaboration of, 8690
in Etruscan religion, 2277, 2871
in folk Judaism, 3158, 3159
gambling by, 3263
in Germanic religion, history of study of, 3458
in Gnosticism, astral, 8425
good and evil, 2275, 2276, 2284
in Greek religion, 2276–2277
in witchcraft, 9770
in Hellenistic religions, magicians and, 3904
in Hinduism, 2276, 2284
(*See also* Asuras; *Deva*)
in Brāhmaṇas, 1027
mythology of, 2368, 4439, 4442–4443
as renounciants, 4442
schools on, 1197
Śiva fighting, 4324
horn symbolism and, 4131
incantations addressed to, 4407, 4408
in initiation rituals, 4486
invisibility of, 2275, 2276, 2280
in Iranian religion, 2276, 2284
in Islam, 2279–2280, 2314–2315
in Japanese religion, Hirata Atsutane on, 4023
in Judaism, 2275, 2277–2278
magical conjuration of, 5579, 5584–5585
magic taught by, 5577
in Maya religion, 5798
in Melanesian religions, 5834
in Minoan-Mycenaean iconography, 4320
as monsters, 6164
in New Guinea religions, 6504
in origin of evil, 2901–2902
origin of term, 2275, 2276
Plutarch on, 2277, 7189, 7200
as possessing spirits, 2928
possession by (*See* Spirit possession)
power of, 2275, 2284
powers of, *daivas,* 2128
in pre-Buddhist Tibetan religion, 9183
in psychoanalysis, 2285
psychological perspectives of, **2282–2286**
in Roman religion, 2277
disease caused by, 3842
serpents associated with, 8459
in shamanism, in initiatory ordeals, 8270–8271
in Sinhala religion, 8412
therianthropic, 9155
universal belief in, 2276
use of term, 2314
in Vedism, Indra fighting, 4467
visual representations of, 2278–2279
Xenocrates of Chalcedon on, 7187, 7189
in Zoroastrianism, 9994–9995
gender and, 3372, 3373
Demophoon, 3118
Demosthenes, oration of, 1532
De motu (Galileo), 7340
De musica (Augustine), 6305, 6309
De natura (Pelagius), 7027
De natura deorum (Cicero), 1786, 1787, 9128
Denck, Hans, biblical exegesis of, 874
Dendera, temple at, Hathor and, 3795
Dendera (Egypt), temple of Hathor at, 2709
Dendrites, 2826
Dendrophoria (Roman celebration), 987
Dene tribes, ablutions among, 11
Deng (spirit), 7443
Deng Huoqu, autobiography of, 701
Dengjie (lantern festival), 1642
Denglu (Lamp Records), 1524, 1604
Deng Xiaoping, 1610, 1611
Buddhism attacked by, 1158
Muslims tolerated under, 4636, 4637, 4638
reform policies of, 4637, 10073
Dengyō Daishi. *See* Saichō
Dengzhen yinjue (Tao), 8996
Denjutsu isshin kaimon (Kōjō), 995
Denk, Hans, 304
Dēnkard, 411, 9993
Ahriman as source of evil and sickness in, 3809
union and solidarity of human race in, 3907
wisdom in, 9752
Denmark
ballet in, 2156
films from, 3098–3099
folklore of, *nis,* 2951
Germanic religion in, boat burials, 990
Inuit religious studies in, 475
Islam in, 4678
Kierkegaard in, 5140–5141
Neolithic religion in, 6465
new religious movements with origins in, 6568
runic inscriptions in, 7941
Dennett, Daniel, 2658
on Darwinism, 8477
Dennis, John, 5356
Denominationalism, **2286–2291**
in Canada, 1711
countervailing attitudes toward, 2289–2290
"denomination" as category, 1866–1867
denomination distinguished from sect, 2084
emergence of, as ecclesiology, 1774–1775
evangelical postdenominational consciousness, 1775
in Judaism, 4868–4869, 4985
membership in the church and, 1778
origin of, 2286, 2287–2288
ridicule of, 4200
vs. sectarianism, 2286
and toleration, 2286–2287
in United States, 1711, 2288–2290
use of term, 2286–2287
Denryaku (text), Shotoku Taishi in, 8375–8376
Densmore, Frances, 754
Densmore, Ruth, 3406
Dentan, Robert, 2486
Dentheleti tribe (Thracian), 9168
Denunciatory, revival and renewal activities described by, 7784
De Nuptiis (Capella), 522
Deoband school (Islam), 4645, 4652, 4654
Deontological approach to ethics, 1650, 1655, 1656
Deontological ethics, desire in, 2303
Deoxyribonucleic Acid. *See* DNA
De pace fidei (Nicholas of Cusa), 7244
Dependence
in essence of religion, 1819–1820
faith as, 2956
Schleiermacher (Friedrich) on, 8166
Dependent arising, in Buddhism, 5098, 7364, 7365
Dependent Co-origination, 7678
Dependent co-origination doctrine. *See Pratītya-samutpāda*
Deposition from the Cross (Rembrandt), 4347
De potestate summi pontificis in rebus temporalibus (Bellarmino), 816
Depression
of James (William), 4777
negative reality and, 6489
religiousness, relationship with, 3875–3876
De primatu Petri (Eck), 2601
Deprivation
in millenarianism, 6033, 6034
ritual (*See also* Asceticism)
ecstatic discipline and, 8703
sacred and profane and, 7971
trances induced by, 8688–8689
Deprivation theory, on spirit possession, 8694
Deprogramming, 1032, 1033, **2291–2293**
by anticult movements, 396, 2085
brainwashing as legal defense and, 5376
coercive, 2292
conservatorship laws and, 5376
debate on, 6566
decline of, 2292–2293

in Europe, 6569
of Family members, 2987
in Japan, 6523
of Jesus Movement members, 4853
lawsuits on, 2292–2293
new religious movements and, 6513, 6522, 6525, 6562
noncoercive, 2291
opposition to, 2292
price of, 2292
of Unification Church members, 6560
unsuccessful, 2292
Depth psychology, 5031–5036
symbolic theory and, 8911–8912
Depth Theology, of Heschel (Abraham Joshua), 1960
De pulchro et apto (Augustine), 624
De purgatorio (Eck), 2601
De Purucker, Gottfried, 7229–7230
Deqing, 1578
Derash (form of exegesis), 867, 868, 7620
Derashah (direct scriptural exegesis), 4482
in tannaitic texts, 3748
Derbent (Dagestan), 4612
Derceto (deity), 7103
De regia protestate (Hugh of Fleury), 7791
De regno Christi (Bucer), 1059, 9110
Deren, Maya, 76, 3099, 3102, 10026
De rerum natura (Lucretius), 7913
De revolutionibus orbium coelestium libri sex (Copernicus)
implications of, 1978, 8182
preface to, 1977, 8182
publication of, 1977
Reformation and, 8182
suspension of, 1978
Derrida, Jacques
and deconstruction, 2245–2248
deconstructionism of, 8752
on difference, 3303
and feminism, 3028, 3035
metaphysics of, 5991
on *différance,* 3028, 5474, 5475, 5482
on phenomenology of religion, 7099
on poetic truth, 7206
and postcolonial theory, 10042
on supplementarity, 3024
on textual interpretation, 5474, 5475–5476, 5487
on time, 7993
Derveni Papyrus, 2965, 6892, 6895
Dervishes
enthusiasm of, 2807
Howling, in Rifā'i Sufism, 8823
Mevlevi order of, 6750
and migration, 6024
and mysticism, 6352
orgy and, 6879
rise of, 6024
trickster-like behavior of, 4214
whirling, 2140, 7935
in Bektashī Sufism, 8823
Deśabhakti (devotion), 829
Desacralization
Canaanite ritual of, 1385
secularization *vs.,* 8215
De sacrificio missae (Eck), 2601
Desaguliers, John Theophilus, as Freemason, 3195
Desana religion (Colombia)
celestial ordering in, 8428
center of the world, 1502
flood in, 3131, 3132
Milky Way in, 2863
tricksters in, 9358
visions in, 9614
De sapientia veterum (Bacon), 733
De satisfactione (Eck), 2601
Descartes, René, **2293–2295**
on animals, 356
Aristotelian world image broken down by, 1996
Christian dualism influenced by, 2649
"Cogito ergo sum," 2293–2294, 2424, 7110
on conscience, 1942
on doubt, 2424
dualism of, 2505, 7282
epistemology of, 2819
as father of modern philosophy, 2293
on free will, 3200
Gilson (Étienne) and, 3492
on God, 3556
existence of, 582, 2294, 7421
on historiography, 4030
as idealist, 4355
on intuition, 4525
on knowledge, 5205–5206
life of, 2293
materialism and, 5776
metaphysics of, 2293, 5990
Neoplatonism and, 6475
on nervous system, 6485
philosophy of, 2293–2294, 7110, 7111
as predecessor of positivism, 7340
on reality, 7137
on Rosicrucians, 7930
Scholasticism and, 8176
skepticism and, 8421
on soul, 2294, 6486
Spinoza (Baruch) on, 8681, 8682
writings of, 2293
Descent
anthropological concept of
kinship and, 5183, 5184–5185
in Yap culture, 5183
of *tsaddiq,* 2768
Descent into the underworld, **2295–2300**
in Greek mythology, 2298, 2299
by heroes and deities, 2297–2299
as literary motif, 2295, 2299
in Maori religion, 2298
with no return, 2295
in North American Indian religions, 2298
in quests, 7553, 7555
reasons for, 2297
with return, 2295
by shamans, 2296–2297
in Siberian mythology, 2296–2297
topographies of, 2295–2296
visionary, 2299–2300
Descent of Man, The (Callicott), 2656
Descent of Man, The (Darwin), 2917
Müller (F. Max) on, 6236
Descola, Philippe, 2486
Description
in phenomenology, 7088, 7090, 7092, 7094, 7096
thick, Geertz (Clifford) on, 8499, 8500
Description (Pausanias), 507
Descriptive confessionalism, definition of, 2056
Desert Fathers
communal eremticism and, 1980
Evagrios of Pontus and, 2886
on knowledge, 5203
prayer of the heart and, 3883
Satan and, 9771
sleeplessness among, 8441
Symeon the New Theologian and, 8920
writings of, 2828
Desert of Cells, 2825
Deserts, **2300–2303**
Christian monastic movement in, 2301, 6117, 6131
demons of, 2277
eremitism in, 2824
in history of religions, 2301–2302
in Islam, 2301
of Judaea, Jesus's retreat in, 7770–7771
in Judaism, 2300–2301
and personal religious experience, 2300–2301
religions founded in, and gardens, 3276–3277
as source of monotheism, 2301–2302
of spiritual solitude, 2301
Teresa of Ávila on meditation in, 8724
Desert Solitaire (Abbey), 2563
Desertum civitas, 2301
Desertum floribus verans, 2301
Desideri, Ippolito, 1311
Designation, in semantics, 8227
Design theorists. *See* Intelligent design
Desire, **2303–2309**
Campbell on, 1379
celibacy and, 1475
in Christianity, 2307–2309
in deontological ethics, 2303
elimination of, in Confucianism, 9674
in enlightenment, 2794
interpreting, 2303
liberation from, 2304
in Buddhism, 2306
in Daoism, 2304, 2306
in Hinduism, 2304–2305, vol. 13 color insert
in mysticism, 2309
power of, 2304
renunciation of, in Hinduism, 5097
Spinoza (Baruch) on, 8684
spiritual importance of, 2304
in Stoicism, 2307
in Sufism, 2309
in Tantrism, 2305
in teleological ethics, 2303
Desjarlais, Robert, 2489
Desmangles, Leslie, 10026
de Soto, Hernando, 6689
Despair
hope as obverse of, 4127
Kierkegaard on, 4127
De Spectaculis (Tertullian), 2437
Despotes hippon (horse-taming god), 4252
Destiny. *See also* Fate; Predestination
in African religions, 89
God's role in, 92, 93
Yoruba, 3571
in Australian Indigenous myths, 656–658
in Baltic religions, 5285–5286
in Etruscan religion, 2873
in Ājīvikas doctrine, 213
Destruction. *See also* Flood, the
in Buddhism (*See Saṃvartānis*)
by creators, disease and, 3808–3809
desecration, 8011–8012
in Hinduism (*See Pralaya*)
play and, 7194
of religion *vs.* of the sacred, 7975
sacrifice and, 7997, 7999, 8000
in South American Indian myths, 8588–8589
by water, 9703

Detachment and nonattachment
entrance of practice in Chan school and, 1521
in Mādhyamika tradition, 1576
wu ("nothing") in early Daoism, 1575
Detective stories, morality in, 3062
De temporum ratione (Bede), 814
Determinism
astrological, Cumont on, 2093–2094
biological, neuroscience and, 8191
in Buddhism, dependent co-origination and, 1527
chance and, 1526–1529
chaos theory in, 7139
definition of, 3199, 3200
vs. fate and fatalism, 2998
free will and, **3199–3202**
genetic, 8187
in Ājīvikas, 213, 3639–3640
in Islam, 3563–3565
in Ash'arīyah, 535, 3563–3565
Ja'far al-Ṣādiq on, 4761
suffering and, 8809
Newtonian physics and, 7137, 7139
vs. predestination, 3202
Deterministic chaos, 1542
Detienne, Marcel, 1014
on Greek religion
memorization in, 5852
sacrifice in, 3669
on sacrifice, 1466, 3669, 8009
Detlavs, Eduards, 765
Det osynligas värld (Andrae), 333
De Trinitate (Augustine). *See On the Trinity* (Augustine)
De Trinitatis erroribus (Servetus), modalistic trinitarianism in, 8232
De triplici via (Bonaventure), 5818
Detschew, Dimiter, 9171
Deukalion
as flood survivor, 3131
and Prometheus, 3132
and Pyrrha, myth of, 2965–2966
Deus otiosus (god at leisure), **2309–2313**
absence of myth and cult of, 2310
Alalu as, 2311
Bunjil as, 2310
Caribbean high gods as, 1426
in creation myths, 757, 2309–2310, 2311, 2312
Daramulun as, 2310
Dyaus as, 2313
Eliade on, 8879
masculine sacrality and, 5760
Mwari as, 2313
Ọlorun as, 2310–2311
Ouranos after castration as, 1450, 2311
Pettazzoni (Raffaele) on, 8878
Puluga as, 2310
sky gods as, 2309–2310, 2311, 2312
study of, 2312–2313
supreme beings as, 8870
as supreme creator, 1993
symbolic characteristics of, 2311–2312
Témaukel as, 2310
withdrawal of God and, 2310–2311
Deussen, Paul, 735, 4446
Deuteronomic history
monarchical prophets in, 7436
premonarchical prophets in, 7435
prophetic authority in, 7433, 7434
prophetic experience in, 7430, 7431, 7432, 7433
prophetic task in, 7435
Deuteronomy, 878
Aaron in, 5423
amulets and talismans in, 299
ancestor worship in, 4743
Aramaic translation of, 888
authority of, 882
authorship of, Smith (W. Robertson) on, 8451
blessings in, 4745
citations from, in *Matthew,* 907
content of, 879, 9232–9233
corporate responsibility in, 4857
covenant theology in, 2048
curses in, 2102–2103, 4745
divorce in, 7822
Hoffmann (David) on, 869
Hosea, affinities with, 4138
human perfectibility in, 7039
Ibn 'Ezra' on, 4266
Ibn Ḥazm on, 7238
idolatry in, condemnation of, 4358, 4359
Jerusalem in, 4839
Josianic reforms and, 4828, 4959
as law code, 1845
laws in, 9233
asylum, 4728–4729
criminal law, 4738
dietary laws, 7508
family law, 4733, 4734
personal status laws, 4731, 4732
state and judiciary law, 4739, 4740
Levites in, 5421–5422, 5425, 5426
on local shrines, 4745
al-Maghribī (Samuel) on, 7239
midrashim on, 6018
Moses in, 6200, 9232–9233
miracles of, 6051
and mystical union, 6339
ocular activity in, 5425
pesher of, 7065
pre-covenant historiography in, 4027
prophetic critique of Israelite religion in, 4748
in Samaritan Bible, 8070
scroll in, 4749
stone pillars proscribed by, 8744
suffering in, 8805, 9115
Temple cult centralization in, 935
Temple procedures in, 927, 932
Ten Commandments in, 9074
tithes in, 9209
in Torah, 9231, 9232–9233
Deuteronomy (D) source, dating of, 6199
Deutsch, Eliot, 51
Deutsch, Nathaniel, 81
on Gnosticism, 3534
Deutsche Mythologie (Grimm), 3111, 3702, 4458
Mannhardt (Wilhelm) influenced by, 5676
Les deux sources de la morale et de la religion (Bergson), 838
Deva. *See* Āryadeva
Deva (spirit), 1027, 1197, 1329, 2276, 2284
asuras conflict with, 9560
Devadāsīs (hereditary dancers), 2448, 7043
Devadatta (Buddha's cousin), 1089
murder attempted by, 8015
Devadatta (breath), 1043, 7363
Devakī(Hindu figure), 743
Devaḷ (mythic figure), 4434
Devalayas (shrines), 7407
Devall, Bill, 2608
Devānaṃpiyatissa (king of Sri Lanka), **2313–2314**
as Aśoka's ally, 2313
Theravāda Buddhism and, 2037, 2313, 9146–9147
Devarāja (god-king cult), 1134–1135, 1138
in Cambodia, 4012
in Khmer religion, 5129
maṇḍalas and, 8644, 8645
Devarim. See Deuteronomy
Devas (rank of god)
devarāja (god-king cult), in Cambodia, 4012
in Sinhala religion and, 8410–8412
sun (Sūrya or Āditya) as, 8135
in Vedic belief system, 3990
Devaśarman
Abhidharma texts attributed to, 10021
on Nāgārjuna, 5552
Devatās (divine powers), 1329, 9094
in Sinhala religion, 8410
Devekut. See Devequt
Development, concept of, in *Wissenschaft des Judentums,* 4876
Development of Religion and Thought in Ancient Egypt (Breasted), 2730
Devendrabuddhi (Buddhist scholar), 1212
Devequt (communion with God), 726, 2320, 2321, 2429, 2430
circle of BeSHT on, 3786
in Hasidism, 3789, 4982–4983, 5017
and mystical union, 6339–6340
Soloveitchik (Joseph Baer) on, 8519
De vera religione (Augustine), 625
De vera religione (Pinard), 7173
Devereux, Georges, 10043
De veritate (Anselm), 373
De veritates (Aquinas), 9375
Devī (Great Goddess). *See also* Kālī
and Tārā, 9000
body symbolism and, 4164–4165
cakras and, 1348
hymns to, 7209
iconography of, 4325–4326
in Navarātri festival, 6444
in Purāṇas, 7500
mythology of, 4443–4444
third eye of, 4326
yoni icons of, 9905, 9906
Devi, Mahasveta, 6742–6743
Devi, Maitreyi, 2760
Deviance, sociological concept of, 8484–8485
Deviationist movements, in Africa, 102
Devībhāgavata (Hindu text), 7499
Devil, the. *See also* Devils
in Christianity, 2276, 2314, 2315 (*See also* Satan)
in Finno-Ugric creation myths, 3108–3109
in Otomí religion, 6927–6928
magic performed with assistance of, 6452
in Nahuatl religion, 6403
Devil, The (Tolstoy), 9221
Devil and Commodity Fetishism in South America, The (Taussig), 9297
Devil in the New World, The: The Impact of Diabolism in New Spain (Cervantes), 9297
Devils, **2314–2316**. *See also* Demons; Satan
in ballets, 2155–2156
in Buddhism, 2315
characteristics of, 2275–2276
in Christianity, in colonial South America, 8609
definition of, 2314
dogs associated with, 2393
dragons as, 2432–2433
gender of, 2315
in Hellenistic religions, dualism with angels, 3904
in Hinduism, 2314, 2315
horn symbolism and, 4131

intercourse with, alleged in witch hunts, 8013
in Jainism, 2315
in Mari and Mordvin religion, 5710
in mirrors, 6064
music invented by, 6277
origin of term, 2275, 2314
origins of, 2315–2316
serpents associated with, 8459
typology of, 2314–2315
use of term, 2314
in Zoroastrianism, 2314, 2315
Devil's Delusion, The (Ibn al-Jawzī), 976
Devils of Loudun (Huxley), 2476
Devīmāhātmya (Hindu text), 7500
Navarātri festival in, 6443–6444
Devir (shrine), 924
De viris illustribus (On famous men) (Jerome), 4834
Devisse, Jean, on Hincmar, 3983
Devlin, Patrick, 5369
Devotio Moderna, 7771–7772
Devotion, **2316–2322**. *See also* Worship and devotional life
art, devotional, human body in, 4170
in Buddhism, 1111–1112
buddhas and *bodhisattvas* inspiring, 1084–1085, 7495
Buddha's relics as object of, 2317, 4383, 7495
as meditation, 2319, 2320
philosophy of, 2321
Southeast Asian, 9827–9828
characteristics of, 2318–2319
in Christianity
characteristics of, 2318
charity in, 2320–2321
Law (William) on, 5324
objects of, 2317
definition of, 2316
in Eastern Orthodox Christianity, 2320
and ethics, 2321
in Hinduism (*See also* Bhakti)
antiritualism of, 7699
characteristics of, 2319
objects of, 2317
philosophy of, 2321
pilgrimage as, 2320
and iconoclasm, 4280
in Shintō, 2317
in Islam
characteristics of, 2318–2319
dhikr as, 2339, 2340
pilgrimage as, 2319
to Muḥammad, 6227–6228
in Judaism
dance as, 2319
Dov Ber of Mezhirich on, 2429–2430
mysticism and, 2320, 2321
language of, 7119
objects of, 2316–2317
philosophy of, 2321
pilgrimage as act of, 2319–2320, 7147
in poetry, 7207–7208
and religious practices, 2318, 2319–2321
scripture, role in, 8199–8200
in Sufism
dance as, 2319
devotional allegiance, 9819–9820
emotional, 2317
images of, 2321
meditation as, 2320
monastic, 2318
mysticism and, 2320
types of, 2317–2318
worldly engagement as, 2673
Devotional, revival and renewal activities described by, 7784–7785
Devotio rites, sacred *vs.* profane and, 7966
"Devourers" (desert gods), in Canaanite religion, 1383
De Vries, Ad, on anchors, 332
De Vries, Peter, 1539
De Wall, Frans, 7850
Dewantara, Ki Hadjar, Tamam Siswa movement and, 8652–8653
Dewaruci (Java), divine beings in, 4816
Déwata Mattanru' Kati (deity), 1317
Déwata Sisiné (Déwata Séuwaé) (deity), 1316–1317
Déwa yajña (offering), 747–748
Dewey, John
aesthetics of, 49
Campbell, influence on, 1378
on experience, 49
on knowledge, 5207
metaphysics of, 5991
on naturalism, 6429, 6430
on pragmatism, 5081
religion, criticism of, 1378
Dewi Sri (deity), in Agami Jawi, 4817
De Witt, Johan, Spinoza (Baruch) and, 8682
Dewitt, John, 6541
"Dew of light" (Jewish concept), soul and, 8557
Dgambara sect, heavens in, 2024
Dge 'dungrub pa (Dalai Lama), 2131
Dge 'dun rgya mtsho (Gendün Gyatso) (Dalai Lama), 1154, 2131
Dge lugs pa order of Buddhism, 1157, 2131, **2322–2324**
and Bon religion, 1009
education in, 2322–2323
emergence of, 8083
foundation of, 2322, 9386, 9387
monasteries in, 8084
monastic morality of, 1218
in Mongolia, 1149, 1228, 2322
philosophy of, 1301
reestablishment of, 2323
reincarnate lama of, 2132
Shugs ldan (Shugden) and, 8381, 8382
spread of, 2322
temples of, 9051–9052
theocracy in, 9109
in Tibet, 1154–1155, 1228–1229, 1232, 2322–2323
Dgra bla (enemy gods), 9185
Dhalang (puppeteers), 2451
Dhamma, 1072, 1073, 1134
Dhammacakkappavattana Sutta (Buddhist text), 1296, 1305
Dhammacakkhappavatana Sutta, 2737
Dhammaceti (king of Chiangmai), 1137, 9149
Dhammachaiyo, Phra (Dhammajayō/Thammachaiyō), 2324
Dhammakāya movement, **2324–2326**
in Cambodia, 5132
controversies over, 2325
origins and growth of, 2324–2325
reform movements in, 9095–9096
significance of, 2326
teachings of, 2325–2326
Dhammapada (Buddhist text), 1198
desire in, 2306
environment and, 2627
Dhammapāla (Buddhist monk), 998, 1199, 1200, 9148
Dhammarāja (king), 1138, 1329
Dhammasaṅgaṇī (Buddhist text), 10021
Dhammayutnikāy sect, in Cambodia, 5131
Dhammayuttika. *See* Thammayut Nikāya
Dhanaṃjaya (breath), 1043, 7363
Dhanasi (dance), 7048
Dhanvantari (deity), in Āyurveda, 714
Dharamsala, Tibetan exile to, 2924
Dhāraṇā (concentration), 9895
aṣṭāṅgayoga (eight-limbed discipline), 8705
Dhāraṇī Piṭaka (Buddhist text), 1114, 5309
in Mahāsāṃghika Buddhism, 5601
Dhāraṇīs (sacred verse), 1263
chanting during meditation, 1291
in Vajrayāna (Tantric) Buddhism, 1121–1122, 1214
in Shingon Buddhism, 1243
Dharma, **2327–2336**. *See also* Enlightenment
Abhidharma theory of, 5308
āśrama and, 7817
avatāra theory and, 4000–4001
Buddhist, 1272, **2331–2336**
ages of, 1276, 5685–5687
Aśoka on, 553–554, 555
Aśoka's commitment to, 1090
Avalokiteśvara teaching, 7408
Buddha as personification of, 2332
in Burmese Buddhism, 1330
celebrating, 1305–1306
in Chinese Buddhism, 1160
classifications of, 2333–2335
conditioned, 2333–2335, 7357
Daosheng on, 2217
as doctrinal teaching, 1104, 1252, 1258, 1261–1262, 1268–1269, 2332
drums as sound of, 2496
embodiment in words, 5309
as empty, 8856, 8857
and entrance of practice, in Chan school, 1521
enumeration of, 2334–2335
as essence, 2332
Huineng on, 4154
in Mahāyāna Buddhism, 1206, 1298, 2332
in Japanese Buddhism, 1182
and *karman,* 5099–5100
law and, 5347
literary sources of, 2333
Maitreya proclaiming, 6984
in missions, 6079
as natural law, 2331
number system used to describe, 6752
presence of, 1277
propagation in Tibet, 3156
protector deities of, 8381
quest for, as goal of pilgrimage, 7163
as reality, 1112, 2332
recitation of, as early canon, 2035
reliance on, 1274
Sarvāstivāda theory of, 2333–2335, 8118

Buddhist *continued*
Sautrāntika view of, 8119, 8137
Stcherbatsky (Theodore) on, 8737
Suzuki Shōsan on, 8887
in Tibetan Buddhism, 3156, 8381
as truth, 2332
turnings of the wheel of, 1275–1276, 2332, 4328
unconditioned, 1197, 2333–2335, 7357
visual symbols of, 4327, 4328
Hindu, **2327–2331,** 3001, 4428 (*See also* Varṇāśramadharma theory of caste)
and authority, 2328
as basic aim, 2305
caste system and, 5289, 5343, 5346
charity and, 1555
chastity and, 1559
concept of, 2327
as cosmological principle, 2327
deterioration of, 2327
as duties of castes, 2329–2330
in environmental activism, 2620, 2623
in epic cosmology, 2017
four sources of, doctrine of, 2328
fulfillment of, 2305
immutability of, exceptions to, 2330
in *Bhagavadgītā,* 853, 4442
of individuals, 5346
in *kṛtayuga,* 6983
in Mīmāṃsā school, 6042
in *kaliyuga,* 6983
king as guardian of, 2328, 5344–5345
Kṛṣṇa as protector of, 854
as law, 2327, 2328, 2330–2331, **5343–5347**
lexical diversity of, 2327–2328
literary sources of, 2327, 2328–2329, 5343–5344
mythic themes of, 4441–4442
principles of, 5344
Puruṣārthas (four goals of humankind) and, 3996
and reincarnation, 7677
Śaṅkara on, 9373
and social reform, 2330–2331
sources of, 2328, 5343–5344
as stages of life, 2329, 2330
Tagore (Debendranath) on, 9318
textual focus on, 2620–2621
topics of, 2329
as tradition, 2328–2329
as truth, 9372
as virtue, 2328
vs. mokṣa, 2621
meaning of, Western study of religion, implications for, 8762
obedience required by, 2955
ṛta as Vedic antecedent of, 2327, 7933
single *vs.* multiple, in Pali *vs.* Sarvāstivādin texts, 2029
in Southeast Asian religions, 5346
vs. mokṣa, 2621
Dharma (deity), 2327, 3001
Dharmacakra mudrā (gesture), 4328, 4329, 4330
Dharmacakrapravartana Sūtra, meaning of name, 1350
Dharmadharmatāvibhaṅga (Buddhist text), 9899
Dharmadhātu (Buddhist concept), 1117, 1120, 1291, 2628–2629, 9019
Sthiramati on, 8739
Dharma Drum Mountain, 1168
Dharmagupta (Buddhist monk), Śubhākarasiṃha and, 8803
Dharmaguptaka school of Buddhism, 1110
doctrines of, 1196, 1197
geographical distribution of, 1195
literature of, 1198
origin of, 1194
Sarvāstivāda and, 8120
Dharmagupta Vinaya, 6760
Dharmākara *(bodhisattva),* 1079, 1114, 6632. *See also* Amitābha
Dharmakāya (body of truth), 2332, 2628–2629
achievement of, 9017
Amida Buddha as, 8355
and *tathāgata,* 9015
of Buddha, 1064, 1065, 1069–1070, 1077, 1117, 1217, 1261, 4416, 4928, 9347, 9962
golden body of Buddha and, 1861
of Amitābha, 1293
similes indicating, 9018
Vajradhara as, 9510
Dharmakāyadhātu (truth-body realm), 9017
Dharmakīrti (Buddhist scholar), **2336–2337**
Atīśa studying under, 1126
and Buddhist epistemology, 1212, 1213, 1301, 2336
and Buddhist logic, 1120, 2336
in curriculum of colleges, 1156, 2323
in Mādhyamika Buddhism, 5554
Nālandā critizing, 1121
Sakya Paṇḍita on, 8052
Stcherbatsky (Theodore) on, 8737
theory of concepts of, 2336–2337
writings of, 2336, 2352
Dharmaksema (Buddhist monk), miracles of, 6053
Dharmamaṅgals (Bengali text), 825
Dharmamudrā (Dharma Seal), 1217, 1218
Dharmapada (Buddhist text), 1146
Dharmapāla (Buddhist monk), **2337–2338**
as founder of Vijñānavāda tradition, 2337
and Buddhist education, 1126
and Buddhist ethics, 1282
followers of, 2337
on lay asceticism, 9152
life of, 2337
Malalasekera (G. P.) and, 5624
as missionary in Britain, 1188–1189
philosophy of, 1301, 2337–2338
and revival of Buddhism, 1187
visiting Indonesia, 1133
at World's Parliament of Religions, 9805
writings of, 2337, 2338
Dharmarāja. *See* Yama
Dharmarakṣa (Buddhist translator), 1147, 1163
Dharmaśāstras (Hindu texts)
in Brahmanism, 9568–9569
in British Indian law, 8123
commentaries on, 2329
content of, 2329
contents of, 5345–5346
dating of, 2329
dharma in, 2329, 5343–5344
Dharmasūtras compared to, 3995
interpretation of, 5345
law in, 5344
overview of, 8122
Puruṣārthas (four goals of humankind) in, 3996
relational discipline and, 8706–8707
studies of, 4450
time in, 2016–2017
varṇāśramadharma theory of caste in, 3995–3996
Dharmaskandha (Buddhist text), 10021
Dharmasūtras (Hindu texts)
āśrama in, 7816
authors of, 2329
in Brahmanism, 9568–9569
classical Hinduism and, 3994
contents of, 5345–5346
dating of, 2329
dharma in, 2327, 2329, 5343–5344
Dharmaśāstras compared to, 3995
Gaṇeśa in, 3274
interpretation of, 5345
law in, 5344
style of, 2329
suicide in, 8831
varṇāśramadharma theory of caste in, 3995–3996
in Vedas, 9554
Dharmasvāmin (Tibetan pilgrim), 1125
Dharmayātrā (journey for truth), 7163
Dharmottarīya school of Buddhism, 1194
Dharm-thmī, 5132
Dhātakīkhaṇḍa (island-continent), in Jain cosmology, 2023–2024
Dhātus (elements of the body), in Āyurveda, 3855
Dhātuvaṃsa (Buddhist text), 1305
Dhaval, Neryōsangh, 9994
Dhawū al-arḥām (distant kindred), 4709
Dhawū furūḍ (Qur'anic heirs), 4709–4710
Dhikr (remembrance), **2339–2342**
as anamnesis, 312–313
attention in, 604
breath control in, 1046
in *ḥadīth,* 2340
in Qur'ān, 2339–2340
Ṣūfī orders and, 8822
in Sufism, 2339, 5818, 9004, 9005, 9006
female-only, 9007
Khufīya, 4635
Naqshbandī, 4616, 4621, 9010
principles of, 2340–2341
Tijānī, 9007
Yahrīyah, 4635
Yasawī, 4616, 4621
types of, 2341
Dhimay (drum), 2497
Dhimma (protection) system, 1673–1674, 4995
Dhimmī (non-Muslim) communities, 6736
in Andalusia, 4593, 4596–4597, 7282
Islamic law governing, 7540
Jews as, 7236
Parsis as, 6997
Zoroastrians as, 10003
Dhīr Mal, 32
Dholak (drum), 7036
Dhorme, Édouard, 5968–5969
on messiah, 5972
Dhruva (deity), North Star represented by, 8734
Dhū al-Nūn al-Miṣrī, poetry and mystical theology of, 8811–8812
Dhū al-Qaʿdah (month in Islamic year), 4714
Dhū Nuwās (Himyarite ruler), 442, 894
Dhup-sarvi (perfume ceremony), 3137
Dhūtanga (wandering ascetic), 9096

Dhuwa religion (Australia), Djan'kawu in, **2378–2380**
Dhyānas (meditation realms), 5820
Asanga on, 5200
destructions and, 2028
development of, 7041
in eightfold path, 2737, 2738
aṣṭāṅgayoga (eight-limbed discipline), 8705
practicing, 7357
stages of, 7357
in Yoga, 9895
Dhyāni-buddhas (meditational buddhas), 1078, 1214
Di. *See* Shangdi
Di (deities), in China, Shangdi and, 8299
Di (deity), 2984
Di (musical instrument), 6293
Dia (deity), Arval Brothers and, 513–514
Diabolical witchcraft, 9770–9774
neopaganism and, 9775
Diabolic root. *See* Peyote
Diaghilev, Sergei, 2161
Diagoras (Greek poet), 971
Diagoras of Melos, as atheist, 3910
Diagrams, vol. 3 color insert
aesthetics of, 55–56
geometric (*See Maṇḍalas*)
Diakonov, Igor M., on *Epic of Gilgamesh,* 3487
Dialectic(s)
Jerome's use of, 4832
Platonic, reflexivity in, 7648
sacred *vs.* profane and, 7976
transcendental, Kant (Immanuel) on, 5077
Dialectica (Abelard), 7
Dialectical dualism, 2508, 2509
Dialectical materialism, 5777
Dialectical method, of Hegel (G. W. F.), 3893, 5777
Dialectical theology
Barth (Karl) and, 790–791
proponents of, 6466
Dialecticians, in China, suppression of, 1590
Dialectic of Sex, The (Firestone), 3311
Dialectic opposition. *See* Binary oppositions; Duality
Dialogi (Abravanel), 4897
Dialogic diversity, 2605
Dialogorum de Trinitate (Servetus), conciliatory efforts in, 8232
Dialogue
in Egyptian literature, 2721
in *Job,* 4931–4932
among religions (*See* Dialogue of religions)
in science and religion typology, 2658
in Zapatismo, 9932–9933
Dialogue, The (Catherine of Sienna), 1461
Dialogue between Theology and Psychology, The (Homans), 7477
Dialogue of a Man with His Soul (Egypt), 2721
Dialogue of a Philosopher with a Jew and with a Christian (Abelard), 7
Dialogue of religions, **2342–2345**. *See also* Ecumenical movement
artificial (imaginative), 2342
Christians in, 2342, 2343, 2344–2345
didactic (controversial), 2342
discursive, 2344
first attempts at, 2342–2343
Hindus in, 2342–2343
human (Buberian), 2344
objectives of, 2343
secular, 2344
spiritual, 2344
after World War II, 2343–2344
written, 2342
Dialogue of Religions, A (Smart), dialogical process in, 8443
Dialogue on Miracles (Caesarius of Heisterbach), 2279
Dialogue on the Two Great World Systems (Galileo), 3257
Dialogues (Gregory I)
bridge in, 1050
life of Benedict of Nursia in, 823, 3688
miracles in, 3688
Dialogues (Hume), 7125
Dialogues concerning Natural Religion (Hume), 390–391, 7124
argument from design refuted in, 4193
Dialogue with Heraclides (Origen), 6888–6889
Dialogue with Trypho (Justin Martyr), 5044
Diamant, Anita, 6021
Diamond, Arthur S., 5325
Diamond Maṇḍala, 5608, 9963
Diamonds, **2345–2346**
in Buddhism, 2345
in Christianity, 2345
in Hinduism, 2345
in Old Testament, 2345
as remedy for snakebite, 2346
in Roman religion, 2345
as symbols, 2345
transmutation of, Indian references to, 2557
Diamond Sūtra, Huineng and, 4154
Diamond World Mandala. See Vajradhātu (Diamond World) *maṇḍala*
Diana (deity), **2346–2348**
Artemis identified with, 506, 2347, 5514
cult of, 2346–2347
under Roman authority, 7898
in form of cat, 1462
in Gaul, 7911
and Juno, 2346
as Lucina, 2346
moon and, 6175
origin of name, 2346
Roman soldiers' cult of, 2347
temple of, 2346–2347
in witchcraft, 9771
Diana Aricina, 2346
Diana Nemorensis, 2346
Diana Tifatina, 2347
Dian Cecht (deity), 1483, 1488, 9390, 9391
Dianetics: The Modern Science of Mental Health (Hubbard), 6530
mental health in, 4149, 8192
Dianic Wiccans, 3022
Dianius (bishop), 797
Dianyi (Heavenly Unity), 9347
Diarchy, Spartan, 5166–5167
Diaries. *See* Autobiography
Diarmaid ua Duibhne (mythic figure), 1495
"Diary" (Edwards), 2699
Diary of the Trojan War *(Ephemeris Belli Troiani),* 3051–3052
Diascalicon (Hugh of Saint-Victor), philosophy and exegesis in, 4151
Diasia (festival of Zeus), 9953
Diaspora
African (*See also* Afro-Brazilian religions; Afro-Caribbean religions)
Garvey (Marcus) and, 7624
gender in, 3404
healing in, **3821–3824**
Creole religions in, 2068
of Eastern Christians, 1673
Eastern Orthodox, social ethics and, 1652
Greek Orthodox, 3659
Jewish
anti-Semitism in, 398
cohesiveness in, 4855
connection to Israel of, 9977
elect status and, 2745
as exile, 2922–2923
halakhah in, 3754
historiography in, 4028
Israeli citizenship and, 4864
Lévi (Sylvain) and, 5419
micrography and, 1369
in Middle Ages, 6308
"people of God" and, 1777
religious education in, 7735
Shemu'el the Amora's guidelines for, 8318
Sibylline Oracles and, 8384
synagogue and, 8923, 8924
Diatessaron (Tatian), 906, 922
Díaz, Bernal, on Moctezuma, 5914
Díaz del Castillo, Bernal, on Aztec human sacrifice, 4185, 4191
Dibble, Charles E., 5939
Dibelius, Martin, 944
on miracles of Jesus, 6054
Dibia afa (healers), 4365
Dibuk, Der (film), 2534
Dicearchus, on transmigration of soul, 7186
Dice games, gambling on, 3260, 3261, 3263
in *Mahābhārata,* 5595
Dice metaphor, in Hinduism, 4440, 7362
Dice oracles, 2370, 2376–2377
Dichotomies, in Western Christian theology, 2589
Dichtung und Wahrheit (Goethe), 3525
Dick, Michael B., 4381
Dickens, Charles, 363, 7322
Bleak House, 5356
Domby and Son, 3059
The Old Curiosity Shop, 3062
The Pickwick Papers, 3059
Dickson, H. R. P., on Arabic hospitality, 4139–4140
Dictates of the Pope (Gregory VII), 6970
Dictionaire historique et critique (Bayle), 7283
Dictionaries, 7642, 7643–7644
Dictionary of All Religions and Religious Denominations (Adams), 30–31
Dictionary of Comparative Religion, A (Brandon), 1040
Didache (Christian church order), 781, 920
baptism in, 9809
Eucharist in, 9810
Didactica magna (Comenius), 1863
Didactic (controversial) dialogue, 2342
Didactic names, Akhenaton and, 218
Didascolion (Hugh of Saint-Victor), magic in, 5577
Diderot, Denis, 2783–2784
in French Enlightenment, 2796
naturalism of, 6434
reductive materialism of, 5776
Didgeridoo, 2379
Didot-Perceval (Robert de Borron), 3649
Dido tribe (Caucasus), 4614
Didron, Adolphe Napoléon, 499
Didymus, Areius, 7188
Dieffenbach, Ernest, on Maori religion, 5679

Diego, Juan, 3064, 7149
  Virgin of Guadalupe appearing to, 5921–5922
Diegueño tribe (North America)
  iconography of, 4308
  weaving in, 939
Diéguez, Manuel de, on monotheism, 6161
Dīeṅ, Samtec Braḥ Sangharāj, 5130
Dieri people (Australia)
  biblical translation for, 686
  mythic themes of, 653
Diermes/Tiermes (deity), 6755
Dieses Volk (Baeck), 737
Dies Parentales, 7909
Diet. *See also* Fasting; Vegetarianism
  in *ahiṃsā,* 197
Dietary laws
  for Caribbean healers, 1430
  Hindu, 7505
  Islamic, slave traditions of, 4682–4683
  Jewish (*See also* Kashrut)
    of Karaites, 5086
Dieterich, Albrecht, **2348–2349**
  and Gnosticism, 3532
Dieterich, Friedrich, Goldziher (Ignácz) and, 3634
Dieterlen, Germaine, **2349–2351**
  anthologies edited by, 116
  on Bambara religion, 116
  on Dogon religion, 116, 2349–2350, 3701
  on Fulbe religion, 3228
  Griaule (Marcel) and, 2349–2350, 3701
  on myths of cosmic egg, 99, 100
Diet of Speyer (1526), 7658
Diet of Speyer (1529), 7656, 7658–7659
Dieux des Germains, Les (Dumézil), 4462
Dieva dēli (sons of god), 758, 760
Dieva dukryte (daughter of heaven), 760
Dievs (deity)
  characteristics of, 757, 763–764
  comparison to Greek and Indian gods, 759–760
  cosmic tree and, 1502
  dancing with Pērkons, 7054
  etymology of term, 757
  Laima and, 5286
  in Latvian folk religion, 769
  Māra and, 5693
  as twins, 9419–9420
Dievturi (Latvia), 763–764, 765–766
Dievturība (Latvia), 763–764, 766
  cult of ancestors in, 328–329
Dievtuŗu cerokslis (catechism), 763
Dievtuŗu Vēstnesis (magazine), 766
Diez del Corral, Luis, on Shintō, 2639
Difference
  cultural, comparativism and, 1879, 1880
  vs. diversity, 3303
  in gender studies, 3303–3304
  genetics and, 3429
  meanings of, 3303
  in women's studies in religion, 9790–9791
Differentiating Consciousness and Wisdom (Rang byung rdo rje), 5102
Difficult Path, in Pure Land Buddhism, 4922
Diffused religion. *See* Popular religion
Diffusion
  Barnard (Alan) on, 8169
  comparative-historical study and, 1869–1870, 4063
  comparative mythology and, 1873–1874
  cultural-historical method and, 5259, 5261
  Cumont (Franz) on, 2093
Diffusionism, 2915
Digambara sect of Jainism, 4765
  enlightenment in, 5610
  food of, 4769
  gender in, 3326–3327, 4765
  Mahāvīra in, 5609–5610
  on *tīrthaṃkaras,* 9207, 9208
  scripture of, 4767
Digests (Roman legal documents), 5333
"Digging Sticks and Spears; or, The Two-Sex Model" (Berndt), 840
Dīgha Nikāya (Buddhist text), 1272
  Ājīvikas doctrine in, 213
  arahant in, 476
  cosmology in, 1134
  great commission in, 6077
Dignāga (Buddhist philosopher), **2351–2352**
  and Yogācāra philosophy, 1212, 1301, 2351
  and Buddhist epistemology, 1120, 1301, 2351
  and Buddhist logic, 1120, 1301, 2351
  on *ālaya-vijñāna,* 2351
  Stcherbatsky (Theodore) on, 8737
  writings of, 1301, 2351
Di gods (China), Shangdi and, 8299
Dii Mauri (Mauretanian gods), 834
Dikka (raised platform), 6208
Dīkṣā (consecration or initiation), 7816, 8992
  in *śrauta* rituals, 3992
Dillard, Annie, nature writing of, as spiritual autobiography, 703
Dillenberger, Jane Daggett, 495, 501
Dillenberger, John, 501
Dilling, Walter J., 937
  on binding, 5196
  on knots, 5196
Dillon, John, 7106, 7189
Dillon, Michele, 7891
Dil mgo Mkhyen brtse Rin po che, 7869
Dilmun (deity), 5955
Dilmun (garden of gods), 6981
Diloggun (divining system), 3065
Dilthey, Wilhelm, **2352–2353**
  Baeck (Leo) studying under, 736
  Gadamer (Hans-Georg) on, 3934
  Heidegger (Martin) on, 3934
  on hermeneutics and cultural sciences, 3930, 3932–3933, 8164
  and liberal Protestantism, 6104
  and naturalism, 6430
  on Schleiermacher (Friedrich), 2352, 2353, 3931, 7738, 8160, 8163
  studies of, 2352
  theory of human sciences by, 2353
  on understanding of religion, 8493
Dilun school of Buddhism, 9901
  textual basis of, 1576
  Zhiyan and, 4146
Di Mambro, Emmanuelle, 9068
Di Mambro, Joseph, 6554, 9067–9068
Dimcock, Edward, 5466
Dimensional approach, of Smart (Ninian), 8444, 8466
Dime people (Ethiopia), chiefs of, 5170
  restrictions on, 5171
DiMicelle, Alice, 2562–2563
Dimock, Edward C., Jr., 827
  on Caitanya, 1346
DIM-PAC. *See* Deceptive and Indirect Methods of Persuasion and Control
Din, Dovid, 4873
Dīnawarī, Abū Bakr al-, Ḥanābilah and, 3766
Diné. *See* Navajo
Diné Bahane' (Navajo creation story), 573–574
  sky in, 8426
Dingaka (healers), 9389
Dingari people (Australia), myths of, Gadjeri as Ganabuda in, 3251
Dingarri-Kuranggara song cycle, 671–672
Dingo, Ernie, 635, 637, 640, 641, 642, 646, 647, 651
Ding ri brgya rtsa (Pha Dam pa), 1227
Dīn-i-ilāhī, in India, Akbar's promulgation of, 217, 4649–4650
Dini ya Msambwa (Religion of the Ancestors), 2578
Dini Ya Msambwa, ancestor worship in, 109
Dinka religion. *See* Nuer and Dinka religion
Dīn Manērī, Sharaf al-, 7770
Dinnshenchas, 1480, 1486, 1495
Di Nola, Alfonso Maria, historiography of, 4050
Dinter, Artur, 3526
Dinur, Ben Zion, on messianism in Hasidism, 3788
Dio: Formazione e sviluppo del monoteismo nella storia della religioni (Pettazzoni), 7074–7075
Dio Cassius
  on Apollonius of Tyana, 6051
  on apostasy, 432
  on Celtic religion, women in, 3387
  on Phoenician religion, 7129
Diocesan Assembly, in Orthodox Church of America, 1766
Diocesan Coordination of Women (CODIMUJ), 3413
Diocesan Council, in Orthodox Church of America, 1766
Dioceses, in church polity
  early church, 1763, 2581
  Episcopal, 1766
  Orthodox, 1766
  Roman Catholic, 1764, 7874, 7887
Diocletian (emperor)
  abdication of, 1966
  astrology banned by, 7915
  Christian persecution by, 2874, 7059–7060
  imperial cults and, 7916
  and Manichaeism, 5660, 5663, 5664
Dio Cocceianus, on Greek art, 4363
Diodore of Tarsus, 2583, 6482
Diodorus (bishop of Tarsus), Cyril of Alexandria, opposition from, 2117
Diodorus Siculus
  on Amazonians, 3383
  on Demeter cult, 2269–2270
  on Etruscan portents, 7336
  on Isis, 4557
  on Nabatean kingdom, 6386
  on Orphic myth, 2965
  on Priapus, 7392–7393
  on Stonehenge, 8835
Diogenes, Antonius, 3053
Diogenes Laertius
  on atheism, 582
  on druids, 2492
  on Pythagoras, 7529, 8709
  on transmigration of soul, 7186
Diogenes of Seleucia-on-the-Tigris (of Babylon)
  national background of, 8742
  Stoicism and, 8740
Diogenes the Cynic, 165
  on breathing, 1041–1042
  on Eleusinian mysteries, 3910
  on world citizenship, 3906
Diognetus, 920
Diola religion (West Africa), **2354–2355**
  agriculture in, 261–262
  Christianity and, 2354
  funeral rites in, 3236, 3237

history of study of, 118
Islam and, 2354
prayer in, 2354
prophets in, 7444–7445
Alinesitoue, 261–262, 2355, 7444
women as, 261, 262
spirits in, 2354
supreme being of (*See* Emitai)
totemism of, 9252
Dione, Assane, vol. 10 color insert
Dione (deity), Hera and, 3914
Dion of Syracuse, 7181
Dionysian path, 2298–2299
Dionysius, Fabricius, 768
on Pērkons cult, 7053–7054
Dionysius Exiguus, 173
Dionysius of Alexandria, on Armenia, 487
Dionysius of Halicarus, on Cybele, 2110
Dionysius the Areopagite (Pseudo-Dionysius), **2355–2356**
on angels, 346, 2356
Anthony of Padua and, 377
on baptism, 2356
and Bonaventure, 1011, 1012
on darkness, 5454
on God, 3554
knowability of, 183, 5203, 6990
Hugh of Saint-Victor on, 4151
on images, 4353, 6347
influence of, 2356
mystical hermeneutics of, 8908
on mystical union, 6336, 6337
mysticism of, 390, 6341, 6347
Neoplatonic traditions and, 6475
on priesthood, 7402
Severus of Antioch as, 8238
and theurgy, 9157–9158
Thomas Aquinas on, 9160
on *via negativa,* 9586, 9587
writings of, 2355–2356
translation of, 2830
Dionysos (deity), **2356–2360**
Adonis assimilated with, 34
Apollo and
opposition between, 426
in partnership, 2357, 2358
Bacchae followers of, rites of, 3383–3384
birth of, 8301
cult of
cathartic orgies, 1459
civic religion and, 3671, 3672–3673
deification in, 2249
drums in, 2498
enthusiasm in, 2807
frenzied behavior in, 3214
initiation ceremony in, 2357, 2358
initiation into, 2249, 6330
lares and, 5320
as mystery religion, 6330
omophagia of, 6821–6824
orgy in, 6865–6866
Rohde (Erwin) on, 7871
sacrifices in, 2357–2358
women in, 2358, 3383–3384, 3672–3673
dance dramas honoring, 2436–2437
death of, 2357
punishment in afterlife for, 165–166
rebirth and, 8302–8303
descent into the underworld by, 2298–2299
dismembered by Titans, 2965, 2983
Euripides on, 2357, 2443, 3383–3384, 9158
festivals of, 375, 2436–2437
Anthesteria, **374–376**
followers of, 9158
functions of, 3680
and gender roles, 3383–3384
goats and, 8311
as god of masks, 2356
as god of wine, 2356
hare associated with, 7590
immortality and, 7871
madness of, 2359
mirrors and, 6064
music and, 6304
as Mustes, 2358
in Mycenaean religion, 42, 3680
on Olympus, Hestia replaced by, 3964
and omophagia, 2357
orgiastic feasts to, 8247
orgies of, 6863
Orphic Gold Tablets and, 6897, 6898
in Orphism, 6891, 6893, 6894–6895
Osiris identified with, 3908
Otto (Walter F.) on, 6933
parousia of, 2358, 2359
as Pelekus, 2359
phallus of, 7079, 7082
as Phanes-Metis, 2357
Ptolemy XIII as incarnation of, 4416
rebirth of, 2249
Sabazios identified with, 7953
shape shifting of, 8302–8303
son of, 7392
strangeness of, 2358, 2359
tattoo symbol of, 1002
temples of, 2356–2357, 2358, 2359
in Thracian religion, 9169–9170
in triad, 9348–9349
and violence, 2358–2359
Diop, Boubacar Boris, 3088
Diophysite (two natures) Christology, 1666. *See also* Monophysitism
Council of Chalcedon and, 1673, 1979–1981, 2040
hupostasi vs. phusis and, 4241–4242
Dioptrice (Kepler), 5112
Diorama Filosofico (supplement), 2905
Dios aisa (Bianchi), 863
Dioscorus (patriarch of Alexandria)
Egyptian bishops and, 1981
on Monophysitism, 6153
Dioscuri (mythic twins), 5994–5995
iconography of, 2123
and Spartan diarchy, 5166
Diószegi, Vilmos, 3109, 3114
Diotrephes (biblical figure), 918
Dīpaṃkara (buddha), 997, 998, 1067, 1077
Dipanagara (Javanese prince), 6547
Dīpavaṃsa (Buddhist text), 1065, 1199
Pāṭaliputra council in, 2037
Dipolarism, in Holocaust response of Cohen (Arthur), 4093
Dippel, Johann Konrad, 7143
Dirac, Paul, 7138
Ḍirār ibn ʿAmr, 3212
on atomism, 6323
in Muʿtazilah, 6318, 6319
Directories, Egyptian, 2724
Direct violence, 9596
Di-ri-mi-jo (deity), 42
Dirks, Nicholas, on colonialism, 1857
Disability
church attendance and, 3876
of Mani, 5647
Disappearing god myths. *See* Vanishing god myths
Discalced Carmelite order, 4942, 6764
Sor Juana in, 4967
Discernment, in eightfold path, 2738
Discernment of the Confessions and Sects (Ibn Ḥazm), 7242
Disciples
of Jesus
as apostles, 435
the beloved, 4943
healing touch of, 9255–9256
historical, 4848–4849
number of, 4848–4849
objections to narratives of, 4846
reciting words of Jesus, 905, 2360
of *gurūs,* 3713–3715
Discipleship, **2360–2364**. *See also* Spiritual discipline; Spiritual guides
community of, 2361–2363 (*See also* Monasticism)
definition of, 2360
and dialogue, 2342
emulation of master in, 2360–2361
heteronomous, 8700
social protocol of, 2361
in Stoicism, 2360
in Sufism, 2360, 2361, 8700, 9005–9006
teachers, types of, 8699
and touch of reverence, 9256, 9257
transformative knowledge in, 2361–2362, 2363
working model of, 2360–2361
Disciples of Christ (Christian Church) (religious group), **2364–2366,** 6561. *See also* Churches of Christ
Campbell in, 1377, 2364–2365
Churches of Christ and, 1780
during Civil War, 2365
division in, 2365–2366
in ecumenical movement, 2365, 2366
journals of, 2365, 2366
Peoples Temple affiliated with, 4953
restorationism of, 1712
sacred meal of, 7455–7456
Discipline. *See also* Asceticism; Spiritual discipline
in Christianity, suffering as, 8807
Discipline and Punish (Foucault), 5374
Discordia (deity), 3001
Discorso del flusso e riflusso del mare (Galileo), 7340
Discourse(s). *See also* Dialogue; Language; Poststructuralism
in Egyptian literature, 2721
Discourse against the Arians (Athanasius), 572
Discourse in Praise of Knowledge (Bacon), 733
Discourse on Comets (Galileo), 3257
Discourse on Method, The (Descartes), 2293, 7340
Discourse on the Origin of Social Inequality (Rousseau), 2236
Discourse on the Origins of Inequality (Rousseau), 7931
Discourse on the Sciences and Arts (Rousseau), 7931
Discourses (Machiavelli), 7790
Discourses concerning Two New Sciences (Galileo), 3257
Discourse to Kātyāyana, 7363–7364, 7365

Discourse to Pope Benedict XII (Barlaam of Calabria), 788
Discours sur l'ensemble du positivisme (Comte), 7339
Discursive dialogue, 2344
Discursive space, Japanese mythology and, 4800–4808
Disease and illness. *See also* Affliction; Healing and medicine
affliction and, 57, 60, 62
in African religions, 60, 62
Akan, 215
causes of, 87
central Bantu, 1508
East African, 2568
Edo, 2697
Kongo, 5220
Lugbara, 5527
Ndembu, 6447
as sacred calling, 87
Shona, ancestor spirits and, 8372
Swazi, 8896
Zulu, 10009
African slave trade and, 1510
in Afro-Surinamese religions, 127
attributed to fairies, 2953
in Australian Indigenous religions, 3871–3873, 3874
Āyurveda theory of, 714, 3855
in Buddhism
in Vajrāyana, Tibetan, 3866
possession and, 9837–9838
cats as cause of, 1463
caves and, in Mesoamerican religion, 1470
in Celestial Masters, 2181
in Chinese religion
precautions against spirits, 1642–1643
qi and, 3859
in Christianity, 3848
Christian Science, 2694–2695
in early church, 3843–3844
cultural *vs.* pathological concept, 3817
dances dealing with, 2138, 2140
in Daoism, 2177, 2179, 2180, 2193
Shangqing, 2195
deities of, 3622–3623
demons as cause of, 3842
diagnosis, 3810–3811
in Egyptian religion, 3826–3827
expulsion of, 2939
genetics of, 3427, 3428–3429
in Greek religion, 3839–3840
in Hittite religion, 3825
in Candomblé, 122
indigenous cultures fragmented by, 2616
in Inuit religion, 7505
in Islam, 3831–3833
in Japanese religion, *jibyō* (inborn chronic illness), 3867
in Judaism, visiting the sick, commandment of, 3828–3829
loss of soul and, 2297
in Mesopotamian religions, 3824–3825
in Navajo religion, 6442
in Oceania, missionaries and, 6792–6793
origins of, in myth, 3808–3809
pollution and, 7505
possession as, 2931
proximate causes of, 3809–3810
as punishment for sin, 7759
in Roman religion, 3841, 3842
saliva and, 8722
in shamanism
explanations for, 8273
soul loss and, 8279
social change, role in, 3815
social management of, 3810, 3814–3815
soteriology and, 8527
in South American Indian religions
of Andes, modern, 8619
of Gran Chaco, in Ayoré religion, 8633
spirit or demon and, 2284
Spiritualism, diagnosis in, 8717
in Tibetan religion
humors and, 3865
spirits as cause of, 3864–3865
trees averting, 9334
in Warao religion, 9688
water as, 9703
Disenchantment, cargo-cult theory and, 1424, 1425
Disfellowshipping, 4821
Disibodenberg (Germany), monastery as, Hildegard of Bingen and, 3979
Disk, winged, migration of symbol of, 3537
Dismemberment, **2366–2368**
in Aztec human sacrifice, 4190
in Dinka religion, 2366
in Germanic religion, 2366–2367
in Hinduism, 4440
logic of, 2367
as repetition of creation, 2366, 2367
in Roman religion, 2366
in shamanistic initiation visions, 8270–8271
social segmentation corresponding to, 2367–2368
Disobedience, as obedience, 6778
Disorder. *See* Order and disorder
Dis Pater, 1485, 1487
Dispensationalism
in Christian fundamentalism, 2889, 2892
Christian Identity movement rejection of, 1658
Disphysite Christological doctrine, Oriental Orthodox churches' rejection of, 1673
Disputationes de controversiis Christianae fidei adversus hujus temporis haereticos (Bellarmino), 816
Disputation hymns, of Ephraem of Syria, 2813
Disputations
Job as, 9758
wisdom in, 9749
Dispute of a Man with His Ba (Egypt), 2711
Dissipating self, in Chinese medicine, 3859
Distant Sanctuary. *See Masjid al-aqṣā, al-*
Distinctive-features theory, structuralism and, 8749
Ditan (deity), in Canaanite religion, 1387
Dithyrambs (drama), 2436–2437
Dittography, 921
Dius Fidius (deity), 3094
Divākara, 3012
Dīvālī (festival), **2368–2369,** 6594
in devotional life, 9824
gift giving in, 3482
in Hindu religious year, 4016
in Marathi religions, 5698
myth of, 2368
rituals of, 2368–2369
Dīvān (Ḥāfiẓ Shīrāzī), *ghazal* form in, 3734
Divan-i Hafiz (Hafiz), 7223
Dīvān-i Shams Tabrīz (Rūmī), 7222, 7936, 7937
inspiration for, 8818
Diversion of Angels (Graham), 2159
Diversity
vs. difference, 3303
in gender studies, 3303–3304
religious (*See* Religious diversity)
Divided Self of William James, The (Gale), 4776–4777
Divinae institutiones (Lactantius), 4361
Divination, **2369–2378**. *See also* Geomancy; Portents; Prodigies
in African religions
ancestor spirits and, in central Bantu religion, 1508
cults of affliction, 61, 62
decision-making process of, 87
diviner-diagnosticians, 3818
Dodoth, 9615
Dogon, 2391
in drama, 2457
East African, 2569, 2570
equipment for, 87
forms of, 87
history of study of, 117
Ifa system of (*See* Ifa divination)
illness diagnosis and, 3810
intuitive, 2370
in Khoi religion, 5136–5137
in Lugbara religion, 5527–5528
Maasai diviners *(il-oibonok),* 2001
mediumistic trance, 2371
vs. mediums, 7443
vs. myths, teachings of, 91
myths about, 94
Ndembu, 9405
northeast Bantu, 2576–2577
Nuer and Dinka, 6744
vs. prophecy, 7443
sacrificial motifs of, 2373–2374
in San religion, 5136–5137
shades and, 8659
Shona, 8372
in Southern Africa, 8659
in Swazi religion, 8896
trickster myths and, 94, 9353
witchcraft and, 9777
Yoruba, 9911
Zulu, 10008, 10009, 10010
in agricultural societies, 2371
in Aztec religion, 5908
in Babylonian religion, 2371
basic forms of, 2369–2370
bibliomancy as, 1528, 8200
in Canaanite religion, 1387
cards for, 1414
in Caribbean religions, 1430
creolization and, 2066
diagnosis with, 3822
in Santería, 8108
cats and, 1463
in Celtic religion, 2374
in Chinese religion
astrology as, 2372
bone oracles, 1582, 1583, 1628, 1891
diviners, 1605, 1617
fortune and, 1527
in Han imperial era, 1575
moon-blocks and divinationslips, 1605
oracle bone, 2374
popular, contemporary practice with wood blocks, 4208
with *Yijing,* 1583–1584, 1906, 2372
yin-yang *wu xing* theory and, 1572
in Christianity, 2373
correspondence systems and, 3810
in death rituals, 3242
definition of, 2369, 5570

deities of, in Yoruba and Caribbean religions, 1434
with entrails (extispicy)
in Canaanite religion, 1387
in Greek religion, 4108
in Southeast Asian religions, traditional, 4108
Essene, 2846
in Etruscan religion, 2873–2874
fortune or chance and, 1528
gambling on, 3259
in Germanic religions, *Seiðr* in Icelandic sagas, 8024–8025
in Greek religion, **2375–2378**
augury, 2370–2371
dice oracles, 2376–2377
dream interpretation, 2376
Homer on, 4108
mantis, 2376
oracles, 2375, 2376
in Persian Wars, 2375, 2376
purpose of, 2375
on Halloween, 3758–3759
heads and skulls used in, 3806
in Hellenistic religions, 3905–3906
in Hinduism, 2370
astrology as, 2372
in Hurrian religion, 4232
of illness, 3810–3811
indigenous theory of, 2369–2370
instructions for, medieval, 5578
intuitive, 2370
in Islam
Ja'far al-Ṣādiq in, 4761
vs. magic, 5583
in Israelite religion, 5425
in Japanese religion
folk, 4795
Hirata Atsutane on, 4023
by Joseph, 4956
in Judaism, 2370, 2373
folk, 3158, 3159, 3160
kledonomancy, 1528
vs. magic, 5570
in Islam, 5583
in Micronesian religions, 6004–6005
mirrors in, 6064
moon in, 6175
in Neopaganism, 6473
onmyōdō, 6827–6830
oracles, 6831–6832
in Greek and Hellenistic religions, 3905–3906
possession, 2370–2371
in Renaissance, 2373
rhapsodomancy, 1528
in Roman religion, **2375–2378,** 7907–7908
augury, 2370–2371
auspices, 2377
haruspices, 2377
in imperial period, 7914–7915
in middle republic, 7903–7904
portents and prodigies, 2377
purpose of, 2375
response to, 2378
Sibylline Books, 2377–2378
sortition, 2375–2376
state control of, 2372, 2377, 2378
templum, 2377
sacrificial motifs of, 2373–2374
science evolving from, 2369
in Scythian religion, 8206
in South American Indian religions
in Andean religions, 8604, 8616, 8619
calendar and, 1364
in Caribbean religions, 2066
diviners in modern era, 8616, 8619
gender and, 3418
pre-Inca, 8604
in Southeast Asian religions, traditional, 8650
Stoics on, 8742
sumbolos (symbolic language) in, 8907
in Tibetan religion *(mo)*
divination charts in, vol. 3 color insert
healing through, 3866
wisdom, 2371–2372, 2374
Divine, Father. *See* Father Divine
Divine, the
Otto (Rudolf) on the holy and, 4096
Socrates' conception of, 8503
Divine Adoratress of Amun, 2709
Divine Antiquities (Varro), 7918
Divine assembly, Near Eastern notion of, 1384
Divine Book ('Aṭṭār), 601
Divine Comedy (Dante), 157–158, 2169, 2170
ascension in, 524
confession in, 1887
content of, 7219
epic narrative of, 7204
Holy Trinity in, 5373
Islamic sources for, 524, 6061
poetic style of, 7219
Sayers (Dorothy) on, 8142–8143
suicide in, 8830
Divine encounters, and new religious movements, founding of, 6529–6530
Divine Horsemen (Deren), 76
Divine-Human Encounter, The (Brunner), 7118
Divine Imperative, The (Brunner), 1054
Divine justice. *See* Justice
Divine kingship. *See* Kingdom of God; Kings and kingship, divine
Divine Legation of Moses Demonstrated (Warburton), 9109
Divine Life Society, 108
Śivānanda in, 546
Divine light. *See* Light
Divine Light Mission, 6568
Divine Liturgy. *See also* Eucharist
in Orthodox Christianity, 2592
in United States, 1713
Divine madness, in Greek religion, 2807
Divine Milieu, The (Teilhard de Chardin), 9032, 9033, 9034
Divine Mind
Hopkins (Emma Curtis) on, 4128
New Thought movement on, 6583
Divine Mother, Ramakrishna on, 7611–7613
Divine Names (Dionysius), 2355
Divine pathos, Heschel (Abraham Joshua) on, 3962
Divine Principle (Moon), 6529, 9466, 9467
the Fall in, 6530
Divine providence, in Christianity, contradictory consequences of, 7791
Divine Science, 6585–6586
central texts of, 6586
founding of, 3096, 6584
Hopkins (Emma Curtis) and, 4128
Divine Science of Light and Sound, 2603
Divine Vengeance, The (Plutarch), 7200, 7201–7202
Divine-voice (hermeneutical) prophecy, 7107
Divine word, in Islam, 7571
Divine Word and Prophetic Word in Early Islam (Graham), 945
Divinity, 7536
contact with, psychedelic drugs as facilitators of, 7467
of eternity, 2855
eye and, 2940–2941
French feminists on, 3029
in Hermetism, 3944
humanity *vs.*
heroes and, 3956–3957
Jesus and, 3957
in Islam, Mu'tazilah on, 5063
of Jesus, 4843, 4844–4845
of Jones (Jim), 4952
in Judaism
Habad Hasidism, 3792
Qabbalah, 7536
Reconstructionist Judaism, 5081
nature of
and afterlife, views of, 128–130
in Eblaite religion, 2597
Eriugena on, 2831
fourfold symbolic structure of, 7550–7551
in Neopagan theology, 6472
numen of, 6753
of Qur'ān, 7571
ordeal and, 6848–6849
revelation of, through dance creation, 2141
in Roman religion, 7899–7900
sacred space and, tension with localization of divinity, 7979–7980
serpents associated with, 8459
in Unity, 9473
water and, 9701–9702
Divinity and Experience (Lienhardt), 117
Divinity schools
in Middle East, 8782–8783
in North America, 8785
Divino afflante Spiritu (Pius XII), 7879
Division of Labor in Society, The (Durkheim), 2527, 2528
Divodāsa, Śiva evicting, 779
Divorce
in Islam, 3368
joking about, 4213
laws on, 4706, 4708–4709
in Israel, 9981
in Israelite religion, laws on, 4733
in Judaism
get of, 7821, 7822
in *halakhah,* 3752, 7589
in rabbinic Judaism, 7589
religious *vs.* civil, 3754
in Orthodox Christianity, 2593
Divyaprabhandam (Nāthamuni), 7210, 10088
Dīwān (Ibn al-Fāriḍ), 4261
Dīwān (Rūmī), 9008
Dixon, John W., 501
Dixon, Joy, 6535
Dixon, Roland B., 6671
Dixon, Suzanne, 3381
Ḍiyā' al-Dīn, 7632
Diyi (Earthly Unity), 9347
Dizang. *See* Kṣitigarbha
Dižvadonis (Grand Leader), 764
Djabo (mythic figure), 663
Djang (spirit), in Australian Indigenous myths, 656–658, 7606
Djanggawul (Berndt), 841, 951
Djanggawul myths
body shapes in, 663
everyday life in, 653, 654

Djanggawul myths ***continued***
fertility in, 659
Wawalag myths
interconnected with, 659–662
Djanggawul sisters (mythic figures), 653
Djan'kawu (ancestral beings), **2378–2380**
dance and ceremonies of, 2380
designs of, 2379–2380
songs of, 2379
Djebar, Assia, 3088
Djilga Kyyryy (ritual), 2395
Djinagarbil sorcerers, counter-sorcery of *mabarns* against, 3873
Ḍjinn (demonic figure), 2279–2280, 2314–2315
characteristics of, 2280
creation of, 2314
in Qur'ān, 2279
possession by, 2402
in Southeast Asian Islam, 4660
subclasses of, 2280, 2314–2315
trees associated with, 9337
Djiwar custom, as hospitality, 4139
Dkon mchog rgyal po (Köngchog Gyalpo, Buddhist scholar), *Hevajra Tantra* and, 3966
Długosz, Jan, 329, 330, 331
Długoszius, Ioannes, 767
Dmitrii (Grand Prince), Sergii of Radonezh and, 8230
DNA. *See also* Genetics
discovery of, 2908–2909
and medical ethics, 5810
functions of, 3427
Do (Marshall Herff Applewhite), Heaven's Gate and, 3889–3891
Doan Minh Huyen, on Maitreya, 5621
Dobberstein, Paul Matthias, vol. 5 color insert
Dober, Leonard, 6191
Dobson, James, 6540, 7714
Dobu Islanders (Papua New Guinea), kinship of, 5185
Docetism, **2381,** 2648
in Catharism, 1457
definition of, 2381
in Gnosticism, 2381
in Mahāsāṃghika Buddhism, 5602
in Manichaeism, 2381
Docta ignorantia. See Learned ignorance
Doctor Admirabilis. *See* Ruusbroec, Jan van
Doctrine, **2381–2385**. *See also* Heresy; Orthodoxy
Buddhist, practice and, 9836
Christian, in ecumenical movement, 2684, 2685
of Christian eremitism, 2826
in comparative religion, 2382–2383
creeds as statements of, 2053
definition of, 2381
disavowal of, in nonreligious spirituality, 8720
dogmatico-theological questions, and heresy, 3922–3923
dualistic (*See* Dualism)
intellectuals developing, 4512–4513, 4514
Islamic
Shī'ī, 2064–2065
Sunni, 2062–2064
Rastafari, 7623
soteriological function of, 8529
and theology, 2383–2384
Zoroastrian, 9994–9997
Doctrine and Argument in Indian Philosophy (Smart), 7093
issues in, 8443
Doctrine and Covenants (Mormon text), 6193
Doctrine of Addai, 6479
Doctrine of the Atonement, The (Hodgson), 597
Doctrine of the Law and Grace Unfolded, The (Bunyan), 1323
Doctrine of the Mean. See Zhongyong
Doctrine of the Trinity, The (Richardson), 7794
Documentary Hypothesis, 869, 883, 9233–9234
Document of the Feast of the Protective Ancestral Spirits, in Canaanite religion, 1384
Dodd, Charles Harold
on Gospels, 4847
on kingdom of God, 4847, 5151
on parables, 6979
Dodds, E. R., 520, 7107
on magic, 5568
on shame in Greek culture, 8405
Dodecapolis, Etruscan, 5167
Dodona, oracle of Zeus at, 6832–6833
Dodoth religion, divination in, 9615
Dodson, Jualynne, 75, 81
Dodson, Patrick, 679
Dog. *See* Dogs
Dōgen (Buddhist monk), **2385–2387**
as founder of Sōtō school, 2385, 2386, 4786
in Caodong school, 1244–1245, 2385
on enlightenment, 6631–6632
life of, 2385
on meditation, 1180, 1293, 2386
philosophy of, 1302
relationship with Keizan, 5109
on universal buddha-nature, 2629
writings of, 1276–1277, 2385–2386
translation of, 2386
in Zen Buddhism, 9944, 9945
Dogma, 2382, **2387–2390**
Catholic
definition of, 2387
development of, 2387–2389
Christian
anticreedalism and antidogmatism, 2060–2061
creeds and confessions of faith *vs.,* 2054
Harnack (Adolf von) on, 3778–3779
Ritschl (Albrecht) on, 7832
Schleiermacher (Friedrich) on, 8165–8166
Spinoza (Baruch) on, 8683
Eastern Orthodox, 2387
Jewish, Albo (Yosef) on, 233–234
in monism, 5207
Protestantism on, 2387, 2388
schism and, 8153
Schleiermacher (Friedrich) on, 8161–8162
Dogmatic Constitution on the Church (*Lumen gentium,* 1964), 9535–9536, 9539–9540
conciliarism and ecumenism in, 2045
ecclesiology in, 1775, 2061
Mary in, 5754, 5755
Dogmatics (Brunner), 1054
Dogmatics, in law and religion, 5359
Dogmatic theology, 9139, 9140
Dogmatism, Erasmus opposed to, 2822
Dogon language, 100–101
Dogon religion (Mali), **2390–2392**
agriculture and, 2390
altars in, 3576
ancestors in, 2390–2391, 3569, 4301
androgynes in, 338
birth in, 2390, 2391, 2392
cave burial, 1472
circumcision rites, 1470, 2391, 2392
clitoridectomy in, 2392
cosmology, 1503, 2350
creation myth in, 1987, 1988
cults in, 2391–2392
culture heroes in, 2091
dance in, 2134, 2138
masquerade, 2140
death rites in, 2138
deus otiosus in, 2309–2310
divination in, 2391
dualism in, 2515
funeral rites in, 2392
gardening in, 3281
God of (Amma), myths about, 2390, 2392
history of study of, 116 (*See also* Griaule, Marcel)
myths in, 99–100, 116, 3701
houses in, 4104
on human beings, 2392
iconography of, 4301, 4303
initiation in, 100–101, 2391
Islam and, 2390
literacy in, 101
mask dance in, 2391, 5768
masks in, 5768
myths of, 99–101
blacksmith, 95, 4301
creation, 97, 100, 325, 2390–2391, 3086, 3569–3570, 4301
depth of, 1992
the Fall in, 2960
history of study of, 99–100, 116, 3701
for initiated men, 100–101
language and, 100–101
trickster, 86
sacred language in, 5303
Sirius (star) in, 8735
and social organization, 2391–2392
speech in, 2392
spirit possession in, 2391
studies of, 2349–2350, 2390
supreme being of (Amma), 100, 325, 3569–3570, 3576
tobacco in, 9217
tricksters in, 9352, 9353
twins in, 9414–9416
weaving in, 938
women in, 2391
Dogs, **2392–2394**
in African religions, 2393, 2394
Anubis as, 403, 2393
Asklepios as, 551
associated with death, 2392–2393
in Australian Indigenous myths, 654
in Buddhism, 2393
in Central Asian religions, 2393
in Christianity, 2393
in creation myths, 2394
domestication of, 2392
in Egyptian religion, 2393
at gate of underworld, 2296
in Greek religion, 2392, 2393 (*See also* Kerberos)
Hekate and, 3900
sacrifice of, 3682
in Hinduism, 2392, 2393, 4438
in Islam, 2393
in Judaism, 2393
in Mesoamerican religions, 2393, 2394
buried with dead, 148, 151, 3244, 5896
myths about, 5938
in North American religions, 2394
as nurse, 2393

qualities and behaviors of, 2392
in Roman religion, 2393
sacrifice of, 2393
in prehistoric religions, 7384
union of human woman and male, 2393–2394
in Zoroastrianism, 2393
Dog Soldiers, 3409
Dohāvadi (Tulsīdās), 9393
Dohm, Wilhelm von, on Jewish people, 5854
Dōjimon (Itō Jinsai), 4753
Dokhma (tower of silence), 9264
Doktor Faustus (Mann), 3528
Dōkyō (Buddhist monk), 1175, 1242
bid for throne by, 8361
Dōkyō, 2215
Dolaha Deviyo (twelve gods), in Sinhala religion, 8410
Dolan, Jill, 2438–2439
Dolci, Danilo, Gandhi (Mohandas) influencing, 3273
Dolgan language, 2394
Dolgan people (Siberia), 468
converting to Christianity, 2394
as nomads, 2394, 2395, 2396
Dolgan religion (Siberia), **2394–2396**
calendar in, 2394–2395
dance in, 2396
hunting in, 2395
rituals in, 2395–2396
shamanism in, 2395–2396
supreme beings in, 2395
Doliche (Turkey), Iupiter cult at. *See* Iupiter Dolichenus
Dolichena (temples), 4754
Dolling, Robert, 9427
Döllinger, Ignaz von, 9528, 9530
Döllinger, Johann, **2396–2397**
Dolls, in Caribbean religion (*wanga* charms), 3823
Dolly (sheep), 5814
Dolmens, 5827
Dolphin
anchor and, 332
brain of, 6488
in North American Indian religions, 6662
religious symbolism of, 3123
Dol po pa Shes rab rgyal mtshan (Dölpopa), 1227
Dol po pa was Rje btsun Tāranātha, 1156, 1227
Dolto, Françoise, 6065
Domby and Son (Dickens), 3059
Dome, 794
Dome of the Rock (Jerusalem), 4836–4837, 6736, 7698
Domes
in mosques, 6209
of stupa *(aṇḍa)*, as dome of heaven, 1796
in Roman temples, as celestial home of gods, 1792
Domestication of animals
of cattle, 1464
of horses, 4132
Domestic church, in Orthodox Christianity, 2593
Domestic cult (China), 323
Domestic deities, 3622
Domestic observances, **2397–2412**. *See also* Home
Buddhist
Japanese, 2409, 2410
Tibetan, 9841
Chinese practices, **2406–2409**
calendrical rituals, 2408–2409
house rites, 2406–2407
life-cycle rituals, 2407–2408
Christian practices, **2399–2401**
Catholic, 2399, 2400
Eastern Christian, 2399, 2400
Jewish practices and, 2400
consecration of homes, 4105
Hindu practices, **2403–2406**
Brahmanic *gṛhya* rites, 3991
hearth fires in, 4106
household observances, 2403–2404, 4429, 7493–7494
and nondomestic observances, 2404–2405
pollution and, 2404, 2405
pūja as, 4105
sacrifices, 9821
house spirits and deities, 4106
in Israelite religion, 4744
Japanese practices, **2409–2412**, 4793, 4797
Buddhist, 2409, 2410
calendrical rituals, 2410, 2411
decline of, 2409, 2411
life-cycle rituals, 2410, 2411
Shintō, 2409, 2410
Jewish practices, **2397–2398**
and Christian practices, 2400
Hasidic, 2398
Marrano, 5718–5719
Orthodox, 2397–2398, 3353
perennial, 2397–2398
periodic, 2397
women in, 2397, 3353
in Micronesian religions, 6004
Muslim practices, **2401–2403**, 3163
rituals and ceremonies, 2402
women in, 2401–2402, 3369
shrines in homes, 4106
Vedic, 9565–9566
Domestic violence
animal abuse and, 358
in Qur'ān, 3368
Dominance, in nature religions, 2663
Dominario ceremony, 284
Domination, Weber's (Max) definition of, 5385
Domingo de Guzmán. *See* Dominic
Dominic (saint), **2412–2413**, 9160
mendicant friars and, 7724
Dominican Republic
Catholic pilgrimage in, 7149
Islam in, 4684
Dominicans, **2413–2415**. *See also specific figures*
and All Saints Day, 2230
and All Souls Day, 2230
architecture of monasteries, 6119
Bruno (Giordano) expelled by, 1055
on conscience, 1941
Eckhart (Johannes), 2603
in England, 2413
founder of, 2412, 2413, 9160
founding of, heresy, correction of, 3928
in France, 2413, 2414
in Germany, 2414
on grace, 3646
growth of, 2414, 6133
Honorius III and, 2413
as inquisitors, 4499, 4500, 4504, 6971
vs. Jesuits, 816
Paul V terminating debate, 6973
Latin American missions, 1695–1697
life of, 2413, 9160
Mantellates, 1461
Maritain (Jacques) in, 5712
mendicancy of, 5856, 6133–6134
in Mesoamerica, 5915
language used by, 5917
missionary activity of, 2414
on nature, 6432
objective of, 2413
polemics against Islam, 7243
preaching by, 6133–6134
reform of, 2414
renewal of, 2414
in Taiwan, 8963
and Thomism, 2414
women as, 2412, 2414, 6135
Dominic's Order of Preachers, 7724
Dominium (lordship), Wyclif (John) on, 9848
Domitian (Roman emperor), 7916
Christian persecution by, 7058
and Isis cult, 4558
Plutarch criticizing, 7200
Dömötör, Tekla, **2415–2415**
Domovoi (family founder spirits), in Slavic religion, 4106
Domus dei (house of god), sanctuary as, 8100
Domus ecclesiae (house of the gathered assembly), sanctuary as, 8101
Dôn, Family of, 1489
Dona Béatrice (prophetess), 1511, 5221
Donald, Merlin, on mimesis, 8278
Donar. *See* Thor
Donatello, 377
Donation of Constantine (document), 1968, 9663
Donatism, **2416–2418**, 4580
Augustine's conflict with, 626, 2417, 7061
baptism in, 782
in Carthage, 1679
cause of, 2416
Circumcellions in, 2417
Council of Arles and, 1966
in early Christian theological issues, 2581
ecclesiastical discipline and, 8155
election in, 2747
enthusiasm of, 2805
leader of, 2416
literature of, 2417
persecution of, 2416–2417, 7060, 7061
political tensions and, 8153
on separation of church and state, 1968
Donatus
Council of Arles and, 1966
Jerome and, 4832
Donatus of Casae Nigrae, 2416
'Don chants, 1535–1536
Dong (caverns), in Daoism, 2637, 9056
Dongjie, 1643
Donglin monastery
factionalism in, 1578
Huiyuan and, 4156
Dongshan doctrine, 994, 1276
Dongshen (Daoist cavern), 2183, 2203
Dongsonian culture (Neolithic), burial practices in, 8642
Dongtian (grotto-heavens), 2637, 9056
Dongxiao (musical instrument), 6293
Dongxuan (Daoist cavern), 2183, 2203
Dongxuan jinyu ji (Daoist text), 2210
Dongying zi. *See* Du Guangting
Dong Yue, 3068
Dongyue Zhenren. *See* Liu Deren
Dongzhen (Daoist cavern), 2183, 2203

Dong Zhongshu, **2418–2419,** 2632
 Confucianism and, 1574, 1898
 life of, 2418
 on Mandate of Heaven, 1592
 moral philosophy of, 1575
 naturalism of, 1591
 philosophy of, 2418, 2419
 on *ren* and *yi,* 7752
 writings of, 2418–2419
 on *yinyang wuxing,* 9889
Doniger, Wendy, 3100, 3322
 on Hindu goddesses, 3607, 7500
 on Hindu view of body, 4164
 on politics and religion, 7252
Donin, Nicholas, 7233
Don Juan, as hero, 3957
Donkey, as symbol of king, 5164
Dönmeh sect, **2419–2420**
Dönmeh Shabbateans, Islam and, 8259, 8261
Donn (deity), 1485, 1487
Donne, John
 on Israelite theocracy, 9108
 poetry of, 7206, 7220
 on suicide, 8830
Donnely, Jack, on human rights, 5362
Donner, Kai, **2420–2421**
 on Arctic religions, 475
Donner, Otto, 2420
Donnotarvos (Brown Bull), 1487
Don Quixote (Cervantes)
 in history of the novel, 3050, 3051
 religious motifs in, 3058–3059
Doom, oracles of, in *Micah,* 6000–6001
Doomsday teachings. *See* Apocalypse
Door of mercy, in Adventist theology, 8235
Doorways. *See* Portals
Doppler shift, discovery of, 2031
Dora (moral concept), 765
Doran, Robert, 901
Dorca (Zulu *sangoma*), 9613
Doré, Henri, 1051
Doresse, Jean, Nag Hammadi Gnostic texts discovered by, 3535
Dorff, Elliot, 3428
 on Jewish medical ethics, 5812
Dorgan, Howard, on religious broadcasting, 7711
Dorian religion, ritual homosexuality in, 4112
Doric columns, 9063
Dormancy, church membership and, 1779
Dormitories, in monasteries, 6118
Dorn, Gerhard, 6434
Dorotheus of Gaza, social orientation of, 2829
Dorris, Michael, 3093
Dorsey, J. Owen, 6670
Dorsey, Thomas A., 6313
Dorson, Richard M., 3142
Dort, Synod of, predestination affirmed at, 2044
Dorzhiev, Agwang, 1150
Dosali (mythic hero), 9606
Doṣas (bodily substances or humors)
 in Āyurveda, 3854–3855
 in Tibet, 3865
Doṣas (faults), *vs. guṇas,* 3709
Dōshaku. *See* Daochuo
Dōshō (Buddhist monk), 1242, 2337, 2338
Dosítheos (patriarch of Jerusalem)
 confession of, 2059
 Confession of Faith by, Roman Catholic perspectives in, 2588
 Cyril *vs.,* 2115
Dōsojin (deity), crossroads and, 2071
Dostoevsky, Fyodor, **2421–2423**
 Bakhtin (M. M.) on, 741–742
 The Brothers Karamazov, 3059, 3062
 on conscience, 1943
 epilepsy of, 2421, 6487
 Golden Age and, 3628
 The Idiot, 3059
 and neoorthodoxy, 6468
 in penal exile, 2421–2422
 The Possessed, 7943
 in Russian Orthodox Church, 7943
 Solov'ev (Vladimir), influence of, 8520
 temperament of, 3060
 Tikhon of Zadonsk and, 9194
 writings of, 2422
Dottin, Georges, 1498
Doty, William G., 3314
Double axes. *See* Axes
Double burial practices, 2239, 2241
Double-consciousness, of African Americans, 67
Double-headed drum, 2497, 7036, 7037
Double justification theory, 1968
Doubleness, **2423**. *See also* Dualism
 mirrors and, 6064
Doubles (second selves), soul and, 8533
Doubt, **2423–2429**. *See also* Belief; Faith
 as act of will, 2427
 analysis of statements of, 307
 as attitude of mind, 2424
 in Aztec religion, 5892
 certainty and, 2428
 as component of belief, 2424–2425, 2427, 2428
 as component of faith, 2428
 in demons, 2280–2281
 as expression of humility, 2428
 in Judaism
  Naḥman of Bratslav on, 6401
  Sa'adyah Gaon on, 7951–7952
 meaning of, 2424
 nihilism and, 2427–2428
 origin of word, 2424
 as philosophical method, 2424
 and religious tolerance, 2428
Douglas, Kelly Brown, 79
Douglas, Mary, 116
 on asceticism, 5372
 on body symbolism, 4162, 4163, 4164
 on food taboos, 3172, 7508
 on gender roles, 7797
 historiography and, 4048
 on liminal beings, 7797
 on liturgy, 5492
 on millenarianism, 6033
 on purification, 7504, 7510, 7513
 on rites of passage, 7797
 on ritual, 7846, 7849
 on sacrilege, 8010
 symbol theory and, 8911
 on tears, 9024
 on witchcraft and sorcery, 9778
Douglass, Frederick, 73, 963
Douglass, James W., on kingdom of God, 5153
Douglass, Mary, on trauma, 8245
Doukhobors, persecution in Europe, 6567
Doussa, John Von, 651, 3392
Doutté, Edmond, 5583
 on sacred prostitution in North Africa, 3970
Dov Ber of Lubavitch
 on mystical union, 6340
 Shne'ur Zalman of Lyady and, 8371
Dov Ber of Mezhirich, **2429–2430**
 disciples of, 3787
 followers of, 2429
 as Hasidic leader, 726, 2429, 3787, 9381
 Levi Yitsḥaq of Berdichev and, 5428
 mystical union and, 6340
 mysticism of, 6354
 Shne'ur Zalman of Lyady and, 8371
 teachings of, 2429, 2430
Dove, 948, 949
 as Christian prefiguration, 6643
Dow, Alexander, 4446
Dow, James, 5929, 5945
Dowie, John Alexander, 103
Dowman, Keith, 9190
Downes, Rupert M., on afterlife, 136
Downriver Man (deity), 5120
Downs, Frederick S., 6072
Downward Journey, The (Lucian), 989
Dowries
 definition of, 5725
 in North African religion, prostitution linked with, among Awlad Nā'il, 3969–3970
Doxography, 1204, 1213
Doxology, in *Psalms,* 7461
Doyle, Arthur Conan, on Kardec (Allan), 5090
Doyle, Clive, 1038
Doyle, Matthew, 646
Dózsa, György, peasant revolt led by, 4226
Dpal spungs (Buddhist monastery), 5223
Dpyad sgom (analytical meditation), 1284
Draco, laws of, 1845–1846
Dracontia (dracontites in brains of dragons), 2346
Dracula (Stoker), 3062
Dragon boat races, 1642
Dragonflies, 4508
Dragon monster, eagle in, 2553
Dragon Rouge, 6568
Dragons, **2430–2434**. *See also* Monsters; Snakes and serpents
 as abductors and devourers, 2431–2432
 brains of, 2346
 caves as, in geomancy, 1468
 chaos and, 1538, 6163
 conquest of, 6165
 in creation myths and eschatologies, 2431, 2441–2442
 definition of, 2430
 as enemies and devils, 2432–2433
 etymology of term, 2430
 in Germanic religion, 8457
 as givers of life, 2433
 in Hinduism, 4438
 image of, 2430
 killing of, in Semitic myths, 1875
 in Mesoamerican iconography, 4311, 4312
 in Mesopotamian iconography, 4316
 in Olmec pantheon, 6818
 as parents and ancestors, 2433–2434
 pearl and, 7024
 rain associated with, 7603
 storms associated with, 5996
 symbolism of, 2430, 2432
 as water figures, 2433, 6439–6440
 as withholders and custodians, 2432
Drakaina (serpent), 2431
Drake, Saint Clair, 74, 75
Drama, **2434–2478**. *See also* Dance; Performance
 aesthetics of, Aristotle on, 45
 African religious drama, **2456–2459**
  characters in, 2458–2459
  divination as, 2457
  elements of, 2456–2457
  funeral rites as, 2457
  initiations as, 2457, 2459

masks in, 2457–2458
in Nyakyusa religion, 6770
origin of, 2456
Balinese dance and dance drama, **2450–2452**
audience of, 2450–2451
characters in, 2451
genres of, 2450
mantras in, 2451
modern Western drama influenced by, 2438
musical instruments used in, 2450, 2451
in Chinese religion, at New Year, 1642
Christian
African American, 2476–2477
Counter-Reformation, 2474
imitating Greek drama, 2467
medieval, 2437, 2467–2471
modern, 2438, 2471, 2475–2477
mystery plays, 2469–2470, 2474
Renaissance, 2438, 2470, 2472, 2473–2474
of Sayers (Dorothy), 8142
South American, 2438
Christian ban on, 2437, 2438, 2467–2468, 2474, 7044–7045
clowns in, 1838, 1840
East Asian dance and theater, **2453–2456**
in Buddhism, 2455–2456
in Confucianism, 2455
in shamanism and animism, 2453–2455
European religious drama, **2467–2473**
characters in, 2469
cycle plays, 2437
Hrotsvit as first female playwright in, 4142–4143
liturgical drama, 2437, 2467–2471
manipulation in, 2469–2470
miracle plays, 2437
modern, 2438, 2471, 2475–2477
morality plays, 2437, 2470
origins of, 2468, 2471, 2473–2474
resurrection plays, 2468–2471
structure of, 2468, 2469
subject of, 2467
vernacular drama, 2471–2472
Greek
Christian imitation of, 2467
magic in, 5575
music in, 6304
origins of, 2436–2437
and Renaissance theater, 2473–2474
ritual elements in, 2443
time in, 6375
Hindu dance and dance drama
costumes for, 1828
Kṛṣṇa and Rādhā in, 5250, 7594
humor in, in East Asia, 4209
Indian dance and dance drama, 2436, **2447–2450**
bhakti in, 2450
mantras in, 2449
music in, 2448, 2449
ritual frames in, 7048
Islamic ban on, 7044
Japanese popular drama, 4798–4799
Javanese *wayang,* **2452–2453**
Jewish ban on, 7044
Mesoamerican dance and drama, **2463–2467**
accessories of, 2466–2467
in art and literature, 2465–2466
elements of, 2464
physicality of, 2464–2465
sex and fertility in, 2463–2464
social politics of, 2465
war dances, 2466
Middle Eastern narrative traditions, **2446–2447**
in Sunnī Islam, 2447
in Shiism, 2446–2447, 4572, 9022–9023
Ṣūfīs opposing, 2446
modern Western theater, 2438, **2473–2478**
African American, 2476–2477
expressionist, 2475, 2476
feminist, 2438–2439
performance theater, 2476
religious, 2438, 2471, 2472, 2475–2477
ritual, 2439
romantic, 2474
social realist, 2474–2475
music in, 6304
Near Eastern ritual drama, ancient, **2440–2446**
components of, 2440
Egyptian, 2435, 2441, 2444
in Hebrew scriptures, 2442–2443
Hittite, 2442, 2445
Mesopotamian, 2441–2442, 2444–2445
origin of, 2440
research on, 2444
North American Indian dance and drama, **2459–2463**
music in, 2459–2460
Northwest Indians, 2460
Plains Indians, 2460
purpose of, 2459
Southeast Indians, 2461
Southwest Indians, 2460, 2461–2463
poetic justice in, appropriate use of, 5356
of religious festivals, 2436
ritual, 2435–2436 (*See also* Performance, and ritual)
components of, 2440
connection to, humor and, 4199
modern, 2439, 2471, 2472, 2475–2476
origin of, 2440
vs. secular, 2436
Sanskrit, 2436, 2447–2448
secular
Christian influence on, 2438
modern, 2438
vs. ritual, 2436
social, 7050
in Southeast Asia, Kawakin poetry and, 4010
Drama of the Medieval Church, The (Young), 2468
Dramatic Universe, The (Bennett), 832, 833
Drang (urge), Scheler (Max) on, 8147
Drang srong (seers of the Vedas), 1009
Draugar (reanimated corpses), 167
Draupadī (deity)
Arjuna and, 487
gambling and, 3263
in *Mahābhārata,* 5595
Karaga festival to, 1807
as local goddess, 3608
modern retelling of story of, 6742–6743
Dravidian culture
cult sacrifices in, 4474
and Hinduism, 4427
iconography of, 4472
and Indus Valley religion, 4468–4470
origins of, 8973
pūjā in, 7493
temple construction in, 8975
Dravya (substance), *guṇas* and, 3709
Dṛḍhamati *(bodhisattva),* 1079
Dṛḍimati *(bodhisattva),* 1077
Dread (Owens), 7628
Dread Act (Dominica), 7625
Dreadlocks, Rastafari and, 7623, 7624, 7626–7627
Dream. *See* Dreams
Dream and Reality: An Essay in Autobiography (Berdiaev), 836
Dream catcher, vol. 3 color insert
Dream drum, 2500
Dreaming, the (Australia), **2478–2482**. *See also* Australian Indigenous religions, myths of
in Aboriginal Theology movement, 675
accounts of, 2479–2480
anamnesis and, 314, 315
ancestors in, 638, 3434, 5704
and art, 2480, 4304–4307
art based on, 639–640, 666, 667, 668, vol. 1 color insert
breaches of laws or taboos, 3872–3873
in Central Desert, 644–645
change and continuity in, 2480–2481
cosmology and, 2002–2004
dogma of, 2478, 2480
genealogy of term, 2478
grounded in history, 2481–2482
law and, 2002, 2003–2004
mana compared to, 5632
in Mardu religion, 5704, 5705, 5706, 5707
meaning of, 638, 5704, 6260
music in, 6260–6261
in New Age movement, 666
new religious movements and, 671
origin of human life and, 5444
origin of terms related to, 637–638, 640
Rainbow Snake in, 7605
sacred geography of, 3434
Seven Sisters stories and, 643–644
Stanner (W. E. H.) on, 8730
terms used for, 2478
tjurungas in, 9212
totemism in, 5705, 9252
unchanging nature of, 639
women in, 3392
Dream of Dumuzi (myth), 5958
Dream of the Earth, The (Teilhard de Chardin), 2610
Dream of the Red Chamber, or *Story of the Stone* (Cao Xueqin), 3057, 3068
Dream of the Road, The (Old English poem), 7940
Dreams, **2482–2491**. *See also* Sleep; Visions
in Acehnese religion, 26
as active experience, 2485–2486
in African religions, southern, 8660
in afterlife, 147
in Ainu religion, 205
in animism, 363–364
as archetypes, 1379
Aristotle on, 2376, 2378, 2485
in Australian Indigenous religions, 2483, 2487
in Buddhism, 2488

Dreams ***continued***
of children, 2484
in Chinese religion, 2484
in Christianity, 2489
cognitive responses to, 2484, 2485–2487
conception, 2489
cross-cultural study of, 2482–2484, 2486
in Daoism, 2489–2490
in Diola religion, 2354
divination by, in Kamba religion, 2577
experience of, 2482, 2489
Freud on, 2376, 2483–2484, 3215, 3216
in Greek religion, 2376
Asklepios and, 551
healing, Asklepios and, 551
in Hinduism, in Upaniṣads, 9482
in Hittite religion, 4072
in incubation oracles, 6833
as individual myths, 5114
interpretation of, 2370, 2373
by Joseph, 4956
as irregular relationships, 6489
in Islam, 2489
in Judaism, 2489
Jung on, 2484–2485
language of, 2485–2487
latent, 2483, 2484
lucid, 2485, 2488
manifest, 2483, 2484
and myths, 2489–2490
nightmares, and horse symbolism, 4134
in North American Indian religions, 2484, 2485, 6650, 6681, 7299
Blackfoot, 960
Cahuilla, 2488
of California, 6713
Delaware, 6683
of Far North, 6678
of Great Plains, 6700
Hopi, 2483
Iroquois, 2483, 4542–4543
Kwakiutl, 2486
Mohave, 2489, 6716
Navajo, 2483, 2489
Pomo, 2488
Yuman, 2489
Zuni, 2484, 2485
as passive observation, 2485–2486
in Polynesian religions, 7306
as portents, 7337
pragmatic responses to, 2484–2485
revelatory, retreats for, 7769
in Roman religion, 2378
in shamanism, 2488, 2490
sharing, 2484, 2487
in Solomon Islands religions, shades and, 8515
soul and, 8533
in South American Indian religions
Amazonian Quechua, 2484
Jivaroan, 2486
Kagwahiv, 2487
Mapuche, 2487
Maya, 2484, 2485, 2489
spiritual responses to, 2484, 2487–2488
Swedenborg (Emanuel) on, 8899
symbol theory and, 8909, 8911
in Ungarinyin religion, 9461
visionary (prophetic), 2483, 2488, 2489
vs. visions, 9611
in Warlpiri religion, 9694
Dream Seekers: Native American Visionary Traditions of the Great Plains, The (Irwin), 9610
Dreamtime. *See* Dreaming, the
Dreamtime, The: Australian Aboriginal Myths in Paintings (Roberts and Mountford), 2480
Dream yogas, 1288
Dreidel (spinning top), Ḥanukkah and, 3774–3775
Dreisch, Hans, Maritain (Jacques) and, 5712
Drennan, Robert, 454
Drenpa Namkha, 2549, 2550
Dresden Codex, Venus table in, 1359–1360
Dress. *See* Clothing; Hair
Dresser, Horatio, 6583
Dreuille, Mayeul de, on monasticism, 6136
Drew, Timothy (Noble Drew Ali), 71–72, 4687, 4688, 6418, 6563
Drewal, Henry, 10033
Drey, Johann Sebastian von
Möhler (Johann Adam) and, 6113
"world religions" used by, 9800
Dreyer, Carl Theodor, 3098, 3100, 3101
Dreyer, Elizabeth, 3312
Dreyfus, Alfred, 2527
Dreyfus, Georges, 9190
Dreyfus, Hubert, 510
Dribidu (culture hero), hair, association with, 3739
Drinking. *See also* Alcoholic beverages
in New Year festivals, 6590
Driver, Tom, 7858
Drobisch, M. W., 6234
Drogin, Marc, on book curses, 2105–2106
Droṇa (brahman)
Arjuna taught by, 487
Buddha's relics and, 7690
Drona stupas (funerary mounds), 7690
Drone pitch, in Indian music, 6279
Dropsie University, Gaster (Theodor H.) at, 3288
Drower, Ethel S., 5635, 5637–5638
Droysen, Johann G., 3599
Drug (confusion), in Zoroastrianism, 9989
Drugom Gyelwa Yungdrung (bru sgom rgyal ba gyung drung), 2549–2550
Drugs. *See also* Herbal medicine; Narcotics; Psychedelic drugs
in Caribbean religions, 1430
in China, sellers of, 3863
ecstasy from, 2679–2680
as elixirs, 2770
mysticism induced by, 6342
psychotropic, in South American religions, 6274
religion originating through, 366
Drug tourism, 7472
Druids, **2491–2493**
calendar and seasons, 1491
Fustel de Coulanges on, 3246
in Greek and Roman literature, 2492
among learned class, 1479
meaning of word, 2491
in medieval Irish literature, 2493
memorization by, 5851
oral tradition of, 1479
Patrick and, 2493, 7010
persecution of, in Roman Empire, 7921
rainmaking by, 7603
re-creations of, 6470
role exaggerated by Romans, 1481
sacred places and, 1491
Stonehenge as temple of, 2493
studies on, 1497, 1499, 2493
transmigration belief of, 9329
women as, 3387
Druj (confusion), gender of term, 3372
Drukhsh Nasush (ghoul), 3372, 3373
"Drum as Love, Fear, and Prayer" (Alexie), 7226
Drums, **2493–2502**. *See also* Percussion
of affliction, 60
in African American traditions, 2495–2496, 2500
in African religions, 2494, 2495–2496, 2500, 7035, 7036–7037
African Independent Churches, 103
functions of, 6257–6258
Balinese, 745
baptism of, 7037
in Buddhism, 2496–2497, 7036
in Chinese religion, 2499, 7036
in Christianity, 2498, 2499
in Coptic Church, 2495
in Cuba, 7037
description of, 2494
in Egyptian religion, 2498
in Garifuna religion, 3284
in Greek religion, 2498
in healing, 7036
in Indian religions, 2448, 2494, 2496, 2499, 7036
in Islam, 2498, 2499, 7036
in Japanese religions, 7036
in Judaism, 2495, 2496, 2498, 2499
in Korean religions, 5229, 7036
in Mesoamerican religions, 6268, 6269, 7036
Aztec, 6269, 6270
in dance drama, 2465
in Mesopotamian religions, 2498, 6276
in Neolithic burials, Southeast Asian, 8642
in New Guinea religions, vol. 13 color insert
in North American Indian religions, 2499–2500, 7035
in drama, 2460
of Śiva, 3442, *3443*
in Polynesian religions, 6263
Rastafarian, 1438
replaced by other instruments, 7035–7036
in Roman religion, 2498
in shamanism, 2494, 2497–2498, 2500, 7035, 7036, 8272, 8284–8285
Korean, 5229
in Mongol religions, 6141
neoshamanic drum journey, 8294–8295, 8296
in South American Indian religions, 2499, 7036
and spirit possession, 2496, 2500–2501, *2501,* 7036
in Sri Lanka, 7036
in Sufism, 2495, 2499, 7036
in Sumerian religion, 2498
symbolism of, 2494–2495
in vision inducement, 9613
Drums of Affliction, The (Turner), 1003, 9405
Drunemeton, 1491
Druze, **2502–2504**
beliefs and practices of, 2504
decline of, 2503
doctrines of, 2502, 2503, 8330
genealogy of, 2502–2503
geographical distribution of, 2502
on *ghaybah* (concealment), 3469
initiated *vs.* uninitiated, 2502
missions of, 2503
number of, 2502
origins of, 226, 2503, 8324
teachings of, 2503
women in, 2502
Dryads, 2951
Dryden, John, 30
on deism, 2251
Drykkeoffer (Viking beer party), 5434

D source. *See* Deuteronomy (D) source
Du'ā' (voluntary prayer), 7342
Dua clans
myths of, 660–661
Wawalag myth of, 9704–9706
Du'āh (missionaries), 4572
Dual inheritance system, 8475
Dualism, **2504–2517**. *See also* Doubleness; Duality; Twins
abstinence and, 1476
in anthropology, 2505–2506, 2507, 2509, 2511
anticosmic, 2508–2509, 2509–2510, 2512
antihylic, 2509
asceticism and, 528–529
in Baltic religion, 758–759
of body and soul/mind, 4158–4159, 4163
in Bogomilism, 2505, 2508, 2509, 2511, 2513–2514, 9415
in Buddhism, Zhenyan (Tantric) school and, 1577
in Catharism, 1456–1458, 2508, 2509, 2513–2514
chaos and transcendent, 1539
in Cheng-Zhu Confucianism, 1577
in Chinese religion, 2508, 6746
Christian critique of, 2507
in Christianity, 2512–2514
in Creation, 2648–2649
conflict, 2509
cosmic (procosmic), 2508–2509, 2509–2510, 2512
in creation, 2505
creation myths and
in Dogon religion, 1987
as theme in, 1989
debunking, 2654–2655
definition of, 2504
Bianchi (Ugo) on, 864
dialectical, 2508, 2509
diffusion of, 2511
in earth diver myths, 1994
in Dogon religion, 2515
earth diver myths and, 1994, 2510–2511
in Egyptian religion, 2514–2515
eschatological, 2508, 2509, 2511
ethical, 2505, 2509
gender
of androcentrism, 334–336
North American Indian rejection of, 3406
gnostic, 2506, 2508, 2509, 2511, 2512–2513
in Gnosticism, 3512, 3522–3523, 6746, 7190
Culianu (Ioan Petru) on, 2079, 2080
of light and darkness, 5452
in Greek religion, 2507, 2508, 2511, 2514–2515
in Hellenistic religions, of angels and devils, 3904
in Hinduism, 2508, 2509, 4427
in *Bhagavadgītā,* 852
Madhva's dualistic Vedānta, 4005 (*See also* Dvaita school of Vedānta)
nondualism (*See Advaita*)
Śaiva sects, dualistic *vs.* nondualistic, 8047–8048
Śaṅkara on, 4003
viśeṣādvaita (qualified dualism) in Vīraśaivism, 8044
in history of religions, 2510–2511
vs. holism, in science and religion, 2659
horizontal, 2509
human body and, 4158, 4161–4162
in Otomí religion, 6927
in Iranian kingship, 5165
in Islam, 2514, 4570
in Jainism, 4768
in Judaism, 2507, 2511–2512
body and soul, in Hebrew scriptures, 4158
condemnation of, 3548
Satan and, 8124
in soul, 8557
of Kant (Immanuel), 7137
in Khoi religion, 5135
knowledge in, 5207–5208
of light and darkness (*See* Darkness; Light)
Löw (Yehudah ben Betsal'el of Prague) on, 5520–5521
in Manichaeism, 2505, 2506, 2508, 2509, 2513, 5652–5653, 5659, 5666–5667, 5668
in Mapuche religion, 5688–5689
in Marcionism, 2506
in Mazdakism, 5800–5801
metaphysical, 2509
mitigated, 1456–1457
moderate, 2507–2508, 2509, 2513
in monism, 2505, 2507
in monotheism, 2506–2507, 2511–2514, 6159–6160
vs. monotheism, 6158–6159
in Neo-Confucianism
in Korea, 8510
of Lu Xiangshan, 5541
in North American Indian religions, 2508, 6728
number two and, 6746
in Orphism, 2508, 2509, 2511
Osage, 6917, 6918–6919
in philosophy, 2505
physical, 2509
in Platonism, 2506, 2507, 2508, 7189, 7190
Plutarch on, 2514–2515, 7200
in polytheism, 2505, 2507
in primitive religion, 8531–8532
prohylic, 2509
in psychology, 2509
radical, 1457, 2507–2508, 2509, 2513, 7189
as religio-historical phenomenon, 2505–2506
sacrilege and, 8010
in San religion, 5135
of Shakers, 8268
in sociology, 2505–2506
soteriological, 2509
in Southeast Asian religions
complementary dualities in, 8648–8649
in cosmology, 8643
spatial, 2509
in Sufism, *coincidentia oppositorum* (conjunction of opposites) doctrine in, 8812, 8813–8814
in Tehuelche religion, 9030
theological, 2509
in Turkic religions, 9398
two-world, 2509
vertical, 2509
war legitimized by, 9680
witchcraft and, 9771
in *yinyang,* 9888
in Zoroastrianism, 2505, 2506, 6746, 9994–9995
cosmic dualism, 2509
as dualist monotheism, 2511
eschatological dualism, 2508
morality and, 7651
origins of, 2510
Plutarch on, 7200
radical dualism, 2507, 9412–9413
Zurvan and, 10014
Dualismo religioso, Il (Bianchi), 863
Dualismus oder Monismus (Stein), 2505
Duality. *See also* Binary oppositions
in Aztec religion, 5891
in Gnosticism, 3512
in Maya religion, 5883
in Mesoamerican religions, 5933–5934
of afterlife, 148
in messianism, 5975
in Oceanic religions, of afterlife, 147
Dual transcendence, 9282–9283, 9284
Düben, Gustaf von, 474
Dubnow (Dubnov), Simon, 4880, 4882
Dubois, Jean-Antoine, 4447
on magic, 5587
DuBois, Thomas A., 3459, 3460
Du Bois, W. E. B.
on Caribbean religions, 10025
on civil religion, 1816
Garvey (Marcus) criticized by, 3287
on identity, 67
religious studies by, 73–74
interdisciplinary approach of, 73
music in, 77
phenomenological, 66–67
Du Bois-Reymond, Emil, 7341
DuBourg, William Valentine, Seton (Elizabeth) and, 8234
Dubowski, Sandi Simcha, 3098
Dubroux, Danièle, 3099
Dubs, H. H., 235
Dubuffet, Jean, 9625–9626
Dubuisson, Daniel, 4455, 4464
Duchesne, Louis, 9814
Duck, 7376
Du culte des dieux fétiches (De Brosses), 365–366, 4363
Dudley, Guilford, 7097
Dudū Miyān, 4651
Duel, ordeal as, 6848–6849
Duel, The (Dollar), 2154
Duende, 2951
Duenov's Brotherhood of Light, 6568
Dufay, Guillaume, 6309
Duffryn, Powell, 833
Duffy, Eamon, 7888
Duggan, Cheryl Kirk, 77, 79
Dughdōvā, 9989
Du Guangting (Daoist scholar), **2517–2518**
writings of, 2185, 2198, 2205, 2206, 2209
Dügü (mashing down the earth) performances, 3284, 3285–3286
Duḥkha (suffering)
Buddha on, 9119
Buddhist philosophy on, 1296–1297, 5200
law and, 5350
causes of, 6391
cessation of, 1296
in Four Noble Truths, 2306, 3178, 3179
karman and, 9112
in Khmer religion, 5132
Nāgārjuna on, 3180, 6391
nirvāṇa as practical solution to, 6628
sukha (bliss) *vs.,* 2029
in Thai Buddhism, 9094
Duhm, Bernard, on anthropomorphism, 389
Duḥṣamā (unhappy period), in Jain cosmology, 2025

Duḥṣamā-duḥṣamā (very unhappy period), in Jain cosmology, 2025
Duḥśāsana, in *Mahābhārata,* 5595
Duisburg, Peter von, on Baltic nature worship, 8131
Dukduk society (Melanesia), as secret society, 8212–8213
Dukhovnyi Reglament (1721), 7418
Dukkha (suffering). *See Duḥkha;* Suffering, in Buddhism
Dulare, Jacques Antoine, on symbols, 8909
Dule Monastery (Buddhist temple), 9047
Dulu bugha (middle world), 9394
Dulungun, 9460
Dumas, Marlene, 813
Duméry, Henri
on knowledge, 5210
phenomenology and, 4237
Dumézil, Georges, **2518–2520,** 2965
and Lévi-Strauss (Claude), 2519, 4463
augmenting work of, 385
on Baldr, 744
on Beyla, 3220
on binding, 937, 5196
on *brahman,* etymology of, 1024
on *brahman* and *flamen,* common etymology of, 3125
on Celtic religion, 1481, 1482, 1491, 4453, 4462, 4463, 4464
and comparative mythology, 2518–2519, 4461–4464
comparative mythology method of, 1874, 1875
critics of, 2519, 2543, 4463
on druids, 2493
on functions of deities, 3452, 3459, 3621
on Germanic deities, 3452, 3453, 3454–3455, 3459
Granet (Marcel) influencing, 3655
and Greek mythology, 3662–3663
on Hindu literature, 5467
on Indo-European religions, 2518–2519, 4440, 4453, 4454, 4461–4464, 10079
influence on scholarship, 3460
on knots, 5196, 5278
life of, 2518
on Mars, 5727, 5728
on memorization, 5851–5852
on Indra as *sahasramuṣka,* 3040
on *Mahābhārata,* 5595
on Týr, 9426
oral tradition and, 6842
on power, 7351–7352
on Roman religion, 4462, 7893, 7901
on savage frenzy, domestication of, 3214
on Siberian religions, 3114
structuralism and, 8758
on Thor, 9166
trifunctional model of society, 1499, 4045
tripartite cognitive model of, 2519
on Vedic mythology, 9559
Wikander (Stig) and, 9735
Dumitrescu, Hortensia, 7380
Dumitrescu, Vladimir, 7380
Dumje ceremony, of Buddhists, 2138
Dumont, Louis, 385
on caste system, 4448–4449
Fustel de Coulanges and, 3246
on magic, 5588
on purification, 7504
on renunciation, 8094
Dumuzi (deity), **2520–2523,** 5957–5958. *See also* Tammuz
Adonis compared with, 34, 2521
aspects of, 5957–5958
death of, 2521, 2522, 5958
in divine bureaucracy, 5951
dove as symbol of, 948
as dying and rising god, 1874, 2521–2522, 2538–2539, 7767
in Holy Wedding, 5162
iconography of, 4317
and Inanna, 2445, 2520, 2521, 2522–2523, 3976, 4403, 4404, 4405, 5949, 5956, 5957, 5958
as officer of underworld, 2520–2521
passivity of, 2522–2523
pastoral association of, 3977
portrait of, 2521
songs about, 2520, 2521
transvestites as consorts of, 3968
as vegetation god, 2522
wedding of, 5958
Dumuzi-Abzu (deity), 5959
as city god, 5949
Dun, Tan, 6313
Dunand, Françoise, 4558
Duna people (New Guinea), female spirits of, 3396–3397
Duncan, Isadora, 2141, 2157
Dundes, Alan
on Campbell (Joseph), 1379
on earth diver myth, 1988–1989
on folk group, 3143
on proverbs, 6976
Dundubhiḥ (drum), 2496
Dundun (drum), 7037
Dung beetle, 4508
Dunham, Katherine, 76, 2164
Dunhuang manuscripts, 2211
Chan Buddhism in, 1520, 1523, 1634
devotion to, 1521
discovery of, 1634, 5669
motivations for copying, 1262, 1263
study of, 9188
Dunjiao (sudden teaching), Huayan perspective on, 4148
"Dunkers," 785
Duns Scotus, John, **2523–2525,** 3183
in exile, 2524
on existence of God, 7421
as founder of Scotism, 2523
Francis of Assisi and, 3185
on free will and predestination, 3203, 3207
Ibn Sīnā's influence on, 4275
on knowledge, 5204
life of, 2523–2524
on merit, 5876
philosophy of, 2524–2525
theology of, 9136
writings of, 2524
Dunstable, John, 6309
Duong Thu Huong, 3078
Duo viri sacris faciundis, 7908
Du Plessi-Mornay, Philippe, Hermetism and, 3946
DuPonceau, Peter, 6670
Duppies (spirits), in Kromanti dance, 1436
Dupré, Louis, 6355, 6356
Dupré, Marie-Claude, on masks, 5768
Dupré, Wilhelm, 4401
on *homo existens, homo symbolicus,* and *homo religiosus,* 4110
Du Préau, Gabriel, Hermetism and, 3946
Dupuis, Charles-François, 4459
Dura-Europos
Cumont (Franz) and, 2093, 2094
Mithraeum (Sanctuary of Mithra) in, 2093
synagogue at, 8923
Durán, Diego, 2464, 2465, 2466–2467, 5294, 5901, 5920, 5939
on Aztec Flowery Wars, 4186
Duran, Profiat, 7234
Durandel (sword), 9686
Duren jing (Daoist text), 1602, 2186, 2205, 2206
Dürer, Albrecht, 4346
German humanism and, 4176
Durgā (deity), 2525–2526
and Tārā, 9000
as Śiva's wife, 2525, 2526, 4444
avatāras of, 708
Bengali worship of, 826
as dangerous goddess, 3607
hymns on, 2526
iconography of, 4325–4326
images of, 2526
Mahiṣāsura defeated by, 2525, 2526
Navarātri festival of, **6443–6444**
Rādhā and, 7593
symbols of, 4435
in virgin-mother-crone triad, 2984
Durgā-Caṇḍī poems, in *Dasam Granth,* 2221
Durgā Hinduism, **2525–2526**
Durgā Pūjā (festival), 826, 830, 2526, 7043, 9824
Durgati (evil existence), 1197
Durgatipariśodhana Tantra, 1214
Durgotsava (festival), 2526. *See also* Navarātri
Durham, William H., 7029
Durham Cathedral (England), Saint Cuthbert's body in, 8376
Durkheim, Émile, **2526–2530**
on African religions
kingship in, 5169
supreme beings of, 3576
and Dumézil (Georges), 2518
on Australian Indigenous religions, 2478–2479, 2528–2529, 4461
mythology of, 686
women in, 3389
Bellah (Robert) compared to, 8498
Celtic religious studies and, 1498
on collective effervescence, 3138
on community *vs.* society, 7716
on conscience collective, 8493
coworkers of, 2528
on deviance, 8484–8485
on dynamism, 2542
evolutionism and, 2916
on food taboos, 3172
functionalism and, 3231–3232, 8493
Fustel de Coulanges and, 3246
Gillen and Spencer influencing, 3490
Granet (Marcel) and, 3655
on grieving processes, 2241
on history, 2527
on individual *vs.* society, 5785
influence on archaeology, 454
influence on contemporary anthropology, 378
influence on Reconstructionist Judaism, 5081
influences on, 8493
journal founded by, 10057
on kingship, in Africa, 5169
on knowledge, 5207
on law and religion, 5325, 5371
legacy of, 2529
Lévy-Bruhl's (Lucien) criticism of, 5429
life of, 2527
on liturgy, 5491
on magic, 5565, 5571
Malinowski (Bronislaw) on, 5629
on *mana,* 2542, 7373
on material interests, religion and, 2669

Mauss (Marcel) and, 5785, 5786
modern social theory, contributions to, 8493
and naturalism, 6430
Otto (Rudolf) contrasted with, 4095–4096
on philosophy, 2527
on politics and religion, 7251
on purification, 7504
Radcliffe-Brown (A.R.) influenced by, 7592
on reflexivity, 7649
on religion as social function, 4163
religion defined by, 7693
on religion *vs.* magic, 6502–6503
on retribution, 5373
revaluation of, 380
on rites of passage, 7800
on ritual, 7043, 7840, 7841, 7850
on sacred and profane, 6359, 7970–7971, 8010
on sanctions, restitutive *vs.* repressive, 1843
Smith (W. Robertson) *vs.,* 8452
on social groups, 8482
social realism of, 2527
on society and religion, 8465, 8487
sociological approach of, 382, 2528
on sociology and religion, 8480–8481
on solidarity, types of, 8488, 8495
Spencer (Herbert), criticism of, 8679
Stanner (W. E. H.) on, 8729
and study of North American Indian religions, 6671
on suicide, 2527, 8828
on the supernatural, 8861–8862
symbol theory and, 8910
on taboo, 7841, 8948
on tears, 9025, 9026
theory of religion, 3231
on totemism, 9250, 9251
Weber (Max) and, 8494
writings of, 2528–2529, 4461
Durt, Hubert, 1313
Durūd (blessing of the Prophet), 9818
Duryodhana (Hindu figure), 743
in *Mahābhārata,* 5595
Dusadh (mythic figure), 4434
Dus gsum mkhyen pa (Dusum Khyenpa), 1226, 5101, 5102
Dushara (deity), 6388–6389
as main Nabatean god, 6388–6389, 6390
temple of, 6386
Zeus identified with, 6386, 6389
Dushun (Buddhist monk), **2530**
Huayan Buddhism and, 4146
on *li,* 5431
Dussart, Françoise, 644, 668, 687, 3390
Dussel, Enrique, 5439
Dusun people (Borneo), 1022
Dutch Guiana. *See* Surinam
Dutch Learning (Japan), 9311
Dutch people. *See* Netherlands
Dutch Reformed church
in Africa, 1722
Arminius (Jacobus) in, 492–493
Chantepie de la Saussaye and, 1530, 5391
in Indonesia, 9241
Leeuw (Gerardus van der) in, 5391
Pietism in, 7142
in South Africa, evangelicals and political activism, 1724
Dutertre, Jean-Baptiste, on Caribbean shamanism, 1431
Du Thet, Gilbert, 9302
Duties of the Heart (Baḥye), 4890
Dutoit, Antonio, 9068
Dutoit, Christopher Emmanuel, 9068
Duṭṭhagāmaṇī (king of Ceylon), **2530–2531**
Buddha images under, 1304–1305
Buddhism under, 1092, 2530–2531, 7261, 9147
relics and, 7690–7691
image of, 2531
Duty, in social roles, 8484
Duvalier, François, Caribbean neo-African cults and, 1434
Duverger, Christian, 5945
Duviols, Pierre, 3416
Duwayrah (small cloister), 9005
Du Wenxiu (Muslim leader), 4633
Dvags po Bka' brgyud (Dakpo Kagyu) Buddhism, Sgam po pa and, 8255
Dvags po Bkra shis rnam rgyal (Dakpo Tashi Namgyel), on *mahāmudrā,* 5598
Dvaita (dualism), 828, 858
Dvaitādvaita, 9548
Dvaita school of Vedānta
influence of, 5551
Madhva in, 5550–5551
metaphysics in, 8547
vs. Advaita Vedānta, 5551
Dvāparayuga (period of time), in Purāṇic cosmology, 2018, 2019
Dvārakā (India), pilgrimage to, 7170
Dvāravatī (Mon Buddhism), 1132, 9147
Dvergar (dwarfs), **2532**
Dvina Karelians, 5092
Dvornik, Francis, 7135
Dvr (communication on God's part), 7777
Dwarfs
in Germanic religion, **2532**
in Olmec iconography, 4311
Viṣṇu in form of, 708, 4325
Dwelling, divine. *See also* Temples
architecture classified as, 461–463
mountains as, 462, 6213–6214
Dwight, Timothy, **2532–2533**
Dwivedi, Hazariprasad, on Gorākhnāth, 3637
Dworkin, Ronald, 5358
Dyaus (deity), 2313, 4466, 9524
Dybbuk (disembodied human spirit), **2533–2535,** 2931
emergence of, 2932–2933
possession by, 2533
etiology of, 2533
locus of, 2533
signs of, 2534
treatment of, 2534
Dybuuk; or, Between Two Worlds, The (Anski), 2933
Dyer, Mary Marshall, 6558
Dying and rising gods, **2535–2540**. *See also* Resurrection; *specific gods*
Adonis as, 34, 2535–2536
Aqhat as, 1874–1875
Attis as, 2536–2537
Baal as, 724, 1874, 2536, 7767
castration of, 1452
comparisons in Semitic myths, 1874–1875
courtesans and, 3968
definition of, 2535
in *dema* myth complex, 4826
Dumuzi as, 1874, 2521–2522, 2538–2539, 7767
in Germanic religion, 744
Marduk as, 2522, 2537–2538, 5703
Melqart as, 5847
in mystery religions, 6328
Osiris as, 1875, 2538
patterns of, 2535
as precursor to resurrection, 7767
theories on, 2522, 2535
vegetation deities and, 6328
Dylan (deity), in *Mabinogion,* 5546
Dylan Eil Don (deity), 1489
D'yly Oduuluur (festival), 2395
Dynamic, revival and renewal activities described by, 7784
Dynamic Laws of Prosperity, The (Ponder), 6585
Dynamism, **2540–2545**
animism and, 362–363, 2540
application of, 2542
classic theories of, 2541–2542
criticism of, 2542–2543
origin of term, 362
in philosophy, 2540
power in, 7348
preanimism and, 2540–2541
remnants of, 2543–2544
in study of religion, 2540, 2541
totemism and, 2542
Dynov, Tsvi Elimelech, 9380
Dyongu Seru (Dogon ancestor), 2391
Dyson, Freeman, 510, 513
Dyson, Michael, 80, 81
Dzieci (troupe), 2476
Dzivaguru (mythic figure), 97
in Karanga religion, 8663, 8664
Dzogchen (Great Perfection), **2545–2550**. *See also* Snying thig
in Bhutan, 5194
Klong chen Rab 'byams pa (Longchenpa) and, 5191, 5194
Kumārāja on, 5192
literature of, 2548, 2549, 2550
origins of, 2545–2547
Rang byung rdo rje on, 5192
in Rnying ma pa (Nyingmapa) school of Buddhism, 7868–7869, 7870
study of, 9190
transformations in, 2546–2547
Dzongs (Buddhist temples), 9052
Dzongsar (Buddhist school), religious education at, 5224

E

Ea (deity), 2962, 2963. *See also* Enki
cosmic tree and, 3449
in *Enuma elish,* 5955
in Eridu, 1502
in Hurrian religion, 4231–4232
as keeper of keys, 5116
in myth of Nergal and Ereshkigal, 6476–6477
in myth of the Flood, 599
Nabu and, 6390
offspring of, 7861
in triad, 9349
as water deity, 9701, 9702
Worm of Sickness and, 3811
"Eagle Poem" (Harjo), 7225
Eagles, 948, 949, **2553–2554,** 7387
in Aztec religion, 5891
deities as, Our Mother Young Eagle Girl (Huichol), 4152
masculine sacrality in, 5760
in North American Indian religions, 6698–6699, 6717, 6724
Odin as, 8522, 8722
in Vedism, Garuḍa as, 8522
Eagleton, Terry, 5474, 5486, 5489
Eannna (deity), 4403

Ea-Oannes (mythical hero), 3123
Earle, Augustus, 7306
Early Dynastic period (Mesopotamia), 5947–5948
Early Translation school of Buddhism. *See* Rnying ma pa (Nyingmapa) school of Buddhism
Earth, **2554–2561**
in African myths, 96–98
supreme being and, 3567
in Swazi religion, 8895
afterlife located on, 137
age of, in creationism, 2911
agriculture as metaphor for, 9578
in astronomy, Copernicus on movement of, 1977
in Aztec religion, 5907
in Baltic religion, 758–759, 769
burial in, symbolism of, 3238–3239
in Chinese religion
heaven, ruptured link with, 1625–1626
landscape in myth, 1625
she, 1584, 1615–1616
in Confucian triad, 2631, 2633
cooking and baking linked to, 3019
in cosmic solidarity of life, 2560
in creation, 2555–2557
death and regeneration and, 2559–2560
deities of (*See* Earth deities)
Egyptian concept of, 2710
in farmers' religion, 3108
feminine sacrality of, 3014–3016, 3020, 3021
first image of, responses to, 2608
Gaia hypothesis of, 3022, **3253–3255**
Heaven and
marriage of, 7602
separation of, 6983
hierophanies (sacred manifestations) of, 3971
in Hinduism, in Purāṇic cosmology, 2018
Lady of the Animals as, 5280
lying on, in birth rituals, 2559
in Maya religion, 5796
image of, 5882–5883
in Mesoamerican religions, 5927
Mother (*See* Earth mothers; Mother Earth)
mountains linking heaven and, 6213
in Osage religion, 6917, 6918–6919
sacralization of, Neolithic religion and, 6459
in secular myths, 5035
as source of life, 2554–2555
worship of, 6440
in ancient religions, 2662
Earth Charter, 2613, 2657
Earth Day, 2650
Earth deities, 3619–3620
in Aztec religion (*See* Tlaloc)
in central Bantu religion, 1508–1509
Chac (Maya), 1469
in Chinese religion, 1911–1912
examples of, 3619–3620
functions of, 3619–3620
masculine sacrality and, 5761
in nature worship, 6440
offerings to, vol. 7 color insert
in Polynesian religions, 7312–7313, 7314
in primordial couple, 1993–1994
Zeme, 9942–9943
Earth diver myths
in Arctic religions, 472, 474
chaos and, 1538
comparison of, 1875–1876
diffusion of dualistic elements in, 1994
and dualism, 2510–2511
insects in, 4508
in North American Indian religions
Asian origins of, 6653
of California and Intermountain region, 6713
Ojibwa, 6660, 6661
of Southeast Woodlands, 6692
as symbolic pattern, 1988–1989
Earth First!, **2561–2566**. *See also* Ecology
deep ecology in, 2561–2562
philosophy of, 2562
as religious movement, 2564
ritual in, 2563–2564
tactics and goals of, 2562
Earth Liberation Front (ELF), 2562
Earth Lodge Cult, 6700–6701, 6718
Earthmaker (deity), in Winnebago religion, 8870
Earth Mother (deity), 5119–5120
Earth mothers, 3619. *See also* Mother Earth
in agricultural rituals, 189, 190
in Aztec religion (*See* Coatlicue)
in Caribbean religions, 1427
and castration of Sky gods, 1450
emergence myths and, 1988
examples of, 3619
in Finno-Ugric religions, 3108
functions of, 3619
in Greek myth, 1450
in Inca religion, 4411
in Iroquois religion, 6682
as sole generative principle, 1993
worship of, 3589
Earth Primitive (dance style), 2158
Earthquake deities, in Lugbara religion, 2568
Earth shrines, Andean. *See* *Huacas*
East Africa and East African religions, **2566–2579**. *See also* Bantu religions; Kamba religion; Maasai religion; Nuer and Dinka religion; Shilluk religion; *specific countries and religions*
African Independent Churches in, 2571
Christianity, 2571–2572, 2578
colonialism in
Christianity as agent of, 2572, 2578
Portuguese, 4607
divinity in, 2566–2567
lesser divinities, 2567–2569
evil in
explanations of, 2569–2570
responses to, 2569–2570
God in, 2566–2567
illness and healing in
conception of illness, 3817
diagnosis in, 3818
surgery, 3820
Islam, 2571–2572, 2578, 4607
architecture of mosques in, 6209
mawlids in, 5789–5790
spirit cults, 2568
traditional cults and, 4609
women in, 4610
myth in, 2566–2567
overview of, **2566–2572**
political movements in, prophets inspiring, 87
population of, 2566
priests of, 2569
prophetic movements in, 2570–2572
prophets in, 7443–7445
rites of passage in, circumcision and, 1799
rituals of, colonial opposition to, 2578
sacrifice in, 2568–2569
East Asia and East Asian religions. *See also* Ainu religion; *specific countries and religions*
ancestor worship in, 323
animism in, drama in, 2453–2455
Buddhism
Avalokiteśvara in, 705–706
drama in, 2455–2456
drums in, 2497
literature of, 1257
Mahāvairocana in, 5607
meditation in, **1290–1295**
nianfo in, 6601–6602
nirvāṇa in, 6630–6632
pilgrimage in, **7164–7166**
schools of, **1246–1251**
tathāgata-garbha in, 9018
temples of, **9045–9049**
worship and devotional life in, **9834–9839**
films from, 3097
journals devoted to, 10058
kingship in, **5178–5181**
lesbianism in, 5415
magic in, **5592–5594**
millenarianism in, 6030
Shamanism in
ancestor worship and, 323
drama in, 2453–2455
East Asia Secretariat, formation of, 1730
Easter, **2579–2580**
archaic elements in, 6593
baptism at, 9810
ceremonies of, 2471 (*See also* Carnival)
domestic observances of, 2399
egg symbolism in, 2702
Irenaeus on, 4538
in liturgical calendar, 1741, 9813–9814
and history, view of, 4053–4054
moon and, 6171
in New Testament, God revealed by, 3544
pilgrimage during, 7154
as preferred time for baptism, 2468
Pueblo celebration of, 6729
waehma, as ritual performance of, 7045
Easter: Its Story and Meaning (Watts), 2702
Easter Bunny, 7590
Easter eggs, 2702, 3170, 7590
Easter Island religion
origin myth of, 7314
Tangaroa in, 8980
Easter lily, symbolism of, 3136
Eastern Buddhist (journal), Suzuki (D. T.) as founder of, 8886
Eastern Catholic churches
establishment of, 2587
Orthodox churches and, property right disputes between, 2588
polity of, 7887
Eastern Christianity, **2580–2595**. *See also* Eastern Orthodox Christianity; Greek Orthodox Church; Russian Orthodox Church
on abortion, 941
on Arianism, 478
biblical exegesis in, 874
branches of, 1765
Byzantine Empire, Christian culture of, 1661–1662
Cassian's theology and, 1448
chanting in, 1534
charity in, 1554
Chrysostom's role in, 1761–1762

church architecture of
body correlated with, 7983
intersection of realms in, 7980
colors, liturgical, 1744
confession in, 1889
development of
charity in, 2582
division with Roman Catholicism, 2585–2588
early, 2580–2582
monasteries in, 2582
organizational, 2581
papal authority in, 2585–2586
schism in, 2586–2587
theological, 2581–2585
doctrine, control over, 1667
domestic observances in, 2399, 2400
in Eastern Europe, 1681–1687
ecclesiology, 1772–1773
on embryonic stem cell research, 941
European Christianity, differences with, 1689–1690
false perceptions of, 2589
on free will and predestination, 3208
God in, 3554–3555
gold color symbolism, 1861
grace in, 3645
heart symbolism in, prayer of the heart, 3883
icons in, vol. 12 color insert
in Latin America, 1703
Lent in, 1743
liturgical calendar, 1741
Palm Week, 1743
membership in the church in, 1777
missions, 6083
in Bulgaria, Moravia, and Russia, 1683
language use, 1662, 1683
Monophysitism in, 6153–6155
non-Chalcedonia (*See* Non-Chalcedonian Orthodox churches)
pilgrimage in (*See* Pilgrimage, Eastern Christian)
prayer in, 1046
Protestants, view of, 8158
recent developments in, 2588–2589
reforms of, Theodore of Studios and, 9122
spirituality of, enthusiasm in, 2808
Symeon the New Theologian in, 8919–8920
textiles in, 9091
theocracy in, 9110
theology in, 9135–9136
tolerance for indigenous religions, 3106
tradition in, 9268
West, split with (*See* Schism)
Western contacts with, 1664
Eastern Europe. *See also* Europe; Southeastern Europe; *specific countries and religions*
academic study of religion in, **8771–8775**
Christianity in, **1680–1687**
early Christianity in, 1682
Great Schism and imperial contention in, 1683–1685
influences in, 1680–1682
in Latvia, 762, 767, 768, 773
legitimization and barbarian inroads, 1682
in Lithuania, 773, 775
missionary efforts, conflicting, 1682–1683
and modern nation-states, 1685–1686
Pentecostalism, 7029
after World War II, 1686–1687
films from, 3098
Islam in, 4676–4677, 4678, 4679, 4680
Jewish studies in, 4884
Judaism in
to 1500, **5011–5014**
Orthodox, 6901–6903
parables of, 6978–6979
since 1500, **5014–5023**
tekhines in, 9037
tsaddiq in, 9380–9382
yeshivot of, 9885
magic in, **5580–5583**
new religious movements in, 6515, 6526, 6567
laws curbing activities of, 6571
native, 6568
study of, 6569–6570
winter solstice in, 9741
Eastern Han period (China), afterlife in, 169, 170–172
Eastern Monastery (Buddhist temple), 9049
Eastern Orthodox Christianity. *See also* Eastern Orthodox Church; Greek Orthodox Church
authority in, 695
Beth (Karl) on, 846
Bulgakov (Sergei) on, 1319–1320
calendar of, 4832
churches of
architecture of, 794, 9265
sacredness of, 7698
devotion in, 2320
eremitism in, 2826–2827
Eucharistic prayer in, 9811
God in
nature of, 2590
personal relationship with, 2592
heterodoxy in, 6912
on homosexuality, 7404
icons in, vol. 10 color insert, vol. 12 color insert
justification in, 5040
Mary in, 5754
ministry in, 6044
monasticism in, 7720
music in, 6310
orthodoxy in, 6912
on Peter the Apostle, 7069
postures and gestures in, 7342, 7343
redemption by Jesus in, 4843
Russian Orthodox Church and, 7942
theology of, in *Pege gnoseos,* 4940–4941
Trinity in, 9350
true images in, vol. 12 color insert
union with Roman Catholicism
Gregory of Cyprus against, 3692
Gregory of Datev against, 3693
Mark of Ephesus against, 5713–5714
Vatican I and, 9528, 9530
at Vatican II, 4946
witch craze and, 9773
Eastern Orthodox Church
autocephalies in, 1765
Calvinism condemned by, 2044
canon law of, Quinisext Synod and, 2041
Cerularios's role in, **1519–1520**
Christ the Saviour Brotherhood and, 4103
clergy in, distinction from laity, 5287
conversion of Khanty people by, 5118, 5125
conversion of Mansi people by, 5118, 5125
corruption in, Catharism as reaction to, 2748
creeds in, 2056–2057, 2059
dance in, 2135
and Days of the Dead, 2230
dogma of, 2387
Easter celebrations of, 2579
ecology and, 2649–2650
in ecumenical movement, with Oriental Orthodox Church, 2589
egg symbolism in, 2702
Epiphany in, 2818
ethics in, 1651, 1652–1653
Eucharist in, 2877–2878
in Finland, 5093
fools in, 4202
gender in, 3358
Greek *vs.* Latin tradition, 1681
healing and medicine in, 3844–3845
hell in, 3885
hesychastic prayer, debate over, 2042
iconography of, 4345, 4386, 4389, 4390
icons, meaning of, 1662
incense offering in, 4420
in India, 1729
laity in, 5287
married *vs.* celibate priests, 1477
merit in, 5876
in Middle East, 1673
monasticism in, *philanthropia* (kindness or love towards others) and, 3844–3845
monophysitism in, Severus of Antioch and, 8238
Ottoman Empire and, Scholarios (Gennadios) and, 8174
polity of, 1765–1766
Protestantism, responses to
Cyril and, 2115
in synods and confessions, 2059
Roman Catholic Church and
division between, 2585–2588
Paul VI and, 7012
in Poland, 2114–2115
sacraments in
overview of, 7960
penance, 1652
Roman Catholic interpretation *vs.,* 1669
spirituality in, Serafim of Sarov, role of, **8229**
startsy (elders) in, 8709–8710
structure of, 1765–1766, 2589
Syriac Orthodox Church, relations with, 8940
theology, tradition, role of, 1652
Uniate churches and, 9462–9463
in United States, 1713
in World Council of Churches, 2685
Eastern Peak, 1619
Eastern Rite Catholicism. *See* Uniate Churches
Eastern Woodlands, indigenous peoples of, manitou and, 5673–5674
Eastern Zhou dynasty (China), 1583, 1623–1624
afterlife and, 169–170
law in, 5352
"Easter Wings" (Herbert), 7204
East India Company, Ahmad Khan (Sayyid) at, 201
Eastman, Charles, 702

East Mountain teaching in Chan Buddhism
Huineng in, 4154
teachers in, 1521
Easton, Stewart C., 734
East Timor, Mambai religion in, creation myth in, 8649
East-West Schism. *See* Great East-West Schism
Eating. *See* Food
Eaton, Richard
on Bengali Muslims, 825, 4642
on South Asian Islam, 4642, 4643
EAT-WOT. *See* Ecumenical Association of Third-World Theologians
Ebadi, Shirin, 3365
progressivism of, 6099, 6100
Eban, Abba, 3288
Ebbo (archbishop of Reims), deposition of, and Hincmar, 3983
Eberhard, Wolfram, 1636
Eberle, Gary, on sabbatical, 7989
Ebers Papyrus, medical material in, 3826
Ebionites, **2595–2596**
Ebionites, Gospel of the, 2596
Ebisu (deity), 2410
Ebla (deity), adopted into Hurrian religion as Hebat, 4230
Ebla (Syria)
city gates of, 7761
Dagan in, 2125–2126
kingship in, 5164
Reshef's cult in, 7760, 7761
written records from, 5161
Eblaite religion, **2596–2599**
archaeology of, 455
foreign gods in, 2597, 9495
pantheon of, 2596–2597
Ebla tablets, 455
Ebner, Ferdinand, 6468
Ebomis, 123
Ebreo, Guglielmo (William the Jew of Pisaro), 2154
Ebussüud, Mehmed, as shaykh al-Islam, 8306
Ecatl (deity), self-sacrifice of, 4187
Ecchellensis, Abraham, 5637
Eccles, John, 6486
Ecclesia. *See also* Church
as category, 1867
definition of, 2084
domus ecclesiae (house of the gathered assembly), 8101
and history, Christian views of, 4052–4053
Ecclesiastes, **2599–2600**
absence of divine justice in, 4749
author of, 9763
canonization and, 1408, 1410
dating of, 9755
ḥokhmah in, 4078
Hugh of Saint-Victor on, 4151
Ibn ʿEzraʾ on, 4265
misogyny in, 9756
proverbs in, 6978
skepticism in, 5202, 9756
Solomon as author of, 8513
theodicy in, 9116
as wisdom literature, 9750, 9759
Ecclesiastical authoritarianism model, in science and religion, 8185
Ecclesiastical Hierarchy (Dionysius), 4353, 7402
Ecclesiastical History (Theodoret), 9123
Ecclesiastical History of the English People (Bede), 814
Ecclesiastical Ordinances (Calvin), 7661
church organization in, 1376
Ecclesiastical Regulation (1721), of Peter the Great, 7942
Ecclesiastical understanding of history, Christian, 4055
Ecclesiasticus. See Ben Sira
Ecclesiology, **1770–1777**. *See also* Schism
Augustine of Hippo on, 1771–1772
comparative, in ecumenical movement, 2684
Constantine and the creeds and, 1771
Cyprian on, 2113–2114
in early church, geographical dispersion, episcopacy, and formation of the canon, 1771
in Eastern Church, 1772–1773
of liberation theology, 5439
in New Testament, 1770–1771
papacy and, 1771–1772
in Reformation and rise of Protestantism, 1773–1775
Roman Catholic
ethics, and teaching function, 1653
Vatican II Council on, 2061, 9540
twentieth-century developments and ecumenism in, 1775–1776
in twenty-first century, 1776
Echevarría, Nicolás, 3099
Echidna Woman (mythic figure), 656
ECHR. *See* European Court of Human Rights
Eck, Diana L., American study of religion, role in, 8787
Eck, Johann, 881, **2601**
Eckankar, **2601–2603**
Eckartshausen, Karl von, 340
Eckhart, Johannes (Meister Eckhart)
asceticism of, 527
condemnation of, 6337
on eternity of world, 9362
on God, 3555–3556, 6147
on images, 6347–6348
on knowledge, 5205
on laughter, 4202
monistic system of, 6146, 6147
on mystical union, 6335, 6337
mysticism of, 6347–6348
Neoplatonism and, 6475
Tauler (Johannes) under, 9022
trial of, 4498
via negativa used by, 6990
Eck Masters, 2601
Eclipse Myth, Inanna in, 5956, 5957
Eclipses
interpretations of, 8835
Mesoamerican calendar and, 1356
monsters as cause of, 6163
techniques for "curing," 8835
Eclogues (Vergil), 9582
Sibylline Oracles and, 8384
Eco, Umberto, 3514
on humor, 4202, 4219
Ecocentric holism, 2656–2657
Ecofascism, 2656–2657
Ecofeminism, in India, 2623
Eco-kosher, 2646, 4870
École Française d'Extrême-Orient (EFEO), Maspero (Henri) in, 5773
École Nationale des Langues Orientales, 2272
École Normale Supérieure, 2527
École Pratique des Hautes Études, Mauss (Marcel) at, 5785
Ecological anthropology, 2664
"Ecological Crisis, The," 2613
Ecological imaginaries, 2611–2612
Ecological justice, World Council of Churches focus on, 2612
Ecological self, in Chinese medicine, 3859, 3860
Ecological Society of America, founding of, 2608
Ecologism, 2663
Ecology. *See also* Earth First!
adaptation in, 2868, 2869
in Australian Indigenous religions, moral ecology, 2004
in Buddhism, **2627–2631**
in Christianity, **2647–2650**
in Confucianism, **2631–2635**
conservation in, 2608
cultural absorption and, 2617
culture, 452–453
in Daoism, **2635–2638**
definition of, 2605–2606
ecotheology, feminist, 4166
Eleventh Commandment Fellowship and, 4103
environmental ethics and, **2654–2657**
green spirituality and, 8719
in Hinduism, **2620–2624**
historical, 2664
in indigenous traditions, **2616–2620**
interdisciplinary nature of, 2614
interreligious nature of, 2614
in Islam, **2651–2654**
in Jainism, **2624–2627**
in Judaism, **2641–2642**
nature religions, **2661–2668**
overview of, **2604–2616**
place-based, 2611
principles *vs.* practices in, 2614
Rappaport (Roy) on, 6507, 10043
"Religions of the World and Ecology" project, 2613–2614
religious communities in, participation of, 2612–2613
rituals and, 7840
science and, **2657–2661**
study of
approaches within, 2609–2610
in North America, 2608–2609
term coined, 2608
witchcraft studied in, 9779
world religions and, **2654–2657**
Ecology in the 20th Century (Bramwell), 2663
Ecomuseums, 6245
Economic analysis, development of, 2668
Economic development
in Africa, religious change among central Bantu and, 1510
cargo cults and, 1419–1420
church involvement in, 2685
in Eastern civilizations, 2674
and religion, collaboration with, 9707
and religion, marketing or revitalization of, 1810
Economic Ethic of the World Religions, The (Weber), 9802
Economic justice
in Earth Charter, 2657
in engaged Buddhism, 2788
Economics. *See also* Wealth
and African American religions, 67
Nation of Islam, 6418–6419
and agriculture, emergence of, 3975
Buddhism and, 9708
of Buddhist monasticism, 6129
Calvinism and, 1692
China's expansion of, Confucianism and, 1924
Christianity and, 9709
cities as ceremonial centers and, 7984
commercial and sacred space in India, 1806–1807
Confucianism and, 1924, 9708

of conversion, in
contemporary Mesoamerica, 5929–5930
Daoism and, 9708
degree of embeddedness of, 2675
and Egyptian religion, 2730
environment threatened by, 2610
feast days and chronology and, 1758
gift giving as basis of, 3479
globalization in, 3497–3498
government role in, 2670
Hinduism and, 9708
Islam and, 9708–9709
in Sunnism *vs.* Twelver Shiism, 8344–8345
Jewish law and, 3749
Judaism and, 9708–9709
legitimation and, 5399
premodern concept of, 2668
and religion, **2668–2677**
in religious lives, 9790–9791
schism and, 8152
shrines as centers of service and commerce, 8378
Smith (Adam) and, 8491
society and, separation of, 2668–2669
Sumerian, urbanization and temples and, 1802–1803
war in, 9679
Zapatismo and, 9930–9933
Economy
global, religions' reactions to, 2676–2677
market
impact on religion, 6498
vs. nonmarket, money in, 6136–6137
principle of, in Eastern Orthodoxy, 1652
Ecstasy, **2677–2683**
ascension linked to, 518–519
in Buddhism, *samādhi* (meditative absorption) and, 8066, 8067
definition of, 2677–2678
discipline, ecstatic, 8703
duration of, 2681–2682
efficacy of, 2681–2682
elixirs for inducing, 2770
genuineness of, 2681
vs. inspiration, 4509
al-Junayd on, 5030
mechanisms for inducing, 3138
in Micronesian religions, 6005
otherworld reached through, 6923
in outsider art, 9627
of prophets
African, 7443
Israelite, 7432
psychedelic drugs as facilitators of, 7467, 7469
in Qabbalah, 4981
reductionist explanations of, 2682
as religious experience, 7695–7696, 7739 (*See also* Religious experience)
sacred *vs.* profane and, 7972
in shamanism, 519, 7349, 8269, 8272
of Mongol religions, 6141
study of, approaches to, 2678–2681
in Sufism, meditation and, 5818–5819
tobacco and, 9216, 9217, 9218
union and, 2681–2682
in visions, 9612
Ecstasy and Healing in Nepal (Peters), 57–58
Ecstatic Qabbalah, 4981, 7534
Ashkenazic Hasidim and, 7538
Ecstatic Religion (Lewis), 57, 2935, 10027
Ecuador, origins of, Atahuallpa in, 568
Ecumenical Association of Third-World Theologians (EATWOT), 3034, 5403, 5442
Ecumenical councils. *See* Councils, Christian
Ecumenical Methodist Conference, 5999
Ecumenical movement, **2683–2691**. *See also* Ecumenism
in Anglicanism, 352–353
Disciples of Christ active in, 2365, 2366
between Eastern and Western Christianity, 2589
extramural developments in, 2688–2689
grace in, shared beliefs about, 3647
intramural developments in, 2687–2688
ministry in, orders of, 6045
neoorthodoxy and, 6466
and priesthood, 7404
structural issues in, 2690
unresolved issues in, 2689–2690
World Missionary Conference as beginning of, 2044
Ecumenical patriarchate
of Constantinople, in early Christian structure, 2581
in Orthodox polity, 1765
Ecumenical theology, 9140
Ecumenism. *See also* Ecumenical movement; World Council of Churches
in Africa, 1722, 1723
in Ondo Yoruba beliefs, 2000
in Asia, Inter-Religio network, 1730
in Australia and New Zealand, organic unions and councils of churches, 1735
Chantepie de la Saussaye on, 1531
Child (Lydia Maria) on, 1569, 1570
Christian ethics and, 1656
church membership and, 1778
Congregationalism and, 1938
Coptic Church and, 1982
Council of the Churches of the Middle East, 1673
Eastern Europe and, 1687
ecclesiology and, 1775, 1776
etymology of, 2683
evangelical postdenominationalism, 1775
full communion agreements, 1769
future prospects, 1776
heresy *vs.*, 3929
Hus (Jan) on, 4234
Jesuit studies of Confucianism and, 1920
in Jewish renewal, 4870
in Latin American Protestantism, 1704
modern, 2683–2684
New Dispensation (of Sen) and, 8227
in Pacific islands, 1739
in Roman Catholicism, 7879, 9534
Second Vatican Council and, 1665, 4946, 7011–7012, 9537–9538
sacraments and, intercommunion issues, 7963
secular, 7012
social ethics and, 1776
Syriac Orthodox Church and, 8940–8941
in United States, polity and, 1769
World Fellowship of Buddhists and, 2038
ʿEdah Ḥaredit (Community of the Pious), 6903
Edaín Echraidhe (deity), 1487, 9391
Ẹdan (chain), 4303, 4304
Eddas, **2691–2694**. *See also* Prose Edda (Snorri)
Baldr in, 744
creation myth in, 3446–3447
dwarfs in, 2532
Heimdallr in, **3898–3899**
Indian narrative compared to, 8522
ocean in, 6807
organization of, 2691–2692
Poetic Edda, 167, 3446
rejuvenation myth in, 7683
seidr ritual in, 8295
sources for, 2693
Thor in, 9165, 9166–9167
Eddic religion, gods and goddesses of, hawks and, 2554
Eddy, Asa Gilbert, 2694–2695
Eddy, Mary Baker, **2694–2696**. *See also* Christian Science
in Christian Science, **1745–1748**
on *Genesis*, 6530
Hopkins (Emma Curtis) and, 4127, 6584
mesmerism and, 3850
modernity and, 6110
and New Thought Movement, 3096, 6582
and origins of Christian Science, 6516, 6535, 6563
as prophet, 7428
teachings as new religious movement, 1714
Eddy, Sherwood, 6611
Ededis, 123
Edelstein, Emma J., 552
Edelstein, Ludwig, 552
Eden, Garden of, 2967–2968, 6981–6982
Adam in, 6982
expulsion of, 30, 6982
role of, 29
rules for, 29–30
androgyny in, 8316
conditions of life in, 6982
Eve in, 6982
gardeners inspired by, 3277
as Golden Age, 4025
human-God relationship in, 4743–4744
in Islam (*See* Paradise)
in New Testament, 6984
nudity in, 6741
river in, 7862
search for, 6982
serpent in, 6982
as source of food, 6982
as source of water, 6982
structuralist analysis of, 8753
Swedenborg (Emanuel) on, 8899
trees in, 6982, 9335
Edessa (Mesopotamia), 786
Christianity in, 2812
early, 2581
theology developed in, 2583
Edfu (Egypt), temple of Horus at, 2709
Edfu Drama, 2441
Edgar, Bob, in environmental issues, 2613
Edgar Cayce (Stearn), 560
Edgar Cayce Foundation, 559
Edgerton, Franklin, 1315
Edgerton, Robert B., African psychiatry, 3818, 3821
Edin (grasslands), deities in, 5949–5950

Edinburgh (Scotland), missionary conference in (1910)
on demise of traditional religions, 109
in ecumenical movement, 2683–2684
Edio (ghosts), 7523
Edison, Thomas, 3097
Edjo (deity), 2712
Edkins, Joseph, 1633
Edo period (Japan). *See* Tokugawa period
Edo religion (Nigeria), **2696–2697**. *See also* Benin religion
ancestor worship in, 322
creation in, 3572
dance in, 2142
deities of, 4301
iconography of, 4301–4302
kingship in, 5170, 7805–7806
reincarnation in, 7677
supreme being (Osanobwa) in, 3572
Edou, Jérôme, 9190
2 Edras, judgment in, 5027
Edsman, Carl-Martin, historiography of, 4043
Edson, Hiram, Seventh-day Adventism and, 8235
Eduardo, Octavio da Costa, 121
Education. *See also* Colleges and Universities; Religious education; Seminaries
Academy Movement in Swedenborgianism, 8904, 8905
in Africa
Christian churches and, 7292
missionaries, dominance of, 8793
in Australia and New Zealand, at denominational schools, 1733
Baiš Ya'akov movement in, 8149
cargo cults and, 1420
"character training," Starbuck (E. D.) on, 8732
Charlemagne and, 1557
in China, pre-classical, 1570
clinical pastoral, 7486
Comenius on, 1862–1863
Congregationalism and, 1938
creeds and, 2054
encyclopedia understood as, 2782
evolution and creationism in, 2911–2912
Greek, 3678
humanism and, 4175, 4177
in India
Ambedkar (B. R.) and, 286
Āyurveda and, 3856, 3857
British rule, effect of, 3856
Japanese, Sōka Gakkai and, 8508
Kenyan school ceremonies and national identity, 1515
in Korea, Confucianism and, 1930
Kosmas Aitolos and, 5239
Lancaster system of education, 1700
by missionaries
in Africa, 1719
in Latin America, 1697, 1700
in Oceania, 6791, 6792, 6793
monastic, in medieval Europe, 3845
Montessori International, 1783
moral, Rousseau (Jean-Jacques) on, 811
new religious movements and, 6542
of North American Indians, 7304
Christian churches and, 7301, 7302
Deloria (Ella Cara) and, 2264
gender and, 3407–3408
at Point Loma Theosophical Community, 7229
of priesthood, 7396–7397
in religious studies, Smart (Ninian) and, 8443–8444
in Russia, Pobedonostsev (Konstantin) and, 7203
Scholasticism and, 8174–8175
secular, of Parsis, 6998
Steiner (Rudolf) on, 8738
in Taiwan, 8963
Tamam Siswa movement (Indonesia) and, 8652–8653
in Tibet, medical colleges, 3865
Waldorf Schools, 8738
for women
at Al-Azhar university, 230
in Jainism, 3328
Jewish, 3354
at theological schools, 3310, 3359
in Zoroastrianism, 3374
Education and Renewal Program Unit (WCC), 2685–2686
Educative theodicy, 9114, 9117
Eduyyot (Mishnaic tractate), 2743
Edward VI (king of England)
on music, 6311
Reformation and, 2051, 7281
Edward, Lord Herbert of Cherbury, on religion, 7702
Edward I (king of England), taxation of clergy by, 1019
Edwards, Bryan, 10024
Edwards, Jonathan, **2698–2701**
on atonement, 597
and Bushnell (Horace), 1337
creating heaven on earth, 6985
Dwight (Timothy) as grandson of, 2532
on free will and predestination, 3204, 3208
Great Awakening and, 1710
civil religion and, 1814
on kingdom of God, 5152
on religious affections, 2808
on religious experience, 7737
Edwards, Jonathan, Jr., 2700
Edwin Smith Papyrus, medical material in, 3826
EEA. *See* Environment of evolutionary adaptation
Eels
in Micronesian religions, 6006
use in necromancy, 6453
EFEO. *See* École Française d'Extrême-Orient (EFEO)
Effect, cause and. *See* Causation
Effigies
in funeral rites, 3234, 3237
of Jester King, in Carnival, 1440
of kings, 5155
in Vanuatu religions, 9520
Effort, in eightfold path, 2738
Effulgence, masculine sacrality in, 5760
Efik people, dances of, 2137
Efile Mukulu (supreme being), 5524
Efod, 4358, 7400
Urim and Tummim associated with, 5425
Efrayim of Luntshits, 867
Egalitarianism
in Carnival, 1440
in communitarian movements, 5399
in vision quest, 9610
Egba religion (Benin), funeral rites in, 3236
Egeria (pilgrim)
on Holy Week rituals, 1742, 1743
on pilgrimage to martyria, 7153
Egersis ritual, 5846–5847, 5849
Eggan, Dorothy, 2483
Eggs, **2701–2702**
in African myths, 98–99, 100, 325
Dogon, 3569
in Australian Indigenous myths, 656–657
in Chinese alchemy, 239
cosmic (*See* Cosmic eggs)
Easter, 3170
as Easter symbol, 2580
in Finno-Ugric creation myths, 3109
primal, in Chinese myth, 1625
symbolism of, 2423
Egill Skallagrimsson, 168
Egils saga Skallagrímssonar, magic in, 8025
Église de Jesus Christ sur la Terre par Le Prophète Simon Kimbangu (EJCSK). *See* Kimbanguist Church
Ego
in Buddhism, *asmimāna* (ego conceit), 8552–8553
Erikson (Erik) on, 7476
experiences of, of Evola (Julius), 2904–2905
Freud (Sigmund) on, 7474, 7476
Gurū Nānak on, 8395
mirrors and, 6064–6065
in Sikhism, *haumai* concept and, 8548
Socrates on, 8503
states of consciousness and, 1949
Ego psychology, 7476, 7482
Egoyan, Atom, 3099
Egungun (ritual), 2435, 2439
Eguṅguṅ paaka (ancestors), 4302
Eguns, in Brazil, rites of, 121
Egypt. *See also* Alexandria; Cairo
anchorites in (*See* Anchorites and anchoritism)
ancient religion of (*See* Egyptian religion)
Arab conquest of, Coptic Church and, 1981
archaeological sites in, 455, 456
Canaanite, 1381
Frankfort (Henri) and, 3188
artisans in, 4296
Ayyūbid rule in (*See* Ayyūbid dynasty)
baptism in, 779, 780
Bleeker on, 4042
British occupation of, resistance to, 6314–6315
Cassian and Germanos in, 1447
cats in, 1462, 1463
chanting and gestures, 1533
Christianity in
Chalcedon statement rejected by, 2584
devotion to Thecla in, 9102
monasticism in, 6117, 6131, 6939–6940
persecution of, 2710
clitoridectomy in, 1825
Coptic Church in, 1675, **1979–1983**
coup in (1952), 7575
Crusades and, 2075, 2076
exorcism in, 2933
family law in, 3368
feminism in, Islamist, 3368
fiction of, 3053, 3054, 3088
films from, 3098
geometry in, *3439,* 3439–3440
Gnosticism in, 3511
Greek Orthodox Church in, 3658
hare myths in, 7590
horses and chariots in, 4132
humor in, 4213, 4215
Ikhwān al Muslimūn in, 108
Islamic identity in, 1982

Islam in, 7575–7576
conversion to, 2710
jihād in, 7257, 7289
mawlids in, 5789
reformist movement, 5068
rites of passage in, 7827
waqf in, 9678
Judaism in, 4990–4991
"prayer places" in, 8920, 8921
Karaite sect in, 5083, 5084
writings of, 5085, 5086
kingship in, 5163–5164
Kush controlled by, 5269
Maimonides in, 4990–4991, 4993
Mamluk sultans and Abbasid caliphate, 1367
Moses in, 6199
in Nag Hammadi, 3941
names in, 6406, 6409
nationalism in, 1982, 6314–6315
Neolithic religion in, 6465
New Kingdom in (1551–1070 BCE)
god-human dogma in, 3903
Re-Atum in, 8837
Seth in, 8234
Ottoman conquest of, 1981–1982
Philistine invasion of, 7101–7102
as river civilization, 7861
rock tombs and temples, 1471
as Roman province, 4558
as sacred national community, 7717
travellers to, documentation by, 2727–2728
women in
lives of, 3381–3382
organizations for, 3365, 3366
writing in, development of, 5161
Egyptian Commission for Population and Development, 3366
Egyptian Feminist Union, 3365
Egyptian Hallel, in *siddur* and *maḥzor,* 8389
Egyptian religion. *See also* Re religion
ablutions in, 10, 11
afterlife in, 9452
in *Book of Going Forth by Day,* 2719
in burial customs, 2703
cosmology of, 2705
divinity in, 2711–2712
geography of, 136, 138
heterodox views of, 2721
importance of, 2716
judgment of the dead in, 128–129, 139, 5025–5026, 5871
justice in, 128–129
multiple conceptions of, 138
nature of humankind in, 130
resurrection of body in, 131
spells in preparation for, 8676
study of, 2731
time in, 132
under Akhenaton, 217–221
alchemy in, 244–247
altars in, 275
amulets and talismans in, 299
analysis and interpretation of, 2729–2730
and apocalypse genre, 411
apotheosis in, 438
archaeology and, 456
art of, under Akhenaton, 219
astral religion in
catasterism in, 8424–8425
Sirius in, 8735
star organization in, 8733
astrology in, 563
belief systems in, interpretation of, 2730–2731
birds in, 948–949
birth rituals in, 2559
Bleeker (C. Jouco) on, 978
bread in, 1041
calendar, 1354, 8836
stars and, 8733
Circuit of the White Wall ceremony, 1503
cosmogony in, water in, 9699
cosmology in, sky in, 8426
creation myth in
sexuality in, 8239
spitting in, 8721
cults of, 2711, 2718
mythology used in, 2720
curse-threats in, 2101–2102
death in, 2242
deities of, 2704–2705, 2711–2712 (*See also specific deities*)
Akhenaton's policies on, 219
egg symbols of, 2701
goddess worship, 3596–3597
as healers, 3826
heart of, 3881
Heliopolitan ennead (family of gods), 3795
Ḥokhmah and, 4079
iconography of, 4317–4318
king's relation to, 2704–2705, 7277
in mortuary texts, 2718
names of, 6409
in Ramessid literature, 2707–2708
study of, 2731
of sun, 5451
sunnaoi theoi system (temple-sharing gods), 3908
theocrasies (combinations of gods), 8930
theranthropic, 9155
warrior, 37
demons in, 7144
divination in, 6835–6836
dogs in, 2393
dragons in, 2431
drums in, 2498
dualism in, 2514–2515
in dynastic propaganda, 2706
eye in, 2940
fasting in, 2996
in First Intermediate Period, 2705–2706
fish symbolism in, 3123
flower symbolism in, 3135
funeral rites in, 3240 (*See also* Pyramids)
grave boats in, 989
iconography of, 4318, 4319–4320
Osiris myth and, 2538
gender in, **3375–3381**
gnosis in, 3508
goddess worship in, 3596–3597
government officials and, tombs of, 2705
healing in, 3826–3827
healers, types of, 3836
infertility treatments, 3836
heart symbolism in, 3881
historical setting of, 2702–2710
history of study, **2727–2737**
iconoclasm in, 4285
iconography of (*See* Iconography, Egyptian)
incantations in, 4407, 4408
incarnation in, 4416
infants in, images of, vol. 13 color insert
information sources on, 2702–2703
insects in, 4508
kings in, 2703–2704, 2711–2712, 5157
Amun-Re associated with, 2706
authority of, 693
eschatology and, 5159
Horus associated with, 2441, 2703–2704, 2706, 4416, 7277
mythology of, 2720
Re associated with, 2704
ritual duties of, 2714
"Son of Re" title of, 7277
Lady of the Animals in, 5280
laws in, 4727
libations in, 5433
lion symbolism in, 5464
and literature, influence on, 3054
literature of, **2717–2727**
modern translations of, 2703
Old Kingdom Pyramid Texts, 3795
religious texts, 2702–2710
lotus symbolism in, 5518, 5519
Maat cosmovision in, 2102
magic in, 2712–2713, 2714
in healing, 2713
mythology used in, 2720
from Re, 2706
religion and medicine mixed with, 3826–3827
texts of, 2721–2722
masks in, 5766
merit in, 5871
metals in, 5987
in Middle Kingdom, 2706
miracles in, 6051–6052
monkeys in, 6151
monotheism in, 219–220, 6157, 6159
music in, 6275–6276
mythic themes in
the Fall, 2959, 2961–2962
the Flood, 3130, 3131
keys, 5116
mythology of, 2720–2721
compendiums of, 2724
permeation of, 2715
in spells, 2722
stories in, 2720–2721
names in, 6409
in New Kingdom, 2706–2707
New Year festival in, 2441
nobility and, tombs of, 2705
ocean in, 6806
in Old Kingdom, 2704–2705
oracles in, Nag Hammadi compared to, 3941
ordination in, 6852
ouroboros in, 1792
overview of, **2702–2717**
phallus in, 7080
pharaoh in
ablution of, 10
as divine, 3902
god-human dogma, 3903
Seth and, 8234
piety in, 2714, 2732
plants in, 9576
Plutarch on, 7201, 7202 (*See also* Isis and Osiris (Plutarch))
politics and, 7277
popular, 2713–2714
postures and gestures in, 7343
priesthood of, 2714, 7277
functions of, 5424
study of, 2731–2732
pyramids in (*See* Pyramids)

Egyptian religion ***continued***
ram cult in, 8311
in Ramessid period, 2707–2708
redemption in, 7640–7641
reincarnation, 7676, 7679
repentance in, 7757
Reshef in, 7760, 7761
resurrection in, 7763
ritual drama in, 2435, 2441, 2444
rituals in
in mortuary texts, 2718
study of, 2731
rivers in, 7861
sacred and profane in, 7969
sacrifice in, 8005
of pigs, 7144
salvation in, 7640–7641
in Second Intermediate Period, 2706
secret symbolic language in, 8907
serpents in, 8456, 8459
soul in, 2711
hawk as symbol of, 2553
spells in, 8676
in *Book of Going Forth by Day,* 2708, 2712–2713, 2719
in Coffin Texts, 2705
purposes of, 2722
in Pyramid Texts, 2718
for transformation, 2716
sun in, 8836–8837
surveys of, 2703
survivals from, 2715–2716
symbolism in, mountain with solar disk, 40, *40*
syncretism in, 217, 2716
Hermetic texts as reflection of, 3942
priesthood and, 8930
tarot cards and, 1414
tattooing in, 1002
temples of (*See* Temples, Egyptian)
textiles in, 9089
theocracy in, 9109, 9110
in Third Intermediate Period, 2709
tithes in, 9209
tombs of, 1471 (*See also* Valley of the Kings)
communications in, 2719–2720
iconography of, 4318, 4319–4320
looting of, 2709
totemism as antecedent of, 9252
trees in, 9335, 9338
triads in, 9349
turtles in, 9408
twins in, 9414, 9415
underworld in, 9452
universe in, 2710
violence and, 9597
water symbolism in, 7602
wisdom in, 2722–2723, 9749–9750, 9754
concept of, 9748
in Hermetism, 3940
Israelite wisdom influenced by, 9755, 9758, 9764
women in, **3375–3381**
writing in, myth of origin of, 269
Egyptians, Gospel of the, hypostasis in, 4242
Egyptocentric Diffusionist school, Smith (Grafton Elliot) and, 8768
Egyptomania or Egyptophilia (European esoteric movements following Egyptian themes). *See also* Rosicrucians
Hermetism and, 3950
Egziabher (deity), in Amhara-Tigriña religion, 2573
Ehecame (wind spirits), 6403
Ehécatl (deity)
fertility and, 719
Quetzalcoatl as, 7557
Ehécatl Quetzalcoatl (deity), 5910, 5911
Ehrenkrantz, Dan, 7639
Ehrenreich, Paul, natural mythology theory of, 2090
Eibingen (Germany), monastery at, Hildegard of Bingen and, 3979–3980
Eidetic vision, in phenomenology, 7088–7089, 7095–7096
Eidōlon (image), 4356, 4357, 4359
Eiei (Buddhist priest), 3275–3276
Eight (number), interpretations of, 6748
Eighteen (number), interpretations of, 6750
18 Rabbit (Waxaklahun-Ubah-K'awil), Maya calendar and, 1358
Eighfold domain of Śiva, cosmos and, 8415
Eightfold Path, **2737–2739,** 2957, 3178
ascetic ideals in, 1104
autonomous discipline and, 8701
and *bodhisattva* path, 3180
Campbell on, 1379
and Four Noble Truths, 2306
nirvāṇa as destination in, 6628
samādhi in, 8066
Theravāda Buddhism on, 3179
turning of the wheel of *dharma* and, 2332
Eighth Day (of Creation), 9813
Eighth Ecumenical Council, 2585
Eight-limbed discipline. *See Aṣṭāṅgayoga*
Eight Systems, of Tibetan Buddhism, 5223–5224
Eight Trigrams uprising, 1609
Eight White Yurts sanctuary, 1645
Eihei kōroku (Dōgen), 2385–2386
Eihei shingi (Buddhist text), 2386
Eilberg, Amy, ordination of, 1964, 7582
Eilberg-Schwartz, Howard, 6741, 7080
Eine Mithrasliturgie (Dieterich), 2349
Einführung in die Religionssoziologie (Wach), 5385–5386
Einführung in die vergleichende Religionsgeschichte (Beth), 846
Eingsaung nat spirits, house protection by, 4106
Einherjar (warriors), 842, 843, 9516
Einhorn, David
Holdheim (Samuel) and, 4080–4081
and Reform Judaism, 7670
Einhorn, Paul, on Baltic religion, 756, 757, 768, 2127
Einleitung in die Geisteswissenschaften (Dilthey), 2353
Einleitung in die Philosophie (Paulsen), 9230
Ein Sof, 7536
Cordovero (Mosheh) on, 1985
God as, 3550–3551
Einstein, Albert, **2739–2740**
cosmological constant of, 2032, 2033
indeterminism, 1527
quantum theory developed by, 7138
relativity theory of, 2031–2032, 7138, 8183–8184
theory of gravity by, 7138
visualization in method of, 6426–6427
Eirene (deity), 7021
Eiríks saga rauða, divination in, 8024, 8025
Eisai (Buddhist monk), 847, 1244, **2741–2742,** 4786, 9075
in Zen Buddhism, 9943, 9944
Eisendrath, Maurice (rabbi), 7671
Eisenstein, Ira, 7636–7638
Eisenstein, Sergei, 3101
Eisland, Nancy, on human body, 4166–4167
Eisler, Robert
on cosmic mantle, 8424
historiography of, 4043
Eison (Buddhist figure), 1180
Eitel, Ernst, 1633
Eizon (Buddhist monk), 1250
EJCSK. *See* Kimbanguist Church
Ejido (communal land), 9930
Ejin (Buddhist monk), 9079
Ekadanta. *See* Gaṇeśa
Eka Dasa Rudra (ceremony), 748
Ekāgratā (sustained concentration), 9894
aṣṭāṅgayoga (eight-limbed discipline), 8704, 8705
Ekalte (Syria), Dagan in, 2126
Ekan (Korean monk), in Mādhyamika Buddhism, 5556
Ekarāja (sovereign king), 1329
Ekavyāvahārika school of Buddhism, 1194
Ekayāna (single path to salvation), in *Lotus Sūtra,* 2029
Ekejimi (my spiritual other), 9911
Ekhirit-Bulagat tribe (Mongolia), 1325–1327
Ekklesia (assembly), 1770. *See also* Church; Ecclesia
Eknāth (poet), 7210
Ekoi religion (Nigeria), 3223
Ekottarāgama (Buddhist text), 1198
Ekphonetic signs, 1533, 1534
Ekron. *See* Eqron
Ekseri (spirit), 9394
Ekstatic Confessions (Buber), 7739
El (deity), **2742.** *See also* Il
and Anat, 319
Athirat (Asherah) as consort of, 590
and Baal, 723, 724, 7129
in Canaanite literature, 1391–1397, 1399
divine kingship of, 5146
in Hebrew scriptures, 3538–3539
in Moabite religion, 6094
passivity of, after creation, 8872
in ritual drama, 2442
Yahveh as, 1397, 4742
in Abraham stories, 14
in Hebrew scriptures, 3538–3539
Ela, Jean Marc
on ancestors, 142, 143
on integration of African and Christian beliefs, 142
Elagbalus (emperor), Sol worship and, 8510
Elal (deity)
cycle of, 9029, 9030–9031
as inventor of weapons, 9029
omnipotence of, 9030
Elam culture (Iran), goddess worship in, 3594–3595
Elamite religion, 4468–4470, 4472, 4473
Élan Vital, 6568
Élan vital (absorbing love), 4534
Elatha (mythic figure), 1488
Elat Hayyim (Jewish Renewal retreat), 4870
El'azar ben 'Azaryah, **2743**
El'azar ben Pedat, **2743–2744**
Abbahu and, 2
El'azar of Worms
on anamnesis (recollection), 313
in Ashkenazic Hasidism, 542–545
eschatology of, 542
on penance, 544
writings of, 544
El Bersha, Coffin Texts of, 2705
Elcasai (Babylonian Jew), 3516
Elcasaite sect
ablutions in, 12
Jesus in, 3516

transmigration belief of, 9329
vegetarianism in, 9329
El Castillo, 1471
Elchaninov, A. V., 3133
Elderly, the
and humor, in Islam, 4212
sacred *vs.* profane and, 7973
Elders
in church polity
in early church, 1763
in Methodist churches, 1767
in Presbyterian churches, 1767
in Eastern Orthodoxy (*See Startsy*)
in Maasai culture, 2000
in North American Indian culture, 7300
in Oceanic religions, 7808
Eleatic school (philosophy), 6995
Eleazar
exorcisms of, 2932
martyrdom of, 5739
Election, **2744–2749**
Barth (Karl) on damnation *vs.*, 3885
ecclesiology and, 1772, 1773
in Islam, *walāyah* and, 9661
in Judaism, circle of BeSHt on, 3786
predestination as, 3202
Puritan belief in chosenness
civil religion and, 1813, 1814
predestination and, 4238
Smith (Joseph) on, 8447
Spinoza (Baruch) on, 8683
Electricity
animatism compared with, 363, 364
mana and, 5631
Elect status (predestination), success as sign of, 2673
Ẹlẹfon festival, 9910–9911
Ẹlẹgba (deity)
foods favored by, 3171
in Santería, 1434
Elema hevehe (cycle play), 7047
Elema people (New Guinea), masks of, 5768
Elementarius dialectice (Eck), 2601
Elementary Forms of Religious Life (Durkheim), 382, 2527, 3389, 3490
on the Dreaming, 2478–2479
on Indo-European religions, 4461
magic in, 5571
on primitive religions, 2528–2529
reflexivity in, 7649
religion defined in, 7251
sacred and profane in, 7971
sociological theory in, 8464, 8480–8481
tears in, 9025
Elements
in Buddhism
as agents of destructions, 2028
five-element stupas in Okunoin cemetery (Japan), 8352
in Chinese religion (*See Wuxing; Yinyang wuxing* philosophy)
in Empedocles' physics, 2776
in Islamic medicine, 3832
Elements (Euclid), 2878
Elements of Theology (Proclus), 7191, 9134
Elenchus, Socratic, 8503
Elephanta (India), cave-temple of Śiva at, 5242
Elephants, **2749–2751**
in Bantu rites of passage, 8667
Gaṇeśa and, 3273–3274, 4438
in Hinduism, mythic themes of, 4438
in Kushite religion, 5269
Eleusinian Mysteries, **2751–2753,** 6329
afterlife and, 8543
civic religion and, 3671–3672
Demeter in, 2269, 2270, 3382–3383, 3671, 6329
Diagoras, criticism by, 3910
Diogenes, criticism by, 3910
ecstasy and, 2678
elixir used in, 2770
and Freemasonry, 3198
Hades in, 3724, 3725
initiation into, 3671–3672, 4477, 6329
musteria (sacraments) in, 7955
origins of, 6329
Orphism and, 6891
Persephone in, 2269, 3382–3383, 3671
pig sacrifice in, 7144
procession and, 7417
public ceremonies of, 6329
purification and defilement in, 1459, 1460, 3684
rituals in, 2751–2752
secrecy of, 3684
Eleutherius (pope), 4538
Elevation of Inanna (myth), 5956
Eleven (number), interpretations of, 6749
Eleventh Commandment Fellowship, ecological awareness and, 4103
ELF. *See* Earth Liberation Front
El Fadl, Khaled Abou, 3367
Elgabalus (emperor), sun worship and, 8840
El Greco, vol. 11 color insert
Eliade, Mircea, **2753–2763**
accuracy of work of, 2760
aesthetics of, 48
on agricultural rituals, 189
on alchemy, 247
American study of religion, role in, 8785
androcentrism of, 9789
and anthropological definitions of religion, 378
and archaeology, 453–454
on archetypes, 458–459, 460
on art and religion, 499–500
on Baltic religion, 759
on binding, 937–938, 5196
biographical details of, 2760
on bisexuality, divine, 4116
on bones, 1015
on bridge symbolism, 1052
on celestiality of divine beings, 5759
on Chinese alchemy, 2771
on collective unconscious, 7476
comparative theology of, 9130
on cosmic hierophanies, 8428
on cosmic *vs.* historical religions, 1821
on cosmogonic myths, significance of, 6361, 6363
criticisms of, 7745
Culianu (Ioan Petru) and, 2079, 2080
on diamonds, 2345
early career of, 2754
on eastern Europe, 5580
on ecstasy, 2679, 2682, 6923, 7349
Encyclopedia of Religion and, 2757
Evola (Julius) and, 2905
on expulsion, 2939
fiction of, 2754, 2755–2756, 2757
on flight, mythic theme of, 3127, 3129
Freud's theories and, 3217
Frye (Northrop) influenced by, 3224
gender in paradigm of, 3301
on Germanic religion, 3460
on Geto-Dacian religion, 3466
hermeneutics and, 3932
historiography of, 4046–4047
"history of religions" approach, 1878
on *homo religiosus*, 4110–4111
on human-divine contact, women and, 3338
illo tempore of, 692, 6372
influences on, 2760
on Jesus as God incarnate, 4417
Kitagawa (Joseph M.) and, 5188, 5189
on knots, 5196, 5197
on kratophany, 7346
Leach (Edmund) on, 5382
Lévi-Strauss and, 6368
on literature, 5466
on *mana*, 7374
on materiality of religion, 10047
on Mesopotamian ceremonial centers, 453–454
methodology of, 2755
in modern academia, 2757–2758
on morphology of religion, 6367
on mortification, 6198
on mystery religions, 6328
on naked body, 6740
in Neopaganism, 2664
on Oceanic religions, 6798
on orgy, 6863
on origins, 8402
on Otto's (Rudolf) work, 7349
on pain, 6947
and Pettazzoni (Raffaele), 7073–7074, 7075
on phenomenology of religion, 7087, 7092, 7094, 10078
political position of, 2758–2760
on politics and religion, 7251–7252
on power in study of religion, 2543, 7349–7350
on primordiality, 1989
forms of, 325
on rejuvenation myths, 7683
religion defined by, 864
on religious experience, 7694, 7743
on rites of passage, 7797–7798, 7801, 7802
on ritual, 7800, 7802, 7834, 7835, 7837
meaning of, 4480
on Roman sacrifice, 1051
on sacred, idea of, 1624, 5436, 7694, 7975, 7977
on sacred and profane, 7976, 8010
on sacred space, 7983
on sacred time, 944, 945, 5898, 7694
on sacrilege, 8010
on sexuality, 8239–8241
on shamanism, 5228, 7769
in Arctic religions, 474
ecstasy in, 519, 7349
enthusiasm in, 2807
paradisial images in, 6983
sacred cord of, 7387
Waugh (Earle H.) influenced by, 946
on shells, 6137
on stones, sacred, 8746
student years of, 2753–2754
as subject of study, 2758–2761
on supreme beings, 8879
on symbolism, 781
on symbolization of religious cultures, 1878–1879

Eliade, Mircea ***continued***
symbol theory and, 8912, 8913
on Tantrism, 8988, 8990, 8991
on Teilhard de Chardin (Pierre), 9034
theological position of, 2761
on totemism, 7251
on twins, 9413, 9414
ultimate orientation and, 1581
on witches' Sabbath, 8249–8250
on yoga, 7350
on Zalmoxis, 9927
Elianus, on Iberian religion, 4254
Eli'ezer ben Hyrcanus, **2763–2764**
ban on, Gamli'el of Yavneh in, 3269
on education for women, 3354
Yehoshu'a ben Ḥananyah and, 9875
Eli'ezer of Touques, *tosafot* of, 9244
Elihu (biblical figure), in *Job,* 4931, 9758
Elijah (biblical figure), **2764–2767**
Baal prophets mocked by, 4200
Biblical traditions of, 2765
days spent in wilderness, 6750
fasting by, 2996
in Finno-Ugric religions, 3108
historicity of, 2764
on kissing holy objects, 9258
literary sources for, 2764–2765
Melqart and, 5847
in New Testament, 2765–2766
presence at circumcisions, 7819
in Slavic religion, 8435–8436
Elijah Muhammad, **2767**
death of, 72, 4689
Malcolm X and, 72, 5626
Nation of Islam under, 70, 4563, 4688, 6418–6419, 6563
teachings of, 6418–6419
violent rhetoric of, 6564
Elijah of Vilna, 9379
Elima (Pygmy festival), 7525
Elimelekh of Lizhensk, **2767–2768**
tsaddiq theory of, 3789–3790, 9378, 9380, 9381
Eliminatory ritual, confession as, 1885
Eli of Shiloh (priest), and Samaritans, origin of, 8068
Elior, Rachel, on mystical union, 6339
Eliot, George, 6181
Eliot, John, evangelization of Indians, 1708
Eliot, T. S., 47, 2470, 2472, 2476
creative dissonance in works of, 7204
Julian of Norwich and, 5029
on Lawrence (D. H.), 5480
on liberalism, 6102
on literary criticism, 3931–3932
as postmodernist writer, 5482
Elisha (biblical figure), **2768–2769**
Elijah and, 2765
healing touch of, 9255
mocked by children, 4200
prophetic actions of, 7432
Elisha' ben Avuyah, **2769**
Me'ir and, 5830
Elixir, **2770–2773**
in alchemy, 236, 5987
Chinese, 239
Islamic, 248
for rejuvenation, 7683
Eliyyahu ben Avraham, on 'Anan ben David, 317
Eliyyahu ben Shelomoh Zalman, **2773–2774,** 4869–4874
biblical exegesis of, 868
Hasidism, opposition to, 3787
on *pilpul* casuistry, 1454
at Reconstructionist Rabbinical College, 7638
as *tsaddiq,* 9383
Eliyyahu de Vidas, on mystical union, 6340
Elizabethan settlement, 7663
Elizabeth I (queen of England)
and Anglicanism, 349
Bacon (Francis) under, 733
Beza (Theodore) and, 851
comets and, 8736
drama outlawed by, 2438
and ministry, 6045
prosecution of heresy under, 973
Puritan reform under, 7518–7519
in Reformation, 7663
Elizabeth II (queen of England), coronation, sun symbolism in, 8836
Elk, in Komi religion, 5218
Elkadi, Ahmed, 5812
Elka dievi (deity), 773
Elkasite community, Mani's renoucement of, 5648
Elkesai (prophet), on repentance, 7758
Elkesaites. *See also* Ebionites
baptism by, 781
Elkin, A. P., 840, 841, 2479
on Australian Indigenous religions
names in, 6409
new movements in, 681, 682
in history of study of Australian religions, 686, 687
Elkin, Adolphus, 671
Elkins, James, 502, 4300
El-Kronos (deity), castration by, 1451
"Elk Song" (Hogan), 7225
Elkunirsha (deity), in Hittite myth, 4070
Ellekilde, Hans, 3459
Eller, Cynthia, 7079
Elliger, Walter, 6238
Ellington, Duke, 6313
Ellis, A. B., on sacred prostitution in West Africa, 3969
Ellora caves, 1472
Ellwood, Robert S., 6522, 6527, 6546
Elmer Gantry (Lewis), 3060
Elm tree, 9337
Eloah (God of Israel), in Hebrew scriptures, 3538
Elohim (deity)
cursing and, 968–969
ghost of, 4743
as God of Israel, 3538, 4742
in Hebrew scriptures, meanings of, 3538
in Raëlianism, 9435
as other gods, 3538
in *Psalms,* 7461
Raël on, 6530
Elohim (extraterrestrial creators of Earth), in Raëlian religion, 7596–7599
Elohist (E) source
on Abraham, 14
dating of, 6199
J source and, 6199
on Moses, 6199–6201
"Elopement of Diarmaid and Gráinne," 1495
El penitente (Graham), 2159
El primer nueva coronica y buen gobierno (Guaman Poma de Ayala), vol. 2 color insert
El Saadawi, Nawal, 3088, 3366
El Santuario de Chimayó, as pilgrimage site, 8377
El Shaddai
God's appearance to Abraham as, 15
in Hebrew scriptures, problems with understanding, 3538
Elsner, Jaś, 4343
Elssler, Fanny, 2155
El Tajín (Totonac ceremonial center), 9254–9255
in Classic period, 5904
Elves, 2952
álfar, **254–255**
Elvin, Mark, 3341
Elvira, Council of (309), 4285
Elvira, Synod of (306), 7403
Elysian Fields, souls of the dead and, 8543
Elysium, Menander on, 8543
El Zapotal (Mexico), in Classic period, 5904–5905
Emadloti (world of spirits), in Swazi religion, 8896
é-mah (exalted house), 2598
Emanation
Jewish doctrine of
in creation, 2642, 5302
and prophecy, 7439
of Kwoth (Nuer supreme being), 7443
Emanational mystical monotheism, 6160
Emanationism
of Servetus (Michael), 8232, 8233
in Sufism, Ibn al-'Arabī on, 8819–8820
Emancipation
Jewish
Hirsch (Samson Raphael) on, 4023–4024
Holdheim (Samuel) on, 4080–4081
political *vs.* human, Marx (Karl) on, 5745
of slaves (*See* Abolitionism)
Emancipation of Massachusetts, The (Adams), 9109
Emandwa. See Embandwa
Emanja (deity), in Caribbean religions, 1434
Emanuel, Christianah Abiodun, in Aladura movement, 104
Emanu-El, Temple (New York), Adler (Felix) at, 33
Emar (city)
Dagan in, 2126
written records from, 5161
Emasculation. *See* Castration
Embalming, 9228
Embandwa (spirits), 4519, 4520, 4521
Ember Days, 2996
Embertides, in Christian liturgical calendar, 1743
Emblem, in visual narratives, vol. 2 color insert
Embron (town), 1486
Embryonic respiration, in Daoist initiation rites, 7683
Embryonic stem cell research, 941–942, 5813–5814
and science and religion questions, 8190
Vatican on, 8190–8191
Emchetta, Buchi, 3088
Emden, Ya'aqov, 7235
Eme-bala (translator), in Eblaite religion, 2599
Emei, Mount, 6213
Emerald, transmutation of, Indian references to, 2557
Emerald Cliff Record, 1524
Emergence myths. *See* Anthropogony
Emerson, Ralph Waldo, **2774–2775**
on church, 785
Coleridge and, 1853
on Confucian China, 1632
on Hermetism, 3951
influence on New Thought movement, 6585
liberalism of, 6105
Müller (F. Max) and, 6236
on poetic imagination, 7206
on religious experience, 7738
and spiritualizing of art, 499
Swedenborgianism and, 8903

in Unitarianism, 9469
E-meter, use in Scientology, 6559
'Emeth (truth), 9372
Emetics
in Cherokee religion, 1564
in purification, 7508
Emet ve-Emunah (Truth and Faith), 1964
Emianga myth, 655–656
Emigration, of Christians, from Middle East, 1676
Émile (Rousseau), 811
religious thought in, 7931
work foreshadowing, 3039
Émile Durkheim: His Life and Work (Lukes), 2529
Eminescu, Mihai, Gnosticism and, 3526
Emin Foundation, 6567
Emitai (deity), 2354
Alinesitoue's revelations from, 261, 262, 7444
prophetic revelations from, 7444
Emitai dabognol (epithet), 7444
Emitai dabognol (rain), 7444
Emmanuel Baptist Rescue Mission (Los Angeles), vol. 7 color insert
Emmer-kai and the Lord of Aratta (Sumerian story), 2962
Emotion(s)
art and, 494
in brain processing and cognition, 6486, 6493
in Christianity
enthusiasm, 2805–2808
legitimacy of, 2700
in existentialism, 2926
of God, in Judaism, 3542–3543
heart and, 3882
and holiness, perception of, 7978
illness caused by, 3810
Langer (Susanne) on, 5301
in religion, neurotheological analysis of, 6494
religion as emotional experience, in Romanticism, 4040
rituals and, in southern African religions, 8660
sainthood, path to, 8037
Scheler (Max) on, 8147
Spinoza (Baruch) on, 8684
Sundén (Hjalmar) on, 8851
Empathic concept of religion, Smart (Ninian) on, 4048
Empathy
imagery and, vol. 11 color insert
in moral reasoning, 6180, 6185–6186
orgy and, 6862
Empedocles, **2775–2776**
ascension by, 520
on cosmos, 2368
on deification, 2248
on dualism, 2507, 2508
on nature, 6431
on reincarnation, 7679
on sacrifice, 1467
on soul, 1041, 4415
on transmigration, 9328
Emperors. *See also specific emperors*
Japanese, divine origin of, 5157
Roman, apotheosis of, 439–440
Emperor's Cult, **2776–2778**
in China, Huangdi in, 4144–4145
in Japan
in Meiji period, 8367–8368
post–World War II occupation and, 8368–8369
Empirical knowledge, in Islam, 3565
Empirical research
Greek philosophy and, 8180–8181
Honko (Lauri) on observation in, 4123
secularization and, 8218
Empirical studies, on psychology of religion, 7477, 7478–7479
Empiricism, **2778–2781**
British
Hume (David), role of, 4192
Kant's (Immanuel) reaction to, 5076
Cārvāka, 1446
criterion of meaning in, 7115–7119
definition of, 7111
in history of religions, 9650
in Indo-European religious studies, 4460–4461
Kant and, 2426, 5076
logical, 7115, 7118
logical positivism and, 5498
metaphysics and, 5991
in phenomenology of religion, 7093, 7097
rationalism and, 5076
Russell (Bertrand) and, 2427
in social science, 9711
of Spinoza (Baruch), 8683
Westermarckian, Harva (Uno) and, 3783
"Empiricism to Metaphysics: In Defense of the Concept of the Dreamtime" (Morphy), 2478
Employment Division, Department of Human Resources of the State of Oregon v. Smith, 7303–7304
Empresses (female Rastafarians), 7624
Emptiness
in Buddhism (See Śūnyam and *śūnyatā*)
mathematical symbol of, 6752–6753
Empusa (female spirit), 2277
Emre, Yunus (poet), 2653
on light of Muḥammad, 6767
Emsheimer, Ernst, 474
Emūṣa (boar), 7356
En (deity), in Komi religion, 5217
En (spouse of deity), 3377, 5947–5948, 5961
Enactments, in Judaism. *See Taqqanot*
Enarees (cultic leaders), in Scythian religion, 8206
Enawenê Nawê people (Brazil), cosmology of, 2012–2013
Enbilulu (deity), in divine bureaucracy, 5951
Enchi Fumiko, 3074
Enchin (Buddhist monk), 1242, **2781–2782,** 9075
Enchiridion (Augustine), 628
Enchiridion (Eck), 2601
Enchiridion (Epictetus), 2307
Enchymoma (inner macrobiogen), 5318
Encomienda system, 1695, 1696
Encounter dialogue style, 1522–1523
Encounters, divine, and new religious movements, founding of, 6529–6530
Encounter stage of conversion, 1972
Encyclopaedia of Buddhism (Malalasekera), 5625
Encyclopaedia of Religion and Ethics
Harva (Uno) and, 3783
Hastings (James) as editor of, 3794
Marett's (R. R.) article in, 5708
Söderblom (Nathan) on holiness in, 4098–4099
Encyclopedia Biblica, Moore's (George Foot) articles in, 6177
Encyclopedia Britannica, 2784
Frazer's contributions to, 3191
Marett's (R. R.) entry in, 380–381
Smith (W. Robertson) and, 8451
Encyclopedia of African and African American Religions, The (Henry), 10028
Encyclopedia of Religion (Eliade, first edition), women's perspectives in, 3313
Encyclopedia of Religion and Nature (Kaplan and Taylor, eds.), 2612
Encyclopedia of the Philosophical Sciences (Hegel)
Christianity and philosophy in, 3895
systematic structure in, 3893
Encyclopedia of Women and World Religion (Young), 3301
Encyclopedias, **2782–2785**
early, 2782–2783
Enlightenment and, 2783–2784
of Judaica, 4883
Mesoamerican religions in, 5944
as reference works, 7642, 7644
Encyclopédie, 2783–2784
Encyclopédie des sciences religieuses, 2784
Ende, Werner, 4718
Endicott, Kirk, 6455
Endocannibalism
exocannibalism *vs.*, 1402
in South America, 1403
End of Creation (Edwards), 2699
End of Days, Qumran sect and, 2234
End-of-life care, 5813
Endogamy, definition of, 5726
Endorphins, in vision state, 9612
Endo Shūsaku, 3072, 3073
Endowment, in Islam. *See Waqf*
Endymion (mythic figure), 6173
Endzelīns, Jānis, on Māra, 5692
Enemy, in warfare, 9681
Enemyway ceremony, 6442
Energy
celibacy and, 1475
Kuṇḍalinī as, 5266–5267
in physics, 2659
subtle energy, in New Age spirituality, healing and, 3850–3851
transfer of, between people, Mesmer on, 1947
vital, in chiropractic, 3850
in yoga, 5266
Energy centers. *See* Cakras
Enfant prodigue, l' (Gardel), 2155
Enfield sermon (Edwards), 2699
Engaged Buddhism, **2785–2791**
gender in, 3333–3334
origins of, 2786–2788, 7264
principles of, 1283
teachings of, 2788–2789
thinkers of, 1283, 7264
Western influences on, 2689, 2787
Engaged Surrender: African American Women and Islam (Rouse), 10039
Enga people and religion (New Guinea)
deities of, 2006
duality in, 147
Engels, Friedrich
Bachofen's (J. J.) influence on, 732
on economy and religion, 2669
Marx and, 5745, 5746, 5747
materialism of, 5777
on Reformation, 7664
on socialism and religion, 8480
on Spinoza (Baruch), 8685

Engels, Friedrich ***continued***
utopianism of, 9492
Engendering, definition of, 3299
Engishiki (Japanese text)
compilation of, 4785
Izanagi and Izanami in, 4755
kami in, 5072
Kiki texts and, 4803
England. *See also* Anglicanism; Britain; Church of England
Anglo-Saxons in (*See* Anglo-Saxons)
Baptist churches in, 783–784, 785
blasphemy cases in, 973, 974
church architecture in, Gothic revival, 795–796
Congregationalism in, 1937–1938
Cromwellian revolution
ecclesiology and, 1774
social activism and, 1750
dance in
in Baroque period, 2155
twentieth-century ballet, 2162
death penalty for blasphemy and heresy in, 973
deism in, 2251
drama in, 2470, 2472, 2474
outlawed, 2438, 2474
Freemasonry in, 3194, 3195
genealogy in, 3425–3426
Hermetism in, 3948, 3950
Hinduism in, Swaminarayan movement in, 8892
Holiness movement in, 4083
Smith (Hannah Whitall) and, 8445–8446
Jewish studies in, 4878, 4883, 4884
Jews in
acculturation of, 5020
medieval, 5013
readmission of, 5016
Judaism in
liberal, 6166–6167
Reform Judaism, 7669–7670
Keswick Movement in, 4083
law in, equity and conscience in, 1941
magic in, decline of, 5568
megalithic religion in, 5823
monasteries in, architecture of, 6120
museums in, 6243, 6245
music in, 6310, 6311
Neolithic religion in, 6465
novel in, claims to invention of, 3051
Parsis in, 6999
poetry in, 7218, 7220–7221
Presbyterianism in, 7389, 7390, 7519
Protestantism in
and ban on theater, 2438
Calvert (Lord Baltimore) and, 1373–1374
Calvinism and, 1692
liberal, 6105
Nonconformists, 1322–1323
non-Separatist Independents, 2287–2288
persecution of, 7061, 7281
and priesthood, 7403
in Reformation, 7662–7663
Separatists, 1054
Puritanism in, 7518–7519, 7520–7521, 7663
concrete assurance of election doctrine, 4238
Hooker (Richard), defense against, 4124
humor, suppression of, 4219
Quakers in, 973, 7547, 7548, 7549
Ranterism in, 973
Reformation in, 7662–7663
Elizabethan settlement and, 7663
Puritanism and, 7663
religious education in, 7732, 7735
Renaissance humanism in, 4176
restoration of Charles II, Congregationalism and, 1937
Roman Catholicism in
Augustine of Canterbury's mission, 623
Bede's *Ecclesiastical History* on, 814
Benedictines, 821, 822
Catholic Apostolic Church, 4543, 4544
Dominicans, 2413
ecclesiology and, 1774
opposition to, 7662
in Reformation, 7662–7663
revolt against papacy, 7281
secularization in, 8217
Sen (Keshab Chandra) on, 8227
Spiritualism in, 8718
sports in, 8725
study of religion in, Mesoamerican religions in, 5941
Swedenborgianism in, 8901–8903
Theosophical Society in, 9142
tombs in, 9227–9228
Unitarianism in, 974, 9469
Victorian, Salvation Army and, 8064
Wyclif (John) and, 9848–9849
Zoroastrianism in, fire in, 570
England, Church of. *See* Anglicanism; Church of England
Engler, Jack, 7479
English Ladies. *See* Institute of the Blessed Virgin Mary
English language
Bible translated into, 9425
biblical phrases in, 8203
Buddhist writings translated into, 1256, 6955–6956
in East Africa, 2566
Germanic and Romanic synonyms in, 4097
globalization of, and gender studies, 3304
glossolalia and, 3505
"holy" and "sacred" in, 4097–4099
journals written in, 10059–10060
Nag Hammadi codices in, 3508, 6395
Pañcatantra translated into, 6960
Rastafari dialect of, 9307
South Asian fiction in, 10036
Zoroastrian texts in, 9994
English Reformation. *See* Reformation
Engnell, Ivan, in Myth and Ritual school, 6381
Engrams (mental aberrations), in Scientology, 8192, 8193
Engžekit (river), 9394
Enhancement, in Hindu ritual, 9821, 9825
Enheduanna (Sargon's daughter), 3377
Enigma, 6986, 6991. *See also* Riddles
Enigma of the Gift, The (Godelier), 3481–3482
Enki (deity), **2791–2792,** 2962, 5953–5955. *See also* Ea
in Akkadian religion, 2791–2792
in *Atrahasis* myth, 5954
and Atrahasis/Utanapishtim, 3131
as city god of Eridu, 5949, 5953
creation by, 3377, 5954
Dagan and, 2126
death of, 2811
in divine bureaucracy, 5951, 5994
drums of, 2498
Enlil's antagonism with, 598, 5954
in *Enuma elish,* 2809–2810
family of, 5951, 5953
functions of, 5953
in Golden Age myth, 3628
iconography of, 4316
and Inanna, 2521, 4403, 4404, 4405, 5957
Marduk and, 2810, 5702, 5703
Mummu castrated by, 1450
in myth of the Flood, 598
Ningirsu and, 5953
Ninhursaga and, 5954–5955, 6624, 6625
Nin-ti created from, 2896
and Ninurta, 6626–6627
sacred tree and, 1502
in Sumerian pantheon, 5964
in triad, 9349
Utu and, 9494
and water, 779, 5953, 9700, 9701
Enki and Ninhursaga (myth), 5954–5955
Enki and Ninmah (myth), 5954
Enki and the World Order (myth), 2791
Enki in, 5951, 5953
Inanna in, 5957
Enkidu (mythic figure)
Bull of Heaven and, 1465–1466
harlot and, 3967
Enkimdu (deity), in divine bureaucracy, 5951
Enkrateia. See Continence
Enlightenment (spiritual state), **2792–2795**. *See also* Nirvāṇa
baptism and, 782
in Buddhism, 2793–2795 (*See also* Salvation, in Buddhism)
autonomous discipline and, 8701
of Buddha (*See* Buddha, enlightenment of)
in Chan school, 1577, 1601
Daochuo on, 2176
Daosheng on, 1576, 2217
emptiness *(śūnyatā)* and, 8856–8857
as end of reincarnation, 7679
evil and, 2903
Mahāyāna Buddhism, 2217, 5105
Māra challenging, 5690–5691
merit making and, 5874
of *mahāsiddhas*, 5604–5605
perfect and timeless, 9020
Pure Land Buddhism, 4922, 4934
Saichō on, 8031
Sgam po pa (Gampopa) on, 8255
Shandao on, 8298, 8299
Shinran on, 8354–8355
subitist *vs.* gradualist, 2217–2218
Suzuki (D. T.) on, 7740–7741
tathatā in, 9019, 9020
in Tendai school, 9077
in Tiantai school, 9174
Vajrayāna (Tantric) Buddhism, 5604–5605
Zhenyan Buddhism, 9961–9962
in Confucianism, 2218
dance as means to, 2140
in Daoist literature, 1588
definition of, 2792–2793
and denial of existence of demons, 2284–2285
drama in, 2474

feminism and, 1754–1755
German, societal construct in, 7716
Herder (Johann Gottfried), criticism by, 3918
and iconography, 4347
in Jainism, 4764, 5610
in Japanese religion (*See Satori*)
of En no Gyōja, 2802
religion defined in, 7702
Sakya Paṇḍita on, 8052
in Scientology, thetan's path to, 8193
sleep as, 8441–8442
Sthiramati on, 8739
superstition, view of, 8866
tea and, 848
Enlightenment, Jewish. *See* Haskalah
Enlightenment, the (historical era), **2795–2799**
aesthetics and ethics *vs.* religion in, 8471
aesthetics in, 46–48, 811
American civil religion and, 1812–1814
anti-Semitism in, 401
Bacon (Francis) as forerunner of, 734
and biblical exegesis
Christian views, 874–876
Jewish views, 869
and blasphemy prosecutions, 973
Christianity and
American civil religion and, 1715
movements to combat secularization, 1664
papacy during, 6973
politics in, 7282–7283
secularism, 1693
comparative theology in, 9128, 9129, 9131
Confucianism and, 1921
Edwards (Jonathan) influenced by, 2699
encyclopedias and, 2783–2784
gender in, 3360–3361
grace in, 3646
Hermetism and, 3950–3951
historiography and, 4040–4041
on human nature, 1693
humor and, 4203
Index of Forbidden Books in, 4506
Indian philosophies influenced by, 4420, 4425
Indian religious studies in, 4446
Jesuits and, 4842
Jews and, 5018
Judaism and, 4982, 4983
kingdom of God concept in, 5150, 5151–5152
liberalism of, 6102
literature in, 5477
Lutheranism in, 5539
Mendelssohn in, 4900
Methodism and, 4083–4084
monasticism in, 6134
morality in, distinction between religion and, 6177
music in, 6312
mythology in, study of, 6366
and natural religion *vs.* traditional religion, 2958
nature viewed by, 2607
occultism and, 6780
Pietism rejected by, 7142, 7143
and politics and religion, 7248, 7249–7250, 7282–7283
and prophecy, 7428
Protestantism and, and ethics, 1656
rabbinate and, 7581
relativism in, 7685
religion in, 2798
Roman Catholicism in, 7878
Romantic movement, interaction with, 4040–4041
Scottish, *Encyclopaedia Britannica* in, 2784
sociology and, 8491
studies in, on origin of religion, 2236
and study of religion, emergence of, 8761
and tourism, 9261
and "two books" metaphor, 9423
and views of desire, 2308–2309
wisdom after, 9764
Enlil (deity), **2799–2801,** 5952
An and, 301, 302
Ashur identified with, 548
communication between worlds by, 5163
death of, 2811
dragon defeated by, 2431
in Eblaite pantheon, 2596
Enki's antagonism with, 598, 5954
family of, 5951, 5952, 5953
functions of, 5952
in general assembly of gods, 5951, 5952, 5994
as god of hoe, 5950, 5952
in Golden Age myth, 3628
kingship and, 1803, 5162
Marduk and, 2810
in myth of the Fall, 2962
in myth of the Flood, 598–599, 2963
Nanna and, 6172, 6414
and Ninhursaga, 6624, 6625
Ninlil as wife of, 5952
and Ninurta, 6626, 6627
in Nippur, 5950, 5952
Nusku and, 5953
in Sumerian pantheon, 5964
in triad, 9349
water held back by, 9700
Enlil and Ninlil (Sumerian myth), 2799
Enma-ō (deity), 5026
Enmeduranna, Enoch identified with, 2803
Enneads, The (Plotinus), 45, 6474, 7191, 7198
doctrine of hypostases in, 4240, 4243
monism in, 6146, 6147
in Muslim Neoplatonism, 7192
mystical union in, 6336
translation of, 7193, 7199
Ennemoser, Joseph, 6435
Enni Ben'en (Buddhist monk), 9944
Ennin (Buddhist monk)
Amitābha's name transmitted to Japan by, 1239
autobiography of, 702
Enchin and, 2781
Esoteric Buddhism studied by, 9075, 9077, 9078
Mingkong's writings transmitted by, 1250
at Mount Wutai, 6213
music of, 6300
Nembutsu cult transmitted by, 1242
Pure Land Buddhism studied by, 9079
and *wuhui nianfo,* 6603
Ennius, 2994
on apes, 6151
on apotheosis, 438
on superstition, 8864
En no Gyōja, **2802**
Shugendō movement and, 8379, 8380
Ennoia, in Gnosticism, 7190
En no Ozunu. *See* En no Gyōja
1 Enoch
ascension in, 522
dating of, 414
in Dead Sea Scrolls, 417
demons in, 2277
Enoch in, 2803
historical apocalypses in, 410, 415, 10050
otherworldly journey of, 410, 414, 416, 417–418
resurrection in, 7765
versions of, 902, 903
2 Enoch
ascension in, 522
Enoch in, 2803
3 Enoch, ascension in, 522
Enoch (biblical figure), **2802–2804**
angels and, 345
ascension of, 522
as Cain's descendant, 1344
Freemasons on, 3194
Enoch, Apocalypse of
afterlife in, 152
judgment in, 5027
messianism in, 5972
preserved by Ethiopian Church, 874
She'ol in, 9454
Enoch, Book of
angels in, 345
descent into the underworld in, 2295, 2299
in Ethiopian Bible, 2859
Enoch, Similitudes of, 410, 417–418
Enodia (deity), Hekate identified with, 3900
Enore (spirits of the sky), in Enawenê Nawê cosmology, 2012–2013
Enqawa, Ephraim, 834
Enriquez, Enrique, 8978
Ensete ventricosum, 2574
Ensi (political ruler), 5948
En Sof (unknowable essence), in Qabbalah, 4981
Enstasy. *See* Nontheistic ecstasy
Entelecheia of phenomena, 7092
Entenga (drum), 2496
Enthusiasm, **2804–2809,** 2831, 6882–6883
revival and renewal activities described by, 7785
Entrail reading, 2377
Entrails, divination with. *See* Extispicy
"Entrance of practice" *(xingru),* 1521
"Entrance of principle" *(liru),* 1521
Entrapment and escape myth, thetan concept in Scientology and, 8193
Entremont, France, Celto-Ligurian sanctuary at, 3807
Entretiens sur la pluralité des mondes (Fontenelle), 7340
Entrudo festival (Portugal), in Carnival, 1442–1443
Entsy Samoyed. *See* Samoyed religion
Énú (spirits), 6003, 6007
Enuma elish (creation epic), **2809–2812,** 2962
and Akitu festival, 223, 549
ancestors in, 325
An-shar in, 548
and apocalypse genre, 410
Apsu in, 3377
body and soul in, 8539
chaos in, 1539, 1987, 2899
death in, 2237
divine kingship in, 5146
dragons in, 2431
dualism in, 2507
Ea in, 5955
Enlil and, 2800
fate in, 3002–3003
goddesses in, marginalization of, 3376–3377
and kingship, authority of, 693

Enuma elish (creation epic) ***continued***
Kumarbi cycle, similarities with, 4231
Marduk in, 1392, 1393, 2537, 5703, 5955
elevation in pantheon of, 5965–5966
victory of, 3377
methods of creation in
manufacture, 3377
procreation, 3377
Mummu castrated by Enki, 1450
parent-offspring tension in, 1987
revolutionary ideas in, 5965–5966
as ritual drama, 2441–2442, 2444–2445, 5961
scapegoat concept in, 8145
sky in, 8428
Tiamat in, 1392, 1393
defeat of, 3377
in form of cow, 1466
tragedy in, 8403
waters in, 3016, 6439, 9700
Enúúnap (deity), 6003, 6004, 6009, 6010
inactivity of, 6010
Environment
in Arctic religions, history of study of, 473
destruction of
Buddhism and, 2630
in Hindu texts, 2621
poverty and, 2653
vs. ecology, 2605
economic threat to, 2610
Gaia hypothesis on, 3253–3254
in goddess worship, 3609
in Islam, terms to denote, 2653
in *Pigs for the Ancestors,* 7618
shamanistic views of, 2618–2619
Environmental activism
in India, 2622–2623
women in, 9791
Environmental ethics
biocentrism *vs.,* 2655–2656
cosmology and, 2604
Daoist, 2637
ecology and, **2654–2657**
Jewish, 2644
in North American Indian religions, 6682
in world religions, 2655
Environmental history, idealizations in, 2605
Environmentalism. *See also* Earth First!; Ecology
Buddhist, 2788
feminist spirituality movement and, 3022
green spirituality and, 8719–8720
in Israel, 2643, 2646
in Japan, 2638
Jewish, 2645–2646
in Jewish Renewal movement, 4870
nature worship as, 2663
Neopaganism and, 6560
as religion, 2663
Romantic influence on, 2607
Wicca and, 9731
Environmental philosophy
agenda for, 2654–2655
of Hippocrates, 2606
Environmental racism, theology and, 2610
Environmental studies
development of, 2609
religious studies linked with, 2613
Environmental virtues, in Judaism, 2644
Environment of evolutionary adaptation (EEA), 2917
Envy, depiction in novels, 3059
Eochaidh Ollathair (deity), 9390
Ẹpa festival, 9910–9911
Epaphras (Paul's associate), 914
Epaphroditus, 914, 7018
Ephedra (plant), 849
Ephedra, in Zoroastrianism, 3775
Ephemerides, calendars and, 1359–1360
Ephemeris Belli Troiani (Diary of the Trojan War), 3051–3052
Ephesiaka (Xenophon of Ephesus), 3052
Ephesians, 913–914, 920
author of, 911, 914
baptism in, 782
blessing in, 982
Colossians compared to, 914
content of, 913–914
Ephesus
Artemis in, 508, 9063
John the Evangelist in, 4944
Lady of the Animals in, 5280
Leo I in, 5410
Paul's missionary journey to, 7017, 7018–7019
under Roman Empire, 7912
Ephesus, Council of (431)
Assyrian Church, dissent of, 1673
on Church of Cyprus, 3658
division in Christianity after, 2582–2584
Eutyches and, 2885
on Mary as *theotokos* (Mother of God), 2040, 4345, 5753, 7884
Nestorianism and, 2040, 2117
Nestorius condemned at, 6480, 6482, 6483
Ephoros, on ritual homosexuality on Crete, 4112
Ephraem of Syria, **2812–2813**
and Bardesanites, 786–787
Christology and, 2581
on cross of Jesus as bridge, 1050
theology of, 9135
Ephthalites, 4491
Epic of Aqhat. *See* Aqhat, Epic of
Epic of Atrahasis, Enlil in, 2800
Epic of Gilgamesh. See Gilgamesh, Epic of
Epic of Kirta
in Canaanite religion, 1386, 1388, 1398–1400
god list in, 1384
parts of, 1390
Epic of Palnāḍu, 2814–2815
Epics, **2813–2818**. *See also specific epics*
of Ainu religion, 207
authority of, 6362
chanting of, 1536
Hegel (G. W. F.) on, 4219
heroic, 2814
Hindu (*See Mahābhārata*)
Homeric (*See Iliad; Odyssey*)
Indian (*See also* Mahābhārata; See also Rāmāyaṇa)
classical Hinduism and, 3994
Puruṣārthas (four goals of humankind) in, 3996
myths in, 6362
oral, 2814
shamanistic accounts, similarity to, 8274
universal appeal of, 2817
Epictetus
canon in writings of, 1406
on desire, 2307
on divine service, 8405
on kingship, 5147
Stoicism and, 8741
on suicide, 8829
Epicureans
canonization and, 1406
charges against, 3910
Hellenism and, 3901, 3910–3911
materialism and, 5776
Epicurus
on belief in gods, 4036
"canonics" in writings of, 1406
on friendship, 3910–3911
materialism and, 5776
on pleasure, 3910
on religion, 3911
Epidaurus
Asklepios in, cult of, 551, 552
inscription at, 1460
Epigenetic mind, in sociobiology, 8475
Epigrams
Egyptian, 2728
in Sufism, of ʿAbd Allāh Anṣarī, 8816–8817
Epigraphy
Daoist, 2208, 2211
Islamic, 6208
Maya, 5886–5887
Epiklēsis (invocation of Holy Spirit), 9810–9811
Epilegomena (Harrison), goal of, 3781–3782
Epilepsy
in Greek religion, 3839–3840
moon and, 6175
temporal lobe, 6487
Epimenides of Crete
ascension by, 520
miracles of, 6050
Zalmoxis and, 9927–9928
Epimetheus (deity), 7419
Epipaleolithic Period. *See* Mesolithic Period
Epiphanes (Gnostic leader), 3516
Epiphanius
on Aion, 208, 209
on Gnostic orgy, 6867–6868
on Mary, 5753
on Montanism, 6167, 6168
on sexual rites, 8247
on Valesianism, 1452
Epiphany, **2818**
in Christian liturgical calendar, 1743–1744, 9814
Epiphany, Feast of, 2400
Epiphany the Wise, on Komi religion, 5217
Episcopacy. *See* Bishops
Episcopal Church, Protestant (U.S.)
African Americans in, ordination of, 4950–4951
formation of denomination, 1712
full communion agreement with Lutherans (ELCA), 1769
liturgical year in, 1744
missions, Crummell (Alexander), role of, 2073
polity of, 1766–1767
Episcopal form of church government, 1763–1767. *See also* Bishops
Episcopalianism, 352–353
African American, 68
in ecumenical movement, 352–353
Eucharist rites in, 2580
homosexuality in, 353, 7404
missionaries of, 352
North American Indian, 2264
in Philippines, 1727
women as priests in, 68, 353, 7404
Episcopius, Simon, in Remonstrant Brotherhood, 493
Epispanic initiation, 9721
Epistemological certainty, 2428
Epistemology, **2818–2820,** 5210–5211. *See also* Mind
Buddhist, 1120, 1212–1213, 1301, 2336, 2351
Mahāyāna, *kṣaṇikavāda* (momentariness) doctrine and, 8119
Cārvāka, 1446
in Chinese thought
Wang on, 1578
Wang's Study of Inner Mind, 1902–1903
Xunzi on, 1588
Copernican revolution and, 1978
hermeneutics and, 3930
Hindu
of liberation, 8417
of Rāmānuja, 7615

historiography and, 4030–4031
Hocking (William Ernest) on, 4076
human experience in, 2778–2780
of Hume (David), 4192
Indian (*See also* Pramāṇas)
in Sāṃkhya Hinduism, 8090
Sakya Paṇḍita on, 8051
Śaṅkara on, 8105–8106
in Islam, in Muʿtazilah, 6324
in Korean Neo-Confucianism, 1931–1932
neuroepistemology, 6488–6492
sacred *vs.* profane and, 7975–7976
in science and religion, 1996
unpredictability in chaos theory, 1542
Epistle of Barnabas, 873, 920
Epistle of Polycarp to the Philippians, 920
Epistle on Resurrection (Maimonides), 24
Epistle to Diognetus, hypostasis in, 4241
Epistle to Rheginos concerning the Resurrection, 3513
Epistle to the Jewish Community of Avignon (Crescas), anti-Jewish massacres in, 2069
Epistle to the Romans, The (Barth), 6466, 6467
Epistle to the Son of the Wolf (Bahāʾ Allāh), 738
Epistle to ʿUthmān al-Battī (Abū Ḥanīfah), 21–22
Epitaphs
Aramean, 450
Islamic, 162
Epithets
in Canaanite literature, 1391
for Anat, 319
in Greek religion, 3678
for Zeus, 3663, 3664
Epithumia (desire), 7184, 9070
Epitome (part of *2 Maccabees),* 901
Epoche (suspension of judgment), 7088, 7092, 7095, 7188
Epona (deity), **2820**, 4253
analogues of, 1487, 1490
gender of worshipers of, 3388
as horse goddess, 4133
origin myth of, 4133
sexuality and, 8239
Epstein, Barukh, 868
Epstein, Jacob, on Shimʿon bar Yohʾai, 8346
Epstein, Jean, 3097, 3100, 3101
Eqron (Ekron) (Philistine city)
excavations at, 7104
inscription from, 7103–7104
Equality
gender
in Catharism, 2748
in early Islam, 6224
in progressive Islam, 6099
genetics and, 3429
Gurū Nānak on, 8395
human rights and, 4181
in Kurozumikyō, 5267
in Islam, 4573, 4575
under law, U.S., 5330
in nature, in Confucianism, 2632
Paul on, 3357
Equilibrium, in African religions
through animal sacrifice, 88
myths about, 91
Equinoxes
in Hindu religious year, 4016, 4017
in Japan, 2411
New Age pilgrimages on, 8429
Stonehenge and, 8835–8836
Equivalence principle, relativity theory and, 2032
Eraclius, as Augustine's successor, 628
Era names, Japanese, 6828
Eranistes (Theodoret), 9123
Eranos group, esotericism studied by, 2843–2844
Erasmus, Desiderius, **2821–2822**
and Bucer (Martin), 1059
on ceremonialism, 8866
on folly, 4201
on free will, 3201, 3207
Luther (Martin) on, 7026
Moralia (Plutarch) translated by, 7202
Neoplatonism and, 6475
northern humanism, role in, 4176–4177
paradox by, 6988
on pilgrimage, 9262
skeptical views of, 8421
Erasmus of Rotterdam, in Reformation, 7657, 7662
Eratosthenes, and Anthesteria, 375
Erdrich, Louise, 3061, 3092
Love Medicine, 3092
poetry of, 7226
Erecteion (deity), 5275
ʿErekh (monetary equivalents), 4738
Eremitism, **2822–2830**. *See also* Anchorites and anchoritism; Hermits; Recluses; Spiritual discipline
in Buddhism, sectarianism and, 8080
communal, Antony and, 1980
in Coptic Christianity, Shenoute the Archimandrite and, 8319
in Eastern Orthodoxy, Sergii of Radonezh and, 8230
Hijiri (Japanese lay ascetics) as hermits, 3978
historical development of, 2826–2828
human solidarity and, 2829
spread of, 2826–2828
Ereshkigal (deity), 2521, 2539, 2984, 3016, 3376, 4403, 4404, 5959, 9452
Hekate identified with, 3900
Nergal and, 6476–6477
Erfahrung (experience), 9651–9652, 9652
Erga (Hesiod), Demeter in, 2268
Ergriffenheit, Frobenius's (Leo) idea of, 5113
Erhu (musical instrument), 6295
Erichthonios (mythic figure), 6958
Eridu (Sumer)
Enki as deity of, 5949, 5953
supplanted by Babylon, 2810–2811
Eridu Genesis (myth), 5954
Erie Canal (New York), 10086
Erie tribe (North America), ballgame played by, 754
Erigone, in Anthesteria, 375
Erikson, Erik
on change, 1413
and Niebuhr (Reinhold), 6612
religious figures analyzed by, 7476, 7482–7483
Erinyes (avenging spirits), 2277, 7782
of beggars, 2100–2101
patriarchal *vs.* matriarchal rights and, 7782
Eritrea, Church of, 2585, 2861
Ériu (deity), 1490
Eriugena, John Scottus, **2830–2831**
on God, 6147
Hincmar and, 3983
monistic philosophy of, 6147
mysticism of, 390
on nature, 6432
realism of, 6644
work of Dionysius the Areopagite translated by, 8908
Erkenntnisproblem in der Philosophie und Wissenschaft der neuern Zeit, Das (Cassirer), 1448
Erkes, Eduard, 1635
Erkes, Edward, 3339
Erlik (deity), **2831–2832,** 9441
in shamanistic descents, 8272
sick souls held captive by, 8273
Erlik/Erklik (warrior), 9398
Erman, Adolf, 2730
Er myth, of Plato, 7680
Ern, V. F., 3133
Erndl, Kathleen, 3608, 3609
on spirit possession, 8695
Ernst, Carl, 3161
on South Asian Islam, 4642
Eros (deity), **2832–2833**
hare associated with, 7590
Eros (love), 2308
Freud (Sigmund) on, 2238
Eroticism. *See also* Homoeroticism
in images of mystical union, 6335, 6352
Kṛṣṇa and, 5249, 5252
lotus symbolism and, 5519
love of God expressed in erotic terms, sainthood and, 8037
in *Proverbs,* 9756
vs. reproduction, 6861
in Sufism, al-Hujwīrī on, 4157
*Erotókritos (*Kornáros), 3053–3054
Erra (deity), 9597
Erring: A Postmodern Altheology (Taylor), 2247
Erru sixing lun (Buddhist text), 994, 1292
Erskine, Thomas, Maurice (Frederick Denison) influenced by, 5783
Erudites *(boshi),* Confucianism and, 1897–1898
Erusin (betrothal), 7821
in Jewish law, 3752
Eryō (Buddhist monk), 1177
Erzä religion (Russia). *See* Mari and Mordvin religion
Esack, Farid, 6099
Esagila temple, in Akitu festival, 222
Esalen Institute, 6568
Esarhaddon (Assyrian king)
Ashur and, 549
loyalty oath of, 2047
Melqart and, 5847
on moon, 6171
oath to, 4728
treaty between King Baal and, 7129–7130, 7134
Esau (biblical figure)
birth of, 4757
Rebecca and, 7634
Eschatological dualism, 2508, 2509, 2511
Eschatological prophet, 7426
Eschatological theocracy, 9111
Eschatological theodicy, 9114, 9116, 9118
Eschatology, **2833–2840**. *See also* Judgment of the dead; Soul
in African religions
Sabbatucci (Dario) on, 5159
Tardits (Claude) on, 5159
Bahāʾī, 739
Berdiaev (Nikolai) on, 836
in Buddhism, 2834
Shandao on *mofa* era, 8298
of Xinxing, 9859
in Chinese religion
Buddhist, 1596
Daoist, 1597

Eschatology ***continued***
in Christianity
and afterlife, 133
Augustine on, 1652
of Churches of Christ, 1780
in *Colossians,* 914
and history, view of, 4053
of Jehovah's Witnesses, 4822
Jerusalem in, 4837
of Jesus, 4846–4847, 4849
in *1 John,* 918
Justin Martyr on, 5045
millenarian, and history, view of, 4055
in Millerite movement, 8235
mustērion as disclosure of God's intention, 7955
Schweitzer (Albert) on, 8179
in *2 Thessalonians,* 915
cosmic, 2834
cosmogony tied to, 6362
on cybernetics and, 2112
in Daoism, 2178, 2205
death in, 2237
definition of, 2833–2834
dragons in, 2431
in Greek religion
ascension and, 521
in mystery religions, 3684–3685
in Hinduism, 4440–4441, 7361–7362
individual, 2834
Indo-European, 4456
Irenaeus on, 4540
in Islam, **2836–2840**
in Ḥanafī creed, 2064
in Imāmīyah, 8337, 8342
in Ismāʿīlīyah, 8326, 8329
in Qurʾān, 5060
Jerusalem in, 4837
soul in, 8568
in Judaism
and afterlife, 133
in Ashkenazic Hasidism, 542
in mysticism, 6352–6354
in Qabbalah, 7538
of Saʿadyah Gaon, 7953
in Second Temple Judaism, 4974–4975
time in Hebrew scriptures and, 4058
in Zionism, 4906–4907
in North American Indian religions, Handsome Lake as ethical-eschatological prophet, 3771
Orphic, 7679
overview of, **2833–2836**
paradise in, 6985–6986
Plutarch on, 7200
relative, 2834
Samaritan, 8070
soteriology and, 8528
Stoic, 8741
of UFO religions, 9434
of West African religions, 9717
in Zoroastrianism, 9996–9997
Saoshyants ("redeemers") and, 8110
universalism in, 3907
Eschenmayer, Carl August von, on nature, 6435
Eschetewuarha (mother of the universe), in Chamacoco religion, 8578–8579
Escobar, Carlos, 2436
Escorial palace-monastery (Madrid), 6120
2 Esdras, 882
messianism in, 5972, 5973
Eshmun (deity), **2840–2842**
Melqart and, 5847
in Phoenician religion, 7129, 7130, 7131
Eshmunazor (king of Sidon), 7130
Eshmunazor II (king of Sidon), 7132
Eshnunna (city), law code of, 1844–1845
Eshnunna (codex), 4727, 4728
Esh Qodesh (Kalonymus), 9382
Eshu (deity), in Caribbean religions, 1435
Eshu-Elegba (deity), 3086
Eskimo. *See also* Inuit
origin of term, 4526
Esna (Egypt), temple of Khnum at, 2709
Ešnuwérta (primordial mother), in Chamacoco religion (South America), 8633–8634
Esoteric Buddhism. *See also* Buddhism, schools of; *See also* Vajrayāna (Tantric) Buddhism
central buddha in, 1068
in China, 1240
homa in, 9838
iconography of, 4330, 5608
in Japan, 1096, 1176–1177, 1243, 9077–9078
living buddhas in, 1068
Mahāvairocana in, 5607, 5608
in Mongolia, 1097
nirvāṇa in, 6632
Saichō and, 8030, 8031
salvation in, 1088
in Tibet, 1096, 1097
Esotericism, **2842–2845**. *See also* Hermetism; Western Esotericism
academic approaches to, 2843–2845
alchemy and, 235
androgynes in, 339–340
of anthroposophy, 392–393
of Ashkenazic Hasidism, 544–545
in Buddhism, Japanese (*See* Shingonshū school of Buddhism)
celibacy and, 1475
Creuzer (G. F.) on, 2070
definition of, 9277
deities of, 3623
of Dogon religion, 101
evolutionism and, 6498
Fludd (Robert) and, 3950
Frye (Northrop) and study of, 3225
Guénon (René) on, 3707
institutionalization of, 2845
in Islam
in Ismāʿīlīyah, 8326
Shīʿah, 4572
Suhrawardī on, 8827
taqīyah in, 8999
Mead (George) on, 3952
meanings of, 2842–2843
mudrās, 6219
and New Age movement, 6497–6498
occultism and, 6780–6781
of Upaniṣads, 9480–9481
of Ouspensky (P. D.), 6935
paradigms of, 2843–2845
in popular religion, 7327
psychology and, 6498
Rosicrucian influence on, 7930
Scientology as, 8192, 8193–8194
secularized, 6497, 6499
spiritual guides and, 8710–8712, 8713
symbolism and, 8908, 8909
tarot cards and, 1414
and tradition, 9278
Western, 2843
worldview of, 6497
E source. *See* Elohist source
ESP. *See* Extrasensory perception
Espinas, Alfred, Durkheim (Émile) influenced by, 2527
Espiritismo, creolization and, 2066–2067
Espiritistas, Puerto Rican, initiation of, 8691
Esposito, John, 7254
Esprit follet, 2951
Esquisse d'un tableau historique des progrès de l'esprit humain (Condorcet), 7340
Esrel (angel of death), 1785
Ess, Josef van, 6445
Essai sur la légende du Bouddha, son caractère et ses origines (Senart), 945
Essai sur la religion bambara (Dieterlen), 116, 2350
Essai sur les données immédiates de la conscience (Bergson), 838
Essay concerning Human Understanding (Locke), 5496
Essay on Human Freedom (Schelling), will in, 8148
Essay on Human Understanding, An (Locke), 7282
Essay on Man, An (Cassirer), 1448
Essays (Bacon), 733
Essays in Zen Buddhism (Suzuki), 2906
Essence(s)
in Buddhism (*See Svabhāva*)
extraction of (yogic practice), 1288
of music, in Yanyuwa religion, 6261–6262
philosophies of, 2925
of religion, classification of religions and, 1819–1820
Essence of Christianity (Feuerbach), 3047–3048
Marx (Karl) influenced by, 5745
sociology in, 8480
Essence of Religion (Feuerbach), 3048
Essence possession, 2140
Essenes, **2845–2848**. *See also* Qumran sect
asceticism of, 7722
baptism of, 780
Christianity influenced by, 2847–2848
eremitism of, 2823
fasting among, 2996
history of, 2846
initiation to, 2846
John the Baptist and, 4943
membership in, 2846
names of, 2845–2846
on predestination, 3203
as Qumran sect, 2234, 7722
on resurrection, 7765
Sabbath liturgy of, 8921
theology of, 2847
underworld beliefs of, 9454
way of life of, 2846–2847
Essentialism
in Enlightenment philosophy, humor and religion, effect on, 4203
genetic, 8187
linguistic, Smith (Wilfred Cantwell) on, 8450
of Mullā Ṣadrā, 6231–6233
postcolonialism and, 1858
subaltern studies against, 8800, 8801
Essex Street Chapel, 9469
Essien-Udom, Essien Udosen, 79
est (movement), 6568
"Established sects," as category, 1866–1867
Estates, settlement of, in rabbinic Judaism, 7589
Estes, Clarrisa Pinkola, 7485
Esther, **2848–2849**
ballet based on story of, 2163
Esther
additions to, 898
anti-Semitism in, 398
celebrating at Purim, 7516, 7517
"Jew" used in, 4856
not found at Qumran, 880, 886
Purim liturgy from, 8390
Shemuʾel the Amoram on, 8318
Esther, Fast of
in Jewish calendar, 4867
in Marrano Judaism, 5718

Estonia and Estonian religion
Estonian Orthodox Church
in Orthodox structure, 2589
vs. Russian Orthodox churches, 1686
goat in folklore of, 8312
Lutheranism in, 1685
Estonian language, 756
Estonian Orthodox Church
in Orthodox structure, 2589
vs. Russian Orthodox churches, 1686
Estonians, 3106
epic poetry of, 3111
Eṣu (deity)
in Edo religion, 2697
as messenger, 1435
sacrifices supervised by, 3571
as trickster, 86, 94, 1435, 9353
in Yoruba religion, 9911–9912
Esu (Ẹlẹgba), in Santería, 1434
Esus (deity), 1483
Etana (Babylonian myth), 5147
Etao (mythic figure), 6011, 6012
Étaples, Lefèvre d', French humanism and, 4176
Eṭemmu (ghost), in Mesopotamian religion, 8535–8536
Eternal Garden: Mysticism, History, and Politics at a South Asian Sufi Center (Ernst), 4642
Eternalist views in Cārvāka, 1446
Eternal Mother, in Chinese millenarianism, 6040
Eternal Sacred Order of the Cherubim and Seraphim of Orimolade, 1720–1721
Eternal Venerable Mother
in White Lotus Sectarianism, 2188
Xi Wang Mu and, 1607
Eternity, **2853–2857**
and afterlife, 133–134
anthropological bias on, 7992
Aristotle on, 480–481, 485
in Australian Indigenous religions, 314
of Church, 4034
God's existence in, Augustine on, 3205
in Islam, 3563
in Judaism, 614
number eight as symbol of, 6748
Osiris as, 6921
Ethelbert, Augustine of Canterbury and, 623
Etheldreda (nun), 822
Ethelwold (bishop), 2437
Ethical Animal, The (Waddington), 2919
Ethical atheism, 7422
Ethical Culture, **2857–2858**
Ethical Culture, New York Society for, Adler (Felix) in, 33
Ethical Culture School, 33
Ethical dualism, 2505, 2509
Ethical monotheism, 9120
historical, 6160–6161
Ethical overlap model, on science and religion, 8186
Ethical Philosophy of Life, An (Adler), 33
Ethical piety, in Judaism, 4902–4903
Ethical prophet, 5384
Ethical religions, as classification, 1818
Ethical theology movement, 1530
Leeuw (Gerardus van der) in, 5391
Ethics. *See also* Morality; Transgression
Adler (Felix) on, 33
aesthetics and
Dewey (John) on, 49
Kant (Immanuel) on, 46
Kierkegaard (Søren) on, 48
in African religions, Yoruba cosmology and, 1999
and afterlife, differentiation of destinies in, 138
and animals, 357–358
Aristotle on, 485–486, 7109
artificial intelligence and, 512–513
bioethics (*See* Bioethics)
Buddhist, **1278–1284**
animals in, 359–360
anthropocentrism of, 2628
buddhas and *bodhisattvas* and, **1083–1087**, 1118, 1280–1282
in Chinese Buddhism, 1161, 1167, 1280
combined with Confucian virtues, 1604
in Mahāyāna Buddhism, 1118, 1280–1282, 8110
in Theravāda Buddhism, 1280, 5098
in Vajrayāna (Tantric) Buddhism, 1282
karman and, 5098
modern, 1282–1283
patterns of, 1278–1280
Sarvāstivādin, 8118–8119
Canaanite, 1388
Cārvāka, 1446
casuistry (principles and choices), **1454–1455**
charity, **1553–1556**
in Chinese thought (*See also* De (virtue); Self-cultivation)
common beliefs on, 1618
Confucian-Buddhist combination, 1604
Confucius on, 1586
Wang on situational ethics, 1578
Christian, **1650–1657**
Brunner (Emil) on, 1054
casuistry in, 1455–1456
contemporary, 1656–1657
early history of, 1651–1652
Eastern Orthodox, 1652–1653
formal approaches to, 1650–1651
Kagawa Toyohiko on, 5053–5054
morality *vs.* ethics in, 1650
Pentecostal, 7032
philosophical ethics, relation to, 1650
Protestant, 1654–1656, 7457–7458
Roman Catholic, 1653–1654, 7457
Schleiermacher (Friedrich) on, 8160, 8164, 8165
social transformation and, 1671
sources of, 1651
of Clement of Alexandria, 7191
Confucian
Kaibara Ekken on, 5055
Mengzi and, 5859
conscience and consciousness in, 1943–1944
creation myths and, 1989–1990
Daoist, 2637
deontological, desire in, 2303
devotion and, 2321
in Earth First!, 2564
ecumenism and social ethics, 1776
in eugenics, 2881
evolution of, 2656
existentialism and, 2927
formal approaches (teleology, deontology, and responsibility), 1650–1651
Golden Rule of, 3630–3633
in Greek religion, charity, 1553–1554
and heresy, development of, 3923
Hindu, 4428
animals in, 359
Hume (David) on, 4192–4193
idealist, 4356
in Ch'ŏndogyo, 1648
Islamic, 1454
ʿAbd Allāh Ansarī on, 8817
Ibn al-ʿArabī on, 8820
Ibn Rushd and, 4272
in Ashʿarīyah, 538
in Sufism, 8817, 8820, 9006–9007
Jaina, 2624
Jewish
casuistry, 1454
medical ethics, 3829
in Musar movement, 6241–6242
of Ashkenazic Ḥasidim, 4913–4914
Reform Judaism, 7666
Kant (Immanuel) on, 5077–5078
in Khmer religion, 5132
Kierkegaard on, 5142
of liberation, 5437
Lincoln (Bruce) on, 8471
medical (*See* Medical ethics)
in Melanesian religions, 5834
moral teaching *vs.*, 1650
mystical union and, 6335–6336
naturalism in, 6428
of Nicostratus, 7189
North American Indian
Anishinaabe, 369
Cherokee, 1564–1565
Handsome Lake as ethical-eschatological prophet, 3771
Zuni, 8016
in Oceanic religions, spirits and, 2007
of Origen, 7191
Plato on, 7110
Plutarch's, 7189
in proofs for existence of God, 7422, 9106
Quaker, 7547
Raëlian, 7598
relativism and, 7685
science and religion and, 2660
sexual, 8245–8246
in Sikhism, 8396
in *Ādi Granth,* 32, 6413
Socrates on, 8504
soteriological function of, 8528
Spencer (Herbert) on, 8679
in Stoicism, 8741, 8742
teleological, desire in, 2303
theological, 9100
vs. philosophical, 1651
Ethics (Abelard), 7
Ethics (Spinoza)
desire in, 2308–2309
monistic system in, 6148
Ethics according to the Stoics (Barlaam of Calabria), 788
Ethika (Plutarch). *See Moralia* (Plutarch)
Ethik des Judentums, Die (The ethics of Judaism) (Lazarus), 4903
Ethiopia, Church of, 2585
Ethiopia Africa Black International Congress, Bobo Dreads of, 7623, 7627
Ethiopia and Ethiopian religions, **2572–2574**. *See also* Aksumite religion
Agaw, 2573
Amhara-Tigriña, 2573

Ethiopia and Ethiopian religions ***continued***
Christianity, 2573, 4606–4607
Chalcedon statement rejected by, 2584
conversion to kingdom to, 1980, 2859
and East African religions, 2571
Roman Catholicism, 2860
civilization in, origins of, 224
commerce of images in, vol. 7 color insert
cosmogony of, written accounts of, 2567
Dime people of, chiefs of, 5170
Gurage, 2573
homes in, vol. 6 color insert
Islam, 2571, 2860, 4606–4607
spread of, 4600
Italian invasion of (1935–1936), 7624
Judaism in (*See* Bēta Esra'ēl)
languages of, 2566
Majangir, 2574
modern movements in
charismatic Christianity in, 106
zaar cult in, 107
Oromo, 2573
spirit possession in, 8691
Ethiopian Church, **2858–2862**
Apocalypse of Enoch preserved by, 874
healing in, 1721
as independent movement, 1719–1720, 8316
Ethiopianism
of African Independent Churches, 103
history of study of, 75
Liele (George) and, 5443
in Rastafarian movement, 1437–1438
in Rastafari movement, 7623
Ethiopian Jews. *See* Bēta Esra'ēl
Ethiopian World Federation (EWF), 7625, 7627
Ethiopic language, biblical translations into, 922
Ethnic groups
in Africa
diversity of, 139
religion tied to, 66, 83
circumcision as marker of, 1798
conflict among, religions contributing to, 2614
genetics and, 3429
identity and cultural hybridity, 1859
in Candomblé, 121–122
Jews as, 4864
in new religious movements, 6563
new religious movements and segmentation of, 1809
in Sahara, 83
secret societies and, 8213
secularization and, 8217
in Surinam, 125–126
Ethnicity, in visual culture, 9620
Ethnic religions, in history of religions approach, 4064–4066
Ethnic studies, Jewish studies and, 4884
Ethnoastronomy, **2862–2866**
Ethnobotany, 2664
Ethnocentrism
cultural relativism and, 2086
sacred time and, 7992–7993
and study of religion, 8761
Ethnographic films, 2350
Ethnographies. *See also* Anthropology; Study of religion
of African societies, 115
archaeological, 452
of Caribbean religions, 10024–10025
Codrington on, 1848
of Finland, Harva (Uno) and, 3783
internal, 384
of Komi society, 5216
of Oceania, 6800
of Osage tribe, 6916–6917
poststructuralist, in South America, 8597
of Rastafari, 7628
of South American Indian religions, 8594–8597
on spirit possession, 8694–8695
Ethnohistorians, South American Indian religions, studies of, 8595, 8597
Ethnology, **378–388**. *See also* Anthropology
contrasted with social anthropology, 7592
definition of, 115
Frobenius (Leo) and, 3222
Jensen (Adolf E.) and, 4824
Kluckhohn (Clyde) on, 5261
kulturkreiselehre, 5259–5262
religious, de Martino (Ernesto) and, 2266–2267, 5261
in ritual studies, 7858
Schmidt (Wilhelm) on, 8168
Schoolcraft (Henry Rowe) and, 6670
Ethnology, U.S. Bureau of, and study of North American Indian cultures, 6670–6671
Ethno-performance theory, spirit possession and, 8697
Ethno-religious groups. *See* Anabaptism; Sectarianism; *specific groups*
Ethology of religion, **2867–2870**
definition of, 2867
history of, 2867
Ethos
of Catholicism, 7887
modern, origins of, 2672
Ēthos, in Greek music theory, 6303–6304
Eto, Silas, 6796
religious movement of, 8516
Etrusca disciplina, 2872
Etruscan religion and society, **2870–2876**
afterlife in, 166
Hades and, 3725
celestial portents in, 7336–7337
deities of, 2870–2871
demons in, 2277
Fortuna in, 3175
funerary cults of, vol. 4 color insert
haruspices in, 2872, 7336
iconography of, 4322
information sources for, 2870
kingship in, 5167
postures and gestures in, 7343
prodigies in, 7337–7338
prophets of, 2872
rituals in, 2873–2874
in Roman empire, 2874–2875
Roman religion influenced by, 7896
sacred books of, 2872–2874
sacred space in, sky and, 8428
sacrifice in, 8006
temples in, 9064
thunderbolt symbolism in, 7603
triads in, 9349
urbanization in, 5167
women in, 2871–2872
Étude comparée des religions, L' (Pinard), 7173
Etymologies (Isidore), 4557
Euá (spirit), 122
Euaggelion, 3640
Euboulus, on Mithraism, 6091–6092
Eubulides of Epimenides, paradox by, 6988
Eucharist, 2876–2878. *See also* Sacraments
altars in, 277–278
in Anglicanism, 350
archetypes in, 459
in Armenian church, 489
Augustine of Hippo on, 837
Berengar of Tours on, 837
Gregory VII and, 3689
Beza's doctrine of "relation" in, 851
bread used in, Azyme Controversy and, 5388
cognates of, in comparative studies, 7956–7957
confession as preparation for, 2592–2593
consecration and, 1956
Cyril of Jerusalem on, 2118
desecration of, in diabolical witchcraft, 9771
divine presence in, 4390
early interpretation of, 792, 7959–7960
at Easter, 2579–2580
in Eastern Christianity, 7960
Cabilas on, 1343
at home, 2399
infants and, 7960
as elixir, 2771
excommunication from, 2920
gift giving in, 3484
hermits and, 2825
as historical rhythm, 4053
history of, 2877
in Holy Order of MANS, 4102
Hus (Jan) on, 4234
Ignatius of Antioch on, 4370
in initiation rituals, 4483
Irenaeus on, 4540
in Jansenism, 7001
Jewish roots of, 7958
Justin Martyr on, 5045
as Lord's Supper
frequency of, 7962
in Protestantism, 7962
in Reformed confessions, 2059
medieval practices, 7961
music in, 6307, 6309
in New Testament, 7959
as orgy, 6867
in Orthodox Christianity, 2592
ordination and, 2593
prayers, Eucharistic, of Syriac Orthodox Church, 8941
presider at
in early Christianity, 7401, 7402
medieval, 7403
in Protestantism, 7455–7456
in Anglican *Book of Common Prayer,* 2051
as communion, 1669
and reconciliation, ritual of, 7959
reforms in *Book of Common Prayer* (Anglican), 2051
in Roman Catholicism, 7882
Mary and, 7884
after Vatican II, 7962
as sacrifice, 7402, 7404
sacrificial meaning of, 8006–8007
Servetus (Michael) on, 8232
Simons (Menno) on, 8401
soteriology and, 8527
terminology for, 5490
theology of, 2877–2878
transubstantiation doctrine, 1669
Trent Council on, 9343
use of bread and wine in, 848, 987, 1040, 1041, 3171
at weddings, 5726
in worship, 9810–9811
Euchee (Yuchi) language, 6697
Eucherius, 1447
Euclid, 2878–2879
geometry of, 3438, 3441, 3443–3444
Gersonides's commentary on, 3462
influence on *falsafah,* 2971
Eudemus, on Babylonian cosmology, 2811
Eudemus (Aristotle), soul in, 484, 8564
Eudorus of Alexandria
as Middle Platonist, 7188

Philo Judaeus influenced by, 7106
Eudoxia (empress), Chrysostom and, 1762
Eudoxus of Cnidus, astrology and, 563
Eugene IV (pope), 6972, 7280
Eugene, Toinette, 79
Eugenics, **2879–2882**
Darwinian model in, 2910
Eugenics Catechism, A, 2881
Eugenius (emperor), 7922
Eugenius III (pope), 839
Eugenius IV (pope)
councils convoked by, 2043
Greeks united by, 8157
on Mark of Ephesus, 5714
Eugnostos the Blessed (Gnostic text), 3517
Euhemerism, **2882–2884**
and animism, 365, 366
attractiveness of, 3910
Chinese mythology and, 1623
Christianity and, 6366
definition of, 6365
in Germanic religion, history of study of, 3458
and manism, 5672
origins of, 6365
of Saxo Grammaticus, 8142
of Snorri Sturluson, 366, 3458, 5672
Euhemerus, **2882–2884**
and animism, 365, 366
on apotheosis, 438
as atheist, 582, 3910
on spirits of the dead, power of, 5672
on Zeus, 4036
Eulogia, 1041
Eulogius (Andalusian martyr), 4593
Eulogius (patriarch), Gregory I and, 3688
Eulogius of Cordova, 7243
Eulogy, blessing as, 981
Eulogy to Atahualipa, A, 567
Eumenides, The (Aeschylus), 7783
Eunomios, Arianism of, 478
Eunuchs. *See also* Castration
as priests, 1451–1452
Euphrates River, 7861, 7862
course of, 5946–5947
Eurasian steppes, prehistoric religions in, **7382–7388**
Euripides, 375. *See also* Bacchae
on afterlife, 3725
on Aphrodite, 407
on catasterism, 8424
Cretans, The, defilement in, 1460
on Dionysos, 2357, 2443, 9158
gender in works of, 3383–3384
on guilt, 8405
on Hades, 3725
Heracles, 5469
on oaths, 971
on repentance, 7756
ritual patterns used by, 2443
on sacrifice, 4456
on scapegoats, 8144
tuchē (fortune) in, 1527
Eurocentrism, historiography in age of, 4042–4047
Europa (mythic figure), 4321
European Baptist Federation, 785
European Court of Human Rights (ECHR)
new religious movements and, 5378
new religious movements appealing to, 6570
Europe and European religions. *See also specific countries, regions, and religions*
in African American religions, 65
anticult legislation in, 1033–1034
anticult movement in, 2085, 2086
archaeology in, 451–452, 456
astrology in, 564
bears in, 5514
Buddhism, 1187, 1188–1191
engaged Buddhism, 2786
cards, history of, 1413–1414
Carnival in, 1440–1443
cave paintings, 1470–1471
central, Jewish migration to, 5016
Christianity, **1680–1694**
Easter celebrations in, 2579
Holiness movement in, 4083
nuns and sisters, 6765
dance in, 2135, 2138–2139
in Baroque period, 2154–2155
Central European, 2159–2160
in Middle Ages, 2153
popular and folk dance, 2144
in Pre-Romantic period, 2154–2155
religious and ceremonial, 2146–2148
in Renaissance, 2153–2154
in Romantic period, 2155–2156
death in
changing attitudes towards, 2239–2240
dances dealing with, 2138–2139
death masks and, vol. 10 color insert
Eckankar in, 2602
epic tradition of, 2815
evil eye, belief in, 3809–3810
folklore of, Christmas and, 1757
folk religion in, discovery of, 3142
geomancy in, 3437
head-hunting in, 3807
Inquisition in, **4498–4502** (*See also* Portuguese Inquisition; Roman Inquisition; Spanish Inquisition)
International Society for Krishna Consciousness in, 4522, 4523
Islam, **4673–4682**
education in, 4675–4676
Mongolian invasion and, 4673–4674
movements and trends in, 4681–4682
Ottoman Empire and, 4674
in politics, 4680
as second largest religion, 4563
settlement and organization of Muslim communities in, 4676–4680
Shiism, 4678, 4681
Sufism, 4681
Sunnī Islam, 4678, 4681
Jewish studies in, 4882–4884
Judaism (*See also* Ashkenazic Hasidism; Sephardic Judaism)
during the Enlightenment, 7581
Karaite sect, 5084
rabbinate in, 7581
Reform Judaism, 7666–7670
ritual in, 4984
tekhines in, 9036–9038
kingship in, models of, 5157
kinship in, 5183
labyrinths in, 5275
magic in, **5577–5583**
medieval (*See also* Middle Ages)
laws in, **5336–5339**
orgy in, **6869–6877**
witchcraft in, spells in, 8677
missionaries from (*See* Missions)
Mongolian invasion of, 4493, 4673
Neolithic religion in, 6459, 6460
new religious movements, **6566–6572**
Old religion, Slavic religion and, 8432
oral tradition of, 6842–6843
orgy in, **6869–6877**
paganism in, history of, 6567
politics of, Crusades, effect of, 2077
popular culture criticism in, 7321, 7322
prehistoric (*See* Prehistoric religions, in Old Europe)
Protestantism, 7447
decline of, 7459
psychology of religion in, 7473–7475
racism in, and nature religions, 2663
Reformation in (*See* Reformation)
religious broadcasting in, 7713–7714
Renaissance in (*See* Renaissance)
sacred geography of, 3434, 3435–3436
secret societies in, 7719
Slavic invasions, 1682
spiritism in, 8715, 8716
Spiritualism in, 8716
Transcendental Meditation in, 9290
witchcraft in, 9770–9773
European Union (EU)
bioethics in, 942
establishment of, Christianity, effect on, 1686
Eurydice (deity), vol. 2 color insert
Eurystheus (deity), Herakles and, 3916
Eurythmy, Steiner (Rudolf) and, 2160
Eusebius (bishop of Caesarea), **2884–2885**
on Andrew in Scythia, 1682, 4038
on Armenia, 487
Basil of Caesarea ordained by, 797
on Baubo, 803
on Canaanite religion, 1380–1381
on Christian persecution, 7059
chronological tables of, 4028
on church history, 4029
on Constantine, 1771
on heretics, 3926
on historiography, 4054
letter of Serapion of Antioch quoted in, 2381
on Luke, 5530
on Matthew the Evangelist, 5780
on Moabite religion, 6094
on Montanism, 6167, 6168, 6169
on Pan, 6958
on persecution in Gaul, 1688
on Phoenician religion, 7131
on rivers, 7862
theology of, 9134
on theurgy, 9157
on wisdom, 5502
Eusebius Hieronymous. *See* Jerome
Eustathius (Astat), 2971
on asceticism, 7723

Eustathius (Astat) ***continued***
Eusebius and, 2885
on sacred circles, 1791
Eustochius, 6474
Euthanasia, 5813
early court cases on, 5810
Euthydemus (Plato), 2273
Euthymius the Great (monk), retreats of, 7771
Eutyches (monk), 2583, 2584, **2885–2886**
Ethiopian Church and, 2859
Eutychianism, Athanasian Creed against, 2057
Evagrianists. *See* Origenists
Evagrios (Evagrius) of Pontus, 2829, **2886,** 5413
Makarios of Egypt and, 5624
on mystical union, 6336–6337
Evangelical Adventist Church, Millerite movement and, 8235
Evangelical Alliance, Spurgeon (Charles Haddon) and, 8727
Evangelical Christianity, **2887–2894**. *See also* Holiness movement
Aboriginal, 677–678
in Africa, South African politics and, 1724
Anglican, 352
in Australia and New Zealand, 1735
in Canada, moral crusades and, 1710
in Caribbean, creolization and, 2067
charismatic influence on, 2893
confessions of faith in, 2058
conversion testimonies in, 1971
definition of, 2887
dramatic worship in, 2473
ecological theory of, 2650
emergence of, 2887–2888
in England, Spurgeon (Charles Haddon), role of, 8727
vs. fundamentalism, 2890
in Garifuna religion, 3286
internationalization of, 2891
Lutheranism, in Finland, 3103
media used in, 5806
men's movements in, 5862–5863
in Mesoamerica, 3414
missions and, in Papua New Guinea, 1741
postdenominational consciousness in, 1775
premillenarianism in, 4055
public activism, 1755
religious broadcasting and, 7710–7711, 7715
religious experience in, 7737
Salvation Army, role of, **8063–8064**
in South America
in Amazon, Baniwa Indians and, 8625
in Andes, 8620
in United States
differences within, 2891
moral crusades and, 1710–1711
Republican Party and, 7713, 7714
Whitefield (George) in, 9726–9727
women and, 1755
Evangelical Confraternity of Latin America (CONELA), 1704
Evangelical Council for Financial Accountability, 7712
Evangelical Lutheran Church of America (ELCA), full communion agreements with other denominations, 1769
Evangelical Marian Sisterhood of Germany, 6765
Evangelical separation, as curse, 2105
Evangelical United Brethren (Methodist church), 5999
Evangelism
advertisement as form of, vol. 7 color insert
in Baptist churches, 785
by Churches of Christ, 1780
Holiness movement and
camp meetings in, 4083
Smith (Hannah Whitall) and, 8446
in Japanese Shintō, *kyōdōshoku* (national evangelists) in, 8366–8367
by Jehovah's Witnesses, 4821
of Quakers, 7548
by Salvation Army, 8063
in Seventh-day Adventism, 8236
in Swedenborgianism, 8905
on television, 5806
Evangelization. *See* Missions
Evans, Arthur, **2894–2895**
on Minoan religion, 37, 38, 40, 5275
Evans, Donald, 307
Evans, Gertrude, 1473
Evans, Susan, 2465
Evans, Warren Felt, Mind Cure (New Thought) movement and, 6583
mesmerism and, 3850
Evans-Pritchard, E. E., **2895–2896**
on African religions, 115, 116–117
kingship in, 5169
Festschrift dedicated to, 3041
historical revaluation by, 380
on left and right symbolism, 5393
on magic, 5563, 5567, 5571
and masks, 5769
methodological critique of, 379
on Nuer religion, 115, 3573–3574, 7443, 7844
on Nuer salutations, 8061–8062
on primitive religions, anthropologists' focus on, 363
on regicide, 5158–5159
on religious communities, 7717
on sacrifice, 8003
theory, distrust of, 4061
on witchcraft, 9777–9778, 9779
Evans-Wentz, Walter Y., 1313
Evara, 6796
Eve, **2896–2897**
as androgyne, 338
in ballet, 2163
expulsion of, 2938
French feminists on, 3029, 3030
in Garden of Eden, 2967, 6982
and gender in Christianity, 3358
in Manichaeism, 2967, 5654, 5667
marriage of, 5724, 5727
Mary as new, 3358, 5753
feminist critique of, 5755
Sistine Chapel and, 8755
monkeys and, 6150, 6151
as mythic ancestor, 325
nudity of, 6741
Nuwaubians on, 6769
sin of (*See also* Fall)
androcentrism in, 335
childbirth pain as punishment for, 6982
temptation and, 9069, 9071
women's subordination as punishment for, 3252, 6982
in Sistine Chapel, 8755
two-seed theory and, 1658
'Eved 'ivri (male slave), 4731
'Even ha-melekh (royal weight), 929
Even ha-shetiyyah (foundation stone), 924
Evenki religion (Siberia), 468. *See also* Shamanism; Siberia and Siberian religions; Tunguz religion
bear myths of, 9394–9395
ceremonies of, 9395
Feast of the Bear in, 8670
shamanism in, 2619
ancestor spirits in, 8284
clan shamanism in, 8282
inheritance of, 8283
Eveny people (Arctic), 468. *See also* Southern Siberian religions; Tunguz religion
Everard, John
on Hermetism, 3949, 3952
quoted by Emerson, 3951
Everlasting, *vs.* eternal, 2853, 2855
Everybody's Story: Wising up to the Epic of Evolution (Rue), 2666
Everyman (medieval drama), 2437
Evgeny Onegin (Pushkin), 3053
Evidential research, *kaozheng* school of, Dai Zhen and, 2129–2130
Evidentials, 2486
Evil, **2897–2904**. *See also* Sin; Theodicy
African concepts of, 90
in central Bantu religion, 1506
in East African religions, 2569–2570
in Hyakyusa religion, 6772
in Lugbara religion, 5528
in Lumpa church movement, 5409
in new religious movements, 102
witchcraft as source of, 8659–8660
in Ainu religion, 206
in Amazonian religions, in Baniwa belief, 8624–8625
animals as, wild, 360
Augustine on, 626, 3205–3206, 3645
Babylonian explanations for, 2962
Basil of Caesarea on, 8406
in Chinese philosophy, Dai on, 1579
in Christianity
in Christian Science, 1746
Cyprian on, 2113
Leibniz (Gottfried) on, 5407
Lonergan (Bernard) on, 5510
defense of God's omnipotence in view of (*See* Theodicy)
empirical form of problem of, 7124, 7125
explanations for
defilement as cause of, 8403
in Hebrew scripture, 8404
individual life as root of, 8403
in Mesopotamian religion, 8403
in the Fall, 2960, 2968
Fox (George) on, 3180
frog associated with, 3223
good and (*See also* Dualism; Twins)
in Catharism, 1456–1457
in Christianity, 3636
in cosmic dualism, 2509
in dialectical dualism, 2508
Hobbes (Thomas) on, 4074
in Islam, 4567, 4570, 8817
in Sufism, 8817
grace and, 3645, 3647
Greek explanations for, 2965
insects as, 4508
in Islam, 4567, 4570
lack of belief as root of, 8808
Mu'tazilah on, 5063

Sufism, 8817
in Israelite religion, human propensity toward, 4744
in Japanese religions, *kami,* 5071
in Judaism (*See also* Holocaust, the)
in Ashkenazic Hasidism, 542, 543
existence of, 4992–4993
God in, 3552
in Hasidism, 3789
Hester panim (hiding the face of God) doctrine and, 4090
in Qabbalah, 6354
in Shabbateanism, 3789
in Korean philosophy, Neo-Confucianism and, 1931
in lamentation, 2897
latent, purgation rites and, 8209
in Manichaeism, 5664
Mengzi on, 1572
in Micronesian religions, 6003
in monotheism, 6158–6159
moral, 2897, 9114
myths of, 2897–2903
natural, 9114
Neoplatonism on, 7190
neurotheology on, 6493
in Orphism, 8405
physical, 2897
protection against, vol. 9 color insert
in Samoyed religion, 8095
Satan associated with, 8123, 8124, 8125
Soloveitchik (Joseph Baer) on, 8519
Solov'ev (Vladimir) on power of, 8520
of sorcery, 90
Spinoza (Barukh) on, 9112
in Stoicism, 8742
trees averting, 9334
typologies of, 2898–2903
warding of
apotropaic hand gestures, 3770
salt for, 8059
of witchcraft, 90
in Zoroastrianism, 203–204, 7778, 9936
Evil and the God of Love (Hick), 9117
Evil eye, 2941–2942
disease caused by, 3809–3810
in East Asia, 5588
in Eastern Europe, incantations against, 5582
in folk Judaism, 3159
protection against, vol. 3 color insert, vol. 9 color insert
in Islam
protection against, vol. 9 color insert
white magic and, 5587
Mesopotamian spells against, 8676
in Middle Eastern popular practice, 3837
Evocatio, 7904, 7911
Evola, Julius, **2904–2907**
Group of Ur and, 8252
Evolution: The Modern Synthesis (Huxley), 2909
Evolution and evolutionary theory, **2907–2920**. *See also* Creationism; Intelligent Design
Adventist rejection of, 8236
African religions in, 113–115
in animism, 362–367
in anthropology, 8485
methodological critique of, 379
Schmidt (Wilhelm) on, 8168
in archaeology, 453–454
of brain, shamanism and, 8279
Breuil (Henri) on, 1048
and Christianity, Teilhard de Chardin on, 9032, 9033
classification of religions and, 1818–1819, 1821
comparative-historical method and, 1870, 5261
and conscience, evolution of, 1944
history of religions approach and, 4064–4065
Schmidt (Wilhelm), argument from, 8876
consciousness, evolutionary model of, 1949
Steiner (Rudolf) on Christ's role in, 8738
vs. creationism, **2907–2913**
on cursing, 2098–2099
Darwinian model of, 2908
Darwinism and religion, **8477–8480**
and decline of "two books" metaphor, 9423
and dynamism, 2540, 2541, 2543
and Esotericism, 6498
in ethology of religion, 2867–2870
evolutionary ethics, 2917–2920
land ethic and, 2656
evolutionism, **2913–2917**
influences on, 2913–2914
of Jevons (F. B.), 4854
Parsons (Talcott) on, 8495
in sociology, 8494
Tylor (E. B.) in, 2914–2915
fundamentalism *vs.,* 2889–2890
Gaia hypothesis of, **3253–3255**
games in, 3266–3267
gene-culture coevolution, 8475
genetic engineering and, "playing God" problem and, 8187
goddess worship in, 3611–3612
Gurdjieff (G. I.) on, 3711
Herder (Johann Gottfried) on, 3919
intelligent design challenging, 4516, 4518
liturgy in, 5490
magic in, 5563–5565, 5571–5572
Malinowski (Bronislaw) on, 5628–5629
masks in, 5764–5765
Müller (F. Max) on, 6235–6236
and myth, study of, 6367
Myth and Ritual school against, 6380, 6382
nature religions influenced by, 2662, 2664
neo-Darwinian theory, 8189
in New Age spirituality, 8186
Nilsson (Martin P.) on, 6622
psychology, evolutionary, 8475–8479
religion and, 2660
and field of science and religion, 8184, 8185–8186, 8189–8190
five positions in, 8189–8190
gradual disappearance of religion, 5325
ritual and religion in, 7850
secularization and, 8216–8217
selfish gene thesis, 8474
social evolution and religious studies, 1872
sociobiology, 8473–8475, 10043
in sociology, 8485
Spencer (Herbert) on, 8466, 8678, 8679
on supreme beings, 8875–8876
syncretism and, 8929
teleological, 9143
theism challenged by, 3558
theism influenced by, 9105
theistic evolution, 2912, 8190
theology and, 2909–2910
totemism in, 9250, 9251–9252
Tylor (E. B.) on, 9424–9425, 10077
Evolutionary ecology, development of, 2608–2609
Evolutionary psychology. *See* Sociobiology and evolutionary psychology
L'évolution créatrice (Bergson), 838, 9032
Evolution of the Idea of God, The (Allen), 5673
Ewen, Stuart, 7321
Ewe religion. *See* Fon and Ewe religion
EWF. *See* Ethiopian World Federation
Exaplōsis epiphaneias sphairas (Ptolemy), 7492
Excalibur (sword), 9686
Excarnation, in megalithic religion, 5825
Excavation, archaeological
Wheeler-Kenyon method of, 5111
Wheeler method of, 5111
"Excavation at Santa Barbara Mission" (Rose), 7226
Excellent Refutation of the Divinity of Jesus Christ (al-Ghazālī), 7242
Exchange. *See also* Gift giving
marriage as system of, 5725
religion as, 10082, 10085–10086
Exchange obligations. *See* Reciprocity
Exclusivism, in soteriology, 8528
Excommunicamus (Gregory IX), 4499
Excommunication, **2920–2921**. *See also* Expulsion; Shunning
as curse, 2105
for heresy, 3927
Jewish, of Spinoza (Baruch), 8681
of Luther (Martin), 5536
Protestant versions of, 2105
Execration Texts (Egypt), 2713
Execution. *See* Death penalty
Exegesis. *See also* Hermeneutics
biblical (*See* Biblical exegesis)
Buddhist, **1268–1278**
Abhidharma as, 1270, 10022
of canon, 1269
categories of, 1271–1272
commentaries and treatises, 1271
of Kuiji, 5258
Mahāyāna, 1270–1271
non-Mahāyāna, 1270
in Gnosticism, Culianu (Ioan Petru) on types of, 2080
in Judaism
on Mishna, 7586
of Rashi, 7619–7620
of Qur'ān (*See Tafsīr*)
Schleiermacher (Friedrich) on, 8164
Exegesis (movement), 6567
Exemplary prophet, 5384
Exhortation to Martyrdom (Origen), 6888
Exhortation to the Heathen (Clement of Alexandria), 4357–4358

Exile, **2922–2924,** 2938
in epics, 2816
voluntary, 2938
Zionism and, 9979–9980
Existence. *See also* Being
definition of, 2925–2926
of God (*See* Proofs for the existence of God)
Heidegger (Martin) on, 3896, 3934
human, Kierkegaard's stages of, 5142
Hypostasis (Greek concept), **4239–4243**
Indian thinking about, *avidyā* in, 710–711
pain in, in Yoga, 9894
planes of, in Amazonian Quechua religions, 283–284
rationalization of, orgy in, 6861
sole reality of, Mullā Ṣadrā on, 6231–6233
Sundén (Hjalmar) on, 8851
transcendence and, 4814–4815
Existentialism, **2924–2927**
atheistic, 7111
Sartre (Jean-Paul) on, 8116
in Buddhism, 2627
Bultmann (Rudolf) and, 1322
Fackenheim (Emil) and, 2950
Gnosticism and, 4948–4949
in hermeneutics of Jonas (Hans), 4061
hope in, 4127
Jaspers (Karl) in, 4814
Judaism and, 4904–4906
Kierkegaard's influence on, 5142
Maritain (Jacques) on, 5713
and neoorthodoxy, 6468
Nietzsche and, 6616
nihilistic elements of, 2428
Otto (Rudolf), influence of, 4101
Sartre (Jean-Paul) on, 8116
soteriology in, 8527
theistic, 7111
Existentialism and Humanism (Sartre), atheism in, 8116
Existential psychology, 7476–7477
Exit counseling, 6562
in Europe, 6569
Exocannibalism
endocannibalism *vs.*, 1402
in South America, 1403
Exodus, 878. *See also* Moses
Aaron in, 1
Abraham in, 15
and Adonis, 34
Athirat (Asherah) in, 590
blasphemy in, 969, 971
blood in, 987
canonizing process in, 882
condemnation of idolatry in, 4358
content of, 9232
divine kingship in, 5148
God in
names of, 3539
origins of worship of, 3539
golden calf, 1466
historicity of, 6199
Ibn Ḥazm on, 7237
Ibn Kaspi (Yosef) on, 867
laws in, 4728, 4729
asylum, 4728–4729
dietary laws, 7508
family law, 4733
al-Maghribī (Samuel) on, 7239
midrashim on, 6018
Miriam in, 6062
Moses in, 6200–6201, 9232
Myth and Ritual school on, 6381
pesher of, 7064
referenced in *Wisdom of Solomon,* 9757
in Samaritan Bible, 8070
story of, in *Matthew,* 907
Temple procedures in, 926, 930, 933
Ten Commandments in, 9074
in Torah, 9231, 9232
unleavened bread in, 5388
victory hymn in, 7460, 7462
violent images of divinity in, 6647
Exogamy, 8948
definition of, 5725–5726
revenge and, 7779, 7781
Exorcism, **2927–2938**
aims of, 8687
in Buddhism, 9837–9838
Sinhala Buddhism, 7197
Thai Buddhism, 2315
in Christianity, 2315, **2928–2931**
miracles of, 6053–6054, 6056
necromancy and, 2279
Vatican II on, 2280
comedy of, 8692
dance and, 2140
demands of the spirit in, 8692–8693
as expulsion, 2939
glossolalia in, 3507
healing through, 3814
in Hinduism, in devotional life, 9825–9826
of homes, 4105
in Judaism, 2534
in Mesoamerican religion, 1470
in Mesopotamian religions
ashipu (exorcist) as healer, 3824–3825
ouroboros serpent used for, 1793–1794
ordination for, 2929
permanent *vs.* transformational, 8688, 8691
salt in, 8059
scholarly interpretations of, 2935–2936
social function of, 8692
spirit-host relationship and, 8692
spirit possession and, 8691–8693
by spitting, 8722
in Sri Lanka, 7836, 8690
techniques of, 8691–8692
zār ceremony for, 2148–2149
Exorcist, The (Blatty), 2931, 2939
Expansionism, Orthodoxy and, 6904–6905
Experience. *See* Religious experience
Experiential wisdom, 9755
Experimentalism, on mysticism, 6357
Experimental psychology, 7473–7474, 9847
Experts, Hijiri (Japanese lay ascetics) as, 3978
Expiation
distinction from liberation, 5435–5436
sacrifices of, 8001, 8006
Explanation
Dilthey (Wilhelm) on, 3932
wisdom and, 2903–2904
witchcraft as, 9769–9770, 9777
Exploitation, Buddhism and, 2630
Exposition of the Law (Philo Judaeus), 16
Exposition of the Methods of Proof (Ibn Rushd). *See Kashf, al-* (Ibn Rushd)
Exposition on the Psalms (Augustine), 4363
Expressionism, drama in, 2475, 2476
Expression of the Emotions in Man and Animals, The (Darwin), 2867
Expressive behavior, 2867–2868
Expressivism, of Smith (Wilfred Cantwell), 8450
Expulsion, **2938–2940**. *See also* Excommunication; Shunning
Expurgation, 2939–2940
Exsecrabilis (1460) (bull), 6972
Exsuperius (bishop), 4495
Exsurge Domine (papal bull), publicity of, 2601
Extension, as attribute of God, Spinoza (Baruch) on, 8684
Exteriorization, in Scientology, 8192
Extispicy (divination with animal entrails)
in Canaanite religion, 1387
Dagan and, 2126
in Greek religion, 4108
in Mesopotamian religion, 8838
in Southeast Asian religions, traditional, 8650
Extraction of essences (yogic practice), 1288
Extrareligious explanations, 1870
Extrasensory perception (ESP), 6057
Extraterrestrial intelligence, 4516
Extraterrestrials, worship of. *See* UFO religions
Extreme unction
cognates of, in comparative studies, 7956
medieval practices, 7961
as sacrament, 1670
Extremism. *See also* Fundamentalism
Islamic, origins of, 225
Exú (spirits), 122
Exultet (poem), 2579
Eye, **2940–2943**. *See also* Evil eye; Tears; Third eye
of Óðinn, 6808
Eye goddess, in megalithic religion, 5824–5825
Eye Goddess, The (Crawford), 5824
Eylot, Sir Thomas, on dance, 2154
Eymeric, Nicolas, 4499
Eyn Gor Sheyne Tkhine (tekhine collection), 9037
Eyrbyggja saga, Christian worldview in, 8024
Eyre, Edward John, 3390
Eyvindr the Plagiarist, 3457
Ezekiel (biblical book), 879
apocalyptic writings in, 4749
divine man in, 3508, 3509
hieros gamos (sacred marriage) opposed in, 3976
Levites in, 5422, 5426
merkavah in, 10050, 10051
messianism in, 5975
pesher of, 7064
priesthood in, 7399
property law in, 4735
purity in, 7513, 7514
resurrection in, 7764
in Shavu'ot liturgy, 8306
siege of Tyre in, 7128
Spinoza (Baruch) on, 8683
structure of, 2943
Tammuz in, 2521
Temple procedures in, 924, 926, 928, 929, 935
Ezekiel (Hebrew prophet), **2943–2946**
on altars, 276
on exile, 2922
prophecy of, 2943–2945
prophetic actions of, 7432
sun idolatry and, 2662
vision of river, 7862
vision of Yahveh's regenerated Temple, 3177–3178, 5424
Ezen (masters), 1325
Ezengi (spirit), 7523, 7524
Ezili (spirit), in Caribbean neo-African cults, 1433
Ezili Danto (Our Lady of Mount Carmel), in Vodou, 9638
Ezili-Freda-Dahomey (sea spirit)
description of, 8690
possession by, 8692
Ezinu (deity), in divine bureaucracy, 5951
EZLN. *See* Zapatista Army of National Liberation

Ezra, 882, 898
Asaph in, 7461
chanting psalms in, 7463
David in, 7461
Koraḥ in, 7461
priests in, 5423
purity in, 7514
Temple procedures in, 924–925, 928, 930, 933
2 Ezra, 898, 900
priests in, 5422
4 Ezra, 902
as apocalypse, 418
resurrection in, 7765
Ezra (Hebrew prophet), **2946–2947,** 6911
commission of, 883
Ibn Ḥazm on, 7238
al-Maghribī (Samuel) on, 7239
relationship to Nehemiah, 6457
Ezra, Apocalypse of, 2947
ʾEzra of Gerona, on mystical union, 6339–6340
Ezra the Scribe, 1532

F

Fabian, Johannes
on ethnocentrism, 7992
on revival and renewal activities, 7788–7789
Fabian (pope), execution of, 7059
Fabian Society, 844
Fabiola, hospital in Rome founded by, 3844
Fabius Pictor (Roman author), 7899, 7900
Fable, A (Faulkner), 5480
Fables, in typology of narratives, 6376–6377
Fabré-Palaprat, Bernard-Raymond, 9067
Fabric. *See* Textiles
Fabricius, Johann Albrecht
on Hermetism, 3951
on Tamil religions, 8978
Face of God, *hester panim* (hiding of), Holocaust and, 4090
Face on the Moon, The (Plutarch), 7200, 7201
Face paintings, masks and, 5765, 5766
Faces of the Chariot, The (Halperin), 10052
Facing Mount Kenya (Kenyatta), 115
Fackenheim, Emil, **2949–2951,** 4985
on Holocaust as new revelation, 4092
Facsimile, cave art and, 1471
Facts
knowledge of
through experience, 2779–2780
verifiability of, 2780
news and, 4961, 4964–4965
in science *vs.* religion, 2658
Faḍāʾil al-Qurʾān (Abū ʿUbayd), 8952
Fa divination. *See* Ifa divination
Faerie Queene (Spenser), 7220
Faerose islanders, folklore of, 2951
Faery Witchcraft, 9730
Fáfnir (dragon), 2532
Fagan, Livingstone, 1038
Fagu, 6295, 8980, 8981
Faguo (Chinese monk), 8995
Fahai guanlan (Zhixu), 9180, 9181
Fa-Hsien. *See* Faxian
Fahua jing (Buddhist text), 9174, 9175
Fahua lunguan (Zhixu), 9179
"Failing Male God, The" (Casadio), 7201
FAIR. *See* Family Action Information and Rescue
Fairbairn, Ronald, 7478
Fairhair, Harald, 842
Fairies, **2951–2954**
in Celtic religion, in mythohistory, 1489
Fairservis, Walter A., 3439
Fairy rings, 2953
Fairy tales. *See also* Folklore
Freud on, 3216
quest motif in, 7554–7556
Russian, 3958
goats in, 8312
shape shifting in, 8302
winter carols and, 9745
Faisal, Shaykh Daoud Ahmed, 4687–4688, 4689
Faith, **2954–2959**. *See also* Belief; Doubt
abandonment of (*See* Apostasy)
Abraham and, 16
as act of will, 2425
Barth (Karl) on, 5208–5209
vs. belief, 2425–2427
Berger (Peter L.) on, 8498
Buber (Martin) on, 1057–1058
in Buddhism, Shinran on, in Pure Land school, 8354, 8355
Bultmann (Rudolf) on, 1322
Calvin on, 1375, 1376, 2426
in Christianity
Christianity as system of, 1666
in ecumenism, 2689
in *James,* 917
meanings of, 1666
in Roman Catholicism, 7882–7883
rule of, 874
as seal of election, 2748
Simons (Menno) on, 8401
Thomas Aquinas on, 2425, 5204–5205, 9163
community of, 2957
confessions of (*See* Confessions of faith)
as credo, 2958
as dependence, 2956
doubt as component of, 2428
as experience, 2956–2957
as faithfulness, 2955
healing through (*See* Faith healing)
Heschel (Abraham Joshua) on, 3962
Hugh of Saint-Victor on, 5204
in Islam
Abū Ḥanīfah on, 21–22
Ashʿarī and Ḥanbalī *vs.* Māturīdīyah and Ḥanafīyah views, 2064
basis of, 5204
in *Fiqh al-akbar,* 5062
in *Waṣīyah,* 5062
al-Māturidī on, 5781
Muḥammad on, 5062
Muʿtazilah on, 5063
suffering as test of, 8808, 8809
in Judaism, Naḥman of Bratslav on, 6401–6402
justification or salvation by, 5041
in Adventist theology, 8236
in Augsburg Confession, 2058
ethics and, 1655
Luther on, 1375, 1667, 5537
Kant (Immanuel) on, 5077, 5079
Kierkegaard on, 5141, 5142
and knowledge, 2426, 2958–2959
Locke (John), 2798, 5496
loss of, autobiographies on, 699
Newman (John Henry) on, 6511
Niebuhr (Reinhold) on, 6612, 6613
as obedience, 2955
paradox of, 6990–6991
and political activity, Niebuhr (Reinhold) on, 6613
vs. reason, Locke on, 2798
Sartre (Jean-Paul) on, 8116
Sharpe (Eric) on, 8305
skepticism and, 8421
Smith (Wilfred Cantwell) on, 8450, 8451
Sozzini (Fausto Pavolo) on, 8673
and tradition, 2958
as trust, 2956
truth of, 9375
Vatican I on, 9531
and works, 2955–2956
and worship, 2957–2958
Faith and Fratricide (Ruether), 2747
Faith and History, modern historiography in, 4032
Faith and Order Commission. *See* World Council of Churches
Faith and Values Media, 7714
Faith and Witness Program Unit (WCC), 2685
Faith communities. *See* Religious communities
Faithful Narrative, A (Edwards), 2699
Faith healing. *See also* Miracles
in Asklepios cult, 3904
in Islam, 3836
necromancy and, 6453
in Pentecostalism, 3847
television ministries and, 7712
Faithist movement, scripture for, 6531
Faith-Man-Nature group, 2610
Faith missions, 2893
Faith of Our Fathers (Gibbons), 3478
Faith schools, religious education in, 7733–7734
Faitlovich, Jacques (Yaʾcov), 5004
Faivre, Antoine, 3041
esotericism paradigm of, 2844–2845
on Western Esotericism, 6527
Fa jia. See Legalism, in Chinese philosophy
Fajie guanmen (Buddhist text), 2530
Fajie ziti chumen (Buddhist text), 9174
Fakhr al-Dawla, 4
Fakhr al-Dīn Zarrādī, 6639
Fál, 1488
Falacer (deity), priest of, 3126
Falaky, Joseph, 1498
Falang (Buddhist monk), 4926
Falaquera, Shem Ṭov ben Yosef ibn, 4266
in *Wissenschaft des Judentums,* 4877
Falardeau, Robert, 9068
Falāshā. *See* Bēta Esraʾēl
Falāsifah. See Falsafah
Falcons, 948
Horus as, 4136
Inca calendar and, 1364
in *maṇḍalas,* 5640
king symbolized by, in Egyptian religion, 2703
Fali people (Cameroon), myths of, 95, 98–99
cosmogony, 9699
the Flood, 3132
Falk, Nancy, 3313
Falkenhausen, Lothar von, 1637
Fall, the, **2959–2970**
androcentrism in, 335
anthropogonic perspective on, 2960
in archaic religions and oral traditions, 2960–2961
Calvin on, 1376

Fall, the ***continued***
in Catharism, 1457
celibacy as reversal of, 9607, 9608
in Chinese myth, 1625–1626
in Christianity, 2968
Augustine on, 8405
grace and, 3645
and history, view of, 4053
Irenaeus on, 8405
Origen on, 8405
cosmogonic perspective on, 2960
in Egyptian religion, 2959, 2961–2962
evil and, origin of, 2900–2901
explanations for, 30
as fate, 2960–2961
in Gnosticism, 2966, 3525
Heidegger (Martin) on, 8402
Herder (Johann Gottfried) on, 3919
in Indian religions, 2963–2964
in Iranian religions, 2964
in Islam, 2969
Jesus's ethics and, 4849–4850
in Judaism, 2967–2968, 5201
in literature, 5479
in Manichaeism, 2966–2967
in Mesopotamian religions, 2959, 2962–2963
as punishment, 2960
results for humanity, 30
in Sistine Chapel, 8755
sleep as Adam's first, 339, 340
temporal and historical conception of, 2959
temptation and, 9069, 9071
theogonic perspective on, 2959–2960
in Unificationist movement, 6530
in Unification theology, 9467
work associated with, 9797
Falla, Ricardo, 5929–5930
Falling stars, 8736
Fall of Jerusalem and the Christian Church, The (Brandon), 1040
Falloux law, 9442
Fāl-nāmas, divination in, 4761
Falsafah (Islamic philosophy), **2970–2978**
Aristotle and, 479
attributes of God in, 621
Corbin (Henry) on, 1984
ecology and, 2652–2653
al-Ghazālī on, 5204, 8815
Greek philosophy and, 2970–2971
Ibn Rushd defending, 4271, 5204
imaginal thinking in, 4552, 4553–4554
in Ash'arīyah, 533
Islamic studies on, 4717–4718
Neoplatonism, 7192–7193
on prophetic *vs.* philosophical truth, 6736
skepticism in, 8420–8421
soul in, 8566, 8569–8570
in Sunnism *vs.* Twelver Shiism, 8344
traditionalism *vs.* rationalism, Ḥanābilah and, 3760–3762
False banana, 2574
False Faces, 5767
False Face Society (Iroquois), 4542
False self, attentional exercises and, 606–607
Falun Dafa. *See* Falun Gong
Falun Gong, **2978–2981,** 6513, 7269–7270
components of, 7269
crackdown on, 1611
in Europe, 6568
ideology of brainwashing and, 2086
Li Hongzhi founding, 7269
in North America, 2980
origins of, 2979
persecution of, 2980–2981, 6518, 6549
practice of, 2980
principles of, 2979–2980
rapid growth of, 1638
suppression in China, 1034, 7270
teachings of, 7269
Falwell, Jerry, 7713, 7714
Familiars, in African witchcraft, 9776, 9777–9778
Family(ies), **2981–2987**. *See also* Ancestors; Kinship
affliction in, 58, 61
African concepts of, ancestors in, 143
ancestors as founders of, 326
and ancestor worship, 2982
Aristotle on, 486
children in, 2982–2983
in Chinese tradition, healing and, 3861–3862
in Christianity
gender and, 3357, 3361
Protestant, 7457
definition of, 2981–2982
in Eblaite religion, 2598
fathers in, 2984–2985
genealogy of (*See* Genealogy)
of Greek deities, 3678–3679
ḥokhmah and, 4078
home and, 4104
in Reiyūkai Kyōdan, 7862
in Islam
endowment for, 9677
ummah and, 9447
in Japan (*See also* Uji)
Kiki texts separate from, 4801
records of, 4802–4803
in Jehovah's Witnesses, 4823
of kings, 5155
marriage for continuation of, 5724–5725
in Mormonism, 6195
mothers in, 2983–2984
new religious movements and, 6562–6563
of Muḥammad (*See Ahl al-bayt*)
in Roman religion, cults of, 7908–7909
servants in, 2986
siblings in, 2985–2986
in Slavic religion, *domovoi* (family founder spirits), 4106
in Zoroastrianism, 10000
Family, the (Children of God), **2987–2989,** 6560
anticult movement against, 396
children in
abuse allegations, 6526, 6540–6541
disciplining of, 6540
homeschooling of, 6542
deprogramming members of, 2291, 4853
in Europe, 6568
free love practiced by, 2987–2988, 6548, 6560
gender roles in, 6516
in Jesus Movement, 4852–4853
Jesus People movement and, 6551
legal defense of, 5378
membership in, 6516
North American religious culture and, 1714
origins of, 6560
second-generation members in, 6538
tensions with society, 6548
world-rejecting orientation of, 6542
Family Action Information and Rescue (FAIR), 6569
Family guardian spirits
in Khanty religion, 5122
in Mansi religion, 5122
Family in Ancient Rome, The (Rawson), 3381
Family law, Muslim. *See* Islamic law
Fanā' (annihilation), 956, 4259, 4569, 5030
Abū Yazīd al-Bisṭāmī on, 8812
'Aṭṭār on, 8818
in mystical union, 6338
question of, 8812
Fanaticism, religious, morality and, 6178
Fanbei (music), 6294
Fane Kantsini (mythic figure), 5937
Fan Feizi (book), morality in, 1897
Fang La, 5669
Fang religion (Gabon)
creation myths in, 93
dances of, 2138
psychedelic drug use of, 7469–7470
souls in, 8532
Fang Shan stones, 1254
Fangshi, 2179, **2989–2991,** 7267
fiction composed by, 3066
Fangyan (Buddhist monk), 9179
Fang Yizhi, 1608
Fan Ning, 1899
Fanon, Frantz
on colonization and indigenous tradition, 1858
liberation theology and, 5438
postcolonial theory of, 10042
Fantasia, 9588
Fantasy literature, 3062
Gnosticism in, 3528
Fanti people (Ghana), spirit possession in, dance and, 2139–2140
Fanum Voltumnae, assembly of Etruscan government at, 5167
Fanwang precepts, Saichō on, 8030, 8031
Fan Xuanzhi (Buddhist monk), 2530
Fan Zhen, 1576
Fan Zhongyan, 1577
Fapudixin zhang (Fazang), 2530
Faqīh (jurisprudent)
in Almoravid dynasty, 4585
Ibn Tūmart challenging, 4585–4586
importance of, 4587
in development of *sharī'ah,* 4697–4698
Mālikī, 4584
polygamy supported by, 4700
power of, 4697
Salafīyah criticizing, 4590
Faqīr (Muhammadan poverty), 2220
Fārābī, Abū Naṣr al-, 2973, **2991–2992**
Aristotle and, 479
on attributes of God, 621
al-Ghazālī's critique of, 2975, 3470
Ibn Sīnā influenced by, 4273
on knowledge, 5203
Maimonides (Moses) influenced by, 5617
political theology of, 2973, 2975
on prophetic *vs.* philosophical knowledge, 6736
on soul, 8569
on wisdom, 7193
Faraday, Michael, chaos theory and, 1541
Faraguvaol (tree), in Island Arawak religion, 1427
Farah, Nuruddin, 3088
Farā'idī movement, 829, 4651
Farajaje-Jones, Elias, 79, 80
Faraji, Salim, 80
Farangī Mahal *(madrasah),* 4645
Farazdaq, al-, poems of, 3210
Fard, Wallace D.
aliases of, 72
Elijah Muhammad and, 2767
in Nation of Islam, 72, 6418, 6419, 6563
Fard Mohammed, Wali, 4688
Far East Broadcasting Company (FEBC), 7713
Farel, Guillaume, **2992–2993,** 7281

"Farewell Sermon" (Edwards), 2699
Farīd al-Dīn Janj-i Shakar, Bābā, shrine of, in Pakpattan, 1806
Fāriḍīyah, al- (Ṣūfī order), 4261
Farissol, Avraham, 7234
Farley, Edward
  on phenomenology, 4237
  on phenomenology of religion, 7087
Farmer, H. H., 7118
Farming. *See* Agriculture
Faro (deity), 98, 776, 3130
Farquar, John Nicol, Sharpe (Eric) on, 8304
Farquhar, J. N., 4447
Farrā', al-, 8952
Farrad, Walli. *See* Fard, Wallace D.
Farrakhan, Louis
  in Million Man March, 5863
  Nation of Islam under, 72, 4689, 6420, 6563
Farrar, Janet, 9729–9730
Farrar, Stewart, 9729–9730
Farrer, Austin, 5487
Farrington, Benjamin, on friendship, 3911
Farriss, Nancy, 5926
  on linear *vs.* cyclical time, 7992
Farrokhsi ritual, 9998
Faru (Buddhist scholar), 994
  and Chan school, establishment of, 1601
Fārūq (king of Egypt), 6315
Farvardigan holidays (Iran), 6731
Fas (permitted acts), *profanus vs.*, 7966
Fasalīs (Parsi community), 6998
Fasciano, Domenico, 3125, 3126
Fascinans, Gennep (Arnold van) on, 7349
Fascism
  de Martino (Ernesto) distancing himself from, 2266
  Evola (Julius) and, 2906
  in Romania, 2754
Fashun. *See* Dushun
Fasi, Isaac al-, 9236
Fāsid marriage (irregular marriage), 4706
Fāsiladas, 2860
Faṣl al-Maqāl (Ibn Rushd), 4271
Fasti, **2993–2995,** 7335
Fasting, **2995–2998,** 3171–3172
  in Agami Jawi, 4817
  in ancient cultures, 2995
  in Armenian church, 489
  in asceticism, 526, 2996, 2997, 3171–3172
    objectives of, 528
  in Aztec religion, human sacrifice and, 4189
  in Buddhism, 2996, 2997
    Tibetan, 9840
  in Christianity, 2996
    in Holy Week, 1742
    in Lent, 1743, 7771, 9814–9815
    in liturgical week, 9813
    at Pentecost, 1742
    as purification, 7508
  in Confucianism and Daoism, 2996
    for *jiao,* 4916
  as devotion, 2320
  in East African religions
    Amhara-Tigriña, 2573
    Qemant, 2573
  in Greek religion, 2995
  in Hinduism, 2403, 3172
    for pilgrimage, 7169
  in Islam, 2996, 2997, 3171
    in devotional life, 9817
    on 'Āshūrā', 549
    during retreats, 7770
    ṣawm, **8140–8141**
    slave practices of, 4682
  in Jainism, 4769
  in Judaism
    days of, 4867–4868
    Marrano, 5718
    on Yom Kippur, 7928
  monasticism and, 2997, 3171–3172
  as mortification, 6197
  in mortification rites, 8208
  in North American Indian religions
    Sun Dance and, 8845
    in vision quest, 9609, 9610
  as penance or purification, 2996–2997
  preparatory, 2995–2996
  in purification, 7508
  in retreats
    for revelatory dreams, 7769
    for spiritual renewal, 7770
    for tribal initiation, 7769
  in Sufism, during retreats, 7770
  as supplication, 2997
  in vision inducement, 9613
  in Yoga, objectives of, 528
Fast of the Firstborn, 4867–4868
Fatalism
  in Baltic religion, 5286
  in Chinese religion, 3004
  definition of, 2998
  divine providence leading to, 7791
  examples of, 2998–2999
  Malay-Indonesian sense of, 3214
  Mozi on, 1571, 6218
  Wang on, 1575
Fatāwā Jahāndārī (al-Baranī), 4643
Fate, **2998–3006**
  in *Aeneid,* 9583
  ambiguity in definition of, 2998, 3000
  ancient and classical concerns with, 3000–3003
  in Australian Indigenous myths, 656–658
  chance and, 1529
  earliest expression in agricultural cultures, 2999
  element of mystery in, 2998
  the Fall as, 2960–2961
  in Greek religion, 8405
  in Hittite religion, 4070
  in Ājīvikas doctrine, 213
  in Islam, 3002, 3003, 3201, 3209
  and mysticism, 3003
  as origin of evil, 2901
  vs. predestination, 3202
  psychological observations on, 2998–2999
  spread of ideas about, 3004–3005
  in Stoicism, 8741–8742
  Sundén (Hjalmar) on, 8851
  tenacity of notions of, 3005
Fate goddesses
  Dēkla as, 769
  Kārta as, 760, 769
  Laima as, 760, 769, 5285–5286
  lunar, 3018
  in Slavic religion, 8436–8437
Fates, the. *See also* Moirai
  in eastern European magic, 5581
Father(s), 2984–2985
  archetypal, Campbell (Joseph) on hero myths and, 3958
  Caribbean *couvade* ritual, 1430
  in Christian Trinity
    Edwards (Jonathan) on, 2700
    in Orthodox theology, 2589–2590
    in Protestantism, 7450
  couvade and, **2046–2047**
  Freud (Sigmund) on, 2238–2239
  God as, in New Testament, 3544, 6407
  in North American Indian religions, Hako ceremony, 6704
  Orthodox Christian, 2593–2594
  primeval, 3015
  in Trobriand Islanders religion, 5184
Father David. *See* Berg, David Brandt
Father Divine, 69, **3006–3007,** 6563
  Daddy Grace and, 2124, 2125
  Jones (Jim) and, 4952, 4954
Father Kosmas. *See* Kosmas Aitolos
Father legends, 6376
Father of Greatness, in Manichaeism, 5654, 5666, 5667
Father Sergii (Tolstoy), 9221
Father Sun (deity), in Huichol religion, 4152
Father Tantras, 1215, 1218
Faṭḥīyah Shiism, schism from Imāmīyah, 8322
Fatihah (Qur'anic verse), recitation of, for remembrance of deceased, 7572
Fatima (Ibn al-'Arabī's wife), 4257
Fatima, hand of. *See* Hand of Faṭimah talisman
Fatima bint Ibn al-Muthanna, 4257
Fāṭimah bint Asad, 256
Fāṭimah bint Muḥammad, **3008–3009**
  Abū Bakr's disagreement with, 257
  as *ahl al-bayt,* 198
  as 'Alī's wife, 256
  cult of, 3008–3009
  mawlid of, 5788
Faṭima of Nīshāpūt, 955
Fāṭimid dynasty
  and Aghlabid dynasty, 4582
  al-Azhar under, 230
  as caliphate, 1366
  Coptic Church and, 1981
  Druze in, 2503
  fall of, 4395
  history of, *Qāḍī al-Nu'mān* on, 7541
  Ismā'īlīyah and, 8324, 8329–8331
  Karaite sect and, 5083
  mawlids in, 5788
  Maymūnīyah movement and, 8327
  Nāṣir-i Khusraw in, 6417
  political power of, 4562
  and Qarāmiṭah communities and, 7543
  Syriac Orthodox Church and, 8939
  victory of, 4583
Fa-tsang. *See* Fazang
Fatum (destiny), in Etruscan religion, 2873
Fatwā
  casuistry, 1454
  muftī issuing, 4697
  of bin Lādin (Usāmah), 6099–6100
  against Rushdie (Salman), 434
  by shaykh al-Islam, 8306
Fauconnet, Paul, 5785
Faulkner, William, 5480
Fauna. *See* Bona Dea
Fauna (deity), 7900
Faunus (deity), 6957, 7900
Faure, Bernard, 3346, 7084
Fauset, Arthur Huff, 74, 6521
Faust (Goethe), 2474
  Gnosticism and, 3514, 3525

Faust (legendary hero), **3009–3010**
historical personage of, 3009
literary treatment of, 3009–3010
origin of legend of, 3009
Renaissance magic and, 5580
Faustus (Manichaean bishop), Augustine and, 624, 5665
Faustus of Riez, as follower of Pelagius, 7026
Fawā'iḥ al-jalāl wa fawāitḥ al-jamāl (Kubrā), 5257
Faxian (Buddhist monk), 1305, 1310, 1577, **3010–3011,** 4490, 7163–7164
on relics of Buddha, 7691
Faxiang school of Buddhism, 1202, 1238, 2337, 2338. *See also* Yogācāra school
Dasheng qixin lun text, 1576
emptiness *(śūnyatā)* in, 8858–8859
founding of, 1577, 5258
Kuiji and, 5258
in Tang dynasty, 1599–1600
Fayan lineage, 1523
Faye, Eugène de, 3532
Fayyūmī, Sa'adyah ben Joseph al-. *See* Sa'adyah Gaon
Fazang (Buddhist monk), 1238, 1302, 2530, **3012–3013,** 6631
Huayan Buddhism and, 1600, 4146
FBI. *See* Federal Bureau of Investigation
FCC. *See* Federal Communications Commission
Fear
deities of, in Dinka religion, 2568
and iconoclasm, 4280
of masks, in women, 5770
and religion, 2998, 2999
Spinoza (Baruch) on, 8683
Fear and Trembling (Kierkegaard), 2425–2426
Feasting. *See* Banqueting
Feasts. *See also* Banqueting; Festivals; *specific feasts*
in ancestor worship, 322–323, 329–331
in Armenian religion, 489, 492
in Chinese religion, sacrifice to Shangdi, 1914
concept of, Carnival and, 1440
Egyptian, 2715
jubilation rites and, 8210
orgiastic, 8247
orgies at, 6863
in Roman religion, for Mars, 5728
timing of, agriculture and, 186–188
Feather gods (wicker images), in rites to Kū gods, 3798
Feathers, in Hopi religion, 6726
FEBC. *See* Far East Broadcasting Company
Febronia (martyr), 6742
Febronianism, 6973
Feces, and pollution, 7504
Fechner, Gustav Theodor
on consciousness, 1947
on contingency in God, 6963
on nature, 6435
Fecundity. *See also* Fertility
of God, Hildegard of Bingen on, 3980
masculine sacrality in, 5761–5762
Fedeli d'Amore, transcendence of sexuality in, 8248
Federal Bureau of Investigation (FBI), and Branch Davidians siege, 1037–1038, 5237, 6554, 7255
Federal Communications Commission (FCC), 7711
Federal Council of Churches, 2684, 7711
Federal Radio Commission (FRC), 7710
Féderation Européene des Centres de Recherche et d'Information sur le Sectarisme (FECRIS), 6569
Federation of American Zionists, Szold (Henrietta) and, 8941
Federation of Reconstructionist Congregations and Havurot (FRCH), 7637, 7638
Federation of University Women, 840
Fedor (tsar of Russia), 6622
Feeblemindedness, eugenics and, 2879–2880
Feeding funnel *(koropata),* in Maori religion, vol. 13 color insert
Feeling
aesthetics and, 46, 48, 494
in art, 494
in liberal Protestantism, 6103
religious
Otto (Rudolf) on the holy as, 4096–4097
Schleiermacher (Friedrich) on, 8165, 8493
Sundén (Hjalmar) on, 8851
Feet
in Buddhism
replicas of, 9830
respect and, 9830
right *vs.* left, preference for, 5393
symbolism of, **3013**
washing of
by Jesus, as hospitality, 4139
ritual of, 3013
Fei, Prince, on morality, 1897
Feigel, Friedrich Karl, on sacred as *a priori* category, 7976
Feil, Ernst, on religion, 7702
Fei Ming, 3070
Feinstein, David, 3013
Feinstein, Moshe, **3013–3014,** 6905
Feis Temhra (Feast of Tara), 1492
Féjérvary-Mayer Codex, space-time symbols in, 1356
Feld, Elliot, 2164
Feld, Steven, 146
Felder, Cain Hope, 80, 5441
Feldhaus, Anne, 3322–3323
Feldman, M. W., on fertility rates, 8475
Felicity, in Buddhism, 9832–9833
Felicity conditions, 980
Felix III (pope), 6967
Felix of Apthungi (cleric), 2416
Fell, Margaret, 3180, 3181
Fellata religion. *See* Fulbe religion
Fellman, Jacob, 5284
Fellowship
in Orthodox Church, 2591
Spener (Philipp Jakob) on, 8680
Fellowship movements, pietistic, revival of, Smith (Hannah Whitall) and, 8446
Fellowship of Christian Unions (FOCUS), 106
Fellowship of Reconciliation, 6648
Female Eunuch, The (Greer), 3310–3311
Female Power and Male Dominance (Sanday), 3421
Female Spirit, in Oceanic religions, 3396–3397
Female Stereotypes in Religious Traditions (Kloppenborg and Hanegraaff), 3301
Feminine Mystique, The (Friedan), 3310
Feminine sacrality, **3014–3023**
contemporary, 3021–3022
in culture, 3018–3020
"female divine" in feminist theology, 4166
in feminist spirituality, 9788
and goddesses, nudity of, 3976
ḥokhmah and, 4078
in nature, 3014–3018
in women, 3020–3021
Feminism (women's movement), **3023–3031**. *See also* Feminist theology
in African religions, 3403–3404
on androcentrism, 3298–3299, 3313, 3719
anthropology and, 386
and art, study of, 502
in Australia and New Zealand, 1736
Berndt (Catherine) and, 840
Besant's (Annie), 844, 845
and biblical exegesis, 877
Stanton (Elizabeth Cady) and, 8731
biblical teachings and, 3297
black, 3311
on body symbolism, 4163–4164, 4166–4167, 4172
on *Book of Ruth,* 7948
in Christianity
on God, 3559
history of, 3301, 3311–3312
influence of, 3356
on patriarchy, 7008
potential for reform, 3301, 3312
vs. thealogy, 9099
conversion, feminist theory on, 1972
and drama, 2438–2439
ecological theology in, 2650
first wave of, 3024, 3297
and Hindu women, 3320
and folk religion, study of, 3147–3148
French, **3027–3031**
Gage (Matilda Joslyn) in, 3251–3252
gender in
concepts of, 3299, 3313
vs. sex, 3420
and gender studies, 3310–3313
development of, 3297–3298
on Goddess (*See* Thealogy)
on goddess worship, 3609, 3613, 3616–3617
goddess worship revival by, 3613–3614
in Grail movement, 3654
gynocentric, **3719–3721**
Hildegard of Bingen and, 3979
and history of religions, 10041–10042
human rights and, 5364–5365
in Iran, Qurrat al-'Ayn Ṭāhirah and, 7575
in Islam, 3366–3368
Islamist, 3367–3368
Muslim, 3366–3367, 3368
secular, 3366
in Japan, 3345–3346, 3348
study of religion in, 8778
Jewish, 3350–3352
history of, 3301, 3311–3312, 3350–3352
Lilith and, 5459
reconstructions of, 3301
vs. thealogy, 9099
in Jewish Renewal, 4869
in Judaism, 4985
ordination of women and, 1963
law and, 5360–5361
liberation theology and, 5402–5403, 5440
on Mary, **5755–5756**
androcentrism and, 5754
on matriarchy
critique of, 3298, 3613
defense of, 3613
Mead (Margaret) in, 5804
and men's studies, 5862
on menstruation, 5867
methodologies of, 3299–3301
and midrash, 6021

on misogyny, 3299, 3311, 3312
on monotheism, 6161
on mysticism, 6358
negative view of, 3032
Neopaganism and, 7830
as nonwhite and non-Western women and, 9791
objectives of, 3298
paradigm shifts in, 3299
on patriarchy, 3298, 3311, 3312, 7007–7008
on politics and religion, 7252
primary concerns of, 3311
psychology of religion criticized by, 7479
on Qabbalah, 8243
and Qur'anic exegesis, 7568
racism in, 3311
radical *vs.* liberal, 1754
Ramabai's (Pandita), 7610–7611
reductionism by, charge of, 3025–3026
religion critiqued in, 9787–9788
religious roots of, 3297, 3310
on rites of passage, 7859
role conflicts and, 8484
role in study of religion, 3024–3025
on sacrifice, 8009
second wave of (women's liberation), 3024, 3034, 3297–3298, 3310–3311
and Buddhist women, 3330, 3334
and gender studies, 3297–3298, 3310–3311
gynocentrism in, 3719
and Hindu women, 3321
and Jewish women, 3351
on patriarchy, 7007–7008
racism in, 3311
religious leaders in, 2614
rise of, 3310–3311
in women's studies, 9785
Seventh-day Adventism and, 8237
sexuality, analysis of, 8243–8244
social movements and, 1754–1755
on spirit possession, 8694–8697
Spiritualism and, 8717
spirituality based in, 9787
Stanton (Elizabeth Cady), role of, 8730–8731
subaltern studies and, 3322
suffrage movement, Stanton (Elizabeth Cady) and, 8731
in theosophy, 9144
third wave of (postfeminism), 3024, 3298
definition of, 3298
on Tibetan Buddhism, 8243–8244
Tibetan studies in, 9190
United Nations and, 4181
in Wicca, 9730
wisdom interpreted through, 9761
zār cult and, 3837
Feminism in the Study of Religion (Juschka), 3301
Feminist Spectator as Critic, The (Dolan), 2438–2439
Feminist Spirituality movement (Goddess movement), 3022, 6537
ancient Mediterranean religions in, 3386
Gimbutas (Marija) in, 3312, 3493
Great Goddess in, 3617
objectives of, 3312
prehistory recreated for, 3312
in women's studies, 9788–9789
Feminist studies. *See also* Women's studies
use of term, 9793
Feminist theology, **3031–3039**
Australian fiction and, 3082
biblical hermeneutics in, 5488
Buddhist, 3032, 3033
Christian, 3031, **3034–3039**
in Grail movement, 3654
on potential for reform, 3312
Confucian and Daoist, 3033–3034
development of, 5440
ecology in, 2610
feminist scholars of religion and, 3025
Hindu, 3033
Jewish, 3032–3033
liberation theology and, 1657
Muslim, 3033
Nightingale's theology and, 6618
origins of, 3031, 3034
rise of, 3301
vs. thealogy, 9099
in women's studies in religion, 9788
Fen (limits), Guo Xiang on, 3710
Fenari, Şemseddin al-, as shaykh al-Islam, 8306
Fénelon, François, **3039–3040**
mysticism and, 6350
and Quietism, 7558, 7559
Fengdao kejie (Daoist code), 7414
Fengguo Monastery (Buddhist temple), 9047
Feng Menglong, 3067
Feng sacrifices, 1590, 1591, 7267
Fengshan (Daoist ritual), 2178
Feng-shui
and ancestor worship, 324
development of, 1594
and domestic observances, 2406
gaining blessings with, 984
in gardens, 3277
as geomancy, 3437
in trees, 9334
Fen guonianqian (money of the passing year), 1641
Feng Wenbing, 3070
Fenian Cycle, 1494–1495
Fenn, Richard K., 7858
Fenrir (mythic wolf), 3456, 3457, 5508, 9426, 9784
Fenrisúlfr (monster), 6165
Fenton, William, 3409, 6672
Fenyang Shanzhao (Buddhist monk), 1276
Feralia (festival), 5321, 6994–6995, 7909
Ferdinand (king of Spain)
Abravanel (Isaac) in government of, 17
and Ignatius Loyola, 4367
Spanish Inquisition created by, 4498, 4500, 4502
Torquemada (Tomás de) as confessor to, 9242
Ferdinand of Aragon
Jews expelled by, 5717
Latin American missions and, 1695
Ferg (anger), 4479
Ferghus mac Roich, **3040**
Fergie, Deane, 3398
Ferguson, Adam, on social systems, 8491
Ferguson, Marilyn, 6496
Feriae (holidays), 7906
Feriae Denecales, 7909
Feriae Latinae (sacrifice), 1466, 2366
bull sacrifice in, 1466, 7898
Feridun (monster), 2432
Fernandes, Gonçalves, 121
Fernandes, Valentim, 112
Fernandez, James, on rites of passage, 7796
Fernandez, James W.
on Bwiti religion, 383
on millenarianism, 6033
on rituals, 7836
Fernández de Santa Cruz, Manuel, 4967
Ferrante I, government of, Abravanel (Isaac) in, 17
Ferrara-Florence, Council of, 2587, 7884
Fertility
in African religions, 7677
central Bantu earth deities and, 1509
herbalism and, 3819
Nyakyusa, 6771
in southern African religions, 8660
Swazi Mhlanga ritual, 8897
in agrarian rites, 2558–2559, 2560
animal horns as signs of, 1481
in Aztec religion, 718–719, 5293, 9213
in Baltic religion, 5285, 5286
Latvian Saule (sun) cult and, 8133
in Batak religion, 799
Canaanite rites of, 1383, 1385
chastity and, 1557
creation from cosmic egg and, 1987
dainas (folk songs) dealing with, 2127
death associated with, 2239
deities of (*See* Fertility deities)
dragons associated with, 2433
egg as symbol of, 2702
in Egyptian tradition
mythology of, 2720
treatments for infertility, 3836
evil eye and, in Middle East, 3837
evolutionary psychology and, 8475
fish associated with, 3122
in Frazer's theory of myths, 6363
of gardens, 3281
of God, Hildegard of Bingen on, 3980
goddess worship associated with, 3584, 3589
hare as symbol of, 7590
horn symbolism and, 4130–4131
and human body, in art, 4170
Indo-European gods of, comparative, 1874
initiation rituals and, 4484, 4485, 4486, 4487
in Japanese religions, *kami* and, 5071
of Leah, 7591
in Madagascar stone cult, 8745
masculine sacrality in, 5761–5762
in Melanesian religions, 5836
in Mesoamerican drama, 2463–2464
in Micronesian religions, 6005–6006
Milky Way linked to, 2863
moon and, 3971
mountains as source of, 6214
in Near Eastern religions, gender and, 3376, 3377–3378
in Neolithic societies, vol. 9 color insert
in Oceanic religions, gender and, 3396
orgy and, 6861
in Persephone myth, 2751
rain as symbol of, 7602, 7603
in ritual sacrifice, 2556
sacrifice and
blood symbolism in, 7998

sacrifice and *continued*
Frazer (James G.) on, 4183
self-control in rites of, 8239–8240
sheep and ram symbolism and, 8310, 8311
in South American Indian religions
human fertility rites, 8583
plant fertility rites, 8582, 8618
tranvestism and, 3968–3969
tree of life and, 9577
Venuses as symbols of, 3584, 6953, 7079
warrior deity and, 9686–9687
witchcraft and, 6871–6872
in Yakkut religion, 9865
yoni and, 9907–9909
in Zulu religions, 10008–10009
Fertility dances, 2135
of Ganda people, 2137
of Sandawe people, 2137
Fertility deities, 3622
Adonis as, 2985
Aphrodite as, 407
in Aztec religion, 718–719
Baal as, 723, 724
in Celtic religion, 1490
Cybele as Great Mother, 1451
Demeter as, 2270
dove as symbol of, 948
examples of, 3622
functions of, 3622
in Germanic religion, 3451
Freyja, 3218
Freyr, 3219, 3220
Njǫrðr, 6642
goddess worship and, 3584, 3589
in Israelite religion, 7602
Jumis as, 761
nāgas as, 6394
in North American Indian religions, 6654
Osiris, 6919–6921, 6922
Pan as, 7079–7080
Pērkons as, 7054
in Phoenician religion, 7129, 7130
prehistoric, 7377, 7378
Priapus as, 7079–7080
Saule as, 759
Ukko, 9438
Ülgen, 9441
yakṣas as, 6394
Zeme as, 760–761, 9942–9943
Fescska, Ede, on opioid-mediated attachment processes, 8278
Fessenden, Larry, 3099
Festinger, Leon, on rites of passage, 7798–7799
Festivals. *See also* Seasonal ceremonies; *specific festivals*
aberration and, 6880
Akan, 215
almsgiving in, 268
Amazonian
Quechua, 284
Tukanoan, 8623
and architecture, 465–466
Baltic, ancestors in, 328, 329, 331
Brazilian, music in, 6272
Chinese, 1641–1644
Christian, 7196
dainas (folk songs) dealing with, 2127
drama of, 2436
Ebliate, 2597–2598
economics and, 1758
etymology of term, 7196
Greek, 3684
Hawaiian, 7308
Hindu, 7196
in devotional life, 9824–9825
fire in, 3117
Hittite, 4071–4072
Inca, 4412–4413
Indian, in Hindi tradition, 3987
in Inuit religion, 4528
Iranian, 6730–6732
in Iroquois religion, 4541–4542, 4543
in Israelite religion, 4972
Jewish, days of, 4867–4868
Korean, 5229
Lao, 5314
Marathi, 5698
Marian, 5753
Neopagan, 6471
orgy in, 6863, 6878
in Phoenician religion, 7131–7132
Plutarch on, 7200
Raëlian, 7598
raw-eating in, 6822
in remembrance of dead, 2244
Roman, 7897–7898, 7906
for ghosts, 166
for *lares,* 5320–5321
Shintō, in Edo period, 8364
Tamil, 8977
timing of, agriculture and, 186–188
Totonac, 9254, 9255
in Wicca, 9731
in Zoroastrianism, 9998–9999
Festschriften, **3040–3042**
Festugière, A.-J.
on alchemy, 245
on Greek religion, 3661
Nock (Arthur Darby) and, 6643
Festus
on *numen,* 6754
on *pontifex,* 7319
Fetal position, burial in, 7344
Fetches (apparitions), 3475
Fete-man (ritual specialist), in Kromanti dance, 1436
Fêtes et chansons (Granet), 3655
Fetiales, 7908
Fetishism, **3042–3047**
in African religions, 67, 74, 3044, 3045
animism and, 366
in Berber religion, 834
cargo-cult theory and, 1424
of commodities, 3045
in cultural studies, 3046
in European philosophical discourse, 3044–3045
European use of term, 113, 366, 4040
and idolatry, 4363
vs. idolatry, 3043–3044
invention of, 3043–3044
original, 67, 74
vs. positivism, 7339
as sexual pathology, 3046
transculturation and, 9296
Fetuses
conception of, life beginning at, 5811, 5812
ensoulment of
life beginning with, 5812
timing of, 5812
in Mesopotamian religion, 8536–8537
Feuchtwang, Stephan, 7266
Feudalism
in China, 1583
in Japan, historiography and, 4026
in papacy, 6970
Feuer, Lewis, on Spinoza (Baruch), 8686
Feuerbach, Ludwig, **3047–3048**
atheism and, 583
Bakhtin (M. M.) on, 742
Essence of Christianity, 3047–3048
Essence of Religion, 3048
on faith as experience, 2957
and French feminists, 3029
on God, 3558, 7422
on knowledge, 5207
Marx (Karl) influenced by, 5745
on origins of religion, 3044
on religious beliefs and practice, 7126
sociology and, 8480
study of religion and, 10076
Theogonie, 3048
Feuerpriester in Kleinasien und Iran (Wikander), 9735
Feuerstein, Georg, 8992
Feu follet, le, 2952
Fèvre, J., 816
Fewkes, J. W., 6670
Feyerabend, Paul, 10044
Fez (Morocco), Judaism in, 4990
Sephardic, 4996
FGBMFI. *See* Full Gospel Business Men's Fellowship International
FGM Task Force, 3366
Fian, 1494–1495
Fianaighecht (Fionn Cycle), 1494–1495
Fichte, Johann Gottlieb, **3048–3049**
and aesthetics, 47
in art history, 499
Atheism Controversy involving, 3049
Attempt at a Critique of All Revelation, 3049
as Freemason, 3195
on nature, 6435
on reflexivity, 7648
Schelling (Friedrich) and, 8148
on will, 4355
Fichter, Joseph H., on membership, 1779
Ficino, Marsilio, **3049–3050**
on angels, 348
on ascension, 522
Corpus Hermeticum translated by, 5579
erotic magic and, 8248
Hermetica, translation of, 3945
Hermetism and, 3946
on humanity, 7141
Italian Renaissance humanism, role in, 4175
on magic, 5579
Neoplatonism and, 3049, 6475
Plato and Plotinus translated by, 7193
on rebelliousness, 7420–7421
in search for origins, 367
of transmission of ancient wisdom, 3950
Fiction, **3050–3094**. *See also* Literature; *specific authors*
aesthetics of, 54
African, 3085–3089
ancient, 3051–3053
Eastern and African influences on, 3054
and political resistance, 3055
Australian, 3079–3082, 3083, 3084
Chinese, 3056–3057, 3066–3071
of Eliade, 2754, 2755–2756, 2757
Greek, 3052, 3053
women in, 3055–3056
Jain, 10034
Japanese, 3056, 3057, 3071–3075
Jewish
by Agnon (Shemu'el Yosef), 180
ancient, 3052
Latin, 3051–3052
Latin American, 3063–3066
Marxist, 10034, 10035
Native American, 3089–3094
Oceanic, 3083–3085
origins of, theories of, 3050–3051
popular, 7322–7323
science, artificial intelligence in, 512
South Asian, **10033–10036**
in Bengali language, 10035
definition of, 10033

in English, 10036
in Hindi language, 10034–10035
origins of, 10033–10034
in Tamil language, 10035–10036
in Urdu language, 10035
Southeast Asian, 3075–3079
time in, 3057
Western, 3058–3063
Fictuld, Hermann, on Hermetism, 3951
Fiddler on the Roof, 2164
Fideism
Christian theology and, 2819
in Islam, 3565
skepticism and, 8421–8422
Wittgenstein (Ludwig) and, 7116, 7119
Fidencio de Jesús Síntora Constantino, José (El Niño Fidencio), 6578
Fide quaerens intellectum (Barth), 791
Fides (deity), **3094,** 7899, 7900
Fides (faith), 2425
Field, Henry, 1002, 1003
Field, Karen, 378
Field, Margaret, 118
Fielding, Henry, 3051
Joseph Andrews, 3059
law in literature of, 5355
Field of Mars. *See* Campus Martius
Fields, Karen, 9297
Fieldston School, 33
Field theory, 1541
unified, 2740
Fiesta (Santa Fe, New Mexico), 1517
Fiestas
in Mesoamerican religions, 5925
in Nahuatl religion, 6402
in South American religions, gender and, 3417–3418
in Tarascan religion, 9001, 9002
Fifteen (number), interpretations of, 6749
Fifteen Sermons (Butler), 1339
Fifth Ecumenical Council, 2584
Fifth Sun era (Aztec), 5888, 5901, 5907, 5935
in creation myth, 1468
human sacrifice and, 4184
Fifty (number), interpretations of, 6750
Fig, sign of (gesture), 7344
Fig tree, 9335, 9337
Figulus, Nigidius, 421, 7530, 7913
Figura, in symbolic time, 8915–8919
Figurative art
African, 90
agriculture and, 188–190, 3584–3585
curse figurines, 5574
Greek, 3662, 3679
in megalithic religion, 5825
Mesoamerican
in Classic period, 5904–5905
in Formative (Preclassic) period, 5880, 5895–5897, 6268
in Teotihuaćan, 5900
Neolithic, goddess worship in, 3584–3585, 3592, 3593
Paleolithic, goddess worship in, 3583–3584, 3593, 3613
Figures, burying of, in mortification rites, 8209
Figurist movement, 1631
Fiji Islands and Fijian religion. *See also* Oceania and Oceanic religions
ablutions in, 10, 11
cannibalism in, 1403, 1404
Christianity, 7298
Methodist missionaries, 1738
Pentecostalism, 1741
as Polynesia *vs.* Melanesia, 5832
purification in, 7509
Tuka cargo movement, 1421–1423, 1425, 7298
Filaret of Moscow, **3094–3095**
Filial piety
in Confucianism
and ancestor worship, 323–324
Kaibara Ekken on, 5055
in Reiyūkai Kyōdan, 7862
Kṣitigarbha and, 5255
Filicchi, Antonio, Seton (Elizabeth) and, 8234
Filicchi, Filippo, Seton (Elizabeth) and, 8234
Filidh class, 1479, 1484, 1488
Filioque ("and from the Son")
controversy over
Barlaam of Calabria in, 3698
Gregory of Cyprus in, 3692
Gregory Palamas in, 3699
Photios in, 7135
Eastern Europe and, 1683
in Nicene-Constantinopolitan Creed, objection to, 2585
in Nicene Creed, 2056
schism and, 8155, 8156
and Western *vs.* Eastern Christianity, 1681
Filippov, Daniil, *lucerna extincta* rite and, 8249
Fillmore, Charles and Myrtle, **3095–3097,** 6536, 6563, 9472
and Hopkins (Emma Curtis), 3095, 3096, 6584
and Unity (Unity School of Christianity), 3095–3096, 6584, 6586
writings of, 6585, 6586
Fillmore, Lowell, 3096
Film, **3097–3103**
artificial intelligence in, 512
and decrease in theater audience, 2473
ethnographic, 2350
Indian, music in, 6286
poetic qualities of, 7208
religion as, 3100–3101
religion in, 3099–3100, 5806, 5808, 7323–7324
ritualized performances of, 3101
Filosofov, Dmitrii, 5869
Final judgment, in Zoroastrianism, 3118
"Final Soliloquy of the Interior Paramour" (Stevens), 5483
Findhorn community (Scotland), 6495, 6568
Finding Space: Winnicott, God, and Psychic Reality (Ulanov), 7483
Findlay, J. N.
on comedy, 4220
monistic philosophy of, 6146, 6149
Findlay, John, 6964
Findly, Ellison Banks, 3313
Fine, Steven, 4343
La fine del Mondo (de Martino), 2268
Fingarette, Herbert, 7476
Finished Work (Baptistic) Pentecostalism, 7029, 7033
Finish Orthodox Church, in Orthodox structure, 2589
Finitude, in existentialism, 2926
Finkel, Note Hirsh, 6242
Finkelstein, Louis, Conservative Judaism and, 1961
Finland. *See also* Finnish religions; Finno-Ugric religions
Christianity in, history of, 1685, 1686
folklore of
Lönnrot's (Elias) work on, 5511–5512
Reguly's (Antal) work on, 7673–7674
folk songs of, 5511
historiography in, 4047
history of, 3103
independence of, 5092
Islam in, 4678
Kalevala epic (*See Kalevala*)
Karelian religion in, 5091–5093
Lutherans in, 5092
moon in, 6173
population of, 3103
saunas in, 800–803
Finlayson, Roderick, 3085
Finn, Celtic legend of, 3123
Finnegan, Ruth, on open *vs.* closed systems of thought, 5567
Finnegans Wake (Joyce), Campbell (Joseph) on, 1378, 1379
Finney, Charles G., 3204
evangelicalism of, 2888
Holiness movement and, 4083
revivalism and, 1710
Stanton (Elizabeth Cady) and, 8730
Finney, Charles Grandison, 2700
Finnis, John, 5370
Finnish Literature Society, 5511
Finnish religions, **3103–3105**. *See also* Finno-Ugric religions
birds in, 948
cosmology in, 3104
deities of (*See* Ilmarinen)
folklore and mythology
Haavio (Martti) on, 3723–3724
Sirius (star) in, 8735
netherworld in (*See* Tuonela)
ocean in, 6806
Finnish Society for Comparative Religion, Honko (Lauri) and, 4122
Finno-Ugric languages, 3105
basis for recognition of, 3110–3111
Castrén (Matthais) on, 1453
Honko (Lauri) on, 4123
Hungarian and, 4224
words for "soul" in, 802
Finno-Ugric peoples, 3105
Finno-Ugric religions, **3105–3116**. *See also* Sami (Lapp) religion
Castrén on, 1453
Chuvash religion and, 1785
creation myths in, 3108–3109
Donner's (Kai) research on, 2421
Harva (Uno) on, 3782–3783
history of study of, 3110–3116
Khanty religion influenced by, 5125
Komi religion (*See* Komi religion and society)
Mansi religion influenced by, 5125
ocean in, 6806
Reguly (Antal) on, 7673–7674
sanctuaries and offerings in, 3109
shamans in, 3109–3110, 3114
Finno-Ugric Society, 2420
Finns, 3103, 3106
epic poetry of, 3111
Finot, Louis, 3177
Finsch, Otto, 474
Finster, Howard, 9626, vol. 14 color insert
Fintan, 1488
Fionn Cycle, 1494–1495
Fionn mac Cumhaill (mythic figure), 1494–1495

Fiorenza, Elisabeth Schüssler, 3036, 3312
on Grail movement, 3654
influence on biblical scholarship, 3356
on patriarchy, 7008
Fioretti, Anthony of Padua in, 377
Fipa religion. *See* Central Bantu religions
Fiqh (religious law). *See also* Uṣūl al-fiqh
ʿAbd al-Jabbār on, 3
blasphemy in, 976
as central discipline, 4587
feminism on, 3368
gender in, 3368
hawzah and, 3801
ijtihād in, 4373
ikhtilaf (legal differences) as result of, 4594
meaning of term, 4692
qāḍī and, 7540
qualification in, 3801
ṣalāt (prayer) in, 8055
sources of, 4695–4697
in Sunnism *vs.* Twelver Shiism, 8342–8343
women in, 3368
Fiqh akbar II (Abū Ḥanīfah), 4400
Fiqh al-akbar (Islamic creed), 5062
Fiqh al-akbar II (Islamic creed), 5063
Fir Bholg, 3164
Firdawsī (Persian author), 5257
al-Bīrūnī and, 954
on Mazdakism, 5801
Shāh-nāmah by, 2814
Firdawsī school (Islam), 4647
Fire, **3116–3121**. *See also* Ashes; Cremation
in African myths and rituals, 94–95
Bantu myths of origin of, 8665
Mbuti culture hero as bringer of, 2091, 7525
Nyakyusa, 6770, 6771
in alchemy, 236
Chinese, 238
Renaissance, 251–252
in altars, 275–276
angels and, 344–345
in Anishinaabe religion, 370
in Armenian religion, 491, 492
in *ateshgah,* 568–570
in Australian Indigenous myths, 654
in Buddhism
destruction by, 2028
in Japanese Shingon, 8352
in Cherokee religion, 1564
in Chinese religion, jumping over, at New Year, 1641
in Christianity, 3119–3120
cultic dimensions of, 3116
in Saka religion, 7385–7386
deities of (*See* Fire deities)
in Demeter Eleusinia cult, 2751–2752
female divinities associated with, 3018
in funeral rites, 3239–3240
in Ge mythology, 3293–3294
in Germanic religion, creation myth of, 3446
in Greek religion, 3669
at Panathenaia, 6958
Prometheus as bringer of, 7419, 7420
in Hinduism
at Holī, 4081
in *Saṃnyāsa* initiation, 8094
in purification, 7507
in Inca religion, spirits manifested in, 5176
in Indian religions, 3116–3117
in Iranian religion, 3116, 3117–3118, 4535, 10002
in Islam, 3120
in eschatology, 2838
in Hell, 9455–9456
in Judaism, 3119–3120
on Sabbath, 5087
in Komi religion, 5218
in Mediterranean tradition, 3118–3119
in Melanesian religions, origins of, 5843
in Mesoamerican religions
in Aztec religion, 5891
in Tarascan religion, 5909
in metallurgy, 5988
in Micronesian myths, 6012
in New Year festivals, 6590, 6592, 6594
in North American Indian religions
Green Corn Ceremony, 6694
healing ceremonies, 6685
home and, 4106
ordeal by, 6850
in purification, 7507
sacred hearth fires, 4106–4107
sacrifice with, 7999
in Sarmatian religion, 8114, 8115
in Shinto, Buddhist influence on, 9836
in South American Indian religions, origin myths of, 8590
in Turkic religions, 9399
in Vedism, 178–179, 9557, 9564–9565
domestic, 9565–9566
in funeral rites, 9566
installation of, 9565
in sacrifice, 9821
of Vesta, 9585
in Vestal cult, 9607
in Vietnamese religion, 9593
in West African religions, worship sites and, 9720–9721
World Fire myth, in South American Indian religions, 8589
in Zoroastrianism, 568–570, 4535, 6997
magi and, 9990
Fire deities
Agni as, **178–179,** 2404, 3990, 7507
in Ainu religion, 206
in Aztec religion, 718
Hestia as, 3964
Fire-rain, Sun of, in Aztec calendar, 1357
Firestone, Shulamith, 3311
Firewalking
in Greek villages, 3120
New Age practice of, 3120
in South India and Sri Lanka, 3117
Fir flathemon (ruler's truth), 1492
Firkovitch, Abraham, writings of, 5085–5086
Firmicus Maternus
astrology of, 563
on Attis, 2536, 2537
on idolatry, 4358, 4361
on mystery religions, 6330
on Orphic myth, 2965
Firmin, Thomas, 9469
Firsoff, Valdemar Axel, 6437
First Amendment, of United States Constitution, 5330
First and last, motif of, Hestia associated with, 3964
First Baptist Church of Savannah, 5443
First Book of Discipline (document of Scottish Reformation), 5212
Firstborn, Fast of the, 4867–4868
First Born Church of Christ, 10054
First Constitution on the Church of Christ, 9532
First fruit rites
Cain and Abel, 1344
in North American Indian religions, 6714–6715
First International Psychology of Religion Congress, 847
First Nations (Canada), 2616
First Philosophy or Ontology (Wolff), 6830
First Principles (Spencer), 5672
First Temple. *See* Solomon's Temple
First Zionist Congress, 9979, 9982
Firth, Raymond, **3121–3122**
on *atua,* 622
Berndts (Catherine and Ronald) studying under, 840, 841
on body symbolism, 4161
on genital operations, 7808
on *mana,* 2543
on spirit possession, mediumship, and shamanism, 8688, 8690
on Tikopia religion, 9195, 9197
Fiṣal (Ibn Ḥazm), 4268
Fischel, Henry, 6019
Fischer, Eberhard, on masks, 5766
Fischer, Johann Eberhard, 3110–3111
Fischer, Michael M. J., 3141
Fish, **3122–3124**. *See also* Fishing
in Australian Indigenous myths, 649, 653
as food, *kashrut* laws on, 5106
Jonah and, 4947
in North American Indian mythology, 6662–6663, 6707
in prehistoric religions, 7377
Viṣṇu in form of, 707
Fish, Stanley, 50
Fishbane, Michael, 6019, 6021
Fisher, Herbie, 677
Fisher, Margaret, 7262
Fisher, Miles Mark, 77
Fisher King (mythic figure), 3649, 3650, 3651, 3652, 7552, 7553
Fishing
in balance of life, in indigenous traditions, 2618
confession and, 1884
in Dolgan religion, 2395
in Inuit religion, 4527
Fishing cultures, New Year ceremonies of, 6591
Fishman, Steven, 1033
Fishman v. United States, 1033, 5376
Fiske, John, 4459–4460
in evolutionary ethics, 2918
Fison, Lorimer, Codrington and, 1847
Fisu Sakio (deity), 3094
Fitnah (disorder), women and, *ṣalāt* (prayer) and, 8055
Fitrah (tax), in Acehnese religion, 25
Fitts, Leroy, 75
Fitzpatrick, Peter, 5328
Five (number), interpretations of, 6747–6748
Five Books on Consideration (Bernard), 839
Five Buddhas, 1078, 1079, 1080
Five Civilized Tribes (North America), 7301
Five Classics/Scriptures. *See Wujing*
Five Dragons Temple (Ruicheng), 9057
Five Dynasties period (China), Manichaeism in, 5669–5670
Five Elements *(wu xing). See Yinyang Wuxing* philosophy
Fiveiskii, F., moral theology, 1653
"Five Kinds of Action" *(Wuxing),* ethics in, 1895, 1896
"Five More Psalms of David," 904
Five Mountains temples, 1180, 1181, 9947
Five Percent Nation (Islamic movement), 4689, 6420

Five Pillars of Islam, 4565, 5062, 5446. *See also* Shahādah (confession of faith)
in Agami Islam Santri, 4818
fasting at Ramaḍān, 8140–8141 (*See also* Ṣawm (fasting))
ḥājj in, 7154–7155
heteronomous discipline and, 8700
humor about, 4215
ṣalāt (prayer) in, 8055
in Sufism, 8817
in worship, 9816
Five Tathāgatas, 1078
Five Terrace Mountain. *See* Wutai, Mount
Fī Ẓilāl al-Qur'ān (Quṭb), 7567–7568, 7576, 8955
Fjellström, Pehr, on Sami bear ceremonies, 8087
Fjörgynn (deity), 3453
Flaccus, Verrius, 2994, 3125
Flacius, Matthias, **3124**
on evidence analysis, 4039
Flags
of Israel, Magen David on, 5559
in Vodou, vol. 8 color insert
Flamen, **3124–3126,** 7900
Flamen, of Quirinus, 7559
Flamen Dialis (Plutarch), 7201
Flamines maiores, 4462
Flamines minores, 7907
Flannery, Kent V., 454, 5902
Flavius, Gnaeus, 2993
Flavius, Josephus. *See* Josephus Flavius
Fléché, Jessé, 9302
Fleischer, Heinrich Leberecht, 3634
Steinschneider (Moritz) and, 4878
Fletcher, Alice, 2540, 6670
Fletcher, Angus, 2276
Flew, Anthony, 5499
Flew, Antony, 9113
Flidhais (deity), 1487
Flight, **3126–3130**
of Deadalus and Icarus, 5274
Flight of the Wild Gander, The (Campbell), origins of myth in, 1378
Flint, Robert, 7340
Flood, Gavin, 742, 7098–7099
on semiotics, 8759
Flood, the, **3130–3133**
biblical story of, 2968, 3131, 3132
in Celtic mytho-history, 1488
chaos and, 1538
in Chinese myth, 1626
as Christian prefiguration, 6643
comparative mythology of, 1876
cosmogonic perspective on, 2960, 3130–3131
Egyptian version of, 3130, 3131
as force of nature, 7604
forms of, 3132–3133
frog associated with, 3223
Greek version of, 2965–2966, 3131, 3132
humanity after, 3131–3132
implications of archetypal flood in, 7604
Indian version of, 2963–2964, 3130, 4440
Iranian version of, 2964, 3130
in Islam, 2969
in Latin American fiction, 3063
Mesopotamian version of, 884, 1876, 2963, 3131, 3132
in *Atrahasis* myth, **598–600**
in *Epic of Gilgamesh,* 7604
mountains in, 6212–6213
in North American Indian religions, 6653, 6660, 6661
and number symbolism, 6750
primordial water and, 3132
as punishment, 7604
in South American Indian myths, 8588–8589
in Ayoré religion (Gran Chaco), 8633
in Makiritare religion (Amazon), 8626
Sumerian version of, 2791
survivors of, 3131, 3133
Ungarinyin version of, 9459–9460
Floods
disease and, 3808–3809
in India, monsoon floods, and religious calendar, 4018
Flora (deity), 3135
priest of, 3126
Florence
Carnival at, 1442
Gregory XI, conflict with, 1461
Platonic academy in, 6475
Savonarola (Girolamo) and, 8139–8140
Florence, Council of (1438), 6475
Florence, Council of (1442), on Trinity, 9362
Florenskii, Pavel, **3133–3134**
Florensov, Antonii, 3133
Florentine Codex (Nahuatl text), 2465, 5917, 5939
Flores, Fernando, 510
Florovsky, Georges, on Florenskii (Pavel) theology, 3134
Flournoy, Théodore
on psychology of religion, 7474
on psychology of the subconscious, 1949
Flower Festival in Genzano, The (ballet), 2156
Flower Garland (Flower Ornament Scripture). See Huayan jing; See Avataṃsaka Sūtra
"Flower of Tulledega, The" (Posey), 7225
Flowers, **3135–3137**
deities associated with, 3135–3136
in gardens
African subsistence, 3281
Eastern cosmic, 3277–3278
Western recreational, 3277
in Mesoamerican drama, 2464, 2466
and rituals, 3136
supernatural power of, 3136–3137
Flowery Wars. *See Xochiyaoyotl*
Flow experience, **3138–3139**
Fludd, Robert
on Hermetism, 3950
graphic representations of, vol. 3 color insert
and nature, 6434
in Rosicrucianism, 7930
Fluehr-Lobban, Carolyn, on matriarchy and goddess worship, 3613
Flute Dance feast, in Arawak religion, 8582–8583
Flutes
Mesoamerican, 6267, 6268
New Guinea, 6265
Flynn, Maureen, 6947
FM radio, religious broadcasting on, 7711
fMRI. *See* Functional magnetic resonance imaging
Focolare (fireplace) movement, 5399, 6568
FOCUS. *See* Fellowship of Christian Unions
Fódla (deity), 1490
Foerst, Anne, 512
Fogong Monastery (Buddhist temple), 9047, 9264
Foguangshan, **3139–3141**
globalization of, 3140–3141, 6568
Foix-Candale, François, Hermetism and, 3946
Fojiao Xiejin Hui, 8967
Fo-Jih Ta-Hui, Master, on time-bound logic, 7988
Fo kwan shan. *See* Foguangshan
Foley, Edward, 7858–7859
Folk art, **9624–9627**
Folk culture
in Europe, 2144
vs. popular culture, 7320
Folk dance, 2141, **2143–2152**
definitions of, 2144–2146
Folklife museum, in Scandinavia, 2145
Folklore, **3141–3149**
Baltic, 756–757, 760, 766, 768, 769–771
in *dainas* folk songs, 8131–8132, 8133–8135
in Brazilian Carnival parades, 1444
bridge motif in, 1050, 1051
cats in, 1463–1464
Celtic, the Grail in, 3651
East African, 2567
European, Christmas and, 1757
Finno-Ugric, 1453
Germanic, in study of Germanic religion, 3458–3459
goats in, 8312
horses in, 4134–4135
humor in, 4194–4195
Hungarian, 2415–2416, 4227
Reguly (Antal) and, 7674
Italian, de Martino (Ernesto) on, 2267
Japanese, 4797–4798
Japanese study of, 8778
Jewish, midrash as, 6020
in Jewish studies, 4880
Karelian, 5093
Latvian, Māra in, 5691–5694
moon in, 6175–6176
nationalism, effect of, 8763
number symbolism in, 6747, 6748
oral tradition in, 8199
primitive religion as source of, 2144–2145
Rip Van Winkley motif in, 8440
Russian, Baba Yaga, **727**
Slavic, 8436–8438
sleep in, 8440
South America, *indigenista* studies in, 8595
swans in, 8894
Folk-Lore (journal), 7372
Folklore Matters (Dundes), 6976
Folklore Studies movement, in China, 1636
Folk religion, **3150–3164**. *See also* Popular religion
Buddhism, **3153–3157**
Catholicism
in Latin America, 6577–6578
in Maya religion, 3413, 5799
in Nahuatl religion, 6402
women in, 3413
in China, law and, 5352
cultural studies approach to, 3146–3147
definitions of, 3142–3143
East Asian, humor in, 4207–4209
in Europe, discovery of, 3142
experience-centered approach to, 3145

Folk religion ***continued***
feminist approaches to, 3147–3148
functionalist approach to, 3143–3144
healing in
Chinese folk healers, 1617
Egyptian spiritist healers, 3836
in Germanic religion, 3845
in Judaism, 3829
Middle Eastern and Islamic, 3833, **3834–3839**
in Roman religion, 3841
Hungarian, 4226, 4227
idealization of, 3141–3142, 3152
Islam, **3161–3164**
ʿAlawīyūn as, 226
in Japan, 9311–9312, 9314
Judaism, **3157–3161**
in Mesoamerica, persistence of, 5920
in Pacific islands, Christianity, folk, 1739
performance studies of, 3145–3146
reflexive ethnographic approach to, 3148
stigmatization of, 3141, 3142, 3152
of Surinam Creoles, 126–127
survivalist approach to, 3143
as undifferentiated community, 1865
wild hunt in, 9771
Yule in, 9741
Folk songs
in Baltic cultures, 2127–2128
ancestors in, 327
of Finland, 5511
Folk Tale, A (Bournonville), 2156
Folk tales. *See* Folklore
Fomhoire, **3164–3165**
in Celtic mytho-history, 1488
in war of foundation, 9686
Fon and Ewe religion (western Africa), **3165–3167**
ancestors of Fon, dances devoted to, 2137
ancestor worship in, 322, 3165–3166
deities of (*See also specific deities*)
Mawu-Lisa, **5790**
divination in, 10032
drums in, 7037
food symbolism and ritual in, 3171
Haitian Vodou, influence on, 1433
Ifa divination in, 87, 94
mediums in, diagnosis of illness by, 3818
sacred objects in, vol. 4 color insert
soul in, 1434, 8533
spirits, 1433
tricksters in, 9352–9353
Fonrobert, Charlotte Elisheva, 7515
Fons/Fontanus (deity), priest of, 3126
Fons vitae (Ibn Gabirol). *See Yanbuʿ al-hayat* (Ibn Gabirol)
Fonte Avellana (hermitage), Damian (Peter) at, 2133
Fontenelle, Bernard Le Bovier de, 3044, 6366
the Enlightenment influenced by, 2795–2796
on scientific progress, 7340
Fontenrose, Joseph
on Euhemerus, 2883
on Greek oracles, 4044
Food, **3167–3175**. *See also* Banqueting; Diet; Dietary laws; Fasting; *specific foods*
ablution of, 12
in African rituals, 88
Nyakyusa, 6770
in ancestor worship, 322–323, 329–331
animals for, 356, 361
in Australian Indigenous religions
knowledge of music compared with, 6262
myths of, 653, 654
cannibalism and, 1403
at Carnival, 1442–1443
in Christianity, 3170, 3171
culture and, 2087
the dead and, in Oceanic religions, 6784
in funeral rites, 3237–3238
globalization and, 3174
in Greek religion
cooking of, 3669–3670
as offering, 3668
in Hinduism, 2404
consecration of, 1955–1956
hospitality and, 4140–4141
human production of, 9578
in *ahiṃsā*, 197
in Islam, 2401, 3170–3171
in Central Asia, 4625
in China, 2401
folk Islam, 3163
at rites of passage, 7828
in Jainism, 4769
women's role in, 3328
in Judaism
domestic rituals of, 2397, 2398
Marrano, 5718–5719
for Roʾsh ha-Shanah meal, 7928
as kinship substance, 5184
magic involved in obtaining, 5566–5567
in Maori religion, 5680–5681
in marriage rituals, 5726
in Mexican religion, spells for cooking, 8678
in Micronesian myths, 6011–6012
in Mongol rituals, 6826
in Neolithic pastoral societies, 1464
in New Year ceremonies, 6590, 6594
in North American Indian religions, 6707, 6710
offerings of
in Buddhism, 3170
in Chinese traditions, 3170, vol. 7 color insert
in folk Islam, 3163
in Hinduism, 3169–3170
in Shintō, 3171
in Judaism, 3169
in North American Indian religions, 6652, 6726
and pollution, 7504–7505 (*See also* Dietary laws)
in Polynesian religions, 7308, 7310
raw *vs.* cooked, 6821–6822
in rituals, 7838
and sacrifice, 3171
sacrificial meals, 7999–8000, 8002–8003
and social justice, 3173–3174
in symbol, myth, and ritual, 3169–3171
taboos on, 3167–3169
in Australian Indigenous religions, 3873
in Chinese traditions, 3169
in Christianity, 3168
in Hinduism, 3167–3168, 7505
in Islam, 3168–3169, 7144
in Judaism, 3167, 7144
in North American Indian religions, 7299–7300
theoretical perspectives on, 3172–3173
trees as, 9335–9336
in Yoruba traditions, 3171
"Fooling God" (Erdrich), 7226
Fools. *See also* Tricksters
antinomian dervishes as, 4214
in Chan/Zen Buddhism, 4207
in Christian traditions, 4202
clowns, affinity with, 1838
as ritual humorists, 4198
Ṣūfīs as, 4202
Thomas Aquinas on, 4219
Fools, Feast of, 266
Carnival and, 1441
dancing at, 2153
humor in, 4198, 4218
inversion in, 1441
Mass as form of reference for, 7194
Fool's Mass, 2476
Foot. *See* Feet
Foote, Julia, 10037
Foote, Peter, 3460
Foot washing
by Jesus, as hospitality, 4139
ritual of, 3013
Forbidden City (China), sacrifice to Shangdi and, 1914–1915
Forbidden Image, The (Besançon), 4380
Ford, Desmond, on sanctuary doctrine, 8237
Forde, Daryl, 116, 473
Fordicidia (festival), 7897
Foreign Missions Conference of North America, 1709
Foreman, Dave, 2562, 2563
Fore people, cannibalism among, 1404
Forest. *See also* Trees
deities of, in Hawaiian religion, 3798
in Khanty religion, 5120, 5121
in Komi religion, 5217–5218
in Mansi religion, 5120, 5121
in Nayaka religion, 5185
in Pygmy religions, 7523–7524, 7525
Forest-dwelling life stage. *See Araññavāsm; Vanaprasthin*
Forest People, The (Turnbull), 2495
Forest recluses, in Tibetan Buddhism, women as, 3332–3333
Forêt interdite (The Forbidden Forest) (Eliade), 2755–2756
Forges, in West African religions, 9720–9721
Forgiveness. *See also* Confession of sins; Grace
in Buddhism, *Pratisaṃharaṇīya-karma* (form of punishment), 2035
in Islam, 8407
For-itself, Sartre (Jean-Paul) on, 8116
Form, human body and, 4170
Formalism, in Ashʿarīyah, 536
Formality, in ceremony, 1513
Forman, Robert K. C., 7745–7746
on mysticism, 6357
Former Prophets, 879
Formes élémentaires de la vie religieuse (Durkheim), Otto's *Idea of the Holy* contrasted with, 4095–4096
Formgeschichte des Evangeliums, Die (Dibelius), 944
Formisano, Ciro. *See* Kremmerz, Giuliano
Forms
Aristotelian, 485
in epistemology, 2819
Platonic, 44–45, 7110, 7181–7182, 7184
Aristotle's rejection of, 484, 7187
in Middle Platonism, 7189
Plotinus on, 7198
Speusippus's rejection of, 7187
Xenocrates accepting, 7187
Formstecher, Solomon, 4901–4902
Formula, in Vedic ritual, 9561–9562
Formula of Agreement, A, 1769

Formula of Concord (1577), 5832
    Augsburg Confession and, 2055
    Lutheranism in, 5539
Fornax (deity), 7560
Forseti (deity), 3451
Fors Fortuna, and Dea Dia, 2232
Forster, Anselm, on merit, 5875
Forsyth, P. T., 6105
Forte, Maximilian, 10028
Forten, James, 264
Fortes, Meyer, 116
    on ancestor worship, 321
    and Dieterlen (Germaine), 2350
    on kingship, in Africa, 5169, 5170
    on kinship, in primitive societies, 5182
Fortin, Ernest, 7246
Fortuna (deity), 3002, **3175–3176**
    Tyche and, 1527, 3175
Fortuna Muliebris temple, 7919
Fortunatus, Augustine's debate with, 626
Fortune. *See* Chance; Fate; Misfortune
Fortune, Reo F., 137, 6801
Fort Wayne, Treaty of (1809), 9028
Forty (number), interpretations of, 6750
Forum Boarium (Rome), 3175
Forum Romanum (Roman Forum), 7897
Fosdick, Harry Emerson, 6106
Fosite (deity), 3451
Fossum, Jarl, 3534
Foster, George, 2611, 5941–5942
    on knowledge, 5207
    on maize myth, 5936
Foster, Lawrence, 6535
    on utopianism and sexuality, 8243
Foster, Robert J., on cargo cults, 1421, 1424
Foster, Steven, 7802
Fotudeng (Buddhist monk), 1164, 2171
    miracles of, 6053
Fotuo (Buddhist scholar), 994
Fotuo (Chinese name for Buddha), 1160
Foucauld, Charles-Eugène, 2828
Foucault, Michel
    on androgyny *vs.* androgynes, 339
    Aristotle and, 45
    deconstruction of, 5413
    discourse, notion of, 2088
    and feminist theology, 3035
    on homosexuality, 8241–8242
    in men's studies, 5863
    on politics and religion, 7252–7253
    and postcolonial theory, 10042
    on punishment, 5374
    on ritual and political power, 1514
    on sexuality, 4163, 5413, 6740, 8241, 8244
        queer theories influenced by, 3300
    structuralism and, 8759
Foucher, Albert, 1312, 4328
Foucher, Alfred, 1063, **3176–3177**
Fouillée, Alfred, 7341
Foulk, T. Griffith, 1248
Foulston, Lynn, 3608
Foundation rites, in consecration of homes, 4105
Foundations (Teresa of Ávila), 9084
Founded religions, 1866
    in history of religions approach, 4066–4067
Founded religious communities, 7717–7718
    development of, 7718
    founders of, 7718
    reform in, 7718
Founders of religions, 944–946
    death of, 1062
    and gender roles in formative period, 3301–3302
    heresy *vs.* orthodoxy and, 3921, 3922
    sacred biography of, 7718
Fountain, **3177–3178**
Fountain of Life, The (Ibn Gabirol). *See Yanbuʿ al-hayat* (Ibn Gabirol)
Fountain of youth, 7683–7684. *See also* Rejuvenation
Four (number), interpretations of, 6747
Four Beasts, in *Daniel,* 2169
Four Beginnings, Korean Neo-Confucianism and, 1931, 1932
Four Books *(sishu)*
    modern use of, 1910
    Nakae Tōju studying, 6403, 6404
    Zhu Xi and, 1900, 1917, 9973
Four Branches (Welsh tales), 5545–5546
Four-Entry Pagoda (Shandong), 9045
Four Great Mission of Compassion Relief, 1789
Four Immeasurable Attitudes, *karuṇā* and, 5105
Fournier, Marcel, 5786
Four Noble Truths, 2628, 2738, **3178–3180**. *See also* Nirodha; *Samudaya*
    autonomous discipline and, 8701
    as central doctrine, 1104, 4428
    charity and, 1555
    Dharmacakrapravartana Sūtra and, 1296, 1350
    early doctrinal schools on, 1197
    and Eightfold Path, 2306
    in enlightenment, 2794
    in Mahāyāna Buddhism, 3179–3180
    in Theravāda Buddhism, 3179
    in Tiantai school, 9177–9178
    turning of the wheel of *dharma* and, 2332
Four Quartets (Eliot), 5029, 5482, 7204
Four Sources. *See Uṣūl al-fiqh*
Foursquare Gospel, International Church of the, 5803
    founder of, 6536
    McPherson (Aimee Semple) in, 5803
    in Pacific islands, 1741
Fourteen (number), interpretations of, 6749
Fourteen Immaculate Ones, Shaykh Aḥmad on, 8307
Fourth Support doctrine, Shaykh Aḥmad on, 8308
Fourth Way, The (Ouspensky), 6935–6936
Four Valleys (Bahāʾ Allāh), 737
Fowler, James, 7479
Fox, C. E., on *mana,* 8515
Fox, Emmet, 6586
Fox, George, **3180–3181**, 6648, 7547
    on authority, 695
    blasphemies of, 973
    as enthusiast, 2805
    on kingdom of God, 5152
    and Penn (William), 7028
Fox, Kate, 6535, 6559
    Spiritualism, role in, 8715
Fox, Margaret, 6535, 6559
    Spiritualism, role in, 8715
Fox, Matthew, on spirituality, 8719
Foxe, John, 7662–7663
Foxes, **3181–3182**
    in African myths, 95, 100
    in Chinese religion, as trickster, 8303
    in Dogon religion, 2390, 3569, 9353
    in Dolgan religion, 2395
    in Japanese religion, 4795
    in North American Indian religions, 7299
Foxing lun (treatise on Buddha nature), 9527
Fox religion (North America), funerary rites of, 6683–6684
Foyer Unitas, 2686
Fozu tongji (Zhipan), 9179
Fractals, 1542, 1543
Fragmenta Hermetica, in Hermetic corpus, 3939
Fragmentary, in postmodern literature, 5482
Fragmentary Targum. *See Targum Jonathan*
Fragmenter i lappska mythologien (Laestadius), 5284
Fragrance offering, in Arabian religions, 445
Frame drums, 2498, 2499, 7036
Frampton, Hollis, 3102
France, Anatole, 3528
France and French religions. *See also specific religions*
    All Fools' Day in, 266
    Annales School and study of religion, 1873
    anticult legislation in, 1034, 9067
    anticult movement in, 2085, 2086
    calendar, revolutionary, 1355
    calligraphy in, 1372
    Catharism in, 1458, 4498
    China, study of, 1632
    colonialism
        in Brazil, 1698
        in Canada, 9299–9300
        in Caribbean, 1706
        Code Noir, 1706
        in North America, 7301
        in Oceania, 7298
        in West Africa, and Alinesitoue's prophecy, 261–262
    dance in, 2154–2155
    drama in, 2469, 2470, 2474
    the Enlightenment in, 2795
    Feast of Fools, 1441
    feminism in, **3027–3031**
    films from, 3099
    folklore of
        esprit follet, 2951
        feu follet, 2952
    Freemasonry in, 3195–3196
    Gallicanism in, 1693, 3258–3259
    Hermetism in, 3946–3947, 3951
    hermits of, 2826, 2827
    historiography in, 4044–4045, 4049–4050
    Islam, 4674–4675, 4676, 4678, 4680
    Jesuits opposed by, 4842
    Jewish studies in, 4884
    Jews in, 5000–5001
        acculturation of, 5020
        medieval, 5013
    Joan of Arc and, 4929–4930
    John XXIII (pope) in, 4945
    Judaism
        anti-Semitism and, 401
        Reform Judaism, 7668, 7670
    missions, in North America, 1708
    museums in, 6243
    national consciousness in, 1941
    naturalism of, 6434–6435

France and French religions ***continued***
new religious movements in, 5377
discrimination against, 6518, 6526, 6541, 6570
native, 6568
Temple Solaire, 9067–9068
nuns and sisters in, 6764
occultism in, 6782
Hermetism and, 3951
philosophical phenomenology in, 7088
poetry in, 7218, 7220
Protestantism, 7662
Reformation in, 7662
Renaissance humanism in, 4176
retreat houses in, 7772
Revolution in (*See* French Revolution)
Roman Catholicism
Benedictines, 822
Dominicans, 2413, 2414
French Revolution and, 7878
Inquisition in, 4498
pilgrimage in, 7148
Romanticism and, 7878
Schmidt (Wilhelm), support from, 8168
secularism of, 4044
study of religion in
institutions for, 10077–10078, 10080
Mesoamerican religions in, 5940
Tibetan Buddhist training center in, 6761
yoni symbols found in, 9906
Francis I (king of France)
as patron of art and literature, 4176
in Reformation, 7662
Francis II (king of France), in Reformation, 7662
Francisca de Jesús (nun), 3417
Franciscan College of Santiago Tlatelolco, 5917
Franciscans, **3182–3184**. *See also specific figures*
Anthony of Padua in, 376–377
architecture of monasteries of, 6119
on artistic expression, 2141
on conscience, 1941
and dance, 2136
devotion of, Heiler (Friedrich) on, 3898
growth of, 6133
as inquisitors, 4499, 4504, 6971
manual labor in, 6133
mendicancy of, 5856, 6133
in Mesoamerica, 5915–5916
in native clergy debate, 5917
native languages used by, 5917
spiritual conquest by, 5915
millenarianism in, 5915–5916
missions of
in China, 1725
in Latin America, 1695–1697, 8623
in North America, 1708, 6729, 8231
in Tlaxcala, 9215
moral theology, 1654
on nature, 6432
performing pageant during Feast of Corpus Christi, 2438
poverty in, 6133
women as, 6135
wounded heart symbolism in, 3883
Francisco, Gabriel Beato, 3079
Francisco, Lazaro M., 3079
Francisco Ximénez, 5797
Francis of Assisi, 3182, **3184–3185**
and Valdès (Pierre), 6648
animals as concern of, 358, 2648
Anthony of Padua and, 376–377
Benedict's rules modified by, 8704
and Bonaventure, 1010, 1011, 1012, 1013
compassion of, 2608, 4844
on desire, 2309
as devotee, 2318
on devotion, 2321
ideals of, 6133
Ifa/Orunmila identified with in Santeria, 1434
on love, 6349
on mendicancy, 5856
on nature, divine in, 2606–2607
Shakpana identified with in Trinidad, 1434
as stigmatic, 1004
Waldensians and, 9662
Francis of Sales, on meditation, 5818
Francke, August Hermann, **3185–3186,** 9190
Franckenberg, Abraham von, 1006
Franginen (fully African), in Vodou, 9635
Frank, Eve, 6873
Frank, Ewa, 3186
Frank, Jacob, **3186–3187,** 5017, 6872–6873
sexual rituals and, 8250
Frank, Jerome, on rites of passage, 7798
Frank, Sebastian, Hermetism and, 3947
Fränkel, Jonah, 6020, 6021
Frankel, Zacharias, **3187–3188**
on 'Aqiva' ben Yosef, 441
Geiger (Abraham) and, 3291
on *halakhah,* origins of, 3748
Historical Judaism of, 4984
positive-historical Judaism movement and, 1957–1958
in Reform Judaism, 7669
Frankenberry, Nancy K., on semiotics, 8759
Frankenstein (Shelley), 811
as rebellion against God, 3059
Frankfort, Henri, 2730, **3188–3189**
on anthropomorphism, 5950
on dying and rising gods, 2522
on kingship, divine, 3902, 5983
on Myth and Ritual school, 6382
on sin, 7757
Frankfurt, Council of (794), 4286, 4290
Frankfurt School, 6883
feminist critique of, 3304
Frankish kingdom
authority of, 696
Boniface as missionary in, 1018
Charlemagne and, 1556, 1557
Christianity in, distinct from Latin-Roman and Greek-Byzantine traditions, 1681
division of, 1683
legal system in, inquisition and, 8013
missions in Moravia, Cyril and Methodius *vs.,* 2116, 2117
Muslim consciousness of threat of, 2077–2078
Rome, alliance with, 1662, 1689, 6967, 7280
Rome-Constantinople schism and, 8155
Frankist movement, 6872–6873. *See also* Frank, Jacob
sexual rituals in, 8250
Shabbateanism and, 3786, 8259, 8262
Frankl, Viktor, 7476–7477, 7482
on hope, 4127
Franklin, Benjamin
autobiography of, 699
Carroll (John) and, 1445
on civil religion and natural law, 1814
influence on New Thought movement, 6585
Spiritualism and, 8715
Franks, R. S., on atonement, 596
Frantellanza Terapeutica e Magica di Myriam, sexual magic and, 8252
Franz, Frederick W., 4821
Fraser, Robert, 381
Frashōkereti, **3189–3190**
microcosm-macrocosm and, 4159–4160
resurrection of body in, 131
Fraternalism, religious. *See* Freemasons
Fraternitas Saturni, sexual magic and, 8252
Fraticelli, 6869
Fratres arvales. See Arval Brothers
Fratricide, theme of, 2985–2986
Frauwallner, Erich, 1063, 1312, 9527
on Sthiramati, 8739
Fravashis (preexistent souls), **3190,** 4537
angels and, 345
feast dedicated to, 6731
Frazer, James G., **3190–3193**. *See also* Golden Bough, The
on African religions, 114
kingship in, 5169, 5170
supreme beings of, 3576
on agricultural rituals, 189
and Dumézil (Georges), 2518
on Baldr, 744
on binding, 937, 5196
on bird, image of, 3127
Celtic religious studies and, 1498
comparative religion and, 1878
cursing research, influence on, 2098
on dance, 2145
on death, 2239
and Donner (Kai), 2421
on dying and rising gods, 2522, 2535, 7767
evolutionism of, 2916
on external soul, 8532
on fertility
cult of, 3376
in myths, 6363
Gaster (Theodor H.) and, 3288–3289, 4044
Gillen and Spencer influencing, 3490
on goddess worship, 3611, 3616
vs. Goldenweiser (Alexander A.), 3634
Graebner (Fritz) on, 3648
on *hieros gamos* (sacred marriage), 3974, 3976
on Indo-European religions, 4461
influence on Frye (Northrop), 3223, 3224
on kingship, 1514, 5157–5158, 5169, 8664
on knots, 5196
Lang's (Andrew) critique of, 5299–5300
on liturgy, 5491
on magic, 2540, 4461, 5373, 5564, 5570–5571, 5588, 7914
Malinowski (Bronislaw) and, 5628
on manism, 5673
Mannhardt (Wilhelm) influencing, 5676
method of, 5381
on mortification of kings, 6198
on mystery religions, 6327, 6328
on myth and ritual, 2444, 3288–3289, 3460

and Myth and Ritual school, 6380
on nature religions, 2662, 6440
and Neopaganism, 6470, 7830
on Nilsson (Martin P.), 6622
on origins and evolution of religion, 10077
on preanimism, 2540
on purification, 7504
Raglan (Lord), influence on, 3958, 3959
religion defined by, 7702
on religion *vs.* magic, 6502
revaluation of, 380, 381
on rituals, 7839
on Roman religion, 7893
on Roman sacrifice, 1051
on sacrifice, 1051, 4183, 8001
on salutations, 8060
Smith (W. Robertson) and, 8451–8452
on soul loss in sleep, 8440
symbol theory and, 8910
on taboo, 2540
on theater, 7050
on totemism, 3634, 9250, 9251
Frazier, E. Franklin, 74
on Afro-Caribbean religions, 10025
debate with Herskovits (Melville), 73, 74
FRC. *See* Federal Radio Commission
FRCH. *See* Federation of Reconstructionist Congregations and Havurot
Frederic Barbarossa, 5337
Frederick II of Hohenstaufen (emperor)
in Crusades, 2075
Innocent III and, 4495–4496
Frederick II of Prussia (king), 5539
Frederick the Great (Prussian king), German Enlightenment under, 2797
Free African Society, 68, 264
Free Christian Church, 9469
Free churches, Protestant
confessions of faith in, 2055
ecclesiologies of, 1774
on separation of church and state, 1968
Free Church of Scotland, Smith (W. Robertson) and, 8451
FREECOG, 9410–9411
Freedberg, David, 4280, 4380
response theory of, 500–501, 502
Freedom
American civil religion and, slavery as constraint to, 1815
Congregationalist emphasis on, 1938
in essence of religion, 1819–1820
in existentialism, 2926
human rights and, 4179–4181
Indo-European concept of, Sabazios and, 7953
Kook (Avraham Yitsḥaq) on, 5226–5227
Niebuhr (Reinhold) on, 6612
obedience and, 6778
Protestant ethics and, 1654–1655
religious
in China, under Communist rule, 5354, 10072
in Europe, 6570
in Japan, 4791, 4792, 4813
laws and, 5329, 5330
legal protection of, 5363
missionary activity and, 6071
new religious movements and, 1714, 5376, 6518, 6541–6542, 6566, 6570
social action and, 1751
United Nations declaration of, 7704
in United States, 5330, 5362, 5376, 6556
Williams (Roger) and, 9739
sin and, in Greek thought, 8405
Freehof, Solomon, 7672
Free Jewish House of Learning, 7926
Free love, the Family and, 2987–2988, 6548, 6560
Freeman, Derek, 5804
Freeman, John, 460
Freemasons, **3193–3199**
Christian opposition to, 3197
Clement XII condemning, 6973
famous members of, 3197, 3198
on God, 3194
Hermetism and Christianity, commonalities with, 3952
history of, 3193–3197
initiation into, 4479, 4482–4483
occultism and, 6783
principles of, 3193
as religious community, 7718–7719
as secret society, 8213
sounds and word, power of, 8675
teachings of, 3197–3198
Free Methodist Church, 5998–5999. *See also* Holiness movement
as first Holiness denomination, 4083
Free Officers movement (Egypt), 6315
Free Religious Association, 1570
Freerks, Sicke, executed for rebaptism, 8401
Free State era (Congo), 5221
Free the Children of God, 396
Freethought movement, 5862
Freethought Publishing Company, 844
Free will
chance and, 1526
in Christianity
Arminius (Jacobus) on, 492
Augustine on, 626–627, 1667, 3645
Cathari doctrine on, 1457
Edwards (Jonathan) on, 2699
grace and, 3645, 3646
merit and, 5876
definition of, 3199, 3200, 3202
and determinism, **3199–3202**
evolutionary ethics and, 2920
genetics and, 3430
as Holocaust paradigm, 4091–4092
Irenaeus on, 4540
in Islam (*See also* Qadar)
ʿAbd Allāh Anṣari on, 8816
ʿAbduh (Muḥammad) on, 5067
Ibn al-ʿArabī on, 8820
Ibn Taymīyah on, 4569
in Ashʿarīyah, 2064, 3563–3565, 8816
Murjiʾah sect on, 4568
in Muʿtazilah, 2064, 8816
questioning of, 8809
Waṣīyah on, 5062
in Judaism
Crescas on, 4897
God's foreknowledge and, 3549
Saʿadyah Gaon on, 4889
Kant (Immanuel) on, 5077
knot symbolism and, 5199
Paracelsus on, 6981
and predestination, **3202–3213**
Christianity on, 3203–3204, 3206–3209
Hinduism on, 3204–3205
Islam on, 3204, 3209–3213
Judaism on, 3203
of spirits, in Kardecism, 5090
in Stoicism, 8742
and theism, 9104
Free Will (Edwards), 2699
Free Will Baptists, 784
Free-will theodicy, 9113–9114
in Christianity, 9117
in Hinduism, 9119
in Islam, 9118
in Judaism, 9115
Frei, Hans W., 6377
Freidel, David, on Maya religion, 5886, 5943
Freidenberg, Ol'ga, 3114
Freie Vereinigung, 194, 195
Freire, Paulo, liberation theology and, 5438
Frelinghuysen, Theodor J., 7143
French, Marilyn, 7008
French Asiatic Society, 1333
French Catholic White Fathers, in Buganda, 2578
French (Gallican) Confession (1559), as Reformed creed, 2058
French language, Nag Hammadi codices in, 3535
French National Center for Scientific Research, 9188
French Polynesia. *See* Oceania; Polynesia
French Reformation, 7662
French Reformed Confession (1559), on free will and predestination, 3208
French Revolution
anti-Semitism and, 401
calendar and, 1355
Catholicism and, 7878
Christianity and, 1693
dance influenced by, 2155
and iconoclasm, 4286–4287, 4347
Jewish citizens in, 4862
Marx on, 5746
against papacy, 6973
Pius IX on, 7180
Romanticism *vs.*, 8492
social movements and, 1752
violence of, remembrance of, 9599
Frenzy, **3213–3215**. *See also* Spirit possession
Freo (deity), 6943
Frequens decree (1417), 6972, 9340–9341
Frères at Avignon, 6874
Fréret, Nicolas, on animism, 4040
Freud, Anna, 7476
Freud, Sigmund, **3215–3218**
on Akhenaton, 220
on ancestor worship, 321
on anchor, 332
animism and, 2914–2915
on art, 7111
atheism of, 7422
on Australian Indigenous women, 3389
bridge symbolism used by, 1051
Campbell, influence on, 1378, 1379
on circumcision, 4481
on conscience, 1944
on consciousness, 1949
on conversion, 1970
on death, 2238
on dreams, 2376, 2483–2484

Freud, Sigmund ***continued***
on ego, 7474, 7476
Eliade on, 4047
evolutionism of, 2916
exorcism studied by, 2935
on faith and experience, 2957
on fatalism, 2998
on fetishism, 3046, 9296
Frazer's (James G.) influence on, 2916
Gillen and Spencer influencing, 3490
on goddess worship, 3611
on Golden Rule, 3632
hermeneutics of, 3933
on homosexuality, 4112
on human beings, 7112
on human body, 4163
on illusion, 7482
on jokes, 4222
Jung and, 5031, 7475, 7484
life and principle works of, 3215–3216
on liturgy, 5491
on magic, 5565
Malinowski (Bronislaw) on, 5628
Marxist criticism of, 7489–7490
on morality, 6178
on Oedipal complex, 7474, 7478
on pain, 6947
paranormal experience and, 6057
on phallus, 7085
psychoanalytic theory of, 3216 (*See also* Psychoanalysis)
on psychology of religion, 7474, 7482
on puberty rites, 7799
on rejuvenation, 7683
on relativism, 7685
on religious phenomena, 2285
on ritual, 7838–7839, 7841, 7858
Róheim (Géza) influenced by, 7872–7873
on sacrifice, 8003, 8004
on Schmidt (Wilhelm), 8169
on superego, 7474
symbol theory and, 8911–8912, 8913–8914
on taboo, 7974
theory of culture and religion, 3216–3217
on totemism, 7872, 9251
on trance, 59
on unconscious, 1949, 7474
nature and, 6437
on upward displacement, 4165
Freudian psychology
charisma and, 1544–1545
hair symbolism in, 3738–3739
initiation rituals in, 4480
and Rank (Otto) on heroes, 3958
Frey, Sylvia, 76–77
Freyja (deity), **3218–3219**
carriage drawn by cats, 1462
Friday named after, 1689
functions of, 3452
hawk's plumage of, 2554
in war with Æsir, 3450
legitimacy of, problem of, 6641
Loki and, 5508, 5509
and Thor, 9166
Freyr (deity), **3219–3221,** 4462
in *Edda,* 2692–2693
in war with Æsir, 3449–3450
legitimacy of, problem of, 6641
in sagas, 8024, 8025
sister of, 3218
Friars
Dominican (*See* Dominicans)
Franciscan (*See* Franciscans)
mendicant, 7724
Friars Minor, 3182–3183. *See also* Bonaventure
Frick, Heinrich, **3221**
Friday (day), Mokosh connected with, 6115
Friday Mosque (Iran), vol. 5 color insert
Fried, Martha, on rites of passage, 7798
Fried, Morton, on rites of passage, 7798
Friedan, Betty, in women's liberation movement, 3310
Friedel, David
on Mesoamerican ballgames, 751
on Mesoamerican funeral rites, 7813
Friedländer, Moritz, 3532, 3533
Friedman, Kajsa Ekholm, on Congolese kingship, 5159
Friedman, Mordecai, on Palestinian marriage law, 3746
Friedmann, Yohanan, 433
Friedrich, Adolf, 475, 1014
Friedrich, Johannes, 2396
Friends, Society of. *See* Quakers
Friendship
Epicureans on, 3910–3911
in *walāyah,* 9656
Friends of Swedish Folk Dance, 2145
Friends of the Western Buddhist Order, 1191
Fries, Jakob Friedrich, 6928, 6929
Frigg (deity), 744, 3218
in death of Baldr, 3455–3456
and fish symbolism, 3122
Friis, J. A., 474
Friis, Jens Andreas, 3112
Frikel, Protasius, on Pura (deity), 8577
Fringe-Masonry, 6783
Frisbie, Charlotte J., 4485, 6672
Fritz, John, 453
Fritz, M. M., 2522
Fritzner, Johan, 474
Fröbe-Kapteyn, O., 3041
Frobenius, Leo, **3222**
on African supreme beings, 3576
Ergriffenheit idea of, 5113
Graebner (Fritz) and, 3648
Jensen (Adolf E.) and, 4824
kulturkreis idea of, 5259–5260
on masks, 5765
Otto (Walter F.) and, 6932
Fróði, 2693
Froebe-Kapteyn, Olga, 6484
Frogs and toads, **3223**
in African myths, 98–99
on amulets and talismans, 299
in prehistoric religions, 7377
Frogwoman (mythic figure), in Cuna creation myth, 2095
From Hegel to Nietzsche: The Revolution in Nineteenth-Century Thought (Löwith), 9294
Fromm, Erich, 7476, 7482
Frömmigkeit der Mystik und des Glaubens (Beth), 846
From Myth to Fiction: The Saga of Hadingus (Dumézil), 5467
From Tradition to Gospel (Dibelius), 944
Front de Liberation du Québec, 9303
Fronzaroli, Pelio, on Eblaite scapegoat rite, 2598
Froude, Richard Hurrell, 6510
Fruitfulness, in Baltic religion, Saule (sun) and, 8133
Fruits, in *ahiṃsā,* 197
Frum, John, 6797
Frumentius, as bishop of Ethiopia, 2859
Fruzzetti, Lina, 3321
Fryar, Robert H., Hermetic Brotherhood of Luxor and, 8251
Frye, Northrop, **3223–3226**
on low mimetic, 3086
FTL. *See* Latin American Theological Fraternity
Fuchs, Ernst, 3544
Fuchs, Stephen, on revival and renewal activities, 7789
Fuda (amulets), 2410, 4532
Fudi (blessed plots), 9056
Fudō (deity), **3226–3227**
Fudō Myōō Sokusai Goma ritual, in Shingon training, 8351
Fuente Avellana, monastic congregation of, 2827
Fuentes, Carlos, on religious ambiguities, 3064
Fu fazang jing (Buddhist text), 9176
Fugard, Athol, 2477
Fu Hao, 1582
Fuji (deity), 3018
Fuji, Mount
as cosmic center, 6212
Maitreya manifested on, 5622
mountain cults and, 8364
pilgrimages to, 2640
as sacred space, 9260
Fujikō (Japan), Maitreya in, 5622
Fujishima Ryōon, 1314
Fujiwara clan
Ame no Koyane venerated by, 289–290
Inbe clan and, 4811
in *Kojiki,* 4810–4811
in *Nihonshoki,* 4810–4811
political power of, 7272
regency of, 4785
Shintō lineage of, 8359
Fujiwara no Michinaga, 1177
Fujiwara no Morosuke, 1178, 9075
Fujiwara no Shunzei, 7216
Fujiwara no Tadahira, 1178
Fujiwara no Teika, 3227
Fujiwara Seika, **3227–3228**
Confucianism and, 1927
Fukaku (nonenlightenment), 9077
Fukami Toshu, Worldmate movement and, 8369–8370
Fukeshakuhachi (musical instrument), 6302
Fuku-Daruma (Daruma of happiness), 995
Fukuyama, Francis, 3428
on human rights, 4178
Fukuzawa Yukichi, 7274
Fulani religion. *See* Fulbe religion
Fulbe religion (Africa), **3228–3230**
Dan Fodio (Usuman) and, 2167–2168
drums of, 2495
in Umarian *jihād,* 9445
myths of, 97
Fulbert, 7
Fulk (bishop), 2412
Fulk of Neuilly, Crusade preaching, 2075
Fuller, Charles E., religious broadcasting of, 7711
Fuller, Lon, 5369
Fuller, Reginald H., on miracles, 6056
Fuller Theological Seminary, 2890
Full Gospel Business Men's Fellowship International (FGBMFI), 7030
Full Moon Visualization, 9834
Fulop, Timothy, 79
Fumihiro, Jōyū, Aum Shinrikyō under, 631, 632
Funan kingdom, Indianization in, 4011
Functionalism, **3230–3233**
in anthropology
British, historiography and, 4043
Leach (Edmund) influenced by, 5381
on rituals, 7840
Brelich (Angelo) and, 4046
Donner (Kai) and, 2420
Durkheim (Émile) and, 3231–3232, 8493
early French school of, 3230
and folk religion, study of, 3143–3144

in history of religion, Haydon (A. Eustace) and, 3803
Malinowski (Bronislaw) and, 3143, 3232, 5628–5629
in South American Indian religions research, 8595–8596
Spencer (Herbert) and, 3231
Stanner (W. E. H.) on, 8729
structural, 8749
Functional magnetic resonance imaging (fMRI), and oral tradition, 6425
Functional spirits, in Haitian Vodou, 1433
Functions, ideology of, warriors and, 9684–9686
Fundamentalism
antievolutionism and, 2910
apologetics and, 429–430
Christian, **2887–2894** (*See also* Evangelical Christianity)
and censorship, 4282
denominationalism and, 1712
dress and, 1832
vs. evangelicalism, 2890
folklorist studies of, 3144
growth of, 1716
historiography and, 4034
impact of, 2891–2893
media used in, 5806
militancy of, 2889, 2890, 2892
and missions in Papua New Guinea, 1741
modesty in, 1832
nature and, 2608
opposing same-sex marriage, 7283
political ideology and, 1517
premillenarianism in, 4055
religious broadcasting of, 7710–7711, 7715
rise of, 2889–2890
science, opposition with, 1995
scientific creationism and, 8185
Seventh-day Adventism and, 8236
women and, 1832, 6844–6845
definition of, 2887
gender in, 3304
in globalization, 3501
Hindu, Swaminarayan movement and, 8892
Islamic, 7286–7290 (*See also* Islamism)
in Africa, 7295
ijtihād in, 4573
in Ṣūfī orders, 8824
leadership in, 7287
neofundamentalism, 4574
of Quṭb (Sayyid), 6227
origins of, 4573, 7286, 7287
political ideology and, 1517, 1518, 7287–7288
popular healing practices, opposition to, 3835–3836
simplification of religion in, 4573
and terrorism, 7288–7290
use of term, 7286–7287
violence and, 9598–9599
Jewish, 4985
liberation theology, reaction to, 8468
in North American Indian religions, 6666–6667
in Northern Ireland, 2892
political ideology and theology, convergence of, 1517
religion and modernity and, 5031–5032
as response to modernity, 6111
theology of, 9139–9140
Fundamentals of the Buddhist Tantras (Mkhas grub rje text), 1217
Fundamental theology, 9139–9140
Fundraising, for missionary and social movements in U.S., 1752
Funeral rites, **3233–3245**. *See also* Burial; Cannibalism; Cremation; Mourning; Tombs
ablutions in, 11
in African religions, 89, 3235, 3236
and afterlife, beliefs about, 140–141
Benin, 3236, 7805–7806
and body, beliefs about, 140
Dogon, 2392
drama in, 2457
East African, for priests, 2569
Edo, 7805–7806
for kings, 5171, 7805
Kushite religion, 5270
Limba, 7806
Luba, 5523
Lugbara, 5527
Mossi of Burkina Faso, 3234, 3235
in southern African religions, 8658
Swazi, 8896
tombless, 9225
in Afro-Surinamese religions, 127
in Ainu religion, 205
in Anglo-Saxon paganism, 6943
in Aramean religion, 450
attendance at death, 3236
in Australian Indigenous religions, 144, 5051
in Australian religions, 7808
in Balinese religion, 748, 9226
in Bemba religion, 817–818
boats in, 989–991
bones in, 1014–1015
in Bornean religions, 1021, 9227
in Buddhism, 3155
burial mounds, 1065
in China, 1098
circumambulation in, 1797
in Japan, 2410
Zen, 9946
in Bugis religion, 1317–1318
burial and, 3238–3239
Canaanite, 1382, 1386
cannibalism in, 3169, 3238, 3239
in Caribbean religions, 1428, 1437
certification of death, 3236
in Chinese religion, 3234, 3236
archaeology on, 1637
clothing for mourning, 1827
domestic rituals of, 2408
Han dynasty, 1592
history of study of, 3703
human sacrifice in, 1570–1571
jade in, 4759
mythic imagery, 1628
prehistoric, 1581–1582
royal tombs, 9225
Shang dynasty, 1582
Xi Wang Mu in, 9860
in Christianity
earth burials, 9226
Orthodox, 2593
pollution in, 7506
Protestant, 7455
understanding of body in, 142
in Chuvash religion, 1785
circumambulation in, 1797
controlling decay in, 3238–3241
cremation (*See* Cremation)
dance in, 2138–2139
in Daoism
for facilitation between realms, 2179
music in, 6295
display of deceased, 3237
in Dobuan religion, 5185
double/secondary burial practices, 2239, 2241
in Egyptian religion, 2703, 2704, 3240 (*See also* Pyramids)
Anubis's role in, 403
ba and *ka* in, 7763
grave boats, 989
iconography of, 4318, 4319–4320
Osiris myth and, 2538
for pharaohs, 5164
shawabtis in, vol. 9 color insert
study of, 2731
Etruscan
sarcophagi in, vol. 4 color insert
women in, 2871
flowers used in, 3136
food in, 3237–3238
fundamental aims of, 3241
in Garifuna religion, 3284
in Germanic religion, 168
in Greek religion, 163–164, 3666, 9226, 9227
in Haitian Vodou, 1434
hare symbolism in, 7590
in Hinduism, 1015, 7815–7816
circumambulation in, 1797
pollution in, 7506
Sati (*See* Sati)
tombless, 9225
total destruction of body in, 7687
in Hittite religion, 4072–4073
in Hun religion, 4228–4229
in Iberian religion, 4250, 4251–4252, 4254
images in, vol. 9 color insert
importance of, 3234
in Inca religion, 4412
in Indonesian religions, 3235, 3237, 9227
integration and cessation of mourning, 3235–3236
interrogation of deceased, 3236, 6452
in Islam, 3239, 7827
in China, 4635–4636
earth burials, 9226
postures and gestures of, 7343
recitation of Qur'ān, 7572, 7827
in Israel, ancient, separation of dead from living, 7687
in Jainism
ritual time and, 7987
tombless, 9225
in Japan, 3136, 3240
poetry of, 7215
in Judaism, 7822–7823
circumambulation in, 1797
domestic rituals of, 2397
in Kushite religion, 5270
liminality and, 2240
in Mandaean religion, 5636
in Maori religion, 3234, 7808
in Mapuche religion, 5689
masks in, 5770
media coverage of, 5809
in Melanesian religions, 5838

Funeral rites *continued*
in Mesoamerican religions, **3241–3245**
Aztec, 3238, 3243–3244, 7813
death in motion and, 148–149
Inca, 3234, 3240
in Teotihuaćan, 149, 5900
Maya, 3242–3243, 3244, 4759, 7813
as rite of passage, 7813
in Micronesian religions, 6005
for Minoan kings, 5166
of Neanderthals, 6950–6951
necromantic practices in, 6452
in Neolithic period, 7375, 7377
in Jericho, 5111
in New Britain religions, 9227
in New Guinea religions, 7808, 9226, vol. 13 color insert
in North American Indian religions, 3237
Fox, 6683–6684
in Haida tradition, 3736
Plains, 6697, 6703
of Nyakyusa people, dances in, 2138
in Oceanic religions, 6784–6785, 7808
in Paleolithic religion, 6952, 7375, 7377
in Papua New Guinea, 7808
in Phoenician religion, 7132, 7134
prehistoric, 7375, 7377, 7381, 7386, 7387
preservation of bodies, 3240–3241
purification and mothering during, 3236–3237
purification through, 1459, 1460
purposes of, 7506
rock tombs, 1472–1473
in Roman religion, 166, 7895
art, funerary, 2094
cremation, 9226–9227
earth burials, 9227
for emperors, 439–440, 5167
Feriae Denecales, 7909
in Samoyed religion, 8096
sati (widow burning) (*See* Sati)
saunas in, 803
separation rites, 3234–3235
Shintō, 2640
in Sikhism, 8397
in South American Indian religions
in Amazonian religion, 8622–8623, 8631
death cults and, 8584, 8585
Goajiro Indians of Venezuela, 3235
in pre-Incan Andean religions, 8603
in Southeast Asian religions
double/secondary burial practices, 2239
traditional, 8651
in Southern Siberian religions, 8671
in Tamil religions, 8973
in Tarascan religion, 9001
textiles in, 9089
in Thracian religion, 9170
in Tibetan religions, 3236, 3238
tombless, 9225
tombless, 9225, 9226
in Tunguz religion, 9395–9396
in Turkic religion, 9399, 9403
in Ungarinyin religion, 9460–9461
in Vedism, 9566
fire in, 178
in Āraṇyakas, 1028
in Vietnamese religion, 3235, 9591–9592
winter carols for, 9742, 9745
women's involvement in, 2242
in Zoroastrianism, 3136, 3238, 10001
dakhma in, 2130
of Parsis, 6998, 7506
Funerary deification, 2250
Funerary rites. *See also* Funeral rites
definition of, 3241–3242
Funerary texts, of Egyptian religion, 2703, 2704, 2728
Funk, Robert, 4847
Furies, the (vengeance deities), 7782
Furlani, Giuseppe, 5969
on *Epic of Gilgamesh,* 3488
Furnaces, in metallurgy, 5987, 5988
Furo (bath), 801
Furor, 3213–3214
of warrior, 9684, 9685
Furphy, Joseph, 3080
Furrina (deity), priest of, 3126
Furst, Peter T., 5896
on drums, 6268
on smoking, Native American, 8454
Further Mosque. *See Masjid al-aqṣā*
Fu Sheng, on Classic of Documents, 1906
Fushidansekkyō (chant), 6301
Fushimi (Japan), Inari shrine at, 4795
Fushō (Buddhist priest), 3275–3276
Fustel de Coulanges, N. D., 3231, **3245–3246**
on ancestors
families founded by, 326
worship of, 321
on society and religion in Western civilization, 8466
Fuṣūs al-Hikam (Ibn al-ʿArabī), 4256, 4258, 9373
Burckhardt (Titus) translating, 1324
Fūta Jalon, in Umarian *jihād,* 9445
Futhark (runic alphabet), 7939
Futūḥāt al-Makkīya, al- (Ibn al-ʿArabī), 4256, 4257, 4258, 4570
Future
eternity and, 2853
theology oriented toward, 5152–5153
Future of an Illusion (Freud), 7474, 7482
morality in, 6178
Future of Man, The (Teilhard de Chardin), 9033
Future of Religion: Secularization, Revival, and Cult Formation, The (Stark and Bainbridge), churches, sects, and cults in, 2084–2085
Future of Science, The (Renan), 7750
Futurism, Evola (Julius) influenced by, 2904
Futūwwa Ṣūfī orders, 9006
Fuxi (Chinese emperor), 2433
Fu Xi (deity)
Nügua and, 1624
as sage-king, 1627
Fylgjur (guardian spirits), **3246–3247**

G

Gabinius, Aulus, John Hyrcanus II and, 8102
Gabon. *See also* Fang religion
Kota people of, 4302
Gabr (hollow), 10003, 10004
Gabriel (angel)
in Christianity, 346
images of, vol. 8 color insert
in Islam, 346, 523
and *miʿrāj,* 6059–6060
Black Stone brought by, 5050
iconography of, 4350, vol. 8 color insert
al-Suhrawardī on, 4555
transmitting Qurʾān to Muḥammad, 4510, 9271
in Trinidadian Shango, 1434
Gad (prophet), 7436
Gadamer, Hans Georg
biblical exegesis of, 876
comparative theology of, 9131
political theology influenced by, 7245
on religious experience, 7738
on Schleiermacher (Friedrich), 8164
on truth, 7206
Gadjari. *See* Gadjeri
Gadjeri (mythic figure), **3249–3251**
as Kunapipi, 3249–3250
regional variations of, 3249–3251
Gaels, 1488–1489
Gaetani, Benedetto. *See* Boniface VIII
Gagaku (music and dance), 6300, 6301
Gage, Henry H., 3251
Gage, Matilda Joslyn, **3251–3253,** 3310
Anthony (Susan B.) and, 3251–3252
Stanton (Elizabeth Cady) and, 3251–3252, 3310, 8731
in suffrage movement, 3251–3252, 3310, 9144
Gager, John G., on kingdom of God, 5152
Gahan (dance), 2462
Gāhānbārs (festivals), 9998
Gahs, Alexander, 474, 475
Gaia (deity), 967, 2984
and castration of Ouranos, 1450
in creation, 1993, 2555
Daedalus and, 5275
daughters of, 7783
and fate, 3001
in Neopaganism, 6472
Zeus and, 3663
Gaia: A New Look at Life on Earth (Lovelock), 2666
Gaia hypothesis, 2564, 3022, **3253–3255**
Lovelock (James) on, 3253
in nature religions, 2666
Gaimard, J. P., 5284
Gain: (sect), 1331
Gaius, on Roman law, 5333–5334
Gaiwiio (good word), 4543
Gaiwiio (Good Word) religion, conversion in, 7756
Gaja-Lakṣmī (deity), lotus associated with, 5519
Gajānana. *See* Gaṇeśa
Gajerrong people (Australia), land claims of, 690
Gakkai, Sōka, 3156
Gakko (Eck Master), 2601
Gakudōyōshinshū (Dōgen), 1277
Gakushōshiki mondō (Saicho), 9079
Ga-lahs (ballgame), 754
Galalkalû (priest), 2520
Galante, Livius, on Hermetism, 3949
Galanter, Marc, 6552, 6553
Galaru (sky-snake), 9458
Galatas (Crete), palace of, 39
Galatea (mythic figure), shape shifting and, 8302
Galatia, 1478
Galatians, 913, 920
Abraham in, 16
allegorical exegesis of, 872, 873
apostleship in, 435
circumcision in, 7017

condemnation of idolatry in, 4359
content of, 913
curses in, 2105
date of, 913
Eastern Christianity on, 874
Jerusalem apostolic conference in, 7016
John in, 910
justification in, 5039–5040
Paul's life in, 7014
Peter the Apostle in, 7067, 7068
Romans compared to, 912
Galatians, Council of the, 1491
Galatur (spirit), 4403
Gale, Fay, 3390
Gale, Richard, on James (William), 4776–4777
Gale, Theodore, on paganism and Judaism, 4039
Gale, William Potter, Christian Identity movement and, 1658, 1659
Galeano, Eduardo, 5438
Galen, **3255–3256**
education of, 3255
influence on *falsafah,* 2971
Maimonides (Moses) on, 5614
medical theories of, 3255
and medicine
astrology and, 3841
Islamic medicine, influence on, 3830, 3832
on monkeys, 6151
on nervous system, 6485
on Priapism, 7393
on secrecy, 235
on tears, 9025
writings of, 3255–3256
translations of, 3256
Galerius (Roman emperor)
on apostasy, 432
Christian persecution by, 7060
Constantine and, 1966
Galeru (Rainbow Snake), 7605
Galgolithic alphabet, creation of, 2585
Galicia (Spain)
atheism in, 4253
Carnival in, 1443
Jews in, 5019
Galicia, Hasidism in, 5247
Galician Church, 9464
Galilean Aramaic Targum, 888
Galilee, pilgrimage to, 7161–7162
Galileo (Brecht), 2476
Galileo Galilei, **3256–3258**
Aristotelianism and, 480, 482, 3257
astronomical findings of, 3256–3257
education of, 3256
exonerated by John Paul II, 8184–8185
on heliocentrism, 1978, 7136
interrogation of, Bellarmino (Roberto) in, 816
martyrdom of, 8183
materialism and, 5776
on natural philosophy, 6431
as predecessor of positivism, 7340
Scholasticism and, 8176
trial of, 3257, 4501
on "two books," 9422
writing his own defense, 7136
Galka (sorcerers), in Australian Indigenous religions, as killers, 3871–3872
Galla religion (Ethiopia)
initiation rites in, 2569
knot symbolism in, 5198
migration of group and, 2860
Gallatin, Albert, 6670
Galli (priests)
in cult of Cybele, 1452
ritual castration of, 1452, 2109–2110
Gallia Cislpina, 1478
Gallican Confession. *See* French Confession
Gallicanism, **3258–3259**
Bellarmino (Roberto) on, 816
Catholic condemnation of, 7877–7878
as conciliarism, 6973
French Revolution and, 7878
nationalism and, 1693
ultramontanism replacing, 3259, 9442
Vatican I against, 6974
Gallican Psalter, 893
Gallic religion. *See* Celtic religion
Gallic Wars (Caesar), 1481, 9329
Gallienus (Roman emperor), Christians tolerated by, 7059
Gallo, Bernardo da, in Kongo society, 5221
Gallows symbolism, al-Ḥallāj and, 3758
Gallus (Roman emperor), Christian persecution by, 7059
Galton, Francis, in eugenics, 2879, 2880
Gamaliel, Gospel of, 3270
Gamaliel of Yavneh. *See* Gamli'el of Yavneh
Gamaliel the Elder. *See* Gamli'el the Elder
Gāmavāsins (Buddhist monks), 1096, 9149
Gambia, childbirth practices in, 3819
Gambling, **3259–3264**. *See also* Chance; Games
deep play in, 3260, 3261
by deities, 3263
Hermes as god of, 1527
by heroes, 3263–3264
origins of, 3260
prohibitions on, 3259, 3262–3263
religious significance of, 3259, 3260
in traditional cultures, 3259–3262
Gamboni, Dario, 4282–4283
Gambuh (dance drama), 2450
Gamelans (metallophones), 2450, 2451, 2452
Gamelans (musical ensembles), 6288
Games, **3264–3269**. *See also* Ballgames; Sports
in Apache religion, 405
artificial intelligence and, 510, 511
in Christianity, 3267
classification of, 3267–3268
cosmic symbolism in, 3260
desacralization of, 3266–3267
evolutionary theory on, 3266–3267
gambling on (*See* Gambling)
in Greek religion, 3265–3266 (*See also* Olympic Games)
labyrinthine, 5276
Olmec, 6819
as play, 3264–3265
in Rome
ludi, 7906–7907
ludi saeculares, 5525–5526
in middle republic, 7903
social life and, 3267–3268
symbolism of cosmic center in, 1503
time and, 1761
Games of the North American Indians (Culin), 752, 3266
Game spirit, 5513
Game theory, 3268
Gamli'el II. *See* Gamli'el of Yavneh
Gamli'el of Yavneh, **3269–3270**
'Aqiva' ben Yosef influencing, 441
patriarchal authority of, 3269–3270
Tefillah and, 8388, 8389
on worship, 9806
at Yavneh academy, 3269
Gamli'el the Elder, **3270**
Gamonal, Ezequiel Ataucusi, 5986, 6547
Gaṇa (demonic figure), 2315
Ganabuda (mythic figure), 3249, 3251
Gaṇadhara (disciples), in Jainism, 4765
Gaṇādhipa. *See* Gaṇeśa
Gaṇakārikā (text), Pratyabhijñā Saivism and, 8049
Ganander, Christfried, 3111
Mythologia Fennica, 3104, 3105, 3111
Ganapati. *See* Gaṇeśa
Gāṇapatyas (Hindu sect), **3270–3271**
Gaṇeśa in, 3270–3271, 3273
Gaṇas (flocks), 778
Gan Bao, 3066
Ganda religion (Uganda). *See also* Southern African religions
African Independent Churches among, 2571
creation story of, 85
creator god of, 2575
dances of, 2137
hero gods of, 2575–2576
Gaṇḍavyūha (Buddhist text), 1114
Gaṇḍavyūha Sūtra. See also Avataṃsaka Sūtra
Huayan Buddhism, role in, 4145–4146
Gandersheim, Abbey of, Hrotsvit at, 4142–4143
Gandhādhara (Hindu logician), 6774
Gandhakuṭī (sweet-smelling chamber), 9042, 9043
Gandhari language, Buddhist writings in, 1145–1146
Gaṇḍhavyuha Sūtra (Buddhist text), Maitreya in, 5620
Gandhi (film), 3273
Gandhi, Indira
Ānandamayī Mā and, 318
assassination of, 6647
military assault on Sikhism by, 7257
Gandhi, Mohandas (Mahatma), **3271–3273**
Ambedkar (B. R.) opposing, 286, 5400
asceticism of, 3272
in ashram revival, 545, 546, 547, 3272
assassination of, 3273, 5400
autobiography of, 700–701
Besant (Annie) disagreeing with, 845
Bhave (Vinoba) as successor of, 861, 3273
Bose (Netaji Subhascandra) disagreeing with, 827
canonization of, 3273
Chipko movement influenced by, 2622
as devotee, 2321
Erikson (Erik) on, 7476, 7482
family of, 3272, 5399
on God, 5399
Gorakhpurians' interpretation of, 8800
Hindi fiction influenced by, 10034
Hinduism of, 3272–3273
"How to Serve the Cow," 1467
hunger strikes by, 3172
on Indian Jews, 5007
King (Martin Luther, Jr.) influenced by, 5145, 5402
leading by example and experiment, 4425
legacy of, 3273
Mirabai and, 6048

Gandhi, Mohandas (Mahatma) ***continued***
Naess (Arne) influenced by, 2561
nationalism of, 3272–3273, 5398, 9319
nonviolence of, 197, 3272, 4425, 6645, 6646, 6648, 7023, 7257
on *satyāgraha,* 9072
on politics, 5399, 7248
on prayer, 4425
prayers of, 2221
principles of, 546, 3272, 5399–5400
religious influences on, 3271–3272
religious transformation of, 3152
sermon on the mount and, 4845
Tagore (Rabindranath) and, 3272, 5400
Tilak's commentary on *Bhagavadgītā* rejected by, 9199
on unity, 4420–4421
vegetarianism of, 3272
writings of, 3272
Gandhism
example and experiment in, 4425
origins of, 4421
Gandhi's Truth (Erikson), 7482
Gandju, Old Man (mythic figure), 654
Gan 'Eden, 153
Gaṇeśa (deity), **3273–3274**
as son of Śiva, 4436
beheaded by Śiva, 8041
birth of, 3273
as elephant, 2750
in Ellora cave art, 1472
festival of, vol. 6 color insert
household consecration ceremony, 1955
iconography of, 4326–4327, 4438
in Gāṇapatyas sect, 3270–3271, 3273
in Purāṇas, 3271, 3273
in Marathi religions, 5697–5698
origins of, 3273
petitions to, vol. 9 color insert
shrines to, 3271
temples to, 8977
Gaṇeśas (troop leaders), 778, 779
Gaṅgā (deity), 3274, 4324, 7861, 7862. *See also* Ganges River
Gaṅgeśa (Hindu logician), 6774
Ganges River, **3274–3275**
ablutions in, 12
as Śakti, 7862
Banaras on bank of, 778, 3274
bathing in, 7862
as blessing, 980
divinity of, 2621, 7861, 7862
in funeral rites, 3240
healing waters of, 7862
as heavenly river, 7861
Hindi traditions and, 3987
in Hindu religious year, 4018
iconography of, 3275
as living waters, 7862
myths of, 3274–3275
pilgrimage to, 3274, 7170
pollution of, 2622–2623
as sacred space, vol. 5 color insert
Ganges Valley, new religions, emergence in, 8039
Gang of Four (China), 1610, 4637
Gangotri shrine (India), nature-culture threshold in, 8377
Gangra, Council of (c. 345), 7723
Gangs, graffiti and, vol. 6 color insert
Gang-san (gong), 7036
Ganio' Daí Io'. *See* Handsome Lake
Ganja. See Marijuana
Ganjin (Buddhist monk), **3275–3276**
Ganshui xianyuan lu (Daoist text), 2208
Gante, Pedro de, 5915
Gao (emperor), Confucianism and, 1897
Gaonate (in Babylonian Judaism), 4988–4989. *See also* Sa'adyah Gaon
H'ai Gaon, role of, **3737–3738**
halakhah and, 3742–3743, 3744–3745, 4988
Karaism and, 4991
meaning of term, 3742
oral Torah and, 6840
prayer books of, 8387
rabbis in, 7579
Talmudic discussion and commentary in, 3744–3745
yeshivot under, 9883
Gaon of Vilna, Hasidism, opposition to, 3787
Gao Panlong
autobiography of, 701
on cultivation, 8704
Gaoseng zhuan (Biographies of eminent monks), Sengzhao in, 8228
Gaoshang shenxiao zongshi shoujing shi (Daoist text), 2205–2206
Gao Xingjian, 3070
Gaozi, 1572
Gaozong, 1600, 4338
Laozi given title of emperor by, 1602
Gaozu (Chinese emperor), 1591, 1599, 2433
Ga people (Ghana)
ghosts and, 3476
spirit possession in, dance and, 2139
supreme being of, 3570
Gapn (mythic figure), in Canaanite religion, 1384, 1394
Garābah (blood relationship), 4706
Garamantes, myths of, 99
Garang (mythic figure), 3573
Garan temple complex (Japan), Shingon Buddhism and, 8352
Garbagṛha (dwelling place), 9265
Garbe, Richard, Glasenapp (Helmuth von) and, 3496
Garbhādhāna (conception rite), 7814
Garbhakośadhātu (Womb World) *maṇḍala*
in Shingon Buddhism, 8351–8352
Shugendō movement and, 8380
García Icazbalceta, Joaquín, 5922
García Márquez, Gabriel
liberation theology and, 5438
One Hundred Years of Solitude, 3063, 5438
Garcilaso de la Vega, 567, 3415–3416
on *huacas,* 8612
on syncretism, 8608
Gardel, Pierre, 2155
Gardell, Mattias, 2663
Garden of Eden. *See* Eden, Garden of
Garden of Empowering Liberation (monastery), 1071, 1072
Garden of the Martyrs, The (Kāshifī), 7632, 9022
Gardens, **3276–3283**. *See also* Agriculture
of Adonis *(kepoi),* 2536
in African myths, 98
alternative understandings of, 3279
in Buddhism, 3277, 3278
Zen, 9947
in Christianity
prayers for, 3280
recreational, 3277
views of, 3276–3277
Eastern, 3276
cosmic, 3277–3278
of Eden (*See* Eden)
feminine sacrality and, 3019
gender roles in, 3280–3281
in indigenous traditions, **3279–3281**
in Islam, **3282–3283**
architectural design of, 6208
history of, 3282–3283
literature of, 3283
modern, 3283
recreational, 3277
views of, 3276–3277
literary anthologies as, 3279
overview of, **3276–3279**
prayers for, 3280, 3281
rituals associated with, 3280, 3281
subsistence, 3278, 3279–3281
symbolism of, 3277
violence implicit in, 3015
Western, 3276–3279
Gardet, Louis, 533, 4717, 4718
on mirrors, 6063
Gardner, Gerald, 3021–3022, 6471, 7829
Crowley (Aleister) and, 2072
esoteric orders associated with, 6568
sexual magic and, 8251
Gardner, Gerald Brosseau, 9728–9729, 9774–9775
Gardner, Helen, 5487
Gardner, Percy, 6105
Gardnerian Wicca, 9729
Gardnerian Witchcraft, 7829
Gardnerian Witches, 6471
Gargoris dynasty (Tartessian), 4250
Garibay, Angel María, 5922
Garifuna language, 3283
Garifuna religion and society (Central America), **3283–3287**
ancestors in, 3284, 3285–3286
ancestry of, 3283
emigration of, 9307
new developments in, 3286
population of, 3283
rituals of, 3284–3286
major, 3285–3286
small-scale, 3284–3285
Roman Catholicism in, 3284
shamanism in, 3283–3284, 3286
transculturation of, 3283–3284, 9307–9308
Garis (stones), 4361
Garmr (mythic dog), 9426
Garner, Helen, 3082, 3084
Garnet, Henry Highland, 68
Garninyirdi (sticks), 2379
Garōdman (Paradise), 1647
Garrard-Burnett, Virginia, 5929, 5930–5931
Garrawurra, Dhalanganda, 679–680
Garrett, John, 6072
Garrigou-Lagrange, Reginald Marie, 583
Garrison, James H., 2365
Garstang, John, archaeological work of, 5111
Garuḍa (mythic eagle), 4438
soma stolen by, 8522
swiftness of, 2554
Garuḍa (mythic serpent), vol. 8 color insert
Garvey, Amy Jacques, 75
Garvey, Marcus, **3287**
black nationalism of, 2767
on Ethiopianism, 75
NAACP criticizing, 3287
Rastafari and, 7623–7624, 7626
Universal Negro Improvement Association formed by, 1438, 3287
Garvie, A. E., 6105
Gasan Jōseki (Buddhist monk), 9947
Gas attacks, by Aum Shinrikyō, 631–632
Gason, Samuel, 687
Gaspraly, Ismail, 4618, 4619

Gassendi, Pierre, 9422
materialism and, 5776
Gasser, Vincent Ferrer (bishop), 9531–9532
Gaster, Moses, 3288
expulsion of, Eliade and, 2759
Gaster, Theodor H., 2444, 2445, **3288–3289**
education of, 3288
Frazer (James G.) and, 3288–3289
on myth-ritualism, 3288–3289, 4044
on rituals, 7844
writings of, 3288
Gatci·"kwae (ballgame), 754
Gateless Barrier, 1524
Gate of the Reward (Nahmanides), 154
Gates of Light (Gikatilla), 9378
Gates of Prayer (prayer book), Reform Judaism and, 8388
Gates of Repentance (prayer book), Reform Judaism and, 8388
Gateways. *See* Portals
Gāthās
Amesha Spentas in, 290
author of, 9934, 9935, 9988
in Avesta, 709
cattle in, 1466
days of, 1355
dualism in, 2506, 2507
European scholars on, 6999
Frashōkereti in, 3189
translation of, 9994
twins in, 9412, 9413
Zarathushtra in, 9935–9936
"Gathered Church" notion
in Congregationalism, 1938
and separation of church and state, 1968
Gatis (destinies), 1092, 1093
Gatlif, Tony, 3098
Gatumdug (deity), 5958
Gatwood, Lynn, 3323
Gauchet, Marcel, on law and religion, 5326
Gauḍapāda (Indian philosopher), **3289–3290,** 9545
on *māyā,* 5795
Gaudium et spes. See Constitution on the Church in the Modern World
Gauḍīya Maṭh
founding of, 1347
Prabhupada in, 7355
Gauḍīya Sampradāya (order)
bhakti movement and, 3985–3986
initiation in, 3986
Kṛṣṇa worshipped by, 5250
Gauḍīya Vaiṣṇavism, 826, 7355. *See also* Vaiṣṇavism
Caitanya and, 1346
Gauguin, Paul, 4347
Gaul
Celts associated with, 1478
hermitages of, 2826
learned classes (druids, bards and *vātis),* 1479
Leo I in, 5410
persecution of Christians in, 1688
Roman conquests in, 7911
Rome sacked by, 7894
women of, 3388
Gaulish language, 1479
Gaulish religion. *See* Celtic religion
Gaulle, Charles de, Maritain (Jacques) and, 5712
Gaunilo, Anselm criticized by, 373, 7123
Gaun ti Kembong (deity), 9241
Gaurī (deity), 4326, 4436, 9089
Gaurico, Luca, 564
Gautama (Vedic man), 9685
Gautama Buddha. *See* Buddha, the
Gautama Indrabhūti, 4765
Gautier, Théophile, 2155
Gautier of Montfaucon, Count, 3649
Gautreks saga, Starkaðr the Old in, 8024
Gavrinis, passage grave of, 5824
Gay, Volney
on Freud (Sigmund), 7839, 7858
ritual studies of, 7858
Gayadhara (Tantric master), 1153, 1224
Gāyatrī Mantra, 5677
as creed, 2053
sacred language of, 5304
Gāyatrīs, 5677
Gay men and lesbians. *See also* Homosexuality
in Afro-Brazilian religions, 121
gay rights movement and, 4117
ordination of, in Episcopal Church, 7404
in Reconstructionist Judaism, 7639
in Reform Judaism, 7673
religion and, 9792
as social category unique to Western culture, 4117
Gayo language, 25
Gayō Maretan (androgyne), 3372, 9995
Gay spirituality, types of, 5864
Gay studies, 5864
differentiation from lesbian studies, 5413, 5414
Gaze, sacred, vol. 11 color insert
Gbaya people (Mali), rites of passage of, 88–89
GBC. *See* Governing Body Commission
Gcod order (Buddhism), 1227, 1228
Gcod rite (Buddhism)
exorcism and, 8273
Ma gcig Lab sgron and, 5557, 5558
Gdaṅ (hymn), 6298
Ge. *See* Ge religions
Geb (deity)
in Egyptian pantheon, 2704
in judgment of the dead, 5026
Gebara, Ivone, feminist theology of, 5440
ecology and, 2610
Mary in, 5755
Gebeleizis. *See* Zalmoxis
Gebelin, Court de, on tarot cards, 1414
Gebet, Das (Heiler), prayer in, 3897
Ge Chaofu, 2205
Gèdè (spirits), 9636, 9637
in Caribbean neo-African cults, 1433
Gedimu Islam (China), 4633, 4635
Gee, Maurice, 3085
Geering, Lloyd, in New Zealand, 8768
Geertz, Clifford, 4718
anthropological study of religion reviewed by, 381–382
on ceremony, 1513–1514
on cockfights, 3260, 3261, 3267, 3268
colonialist agenda and, 8639
on cultural system, religion as, 8467–8468
on dismissal of religion, 6369
film studies influenced by, 3100
hermeneutical approach of, 8499–8501
on liturgy, 5492
on peasant religion, 3151
on reflexivity, 7649
on religion, 7702
religion defined by, 378, 7328
Ricoeur (Paul), influence of, 8499
on ritual, 7833, 7842, 7850
on thick description, 8499, 8500
Geez language, 3085
Ethiopian liturgy in, 2861
Gefjun (deity), 3453
parallels between Freyja and, 3218
Gehenna (Hell), 153, 9453–9454
in Christianity, development of concept, 8564
Hades *vs.,* 8564
in Islam, 6984, 9455–9456
eschatology, 2837
in Qur'ān, 3885
in Judaism, 6984
Ge Hong (Chinese writer), 1575, 1597, **3290–3291**
and Celestial Masters religion, 2181–2182
Laozi described by, 5319
on miracles, 6052
Tao Hongjing and, 8996
Geiger, Abraham, **3291–3292**
Adler (Felix) studying under, 33
Goldziher (Ignácz) studying under, 3634
Kohler (Kaufmann) studying under, 5214
on Pharisees, 4877
on prophecy, 7441
in Reform Judaism, 3291–3292, 4902, 5019, 7668–7669, 9238
writings of, 3291–3292
Geihinnom (Hell). *See* Gehenna
Geiji (bells), 7036
Geist. See Spirit(s)
Geisteskrankheit (spirit-illness), 2284
Geisteswissenschaften (human sciences), 2353. *See also* Cultural sciences
Ge language groups, 3292. *See also* Ge religions
Gelasius I (pope), 6967
Gelassenheit ("releasement"), Heidegger (Martin) on, 3896
Gelder, Ken, 690
Gẹlẹdẹ society
festival of, 9910
masks of, 90, 2458
masquerade dances of, 2140–2141
Geller, Jay, 3046
Gellius, Aulus, 3125
Gello (female spirit), 2277
Gelugpa Buddhism. *See* Dge lugs pa order of Buddhism
Gelukpa Buddhism. *See* Dge lugs pa order of Buddhism
Gemara' (Mishnah commentary), 4976
Gematria, 272
Gemeinschaft and Gesellschaft (Tönnies), 9230
Ge ming (breaking of the mandate), 7790
Geming geji (revolutionary song), 6292
Geminus, on Greek calendar, 6171
Gems, of Dacian Riders, 2123, 2124
Gender, **3295–3423**. *See also* Androgyny; Feminism; Gender studies; Men's studies; Women
in Acehnese religion, 25–26
affliction and, 56, 57, 58
in African American religions, **10036–10041**
in African religions, **3400–3406**
central Bantu, 1510
of healers, 3818
Mami Wata and, 5630
Swahili females, resistance by, 1515

Gender *continued*
ancestor worship and, 324
artistic expression of, 4170
in Australian Indigenous religions, 638–639, 645, **3389–3395**
history of study of, 686–687
myths of, 654
problems with sources on, 3389–3390
and beauty, 810, 811, 812–813
blurring of, in cosmologies, 4115–4116
in Buddhism, **3330–3335**
Chinese, 3343–3344
Japanese, 3346, 3348
sanctuary access and, 9830
cannibalism and construction of gender, 1404
in Celtic religion, **3387–3389**
in Chinese religion, **3338–3345**
healing and, 3859–3860
in Christianity, **3356–3364**
Eriugena on, 2831
nature and, 2647
clothing and, 1827
in Confucianism, 3340–3341, 3346
and conversion, experience of, 1972
dance as vehicle for conveying, 2136
in Daoism, 3341–3342
of deities
and functions, 5758
in Roman religion, 7900
shift of, in Semitic mythology, 1874
of devils, 2315
equality of
in early Islam, 6224
in progressive Islam, 6099
feminist understanding of, 3299, 3313
in Fundamentalism, 3304
gap, documentation of, 3296
in gardening, 3280–3281
in gay studies, 5414
of God, in Qabbalah, 4981
of heroes, 3958, 3959
in Hinduism, **3318–3326**
Śiva and, 8417
in Swaminarayan movement, 8890, 8892
history of study of (*See* Gender studies)
homosexuality, gender-reversed, 4115–4116
human body and, 4163–4167
humor and, 4198–4199
in Candomblé, 122–123
in Indus Valley religion, male animals and goddess in, 3989
in Raëlian religion, 7598
in Islam, **3364–3371**
progressive, 6099
in Jainism, **3326–3330**
in Japanese religions, **3345–3350**
in Japanese study of religion, 8778
in Judaism, **3350–3356**
in *Genesis* creation account, 8316
in Qabbalah, androgyny of God in, 8315
synagogues, gender separation in, 3750, 8922
law and, 5360–5361
leadership and, 5387
meanings of term, 3296–3297, 3330
in Mediterranean religions, **3381–3387**
in Melanesian religions, segregation of, 4115
in Mesoamerican religions, **3411–3415**
in Mesopotamian religions, **3375–3381**
in Minoan religion, 38–39
monasticism and, 6756 (*See also* Nuns)
in mysticism, 6358
nationalism and, 9631
in Near Eastern religions, **3375–3381**
in Neopaganism, 7831
in New Guinea religions, 6505, 6508
new religious movements and, 6516, 6533
in North American Indian religions, **3406–3411**
in Oceanic religions, **3395–3400,** 7808–7809
mana and, 8515–8516
overview of, **3296–3310**
in Paleolithic cosmology, 1470
prophecy and, 8695
puberty exclusion of girls, in Upper Xingu religion (Brazil), 2011
in puberty rites, 7798
public *vs.* private spheres and, 4107
in rites of passage, 7797, 7798, 7808–7809
roles, **3420–3423**
challenges to, 3422
definition of, 3420
nature *vs.* culture in, 3421–3422
in rites of passage, 7797
sex *vs.* gender in, 3420–3421
in Sikh Dharma and 3HO, 3879
slavery and, 7627–7628
in Roman religion, of deities, 7900
sacrifice and, 8009
in secret societies, 8211
in Selk'nam religion, 8224–8225
vs. sex, 3296–3297, 3299, 3420–3421
sexuality and, 8244–8245
in Sikhism, **3335–3338**
in South American religions, **3415–3420**
spirit possession and, 8694–8697
in Syrian religions, **3375–3381**
of tricksters, 9351, 9357–9358
in Unarius, 9449
of untouchables, 9476
virginity and, 9607
vs. women, 3296, 3330
in women's studies in religion, 9787–9788
in Zoroastrianism, **3371–3375**
Gender, Religion and Diversity (King and Beattie), 3301, 3315
Gender and Salvation (Jani), 3326
Gender Development Index, 3296
Gender gap, documentation of, 3296
Gender of the Gift, The (Strathern), 3396
Gender studies, **3310–3318**. *See also* Feminism; Women's studies
in African religions, 3400–3404
in Chinese religion, 3338–3339
development of field, 3296–3297, 3313–3314
three-phase pattern in, 3319
difference and diversity in, 3303–3304
feminism and, 3310–3313
development of, 3297–3298
globalization and, 3304
in goddess worship, 3613
in Hinduism, 3321–3324
in Islam, 3365–3368, 3369–3370
in Japanese religions, 3345–3348
Jewish studies and, 4885
methodologies of, 3298, 3299–3301
multidisciplinary nature of, 3298
in Near East studies, 3375
non-Western, 3314–3315
paradigm shifts and, 3299
postcolonialism in, 3314–3315
Hinduism and, 3321–3322
queer theory in, 3300, 3314
recognition of value of, 3296
in religion, 9792–9793
research themes in, 3301–3303
language and symbolism, 3302
religious experience, 3302–3303
roles and status, 3301–3302
violence and, 3304
vs. women's studies, 3296
women's studies and, 9792–9793
in Zoroastrianism, 3371–3372
Gender Trouble (Butler), 3296, 3420–3421
"Genealogical Method as Anthropological Inquiry, The" (Rivers), 2421
Genealogy, **3423–3427**. *See also* Kinship
Cain's descendants, 1344
two-seed theory, 1658
colonialist constructed genealogies of indigenous people, 1856
in *Genesis,* 884
of Greek deities, 3678–3679
in Hinduism, in Purāṇas, 4025
in Maori religion, 5682–5683
Melanesian, 6501
principles of, 3423–3424
systems of, 3424–3426
Genealogy of Morals, The (Nietzsche), 7490
General, in Buddhism, 2628
General Anthroposophical Society, Steiner (Rudolf) and, 8738
General assemblies
in Mesopotamia, 5947, 5951
in Presbyterian polity, 1767–1768
General Church of the New Jerusalem, 8904–8905. *See also* Swedenborgianism
General Conferences, in United Methodist Church, 1767
General Convention of the Church of the New Jerusalem, in Swedenborgian movement, 8903
General Conventions, in Episcopal Church, 1766–1767
General Council of Burmese Associations, 1140
General Introduction to Religious Studies (Anesaki), 342
Generalization
comparative-historical method and, 1871
comparative religion and, 1877
General Jewish Congress, 6899
General relativity, theory of, 2740, 2879
General Synod, in United Church of Christ, 1768
General Theory of Magic (Mauss), 2541–2542
Generation names, in Papua New Guinea, 7809
Generation of the Soul in the Timaios, The (Plutarch), 7200
Genesis, 878, 879
Abraham in, 14–15
Adam in, 29–30

allegorical exegesis of, 872, 873
ancestors in, mythic, 325
androcentrism in, 334
androgynes in, 338
animals in, 360
ʿAqedah (binding) of Isaac in, as Holocaust paradigm, 4088
Aramaic translation of, 887
ascension in, 518
Athirat (Asherah) in, 591
ballet based on themes from, 2163
blood in, 986
body and soul dualism in, 4158
Cain and Abel, **1344–1345**
Canaanite parallels, 1396–1397
chaos in, 1537
circumcision in, 7080, 7818
content of, 9232
creation stories in, 2967, 4743, 4744, 5445
gender and, 8316
literal interpretation of, 2910
sky in, 8428
water in, 9698
death as returning to dust in, 4158
dietary laws in, 7508
Documentary Hypothesis on, 883
Eddy's (Mary Baker) exegesis on, 2695
Enlightenment and interpretation of, 874–875
Enoch in, 2802
1 Enoch story based on, 416
Enuma elish compared to, 2811
Eve in, 2896
evil and sin in, 8404
expulsion in, 2938
the Fall in, 2967–2968, 5201
the Flood in, 2968, 3131, 3132
Garden of Eden in, 6981–6982
gender in, 3358
genealogies in, 884
Gnostic interpretations of, 3525
God in
compassion of, 6185–6186
involvement with humans by, 3540
names of, 3539
origins of worship of, 3539
will of, 6183
Herder (Johann Gottfried) on, 3919
Hermetic interpretation of, 3941–3942
Hoffmann (David) on, 869
humor in, 4196
Ibn ʿEzraʾ on, 4266
Ibn Ḥazm on, 7237
Irenaeus on, 4540
Isaac in, 4544
Ishmael in, 4552
Judah and Tamar in, 34
knowledge in, 5201
Leah in, 7591
Levites in, 5422
liberation from habits of mind in, 6364
al-Maghribī (Samuel) on, 7239
marriage in, 4733, 5725
meat in, 6982
Messiah in, 7231–7232
Middle Platonist interpretation of, 7191
midrash on, 6015
morality in, 6183
myth about death in, 2237
Nahmanides (Moses) on, 867
new religions' reinterpretations of, 6530–6531
Nissim of Gerona on, 867
pesher of, 7065
Philistines in, 7102
Philo Judaeus on, 7191
Pico della Mirandola on, 7141
"primeval history" in early chapters of, 4058
Qirqisānī (Yaʿqūb al-) on, 5085
Qurʾān compared with, 2969
Rachel in, 7591
Rashbam on, 866
Sarah in, **8112**
Sforno (ʿOvadyah) on, 867
shrines in, 4746
sinfulness in, 9115
Soloveitchik (Joseph Baer) on, 8519
sources for, 14, 15
Spencer (Herbert) on, 8678
stones in, 8744
Swedenborg (Emanuel) on, 8899
Temple sanctity in, 933
temptation in, 9069, 9071, 9072
theft in, 4738
tithes in, 9209
in Torah, 9231, 9232
Trees of Knowledge and Life in, 9335, 9577
Genesis Apocryphon, 887
Genesis Rabbah, on Abraham, 16
Genetic engineering, 942
in Raëlian religion, 7597, 7599
Genetics, **3427–3431**. *See also* Sociobiology and evolutionary psychology
ethical and theological issues in, 8190–8191
eugenics and, 2879–2882
in evolutionary ethics, 2919–2920
gender and, 3420
gene-culture coevolution, 8475
medical ethics and, 5810–5811, 5813–5814
in neo-Darwinism, 2909
"playing God" problem and, 8187
and pride, warnings against, 8187
religion instinct and, 2916
Roman Catholicism, position of, 8190–8191
"selfish gene" thesis, 8474
Geneva
Calvin and, 1375, 7281, 7661
Knox (John) in, 5212
Genevan Confession of Faith, 7281
Genghis Khan. *See* Chinggis Khan
Gengshen day, 2188
Genii (spirit), 2277
Geniocracy, 7597
Genitals
bloodletting, Maya, 1358
discharges from, and pollution, 7511, 7513
in Maori religion, 5681
mutilation of (*See* Castration; Circumcision; Clitoridectomy)
Genita Mana (deity), 5321
Genius loci (spiritual places), 777
Genizah (storehouse) of Cairo, legal documents found at, 3746, 4980, 4989
Genkōshakusho (Buddhist text), 995
Gyōgi in, 3721
Gennadius of Marseilles, 1448
on Makarios of Egypt, 5624
Gennep, Arnold van, **3431–3432**
on dynamism, 362
education of, 3431–3432
on initiation rituals, 118, 4480, 4481
Lévi-Strauss on, 3432
on liminality, 7844
on liturgy, 5491
on power, 7348, 7349
on rites of passage, 3432, 7797, 7801, 7802, 7804, 7806–7807, 7811, 7844
liturgy in, 5492
phases of, 5460
on ritual, 2436, 7049–7050
on the sacred and the profane, 7842
on salutations, 8060
on spirit possession, 8691
structuralism and, 8752
on taboo, 3432
on tears, 9024
on totemism, 3432, 9251
Turner (Victor) and, 118, 381, 7049, 9405–9405
writings of, 3432
Genocide. *See also* Holocaust, the
in Moses' story, 6200
statistics on, 4180
Genovese, Eugene, 77
Genroku period (Japan), Kokugaku movement in, 5214
Genshin (Buddhist monk), **3432–3433**
and Amitābha, 292
and Hōnen, 1243, 3433
hell, descriptions of, 2029
on Impure Lands, 7503
music of, 6300
and Pure Land Buddhism in Japan, 4119
and recitative *nianfo,* 6602
Ryōgen and, 3432, 9077
writings of, 9079
Gensō ("returning"), Shinran on, 8354
Gentile, Giovanni, 9391
on knowledge, 5207
Gentile Impurities and Jewish Identities: Intermarriage and Conversion from the Bible to the Talmud (Hayes), 7514
Gentiles
election of, 2746–2747
Paul on, 7014, 7016
Samaritans as, Abbahu and, 2
Geoffrey of Monmouth
and *Mabinogion,* 5546
on Merlin, 5878
Geographical classification of religions, 1819
Geography
ecological studies in, 2611
Islamic scholarship on, 8782
of religions, *vs.* cultural ecology, 2611
sacred, **3433–3437**
divisions of geographic space in, 7982
Geography (Ptolemy), 7492
Geography (Strabo), 9128
Geography of Religion, The (Soper), 2611
Geomancy, 2406, **3437–3438**
and ancestor worship, 324
Arab, 3437
caves and mountains in, 1468
Chinese, 3437–3438 (*See also* Feng-shui)
in *onmyōdō,* 6828–6829
Western, 3437
Geometry, **3438–3445**
and dance, in Renaissance, 2154
Euclid in, 2878–2879
in Islamic architecture, 6208
of Ptolemy, 7492
Geonic period of Judaism. *See* Gaonate
George (saint)
day dedicated to, in Balto-Finnic areas, 3108

George (saint) ***continued***
as dragon slayer, 2432
George II (king of England), 1339
George, Carol V. R., 68–69
George, David, 5443
George, Stefan, 9651
George Adamski Foundation, 9433
George of Alexandria, on Chrysostom, 1761
Georgetown, Madras, India, sacred and commercial space in, 1806–1807
Georgetown College, Carroll (John) and, 1445–1446
Georgi, J. G., 3110
Georgi, J. P., 5709
Georgia (country). *See* Caucasus
Georgia, Cherokee Nation v., 7301–7302
Georgia, Worcester v., 7301–7302
Georgian language
alphabet of, 5764
biblical translations into, 922
Georgian Orthodox Church
in Orthodox structure, 2589
political involvement of, 2588–2589
Georgics (Vergil), descent into the underworld in, 2297–2298
Georgiev, Vladimir, 3466
Gepids, 4492
Gerald de Barri. *See* Giraldus Cambrensis
Gerald of Wales. *See* Giraldus Cambrensis
Geranium, symbolism of, 3135
Geranos (dance), 5277
Gérard d'Abbeville, 9161
Gerard of Cremona, 250, 7492
Gerard of Zutphen, 7772
Gerber, Jane, 2922
Gerðr (giantess), 2692, 3219–3220
Ge religions (South America)
cosmology in, 8587–8588
death cults in, 8584–8585
geography of, 8575
Ge-Timbira religion, 8629–8631
mythology of, **3292–3295**
analysis of, 3294–3295
content of, 3293
vs. cosmology, 3293
humor in, 6364
lord of the animals in, 5515–5516
messianism in, 5985
narrative styles of, 3292–3293
settings for, 3293
transformation, 3293–3294
origin of agriculture in, 8590
solar and lunar gods in, 8578
Gerhaert, Nicolaus, vol. 13 color insert
Gerim (resident alien), 4731
Gerima, Haile, 3098
Geringsing (cloth), 9088, 9090
Gerizim, Mount
as "navel of the earth," 1501
pilgrimage to, 8070
Samaritans on, 8067, 8068, 8069, 8070
Gerlach, Franz Dorotheus, 730
Germain (saint), 4245, 4246
German Confessing church, kingdom of God in, 5150–5151
German empire, Jews under, 5013–5014
German Enlightenment, societal construct in, 7716
Germania (Tacitus), 767, 2366, 3447, 3450, 9128
Germanic religion, **3445–3461**
afterlife in, **167–169,** 3448, 3456
ages of world in, 176
álfar (elves) in, **254–255**
and Anglo-Saxon paganism, 6942, 6943
apocalypse in, 3456–3457
axis mundi in, 3449
berserkers in, **842–843,** 4478
burials in, 3457
boat, 989–990, 3457
cats in, 1462, 1463
chaos in, 1537
Christianity in
development of, 1681
influences of, 3457, 3460
sagas, effect on, 8024, 8025
cosmology of, 3447–3448
creation in, 3446–3447
of earth, 3446–3447
of man, 3454–3455
microcosm-macrocosm homologization in, 4159
spitting in, 8721–8722
deities of, 3449–3454 (*See also* Baldr; Heimdallr; *See also* Æsir; *See also* Óðinn; Thor; *specific deities*)
Christian days named after, 1689, 1873
of esoteric knowledge and magic, 3623
female, 9517
fertility, 3218–3221, 6642
marriage among, 3460
origin of, 3446–3447
Saxo's euhemerization of, 8142
sources on, 3446
sovereignty of, 5995
status in pantheon, 3452–3454
dragons and serpents in, 8457, 8458
dvergar (dwarfs) in, **2532**
end of world in, 3456–3457
eschatology of, 2835–2836
eyes in, 2941
fate in, 3001
giants in, 4960
Golden Age in, 3628
Grimm (Jacob) on, 4458
guardian spirits in, *Fylgjur,* 3246
Hartland (E. Sidney) on, 3782
Hininbjörg as heavenly mountain, 1501
history of study of, **3458–3461**
demonism in, 3458
euhemerism in, 3458
historicism in, 3459
place-name approach in, 3453, 3459
household spirits in, 4106
initiation in, 4478–4479
literature of (*See* Eddas; *Prose Edda*)
in Migration and post-Migration periods, 3451
mythology of
horses in, 4134, 4135
origin of mead, 3455
rejuvenation, 7683
Snorri Sturlson on, 8460
nature worship in, 6439
necromantic practices in, 6452
neoshamanism and seidr ritual, 8295
number nine in, 6748–6749
oath-taking in, 9640, 9641–9642
ordeal in, 6847
origin of mead, 849, 3455
overview of, **3445–3458**
practices of, 3457–3458
Prose Edda cosmogony, 1451
rejuvenation in, 7683
resurrection in, 744
and Roman Empire, invasions of, folk beliefs, diffusion of, healing practices in, 3845
in Roman period, 3450–3451
runes in, 7938–7941
sacrifice in, dismemberment in, 2366–2367
sagas in, **8023–8026**
Sami religion and, 474
shamanism in, 8273
sources on, 3445–3446
springs in, 3178
sun worship in, 8836
transition to Christianity, 168–169, 3445
tree symbolism in, 1502, 9335 (*See also* Yggdrasill)
cosmic, 3448–3449, 3456
valkyries in, 3001
value system of, 3457–3458
in Viking age, 3451–3452
waters in, 6439
winter solstice in, 9740–9741
writing's origins and, 270
Germanic tribes, origins of names of, 3447
Germanicus (Roman emperor), 4558
German Idealism
Kant's (Immanuel) contributions to, 5076
post-Kantian contributions to, 5080
German Ideology, The (Marx), 5745–5746
Germanische Mythen (Mannhardt), 5676
German language
heilige as "holy" or "sacred" in, 4099
and "holy," concept of, 7969
Pentateuch translated into, 5854
German Oriental Society, 2263
Germanos, Cassian and, 1447
Germanos I (Byzantine patriarch), 4289, 4290, 4353, 6619
German philosophy
knowledge in, 5209
Krochmal (Naḥman) influenced by, 5247
German Sermon (Eckhart), 6337
German Social Democratic Party, 2671
German Sociological Society, 9230
Germany and German religions. *See also* Germanic religion
Agudat Yisra'el in, 194–195
Anabaptism in, 304, 7660
anti-Semitism in, Hoffmann (David), defense by, 4077
Buddhism, 1187, 1188, 1189, 1190
calligraphy in, 1372
Canisius as second apostle of, 1402
Carolingian dynasty, missionary efforts, 1683
China, study of, 1635
Christmas traditions in, 1757
colonies of
in New Guinea, 1417, 1418, 1419
in Ngarambe, 5181
demonic possession in, 8687
drama in, 2474, 2475
economics and religion in, critiques of, 2669–2670
the Enlightenment in, 2795, 2796–2797
Evangelical Marian Sisterhood of, 6765
folklore of
das Irrlicht, 2952
der Kobold, 2951
Gnosticism in, 3524–3525
history of study of, 3514, 3532–3533
Grail movement in, 3653
Hermetism in, 3947–3948, 3950–3952
hermits of, 2828
historiography in, 4042–4043, 4048
Holiness movement in, 4083
Idealism in, Fichte (Johann Gottlieb) and, 3048–3049
Indological studies in, 4446
Inner City Movement in, 8446
Islam, 4674, 4675, 4676, 4678, 4680
Islamic studies in, 4723
Jewish studies in, 4874–4879
Jews in
emancipation of, 5019

integration of, 5019
Judaism (*See also* Ashkenazic Hasidism)
iconography of, 4340
Jewish peoplehood in, 4862–4863
medieval Jewish persecution, 7055, 7057
Orthodox, 6900–6901
rabbinical seminaries in, 7581
rabbis in, 7579–7580
Reform Judaism, 7668–7669
science of (*See Wissenschaft des Judentums*)
Kulturkampf, 1693
Landeskirchen (territorial churches), 1773
Mennonites in, 5860
Moravians in, 6191
museums in, 6246
nationalism in, Strauss (David Friedrich) and, 8748
nature in, philosophy of, 6433–6437
Nazi period (*See also* Nazism)
astrology in, 2372
Baeck (Leo) on, 736–737
Barmen Declaration (1934) in, 2061
Barth (Karl) fighting, 789, 791
Bonhoeffer (Dietrich) fighting, 1016–1017
Christianity, conception of, 1693–1694
New Year festival in, 6593
occultism in, 6782
philosophical phenomenology in, 7088
poetry and drama in, Hrotsvit, role of, 4142–4143
poetry in, 7219, 7220
Protestantism
Baptist churches, 785
liberal, 6104
Pentecostalism, 7029
Pietism in, 7142
Reformation in (*See* Reformation)
religious studies in, 1872
Renaissance humanism in, 4176
Roman Catholicism
Benedictines, 821, 822, 1018
Dominicans, 2414
Inquisition in, 4498, 4500
pilgrimage in, 7148
during Reformation, 7657
Romantic movement in (*See* Romanticism, German)
sociology in, 8493–8494 (*See also specific scholars*)
Strauss (David Friedrich) on, 8748
study of religion in
Clemen's role in, 1822
Mesoamerican religions in, 5940, 5941
scholars of, 10081
Transcendental Meditation in, 9290
in World War I, Protestant support for, 790
in World War II (*See also* Nazism)
and Karaite sect, 5084
Gernet, Jacques, 267, 1314
Gernet, Louis, 3662, 3672
Gero Crucifix, 4345
Gerondi, Yonah
Adret (Shelomoh ben Avraham) studying with, 36
ethics of, 4912–4913
Geronimo, 574
Gershom ben Yehudah, **3461**
legal decisions of, 5011
polygyny banned by, 3352, 3461, 3749–3750
responsa by, 3461
women affected by policies of, 3352, 3461
Gerson, Jean de
on mystical theology, 6341
on mystical union, 6337
Gersonides (Levi ben Gershom) (Jewish philosopher), **3461–3463**
Abravanel (Isaac) opposing, 17
on Aristotle, 480, 481, 3462
biblical exegesis of, 866
commentaries of, 3462
condemnations of, 3462
cosmology of, 3462–3463
on creation, 2642, 3549
on God's knowledge, 3462, 3549, 6962
in Jewish thought and philosophy, 4894–4896
on prophecy, 7440
writings of, 3462
Gerson-Kiwi, Edith, 6251
Gertrude the Great (nun), 822
Gerusalemme conquistata (Tasso), 7220
Gerusalemme liberata (Tasso), 7220
Gervase of Tilbury, on devils, 2316
Geryon (monster), 6165
Geryon dynasty (Tartessian), 4250
Geryoneia (Stesichorus of Himera), 4250
Gesammelte Schriften (Troeltsch), 9366
Gesar epic (Tibet), 2814, **3463–3465**
appropriation of, 3464
bards transmitting, 3464
Buddhism and, 3463, 3464
episodes of, 3463–3464, 9185
origins of, 3463
study of, 9190–9191
versions of, 3463
Geschichte der Römer (Bachofen), 730
Gesellschaft fuer Juedische Volkskunde, 4882
Gesellschaft zur Förderung der Wissenchaft des Judentums, 4882
Geser Khan (epic hero), 6142
Geshtinanna (deity), 3594, 4403, 5958, 9417
Gessa (taboos), 1492
Gesta Danorum (Saxo Grammaticus), Sventovit cult in, 8888–8889
Gestation. *See* Pregnancy
Gestefeld, Ursula, 6536
Gestures. *See* Postures and gestures
Get (bill of divorce), 7821, 7822
Getae people. *See* Geto-Dacian religion
Gethin, Rupert, 6956
on consciousness in Buddhism, 8548
Ge-Timbira religion (Amazon), 8629–8631
Canela in, 8629
Kayapó in, 8630
Krahó in, 8629–8630
Xikrin in, 8630–8631
Geto-Dacian religion (Thrace), **3465–3468,** 9168, 9169
calendar of, 3467
calendar temple in, 3467
Christianity and, 1682
and Dacian Riders, 2123
and immortalization, 2248
kingship in, 3466, 3467
language of, 9169
priesthood in, 3466, 3467
in Romanian culture, 2754
tattooing among, 9928
territory of, 9168
warrior rites of, 9926
Zalmoxis and, 9926–9928
Gēush Urvan (deity), 4535
Gezerah shavah method, *halakhah* and, 3748
Gezerot (decrees)
in *halakhah* system, 3749
repeal of, 3750
Ghadīr Khumm, Muḥammad's sermon at, 257
Ghai, Subhash, 3098
Ghana and Ghanian religions. *See also* Akan religion; Ashanti religion; Fon and Ewe religion
agriculture in myths of, 191
Christianity in, political theology, 1723
ghosts in, 3476
hierodouleia (sacred prostitution) in, 3969
Islam in, 4601
LoDagaa people of
ancestor worship by, 321–322
myths of, 91, 95, 99
museums in, 6245
Nzema people of, history of study of, 117
spirit possession in, 2139–2140
Ghandhavyūha Sūtra (Buddhist text), 7503
Ghare Bhine (Tagore), 10035
Gharrār (demonic figure), 2315
Ghasaq (darkness), 4554
Ghāṭs (stone steps), 778
Ghaybah (concealment), **3468–3469**
Ghaylan al-Dimashqi, and Qādāri ideas, 3210, 3211
Ghaythī, al-, on *mi'rāj,* 6061
Ghazal (poetic form), 4641, 7222–7223
Ḥāfiẓ Shīrāzī and, 3734
Ghazālī, Abū Ḥāmid al-, **3469–3472**
on almsgiving, 267, 268
on attributes of God, 620–621
Augustine compared with, 3221
autobiography of, 700, 3469–3470
on blasphemy, 976
critique of *falsafah,* 2974–2975
death of, 3471
education of, 3469
on fasting, 8141
hermeneutics of, 5485
Ibn Rushd's reply to, 2976–2977, 4271–4272
in Ash'arīyah, 534, 537–538, 3469, 3470, 4569
influence of, 3471–3472, 4563
Iqtiṣād of, 5066
on *istikharah,* 7572
Jamā'ī Sunni legalism and, 8855
kalām of, 5066
on knowledge, 5204, 7734–7735
life of, 4570
and modernism, 6097
on mystical union, 6339
mysticism of, 3471–3472, 6349, 6351
on Neoplatonism, 3470, 3472
Nizārī Ismā'īlīyah attacked by, 558
on Fārābī (Abū Naṣr al-), 3470
on Ibn Sīnā, 3470, 4273, 4274, 4275
on *ijmā'* doctrine, 8265
on Ismā'īlī Shiism, 3470
on light of Muḥammad, 6767
on *mi'rāj,* 6060–6061
on rejected *ḥadīths,* 3732

Ghazālī, Abū Ḥāmid al- ***continued***
on *sharīʿah,* 4699
polemics against Christianity, 7242
on prayer preparation, 5447
on religious education, 7734–7735
on resurrection, 8568–8569
skeptical views of, 8421
on soul, 8567, 8570
Sufism, role in, 8815–8816
Sufism of, 3470, 3472, 4569–4570
tafsīr of, 7573, 8955
theodicy of, 9118
on theology, 2383
writings of, 537, 3471, 4569–4570
Ghazālī, Aḥmad
ʿAṭṭār, Farīd al-Dīn and, 601
al-Suhrawardī as pupil of, 9008
Ghazālī, Zaynab al-, 3368
Ghazū (raids), Muḥammad's use of, 6225
Ghazwānī, ʿAbdallāh al-, on God, 3561
Ghelderode, Michel de, 2476
Ghināʾ (singing), 6277
Ghiyāth al-Dīn, 4372
Ghosananda, Mahā, 5133
Ghose, Aurobindo. *See* Aurobindo Ghose
Ghosh, Amitav, 10036
Ghost bear, 807
Ghost Dance, **3472–3475,** 6700–6701
of 1870, 3473, 6666, 6718
of 1890, 3473, 6666, 6718
ban on, 7248
Black Elk in, 957
in California and Intermountain region, 6718
cargo cults compared with, 6666
definition of, 3473
drums in, 2499
Lakota in, 5295
messianism in, 5973
as nativist millennial movement, 6547
principles of, 2139
roots of, 3473–3474, 6513, 6514
shamanism and, 8289
spread of, 3473, 6718
study of, 6670, 6671
Wodziwob's, 3473, 5973, 6718
Wounded Knee massacre and, 6548, 6701
Wovoka's, 3473, 3474, 6701, 6718, 9846–9847
Ghost Festival, 4797, 9835
in Zen Buddhism, 9946
Ghosts, **3475–3478.** *See also* Ancestors; Shades; Spirit(s); Spirit possession
in African religions, 89, 3476–3477
interlacustrine Bantu religions, 4519, 4520
Lugbara religion, 5527
northeast Bantu, 2576
in Buddhism, 3477
feeding of, 9835
in Caribbean religions, 1428
in Chinese religion, 3477
Cheng Hao on, 1561
Cheng Yi on, 1563
Confucius on, 1571
popular tradition, 1605, 1606, 1614, 1618–1619
season festivals and, 1641, 1642–1643, 5231
in Christianity, 3475–3476
in Chuvash religion, 1785
definitions of, 3475
fairies and, 2954
in Greek religion, 164
Hekate as deity of, 3899–3900
in Hittite religion, 4073
in Indian religions, 3477
in Islam, 3476
in Israelite religion, 4743
in Japanese religion, 3477–3478
Hijiri ascetics as protectors against, 3978–3979
at jubilation rites, 8210
in Melanesian religions, 5833, 5838
in Negrito religions, 6455
in New Guinea religions, 6503, 6504, 6505
in North American Indian religions, 6651
in Oceanic religions, 145–146, 2006
in Solomon Islands religions, 8514
and origins of religion, 2238
as possessing spirits, 2928, 2929, 2934
in Roman religions, 166
in Sami religion, 8087–8088
in Samoyed religion, 8096
soul-ghosts, Tylor (E. B.) on, 4183
in South American Indian religions
Andean *supaya,* 8616–8617, 8618–8619
in Juruna religion (Amazon), 8629
in Sumerian religion, 8537
in Vanuatu religions, 9520
at winter solstice, 9741, 9742–9743
Ghost Story (Egypt), 2711
Ghost theory. *See* Manism
Ghouls, in Islam, 3476
Ghūl (demonic figure), 2280, 2315
Ghulām Aḥmad, Mirza, 6738
Aḥmadiyah founded by, 72, 108, 200, 4573, 4650
as Islamic reformer, 72
as *mahdi,* 200
as prophet, 200, 4573
Ghulāt (heretical extremists), 4572, 4760
ʿAlawīyūn as, 225
beliefs of, 259
Ghulūw (zeal), 225
Ghumārah tribe, 835
Ghurar akhbâr mulûk al-Furs, Mazdakism in, 5801
Ghurar al-ḥikam, 260
GI (deity), 5797
Giadruvava (hero), in Caribbean religions, 1429
Giaia (mythic figure), in Caribbean religions, 1429
Giaiael (mythic figure), in Caribbean religions, 1429
Giak (dance), 2455
Giant panda, 808
Giants
chaos and, 1538
in Germanic religion (*See also* Loki)
creation myth of, 3446–3447
in Lengua religion (Gran Chaco), 8634
in Scandinavian mythology, 4959–4960, 6808–6809
Giay, Benny, 6507
Gibb, H. A. R., 4718, 6071
Gibbon, Edward, 2589
as Freemason, 3195
Gibbons, James, **3478–3479**
Gibbons, Rawle, 10027, 10028
Gibbor, Judah, writings of, 5085
Gibbs, Philip, 3398
on God Triwan movement, 6509
Gibbs, Robert, 3428
Gibran, Kahlil, parables of, 6979
Gibson, Edmund, 9726–9727
Gibson, Mel, 3097, 7323
Gicelamu'kaong (deity), in Algonquian religion, 8870–8871
Gichtel, Johann Georg, on angels, 348
Gidatl people (Caucasus), 4614
Gidda (Punjabi folk dance), in Sikhism, 8397
Gidim (ghost), in Sumerian religion, 8537
Gifford, John, 1322
Gift, The (Mauss), 267, 3479
Gift giving, **3479–3486**
in African myths, 93
almsgiving as, 266–269, 3483
in Buddhism, 3482–3483
merit making through, 5873
in Chinese religion, 3483–3484
in Christianity, 3484–3485
at Christmas, 1757
gold and silver in, 6138
in Hinduism, 3482
history of study of, 3480–3482
hospitality and, 4140
in Islam, 3485
in Judaism, 3484
marriage as, 5725
money and, 6137, 6138
in Oceania, women in, 3480–3481
potlatch as model for, 3479–3480
reciprocity in, 267
sacrificial, 7998–7999, 8002
vows and oaths as, 9639–9640
Gift in Sixteenth-Century France, The (Davis), 267
Gigaku (dance drama), 2455, 6300
humor and, 4209
Gihon (river), 7862
Gikatella, Joseph, 9378
Gikuyu people (Kenya). *See* Kikuyu religion
Gilbert, Kevin, 680
Gilbert, William, Hermetism and, 3950
Gilbertines of England, and women, 6763
Gilbert Islands
masculine sacrality in, 5760, 5761
Nauru people of, knotted ropes of, 5197
prophet movements in, 2007
Gilbert of Poitiers, Peter the Apostle on, 7066, 7067
Gilbert of Sempringham, 6763
Gildas, 509
Gilfaethwy (deity), 1489
Gilgamesh (epic hero), **3486–3489**
initiation rituals of, 4477
and Ninhursaga, 6625
quest of, 7553
and rejuvenation, 7684
sun god and, 8837
Gilgamesh, Epic of, **3486–3489**
ancestor veneration in, 2982
Atrahasis in, 598
ax in, 967
bread in, 1040
Bull of Heaven slain by Enkidu, 1465–1466
as combination of literature and religion, 5466
contents of, 3486–3487
descent into the underworld in, 2295, 2298, 2539, 4403
Enlil in, 2800
the Flood in, 598, 884, 2963, 3132, 5963, 7604
harlot in, 3967, 3968
in history of fiction, 3053
Huwawa in, 5276–5277
immortality in, 2770
incense offering in, 4419
initiation ordeals in, 2814, 4477
interpretations of, 3487–3489
justice in, 128, 5962–5963
lovers of Inanna in, 4405

parallels to, 1398
versions of, 3486, 5963
waters of death in, 7863
crossing, 988–989
Gilgul (metempsychosis), 155
Gilhus, Ingvild Saelid, on laughter, 4219
Gilkes, Cheryl Townsend, 75, 79
Gilkey, Langdon, 7882, 9130
Two Language model and, 8184
Gill, Brendan, on Campbell (Joseph), 1380
Gill, Lesley, 3418
Gill, Sam D., 668, 6672
on contextual research, 8786
ritual studies of, 7857
Gillen, Francis James, **3489–3491**
on Australian Indigenous religions, 3489–3491
burial rituals of, 688
as first phase of study, 683
totemism, 9251
transmigration, 9326–9327
women in, 3390
Spencer's (Baldwin) work with, 3489–3491
Gillette, Douglas, 5862
Gilligan, Carol, 813
Gillison, Gillian, 3397
Gilmore, David D., 3314
Gilson, Étienne, **3491–3492**
Aristotle's metaphysics and, 5990
atheism and, 583
on Ibn Rushd, 4272
on knowledge, 5204, 5209
Gimbutas, Marija, **3492–3494**
archaeology of, 456, 3492–3494
archaeomythology of, 3493
on Baltic religion, 327, 756, 764, 771
evaluations of work of, 3493–3494
on female-male polarity in prehistoric art, 3974
in Feminist Spirituality movement, 3312, 3493
on goddess worship, 3616–3617, 9601–9602
on Kurgan culture, 4453
Kurgan theory of, 3493
on matriarchy, 7009
on matrifocal societies, 950
methodology of, 3493
on "Old Europe," 5281
Gimi people, cannibalism among, 1404
*Ginān*s (Islamic poems), **3494**
themes of, 3494
Ginen, 9635, 9636
Ginés de Sepúlveda, Juan, 5322
Ginibi, Ruby Langford, 667
Ginkgo tree, 9337
Ginneken, Jacques van, in Grail movement, 3653
Ginnungagap (primordial void), 1537
in Germanic creation myth, 3446
Ginsberg, H. L., 935
Ginsberg, Louis, Jewish Theological Seminary of America and, 1958
Ginsburger, Moses, 888
Ginza (Mandaean text), **3494–3495,** 5635
Adam in, 3494, 5634
date of, 5638
John the Baptist in, 3495, 5634
Manda d'Hiia in, 3495, 5634
origins of, 3494
structure of, 3494–3495, 5635
translations of, 3495
Ginzberg, Asher, **3495–3496**
influence of, 3496
writings of, 3495–3496
Zionism of, 3495–3496, 4906, 5021, 9980
Ginzburg, Carlo, 5647, 7327
on witches' Sabbath, 8250
Giordano Bruno and the Hermetic Tradition (Yates), 2843
Giorgio, Francesco (Zorzi)
Hermetism and, 3947
Mersenne (Marin) on, 3949
Giotto (artist), color and, 1861–1862
Giovanni da Pian del Carpini (John of Plano Carpini)
historiography of, 4038
on Mari and Mordvins, 5709
Giovanni di Fidanza. *See* Bonaventure
Giovaua (grotto), in Caribbean religions, 1429
Gippius, Zinaida, 5869
Giraldi, L. G., 6088
Giraldus Cambrensis (Gerald of Wales; Gerald de Barri)
on Brighid, 1484
on Celtic inauguration ceremony, 1493
on horse sacrifice, 8239
on prophecy, 4038
Girard, René
Gnosticism and, 3527
on heroes, 3960
on origin of the sacred, 7974
on pain, 6944, 6947
on ritual, 7854
on sacrifice, 8004–8005, 8009
on scapegoat, 8145
Giraud-Teulon, Alexis, 731–732
Girgensohn, Karl, 7474
Giriama movement (Kenya), 2571
healing in
classifications of healers, 3819
diviners, diagnosis by, 3818
Girls' Day (Japan), 2411
Girō, Seno'o, 6608
Gisalo dance songs, 6265–6266
Giselle (ballet), 2155–2156
Gishin (Buddhist monk), 9075
Gīsūdarāz, Muḥammad, on creation, 8705
Gisu religion (Uganda)
creator god of, 2575
divination in, 2577
initiation rites of, 2577
shrines of, for spirits, 2576
Gītā. *See Bhagavadgītā*
Gītagovinda (Sanskrit poem), 826, 4819–4820, 5252, 7209, 7211
Rādhā in, 7593
Gitai, Amos, 3098
Gītāmāhātmya (Hindu text), 854
Gītamitra (Buddhist translator), 1146
Gītāñjali (Tagore), 829, 8958
Gītā Rahasya (Tilak), 854, 9199
Gītārthasaṅgraha (Hindu text), 854
Gītāvali (Tulsīdās), 9393
Gitgaát tribe (North America), on bears, 807
Giuliani, Rudolf, Brooklyn Museum of Art funding withdrawn by, 4282
Giving and receiving. *See also* Gift giving
in vows and oaths, 9639–9640
Gizzida (deity), 2520, 2522. *See also* Dumuzi
Gjessing, Gutorm, 474
GLA. *See* God Light Association
Glacken, Clarence, 2663–2664
Glad Ghosts (Lawrence), 5480–5481
Gladigow, Burkhard, historiography of, 4048, 10080
Gladstone, William, 6510
Glámr, 167
Glancy, Diane, 3093
Glaphura (christological references in Old Testament), Cyril of Alexandria on, 2117
Glasenapp, Helmuth von, **3496–3497**
Glasgow (Scotland), museums in, 6244, 6246
Glass beads, as money, 6137
Glass-Coffin, Bonnie, 3418
Glassman, Bernie, on wisdom and compassion, 2788
Glaṭ kosher, 5107
Glauben und Mystik im Schatten des Höchten Wesens (Preuss), 7392
Glaubil, Antoine, 1631
Glaude, Eddie, 79
Glavendrup inscription, 7940
Glazier, Stephen D., 10028
Glen, James, Swedenborgianism, role in, 8901
Glh (to uncover or unveil), 7776
Gli eroi greci (Brelich), 1047
Glinka, Mikhail, 6312
Glissant, Edouard, 9297
Global Ethic Project, 3499, 3502
Global Forum of Spiritual and Parliamentary Leaders, environmental focus of, 2613
Globalization, **3497–3498**
and art, 502
conversion, globalization theory of, 1971
definitions of, 3497–3498
economic, 3497–3498
and food, 3174
gender studies and, 3304
human condition and, 3502–3503
implicit meaning of, 9931
of local religion, 110
media and, 5807–5808
in Mesoamerica, 5924
migration in, 3500–3501
of music, South Asian, 6286
negative interpretations of, 3498, 3502–3503
origins of, 3498
political, 3498
positive interpretations of, 3498, 3502–3503
religious perspectives on, 3498–3499
role of religion in, 3499–3502
social movements and, 1754
spirituality and, 8719
state role in, 3498
in study of religion, 8766–8767
and tradition, 9280
urban religion and, 1810
World Council of Churches focus on, 2612
of Zoroastrianism, 10004–10005
Global theology, 9126
Globus (journal), 7372
Glocalization, 110
media and, 5807–5808
Glock, Charles T., 6522
Glory of the Lord, The (von Balthasar), 5482
Glosae super Trismegistum, medieval commentary on, 3945
Glossolalia (speaking in tongues), **3504–3507**
in Charismatic movement, 7031
Caribbean creolization and, 2067
cross-cultural similarities in, 3505
as divination, 2370
as enthusiasm, 2807
as evidence of Spirit Baptism, 7029, 7031
as language, 3505

Glossolalia (speaking in tongues) *continued*
as learned behavior, 3505–3506
in Montanism, 6167, 6168
Paul the Apostle on, 7019
in Pentecostalism, 70, 3504–3505, 6844, 7029, 7031, 8254
segmental structure of, 3505
spirit possession and, 3506–3507
as spiritual gift (charism), 1550
syllables in, 3505, 3506
trance and, 3505, 3506
Gloucester, James, 68
Glover, George Washington, 2694
Glover, T. R., liberal Protestantism of, 6103, 6105
Glucklich, Ariel, 6947
Gluckman, Max, 1516
on ancestor worship, 322
on kingship in Africa, 5169
on rites of passage, 7800
on ritual, 7845
on ritual of rebellion, 8656
Glud (ransom), 9185
Glueck, Nelson, 7671
Gluttony
at Carnival, 1442–1443
depiction in novels, 3059
Gmelin, Johann Georg, 3110
Gnas skor ba (pilgrim), 7166
Gnesio-Lutherans, *vs.* Philippists, 5539
Gnoli, Gherardo, 3535
Gnomes, 2952
Gnosis
in comparative religion, 3507
in election, 2748–2749
esotericism as, 2843
vs. faith, 5202
vs. gnosticism, 3508, 3515
in Hinduism, 4925
in Islam *(ma'rifah)*
Ibn al-'Arabī on, 8819–8820
Suhrawardī on, 8827
in modern scholarship, 3507, 3528
origin of term, 3507
pre-Christian, 3507–3508
as revelation, 7774
wisdom in, 9751–9753
Gnosis und Späntantiker Geist (Jonas), 4948
Gnostic deification, 2249–2250
Gnosticism, **3507–3537**. *See also* Mandaean religion; Manichaeism; Marcionism
Adam in, 5202
aeons in, 7190
aiones in, 209
alchemy and, 244–245
amulets and talismans in, 300
anamnesis (recollection) in, 311–312
angels in, 344, 347, 3525
anti-Semitism and, 3526
apocalypses of, 412
apocatastasis in, 421–422
apostles in, 436
ascension in, 521, 523
astral demons in, 8425
atheism in, 582
Australasian study of, 8771
baptism in, 780, 3515
and Bardesanite ideas, 787
Bianchi (Ugo) on, 864
biblical exegesis in, 874, 3525
biblical wisdom and, 9750
breath in, 3510
celibacy and, 1476
Christian, 3511–3513, 3516–3520
in Roman Empire, 5334
as Christian heresy, 3514, 3515, 3522–3524, **3529–3531**
Christians, Gnostics as, 3923
Christian theology and, 2819
Clement of Alexandria's criticism of, 1823
creation myth in, 8239
Culianu (Ioan Petru) on, 2079–2080
dance in, 2153
decline of, 3519
definitions of, 3508, 3515, 3522, 6397–6398
Demiurge of, 2274, 3511
divine man in, 3508–3509, 3526
docetism in, 2381
dualism in, 2506, 2508, 2509, 2511, 2512–2513, 5452, 6746, 7190
of Elisha' ben Avuyah, 2769
emergence of, 3515–3517
exile in, 2923
eye in, 2942
the Fall in, 2966, 3525
in fantasy literature, 3528
on fate beyond God, 3003
fire in, 3119
vs. gnosis, 3508, 3515
gnosis in, ecclesiastical *vs.* heretical, 3924
God in
dualism of, 3522
knowability of, 182, 3554
unknown, 3510, 3512
gospels, Egyptian influence on, 3054
as heresy, 3923–3924
emergence as heresy, 3921
Hindu, 4925–4926
history of study of, **3531–3537**
challenges to, 3528
in Germany, 3514, 3532–3533
Nag Hammadi codices in, 3515, 3535, 6397–6398
roots of, 3514, 3531
in Holy Order of MANS, 4102
hypostasis in, 4241, 4242
intuition in, 4525
Irenaeus against, 4539
Ishrāqīyah influenced by, 4554
in Islam, 3511, 3523
Ḥasan al-Baṣrī and, 8810
Maymūnīyah movement and, 8327
on Jesus as Logos, 4417
on Jesus' male lover, 7081
Jewish, 3510–3511, 3516, 3523
Jonas (Hans) and, 4948–4949
Jung Codex of, 3512–3513
knowledge in, 5202–5203
letter mysticism in, 272–273
light and darkness symbolism in, 5452
magic in, 5576
Mani influenced by, 5648
Mary Magdalene in, 5757–5758
and Mazdakism, 5800, 5801
in Middle Ages, 3514, 3522
modern, 3514, 3527–3528
monism and dualism in, 3522–3523
mustērion as quest for insight in, 7955
mystery religions and, 6333
Naaseene Gnostic interpretation of Attis myth, 1452
in Nag Hammadi, 3941, 6397–6398
nature in, 6432
number symbolism in, 6746, 6749
orgy and, 6867–6868
origins of, 3515–3517
history of study of, 3531–3532, 3533–3535
modern theories of, 3508, 3514
otherworld in, 6924
Paul the Apostle on, 7018
2 Peter opposing, 917
in philosophy
Greek, 3532, 3534–3535
modern and postmodern, 3526–3527
Platonism and, 7190
Plotinus against, 7199
Qabbalah and, 3524, 6353
Scholem (Gershom) on, 8178
in Roman Empire, 7921
Romanticism and, 3525–3526
salvation in, 3520
Satan in, 8125
in science, 3528
Scientology as, 8192
search for pearl in, 7024
sects in, 3515, 3519
sexuality in, 3512, 8240–8241
sexual rites in, 8247
sexual symbolism in, 7081–7082
Simon Magus and, 3926
snake symbolism in, 3518–3519
Sophia (wisdom) in, 3509–3511, 3517, 3518, 8523, 9751
soul in, 4415
ascension of, 521
syncretism in, 8932–8933
texts of, 3515
discovery of, 3508, 3515, 3535
2 Timothy and, 915
transmigration in, 9329
universal religions and, 4067
virginity in, 9605
in Western culture, 3522
Wikander's (Stig) study of, 9736
words of power in, 8676
Gnostic Problem, The (Wilson), 3533
Gnostic Religion, The (Jonas), 2506, 4948
Gnostikos (Evagrios of Pontus), 2886
Gñya'-khri Btsam-po (mythical king), heavenly descent of, 5180
Gnyos Lo tsā ba (Nyö Lotsāwa), Mar pa and, 5715
Goajira people (Colombia), pastoral mode of life of, 2302
Goajiro people (Venezuala), funeral rites of, 3235
Go'a-mëe (phallic image), as center of the world, 1502
Goats. *See* Sheep and goats
Gobbán Saer/Gobán Saor (deity), 1485
Gobbi, Stefano, 6216
Gobind Singh. *See* Singh, Gobind
Gobir dynasty, Islam and, 2167–2168
Goblet d'Alviella, Eugène, **3537**
on idols, 4357
Goblins, 2952
in Slavic religion, 8438
Gocari (grazing), 4769
God, **3537–3579**. *See also specific religions*
as absent or withdrawn (*See also* Deus otiosus)
clockmaker metaphor, 1541, 8183
Holocaust responses and, 4090, 4093–4094
as Absolute, Hegel on, 3895
as Absolute Mind, Hocking (William Ernest) on, 4076
activity of, physics challenging, 7137
as androgyne, 337
anthropocentric model of, challenged, 2610
anthropomorphism of, 388–391
Kant (Immanuel) on, 5078
a priori concept applied to, 7975–7976
Aristotle on, 7114
asexuality of, in Abrahamic traditions, 4196
attributes of (*See* Attributes of God; *specific attributes*)

awareness of, 9282
Heschel (Abraham Joshua) on, 3962
belief in (*See* Theism)
in cargo cults, 1418
color of, in black theology, 5441
compassion of, 9282–9283
concept of, 7123
Nightingale on, 6618
contingency in, *6961,* 6961–6962, 7124
in cybernetics, 2112
as dead
as Holocaust response, 4094
spirituality trends and, 8721
in Dead Sea Scrolls, as master of time, 7990
death of, 2247–2248
theology of, 584–585, 3552, 3558, 5489
Derrida (Jacques) on, 2247–2248
distinction from deity, 2254
dwelling of (*See* Dwelling, divine)
eternity as, 2855
evil and, 2900
existence of (*See* Proofs for the existence of God)
face of, *hester panim* (hiding of), Holocaust and, 4090
fasting as supplication to, 2997
fate beyond, 3003
feminine aspect of, in Sophia, 8523
freedom of, ethics and, 1654–1655
Gandhi on, 5399
gender of, in Qabbalah, 4981
goodness of, **3635–3636**
denials of, 9112
as ground of being, Philo on *hypostasis* and, 4240–4241
human encounter with, 7118
Husserl (Edmund) on, 4237
as "I Am," New Thought meditation on, 1782
idolatry and, 4363
image of, 4296
Adam made in, 29
androcentrism of, 334, 335
and doctrine of sin and grace, 1667
ethics and, 1652
in Ethiopian theology, 2860
humans made in, 2590
as white male, 3559
incarnation in Jesus (*See* Incarnation)
infidelity to, in *Ezekiel,* 2944
as infinite and inclusive, neurotheology on, 6494
in justification, 5039
Kabīr's notion of, 5052
Kant on, 5078–5079, 8161
Kierkegaard on, 5142
kingdom of (*See* Kingdom of God)
kingship of, 2812
knowledge of (*See* Knowledge, of God)
in literature, postmodern, 5483–5484
love of
dually transcendent, 9282–9283, 9284
pure, in Sufism, 7591
reality of, 9285–9286
maleness of, androcentrism of, 335
manifestation of (*See* Theophany)
mercy of
in *Jonah,* 4947
justice and, 613–614
merit calculated by, 5871
in metacosmology, 2256
mind of, in Stoicism, 8741
monotheistic view of (*See* Monotheism)
as mystery, as Holocaust response, 4094
mystical union with (*See* Mystical union)
names of (*See also* Names and naming)
derivation of, 2253
as sacred word, 5304
in natural selection, 2909
nature and, 2830–2831
nature of (*See* Attributes of God)
necessity in, *6961,* 6961–6962
in negative theology, 7774
neuroscience on, 6490
Nietzsche on, 6615
oneness of, 1666 (*See also* Monotheism)
oneness with, in Ch'ŏndogyo, 1648
origins of concept of
Africa in search for, 115
Schmidt (Wilhelm) on, 8168–8169
Pascal on, 7002, 7421
as personal *vs.* impersonal, 128
anthropomorphism and, 389
Plato on, 7182
Plutarch on, 7200–7201
power of
in creation, 1986
ordained *vs.* absolute, 9738
presence of, Jews as, 4860
proofs for existence of (*See* Proofs for the existence of God)
retribution and, 7784
revelation of, natural revelation, 7774
Sartre (Jean-Paul) on, 8116
Scheler (Max) on, 8147
Schleiermacher (Friedrich) on, 8162
silence of, as Holocaust response, 4094
Smith (W. Robertson) on, 8452
society identical with, 2528
Solov'ev (Vladimir) on, 8520
sovereignty of, in Islam, 2064
Spinoza (Baruch) on, 8683–8684
as supreme being (*See* Supreme beings)
swearing by, 6848
symbol of, Tillich (Paul) on, 9204
union with (*See* Mystical union)
universality of, and election of Israel, 2744–2745
as Unmoved Mover, 7775
Vatican I on, 9531
visions of, and afterlife, 128
Viṣṇu as, forms of, 9619
water from, 9698
will of (*See* Will, of God)
wisdom of, 9747
feminine symbolism of, 335–336
withdrawal of, Hobbes (Thomas) on, 4075
in writing's origins, 270
Xenophanes on, 9855
God A, 150–151
Go-Daigo (Japanese emperor), Musō Sōseki and, 6316, 6317
Godān (Premcand), 10034, 10035
God and Man at Yale (Buckley), 3637
Godānīya (mythic island), in Buddhist *cakravāla* cosmology, 2026, 2027
Godan Khan, 1154
Sakya Paṇḍita and, 8051
Godāvārī (river), 7861
divinity of, 2621
God-Being, in Holy Order of MANS, 4102
Goddard, Dwight, 1313
Goddard, Henry H., 2880
Goddess (Daly), 9099
Goddesses, Whores, Wives, and Slaves (Pomeroy), 3381
Goddess feminism. *See* Thealogy
Goddess movement. *See* Feminist spirituality movement
Goddess worship, **3583–3616**. *See also* Gods and goddesses; *specific goddesses*
analytical psychology of, 7485
Bachofen (J. J.) on, 731, 3611, 3612–3613, 3616
in Baltic religions, motif of goddess in the tree, 8132–8133
in Bengal, 826
in Buddhism, 1079–1080, 1081, 1082, 3587, 4330, 9000
cakras and, 1348
in Chinese religion, 3587
in Christianity
lack of, 7082
Roman Catholicism, 3587–3588
contemporary patterns and themes of, 3587–3591
in Elamite religion, 4469, 4470
feminist revival of, 3613–3614
feminist spirituality movement and, 3022, 4166, 9788
feminist studies of, 3609, 3613, 3616–3617
feminist theology and, 3036
fertility and, 3584, 3589
in figurative art, 3583–3585, 3592–3593
French feminists and, 3029
in Greek religion, 3587, 3601–3602
healing and, 3589–3590
in Hellenistic religions, **3599–3607**
hierodouleia (sacred prostitution) and, 3966–3969
in Hinduism, **3607–3611**
bhakti synthesis and, 3998, 3999, 4000, 4001–4002
Durgā worship, 2525–2526
gender studies on, 3323
in Purāṇas, 7500
in *Śākta* Tantrism, 8547
in Trika Śáivism, 8046
local *vs.* universal, 3608
male deities and, 3585
nationalism and, 3609
Navarātri festival in, 6443–6444
nurturing *vs.* dangerous, 3607–3608
origins of, 3608–3609, 4427
outside India, 3609–3610
in popular Hinduism, 4007
Śakti worship, 857, 2526
studies of, 3607, 3608
Tantric, 3609, 4002, 4003
violence in, 3590
virginity in, 3588
and women's role, 3609, 3613

Goddess worship ***continued***
history of study of, 3611–3615
contemporary issues in, 3612–3615
early perspectives in, 3611–3612
Hindu, 3323, 3607, 3608
in Iberian religion, 4252, 4253
in India, 3585
in Indus Valley religion, 3989, 4427, 4468, 4470–4472, 4473
in Israelite religion, 3586
in Japanese religions, 3587
Mary as repository for, 9605
matriarchy's relationship to
contemporary debate over, 3612–3613, 7009
early theories on, 3611–3612
in megalithic religion, 5822–5826
in Melanesian religions, 5834
motherhood and, 2983–2984, 3588
Mother Tantras, 1349
in Nabatean religion, 6386, 6389
in Near Eastern religions, **3592–3599**
in development of civilizations, 3585–3587
evidence regarding, 3592–3593
gender and, 3376–3377, 3592
in Neolithic religion, 950, 3584–3585, 3593, 6462, 7377, 7378
overview of, **3583–3592**
in Paleolithic religion, 3583–3584, 3593, 3613, 7375, 7377, 7378
polarization in, 2984
prehistoric, 7376–7378, 7382–7383, 7386
protection in, 3589
in Roman Catholicism, 3587–3588
in Roman religion, 3587
in rural Indian religions, 4432–4433
sainthood and, 8037
specialization in, 2984
themes of, 3588–3591
theoretical perspectives on, **3611–3616**
in Vedism, 2525–2526
violence/anger and, 3590
virginity in, 3588, 9601 (*See also* Virgin goddess)
in Wicca, 9730
wifehood in, 3588–3589
and women, empowerment of, 8243
women dominant in, 9787
women's roles indicated by, 3609, 3613
yoni and, 9907
Gödel, Kurt, 6057
Godelier, Maurice, 3481–3482
Godfrey of Saint-Victor, in Victorine tradition, 4151
Godhead
distinction from God, 2254
in Qabbalah, 7536
Godianism, 109–110
God-image, in psychoanalysis, 7483
God in Search of Man (Heschel), modernity in, 3962
God Light Association (GLA), 6574
God-man, Kierkegaard on, 5142
Gododdin (Welsh poem), Arthur in, 508–509
God of the Oppressed (Cone), 965
God of the Witches (Murray), 9729
Godparenthood, in Nahuatl religion, 6402
"Gods, Ghosts, and Ancestors" (Wolf), 322
Gods and goddesses, **3616–3624**. *See also* Goddess worship; *specific deities and religions*
in *Aeneid,* 9583
affliction by, 56–57
in Agami Jawi, 4816–4817
anthropomorphism of, 388–391
Xenophanes on, 4108
of "Axial Age," 9603
binomial, 1383
birds as epiphanies of, 948, 949
capturing of, 5198
in cargo cults, 1418
of caves (Mesoamerican), 1468–1469
communion with, orgy as, 6865
comparative mythology of, Greek and Roman names applied to others, 1873
compelling (*See* Theurgy)
cultural context of, 3616, 3617
descent into the underworld by, 2297–2299
desire in lives of, 2305
Deus otiosus (inactive gods), 1426
disease attributed to, 3808–3809
double-headed, 2423
in epics, 2815–2817
equation or equivalence of
as form of syncretism or mingling *(theokrasia),* 3907–3909, 8931–8932
in Greek thought, 1878
in Hellenism, 3907–3909
interpretation test of, *vs.* heresy, 3921
flowers associated with, 3135–3136
food from, 9579
functions of, 3618–3623
challenge of determining, 3616
masculine sacrality in, 5758–5763
gambling by, 3263
goodness of, 3635
heroes and, 2815–2816
high (*See* High gods)
horned, 4131
humanism and domestication of, 827
images of, 9623
at leisure (*See Deus otiosus*)
man as creator of, 2250
manifestation of (*See* Theophany)
morphology of, 3617–3618
names including, 1387
in novels, 3057
Greek, 3056
as objects of devotion, 2316–2317
in origin of evil, 2901–2902
origins of, 2882–2884
in manism, 5672–5673
shamans as, 2869
pairings of, 1383–1384, 1387
Plato on, 7183–7184
in polytheism (*See* Polytheism, gods in)
sleeping, 8440
social implications of, 3616
speaking names of, 2597
specialization of, supreme beings and, 8871
syncretism in formation of divine personalities, 8936–8937
theocrasies (combinations of), syncretism and, 8930–8931
therianthropism of, 9155–9156
typologies of, 3618–3623
cosmic, 3618–3620
social, 3618, 3620–3623
violent, 9597
vision of, and afterlife, 128
walking with, in procession, 7417–7418
Xenocrates of Chalcedon on, 7187
God's Chosen People (Bühlmann), 2748
God self, in New Thought teachings, 1782
Gods of the Blood: The Pagan Revival and White Separatism (Gardell), 2663
God's Phallus (Eilberg-Schwartz), 7080
God Triwan movement, 3398
Godwin, Joscelyn, 6527
God Worshipers Society (China), 1609–1610. *See also* Taiping Rebellion
establishment of, 6041
Goebbels, Joseph, *Kristallnacht* riots and, 4085
Goehr, Alexander, 6312
Goel, Sīta Ram, 547
Go'el ha-dam (blood redeemer), 4742
Goethals, Gregor, 7859
Goethe, Johann Wolfgang von. *See also* Sturm und Drang movement
in art history, 499
on conscience, 1943
on faith as trust, 2956
Faust, 2474, 3010
Gnosticism and, 3514, 3525
as Freemason, 3195
Herder (Johann Gottfried) and, 3918, 3919
on nature, 6436
on Spinoza (Baruch), 8685
Steiner (Rudolf) and, 8738
on surrender of self, 8715
Goetheanum, the, Steiner (Rudolf) and, 8738
Goetz, J., 4357
Gofannon (deity), 1485, 1489
in *Mabinogion,* 5546
Goffman, Erving
on ceremony, 1512
on games, 3268
on procession, 7417
Goffman, Erwin, on memorization, 5850
Gog (hostile power), origin of name of, 7102
Gogarten, Friedrich
on history as foundation of religion, 7117
and neoorthodoxy, 6466, 6467, 6468, 6469
Sölle (Dorothee), influence on, 8511
Gogdu gagsi (puppet play), 2454
Gogh, Vincent van, 4347
on creative discipline, 8702
Gog of Magog, 2945
Gogo religion (Tanzania)
dances of, 2137, 2139
initiation rites of, 2577
knotted ropes of, 5197
rituals of, 2576
Gohei (paper streamers), 2410
Gohonzon Maṇḍala, in Sōka Gakkai, 8508
Goibhniu (deity), 1483, 1485, 9390
Goidelic languages, 1478
Gokak, V. K., Bangalore Consultation presentation, 8790
Gökalp, Ziya, **3624–3625**
nationalism of, 3624
Gokulika school of Buddhism, 1194
Golah ve-nekhar (Kaufmann), 5108
Gola people (Liberia), dances of, 2141
Gold, **3625–3626**
in Buddhism, 7386, vol. 9 color insert
color symbolism, 1861–1862
cowrie shells and, 6137
cult of, in Saka religion, 7386
in Egyptian religion, 5987
in Hinduism, 7386
in mines, 5987
as money, 6138
in rejuvenation myths, 7683

Scythian festival of golden sacred objects, 8205
sun and, 8836
symbolism of, 3625–3626
turning metal into (*See* Alchemy)
in winter carols, 9745
Gold, Ann Grodzins, 3322
on spirit possession, 8694, 8696–8697
Gold, Thomas, steady state theory and, 2032
Goldammer, Kurt, phenomenology of, 4043
Goldberg, Ellen, 3323
on androgyny, 8243
Golden Age, **3626–3630**
in Chinese religion, 1628
millenarianism of, 6030, 6038
definition of, 3626
in Egyptian religion, 2961
in Greek religion, 2964, 3626–3627
Hesiodic myth of, 3626–3628
in historiography, 4025
in Indian religion, 2963
in Iranian religion, 2964, 3629–3630
in Islam, 6223
kingship and, 3629–3630
in Manichaean religion, 2966
millenarianism and, 3628–3629, 6030, 6038
myths of origin in, 3628
nostalgia expressed in, 2969
origins of term, 2964
in periodization systems, 175
in Sai Baba movement, 8028–8029
in Summit Lighthouse teaching (New Age), 1782
Vergil on, 9582–9583
Golden Ass, The (Apuleius). *See Metamorphoses* (Apuleius)
Goldenberg, Myrna, 3352
Goldenberg, Naomi, 9098
on female body, 4164
Golden Bough, The (Frazer), 380, 381, 2421, 2518, 2535, 2540, 2664, 3191–3192, 4461, 5381
comparative religion and, 1878
cursing research, influence on, 2098
dance in, 2145
death in, 2239
dying and rising gods in, 7767
evolutionism in, 2916
external soul in, 8532
fertility cult in, 3376
Gaster's (Theodor H.) version of, 3288
goddess worship in, 3616
kingship in, 5157
magic in, 5570
Malinowski (Bronislaw) influenced by, 5628
Mannhardt (Wilhelm) influencing, 5676
mortification of kings in, 6198
and Myth and Ritual school, 6380
nature symbolism in, 8910
popularity of, 4100
regicide in, 5157
sleep in, 8440
Golden calf
Aaron's role in, 1–2
dance around, 2153
as moon, 6172
worship of, 5422
Golden Dawn. *See* Hermetic Order of the Golden Dawn
Golden Elixir Way (Jindandao), 1603, 1607
Golden Hall (Buddhist temple), 9049
Golden Horde
in Caucasus, 4613
in Europe, 4673
and Il-khanid dynasty, 4493
in Middle Volga, 4616
Golden Lord. *See* World-Overseeing Man
Golden Lotus, The (Chinese novel), gift giving in, 3483
Golden Rule, **3630–3633**
evolution and, 2660
Hillel (Jewish sage), version of, 3981
retribution in, 7779
Sorokin (Pitirim Aleksandrovich) on, 8524
as universal morality, 7652
versions of, 3630–3633, 6185
Golden Temple at Amritsar, India (Sikh), *seva* (service) of American Sikh women at, 3879–3880
Golden Temple at Punjab, India (Sikh), vol. 14 color insert
Golden Verses (Pythagoras), 2248
Golden Way Foundation, 6554, 9067
Goldenweiser, Alexander A., **3633–3634,** 6671
on magic, 5564–5565
on totemism, 9251
Goldenweiser, Alexander Solomonovich, 3633
Goldfrank, Esther, 6671
Goldin, Judah, 6019
on Hillel (Jewish sage), 3982
Golding, William, 5478–5479
Goldman, Irving, 6672, 7345
Goldstein, Daniel, vol. 12 color insert
Goldstein, Diane E., 3146
Goldstein, Jonathan A., 900, 901
Goldstein, Melvyn, on mass monasticism, 8083
Gold Woman (deity), 5120
Goldziher, Ignácz, **3634–3635**
Andrae (Tor) and, 333
education of, 3634
Islamic studies of, 3634–3635, 4716, 4717, 8951
Muḥammad biography by, 945
on authenticity of *ḥadīths,* 3727
Golem. *See* Löw, Yehudah ben Betsal'el of Prague
Golem (image or substance), 5521
in Qabbalah, 8676
Golgotha, as cosmic mountain, 1502
Goliath (biblical figure), origin of name of, 7102
Golijov, Osvoldo, 6313
Golubeva, Leonilla A., 3114
Gomarus, Franciscus, Arminius (Jacobus) and, 493
Gombrich, Ernst H., 4297
Gombrich, Richard
on *Jātaka* tales, 6993
on Theravāda Buddhism, 1313
in Pali Text Society, 6956
on *pinkama,* 4140
Gomer, daughter of Diblaim, Hosea, marriage to, 4136–4137
Gōmēz (cattle urine), 4535, 9997
Gomez, Luis, 7479
Gomez, Michael, 81
Go-Mō jigi (Itō Jinsai), 4753
Gomorrah, Sodom and, 14, 15
Goncharov, Ivan, 3059
Gonda, Jan, 1024, 1025
on *gurus,* 8711
on magic, 5588, 5590
on Rudra-Śiva, 8039, 8414
Go-neno-hodi (Deity), in Caduveo religion, 8636
Gong (palace), 9056
Gongan (precedents). *See also* Huatou method
as anecdotes, 1524
meditation on, 1520, 1604
Gongdzö (dgongs mdzod), 2549, 2550
Gonggong (chaos monster), 1625
Gongguan beizhi (Daoist text), 2208
Gongs
in Mesoamerican music, 6268–6269
in Southeast Asian music, 6287–6288
Gongsun Long, 1572, 1573, 1575
Gongsuo (common-origin association), 1616
Gongūji (chief priest), 7410, 7412
Gongyang Commentary, 1574–1575
overview of, 1907
Gonorrhea, in Melanesia, 6787
Gonuklisia ("the bending of the knee") service, 1742
González, Yolotl, 5943, 5944
González de Mendoza, Juan, 1630
on China, 4039–4040
Good, the, **3635–3636**. *See also* Goodness
aesthetics and, 46
in Christianity, 3635–3636
ethics and, 1654
complete *(summum bonum),* Kant (Immanuel) on, 5077–5078
criteria for, 3635–3636
evil and (*See* Evil, good and)
in Islam, in Muʿtazilah, 5063
in Japanese religions, *kami,* 5071
in Judaism, in Hasidism, 3789
in Neoplatonism, 6474
neurotheology on, 6493
in New Thought movement, 6583
origin of, *vs.* origin of evil, 2899–2900
Plato on, 5201
Plotinus on, 7191, 7198
in Roman Catholicism, medical ethics and, 5811
Schleiermacher (Friedrich) on, 8164–8165
Socrates on, 8503
in Zoroastrianism, 203–204, 7778, 9936
Good, Anthony, 3323
Good, Battiste, vol. 2 color insert
Good, Byron, 2611
Good, John Mason, 9423
Goodale, Jane, on Australian Indigenous women, 3391
Goodall, Jane, 361
Good and Peaceful movement, 5683
Goodblatt, David, 294, 843–844
Goodbye, meaning of, 8062
Goodenough, Erwin R., **3636–3637**
education of, 3636–3637
on Hellenization of Judaism, 4044
on Jewish art, 4343
Goodenough, Ruth Gallagher, 3313
Goodenough, Ursula, 2666
Good Friday. *See also* Crucifixion
in Christian liturgical calendar, 1742
Holocaust as analogous to, 4089–4090
Gooding, D. W., 7106
Gooding, Susan Staiger, 5340
Goodison, Lucy, on goddess worship, 3617
Goodman, Howard, 7267
Goodman, Lenn, 2652
on monotheism, 6162
Goodman, Nelson, metaphysics of, 5991
Goodman-Martinez-Thompson correlation, in calendrical calculation, 1357
Goodness. *See also* Good, the
of creation, 1344, 3636

Goodness *continued*
criteria for, 3635
of God, 1344, 3635–3636
denials of, 9112
of humans, 3635
Kant (Immanuel) on, 5079
in Neo-Confucianism, 5541
"Good News Is No News: Aretalogy and Gospel" (Smith), 946
Goodpaster, Kenneth, 2655
Goodrich, Peter, on law and religion, 5326
Goodrick-Clarke, Nicholas, 2663
Good Shepherd Independent Episcopal Church, establishment of, 3287
Goodspeed, Edgar J., 897
Good Word (Gaiwiio) religion, conversion in, 7756
Goody, Jack, 1516
on ancestor worship, 321–322
on memory, 5850
Goonan, Michael, 3082
Goose, 4438, 6959
Gopāla. *See* Kṛṣṇa Gopāla
Goparam (gateway), 9265
Gor (deity), 5514–5515
Gorá (deity), creation by, 2013
Gorā (Tagore), 10035
Gorākhnāth (Hindu scholar), **3637–3638**
poetry of, 7211
uncertainty about life of, 3637–3638
writings attributed to, 3638
Gorakṣanātha. *See* Gorākhnāth
Gorakṣa-śataka (Hindu text), 3638
Gorbachev, Mikhail, and revival of Islam in Central Asia, 4626
Gordian (Roman emperor), and Plotinus, 7198
Gordon, Aharon David
on nature, 2645
Zionism of, 4906, 9980
Gordon, Eli'ezer, 6241–6242
Gordon, Richard, on Cumont (Franz), 2093
Gore, Al, Foguangshan and, 3140
Goree, B. W., Jr., 6168
Gorgias (Plato), 2273, 2427
Gorgias (Sophist), skeptical views of, 8420
Gorgias of Leontini, 3052
Gorgons (mythic figures), 2277
in Greek mythology, 6165
Göring, Hermann, anti-Semitism policies and, 4085
Goriyaku (benevolent function of deities and buddhas), health and, 3870
Gorky, Maxim, *Childhood,* 2951
Görres, Joseph von, **3638–3639**
on nature, 6435
Gorton, Samuel, 6557
Gortyn (city), laws of, 1846
Goryō (spirits), 4785–4786, 7272
Goryōshin (spirits), 4796, 5073
Hijiri (Japanese lay ascetics) as protectors against, 3978–3979
Gośāla (Indian ascetic), **3639–3640**
asceticism of, 3639
death of, 212
eremitism of, 2823
in Ājīvikas, 211–212, 3639–3640
Mahāvīra and, 211–212, 3639, 5610
teachings of, 213, 3639–3640
variations of name, 3639
Goshen-Gottstein, Moshe H., 894
'Gos Lo tsā ba Gzhon nu dpal (Gö Lotsawa) (historian), 1223
on Karma pas, 5103
on Shamar pas, 5103
Gospel, **3640–3642**. *See also* Gospels, the Four
Harnack (Adolf von) on, 3779
as literary form, 5470
origin of term, 3640
in Reformation creeds, 2057, 2058
use of term
in New Testament, 3640–3642
in Septuagint, 3640
Gospel and the Church, The (Loisy), 6106
Gospel music, 2477
in African American religions, 6313
women in, 10039
Gospel of Barnabas, 7243
Gospel of Buddha According to Old Records, The (Carus), 1313
Gospel of Gamaliel, 3270
Gospel of Philip (Gnostic text)
Mary Magdalene in, 5757
sexuality in, 8247
Gospel of the Ebionites, 2596
Gospel of the Egyptians, hypostasis in, 4242
Gospel of Thomas (Gnostic text), 906, 920, 3517
knowledge in, 5202
Mary Magdalene in, 5757
in Nag Hammadi codices, 6396, 6397, 6398
publication of, 6395
vs. New Testament Gospels, 6396, 6398
Thomas Christianity based on, 6397
virginity in, 9607–9608
wisdom in, 9760
Gospel of Truth (Gnostic text), 3513, 3530
knowledge in, 5202
Gospel of Wealth (Carnegie), 6585
Gospels, the Four, 905–911. *See also* John; *Luke; Mark; Matthew;* New Testament
Antichrist in, 394
and anti-Semitism, 398–399
apocatastasis in, 422
atonement in, 595
canonization and, 1410
canon of, 920, 921
death of Jesus in, 7766
different pictures of Jesus in, 905–906, 911
emergence of, 920
gender in, 3358–3359
Golden Rule in, 3630, 3632
as "gospel," 3641–3642
historicity of, 4846–4847
and history, Christian views of, 4052, 4053
hospitality in, 4139
humor in, 4196–4197
inconcinnities in, 4845–4846
Jesus as rabbi in, 7578
Jesus as wisdom in, 9760
John the Evangelist in, 4943
literal interpretation of, 4845
Mary in, 5751, 5752
miraculous healing in, 3843
Moses in, 6203
mysticism in, 6346
vs. Nag Hammadi gospels, 6396, 6398
peace in, 7021–7022
resurrection of Jesus in, 7766
as sacred biography, 944
Sanhedrin in, 8103
Satan in, 8124
structuralist analysis of, 8754
suffering of Jesus in, 8807
two-source theory of, 906–907
variants of, 921–922
women in, 3358–3359
Gospel Tabernacle (Chicago), religious broadcasting and, 7710
Gossaert, Jan, vol. 12 color insert
Gossen, Gary, 5943
Gosvāmins (religious teachers)
Bengal, influence in, 1347
Caitanya and, 9505
theological works by, 1346
Goswami, Bijoy Krishna, 9318
Go Tell It on the Mountain (Baldwin), 3060
Gothic church architecture, 793–794, 9265
body correlated with, 7983
as image of heavenly city, 7983
Gothic iconography, 4346
Gothic language
biblical translations into, 922
and "holy," concept of, 7969
Gothic marginalia, in micrography, 1372
Gothic revival, 795–796
Goths. *See also* Visigoths
Christianity among, 1682, 1689
Roman Empire, attacks on, 1682
Go-Toba, Cloistered Emperor, Jōdoshū Buddhism and, 4120
Götterdämmerung (Wagner), horse symbolism in, 4134
Götternamen: Versuch einer Lehre von der religiösen Begriffsbildung (Usener), 9487
Gottlieb, Alma, 5866
Gottlieb, Roger, 2610
Gottlund, Carl Axel, 3105
Gottschalk of Orbais
Hincmar, criticism by, 3983
on predestination, 3203, 3207
refutation of, 2830
Gould, Janice, 7226
Gould, Stephen Jay
in science and religion, 2658
on sociobiology and evolutionary psychology, 2917
Gouldner, Alvin W., on games, 3265
Goulet, Jean-Guy A., 6678
"Gourd Dancer, The" (Momaday), 7225
Gourd of Lono, in Makahiki ceremony, 3798
Gourd rattles, in South American shamanism, 8291
Govardhana, Mount, 5249
Governance of churches. *See* Church polity
Governing Body Commission (GBC), 4522, 4523
Government. *See also* Church polity; Politics
in Daoism, 9969–9970
economic role of, 2670
nature of
Hobbes (Thomas) on, 5367
Locke (John) on, 5367–5368, 5496
Zwingli on, 10016
Govindanātha (Hindu teacher), Śaṅkara and, 8014
Govorov, Feofan, 7943
Gowariker, Ashutosh, 3098
Gozan bunka (artistic forms), 9947
Gozan Zen, **3642–3644**
in Ashikaga regime, 4787
Ikkyū Sōjun studying, 4377
Grabar, André, 501, 4287
Grabar, Oleg, 4283
Gräbersymbolik (Bachofen), 730, 731
Gracchus, T. Sempronius, 7897
Grace, **3644–3648**
in Buddhism, 3647
in Christianity, 3644–3647
Arminius (Jacobus) on, 492
Augustine on, 627, 3645, 8406
development of theology of, 3645–3646
domestic rituals of, 2399
good conscience and, 1942
history of doctrine, 1667
Jansenism *vs.* Molinism, 7001
Kant (Immanuel) on, 5079–5080

Luther (Martin) on, 5537, 5538, 7454
merit and, 5876, 5877
in Middle Ages, 5110
Paul on, 3644–3645, 6188
Pelagius on, 7025
predestination and, 3203, 3207
prospects in theology of, 3647
in Protestantism, 158, 3646, 7454
Protestant *vs.* Catholic, 158, 3646
Rahner (Karl) on, 7600
in Roman Catholicism, 158, 3646, 7876, 7880, 7881, 7883, 7885
sacraments and, 7885
salvation by, 1375
Servetus (Michael) on, 8232
Spurgeon (Charles Haddon) on, 8727
Thomas Aquinas on, 158, 3645–3646, 7737, 9163
definitions of, 3644
deities and spirits of, in Haitian Vodou, 1433
in Hinduism
in Śrī Vaiṣṇavas Sampradāya, 8728
Rāmānuja on, 7616
in Judaism
and atonement, 593–594
on Passover, 7004
Sa'adyah Gaon on, 4888
and morality, 6188
Niebuhr (Reinhold) on, 6613
redemption and, 7640
Servetus (Michael) on, 8232
in Sikhism, in *Ādi Granth,* 32
Grace, Charles M. "Daddy." *See* Daddy Grace
Grace, Patricia, 3085
Grace Abounding to the Chief of Sinners (Bunyan), 698–699
Graces, the (goddesses), charity and, 1554
Grade Abounding to the Chief of Sinners (Bunyan), 1323
Gradin, Carlos J., 9029–9030
Graduate Theological Union
Center for Theology and the Natural Sciences (CTNS) at, 8184
Swedenborgianism and, 8904
Graebner, Fritz, **3648–3649**
culture-historical method of, 3648, 5260, 5261
education of, 3648
on Oceanic cultures, 3648
and Pinard de la Boullaye, 7173
Graetz, Heinrich, 3532, 7056, 10052
Graf, Fritz, 2271, 7201
Graffiti
Christian, 4845
Egyptian, magic in, 2714
gangs and, vol. 6 color insert
Grags pa rgyal mtshan, 1225
Shugs ldan (Shugden) and, 8381–8382
Grags pa sengge (Shamar pa), 5103
Graham, Billy
on knowledge, 5199
media used by, 5806
in neoevangelicalism, 2890
Niebuhr's criticism of, 6612
revivalism and, 1710
television ministry of, 7711, 7712
Graham, David Crockett, 1635
Graham, Isabella Marshall, Seton (Elizabeth) and, 8234
Graham, Martha, 500, 2142, 2158, 2159
in *Le sacre du printemps,* 2161
Graham, Sylvester, 3173
Graham, William A., 945
Grail, the, **3649–3653**
angels and, 348
diachronic view of, 3650–3651
as elixir, 2772
origin of term, 3649–3650
quest for, 7552
synchronic view of, 3650
Grail movement, **3653–3654**
Gráinne (mythic figure), 1495
in megalithic religion, 5825
Grains
deities of, in Confucianism, 1913
in Demeter Eleusinia cult, 2751–2752
offering of, in Israelite religion, 926
Grāmadevatas (or *gramadevatas,* village deities)
festivals for, 4018
as impure gods, 4006
Grāma mātṛkās (village mothers), 4435
Grammar of Assent (Newman), 9427
Gramsci, Antonio
on hegemony, 2088
and postcolonial theory, 10042
subaltern studies and, 8800–8801
Grām swarāj, 861, 862
Gran Brijit (first woman buried in cemetery), 9637
Gran Chaco region of South America, **8632–8637**
animal dances in, 8581
Chané Arawak, 8637
cosmology in, 8587
death cults in, 8585
geography of, 8576, 8632
Guiacuru-Caduveo peoples (Pilagá, Toba, Caduveo, and Mocoví), 8636–8637
initiation rites in, 8585
Lengua-Mascoy peoples (Angaité, Lengua, Kaskihá, and Sanapaná), 8634–8635
Mataco-Makka peoples (Mataco, Chulupí, Choroti, and Makká), 8635–8636
mythic narratives, ontological structure of, 8632–8633
Tupi-Guaraní peoples (Chiriguano, Tapuí, and Guasurangwe)
dancing and soul movement in, 8533
overview of, 8634
supreme beings of, 8577–8578
World Fire myth in, 8589
Zamuco peoples (Ayoré and Chamacoco), 8633–8634
Grand Avenue: A Novel in Stories (Sarris), 3092–3093
Grandchamp, ecumenical communities of, 6765
Grande Chartreuse, La (monastery), 6119
Grande Sertão: Veredas (Guimarães Rosa), 3064
Grandier, Urbain, 2930
Granet, Marcel, **3654–3656**
on agricultural rituals, 190
and Dumézil (Georges), 2518, 4461
on Ba Zha festival, 4140–4141
on Chinese religion, 3654–3656
Chinese texts analyzed by, 3655
on Daoism, 2213
education of, 3655
on gift giving, 3484
on left and right symbolism, 5394
Maspero (Henri) and, 3655, 5773
Mauss (Marcel) and, 3655
methodology of, 1634, 3655–3656
on women, 3339
on yin and yang, 3266
Graniceros, 1470
Grannus (deity), 1483
Grant, Jacquelyn, 79
Grant, Joan, 560
Grant, Robert M., on Gnosticism, 3534
Grant, Ulysses S., Native American policy of, 7302
Granthis (knots), cakras and, 1348
Granth Sāheb. See Ādi Granth
Grapes of Wrath, The (Steinbeck), 5479–5480
Graphology, 2373
Grässer, Erich, on kingdom of God, 5152
Gratian (Franciscus Gratianus, Christian canonist), 1406, 5336–5337
Gratian (Roman emperor), 7922
Graulich, Michel, 5934, 5938, 5943
Grave boats, in Egyptian religion, 989
Grave goods, 9225–9226
in Germanic religion, 167–168
Gravely, Will B., 68
Grave-post, Feast of the (Chuvash), 1785
Graves. *See* Burial; Tombs
Graves, Robert, 9774
and Neopaganism, 6470
Gravesites, visits to, 2241
Graveyards, 9227–9228. *See also* Tombs
Gravitational mass, relativity theory and, 2032
Gravity
discovery of, Darwin on, 2909
Einstein on, 7138
Einstein's cosmological constant and, 2032
Newton on, 7138
Gray, John, 5862
Great Abbot Bodhisattva. *See* Śāntarakṣita (Buddhist monk)
Great Awakening, First
African American slaves in, 66
civil religion and, 1814
confession of sins in, 7755
Congregationalism and, 1938
denominational theory popularized by, 2288
Edwards (Jonathan) in, 2698
evangelicalism in, 2887
and growth of Baptist churches, 784
revivalism and, 1710
Great Awakening, Second, civil religion and, 1814
Great Bath (Mohenjo-Daro structure), 4472
Great Bear constellation, in Caribbean religions, 1429
Great Blessing of Water, in Orthodox Christianity, 2593
Great Britain. *See* Britain
Great Carnivalesque Societies, parades sponsored by, 1443
Great Commission, Trinity and, 1666
Great Court in Jerusalem
halakhah, and rulings of, 3748
rabbinical legislation and, 3749
Great Depression
in Australia and New Zealand, 1734

Great Depression ***continued***
Conservative Judaism and, 1959
in Jamaica, 1437
Great Doubt, in Zen Buddhism, 9949
Great East-West Schism (11th century). *See also* Great Western Schism
Azyme Controversy preceding, 5388
Cerularios, role of, 1519
Crusades, effect of, 8156–8157
Cyprian on, 2113
ecclesiology and, 1772–1773
events of, 1664, 1683
filioque doctrine and, 1681, 8155, 8156
Florentine decree on, 2043
fourth marriage controversy, 8155–8156
Great Schism, 8156
Monophysitism in, 6153–6155
Photian schism, 8155
roots of, 3657
Scholarios (Gennadios) on, 8174
second council at Lyons and, 2042
union efforts, 8157
Greater Antilles. *See also* Caribbean religions
Island Arawak in, 1426
Greater Moravia, missions to, from Church of Constantinople, 2585
Great Expanse, Seminal Essence of the, 7869
Great Fifth. *See* Nag dban rgya mtsho
Great goddess (mother goddess). *See also* Devi; Goddess worship
existence of, scholarly debate over, 3616–3617
generatrix as characteristic function of, 3975
hieros gamos (sacred marriage) and, 3975–3976
in Hinduism
bhakti synthesis and, 3998, 3999, 4000, 4001–4002
cakras and, 1348
in creation story, 3999
existence of, 3617
Indus Valley religion practices as precursor to, 3989
mokṣa, bestower of, 3999
Parā śakti as, in Tantras, 4020
Ḥokhmah/Sophia as, 8523
of Maltese religion, 6465
of Minoan religion, *37,* 37–38
power and love of, 3977
prehistoric, 7378
tree of life and, 9577
Great God Engineer cult (Mexico), 6576
Great Hallel, in *siddur* and *maḥzor,* 8389
Great Hare (Algonquin mythical figure), 7590
Great Horse Dance, 957
Great Japan Association for the Worship of Bodhisattva Kannon, founding of, 8369
Great Lakes, indigenous peoples of, manitou and, 5673–5674
Great Learning (Daxue), 1909
Jesuits and, 1918
on moral cultivation, 2632
Great Man view of history, heroes and, 3956
Great Medicine Society. *See* Midewiwin
Great Mother (Magna Mater)
archetypes of, Neumann (Erich) on, 3612
Cybele as, 1451, 2108
in Latvian religion, 5691–5694
Great Mother, The (Neumann), 3612, 3616
Great Pandanus Tree Rite, cannibalism and, 1404
Great Perfection. *See* Dzogchen
Great Persecution
Eusebius and, 2884, 2885
in Korea, 5234
Great Plains of North America. *See* Plains peoples
Great prayer *(mahā-mantra),* chanting of, 1347
Great Pyramid (Giza), 7527
Great Qing Code (Chinese code of law), 5353
Great religions
mundane *vs.* transmundane worlds in, 7726
vs. pagan religions, 7725–7726
Great Revival (Jamaica 1861–1862), 1437
Great Rite (Neopagan ritual), 7830
Great Rosary, The (Schön), vol. 3 color insert
Great Sacrifice, in Chinese cult of heaven, 1911–1913
Great seal, in Buddhism. *See* *Mahāmudrā*
Great Seal Prayer, 5102
Great seal writing, calligraphy and, 1370
Great Sphere, revelation of, 5195
Great Star (Hawaiian). *See* Hokuloa
Great Sun Buddha. *See* Mahāvairocana
Great Temple (Aztec), expansion of, 5173
Great Temple (Petra), 6387
"Great Vehicle." *See* Mahāyāna Buddhism
Great Western Schism (14th century). *See also* Great East-West Schism; Papacy, division of
conciliarist theory and, 2042, 6971
councils and, 1763, 6971
events of, 6971
overview of, 8157–8158
Great White Brotherhood, Holy Order of MANS priests ordained under, 4102
Great Work, The (Teilhard de Chardin), 2610
Great Zimbabwe, ruins of, 84
Grebel, Conrad
in Anabaptism, 304–305
Müntzer (Thomas) and, 6239
Greco-Turkish war (1922), 3658
Greece. *See also* Greek Orthodox Church; Greek religion
ancient
African religions studied in, 111
anti-Semitism in, 398
archaeological study of, 456
atheism in, 581–582
enlightenment of, 9855
eremitism of, 2823
geometry in, 3441–3442
hare myths in, 7590
Jerusalem under, 4835
Jewish persecution in, 7055
kneeling in, 5195, 5196
law codes in, 1845–1846, 4727
literature of, 3052, 3053, 3055–3056
love and courtship in, 3055–3056
money in, 6138
monism in, 6146
myth and history in, 6373–6375
scientific history and, 8180–8181
slaves in, 7079
social position of women in, 4298–4299
study of myths in, 6365
women in, 9602–9603
Islam in, 4674, 4677, 4678
Dönmeh sect, **2419–2420**
Judaism in, divine kingship in, 5148
prehistoric culture in, 7379
Greece, Church of, 3657–3658. *See also* Greek Orthodox Church
Greek art
Asklepios in, 552
Muses presiding over, 6242
vases, 4296, 4298
Greek Christianity. *See also* Greek Orthodox Church
in Byzantine Empire, 3656–3657
development of, 3656
vs. Latin Christianity, 3656
Greek drama
Christian imitation of, 2467
magic in, 5575
music in, 6304
origins of, 2436–2437
and Renaissance theater, 2473–2474
ritual elements in, 2443
time in, 6375
Greek Fathers, on knowledge, 5203
Greek Folk Religion (Nilsson), 7327
Greek Greek art, figurative, 3662, 3679
Greek language. *See also specific terms*
alphabet of, mystical speculation on, 270–272, *273*
biblical literature in, 889–892 (*See also* Septuagint)
Apocrypha, 896, 899, 900, 901
New Testament, 874, 921, 922
in early Christianity, 2581
Hellenism and, 3900–3901
sacred and profane in, 7966–7967
scripture, terms for, in, 8196, 8197
Greek literature, 5466–5469. *See also* Greek drama
magic in, 5574–5575
magi in, 5559–5560, 5561
Greek Magical Papyri, 5433, 5451–5452, 5573
Greek Orthodox Archdiocese (United States), 2589
Greek Orthodox Church, **3656–3659**
autocephalous status of, 2588
biblical canonicity in, 881
in Byzantine Empire, 3656–3657
Byzantium and, 1662
Cabasilas and, **1343–1344**
and Days of the Dead, 2230
diaspora of, 1652, 3659
doctrinal formulations and Greek tradition, 1681
ethics, 1652, 1653
and fasting, 2997
Florentine decree repudiated by, 2043
icons of, 4392
in Latin America, 1703
mendicancy in, 5856
missionary policy of, 3657
modern, 3657–3659
origins of, 3656–3657
in Orthodox structure, 2589
in Ottoman Empire, 3657
patriarchates of, 3657–3659
polity of, 1765
Pyrovasia rite in, 7654
Roman Catholicism and
Barlaam of Calabria's attempt at reconciliation, 788
roots of schism between, 3657
Syriac Orthodox Church, relations with, 8940
in United States, 1713

Greek philosophy
- Adret's (Shelomoh ben Avraham) ban on, Asher ben Yeḥi'el on, 539
- in apologetics, Christian, 427–428
- asceticism and, 7722
- as source of *kalām,* 5061
- atheism in, 581–582
- catharsis in, 1460
- charity in, 1554
- Christianity, influence on, Harnack (Adolf von) on, 3778
- on doubt, 2424
- eternity in, 2854–2855
- and *falsafah,* 2970–2971
- on free will, 3200
- Gnosticism and, 3532, 3534–3535
- Golden Rule in, 3632
- Greek religion questioned by, 3685
- heart in, 3882
- Hellenism and, 3910–3912
- historiography and, 4035–4037
- history separated from, 4035
- *hypostasis* in, 4240
- infinite in, 2854
- in Islamic philosophy (*See Falsafah*)
- light and darkness symbolism in, 5452
- *Logos* in, 5501–5502
- on magic, 5575
- mathematics and, 8180–8181
- suicide in, 8828–8829
- on truth, 9374
- and Western philosophy, 7109–7110

Greek Questions (Plutarch), 7201

Greek religion and mythology, **3659–3687**. *See also* Hellenistic religions
- ablutions in, 11, 780
- afterlife in, **163–166,** 3678, 7697
  - ferry across waters of death in, 989
  - immortality of the soul in, 3884
  - judgment of the dead in, 5026–5027
  - soul of the dead and, 8542–8543
- ages of world in, 176
- *agnōstos theos* in, 181–182
- *agōgē* in, 183–184
- agriculture in, 191
- *aion*/Aion in, 207–208
- altars in, 275
- ancestors in, 326
  - heroes as, 3665–3666
  - worship of, 321
- androgynes in, 338
- angels in, 344
- animal sacrifice in, 3667–3670, 3682–3683
  - to Asklepios, 551
- animals in, 358
- anthropomorphism in, 389, 3679
- and apocalypse genre, 410–411
- apostasy in, 431–432
- apotheosis in, 437–438
- archaeology and, 456
- art in (*See* Greek art)
- ascension in, 520–521
- astrology in, 563–566
- atheism in, 581–582
- auspices in, 7335–7336
- baptism in, 780
- beggars, avenging spirits of, 2100–2101
- birds in, 948, 949
- blades in, 967, 968
- blood in, 986
- bread in, 1040–1041
- breath and breathing in, 1041–1042
- bull-roarers used in, 1320
- calendar of, 1355
  - agriculture and, 186
  - festivals of Dionysos in, 375
  - moon and, 6171
- catharsis, **1458–1461**
- chance, views on, 1526–1527
- chariot in, 6995–6996
- charity in, 1553–1554
- children in, 1568–1568
- circle symbolism in, 1791, 1793
- civic nature and role of, 3665–3667, 3677
- cocks in, 1841–1842
- confession in, 1887
- corporate (body) symbolism in, 4161
- cosmogony
  - chaos in, 1537
  - Eros in, 2832
  - Okeanos in, 6805
- cosmology, circle symbolism in, 1791
- creation myth of
  - Hesiod on, 3963
  - parthenogensis in, 2555
- Creuzer (G. F.) on, 2070
- crossroads in, 2071
- Cumont (Franz) on, 2093–2094
- dance in, 2135, 2143
  - modern dance influenced by, 2157
- decline of, 3685
- deification in, 2248–2249
- deities of, 3663–3665, 3677–3681 (*See also specific deities*)
  - anthropomorphism in, 4108
  - complexity of relationships among, 3663–3664, 3678–3681
  - depicted as human beings, 4321, 4363
  - doctrine of equivalence of the gods, 1878
  - eagles as messengers of, 2554
  - Epicureans on, 3911
  - in Etruscan pantheon, 2870–2871
  - eyes of, 2941
  - figurative representations of, 3662, 3679
  - followers of (*See Thiasoi*)
  - functions of, 3663, 3679–3681
  - goddess worship, 3587, 3601–3602
  - Hesiod's genealogy of, 3963
  - historiography and, 4027
  - Homer on, 4107–4108
  - humor and, 4195
  - Hypnos as sleep in, 8439
  - iconography of, 4321–4322, 4363
  - knowledge of, 181–182
  - in literature, 5468–5469
  - local connections of, 4108
  - Minoan deities and, 38, 3664, 4320–4321
  - mortals' relationship with, 3666
  - Mycenaean deities and, 41–42, 3665, 3678, 4320–4321
  - names applied to other cultures, 1873
  - three-headed, 3804
- demons in, 2276–2277
- descent into the underworld in, 2298, 2299
- *deus otiosus* in, 2311
- divination in (*See* Divination, in Greek religion)
- divine beings in, classes of, 3667
- divine kingship in, 5146–5147
- dogs in, 2392, 2393
- dragons in, 2431, 2432, 2433
- dreams in, 2376
- drums in, 2498
- dualism in, 2507, 2508, 2511, 2514–2515
- education in, 3678
- as embedded in society, 3677
- enthusiasm in, 2807
- eschatology of, ascension and, 521
- evil in, 2898–2901
- the Fall in, 2964–2966
- fasting in, 2995
- fate in, 3000, 3001, 3004
- festivals in, 3684 (*See also specific festivals*)
- fire in, 3118
  - at Panathenaia, 6958
  - Prometheus as bringer of, 7419, 7420
- the Flood in, 2965–2966, 3131, 3132
- flowers in, 3137
- free will and predestination in, 3203
- funeral rites in, 163–164, 3666, 9226, 9227
- games in, 3265–3266
- gender in, **3375–3381**
- goats in, 8311
- goddess worship in, 3587, 3601–3602
- Golden Age in, 3626–3627
- *hairesis* as philosophical school in, 3920
- Harrison (Jane E.) on, 3781
- haruspices in, 7336
- hawk symbolism in, 2554
- head hunting in, 3805
- head symbolism in, 3804
- healing in, **3839–3842**
  - Hippocratic, 4021–4022
- heart symbolism in, 3882
- Hellenistic (*See* Hellenistic religions)
- heroes in, 3665–3667, 3681 (*See also specific figures*)
  - cults of, 3665–3667, 3681
  - initiation rituals for, 184
  - local association of, 3667, 3681
  - as mortals, 3666
  - sacrifices to, 3683
  - worship of, Alexander the Great and, 3902–3903
- historiography in, 4026–4027, 4030, 4035–4037
- history and, 6371–6372, 6373–6375
- history of study of, 3660–3663, 3677
  - classical, 6365
  - Müller (Karl Otfried) in, 6237
  - Nilsson (Martin P.) and, 6622
  - Otto (Walter F.) in, 6932–6933
- Homer, influence of, 4108
- homosexuality in, 7079
  - age-structured, 4112–4113
  - in initiation rituals, 184
  - role-specialized, 4116
- horses in, 4382
  - fertility cult associated with, 4132
  - in mythology, 4133
- hospitality in, 4138–4139
- human body in
  - cult of perfection in, 4171
  - divine beauty and, 4168, 4169

Greek religion and mythology *continued*
human sacrifice in, Artemis and, 507
iconography of (*See* Iconography, Greek)
immortality in, 3664, 3666
incarnation in, 4415
initiation rituals in (*See* Initiation, in Greek religion)
inspiration in, 4509–4510
Isis cult in, 4557, 4558, 4559
journals devoted to, 10059
Kerényi's (Károly) study of, 5113, 5114
keys in, 5116
kingship in, divine, 5146–5147
kissing holy objects in, 9258
knowledge in, 5201
Lady of the Animals in, 5282
libations in, 5433
light and darkness symbolism in, 5452
literature of, 5467–5469
as literature *vs.* religion, 3660–3663
magic in, 3678, **5572–5577**
sources on, 5573–5575
sun and, 8839
memorization in, 5852
milk and honey in, 847
Minoan-Mycenaean myths and, 4320–4321
miracles in, 6050–6051
mirrors in, 6064
money in, 6138
monkeys in, 6150
monotheism in, 6156
moon in, 6171, 6173, 6175
morality in, 6187
mountains in, 6213
Muses in, 6242
music in, **6302–6306**
and early Christian music, 6305
magic power of, 6303
of Muses, 6242
relics of, 6304
in sacrifice, 3682, 6303
theory of, 6303–6304
mustērion as sacrament in, 7954–7955
mystery religions (*See* Mystery religions)
mysticism in, 3670–3675
in Native American poetry, 7225
necromantic practices in, 6452
oaths in, 9640
oracles in
features of, 3905–3906
heads, oracular, 3806
Sibylline Oracles, **8382–8386**
oral tradition in, 3660
Ouranos, castration of, 1450, 1451
paradise in, 6984, 6985
phallus in, 7079–7080
of Dionysos, 7079, 7082
philosophical critique of, 3685
Pleiades in, 8735
Plutarch on, 7201
poetry of, 3660, 3678
politics and, 7275, 7277–7278
pollution in, 3677–3678, 7506
polytheism of, 7317
postures and gestures in, 7344
prayer in, 3683–3684
priesthood in, 7277
procession in, 7417, 7420
prodigies in, 7337
prophecy in, 7424
prostitution in, 7079
purification in, 7144, 7507, 7509
rain in, 7602, 7603
rape in, 7079
reincarnation in, 7528, 7676, 7679–7680, 9328–9329
rejuvenation myths in, 7684
relativism in, 7685
relics in, 7687
religious communities in, 7700
repentance in, 7756
retribution in, 7783
riddles in, 6986–6987
ritual in, 3662, 3681–3683
Homer on, 4108
role of, 3662
rivers in, 7862
sacrifice in, 3667–3670, 3682–3683, 8006
altars of, 4381
animal bones, 1014
to Artemis, 506–507
bridge and, 1051
Burkert (Walter) on, 8008–8009
of cattle, 1466–1467
in Demeter cults, 2270
Detienne (Marcel) and Vernant (Jean-Pierre) on, 8009
in Dionysos cult, 2357–2358
goals of, 6302
Homer on, 4108
of horses, 4132
humans and gods in, 9579
of locks of hair, 3740
origin of, 3669–3670, 3683
at Panathenaia, 6958
of pigs, 7144, 9156
Pythagoras on, 7529
of sheep, 8310
social significance of, 3667–3670
scapegoat in, 8143–8144
seers in, Zalmoxis and, 9927–9928
serpents in, 8457, 8458, 8459
shamanism in, 8273
shame and guilt in, 8405
shape shifting in, 8301, 8302–8303
sheep in, 8310
ship symbolism in, 991–992
Sōphrosunē as chastity, 1558
soul in, 4415, 7871–7872 (*See also* Psuchē)
spells in, 8676–8677
spiritual guides in, 8708–8709
sports and, 8723
stones in, 8745
structuralist analysis of, 8758
suicide, attitudes toward, 8828–8829
sun in, 8836, 8839–8840
swans in, 4135, 8894
syncretism in, 8931, 8937
temples (*See* Temples, Greek)
textiles in, 9088, 9090
theurgy in, 9156–9157
tithes in, 9209–9210
transmission of, 3660, 3678
trees in, 9337, 9338
triads in, 9348–9349
tricksters in, Prometheus as, 7419, 7420
tuchē (fortune) in, 1527
turtles in, 9408
twins in, 9416–9417
underworld in, 9452–9453
vagina in, 7079
vegetarianism in (*See* Vegetarianism, in Greek religion)
virginity in, 9602–9604, 9606
warfare in, 9597
wisdom and, 9747
witchcraft in, 9770
women in, **3375–3381**
Artemis and, 506, 507–508
in Dionysos cult, 2358
inferior position of, 3677
as priestesses in Demeter cult, 2270–2271
as sexual possessions, 7079
writing's origins in, 270
Xenophanes on, 9855
Greek vases
anonymity of makers of, 4296
death depicted on, 4296, 4298
paintings on, 4296, 4298
Greeley, Andrew, 6057
Greeley, Dana McLean, 9471
Green, Arthur, 7638
in Jewish ecology, 2646
in Jewish Renewal, 4869, 4871–4874
retreat centers established by, 9383
Green, Dorothy, 3080, 3081
Green, Linda, 3414
Green, Ronald, 3430
Green, William Scott, 7253
Green (color), symbolism of, 1861
Greenbaum, Lenora, 2371
Greenberg, Irving, on new age after Holocaust, 4092–4093
Greenberg, Moshe, 869
Green Corn ceremony, 1564, 1565, 1566, 2461, 4542, 4543, 6694
Green Dragon Monastery, Kūkai at, 8349
Greene, Graham
Monsignor Quixote, 3059
Roman Catholic thought behind work of, 3060
Greene, William Chase, 3001
Greenland
Eskimo religions in (*See* Inuit religious traditions)
moon in, 6173
Greenless, Duncan, on Hermetism, 3953
Green Space, Green Time: The Way of Science (Barlow), 2666
Green Table, The (Jooss), 2160
Greenville, Treaty of (1795), 9028
Greer, Germaine
on menstruation, 5867
in women's liberation movement, 3310–3311
Greeting, ritual of, 2868
Greeting cards, and secularization of salutations, 8062
Gregoras, Nikephoros, Gregory Palamas and, 3699
Gregorian calendar
Inca calendar compared to, 1361
in Japan, 1355
Maya calendar compared to, 1357
Orthodox rejection of, 4832
Gregorian chant, 1534
named after Gregory I, 3688
origins of, 3688, 6309
revival of, 6313
Gregorian Reform, 3691
law and, 5336
Gregorius, Gregor A. (Eugen Grosche), Fraternitas Saturni and, 8252
Gregory (Armenian catholicos), 488
Gregory IX (pope)
Anthony of Padua and, 377
Dominic canonized by, 2413
Franciscans and, 3182
and Inquisition, 4499, 6971
seeking reform of monasticism, 821
Gregory I (Gregory the Great) (pope), **3687–3689,** 6967
administrative skills of, 3687, 6967
on angels, 347
on Anglo-Saxons, 6943
on Antichrist, 394
Augustine of Canterbury under, 623, 3688
and Benedictines, 821, 3687, 3688
on Benedict of Nursia, 823
biblical exegesis of, 3688
bridge image used by, 1050

chanting and, 3688, 6309
on conversion, gradualist approach to, 8865
correspondence of, 3687
ecclesiology of, 1777
education of, 3687
on healing, 3845
on images, 4385, 4389
on *Job,* 3688
and language of fire, 3120
Lenten fast prescribed by, 2702
on Mary Magdalene, 5757
missions under, 6083
monasticism of, 3687
on morality, 1651
as religious and secular leader, 7254
Gregory II (patriarch). *See* Gregory of Cyprus
Gregory II (pope)
Gregorian chants and, 3688
Leo I condemned by, 6967
Gregory IV (Armenian catholicos), 490
Gregory VI (pope)
and All Saints Day, 2228
Gregory VII and, 3689
Gregory VII (pope), **3689–3692**
authority of, 697, 3690–3691
on celibacy, 7403
early Western Christianity influenced by, 2582
on ecumenical councils, convoking of, 2041
education of, 3689
election of, 3690
in eucharist controversy, 837
exile of, 3689, 3691
Henry IV excommunicated by, 697, 3691, 7280
Henry IV in conflict with, 697, 1690, 1772, 3690–3691, 6970, 7254
investiture controversy and, 7876
on membership in the church, 1777
monasticism of, 3689, 7724
on papal power, 1772, 9340
papal power restored by, 7876
political influence and, 2586
reform of, 839, 1663, 3690–3692, 6970
Gregory VIII (pope), 6972
Gregory X (pope)
Bonaventure named bishop by, 1011
in Council of Lyon, 2587, 6971
and Thomas Aquinas, 9162
Gregory XI (pope)
Great Western Schism and, 8157
return to Rome, 1461, 6971
Gregory XII (pope), 6971
divided papacy and, 4233
Gregory XIV (pope), Hermetism and, 3948
Gregory XVI (pope)
Romanticism and, 7878
and ultramontanism, 6973
Gregory, Peter, 1250–1251
Gregory Bar Hebraeus, Syriac Orthodox Church and, 8939
Gregory Nyssen. *See* Gregory of Nyssa
Gregory of Cyprus (Gregory II) (patriarch), **3692–3693**
abdication of, 3692–3693
in *filioque* controversy, 3692
Gregory of Datev (theologian), **3693–3694**
Gregory of Narek (poet), **3694**
Gregory of Nazianzus, **3694–3696**
Apollinaris of Laodicea and, 423, 424, 3695
on Arianism, 3695
on baptism, 782
Basil of Caesarea and, 797, 798, 3695
on dance, 2139
Evagrios of Pontus and, 2886
family of, 3694–3695
heresies opposed by, 3694–3695
hymns by, knowability of God in, 183
on knowledge, 5203
Neoplatonic traditions and, 6475
poetry of, 3695–3696
Gregory of Nyssa, **3696–3697**
on anthropological dualism, 2507
on Apollinaris of Laodicea, 424
against Arianism, 3696–3697
on asceticism, 3696
Basil of Caesarea and, 3696
ecology and, 2650
family of, 3696
on heart, 3882
on mysticism, 6347
Neoplatonic traditions and, 6475
Nersēs of Cla commentary on, 6478
on pain, 6946
on *Song of Songs,* 9763–9764
on souls, 8564
on Trinity, 3696–3697
Trinity and, 2582
Gregory of Sinai, 2587, **3697**
Gregory of Tours
on healing, 3845
on Seven Sleepers of Ephesus legend, 8440
Gregory Palamas, **3698–3700**
and Barlaam of Calabria, 788, 789, 3698
Cabasilas and, 1343
Eastern Christianity influenced by, 2582
on God, 3554, 3698
vision of, 3699
on hesychasm, 3698, 3699
homilies of, 3699
influence of, 3699
on knowledge, 5205
Makarios of Egypt and, 5624
monasticism of, 3698
synods of Greek church and, 2042
theology of, 2587, 3699, 9136
Gregory the Elder, 3694–3695
Gregory the Great. *See* Gregory I
Gregory the Illuminator, **3700**
and Nersēs the Great, 6479
in Armenian church, 488, 492, 3700
Tiridates III converted by, 488, 3700
Gregory the Theologian
on charity, 1554
charity taught by, 2582
Trinity and, 2582
Greimas, A. J., structuralism and, 8749–8750, 8755
Gremlins, 2952
Grenada
Big Drum Dance in, 1436
Shango cult in, 1435
Gressmann, Hugo
on *Epic of Gilgamesh,* 3487
on narrative forms, 6376
Old Testament studies of, 7707
Grettir, 167
Grey, George, colonial administration system of, 1856
Gṛhasthin (householder), 2330, 4421, 4441–4442, 4521, 4522. *See also* Āśramas
celibacy/chastity and, 1476, 1477, 1559
host role in, 4140
rites for, 9822
Gṛhya (domestic) rites, in Brahmanic religion, 3991
Gṛhyasūtras (ritual manual)
dharma in, 2328–2329
domestic rites in, 3991
magic in, 5590–5591
marriage in, 7814
saṃskāras in, 8884
in Vedas, 9554
Griaule, Marcel, **3700–3702**
critics of, 3701
Dieterlen (Germaine) on research team of, 2349–2350
on Dogon religion, 116, 2349–2350, 2390, 3700–3701
gardening in, 3281
masks in, 5768
myths of, 99–100, 116, 3701
Ogotemmêli's revelations to, 100, 116, 3701, 7329
ethnographic research in Africa by, 3700–3701
methodology of, 3701
on tobacco, 9217
Gribova, Ljubov S., 3114
on Komi religion and society, 5216
Griechische Roman und seine Vorlaufer, der (Rohde), 7871
Grief. *See* Mourning
Grieving process, 2241
in Australian Indigenous religions, 5051
Griffin (creature), 6164
Griffin, Susan, gynocentrism of, 3719
Griffith, D. W., 3097, 3100
Grigor Narekatsi. *See* Gregory of Narek
Grigoros, Nikephoros, 788
Grigor Tatevatsi. *See* Gregory of Datev
Grim, John, 2613, 2665, 6672
Grimble, Sir Arthur, 6004
Grimes, Ronald, 1512, 1513, 1517
on rites of passage, 7801, 7802
on ritual, 7857, 7858, 7859
on ritual failure, 7803
Grimm, Georg, 1188
Grimm, Jakob Ludwig Karl, 3053, **3702,** 4458
Deutsche Mythologie, 3111, 3702, 4458, 5676
fairy tale collection of, 7325
on Germanic mythology, 3458, 3702
on law, 5328
Mannhardt (Wilhelm) influenced by, 5676
Grimm, Wilhelm Karl, 3053, **3702,** 4458
fairy tale collection of, 7325
on Germanic mythology, 3458, 3702
Grimme, Hubert, 4717
"Grimm's law," 4458
Grímnir, 2692, 6808
Grímnismál, 2692, 6808
Grindal, Edmund, 7518–7519
Grīns, Margers, 765
Grintz, Y. M., 869
Griphos (riddle), 6986
Grisward, Joël, 4463
Grizzly bear, 807, 808–809
Groans, 7037
Gro bonanj (soul), in Caribbean neo-African cults, 1434
Grocyn, William, humanism and, 4176
Groethuysen, Bernhard, on French bourgeoisie, 8467
Grof, Stanislav
on paranormal phenomena, 7478
on states of consciousness, 1952

Grönbech, Vilhelm, 3459
and Myth and Ritual school, 6380
Gröndahl, Frauke, on Canaanite religion, 1387
Gronovius, Jacob, on Spinoza (Baruch), 8682
Groot, Gerhard, Devotio Moderna and, 7771–7772
Groot, Huigh de. *See* Grotius, Hugo
Groot, J. J. M. de, 1050, 1314, 1633–1634, **3702–3703**
on funeral rites, 3703
on religion, 7692
on univerism, 3703
Groper Ancestor (ancestral being), journey of, 2003
Grosche, Eugen. *See* Gregorius, Gregor A.
Gross, Darwin, 2602, 2603
Gross, Rita, 3313, 6536
on politics and religion, 7252
on *Religionswissenschaft* school, 9789
on study of women's religious lives, 9786
on women in Buddhism, 3330
Grosse Täuschung, Die (Delitzsch), 2263
Grosseteste, Robert
Aristotle translated by, 5990
and Bacon (Roger), 734
on nature, 6432
Grossfeld, Bernard, 889
Grotesque, humor of, 6365
Grotius, Hugo, **3703–3704**
on atonement, 597
on human rights, 5331
on natural law, 3703, 8491
in Remonstrant Brotherhood, 493
on war, 3703
Grotowski, Jerzy, 2438, 2476, 7051
Grottanelli, Cristiano, 4454
Grottanelli, Vinigi, 117
Grottasöngr, 2693
Grotto of Balankanché, 1469
Grotto of the Redemption (Iowa), vol. 5 color insert
Ground Crew, 9434
Ground of being, God as, Philo on *hypostasis* and, 4240–4241
Group of Ur, 2905
sexual magic and, 8252
Grousset, René, 3706
Grove, Lilly, 2145
Grube, Nikolai, 2435–2436, 2466
Gruber, Loren, 3460
Grub mtha' (Buddhist lineage), 1223
Gruenwald, Ithamar, 10052
Gruffydd, William John, 1498
on *Mabinogion,* 5545
Grunau, Simon, 767
Grundkurs des Glaubens (Rahner), 7601
Grundtvig, Nikolai Frederik Severin, **3704–3706**
and ecumenical Lutheranism, 5539
on heart's voices, 3704–3705
hymns of, 3705
Grundtvig Initiative, 3705
Grunebaum, Gustav Edmund von, 4716, 4722
Grünewald, Matthias, 495, 4346
Grunwald, Max, 4880
Grünwedel, A., 4492
Gsang ba'i sniying po (Tibetan Tantra), 9515
Gsang ba snying (Buddhist text), Klong chen Rab 'byams pa (Longchenpa) on, 5193
Gsang skor (Secret Cycle), 2547
Gsell, Stéphanie, 111, 4580
Gsusl (ritual bath), requirements for, 8057
Gter bdag gling pa, 7869
Gter bdag gling pa, Rig 'dzin, 1232
Gter chos (treasure-doctrines), 7868
Gter ma (treasures). *See* Treasure tradition
Gter ston (treasure finder), 1009, 9331
in Rnying ma pa (Nyingmapa) school of Buddhism, 7868–7869
Gtong len (giving and taking meditation), 1285
Gtsang pa Rgya ras pa (Tsangpa Gyarepa), on *mahāmudrā,* 5598
Gtsang (Tsang) school of Buddhism, emergence of, 8083
Gtsang smyon Heruka (Tsangnyon Heruka)
on Mar Pa, 5716
on Mi la ras pa, 6027
on *mahāmudrā,* 5598
G tumo Yoga (Tibetan), altered states of consciousness and, 1952–1953
Gu (musical instrument), 6293
Gu (shamanic witchcraft), 5592–5593
Guabancex (deity), in Island Arawak religion, 1427
Guacarapita (deity), in Island Arawak religion, 1427
Guadalupe, Virgin of. *See* Virgin of Guadalupe
Guagnini, Alexander, 331, 768
Guagnino, Alessandro, 3110
Guaman (falcon), Inca calendar and, 1364
Guaman Poma, 1854
Guaman Poma de Ayala, Felipe, 3415–3416, 5983, vol. 2 color insert
Guamaonocon (deity), in Island Arawak religion, 1426–1427
Guan (emperor), 1619
Guan (monastic communities), 9056, 9845
//guanab (deity), 5136
Guanajuato (Mexico), dances in, 2139
Guandi (deity), 2187
military cult and, 1913
Guanding (Buddhist monk)
writings of, 9176, 9178, 9179
as Zhiyi's successor, 9179
Guangcheng. *See* Du Guangting
Guangcheng ji (Daoist text), 2209
Guangsheng Monastery (Buddhist temple), 9047
Guangwu (emperor), on Confucius, 1898
Guan Sheng Da Di, birthday of, 1644
Guanyin (deity)
Avalokiteśvara as, 704, vol. 8 color insert
birthday of, 1644
flower associated with, 3135
gender and, 3343, 3344
Kṣitigarbha compared with, 3155
in Pure Land Buddhism, 292
sacrifices to, 1643
Guanzi (Chinese text), 1588, 5395
Guaraní-Apapocuvá religion (South America). *See also* Tupi-Guarani religion
deities of, 8578
World Fire myth in, 8589
Guaraní religion (South America)
flood myth of, 3131, 3132
music of, 6273
quest for paradise, 6983
Guarasu religion (Bolivia), lord of animals in, 8580
Guarayo religion (South America). *See also* Tupi-Guarani religion
messianic movements in, 8578
Guardian, in *walāyah,* 9656
Guardian Angels, The (Cortona), vol. 8 color insert
Guardian beings and spirits
angels as, vol. 8 color insert
in Igbo religion, 4365
in Mari and Mordvin religion, 5710
North American Indian, 6651–6652
Dakota, 8534
iconography of, 4307–4308
Iroquois, 4543
Nez Perce, 6595–6596
Northwest Coast, 6707–6708
in Old Norse tradition *(fylgjur),* 3246–3247
in Sami religion, 8087
Guardian's Office, in Scientology
attacks on the church and, 8193
legal problems with, 4149
Guardini, Romano, 310
Guasurangwe people (Paraguay), 8634
Guatauva (deity), in Island Arawak religion, 1427
Guatavita, Lake of, 6230
Guatemala. *See also* Mesoamerica
birth rites in, 7812
Catholic Action in, 5930
Christianity in, priest shortages, 1701
coup in (1982), 5931
liberation theology in, 5930, 5931
Maximón in, 5790–5792, 5926–5927
Maya religion in, 5796, 5799, 5882
government campaign against, 5931
Naj Tunich cavern, 1473
Protestantism in, 5928–5929
Guaticabantu (Caribbean chief), 10024
Guattari, Félix, and schizoanalysis, 7488–7491
Guayaki people (Paraguay)
pregnant women of, as diviners, 2557
sacred time and, 7986
Gudea (king), *hieros gamos* rite and, 3976
Gudea (ruler of Lagash), 5950, 5951, 5962
Guédon, Marie-Françoise, 6678
Guénon, René, **3706–3707**
and Burckhardt (Titus), 1324
on esotericism, 3707
on occultism, 6780–6781
writings of, 3706–3707
Guenther, Herbert, 1315, 8987, 9189
Guéranger, Prosper, 822
Guercino, Giovanni Francesco, vol. 13 color insert
Guernica (Picasso), 56, 4348
Guerrero, José Luis, 5922
Guerrero (Mexico), Formative (Preclassic) period in, 5896–5897
Guests. *See also* Hospitality
curses and, 2100–2101
gods as, in Greek myth, 4139
greeting of, 8060
Jesus as, 4139
Gu ge, Ye shes 'od (Yeshe-ö), 1224
Guha, Ramachandra, 2623
Guha, Ranajit, subaltern studies and, 8800
Guhyagarbha (Buddhist text)
Klong chen Rab 'byams pa (Longchenpa) on, 5193
in Rnying ma pa (Nyingmapa) school of Buddhism, 7870
Guhyasamāja Tantra (Buddhist text), **3708–3709**
Atīśa and, 1224
Candrakīrti's commentary on, 1216, 1275, 1401, 3708
exegesis of, 3708
horrific buddhas in, 1081
Līlavajra's commentary on, 1216
mahāmudrā in, 5596
Maitreya in, 5619
practice based on, 3708–3709

rituals in, 1219
sexuality in, 3708
as Tantric text, 1215, 8987
translations of, 3708
Tsong kha pa on, 1228, 2323
Gui (negative spirits or demons), soul and, 8555
Guiacurú-Caduveo peoples (South America)
geography of, 8576
religion of, 8636–8637
Guiart, Jean, on masks, 5766
Guida Spirituale (Molinos), 7558
Guide, spiritual. *See* Spiritual guides
Guide, The (Narayan), 10036
Guide of the Perplexed (Maimonides), 4892–4894, 5616–5617
Abravanel (Isaac) on, 17
audience of, 5616–5617
biblical exegesis in, 866
and Ibn Daud's (Avraham) writings, 4264
Kimḥat (David) on, 5145
knowledge in, 5203
Nahmanides (Moses) on, 6400
prophecy defined in, 7439
souls in, 8559
Torah as law in, 9236
translation into Hebrew, 5616
Guide to the Way to the Heavenly Kingdom, A (Innokentii), 4497
Guigemar (Marie de France), 991
Guignebert, Charles, 987
Guilds, professional, in China, 1616
Guillaume de Trie, Servetus (Michael) and, 8233
Guillaumont, Antoine, 3535
Guillen, Michael, 7599
Guillot of Tudela, 3652
Guilt, **8402–8407**. *See also* Conscience; Sin
in Christianity, conscience *vs.*, 1940
deities of, in Dinka religion, 2568
evil and, 2897
in Greek religion and mythology, 7756
in Judaism, 7757
punishment as compensation for, 7780, 7782–7784
repentance and, 7755–7756
revenge and, 7781
Guilt cultures, *vs.* shame cultures, 7755–7756
Guimarães Rosa, João, 3064
Guimazoa (deity), in Island Arawak religion, 1427
Guise (cardinal), in Reformation, 7662
Guiyang lineage, 1523
Gujarat (India)
Akbar's defeat of, 216
Parsis settling in, 6997
Śvetāmbara Jainism in, 4765–4766
Swaminarayan movement in, 8889–8892
Gujari (Sikh woman), 3336
shrines to, 8395
Gūji (chief priest), 7410, 7412
Gu Jiegang, 1636, 3339
Guji Oromo religion (Ethiopia), 2573
Guk (prophet), 7443
Gukanshō (Jien), 1178, 4917
Ame no Koyane in, 289–290
Gula (deity), 3376
Gulf of Mexico region, in Classic period, 5904–5905
Guliang Commentary, overview of, 1907
Gulick, Luther, 6001–6002
Gulingi (rain), 9458
Gulistān (Saʿdī), 2341
dating of, 8022
material in, 8023
Gullveig (deity), in apocalypse, 3456
Gu Long, 3070
Gu Louguan ziyun yanqing ji (Daoist text), 2208
Gulshan-i raz (al-Shabistarī), 8262, 8263
Gun (mythic figure), 1626
Gunabibi cult (Australia), 671–672, 6598–6600. *See also* Kunapipi
Guṇāḍhya (South Asian writer), 10033
Guṇamati (Buddhist monk)
on Nāgārjuna, 5552
Sthiramati and, 8739
Gunaprabhā (Buddhist scholar), 2322
Guṇas (qualities or energy fields), **3709**
desire in, 2305
in Pāñcarātra cosmology, 9508
in Sāṃkhya Hinduism, 2016, 3709, 3998, 7361, 8089
in Upaniṣads, 9346
in Vaiśeṣika school, 3709
in Jainism, 3709
puruṣa driven by, 853
Guṇaśri, on Nāgārjuna, 5552
Guṇavarman (Buddhist monk), 1133
Guṇavrata (Subsidiary Vows), 4770
Gundam Raul (deity), Ṛddhipur as pilgrimage site for, 7978
Gundel, Wilhelm, on catasterism, 8424
Gundestrup Caldron, 1481
Gundissalinus, Dominicus, 4266, 4275
Gundolf, Friedrich, 9651
Gung ru mkha' 'gro ma, 1233
Gunkel, Hermann
on *Epic of Gilgamesh,* 3487
and Myth and Ritual school, 6380, 6381
on narrative forms, 6376, 6377
Old Testament studies of, 7707
on origins of Christianity, 7707
on psalm types, 7463
in Religionsgeschichtliche Schule, 7706, 7707
on tradition history, 7708
Gunki (military texts), 4805
Gunn, Giles, 3073
Gunn, Mrs. Aeneas, 3390
Güntert, Hermann, 4456
Günther, Anton, Hegelianism and, 8176
Gunther, Erna, 6671
Gunton, Colin, 6161
Gunwinggu people (Australia), Rainbow Snake and, 7606
Guo Moruo, 3070
Guonian (New Year's Eve), 1641
Guo Xiang, 1575, **3710**
on *Zhuangzi,* 3710
Zhuangzi revision by, 9968
Gupta, Aghore Nath, 9318
Gupta, Bijaya, 825
Gupta, Dipankar, on subaltern studies, 8801
Gupta, Murāri, Caitanya and, 1346
Gupta dynasty (India)
Ajanta caves and, 1471
Aryanization of Bengal under, 824–825
Buddhist monasticism under, 1115, 4383, 6129
empire, image of, 1351
Hinduism in, 4429
Śaiva sects emerging in, 8041
Tantrism under, 8984
Gurage religion (Ethiopia), 2574
Gurdjieff, G. I., 2160, **3710–3712**
on attention, 604
and Bennett (John G.), 832–833
Brook (Peter) inspired by, 2476
on consciousness, 3711
Ouspensky (P. D.) and, 3711, 6935
students of, 3711
Gurdjieff Foundation, 3711
Gurdjieff International Review (periodical), 3712
Gurdwārās (Sikh shrines)
Ādi Granth in, 3716
Harī Mandir (Golden Temple), 8394–8395
to Mata Gujari, 8395
religious education at, 7733, 7734
Gurindji people
in new religious movements, 673–674
strike by, 673
Gurion, Ben, on Spinoza (Baruch), 8685
Guri ri Selle' (Bugis mythical figure), 1317
Gurney, Dorothy Frances, 3279
Gurney, Edmund, on phantasms, 3475
Gurney, Oliver R., 2522
Gurpurabs (days of the gurū), in Sikhism, 8396–8397
Gurteen, Stephen Humphreys, 7487
Gurū (Batak sorcerer), 799
Gurū Gobind Singh. *See* Singh, Gobind
Gurū Granth Sāhib (Sikh text), **3715–3718,** vol. 10 color insert, vol. 14 color insert. *See also* Ādi Granth
Gurukulas (guru schools), 4523
Gurū Nānak. *See* Nānak
Gurūs (spiritual masters), **3712–3715**. *See also* Spiritual guides
in *bhakti* movements, as saints, 8036
in Brahmanism, 9572
charisma of, 1548–1549
deification of, 8712
disciples' relationship with, 3713–3715
false, 3714
with followers as subcommunities, 1867
functions of, 3714
in Hinduism, 3712–3715
insights by, 2370
in sectarian movements, 4004
in Advaita Vedānta, 3714
in Śaivism, 4430
inŚrī Vaiṣṇavas Sampradāya, 8728
in Vajrayāna (Tantric) Buddhism, 1216, 1286, 3714
transcendental union, teaching on, 8016
in Vīraśaivism, 8043, 8044
married *vs.* celibate, 1477
modern developments in, 3714–3715
renunciate sects founded by, 8019–8020
roles of, 3714
in Sikhism, 32, 3714, 3878, 8393–8395
Ādi Granth as, 3716–3717
portraits of, vol. 10 color insert
women and, 3335–3336
as spiritual guides, 8711–8712
women, 3715
Guruvandaṇa (homage to the teacher), 4769
Guruvāyūr Temple (India), 2448, 5254
Gurvich, I. S., 475

Gurzah (stone idol), 835
Gurzil (stone idol), 835
Gush Emunim (bloc of the faithful), 5227, 9981
Gushri Khan, 1154, 2322
Gusinde, Martin, on supreme beings, 8577, 8579, 8877
Gustafson, James, 5811, 5813
Gutaal (singer), 10070
Gutenberg, Johann, 893, 7456
Güth, Anton, 1187
Guthrie, Stewart
 on animism, 8277
 on culture and religion, 2089
Guthrie, William Norman, 2164
Gutiérrez, Gustavo
 on kingdom of God, 5153
 liberation theology of, 5438, 5439, 5931
  in progressive Islam, 6098
Gutiérrez Alea, Tomás, 3099
Guttman, Alexander, on Hillel (Jewish sage), 3982
Guttman, Allen, on sports, 8724–8725
Güüshi Khan, 1149
Guyana
 cannibalism among sorcerers in, 1404
 funeral rites in, 3236
 Jonestown group in (*See* Jonestown and Peoples Temple)
Gu Yanwu (Gu Yinglin), 1579, **3718–3719**
 Confucianism of, 3718
 family of, 3718
 Han Studies *(Hanxue)* movement and, 1903
Guyart, Marie. *See* Marie de l'Incarnation
Guyon, Jeanne-Marie de la Motte
 mysticism and, 6350
 and Quietism, 6350, 7558–7559
Guyon, Madame, 3039
 enthusiasm of, 2805
Gwaltney, John, 77
Gwek (prophet), 2570, 6745, 7443
Gwo bananj (big guardian angel), 9636
Gwydion (deity), 1489
 in *Mabinogion,* 5546
Gwynn ap Nudd, 372, 1494
Gyarmathi, Samuel, 3111
Gyatso, Janet, 701, 9189, 9190
Gyatso, Tenzin, 9189
Gyi jo Lo tsā ba Zla ba'i 'od zer, 1227
Gylfaginning (Eddic poem), 2692, 5509, 8460
Gylfi, 2692
Gymnastics, *daoyin,* 5734, 5735
Gynecocracy, 731
 female concepts of sacredness and, 3407
Gyn/Ecology (Daly), 7008
Gynocentrism, **3719–3721**
 critiques of, 3720
 definition of, 3298, 3719
 theories of, 3719–3720
Gynocritics, 3719
Gyōgi (Buddhist monk), 1176, 1177, **3721,** 4795
Gyōnen (Buddhist monk)
 on Buddhist schools, 1246, 1247, 1249, 1250
 and Japanese Buddhism, 1183
 writings of, 1179

H

Haab (year), in Maya calendar, 1356
Ha'ameq davar (Berlin), 868
Ha-'anaq (Ibn Gabirol), 4266
Haas, Mary R., 754
Haasan, Kamal, 3098
Haavio, Martti, 3104, 3114, **3723–3724,** 5512
Habad (Lubavitcher) Hasidism, **3792–3793**
 God in, 3551
 Habad, meaning of, 8171
 in Jewish Renewal movement, 4869
 messianism in, 3788, 8173
 mystical union in, 6340
 outreach organization and education, 8172
 Return to Judaism movement, 8172
 Schneerson (Menachem), role of, **8171–8173**
 Shne'ur Zalman of Lyady, role of, **8371**
 tsaddiq doctrine in, 3790–3791
 tsimtsum concept in, 3551
 in United States, 6905
Habakkuk (prophet), 7436
Habakkuk, Book of, 879
 Canaanite parallels, 1392
 faith in, 7017
 pesher of, 872, 889, 7063
 prayer in, 7461
Habel, Norman, at University of South Australia, 8770
Habib, Samuel, vol. 3 color insert
Habibie, B. J., 4670
Habilitation (Klimkeit), 5190
Habilitationsschrift (Dilthey), 2352
Habis dynasty (Tartessian), 4250
Habitation, religion as, 10082, 10084
Habits (clothing of nuns), 1832
Habitus, Bourdieu's notion of, 2088
Hablador, El (Vargas Llosa), 3064
Haboush, Jahyun Kim, 3346
Hachas (carved stone), 749–750
Hachiman (deity)
 as *bodhisattva,* 4783–4784
 in Kamakura period, prominence of, 4786
 as *kami*-buddha amalgamatio, 8360
Hachlili, Rachel, 4342
Hacilar (Anatolia), Neolithic settlement of, 6462
Hacker, Paul, 4450
 on Śaṅkara, 8105
Hackett, Rosalind, 117
Hadad (deity), **27–29**. *See also* Adad
 in Aramean religion, 27–29, 447–450
 Iupiter Dolichenus derived from, 4753
 in Phoenician religion, 7130
Hadaka matusuri, fertility of earth and, 2559
Ḥaḍānah (custody), 4711
Hadassah. *See* Esther
Hadassah (Zionist organization), Szold (Henrietta) as founder of, 8941
Hadd. *See* Adad
Hadda. *See* Adad
Haddad, Yvonne Yazbeck, 3313
Hadden, Jeffrey, 6524
Haddon, A. C., 2420, 2421
 on revival and renewal activities, 7788
Hades (deity), 164, **3724–3726**
 functions of, 3680, 9952
 Hermes and, 3937
 judgment of the dead by, 5026
 Persephone as bride of, 2269, 2271, 3382
 Persephone kidnapped by, 2751
 souls of the dead and, 8542–8543
Hades (underworld), **3724–3726,** 9453. *See also* She'ol
 afterlife in, 164–165
 descent into, labyrinth as symbol of, 5274
 Gehenna *vs.,* 8564
 Hermes as messenger to, 3937
 judgment in, 165
 Kerberos as guardian of, 3804
 in Nag Hammadi, 3941
 Odysseus's visit to, 6452
 punishment in, 165
 river Styx in, 7863
 water in, 9703
Ḥad Gadya' (song), 7004
Hadhōkht Nask (Zoroastrian text), 7763
Hadhramautis, in Arabia, 443
Hadi, Syed Sheikh bin Ahmad al-, 3078
Hādī ilā al-Ḥaqq, al-, and Mu'tazilah, 6320
Hadingus, saga of, Saxo Grammaticus on, 8142
Ḥadīth (sayings of the Prophet), **3726–3733**. *See also* Ahl al-ḥadīth; *Sunnah*
 'Abd al-Jabbār on, 3
 ablutions in, 10
 acceptance of, 4566
 afterlife in, 161
 Ahmad Khan on, 202
 al-Ash'arī and, 530, 531
 as source of *kalām,* 5060
 authenticity requirements, 3731, 4565–4566, 4694, 4696, 4704
 authority of, 695–696
 al-Bukhārī on, 1318–1319
 caliphate in, 4393
 as canonical, 1409, 9274–9275
 Chirāgh 'Alī on, 4652
 codification of *sunnah* into, 4565
 collections of, 3729–3730
 creed of Islam and, 2053
 criticism on, 3730–3731, 4565, 4566, 4704
 on days of the week, 4712
 dhikr in, 2340
 on disease and medicine, 3831–3832
  prophetic medicine drawn from, 3833, 3834
 during Muḥammad's time, 7562
 in formulation of law, 4566
 gift giving in, 3485
 God in, 3565
  attributes of, 617, 618
 gold and silver in, 3626
 humor and, 4211, 4215
 Ibāḍis on, 4249
 Ibn Ḥazm on, 4268
 Ibn Hubayrah on, 3767
 Ibn Khaldūn on, 4269
 Ibn Taymīyah devoted to, 4276
 iconoclasm in, 4349
 idolatry condemned in, 4385
 ijtihād in, 4373–4374
 īmān and *islām* in, 4398, 4399
 in Sunnī Islam, 4565, 4696, 9268
  vs. Twelver Shiism, 8342, 8344
 Islamic studies on, 4717
 isnād (chain of transmission) and, 3727, 8821
 Jerusalem in, 4840
 on Jews, 7237
 Jihād in, 4918
 light of Muḥammad in, 6766
 madhhabs (schools of law) disagreeing on, 5549
 magic in, 5583
 mahdī in, 5980
 Mālik ibn Anas on, 5627
 meaning and terminology, 3726–3727
 menstruation in, 5866
 and messengers of God, 6735
 messianism in, 5979–5980
 mi'rāj in, 6060
 mirrors in, 6063
 modern attitudes toward, 3731–3732
 Mu'tazilah rejection of, 4567, 5063
 on nature, 2651
 predestination in, 3211
 reception and documentation of, 3727–3728
 ṣalāt (prayer) in, 8054–8055
 salutation in, 8061
 in Shiism, 3732–3733, 4565
  al-Ḥillī, methodology of, 3982
 soul in, 8567

in Southeast Asia, 4663
on state functions, 7285
suicide prohibited by, 8830
Sunnat al-nabī (inspired prophetic example) and, 8852–8853
al-Ṭabarī's collection of, 8944
tafsīr based on, 8950
types of, 3728–3729
waqf in, 9676–9677
Western scholarship on, 9275
Hadīth qudsī (divine sayings), Ibn al-ʿArabī's collection of, 4257, 4259
Hadot, Pierre, 6475
Hadrah (Sufi dance), 2139, 2933
Hadrian (Roman emperor)
apotheosis of, 440
Christian persecution by, 7059
and Isis cult, 4559
Jerusalem rebuilt by, 4836
Jewish persecution by, 7055, 7056
Mausoleum Hadriani, circularity of, 1792
Rome as goddess and, 7913
temples built by, 9065
Hadza people (Tanzania)
hunting/gathering system of, 2566
mortuary rites of, 2569
Haeberlin, Herman, 6671
Haeckel, Ernst
on death, 2239
"ecology" coined by, 2608
nature worship of, 2663
Haekel, Josef, 475, 6671
on lord of the animals, 5515
on supreme beings, 8877
South American, 8577
Haeterism, 731
Haewŏl, Ch'oe, 1647
Ḥafets Ḥayyim (Kagan), 5053
Hafgan (deity), 1490
Hafiz (poet), 7223
Ḥāfiẓīyah movement, origin of, 8331–8332
Ḥāfiẓ Shīrāzī, **3733–3735**
Häfker, Hermann, on *Epic of Gilgamesh,* 3487
Ḥafṣ (reciter of Qur'ān), 9200
Ḥafṣah, as Muḥammad's wife, 6224
Hafsid dynasty, 4587
Haftarah (concluding reading), in Shabbat services, 8257–8258
Hafuri (liturgist), 7411
Hafuribe (liturgist), 7411
Ḥag (pilgrim festival), 934, 7153
Hagar (biblical figure)
feminist reading of story of, 3036–3037
Ishmael as son of, 4551
Sarah and, 8112
Hag archetype, 9773–9774
Hagen, Mount, cargo cults and, 1418, 1419
Haggadah (prayer book), Kaplan's (Mordecai), 7636
Haggadah (telling), 7003–7004
Haggai, 879
prophecy in, 5426
Ḥag ha-Matsot (Feast of Unleavened Bread), 1040, 5388
Hagia Sophia (Istanbul), 6246–6247
Hagia Sophia, Synod of (815), 6619
Hagia Triada (Crete)
religious art in, 38–40, *39*
sarcophagus from, 39–40, 5433
Hagin, Kenneth, 7030
Hagiographa Chaldaice, 889
Hagiography
in Bengali language, 10035
Daoist, 2206–2207
in English, 10036
in Hindi language, 10034
Islamic, 4584
of Yeshe Tsogyal, 9882
Zoroastrian, 9989
Hagioretic Tome (Gregory Palamas), 3698, 3699
Hagios, Greek concept of, 7966, 7967
Hagnos, Greek concept of, 7967
Hagoromoi (Japanese folk tale), 4798
Haguenaur, Charles, on female shamans, 8273
Haguro, Mount, 6439
Haha (domestic spirits), in Samoyed religion, 4106
Hahn, Eduard, 1464
Hahn, Michael, 340
Hahunga ceremony (Maori), 7808
Haichaoyin (journal), 8967
Haida religion (North America), **3735–3737**
area covered by, 6656
body marks in, 1004
cultural renaissance in, 3736–3737
mosquitoes in, 4508
myths and stories in, 3735
potlatch in, 3736
repatriation of sacred objects, 6711
salmon tales in, 6662–6663
servitude as positive attribute in, 2986
social organization of, 3735–3736
story of Shining Heavens, 2983
supernatural in, 3735
trees in, 9334
H'ai Gaon, **3737–3738,** 4989
prayer book by, 8387
Haigon ryūjitsu (ultimate teaching), 9076
Haiku (poetic form), 7207
interactive discipline and, 8702
Haile, Berard, 6672
Haile Selassie, 9306–9307
Rastafari and, 7622, 7623, 7624, 7625, 7627
Rastafarianism and, 1437–1438
Haimavata school of Buddhism, 1194
Hain ceremony, in Selk'nam religion, 8224–8225
Hainuwele (mythic figure), 191
food from, 9578–9579
murder of, 2091–2092, 5277, 5444
Persephone and, 4825
Hair, **3738–3741**
in Chinese tradition, 1827
covering of, by Jewish women, 1831, 1832, 1837
in Freudian theory, 3738–3739
haircutting, social control, and initiation, 3739–3740
in Mesoamerican religions, rites of passage and, 7812
as relic of life force, 8533
ritual changes to, 7844
sacrifice of, 7999
shaving of
Muslim pilgrimage to Mecca and, 1832
Roman Catholic nuns, 1832
as symbol of animality, strength, and the supernatural, 3739
use in magic, sacrifice, and mourning, 3740–3741
Hairesis (philosophical school, or heresy), in Greek thought *vs.* New Testament, 3920, 3926
Hair shirts
development of, 6197
in mortification, 6197
Haiti and Haitian religions
antisuperstition laws in, 3823
Arawak of, 1428
Christianity
demographics, 1707
Roman Catholicism, 1706
creolization in, 2067
diaspora of, 9638
Vodou in, 9634
funeral rites in, 3238
ghosts in, 3476–3477
history of study of, 76, 10026
necromancy in, 6453
origin myths in, 1429
Taino Indian religion
deluge myth in, 8588
high god in, 8589
Vodou (*See* Vodou)
Haituka schools of Hinduism, and classical Hinduism, development of, 3997–3998
Haizmann, Christopher, possession of, 2935
Haja kensei campaign, 4791
Hajat (ceremonial meal), in Sudanese religion, 8850
Ḥājj (pilgrimage to Mecca). *See also* Pilgrimage
Abrahamic origins of, 7155–7156, 7159
accounts of, 7157
arms forbidden in, 6226
by Muḥammad, 6226
in calendar, 4712, 4714, 7155, 7157
from China, 4633, 4637
circumambulation *(ṭawāf)* of the Kaʿbah in, 1797, 7158, 7160
clothing for, 1832–1833, 7158
in devotional life, 9816, 9817–9818
etymology of term, 7155
in Five Pillars, 7154–7155
forgiveness through, 8407
gestures during, 7158, 7343, 7344
guides for, 7157
al-Hujwīrī on, 4157
iḥrām for, 7157–7158
in Qur'ān, 7155
interpretation and meaning of, 7160–7161
joke about old lady and, 4212
local variations in customs, 7824
manuals of, 7155, 7157, 7158, 7159
in Middle Ages, 7157
prayer during, 7157–7158
pre-Islamic, 7155
preparations for, 7156–7157
purification before, 7157
requirements for, 7156
sacrifice during, 4714, 7159, 7160
in Shiism, 7155
Snouck Hurgronje (Christiaan) on, 8460
from Southeast Asia, 4660
space and time collapsed in, 7984
stations of, 7155, 7157, 7159–7160
symbolism of, 7155, 7156–7157
Ḥajj al-akbar, al- (greater pilgrimage), 4565
Hajjī Sharīʿat Allāh, 4651
Hajj ʿUmar, al-, 4606
Hakamaya Noriaki, 1247, 1250
Hakata (dice), 2370
Hakham (wise), as class *vs.* division, 9761
Ḥākim, al-
and al-Azhar, 230
Church of the Holy Sepulchre burned by, 4837
Druze movement and, 2503, 8330
ghaybah (concealment) of, 3469

Ḥakīm al-Tirmidhī, 4569
Hakimiyya (sovereignty), Qutb (Sayyid) on, 7576
Hako ceremony, 6704
Hákon (king), Snorri Sturlson and, 8460
Hakuin (Buddhist teacher), 1085, 1277, 1293, **3741–3742,** 9949
on meditation, 3742, 8714
Hakuyu (Buddhist monk), Hakuin and, 8714
Halakhah (Jewish law), 888, **3742–3755**. *See also* Talmud; *Yeshivah/Yeshivot*
vs. aggadah, 6015
areas of law in, 3751–3753
Asher (Ya'aqov ben) on, 5104
Avraham ben David on, 711
Babylonian Gaonate and, 4988–4989
Beit Hillel and, 815
casuistry and, 1454
on children on non-Jewish fathers, 7666
on clothing and modesty, 1831, 1832
Conservative Judaism and, 1960–1961, 1964
conversion from Judaism in, 4860
conversion in, 7824
on cremation, 7823
vs. election, 2746
Eli'ezer ben Hyrcanus and, 2764
Enoch and, 2803
gezerot (decrees), 3749
repeal of, 3750
H'ai Gaon, role of, **3737–3738**
Hasidic, 5017
healing and medicine in, 3829
Heschel (Abraham) on, 4908
Hillel ("the Elder"), role of, 3981, 3982
history of, **3742–3747**
chronological periods, centers, and authorities of, 3742–3744
literary genres and intellectual currents in, 3744–3746
modern scholarship on, 3746–3747
Israeli law (modern) and, 3753–3754, 9982
Jewish identity, patrilineal *vs.* matrilineal, 3751–3752
justice and, 10063
Karo (Yosef) on, 5104
Kook (Avraham Yitsḥaq) on, 5226
literary conventions of, 5356
Maimonides on, 4894, 5616, 5617, 5618
marriage in, 4859
midrash on, 6014–6015
minhag (custom) in, 3750
miqveh in, 6047
moral norms in, 6181–6182
Moses in, 6203
oral Torah and, 9235
origins of, 3747–3748
in Orthodox Judaism, 6898
outside influences on, 3746–3747, 3751
and Qabbalah, 7533
Rabbah bar Nahmani on, 7577
rabbinate and, 7578–7579
in rabbinic Judaism, 7588–7589
Reform Judaism and, 4983
responsa literature on (case law), 3746
by Adret (Shelomoh ben Avraham), 36
by Asher ben Yeḥi'el, 540
by Feinstein (Moshe), 3013–3014
by Gershom ben Yehudah, 3461
by H'ai Gaon, 3737
by Karo (Yosef), 5104
medical ethics in, 5811
medical issues in, 3829
by Me'ir ben Barukh of Rothenburg, 5831
modern commentary on, 3744
by Nahmanides (Moses), 6399
by Rashi, 7620
by Sherira' Gaon, 8320
of Spektor (Yitshaq Elhanan), 8674
by Tam (Ya'aqov ben Me'ir), 8972–8973
Rosenzweig (Franz) on, 7927
Sa'adyah Gaon on, 4888–4889
on types of law, 7952
Sadducees *vs.* Pharisees on, 8018
salvation and, Paul on, 2746
Samaritan, 8070
Sherira' Gaon on, 8320
sin in, 1888
Soloveitchik (Joseph Baer) on, 8518–8519
structure of, **3747–3755**
current role of, 3753–3754
influences, external, 3751
origins of, 3747–3748
rabbinic law in, 3748–3750
scriptural exegesis and, 3748
subdivisions of, 3751–3753
taqqanot (or *taanot,* enactments), 3746, 3749–3750
of Hillel ("the Elder"), 3981
power of repeal, 3750
on Torah as law, 9235–9236
tosafists producing, 9248
tosafot in deciding, 9246
worship in, 9805–9806
Halakhic Man (Soloveitchik), Talmudic interpretation in, 8518
Halakhic Mind (Soloveitchik), cognitive religion in, 8519
Halakhot gedolot (Major *Halakhot*), 4989
as monograph-codes, 3745
Halakhot pesuqot, 4989
Ḥalāl ("permitted"), and profane, concept of, 7968
Halaqah (study circles), 4666
Halāyudha. *See* Balarāma
Halbfass, Wilhelm, 7740
Halbwachs, Maurice, 5850
Haldar, Alfred, in Myth and Ritual school, 6381
Haldi spirits, in Sami religion, 8087
Hale, Horatio, 6670
Hale, Janet Campbell, 3093
Hale, Matthew, on law and religion, 5326
Hale Bopp comet, 6555, 6561
Haleluyah (hymn to the Lord), in Qabbalah, 8676
Halevy, Judah. *See* Yehudah ha-Levi
Half-Moon Ceremony, 10053–10054
Half-Way Covenant
church membership and, 1938
Mather (Richard) and, 5778
Ḥālī, Alṭāf Ḥusayn, 4652
Hall, G. Stanley, **3755**
on adolescence, 7796
on psychology of religion, 7475
Starbuck (E. D.) and, 8732
Hall, John R., 6525, 6553
Hall, Palmer, on Hermetism, 3953
Hall, Prince, 68
Hall, Stuart, on Afro-Caribbean identity, 1859, 10025
Ḥallāj, al- (al-Ḥusayn ibn Manṣūr), **3755–3758**
ecstatic utterances of, 8812–8813
execution of, 976, 4569, 7427, 8813
on God, unity of, 3566
love mysticism of, 6351
Massignon (Louis) on, 5774–5775
on mystical union, 6338, 6339
mysticism of, 7740
on light of Muḥammad, 6766
on *mi'rāj,* 6061
sayings of, 976, 4511
Hall cult (China), 323
Hallel (praise), on Jewish holy days, 4866
Hallels, in *siddur* and *maḥzor,* 8389
Hallelujah psalms, 7461
Hallen, Barry, 10032
Halley, Edmond, 6588
Halligan, Marion, 3082
Hal Lindsey (television program), 7714
Hallinskíði. *See* Heimdallr
Halloween, **3758–3759**. *See also* Samhain
development of, 2230
as ritual of reversal, 7844
in Wicca, 9731
Hallowell, A. Irving, 474, 5514, 6672, 6691
Hallstatt culture, 1479
Hallucination, *vs.* vision, 9612
Hallucinogens. *See* Psychedelic drugs
Halo. *See* Nimbus
Halperin, David, 10050, 10052
Halprin, Anna, 2161, 7047, 7051
Ḥalqa (circle school), 7735
Ham
at Easter Sunday meal, 2580
Nuwaubians on, 6769
Ḥamadānī, Yūsuf, 4621
Hamadhānī, 'Ayn al-Quḍāt al-, 5739
Hamadsha brotherhood (Morocco), spirit possession in, 8691
Hamadsha dances, 2139
Hämäläinen, Albert, 5709
Haman (biblical figure), in *Esther,* 2848
Hamangia culture, 6464
Hamann, Johann Georg
skepticism and, 8421
on symbol theory, 8908
Hamartia, 5469
Ḥamās (Palestinian movement), 7257
Hamaspathmaēdaya (feast), 6731
Hamatsa (performance), 7048
Hamatsa dancer ceremony, cannibalism and, 1403
Hamawi, al-, on African religions, 111
Hambleton, Ronald K., 50
Hambly, Wilfrid D., 1001
on African religions, secret societies in, 7719
Hamburg Ballet, 2162
Hamburg Prayer Book, significance of, 8388
Hamburg temple, 7668, 7669
Ḥamd (thankful praise), 2318
Ḥamdān al-Qarmaṭ, 7542
Hamdani, Husayn, 4375
Hamdullāhi
caliphate of, 3229
'Umar Tāl *vs.,* 9445
Hamelin, Octave, Durkheim (Émile) influenced by, 2527
Hamer, Fannie Lou, 10039
Ḥamets (leaven), 7003
Hami, Tassi, on head scarfs, 4212
Hamid, Yusuf Muzaffaruddin, 4689
Hāmidīyah Shādhilīyah (Ṣūfī order), 9009
Hamilton, Annette, 648, 686–687, 3390, 3392
Hamilton, Kenneth G., Eliade (Mircea), critique of, 4111

Hamilton, William
on death of God, 585
evolutionary ethics influenced by, 2919
on phallus, 7085
on phenomenology, 7087
Ḥā-Mīm (Berber writer), 835
Hamitic languages, in East Africa, 2566
Hamlet (Shakespeare), ghosts in, 3475
Hammād ibn Abī Sulaymān, Abū Ḥanīfah as student of, 21
Hammadid dynasty, 4582
Hammers
in Celto-Roman religion, 1481, 1485
in metallurgy, 5988
of Thor, 9166, 9167
Hammurabi (Babylonian ruler)
reign of, 5948
on Shamash (sun god), 8838
social justice and, 1553
studies of, 5968
Hammurabi, Code of
Adad in, 27
An in, 301–302
Babylonian pantheon in, 5965
codification and, 1842, 4727
compared to other codes, 1844–1845
cursing in, 2102
divine kingship in, 5147
divorce in, 4733
false accusations in, 4740
vs. Hebrew scriptures, 3540–3541
as law of talion, 7782
ordeal in, 6847
social classes in, 4730
Hamod, H. S., on humor, 4212
Hampaté Ba, Amadou, 116, 3228
Hampden, Renn Dickson, 6105
Hampl, Patricia, 703
Hampson, Daphne, 3035
Hamsa (protective symbol), vol. 3 color insert, vol. 9 color insert
Hamzah (Druze founder), *ghaybah* (concealment) of, 3469
Ḥamzah Fanṣūrī
mysticism of, 25
writings of, 4663
Ḥamzah ibn ʿAlī, 2503
Druze movement and, 8330
Han (anger, just indignation), in *Minjung* theology, 5441
Ḥanābilah (school of Islamic law), **3759–3769,** 9489
Aḥmad Ibn Ḥanbal and, 3762–3763, 5548
al-Ashʿarī and, 531
on attributes of God, 617–618
current status of, 5549
development of, 5548–5549
doctrine of, 5548–5549
doctrines of, 4695
emergence of, 3759–3762
followers of, 3763–3768
Ibn ʿAbd al-Wahhāb studying, 4254–4255
Ibn Taymīyah and, 4277
ijmāʿ in, 4697
imamate in, 4393, 4394
inheritance in, 4709
liberal aspects of, 5548–5549
in Saudi Arabia, 4698, 4703
Ḥanafī school of Islamic law. *See* Ḥanafīyah
Ḥanafīyah (school of Islamic law), 9489
Andalusian rejection of, 4593, 4594
bequests in, 4710
blasphemy in, 975
in Caucasus, 4614
in Central Asia, 4620, 4627
in China, 4633
creed of, 2063–2064
current status of, 5548
development of, 5547–5548
Abū Ḥanīfah in, 22–23, 24–25, 4695, 5547
Abū Yūsuf in, 22, 24–25, 4695, 5547
Shaybānī in, 22, 24, 4695, 5547
divorce in, 4708, 4709
doctrine of, 5547
government adoption of, 22–23, 5548
imamate in, 4393, 4394
inheritance in, 4709
ʿiṣmah in, 4725–4726
kafāʾah in, 4706
on marriage, 4706
Māturidī school and, 5781
in Ottoman Empire, 4698
paternity in, 4710
prayer in, 4396
prevalence of, 4567
qiyās in, 7546
al-Shāfiʿī on, 8263–8264, 8265
in South Asia, 4644, 4645
al-Taftāzānī on, 8957
and traditionalism *vs.* rationalism, 3761–3762
vs. Ḥanābilah, 3761–3762
on *waqf,* 9677
wife waiting for missing husband in, 4566–4567
Ḥanan'el ben Ḥushi'el, 4990
Hananim (deity), as Maitreya, 5621
Hanan Raymi (festival), 4412
Ḥananyah ben Teradyon, 843
on *shekhinah,* 8314
Ḥanbal ibn Isḥāq, Ḥanābilah and, 3763
Ḥanbalī school of Islamic law. *See* Ḥanābilah
Hanbleceyapi (Lakota sacred rite), 5296
Handarz, as wisdom literature, 9751
Handball, 749, 750, 751
Handbook of American Indians (Boas), 2542
Handbook of Middle American Indians, 5942
Handbook of Modern Item Response Theory (van der Linden and Hambleton), 50
Handbooks, magical, 5574
Handbuch der Methode der kulturhistorischen Ethnologie (Schmidt), systematic form in, 8168
Handclapping, 7038
Handel, George Frideric, 6252
oratorios of, 6311
Handelman, Susan, 5485, 6020
Handfasting (Neopagan marriage), 7829
Hand of Faṭimah gesture, 7344
Hand of Faṭimah talisman, 6747–6748
in Middle Eastern popular tradition, 3837
symbolism of, 3769
Hands, **3769–3771**. *See also* Postures and gestures
apotropaic and magical uses of, 3770
in blessings, oaths, and consecrations, 3770
cheironomy (melody movements), 1533
gestures of (*See Mudrās*)
handprints in cave art, 1469
in Judaism, "defiling the hands" concept in, 1406, 1408
laying on of, 3770
in Catharism, 1457
in Christianity, 1956, 7959
by Kambangu (Simon), 5143
returning heretics and, 2113
by Roberts (Oral), 7712
right
in blessing, 980
vs. left, preference for, 5393
ritual avoidances and mutilations, 3770–3771
as symbols of deity, 3769
votive gestures of, in Sabazios cult, 7954
in worship, prayer, and meditation, 3769–3770
Handshaking, 9259
Handsome Lake (prophet and shaman), **3771–3772,** 6667, 6686
ballgame for, 754
influence of, 4541
revelations given to, 4543, 7756
study of, 6671
Handy, E. S. Craighill, 622, 8980
on *mana,* 8515
Han dynasty (China)
afterlife during, 170–172
Buddhism in, 1160, 1163, 1170, 1575–1576, 4383
temples of, 9045, 9046
"common religion" in, 1614
Confucianism in, 1897–1898, 2632, 3341, 4337, 7267
Confucian texts in, 1908
cosmology in, 2178
Daoism in, 2179–2180, 2192, 4332, 7165, 7257, 7268, 9670–9671
temples of, 9056
divination in, 2372
fall of, 2180
and Ge Hong, 3290
homosexuality in, 4114
Huangdi (Yellow Emperor deity) in, 4144
imperial religion of, influences on Daoism, 2179–2180
Islam in, 4631
kingship in, 5179
Legalism in, 5396
magic in, 5592, 5593
middle-level cults in, 1913
music in, 6293
mythology, 1622
overview of, 1590–1594
pantheon, development of, 1910
philosophy in, 1574
poetry in, 7213
sacrifice in, 7267
taiping in, 8961
Taiwan in, 8962
utopian visions in, 1628
Vietnam, conquest of, 8643
wuxing (five phases) philosophy in, 3860
Hanegraaff, Wouter J.
on alternative religions, 6527
on esotericism and Faivre (Antoine), 2844–2845
on Hermetism and Yates (Frances), 3954
on occultism, 6781
Han Fei-Tzu. *See* Han Fei Zi
Han Fei Zi, 1573–1574, **3772–3774,** 5395
Hangest, Charles de, Calvin (John) and, 1374
"Hanging Odes" (Zuhayr), 7221
Hangings (textile), 9092
Hani, Jean, on kingship, 5160
Ḥanina' ben Dosa', 3158
miracles of, 6051
Hanks, William F., 6845
Hannahanna (deity), 3595
Hanshan (poet), 2629, 7214
on mountains, 6212, 6213
Hanshan Deqing, 1607
Han Shantong, in White Lotus, 6040
Hanslick, Eduard, 6312
Han Studies *(Hanxue)* movement, 1903

Han Tianshi shijia (Daoist text), 2206
Hantu (ghosts), possession by, 8696
ḥanukat-habayit (dedication the home), in Judaism, 4105
Ḥanukkah, **3774–3775**
celebration of, in Apocrypha, 901
commercialization of, 2398
domestic observances of, 2397, 2400
gift giving in, 3484
in Jewish calendar, 4866–4867
maḥzor liturgy for, 8390
Hanullim (deity), 1648
Hanumān (monkey god), **3775**, 4438
Balaji temple of, exorcisms at, 2934
in Buddhism, 6152
cult of, 6150
functions of, 6152
as guardian against ghosts, 3477
iconography of, 6152
in *Rāmāyaṇa*, 6152
and magic plant, 4439
in North India, 3987
origins of, 6152
punishment of, 6151
in puppet theater, 2452
Ḥanuyyot (stores), 925
Han Wŏnjin, in Nak-Ho debate, 1932
Han Wudi (Chinese emperor), 2990
magic in court of, 5465
Han Yu, 1165
campaign against Buddhism, 1577, 1602
poetry of, 7214
on relics, 7691
on *ren* and *yi*, 7752
on "Transmission of the Way" *(daotong)*, 1900
Xunzi and, 1573
Hao Datong, 2210
Haoma (deity), **3775–3776**
Haoma (substance), **3775–3776**, 4455
and ascension, 519
fire in offerings, 3116
and immortality, 849
and inspiration, 4509
as libation, 5434
preparation of, 849, 4535
as sacrifice, 849, 4535
redemption and, 7641
soma compared to, 8521–8522
symbolic importance of, 850
as water, 9577–9578
Haotian (heaven), 9172
Haoxiong (spirits), 1641
Hapi (deity), 3123
Nile River associated with, 7861
Haplography, 921
Happiness
in Greek thought, 8405
in Kurozumikyō, 5267
in Sōka Gakkai, 5400
Kant (Immanuel) on, 5078
Sa'adyah Gaon on, 7952
serpents as bestowers of, 8457
Spinoza (Baruch) on, 8684
in Stoicism, 8741
Haqā'iq al-tafsīr (al-Sulamī), 8954
Ḥaqīqah (reality), 4400, 4416
Ja'far al-Ṣādiq and, 4761
Ḥaqīqah Muḥammadīyah. *See* Nūr Muḥammad
Haqq (divine truth), 2652
Haqqafot (circumambulation), 1796, 1797
Hara, Mount, as cosmic center, 6212
Harakas, Stanley S., ethics, 1653
Harakhti (deity), Akhenaton and, 217–218, *218*
Harald Bluetooth (king), 7940
Haraldskvaði (Norse poem), 842
Haram al-sharif, al- (Sacred Precinct), 4841
Ḥaram and *ḥawṭah* (sacred enclaves), **3776–3778**
female seclusion as, 1559
hirjah concept and, 3777–3778
and holy, concept of, 7968
in *ḥājj*, 7158
inviolability of the enclaves, 3777
meaning of terms, 3776–3777
nature in, 2604
popular healing practices as, 3835
Ḥaram Mosque (Mecca), vol. 3 color insert
Haran (city), moon worship in, 6172
Haran Gawaita (Mandaean text), 5634, 5638, 5639
Harappa (India), 4427, 4433, 4470, 4471–4472, 4473. *See also* Indus Valley religion
Hárbarðr, 2692
Hárbarðsljóð, 2692
Hárbarzljóð (Eddic poem), 9165
Ḥarbī, Ibrāhīm al-, Ḥanābilah and, 3763
Harbin (Manchuria), Judaism in, 5008
Hardacre, Helen, 3346, 7274
on women in Japanese new religious movements, 8695
Hardeman, Charlotte E., 6527
Hardenberg, Friedrich von. *See* Novalis
Harding, Chester, 31
Harding, Rachel, 80
Harding, Sarah, 9189
Harding, Stephen, Cistercian reforms and, 1800
Harding, Vincent, 76, 965
Hardt, Hermann van der, on Hermetism, 3951
Hardy, Peter, 4642
Hard Yam Woman (mythic figure), 653
Hare (animal). *See* Rabbits and hares
Hare (culture hero)
in Khoi myth, 2091
in North American Indian trickster tales, 6661
Hare, David, 2477
Hare, R. M., 307, 5499
Haredi movement, 6907
Hare Kṛṣṇa mantra, 4522, 5678. *See also* International Society for Krishna Consciousness
Haremhab, 219
Harepo (orators), 5850
Hareven, Shulamit, 6021
Hargobind, and *Ādi Granth*, 32
Hargrave, Catherine P., on cards, 1414
Hari-bhakti-vilāsa, Gōsvamins and, 1346
Hardivār (India), Kumbha Melā at, 5265
Harihara (deity), 5129
Hari-Hara (deity), in Southeast Asian Hinduism, 4012
Hariharan, Gita, 10036
Ḥarim (protected zone), 2652
Harī Mandir (Golden Temple), design of, 8394–8395
Häring, Bernhard, on moral theology, 1654
Hariścandra, Bhāratendu, 10034
Ḥārith, 'Abd Allāh ibn al-, Shī'ī doctrines originating from, 8321
Hariti (deity), 3135
Harivaṃśa
avatāra theory in, 4000–4001
Balarāma mentioned in, 743
bhakti synthesis in, 3998–4002
caste in, 4001
Durgā in, 2526
Harivaṃśa Purāṇa, Kṛṣṇa in, 5456
Harivarman (Buddhist writer), 1200, 1201
Mahāsāṃghika Buddhism and, 5602
Harjo, Joy, 702, 7225
Harlan, Lindsey, 3322
Harlem
Peace Mission in, 3007
United House of Prayer in, 2125
Harley, Gail M., 6582
Harmenszoon, Jacob. *See* Arminius, Jacobus
Harmon, Ellen Gould. *See* White, Ellen Gould
Harmonial philosophy, in Spiritualism, 8715
Harmonia mundi, 6746
Harmonics, geometry of, 3441–3442
Harmonium (instrument), 6285
Harmonization, syncretism and, 8929
Harmony
in Chinese religion
Heaven and, 3888
qi and, 8555
Doctrine of the Mean on, 2634
in Greek music, 6303
between universe and humankind, music in, 6277–6278
Harmony Society, 6558
Harnack, Adolf von, **3778–3779**
antidogmatism of, 2060
Baeck's (Leo) rebuttal of, 736
Barth (Karl) studying under, 789
Bonhoeffer (Dietrich) studying under, 1016
on early Christian charity, 3844
Eastern Christianity depicted by, 2589
on essence of Christianity, 7235
on Gnosticism, 3514, 3532
on knowledge, 5208
on leadership, 5384
and liberal Protestantism, 6104
Loisy (Alfred) and, 5507, 6106
on Marcion, 5701
Ritschlianism of, 6104
Harner, Michael
on cannibalism, 1403
on core shamanism, 8275
neoshamanism and, 8294, 8295
Haroeris (deity), and Sobek, Kom Ombo temple of, 2709
Ḥaroset (paste), 7004
Harper, Edward B., on caste system, 7843
Harper, William Rainey, 5188
Harpers' songs, in Egyptian literature, 2721
Harpies (monsters), 2277, 6165
Harps
Greek, 6304
Middle Eastern, 6276
Harpy eagles, in South American shamanism, 8291
Ḥarrān, Qāḍī, Ḥanābilah and, 3765
Harran (province), Aramean religion in, 447–448
Harranians, 2971
Harrell, Stevan, 3314
Harrington, J. P., 6672
Harris, Barbara, 353
Harris, Charles, 675–676, 678–679
Harris, Ian, on modern Buddhist institutions, 2787
Harris, Joseph, 3458
Harris, Marvin, 1467
on cannibalism, 1403
on ecology of religion, 10043
on Jewish food taboos, 3172
on *Kulturkreiselehre*, 5259
on religion, adaptation of, 2868
on Schmidt (Wilhelm), 8169
Harris, Roy, on Saussure, 8758
Harris, William T., on Ngewo, 3570

Harris, William Wade, **3779–3781**
prophetic movement, 1720
teachings of, 104
vocation of, 9633
Harris Magical Papyrus, egg symbolism in, 2701
Harrison, Greg, 3099
Harrison, Jane E., 3001, **3781–3782**
on games, 3266
on homosexuality, 4115
on Lady of the Animals, 5280
methodology of, 3381
Neopagans influenced by, 7830
on theater, 7050
Harrison, Paul, 1085
Harrist Church, in Ivory Coast, 3780–3781
Harrowing (play), 2471
Har Sinai (synagogue), 7670
Hart, C. W. M., 3391
Hart, H. L. A., on law, 5369
Hart, Herbert, on law and religion, 5326
Hart, William D., on Said (Edward), 8032
Hartford (Connecticut), founding of, 4125
Hartland, E. Sidney, 2542, **3782**
Hartley, David, Martineau (James) and, 5737
Hartley, Hal, 3099
Hartley, Thomas, Swedenborgianism and, 8901
Hartman, Geoffrey, 5473
Hartman, Olov, 2477
Hartmann, Eduard von, 6437, 7087
Hartmann, Heinz, 7476
Hartmann, Olga de, 3711
Hartmann, Thomas de, 3711
Hartshorne, Charles, 3201
atheism and, 584
on God, 3560, 6161
on monotheism, 6161
Hārūn al-Rashīd (caliph)
Abū Yūsuf appointed chief judge by, 24
Mālik ibn Anas and, 5627
and Mu'tazilah, 6319
Ḥarūrīyah. *See* Khārijīs
Haruspices, 2377, 2872, 7336, 7337–7338
books of, 2873
in Roman religion, 7903
Haruwen territories, in Selk'nam and Haush culture, 8224
Harva, Uno Holmberg, 474, 3104, 3113, **3782–3784**
on Arctic religions, 475
on Komi religion and society, 5216
on Mari and Mordvin religion, 5709
Harvard Divinity School, women's studies at, 3313, 9786
Harvard Forum on Religion and Ecology, 2614
Harvard Memorial Church, Daly (Mary) at, 3312
Harvard Theological Review, 10057
Moore (George Foot) in, 6177
Harvard University
Gimbutas (Marija) at, 3492
Goldenweiser (Alexander A.) at, 3633
Goodenough (Erwin R.) at, 3637
Mather (Cotton) at, 5779
Mather (Increase) at, 5778, 5779
Mather (Richard) at, 5778
Moore (George Foot) at, 6176
Harvest. *See also* Agriculture
festivals of, 187–188
in Celtic religion, 3758
communal meals associated with, 7957
in Germanic religion, studies of, 5676
rituals of, 188–189
sacrifice at, 8000
Harvey, John W., translation of Otto's *Das Heilige,* 4098
Harvey, Richard, 564
Harwood, Alan, 9778–9779
Ḥasan, al-
as *ahl al-bayt,* 198
al-Ḥusayn ibn 'Alī and, 4234, 4235
Ḥasan al-Bannā'
assassination of, 6315
movements inspired by, 108
in Muslim Brotherhood, 6314–6315
Ḥasan al-Baṣrī, 2446, **3784–3785**
'Amr ibn 'Ubayd and, 6318
and Rābi'ah al-'Adawīyah, in fables, 8811
asceticism of, 8810–8811
as Fāṭimah's son, 3008
Baḥye influenced by, 740
eschatology of, 2838–2839
fire handling by, 3120
on free will and predestination, 3210–3211
mysticism of, 6350
Rābi'ah al-'Adawīyah and, 7591
on sacred time, 7987
Ḥasan 'Alī Shāh. *See* Aga Khan I
Ḥasanāt al-'Ārifīn (Dārā), 2219
Ḥasan (fair) *ḥadīth*
in Shī'ī collections, 3733
in Sunni collections, 3728–3729
Ḥasan ibn Mūsā, and Mu'tazilah, 6320
Ḥasan-i Ṣābbāḥ
murder of, 8332
Nizārī Ismā'īlīyah led by, 558
Nizārīyah and, 8332
order of Assassins founded by, 8831
Hasan-Rokem, Galit, 6020
Hasbany, Richard, 3314
Haseltine, W. G., 3096
Hashagakari (suspension bridge), 7048
Hāshimī, al-, 7242
Hāshimīyah movement
Abbasid revolution and, 8321
offshoots of, 8321
Hashish, Assassins' use of, 557
Ḥashwīyah, on attributes of God, 617–618, 619
Hasidism, **3785–3794,** 4982–4983, 4993–4994
American culture and, 4869
angels in, 345
Ashkenazic (*See* Ashkenazic Hasidism)
Ba'al Shem Tov as founder of, 726
Bratslav school, messianism in, 3790
Buber (Martin) on, 1055–1056
charismatic expression in, 1546
contemplation in, 5817
dance in, 2137, 2146–2147
decline and accommodation of, 9382
disputing with God in, 968
domestic rituals in, 2398
Dov Ber of Mezhirich as leader of, 726, 2429
dress code in, 1831–1832, 1836–1837
Elimelekh of Lizhensk in, 2767–2768
"empire" of, Shne'ur Zalman of Lyady and, 8371
ethics of, modern trends and, 4914–4915
European, 5017
fire symbolism in, 3119–3120
founding of, 4982
God in, 3551
Habad (*See* Habad Hasidism)
history of, 3786–3787
in Hungary, Sofer (Mosheh) and, 8507
internal dissent in, 9381
in Jewish ecology, 2646
Jewish Renewal and, 4869–4871, 4873, 4874
leadership in, 9379–9380
Levi Yitsḥaq of Berdichev and, 5428
literature of, 3791
messianism in, 3786, 3788–3789, 5978
misconceptions about, 3791
music in, 6310
mystical union in, 6339, 6340
mysticism in, 6352–6353, 6354
redemption in, 7641
nature in, 2643
opposition to, 3787, 9379, 9381–9382
by Eliyyahu ben Shelomoh Zalman, 2773–2774
Shne'ur Zalman of Lyady and, 8371
in Orthodox Judaism, Hungarian, 6899
Orthodoxy and, 6901
overview of, **3785–3792**
post-Holocaust, 9382–9383
prayer in, attention in, 606
Purim in, 7517
rabbinate in, 7583
rebe as spiritual guide in, 8709
revelation in, 7777
roots of movement, 3785–3786
Satmar school, **3793–3794**
Schenirer (Sarah), role of, 8149
Scholem (Gershom) on, 726
in Speyer, 5012
spirit possession in, 2533–2534, 8695
spread of movement, 3787–3788
Suffering Servant doctrine in, 4089
theology and ethics, 3788–3789
Torah study in, 9239
transmigration in, 9330
Tsaddiq doctrine in, 3789–3791, 9377–9386
women in, 9381
as spiritual masters, 5611–5612
Zion and, 9978
Hasidut Ashkenaz. *See* Ashkenazic Hasidism
Haskalah (Jewish Enlightenment). *See also* Jewish thought and philosophy
on Christianity, 7235
and decline of Jewish folk religion, 3160
Galician phase of, 5247
Krochmal (Naḥman) and, 5247–5248
vs. Musar movement, 6241
nature and, 2643
Northern European, 5017–5018
Russian, 5019
Spektor (Yitshaq Elhanan) against, 8674
in Zionism, 9978–9979
Hasmonaean period, *miqveh* in, 6046
Hasmonean priesthood, Sadducees and, 8018

Hassagot, Avraham ben David and, 711
Hassan, Riffat, 3370
Hassan II Mosque (Casablanca), 6210
Hasshū kōyō (Gyōnen), 1246
Hastavāla-prakaraṇa (Dignāga), 2351
Hastings, James, **3794**
Hastings Center, 940
Ḥatam Sofer. *See* Sofer, Mosheh
Hatara varan dēviyō (gods of four warrants), in Sinhala religion, 8411–8412
Hataria, Manekji Limji, 6998
Haṭha Yoga, Kuṇḍalinī in, 5266
Haṭhayoga, **3794–3795**
  breath in, 1043, 1044, 7363
  in devotional life, 9822
  Gorākhnāth as teacher of, 3637, 3638
  in Hindu Tantrism, 4003
Hathor (deity), **3795–3796**
  Dendera temple of, 2709
  in Egyptian cosmogony, 2710
  in Egyptian pantheon, 2704
  feast of, 2715
  iconography of, 4318
  Isis and, 4557
  in Kushite religion, 5269
  as Lady of the Animals, 5280
  music and, 6275
  Re and, 7634
  worship of, 3597
Ḥathth ʿalā al-baḥth, al- (Ashʿarī), 531
Hatraʾah institution, capital punishment and, 3752
Hatshepsut (queen of Egypt), 1472, 2706–2707, 4285
  claim to throne, 3381–3382
Hatt, Gudmund, 474
Ḥaṭṭaʿt (offering), 927, 4747, 7514
Háttatal, 2692
Hattians
  deities of, in Hittite religion, 4068, 4069, 4072
  mythology of, in Hititte myths, 4069
Hattic religion (Anatolia), goddess worship in, 3595
Hattishili III (king), 5165
Hattori Nakatsune, astronomical method of, 4022–4023
Hattushash (Hittite city), cuneiform texts from, medicine in, 3825
Hauck, Dennis William, on *Tabula Smaragdina (T.S.),* 3954
Hauck, Karl, 3459
Haudenosaunee religion. *See* Iroquois religion
Hauerwas, Stanley, 3429
Haugen, Einar, 3460
Haught, John F., 2912
Hauhet (deity), in Egyptian pantheon, 2705
Haumai (illusion of independence), *karma* and, 8548
Haumea (deity), 7315
Haumia (deity), 7313, 7314
Hauʾofa, Epeli, 3085
Haupt, Erich, on apostles, 435
Haurvatāt (spirit), 290
  in Armenian religion, 492
  gender of, 3372
Hausa-Fulani tradition in mosques, 6209
Hausaland
  establishment of, 4604
  Islamic revolution in, 3229, 4605–4606
  Islam in, 4604–4605
  women in, 4610
Hausa language
  Islamization of, 4611
  literature in, 3086
Hausa people
  calendar, 1353
  Dan Fodio (Usuman) and, 2167–2168
  drums of, 2495
  revenge and, 7780
Haush religion (Tierra del Fuego)
  Selkʾnam and, 8223–8224
  social order in, 8226
Hávamál (Old Norse text), 2692, 7939
Havasupai people (North America), 6721
Hável, Vaclav, Capps on, 1413
Havelock, E. A., on memorization, 5850, 5852
Haveng, Philipp van, 175
Havice, Doris Webster, 7486
Havnevik, Hanna, 9190
Ḥavurah/ḥavurot Judaism, 4985
  origins of, 1963
  in Reconstructionist Judaism, 7637, 7638
Havurat Shalom (Jewish community), 4869
Hawaii and Hawaiian religion, **3796–3800**. *See also* Oceania and Oceanic religions
  Buddhism, Shingon, 8352–8353
  cannibalism in, 1403
  chiefs in, 7307
  Christianity, beginnings of, 3083
  Christian missions in, 1738
  Cook (James) in, 9320
  creation myths in, 7313–7314
  deities of, 3796, 3797–3799
  drums in, 2500, 6263
  festivals in, 7308
  fiction of, 3085
  Hinduism, Śaivism in, 8419
  Hokuloa (Great Star), Venus as, 8427
  human sacrifice in, 7309
  kauwa in, 2986
  law in, 5341–5342
  Māui in, 5782–5783
  music in, 6263, 6264
  origin myth of, 7315
  planets in, 8427
  priesthood and places of worship, 3796–3797
  protective figures in, vol. 9 color insert
  rainbow symbolism in, 7604
  rituals in, 7308, 7310
  sacrifice in
    human sacrifice, 4184
    royal sacrifice, 8009
  settlement of, 3083
  sovereignty of, 5341–5342
  state religion in, 3799
  Tangaroa in, 8980
Hawes, John C., 2828
Hawkes, David, 7213
Hawkes, Jacquetta, on gold, wheels, and the sun, 8836
Hawkins, Edward, 6510
Hawkins, Erick, 2160
Hawkins, Gerald, 453
  on Egyptian temples, 8734
Hawks, 948, 949, **2553–2554**
  in Australian Indigenous myths, 654
Ḥawṭah. See Ḥaram and *ḥawṭah*
Hawthorn, symbolism of, 3136
Hawthorne, Nathaniel, 3061
Hawzah (seminary), **3800–3802**
  educational schedule in, 3801
  hierarchical order in, 3801–3802
  in Iran, 3801
Hay, Deborah, 2161
Haya (deity), 5952
Hayah (soul), 9378
Hayākil al-nūr (temples of light), 4554
Hayashi Razan, **3802–3803**
  Confucianism and, 1927, 8363
  shogunate and, 4789
Ḥay ben Meḳiẓ (Ibn ʿEzraʾ), 4265
Hayden, Maria Trenholm, Spiritualism and, 8716
Haydn, Joseph
  as Freemason, 3195
  music of, 6312
Haydon, A. Eustace, **3803**
Hayes, Christine E., 7514
Hayes, Diana, 79
Hayes, Rutherford B., and African Americans, 69
Haynes, Jeff, on religion, relevance of, 4179
Haywood, Garfield T., 7029
Ḥayy Ibn Yaqẓān (Ibn Sīnā), 4553
Ḥayy Ibn Yaqẓān (Ibn Ṭufayl), 4270
Ḥayyim Vital. *See* Vital, Ḥayyim
Hazael, 929
Hazelton, Roger, 495
Hazi (musical instrument), 6294
Hazra, R. C., 7497
Ḥazrat Amīr Khusraw. *See* Khusraw, Amīr
Hazzan (cantor), in Sephardic Judaism, 7582
HCJB (radio ministry), 7713
Head(s), **3803–3808**. *See also* Crowns
  beheading, 3804–3806 (*See also* Decapitation)
  Celtic head cult, 3805, 3806, **3807**
  honored heads, 3806
  multiple, 3804
  shrunken (*See Tsantsa*)
  surgery on, in African traditions, 3820
  symbolism and ritual use of, **3803–3807**
    Freudian symbolism, 3738
Headdresses
  African, 90
  as masks, 5765, 5766
Headhunting, 3805, 3807
  in Bornean religion, 1022
  in Southeast Asian religions, traditional, 8651
Head of Christ (Sallman), 4348, vol. 12 color insert
Healing and medicine, **3808–3875**. *See also* Bioethics; Disease and illness; Health; Medical ethics
  for affliction, 57–59, 60–63
  in Africa, **3816–3821**
    in Akan religion, 118, 215
    childbirth in, 3819
    Christianity and, 1721
    conversion and, 2571
    diviner-diagnosticians in, 3818
    by diviners, 2569
    in East African religions, 2569, 2571
    in Edo religion, 2697
    Ethiopian Church movement and, 1719–1720, 1721
    ethnopsychiatry in, 3820–3821
    by healing touch, 9256
    health in, 3817
    herbalists in, 3818–3819
    history of study of, 118
    in Igbo religion, 4365, 4366
    in Khoi religion, 5136–5137
    by Kimbangu (Simon), 5143
    in Kongo religion, 5221
    in Luba religion, 5524
    by mediums and diviners, 87
    Muslim, 4609
    prophets and, 7443
    protection rituals in, 3820
    religious background of, 3816–3817
    in San religion, 5136–5137
    social context of, 3819
    surgery in, 3819–3820
    in West African religions, 9720
    witchcraft and sorcery in, 3820, 9777
    by women, 3401
  in African diaspora, **3821–3824**
    ashe energy, raising, 3823

diagnosis and theory of parallel causalities, 3822–3823
leaves (herbs) used in, 3822
poisons in, 3823
wanga dolls in, 3823
in Andean religion
modern, 8619
pre-Inca, 8603–8604
in Apache religion, 405–406
in Assyrian religion, spells of, 8676
in Australian Indigenous religion, **3870–3875**
bush medicines in, 3874
healers in, 3873–3874
sorcery and, 3871–3873
women in, 3874
in Baltic religions, Māra in, 5692–5693
Buddha of (*See* Bhaiṣajyaguru)
in Buddhism, 9837
in Vinaya literature, 1260
in Byzantine Empire, 3845
in Caribbean religions, 1430
catharsis and, 1459
by Cayce (Edgar), 559, 1474
in China, **3859–3864**
alchemy in, 239
fangshi and, 2990
folk healers, 1617
personal and social contexts of, 3861–3862
Tao Hongjing and, 8997
types of healers, 3862–3864
yinyang wuxing philosophy and, 3859–3861
in Christianity, **3843–3848**
in early church, 3843–3844
faith healing in, 3847
giving thanks for, vol. 7 color insert
Lourdes pilgrimage site and, 8378
at Saint Joseph's Oratory, 5196
themes in, 3847–3848
in Christian Science, 1714, 1745–1746, 1747, 2695–2696
Hopkins (Emma Curtis) on, 4128
Daddy Grace and, 2125
dance and, 2140
in Daoism, 2180
Celestial Masters, 2204
Daofa huiyuan, 2206
Tianhsin/Tianxin Zhengfa, 2198, 2206
deities and spirits of, 3622–3623
Asklepios as, 550–552, 3840
in Celtic religion, 1484
Eshmun, 2840–2842
examples of, 3622–3623
functions of, 3622–3623
in Haitian Vodou, 1433, 1434
in Hawaiian religion, 3797–3798
diagnosis, 3809–3811
in African diaspora religions, 3822–3823
in African religions, 3809–3810
drums in, 7036
in Eastern Orthodoxy, 3844–3845
in Egyptian religion, 2713
spells for, 2722
texts of, 2725
embryonic stem cell research in, 941–942
ethics of (*See* Medical ethics)
excommunication used as, 2921
flowers and, 3137
Galen in, 3255–3256
genetics in, 3428–3429
in goddess worship, 3589–3590
in Greece and Rome, **3839–3842**
Apollo's role in, 425
Hippocratic, 4021–4022
hair used in, 3740
hands and, 3770
in Hawaiian religion, *kahuna* and, 3799
healers, 3813–3814
in Hellenistic religions, magicians and, 3904
Hermetism and, 3949
in Hinduism
Āyurveda system of (*See* Āyurveda)
in devotional life, 9825–9826
images and, vol. 9 color insert
in Āyurveda (*See* Āyurveda)
in India, 713–715
in Inuit religion, 4528
in Islamic texts and traditions, **3831–3833**
customary medicine, 3832–3833
Greco-Islamic medicine, 3832
modern medicine, 3833
in popular traditions, 3833, 3834–3836
prophetic medicine, 3833, 3834
Qur'ān and, 7572
in Israelite religion, 5425
priests in, 7400
jade for, 4759–4760
in Japan, **3867–3870**
evangelical Shintō-style movements in, 8369
health, notions of, 3867–3868
kampō system, 3868, 3869
Konkōkyō, 5225
pluralistic system of, 3868
temples and shrines, role of, 3868–3870
in Judaism, **3828–3831**
divine healing in, 3828
folk healing, 3829
health wisdom in, 3828
professional medicine and, 3829–3830
religion and health in, 3830
religious law and, 3829
sickness and spirituality, contemporary developments on, 3830–3831
visiting the sick in, 3828–3829
in Lao religion, 5313
Lourdes pilgrimage as rite of passage, 1470
lying on soil in, 2559
magical, instructions for, 5578
by Mani, 5647–5648
Mesmer on magnetism and, 1947
in Mesoamerican religions
Aztec religion, medical specialties in, 3813
in Cuna religion (Panama), 2095
in Huichol religion, 4153
spell for intestinal maladies, 8677
microcosm-macrocosm in, 4159
in Micronesian religions, 6005
Middle Eastern cultures, popular healing practices in, **3834–3839**
amulets and evil eye in, 3837
cupping and cautery in, 3836–3837
history of prophetic (Islamic) medicine, 3834
Islam and, 3835–3836
saint veneration and healing pilgrimages in, 3834–3835
spirit possession and the *zār* cult in, 3837–3838
women, pilgrimage, and healing in, 3835
in millenarianism, 6031
miracles in
in Christianity, 6053–6054, 6056
in Egyptian religion, 6051–6052
in indigenous religions, 6049–6050
in Mediterranean religions, 6051
by missionaries, in Oceania, 6792–6793
modern biomedical
Australian Indigenous religions and, 3872, 3873–3874
Āyurveda and, 3856–3857
Chinese medicine and, 3863–3864
Christian views of, 3836, 3848
genetic engineering in, 8187–8188
Hippocrates, role of, 3830, 3839–3840
Islam and, 3833
Japanese medicine and, 3868
Judaism and, 3830
orthodoxy of, 3848–3849
physicians, status of, 3814
"playing God" problem in, 8186–8187
religion, inclusion *vs.* exclusion of, 3876–3877
Schweitzer (Albert) and, 8178–8179
in Near East, ancient, **3824–3827**
Egyptian, 3826–3827
Hittite, 3825
Mesopotamian, 3824–3825
in Negrito religions, 6455
in Neopaganism, 6473
in seidr ritual, 8295
New Age alternative medicine, **3848–3852**
energy healing systems in, 3850–3851
holistic health and human potential movements in, 3851–3852
metaphysics of health and healing in, 3849–3850
spiritual energy and, 3852
in new religious movements, in Japan, 6573
in New Thought movement, 6584
in North American Indian religions, 7300
gender and, 3408
medicine men and, 6652
in poetry, 7226
shamanism and, 8288
in Oceanic religions, gender and, 3397–3398
origins of cure, myths of, 3811
overview, **3808–3816**
pain as, 6946
Paracelsus on, 6980
pearl in, 7024
in Pentecostalism, 7030

Healing and medicine
continued
in Phoenician religion, 7130
at pilgrimage centers, 7146, 7151, 7154
plants for, 9575
in Protestantism, 3846–3847
relics and
in Christianity, 7690
in Greek religion, 7687
rites of passage for healers, 1470
in Roman Catholicism, 3845–3846, 3847
in sacred space, 7981
sacred *vs.* profane and, 7973
saints and
contagious magic and, 3811–3812
illnesses connected to specific saints, 3812
in medieval Catholicism, 3845
ziyārāt pilgrimage and, 3834–3835
saliva in, 8722
in Selk'nam religion, 8225
in Seventh-day Adventism, 9724
water cures, 8236
in shamanism, 2619, 8273, 8276
in Mongol religions, 6143
in neoshamanism, 8295
North American, 8288
therapeutic mechanisms, 8278–8279
shrines and, 8378
social body and community in, 3810, 3814–3815
in Africa, 3819
in Australian Indigenous religions, 3872–3873
in China, 3861–3862
in Japan, 3867–3868
sorcery for, 9769
soteriology and, 8527
in South American religions, gender and, 3417–3418
in South Asian religions, magic in, 5588
spirit possession and, 2140
in Sri Lankan religions, spirit possession and, 2140
Ṣūfī saints and, 1547
surgery, in Africa, 3819–3820
techniques, 3811–3813
popular practices in Middle East, 3836–3837
television ministries and, Roberts's (Oral), 7712
in Tibet, **3864–3867**
a mchi medical tradition in, 3865–3866
astrology and, 3865
doctors, traditional, 3864
life-force, soul, and well-being in, 3865
modernity, effects of, 3866
spirit causation of illness in, 3864–3865
Tantric Buddhist medicine and divination in, 3866
with touch, 9255–9256
trees in, 9334
in Tswana religion, 9389
in Unarian philosophy, 9449
vimbusa healing dance, 2140
through violence, 9599
in Vodou, 9638
deities and spirits of, 1433, 1434
in Warao religion, 9688
water and, 7862
water associated with, 9702
Western, in Korea, 5234
in Yakkut religion, 9866
Zalmoxean, 3466
in Zulu religion, 10009
Healing of the Greek Passion (Theodoret), 9123
Health. *See also* Disease and illness; Healing and medicine; Rejuvenation
in African religions, 3817
cakras and, 1348–1349
in Chinese religion, *yinyang wuxing* philosophy and, 3859–3861
holistic, 3851–3852
in Āyurveda, 3854–3855
in Islam, 3831
in Japanese religion, 3867–3868
in Judaism, 3828
in Orphism, 6894
religious experience and, 6493
religiousness, relationship with, **3875–3877**
critics, concerns of, 3876–3877
historical connection, 3875
mental health and, 3875–3876
physical health and, 3876
and spirituality *vs.* religion, 3875
in Tibetan religion, 3865
in Tiv religion, 9210, 9211
Health care, of children, in new religious movements, 5377
Healthy, Happy, Holy Organization (3HO), **3877–3880**
controversies and issues in, 3879
gender roles in, 3879
practices and rituals of, 3879
recent history of, 3879–3880
worldview and beliefs of, 3878–3879
Heap, Jane, 3711
Hear O Israel. *See* Shema'
Hearst, Patty, 1034
Heart(s), **3881–3884**
in Aztec human sacrifice, 4185, 4190
discipline of the, 8705–8706
Scheler (Max) on, 8147
voices of, Grundtvig's (Nikolai Frederik Severin) theology of, 3704–3705
Hearth
altar as, 275–276
cult of, in Neolithic religions, 6463, 6464
deities of
in Chinese and Japanese religion, 4106–4107
Hestia as, 3964
lares of, 5321
sacred hearth fires, 4106–4107
in southern African religions, 8657
Vesta as goddess of, 9585
Heartland of Cities (Adams), 454
Heart of Matter, The (Teilhard de Chardin), 9034
Heart of the Sky (creator being), 5797
Hearts, Patty, 6522
Heart-souls, in Caribbean religions, 1428
Heat. *See also* Thermodynamics
Agni as god of fire and, 178, 179
Heaven(s), **3884–3889**. *See also* Afterlife; Cosmology; Hell; Paradise; Sky
as "above," 3884
in African myths, 92, 95, 96–97
in Arctic religions, 469, 472
in Baltic religion, 757–760
in Buddhism, 3886–3888
in *cakravāla* cosmology, 2027
in cargo cults, 1418
center of, 6886
in Chinese religion (*See* Shangdi; *Tian*)
in Christianity, 3884–3885
Catholicism, 157–158, 7885–7886
medieval, 157
in Confucianism, Xunzi on, 9862
in Confucian triad, 2631, 2633
in Cuna religion (Panama), 2096
and earth
marriage between, 7602
mountains linking, 6213
earth connected to, in temples, 7980
as garden, 3277
geography of, 138
in Han imperial religion, 2179–2180
in Hinduism, 3885–3886
intermediate state before, 134
in Islam (*See* Paradise, in Islam)
Itō Jinsai's definition of, 4752
in Jain cosmology, 2022–2025
in Japanese religion, 3888
Ame as, 3888
in Judaism, 3884
in Korean religion, 5229
Milky Way as ladder to, 8871
multiple
in Buddhism, 3887
in Jain cosmology, 2024–2025
in Judaism, 3884
soteriology and, 8529–8530
in otherworld, 6923, 6924
rewards in, structure of universe and, 134
sacred space and, 7983
separation of Earth and, 6983
shamanic ascents to, 8272
in shamanism, Korean, 5229
soteriology and, 8529–8530
spatial conceptions of, 134
supreme beings as resident in, 8870
in Toraja religion, 9241
in Zoroastrianism, 9996
Heaven and Hell (Swedenborg), influence of, 8901
Heavenly book, concept of, and scripture, development of, 8195
Heavenly Masters. *See* Celestial Masters/Heavenly Masters
Heaven of the Thirty-three Gods shrine, ordering of sacred space and, 7982
Heaven's Gate, **3889–3892,** 6555, 6561, 9435
aftermath of, 3891
development of, 3890–3891
as fragile movement, 6517
group suicide by, 6545, 6555–6556, 6561
origins of, 3889–3890
suicides in, 3891
traditions blended in, 6551
and violence, conditions leading to, 6553
Heavy metal music, Satanism scare and, 8127, 8128
Hebat (Hepat) (deity), 3595, 9087
in Hurrian religion, 4230
Hebet (ritual book), 2723
Hebräische Melodien (Heine), 4875
Hebraist movements, in Africa, 102
Hebrew (Jewish person), 4856
Hebrew bible. *See* Hebrew scriptures
Hebrew language. *See also specific terms*
accents in, 1533
alphabet of
meditation based on, 5817
mystical speculation on, 271–272, *273,* 544, 8221
in Andalusia, 4593
biblical literature in, 885–887, 890–893 (*See also* Hebrew scriptures)
Apocrypha, 900
"canon," relation to, 1406

Conservative Judaism and, 1957, 1959
ethical works in, 4912–4913
healing power in, 3829
Karaite literature translated into, 5085
names for demiurge in, 2274
Pañcatantra translated into, 6960
pronunciation and cheironomic signs, 1533
Reform Judaism and, Holdheim (Samuel) on, 4080
sacred *vs.* profane in, 7967–7968
scripture, terms for, in, 8196, 8197
Hebrew literature
by Agnon (Shemu'el Yosef), 179–180
apocalyptic (*See* Apocalypse, Jewish)
diversity of authorship in, 4874
Enoch in, 2803
poetry, 7207
Hebrew people. *See* Jewish people
Hebrew religion. *See* Judaism
Hebrews, 916
allegorical exegesis of, 873
anchor in, 332
audience of, 916
author of, 916
baptism in, 782
canon of, 920, 921
date of, 916
faith in, 2425
Moses in, 6204
pain in, 6946
structure of, 916
Hebrew school
Conservative Judaism and, 1962
Ibn Ḥazm on, 7238
Hebrew scriptures (Old Testament), **896–905**. *See also* Septuagint; *specific books*
accents in, 1533
amulets and talismans in, 299
angels in, 345, 346
anthropomorphism in, 389, 390
anti-Semitism in, 398
apocalypse in, 414
apocrypha to (*See* Apocrypha)
architecture in, 461–462
Astarte in, 561, 562–563, 7103
Athirat (Asherah) in, 590–591
atonement in, 594
attributes of God in, Jewish understanding of, 613, 614
authority of (*See* Biblical literature, authority of)
authorship of, Hoffmann (David) on, 4077
Baal in, 724
Baal Zebub in, 7103
baptism in, 781
Bauer (Bruno) on, 804
Bertholet (Alfred) on, 843
on birth, 953
blasphemy in, 968–970, 971–972
blessing in, 982
body and soul dualism in, 4158
books of, 878–879 (*See also* Pentateuch; Torah; *specific books*)
number of, 881–882
on breath and breathing, 1042
calligraphy and, 1372
Canaanites in, 1380
Canaanite text parallels, 1391, 1392, 1396–1397, 1399–1400
canonization, 1406–1407, 1408, 1409–1410
canonizing process, 882–883
canon of, 878–882, 7426
Alexandrian, 880
Christian, 880–881, 891, 896
of Dead Sea Scrolls, 880, 2233–2234
Ecclesiastes of, 2599–2600
ending biblical prophecy period, 7438
law in, 5355
meaning and origin of word, 878
Samaritan, 879–880
of Torah, 9232–9234
tripartite, 879, 881
cantillation of, 1532–1534
Cathari view of, 1456
chaos in, 1537
charismatic leadership in, 1545
charity in, 1553
Christian censorship of, 968
Christian identity and, 871–872
Christian Identity movement and, 1658–1659
Christian interpretation of, 873, 874–875
oral Torah and, 6840
in Christianity, 4858–4859, 7230
in Protestantism, 7449, 7450–7451
Christian polemics on, 7231–7233
christological references (*Glaphura*) in, Cyril of Alexandria on, 2117
circles in, 1793
circumambulation in, 1796
citations from
in Jewish literature, 885
in *Matthew,* 907
clay tablets in, 1842
codices of, 890, 891
compilation and redaction of, 883–884
conscience in, 1939–1940
covenant and contract in, 2047–2048
curses in, 2102–2104
creeds, declarations as, 2054
Dagon in, 7102, 7103
death in, 7822
as returning to dust, 4158
demons in, 2277, 2284, 2314, 3158
desert in, 2300–2301
desire in, 2307
diamond in, 2345
divination in, 3158
divine justice in, 129
divine kingship in, 5147
as divine law, 4859
Documentary Hypothesis regarding, 869, 883, 9233–9234
drama in, sacred, 2442–2443
dreams in, 2489
Enoch in, 2802–2803
eschatology of, 2834
evil in, 8123–8124
exegesis of (*See* Biblical exegesis)
eye in, 2942
faith in, 2425
fate in, 3003
female deities in, 3541
fire in, 3119
firmament in, 8426
the Flood in, Mesopotamian version compared to, 1876
folk beliefs and rites in, reference to, 3157
funeral rites in, 7822
gender in, 3351, 3358
ghosts in, 3475
gift giving in, 3484
glossolalia in, 3504
God in, **3537–3543**
attributes of, Jewish understanding of, 613, 614
Christian understanding of, 3553
descriptions of body of, 6741
imagery of, 3542–3543
monotheistic worship of, 3539–3541
names of, 3537–3539, 6406–6407
origins of worship of, 3539
perfection of, 7039
Golden Rule in, 3632
gold in, 3626
gospel in, 3640
Greek translation of (*See* Septuagint)
Gunkel (Hermann) on, 7707
hair symbolism in, 3740
healing in, 3828, 3829
healing touch in, 9255
heart in, 3882
heaven and hell in, 3884
henotheism in, 7318
Herder (Johann Gottfried), hermeneutics of, 3919
Hermetism, influences on, 3940
hierodouleia (sacred prostitution) in, 3966–3967, 3968
hieros gamos (sacred marriage) opposed in, 3976
historical complexity of text of, 885–886
historical study of, 9714
historiography in, 4027–4028
Christian view of, 4054
in Muslim tradition, 4029
history, conception of, in, 4057–4058
ḥokhmah in, 4077–4079
Holocaust responses and, 4088–4090
"holy" in, 7967–7968 (*See also* Qadosh)
homosexuality in, 4113
honey in, 847
Horites in, 4229
hospitality in, 4139
humor and ridicule in, 4196, 4200
on idolatry, 4357, 4358–4359, 4385
immoral world of, Delitzsch (Friedrich) on, 2263–2264
in Islam, 7230
Muslim polemics on, 7237–7240
Jerome influenced by, 4833
Jesus in, prediction of, 873
in Karaism, 4991
Karaites on, 5082, 5083
Kemosh in, 6094
law of talion in, 7782
Levites in, 5420–5423
libations in, 5434
life in, 5445
light and darkness symbolism in, 5453
lion symbolism in, 5464
literalness of, Maimonides on, 4893
literary genres in, 6375
love in, 8706
magic in, 5575
in Maori religion, 5683
Marcion rejecting, 5701
marriage in, 5725
martyrdom in, 7056
Mary in, 5751
Masoretic text of, 885, 886–887
menstruation in, 5866
messianism in, 5972, 5974
Micah in, 5420
milk in, 847
miqveh in, 6046
Moabite religion in, 6093, 6094

Hebrew scriptures (Old Testament) ***continued***
monotheism in, historical problem of, 3539–3541
monsters in, 2431
Moses in, 6199–6202
mountain symbolism in, 1501
mourning in, 7822
music in, 6276, 6307
mystery religions and, 6332
myth and history in, 6375–6379
Myth and Ritual school on, 6380, 6381
names for, 1406–1407
names taken from, 6409
narrative forms in, 6375
Nathan in, 6417
and Near East, ancient, 884–885
number symbolism in, 6748
oaths in, 9642–9643
pain in, 6944
paradise in, 6981–6982
peace in, 7021
"people of God" in, 1777
Philistine religion in, 7102, 7103, 7104–7105
pilgrimage in, 7152
pillars in, 8744
poetry of, 7204, 7218
Herder (Johann Gottfried) on, 3919
possession by figures of, in Revival Zion (Jamaica), 1437
power in, 7346–7347
priesthood in, 7399
prophetic experience in, 7430, 7431, 7432, 7433
proverbs and parables in, 6978
pseudepigrapha to (*See* Pseudepigrapha)
purity in, 7511–7513
Rashi's commentaries on, 7619–7620
Rastafarian interpretation of, 1438
rejuvenation in, 7684
resurrection in, 7764, 8557
revelation in, 7776–7777
riddles in, 6987
sacrifice/offering in, 926, 927, 8006
critique of, 8004–8005
salt in, 8059
Samaritans and, 8068, 8069
Satan in, 2314, 8123–8124
Saul in, 8131
scapegoat in, 8144
Schopenhauer (Arthur) on, 4447
as scripture, 8196
scripture, terms for, in, 8196
scrolls of, 879, 890
serpents in, 8456
Shabbat in, 8256
shaping of, 4972
shekhinah in, 8313
She'ol (grave) in, 3725, 8557
sin in
confession and, 1888
guilt and, 8403–8404
soul in, 8556–8557
stones in, 8744
suffering in, 8805, 8806
suicide in, 8829
Temples in, 924–926, 928–931
Ten Commandments in, 9074
theodicy in, 9115–9116
time in
conception of, 6378–6379
linear *vs.* cyclical, 4058
tradition in, 9276
translations of (*See* Biblical literature, translations of)
tranvestism, interdiction against, 3968
tsaddiq in, 9377–9378
"two books" metaphor originating from, 9421
violent images of divinity in, 6647
vows in, 9640–9641
wisdom in, 884–885, 5502, **9754–9762**
in *Wissenschaft des Judentums,* 4877
women in, 3351
in worship, 9807
"Zion" in, 9977
Hebrew Union College
Kohler (Kaufmann) as president of, 7671
ordination of women and, 1963–1964
Wise's (Isaac Mayer) founding of, 7582, 7670
Hebrew Union College-Jewish Institute of Religion (HUC-JIR), 7665
Zionism and, 7672
Hebrew University of Jerusalem
Fackenheim at, 2949
in Jewish studies, 4882
Hebron, Sarah's burial site in, 15
Hecataeus
on Celts, 1478
on Massagetae religion, 7387
Hecataeus of Abdera, on gods, categories of, 4036
Hecataeus of Miletus, in transition from myth to history, 6373–6374
Hecate (deity). *See* Hekate
Heckewelder, John, 6458
Hector (mythic figure), 4321
Heda, Willem Claesz, vol. 1 color insert
Heddawa cult of cats, 1463
Hedgehogs, **3892,** 4508
in prehistoric religions, 7377
Hedgewar, K. B., 5699
Hedonism
Kang Yuwei on, 5075
in *Satanic Bible* (LaVey), 8127
of Yang Zhu's followers, 1571–1572
Heelas (Self Religion), 6498
Heesterman, J. C., on human sacrifice, 4184
Hefta monastery, heart symbolism at, 3883
Hegel, G. W. F., **3892–3895**
aesthetics of, 47
African religions dismissed by, 113
on anthropomorphism, 389
Bauer (Bruno) and, 804
Baur (F. C.) and, 805
Chantepie de la Saussaye on, 1531
characteristics of, 3893
on China and Confucianism, 1631
classification of religions by, 1819
on colonialism, 1854
on comparative method, 4458
on conscience, 1943, 1944–1945
dialectic method of, 3893, 5777
Eastern philosophy influencing, 7112
Eckhart (Johannes) and, 2603
evolutionism influenced by, 2913
Fackenheim (Emil) study of, 2949
on fetishism, 3045
Feuerbach's criticism of, 3047
on freedom and necessity, 3200
Frye (Northrop) study of, 3224
Gimbutas (Marija) and, 3493
Gnosticism and, 3526–3527
on God, 3557, 7422
Hegelianism and, 3895
on heroes, 3956
history, philosophy of, 4031–4032
on Indian religions, 4447
on Jewish art, 4342
in Jewish thought
modern, 4901–4902
about Torah, 9237, 9238
Kierkegaard's criticism of, 5141, 5142
on knowledge, 5206, 5207
language use by, 3893
life of, 3892–3893
Marx (Karl) studying, 5744–5745
on materialism, 5777
metaphysics of, 5991
monistic philosophy of, 6146, 6148–6149
on myth, 6366
on nature, 4355–4356
philosophy of, 5777, 6431
on nature religions, 2662
Neoplatonism and, 6475
ontology of, 6830
panentheism of, 6963
on phenomenology, 7087
on reflexivity, 7648
on religion, 3893–3895
on religious beliefs and practice, 7126
Schelling (Friedrich) and, 8148
on Spinoza (Baruch), 8685
systematic thinking of, 3893
on theocracy, 9109
on theology, 9129, 9130, 9136
Tillich's (Paul) theological method influenced by, 7120
on tragedy *vs.* comedy, 4219–4220
Hegelianism
Günther (Anton) and, 8176
Hegel and, 3895
Hegemony
counterhegemony and, 2088
culture and, 2088
Heglen (moose), 9395
Hegumen, in cenobitic monasticism, 6939, 6940
Hehaka Sapa. *See* Black Elk
Heiankyo (Japan), 4784
Heian period (Japan)
Buddhism in
impact of ruling family on, 1175
Maitreya in, 5622
Shingon school, 1176–1177, 1243
Tendai school, 1176, 1178, 1242, 9077, 9079
women in, 1179
calligraphy in, 1371
En no Gyōja's influence on, 2802
onmyōdō in, 6828–6829
pilgrimage in, 7165
poetry in, 7216
political power of, 7272
religion in, 4784–4786
Ritsuryō state during, 5073
temples in, 9049
Heiau (religious centers), in Hawaiian religion, 3796–3797
Heidegger, Martin, **3895–3897**
aesthetics of, 50
on Aristotle's metaphysics, 485
on art, 501
Bultmann (Rudolf) and, 1322
on conscience, 1944
and deconstruction, 2246
on Dilthey (Wilhelm), 3934
early thought of, 3896
Eckhart (Johannes) and, 2603–2604
epistemology and, 2819
in existentialism, 2925–2927
on "fall," 8402
Gnosticism and, 3527
hermeneutics and, 3930, 3933–3934
human being defined by, 7111
on humanity, 4417–4418
Jonas (Hans) and, 4948
on language, 7112
later thought of, 3896
metaphysics of, 5991

Müller's henotheism and, 3913
and Nazism, 6637
ontology of, 6831
on phenomenology of religion, 7099
on ritual, 7842
Rosenzweig (Franz) and, 7927
on soteriology, 8527
on Suzuki (D. T.), 8887
theology, impact on, 3896–3897
tradition rejected by, 9273–9274
on truth, 7206
Wittgenstein (Ludwig), affinities with, 3935
Heidel, Alexander, on *Epic of Gilgamesh,* 3488
Heidenheim, Olf, annotated liturgy printed by, 8387
Height, masculine sacrality in, 5759–5760
Heike monogatari (Japanese epic), 4804, 7216
Heikhal (great hall), 924, 931
Heikhalot mysticism. *See also* Merkavah mysticism
in Ashkenazic Hasidism, 10050–10051
meditation in, 5817
Heikhalot Rabbati, 10051, 10052
Heikhalot Zutarti, 10050
Heikyoku (music), 6302
Ḥeil (wall), 925
Heilbringer. See also Culture heroes
introduction of term, 2090
Heiler, Friedrich, **3897–3898**
and dialogue of religions, 2343
on monolatry and henotheism, 3913
phenomenology of, 4043
on phenomenology of religion, 7091–7092
on prayer, 7368
Schimmel (Annemarie) and, 8149, 8150
Heilige, Das (Otto). *See Idea of the Holy (Das Heilige)* (Otto)
Heilige im Germanischen, Das (Baetke), 7373
Heilman, Samuel C., on joking, 4203–4204
Heilsgut (fruit of salvation), 4729
Heim, Karl, 3559
Heim, Mark, on Smith (Wilfred Cantwell), 8451
Heimdallr (deity), **3898–3899**
Loki and, 5509
Rígr and, 2693
role in Germanic pantheon, 3452
Heimskringla (Norse saga), 842
parts of, 8460
Heine, Heinrich, 4875
Heine, Steven, 1292
Heine-Geldern, Robert, 5261, 5826
on prehistoric Southeast Asian religions, 8642
Heinemann, Joseph, 6017, 6020
Heinlein, Robert, 6471
Heisenberg, Werner, 6057, 7138
Heisenberg's uncertainty principle, 1542, 1543
Heisha (celestial general), protection from, 2185
Hejaz region (Arabia), pre-Islamic history of, 443, 444–445
Hekabe (mythic figure), 4381
Hekataios, on Greek religion, 3660
Hekate (deity), 3020, **3899–3900**
associated with dogs, 2392
castrated priests, 1451
crossroads as domain of, 2071
and gender roles, 3383
spell addressed to, 8676–8677
three heads of, 3804
Hekate lodge, Viennese, sexual magic and, 8252
Hekay (magician), 2722
Hel (deity), 3016, 5508
Hel (Germanic world of dead), 167
in apocalypse, 3456
Baldr in, 3456
in cosmology, 3448
Helena of Constantinople (saint), 4836
Helene (queen of Adiabene), 929
Helfagell (Holy Mountain), in sagas, 8025
Helfgott, Benjamin, 2745
Heliades (deity), Parmenides on, 6995, 6996
Helimski, E. A., 3113
He Lin, New Confucianism and, 1924
Heliocentric hypothesis (Copernicus)
overview of, 1976–1978
Roman Catholic Church against, 7136
science and religion and, 8182–8183
Heliodoros, 9502
Heliodorus of Emesa, *Aithiopika,* 3052, 3054, 3055
Heliopolis (Egypt)
Atum in, 623
cult of Re in, 7634
in magical Papyrus Oslo, 3909
sun worship and, 8837
utopianism and, 3906
Heliopolitan ennead (family of gods in Egypt), 2704, 2718
Hathor as personification of, 3795
Helios (deity)
Aion compared to, 208
cattle of, 1466
cult of, on Rhodes, 8839
as sun god, 8839
Hell, **3884–3889**. *See also* Cosmology; Gehenna; Underworld
in Buddhism, 3886–3888, 3887
Genshin on, 2029
in *cakravāla* cosmology, 2027
in Chinese tradition, 3888
in folk religions, 5352
in Christianity, 3884–3885, 9454–9455
Catholicism, 157–158, 3885, 7886
Dante on, 8426
development of concept, 8564
Eastern Orthodox, 3885
existence of, 9455
Jesus's descent into, 4843
medieval, 157
in *Commedia* (Dante Alighieri), 2170
devouring mouth image and, 4165–4166
geography of, 138
Hesiod on, 8426
in Hinduism, 3885–3886, 9456
intermediate state before, 134
in Islam, 3885
in Ḥanafī creed, 2064
in Sufism, 2839
in Jainism, 2022–2025
in *loka* cosmology, 2022–2023, 2024
in Japanese religion, 3888
Yomi as, 3888
in Judaism, 3884, 6984
meaning of term, 3884
monsters associated with, 6164
punishment in, structure of universe and, 134
in Samoyed religion, 8095
soteriology and, 8530
spatial conceptions of, 134
in Zoroastrianism, 9996
Helladius, 1447
Hellanicus (historian), 9170
Hellenism, 3599–3601
ancient Iran and, 10002
and Christianity, 6474
culture of, 3599–3600
definition of, 3599–3600
fundamental tendencies of, 3600–3601
Israelite wisdom influenced by, 9750, 9757, 9759
in Jerusalem, 4835
temples in, 9063, 9064
transformation brought by, 4973
Hellenistic Judaism. *See also* Philo Judaeus
afterlife in, 152
body and soul in, 8557
Enoch in, 2803
eremitism in, 2823
God in, knowability of, 182
Goodenough (Erwin R.) on, 4044
history, view of, 4058
hypostasis in, 4240–4241
iconography of, 4340, 4352
Logos in, 5302, 5502, 5503
Moses in, 6202–6203
as origin of Christianity, 7707
pneuma (breath) in, 8542
Sadducees, role of, 8018
Stoicism and, 8742–8743
virginity in, 9605
wisdom in, Torah as, 9763
Hellenistic religions, **3900–3913**. *See also* Christianity, hellenization of; Greek religion
afterlife in, 8543–8544
agnōstos theos in, 181–182
aion in, 208
alchemy in, **244–248**
Alexander the Great and Hellenism, 3900–3902
ascension in, 521–522
astrology in, 563
deification in, 2249
deities of
knowledge of, 181–182
theocrasies (combinations of), 8931
Étaples on, 4176
gender in, **3375–3381**
goddess worship in, **3599–3607**
Hermetism, influence on, 3940
historiography in, 4027, 4036
homosexuality, age-structured, in, 4112–4113
iconography of, 4322–4323
kingship in, 5165–5167
magi, Hellenized, Cumont on, 2094
magic in, 3903–3905, 5572–5573
Meter in, cult of, 2109–2110
miracles in, 3903–3905, 6050–6051
mustērion as sacrament in, 7954–7955
mystery cults in, healing and, 3840
oracles and divination in, 3905–3906
Osiris in, 6921–6922
philosophy and
Epicureanism and, 3910–3911
Stoicism and, 3901, 3906–3907, 3910, 3911–3912 (*See also* Stoicism)
rejection of religion in, 3909–3910
ruler, cult of, 3902–3903, 4036
soul in, 8542, 8543–8544
syncretism in, 3907–3909, 8928–8929

Hellenistic religions ***continued***
theurgy in, 9156–9157
universalism, cosmopolitan, 3906–3907
women in, **3375–3381**
"Hellenistic Synagogal Prayers," 904
Helm, June, 576
Helm, Karl, 3459
Helmholtz, Hermann von, 6485
Helmold (German historian), on Perun, 7062
Helms, Mary, 9292, 9293
Héloïse, 7
Helvetic Confession, Second (1566), on free will and predestination, 3208
Helvétius, Claude-Adrien, in French Enlightenment, 2796
Helvidius, 4833
Helwys, Thomas, 783
Hemacandra, in Gujarait Jainism, 4766
Hē mathēmatikē syntaxis (Ptolemy). *See Almagest* (Ptolemy)
Hemenway, Robert, 3142
Hemerologies, Egyptian, 2724
Hemingway, Ernest, 5481
Hemming, Steven, 2481
Hem-netjer (servant of the god), 2714
Hemodialysis, 5810
Hemu-ka (servant of the *ka*), 2714
Henads (Unities), Proclus on, 7191–7192
Henderson, John B., on Confucian classics *vs.* commentaries, 1905
Hengist (deity), 9420
Henjō nanshi doctrine, 3346
Henki (soul), 802
Henkin, Louis, 5363
Henna, in Islam
in circumcision ceremony, 7826
in marriage ceremony, 7827
in naming ceremony, 7825–7826
Henning, Salomon, 767
Henninger, Joseph, 1014
on Supreme Beings, 8170
Henotheism, **3913–3914**
definition of, 6158
in Eblaite religion, 2597
etymology of term, 7318
in Hebrew Bible, 7318
Hermes and solar henotheism, 3937
in Israelite religion, 4743
vs. monotheism, 6158
in Vedism, 9555
Henoticon (Chalcedonian formulations), schism and, 8155
Henri, Claude, 3230
Henrici, Peter, on Hobbes (Thomas), 4075
Henrici chronicon Livonia, 767
Henry (abbot of Clairvaux), 1458
Henry I (king of England)
Anselm and, 372
Jews under, 5013
Henry, Francis, 10028–10029
Henry, Maurice, androgynes of, 339
Henry, Michel, 7099
Henry, Victor, on magic, 5588
Henry II (king of England), Jews under, 5013
Henry II (king of France), in Reformation, 7662
Henry III (Roman emperor), control of papacy by, 696–697
Henry IV (German king and Holy Roman emperor)
excommunication of, 697, 3691, 7280
Gregory VII in conflict with, 697, 1690, 1772, 3690–3691, 6970, 7254
Henry IV (king of France), 851
Henry VI (Holy Roman emperor), 4495
Henry VIII (king of England)
conscience of, 1942
marriage, annulment of, 2051, 7662
Protestants persecuted by, 7061
in Reformation, 7662
reforms of, 2051
title of, 349, 7281
Henry of Suza. *See* Hostiensis
Hens. *See* Chickens and hens
Henschel, Milton G., 4821
Hentze, Carl, 1635
Hepat (deity). *See* Hebat
Hepatina (the middle place), 1469
Hepatoscopy (liver divination), in Etruscan religion, 2873
Hepding, Hugo, 181
Hephaestus (Hephaistos) (deity), 35
Athena and, 586, 587, 6958
Baal identified with, 7129
Deadalus and, 5275
functions of, 3680
Hera and, 3914
Pandora fashioned by, 7419
sun and, 8839
Hephaistos. *See* Hephaestus
Heptaplus (Pico), 7141
Hera (deity), **3914–3916**
Argos cult of, 3915
Astarte identified with, 7130
family of, 2982, 3679
functions of, 3679
and gender roles, 3383
and girls, education of, 3914
Herakles and, 3916
Hermes and, 3937
iconography of, 4321
marriage, as goddess of, 3914–3915
Samos cult of, 3915
southern Italy cult of, 3915
temple of, 9063
as virgin, 9604
worship of, 3601
Zeus and, 3663, 3679
Herabkunft des Feuers und des Göttertranks, Die (Kuhn), 4460
Heracleides Ponticus, and ascension, 520–521
Heracles (Euripides), 5469
Heraclitus (Greek philosopher), 1042
on *aion,* 207
as time, 2855
on catasterism, 8424
on change, 5452, 8420
on charity, 1554
on destiny, 8405
on Dionysos, 2357
on dualism, 2507
fire in worldview of, 3118, 3119
Greek religion criticized by, 3685
on images veneration, 4380, 4382
on *Logos,* 5201, 5501, 5503
paradoxical statements by, 6988
on sibyls, 8382–8383
Heraclius (Byzantine emperor)
Maximos the Confessor and, 5792
Monophysitism under, 6155
Herakles (Heracles, Hercules) (legendary hero), **3916–3918**
apotheosis of, 2298
as cattle raid hero, 1465
Celtic parallels, 1485
cults of, 3917
Etruscan, 2871
as deity in Germanic religion, 3450
as founder of Olympic Games, 3266
as human, not divine, 3957
identifications with local gods, 3917
Melqart identified with, 5846–5849
mythology of, 3916–3917
name of, 3916
Pindar on, 7174
on pyre of Mount Oeta, 3240
sins of, 9685
sun symbolism and, 8836
temples to, 1792
Herbal medicine. *See also* Healing and medicine
in African diaspora religions, 3822
poison and, 3823
in African religions, 3818–3819
in China, 3864
in Christianity, Hildegard of Bingen and, 3980
in Cuna religion (Panama), 2095
in Egyptian religion, specialists in, 3836
in Manus religion (New Guinea), origin myths of, 3811
in Mesopotamian religions, 3824
Qolla-huaya healers (Bolivia), 3811
Herbart, Johann, 6235
Herberg, Will, on civil religion, 1813, 1815
Herberstein, Sigismundus, 3110
Herbert, George, 5471, 7204, 7220
Herbert, Thomas, 6231
Herbert of Cherbury, on natural religion, 8762
Hercules (legendary hero). *See* Herakles
Hercus, Luise, 643–644
Herder, Johann Gottfried, **3918–3920,** 4457
background of, 3918
as Freemason, 3195
Geiger (Abraham) influenced by, 7669
on Hermetism, 3951
historiography of, 4031
Müller (Karl Otfried) and, 6237
on myth, 6366, 6367
nationalism and, 8763
philosophy of, 3918–3919
on popular religion, 7325
on relativism, 7685
on Spinoza (Baruch), 8685
on symbol theory, 8908
theology of, 3919
Herding societies. *See* Pastoral societies
Herdsmen, in winter carols, 9744
Herdt, Gilbert, 2487, 6508
on birth rituals, in Oceanic religions, 7807
Hereditary process in history, Schmidt (Wilhelm) on, 8169
Heredity
Darwinism and, 2908–2909
in eugenics, 2879–2880
in Yoruba religion, 9910
Ḥerem (ban)
of Eli'ezer ben Hyrcanus, 2763–2764
as excommunication, 2921
Ḥerem (dedicated to God), 4738
Herero people (southwest Africa), supreme being (Mulungu) of, 3574
Heresy, **3920–3930**
abandonment of faith (*See* Apostasy)
blasphemy equivalent to, 972–973, 975
in Christianity, **3925–3930** (*See also* Antinomianism; Arianism; Cathari sect; Docetism; Donatism; Ebionites; Gnosticism; Manichaeism; Marcionism; Monophysitism; Montanism; Nestorianism; Pelagianism; Waldensians)
of Apollinaris of Laodicea, 424, 3695
baptism of heretics, validity of, 2113
challenges to concept of, 3928–3929

Constantine's quest for unity, and, 1967, 7060
in Cyrenaica, 1678
Cyril of Alexandria on, 2117
death penalty for, legal system and, 8014
early assessment of, 3926
fornication and debauchery attributed to, 8249
Gnosticism as, 3514, 3515, 3522–3524, **3529–3531,** 3923–3924
Gregory of Nazianzus opposing, 3694–3695
in Hungary, 4225–4226
of Hus (Jan), 4233–4234
Jerome accused of, 4833–4834
medieval heresies, 3927–3928
Novgorod-Moscow (Judaizer) heresy, 8525
piety and, 9662
in Protestantism, 7449, 7450
Reformation and, 3920, 3928
ridicule of, 4200
Roman persecution of, 7060, 9124
stabilization of the church and, 1661
suppression of, 7060–7061 (*See also* Inquisition)
Tertullian against, 9086
tools against, 3926–3927, 3928
treatment and suppression of heretics, 3927
Wyclif (John) charged with, 4233
creeds as defense against, 2054–2055
history of study of, 3920–3921, 3928–3929
in Islam (*See also* Ismāʿīlī Shiism, schisms in)
Khārijīs, 4693
Milal wa Nihal studies on, 8780–8781
al-Shahrastānī on, 8267
Joseph of Volokolamsk on, 4957
in Judaism, 970
Habad messianism as, 3793
meaning and development of term, 3920
meaning of term, 3920, 3929
morphology and development of, 3921–3923
overview of, **3920–3925**
in *Pege gnoseos,* 4940
as philosophical school, 3920
sacrilege and, 8013
schism and, 8151
secularization and, 8216
witchcraft as, 9771–9772
Hergu bugha (underworld), 9394
Herihor (High Priest of Amun), 2709
Herman (monk), 7942
Hermandades (brotherhoods), 9215
Hermann, Elfriede, 5380
Hermanrich of Passau (bishop), Methodius, opposition to appointment of, 2117
Hermansen, Gustav, on Mars, 5728
Hermanubis (deity), as Hermes and Anubis fused, 3938
Hermaphroditism, androgynes and, 341
Hermeneutical (divine-voice) prophecy, 7107
Hermeneutics, **3930–3936,** 5484–5489. *See also* Biblical exegesis; Historiography; Poststructuralism; Structuralism
as analytic and mediating practice, 3934–3935
Antiochene school of, Cyril of Alexandria, opposition of, 2117
biblical, liberation theology and, 5441
Buddhist, **1268–1278**
Abhidharma as, 1270, 1273, 1275
and apologetics, 1277
Buddhadāsa and, 1073
criteria of authenticity, 1273, 1274
fundamental questions of, 1272
principles of, 1273–1275
progressive, 1275–1276
Tantric, 1123, 1275
and Western thought, 1277
Zen, 1276–1277
Christian, 5485, 5486
Alexandrian *vs.* Antioch school of, 5486
contemporary, 5488–5489
in feminist theology, 5486
in Germany, 5486
and Christian exegesis, 876
classical, 5486
Copernican revolution and, 8183
cultural sciences, foundation of, 3932–3933
and deity, 2257
distinguished from exegesis, 865
double hermeneutical approach, Schleiermacher (Friedrich) on, 8163
Geertz (Clifford) on, 8499–8501
of Herder (Johann Gottfried), 3919
Hindu, of Mīmāṃsā school, hermeneutics of, 5345
historiographical methods and, 4041
history of, 3930–3931
in history of religion, 9650
history of religions approach *vs.,* 4061
human existence as hermeneutical, Heidegger (Martin) on, 3896
in Islam
of Qurʾān, 5485
Shīʿī imamate and, 8337
of Jonas (Hans), 4948
in Judaism
halakhah and, 3748
pilpul method of, 5533
in Qabbalah, 7538
of Torah, 5485
of law, 5328–5329
legal, 5356, 5359
literalism, in Churches of Christ, 1780
meaning of, 3930
mystical, of Dionysius the Areopagite, 8908
and naturalism, 6430
in Orientalism, 6883
Plutarchian, 2514–2515
sacred and profane in, 7976–7977
Said (Edward) on worldliness of the text, 8032
Schleiermacher (Friedrich) on, 8163–8164
scripture and, 8202–8203
subaltern studies and, 8802
symbol theory and, 8908, 8913
Tantric, in *Hevajra Tantra,* 3965
texts, inquiry into interpretation of, 3931–3932
in theology, 9131–9132, 9138
theology challenged by, 7245, 7246
understanding, reflection on conditions of, 3933–3934
Vernant (Jean-Pierre) on, 4045
of Weber (Max), 9711
Hermes (deity), **3936–3938**
angels and, 344
in astrology, origins of, 563
cattle stolen by, 1465
crossroads and, 2071
functions of, 3680
as gamblers' god, 1528
in Hades, 165
hermeneutics associated with, 3930, 5484
herms to
as border stones, 8745
as phallic symbols, 2071, 3936, 3937, 7079
Hestia paired with, 3964
images of, vol. 2 color insert
Pan as son of, 7079
as ram, 8310
Thoth identified with, 9168
Hermes, Georg, Kantianism and, 8176
Hermesias (drink), 847
Hermes Trismegistos, **3938–3944**. *See also* Hermetism
on apocatastasis, 421
on gnosis, 3508
and the Grail, 3652–3653
monkeys and, 6151
in Nag Hammadi, 3941
as oracle, 3941
Order of the Golden Dawn influenced by, 7930
teachings of (*See* Hermetism, literature of)
as theocrasy (combinations of gods), 8931
Hermetic Brotherhood of Light, sexual magic and, 8251
Hermetic Brotherhood of Luxor, sexual magic and, 8251
Hermetic Corpus. See Corpus Hermeticum
Hermeticism
and Freemasonry, 3196
light and darkness symbolism in, 5452
Hermetic Order of the Golden Dawn, 6470, 6471
angels in, 348
Crowley (Aleister) and, 2071–2072
Hermetism in, 3952
Rosicrucian influence on, 7930
Hermetism, **3944–3956**. *See also* Hermes Trismegistos
in 17th century, 3949–3950
in 20th century (after occultism), 3951–3953
alchemy and, 244–245, 247, 252
ascension in, 521
astrology in, 563
baptism and, 780
on demons, 2277
dualism in, 2513
in Enlightenment and Romantic period, 3950–3951
esotericism as, 2843
gnosis in, 3508
Gnosticism and, 3519, 3523
God in, 3556, 3942
knowability of, 182
the Grail and, 3652–3653
imagery of, vol. 3 color insert
on intellect, 7190
in late antiquity and Middle Ages, 3944–3945
literature of (Hermetica) (*See also* Nag Hammadi)
Hellenic and Judaic influences on, 3940
overview of, 3938–3942

literature of (Hermetica) ***continued***
in Renaissance, 3946–3948
in Roman Empire, 7921
Tabula Smaragdina, text of, 3948
on Logos, 7190
nature in, 6432
Neo-Alexandrian
definition of, 3944
other esoteric movements and, 3953
occultist movement (1850–1920) and, 3951–3953
origins of religion in, 367
Platonism and, 7190–7191
in Renaissance, 2843, 3945–3948
repentance in, 7756
terminology of, 3944
Hermetis Trismegisti Erkanntunusz der Natur (Aletophilus), *Corpus Hermeticum* and, 3950–3951
Hermias of Alexandria, on Hermes Trismegistos, 3938
Herminones (Germanic tribe), 3447
Hermits. *See also* Eremitism; *Vanaprasthin*
celibacy and, 1477
in Christian monasticism, 6133
dwellings of, 2826
eremitism of, 2822, 2823
female, 6763
and gnostic deification, 2249–2250
in Islam, 2828
Maronite, 2827
Hermits of Saint Augustine, 2827
Hermóðr (son of Óðinn), 744
after death of Baldr, 3456
Hermon, Mount, 6213
Hermopolitan Ogdoad, 2704, 2706–2707
Hermotimos of Clazomenae
ascension by, 520
wandering soul of, 8541
Herms, 8745
as phallic symbols, 2071, 3936, 3937, 7079
Hernández, José Gregorio, 6579
Herod (king of Judaea)
Jerusalem under, 4835
John the Baptist executed by, 4943
Salome's dance for, 2135, 2153
Temple renovations under, 925, 4835
Herod Agrippa (king)
Christian persecution by, 7058
loan to, 7105
Herodotus
on Africans, 111
on Aphrodite's cults, 408
on Arimaspeans, 6165
on Armenians, 491
on Bendis, 819
on Berber religion, 834
on Celts, 1478
on chariot of the sun, 8838
comparative theology of, 9128
dēmiourgos used by, 2272
on Dionysos, 2357, 2358
on geometry, 3439
goal of writings, 6374
on Greek deities, 4321
on Greek heroes, 5468
on Greek literature, 5467
on Herakles, 3917
history of, myth and, 6373–6375
on incense offering, 4419
on Iranian religions, 4535, 4536
on Isis, 3604
on magi, 5559, 5573
on Melqart, 3917, 5846, 5847, 5848
on Mesopotamian temples, 9062
on Allāt, 6389
on origin of writing, 270
on Pan, 6957
on Persian religion, 8838
Plutarch against, 7201
on prayer, 3683–3684
on reincarnation, 7679
on sacrifice, music in, 3682
on Saka religion, 7384, 7387
on Scythian religion, 4489, 8205, 8206
on souls, 8541
on study of religion, 4036
syncretism of, 3908
on Thracian religion, 9168, 9169, 9170
time in works of, 6375
on transmigration of soul, 7186
on Zalmoxis, 3466, 9926–9927
on Zoroastrianism, 9990
Herod's Temple, 4835–4836
Heroes, **3956–3961**. *See also* Culture heroes; *specific figures*
in African myths, 86, 97
in Ainu religion, 207
in Athapaskan sacred stories, 573
birth and childhood of, 1568
in Buddhism, buddhas and *bodhisattvas* as, 1083–1085
Campbell on myths of
on birth of, 1568
as universal narrative formula, 1379–1380
view of Rank (Otto) compared to, 3958–3959
in Canaanite epics, 1391
Carlyle (Thomas) on, 3956–3957
catasterism of (becoming stars), 8733
of cattle raids, 1465
in Celtic literature, 1493–1494, 1499
Chinggis Khan as hero-king, 1645
comedy and, Hegel (G. W. F.) on, 4220
culture (*See* Culture heroes)
descent into the underworld by, 2297–2299
divinity *vs.* humanity of, 3956–3957
in epics, 2813–2815
Freudian interpretation of, 3958
gambling by, 3263–3264
Girard (René) on, 3960
as gods, in northeast Bantu religions, 2575–2576
"Great Man" view of history and, 3956
in Greek religion, 3665–3667, 3681
cults of, 3665–3667, 3681
initiation rituals for, 184
in literature, 5468
local association of, 3667, 3681
origin of, 3681
parentage of, 3902
sacrifices to, 3683
Hegel (G. W. F.) on, 3956, 4220
in Hinduism, rural traditions, 4435–4436
Hook (Sidney) on, 3956
hubris of, in paradigm of evil, 2899
in Jainism, women as, 3327
in Judaism
Samson as, 8099
Samuel as, 8099–8100
tsaddiqim as, in Hasidism, 3791
Jungian interpretation of, 3958–3959
as male, 3958, 3959
martyrs as, 5740
modern, 3957
in Oceanic religions, 6788, 6789
parentage of
in Freudian approach, 3958
in Greek myth, 3902
powers of, 3957
quests of, 7552–7553
Raglan (Lord) on, 3958–3959
Rank (Otto) on, 3958
shamans as, 8274
sleep in tales of, 8440
in southern African religions, 8656
Spencer (Herbert) on, 3956
suicide, heroic, 8828–8829
sun and, 8836
superhuman *vs.* subhuman, 2815
theories on, 3957–3960
trickster-transformer-hero motif, 1988–1989
underworld journeys of, 9451
Väinämöinen as, 9497
in winter carols, 9745
worship of, 3956–3957
Alexander the Great and, 3902–3903
wreaths honoring, 2073
Heroes (spirits), 2277
Hero legends, 6376
Héros civilisateur. See Culture heroes
Hero Twins, 751
in Maya creation myth, 5797
Hero with a Thousand Faces, The (Campbell), 7476
Jungianism in, 3958
overview of, 1378, 1379
Herpyllis, 3053
Herr, Lucien, 2527
Mauss (Marcel) and, 5785
Herrera y Tordesilla, Antonio de, on Caribbean religions, 1430
Herrigel, Eugen, 1189
Herrmann, Wilhelm
Barth (Karl) studying under, 789
Bultmann (Rudolf) and, 1322
on history as foundation of religion, 7117
on knowledge, 5208
Ritschlianism of, 6104
Herrnhut (Germany), 6191
Herrnhutian community, Schleiermacher (Friedrich) and, 8159–8160
Herrnstein, Richard J., 2882
Herschel, William, Milky Way, discovery of, 2031
Herskovits, Frances, 115
Herskovits, Melville J.
on Afro-Brazilian religions, 121
on Afro-Caribbean religions, 10025–10026, 10028
debate with Frazier (E. Franklin), 73, 74
Dunham (Katherine) trained by, 76
focus of studies, 74, 75, 76, 115
on Tempels (Placide), 116
Hertz, Joseph, 869
Hertz, Robert, 682, 1021, 3239, 3240
on death, 2239
on left and right symbolism, 5393, 7837
on sin, 8402
Hertzberg, Arthur, on exile, 2923
Heru. *See* Horus
Herzl, Theodor
Ginzberg (Asher) as nemesis of, 3496
Mohilever (Shemu'el) and, 6113
Reines (Yitsḥaq Ya'aqov) as supporter of, 7681
in Zionism, 4906, 5021, 9979
He Sapa (Black Hills), 5295
Heschel, Abraham Joshua, **3961–3963**
and contemporary Hasidism, 9382, 9383
Depth Theology of, 1960

on God, 3552
in modern Jewish thought, 4908
on nature, 2646
on prayer, 7370
on prophecy, 7442
Heshshi the Hunter, in Hurrian and Hittite myth, 4070
Hesiod, **3963–3964**
on Africans, 111
on altar fire, 3118
and An, 302
on Aphrodite, 407, 408
on Apollo, 424
on Artemis, 506
on chaos, 1537, 1538
on charity, 1553–1554
on classes of divine beings, 3667
on creation
of man, 3454
parthenogenesis in, 2555
successive cosmic rulers in, 3963
deities described by, 4321
on Demeter, 2268
on demons, 2277
on Dionysos, 2357
on disease, 3839
on divinity, 5468
on fate, 3000
on genealogy of deities, 3679, 3963
on gods, 7317
Golden Age myth of, 3626–3628
on harpies, 6165
on Hekate, 3899, 3900
on Helios, 8839
on heroes, 3666
on history, 4035–4036
on Hypnos, 8439
influence on Greek religion, 3660
on moon, 6174
on Muses, 6242
and myth of the Golden Age, 2964, 2965
on Ouranos and Gaia, 1450, 3963
on Persephone, 2269
on primeval mother and father, 3015
on Prometheus, 1014, 7419, 7420
on sacrifice, 3683
on Styx (river), 3016
time in works of, 6375
on tradition, 9267
Xenophanes, criticism from, 4108
on Zeus, 3663
Hess, Moses, 9979
Hesse, Hermann, 949
Brahmanic and Buddhist asceticism in works of, 3061
Gnosticism and, 3527
Hesse, Mary, on hermeneutics and philosophy of science, 3934
Hessel, Dieter, 2610
Hester panim (hiding the face of God) doctrine, as Holocaust paradigm, 4090
Hestia (deity), 3018, **3964–3965**
eternal flame of, 3118
as virgin, 9603–9604
Hēsuchia (serenity of solitude), 2301
Hesychasm, 1046
Christian, in early Eastern Christianity, 2582, 2587, 2826–2827
debated at synod of Constantinople, 2042
Gregory Palamas' defense of, 3698, 3699
of Isaac the Syrian, 4545
Jesus Prayer in, 5818
prayer of the heart as, 3883
Russian
in Optino community, 5187
Velichkovskiy (Paisiy) and, 7943
schism and, 8157
Sergii of Radonezh and, 8230
Sorskii (Nil) on, 8525
spiritual guidance in, 8710
Hesychius of Alexandria, 9170
Hetata, Atef, 3098
Heterodoxy, **6909–6913**. *See also* Orthodoxy
in Axial Age civilizations, 7730
Indian (*See also* Ājīvikas) atheism in, 578–579
Heteronomous discipline, 8700
Heteronomy, of culture, 5482–5483
Hetubindu (Dharmakīrti), 2336
Hetucakraḍamaru (Dignāga), 2351
Hetumukha (Dignāga), 2351
Heung Jin Nim, 9467
Heuristical reason, Schleiermacher (Friedrich) on, 8162
Heusch, Luc de, 1506
on myths, 97
on regicide, 5159
on sacrifice, 7845
Hevajra (deity), **3965–3966,** vol. 11 color insert
Hevajra Tantra (Buddhist text), 1215, 1216, 1224–1225, 5102
cakras and, 1348
Hevajra in, 3965–3966
Lamdre system derived form, 5223
Hevel (emptiness), 4749
Ḥevrah' qaddisha' (holy brotherhood), 4868
Ḥevra kaddisha (burial society), 7823
Hewitt, J. N. B., 2541, 6670, 7348
Hewitt, Marsha, 3304, 3314
Hexaemeron literature, 2606
Hexagrams
in *maṇḍalas,* 5642
in Magen David (Star of David), 5558–5559, 5642
in *Yijing,* 1583–1584, 1906–1907
Hexapla (edition of Old Testament), 892, 893, 894, 6888
Hexateuch, covenant and, 2048
He Xinyin, 1578
He Xiu, 1575
Heyden, Doris, 5943
Hezekiah (king of Judah), 924, 934, 4546, 4828
He Zhiyuan, 2209
Hezmalhalch, Thomas, 7030
Hiatt, Lester R., 687, 3392
Ḥibbat Tsiyyon (Love of Zion), 7681, 9979
Mohilever (Shemu'el) in, 6113
Hibil (Mandaean figure), in *Ginza,* 3495
Hibiscus tree, 9334
Hick, John
comparative theology of, 9130
on knowledge, 5211, 5499
theodicy of, 9117–9118
Hicks, Edward, 5152
Hidalgo, Cristina Pantoja, 3079
Hidāyah, al- (Ibn Bābawayhi), 4262
Hidāyah ila farā'id al-qulūb, al- (Baḥye), 740
Hidden Half, The (Alber and Medicine), 3410
Hidden Wisdom (Stroumsa), 2514
Hidden Words (Bahā' Allāh), 737
Hides, Jack, 146
Hideyoshi, Toyotomi, 4788, 6607, 7273, 9310
Hiei, Mount, 6214
Mahāyāna Buddhism at, 2801
monasteries at, 9075–9076, 9078, 9079
Saichō and, 8029, 8030
Sannō Shintō at, 8361–8362
pilgrimage to, 9835
Tendai Buddhism at, 4784
Hiera Anagraphē (Treatise on Sacred Matters) (Euhemerus), 2883
Hiereiai (priestesses), 2270
Hiereus (priest), 7275
Hieria Council (754), 4290
Hierocracy, 9109
Hierodouleia (sacred prostitution), **3966–3970**
Hierogamy, in creation myths, 2555–2556
Hieroglyphic writing
Egyptian, 4317
consistency of, 2703
development of, 5161
interpretation of, 2729
Mayan, 4312
Monte Albán, 4312
Hierography, definition of, 3537
Hierology, definition of, 3537
Hieronymous, on Buddhism, 1310
Hieronymus, on covenant *(foedus/pactum),* 2047
Hierophany (manifestation of the sacred), **3970–3974**
animals and, 10065
archetypes and, 458
cities founded after, 326
definition of, 7346
elements of, 7346
Eliade's concept of, 2755, 7743, 8879
forms of, 3971–3972
and material world, 10047
meaning of, 3970–3971
sacred space and, 1504
sacred *vs.* profane and, 7976
sky and, 8428–8429, 8879, 10065
space, impact on, 3972
structure and dialectic of the sacred, 3971–3972
symbolism and, 3973–3974
theophany and kratopany as, 3972
time, impact on, 3973
Hieros, as Greek concept, 7966–7967
Hieros gamos (sacred marriage or union), 2445, 2520, 2521, 2982, **3974–3978**
agriculture and, 3975–3976
city states, royal rites in, 3976–3977
in Finno-Ugric religions, 3108
in Frankist Qabbalah, 8250
in Gnosticism, 8247
as invigoration rite, 8210
in Mesopotamian religions, 3377
power and love of the goddess and, 3977
prehistoric, 3974–3975
Hieros logos (sacred poem), 933
Hierosophy, definition of, 3537
Higginbotham, Evelyn Brooks, 75, 10038
Higginbotham, Leon, 77
Higginson, Francis, 2288
Higginson, Thomas Wentworth, 3361
High Caste Hindu Woman, The (Ramabai), 7610
High cultures
history of religions approach and, 4065
Schmidt (Wilhelm) on, 8168
Higher Consciousness Society, 2603
Higher criticism. *See* Biblical literature, higher criticism of
Higher-Life theology. *See also* Holiness movement
Calvinism and, 4084

High gods. *See also* Supreme beings
African, Christianity and, 1721
Caribbean, 1426
Chinese (*See* Shangdi)
in Indo-European religions, sky god as, 8838
and monotheism, origins of, 6156
in New Guinea, 2006, 2007
Schmidt (Wilhelm) on, 8877
Söderblom (Nathan) on, 8878
in South American Indian religions, 8589–8590
supreme beings and, theoretical debate on, 8877–8878
High Magic's Aid (Gardner), 9728
Ḥijābs (head scarfs)
cultural tension and humor over, 4212–4213
feminism and, 9792
Hijāda role, gender reversal in, 4116
Hijiri (Japanese lay ascetics), **3978–3979,** 4795
Hijrah (migration), 4561
of Muḥammad, to Medina, 6223
of Muḥammad Aḥmad, 6228–6229
Hijrah/hijar (protected enclave), *ḥaram/ḥawṭah* and, 3776, 3777–3778
Hijras (multiple-gendered people), 3422
community of
castration in, 3968–3969
transvestism in, 1827, 3968–3969
Ḥikam (Ibn ʿAṭāʾ Allāh), aphorism in, 8823
Ḥikam al-ʿAṭāʾīyah, al- (Ibn ʿAṭāʾ Allāh), 4663
Ḥikmah (wisdom), 2504
Ibn Rushd on, 4271
Ḥikmat al-ishrāq (Suhrawardī), 4276, 4552
commentaries on, 4555
Ḥikmat al-mashriqīyah, al- (Ibn Sīnā), 4553
Hikule'o (deity), 7314
Híkuri. See Peyote
Hilāl (crescent), 4350–4351
Hilary of Arles (bishop), 5410
Hilary of Poitiers (saint)
as dragon slayer, 2432–2433
poetry of, 7218
Hilda (nun), 822, 6763
Hildebrand. *See* Gregory VII
Hildegard of Bingen, 2471, **3979–3980**
contributions of, 3980
hymns of, 7207
life of, 3979–3980
monasteries under, 3359
musical compositions of, 6309
visions of, 3979, 3980
Hildesheimer, Esriel, **3980–3981,** 6899–6900
Hoffmann (David) and, 4076
Hilgenfeld, Adolph, 3532
Hilger, B. J., on Hermetism, 3951
Hill, Geoffrey, 5483
Hill, Napoleon, 6582, 6585
Hill, Robert, 75
Hillah (Iraq), hawzah of, 3801
Hillel (Jewish sage), **3981–3982**
Gamli'el the Elder in family of, 3270
Golden Rule of, 3631, 3981
house of, on afterlife, 153
Passover traditions of, 7004
school of (Beit Hillel), **815–816**
Ḥillī, al- (ʿAllamah, "sage"), **3982**
Hillman, James, 7476, 7485
Hill of the Crosses (Kryžių kalnas), 775
Hill of the Star (Mexico City), astronomy and, 1356–1357
Hills, in Baltic religion, 775
Ḥilluqim (distinctions), 9246
Hiltner, Seward, 7487
Hilton, R., subaltern studies and, 8800
Ḥi ma (protected sanctuaries), 2604, 2652
Himalayan Buddhism, 1126
art of, 1232–1233
drums in, 2497
female incarnations in, 1233
iconography of, 4330
kingship in, 1230, 1232, 7262–7263, 8985
literature of, 1253
missions and, 1099
pilgrimage in, 1234, 7166–7167
schools of, **1230–1235**
spread of, 1230, 1231
studies on, 1311, 1313
stupas in, 1234, 9264
temples of, 9050
Himes, Joshua, on Millerites, 8235
Himiko (Japanese queen), 4780, 4809
Himmelfarb, Martha, 10052
Himmler, Heinrich, anti-Semitism policies and, 4085
Ḥimyarī kingdom, Abyssinian invasion of, 442, 443
Hina (deity), 3397, 7313, 7314, 7315, 8980
overview of, 3798–3799
Hīna, 996
Hinagata (model life), 9082
Hina Matsuri (Girls' Day), 2411
Hīnayāna Buddhism
arhats in, 1080, 1192
bodhisattvas in, 1068, 1076, 1085, 1116
Chinese, translation of texts into, 1576
clothing, monastic, 1829
cosmology in, 1092
sāhasra, 2026, 2027–2030
early *nikāyas* and, 8074
future buddha in, belief in, 1067, 1076, 1092
Huayan school on truth in, 4148
in Japan, 1241–1242
knowledge in, 5200
literature of, 1092, 1093
meaning of term, 1192
meditation in, 1118
techniques of, 2171
merit in, 5874, 5875
morality in, 7651
mysticism in, 6344, 6345
origin of term, 1088
previous buddhas in, 1067
sāhasra cosmology in, 2026, 2027–2030
salvation drama in, 2028–2030
salvation in, 1088
samādhi in, 8066
Sarvāstivāda and, 8117, 8120
in Southeast Asia, 1132, 1133, 1202
stupas and, 8797
and Tendai school, 9078
Vasubandhu in, 9525–9527
vs. Mahāyāna Buddhism, 996, 1076, 1081, 1088, 1113, 1118, 8798
Weber (Max) on, 8152
Hincmar (archbishop of Reims), 2830, **3983**
on magic, 5577
Hincmar of Laon, Hincmar (archbishop of Reims), opposition with, 3983
Hindi, Augustine, 6480
Hindi language
Eckankar use of, 2602
fiction in, 10034–10035
study of, 4458
Urdu and, 3983–3984
Hindi religious traditions, **3983–3988**
bhakti poetry in, 3984–3987
communities and orders in, 3985–3987
Hanumān in, 3987
Hindi *vs.* Urdu language and, 3983–3984
performance in, 3985
pilgrimage in, 3987
ritual in, 3987
saint-singer tradition in, 4005
Hindmarsh, Robert, Swedenborgianism, role in, 8901, 8902
Hindmarsh Island bridge, 649–651, 667
Hinduism, **3988–4009,** 4427–4428. *See also* India and Indian religions; *specific countries, doctrines, movements, and regions*
ablutions in, 12, 2403–2404
aesthetics in, 50–51
afterlife in
community in, 131
heaven and hell in, 3885–3886
justice and judgment in, 129
nature of humankind in, 130, 140
time in, 132
vision of divine in, 128
alchemy in, 241–244
alcohol in, Balarāma's addiction to, 743
altars in, 275–276, 9038, 9039–9040
ancestor worship in, 322–323
animals in, 359
mythic themes, 4437–4438
anthropogony in, 4439–4440
anthropomorphism in, 391
art of
attitudes toward, 496
Bengali, 824
cave, 1472
earth symbolism in, 3014–3015
asceticism in, 527, vol. 13 color insert
fasting in, 2996
ashrams in, 545–547
astrology in, 2372, 3000, 3002
atheism in, 577, 578, 580–581
autobiography in, 700–701
Āyurveda in (*See* Āyurveda)
in Bali (*See* Bali and Balinese religion)
birds in, 4437, 4438, 7387
birth in, 951–952
blades in, 967, 968
blessing in, 980, 983–984
blood in, 986, 7083
Brahamanic period, 3991–3992 (*See also* Brahmanism; *See also* Brāhmaṇas)
Brahmanism and, 9568
breath and breathing in, 1043–1045, 5443, 7362–7363
bridges in, 1049
Buddhism and, 4429
appropriation of ideas from, vol. 8 color insert
comparison of doctrines, 6344
and decline of Buddhism, 1095, 1121, 1125–1126, 6072
and rituals, 1113–1114, 1115
siddha teachers and *Cackrasamvara,* 1349–1350
in Southeast Asia, 1133, 1135, 1138
Theravāda Buddhism and, 9148, 9150
Campbell and, 1379–1380
in Caribbean religion, creolization and, 2068
caste system and, 9522 (*See also* Castes; See also Varṇa and *jāti*)
authority of, 8483

potlatch compared with, 3480
religious power above political power in, 7254
taboos and, 7843
cave art, 1472
celibacy and, 1475, 1476–1477, 7083
chanting in, 1535
charisma in, 1548–1549
charity in, 1555
chastity in, 1559
Christianity and, 828
Sen (Keshab Chandra) on, 8227, 8228
circumambulation in, 1795–1796, 1797
classical
bhakti in, 3998–4002
consolidation of, 3994–4002
darsanas (viewpoints) and paths to salvation in, 3997–3998
four puruṣārthas (goals of humankind) in, 3996–3997
Śruti and *smṛti* texts in, 3994–3995
varnasramadharma theory of castes in, 3995–3996
classification of, 1867
clothing in, 1829–1830
cognitive elements of, 5200
colonialism and, 10042
consecration in, 1957
cosmology in (*See* Cosmology, Hindu)
cows in
mythic themes of, 4438
sacred, 1467
creation stories in, 3016, 4439–4440, 5447
bhakti synthesis and, 3999–4000
humor of, 6364
language in, 5302
creed in, 2053
dance in (*See* Dance, Hindu)
death in, 4440–4441
in Banaras, 779
sati in (*See* Sati)
deep ecology influenced by, 2608
deities of (*See also specific deities*)
as *avatāras,* **707–708**
creation of, 4440
vs. demons, 4439, 4442–4443
in Epic cosmology, 2016
gender studies on, 3323
images, consecration of, 1955
īśvara, 4751–4752
mythology of, 4443–4444
names of, 6408
pure *vs.* impure, 4006, 4007
self-transforming, 7195–7196
sleeping gods, 8440
in Southeast Asia, 4012
Vedic pantheon, 3990–3991
worship of, 9823
deity in, 2256
demons in (*See* Demons, in Hinduism)
desire in, 2304–2305, vol. 13 color insert
devils in, 2314, 2315
devotional, antiritualism of, 7699
devotion in (*See Bhakti;* Devotion, in Hinduism)
dharma in (*See Dharma,* Hindu)
in dialogue of religions, 2342–2343
diamond symbolism in, 2345
diversity in, lack of dogma and, 8153
divination in, 2370
astrology as, 2372
divine inhabitation in humans in, heart as symbol of, 3881
divine triad in, 6747
doctrine in, 2382
dogs in, 2392, 2393, 4438
domestic observances in (*See* Domestic observances, Hindu practices)
drums in, 2499
dualism in, 2508, 2509, 4427
in *Bhagavadgītā,* 852
ecology and, **2620–2624**
economics and, 9708
ecstasy in, 2678, 2680
egg symbolism in, 2701
elephants in, 2750
mythic themes of, 4438
elixir used in, 2770–2771
enlightenment in, 2793
eremitism of, 2823
eschatology in, 2834, 4440–4441, 7361–7362
ethics of, 4428
animals in, 359
evil in
mythology of, 2901–2903
origin of, 2901–2902
eye in, 2942–2943
fasting in, 2403, 3172
feminist analysis of, 3033
festivals in (*See specific festivals*)
fire in, 3117
fire sacrifices in, 3170
food in, 2404
food offerings in, 3169–3170
consecrated food, 1955–1956
food taboos in, 3167–3168, 7505
violations as spiritual practices in, 3170
free will and determinism in, 3200–3201
free will and predestination in, 3204–3205
funeral rites in, 1015, 7815–7816
tombless, 9225
gambling in, 3262–3263
games in, 3266
Gāṇapatyas sect of, **3270–3271,** 3273
gender in, **3318–3326**
gender studies in, 3321–3324
gift giving in, 3482
gnosis in, 4925
goddess worship in, **3607–3611**
of Great Goddess, 3608, 3617
in Purāṇas, 7500
local *vs.* universal, 3608
male deities and, 3585
nationalism and, 3609
Navarātri festival in, 6443–6444
nurturing *vs.* dangerous, 3607–3608
origins of, 3608–3609, 4427
outside India, 3609–3610
studies of, 3607, 3608
Tantric, 3609
violence in, 3590
virginity in, 3588
women's roles and, 3609, 3613
God in (*See also* Īśvara)
acts of (*See Līlā*)
as bridge, 1049
in humans, heart as symbol of, 3881
name of, 6406, 6408
Rāmānuja on, 7615–7616
in sectarian movements, 4004
three modes of, 1346
Golden Rule in, 3632
gold in, 7386
gurūs in, 3712–3715
heart symbolism in, 3881–3882
heavens in, soteriology and, 8529–8530
heresy in, 3922
heterodoxy in, 6909–6910
hierodouleia (sacred prostitution) in, 3967, 3968
"Hinduness" *(Hindutva)* in electoral politics, 1858
holidays and religious year in, **4014–4019**
Holi festival in, 7654
horses in, 4438
hospitality in, 4140
human perfectibility in, 7040–7041
iconoclasm in, 4282, 4283–4285
iconography of (*See* Iconography, Hindu)
idolatry in, Roy (Ram Mohan) on, 7932, 7933
immortality in
in *Bhagavadgītā* on, 852–853
Brahmā and, 1024
incarnation in, 4415–4416
Indus Valley religion as precursor, 3988–3989 (*See also* Indus Valley religion)
initiation in, 4483
Tantric, 8992
insects in, 4508
inspiration in, 4509
Islam and
Dārā Shikōh (Muḥammad) and, 2219
Islamic influences in, 4007–4008
parallels between, 3163
relations with, 4575
in South Asia, 4641, 4643–4644
and tensions, 4431
territorial disputed and desecrations, 8011
Jainism and, 4429, vol. 8 color insert
Jesus in, 4845
jīvanmukti in, 4925–4926
Judaism and, common aspects, 1880
Kabīr as saint in, 5052
karman in (*See Karma,* Hindu)
kingship in
Cakravartin ideal, **1350–1352**
king as guardian of *dharma,* 2328
labyrinth symbols in, 5275
laity in, 5289
laws in, **5343–5347** (*See also* Dharma; *Laws of Manu)*
under British colonial rule, 5346
enforcement of, 5344–5345
interpretation of, 5345
Southeast Asia influenced by, 5346
lesbianism in, 5414, 5415
life in, 5443, 5447–5448
life stages in, 1476
lightning bolt in, 7603–7604
līlā in, 5455–5458
literary theory and interpretation in, 5484–5485
literature of (*See* Hindu literature)
liturgy in, heart, liturgy of, 3881
lotus symbolism in, 5518, 5519
magic in, 5587–5588

Hinduism *continued*
maṇḍalas in, **5640–5641**
Banaras as, 779
mantras in, 5676–5678
Manu in, 3131
in Marathi religions, 5696–5699
marriage in (*See* Marriage)
masculine sacrality in, 5759, 5760, 5761
māyā in, 5794–5795
meditation in, 5819–5820
mendicancy in, 5855
men in, duties of, 2403, 2404
menstruation in, 5866
on mind-body relation, 6486
missions, 6070
modern, 9630–9631
monasticism in, 7769–7770
vs. Christian monasticism, 6135
temporary, 6122
monism in, 6144–6145, 6156, 6964
monkeys in, 4438, 6150–6152
monotheism in, 6156–6157, 6160
morality in, 6182–6188
mortification in, 6197
mountain symbolism in, 1501, 4439, 6212
mudrās in, 6219–6220
music in, 6278–6282
classification of, 6279–6280
hierarchy of, 6280, 6281
influence on Indian music, 6280–6281
of Mirabai, 6048–6049
retention of traditional, 6279
role in devotion, 6278, 6282
in Southeast Asia, 6288–6289
structure of, 6281–6282
mysticism in, 6342–6344
names in, 6408, 6410
and nationalism, 7255–7256
Navarātri festival of, 6443–6444
new religious movements in, Swaminarayan movement, **8889–8893**
New Year celebrations in, 6594
nonviolence in, 6646
obedience in, 6777, 6778
ocean in, 6806
offerings in, 4419
oṃ in, 6821
ordination in, 6853–6854
origins of, 4427
orthodoxy in, 6909–6910
orthopraxy in, 6914–6915
otherworld in, 6924
pain in, 6946
pantheism in, 6964–6965
paradise in, 6983, 6985
peace in, 7022–7022
performance and ritual in, 7043, 7044, 7046–7047
pilgrimage in (*See* Pilgrimage, Hindu)
pluralism in, 2620
pollution in, 2404, 2405
popular form of, 4006–4007
power in, 7347, 7350
prayer in, Rūmī (Jalāl al-Dīn) on, 7937
priesthood in (*See* Priesthood, in Hinduism)
primoridal elements of, 4512
purification in (*See* Purification, in Hinduism)
quaternity in, 7550
quests in, *Rāmāyaṇa,* 7553
rainbow symbolism in, 7604
ram in, 8311
reference works on, 7646
reform movements in
Ārya Samāj, **515–516**
and ashram revival, 545–546
Roy (Ram Mohan) and, 7932–7933
reform movements of 19th century ("Hindu renaissance")
Christian missionaries and, 4007–4008
ideology and, 4008
reincarnation in, 7676, 7677–7678 (*See also* Saṃsāra)
animals and, 359
relics in, opposition to, 7687
as religion, 7692
religious communities in, 7699, 7700
religious education in, 7733, 7734
religious experience in, 7694, 7695, 7700, 7737, 7740, 7742
revelation in, 7778–7779
revival of, 4430–4431
riddles in, 6987
rites of passage in, **7813–7818**
āśrama, 7816–7817
Saṃskāras, 7814–7816 (*See also* Saṃskāras)
śūdras, 7817
of women, 7817
rituals in
in devotional life, 9822
gender studies on, 3323
in Śrautasūtras, 3991, 8883–8884
performance by priests, 7835
philosophy of, 7835
renunciation of, 8094
rituals of reversal, 7844
sacrificial rituals, 7699
rivers in
Ganges, 3274–3275, 7861, 7862
as objects of devotion, 2317
Vaitaraṇī, 7863
sacraments in, mysticism and, 7955
sacred city of (*See* Banaras)
sacred language in, 5303, 5304
sacred stones in, vol. 4 color insert
sacrifice in
bridge and, 1049
mysticism and, 6343
redemption and, 7641
ritual patterns of, 7699
sacrilege in, 8014–8015
salutations in, 8060–8061
salvation in, 527, 6344, 7112
through knowledge, 5199–5200
līlā in, 5457–5458
Sāṃkhya (*See* Sāṃkhya school)
sampradāya in, 5251, 5252
as cult-based community, 7719
saṃskāras in (*See Saṃskāras*)
sectarian, 4004–4006
under Islamic rule, 4007
sects in, 7730
secularization and, 8219
servitude as positive attribute in, 2986
sexual themes in, 7082–7083
snakes and serpents in, 4437–4438, 4439, 7500, 8456, vol. 8 color insert
social classes of, *dharma* in, 2622
society, relations with, 8463, 8466
soul in (*See* Soul(s), Hindu concepts of)
sound in, 6278
space in (*See* Space, in Hinduism)
spiritual guides in, 8711–8712
sports in, 8723–8724
stones in, 4326, 7494
storytelling in, 3145
suffering in, 9112, 9113, 9119
suicide, attitudes toward, 8831
sun in, 8838–8839
swan iconography in, 8894
symbols in, 7697
taboos in, caste system and, 7843
Tantrism, development of, 4002–4003 (*See also* Tantrism, Hindu)
tapas in, 8998
temples in (*See* Temples, Hindu)
textiles in, 9089, 9090, 9092
theodicy in, 9112, 9113, 9119–9120
theogony in, 4439–4440
thunderbolt in, 7603–7604
time in (*See* Time, in Hinduism)
touch of reverence in, 9256
traditionalism in, 7697
tradition in, 9270, 9276–9277
trees in, 4439, 9334, 9335, 9337, 9338, vol. 5 color insert
triads in, 9345–9346
truth in, 9372
underworld in, 9456–9457
Upanisadic period, 3992–3994 (*See also* Upaniṣads)
Vallabha sect of, worship of divine child by, 2983
Vedic period, 3989–3991 (*See also* Vedas; Vedism)
Vedism and, 4427
reaction against, 1407
via negativa in, 9587
votive offerings in, 3163
as way of life, *vs.* as religion, 7705
wealth and, 9708
weaving in mythology of, 9713
Western interest in, swamis and gurus with popularity abroad, 4008
Westernization, responses to, 4007–4008
woman question in, 3319–3321
women in, **3318–3326**
ascetics, 6758
duties of, 2403, 2404
goddess worship and, 3609, 3613
ordination of, 6854
Ramabai (Pandita) on, 7610
rites of passage of, 7817
rural traditions, 4435
Vivekananda on, 10090–10091
women's studies in, 3321, 3322–3324
at World's Parliament of Religions, 9805
worship and devotional life in, **9820–9826**
yantras in, 9871–9872, vol. 3 color insert
yoni in, 9905–9909
Hindu literature. *See also* Scripture; *See also* Bhagavadgītā; *See also* Brāhamaṇas; See also Mahābhārata; *See also* Purāṇas; See also Rāmāyaṇa; *See also* Śāstra literature; *See also* Upaniṣads; Vedas
fiction, 10034, 10035
poetry (*See* Poetry, Hindu)
sacred texts
focus on, 2620
nature in, 2620–2621
studies of, 4446
Tantric, Bengali, 825
women in, 3318–3319
Hindu Manners, Customs, and Ceremonies (Dubois), 4447
Hindu religious year
Dīvālī in, **2368–2369**

Navarātri festival in, **6443–6444**
pilgrimage in, 7171
Hindu Renaissance, 9319
Hindutva nationalist movement
missionary activity of, 6070
Shiv Sena (army of Śiva) party and, 8418
Hindu View of Life, The (Radhakrishnan), 7742
Hine, Virginia H., on glossolalia in Pentecostalism, 3504–3505
Hine-nui-te-po (deity), 2298–2299, 3016, 7311
Hinin (non-person), 1180, 1181–1182
Hinkins, John-Roger, 2603
Hinn, Benny, 7712
Hinna' rite, in Morocco, 7803
Hinukan (hearth deity), 6813
Hipball, 749–751
Hipparchus, astrology and, 563
Hippias Maior (Plato), 2273
Hippie movement
and the Family, 2987
and Jesus Movement (Jesus freaks), 6560
utopian communities in, 7721
Hippocrates, **4021–4022**
Asklepios and, 551
on children, 2982
environmental philosophy of, 2606
Galen and, 3255
on Inner Asian religions, 4488
on medicine
role in roots of, 3830
theoretical basis for, 3839, 3840
Hippocrates of Chios, 6748
Hippocratic Oath, 5810
history of, 4021
Hippocratic treatises, history of, 4021
Hippodamos of Miletus, 3052
Hippolytus of Rome
on Antichrist, 394
on bishops, 7401
on bread, 1041
in exile, 7059
on Gnosticism, 3518, 3532, 5202
on *Logos,* 5504
on Mary Magdalene, 5757
on resurrection, 7765
Hipponax of Colophon, on scapegoats, 8143
Hippopotamus, in Bantu rites of passage, 8667
Hira, Mount, 6213, 6221
Hiragana writing, in Heian court, 1371
Hirai Naofusa, on Shintō, 8356–8357
Hiram (king of Tyre), 3195, 7128, 7129
Melqart and, 5846
Hiram Abiff, 3195, 3197, 4482–4483
Hiraṇyākṣa (demon), 7144, 7501
Hirata Atsutane, **4022–4023**
Kokugaku movement and, 5215–5216, 8365
Hirata school of Shintō, overview of, 8365
Hirata Tokuboku, 3072
Hirhib (deity), in Canaanite religion, 1395
Hirohito
divinity denied by, 4813–4814
enthronement ceremony, 1515
Hiromi, Maeda, 2641
Hiroshima (Japan), bombing of, Raëlians influenced by, 7597, 7598
Hirsch, Bernard, 3091
Hirsch, Christoph. *See* Stellatus
Hirsch, E. D., Jr., on hermeneutics, 3932
Hirsch, Emanuel, on kingdom of God, 5151
Hirsch, Hans, 5969
Hirsch, Samson Raphael, 3188, **4023–4024,** 5020
biblical exegesis of, 868–869
in German Orthodoxy, 6900
Hoffmann (David) criticized by, 4077
Kohler (Kaufmann) as student of, 5214
on nature, 2645
on revelation, 7441
torah 'im derkh erets philosophy, Hildesheimer (Esriel), support from, 3980
Hirsch, Samuel, 4901–4902
Hisamatsu Shin'ichi, 501
Hisham (caliph), 3210
Hishām ibn al-Ḥakam, 4725
as Shī'ī theologian, 4571
on free will and predestination, 3212
Hispaniola. *See also* Caribbean religions; Dominican Republic; Haiti
conquest of, 5322
creation legend, 1468
Hissink, Karin, on jaguars, 8291
Histoire (Lamotte), 1062
Histoire ancienne de l'Afrique du nord (Gsell), 111
Histoire des origines du christiaisme (Renan), 7750
Histoire du bouddhisme indien des origines à l'ère Śaka (Lamotte), 5298
Histoire du peuple d'Israël (Renan), 2301
Histoire générale des langues sémitiques (Renan), 2301
Historia Augusta, on female druids, 3387
Historia Brittonum, Arthur in, 508, 509
Historia de la nación mexicana, Huitzilopochtli in, 4155
Historia ecclesiastica (Eusebius), 2884–2885
Historia Lettica (Einhorn), 768, 2127
Historia regum Britanniae (Geoffrey of Monmouth), Merlin in, 5878
Historia religionis veterum Persarum (Hyde), 2505
Historia Religionum (handbook), 979
Historical art, reality status of, 54
Historical Atlas of World Mythology (Campbell)
historical analysis in, 1379
origin of myth in, 1378
Historical consciousness, Judaism and, 4901–4902
Historical creativity, 1047
Historical-critical method
advocated by Harnack (Adolf von), 3778, 3779
Barth (Karl) on, 5487
Religionsgeschichtliche Schule and, 7706
Historical Dictionary of All Religions (Broughton), 30
Historical ecology, 2664
Historical ethical monotheism, 6160–6161
Historical Judaism
founder of, 3187–3188
modernity and, 4984
Historical materialism, 5777
Historical-reconstructionist school, Hungarian folklorists and, 4227
Historical religious orientation, Eliade on, 1821
"Historical Roots of Our Ecologic Crisis, The" (White), 2608, 2649
in environmental ethics, 2654
Historical science, emergence of, 4032–4034
Historical societies, Jewish, 4879
Historical Study of African Religion, The (Ranger and Kimambo), 117
Historicism
Bianchi (Ugo) opposing, 863
cyclical organic model of history and, 4031
Eliade's opposition to, 4046
in Germanic religion, studies of, 3459
history of religions approach *vs.,* 4061
religion and, 2761
in *Wissenschaft des Judentums,* 4902
Historicity, Vatican II influenced by, 9539–9540
Histories (Herodotus)
goal of, 6374
magi in, 5559
in transition from myth to history, 6373, 6374
Historiography, **4024–4052**
anthropocentric, 4030–4035
autobiography, role of, 4038
biblical, and David, 2224
Chinese, 4026, 4030
Christian
anthropocentric, 4030–4035
history, views of, **4052–4057**
traditional, 4028–4029
Daoist, 2208–2209
definition of, 6373
Fāṭimid, 7541–7542
Greek and Roman, 4026–4027, 4030
historical science, German, 4032, 4033
Indian, 4025–4026, 4030
Islamic, 4029–4030
Japanese, 4026, 4030
Jewish, 4027–4028
history, views of, **4057–4060**
Krochmal (Naḥman) and, 5247
myth and, relation between, 6372, 6373–6379
mythical stage of, 4024, 4025
overview, **4024–4035**
of Reformation, 7664
of Scholem (Gershom), 8178
secularization on, 4032–4034
time in, 6373, 6374–6375, 6378–6379
traditional, 4025–4030
in Western studies, **4035–4052**
by ancient Greeks, 4035–4037
in Baroque age, 4039–4040
Christian-pagan polemics and, 4037–4038
in early 20th century, 4042–4047
in Enlightenment and Romantic period, 4040–4041
historical and philosophical dichotomy, 4035
in Middle Ages, 4038
in Renaissance, 4038–4039
in Roman thought, 4037
since World War II, 4047–4051
Historische und legendarische Erzählungen: Zusätze zu Esther (Bardtke), 898
Historismus und seine Probleme, Der (Troeltsch), 9366
History, **4052–4060**
biblical paradigm for, Schmidt (Wilhelm) on, 8169

History *continued*
cargo cults as history making, 1422
in Chinese philosophy
historical perspective *vs.* historical constancy, Han Fei Zi on, 3773
Mandate of Heaven and, 4026
Christian views of, **4052–4057**
ages of, in Paul, 4053
ecclesiastical understanding of, 4055
Hobbes (Thomas) on biblical history, 4075
Judaism in, 4970
millenarian understanding of, 4054–4055
mystic understanding of, 4055
reform/revivalist understanding of, 4055
creation from nothing and, 1986
cultural, Schmidt (Wilhelm) on, 8168
definitions of, 6372, 6373
dialogical, 1421
Dilthey (Wilhelm) on, 3933
division into ancient, medieval, and modern periods, 4030
Durkheim (Émile) on, 2527
in ecology and religion, study of, 2604, 2609
ethology and, 2869
existentialist view of, 2927
exorcism studied in, 2936
as foundation of religion, 7117
Great Man view of, heroes and, 3956
Harnack (Adolf von) on, 3778
hereditary process in, Schmidt (Wilhelm) on, 8169
vs. history-like narratives, 6375, 6377
Italian Renaissance humanist emphasis on, 4175
in Jewish studies, 4874–4875
Jewish views of, **4057–4060**
Abravanel (Isaac) on, 18
Greenberg (Irving) on Holocaust and, 4092–4093
myth and, 6375–6379
Jihād in, 4919
linear *vs.* cyclical
in Hebrew scriptures, 4058
in historiography, 4031
and history, Christian views of, 4053
sacred time and, 7991–7992
as literary activity *vs.* lived experience, 6372, 6373
Maya view of, 1357, 1358
and myth, **6371–6380**
Eliade on, 1821
among traditional peoples, 6658
neoorthodoxy on, 6467
Niebuhr's (Reinhold) doctrine of, 6613
in phenomenology of religion, 7094, 7097
philosophy of (*See also* Historiography)
emergence of, 4031
Herder (Johann Gottfried) on, 3919
Qarmaṭī views of, 7543
reform/revivalist understanding of, 4055
mystic understanding of, 4055
of religions (*See* History of religions)
of religions approach (*See* History of religions approach)
secularization as historical process, 8216–8217
sociology of, 8494–8495
of study of religion (*See* Study of religion)
theologies of, 4928, 6378
three ages theory of
in Christian historiography, 4028
Greenberg (Irving) on Holocaust and, 4092–4093
He Xiu and, 1575
salvation by faith and, 1576
time and, 1760
time in, 6373, 6374–6375, 6378–6379
in typology of narratives, 6375–6377
Weber's "great man" approach to, 1544
witchcraft in, 9770
in women's studies, 9791
Zhang's unity of knowledge, 1579
History museums, 6244–6245
History of Divine Love (Theodoret), 9123
History of Indian Philosophy (Dasgupta), 4420
History of Joseph, 903
"History of Latvia" (Einhorn), 757
History of Mathematics, A (Boyer), 3438
History of My Misfortunes, The (Abelard), 698
History of Philosophy (Hegel), 7112
History of Phoenicians (Dio), 7129
History of Playing Cards, A (Hargrave), 1414
History of Rationalism (Lecky), 9109
History of Religion (journal), 2756
History of religions, 7702–7703, **10041–10047**. *See also* History of religions approach; Study of religion; Theology, comparative
Anesaki Masaharu on, 343
Beth (Karl) on, 846
Bianchi (Ugo) on, 863
Brandon (S. G. F.) on, 1039–1040
Brelich (Angelo) on, 1047–1048
cognitive approaches to, 10043–10044
comparative-historical method, Pettazzoni (Raffaele) developing, 7073
cosmological imagery and, 1991–1992
deserts in, 2301–2302
dualism in, 2510–2511
of ecstasy, 2678, 2681
Eliade on, 2755, 2756
Eliade on value of, 459
Eliade's dialectic approach and, 7976
feminist approaches to, 10041–10042
Feuerbach (Ludwig) on, 3047
Frazer (James) and, 3192
functionalist approach to, Haydon (A. Eustace) and, 3803
in Hegel and Chantepie de la Saussaye, 1531
heresy, development of, 3920–3923
history of, 2756–2757
hypostases concept in, 4242–4243
and initiation rituals, 4480, 4484
Islamic studies of, 8781
Kerényi (Károly) on, 5112–5115
Kraemer (Hendrik) on, 5241–5242
Kristensen (W. Brede) on, 5246–5247
Leach (Edmund) on, 5382
materiality and, 10048–10049
Otto (Rudolf) in, 6930
Pettazzoni (Raffaele) on, 7072–7077
and phenomenology of religion, 7089
and philosophy of religion, 7126–7127
postcolonial approaches to, 10042–10043
religious studies preceded by, 2608
ritual defined in, 7833–7834
Roman Catholicism against, 7073
romanticists *vs.* rationalists in, 2070
sacred *vs.* profane and, 7973–7975
science and humanities combined in, 1991
secularization in, 8216–8217
Sexuality in, 8241
Sharpe (Eric) on, 8305
sociobiological approaches to, 10043
tears in study of, 9024, 9025, 9026
as theoretical approach (*See* History of religions approach)
Tiele (C. P.) on, 9192
Wach (Joachim) in, 9649–9651
Widengren (Geo) in, 9732–9733
wisdom in, 9764–9765
Zaehner (R. C.) in, 9923–9924
History of Religions (journal), 10057
History of Religions (Moore), 6177
History of Religions (Smith), 1879
"History of Religions and a New Humanism" (Eliade), 2756
History of religions approach, **4060–4068**. *See also* Comparative-historical method; Study of religion
Chicago approach to, Kitagawa (Joseph) and, 4044
historical typology, 4063–4067
holistic approach in, 4063
Japanese study of religion compared to, 8778
Kitagawa (Joseph M.) and, 5188, 5189
mystery religions in, 6327
other approaches contrasted with, 4061, 4063, 4064
Religionsgeschichtliche Schule and, 7706–7709
theoretical and methodological overview, 4060–4063
typology of religion in, 4063–4067
History of Religions in the Caribbean (Bisnauth), 10023–10024
History of Religious Ideas, A (Eliade), 2756–2757
History of Sexuality (Foucault), 5863
History of Spiritism (Doyle), 5090
History of the English Church and People (Bede), 6942–6943
History of the Jews (Adams), 30
History of the Negro Church, The (Woodson), 74
History of the Rechabites, 903
History of the Work of Redemption, A (Edwards), 2699
History of Tom Jones, A Foundling, The (Fielding), 5355
History or Classification of the Sciences (Flint), 7340
Hitbodedut (conversation), 6401
Hitchcock, Alfred, 3100
Hitler, Adolf. *See also* Nazism
anti-Semitism of, 402, 4085
assassination attempt on, 1016–1017

Baeck (Leo) on, 736
Barth (Karl) opposing, 789, 791
as charismatic leader, 6515
consolidation of power of, ecumenical movement and, 2684, 2685
Grail movement suppressed by, 3653
inner circle of, 6547
as monster, 6166
nationalism and, 5398
rise to power of, 4085
Hitnabbe' (prophetic action), 7432
Hitsudan (form of writing), practice of, 1371
Hittite religion and society, **4068–4073**. *See also* Anatolia and Anatolian religions
and An, 302
Babylonia conquered by, 5948
blessing and cursing in texts of, 2102
deities of (*See also* Athirat; Teshub)
functions of, 4068–4069
goddess worship, 3595
Hurrian deities and, 4230
Indo-Aryan gods and, 4230–4231
Kubaba Great Mother, 2109
names, and languages of origin, 4068
nature of, 4068
pantheon of, 4068, 4069
deus otiosus in, 2311
dragons in, 2431, 2442
goat sacrifice in, 8311
goddess worship in, 3595
healing in, 3825
kingship in, 5165
Kumarbi myth, 1450–1451
laws in, 1844
mythology in, 4069–4070
revelation in, 4072
ritual drama in, 2442, 2445
sacred and profane in, 7969
sacrifice in, 8005
scapegoat in, 8143, 8144
sin, death, and afterlife in, 4072–4073
Soldiers Oath, 2099
temple worship in, 4070–4072
Hittman, Michael, 3474
Hiu-wan (Buddhist nun), 6761
Ḥizb ut-Taḥrīr (Islamist organization), 4628, 4629–4630, 6568
Ḥizzuq emunah (Troki), 5085
HKBP. *See* Huria Kristen Batak Protestan
Hmong. *See* Miao
Hoa Binh culture (Thailand), 6459
Hoang, Arcade, 1631
Hoang, Pierre (Huang Bailu), 1633
Hoasca (hallucinogen), 7470
Hobart, John Henry, Seton (Elizabeth) and, 8234
Hobbes, Thomas, **4073–4076**
on biblical history, 4075
on free will, 3200
on Golden Rule, 3632
on human nature, 5367
on laughter, 4221–4222
on law and morality, 5367
on laws of nature and the sovereign, 4074
life of, 4073–4074
materialism of, 5776
on necessary acts, 3203
on political theology, 4075
on scripture, abuses of, 4074–4075
on state of nature, 4074
Hobgoblin, 2952
Hōbōgirin (Sino-Japanese encyclopedia), Seidel (Anna) on, 8222
Hobsbawm, Eric J., 7330, 9273
Hocart, A. M., 381
on flight, human fascination with, 3127
on gods in Solomon Islands religions, 8514
on iconoclasm, 4386
on kingship, 1514
manism and, 5673
on *mana,* 2542
Hōchibō Shōshin, 818
Ho Chi Minh, 7264
Hochmann von Hochenau, Ernst Christoph, 7143
Hochschule für die Wissenschafe des Judentums (rabbinical seminary in Berlin), 7581
Hock, Ronald F., 7014
Hockewelder, John, on emergence beliefs of Deleware Indians, 2557
Hocking, William Ernest, **4076,** 9130–9131
liberal manifesto of, 2343
panentheism of, 6963
on psychology of religion, 7475
Hocquenghem, Anne-Marie, 3416
Hodayot (Dead Sea composition), 7461
Hodegetria (icon), 4390
Hodge, Charles, 3204
Hodgkin, Thomas, 4605
Hodgson, Brian, 1078, 1311, 1333
Hodgson, Leonard, on atonement, 597
Hodgson, Marshall G.
on iconoclasm, 4280–4281, 4282, 4284
Islamic studies of, 4577, 4716
on *ṭarīqah,* 9004
Hod'im (Bene Israel identity), 5007
Hǫðr (deity), Baldr killed by, 744, 4461
Hoe, Enlil as god of, 5950, 5952
Hœrnir (deity), in creation of man, 3454–3455
Hoffman, Barbara, 4282
Hoffman, W. J., 6670
Hoffmann, David, **4076–4077**
biblical exegesis of, 869
Hoffmann, Herbert, 4298
Höfler, Otto, 3459, 9735
Hofmann, Melchior, in Anabaptism, 304, 7660
Hogan, Linda, 702, 3093, 7225
Hogbin, Ian, on *mana,* 8515
Hoge, Dean R., on schism, 8152
Hogg, James, 3060
Hogon (Dogon priest), 95, 99–100, 2391, 4301
Hohokam culture (North America), 6654
Hōjō (hut), 9049
Hōjō Shigetoki, 6604
Hōjō Tokiyori, Suzuki (D. T.) and, 8884
Hokan linguistic family, 9228
Ḥokhmah, **4077–4080,** 9750, 9756
ancient understanding of, 4078–4079
in biblical piety, 4077–4078
female personifications of, 4078
as great goddess, 8523
as hypostasis, 4243
in late antiquity and Middle Ages, 4079–4080
meaning of, 4077
as Sophia, 8522
Hokke Shintō, 6607
Hokkeshū (Hokke or Lotus sect), 6606–6607
Hokku (verse form), 7217
Ho Kojī, *haiku* of, 8702
Hokuloa (Great Star), in Hawaiian religion, 8427
Holbach, Paul-Henri d'
in French Enlightenment, 2796
materialism of, 5776
Holcan Ok'ot (war dance), 2466
Hölderlin, Friedrich, 7206
Holdheim, Samuel, **4080–4081**
Geiger (Abraham) compared to, 3292
in Reform Judaism, 7669
Holekreish (naming ritual), 7819
Holī (Hindu festival), **4081–4082,** 7654, 7844, 9824–9825
in Hindu religious year, 4017
Holidays. *See also* Festivals; *specific holidays*
in Jehovah's Witnesses, 4823
in Khanty religion, 5124
in Mansi religion, 5124
Holikā (demon), fire and, 4081
Holiness
God's, in Judaism, 614
Kook (Avraham Yitsḥaq) on, 5227
sin as deviation from, 8403–8404
Holiness Code (biblical law), on purity, 7512, 7513, 7514
Holiness movement, **4082–4084**
among African Americans, 1709, 10038
in Caribbean, 1437
creolization and, 2067
and Daddy Grace, 2124
in Europe, 4083
evangelical, 2888
and the Family, 2987
formative years of, 4082–4083
institutionalization of, 4083–4084
Methodist roots, 1713–1714
origins of, 70, 6557
Pentecostalism and, 70
religious broadcasting and, 7711, 7712
post-Civil War revival of, 4083
Quakers and, 7548
revivalism and, 1710
Seymour (William J.) and, 8254
Smith (Hannah Whitall) and, 8445–8446
in United States, 7029
Holism, 863
vs. dualism, in science and religion, 2659
in history of religions approach, 4063
New Age, healing in, 3851
Holistic methodology, structuralism and, 8759
Holl, Karl, Pauck (Wilhelm) studying under, 7010
Holland. *See* Netherlands
Hollenbeck, Jess Byron, 7747
Hóŀŀi icósi (ballgame), 754
Hollis, Alfred C., 115
Hollis, Martin, 5568
Hollis, Thomas, 2287
Holloway, Joseph, 76
Holly, James, 68
Hollywood, Amy, 386
on bodily experience, 4166
Holm, Bill, on masks, 5767
Holm, Gustav, 475
Holm, Nils G., historiography of, 4047
Holmberg, Bengt, 7013
Holmberg, H. J., 475
Holmberg, Uno. *See* Harva, Uno
Holmes, Ernest S., 6584, 6586
Holmes, Fenwicke, 6574
Holmes, Guiteras, 5942
Holmes, John Haynes, on Gandhi (Mohandas), 3273

Holmes, Oliver Wendell, Spinoza (Baruch), influence of, 8685–8686
Holmes, Trevor, 680
Holocaust, the, **4084–4095,** 5022
  Agudat Yisra'el in, 195
  anti-Semitism of, 402, 4863, 4984
  and Auschwitz as pilgrimage site, 8377
  in 'Avodah (poetic saga), 8391
  and decline of Purim, 7517–7518
  destruction of seminaries during, 7582
  as expulsion, 2939
  gender and, 3352
  God in history and, 3552
  Hasidism after, 9382–9383
  history of, **4085–4087**
  in Jewish studies, 4885
  Jewish theological responses to, **4088–4095,** 4984–4985
    'Aqedah/martyrdom paradigm, 4088
    Cohen (Arthur A.), 1849, 4093–4094
    Fackenheim (Emil), 2949–2950, 4092
    free will defense, 4091–4092
    Greenberg (Irving), 4092–4093
    Hester panim (hiding the face of God) paradigm, 4090
    Job paradigm, 4088–4089
    Maybaum (Ignaz), 4089–4090
    mippenei hata'einu (because of our sins) paradigm, 4090–4091
    mystery and silence of God paradigm, 4094
    Rubenstein (Richard L.), 4094
    Soloveitchik (Joseph Baer) on, 8519
    Suffering Servant paradigm, 4089–4090
  memorialization of dead, 7823
  modern dance/ballets about, 2163
  in modern Jewish thought, 4909
  modern Judaism and, 4984
  motivation behind, 4085, 4088
  Nazi officers prepared for killing, 5743
  novels about, 3059
  victims of, as martyrs, 5741
"Holocaust" *('olah),* as type of sacrifice, 926
Holocaust Day (Yom ha-Sho'ah), 4868
Holographic worldview, afterlife in, 147
Holt, John Dominis, 3085
Holtved, Erik, 475
Holwell, John Z., 4446
Holy, idea of the, **4095–4101**. *See also* Holiness; Sacred
  in Arabic language and thought, 7968
  definition of, 7692
  in definition of religion, 7694
  in Greek thought and language, 3677, 7966–7967
  Handsome Lake on, 3771
  in Hebrew language and thought, 7968
  linguistics of, 7969, 7970
  in North American Indian religions, 6703
  Otto (Rudolf) on, 48, 6928–6930, 7090
    descriptive and interpretive tendency in, 4064
    legacy of, 4100–4101
    as mysterious, 8493
    as religious feeling, 4096–4097
    semantics and translations of, 4097–4100
  phenomenon *vs.* language of, 4100
  in Salvation Army, 8063
  scripture and, 8201
  typology of religions and, 4064
  Windelband (Wilhelm) on, 4096
Holy, Ladislav, on kinship, 5183
Holy City Old Man (deity), 5120
Holy Communion. *See* Eucharist
"Holy dimension," Heschel (Abraham Joshua) on, 3962
Holy Face, The (Zurbarán), vol. 12 color insert
Holy Fire (Eastern Orthodox ceremony), 7154
Holy Ghost. *See also* Holy Spirit
  as Wisdom, 5502–5503
Holy Grail. *See* Grail, the
Holy Koran, The (Moorish Science booklet), 72, 4687
Holy of Holies, 924, 934
Holy oil, in Orthodox sacraments, 2592–2593
Holy Order of MANS, **4101–4104,** 6545
  women in, 6563
Holy Path Buddhism, *vs.* Pure Land Buddhism, 4796
Holy Piby, The, 6531
Holy places. *See* Geography; Pilgrimage; Sacred space
Holy Reich: Nazi Conceptions of Christianity, The (Steigmann-Gall), 2663
Holy Roman Empire
  Charlemagne and, 1557
  Constantinianism and, 1968
  creation of, 7876
  Jews in, 5016, 5019
  political power of, 7254
  Reformation and, 7656
  separation from Eastern empire, 1662
  theocracy in, 9110
Holy See. *See* Papacy; Pope
Holy Spirit. *See also* Trinity
  in African American religions, 67
  age of
    in Christian historiography, 4028
    Schelling (Friedrich) on, 8148
  Augustine on, 628
  baptism in (*See* Spirit Baptism)
  Bernard on, 839
  Calvin (John) on, 7454
  Congregationalist views of, 1938
  Council of Constantinople on, 2040
  Cyprian on, 2114
  divine energies associated with, Basil of Caesarea on, 3554
  dove as symbol of, 949
  Edwards (Jonathan) on, 2700
  filioque doctrine (*See Filioque*)
  gifts of
    charisma and, 1549–1550
    Pentecostalism and, 1714, 7028–7029
  history of doctrine on, 1666
  inspiration given by, 4510
  as interpreter of scripture in Calvin, 1375
  Justin Martyr on, 5044
  in Montanism, 6167
  in New Testament, as *pneuma,* 8562
  Origen on, 873
  in Orthodox theology, 2589–2590
  Photios on, 7135
  possession by
    in Afro-Caribbean revivalist cults, 1437
    and glossolalia, 3506
  in Protestantism, 7450
  in Roman Catholicism, 7884
  Servetus (Michael) on, 8232
  as Sophia, 8522, 8523
  symbol of, Tillich (Paul) on, 9204
  Symeon the New Theologian on, 8920
Holy Spirit Association, Molko and Leal v., 1033
Holy Spirit Movement, Lekwena (Alice) in, 106
Holy Spirit's Feast, music in, 6272
Holy Synod
  in Orthodox Church of America, 1765
  of Russian Orthodox Church, 7945–7946
Holy Tabernacle Ministries, 6769
Holy Trinity-Saint Sergii Monastery, Sergii of Radonezh and, 8230–8231
Holy unction, in Orthodox Christianity, 2593
Holy Virgin Mary, The (Ofili), 4282, 4287
Holy War. *See* Crusades; *See Jihād*
Holy War, The (Bunyan), 1323
Holy Wedding, in Mesopotamia, 5162
Holy Week
  in Christian liturgical calendar, 1742–1743
  in Orthodox Christianity, holy unction during, 2593
Homa (fire offering), 9836, 9838
Homage, as sacrificial intention, 8001, 8002
Homans, Peter, 7477, 7478, 7480
Hombahomba (diviners), 2370
Home (house), **4104–4107**. *See also* Domestic observances
  in Acehnese religion, 25–26
  as center of the world, 1503, 1504
  consecration of, 4105
  death and, 4105–4106
  deities of, 3622, 4106
  in Ethiopia, vol. 6 color insert
  guardians of, in Slavic religion, 8436
  hearth fire, sacred, 4106–4107
  homelessness, 4104–4105
  in Micronesian religions
    rituals in, 6004
    shrines in, 6004
  in Oceanic religions, spiritual presences in, 2006
  in Orthodox Christianity, prayer in, 2593
  pollution of, 4105
  Protestant, in Ethiopia, vol. 6 color insert
  purification of, 1459, 4105
  secularization of, 4107
  serpents as protectors of, 8457
  shrines in, 4106
  sleep location in, 8441
  in southern African religions, 8657
  spirits of, 4106
    in Khanty religion, 5122
    in Komi religion, 5218
    in Mansi religion, 5122
Home, Daniel Dunglas, Spiritualism and, 8716
Home and the World, The (Tagore), 8958
Ho megale syntaxis (Ptolemy). *See Almagest* (Ptolemy)
Homelessness, 4104–4105
  shelters for, 4102
Home of the Holy Spirit, 7929. *See also* Rosicrucians
Homeopathy
  in India, politics of, 3856
  in magic, 5571, 5588
Homeostatis, in eternity, 2855
Homer, **4107–4109**. *See also* Iliad; *Odyssey; specific works*
  on *aion,* 207
  on altar fire, 3118

on Aphrodite, 407
on Apollo, 424
on Artemis, 506
atheism and, 581
on deities, 4107–4108
deities described by, 4321, 5468
on Delphic oracle, 2265
on Demeter, 803, 2268, 2443
on *dēmiourgos* used by, 2272, 2273
on demons, 2277, 2283
on descent into the underworld, 2295
eidōlon (image) used by, 4357
Epic of Gilgamesh and, 3487
on fate, 3000, 3001
on Helios, 8839
on Hera, 3679
Herder *vs.* Lessing on, 3918–3919
on human nature, 5468
influence on Greek religion, 3660, 3678, 4108
on kingship, 5166
on magic, 5574
memorization of works of, 5852
on paradise, 6984
on Poseidon, 7338
on Prometheus, 7420
on retribution, 7783
ritual patterns used by, 2443
on sacrifices, 3682
on souls, 8541
on Thracian religion, 9169, 9170
time in works of, 6375
on tradition, 9275
on twins, 9417
Xenophanes, criticism from, 4108
on Zeus, 5994
Homer, Michael, 6542
Homeric Hymns
chariot of the sun in, 8839
independence from local traditions in, 4108
Lady of the Animals in, 5280
magic in, 5574
Meter (Mother) in, 2109
Homeric Hymn to Aphrodite, 506
Athena in, 586
Homeric Hymn to Apollo, 506
Homeric Hymn to Demeter, 803, 2269, 2443, 2751, 3382, 3671, 3678, 3684
in Eleusinian mysteries, 6329
Hades and Persephone in, 3724
magic in, 5574
secret rites in, 8543
Homeric Hymn to Helios, chariot of the sun in, 8839
Homeric Hymn to Hermes, 1465
Hermes in, 3936
Homer's Ancient Readers (Lamberton and Keaney), 7106
Home schooling, 5377
in Jesus Movement, 4853
Homes of Truth, founder of, 6584
Homiak, John P., 10027
Homicide. *See* Murder
Homilies
of Elimelekh of Lizhensk, 2767–2768
of Ephraem of Syria, 2812–2813
of Jerome, 4833
of Origen, 6888
Homililes on the Hexaemeron (Basil of Caesarea), 798
Hominids, 6951
Homme devant la mort (Ariès), 2240
Homo erectus, archaeology on, 454
Homoeroticism, 5414
in Christianity, 7082
in Islam, lack of, 7082
in Judaism, 7080
Homo faber, 5199
Homo Hierarchicus: The Caste System and Its Implications (Dumont), 4448–4449, 7504
Homoioteleuton, 921
Homo Ludens (Huizinga), 3265
Homo modernus, homo religiosus vs., 4110–4111
Homoousios ("of the same substance") doctrine. *See also* Arianism
Athanasius as champion of, 1979
Cyril of Jerusalem's avoidance of term, 2118
hypostasis vs. ousia and, 4241
Homo religiosus, **4109–4111**
archetypes and, 458, 459
early humans as, 6954
Erikson (Erik) studying, 7482
feminist critique of, 3025
gender in, 3301
homo modernus and, 4110–4111
idolatry and, 4357, 4363–4364
initiation and, 4482
as religious humanity, 4110
as religious leader, 4109–4110
in study of religion, 4111
Homosexuality, **4111–4118**. *See also* Bisexuality; Gay men and lesbians; Lesbianism
in Afro-Brazilian religions, 121
age-structured, 4112–4115
in Anglicanism, 353, 5808, 7404
Eastern Orthodox Christianity on, 7404
Foucault (Michel) on, 8241–8242
gender-reversed, 4115–4116
in Greek religion, 7079
initiation rituals of, 184
hierodouleia (sacred prostitution) *and,* 3969
in Hinduism, 3969
in Raëlian religion, 7598
meaning of term, 4111
in men's studies, 5862, 5864
in Mesopotamian religions, gender and, 3378–3379
in North American Indian religions, gender and, 3410
prohibitions on, 5415
role-specialized, 4116–4117
Roman Catholicism and, 7404, 8244–8245
sublimation and, 8244–8245
as universal *vs.* cultural, 4112
in Wolfenden Report (1957), 5369
Homosexuality and Religion (Hasbany), 3314
Hōm Yasht (Zoroastrian text), 850
Haoma in, 3776
women reciting, 3373
Hondo, Med, 3098
Hōnen (Buddhist monk), **4118–4121**
and Amitābha, 292, 6408
as disciple of Benchō, 818
Genshin influencing, 3433
Jōdoshū school of Buddhism and, 1243–1244, 4119–4120, 4937–4938, 9080
on meditation, 1294
and merit, 5872
on morality, 1281–1282
on music, 6301
on *nenbutsu,* 1179
on *mappō,* 5687
in popular religion, 4796
and recitative *nianfo,* 6602–6603
Shinran and, 4934, 8354
Tendai Buddhism and, 4118–4119, 9075
Honey, 847
in Australian Indigenous myths, 660–661
kashrut laws on, 5106
Honey bear, 808
Hong, Nansook, 9468
Hoⁿ'ga (earth), 6917, 6918–6919
Hōn'ga (orchestra), 6296, 6297
Hongaku (original enlightenment), 2781
Hongaku shisō (original enlightenment thought), 1291–1292, 9077, 9079
Honganji (Original Vow Temple), 4935–4936, 7752, 7753
Hong Kong
Catholicism in, 2228
Daoism in, music in, 6295
Judaism in, 5008
study of religion in, 1620
Zoroastrianism in, fire in, 570
Hong Mai, 3067
Hongo (spirit), 7443
Kinjikitile possessed by, 2571, 5181
Hongren (Buddhist teacher), 1302, 1521–1522
Huineng and, 4154
students of, 1601
Hongshan people, jade carvings of, 4758
Hongwu (Chinese emperor), Muslims under, 4632
Hong Xiuquan, 1609–1610, 7719
as leader of Taiping Rebellion, 6041, 7022, 8961
millenarianism of, 6041
Hongzhi Zhengjue, 1604
Hongzhou school, 1522–1523
Honigman, John, 576
Honi ha-Me'aggel (Circle-Drawer), 1793
Honi the Circle Maker, 3159
Honjisuijaku theory, **4121–4122,** 4796
Honko, Lauri, 2285, 3104, 3106, 3109, 3110, 3113, **4122–4123,** 10081
and comparative mythology, 3114
historiography of, 4047
Honkyōgaihen (Hirata Atsutane), *kami* and afterlife in, 4022
Ho no Ninigi no Mikoto. *See* Ninigi
Honoratus, 1447
Honorius (Roman emperor), Donatist revolt against, 2416–2417
Honorius III (pope), 5337
administrative affairs of, 6971
and Dominicans, 2413, 9160
Francis of Assisi and, 3184
seeking reform of monasticism, 821
Honti, János, 2415
Hood, J. W., 75
Hood, Robert, 80
Hoodoo. *See also* Vodou
as derogatory term, 9634
folklorists' perspectives on, 3142
history of study of, 73, 76
in New Orleans, Catholic elements in, 3143
Hook, Sidney, on heroes, 3956
Hooke, Robert, 6588
Hooke, S. H., 5969
in Myth and Ritual school, 6380–6381
Hooker, Richard, **4123–4124**
on Anglicanism, 7663
on free will and predestination, 3208
Hermetism and, 3948
influence of, 350
on revolution, 7790
theology of, 9138
Hooker, Thomas, 2288, **4125**

Hooks, bell, on beauty, 812
Hoover, Herbert, religious broadcasting and, 7710
Hoover, Stewart, 3101
Hope, **4125–4127**
in *Jeremiah,* 4830
Hopewell culture (North America), 6654
Hopi religion (North America)
ballgame played in, 752
Basket Dances in, 6726
cave myth in, 1469
clowns in, 1838, 1839
cosmology of, 6722
creation story in, 1469, 6660
deities of, 6723, 6724
drama in, 2461
dreams in, 2483
economic patterns and, 6720
geographical distribution of, 6720
iconography of, 4309, 4310
identification of food and people in, 3169
kachina ceremonies in, 6725
Lady of the Animals in, 5280
maize symbolism and ritual of, 6726
marriage in, 5724
medicine men in, 6721
Mesoamerican influences on, 6654
narratives in, types of, 6658
poetry in, 7226
proverbs in, 6977
rain dance in, 7603
religious societies in, 6724–6725
seasonal divisions and, 6724
Snake-Antelope rites in, 6725
Thunderbird in, 1471
weaving in, 939
winter solstice ceremony in, 6725
Hopkins, E. Washburn, on rejuvenation myths, 7683
Hopkins, Emma Curtis, **4127–4129,** 6536, 6563
and Eddy (Mary Baker), 6584
and Fillmore (Charles and Myrtle), 3095, 3096, 9472
and New Thought movement, 6582, 6583, 6584
students of, 6584
Hopkins, Grace, on Baltic religion, 757
Hopkins, Jeffrey, 9190
Hopkins, John, 6310
Hopkins, Samuel, Edwards' (Jonathan) influence on, 2700
Hopkins, Sarah Winnemucca, 702
Hopkins College of Christian Science, founding of, 4128
Hopkins Metaphysical Association, New Thought and, 4128
Hoppál, Mihály, 3109, 3114
Hopstein, Israel, 9381
Hopwood, Derek, 4720
Ḥoq ha-Shevut (Israeli Law of Return)
halakhah and, 3754
Samaritans, status of, 8071
Horace
on Diana, 2346
on golden age, 2964
on music, 6304, 6305
music composed by, 6304
on Priapus, 7392
ship symbolism of, 992
on witchcraft, 9770
Horae (goddesses), role of, 3000
Horagalles (deity), sacrifices to, 8088
Horeb, Mount, 6213
Horemheb (Egyptian king), religion under, 2707
Horesman. *See* World-Overseeing Man
Hori Keizan, Motoori Norinaga and, 6211
Horites, Hurrians and, 4229
Horizontal dualism, 2509
Horkheimer, Max, 3527
on popular culture, 7321
Hormisdas (pope), 9205
Hormizd, Yūḥanna (John), 6480
Hormīzd I (king of Persia), Mani and, 5655, 5659, 5665
Hormīzd II (king of Persia), Manichaeism under, 5660
Horn, J., 3531
Horner, I. B., **4129–4130**
in Pali Text Society, 6956
translations by, 6126, 6128
on women in Buddhism, 3330
Horn of Africa, Islam in, 4606–4607
Horn of Plenty. *See* Cornucopia
Horns, **4130–4131**. *See also* Antlers
in Celto-Roman art, 1481
in Minoan religion, 39, 40, *40*
Horns, sign of (gesture), 7344
Hornung, Erik, 2730
Horodetzky, Shmuel Abba, 5611
Ḥoron (deity)
Kirta and, 1399
in Moabite religion, 6094
Horowitz, Aharon Halevi, on mystical union, 6340
Horowitz, Leah, 9037
Horrocks, Roger, 3314
Horsemen, Dacian Riders, 2123–2124
Horses, **4131–4136**
in Baltic religion, 757, 758
in Celtic religion, 1487, 1493
Epona, 2820
myths of, 4133
sacrifice of, 1493, 4132, 4133, 8239
chariots and, 4132
evil mare myth, European, 4133–4135
in Gallic religion, deities associated with, 4133
in Greek religion, 4382
myths of, 4133
sacrifice of, 3682–3683
in Hinduism, 4438
in Indic religion, sacrifice of, 1350, 1493, 4132, 4133, 4135, 8239
in Indo-European religions, 4452
myths of, 4133
sacrifice of, 4132–4133
in Inner Asian religions, 4488
mouth of, 4135
Poseidon associated with, 7339
in prehistoric religions, sacrifice of, 7384
in Roman religion, 4132, 4133
sacrifice of, to sun, 8838
in Saka religion, cult of, 7385, 7387
in Scandinavian religion, deities associated with, 3220
in Scythian religion, sacrifice of, 4489
in Siberian religions, sacrifice of, 6755
sun associated with, 8835, 8838
in Vedism, 1025, 4132, 4133
sacrifice of, 9563–9564
white stallion myths, 4135–4136
Horst (deity), 9420
Horst, Louis, 2158
Hortensius (Cicero), 624
Horticulturalists, visions of, 9615
Horton, Lester, 2159
Horton, Robin, 118
on African religions, 3087
Festschrift edited by, 3041
intellectualist theory, microcosm, macrocosm, and conversion, 1971
on magic, 5567
on rituals, 7839
Horus (Heru) (deity), **4136**
in African American religion, 80
on amulets and talismans, 299
Atum and, 623
Canopic jars associated with, 4319
conception of, 6920
Edfu temple of, 2709
in Egyptian religion
cosmology of, 2710
Hathor and, 3795
Isis and, vol. 8 color insert
pantheon of, 2704
eye of, 2940
hawks in depiction of, 2553
as healer, 3826
kings identified with, 693, 2441, 2703–2704, 2706, 2711–2712, 2720, 4416, 5163, 7277
in Kushite religion, 5269
lotus associated with, 5518
pigs sacrificed to, 7144
Reshef and, 7761
Seth emasculated by, 8233
as son of Isis, 4557, vol. 8 color insert
struggle with Seth, 5163
sun and, 8836–8837
Thoth restoring injured eye of, 9168
in triad, 9349
Hose, Charles, 1022
Hosea (biblical book), 879, **4136–4138**
authorship of, 4138
condemnation of idolatry in, 4358, 4359
Israelite religion criticized in, 4747–4748
language of, 935, 4138
Melqart in, 7129
pesher of, 7065
quotation from, in *Matthew,* 907
resurrection in, 7764
structure of, 4138
Hosea (prophet), **4136–4138**
on kissing holy objects, 9258
prophetic actions of, 7432
Hosha'nah Rabbah (day of Sukkot), practices on, 8834
Hōshang (mythic figure), 3629
Hoshino Tenchi, 3072
Hoshiuta (songs), 6300
Hosios (right behavior), in Septuagint, 7967
Hoskins, Janet, on Kodi healing rituals, 3815
Hospices. *See also* Khānagāh
in Byzantine Empire, 2582
Hospitality, **4138–4142**. *See also* Charity; Guests
as agricultural value, 192
Chabad House concept (Hasidic), 8173
curses and, 2100–2101
dharma of, in Hindu epic cosmology, 2017
in Hinduism, 2404
in Islam, 2401–2402
Hospitallers, women in, 6763
Hospitals
birth in, ritualization of, 7803
in Byzantine Empire, 2582
Christian, creation of, 3844
of Compassion Relief (Ciji), 1788
Islamic, history of, 3832
religious founding of, 1750
Hosso Buddhism, 5258
Hossori (chant), 6297–6298
Hossō school of Buddhism. *See also* Yogācāra school of Buddhism
Dharmapāla and, 2337, 2338
Saichō, criticism by, 8030
śūnyatā (emptiness) in, 8858–8859
vs. Tendai school, 1242, 9075, 9076, 9077
Hostiensis (cardinal-bishop), 5338
Host of Heaven (Israelite deities), 4742

Hosts. *See also* Hospitality; Potlatch
Abraham as patron saint of, 4139
Hot and cold. *See* Thermodynamics
Hotei (Laughing Buddha), humor and, 4208–4209
Høtherus (deity), 744
Hotṛ priests, 7405
Ṛgveda as province of, 3991
Hottentots. *See* Khoi and San religion
Hǫttr (hero), 9166
Houji (ancestor spirit)
star god associated with, 1591
worship of, 1583
Hou Ji (Lord Millet), 1625
and Zhou dynasty origin, 5178
Hourani, Albert, 4720
Hourglass drum, 2497, 2499
Hourglass figures, in megalithic religion, 5825
Houris (virgins)
in garden of paradise, 3282
in Qur'ān, 160
Hour of Decision (radio program), 7712
House. *See* Home
Householder life stage. *See* *Gṛhasthin*
Household guardians, in Slavic religion, 8436
House Made of Dawn (Momaday), 3091, 7225
House of Bishops, in Episcopal Church, 1766
House of Deputies, in Episcopal Church, 1766
House of Islam, The (Cragg), 9118
House of Judah, child abuse in, 6540
"House of Life" (Egypt), 2723, 2724
House of Love and Prayer (San Francisco), 4869
House of Nyahbingi, 7623, 7626
"House of Papa"
heiau and, 3796
in ceremony to Kū, 3799
Houses. *See* Home
Houston, Jean, 560
Houston, Stephen, 5943
on Mesoamerican ballgames, 751
Houteff, Victor, 1036, 5237, 6561
Hovevei Zion, Ginzberg (Asher) in, 3495
Hovhannes of Orot'n, Gregory of Datev and, 3693
Ḥovot ha-levanot (Baḥye), 313, 740
Hovsep I (Armenian catholicos), 488
Howard, Elizabeth, 833
Howard, James G., 6672
Howard, James H., 6672
Howe, LeAnne, 3093
Howell, Donna Wyant, 77
Howell, Leonard, 7623, 7624
Howell, Vernon. *See* Koresh, David
Howitt, A. W., **4142**
on Australian Indigenous religions
All-Father in, 265, 4142
existence of, 681
as first phase of study, 683
initiation ceremonies of, 681, 683
myths of, 663
new movements in, 682
on violence of colonialism, 680
Howling Dervishes, in Rifā'i Sufism, 8823
How to Eat to Live (Elijah Muhammad), 4688
"How to Remodel the Interior of a Catholic Church" (Alexie), 7226
"How to Serve the Cow" (Gandhi), 1467
Hoxha, Enver, 4677
Hoyle, Fred, steady state theory and, 2032
Ḥozeh (prophet), 7431
Hózhó (beauty or harmony), 4485, 6442
body symbolism and, 4160
Hózhóójí ceremony, 6442
Hpaya:laung (bodhisattva), 1329
Hrafnkels saga
Christian worldview in, 8024
pagan elements in, 8025
Ḥrm (sanctuary), *ḥaram* and *ḥawṭah* and, 3776–3777
Hrólfr (mythic figure), 9166
Hrólfs saga kraka (Germanic myth), 9166
Hrotsvit (Saxon canoness), **4142–4144**
Hrungnir (giant), 9166
Hsiao. *See* Xiao
Hsiao Pao-Chen. *See* Xiao Baozhen
Hsien. *See* Xian
Hsin-Hsing. *See* Xinxing
Hsi-Wang-Mu. *See* Xi Wang Mu
Hsu, Francis L. K., 1636
Hsüan-Tsang. *See* Xuanzang
Hsün-Tzu. *See* Xunzi (Xun Qing)
Hua, Mount, 5240
Hua (New Guinea), cannibalism among, 3169
Huacas (earth shrines or divinities), 4384–4385, 4386, 4411, 4412
Ayllus and, 8617–8618
and Catholic cult of saints
in colonial period, 8605–8606, 8609–8612
in modern period, 8619–8620
messianism and, 8604
in modern Andean religions, 8616, 8619
in pre-Incan Andean religions, 8602–8603
Spanish perceptions of, 8606–8609
veneration of, 5177
Huahu (conversion of the barbarians), Laozi and, 5317
Huahu jing (Daoist text), 2186, 2194, 5319
Huainan (China), 5493–5494
Huainanzi. *See* Liu An
Huainanzi (book)
authorship of, 5494
as comprehensive mythic history, 1623
contents of, 5494
Daoism represented in, 1574, 5494
li in, 5430–5431
paradox in, 6991
presented to emperor, 1590
Yi the archer in, 1627
zhenzen in, 9959
Huairang, Nanyue (Buddhist figure), 1292
Huairang (Buddhist monk), Mazu and, 8713–8714
Huaji (Chinese concept), acrobats and jesters as, 4205
Huang Bailu (Pierre Hoang), 1633
Huangbo school of Buddhism, 1524
Huangdi (Yellow Emperor deity), **4144–4145**
Huang-Lo school and, 1590
as model emperor, 1627
as patron deity of immortality, 1592
Shangdi and, 8299
Huangdi chi (August Earth God), earth cult and, 1911–1912
Huangdi neijing suwen (medical text), Huangdi and, 4144
Huang Kan, on *Analects,* 1899
Huanglao cult, 7719
Huang-Lao Dao (sacred teachings), Huangdi (Yellow Emperor deity) and, 4144
Huang Laojun, 1593
Huang-Lao school, 1590, 1591
Huang Lingwei, 2184
Huanglong sublineage, 1523
Huangmei monastic complex, 1521
Huangtian (heaven), 9172
Huang Tingjian (poet), 7214
Huangting jing (Scripture of the Yellow Court), 2205
Huang Zongxi, 1579
historical scholarship and, 1917–1918
on Study of Inner Mind, 1903
Huan Tan, 1592
Huanyuan (promise), 1620
Huari culture, llama sacrifices in, 1364
Huascar (Inca ruler), 566–567, 568
Huashan ji (Daoist text), 2208
Huastec religion (Mexico)
deities of, 5910
in Postclassic period, 5910
rituals in, 5910
Huatou method, 1293, 1524, 1646
Huayan jing (Buddhist text). *See also* Avataṃsaka Sūtra
Huayan Buddhism, role in, 4145–4147
Huayan school of Buddhism, 1238, **4145–4149**
buddhahood in, 1069
Dasheng qixin lun text, 1576
development of, 1094
doctrines of, 1163
Dushun as patriarch of, 2530
emptiness *(śūnyatā)* in, 8859
Faxiang school replaced by, 1600
Fazang and, 3012
history of, 4146–4147
in Korea, 1646
and Korean Buddhism, 1171
li in, 5431
masters of, 1577
nirvāṇa in, 6630–6631
philosophy of, 1302, 9177–9178
scriptural foundation of, 4145–4146
teachings of, 4147–4148
Zhiyan in, 9964–9965
Zongmi in, 9987
Huayana Cápac (Inca emperor), 566–567, 6576
Hubal (deity), 444
Hubbard, L. Ron, **4149–4150,** 6559
Scientology and, **8192–8194**
works of, 6530
Hubbard Dianetic Research Foundation, founding of, 4149
Hubble, Edwin, on Doppler shift and expanding universe, 2031
Hubbs, Joanna, 3587
Hubert, Henri, 2436
Durkheim (Émile) and, 2528
Mauss (Marcel) and, 5785
on sacrifice, 4183, 7844–7845, 8003
Hubias (spirits), in Caribbean religions, 1428
Hubris, in paradigm of evil, 2899
HUC-JIR. *See* Hebrew Union College-Jewish Institute of Religion
Hucks, Tracey, 79, 80–81
Huḍaybī, Ḥasan Ismā'il al-, 6315
Ḥudaybiyah, treaty of (628), 6226
Hu Dengzhou (Muslim scholar), 4632

Hudson, Charles M., 6672, 6694–6695
Hudson, W. H., Spencer (Herbert) and, 8679
Ḥudūd (punishment), 4566
Ḥuḍūr (presence), 4554
Huehuecoyotl (deity), 2464
Huehueteotl (deity), 5890, 5895, 5906
Huehuetls (drums), 7036
Huemac (king), 5889
Huet, Daniel, Hermetism and, 3950
Huet, Pierre-Daniel, 3050–3051
  on paganism and Judaism, 4039
Huffman, Thomas, on Zimbabwean stone birds, 8665
Hufford, David J., 3145, 3148
Hügel, Friedrich von, **4150,** 5207
Hugh (Benedictine monk), 821
Hughes, Langston, 3142
Hughes, Thomas, 3361
Hugh-Jones, Christine, structuralism and, 8751
Hugh of Fleury, on revolution, 7791
Hugh of Saint-Victor, **4150–4152**
  biblical exegesis of, 873–874
  on church and state relationship, 5150
  on knowledge, 5204
  on magic, 5577
  on mystical union, 6337
  numerology and, 6746
  theology of, 2384
  on "two books," 9422
  on world ages, 4028
Hugo, Gustav, 730
Hugo, Victor, 3062
  Gnosticism and, 3525
Hugolno di Segni (cardinal). *See also* Gregory IX
  and Franciscans, 3182, 3183
Hugo Sanctelliensis, on Hermetism, 3945
Huguenot Camisards, enthusiasm of, 2805
Huguenots
  Beza (Theodore) and, 851
  colony in Brazil, 1698
  in Reformation, 7662
Huh (deity), in Egyptian pantheon, 2705
Hui (guilds), 1616
Huichol religion (Mexico), **4152–4153**
  Christian elements in, 4152
  confession in, 1886, 7759
  deities of, 4152
  dogs in, 2394
  healing rituals of
    lying on soil in, 2559
    peyote in, 4153
  myths of
    animals in, 5938
    pilgrimage in, 5938
  paradise of, 3136
  peyote in, 7471, 9216
  ritual journey of, 5197
  sacred spaces in, 4152–4153
  tobacco in, 8456, 9216
  tricksters in, 9357
  truth in, 9370
Huidong (Chinese philosopher), Dai Zhen influenced by, 2129
Huiguan (common-origin association), 1616
Huiguan, on enlightenment, 2217
Huiguo (Buddhist monk)
  Kūkai and, 8349
  Shingon Buddhism and, 8351
Huihu jiao (Chinese term for Islam), 4631
Huike (Buddhist scholar), 1292, 1521
Hui Mālama I Nā Kūpuna O Hawai'i, 5342
Hui Muslims (China)
  clothing of, 4631
  economic status of, 4639
  education of, 4633–4634
  language of, 4630–4631, 4632
  in Ming period, 4632
  in Ningxia, 4638–4639
  persecution of, 4636–4637
  rebellion of, 4633
  religious practices of, 4638–4639
  Śūfī, 4635
  in Xinjiang, 4640
Huineng (Buddhist teacher), **4153–4155**
  on awakening, 5200
  on enlightenment, 6631
  and iconoclasm, 4284
  oral teaching and, 8713
  as sixth patriarch of Chan Buddhism, 1522, 1601, 4154
  on spiritual guides, 8708
  writings of, 1302
Huiopatoria doctrine, Cyril of Jerusalem on, 2118
Hui Shi, 1572
Huisi (Buddhist monk), 1249, 9174
Huitu (Impure Lands), 7502
Huitzilopochtli (deity), **4155–4156**
  androgynous deities replaced by, 3411
  birth of, 5890, 5892, 5937
  bread in shape of, 1041
  cosmic sacrifice of, 4187–4188
  cosmogony of, 716
  Coyolxauhqui and, 4188
  as culture hero, 5937
  deification of, 5890
  eagle as symbol of, 2553, 4155
  human sacrifice for, 719
  and migration, 718, 5890, 5937
  moon and, 6174
  as sun god, 8842
  temples to, 5891, 9266
  Templo Mayor of, 5892
  tobacco and, 8455
Huiwen (Buddhist monk), 9174
Huiyan, in Pure Land Buddhism, 4922
Hŭiyang-san school of Buddhism (Korea), 1172
Huiyuan (Buddhist monk), 1163–1164, 1236, **4156–4157**
  and Amitābha
    cult to, 1596
    popularization of, 3155
  Dao'an and, 1576
  Huayan Buddhism and, 4146
Huizinga, Johan, on play, 3265, 3266, 4201–4202, 7194, 8725
Huizong (Chinese emperor), 1602, 2186, 7267, 9057
  and music in Korea, 6296
Ḥujaj al-nūbuwah (al-Jāḥiẓ), 4371
Ḥujjah (proof), 4395
Ḥujjatul-Islām (proof of Islam), as hawzah classification, 3801
Hujwīrī, al-, **4157**
  on God, unity of, 3566
  on 'Alī ibn Abī Ṭālib, 260
  on *mi'rāj,* 6061
  on *quṭb* (axis) and cosmic hierarchy, 8821
  on *samā'* (listening parties), 8065
  on *ṣuḥbah* ("companionship"), 8826
  Ṣūfī manual by, 956, 4647
Ḥukm (divine injunction)
  in Sikhism, in *Ādi Granth,* 32
  in Sunnism *vs.* Twelver Shiism, 8342–8343
Hūlegū (Mongol ruler of Iran), 9408–9409
Hu-ling (mountain), 1501
Huli religion (Papua New Guinea), deities of, 2006
Hulme, Kathryn, 3711
Hulme, Kerri, 3085
Hulme, Peter, 9295
Hultkrantz, Åke, 2543, 2611, 9414, 9418
  on goddesses, 3588, 3589
  historiography of, 4047
  on knowledge, 5199
  on North American Indian religions, 6671, 6721
  on phenomenology of religion, 7086
  on Sun Dance, 8844
Ḥulwānī, al-, Ḥanābilah and, 3765
Humanae vitae (Paul VI), 6975, 7012–7013, 9540
Human beings and human nature. *See also* Human body
  Adam and, 30
  in African religions, 84, 85, 89, 142
    in Luba religion, 5523
    in Lugbara religion, 5527
  and afterlife, beliefs about, 130–131, 140–141
  as aid to gods' greatness, 2137
  alchemy's conception of, 236–237
  in Amazonian religions, in Baniwa religion, 8624
  ambivalence of, Jung (C. G.) on, 5114
  animals as distinct from
    in myths, 5198
    religion in, 2913
  as "animal symbolicum" in Cassirer, 1448
  Aristotle on, 7111
  attribution of qualities of, to natural objects, 5185
  Augustine on, 627, 7025, 7026, 7027, 7353
  behavior of
    natural selection of, 2916–2917
    universals in, 2867–2868
  bonds of, 5198
  in Buddhism, 5448, 7364–7365, 7366, 7678
    elements of, 8551
    in Yogācāra Buddhism, 9900
    Werner (Karel) on, 8548
  in Chinese tradition
    Cheng Hao on, 1561
    Han Fei Zi on, 3772–3773
    Mengzi on, 1572, 5857–5858, 5859
    in myth of Yu, 1626
    as psycho-physical whole, 1589
    qi and, 8555
    xian, 9856
    Xunzi on, 1573
  in Christianity
    Gaia hypothesis and, 3253–3254
    gender and, 3357
    memento mori and, vol. 1 color insert
    nature subjugated by, 2648
    Ruusbroec (Jan van) on, 7948–7949
  comparativism at level of, 1880
  in Confucianism, 2631–2634, 9674
    Old Text school, 1575
    self-transformation, 1895–1897, 1900–1901
    Zhu Xi on, 9973
  as constellations, in ethnoastronomy, 2863
  corruption in, in Judeo-Christian tradition, 8404
  cosmologies, prominent place in, 1992–1993
  creation/origin of
    in Qur'ān, 5060
    myths on (*See* Anthropogony)
  Dai Zhen on, 2129
  in Daoism, 2177
  deity as symbol of perfection of, 2256
  destruction of, in Egyptian mythology, 2720

development of
Freud (Sigmund) on, 2239
Haeckel (Ernst) on, 2239
in Dogon religion, 2392
earth and, relation with (*See* Ecology)
Eckhart (Johannes) on, 2603
Eddy (Mary Baker) on, 2696
Edwards (Jonathan) on, 2699–2700
Egyptian concept of, 2710–2711
elephants and, 2750
encounter with God, 7118
the Enlightenment on, 1693
environmental dependence of, in religious tradition, 2606
equivocal position of, between nature and culture, 7796
eremitism and, 2829
Eriugena on, 2831
eternity and, encounter with, 2854–2855
evil, inclination toward, in Judeo-Christian tradition, 8404
evil in condition of, 2898–2899
evil initiated by, 2899–2900
existence of, 2925–2926
Freud (Sigmund) on, 7112
globalization and, 3502–3503
as good, 1344
Greek gods depicted as, 4321, 4363
Heidegger (Martin) on, 7111
heredity in, 2879–2880
hermeneutics and, 3933
as heroes, 2816
in Hinduism
animals and, 359
nature of, 5447
Hobbes (Thomas) on, 5367
Hocking (William Ernest) on, 4076
as *homo religiosus,* 4110
imago Dei (image of God)
consciousness of sin and, 8403
Irenaeus on, 8405
immortality of
former, 2770
Gersonides on, 4895
Ibn Rushd on, 4895
imperfection of, 7039, 7040
in African religions, 84
in Ch'ŏndogyo, 1648
individual *vs.* collective nature of, 7796–7797
as information systems, in cybernetics, 2111–2112
in Konkōkyō, 5225
in Otomí religion, 6927
in Upaniṣads, 9544
in Islam
'Abduh (Muḥammad) on, 5067
Mu'tazilah on, 6323–6324
philosophy on, 2652
Qur'ān on, 4564
Waṣīyah on, 5062
in Israelite religion, 4743–4744
jaguars and, 4762
in Jainism, 2625
in Judaism
environmental responsibilities of, 2643–2644, 2645
God's relation to, 4894
in justification, 5039
Kant (Immanuel) on, 5077, 5079, 7109
Kierkegaard on, 5142, 7117
in Korean thought, Neo-Confucianism and, 1931
Lessing (G. E.) on, 5417
life of (*See* Life)
Locke (John) on, 5368
in Malay religion, makeup of, 3810
in Manichaeism, 5652
Marx (Karl) on, 7112
Maximos the Confessor on, 5793
monkeys as degraded, 6150–6151
as monsters, 6163, 6165
names of, 6409–6411
in New Age teachings, Summit Lighthouse, 1782
Nietzsche on, 6616
in North American Indian iconography, 4310
as oracles, 6834–6836
order accessible to, in *Ecclesiastes,* 2600
Origen on, 6889, 8406
origins of (*See* Anthropogony)
in Orthodox theology, 2590
in otherworld, 6925
Pascal on, 7002–7003
Pelagius on, 7025, 7026, 7027, 7353
perfectibility of (*See* Perfectibility, of human beings)
in Protestantism, 7454
and quests, 7553
reflexivity of, 7648
responsibility of
to creation, 2654
ethic of, 4949
in Roman Catholicism, 7454
and medical ethics, 5811
Sartre (Jean Paul) on, 7117
sociality of, religion in, 2669
Soloveitchik (Joseph Baer) on, 8518–8519
Sozzini (Fausto Pavolo) on, 8673, 8674
in Sumerian religion, 5964
Swedenborg (Emanuel) on, 8899
Teilhard de Chardin (Pierre) on, 9033–9034
Tillich (Paul) on, 7111
in Unity, 9473
unity among, and Christian unity, 2689
violence innate in, 9598
in Vodou, 9636–9637
work by, 9797–9798
in Yap culture, 5183
in Zoroastrianism, 9995–9996
Human body, **4157–4174**. *See also* Human beings and human nature
in African religions, of king, 5170
African views of
and afterlife, 140–141
in art, 4302, 4303
house correlated with, in Dogon religion, 4104
in Luba religion, 5523
Amazonian longhouses and, 8622
as art, 499
art and, **4168–4174**
ashes on, 540
Australian views of
and afterlife, 144
in myths, 662–663
Āyurvedic view of, 3854–3855
in Baltic religion, 763–764
beauty of, 811–813
celibacy and low view of, 1475
as charisma, 1548
Chinese view of, 3859–3861
"three corpse worms" and, 3862
in Christian Science, 1746, 2696
Christian views of
and dance, 2135, 2152–2153
in funeral rites, 142
gender and, 3357–3358
health and, 3848
as incidental or detrimental, 142
negative *vs.* positive, 3357
original sin and, 4164
in Orthodox deification, 2591
Paul on, 156, 2135, 2153, 7018
corporate (social) symbolism, 4161–4162, 4169
cosmology represented by, 1503, 4159–4160, 4171
in Daoism, 2177–2178, 2183
environment and, 2635–2636
longevity of, soul and, 8556
in ritual practices, 9843
dichotomy between spirit/soul and
and afterlife, 130, 140, 168–169
and asceticism, 528–529
disabilities and, 4166–4167
discipline of the, 8704–8705
dualism of body and soul, 4158–4159
female
in religious writings, 4163–4166
spirit possession and, 8696
theological significance of, 3037
in feminist spirituality, 9788
gender and, **4163–4168**
female body in religious writings, 4163–4166
personhood accounts and, 4163
"return to the body" theorizing, 4166–4167
in gender studies, 3300
in gender *vs.* sex, 3420–3421
Greek view of divine beauty and, 4168, 4169
hierophany (manifestation of the sacred) and, 3971
Hindu view of
cosmology and, 2015, 2016
mother goddess and, 4164–4165
pollution and, 4164
Rāmānuja on, 7615–7616
in Tantrism, liberation through, 4003
humors of (*See* Humors of the body)
images of, vol. 13 color insert
and iconoclasm, 4281
as microcosm, vol. 3 color insert
in Islam, 2153
soul and, 8567
Japanese view of
balance/imblance and purity/impurity, 3867–3868
natural state of, 3868
in Judaism, 2153
body and soul in, 3831
Sa'adyah Gaon on, 7953
kinship and, 5183–5184
in Langkawi culture, 5184
maṇḍala mapped onto, 1350
marking of (*See* Bodily marks)
as medium of belief, vol. 13 color insert
Mesoamerican views of, and afterlife, 149–151
as microcosm of universe, vol. 3 color insert
as model of cosmos, 7837
myths and symbolism of, **4158–4163**
in art, 4169–4170

Human body *continued*
naked (*See* Nudity)
organic matter, problematic of, 4158
in Orphism, evil in, 8405
painting of, vol. 13 color insert
posture and, 4171
qi and, 1589, 1597
resurrection of (*See* Resurrection)
in rites of passage, 7859
in rituals, 7834, 7844, 7853
in Roman Catholicism, and medical ethics, 5811
sacred space, body symbolism in, 7982–7983
separation from, in Heaven's Gate movement, 3890–3891
as ship, 991, 992
soul flight as body-based metaphor, 8277
soul located in, 8532, 8533
in Spiritualism, 8717
in Tantrism, 8991–8993
as vehicle for religious experience, 7834
Western cultural attitudes (classical, medieval, and modern), 4168
in Zoroastrianism, 9996
Human cloning. *See* Cloning
Human condition
Buddha on, 8547
soteriology and, 8526
Human consciousness, of deity, 2258–2261
Human (Buberian) dialogue, 2344
Human Direction, The (Peacock and Kirsch), 379
Humaneness *(ren). See Ren*
Human ethology, 2867–2868
Human flourishing, in Buddhism, ecology of, 2629
Human Genome Project, 2882, 5813
Humani generis (Pius XII), 6974
Human Individual Metamorphosis (HIM) movement, Heaven's Gate and, 3890
Humanism, **4174–4178**. *See also* Secular humanism
of Benedict (Ruth), 820
of Bucer (Martin), 1059
of Calvin, 1374, 1375
civic, 4175
Culianu (Ioan Petru) on, 2079
of Eck (Johann), 2601
of Eliade, religion as key to, 2755
in Ethical Culture, 2858
Haydon (A. Eustace) as founder of, 3803
in Hungary, 4226
Islamic, 6099
Judaism influenced by, 5016
meaning of term, 4174
northern (in Europe outside Italy), 4176–4177
Hermetism and, 3948
Servetus (Michael) and, 8231
skepticism and, 8421
in Orientalism, 6882
of Pico della Mirandola (Giovanni), 7141
of Pius II, 6972
radical, of Ibn al-ʿArabī, 4570
Reformation and, 4177, 7657
and reformed theology, 7388–7389
of Renaissance
Culianu (Ioan Petru) on, 2079
historiography in, 4039
intellectuals and, 4514
overview of, 4174–4176
textual criticism in, 4029
traditions attacked by, 1691
in Solomonic works, 9763
and tourism, 9261
of Wang Yangmin, 9675
Humanism and Democratic Criticism (Said), 6881–6882
Humanistic Buddhism, Foguangshan and, 3139–3140
Humanistic psychology, 7476–7477, 7485
Humanitarianism, Schweitzer (Albert) and, 8179
Humanities
in ecology and religion studies, 2609
in environmental studies, 2609
study of religion in, 2761
Human Knowledge (Russell), 2427
Human life, length of, 2236–2237
Human nature. *See* Human beings
Human Nature (Hobbes), laughter in, 4221–4222
Human Phenomenon, The (Teilhard de Chardin), 9032, 9033
Human potential movement, 6568
child socialization and education in, 6542
holistic health and, 3851–3852
Human rights, **4178–4182**
collective rights *vs.*, 5341, 5364
culture and, 5364
definitions of, 5362
as ecumenical concern, 2685
engaged Buddhism and, 2785
equality, and tensions among worldviews, 4181
international declarations on, 4178, 4179–4180
international developments in, 5362, 5363
in Latin America, 5364
laws concerning, 5330–5331, **5362–5366**
legal protection of, 5363
naturalization of, 5365
origins and evolution of, 5362
religion and, 5330–5331, **5362–5366**
compatibility/incompatibility arguments on, 5363–5364
proselytization and, 5364
religious issues in, 4179–4181
United Declaration of, 7704
Universal Islamic Declaration of Human Rights, 7704
for women, in Muslim countries, 3366, 3367
women's rights and, 5364–5365
and world politics, place of religion in, 4178–4179
Human Rights Watch, focus of, 4181
Human sacrifice, 2242–2243, **4182–4191**
in Africa
Bunyoro, 2577
for Luba chief, 5171
in myths, 95–96, 99
for Rukuba king, 5170
as agricultural rite, 9578
in Arabian religions, 445
in Athens, 1459
in Aztec religion, 719, 2242, 3244, **4185–4191,** 5891–5892
as agricultural ritual, 9578
cannibalism and, 1403
caves and, 1469
charisma and, 1548
controversy over, 4190–4191
cosmic time and, 7988
cosmology of, 4187
decapitation and, 3805–3806, 4190
as deity impersonation, 4189, 7957
description by Díaz del Castillo, 4185
functions of, 719
Huitzilopochtli and, 4155, 4187–4188
mass, 719
practice and paraphernalia of, 4188–4190
as sign of power, 5173
and social world of center and periphery, 4186–4187
themes in, 4184
Brundage (Burr) on, 4185
cannibalistic (*See* Cannibalism)
Carrasco (David) on, 8009
in Chinese religion, 169
in foundation rites, 4105
Keightley (David) on, 4183
to royal ancestors, 1570–1571
dismemberment in, 2366, 2367
divine sacrifice and, 7957
Europe, infant sacrifices in
in Black Masses, 8250
in Khlysty sect, 8248
in foundation rites, 4105
in goddess worship, 3590
in Greek religion, Artemis and, 507
in Hawaiian religion
heiau and, 3796, 3797
in *luakini* ritual, 3798–3799
themes in, 4184
head hunting and decapitation in, 3805–3806, 3807
heart in, 3881
in Hinduism, sati (*See* Sati)
in Hun religion, 4229
in Igbo religion, 4366
in Inca religion, 1364
gender in, 3417
heart symbolism in, 3881
in Indo-European religions, 4454
in Indonesia, for agricultural reasons, 5277
in Japanese religion, 4183–4184
in Jonestown, Guyana, 4184
martyr as, 5738
in Maya religion, 1472–1473, 2242, 3243, 4187, 5884
in Mesoamerican religions
afterlife and, 149
heart symbolism in, 3881
in Huastec religion, 5910
in Otomí religion, 5909
to Tlaloc, 9214
in Tlaxcalan religion, 9215
in Toltec religion, 9222, 9223
in Totonac religion, 5911, 9254
in Moabite religion, 6094–6095
in Neolithic religions, Near Eastern, 6461
in North American Indian religions, 6654
Oceanic religions and, 6789
overview, **4182–4185**
in Phoenician religion, 4580, 7132, 7134
in Polynesian religions, 7309
in purification, 7509
purposes of, 4183
in Scythian religion, 4489
in South American religions
in Andean religions, pre-Inca, 8603
in Muisca religion, 6230
substitutions for, 7999
themes of, 4183–4184
theoretical perspectives on, 4183
in Thracian religion, 9169
to Óðinn, 6809

in Vedism, 9564
Agnicayana (fire sacrifice), 4184
violence of, 9598–9599
Human sciences, Dilthey's (Wilhelm) theory of, 2353
Humāyūn (Mughal emperor), 4646, 4647
Humbach, Helmut, 9412
Humbard, Rex, television ministry of, 7711–7712
Humbert of Moyenmoutier, Gregory VII and, 3689
Humbert of Romans, manual for Crusade preachers by, 2076
Humbert of Silva Candida
Cerularios excommunicated by, 2586
oath formulated by, 837
Humble Attempt, An (Edwards), 2699
Humboldt, Alexander von, on relativism, 7685
Humboldt, Wilhelm von
on androgynes, 340
on Mesoamerican religions, 5940
Hume, David, **4191–4194**
and animism, 364, 365
on atheism, 577, 583
British empiricism and, 4192
in British Enlightenment, 2797
on causality, 3557
on chance, 1527
empiricism and, 2778–2780
on existence of God, 7124–7125
on experience, 7118
on free action, 3200
historical and philosophical approaches to religion, 4035, 4040, 10076
Kant on, 4192
on knowledge, 2427, 5206
on law and morality, 5368
metaphysics of, 5991
on miracles, 1528, 4193
moral philosophy of, 4192–4193
on mysticism, anthropomorphism and, 390–391
and mythology, study of, 6366
on reason, 8492
refutation of Lucretius' reflections on chance, 3002
on relativism, 7685
on religion, 4193, 7125
skepticism and, 8421
on source of religion, 3044
on suicide, 8830
on transcendence of God, 9283
on "two books," 9423
Humiliation of the Saints ritual, in Benedictine monasteries, 2105
Humility
doubt as expression of, 2428
laughter as expression of, 2428
in poems, 7219
Hummel, Siegbert, 5645
Humor, **4194–4223**. *See also* Laughter; Tricksters
in Anishinaabe religion, 369
anticlerical, 3162
arts and, 4209
in Buddhism, 4199–4200, 4202, 4207
children and, 4199, 4211–4212
in Christianity
in Carnival, 4198
folly and, 4202
in New Testament, 4196–4197
in popular theology, 4203
rejection of humor in, 4200
ridicule and, 4200
in rituals, 4197
clowns and, 1839, 4198
and congruity *vs.* incongruity, 4194, 4221, 4222
in Daoism, 4206–4207
dark side of, 4199–4201
in divinatory practices, East Asian, 4208
in East Asian contexts, **4205–4210**
and everyday life *vs.* religion, 4211
in exorcism, 8692
in Islam, **4210–4218**
in *adab* literature, 4214–4215
critiques and dialog, 4215–4216
curses and, 4213
in everyday life, 4211–4213
in Qūr'an and *ḥadīths,* 4197, 4211, 4212
subaltern resistance and, 4213
in Sufism, 4202, 4211
tricksters in, 4210–4211, 4213–4214
in Judaism, 4195–4196, 4202–4204
in myths, 4194–4197, 6363–6365
as overlooked, 4203–4204
overview, **4194–4205**
reappraisal and celebrations of, 4201–4203
ridicule and satire, 4200–4201
ritual and, 4197–4199
in sacred texts, and literature, 4194–4197
trickster figures and, 4194–4195
in Western theology and philosophy, **4218–4223**
in 20th century, 4211–4222
condemnation of laughter in, 4218
Feast of Fools and, 4198, 4218 (*See also* Fools, Feast of)
Hegel (G. W. F.) on, 4201, 4219–4220
Kierkegaard (Søren) on, 4220–4221
in Reformation and Protestantism, 4219
Thomas Aquinas on, 4218–4219
Humors of the body
doṣas in Āyurveda, 3854–3855
as Tibetan *nyes pa,* 3865
in Islamic medicine, 3832
tears in, 9025
Humphrey, Caroline, 7853
Humphrey, Chuck, 6556
Humphrey, Doris, 2158–2159
Humphrey, Hubert, 6613
Humphreys, Christmas, 1188
Hun (heavenly aspect of soul), 1043
death and, 1589
ghosts and, 1605
yinyang and, 8554, 8555
Hunahpu (mythic figure), 5797, 5935
as culture hero, 5937
Ḥunayn ibn Isḥāq, 2971
Arabic translation of Bible by, 894
Galen's works translated by, 3256
Greek philosophers translated by, 7192
Hundred Days Reform, defeat of, Kang Yuwei and, 5075
Hundred Letters (al-Dīn Manērī), 7770
Hundred Schools, 1572
Hundred Years' War, Joan of Arc in, 4929–4930
Hundun (chaos), 1540, 1624–1625
Hunfalvy, Pál, 3112
Hungarian Diet (1579), 973
Hungary and Hungarian religion, **4224–4228**. *See also* Finno-Ugric religions; Slavic religion
Austro-Hungarian dual monarchy and, 1685
birds in, 948
cattle herding in, 3108
Christianity
establishment of, 4224
history of, 1684
Mary in, 4225
overview of, 4225–4226
pagan uprisings against, 4225
Protestantism, 1685
Reformation and Counter-Reformation in, 4226
women's monasteries, 6763
Chuvash religion and, 1785
Dömötör (Tekla) studying, 2415–2416
early religion, 4224–4225
Finno-Ugric comparative linguistic research in, 3111, 4224–4225
folk beliefs in, 4226, 4227
folk customs of, 2415–2416
folklore and mythology of, Reguly (Antal) and, 7673–7674
historiography in, 4046
history of study of, 4226–4227
humanism, occulting, and alchemy in, 4226
Islam, 4224, 4678
Judaism
Holocaust and revival of, 4227
kashrut laws of, 5107
migrations and expulsions, 4224
Orthodox, 3793, 6898, 6899–6900
Satmar Hasidism in, 3793
Sofer (Mosheh) and, 8507
tsaddiq in, 9382
May Day in, 1515
new religions in, 4226, 4227
prehistoric, 4224, 7378, 7379
shamanism in, 2415
sorcerers in, 1785
studies of, 3112
study of religion in, 8772, 8773, 8774, 8775
Uniate church in, 9464
Hungwe religion (Africa), origin myth in, 8663
Hun Hunahpu (mythic figure), 5935
Hunkapi (Lakota sacred rite), 5297
Hun religion, **4228–4229**. *See also* Inner Asia
Huns, 4490–4491
invading Europe, 4490
language of, 4491
Romans and, 4490–4491
sources on, 4490
Hunsinger, Deborah van Duesen, 7487
Hunt, Eva, 1517, 9357
on Mesoamerican religions, 5943
Hunt, George L., 6671
Hunt, Harry, on shamanistic visions, 8277
Hunt, Lynn, on social categories, 8470
Hunt, Robert, 2952
Hunt, Stephen J., 6527
Hunter, Edward, 1030

Hunter, Tera, 10038
Hunter-gatherer communities
of Australian Indigenous people, 636
communal meals in, 7957
consciousness of, 2282
and dreams, 2488
in East Africa, 2566
in Japan, *kami* in, 5072
Mesoamerican, 5880
monotheism and, Schmidt (Wilhelm) on, 8168–8169
in Paleolithic period, 6948, 6951
prayer and sacrifice in, 3173
psychedelic drug use in, 7468–7469
in rural India, 4432
sacrifice in, 7997, 8003
Schmidt (Wilhelm) on, 8168
shift to agriculture, 186
visions of, 9614–9615
Hunting
in African religious drama, 2456, 2457
animal skulls in rituals and, 3804
in Anishinaabe religion, 369
by Arctic people
animal ceremonialism in, 471, 9394
culture of, 468, 472, 4527
by Artemis, 506–507
in balance of life, in indigenous traditions, 2618
in Buriat religion, 1325
central Bantu cults of, 1509, 1510
confession and, 1884
cults of affliction and, 62
deities associated with, 3622
morphology of, 3617
in Dolgan religion, 2395
and Finno-Ugric religions, 3107
gardening and, 3279–3280
and gender roles, 3421
Japanese prehistoric, mountain cults and, 8379
in Komi religion, 5218
by Lipan Apaches, 404
lord of the animals and, 5513–5516
in Mesopotamian iconography, 4315
and New Year festivals, 6590–6591
in North American Indian drama, 2459
in North American Indian religions, 6653–6654
in Pygmy religions, 7524, 7525
and ritual care of animal bones, 1014
sacrifice as rooted in, 8008–8009
in Sami religion, 8087
sexual imagery and, 3974
in South American Indian religions
animal dances and, 8581
rituals over slain animals, 8582
in Southern Siberian religions, 8669–8672
as symbolic ritual, 2606
in winter carols, 9743, 9744
Huntington, Samuel
on clash of civilizations, 3502
on value system conflicts, 4178
Hunyuan huangdi sheng ji (Daoist text), 5319
Hunyuan shengji (Daoist text), 2209
Huoiou (deity), in Island Carib religion, 1427
Huot Tath, 3077
Hupashiya (mythic figure), Inara and, 4069, 4070
Hupa tribe (North America), 574
ballgame played by, 752
Hupostasis. See Hypostasis
Ḥuppa (wedding canopy), 7821–7822
Ḥūr (wives), in Islamic paradise, 2837
Hurā (drink), 849
Huracán (deity), 3063, 9255
Hurā Purā (hero), 4436
Hurgronje, Christiaan Snouck. *See* Snouck Hurgronje, Christiaan
Huria Kristen Batak Protestan (HKBP), 800
Hurley Burly (Rabe), 2477
Hurll, Estelle, 499
Huron religion (North America)
ballgame played in, 753–754
concept of *oki* in, 6680
creation story of, 3223
moon in, 6173–6174
dice games of, 3261
Feast of the Dead in, 6684
funerary rites in, 6684
masks of, 4542
Midwinter festival of, 4543
naming ceremony of, 6683
power charms in, 6684
shamanism in, 6686
study of, 6672
transmigration belief of, 9326
Hurray, Lady, Canaanite religion and, 1398–1399
Hurrian religion, **4229–4233**. *See also* Anatolia and Anatolian religions; Hittite religion and society
assimilations in, 4229–4230
deities of (*See also specific deities*)
adopted into Canaanite religion, 1384
adopted into Hittite religion, 4068, 4069
in Eblaite religion, 2597
pantheon in, 4230–4231
deus otiosus in, 2311
Heshshi the Hunter in, 4070
myth cycles in, 4231–4232
Reshef in, 7760
at Ugarit, 1381
worship in, 4232
Hurricanes, attributed to monsters, 6163
Hursag (deity), 5953
anthropomorphism of, 5950
Enlil and, 5952
Hurston, Zora Neale, 76, 77
on hoodoo, 3142
Ḥurūf al-Ḥayy, 728
Hurūfī sect of Islam, letter mysticism in, 274
Hurun, Mount, cargo cults and, 1418
Hurwitz, Jacob Isaac, 9380
Hurwitz, Yosef Yosl, 6242
Hus, Jan, **4233–4234**
death of, 6190
execution for heresy, 4233–4234
martyrdom of, 5739
and Moravians, 6190
teachings condemned by council at Constance, 2043
Ḥusām al-Dīn, Rūmī (Jalāl al-Dīn) and, 7936
Ḥusayn, Ṣaddām, 5088–5089
Muslim Brotherhood under, 6316
Ḥusayn, Ṭāhā, Qur'anic exegesis of, 7568
Ḥusayn I (shah of Iran), al-Majlisī under, 5623
Ḥusayn Bāyqarā, ʿAlī Shīr Navāʾī and, 263
Ḥusaynī, Shāh Karīm al-. *See* Aga Khan IV
Ḥusayn ibn ʿAlī, al-, **4234–4236**
as *ahl al-bayt,* 198
as Fāṭimah's son, 3008
burial of, in numerous places, 7687
death of, as self-sacrifice, 8830–8831
devotional allegiance to, 9819
history of, 4234–4235
Imāmīyah lineage traced through, 8321
legacy, martyrology, and commemoration, 4235–4236
martyrdom of, 1517, 4235, 5088, 5089, 5740
and ʿĀshūrāʾ, 549–550, 7285
commemoration of, 4572
in Shīʿī eschatology, 2838
mahdī after, 5982
public lamentation for, 7631, 7632
Zaynab and, 9937–9938
Ḥusayn ibn Mansur. *See* Ḥallāj, al-
Ḥusayniyah movement, Muṭarrifīyah *vs.,* 8325
Húsdrápa, Baldr in, 743–744
Hu Shi, 1579
on Dai Zhen, 2129
ru, reconception of (Confucianism), 1922
Hu Shi (Chinese intellectual), 1167
Ḥushiʾel, 4990
Husk Faces (Iroquois), 4542
Huss, John. *See* Hus, Jan
Husserl, Edmund, **4236–4238**
conversion of, 4237
Gnosticism and, 3527
metaphysics of, 5991
ontology of, 6831
on phenomenology, 7088, 7089, 7098–7099
Hussites
Hus (Jan), influence of, 4234
pacifist teachings of, 6648
Hut, Hans, 304
Hutash (deity), 6662
Hutcheson, Francis, on humor, 4201
Hutchinson, Anne, **4238**
Hutten, Ulrich von, on humanism *vs.* Scholasticism, 4176
Hutter, Jacob
and Anabaptism, 304, 4239
Hutterian Brethren and, 4239
Hutterian Brethren (Hutterites), **4238–4239**
dress code and social control among, 1835–1836
ecclesiology of, 1774
membership in, growth of, 6538
origins of, 304
persecution in Europe, 6567
on separation of church and state, 1968
Hutu (deity), 2298
Huve (mythic figure), 94
Huveane (mythic figure), 94
Huwaydī, Fahmī, on *ḥadīths,* 3732
Huxley, Aldous, 2476, 2679, 3061
on religious experience, 7695
on spirit possession, 8691
Huxley, Julian, 2909, 7049, 9032
evolutionary ethics of, 2919
Huxley, T. H., 6243
Huxley, Thomas, 2909–2910
and agnosticism, 5208
evolutionary ethics opposed by, 2918
Hu Yaobang, 1158
Huygens, Christiaan, 6588
Spinoza (Baruch) and, 8682
Huysman, Roelof, German humanism and, 4176
Huysmans, Joris-Karl, 3062
Hwach'ŏng (chant), 6297
Hwadam. *See* Sŏ Kyŏngdŏk
Hwadu method, 1646. *See also* Huatou method
Hwang-wung (Korean ruler), heavenly descent of, 5179
Hwanin (deity), 5229
Hwaŏm school of Buddhism, 9437. *See also* Huayan school of Buddhism
Chinul and, 1646
Hwarang movement (Korea), 1171

Hyacinthus, 425
Hyades (constellation), in ethnoastronomy, 2865, 2866
Hyakumantō darani (Dhāraṇī of one million pagodas), 4810
Hybridity
colonial, 1858–1859
syncretism *vs.,* 8936
Hybrid religions. *See* Syncretism
Hyde, Thomas, on dualism, 2505
Hyder, Qurratulain, 10035
Hydra (mythical monster), 6165
killed by Herakles, 3916
Hyenas, in African myths, 92
Hyers, M. Conrad, on humor in Islam, 4211
Hyksos kings (Egypt), 2706
Joseph and, 4956
Hyma, Albert, 9159
Hymes, Robert, 7268
Hymir (giant), 2692, 9165
Hymiskviða, 2692, 5509
Hymn from Kyme, Isis in, 3606
Hymn of the Pearl, 7024
Hymns. *See also* Music; *Psalms*
in African Independent Churches, 103
Shembe (Isaiah) and, 8316
Anishinaabe, 370
in *bhakti,* 9572
Buddhist, 1111
in Chinese Classic of Odes, 1906
Christian
in Africa, 6259
Ambrose and, 288
in China, 6292
of Ephraem of Syria, 2813
at funerals, 142
of Grundtvig (Nikolai Frederik Severin), 3705
of John of Damascus, 4941
poetry of, 7207, 7218
in Protestant worship, 1668–1669
in sacraments, 2592
of Symeon the New Theologian, 8920
of Syriac Orthodox Church, 8941
of Wesley (Charles), 5998
devotion in, 2319
Egyptian, 2716, 2723–2724
to Amun, 301
Hindu
and *bhakti,* 858
by Māṇikkavācakar, 5671
in Vaiṣṇavism, 9501
Jain, 4771
women and, 3329
Jewish
on Passover, 7003–7004
in Pseudepigrapha, 904
kingdom of God in, 5152
in magic, Greco-Roman, 5574
scripture in, 8200
Sikh, 8394
of Nānak, 6413
Vedic, 9550–9551 (*See also* Vedas)
ceremonial use of, 4426–4427
to Indra, 4467
Zoroastrian, in Avesta, 709
Hymns against Heresies (Ephraem of Syria), 786, 787
Hymnscroll (Manichaean text), 5669
Hymn to the Aton (Egypt), 2711
Hymn to Zeus (Callimachus), 3664
Hyndla, 2693
Hyndluljóð, 2693
Hypatia (Neoplatonist philosopher), 2710
Synesius of Cyrene and, 1677, 1678
Hyperion (moon of Saturn), 1543
Hypnos (deity), as sleep personified, 8439
Hypnosis
of Cayce (Edgar), 559
in shamanic healing, 8278
Hypnotic trance, 7048
Hypogea (rock tombs), 1472
Hypostasis (Greek concept), **4239–4243**
in Christology, 2583
in early Christianity, 4241–4242
in Gnosticism, 4241, 4242
in Greek philosophy, 4240
in history of religions scholarship, 4242–4243
meaning of term, 4240
Philo's use of, 4240–4241
sacrifice as, 8003
in Septuagint, 4240
time and, 7991
in Trinity, 2583
wisdom as, 4079
Hypostasis of the Archons, The, reality in, 4242
Hypostyle mosques, 6208–6209
Hypotheseis tōn planōmenon (Ptolemy), 7492
Hypothetical consonance model, on science and religion, 8186
Hysteria
accusations of, women marginalized through, 2694
trance compared to, 59

I

I, Robot (Asimov), 512
Iah (deity), 2706–2707
IAHR. *See* International Association for the History of Religions
Ialdabaoth (demiurge), 2274
Iambe (mythic figure), 803
Iamblichus
Babyloniaka, 3053
on contact with the dead, 1459
on fasting, 2996
on hypostases, 4240
metaphysics of, 5990
on numbers, 6746
as Porphyry's pupil, 7191
on Pythagoras, 6050
on Pythagoreanism, 7530
on secret symbolic language, 8907
and theurgy, 6474, 9157
on unity, 6474
I Am movement, **4245–4247**
beliefs of, 4246
breakaway groups of, 4247, 7445
critics of, 4246
history of, 4245–4246
lawsuits against, 4246–4247
UFO religions and, 9433
I and You (Buber). *See Ich und Du* (Buber)
Ianus. *See* Janus
Iao. *See* Yahveh
Iatmul people (New Guinea), cosmology of, 7195, 7196
Iatromanteis (shaman-like healers), travels of, 3839
IATS. *See* International Association of Tibetan Studies
Iawôs, 123
Ib (heart), in Egyptian religion, 2711
Ibāḍ, ʿAbd Allāh Ibn, 4248, 5127
ʿIbādah (worship), 2318, 9816
ʿIbadāt (religious obligations), 4692–4693, 4700, 4760
Ibāḍiyya sect (Islam), **4247–4249,** 5126, 5127
doctrines of, 4248–4249
geographical distribution of, 4699
and *imam,* 4248, 4249, 4396
origins of, 4248
vs. Shiism, 4248, 4249
vs. Sunnī Islam, 4248, 4249
Ibāḥah (permissibility), in Ḥanbalī school of law, 5548–5549
Ibānah ʿan uṣūl al-diyānah, al- (Ashʿarī), 530–531
Iban people (Borneo), 1021–1022
Ibas (bishop of Edessa), 6483
ʿIbbur (pregnancy), 2932
Ibeji (deity), in Caribbean religions, 1434
Iberian Peninsula. *See also* Andalusia; Portugal; Spain
Arab conquest of, 4581, 4591, 4592
conversion of Jews in, 400
expulsion of Jews from, 5104
Neolithic religion on, 6464–6465
Iberian religion, **4249–4254**
archaeological data on, 4249–4250, 4251
deities of, 4252–4253
funeral rites in, 4250, 4251–4252, 4254
literary data on, 4250, 4251
Phoenecian religion and, 4249–4250
priesthood in, 4252, 4253
rituals in, 4251–4252, 4253–4254
sacrifice in, 4249–4250, 4252–4253
sanctuaries in, 4250–4251, 4253
Ibis, 9168
Iblīs (the Devil), 2280, 2968
ʿAyn al-Quḍāt on, 8813–8814
al-Ḥallāj on, 3757, 8813
sin modeled by, 8406
Ibn ʿAbd al-Hādī, Yūsuf, Ḥanābilah and, 3768
Ibn ʿAbd al-Salam, ʿIzz al-dīn, 2652
Ibn ʿAbd al-Wahhāb, Muḥammad, **4254–4255,** 9653–9654. *See also* Wahhabiyah
Ibn Taymīyah's influence on, 4278, 4699
influence of, 4255
studies of, 4254–4255
teachings of, 4255, 4573
writings of, 4255
Ibn Abī Bishr. *See* Ashʿarī, (Abū al-Ḥasan) al-
Ibn Abī Duwād, 6319
Ibn Abī Laylā, 22
Ibn Abī Yaʿlā, 3765
Ibn Abi Yaʿlā, Abū Kāzim, 3766
Ibn al-ʿArabī, 2977, **4255–4260**
and anamnesis, 312
as blasphemous, 976, 4260
Burckhardt (Titus) translating works of, 1324
children of, 4258
on creation, 2653
on *dhikr,* 2340, 2341
on gnosis *(marʿrifah),* 8819–8820
on God
nature of, 128
unity of, 3566, 4255, 4258–4259, 4570
on Golden Rule, 3633
imaginal thinking of, 4552
influence of, 4259–4260, 4663, 8820
life of, 4256–4258, 8818–8819
love mysticism of, 6351–6352
monism of, 6146, 6352
on music, 6277
on mystical union, 6339
on nature of divine, 4259
Nyberg (H. S.) on, 6774
on *miʿrāj,* 6061
on *nūr Muḥammad,* 6767–6768

Ibn al-ʿArabī ***continued***
on *quṭb* (axis) and cosmic hierarchy, 8821
on *waḥdat al-wujūd* (unity of being), 8819, 8820
on *walāyah,* 9661
on Perfect Human Beings, 8711, 8819–8820
pilgrimage of, 4257
Quṭb al-Dīn Shīrāzī on, 4555
radical humanism of, 4570
Rūmī (Jalāl al-Dīn) influenced by, 7937
on soul, 8570
tafsīr (Qurʾanic exegesis) of, 7566, 7567
teachers of, 4256–4257
teachings of, 4255–4256, 4258–4259
on transcendence of number, 3566
on truth, 9373
visions of, 4256, 4257, 8819
wives of, 4257, 4258
on women, 4257, 9007
writings of, 4256, 4257, 4258, 7222
Ibn al-ʿArabī, Muḥammad, retreat of, 7770
Ibn al-Bawwab, calligraphy and, 1373
Ibn al-Fāriḍ, **4260–4261**
commentaries on, 4261
on mystical union, 6339
poems of, 4261, 7222
on recollection, 312–313
Ibn al-Farrā, Abū Yaʿlā, 5787
Ibn al-Habbārīyah, 6641
Ibn al-Ḥajj, 4589
Ibn al-Hajjāj, Muslim, 3729–3730
Ibn al-Haytham, Abū ʿAli al-Hasan, on medicine, 3832
Ibn al-Hītī, David, writings of, 5085
Ibn al-Ḥusayn, Ṣadaqah, 3767
Ibn al-Jawzī, 976, 6641
on Ḥanābilah, 3763, 3767
Ibn al-Kalbī, 4361
on Arabian religion, 444, 445
Ibn al-Khammār, 2971
Ibn al-Manabbih, Ḥammām, 3727
Ibn al-Muqaffaʿ, 4699
and Mazdakism, 5800
Ibn al-Nadim
on Mani, 5651
on Mālik ibn Anas, 5627
Ibn al-Raqīq, Ibrāhīm, 4584
Ibn al-Rāwandī, on al-Jāḥiẓ, 6320
Ibn al-Ṣaghīr, 4583
Ibn al-Sarrāj, 2973
Ibn al-Zakī, 4258
Ibn ʿAqil, 3766
Ibn ʿAsākir, 4277
Ibn ʿAṭāʾ Allāh, **4261–4262**
on *dhikr,* 2340, 2341
Shādhilīyah and, 8823–8824
writings of, 4261, 4663
Ibn Attar, Ḥayyim, 867
Ibn Avi Zimra, David, on authority of *Zohar vs.* Talmud, 3751
Ibn Bābawayhi, **4262–4263**
ḥadīth collection of (*See* Imāmī Shiism)
on *ʿiṣmah,* 4725
Ibn Bājjah, 2975–2976, **4263**
Ibn Baqqāl, Ḥanābilah and, 3764
Ibn Baṭṭah, Ḥanābilah and, 3764
Ibn Baṭṭūṭah
in Aceh (Indonesia), 25
on ʿAlawīyūn, 226
on Pasai sultanate, 4659
on South Asian Islam, 4644
travel accounts of, 8782
Ibn Batuta, 4602
Ibn Bazzāz, 601
Ibn Daud, Avraham, 255, **4264–4265**
Ibn Gabirol's work criticized by, 4267
soul, theory of, 8559
writings of, 4264–4265
Ibn ʿEzra,ʾ Avraham, **4265–4266**
biblical exegesis of, 865, 866, 867, 868, 4265–4266
on *Isaiah,* 4546
on mystical union, 6339
Nahmanides' (Moses) critique of, 6399
on *Sefer yetsirah,* 8221
on using God's name in vain, 970
writings of, 4265–4266
Ibn ʿEzra,ʾ Mosheh, soul, theory of, 8559
Ibn Faḍlān
on Germanic religion, 3446, 3457
on Khazars and Bulgars, 4492
on Norse boat burials, 990
Ibn Fadlan, Ahmed, 168
Ibn Funduq, 6641
Ibn Fūrak, Abū Bakr
in Ashʿarīyah, 534, 536
writings of, 534
Ibn Gabirol, Shelomoh, **4266–4267**
Ibn Daud's critique of, 4267
Neoplatonism and, 6475
philosophy of, 4266–4267
poetry of, 4266
soul, theory of, 8559
Ibn Giqatilla, 867
Ibn Ḥāmid, Ḥanābilah and, 3764
Ibn Ḥanbal, Aḥmad. *See* Aḥmad ibn Ḥanbal
Ibn Ḥasan, Saʿīd, 7240
Ibn Ḥawqal, on Qarāmiṭah, 7543–7544
Ibn Ḥazm, Ahmad, **4267–4269**
Adret (Shelomoh ben Avraham) response to, 36
al-Milal wa al-Nihal work of, 8780–8781
polemics against Christianity, 7242
polemics against Judaism, 7237–7239
political activities of, 4268
writings of, 4268, 7237, 7238
Ẓāhirī school and, 4268, 4593, 4595, 4699, 7238–7239, 9490
Ibn Hishām, on *miʿrāj,* 6059
Ibn Hubayrah, Ḥanābilah and, 3767
Ibn Isḥāq
on life of Prophet, 7243
on Abū Bakr, 19
on *miʿrāj,* 6059
sīrah of, 6735, 6736
tafsīr of, 8952
Ibn Ismāʿīl, Muḥammad
Ismāīlīyah and, 8324, 8326
return of, 8326
Ibn Jannaḥ, 865
Ibn Kammūnah, polemics against Islam, 7240–7241
Ibn Kaspi, Yosef, biblical exegesis of, 866, 867
Ibn Kathīr, 4277
Qurʾanic exegesis of, 7565
Ibn Khafīf, al-Ḥallāj and, 3756
Ibn Khalaf, Dāwūd, 4695
Ibn Khaldūn, 2977, **4269–4270**
at Al-Azhar university, 230
on alchemy, 250
on Berber religion, 834, 835
on demons, 2280
on *fiqh,* 4587
kalām of, 4587–4588, 5059, 5064
life of, 4269
on magic, 5584, 5585, 5586
on medicine, 3832–3833
on messianism, 5980
on Ashʿarīyah, 533
pilgrimage of, 4269
on rationalism and traditionalism in Islamic history, 4029
on rural and urban civilization, 4588, 4590
writings of, 4269
Ibn Killis, and al-Azhar university, 230
Ibn Kullāb, and Ashʿarīyah, 531, 532
Ibn Mājah (Muhammad ibn Yazīd al-Qazwīnī), *sunan* collection of, 3730
Ibn Masarrah, 2975
Ibn Masʿūd, crossing bridge, 1050
Ibn Migash, Yosef, 255
Ibn Muḥammad, Marwān, 4612
Ibn Mujāhid, 9200–9201
Ibn Muqlah, calligraphy and, 1368, 1372–1373
Ibn Nafis, on medicine, 3832
Ibn Nagrela, 7238
Ibn Naʿīah al-Ḥmṣī, 2971
Ibn Nujaym, 4699, 4701
Ibn Nuṣayr, Muḥammad, in ʿAlawīyūn, 226
Ibn Qāsim, Muḥammad, 4641
Ibn Qayyim al-Jawzīyah
as Ibn Taymīyah's disciple, 4278, 4699
copying al-Maghribī's works, 7240
on fasting, 8141
Ḥanābilah and, 3768
on prayers for the dead, 8568
prophetic medical text of, 3833
soul, doctrine of, 8567–8568
Ibn Qutaybah, 2783
on Ḥasan al-Baṣrī, 3210–3211
tafsīr of, 8952
Ibn Rajab, 4277
Ibn Rāshid, Buhlūl, 4584
Ibn Rashīq, Ḥasan, 4584
Ibn Rushd (Averroës), **4270–4273**
Almohad religious policies and, 4596
and Ibn al-ʿArabī, 4256, 8819
Aristotle and, 479, 481, 4270–4271, 4272
on blasphemy, 976
defending philosophy, 4271, 5204
and double-truth theory, 6475
and ethics, 4272
in exile, 4270
and *falsafah* thought, 2975, 2976–2977
Gersonides's commentary on, 3462
on God
attributes of, 621, 3564
existence of, 7422
Ibn Sīnā criticized by, 4274
influence of, 4272–4273, 4597
in Jewish thought and philosophy, 4894–4896
on knowledge, 5204
life of, 4270
Neoplatonism opposed by, 7192
on occasionalism, 6779–6780
on *jihād,* 5738, 5742
Pecham (John) opposing, 7025
and politics, 4272
rebuttal of *Tahāfut al-Falāsifah* (al-Ghazālī), 4271–4272
skeptical views of, 8421
on soul, 8570
studies of, 4270
and theology of analogy, 391
writings of, 4270–4271, 4595
translations of, 4272, 4597
Ibn Sabʿin, 2977
Ibn Saʿīd ibn Sharaf, Muḥammad, 4584
Ibn Saʿūn, Ḥanābilah and, 3764
Ibn Shannabūdh, retraction of, 3761
Ibn Shihāb (Abū ʿAlī al-ʿUkbarī), Ḥanābilah and, 3764
Ibn Sīnā (Avicenna), **4273–4276**
ʿAbd al-Jabbār and, 4
Afghānī (Jamāl al-Dīn al-) and, 64
on alchemy, 249–250
and *miʿrāj,* 6061

on angels, 4554
Aristotle and, 479, 4274, 4275, 4553
al-Bīrūnī and, 954
on blasphemy, 976
on breath and breathing, 1042–1043
on causation, 2975
on demons, 2280
disciples of, 4275
education of, 4273
and *falsafah* thought, 2973–2974
followers of, 8827
al-Ghazāli criticizing, 2975, 3470, 4273, 4274, 4275
on God
attributes of, 621
existence of, 7422
Ibn Rushd criticizing, 4274
imaginal thinking of, 4553
influence of, 4275–4276, 4552–4553
Kindī (Abū Yūsuf Ya'qūb al-) and, 2972
on knowledge, 5203
on magic, 5587
on medicine, 3832
Mullā Ṣadrā on, 6233
philosophy of, 4274–4275, 4552–4553
and physics, 7136
political activities of, 4274
Rāzī (Fakhr al-Dīn al-) criticism of, 7633
on soul, 8567, 8569–8570
al-Suhrawardī on, 6231–6232
writings of, 4274, 4276, 4553
translations of, 4275, 4276
Ibn Sudun al Busbugawi, on humor, 4215–4216
Ibn Sulaymān al-Jazūlī, Muḥammad, 4588
Ibn Tamīm, Abū al-'Arab Muḥammad, 4584
Ibn Taymīyah, Aḥmad, **4276–4279**
Ash'arīyah opposed by, 4277–4278, 4568–4569
on character of caliph, 7285
early career of, 4276–4277
on free will, 4569
on good and evil, 4570
Ḥanābilah and, 3768
imprisonment of, 4278
on *mawlids,* 5789
on 'Alawīyūn, 226
on *īmān* and *islām,* 4399
on *'iṣmah,* 4726
on *samā'* (listening parties), 8065
polemics against Christianity, 7242
sainthood and, 8035
studies of, 4276
against Sufism, 4277, 4570
on *taqlid,* 4699
on Zoroastrianism, 4569
Ibn Ṭufayl, 2975, 2976
Ibn Rushd and, 4270
on Ibn Bājjah, 4263
on soul, 8570
on ultimate truth, 6736
Ibn Tūmart, Muḥammad, 4585–4586, 6737
Almohad movement founded by, 4592
disciples of, 4586–4587
faqihs challenged by, 4586
ijtihād promoted by, 4586
on *tawḥīd,* 4586
Ibn-ul-Vaqt (Ahmad), 10035
Ibn Zur'ah, 2971
Iboga (hallucinogen), 7469–7470
Ibo religion. *See* Igbo religion
Ibrāhīm. *See* Abraham, in Islam
Ibrāhīm al-Ḥakīm, on *mi'rāj,* 6061
Ibrāhīm ibn Adham, quietism and asceticism of, 8811
Ibsen, Henrik, 2472, 2474
Iburi Izō, 9082, 9083
Ibuse Masuji, 3073, 3074–3075
Icaka calendar, 748
Icarian II/Incline (Goldstein), vol. 12 color insert
Icarus, story of, 3126, 5274
ICCPR. *See* International Covenant on Civil and Political Rights
Ice Age. *See* Paleolithic Period
Iceland. *See also* Germanic religion
Christianity in, women's monasteries, 6763
history of, Snorri Sturluson, role of, **8460**
Landvættir myths in, 5299
Loki myths in, 5507–5509
rejuvenation myths in, 7683
sagas of, **8023–8026**
ICESCR. *See* International Covenant on Economic, Social and Cultural Rights
Icheiri (deity), in Island Carib religion, 1427–1428
Ichijyo (Japanese emperor), music under, 6300
Ichikawa Hakugen (Buddhist monk), 9950
I-Ching (book). *See Yijing*
I-ching (Chinese traveler), on Buddhist schools, 1132, 1133
Ichon, Alain, 5942
Ich und Du (Buber), 1057, 2343, 7118
ICMI. *See* Indonesian Association of Muslim Intellectuals
ICNA. *See* Islamic Circle of North America
Icon(s), **4352–4354,** vol. 10 color insert. *See also* Iconography
assists (golden rays) in, 1861
corner of, 2399
cult of, 4379
diffusion of, 4353–4354
origins of, 4352
cult of saints and, 2081
in Eastern Christianity, vol. 10 color insert, vol. 12 color insert
debate over, 3554–3555
in Ethiopian Church, 2860
gold in, 1861
honored as living beings, 4380
vs. image, 4388–4389
as images, power of, 9623
importance and meaning of, 1662
in Jainism, 4771
media of, 4345, 4352
painters of, 4353, 4354, 4392
reality status of, 54
subject matter of, 4345
textiles as, 9090
theology of, 4352–4353
use of term, 4388
of *yoni,* 9905
in Zoroastrianism, 9935
Iconic (figurative) images, 4389
Iconoclasm, **4279–4291,** vol. 11 color insert
in Buddhism, 4284
Byzantine, 1662, 4285, **4289–4291,** 4352, 4353, 4385, 4386
Carolingian, 4286, 4290
Nikephoros's role in, 6619
origins of, 4289
perception of, 4280
phases of, 4289–4290
prejudices about, 4281
Theodore of Studios fighting, 9122
in Christianity, 4285–4287, 4385 (*See also* Iconoclasm, Byzantine)
colonialism and, 4386
early Eastern, 2582, 2585
Protestant, 7449, 7459
Puritans and, 4347
Reformation and, 4281, 4286, 4346, 4361, 4386, 4392
silent (passive), 4283, 4392
in Confucianist Han Studies movement, 1903
councils on, 2041
as cultural idea, 4279
defining, 4279, 4282–4283
Eastern, 4280, 4283–4285
in Egyptian religion, 4285
in Hawaiian religion, 3799
in Hinduism, 4282, 4283–4285
as historical event, 4279
in Islam, 4281, 4287, 4349
in Jainism, 4282, 4285
in Judaism, 4281, 4285
meaning of word, 4279
in monotheism, 4279, 4281, 4283, 4285
motives of, 4280, 4285, 4297, 4392
perceptions of, 4280–4287
prejudices about, 4281–4282
in *Satanic Bible* (LaVey), 8127
silent (passive), 4282, 4283, 4284, 4285, 4392
Western, 4279, 4285–4287
perception of, 4280
prejudices about, 4281
Iconographic deification, 2250
Iconography, **4295–4352,** vol. 10 color insert. *See also* Icon(s); Images; Symbol and symbolism; *specific symbols*
African, **4300–4304**
of ancestors, 89, 4301–4303
form and meaning in, 4302–4303
of kings, 4301–4302
in rituals, 4303–4304
approaches to, 4297–4299
appropriation of, vol. 8 color insert
in art history, 9621
Australian Aboriginal, **4304–4307**
interpretation of, 4306–4307
representation of, 4305–4306
tjurungas, 9212–9213
Baltic
of cult of ancestors, 331
of Laima, 5286
Buddhist, **4327–4331,** 4389 (*See also* Temples, Buddhist)
bodhisattva images in, 1111, 4327, 4329
Buddha images in (*See* Buddha, the, images of)
celestial buddhas in, 4329
consecration of, 4389–4390
as divine presence, 4390
Esoteric, 5608
of Hevajra, in Indian art, 3965
in Risshō Kōseikai, 7795
light symbolism in, 5454
of Maitreya, 5620
of Amitābha, 292, 5454
of Kālacakra, 5058
of Kṣitigarbha, 5256
of Mahāvairocana, 5608
of Mañjuśrī, 5675
of Vajrapāṇi, 9513
and religious conversions, 4391
ritual uses of, 4330–4331, 4391
saints, *arhats,* and monks in, 4330
veneration of, 4382–4383
wisdom goddesses in, 4330

Buddhist *continued*
wrathful figures in, 4329–4330
Celto-Roman, 1481–1487
Chinese, Xi Wang Mu in, 9860
Christian, **4344–4349**
in 17th and 18th century, 4346–4347
in 19th century, 4347
in 20th century, 4347–4348
of angels, 346
of Anthony of Padua, 377
Byzantine, 4345, 4352–4354
as divine presence, 4390
early, 4297, 4344
function of, 4348
of Hugh of Saint-Victor, 4151
imperial, 4344–4345
interest in, 4348–4349
lions in, 5464
medieval, 4345–4346, 9265
memento mori in, vol. 1 color insert
nimbus in, 6624
Orthodox Christian, 2591, 2594, vol. 10 color insert
popular art, 7322, 7323
Protestant, 4346–4347, 7456, 7459
Reformation and, 4346
and religious conversions, 4391
Renaissance, 4346
ritual uses of, 4391
in Sistine Chapel, 8755
colonialism influencing, 7322
Communist, 4348
Confucian, **4336–4339**
20th-century trends of, 4338–4339
calligraphy, 4338
divinities and mythic beings in, 4336
early, 4336–4337
paintings, 4338
physical appearance of, 4337
political and societal acceptance of, 4337–4339
sculptures, 4338
of Dacian Riders, 2123, 2124
Daoist, **4331–4336**
Buddhist iconography and, 4333, 4334
deities in, 4334–4335
early, 4332–4333
origins of, 4331–4332
paintings, 4334–4335
in popular art and religion, 4335
popular culture, 7322
sculptures, 4333–4334
definition of, 500
Egyptian, 4298, **4317–4320**
consecration of, 4389
deities in, 4317–4318
as divine presence, 4390
funerary, 4318, 4319–4320
narrative cycles in, 4318–4319
netherworld in, 4319
symbolic motifs in, 4319
in temples, 4318–4319
in Elamite religion, 4468, 4469, 4472, 4473
Etruscan, 2870
feet in, 3013
Greek, 4298, **4320–4323**
of Aphrodite, 408–409
architecture, 4322
deities in, 4321–4322, 4363
of Dioscuri, 2123
Hekate in, 3900
Minoan-Mycenaean iconography and, 4320–4321
nimbus in, 6624
of Prometheus, 7421
sculpture, 4322
on vases, 4296
veneration of, 4381–4382
hands in, 3769
Hindu, 4296, **4323–4327,** 4389, 4429 (*See also* Temples, Hindu)
animal themes, 4438
consecration of, 4389–4390
as divine presence, 4390
mūrti in, 6239–6240
of Devī, 4325–4326
of Gaṇeśa, 4326–4327, 4438
of Kṛṣṇa, 5248–5249
of Śiva, 4323–4324, 4383, 4384
of Viṣṇu, 4324–4325, 4383, 4384, 9618
popular culture, 7322
ritual uses of, 4391
rural traditions, 4433, 4434, 4435
veneration of, 4383–4384
in Iberian religion, 4252, 4253
vs. iconology, 500
in Indus Valley religion, 4472–4474
Islamic, 4297, **4349–4352**
angels in, 4350
calligraphy, 4350, 4351
imagery of, 4350
paintings, 4350
pilgrimage sites in, 4351
Jewish, 4296, **4340–4344**
Hellenistic, 4340, 4352
lions in, 5464
in Middle Ages, 4340
in Qabbalah, 4340–4341
studies on, 4341–4343
in Khmer religion, 5130
light symbolism in, 5454
meaning of, 4295
Mesoamerican, **4311–4315**
afterlife in, 149
in Aztec religion, 5891
birds in, 4312
dragons in, 4311, 4312
dwarfs in, 4311
in Teotihuaćan, 5888, 5900–5901
interpretation of, 4311
music in, 6267
in Olmec religion, 5881
water in, 9213–9214
Mesopotamian, **4315–4317**
animal combats in, 4315–4316
banquet scenes in, 4316
consecration of, 4389
deities in, 4316–4317
as divine presence, 4390
unidentifiable figures in, 4317
urban imagery in, 4316
veneration of, 4380–4381
new perspectives on, 4299, 4300
nimbus in, 6624
North American Indian, **4307–4310**
abstract symbols in, 4310
animal beings in, 4309
astronomical beings in, 4309
cosmologies in, 4307
geological beings in, 4310
guardian beings in, 4307–4308
human beings in, 4310
meteorological beings in, 4309
monsters in, 4309
supreme beings in, 4307
tricksters/culture heroes in, 4307
vegetation beings in, 4309–4310
Olmec, 6817–6818
Phoenician, of Melqart, 5846, 5848
Polynesian, 7309
in popular culture, 7321, 7322, 7323
prehistoric, 7376, 7380–7381
Rastafari, 7626–7627
Roman, 4296, 4298, **4320–4323**
of *lares,* 5320
nimbus in, 6624
sacred time in, vol. 1 color insert
Scythian, 8205–8206
South American Indian, in pre-Incan Andean religions, 8602
as visible religion, **4295–4300**
Iconology, 4297–4299
definition of, 500
Iconomachy, 4279
Iconophobia, 4280–4281
Iconostasis, 794
in Byzantine churches, 7980, 7984
ICR. *See* Institute for Creation Research
Id. *See* Unconscious
Iḍā (mythic figure), 5678, 5679
Ida, Mount, 7602
Idā dance, 2136
ʿĪd al-Aḍḥā, 4712, 4714, 9818
women's attendance at, 3369
ʿĪd al-Fiṭr festival, 830, 4712, 4714, 9202, 9817
religious and social aspects of, 8141
women's attendance at, 3369
ʿIddah (waiting period)
after death of spouse, 4706
after divorce, 4706, 4708
Idea(s)
in epistemology, 2819
experience as origin of, 2778, 2819
God as, Husserl (Edmund) on, 4237
innateness of, 2819
Idealism, **4354–4356**
Absolute, Hegelianism as, 3895
in American culture, new religious movements and, 1714
in Buddhism, Stcherbatsky (Theodore) on, 8737
in Chinese philosophy, 1576
in Neo-Confucianism, 1603
definition of, 4354, 7111
and ethics, 4356
German
Evola (Julius) influenced by, 2904–2905
Fichte (Johann Gottlieb) and, 3048–3049
in Hinduism, in Trika Śáivism, 8046
historiography and, 4032
Hocking (William Ernest) on, 4076
in Ishrāqīyah, 4555
mystical, of Merezhkovskii (Dmitrii), 5869
nature in, 4354–4355
in New Thought movement, 6582, 6583
objective, 4355–4356
of Śaṅkara, 4430
realistic, 9282
religious experience and, 7742
subjective, 4355
of Trubetskoi (Sergei), 9368
Idealist View of Life, An (Radhakrishnan), 7742
Ideal time, and afterlife, views of, 132
Ideal-types, in comparative religion, 5436
Idea of God in Early Religions (Jevons), 4854
Idea of Purity in Ancient Judaism, The (Neusner), 7513–7514

Idea of the Holy (Das Heilige) (Otto), 48, 500, 2266, **4095–4101,** 6929–6930, 7090, 7348, 7374, 7835
Durkheim's *Les Formes élémentaires de la vie religieuse* contrasted with, 4095–4096
legacy of, 4100–4101
a priori concept in, 7976
translation of, 4098
Ideas (Husserl), phenomenology in, 4236
Ideational supernaturalism, Sorokin (Pitirim Aleksandrovich) on, 8523
Ideen zur Philosophie der Geschichte der Menschheit (Herder), philosophy of history in, 3919
Idel, Moshe, 7739
on mystical union, 6339
Identification, attention and, 607
Identity
aesthetics and, Schelling (Friedrich) on, 47
African American, 65
history of study of, 67, 79
artificial intelligence and, 513
Australian Indigenous, 637, 667
autobiography and, 703
in Christianity
covenant and, 8464
creeds and, 2055–2056
clothing and, 1826–1828, 1834, 1835
in Sikh Dharma, 3879
conversion and identity theory, 1971
cultural hybridity and, 1859
desecration and, 8011
in exorcism, 2930, 2932, 2934, 2936
Foucault (Michel) on homosexuality and, 8241–8242
genetics and, 3428, 3429
images and, vol. 6 color insert, vol. 8 color insert
Japanese, modernization and, 8778
Jewish
clothing and, 1831–1832
Greenberg (Irving) on Holocaust and, 4092–4093
Israeli Law of Return and, 3754
patrilineal *vs.* matrilineal, 3751–3752
Schneerson (Menachem) on, 8172
Torah and, 8012–8013
media and, 5807
men's, in men's studies, 5863
vs. mental flow, 608
Muslim
imitation of Muḥammad in, 6227
Islamic states and, 8462
mystical, 6335–6340
nature and, 6436
secret societies and, 8212
sexuality and, 8241–8242
social differentiation and, 8472
women's, in feminism, 3311
in women's studies in religion, 9790–9791
Identity Christians, 6549
Identity Crisis in Black Theology (Cone), 78, 965
Ideograms. *See also* Calligraphy
cosmognic myths and, 1989
"great seal" style, 1370
sacred *vs.* profane and, 7976–7977
written talismans and, 8677
Ideographic research, comparative-historical method *vs.,* 4063
Ideologies
as distinct cultural realities, and martyrdom, 5737–5738
schism and, 8151–8152
Smart (Ninian) on, 8443
Ides, Y. E., 3110
Ides of March, in Roman calendar, 1354
Ides of September, in Roman calendar, 1353
Idinopulos, Thomas A., 7745
Idiophones, 6251, 7037
Idiot, The (Dostoevsky), 3059
Idol
definition of, 4357
use of term, 4388
Idolatry, **4356–4365**. *See also* Images, veneration of
apologists on, 4360–4361
Augustine of Hippo on, 834, 4358, 4361, 4363–4364, 4385
Bengali, 828–829
in Christianity, Jewish trade and, 5016
colonial efforts against, in South America, 8593, 8608–8609
concept of, 4357
condemnation of, 4296, 4297
Christian, 4358, 4359–4361, 4380, 4385, 7014, vol. 4 color insert
and iconoclasm, 4285, 4297
Islamic, 4361–4363, 4385–4386, 4561
Israelite, 4385, 4737–4738
Jewish, 4340, 4357, 4358–4359, 4380, 4385, vol. 4 color insert
Sikh, 4431
cult of saints as, 2083
definitions of, 4356–4357, 4363
fetishism and, 3043–3044, 4363
in Hinduism, Roy (Ram Mohan) on, 7932, 7933
historical semantics of, 4357–4358
and *homo religiosus,* 4357, 4363–4364
in Islam (*See also* Shirk)
in Druze movement, 8330
in Israelite religion, 4358–4359, 4744
in Judaism
Christianity as idolatry, 3753
Noahic prohibition against, 3753
as sacrilege, 8012
the state and, 4907
laws and, 5329–5330
and pollution, 7513
rites and symbols in, 4364
in Roman Catholicism, 4361, 4386, 4389, 4390, 4392
sacraments and, 7881
in Slavic religion, 8433–8434
Smith (Wilfred Cantwell) on, 8450
use of term, 4388
Vivekananda on, 828–829
Idowu, E. Bolaji, 117, 140, 5449
Idrimi (king of Alalakh), 28
Idris, Jafar Sheikh, on *Khalīfa,* 2651
Idrīs, Sayyid, 6737
Idrīs, as Enoch, 2803–2804
Idumeans, 9940
Iðunn (deity), Loki and, 5508
Iduq yer sub (sacred lands and waters), 9401, 9402
Idus (festival days), 7906
Idylls (Theocritus), 6957
Iella (deity), in Island Arawak religion, 1427
Iemanjá (spirit), 122, 123
Ieru (deity), 834
Ifa (god of divination), 4304, 10032
in Santería, 1434
signature of, 10032
Ifa: An Exposition of Ifa Literary Corpus (Abimbola), 80, 117, 10032
Ifaḍāh (pouring forth), 7159
Ifa divination, **10032–10033**
determinism in, 1528
handclapping in, 7038
history of study of, 117
iconography of, 10033
in Santería, 8108
and Latin American fiction, 3065
myth about origins of, 94
paraphernalia of, 10032, 10033
poetry in, 87, 10032
procedures of, 87, 3437, 10032
studies on, 10032–10033
Ifa Divination: Communication between Gods and Men in West Africa (Bascom), 10032
Ifa Divination Poetry (Abimbola), 10032
Ifat (Muslim state), 4606
Ife (Nigeria)
bronze heads of, 84
in Yoruba religion, 9909–9910
IFEES. *See* Islamic Foundation for Ecology and Environmental Sciences
Ifḥām al-Yahūd (al-Maghribī), 7239
'Ifrīt (demonic figure), 2280, 2314–2315, 3476
Ifṭār (breaking fast), 9817
at Ramaḍān, 8140
Iftitāḥ al-da'wah (Qāḍī al-Nu'mān), 4584, 7541–7542
Igala people (Nigeria), Ifa divination by, 87
Igalima (deity), family of, 5951
Igbo (Ibo) religion (Nigeria), **4365–4367**
ancestors in, 4365–4366
Aro influence on, 66
Christian missionaries influencing, 4365
creation in, 3572
cultic sexual activity in, 3969
dogs in, 2393
God of, 4365, 4366, 5445
healing in, 4365, 4366
iconography of, 4303
Ifa divination by, 87
masks in, 2458, 5768
myths of, 97–98
prayer in, 4366
sacred language in, 5304
sacrifice in, 4366
shrines in, 3572
spirits in, 4365–4366
supreme being (Chukwu) in, 97–98, 3572
Iggeret ha-Shabbat (Ibn 'Ezra'), 4265
Iggerot Mosheh, 3013–3014
Iggrat (demon), 3158
Iglesia Fidencista Cristiana (Mexico), 6578
Iglesia Filipina Independiente (IFI or Philippine Independent Church)
as new movement, 8654
Unitarianism and Anglicanism in, 1727
Iglulik religion (Inuit), shamanism in, initiation in, 8271
Ignatius a Jesu, 5637
Ignatius Loyola, **4367–4369**. *See also* Jesuits
as bishop, 4369
education of, 4367

Ignatius Loyola ***continued***
execution of, 4369
letters of, 4369–4370
life of, 4367
on meditation, 5818
Pinard de la Boullaye on, 7173
poetry of, 7207
retreats of, 7770, 7772
spiritual life of, 4367–4369
as superior general of Jesuits, 4367, 4368–4369
Xavier (Francis) and, 9853–9854
Ignatius of Antioch, **4369–4370**
anti-docetic views of, 2381
on Christianity in Antioch, 8938
on election, 2747
epistles of, 920
on Eucharist, 4370
on "gospel," 3641
on heresy, 3926
on local bishop, centrality of, 8154
on *Logos,* 5505
on martyrdom, 4183, 7057–7058, 8807, 8830
martyrdom sought by, 5741
on Mary, 5753
on *Matthew,* 907
on Roman church, 6966
on unity of church, 4370
Ignatius of Constantinople
abdication and reinstatement of, 2041, 7135
Photian schism and, 8155
restoration of, 2585
Ignis fatuus, 2952
Ignorance. *See also* Knowledge
in Buddhism (*See Avidyā*)
learned (*See* Learned ignorance)
sleep as, 8441
in Yoga, 9894
Igorot (Philippines), 2616
drums of, 7036
Iguvium (Italy), pantheon of, 7894
Igwe (deity), 3572
Ihimaera, Witi, 3085, 5682
Iḥkām fī uṣūl al-aḥkām, al- (Ibn Ḥazm), 4268
Iḥrām (sacred state required for *ḥājj*), 7157–7158
Iḥsān (state of being perfected), 4398, 4399
Iḥtisham (modesty), 1559
Iḥyā' 'ulūm al-dīn (Ghazālī), 3471, 4570, 4699, 6097
Ijaw religion (Nigeria), children in, 4199
I'jāz (miraculousness of Qur'ān), **4370–4371,** 4564, 8952, 8956
I'jāz al-Qur'ān (al-Bāqillānī), 4371
Ijbār (marriage guardian), 4706
Ijca people (Columbia), 7759
Ijele (mask), 5768
Ījī, 'Aḍud al-Dīn al-, **4371–4372**
in Ash'arīyah, 538
kalām of, 5059, 5066–5067
Ijmā' (consensus), **4372–4373**
as source of *kalām,* 5060
in *fiqh,* 9488–9489
in Sunnī Islam, 4373–4374, 4697
on *mawlids,* 5789
al-Shāfi'ī on, 5548, 8265
as source of law, 4372–4695, 4566, 4695
sunnah and, 8854
Ijo Orunmila, 109
Ijtihād (strenuous endeavor), **4373–4375**
expanding definition of, 6096
in fundamentalist movements, 4573
and gender in Islam, 3365
Ibn Tūmart promoting, 4586
in Wahhābīyah, 9654–9655
Iqbāl (Muḥammad) promoting, 4534, 4652
jurists making, 4566, 4697
madhhabs (schools of law) disagreeing on, 5549
in modernism, 6096
qiyās identified with, 4374, 4566
qualification of, 3801
rejection of, 4699
al-Shāfi'ī on, 8264–8265
in Sunnism *vs.* Twelver Shiism, 8343
tasks of, 4373–4374, 4697
Ikarios, in Anthesteria, 375
Ikeda Daisaku, 6574
Ikega (Cult of the Hand), 4302
Ikegobo (Cult of the Hand), 4302
Ikenipke (festival), 9394, 9395
Ikhtilaf (legal differences), 4594
Ikhtilāf al-fuqahā' (al-Ṭabarī), 8944
Ikhwān al Muslimūn. *See* Muslim Brotherhood
Ikhwān al-Ṣafā' (Brethren of Purity), **4375–4377**
on *mi'rāj,* 6060
Rasā'il Ikhwān al-Ṣafā' by, 4375–4377
authorship and dating of, 4375
contents of, 4375–4376
parables and animal stories in, 4376
philosophical system of, 4376–4377
sources of, 4376
on study of nature, 2652
Ikki, Kita, 6608
Ikkō ikki (popular uprisings), 7753
Ikkyū (Buddhist monk), 847
in Zen Buddhism, 9947
Ikkyū Sōjun (Zen eccentric), **4377–4378**
Gozan Zen criticized by, 3643
Ikmāl al-dīn wa-itmām al-ni'mah (Ibn Bābawayhi), 4262
Ikṣvāku (mythic figure), 5678
Iktomi (trickster), 5296, 5297
Il (deity). *See also* El
in Canaanite religion, 1382, 1383–1384, 1386, 1387, 1388
'Ilal al-sharā'i' (Ibn Bābawayhi), 4262
Ila religion (Zambia). *See also* Central Bantu religions
ghosts in, 3476
myths of, 97
Ilat, in Canaanite religion, 1383
Il combattimento di Tancredi e Clorinda (Monteverdi), 2154
Ile-Ịfe (Yoruba city), 9910
Ilha'u (mythic figure), in Canaanite religion, 1399
Il'ia (saint), in Slavic religion, 8435–8436
Iliad (Homer)
allegorical interpretation of, 6365
Artemis in, 506
Athena in, 586
authorship of, 4107
battle in, 2816
circles in, 1791
Delphic oracle in, 2265
Demeter in, 2268
eagles in, 2554
eye imagery in, 2941
fate in, 3000
Hades in, 3724, 3725
healing in, 3839
Hera in, 3679, 3914
hospitality in, 4139
human-divine relations in, 4108
image veneration in, 4381
in Indo-European language study, 4458
kingship in, 5166
letter mysticism on, 271, 272
magic in, 5574
Mahābhārata cognate to, 4465
music in, 6303
Night in, 3017
Poseidon in, 7338
Rāmāyaṇa to, 4465
ritual practice in, 4108
time in, 6375
underworld in, 9452
warrior prestige in, 9679–9680
Zeus in, 3663, 3679
Ilib (deity), Mount Sapan and, 1382
Ilibemberti (spirit), in Samoyed religion, 8095
Ilima naimima (gracious gods), in Canaanite religion, 1386, 1395
Ilimilku (scribe), in clay tablets, 1390–1391
Il-khanid dynasty (Iran), 4371–4372, 4493
in Caucasus, 4613
Illapa (deity), 4411, 4413
ambivalence of, 5993
as high god, 8590
Inti and, 8602
legitimacy of Inca kings and, 5176
male shamans and, 3418
overview of, 8601–8602
Pachamama paired with, 3416
Illness. *See* Disease and illness; Healing and medicine
Illumination. *See also* Light
in Christianity, Servetus (Michael) on, 8232
distinction from liberation, 5435
in Holy Order of MANS, 4102
in Islam, Suhrawardī's philosophy of, 8827
mysticism of, 5454
in Vedism, bestowed by Agni, 3990
Illuminist current, in Western esotericism, 2843
Illusion
analytical psychology of, 7484
in Buddhism, sacrilege and, 8015
Freud (Sigmund) on, 7482
in Hinduism (*See Māyā*)
māyā as, 5794
mirrors and, 6063
psychoanalysis of, 7481, 7482, 7483
time as, 7989
Illusionist stage magic, 6452
Illuyanka (serpent), 2431, 2442
Hittite myth of, 4068–4070
'Ilm (knowledge), 4374
'Ilm al-fiqh (science of positive law), 9490
Ilmarinen (deity), **4378–4379**
Ilm-e Khshnum (Knowledge of joy), 9991
Ilmer (deity), 448
'Ilm usul al-fiqh (science of derivation of positive law), 9490–9491
Ĭł Mŭw Ĭki (deity). *See* Lower-Earth Old Man
Il Terribile. *See* Julius II
Ilu (personal gods), in Mesopotamian religion, 8536
Iluwer, 28
Ilwer (deity), 448
Ilyās, Mawlāna Muḥammad, 4653
Ilyina, Irina Vasiljevna, on Komi religion, 5217
Image (Mani), 5649, 5651
Image and Pilgrimage in Christian Culture (Turner and Turner), 7163, 9406
Imagen de la Virgen Maria, Madre de Dios de Guadalups (Sánchez), vol. 12 color insert
Images, **4379–4393**. *See also* Art; Icon(s); Iconography; Visual culture
achieropaeic (not made by hands), 4286, 4352, 4392
aesthetics and, 53–56
aniconic (abstract), 4389
appropriation of, vol. 8 color insert
as *mūrti,* 6239–6240

attitudes toward, 496
as blessings, 980
in Buddhism
in devotion, 9828–9830
prostration before, in Theravāda, 8061
Canaanite, 1387
in Christianity (*See also* Icons)
of God, 3559
miracles and pilgrimage associated with statues, 2082
in Spanish colonial South America, 8610–8611
commerce of, vol. 7 color insert
commissioning and making of, 4391–4392
community and, vol. 6 color insert
consecration of, 4389–4390
cosmic visions, vol. 3 color insert
deities and humans joined through, 7980
destruction of (*See* Iconoclasm)
divine *(acheiropoetic)*, vol. 12 color insert
as divine presence, 4390–4391
efficacious, Vol. 9 color insert
functions of, 4389, vol. 9 color insert
in funeral rites, vol. 9 color insert
goddesses in (*See* Goddess worship)
in Hawaiian religion, feather gods (wicker images), 3798
in Hinduism, consecration of, 1955
of human body, vol. 13 color insert
iconic (figurative), 4389
vs. icons, 4388–4389
identity and, vol. 6 color insert, vol. 8 color insert
in Jainism, 4771
in Judaism, of God, 3542–3543
justification of, 4392
meaning making and, 493–494, 9622–9623
and miracles, 4390–4391
in mirrors, 6063–6065
misconceptions of, 9623–9624
mistrust of, 4280–4281, 4282
multiplication of, 4389, 4390–4391
of mystical union, 6335
mysticism of, 6346–6348
in oral tradition, 6425–6426
origin of term, 4379
Plato on, 4283
portraits, vol. 10 color insert
power of, 4280, 4281, 4282
in African religion, 4302–4303
and religious conversions, 4391
ritual uses of, 4389–4390, 4391
sacred, categories of, 497
of sacred time, vol. 1 color insert
in storytelling, vol. 2 color insert
symbolic, vol. 14 color insert
theology of, 4352–4353
true, vol. 12 color insert
types of, 4388–4389
understanding, 9622–9623
use of term, 4388
veneration of, 497, **4379–4388** (*See also* Idolatry)
categories of images meriting, 497
consecration ceremonies in, 497
critiques of, 4380, 4385–4386
forms of, 497
in Inca religion, 4384–4385, 4386, 4410
in Jainism, 4382, 4389, 4390, 4391
origin of term, 4379
rituals of, 4380
in secular world, 4386–4387
violence and, 9599
in visual culture, 9621–9622
as visual narrative, vol. 2 color insert
vows taken before, 4391
and words, 4295–4297
vs. words, primacy of, 494, 495
words incorporated in, 9623, vol. 14 color insert
of Zarathushtra, 9935, 9989
Imagetexts, vol. 14 color insert
Imaginal thinking, in Islamic philosophy, 4552, 4553–4554
Imaginal world *(mundus imaginalis)*, Corbin (Henry) on, 1984
Imagination
Coleridge (Samuel Taylor) on, 47
in esotericism, Faivre paradigm of, 2844
Kant (Immanuel) on, 46
mythic
neoshamanism and, 8296
social formation and, 8471
and play, 7194
poetic, 7206
and prophecy, 7439, 7440
Schleiermacher (Friedrich) on, 8163
seeing, imaginative, Steiner (Rudolf) on, 8738
Spinoza (Baruch) on, 8683, 8684
Imaginative (artificial) dialogue, 2342
"Imagining 'Korean Buddhism': The Invention of a National Religious Tradition" (Buswell), 1248–1249
Imago Dei (image of God)
consciousness of sin and, 8403
Irenaeus on, 8405
Imago mundi, tree as, 9576–9577
Īmām, al- (Ashʿarī), 530
Imāmah, nubūwah and, 6737
Imamate, **4393–4397**. *See also* Imāms
in Sunnī Islam, 4393–4394
ʿiṣmah in, 4724, 4725, 4726
Khārijī doctrine of, 4396
as leadership of ritual prayer, 4393, 4396–4397
of Khārijīs, 5127
Shīʿī doctrine of, 259, 7565–7566, 8035
Imāmīyah and, 8321, 8322, 8337–8338
in Shiism (*See* Shiism, imamate in)
as supreme leadership of Muslim community, 4393–4396
Imāmī (Twelvers) Shiism, **8337–8346**
ʿAlawīyūn and, 225, 226, 227
branches of, 5549
in Caucasus, 4614
in Central Asia, 4620
Corbin (Henry) on, 1984
current distribution of, 8323
development of, 8338–8342
doctrines of, 2064–2065, 5549
free will and predestination in, 3213
Ibn Bābawayhi in, 4262–4263
ijmāʿ in, 4697
ijtihād in, 4374, 4697
imamate in, 4394–4395, 4693, 8344, 9659
centrality of, 8337–8338
doctrine of, 8322, 8337
Hidden Imam, 8337–8338, 8344
tombs, pilgrimage to, 8345
twelve, 8337
imams in, 5549
ghaybah (concealment) of, 3468–3469
as saints, 8035
in Iran, 4698, 4700, 4703
Islamic Revolution in Iran and, 8340
Jaʿfar al-Ṣādiq in, 4760–4761, 8322
jurisprudence in, 8342–8343
knowledge in, 5204
law of, 4571–4572
madhhabs of, 9490
mahdī in, 5982
Muʿtazilah in, 6320–6321
Öljeitü Khudā-Banda (sultan of Persia), conversion of, 3982
on Qurʾān, 4696
origins of, 8338
Pahlavi rule and, 8340
philosophy and theosophy, 8343–8344
political and social thought in, 8344–8345
political power of, 4462
political quietism in, 8338–8339
prayer in, 4397
prevalence of, 4567
qiyās in, 4696–4697
religious practices in, 8345
renewal in, 8339–8340
Savafid state and, 8339
schisms over successions in, 8322–8323
Shaykhīyah school in, **8307–8309**
in South Asia, 4645, 4646–4647
Sunni doctrine *vs.,* 8342–8345
tafsir (Qurʾanic exegesis) in, 7565–7566, 8954
thought, development of, 8340–8342
Twelvers, development of, 8322–8323
vengeance for al-Ḥusayn in theology of, 4235
walāyah and, 9659–9660
Zaydīyah *vs.,* 8322
Īmām khaṭīb, 9817
Imāms (leaders). *See also specific figures*
as *ahl al-bayt,* 198, 199
ʿAlī ibn Abī Ṭālib as, 259
authority of, 695–696
in China, 4633, 4634, 4635, 4637
devotional allegiance to, 9819–9820
in formative period, afterlife affected by, 160
ghaybah (concealment) of, **3468–3469**
hidden, 8334, 8337–8338, 8711
Ḥusayn as, 7632
Ibāḍīs and, 4248, 4249
ignorance or disobedience of, 4394
immunity of, 4262
in ʿAlawīyūn, 225, 226
incarnation of, 4416
infallibility of, *ḥadīth* collections and, 3733
in Nizārī Ismāʿīlīyah, 557, 558

Imāms (leaders) ***continued***
in Shī'ī eschatology, 2838
Ja'far al-Ṣādiq, 4760, 4761
jihād and, 4918–4919
meaning of term, 4393
miracles and supernatural powers of, 4394–4395
on *ṣalāt* (prayer), 8055
ordination of, 6858
role of, 4761
sayings of included in *ḥadīth,* 3726
Shaykh Aḥmad on, 8307–8308
succession of, 4394
Sunnah of the Prophet, knowledge of, 3726
tombs of, pilgrimage to, 8345
ummah and, 9447
walāyah and, 9658–9659
zakāt and, 9925
Īmān (faith), **4397–4400**. *See also* Faith, in Islam
elements of, 4565
in *ḥadīth,* 4398, 4399
in Ḥanafī creed, 2064
in Qur'ān, 4397–4398, 4400
in Muslim theology, 4398–4400
origin of word, 4560
Imana (Tutsi God), 4519
in paradise lost myth, 139–140
Imaymana (deity), 4412
Imayō (songs), 6301, 7216
Imbeleko (sacrifice), 10010
Imbolg
Brighid and, 1484
in Celtic calendar, 1491
Imdugud, eagle as, 2553
Imhotep (architect)
cult of, 2712
pyramid built by, 7527
Imikhondo (tracks), 10009
Imitation
in constructive discipline, 8703–8704
of Jesus Christ, 1670, 8704
of Mary, 8704
of Muḥammad, 6227
Plato on, 45
Imitation of Christ (Thomas à Kempis), 4844, 9159–9160
influence of, 1670
teachings in, 8704
Immaculate conception, in Roman Catholicism, 5754
Immaculate Heart Sisters of Mary, Holy Order of MANS and, 4102
Immanence. *See* Transcendence and immanence
Immediacy, superhuman, in rituals, 7851
Immersion
ablution through, 9, 10, 12
in *miqveh,* 6046–6048
in mortification, 6198
Immigration
of Christians, from Middle East, 1676
eugenics and, 2880
to Europe, of Muslims, 4674–4680
to Israel (ancient), laws on, 4731
to Latin America, 1699
memory and, vol. 1 color insert
to United States
development of American religions and, 10082–10087
of Muslims, 4686, 4690–4691
Reform Judaism and, 7670
Immigration Act of 1924, 2880
Immigration and Naturalization Act (1965) (US), 830
Immolation, of Hindu widows, 3320
Immortality. *See also* Deification; Mortality; Rejuvenation
in African religions, living dead and, 141
afterlife and, views of, 133
in alchemy, 235
Chinese, 235, 237–238, 3625
ancestor veneration associated with, 2982
artificial intelligence and, 513
astral, 8424–8425
in Babylonian religion, 989
in Bambara religion, 777
baptism and, 780
birds as symbol of, 948–949
in Chinese religion
Confucian-Daoist debate, 1576
Confucian notion of, 8555
cults of, 7719
Daoism and Pure Land in, 3887–3888
deities of, 1592–1593
myth and, 1628
quest for, 1588–1589, 1590, 1592, 1597, 1603, 7267
Sima Chengzhen on, 8400
xian, 9857
zhenren (perfected people), 1588
in Christianity
biblical, 157
Feuerbach on, 3047
Lateran Council of 1513 on, 2280–2281
Paul on, 8563–8564
Swedenborg (Emanuel) on, 8898
cybernetics and, 2112
in Daoism, 4332, 8556
descent into the underworld and, 2298–2299
diamond as symbol of, 2345
dragon as custodian of, 2432
in Egyptian religion, 2237
from elixir, 2770–2772
eternity and, 2855
through eugenics, 2881
before the Fall, 2960, 2961
fountain of youth and, 3177
in Geto-Dacian religion, 3466
in Greek religion, 3664, 3666, 7871
in Hinduism
in *Bhagavadgītā* on, 852–853
Brahmā and, 1024
of humans
Gersonides on, 4895
Ibn Rushd on, 4895
in Raëlian religion, 7597, 7598
in Judaism, 4858
afterlife and, 152
in Apocrypha, 900
forms of, 3884
suffering and, 8806
of kings, 5159
"nectar of," in *khecarī* technique, 3795
in pagan religions, 7726
Plato on, 7182, 7184
in primordial paradise, 6983
quest for, *fangshi* and, 2989, 2990
ritual barter of, 7836–7837
in Roman religion, Cumont (Franz) on, 2094
in Semitic myths, 1875
serpents associated with, 8458–8459
shape shifting and, 8302
soma and *haoma* and, 849, 4439
of soul
in Greek religion, 7871
Kant (Immanuel) on, 5077
Sozzini (Fausto Pavolo) on, 8673
Spinoza (Baruch) on, 8681, 8684
as symbol of rebirth, 809
from water, 9702
Immortals *(Xian),* in Daoism, 2178, 2179, 2182
Immortal Zhongli Quan, The (Zaho Qi), vol. 10 color insert
Imo no chikara (Yanagit), 3347
Impartial History of the Churches and Heresies (Arnold), 3514
Impartiality, in moral reasoning, 6180, 6185–6186
Imperative of Responsibility (Jonas), 4949
Imperial Academy (Han Chinese), establishment of, 1897, 1917
Imperial cult. *See* Emperor's Cult
Imperial Eyes: Travel Writing and Transculturation (Pratt), 5928, 9292
Imperialism. *See also* Colonialism
cultural, missions and, 6071
Japanese, 8777
religion and, 9791
Said (Edward) on, 8032
Imperial Manuscript Library (Siku Quanshu), 2129
"Imperial Message, An" (Kafka), 6979
Imperial Rescript on Education (Japan), 4790, 4791, 4813
Imperial Shrine (Forbidden City), sacrifice to Shangdi in, 1914–1915
Imperial Temple (China), cult of imperial ancestors in, 1912
Imperial-way Buddhism, 2787
Império do Belo Monte (Brazil), 6577
Implicit religion, **4400–4402**
concept of, 4400–4401
factors of, 4401–4402
origins of, 4401
study of, 4400, 4401
Imprinting, 10043
Imps, 2952
Impure Lands (Buddhist concept), **7502–7503**
Impurity. *See also* Pollution
of death
in Hinduism, 7687
in Judaism, 7687
duration of, 7511
illness caused by, 3810
in Israelite religion, 4973
states of, 7511
transferable, 7511
of transgressive behavior, 7513–7514
of untouchables, 9474
Impurity and Sin in Ancient Judaism (Klawans), 7512, 7514
Im Sŏngju, on principle and material force, 1932
I myrtenträdgården (Andrae), 333
Inalienable Possessions (Weiner), 3480–3481
In an Antique Land (Ghosh), 10036
In and yo. *See* Yin and yang
Inanna (deity), 2596, 3003, **4402–4406,** 5956–5957. *See also* Ishara; Ishtar
Amaushumgalana and, 5951
anthropomorphism of, 5950
aspects of, 5956–5957
in cuneiform tablets, 3586
death of, 5957
descent into underworld by, 2521, 2539, 4403–4404, 5957
and Dumuzi, 2445, 2520, 2521, 2522–2523, 3976, 4403, 4404, 4405, 5949, 5956, 5957, 5958
and Enki, 2521, 2791, 4403, 4404, 4405, 5957
eyes of, 2940
family of, 5951
functions of, 5956–5957
gender of, 3594
as harlot, 5956–5957
hierodouleia (sacred prostitution) and, 3967
in Holy Wedding, 5162
iconography of, 4316, 4317
kings in sacred marriage with, 3377
lovers of, 4404–4405

manifestations of, 3594
marriage of, 5956
origins of, 3586
power sought by, 5957
prominence of, 3586, 3594
vs. other goddesses, 3376
rape of, 4404–4405
rituals of, 4470
Shaushka associated with, 4230
songs about, 2520, 2521
stealing divine powers from Enki, 4404
takes command of heaven, 4402–4403
in Uruk, 3586, 3594, 5949, 5956
as virgin, 9604
warlike qualities of, 4404, 5956
wifehood of, 3589
worship of, 3586, 3589, 3594
Inanna and the Parse (myth), 5957
Inanna's Descent to the Netherworld (myth), 5957
Inar (deity), 3595
Inara (deity), storm god and, 4069, 4070
Inari (deity), 4795
In a State of Siege (Hariharan), 10036
Inaw (carved wood offerings), 9334, 9338
Inaw (family spirit), as household spirit, 4106
Inbal Dance Theater, 2164
Inca. *See* Inca religion
"Inca Culture at the Time of the Spanish Conquest" (Howe), calendar in, 1362
Incantation, **4406–4410**. *See also* Chanting; Cursing; *Mantras*
Aramaic incantation bowls, 5458–5459
in Buddhism, 4407–4408, 5309
in Canaanite religion, 1387
in Cherokee religion, 4407, 4408, 4409
in Chuvash religion, 1785
in Daoism, 4407
defensive, 4408
in Egyptian religion, 4407, 4408
forms of address in, 4407–4408
in Ch'ŏndogyo, 1648
in Java, 4407, 4409
in Judaism, against Lilith, 5459
in magic
Eastern European, 5581–5582
Greco-Roman, 5574
Islamic, 5583
malevolent, 4409
in Maori religion, 5680
in Maya religion, 4407
in Polynesian religions, 7309, 7311
power of, 4406–4407
vs. prayer, 4406
productive, 4408–4409
purposes of, 4408–4409
rituals of, 4407
spells, **8675–8678**
of Trobriand Islanders, 4406, 4408
in Vedism, 4408
Incarceration, as punishment, 5374
Inca religion and society (South America), **4410–4414**. *See also* Andean religions; Peru; South American Indian religions
afterlife in, 4412
agriculture in, 4524
ancestors in, 4412
archaeology of, 454
under Atahuallpa, **566–568**
ayllus in, 5176
bears in, 808
calendar, **1360–1365,** 4410
ethnoastronomy in, 2865
chronicles of, 1361–1362
colonialism and, 4410, 4411
confession in, 1886
converting to Christianity, 4501
cosmology in, 4410–4411
creation in, 4524, 5292, 5633
creator god of, 9600–9601
Cuzco as sacred city in, 1503
deities of, 4410, 4411–4412 (*See also specific deities*)
gender of, 3416
images of, 4384–4385, 4410
storm, ambivalence of, 5993
sun gods in, 1364, 8576, 8842–8843
temple of, 4384, 4411, 4524
drums in, 2499, 7036
dynastic legends in, 1363–1364
education in, 5850–5851
expansion and conquest by
gender in, 3416–3417
Pachacuti (Cusi Yupanqui) and, 5176
fasting in, 2997
festivals in, 4412–4413
funeral rites in, 3234, 3240, 4412
gender in, 3415–3417
huacas in, 5177
human origin myth in, 8589
human sacrifice in
gender in, 3417
heart symbolism in, 3881
image veneration in, 4384–4385, 4386, 4410
kingship in, 1362–1363, 5175–5177, 5983–5984
divinity of, 5176
mummification and, 5176–5177
panaqa of, 5177
knots in record keeping of, 1364, 4410
under Manco Capac, **5633–5634**
meanings of *Inca* in, 5175
messianism in, 5983–5984
mummies in, 5176–5177
nativistic movements, 6576
necromancy in, 6453
origin myths in, 5175–5176
origins of, 4410
Pizarro (Francisco) and, 5175
Pleiades in, 1362, 8735
prayer in, 4412
priesthood in, 4412
rituals in, 4410, 4412–4413
sacrifices, 1364, 4411, 4412–4413
scope of, 5175
sinchis in, 5176
social and political divisions, 1362–1363
soul in, 4412
Spanish conquest of, 567, 1695, 5175, 5177
Spanish rule of
gender during, 3415–3417
resistance to, 567
sun in, 8842–8843
temples of, 4384, 4410, 4411, 4413
water in, Lake Titicaca, 5291–5292
women in, 3415–3417, 4411–4412
Incarnation, **4414–4418**. *See also* Theophany
architectural expression of, 794
in Buddhism, 2131, 4416–4417
female, in Himalayan Buddhism, 1233
in Christianity, 4414, 4417
Jewish polemics on, 7232
nature in, 2647–2648
concept of, 4414
definition of, 4414
divine kings and, 3902–3903
in Egyptian religion, 4416
evil identified with, 2899
of God in Jesus
Arianism on, 478
Athanasius on, 572
in atonement, theories of, 596
Bultmann (Rudolf) on, 8807–8808
and history, Christian views of, 4054
Kant (Immanuel) on, 5079
in New Testament, 3545–3546
in postbiblical Christianity, 3553
Servetus (Michael) on, 8232
Solov'ev (Vladimir) on, 8520
time and, 3973
in Greek religion, 4415
Hegel (G. W. F.) on, 4220
in Hinduism, 4415–4416
in Iranian religion, 4416
in Islam, 4416
kingship and, 4416
mystery of, 3553
negative interpretation of, 4414
positive interpretation of, 4414
in primitive religion, 4414–4415
scientific history and, 8181
as shape shifting, 8303
shekhinah concept and, 8315
Simons (Menno) on, 8401
twentieth-century views of, 4417–4418
Incense (St. Denis), 2157
Incense and incense offerings, 3137, **4418–4420**
in Arabian religions, 445
in Buddhism, 4419
Japanese, at Nakayama-dera Temple, 3869
Southeast Asian, 9827
in Chinese religion, 2408, 4419, vol. 7 color insert
in Christianity, 4420
in Daoism, 4419
in Hinduism, 4419
in Islam, 4420
in Israelite religion, 927, 931–932
in Judaism, 4419–4420
meaning of term, 4418
in Mesoamerican drama, 2467
in Mesoamerican religions, 5895–5896
in Mongol shamanism, 6142
in Near East, ancient, 4419
in purification, 4418–4419, 7507
in Vietnamese religion, 9593
Incest
chaos and, 1538, 1624
Freud on, 2239, 7974
kings and, 5155
moon and, 2863
and pollution, 7506
prohibitions on, exogamy in, 5726
as taboo, 8949
as universal mythologem, 2985
in Wawalag myth, 9705
Inclusivism, Smith (Wilfred Cantwell) on, 8451

Incomprehensibility, of God, in postbiblical Christianity, 3553–3554
Incongruity, humor as, 4194, 4221
Increase rite, in Mardu religion, 5706
Incubation, 464–465
 Asklepios and, 551, 552, 6051
 sleep and, 8441
Incubation oracles, 6833
Incubi (monsters), 6164, 6165
Incubus (demon), 2278
Inculturation theology, 142
 in Asia, 1730
In Darkest England and the Way Out (Booth), 1020
 Victorian society in, 8064
Independence, political
 in Africa, and new religious movements, 105–106
 in Oceanic, 6797
Independence Day (Israel), 4868
Independence day celebrations, 1515
Independence model of science and religion. *See* Two Language model
Independent Labour Party (India), 286
Independents. *See* Congregationalism
Indeterminism
 chance and, 1527
 quantum, 7139
Index of Forbidden Books
 during Enlightenment, 4506
 heresy and, 3928
 Lettres provinciales (Pascal) on, 7001
India (al-Bīrūnī), 954, 955
India and Indian religions, **4426–4451**. *See also* Hinduism; Jainism; Vedism; *specific religions*
 academic study of religion in (*See* Study of religion, in South Asia)
 affliction in, 57
 Aga Khan I in, 173
 ages of world in, 176–177
 ahiṃsā doctrine, 1467
 Aḥmadiyah in, 200
 alchemy in (*See* Alchemy, Indian)
 altars in, 275–276
 ancestor worship in, 322–323, 2982
 androgynes in, 338, 339
 animals in, 359–360
 archaeology in, 455–456
  Foucher (Alfred) and, 3176
 ashrams in, 545–547
 astrology in, 564
 astronomy in
  comets in, 8736
  falling stars in, 8736
  stars, system of, 8733
 asuras in, 204–205
 atheism in, 578–581
 attention in, 603
 authority in, 692–693
 autobiography in, 700–701
 avidyā in, **710–711**
 Āyurveda in, 713–715
 bhakti cults, 3002
 birth in, 951–952
 British role in classifying, 1855
 British rule in
  Ahmad Khan on, 201
  Aurobindo Ghose opposing, 633
  Āyurveda and, 3856
  and Buddhism, 7262–7263
  caste system, effect on, 1858
  Christianity and, 1729
  and Hinduism, 10042
  and iconoclasm, 4284
  Indological studies, 4446
  and Islam, 4641, 4645, 4651–4653
  and Islamic law, 4701
  legal system under, 5346
  opposition to (*See* India and Indian religions, nationalism in)
  and Orientalism, 9316–9317
  and Parsis, 6998
  partition of India, Smith (Wilfred Cantwell) on, 8450
  religious control exerted in, 1855
  sati outlawed in, 8130
  Sen (Keshab Chandra) on, 8227
  and social reform, 2330–2331
  Swaminarayan movement and, 8889–8890
  and Western influences on Hinduism, 4007–4008
  and woman question, 3319–3320
 Buddhism, **1101–1131,** 4428–4429
  Ajantā cave paintings, 1471–1472
  ālaya-vijñāna in, 228–229
  Ambedkar's (B. R.) conversion and, 286–287
  Aśoka's impact on, 553–556, 1089, 1090–1091, 1145, 1161
  Bodhidharma and, 994
  bodhisattvas in, 1082
  under British rule, 7262–7263
  Cakrasamvara Tantra, **1349–1350**
  celebrations in, 1304, 1305
  and Chinese Buddhism, 1094–1095, 1160
  councils of, 2035–2037
  decline of, 1125–1126, 6072
  ethics of, 1280
  Guhyasamāja Tantra in, 3708
  Hīnayāna Buddhism, 1093
  Hinduism and, 1108–1109, 1121, 1125–1126
  human perfectibility in, 7040–7041
  iconography of, 4328, 4329, 4330
  incense offering in, 4419
  instability of, 1094, 1095, 1108–1109
  Kālacakra tradition in, 5056–5058
  and Korean Buddhism, 1170
  Kṣitigarbha in, 5255
  of lay people, 1107, 1114–1115
  literature of, 1198, 1199, 1200, 1260, 1271
  mahāmudrā in, 5596–5597
  Mahāsāṃghika Buddhism, 1195
  Mahāyāna Buddhism, 1093
  Mahīśasaka school, 1195
  maṇḍalas in, 5642–5643
  Middle Way, 5070–5071
  missions and, 1099
  monasteries, 1095, 1105–1107, 6127, 6129
  monasticism in, 6127, 6128, 6129
  music in, 6282–6283
  origins of, 1102–1105
  philosophy of, 1295–1301
  pilgrimage in, 7163–7164, 7166
  pūjā in, 7496
  revival of, 1126–1127
  Sammatīya sect, 1195
  schools of, 1109–1110, 1112–1115, 1195, 1200
  spread of, 1091–1092, 1093
  stupa complex as monumental religious architecture, 1805
  stupas in, 9264
  Theravāda Buddhism, 9147–9148
  and Tibetan Buddhism, 1153, 1154, 9184
  universities and, 1118–1121
  Vajrayāna (Tantric) Buddhism, 1093, 1121–1125, 1153, 1214, 1221, 5056–5058
  Vibhajyavāda school, 1195
  vs. Nyāya, 6773
  weaving symbolism in, 9713
  Yogācāra Buddhism, 9897–9901
 caste system in (*See* Castes)
 castrated priests, 1451
 cattle and the sacred cow, 1465, 1467
 caves, painted, 1471–1472
 chanting in, 1535
 charisma in, 1548–1549
 Chinese Buddhist pilgrims to, 3010–3011
 Christianity, 1729–1730, 4431
  caste and, 9476–9477
  Hinduism, relations with, 1855
  missions, 6084, 6086
  music in, 6285
  Nestorian church, 6480
  Pentecostalism, 7030
  reasons for conversion to, 6084
  Roman Catholicism, 1729, 1730
  Syriac Orthodox Church in, 8940
 circumambulation in, 1796
 cities in, sacred space and, 1805–1807
 confession in, 1886
 constitution of, untouchables in, 286
 cosmology in, 1995
 creation in, of man, 3454
 dance in, 2137, 2140
 dance of, ecological concerns raised through, 2623
 deities of (*See specific deities*)
 dice games in, 3263
 Dīvālī festival in, 6594
 drums in, 2448, 2494, 2496, 2499, 7036
 ecology and, **2620–2624**
 education in, Ambedkar (B. R.) and, 286
 elephants in, 2750
 Eliade in, 2753–2754, 2760
 environmental activism in, 2622–2623
 eremitism in, 2823
 eschatology in, 2834
 exorcism in, 2933–2934
 films from, 3098
 fire in, 3116–3117
 funeral rites in, 3240
 gambling in, 3263
 gender studies in, 3321–3324
 ghosts in, 3477
 goats in, 8311–8312
 goddess worship in, 3585
 God in, nature of, 128
 heterodox (*See* Ājīvikas)
 hijāda gender reversal in, 4116
 Hijras community, cross-gender dressing in, 1827
 Hinduism (*See* Hinduism)
 historiography, traditional, 4025–4026, 4030
 history of study of, **4445–4451**
  beginnings of, 4445–4446
  classical, 4446–4447

Glasenapp (Helmuth von) in, 3496–3497
philosophical, 4447–4448
recent trends in, 4449–4451
scientific, 4448–4449
horse myths in, 4133
horse sacrifice in, 4132–4133
sexuality and, 8239
humor in, 4195
independence movement in
Besant's (Annie) role in, 845
Bhave's (Vinoba) role in, 861–862
International Society for Krishna Consciousness in, 4522
interplay with Western religions, Radhakrishnan (Sarvepalli) on, 7595
Islam
under Akbar, 216–217, 4647, 4648–4649, 4649–4650
Ameer Ali (Syed) on, 288–289
architecture of mosques in, 6209
under British rule, 4641, 4645, 4651–4653
caste and, 9476
Hindu influence on, 4007–4008, 4641, 4643–4644
Jainism and, 4766
law, 4644
literature, 4644
madrasahs, 4645
mosques in, 6209
music in, 6278, 6279, 6283–6284
Muslim identity in, 4653–4654
Muslim minorities, 4641, 4655
Nizārīyah movement in, 8334
personality cults in, 4649–4650
reform movements in, 4650–4651
role of culture in, 4643–4644
sacred and commercial urban space in, 1806
Schimmel (Annemarie) on, 8150
Shiism, 4646, 4647
Sirhindī (Aḥmad), role in, 8413–8414
Sufism, 4647, 4648–4649
Sunnī Islam, 4644–4645
Ṭayyibīyah movement in, 8335–8336
Walī Allāh (Shāh) in, 9666
Jainism (*See* Jainism)
jihād doctrine in, 4919
Judaism, 5005, 5006–5007
music in, 6285
judgment of the dead in, 5026
Karaga festival in Bangalore, 1807
karman in, **5093–5097**
kingship in
Cakravartin ideal, **1350–1352**
rural traditions of, 4434
knowledge in, 5199–5200
Lady of the Animals in, 5280
law in
secular *vs.* religious, 5330
Southeast Asia influenced by, 5346
lesbianism in, 5415
liberation theology in, 5442
literature and religion in
fiction, 10033–10036
interrelations of, 5466–5467
little kingdoms in
Muslim rule and, 4007
popular Hinduism and king as *jajmān* in, 4007
logic in, 5497
lotus symbolism in, 5518
magic in, 5587–5591
Marathi religions, **5696–5700**
martial arts in, 5730–5731
medicine and healing in, 713–714 (*See also* Āyurveda; *See also* Ūnānī; Siddha medical system)
meditation in, 5819–5821
merit in, 5870
migration in, 6023–6024
millenarianism in, 6030
miracles in, 6052
mirrors in, 6064
mokṣa in, **6115–6117**
money in, 6137
monism in, 6144
monkeys in, 6150–6152
moon in
death and, 6174
myths about, 6172–6173
time and, 6171
morality in, 6187
mountains in, as divine dwellings, 6213
mudrās in, 6219–6220
museums in, 6245
music in, **6278–6287**
classification of, 6279–6280, 6285
retention of old, 6279
ritual meaning of, 6279
sound and, 6278–6279
structure of, 6279
mysticism in, chaos and, 1539–1540
mythic themes in, **4437–4445**
animals, 4437–4439
cosmic ages, 176–177
deities, 4443–4444
dharma, 4441–4442
eschatology and death, 4440–4441
the Fall, 2963–2964
the Flood, 2963–2964, 3130, 4440
Ganges River, 3274–3275
gods and demons, 4439, 4442–4443
illusion, 4443
Manu in, 5678–5679
mokṣa, 4440, 4441–4442
totemism and, 4437
trees and mountains, 4439
nationalism in
and ashram revival, 545–546
Aurobindo Ghose and, 633
feminine sacrality associated with, 3021
Gandhi (Mohandas) and, 3272–3273, 5398, 9319
goddess worship and, 3609
religious, 7255–7256
Tagore (Rabindranath) on, 8958, 9319
Theosophical Society in, 9143
Tilak (Bal Gangadhar) in, 9198–9199, 9319
Vivekananda in, 7255–7256, 9319, 9631
woman question in, 3320
new religious movements with origins in, 6568
nonviolence in, 6645–6646
North India (*See* Hindi religious traditions)
North Star in, 8734
nudity in, 6740–6741
number symbolism in, 6747, 6748, 6749
number system in, 6752
orgy in, 6878–6879
Pāñcarātra in, 9509
politics in
Āyurveda and, 3856
Shiv Sena (army of Śiva) party, 8418
rainbow symbolism in, 7604
reformers, Christianity and, 1730
religious broadcasting and, 7714
religious studies in, **8789–8792**
renunciates in (*See Sadhus/Sadhvis*)
resurrection in, 7763
ritual calendar of, agriculture and, 187
rivers of, 7861–7862
female sacrality of, 3016
Ganges, 12, **3274–3275,** 7861
Seven Gaṅās, 7861
royalty of, Jainism and, 4765
rural traditions in, **4432–4437**
cultural groups in, 4432, 4433–4434
epic poems, 4434
goddess worship, 3608, 4432–4433
heroes and ancestors, 4435–4436
iconography, 4433, 4434, 4435
kingship, 4434
music, 4434–4435
priesthood, 4435
women, 4435
sacred space in, land east of Sadanira River as, 7979
salutations in, 8060–8061, 8062
Schlegel (Friedrich) on, 8159
secularization in, 8219
sexual themes in, 7082–7084
Freud on, 3217
Sharpe (Eric) on, 8304
Sikhism
gender in, 3335–3338
idolatry condemned in, 4431
rebellion of, 7257
social reform in
Ārya Samāj in, 516
Gandhi (Mohandas) in, 3272–3273
soul concepts in, **8544–8550**
sound in, 6278–6279
spells in, 8677
spirit possession in, 2140, 8694, 8697
spread to Southeast Asia, 5128
subaltern studies and, 8800–8802
Sufism, Chishtī order, 6638–6639
temples in (*See also* Temples, Hindu)
heaven and earth connected in, 7984
Theosophical Society in, 7228, 9142
theosophy in, 6815–6816
transculturation of, **9316–9320**
tree symbolism in, 3449
tribal communities of (*See Ādivasis*)
turtles in, 9407
untouchables of (*See* Untouchables)
Vaiṣṇavism in, 9500
Vajrasattva in, 9514–9515
Vedas, role in, 8545
violence in
in public life, 6646–6647
religious, 1808
virginity in, 9607
wisdom in, 9752–9753

India and Indian religions *continued*
woman question in, 3319–3321
women's studies in, 3321, 3322–3324
Xuanzang in, 9861
yuni pilgrimage sites in, 9906
Zimmer (Heinrich) on, 9975
Zoroastrianism (*See also* Parsis; Zoroastrianism)
fire in, 570, 6997
magi in, 9991
India and Its Faith: A Traveler's Record (Pratt), 7367
Indian Association for the Study of Religion (IAHR)
Marburg Congress (1960), 8789
Regional Conference (Delhi, 2003), 8791
Indian Boy Scouts Association, 845
Indianization, 5128
of China, by Buddhist missions, 6071, 6072
music and, 6279
Indian Journal of Gender Studies, 3322
Indian languages, in *Ādi Granth,* 32
Indian Medicine Central Council Act (IMCCA), 3856
Indian National Congress
Ahmad Khan opposing, 201
Besant (Annie) as president of, 845, 9143
Indian philosophies, **4420–4426**
atheism in, 578–579
Cārvāka, **1446–1447**
Dvaita Vedānta school of, Madhva in, 5550–5551
European Enlightenment and, 4420, 4425
heterodox systems of, 4420–4422, 4428–4429
history of, 4420
jñāna, karma, and *bhakti* in, 4421, 4423
Nyāya, **6772–6774**
orthodox systems of, 4420–4421, 4423
Smart (Ninian) on, 8443
Stcherbatsky (Theodore) on, 8737
texts of, 4423–4424
unity and plurality in, 4420–4421, 4422–4423
Vaiśeṣika (*See* Vaiśeṣika school)
Indian Renaissance, 6816
Indian Reorganization Act (1934). *See* Wheeler-Howard Act (1934)
Indian Revolution (1857), Ahmad Khan on, 201, 202
Indians, American. *See* Mesoamerica; North American Indian religions; South American Indian religions; *specific tribes*
Indian Shakers (Pacific Northwest), 6667, 6718–6719
confession and, 7759
study of, 6671
Indian Systems of Medicine and Homeopathy (ISM&H), 3856. *See also* Āyurveda; *See also* Ūnānī; Siddha medical system
Indifference, of supreme beings, 8870
Indigeneity, postcolonial, 1858
Indigenism, 2617
Indigenista studies, in South America, 8595
Indigenization, of Orthodox Churches, 2589
Indigenous Church, The (Allen), 677
Indigenous peoples and religions. *See also specific countries, peoples, and regions*
colonialism influencing, 10047
definition of, 2616, 5340–5341
ecology and, **2616–2620**
feminist spirituality movements and, 9789
gardens of, **3279–3281**
laws of, **5339–5343**
approaches to study of, 5339–5340
liberation theology and, 5440
magic in, **5569–5572**
political function of, 7295–7296
precontact, 2616
soul in, **8531–8534**
destiny of, 8533–8534
origin of, 8533
theoretical elaborations on, 8531–8532
varieties of, 8532–8533
study of, 10064–10065
voices of, 2617
Indigenous resistance. *See* Zapatismo and indigenous resistance
Indigitation, 2232
Indiki (spirit possession), 10010–10011
Individual, interdependence with collective, 7796–7797
Individual and His Religion, The (Allport), 7476
Individual eschatology, 2834
Individualism
in Africa, 143
Bellah (Robert) on, 8489
in Brahmanism, 9571–9572
Campbell on, 1379
community interests superseding, vol. 6 color insert
congregational polity and, 1939
Durkheim *vs.* Weber on, 8488
in existentialism, 2926–2927
in faith, 2957
in fiction, 3055
in Hellenism, 3600, 3901
hope and, 4127
human body and, 4171
in modern society, 7799–7800
music and, 6249
in New Age movement, 6496, 6498–6499
in new religious movements, in Japan, 6575
privatized, modern religion, 8472
in Protestantism, 7453, 7457
Puritanism and, 5399
schism and, 8152
Spiritualism and, 8715
in Sufism, in Malāmatīyah branch, 8821
Tönnies (Ferdinand) on, 8466–8467
vision quest and, 9610
Individuality, Cassirer (Ernst) on, 1448
Individuation
Buddha on, 8551
Jung on, 1950, 7475
Indlovukah (elephant/queen), in Swazi religion, 8895
Indo-Aryan religion, deities of, Hittite religion, adoption into, 4230–4231
Indo' Belo Tumbang (deity), 9241
"Indo-European," basis of, 9801
Indo-European languages
family of, 4452, 4457–4458
and "holy," concept of, 7969
study of, 4458, 10076
supreme beings in, 8875
word for God in, 4452, *4453*
Indo-European religions, **4452–4466**. *See also specific religions*
birds in, 948
calendar, 1353
Celtic literature and, 1495, 1499
comparative mythology, 1874
cosmology in, 4454, 4464
creation myths in, 4439–4440, 4453, 4454
death and resurrection in, 4456
deities of, 4454, 4456
in Slavic pantheon, 8434–8436
with three heads, 3804
dragons in, 2431–2432
Dumézil (Georges) on, 2518–2519, 4440, 4453, 4454, 4461–4464, 10079
epic traditions in, 2815
eschatology in, 4456
Frazer (James G.) on, 4461
and freedom, idea of, Sabazios associated with, 7953
head hunting in, 3805
history of study of, 4452, **4457–4466**
in 19th century, 4446, 4458–4459, 10076–10077
anthropological, 4460
empirical, 4460–4461
first paradigm of, 4459–4460
naturistic, 4459–4460
neo-comparative, 4461
origins of, 4457–4458
recent developments in, 4464–4465
second paradigm of, 4461–4464
homosexuality in, 4113
horses in, 4132, 4452
myths of, 4133–4135
sacrifice of, 1493, 4132–4133
marriage in, 4455
microcosm-macrocosm homologization in, 4159
oral traditions of, 6842–6843
prehistoric (*See* Prehistoric religions, in Old Europe)
priesthood in, 4453, 4454, 4455
rituals in, 4454–4456
sacrifice in, 4454–4455, 4456
sexual images, destruction of, 3975–3976
sky gods in, 8424, 8838, 8875
Slavic religion and, 8432
social structure in, 4453–4454
soul in, 4456
sun in, 8838–8839
sun-myth in, Latvian Saule (sun) cult and, 8134
twins in, 9416–9417
war and warriors in, 4453–4454, 4455, **9683–9687**
Zeus derived from, 3663, 3664
Indo-Iranian religion
cattle in, 1466, 1467
Christensen on, 1649
prehistoric, **7382–7388**
sacrifice in, 8006
Sarmatian religion, **8114–8115**
Scythian religion and, 8205
Slavic religion, influence on, 8432
sun in, 8838
Indologica Taurinensia (journal), 10058
Indombe (mythic figure), 93, 97
Indonesia and Indonesian religions. *See also* Acehnese religion; Southeast Asia and Southeast Asian religions; Sumatra; Toraja religion
agricultural myths in, 5277
animal symbolism and beliefs, cats, 1463
Batak religion, **799–800**
Christianity in, 1729
textiles in, 1828, 9089
blood in, 987
boats in, 991
Buddhism
missions and, 1099
origins of, 1133
schools of, 1201

Bugis religion, **1316–1318**
cargo cults in Irian Jaya, 1414
Ceramese people, Hainuwele story of, 2091–2092, 3015, 3018
Christianity, 1729
conversion to, 1973
Pentecostalism, 7030
demographics, religious, 8647
fiction of, 3078
the Flood in mythology of, 3130
funeral rites in, 3235, 3236, 9227
government recognition of religions, 8647–8648
history of study, colonialist agenda in scholarship on, 8638
hypereridic rage reactions (amok) in, 3214
illness in, saliva and, 8722
independence of, 4669
Indonesian Communist Party (PKI), coup attempt (1965) and, 1973
Islam, 4671 (*See also* Bugis religion)
academic neglect of, 8638
architecture of mosques in, 6209
conversion to, 4661
feminism in, 3367
in politics, 4668–4670
reform movements in, 4665, 4667–4668
spread of, 4563, 4658
as state religion, 4669
ṭarīqah in, 9012
Kodi religion in, communal performances of healing in, 3815
languages in, 25, 4657
life in, 5444–5445
martial arts in, 5732–5733
megalithic religion, 5827–5828
millenarianism in, 8648
music in, 6287, 6288, 6290, 6291
mysticism in, 25
new religious movements in, 8652–8653
religious revolts in, 4669
ritual clothing in, 1828
Snouck Hurgronje (Christiaan) on, 8460
textiles in, 9088, 9090
traditional religions in, government policies and, 8648
Indonesian Association of Muslim Intellectuals (ICMI), 4670
Indonesian language, 25
Indo' Ongon-ongon (deity), 9241
Indra (deity), **4466–4468**
and ants, 4508
as archdemon, 2128
Arjuna as son of, 486–487
as *sahasramuṣka,* 3040
at Kurukṣetra, 5268
and binding, 937
birth of, 4440, 4467
in Buddhist mythology, 4467
castration of, 4467
cattle recovered by, 1465
characteristics of, 4466–4467
Chinggis Khan as son of, 1645
doubt about existence of, 577
dragon defeated by, 2431, 4439, 4467
drinking *soma,* 4466, 4467
functions of, 5758–5759
in Hindu mythology, 4467
hymns to, 4467
in Āyurveda, 714
lightning of, 7603
magic of, 5590
masculine sacrality exemplified in, 5758–5759
Mithra and, 6087
net of (metaphor), in Huayan Buddhism, 4147
physical power of, 7351–7352
as ram, 8311
sins of, 9684–9685
soma and, 3455, 4439, 4466, 4467, 8521, 8522
sovereignty of, 5995
suffering inflicted by, 9119
symbols of, 5758–5759, 5993
tapas generated in, 8997
thunderbolt of, 967, 9511–9512
Triśiras, struggle with, 3804
values represented by, 5758–5759
Vedas on, 577
in Vedism, 9556, 9560
violence of, 8872
Viṣṇu and, 9617–9618
Vṛtra slain by, 9645–9646
as warrior, 4466, 4467
wife of, 4467
Inductive logic, 5497
Indulgences, vol. 7 color insert
Crusade indulgences, 2074, 2076
Hus (Jan), opposition from, 4233
definition of, 158
in Luther's Ninety-five Theses, 5535, 7657
merit and, 5877
origins of concept, 158
Protestant rejection of, 158, 7657
Indus River, 3274, 7861
Industrialization
economistic responses to, 2675–2676
implicit meaning of, 9931
in Latin America, 1700
religion and, 2669
Roman Catholicism and, 7878
secularization and, 8218
social reform and, 1750, 1752
sociology and, 8481
Industrial revolution
gender and, 3361
occultism and, 6782
Indus Valley religion, **4468–4475**
animals in, 4473–4474
archaeology and, 456
goddess worship in, 3608, 4427, 4468, 4470–4472, 4473
great goddess and sexuality in, 3975
iconography in, 4472–4474
origins of, 4468–4470
as precursor to Hinduism, 3988–3989
proto-Paśupati seals from, 8039
rivers in, 7861
urbanization and, 4470–4472
yoni icons in, 9905–9906
Ineffability, in mystical states, James (William) on, 1948, 6341
Inequality, human rights and, 4181
Inerrancy, biblical, in Adventist theology, 8236
Inertial mass, relativity theory and, 2032
Infallibility
of church, in ecumenism, 2689
of Shīʿī *imāms, ḥadīth* collections and, 3733
of the Pope
ultramontanism and, 9442
Vatican Council I on, 2044, 9528–9532
Infanticide, 2982
in diabolical witchcraft, 9771
Infants
baptism of, 782
confirmation and, 7956
in Orthodox Church, 2592
in Protestantism, 7455
in Christianity, initiation of, in Eastern Orthodox tradition, 7960
ghosts and, in Kaguru religion, 2576
images of
in Egyptian religion, vol. 13 color insert
in Olmec religion, vol. 13 color insert
sacrifice of, for Rukuba king, 5170
Inferno (Dante), 4275, 9455
Infertility
metaphor of, 7078, 7080
trees healing, 9334
Infibulation, 1824, 1825. *See also* Clitoridectomy
Infidelity, in Islam, blasphemy overlapping with, 975, 976
Infidels, in Islam, judgment of, 3885
Infinite, in Greek philosophy, 2854
Inflation (boiling) of the universe, 2033–2034
Influenza, and Aladura movement, 104
Influx, spiritual, in metaphysical movements, healing and, 3849, 3850
INFORM. *See* Information Network Focus on Religious Movements
Information Network Focus on Religious Movements (INFORM), 6524, 6569
Ing (deity), 6943
Ingalls, Daniel H. H., on Rudra-Śiva, 8414
Inge, Dean, on knowledge, 5207
Inge, W. R.
on ecstasy and union, 2682
and liberal Protestantism, 6105
on mysticism, definitions of, 6341
Ingemann, Frances J., 5709
Ingerman, Sandra, on soul loss, 8279
"Ingesting the Marvelous" (Campany), 2637
Ingestion, for healing, 3812
Ingolstadt, Eck (Johann) at, 2601
Ingrians, Lutheranism of, 5092
Inguaeones (Germanic tribe), 3447
Ingwenyama (lion/king)
Ncwala ritual and, 8897
in Swazi religion, 8895
Inheritance
and ancestor worship, 323
Holdheim (Samuel) on, 4080
in Islam
gender and, 3368
in *walāyah,* 9656, 9657
laws on, 4564, 4707, 4709–4710
waqf and, 9677
in Israelite religion, laws on, 4732, 4735–4736
in North American Indian religions (*See* Potlatch)
In His Steps (Sheldon), 4844
Iñigo López de Loyola. *See* Ignatius Loyola
Inikagapi (Lakota sacred rite), 5296
Inipi (bath), 801
Inipi (Lakota sacred rite), 5296
Inis Tarbhnai, 1485
Initiated Druze, 2502
Initiation, **4475–4488**. *See also* Rites of passage
ablution as, 10
into adulthood (*See* Puberty rites)
in African religions
Agikuyu, 7805

in African religions *continued*
in Benin, 3806
central Bantu, 1507
into cults of affliction, 61, 4478, 4520
dance in, 4483, 4485
Dogon, 100–101, 2391
as drama, 2457, 2459
Fulbe, 3228–3229
for girls, 818, 4478, 4484–4485
history of study of, 118
iconography in, 4303
interlacustrine Bantu, 4520
Kongo, 5220
Ndembu, 6446–6447, 9405–9406
in Ndembu Chihamba cult, 4197–4198
psychedelic drugs in, 7470
purification in, 4486
rites of passage for, 88–89
sexuality in, 4484, 4485, 4486
of Swazi diviners, 8896
Tswana, 9389
in Afro-Brazilian religions, Candomblé, 122, 123
into alchemy, 235
allotactic, 9721
anthropologists on, 4480
in Australian religions
Aboriginal, 6590
for boys, 4476, 4477, 4480, 4481
for girls, 4478
history of study of, 681, 682
Howitt (A. W.) on, 4142
for medicine men, 4477
mimicking of maternal role in, 2985
ordeals of, 4477
psychedelic drugs in, 7468–7469
Rainbow Snake and, 7605
into secret cults, 4478
tjurungas in, 9212
in Bambara religion, 777
biological roots of, 2868
blacksmiths' role in, 5988–5989
blood in, 4481
Brelich (Angelo) on, 1048
in Buddhism, 4483
in Tibetan Buddhism, 8713
catharsis in, 1460
caves and, 1470
in Chinese religion, of king, 5179
in Christianity, 4479, 4482–4483
baptism as, 1669, 9809–9810
catechumenate, restoration of, 7961–7962
as Eastern Orthodox rite, 7960
mystagogical catecheses of Cyril of Jerusalem, 2118
Protestant, 7454–7456
in Dacian Riders, 2124
in Daoism, 2195, 7683
death and rebirth symbols in, 2237
in East African religions, 2569
northeast Bantu, 2577
in Eleusinian mysteries, 2751–2752
epispanic, 9721
to Essene sect, 2846
feminine sacrality in, 3018
in Finno-Ugric communities, 3107
fish symbolism in, 3123
genital mutilation, 1451, 4481 (*See also* Circumcision; Clitoridectomy)
in Germanic religion, 4478–4479
in Greek religion, 4482
agōgē, 183–184
in cult of Sabazios, 7953
in Dionysos cult, 2357, 2358
Hera and, 3915
homosexuality in, 184
martial and heroic, 4478
haircutting in, 3739–3740
in Hinduism, 4483, 7815
circumambulation in, 1797
in *Saṃnyāsa*, 8093–8094
Tantric, 8992
historians of religion on, 4480, 4484
in Holy Order of MANS, 4102
in Inca religion, 4412
in Indian religions, in Gauḍīya and Vallabha orders, 3986
into Kālacakra tradition, 5057–5058
as invigoration rite, 8210
in Iranian religion, 4537
of kings, 5165
in Islam, in Sufism, 9006, 9011
in Israelite religion, 4744
in Jainism, 4769
in Japanese religions, in Shugendō, 8380
in Judaism, 4482
key symbolism in, 5116–5117
liminality phase of rites, 5461
in Mardu religion, 5705
Masonic, 3197
meaning of term, 4475–4476, 4480
in Melanesian religions, 4478, 5837
homosexual practices in, 4114–4115
men's, 951, **4480–4484**
Australian Indigenous, 4476, 4477, 4480, 4481
Buddhist, 1098
bull-roarers in, 1320
Dogon, 2391
Hindu, 952
martial and heroic, 4478–4479
ordeals of, 4477–4478
into secret societies, 4476, 4478, 4482–4483
vs. women's, 4484, 4487
monastic, retreats of, 7769–7770
in Mordvin religion, 4478
mortification in, 6197–6198
in mystery religions, 6327
in Neopaganism, 6471, 7829
in New Guinea religions, 4477, 6505, vol. 9 color insert
in New Year ceremonies, 6590
in North American Indian religions
California, 6713, 6715, 6716
as drama, 2461, 2462
Navajo, 6659–6660
into secret cults, 4478
Sun in, 4485–4486
women in, 3408, 4485–4486, 6659–6660, 10069–10071
novels as, 3056
in Oceanic religions, 4478, 6802, 7296, 7807
ordeals in rituals of, 4477–4478, 4481–4482, 6850
pain in, 6945
as paradigm for rites of passage, 7801
psychologists on, 4480, 4481
vs. puberty rites, 7807
religious communities and, 1864
into religious vocation, 4476, 4477, 4483
resurrection in, 4476, 4477–4478, 4480–4481, 4482–4483
retreats of, 7768, 7769
reversal of time in, 7683
in Samoyed religion, of shamans, 8096
in secret societies, 4476–4477, 8211
Christian, 4479, 4482–4483
female, 4476, 4478
male, 4476, 4478, 4482–4483
in shamanism (*See* Shamanism)
in Sikhism, 3878
Amrit initiation, 8395, 8397
sociologists on, 4480, 4481
in South American Indian religions
overview of, 8585
into secret cults, 4478
in Selk'nam religion, 8224–8225
in spirit possession, 8690–8691
supreme beings in, 8873–8874
symbolic death in Kwakiutl religion, 1503
tarot cards and, 1414
tattooing as, 1001, 1002, 1003
as transitional sacrament, 7956
trees in, 9339
in Turkic religion, 9400
underworld journey as, 9451
in Ungarinyin religion, 9461–9462
in Vanuatu religions, 9520
in visions, 9614
in Vodou, vol. 6 color insert
in Warlpiri religion, 9695–9696
in West African religions, 9721
knowledge in, 9720
women's, 951, **4484–4488**
African, 4478, 4484–4485
Australian Indigineous, 4478
Bemba, 818
in California religions, 6715
cicatrization, 1003
lack of studies on, 4484
vs. men's, 4484, 4487
in Navajo religion, 6659–6660
in North American Indian religions, 4485–4486, 10069–10071
purification in, 4484, 4485, 4486
rituals of, 4484, 4487
into secret societies, 4476, 4478
and sexuality, 4484, 4485, 4486
winter carols and, 9743
in Yurupary cult, 9919–9920
in Zoroastrianism, 9999–10000
Initiatory deification, 2249
In-itself, 8116
Injannashi (Buddhist writer), 1150
Inkarri (mythic figure), 567
and Kechwa nativistic movements, 6576
messianism of, 5984, 8604
iNkosazana. *See* uNomkhubulwana
Inkosazana yase zulweni (mythic figure), 3281
iNkosi yeZulu (deity)
vs. uNkulunkulu, as supreme being, 96
in Zulu religion, 10008
Inner alchemy, 2185, 2187, 2188
in China, Liu An and, 5494–5495
in Korea, 2189
writings on, 2211

Inner Asia and Inner Asian religions, **4488–4494**. *See also specific countries and religions*
ancient views of, 4488–4489
vs. Central Asia, 4488
ecology of, 4488
history of, 4489–4494
Hun religion, **4228–4229**
languages in, 4488
medieval views of, 4489
oral sources of, 4488
prehistoric religions in, **7382–7388**
shamanism in, **8280–8287**
turtles in, 9407
warriors in, 4489, 4490, 4494
written sources of, 4488
Inner City Movement (Germany), Holiness movement and, 8446
Inner life, orientation towards, salvation and, 7697
Inner light theory
conscience and, 1943
Symeon the New Theologian on, 8920
Inner logos, 5503–5504
Inner Reaches of Outer Space (Campbell), lectures in, 1378
Inner Winds. *See Angina*
Inner World, The (Kakar), 7478
Inness, George, Swedenborgianism and, 8903–8904
Innocence, sacred *vs.* profane and, 7973
Innocente, Geraldine, 4247
Saint Germaine Foundation and, 1782
Innocent I (pope), **4494–4495**
letters of, 4495
life of, 4494–4495
Pelagius condemned by, 7026, 7027
Innocent II (pope), 839
Innocent III (pope), **4495–4497**
administrative and judicial affairs of, 4496, 6971
authority of, 9110
Catharism, crack down against, 1458, 2412
conflict with King John, 7280
Constantinianism and, 1968
Crusades and, 2075, 4496, 4499
excommunication used by, 2921
and Francis of Assisi, 3184
Frederick II and, 4495–4496
and Inquisition, 4496, 4498–4499
Lateran IV and, 5337, 5338
life of, 4495
liturgical color system of, 1744
on Pērkons cult, 7053
papal power restored by, 7876
pastoral care and reforms of, 821, 4496
schism and, 8157
seeking reform of monasticism, 821
writings of, 4495
Innocent IV (pope), 4493, 6971
Innocents, Feast of. *See* Fools, Feast of
Innocent VIII (pope)
on astrology, 564
on Pico della Mirandola, 7141
Innocent X (pope)
on grace, 6973
Jansenism condemned by, 7001
against Peace of Westphalia, 6973
Innocent XI (pope)
Benedictine College of Sant'Anselmo founded by, 822
halting Muslim expansion of Europe, 6973
Louis XIV's conflict with, 6973
Gallicanism and, 3258
and Quietism, 7558, 7559, 7876
Innocent XII (pope)
nepotism banned by, 6973
Quietism disapproved by, 6973
Innokentii Veniaminov, **4497,** 7942–7943
Innovation
in Confucianism, 2633
North American Indian, 6426
Inoue Hisashi, 3073
Inoue Tesujirō
Anesaki Masaharu influenced by, 342
and study of religion in Japan, 8777
In Our Time (Hemingway), 5481
Inouye, Daniel, 7303
Inquisition (Catholic), **4498–4507**
criminal justice and, 8013–8014
manuals of, 9772
Marranos in, 5717–5718, 5719, 5720–5722
in the New World, 1698, **4502–4507,** 5917–5918
activities and offenses of, 4505–4506
development of, 4503–4504
exemptions granted in, 5918
origins of, 4502–4503
purpose of, 4503–4504
victims of, 4504, 4505
visitations and autonomous tribunals in, 4504–4505
in the Old World, **4498–4502**, 6971 (*See also* Portuguese Inquisition; Roman Inquisition; Spanish Inquisition)
in Hungary, 4226
influence of, 4502
medieval, 4498–4500
modern, 4500–4501
opposition to, 4498
origins of, 4496, 4498–4499, 6971
purpose of, 4498
records of, reliability of, 5717–5718
Roman criminal law revived in, 8013
Servetus (Michael) executed by, 8233
superstition and the diabolical pact theory in, 8865
witchcraft in, 9772
Inquisition (Islamic)
Muʿtazilah in, 6319
traditionalists *vs.* rationalists and, 3760, 3761
Inṣāf, al- (Ibn Sīnā), 4274, 4276
Insān al-kāmil, al- (Perfect or Complete Man), 4256, 4259, 4650
Ibn ʿArabī and, 8819–8820
as saint, 8821
as spiritual guide, 8711
in Sufism, 2653
Inscription on Laozi (Bian Shao), 5316
Inscriptions
on bronze, in Zhou dynasty, 5352
on Egyptian temples, 2725–2726
on jade, in Chinese religion, 5352
Maya, 5797, 5886–5887
Nabatean, 6385, 6386
runic, 7938–7941
Insects, **4507–4509**
as creators, 4507, 4508
as culture heroes and tricksters, 4507, 4508
kashrut laws on, 5106, 5107
Insecurity of Freedom, The (Heschel), 7370
Insei (rule by retired monarchs), 4785
INSETs. *See* Integrated National Security Enforcement Teams
Inshāʾallāh Khān, 10034
Insh ilm (Ugaritic term), in Canaanite religion, 1387
Insiders and outsiders
African scholars on, 8793
Smith (Wilfred Cantwell) on, 8451
Inside space, in Japanese religion, healthiness and, 3867–3868
Insight, quest for, in Gnosticism, *mustērion* as, 7955
Insight Meditation Society, 1191
Insitutiones theologiae moralis (moral teaching manuals), moral theology and, 1654
Inskip, John, Holiness promotion and, 4083
In Sorcery's Shadow (Stoller), 118
Inspiration, **4509–4511**. *See also* Enthusiasm
acceptability of, 2808
in Buddhism, 4509
canonization and, 1406, 1408
in Christianity, 4510
definition of, 4509
vs. ecstasy, 4509
in Greek religion, 4509–4510
in Hinduism, 4509
Irenaeus on, 4539
in Islam, 4510–4511
in Judaism, 4510
poetic, 4509–4510
prophetic, 4510
of scripture, 8201–8202
use of term, 4509
in Vedism, 4509
Inspired oracles, 6833–6834
Instant of My Death, The (Jabès), 5483
Instinct
archetype as, 459
culture contrasted with, 2086–2087
Starbuck (E. D.) on, 8732
Instinctive behavior, evolution in, 2867–2868
Institute for Creation Research (ICR), 2910
Institute for the Harmonious Development of Man, 832
Institute for the Study of American Religion (ISAR), 6524
Institute for the Study of Ethics and the Life Sciences, 940
Institute of Aboriginal Studies, 841
Institute of Archaeology, of University of London, 5110
Institute of Education by Radio, 7711
Institute of the Blessed Virgin Mary, 6764, 9691–9692
Institute of World Religions, 10074
Institutes of Christian Religion (Calvin), 9137
Institutes of the Cenoby and the Remedies for the Eight Principal Vices (Cassian), 1447
Institutes of the Christian Religion (Calvin), 7661
election in, 2748
theology in, 1374–1376
Institutional bioethics, 940
Institutionalization
of African American religions, 68–69
of religion, and invisible religion, 4531
Institutionalized sects, 1866–1867

Institutiones theologie Christianae dogmaticae (Wegscheider), 9137
Institutions (Roman legal documents), 5333
Instituto Italiano per il Medio ed Estremo Oriente (IsMEO), 9391
Instruction for Merikare (Egypt), 2706, 2711, 2722
judgment of the dead in, 5026
Instructions
Egyptian
Israelite wisdom influenced by, 9761
wisdom in, 9749, 9754
in *Proverbs,* 9757–9758
Instructions (Serafim of Sarov), teachings in, 8229
Instructions to Hesychasts (Gregory of Sinai), 3697
Instruments. *See* Musical instruments
In summulas Petri Hispani (Eck), 2601
INTA. *See* International New Thought Alliance
Integralism, 9534
Integral Perfection order of Daoism. *See* Quanzhen Daoism
Integral Tradition, Evola (Julius) in, 2905
Integral Yoga, 634
Integrated National Security Enforcement Teams (INSETs), 4686
Integration, in mysticism, 6342
Intellect
Aristotle on, 481–482
Hermetism on, 7190
Ja'far al-Ṣādiq on, 4761
Plato on, 7182
Plotinus on, 7184, 7191, 7199
Plutarch on, 7200
and prophecy, 7439, 7440–7441
Intellects, Ten
al-Ḥāmidī on, 8335
al-Kirmānī on, 8331
Intellectual activity, in monasticism, 6124
Intellectual Adventure of Ancient Man (Frankfort), 2730
Intellectualism
in anthropology of religion, 2914
in early Eastern Christianity, 2582
Intellectualist theory, on conversion, 1971
Intellectuals, **4511–4515**
definition of, 4511–4512
humanistic, 4514
religious, 4511–4515
developing doctrines, 4512–4513, 4514
lay (amateur), 4513
originality of, 4513–4514
in priesthood, 4513–4514
in primordial religions, 4512
prophets as, 4514
responsibilities of, 4514–4515
tradition in activities of, 4513–4514
in world religions, 4512
Romanian, 2759
secular, 4513, 4514–4515
Intellectus fidei (understanding of faith), 9136
Intelligence
artificial, **509–513**
definitions of, 509–510
extraterrestrial, 4516
race and, 2882
signs of, 4515
defining, 4516–4517
study of (*See* Intelligent design)
Intelligent design, 2911–2912, **4515–4518**. *See also* Creationism
anthropic principle and, 8189
arguments of, 8185–8186
challenging Darwinism, 4516, 4518
compatible with special creation, 4516, 4517–4518
controversy over, 4515–4516
definition of, 4515
of nature, 4516, 4517–4518
and religion, 4517–4518
Intelligent Man's Gift to Christians (al-Turjumān), 7242–7243
Intelligent matter, 6437
Intention
of actions, in Buddhism, 5098
in morality, 6184
in oaths, 9642
Intentionality
of God, in Islam, 3565
in phenomenology, 7088, 7094–7095
in symbolic time, 8915
Interaction, strategies of, 2867–2868
Interaction stage of conversion, 1972
Interactive discipline, 8701–8702
Intercalation
moon and, 6171
in Roman calendar, 1354
Intercession
in African religions, by spirits, shades, or ancestors, 3816, 3817
afterlife and, 129–130, 161
forms of, 129
in Islam, by prophets, on Last Day, 2064
of martyrs, 2081
of saints, 2083
Interchurch Holiness Convention, anti-modernism of, 4084
Interchurch World Movement (1919-1920), 2289
Interconnectedness, Paul on, 2650
Interdependence
in engaged Buddhism, suffering and, 2689
Socrates on, 8504
Interdimensional physics. *See* Unarius Academy of Science
Interdisciplinarity, in women's studies in religion, 9792
Interfaith communication, Kraemer (Hendrik) on, 5241
Interfaith Partnership for the Environment (IPE), 2613
Interfaith Peace Prayer Day, 3HO and Sikh Dharma sponsorship of, 3879
Inter Insignores, 9541
Interior Mansions (Teresa of Ávila), 9084
Interlacustrine Bantu religions, **4518–4521**
cults in, 4519, 4520, 4521
decline of, 4520–4521
Islam, 4607
sacrifice in, 4519
spirits in, 4519–4520
International Academy for Continuous Education, 833
International Archive for the Psychology of Religion (journal), 10059–10060
International Association for the History of Religions (IAHR)
Bianchi (Ugo) in, 862–863
Bleeker (C. Jouco) as secretary-general of, 979
Brandon (S. G. F.) as secretary-general of, 1040
Delhi (India) Conference of, 8791, 8792
in Eastern Europe, 8775
historiography and, 4042
Leeuw (Gerardus van der) as president of, 5391
Marburg (Germany) Conference of, 8789
Pettazzoni (Raffaele) as president of, 7072, 7074
in United States, 8788
women's studies in, 3313
International Association for the Study of Pain, 6944
International Association of Sufism, 9013
International Association of Tibetan Studies (IATS), 9188, 9191
International Bibliography of the History of Religions (Bleeker), 7074
International Bill of Human Rights, documents contained in, 4178
International Central Gospel Church, political theology and, 1723
International Churches of Christ (ICOC), 1781, 6561
in Europe, 6568
International Council of Unitarian and Other Liberal Religious Thinkers and Workers, 2343
International Covenant on Civil and Political Rights (ICCPR), 5363, 5364
International Covenant on Economic, Social and Cultural Rights (ICESCR), 5363
International Dhamma Hermitage, 1072
Internationales Jahrbuch für Wissens- und Religionssoziologie (journal), 10057
International Ethical Union, 2857–2858
International Get Acquainted Club, 9433
International Humanist and Ethical Union, 2858
International Islamic University (Kuala Lumpur), 4668, 4671
International Journal of Ethics, 33
International Missionary Council, 2343
East Asia Secretariat and, 1730
in ecumenical movement, 2684, 2685
International New Thought Alliance (INTA), 6586–6587
Declaration of Principles of, 6583
predecessor of, 6585
International Order of Chivalry-Solar Tradition. *See* Temple Solaire
International Raëlain Movement. *See* Raëlians
International Religious Freedom Act (U.S. 1998), 5362
human rights and, 4181–4182
International Review of Sociology of Religion (journal), 10057
International Society for Krishna Consciousness (ISKCON), **4521–4524,** 5250, 6513, 6560
brainwashing civil suit against, 1033
chanting in, 4522
child abuse in, 6516, 6526, 6541
children in, 4523
child socialization and education in, 6542
defamation of, 5378
ethnic makeup of, 6563
in Europe, 6568, 6571
expansion of, 4522
founder of, 826, 4521, 7354, 7355
Hindu traditions and, 6551
institutionalization of, 4523–4524
internal crises in, 4522–4523
mantra, 1347
membership in
decline of, 6538
second-generation, 6541
opposition to, 4522
origins of, 6560
religious practices of, 4522
solicitation laws and, 5378
in Soviet Union, 6567
temples of, 4522
women in, 4523, 6536, 6563

International Society for Science and Religion, founding of, 8185
International Society for the Sociology of Religion, 10057
Internet. *See also* Websites
Caribbean religious studies on, 10028
devotional sites of, vol. 11 color insert
and Japanese Buddhism, 1184
and Neopaganism, 6472, 6473
and popular Buddhism, 1191
and Tibetan religious studies, 9188
Internment camps, during World War II, 5188
Interpretatio Graeca and *Romana,* 1873
syncretism and, 8931
Interpretation. *See* Hermeneutics
Interpretation of Cultures, The (Geertz), thick description in, 8500
Interpretation of Dreams, The (Freud), 2483
Interpretation of the Holy Liturgy (Cabilas), Divine Liturgy in, 1343
"Interpreting Hasidism" (Buber), 1056
Interregnum
dangers of, 5155, 5158
modernity as, 5160
Inter-Religio network in Asia, establishment of, 1730
Interstellar dust, in Milky Way, in ethnoastronomy, 2864
Interventionism, as response to classical physics, 7137
In the Beginning Was Love (Kristeva), 3028
In the Name of the Almighty (calligraphic image), vol. 14 color insert
In the Trail of the Wind (Bierhorst), 7224
Inti (deity), **4524–4525**
effigy of, 5292
Illapa and, 8602
kings as living spirit of, 5177
portrayal of, 8576
sinchis relationship to, 5176
as sun, 8600–8601
Viracocha, relationship with, 1364, 4524
Intichiuma ceremonies, totemism and, 8003
Intichiuma religion (Australia), fasting in, 2997
Intimate Enemy, The (Nandy), 3319
Inti Raymi (festival), 4412
Intolerance, in Middle East, 7654
Intoxicants. *See also* Alcoholic beverages
engaged Buddhism and, 2788
in Indo-European religions, 4455
religion originating through, 366
from trees, 9338
visions from, 9614
Intrareligious explanations, 1870
Intrinsic value, of animals, 2655
Introducing Liberation Theology (Boff), 6099
Introduction to Platonic Philosophy (Albinus), 7189
Introduction to the Devout Life (Francis of Sales), 5818
Introduction to the History of Religion, An (Jevons), 4854
Introduction to the Science of Religion (Müller), 9125
Introversionist movements, in Africa, 102, 105
Introvigne, Massimo, 6524
Intuition, **4525–4526**
in divination, 2370
Duns Scotus (John) on, 2525
Emerson (Ralph Waldo) on, 7738
origin of term, 4525
in philosophy, 4525
Radhakrishnan (Sarvepalli) on, 7742
in religion, 4525–4526
Schleiermacher (Friedrich) on, 7738, 8163
Spinoza (Baruch) on, 8684
Suhrawardī on, 8827
types of, 4525
Wang's Study of Inner Mind and, 1902
Inua (soul), 4527, 4528
Inuit Circumpolar Conference, 4526
Inuit language, 4526
Inuit religious traditions, **4526–4529,** 6655
ablutions in, 10–11
animals in, 4527
children in, 4528
Christianity and, 4527
confession of sins in, 7505, 7509, 7759
culture hero myth in, 2092
death in, 4528
deities in, 469–470, 4528–4529
supreme, 469
development of, 472
festivals in, 4528
frenzied behavior in, 3214
healing in, 4528
history of study of, 475
hunting culture in, 472, 4527
hunting rituals in, 6655
illness in, 7505
incarnation in, 4415
lady of animals in (Sedna), 470, 3017, 4528, 5280, 5515, 6655, **8220–8221**
lord of the animals in, 5515
meteorological beings in, 5992
miracles in, 6050
New Year ceremonies in, 6590
on origin of human races, 2394
rites of passage in, 4527–4528
rituals in, 4527
sacrifices in, 470
shamanism in, 4528, 7505, 7509, 8288–8289
initiation in, 8271
Siberian counterparts of, 6653
social structure in, 4526
soul in, 4527
spirits in, 469–470, 4528
taboos, amulets, and songs in, 4527
tattooed flying heads in, 3806
transmigration in, 9326
tricksters in, 4528
underworld in, 472
whales in, 471
Inuus (deity), 6957
Invasion possession, 2140
Invention of Africa, The (Mudimbe), 111
Inventories of wisdom, 9749
Inverse effects, in humor, 6364
Inversion of social norms
at Carnival, 1440, 1444
clowns and, 1838, 1839, 8016–8017
Investiture Conflict, 3691
Investiture controversy
ecclesiology and, 1772
Gregory VII and, 7876
Investiture of the Gods (Daoist novel), 3068–3069
Invigoration rites, seasonal, 8209–8210
Invisibility, in art, 53
Invisible religion, 4401, **4529–4532**
concept of, 4529
secularism and, 4529–4530
Invisible Religion, The: The Transformation of Symbols in Industrial Society (Luckmann), 4529, 4531
Invitation possession, 2139–2140
In vitro fertilization (IVF), 941, 942
Invocation. *See also* Mantras
in Minoan religion, 39–40
sacred language of, 5307
Inyak-Uyu structure, on Koati Island, 5291
Ioann of Kronstadt, 2588, **4532,** 7943
Iocauna (deity), in Island Arawak religion, 1426–1427
Ionescu, Nae
anti-Semitism of, 2759
Eliade and, 2753, 2754
Ionia, Anthesteria festival in, 374, 375
Ionian alphabet, mystical speculation on, 271
Ionic columns, 9063
Ionic Enlightenment, 6373
Ioskeha (deity), 2985
Iou (deity), 7894
Iousheka (deity), 6680
Iouskeha (deity), 9413
Ipaina Huitzilopochtli ritual, human sacrifice in, 4155
IPE. *See* Interfaith Partnership for the Environment
Ipelele (mythic figure), in Cuna creation myth, 2095–2096
Ipelerkan (lord shamans), in Cuna creation myth, 2096
Ipeorkun (culture hero), in Cuna creation myth, 2096
Iphigeneia (mythic maiden)
Artemis and, 9604
Hekate identified with, 3899
ʾIpnúucililpt ritual (Nez Perce), 6596–6597
Ipolyi, Arnold, 3112
Ippen (holy man), **4532–4533,** 4938–4939
music of, 6301
ʿIqāb al-aʿ māl (Ibn Bābawayhi), 4262
Iqāmah (call to prayer), overview of, 8056
Iqbāl, Muḥammad, **4533–4535**
education of, 4533
Gökalp (Ziya) influencing, 3625
on Islamic identity, 4644
life of, 4533
modernism of, 6098, 6101
as neofundamentalist, 4574
on al-Ḥallāj, 3758
on light of Muḥammad, 6767
on *miʿrāj,* 6061
on Niẓām al-Dīn Awliyāʾ, 6638
philosophy of, 4534, 6964
poetry of, 4533–4534
as spiritual founder of Pakistan, 4652, 4654
on Sufism, 8824
on Western understanding of Islam, 4574
Iqrār (verbal acknowledgment), 4399, 4711
Iqtiṣād (al-Ghazālī), 5066
Iqtiṣād fī al-Iʿtiqād (Ghazālī), 620–621
Iraivan/Kadavul temple (Kauai), Śaivism and, 8419
Irama, Rhoma, 6291
Iran and Iranian religions, **4535–4538**. *See also* Indo-Iranian religion; Persia; Zoroastrianism
Aga Khans in, 172–173
ahuras in, 204–205
Airyana Vaējah in, 210
apostasy in, 433–434
architecture of, fire in, 569–570
artisans in, 4296

Iran and Iranian religions *continued*
ascension in, 519–520
'Āshūrā' in, 550, 1517
Bābīs in, 729
Bahā'īs in, 739
birthrate in, reduction of, 2653
bridges in, 1049
Christensen's history of, 1649–1650
clothing, sacred *vs.* secular, 1833, 1835
Corbin (Henry) on, 1983–1984
cosmology in, 4536
creation in, 4536
daivas in, 2128–2129
dakhma in, 2130
dates eaten in, 2401
death in, 4537
deities of, 4535 (*See also* Mithra; *See also* Anāhitā)
goddess worship, 3594–3595
demons in, 2276, 2284
dragons in, 2431–2432
Dumézil (Georges) on, 4462
the Fall in, 2964
family law in, 3368, 4703
feminism in, Qurrat al-'Ayn Ṭāhirah and, 7575
festivals in
New Year, 6592, 6594
Nowrūz, 6730–6732
films from, 3098
fire in, 3116, 3117–3118, 4535
the Flood in, 2964, 3130
frog in, 3223
Gnosticism originating in, 3508, 3514
goddess worship in, 3594–3595
Golden Age in, 3629–3630
the good in, 3635
haoma in, 849–850, 4535, 5434
hawzahs in, 3801
incarnation in, 4416
initiation in, 4537
Islam
architecture of mosques in, 6209
and Central Asian Islam, 4629
domestic observances in, 2402
Imāmī (Twelvers) Shiism, 4698, 4700, 4703
madrasahs in, 5556
Mu'tazilah in, 6319
Ni'matullāhīyah, 9011
Nizārī Ismā'īlīyah, 557–558
priesthood, 4574
ta'ziyah in, 9022–9023
'ulamā' in, 4702
in Umayyad caliphate, 4562
women in, 3367
Zoroastrianism and, 9990, 10002–10004
Islamic Revolution in
Imāmīyah and, 8340
media and, 4964
walāyah and, 9660
Zoroastrianism and, 10004
Jewish community in, Karaite sect, 4991, 5083
kalām in, 5061
khvarenah in, 5139–5140
kingship in, 5165
Kubrawīyah order in, 5257
libations in, 4535, 5434
light and darkness symbolism in, 5451
light in, 4537
magi in, 5559–5562
Manichaeism, **5659–5662**
persecution of, 5660–5661
spread of, 5660
martyrs in, public lamentation for, 7632
merit in, 5871
microcosm-macrocosm homologization in, 4159–4160
Mongol invasion of, 4613
moon in, 6173
Muslim conquest of, 6997
neofundamentalist government in, 4574
Neolithic, 6461
Nestorian Church in, 2584
number symbolism in, 6748
offerings in, 4535
Pahlavi period in, Imāmīyah and, 8340
political revolution in, 7257
prehistoric (*See* Saka religion)
purification in, 4535
religious studies in, 8783–8784
sacrifice in, 4535
sheep in, 8311
Söderblom (Nathan) on, 8506
soul in, 4537
study of, 10079
twins in, 9416, 9420
votive offerings in, 3163
water in, 4535
wisdom in, 9751–9752
concept of, 9748
world-periods in, 174
writing in, 1373
written records from ancient, 5161
Zoroastrianism (*See* Zoroastrianism)
Irani, Mehera J., 5829
Irani, Merwan Sheriar. *See* Meher Baba
Iran-Iraq war (1980), 5089
Iraq and Iraqi religions. *See also* Mesopotamia
archaeology of, Frankfort (Henri) and, 3188
Assyrian Christians (Nestorians) in, 1675, 6480, 6481
Ba'ath government, hawzahs and, 3801
creation of, 5088
hawzahs in, 3800–3801
Islam
Imāmī (Twelvers) Shiism in, 4698
Mu'tazilah, 6317–6321
Islamic conquest of, 20
Jewish community in, Karaite sect, 5083
Karbala in, 5088–5089
Mandeaen religion in (*See* Mandaean religion)
Muslim Brotherhood in, 6316
Nestorian Church in, 2584
polygamy in, 4707
Qarāmiṭah in, 7543
Sufism in, Rifā'ī and Suhrawardi schools of, 8823
wars, and Christian emigration, 1673
Iraq-Iran war (1980), 5089
Ireland, John, Gibbons (James) and, 3478
Ireland and Irish religions. *See also* Celtic religion
Anglicanism, 350
cattle raids, tales of, 1465, 8960
Celtic settlement, 1478
Christianity introduced to, 1479
devil in form of cat, 1463
folk culture of, Clamor and Humiliation of the Saints rituals in, 2105
folklore of
banshee, 2952
places associated with fairies in, 2954
hermits of, 2826
Islam, 4678–4679
learned classes *(druïdh, filidh,* and *baird),* 1479
literature of, 1479–1480
Audacht Morainn, 1492
debate over pre-Christian representation, 1499–1500
druids in, 2493
Fionn Cycle, 1494–1495
mythology and folklore, 1483
order and incoherence in, 1481–1482
Ulster Cycle, 1493–1494
women in, 3388
megalithic passage tombs in, 5823
circle symbolism and, 1791
megalithic religion in, 5823, 5825
monasticism in, confession in, 1889
mytho-history, 1487–1489
paganism in, Lugh and (*See* Lugh)
pagan religion of (*See* Celtic religion)
personified in deities, 1490
place names in, 1480
Presbyterianism, 7390
Roman Catholicism
Brighid and, 1052–1053
Patrick and, 7009–7010
tuath in law of, 1482
Irenaeus (bishop of Lyons), **4538–4541**
on *aiones,* 209
on archetypes, 458
on baptism, 4540
canons mentioned by, 1406
on church unity, 8154
on Easter, 4538
"Ebionite" coined by, 2595
on Eucharist, 4540
on Fall, 8405
on free will, 4540
on *Genesis,* 4540
on Gnosticism, 3515, 3517, 3518, 3529, 3530, 3923–3924, 3926, 4539, 6396, 6397
on *hypostasis,* 4242
influence of, 4540
on *John,* 910, 4539, 4943–4944
life of, 4538
on *Logos,* 5501–5502, 5504
on Luke, 908, 5530
on Marcion, 4539
on Mary, 5753
as Eve, 3358
on Matthew the Evangelist, 5780
"New Testament" used as term by, 1406
on Roman church, 6966
on scripture, 8196
on Simon Magus, 3515
theodicy of, 9117
theology of, 4539–4540, 9135
on Valentinius, 6397
writings of, 4538–4539
Irene (Byzantine empress), 4290, 4386
Irene (Roman empress), icon veneration supported by, 2585
Ireneus on Lyon, on unity of Testaments, 2049
Irezumi, 1002
'Irfān (Islamic philosophy), 4552
imaginal thinking in, 4553
Irian Jaya. *See also* New Guinea
Asmat people of, masks of, 5769
cargo cults in, 1414
Irigaray, Luce, 3027, 3314
on biblical exegesis, 5488
consideration of non-Western traditions by, 3030
on female mystical experience, 3029
and feminist theology, 3035
on lack of studies on vagina, 7077

on law and religion, 5360–5361
on Mary, 5755–5756
on motherhood, 3028
on subjectivity and divinity, 3029
Irish Articles (1615), on free will and predestination, 3208
Irish Folklore Commission, 1498
Irish religion. *See* Celtic religion; Ireland and Irish religions
Irmandade da Nossa Senhora da Boa Morte. See Sisterhood of Our Lady of the Good Death
Iroke (fly-whisk), 10033
Iron Age
graves from, 990, 5320, 7895
Roman religion in, 7894–7895
Iron and ironworking, 5986–5987
and African religions, 83–84
myths of, 94–95
discovery of smelting and, 5987
in Egyptian religion, 5987
industrialization of, 5987
from meteorites, 5986–5987
Iron Guard. *See* Legion of the Archangel Michael
Irony. *See also* Humor
Kierkegaard on, 4220–4221
Iroojrilik (deity), 6009
Iroquois, League of, 4541
Iroquois, Six Nations of, 4541, 7300–7301
Iroquois Confederacy, 6665
Iroquois language, 4541
Iroquois religion and society (North America), **4541–4543**
on agriculture, origins of, 6682
ballgame played in, 753, 754
in Beaver Wars, 6664
blood in, 986
calendrical ceremonies in, 3280, 4541–4542, 4543
color symbolism in, 1862
community rituals in, 4541–4542
concept of *orenda* in, 6680
conversion in, 7756
cosmology in, 4541
creation story in, 3169
drama in, 2460
dreams in, 2483, 4542–4543
False Face society of, 6684, 6685
formation of United States and, 10086, 10087
gardening in, 3279–3280
gender in, 3407, 3408–3409
Handsome Lake as prophet in, **3771–3772,** 4541, 4543, 6667
harvest festivals in, 188
individual in, 4542–4543
masks in, 5767
medicine societies in, 4542, 6685
menstrual cycle in, 3018
Midwinter ceremony of, 6682
naming ceremony of, 6683
puberty rites of, 6683
regions occupied by, 6655, 6679
relations with other Native nations, 6665
scalping in, 3805
shamanism in, 4542, 6686
soul in, 4543
spirits in, 4541, 4542–4543
study of, 6670, 6672
tobacco in, 9218
tricksters in, 9355
twin gods in, 2092, 2985
twins in, 4541, 9413–9414, 9418
water in, 10086
witchcraft in, 7755
women in, 3019, 4541, 4542, 6682
IRP. *See* Islamic Rebirth Party
Irra Epic (myth), 5959–5960
Irrationality, in Daoism, humor and, 4207
Irreducible complexity, 4517
Irrigation systems, Cambodian temples and, 4013
Irrlicht, das, 2952
Irshād (al-Juwaynī), 5066
Irshappa (deity), 7760. *See also* Reshef
Iruak religion (Central Asia), disanimation myth in, 8532
Irving, Edward, **4543–4544**
on liberalism, 6102
Maurice (Frederick Denison) influenced by, 5783
Irwin, Lee, 6693, 9610
Iryon (Buddhist monk), on Korean religion, 5229–5230
Is (soul), 5122
Isaac (biblical figure), **4544**
Abraham's sacrifice of, 15, 16, 4544
altar in, 277
as Holocaust paradigm, 4088
birth of, 14, 15
Canaanite parallels, 1396
circumcision of, 4544, 7818
matchmaking for, 15, 4544
Rebecca as wife of, 7634
Sarah as mother of, 8112
Isaac, Jules, 7235
Isaac ben Asher, 9248
Isaac ben Moses, 9248
Isaac of Acre, on mystical union, 6340
Isaac of Dampierre. *See* Ri
Isaac of Komarno, 9381
Isaac of Nineveh. *See* Isaac the Syrian
Isaac the Syrian (bishop), **4544–4545**
influence of, 4545
life of, 4545
writings of, 4545
ʿIsā al-Masīḥ (Jesus the Messiah), 5979–5980
Isabella of Castile
Abravanel (Isaac) in government of, 17
Jews expelled by, 5717
Latin American missions and, 1695
Spanish Inquisition created by, 4498, 4500, 4502
Torquemada (Tomás de) as confessor to, 9242
Isāf (deity), 444
Isafan, Persia, as center for Islamic sciences and arts, 3801
Isagoge (Porphyry), 5990
Isaiah (biblical book), 879
Abbahu's exegesis on, 2
Abraham in, 15
Adonis in, 34
apocalypse and, 415, 416
authors of, 4545–4546
blasphemy in, 971
blood in, 986
Canaanite parallels, 1400
composite nature of, 4545–4546
condemnation of idolatry in, 4385
dating of, 4546
demons in, 2277
desert in, 2301
early sources on, 4545
on exile, 2922, 4857
First, 4545, 4546–4547, 4548
political context of, 4548
speeches in, 4546–4548
style of, 4547
found at Qumran, 4545, 4550
gambling in, 3262
ghosts in, 3475
historical setting of, 865, 4546
Lillith in, 5458
Luzzatto (Shemuʾel David) on, 869
merkavah in, 10050, 10051
Messiah in, 7232
messianism in, 5972, 5973, 5974, 5975
Micah compared with, 6001
music in worship in, 7463
papyrus in, 1842
pesher of, 7063, 7064, 7065
prediction of Jesus in, 873
prophecies in, 4546, 4547–4548, 4549, 4550
al-Rāqilī on, 7240
reinterpretation of, in *Daniel,* 2169
resurrection in, 7764, 8557
sacred space in, 4857
sacrifice criticized in, 4748
Second, 4545–4546, 4548–4550
apocalyptic writings in, 4749
gospel in, 3640
political context of, 4549
speeches in, 4549
style of, 4549–4550
theodicy in, 9116
suffering in, 9115
Suffering Servant doctrine in
as Holocaust paradigm, 4089
vicarious suffering and, 8806
thanksgiving psalm in, 7461
Third, 4546, 4550
variants of, 886
virgin birth in, 7233
Isaiah (biblical figure), **4545–4551**
on amulets and talismans, 299
ascension of, 523
as healer, 4546
and King Ahaz, 4546, 4547, 4548
and King Hezekiah, 4546
life of, 4546
Micah and, 6000–6001
on morality, 7652
on perfection of God, 7039
political issues addressed by, 4545, 4547, 4548
prophecy of, 4546, 4547–4548
prophetic actions of, 7432, 7436
Rastafarian reincarnations of, 1438
religious experience of, 7694, 7700
vocation of, 9632–9633
Isaias, 2824
ISAL. *See* Church and Society in Latin America movement
ʾIsánáklésh (deity), 404, 405, 574, 10069, 10070
ʾIsánáklésh Gotal (initiation ceremony), 10069–10071
ISAR. *See* Institute for the Study of American Religion
Isasi-Díaz, Ada Mariá, 9791
Iṣatprāgbhāra ("Slightly Curving Place"), in Jain cosmology, 2025
Isekagura (dance), 6300
Ise religion, Konkō Daijin influenced by, 5224–5225
Ise Shintō movement, 4786–4787
Ise Shrine (Japan)
ancestor worship at, 2639
Buddhism and Ryobu Shinto and, 8361
as imperial shrine, 4783
Outer Shrine of, 4801
pilgrimage to, 4798, 8364
priests of, 7410, 7411
as national officials, 7411

Ise Shrine (Japan) ***continued***
rebuilding of, 2640
reconstruction of, 8841
saigu (shrine virgins) at, 1528
Isfahan, School of, Corbin (Henry) on, 1984
Isfara'ini, Abū Isḥāq al-
in Ash'arīyah, 534
writings of, 534
"Is Female to Male as Nature Is to Culture?" (Ortner), 7079
Isfet (defect), Egyptian pharaohs and, 5163
Is God a White Racist (Jones), 78
Ishanism (Ṣūfī order), 4622, 4625
Isḥāqīyah movement, as *ghulāt* (extremist), 8323
Ishara (deity), 4316
Ishārāt (hints), al-Junayd and, 3756
Ishārāt wa-al-tanbīhāt (Ibn Sīnā), 4274
Isheh (offering), 926
Isherwood, Lisa, on body theology, 4167
Ishhara (deity), in Canaanite religion, 1384
Ishida Baigan, **4551,** 6572
Ishikiri Shrine, Japan, healing in, 3869
Ishin Suden (monk), 3644
Ishkur (deity), 5949, 5956
in divine bureaucracy, 5951
Ishmael (biblical figure), **4551–4552**
circumcision of, 4552
construction of the Ka'bah by, 5050
in Islam, 4362, 4552
Sarah and, 8112
Ishmaelites, 4552
'Ishq (absorbing love), 4534
Ishrāq (illumination), 4552
Ishrāq, al-, 2977
Ishrāqīyah (Islamic school of philosophy), **4552–4556**
exile in, 2923–2924
founder of, 4553–4555
Ibn Sīnā's influence on, 4275–4276, 4552–4553
idealism in, 4555
imaginal thinking in, 4552, 4553–4554
lights in, 4554–4555
post-Suhrawardian developments of, 4555–4556
Ishtanu (deity), as dispenser of justice, 4069
Ishtar (deity), 2984. *See also* Inanna
Anat, fusion with, 1383, 1398
Astarte and, 561
ballet about, 2162
Dagan and, 2126
descent into the underworld by, 2298, 2538–2539
Eblaite equivalent of, 2596
eunuch priests of, 1451
iconography of, 4317
Inanna identified with, 3586, 3594
Kemosh and, 6094
lovers of, 4405
in myth of the Flood, 2963
polarization with Ereshkigal, 2984
prominence of, *vs.* other goddesses, 3376
shape shifting of, 8303
son-consort of, 2983
temple to, 9062
as Venus, 8427
as virgin, 9604
worship of, 3586
Ishwara Totāpurī, Ramakrishna as student of, 7612, 7613
Isidore of Seville (bishop), **4556–4557**
on magic, 5577
Isidorus
on ascension, 521
on sacred space, 8428
Isis (deity), **4557–4560**
in alchemy, 245, 246
and ancient novels, 3054
Apuleius on, 4558, 4559, 7189
areatalogies of, 7917
castration of Osiris, 1451, 4557
cult of, 2709–2710, 4557–4559
deification in, 2249
dissemination of, 4558
in Greek religion, 4557, 4558, 4559
initiation into, 2249, 4559
religious practices of, 4559
in Roman religion, 4558–4559
women in, 3384–3385
Demeter identified with, 3908, 4557
drums of, 2498
in Egyptian pantheon, 2704, 6331
festivals of, 4559
and gender roles, 3384–3385
in Germanic religion, 3450
Hathor and, 4557
in Hellenistic religions, 3604–3606, 4557, 4558, 4559
helping women in childbirth, 4557
hieroglyph of name of, 4557
Ḥokhmah as parallel to, 4079
Horus as son of, 4557, vol. 8 color insert
kingship associated with, 3586
in Kushite religion, 5269
as Lady of the Animals, 5280
Lucius and, 3904–3905, 3908
marriage of, 5727
miracles of, 6051–6052
monotheism and, 6156
multiple symbolism of, 3021
mystery religion of, 6330–6331
ecstasy in, 2678
spread of, 6331
in Nabatean religion, 6386, 6389
Nile River and, 7861, 7862
Osiris and, 6920
marriage of, 3604, 3605, 4557, 5727
Philae temple of, 2709
Plutarch on, 2514–2515, 2538, 4557, 7201, 7202
Re and, 4557
resurrection of Osiris by, 7767
in Roman religion, 7913–7914, 7917
Sarapis and, 4559
Sothis (Sirius) and, 4557
in *Stobaei Hermetica,* 3940
temple of, 4557–4558, 4559
and Thoth, 4557
in triad, 9349
worship of, 3596, 3604–3606
Isis and Osiris (Plutarch), 2514–2515, 2538, 4557, 7201, 7202
universalism in, 3907
Isis Book (Apuleius), 3651–3652
Isis Unveiled (Blavatsky), 977, 5023, 9142
Is It Too Late? A Theology of Ecology (Cobb), 2610
Iskandar Muda, 25, 4660, 4663
Iskandar Thānī, 25
ISKCON. *See* International Society for Krishna Consciousness
Iṣlāḥ (reform of Islam), in messianism, 5980–5981
Islah al-akhlaq (Ibn Gabirol), 4266
Islam, **4560–4691**. *See also specific countries, doctrines, sects, and regions*
ablutions in, 10, 11, 2401, 7157
abortion in, 5813
Abraham in (*See* Abraham, in Islam)
Adam in, 4564
African Americans in, 6418, 6563 (*See also* African American religions; Nation of Islam)
African movements derived from, new, 107–108
afterlife in (*See* Afterlife, in Islam)
alchemy in, **248–250**
Almond (Philip) on, 8769
almsgiving in, 267, 268
amulets and talismans in, 300
angels in, 346
Ibn Sīnā on, 4554
iconography of, 4350, vol. 8 color insert
magic and, 5583
al-Suhrawardī on, 4554–4555
animals in, speech of, 2651
animal symbolism and beliefs in, 361
Antichrist in, 394–395
anti-Semitism in, 402
apocalypse in, 413
Qur'ān on, 159–160, 413
apocalyptic, millenarian, and reformist figures in, titles adopted by, 6737–6738
apologetics in, 428–429
apostasy in, 433–434, 4575
apostles in, 436
art of (*See* Art, Islamic)
ascension in, 523–524, 3129 (*See also* Mi'raj)
asceticism in
pain in, 6946
Ṣūfī, 9004
attention in, 604
attractiveness of, 1973
authority in, 695–696
modernism in struggle over, 6097
autobiography in, 699–700
Bedouin religion and, 4561
binary periodization in, 173
bioregional center of, 2605
birds in, 948, 949
birth in, 953, 7825–7826
blasphemy in (*See* Blasphemy, Islamic concept)
blessing in, 982, 983
blood in, prohibition on consuming, 986
body marking forbidden in, 1001
body marks of divine election in, 1004
bread in, 2401
breath and breathing in, 1042–1043, 1046
bridges in, 1049–1050, 1051
Buddhism and
and decline of Buddhism, 1095
relations with, 4575
in Southeast Asia, 4657
calendar, 1353–1354, **1372–1373**
'Āshūrā' in, **549–550**
moon in, 6171
caliphs (*See* Caliphate)
calligraphy, 1368, 1369, 1372, 4350, 4351
canon in, 1407, 1409
ḥadīth, 9274–9275
cats in, 1463
chanting in, 1535
charismatic leadership in, 1546–1547
charity and the *waqf,* 1555
chastity in, 1559
children in
ḥājj of, 7156
humor and, 4211–4212
inheritance to, 4709
paternity of, 4710–4711
Christianity, relations with, 4575
in Africa, 1724
in Andalusia, 4591, 4592

Christian-Muslim polemics in, **7242–7244**
in Chuvash religion, 1784, 1785
circumcision in (*See* Circumcision, in Islam)
classification of, 1867
clitoridectomy and, 1825
on cloning, 5814
clothing in, 1829, 1831, 1833, 1835
cocks in, 1842
community in, eremitism and, 2828
conferences, 4574–4575
Constantinople, capture of, 1664
conversion to (*See* Conversion, to Islam)
creation story in (*See* Creation and cosmogonic myths, in Islam)
creed in (*See* Creeds, in Islam)
crescent as symbol of, 4350–4351
dance in, 2135
for initiations, 2136
David in, 2223
da'wah (missionary) aspect of, 2225–2226
death in, 7827
demons in, 2279–2280, 2314–2315
desert in, 2301
determinism in, 3563–3565
devotion in (*See* Devotion, in Islam)
and Diola religion, 2354
as doctrine and method, Qutb (Sayyid) on, 7576
doctrine in, 2382
and Dogon religion, 2390
dogs in, 2393
domain of, 7562
domestic observances in (*See* Domestic observances, Muslim practices)
dreams in, 2489
drums in, 2498, 2499, 7036
dualism in, 2514, 4570
Eastern Christianity and, 2582, 2583, 2584
ecology and, **2651–2654**
economics and, 9708–9709
ecstasy in, 2678
education in (*See* Religious education, Islamic)
election in, 2748–2749
elixir in, 2771–2772
Enoch in, 2803–2804
environmental issues addressed by, 2610–2611
eremitism in, 2828
eschatology of, 2835, **2836–2840**
ethics in (*See* Ethics, Islamic)
European history of, 6567
evil eye and, 2942
Ezra in, 2947
faith in
basis of, 5204
as dependence, 2956
in *Fiqh al-akbar,* 5062
in *Waṣīyah,* 5062
Muḥammad on, 5062
the Fall in, 2969
fasting in, 2996, 2997, 3171
on 'Āshūrā', 549
fate in, 3002, 3003, 3201, 3209
feminism in, 3366–3368
Islamist, 3367–3368
Muslim, 3366–3367, 3368
secular, 3366
feminist analysis of, 3033
and fiction, African, 3086, 3087, 3088
and film, 3098
fire in, 3120
Five Pillars of Faith in, 2956, 4565, 5062, 5446
the Flood in, 2969
flower symbolism in, 3135
folk traditions in, 3161–3164
food in, 2401, 3170–3171
food taboos in, 3168–3169, 7144
in Central Asia, 4625
in China, 2401
as founded religious community, 7718
free will and determinism in, 3201
free will and predestination in, 3204, **3209–3213,** 4568
free will in, Ibn Taymīyah on, 4569
funeral rites in (*See* Funeral rites, in Islam)
Gabriel in (*See* Gabriel, in Islam)
gambling in, 3262
Gandhi (Mohandas) influenced by, 3272
gardens in, **3282–3283**
architectural design of, 6208
history of, 3282–3283
modern, 3283
recreational, 3277
views of, 3276–3277
gender in, **3364–3371**
in progressive Islam, 6099
gender studies in, 3365–3368, 3369–3370
geographical distribution of, 1819
ghosts in, 3476
gift giving in, 3485
global economy and, reaction to, 2676–2677
Gnosticism in, 3511, 3523
and Gobir dynasty, 2167–2168
God in, **3560–3567**
attributes of, **616–622,** 4563, 4568
belief in, in Five Pillars, 4565
consciousness of otherness from, 4569
creation by, 3565
determinism and, 3563–3565
development of, desert and, 2301
environment as, 2651
exceptionalism of, 3562–3563
falsafah concepts of, 2972, 2974
friends of (*See Walāyah*)
Ibn al-'Arabī on, 4258–4259, 4570, 8819
Ibn Bābawayhi on, 4262
Ibn Bājjah on, 4263
Ibn Sīnā on, 8569
immanence of, 3566
in Ḥanafī creed, 2063
in Ismā'īlīyah, 8326
in Qarāmiṭah Shiism, 8328
in *Rasā'il Ikhwān al-Ṣafā',* 4376–4377
insulting, 974–975
intentionality of, 3565
justice of, 129, 3562–3563
knowledge of, 3563, 3565, 5203–5204
as light of lights, 4554
Mu'tazilah on, 4567–4568, 5063
names of, 619–620, 621, 2340, 2341, 3562, 6406, 6407, 8822
power of, 3562, 4563
and predestination, 3209
proofs for existence of, 7422
rejection of, 975
remembering, 2339–2341
transcendence of, 3566, 4563
unity of (*See Tawḥīd*)
vision of, 128
gold and silver in, 3626
Golden Age in, 6223
Golden Rule in, 3630, 3631
great tradition *vs.* little tradition in, 2148
haircutting in, 3739–3740
hare myths in, 7590
healing (*See* Healing and medicine)
heresy in
Khārijīs, 4693
religio-political movements and, 3923
heterodoxy in, 6912–6913
Hinduism and
Dārā Shikōh (Muḥammad) and, 2219
influence on Hinduism, 4007–4008
parallels between, 3163
relations with, 4575
in South Asia, 4641, 4643–4644
and tensions, 4431
territorial disputed and desecrations, 8011
historiography
modern, 4032–4033
traditional, 4029–4030
homosexuality in, 4113–4114
hospitality *(djiwar)* in, 4139–4140
human body in, 2153
human rights in, 5364
humor in (*See* Humor, in Islam)
Hurūfī sect of (*See* Hurūfī)
iconoclasm in, 4281, 4287, 4349
iconography of (*See* Iconography, Islamic)
ideal state for, 4774
idolatry condemned in, 4361–4363, 4385–4386, 4561
images in
appropriation of, vol. 8 color insert
words incorporated into, vol. 14 color insert
incarnation in, 4416
in Indonesian literature, 3078
initiation in, in Sufism, 9006, 9011
in Jamā'at-i Islāmī, 4774
insects in, 4508
inspiration in, 4510–4511
intolerance in, 6186
intuition in, 4526
Islamist movements, and emigration, 1676
Jerusalem in, 4836–4837, **4838–4841**
Jesus in, 4845
and *ghaybah* (concealment), 3468
as Messiah, 5979–5980
Jewish people in, attitudes toward, 6226
Jewish Renewal and, 4871
Jewish status in, 4979
jihād in, 6648
journals devoted to, 10059
Judaism and, 3032
comparison of, 4855
Jewish persecution, 7055
Muslim-Jewish polemics, **7236–7242**
relations with, 4575
status of, 4995
judgment of the dead in, 5027

Islam *continued*
Khārijīs (*See* Khārijīs)
khilāfah (*See* Caliphate)
kissing holy objects in, 9258
kissing holy people in, 9259
knowledge in, 5203–5204
laity in, 5290
left and right symbolism in, 5393–5394
lesbianism in, 5414, 5415
letter mysticism in, 273, 274
libations in, discontinuation of, 5288
life in, 5446–5447
light symbolism in, 5454
literature of (*See* Drama; Islamic literature; Poetry)
magic in, **5583–5587**
black, 5583–5585
literature on, 5578–5579
talismanry, 5585–5586
white, 5586–5587
magic phrases in, 8676
Mandaean religion and, 5639
in Marathi religions, 5699–5700
marriage in (*See* Marriage, in Islam)
martyrdom in
as exemplary, 5738
in self-determining societies, 5740
social control of, 5742
masks and, distribution of, 5766
media and, 5805, 5807
medical ethics in, 5812–5814
meditation in, 5818–5819
memorization in, 5852–5853
mendicancy in, 5856
menstruation in, 5866
merit in, 5871
messianism in, 5973, **5979–5983,** 6545
false messiah in, 5979, 5980
Jesus in, 5979–5980
mahdī in, 5973, 5979, 5980–5982
migration in, 6023–6024
millenarianism in, 6030
millennialism in, 6545–6546
millet (nation) system, 1674, 1684
miracles in, 6054
mirrors in, 6063
missions in (*See* Missions, Islamic)
modern, 4573–4575, 4577–4579
studies on, 4718
modernism in, **6095–6102**
gender and, 3365, 3369–3370
monasticism banned in, 6024
monism in, 6146
monkeys in, 6150
monotheism in, 6160, 6161
moon in, 6171
morality in, 6181–6188
in Qur'ān, 4564
Moses in, 6204
in *mi'rāj,* 6060
mosques of (*See* Mosques)
mountains in
revelation on, 6213
symbolism of, 1501–1502
music in, 6276–6277
in Africa, 6258
in China, 6292
debate over, 6277
definitions of, 6250
Hindu music and, 6278, 6279
in South Asia, 4642
in Southeast Asia, 6283–6284, 6289, 6290–6291
in Sufism, 9004–9005
theories on origins of, 6277
mystical union in, **6334–6341**
origins of, 6336
mysticism in, 2977 (*See also* Sufism)
calendar of, 4714
ecstasy of, 2680
in Javanese Islam, 4816
letter, 273, 274
love, 6350
origins of, 5204
poetry in, 7222
prophets in, 7427
religious experience and, 7739–7740
ṣalāt and, 9817
studies on, 4718
Ṭabāṭabā'ī's contribution to, 8946
whirling dervishes and, 2140
Nabatean religion and, 6389–6390
as "natural" religious community, 1866
nature in, 2604
ambivalence about, 2607
Neoplatonism and, 6475
New Year observances in, 6594
Noah in, 2969, 6643
non-Muslims in Muslim countries, 1673–1674
nonviolence in, 6648
nubūwah in, 6733–6739
number symbolism in, 6747–6748, 6749, 6750
obedience in, 6777, 6778, 6779
occasionalism in, 6779–6780
offerings in, 4420
oral tradition of, 6843–6844
ordination in, 6858
in Orientalism, 6882–6883
origins of, 4561–4563
Renan (Ernest) on, 7750
orthodoxy in, 6912–6913
development of, 7730
heretical elements, incorporation of, 3924
orthopraxy in, 6914–6915
otherworld in, 6924
pain in, 6946
paradise in (*See* Paradise, in Islam)
peace in, 7021
performance and ritual in, 7044
phallus in, 7082
phenomenological approach to, Schimmel (Annemarie) on, 8150
philosophy of (*See Falsafah*)
pilgrimage in (*See Pilgrimage, Muslim; See Ḥājj)*
pillars of faith in, 4692–4693
political ideology and fundamentalism, 1517
political movements in, imitation of Muḥammad and, 6227
politics and (*See* Politics, and Islam)
postures and gestures in (*See* Postures and gestures, in Islam)
prayer in (*See Dhikr;* Prayer, in Islam)
predestination in
Murji'ah sect on, 4568
Waṣīyah on, 5062
priesthood in (*See* Priesthood, in Islam)
progressive, 6098–6100
afterlife in, 162
prostration in, 5195
purification in (*See* Purification, in Islam)
Qādāri heresy in, 3210–3211
radical groups in, Qutb (Sayyid) as inspiration of, 7576
redemption in, 7641
reference works on, 7646–7647
reform movements in
in Africa, 107–108
and *ṭarīqah,* 9011, 9012
modernism and, 6095–6096
Rashīd Riḍā (Muḥammad) and, 7621
reincarnation in (*See* Reincarnation, in Islam)
relics in, 7687
religious broadcasting and, 7714
religious communities in, 7700, 7716
religious education in, 7734–7735
faith schools, 7734
supplementary schooling and, 7733
religious experience in, 7700, 7739–7740
repentance in, 7756, 7757–7758
resurrection in, 7766–7767
retreats in, for spiritual renewal, 7770
retribution in, 7782–7783
revelation in, 7778
rites of passage in, **7824–7828**
birth, 7825–7826
circumcision, 7826, 7828
death, 7827
local variations in, 7827–7828
marriage, 7824, 7825, 7826–7827
naming, 7825–7826
rituals in, *ummah* and, 9446–9447
sacred biographies in, 945–946
sacrifice in (*See* Sacrifice, in Islam)
sacrilege in, 8014
Said (Edward) on, 8032
salutations in, 8061, 8062
Satan in, 2280, 2314–2315, 4564, 8124, 8125–8126
science in, 8181
cultivation of, 4574
secularization and, 8219
as Semitic religion, 9801
Shī'ī (*See* Shiism)
sin in (*See* Sin, in Islam)
social justice in, as cardinal virtue, 6222
society, relations with, 8462
soul in (*See* Soul, Islamic concepts of)
sources of (*See Sunnah*)
and spirit possession, 2148
spirit possession in, 2402
spiritual guides in, 8710–8711
spread of
Christianity, impact on, 1662
and *da'wah,* 2225–2226
da'wah and, 2225–2226
early military expansion, 6546
into Egypt, 1981
medieval, 4860
studies of, Jewish and Christian, 8782
suicidal missions in name of, 2999
suicide, attitudes toward, 8830–8831
Sunnī (*See* Sunnī Islam)
supremacy of, *dhimma* system and, 1673–1674
systematic content of, 4563–4576
taxation in (*See* Taxation, Islamic)
textiles in, 9090, 9091
theater forbidden in, 7044
theism in, 6964
theocracy in (*See* Theocracy, Islamic)
theodicy in, 9118–9119
theology of, 4567–4569
Ja'far al-Ṣādiq in, 4761
kalam (*See Kalām*)
traditionalism in, 7696
tradition in, 9268, 9270, 9274–9275

transnationalism of, 3499, 3500
triadism rejected by, 9349, 9350
Trinity rejected in, 5979
truth in, 9371, 9372
ʿulamāʾ in, 9438
underworld in, 9455–9456
vernacular traditions in, 9818–9820
Vietnamese religion influenced by, 9591
visionary journeys in, 9616
vocabulary of, 5774
vows in, 9641
warfare in, 9597 (*See also* Jihād)
wealth and, 9708–9709
in West, humor in, 4212–4213
women in (*See* Women, in Islam)
work and belief integrated in, vol. 7 color insert
world domination and, 4919
as world religion, 9801–9802
worship and devotional life in, **9815–9820**
Zoroastrianism and, 10002–10003
relations with, 4575
Islām, **4397–4400**
in *ḥadīth,* 4398, 4399
in Qurʾān, 4397–4398, 4400
meaning of word, 4577
in Muslim theology, 4398–4400
origin of word, 4560
use of term, 4715
Islam (Rahman), 9275
Islam, Kazi Nazrul, 829, 830
Islam and the Malay-Indonesian World (Riddell), 4671
Islāmī, ʿAbd al-Ḥaqq, al-, 7240
Islamic Association of China, 4636, 4637
Islamic Brotherhood (United States), 4687–4688
Islamic Circle of North America (ICNA), 6100
Islamic empire
Abū Bakr as founder of, 19, 20
Christian missions and, 6083
Judaism in, 4979, 4982
Mandaean religion in, 5635
Manichaeism in, 5656
migration of Muslims in, 6023
under ʿUmar ibn al-Khaṭṭāb, 9444
Islamic Foundation for Ecology and Environmental Sciences (IFEES), 2613
Islamicization, in music, 6283
Islamic law *(sharīʿah),* 2382, 4566–4567, **4691–4712**. *See also* Fiqh; See also Uṣūl al-fiqh
in 19th century, 4700–4701, 4702, 4703
in 20th century, 4701, 4702, 4703–4704
in Abbasid caliphate, 4695
ʿAbd al-Rāzīq (ʿAlī) on, 5
on ablutions, 8057
in Andalusia, 4593–4595
and imitation of Muḥammad, 6227
Arabic language essential to, 4698
blasphemy in, 975–976
caliph as guardian of, 1365, 1367
in Central Asia, 4620, 4627
in central place in Islam, 4566
in China, 4633
classification of acts in, 4692
colleges of, religious studies and, 8783
contemporary reformulations of, 4703–4704
on conversion and intermarriage, 1674
criminal law, 4575
development of, 4566
dhimma system for other religions, 1673–1674
divorce in, joking about, 4213
earliest stage of, 4693–4694
ecology in, 2652
family
gender in, 3368
in Ottoman Empire, 4701, 4704
walāyah in, 9657
fiqh (Islamic positive law), *qāḍī* and, 7540–7541
flexibility of, 4566
governments based on, as religious communities, 1866
hawzah and, 3801
historical development of, 4693–4698
ʿibadāt in, 4692–4693, 4700
Ibn Hazm (Ahmad) on, 8781
Ibn Rushd on, 4271
ijmāʿ as source of, **4372–4373,** 4566, 4695
ijtihād as endeavor to derive rule of, 4373, 4697
inheritance in, 9657
interpretation of (casuistry), 1454
and Islamic theology, 4692
Islamization campaigns and, 4703
ʿsmāʿīlī, development of, 7541
Jaʿfar al-Ṣādiq in, 4760
Jamāʿī Sunni emphasis on, 8855
jihād in, 4918–4919
judgment of life and, 5446
judiciary law, 4575
jurists in development of, 4697–4698
at *madrasahs,* 5556
maṣlaḥah (public interest) in, 5772–5773
meaning of term, 4691
medical ethics based on, 5812
muʿamalāt in, 4693, 4700
on murder, 4566
in Muslim Brotherhood mission, 6315–6316
Muslim feminists on, 3367
on *niyyah* (intention), 8057
on *ṣalāt* (prayer), 8055, 8057
origins and nature of, 4692–4693
personal law, **4705–4712**
on adultery, 4566
on bequests, 4710
on divorce, 4706, 4708–4709
on inheritance, 4564, 4707, 4709–4710
on marriage, 4705–4708
on paternity, 4710–4711
on polygamy, 4700, 4707
personal *vs.* geographical schools of juriconsults, 3760
and politics, 4692, 4703
on poor people, 4564
principal figures in, 4699–4700
principal subjects in, 4700
qiyās as source of, 4372, 4696–4697
Qurʾān as source of, 4372, 4566, 4692, 4693, 4695, 4696
Qurʾanic exegesis and, 7563
ṣawm (fasting) in, 8141
schools *(madhhabs)* of, **5547–5550** (*See also specific schools*)
ancient, 4694
emergence of, 3759–3762, 5547
establishment of, 4566–4567, 4694–4697
geographical distribution of, 4698–4697
mature, 4698–4700
on *ḥadīth,* 4566
talfiq (patchwork) procedure in, 4566–4567
al-Shāfiʿī on, 8263–8265
shaykh al-Islam, role of, 8306
on slaves, 4564
Smith (Wilfred Cantwell) on, 8450
studies on, 4717
in Sufism
Ibn al-ʿArabī on, 8820
transcendence of, 8817
sunnah as source of, 4372, 4694, 4696, 8853, 8854
Sunnī, *qiyās,* 7545
in Sunnism *vs.* Twelver Shiism, 8342
tafsīr on, 8952
talion in, 7782–7783
taqīyah in, 8999
on theft, 4566
traditionist movement in, 4694
Twelver Shiism, 4571–4572
ummah in, 9446–9447
uṣūl (sources of), al-Shāfiʿī on, 8264–8265, 8854
walāyah in, 9657–9658
waqf in, 9677
westernization of, 4701–4703
on women, 4564, 4573
Islamic literature
Andalusian, 4595–4596, 4597
Bengali, 825
Central Asian, 4629–4630
Chinese, 4639
fiction, 10035
gardens in, 3283
ḥājj manuals, 7155, 7157, 7158, 7159
ijtihād as authentication of, 4373–4374
magic in, 5578–5579
North African, 4583–4584, 4586–4587, 4589
South Asian, 4641, 4642, 4644, 4649, 10035
Southeast Asian, 4662–4665
sub-Saharan African, 4600, 4603, 4611
Tatar, 4618
Islamic Movement of Uzbekistan, 4628, 4630
Islamic Party of North America, 4689
Islamic philosophy. *See Falsafah*
Islamic Rebirth Party (IRP) (Tajikistan), 4626, 4627
Islamic reformation, 6100–6101
Islamic religious year, **4712–4715**
ḥājj in, 4712, 4714, 7155, 7157
in Java, 4661
lunar-based, 4712
Mawlid al-Nabī, 4713, 9202
Nawrūz, 4714
tilāwah in, 9202
Islamic Revolution (Iran)
media and, 4964
Zoroastrianism and, 10004
Islamic Society. *See* Jamāʿat-i Islāmī
Islamic Society of North America (ISNA), 6100
Islamic studies, **4715–4724**
in Andalusia, 4597
on art and architecture, 4718
in Canada, 4723
comparative religion and, 8782, 8783
contemporary, 4718–4721, 4723–4724

Islamic studies ***continued***
Eurocentric pattern of, 4721–4722, 4723
on *falsafah,* 4717–4718
in Germany, 4723
Goldziher (Ignácz) in, 3634–3635, 4716, 4717, 8951
history of, 4715–4718
on Islamic law, 4717
Jewish and Christian studies of Islam, 8782
on modern developments in Islam, 4718
on Muslim life, 4718
on mysticism, 4718
nonnormative, 4715, 4716–4718
normative, 4715
on *ḥadīth,* 4717
on *kalām,* 4717
on Muḥammad biographies, 945–946, 4716–4717
on Qur'ān, 4717, 4719
on *tafsīr,* 8951
Rahman (Fazlur) in, 4577–4579, 4719
on religious institutions, 4718
scope of, 4715
in Soviet Union, 4723
in sub-Saharan Africa, 4600
in United States, 4723
Waldman (Marilyn) in, 9664
Wensinck (A. J.) in, 9715
Islami nāvil (Islamic novel), 10035
Islamism
family law in, 3368
feminism in, 3367–3368
women in, 3365–3366, 3367–3368
Islamization theory, conversion in, 1972–1973
Islam Santri. *See* Agami Islam Santri
Islam wa-usul al-hukm, al- ('Abd al-Raziq), *5*
Island, The (Fugard), 2477
Island Arawak, **1426–1432**
Island Carib, **1426–1432**
Island Pond, Vermont, community, 6540
Islands
in Buddhist *cakravāla* cosmology, 2026
in Purāṇic cosmology, 2017
paradise as, 6985
Isle of Man, 7941
'Iṣmah (immunity from sin), **4724–4726**
Isma'il (viceroy of Egypt), al-Azhar university under, 231
Ismā'īlī (Seveners) Shiism, **8325–8337**
Aga Khans in, 172–173, 4572, 4698–4699
Assassins, order of (*See* Assassins)
calendar in, 4712
in Central Asia, 4621
in China, 4634
da'wah (missionary) aspect of, 2225
dissident group from, 7542–7544
doctrine in, 2064
early doctrines, 8326–8327
esoteric, 8330
in Ṭayyibīyah, 8335
"new preaching," 8333
qiyāmah, 8332–8333
emergence of movement, 8327–8328
establishment of, 4572
Fatimid age, 8328–8332
free will and predestination in, 3213
ghaybah (concealment) in, 3469
Ghazālī (Abū Ḥāmid al-) on, 3470
Gnosticism in, 3523
God in, 8326
ideology of, 4562
imamate in, 4395, 4572
imams, holiness of, 8035
in India, 8334, 8335–8336
Ja'far al-Ṣādiq in, 4760
jurisprudence of, 7541
Malikshāh ibn Ālp Arsalān and, 6640
Maymūnīyah movement and, 8327
missionaries in, 4572
Musta'lī branch of (*See* Musta'lī Ismā'īlīyah)
Nizārī branch of (*See* Nizārī Ismā'īlīyah)
number symbolism in, 6748
overview of, 8324
post-Fatmid era, 8332–8336
pre-Fatimid age, 8326–8328
prophets in, 8326
Ramaḍān in, 4714
Rasā'il Ikhwān al-Ṣafā' written by, 4375
schisms in
Druze, 8324, 8330
Fatimid, 8324, 8329–8331
from Imāmīyah, 8322
Ḥāfiẓīyah (Majīdīyah), 8331
Ḥusaynīyah, 8325
Muḥammad-shāh *vs.* Qāsim-shāh, 8333
Muṭarrifīyah, 8325
Naṣirīyah, 8325
Nizārīyah, 8324, 8331, 8332–8333
Qarāmiṭah, 8327, 8328–8329
Qāsimīyah, 8325
Ṭayyibīyah, 8324, 8334–8336
schools of law in, 5549
in South Asia, 4644, 4645, 4646
Sufism and, 8333
tafsīr (Qur'anic exegesis) in, 7566, 8954
al-Ṭūsī (Nāṣir al-Dīn) in, 9408
walāyah and, 9659
ẓāhir (exoteric) and *bāṭīn* (esoteric) aspects of, 8326
Zaydīyah, 8324–8325
Ismāīlīyah. *See* Ismā'īlī (Seveners) Shiism
Ismā'īl Safavī, as *mahdī,* 5982
Ismenos, 2985
IsMEO. *See* Instituto Italiano per il Medio ed Estremo Oriente
ISNA. *See* Islamic Society of North America
Isnād (chain of transmission), 1318–1319, 4374
authenticity requirements, 3731, 8944
in collections, 3729–3730
ḥadīth supported by, 3727, 4565, 8821, 8854
sunnah and, 8854
Isnati Awicalowanpi (Lakota sacred rite), 5297
Isocrates
oration as musical, 1532
on piety, 3677
Isokelekel (mythic figure), 6010–6011
Isolation
of retreats, 7768
for monastic initiation, 7769
for revelatory dreams, 7769
for shamanistic initiations, 7769
for tribal initiations, 7769
in rites of passage, 5461, 7798
Ispahbad (commander-in-chief), 4555
Isra' (Muḥammad's nocturnal journey), 6222–6223
mi'rāj and, 6058–6059
Israel. *See also* Judaism
Agudat Yisra'el in, 195–196
ancient (*See* Israelite law; Israelite religion)
archaeology in, 2224
as belonging to Jewish people, Rashi on, 7620
Bene Israel emigration to, 5007
Bēta Esra'ēl emigration to, 5004
as bride of God, 7080
Bukharan emigrants to, 5009
capital of (*See* Jerusalem)
chosenness of, 4860, 4861
Christians as, 4859
Christian views on, 7236
citizenship in, 4864
covenant in origin of, 2048–2049
creation of, 4864, 4906–4907
anti-Semitism and, 402
and arrival of messianic age, 5069
dance in, 2164
David as king of, 2221–2224
historical accuracy of, 2224
destiny of, Abraham in, 15
divine kingship in, 5147, 5148
Druze in, 2502
earliest Egyptian reference to, 2708
as end of exile, 2922
environmentalism in, 2643, 2646
films from, 3098
gender in, 3351
God's favoritism toward, 3548
halakhah in, 3753–3754
Hasidism in, 3788, 9382
Hirsch (Samson Raphael) on, 4023–4024
Holocaust and, 4984
Ḥoq ha-Shevut (Law of Return) in, 3754
Independence Day in, 4868
Jewish Renewal in, 4873
as "Jewish state," 9982
Jewish studies in, 4885
Judaism in, 4985
Karaites in, writings of, 5086
kingship in, 5164–5165
Kook's (Avraham Yitsḥaq) influence on, 5227
life of, maintenance and revitalization of, 5445
Magen David in, 5559
Masorti movement in, growth of, 1961
messianism in, 5978
in midrash, 6016–6017
national growth of, Krochman (Naḥman) on, 5248
as "natural" religious community, 1865
in Orthodox Judaism, Hungarian, 6899
Orthodox Judaism in, 6903–6905
Palestinian conflict with (*See* Arab–Israeli conflict)
pilgrimages in, 7161–7162
rabbinate in, 7582–7583
rabbinic Judaism in, 7583
Raëlian embassy in, demand for, 7599
Reconstructionist Judaism in, 7637
Reform Judaism in, 7672
religion and state in, 9981–9982
Bar-Ilan (Me'ir) on, 788
religious education in, 7735
religious nationalism in, 7255
Samaritans, status of, 8070
scientific history and, 8181
secularization in, 8219
Spinoza (Baruch) on, 8683
supermundane nature of, 4862
supernatural nature of, 4862
supporters of, blessings promised to, 2892
as symbol of survival, 4909
synagogues in, 7582–7583

Teitelbaum (Yo'el),
opposition to statehood by, 3793
as vassal of Yaveh, 4830–4831
women in, 3351, 3354
yeshivot of, 9885
Zionism and, 788, 4984, 6903–6904
Israel (Albanian bishop), and Huns, conversion of, 4229
Israel (biblical figure), 4757, 4758
Israel (mythic sacrificial victim), 99
Israel, Adrienne, 80
Israel, Jonathan, on Spinoza (Baruch), 8681, 8685
Israeli, definition of, 4856
Israeli, Isaac, medical ethics of, 3830
Israeli Independence Day, 7672
Israeli Renewal, 4873
Israelitas (Israelites of the New Universal Covenant, Peru), 6547
Israelite, definition of, 4856, 4971
Israelite law, **4727–4742**
apodictic, 4728
casuistic, 4728
codification of, 4727
criminal law, **4737–4739**
crimes against king, parents, and authorities, 4737
homicide and manslaughter, 4738
idolatry, 4737–4738
and sacred law, 4738
sexual offenses, 4737
talion, 4738, 4742
theft, 4738
death penalty in (*See* Death penalty, in Israelite religion)
family law, **4733–4734**
adultery, 4733–4734, 4737, 4738, 4740
divorce, 4733
marriage, 4733, 4736
functions of, 4727–4728
as God's will, 4727, 4729
history of, 4727–4730
vs. Mesopotamian law, 4728
personal status law, **4730–4733**
king, 4732, 4737, 4739–4740
minors, 4731–4732
poor people, 4731
resident aliens, 4731
slaves, 4731
priests and, 7400
property law, **4734–4737**
conveyance of property, 4734–4735
inheritance, 4732, 4735–4736
redemption of hereditary land, 4735
tithes, 9209, 9210
on purity, 7511–7513
state and judiciary law, **4739–4742**
decision making, 4740
execution of decision, 4740–4741
expiation, 4739, 4741
jurisdiction, 4739–4740
Ten Commandments and, 4745, 9074
Torah as (*See* Torah, as law)
on women, 4731, 4732–4734, 4736
Israelite religion, **4742–4750**. *See also* Biblical Temple; Hebrew scriptures
Aaron in, 1
altars in, 276–277
amulets in, 4742
ancestor worship in, 4743
angels in, 4742
anti-Semitism and, 397–398
apocalypse in, 4748–4749
Assyrian religion and, 4359
in Babylon
destruction of Solomon's Temple, 923, 935, 4549
Isaiah on, 4548–4549
biblical literature of (*See* Hebrew scriptures)
bread in, 1040, 1041
Canaanite religion and, 4742
circumcision in
of Isaac, 4544
of Ishmael, 4552
collective existence in, 4856–4858
confession in, 1888
covenant in, 4745–4746
cult of Jerusalem Temples in (*See* Biblical Temple)
deities of, 4742–4743
lesser deities (Sons of God), 4742
origins of, 4742
divination in, 5425
domestic observances in, 4744
ecstasy in, 2678
election in, 2744
eschatology in, 4974–4975
extrabiblical sources on, 4972
as family religion, 4742, 4744
fertility gods in, 7602
ghosts in, 4743
goddess worship in, 3586
God in, **3537–3543**
relationship with, 2642
healing and medicine in, 5425
henotheism in, 4743
human beings in, 4743–4744
idolatry condemned in, 4385, 4737–4738
idolatry in, 4358–4359, 4744
immigrants in, laws on, 4731
initiation in, 4744
kingship in, 6380–6382
laws on, 4732, 4737, 4739–4740
and prophets, 7436
as son of God, 4743
Temple maintained by king, 4745
kissing holy objects in, 9258
kneeling in, 5195–5196
libations in, 5434
as local religion, 4745
magic in, 5575
merit in, 5871
migration in, 6024, 6025
monolatry in, 3539–3542, 4743, 6157
monotheism of, 6157–6158
historical problem of, 3539–3541
as monarchic, 6159
Moses and, 6201–6202
rise of, 3541–3542
Moses as founder of, 6201–6202
music in, 6276
myth and history in, 6375–6379
Myth and Ritual school on, 6380–6382
New Year festival in, 6593
offerings in (*See* Offerings, in Israelite religion)
ordination in, 6852
persecution of, 925, 7055–7056
Pesaḥ ritual in, 6593
pilgrimage in, 934, 935, 936, 7152, 7161
politics in, Levites and, 5426
polytheism of, 3539–3541
postscriptural, 4858–4859
priesthood in (*See* Levites; Priesthood, in Israelite religion)
prophetic critique of, 4747–4748
prophets in, 7424–7425
purification in, 4732–4733, 4747, 7511–7513
ritual calendar of, 186
rituals in, 4972–4973
Sabbath in, 4548, 4550
sacrifices in (*See* Sacrifice, in Israelite religion)
scriptualization of, 4749–4750
scripture in, 4974–4975
social classes absent in, 4730–4731
as state religion, 4742, 4744–4745
suffering in, 4748–4749
temptation in, 9070–9071
terafim skulls in, 3806
theocracy in (*See* Theocracy, Israelite)
theodicy in, 9115–9116
time in, 6378–6379
wisdom in, 9750, **9754–9762,** 9755
women in, 3351
excluded from Temple in, 934–935
exclusion of, 3541
laws on, 4731, 4732–4733, 4733–4734, 4736
as priestesses, 5420
as prophets, 7435
Yavheh in identity of, 4856–4857
Zion and, 9977
Israelites of the New Universal Covenant, 5986
Isrāfīl, 2838
Isserles, Mosheh (RaMa), **4750–4751**
Shulḥan 'arukh (law code), 3159, 4751, 5104
education of, 4750
halakhah and, 3743–3744
Me'ir ben Barukh of Rothenburg and, 5831
in Polish Judaism, 5015
synagogue built by, 4750
writings of, 4751
Issyk royal headdress, 7386–7387
Iṣṭadevatā (deity of choice), Śaṅkara on, 4004
Istaevones (Germanic tribe), 3447
Istanbul (Turkey). *See also* Constantinople
Hagia Sophia in, 6246–6247
heritage politics and religion in, 1810
Iṣṭāpūrta, distinction from *karman,* 5094
Isthmian games, 8723
Iṣṭi (sacrifice), 9562, 9563
Istiḥsān (preference), 9489
Istikharah, 7572
Istiṣlāḥ (consideration of public interest), 5772, 5773, 9489
Istoria della città di Viterbo (Covelluzzo), cards in, 1413–1414
Istorica descrizione de' tre' regni Congo (Cavazzi), 112
Isutzu, Toshihiko, 3561
Īśvara (personal god), **4751–4752**
bhaktimārga leading to, 856
in *rājayoga,* 3998
in Vaiśeṣika, 9498
in literature, 4751–4752
monism and, 6144, 6145
origin of term, 4751
in philosophy, 4752
Śaṅkara on *brahman* as identical with, 4004
in Yoga, 9896
Īśvaragītā (Hindu text), 854
Īśvarakṛṣṇa, 7361, 7522
Īśvarapratyabhijñāvimarśini (Abhinavagupta), 9
Īśvarapratyabhijñāvivṛtivimarśini (Abhinavagupta), 9

Italian Bacchanalia, persecution of, 7909
Italian Discorso (Luzzatto), 7107
Italy. *See also* Papal States; Roman Catholicism
All Saints Day in, 2230
All Souls Day in, 2230
ancient (*See* Roman Republic and Empire)
benandanti cult in, 8250
Byzantine territories of, Norman conquest of, 2586
Carnival in, 2147–2148
Catharism in, 1458
Celts in, 1478
commedia dell'arte and Carnival, 1441–1442
dance in, 2154
drama in, 2470
ethnology in, 5261
Etruscan urbanization in, 5167
folklore of, de Martino (Ernesto) on, 2267
Greek colonization Southern Italy
Hera cult in, 3915
Herakles cult in, 3917
Hermetism in, 3945–3946, 3949, 3951
hermits of, 2826, 2827
historiography in, 4045–4046, 4050–4051
history of religions in, Pettazzoni (Raffaele) and, 7072–7077
Inquisition in, 4498
invasion of Ethiopia by (1935-1936), 7624
Islam in, 4679
Jews in, forced conversion of, 5722
Judaism in
iconography of, 4340
rabbis in, 7580
kingship in
Etruscan, 5167
Roman, 5167–5168
legal system in, inquisition and, 8013
Melqart in, 5848–5849
new religious movements in, study of, 6524
new religious movements with origins in, 6568
New Year festival in, 6593
poetry in, 7220
prehistoric culture in, 7381
Protestantism in, Pentecostalism, 7029
Qabbalah in, 7535, 7537
Renaissance in (*See* Renaissance)
Roman religion and, 7893–7903
Tuscan region of, *veglia* (social event) in, 2147–2148
Itang (priest-chiefs), 6008, 6009
It Does Not Die (Eliade), 2760
Itelmen people (Arctic), 468
Ithna Ashariyah. *See* Imāmī (Twelvers) Shiism
I–Thou relationship
Buber (Martin) on, 1057, 1058, 2343, 4905, 7118
Fackenheim (Emil) on Holocaust and, 4092
Rosenzweig (Franz) on, 4904–4905
Itihāsa (history), 4423, 4424
Itihāsa-Purāṇa tradition, historiography as epic history in, 4025
Itiriti plant, 9575
Itkonen, T. I., 474
Ito Jikigyō, *Miroku-ha* (Maitreyism) teachings of, 8364
Itō Jinsai, **4752–4753**
cosmology of, 4752–4753
influence of, 4753
Kogidō (School of Ancient Meanings) and, 1928, 4752
philosophy of, 4752
as teacher, 4752, 4753
writings of, 4753
Itonde (mythic figure), 93, 97
Ito Shinjo, 6574
Ito Tomoji, 6574
Itsumadegusa (Hakuin), 1085
Ittiṣāl (conjunction with the divine), 4263
itu er-me festival, 2598
itu hu-lu-mu festival, 2598
Itzamná (deity), 5883
Itzamna festival, 7603
Itzamnah (deity), 5798
Itzcoatl (Aztec ruler), restructuring of Aztec government by, 5173
Itzpapalotl (deity), 5906
Itztli (deity), 717, 718, 9093
Iulius Solinus, 1484
Iupiter (Jupiter) Dolichenus (deity), **4753–4754**
Adad identified with, 28
cult of, 4753, 4754
iconography of, 4753
origin of, 4753
in Rome, 7914, 7917–7918
Iurung Aiyy Toion (White Lord Creator), 9865
Ius canonicum. *See* Canon law
Ivan (Saint John), in Slavic religion, 8435
Ivanov, Lev, 2156
Ivanov, S. V., 3114
Ivanov, Vjačeslav, 771, 9421
on Māra, 5691
Ivan the Terrible (Russian tsar), and Tatar conversion, 4616–4617
IVF. *See* In vitro fertilization
Ivory Coast. *See also* Akan religion
Christianity in, Harris (William Wade) and, 3780
funeral rites in, 3236
ghosts in, 3476
Harrist Church in, 3780–3781
myth of the Fall from, 2960
Nafana people of, masquerade dances of, 2141
Wan people of, dances of, 2138
'Ivri (Hebrew), 4856
'Ivri, ha- (weekly), 788
Ivy, 9337
Iwainushi no Mikoto (deity), 289
Iwamoto Yoshiharu, 3072
Iwans (vaulted open porches), mosques with, 6209
I Will Praise the God of Wisdom (Babylonian text), 4931
Ixchel (deity), 5883, 7812
Ixcuina (deity), 5910
Ixiptla (deity impersonator), 9093
Ixquimilli-Itztla-coaliuhqui (deity), 9093
Iya (female leaders), 10027
'Iyād, Qāḍī, 4585
Iya Mi group, of Yoruba, 3401
Iyatiku (deity), 6724
Iyerosun (divining powder), 10032
Iyō. *See* Kamo no Mabuchi
Izanagi (deity), 3016, **4754–4755**
and Amaterasu Ōmikami, 280
creation by, 7978–7979
descent into the underworld by, 2298, 4755
in Japanese creation, 2555, 4801
marriage of, 5727
worship of, 4755
Izanami (deity), 3016, **4754–4755**
creation by, 7978–7979
death of, 4754
Izanagi searching for, 2298, 4755
in Japanese creation, 2555, 4801
marriage of, 5727
worship of, 4755
Izapa (Mexico), monuments in, 5882
Izapan religion (Mesoamerica), iconography of, 4311–4312
Izibidi (soul), 146
Izō Iburi, 6405
'Izrā'īl (angel of death), 1785
Izumo (Japan), 4811, 6814
Izumo fudōki (records of wind and earth), 4811
Izumokagura (dance), 6300
Izzi Dien, Mawil, 2652

J

J (source). *See* Yahvist source
Jaapu (hymn from *Dasam Granth*), 2221
Jabès, Edmund, 5483
Jābir ibn Ḥayyān
alchemy and, 248–249
on number seventeen, 6750
Jābir ibn Zayd, 4248, 5127
Jabotinsky, Vladimir, 9980
Jabrīyah (school of Islam), power of God in, 3562
Jackal
Anubis represented as, 403
in *Pañcatantra,* 6959–6960
Seth represented as, 8233
Jack-o'-lantern, 2952
Jacks, L. P., 6105
Jackson, Bernard, 5373
Jackson, Jesse, Nation of Islam and, 6420
Jackson, Natasha, 1189
Jackson, Roger R., 9190
Jackson, Sheldon, 573
Jackson, W. T. H., 2816
Jack Van Impe Presents (television program), 7714
Jacob (biblical figure), **4757–4758**
angels and, 345
Canaanite parallels, 1396–1397
goat breeding by, 3427
as Israel, 4757, 4758, 4856
Rebecca and, 7634
vow of, 4746
wives of, 7591
Jacob (bishop of Edessa), 894
Jacob, Benno, 869
Jacob, Rayda, 3088
Jacob Baradeus, Syriac Orthodox Church and, 8939
Jacob ben Asher, 9236
Jacobi, Friedrich, on Spinoza (Baruch), 8685
Jacobi, Hermann
Glasenapp (Helmuth von) and, 3497
Jain studies by, 4447
on *Rāmāyana,* 7617
Stcherbatsky (Theodore) and, 8737
Jacobins. *See* Dominicans
Jacobite Syrians. *See also* Syriac Orthodox Church of Antioch
origin of name, 8939
Severus of Antioch and, 8238
Jacobovitz, Immanuel, on medical ethics, 3829
Jacobs, Claude, 75
Jacobs, Jane M., 690
Jacobs, Melville, 6671
Jacobsen, Doranne, 951
Jacobsen, Thorkild, 2520, 2522
archaeological research of, 455
on *Epic of Gilgamesh,* 3487
on Mesopotamian religion, 5969, 5971
on myth of Enki and Ninhursaga, 6625
Jacobson, Doranne, 3321
Jacobson, Israel, 7668
Jacolliot, Louis, comparative religion and, 8716
Jacquot, Benoît, 3099
Jade, **4758–4760**
Chinese cult of the dead and, 1582
inscriptions on, in Chinese religion, 5352
in Mesoamerican drama, 2466
Jade Emperor (deity), 1606, 1619, 9593. *See also* Yuhuang
Jadeite. *See* Jade

Jadid renaissance (Tatar), 4617, 4618–4619
Jadīds (Muslim reformists), in Central Asia, 4623
Jādi Rānā (Silhara ruler), 6997
Ja'far al-Ṣādiq, **4760–4762**
  Abū Ḥanīfah and, 21
  on *ahl al-bayt,* 199
  alchemy and, 248
  Imāmīyah and, 8322
  in *ṭarīqah* heritage, 9005
  on mystical union, 6338
Jafarey, Ali, 9991–9992
Ja'farī madhhab, 4760
Jaffee, Martin, 6020
Jagaddhātri (deity), Bengali worship of, 826
Jannātha (deity)
  Caitanya absorbed into image of, 859
  Caitanya and, 826, 1345–1346
  consecration of image of, 4390
  devadāsīs of temple of, sexual activity of, 3967
  Jayadeva and, 4819
  Kṛṣṇa and, 5253
Jāgaritṛ (wakefulness), 4435
Jagat tarinī (deliverer of the world), 4330
Jäger, Johann, on humanism *vs.* Scholasticism, 4176
Jagganāth (India), pilgrimage to, 7170
Jaguar, Sun of, in Aztec calendar, 1357
Jaguar priest, throne of, 1469
Jaguars, **4762–4764**
  in ethnoastronomy, 2864
  in Olmec iconography, 4311, 5881, 6818
  in South American religions
    in fire origin myths, 8590
    in Ge mythology, 3293–3294
    in myths on origin of sun and moon, 8588
    in shamanism, 8291, 8292
    veneration of, 8581–8582
    water jaguar myths in, 8292
Jahāmgīr (Mughal emperor), 4350
Jahāngīr (Mughal emperor), 4646, 4647, 4650
Jahannam. *See* Gehenna, in Islam
Jahikā (spirit), 3372–3373
Jāhilīyah, 442, 5203
  polytheism of, 7155
Jahiliyya (paganism), Qutb (Sayyid) on, 7576
Jāḥiẓ, al-, 2446, 4371, 7242
  book on Mu'tazilah, 6320
  al-Naẓẓām and, 6445
Jahiz (scholar), satire by, 4215
Jahn, Robert F., 6057
Jahner, Elaine A., 6672
Jaimini
  and Bādarāyaṇa, 735–736
  atheism and, 580
  on *dharma,* 2328
  Mīmāṃsā Sūtra compiled by, 6042
Jaina Path of Purification, The (Jaini), 5870
Jaina Rāmāyaṇa (Hemacandra), 7609
Jaini, P. S., 5619
Jaini, Padmanabh S.
  on merit, 5870
  on *sallekhanā,* 8831
Jainism, 4429, **4764–4772**. *See also* India and Indian religions; *specific countries and doctrines*
  ablutions in, 10
  ahiṃsā in, 197, 2624–2625, 4429, 5096, 6646, 7023
  alchemy in, 241
  arhat in, 476
  asceticism in
    dependence on laity and, 5288
    dualism and, 528
    vs. normal behavior, 529
    objectives of, 527, 528
  atheism of, 578, 579
  beginnings of, 4764
  blessing in, 980
  Buddhism and, 1102, 1125–1126, vol. 8 color insert
  castes criticized by, 4421
  cave art, 1472
  charity in, 1555
  confession in, 1886
  contemporary, 2626
  cosmology in, **2022–2026,** 2625, 8548
    ethical system from, 2624
  deities of (*See also specific deities*)
    gender of, 3327
    in Lower World, 2024
    Sarasvatī as, 8113
  devils in, 2315
  ecology and, **2624–2627**
  enlightenment in, 2793, 5610
  eremitism of, 2822, 2823
  fasting in, 2996, 2997
  fiction in, 10034
  food taboos in, 3168
  founders *(tīrthaṃkaras)*
    cakravartin ideal and, 1350
    Mahāvīra, 4429
  funeral rites in
    ritual time and, 7987
    tombless, 9225
  Gandhi (Mohandas) influenced by, 3272
  gender in, **3326–3330**
  God in, 4770
  guṇas in, 3709
  as heterodoxy, 6909–6910
  Hinduism and, 4429, vol. 8 color insert
  historiography in, 4025
  history of, 4765–4766
  iconoclasm in, 4282, 4285, 4392
  image maps in, vol. 3 color insert
  image veneration in, 4382, 4389, 4390, 4391
  initiation rites in, 7816
  karma in, 5096, 9207
    vs. in Buddhism, 1887
    as central power, 4429
    rebirth and, 8098
    reincarnation and, 7679
  laity of, 4770, 5288
  mantras in, 5676–5677
  merit in, 5870
  modern, 4771
  music in, 6285
  nirvāṇa in, 9207
  nonviolence in, 6646
  nudity in, 6740–6741
  nuns in, 6757
  offerings in, 4382
  ordination in, 6854
  peace in, 7023
  poetry of, 7212
  portraits in, vol. 10 color insert
  reincarnation in, 7676, 7679
  religious communities of, gender in, 3327–3328
  renunciant practice of, 4768–4770
  rituals in, 4769
  sallekhanā (austere penance) in, as suicide, 8831
  salvation in, women and, 3326, 7084
  saṃsāra in, 8098
  scriptures of, 4766–4767
    Ājīvikas in, 3639
  self-discipline in, 8548
  sexual themes in, 7083–7084
  social classes in, 4421
  soul in, 8548
  studies of, 4447
  teachings of, 4767–4768
  temples of, 4429
  time in, 2025
  tolerance in, 4429
  Vedic tradition criticized by, 4421
  vegetarianism in, 2625, 4770, 5610, 6646
  women in, **3326–3330**
    in myths, 3326–3327
    salvation of, 3326, 7084
Jajmān, king as, in popular Hinduism, 4007
Jajmāni (sacrificer-patron) relationship, 7406
Jaki, Stanley L., on incarnation and scientific history, 8181
Jakobson, Roman, 3114, 5381
  distinctive-features theory of, 8749
Jalāluddīn Rūmī, on nature, divine in, 2606–2607
Jālandhara (India), 1110
Jalp-ūs Ōjka (deity). *See* Holy City Old Man
Jam' (union), in mystical union, 6338
Jama'a Islamiyya (Muslim group), 4671–4672
Jamaa movement, 7788–7789
Jamā'āt (groups), Muslim Brotherhood and, 6315, 6316
Jamā'at-i Islāmī, 830, 4681, 4772–4774
  Mawdūdī in, 107, 5788
Jamaica and Jamaican religions
  ancestral cults in, 1435–1436
  black Baptists in, Liele (George) and, 5443
  Christianity, 1706, 1707
    missionaries in, 2067
  creolization in, 2067
  Ethiopianism, 7623
  Great Depression, unrest caused by, 1437
  Rastafari (*See* Rastafari)
  Revival Zion, 1436–1437
  transculturation of, 9306–9307
Jamaican Revival, 7623
Jamā'ī-Sunnism, emergence of schools of, 8854–8855
Jamal, Battle of al- (656), 211, 258
Jamāl Hānswī (Ṣūfī sage), on women, 4165
Jambho-ji, in Bishnoi movement, 2622
Jambū, 4765
Jambudvīpa ("Rose Apple Island")
  in Buddhist *cakravāla* cosmology, 2026, 2027
  in Purāṇic Hindu cosmology, 2017
  in Jain cosmology, 2023–2024
'Jam dbyang Mkhyen brts'i dbang po, 5222, 5223, 5224, 7869
Jameikis, Stasys, 764
James (biblical book), 916–917
  Abraham in, 16
  audience of, 916–917
  author of, 916
  canon of, 920, 921
  purpose of, 916, 7020
  against teachings of Paul, 917
  temptation in, 9070, 9071
James (Jesus' brother), 916
James (New Testament figure, saint)
  Illapa identified with in Andean religions, 8601–8602
  liturgy of, 2592
  Ogou Ferraille identified with in Vodou, 1433
  relics of, 7689
James I (king of England)
  Bacon (Francis) under, 733
  Bellarmino (Roberto) and, 816

James I (king of England) ***continued***
Calvert (Lord Baltimore) and, 1373, 1374
magic prohibited by, 6453
witchcraft under, 9773
James II (king of England), 1323, 3195
James, Apocryphon of, 3513, 6396
James, E. O., 2542, **4774–4775**
on goddess worship, 3612, 3616
on sky gods, 8424
James, Fannie Brooks, 6585
James, Letter of, wisdom in, 9751
James, Simon, 1499
James, William, **4775–4778**
American study of religion, role in, 8785
atheism and, 584
and Bergson (Henri), 838
on Bunyan (John), 1323
on doubt, 2427
on ecstasy, 3138
influence of, 6636
on knowledge, 5208
metaphysics of, 5991
Myers (F. W. H.) influenced by, 7474
on mysticism, 6356, 7741–7742
characteristics of, 6341–6342
on mystic state, marks of, 2681
on new religions, 6520
on New Thought movement, 6584
Otto (Rudolf) and, 7742
paranormal experience and, 6057
on polytheism, 378, 386
on pragmatism, 5081
Pratt's (James) critique of, 7366
on prayer, 7370
on psychology of religion, 7475
on religion, 7113, 7126–7127
religion defined by, 7693, 7741
on religious experience, 6487, 7738, 7741–7742
on saints, 8033
on science and religion, 7341
Starbuck (E. D.) and, 8732
on states of consciousness, 1947–1948
theology of, 9137
Tönnies (Ferdinand) influencing, 9230
James I (king of Aragon), Nahmanides (Moses) and, 5976, 6400
Jameson, Anna Brownell, 499
Jameson, Fredric, on reflexivity, 7649
James the Elder (saint), in Vodou, 9638
Jamet, François, and Marie de l'Incarnation, 5712
Jāmī, ʿAbd al-Raḥmān
on *ahl al-bayt,* 199
on light of Muḥammad, 6768
on Naqshbandīyah, 9010
Jamia al-Azhar, 6206
Jāmiʿ al-bayān ʿan taʾwīl āy al-Qurʾān (Ṭabarī), 4400, 7565, 8943–8944, 8945, 8950, 8953
Jāmiʿ al-ṣaḥīḥ, al- (al-Bukhārī), 1318–1319
in *ḥadīth* literature, 3728, 3729–3730
Jamme, Albert, 443
'Jam mgon Kong sprul Blo gros mtha' yas, 7869
on *mahāmudrā,* 5598
Jamshēd (mythical Iranian king), feast dedicated to, 6730
Janaka (king), in *Rāmāyaṇa,* 7617
Janamsākhīs (birth stories), 6413
Janet, Pierre
on psychology of religion, 7474
on psychology of the subconscious, 1948–1949
Jangchup Gyaltsen, Tai Situ, Klong chen Rab 'byams pa (Longchenpa) and, 5193–5194
Jangnāma (Bengali stories), 825
Jāṇi (summer solstice), 768
Jani, Padmanabh S., 3326
Janiger, Oscar, 7472
Jānis (deity), 9420
Janissary corps, and Bektāshi Sufism and, 8823
Jānn (demonic figure), 2314–2315
Janna (garden), 6984
Jannabi, Abu Saʿid, al-, 7542
Jannah (garden), in Islamic eschatology, 2837
Sunnī, 2838
Jansen, Cornelis
on grace, 7001
on predestination, 3204, 3208
Jansenism, 7877–7878
and dance, 2155
enthusiasm of, 2805
on Eucharist, 7001
Pascal as, 7001
Jansenius. *See* Jansen, Cornelis
Janson, Horst, 6151
Jansons, Jānis Alberts, 770
Jantzen, Grace, 3025, 3314, 3360, 7008
on natality, 4166
on politics and religion, 7252
Janus (deity), **4778–4779**
as keeper of keys, 5116
place in Roman pantheon, 7899, 7901
Janzen, John, on Ngoma shrine of affliction, 118
Janzen, John M., 58
Jaoel (angel), 3510
Jāpā (prayer beads), 4522
Japal (big meeting), 5706
Japaljari, Andrew, 669
Japan and Japanese religions, **4779–4819**. *See also specific religions*
abortion in, 3869
academic study of religion (*shūkyōgaku*) in, **8775–8780**
early developments in (1905–1945), 8776–8777
prehistory of, 8762, 8775–8776
recent developments in (since 1945), 8777–8779
aesthetics in, 51
in African religious movements, 108–109
afterlife in, heaven and hell in, 3888
amulets and talismans in, 300
ancestors in, 2410–2411
health and, 3867
worship of, 324, 2982
art in
in Ashikaga period, 4787
Buddhism and, 4782
asceticism in, Shugendō and, 8352, 8379, 8380
in Ashikaga period, 4787
Aum Shinrikyō (*See* Aum Shinrikyō)
autobiography in, 702
baths in, 801
birds in, 948
bodhisattvas in, 1175
buddhas in, 1175
Buddhism (*See* Japanese Buddhism)
calligraphy in, 1368–1369, **1370–1371**
cats in, 1463
China and, Empress Suiko and, 5180
Chinese religion, study of, 1635–1636
Chinese script used in, 4782
Christianity, 1726–1727
in Japanese philosophy, 9314–9315
Kagawa Toyohiko's influence on, 5053–5054
kami in, 5074, 8365
in Meiji restoration, 4791–4792
missions and, 1186
Pentecostalism, 7030
persecution of, 9310
Roman Catholicism, 1727, 4787–4788, 4791–4792, 7273, 9310
Russian Orthodox Church, 7943, 7946
Russian Orthodox missions to, 2588, 4497
Uchimura Kanzō, 9431
concept of religion in, 1580
Confucianism, **1926–1929,** 4782
early history of, 1926–1927
Fujiwara Seika and, 3227–3228
Hayashi Razan, role of, **3802–3803,** 8363
Itō Jinsai's role in, 4752–4753
modern, 1928–1929
music in, 6300
in popular religion, 4795, 4797
Shintō and, 8363, 8375
in syncretic religions, 5073–5074
texts of, 4813
Tokugawa Confucianism, 1927–1928
in Tokugawa period, 1927–1928, 3802–3803, 4789, 8363
Tominaga Nakamoto on, 8776
under Shōtoku, 4782
Yamaga Sokō in, 9868
cosmogony of, 4801–4802
court in, *Kani'i junikai* ranks of courtiers in, 8375
creation myths in, sacred space and, 7978–7979
cultural identity in, 5216
dance in
and cultural identity, 2164
music with, 6299–6300
Daoism, 2188–2189, 2213, 2214–2215
Shugendō movement and, 8379
in syncretic religions, 5073–5074
deities of (*See also specific deities*)
crossroads and, 2071
goddess worship, 3587
goriyaku (benevolent functions) of, 3870
honjisuijaku theory and, 4121–4122
nature and, 2639
origin of, 2555
supreme (*See* Amaterasu Ōmikami)
divination in, shrine virgins and, 1528
domestic observances in, **2409–2412,** 4793, 4797
drama in, 2454, 2455–2456, 7042, 7048
humor and, 4209
drums in, 7036
ecology and, 2638–2639
emperor worship in
enthronement ceremony, 1514–1515
historiography and doctrine of divine descent, 4026
in Meiji period, 8367–8368
Ōmotokyō and, 6824–6825

post–World War II occupation and, 8368–8369
epic tradition of, 2815
family register of, 4785
films from, 3097
fish symbolism in, 3123
flower arrangement in (ikebana), 3135
folklore of, 4797–4798
fox in, 3182
folk religion, 9311–9312, 9314
food in, identification with people, 3169
funeral rites in, 2240, 2241, 3136, 3240
poetry of, 7215
gardens in, cosmic, 3277–3278
gender in, **3345–3350**
gender studies in, 3345–3348
genealogy in, 3425
ghosts in, 3477–3478
goddess worship in, 3587
government of, religion in, 4781–4782, 4783
hadaka matsuri in, fertility of earth and, 2559
healing in (*See* Healing and medicine, in Japan)
Hijiri (lay ascetics) in, **3978–3979**
historiography
modern, 4032
traditional, 4026, 4030
homosexuality in, 4114, 5415
humor in, 4203
imperial family of
divinity of, 4781–4782, 4783, 4785, 4810, 4813
divinity denied by, 4792, 4813–4814
Kiki texts and, 4802, 4804–4806
queens in, 4780
imperialism in, Confucianism and, 1928–1929
incense in, 3869
indigenous (*See* Shintō)
insects in, 4508
journals devoted to, 10058
Judaism, 5008
in Kamakura period, 4786–4787
kami in, 5071–5074
kingship in, 5157, 5178
emergence of, 5180
Kitagawa (Joseph M.) and, 5187–5189
Kokugaku movement (*See* Kokugaku)
Konkōkyō, **5224–5226**
Shintō and, 8367
Korean influences in, Shotoku Taishi and, 8375
Korea ruled by, 5233
Kṣitigarbha in, 5255–5256
Kurozumikyō, 5267–5268
Lady of the Animals in, 5280
laity in, 5289–5290
literature of
Buddhist, 1175, 1176, 1177, 1178, 1181
fiction, 3056, 3057, 3071–3075
poetry (*See* Poetry, Japanese)
Westernization and, 9315–9316
in lower classes, 4785
magic in, 5592, 5593–5594
marriage in, 5727
martial arts in, 5732
Meiji period in (*See* Meiji period; Meiji Restoration)
migrations to, 4779
miracles in, 6052–6053
mirrors in, 6063
missionaries in, Jesuit, 1355
modern, 4790–4793, 4813–4814
Jōdoshū Buddhism in, 4939
modernization of, 9312–9316
monkeys in, 6150, 6152
monsters in, 6165
moon in, 6173
mountains in, 8379
as cosmic centers, 6212
divine power of, 6214
Fuji-kō associations and, 8364
persistence of, 6214
prehistoric, 8379
women excluded from, 3348
museums in, 6245
music in, **6299–6302**
myth of the Japanese state in, *kami* in, 5073
mythology of
androgyny in, 2555
in medieval period, 4803–4806
study of, **4800–4809**
nationalism in, 7271, 7272, 7273–7274
nature worship in, 6439
Neo-Confucianism
Kumazawa Banzan and, 5264
in Tokugawa period, 9310, 9311
Neolithic culture in (Jomon culture), 6459, 6465
New Age religion, 4793
Worldmate movement and, 8369–8370
new movements in (*See Shinkō shūkyō*)
New Year festival in, 6594
Obon festival in, 3155
occupation of, 4792
ocean in, 6806
offerings in, 2410
orgy in, 6879–6880
overview of, **4779–4794**
periods of (*See specific periods*)
politics in (*See* Nationalism, Japanese; Politics, in Japan)
popular religion, **4794–4800**
institutionalization of, 4799–4800
Kiki texts and, 4802
prayer in, 4785
prehistoric background on, 4779–4780
rabbit symbols in, 7590
rainbow symbolism in, 7604
regency of, 4785
rejuvenation myths in, 7683–7684
religion, problematic meaning of, 8762
religious documents, **4809–4814**
religious experience in, 7740–7741
religious studies in
Anesaki Masaharu and, 342–343
gender in, 3345–3348
religious year, domestic observances in, 2410, 2411
retired monarchs of, rule by, 4785
Risshō Kōseikai, 7794–7795
rituals in
decline of, 4806
serious and comic modes of, 4198, 4208
under Yamato kingdom, 4781–4782
ritual texts in, 4803, 4806, 4809–4810
rivers in, 7863
sacred and profane in, 7970
sacred space in, 7978–7979
seclusion of, 9310
secularization and, 8219
seppuku (ritual suicide) in, 4183–4184, 8832
servitude as positive attribute in, 2986
Seventeen-Article Constitution (604), Confucianism and, 1927
shamanism in
charisma and, 1548
female, 8273
health care and, 3867
women in, 4795, 4921
shinkoku (land of the gods), Japan as, 8362
Shinto (*See* Shintō)
Shotoku as regent in, 8375
shrines and temples in, healing and, 3868–3870
Shugendō, Shingon Buddhism and, 8352
socialization in, healthiness and, 3867–3868
Sōka Gakkai movement in, urbanization and, 1809
Southeast Asia occupied by, 4668–4669
spirit possession in, 8695, 8696
studies of, Anesaki Masaharu and, 342–343
sun deity in, 4781–4782
sun in, 8841
supreme deity in (*See* Amaterasu Ōmikami)
Swedenborgianism in, Suzuki (D. T.) and, 8885–8886
syncretism in, 3868–3869, 8929
kami and, 5073–5074
Taiwan, occupation of, 1726, 8962
tattooing in, 1002
tea ceremony *(chanoyu)* in, as hospitality, 4141
tea drinking in, 847–848
Tenrikyō, 3005
theocracy in, 9109
tradition in, 9277
transculturation of, **9309–9316**
trees in, 9334, 9337, 9338
as unified religion, 4793
utopian communities in, 7720
Vajrasattva in, 9515–9516
under warrior rule, 4786–4787
Westernization of, 9312–9316
women in, **3345–3350**
Buddhism spread by, 4785
exclusion from sacred sites, 3348
work ethic in, Bellah (Robert) on, 8489
in World War II
cargo cults and, 1417, 1418
kamikaze pilots, 7270–7271
writing of, 4782
yamabushi (mountain ascetics) in, 3156
under Yamato kingdom, 4780–4782
Zen Buddhism, rock gardens of, vol. 5 color insert
Japan Association for Healing through Purification, founding of, 8369
Japanese Autonomous Orthodox Church, 7946
Japanese Buddhism, **1174–1186,** 8379. *See also* Jōdoshū school; *See also* Nichirenshū; *See also* Shingonshū school; *See also* Sōka Gakkai; Zen Buddhism
abortion and, 2241
Amitābha in, 292, 1179
Bodhidharma and, 995
bodhisattvas in, 1175, 1176, 1177, 1179, 1244, 5255
in Brazil, 1188, 1190
buddhas in, 1175, 1176

Japanese Buddhism ***continued***
bushidō in, 1247, **1334–1337**
canon, 1256
capitalism and, 1098
celebrations in, 1304, 1306, 1308
Chinese Buddhism and, 1176, 1179–1180, 1242, 1244, 4783–4784, 9075, 9076, 9077
Christian missionaries and, 1098, 1186
clothing, monastic, 1829
in colonial era, 7263
decline of, 1095
deities of, 3226
desire in, 2306
domestic observances of, 2409, 2410
drums in, 2497
effect on *kami,* 5072
emperor Yomei, acceptance by, 8374
enlightenment in, 1175–1176
Esoteric Buddhism, 1096, 1176–1177, 1243
ethics of, 1281, 1282
folk, 3155–3156
funeral rites, 2410
Gyōgi in, 3721
Gyōnen on, 1246
in Heian period (*See* Heian period, Buddhism in)
Hīnayāna Buddhism, 1241–1242
honjisuijaku theory in, **4121–4122**
Hosso Buddhism, 5258
Huayan school in, 4146, 4147
iconography of, 4329, 4330
Impure Lands in, 7503
incense offering in, 4419
influence of, 4782
introduction of, 4781
in Kamakura period (*See* Kamakura period, Buddhism in)
kami in, 2639–2640, 5073, 8356
karma in, 1175–1176
kingship in, 1241, 1242, 7262, 7271–7274
Korean Buddhism and, 1170, 1173, 4782
law and, 5349
of lay people, 1178, 1182
literature of, 1175, 1176, 1177, 1178, 1181
local spirits assimilated into, 8360
Mādhyamika Buddhism, 5555–5556
Mahāyāna Buddhism, 1176, 1183, 1202, 1242
Maitreya in, 5621–5622, 7503
maṇḍalas in, 5644
mappō in, 5685–5687
Māra in, 5690–5691
married monks in, 1182, 1183
meditation, 1096, 1290–1294
in Meiji period, 1183, 1245, 9313, 9314
in Meiji restoration, 4790
Miroku-ha (Maitreyism) teachings in, 8364
modern, 1184, 1245, 4790–4791, 4792–4793, 7264
monasteries, 1095, 1175, 1177, 1180–1184, 1241–1243
monks and nuns in, 6761
in Morumachi period, 1181–1182, 1245
music in, 6300–6302
in Nara period (*See* Nara period, Buddhism in)
nationalization of, 1182–1183
nembutsu in, 3155–3156, 6602–6603
Nichiren and, 6603
Nihonshoki interpreted in, 4805–4806
nirvāṇa in, 6631–6632
persecution of, 9075–9076
philosophy of, 1302
pilgrimage centers of, 1097, 1183, 1184, 7165–7166
politics and, 7260
in popular religion, 4795–4797
priesthood in, 7408, 7409
Pure Land Buddhism (*See* Pure Land Buddhism, in Japan)
Pure Lands in, 7503
rebirth in, 1175–1176
reformation of, 2741
Reiyūkai Kyōdan, 7861–7862
religious texts of, 4811–4813
rituals of, 1176, 1177, 1178, 1179, 1180, 1184
Saichō, role of, **8029–8031**
schools of, 1201–1202, **1241–1246,** 1247, 1248, 1249
shinkoku doctrine and, 8362
Shintō, relationship with (*See* Shintō)
Shotoku Taishi and, 8375
Shugendō and, 8352, 8379, 8380
sports and, 8724
spread of, 1093, 1094, 1164, 1174–1175, 1241, 4391
as state religion, 1241, 1245
studies on, 1235, 1246, 1247, 1248, 1249–1250, 1311, 1314
śūnyatā (emptiness) in, 8858–8859
in syncretic religions, 5073–5074
synthesis of indigenous religions and, 3154
and Taiwanese Buddhism, 8962
temples in, 4783–4784, 9048–9049
healing at, 3868–3870
Nakayama-dera Temple, 3869
sacredness of, 7698
Tendai, 2781, 4784–4785
in Tokugawa period (*See* Tokugawa period, Buddhism in)
under Shōtoku, 4782–4783
in United States, 1187–1188, 1189
Vajrayāna (Tantric) Buddhism, 1093–1094, 1096, 1214, 1215, 1217, 1243, 8985
Vinaya school of, 3275–3276
visions of descent into the underworld in, 2299
women in, 1180, 1183, 3346, 3348
domestic duties of, 2410, 2411
Yogācāra Buddhism, 9901
Japanese language, Buddhist chanting in, 6301
"Japaneseness," 5216
Japanese Society for Historical Research on Chinese Buddhism, 1635
Japjī, 2601
Japji (prayer of Nānak), opening words as Sikh creed, 2053
Jarḥ, al- (impugnment), in *ḥadīth* criticism, 3730–3731
Jarḥ wa' l-ta' dīl, al-. See Naqd al-ḥadīth
Jarir, poems of, 3210
Jarīrīyah, 8944
Jarl (mythological figure), 2693
Jarman, A. O. H., 5878
Jarmusch, Jim, 3099
Jarnail Singh Bhindranwale, 7257
Jarry, Alfred, 2475
Jarvie, Ian, on cargo cults, 1416
Jason of Cyrene, 900, 901
Jaspers, Karl, **4814–4815**
on "Axial Age," 378, 9603
on knowledge, 5209
Jastorf culture (Europe), 3445
Jastrow, Morris, 5968
Jātaka literature, 1111
Jātaka tales, 3075, 3076, 3156
bodhisattva in, 1076
in cave art, 1471
karuṇā in, 5105
norms for reading, 6993–6994
rebirth stories in, 998
as sacred biography, 945, 1064
stupa inscriptions of, 8797
suicide or self-sacrifice of Buddha in, 8832
Jātavedas, Agni as, 178–179
Jāti. See Varṇa and jāti
Jauhar (ritual suicide), by Rajputs, 8129
Jaurès, Jean, 2527
Java and Javanese religions, 4815–4819
Buddhism, 4657, 4816
temples of, 9044, 9052–9053, 9054–9055
Tengger Neo-Buddhism in, 8653
cats in, 1463
childbirth in, 7827
Christianity
conversion to, 1973
Pentecostalism, 7030
circumcision in, 7828
court attire in, 1830
fiction of, 3076
Hindu-Buddhist kingdoms in, 745
Hinduism, 4816
incantation in, 4407, 4409
Islam, 4815–4816
architecture of mosques in, 6209
calendar, 4661
in colonial era, 4660
conversion to, 4661–4662
evidence for, 4659
literature, 4664
marriage in, 5726
mawlids in, 5789
reform movements in, 4665, 4666, 4667
spread of, 4563, 4658
sultanates in, 4660, 4661
marriage ceremony of, 3136, 5726
Muḥammadīyah movement in, 4667, 4818, 8653
music in, 6287, 6288
new religious movements on, 8652–8653
political ceremony in, 1513–1514
postures and gestures in, 7344
Prambanan temple complex in, 4012
rainmaking in, 7603
rebellion against Dutch, 6547
stupas in, 1502
trees in, 9339
wayang (shadow theater) in, 8649
Javanese language, 4657, 4662
Java War (1826–1830), 4665
Jāvīd-nāmah (Iqbāl), 4534
Jawab (Iqbāl), 4534
Jawhar, al-Azhar founded by, 229
Jawharī, Ṭanṭāwī
scientific exegesis of, 7567
tafsīr of, 8956
Jawīsh, ʿAbd al-ʿAzīz, 7244
Jay, Nancy, 3037
on sacrifice, 8009
Jayadeva (poet), 826, **4819–4820,** 7209, 7211
on Rādhā, 7593
Jayadratha Yāmala, cult of Kālasaṃkarṣaṇī introduced in, 4020
Jaya jaya cankara (Jeyakāntan), 10036
Jayanāsā (Buddhist monarch), 1133
Jayarāśi, 1446
Jayavarman (Angkor king), 1133, 1135, 1138
Jayavarman II (Angkor king), 1134–1135, 5129
Jayavarman VII (Angkor king), 1133, 1135, 5129

Jayawardene, J. R., 7264
Jay Yaudheya (Pāṇḍey), 10034
Jazz music, 6313
Jealousy
of God, in Judaism, 3542
of Hera, 3914
Jean, Charles F., 5969
Jean de Meung, on nature, 6432
Jean de Rupescissa, on nature, 6433
Jeanmarie, Henri, on exorcism, 8687
Jean Paul, on humor, 6364
Jebe (Mongolian general), 4493
Jebel al-Aqra, Mount Sapan and, 1382
Jebel el Arak, knife of, 5277
Jebro (mythic figure), 6002
Jedidim, 5722–5723
Jedrej, M. C., on masks, 5765
Jefferson, Thomas
and blasphemy prosecutions, 974
Louisiana Purchase signed by, 7283
religious rhetotic used by, 7257
and religious tolerance, 7283
and study of North American Indian cultures, 6670
Jeffery, Arthur, 4717
Jeffries, Richard, mysticism of, 6342
Jehoiachin of Judah, exile of, 2943
Jehoiakim (king of Judah), 4830
Jehovah's Witnesses, **4820–4824,** 6558–6559
appeals to European Court of Human Rights, 6570
health care and, 5377
in Japan, 6574
in Latin America, 6579
millennialism of, 6552
pacifism of, 6648
in Russia, 6518, 6571
Jelles, Jarig, Spinoza (Baruch) and, 8681, 8682
Jelling Stone, 7940, 7941
Jemaluut (mythic figure), 6011
Jem Woš Iki (deity). *See* Holy City Old Man
Jenar, Siti, 4662
Jenkins, David, on knowledge, 5210
Jenkins, Jerry, 7324
Jenness, Diamond, 475
Jennings, Hargrave, on Hermetism, 3952
Jennings, Theodore, 7081
Jennings, Theodore W., Jr., 7859
Jensen, Adolf E., **4824–4826**
on agricultural myths, 191, 5277, 7835, 9578–9579
on Ceram culture hero myth, 2091–2092
cultural historical model of, 4043
on *dema* deity, 4464
on epochs of human history, 7835
on mystery religions, 6328
on mythic ancestors, 325
Preuss (Konrad) criticized by, 2543
on rituals, 7839
on sacrifice, 8004
on solar gods, 8578
and study of North American Indian religions, 6671
Jensen, Jeppe Sinding
on semiotics, 8759
on structuralism, 8758
Jensen, Peter, 989
on *Epic of Gilgamesh,* 3487
Jen-t'ien yen-mu (Buddhist text), 1276
Jeremiah (biblical book), 879, 4826–4827
Abravanel (Isaac) on, 868
Canaanite parallels, 1393
Christological interpretation of, 878
condemnation of idolatry in, 3485, 4358
heart in, 3882
historical background of, 4828–4830
on Inner Asian religions, 4489
Letter of Jeremiah inspired by, 897
messianism in, 5975
Moabite religion in, 6095
monotheism in, 3541–3542
personal status laws in, 4731
self-scrutiny in, 1939–1940
Spinoza (Baruch) on, 8683
Jeremiah (biblical figure), 2944, **4826–4831**
biography of, 4826–4827
Israelite religion criticized by, 4748
in Josianic reform, 4828–4829
on monotheism, 3541–3542
personality of, 4830
position of, 4828–4830
prophecies of, public readings of, 4827, 4830
prophetic actions of, 7432
prophetic authority of, 7434
prophets condemned by, 7433–7434
Rastafarian reincarnations of, 1438
Jeremiah, Letter of, 897
Jeremiah (book in Hebrew Scripture), micrographs of, vol. 14 color insert
Jeremiah Mourning the Destruction of the Temple in Jerusalem (Reiss), vol. 14 color insert
Jeremias, Joachim, on Jesus, 4847
Jeremias II (patriarch of Constantinople), **4831–4832**
correspondence with Lutheran theologians, 2587–2588
Lutheranism, response to, 2059
Jericho
agriculture in, origins of, 185
archaeology in, 1802
Kenyon's (Kathleen) work on, 5111
burial practices, 1802
Joshua's circumambulation of, 1796
Jeroboam I (king of Israel)
calves of, 2
oracle legitimating, 7436
Jeroboam II (king of Israel), Amos and, 295
Jerome, **4832–4834**
on Adonis, 35, 2536
on Apocrypha, 896
Apollinaris of Laodicea and, 424
on asceticism, 7723
Augustine and, 625
chanting *Psalms,* 7464
on chastity, 1558
commentaries of, 4833
on demons, 2277
Eastern influence on, 2582
Europe, connections to, 1688
on Hebrew scriptures, 881, 7205
homilies of, 4833
on Huns, 4490
conversion of, 4229
on Innocent I, 4495
Latin translation of Hebrew Bible by (*See* Vulgate Bible)
on mendicancy, 5856
on Montanism, 6167, 6168
and Paula, 6763
Pelagius criticized by, 7026
on Roman Empire's fall, 628
Shakpana identified with in Trinidad, 1434
ship symbolism of, 992
on Tertullian, 9085
translating works of Pachomius, 6940
on wisdom, 5502
Jerusalem, **4834–4841**
Abraham and, 4839
apostolic conference at (53 CE), 7016
archaeology in
Kenyon's (Kathleen) work on, 5111
tenth-century, 2224
Armenian patriarch of, 489
as capital
of Israel, David and, 923, 4839
Jewish, 4834–4835, 4837
in Christianity, **4838–4841**
in early structure, 2581
symbolism of, 4836
Church of the Holy Sepulcher in, 8377
Crusades and, 2074, 2075
Dome of the Rock in, 4836–4837, 6736, 7698, 8377
Easter in
lamp lighting during, 2579
octave celebration during, 2580
elderly Jewish women in, study of, 3147
Ethiopian Church in, 2861
Ezekiel's prophecies on, 2943–2944
Ezra in, 2946
in Greek empire, 4835
Greek Orthodox patriarchate of, 3658
heavenly prototype of, 7983
Hellenization of, 4835
in Islam, **4838–4841**
as holy place, 7979
ṣalāt (prayer) and, 8056
significance of, 6205
Jesus in, 4836, 4851
in Judaism, **4838–4841**
Mandaeans in, 5638
maps of, 3436
Masjid al-aqsa in, 6059, 6205
miqveh in, 6046
overview of, **4834–4838**
paganism at, 4839
Paul the Apostle's missionary journey to, 7019–7020
under Persia, 4835
pilgrimages in, 1808, 8377
Christian, 7152–7153, 9293
Eastern Christian, 7153–7154
Israelite, 7152, 7161
Jewish, 7161
pre-Israel, sanctity of, 4839, 4841
Qabbalah in, 7534
rebuilding walls of, Nehemiah and, 6457
religious traditions centered on, diversity among, 2605
rival patriarchs and bishops of, 2586
Roman destruction of (70)
Jewish apocalypses after, 417, 418
Josephus Flavius at, 4957
under Roman Empire, 4836
sacred geography of, 3436
sacred places in, 7698
sanctity of, 933, 4838–4841
schism in, 2586
siege of, Ezekiel in, 2944
symbolism of, 4835, 4837
as sacred space, 4838
Temple in (*See* Biblical Temple)
Temple Mount in
Masjid al-aqsa as, 6205
in multiple religious traditions, 6214
urbanization of, 4973
Western Wall in, 8377
pilgrimage to, 7161
as sacred space, 9261

Jerusalem (Mendelssohn), 5854
Jerusalem, Confession of (1673), on free will and predestination, 3208
Jerusalem, Council of (415), 7026, 7081
Jerusalem, Council of, Roman Catholic influences on, 2588
Jerusalem, Synod of (1672)
  confessions and catechisms endorsed by, 2059
  Cyril and, 2115
Jerusalem oder über religiöse Macht und Judentum (Mendelssohn), 4900
"Jerusalem Syndrome," 4841
Jerusalem Talmud. *See* Talmud, Jerusalem
Jerusalem Targum. *See Targum Jonathan*
Jerusalem Temple. *See* Biblical Temple; Second Temple; Solomon's Temple
Jester King, Carnival and, 1440
Jesudason, Savarirayan, in ashram movement, 546–547
Je suis un Phénomène (Brook), 2476
Jesuits (Society of Jesus), **4842–4843**. *See also specific figures*
  accommodationism of, 1918, 1919
  on Baltic religion, 761
  Benedict XIV on, 6973
  in Canada, 9302
  Canisus, role of, 1401–1402
  casuistry of, 1455
    Pascal's attack on, 7001
  Catholic Reformation and, 1663, 1692, 7877
  in China, 1355, 1608, 1609, 1630–1631, 1633–1634, 1725, 6084
    Confucianism, study of, 1918–1921
    Hermetism used as tool in, 3950
    of Ricci (Matteo), 7792–7793
  colleges of, 1402
    in Latin America, 1697
  and dance, 2136
    in Baroque period, 2155
  decline of, 6134
  vs. Dominicans, 816
    Paul V terminating debate, 6973
  dramas used by, 2474
  establishment of, 6134, 6972
  in Ethiopia, 2860
  on free will and predestination, 3204
  on grace, 3646
  growth of, 6134
  history of, 4842–4843
  humanism and, 4177
  as inquisitors, 4505
  Institute of the Blessed Virgin Mary and, 9692
  in Japan, 1355, 1726, 7273
  in Korea, 5233–5234
  in Latin America, 1696, 1697
  monastic community of, 7720
  in North America, 1708, 6422, 7301
    study of North American Indian religions, 6669
  organization of, 4842
  Pius XII on, 6973
  purpose of, 4842
  Rahner (Karl) in, 7600
  as religious order, 7721
  rites controversy, 1608, 1609, 1631, 1921
  in Romania, 9464
  Suárez (Francisco) in, 8799
  suppression by Clement XIV, 1445, 1921, 4842, 6973
  in Tamil, 8978
  Thomism in, 8175–8176
  Xavier (Francis) in, 9853–9854
Jesup Expedition, 475
Jesus (Christ), **4843–4852,** 4847. *See also* Christology; Trinity
  abandonment by God, 4845
  Abraham and, 16
  as Adam, new, 30, 3358
  Adam and, Paul on, 4052
  in ages of world, 173, 175
  Alexandrian theologians on, 6482
  androcentrism of, 335
  androgyny of, 341
  anointing of, 9809
  Anthony of Padua on, 377
  Antiochene theologians on, 6482
  as apocalyptic prophet, 411–412, 417, 6545, 6546
  Apollinaris of Laodicea on, 423–424
  as apostle, 436
  Aramaic spoken by, 887, 906
  in Arianism, 478
  arrest of, 4851
  ascension of, 523
  asceticism and, 7722
  Asklepios in competition with, 552
  as Raëlian prophet, 7597
  astrology and, 465
  Atahuallpa compared with, 567
  in atonement, 595–597
  on atonement, 595
  authority of, 694
  baptism of, 781, 4848, 9809
    Epiphany and, 1743–1744, 9814
    Holy Spirit and, 8562
    retreat after, 7770–7771
    vocation and, 9633
  beauty of, 812–813
  beliefs about God, 3543–3544
  bestowing power upon Peter, 6966, 6974, 7068
  birth of
    docetic descriptions of, 2381
    Epiphany and, 9814
  body of
    denial of physical body, 2381
    female embodiment and, 3037
    Thomas Aquinas on, 3170
  Bonaventure on, 1011–1012
  Bonhoeffer (Dietrich) on, 1017
  brides of Christ, 1476
  brother of, 916
  Buddha identified with, 1570
  in cargo cults, 1415, 1418, 1419
  charismatic leadership of, 9271
  as child, 1567
  as Christ
    as bridegroom, 9608
    brides of, 1476
    wisdom revealed in, 9751
  on circumcision, 7081
  citing *Psalms* 22:1, 887, 7464
  color of, in black liberation theology, 5441
  commands of, 1455
  compassion of, 4844
  condemnation of, by Sanhedrin, 972
  crucifixion of (*See* Crucifixion)
  cursing, 972
  days spent in wilderness, 6750
  death of
    anticipation of, 4851
    docetic descriptions of, 2381
    Eucharist and, 2877
    as saving act of God, 3544
    in worship, 9809
  denial of physical body of, 2381
  depictions of
    aureole in, 6624
    feet in, 3013
    as shepherd with lamb on his shoulders, 4297
  descent in the underworld by, 2299
  diamond as symbol of, 2345
  different pictures of, in Gospels, 905–906, 911
  disciples of (*See* Disciples)
  divinity of, 4843, 4844–4845
  doctrinal controversies concerning, 7876
  eagle as symbol of, 949
  early Church on, 1660
  earthly ministry of, in Orthodox theology, 2590
  Ebionite view of, 2595–2596
  ecclesiology and, 1770
  Eddy (Mary Baker) on, 2695–2696
  election through, 2747
  as enthusiast, 2807
  eremitism and, 2824
  eschatology of, 4846–4847, 4849
  and ethic of love, 6647, 6648
  in eugenics, 2881
  evolution of consciousness, role in, 8738
  exorcism by, 2928
  as face of God, 4844–4845
  family of, in New Testament, 5752
  the Family on, 2988, 2989
  Ficino (Marsilio) on, 3050
  in film, 3097
  fish symbolism and, 3123
  Freemasons on, 3195
  Freud on, 3216
  gardens associated with, 3277
  as ghost, 3475
  on gnosis, 3507–3508
  as God incarnate, 4417
  on God's name, 6407
  God's relation to
    in New Testament, 3543–3546
    in postbiblical Christianity, 3553
  grace in, 3644–3645
  healing by, 3813, 3843
    of palsied man, 6988
    spittle and, 8722
  heart of
    in mysticism, 3882–3883
    Sacred Heart of Jesus, 3883
  Heaven's Gate view of, 3890, 6555
  as hero figure, 7552, 7553
  historical, 4845–4848
    reconstruction of, 4848–4852
    Schweitzer (Albert) on, 8179
    Strauss (David Friedrich) on, 8748
  historiography of, 4032
  and history, Christian views of, 4028
  in Holy Order of MANS, 4102
  hospitality of, 4139
  humanity of, 2381
    nature and, 2648
  on human perfectibility, 7039
  humor and, 4196–4197, 4200
  in hymns of Ephraim of Syria, 2813
  identified with God, 1666
  images of
    in Byzantine art, 4345
    controversy over (*See* Iconoclasm)
    in early Christianity, 4344, 4352, 4353
    at Last Judgment, vol. 1 color insert
    on mandylion, vol. 12 color insert
    medieval, 4345–4346
    modern, 4348
    with phallus, 7081, 7082
    popular art, 7322
    Protestant, 4347, vol. 12 color insert

Renaissance, 4346, 7082
in Roman Empire, 4344–4345
suffering in, vol. 13 color insert
veneration of, 4386
imitation of Christ, 1670, 8704
incarnation of (*See* Incarnation, of God in Jesus)
intercession by, 129
interpretation of, in eschatological terms, 2835
interrogation of, 4851
in Islam
as *walāyah,* 9660
in eschatology, 2838
and *ghaybah* (concealment), 3468
as messenger, 6735, 6736
as Messiah, 5979–5980
as prophet, 5979
in Jehovah's Witnesses theology, 4820, 4822
in Jerusalem, 4836
in Jewish folk tales, 7231
as Jewish messianic pretender, 875
Jewish polemics on, 7231–7233, 7234
Jewish reevaluation of, 7235–7236
Jewish rejection of, 972
Christian view of, 399
exile attributed to, 2923
Jewish tradition confronted by, 9271
John the Baptist and, 4848, 4943
as judge of the dead, 5027
judgment of, 4844
Julian of Norwich on, 5029
in *Kalevala* (Finnish epic), 3104
as king, 4851
on kingdom of God, 5148–5149, 5151, 7024
kisses of, 5757
as "Lamb of God," 987
liberal lives of, 4846
in liberal Protestantism, 6104
lineage of, from David, 2223
lion associated with, 5464
as Logos, 992, 4417
as Lord of Chalma (Mexico), 1469
Luther (Martin) on, 7450
male lover of, 7081
in Mandaean religion, 5636
in Manichaeism, 2967, 5666, 5667
marriage associated with, 5724
as martyr, 8807
Mary Magdalene and, 5756–5757
Matthew the Evangelist and, 5780
as mediator, in Calvin, 1376
Mennonites on, 5860
menstruation and, 5866–5867
as messiah, 5972–5973, 6547
Gospels and, 4851
in Islam, 5979–5980
paradox of, 8260
in millenarianism, 6032
miracles of, 4850, 6053–6054, 6056
healing by, 3843
vs. magic, 5576
missions originating in, 6082
monotheism and, Justin Martyr on, 5044
on morality, 7652
as moral model, 4844
mortification and, 6197, 6198
Moses compared to, 6203–6204
as mother hen, 953
on mountain, 6213
mysticism of, 6346
as mythological figure, 4846
Jung on, 5034
in Nag Hammadi codices, 6396, 6398
name of, 6407
to ward off evil, 8676
and Narcissus, association between, 3064
nature of (*See* Arianism; Christology)
neoorthodoxy on, 6467, 6468
Nestorianism on, 6482–6483
Noah prefiguring, 6643
nonviolence of, 6647
nudity of, 6742
in Orthodox Christianity, 2590
pain of, 6946
passion of, 9814
on peace, 7021
on persecution, 7058
phallus of, 7081, 7082
philosophy of, 2821–2822
pilgrimage of, 7152–7153
on political power, 7279
prayer to, Sozzini (Fausto Pavolo) on, 8673, 8674
prediction of, in Hebrew scriptures, 873
presence and power of, in sacramental theology, 7959
as priest, 7403
on priesthood, 7401
as prophet, 875, 7425
apocalyptic, 411–412, 417, 6545, 6546
eschatological, 7426
in Islam, 5979
in Protestantism, 7450
proverbs and parables of, 6979
as rabbi, 7578, 7584, 8709
redemption and, 7640
relics of, 7689–7690
on repentance, 7758
repudiation of, in diabolical witchcraft, 9771
on resurrection, 156
resurrection of, 7765–7766
Barth (Karl) on, 790
Bultmann (Rudolf) on, 8807–8808
and history, Christian views of, 4052
Lessing (G. E.) on, 5417
as miracle, 6056
Paul on, 156, 7014
Strauss (David Friedrich) on, 8747
theories of, 4851–4852
in worship, 9809
retreat in Judaea of, 7770–7771
return of (*See* Eschatology; Millenarianism; Parousia)
revelations and, 7778
Ritschl (Albrecht) on, 7116
in Roman Catholicism, 7876, 7880, 7881, 7883–7884
Satan as brother of, 9415
Satan as personal adversary of, 2278
as savior, 4843–4844
as scapegoat, 8005, 8145
Origen on, 8144, 8145
search for real, 875, 944
second coming of
in cargo cults, 1415
imminence of, 2835
Seventh-day Adventists on, 1036
self-conception of, 4850–4851
Smith (Wilfred Cantwell) on, 8450
as solar metaphor, 4459
as Son of man, 2835, 4850–4851
as spiritual guide, 8709–8710
suffering of, 8807, 9116–9117
anticipation of, 4851
asceticism based on, 528
sun and
solar imagery of, 8841
as solar metaphor, 4459
as Sol Iustitiae (sun of justice), 8511
Swedenborg (Emanuel) on, 8899
in Talmud, 7231
as teacher, 875
Teilhard de Chardin (Pierre) on, 9033, 9034
on temptation, 9070, 9071
temptation of, 4848, 7771, 9071–9072, 9073
as thaumaturge, 6053–6054
three births of, 2861
Tillich (Paul) on symbol of, 9204
Torah superseded by, 4858–4859
touch of
healing, 9255
of power, 9257
transfiguration of
Elijah at, 2765–2766
as shape shifting, 8303
Troeltsch (Ernst) on, 9364, 9366
in Unification theology, 9467
virgin birth of, 953
washing of feet by, 4139
will of, in monothelitism, 5792, 5793
wisdom attributed to, 9760
woes and curses by, 2104
Jesus, the Christ, in the Light of Psychology (Hall), 7475
Jesus and the Disinherited (Thurman), 963
Jesus and the Zealots (Brandon), 1040
Jesus Army, 6568
Jesus Christ Superstar (Webber), 2470
Jesus ein geborener Jude Sei, Dass (Luther), 7234
Jesus Movement, **4852–4854,** 6560
exorcism in, 2928
Jesus Only (Oneness) Pentecostalism, 7029, 7030
Jesus People movement, and the Family, 6551
"Jesus Prayer," 2587
meditation in, 5818
origins of, 5818
Jesus Seminar, 4847
Jesus the Magician (Smith), controversy over, 8449
Jetavanīya school of Buddhism, 1194, 9147
Jetté, Jules, 575
Jeu des tarot, Le (Gebelin), history of tarot in, 1414
Jevons, F. B., **4854**
JewBu (Jewish-Buddhist), 4873
Jewels, in Mesoamerican drama, 2466–2467
Jewish Antiquities (Josephus), 898, 4957–4958
Enoch in, 2803
Sanhedrin in, 8102
Jewish Art (Roth), 4342
Jewish Center (New York City), 5082
Jewish Christian sects
Ebionites, **2595–2596**
gospels of, 2596
Jewish Daily Post, 3288
Jewish Encyclopedia, 4879
Jewish Enlightenment. *See* Haskalah
Jewish Historical Society of England, 4879
Jewish Identity in Modern Art History (Soussloff), 4342
Jewish Institute of Religion, 7671

Jewish law. *See also* Halakhah; Mishnah
on blasphemy, 968, 969
Christian polemics on, 7232
codification of, 1843–1844, 1845
Ebionite observation of, 2595–2596
Ezra's reading of, 2946
on martyrdom, 7056
Mendelssohn (Moses) on, 5854
Muslim polemics on, 7238, 7239
observance of, *Judith on,* 897–898
Paul the Apostle on, 7016, 7019
prophecies in, 7440
on purity, 7511–7513
Ṭarfon on, 9003
tithes in, 9210
Torah as (*See* Torah, as law)
Jewish people, **4854–4865**. *See also* Judaism
anti-Semitism against (*See* Anti-Semitism)
Aramaization of, by Assyrian kings, 887
in Aryan myth, 3526
Ashkenazic (*See* Ashkenazic Hasidism)
chosenness of, 4860, 4861
as chosen people, Kaplan (Mordecai) on, 7636
Christendom and, communal bond of, 4855
Christian imagery of, anti-Semitism in, 400
in Christianity, 4855
community of, Buber (Martin) on, 1058
concept of, in modern Jewish thought, 4900, 4907
cultural identity of, dance and, 2163–2164
culture of, Ginzberg (Asher) on, 3495–3496
in defining Judaism, 4968–4970
definitions of, 4971
in diaspora (*See* Diaspora, Jewish)
emancipation of
Hirsch (Samson Raphael) on, 4023–4024
Holdheim (Samuel) on, 4080–4081
Sofer (Mosheh) on, 8507
exile of, 2922–2923 (*See also* Babylonia, Jewish exile to)
Jewish-Christian polemics on, 7234
formation of, 4856
Freemasonry and, 3197
history of, Ibn Daud on, 4264
international community-building by, 4863
in Islam, 4855
Islam compared to, 4855
Islamic view of, 6736
Marranos, **5716–5724**
medieval, 4860–4861
in Medina, Muḥammad and, 6224, 6225–6226
membership in, 4854–4855, 4858–4864
modern concepts of, 4862–4864
names of, 4856, 6409
in nation-state, 4862
persecution of (*See* Persecution, of Jews)
as presence of God, 4860
restoration of, 2945
in Roman empire, expulsion of, 4558
sacred history of, 4971–4972
secular loyalty of, 4862–4863
subcultures of, 4860
terms for, 4971
walāyah and, 9657
Westward migration of, 5016–5017
Jewish priesthood. *See* Priesthood, in Judaism
Jewish Publication Society of America, Szold (Henrietta) and, 8941
Jewish Quarterly Review, 4879
Montagu (Lily) in, 6166
Jewish Religious Union (JRU), 6166–6167
Jewish Renewal movement, **4868–4874**, 7638
challenges facing, 4874
in contemporary Judaism, 4985
ideology of, 4872
impact of, 4872–4873
influences on, 4869–4872
origins of, 4868–4869
personalities in, 4873–4874
ritual in, 4869
Jewish socialism, anti-Semitism and, 5021
Jewish studies, **4874–4886**. *See also* Wissenschaft des Judentums
from 1818 to 1919, **4874–4882**
academic standing of, 4878–4879
of Ginzberg (Asher), 3495–3496
since 1919, 4882–4886
Jewish Symbols in the Greco-Roman Period (Goodenough), 3637
Jewish Theological Seminary (Breslau), 7581
Wissenschaft des Judentums at, 4878
Jewish Theological Seminary of America (New York)
Conservative Judaism and, 1958–1959
Kaplan (Mordecai) teaching at, 7636
Morais's (Sabato) founding of, 7582
Schechter (Solomon) and, 1958–1959, 8146
women at, 7582
Jewish thought and philosophy, **4886–4915**
apocalyptic, and Gnosticism, 5202
Aristotelian, 479
afterlife in, 154
Gersonides and, 480, 481, 3462
Ibn Daud and, 4264
opposition to, 17, 18, 481
soul in, 8558, 8559
ethical literature in, **4911–4915**
fundamental principles of, rejection of concept of, 18
Holocaust and
Fackenheim (Emil) response to, 2949–2950
theological responses to, **4088–4095**
Jewish Enlightenment in (*See* Haskalah)
medieval, 4886–4889, 4980
on God, 3548–3550
modern, **4899–4910**
oral Torah in, 6839–6841
peoplehood in, 4861
premodern, **4886–4899**
Gersonides in, 3461–3463
revival of, 4992–4993
skepticism in, 8420–8421
soul in, 8558–8560
Spinoza in, 4900
Jewish War, The (Josephus), 4957
Sanhedrin in, 8102
Jewison, Norman, 3097
Jews. *See* Jewish people
Jeyakāntan, Taṇṭapāṇi, 10036
Jezebel (Ahab's wife), 969
Melqart and, 5847
Jezreel (biblical figure), name of, 4137
Jhana. See Dhyānas
Ji (deity), cult of, 1913
Jia (house/family), 2406
Jiajing reforms, 1911
Jianfu cao (office to oversee merits), 8995
Jiang Qing, 1610
in Gang of Four, 4637
Jiangyong (Chinese philosopher), as teacher of Dia Zhen, 2129
Jianwu ji (Daoist text), 2210
Jianxing, in Zen Buddhism, in enlightenment, 2795
Jianzhen (Buddhist monk), 9075
Jiao (dragon), storms and, 5996
Jiao (sacrifice), **4915–4917**
in devotional life, 9844
incense in, 4419
music in, 6295–6296
revived by Emperor Wu, 1591
Jiao (teaching and learning), 10072–10073
Jiaoguan kangzong (Zhixu), 9178–9179
Jia Pingwa, 3070
Jia Shanxiang, 2209, 5318
JIATS. *See Journal of the International Association of Tibetan Studies*
Jiaxiang temple, 4926
Jia Yi, 1590
Han cosmology and, 1897–1898
Jiba (sacred spot), 9082, 9083
Jibyō (inborn chronic illness), health and, 3867
Jicarilla Apaches (United States), culture hero myth of, 2091
Jie, 1640
Jien (Buddhist priest), 1178, **4917**
on Ame no Koyane, 289–290
on historiography, 4026
Jigme Singye Wangchuck (king of Bhutan), 7263
'Jigs med dpa' bo, 1232
'Jigs med gling pa (Jigme Lingpa), 7869, 9333
'Jigs med rnam rgyal, 1232
Jihād, **4917–4920**
in Africa, Fulbe and, 3229
Aḥmadiyah interpretation of, 200
Bābī interpretation of, 728, 729
in Caucasus, 4614–4615
concept of, 6648
contemporary significance of, 4919–4920
Crusades, effect on, 2077
of Dan Fodio (Usuman), 2167–2168
definition of, 4917–4918
as exemplary, 5738
globalization of, 7289–7290
Ibn Rushd on, 5738, 5742
in Qur'ān, 4562, 7289–7290
interior/personal, 6225
migration in, 6023
Muḥammad on, 6225
of bin Lādin, 7290
progressive Islam on, 6099–6100
purpose of, 4562
Quṭb (Sayyid) on, 7257, 7289, 7576
social control of, 5742
as struggle *vs.* holy war, 6225, 6227
in sub-Saharan Africa, 4604, 4606
in Sufism, 4563, 6648
terrorism in, 7257–7258, 7288–7290
Umarian, 9445
use of term, 7289
Jijinmōsō (music), 6302
Jijiu (libationer), 7413
Jikidō (direct path), 9077
Jikkyō-kyō Shintō, Shibata Hamamori and, 8364
Jilakata's Recourse *(huaca),* names of, 8616
Jildakī, Aydamir ibn 'Alī al-, 249
Jilek, Wolfgang, 2490
Jīlī, al-, on Perfect Human Beings, 8711

Jiménez de Cisneros, Francisco, 7772
Jimmu (mythical Japanese emperor), 948, **4920,** 5434
Jimon branch, 2781–2782
Jimsonweed, 4309
Jinacarita (Buddhist text), 1199
  Mahāvīra in, 5610
Jīnakālamāli (Buddhist text), 1137
Jinarajadasa, Curuppumullage, 9143
Jinas (conquerors). *See also* Tīrthaṃkaras
  devotion to, 4770
  as Jain authorities, 4764
  portraits of, vol. 10 color insert
  praise to, 4769
Jindandao sect, 1603, 1607
Jin dynasty (China), 1602
  Buddhism in, 1254
    Maitreya in, 5620
    temples of, 9047
  Daoism in, 2186, 2203, 5495–5496
    temples of, 9057
  Ge Hong in, 3290–3291
  law in, 5352
Jinenchishu (Nature Wisdom school of Buddhism), 4784
Jingikan (Ministry of Kami Affairs), in Meiji period, 8366
Jing-jing (missionary), Manichaean texts translated by, 5669
Jĭngk Wurt (deity). *See* Water King
Jĭngk Xon (deity). *See* Water King
Jingming Dao (Way of Purity and Perspicacity), 2207
Jingō, **4921**
Jingshi (temple), 9056
Jingtu (Pure Land), **4921–4925,** 7502
Jingtu Buddhism. *See* Pure Land Buddhism
Jingtu shiyao (Zhixu), 9180
Jingūji (Buddhist temples), 1176
Jingyuan Islamic Association (China), 4635
Jing zuo (quiet sitting), constructive discipline and, 8704
Jinimin, 672–673
Jinin (divine attendant), 7411
Jinja (shrines), for Shintō ancestor worship, 2639
Jinlian zhengzong ji (Daoist text), 2206
Jinlian zhengzong xianyuan xianzhuan (Daoist text), 2207
Jinmu (Japanese emperor), 4810
Jinn (spirits), 3476
  exorcism of, 2933
  magic and, 5583, 5584–5585
  vs. zār masters, 2933
  worship of, in Qemant religion, 2573
Jinnāḥ, Muḥammad ʿAlī, 4654
Jinsei (total capacity of the mind), 4551
Jin state, 1523, 1597
Jin Yong, 3070
Jinzen (Buddhist monk), 9075
Jipae ritual, 5769
Jiriki (self-power), 819
Jisha engi (temple and shrine histories), 4805
Jishū (Buddhist order), 1181–1182, 4532, 4533
Jitāri, writings of, 5555
Jitoji (Sikh woman), 3336
Jiuhua, Mount, 6213
Jiujing (nine classic works), and Confucianism, construction of, 1916
Jīva, theological works by, 1346
Jīva (soul or life), 4764, 4768, 9328. *See also* Ātman
  Caitanya on, 1346
  in Ārya Samāj, 516
  karman of, in Jainism, 5096
  in Kevala Advaita, 9546, 9547
  liberation of, 8548
  Mahāvīra on, 5610
  meanings of, 8551
  saṃsāra and, 8098
  Śaṅkara on, 8105
  in Sikhism, *Ādi Granth* on, 33
  in Swaminarayan movement, 8891
"Jivaka's Mango Grove," ruins of, 1106
Jīvanmukti (liberation), **4925–4926,** 8990
Jivaroan religion and soceity (South America), 281–284
  agrarian rites of, women in, 2558
  arutam souls in, 8533
  dreams in, 2486
  flood in, 3131
  Nunkwi earth mother cult in, 8583
  plants in, 9575
  shrunken heads *(tsantsa)* in, 8583
Jīva Vicāra Prakaranam, 2624–2625
Jiver, Jacob, 928, 930
Jiv Goswami, Mirabai and, 6048
Jizang (Buddhist monk), 1247, 1301, **4926–4927,** 9018
  in Mādhyamika Buddhism, 5556
  on emptiness *(śūnyatā),* 8859
Jizō *(bodhisattva). See* Kṣitigarbha
Jizōkō (ceremony), 5255
Jizya/Jizyah (poll tax), 4562, 6997, 6998
  for Jews, 4995
  jihād and, 4919
  for Zoroastrians, 10003
Jñāna (cognitive event), 1274, **4927–4928,** 9507
  and *karma* and *bhakti,* 4421, 4423
  types of, 7357–7358
  vs. prajñā, 7359
  as wisdom, 9752
Jñānagarbha (Buddhist scholar), 1120
Jñāna-karma-samuccayavāda, 4928
Jñanamudrā (seal of knowledge), 1218, 1219
Jṇānapada school, on *Guhyasamāja Tantra,* 3708
Jñānaprabha (monk), Śīlabhadra, conflict with, 8399
Jñānaprasthāna (Buddhist text), 1270
  commentaries on, 10022
  Mahāvibhāṣā commentary on, 2037
Jñānayoga (way of knowledge)
  desire and, 2305
  in *Bhagavadgītā,* 853, 4928
  mokṣa and, 6116
  reincarnation and, 5200
Jñāndev (Indian author), 3638, 9504
Jñāneśvar (poet-saint), 7210
  commentary on *Bhagavadgītā,* 5696
  on worship of *guru* Nivritti, 8036
Jnun (spirits), 834
Joachim, Georg, Copernicus, publishing agreement with, 8182
Joachim of Fiore, **4928–4929**
  on ages of world, 175, 4028
  in apocalypticism, 412
  millenarian prophecy of, 6747
Joan of Arc, **4929–4930**
  execution of, 7427
  vocation of, 9633
João, Prince, marriage o, 1443
João do Rio, 121
Joaseiro do Notre (Brazil), 6514, 6577
Joash (biblical figure), 929, 931
Job (biblical book), **4930–4933**
  Aramaic translation of, 887, 889
  blood in, 986
  Canaanite parallels, 1392
  dating of, 9755
  demons in, 2278
  divine victory over chaos in, 4749
  Gregory I on, 3688
  ḥokhmah in, 4078
  as Holocaust paradigm, 4088–4089
  lion symbolism in, 5465
  paradox in, 6990
  power in, 7346–7347
  property law in, 4736
  proverbs in, 6978
  Saʿadyah Gaon, commentary of, 7952–7953
  Shimʿon ben Laqish on, 8348
  skepticism and, 9756
  suffering in, 5372
  temptation in, 9071
  theodicy in, 9115
  wisdom in, 2904, 9750, 9758–9759
Job (biblical figure), **4930–4933**
  Abraham compared to, 15
  ashes used by, 541
Job, a Masque for Dancing (Valois), 2162
Jobes, Evelyn, on anchor, 332
Job's Daughters, 3198
Jōbutsu (awakening), in Shingon Buddhism, 8350–8351
Jocakuvaque (deity), in Island Arawak religion, 1427
Jochebed (mother of Aaron), 1
Jochelson, Waldemar, 474–475
  on shamanic initiatory illness, 8283
Jochi (son of Chinggis Khan), 4493
Jōdo Shinshū school of Buddhism, 1244, **4933–4936**
  Amitābha in, 292
  in Europe, 1189
  Genshin as patriarch of, 3433
  Ippen influenced by, 4533
  Jōdoshū and, 4939
  music in, 6301
  Ninkū in, 9079
  Rennyo and, 7752–7753
  Shinran as founder of, 1244, **8354–8356,** 8981, 9080
  Takada branch of, 7753
  texts of, 4934
Jōdoshū school of Buddhism, 1243–1244, **4937–4940**
  attacks against, 4120
  Benchō as second patriarch of, 818
  Hōnen as founder of, 1243, 4119–4120, 9080
  Jōdo Shinshū and, 4935
  schisms in, 4938–4939
  texts of, 4937
Joel, 879
  gambling in, 3262
Joffrey, Robert, 2162
Joffrey Ballet, 2162
Jo-ga-oh (little people), 4542
'Jog sgom (stabilizing meditation), 1284
Johanan bar Nappaha. *See* Yoḥanan bar Nappaḥa'
Johanan bar Zakkai. *See* Ỵohanan ben Zakk'ai
Johansen, Baber, 4723
Johansons, Andrejs, 770–771
John (apostle). *See* John the Evangelist
John (Gospel), 910–911. *See also* Gospels, the Four
  adultery in, 921–922
  afterlife in, 156–157

John (Gospel) ***continued***
anti-docetic text of, 2381
apostasy in, 431
apostles in, 436
Augustine on, 1051
author of, 910, 4943–4944
Baur (F. C.) on, 805
biblical exegesis in, 870
Bonaventure on, 1011
canonization and, 1410
and Christian exegesis, 872
Christology of, 911, 918, 3546
date of, 910–911
eternal life in, 2856
exile in, 2923
gambling in, 3262
geometry in, 3441
gnosis in, 3507–3508
God in, 3546
incarnation in, 8303
Irenaeus on, 910, 4539
Jesus and Peter in, 6966
Jesus as God incarnate in, 4417
Jesus' male lover in, 7081
Jesus' pilgrimage in, 7153
judgment in, 5027
Logos in, 5505
Luther (Martin) on, 874
martyrdrom in, 7057
Mary in, 5752
messianism in, 5973
in Montanism, 6167
Moses in, 6203
mysticism in, 6346
Peter the Apostle in, 7068
purpose of, 911
resurrection in, 7766
revelation in, 7778
rivers in, 7862
Satan in, 2278
Sistine Chapel reference to, 8755
Sozzini (Fausto Pavolo) on, 8673
spirit and flesh in, 8562
status of, 4944
synoptic gospels and, 910, 911
Tertullian on, 9087
typological exegesis of, 872
variants of, 921–922
virgin birth absent in, 7081
John (king of England), and Magna Carta, 7280
John II (pope), 6967
John V Palaeologus (Byzantine emperor), Gregory Palamas and, 3698
John VI Cantacuzenos (Byzantine emperor)
Cabilas and, 1343
Gregory Palamas and, 3698–3699
John VIII (pope), 2585, 6967, 7135
John VIII Palaeologus (Byzantine emperor), 2587, 7280
Mark of Ephesus and, 5714
John XXII (pope)
administrative affairs of, 6971
Barlaam of Calabria negotiating with, 788
Eckhart's (Johannes) heresy pronounced by, 2603
Franciscans and, 3183
on Marsilius of Padua, 5729
on mirrors, 6064
and music, 6311
John XXIII (pope), **4944–4946**
ecumenism under, 2686, 6974
election of, 6971
indulgences, opposition of Hus (Jan) to, 4233
leadership style of, 6974
and social doctrine, 7878
Vatican II under, 4945–4946, 6975, 7011, 7879–7880, 9534–9535
1 John, 917–918, 920, 4944
2 John, 917–918, 920, 921, 4944
3 John, 917–918, 920, 921, 4944
John, Apocryphon of, 521, 3510, 3511, 3517
hypostasis in, 4242
Irenaeus of Lyons and, 6397
Sophia in, 8523
John, Monastery of Saint, 2826
John Calecas (patriarch), Gregory Palamas and, 3698
John Cassian
Eastern influence on, 2582
Egyptian monasticism and, 2710
eremitism of, 2826
as follower of Pelagius, 7026
John Chrysostom. *See* Chrysostom
John Frum movement, cargo cults and, 1414
John Hyrcanus I
in *1 Maccabees,* 900
Samaritan temple destroyed by, 880
on *Targum Jonathan,* 888
John Hyrcanus II, powers stripped and restored, 8102
John Mark, 907–908
John Mark of Jerusalem, Mark the Evangelist as, 5714
John of Antioch, Christology and, 2583
John of Damascus, **4940–4941**
Eastern Christianity influenced by, 2582
on God, 3554
icon veneration defended by, 2585
on images, 4290, 4353, 4386, 4391, 6619
on morality, 1652
John of Giscala, 9940
John of Husinec. *See* Hus, Jan
John of Jandun, Marsilius of Padua and, 5729
John of Kronstadt. *See* Ioann of Kronstadt
John of Monte Corvino, in China, 1725, 6083
John of Nicopolis, 2825
John of Odzun, 490
on *lucerna extincta* rite, 8249
John of Patmos, on millennium, 6028
John of Plano Carpini. *See* Giovanni da Pian del Carpini
John of Salisbury, 6748
on magic, 5577
on music, 6311
John of Stobi, and *Corpus Hermeticum,* 3515
John of the Cross, 3003, **4941–4942**
on darkness, 5454
on desire, 2309
as devotee, 2320
and language of fire, 3120
on learned ignorance, 6990
on meditation, 5818
on mystical union, 6338
mysticism of, 6349–6350
attention in, 604
on phallus of Jesus, 7081
poetry of, 7208
on truth, 9373–9374
John of Vercelli, Albertus Magnus and, 232
John Paul I (pope)
election of, 6975
selecting double name, 6967
John Paul II (pope)
Anglican dialogue with, 353
on bishops, 1763
on cloning, 7599
and Dalai Lama, 2133
ecumenism of, 9539–9540
on Francis of Assisi, 3184
Galileo exonerated by, 8184–8185
on Galileo's trial, 3257
and gender, 3362
Juan Diego canonized by, 5922
kissing ground, 7344
on Mary, 5754
on pain, 6944
popularity of, 6975
reform of, 6975
and social doctrine, 7878
travels of, 6975
on "two books," 9421
writings of, 6975
John Philoponus, on Aristotle, 479
Johnson, Clifton, 77
Johnson, Colin (Mudrooroo), 3079
Johnson, Dianne, 668
Johnson, Douglas, 117–118
Johnson, E. Pauline, 7224, 7225
Johnson, Edward, calligraphy and, 1369
Johnson, Elizabeth, 3035, 3036
on monotheism, 6161
Johnson, Ford, 2603
Johnson, James Weldon, 77
Johnson, Julie, plagiarism of, by Twitchell (Paul), 2602
Johnson, Paul, 7487
Johnson, Philip, 796
Johnson, Roswell, 2881
Johnson, Samuel, 5356, 7220
John Templeton Foundation, 2661
John the Almsgiver, charity taught by, 2582
John the Apostle. *See* John the Evangelist
John the Baptist, **4942–4943**
asceticism of, 7722
departure from official practice by, 780–781
Elijah identified with, 2765
and Gnosticism, 3515
going to the desert, 2301
historical, 4848
in Islam, as *walāyah,* 9660
in Mandaean religion, 5635, 5636, 5638
Ginza of, 3495, 5634
Ogun (Yoruba and Santeṛia), 1434
as prophet, 6546
relics of, 7689
on repentance, 7758
Salome and, 2135
title of, 8709
in Unification theology, 9467
John the Deacon, biography of Gregory I by, 3687
John the Evangelist (apostle), 910, 917–918, **4943–4944**
eagle as symbol of, 949
ecstasy of, 2678
iconography of, 4345
on knowledge, 5202
on revelation, 7778
Shango identified with in Trinidad, 1434
in Slavic religion, 8435
touch of, 9257
Jōjitsu sect I(Buddhist), 1202, 1242
Jok (deity), 5445. *See also* Nhialic
Jōkei (Buddhist monk), 1179
Jo khang (Buddhist temple), 7167, 9050
Joking. *See also* Humor
popular culture of, in Carnival, 1440
Joli-Mā Angkw (deity), 5119–5120
Jolley, Elizabeth, 3082, 3084
Joma (Mishnah treatise), scapegoat in, 8144
Jomon period (Japan), 4779–4780, 6459
kami in, 5072
Jonah (biblical book), 879, **4947**
chanting psalms in, 7464
scapegoat concept in, 8145
in Yom Kippur services, 7929
Jonah (biblical figure), **4947**
as hero figure, 7553
iconography of, 4344
as transition symbol, 3123
Jo nang pa order (Buddhist), 1227, 1228
Jonang school of Buddhism, 5224
Jonas, Hans, **4947–4950**
on dualism, 2506
existentialist categories, application of, 4061
on Gnosticism, 3514, 3527, 3528, 3533

  on metaphor of vision, 1296
  on sacred and profane, 7976
Jonas, Regina, 3351, 7582
Jonathan (high priest), 7103
Jonathan ben Uzziel, 889
Jonayaiuin (culture hero), in Jicarilla Apache myth, 2091
Jones, Absalom, **4950–4951**
  Allen (Richard) and, 264
  as priest of Saint Thomas's Protestant Episcopal Church, 68
Jones, Alonzo T., Seventh-day Adventism and, 8236
Jones, Charles B., 1638
Jones, Evan, 1565, 1566
Jones, Jim, **4951–4952,** 6515, 6561, 7255. *See also* Jonestown and Peoples Temple
  inner circle of, 6547
  mass suicide of followers of, 6023
  rereadings of *Genesis,* 6531
  on suicide, 4184
Jones, Major, 77
Jones, Major J., 965
Jones, Rufus, 7549
Jones, William (of East India Company)
  on Buddha, 1312
  on Indo-European languages, 4452, 4459
  studying Sanskrit language, 4446, 4458
Jones, William (scholar), 78
  on Fox Indians, 6682
Jones, William R. (theologian), 966
Jonestown and Peoples Temple (Guyana), **4952–4956,** 6561. *See also* Jones, Jim
  charismatic leader of, 6515, 6547
  God in theology of, 4953
  mass suicide at, 6561, 7255
    European reaction to, 6570
    fragile movement characteristics and, 6517, 6549
    as human sacrifice, 4184
    justification of, 8828
    study of, 6525, 6551
  media and, 4964
  museum collection related to, 6524
  objective of, 7255
  rereadings of *Genesis,* 6531
  scriptural text of, 6531
  secondary leaders of, 6547
  study of, 6525
  and violence, conditions leading to, 6553
Jonestown Institute, 6524
Jonge, Marinus de, 903
Jonson, Ben, 236, 5987
Jonte-Pace, Diane, 7479
Jooss, Kurt, 2160, 2163
Jorai religion (Indochina), on original humanity, 2960
Joralemon, Peter D., 6817, 6818
  on Olmec iconography, 5881
Jörð (deity), 3453
Jordan
  Nabatean religion in, **6385–6390**
  Nabetean rock city, 1472
Jordan, David, 1638
Jordan, Ivan, 640, 645–646
Jordan, Louis Henry, 31
  on Müller (F. Max), 6235
Jordan, Mark, on sexuality in Roman Catholicism, 8244, 8245
Jordanes (historian)
  on Geto-Dacian religion, 3467
    Zalmoxis in, 3466
  on Hun religion, 4229
  on Mordvins, 5709
  on Æsir, 3449
Jordan River, 7862, 7863
Jordanus (Dominican friar), on Parsis, 6997
Jǫrmungandr (mythic serpent), 5508
Jōsai Daishi. *See* Keizan
Joseph (biblical figure), **4956**
  ballet based on story of, 2163
  feast dedicated to, folklorist study of, 3147
  Ogou Balanjo identified with in Vodou, 1433
  prophetic dreams of, 2489
  tale of wolf and, 4215
Joseph II (Holy Roman Emperor), 5019
Joseph II (patriarch), 2587
Joseph and Aseneth, 903
Joseph and His Brothers (Mann), 6021
Joseph Andrews (Fielding), 3059
Joseph d'Arimathie (Robert de Borron), 3649–3653
Josephides, Lisette, 3396
Josephism, 6973
Joseph of Volokolamsk, **4956–4957**
  Trans-Volgan elders and, 8526
Joseph tribes, Rachel as mother of, 7592
Josephus Flavius, **4957–4958**
  on Abraham, 15–16
  apologetics of, 427, 428
  apostasy and, 431
  Athirat (Asherah) and, 590, 591
  on Baal Zebub, 7103
  on biblical canon, 879
  on Essenes, 2846
  on exorcism, 2932
  2 Ezra used by, 898
  on Geto-Dacian religion, 3466
  on Hebrew scriptures, 881, 886
  on Israelite religion, 4974
  on Israelite theocracy, 9108–9109
  and Jewish view of history, 4058
  on Jews, 4036
  on mass suicide at Masada, 8829
  on Melqart, 5846
  on *mitsvot,* 3201
  on Moses, 6202
  on *agnōstos theos,* 182
  on Pharisees, 3203
  on priests, 7399
  on resurrection, 152, 7765
  on rivers, 7862
  on Sadducees, 3203, 8018
  on Samaritans, 8068
  on Sanhedrin, 8101, 8102–8103
  on scripture, 8197
  on Solomonic works, 9763
  Temple procedures in, 925, 929, 930
  on theocracy, 10061
  on Tiberius Julius Alexander, 7105
Joshua (biblical book), 879, **4958–4959**
  Abravanel (Isaac) on, 867
  circumambulation of Jericho in, 1796
  condemnation of idolatry in, 4358–4359
  laws in, 4729
  Levites in, 5421
  monotheism in, 3540
  pesher of, 7065
  Torah in, 9231
Joshua (biblical figure), **4958–4959**
  circumambulating, 7417
  covenant of JHWH with, 2048–2049
  Freemasons on, 3195
  God's covenant with, 3540
  military leadership of, 6200–6201
  Rastafarian reincarnations of, 1438
Joshua, Apocryphon of, 7063, 7065
Joshua ben Hananiah. *See* Yehoshuʿa ben Ḥananyah
Joshua ben Levi. *See* Yehoshuʿa ben Levi
Josiah (king of Judah), 924, 929, 934–935, **4959**
  Levites and, 5422
  religious reforms of, 4828, 4959
  sun idolatry under, 2662
Josianic reform, 4828–4829, 4959
Jōsō (poet), *haiku* of, 8702
Josquin Des Prez, 6309
Jötnar, **4959–4960**
Jou-jan people. *See* Ruanruan people
Jouret, Luc, 6554, 9067–9068
Journal asiatique (journal), 10056
Journal de psychologie, Mauss (Marcel) in, 5786
Journal for the Scientific Study of Religion (journal), 10057
Journalism, **4960–4967**
  emergence of mass press and, 5806
  presentation of religion through, 5806
  storytelling in, 4961–4962
Journal of al-Azhar, 231
Journal of American Folk Lore, 820
Journal of a Soul (John XXIII), 4946
Journal of a Ten Months Residence in New Zealand (Cruise), 7307
Journal of Biblical Literature, Goodenough (Erwin R.) at, 3637
Journal of Dreams (Swedenborg), interpretation in, 8899
Journal of Indian Philosophy (journal), 10058
Journal of Religion (journal), 10057
Journal of Ritual Studies (journal), 10058
Journal of the American Academy of Religion (journal), 10057, 10060
Journal of the American Oriental Society (journal), 10056
Journal of the International Association of Tibetan Studies (JIATS), 9188
Journal of the Royal Asiatic Society (journal), 10056
Journal of Transpersonal Psychology, 7478
Journals, **10056–10060**
  languages of, 10059–10060
  price of, 10060
Journey(s). *See also* Ascension; Pilgrimage
  in apocalypses, 410–411
    Jewish, 410, 416, 418
  in Australian Indigenous religions, land identified with, 2003
  figurative, in Christian view of history, 4053
  of healers, 3813–3814
  in horticulturalist visions, 9615
  in Islam (*See also* Ḥājj) *ṣuḥbah* ("companionship") and, 8826
  life and death as
    African views on, 140
    Oceanic views on, 146
  macrocosm and microcosm in, 7983
  in shamanism
    in Baniwa religion (Amazon), 8625
    neoshamanic drum journey, 8294–8295

in shamanism ***continued***
soul flight, 8272, 8278, 8286
in Southeast Asian religions, traditional, 8651
spiritual (*See* Quests; Visionary journeys)
spiritual discipline as, 8699
Journey Drama (Mesopotamia), 5961
Journeys of the Gods (Sumerian myth), 2799–2800
Journey to the West (Chinese novel), 3057, 3070
Jowett, Benjamin, 6105, 6618
Jowo (statue), 1151
Joy(s)
four joys (*See Caturānanda*)
natural (*See Sahajānanda*)
Joy, Bill, 512–513
Joyce, James
Campbell, influence on, 1379
Petronius' influence on, 3051
Roman Catholic thought behind work of, 3060
Joyce, Rosemary, 2466
JRU. *See* Jewish Religious Union
J source. *See* Yahvist source
Juana Inés de la Cruz de Asbaje y Ramirez, **4967–4968**
association between Christ and Narcissus, 3064
Jubal (biblical figure)
as Cain's descendant, 1344
music invented by, 6276, 6277
Jubbā'ī, Abū 'Alī al-
'Abd al-Jabbār and, 4
on God
attributes of, 6322
proofs for the existence of, 6324
in Mu'tazilah, 6320
on Abū al-Hudhayl al-'Allāf, 19
Jubbā'ī, Abū Hāshim al-
'Abd al-Jabbār and, 3, 4
on God, attributes of, 6322
in Mu'tazilah, 6320
Jubilation rites, seasonal, 8210
Jubilee (sabbatical year)
calendar and, 1355
debt-slaves released in, 4731
Jubilee 2000, 2614
property laws on, 4735
Jubilees, Book of
Abraham in, 15
dating of, 903–904
Enoch in, 2803
in Ethiopian Bible, 2859
Moses in, 6203
periodization in, 175
Torah in, 9233, 9234
Judah (biblical figure), 34
under Assyria, 4828
David as king of, 2221–2224
Levites as clan of, 5420
Judah I (patriarch), 7006
Judah II (patriarch), 7006
Judah III (patriarch), 7006
Judah, J. Stillson, 6527, 6583
Judah ben Barzillai, 7579
Judah ha-Levi (Hebrew poet), 7207
Judah Halevi: The Kuzari (Slonimsky), 2746
Judah the Galilean, 9939
Judaism, **4968–5023**. *See also* Jewish people; *specific countries, doctrines, movements, and regions*
ablutions in, 10, 11, 780
abortion in, 941, 5812–5813
Abraham in, 14–16
action in, 4986
African Americans and, 6563
afterlife in (*See* Afterlife, in Judaism)
ages of world in, 174–175
aḥaronim ("later ones"), *halakhah* and, 3743–3744
aion in, 207–208
almsgiving in, 267–268
altars in, 276–277
amulets and talismans in, 299, vol. 14 color insert
ancestors in, 9940–9941
androcentrism in, 334–336
androgynes in, 338
angels in, 345–346, 2275
tsaddiq as, 9378
animal sacrifice in, human atonement through, 360
animals in, 360
Antichrist in, 394
apocalypses in, 4975
apostasy in, 431
ascension in, 522–523
historical, 409–410, 414–416, 417–418
medieval, **419–420**
Moses in, 6203
otherworldly journey in, 410, 416, 418
to rabbinic period, **414–419**
apologetics in, 427
apostasy in, 430–431
architecture of, classification of, 461–462
ascension in, 522–523, 3129, 4979
asceticism in, 7722
Baḥye on, 741
assimilation and, 4985
atonement in, **593–594** (*See also* Yom Kippur)
Cohen (Hermann) on, 4903
attention in, 604, 606
autobiography in, 703
baptism in, 780–781
baths in, 2398
Bēta Esra'ēl, **5002–5004**
biblical, 4971–4973
definition of, 4970
biblical exegesis in (*See* Biblical exegesis, Jewish views)
biblical heritage of, 4971–4973
bioregional center of, 2605
birds in, 949
birth in, 953
blasphemy in (*See* Blasphemy, Jewish concept)
blessings in, 982–983
recitation throughout day, 7841
blood in, 985, 987
prohibition on consuming, 986
sacrificial blood in Temple, 926, 927
body marking forbidden in, 1001, 1002
bread in, 2398, 5388, 7003
breath and breathing in, 1042
bridges in, 1049
burial rites in, in Reform Judaism, 7667, 7668
calendar of, **4865–4868**
of Karaites, 5086
of Rabbanites, 5086
canonization in, 1406–1407, 1408, 4975
cantillation (chanting) in, 1532–1534
celibacy in, 1476
charismatic, 1545–1546
charity in, 1553
chastity in, 1558–1559
chosenness in, 4860
Christianity and
affinities between, 1660
Baeck (Leo) on, 737
Christian missionary efforts, 7235
Christian persecution, 7058
church challenged by, 2747
conversion to, 3186
election challenged by, 2745
Jewish-Christian polemics, **7230–7236**
Jewish persecution, 7055–7056
Marcion on, 5701
origins within, 2595
Paul VI and, 7012
Reformation, 7234–7235
Roman Catholicism, 7012, 7234–7235
circular symbolism in, 1793–1794
circumambulation *(haqqafot)* in, 1796, 1797
circumcision in (*See* Circumcision, in Judaism)
as civilization, Kaplan (Mordecai) on, 7635–7636
on cloning, 5814
clothing in, 1831–1832
cocks in, 1842
confession in, 593, 1888, 7757
consecration in, 1957
Conservative (*See* Conservative Judaism)
contemporary, 4985–4986
conversion from
to Christianity, by Marranos, **5716–5724**
in *halakhah,* 4860
to Islam, 2419, 2420
conversion to, 4859, 7757, 7823–7824
baptism of proselytes, 780
debate over, 3754
Khazars, 4492
nudity in, 6740
Reform Judaism, 7666
cosmology of
Abravanel (Isaac) on, 18
circles in, 1793
Gersonides on, 3462–3463
covenant in (*See* Covenant and covenant theology, in Judaism)
creation stories in, 2967, 5445
divine order of, 2607
cultural *vs.* religious orientation to (*See* Reconstructionist Judaism)
cursing in, 2098, 2104
Dalai Lama and, 2924
dance in, 2135, 2136, 2143–2144, 2319
Hasidism, 2146–2147
sacred, 2165
Tanzhausen and, 2154
for worship and honor, 2137
David in, 2223
Day of Atonement in (*See* Yom Kippur)
Day of Remembrance (Yom ha-Zikkaron) in, 6593
Day of Sounding the Shofar (Yom Teruah) in, 6593
death in, 5445, 7822–7823
defense of, 4891–4892, 9878
definitions of, 4969–4970, 7583
demons in, 2275, 2277–2278
denominationalism in, 4868–4869
desert in, 2300–2301
devotion in (*See* Devotion, in Judaism)
dietary laws in (*See Kashrut*)
divination in, 2370, 2373
divine kingship in, 5147, 5148
divorce in, 7821, 7822
doctrine in, 2382
dogs in, 2393
domestic observances in, **2397–2398**
dragons in, 2431, 2432
dreams in, 2489
drums in, 2495, 2496, 2498, 2499
dualism in, 2507, 2511–2512
early modern, 4982–4985
definition of, 4970
ecology and, **2641–2642**
economics and, 9708–9709
ecumenical developments with, 2688, 9539
education in (*See* Religious education, Jewish)
egg symbolism in, 2701–2702

election in, 2744–2746
challenged by Christianity, 2745, 2746–2747
on embryonic stem cell research, 941
environmentalism in, 2644, 2645–2646
eschatology of, 2834–2835
essence of, 4969
ethical piety in, 4902–4903
evil in, concept of, 3552
exile in, **2922–2923**
exorcism in, 2534, 2931–2933
Ezra in, 2947
faithful remnant in, 2765
the Fall in, 2967–2968
fasting in, 2996, 2997, 3171, 4867–4868
fate in, 3002, 3003
feminism in, 3350–3352, 4985
history of, 3301, 3311–3312, 3350–3352
reconstructions of, 3301
feminist analysis of, 3032–3033
festivals of, 4867–4868 (*See also specific festivals*)
and fiction, Australian, 3084
fire in, 3119–3120
fish symbolism in, 3123
the Flood in, 2968
folklore in, healing in, 3829
folk traditions in, **3157–3161**
Kaplan (Mordecai) on, 7636
food in
domestic rituals of, 2397, 2398
early, 3171
in myths and rituals, 3169
food taboos in, 3167
pork, 7144
founding of, 2946
free will and determinism in, 3201
free will and predestination in, 3203
funeral rites, 7822–7823
domestic rituals of, 2397
gambling in, 3262, 3263
gender in, **3350–3356**
genetics and, 3428, 3429, 3430
Geonic period of (*See* Gaonate)
gift giving in, 3484
Gnosticism in, 3510–3511, 3516, 3523
goddess worship in, 3586
God in, **3537–3543, 3547–3552**
on Aaron in priesthood, 1
anthropomorphism of, 389, 390, 3543, 3547–3548
attributes of, **613–615**
Baal, parallels with, 1392
biblical, **3537–3543**
bringing disrepute upon, 970–971
Canaanite influence on, 724
Cohen (Arthur A.) on, 1849
covenant with (*See* Covenant, in Judaism)
as creator, 2641, 2642, 3549
cursing, 968–969
dance as communication with, 2137
descriptions of body of, 6741
disputing with, 968
dualism of, condemnation of, 3548
as El, 1397
election by, 2744–2746
emotions of, 3542–3543
feminine traits excluded from, 3541
flashing sword of judgment of, 967
Freud on, 3216
gender of, 3350, 3541
Hasidic concept of, 4982–4983
Heschel (Abraham Joshua) on, 3962
homoerotic relationship with, 7080
imagery of, 3542–3543
Israel favored by, 3548
jealousy of, 3542
Jews as presence of, 4860
Kaplan (Mordecai) on, 4907, 7636
kavod of, 3542
kingship of, 3542, 3548
life of, 5445
Maimonidean concept of, 4894, 4980–4981
medieval Judaism, 4980
modern approaches to, 3551–3552
names of, 3537–3539, 3547–3548, 6406–6407
origins of worship of, 3539
perceived humiliation of, 2944–2945
perfection of, 7039
philosophical approach to, 3548–3550, 5247–5248
postbiblical, **3547–3552**
problems with monotheism and, 3539–3541
pronouncing name of, 970, 3547
proofs for existence of, 7422
Qabbalah, 615, 1985, 3550–3551, 4981
rabbinic approach to, 3547–3548
rabbinic ways of, 7584
Reconstructionist Judaism, 5081
sanctification of, 971
saying inappropriate things about, 970
scrutiny of, 1939
spouse of, 8523
suffering of, 8806
Torah study by, 7584
transcendence of, 3542, 3543, 3548
using name of, in vain, 969–970
Golden Rule in, 3630, 3631, 3632, 3633
gold in, 3626
golem legend in, 5521
grace in, and atonement, 593–594
guilt in, 7757
ḥanukat-habayit (dedication the home) in, 4105
Hasidic (*See* Hasidism)
Havurah/havurot movement, origins of, 1963
healing and medicine in (*See* Healing and medicine)
Hellenistic (*See* Hellenistic Judaism)
heresy in, 970
Hermetism, influences on, 3940
heterodoxy in, 6911–6912
Hinduism and, common aspects, 1880
Historical
founder of, 3187–3188
modernity and, 4984
historical societies of, 4879
historiography, traditional, 4027–4028
history, views of, **4057–4060**
history of
changes over time, 7635
Christianity on, 9295
Dead Sea Scrolls and, 2234–2235
holy days in, 4866–4867
hospitality in, 4139
human body in, 2153
human perfectibility in, 7039
humor in, 4195–4196, 4202–4204
iconoclasm in, 4281, 4285
iconography of (*See* Iconography, Jewish)
idolatry condemned in, 4340, 4357, 4358–4359, 4380, 4385, vol. 14 color insert
immortality in
afterlife and, 152
in Apocrypha, 900
initiation in, 4482
inspiration in, 4510
Islam and, 3032
Jewish persecution, 7055
Muslim-Jewish polemics, **7236–7242**
relations with, 4575
Islamic eschatology and, 2836
Jerusalem in, **4838–4841**
Jesus in, images of, 4845
Job in, 4932–4933
jubilee, 1355
as "Judaisms," 4969
judgment of the dead in, 5027
justice and righteousness in, 1748, 7589, 10063
justification in, 5039
Kant on, 4902–4903
Karaite sect of (*See* Karaites)
key symbolism in, 5116
kingship in, 10062
kissing holy objects in, 9258
knees/kneeling in, 5195–5196
knowledge in, 5201–5202
knowledge of God in, 7776–7777
laity in, 5288
laws (*See* Jewish law)
lesbianism in, 5414
letter mysticism in, 271–273, 6353
libations in, discontinuation of, 5288
liberal, origins of, 6166–6167
life in, 5445
light symbolism in, 5453
liturgy of, 9808 (*See also* Liturgy, Jewish)
election in, 2745–2746
Zion in, 9977
Magen David (Star of David) in, 5558–5559
magic in, 5575–5576, 5579
Mani influenced by, 5648
marriage in (*See* Marriage, in Judaism)
martyrdom in (*See* Martyrdom, in Judaism)
masculinity in, 3351, 5863–5864
media in, 5805
medical ethics in, 5810–5814
medieval (*See* Middle Ages, Judaism in)
meditation in, 5817
memorization in, 5852
men's studies in, 5863–5864
menstruation in, 5866
merit in, 5870, 5871
Mesopotamian religions and, 2967, 2968
messianism in (*See* Messianism, Jewish)
micrography, 1369, **1371–1372**
miqveh (ritual bath) in, **6046–6048**
miracles in, 6051
modern, 4982–4985
definition of, 4970
rabbinate in, **7581–7583**

Judaism ***continued***
modern historical consciousness and, 4901–4902
monism in, 6146–6148
monkeys in, 6150, 6151
monolatry in, 3913
monotheism of
historical ethical, 6160
historical problem of, 3539–3541
rise of, 3541–3542
Roman ruler cult as problem for, 3902
moon in, 6171
morality in, 6181–6188, 7651–7652
moral theology and, 4902–4904
Musar movement in, **6241–6242**
museums of, 6245
music in, **6307–6314**
early, 6276–6278, 6307–6308
instruments excluded from, 6276–6277
medieval, 6308–6309
modern, 6312
Renaissance, 6309–6310
theories on origins of, 6277
in Muslim countries, 1673–1674
mystical and poetic influences in, Wasserstrom (Steven M.) on, 8786
mystical union in, **6334–6341**
origins of, 6336, 6339
mysticism in (*See Heikhalot* mysticism; *Merkavah* mysticism; Mysticism, Jewish; Qabbalah)
mythic narrative in, soteriology and, 8528
Nabatean religion and, 6389
names of, 4856
natural religion *vs.* revealed law, Ascher (Saul) on, 7667
nature in
ambivalence about, 2607
sacred texts on, 2642–2643
scientific interest in, 2642
in New Testament
James, 916–917
Romans, 912
New Year festival in (*See* Ro'sh ha-Shanah)
nonviolence in, 6647
number symbolism in, 6746, 6749, 6750
Oceanic religious movements influenced by, 6795–6796
offerings in, 4419–4420
ordination in, 6856–6857
orgy and, 6872–6873
Orthodox (*See* Orthodox Judaism)
orthodoxy in, 6911–6912
orthopraxy in, 6914–6915
overview of, **4968–4988**
owl symbol in, 6936
paganism and
in early modern historiography, 4039
Rubenstein (Richard) on Holocaust and, 4094
paradise in, 6981, 6984
particularism of, 4855–4856
peace in, 7021
peoplehood in, 4968–4970 (*See also* Jewish people)
"people of God" notion, 1777
performance and ritual in, 7043, 7516–7518
phallus in, 7080–7081, 7085
philosophy in (*See* Jewish thought and philosophy)
pilgrimage in (*See* Pilgrimage, Jewish)
Plutarch on, 7201
poetry of, 7207, 7208
politics and, **10060–10064**
secularizing conceptions of, 10061–10063
theocratic conceptions of, 10061–10063
positive-historical, 1957–1958
postbiblical
Abraham in, 15–16
Elijah in, 2766
Moses in, 6202–6203
post-Holocaust, 5022
postures and gestures in, 7343, 7344
power in, 7346–7347
prayer books of, 4989
prayer in
as devotion, 2319
domestic rituals of, 2397–2398
Dov Ber of Mezhirich on, 2430
pre-modern
origins of, 7578
rabbinate in, **7578–7581**
pre-Talmudic, in Ethiopia, 2573
priesthood in (*See* Priesthood, in Judaism)
primordial elements of, 4512
proverbs and parables in, 6978–6979
public respect for, through *Wissenschaft des Judentums,* 4875
purification in (*See* Purification, in Judaism)
quaternity in, 7550
rabbinate in (*See* Rabbinate)
rabbinic (*See* Rabbinic Judaism)
rainbow symbolism in, 7604
rainmaking in, 7602–7603
reason in, Mendelsson on, 4900–4901
Reconstructionist (*See* Reconstructionist Judaism)
redemption in, 7640
reference works on, 7647
Reform (*See* Reform Judaism)
religious communities in, 7700
religious education in, 7735
faith schools, 7734
supplementary schooling and, 7733
religious experience in, 7700, 7737, 7739–7740
religious reform in, 7654, 7666–7667 (*See also* Reform Judaism)
religious year in, **4865–4868**
and domestic observances, 2397
liturgical use of *Psalms* in, 7464
Renewal, 7638
repentance in, 7756, 7757
resurrection in, 152, 153, 154, 7764–7765
in Apocrypha, 900
vs. Christianity, 156
retribution in, 7782
revelation in, 7776–7777 (*See also* Revelation)
Buber (Martin) on, 4905
in existential theology, 4904
at Mount Sinai, 7584
nature and, 2641
Orthodox Judaism, 7666
progressive, 7666
purpose of, 7777
reason and, 4904
Reform Judaism, 7666
Rosenzweig (Franz) on, 4904–4905
Steinheim (Solomon) on, 4904
verbs describing, 7776–7777
riddles in, 6987
Ri'shonim ("first ones"), halakhic development and, 3743
rites of passage in, **7818–7824**
bar and bat mitzvah, 7820–7821
circumcision, 7818–7819
conversion, 7823–7824
death, 7822–7823
of girls, 7819
marriage, 7821–7822
memory books, 7823
mourning, 7822–7823
redemption of firstborn male, 7819–7820
ritual in
contemporary, 4986
modern, 4984
nature in, 2644–2645
ritualization of consciousness in, 7841
ritual law in, 3751 (*See also* Halakhah)
sacred and profane in, 7967–7968
sacred language in, 5304
sacred matter in, vol. 4 color insert
as sacred national community, 7717
sacrifice in
blood in, 7845
criticism of, 8007
Hubert (Henri) and Mauss (Marcel) on, 8003
Kalischer (Tsevi Hirsch) on, 5069
Levenson (Jon) on, 8009
sacrificial expiation in, 7757
sacrilege in, 8012–8013
Samaritans, view of, 8070
scapegoat in, 8144–8145
Scholem (Gershom) on Shabbateanism, effect of, 8178
scriptures of (*See* Hebrew scriptures)
Second Temple period of (*See* Second Temple Judaism)
sectarianism in
during Second Temple period, 5083
in *Wissenschaft des Judentums,* 4876–4877
secularization and, 8219
Sephardic (*See* Sephardic Judaism)
sexual activity in, 2397, 2398
Shema' (Hear O Israel) as creed in, 2052
sin and guilt in, 8403–8404
social work in, 7487
society, relations with, 8463–8464
soteriological path in, 8528–8529
soul in (*See* Soul, Jewish concepts of)
spirit possession in, 2533–2534
spiritual guides in, 8709
on stem cell research, 5814
Ṣūfī influences in, Maimonides (Abraham) and, 5612–5613
suicide, attitudes toward and instances of, 8829–8830
taboos in, 7842
Tacitus on, 7201
temptation in, 9069, 9070–9071
textiles in, 9088–9089, 9092
theater forbidden in, 7044
theodicy in, 9115–9116
tradition in, 9268
transmigration in
in Hasidism, 9330
in Qabbalah, 9330
rejection of, 9330
travel in, to supplement education, 7821
triadism rejected by, 9349–9350, 9360
truth in, 9372, 9375
underworld in, 9453–9454
Union for Traditional Judaism, 1964
universalism of, 4855

utopian communities in, 7720–7721
vagina in, 7080
violent images of divinity in, 6647
visionary journeys in, 9616
vows in, 9641
warfare in, 9597
wealth and, 9708–9709
weddings in
dancing at, 2137
domestic rituals of, 2397
wisdom in, 5502, 9750
women in, **3350–3356**
bat mitzvah and, 7820–7821
in domestic observances, 2397
Gamli'el the Elder on, 3270
limitations on, 3541
ordination of, 6857
as prophets, 3541
reciting tekhines, 9036–9038
as victims of *dybbuk* possession, 2534
worship and devotional life in, **9805–9809**
Smith (W. Robertson) on, 8466
zealots of, 9939–9940
Zionism in (*See* Zionism)
Zoroastrianism and, 2277
Judaism as a Civilization (Kaplan), 2746, 5081, 7635, 7636
Judaism in the First Centuries of the Christian Era (Moore), 6176
Judaizers, Sorskii (Nil) on, 8525
Judas (Essene prophet), 2846
Judas Iscariot, in Mesoamerican religions, 5926
Jude, 918
author of, 918
canon of, 920, 921
content of, 918
opponents of, 918
2 Peter borrowing from, 917
purpose of, 7020
Jude (saint), vol. 7 color insert, vol. 9 color insert
Judea, Hellenization of, 4973
Judge, William Q., 845, **5023–5025,** 7228, 9143, 9205
Judges (biblical book), 879
Aaron in, 2
Athirat (Asherah) in, 590, 591
criminal law in, 4738
Dagon in, 7103
Levites in, 5420, 5421
Samson in, **8099**
Judges, rabbis as, 7578, 7579
in rabbinic Judaism, 7588–7589
Judges, secular reading of, 10062
Judgment
aesthetic, Kant (Immanuel) on, 46–47
in afterlife (*See* Judgment of the dead)
in Akkadian religion, by river, 2791
in Christianity, of Jesus, 4844
in Islam, 2837–2838, 9455–9456
ordeal, 6846–6849
Utu as god of, 9494
in Vedism, 9524–9525
Judgment of the dead, 128–129, **5025–5028**. *See also* Eschatology
in African religions, 139, 142
in Buddhism, 129, 5026
in Christianity
death as sleep and, 8565
and history, view of, 4053, 4054
Swedenborg (Emanuel) on, 8899
in Egyptian religion, 128–129, 139, 2719, 5871
in eschatology, 133
in Greek religion, 9453
in Hinduism, 129
imagery of, vol. 1 color insert
in Islam, 5446
Heaven and Hell in, 3885
in Ḥanafī creed, 2064
in Qur'ān, 4564, 4565
souls in, 8567
in Judaism
messianism and, 3884
Sa'adyah Gaon on, 7953, 8559
merit and, 5871
in Micronesian religions, 6007
in Roman religion, 9453
in Samaritan belief, 8070
soteriology and, 8530
Judicial systems, oath-taking in, 9641–9642
Judicial wisdom, of Solomon, 9755
Judiciary ordeal. *See* Ordeal
Jüdisch-Theologisches Seminar, 1958
Judith, 897–898, 900
Judson, Adoniram, 785
missions to Burma, 1728
Juergensmeyer, Mark, 383
Juha (trickster)
irreverance and, 4213–4214
Tunisian tale of, 4210–4211
Juhachidō ritual, in Shingon training, 8351
Juhhāl (uninitiated Druze), 2502
Jūjūshinron (Kūkai), 1243
Jukun people (Nigeria), kingship of, 5155, 5158, 5159, 5171
Jukurrpa (Warlpiri concept), 9693–9694
Julāhā, Kabīr as, 5052
Julian of Eclanum (bishop), 7026
Julian of Halicarnassus, **5028**
Severus of Antioch *vs.,* 8238
Julian of Norwich, **5028–5029**
eremitism of, 2827
Julian the Apostate (Roman emperor)
Adonis shrine rebuilt by, 34
Apollinaris of Laodicea and, 423
apostasy by, 432
on castration of Attis, 1452
Cumont (Franz) on, 2094
on images, 4352
and Neoplatonism, 6474
persecution of heretics by, 7060
on relics, 7688
sun worship and, 8841
Julian the Chaldean, 9156
Julian the Theurge, 9156–9157
Julius I (pope), Athanasius and, 571
Julius II (pope) (Il Terribile), 6972, 9341
Julius III (pope)
election of, 9343
Nestorians and, 6480
and Trent Council, 9343–9344
Julius Africanus, on chronology, 4054
Julius Caesar. *See* Caesar, Julius
Jullian, Camille, 1479
Julurru cult, 673–674
Jumādā al-Ākhirah (month in Islamic year), 4713
Jumādā al-Ūlā (month in Islamic year), 4713
Jumadil Kubra, 5257
Jum'ah masjid (great mosques), *ṣalāt* (prayer) in, 8058
Jumala (deity), 9419–9420
Jumat Imam, Al-hajj, 107
Jumbies (spirits), in Kromanti dance, 1436
Jumis (deity), 761, 2423, 9419–9420
Jumishipas (deity), 5710
Junayd, al-, **5029–5031**
on God, 3565–3566
consciousness of otherness from, 4569
unity of, 3566, 6339
al-Ḥallāj and, 3756
love mysticism of, 6350, 6351
on mystical union, 6339
silsilah lineage of, 8820
Jundīshāpūr (Persia), Nestorians of, 2971
June Festivals, music in, 6272
Jung, Carl Gustav (C. G.), **5031–5036**
on alchemy, 246, 247
on androgynes, 341
on archetypes (*See* Archetypes)
bridge symbolism used by, 1051–1052
Campbell, influence on, 1378
categorizing, 5032–5033
on collective unconscious, 1950, 7475, 7485
comparative theology of, 9131
on development of consciousness, 2282
on divination, 2373
on dreams, 2484–2485
on earth spirit, 3014
Esotericism and, 6498
on feet, symbolism of, 3013
Festschriften dedicated to, 3041
as founder of analytical psychology, 7474–7475, 7476, 7484
Freud and, 3215, 7475, 7484
on Gnosticism, 3514, 3527, 3535
on goddess worship, 3611–3612
on the Grail, 3650
on individuation, 7475
influence on Frye (Northrop), 3224
Kerényi's (Károly) collaboration with, 5113–5114
on lion symbolism, 5465
on mysticism, 6345
on nature and the unconscious, 6437
Neumann (Erich) and, 6484
on otherworld, 6925
on paranormal experience, 6057–6058
on possession, 59
on psychology of religion, 7474–7475, 7484–7485
on quaternity, 6747
on science and religion, 5033–5034
on states of consciousness, 1949–1950
symbol theory and, 8912, 8913
on synchronicity, 1528, 6057–6058
Yijing translation, patronage of, 1635
Zimmer (Heinrich) and, 9975
Jung Codex, 3512–3513, 6395
Jungianism, Campbell (Joseph) on hero myths and, 3958–3959
Jungian psychology, ritual symbolism in, 7839
Jung in Context (Homans), 7478
Jun.gun (Owlet Nightjar), 9460
Junius Brutus, 5321
Juno (deity), 3017, **5036–5037**
and Diana, 2346
Jupiter and, 5037
Minerva and, 6043
moon and, 6170
music and, 6304
in triad, 7900, 7901, 9349

Junod, Henri A., 113
on memory, 5850
Juno Lucina (deity), 7909
Juno of Carthage (deity), 7911
Juno Regina (deity), 7904
Junrei (pilgrimage), 7165
Junta Apostólica (1532), 5917
Junta Apostólica (1544), 5917
Junzi (superior men or noble ideal), 1586
Confucius on, 1894, 1895
Mengzi on, 1896
Juok (deity), in Shilluk religion, 2567
in cosmogony, 2567
Jupiter (deity), **5037–5039**
Brelich (Angelo) on cult of, 1048
and Fides, 3094
in Gaul, 7911
iconography of, 4322
Mars and, 5727, 5728
Minerva and, 6043
moon and, 6170
priest *(flamen)* of, 3125–3126
Quirinus in relation to, 7559, 7560
sovereignty of, 5994, 5995
in triad, 7900–7901, 9349
Zeus compared with, 3663
Jupiter, Mars, Quirinus (Dumézil), 4462
Jupiter (planet), deities of, 8428
Jupiter Dolichenus (deity). *See* Iupiter Dolichenus
Jupiter Heliopolitanus (deity), Adad identified with, 28
Jupiter Latiarus (deity), 7898
Jupiter Pluvius (deity), 7603
Jupiter Turmasgades (deity), 4754
Jurajni, al-, and *kalām*, 5066–5067
Jurchen people, 1602, 4493
Jurema (beverage), 120
Jurema (plant), 6274
Juridictional Conferences, in United Methodist Church, 1767
Jurijuri (spirit), 282
Jurisdiction, in Israelite law, 4739–4740
Jurisprudence. *See* Law
Jurists, in Roman legal system, 5332–5333
Jurjānī, al-, on *walāyah*, 9657
Jurji, Layla, 10055
Juruna people (Amazon), 8628–8629. *See also* Tupian religions
Jushamī al-Bayhaqī, al-, 3
Jushe school of Buddhism, 1202
Sarvāstivāda and, 8120
Jushi (sorcerer), 2455
Justice. *See also* Suffering
in black theology, 78
divine (*See also* Theodicy)
Muʿtazilah on, 5063
Saʿadyah Gaon on, 7952–7953
Duns Scotus (John) on, 2524–2525
in *Ecclesiastes*, 2600
genetics and, 3429, 3430
of God
and afterlife, 128–129
in *Ben Sira*, 9759
denials of, 9112
in Islam, 129, 3562–3563
and *Job*, 4932
mercy and, 613–614, 615
Golden Rule and, 3632–3633
in Grail movement, 3654
in Greek religion and mythology, 7783
in Judaism, 7589
as core value, 10063
suffering and, 8806
Jupiter associated with, 8428
in kingships, 5164
Marsilius of Padua on, 5729
myth and, 6361
Niebuhr (Reinhold) on, 6613
racial, Christian social movements and, 1753
retribution and (*See* Retribution)
Smith (Wilfred Cantwell) on, 8450
social (*See* Social justice)
in Zapatismo, 9932
of Zeus, 3663
Justice, Peace and Integrity of Creation program, 3502
Justice and Service Program Unit (WCC), 2685
Justification, **5039–5042**. *See also* Salvation
in Christianity
in Augsburg Confession, 2058
Contarini (Gasparo), double justification theory of, 1968
Council of Trent on, 2060, 9343
ethics and, 1655
history of doctrine, 1667–1668
Luther (Martin) and, 5538
merit and, 5877
works *vs.* faith, superstition, charges of, 8866
Justification and Reconciliation (Ritschl), 597
Justin I (Byzantine emperor), and Monophysitism, 6154
Justinian, Code of (534), apostasy in, 433
Justinian I (emperor), **5042–5043**
and Avars, 4491–4492
Caesaropapism and, 1661
church architecture under, 794
Codex Iustinianus/Justinianus, 5333, 5334–5335
coerced conversion under, 6083
heresy suppressed by, 1679
and Monophysitism, 6154
Origen condemned by, 6890
persecution of Manichaeism under, 2513
Plato's Academy closed by, 6474
Severus of Antioch and, 8238
Stoicism suppressed by, 8741
Justin II (emperor), 4492
on Monophysitism, 6155
Justin Martyr, **5043–5045**
apologetics of, 428
on baptism, 782
on God, 3553
Goodenough (Erwin R.) on, 3637
gospels known by, 920
"gospels" used by, 3642
on Hebrew scriptures, 873, 3553
on idols, 4357, 4358, 4360, 4385
on inspiration, 4510
Irenaeus studying under, 4538, 4539, 4540
on knowledge, 5202
on Liturgy of the Word, 9811
on *Logos*, 5503, 5505
on *lucerna extincta* rite, 8249
on Mary as Eve, 3358, 5753
"Sayings of the Lord" cited as authoritative, 1406
on *Sibylline Oracles*, 8384
and Trinity doctrine, 9361
on wisdom, 5502
Juvenal, on Bona Dea, 3386
Juwaynī, ʿAbd al-Malik al-, Ghazālī (Abū Ḥāmid al-) and, 3469
Juwaynī, Abū al-Maʿālī al-
on attributes of God, 617, 619, 620
in Ashʿarīyah, 534, 537
writings of, 534
Juwaynī, al-, 5064
Irshād of, 5066
Juwaynī, al-Ḥaramayn al-, 6640
Jyōruri (chant), 6301
Jyotibā (deity), in Marathi religions, 5697
Jyotirliṅga (pillar of light), 778, 779
Jyotiṣas, cosmology of, 2019

K

Ka (figures)
in Egyptian magic, 2713
in Egyptian religion, 2710
Ka (vital force)
of Egyptian pharaohs, 5163–5164
and resurrection, 7763
Kaang (culture hero), animals and, 2091
Kaanthos, 2985
Kaapora (deity)
as lord of the animals, 5515
as master the animals, 8580
Kaata, Mount, 6885–6886
Kaʿb (poet), 7221–7222
Kaba Aye Pagoda, 9479
Kaʿbah (shrine in Mecca), **5049–5050**
Abraham in founding of, 16, 7155, 7156
in Arabian religion, pre-Islamic, 444, 445, 5049–5050
architecture of
classification of, 462
dimensions of, 5049
reconstruction of, 5050
Black Stone of, 5049, 5050, 7158, 7344, 7980–7981, 9258
as center of the world, 1501–1502, 5050, 7155
comparison with Jerusalem Temple, 5050
four corners of, 7158
heavenly counterpart of, 5050, 9577
and holy, concept of, 7968
in *ḥajj*, 9817–9818
in Muḥammad's life, 6220
in Qurʾān, 6205, 6207–6208
in Islam, 6222
kiswah (black curtain) of, 7158, 7160, 7222, 9090
localization of deity negated in, 7980
as meteorite, 8736
as pilgrimage site, 1808, 5049, 5050, vol. 5 color insert
in Five Pillars, 4565
ḥājj, 7155, 7158, 7160
maps to, vol. 3 color insert
ʿumrah, 7158
in prayer, 9816–9817
purification of, 7160
as sacred space, 7158, vol. 5 color insert
ṣalāt (prayer) and, 8056
shrines adjacent to, 7158–7159
stone flooring of, 7158
stone worship and, 8744
Kaʿb al-Aḥbār, 7237
Kaballah. *See* Qabbalah
Kabana people (Papua New Guinea), 7808
Kabardins (Caucasus), 4613
Kabbalah. *See* Qabbalah
Kabeiroi (deities), mysteries of, 6329–6330
Kaberry, Phyllis M., 684, 690, 840, 3390, **5050–5051**
on Rainbow Snake, 7605
Kaʿbī, Abū al-Qāsim al-, in Muʿtazilah, 6320
Kabilsingh, Chatsumarn, 6760
Kabilsingh, Voramai, 6760
Kabīr (Indian saint and mystic), **5051–5053**
in *bhakti* poetry tradition, 3985
birth of, 5052
on caste, 3986
death of, 5052
in *Guru Granth*, 5052
on *gurus*, 8712

in *Ādi Granth,* 32
Islamic Sufism and Hindu *bhakti* combined by, 4007
Kabīrvāṇīs of, 5052
on localization of divinity, 7979
poetry of, 7211
Sai Baba movement and, 8026–8027
Vaiṣṇava *bhakti* cult and, 9500
world view of, 4431, 5052–5053
Kabīr Granthāvalī, 5052
Kabīr Panth community, extent of, 3986
Kabīrpanthīs, 5052
Kabīrvāṇīs, 5052
Kabrousse (Senegal), Alinesitoue in, 261–262
Kabuki theater, 2455
calligraphy by actors in, 1371
Kabyle people, revenge and, 7780
Kachchāf' an ḥaqā'iq ghawāmiḍ al-tanzīl, al- (al-Zamakhshari), 9929
Kachinas (deities)
dance/ceremony for, 2461, 6653, 6725
in Pueblo religion, 6723
Zuni rituals of, clowns, transgressive behavior of, 8016–8017
Kachin people (Burma), 5380–5381
Kachō (familial records), *Kiki* texts and, 4801
Kācumalai (Putumaipittan), 10036
Kada Azumamaro
Kamo no Mabuchi as student of, 5074
Kokugaku movement and, 5214, 8365
Kadai (deity), 6454
Kadaitcha or *kwertatye* (sorcerer), in Central Australian religion, as killer, 3871–3872
Kadampa. *See* Bka' gdams pa order
Kaddish (mourning prayer), 7823
for Holocaust victims, 7823
Kad ha-qemaḥ (Baḥya), 4913
Kadjeri. *See* Gadjeri
Kadmīs (Parsi community), 6998
Kadmos (mythic figure), 2433
Kadō (way of poetry), 7216
Kaelber, Walter, 6757
Kaenzig, Thomas, 7599
Kafā'ah (equality), 4706
Kaffārah (atonement), for infractions against *ṣawm* (fasting), 8140
Kāfī (devotional song), 6284
Kāfir (infidel), 4362, 4398, 4399, 4567
Kafka, Franz, 30, 5360
parables of, 6979
Kaftan, Julius
on knowledge, 5208
Ritschlianism of, 6104
Kaga Ikkō Ikki, 7753
Kagame, Alexis, 117
Kagami no ma (mirror room), 7048
Kagan, Yisra'el Me'ir, **5053**
Kaga Otohiko, 3074
Kagawa Toyohiko, **5053–5054**
Kaghan (emperor), 9401, 9402
Kagura (music), 2454, 6300
Kagura Zutome (salvation dance service), 9082
Kaguru religion (Tanzania)
initiation rites of, 2577
sacrifices in, for spirits, 2576
Kagutsuchi (deity), 4754
Kagwahiv people (Brazil), dreams of, 2487
Kagyu order. *See* Bka' brgyud pa order
Kahana, Kalman, 7515
Kahana, Menahem, 6019
Kāhinah, al- ("the sorceress"), 4581
Kähler, Martin, 6468
Kahn, Tobi, vol. 11 color insert
Kaḥ thog (monastery), 7868
Kaḥ thog Rig 'dzin chen po, 1232
Kahuna (priests)
in Hawaiian religion, 3796
in ceremony to Kāne, 3797
in ceremony to Kū, 3799
medical, 3799
Kahun Papyrus, medical material in, 3826
Kaibara Ekken, 2633, **5054–5055**
Kaifeng (China), Jews of, 5005–5006
Kaihōgyō (circumambulation), 9078
Kaikanjō (consecrated ordination), 9079
Kaikeyī, in *Rāmāyaṇa,* 7617
Kailash temple, 1472
Kaingán-Aweicoma religion (Brazil)
death cult in, 8585
hunting rituals in, 8582
Kairites, Jesus and, 4845
Kairos (Greek concept), meaning of, 7992
Kairouan (North Africa), Sherira' Gaon's epistle to, 8320
Kairouan (Tunisia), Judaism in, 4989–4990
Kaivalya, in enlightenment, 2793
Kajirri (initiation), 9696
Kakar, Sudhir, 58
on object-relations theory, 7478
on psychotherapy, 382
Kakawin poetry, in Southeast Asian theatrical performances, 4010
Ka kha sum cu (Longchenpa), 5193
Kakinomoto no Hitomaro (poet), 4811
Kakizome (brush writing), seasonal practice of, 1371
Kakkab (deity), 2597
Kakkar (five emblems), in Sikhism, 8395, 8408
Kakora (deity), birth by, 2985
Kakua (Buddhist monk), 9944
Kakuban (Buddhist monk), Shingon, role in, 8350
Kakugyō (Japanese priest), 5622
Kakukai (Buddhist monk), Shingon Buddhism and, 8350
Kakunyo (Buddhist leader), 4935
Kakusan (Buddhist figure), 1180, 9077
Kakushinni (Buddhist leader), 4935
Kakutarō, Kubo, 6574
KAL (deity), in Kumarbi cycle, 4232
Kalābādhị, al-, **5055–5056**
Kalabari people (Nigeria)
dances of, 2137, 2139
spirit possession in, 2139
dress and modesty among, 1833
Kāla Bhai-rava, 779
Kālacakra (deity), **5056–5059**
iconography of, 5058
names of, 5056
Kālacakra Tantra (Buddhist treatise), 1122, 1123–1124, 1215, 1227, 1228, 1306, 2548, 5056
content of, 5057–5058
Alternative Kālacakra, 5057–5058
Inner Kālacakra, 5057
Outer Kālacakra, 5057
history of, 5056–5057
yoga system of, 5056, 5058
Kālacakra tradition
definitions of, 5056
history of, 5056–5057
initiation into, 5057–5058
maṇḍala of, 5057–5058
Kalala Ilunga (mythic figure), 97
Kalām ('il al-kalām) (Islamic speculative theology), 2382, **5059–5069**
'Abd al-Jabbār on, 3, 4
Ahl al-kalām (rationalism), 3760–3761, 3765, 4029
Ash'arīyah on (*See* Ash'arīyah)
causation according to, 2974–2975
definitions of, 5059
development of, 3212
discussions on free will, 3212
vs. falsafah, 2970, 2974
Ghazālī (Abū Ḥāmid al-) on, 620–621
history of, 5061–5068
early creeds, 5061–5063
Mu'tazilī problematics and creeds, 5063–5064
reformist period, 5067–5068
rigid Ash'arīyah, 5067
from *via antiqua* to *via moderna,* 5064–5066
via moderna, 5066–5067
Ibn Bābawayhi opposed to, 4262
Ibn Rushd opposed to, 4271
Ibn Taymīyah opposed to, 4277
in Jamā'ī-Sunnism, 8854–8855
Islamic studies on, 4717
Judaism influenced by, 4992
Maimonides and, 4893
Mu'tazilah on (*See* Mu'tazilah)
of Ibn Khaldūn, 4587–4588
origins and sources of, 5060–5061
Christianity as, 5061
Greek philosophy as, 5061
ḥadīth as, 5060
ijmā' as, 5060
Manichaeism as, 5061
Mazdakism as, 5061
political dissensions as, 5061
Qur'ān as, 5060
reason as, 5060–5061
proof of existence of God using, 7952
Sa'adyah Gaon influenced by, 4887
adoption of methods, 7951–7952
scientific history and, 8181
in Shiism, 5068
soul in, 8566, 8568–8569
sunnah and, 8853
in Sunnism *vs.* Twelver Shiism, 8343, 8344
tafsīr (Qur'anic exegesis) based on, 7566
Kalām Allāh (word of God), etymology of, 5059
Kālāma Sutta (Buddhist text), 1269
Kālāmukha sect, 8990
Lakulīśa Pāśupata system, influence of, 4019, 8049
location of, 8049
Kaḻarippayattu (martial system), 5730–5731
Kalaśa (water pot), 9265
Kālasaṃkarṣaṇī (deity), cult introduced in *Jayadratha Yāmala,* 4020
Kalberg, Stephen, 378
Kaleri-kalering (mythic figures), 3249
Kaleru (Rainbow Snake), 7605
Kalevala (Finnish epic), 2814, 3103
baths in, 801

Kalevala (Finnish epic) ***continued***
creation story in, 3016
Ilmarinen in, 4379
importance to Finland, 5512
importance to Karelians, 5093
Jesus in, 3104
Lemminkäinen in, **5407–5408**
death and rising of, 1875
Lönnrot version of *(New Kalevala),* 3104, 3111, 5407, 5511, 5512
rejuvenation in, 7682
ritual chanting in, 7838
Väinämöinen in, 9496
Kalevi-poeg (folk hero), 3111
Kālī (deity), 2984, 3020
Bengali worship of, 826
body symbolism and, 4164–4165
in dance drama, 2448–2449
French feminists on, 3030
humanism and domestication of, 827
images of, vol. 9 color insert
in *Jayadratha Yāmala,* 4020
in Śaivism
in Trika Śáivism, 8046
in Kashmir, 8047–8048
Krama Śaivism and, 8045–8046
kaula style of worship of, 4020, 8047–8048
Ramakrishna as priest of, 7611
Ramakrishna's devotion to, 9629, 10067
sword of, 968
temple of, at Dakshineshwar, 7611
violence of, 3590
Kālidāsa (poet), 9346
on Murukan̲, 6240
Kalikan̲r̲i (poet), 8974
Kalimah (word of belief), 9816
Kaliña (deity), 9415
Kalinga (modern Orissa), India, migration to Southeast Asia from, 4011
Kalischer, Tsevi Hirsch, **5069,** 9979
Kālī's Child (Kripal), 7479, 7613–7614
Kālī-varjyas, doctrines of, 2330
Kalivilakku (bronze oil lamp), 7048
Kāliya (deity)
as prince of serpents, 8456
tamed by Kṛṣṇa, 5249
Kaliyuga (Kali age)
dharma in, 6983
duration of, 7499
in Purāṇic cosmology, 2018, 2019
as present evil age, 858, 4440, 6983
society of, 4422
Tamil poetry saints in, 857
Kalki (deity), 4416
Viṣṇu in form of, 708
Kalkú (witch), in Mapuche religion, 5689
Kállay, Ferenc, 3112
Kallenbach, Hermann, 3272
Kallinikos ("He of the Beautiful Victory"), Herakles as, 3917
Kallistos I (patriarch), 3697
Kallu (ritual expert), in Oromo religions, 2573
Kalonymus Kalmish of Piasetzna, 9382
Kalophonic music, 6309
Kalou (power), 7373
Kalpas
in Hinayana Buddhist cosmology, 2028
in Jain cosmology, 2024–2025
in millenarianism, 6030
Kalpa Sūtra, 9554
categories of, 3994, 8883–8884
in Jain scriptures, 4767
Kaltenmark, Max, 6052
Kalteś (deity), 5120, 5125
Kaluli people (New Guinea)
afterlife of, 146, 147
homosexuality among, 4115
illness and spirit séances, 3810
music of, 6265–6266
taboos of, 8949
virginity among, 9606
Kalwadhaṇī, Abū al-Khaṭṭab al-, Ḥanābilah and, 3766
Kalwadi (mythic figure), Gadjeri as, 3249
Kalyāṇamitra (guide or teacher), 1083, 1279
humanity of, 8712
Kalym (bride price), 4625
Kāma (deity), 3002
festival to, Holī, similarities to, 4081–4082
flowers associated with, 3135
in conflict with Śiva, 2305
killed by Śiva, 8415
laughter of, 4195
lotus associated with, 5519
Kāma (desire), 748, 2305
tapas and, 8997, 8998
Kamakura period (Japan)
Buddhism in, 5213
Jōdo Shinshū school, 1244
Jōdoshū school, 1243–1244
Kōben and, 5213
Nichiren school, 1180, 1244
Pure Land Buddhism, 1096, 1243–1244
Shingon school, 1178, 1179, 1180
Tendai school, 1178, 1179, 1180, 1181, 9079
Zen Buddhism, 1244–1245, 2741
kami in, 5073
pilgrimage in, 7166
poetry in, 7216
political power of, 7272–7273
religion in, 4786–4787
temples in, 9049
Kamalaśīla (Buddhist scholar), **5069–5071**
on *bodhisattva* path, 998–999
death of, 5070
in debate at Bsam yas, 5069–5070
in debate with Moheyan, 1152
on illumination of middle way, 5070–5071
at Lhasa council, 2038
on logic, 5311
on meditation, 5070
philosophy of, 1213, 1300
Śāntarakṣita and, 1300, 8107
writings of, 1120, 5554, 5555
Kāmaloka (lower universe), heavens and hells in, 3887
Kama no kami (deity), 2410
Kāmaṣāstra literature, overview of, 8122–8123
Kāma Sūtra, 2305
lesbianism in, 5415
magic in, 5591
overview of, 8122–8123
Puruṣārthas (four goals of humankind) in, 3996
Kambala, writings of, 5555
Kamba religion (East Africa)
creator god of, 2575
disease and illness in, 3817
diviners in, 2577
medicine women in, 3818
supreme being (Ngai) of, 3574
Kamehameha I (king), state religion and, 3799
Kamehameha II (king), religious reform by, 3799
Kamenetz, Rodger, 2924
Kami (deities), **5071–5074**
buddhas, amalgamation with, 8359–8361
in Buddhism, 1175, 3154, 4796–4797, 5073, 8356, 8366
Jien and, 4917
characteristics of, 5071–5073
invisible and concealed, 5071–5072
itinerancy, 5072
locative type, 5072
multiplicity of, 5072
in prehistoric cultures, 5072–5073
Utopian type, 5072
Christianity tied to, 8365
Confucianism and, 8363
in early Japanese religion, 4781
as folk deities, 4797
in folk religion, 4795
Hirata Atsutane on, 4022
honjisuijaku theory on, 4121–4122
in Kurozumikyō, 5267
in Shintō, 2639, 7274, 8356, 8366
norito addressed to, 6649–6650
Japan as created and protected by, 7979
Jingikan (Ministry of Kami Affairs) and, 8366
in Kamakura period, 4786
Maitreya as, 5621–5622
as manifestation of buddhas and *bodhisattvas,* 1176
Motoori Norinaga on, 5215, 6211
mountains and, 6214, 8379
Mount Fuji and, 8364
in myth of the Japanese state, 5073
neotraditionalist view of, 8357
origin of, 4801
power of, 1180
salvation of, 1177
shinkoku doctrine and, 8362
Shintō defined as worship of, 8357
Shotoku Taishi and, 8375
shrines as dwelling places for, 7980
sovereign as, 4783
and syncretism in Edo period, 8362
Worldmate movement and, 8369–8370
worship of
prehistoric, 2640
separation from buddhas, 1183
social roles of, 2640–2641
system of, 7271
Yamato court references to, as *jingi-ryo,* 8359
Kamidana (shelf), 2410
Kamigakari (*Kami* possession), 4795
Kamikaze pilots, 7270–7271
Kamilaroi (deity), 2984, 4481
Kamish (deity)
Eblaite festival of, 2597
Kemosh identified with, 6093
Kamitsu Miya. *See* Shotoku Taishi
Kamm, William, 6216
Kamma, Freerk
on cargo cults, 1416
on memorization, 5852
Kammu (emperor), Saichō and, 8030
Kamo no Chōmei, autobiography of, 702
Kamo no Mabuchi, **5074–5075**
Kokugaku movement and, 5214–5215, 8365
Motoori Norinaga and, 6211
Kamōsho (Hirata Atsutane), criticism of Dazai Jun in, 4022
Kampala, urban nature of, 2566
Kampō healing system, in Japan
overview of, 3868
temples and shrines and, 3869
Kampuchea, Buddhism in, 5133
Khmer Rouge eradication of, 5132–5133
Kamrushepa (deity), 3595
in Hittite religion, 4069

Kamu-yamato-iwarehiko. *See* Jimmu
Kamuy Fuchi (deity), 9337
Kāmya pūjā (*pūjā* undertaken by choice), 7494
Kan, Sergei, 6423
Kanaimà sorcerers, creation as mythic struggle and, 2013
Kanaloa (deity)
overview of, 3797
in Polynesian creation myths, 7313–7314
in Polynesian origin myths, 7315
Kanalu order of priests, rituals of, 3796
Kan'ami Kiyotsugu, 2455
Kanati (deity), 1564
Kanbar-ata (saint), 4622
Kāñcanamayībhūmi (golden earth), in Buddhist *cakravāla* cosmology, 2027
Kanchipuram (India), migration to Southeast Asia from, 4011
Kanda empat (birth spirits), 748
Kaṇḍarīya Mahādeva Temple (Hindu temple), 9041, vol. 2 color insert
Kande Deviyo (deity), in Kandyan religion, 8410
Kandē Yakā (deity), in Vädda religion (Sri Lanka), 8409–8410
Kandinsky, Wassily, 4348, 9144
on color, 1860
Kandori Genshichi. *See* Konkō Daijin
Kandra, Kabos, 3112
Kandyan kingdom. *See also* Sinhala religion
Vädda religion in, 8409–8410
Kāne (deity)
overview of, 3797
in Polynesian creation myths, 7313–7314
in Polynesian origin myths, 7315
Kane, Cheikh Hamidou, 3087
Kane, Mohammadou, 3086
Kāne, P. V., 2328, 4450
Kanem-Bornu (African trading empire), Islam in, 4604–4605
Kanezane regency (Japan), Tendai under, 4917
Kangosan (chanting), 6301
Kangsinmu (Korean shaman), 5234, 5235
Kangxi, 1608
Kang Youwei (Chinese scholar), 946, 1579, 1608, 1610, **5075–5076**
on Konzi (Confucius), 1904
Kanhua (contemplating the phrase), 1292–1293
Kaniṣka (Kushan king), 1032, 1092, 1109, 1145, 4490
council of, 2037
Sarvāstivāda and, 8117
Kanji, Ishiwara, 6608
Kan jing, in Zen Buddhism, in enlightenment, 2795
Kankāl (Prasād), 10034
Kankarlu (initiation), 9696
Kanmu (Japanese emperor), 1176
Kannagi (deity), virginity of, 3588
Kanna meditation, 1293
Kanna-zen (meditation on words), 5311
Kanne, J. A., 6484
Kannisto, Artturi, 3112
Kannon *(bodhisattva),* 4329. *See also* Guanyin; *See also* Avalokiteśvara
Seikai kyūsei-kyō movement and, 8369
Shotoku as incarnation of, 8375–8376
Kannushi (master of divinities), 7410
Kano, Nigeria, economics and Muslim identity in, 1810
Kanōn. See Canon
Kanpeisha (shrines), 7411
Kānphaṭā Yogīs (Hindu sect)
doctrinal basis of, 8041
Gorākhnāth in, 3638
Kanrodai sekai (perfect divine kingdom), 9082
Kansaoya, Lake, Saoshyants and, 8110
Kanshō no Hōnan (persecution of the Kansho period), 7752
Kant, Immanuel, **5076–5081**. *See also* Kantianism; Neo-Kantian philosophy
Adler (Felix) influenced by, 33
aesthetics of, 46–47, 48, 810, 811, 812
Anselm criticized by, 7123
and art, history of study of, 499
on atheism, 583
Baeck (Leo) influenced by, 7670
Barth (Karl) studying, 789
biography of, 5076
categorical imperative of, 3557, 7652
on Christianity, 5078–5079
Cohen (Hermann) on, 1850–1851
on conscience, 1944
on consciousness, 1943
criticism of, 5079–5080, 7115–7116
on design argument, 4517
Dilthey (Wilhelm), influence on, 3932
dualism of, 7137
Durkheim (Émile) influenced by, 2527
on Enlightenment, 2798
epistemology of, 2819
on ethics, 1455, 4356
Fackenheim (Emil) study of, 2949
on facts, knowledge of, 2779–2780
faith, room created for, 4100
on faith as obedience, 2955
on fetishism, 3044–3045
Fichte (Johann Gottlieb) and, 3048–3049
on free will and determinism, 3200
in German Enlightenment, 2797
on God, 3557–3558
existence of, 583, 7123, 7125, 7422
God, idea of, 8161
Hamann (Johann Georg) *vs.,* 8908
Herder (Johann Gottfried) and, 3918
on humanity's main questions, 7109
on Hume (David), 4192
on humor, 4201, 4221
as idealist, 4355, 4356
influence of, 5079–5080
on poetry, 7206
on intuition, 4525
on Jewish art, 4342
and Jewish thinking about Torah, 9237
on Judaism, 4901, 4902–4903
on kingdom of God, 5151, 7776
on knowledge, 5206
on knowledge and faith, 2426, 2959
on law and morality, 5368
on Lord's Prayer, 7370
Maritain (Jacques) on, 5713
on metaphysics, 7110
metaphysics of, 5991
on Milky Way, 2031
on morality, 6102–6103
philosophy of religion and, 6181
religion's role in, 6178
on nature, 6435
ontological argument criticized by, 7422
ontology of, 6830
on phenomena, 7087
phenomenology of, 1542
and philosophy and religion, 7115–7119
on politics and religion, 7250
positivism as response to, 7115
Protestant theology influenced by, 2649
on reflexivity, 7648
religion of, 2797
on religious beliefs and practice, 7125
on revelation, 3049, 5079, 7441, 7776
Rousseau's influence on, 7932
Schleiermacher (Friedrich), opposition of, 8160
skepticism and, 8421
Stoicism and, 8741
on sublime, 47, 48
on Swedenborg (Emanuel), 8899
on temptation, 9070
and theological liberalism, 6102–6103
and Troeltsch (Ernst), 9365
on "two books," 9423
on *Weltanschauung* (worldview), 1992
Kantianism. *See also* Neo-Kantian philosophy
animal rights based on, 2655
God in, 5078–5079
Hermes (Georg) and, 8176
as moral view, 5077
Otto (Rudolf) on knowledge of the transcendent, problem of, 4096–4097
religion in, 5078–5079
Schleiermacher (Friedrich), struggle with, 8160
as worldview, 5076–5077
Kantu (deity), in Nyoro religion, 2574–2575
Kantu (small pillar), 8973
Kantule, Nele, Spanish conquest, resistance against, 2096
Kantuzzili prayer (Hittite), afterlife in, 4072
Kanungu (Uganda), Movement for the Restoration of the Ten Commandments of God in, 105–106, **6215–6217**
Kāṇva dynasty, Buddhist community under, 6128
Kaozhao ritual, 2185
Kaozheng school of evidential research
Dai Zhen and, 2129–2130
Gu Yanwu in, 3718
Kapadia, Karin, 3323
Kāpāla-ḍamaru (drum), 2497
Kapaladharin ("skull cup–bearing") *maṇḍala,* in *Hevajra Tantra,* 3965
Kāpālika Śaivism, 8041, **8049–8050,** 8990
Cakrasamvara and, 1349–1350
Kaula system and, 4020
Krama Śaivism and, 8045
Lakulīśa Pāśupata system, influence of, 4019
Kapferer, Bruce, 58, 382
on exorcism, 8692
on exorcism rituals, 7836
Kapha (phlegm), in Āyurveda, 3854–3855
Kapila (deity), 4415
Kapilavastu (pilgrimage site), 1064
Kapingamarangi religion (Polynesia)
birth in, 7311
gods of, 7305

Kapingamarangi religion (Polynesia) ***continued***
religious practices of, 7305, 7310
Kaplan, Aryeh, 604
in Jewish Renewal, 4873–4874
Kaplan, Jeffrey, 2612, 2663
Kaplan, Martha, on cargo cults, 1421, 1422–1423
Kaplan, Mordecai, **5081–5082**
bat mitzvah, creation of, 1962
in Conservative Judaism, 4983–4984
as creator of Reconstructionist Judaism, 7635–7636
on election of Israel, 2746
Ginzberg (Asher) influencing, 3496
on God, 3551
on Jewish peoplehood, 4864
Jewish Theological Seminary of America and, 1958
in modern Jewish thought, 4907
reconstructionism of, 4870–4871
at Reconstructionist Rabbinical College, 7637
theology of, 1960, 7636, 7639
on tradition, 7636
Kapleau, Philip, 1189
Kapnobatai (walkers on smoke), 9170
Kapp, Gary, vol. 2 color insert
Kapparoh (atonements), 7928
Kappiyam (poetic form), 7223
Kapporet (cover), 9092
Kaprow, Allan, 7051
Kapucha toli (ballgame), 755
Kapu Māte (grave mother), 2127
Kapuralas (priests), 7407, 7409
Kapu svētki, 328
Kapu (taboo) system (Hawaii), 8947. *See also* Taboo
abolished by Kamehameha II, 3799
legendary origins of, 3796
priestly failure and, 3796
sacrifice of breakers of, 3798–3799
women and, 3799
Kapwangwa Kapwicalo (deity), 6501
Karady, Victor, 5786
Karaga festival, 1807
Karahprashad sacrament, in Sikh worship, 8396
Kāraikkāl Ammaiyār, 8974
Karaites and Karaism, **5082–5088**
'Anan ben David as founder of, 317, 5083
anti-Christian arguments in, 7235
Arabic Bibles of, 894
and biblical exegesis, 865
codes of law of, 5084, 5085
development of, 5083–5084
dogma of, 5086–5087
historiography of, 4058–4059
in Judaism, 4991–4992
legislation of, 5086
literature of, 5084–5086
translation into Hebrew, 5085
oral Torah and, 6839–6840
on postbiblical writings, 5086
practice of, 5086–5087
and Rabbanites, 5083, 5084, 5086
and Rabbinites, 865, 4861, 4979
Shabbat law and, 8257
in *Wissenschaft des Judentums,* 4876–4877
Karak (city), origin myth of, 5179
Karakia (ritual incantations), 5680
Karam, Azza, 3367
Karāmāt. See Miracles, in Islam
Karāmat 'Alī Jawnpurī, 4651
Karamojong religion (East Africa)
funeral rites of, 3237
initiation rites of, 2569
Karamustafa, Ahmet, on tricksters, 4214
Kāraṇḍavyūha (Buddhist text), 1079
Karanga religion (Africa)
founding myth and sacred kingship in, 8665
myths in, 8663–8664, 8665
Karanovo culture (prehistoric), 7380–7381
Karatala (cymbals), 7036
Karbala (Iraq), **5088–5089**
etymology of word, 5088
hawzah of, 3801
martyrdom of Ḥusayn at, 5088, 9938
pilgrimage to, 5088
shrine of al-Ḥusayn in, 4236
shrines in, 5088
under Ḥusayn (Ṣaddām), 5088–5089
Karbala, Battle of (680), and 'Āshūrā', 550
Kardec, Allan, **5089–5091,** 6578
biography of, 5089–5090
and Brazilian religions, 119, 9308
name of, 5090
spiritism of, 8716
Kardecism, **5089–5091,** 6578
in Brazil, 5090–5091
doctrine of, 5090
God in, 5090
Kardēr. *See* Kerdīr
Karei (deity), 6454, 6457
Karelian language, 5092
Karelian literature, 5092–5093
Karelian Rebellion (1921-1922), 5092
Karelian religion, **5090–5093**. *See also* Tuonela
Karelians, 3106
Karenga, Maulana, 80
Karen people (Burma), Christianity and, 1728
Karen religion (Burma), healing in, 8273
Kari (deity), disease attributed to, 3808
Karīm Khān Kirmānī, Ḥājj Muḥammad, Shaykhīyah movement and, 8308
Karimov, Islom, 4628, 4629
Karin (spirit), 2280
Karinga initiation guilds, 109
Karjala. *See* Karelian religion
Karjalainen, K. F., 475
on folk songs, 8134
Karjalainen, Kustaa Fredrik, 3113, 6754, 6755
Karkar Island, cargo cults and, 1418, 1419
Karl (mythological figure), 2693
Karl XII (king), Swedenborg (Emanuel) and, 8898
Karlekar, Malavika, 3322
Karlgren, Bernhard, 1622, 1635
Karlstadt, Andreas
and Anabaptism, 304, 305
disagreement with Luther (Martin), 7659
in Leipzig Disputation, 2601
on religious art, 4286
Karmabhumi (earth of ritual activity), cosmological time and, 4015
Karma Bka' Brgyud (Karma pa), 5103
Karma Densa (Tibetan Buddhist monastery), 5102
Karma Gon (Tibetan Buddhist monastery), 5102
Karma Kamtshang school, 5101, 5103
Karma/karman, **5093–5101**
aesthetics and, 51
and *jñāna* and *bhakti,* 4421, 4423
Brahmanic notion of, 5094, 5095, 9570
in Buddhism, 1103, 1155–1156, 2627–2628, 2737, 3001, 4428, **5097–5101**
of *bodhisattvas,* 5100
Buddha on, 8547
in Burmese Buddhism, 1330
consequences of, 9094, 9095
healing and, 3863
heavens and hells and, 3887
in Mahāyāna Buddhism, 5100
in Sarvāstivāda, 5099–5100, 8118–8119
Jainism and Brahmanism *vs.,* 1887
in Japanese Buddhism, 1175–1176
law and, 5350
law of, 2333
merit and, 5870, 5872–5874
and personhood, continuity of, 8547–8548, 8551–8552
recitative practices for, 9837
reincarnation and, 7678–7679
rest from, 1103
Sautrāntika view of, 8119, 8137
in Tibetan Buddhism, 1155–1156, 9840
in caste, 9524
decline of human condition explained with, 2963
definition of, 3002, 5094, 5872–5873
divine justice and judgment in, 129
ethicitization of, in Theravāda Buddhism, 5098
in Falun Gong, 2979
fasting and liberation from, 2997
freedom within, 3200–3201, 3204
god-creation in, 8409
in Hinduism, 4428, **5093–5097**
animals and, 359
caste system and, 5289
charity and, 1555
in *Bhagavadgītā,* 853, 5096–5097
in Śaiva Siddhānta, 8547
in Upaniṣads, 3993, 5095, 5096
Madhva on, 8547
as punishment for breaking laws, 5327
Rāmānuja on, 7616
reincarnation and, 7677
release from, 4925
sati (widow burning) and, 8130
and soul's passage, 3886, 4440
in Reiyūkai Kyōdan, 7862
in Jainism, 2624, 4768, **5093–5097,** 9207
as central power, 4429
colors in doctrine of, 2024–2025
hells and negative karma, 2024
reincarnation and, 7679
soul and, 8548
in Khmer religion, 5132, 5133
in Lao religion, 5314
and liberation, 5099
materialistic notions of, 5096
mokṣa and, 6116
moral quality of acts in, 5098–5099
moral retribution in, 6187
need to justify God eliminated by, 9112
in Neopaganism, 6473
in New Age movement, 6498
and nonviolence, 6645
ontological notions of, 5096
origin of evil and, 2901–2902
prevalence of belief in, 6187
Rāmānjua on, 8547
renunciant notion of, 5094–5095

saṃsāra and, 8098
Śaṅkara on, 8105
in Sikhism, in *Ādi Granth,* 32
in Sinhala religion, 8409, 8411
soul and, 8544–8545
theistic notion of, 5096–5097
theosophical form of, 6535
in theosophy, 9143
transformation of, Bhaiṣajyaguru and, 856
in Vedic texts, 3001, 9553
in Vedism, 4442, 5094, 5098
Western society and, Steiner (Rudolf) on, 8738
vs. wisdom, 9752
in Yoga, 5095
Karma Mīmāṃsā. *See* Pīrva Mīmāṃsā
Karmamudrā (Action Seal), 1217, 1218, 1219
Karmamudra (sexual Yoga), 6879
Karma Pakshi (Karma pa), 5102
Karma pas (Tibetan Buddhism), 1155, **5101–5104**
lineage of, 5103
Karmāśaya, 5095
Karmay, Samten, 2549, 9189, 9190
Karmayoga
desire and, 2305
in *Bhagavadgītā,* 853, 4928
Karṇa (hero)
Arjuna and, 486–487
birth of, 1568
in *Mahābhārata,* 5595
Karnak (Egypt)
Akhenaton's religion in, 217, 218
Amun-Re's temple in, Theban kings devoted to, 2706–2707
Amun's temple in, 301, 9061
Karnataka, bhagavatas of, 9503–9504
Karo, Yosef, **5104–5105,** 9236
Shulḥan ʿarukh (law code), 3159, 4751
as follower of Qabbalah, 5104–5105, 7534
halakhah and, 3743–3744
influence of, 4998
on Alfasi (Yitsḥaq ben Yaʿaqov), 255
ordination as rabbi, 7580
on ritual law, 3751
on synagogues, 8925
Karo Batak people (Indonesia), 799, 800
Karpelés, Susanne, Buddhist Institute founded by, 5132
Karrāmīyah (Ṣūfī brotherhood), 9005
educational institution of, 5556
Kārta (deity), 760, 769
Kartāpur dī bīṛ, 32
Karter (high priest), 7398
Kartinyeri, Doreen, 650
Kartinyeri, Doris, 3391
Kartosuwirjo (Indonesian *imām*), 4669
Karuk tribe (North America)
ballgame played by, 752
and trees, 9336
trickster tales of, 6661–6662
Karulis, Konstantīns, on Māra, 5691
Karuṇā (compassion), 1555, **5105–5106**
meditation on, 1284, 1285
prajñā and, 6629
Karuṇāpuṇḍarīka Sūtra, 7502, 7503
Karunga (supreme being), 3574
Karusakaibe (deity), in Mundurucú religion, 8577
Karuten (deity), 9030
Kasatkin, Nikolai, 4497, 7943
Kasaya (patchwork mantle), 1829
Kasb (acquisition), debates on meaning of, 3212
Kashaku, Paul, 6215
Kasher, Menaḥem Mendel, 868
Kashf, al- (Ibn Rushd), 4271
Kashf al-maḥjūb (al-Bisṭāmī), *walāyah* in, 9660
Kashf al-maḥjūb (al-Hujwīrī), 956, 4647
Kashfīyah. *See* Shaykhīyah
Kāshgharī, al- (Inner Asian army), 4489
Kāshgharī, Maḥmūd al-, 9081
Kāshifī, Ḥusayn Vāʿiẓ, 2446
Kashiway, Jonathan, 10054
Kashmir
Buddhism in, 1230
Sarvāstivādin teachings, 8119
Kubrawīyah order in, 5257
migration to Southeast Asia from, theory on, 4011
Śaivism in, **8047–8048** (*See also* Trika Śaivism)
bhakti in, 858
Krama Śaivism in, 8045, 8046
philosophy in, 8417
Pratyabhijñā Saivism in, 8048
Sufism in, 4647
Kashrut (Jewish dietary laws), 3167, **5106–5108**
biblical laws on, 5106, 7508
and domestic observances, 2398
eco-Kosher, 4870
healthiness and, 3829
in Marrano Judaism, 5718–5719
purpose of, 7504–7505
rabbinical interpretation of, 4978, 5106–5107
rabbinical legislation of, 5107
theological interpretation of, 5107–5108
Kashshāf ʿan ḥaqāʾiq ghawāmiḍ al-tanzīl, al- (al-Zamakhshari), 8953
Kāśī. *See* Banaras
Kāśī Khaṇḍa (Hindu text), 778, 779
Kasimil (evangelist), 5695
Kasiṇa disks, *maṇḍalas* and, 5645
Kasiṇas (visualization), 9834
Kaskihá people (Paraguay), religion of, 8635
Kasō Sōdon (Buddhist monk), 4378
Kasparov, Garry, 511
Kasr (cupping), in Middle East, 3836
Kass, Leon, 3428, 3429, 3430
Kassites, Babylonia under, 5948
Kassovitz, Mathieu, 3099
Kasuga Shrine (Nara, Japan), Ame no Koyane at, 289, 290
Kasuga Taisha Shrine (Nara, Japan), trees of, 2639
Kasulis, Thomas P., 3300
Kāśyapa (monk), Rājagṛha council and, 2035
Kāśyapīya school of Buddhism
doctrines of, 1196
geographical distribution of, 1195
literature of, 1198
origin of, 1194
Katagoge (festival), 2270
Katami (Japanese memorial object), 2241
Kathakali (all-male dance companies), 2136–2137, 2436, 2448, 7048
Katharsis. See Catharsis
Kathāsaritsāgara (Somadeva), 10033–10034
Kaṭha Upaniṣad, Puruṣa in, 3993–3994
Kathāvatthu (Buddhist text), 1110, 1198, 9146
Pāṭaliputra council in, 2037
rejection of, 10021
Kathenotheism
Müller (F. Max) on, 3913
in Vedism, 9555
Kathina (ceremony), 1107, 1307
Kathmandu, Tibet, sacred space in, 7982
Kathmandu Valley, *maṇḍala* mapped in, 1350
Katonda (deity), 4519
in Ganda religion, 2575
Kato religion
bears in, 809
trout myth in, 5198
Ka To Souma (deity), 6501
Katsuragi, Mount, En no Gyōja at, 2802
Kattowitz Conference (1884), Mohilever (Shemu'el) in, 6113
Kattowitz Conference (1912), 194–195
Katuns (division of time), in Maya calendar, 1358
Kātyāyana, 7005, 10021
Katz, Jacob, on Jewish law, 3746
Katz, Steven, on mysticism, 6357
Katz, Steven T., 7745, 7746
Katzenelson, Berl, 9980
Katz v. Superior Court, 1033, 5376
Kaua religion (South America), fertility rites in, 8583
Kaufman, Gordon, ecotheology of, 2610
Kaufmann, David, 4343
Kaufmann, Yeḥezkel, **5108–5109**
biblical exegesis of, 869
on Israelite monotheism, 3539
Kauket (deity), in Egyptian pantheon, 2704
Kaulism, in Tantric Hinduism
in Trika Śáivism, 8046–8047
Kāpālika sect and, 4020
in Kashmir, 8047–8048
Kaum (rebel leader), 7756
Kaum Muda (new faction) movement, in Southeast Asia, 8653
Kaum Tua (old faction) movement, in Southeast Asia, 8653
Kaunda, Kenneth
evangelical Christians and, 1723
United National Independence Party founded by, 5408
Kauṇḍinya (Buddha's disciple), 1104
commentary on *Pāśupata Sūtras,* 4019
Nāga princess, marriage to, 4010
Kaur, Shakti Parwha, on White Tantric Yoga, 3878
Kauravas (Hindu figures)
Balarāma and, 743
in *Mahābhārata,* 5595
war between Pāṇḍavas and, 852
Kauśika Sūtra, magic in, 5590
Kauṣītakī Brāhmaṇa Upaniṣad, karman in, 5096
Kautantowwit (spirit), 6680
Kauṭilya
on *cakravartin,* 1351
on *dharma,* 2329
Kautsky, Karl
biblical exegesis of, 876
on economics, 2671
Marx notes published by, 5747
Kautzsch, Emil, 901
Kauwa, 2986
Kauymali (mythic figure), as trickster, 5937
Káuyúumaari (trickster), 9357
Kava (plant), 7315, 9196
elixir from, 2770
Kavād (Sasanian king), Mazdakism under, 5800
Kavanagh, Maggie, 642–643
Kāverī (Cauvery) River, 7861
divinity of, 2621

Kāverī (Cauvery) River
continued
Śiva and, 7979
Kavitāvali (Tulsīdās), 9393
Kavod, 4266
of Yahveh, 3542
Kavvanah/kavvanot (frame of mind), 726
in Hasidism, 3789, 3790
in Qabbalah, 5304
in Talmudic writings, 5304
Torah study and, *shekhinah* concept and, 8314–8315
Kāvya (great poem), 7205, 10034
Kavya (style of writing), 5467
K'awil (deity), 2466, 5798
Kawi language, Balinese use of, 746
Kawsaj, al-, Ḥanābilah and, 3763
Kaya. *See* Karak
Kayai (deity), 6454
Kāyaka (orderly conduct of life), 4424
Kayan people (Borneo), 1022
Kayapó people (Amazon). *See also* Ge religions
cosmology of, 8587–8588, 8630
mythology of, 3295
origin of agriculture in, 8590
religion of, 8630
Kāyasthas (caste), in Bengal, 825, 826
Kāyotsarga (laying down the body), 4769
Kaysānīyah movement
on *ghaybah* (concealment), 3468
Shiism and, 8321
Kayserling, Meyer, 4879
Kāytāks (Caucasus), 4613, 4614
Kazakhstan, 4620. *See also* Central Asia and Central Asian religions
Islam in
in post-Soviet era, 4627, 4628
reform movement of, 4623
in Soviet era, 4624
Sufism, 4621
under tsarist rule, 4622–4623
prehistoric religion in (*See* Saka religion)
Kazamaki Keijirō, 4807
Kazan (city in Tatar khanate), 4616, 4617
Kazanskii, Benjamin, 9193
Kazan Theological Academy, 4617
Kazi-Kumukh (Dagestan), 4614
KBW. *See* Kulturwissenschaftliche Bibliothek Warburg
KDKA radio station (Pittsburgh), religious broadcasting on, 7709–7710
Keakea-lani-wahine (chief), gender and, 3799
Keane, A. H., 379–380
Keane, John, Gibbons (James) and, 3478
Keaney, John J., 7106
Keating, Thomas, 604
Keats, John, 5631
Kebatinan
in Java, 8653
path of, 5733
Kebatinan kejawen (spiritual movements), 4818
Keber moiety, in Qemant religion, 2573
Keble, John, 6510
Kedáreśvara *(liṅga),* 779
Keddie, Nikki R., 4718
Keeble, Marshall, in Churches of Christ, 1780–1781
Kee-khwei (prophet), 5985
Keeling, Richard, 575
Keen, Ian, 647, 648, 668, 2481
Keen, Sam, 7831
Keene, Donald, 51
Keepers of the Earth. *See* Shomrei Adamah
Keepers of the Flame Fraternity, 7445, 7446
Summit Lighthouse and, 1782
Keesing, Roger, 5835
on *mana,* 8515
on social structure, 8516
Keetan'to-wit (spirit), 6680
Keetoowah Society, 1565
Kefalaia gnostika (Evagrios of Pontus), 2886
Kegon school of Buddhism (Japan), 1177, 1179, 1242. *See also* Huayan school of Buddhism
Kōben and, 5213
Keichū (Buddhist monk), 5214
Motoori Norinaga and, 6211
Keightley, David, 455
on human sacrifice, 4183
on Shang mentality, 1637
Keisō dokuzui (Hakuin), 1277
Keith, A. B., on Rudra-Śiva, 8039
Keizan, **5109–5110,** 9947
Kelal Yisra'el (the wholeness of the people of Israel), 4864
Kele ceremony, as ancestral cult, 1436
Kelimat ha-goyim (Duran), 7234
Keli yaqar (Efrayim of Luntshits), 867
Keller, Carl-Albert, historiography of, 4049–4050
Kellis (Egypt), Manichaeism in, 5663
Kellner, Carl, Ordo Templi Orientis (OTO) and, 8251
Kellogg, John Harvey, 3173
Seventh-day Adventism and, 8236–8237
Kellogg, Susan, 3412
Kelly, Elizabeth, 3148
Kelly, Galen, 2292
Kelly, George Armstrong, 7249
Kelly, Isabel, 5945
Kelly, John D., 9297
Kelly, Ned, in Australian Indigenous religions, new movements of, 674
Kelly, Raymond C., on kinship, 5183
Keloids, 1001, 1003
Keluskar, K. A., 286
Kelvin, Lord, 7138
Kemal, Mustafa. *See* Atatürk, Mustafa Kemal
Kemosh (deity)
characteristics of, 6094
in Moabite religion, 6093–6095
popular worship in Israel, 3157
in Syrian religions, 6093
Kemp, Martin, 4300
Kempe, Margery, **5110**
Kemper, Steven, 7263
Kenana (prophet), 5683
Keneally, Thomas, 3081, 3082, 3084
Kenekuk (prophet), 6686
Keneset Yisra'el. See Jewish people
Kenesiyyah Gedolah, 195
Kenji, Miyazawa, 6608
Kenjutsu (sword art), 5732
Kenmitsu (Buddhist lineage), 1178, 1180, 1181, 1182
Kennan, George, 6611
Kennedy Institute of Ethics, 940
Kenny, Chris, 3392
Kenny, Maurice, 7226
Kennyo (Buddhist leader), 4936
Kénos (culture hero), rejuvenation myth of, 7683
Kenosis (Christ's negation of divine power), 5454
Ken'ō Sōi (Buddhist monk), 4377–4378
Kenshō (true nature), Hakuin's teaching on meditation and, 3742
Kentoshi (Japanese envoy), 6300
Kenya. *See also* Kikuyu religion; Luo people
African churches founded in, 2578
African Independent Churches in, 103
Agikuyu people of, initiation rites of, 7805
charismatic Christianity in, 106
Christian missions to, colonial government established by, 2578
Legio Maria movement in, 105
Mau Mau resistance movement in, 87, 109
as secret society, 8213
neotraditionalist movements in, 109
schools and national identity, 1515
Kenya, Mount
Molungu located at, 2575
Ngai located at, 2567, 2575, 3574
Kenyah people (Borneo), 1022
Kenyatta, Jomo, 115
on Kikuyu initiation rites, 2577
Kenyon, Kathleen, **5110–5111**
Near Eastern excavations by, 455
Kenzuishi (Japanese envoy), 6300
Keoke, Emory, 6426
Keown, Damien, 5810
Kepha. *See* Peter the Apostle
Kephalaia (Manichaean text), pearl in, 7024
Kepler, Johannes, **5111–5112**
astrology and, 564
on craters of moon, 4516
on elliptical orbits, 1978
Galileo Galilei and, 3257
geometry of, 3443
on God, 7136
on science and religion, 8182
theology of, 5205
Kepoi (gardens of Adonis), 2536
Keppel-Compton, Ursula, 6611
Kerala ritual, Kṛṣṇaism in, 5254
Kerberos (mythic figure), 165, 2393
three heads of, 3804
Kerdīr (priest), Mani and, 5659–5660, 5665
Kereit tribe (Mongolia), 4493
Keremet (deity), 5710
Kerensky, Alexander, Sorokin (Pitirim Aleksandrovich) and, 8524
Kerényi, Karl, 3056
Kerényi, Károly, **5112–5116**
Brelich (Angelo) studying under, 1047
historiography of, 4046
Jensen (Adolf E.) and, 4825
on labyrinths, 5276
on Prometheus, 7419, 7420
Keres (powers of evil), 2277
Keresan Pueblo religion (North America), 6727–6728
cosmology of, 6722
Keres tribe (North America), ballgame played by, 752
Kermode, Frank, 5473, 5487–5488
Kermode bear, 807
Kern, Hendrik, 945
Kerner, Justinus, 6435
on spirit possession, 8687
Kernis, Aaron Jay, 6312
Kernos (sacred vessel), 7144
Kerong (diviner), 6004–6005, 6007
Kerr, Justin, on war dance, 2466
Kerugmata Petrou, 7069
Kerygma of Peter, 7068
Kesari (newspaper), 9198
Keseg mishhen (Karo), 5104
Keshab Chandra Sen. *See* Sen, Keshab Chandra
Kesselman, Jonathan, 3099
Kessler, Konrad, 3532
Kesteloot, Lilyan, 3088
Keswick movement, 2888, 2889
Holiness movement and, 4083
Smith (Hannah Whitall) and, 8446
Keter malkhut (Ibn Gabirol), 4266

Ketiv (Masoretic text), 868
Ketou (kowtow), 1642
Ket religion. *See* Southern Siberian religions
Kettanagai (mythic figure), 939
Kettledrum, 2495, 2497, 7036
Ketton, Robert, 4715
Ketubba (marriage contract), 7821
Ketuvim ("Writings" section of Hebrew scriptures), 879, 889
as scripture, 1406
Keuls, Eva, 7079
Kevala Advaita (absolute nondualism), 9545–9547
Kevalajñāna (omniscience), 2793
Kevesh (altar), 925
Keynes, John Maynard
on government role in economics, 2670
on Newton, 6589
Keys, **5116–5117**
Key to Theosophy, The (Blavatsky), 977, 9142
KFSG (Kalling Foursquare Gospel) radio station (Santa Monica), religious broadcasting and, 7710
Khabar/akhbār ("news"), *ḥadīth* and, 3726
Khādi (self-spun cloth), 861
Khadījah bint Khuwaylid
Abū Bakr and, 19
daughters of, 3008, 6220
death of, 6222
Muḥammad's marriage to, 6220, 6223
on Muḥammad's revelation, 6221
Khafre (Egyptian king), statue of, symbolism of, 2704
Khalafallah, Muḥammad, Qur'anic exegesis of, 7568
Khālid ibn al-Walid, army under, 20
Khālid ibn Yazīd, alchemy and, 248, 250
Khalīfa (vice-regent), in creation, 2651
Khalīfah, on magic, 5583–5584, 5585, 5586
Khalīfat Allāh, title of, 1367
Khalīfat rasūl Allāh, Abū Bakr as, 1365
Khallāl, Abū Bakr al-, Ḥanābilah and, 3763–3764
Khalq (that which is created), 2652
Khālsā (Community of Pure)
creation of, 8395
Singh (Gobind) and, 8408
Khālsā Council, of Sikh Darma Brotherhood, 3878
Khālsā Sikhs, initiation of, 3878
Khālsā Women's Training Camp, 3879
Khalwah (Druze house of prayer), 2502
Khalwatīyah Ṣūfī order, 4571, 9009
Khammaan Khonkhai, 3077
Khamrīyah (Ibn al-Fāriḍ), 4261, 7222
Khan. *See* Aga Khan; Ahmad Khan, Sayyid; Chinggis Khan; Kublai Khan
Khan, Abdul Ghaffir, 6648
Khan, Abrahim, on *dharma,* meaning of, 8762
Khan, Nusrat Fateh Ali, 6286
Khan, Sayyid Ahmad. *See* Ahmad Khan, Sayyid
Khānagāh (hospice), **5117–5118**
Akbar (emperor) establishing, 4649
alternative terms for, 9005
formation of, 4647
function of, 9006
Ḥamadānī (Yūsuf) establishing, 4621
Mu'īn ad-Dīn Chishtī establishing, 9009
samā' khānahs (music halls) in, 8065
shaykhs in, 4648
Khaṇḍas (sector), 779
Khandhaka (section of Vinaya), 5348
Khaṅḍobā (deity), in Marathi religions, 5697
Khanty (Ostiaks), 3106. *See also* Khanty and Mansi religion
Khanty and Mansi religion, **5118–5126**. *See also* Ob-Ugrian religion; Southern Siberian religions
afterlife in, 5123
aquatic sphere in, 5121
bears in, 807, 5125
cult of, 5120–5121
cosmology of, 5119–5121
deities of, 469
sky, 3107, 6754–6755
family guardian spirits in, 5122
forest-settlement opposition in, 5121
forest sphere in, 5120
mirroring of social structure in, 5121
human sphere of, 5121–5124
land-water opposition in, 5120–5121
mediator spirits in, 5122
middle world of, 5120–5121
mythology of, 5119–5120
nonindigenous influences on, 5125
sacrificial ceremonies in, 5124–5125
shamanism in, 3109, 5123–5124
soul in, 5122–5123
studies of, 3112
totemic ancestor in, 3107
underworld in, 472
warlord guardian spirits in, 5120
during bear festival, 5121
function of, 5121
hierarchy of, 5122
Khanty language, 5118–5119
Khanty people (Arctic), 468
Khaqani (poet), 6767
Khārijīs, **5126–5127**
Abū Ḥanīfah opposing, 21
on afterlife, 161
caliphate, interpretation of, 1366
declaring war on Muslim community, 4562
doctrines of, 4248
on free will and predestination, 3211
geographical distribution of, 4699
as heretics, 4693
imamate in, 4396, 4583
īmān and *islām* in, 4398–4399
literature of, 4583
Murji'ah sect opposing, 4568
in North Africa, 835, 4583, 4600, 4601
prevalence of, 4567
sects of, 5126
tafsīr (Qur'anic exegesis) of, 7566
on true Muslim, 4567
walāyah and, 9658
Kharjas (verses), 4597
Kharrāz, Abū Bakr al-, on union with God, 3757
Khaṣībī, Ḥusayn ibn Ḥamdān al-, 226
Khaṭīb (preacher), 4397, 4645
Khaṭīb, 'Abd al-Karīm al-, 4371
Khatm al-awliyā' (Ḥakīm al-Tirmidhī), 4569
Khatrī, Devakīnandan, 10034
Khatri (merchant) caste, Sikh Panth and, 3986
Khaṭṭābī, al-, 4371
Khaṭṭābīyah movement
as *ghulāt* (extremist), 8323
Twelvers doctrine, role in, 8326
Khattiya (lord), 1134
Khātūn, Turkān, 6640
Khawājah Shams al-Dīn, 6638
Khawatir (internal impulses), in Sufism, 8815
Khaybar, Battle of (629), 'Alī ibn Abī Ṭālib in, 256
Khayr, Abū Sa'id ibn Abī al-
and Niẓām al-Mulk, 6640
khānagāh of, 5117
Khayyām, 'Umar (Omar), 6731
Khayyāt, al-, 6774
Khaz (Armenian ekphonentic signs), 1534–1535
Khazar kingdom
Judaism in, as state religion, 4860
missions to, from Church of Constantinople, 2585
Khazar people (Russia)
Arab conquest of, 4612
conversion to Judaism, 4492
Cyril and Methodius, mission to, 2116
Khāzin, al-, 4662
Khazneh (Petra), 6386
Khecarī (deity), 1226
Khecarī ("she who moves the sky") technique, in *Haṭhayoga,* 3795
Kheiralla, Ibrahim George, 738
Khemaka (elder), "I am" and, 8553
Kheper (scarab), 2713
Khepri (deity)
Atum and, 623
birth by, 2985
scarab identified with, 4508
Khereg (private sacrifice), 1326
Khidr (mythic figure), in Sufism, Ibn al-'Arabī's vision of, 8819
Khilafah. See Caliphate
Khilāfat reform movement, 4654
Mawdūdī in, 5787
Khiraqī, al-, Ḥanābilah and, 3764
Khirqah (pathwork cloak), 9005
Khivi (Sikh woman), 3335
Khlyst (people of God) sect
orgy and, 6873–6874
sexual rites of, 8248
Khmel'nitskii uprising, 5016
Khmer literature, 5130
Khmer religion, **5127–5135**. *See also* Cambodia and Cambodian religions
founding stories in, 4010
in Vietnamese religion, 9591
Khmer Rouge, 5132–5133
as revolutionary millennial movement, 6546, 6549
Khmwum (deity), 5514
Khnemu (deity), 7861
Khnum (deity), 2709
Khoi and San religion (Southern Africa), **5135–5157**
cosmology of, 5135
culture hero myth of, 2091
death, myth of origin of, 2091
history of study of, 112
myths of, 94, 5135–5137
rabbit symbols in, 7590
rituals in, 5136–5137
shamanism of, 83, 5136
Khoisan languages, in East Africa, 2566
Khojas. *See* Nizārī Ismā'īlīyah
Khojiev, Jumabai, 4628
Khola (drum), 7036
Khomeini, Ruhollah
on *walāyah,* 9660
on Rushdie (Salman), 434
Khomiakov, Aleksei, **5137–5138**
and Florenskii (Pavel), 3134

'Khon Dkon mchog rgyal po (Khön Könchog Gyalpo), 1225
Khond people (Bengal), ritual sacrifice practiced by, 2556
Khonkhai, Khammaan, 3077
Khonsu (deity)
in Kushite religion, 5269
Theban kings and, 2706
Khormusta Tengri (deity)
Ahura Mazdā as, 6140
Chinggis Khan as son of, 1645
as hedgehog, 3892
Khosrow I (king of Persia), 5661
Khrapovitskii, Antonii, 7203
Khri 'Dus srong (Tibetan emperor), 1151
Khri Lde gtsug btsan (Tibetan emperor), 1151
Khri Srong lde btsan (Tibetan emperor), 7867
and Bodnath stupa, 7166–7167
as Buddhist benefactor, 1151–1152
Buddhist disputes and, 2038
Buddhist texts under, 1223, 1266
and debate at Bsam yas, 5069–5070
Lhasa council sponsored by, 1095
and Padmasambhava, 6940–6941, 7167
temples built by, 9050
Khro bcu (Tibet), 1009
'Khrul zhig rin po che (Trulshig Rinpoche), Ani Lochen and, 355
Khshathra, divine kingship of, 5147
Khshathra Vairya, 290, 2128
Khshnumism, 9991
Khubilai Khan. *See* Kublai Khan
Khuddaka Nikāya (Buddhist text), 1198, 1269
Khudī (self), 4534
Khüdkhe (disordered state), 1326
Khufīya (Ṣūfī order)
in China, 4635
dhikr of, 4635
Khul' (divorce), 4708
Khūlī, Amīin al-, Qur'anic exegesis of, 7568
Khum (deity), in Kushite religion, 5269
Khums (religious tax), hawzah and, 3801
Khunrath, Heinrich, 252
Khusrau I (Sasanian king), Mazdakism under, 5800
Khusraw, Amīr, **5138–5139**
and Niẓām al-Dīn Awliyā', 6638, 6639
qawwālī music of, 6284
Khuṭab al-shaykh (Ibn 'Abd al-Wahhāb), 4255
Khuṭbah (official sermon), 4397
Khvarenah (splendor), 4537, **5139–5140**
Khwaday-nāmag (Iranian text), Mazdakism in, 5800, 5801
Khwāfī, Faṣīḥ-i, 601
Khwan (vital essence), 9094
Khwari, Ahmad, 'Aṭṭār (Farīd al-Dīn) and, 601
Khwurdag Abestāg (Avesta text), 9992
Khyung po Rnal 'byor (yogin), 1226
Ki (material force). *See Qi*
Kiarostami, Abbas, 3098
Kibbutz movement
charismatic leadership and, 1546
in Palestine, 7721
Kibeho (Rwanda), Movement for the Restoration of the Ten Commandments of God and, 6215, 6216
Kibwetere, Joseph, in Movement for the Restoration of the Ten Commandments of God, 105, 6215–6217
Kickapoo religion (North America)
Prophet movement in, 6667, 6686
puberty rites in, 6683
religious societies of, 6685
Kidd, Benjamin, Anesaki Masaharu influenced by, 342
Kidder, Daniel, on Carnival, 1443
Kiddushin (engagement), 7821
Kido (prayer), 1648
Kido Kōichi, 6637
Kidwell, Clara Sue, 6423, 6424
Kieckhefer, Richard, 2279
Kiengir. *See* Sumer
Kiepja, Lola
as last women Selk'nam shaman, 8224
song of, 8225
Kierkegaard, Michael Pedersen, 5140
Kierkegaard, Søren, **5140–5143**
on "absolute paradox," 6990–6991, 7116
aesthetics of, 47–48
anticlericalism of, 2474
attack on Danish church by, 5140–5141
Barth (Karl) on, 790
on Christian truth, 7675
communication method of, 5141–5142
on conscience, 1943
criticism of *Corsair* by, 5140–5141
on despair, 4127
on doubt, 2424–2425
in existentialism, 2925–2927
Fackenheim (Emil) study of, 2949
on faith, 2425–2426
on human beings, 7117
on humor and irony, 4201, 4220–4221
influence of, 5142–5143
on film, 3098
on knowledge, 5208
on learned ignorance, 6990
life of, 5140–5141
Maurice (Frederick Denison) compared to, 5784
metaphysics of, 5991
on morality, 6178
and mythology in modern world, 6369
and neoorthodoxy, 6468
parables of, 6979
on paradox, 6988
on religion, 7116–7117
on religious beliefs and practice, 7126
on Socrates, 8708
Sölle (Dorothee) on, 8511
works of, 5141
Kieser, Dietrich Georg, 6435
Kieslowski, Krzysztof, 3099
Kiev
conversion of, to Eastern Christianity, 2585
Orthodox Christianity in, 1684, 7941, 7942, 9632
Kievan Monastery of the Caves, 7941
Kievan pantheon
Dazhbog in, 2231
Mokosh in, as only female deity, 6115
Kiev school, ethics, 1652–1653
Kifāyat al-'abidin (Maimonides), 5612
Kigal (underworld), 9452
Kiki texts (Japan). *See also* Kojiki; *Nihonshoki*
academic essays on, 4806–4807
audience of, 4802
commentaries on (*See Nihongi kōsho*)
court political decline and, 4804–4805
as history, 4800–4801, 4802–4803, 4807
as mythology, 4807
as national memory, 4806–4808
popular propagation of, 4806
ritual texts and, 4803
Kikuyu (mythological figure), 2575
Kikuyu (Gikuyu) religion (Kenya)
in African Independent Churches, 2571
in African Independent Pentecostal Church, 103
ancestors in
Christian missions and, 142
status of, 141
childbirth practices in, 3819
confession in, 1884
creator god of, 2567, 2574, 2575
divination in, 2576–2577
high deity in, 2567
initiation rites of, 2569, 2577
priesthood of, 2569
revenge in, 7780
studies of, 115
supreme being (Ngai) of, 3574
Kilamuwa (king of Ya'adi), 7130
Kilborne, Benjamin, 2483
Kilibob (deity), 6788
cargo cults and, 1418, 1419
Kilimanjaro, Mount, Molungu located at, 2575
Killer-of-Enemies, 405
Killer Whale, in Haida myth, 3735
Kilson, Marion, 6257
Kilumba (healer), 9370
Kim, Oon Young, 6536
Kimambo, I., 117
Kimball, Solon, on individualism, 7800
Kimball, Spencer W., 6195
Kimbangu, Simon, **5143–5144**
government persecution of, 103, 5143
messianism of, 5973
popularity of, 103
as priest-diviner, 2001
prophetic movement, 1720, 5221, 7443
syncretism, 1511
teachings of, 103
Kimbanguist Church, 5143
establishment of, 103
indigenous cosmology in, 2001–2002
membership in, 5144
teachings of, 103
Kimberley (Australia), Ungarinyin religion in, 9458–9462
Kim Hak, 3077
Kim Heshang. *See* Musang
Kimḥi, David, **5144–5145**
biblical exegesis of, 866–867, 868, 5144–5145
Kimḥi, Mosheh, 5144
Kimḥi, Yosef, 5144
Kimi, Kotani, 6574
Kimmei Reigakkai, 6824–6825
Kimmel, Michael S., 3314
Kim Nam Ha (Korean poet), 5441
Kimon school, Confucianism and, 1927
Kimpa, Dona Beatrice, 67
Kimpasi, initiation rites of, 5220
Kimpa Vita (prophetess), 5221
Kin. *See* Kinship
Kin (time, day, sun)
as Maya deity, 5883
in Mesoamerican calendar, 1356, 1358, 5885
in periodization systems, 177
Kinaaldá ceremony, 3408, 4485–4486
Kinar (deity), in Canaanite religion, 1384
Kindaichi, Kyosuki, 5514
Kindī, Abū Yūsuf Ya'qūb al-, 2970, 2971–2972
Aristotle and, 479
on Christianity, 7242, 7243
on knowledge, sources of, 6097
on Philoponus, 5203
philosophy of, 7192
on prophetic and philosophical truth, 6736
on soul, 8569

Kinetography Laban, 2160
King, Coretta Scott, on kingdom of God, 5153
King, Godfré Ray. *See* Ballard, Guy
King, H. C., 6105
King, John H., 2541
King, L. W., 5969
King, Martin Luther, Jr., **5145–5146**
charisma of, 5402
Gandhi (Mohandas) influencing, 3273, 5402
and kingdom of God concept, 5153
Malcolm X's rejection of, 72
nationalism of, 5398
Nation of Islam opposing, 4688–4689
on nonviolence, 7257
nonviolence of, 6648
Pentecostalism and, 70
principles of, 5401–5402
progressive Islam influenced by, 6100
religious studies on, 80
Southern Christian Leadership Conference and, 1753
King, Richard, on religious and postcolonial studies, 8801
King, Ursula
on gender and religious studies, 3311, 3313, 3314, 3345
on non-Western gender studies, 3315
on women in theological schools, 3310
King, Winston, on religious experience, 7701
King, Winston L., on *saṃsāra*, 5401
Kingdom Halls, 4820, 4821, 4822, 4823
Kingdom of God, **5146–5154**
in Christianity, 5149–5153
in Lord's Prayer, 5517
Roman Catholicism, 7885
church as reflection of, 2700
entering into, 5149
Jesus on, 4849–4850
Kant (Immanuel) on, 5079
as kingdom of righteousness and peace, 5152–5153
as object of search or struggle, 5149
Rauschenbusch (Walter) on, 5152, 7630
Schleiermacher (Friedrich) on, 8166
in words of Jesus, 5148–5149, 7024
Kingdom of God in America, The (Niebuhr), 2290
"Kingdom of God is at hand, the," 5148–5149
Kingdom of God Is Within You, The (Tolstoy), 9220
Kingdom of Heaven, in Christian Science, 1746
Kingdom of Kongo, The: Civil War and Transition, 1641-1718 (Thornton), 10027
Kingfisher dance (Australia), 2380
King James Bible
apocryphal books in, 881
"holy" and "sacred" in, 4098
King Lear (Shakespeare), Tate's (Nahun) revision of, 5356
King-lists, 2724
Kingo, Thomas, 3705
King of Chaos, Carnival and, 1440
King of Fools, Carnival and, 1441
"King of kings," 5147–5148
King of Terqa. *See* Dagan
"King of the gods," 5146–5147
Kings, 879, 882
Levites in, 5422
Temple procedures in, 928, 929
1 Kings
Asherah in, 4743
Baal in, 7129
Baal prophets mocked in, 4200
criminal law in, 4738
David in, 2221–2222
Documentary Hypothesis on, 883
Elijah in, 2764–2765
heterodoxy in, 934
priests in, 5421
sanctity of Jerusalem in, 933
shekhinah concept and, 8313
Solomon in, 34–35, 8512–8513
Temple procedures in, 924, 931, 935
2 Kings
Baal Zebub in, 7103
blasphemy in, 972
Elijah in, 2764–2765
heterodoxy in, 934
Isaiah in, 4546
Levites in, 5426
scroll in, 4749
Temple cult centralization in, 935
Temple procedures in, 924, 931
Torah in, 9231
Torah reading in, 882
Kings and Councillors (Hocart), 4386
Kings and kingship, **5154–5181**. *See also* Chiefs; Kingdom of God; Leaders; Political philosophy; Royalty; Theocracy
in African religions
Benin, 7805–7806
divinity of, 84
Edo, 7805–7806
iconography of, 4301–4302
interlacustrine Bantu, 4520
Kongo, 5220
Luba, vol. 13 color insert
myths about, 95–96, 97, 5171
northeast Bantu, 2577
Ondo Yoruba cosmology and, 2000
relics of, 5170–5171
role of, 84
royal spirits in central Bantu religion, 1509
in Southern Bantu religion, 8664–8665
sub-Saharan, **5169–5172**
in Swazi religion, 8864, 8865, 8895–8896, 8897
anointing of, in Ebla, 5164
in Assyria, 5162–5163, vol. 8 color insert
authority of, 693
in Aztec Mexico, 5172–5174
Babylonian
in Akitu festival, 222, 223, 2537–2538
divinity of, 7276–7277
Dumuzi and, 2522, 2523
hieros gamos rite and, 3976
negative confession of the king, 1887–1888
sky imagery and, 8428
birds as symbols of, 948
in Buddhism, 1091–1092, 1161
Aśoka as ideal king, 556, 1135, 7261
in Bhutan, 7262–7263, 8985
the Buddha as heir to, 5347
in Burma, 1328–1330, 7261–7262
in China, 1161, 1164, 1166, 7267, 8994–8995
function of monarch in, 7262–7263
in India, 1105
in *Sutta Piṭaka,* 5348
in Vajrayāna (Tantric) Buddhism, 1221
in Japan, 1241, 1242, 7262, 7271–7274
in Laos, 7262
and monastic power, 1095
nāgas and, 6394–6395
and national integration, 1099
in Nepal, 7262, 8985
saṃgha, affinity with monarchy, 8078–8079
in Sikkim, 7262
in Southeast Asia, 1133–1135, 1139, 5346, 7261, 9150
in Sri Lanka, 2530–2531, 7261
in Thailand, 7262, 9095
in Tibet, 1230, 1232, 7262, 8985, 9183–9184
yakṣas and, 6394–6395
in Bugis religion, 1317
Cakravartin (universal king) ideal, **1350–1352**
history of ideal, 1350–1351
in *Arthaśāstra,* 8122
religious dimensions of, 1351
saṃgha and, 8078
calendars and, 1355
Canaanite, 1384, 1385, 1386, 1399–1400
in Carnival, 1440
in Celtic religion, 1483, 1488, 1490, 1491–1495
horse sacrifice and, 8239
in Central Asia, 5179
ceremony and, 1513–1514, 1517
Charlemagne and, 1556
in Chinese religion (*See also* Huangdi; Mandate of Heaven; Shangdi)
authority of, 693
Buddhist perspective, 1161, 1164, 1166, 7267
and cities as celestial order recreated on earth, 7984
Confucian imperial cult sacrifices, **1910–1916,** 7267
Confucius on, 1571
Daoist perspective, 1590, 7267
in Han dynasty, 5179
Han Fei Zi on, 3773
immortality quest in, 7267
jade and, 4759
law and, 5352–5353
Mengzi on, 1572
in Qin dynasty, 5179
sage kings and model emperors in myth, 1627
in Shang dynasty, 1582, 5178
in Zhou dynasty, 1583, 1584, 5178
in Christianity, 6814–6815
consecration and, 1956
confession by kings, 1885
in Confucianism, 1161, 1540
consecration and, 1956
in Crete, 5165–5166
crown symbolism, **2072–2073**
in Daoism, 1161, 7267
death of, 5155–5156
in African religions, 5170
in Egypt, 5164
in Hittite religion, 5165
in Ugarit, 5164
definition of, 5154–5155
deification of, in manism, 5673

Kings and kingship ***continued***
diffusionist view of, 5158
distinction between person and office, 5159
divine, 5157–5159
in Africa, 5169
criteria for, 5158
in East Asia, 5178
in Egyptian religion, 5163
Frazer (James G.) on, 5169, 5170
in Iran, 5165
Mesopotamian, 5162
and ritual regicide, 5158
divine right of kings doctrine, Suárez (Francisco) on, 8799
in East Asia, **5178–5181**
effigies of, 5155
in Egyptian religion, 5163–5164
authority of, 693
Circuit of the White Wall ceremony, 1503
divinity of, 2703, 2706, 2711–2712, 5163, 7277
Horus and, 2441, 4136, 4416, 7277
iconography of, 4318–4320
mythology of, 2720
pyramids symbolic of, 2704
ritual duties with, 2714, 5164
"Son of Re" title of, 7277
sun and, 8837
elephant as symbol of, 2750
establishment of, via conquest, 5156–5157
Ethiopian, conversion to Christianity, 2859
Etruscan, 5167
evolutionary stages of, 5158
foreign, legitimacy of, 5157
in Geto-Dacian religion, 3466, 3467
Golden Age and, 3629–3630
in Greek religion, 5165–5167
Herakles as symbol of, 3917
in Hellenistic religions, 5165–5167
cult of the ruler, 3902–3903, 4036
in hero myths, 3958, 3959–3960
hieros gamos (sacred marriage) and, 3976–3977
in Hinduism
caste system and, 3996
dethroning of, 5345
enforcement of law by, 5344–5345
king as guardian of *dharma,* 2328, 5344–5345
king as *jajmān* in popular religion, 4007
semidivinity of, 5345
in Hittite religion, 5165
Kumarbi myth and, 4070
Homeric, 5166
and incarnation, 4416
in Inca society, 1362, 1363–1364, 5175–5177
in Indian religions
Cakravartin ideal, **1350–1352**
consecration and, 1956
genealogies and, 4025
Manu as first, 5678–5679
performance of, in Vijayanagara, 1806
rural traditions of, 4434
sexual activity, and power of, 3968
in Indo-European religions, 4453
gods of, comparative, 1874
horse sacrifice and, 4133
interregnum of, 5155, 5158
in Iran, 5165
in Islam, in sub-Saharan Africa, 4602–4603
in Israel, 5164–5165
in Israelite religion, 6380–6382
election and, 2744
laws on, 4732, 4737, 4739–4740
and prophets, 7436
as son of God, 4743
Temple maintained by king, 4745
jaguars identified with, 4762
in Japan, 5157, 5178, 7271–7274
emergence of, 5180
enthronement ceremony, 1514–1515
Yamato clan and, 8358
in Judaism
of God, 3542, 3548
Hosea on, 4137
in Mishnah, 10062
judgment by, 6847–6849
justice in, 5164
in Khmer religion, 5129
killing of, 5157–5159
kneeling before, 5196
in Korea, 5178, 5179
legitimacy of, 5156, 5162–5163
on Madagascar, coronation stones and, 8745–8746
in Maya society, 1358, 5175, 5798–5799
ancestors of, 5798
divine, 5798
inscriptions on, 5798, 5886–5887
souls of, 5798
in Mediterranean world, ancient, **5161–5169**
in Mesoamerica, **5172–5178**
in Mesopotamian religion, 5161–5163
divinity and, 3902, 5162, 5965, 7276–7277
goddesses's role in, 3377
hieros gamos rite and, 3976
illness of king tied to epidemic, 3825
relation to gods, 5162
sexual activity, and power of, 3968
in messianism
Jewish, 5972
South American, 5983–5984
Minoan, 5166
in modernity, 5160
monarchy distinguished from, 5154, 5156
mortification of, 6198, 8208
Mycenaean, 5166
Myth and Ritual school on, 6380–6382
mythology surrounding, 5157
"natural" religious communities and, 1865–1866
Near Eastern
ancient, **5161–5169**
goddess worship in, 3586
in Okinawan religion, 6812
origin of, 5156–5157
external origin, 5156
ritual origin, 5156
in Palestine, 5164–5165
papacy and
Gallicanism on, 3258–3259
tension between, 696–697, 3691
in Phoenician religion, 7132
prehistoric, 7385, 7386–7387
priesthood in, 7398
in primitive societies, 10065
qualifications of, 5156–5157
reverence for, in Ethiopian Church, 2860
ritual regicide, 5157–5159
in Africa, 5169, 5171
in Rome, 5167–5168, 7901
sacred, 5156, 5158, 5160
in Africa, 5169
in Aztec society, 5172–5174
in Inca society, 5175–5177
in Japan, 5180
in Maya society, 5175
sacred national communities and, 5164
in Scythian religion, 8205
separateness from general populace of, 5155
in Sinhala religion, 8411–8412
sonship and, 1399–1400
in South America, **5172–5178**
in Southeast Asian religions
devarāja (god-king) cult, 4012, 8644
semi-divine marriage narrative in, 4010
women rulers, 4011
Spanish and Portuguese colonialism and, 1695
state distinguished from, 5156
in sub-Saharan Africa, **5169–5172**
successor to, 5155
Sumerian
city of, 2810
Enlil's role in, 598
urbanization and, 1802–1803
sun symbolism and, 8836
swords and, 967–968
in Syria, 5164–5165
in Tibet
heavenly origin of, 5179–5180
pre-Buddhist, 9182–9183
tombs of, 9225
touch of, 9257–9258
and transcendence, 5159–5160
two bodies of, 5155
in Vedism
ritual coronation, 1350
royal consecration, 7816
vs. warrior, in epics, 2816
Zeus and, 3663
Kingsborough, E. K., 5941
Kingsford, Anna, 361
on Hermetism, 3952
Kingship (Hocart), 5673
Kingship, Religion and Rituals in a Nigerian Community (Olupona), 117
"Kingship from heaven," 5147
Kingship in Heaven. See also Kumarbi
in Hittite religion, 4068, 4070, 9087
"Kingship of heaven," 5148
Kingship of the God Lamma, The, in Hittite religion, 4068, 4070
Kingsley, Charles, 3361
attacks on of Newman (John Henry), 6510
in Christian Socialist movement, 5784
Maurice (Frederick Denison) and, 5784
Kings of Disaster (Simonse), 5159
Kingston, Maxine Hong, 701
Kinhin (walking meditation), 7417
K'inich Ajaw (deity), 5798
K'inich Janab Pakal (Maya king), 5798
K'inich Yax K'uk' Mo' (king of Copan dynasty), 2465, 5798
Kinirsha (Iraq), Dumuzi-Abzu as deity of, 5949
Kinjikitile (religious leader), 2571, **5181–5182,** 7443–7444
death of, 5181
Kinkhimba, initiation rites of, 5220
Kinmei (Japanese emperor), 7271
Kinnikinnick, smoking of, 8454
Ki no Tsurayuki (poet), 7215
Kinship, **5182–5186**. *See also* Ancestors; Family; Genealogy
ancestors and, 5184–5185
biological, 5182–5183
vs. social, 5182–5183
blood as substance of, 5184

body and, 5183–5184
cannibalism and, in Oceania, 1404
in clans, 5185
concept of, 5182
definition of, 5183
descent and, 5184–5185
in Yap culture, 5183
in East African religions, witchcraft and, 2570
family and, 2982
in Finno-Ugric culture, Harva (Uno) on, 3783
Fortes (Meyer) on, 5182
gender roles in, 3420
in Germanic religion, Ragnarók and, 5509
humor and, 4198
in *walāyah,* 9656
in Kongo society, 5220, 5221–5223
in Lakota religion, 5297
Lévi-Strauss (Claude) on, 8751
life-cycle rituals and, 5184
lineages and, 5185
in Melanesia, 5184
modern concepts of, 5184
morality of, extension of, 5185
in Nyakyusa religion, 6770
in Oceanic religions, 7295–7296
person and, 5183–5184
in primitive societies, 7717
Fortes (Meyer) on, 5182
revenge and, 7781
social, 5182
vs. biological, 5182–5183
in Southern African religions, rituals of, 8657–8659
Strathern (Marilyn) on, 5183–5184
in Tswana society, 7805
in Warlpiri religion, 9694, 9695
Kinsley, David, 3609, 9789
on green spirituality, 8719
Kintu (hero), 2575
Kipling, Rudyard
as Freemason, 3198
Tylor (E. B.) compared to, 363
"The White Man's Burden," 3005
Kippah (yarmulke), in Reform Judaism, 7666
Kippenberg, Hans Georg, historiography of, 4048
Kipper, 593
Kirchenrecht (Sohm), canon law in, 8507
Kircher, Athanasius, 2729
Egyptomania of, 3950
on pagan civilizations, 4040
Kirchliche Dogmatik (Barth), 6468–6469
Kirda (patrimoiety), 9694
Kirdīr, 520, 9990
Kireevskii, Ivan, **5187**
and Florenskii (Pavel), 3134
Kiremets (spirits), 1785
Kirghiz confederacy, 4492
Kiri Ammā (deity), in Sri Lankan religions, 8410
Kiribati (Micronesia)
dance in, 6007
household rituals in, 6004
myths in, 6009
creation, 6009–6010
fire in, 6012
sun and moon in, 6002, 6010
Kirirsha (deity), 3594, 3595
Kirishitan (Catholic missionaries), 4787–4789, 4791
publications of, 4812
Kirjokansi (brightly worked cover), 4379
Kirk, David, 675–676, 677–678, 679
Kirk, Geoffrey S., on *Epic of Gilgamesh,* 3487
Kirk, Kenneth E., 1455
Kirk, Robert, 2953
Kirmānī, Ḥamid al-Dīn al-, in Ismā'īlīyah, 8330–8331
Kirmānī, Ḥarb al-, Ḥanābilah and, 3763
Kirmānī Shaykhīyah, Bābī movement and, 8308
Kirsch, A. Thomas, 379
Kirshna Society. *See* International Society for Krishna Consciousness
Kirta cycle. *See* Epic of Kirta
Kīrtana (musical worship), 6282
Kirtland (Ohio), Mormons in, 6193
Kisaburō, Ueda, 6573
Kisā'ī, al-, 6736, 8952
Kish (Mesopotamia), 5947
Kishimojin (deity), 3135
Kishwar, Madhu, on women, 3321
Kisi Kaamy Gynan (ritual dance), 2396
Kiskanu (tree), 1502, 3449, 9335, 9576
Kismet (machine), 511
Kissayōjōki (Eisai), 847
Kisse ha-kavod (throne of glory), 4266
Kissing, 9258–9259
of holy objects, 9258
of holy people, 9259
osuculum infame (kiss of infamy), 8013
sacramental value of, 9259
in worship, 7343–7344
Kiss of the Yoginī (White), 7083
Kister, Menahem, 6019
Kiswah (curtain), of the Ka'bah, 5049, 7158, 7160, 7222, 9090
Kitāb akhbār al-Rustumīyīn (Ibn al-Ṣaghīr), 4583
Kitāb al-aḥkām al-sulṭānīyah (al-Māwardī), 5787
Kitāb al-akhlāq wa-al-siyar (Ibn Ḥazm), 4268
Kitāb al-amanat wa-al-I' tiqādāt, 4992–4993
Kitāb al-anwār wa'l-marāqib (al-Qirqisāni), 4992, 5085
Kitāb al-aṣnām (Ibn al-Kalbī), 4361
Kitāb al-fiṣal wa-al-niḥal (Ibn Ḥazm), 7237
Kitāb al-'Ibar (Ibn Khaldūn), 4269
traditionalism and rationalism in, 4029
Kitāb al-Isrā (Ibn al-'Arabī), 4257
Kitāb al-Kashf (Isma'ili text), Gnosticism and, 3523
Kitāb al-kharāj (Abū Yūsuf), 24
Kitāb al-khiṣāl (Ibn Bābawayhi), 4262
Kitāb al-mādarik ('Iyād), 4585
Kitāb al-Majd ('Abd al-Jabbār), 4
Kitāb al-mawāqif (al-Ījī), 4372
Kitab al-milal wa-al-nihal (al-Shahrastānī), heresiography in, 8267
Kitāb al-muḥallā (Ibn Ḥazm), 4268
Kitāb al-muqāwamāt (Suhrawardī), 4552
Kitāb al-muṭāraḥāt (Suhrawardī), 4552
Kitāb al-radd 'alā 'Anan, 4992
Kitāb al-riyāḍ wa'l-ḥadā'iq (al-Qirqisāni), 5085
Kitab al-ruh (Ibn Qayyim), soul in, 8567
Kitāb al-sab'ah (Ibn Mujāhid), 9200–9201
Kitāb al-ṣārim al-maslūl 'alā shātim al-rasūl (Ibn Taymīyah), 4277
Kitāb al-shifa' (Ibn Sīnā), 4553
Kitāb al-sīrah wa-akhbār al-a'immah (Abū Zakarīyā'), 4583
Kitāb al-ta'arruf li-madhhab ahl al-taṣawwuf (al-Kalābādhī), 5055
Kitāb al-tahdhīb fi al-tafsīr (al-Bayhaqī), 4662
Kitāb al-talwīḥāt (Suhrawardī), 4552
Kitāb al-tamhīd (Bāqillānī), 619
Kitāb al-ṭawāsīn (al-Ḥallāj)
"Anā al-ḥaqq" ("I am the Creative Truth") in, 3756
moth and candle parable in, 3757
Prophet described in, 3757
Kitāb al-tawḥīd (Ibn 'Abd al-Wahhāb), 4255
Kitāb al-tawḥīd (Ibn Bābawayhi), 4262
Kitāb al-'umdah (Ibn Rashīq), 4584
Kitāb al-umm (al-Shāfi'ī), legal system in, 8264
Kitāb al-wujūh wa-al-naẓā'ir (Muqātil), 8952
Kitāb-i 'Ahd (Bahā' Allāh), 738
Kitāb-i Aqdas (Bahā' Allāh), 737–738, 739
Kitāb-i Badī' (Bahā' Allāh), 737
Kitabi Dedem Qorqut (epic), 2814
Kitāb taḥqīq mā lil-Hind min maqbūlah lil-'aql aw mardhūlah (al-Bīrūnī), 954, 955
Ki Taesŭng, Four-Seven debate with T'oegye, 1931
Kitagawa, Joseph M., **5187–5189**
academic career of, 5188–5189
biography of, 5187–5188
Chicago approach and, 4044
classification of religions by, 1821
on *kami,* 5072
on religious experience, 7743
scholarly contributions of, 5189
Kitamura Sayo, Tenshō kōtai jingū kyō movement and, 8369
Kitamura Tōkoku, 3071, 3072
Kitans (Mongolia), 4492, 4493
Kitara people (Africa), metallurgy of, 5988
Kitaribaabo, Dominic, in Movement for the Restoration of the Ten Commandments of God, 105, 6216–6217
Kitasoo tribe (North America), on bears, 807
Kitchanukit (Thiphakorawong), 1139
Kitchen gods, in Japanese religion, 4106
Kitmān (concealment), 8999
Kitsi Manitu (supreme being), 4308
Kitsirimeghavaṇṇa (king of Sri Lanka), 1305
Kittiwutthō Phikkhu, 9097
Kiuas (stones), 801
Kivas
as artificial caves, 1469
in Pueblo religion, 6726
Kiwai people (New Guinea)
myths of, agricultural, 191
vaginal fluid beliefs of, 9907–9908
Kiwanuka, Joseph, appointed bishop, 1719
Klages, Ludwig, 732
Klaproth, Julius von, 1311
Klass, Morton, 10026
Klaus, Bruno, 9067, 9068
Klaus, Rose-Marie, 9067–9068
Klausner, Joseph, on Hillel (Jewish sage), 3982
Klawans, Jonathan, 7512, 7514
Kledonomancy, 1528
Klee, Paul
on angels, 348
on color, 1860
on creative discipline, 8702
Kleebatt, Norman, 4342

Klein, Anne, 6536
Klein, Cecelia, on Aztec autosacrifice, 4189
Klein, Isaac, *A Guide to Jewish Religious Practice,* 1964
Klein, Melanie, 7478
Kleinman, Arthur, 59, 2611
Kleitophon and Leukippe (Tatius), 3050, 3052
Klemp, Harold, Eckankar led by, 2602
Klenke, M. Amelia, 3650
Kleśa, 5095
Klimakos, John, 518
Klimkeit, Hans Joachim, 5189–5191
historiography of, 4048
Kliṣṭamanas (afflicted mentality), 9018
Klong chen Rab 'byams pa (Longchenpa), 2548, **5191–5195,** 9333
Ani Lochen and, 354
in Bhutan, 5194
death of, 5194
early years of, 5192
incarnational line of, 5194–5195
influence of, 5194–5195
reincarnation of, 5192, 5194–5195
Snying thin (Seminal Essence) system and, 7869
social and political conflicts involving, 5193–5194
teachings of, 5192–5193
visionary presence of, 5195
writings of, 5192–5193, 5194
Klor de Alva, Jorge, 5915
Klu (subterranean beings), 9183, 9185
Kluckhohn, Clyde
on culture, 2087, 2088, 5261
on illness, 6442
on *kulturkreiselehre,* 5261
on witchery, 2100
Knappert, Jan, 6977
Kneeling (posture), 5195–5196
in Christian worship, 7342, 7343
symbolism of, 7343
Knees, **5195–5196**
Knesset, Agudat Yisra'el in, 195–196
Knight, Charles F., 1189
Knight, Chris, 9706
Knight, J. Z., 6532
Knight, Richard Payne, 7085
Knights, in the Grail stories, 3649
Knights of Columbus, 3198
Knights of Labor, Gibbons's (James) defense of, 3478
Knights Templar
accusations against, 6869
Council of Vienne, 2042
Crusades and, 2077
and Freemasonry, 3196
and Solar Temple, 6554
and Temple Solaire, 9067
women in, 6763
Knitter, Paul, 9130
Knivet, Antonio, on Tupi religion, 8593
Knoche, Grace F., 7230
Knockers, 2952
Knorosov, Yuri, 5886
Knorr, Nathan Homer, 4821
Knossos (Crete)
excavation by Evans (Sir Arthur) in, 37, 38, 2894–2895, 5275
palace of, 37, 39, 41, 5275
Knots, 937, **5196–5199**. *See also* Binding
labyrinths and, 5278
of Varuṇa, 5275, 5278
Peruvian *quipus,* 1360–1361, 4410, 5197
in ropes, 5197
symbolic nature of, 5197
time computation with, 1353, 5197
Knowledge, **5199–5211**. *See also* Epistemology; Gnosis; Truth; Wisdom
in Amazonian Quechua religions, 282–283, *283*
in Australian Indigenous religions, 639, 648, 650, 689–690
of music, 6261, 6262
restricted *vs.* unrestricted, 6260–6261
al-Bājūrī on, 5059–5060
in Bambara religion, 777
Barth (Karl) on, 5208–5209
belief and, 2427
Bonaventure's theory of, 1012–1013
in Buddhism, 5200
in Mādhyamika Buddhism, 5554–5555
in Sarvāstivāda school, 5554
mirror, 6064
threefold, 7357
Bultmann (Rudolf) on, 5209
in Cartesianism, 5205–5206
chance and unknowability, 1528–1529
Chantepie de la Saussaye on, 1531
in Christianity, 5202
Comenius's pansophia philosophy, 1863
Comte (Auguste) on, 5206
in Confucianism, 5201
conscience as shared knowledge, 1944
in *Dao de jing,* 1574
in Daoism, 5201
disclosure of, in initiation rituals, 4481
in dualism, 5207–5208
in Egyptian religion, 3508
eightfold path and, 2739
encyclopedia understood as, 2782
epistemology and, 5210–5211
faith and, 2426, 2958–2959
female personification of, 3019
gnosis as, pre-Christian, 3507–3508
in Gnosticism, 5202–5203
of God (*See also* Revelation)
in afterlife, 157
agnōstos theos and, 181–183
Aristotle on, 6960, 6961, 6962
in Calvin, 1375–1376
Gersonides' theory of, 3462, 3549, 6962
in Islam, 3563, 3565
in Judaism, 3462, 3549, 7776–7777
Kant (Immanuel) on, 7776
in logical positivism, 5499
nature in, 6432
Plato on, 6960, 6961
Spinoza (Baruch) on, 8684
Thomas Aquinas on, 7775–7776
via negativa, 6990, 9587
of good, Socrates on, 8503
of good and evil, Spinoza (Baruch) on, 8684
of Greek Fathers, 5203
in Greek religion and mythology, 5201
Hegel (G. W. F.) on "absolute knowing," 3894
in Hinduism, 5200–5201
heart knowledge in, 3881
in Pratyabhijñā Saivism, 8048
in Śaivism, 8417–8418
Rāmānuja on, 7615
ritual and, 9822
in human immortality, 4895
in Candomblé, 123
in India, 5199–5200
in Vedānta, 5200–5201
in Islam, 5203–5204
empirical, 3565
modernism and, 6097
purity of sources of, 6097
types of, 3565
Jaspers (Karl) on, 5209
in Judaism, 5201–5202
Kant (Immanuel) on, 5077, 5206
of Latin church fathers, 5203
Locke (John) on, 5496
in monism, 5207
moral principles, 1454
in mystical union, 6335, 6337
of Native American Indians, ancient, 6425–6427
natural wisdom *vs.* revealed truth, 5202
in Neo-Confucianism, Lu Xiangshan on, 5541–5542
neuroepistemology on, 6491
oral *vs.* written, 6842
Origen on, 6889
Paracelsus's theory of, 6981
paradox of, 6989–6990
in philosophy, 2818–2819
of primal peoples, 5199
a priori *vs.* a posteriori, Kant (Immanuel) on, 5077
in Protestantism, 5205, 5206–5207
Pythagoreans on, 5201
recollection of (anamnesis), 309–316
Plato on, 309–311, 315–316, 5990
religion, kinds of knowledge about, 8761
in Roman Catholicism, 5205, 5209–5210
sainthood, path to, 8037
Schleiermacher (Friedrich) on, 8164
in Scholasticism, 5204–5205, 8175
of self, through asceticism, 527
Spinoza (Baruch) on, 8684
subjectivity *vs.* objectivity of, 6425
supreme beings, unknowability of, 8868
three-state law of, positivism and, 7339–7340
tradition as source of, 9267, 9268
of transcendent, problem of, Otto (Rudolf) on, 4096–4097
transformative, 2361–2362, 2363
tree of, 9335, 9577
as virtue, Plato on, 310
Wang Yangming on, 9674
of water, 9702
in West African religions, 9719–9720
written books and, 6839
in Yoga, 9895–9896
in Yurupary cult, 9919
in *Zhuangzi,* 9969
Zhu Xi on, 9974
Knowledge, Belief, and Witchcraft (Sodipe and Hallen), 10032
Knowledge and Secrecy in an Aboriginal Religion (Keen), 648
Know-Nothing Party, as anticult movement, 395
Knox, Elizabeth, 3084
Knox, John, **5211–5212**
ecclesiology of, 1774
museum of, 6245
Reformed Church of Scotland and, 1692, 7281
Knox, Ronald
on enthusiasm, 2805–2806, 2808
on religious experience, 7739
on revival and renewal activities, 7788
Knutson, Karl, on Kallu institution, 2573
Kō (religious confraternities)
in Edo period, 8364
Mount Fuji and, 8364
pilgrimage and, 8362
Ko, Dorothy, 3346

Kōan, 1277, 9946
meditation, 1292–1293, 2306, 2386, 6987–6988
in Rinka monasteries, 9947
as sacred text, 5311
zazen and, 6987
Kōan Zen
Hakuin and, 3741–3742
lists as canonical, 1407
revelation and sacred time in, 7988
Koati Island, 5291, 5292
Kōben, **5213**
Kōbō Daishi. *See* Kūkai
Kobold, der, 2951
Kobunjigaku (school of ancient words and phrases), Ancient Learning movement and, 1928
Koch-Grünberg, Theodor, on jaguars, 8291
Kochi (India), Jews in, 5005
Kodiak bear, 807
Kodi religion (Indonesia), communal performances of healing in, 3815
Kōdō Ōmoto, 6825
Kōen (Buddhist monk), 9079
Koenig, Harold, 7487
Koep, Leo, on heavenly book concept, 8195
Koepgen, Georg, on androgynes, 341
Koerbagh, Adrian, Spinoza (Baruch) and, 8682
Koestler, Arthur, 6437, 7194
on humor, 4202
Kōfukuji order, Jōdoshū Buddhism, attacks on, 4120
Kofuku no Kagaku, 6574–6575
Kofun period (Japan), 4780–4781
Kogaku. *See* Ancient Learning
Kogakusensei bunshu (Itō Jinsai), 4753
Koghi religion (South America), creation myth in, 8587
Kogidō (School of Ancient Meanings)
Confucianism and, 1928
founder of, 4752
Kogi people (Columbia)
cosmology of, 2010–2011
priests *(mama)* of, 2011
Kogoshūi (Inbe clan chronicle), 4811
Nihonshoki in, 4802
Kohamin, 5419–5420. *See also* Levites
Kohen (priest), 7399
Kohen, Sha'ul ha-, 17
Kohler, Kaufmann, **5214,** 7671
on sin and the body, 8557
Kohn, Livia, 1638
Kōhō Kennichi, Musō Sōseki and, 6316
Ko Hung. *See* Ge Hong
Kohut, Heinz, 7478, 7484
Koi priestesses, prostitution by, 3969
Kojiki (Japanese text)
age of the *kami* in, 7978–7979
ancient poetry style preserved in, 7214
compilation of, 4783, 4809–4811
creation myths in
androgyny in, 2555
water in, 9698
descent into the underworld in, 2298, 4755
as history, 4801
imperial system in, 7271
Izanagi and Izanami in, 2298, 4754–4755
kami stories in
on invisibility of *kami,* 5071
on multiplicity of *kami,* 5072
on myth of Japanese state, 5073
in modern period, 4813
Motoori Norinaga and, 5215, 8365
mythology in, 4800
as national memory, 4806–4808
Ninigi stories in, 5180
tears in, 9026
theater in, 2454
time in, 4807
translation of, 4812
triads in, 9348
Yamato Takeru in, 9868–9869
Koji ruien (Classified collection of old documents), 4813
Kōjō (Buddhist monk), 995, 9078
Kokan Shiren (Buddhist monk), 995
Köke Möngke Tengri (deity), 6142
Kōken (Japanese empress), 1242
Kokka Shintō, 2639
Kokkinakis, Minos, 6570
Kokoro (soul, spirit)
Ishida Baigan on, 4551
Kamo no Mabuchi on, 5074–5075
Kokoschka, Oskar, 2475
Kokuchūkai (Pillar of the nation society), 6608
Kokugaku (Japanese intellectual movement), 2640, 4812, 4813, **5214–5216,** 7274
folklore studies and, 8778
Motoori Norinaga in, 6211
Shintō and, 8364–8365
Kokuheisha (shrines), 7411
Kokutai (national polity), 4813, 7273–7274
Kokutai no hongi, 1336, 4813
Kokyanguruti. *See* Spider Woman
Kolakowski, Leszek, 9072
Kolelim (institution of study), 9885
Kol Ha-neshamah (prayer book series), 7638–7639
Kolig, Erich, 671, 672
Kollyvades movement, 6621
Kol Nidrei (all vows), in Yom Kippur services, 7929
Kol puping. See Family guardian spirits
Kolyo (deity), 4456
Komata Chettiar merchants, Beeri Chettiars, competiton with, 1806–1807
Komba (deity), 7524
Kōmei Party (Japan), Sōka Gakkai and, 8509
Komenský, Jan Amos. *See* Comenius, Johannes Amos
Komi (Zyrians), 3105
Komi religion and society, 468, **5216–5219**
cosmogony of, 5217
cults in, 5218–5219
Khanty religion influenced by, 5125
Mansi religion influenced by, 5125
Komo (Bambara society), 777
Komokums (deity), 6713
Komparu Zenchiku, 2456
Kōmyō (Japanese emperor), 1175
Kōmyō (light), Shinran on, 8355
Kōmyō Shingon (Clear Light Mantra), in Shingon Buddhism, 8351
Konākamana (buddha), 1066
Konarak (India), sculptures at, 7042
Konde people (Africa), sky divinities of, 6438
Kondō (Buddha image hall), 9048
Kondoy (mythic figure), 5937
Konfuzianismus und Taoismus. See Religion of China, The (Weber)
Kong Fuzi. *See* Confucius
Kongjiao (Kong teaching), 1917
repudiation of, 1922
Kong Li (Boyu), 1935
Kongōkai ritual, in Shingon training, 8351
Kongo religion and society (Central Africa), **5219–5222.** *See also* Central Bantu religions
Christianity in
Kimbanguist movement, 1720
missions, 1718
Christianization of, 5221
cosmogony of, 2960
cosmology, 2001–2002
cults of affliction in, 62–63
current beliefs and practices, 5220–5221
history of, 5220–5221
kingship in, 5170
messianism in, 5973
minkisi in, 3043
new religions, 1511
spirit possession in, 67
Kongōsatta, 9515
Kong Qiu. *See* Confucius
Kong sprul Blo gros mtha' yas (Kongtrul Lodro Taye), 1223, **5222–5224,** 7869, 9333
Kongtrul Lodro Taye. *See* Kong sprul Blo gros mtha' yas
Kongzi. *See* Confucius
Koni (mythic figure), 776
Königsberg university, Glasenapp (Helmuth von) at, 3497
Konjaku monogatari (Buddhist folk tales), 4798
Konjin (deity), 5225, 6824
Konkani. *See* Bene Israel
Konkō Daijin, 5224
Shintō and, 8367
Konkōkyō (Konko religion), **5224–5226,** 6573
founding of, 5073–5074, 9312
relation to Shintō, 5225
Shintō and, 8367
teachings of, 5225
Konner, Melvin, materialism of, 6056–6057
Kono (Bambara society), 777
Konoe Ayamaro (Fumimaro), 6637
Ko-no-hana-sa-kura-hime (fairy), 3135
Konsing Ōjka (deity). *See* Holy City Old Man
Konstan, David, 3055
Kontakia (poetic form), 7205
Kontakion, 1534
Konti Vo'o (stations of the cross), 7045
Kony, Joseph, 106
Kooch (deity), 9029, 9030
Kook, Avraham Yitsḥaq, **5226–5228**
and contemporary Hasidism, 9382
in expansionism, 6904
on freedom, 5226–5227
on God, 3551–3552
on holiness, 5227
and messianism, 5978
and Qabbalah, 5226, 7535
on repentance, 5226
writings of, 5226
Zionism movement and, 5226, 5227
Zionism of, 4906, 9981
Koori people (Australia), 646–647
dance by, 646–647
Kopernik, Mikołaj. *See* Copernicus, Nicolaus
Kopp, Hermann, 252
Koppers, Wilhelm
on mystery religions, 6328
Schmidt (Wilhelm) and, 8168
on supreme beings, 8877
Kopytoff, Igor, on ancestor worship, 322
Koraḥ, as author of *Psalms,* 7461
Korè (Bambara society), 777

Kore (deity). *See also* Persephone
in Eleusinian mysteries, 6329
as virgin, 9603
Korea and Korean religions, **5228–5237**
in African movements, modern, 109
alchemy in, 2189
ancestor worship in, 324
Buddhism, **1169–1174,** 5230–5232
Amitābha in, 292
buddhas in, 1171
celebrations in, 1306, 1308
Central Asian Buddhism and, 1170, 1171
Chan Buddhism, 1172
Chinese Buddhism and, 1170, 1171, 1172
Chŏng's challenge of, 1930
Chosŏn Buddhism, 1172–1173, 5232
communism and, 1098, 1100
cosmology, 5232
decline of, 1095
Hwaŏm (Huayan) school of, 4146
Hwarang movement in, 1171
iconography of, 4329
incense offering in, 4419
Indian Buddhism and, 1170
and Japanese Buddhism, 1170, 1173
Japan influenced by, 4782
Koryŏ Buddhism, 1171, 1172
law and, 5349
literature of, 1254–1255
Maitreya in, 1170, 1171, 5621
missions and, 1170, 1173
modern, 1173
monasteries, 1095, 1170, 1171, 1173
mortuary rites, 5231
music in, 6296, 6297–6298
nirvāṇa in, 6631
nuns in, 6757, 6761
politics and, 7260
spread of, 1170, 4391
as state religion, 1170–1171
studies on, 1248–1249
temples of, 9048
Three Kingdoms Buddhism, 1170–1171
Tibetan Buddhism and, 1171
Ŭich'ŏn in, 9436
Ŭisang in, 9437
Wŏnhyo in, 9796–9797
Ch'ŏndogyo, **1647–1648**
Christianity, 1727
music in, 6296
persecution of, 5234
Protestantism, 5234
Roman Catholicism, 1648–1649, 5233–5234
transmission of, 5233–5234
communism in, 5235
Confucianism, **1929–1933,** 5232–5233
music in, 6296–6297
Neo-Confucianism in, Sŏ Kyŏngdŏk, role of, **8510**
scholarship, development of, 1930–1933
Tasan's theistic interpretation of, 1648, 1649
Yi Neo-Confucian polity, founding of, 1930
Yi T'oegye in, 9891–9892
Yi Yulgok in, 9892–9893
Daoism, 2189
dreams in, 2489
drama in, 2453, 2454, 2455
drums in, 7036
dynasties in (*See specific dynasties*)
hwarang (flower boys) and homosexuality in, 4117
Japanese rule of, 5233
kingship in, 5178, 5179
magic in, 5592, 5593–5594
Minjung theology, 5236, 5441–5442
modern era of, 5233–5236
music in, **6292–6299**
new religious movements in, with Japanese origins, 6574
Sandae (masked drama) in, 4209
shamanism in (*See also* Musok)
charisma and, 1548
consecration in, 4105
kut ritual, and humor, 4208
women in, 5235
Sirhak (Practical Learning) movement, 1648, 1649, 1932–1933
spirit possession in, 2140
state formation of, 5228–5230
tigers in, 4208
women in, as shamans, 5235
in Yamato (Japanese) kingdom, 4781
Korean War
American prisoners during, brainwashing programs of, 1030, 1031
Japan affected by, 4792
Koreeda, Hirokazu, 3097
Korekore people (Zimbabwe), myths of, 97
Kore Kosmou, translations of, 3952
Koresh, David, 1036, 1037, 1038, **5237–5239**
Branch Davidians under, 6553–6554, 6561
child abuse allegations against, 6541
as messiah, 6547
raid on Branch Davidians and, 6518
sexual relationships of, 6516, 6517, 6541, 6554
teachings of, 6548
Kores Tōrem (folklore figure), 5120
Koriak religion (Arctic), 468. *See also* Shamanism; Siberia and Siberian religions
animal ceremonialism in, 471
New Year ceremonies of, 6591
occupational shamanism in, 8282
trickster myths of, 472
whale feasts of, 6655
Koriwn (historian), 5763
on Sahak Parthev, 8026
Kornáros, Vitzéntzos, *Erotókritos,* 3053–3054
Kornfield, Walter, on hierodouleia (sacred prostitution) in Israelite religion, 3967
Koropata (feeding funnel), in Maori religion, vol. 13 color insert
Kőrösi Csoma, Sándor, 1311, 9188–9189, 9190
Korupira (deity), as "lord of the beasts," 2091, 5515, 8580
Koryŏ dynasty (Korea)
Buddhism in, 1171, 1172, 1255, 5231
Maitreye in, 5621
Confucianism in, 1929–1930
and drama, 2455
Daoism in, 2189
musok in, 5228
Kośa. See Abhidharmakośa (Vasubandhu)
Kōsai (Buddhist monk), 4938
Kosambi, D. D., on Paśupati (Lord of the Animals), 8039
Kośar Tōrem (folklore figure), 5120
Kose (spirits), 7524
Kōseikai, Risshō, 3156
Kōsen (Buddhist teacher), Suzuki (D. T.) and, 8885
Koshchei Bessmertnyi, 727
Kosher. *See Kashrut*
Kōshin day, 2188
Koshi no Obito. *See* Gyōgi
Kōshō. *See* Kūya
Koshōgatsu (Little New Year), 2411
Kosinski, Jerzy, 3059
Koskinen, Yrjö, 3104
Koslowski, Peter, Gnosticism and, 3527
Kosmas Aitolos, **5239**
Kosrae (Micronesia)
colonialism in, 6002
geology of, 6002
government of, 6002
grand rituals in, 6006–6007
Kōtai (poet), 8974
Kotani Kimi
Maitreya identified with, 5622
Reiyūkai Kyōdan founded by, 7861, 7862
Kotani Sanshi Rokugyō, on Mount Fuji, 8364
Kota people (Gabon), 4302
Kothar (deity), 7129
in Canaanite religion, 1384, 1387, 1388
Kotharatu (Wise Women), in Canaanite religion, 1384, 1395, 1396
Kothar-wa-Hasis
Baal helping, 724
in Canaanite religion, 1384, 1391, 1392
Kotler, Aharon, **5239–5240**
Koto (musical instrument), 6300
Kotodama (magico-religious power), 7214
Kōṭṭe kingdom, four gods and four shrines in, 8411
Koua, Mount, 6214
Koumen (initiation ceremony), 3228–3229
Kou Qianzhi, 1598, 2183, 2194, 4333, **5240–5241,** 5317, 7413, 8994–8995
Cui Hao and, 5240
Laozi's appearance to, 5240
systematization of Daoism by, 7719
Kouros (figure), 4322
Kourotrophos (nursing mother), 2270
Kourouma, Ahmadou, 3088
Kourtesios, Georgios. *See* Scholarios, Gennadios
Kouyaté, Dani, 3098
Kou-zaun nats (spirits), 1330
Kowtow, 1642
Kōya. *See* Kūya
Kōya, Mount
identified with Pure Land of Bliss, 8350
pilgrimage to, 9835
in Shingon Buddhism, 4784, 8352
Koyemshi (dancers), 2461–2462
Ko-yi Buddhism, 5485
Koyukon people (Alaska), conservation ethic of, 2618
Kōzanji (Buddhist monastery), 5213
Kōzen gokokuron (Eisai), 2741
Kra (soul), in Akan religion, 214
Kracauer, Siegfried, 3101
Kracke, Waud, 2483, 2487
Kraemer, David, 6021
Kraemer, Hendrik, **5241–5242,** 7452
comparative theology of, 9130
writings of, 5241
Kraemer, Jörg, 4716
Kraemer, Ross, 3352
Krafft-Ebing, Richard, 3046
Krahmer, Gerhard, 4298

Kraho people (Brazil), 8629–8630. *See also* Ge religions
earth in death of, 2559–2560
messianism of, 5985
Krama, Abhinavagupta on, 9
Krama Śaivism, **8045–8046**
in Kashmir, 8047
kaula style of worship of Kālī in, 4020, 8047–8048
Kramastotra (Abhinavagupta), 9
Krämer, H. J., 182
Kramer, Samuel Noah, 2538, 2962, 2999
archaeological research of, 455
on *Epic of Gilgamesh,* 3486
Kramrisch, Stella, **5242–5243**
on Hindu art, 501
on Hindu temples, 9038
Krappe, Alexander, 3141
Kratophany (appearance of a supernatural power)
Eliade (Mircea) on, 7346
as form of hierophany, 3972
sacred place and, 1504
Kraus, F. A., 5963, 5964
Kraus, Paul, 5586
Krause, K. F., 6963
Kremer, Alfred von, 3634
Kremmerz, Giuliano (Ciro Formisano)
Frantellanza Terapeutica e Magica di Myriam and, 8252
on Hermetism, 3951
Kremser, Manfred, 10028
Kretschmer, Paul, 3466
Kreutzer Sonata (Tolstoy), 9221
Kreutzwald, Reinhold, 3111
Krieger, Dolores, therapeutic touch healing and, 3850–3851
Kriegsmann, Wilhelm Christoph, on Hermetism, 3949
Kripal, Jeffrey, 7479
Kripal, Jeffrey J., on Ramakrishna, 7613–7614
Krippner, Stanley, 560
on religious experience, 7747
Kris, Ernst, 7476
Krishna. *See* Kṛṣṇa
Krishna, Gopi, 5266
Krishnamurti, Jiddu, **5243–5246**
on attention, 604
Besant (Annie) sponsoring, 9143
charisma of, 1549
lectures of, 5245
as Maitreya, 845, 5244, 5245
as messiah, 6547
in Order of the Eastern Star, 9143
psychic experiences of, 5245
schools of, 5245
as World-Teacher, 844, 845, 5244, 5245
Krishnamurti Foundation, 5245
Krishna Society. *See* International Society for Krishna Consciousness
Krishnaswami, Arcot, on human rights, 5363
Kriss, Rudolf, 4718
Kriss-Heinrich, Hubert, 4718
Kristallnacht riots, Nazism and, 4085
Kristensen, W. Brede, 978, **5246–5247**
classification of religions by, 1820
on phenomenology of religion, 7086–7087, 7090
on rituals, 7837
on sacrifice, 7845
Kristeva, Julia, 741, 3027
In the Beginning Was Love, 3028
and feminist theology, 3035
and gender studies, 3314
on Mary, 5755–5756
theorization of abjection by, 3029
Kristiania Bymission, 7029
Kriti (musical composition), 6279, 6281
Kritik der evangelischen Geschichte der Synoptiker (Bauer), 804
Kritische Gesamtausgabe (Schleiermacher), theology in, 8160
Kritische Wälder (Herder), Homer in, 3918
Krive krivaitis (high priest), 767, 774
Krivis (high priest), 765
Kriyā (action), 9507
Kriyā Tantras, 1215–1216, 1217
Kṛkara (breath), 1043, 7363
Krochmal, Avraham, on Spinoza (Baruch), 8685
Krochmal, Naḥman, **5247–5248,** 7107, 9238
on *Wissenschaft des Judentums,* 4902
Krodha (anger), 748
Kroeber, A. L., 475, 6671
on Chumash Indians, 9228
on culture, 2087, 2088
on secret societies, 574
Krohn, Julius, 3113
Krohn, Kaarle, 474, 3112
Haavio (Martti) and, 3723
Harva (Uno) and, 3783
Kromanti Dance, in Caribbean, 1436
Krom Luang Prichit Prichakon, 3077
Kronia (festival), 6864–6865
Kronos (deity)
Astarte and, 562
bull-roarer as symbol of, 1320
castration of Ouranos by, 1450
deposed by Zeus, 9952
Kumarbi compared to, 4231
and Ouranos, 986
sickle of, 967
Kṛṣṇa (deity), **5248–5251**. *See also* Mahābhārata
Arjuna and, 487, 852–853, 854, 2317, 2321, 5249, 5268, 7553
bhagavān, 1346
as guide to *mokṣa,* 854, 6116–6117
as Māyōn (Māyavan), 4434
Balarāma paired with, 743
Bengali devotion to, 826
in *bhakti,* 9572
bhakti synthesis and, 3998, 4000–4002
birth of, 952
as both human and divine, 8036
as *brahman,* 5252, 5253–5254
Braj Bhāṣā poetry devoted to, 3984
Caitanya and, 826
celebration of, 2368–2369
celibacy and, 1476
as child, 1568, 5249, 5250
creation and, 5447
cult of, 5250
dances devoted to, 2136, 2137, 5250
devotion to, 859, 2320 (*See also* International Society for Krishna Consciousness)
Caitanya on, 7354
in Vaiṣṇavism, 4428
Sūrdās, poetry of, 8881–8882
as divine child, 2983
on divine love, 8706
as divine lover, 5249
dramas celebrating life of, 2436, 2448, 2449–2450
erotic devotional poetry to, in saint-singer tradition, 4005
erotic nature of, 5249, 5252
festivals for, 5250
free from desire, 2305
on gambling, 3263, 3266
games and, 3266
gift giving and, 3482
history of, 5248–5249
humanism and domestication of, 827
iconography of, 4325, 5248–5249, vol. 2 color insert
in *Gītagovinda,* 4819–4820
in *śuddhādvaita,* 9518
in Vaiṣṇavaism, 5248
Janmāṣṭamī (birthday) festival of, performance of poetry at, 3985
līlā and, 5455–5458
in *mantras,* 5678
in Marathi religions, 5696–5697
meditation on, 5819
milkmaids and, 854, 5249, 5250, 5252
Mirabai's devotion to, 6048
Mīrā Bāī's devotion to, 859
music and, 6280
origins of, 5248–5249
poetry for, 5250, 5252, 5253, 7211, 8974, 8977
as protector of *dharma,* 854
in puppet theater, 2453
Rādhā and
equal status of, 3608
erotic liaison, 4444
love of, 5250, 5252, 5253–5254, 7593, 7594
poetry on, 7211
reincarnated as cow, 359
rituals of, 5250
rural tales of, 4434
on salvation, three ways to, 4001
shape shifting of, 8303
supremacy of, 5249
as Supreme Being, 4751
in *Bhagavadgītā,* 853, 854
in Swaminarayan movement, 8891
as thief, 5250
on time, 2017
Vaiṣṇava *bhakti* cult and, 9500
Viṣṇu as, 708, 4415, 5248, 5251, 7501
Vṛndāvana and, 9644–9645
as youth, 5249–5250
Kṛṣṇa Bhagavadism, 9504
Kṛṣṇa-Caitanya. *See* Caitanya
Kṛṣṇa-Caitanya-caritāmṛta, Caitanya in, 1346
Kṛṣṇacaritra (Bankimcandra), 827
Kṛṣṇa Kavirāja (Bengali writer), 826
Caitanya in, 1346
Kṛṣṇa Gopāla, 5249, 9499
līlā and, 5455, 5456
as supreme being, 5249
Kṛṣṇaism, **5251–5255,** 9499
Brndavan and, 5253–5254
early, 5251
in northern India, 5252–5253
regional forms of, 5253
in southern India, 5251–5252
Kṛṣṇa-karṇāmṛta (Vilvamaṅgala), 5252
Kṛṣṇarājī (Black Fields), in Jain cosmology, 2025
Kṛṣṇattam (dance drama), 2448
Kṛṣṇa Yarjurveda (Veda), 9551–9552, 9554
Kṛtayuga (period of time)
dharma in, 6983
in Purāṇic cosmology, 2018, 2019
as paradise, 6983
Kṛttivāsa (Bengali poet), 825, 827
Kṛtyakalpataru (Hindu text), 7169
Krūgis (deity), 770
Krupp, Edwin C., on Egyptian temples, 8734
Krusche, Rolf, 6671
Kruschev, Nikita, Russian Orthodox Church under, 7944

Kruse, Albert, on Pura (deity), 8577
Krywyen (crooked), 774
Kryžius (vertical post), 775
Kṣaṇikavāda (momentariness), Sautrāntika doctrine of, 8119
Kṣatriya (warrior class), 9522–9523
as *männerbund,* 9684
authority of, 7254
cakravartin ideal and, 1351
in caste system, 3996
development as class, 3990
Indra as supreme god of, 4467
initiation of, 7815
in Kurukṣetra, 5268
king as *jajmān* and, 4007
social duties of, 2329–2330, 5289
Kṣemarāja, 9
Kṣetrapal (guardian of the field and womb), 4435, 4436
Kṣitigarbha *(bodhisattva),* **5255–5256**
in Central Asian Buddhism, 1079
in China, 5255
in Chinese Buddhism, 1079, 1162
delaying entry into *nirvāṇa,* 7408
iconography of, 5256
in India, 5255
in Japan (Jizō), 2410, 3155, 5255–5256
at Nakayama-dera temple, 3869
pearl as symbol of, 7024
in Tibet, 5255
varieties in cults of, 9838
Ktahandowit (spirit), 6680
Kū (deities, Hawaiian)
Kū-moku-hāli'i as forest god, 3798
overview of, 3798–3799
priests of, 3796
Ku (deity, Chinese), as model emperor, 1627
Kū (deity, Polynesian), in creation myths, 7313–7314
Kuai (culture hero), origin of disease and, 3809
Kuan wu-liang-shou-fo ching. See Amitāyur-dhyāna sūtra
Kuan-yin *(bodhisattva),* 4329
lotus associated with, 5520
Kubaba (deity). *See also* Cybele
as Great Mother, 1451
as Lady of the Animals, 5280
Phrygian Mother goddess, similarity to, 2109
Kuba religion. *See* Central Bantu religions
Kublai Khan, 1603
concept of dual Buddhist world state and, 1645
and Daoism, 2186, 2203
invasion of China by, 4494
Nichiren's response to, 6604
shamanism under, 6141
spiritual preceptor of, 1225
Kubler, George, 457, 4297, 5943
Kubo Kakutarō, 5622
Reiyūkai Kyōdan founded by, 7861–7862
Kubrā, Najm al-Dīn, **5256–5258,** 9616
successors of, 5257
tafsīr of, 5257
writings of, 5256–5257
Kubrawī Ṣūfī order, 5256
in Central Asia, 4621
in China, 4635
establishment of, 9006
in South Asia, 4647
Kubrick, Stanley, 3100
Kūbu (fetus), in Mesopotamian belief, 8537
Küchlüg (Naiman leader), 4493
Kūčios, 328
Kudurru (boundary-stone inscriptions), oath/curse formula and, 2102
Kufa (Iraq), school of law in, 5547
Kufan revolts, Shiism and, 8320–8321
Kufic calligraphy, development of, 1372–1373
Kufr (rejection), 4399
Kugel, James, 6019, 6020
Kugu Sorta movement, 5710–5711
Kuhlman, Kathryn, 7712
Kuhn, Adalbert, 3458, 4460
on supreme beings, 8875
Kuhn, Thomas S., 4459, 4723, 5499, 6057
on deconstruction, 2246
Kuiji (Buddhist monk), **5258–5259**
Asaṅga and, 517
Faxiang school and, 1577, 1600
Sthiramati on, 8739
Kuiper, F. B. J., on Vedic mythology, 9559
Kuji, Mount, 5179
Kujika (song cycles), 6261
Kujō (priest), 7412
Kuk (deity), in Egyptian pantheon, 2704
Kūkai (Buddhist monk), 1176
and *maṇḍalas,* 5644
as buddha, 1068
on enlightenment, 6632
Esoteric Buddhism studied by, 9075, 9077, 9078
as founder of Shingon school, 1177, 1214, 1217, 1243
imperial favor for, 4784–4785
Japanese poetry influenced by, 7215
on Maitreya, 5622
on *mantras,* 5310
on meditation, 1294
on Mahāvairocana, iconography of, 5608
Saichō and, 8030
Shingon, founding of, 8349–8350
texts collected by, 4809
tomb of, 8352
on universal buddha-nature, 2629
Kukeōn, 803
in Eleusinian mysteries, 2752, 2770
Kuki tribe, Jewish conversion of, 5007
Ku Klux Klan
as anticult movement, 395
as secret society, 7719, 8213
Kukn (deity), 9030, 9031
Kuksu cult (North America), 6717, 6719
Kukukuku myth (Papuan), hair symbolism in, 3739
Kukulcan (deity). *See also* Quetzalcoatl
Maya calendar and, 1359
K'uk'ulkan (deity), 2464
K'uk'ulkan (quetzal-feathered serpent), 9222–9223
Kul' (deity), in Komi religion, 5217
Kul (folklore figure), 5119
Kuladevatās (or *kuldevatas,* lineage deities)
festivals for, 4018
as impure gods, 4006
Kularatne, Patrick de Silva, 5624–5625
Kula ring, of Trobriand Islanders, 6137
Kularnava Tantra, Parā Śakti in, 4020
Kulcsar, Zsuzsanna, on opioid-mediated attachment processes, 8278
Kulīna castes, 1029
Kulina religion (Brazil), transformation and metamorphosis in, 2012
Kulin religion (Australia), deities
Bunjil, 1471
deus otiosus, 2310
Kulitta (deity), in Hittite religion, 4071
Kuloscap (deity), shape shifting of, 8301
Kulp, Daniel, 1635
Külpe, Oswald, on psychology of religion, 7474
Kultrūn (drum), 7036
Kultur, German approach to religion and, 1872
Kulturkampf, 1693
Kulturkreiselehre (doctrine of culture circles), **5259–5262**
African religions in, 114
methodological debate in, 5261–5263
Schmidt (Wilhelm) on, 8876
Schmidt's (Wilhelm) contributions to, 5260–5261
Kulturwissenschaftliche Bibliothek Warburg (KBW), 9689–9691
Kulu (spiritual power), 7524
Kuma (deity), in Yaruro religion, 8579
Kumai, Kei, 3097
Kuma people (New Guinea), gardens of, 3281
Kumaphari (deity), as jaguar god, 8581–8582
Kumāra (deity), in Tamil religions, as Murukaṉ, 6240
Kumāra Gupta I, 1115
Kumārāja (Buddhist teacher), Klong chen Rab 'byams pa (Longchenpa) as student of, 5192
Kumārajīva (Buddhist monk), 1164, **5262–5264**
Buddhist translations by, 1147, 1236, 1246, 1266, 1291, 5262, 5263, 5555–5556
in Mādhyamika Buddhism, 5555–5556
and Sengzhao, 1301
Sengzhao and, 1576, 8228
transmission of *Sanlun* school to China by, 1596
Kumārapāla (Indian king), Jainism under, 4766
Kumārasambhava (Kālidāsa), 9346
Kumarbi (deity), 2311, 9087
myth of
Enuma elish, similarities with, 4231
Hurrian religion and, 4230, 4231–4232
kingship in, 4070
Ouranos narrative, similarities with, 1450–1451, 4231
Kumari (deity), as virgin, 9605
Kumārila, on atheism, 580
Kumazawa Banzan, **5264**
writings of, 5264
Kumbhaka (breathing), 1044
Kumbha Melā festival, **5264–5266,** 7862
Prayāga as location of, 3987
Kumbha Parva. *See* Kumbha Melā
Kumbha Yoga. *See* Kumbha Melā
Kumbi Saleh (Ghana), 4601
Kumbum (stupa), 9052
Kume Kunitak, on Shotoku Taishi, 8374
Kumiks (Caucasus), 4614
Kumina ancestral cult, in Jamaica, 1435
Kümmel, Werner G., on kingdom of God, 5152
Kumu (priest), in Tukanoan religion, 8623
Kumulipo chant, 5783
Kun (earth), 1583, 1584
Küna (king of Chiangmai), 1137
Kunal Cakrabarti, 826
Kunanbayev, Abai, 4623
Kunapipi (Berndt), 951
Kunapipi (mythic figure)
cult of
history of study of, 683
sexuality in, 8239
Gadjeri as, 3249–3250
Kundakunda (Jain teacher), 4770
Kuṇḍalinī, **5266–5267**
cakras and, 1348, 1349, 5266
dangers of, 5266

in Healthy, Happy, Holy Organization (3HO), 3877, 3878
in Holy Order of MANS, 4102
in *Haṭhayoga,* 3795
meditation in, 5820
percussive breathing in, 7038
Kuṇḍalinīyoga, 5266–5267
in Hindu Tantrism, 4003
Kun dga' legs pa, 1232
Kundurī, ʿamīd al-Mulk al-, 6640
Küng, Hans, 2657
comparative theology of, 9130
on kingdom of God, 5152
on religion's role in globalization, 3499, 3502
Kung-an (enigmatic verses), 1096
Kung fu, development of, 8724
!Kung San
duality in, 5135
shamanism of, 83
spirit possession in, 2140
!Kung tribe, birth in, 950
K'ung-tzu. *See* Confucius
K'ung-tzu chia yü, 946
Kunikida Doppo, 3071–3072
Kuni no miyatsuko (provincial governor), 7410
Kuni no Tokotachi no Mikoto (deity)
in Ōmotokyō, 6824–6825
Ise Outer Shrine and, 4801
Kunio, Yanagita, on folklore and humor in Japan, 4208
Kūnī principle, in Ismāʿīlīyah, 8326
Kunlun (mountain), 1501
Kŭnšeng Ĭki (deity). *See* Holy City Old Man
Kunstwollen (artistic intention), 4298
Kuntianaks (ghosts), in Sudanese religion, 8850
Kuntur Qutu (Mountain of the Condor), 6886
Kunz, Dora, therapeutic touch healing and, 3850–3851
Kuo Hsiang. *See* Guo Xiang
Kuo Xiang, on *li,* 5431
Kuper, Adam, 6369
Kupyamika (ceremony), 817
Kura (deity), 2597, 2598
Kuraishi Atsuko, 3347
Kurawas (Hindu figure), in puppet theater, 2452
Kurdiji (ritual cycle), 9695
Kurdish religion
Islam in, Ahl-i Ḥaqq movement in, 8324
Wikander's (Stig) study of, 9736
Kurdistan, Nestorian community in, 6480, 6481
Kurdukurdu (sacred), 6260–6261
Kurdungurlu (opposite patrimoiety), 9694
Kurgan (burial mound), 7384, 7385, 7386, 7387
Kurgan culture, 4453
Kurgan theory, 3493
Kurgarra (spirit), 4403
Kurgarru, 1451
Kuripako people (Amazon), 8624–8625. *See also* Arawak Indians; Baniwa religion
Kūrma (avatāra of Viṣṇu), 4325, 7500
Kūrma (breath), 1043, 7363
Kūrma Purāṇa (Hindu text), 7500
Kurnai religion (Australia)
the Flood in, 3223
myths of, 654
Kuroda Toshio, on Shintō, 8357
Kurosawa, Akira, 3097, 3100
Kurozumikyō, **5267–5268,** 6513, 6573
founding of, 5073–5074, 9312
Shintō and, 8367
Kurozumi Munetada, 6573
Kurruwalpa (life force), 9693
Kursīte, Janīna, 328, 771
on Māra, 5691
Kurtachi people (Pacific), couvade among, 2046
Kurtz, Stanley, 3608
Kuru (king), 5268
Kurukṣetra (India), **5268–5269**
Kuru sickness, 6784
Kuruwari: Yuendumu Doors (Aboriginal stories), 2480
Kuruwarri (life force), 9693
Kurzah (stone idol), 835
Kurze Darstellung des theologischen Studiums (Schleiermacher), theology in, 8165
Kurzweil, Ray, on cybernetics, 2111, 2112
Kurzweil, Raymond, 512, 513
Kūṣāṇa dynasty, Buddhist community under, 6128–6129
Kusanagi sword (Japan), 4803–4804
Kusaylah (Berber chief), 4581
Kush (Africa), 5269–5270
Kushan empire, Buddhism in, 1092, 1109, 1132, 1145–1146, 4490
Kusha sect (Buddhist), 1242
Kushite religion, **5269–5270**
Kustī(cord)
in funeral rites, 10001
in initiation, 9999–10000
Kusturica, Emir, 3098
Kusunoki Masashige, 1336
Kut (deity), 5120
Kut (Korean ritual), 5232–5233, 5235–5236
humor in, 4208
Kūṭastha(immovable), 853
Kutbā, al- (deity), in Nabatean religion, 6389
Kutenai people (North America), 6714
Kuth (spirits), in Nuer religion, 5445
Kutiyattam (performance), 7048
Kuttāb (Qur'ān school), 9201
Kuttambalamas (theaters), 2448
Kutter, Hermann, 6468
Kuttiyattam (ritual dance drama), 2448
Kuttner, Fritz, 7036
Kuttner, Stephan, 5338
Kutu (underworld), 9452
Kuwai (deity), Baniwa myth of, 8624
Kūya (Kōya) (Japanese monk), 3155, **5270–5271,** 9080
and Amitābha, 292, 5270
Kuzari (ha-Levi), 4891–4892, 9877, 9878–9879
Kvaerne, Per, 9190
Kvas (intoxicant), 849
Kvasir (mythic figure), 744, 849
creation of, 8721–8722
in war with Æsir, 3449
Kwakiutl religion (North America)
animal bone rituals in, 1014
bears in, 807
Canibal society of, 6656
cannibal symbolism in, 1403
drama in, 2460
dreams in, 2486
genealogy in, 3424–3425
Hamatsa dancer ceremony, 1403, 6710
houses and death in, 4105–4106
initiation ceremony in, 6652
masks in, 5767
mythic ancestors in, 325
Post of the World in, 8873
potlatch in, 3479–3480
parody of, 4198
repatriation of, 6711
spirits in, 6707
stratified social structure and, 3479
study of, 6672
symbolic death in, 1503
winter ceremonials of, 6709–6710
Kwalluk (monk), Confucianism in Japan and, 1927
Kwangdae (shaman), 2454
storytelling by, 5233
Kwan Yin (deity), as Lady of the Animals, 5280
Kwasi (diviner), 126
Kwoaim (warrior hero), 2982
Kwon-Taek, Im, 3097
Kwotaḥ (drum), 2497
Kwoth (deity), 3573–3574, 6744
attributes of, 3573
vs. Christian and Muslim God, 3573–3574
creation of life and, 5445
emanations of, 7443
judgment by, 3573
in Nuer religion, 2567, 2568
Kyala (deity), in Nyakyusa religion, 2567
Kyala (founding hero), 6771, 6772
Kyanzittha (king of Pagan), 1135, 1329, 7261–7262, 9053
Kybele. *See* Cybele
Kyeiwaa (mythic figure), 3570
Kyeyul-chong school of Buddhism (Korea), 1171
Kylian, Jiri, 2163
Kymris lodge, sexual magic and, 8252
Kyōdan (United Church of Christ in Japan), Protestantism in Japan restricted to, 1727
Kyōdōshoku (national evangelists), Shintō and, 8366–8367
Kyogen (play), 7048
Kyōgyōshinshō (Buddhist text), 4934
Shinran on, 8354
Kyoha Shintō, 4790
Kyōiku chokugo. See Imperial Rescript on Education
Kyōka, Izumi, 3073
Kyōkai (Buddhist monk), 1175–1176
Kyon (slaves), 1330
Kyo school of Buddhism (Korea), 1173
Ch'ŏnt'ae school and, 9436
Kyot (source for the Grail story), 3652
Kyoto (Japan)
as capital, establishment of, 4784
Gozan Zen in, 3643, 3644
Kyoto school, and Japanese imperialism, 8777
Kyoto school of Buddhism, 1302, 7273, 9049
Kyoto school of philosophy, 6635
Kyōunshū (Ikkyu), 4378
Kyrgyzstan, 4620. *See also* Central Asia and Central Asian religions
Islam in
in post-Soviet era, 4626–4630
in Soviet era, 4624
Kyriarchy, 7008
Kysogan Tengere (deity), 9081
Kyungu (founding hero), 6771
Kyyryy (shamanic séance), 2395

L

Laban (biblical figure), 4757
Laban, Rudolf, 2160
Laban Movement Analysis, 2160
Labanotation, 2160
La Barre, Weston, 2869, 6671
on hallucinogens, 8293
on neoteny, 10043
Labbu (monster), 2431
Laberthonnière, Lucien, 985
Modernism of, 6106
Labiadectomy, in East African religions, northeast Bantu, 2577
Labietis (magazine), 764

Labor. *See* Birth; Work
Labor movement
Garvey (Marcus) in, 3287
Gibbons (James) and, 3478–3479
Labor unionism, Roman Catholic Church on, 2670
Labor Zionism, 6904, 9980
nature and, 2645
Labyrinth, **5273–5279**
celestial city and, 5279
center of, 5276
in churches, 5275
dance and, 5276, 5277
definitions of, 5273
earth mother and, 2558
in games, 5276
left and right symbolism in, 5275–5276
Minoan, 5273–5274
as prison, 5277–5278
rocks left at, vol. 4 color insert
sacred gaze and, vol. 11 color insert
symbolic meanings of, 5274–5276
ascent to the sacred mountain, 5275–5276
defense, 5275
descent into Hades, 5274
descent into unconscious, 5274
intestine/abdomen, 5276–5277
meeting the monster, 5274–5275
regressus ad uterus, 5274
snakes and serpents, 5277
temenos, 5275
types of, 5276–5279
cross, 5277–5278
maṇḍala, 5278–5279
Ringwallbilder, 5276
serpentine linear, 5276
spiral, 5276–5277
thread and the knot, 5278
Labyrinth, The (Hooke), 6380
Lacan, Jacques
and French feminists, 3027–3028
on mirror stage, 6065
and postcolonial theory, 10042
on reflexivity, 7649
Lacandon Maya religion, tobacco use by, 8455
Lachatañeré, Romulo, 9305
Laches (Plato), 2273
Lachesis (deity), 3001, 9088. *See also* Moirai
Tyche and, 1527
Lachmann, Karl Wilhelm, 730
Lackner, Franz, 9139
Laclos, Choderlos de, 9072
Lacnunga (Anglo-Saxon text), 4406
magical medicine in, 5578
LaCoque, André, 5487
Lāčplēsis (Pumpurs), 762
Lactantius, 4361
Constantine and, 1679
on Hermetism, 3944, 3945
on *Sibylline Oracles,* 8384
Lactation, death-in-life/life-in-death metaphor of, 2238
LaCugna, Catherine Mowry, 3036
Ladders
on amulets and talismans, 299
in ascension, 518, 522
mi'rāj as, 6059
Ladurie, Emmanuel Le Roy, 3514, 7330
Lady Athirat of the Sea. *See also* Asherah; Athirat
in Canaanite religion, 1383–1384
Lady of the Animals, **5279–5283**
in Africa (Osun/Mami Wata), 5280
Algonquin (Nokomis), 5280
in Anatolia, 5279
Aphrodite as, 5279, 5282, 9604
Artemis as, 506, 5279, 5282, 5513–5514, 9604
in Asia Minor (Kubaba/Cybele), 5280
Athena as, 5279, 5282
in Canaan (Ashtoret/Astarte), 5280
in China (Kwan Yin), 5280
in Christianity, 5280
as Earth, 5280
in Egypt (Isis/Hathor), 5280
in Ephesus, 5280
in *Homeric Hymns,* 5280
Hopi (Kokyanguruti/Spider Woman), 5280
in Çatalhüyük, 5281–5282
in India (Tārā/Parvati), 5280
Inuit (Sedna), 470, 3017, 4528, 5280, 5515
in Japan (Amaterasu), 5280
in Mexico (Chicomecoatl/Heart of the Earth), 5280
in Minoan Crete, 5280, 5282
names of, 5280
in Old Europe, 5281
origins of, 5279–5280
in Paleolithic Age, 5280–5281
in Sumer, 5280
virginity and, 9601–9602
Lady Xoc, 5886
Laertes (Odysseus's father), power of, 5166
Laestadian Lutheran revivalist movement, 5283
Laestadius, Lars Levi, 3105, 3112, **5283–5284**
on Sami bear ceremonies, 8087
Laetentur caeli (1439) (decree), 6972
Lafaye, Jacques, 3064
Lafitau, Joseph François
on paganism, 4039
on scalping by Plains Indians, 3805
study of North American Indian religions, 6669
La Flesche, Francis, 6670, 6916–6917
La Fontaine, Jean, 6524
La galigo (Bugis epic), 1316–1317
Lagarde, Paul de, 889, 9364
Lagarriga, Isabel, 5945
Lagash (Sumerian city), economy of, 1803
Lagatea (deity), 7313
Lag ba-'Omer (holiday), 2701
Shim'on bar Yoh'ai and, 8347
Lagerway, John, 1638
Laghusamvara (Buddhist text), divine couple in, 1349
Lagi (deity), 7313
Lagobolon (shepherd's crook), 6957
LaHaye, Tim, 2892, 7324
Lahore Resolution, 4773
Lāhōrī, Muḥammad 'Alī, **5284–5285**
Lāhōrī branch of Aḥmadiyah, 200, 4573, 5284–5285
Laibon (prophet), 7443
Laibons, in Massai priesthood, 2569
Laicization, secularization *vs.,* 8215
Laidlaw, James, 7853
"La ilaha illa Allah" ("There is no god but God"). *See also* Shahādah (confession of faith)
'Ayn al-Quḍāt on, 8812
Lailoken (mythic figure), 5878
Láiluka (sages), in Selk'nam religion, 8226
Laima (deity), 760, 769, **5285–5286**
dainas (folk songs) devoted to, 2127
Māra and, 5691
Laird, Carobeth, 6672
Laity, **5286–5291**
Buddhist, 1095, 5288, 5348
in China, 1161, 1162, 1168
gender and, 3330, 3331, 3333–3334, 3343–3344
in Theravāda Buddhism, 9152
in Japan, 1178, 1182
Mahāyāna texts on, 1114–1115
merit making in, 5873
in Mongolia, 1149–1150
morality of, 1280
in priesthood, 7408–7409
rituals of, 1107
roles of, 1096, 1097
in Southeast Asia, 1142
stupas erected by, 9041
in Taiwan, 8963, 8964–8965
in Tibet, 9184–9186
Tibetan, 9839–9840
Christian, 5287–5288
Eastern Orthodox Church, 5287
in monasticism, 6122, 6133
Protestantism, 5287–5288, 5288, 7452
Roman Catholicism, 5287, 7889, 7890, 9533, 9540–9541
in Confucianism, 5288–5289
Daoist, 7415–7416
posthumous ordination of, 9846
definition of, 5286
etymology of term, 5286–5287
in Hinduism, 5289
in Islam, 5290
Jain, 4769, 4770, 5288
gender of, 3328–3329
in Japanese religions, 5289–5290
in Judaism, 5288
leadership of, 5384
in Manichaeism, 5656
origins of concept, 5286–5287
popular religion of, 7326–7327
in Reformation, 7664
religious reform and, 7653–7654
Zoroastrian, 9991–9992
Lajjā (Nasreen), 10035
Lake, John G., 7030
Lakes, **5291–5295**
in Aztec religion, 5292–5294
in Baltic religion, 774–775
deities of, 3620
in Inca religion, 5291–5292
Lakh people (Caucasus), 4614
Lakota religion, **5295–5298**. *See also* Black Elk
as Bahā'īs, 739
ballgame played in, 752, 5297
Black Elk in, 957–958
circle symbolism in, 1794
circumambulation in, 1796
color symbolism in, 1862
contemporary practice, 5297
cosmic order, 1794
creation story in, 5296, 6662
deities in, 5296
Deloria (Ella Cara) studying, 2264–2265
drama in, 2460
fasting in, 2996
federal assault at Wounded Knee, 6551
four generations in, 5297
gender in, 3407, 3408, 3409
Ghost Dance in, 3473, 5295
Ghost Keeping in, 6703
He Sapa (Black Hills) in, 5295
iconography of, 4308
identification of food and people in, 3169
Iktomi (trickster) in, 5296, 5297
life in, 5444
pipe ceremony in, history of, 6662
Roman Catholicism in, Black Elk and, 957, 958

sacred history of, 6662
sacred pipe in, 5295, 5296, 5297
Seven Sacred Rites, 5296–5297, 5444
Hanbleceyapi (vision quest), 5296
Hunkapi (making relatives), 5297
Inikagapi/Inipi (sweat lodge), 5296
Isnati Awicalowanpi (puberty ceremony), 5297
Tapa Wankayeyapi (throwing the ball), 5297
Wanagi Wicagluha (spirit keeping), 5296–5297
Wiwanyang Wacipi (Sun Dance), 5297
soul in, 5297
spiritual leaders of, 6699
study of, 6672
by Walker (James), 9667–9668
Sun Dance in, 6700, 8846, 8848–8849
self-mutilation in, 6652
sweat lodge in, cosmic order in, 7981–7982
trees in, 9336
tricksters in, 9355
vision quest, 9609–9610
wakan concept in, 6650
Wakan Tanka/Tunkashila in, 5295–5296
White Buffalo Calf Woman in, 9725–9726
White Buffalo Woman myth, 6662
winter counts, vol. 2 color insert
Lakṣaṇa (characteristics), 9898
Lakṣmaṇa (brother of Rāmā), 7609, 7617
Lakṣmī (deity), 3017. *See also* Srí
accessibility of, 3977
as consort, 9618
devadāsīs of temple of Jagannātha as, sexual activity of, 3967
elephants of, 4438
festival of, 2368
iconography of, vol. 8 color insert
in Pāñcarātra cosmology, 9508
lotus associated with, 5518–5519
married women as incarnations of, 3020
as nurturing goddess, 3607
Rādhā and, 7593
shrine to, vol. 11 color insert
sovereignty and, 9908
wifehood of, 3589
Lakulīśa (incarnation of Siva). *See also* Pāśupata Śaivism
as founder of Pratyabhijñā Saivism, 8049
influence of, 4019
Lakwa Bawon (Bawon's Cross), 9637
Lālah (tulip), 4350
Lal Ded (poet), 7210
Lalita, K., 3322
Lalitāditya, 8
Lalitavistara (Buddhist text), 1064, 1200, 1305
birth of Buddha in, elephant in, 2750
Lallā Dēd (poet), on Śiva, 8417
Lalou, Marcelle, 1313, 9188
Lāl salu (Walliullah), 10035
Lāl Śrīnivās Dās, 10034
Lama (deity), in Sumerian religion, 8538
Lamaism. *See* Tibet and Tibetan religions, Buddhism
Lamartine, Alphonse de, 3525
Lamas. *See also* Dalai Lama
in Mongolia, 6142
in Tibetan Buddhism, 7407
astrological charts used by, vol. 3 color insert
emergence of, 1153
establishment of leadership of, 8083
medicine and, 3864, 3866
role of, 9182
as saints, 8037
as spiritual guides, 8713
veneration of, 9841
Lamashtu (demon), 5458, 7144
Lamb. *See also* Sheep and goats
at Easter Sunday meal, 2580
of God, 987
Jesus as, and atonement, 595
Lamb, Matthew, 7246
Lamba religion, 1505
Lambek, Michael, 379
Lambert, Johann Heinrich, 7087
Lambert, Pierre, 6501
Lambert, W. G., 3486, 5963
Lamberton, Robert, 7106
Lambeth Conferences, 352, 353
Anglican polity and, 1766
Lambo, T. A., psychiatric treatment by, 3821
Lambodara. *See* Gaṇeśa
Lam 'bras bu dang bcas pa order (Buddhist), 1224–1225
Lambrechts, Pierre, 1482, 1483
Lamdre system of Buddhism, 5223
Lamech (biblical figure)
Cain killed by, 1345
Freemasons on, 3194
music invented by, 6277
Lame Deer, on psychedelic drugs, 9614
Lamennais, Félicité de, 9442
Lamentations
evil in, 2897
in Finno-Ugric religions, 3110
or Shīʿī martyrs, 7631–7632
in funeral rites, 3236
myth as response to, 2897–2898
Lamentations (biblical book), pessimism of, 4549
Lamentations of Khakheperreseneb (Egypt), 2711
Lament for Ur, Enlil in, 2800
La Mettrie, Julien de
chaos theory and, 1541
in French Enlightenment, 2796
materialism of, 5776
Lamia (female spirit), 2277, 9770
Lammers, Arthur, 1474
Cayce (Edgar) and, 559
Lamotte, Étienne, **5298–5299**
on Buddha biographies, 1061–1062, 1063, 1312
on Buddha's previous lives, 1064
exegetical works of, 5298
translations by, 1313, 5298
Lampe, Friedrich Adolph, 7142
Lamphere, Louise, 6442, 6672
Lamp Records *(denglu),* 1524, 1604
Lamprias, 521
Lam rim chen mo (Tsong kha pa), 1228, 1286, 2322, 9387
Lan, David, on spirit possession, 8695
Lancaster system of education, 1700
Lancaster University
Smart (Ninian) and, 8442
women's studies at, 3313
Land. *See also* Sacred space
in Andean religion, 8617–8618 (*See also* Huacas)
in Australian Indigenous religions
history of study of, 688–690
myths of, 662
new movements of, 673–674
political struggle for, 640–641, 648, 649–651, 690
politics of, 640–641
women and, 689, 3390–3391, 3392
of Cistercians, 6132–6133
degradation of, 2609
ethical relations with, among Maori, 2618
in Israelite religion
Abraham stories of, 14, 15
and monotheism, 3540
in Judaism
commandments based on, 2644
Yahveh in ownership of, 4857
in Maori religion, 5683–5684
in Micronesian myths, 6011–6012
monastic, secularization of, Sorskii (Nil) on, 8525–8526
in North American Indian religions, 6680–6681
religious importance of, 6507–6508
as sacred space, in traditional cultures, 7978
in Sami religion, *seite* (sacred landscape), 8087
vengeance and, 7781–7782
in Warlpiri religion, 9694
in West African religions, worship sites and, 9720
Landa, Diego de
on calendar in Yucatan, 1355–1356
in Inquisition, 4504, 5917–5918
and Maya alphabet, 5886
on Maya architecture, 5882
on Maya cremation practices, 3244
on war dances, 2466
writings of, 5939–5940
Land and Freedom Party (Kenya), 7627
Landauer, Gustav, 1058
Landes, Ruth, 121, 3406, 6672, 10027–10028
Landeskirchen (territorial churches), 1773
Land ethic, 2609, 2656
Land Gift movement. *See* Bhoodān movement
Landgrave Philipp of Hesse, 7660
Landmark Forum, 6568
Landmarkism, 786
Landnámabók (Icelandic book of settlements), 5299
divination and magic in, 8025
histories in, 8023
priestesses in, 8024
Land of Israel. *See* Israel
Land of the Rainbow Snake (Berndt), 841
Land of the Western Paradise, in Pure Land Buddhism, 3887–3888
Landresse, Charles, 1311
Landsberger, Benno, on *Epic of Gilgamesh,* 3487, 3488
Landtman, Gunnar, 5770
Landvættir (guardian spirits), **5299**
Land Wars (1860–1872), 5683
Land-water opposition
in Khanty religion, 5120–5121
in Mansi religion, 5120–5121
"Land Without Evil" movements (Brazil), 6576
Lane, Beatrice Erskine, Suzuki (D. T.) and, 8885

Lane, Edward, on humor in Egypt, 4213
Lanfranc, Anselm and, 372
Lanfranc of Bec, 837
Lang, Andrew, **5299–5300**
on African religions, 114
on Andaman religion, 8170
animism theory, criticism of, 4061, 8168
on deity, 2255
Frazer (James G.) critiqued by, 5299–5300
on Germanic religion, 3458
on God, 5300
Indo-European religious studies of, 4460
on magic, 5299–5300, 5564
on manism, 5672–5673
Marett (R. R.) influenced by, 5708
on mythology and folklore, 5299
on Müller (F. Max), 5299, 6234
on origin of religion, 2541, 7372, 10077
on psychic phenomena, 5300
and study of North American Indian religions, 6671
on supreme beings, 7074, 8874, 8876
Tylor (E. B.) criticized by, 2915, 5300
Lang, Pearl, 2163
Langar (community meal), in Sikhism, 8393
Langdon, Stephen Herbert, 2522
Lange, Friedrich, Adler (Felix) influenced by, 33
Langer, Susanne, 4295, **5300–5301,** 5491
symbol theory and, 8912, 8913
Langkawi (Malaysia), kinship in, 5184
Langone, Michael, 6539
Lango people (Uganda), spirit possession in, 2140
Language, **5301–5313**. *See also* Linguistics; Poststructuralism; Structuralism; Translation; Writing; *specific languages*
in Buddhism, **5308–5313**
doctrinal background of, 5308–5309
Prāsaṅgika *vs.* Svātantrika school, 8858
interpretive frameworks of, 5311
in religious practice, 5309–5311
sacred, 5307
sectarian manifestations of, 5310–5311
classification of religions by, 1818
comparative mythology, linguistic, 1873, 1874
comparison of Christianity and Confucianism with, 1920
as component of blessing, 980, 981–982, 984
conversion and, 1972
cosmopolitanism and, 4098
of creation myths, 5302, 6363
creolization, **2065–2068**
cursing, **2097–2108**
deceptive nature of, 5308–5309, 5311
and deconstruction, 2245–2248
Derrida (Jacques) on, 2245–2248
of disease and cure, 3815
distinctive-features theory of, 8749, 8750
as expressive gesture, 2868
gender studies on, 3302
about God, and existence of God, 583, 585
Hegel (G. W. F.), use of, 3893
Heidegger (Martin) on, 3896
Herder (Johann Gottfried) on, 3918, 3919
hermeneutics and, 3930, 3931, 3935
"holy" and "sacred," semantics and translations of, 4097–4100
inner *vs.* spoken, 5503–5504
of Jewish subcultures, 4860
of journal articles, 10059–10060
Karelian, 5092
Langer (Susanne) on, 5301
law, interpretation of, 5355
in literature, 5472–5475
of liturgy, 5491, 5492
Müller's (F. Max) work on, 6234–6236
multitude of tongues, universalism and, 3907
about mystical union, 6334–6335, 6337, 6338
object language, sacred *vs.* profane and, 7965
in Orthodox Christian worship, 2591
performative, Austin (John) on, 2099
philosophy of, 7112, 7115–7116, 7119, 7127
pidgin, 2065
power of words (*See also* Spells)
in healing, 3811, 3829
in Hebrew, 3829
in Sanskrit tradition, 2099
in scripture, 8200–8201
in spells, 8675–8676
of prayer, 7369
Rappaport (Roy A.) on, 7619
reflexivity and, 7649
ritual and
Bellah (Robert) on, 8470
coevolution of, 2868
of rituals, 5328, 7851, 7858
sacred, **5301–5308**
in Buddhism, 1093, **5308–5313**
context of, 5305
creation and, 5302
functions of, 5305–5307
hearer of, 5304
as manifestation of the sacred, 5302–5304
medium of, 5304–5305
sacred language (e.g. language of the Qur'ān), 5303
as sacred substance, 5302–5303
sets of sacred words, 5304, 5309
speaker of, 5304
spoken, 5301–5302
for transformation, 5305–5306
of Vedas, 5467
for worship, 5305, 5306–5307
sacred and profane in, 7964–7970
Saussure (Ferdinand de) and, 2245–2248
Schleiermacher (Friedrich) on, 8163, 8164
scripture and ritual language, 8199
scriptures, impact of, 8203
semantics, **8226–8227**
signified to signifier relationship in, 5303
Smith (Wilfred Cantwell) on, 8450
in Southeast Asia
diversity in, 8641, 8647
parallelism in ritual language, 8649
speaking in tongues (*See* Glossolalia)
spirit possession and speech, 8695–8696
Steiner (Rudolf) on, 8738
study of religion and, 8762
syncretism, linguistic, 8928
theological, feminist critique of, 3036
time and, 7991
and transculturation, 9296
translations, early modern, and historiography, 4039–4040
vernacular, 5303
vernacular, scriptures in
conversion and, 1972
schism and, 8152
visualization of, vol. 14 color insert
Wittgenstein (Ludwig) on, 3935, 7112, 7115–7116, 7119, 7375
Language, Truth, and Logic (Ayer), 7118
Language and Art in the Navajo Universe (Witherspoon), 5762
Languedoc, 1458
Langxian, stories written by, 3067–3068
Lanka Dharmaduta Society, 1189
Laṅkāvatāra Sūtra (Buddhist text)
Buddha transmitting to Huike, 994
desire in, 2306
mantras in, 1214
meaning and negation in, 5308
mind in, 5731
natural law in, 2332
nirvāṇa in, 6629
on silence of Buddha, 1270
tathāgata-garbha in, 9018
three (number) in, 9347
transmission of, 5731
turnings of the wheel in, 1275
Lankford, Sarah, Holiness movement and, 4082
Lankolo (void), 776
Lannoy, Ghillebert de, 767
Lanternari, Vittorio, 190, 6590, 6591, 7075
comparative historical method of, 4046
on messianism, 5973
on sacrifice, 8004
on spirit possession, 10027
Lantis, Margaret, 475
Lanzhou, on Dao, atheism and, 577
Laocoon (king of Troy), vol. 2 color insert
Lao Dan. *See also* Laozi
as teacher of Confucius, 5315–5316
Laodicea, Council of (336), on angels, 346
Laojun (deity), 1624
Laojun yibai bashi jie (Daoist code), 7413
Laojun yinsong (Daoist text), 5240
Laojun yinsong xinke jeijing (Daoist code), 7413
Laojun zhong jing (Classic on the center of the person), *zhenzen* in, 9959
Lao religion, **5313–5315**. *See also* Southeast Asia and Southeast Asian religions
agricultural rite in, 8643
Buddhist influences on, 5313–5314
monasteries, 5314
Theravāda Buddhism, 5313
festivals in, 5314
healers in, 5313
karman in, 5314
master of rituals in, 5313, 5314
Phī cult, 5313, 5314
Laos
Buddhism in
celebrations in, 1307
colonial influences and, 1139
communism and, 1143
future of, 1131
imperial, 1134
kingship in, 7262

mediation in, 9152
modern, 1140
monasteries, 1096, 1142
Mon Buddhism, 1138
politics and, 9153
reforms in, 9151
revival of, 9149–9150
Theravāda Buddhism, 1137–1138, 1195
fiction of, 3076, 3077
music in, 6287, 6289, 6290
Neolithic burial sites in, 8642
Laotianye (deity), 9172
Lao-tzu. *See* Laozi
Laoust, Henri, on Ḥambālī *madhhab,* 3760
Laozi (book). *See Dao de jing*
Laozi (Lao-tzu), **5315–5320**
apparitions/visions of
and Celestial Masters, 2180, 9843
to Kou Qianzhi, 5240
in Tang Dynasty, 2184
biographies of, 946, 5316, 5318, 5319
birth of, 5318
as Buddha, 2194, 2199, 5317
canonization writings, 1408
Celestial Masters and, 5317
charisma of, 1549
as creator of Buddhism, 2179
Dao de jing attributed to, 5315, 5316
deification, posthumous, 1408, 2179
as deity Huang Laojun, 1593
devotion to, patterns of, 5318–5319
divinity of, 5315
divinization of, 5316
as embodiment of *Dao,* 5318
on equivalence of saint and ruler, 4332
as fictional figure, 1574
as focus of history, 5317–5318
Huangdi associated with, 4144
iconography of, 4333–4334, 4337, 5318–5319
as Lao Dan, 5315–5316
as Li Er (Li Dan), 5316, 5318
longevity of, 5316
messianism of, 2195, 5317
millenarianism of, 6038
monism of, 6146
as perfect ruler, 7267
physical description of, 5319
reincarnations of, 5317–5318
Seidel (Anna) on, 8222
tea ceremony and, 4141
teachings of, 5318–5319
visualization of, 5319
Yin Xi as disciple of, 5316
Zuanzong and, 2197
Laozi bianhua jing (Daoist text), 5317, 5318
Laozi huahu jing (Wang Fou), 5317
Laozi ming (Bian Shao), 5316
Lapide, Pinchas, on Jesus, 4845
Lapie, Paul, 5785
Lapis lazuli
Bhaiṣajyaguru and, 855
blue symbolism and, 1861–1862
LaPlace, Pierre Simon de
and atheism, 582
on chance, 1527
chaos theory and, 1541
determinism of, 7137
Laporte, Pierre, 9303
Lappe, Francis Moore, 3174
Lapp religion. *See* Sami (Lapp) religion
Laprune, Léon Ollé, 985
Lapsi (backsliders), Decian persecution and, 2112
Lara (deity), 5321
Lara, Simón de, 5921
Larcher, Chrysostome, 900
Larentalia (deity), 5321
Larentia (deity), 5321
Lares (deified souls of ancestors), 2277, **5320–5322**
Lares domestici, 5321
Larger Sukhāvatīvyūha Sūtra, 2176
Larios, Juan, 406
Lari tribe, in Mouvement Croix-Koma, 105
Larkin, Clarence, vol. 1 color insert
Larlan (rain clouds), 9459
Laroui, Abdallah, 4720
Larsen, Robin, on Campbell (Joseph), 1380
Larsen, Stephen, on Campbell (Joseph), 1380
Larson, Daniel, 9229
Larunda (deity), 5321
Las Casas, Bartolomé de, **5322–5323**
Lascaux caves (France), 9906
paintings in, horses in, 4131–4132
Lash, Nicholas, on knowledge, 5211
Las Higueras (Mexico), in Classic period, 5905
Łasicki, Jan, 330, 331, 768
Laski, Marghanita, on religious experience, 7695
Lassen, Christian, 1333
Lasso, Orlando di, 6311
Last and first. *See* First and last, motif of
Last Day, in Islam
in Ḥanafī creed, 2064
in Qur'ān, 4564, 4565
opposition to, 6222
wealth in, 6222
Last Journals of David Livingstone in Central Africa (Livingstone), 1003
Last Judgment. *See also* Eschatology; Judgment of the dead
imagery of, vol. 1 color insert
Last Judgment (Michelangelo), 4346
"Last Priest Didn't Even Say Goodbye, The" (Welch), 7226
Last supper
atonement in, 595
hospitality in, 4139
leavened *vs.* unleavened bread in, 5388
Last Supper (Leonardo da Vinci), 4346
Latakia, Canaanite religion and, 1381
Late antiquity, definition of, 7583
Late Great Planet Earth, The (Lindsey), 413, 2892
La Tène culture, 1478–1479
Latent dreams, 2483, 2484
Lateran Council (746), on angels, 347
Lateran Council (769), on images, 4290
Lateran Council (1123)
on Catharist/Albigensian heresy, 2042
on celibacy, 7403
on church hierarchy, 2041–2042
Lateran Council (1139)
on Catharist/Albigensian heresy, 2042
on church hierarchy, 2041–2042
Lateran Council (1179)
on Catharist/Albigensian heresy, 2042
on church hierarchy, 2041–2042
on papal elections, 6971
Lateran Council (1215)
on confession, 1941
on demons, 2278
on Fifth Crusade, 4496
jurisprudence and, 5337–5338
overview of, 2042
in reform of monasticism, 821, 2412, 7724
on theology of analogy, 391
unity of the church at, 1690–1691
Lateran Council (1511–1517), overview of, 2043
Lateran Council (1512–1517), decrees produced by, 9341
Lateran Council (1513), on human immortality, 2280–2281
Latifeh (anecdotal literature), 10035
Latihan (conscience), 833
Latimer, William, humanism and, 4176
Latin America, journals devoted to, 10058
Latin America and Latin American religions. *See also specific countries and religions*
in 20th century, 1700–1704
artistic expression in, 2141
Christianity, **1694–1705,** 1703 (*See also* Liberation theology)
church and national states in, 1698–1703
indigenous religions and, 3063–3064
indigenous theology of, 2689–2690
Inquisition, 1698
liberation theology of, 2676, 5302–5304, 5438, 5439, 5440
nuns and sisters, 6765
Pentecostalism, 1702, 1704, 1973, 6579–6580
pilgrimage to El Santuario de Chimayó, 8377
Reformation and, 1664
Sor Juana, 4967–4968
conquest and colonialism in
Christianity and, 1694–1698
Requirement formula and, 1854
demographics at end of colonial period, 1698
devotional dances in, 2137
drug tourism in, 7472
festivals in, 3136
fiction of, **3063–3066**
films from, 3099
homosexuality and gender roles in, 4117
human rights in, 5364
immigration to, 1699, 1702
kingdom of God in, 5153
new religious movements in, **6575–6582**
folk-saint, 6577–6578
nativist, 6576–6577
Protestant-related, 6579–6580
spiritist, 6578–6579
number of Indians at time of conquest, 1696
popular culture criticism in, 7321, 7322
Protestantism, 1698, 1699–1700, 1702–1703, 1704, 6579–6580, 7447
religious and cultural syncretism in, 3064
religious broadcasting in, 7714
revolutionary period, 1698–1700
Roman Catholicism
19th and 20th centuries, 1700–1702, 1703–1704
colonial period, 1695–1698

Roman Catholicism *continued*
folk, 6514, 6577–6578
revolutionary period, 1699
secularization in, 8218–8219
Latin American Association for Jewish Studies, 4885
Latin American Church Council (CLAI), 1704
Latin American Council (1899), 1700
Latin American Council of Bishops (CELAM), 1701, 1703–1704
Latin American Theological Fraternity (FTL), 1704
Latin Christianity, *vs.* Greek Christianity, 3656–3657
Latin language
in Andalusia, 4593
Aristotle's works translated into, 480
Bible translated into (*See* Vulgate Bible)
as Catholic common language, Vatican II on, 9536
in early Christianity, 2581
importance under Charlemagne, 1557
as metalanguage, 7965
Pañcatantra translated into, 6960
sacred and profane in, 7964, 7965–7966
sanctum and *sacrum* as "holy" in, 4099
Scholastic method and, 8175
scripture, terms for, in, 8196, 8197
Latin League, 1466, 7895
Latin Patriarchate of Jerusalem, 1673
Latitudinal order of angels, 4554–4555
Latitudinarianism, humanism and, 4177
La Toge'langi' (Bugis mythical figure), 1317
La Torre (journal), 2905
Latrines, in Maori religion, 5681–5682
as ritual space, 7978
Latse Contemporary Tibetan Cultural Library, 9188
Latte, Kurt, 7896–7897
Latter-Day Saints. *See* Mormonism
Latter Prophets, 879
Latvia and Latvian religions
ancient religion of (*See* Baltic religion)
Christianization of, 762, 767, 768, 773
cult of ancestors in, 327–331
dainas (folk songs) in, 2127, 8131–8132, 8133–8134
folklore of, 766
Māra in, 5691–5694
Lutheranism, 1685
Pērkons cult in, 7053
Roman Catholicism, 773, 775
Saule (sun) cult in, **8131–8135**
twins in, 9419–9420
Latvian Christian Congregation, 763
Latvian Christian Society, 763
Latvian language, 768
Latviešu folklora mītu spogulī (Kursīte), 771
Latviešu pasakas un teikas (Šmits), 770
Latvijas Dievtuŗu Sadraudze, 763
Latvijas Viedas Sadraudzība, 766
Latvju Dievtuŗu Draudze, 763, 765
Lau, D. C., 946
Laud, William, Arminianism and, 493
Laufer, Berthold, 1635
Laufer, Carl, on masks, 5767–5768
Laughlin, Charles, on body-based metaphor, 8277
Laughlin, Harry H., 2880
Laughter. *See also* Humor
Aristotle on, 4199, 4221
Bergson (Henri) on, 4222
Cicero on, 4199
condemnation of, in Western tradition, 4218
culture of, in Carnival, 1440
as expression of humility, 2428
Feast of Fools and, 4218
Freud on, 4222
Hobbes (Thomas) on, 4221–4222
Japanese festivals devoted to, 4208
of Jesus, 4196–4197
Ludovici (Anthony) on, 4222
Meister Eckhart on, 4202
Plato on, 4199
of Sarah, in Hebrew scripture, 4196
Thomas Aquinas on, 4218–4219
in Zen Buddhism, 4207
Laukikabhāsya (empirical speech), 7005
Laum, Bernhard, 6138
Lauras (Eastern Orthodox monasteries), 2826–2827
Laurel, 9337
Lauren, Paul Gordon, on human rights, 5362
Laurentius of Amalfi, Gregory VII and, 3689
Laurinkienė, Nijolė, 771
Lausanne, Treaty of (1923), 3658
Lautenbahs, Jēkabs, 769
La Vallée Poussin, Louis de, 1087, 1313, 5298, **5323–5324**
and Franco-Belgian school of Buddhology, 1634
on Cārvāka, 1446
Stcherbatsky (Theodore) and, 8737
Lavater, Johann Kasper, Mendelssohn (Moses) responding to, 5854
La Venta (Mexico), 6819
Olmec culture in, 5880–5882
La Vestale (Viganó), 2155
LaVey, Anton
Church of Satan and, 8126–8127
The Satanic Bible, 6530, 6531
Lavinium (Italy), relations with Rome, 7898–7899
Law(s), **5325–5379**. *See also* Codes and codification
architecture of, 5360
Austin (John) on, 5369
in Australian Indigenous religions, dreamtime and, 2002, 2003–2004
Bentham (Jeremy) on, 5368
bias in, 5361
in Buddhism, **5347–5351**
the Buddha and, 5347–5348, 5350
duḥkha and, 5450
foundational concepts and, 5349–5450
karman and, 5450
legal pluralism and, 5349
monasticism, 6129–6130
of *saṃgha*, 8072–8073
procedures for, 5348
punishments in, 5348
ritual practices and, 5350
transmission of, 5348–5349
Vinaya Piṭaka and (*See* Vinaya Piṭaka)
canon of (*See* Canon law)
in Caribbean, colonialist antisuperstition laws, 3823
in Chinese religion, **5351–5355**
under Communist rule, 5353–5354
Legalism movement, 5394–5396
li and, 5351
religion and, 5351
religious authority and, 5353
rituals and, 5353
spirit realm and, 5351–5353
types of, 5351
in Christian tradition
canon law, 5336–5337
conscience and, 1940
divine origins of, 5358
ecclesiastic *vs.* criminal justice, witch hunts and, 8013–8014
ethics and, 1652
Hooker (Richard) on, 4124
Inquisition, 4499
Marsilius of Padua on, 5729
New Testament on, 1670
obedience and, 1670
Suárez (Francisco), role of, 8799
class interests in, 5361
closed *vs.* open nature of, 5328
codes and codification, **1842–1847**, 5328–5329
common-law, 5326, 5329
contract, covenant notion and, 2047–2049
critical theory and, **5358–5361**
custom *vs.*, 1843
definitions of, 5326–5327
divine, *vs.* natural, 5326
Egyptian, 4727
enforcement of, flexibility in, 5327
feminism and, 5360–5361
Finnis (John) on, 5370
Fuller (Lon) on, 5369
gender bias in, 5360–5361
Greco-Roman, on magic, 5575
Greek, 4727
Gregorian Reform and, 5336
Habermas (Jürgen) on, 5370
Hart (H. L. A.) on, 5369
Hebrew, Albright (William Foxwell) on, 2098
hermeneutics of, 5328–5329, 5356
in Hinduism, **5343–5347** (*See also* Dharma; *Laws of Manu*)
in colonial period, 5346
enforcement of, 5344–5345
interpretation of, 5345
salutations in, 8060–8061
Hittite, medical expenses, payment of, 3825
Hobbes (Thomas) on, 5367
human rights and, 5330–5331, **5362–5366**
Hume (David) on, 5368
and I Am movement, 4246–4247
idolatry and, 5329–5330
in indigenous cultures, **5339–5343**
approaches to study of, 5339–5340
definitions of indigenous and, 5340–5341
in Hawaii, 5341–5342
human rights *vs.* collective rights in, 5341
relativism *vs.* universalism in, 5341
international, 5329
human rights and, 5363
interpretation of
dogmatics and, 5359
language and, 5355
Islamic (*See* Islamic law; *See Uṣūl; See Uṣūl al-fiqh*)
Israelite (*See* Israelite law)
Japanese
compilation of, 4783
Ritsuryō system of, Shintō and, 8358–8359, 8360
under Tokugawa regime, 4788

Jewish (*See Halakhah;* Mishnah)
Kant (Immanuel) on, 5368
language of, interpretation and, 5355
lawyers and, 5360
legal positivism and, 5326, 5330
literature and, 5328, **5355–5358**
canon and, 5355
Cover (Robert) on, 5357
Dworkin (Ronald) on, 5358
Levenson (Jon D.) on, 5357–5358
modern literature, 5355
Posner (Richard) on, 5356, 5357
White (James Boyd) on, 5356–5357
Locke (John) on, 5367–5368
in medieval Europe, **5336–5339**
canon law, 5336–5338
Fourth Lateran Council and, 5337–5338
human *vs.* divine law, 5337
Mesopotamian
codification of, 4727
vs. Egyptian law, 4727
vs. Israelite law, 4728
medical malpractice in, 3825
morality and, **5366–5371,** 7652
in classic modern theory, 5367–5368
in later theory, 5369–5370
in modern jurisprudence, 5368–5369
myths and, 5328
natural (*See* Natural law)
new religious movements and, **5375–5379**
anticult movements and, 396–397, 1033–1034
brainwashing cases, 1033, 1034
deprogramming and, 2292
normative function of, 5359–5360
oaths and, 9641
oral *vs.* written, 5329
in orthopraxy, 6914–6915
Persian, 4727
poetry in, 5328
positive, 5367, 5368, 5369
pre-Islamic (*See* Constitution of Medina)
punishment and, **5371–5375**
racial bias in, 5361
and religion, **5325–5332** (*See also* Religion)
conflicts between, 5325
critical theory and, **5358–5361**
in indigenous cultures, 5339–5440
legal positivism and, 5326
literature and, **5355–5358**
morality and, **5366–5371**
punishment and, **5371–5375**
separation of, 5325–5326
religious (*See also specific religions and types of law*)
asceticism in, 5371–5372
authority of, 5327
letter *vs.* spirit of, 5328
punishment in, 5327, 5371–5372
retribution in, 5372–5374
sin in, 5327
religious *vs.* secular, 5326–5329
differences between, 5326–5327
genealogical connections between, 5329–5330
parallels between, 5327–5328
in Renaissance, 5358–5359
revenge and, 7779, 7782–7783
rituals and, 5327–5328
Roman, 5329, **5332–5336**
Christian Inquisition and revival of, 8013
Christianity and, 5333–5335
codes of, 5334–5335
Codex Iustinianus, 5334–5335
Codex Theodosianus, 5333, 5334
Corpus Iuris Civilis, 5333, 5358–5359
development of, 5332–5333
divine nature of, 5358–5359
efficacy of, 5333
Fourth Lateran Council and, 5337–5338
impact on Christianity, 5332
influence on future societies, 5336–5337
ius sacrum (sacred law), 7913
law making, 5332
mirror punishments in, 7782
on private associations, 5333–5334
on private rituals, 5333
procedures during empire, 5332–5333
public *vs.* private law, 5332
religious *vs.* secular, 5332
on ritual practices, 5333
Twelve Tables, 5332, 5333–5334, 7782, 7902–7903
sanction of, 5367
secular
authority of, 5327
punishment in, 5327
religious genealogies of, 5329–5330
secularization of, 5325–5326
sources of, 5358–5359
study of, hermeneutics and, 5356, 5359
Tocqueville (Alexis de) on, 5368
validity of, morality and, 5369
Weber (Max) on, 5330, 5369
Law, Liberty, and Morality (Hart), 5369
Law, William, **5324–5325**
on the supernatural, 8861
Lawless, Elaine J., 3147–3148
Law of Causation, in Buddhism, 7678
Law of Consecration and Stewardship, Smith (Joseph) and, 8447
Law of Correspondence, of Delsarte, 2156
Law of Religious Associations (Soviet Union), 4624
Law of Return. *See* Ḥoq ha-Shevut (Israeli Law of Return)
Law of talion, 5372–5374, 7779, 7782–7783
Law of Thelema. *See* Thelema, law of
Law of Threefold Return, 9731
Law of Trinity, of Delsarte, 2156
Law of Zeus, Cleanthes on, 8743
Lawrence, D. H., 5480–5481
Lawrence, Peter, **5379–5380**
on cargo cults, 5380, 7788
on New Guinea religions, 6507, 6508
religion defined by, 5379–5380
Laws (Plato)
dance in, 2143
Demiurge in, 2273
dualism in, 2510, 2515
gods in, 7184, 7186
magic in, 5575
music in, 6303
Laws of Ecclesiastical Polity. See Of the Laws of Ecclesiastical Polity (Hooker)
Laws of Manu *(Manusmṛti, Mānava Dharmaśāstra),* 5289, 5346
ancestor worship in, 322
asceticism in, 5372
as ideal of Dharmaśāstra, 8122
āśrama in, 7817
commentaries on, 2329
cosmology in, 5328
dating of, 2329
dharma in, 2327, 2329, 5344, 9372
economy in, 9708
enforcement of, flexibility in, 5327
golden egg in, 1024
law of talion in, 5373
magic in, 5591
mokṣa in, 6115
relational discipline and, 8707
sexuality in, 5415
tears in, 9024
touch in, 9256, 9258
vegetarianism in, 5327, 5373
women in, 3318–3319, 4435
Lawson, E. Thomas, 7851, 7858
cognitive approach to history of religions by, 10043
structuralism and, 8759
Lawson, Henry, 3080
Lawwāmah souls, in Islam, 8567
Lawyers
role of, 5360
as social class, 5361
Lax, Robert, Merton (Thomas) and, 5879
Layard, John, 5278
on phallic worship, 4114
Laye, Camara, 3086
Layenne movement, 107
Laying on of hands. *See* Hands, laying on of
Laylat al-Barā'ah (Muslim feast), 4713
Laylat al-Qadr (night of power), 4714
Laymen. *See* Laity
Laymen's Foreign Mission Inquiry (1930-1932), 2289
Layne, Al C., 1474
Lay of Grímnir (Germanic poem), 3446, 3448, 3451
cosmic tree in, 3456
Lay of Vafþrúðnir (Germanic poem), 3446, 3448
apocalypse in, 3457
Lay people. *See* Laity
Lay religion. *See* Popular religion
Lazaris, teachings of, 6532
Lazar of P'arpi, on Sahak Parthev, 8026
Lazarus (biblical figure), 9454
as ghost, 3475
Shakpana identified with in Santeria, 1434
Lazarus, Moritz, 4903
Lazzarelli, Lodovico, Hermetism and, 3946
Leabhar Gabhála Éireann, 1480, 1485, 1488
references to Fomhoire in, 3164
Tuatha Dé Danann in, 9390
Leach, Edmund, **5380–5383**
on dialectics, 386
life of, 5380–5381
on memorization, 5851
on myth, 5382
on religion, 5382

Leach, Edmund ***continued***
ritual defined by, 7833
structuralism and, 8755, 8757
theory and method of, 5381
Leadbeater, Charles W., 845
Krishnamurti (Jiddu) and, 5244
Leade, Jane, 1006, 9470
on androgyny, 8523
Leaders and leadership, **5383–5388**. *See also* Chiefs; Kings and kingship; Spiritual guides
charisma and, 1544–1549, 5385, 5387
heresy and, 3923
of Jesus, 9271
charismatic
move to collective administration, 6564–6565
in new religious movements, 6515, 6523, 6546, 6562
and violence, speculations about, 6552, 6553
in Chinese popular tradition, 1606
in Christianity, in *1 Clement,* 1824
definition of, 5383
domination by, 5385
followers as, 5387
gender and, 5387
homo religiosus as religious leader, 4109–4110
in Islam, *nubūwah* and, 6736–6737
in Judaism, *tsaddiq* doctrine in Hasidism, 3789–3791
laity of, 5384
legitimation of authority, 5385–5386
magicians as, 5383, 5384
in Neopaganism, 6560–6561
in New Guinea religions, 6506
New Leadership movement, 1545
in new religious movements, controversy over, 6562
origins of, 5386
Osage, 6918
personal traits of, 5386
priests as, 5383–5385
in primitive societies, 10065–10066
prophets as, 5383–5385
in religious communities, 1864, 1865
revolution and, 7791, 7792
social sources of, 5386
successors of, 5385
typology of
variety in, 5386
Wach's (Joachim), 5386
Weber's (Max), 5383–5385
Wach (Joachim) on, 5385–5386, 5387
Weber (Max) on, 5383–5385
by women, 9787
women's exclusion from, androcentrism of, 336
League of Nations
Aga Khan III in, 173
Commission for Intellectual Cooperation of, 838
Le'ah. *See* Leah
Leah (biblical figure), **7591–7592**
Leah tribes, 7592
Leakey, Caroline, 3084
Leal, Tracey, 1033
Learned ignorance, 6989–6990
John of the Cross on, 6990
Kierkegaard on, 6990
Nicholas of Cusa on, 6989, 7193
Pascal on, 6990
Socratic tradition of, 6989
Learning
culture and, 2087
in rites of passage, 7798–7799
Leary, Timothy, 2680, 7471–7472
Leaven, **5388–5389**. *See also* Bread
prohibition on, on Passover, 7003
Leavis, F. R., 7321
Leavis, Q. D., 7321
Lebanon
Christians in, 1675, 1676
civil war and emigration, 1676
Druze in, 2502
Imāmī (Twelvers) Shiism in, 4698
Le Baron, Ervil, 6551
Lébé (mythic figure), 95, 100, 2391
Leben Schleiermachers (Dilthey), 2353
Lebensphilosophie, Nietzsche and, 6616
Lébé Seru (Dogon ancestor), 2391
Lebhor na hUidhre, 1480, 8960
Lebhor na Nuachongbála, 1480
Le Bourdellès, Henri, 3125
Lechte, John, on structuralism, 8757
Lecky, W. E. H., 9109
Le Conte, Joseph, 9423
Le Coq, Albert von, 4492
Lecourt, Dominique, 5360
Lecs, Juris, 763
Lectio divina, meditation as basis of, 8199
Lectisternia (Roman ritual), 7905
Lectorium Rosicrucianum. *See also* Rosicrucians
Rijckenborgh (Jan van) as founder of, Hermetism and, 3953
Lectures in Metaphysics (Hamilton), 7087
Lectures on Romans (Luther), Pauck (Wilhelm) on, 7011
Lectures on the Origin and Growth of Religions (Sayce), 5968
Lectures on the Philosophy of Religion (Hegel), classification of religions in, 1819
Leda (mythic figure), 4321
Ledgerwood, Judy, on Khmer religion, 5133
Lee, Ann, **5389**
harassment of, 6548
as messiah, 6547
role in Shaker religion, 6516, 6534, 6557, 6563
Shakers and, 8268
Lee, Benjamin, 386
Lee, Jarena, 10037
Leenhardt, Maurice, **5389–5390,** 6801
experiential concept of myth of, 5389–5390
as missionary, 9324
on New Caledonia religion, 6500
on paradox of death, 146
Leeser, Isaac, 7582
Leeuw, Gerardus van der, **5390–5393**
aesthetics of, 48
animism's influence on, 363
on art and religion, 496, 499–500
and Bleeker (C. Jouco), 978
classification of religions, phenomenological, 1820
on community, 7716
dynamism of, 2542
Eliade and, 2755
ethical theology of, 5391
on Gestalt psychology of religion, 8878
historiography of, 4042
on *homo religiosus,* 4110
on human body, 4172
as initiator of Amsterdam congress, 843
life of, 5390–5391
on magic, 5565
on myth, 6367
Nilsson (Martin P.) and, 6622
phenomenology of, 1531
on phenomenology of religion, 7086–7087, 7091, 7094
phenomenology of religion and, 5391–5392
on power, 7350–7351
on revelation, 7774
on sacrifice, 8003
on supreme beings, 8878
works of, 5391
Lefall, Dolores, 74
Le Fevre, Dominique, 2155
Lefevre, Gustave, 2731–2732
Lefèvre, Jacques, 2992
Le Fèvre, Nicolas, 253
Lefèvre, d'Étaples Jacques
on Hermetism, 3946
and Reformation, 7662
LeFleur, William, 1084
LeFranc, Jeanne, 1374
Left and right, **5393–5394**
in body symbolism, 4161
in Buddhism, Southeast Asian, 9830
for gesturing, 7344
hands and, 3770
in *ḥājj* symbolism, 7156–7157, 7159
in Mandaean religion, 5635
Ginza of, 3494–3495, 5634, 5635
symbolism of
in African religions, 5394
in China, 5394
in Islam, 5393–5394
in labyrinths, 5275–5276
male/female differentiation in, 5394
in rituals, 7837
in Vedic cults, 9559, 9566
in Vodou, 9638
Left Behind book series, 2892
Legal Imagination, The (White), 5356–5357
Legalism, **5394–5396**
in Chinese philosophy *(Fa jia),* 1574
dao in, 5395
in Han dynasty, 5396
Han Fei Zi and, 3772–3773, 5395
in Qin empire, 1590, 5396
Shang Yang and, 5395
Xunzi on, 1587, 5395
Eastern Orthodox guard against, 1652
Lega people (Africa), kingship of, 5170
Legates, papal, in Roman Catholic polity, 1764
Legatio (Athenagoras), 589
Legba (deity)
in Haitian Vodou, 1433
description of, 8690
in Latin American fiction, 3065
transcendence in sacred time and, 7987
as trickster, 9352–9353
Légendes epiques, Les (Bédier), 7218
Legends
vs. myths, 6376
in typology of narratives, 6376–6377
Léger, Fernand, abstract art of, 55
Legge, F., 208
Legge, James, 1633, 1635
in religious studies, 2608
Legio Maria movement, 105
Legion, 2928
Legion of Mary, 105
Legion of the Archangel Michael
Eliade and, 2758, 2759–2760
Evola (Julius) and, 2905
Legitimation, **5396–5404**
in Buddhism, 5400–5401
decline of authority and, 5397–5398
definition of, 5396
liberation theology, 5402–5403

nationalism and, 5398
philanthropy and, 5397
pluralism and, 5397, 5398
praxis and, 5398–5404
religiously-based, 5396–5397
royal genealogies and, in Indian historiography, 4025
social action and, 5396–5397
Socialism and, 5399
values and, 5397
Le Goff, Jacques, 7254
Legs bshad snying po (Tsong kha pa), 1276, 9387
Legs ldan 'byed pa. *See* Bhāvaviveka
Le-he-he. *See* Tenes
Lehmann, Edvard, **5404–5405**
Lehmann, F. R., preanimism criticized by, 7373
Lehrbuch der Dogmengeschichte (Harnack), dogma in, 3778
Lehrbuch der Religionsgeschichte (Chantepie de la Saussaye), 363, 1531
Lehrhaus (Free Jewish House of Learning), 7926
Lehtisalo, Toivo, 1453
on Arctic religions, 475
Leibniz, Gottfried Wilhelm, **5405–5407**
and binary number system, 6751–6752, 6753
on chance, 1527
on Chinese rituals, 1921
on dualism, 2505
Eastern philosophy influencing, 7112
on evil, 5407
on existence of God, 5406, 7421
on free will, 3200
on knowledge, 5205, 5206
mathematic works of, 5406
Mendelssohn (Moses) and, 5854
metaphysical thesis of, 5407
metaphysics of, 5990–5991
Neoplatonism and, 6475
and Newton, 6588
Nicholas of Cusa's influence on, 6610
on philosophy of nature, 6431
realistic idealism of, 9282
reunion projects of, 5405, 5406
on Rosicrucians, 7930
as subjective idealist, 4355
theodicy coined by, 9112
writings of, 5406–5407
Leibowitz, Jakob (Frank). *See* Frank, Jacob
Leibowitz, Nehama, 869
Leibowitz, Yeshayahu, 4906–4907
Leiles, George, 68
Leiman, Sid, on canon, 1408
Leinaweaver, Richard, 2436
Leipzig Disputation, Eck (Johann) in, 2601
Leisegang, Hans, on Gnosticism, 3532–3533
Leivestad, Ragnar, 596
Leizistic study of religion, in Poland, 8772–8773
Lejeune, Philippe, 698
Lekganyane, Ignatius, prophetic movement, 1720
Lekwena, Alice, 106
Leland, John, 784
Lele religion. *See* Central Bantu religions
Lelu (Micronesia), grand rituals at, 6006–6007
Lemba religion, 84
Haitian Vodou, influence on, 1433
Lemminkäinen, **5407–5408**
death and rising of, 1875
death of, 5408
Lenaia festival, 375, 3383
Lenat, Douglas, 510
Lencquist, Erik Christian, 3111
Lengqie shizi ji (Buddhist text), 994
Lengua people (Paraguay)
initiation rites of, 8585
religion of, 8634–8635
Lenin, V. I., on Muslims, 4624
Lenni Lenape. *See* Delaware religion
Lenoble, Robert, on the supernatural, 8861
Lenormant, François, 2964
on Mesopotamian religions, 5968
Lenshina, Alice, **5408–5409**
Lumpa church founded by, 105, 5408–5409
prophetic movement, 1720, 7443
syncretism, 1511
Lent, 3171. *See also* Carnival
in Christian liturgical calendar, 1743, 9814–9815
domestic observances of, 2399
fasting during
eggs and, 2702
as purification, 7508
Zwingli (Huldrych) on, 7659
origins of, 7771
Orthodox liturgies during, 2592
pilgrimage during, 7154
retreats during, 7771
in *Rule of the Master,* 7771
waehma, as ritual performance of, 7045
Lenten, 2996
Lenzoni, Carlo, on Hermetism, 3951
Leo (constellation), 5464
Leo (zodiacal sign), 5464
Leo I (Eastern Roman emperor), 6967
Leo I (pope), **5409–5410,** 6966–6967
at Council of Chalcedon, 6966–6967
angry response to, 5410
declared mouthpiece of Peter, 1688
two-nature Christology articulated by, 2040, 4242
as deacon, 5409
against Manichaeism, 5667
as successor of Peter, 5409–5410
Leo III (Byzantine emperor)
Charlemagne and, 696, 1557
and Germanos I, 4289
iconoclasm of, 2041, 2585, 4386
Leo III (pope)
Charlemagne and, 6967, 7280
filioque addition opposed by, 2585
Leo IV (Byzantine emperor), 9003
Leo V (Byzantine emperor)
and iconoclasm, 4289, 4290
Nikephoros's exile under, 6619
Leo VI (emperor), fourth marriage controversy, 8155–8156
Leo IX (pope)
filioque doctrine and, 8156
Gregory VII and, 3689
reform under, 3689, 3690, 6967
Leo X (pope)
and Franciscans, 3183
and Henry VIII, 7662
Reformation underestimated by, 6972
Leo XIII (pope), **5410–5412**
and Benedictines, 822
ethical teachings, 1654
Gibbons (James) and, 3479
on industrialization, 7878
Mercier (Désiré Joseph) and, 5868
modernity and, 5411
and Newman (John Henry), 6510
in Perugia, 5411
Scholasticism and Leonine Thomism, 8176–8177
on social transformation, 1671, 1752–1753, 5411–5412
on Thomism, 5411
Thomism revived by, 9164
and ultramontanism, 6974
León, Alonso de, 406
León, Ponce de, 7683
Leonard, Ellen, 7071
Leonardo da Pistoria, Hermetism and, 3945
Leonardo da Vinci, 4346
León-Portilla, Miguel, 5915, 5942
Leontius of Byzantium, **5412–5413**
Leo of Rome
Christology and, 5042
theological issues addressed by, 2582
Leopardi, Giacomo, 3526
Leopard-skin priests, in Nuer religion, 2569
Leopold, Aldo, 2563, 2609, 2656
Leo the Great. *See* Leo I (pope)
Leovigild (Visigothic king), 4556
Leowitz, Cyprianus von, 564
Lepenski Vir culture, 6463
Lepeschchin, I., 5709
Le Play, Frédéric, on religion and the worker, 8480
Lepowsky, Maria, 3396
Leprechaun, 2951
Leprosy. *See also* Scale disease
of Miriam, 6062
Lequier, Jules, 6963
Lerner, Gerda, 3360
Leroi-Gourhan, André
Granet (Marcel) influencing, 3655
on horse symbolism at Lascaux, 4131
on memorization, 5850
on Paleolithic coherence of expression, 3974
Le Roux, Françoise, 1483, 1499
leRoux, Pieter Louis, 7030
Le Roy, Édouard, 5207
Modernism of, 6106
Léry, Jean de
on musical rituals, 6272
on Tupinambá Indians, 8593
Lesa (deity), 1507
in Bemba religion, 817
Le Saux, Henri, 547
Lesbianism, **5413–5416.** *See also* Gay men and lesbians; Homosexuality
biological *vs.* social construction of, 5413–5414
in China, 4117
definitions of, 5414
prohibitions on, 5415
religion and, 9792
in Sparta, 4113
Lesbian studies, 5413
differentiation from gay male and queer studies, 5413, 5414
writings on, 5413
Leser, Paul, 5261
Lese- und Schreibfehler im Alten Testament, Die (Delitzsch), 2263
Lesky, Albin, 5466
Leslie, Julia, 3321
Lessa, William A., 379
Lesser, Alexander, on games, 3268
Lesser, Isaac, **5390**

Lesser Antilles
Columbus at, 1429
Island Carib in, 1426
Lesser Eastern Churches, 2584
Lesser Mysteries at Agrai, 6329
Lesser Mysteries of Agra, 1459
"Lesser Vehicle." *See* Hīnayāna Buddhism
Lessing, Ferdinand D., 9189
Lessing, G. E., **5416–5418**
belief in reincarnation, 9330
biblical exegesis of, 875
on Christianity *vs.* rationalism, 5416–5417
Faust story and, 3010
in German Enlightenment, 2797
Herder (Johann Gottfried) *vs.*, 3918–3919
on Homer, 3919
Mendelssohn (Moses) and, 5854
Reimarus (Hermann Samuel) published by, 4846
Reimarus's (Hermann Samuel) influence on, 7675
on revealed religion, 5416–5417
on Spinoza (Baruch), 8685
writings of, 5416
Lessons in Truth (Cady), 6586, 9472–9473
Lethe (river), 3016
Leto (deity), Artemis as daughter of, 506
Let Our Children Go! (Patrick), 2291
Letter Concerning Toleration (Locke), 2288, 5368, 7250, 7282
"Letter from Birmingham Jail" (King), 5402
Letter Killeth, The (Jones), 4952
Letter of Aristeas, 886, 926, 5426
Letter of Jeremiah, 897
Letter of Menoeceus (Epicurus), religion and death in, 3911
Letter of Peter to Philip, 7069
Letters (alphabetic)
on amulets and talismans, 298–299
mystical speculation on, 270–272, 6353
shape of, 270–271
Letters, as literary form, 5470
Letters and Papers from Prison (Bonhoeffer), 1017
Letters on Sunspots (Galileo), 3257
Letters on the Gospel (Adams), 30
Letters That Have Helped Me (Judge), 5023–5024
Letter to Anebo (Porphyry), 9157
Letter to a University Professor (Tyrrell), 9428
Letter to His Wife Marcella (Porphyry), 7191
Letter to the Emir of Damascus (Nicetas), 7243
Letter to the Hebrews
Abraham in, 16
God in, 3545
Letter to the Romans. See Romans
Letter to the Soldiers of Coroticus (Patrick), 7009, 7010
Lettres provinciales (Pascal), 7001
Leuba, James H., **5418**
American study of religion, role in, 8785
on psychology of religion, 7475
Leucippus, materialism and, 5776
Leuken, Veronica, 6548
Leukippos, 184
Leupp, Quick Bear v., 7302
Leur, J. C. Van, 745
Levack, Brian, on witch hunts, 8249
Levanon, Ha- (periodical), Mohilever (Shemu'el) in, 6113
Levant
goddess worship in, 3595–3596
region defined, 1390
Leve. *See* Ngewo
Levenson, Jon, on sacrifice, 8009
Levenson, Jon D., 5357–5358
Levey, Howard Stanton. *See* LaVey, Anton
Levi (priest), 7399
Lévi, Sylvain, 1313, 1634, **5418–5419**
and Foucher (Alfred), 3176, 3177
Levi, tribe of, 5422
Levi, Yisḥaq Eiziḳ ha-, 194
Levi (biblical figure), Matthew the Evangelist as, 5780
Leviathan (Ascher), 7667
Leviathan (Hobbes), 5367
abuses of the scripture in, 4074–4075
biblical history in, 4075
importance of, 4073
laws of nature in, 4074
state of nature in, 4074
Leviathan (sea monster), in Canaanite literature, 1384, 1392
Levi ben Gershom. *See* Gersonides
Levinas, Emmanuel, 2951
on ethics, 5482
and French feminists, 3028
on law and justice, 1945
in modern Jewish thought, 4909
on Orientalism, 6884
on phenomenology of religion, 7099
postmodern writings of, 9238
on prophecy, 7442
Rosenzweig's (Franz) influence on, 7927
on suffering, 3429
Levine, Baruch, 7513
Levine, Lawrence, 76
Levine, Lee, 6019
Levinson, Bernard M., 4729
Levinson, David, 106
Levirate, 5724
Lévi-Strauss, Claude
on Amazonian religion, 8596
on bone rituals, 1014
on bull-roarers, 1320
comparative mythology of, 1876
on cultural analysis of religion, 8470
on culture, 8750
on dualism, 2506
Dumézil (Georges) and, 2519, 3460, 4463
on ecstasy, 2679
Eliade and, 6368
on equivocal position of humans, 7796
on ethnoastronomy, constellations in, 2865
on food
raw and cooked, 6821–6822
rules for, 3173
and French feminism, 3028
on games, 3266
on Ge mythology, 3292, 3293–3295
on Gennep (Arnold van), 3432
Godelier's (Maurice) critique of, 3481
on Goldenweiser (Alexander A.), 3634
Granet (Marcel) influencing, 3655
Leach (Edmund) on, 8757
on magic, 5568, 5569, 5572
Mauss (Marcel) and, 5786
on memorization, 5851
methodological critique by, 379
methods of, 5381
on myth, 8753
on myths
comparative analysis of, 3294
similarities among, 3292
on nature, worship of, 6440
Penner (Hans H.) on, 8758
praising Berndt's (Catherine) work, 840
on primitive societies, 8751
Radcliffe-Brown (A. R.) *vs.*, 8749
on reality and the mind, 8751, 8752, 8759
on reflexivity, 7649
religion dismissed by, 6368, 6369
on rituals, 7839
the sacred in work of, 6368
Saussure (Ferdinand de) and, 8750, 8751
structuralism of, 4045, 6368, 8749–8750, 8751
and study of North American Indian religions, 6672, 6709
on symbols, 4298
symbol theory and, 8911, 8913
on totemism, 1422, 9250, 9251–9252
universalism of, 8752–8753
on validity, 8751
Levi-Tanai, Sara, 2164
Levitation, 3127, 3128–3129
Levites, **5419–5428**
Aaron as, 1, 5423
administrative functions of, 5426
as beneficiaries of tithe, 9209
biblical references to, 5420–5423
cultic functions of, 5424–5425
definition of, 5420
distinction from priests, 5422
functions of, 5424–5427
instructional functions of, 5426
judicial functions of, 5426
laws on, 4731
lineages of, 5421
marriage of, 5424
in monarchic period, 5421–5422
oracular functions of, 5425
organization of, 5423–5424
origin of, 5419
political functions of, 5426
in postexilic period, 5426–5427
priesthood reserved to, 7395, 7399
purity of, 5424
sacrificial functions of, 5424–5425
support systems for, 5424
Temple singing by, 927–928
therapeutic functions of, 5425–5426
as tribe of Levi, 5422
vestments of, 5424
Leviticus, 878
Aaron in, 1, 5423
ablutions after childbirth in, 11
altars in, 277
'Aqiva' ben Yosef on, 442
asceticism in, 5372
blasphemy in, 971–972
blessings and curses in, 4745
content of, 9232
Douglas (Mary) on, 7513
Eliyyahu ben Shelomoh Zalman on, 868
Golden Rule in, 3632, 3633
Hoffmann (David) on, 869
Karaites and Rabbinites divided over, 865
law of talion in, 5373–5374
laws in, 9232
criminal law, 4738
dietary laws, 7508
personal status laws, 4731
property law, 4734, 4735
purity laws, 7511
Levites in
tax exemptions for, 5421
therapeutic functions of, 5425–5426
Malbim on, 5626
menstruation in, 5866
midrashim on, 6018
Milgrom (Jacob) on, 7512–7513, 7514
mystical union and, 6340
pesher of, 7065

priesthood in, 7399, 7400
purification in, of homes, 4105
qiddush ha-shem in, 7056
scapegoat in, 8144
scapegoat rite described in, 2598
tattooing in, 1002
Temple procedures in, 926, 927, 929, 933, 934
tithes in, 9209, 9210
in Torah, 9231, 9232
Yishma'e'l ben Elisha' on, 442
Levi Yitsḥaq of Berdichev, **5428**
Leviyyim. *See* Levites
Levtzion, Nehemia, 4662
Lévy, Bernard-Henri, on monotheism, 6161–6162
Levy, Gertrude R., 5281
Lévy, Paul, on Buddhism, as mystery religion, 6327
Levy, Robert, on genital operations, 7808
Lévy-Bruhl, Lucien, **5429**
on African religions, supreme beings of, 3576
animism's influence on, 363
Durkheim (Émile) criticized by, 5429
on dynamism, 2542
Evans-Pritchard (E. E.) and, 2895–2896
evolutionism and, 2916
on humor of "primitives," 4201
on magic, 2267, 5563, 5565, 5567, 5571–5572
on *mana* as soul, 8531
Mauss (Marcel) and, 5785
on myth, 5389–5390
on "participation mystique," 2282
on primitive *vs.* civilized mentality, 5429
on purification, 7504
revaluation of, 380
on revenge, 7780
on society and religion, 8465
and study of North American Indian religions, 6671
on the supernatural, 8862
symbol theory and, 8911
Lewald, Ernest Anton, 3531
Lewandowski, Louis, 6312
Lewandowski, Martha, 1850
Lewis, Bernard, 4716, 4720, 4722
on modernism, 6096
Lewis, Bonnie Sue, 6421
Lewis, C. S., **5429–5430**
atheism of, 5430
autobiography of, 699, 5430
on miracles, 6056
morality in work of, 3062
on moral rules, 6183
on myths, 5430
on pain, 6944
posthumous works attributed to, the Family and, 2988
Tolkien (J. R. R.) and, 5430
Lewis, Gilbert, on ritual symbols, 7839
Lewis, Harvey Spencer, religious broadcasting and, 7710
Lewis, I. M.
on affliction, 57
on charisma, 1547–1548
on ecstasy, 2679
on exorcism, 2935
on new religious movements, 670
on sex roles, 10027–10028
on spirit possession, 8687, 8690, 10027
on *zaar* cult, 107
Lewis, James R., 6523, 6527
Lewis, Matthew Gregory, 3061
Lewis, R. W. B., 6985
Lewis, Sinclair, 3060
Lewis, Todd T., 9277
Lewontin, Richard C., on evolutionary psychology, 8475
Lewu Liau, 138
Lex, Barbara W., 3506
Lex Coloniar Iuliae Genetivae Ursonensis, 7909
Lex Cornelia, 5333, 7907
Lexikon der Ägyptologie, 2732
Lex Julia, 7907
Lex Ogulnia, 7907
Lex orandi, lex credendi (the church prays, so the church believes), 9540
Lex Proprio (papal document), 822
Lex talionsis principle
in Israelite religion, 4738, 4742
pain in, 6946
Lezghians (Caucasus), 4614
Lha-Bzaṅ Khan (Dalai Lama), 2132
Lhacam (Tibetan princess), reincarnation of, 5192
Lhag mthong (insight meditation), 1284
Lha'i rnal 'byor (deity yoga), 1286–1287, 2323
Lha lung Dpal gyi rdo rje (Buddhist monk), 1152
Lhalungpa, Lobsang P., on Milaraspa and Marpa, 8713
Lhamarnda (secular), 6260–6261
Lhasa (Tibet)
pilgrimage to, 7167, 9185
Potala (palace of Dalai Lama) in, 2131, 9051–9052, 9184
Lhasa council
Khri Srong Ide'u btsan sponsoring, 1095
overview of, 2037–2038
Lha Tho tho ri (king of Yar lung), 1151
Li (principle or rites), **5430–5432**
in Buddhism, 2628, 5431
Cheng Hao on, 1561
Cheng Yi on, 1563
in Confucianism, 2631, 2633, 5431
Confucius on, 1586, 1894, 1936
Daosheng on, 2217
homophones of, 5430
in *Huainanzi,* 5430–5431
laws and, 5351
in *Mengzi,* 5430
in Neo-Confucianism, 1603, 9311
as principle, 5430–5431
as rite, 5431
sagehood and, 8037
salutations and, 8060
in *Shi jing,* 5430
suicide and, 8832
tian li (heavenly *li*), 5431
Wang Fuzhi on, 9673
Wang on, 1578
yi and, 7751, 7752
zhi li (ultimate *li*), 5431
Zhu on, 1578
Zhu Xi on, 9973
Li, Andrew, diary of, 1725
Lia Fáil (Stone of Fál), 1492
Liaisons dangereuses, Les (Laclos), 9072
Li'ān (imprecation procedure), 4710–4711
Liandu (Daoist ritual), 2186
Liang Wudi (Emperor Wu of Liang dynasty), **5432**
Bodhidharma's encounter with, 995
Buddhism supported by, 1596, 5432
Buddhism under, 1163, 1164, 1236, 5432
and Buddhist/Doaist conflict, 2183–2184, 2194, 5432
Chan Buddhism and, 1521
Confucianism institutionalized by, 1897
Dong Zhongshu and, 2418
immortality, quest for, 1592
lectures by, 1249
overthrow of, 5432
Paramārtha and, 6992
quest for immortality of, 4332, 7267
religious practices established by, 1591, 5432
Liang Wu-ti. *See* Liang Wudi
Liang Yusheng, 3070
Liangzhu people, jade carvings of, 4758
Li Ao, 1577
Liao dynasty (China)
Buddhism in, 1254, 1255
temples of, 9047
Daoist temples in, 9057
Liao state, 1523
kingship of, 5179
Li Baichuan, 3068
Libanius (pagan rhetor), 797
Libation, **5432–5435,** 9561–9562
in Assyrian religion, 5433
in Babylonian religion, 5433
in Celestial Masters/Heavenly Masters community, 2180, 2181, 2192, 2193
in Chinese religion, 5434
discontinuation of use, 5434
in Egyptian religion, 5433
etymology of word, 5433
in Greek religion and mythology, 5433
in Shintō, 5434
in Iranian religions, 4535, 5434
in Israelite religion, 927, 5434
meanings of, 5433
in Vedism, 5434
of Vikings, 5343
in West African religions, 9719
Libationers, in Villa of the Mysteries fresco, vol. 2 color insert
Libel, against new religious movements, 5378
Libellatici, Decian persecution and, 2112
Libellus (Athenagoras), 4360
Libellus responsionum (Gregory I), 3688
Liberal Catholic Church, 5244
Liberal Catholicism, definition of, 6102
Liberalia (festival), 5321
Liberalism
Christian, 6102–6107
assessment of, 6106–6107
Barth (Karl) against, 6104, 6107
common characteristics of, 6103
definitions of, 6102
Kant and, 6102–6103
use of term, 6102
in Jewish Renewal, 4871
Pius IX against, 7179, 7180
as response to classical physics, 7137
of Trubetskoi (Evgenii), 9367
Vatican I and, 9529–9530
Liberal Judaism, 4983. *See also* Reform Judaism
Montagu (Lily) in, 6166–6167
Liberal lives of Jesus, 4846
Liberal Protestantism, 6103–6106. *See also* Schleiermacher, Friedrich
definition of, 6103
ethics and, 1656
Harnack (Adolf von), role of, 3778–3779
hermeneutics and, 3931
homo religiosus and, 4109
Neoorthodoxy as reaction against, 6466, 6467

Liberal Protestantism
continued
Otto (Rudolf) attack on, 8493
vs. Protestant liberalism, 6103, 6105
vs. Reform Judaism, 7235
religious experience in, 7738–7739
Schleiermacher (Friedrich) as founder of, 3931
Spiritualism and, 8716
in United States
in Congregationalism, 1938
denominationalism and, 1712
fundamentalism *vs.*, 2889
Liber antiquitatum biblicarum, resurrection in, 7765
Liber apologeticus martyrum (Eulogius), 7243
Liberating Rites (Driver), 7858
Liberation, **5435**
in black theology, 5441
in Buddhism (*See Mārga*)
deliverance distinct from, 5435
expiation distinct from, 5435–5436
in Hinduism (*See Mokṣa*)
illumination distinct from, 5435
in Jainism (*See Siddha*)
karman and, 5099
in kingdom of God, 5153
living, 8527
morality and, 6188
parallel concepts of, 5435–5438
rescue distinct from, 5436
by shape shifting, 8302
in soteriology, 8526
transcendence and, 5437–5438
women's (*See* Feminism)
Liberation and Reconciliation (Roberts), 77–78
Liberation Ecologies: Environment, Development, and Social Movements (Peet and Watts), 2611
Liberation theology, **5438–5442**
in African American religions, 77–78, 5440–5441, 10040
in African religions, 5442
in Asian religions, 5442
base communities in, 1775–1776, 5439
Bible movement and, 5440
black (*See* Black Theology)
Catholicism and, 9540
charisma in, 5439
Christology of, 5439
definition of, 5438
development of
diversification stage, 5439–5440
formulation stage, 5438–5439
preparation stage, 5438
systematization stage, 5439
ecclesiology of, 5439
economics in, 2676
ecumenism from, 2687
ethics and, 1656–1657
feminism and, 5402–5403, 5440
formulation and precepts of, 1704
goals of, 7245–7246
God in, 3559, 5439
of Grail movement, 3654
historiography and, 4032
and history, view of, 4055
indigenous peoples and, 5440
in Latin America, 5302–5403, 5438, 5439, 5440
and legitimation, 5402–5403
in Mesoamerica, 5930–5931
Minjung feminist theology, 5236, 5441
Nightingale's theology and, 6618
political theology and, 5440
in progressive Islam, 6098–6099
Protestant contribution to, 1704
religion-society relations and, 8468
scripture in, 5402–5403
social movements and, 1754
Sölle (Dorothee), role of, 8512
in United States, 5442
wealth and, 9709
women's studies and, 9792
zeal of evangelization and, 3063
Liber de causis, 6475
Liber de sex rerum principisi, medieval commentary on, 3945
Liber hebraicarum quaestionum (Hebrew questions) (Jerome), 4834
Liberia
African American emigration to, 4951
Christianity in, Crummell (Alexander), role of, 2073–2074
Dan people of, masks of, 5766, 5767
Gola people of, dances of, 2141
Harris (William Wade) and, 3780–3781
Liber Linteus (Linen book) of Zagreb, 2870
Liber locorum (Book of places) (Jerome), 4834
Liber officialis (Amalarius), 2468
Liber Pater (festival), 5321
Liberty Hall (Harlem), 3287
Liber viginti quattuor philosophorum, medieval commentary on, 3945
Libraries
Charlemagne's court library, 1556–1557
of Egyptian temples, 2715, 2723–2725
Mesopotamian, 5161
in monasteries, 6118
Libri poenitentiales, 1652
Libri sibyllini. See Sibylline Oracles
Libya
Cyrenaica, Christians in, 1677–1678
Islam in
Islamic law in, 4703
neofundamentalist, 4574
as state religion, 4590
Licet ab initio (Paul III), 4501
Lichtenberg, Georg Christoph, on symbol theory, 8908–8909
Lichtenberger, Johann, 564
Lidai diwang chongdao ji (Daoist text), 2209
Līdaks, Osvalds, 327
Li Dan (Li Er), 5316, 5318. *See also* Laozi
Lidzbarski, Mark
Ginza translated by, 3495
on Mandaean religion, 3532, 5637, 5638
Lie, as cause of the Fall, 2964
Liebman, Charles, on Reconstructionst Judaism, 7637
Liedtke, Ralph, on *Corpus Hermeticum,* 3953
Liele, George, **5442–5443**
in Jamaica, 1706
Lienert, Tania, 5414
Lienhardt, Godfrey, 117
on afterlife, 136
on Dinka religion, 2366, 2367, 7842
on Shilluk religion, 2567
on spirit possession, 8689
Li Er (Li Dan), 1574, 5316, 5318. *See also* Laozi
Lietzmann, Hans, on Eastern creeds, 2056
Liexian zhuan (Biographies of the immortals), 5316, 9843
zhenzen in, 9959
Liezi (book), 1575
LIFE. *See* Lighthouse of International Foursquare Evangelism
Life, **5443–5450**
in African religions, 5445
in Australian religions, 5444
breath as sign of, 5443
in Buddhism, 5448
in Chinese religion, Wang Chong on, 9671–9672
in Christianity, 5445–5446
in Confucianism
productivity of, 2632
protection of, 2632–2633
cosmic solidarity of, 2560
death as fact of, 2235
distinction from afterlife, 5449
dragons as givers of, 2433
eagle and hawk associated with, 2553
egg as symbol of, 2701, 2702
elephant associated with, 2750
eternity as, 2854
ethical relations with, among Maori, 2618
in Gnosticism, as exile, 2923
hierarchical view of, 2606
in Hinduism, 5443, 5447–5448
indications of, 5443
in Indonesian religions, 5444–5445
interrelatedness of, in deep ecology, 2561
in Islam, 5446–5447
medical ethics regarding, 5812
in Jainism, 2624
in Judaism, 5445
length of (*See* Longevity)
light as symbol of, 5451
meaningful, interpretations of, 5449
medical advances affecting, medical ethics and, 5810–5811
of the mind, in eternity, 2854
mother earth and, 2557–2559
myth complexes on, 4825
in Native American religions, 5444
in oath-taking, 9640
organic matter, problematic of, 4158
orgy and, 6861, 6864
phases of (*See also* Rites of passage)
ablutions relating to, 9
"playing God" problem and, 8187
profane *vs.* sacred, 5444
religious, characteristics of, 7696–7700
in religious ecology, 2606
reverence for, Schweitzer (Albert) on, 8179
in Roman Catholicism
medical ethics regarding, 5811
sanctity of, 5811
serpents associated with, 8458–8459
source of, earth as, 2554–2555
tree of (*See* Tree of life)
in Warlpiri religion, 9693
water identified with, 9699, 9702
words designating, 5443
Life (Teresa of Ávila), 9084
Life after Life (Moody), 6925
Life and Death of Mr. Badman, The (Bunyan), 1323
Life and Death of Saint Malachy, The (Bernard), 839
Life and Teachings of the Masters of the Far East, The (Spaulding), 4246
Life crisis, rites of passage at times of. *See* Rites of passage
Life cycle
Brahmanic Hindu rites of (*See Saṃskāras*)

dainas (folk songs) dealing with, 2127
religious integration with, 2604
rituals of (*See also* Rites of passage)
in Judaism, 7818
kinship and, 5184
Life is Worth Living (television program), 7712
Life of Antony (Athanasius), 7769–7770
Life of a South African Tribe, The (Junod), 113
Life of Brainerd (Edwards), 2699
Life of Buddha as Legend and History, The (Thomas), 945, 1312
Life of Christ (Nolde), 4348
Life of Constantine (Eusebius), 2884
Life of Gregory the Great, 6943
Life of Jesus (Renan), 7750
Life of Jesus (Strauss), 805, 5745
influence of, 8748
themes of, 8747–8748
Life of Mahomet and History of Islam, to the Era of Hegira, The (Muir), 945
Life of Patrick (Muirchú), 2493
Life of Saint Thierry, The (medieval text), 2489
Life of Saint Wilfrid, 6943
Life of the mind, in eternity, 2854
Life readings, 1473, 1474
Life stages, in Hinduism. *See Āśramas*
Life support, 5813
Life Together (Bonhoeffer), 1017
Lifeways
definition of, 2617
rights to, religion and ecology in, 2617
Lifeworld
Husserlian notion of, 4236
in Maasai cosmology, 2000
Lifton, Robert, 1031
Light, **5450–5455**. *See also* Darkness
in bright sky, omniscience of supreme beings indicated by, 8869
in Buddhism, 5453
rays from body of the Buddha, 2030
Shinran on *kōmyō,* 8355
in Chinese religion, 5453
in Christianity, 5453
at Easter Vigil, 2579
inner light, Symeon the New Theologian on, 8920
light ritual at Paschal vigil, 1742
complementary to *vs.* opposition to darkness, 5450–5451
in creation myths, 5450–5454
emergence from darkness, 5450
in esotericism, 5454
eye linked with, 2940
festivals of, 5453–5454
in Gnosticism, 5452
in Greek philosophy, 5452
in Hermeticism, 5452
in iconography, 5454
in Ishrāqīyah, 4554
in Iranian religion, 4537
in Islam, in Qur'ān, 5454
in Judaism, 5453
Ḥanukkah as festival of, 3774
in Hasidism, 3788, 3792
Kimḥat (David) on, 5145
in Mandaean religion, 5452–5453
in Manichaeism, 5452–5453, 5648, 5652, 5666
millenarianism of, 6040
in Mazdakism, 5800
in Mesoamerican religions, 5451
Mithra as god of, 6087
in mysticism, 5454
in nature, philosophy of, 6433–6434
of Muḥammad *(nūr Muḥammad),* **6766–6768**
ouranic deities associated with, 5451
in South American cosmologies, 2013, 8588
in Maku religion (Amazon), 8625
in Muisca religion, 6229–6230
al-Suhrawardī on, 2977, 4554–4555
sun as source of, 5451
supreme beings and, 8871
as symbol of life, 5451
in Vedism, Agni as god of, 3990
of warrior, 9684
Lightfoot, Joseph B., 4369
Lighthouse of Freedom, 1781, 4247, 7445
Lighthouse of International Foursquare Evangelism (LIFE) Bible College, 5803
Light in August (Faulkner), 5480
Light-Mind (Light-Nous), in Manichaeism, 5666, 5667
Lightning, 7603–7604
in Greek mythology, guilt and punishment symbolized by, 7783
as portent, 7336
in shamanism, 5992
spirits of, in Haitian Vodou, 1433 (*See also* Shangbo)
swords as symbol of, 967
of Zeus, 5994
Lightning deities, 5992–5996
Illapa as, 4411
in Lugbara religion, 2568
Zeus, 9952
Light of Asia, The (Arnold), 1187
Campbell (Joseph) and, 1378
Light of Lights, Shaykh Aḥmad on, 8307
Light of the Lord, The (Crescas), 154
Aristotelianism, assault on, 2069
influence of, 2070
Lightworld (Mandaean heaven), 5635–5637
in *Ginza,* 5634
Li Gonglin (artist), 4338
Liguori, Alfonso, 1455
on Mary, 5754
Li Ho (poet), 7214
Liholiho. *See* Kamehameha II
Li Hong/Li Hung, 1594
messianism of, 2195, 2205
millenarianism of, 6039
Li Hongzhi, 1611, 2978, 2979
immigration to U.S., 2980
message after campaign against Falun Gong, 2981
teachings of, 2979–2980, 7269
writings of, 2980
Li-ism (group), 8965
Liji (Book of Rites) (Confucian text), 5431
Cheng Hao on, 1561
dates of, 1591
Lao Dan in, 5315
millenarianism in, 6038
as one of the Five Scriptures, 1585
rain in, 7604
ren in, 7752
shamans in, 2454
Likitanir (mythic figure), 6002
Liktanur (mythic figure), 6002
Likud, coalition of, Agudat Yisra'el in, 196
Līlā (sport or play), **5455–5458,** 7046, 7195
in meditation, 5456–5457
mythology of, 5456
in salvation, 5457–5458
theology of, 5455–5456
Līlavajra (Buddhist scholar), 1216
Lileng łungx. See Mediator spirits
Liling puping. See Mediator spirits
Lilith (demon), 2277, 2896, 3158, **5458–5460**
Lilliston, Lawrence, 6539
Lilly, Eli, Sorokin (Pitirim Aleksandrovich) and, 8524
Li Longji, 2184
Lilungu (spirit), 7443
Lily of the valley, symbolism of, 3135
Lim, Paulino, 3079
Lima, Mesquitela, 3043
Lima councils I and III, 1695–1696
Lima Document on Baptism, Eucharist, and Ministry (1982), as ecumenical creed, 2061
Li Madou. *See* Ricci, Matteo
Limba people (Sierra Leone), funeral rituals of, 7806
Limbo, in Zoroastrianism, 9996
Limborch, Philippus van, in Remonstrant Brotherhood, 493
Limerov, Pavel Fedorovich, on Komi religion, 5217
Limière, Louis, 3097
Liminality, **5460–5463**
death and, 2240, 7815
definition of, 5460
in initiation, 4481
in modern society, 5461–5462
negative, 5462
preindustrial rites of, 5460–5461
reflexivity and, 7649
in rites of passage, 7797, 7801–7802
Agikuyu initiation rites, 7805
Tswana marriage rituals, 7805
ritual process and, 7049–7050
in rituals, 7844
Turner (Victor) on, 4481, 5461, 7330, 7797, 7801, 9406, 9407
Limitation, in hierophany (manifestation of the sacred), 3972
Limitless Ocean Cycle (Karma Pakshi), 5102
Limon, J. E., 3146
Limón, José, 2160
Linacre, Thomas, humanism and, 4176
Linares, Juan Vidarte de, 5899
Lin-Chi. *See* Linji
Lincoln, Bruce, 386, 3447, 4464, 7249, 7250, 7258
American study of religion, role in, 8786–8787
on *Táin Bó Cuailnge,* 8960
polythetic model of religion, 8471
on rites of passage, 7801, 7802
Lincoln, C. Eric, 74, 77
Lincoln, Kenneth, 3091
Lindberg, David C., on Thomas Aquinas, 8182
Lindblom, Gerhard, 115
Lindgren, J. Ralph, 7858
Lindow, John, 3458, 3460
Lindsay, Vachel, 3101
Lindsey, Hal, 413, 2892
Lindstrom, Lamont, on cargo cults, 1421, 1423–1424
Lineage. *See also* Ancestors; Genealogy; Matrilineal descent; Patrilineal descent
in central Bantu religion, 1520

Lineage ***continued***
in Chan Buddhism, 1523, 1601 (*See also* Caodong lineage; Linji lineage)
Huineng and, 4155
patriarchal structure in, 1520
teaching methods and, 8713–8714
in Chinese folk religion, 1616
in Confucianism, gender and, 3341
in Hasidism (*See Shoshalot*)
in Hinduism, lineage deities *(kuladevatās)* in, 4006
kinship and, 5185
portraiture establishing, vol. 10 color insert
Samaritan *Shalshāla* (Chain of High Priests), 8070
in Shingon Buddhism, 8349
in Southeast Asia
brahmans in, 4013
Khmer, 4010
in Sufism, 8710–8711, 8820–8821
in Tibetan Buddhism, 5223
history of ordination lineages, 8082
Lineage sacrifice, in East African religions, 2568–2569
Linear A, 38, 2894
Linear B, 41, 42, 43, 2894
Linear time, *vs.* cyclical time, 6373, 6374
Ling (spiritual power)
in Chinese popular religion, 1618
soul and, 8555
Ling, Trevor, 7261
Liṅga
as Śiva's symbol, 778–779
at Ellora caves, 1472
iconography of, 4323–4324
in Purāṇas, 7500
made of stone, 4326, 7494, vol. 4 color insert
as phallus, 4323, 7083
and pilgrimage, 7170
rural traditions of, 4436
double significance of, 8416
earliest example of, 8041
as explicit sexual phenomenon, 7077
in *Haṭhayoga,* 3795
as object of meditation, 4423
origin of, 8040
plurality of, 4422
precursors in Indus Valley religion, 3990
in Puranas, 8415
at Wahiawa temple (Oahu), 8419
Liṅga Purāṇa (Hindu text), 7500
Liṅga Śarīra. See Subtle body
Liṅgāyat (cult), 7719
Lingbao bifa (Daoist text), 2211
Lingbaojing, the (Scripture of the Sacred Jewel), 1597
Lingbao pian (Daoist text), 2211
Lingbao scriptures (Daoist), 2183, 2186, 2194, 2196, 2205
Lu Xiujing and, 5542, 5543
organization of, 2183, 2186, 2194, 2196
Ling Dro Dechen Rolmo (dance ritual), 2140
Lingfeng Yuyi Dashi (Zhixu), 9181
Ling Mengchu, 3068
Lingpa, Jikmé, visions of, 5195
Lings, Martin, on Ṣūfī election, 2749
Linguistic philosophy, liturgy in, 5492
Linguistics. *See also* Structuralism
analytic philosophy of, 306–308
Arabic, 7563
deconstruction and, 2245–2248
Derrida (Jacques) and, 2245–2248
of glossolalia, 3505
and history of religions, 10043–10044
Saussure (Ferdinand de) and, 2245–2248
Schleiermacher (Friedrich) on, 8163
Schmidt (Wilhelm) on, 8168
Southeast Asian, 8641
symbol theory and
Malinowski (Bronislaw) and, 8910–8911
Saussure (Ferdinand de) and, 8913
Vienna Circle and, 8913
syncretism, linguistic, 8928
Lingyan (charisma), 1549
Liṅgāyat Saivism. *See* Vīraśaivism
Lini, Walter, 7297
Linji (Buddhist monk), **5463–5464**
sayings of, 5464
teaching methods of, 5463–5464, 8714
Linji lineage, 5464
Huineng and, 4155
Japan, transmission to, 1523
meditation, approach to, 1604
origination of, 1522
shocks and puzzles in, 1577
Linji lu (Buddhist text), 5464
Linji school of Buddhism, 1240, 1293, 8967
Linji Yixuan, 1276, 1522, 1524
Lin Lingsu, 1602, 2186, 2205
Linnaeus, Carolus, 2909
Linqov (to enunciate), 971
Linton, Ralph, on nativistic movements, 670
Linzey, Andrew, on animals, 360
Lin Zhao'en, 1608, 3069
merging of Confucianism, Daoism, and Buddhism by, 2187
Lioba (nun), 822, 6763
Lion Dance, 2454, 2455
Lions, **5464–5465**
in astrology, 5464
in Bantu rites of passage, 8666
Herakles, lion of Nemea killed by, 3916
as Mark the Evangelist's symbol, 5715
in Mesopotamian iconography, 4315
in Minoan-Mycenaean iconography, 4321
royalty associated with, 5464
sun associated with, 5464, 8835
Lionza, María, spirit possession cult of, 6578–6579
Lipan Apache religion, 404–406
Lip bear, 808
Lipit-Ishtar (king), laws of, 1844
Lipkin, Yisra'el. *See* Salanter, Yisra'el
Li Po (poet), 7213
Lippert, Julius, manism and, 5673
Lips, in gestures, 7343–7344
Lipscomb, David, 1780
Lipscomb University, 1780
Lipsius, Richard Adelbert, on Gnosticism, 3532
Li Ruzhen, 3068
Lisa (deity), 3166, 5790. *See also* Mawu-Lisa
Li-sao (Qu Yuan), 7213
Li Shang-yin (poet), 7214
Li Shao-Chün. *See* Li Shaojun
Li Shaojun, **5465–5466**
Li Shaoweng, 5592
Lishi zhenxian tidao tongjian (Daoist text), 2206
Li Si, 1573–1574
Lispector, Clarisse, 3064
Listen to the Heron's Words (Gold and Raheja), 3322
Listing, Jacob B., 937
List wisdom, 9749
Lisu minority group (China), Christianity and, 1726
Liszt, Franz, 6312
Litan (Leviathan). *See also* Leviathan
in Canaanite religion, 1384
Literacy
in Dogon religion, 101
oral tradition and, 6842–6843
orthodoxy and heterodoxy and, 6909
primitive religions and, 2896
among slaves, 66
women and calligraphy, 1369
Literalism
in Churches of Christ, 1780
in Islamic eschatology, 2839
on magic, 5563, 5566
Literary criticism, 5472–5475, **5484–5489**
anthropology and, 383–384
Literature, **5466–5489**. *See also* Drama; Fiction; Sacred texts; *specific types*
apocalyptic (*See* Apocalypse)
of Armenian church, 6478
autobiographical, **697–704**
biblical (*See* Biblical literature)
Buddhist (*See also* Buddhist books and texts)
folk, 3156
theory and interpretation of, 5484–5485
Chinese (*See* Chinese literature)
Christian, 5469–5472
in modern Western society, 5477
critical theory and religious studies, **5484–5489**
curses in, 2106
Daoist (*See* Daoist literature)
deities of, in Chinese religion, 1608
divinity of, 5467
in the Enlightenment, 5477
fantasy, Gnosticism in, 3528
grace as theme in, 3647
Greek (*See* Greek literature)
Hindu, theory and interpretation of, 5484–5485
in Indian religions
interrelations of, 5466–5467
types of, 5467
interrelationship with religion, 5466, 5477
Islamic (*See* Islamic literature)
Japanese, of Kagawa Toyohiko, 5054
Jewish (*See* Hebrew literature)
of Karaites, 5084–5086
Karelian, 5092–5093
Kierkegaard's influence on, 5143
language in, 5472–5475
law and, 5328, **5355–5358**
canon and, 5355
Cover (Robert) on, 5357
Dworkin (Ronald) on, 5358
Levenson (Jon D.) on, 5357–5358
modern literature, 5355
Posner (Richard) on, 5356, 5357
White (James Boyd) on, 5356–5357
liturgy as, 5490
modern Western, **5477–5484**
Christic images in, 5479–5480
the Fall in, 5479
law and, 5355
secularization of, 5477–5478
Neopagan, 6471
of new religious movements, 6528
Nobel Prize for, Bergson (Henri), 838
periodical, **10056–10060**
popular
morality in, 3062
Sen (Keshab Chandra), use by, 8227

postmodern, 5482–5484
characteristics of, 5482–5483
fragmentary in, 5482
God in, 5483–5484
qabbalistic, 7538
Quaker, 7547
quests in, 7554
religion and, as field of study, 5356
of Romantics, 5477
scripture, influence of, 8203–8204
study of, 5472–5475
Deconstruction and, 5475–5476
Derrida (Jacques) on, 5474, 5475–5476
Heidegger on, 5474
language in, 5472–5475
New Criticism approach to, 5474
textual criticism *vs.* textual interpretation, 5472–5473
testimony of, 5466–5472
translation of, interpretation and, 5485
Wach's (Joachim) interest in, 9650–9651
Lithai, Phya, 3076
Lithuania and Lithuanian religions
ancestors in, cult of, 327–331
ancient religion of (*See* Baltic religion)
birth in, earth mother in, 2557
Christianization of, 773, 775, 1684–1685
dainos (folk songs) in, 2127
Judaism
Karaite sect, 5084, 5085
in middle ages, 5014
Musar movement in, **6241–6242**
Tamudic study in, 5015–5016
rainmaking in, 7603
Roman Catholicism, 775
twins in, 9420
Unitarianism, 9469
Lithuanian language, 756
Lithuanian Mythology (Narbutas), 762
Litigation, in Judaism, rabbinic Judaism, 7589
Li Tongxuan, Huayan Buddhism and, 1646, 4146
Little, David, on human rights, 5362
Little, Earl, 5626
Little, Lester, on maledictory formulas in monasteries, 2105
Little, Malcolm. *See* Malcolm X
Little, Meredith, 7802
Little, Robert Wentworth, 7930
Little, Stephen, 1638
Little Book of Enlightenment (Ruusbroec), 6337
Little Flowers. *See Fioretti*
Little Flowers (Francis of Assisi), 2309
Little Genesis. See Jubilees, Book of
Little People Society (Iroquois), 4542
Little Water Medicine Society (Iroquois), 4542
Little Women (Alcott), 7323
Littman, Lynn, 6326
Littré, Émile
Comte and, 1882
reducing philosophy to scientific thought, 7341
Liturgical calendar. *See* Calendars, Christian
Liturgical dance, 2136, 2152, 2164–2165, **2166–2167**
Liturgical drama, 2437, 2467–2471
at Easter, 2580
Liturgical movement
in Catholic Church, 9533
in Catholicism, 5490, 7879
Liturgical year, Christian, **1741–1745,** 9812–9815
Advent in, 1744
Christmas and Epiphany in, 1743–1744
and colors, liturgical, 1744
domestic observances in, 2399–2400
Easter in, 1741
Lent and Palm Sunday in, 1743
paschal fast in, 1742
paschal vigil in, 1742
Pentecost in, 1742–1743
sanctoral cycle in, 1744
since Reformation, 1744
Liturgy, **5489–5493**
of African Independent Churches, AmaNazaretha, 103
of Armenian church, 489–490
Austin (J. L.) on, 5492
Bergmann (Gustav) on, 5492
Buddhist
music in, 6294
siddhas and, 5605
Southeast Asian, 9827–9828
Tibetan, 9840
chanting of, 1532–1536
Christian
Anglican, 350, 5490 (*See also* Book of Common Prayer)
Cabilas on, 1343
Church of England, 5490
color symbolism in, 1861
controversies over, 5490
creeds in, 2054, 2056
in early Eastern Christianity, 2582
Eastern Orthodox
theology of, 7960
in ecumenism, 2689
Ethiopian, 2859
for exorcism, 2929–2930
hermits and, 2825
Justin Martyr on, 5045
language of, 1662
Lord's Prayer in, 5516
in Lutheranism, 5538
origins of, 7698–7699
pilgrimage themes in, 7153
Presbyterian, 7389
Roman Catholicism, 796–797, 5490, 7879
in Slavic language, 2116
standard service texts under Charlemagne, 1557
Syriac Orthodox, 8941
at Vatican II, 4946, 9540–9541
in vernacular, 9540–9541
in worship, 9811–9812
cultural anthropology and, 5491–5492
definition of, 5489–5490
Egyptian, inscriptions of, 2725–2726
Frazer (James G.) on, 5491
Freud (Sigmund) on, 5491
Hindu, heart, liturgy of, 3881
internal *vs.* external, 5490–5491
Jewish, 5490, 9808
election in, 2745–2746
Geonic, 3743
in rabbinic Judaism, 4978
at Shavu'ot, 8305–8306
Shemu'el the Amoram on, 8318
siddur and *maḥzor* (prayer books), **8386–8392**
and synagogue, history of, 8921–8922
Zion in, 9977
language of, 5491, 5492, 7119
in linguistic philosophy, 5492
as literature, 5490
Manichaean, 5656
metaphysics of, 5491–5492
neo-Marxist approach to, 5491
pattern *vs.* spontaneity in, Heschel (Abraham Joshua) on, 3962
poetry of, 7207–7208
religious *vs.* secular, 5490
Ricoeur (Paul) on, 5492
of rites of passage, 5492
as ritual, 5490–5491
Samaritan, 8070
sin, liturgical understanding of, in Israelite religion, 8404
sociology and, 5491
study of, future of, 5493
Tylor (E. B.) on, 5491
visual, 497
Wittgenstein (Ludwig) on, 5492
Zoroastrian, 9998
"Liturgy of Saint Basil," 798
Liturgy of the Hours, 9812
Liturgy of the Word, 9811–9812
Lituus (curved stick), 7336
Liu (Chinese princess), 2433
Liu An (king), **5493–5495**. *See also* Huainanzi
fangshi and, 2990, 5494
inner alchemy and, 5494–5495
as patron, 5494
Liu Chang, 5493
Liu Che, magic under, 5592–5593
Liu Chuxuan, teachings of, 2210
Liu Dabin, 2208
Liu Deren, **5495–5496**
Liu E, 3069
Liu Jun, on karma, 1899
Liu Ling, as eccentric, 4207
Liu Ming, 7416
Liu Pang, 5493
Liu Shipei, 2213
Liu Te-Jen. *See* Liu Deren
Liu Xiang, 5316
Liu Xie, on humor, 4199, 4206
Liu Xiu, 1592
Liu Yu, 2207
Liu Zhi (Muslim scholar), 4632
Livelihood
in eightfold path, 2738
in engaged Buddhism, 2788
Liver, in animal sacrifice, 2873
Liver of Piacenza, 2873
Lives of Dion and Brutus (Plutarch), 7200
Lives of Famous Men (Jerome), 9085
Livets Ord, 6568
Living and the Dead: A Study of the Symbolic Life of Americans, The (Warner), 7836
Living buddhas. *See* Buddhas, living
Living dead, in African religions, 141, 577
Living Flame of Love, The (John of the Cross), 2309, 4942
Living Gospel (Mani), 5649, 5651, 5666
Living religions. *See* World religions
Living Spirit (being), in Manichaeism, 5654, 5666–5667
Livingstone, David, 1001, 1003
on African religions, supreme beings of, 3576
Livius Andronicus, music and, 6304
Livonia, 767, 773
Livonicae Historicae (Dionysius), 7053–7054

Livre des espirits, le (Kardec), 5090
Livy
on apostasy, 431
on Bacchanalia, 6866
on Christian persecution, 7058
on Diana cult, 2346
on Dionysos, women in cult of, 3384
on Italian Bacchanalia, persecution of, 7909
on Lavinium, 7899
on *lucerna extincta* rite, 8248–8249
on music, 6304
on *religio,* 7894
on sacred space, 8428
on war rituals, 7896
Liwā, al- (Jawīsh), 7244
Li Yuan, as Perfect Lord, 2184
Lizards, 7305, 7307
in North American Indian mythology, 6661
Li Zhi, 1578
Llamas
Inca calendar and, 1364
Pachamama and, 5515
Lleu (deity), 1483. *See also* Lugh
Lleu Llaw Gyffes (deity), 1489
Llewellyn, Uthman, 2652
Llew Llaw Gyffes (deity), 5528
Lloyd, G. E. R., on magic, 5563, 5568
Llull, Ramón. *See* Lull, Ramón
Llŷr, Family of, 1489–1490
Lo'-'ammi (biblical figure), name of, 4137
Lobeck, Christian A., 6367
Lobha (greed), 748
Lobi religion (Burkina Faso), funeral rites in, 3236
Local Councils, of Russian Orthodox Church, 7945
Lo chen Dharmaśrī, 7869
Loch Ness monster, 6165
Locke, John, **5496–5497**
Channing (William Ellery), influence on, 1530
in Church of England, 5496
denominational theory popularized by, 2288
as empiricist, 7111
the Enlightenment influenced by, 2796
in exile, 7282
on experience, ideas derived from, 2778
on faith *vs.* reason, 2798
on free will and determinism, 3200
on government, 5496
on knowledge, 5496
on law and morality, 5367–5368
Mendelssohn (Moses) and, 5854
metaphysics of, 5991
on natural law, 8491
on Newton's *Principia,* 6588
on politics and religion, 7248, 7250, 7282–7283
on religious experience, 7737
on religious tolerance, 7282–7283
on religious toleration, 5368, 5496
Lockhart, James, 5922
Lockot, Hans Wilhelm, on Haile Selassie, 7626
Lockyer, J. Norman, on Egyptian temples, 8733
Locus consecratus, 1491
Locus dei (place of god), Symeon the New Theologian on, 8920
LoDagaa people (Ghana)
ancestor worship by, 321–322
myths of, 91, 95, 99
Lodensteyn, Jodocus van, 7142
Lodges, Native American, in Sun Dance, 8845–8846
Lóðurr (deity), in creation of man, 3455
Logan, J. W., 68
Log drums, 2494
Logic, **5497–5498**
Abelard (Peter) on, 7
Aristotle on, 480
Buddhist, 1120, 1301, 2336, 2351
Prāsaṅgika *vs.* Svātantrika school, 8858
Sautrāntikas and, 8119–8120
deductive, 5497
Husserl (Edmund) on, 4236
Indian
Nyāya, **6772–6774**
Sakya Paṇḍita on, 8051
Stcherbatsky (Theodore) on, 8737
inductive, 5497
lack of content of, 7109
modal, 6961–6962, 7123
Nicholas of Cusa on, 6610
Nishida Kitarō on, 6636, 6637
in process theology, 5497
in Scholasticism, 5497, 8174, 8175
in Stoicism, 8741
Thomas Aquinas on, 9162
Logical (mathematical) certainty, 2428
Logical empiricism. *See* Logical positivism
Logical Investigations (Husserl), phenomenology in, 4236
Logical paradox, 6988, 6989
Logical positivism, 2780, **5498–5500**
analytic philosophy and, 306, 307
definition of, 5498
empiricism and, 5498
meaning in, 5498–5499
positivism and, 5498
science in, 5498–5500
Vienna Circle and, 5498–5500
Wittgenstein (Ludwig) and, 5498, 5500
Logische Problem der Geschichtsphilosophie, Das (Troeltsch), 9366
Logogenic cantillation style, 1534
Logographs, Chinese, 1370
Logos, **5500–5506**
Apollinaris of Laodicea on, 423–424
in Christianity, 5502–5506
Christian Middle Platonists on, 7191
Clement of Alexandria on, 1823
as creative force, 5504
definitions of, 5500–5501
eagle representing, 949
functions of, 5504–5505
giving order to nature, 5302, 5501
in Hellenistic Judaism, 5302, 5502
Heraclitus on, 5201, 5501
Hermes as, 3937
Hermetic *logoi,* 3940
Hermetism on, 7190
inner, 5503–5504
Irenaeus on, 4539
Jesus as, 992, 4417
in *1 John,* 918, 5505
Justin Martyr on, 5503, 5505
vs. myth, 6359
in Neoplatonism, 5501
Origen on, 5502, 8406
of phenomena, 7092
Philo Judaeus on, 5302, 8558
in Platonism, 5504–5505
Plotinus on, 5501
Plutarch on, 5202
seminal, 5503
doctrine of, 3119
Servetus (Michael) on, 8232
Solov'ev (Vladimir) on, 8520
soul and, 8558
spoken, 5503–5504
in Stoicism, 3911, 5501–5502, 8405, 8741
inner *vs.* spoken, 5503
seminal logos, 5503
and wisdom, 5502–5503
in wisdom literature, 9759–9760
Logos spermatikos. See Seminal logos
Logos Teleios (text). *See also* Asclepius (text)
in Hermetic corpus, 3939
Logotherapy, 7476–7477
Logun-Ede (spirit), 122
Lohengrin legend, horse/swan god in, 4135
Lohmann, Roger Ivar, 6508
Lohri (Sikh ritual), gender in, 3337
Loisy, Alfred, 5506–5507
Hügel (Friedrich von) and, 4150
as Modernist, 6106
Loka (universe), Jain cosmology of, 2022–2025
Lokakṣema (Buddhist translator), 1291
Lokamanya. See Tilak, Bal Gangadhar
Lokapaññatti (Buddhist text), 1199
Lokaprajñapti (Buddhist text), 1199
Lokasenna, 2692, 5509
Lokāyata, 1446–1447
Lokeśvara, 1079
in Bayon temple, 5129
Loki (mythic figure/giant), **5507–5510**
and Njǫrðr's marriage to Skaði, 6641–6642
Baldr and, 744, 3452, 4461
death of, 3456, 5509
Bragi and, 3453
and dwarfs, 2532
in Eddas, 2692–2693
Fenrir as son of, 9426
Freyja and, 5508, 5509
Heimdallr and, 3898–3899, 5509
Iðunn and, 5508
Lóðurr and, 3455
in *Lokasenna,* 5509
Óðinn and, 5508, 5509
punishment of, for Baldr's death, 5509
role in Germanic pantheon, 3452, 5508, 5509
shape shifting of, 8301
Sif and, 3454, 5508
Skaði and, 5508
Þjazi and, 5508
Þórr and, 5508, 5509, 9166, 9167
as trickster, 5508
Loki, Aulis J., 1453
Lokottaravāda school of Buddhism
dharma in, 2335
doctrines of, 1196, 5602
geographical distribution of, 1195, 5602
literature of, 1198, 1200
origin of, 1194, 5602
split from Mahāsāṃghika Buddhism, 5602
Lok sevaks (servants of the people), 862
Lola, Mama (Vodou priestess), in New York, 1809
Lollards, pacifist teachings of, 6648
Lollianos, 3053
Lolo religion (China), healing in, 8273
Lombard, Denys, 4656–4657
Lombard, Peter. *See* Peter Lombard
Lombards, 4492, 6967
Lommel, A., 671, 672
Lommel, Herman, 203, 1049
Lomotal (deity), 6009
London (England)
Aḥmadiyah in, 200
Augustine of Canterbury in, 623
London Confession (1644), 784
London Ethical Society, 2857

London Medical Papyrus, 2840–2841
London Missionary Society
  China, Morrison sent to, 1608
  modern practices influenced by, 6074
  Morrison (Robert) in, 6196
  Pacific islands missions, 1738, 6791–6792, 9322, 9323, 9324
London Polyglot, 889, 895
London School of Economics, 841
  Malinowski (Bronislaw) at, 5628
London Theosophical Society (Swedenborgian)
  British Conference of the New Church and, 8902
  formation of, 8901
London University, 844
Loneliness, medical consequences of, 6057
Lonely Man of Faith (Soloveitchik), Talmudic interpretation in, 8518–8519
Lonergan, Bernard, **5510–5511**
  on God, 3558, 5510, 7423
  on religion, 5510
  on religious experience, 5510–5511
  theology of, 7246, 9138
Long, A. A., 7106
Long, Charles H., 67, 75, 965
  American study of religion, role in, 8786–8787
  on black theology, 78, 79
  on civil religion and African Americans, 1815–1816
  historiography of, 4049
  Kitagawa (Joseph M.) and, 5188
  on materiality of religion, 10047
  on religious experience, 7743
  on transculturation, in United States, 10087
Long, James A., 7230
Long, John, 6670
Long (dragon), storms and, 5996
Longar, Aiwel, 6744
Long Cave, 1469
Longchenpa. *See* Klong chen Rab 'byams pa
Long Count calendar system, 5796–5797, 5885–5886
  in inscriptions, 5882
  kings in, 5799
Longevity, Āyurveda and, 3854
Longhouse (Handsome Lake) religion, 4543
  origins of, 4541
  religious structure of, 3771
Longhouses, in Amazonian religion, 1503
  as universe or body, 8622
Longhu, Mount, importance in Daoism, 2198–2199
Longitudinal order of angels, 4554–4555
Longley, Charles Thomas, 352
Longmen branch, of Quanzhen Daoism, 2188
Longmen caves (China), Maitreya in, 5620
Longmen Grottoes, 1472
Longobardo, Niccolò, Confucianism, study of, 1919
Long Search, The (TV), Smart (Ninian) and, 8443
Longus, 3052
Long-wang (dragon), storms and, 5996
Longwood, W. Merle, 3314
Longxing Monastery (Buddhist temple), 9047
Loṇkā, 4766
Lönnrot, Elias, 4379, 5093, **5511–5512**
  version of *Kalevala (New Kalevala),* 3104, 3111, 5407, 5511, 5512
Lono (deity)
  Cook (James) as, 9320
  overview of, 3797–3798
  in Polynesian creation myths, 7313–7314
  priests to, 3796
Lono-i-ka-makahiki (god/chief), Cook (James) as, 3797–3798
Lontar manuscripts, 746, 747
Lööw, Heléne, 2663
Lopatin, Ivan A., 475
Lopatin, L. M., 3133
Lopes, Duarte, 112
Lopez, Donald, 9190
López Austin, Alfredo, 5934, 5935, 5936, 5938, 5943, 5945
  on Aztec human sacrifice, 4189
López Beltrán, Lauro, 5922
López Luján, Leonardo, 5944, 5945
Lophophora williamsii. See Peyote
Loraux, Nicole, 3601
Lord, Albert, on Latvian *dainas,* 8134
Lord, Albert B., 2816, 3145, 6843
Lord, Dagan as, in Eblaite religion, 2597
Lord, Frances, 6584
  on New Thought and prosperity, 4128
Lorde, Audre, 5413
Lord Lao. *See* Laozi
Lord of Chalma, 1469
Lord of the animals, **5512–5516**
  forms of, 5512, 5513
  functions of, 5512–5513
  history of, 5512
  hunting and, 5513–5516
  Rudra as, 7934
Lord of the flies. *See* Baal Zebub
Lord of the Flies (Golding), 5478–5479
Lord of the Rings (Tolkien), 3528
Lord of Tuttul. *See* Dagan
Lord's Day, the, 9813
Lord's Prayer, **5516–5518**
  in Christian worship, 5516
  commentaries on
    classical, 5516–5517
    contemporary, 5517
    recurrent themes in, 5517
  Cyprian on, 2113
  Eddy (Mary Baker) on, 2695
  and history, Christian views of, 4054
  Kant on, 7370
  variants of, 921, 5516
Lord's Prayer, The, kingdom of God in, 5149
Lord's Resistance Army, 106
Lord's Supper. *See also* Eucharist
  Calvin (John) on, 7389
  frequency of, 7962
  in Jehovah's Witnesses, 4823
  Luther (Martin) on, 7660
  nonsacrificial character of, 8007
  as Protestant rite, 7962
  in Reformed confessions, 2059
  Zwingli (Huldrych) on, 7660
Lorenz, Edward, 1541
Lorenz, Konrad
  on imprinting, 10043
  instinctive behavior investigated by, 2867
  on pain, 6947
  on violence, 9596
Lorik (mythic figure), 4434
Lorikagan (Indian ballad), 4434
Lo'-ruḥamah (biblical figure), name of, 4137
Lo (Wuwei) sect, 3155
Los Seises (ritual dance), 2153
Lossky, N. O., 3134
Lossky, Vladimir
  on Florenskii (Pavel) theology, 3134
  on tradition, 2958
Lost Teachings of Jesus, The (Prophet), 6529
Lot (biblical figure), Abraham and, 14, 15
Lot-Falck, Eveline, 475
Lothair I (emperor), Hincmar and, 3983
Lothair II (king of Lorraine), Hincmar and, 3983
Lothar of Segni. *See* Innocent III (pope)
Lothlorien (Indiana), 6472
Lotman, Yuri, on minds, 8759
Lot oracles, 6832–6833
Lots
  casting of
    in Bible, 3262
    in Israelite religion, 5425
  judgment by, 6847
Lotus, **5518–5520,** 7697
  as Lakṣmī symbol, 5518–5519
  as Viṣṇu symbol, 4325, 4439, 5518
  in Buddhism, 5518, 5519, 5520
  in Chinese religion, 5519
  cosmic fertility and, 9577
  as creation symbol, 5518
  in Egyptian religion, 5518, 5519
  in funeral rites, 3136
  in Hinduism, 5518, 5519
  in *maṇḍalas,* 5518
    Buddhist, 5642, 5643
    Hindu, 5641, 5642
  as moon symbol, 5518
  as solar symbol, 5518
  symbolism of, 3135, 5642
  as symbol of beauty, 5519
Lotus Circles (Theosophical Society), 7228, 9206
Lotus Position, 7343
Lotus Sūtra. See Saddharmapuṇḍarīka Sūtra
Loubère, Simon de la, 1311
Loudon (France), possession of nuns at, 2930
Loudun, nuns of, spirit possession among, 8695
Lou Guan (Tower Abbey), 2196, 2199
Louguo (mythic figure), in Caribbean religions, 1429
Louis, Adrian C., 3093
Louis (Shaker leader), confession of sins to, 7759
Louis I (Holy Roman emperor), 1557
  and Benedictines, 821
Louis IV of Bavaria (German king), Marsilius of Padua and, 5729
Louis VII (king of France), Crusades and, 2075
Louis IX (king of France)
  in Crusades, 2076
  relics sought by, 7689
Louis XIV (king of France)
  and dance, 2154
  dedication of *Confucius Sinarum philosophus* to, 1920, 1921
  Fénelon (François) and, 3039
  Innocent XI's conflict with, 6973
    Gallicanism and, 3258
  witch hunts ended by, 8250
Louisiana Purchase, 7283
Louisville Abstract of Principle (1859), on free will and predestination, 3208
Loukaris, Kyrillos. *See* Cyril I
Lou Movement, 6568
Lourdes, grotto and shrine of Virgin Mary at
  as center of medical services, 8378
  number of visits to, 7149
  pilgrimage as rite of passage, 1470

Lourdes, grotto and shrine of Virgin Mary at ***continued***
sacredness of, 7698
Louvre, Museé du (Paris), 6243
Lov (soul breath), in Komi religion, 5219
Love
beauty and, 810, 811, 812, 813
in Christianity
charity, *agape* as, 1554
Fedeli d'Amore and, 8248
God's goodness and, 3636
Grundtvig (Nikolai Frederik Severin) on, 3705
Jesus and ethic of, 6647, 6648
love of God, and morality, 1652
mysticism of, 6348–6350
Paul on, 1550
Suárez (Francisco) on, 8799
Swedenborg (Emanuel) on, 8899
comparison with *karuṇā,* 5105
dainas (folk songs) dealing with, 2127
discipline of the heart and, 8705–8706
dove as symbol of, 948
Eros as god of, 2832–2833
Ficino (Marsilio) on, 3050
of God
discipline of the heart and, 8705–8706
dually transcendent, 9282–9283, 9284
reality of, 9285–9286
Spinoza (Baruch) on, 8684
Greeks on, 3055
Greek virtues as forms of, 2307
hare as symbol of, 7590
in Hinduism (*See also* Bhakti)
mādhurya, 5249
of Kṛṣṇa and Rādhā, 5249–5250, 7593, 7594
vātsalya, 5249
in Islam
Rābiʿah al-ʿAdawīyah on, 8811
Schimmel (Annemarie) on, 8149
in marriage, alliance and, 5725
in mystical union, 6335, 6337
in mysticism, 6347, 6348–6350
in Neoplatonism, 6474
Niebuhr (Reinhold) on, 6613
in Roman Catholicism, Day (Dorothy) and, 2226
sacrificial, Christian concept of, 6645
sainthood, path to, 8037
Scheler (Max) on, 8147
in Sikhism, Singh (Gobind) and, 2221
Sorokin (Pitirim Aleksandrovich) on, 8524, 8525
in Sufism
dangerous power of, 3758
in Rūmī's poetry, 7937
pure love of God, 7591
Teilhard de Chardin (Pierre) on, 8525
Lovedu religion (Africa)
kingship in, death of king in, 5170
sacred kingship in, 8665
Lovejoy, Arthur, on paradox, 6989, 6990
Lovell, John, Jr., 77
Lovelock, James, Gaia hypothesis of, 3022, **3253–3255**
in Earth First!, 2564
in nature religions, 2666
Love Medicine (Erdrich), 3092
Lovers, great goddesses as, 3977
Löw, Yehudah ben Betsal'el of Prague, **5520–5521,** 9247
Lowa (mythic figure), 6009
Lowdermilk, Walter, 2609
Lowe, Scott, 6546
Lowenthal, Leo, 7321
Lower, Thomas, 3181
Lower Earth Mother (deity), 5119–5120
Lower-Earth Old Man (deity), 5120
Lower World
in Jainism (*See Adholoka*)
in neoshamanism, 8294
Lowie, Robert H., **5521–5522,** 6671
on Arctic religions, commonalities among, 469, 474
on culture, 5261
on primitive religion, 5522
revaluation of, 380
on Sun Dance, 8844
on supreme beings, 8878
Löwith, Karl, 9294
Loyal League, Stanton (Elizabeth Cady) and, 8731
Loyalty Islands, 6501–6502
Loyalty oaths, as covenants, 2047–2048
Lóyly (spirit/soul), 801–802, 9396
Loyola, Ignatius. *See* Ignatius Loyola
Lozen (Apache warrior), 574
Lozi religion (Zambia). *See also* Central Bantu religions
the Fall in, 2961
myths of, 92
Lozovan, Eugen, 3467
LSD (lysergic acid diethylamide)
ecstasy from, 2679–2680
experiments on, 7471–7472, 7477
states of consciousness and, 1951, 9291
Luahiwa, Robert, on ceremony to Kāne, 3797
Luakini (type of *heiau*)
function of, 3797
rituals to Kū gods in, 3798
Luang Phu Khao, 6245
Luantan (Phoenix Halls), 1608
Lubaale (hero gods), in Ganda religion, 2575
Lubāb al-ta'wīl fī ma'ānī al-tanzīl (al-Khāzin), 4662
Lubac, Henri de, 6114
Lubale (priests), 4520
Lubale religion. *See* Central Bantu religions
Luba religion (central Africa), **5522–5525**. *See also* Central Bantu religions
Bakwa Luntu, 5522
Bene Luluwa, 5522
creation in, 5524
the Fall in, 2961
human beings and human nature in, 5523
human body in art of, vol. 13 color insert
iconography of, 4302–4303
kingship in, 5171, 5522, vol. 13 color insert
lineage in, 5523
Luba Hemba, 5522
Luba Kasai, 5522
Luba Songye, 5522, 5523, 5524
medicine in, 5524
myths in, 92, 97
political organization in, 5522
python cult in, 8663
rituals of, 5524
sacred time in, vol. 1 color insert
sorcery in, 5524
soul in, 5523
unity of spiritual and physical worlds in, 5523
witchcraft in, 5524
women in, vol. 13 color insert
world of the dead in, 5523–5524
Lu-Bat (Saturn), in Sumerian religion, 8428
Lubavitcher Hasidism. *See* Habad Hasidism
Lubavitcher Rabbi. *See* Schneerson, Menachem Mendel
Lubbock, John
on African religions, 114
on fetishism, 3045
Indo-European religious studies of, 4460
on nature religions, 2662
on supreme beings, 8875
Lüber, Thomas, 6981
Lucan
on Celtic afterlife beliefs, 8392
on Teutates, 1482, 1483
Lucanus, on Iberian religion, 4254
Lucar, Mark, 783
Lucas, George, 3100
Campbell (Joseph) and, 1378
Lucas, Phillip Charles, 6518
Lucerna extincta rite, accusations of, 8248–8249
Luchta the Wright (deity), 1485
Lucia, Feast of Santa, 2400
Lucia cakes, 2400
Lucian
on Adonis, 34, 2536, 7131–7132
on ascension, 523
on Atargatis, 449, 3602–3603
on Charon's boat, 989
Cynic tradition and attacks on religion, 3910
on Gaulish deities, 1485
parody of utopias by, 3906
on Roman religion, 7920–7921
Lucian of Antioch, Greek Bible of, 892
Lucian of Samosata, 3052
on Astarte, 562–563
on magic, 5575
satire by, 4200
Lucian of Samothrace
on Phoenician religion, 7129
Syrian Goddess attributed to, 1381
Lucianus, on Adonis, 35
Lucid dreaming, 2485, 2488
Lucifer (Bishop of Sardinia), 4833
Lucifer (journal), 5023
Lucifer, in Catharism, 1456
Lucina, Diana as, 2346
Lucius (Arian bishop), Makarios of Egypt exiled by, 5624
Lucius (deity)
initiation into cult of Isis, 3908
restoration by Isis, 3904–3905
Luck. *See also* Chance
chance and, 1526
spitting and, 8722
Luckert, Karl W., 6672
Luckmann, Thomas
on invisible religion, 4529–4531
on symbolic self-transcendence, 8468
Lucretius. *See also* Epicureans
on fate and chance, 3002
on friendship, 3910
materialism and, 5776
on myths, rational explanations of, 6365
on nature of gods, 7913
on religion, 3911
on superstition, 8864
Lucumis (Afro-Cubans), in Santería and, 1434
Lü Dalin, 1560
Luder, Hans, 5534
Ludi (games), 7906–7907
Ludi Magni, 7907
Ludi Plebei, 7907
Ludi Romani, 7907
Ludi saeculares, **5525–5526**
Ludism, orgy and, 6860
Ludlow, John Malcolm
in Christian Socialist movement, 5784

Maurice (Frederick Denison) and, 5784
Lü Dongbin (saint), 1619, 2187, 2200
temple dedicated to, 9057
Ludos Troiae, ritual games of, 5277
Ludovici, Anthony, on laughter, 4222
Ludus (play), time and, 1761
Ludwig, Emil, on African religions, supreme beings of, 3576–3577
Luelen, Bernart, 6004
Lugal (great householder), 5947–5948
Lugalbanda (deity), 5949, 5958
Lugale (Mesopotamian myth), Ninurta in, 5952–5953
Lugbara religion (East Africa), **5526–5528**
cult of the dead in, 5527
culture hero myth in, 3739
deities of, lesser, of lightning and earthquake, 2568
divination and oracles in, 5527–5528
evil in, 5528
high deity in, 2567
history of study of, 117
lineage sacrifice in, 2568
magic in, 5528
mortuary rites of, 2569
myths in, 5526–5527
creation myth, 5526
culture hero myth in, 5526–5527
political organization of, 5526
possession in, 2568
priesthood of, 2569
prophets in, 2570, 5528
rainmakers in, 5528
sorcery in, 5528
witchcraft in, 5528
Lugbara Religion (Middleton), 117
Lugh (deity), **5528–5529**
Balar, defeat of, 1494, 5528–5529
in battle, 1488, 1489, 5528–5529, 9390
prophecy spoken by, 1492
Roman religion and, 1483
Lughaidh mac Con (deity), 1491
Lughnasa (festival), 5528
Lughnasadh
in Celtic calendar, 1491
Lugh and, 1483
Lugus (deity), 1483, 4253, 5528
Lu Gwei-djen, 237–238, 241
Luheng (Critical disquisitions), *zhenzen* in, 9959
Luhmann, Niklas, 3233
Lu Hsiang-shan. *See* Lu Xiangshan
Lu Hsui-ching. *See* Lu Xiujing
Luhya people (Kenya), African Independent Churches among, 2571
Luiseŋo religion (North America)
bears in, 808
creation story of, 6713
iconography of, 4308
Lu Jiuyuan. *See* Lu Xiangshan
Luk (deity), 6003, 6004
Lukács, Georg, on the novel, 3058
Lukasa (memory board), in Luba religion, vol. 1 color insert
Luke (apostle). *See* Luke the Evangelist
Luke (Gospel), 908–910
Acts separated from, 1410
ascension of Jesus in, 523
audience of, 909
author of, 908–909
banquet in, millenarianism based on, 5916
Bonaventure on, 1011
exorcism in, 2928
ghost in, 3475
"gospel" in, 3641
humor in, 4196
Jesus on *Psalms* in, 7465
Jewish polemics on, 7233
kingdom of God in, 5149
Lord's Prayer in, 5516
Mary in, 5752
Mary Magdalene in, 5756–5757
Matthew the Evangelist in, 5780
Moses in, 6203
mysticism in, 6346
outline of, 908
paradise in, 6984
parallelism in, 909–910
Peter the Apostle in, 7068
proverbs and parables in, 6979
purpose of, 909
Satan in, 2278
sources of, 906–907
suffering in, 8807
on tripartite canon, 879, 881
variants of, 921, 922
Luke (saint), Mother and Child painted by, vol. 12 color insert
Lukeni (African warrior), 5157
Luke of Prague, 6190
Lukes, Steven, 378, 1512, 2529
Luke the Evangelist, 908–909, **5529–5530**
on apostles, 435
on ascension of Jesus, 523
as companion of Paul, 908, 5529–5530, 7015
Lukuman, 126–127
Lull, Ramón, 1055, **5530–5531,** 7243
on nature, 6433
Lull, Raymond (Christianus Arabicus), 4597
Lullo, Raimondo, on angels, 348
Luma', al- (Ash'arī), 530, 534
Lumbholz, Carl, 5941
Lumen gentium. See Dogmatic Constitution on the Church
Luminosity, masculine sacrality in, 5760
Lummi tribe (North America), rainmakers in, 7300
Lumpa church (Zambia), 105
Lenshina (Alice) as founder of, 5408–5409
as prophetic movement, 1720–1721
syncretism, 1511
Lunar calendar, 6170–6171
Buddhist, 9831
Hindu, 9825
Incan, 1361
Jewish, 4865–4968
overview of, 1353–1354
Lunar eclipses, Mesoamerican calendar and, 1356
Lunar sacrality, 3017–3018
Lund, Allan, 3450
Lunda religion (Zaire). *See* Central Bantu religion; Ndembu religion
Łungx-type spirits
in Khanty religion, 5120, 5121
in Mansi religion, 5120, 5121
Lunisolar calendars, motivations for, 1354
Lunyu. See Analects of Confucius
Luomala, Katharine. *See* Maui
Luo Maodeng, 3068
Luo people (Kenya)
African Independent Churches among, 2571
confession of adultery among, 1884
in Legio Maria movement, 105
mortuary rituals of, 141
Luoyang, China, 1472, 1594
Luoyang qielan ji (Buddhist text), 994
Lü Peilin. *See* Taixu
Lupercalia (festival), **5531–5532,** 7896, 7923
Luperci (officiants at Lupercalia), 5531, 7896, 7908
Luperino, Baldo, 3124
Lupinda (Ndembu figure), 1004
Luria, Isaac, 4981, **5532–5533**
on dualism, 2512
ethics of, 4914
Gnosticism and, 3524
on God, 3550–3551
on good and evil, 3789
and messianism, 5977
messianism of, 8258
metempsychosis, doctrine of, 8560
and music, 6309–6310
mystical theory of, 6353–6354
mysticism of, 4998
Qabbalah system of, 5532–5533, 7534–7535
on *tiqqun* (mending/restitution of life), 5533
as *tsaddiq,* 8035
on *tsaddiq,* 9378, 9379
on *tsimtsum* (divine self-contraction), 3788, 5532, 6353
Vital (Ḥayyim) and, 9628
Luria, Shelomoh, **5533–5534**
on Me'ir ben Barukh of Rothenburg, 5831
Lurianic Qabbalah, 5532–5533, 7534–7535
good and evil in, 3789
Hasidism, relation to, 3788
historiography in, 4059
messianism in, 5977
Scholem (Gershom) on, 8178
sefirot in, 7536
Shabbateanism and, 8261
Shabbetai Tsevi and, 8260
Shne'ur Zalman of Lyady and, 8371
theurgy of, 7536–7537
Vital (Ḥayyim) in, 9628
Lurie, Nancy Oestreich, 702
Lü school of Buddhism, 1202
Lüshan Huiyuan. *See* Huiyuan (Buddhist monk)
Lushi Chuqiu (Chinese text), 5396
Lu Shizhong, and Rites of the Jade Hall, 2185
Lust, depiction in novels, 3059
Lu state, Confucius in, 1934, 1936
Lusthaus, Dan, 1250
Lustratio, **5534**
Lutgard of Aywières, on heart of Jesus, 3883
Lü Thai (king of Sukhōthai), 1139–1140
Luther, Martin, **5534–5538**
on afterlife, 158–159
on alchemy, 252
and Anabaptism, 304, 305
on Antichrist, 395
anti-Semitism and, 400–401
on astrology, 3002, 8182
astrology-based prophecies regarding, 564
Augustine's influence on, 629
on authority, 695
and biblical canonicity, 881
biblical exegesis of, 874, 5486
on blasphemy, 973
and Bucer (Martin), 1059, 5832
Calvin and, 1375
Catholic Church's reaction to, 7663
on church and state relationship, 5150
on Communion, 5536, 5537
condemnation of, Edict of Worms, 7657, 7658
on congregational form of polity, 1768
on conscience, 1942, 1945
Copernican revolution and, 8182

Luther, Martin ***continued***
on cult of saints as idolatry, 8034
and deconstruction, 2246
defying inquisitors, 4500
on desire, 2308
disagreements with, 7659
on doctrine, 2382
ecclesiology of, 1773
Eck (Johann) and, 2601
on Erasmus, 7026
Erasmus and, challenge to, 2821
Erikson (Erik) on, 7476, 7482
on ethics, 1654, 1655
excommunication of, 5536
exile of, 2938
on faith, 2425, 5537
as trust, 2956, 2958
and Flacius (Mathias), 3124
on free will and determinism, 3201
on gospel, 2057
vs. law, 3642
on grace, 3646, 5537, 7454
on heresy, 3920
on hierarchy of church, 5288
on human perfectibility, 7040
and iconography, 4346
images of, vol. 14 color insert
on indulgences, sale of, 158, 7657, vol. 7 color insert
on Jesus, 7450
on justification by faith, 1667, 5041, 5877
Council of Trent on, 9343
on kingdom of God, 5150, 5151
on knowledge, 5205
on language, 5303
on Lord's Supper, 7660
at Marburg colloquy, 7660
marriage of, 5536
on Mary, 5753
Melanchthon (Philipp) and, 5831, 5832
on merit, 5877
and ministry, 6044–6045
on miracles, 6056
monasticism of, 5535
monasticism questioned by, 6134
Moravians and, 6190
on mountains, 6212
Müntzer (Thomas) and, 6238, 6239
on music, 6310
mysticism of, 390, 2603
on nature, character of, 2607
Ninety-Five Theses of, 5535–5536, 7657
on papacy, 1773
on papal authority, 8158
Paracelsus compared to, 6981
on paradox of redemption, 6990
Pauck (Wilhelm) on, 7011
on peasant rebellions, 7659
on predestination, 3204, 3207–3208
as priest, 5535
on priesthood, 7403
Reformation principles *sola gratia, sola fide, sola Scriptura* (only grace, only faith, only Scripture), 1691, 9343
on religious art, 4286
religious experience of, 5535
on Renaissance, 4177
on revelation, 7775
on salvation, 158–159, 695
satire by, 4200
scripture in theology of, 5486, 5537
on temptation, 9070
theological studies of, 5535
theology of, 5535–5536, 5537, 9136–9137
Thomas á Kempis's influence on, 9159
Troeltsch (Ernst) on, 9364
two kingdoms doctrine of, 8464
on world, as monastery, 2672
Zwingli (Huldrych) opposed to, 5536, 7658, 7659–7660
Lutheran Book of Worship, Paschal vigil in, 1742
Lutheran Church in America, 5540
Lutheran Council in the United States, 5540
Lutheranism, **5538–5540**. *See also* Evangelical Lutheran Church of America
Anglicanism's dialogue with, 353
Augsburg Confession
Formula of Concord and, 2055
importance of, 2057–2058
Reformation and, 5536, 5539, 7658–7659
baptism in, 5538
Book of Concord (1580) of, 5538
creeds in, 2057
doctrine in, 2055
Catholicism and, vol. 14 color insert
church architecture of, 795
Communion in, 5538
in Eastern Europe, 1685
ecumenical body of, 2684
in the Enlightenment, 5539
Eucharist rites in, 2580
Evangelical, in Finland, 3103
in Finland, 5092
in Formula of Concord (1577), 5539
in Germany, 5538, 5539
Barmen Declaration (1934) and, 2061
history of, 5538–5540
iconoclasm in, 4283, 4392
images in, vol. 14 color insert
Laestadian Lutheran revivalist movement, 5283
law *vs.* gospel in, 5538
liturgical year in, 1744
liturgy in, 5538
ministry in, 6044–6045
missions, 6084
in New Guinea, 1738
in West Indies, 1706, 1707
Nazism and, 5540
Neo-Lutherans, 5539
orgy and, 6871
orthodoxy, 5539
Peace of Augsburg (1555) and, 2057, 5539, 7659
Philippists *vs.* Gnesio-Lutherans, 5539
Pietism in, 7142
polity of, 1768–1769, 7452
Roman Catholicism and, 5540
in Russia, 5092
sacramental theology in
Calvinist perspective *vs.,* 7963
sacrifice in, 8007
sacraments in, 5538, 7455
Smalcald League and, 5536, 5539, 7659
Sohm (Rudolf) on, 8507
Spener (Philipp Jakob) and, 8679–8680
teachings of, 5538
two-realm theory, ethics and, 1655
in United States, 5539–5540, vol. 1 color insert
worship in, 5538
Lutheran Pietism, 5539
Francke (August Hermann) and, 3185
Lutheran World Federation, 2684, 5540
Luthuli, Albert, Gandhi (Mohandas) influencing, 3273
Lutz, Christine, 9072
Lutzker, Adam, 386
Lu-Wang school of Confucianism, 1603
Mengzi and, 5858–5859
self-cultivation in, 5858
Luwu' couple (Bugis mythical figures), 1317
Luxembourg, Islam in, 4679
Lu Xiangshan (Lu Jiuyuan), 1578, 1603, **5540–5542,** 9675
criticism of, 1901
on *dao,* 5541
dualism of, 5541
on mind-heart, 5540–5542
Neo-Confucianism and, 5540–5542
Zhu Xi and, 5541, 5542
Lu Xiujing, 1597, 2637, **5542–5543**
catalog of Daoist texts of, 2183, 2202, 5542
Ge Hong and, 3291
Lingbao scriptures and, 5542, 5543
on sculpted images, 4333
Tao Hongjing as disciple of, 8996
and Three Caverns, 7414
Lux Perpetua (Cumont), importance of, 2094
Lu Xun, 3068, 3070
Lụ Yan, 2207
Lu Yü (tea master), 847
Lu Yuanzhe (governor of Fuchun), 6992
Luz del Mundo, La (Light of the World, Mexico), 6579, 6580
Lu Zijing. *See* Lu Xiangshan
Luzzatto, Shemu'el David
biblical exegesis of, 869, 4877
on Spinoza (Baruch), 8685
on suffering, 8805
on *Wissenschaft des Judentums,* 4902
Luzzatto, Simone, 7107
Lwa (spirits), 9636–9637
in Haitian Vodou, 1433–1434
characteristics of, 8690
Lwembe (founding hero), 6771
Lycanthropy (werewolfism), 9784–9785
Lydda, Council of (415), 7026
Lyden, John, 3100
Ly dynasty (Vietnam), Buddhism in, 1138
Lykurgos (mythical figure), 2359, 4478, 9170
Lynch, James J., 6057
Lyng v. Northwest Indian Cemetery Protective Association, 7303
Lynn, Steven Jay, on religious experience, 7747
Lyon, Patricia J., 3416
Lyons
Christian persecutions at, 9597
Waldensians at, 9662
Lyons, Council of, 2587
Lyons, Council of (1245), 4493
overview of, 2042
Lyons, Council of (1274)
Gregory X and, 9162
on law of conclave, 6971
mendicant orders approved by, 5856
overview of, 2042
Lyotard, Jean-François
on deconstruction, 2246
on gendering beauty, 811
on modernity, 5482
and postcolonial theory, 10042
Lyres
in Greek music, 6304
in Middle Eastern music, 6275, 6276
Lysaght, Patricia, 1498
Lysander, 437
Lysergic acid diethylamide. *See* LSD
Lysis (Plato), 7775
Lysistrata (Aristophanes), 4487

M

Ma (principle), time and spaced opened by, 7989
Ma'a (sacred textile), 9090
Ma'alim fi al-Tariq (Quṭb), 108

Ma'alot (ascents), 7461
Ma'alot ha-middot (Yeḥie'el), 4913
Ma'amar 'al Yishma'e'l (Adret), 7239
Ma'amar qatser (Abravanel), 17
Ma'aminim (believers), 2419
Mā Angkw (deity), 5119–5120
Ma'ānī (meanings), 8950
Ma'ānī al-akhbār (al-Kalābādhī), 5055
Ma'ānī al-Qur'ān (al-Farrā'), 8952
Ma'arekhet haElohut, 9378
Ma' ārif (Bahā' al-Dīn), 7935
Ma'arrī, Abū al-'Alā' al-, on *mi'rāj,* 6060
Ma'arufyah (Jewish trade monopoly), 5011
Maasai religion (East Africa)
 cosmology in, 2000–2001
 cow's milk in, 847
 diviners *(il-oibonok),* 2001
 elephants in, 2750
 the Fall in, 2961
 initiation rites of, 2569
  circumcision in, 1799
 priesthood of, 2569
 prophets of, 7443
 ritual ceremonies in, 2001
 supreme being (Ngai) of, 3574, 5993
 Yoruba, similarities with, 2001
Maasawu (deity), 6723
Ma'aseh Merkavah, 10050, 10051
Maasina movement, 6797
Maat (deity), 4319, 9749–9750
Maat (justice and order), 4727
 in afterlife, 128–129
 under Akhenaton, 221
 Egyptian pharaohs and, 5163
 eternal principles of, 9110
Ma'bad al-Juhani, and Qādāri ideas, 3210, 3211
Ma'barī, Zayn al-Dīn, al-, 4644
Mabarn healers, overview of, 3873–3874
Mabillon, Jean, historiography of, 4030–4031
Mabinogion (Welsh tales), 1489–1490, **5545–5547**
 Annwn in, 371
 Four Branches of, 5545–5546
 Gruffyyd on, 1498
 Rhiannon in, 2820
Mabo case, 636, 640, 690
Ma Bohua (Muslim leader), 4637
Mabon. *See* Maponos/Mabon
Mabouia (deity), in Island Carib religion, 1427–1428
Mabuiag, warrior hero of, 2982
Macaque, 6151, 6152
Macarii monks, Evagrios of Pontus with, 2886
Macarius (Egyptian monk), and mystical union, 6336
Macarius of Jerusalem (bishop), 792
 on pain, 6946
Macassans, annual visits with Yolngu people, 647–648
Macaulay, Thomas Babington, 9319
Macauliffe, Arthur Max, 3717
Macbeth (Shakespeare), necromancy in, 6453
Maccabean revolt, 6647
 ritual law and, 3751
 Sadducees and, 8018
Maccabees
 history, view of, in, 4058
 in various canons, 879, 880
1 Maccabees
 blasphemy in, 971
 content of, 900
 Dagon in, 7103
 dating of, 900
 Ḥanukkah and, 3774
 messianism in, 5972
2 Maccabees
 blasphemy in, 969
 content of, 900–901
 dating of, 900
 David in, 7461–7462
 Ḥanukkah and, 3774
 language of, 896
 resurrection in, 7765
 Temple procedures in, 928
3 Maccabees, 900, 904
4 Maccabees, 904
Mac Cana, Proinsias, 1499
MacCauley, Clay, 6670
Macchioro, Vittorio, 2266
MacCulloch, John Arnott, 1498
Macdonald, Ariane, 9188
Macdonald, Dwight, 7321
Macdonell, A. A., 6414
MacDougall, David, 3098
Mace, as Viṣṇu symbol, 4325
Macedonia. *See also* Slavic religion
 breakup of Yugoslavia and, 1686
 imperialism of, 3901 (*See also* Hellenistic religions)
 Islam in, 4674, 4677
 Neolithic religion in, 6463
 Paul's missions to, 1682
 prehistoric culture in, 7379
Macedonian heresy, Niceno-Constantinopolitan Creed against, 2056
Macehuallatolli (language of commoners), 2465
MacGaffey, Wyatt, 3043
Mach, Ernst, 7341
 logical positivism and, 5498
Macha (deity), 2820, 2984
 Celtic head cult and, 3807
 curse by, 1493
 Dumézil (Georges) on, 1491
 horses and, 1487
 as war goddess, 1490
Macha Oromo religion (Ethiopia), 2573
Máchi (shaman), in Mapuche religion, 5688–5689
Machiavelli, Niccolò, 7249
 on law and morality, 5367
 on religion, 7790
Machiganga people (Peru), moon in myths of, 6173
Machig Labdron. *See* Ma gcig Lab sgron
Machiluwún rite, 5689
Machoveč, Milan, 4845
Maciejko, Pawel, 3187
Mac ind Óg (deity), 1484, 1486
  Maponos identified with, 5685
Macintosh, Douglas Clyde, in knowledge, in Protestantism, 5206–5207
Mack, Burton
 on sacrifice, 8009
 on theory of religion, 8471–8472
Mackay, George L., 8963
Mackie, J. L., 9113
Mackie, Mary, 3092
Mackintosh clan of Scotland, 1463
MacLaine, Shirley, 6496
MacLean, Paul, on brain evolution, 8279
Macmillan, James, 6313
Macmillan, Kenneth, 2163
Macmurray, John, Smith (Wilfred Cantwell) on, 8450
MacNeill, Máire, 1498
Maco Capac, founding of Inca empire by, 5175–5176
Macpherson, James, 1497
Macquarrie, John, on history as foundation of religion, 7117
Macrina, Trinity and, 2581–2582
Macrina the Younger, 6763
Macrobiotics, in Chinese alchemy, 240
Macrobius, 28, 2994
 on ascension, 521, 522
 on catasterism, 8424
 on Iberian religion, 4253
 on Roman religion, 7923
Macrocosm and microcosm. *See also* Qabbalah
 Amazonian longhouse and, 8622
 Āyurveda and, 3854
 in Chinese religion, medicine and, 3859
 in churches and temples, 7983
 in cosmologic myths, 1994
 in Hermetism, above and below in, 3948
 human body in, 4159–4160, 4171
 images of, vol. 3 color insert
 intellectualist theory and, 1971
 ritual actions reflecting, 4159
 sacred places as icons of the world, 7981–7982
 sky mythology and, 8426
 in Southeast Asian traditional religion, 8650
 stars and, 8736
Macrocoti (deity), in Island Arawak religion, 1427
Macropaedia, 2784
Macuch, Rudolf, 5635, 5638, 5639
Macuilxochitl (deity), drums and, 6269, 6270
Macumba religion (Brazil), 120
 spirit possession in, dance and, 2139
Macuna religion (Colombia)
 cosmology of, 8587
 Yurupary in, 8591
Macurgum (deity), 834
Macy, Joanna, 2563, 6536
 on Buddhist environmentalism, 2788
Mada (intoxication), 748
Madagascar
 funeral rites in, 3235
 stones cult in, 8745–8746
Madah (poetic form), 7223
Madang cargo movements, 6801–6802
Madanī, Ḥusayn Aḥmad, 4654
Maddock, Kenneth, 3390, 6600
Madd wa gazr-i Islām (Ḥālī), 4652
Madech (Movement for Welcoming the Elohim, Creators of Humanity), 7597
Mādhava (Buddhist writer), 1295, 8976
 metaphysics of, 8547
 on Āyurveda, 3853
Mādhavadeva (poet), 7211
Madhhab alh al-bayt, 4760
Madhhab 'irfānī. See Druze
Madhhabs (schools of law), **5547–5550**. *See also* Ḥanābilah; *See also* Ḥanafīyah; *See also* Mālikīyah; *See also* Shāfi'īyah
 classical theory of, 9489
 divergence among schools, 5549–5550
 doctrines of, 5547–5550
 emergence of, 3759–3762, 5547, 8854–8855
 ṣalāt (prayer) in, 8058
 traditionalism *vs.* rationalism and, 3761–3762
 translations of term, 5547
Madhi, al- (Muḥammad Ahmed Ibn Abdullāh), 6768
Mādhurya (sweet love), 5249
Madhva (Hindu philosopher), **5550–5551**
 bhāgavatas and, 9503–9504
 on dualism and nondualism, 6623
 dualistic Vedānta of, 4005
 on *mokṣa,* 6116
 on predestination, 3204, 8529
 Vedanta of, 9549

Madhyaloka (Middle World), in Jain cosmology, 2023–2024
Madhyama Āgama (Buddhist text), Sarvāstivāda and, 8117–8118
Madhyamakakārikā (Nāgārjuna), 5551
commentaries on, 5552–5553
dilemmas and tetralemmas in, 5552
Four Noble Truths in, 3180
Madhyamakālaṃkāra (Śāntarakṣita), 5070, 5554
levels of analysis in, 8107
Madhyamakāloka (Kamalaśīla), 5070–5071
Madhyamakāvatāra (Candrakīrti), 1285, 1300, 2322
commentary in, 1401
Madhyamakāvatāraprajñā (Candrakīrti), Tantrism in, 1401
Madhyamārthasaṃgraha (Bhāvaviveka), 860
Mādhyamika Buddhism, 1119, **5551–5556**
Āryadeva in, 5552
Bhāvaviveka's reinterpretation of, 860, 1119
bodhisattva path in, 1300
on buddha nature, 1156
Buddhapālita's role in, 1075
Candrakīrti, role of, **1401**
in China, 1164, 1202
multiple truth in, 1576
popularity in, 1576
Sengzhao, role of, **8228**
śūnyatā (emptiness) in, 8858–8859
transmission to, 1596
dharma in, 2335
early period of, 5551–5552
on emptiness, 1156, 1209, 1276, 1299
founder of, 1092, 1119, 5551–5553, **6390–6394** (*See also* Nāgārjuna)
freedom from pain in, 3201
intuition in, 4525
knowledge in, 5200, 5554–5555
language in, 5308, 5311
last period of, 5554–5555
literature of, 1119
middle period of, 5552–5554
mysticism in, 6344, 6345
nirvāṇa in, 6629
origins of, 1093, 1208–1210, 5551–5552
philosophers of, 1119, 1120, 1212–1213, 5551–5555
philosophy of, 1299–1300
prajñā in, 7358–7359
realities in, 1208–1210, 5554–5555
Śāntideva, role of, 8109–8110
Stcherbatsky (Theodore) on, 8737
subschools of, split into, 5552
śūnyatā (emptiness) in, 5551–5552, 6391–6393, 8857–8858
Madhyāntavibhāga (Buddhist text), 1300
in Tibetan Buddhism, 9899
Madhyāntavibhāgaṭīkā (Sthiramati), 8739
Madison, James, Morrison (Robert) and, 6196
Madison Square Garden Crusade, 7712
Madkhal, al- (Ibn al-Ḥajj), 4589
Madman, The: His Parables and Poems (Gibran), 6979
Madness
of Dionysos, 2359
ritual, 1459
Madonna (performer), 5808
Madonna and Child paintings, vol. 12 color insert
Madonna del Granduca (Raphael), 4346
Madras, India, commercial and sacred space in, 1806–1807
Madrasah (school), 9439. *See also* Hawzah
Madrasah-i Raḥīmīyah, 9666
Madrasahs (religious colleges), **5556–5557,** 7396
architecture of, 5556
in Baghdad, 5557
Ḍiyā-īyah, 3768
first (of al-Jīlānī), 3766
in Central Asia, 4621, 4623, 4624, 4625, 4626
in China, 4633–4634, 4638, 4640
decline of enrollment in, 7000
Hawzah (seminary), **3800–3802**
libraries added to, 3761
in Marinid dynasty, 4587
in Middle Volga, 4618
modern, 5557
modernity in, 6097
Niẓām al-Mulk as sponsor of, 6641
origin of, 5556
patronage supporting, 5556–5557
religious education at, 7733, 7735
in South Asia, 4645
subjects taught at, 5556, 5557
Sufism and, 8820
teacher-student relationship in, 9005
Madrasa-i Raḥīmiyya *(madrasah),* 4645
Madrid (Spain), Escorial palace-monastery in, 6120
Madrid Codex, Maya calendar and, 1360
Madsens, William, 5942
Madurese language, 4657
Maeda Eun, 1277
Mãe de santo (Candomblé priestess), 122
Maenadism, 3672–3673
Maengue people (New Britain), revenge and, 7780
Mafātīḥ al-ghayb (al-Rāzī), 4400, 4665, 8953
Mafdal. *See* National Religious Party
Maffesoli, Michel, on sexual ritual, 8252–8253
Maffly-Kipp, Laurie, 75
Mafia, as secret society, 8213
Māgadhi, as probable language of Buddha, 1108
Magahar, Kabīr's burial at, 5052
Magazin (journal), 769
Ma gcig Lab sgron (Machig Labdron), 1227, **5557–5558**
Ani Lochen as emanation of, 354
Gcod rite of, 5557, 5558
and gender in Buddhism, 3333
Pha Dam pa Sangs rgyas as teacher of, 5558
Magdeburg Centuries (Wigand), Lutheran historiography in, 1402
Magen David (Star of David), **5558–5559**
maṇḍalas and, 5642
Mages hellénisés, les (Cumont and Bidez), on Hellenized magi, 2094
Magga (path), 1296
in Four Noble Truths, 3178, 3179
Maggid (preacher), 2429
Maggid mesharim (Karo), 5105
Maggid mishneh (Vidal), 5104
Maggid of Mezeritch, 3119–3120
Maghili, al-, 4605
Maghreb. *See* North Africa and North African religions
Maghribī, Samuel al-
polemics against Judaism, 7239–7240
writings of, 5085
Maghribi calligraphy
marriage and, 1369
style of, 1373
Magh Tuiredh, Battle of, 1483, 1488, 9390
Magi, **5559–5562**
in Christianity, 5561–5562
cults of, 2818
Epiphany and, 9814
feast of, 2818
as Zoroastrian magi, 9990, vol. 8 color insert
Epiphany and, 1743–1744
functions of, 5559–5560
in Greek literature, 5559–5560, 5561
Hellenized, Cumont on, 2094
magic and, 5561, 5573
meanings of, 5559, 5561
Zoroastrian, 5559–5561, 9991, vol. 8 color insert
Magic, **5562–5594**. *See also* Cursing; Sorcery; Witchcraft
in African religions
in Azande religion, 5567, 5571
good an evil in, 3820
Lugbara religion, 5528
nganga (magicians) in Kongo religion, 2001
in Sudan, spells in, 8677
in Andean religion, pre-Inca, 8604
in Athapaskan religious traditions, 576
in Aztec religion, 5908–5909
Bacon (Roger) advocating use of, 735
belief in, despite failures, 5567
binding and, 937, 938
black
in Islam, 5583–5585
vs. white, in Hellenism, 3904
in Buddhism, 5592–5594
and *mahāsiddhas*, 5605
folk Buddhism, 3154
in Canaanite religion, 1387
cannibalism and, 1404
Cassirer on, 1448
causality in, 5570, 5571
cave art as sympathetic magic, 1470, 1471
ceremonial magicians, 6471
in Chinese religion, Li Shaojun and, 5465
in Christianity
early, 5576
medieval and Renaissance, 5577–5580
Roman Catholicism, mediation and, 7881
sources on, 5577
circles in, 1792–1793
confession as, 1884–1885
contagious, 5571
healing and, 3811–3812
relics and, 7686
content of, 5562
in Daoism, 5592–5593
decline of, 5568–5569
definitions of, 5562, 7914
deities associated with, 3623
in Hattic and Hittite religions, 4069
Hekate, 3899
demonic, necromancy as, 6452
in East Asia, **5592–5594**
economic basis of, 2671
in Egyptian religion, 2712, 2714
and afterlife, 128–129
in healing, 2713
healing and, 3826–3827
mythology used in, 2720
from Re, 2706
texts of, 2721–2722
of Empedocles, 2776
esotericism and, Fludd (Robert) and, 3950
in Europe
Eastern Europe, **5580–5583**
medieval and Renaissance, **5577–5580**
popular, campaign against superstition and, 8865–8866

sexual magic, in satanic clubs, 8250–8251
evidence for, 5563
of evil eye, 2941–2942
in evolutionary theory, 5563–5565, 5571–5572
formulas, writing of, 1793
Frazer (James G.) on, 2540, 4461, 5373, 5564, 5570–5571, 7914
in gardening, 3280
in Germanic religions, in sagas, 8025
in Greek religion, 3678, **5572–5577**
of music, 6303
sources on, 5573–5575
sun and, 8839
hair, use of, 3740
hands and, 3770, 3771
Hartland (E. Sidney) on religion and, 3782
in Hellenistic religions, 3903–3905, 5572–5573
syncretism in, 3909
in Hermetism, in Hermetic texts, 3938–3940
in Hinduism, 5587–5588
yantras in, 9872, vol. 3 color insert
homeopathic, 5571, 5588
illusionist, 6452
in indigenous societies, **5569–5572**
in Islam, 5578–5579, **5583–5587**
black, 5583–5585
Rāzī (Fakhr al-Dīn al-) on, 7633
talismanry, 5585–5586
white, 5586–5587
Jevons (F. B.) on, 4854
in Judaism, 4979, 5575–5576, 5579
folk Judaism, 3158, 3159–3160
of rabbis, 7587
in Khanty religion, 5119, 5123
of kings, 5157
literalist interpretations of, 5563, 5566
literature of instructions on
Greco-Roman, 5574
medieval, 5578–5579
by magi, 5561, 5573
magicians as leaders, 5383–5384
Malinowski (Bronislaw) on, 2543, 5563, 5566, 5567, 5568, 5570, 5571, 5629
mana as, 5566–5567, 5568, 5571, 5632
in Mansi religion, 5119, 5123
in Melanesian religions, 5562, 5566
deities' role in, 5834
specialists in, 5835
women and, 5836
in Micronesia, 6008
by Mi la ras pa, 6027
in mirrors, 6064
moon and, 6175
of music, 6303
in Neopaganism, 6471, 6472
of En no Gyōja, 2802
origins of, 8402
in Orphism, 6892
owl as symbol of, 6937
and power, 7352
of prayer, 7838
prayer and, 9768
in primitive religion, 2267, 5562–5565, 7695
public *vs.* private, 9769
rainmaking (*See* Rainmaking)
Reinach (Salomon) on, 7676
and religion, Marxist view of, 7974
vs. religion, 2541, 6502–6503, 6952, 6954, 7352
religion's relationship to, 5562, 5563, 5568, 5571, 5572
vs. revelation, 7774
ritual, in Wicca, 9729
rituals and, 7699, 7858
in Roman religion, **5572–5577**
in imperial period, 7914
laws concerning, 5333
sources on, 5573–5575
runes and, 7940, 7941
sacrifice as, 8003–8004
in scientific revolution, 2843
secularization and, 8216
sexual
in European satanic clubs, 8250–8251
modern, 8251–8252
in Renaissance, 8248
shamanism *vs.*, 8269
similarity and contiguity in, 5373
Smith (Morton) on, 8449
sociology of, 5565–5566
in Sophistic movement, 3905
in South Asia, **5587–5592**
spells, **8675–8678**
studies of, 5562–5569
bias in, 5562–5563
evidence in, 5563
objectivity in, 5563
symbolist interpretations of, 5563, 5567–5569
sympathetic, 5571
healing and, 3811–3812
theories of, **5562–5569**
vs. theurgy, 9156
in Vanuatu religions, 9521
in Vedism, 9566
Vodou and, 9638
Weber (Max) on, 8488
in Western societies, 5562
in Wicca, 9729
writing in, 6844
Magic, Science and Religion (Malinowski), 6800
Magical activism, in neoshamanism, 8296
Magical deification, 2250
Magical devices (yogic practice), 1288
Magical idealism, 2904–2905
Magical worldview, 9768
Magic and Religion (Lang), 5299–5300
Magick, Crowley (Aleister) on, 2072
Magic Mountain (Mann), Campbell (Joseph) on, 1379
Magico-religious, coining of term, 5564
Magic Presence, The (Ballard), 4246
Magid (preacher), 9380, 9381
Magisterium, canon and, 1408
Magna Carta, 7280
Magna Mater (deity). *See also* Cybele
cult of
taurobolium and, 7917, 7922
women in, 3385
Cybele as, 1451, 2110, 3587, 7905–7906, 7917
and gender roles, 3385
Megalesia festival of, 2110
Magna moralia in Job (Gregory I), 3688
Magnes, Judah, Ginzberg (Asher) influencing, 3496
Magnetic resonance imaging, functional (fMRI), and oral tradition, 6425
Magnetism
animal (*See* Animal magnetism)
Kardec's (Alan) involvement with, 5089–5090
Magnus, Olaus, 3110
Magog (hostile power), origin of name of, 7102
Magoun, Francis Pl, 6843
Magpie (mythic figure), 663, 664
Magritte, René, vol. 11 color insert
Maguey (plant), in myths, 5936
Magus, in Zoroastrianism, 9989–9991
Magyars (Hungary), 948
Mahābhārata (Hindu epic), 5467, **5594–5596**. *See also* Bhagavadgītā
animal mythic themes in, 4438
Arjuna in, 486, 5595
as *kāvya* (great poem), 7205
avatāra theory in, 4000–4001
Balarāma mentioned in, 743
bhakti synthesis in, 3998–4002
in Brahmanism, 9568–9569
caste in, 4001
composition of, 5594
cosmology in, 2016–2017
dance drama based on, 2448, 2449
dharma in, 2328, 2329, 2621, 5343, 5345
Dharmarāja in, 3001
Durgā in, 2526
flood in, 3130
gambling in, 3263, 5595
games in, 3266
Garuda in, 2554
Goddess in, 4000, 4002
Golden Rule in, 3631
hell in, 9456
historiography in, 4025
Iliad cognate to, 4465
in Indo-European language study, 4458
Indra's thunderbolt in, 967
in Vaiṣṇavism, 4428, 9500–9501
īśvara in, 4751
in Javanese shadow theater, 8649
Karna, birth of, 1568
Kauravas in, 5595
Kṛṣṇa in, 5251
Kurukṣetra in, 5268
magic in, 5591
māyā in, 5795
mokṣa in, 4004, 6115
Murukan̠ in, 6240
names for story, 5594
Odyssey cognate to, 4465
Pañcarātras sect in, 4020, 9507
Pāṇḍavas in, 5595
past remembered in, 2816
pilgrimage in, 7169
plot of, 5595
prakṛti in, 7360–7361
puppet theater based on, 2450, 2452, 7044
reincarnation in, 7678
rejuvenation myth in, 7683
riddles in, 6987
Rudra-Śiva in, 8039
Śaivism reflected in, 8041
Sarasvatī in, 8113
sati (widow burning) in, 8129
scope of, 2813–2814
Śiva in, 8415–8416
in Southeast Asia
in bas reliefs, 4013
versions of, 3076
studies of, 4446, 5594
Trimūrti in, 9346
turtle in, 9407
Vedic gods in, 9736
vernacular Hindi adaptations of, 3984
violence in, 1027
wisdom in, 9752
Yudhiṣṭhira in, 852, 4438, 7362
Mahābhāṣya (Patañjali), 7005
Mahā Bodhi Society, 1126, 1187, 1188–1189, 9144
establishment of, 6080
Mahācattārīsaka Sutta, 2738–2739
Mahādev (deity), 4436

Mahādeva (monk)
  Five Points of
    in Mahāsāṃghika Buddhism, 5601–5602
    and monasticism, 6128
  Pāṭaliputra council and, 2036
Mahadevan, T. M. P., 3289
  Bangalore Consultation presentation, 8790
Mahādevi (Buddha's mother), 1304
Mahādevī (Hindu deity), goddesses as aspects of, 3608
Mahādēviyakka (poet), on Śiva, 8417
Mahady, Frank, 9411
Maha-giri (spirit), 1330
Mahā-Kālī (deity), sword of, 968
Mahākalpa (division of time), in Hinayana Buddhist cosmology, 2028
Mahākaruṇā (great compassion), 5105
Mahākāśyapa (Buddha's disciple), 1105
Mahā Kumbha Melā, 5265
Mahāmāyā (great creator), 4433
Mahamba spirits, 1510, 4302
Mahāmudrā (great seal), 1217, 1218, 1219, **5596–5601**
  basis, path, and result of, 5598–5599
  complexity of concept, 5596
  controversies over, 5599
  in Indian Buddhism, 5596–5597
  Mar pa on, 5597–5598, 5716
  Rang byung rdo rje on, 5102, 5598
  Sgam po pa (Gampopa) on, 8255
  in Tibetan Buddhism, 5596, 5597–5599
Mahan, Asa, Holiness movement and, 4083
Mahanavami festival, Vijayanagara as sacred space and, 1806
Mahānidāna Sutta (Buddhist text), 5200
Mahāniddesa (Buddhist text), 1062, 1270
Mahānikāya sect, 5130, 5131, 9095, 9151
Mahanta (Living Eck Master), 2601
Mahānubhāva sect, 5696, 9504
Mahāpadesa Suttanta (Buddhist text), 1269, 1272
Mahāpadma (king), Pāṭaliputra council and, 2036
Mahāpajāpatị (Buddha's foster mother), 6759
Mahāparinibbāna Sutta, 2738
  relics of Buddha in, 7690
Mahāparinibbāna Suttanta, stupas in, 8796
Mahāparinirvāṇa Sūtra (Buddhist text), 2216–2217
  bathing of Buddha in, 1305
  Buddha preaching, 9177
  dharma in, 2333
  drums in, 2496
  Niepan school based on, 1576
  permanence in, 1117
  pūjā in, 7495–7496
  stupas in, 7163
  tathāgata-garbha in, 9018
Mahāprajāpati (Buddha's disciple), 1105
Mahaprājña, Ācārya, 2626
Mahāprajñāpāramitā Śāstra (Buddhist text)
  norms for reading, 6993
  on great concentrations of Śākyamuni, 2030
Mahāprajñāpāramitā-upadeśa Sūtra (Buddhist text), 1271, 1272
Mahāprasthāna (pilgrimage unto death), 7169
Mahāpurāṇas (sacred texts), 7498
Mahāpuruṣa (cosmic person), 1063, 1065, 9207
Māharāj, Śivāndanda Sāraswāti, 108
MaHaRaL. *See* Löw, Yehudah ben Betsal'el of Prague
Maharal of Prague. *See* Löw, Yehudah ben Betsal'el of Prague
Maharam of Rothenburg. *See* Me'ir ben Barukh of Rothenburg
Maharashtra (India)
  affliction in, 56, 57, 58
  bhaktas of, 9504
  culture of, 5696
  Gaṇeśa in, 3271
  household consecration ceremony for Gaṇeśa in, 1955
  Kṛṣṇaism in, 5253
  Marathi religions in, **5696–5700**
Maharishi European Research University, 9290
Maharishi Mahesh Yogi
  education of, 9289
  Transcendental Meditation of, 9289, 9290–9291
  Western missions of, 9290
Mahārs, Ambedkar (B. R.) and, 285, 9477
MaHaRSHaL. *See* Luria, Shelomoh
Mahasamghika (Great Assembly), Pāṭaliputra council and, 2036
Mahāsāṃghika Buddhism, 1110, **5601–5603**
  and Mahāyāna Buddhism, 1113, 1120, 5601
    formation of, 8120
  antarābhava in, 1197
  arhat in, 1195–1196, 5601–5602
  development of, 5601–5602
  dharma in, 2335
  docetism in, 5602
  doctrines of, 5601–5602
  Five Points of Mahādeva in, 5601–5602
  Four Noble Truths in, 1197
  geographical distribution of, 1195
  influence of, 5602–5603
  on interpreting scriptures, 1274
  literature of, 1198, 1200, 1270, 5601
  Maitreya in, 5619
  monastic discipline in, 5601
  nirvāṇa in, 1195–1196, 1197
  origins of, 1090, 1132, 1193–1194, 5601
  pāramitās in, 6993
  prajñtilde;ā in, 5602
  schism leading to, 5601, 6128
  schools developed from, 1194, 5602
  tathāgata in, 9015
  vs. Sthaviravāda Buddhism, 9145
Mahāsammata (ruler), 1134
Mahāsattva (one capable of greatness), 996
Mahāsattva Sūtra (Buddhist text), 1305
Mahāsiddhas (great adepts), 1215, **5603–5606**
  biographies of, 5604–5606
  characteristics of, 5604–5605
  enlightenment of, 5604–5605
  historical existence of, 5605
  historical role of, 5605–5606
  magic and, 5605
  miracles of, 6052
  Nā ro pa as, 6415
  on *mahāmudrā,* 5597
  sources on, 5603, 5604
  writings of, 5606
Mahāśivarātri (Great Night of Síva), 9824
  in Śaivism, 8417
Mahāsthāmaprāpta
  Amitābha and, 291
  Avalokiteśvara and, 705, 706
Mahāsthaviras (monastic head), 9149
Mahāsvami (monastic head), 9149
Mahāthera, Uttarajīva, 1136
Mahātissa (Buddhist monk), 9147
Mahatma Gandhi. *See* Gandhi, Mohandas
Māhātmya (praise literature), 778, 7169, 7498
Mahāvadāna Sutta (Buddhist text), 1066
Mahāvagga (Buddhist text), 1260, 1307
  Buddha in, 3154
    great commission of, 6077
  Buddhist message in, 5200
Mahāvaipulya Buddhāvataṃsaka Sūtra. See Avataṃsaka Sūtra
Mahāvairocana (buddha), 1162, 1217, 1243, 4417, **5607–5609**
  constructed by Shandao, 8298
  as Cosmic Buddha, 5608
  in Esoteric Buddhism, 5607, 5608
  Fudō identified with, 3226
  iconography of, 5454, 5608
  in Vajrayāna (Tantric) Buddhism, 5607, 5608
  in literature, 5607
  Pure Land of Esoteric Grandeur of, 8350
  religious meaning of, 5608
  in Shingon Buddhism, 5608, 8349, 9515
  worship of, 5608
  in Zhenyan Buddhism, 9963
Mahāvairocana Sūtra (Buddhist text), 5607, 9077, 9078, 9961–9962
  in Shingon Buddhism, 8348, 8349, 8351
  Śubhākarasiṃha on, 8804
  in Tendai Buddhism, 8350
  translations of, 5607
Mahavajradhara, Śaiva deities and, 1350
Mahāvaṃsa (Buddhist text), 1199
  Buddha biography in, 1065
  Buddhaghosa in, 1073
  Buddha's relics in, 7690–7691
  content of, 9146
  Devānaṃpiyatissa in, 2313
  Duṭṭhagāmaṇī in, 1304–1305, 2531, 9147
  historiography in, 4025–4026
  Pāṭaliputra council in, 2037
  saṃgha in, 8079
Mahāvastu (Buddhist text)
  bodhisattva path in, 997
  Buddha biography in, 1064, 1198
  Buddha in, 5601
  in Mahāsāṃghika Buddhism, 5601
  language of, 1198, 1200
  Maitreya in, 5619
  pāramitās in, 6993
Mahāviarocana, as subject of *nianfo,* 6601
Mahāvibhāṣā (Buddhist text), 1092, 1110, 1199, 1270, 1298
  Kaniṣka council and, 2037
  Sarvāstivāda and, 8118
Mahāvideha. *See* Videha
Mahāvihāra tradition (Buddhist)
  as *tīrthaṃkara,* 9207
  Devānaṃpiyatissa and, 2313
  foundation of, 9146–9147
  literature of, 1199
  sources on, 9148
  spread of, 1136
Mahāvīra (Jain teacher), **5609–5611**
  asceticism of, 5609
  as *tīrthaṃkara,* 5609
  birth of, 5609
  as *buddha,* 1060, 1067
  conception of, 5609
  family of, 5609
  and food taboos, 3168
  as founder of Jainism, 4429
  Gośāla and, 211–212, 3639, 5610
  as Jaina ideal, 2624
  in Jainism, 4764

on liberation of the soul, 8548
life of, 5609–5610
in literature, 5609
loka cosmology and, 2022
nirvāṇa of, 5610
on reincarnation, 7679
significance of, 5610–5611
teachings of, 5610
veneration of image of, 4382
women in life of, 3327, 5609
Mahāvrata (festival), in Āraṇyakas, 1028
Mahavrata (Great Vow), of Śiva, 8040, 8050
Mahāvrata soma (sacrifice), 9567
Mahavratins. *See* Kāpālika Śaivism
Mahāyāna (monk), at Lhasa council, 2038
Mahāyāna Abhidharma Sūtra (Buddhist text), 5102
Mahāyāna Buddhism, **1203–1213**. *See also* Nāgārjuna
Absolute Body in, 1077–1078, 1117
Amitābha in (*See* Amitābha)
and Theravāda Buddhism, 9150
arhats in, 1080, 1085, 1114, 1192
asaṃkhyeya cosmology in, 2026, 2030
authority in, 694
in Bengal, 824
Bhaiṣajyaguru in, **855–856**
Bodhidharma studying, 994
bodhisattvas in, 1083, 1192, 6630 (*See also Bodhisattvas; See also* Avalokiteśvara; *See also* Mañjuśrī)
bodhisattva path, 996–997, 998–999, 1116
celebration of, 1307
development of, 1076
doctrine of, 1076, 1077, 1115–1117
ideal of, 1298–1299
king as *bodhisattva,* 1068
names of, 1079
roles of, 1113
as saints, 8036–8037
saving power of, 3887
as spiritual guides, 8712
sūtras on, 1093
traveling between buddha fields, 1077
Buddha bodies in (three), 8349
buddha fields in, 1077, 1079, 1114, 1117, 1207
buddhahood in, 1069, 1120, 1207
Buddha in, name of, 6408
Buddha portrayed in, 1064
Buddhist universities and, 1118–1121
celestial buddhas in, 1067, 1081, 1117
in Central Asia, 1145, 1146
Chan Buddhism and, 1601
charisma in, 1549
in China, 1202, 1595, 1596, 1605 (*See also* Huayan school; Tiantai school)
clothing, monastic, 1829
compassion in, 6630
consciousness in, rebirth and, 8552
cosmology in, 1077, 1078, 1092, 1117
critique of, 1206, 1207–1208, 1280
and debate at Bsam yas, 5069–5070
decline of, 1121
desire in, 2306
development of, 1113, 1115–1118, 1207–1212
dharma in, 1206, 1298, 2332
dharmakāya in, 1069–1070
doctrines of, 1205–1208
drums in, 2496–2497
early *nikāyas* and, 8074
in East Asia, 6630–6631
eightfold path of, 2739
emptiness *(śūnyatā)* in, 1117, 1119, 1209, 1211, 1298, 6391–6393, 8856–8857
enlightenment in, 2217, 2794
ethics of, 1280–1282
female imagery in, 3033
Five Buddhas in, 1078
Four Noble Truths in, 3179–3180
gender in, 3331–3332
Hinayānā, division with, Weber (Max) on, 8152
Hinduism and, 1113–1114, 1115
horrific buddhas in, 1081
Huayan school on truth in, 4148
human perfectibility in, 7041
iconography of, 4327, 4329, 4330, 5454
images as divine presence in, 4390
in India, 1112–1121
in Japan, 1176, 1183, 1202, 1242
judgment of the dead in, 5026
karman in, 5100
karuṇā in, 5105
Khmer religion influenced by, 5129
knowledge in, 5200
of lay people, 1114–1115, 1115
literature of, 1113, 1114–1115, 1120–1121
on *bodhisattvas,* 1093
canonization, 1253, 1407
Chinese translations of, 1198, 5262, 5263
early, 1092
on emptiness, 1117
exegetical, 1270–1271
hermeneutical, 1274, 1275
Japanese, 7216
Mahāparinirvāṇa Sūtra, 2216–2217
philosophical, 1204, 1205
production of, 1262
recitation of, 1263
revisions of, 1200
on rituals, 1118, 1119
textual embodiment of Buddha in, 1261–1262
transformative agency of, 1264
translation into Chinese, 1594, 5262, 5263
Wuliang duren jing, 2194
mahākaruṇā in, 5105
Mahāsāṃghika Buddhism and, 5601
Maitreya in, 5619
mappō in, 5686
māyā in, 5794
meaning of term, 1192
meditation in, 1117–1118, 1290
merit in, 5874
transference of, 1113
mirrors in, 6064
missions of, 6071
monasticism in, 1115, 1118, 7720
monism in, 6145
monotheism in, 6157
music in, 6296
mystical experience in, 6344–6345
Sufism, similarities in, 1869–1870
New Year celebrations in, 6594
nirvāṇa in, 1116, 1207, 1208–1210, 1211, 1299, 6393, 6629–6630
ordination in, 6855
origins of, 1112–1115
pantheism in, 6965
paradox in, 3068, 6989
pāramitās in, 6993, 6994
perfection of donation tradition in, 4140
phallus and vagina in, 7084
philosophy of, 1204, 1205, 1298–1299
politics and, 7260, 7262
polytheistic elements of, 7318–7319
prajñā in, 7358, 7359
pūjā in, 7496–7497
and Pure Land Buddhism, 2176
Pure Lands in, 7502–7503
quaternity in, 7551
realities in, 1208–1212
Nāgārjuna on, 6391–6392
reincarnation in, 2131
rituals in, Śāntideva on, 8110
salvation drama in, 2030
salvation in, 1088, 7641
saṃgha in, 8075
saṃsāra in, 1207, 1209, 1210, 1299
Sanskrit language used in, 1205
Śāntideva on, 8109–8110
Sarvāstivāda and, 8120
Sautrāntikas and, 8119–8120
schools of, 1119–1121, 1204, 1207–1213
social impact of, 8463
in Southeast Asia, 1132, 1133, 1137–1138, 1202
temples with stupas in, 4012
studies on, 1313
stupas in, 8797, 8798–8799 (*See also* Stupas and stupa worship)
sūtras as scripture in, 8198
Tārā in, popularity of, 3977
tathāgata-garbha in, 1070, 1120, 9017
tathāgata in, 9015, 9016
temples in, 9053
texts of, 6391
in Thailand, 9094
trikāya in, 1063, 1069, 9346–9347
upāya in, 9484–9485
Vajrapāṇi in, 9512
Vasubandhu in, 9525–9527
in Vietnam, 9592
vs. Hīnayāna Buddhism, 996, 1076, 1081, 1088, 1113, 1118, 8798
wisdom in, 9752–9753, 9764
women in, 3331–3332, 3333
Yogācāra school of (*See* Yogācāra school)
yoga in, 1157
Mahāyāna-mahāparinirvāṇa Sūtra (Buddhist text), 1270–1271
Mahāyāna Prajñāpāramitā literature, 2171. *See also* Prajñāpāramitā Sūtras
Mahāyānasaṃgraha (Asaṅga), 517
Paramārtha translating, 6992
trisvabhāva in, 9900
vijñaptimātra in, 9900
Mahāyānasūtrālaṃkāra (Buddhist text), 9898–9899
Mahāyoga (Great Yoga), 7868, 7870
Mahdawī, ʿAbd al-ʿAzīz al-, 4257
Mahdesi (one who has seen death), 7154
Mahdi
Abū Ḥātim al-Rāzī on, 8328–8329
iconography of, vol. 1 color insert
in *jihād,* 4919
in Qarāmiṭah Shiism, 8328–8329
in Shiism *vs.* Sunnī Islam, 5981–5982

Mahdi *continued*
in Islamic eschatology, 2835
Sunnī, 2838
in messianism, 5973, 5979, 5980–5982
people earning title of, 5981
persons claiming to be, 5982
Al-Mahdī, 8329
Ghulām Aḥmad (Mirza), 200
Muḥammad Aḥmad, 5982, 6228–6229
the Bāb, 728
sub-Saharan expectations of, 4605
use of term, 5980, 5981
Mahdi, al-. *See* Muḥammad Aḥmad
Mahdī, al- (caliph)
as Mahdhī, 8329
Ismāʿīlīyah and, 8327
Mahdism (millenarianism). *See also* Messianism
in Africa, 107
Mahdiyya movement, 107
women in, 4610
Mahendra (Buddhist monk), 1252
Ma Hezhi (painter), 4338
Mahikari, 6568
Mahinda (Buddhist monk)
Buddhism established in Sri Lanka by, 2313
fourth Theravādin council and, 2037
missionary goal of, 9146
Moggaliputtatissa and, 6112
Mahīśāsaka school of Buddhism
doctrines of, 1110, 1196, 1197
geographical distribution of, 1195
literature of, 1198
origin of, 1194
Sarvāstivāda and, 8117, 8119
Mahiṣāsura (demon), Durgā's victory over, 2525, 2526
Mahler, Gustav, 6312
Maḥmal (ornate box), 7160, 9091
Maḥmūd Gāwān (Persian minister), 4645
Maḥmūd of Ghaznah, 954
Mahr (bride price), 4625, 4706–4707
Mahu role, gender reversal in, 4116
Mahya (martyr), 6742
Maḥzor. See Siddur and *Maḥzor* (prayer books)
Maḥzor for Rosh Hashanah and Yom Kippur, Conservative Judaism and, 8388
Mai, Cardinal Angelo, on *Sibylline Oracles,* 8384
Mai (creature), in reference to Rainbow Snake, 7606
Mái (immortal beings), Araweté religion (Amazon), 8628
Maia (deity), 1483
Maiden. *See also* Virgin goddess
in goddess worship, 9601–9602
Maid of Ludmir, **5611–5612**
in oral tradition, 5611
as *tsaddiq* or *rebbe,* 3351, 5611–5612
Maid of Orléans. *See* Joan of Arc
Maidu people (California), knot symbolism of, 5198
Maier, Bernhard, 1499
Maier, Heinrich, Heschel (Abraham Joshua) and, 3961
Maier, Johann. *See* Eck, Johann
Maier, Michael, 7930
Maimon, Salomon, on Spinoza (Baruch), 8685
Maimonides, Abraham, 4994, **5612–5613**
Maimonides (Moses) as father of, 5612–5613, 5614
skeptical views of, 8421
Ṣūfī influences on, 5612–5613
writings of, 5612–5613
Maimonides, Moses, **5613–5618**
Abravanel (Isaac) on, 17
Abulafia (Me'ir) criticizing, 24
on afterlife, 153, 154
Albo (Yosef) on, 233, 234
Alfasi (Yitsḥaq ben Yaʿaqov) and, 255
on almsgiving, 268
on anthropomorphism, 390
on apocalypse, 420
apologetics of, 428, 429
Aristotle's influence on, 479, 481, 4993, 5617
on astrology, 2373
on belief in demons, 2280
biblical exegesis of, 866, 867, 868
on blasphemy, 969, 970
on charity, 1553
almsgiving in, 268
code of law of, 5104, 5614
on creation, 2642, 3549
Crescas (Ḥasdai), opposition by, 2069
in Egypt, 4990–4991
ethics of, 4912
and folk Judaism, 3159
on food taboos, 3172
on free will, 3549
and predestination, 3203
on gambling, 3262
Gerondi (Yonah) and, 4913
Gersonides and, 3462
on God, 3549
attributes of, 614
existence of, 7422
halakhah and, 3745, 3747
on Noahic laws, 3753
philosophy fused with, 5616, 5617, 5618
on repeal of enactments, 3750
theory of origins of, 3748
history, approach to, 4038, 4059
Ibn Bājjah's influence on, 4263
Ibn Daud's influence on, 4264
intellectualism of, critics of, 154
on Islam, 7230
Isserles (Mosheh) on, 4750
on Jewish people, membership in, 4861–4862
in Jewish thought and philosophy, 4892–4894
on Karaite-Rabbanite differences, 5084
on *kashrut* laws, 5107, 5108
Kimḥat (David) on, 5145
on knowledge, 5203
legacy of, 5618
life of, 5613–5614
Maimonides (Abraham) as son of, 5612–5613, 5614
on martyrdom, 5742
medical practice of, 5614
on medicine and healing, 3830
in medieval Judaism, 4980
Mendelssohn (Moses) studying, 5854
on messianism, 5976
on miracles, 481
on Mishnah, 5615–5616
Nahmanides' (Moses) critique of, 24, 6399, 6400
Neoplatonism and, 6475
on oral Torah, 6840
parables of, 6978
philosophy of, 5613–5618
polemics against Islam, 7240
on politics, 10062
on polytheism, 7316
on principles of Jewish faith, 3549, 5615
on prophecy, 7439–7440
Ptolemy criticized by, 7492
on purity, 7512
on rabbinic ordination, 7578
on resurrection, 154, 8560
on scriptural *vs.* rabbinic law, 3748, 3749
soul, theory of, 8559–8560
Spinoza (Baruch) on, 8683
on Sukkot, 8834
Talmudic commentary of, 3745, 5615–5616
on tattooing, 1002
on Ten Commandments, 5615
on Torah, 5614
as law, 9236
writings of, 5613–5617
young readers of, Adret (Shelomoh ben Avraham) and, 36
on Zion, 9978
Maine, Henry, 2983
on ancient law codes, 1842, 1843
on law and religion, 5325
on matriarchy, 3611
Main Problems of Gnosis (Bousset), 3514
Mainz (Germany), Jewish elite of, 5011, 5012
Maiolcuita (confession), 9254
Mairs, Nancy, 703
Maitatsine movement, 107
Maithuna (sexual intercourse, Tantric), 8991
semen withheld in, 4003
spiritual perfection and, 8240
Maitland, Edward, on Hermetism, 3952
Maitland, Frederic William, on retribution, 5373
Maitreya *(bodhisattva),* 1092, **5618–5623**
and Asaṅga, 517
Besant (Annie) on, 845, 5244
as *bodhisattva,* 1067, 1076, 5619
Budai as, 4209
in cave paintings, 5620
in Chinese Buddhism, 1162, 1166, 5620–5621, 7503
millenarianism of, 6039, 6040
coming of, 2834
cult of, 1076, 1082, 1117, 1145, 1147, 5620–5622
Dao'an and, 2171
dharma proclaimed by, 6984
Empress Wu Zhao as manifestation of, 1600, 5620
as future Buddha, 5618, 5620
iconography of, 4329, 5620, 5621
images of
in China, 1596, 5620
in Korea, 5621
incarnations of, 5618
in Yogācāra Buddhism, 9898–9899
in Japan, *Miroku-ha* (Maitreyism) teachings, 8364
in Japanese Buddhism, 5621–5622, 7503
in Korean Buddhism, 1170, 1171, 5621
Kotani Kimi as, 7682
Krishnamurti as, 845, 5244, 5245
Leadbeater (Charles W.) on, 5244
in literature, 5618–5620
messianic traditions and, 2028, 5621
millennialism and, 6545
and popularization of Buddhism, 3155
relics of the Buddha and, 7691
roles of, 1067
as subject of *nianfo,* 6601
in Tibetan Buddhism, 9898–9899
tower of, 9053
White Lotus sect and, 1607
Yogācārabhūmi attributed to, 9898
Maitreyasamitināṭaka (Buddhist text), 1147

Maitreyi (Eliade), 2760
Maitrī (friendliness), in Buddhist meditation, 5105
Maitrīpa (Buddhist scholar), 1225
on *mahāmudrā*, 5597
Maitrisimit (Buddhist text), 1147
Maitrī Upaniṣad
cakravartin in, 1350–1351
gurūs in, 3713
on heterodoxy, 6909–6910
lotus symbolism in, 5518
three (number) in, 9346
Maize. *See* Corn
Majangir religion (Ethiopia), 2574
Majāz al-Qur'ān (Abū ʿUbaydah), 8952
Majd al-Dawla, 4
Majd al-Dīn al-Jīlī, 7632–7633
Majduddīn Isḥāq al-Rūmī, 4258
Majestic Man, Soloveitchik (Joseph Baer) on, 8519
Majidi, Majid, 3098
Majīdīyah. *See* Ḥāfiẓīyah movement
Maji Maji rebellion, 2571
Maji Maji Wars, 5181
Majjhima Nikāya (Buddhist text)
animals in, 356, 359
arahant in, 476
in Hinayana Buddhist cosmology, 2027
nirvāṇa in, 6628
quotation from, 1072
Upāli in, 1062
Majlis (Druze house of prayer), 2502
Majlisī, al-, **5623,** 6731
Majmaʿ al-Baḥrayn (Dārā), 2219
Majolus (Benedictine monk), 821
Major, H. D. A., 6105
Majorinus (bishop of Carthage), 2747
Majrīṭī, Maslamah al-, 249
on magic, 5584, 5586, 5587
Majumdar, R. C., 745
Ma Junshi (Muslim scholar), 4632
Majusi, ʿAli ibn al-ʿAbbas al- (Haly Abbas), on medicine, 3832
Makahiki ceremonial period, Lono and, 3797, 3798
Makah people (North America), repatriation of sacred objects by, 6711
Makara (Capricorn) Saṃkrānti (transiting), in Hindu religious year, 4016
Makarios of Alexandria, 2824
Makarios of Corinth, 6621
Makarios of Egypt, 2824, **5623–5624**
Makarios the Great. *See* Makarios of Egypt
Makasar people (Indonesia), creation myths of, marriage in, 5727
Makemie, Francis, 7390
Make Prayers to the Raven (Nelson), 2618
Mākhiṃ (drum), 2497
Makhmalbaf, Mohsen, 3098
Makhzan (state government), 4587
Makiguchi Tsunesaburō, 4799
Sōka Gakkai and, 8508
Making of Religion, The (Lang), 114, 7372
Supreme Being in, 8168
Making of the Golden Bough, The (Fraser), 381
Makiratare people (Amazon), 8626. *See also* Carib Indians
Makiritare people (Venezuela), 2312
Makká religion (Argentina), 8636
Makkhali Gośāla. *See* Gośāla
Mako (mythic figure), in Cuna creation myth, 2095
Makonde people, masquerade dances of, 2140
Makota ʿĀlam. *See* Iskandar Muda
Maktab, 7735
Maktūbāt-i Aḥmad Sirhindī (Sirhindī), 4570
Makua people, masquerade dances of, 2140
Maku people (Amazon), 8625
Makwa people (Africa), 1003
Māl (deity), Āḻvārs on, 279
Mala (bodily secretion or excretion), in Āyurveda, 3855
Malabar (India), Jesuits in, 4842
Malabar Church (India), 9465–9466
Malacca, sultanate of (Malaysia), 4659–4660, 4661, 4662, 4664
Malachi, 879, 933
apocatastasis in, 422
Elijah in, 2765
Malaise, Michel, 4558
Malaitan religion. *See* Solomon Islands religions
Malak (angelic force), *nafs* (lower souls) *vs.*, 8815
Malakbēl (deity)
in Aramean religion, 449
birth of, 34
Malalasekera, G. P., **5624–5625**
on denial of soul in Buddhism, 8550
on life, 8551
in World Fellowship of Buddhists, 5624, 5625
Malamala (death), 9696
Malāmatīyah branch of Sufism, individualism in, 8821
Malankara, Church of, 2585
Malankara (India), Christianity in, Chalcedon statement rejected by, 2584
Malankara Syrian Orthodox Church
formation of, 1729
Syriac Orthodox Church of Antioch, relations with, 8941
Malawi. *See also* Central Bantu religions
Apostolic Church of John Maranke in, 5695
Chewa people in, *vimbuza* healing dance of, 2140
hypereridic rage reactions (amok) in, 3214
Lozi myth from, 2961
Mbona (deity) in, 5802
Ngonde people of, 6770
Tumbuka people in, *vimbuza* healing dance of, 2140
Malay Annals, The. See Sejarah Melayu
Malay language, 25, 4657
Arabic language influencing, 4657
literature in, 4662, 4663, 4664, 4665
Malayo-Polynesian language family, 745
Malaysia and Malaysian religions. *See also* Borneo; Southeast Asia and Southeast Asian religions
Daoism in, 2190
head hunting in, 3805
human beings, makeup of, and illness, cause of, 3810
hypereridic rage reactions (amok) in, 3214
Islam, 3076, 4671
architecture of mosques in, 6209
birth rituals, 2983
in colonial era, 4660
conversion to, 4661, 4662
evidence for, 4659
incantation in, 4408
as national religion, 4668, 4670
in politics, 4668
reform movements in, 4666
spread of, 4563, 4658
sultanates in, 4659–4660, 4661, 4662, 4664
kinship in, 5184
languages in, 4657
literature of, fiction, 3076, 3078
music in, 6287
Negrito religions, **6456–6457**
Sai Baba movement in, ethnic identities and, 1809
Semang of Kedah, origins of disease in, 3808
spirit possession in, 8696
Malbim, **5625–5626**
biblical exegesis of, 868–869, 5626
Malcarne, Vanessa, 6540
Malcolm, Noel, on Hobbes (Thomas), 4073
Malcolm, Norman, 7123
Malcolm X, **5626–5627**
assassination of, 72, 5626
autobiography of, 700
conversions of, 72, 5626
as national leader, 72, 4688, 5626
in Nation of Islam, 72, 2767, 5626
religious studies on, 80
Male. *See* Androcentrism; Gender; Men
Mâle, Émile, 500, 501, 3177
Malebranche, Nicolas, 7421
on knowledge, 5205, 5206
on "occasions," 6779
Malecite Indians (United States), myth of Aglabem monster, 2091
Maleficium (magical harm), diabolical pact theory and, 8865
Malefic powers, *daivas*, 2128
Malekula religion
corpses in, 6784
funeral symbolism of, labyrinth in, 2558
mythology of, land of the dead in, 3016, 5278
Malenda, Ta, 105
Malevich, Kasimir, vol. 11 color insert
Malfatti, Giovanni, 6435
Malḥūn (poetry), 4589
Mali. *See also* Bambara religion; Dogon religion
drums in, 7037
Gbaya people of, rites of passage of, 88–89
Islam in, 4601–4603
scholars and, 4602–4603
spread of, 4601
kingship in, 4602
Nya cult in, 107
Sundiata epic of, 3086
Tellem people, 1472
Mali-Baining people, masks of, 5767–5768
Malik (deity). *See also* Molech
in Canaanite religion, 1384, 1387
Mālik, Imām, *ḥadīths*, collection of, 3727, 3728
Malik al-Saleh (Sumatran ruler), 4659
Mālik ibn Anas, **5627–5628**
Abū Ḥanīfah compared with, 22
Abū Yūsuf and, 24, 5627
on apostasy, 433
in Mālikī school of law, 5627–5628
development of, 5548, 5627
legal scholarship of, 5627
al-Shāfiʿī studying with, 8263
writings of, 5627

Mālikīyah (school of Islamic law), 9489
in Andalusia, 4593, 4594–4595
blasphemy in, 975, 976
current status of, 5548, 5628
development of, 5548, 5627
divorce in, 4709
doctrine of, 5548
establishment of, 4694–4695
marriage in, 4706
maṣlaḥah (public interest) in, 5772
in North Africa, 4579, 4584, 4585, 4601, 4698
paternity in, 4710
prevalence of, 4567
al-Shāfiʿī on, 8263, 8264
in sub-Saharan Africa, 4603
wife waiting for missing husband in, 4567
Malik Muḥammad Jaʾisi, 7223
Malikshāh ibn Ālp Arsalān, 6639, 6640
Malikum (deified kings), in Canaanite religion, 1384, 1386
Malinalco rock temple, 1470
Malines, Council of, and orthodoxy *vs.* superstition, 8866
"Malines Conversations," Mercier (Désiré Joseph) in, 5868
Mālinīvijayottara Tantra, Abhinavagupta on, 8, 9
Malinowski, Bronislaw, **5628–5629**
on calendars, 1352
and Donner (Kai), 2420, 2421
on earth symbolism, 3015
education of, 5628
ethnography of, 6800–6801
on exchange, 1423
as first ethnographer, 8763
and Firth (Raymond), 3121
on food customs, 3173
and functionalism, 3143, 3232
functionalist approach of, 4043, 5628–5629
on gardens, 3280
generalizations of, 5628
on initiation rituals, 4480
on magic, 2543, 5563, 5566, 5567, 5568, 5570, 5571, 5629
methodology of, 5628–5629
methods of, 5381
on Milamala festival, 6591
on money, 6137
on myths, 5629
authority of, 692
on religion *vs.* magic, 6502
revaluation of, 380
on society and religion among Trobriand Islanders, 8467
Stanner (W. E. H.) and, 8729
symbol theory and, 8910–8911
on Trobriand Islanders, 5628–5629
magic of, 5566, 5567, 5571
sexuality of, 5628
Malinowski, Elsie, 5628, 5629
Malkhut (sovereignty), 3550
Shekhinah and, 8315
Mallarmé, Stéphane, 3224
symbol theory and, 8909
Malleus maleficarum (The Hammer of Witches), 9772
Malli (Jina), gender of, 3326–3327
Mallmann, Marie-Thérèse de, 704
Mallquis (Inca mummies), oracular communication with the dead and, 5176
Maloca (familial residence), 4486
Maloney, Newton, 6522
Malouf, David, 3084
Malqot (flagellation), 7928
Malraux, André, 502, 5480
Malta
Melqart in, 5848–5849
Neolithic religion in, 6465
Malu (tattoo), 7807–7808
Malua Satene (deity), 5277
Mālunkyaputta (Buddhist figure), 1296
Mam (deity), 5791–5792, 5910
Saint Peter and, 5926
Mamacocha (deity), 3416
Mama Huaco (queen), 3417
Mamaia movement, 6795
Mama Latay, in Shango cult, 1434
Mama Ocllo, **5633–5634**
in human origin myth, 8589
Mama Quilla (moon deity), 5292
Mamau (mothers), 1486
Mambai religion (East Timor), creation myth in, 8649
Mamikonian, Vartan, 488
Ma Mingxin (Muslim leader), 4635
Mami Wata (divinities), **5629–5631**
as Lady of the Animals, 5280
Mamiya, Lawrence, 74, 81
Mamluk sultans
Abbasid caliph and, 1367
Coptic Church and, 1981
Schimmel (Annemarie) on, 8149
Mamma Quilla (deity), 3017
Mammy Water cult, 2697
Mamona (deity), in Island Arawak religion, 1427
Maʾmūn, al- (caliph)
court of, Abū al-Hudhayl al-ʿAllāf in, 18
and Muʿtazilah, 3212, 6319
and translation movement, 2970
Man. *See* Gender; Masculine sacrality; Masculinity
Man, Play, and Games (Caillois), 3267
Mana (supernatural power), **5631–5633**
and animatism, 364–365, 7372–7373
Baetke (Walter) on, 7374
Benedict (Ruth) on, 820
charismatic power and, 1547, 7353
Codrington (R. H.) on, 1847–1848, 2540, 2915, 7347–7348, 7372
Durkheim (Émile) on, 2542, 7373
Eliade (Mircea) on, 7374
evangelistic discourse on, 8767
Firth (Raymond) on, 2543
genealogy of, 3425
Hocart (Arthur M.) on, 2542
King (John H.) on, 2541
as magic, 5566–5567, 5568, 5571, 5632
manism not related to, 5671
in Maori religion, 5631, 5632, 5633, 5683, 5684
Marett (R. R.) on, 2541, 5708, 7372, 7373
as "marker" for concept, 5631
Mauss (Marcel) on, 2541–2542
meanings of, 5631–5633, 5683
in Melanesian religions, 5835
morality of, 5631–5632
Nilsson (Martin P.) on, 6622
and *numen,* 6754
in Oceanic religions, 6786, 6800
gender and, 3397
gift giving and, 3481
political power and, 7296
in Polynesian religions, 5631–5633, 7307–7308
of chiefs, 7296, 7307, 8947
primary element of, 7307
as positive attitude toward power, 7346, 7373
and preanimism, 7372–7374
Radin (Paul) on, 2542
sacrifice and, 8003
śakti as, 2542
similar concepts, 7348, 7373, 8947
in Solomon Islands religions, 8515–8516
as soul, 8531
vs. taboo, 5632
and *tapu,* 8947
in Tikopia religion, 9195
totem and, 9251
women and, 8516
Manabozho (culture hero), birth of, 2091
Manājat (intimate converse), 2318
Mānakdīm Shishdev. *See* Aḥmad Abū Hāshim al-Ḥusaynī
Man and God in Art and Ritual (Brandon), 1040
Man and His God, A (Sumerian text), 4931
Manannán mac Lir (deity), 1489, 6806
Manāqib (hagiography), 4584
Manār, al- (journal), 4666, 4684, 7621
Manas (epic), history in, 2814
Manasā (deity)
Bengali worship of, 826
forms of, 3608
Manasābijay (Bipradāsa), 825
Manasāmaṅgal (Gupta), 825
Manāsik al-ḥajj (Ibn Taymīyah), 4277
Manasseh (king of Judah), 924, 934, 935, 4359, 4828, 4829
Manāt (deity), 444
Muḥammad's ban on, 6222
Manatee, in ethnoastronomy, 2864
Mānatuṅga (poet), 7212
Mānava Dharmaśāstra. See Laws of Manu
Manawydan (deity), 1489–1490
in *Mabinogion,* 5546
Mānbhāv movement, 5253
Manchevski, Milcho, 3098
Manchuria, Protestantism in, 5234
Manchurian Candidate, The (film), 1031
Manchus
Buddhist temples under, 9048
Confucian temples under, 9059
Gu Yanwu under, 3718
Muslims under, 4632–4633
Qing dynasty and, 1609
Manco Capac (Inca ruler), 4524, **5633–5634**
in human origin myth, 8589
Manco II (Inca ruler), 567
Man Cures, God Heals (Appiah-Kubi), 118
Manda d'Hiia, **5634,** 5636
in *Ginza,* 3495, 5634
Mandaean language, 5634–5635, 5637
earliest writing in, 5639
Mandaean religion (Middle East), **5634–5640**
ablutions in, 11–12
Adam in, 3494, 5634, 5635–5636
afterlife in, 3494–3495, 3511
angels in, 347
baptism in, 780, 781, 5636
Christianity and, 5635, 5638, 5639
confession in, 1889
creation in, 3494, 3495
history of study of, 3532, 5637–5638
influences on, 5638–5639
under Islamic rule, 5635
Jesus in, 5636
John the Baptist in, 3495, 5635, 5636, 5638
knowledge in, 5203
light and darkness symbolism in, 5452–5453

literature of, 5635
Ginza, **3494–3495,** 5634, 5635
Manda d'Hiia in, **5634,** 5636
Manichaeism and, 5635, 5639
migration and, 5634–5635, 5638
mythology of, 5635–5636
North Star in, 8734
oral tradition in, 5637–5638
origins of, 5634, 5638, 5639
pearl in, 7024
rituals of, 5636–5637
Zurvan in, 10014
Mandaeism. *See* Mandaean religion
Mandailing Batak people (Indonesia), 799
Maṇḍalas (geometric designs), **5640–5646**
Buddhist, **5641–5646**
of *bodhisattvas,* 1076
body, 1350, 5642
cause and effect and, 5448
composite, 5642, 5644
design of, 5641–5642, 7550
erasure of, vol. 11 color insert
in Esoteric Buddhism, 1068, 5608
fivefold, 1078
Gohonzon in Sōka Gakkai, 8508
Hevajra as deity of, 3965
in *Hevajra Tantra,* 3965
in Kālacakra tradition, 5057–5058
kapaladharin ("skull cup–bearing") *maṇḍala* in, 3965
lotus in, 5642, 5643
Mahāvairocana in, 5608
mind, 5642
of Tārā, 9000
origins of, 5644–5645
Padmasambhava as central figure in, 6942
speech, 5642
Tantric, meditation and, vol. 11 color insert
temples based on, 9047, 9050, 9051, 9052
Vajrapāṇi in, 9513
Vajrsattva in, 9514
Zhenyan, 9961, 9962–9963
Buddhist, Tantric, 5641, 5642, 5643, 5645
Śākyamuni at center of, 1081, 1214
central divinity of, 1079, 1287
complexity of, 1081, 1124
consistency of, 1218
as energy grid, 8985–8986
as heavenly palace, 1157
influence of, 1215
origins of, 8984
rituals of, 1219–1220, 1286
in Shingon school, 1217
symbolism of, 1080, 1124
Cakrasamvara, **1349–1350**
Hindu, **5640–5641**
Banaras as, 779
lotus in, 5641, 5642
rural traditions of, 4435, 4436
temples based on, 9040, 9041
in Risshō Kōseikai, 7795
interior *vs.* exterior, 1503
in Japanese religion
in Shugendō, 8380
in Shingon Buddhism, 8351–8352
labyrinth as, 5278–5279
lotus symbolism of, 5518
as magical tool, 5589
meanings of, 5640, 5641
Mount Meru in, 5644, 6212
in Southeast Asia, *devarāja* (god-king) cult and, 8644, 8645
Maṇḍalaśa (deity), 5641
Maṇḍana Miśra, 9547
Mandang province (Papua New Guinea), cargo cults in, 1414–1420
Mandan religion (North America)
cedar post as center in, 1502
Okipa ceremony in, 6652
Sun Dance of, 6699
trees in, 9337
Mandapa (canopy), 7408
Mandara (sacred mountain), 4439
Mandate of Heaven *(tianming)*
charisma and, 1549
Chinggis Khan and, 1645
in Classic of Documents, 1906
in Daoism, 2178–2179
in Han dynasty, 1591
Huangdi (Yellow Emperor deity) and, 4144
king's authority based on, 5178
in Ming dynasty, 1607
mythic prototype for, 1625
revolution and, 7790
in Shang dynasty, 5178
Tian as source of, 9172
in Zhou dynasty, 1571, 1585, 1891–1892, 5352, 7266–7267
Mandell, Arnold, on altered states of consciousness, 8276
Mande people (Sudan), 5514
Mander, Jane, 3085
Mandeville, Bernard, satire of, 8491
Mandinka, in Umarian *jihād,* 9445
Māṇḍukya Upaniṣad
mysticism in, 6343
sleep as enlightenment in, 8442
Mandylion, origin of, vol. 12 color insert
Mandylion of Edessa (portrait), 4286
Mandylion of Edessa with Scenes of the Legend of King Abgar (painting), vol. 12 color insert
Manekshaw, Sam H. F. J., 6998
Manes (spirits), 2277
fravashis compared with, 3190
Manethon
on Hermes Trismegistos, 3938
as source of Plutarch, 7201
Manetti, Giannozzo, on civic humanism, 4175
Manga (comics), and Japanese Buddhism, 1184
Māṅga-ladīpaṇi (Buddhist text), 1137
Maṅgala Sutta (Buddhist text), 1280
Maṅgal-kāvyas (poems), 825, 827, 829
Manghon-il (Day of the Dead), in Korea, 5231
Mangi (Bear), 9394, 9395
Mangu (witch substance), 9778
Mangulbere (drum), 2497
Mangunyjanu rituals, 5706
Mani, 2966, **5646–5650**
ablutions and, 12
angel of, 347
as apostle, 436, 5647, 5665, 5666
art of, 5649–5650
ascension into heaven of, 5649
against Bardesanite ideas, 787
birth of, 5646, 5665
church of (*See* Manichaeism)
condemnations of, 5648, 5650
death of, 5649, 5660, 5665
on dualism, of body and soul, 4158
Elcasaite sect and, 3516
epithets of, 5646, 5647, 5649, 5666
family of, 5646–5647, 5659, 5665
healing powers of, 5647–5648
influences on, 5646–5647, 5648, 5665
life of, 5646–5648, 5659–5660
Mandaean religion and, 5639
missionary work of, 5648–5649, 5655, 5665
name of, 5646
physical appearance of, 5647
as prophet, 7425, 7426
revelations of, 5648, 5655, 5665
as social critic, 7425–7426
teachings of, 3513, 5648–5650, 5659
spread of, 5649, 5655
"twin" of, 3513, 5648, 5655
vocation of, 9633
writings of, 5649, 5651, 5665–5666
illustrations with, 8198
language of, 5649, 5651
pictures in, 5650
as scripture, 1408, 1409
Mani, Lata, 3321
Mania (deity), 5321
Manichaean Book of Prayer and Confession, confession in, 1889
Manichaeism, 2966–2967, **5650–5670**
anamnesis (recollection) in, 312, 5653
angels in, 347, 5655
anthropogony of, 5653–5654, 5666–5667
as apostasy, 432–433
apostles in, 436
as source of *kalām,* 5061
Augustine in, 624, 5653, 5663, 5665, 5667
Augustine opposing, 626, 5652, 5663–5664, 5667, 9325–9326
Bardesanite thought and, 787
in Central Asia and China, 1598, **5668–5670**
arrival of, 5656, 5668
early history of, 5668–5669
laws concerning, 5353
persecution of, 5656, 5669, 5670
as secret religion, 5669–5670
vs. western Manichaeism, 5666
as Christian heresy, 5654, 5656, 5665
Christianity and, **5665–5668**
clergy of, classes of, 5656, 5665
confession in, 1889
cosmogony of, 5653–5654, 5666–5667
critics of, 5651
disappearance of, 9329
docetism in, 2381
doctrines of, 5652–5654, 9329
dualism in, 2505, 2506, 2508, 2509, 2513, 5652–5653, 5659, 5666–5667, 5668
of body and soul, 4158–4159
eremitism of, 2822, 2823
the Fall in, 2966–2967
fate in, 3004
gnosis of, 5648, 5650–5651

Manichaeism ***continued***
Gnosticism of, 3513–3514, 5653
human condition in, 5652
in Iran, **5659–5662**
Jesus in, 5666, 5667
Klimkeit (Hans-Joachim) on, 5190
light and darkness symbolism in, 5452–5453
literature of, 5651, 5662–5663
canon, 5665–5666
rediscovery of, 5662, 5663, 5666, 5669
as scripture, 1408, 1409
translations of, 5662–5663, 5668, 5669
on lying and deceit, 2964
Mandaean religion and, 5635, 5639
in Middle Ages, 3514, 5667–5668
millenarianism in, 6030, 6040
Mongol religions influenced by, 5670, 6140
moon in, 6174–6175
mythology of, 5653–5654, 5666–5667
number symbolism in, 6747
organization of church, 5665
origins of, 5650–5651, 5654–5655
overview of, **5650–5659**
persecution of, 5655–5656, 5660, 5667, 5669, 5670
under Justinian I, 2513
reincarnation in, 7676
in Roman Empire, **5662–5665**
persecution of, 5656, 5664, 5667
salvation in, 5653
purification of the body and, 4158–4159
schism in, 5668
self-castration in, 1452
sources on, 5651–5652
spread of, 5649, 5655, 5656, 5660, 5667–5668, 9329
suffering in, 9112
surviving elements of, 5656–5657, 5667–5668
syncretism in, 8929, 8932
transmigration in, 9325, 9329–9330
twins in, 9413
Zoroastrian opposition to, 5655, 5660–5661
Zurvan in, 10014
Manifest destiny, 3005
Manifest dreams, 2483, 2484
Manifesto (Marx and Engels), 5746
"Manifesto of the Intellectuals," Barth (Karl) disturbed by, 790
Māṇikkavācakar (Hindu poet), **5670–5671,** 7210, 8974
as Nāyaṉār, 8044
Manila (Philippines), Judaism in, 5010
Maning, F. E., 7372
Manipulationist movements, in Africa, 102
Maṇipūra cakra, location of, 1348
Manism, **5671–5673**
critics of theory, 5672–5673
dynamism and, 2540
Spencer's (Herbert) theory of, 5671–5673
Man is Not Alone (Heschel), modernity in, 3962
Manitou (spirit), **5673–5675,** 7348, 7373
Algonquian concept of, 6650, 6680
Manjur (rattle-belts), 7035
Mañjuśrī *(bodhisattva),* **5675**
Buddhapālita's vision of, 1075
Dushun as incarnation of, 2530
feminine expression of, 1079
Gyōgi as manifestation of, 3721
iconography of, 4329, 5675
in Mahāyāna Buddhism, 9512–9513
as leading *bodhisattva,* 1082, 5675
Longchenpa as divine emanation of, 5192
Maitreya and, 5619
mantra of, 1079
mountain associated with, 5675, 6213
names of, 5675
origin of, 1077
as prince, 1078
role of, 1117, 5675
sacred site of, 7165
Tsong kha pa as emanation of, 9387
venerated by Manchus, 1609
wisdom of, 5675
at Wutai Shan, 5675
Mañjuśrīmūlakalpa (Buddhist text), 1076, 1079–1080, 9514–9515
mahāmudrā in, 5596
Mañjuvajra *(bodhisattva),* 1082
Manker, Ernst, 474, 3107
Man lā yaḥḍuruhu al-faqīh (Ibn Bābawayhi), 4262
Manley, Michael, 7625
Man-lion, Viṣṇu in form of, 707–708
Mann, Gurinder Singh, 3717
Mann, Thomas, 742, 3061
Campbell (Joseph) and, 1379
Gnosticism and, 3528
Kerényi's (Károly) correspondence with, 5113
midrash and, 6021
Manners and Customs of the Dieyerie Tribe of Australian Aborigines (Gason), 687
"Manners and Fashion" (Spencer), 5672
Mannhardt, Wilhelm, 3458, **5676**
on agricultural rituals, 189
on Baltic religion, 327, 759, 769
on Saule (sun) worship, 8131, 8133–8134
on Germanic religion, 3459, 5676
on *hieros gamos* (sacred marriage), 3974, 3976
on Indian religions, 5676
on law of similarity, 3192
on masks, 5764
methodology of, 5676
and Myth and Ritual school, 6380
questionnaire of, 5676
Mannheim, Karl, 9109
on utopianism, 8467
Manning, F. E., 3121
Manning, Henry, 6510
Manning, Henry Edward, 9529
Mannus (mythic figure), creation of, 3447
Manobos people (Philippines), vegeance of the dead and, 7781
Manoplas (handstones), 750, 751
MANS, Holy Order of. *See* Holy Order of MANS
Manṣab (lord), *ḥaram/ḥawṭah* and, 3776, 3777
Mansfield, Katherine, Gurdjieff (G. I.) and, 3711
Mansfield, Ralph. *See* Oldfield, Roger
Mansi language, 5118–5119
Mansi people, 468, 3106. *See also* Khanty and Mansi religion
Manslaughter. *See* Murder
Manso, Alonso, 4503, 4504
Man's Quest for God (Heschel), 7370
Mansren people, cargo myth, 1414
Manṣūr, al- (Almohad ruler), 2976
insurrection against, Mu'tazilah in, 6318
Manṣūr, al-Ḥusayn ibn. *See* Ḥallāj, al-
Mansuri Hospital (Cairo), 3832
Manṣūr Ushurma, Imām, 4615
Manteis (diviner), 2376
Mantellates, Catherine of Sienna accepted by, 1461
Manticore (monster), 6164
Manṭiq al-mashriqīyīn (Ibn Sīnā), 4553
Manṭiq al-ṭayr ('Attar), 949, 7222
as fable of Ṣūfī path, 8817–8818
Mantis (diviner), 2376
Mantra mārga (*mantra* path), in Śaiva canon, 4019, 4020
Mantra pīṭha (seat of *mantras*), Bhairava Tantras as, 4020
Mantras, **5676–5678**
Amida, 3155–3156
and attention, 604
as blessing, 980
in Buddhism, 5676–5678
Cakrasamvara Tantra, 1349–1350
in dance drama, 2449, 2451
functions of, 5677
Great prayer *(mahā-mantra),* 1347
in *Hevajra Tantra,* 3965
in Hinduism, 5676–5678
in Hindu Tantrism, 4430
aṣṭāṅgayoga (eight-limbed discipline), 8705
in Dhammakāya movement, 2325
in *Haṭhayoga,* 3795
in Vajrayāna (Tantric) Buddhism, 1217, 1221, 5310, 5677–5678
evidence for, 1121–1122
example of, 1220
function of, 1157
origins of, 8984
pronunciation of, 8986
of Vajrasattva, 1286
language of, 5677
as language of creation, 5302
as magical tool, 5589
in meditation, 5820
mudrās accompanying, 6219
names in, 6408
of Avalokiteśvara, 1079, 1157, 1217, 9184
poems with, 7215
power of words and, 2099, 8200
of praise, 5307
and purification, 7509
recitation of, 1263
variations in, 5305
sacred language of, 5304, 5311
sacredness of, 9371
in Shingon Buddhism, 8348
in Tibetan Buddhism, 9840
transformative agency of, 1263, 1264
translations of term, 5676
in Vedic texts, 4426, 4433, 9553
in Zhenyan Buddhism, 9960
Mantra Upaniṣads, 9483
Mantrayāna school of Buddhism, 1214. *See also* Shingonshū school of Buddhism
Mantua, council at (1537)
failure of, 9342
overview of, 2043
Mantz, Felix, in Anabaptism, 304
Manu (mythic figure), 3131, **5678–5679**
on *dharma,* 2327, 2329, 2330, 5679
as first king, 5678–5679
as first man, 5678
on *oṃ,* 6821
origins of, 5678
Manu, Laws of. See Laws of Manu
Manual of Discipline, 780
Manual of Discipline (Qumran sect text), 2234
Manuals, in Sufism, as spiritual guides, 8814
Manuel I (king of Portugal), Jews under, 5717
Manuel I Commenus (Byzantine emperor), 6478

Manup (deity), 6788
cargo cults and, 1418, 1419
Manuscripts
Japanese, 4809, 4812
preservation of, in monasteries, 2582
Manushi (journal), 3321
Manuṣia yajña (rites of passage), 748
Manus Island religion, 6801
afterlife in, 137
Manusmṛti (text). *See Laws of Manu*
Manus people (Admiralty Islands)
ghosts and, 5833, 5834
healing herbs, origin myths on, 3811
Manus Religion (Fortune), 137
Manvantaras (periods of Manu), 5679
Man Who Was Tired of Life (Egypt), 2712
Man'yōshū (Japanese poetry), 4811, 5074–5075, 7214–7215
in early religion, 4783
in modern period, 4813
Manzan Dōhaku (Buddhist monk), 2386, 9949
Manzat (deity), 3594, 3595
Mao Dun, 3070
Maori religion (New Zealand), **5679–5685**. *See also* Oceania and Oceanic religions
agriculture in myths of, 192, 5680, 5681
allusions to, in Oceanic fiction, 3085
assimilative policies and, 1734
atuas in, 5679–5682
Best (Elsdon) on, 8768
British settlers and, 5679, 5682, 5683
cannibalism in, 1404
Christianity in, 1731–1737, 5682, 5683, 7297
cosmology of, 2005
place in, 2618
creation myths of, 5683, 7305–7306, 7313
Christian influences on, 1876
hierogamy in, 2555
death by sorcery in, 2099
deities of, 5679–5682
descent into the underworld in, 2298
dreams in, 7306
and earth, sacredness of, 3971
Firth (Raymond) and, 3121
funeral rites in, 3234, 7808
Hauhau "extremists," prophets and, 2007
independent churches of, 6797–6798
insects in, 4508
jade in, 4760
koropata (feeding funnel in), vol. 13 color insert
mana in, 5631, 5632, 5633, 5683, 5684
Māui in, 5782
modern, 5682, 5684
music in, 6264
new religious movements in, 6795
ocean in, 6807
oral genealogies of, 5682–5683
origin myth, 1450, 7314
Pai Marire movement, 6547
parenthood in, 7807
purification in, 7509
reactive movements, 1732
reality in, 5679
rituals in, 7309, 7310
sacred space in, 5682
latrine as ritual place in, 7978
social issues, 1735, 5684
tapu in, 5679–5682, 5683, 5684, 6786, 7307
underworld in, 9451
vengeance of the dead in, 7781
weaving in, 938–939
women in, 7311
ritual roles of, 5681
Maorocon (deity), in Island Arawak religion, 1427
Maoshan (Mount Mao) Daoism, 1597, 2637
in Tang dynasty, 1602
Tao Hongjing in, 8996
Maoshan zhi (Daoist text), 2208
Maotchi (trickster), 9358
Mao Zedong
Buddhism attacked by, 1158, 1167
Cultural Revolution and, 1610
death of, 4637
Islam attacked by, 4636
propaganda of, vol. 6 color insert
revolutionary millennial movement of, 6546
Mao Ziyuan, 1606
White Lotus group of, 6040
Map, Walter, on kiss of infamy, 8013
Maparnjarra healers, overview of, 3873–3874
Maponos (Mabon) (deity), **5685**
conception of, 5685
as hunter, 1484
Mabinogion and, 5545
Modron paired with, 1490
parallels to, 1486, 5685
Mappah (Isserles), 4751
Mapplethorpe, Robert, 4282
Mappō (Mofa) (Buddhist age), 1243, 1245, 4785–4786, **5685–5688,** 9859
in Pure Land Buddhism, 4937–4938
Shandao on, 8298
Mappō tōmyōki (Saichō), 5686–5687
Maps, diagrams as, vol. 3 color insert
Mapuche religion (South America), **5688–5690**. *See also* Araucanian religion
deities of, 5688–5689, 8580
storm, ambivalence of, 5994
dreams in, 2487
drums in, 7036
dualism in, 5688–5689
rites of, 5689
rituals in, 5689
Maqāmāt (spiritual stations), 4569
Maqām Ibrāhīm (shrine), 7159
Maqātil (accounts of martyrdom), in Shiism, 4235
Maqdisī, Ḍiya al-Dīn al-, *madrasah* of, 3768
Maqlu tablets (Mesopotamian), counter-witchcraft directives on, 2098
Maqom (cult site), 934
Maqrīzī, al-, on al-Azhar university, 230
Maqṣad al-aqṣā, al- (Ghazālī), 620–621
Maqtal Ḥusayn (genre of poetry), 4712
Maquet, Jacques, 116
Māra (deity), 2793, **5690–5694**
in Baltic religion, 769, 770
in Buddhism, 2315, **5690–5691**
Buddha challenged by, 1078, 5690
evil of, 2902–2903
as impediment to enlightenment, 5690–5691
magic and, 5593
mudrā of defeat of, 9257
in Latvian folklore, **5691–5694**
functions of, 5691, 5692–5693
origins of, 5691–5692
studies of, 5691
Mara'akáme (shaman), 9370
Marabout movement (Islam), 4588, 4589
Marabouts, as saints, 8035
Maracatus, in Carnival, 1443
Maracci, Ludovico, 7244
Marae (open space), 5682–5683, 5684
Balinese temples and, 5828
Mar Ammo, Manichaeism under, 5668
Maranant'a (Buddhist monk), 1170
Maran Atha, das Buch von der Zukunft des Herrn (Herder), poetic explanation of *Revelation* in, 3919
Maranke, Abel, 5695
Maranke, John, **5694–5696**
Apostolic Church of, 5694–5696
death of, 5694, 5695
prophetic movement, 1720, 7443
syncretism, 1511
visions of, 5694
Maranke, Makebo, 5695
Marassa (spirits), in Caribbean neo-African cults, 1433
Maratha (newspaper), 9198
Marathi language, 5696
Marathi religions (India), **5696–5700**
Buddhism, 5699
Christianity, 5700
deities of, 5697–5698
development of, 5696–5697
Hinduism, 5696–5699
Islam, 5699–5700
literature of, 5696
modern, 5699
rituals of, 5698–5699
sects of, 5696–5697
women in, 5699
Māravaiyā, A., 10036
Marbode of Renne, 5578
Marburg, Germany, IAHR Conference in (1960), 8789
Marburg colloquy, 5536, 7660
Marburg School of Neo-Kantianism, Cohen's role in, **1850–1852**
Marcel, Gabriel, 2926
Marcel, Mujanaie, in Apostolic Church of John Maranke, 5695
Marcellinus (Roman commissioner), 2417
Marcellinus, Ammianus (pagan historian), 7922
Marcellus, on falling stars, 8736
Marcellus II (pope), 6967
Marcellus of Ancyra, on *Logos,* 5504
Marcellus of Paris (saint), as dragon slayer, 2432
Märchen (Grimm brothers), 7325
March for Justice, Freedom and Hope (Australia, 1988), 679
Marching Rule movement, 6797
cargo cults and, 1414
Marchmounts (mountains), in Daoism, 2178
Marcion, **5700–5702**. *See also* Marcionism
Bible of, 906, 5701, 5702
biblical exegesis of, 873, 5701, 5702
as Christian heretic, 5701
Gnosticism of, 3511, 3512, 3518, 5701
on God, 5701
Irenaeus criticizing, 3530, 4539
on Judaism and Christianity, links between, 5701
last two chapters of *Romans* removed by, 911

Marcion *continued*
life of, 5700–5701
Mani influenced by, 5648, 5665
Paul's epistles collected by, 920
roots of Christianity and, 2648
on "two books," 9421
Marcionism, **5702**. *See also* Gnosticism
celibacy and, 1476
critics of, 5702
development of, 5701, 5702
doctrines of, 5701, 5702
dualism in, 2506
God in, 5701, 5702
repentance in, 7758
as rival to Roman Catholicism, 5701, 5702
Tertullian against, 9086
Marcos, Subcomandante Insurgente, 9932
Marcossius, G. P., 3531
Marcovich, Miroslav, 3532
Marcus, George E., 3141
Marcus, Joyce, 453, 5902, 5903
Marcus (Gnostic teacher), on *hypostasis* and *ousia,* 4242
Marcus Aurelius (Roman emperor)
Christian persecution by, 7059
Galen and, 3255
on Golden Rule, 3632
and Isis cult, 4559
on *Logos,* 5501
on reason, 8405
Stoicism and, 8741
theurgy under, 9156
Marcus Poricus Cato the Elder, on decadence in Rome, 4027
Marcus Terentius Varro, on ancient virtues, 4027
Mardayin (ancestral law), 2380
Mardi Gras, 3171
Marduk (deity), 2962, **5702–5703,** 5955. *See also* Bel
in Akitu festival, 222–223, 2522, 6390
angels and, 345
An replaced by, 301, 302
Asalluhe identified with, 5955
Ashur and, 548, 549
in Babylon, 5950, 5955
Canaanite parallels, 1392, 1393
chaos and, 1539
as city god, 5950, 5955
cult of, restored by Cyrus II, 2119
and decapitation of primordial man, 3805
divine kingship of, 5146
Enki and, 5702, 5703
Enlil and, 2800
Enlil replaced by, 5952
in *Enuma elish,* 2809–2810, 3377, 5703, 5955, 5965–5966
iconography of, 4316, 4380
imprisonment of, 2537
kingship controlled by, 5965
kings representing, 693
in literature, 5703
as Mercury, 8428
monsters defeated by, 2431, 2441–2442
Nabu associated with, 6390
names of, 2445, 5702, 5703, 5955
as national deity, 7276–7277
under Nebuchadrezzer I, 5948
orgiastical rites, 1451
resurrection of, 222–223, 2522, 2537–2538
rise to head of pantheon, 5702–5703, 5948, 5955
rivers associated with, 7861
rule of, 3977
sex changes of, 2985
in Sumerian religion, introduction of, 5965–5966
sun and, 8838
tensions between creators and, 325, 952–953
Mardu people (Australia)
geographic distribution of, 5703, 5704
language of, 5704
population of, 5703–5704
Mardu religion (Australia), **5703–5707**
Christianity in, 5705
the Dreaming in, 5704, 5705, 5706, 5707
life cycle in, 5705
male initiation in, 5705
mythology of, 5705, 5707
portable objects in, 5707
rituals of, 5706–5707
song sequence in, 5705–5706, 5707
totemic beliefs in, 5704–5705
women's role in, 5705
Marebito (sacred visitors), 4781
Maréchal, Joseph, 5713
on subconscious, 7474
Mar Eliyya XI of Alqosh, 6480
Marett, R. R., animatism of, 10077
Marett, Robert Ranulph (R. R.), 114, **5707–5708**
dynamism of, 2541
on magic, 5564
on *mana,* 2541, 5708, 7372, 7373
on myths, 1986
preanimism (animatism) of, 362–363, 5708, 7372, 7373, 8531
power and, 7347–7348
problems with, 364–365
on religious experience, 7738
revaluation of, 380–381
and study of North American Indian religions, 6671
on the supernatural, 2541, 8862
symbol theory and, 8911
Tylor (E. B.) and, 2915, 5708
Mārga (path to liberation), 1296, 5436
Marga (patrilineal clans), 799
Margaret of Angoulême, French humanism and, 4176
Margaret of Antioch (saint), vol. 13 color insert
Marginalia, Gothic, in micrography, 1372
Marginality, of society
liminality of, 5461–5462
social change stemming from, 5397
Marginalized shamanism, 1327
Margiregir (mythic figure), 6002–6003
Marguerite of Navarre, 2992
Mar Ḥānania Dinkha IV, 6481
Marheineke, Philipp, Möhler (Johann Adam) and, 6113, 6114
Mari (Syria)
Canaanites and, 1381
Dagan in, 2126
kingship in, 5164
oracles of, 7429–7430
written records from, 5161
María de la Candelaría, 5921
Marīāī (deity), 5698
Maria Legio. *See* Legio Maria
Mariamman (deity), 8979
Mariana Islands. *See also* Oceania and Oceanic religions
Roman Catholicism in, 1738
Mari and Mordvin religion (Russia), 3105, **5708–5711**
ages of world in, 175
birds in, 948
Christianity and, 5709, 5710–5711
creation in, 5710
cult priests of, 3110
decline of, 5709
deities of, 5710–5711
initiation rituals in, 4478
life and death in, 5709–5710
nature in, 5710
rural ritual feasts of, 3108
sources on, 5709
Marianismo/machismo dichotomy, 3411
Marian Trinitarian Spiritualism, 6578
Marianus, 245–246
Maria Prophetissa, 245–246
Marid (demonic figure), 2280, 2314–2315
Marie de France, 991
Marie de l'Incarnation, **5711–5712**
writings of, 5711–5712
Ma'rifah (gnosis)
Ibn al-'Arabī on, 8819
Suhrawardī on, 8827
Marijuana
Rastafari and, 1438, 7623, 7624, 7626
in Thracian religion, 9170
Marikitari religion (South America), cosmology in, 8587
Marillac, Louise de, 6764
Marillier, Léon, 5785
Marin, Louis, structuralism and, 8752, 8755
Marina (serpent), 770
Marind-anim people (New Guinea), 725
homosexuality among, 4115
Marine Corps War Memorial (Washington, D. C.), vol. 6 color insert
Marinid dynasty, 4587
Marino, Giambattista, 7220
Mariology. *See also* Mary
development of, 5753
feminist critique of, 5754, 5756
in Protestantism, 5753–5754
in Roman Catholicism, 5754
Marion, Jean-Luc, 5483
on phenomenology of religion, 7087, 7099
Maris, Hyllus, 3391
Mar Ishā Shimon XXI, 6481
Marist order, Oceanic missions of, 6791
Maritain, Jacques, **5712–5713**
on aesthetics, 5713
Aristotle's metaphysics and, 5990
on art, 501
atheism and, 583, 5712
Guénon (René) and, 3706
Neo-Thomism of, 5712–5713
on Gilson (Étienne), 3492
Roman Catholicism of, 5712
writings of, 5712–5713
Maritain, Raïssa, 5712
Marius (Roman leader), 7912
Mariya Devi Khristos' White Brotherhood, 6568
Māriyamman (deity)
as dangerous goddess, 3607–3608
regional differences in, 3608
Marja' (supreme religious leader), hawzah and, 3801
Marja'iyyat (Shi'i office of supreme religious authority), hawzah and, 3801
Mark (apostle). *See* Mark the Evangelist
Mark (Gospel), 907–908. *See also* Gospels, the Four
audience of, 908, 5715
author of, 907–908, 5714
blasphemy in, 972
Christology of, 906
date of, 908
ending of, 908
exorcism in, 2928
as first written gospel, 906
"gospel" in, 3641
John in, 910
martyrdrom in, 7057
Mary in, 5752
Matthew the Evangelist in, 5780
messianism in, 5973
miracles in, 6053–6054
Peter the Apostle in, 7068
proverbs and parables in, 6979
Satan in, 8124

Smith (Morton) on, 8448–8449
as source for *Matthew,* 5780
sources of, 906–907
structure of, 908
variants of, 921
virgin birth absent in, 7081
Mark-Age, 9434
Maṟkali. *See* Gośāla
Mārkaṇḍeya Purāṇa (Hindu text), 7500
Markasu (rope), 5198
Marker, Jamsheed, 6999
Market economy, impact on religion, 6498
Mark Eugenikos
at Council of Ferrara-Florence, 2587
Florentine decree, opposition to, 2043
Markharm, Clements R., on Inca calendar, 1362
Mark of Ephesus, **5713–5714**
antiunionism of, 5713–5714
Marks, Morton, 77, 7037
Markschies, Christoph, on Gnosticism, 3534
Mark the Evangelist, 907–908, **5714–5715**
Coptic Church and, 1979
in Cyrenaica (Libya), 1677
as founder of Alexandrian church, 5410
iconography of, 5464
as John Mark of Jerusalem, 5714
lines of succession to, 1979–1980
lion as symbol of, 5715
liturgy of, 2592
on retreat of Jesus, 7770–7771
"secret gospel" of, 8448–8449
Marler, Joan, 3493
Marley, Bob, 7628
Marlowe, Christopher, *The Tragicall History of Doctor Faustus,* 2438, 3010, 5580
Marmorstein, Arthur, 5871
Maron (monk), 9463
Maronite Christians, 9463
in Egypt, 1675
in Lebanon, 1676
in Middle East, 1673
monasticism of, 2827
Maroon religions, 126, 127
Kromanti Dance in, 1436
Maror (bitter herb), 7004
Marot, Clément, 851
Mar pa (Mar pa Chos kyi blo gros) (Buddhist scholar), 1153, 1215, 1225, 5223, **5715–5716**
on chain of instruction, 8713
education of, 5715
family of, 5715, 5716
on *Hevajra Tantra,* 3966
Mi la ras pa and, 5715–5716, 6027
Nā ro pa and, 5715, 6415, 6416
on *mahāmudrā,* 5597–5598, 5716
portrait of, 5715–5716
Mar pa bka' brgyud order. *See* Bka' brgyud pa order
Marpeck, Pilgram, 304
Marquesas Islands, religion in
human sacrifice in, 7309
rituals in, 7310, 7311
taboo in, 8948
Tangaroa in, 8980
Marr, Wilhelm, 402
Marrakesh (Morocco), rites of passage in, 7825
Marranos, **5716–5724**. *See also* Sephardic Jews
definition of, 5716
Esther and, 2848
impact of, 5721–5722
Jewish practices of, 5718–5719
loyalty to Judaism, 5718–5719, 5721
messianism of, 5719
migration by, 5721
non-Iberian, 5722–5723
reasons for conversion, 5717
rejection of Christianity by, 5719
scholarly interpretations of, 5721
sources on, 5717–5718
transmission of beliefs of, 5719–5720
in Western Hemisphere, 5723
women, 5719, 5720
Marriage, **5724–5727**. *See also* Divorce; Weddings
ablutions in, 11, 12
in Acehnese religion, 26
in agricultural rituals, 189–190
in Australian Indigenous religions, circumcision and, 1799
in Bali, 7796
in Baltic religion, 760
Laima and, 5285–5286
in Batak religion, 799
in Branch Davidians, 5238
bride-price in, 5725, 7780
cannibalism and, in Fiji, 1404
in Celestial Masters religion, 2181
Celtic ritual marriage of kings, 1492–1493
Charavilh tax on remarriage, 1441
in China, 2407
in Christianity, 5724
ceremony of, 5726
consummation of, 5726
Council of Trent on, 4505
in early church, 7959
in Eastern Orthodox Church, 7960
medieval practices, 7961
in Orthodox Christianity, 2593
Paul the Apostle on, 7018
Protestant, 7455, 7963
in Roman Catholicism, 3362, 7962
as sacrament, 1670, 5726, 7956
women's role in, 3360
"common law," 5726
"complex," in Oneida Community, 6535, 6558, 6563, 6732
consummation of, 5726
contracts, decorated, 1372
"cosmic," in Solar Temple, 6554, 6555
in creation (*See* Hierogamy)
creation myths and, 5727
dainas (folk songs) dealing with, 2127
dowry in, 5725
in Eastern European religions, magic and, 5581, 5582
eugenics and, 2881
in Eve story, 2896
Finnish, 802
flowers in, 3136
forms of, 5724–5726
Geertz (Clifford) on, 8500–8501
in Germanic religion, among deities, 3460
in Greek religion
Aphrodite's role in, 407
Hera's role in, 3679
initiation before, 184
group, in Oneida Community, 6558
of Heaven and Earth, 7602
Hera as god of, 3914–3915
hieros gamos (sacred marriage or union), **3974–3978**
as invigoration rite, 8210
in Hinduism, 5724
caste system and, 3996
child marriage, 7610
dowry in, 5725
life stages and, 1476–1477
as rite of passage, 7814
validation of, 5726
women's role in, 3318–3319
home and, 4104
in India
child marriage, Sen (Keshab Chandra) on, 8227
jāti in, 9523–9524
in Indo-European religions, 4455
in Reiyūkai Kyōdan, 7862
interfaith
Karaite-Rabbanite, 5083
in Reconstructionist Judaism, 7639
in Reform Judaism, 7666, 7673
in Islam, 7826–7827 (*See also* Polygamy)
in Central Asia, 4625
dower in, 4625, 4706–4707
guardianship in, 4706
impediments to, 4706
law on, 4705–4708
local variations in, 7824, 7825
Muslim feminists on, 3367
Qur'ān on, 4564, 4573
requirements for, 4705–4706
types of, 4706
walāyah and, 9657
in Israel, 9981
in Israelite religion, laws on, 4733, 4736
in Judaism, 5724, 7821–7822
breaking of glass in, 7822
ceremony of, 5726
equality in, 7822
Gershom ben Yehudah on, 3352, 3461
in *halakhah,* 3752
Holdheim (Samuel) on, 4080
of Hosea, 4136–4137
intermarriage issue, 1964, 7514
Karaite-Rabbanite, 5083
ketubba of, 7821
of Levites, 5424
Palestinian marriage law, 3746
rabbinic, 3352
seven blessings of, 7822
in *Song of Songs,* 8706
in Karaite sect, consanguinity and, 5086–5087
kinship based on, 5182
in Komi religion, 5218
liturgy of, 5492
in Mazdakism, 5801
in Mesoamerican religions, 7812–7813
in Mesopotamian religions
gender roles in, 3378
between humans and deities, 3377
sacred, 2445, 3377, 5961
of monks, in Japanese Buddhism, 1182, 1183
in Mormonism, 6193, 6194
in Morocco, 7803
in Ndembu religion, 5726, 6446
Neopagan, 7829, 7830
new religions and alternatives to, 6534–6535, 6558, 6563
in North American Indian religions, 6682
in Haida tradition, 3736
in Nuer religion, woman-woman, 3420, 5724–5725

Marriage *continued*
in Oceanic religions, 6785
gender roles in, 3397
origins of, 5724, 5727
in Osage religion, 6919
in priesthood, 7395
purposes of, 5724–5725
as rite of passage, 5726
in Bali, 7796
in tribal societies, 7796
ritual language of ceremony, 5328
rituals of, 5726
in Roman religion
gender roles in, 3382
lares in, 5321
same-sex, U.S. dispute on, 7283
of siblings, 2985
in Sikhism
Ādi Granth in, 3716
gender roles in, 3337
in United States, 3879
in South American religions, gender roles in, 3417–3418
in Southern Siberian religions, 8670
as subordination, 9603
in Syrian religions, gender roles in, 3378
taboos and, 1460
Thracian goddess of, 819
in Tswana religion, 7805
in Unification Church, 6536
in Unification theology, 9467
in untouchables religions, 9476
in Vedism, fire and, 178
virginity and, 9607
in Warlpiri religion, 9696
in winter carols, 9743
in Zoroastrianism, 3373–3374, 10000–10001
of Parsis, 6998–6999, 7000
in Zulu religion, 5724–5725, 10009
Marriage of Hell and Heaven (Blake), 348
Marriage tree, 9339
Marriott, McKim, 4448
on Holī, 4081
on universalization and parochialization of Hindu holidays, 4014
Marrnggitj healers, overview of, 3873
Mars (deity), **5727–5729**
Augustus and, 7913
Campus Martius, 5534, 7897
Celtic parallels, 1483
cult of, 5728
feasts for, 5728
in Gaul, 7911
in Germanic religion, 3450
as god of agriculture, 5728
as god of war, 5727–5728
iconography of, 4322
in Jupiter, Mars, Quirinus triad, 7900–7901
names of, 5727
Quirinus in relation to, 7559, 7560
sacrifices to, 5728
in Thracian religion, 9169
Mars (planet)
deities of, 8428
Dresden Codex (Maya) and, 1360
Mar Saba manuscript, Smith (Morton) and, 8449
Marsanes (Gnostic text), *hypostasis* in, 4242
Marsden, Samuel, 3083
and Maori religion, 5682
Marseilles, France, Cassian venerated in, 1448
Marsh, Adam, 734
Marshack, Alexander, 3439
on goddesses, 3589, 3613
Marshall, Donald, 9303–9304
Marshall, George, on proto-Paśupati seals, 8039
Marshall, John, 3176
Marshall Islands (Micronesia)
geology of, 6002
myths of, 6009
charter, 6002
creation, 6004, 6009
trickster, 6011
Marshman, Joshua, 828
Marsilius of Padua, **5729–5730**
political theory of, 5729–5730
Marston, John, on Khmer religion, 5133
Mart (deity), 7894
Martel, Charles, 4673
Marti, Palau, 9416
Martī, Ramōn, 7243
Martial arts, **5730–5736**. *See also* Sports
Buddhism in, 5736
Chinese, 5731–5732, **5733–5736**
Daoism in, 5731–5732, 5735
in India, 5730–5731
in Indonesia, 5732–5733
in Japan, 5732
kung fu, development of, 8724
novels about, 3070, 5735
origins of, 5730
overview, **5730–5733**
qi in, 7544
yoga and, 5731
Martin V (pope)
conciliarism and, 2043, 6971
and monastery architecture, 6118
Martin, Calvin, 6671
Martin, Clarice, 80
Martin, Claude, 5711
Martin, Dan, 9190
Martin, Frank, 6313
Martin, Joan, 79
Martin, Joel W., 3100, 6690
Martin, Richard M., 6964
Martin, Tony, 75
Martin, Wallace, Campbell (Joseph) and, 1379
Martin I (pope), Maximos the Confessor and, 5792
Martin IV (pope), Michael Palaeologus excommunicated by, 2042
Martineau, Harriet, 5737
Martineau, James, **5736–5737**, 9469
Protestant liberalism of, 6105
Martini, Raymund, 7233
Martinist Order, 6782, 6783
Martin of Braga, 6943
on superstition, 8865
Martin of Tours
eremitism of, 2826
monasticism and, 7723
Martinov, A. I., 3114
Mārtiņš (deity), 9419
Marty, Martin
American study of religion, role in, 8787
on Mormonism, 6194
Marty, Martin E., 2290
Martyrdom, **5737–5744**. *See also* Persecution; Suicide; *specific martyrs*
authority associated with, 5738, 5739
in Christianity
in Andalusia, 4593
apologetics and, 428
at Carthage, 1678–1679
cephalophoric (headless) saints, 3806
concept of, 7058
cult of saints and, 2081
early, 6647
as human sacrifice, 4183
Ignatius of Antioch on, 4183, 8807
Jesus as martyr, 8807
monasticism replacing, 6125, 7723
New Testament on, 7057
and nudity, 6742
proposed substitutions for, 1651
relics of, 7688
and sainthood, 2228
sainthood and, 8034
Sanctoral cycle in liturgical calendar, 1744
suffering and, 8807
confession of faith and, 1883
in Confucianism, women in, 3341
in crescive societies, 5739–5740
crowning of martyrs, 2073
in decaying societies, 5740–5741
definition of, 5737
effects on society, 5737
Galileo as scientific martyr, 8183
gender and, 5741
in Islam, 4235–4236
as exemplary, 5738
in *jihād*, 4918
of al-Ḥusayn ibn ʿAlī, 4234, 4235–4236
politics and, 1517
public lamentation for, 7631–7632
Qurrat al-ʿAyn Ṭāhirah as, 7574–7575
Shīʿī *Maqātil* (accounts of martyrdom), 4235–4236
in *taʿziyah*, 9022–9023
in Judaism, 7056–7057
in Apocrypha, 901
apostasy and, 431
atonement through, 8035
control of martyrs, 5742
in crescive societies, 5739
during Crusades, 542–543, 7055, 7056–7057
in decaying societies, 5740–5741
Hebrew scriptures on, 7056
and history, view of, 4058, 4059
Holocaust as, 4088
kashrut laws and, 5108
nonviolence and, 6645, 6647
questioning of, 8806
transgression of the law *vs.* death, 3751
motives for, 5741
origins of, 5737
pain in, 6946
producing candidates for, 5741–5742
public nature of, 5738
records of, destruction of, 5743
restrictions on, 5742
sainthood, path to, 8037
in self-determining societies, 5740
social theory of, 5737–5743
vs. suicide, 5737
suppression of, by dominant group, 5742–5743
symbolism of, 5738
violence in, 9599
women in, 3341, 5741
Martyrdom and Ascension of Isaiah, 903
Martyrdom of Polycarp, 920
Martyria (church built on tomb of martyr), pilgrimage to, 7153
Martyrology of Saints Justa and Rufina, Adonis in, 34
Martyrs, The (Tertullian), 9085
Martyrs' Mirror, Mennonites in, 5860
Martz, Louis, 7220
Maru (ritual elders), 9195
Marudevī (mythic figure), 3327
Marunda (mythic figure), 939
creation of first human and, 5198
Marutha of Miya-farqin, 6479
Maruts (spirits)
fravashis compared with, 3190
lightning bolts of, 7603
Rudra's association with, 7934
shape shifting of, 8301
in Vedism, 9556
Marvell, Andrew
on Milton (John), 5486

on paradise, 3277
Marwazī, al-, Ḥanābilah and, 3763
Marx, Jenny, 5744, 5745
Marx, Karl, **5744–5747**. *See also* Marxism
atheism and, 583, 7422
Bachofen's (J. J.) influence on, 732
on capitalism, 5746–5747
on economy and religion, 2669, 5745, 5746–5747
education of, 5744–5745
Eliade on, 4047
Engels and, 5745, 5746, 5747
family of, 5744
on fetishism, 3045, 9296
Feuerbach's influence on, 3047, 5745
Gnosticism and, 3527
Hegel and, 5744–5745
on human beings, 7112
on knowledge, 5206
materialism of, 5777
modern social theory, contributions to, 8494–8495
on morality, 6178
on politics and religion, 7250–7251
on relativism, 7685
on religion, 8480
religion criticized by, 7250
on religious beliefs and practice, 7126, 7490
on sin, 7246
on social class, 8484
on societal organization, 7716
utopianism of, 9492
Marxism
Berdiaev (Nikolai) criticizing, 836
and biblical exegesis, 876
cargo cults, interpretation of, 1416
in China, 1579, 10074
Christianity and
in Eastern Europe, 1686
in ecumenical movement, 2688
clitoridectomy, interpretation of, 1825
criticized by Latin American bishops, 1704
Di Nola (Alfonso Maria), neo-Marxist methodology of, 4050
Durkheim's theories as alternative to, 2529
in ecological study, 2611–2612
fiction in, 10034, 10035
Freudian psychoanalysis criticized by, 7489–7490
and functionalism, 3232
in historical context, 2267
and Japanese philosophy, 6636
on Jesus, 4845
Lanternari (Vittorio) and, 4046
legitimation and, 5399
in liberation theology, 2676, 5439, 5931, 7246
and popular culture, 7321
on primeval magic and religion, 7974
on Reformation, 7664
reinterpretation of, Weber (Max) and, 9711
religion according to, 3232
religion-society relations and, 8468
religion *vs.*, in Japan, 8777
on rituals, 7838, 7845
social movements and, 1752
subaltern studies and, 8800–8801, 8801
as utopianism, 9492
Marxist Looks at Jesus, A (Machovēccaron;), 4845
Mary, **5751–5756**
Alexandrian *vs.* Antiochene theologians on, 6482–6483
Ambrose on, 287
Anthony of Padua on, 377
apparitions of
avertive apocalypticism of, 6548
in Mesoamerica, gender and, 3412–3413
in Movement for the Restoration of the Ten Commandments of God, 105, 6215–6216
pilgrimage to places sanctified by, 7148, 7149–7151
assumption of, 5754, 7884
churches to, by Zeno, 8069
contemporary writings on, 5755–5756
in Creole religions, 2068
cult of Fāṭimah compared with, 3009
devotion to, in Roman Catholicism, 5754, 5755, 7884, vol. 7 color insert
as dragon slayer, 2432
in ecumenism, 2689
as Eve, new, 3358, 5753
feminist critique of, 5755
Eve compared to, 2897
as female archetype, 9773–9774
feminist perspectives on, **5755–5756**
androcentrism and, 5754
feminist theology on, 3036
festivals for, 5753
flowers associated with, 3136
and gender in Christianity, 3358
as goddess, 5755
in Hebrew scriptures, 5751
in Holy Order of MANS, 4102
in Hungary, 4225
images of
with baby Jesus, vol. 8 color insert, vol. 12 color insert
early icons, 4352
medieval, 4346
miracle stories about, 4390
popular art, 7322
in Roman Empire, 4345
veneration of, 4386
imitation of, 8704
immaculate conception of, 7884
as dogma, 5754
in Amhara-Tigriña religion, 2573
in Latin American Christianity
in colonial Andes, 8610–8611, 8611, 8612
Pachamama associated with, 8615
Māra linked with, 5691, 5692, 5694
as Mediatrix, 7884
in Mesoamerica
gender and, 3412–3413
moon associated with, 5927
in Tzeltal Revolt, 5921
motherhood of, 3588
in New Testament, portrayal of, 5751–5753
overview of, **5751–5755**
piety regarding, 5753–5754
in Protestantism, 5753–5754
relics of, 7689
in Roman Catholicism, 5754, 5755, 7882, 7884
sacrament and, 7884
Servetus (Michael) on, 8232
shrines of, pilgrimage to, 7148
Simons (Menno) on, 8401
sinlessness of, 5753, 5754
Sistine Chapel dedicated to, 8755
syncretism in worship of, 3588
terminology used for, in division of Christianity, 2583
theotokos (Mother of God), 5753
Council of Ephesus and, 2040, 5753, 7884
Nestorius *vs.* Arian and Apollinaristic factions on, 2117, 5753, 6482–6483
virginity of, 3588, 9605, 9608 (*See also* Virgin birth)
as asexual, 4164
in Ebionism, 2596
feminist critique of, 5755
Jerome on, 4833
in New Testament, 5752
in postbiblical Christianity, 5753
Mary I (queen of England)
Catholicism of
attempt at restoration, 7662–7663
Elizabeth I opposing, 349
English reformation and, 2052, 7662–7663
Protestants persecuted by, 7061
Maryam (deity), in Amhara-Tigriña religion, 2573
Maryam (mother of Jesus), in the Ka'bah, 5050
Maryknolls, in Mesoamerica, 5930, 5931
Maryland
Catholicism in, 1445, 1711
colonial, Calvert (Lord Baltimore) and, 1373
as paradise, 6985
religious tolerance in, 1711
Mary Magdalene, **5756–5758**
as apostle, 5757
eremitism of, 2828
in New Testament, 5756–5757
in non-canonical literature, 5757–5758
Mary of Bethany, as Mary Magdalene, 5757
Mary of Egypt, 2825
Mary of Jesus Crucified, Sister, 3127
Mary Stuart (queen of Scots), martyrdom of, 5738
Mar Yūsuf (Joseph) of Diyarbakir, 6480
Marzih feast, in Canaanite religion, 1382, 1386, 1387
Masa (people), Tukanoan notion of, 8623
Masabe spirits (Africa), 1510
Masaccio (Italian painter), vol. 2 color insert
Masada, Israel, mass suicide at, 8829
Masā'il al-intiqād (Ibn Sa'id ibn Sharaf), 4584
Masai religion. *See* Maasai religion
Masala films, 3098
Masalai (spirits), 5833–5834, 5839, 5840, 9252
Masao Abe (Buddhist monk), 9950
Masar Pušě (angel of death), 1785
Masbuta (baptism), 12
Maschio, Thomas, 146
Masculine sacrality, **5758–5763**
in acculturation, 5762
definition of, 5758
in effulgence, 5760
in fecundity, 5761–5762
in height, 5759–5760
in immanence, 5760–5761
in primordiality, 5759

Masculinity. *See also* Gender; Men
in Judaism, 3351, 5863–5864
in men's studies, 5862–5864
studies of, 3314
of Trinity, 9363
Masgid (prayer house), 5002
Mashāhid al-asrār (Ibn al-ʿArabī), 4257
Mashāʾikh (Ṣūfī masters), *khānagāh* of, 5117–5118
Mashal (literary form), 6020–6021, 6978
Ma Shaomei (Muslim leader), 4637
Mashco religion (Amazon), World Fire myth in, 8589
Mashhad (Persia), Jews of, forced conversion of, 4999
Mashmiʿa yeshuʿah (Abravanel), 17
Mashṣāsura (buffalo demon), Indus Valley religion, suggested precursors in, 3989
Mashtotsʿ, Mesrop, **5763–5764**
Armenian alphabet of, 492, 5763–5764
Mashya (mythic figure), 9995
and gender perceptions, 3372, 3373
Mashyāna (mythic figure), 9995
and gender perceptions, 3372
Masīḥ al-dajjāl, al- (false messiah), 5979, 5980
Masinde, Elijah, 109
Masiqta ritual, 5636
Maʿṣiyah (transgression), 4707
Masjid. See Mosques
Masjid al-aqsa (remotest or further mosque), 4836–4837, 6059
in Qurʾān, 6205
location of, 6205
Masjid al-ḥaram (sanctified mosque), in Qurʾān, 6205
Masjid al-jamiʿ (place of assembly), 6206, 6207
Masjid al-Kuba, 6205–6206
Masjid al-Nabi, 6206
Maskarin Gośāla. *See* Gośāla
Maskilim (Haskalah Jews), 5019, 9381
charisma of reason and, 1546
Mohilever (Shemuʾel) on, 6113
Masks, 1000, **5764–5772**. *See also* Clowns
African, 90, 116
distribution of, 5766
in Dogon religion, 2391, 5768
in drama, 2457–2458
figures in, 5768
as sacred objects, vol. 4 color insert
in secret societies, vol. 6 color insert
Carnival and, 1441–1442, 1443, 5765
the dead and, 5769–5770
definitions of, 5765–5766
dragon, 2433
in evolutionary theory, 5764–5765
figures depicted in, 5767–5768
geographic distribution of, 5766
gold, 3625
in Greek religion, Dionysos as god of, 2356
in incarnation, 4414
in Japanese drama, 7048
making and destruction of, 5768
in Mayan dance, 2435–2436
Melanesian, 5769, 5839, vol. 6 color insert, vol. 9 color insert, vol. 10 color insert
Mesoamerican
death in motion in, 148
in drama, 2464
mortuary, vol. 9 color insert, vol. 10 color insert
North American Indian, 2460, 2461, 2462, 4542, 5767
sacred, 6684, vol. 4 color insert
orgy and, 6862–6863
origins of, 5767
as portraits, vol. 10 color insert
secret societies and, 5770–5771
in Siberian shamanism, 1827
skull, 5769
studies of, 5764–5765
wearers of, 5768–5769, 5771
women and, 5770–5771
Zapatista, 9932–9933
Masks of God, The (Campbell)
comparative mythology in, 1378
goddess worship in, 3612
monism in, 1379
Maṣlaḥah (public interest), 4567, 4697, **5772–5773**
Rashīd Riḍā's (Muḥammad) use of, 7621
Maslamah ibn ʿAbd al-Malik, 4612, 4613
Maslow, Abraham
on ecstasy, 2681
hierarchy of needs, 7477, 7478, 7485
states of consciousness and, 1950
on peak-experiences, 7477
on religious experience, 7695
Maslow, Sophie, 2164
Masnawi (poetic form), 7222, 7223
Mason, Charles Harrison, 10038
Mason, J. Alden, 576
Masonic chart, vol. 2 color insert
Masonic Orders. *See also* Freemasons
ancient origins, claims of, 8213
Masorah, 888, 894
calligraphy and, 1372
as tradition, 9268
Masoretic text of the Bible, 885, 886–887
Astarte in, 562
Jeremiah in, 4827
pronunciation symbols, 1533
standardization and, 1410
Masoret seyag la-Torah (Abulafia), 24
Masorti movement. *See also* Conservative Judaism
growth of, 1961
Masowe, John
prophetic movement, 1720
syncretism, 1511
Maspero, Gaston, 5773
Maspero, Henri, 1291, 2272, **5773–5774**
China, study of, 1634–1635
on Chinese religion, 5773
women in, 3339
on Daoism, 2213, 5773, 8222
sexual control in, 8240
death of, 5773
Granet (Marcel) and, 3655, 5773
on Thai religion, 5773
Masquerade dances, 2140–2141
Masquerades
Buddhist masked dramas, 4209
at Carnival, 1442
in Yoruba religion, 9910
Masques dogon (Griaule), 116
Mass. *See also* Eucharist
carnivalization of, 1441, 4198
Catholic
for the dead, 142
as drama, 2468, 2469, 7043
as form of reference for Feast of Fools, 7194
kissing holy objects in, 9258
liturgical dramas developed from, 2437
ordo of, 2468
personal prayers in, 7845
relics in, vol. 4 color insert
children's enactment of, 4199
Council of Trent on, 795, 9344
during Counter-Reformation, 795
for the dead, 142, 2241
Fool's, 2476
music in
classical, 6312
settings of, 6254–6255, 6311
private, 2877
relativity theory and, 2032
sacrificial character of
Augsburg Confession on, 2058
Council of Trent on, 2060
Simons (Menno) on, 8401
Mass (Bernstein), 2470
Massaʾ (burden), 7433
Massachusetts Bay Colony
Congregationalism and, 1938
denominational concept in, 2288
Hutchinson (Anne), and antinomianism, 4238
law in, 5372
Mather family in, 5778–5779
Puritans in, 7520
Quakers prosecuted for blasphemy in, 973
theocracy in, 9110
Williams (Roger) exiled from, 784, 7520
Williams (Roger) in, 9739
Wise (John) in, 9766
Massa confusa, 1540
Massagetae religion, 7384, 7387
Massage therapy, Association for Research and Enlightenment in, 560–561
Mass communication, globalization theory of conversion and, 1971
Mass culture
vs. popular culture, 7320
use of term, 7320
Mass Culture: The Popular Arts in America (Rosenberg and White), 7321
Massé, Enemond, 9302
Mass graves, 9226
Massignon, Louis, 956, 4718, **5774–5775**
on Arabic Hermetic writings, 3939
Corbin (Henry) and, 1983
on Islamic mysticism, 7739–7740
on Islamic vocabulary, 5774
on al-Junayd, 6351
on mirrors, 6063
on al-Ḥallāj, 3756–3757, 3758, 5774–5775
religious beliefs of, 5774
Massine, Léonide, 2161, 2162
Massive Offerings (La Venta), 6819
Mass media. *See* Media
Masson, J. M., on ecstasy, 2679
Masson-Oursel, Paul, 4447
"Mass on the World" (Teilhard de Chardin), 9032
Mass suicide. *See* Suicide
Master Harold and the Boys (Fugard), 2477
Master of Healing vow, 855
Master of Life (Iroquois creator), 4541
Master of Life, in Ganda religion, 2575
Master of the Three Teachings, 1608
MasterPath, 2603
Masters, ascended. *See* Ascended masters
Masters, R. E. L., on witches' Sabbath, 8249
Masters of the Fishing Spear, in Dinka priesthood, 2569, 2570
Mastorava (spirit), 5710
Mastoubios of Armenia, 5764

Masud, Tareque, 3097
Mas'ūdī, al-, on the Flood, 2964
Mas'ūd of Ghaznah, 954
Masyumi. *See* Consultative Assembly of Indonesian Muslims
Matachin (dancers), 7045
Mataco-Makká religion (Argentina), 8636
cosmology in, 8587
death, myths of origin of, 8591
deluge myth in, 8588
fire origin myths in, 8590
origin of agriculture in, 8590
overview of, 8635–8636
World Fire myth in, 8589
Mataco people (South America)
Golden Age myth of, 3629
tricksters of, 9358
Maṭāf (stone flooring), 7158
Maṭam (monastic center), 8976
Matapule (talking chief), 6786
Matar. *See also* Cybele
in Anatolian religion, 2108–2109
Mataram (Java), 4816
Mataram, sultanate of (Java), 4660, 4661
Mataram kingdom. *See* Sanjaya kingdom
Matarata (purgatories), 5636
Mataruka, Ruka, 5694, 5695
Matchmakers, in Mesoamerican religions, 7812–7813
Māte (mother), 760–761
Mateo, Olivorio, 6577
Mater Dolorosa, Ezili identified with in Vodou, 1433
Material cause, Aristotle on, 45
Material culture, Buddhist devotion and, 9830–9831
Material force, principle and, in Korean Neo-Confucianism, 1931–1932
Material Force, school of, 1931–1932
Materialism, **5775–5778**. *See also* Matter
cargo cults, **1414–1421**
Cārvāka school, **1446–1447**
Christianity and, 5777–5778
in cybernetics, 2112
definition of, 5775
dialectical, 5777
in Enlightenment historiography, 4040
historical, 5777
and iconoclasm, 4286
miracles rejected in, 6056–6057
monistic, 844, 5777
naturalism and, 5775, 5777, 6429
neo-Darwinism and, 8189
origins of, 5775–5776
otherworld in, 6925
reductive, 5776–5777
in Renaissance, 5776
in science and religion, 2659
sensate, Sorokin (Pitirim Aleksandrovich) on, 8523, 8524
Smith (W. Robertson) on, 8453
on spirit possession, 8696
Spiritualism *vs.*, 8716, 8718
theism rejected in, 5775
Vatican I on, 9531
Materialist psychiatry, 7488–7491
Materiality, **10047–10050**
and history of religions, 10048–10049
and place of religion, 10048
Mater Larum (deity), 5321
Mater Magna. *See* Magna Mater
Mater Matuta, temple in Rome, 3175
Maṭhas (monasteries)
inŚrī Vaiṣṇavas Sampradāya, 8728
in Vīraśaivism, 8043
sadhus/sadhvis in, 8019
saint-singer tradition and, 4005
Śaṅkara's establishment of Advaita Vedānta and, 4004
influence of, 4005
Mathematical (logical) certainty, 2428
Mathematics. *See also* Geometry; Numbers
cards and, 1413
history of
in Asia, 8180
in Greece, 8180–8181
Husserl (Edmund) on, 4236
Leibniz and, 5406
Maya, 1357
of millenarianism, 6029
nature ordered by, Kepler (Johannes) on, 5112
Plato on, 2878
of Ptolemy, 7491, 7492
Mather, Cotton, **5778–5779**
as clerical physician, 3846
on Golden Age, 3628
Mather, Increase, **5778–5779**
Mather, Richard, **5778–5779**
Mather family, **5778–5779**
on denominations, 2287
Mathews, John Joseph, 3090
Mathews, Robert Hamilton, 265
on Australian Indigenous religions
as first phase of study, 683
initiation ceremonies of, 681
new movements in, 682
on Seven Sisters, 643
Mathews, Shailer, 6106
Mathnavī (poetic genre)
of 'Aṭṭār, 8817–8818
of Rūmī, 4570, 7936–7937, 7938, 8818, 9004, 9008
al-Ḥallāj in, 3757
themes and structure of, 8818
of Sanā'ī, 8817
Mathnawi-yi ma'nawi (Rūmī), 7222
"Math Son of Mathonwy" (deity), 1489
Mathūra, Jainism in, 4765
Math vab Mathonwy, 1483
Mathy, Francis, 3073
Matiel (king), 448
Melqart and, 5847
Matière et mémoire (Bergson), 838
Matilal, Bimal Krishna, 6773
Mati Syra Zemlia (deity), in Slavic religion, 8437
Matlacihuatl (trickster), 9357–9358
Matlala religion (Africa), rites of passage in, 8666
Matory, J. Lorand, 10027
Matos Moctezuma, Eduardo, 5944
Matouš, Lubor, on *Epic of Gilgamesh,* 3488
Matralia (deity), 3175
Mātrāprāmāṇa (breathing), 1044
Mātṛceṭa (Buddhist poet), 1111, 7211
Matres (goddesses), 2984, 4253, **5779–5780**
in Celtic religion, 1485–1486, 5779
in Germanic religion, 3450–3451
Matres lectionis (use of weak letters), 886
Matriarch, The (Ihimaera), 5682
Matriarchy, **7007–7009**
Bachofen (J. J.) on, 731, 3611, 3612–3613, 3616, 7008–7009, 7079
definitions of, 3611
feminist critique of, 3298, 3613
feminist defense of, 3613
in Feminist Spirituality, recreation of, 3312
goddess worship and, 3611–3613, 7009
lack of evidence for, 7008–7009, 7079
masks in, 5765
in Mesopotamian religion, 6625
in Minoan religion, 37–38
retribution rights and, 7783
scholarly debate over
contemporary, 3612–3613, 7008–7009, 7079
early, 3611
in South America, 7008
terminology of, 7008, 7009
Matrifocal, 7009
Matrilineal descent, 7008
in Cambodia, 4013
Jewish identity and, 3751–3752, 4859, 4971
in Reform Judaism, 7666, 7673
in Kongo society, 5220, 5221–5222
of Ndembu people, 6446
in North American Indian traditions, 6654
Schmidt (Wilhelm) on, 8877
Matrilocality, 7008
Matritense Codex, 5889, 5939
Mātṛkā (doctrinal matrices), 1109, 1111, 1252, 1269, 1270
Mâtronae. *See Matres*
Matronalia (festival), 7909
Matrones, 2984
Matsah (unleavened bread), 926, 7003, 7004
Matsarya (jealousy), 748
Matsigenka shamans (South America), bird and, 8291–8292
Matsliaḥ ha-Kohen ben Shelomoh, 4990
Matsot (festival), 934
Matsudaira Sadanobu, *bakufu* college reforms, 1928
Matsumoto Shirō, 1247, 1250
Matsuri (rituals), 4781–4782, 4795, 6880
Matswa, Andre, messianism of, 5973
Matsya (avatāra of Viṣṇu), 4325
Matsya Purāṇa, dharma in, 2621
Matsyendranāth (Hindu guru), 3637–3638
Matter. *See also* Materialism; See also Prakṛti
Aristotle on, 485, 4355, 5775–5776, 7119–7120
dualism between spirit and, and asceticism, 528–529
intelligent, 6437
Numenius on, 7189
perfectibility of, in alchemy, 242
in physics, 2659
Plato on, 4355, 7119–7120
primal, 4377
in alchemy, 245
in Gersonides' cosmology, 3462–3463
sacred, vol. 4 color insert
scientific view of, relativity and, 2032
as secondary feature of creation, gender and, 3358
unreality of, in Christian Science, 1746
Valentinians on, 7190
Matter, Jacques, 3531
Matthäi, Hildegard, on bird in shamanism, 8291
Matthew (apostle). *See* Matthew the Evangelist
Matthew (Gospel), 907. *See also* Gospels, the Four
anti-Mosaic teachings in, 9271

Matthew (Gospel) ***continued***
author of, 907, 5780
Baur (F. C.) on, 805
blood in, 986
Christology of, 906
date of, 907, 5780
exorcism in, 2928
"gospel" in, 3641
humor in, 4196
Jesus and Peter in, 6966
Jewish dimension of, 5780
Jewish polemics on, 7233
judgment in, 5027
Lord's Prayer in, 5516
Mark as source for, 5780
Mary in, 5752
Matthew in, 5780
merit in, 5876
messianism in, 5972, 5973
Moses in, 6203
Peter the Apostle in, 7069
proverbs and parables in, 6979
sources of, 906–907, 5780
structure of, 907
suffering in, 8807
Temple funding in, 930
Thomas Aquinas on, 9161
variants of, 921
wisdom-Torah in, 9763
Matthews, Donald, 80
Matthews, Washington, 6670
Matthews, William H., 5275
Matthew the Evangelist, 907, **5780**
Matthiessen, F. O., 5472
Matthiessen, Peter, 703
Matumbi country (Tanganyika), Maji Maji Wars in, 5181
Māturidī, al-, **5780–5782**
Abū Ḥanīfah and, 22
as founder of *kalām,* 5059, 5064
epistemology of, 5781
on faith, 5781
on free will and predestination, 3212
on God, 5781
attributes of, 619, 3565, 5781
creation by, 3565
intentionality of, 3565
in Ḥanafī, 4568
life of, 5781
tafsīr of, 8950
al-Taftāzānī and, 8957
teachings of, 4568
Māturīdīyah (school of Islamic theology), 5780–5781
development of, 5781
on free will and predestination, 3212
God in, 3565
attributes of, 2063
ḥadīth and, 8855
spread of, 5781
Maturity rituals. *See* Rites of passage
Maudgalyāyana (Buddha's disciple), 1063, 1105, 4382
Abhidharma texts attributed to, 10021
and ancestor worship, 323
Māui (hero), **5782–5783**
as ancestor, 5783
birth of, 7313
in creation myths, 7306, 7313
death of, 5681, 7311
gender in stories of, 3397, 5681
music and, 6264
in origin myths, 7314
quest for immortality of, 2298
underworld journey of, 9451
worship of, 5783
Māui-of-a-Thousand-Tricks (Luomala), 7315
Maulbronn, Abbey of, 6119
Mau Mau resistance movement (Kenya), 87
divination used in, 2577
Mungiki movement influenced by, 109
as secret society, 8213
Mauny Thursday, in Christian liturgical calendar, 1742
Maurice, Frederick Denison, **5783–5785**
in Christian Socialist movement, 5784
and liberal Protestantism, 6105
Maurice, Michael, 688, 5783
Maurice, Priscilla Hurry, 5783
Maurice of Nassau, 493
Mauricio, Rufino, 6006
Maurin, Peter, 2226
Maurists, historiography of, 4030–4031
Mauritania, films from, 3098
Maurus, Rabanus, 821
Mauryan dynasty (India)
Ājīvikas sect in, 212
Aśoka in, 553–556
Buddhism in, 1108
Hinduism in, 4429
Mausoleum Augusti, circularity of, 1792
Mausoleum Hadriani, circularity of, 1792
Mausoleums, 9227
Mauss, Marcel, **5785–5786**
Dieterlen (Germaine) studying under, 2349
Durkheim (Émile) and, 2527–2528, 4461, 5785, 5786
education of, 5785
on exchange, 1423
on fetishism, 3043
on gift giving, 267, 6508
Godelier's (Maurice) critique of, 3481
at potlatch, 3479, 3480
Granet (Marcel) and, 3655
on Hartland (E. Sidney), 3782
Leenhardt (Maurice) and, 6500
on magic, 383, 5565, 5571, 5785
on *mana,* 2541–2542, 5785
on memorization, 5850
on money, 6137
on Lévi (Sylvain), 5418
on potlach, 4141
on Prometheus, 7420
on ritual, 2436
on sacrifice, 7844–7845
on sacrifice and offering, 725, 4183, 8003
socialism of, 5785, 5786
on society and religion, 8467
and study of North American Indian religions, 6671
on tears, 9024
Mau tham ("experts in reciting words"), as exorcists, 3814
Mauthner, Fritz, on wisdom, 9747
Mavalankar, Damodar K., 5023–5024
Mawangdui (archaeological site), 1628, 1634, 1637
Mawāqif (al-Ījī), 5066–5067
Māwardī, al-, 4393, **5786–5787**
Mawasim (annual fairs), 4586
Mawdu'at (forgeries), *ḥadīths* as, 3732
Mawdūdī, Sayyid Abū al-A'lā, **5787–5788**
on fasting, 8141
influence on African movements, 107–108
in Jamā'at-i-Islāmī, 107, 4772, 5788
journalism of, 5787–5788
tafsīr of, 8955
teachings of, 5788
Mawlā, 9656, 9658
Mawlānā. *See* Rūmī, Jalāl al-Dīn
Mawlawī. *See* Rūmī, Jalāl al-Dīn
Mawlawīyah (Ṣūfī order), 9008–9009
characteristics of, 8822–8823
Mawlid al-Nabī (birthday of the Prophet), 4713, 9202
Mawlids (birthdays), **5788–5790**
humor and, 4215
Mawu (deity), 3166, 5790
Mawu-Lisa (deity), 3166, **5790**
Maxentius (emperor), Constantine and, 1966
Maxim, as wisdom, 9748
Maximian (cleric), 2416
Maximian (emperor)
abdication of, 1966
imperial cults and, 7916
Maximilla (prophet), in Montanism, 6167, 6168
Maximinus the Thracian (Roman emperor)
Christian persecution by, 7059
and Iupiter Dolichenus cult, 4754
Maxim of Tyre, on idolatry, 4363
Maximón (deity), **5790–5792**
contemporary worship of, 5926–5927
forms of, 5791
functions of, 5790, 5791, 5792, 5927
gender of, 5927
Judas and, 5926, 5927
origins of, 5790–5791, 5927
Maximos the Confessor, **5792–5794**
Council of Constantinople III and, 2040, 5794
exile of, 5792
on God, 5793
knowability of, 183
on knowledge, 5203
life of, 5792
against monothelitism, 5792, 5793
on souls, 8564
teachings of, 5793–5794
and theurgy, 9158
writings of, 5792–5793
Maximum Illus, political mission in, 8169
Maxwell, James Clerk, chaos theory and, 1541
Maxwell, James L., 8963
Maxwell, Mary, 738
Maxwell, T. S., 9039
May, John R., 3100
Māyā (Indian concept), **5794–5795,** 9481
aesthetics and, 50–51
development of, 5794
dualism and, 2507, 2508
epistemological aspect of, 5795
humor and, 4195
as illusion, 5794
in Śaiva Siddhānta, 8547
meanings of, 5794–5795
metaphysical aspect of, 5794–5795
mythology of, 4443
products of, 7195
Śaṅkara on, 4003
as subjective idealism, 4355
in Swaminarayan movement, 8891
universe as, 4422
Varuṇa identified with, 9525
Mayahuel (deity), 5906
Māyā-līlā (illusion and play), 7044
Maya religion and society (Mesoamerica), **5795–5800**. *See also* Mesoamerica and Mesoamerican religions; Toltec religion
afterlife in, 149–151
ages of world in, 177, 5934
agriculture in, 5796
myths of, 191, 192
ancestors in, 5798
animals in, myths about, 5938
architecture in, 5796, 5799, 5882, 5886
art of, 5799
astrology and astronomy, 1356–1357, 1358–1359, 1360
stelae at Copán linked to, 2009–2010
ballgames played in, 750, 751

bloodletting in, 5799, 5886
of rulers, 1358, 1804
calendar of, 1355–1360, 1473, 5796–5797, 5884–5886
astronomy and, 2009–2010, 5884
deities in, 5884
kings' role in, 5799
Long Count, 5796–5797, 5799, 5882, 5885–5886
caves in, 1469, 3434, 5796
cenotes, 1472–1473
Christianity in, 5799
cities as ceremonial and sacred centers, 1804–1805
codices and almanacs, 1359–1360
colonial period in, Christian priests in, 5916
confession of sins in, 7759
cosmic rites of passage in, 7813
cosmology of, 2009–2010, 5796–5797
creation in, 5797, 5934, 5935
culture of, 5882
dance in, 2435–2436, 2439, 2465–2466
death in, 2242
deities of, 5797–5798, 5883–5884 (*See also specific deities*)
Maximón derived from, 5790–5791
smoking by, 8455
dogs in, 2394
drama in, 2465–2466
dreams in, 2484, 2485, 2489
drums in, 7036
duality in, 5883
earth in, 5796, 5882–5883
evangelicalism in, 3414
floods in, 3130
folk Catholicism in, 5799
women in, 3413
funeral rites in, 3242–3243, 3244, 7813
gender in, 3412–3413, 3414
geographic boundaries of, 5882
hieroglyphic writing in, 4312
history of study of, 5941
archaeological, 452
inscriptions in, 5886
human sacrifice in, 1472–1473, 4187, 5884
iconography of, 4312
afterlife in, 149
ceramic vessels, 4312
dragons in, 4312
illness ceremony in, 3137
incantations in, 4407
inquisition against, 4504, 5917
inscriptions of, 5886–5887
creation myth in, 5797
deciphering, 5886
kings and ancestors in, 5798, 5886–5887
jade in, 4759
jaguar in, 4762–4763
kings in, 5798–5799
ancestors of, 5798
divine, 1804, 5798
inscriptions on, 5798, 5886–5887
souls of, 5798
light and darkness symbolism in, 5451
modern, 5799
mountains in, 3434, 5796
music in, 6268
new religious movements in, 6576
Pan-Mayanism, 5932
pre-Columbian, 5882–5887
Classic period of, 5882
Postclassic period of, 5882
priesthood in, 5799, 5884, 5886
psychedelic drugs in, 7470
pyramids of, 5799
quaternity in, 5796
religious specialists in, 5799
revivalism in, 5799
Ríos Montt's campaign against, 5931
rites of passage in
birth rites, 7812
cosmic rites, 7813
funeral rites, 7813
ritual clowns in, 2464
rituals in, 5799
sacred geography of, 3434–3435, 5796
the sacred in, concept of, 5797–5799
sacred language of, 5303
sacred space in, 8428
souls in, 5798
sources on, archaeological and textual, 5795, 5882
Spanish conquest, 1695
Stela D monument, 1358
sun in, 8842
temples in, 9066
time in, 177, 5882
deep, 5796–5797
tobacco and smoking in, 8454–8455
towers in, 9266
tree symbolism in, 1502, 9335, 9338, 9339
Tzeltal Revolt in, 5921
violence in, 5175
women in, 3412–3413, 3414
worship in, forms of, 5884
Maya Society under Colonial Rule (Farriss), 5926
Maybaum, Ignaz, on Suffering Servant and the Holocaust, 4089–4090
May Day, political ceremony and, 1515
Ma'yenei ha-yeshu'ah (Abravanel), 17
Mayer, Jean-François, 106
Maymūn al-Qaddāḥ, extremism and, 8327
Maymūnī, al-, Ḥanābilah and, 3763
Maymūnīyah movement, Ismāʿīlīyah and, 8327
Mayo, Katherine, 3320
Mayo millenarian movement, 6576, 6721
Māyōṉ (deity), 4434, 5251–5252
Mayordomías (stewardships), 9215
Mayo religion (Mexico), clowns in, 1839
Mayr, Ernst, on animals, 356, 358
Mays, Benjamin Elijah, 67, 74
Mays, Blaine C., 6587
Ma Yu, writings associated with, 2209, 2210
Ma Yuan, vol. 11 color insert
Maẓālim court, jurisdiction of, 7540
Mazar, Benjamin, 925
Mazārs (tomb-shrines), 4649
Mazdaism
as source of *kalām,* 5061
redemption in, 7641
Mazdak, 5800, 5801
Mazdakism, **5800–5802**
doctrine of, 5661, 5800–5801
Manichaeism and, 5657, 5661
origins of, 5800
sources on, 5800, 5801
women in, 5800, 5801
Mazdean theology. *See* Ahura Mazdā; Zoroastrianism
Mazes. *See also* Labyrinth
in North American Indian religions, 1469
Mazhan, as Armenian priest, 491
Māziyārīyah, pacifism of, 6648
Mazo Daoyi (Buddhist figure), 1292
Mazu (Buddhist monk), 6631
violent methods of, 8713–8714
Mazu (deity), 1619
birthday of, 1644
Mazu Daoyi, 1522, 1523
Mazurka, at a *veglia,* 2148
Mazzikim (demon), 2533
Mbatsav (people with talent), 9211
Mbiikawane ceremony, 5770
Mbiti, J. S., on life, 5445
Mbiti, John, 117
on Living-Dead, 141
on medicine men, 3820
Mbiti Kiluwe (mythic figure), 97
Mbona (deity), **5802–5803**
cult of, 5802
creator in, 1507
death of, 5802
Mbori (deity), in Azande religion, 2567
MBTI. *See* Meyers-Briggs Type Indicator
Mbua religion (Brazil), soul in, 8532
Mbulungulu (image of the dead), 4302
Mbuti Pygmies, 7524–7525
culture hero myth of, 2091, 7525
drums of, 2495
myths of, 92, 94
rituals of, 7525
McAlister, Elizabeth, 81
McAllester, David P., 6672
McAllister, Harold S., 3091
MCC. *See* Mennonite Central Committee
McCall, Daniel F., 3588
McCarthy, Dennis, on curses in Near Eastern treaty textis, 2102
McCarthy, John, 510
McCauley, Robert N., 7851, 7858
cognitive approach to history of religions by, 10043
structuralism and, 8759
McClenon, James, on shamanic hypnosis, 8278
McClintock, Anne, 3046
McCloud, Aminah Beverly, 81
McCollough, "Sweet Daddy" Walter, 2125
McCone, Kim, 1499
McConnel, Ursula H., 684
on Rainbow Snake, 7607
McCormick, Richard, 5811, 5813
McCoy, Isaac, 785, 7301
McCullough, Colleen, 3061, 3080
McDannell, Colleen, 502
McDougall, William, 1022
McDowell, Nancy, on cargo cults, 1422
McFague, Sallie
on ecotheology, 4166
feminist ecotheology of, 2610
McFarland, H. Neill, 6521
McGann, Jerome, 5472, 5473
McGehee, Fielding, III, 6524
McGiffert, A. C., 6106
McGill Pain Questionnaire, 6944
McGinn, Bernard, on mystical union, 6339
McGlynn, Edward, 3478
McGuire, George Alexander, 3287
Mchod rten (reliquary), 9840
Mchog ldan mgon po, Rig 'dzin, 1233
McIntire, Carl, 2890
McIntosh, Ian, 647–648
McIntyre, Greg, 689
McKay, Alex, 9191
McKay, Mabel, 3092
McKean, Kip, 6561
McKee, Ruth Eleanor, 3085
McKenzie, Donald A., 4739

McKenzie, Vashti Murphy, 10040
McKinnell, John, 3460
McLennan, J. F.
on matriarchy, 3611
and Smith (W. Robertson), sacrificial theory of, 8002
McLennan, John, 4460
McLeod, Beverly Aminah, 10039
McLeod, Don, 672, 673
McLeod, Hew, 3717
McNally, Michael D., 370
McNamara, Jo Ann Kay, 6756
McNelley, James Kale, 575, 576
McNemar, Richard, Shakers and, 8268
McNicholas, John T., 3653
McNickle, D'Arcy, *The Surrounded,* 3091
McPherson, Aimee Semple, **5803,** 6536
religious broadcasting and, 7710
McQueen, Clyde, 74
McRae, John, 1246
McVeigh, Timothy, 1039, 6549
Mda, Zakes, 3088
Mdo dgongs pa 'dus pa (Buddhist text), 7870
Mdos rituals (Tibet), 3156
Mdzod bdun (Longchenpa), 5192–5193
Meacham, Joseph, Shakers and, 8268
Mead, 849, 4455, 9338
in Germanic religion, as poetic inspiration, 3455, 5509
of Odin, 8722
Mead, George Herbert
on games, 3268
on reflexivity, 7648–7649
Mead, George R. S.
on Hermetism, 3952
Theosophical Society and, 3952
Mead, Margaret, **5803–5804**
on Balinese rituals, 747, 5804
education of, 5803
on gender relations, 3395, 3420, 6508
Mead, Sidney E.
on civil religion, 1813, 1815, 7327
on denominationalism, 2290
Meadville-Lombard Theological School, 846
Meals, communal, of Essenes, 2847
Meaning. *See also* Hermeneutics; Symbol and symbolism
empiricist criterion of, 7115–7119
Geertz (Clifford) on cause and, 8499–8500
in logical positivism, 5498–5499
play altering, 7194
Meaning and Pattern *(yili)* commentaries, 1907
Meaning of God in Human Experience (Hocking), idealism and pragmatism combined in, 4076
Meaning of God in Modern Jewish Religion, The (Kaplan), 7636
Meaning of Health, The (Tillich), 7477
Meaning of Other Faiths, The (Oxtoby), 10056
Meaning of Religion, The (Kristensen), classification of religions in, 1820
Meaning of the Creative Act, The (Berdiaev), 341
Meaning of Witchcraft, The (Gardner), 9729
Measurements, in Jain cosmology, 2023
Meat
in *Genesis,* 6982
in Greek religion
cooking of, 3669–3670
distribution of, 3667–3668, 3682
kashrut laws on, 5106–5108
Meat industry, animal suffering in, 2655
Mebius, Hans, 474
Mecca
Abraham's house of God in, 6734
as *ḥarīm* (inviolable), 7968
ḥaram of, 3777–3778
Jerusalem and, significance of, 6205
Ka'bah in (*See* Ka'bah)
Muḥammad and, 4561, 5050
Muḥammad in, 19, 20, 6220–6223
early life of, 6220
opposition to, 6222
victory of (630), 6226
Muslim World League headquartered in, 4574
persecution of Muslims in, 6222–6223
pilgrimage to, 2319–2320, 4562 (*See also* Ḥājj; *'Umrah*)
maps for, vol. 3 color insert
pre-Islamic, 3777–3778
in prayer, 9816–9817
in pre-Islamic Arabia, 443, 5049–5050
as sacred city, 9260
Sacred Mosque in, 7158, 7159, 7160
school of law in, emergence of, 5547
Snouck Hurgronje (Christiaan) on, 8460
Mechanics, and materialism, 5776–5777
Mechanism, Newtonian, 7136–7137
Mechthild of Hackeborn, 822
Mechthild of Magdeburg, 822
on heart of God, 3883
writings of, 3359
Meddahs (dramatic storytellers), 2447
Medellín CELAM conference, 1703, 5438
Medem, Julio, 3099
Medes people (Iran)
and Armenian religion, 491, 10001
Assyria destroyed by, 5948
magi as tribe of, 5559
and Zoroastrianism, 9990
Medhbh (deity), 1490, 1493
and Ferghus mac Roich, 3040
Media, **5804–5810**. *See also* Journalism; News; Religious broadcasting
commerce of images and, vol. 7 color insert
convergence with religion, 5806–5807
effects on religion, 5808–5809
emergence of mass, 5805
entertainment, 5806
evangelicalism in, 2891
globalization and, 5807–5808
identity and, 5807
interaction with religion, 5807
Jesus Movement in, 4852–4853
New Thought's use of, 6585
print *vs.* nonprint, 5805
religion used by, 5806
religion using, 5805–5806
ritualized reception of, 3101
as symbolic matrix, 4961
Mediation
in African religions, myths about, 91, 93–96
in Daoism, 2177, 2178
in esotericism, Faivre paradigm of, 2844
in North and Mesoamerican religions, cosmology and, 2008–2010
qi in, 2177
in Roman Catholic theology, 7881–7882
ethics and, 1653
Mary and, 7884
in soteriology, 8529
Mediators. *See* Angels; Shamanism; Spiritual guides
Mediator spirits, in Khanty and Mansi religion, 5122
Mediatrix, Mary as, 7884
Medical Anthropology (Foster and Anderson), 2611
Medical anthropology, ecology in, 2611
Medical ethics, **5810–5816**. *See also* Bioethics
advances in medicine and, 5810–5811
approaches to, 5810–5811
casuistry and, 1455–1456
in Christianity, 5810–5814
in medieval monasticism, 3846
Protestantism, 3846–3847, 5810–5814
Roman Catholicism, 5810–5814
definition of, 5810
genetics and, 5810–5811, 5813–5814
Hippocratic Oath and, 4021
Hippocratic oath and, 5810
in Islam, 5812–5814
in Judaism, 3829, 3830, 3831, 5810–5814
"playing God" problem and, 8186–8188
religiousness and health, issue of, 3876–3877
Médici, Catherine de, 851
Medici, Cosimo de'
Ficino (Marsilio) and, 3049, 5579
Hermetism and, 3945
and Platonic Academy, 4175, 6475
Medici, Lorenzo de', 3627
Savonarola (Girolamo) and, 8139
Medici, Piero de', Savonarola (Girolamo) and, 8139
Medicine. *See* Healing and medicine
Medicine, Beatrice, 3407, 3410
Medicine, Rationality and Experience (Good), 2611
Medicine bags (sacred bundles), in North American Indian religions, 6652, 6682
Medicine Lodge. *See* Sun Dance
Medicine men. *See also* Shamanism
in Australian Indigenous religions, counter-sorcery of, 3873–3874
in Caribbean religions, Arawak curing procedures, 1430
Chuvash *yumśă,* 1785
in Iroquois religion, 4542
miracles by, 6049
as sorcerers, 9769
in Sun Dance, 8845, 8847
tobacco used by, 9217
women as, 3408
Medicine wheels, as circles, 1794
Medina (formerly Yathrib)
Golden Age in, 6223
ḥaram at, 3777
Ja'far al-Ṣādiq at, 4760
Jews of, Muḥammad and, 6224, 6225–6226
Muḥammad in, 19, 20, 4561, 6205–6206, 6223–6227
migration to, 6223
mosque built by, 6205–6206, 6208, 6223
war against, 6225–6226
school of law in, 5547
walāyah and, 9656–9657
Medinese, in Mālikī school of law, 5548
Medinet Habu (Egypt)
Amun and, 2706–2707
Ramses III commemorated at, 2709

Melanchthon, Philipp
continued
Luther (Martin) and, 5831, 5832
theology of, 5831–5832
Melanesia and Melanesian religions, **5832–5846**. *See also* New Caledonia religion; New Guinea; Oceania; Solomon Islands religions; *specific Melanesian islands*
absence of term for religion in, 6502
afterlife in, 146, 147
ancestor worship in, 322, 2005, 5833, 5834, 5839, 5844, 7144–7145, 9907
music in, 6265
art in, 5838–5839, vol. 6 color insert
Australian scholarship on, 8769, 8770
calendar, 1353
cannibalism in, 1403–1404
cargo cults, **1414–1425,** 5380, 7789, 9321
cosmologies and, 2007
messianism of, 5973
caves in, 2006, 2007
chiefs in, 7296
Christianity
missions, 1738, 5832, 9197
separatist and independent churches, 1740
traditional culture merged with, 7297, 9323–9324
Codrington in, **1847–1848**
colonization of, 6784
cosmologies in, 2004–2007, 5843
dance in, 6265
definition of, 5832
deities of, 5834 (*See also specific deities*)
female, 5834
supreme, 5842
diversity in, 2004, 5832
drums in, 2500
Dukduk society in, 8212–8213
gender in, **3395–3400**
geographic boundaries of, 5832
ghosts in, 5833, 5838
homosexuality in, 4114–4115
incarnation in, 4414
initiation in, 4478, 7296
kinship in, Strathern (Marilyn) on, 5183–5184
knot symbolism of, 5197, 5198
magic in, 5562, 5566
deities' role in, 5834
specialists in, 5835
women and, 5836
mana in, 1547, 1847–1848, 5835, 7347–7348
masks in, 5769, 5839, vol. 6 color insert, vol. 9 color insert, vol. 10 color insert
mediums in, 5834–5835
millenarianism in, 6034
missionaries and, 5832
mortuary rituals in, 5837–5838, vol. 9 color insert, vol. 10 color insert
music in, 6265
myths of, **5841–5846**
characters in, 5842
creation in, 5842–5843
culture heroes in, 5834, 5843–5844
origins of humanity in, 5843
society and culture in, 5843–5844
spirits in, 5833–5834
studies of, 5841–5842, 5844
New Year festivals in, 6591
as Oceanic cultural area, 6784
overview of, **5832–5841**
paradise in, 6985–6986
pig festival in, 6591–6592, 7840
vs. Polynesia, 5832
religious specialists in, 5834–5835
research on, 6800
rites of passage in, 5837–5838
ritual symbols in, 7839
sacred and profane in, 5839–5840
serpents in, 8457
shades and souls in, 8514
souls in, 5833, 5836
spirit world in, 2006, 5833–5834
taboos in, 5835–5836
tamaniu doubles in, 8533
totems in, 5835–5836
transculturation of, 9320–9325
transmigration in, 9327
women in, **3395–3400,** 5836–5837
goddess worship and, 5834
rites of passage for, 5837
Melanesian Brotherhood, in Solomon Islands, 1739, 8517
Melanesians, The (Codrington), 2540, 5835
Melania the Elder, 6763
Melās (religious fairs), 9824
Melatti, Julio César, 5985
Melchior, Nicholas, 252
Melchizedek
Abraham and, 16
as allusion to Jerusalem, 933
eschatological role of, 7065
Meleager, 991
Meletians, ecclesiastical discipline and, 8155
Meletios of Lycopolis, 571
Melikraton (drink), 847
Melkite Catholics, 9463
Mellaart, James
excavations by, 455
female figures in, 3585, 5281–5282
in Çatalhüyük, 5281–5282
on goddess worship, 3616
Mellon, James, 77
Melodies, 6250–6251
Melqart (deity), **5846–5849**
in African religion, 5848
Astarte and, 562, 5846, 5847, 5848
in Cyprus, 5847–5848
death and resurrection of, 5847, 5849
Eshmun associated with, 2841
in Greek religion, 5848
Herakles identified with, 3917, 5846–5849
iconography of, 5846, 5848
in Phoenician religion, 5846–5847, 7129–7130
in Spain, 5848
spread of cult, 5847–5849
in Syrian religion, 5846–5847
Melton, J. Gordon, 6523, 6525, 6527, 6582, 9434
Melville, Herman, 3059
Melville J. Herskovits (Simpson), 76
Melzack, Ronald, 6947
Membership, *vs.* alienation, in sociology, 8482
Membership in the church, **1777–1779**. *See also* Community; Denominationalism; Excommunication; Religious communities
creeds and, 2053
dress and, 1831–1832
in early church, 1777
Half-Way Covenant (New England) and, 1938
juridical aspects of, 1778–1779
in Middle Ages, 1777
in modern period, 1778
in New Testament, 1777
in Old Testament, 1777
in Reformation and Counter-Reformation, 1778
sociological aspects of, 1778–1779
Membertou (Mi'kmaq chief), 9302
Membranophones, 6251
Memento mori, vol. 1 color insert
Memorial days, 2243
Memorials
architecture of, classification of, 463–464
collective identity and, vol. 6 color insert
importance of, 2243
Memorization, **5849–5853**. *See also* Anamnesis; Oral tradition
mechanical *vs.* deliberate, 5849–5850
of Qur'ān, 5852–5853, 7572
oral memory *vs.* writing in, 5850
specialists in, 5850–5851
techniques of, 5851, 5852
Memory
art of, 3196, 5852
in Buddhist liturgy, 9828
in Greek underworld, 9703
history and, 6374
Hopkins (Emma Curtis) on, 4128
Hubbard (L. Ron) on, 8192
images used in, 9623
in North American Indian oral tradition, 6425–6426
sacred time and, vol. 1 color insert
social, 5850
Memory board *(lukasa),* in Luba religion, vol. 1 color insert
Memory books, in Judaism, 7823
Memphite Theology (Egypt), 2720
Memphite Theology (Memphis Drama), 2441
Men. *See also* Gender; Masculinity; Men's studies
in Acehnese religion, 25–26
in Australian Indigenous religions, Ngukurr, 6599
beauty of, 811, 812–813
couvade and, **2046–2047**
dancing by, 2136–2137
among Chewa people, 2141
among Hamadsha people, 2138
in Căluş ritual, 2147
in Gẹlẹdẹ society, 2141
Sun Dance, 2138
dominance of, in religion, 9787
in gender studies, 3296
Hamadsha, dances of, 2138
in Hinduism, duties of, 2403, 2404
initiation rituals of (*See* Initiation, men's)
in Raëlian religion, 7598
in Islam, majority age for, 4705
in Judaism
divorce and, 7821
marriage and, 7821
naming of, 7819
"low male salience," 2046
in Minoan religion, 38–39
mockery by women, 4199
priesthood restricted to, 7395–7396
rites of passage of
in Agikuyu religion, 7805
in modern society, 7802–7803
Neopagan, 7830
in tribal societies, 7796, 7799, 7801
and sacrifice, powers of, 8009
secret societies of, in tribal communities, 7717
sexual activity of, life-in-death/death-in-life metaphor of, 2238
sexual mores of, in Hinduism, 2136
in Sikh Dharma and 3HO, 3879

in Twelve Tribes, 9410
winter caroling by, 9741
in Zoroastrianism, funeral rites for, 2130
Men (deity), as moon god, 6172
Menahem (Essene prophet), 2846
Menahem (king), Hosea and, 4137
Menand, Louis, on James (William), 4777
Menander (Greek king), 1109, 1186, 1199, 1298
Menander (rhetorician), on afterlife, 8543
Menander of Ephesus, on Melqart, 7129
Men and Religion Forward movement, 5862
Ménard, Louis, on Hermetism, 3952
Menas (saint), pilgrimage to shrine of, 1980, 1981
Menasseh ben Israel, 5086
Shabbateanism and, 8261
Spinoza (Baruch) and, 8681
Menchú, Rigoberta, 3413
Mencian school, 1587. *See also* Mengzi
Mencius (book). *See Mengzi*
Mencius (philosopher). *See* Mengzi
Mendel, Gregor, 2879, 2908–2909, 3427
Mendelson, Michael E., 5942
Mendelssohn, Felix, 6312
Mendelssohn, Moses, **5853–5855**
biblical exegesis of, 869, 5854
on burial rites, 7667
on Christianity, 7235
education of, 5854
on existence of God, 7422
as first modern Jew, 4900–4901
in German Enlightenment, 2797
influence of, 5854–5855
Judaism of, 5854
legacy of, 4901
metaphysics of, 5854
on Spinoza (Baruch), 8685
Wach (Joachim) and, 9649
writings of, 5854
Mende religion (West Africa)
birth in, 951
creation in, 3570–3571
iconography of, 4303
supreme being (Ngewo) in, 3570–3571
Mendes, David Franco, on Spinoza (Baruch), 8681
Mendez, Alphonsus (Catholic patriarch), 2860
Mendicancy, **5855–5857,** 7724
in Buddhism, 5855, 6855
in Christianity, 5855–5856
monasticism of, 5855–5856, 6133–6134
in Hinduism, 5855
in Islam, 5856
Mendieta, Gerónimo de, 5916
Mendis. *See* Bendis
Mendoza Codex, Huitzilopochtli in, 4155
Menelaus (Jewish high priest), and apostasy, 430
Menelaus (mythic figure), afterlife of, 165
Menenius Agrippa, corporate imagery used by, 4161
Menes (Egyptian king), 2703–2704
Mēness (deity), 758–759, 760, 769
Mengele, Joseph, 6166
Mengk people
in Khanty religion, 5121
in Mansi religion, 5121
Menglǫð (deity), 3218–3219
Mengrai (king of Sukhōthai), 1136, 1137
Meng-tzu. *See* Mengzi
Mengzi (book), 5857–5859
author of, 5857
Buddhist ideas in, 1909
canon, elevation to, 1909, 5857
on human nature, 1895–1897, 5858
li in, 5430
in Neo-Confucianism, 5858
ren in, 7751
on *Spring and Autumn,* 1907
structure of, 5857
Mengzi (Mencius) (Chinese philosopher), **5857–5860**
Cheng Hao and, 1572
Confucianism of, 5857–5859
on *de,* 2173
on Golden Rule, 3632, 3633
on goodness, 5541
on heaven, 5859
on humanity, 9674, 9675
on human nature, 5857–5858, 5859
on *jinsei,* 4551
on *li,* 5431
philosophy, overview of, 1572, 1587
on *ren,* 7751
on sages, 8037
on self-cultivation, 2634, 5858
on *xiao,* 9593
Xunzi's opposition to, 1573
on *yi,* 7751
Menhirs (stone monuments), 5116, 5822, 5827. *See also* Stonehenge; Stones
on Madagascar, 8746
Mokosh connected with, 6115
Meni (deity), in Tucanoan religion, 8591
Menjo ritual, in Agikuyu religion, 7805
Menninger, Karl, 7487
on temptation, 9072, 9073
Mennonite Central Committee (MCC), 5861
Mennonites, **5860–5861**. *See also* Anabaptism
and adult baptism, 782
Bible and, 5860
doctrine of, 5860–5861
dress code and social control among, 1835–1836
ecclesiology of, 1774
on ethics, 1655
history in U.S., 6557
modern, 5861
origins of, 783, 5860
pacifism of, 6648
persecution of, 5860
in Europe, 6557, 6567
Reformation critiques, 1663
Simons (Menno), role in, **8400–8402**
Mennonite World Conference, 5861
Menno Simons, Mennonites led by, 5860
Meno (Plato)
anamnesis (recollection) in, 5990
Orphism in, 7186
transmigration in, 9329
virtues in, 310
Menocchio. *See* Scandella, Domenico
Men of Divinity, in Dinka religion, 2570
Mēnōg ī Khrad (Spirit of Wisdom), 9751–9752, 10012
Menominee (Menomini) religion (North America)
ballgame played in, 753, 754
bears in, 809
culture hero myth of, 2091
hunting rituals of, 6682
Medicine rite of, 6681
naming ceremonies of, 6683
origin myth of, 6680
shamanism in, 6685
Menopause, sacred power of, 3020
Menos (Greek concept), 8541
death and, 8542
Mensching, Gustav
Klimkeit (Hans-Joachim) and, 5190
on religion as social coordination, 8467
religious typology of, 4043
Men's movement, 5862–5863
vs. men's studies, 5862
Neopaganism and, 7831
origins of, 5862
Men's studies, **5861–5866**
vs. gay and queer studies, 5864
historical precedents for, 5862
methodologies of, 3300, 5861–5862
need for, 3296, 5862
origins of, 5862
reclaiming religion and faith in, 5862–5863
spiritual and confessional writings in, 5863
theological and biblical investigations in, 5863–5864
Menstrual Purity: Rabbinic and Christian Reconstruction of Biblical Gender (Fonrobert), 7515
Menstruation, **5866–5868**
affliction during, 57
in African religions, 3403
blood taboo and, 1459
in Buddhism, 5866
calendar and, 1353
in Christianity, 5866–5867
death-in-life/life-in-death metaphor of, 2238
feminism on, 5867
in Hinduism, 5866
as impurity, 987, 2404, 4164, 4732, 7082
in Bēta Esra'ēl, 5003, 5004
and initiation ceremony, 4478, 4484
Apache, 10070
Bemba, 818
Navajo, 4485
in Islam, 4708, 5866
in Judaism, 5866
marriage and, 7821
and *miqveh,* 6047
in Lakota religion, 5297
male envy of, 7808
in Melanesian religions, 5836, 5837
Milky Way linked to, 2863
moon linked to, 2863, 3018, 6170
in Neopaganism, 7830
in North American Indian religions, 6682, 6683, 6703, 6715, 10070
and pollution, 5866, 7504, 7505, 7511
contamination from, 7505
in Hinduism, 2405
in Israelite religion, 4732
in Judaism, 7511, 7512, 7514–7515, 10052
in Polynesian religions, 7311
in Rastafari, 7627
ritual use of blood of, 7083
sacred power of, 3020
in Samoan women, 7796
in Sikhism, 3336
in South American religions, 3418
taboos on, 3173, 5866–5867
in Tikopia religion, 9198
in untouchables religions, rituals of, 9476
in Zoroastrianism, 3373, 3374
Mental disease
art produced in, 9625
diagnosed as possession, 2931

Mental health
Hubbard (L. Ron) on, 4149, 8192
New Thought movement and, 6584
religiousness, relationship with, 3875–3876, 6487
Mentalism, structuralism *vs.*, 8759
Mentally Ill Person as Artist, An (Morgenthaler), 9625
Mental Science, founder of, 6584
Mental work, 9798–9799
Mentuhotep II (Egyptian king), 2706
Menzies, A., on supreme beings, 8876
Mercator (Plautus), 7027
Mercedarians, Latin American Missions, 1696, 1697
Mercenaries
in India, *nāgā sāṃyāsīn* as, 8021
missionaries and, 6073
Merchant, Carolyn, feminist ecotheology of, 2610
Merchants
khatrī caste in India, Sikh Panth community and, 3986
Mercurius as god of, 3937
as missionaries, 6073
Mercier, Désiré Joseph, **5868–5869**
Mercier, Sebastian, 9492
Mercurius. *See* Hermes Trismegistos; Mercury
Mercury (element), in alchemy
Indian, 242, 243, 244
Islamic, 249
Mercury (Mercurius, deity). *See also* Hermes
Celtic religion and, 1482, 1483
cult of, in Rome, 3937
in Gaul, 7911
in Germanic religion, 3450
Hermes as, 3937
Mercury (planet)
animals associated with, 8428
celestial metaphors of, 8428
Mercy
God's justice and, 613–614, 615
in *Jonah,* 4947
Mercy, Mount of (Saudi Arabia), 7159
Merezhkovskii, Dmitrii, **5869–5870**
Mergen Tengere (deity), 9081
Meriah, in Khond ritual sacrifice, 2556
Merici, Angela, 6764
Merikare (Egyptian king), 2706
Merimde culture, 6465
Merina of Madagascar, 1015
Merit, **5870–5878**
in Buddhism, **5872–5875**
development of concept, 5870, 5872
karman and, 5099, 5870, 5872–5874
making of, 5870, 5872–5875
Thai, 9829
Tibetan, 9840
transference of, 1113, 5874–5875
in Chinese religion, 5870
in Christianity, **5875–5878**
medieval view of, 5876–5877
patristic view of, 5876
Reformation and, 5877
rise of concept, 5870, 5871, 5872, 5875–5876
in Roman Catholicism, 5875, 5877
in Islam, 5871
in Jainism, 5870
in Judaism, 5870, 5871
overview of, **5870–5872**
religions without concept of, 5872
salutations as act of, 8061
use of term, 5870
Meritaton, 217, 219
Merkavah mysticism, **10050–10053**. *See also* Heikhalot mysticism
antecedents and parallels in, 10050
ascension in, 522–523
in Ashkenazic Hasidism, 10050–10051
eschatology of, 6352
in rabbinic Judaism, 10050
as religious phenomenon, 10052–10053
in *Sar-Torah,* 10050, 10051–10052
in *Shi'ur Qomah,* 10050, 10052
studies of, 10050
Merkelbach, Reinhold, 3056
on mystery religions, 6332
Merker, Barbara, 3527
Merkorios, Abune, 2861
Merlan, Francesca, 687, 3392
Merleau-Ponty, Maurice
atheism of, 7422
on time, 7987
Merlin (legendary figure), **5878**
as child of *incubus,* 2278, 5878
Merlo, Eduardo, 5902
Mermaid language, 3506
Mermaids, Mami Wata as, 5630
Merneptah (Egyptian king), 2708
Mernissi, Fatima, Qur'anic exegesis of, 7568
Merodakh. *See* Marduk
Merok (feast), 9242
Meron (Galilee), pilgrimage to, 7162
Merriam, Alan P., 2496
on music
origin of, 6252
time in, 6255
Merrill, William, 2485
Mersenne, Marin, 2293
on Zorzi, 3949
Merton, Owen, 5879
Merton, Robert, 3232
on authority, 8483
Merton, Ruth Jenkins, 5879
Merton, Thomas, **5879**
autobiographical writings of, 699, 5879
education of, 5879
eremitism of, 2828
and exterior world, 2829
monasticism of, 5879, 6125
mysticism of, 6348
in social protest, 5879
Strict Observance and, 1801
Meru, Mount (mythic mountain), 1501
as *axis mundi,* 6212
in Hinduism, 4439
in Buddhist *cakravāla* cosmology, 2026
in *maṇḍalas,* 5644, 6212
in Purāṇic Hindu cosmology, 2017, 2018
Merula, Cornelius, 3126
Meru religion (Kenya), priesthood in, 2569
Mesa divination
cosmological systems and, 3810
healing and, 8619
Mesas (ritual meals), in Andean religion, 8616
Mescalero Apaches, 404–406, 10069–10071
Mescaline (hallucinogen), 7471, 9216, 9218
Mescaline, South American shamanism and, 8292
Mesha (Moabite king), 6093, 6094, 6095
Meshekh ḥokhmah (Me'ir Simḥah), 868
Meskell, Lynn, 2732
Meslamtaea (deity), 5950. *See also* Nergal
Meslin, Michel, historiography of, 4050
Mesmer, Franz Anton
on animal magnetism, 1947, 3849–3850
on consciousness, 1947
and secularization of Western Esotericism, 6497
Mesmerism
healing and, 3849–3850
Kardec's (Alan) involvement with, 5089
and New Age movement, 6497
Mesoamerica and Mesoamerican religions, **5879–5946**. *See also* Aztec religion; Latin America; Maya religion; Mexico; *specific countries and religions*
afterlife in, **148–152**
ages of world in, 177
animals in, myths about, 5938
archaeology in, 452, 456–457, 9066
art of
afterlife in, 149
earliest, 5880
in Formative (Preclassic) period, 5880, 5895–5897
in Teotihuaćan, 5899–5900
ballgames in, **749–752**
ballcourts for, 750–751
balls for, 750
cosmic symbolism in, 3260
equipment for, 749–750
rules of, 751
social, political, and religious significance of, 751
temporal and regional diversity of, 749
calendar in, 1353, **1355–1360,** 7811
origins of, 5881–5882
caves in, 1468, 1470
Christianity
in colonial period, 5914–5922
contemporary, 5924–5932
folk religion in, 5920
resistance to, 5920–5921
circles in, 1794–1795
cities of
as ceremonial and sacred centers, 1803–1805
death in, 149
Classic period in, **5897–5906**
music of, 6268
cofradías in, 5918–5919, 5925–5926
colonial period in, **5914–5923**
afterlife in, 151
churches established during, 5916
conversions questioned in, 5919–5920
elite hierarchy in church life, 5918
folk religion in, 5920
Franciscans in, 5915–5916, 5917
gender in, 3411, 3412–3413
Inquisition in, 5917–5918
languages used in, 5916–5917
native clergy debate in, 5917
Spanish conquest and, 7810
Spanish priests in, 5915–5920
spiritual conquest during, 5915, 5924
studies of, 5939–5940
uprisings during, 3412–3413, 5920–5921
color symbolism, 1860–1861
confession in, 1885–1886
contemporary, **5923–5933**
gender in, 3413–3414
conversion in
colonial, sincerity of, 5919–5920
economics of, 5929–5930

as social backlash, 5929–5930
cosmogony of, 5934, 7557
cosmologies in, **2008–2010,** 5923–5924
costumbre in, 5924–5925
creation in, 1357–1358, 5934–5935
culture heroes in, 5936–5937
death in, 148–149
definition of, 148, 5879
deities of (*See also* Quetzalcoatl; *specific deities*)
calendar and, 1357, 1359
caves associated with, 1468–1469
contemporary, 5926–5928
creation by, 5934–5935
duality of, 5933–5934
gender of, 3411, 3412, 3413
origins of, 5881
sacrifices by, 1358
saints identified with, 5926
dogs in, 2393, 2394
drama in (*See* Drama, Mesoamerican dance and drama)
drums in, 2465, 6268, 7036
fiesta system of, 5925
Fifth Sun era in, 5888, 5901, 5907, 5935
Formative (Preclassic) period in, **5895–5897**
Early, 5880, 5882, 5895
Late, 5882, 5895–5896
Middle, 5895
music of, 6267–6268
funeral rites in, **3241–3245,** 7813
death in motion and, 148–149
gender in, **3411–3415**
geographic boundaries of, 5879–5880
globalization in, 5924
hierodouleia (sacred prostitution) in, 3969
high culture of, 5880–5882
historical periods of, 148
history of study of, **5939–5946**
contemporary, 5941–5943
early texts in, 5939–5940
national schools of thought in, 5940–5941
types of study, 5943–5946
human sacrifices in, 2242
iconography of (*See* Iconography, Mesoamerican)
influence on North American Indian religions, 6654
Inquisition in, 5917–5918
jade in, 4759
jaguars in, 4762–4763
Judas in, 5926
kingship in, **5172–5178**
liberation theology in, 5930–5931
light and darkness symbolism in, 5451
literature of, 5893
pre-Columbian, 5893
local orientation of, 5924, 5927–5928
lord of the animals in, 5515
matriarchy in, 6625
messianism in, 5983
music in, **6266–6271**
in colonial period, 5918
sources on, 6266–6267
myths of, **5933–5939**
animals in, 5938
creation in, 5934–5935
culture heroes in, 5936–5937
pilgrimage in, 5937–5938
plants in, 5936
sacrifice in, 5935–5936
tricksters in, 5937
twins in, 5937
ocean in, 6807
origins of, 5880
Postclassic period in, **5906–5914**
music of, 6268–6269
pre-Columbian, **5879–5914**
gender in, 3411–3412
Protestantism, 5928–5930
conversion to, 5929–5930
gender and, 3413–3414
introduction of, 5928–5929
pyramids in, 7526, 7527, 9065–9066, 9266
rainmaking in, 7603
rites of passage in, 1470, **7810–7813**
birth rituals, 7811–7812
childhood development, 7812
cosmic, 7813
funeral rites, 7813
historical documentation of, 7810–7811
marriage, 7812–7813
Roman Catholicism
creolization and, 2066
emergent identities in, 5930
gender and, 3412–3413
progressive, 3413
saints of, 5926
Traditionalism, 3413
sacrifice in, 5935–5936
saints in, 2228, 5926
secular movements in, 3414
uprisings in, 3414
shamanism in
colonial, 5920
contemporary, 5928
as single religion *vs.* multiple religions, 5880, 5913, 5942–5943
social structure of, 5880
spells in, 8677–8678
spirits, lost, 1470
sports in, 8723
sun in, 8842
syncretism in, 5893, 5920, 5928
temples in (*See* Temples, Mesoamerican)
trees in, 9335, 9338, 9339
tricksters in (*See* Tricksters)
women in, **3411–3415**
Mesocosm, 9043
Mesolithic Period, 6948
Mesopotamia and Mesopotamian religions, **5946–5971**. *See also* Assyrian religion; Babylonian religion; Iraq; Sumerian religion
academic knowledge in, 3824
afterlife in
judgment of the dead in, 5025
justice in, 128
vision of gods in, 128
agriculture in, 5946, 5947
Akitu festival in (*See* Akitu festival)
amulets and talismans in, 299
angels in, 345
anthropogenesis in, 8535–8538
anthropomorphism in, 5950–5951
archaeology of, 453–454
architecture in, 5960
art of, gender in, 3379
Christianity in, Council of Ephesus rejected by, 2583
cities in, 1802–1803, 5946, 5947, 7984
earliest, 5947, 6172
creation myth in (*See Enuma elish*)
death in, 7684
deities of, 5948–5962 (*See also specific deities*)
adoption into Hurrian religion, 4230
anthropomorphism of, 5950–5951
cities dedicated to, 3593, 5949–5950
communal *vs.* private cults of, 5961–5963
divine bureaucracy of, 5951, 5994
families and households of, 5951
female, 3376–3377, 3593–3594
general assembly of, 5951
iconography of, 4316–4317
meteorological, 5994
moon, 6171–6172
mother-goddess, 6624–6625
pantheon of, 5951–5960
personal gods in, 8536
physiomorphism of, 5949–5950
of rain, 7602
of sky, 7602, 8837–8838
sociomorphism of, 5951
of sun, 8837–8838
theranthropic, 9155
of underworld, 3900, 6476–6478
vision of, 128
war, 6626–6627
deus otiosus in, 2311
drums in, 2498
dynasties in, 5947–5948
eremitism in, 2826
fate in, 3002–3003
gender in, **3375–3381**
geographic boundaries of, 5946
ghosts *(eṭemmu)* in, 8535–8536
goddess worship in, 3586, 3593–3594
decline of, 3594
evidence regarding, 3592
Golden Age in, 3629
hare myths in, 7590
healing in, 3824–3825
hierodouleia (sacred prostitution) in, 3967, 3968
history of, 5946–5948
history of study of, **5967–5971**
homosexuality in, 4113
gender and, 3378–3379
iconography of (*See* Iconography, Mesopotamian)
incense offering in, 4419
influence on biblical stories, 2967, 2968
kings in, 5161–5163
authority of, 693
divinity of, 3902, 7276–7277
nomadic, 5157, 5162
kūbu (fetu) in, 8537
law codes, 1842, 1844–1845
codification of, 4727
vs. Egyptian law, 4727
vs. Israelite law, 4728
literature of, medical texts, 3825
Maqlu tablets on witchcraft, 2098, 2100
marriage in
gender roles in, 3378
sacred, 3377, 5961
melammu (divine splendor) in, 8537
merit in, 5871
monolatry in, 3540
moon in, 6171–6172
mother goddesses in, 3594
mountain symbolism in, 6213
music in, 6275–6276

Mesopotamia and Mesopotamian religions ***continued***
myths of (*See also* Enuma elish)
dying and reviving god, 1874–1875
Enki and Ninhursaga, 6624, 6625
the Fall in, 2959, 2962–2963
the Flood in, 598–600, 1876, 2963, 3131, 3132
keys, 5116
Ninurta and Anzu, 6627
in Neolithic period, 6459
numinous experience in, 5948–5949
ouroboros serpent in, 1793–1794
overview of, **5946–5967**
political leadership in, 5947–5948
politics and, 7276–7277
primitive democracy in, 5947
prophecy in, 7424
pyramids in, 7527
rainbow symbolism in, 7604
repentance in, 7756
ritual drama in, 2441–2442, 2444–2445
as river civilization, 7861
sacred marriage in, 2445
as sacred national community, 7717
sacrifice in, 8005
of pigs, 7144
settlement of, origins of, 5947
shape shifting in, 8303
sin and guilt in, 8403
social structure of, 3375–3376
soul concepts in, 8535–8537
spells in, 8676
sun in, 8837–8838
temples in, 5960–5961, 9062
rituals performed at, 9062
role in society, 3375
structure of, 9062
on top of ziggurats, 9062
theocracy in, 9109
triads in, 9349
wisdom in, 9748–9749, 9754
Israelite wisdom influenced by, 9764
women in, **3375–3381**
writing in, development of, 5161
"Mesopotamian *mīs pī* Ritual, The" (Walker and Dick), 4381
Mesrob. *See* Mashtots', Mesrop
Message to The Black Man (Elijah Muhammad), 4688
Messenger (being), in Manichaeism, 5654, 5666, 5667
Messer Leon, David (rabbi), 7580
Messerschmidt, D. G., 3110
Messhepeshu. *See* Michibizhii
Messiaen, Olivier, 6313
Messiah
definition of, 6547
millennialism and, 6546, 6547
origins of term, 5972, 5974
vs. prophet, 5973
Messianic churches, African, Shembe (Isaiah) and, 8316
Messianic Communities. *See* Twelve Tribes
Messianism, **5972–5986**
Abulafia's (Avraham), 7537
apocalypse and, 410
Besant's (Annie), 846
in Branch Davidians, 5237–5239
Buddhist, Maitreya in, 2028, 5621
Christian, 5972–5973
kingship and, 5164
Strauss (David Friedrich) on, 8747–8748
suffering servant doctrine and, 8807
Daoist, 1594, 1597, 2195–2196, 2205, 5317
definition of, 5974, 5979
Derrida (Jacques) on, 2247
duality in, 5975
eschatology and, 2834
in Heaven's Gate cult, 3889–3890
Islamic, 5973, **5979–5983,** 6545
of Aḥmadiyah, 200
of Qarāmiṭah, 7543
in Japan, 4790
Jewish, 5972, **5974–5979** (*See also* Shabbateanism)
Abravanel (Isaac) on, 18
in apocalypses, 419–420
apocalyptic *vs.* rationalist, 5976
charisma and, 1546
Cohen (Hermann) and, 1851, 1852
corporate salvation and, 4858
development of concept, 5972, 5974–5975
double messiah in, 5975
Ebionites and, 2596
Hasidism and, 3786, 3788–3789, 3790, 3793, 4983, 5978
in Jewish Renewal, 4872
kingship and, 5165
of Marranos, 5719
polemics on, 7231–7232, 7233
rabbinic Judaism and, 7583, 7586
redemption in, 7640
resurrection and judgment associated with, 3884
under Roman Empire, 4975–4976
Schneerson (Menachem) on, 8173
sects of, 6872
Sephardic, 4998–4999
Shemu'el the Amora on, 8318
in *siddur,* 5165
Sofer (Mosheh) on, 8507
Teichthal (Issachar) on Holocaust and, 4091
Zionism and, 4906–4907, 9978, 9979, 9981
Kagan's (Yisra'el Me'ir), 5053
Kalischer's (Tsevi Hirsch), 5069
Koresh's (David), 5237–5239
in nativistic movements, 5973
origins of term, 5972, 5974
overview of, **5972–5974**
vs. prophetic movements, 5973
revival and renewal activities in, 7785
soteriology and, 8528
South American, **5983–5986**
conditions for emergence of, 3063
ethnohistorical studies of, 8597
pre-Incan Andean, 8604
Spanish view of, 8593
Taubes (Jakob) on, 9021
in Unification theology, 9467
Zoroastrian, Saoshyants and, 8110–8111
Messina Congress, on Gnosticism, 3508, 3515, 3534
Messorodi, Moses, writings of, 5085
Mesters, Carlos, 5440
Meta-anthropology, deity in, 2256
Metacosmology, deity in, 2255–2256
Metals and metallurgy, **5986–5989**
in Africa, 5988
in blacksmith myths, 94–95, 98–99, 4301, 5988
deities of, in Edo religion, 2697
in Hinduism, 4326
in Mesopotamian religions, 4315
from meteorites, 5986–5987
from mines, 5987–5988
rituals associated with, 5987–5988
turning into gold (*See* Alchemy)
Metameleia (repentance or conversion), 7758
Metamorphoses (Apuleius), 3051, 3604–3605, 3651
initiation of Lucius into cult of Isis in, 3908
Isis worship in, 3054, 4558, 4559, 7189
restoration of Lucius in, 3904–3905
themes in, 3903
Metamorphoses (Naso), 9330
Metamorphosis. *See also* Shape shifting; Transmigration
in Hellenistic religions, 3903
in Kulina religion (Brazil), 2012
sacred *vs.* profane and, 7975
of shamans, totemic figures portraying, vol. 1 color insert
in winter carols, 9743
Metamorphosis (Ovid), chaos in, 1537
Metanexus Institute, 2661
Metanir (Greek queen), 803
Metanoia (repentance or conversion), 7758
Meta-ontology, deity in, 2256–2257
Metaphysical dualism, 2509
Metaphysical movements
doctrines of correspondence and influx in, healing and, 3849
holistic healing and, 3851
in North America, 1714
Metaphysical philosophy of religion, Chantepie de la Saussaye on, 1531
Metaphysical poetry, 7220–7221
Metaphysics, **5989–5992**. *See also* Idealism; Reality; Soul(s)
of Aristotle, 484–485, 5990
in Buddhism, 51
"emptiness," Chinese interpretation of, 1595
"net of Indra" in Huayan Buddhism, 4147
Sautrāntikas and, 8119–8120, 8137–8138
soul and, 8547–8548
Tang school, 1577
chaos theory and, 1542–1543
in Christianity
bioethics and, 8190–8191
in Christian Science, 1746
o fSuárez (Francisco), 8799
of Swedenborg (Emanuel), 8899
in Confucianism
Hwadam on, 8510
in Song dynasty, 1578
Daoist (*See Yinyang Wuxing* philosophy)
definition of, 5989, 7110, 7114
of Descartes, 2293, 5990
Eastern, 5989
epistemology and, 2818
eternity in, 2854, 2856
general, 7110 (*See also* Ontology)
in Hinduism
in Advaita Vedānta, 8105–8106, 8546
in Dvaita Vedānta, 8547
in Śaiva Siddhānta, 8547
in Sāṃkhya school, 8089–8090
in Islam
soul and, 8568
waḥdat al-wujūd (unity of being) in, 3756, 8819
of James (William), 4776–4777
Kant (Immanuel) on, 7110
of Leibniz (Gottfried), 5407
of liturgy, 5491–5492

logical positivism and, 5498
modern, 5990–5991
in Neoplatonism, 5990
ontology and, 6830
of Parmenides, 5989–5990
of Plato, 5990
vs. positivism, 7339
psychology and, 5033
of Scheler (Max), 8147
in science and religion, 2658
in Sikhism, in *Ādi Granth,* 6413
special, 7110
Stoic, 8741, 8742
of Thomas Aquinas, 9163
of Tillich (Paul), 7120
of Valentinus, 7190
Western, 5989–5991
of Whitehead (Alfred North), 7121
Metaphysics (Aristotle), 484–485, 2855, 7110
Albertus Magnus on, 232
chance in, 1526
eternity in, 2855
influence on medieval theology, 480
prime mover in, 485
substance in, concept of, 485
Themistius on, 479
Metaphysics (Ibn Sīnā), Mullā Ṣadrā on, 6233
Metaprayers, 7370
Metatheology, 6494
Metatron (angel), 345
Elishaʿ ben Avuyah and, conversations with, 2769
Enoch as, 2803
Metempsychosis, 2504
and deification, 2248
in Greek religion and mythology, 7679
Luria (Isaac) on, 8560
Pythagoras on, 8541
in Qabbalah, 7538
Meteorites, 8736
in Greek religion, 8745
metals from, 5986–5987
Meteorological beings, **5992–5996**
animals, 5995–5996
deities, 3618–3619, 5992–5996
creativity and chaos of, 5993–5994
examples of, 3618–3619
functions of, 3618–3619, 5992–5993
sovereignty of, 5992, 5994–5995
specialization of, 5992–5993
as supreme beings, 5993
Meteorology
in *onmyōdō,* 6828–6829
theoretical, 1541
Meteors, 8735–8736
Meter, in Indian music, 6279
Meter (deity), Cybele as, 2109
Methi (cumin seed), 4433
Method and Theory in the Study if Religion (journal), 10057
Methodism
on free will and predestination, 3204, 3208
origins of, 6557
religious experience in, 7737
in Taiwan, 8963
Wesleyan
in development of capitalism, 2669
founding of, 9715–9716
Methodist Church, establishment of, 5998, 5999
Methodist churches. *See* Methodist denominations
Methodist Church of Australasia, 1732
Methodist denominations, **5996–5999**. *See also* Salvation Army; United Methodist Church; *specific denominations*
Aboriginal Christianity and, 676–677
in Africa, 1722
in Sierra Leone, 1718
African American, 68, 69, 1709, 5998
Arminianism and, 493
in Australia and New Zealand, 1732, 1733
in Canada, 1713
among Cherokee, 1566
church architecture of, 796
Coke (Thomas), role of, **1852–1853**
Conferences of, 5999
early, 5997
as *connexion,* 5997, 5998
consolidation among, 5999
development of, 5996–5998
criticism of, 5997
preachers in, 5997–5998
divisions in, 5998–5999
doctrines of, 5997
on embryonic stem cell research, 941
Enlightenment theology in, 4083–4084
Holiness movement and, 4082, 4083–4084
hymns of, 5998
international, 5999
membership in
conditions for, 5997
size of, 5999
ministry in, orders of, 6045
missions, 5998
to American slaves, 1709
in Australia and New Zealand, 1732
in Caribbean, 1706, 1707
in Pacific islands, 1738, 9323
origins of, 5996–5997
perfection in, 5997
perfectionism, and Holiness movement, 1713–1714
polity of, 1767, 5998
proposed covenant with United Reformed Church in England (1980–1982), 1939
Shaker cult in St. Vincent and, 1437
slavery in, 5998
in United States
development and growth, 1712, 5997–5998
divisions in, 5998–5999
Wesley (John) in, 5996–5998
Methodist Episcopal Church
Asbury (Francis) in, 518
divisions in, 5998
founding of, 5998
Holiness movement and, 4083
slavery in, 5998
Methodist Episcopal Church South, 5998
Methodist Missionary Society, in Caribbean, 1706
Methodist New Connexion, 5998
Methodius. *See* Cyril and Methodius
Methodius of Olympus, on Athenagoras, 589
Methodological reductionism, in science and religion, 2658
Methods of Ethics (Sidgwick), 2918
Metiochos and Parthenope, 3053
Metis (deity), Zeus and, 3663
Métis (descendants of Catholic men and Indian women), 9302–9303
Metivot. See Yeshivah/Yeshivot
Meton (astronomer), 6171
Métraux, Alfred, 75, 76
on messianism, 5985
on oral tradition, memorization of, 5850
on supreme beings, 8577–8579, 8580
Metre. *See* Meter
Metrology, in Japanese religion, Hirata Atsutane on, 4023
Metropolitans, in church polity
Greek Orthodox, 1765
in Roman Empire, 1763
Metta/maitri (kindness), 1555
Mèt-tet (master of the head), 9636–9637
Metteyya, Ananda, 1187
Meturgeman (translator), 887
Metz, J.-B., 429
on God, 3559
political theology of, 7245
Rahner (Karl) criticized by, 7601
Metzger, Bruce M., 900
Metzger, Max, 2686
Meulenbeld, Jan, on Indian medical texts, 3854
Meuli, Karl, 474, 520, 1014
cultural historical model of, 4043
on evolution in religion, 2867, 10043
on masks, 5765
Meunasah (dormitory), 25, 26
Mevlevi order (Whirling Dervishes), 6750, 7936
Mevlevi order of Sufism
dance in, ecstasy induced by, 5818–5819
samāʿ (listening parties) in, 8065
Mexican Provincial Council, First (1555), 5916, 5917
Mexica people. *See* Aztec religion and society
Mexico, Valley of, 5292–5294
Mexico and Mexican religions. *See also* Aztec religion; Huichol religion; Mesoamerica; Mixtec religion; Nahuatl religion; Tlaxcalan religion; Toltec religion; Totonac religion; Zapotec religion; *specific religions*
astrology in, 8426
ballgames played in, 749
codices of, Maya calendar and, 1360
crisis cults in, 2139
cult of Quetzalcoatl in, 7556–7557
dance in, 2137, 2139
Day of the Dead in, 2230, 3238
films from, 3099
folk-saint movements in, 6577–6578
Formative (Preclassic) period in, 5895–5897
funerary practices in, 3242, 3244–3245
history of study of, 5939–5946
Inquisition in, 4503–4504, 4505
Islam, 4684
jaguar in, 4763
Lady of the Animals in, 5280
monasteries in, 6119
mountains in, 6214
new religious movements in, 6514, 6576, 6577–6578
nativistic, 6576
spiritist cults, 6578
noise in, 7037
Protestantism, 5929, 6579, 6580
redemption in, 7641
revolution in, 1700
Roman Catholicism, pilgrimage in, 7149, 7150–7151
saints in, 2228
Sor Juana in, 4967–4968
Spanish colonial mission in, 1696–1697
spells in, 8677–8678
tattooing in, vol. 6 color insert

Mexico and Mexican religions ***continued***
temples in, 9066
tobacco in, 9216, 9217, 9218
Virgin of Guadalupe in, 3064, 5922
Zapatismo of, 9930–9933
Zapatista Army of National Liberation in, 3414
uprising of (1994), 5931–5932
Mexico City
convents in, 3412
Franciscans in, 5915
Hill of the Star, 1356–1357
Virgin of Remedies in, 5921
Mexico councils I and III, 1695–1696
Meyendorff, John, on Great Schism, 8156
Meyer, Elard Hugo, 3459
Meyer, Johann Friedrich von, 6435
Meyer, Kuno, 4456
Meyer, Lodewigk, Spinoza (Baruch) and, 8682
Meyer-Ochsner, Heinrich, 730, 731
Meyers-Briggs Type Indicator (MBTI), 7476, 7477
Meykaṇṭār (Hindu theologian), **5999–6000,** 8976
Meykaṇṭaśāstra (Śaiva canon), 9443–9444
Civaṉāṉapōtam (Meykaṇṭār) in, 5999
in Śaiva Siddhanta, 8042
Meykaṇṭa Tēvar, Śaiva Siddhanta and, 8042
Meyrink, Gustav, 348
Mezgana (deity), in Qemant religion, 2573
Mhānubhāv sect, Ṛddhipur as pilgrimage site for, 7978
Mhlakaza (Xhosa chief), 7444
Mhlanga ritual, in Swazi religion, 8897
Mḥrm (sanctuary), *ḥaram* and *ḥawṭah* and, 3776–3777
MI. *See* Moabite Inscription
Miami religion (North America)
religious societies of, 6685
transvestite visionaries ("whitefaces") in, 6686
Miao (Hmong), funeral rites of, 3236, 3237
Miao (temple), 9056–9057
Miaodao (Chan nun), 1524
Miaofa lianhua jing su (Buddhist text), 1271
Miaofa lianhua jing su (Daosheng), 2218
Miaofa lianhua jing wenzhu (Zhiyi), 9175–9176
Miaofa lianhua jing xuanyi (Zhiyi), 9175, 9176
Miaohui (temple festival), 1620
Miao Shan (narrative figure), 3344
Miaoshengding jing (Buddhist text), 9174
Miaoying Monastery (Buddhist temple), 9048
Micah (biblical book), 879, 6000–6001
Aaron in, 1
Isaiah compared with, 6001
messianism in, 5975
Miriam in, 6062
oracles of doom in, 6000–6001
pesher of, 7064, 7065
salvation in, 6000–6001
Micah (prophet), **6000–6001,** 7436
Isaiah and, 6000–6001
on Levites, 5420
life of, 6000
on morality, 7652
Miccosukee (Mikasuki) people (North America), 6691
Green Corn Dance of, 6694
Michael (angel)
cult of, 347
as dragon slayer, 2432
Michael, Émile, 2396
Michael Cerularios (patriarch of Constantinople)
excommunication of, 7877
filioque doctrine and, 8156
Humbert of Silva Candida excommunicated by, 2586
Michaëlis, Sebastian, 2315
Michaelmas, in Balto-Finnic areas, 3108
Michael Psellus. *See* Psellus, Michael
Michaels, Eric, 639
Michaelson, Truman, 6670
Michael the Great (patriarch), Syriac Orthodox Church and, 8939
Michael VII Ducas (Byzantine emperor), 7467
Michael VIII Palaeologus (Byzantine emperor), 2587
excommunication by Pope Martin IV, 2042
at Lyons council, 2042
Michalowski, Piotr, on Enlil, 2799
Michel, Anneliese, 3506, 3507
Michel, Patrick, 6246
Michelangelo
Jesus' phallus in works of, 7082
Sistine Chapel of, 4346
Creation of Adam, 30
iconography of, 8755
reality in, 53
Michelet, Jules, on witchcraft, 6871
Michibizhii, in Anishinaabe religion, 368
Micmac people
calendar, 1353
shape shifting in mythology of, 8301
Microcosm. *See* Macrocosm and microcosm
Micrography, Hebrew, **1371–1372,** vol. 14 color insert
calligraphy *vs.,* 1369
Micronesia and Micronesian religions, **6001–6013**. *See also* Oceania; *specific islands*
afterlife in, 6007
ancestors in, 6003, 6005, 6007, 6010–6011
birth rites in, 7807
Christianity, 7297
colonialism in, 6001–6002, 6008
cosmologies in, 2004–2007, 6002–6004
dance in, 6007
deities of (*See also specific deities*)
inactivity of, 6010
types of, 6003–6004
diversity in, 2004, 6001, 6002, 6008
divination in, 6004–6005
fertility in, 6005–6006
gender in, **3395–3400**
geographic boundaries of
debate over, 6001
origins of, 6001
geology in, 6002
kinship in, 5183
magic in, 6008
medicine in, 6005
music in, 6264–6265
myths of, **6009–6013**
ancestors in, 6010–6011
charter, 6002–6003
creation, 6004, 6009–6010
fire and technology in, 6012
land and food in, 6011–6012
trickster, 6003, 6011
as Oceanic cultural area, 6784
overview of, **6001–6009**
paradise in, 6985–6986
practitioners or leaders of, 6007–6008
rituals in, 6004–6007
Roman Catholicism, and rituals, 6007
sacred and taboo in, 6008
sacred places in, 6004
spirit possession in, 6003, 6004, 6005
spirits in, 2007, 6002–6004, 6007
transculturation of, 9320–9325
transmigration in, 9327
Western influences on, variation in, 6001–6002
women in, **3395–3400**
role in rituals, 6005
Micropaedia, 2784
Mictlan (river), 7863
Mictlantecuhtli (deity), 150
and Quetzalcoatl, 7557
Middle Ages
belief in demons in, 2278
Carnival in, 1440, 4218
Christianity in, 1689–1690
All Souls Day, 2229
church architecture in, 793–794, 9265
dance in, 2136, 2153
gender in, 3359–3360
healing and medicine in, 3845–3846
iconography of, 4345–4346, 9265
Jewish persecution in, 7055–7056
justification in, 5040–5041
Kempe (Margery) on, 5110
liturgical use of *Psalms* in, 7464
merit in, 5876–5877
nuns during, 6763–6764
papacy in, 6967–6971
persecution of heretics in, 7061
poetry of, 7218–7219
priesthood in, 7402–7403
relics in, 7689–7690
religious and political power in, 7254
sacraments, changes to, 7960–7961
theology in, 9134, 9136
views of desire in, 2308
church membership in, 1777
drama in, 2437, 2467–2471
dualism in, 2513–2514
encyclopedic works of, 2783
faith in, 2425, 2426
geomancy in, 3437
Gnosticism in, 3514, 3522
heresy in, 3927–3928
historiography in, 4038
initiation in, 4479
Islam in, 4562–4563
on Christianity, 7242–7243
ḥājj in, 7157
Judaism in, 4860–4862, 4979–4982
on Christianity, 7234
circumcision in, 7819
definition of, 4970
definition of medieval, 4970
developments in, 5011–5013
ethical literature of, 4911–4912
exile in, 2922
expulsion and resettlement in, 5013–5014
worship in, 9808
yeshovot in, 9883–9884
Zionism in, 9977–9978
law in, **5336–5338**
Magen David in, 5558
magic in, **5577–5580**
Manichaeism in, 5667–5668
disappearance of, 3514
music in, 6308–6309
nature in, 6432–6433
necromancy in, 6452
Neoplatonism in, 6475
origin of bioethics in, 939
perception of artists in, 4283
sacred geography in, 3434, 3435–3436

Scholasticism in, 8174–8175
scientific history and, 8181–8182
spells in, 8677
superstition, views on, 8865–8866
syncretism in, 8933
tales of boats in, 991
Tamil religions in, 8975–8977
universities in, Scholasticism and, 8174–8175
witchcraft in (*See also* Witch hunts and trials)
spells in, 8677
women in, rites of passage of, 7802
Zoroastrianism in, 10003–10004
Middle Babylonian period, Dagan in, 2126
Middle East and Middle Eastern religions. *See also* Near East; *specific countries and religions*
academic study of religion in, **8780–8784**
Christianity, **1672–1677**
contemporary crisis in, 1675–1677
non-Muslim status in Muslim countries, 1673–1674
plurality in, 1672–1673
Roman Catholicism, 1673
social and political dynamics of, 1674–1675
dance in, 2148–2149
emigration from, 1676
Islam
jihād doctrine in, 4919–4920
waqf in, 9678
Judaism
to 1492, **4988–4995**
ecstatic Qabbalah in, 7537
emigrants from, 4985
origins of, 4988
since 1492, **4995–5002**
music in, **6275–6278**
New Year festival in, 6592
popular healing practices in, **3834–3839**
religious broadcasting in, 7713, 7714
secularization in, 8219
Middle Platonism, 6474, 7188–7190
Aristotle interpreted by, 7189
Christian, 7190–7191
comparative theology of, 9128
on Demiurge, 7188–7189
eclecticism of, 7188
gnosis (knowledge) in, 3508
and Hermetism, 7190
on Platonic forms, 7189
on *Timaeus* (Plato), 7188, 7189
on World Soul, 7189
Middle Stone Age. *See* Mesolithic Period
Middleton, John, 117
Middle Volga
animism in, 4616
Christianity in, 4616, 4617–4618
Islam in, **4612–4620** (*See also* Tatars, in Middle Volga)
and persecution, 4617, 4619
Sufism, 4616, 4618–4619
Middle Way (Buddhist principle), 1073, 1119, 1296
Kamalaśīla on, 5070–5071
societal influence of, 8463
Middle world
in Jainism (*See Madhyaloka*)
in Khanty religion, 5120–5121
in Mansi religion, 5120–5121
Middot (exegetical principles). *See* Biblical exegesis, Jewish views
Mide secret society, 4308
Midewiwin (Great Medicine Society)
in Anishinaabe religion, 370
in drama, 2460–2461
iconography of, 4308
shamanism and, 8289
Miðgarðsormr (serpent), 9165, 9426
Mīdhuṣī (deity), 7934
Midimu masked dance, 2140
Midrash, **6013–6023**
aggadic, 6014–6017
Cain and Abel in, 1345
composition of, 6017–6018
contemporary scholarship on, 6019
critical editions of, 6019
definitions of, 5485
feminism and, 6021
as folklore, 6020
goals of, 6016
God in, 3547–3548, 6016
attributes of, 614
names for, 3547–3548
halakhah and, 3748
halakhic, 6014–6015
as history *vs.* literature, 6020
Hoffmann (David), studies of, 4077
humor in, 4196
Israel in, 6016–6017
at Kairouan, 4989–4990
meanings of, 6013–6014
as narrative, 6021
orality of, 6020
origins of, 6014, 6019
postmodern literary theory and, 5487–5488
principal compilations of, 6018
Psalms in, 7465
in rabbinic Judaism, 4976
Rashi's use of, 7620
Samaritan, 8069, 8070
Shim'on bar Yoh'ai, compilations by, 8347
soul in, 8557
subcategories of, 6020–6021
suffering in, 8805, 8806
themes of, 6016–6017
Torah in, 6017
Torah personified in, 4079
translations of, 6019–6020
visiting the sick in, 3828–3829
Midrash dance, in Western religions, 2136
Midrash ha-gadol, 4991, 6018
Midrash ha-ne'elam (*Zohar* section), 9984
Midrashim, 868–869, 889
riddles in, 6987
Midrash Rabbah, 6018
Midrash Tanḥuma', holiness of Jerusalem and the Temple in, 7983
Midrash Tehillim, 6018
Midwinter festival, in Iroquois religion, 4541–4542, 4543
Midwives
African
as healers, 3819
in Ndebele birth ritual, 7804
Egyptian, as class of healer, 3836
Mesoamerican, 7811–7812
South American, 3418
Miechow, Mathias de, 3110
Mieder, Wolfgang, 6976
Miescher, Johann Fredriech, 2908–2909
Miettienen, Timo, 3104
Mif' alot Elohim (Abravanel), 17
Mighty Stories, Dangerous Rituals (Anderson and Foley), 7858
Migration, **6023–6026**. *See also* Immigration
of African Americans, 6418
in Aztec religion, 718, 5890, 5937
of Christians, 6023–6024
in Crusades, 6023
in globalization, 3500–3501
of Indians into Southeast Asia, 4011
of Mandaeans, 5634–5635, 5638
of Maoris, 5679, 5682
of Marranos, 5721
megaliths and, 5826–5827
of Mennonites, 5860
in millenarianism, 6031
of Mormons, 6023, 6193, 6194
of Muslims, 6023–6024
in conquests, 6023
to Medina, 6223
of North American Indians, Anishinaabe, 368
religious motives for, 6023–6024
secular motives for, 6024–6025
of Sikh women, 3337–3338
in Southeast Asia, 8647
tribal, 7716–7717
Migration des symboles, la (Goblet d'Alviella), 3537
Mi 'gyur dpa sgron, 7869
Mi 'gyur dpa sgron, Rje btsun, 1232
Mihardja, Achdiat Karta, 3078
Miḥnah (Inquisition)
Mu'tazilah in, 6319
traditionalists *vs.* rationalists and, 3760, 3761
Miḥrāb (prayer niche), 4396, 4608, 4634, vol. 5 color insert
Mihrijja branch of Manichaeism
in Central Asia, 5668
origins of, 5668
Mijiao Buddhism. *See* Zhenyan Buddhism
Mikado (Japanese emperor), divine origin of, 5157
Mikagura (music), 6300
Mikagurauta (Nakayama), 9082, 9083
Mikalson, Jon D., 7327
Mikannagi (priestess), 7411
Mikhah. *See* Micah
Mikhailov, Georgi, 9169
Miki, Nakayama, 6573
Mikkyō, 2801
Miklouho-Maclay, Baron
on cargo cults, 1417
cargo cults and, 1418
Mi'kmaq Indians (Canada), 9299, 9300, 9302
Miko, 2454, 4795, 7411
Mikokagura (dance), 6300
Mikom iyool movement (Africa), 1511
Míl, Sons of, 1489
Milagros (charms of body parts), sympathetic magic in, 3812
Milal wa Nihal studies ("Sects and Heresies"), in comparative religion, 8780–8781
Milan, Edict of (313), 6966, 7723
Mi la ras pa (Milarepa), **6026–6028**
biography of, 9189–9190
in Bka' brgyud pa (Kagyu) order, 6026
as cultural hero, 1225
disciples of, 6027–6028
disobedience of, 6778
followers of, 1153, 1230
Gtsang smyon Heruka on, 6027
Hevajra Tantra and, 3966
holy sites of
in Nepal, 7262
as pilgrimage sites, 7167
life of, 6026–6027
magic practiced by, 6027

Mi la ras pa (Milarepa)
continued
Mar pa and, 5715–5716, 6027
music of, 6027–6028, 6252
names of, 6026–6027
Nā ro pa and, 1215, 6415
on *mahāmudrā,* 5597–5598
ordeals of, 8713
as saint, 8037
Sgam po pa and, 8255
and shamanism, 3155
writings on, 6027, 6028
Milcom (deity), popular worship in Israel, 3157
Miles, Howard, 677
Miles, Margaret R., 502, 3313, 6742
Milesian system of numerology, 272, *273*
Míl Espáine, 1488
Miletus, sacred law of, omophagia in, 6823
Milfoil divination, 1583–1584
Milgrom, Jacob, 7512–7513, 7514
Milhamot ha-shem (Maimonides), 5612
Mīlī, Mubārak al-, 4589
Milik, J. T., 902
Milikofsky, Yaakov David, 9382
Milikowsky, Chaim, 6019
Milindapañha (Buddhist text), 1199, 1285, 1298
ghosts in, 3477
Militancy
in Christianity, 2889, 2890, 2892
in Judaism, 4985
in religious nationalism, 7791
revival and renewal activities described by, 7784
Military
Hellenic, homosexuality in, 4112–4113
Hittite Soldiers Oath, 2099
Jehovah's Witnesses and, 4823
sacrifice by, to Eros, 2832
Salvation Army, military structure of, 8063
Military orders. *See also* Knights Templar
ascectic *akhāḍā* in India, 8021
Crusades and, 2077
Militz, Annie Rix, 6584
on ascension, 1782
Christian Science Theological Seminary and, 4128
Milk, 847
in Hinduism, narrative of churning of the ocean of milk, 4013
kashrut laws on, 5106–5107
in Ndembu religion, 6446
as offering, in Islam, 5434
as sacrifice, 7998
Mil'kovich (surveyor), 5709
Milk tree, 9336
Milky Way
as center of heaven, 6886
discovery of, 2031
in ethnoastronomy, 2863
in Inca religion, 4412
as ladder to heaven, 8871
Nile River associated with, 7861
in North American Indian religions, 6651, 6703, 6722
as semen, 8871
and stars as land of the dead, 8733
in Ungarinyin religion, 9460
Mill, John Stuart, 5368, 6618, 7339, 7341
Millenarianism (millennialism), **6028–6042**. *See also* Eschatology; Soteriology
in Adventist theology, 8235
in Amazonian nativistic movements, 6576
apocalypse compared with, 410
avertive apocalypticism, 6547–6548
Besant's (Annie), 844, 846
of Branch Davidians, 1036, 1037, 1039
in Buddhism, 1100, 1331–1332, 6030, 9152
Chinese, 6039, 6040
forest dwellers and, 8080–8081
Maitreya in, 5620–5621, 6039, 6040
Bunyan's (John), 1322
cargo cults, **1414–1425**
cargo cults and, 6034
catastrophic (apocalypticism), 6545–6546, 6564
in Chinese religion, **6038–6042**
Golden Age in, 6030, 6038
He Xiu's three stages of history and, 1575
Taiping rebels and, 4144
in Christianity
Christian Identity movement and, 1658
Servetus (Michael) on, 8232
colonialism and, 6514
conversion and, 7756
definition of, 6028
definitions of, 6517, 6544–6545
enthusiasm in, 2808
the Family and, 2987
followers in, 6547
of Franciscans, 5915–5916
Golden Age and, 3628–3629, 6030
in Gorakhpurians' interpretation of Ghandi, 8800
and history, Christian views of, 4054–4055
increase in 1990s, 6524
interpretive theories on, 7787–7789
Irving's (Edward), 4544
in Islam, 6030
in Africa, 107
in Bābism, 8308–8309
in Shaykhīyah movement, 8308
Jehovah's Witnesses, 4821, 4822, 4823
leadership in
charismatic, 6546–6547
secondary, 6547
Luther (Martin) rejecting, 159
"managed," 6549
migration and, 6031
in Millerite movement, 8235
movements in, 6031–6036
explanations for, 6033–6035
patterns of, 6035–6036
phases of, 6032
types of, 6032–6033
Myalism in Jamaica, 1437
nativist movements, 6547
New Age movement and, 6495, 6496
in new religious movements, 6513, 6517, **6544–6551,** 6563–6564
in North American Indian religions, 6718
overview of, **6028–6038**
progressive, 6546, 6564
Rastafarian, 1438
repentance and, 7756
revival and renewal activities in, 7785–7787
revolutionary, 6549, 7791, 7792
rituals in, 7843
in Sai Baba movement, 8028–8029
secular ideologies of, 8527
Shabbateanism and, 8260
significance of, 6036
soteriology and, 8528
in Southeast Asia, traditional religion and, 8648
study of, 6524–6525
tensions with society, 6548
thought of, 6028–6031
time in, 6029
in Transcendental Meditation, 9291–9292
of Unarians, 9448
in United States, 1715
civil religion and, 1814
utopia in, 6030–6031, 6036
utopianism and, 9493
and violence, 6545, 6546, 6548–6549, 6552
women in, 6034
Millennial Dawn (Russell), 4820
Millennial Harbinger (journal), 2365
Campbell (Alexander) and, 1377
Millennialism. *See* Millenarianism
Millennium, definition of, 6028
Millennium World Peace Summit of Religious and Spiritual Leaders, 2613
Miller, Albert G., 80
Miller, David, on monotheism, 6161
Miller, David L., on games, 3267
Miller, Dean A., 4464, 4465
Miller, Hugh, 9423
Miller, Mary Ellen, 5944
on Maya religion, 5886, 5943
on Mesoamerican ballgames, 750, 751
Miller, Perry, Earth First! influenced by, 2562
Miller, Timothy, 6527
Miller, William, 412–413, 1036, 6558
Seventh-day Adventism and, 8235
Millerite movement
comets and, 8736
"great disappointment" in, 8235
and Shakers, defection to, 8268
Seventh-day Adventism and, 8235
Millet, Kate, 3311, 7007–7008
Millet beer, in West African libations, 9719
Millet flour, in West African libations, 9719
Millet (nation) system, 1674, 1684
and Greek Orthodox Church, 3657
Milli Görüş movement, 4681
Million Man March, 5863
Nation of Islam in, 6420
Millon, Clara, 5899
Millon, René, 5898, 5901
Mills, Edgar W., 5386
Mills, Kenneth, 502
Mills, Kevin, 5488
Mills, Margaret, 3145
Milman, H. H., 6105
Milne, William, 6196
Miltiades (pope), 2416
Milton, John
on divine providence, 7791
on freedom of choice in salvation, 3205
Hermes Trimegistos cited by, 3950
literary accomplishments of, 5471–5472
Paradise Lost, 30, 3525
images used in, 6985
influence of, 5478
Shelley (Mary) references to, 3059
poetic style of, 7204, 7220–7221
as Protestant writer, 7459, 7521
Milvian Bridge, Battle of the, conversion of Constantine and, 1688–1689
Mīmāṃsā school of Indian philosophy, **6042–6043**
atheism in, 580
and classical Hinduism, development of, 3997
development of, 6042
dharma in, 6042

hermeneutics of, 5345
īśvara in, 4752
on *karman*, 5094
mantras in, 5677
on *prāmāṇya*, 6773
origins of, 6042
subschools of, 6042–6043
truth in, 9371
unity and plurality in, 4421
Mīmāṃsā Sūtra (Jaimini)
Bādarāyaṇa in, 735
commentaries on, 2328
compilation of, 6042
dharma in, 2328
Mimana. *See* Karak
Mimbar (pulpit), 6208
Mimesis, in shamanism, 8278
Mímir (deity), in war with Vanir, 3449
Mimixcoa (mythic figures), 5935–5936
Mimnermus (poet), on sun, 8839
Mimosa tree, 9334
Min (deity), 301
Pan assimilated into, 6957
Reshef and, 7762
Minā (Saudi Arabia), as station of *ḥājj*, 7157, 7159
Minaeans, in Arabia, 443
Minakata Kumakusu, 9313
Mīnākṣī (deity), 3608
Minamata disease, 2638
Minamoto Yoritomo, 1335
Mīnanāth (Hindu guru), 3638
Minangkabau people (Sumatra), music of, 6289
Minar (tower), 9266
Minarets, in mosques, 6208, 6209
Minault, Gail, 3161
Mind. *See also* Consciousness; Epistemology
body-mind dualism, 4163
in Chinese philosophy
and Confucian Way, in Xunzi, 1573
universal mind, 1577, 1578
of wise man, in *Zhuangzi*, 1573
in Confucianism, 9673–9674, 9973
discipline of the, 8705
epigenetic, 8475
in Hinduism, in Upaniṣadic cosmology, 2016
Hocking (William Ernest) on, 4076
Hubbard (L. Ron) on, 8192
in Islamic philosophy, Ibn Sīnā on God as, 8570
in Korean philosophy, Neo-Confucianism and, 1931–1932
materialist views of, 5777
in New Age movement, disease and, 3850
Nicholas of Cusa on, 6610
in structuralism, 8759

Mind (journal), 5672
Mind, Neo-Confucian School of, sagehood in, 8037
Mind, Self, and Society (Mead), 7648–7649
"Mind, The" (Edwards), 2699
Mindaugas (Lithuanian prince), 773
Mind-body relation, neuroscience on, 6486–6487
Mind-body-spirit movement, 9788
Mind control. *See* Brainwashing
Mind Cure movement, 6582
Mindfulness
in Buddhist meditation, 5820
in eightfold path, 2738
Mind-heart, in Neo-Confucianism, 5540–5542
Mind *maṇḍala*, 5642
Mind of the Maker, The (Sayers), trinitarian theology in, 8142
Mindon Min (king), fifth Theravādin council and, 2038
Mind over Machine (Dreyfus), 510
Mind-to-mind transmission, 1524
Miner, Horace, on body symbolism, 4162
Minerals, transmutation of, Indian references to, 2557
Minerva (deity), **6043–6044**
Celtic parallels, 1484
Jupiter and, 5037
owl as symbol of, 6936
in triad, 7900, 7901, 9349
Mines, 5987–5988
Mingalazedi (stupa), 1135
Ming Chengzu (emperor), spirit tablets of, in Imperial Temple, 1912
Mingdao, Master, 1560
Ming dynasty (China), 1607–1609
Buddhism in, 1154, 1166–1167, 1255
Chan Buddhism, 1524
Zhuhong in, 9971–9972
Confucianism in, 1902–1903, 4336, 4338
temples in, 9060
court, and middle cults, 1913–1914
Daoism in, 2186–2188, 2201
divination in, 2372
Gu Yanwu and, 3718
Islam in, 4632
law in, 5353
martial arts in, 5734–5735
millenarianism in, 6040
Neo-Confucianism of, 2632
philosophy in, 1578
taiping in, 8961
Mingjiao, 1598
Mingkong (Buddhist monk), 1250
Ming Shizong (emperor)
imperial ancestors and, 1912
reforms of, 1911

Ming Taizong. *See* Ming Chengzu
Ming Taizu (Zhu Yuanzhang), 1607, 1608
spirit tablets of, in Imperial Temple, 1912
Mingtang (calendar house), seasons represented by walls in, 7984
Minhag (custom), rabbinic law and, 3750
Minḥah (prayer), 926, 4746
Minim (heretic), 7230
Minim, Ebionites identified with, 2595
Minima Moralia (Adorno), 3527
Mining
Australian Indigenous religions and, new movements in, 672–674
and New Guinea religions, 6507–6508
Minister as Diagnostician, The (Pruyser), 7486
Ministry, **6044–6046**. *See also* Clergy; Priesthood
African Americans in, 66, 68–69
definitions of, 6044
offices of, 6044, 6045
World Council of Churches report on, 1769, 6045
Minjung theology, 3035, 5236, 5441
Minnui. See Ordination, of rabbis
Minoan civilization
culture of, 37, 38
discovery of, 2894–2895
kingship in, 5166
language of, 37, 38
Minoan labyrinth, 5273–5274
Minoan-Mycenaean Religion and its Survival in Greek Religion, The (Nilsson), 38
Minoan religion, **37–43**
art depicting, *37, 38,* 38–40, *39*
deities of, 37–43 (*See also* specific deities)
character of, 38
gender-oriented patronage of, 38–39
Greek religion and, 38, 3664
vs. Mycenaean deities, 41–43
Evans (Sir Arthur) on, 37, 38, 40
iconography of, 4320–4321
Lady of the Animals in, 5280, 5282
libations in, 5433
light and darkness symbolism in, 5452
Nilsson (Martin P.) on, 38, 40
rituals of, 39–40
Minority populations
Jews as, 4861

martyrdom in, 5739–5740
Minority religions, media coverage of, 4964–4965
Minor Prophets, 879, 882
Minor Reformed Church of Poland. *See* Polish Brethren
Minoru, Sonoda, 2640
Minos (king), 165, 5273–5274
throne of, 5282
Minotaur, 6165
creation of, 5274
horns of, 5275
revenge of, 5278
Mintz, Moses (rabbi), 7580
Mintz, Sidney, 10025
Minucius Felix, 792
on idolatry, 4360–4361
on *lucerna extincta* rite, 8249
Minyan (quorum of ten), 9806
Minyas (Greek epic), 989
Minymaku Way (film), 642, 643
Mi pham rgya mtsho, 7869
Mippenei Hata'einu (because of our sins), as Holocaust paradigm, 4090–4091
Miqdash (sanctuary), *shekhinah* concept and, 8313
Miqlasijja branch of Manichaeism in Central Asia, 5668
origins of, 5668
Miqra', as scripture, 878, 1406
Miqra' (recitation), of scriptures, 8198
Miqra'ot gedolot (rabbinical textbook), 867
Miqsat Ma'ase Hatorah (scroll), 7514
Miqveh (ritual bath), 2398, **6046–6048,** 7928
purification in, 6046–6048
requirements for construction of, 6046–6047
women in, 6047
Mirabai (Hindu saint), **6048–6049**
absorbed with Kṛṣṇa's image, 859
and *Ādi Granth*, 3717
in *bhakti* poetry tradition, 3985
poetry of, 5254, 7207, 7211
Miracle on the Gorbals (Helpmann), 2162
Miracle plays, 2437
of Middle Ages, dance in, 2153
Miracles, **6049–6058**
Aristotle on, 481
by art, 497
attributed to Albertus Magnus, 232
attributed to imams, 4394–4395
in Buddhism, 6053
relics of the Buddha and, 7690–7691
chance and, 1528

Vol. 1: 1–610, Vol. 2: 611–1340, Vol. 3: 1341–2120, Vol. 4: 2121–2850, Vol. 5: 2851–3580, Vol. 6: 3581–4292, Vol. 7: 4293–5046, Vol. 8: 5047–5748, Vol. 9: 5749–6448, Vol. 10: 6449–7176, Vol. 11: 7177–7864, Vol. 12: 7865–8572, Vol. 13: 8573–9286, Vol. 14: 9287–10018, Appendix: 10019–10091

ENCYCLOPEDIA OF RELIGION, SECOND EDITION

Miracles ***continued***
in Christianity, 6053–6054, 6056
cult of saints and, 2082, 2083
disbelief in, 4846
God's role in, 3557
Gregory I on, 3688
of healing, 3843, 3846, 3847, 6053–6054, 6056, 8722
vs. magic, 5576
Strauss (David Friedrich) on, 8747
definition of, 6049
of Elijah, 2765, 2766
of Elisha, 2768
in Hellenistic religions, 3903, 3904–3905, 6050–6051
Hume (David) on, 4193
images and, 4390–4391
in indigenous religions, 6049–6050
in Islam, 2652, 6054
in Ashʿarīyah, 3564
vs. magic, 5584
of prophets *vs.* of Ṣūfī saints, 8815, 8821
of Jesus, 4850
in Judaism, Saʿadyah Gaon on, 7952
Kant (Immanuel) on, 5079
vs. magic
in Christianity, 5576
in Islam, 5584
materialism and, 6056–6057
modern perspectives on, **6055–6058**
overview of, **6049–6055**
paranormal experiences as, 6057–6058
quantum theory and, 8188
sacred *vs.* profane and, 7973
scientific study of, 6057–6058
witnesses of, 6049
Miʿrāj (ascent of Muḥammad), 523, 3127, 4713, **6058–6062**
iconography of, 6060
in Qur'ān, 6058–6059
interpretations of, 6060–6061
Masjid al-aqsa in, 6059, 6205
in narrative lore, 6059–6060
prayer in, 8056
ṣalāt (prayer) and, 8056
Mīr Dāmād
doctrine of *al-ishrāq* and, 2977
Ibn Sīnā's influence on, 4276
Mullā Ṣadrā and, 6231
Mire of Sin (B. D.), vol. 7 color insert
Mīr Findiriskī, 6231
Mirgeler, Albert, on holiness, semantics of, 4099
Miri (thought), 776
Miriam (prophet), 1, **6062,** 7435
Mirikus, Hermes as, 3937
Miriru (mururu) (*barnmarn* power), 9461
Miriuwung people (Australia), land claims of, 690
Mirkevet ha-mishneh (Abravanel), 17
Miroku. *See* Maitreya
Mirror of Simple Annihilated Souls (Porete), 6337
Mirrors, **6063–6065**
broken, 6064
Chinese, 6063, 6064
maṇḍalas and, 5645
divination by, 6064
in initiation ceremonies, 7796
in Japanese mythology, Amaterasu Ōmikami and, 280–281, 6063
moon and, 6174
Olmec, 6819
self-knowledge and, 6064–6065
Mīr Šawijti Xu (deity). *See* World-Overseeing Man
Mir Susne Xum (deity). *See* World-Overseeing Man
Miryam. *See* Miriam
Mīrzā Ḥusayn ʿAlī Nūrī. *See* Bahā' Allāh
Mīrzā Yaḥyā Nūrī. *See* Ṣubḥ-i Azal
"Miscellanies" (Edwards), 2699
Miserere (Rouault), 4348
Misfortune
in African religions
caused by gods and ancestors, 89
caused by witches and sorcerers, 90
cults of affliction and, 60–61
Kongo religion, 5221
Ndembu, 6447
rituals for overcoming, 84
in Greek religion and mythology, causes of, 7756
in Japanese religions, 4797
protection against, vol. 9 color insert
in South American religions, gender and, 3418
Mishima Yukio, 3074, 9315–9316
Mishkāt al-anwār (Ibn al-ʿArabī), 4257
Mishkāt al-maṣābīḥ (Islamic text), gift giving in, 3485
Mishna berurah (Kagan), 5053
Mishnah (Jewish legal code), **6065–6068**. *See also* Talmud; Tosefta
Abbaye on, 3
Avot, Hillel's sayings in, 3981
canonization of, 9275
circle-drawer in, 1793
circumcision in, 7818–7819
commentaries on, 4989
compilation of, 6067–6068
'Aqiva' ben Yosef in, 441
Yehudah ha-Nasi' in, 6065
contents of, 6066–6067
context of, 6067–6068
creation of, 9881
divisions of, 6066–6067
Elʿazar ben ʿAzaryah in, 2743
Eliʿezer ben Hyrcanus in, suppression of, 2764
gambling in, 3262
Gamli'el the Elder in, 3270
healing in, 3829
history in, 7585–7586
Me'ir in, 5830
New Testament compared with, 6065–6066
as oral law, not scripture, 1406
oral Torah in, 6838
on Passover, 7004
priesthood in, 7399–7400
priests in, 5424
purity in, 7512
Rabbah bar Nahamani on, 7577
rabbinate in, 7584
in rabbinic Judaism, 4976–4977, 7583, 7585–7586, 7589
Rava' on, 3, 7631
Rav on, 7630
reaction against, 7586
on repeal of decrees, 3750
resurrection in, 152
sages in, 7585
scapegoat in, 8144
on scripture in the synagogue, 8922
Shemu'el the Amora, role of, 8318
Sherira' Gaon on, 8320
Shimʿon bar Yoh'ai, role of, 8346
significance of, 6065–6066
suffering in, 8806
tannaitic texts in, 8983
Temple procedures in, 925, 926, 927, 930, 931
vows in, 9641
women in, 3352
Yehudah ha-Nasi' and, 9881
Yoḥanan ben Zakk'ai and, 9903
Yom Kippur in, 7928
Mishnah, kingship in, 10062
Mishneh Torah (Maimonides), 3549, 4980, 5615–5616
Arbaʿah ṭurim and, 9864
classification in, 5616
codification in, 9236
codificatory form of, 5616
halakhah and philosophy fused in, 5616
health and healing in, 3829, 3830
language and style of, 5616
law code in, 3745
Luria's (Shelomoh) objections to, 5533
Noahic laws in, 3753
scope of, 5616
Mishpaṭ ʿivri ("Hebrew Law") school, *halakhah* analysis by, 3747
Mishra, Veer Bhadra, 2623
Misimbwa (hero gods), in Soga religion, 2575
Misinghalikun (deity), 5515
Miskito Indians, Christianity, conversion to, 1700
Misogyny
in Buddhism, 3331
feminism on, 3312
vs. androcentrism, 3299
as key concept, 3311
in Judaism
rabbinic, 3352
in wisdom literature, 9756
in witchcraft accusations, 9773–9774
Mišpatim (casuistic laws), 4728
Mis people
in Khanty religion, 5121
in Mansi religion, 5121
Mīs pī (opening the mouth), 4380, 4381, 4389
Miśra, Vācaspati, 6774
Miśra, Viśvambhara. *See* Caitanya
Missionary societies
in evangelicalism, 2888
in Oceania, 6790–6791
Mission of Sōtō Zenshū (Brazil), 1188
Missions, **6068–6087**. *See also* Conversion; Crusades
Buddhist, 1099, **6077–6082**
Aśoka and, 9145–9146
in China, 1093, 1163, 6072
vs. Christian missions, 6078
Ciji (Compassion Relief), **1787–1790**
development of, 6078–6080
in Korea, 1170, 1173
modern, 6080–6081
in Mongolia, 6142
origins of, 6077
premodern, 6077–6078
reception of, 6072
social and cultural elements of, 6070–6071
in Sri Lanka, 1090, 1093
in Thailand, 9094
Western writings on, 6077
Christian (*See* Christian missions)
cultural imperialism in, 6071
definition of, 6082
Druze, 2503
dynamics of, 6070–6071
among elites *vs.* people, 6072–6073
Ethiopian Church and, 2861
folk religions and, 3152
funding for, 6074
Hindu, 6070
to the West, 2342–2343
home *vs.* foreign, 6069–6070
institutional support for, 6073–6074
Islamic
in Africa, 107–108, 4583
and African Americans, 71, 72
Arabic culture in, 6071
in Central Asia, 4629

vs. Christian missions, 6083
da'wah and, 2225–2226
from Aḥmadiyah, 72
imperialism and, 6071
Ismāʿīlī, 4572
in Melanesia, 5832
of Muʿtazilah, 6318
Shīʿīte, 4583
Islamic restrictions on, 1674
modern, 6074–6075
Mongolian empire and, 1606
motivations for, 6069–6070, 6085
museum items from, 6246
origins of, 6069–6070
reactions to, 6071–6073
resistance to, 6072–6073
salvation in, 6070
social implications of, 6070–6071
by societies *vs.* churches, 6074
of Summit Lighthouse, 1782
and transculturation, 9293
translation of scriptures and, 8203
types of missionaries in, 6073–6074
universality of vision of, 6069–6071
Mississippian culture, influence on North American Indian religions, 6651, 6654
Mississippi Freedom Democratic Party, 10039
Mistè. *See Lwa*
Mistletoe, 774
in death of Baldr, 3455–3456
Mistress of the Animals. *See* Lady of the Animals
Mitanni kingdom. *See* Hurrian religion
Mitchell, Basil, 5499
Mitchell, Henry H., 6977
Mitchell, Stephen, 7484
Mithāq, al- (Druze text), 2503
Mithra (deity), **6087–6088**
as *ahura,* 205
in Armenian religion, 491, 492
and ascension, 522
Asklepios and, 552
ateshgah and, 569
bull killed by, 6088, 6089, 6090, 6091
as celestial light, 8838
Chinvat Bridge and, 1647
functions of, 6087
incarnation of, 4416
khvarenah of, 4537, 5139–5140
lightning of, 7603
morality and, 7651
mystery religion of (*See* Mithraism)
origins of, 4536
as personification of "contract," 4461
Roman cult of (*See* Mithraism)
in Roman religion, 7917
Shamash identified with, 8838
Sol identified with, 8511
Mithraeum (Sanctuary of Mithra), 6089–6092
discovery of, 2093
Mithraic Birthday of the Invincible Sun, 7654
Mithraism, 4482, 6087, **6088–6093**
Cumont (Franz) on, 2093, 6088, 6089, 6090
and Dacian Riders, 2123–2124
deification in, 2250
ecstasy in, 2678
Hellenistic attitude toward, 3908
history of study of, 6088–6089
initiation into, 6332
key symbolism in, 5116–5117
Mercurius as herald of the sun god, 3937
music in, 6305
as mystery religion, 6090, 6331–6332
origins of, 6089–6090, 6331
in Rome, 7917
Sol Invictus and, 8511
sources on, 6088, 6331
spread of, 6087, 6331
in Roman Empire, 8840
syncretism in creation of, 8936
Mithrakāna festival, 6087, 6089–6090
Mithras. *See* Mithra; Mithraism
Mithridates, Flavius, and Christian Qabbalah, 7535
Miti e leggende (Pettazzoni), 115, 7075–7076
Mitigated dualism, 1456–1457
Mitima (collaborators), 4411
Mītiskais folklorā, literatūrā un mākslā (Kursīte), 771
Mitler, Matt, 2476
Mitnagdic (anti-Hasidic), 9379
Mitnaggdim, ethics of, 4915
Mito Confucianism, in Japan, 4789
Mitotes, peyote at, 406
Mitra (deity). *See also* Mithra
as Āditya, 9556
as guardian of *ṛta,* 3001, 7352
Dumézil (Georges) on, 937, 7352
inspiration given by, 4509
meaning of, 8838
Varuṇa and, 9524
Mitra, Rajendralal, 4446
Mitsvot (religious commandments)
in rabbinic Judaism, 4977–4978
Rosenzweig (Franz) on, 4905
Mitsvot/mitzvah (commandments), 4981. *See also* Ten Commandments
bar and bat mitzvah (*See* Bar mitzvah; Bat mitzvah)
circumcision as, 7818
Fackenheim (Emil) on Holocaust and new commandment, 4092
Habad Hasidism on, 3792
relational discipline and, 8706
Saʿadyah Gaon on, 7952
Miura Ayako, 3073
Miwok people (California), knotted ropes of, 5197
Mixcoatl (deity), 5906
in Huastec religion, 5910
Mixcoatl, Andrés, 5919, 5920
Mixcoatl Camaxtli (deity), 5909
Mixteca (shrine), 5911–5912
Mixtec religion (Mexico)
afterlife in, 151
ancestors in, 5911
calendar in, 5887, 5911
codices of, 1360, 5887
in colonial period, translation of Christian doctrine for, 5917
creation in, 5911
deities of, 5887, 5911
drama in, 2464, 2466
fertility god in, 9213
funeral rites in, 3243
iconography of, 4313–4314
pre-Columbian, 5887
in Postclassic period, 5911–5912
priesthood in, 5912
rituals in, 5911
temples in, 5911–5912
worldview of, 5887
Miyabi, 51
Miyanmin people, cannibalism among, 1404
Miyaza (local parish), 7411
Miyazaki, Hayao, 3097
Miyazawa Kenji, 3072, 3073
Mizainhpa-zain nats (spirits), 1330, 1331
Mizan (balance), nature in, 2604
Mīzān fī Tafsīr al-Qurʾān, al- (Ṭabāṭabāʾī), 8945–8946
Mizhavu (drum), 2448
Mizrach (indicator of direction toward Jerusalem), vol. 3 color insert
Mizraḥi
Bar-Ilan (Meʾir) as leader of, 788
Mohilever's (Shemuʾel) influence on, 6113
Reines (Yitsḥaq Yaʿaqov) as leader of, 7681
in Zionism, 4906, 9980–9981
Mizuko kuyō, 3348
Mkhas grub rje school of Buddhism, 1217, 1218
Mkhas pa 'jug pa'i sgo (Sakya Paṇḍita), Sankritic ideals in, 8051
Mlanjeni (prophet), 7444
Mlk (offering). *See Mulk*
Mnemonics, 5851
Mngaʾ bdag Sems dpaʾ chen po, 1232
Moabite Inscription (MI) (Moabite text), 6093–6095
Moabite religion (Middle East), **6093–6095**
deities of, 6093–6095 (*See also* Kemosh)
sacrifices in, 6094–6095
sources on, 6093
Moatsu feast, 187
Moazzam (emperor), Singh (Gobind) and, 8409
Mobandi (Pygmy ritual), 7524
Mobeds (magi). *See* Magi, Zoroastrian
Moberly, Robert C., on atonement, 597
Mobility, 10048
Moby Dick (Melville), 3059
Moccasin Game, 405
Mochizuki Shinkō, 1314
Mockery. *See* Humor
Mocovi people (South America), religion of, 8637
Moctezuma I (Aztec king)
decrees of, 5173
restructuring of Aztec government by, 5173
Moctezuma II (Aztec king), 3013
abdication of, 5174
Cortés (Hernán) and, 5174, 5914
diviners and, 5909
Flowery Wars and, 4186, 4187
pomp surrounding, 5173
Moctezuma's oracle, 1468
Modalistic trinitarianism, Servetus (Michael) and, 8232
Modal logic, 6961–6962, 7123
Mode
in Byzantine musical theory, 6306
in Greek musical theory, 6303
Modekngei movement, 6797
Modekngei religion (Micronesia), 6005
Model emperors (Wu Di), 1627
Moderate dualism, 2507–2508, 2509, 2513
Moderation, of Elʿazar ben ʿAzaryah, 2743
Modern, definition of, 6108
Modern Art: Nineteenth and Twentieth Centuries (Schapiro), 53
Modern Churchmen's Union, 6105
Modern dance
Central European, 2159–2160

Modern dance ***continued***
cultural identity in, 2163–2164
first generation of, 2157–2160
second generation of, 2160–2161
Modern India and the Indians (Monier-Williams), 4447
Modernism, **6095–6108,** 6467. *See also* Enlightenment, the
anti-Semitism, 4085
Catholic, 6102, 6106, 7878–7879
Loisy (Alfred) on, 5506–5507
religious experience in, 7739
Catholic antagonism toward, 2670, 4944
Christian, **6102–6108**
vs. cultural change, 6109
definitions of, 6095, 6102, 6108
in evangelicalism, 2888–2889
expulsion for, 2938
in Finnish Poetry, Haavio (Martti) and, 3723
Gnosticism and, 3526–3527
Hügel (Friedrich von) and, 4150
Islamic, **6095–6102**
20th-century figures in, 6097–6098
challenges to, 6101
definition of, 6095
on gender, 3365, 3369–3370
as Islamic reformation, 6100–6101
on Qur'ān, 6096–6097
progressive Islam in, 6098–6100
on religious authority, 6097
Smith (Wilfred Cantwell) on, 8450
in Southeast Asia, 8653
Westernization and, 6096–6097
Jewish thought and, 4899–4910
liberal Protestantism in, 6103–6106
vs. modernization, 6108
Nietzsche's critique of, 7245
Schmidt (Wilhelm) on, 8168
use of term, 6102
Modernism: Its Failures and Its Fruits (Petre), 7070
Modernity, **6108–6112**
authority in, 5397–5398
Buddhism and, Southeast Asian, 9833
Christianity and (*See also* Political theology, Christian)
European, 1692–1694
cultural change and, 6109
definitions of, 6108–6109
fundamentalism and, 6111
Heschel (Abraham Joshua) on, 3962
Hobbes (Thomas) and, 4075
homo religiosus vs., 4110–4111
hope and, 4127
impact on religion, 6109–6111
as interregnum, 5160
in Islamic education, 6097
Judaism and, 4982–4985
Conservative Judaism and, 1957
Near Eastern, 4999–5001
Orthodox Judaism, 6902, 6905, 8518
"organized religion" and community in, 1863–1864
reification of term, 6109
religion and, 7700–7701
analytical psychology, 5031–5032
economics in, 2674–2677
origins of, 10047
Weber (Max) on, 9711–9712
responses to, 6110–6111
rites of passage in, 7799–7800, 7802–7803
liminality in, 5461–5462
in Oceanic religions, 7809–7810
rituals in, 7846
social structure of, Weber (Max) on, 5369
and study of religion, emergence of, 8763
and tradition, 9279
warfare and, 1694
women's movement in, 3297
Modernization. *See also* Secularization
cargo cults and, 1424
definition of, 6108
games and, 3267
implicit meaning of, 9931
in Japanese study of religion, 8778
vs. modernism, 6108
money cults and, 9324
Nahḍa movement among Arabs, 1674–1675
schism and, 8152
secularization and, 6109
social classes fragmented by, 8484
Sufism *vs.,* 8824
Modernization theories, religious and economic change in, 2675–2676
Modern Man in Search of a Soul (Jung), consciousness in, 1949
Modern Mythology (Lang), 5299
Modern Religious Movements in India (Farquhar), 4447
Modern Spiritualism. *See* Spiritualism
Modern Synthesis, 2909, 2919
Modern Thought (publication), 3096
Modesto, Ruby, 2488
Modesty
clothing and, 1831–1832, 1833, 1836
in Islam, humor and, 4212
Modimo (supreme being), 9388
Modoc people (North America), creation story of, 6713
Modron (deity), 1490
Moehler, Johann Adam, 805
Moerdowo, R., 2451
Moesi tribe (Thracian), 9168
Mo'etset Gedolei ha-Torah, 194–195, 196
Mofa. See Mappō
Moffat, Robert, on Tswana concept of God, 8656
Moffatt, Tracey, 3097
Mogadishu
sultanate of, 4606
urban nature of, 2566
Moggaliputtatissa (Buddhist monk), **6112,** 9145, 9146
Abhidharma texts attributed to, 10021
Pāṭaliputra council and, 2037
Moghila, Petr. *See* Petr Moghila
Mogk, Eugen, 3459
Moha (error), 748
Mohamed, Khalid, 3098
Mohammad Ershad, Hussain, 830
Mohammed, Druse, 4687
Mohammed: The Man and His Faith (Andrae), 945
Mohammed, W. Deen, 6563
Mohanty, Chandra Talpade, 3314, 3315
Mohanty, J. N., 4420
Mohanty, Jitendranath, 6773
Mohave tribe (North America), dreams of, 2489, 6716
Mohawk religion. *See also* Caniengas Mohawk religion; Iroquois religion
ballgame played in, 753, 754, 755
poetry in, 7224, 7226
turtles in, 9407
Mohel (circumcision specialist), 7819
Mohenjaro-Daro (ancient city). *See also* Indus Valley religion
Indus Valley religion in, 3988–3989
Mohenjo-Daro (India), 4427, 4433, 4470, 4471–4472, 4473, 4474
water in, 7861
Moheyan (Buddhist scholar), 1152
Mohe zhiguan (Zhiyi), 1291, 9174, 9175, 9176, 9178
Mohilever, Shemu'el, **6113,** 9980
Mohism, founded by Mozi, 6217
Möhler, Johann Adam, **6113–6115**
on tradition and progress, 4032
Mo-ho-chih-kuan (Buddhist text), 5436
Moiety organization, kinship and, 5185
Moirai (goddesses of fate), 2984, 3002
chance and, 1527
individual names of, 3001, 9088
justice and, 7783
moon associated with, 3018
number symbolism and, 6747
role of, 968, 3000, 9088
weaving of, 9713
Moism, 1571, 1572, 1590
Moist Mother Earth (deity), in Slavic religion, 8437
Mojo religion (South America)
Alligator Jump dance in, 8583
jaguar cult in, 8582
Mokichi, Okada, 6574
Mokkha. See Mokṣa
Mǫkkurkálfi (clay warrior), 9166
Mokondi (Pygmy ceremony), 7524
Mokosh (deity), **6115**
Mokrida ritual, 6115
Mokṣa (release or liberation), 2793, 4415, 4925, **6115–6117**
and *svārāj* (self-rule), 3201
ascetic concern for, 857
avatāra theory and, 4001
as basic aim, 2305, 4423, 4428
bhaktimārga leading to, 856
Brahmā and, 1024
in Brahmanism, 9569
in Buddhism, 8739, 8740
Cārvāka rejecting, 4421
development of concept, 6115–6116
vs. dharma, 2621
eight limbs of Yoga to, 3998
as end of death, 2237, 7678
as epistemological, 8546
eschatology of, 2834
and fulfilling *dharma,* 853
Goddess as bestower of, 3999
gurūs and, 3713
in Advaita Vedānta, Śaṅkara on, 4003–4004
in Ārya Samāj, 516
in *Puruṣārthas* (four goals of humankind) in, 3996
in Śaiva Siddhānta, 8547
in Śaivism
epistemology of, 8417
in Kashmir Śaiva school, 4006
in Upaniṣads, 3993, 9544
in Jainism
laity of, 4770
self-discipline and, 8548
in Kevala Advaita, 9546
knowledge of *Bhagavadgītā* leads to, 852
Kṛṣṇa as guide to, 854, 6116–6117
Madhva on, 8547
mythic themes of, 4440, 4441–4442
origins of concept, 6115
paths to, 6116, 9276
Saṃnyāsa and, 8093
Śaṅkara on, 8105

in Sikhism, soul and, 8548–8549
soul and, 8544–8545
Mokṣadharma, prakṛti in, 7360–7361
Mokṣala (Buddhist translator), 1146
Mokša religion (Russia). *See* Mari and Mordvin religion
Mokshin, N. F., 5709
Mok'tak (drum), 6297
Mokugyō (drum), 2497
Mokusha. *See* Mokosh
Mokysha. *See* Mokosh
Molech. *See* Malik
Molech (offering), 4744
Molesmes, Benedictine community at, 1800
Mo Letters, 4853
Mo lha (female god), 9185
Molière, 2474
Molimo (Pygmy ritual), 7525
Molina, Cristóbal de, on Inca calendar, 1361–1362
Molina, Juan Ignacio, 5994
Molina, Luis de
on free will and predestination, 3204, 3208
on grace, 7001
as Pelagian, 7026
Molinism, 7001
Molinos, Miguel de
mysticism and, 6350
and Quietism, 6350, 7558
Molkho, Shelomoh
influence on Karo (Yosef), 5104
messianism of, 4998
Molko, David, 1033
Molko and Leal v. Holy Spirit Association, 1033
Moller, Martin, 1006
Moltmann, Jürgen
on God, 3559, 6161
on kingdom of God, 5153
political theology of, 7245
Molungu (deity), in Kamba religion, 2575
Moma (deity), 2311
fertility and, 8583
in Witóto religion, 8576–8577, 8870
Momaday, N. Scott, 702, 3090, 3093
"Gourd Dancer, The," 7225
House Made of Dawn, 3091, 7225
on knowledge, 5199
Mombaer, John, 7772
Mombasa
Christianity in, 2578
Islamic influence of, 2578
urban nature of, 2566
Moment, The (Kierkegaard), 5140–5141
Momigliano, Arnaldo, 6374
Mommsen, Theodor, 730, 731
on ancient religions, 5332
on Festschriften, 2993, 3041
on myth, 6367
Momo no Sekku (Girls' Day), 2411
Mon (Burma). *See* Mon people
Monachism. *See* Monasticism
Monarchic monotheism, 6159–6160
Monarchy
distinction from kingship, 5154, 5156
in Rome, 5167
Monasteries. *See also* Temples
architecture of, **6117–6121**
Buddhist
in caves, 1471–1472
Chan, 1523, 1524, 1604
Eisai in, 2741
Karma Gon, 5102
in Lao religion, 5314
natural settings of, 2629–2630
political support for, 6128–6129
role in community, 5348
rules of order of, 5348
Rumtek, 5103
in Thailand, 7720
Tsurphu, 5102
Christian
architecture of, 6117–6120
Ethiopian, 2861
origins of, 6117
women in, 2827–2828
as communities, 1863
components of, 6118–6119
Daoist, 2637–2638
definition of, 6117
Hindu, Advaita *maṭhas* established by Śaṅkara, 4004, 4005
Irish, manuscripts of, 1480
modern, 6120
silence in, 823
as subgroups, 1867–1868
work in, 824
Zen Buddhist
Daijōji, 5109
Gozan, **3642–3644**
Sōjiji, 5109
Tōkoku-san Yōkōji, 5109
Monasticism, **6121–6136**. *See also* Asceticism; Eremitism; Nuns; Religious communities; Spiritual discipline
activities in, 6123–6125
Buddhist, **6126–6131,** 7720 (*See also* Saṃgha)
adaptability of, 6127
advantages of life in, 6126
Aśoka's impact on, 1091
Āyurveda and, 3853
in Britain, 1189
Buddha as model for, 6126–6127
Buddhadāsa and, 1071, 1072
celibacy and, 1475
in Central Asia, 1095, 1146, 1147
children in, 1156
in China, 1095, 1162, 1163, 1164, 1165, 1167–1168, 1238, 1240, 1524, 1594, 1600, 1604
colonial impact on, 1098, 1099
consecration of space in, 1954–1955
daily activities of, 4429
decline of, 1095–1096
earliest permanent structures for, 1106
economics of, 6129
feeding of monks, as act of merit *(pinkama),* 4140
financial support of, 9708
funding for, 6129
gender in, 3330–3331
under Gupta dynasty, 1115, 4383
iconography of, 4330
in India, 6127
initiation rituals in, 4483
in Japan, 1175, 1177, 1180–1184, 1241–1243, 4784, 8354
karman and, 5099
Keizan on, 5109
in Korea, 1170, 1171, 1173
legal system of, 6129–6130
mendicancy in, 5855
missions and, 6077
Moggaliputtatissa's impact on, 6112
in Mongolia, 1149, 1150
monks *vs.* nuns in, 3330, 3331
moral development in, 1279
mountain locations of, 4796
music in, 6294
ordination in, 6854–6855
origins of, 6126
political support for, 6128–6129
rituals of, 1105–1106, 1107–1108, 1118
role of, 1095
rules of, 1108, 1258, 1259, 1260
schism in, 6128
and schools, 1205
shamanism associated with, 3155
social reform and, 7652–7653
societal influence of, 8463
in Southeast Asia, 1133–1142, 9828, 9831
spread of, 6127–6128
Tantric, 1121
in Thailand, 1096, 1137, 1139–1140, 1141, 9094, 9095, 9097, 9151
Theravāda, 1954–1955, 9148, 9149, 9150, 9151, 9153
Tibetan, 9839
transition of, 1094, 1097
Zen, 6317, 9945–9946, 9949
calligraphy and, 1369
Cassian on, 1447–1448
cenobiotic, development of, 7723
charismatic leadership in, 1549
Chinese, medicine and, 3862
Christian, **6131–6136,** 7720 (*See also specific orders*)
asceticism and, 1688–1689, 6135
Benedict of Nursia as father of, 822–823, 7724
body discipline in, 8704
canons regular in, 7724
celibacy and, 1477
as civilizing force in Middle Ages, 1662–1663
clothing in, 1831
Cluniac, 6132, 6135
communal eremitism, 1980
comparative study of, 6135–6136
control of desire in, 2308, 2309
corruption of, 821
Council of Trent on, 822
decline of, 6134
in the desert, 2301, 6117, 6131
desert ideal in, 1980
devotion in, 2318, 2320
education and, in medieval Europe, 3845
in Egypt, 6939–6940
of Ephraem of Syria, 2812
grace in, 3645
hermits in, 6133
initiation into, 7770
labor in, 2648, 6132, 6135
lands, secularization of, Sorskii (Nil) on, 8525–8526
lay participation in, 6122, 6133
Lent and, 7771
maledictory formulas in, 2105
martyrdom replaced by, 7723
mendicancy in, 5855–5856, 6133–6134
music in, 6309

Christian ***continued***
and Nag Hammadi codices, 6396
obedience in, 6778
origins of, 6117, 6131, 7723
Pachomian or cenobitic, 1980
Reformation and, 822, 6134
reform of, 821–822, 839, 2412, 6134
reforms of, 1663, 7724
Roman Catholic, 7875–7876
rule of Basil and, 798
scripture in, 8199
social movements and, 1749
social reform and, 7652–7653
Symeon the New Theologian in, 8919–8920
transition from anchoritic to cenobitic, hospitals and, 3844
women in, 6134–6135 (*See also* Nuns)
common features of, 6121–6122
comparative studies of, 6135–6136
contemporary, 6125
Coptic (Egyptian), 1980, 1982, 2710
Shenoute in, **8318–8320**
Daoist, 1162, 1603, 2196–2197, 9845
in Quanzhen Daoism, 2186
Sima Chengzhen and, 8399–8400
during Tang dynasty, 2184
temples of, 9056
death in, 6124–6125
definition of, 6121
devotional aspect of, 2320
as discipleship communities, 2361–2363
in Eastern Christianity, development of, 2582
Eastern Orthodox, 7720
Christ the Saviour Brotherhood and, 4103
Palamas's doctrine on prayer and, 2042
Serafim of Sarov and, 8229
and fasting, 2997, 3171–3172
female body and, 4165
frequent features of, 6122–6123
and gender, 6756
Hindu, 7769–7770 (*See also* Ashrams; See also Saṃnyāsa)
vs. Christian monasticism, 6135
temporary, 6122
in India, *bhakti* poetry in, 3985–3986
initiation into, retreats of, 7769–7770
Jain, 4765, 4768–4770
gender in, 3327–3328
monks *vs.* nuns in, 3327–3328
nakedness in, 6123
ordination in, 6854
migration in, 6023–6024
missionary, 6073, 6083
motivations for entering, 6124
New Age, Holy Order of MANS in, **4101–4104**
in North African religions, 7724
numbers of, 2201
nuns in (*See* Nuns)
Orthodox Christianity, 2593
overview of, **6121–6126**
Philo Judaeus on, 7652–7653
of Ramakrishna Mission, 9629
Reformation as against, 1663
religious communities and, 7700, 7719–7720
Russian
Skobtsova (Mother Maria) on, 8422
Sorskii (Nil) and, 8525–8526
Russian Orthodox, 2826–2827, 4957
secret societies compared to, 8212
sleep interruption in, 8441
as socially marginal communities, 5397
Syriac Orthodox, 8940
variety of forms of, 6121
women in (*See* Nuns)
Monberg, Torben, 622
Mon Buddhism (Burma)
in Burma, 1135–1136, 1329, 1332
in Cambodia, 1137–1138
decline of, 9148
Dvāravatī, 1132, 9147
in Laos, 1138
origins of, 1135
in Thailand, 1136–1137
traditions preserved by, 9149
Monchanin, Jules, 547
Mondari people (Sudan), sickness attributed to Ngun Ki in, 3808
Mondō (sacred text), 5311
Il mondo magico (de Martino), 2266–2267
Mondrian, Piet, 55, 4348, 9144
Moneo, Teresa, 4251
Monepiscopacy, 6966
Money, **6136–6139**. *See also* Wealth
cargo cults and, 1421, 1424
Chinese festivals and, 1641
forms of, 6137–6138
role of
in market *vs.* nonmarket economies, 6136–6137
in United States, 10086
Money cults, 9324
Möngke Khan, 1148
Mongkut (king of Siam), **6139–6140**
and Theravāda Buddhism, 1200–1201, 1202, 6139
Buddhist studies by, 1310, 6139
modernization by, 1139–1140, 2326, 6139–6140
monasticism of, 6139
Prātimokṣa composed by, 1306
reform movements of, 6139–6140, 9095, 9151
Mongolian language
Buddhist writings in, 1149
epic of Gesar translated into, 3463
Xianbei people speaking, 4491
Mongol religions, **6140–6143**. *See also* Buriat religion; Chinggis Khan; Southern Siberian religions; Turkic religions
birds in, 948
blood in, 986
bridge in, 1052
Buddhism, **1148–1150**
Altan Khan and, 1149, 1228, 6142
art, 1149
Chinggis Khan and, 1148
communism and, 1098, 1100, 1148, 1150, 1189
Dge lugs pa Buddhism, 1149, 1228, 2322
dreams in, 2488
Esoteric Buddhism, 1097
introduction of, 6140, 6142
of lay people, 1149–1150
literature of, 1148–1149
missions of, 6142
monasteries, 1149, 1150
persecution of shamans in, 6142
revival of, 1148
in Russia, 1189
schools of, **1222–1229**
spread of, 1148, 6142
studies on, 1311, 1312
Tibetan Buddhism, 1148, 1149, 1150, 1154, 1155, 3966, 9182
Vajrayāna (Tantric) Buddhism, 1097
Christianity, missions and, 1150, 1186, 6140
cosmological ideas in, 2999
deities of, 6142–6143 (*See also specific deities*)
elixir in, 2771
Erlik in, 2831
Judaism and, 5009
Manichaeism influencing, 5670, 6140
Nestorian Church influencing, 6140
ongon in, 6826–6827
prehistoric (*See* Saka religion)
shamanism in, 6140–6143
development of, 6140–6141
dominance of, 6140
persecution of, 6142
prayers in, 6142
studies of, 6140
tools and techniques of, 6141
textiles in, 9090, 9091
Umai in, 9443
Mongols. *See also* Chinggis Khan
army of, 4493
in Baghdad, 1367
Caucasus invaded by, 4613–4614
Central Asia invaded by, 4493
China ruled by, 1606, 4494, 4632, 7165
Europe invaded by, 4493, 4673
Il-khanids in conflict with, 4493
Kiev, conquest of, 1684
kingship of, 5179
Korea invaded by, 1930
Korea ruled by, 5230
Middle Volga invaded by, 4616
number nine for, 6749
religions of (*See* Mongol religions)
rise of, 4493
Tibet controlled by, 1154–1155, 1228
Monica (Augustine's mother), 624–625
Monier-Williams, Monier, 4447, 5588
Monism, **6143–6150**
in Asian traditions, 6143–6146
Besant's (Annie), 845
in Buddhism, 6145
Stcherbatsky (Theodore) on, 8737
Zhenyan (Tantric) school and, 1577
Campbell on, 1379
chaos and, 1539
in Confucianism, 1577
definition of, 6143
dualism in, 2505, 2507
in Gnosticism, 3522–3523
in Hinduism, 6144–6145, 6156, 6964
and mysticism, 6343–6344
knowledge in, 5207
Kook (Avraham Yitsḥaq) and, 5226
materialism and, 844, 5777
vs. monotheism, 6159
mystical union and, 6334–6335
mysticism and, 6143
problems with term, 6143
in Sufism, 4570
and theism, 9103–9104
in Vedism, 9561

in Western traditions, 6143–6144, 6146–6149
Yoruba, 9912
Monistic pantheism, 2664, 6961
Monk, Meredith, 2161
Monk, The (Lewis), 3061
Monkeys, **6150–6153**
brains of, 6488
cults of, 3070, 6152
as degraded humans, 6150–6151
in Hinduism, 6150–6152 (*See also* Hanumān)
in Mesoamerican religions, myths about, 5938
monsters and, 6166
as tricksters, 6152
veneration of, 6150, 6151–6152
in *Xiyouji* narrative, 4209
Monkeywrench Gang, The (Abbey), 2563–2564
Monks. *See* Monasticism; Religious communities; *specific monks*
Mono (spiritual entities), 4781
Monod, Gabriel, Durkheim (Émile) influenced by, 2527
Monod, Jacques, on chance, 1527, 3558
Monoemus the Arab, on *hypostasis,* 4242
Monogamy, definition of, 5725
Monograph-codes, in geonic *halakhah,* 3744–3746
Monographs, on African religions, 115
Monoimi (abstainer), 7411
Monolatry
definition of, 2302, 3540, 6158
henotheism *vs.,* 3913, 6158
Israelite, 3539–3542, 4743, 4971–4972, 6157
conception of history and, 4058
vs. monotheism, 6158
Near Eastern, 2302, 3540
Monoliths, Stela D (Maya), 1358
Monologen (Schleiermacher), ethics in, 8160
Monologion de ratione fidei (Anselm), 373
Mono-myths, Joyce (James) on, 1379
Mono no aware, 6211
Mononobe clan (Japan), Soga clan *vs.,* 8374
Monophysite churches, 2584. *See also* Non-Chalcedonian Orthodox churches
Monophysitism, **6153–6155**. *See also* Diophysite Christology; Ethiopian Church
Coptic Church and, 1979–1981, 6155
Council of Chalcedon (451) on, 4354, 6153
Council of Constantinople III and, 2040
definition of, 6153
doctrine of, 7876
Eutyches in, 2885–2886
forms of, 6155
and *hypostasis vs. phusis,* 4242
in Amhara-Tigriña religion, 2573
of Julian of Halicarnassus, 5028
Nestorian Church and, 2584
Severus of Antioch and, 8238
struggle over, 6153–6155
Syriac Orthodox Church and, 8938–8939
Timothy Ailuros promoting, 9205
Monotheism, **6155–6163**. *See also* Panentheism
in African religions, 85, 86
pantheon of intermediaries and, 3816–3817
apologetics' defense of, 427–428, 3545
biocentrism opposed to, 2561–2562
birth in, 952–953
in Buddhism, 6157
in Celtic religion, theory of, 1482–1483
in China
debate over, 1631
Jesuit study of Confucianism and, 1918–1919, 1920
in Christianity, 2228, 6160–6161
contemporary scholarship on, 6161–6162
creation from nothing in, 1986
Creuzer (G. F.) on symbol and, 2070
definition of, 6155
deity in, 2258
deserts as source of, 2301–2302
development of, secularization and, 8216
vs. dualism, theistic, 6158–6159
dualism in, 2506–2507, 2511–2514
dualistic, 6159–6160
in Egyptian religion, 219–220, 2711, 6157, 6159
emanational mystical, 6160
ethical, 9120
female deities in, lack of, 3586–3587
Freud on, 3215
in Greek religion, 6156
vs. henotheism, 6158
Henotheism and, 3913
Hermetism and, 3950
in Hinduism, 6156–6157, 6160
Islamic and Christian influences in, 4007–4008
Roy (Ram Mohan) and, 7932, 7933
Rudra-Śiva in, 8040
historical ethical, 6160–6161
history of religions approach on, 4065–4066
iconoclasm in, 4279, 4281, 4283, 4285
in Islam, 6160, 6161
in Qurʾān, 6222
in Shahāda, 8266
in Israelite religion, 6157–6158
historical problem of, 3539–3541, 4857
as monarchic, 6159
Moses and, 6201–6202
in Judaism, 6160
history, view of, 4058
law and, 5359
monarchic, 6159–6160
vs. monism, 6159
vs. monolatry, 6158
nation-state, and concept of, 1425
origin of religion and, Schmidt (Wilhelm) on, 8168–8169
origins of, 6156, 7316
patriarchy and the male creator, 1993
Pettazzoni (Raffaele) on, 7074–7075, 8170
Plato on, 427, 6156
vs. polytheism, 6158
polytheistic elements in, 7318
polyvalence and polymorphism, 1482–1483
vs. positivism, 7339–7340
primitive monotheism *(Urmonotheismus)* doctrine, 2090, 6156, 10065, 10077
in primitive religions, 2915
problems with term, 6156
in Roman religion, 7919
ruler cults and divine kings as problem for, 3902
in Sikhism, 6158, 6160
Söderblom (Nathan) on, 8878
Swanson (Guy E.) on, 8170
vs. theism, 6156
use of term, 6156
violence and, 9598
in Zoroastrianism, 6157, 6160
Monothelitism, Maximos the Confessor against, 5792, 5793
Mon people (Burma)
Buddhism of, 1132, 1135–1138, 1329, 1332
Mongkut's interaction with, 6139
Monsignor Quixote (Greene), 3059
Monsoons, spirits associated with, 6456
Monsters, **6163–6166**. *See also* Dragons
in Chinese myth, Gonggong as chaos monster, 1625
in creation myths, 1986
on Dayak shields, 9682–9683
definition of, 6163
horns and, 4131
in initiation rituals, 4477
in Mesoamerican religions, iconography of, 4312
natural phenomena linked to, 6163
in North American Indian religions
iconography of, 4309
in Malecite myth, 2091
pearl and, 7024
problems blamed on, 6163–6164
in Semitic myths, killing of, 1875
three-headed, slaying of, 9685
types of, 6163–6166
underwater horses as, 4133–4134
water, 6439–6440, 9703
Windigo, in Algonquian legend, 1403
Monstrance, reliquary, vol. 4 color insert
Montagu, Ellen Cohen, 6166
Montagu, Lily, **6166–6167**
in Liberal Judaism, 6166–6167
Montagu, Samuel, 6166
Montague, W. P., 6964
Montaigne, Michel de
on anthropomorphism, 390
autobiographical essays of, 698
on conscience, 1942
French humanism and, 4176
on Plutarch, 7202
on relativism, 7685
skeptical views of, 8421
Montalembert, Charles de, 9442
Montanism, **6167–6168**
charismatic authority and, 1550
ecstasy in, 6866
enthusiasm of, 2805
inspiration in, 872
opposition to, 6167–6169
origins of, 6167, 6168
prophecy in, 6167–6168
repentance in, 7758
Tertullian in, 6167, 6168, 9085, 9086, 9087
writings on, 6167
Montanus, **6168–6169**
life of, 6168
Montanism founded by, 6167, 6168

Monte Albán (Mexico)
calendars at, 5881, 5882
in Classic period, 5902–5904
iconography of, 4312
musical instruments at, 6268
rise of, 5902
tombs at, 3243, 5903
Monte Cassino, 822, 823
monastery at, architecture of, 6117
Montecroce, Ricoldo da, 5637
Montefiore, Claude
in Liberal Judaism, 6166, 6167
Schechter (Solomon) and, 8146
Monter, William, 3360
Montespan, Marquise do, Black Masses and, 8250
Montesquieu, Baron de, in French Enlightenment, 2796
Montessori International, Summit Lighthouse founding of, 1783, 7445–7446
Monteverdi, Claudio, 6311
Montgomery, Ruth, 560
Montgomery, William, 74
Month (periodical), 9427
Montini, Giovanni Battista. *See* Paul VI (pope)
Montolinía, Toribio, 5939
Montreuil, Jean de, French humanism and, 4176
Montu (deity), 301
Montúfar, Alonso de, 4504
Monuments. *See also* Stupas and stupa worship; *specific monuments*
architecture of, classification of, 463–464
collective identity and, vol. 6 color insert
megalithic (*See* Megalithic religion; Menhirs)
vs. museums, 6245
Nabatean, 6386
Pyramid of the Sun (Mexico), 1468
Stela D (Maya), 1358
Monzeki (cloister), 9075
Moody, Campbell N., 8964
Moody, Dwight L., **6169**
evangelicalism of, 2888
revivalism and, 1710, 6169
Mooki, David, New Church of Southern Africa (Swedenborgian) and, 8902
Mooki, Obed S. D., New Church of Southern Africa (Swedenborgian) and, 8902
MoʻoKū. *See* Kū
Moon, **6170–6176**
in African religions
in Bantu rites of passage, 8666, 8667
Dogon, 3570
in Karanga religion (Bantu), 8665
in Swazi religion, 8895
animals associated with, 6170
in Australian Indigenous myths, 663
in Berber religion, worship of, 834
binding of, myths of, 5198
in Canaanite religion, 1384, 1395
in Caribbean religions, 1427, 1429
in Chinese tradition, 1625
goddess of, 1643
rabbit living in, 7590
craters of, Kepler (Johannes) on, 4516
creation of, myths about, 6173–6174
death and, 6170, 6174–6175
deities of (*See* Moon deities)
eclipses of, 1356
in ethnoastronomy, 2862–2863
eye as, 2941
feminine sacrality of, 3017–3018, 3021
in folklore, 6175–6176
frogs associated with, 3223
full, 6176
in gardens, Eastern *vs.* Western, 3278
in Greek religion, 6171, 6173, 6175
hierophany (manifestation of the sacred) and, 3971
in Hinduism
calendrical system and, 4015
Holī and (*See* Holī)
holidays and full moon, 4016–4017
in Purāṇic cosmology, 2018
lotus associated with, 5518
in Inca religion, 4411–4412
gender of, 3416
origins of, 5292
in Indian religions, 6171, 6172–6173, 6174
in Inuit religions, 5515
in Islam, 6171
in Japanese religion, 6173
rabbit living in, 7590
in Jewish calendar, 4866
in Khoi religion, 5136, 7590
in Komi religion, 5217
in Mesoamerican religions
contemporary worship of, 5927
creation of, 1468, 5935
in Teotihuaćan, 5888–5889
in Mesopotamian religions, 6171–6172
iconography of, 4316
in Micronesian religions, 6002, 6010
in mythology, 6172–6174
in Negrito religions, Andaman, 6456
in Neolithic and Bronze Age religions, circle symbolism and, 1791
in Neolithic religions, 6464, 6465
in North American Indian religions, 6651
iconography of, 4309
Iroquois, 6682
Pueblo, 6722, 6723
number associated with, 6749
in occultism, 6175
phases of, 6170
in primitive religions, 10065
rabbit living in, myths of, 7590
in Roman religion, 6170–6171 (*See also* Diana)
in San religion, 5136, 7590
in Slavic religion, 8435
in South American Indian religions
in Ge-Timbira religions, 8629
origin of, 8588
in Selk'nam religion, 8224
spots on, 6175–6176
sun paired with, 6170
technomorphic representations of, 8424
in Tehuelche religion, 9029
time and, 1760, 6170–6171
in Vanuatu religions, 9521
women and, 6170
worship of, 6439
Moon, Sun, and Witches (Silverblatt), 3416
Moon, Sun Myung, 9466–9468
church founded by (*See* Unification Church)
Divine Principle, 6529
marital relations of, 6536
mission of, 6530
teachings of, 6560
and U.S. politics, 6560
Moon bear. *See* Asiatic black bear
Moon-blocks, 1605
Moon deities, 3619, 6171–6172
as anthropomorphic representation, 8424
in Arabian religion, 443
in Aramean religion, 447
in Arctic religions, 469
examples of, 3619, 6172
functions of, 3619
Mēness as, 758–759, 760, 769
in Mesopotamian religions, 6171–6172, 7602
Nanna as, 6172, 6414–6415
in nature worship, 6439
prehistoric, 7383
Soma as, in Southeast Asia, 4010
in South American Indian religions
in Ge religion, 8578
Pachamama-Quilla as, 8601
Thoth as, 9167, 9168
Mooney, James, 3473, 6670
Moonies. *See* Unification Church
"Moon of Pejeng" (Balinese drum), 745
Moon Old Man (deity), 5119
Moore, Carey A., 897
Moore, G. E.
analytic philosophy of, 306
evolutionary ethics opposed by, 2918–2919
Moore, George Foot, **6176–6177**
on afterlife, 152
influence of, 6177
writings of, 6176–6177
Moore, O. K., 2374
Moore, Rachel, 3101
Moore, Rebecca, 6524
Moore, Robert, 5862, 6527
Moore, Sally F., 1513, 1517, 6326
Moore, Thomas, on spirituality, 8720
Moorish Science Temple, 71–72, 6563
doctrines of, 6418
foundation of, 4687
growth of, 4689
vs. Islamic Brotherhood, 4688
Nuwaubians compared with, 6768, 6769
as secret society, 8213
teachings of, 4687
Moos, Kaj, 6539
Moose, 9395
Morais, Sabato, 7582
Moral community, church as, 1776
La Morale (Durkheim), 2527
Moral Essays (Plutarch). *See Moralia* (Plutarch)
Moral evil, 2897, 9114
Moralia (Basil of Caesarea), 798
Moralia (Plutarch), 7200, 7202
Moralia on Job (Pope Gregory), 4932
Moralism
in Chinese philosophy, 1571–1572, 1573, 1578 (*See also* Confucianism)
Buddhist school of names, 1595
in Christianity, evangelicalism and moral crusades, 1710–1711, 1715
Solov'ev (Vladimir) on, 8520
Morality, **6177–6189**. *See also* Conscience; Ethics
in African religions, Hyakyusa, 6771
assessments of, 6184
in Australian Indigenous myths, 664
biblical, 6182
in Buddhism, 7651
monastic discipline as form of, 8073
violation of moral precepts, 8015
Cassirer on, 1448
casuistry (principles and choices), **1454–1455**
charity and, **1553–1556**
in Kardecism, 5090
in Chinese religion, 6187
Confucius on, 8462
Han Fei Zi on, 3772–3773
Heaven and, 3888

Kang Yuwei on, 5075–5076
Mengzi on, 5857–5858
in Christianity, 7651–7652
early, 6182
Roman Catholicism, 7885
clothing and, 1832
in Confucianism, 7651, 7751–7752, 9674–9675
in Daoism, 2179, 2183, 2193
definitions of, 6178–6179
differences in, among traditions, 6184–6185
distinction between religion and, 6177–6179
divine command in, 6183
Durkheim (Émile) on conscience collective, 8493
in early Christianity, 1651–1652
earth mother as patroness of, 2560
equated with religion, in Kant's (Immanuel) philosophy, 5078
ethics *vs.*, 1650
evolution of (*See* Evolution, evolutionary ethics)
expression of truth through, 9372
as foundation of religion, 7116
foundations of, Durkheim (Émile) on, 3231
Golden Rule of, 3630–3633, 6185
and heresy, development of, 3923
in Hinduism, in Swaminarayan movement, 8891, 8892
in Kurozumikyō, 5267
in Islam, 6186
in Qur'ān, 4564, 5060
in Japan, under Tokugawa regime, 4788
Jesus as model of, 4844
in Judaism, 6181–6182, 7651–7652
and Kantian morality, 4903
kashrut laws and, 5108
medical ethics and, 3829
rabbinic Judaism, 7589
Reform Judaism, 7651
Kant on, 5077–5080, 6102–6103
justification for, 6181
philosophy of religion and, 6181
religion's role in, 6178
karman in, 5098–5099
in Khmer religion, 5132
Kierkegaard on, 6178
of kinship, extension of, 5185
laws and, **5366–5371,** 7652
in classic modern theory, 5367–5368
in later theory, 5369–5370
in modern jurisprudence, 5368–5369
of *mana,* 5631–5632
in Manichaeism, 5656
Marx on, 6178
in medicine (*See* Medical ethics)
motivations for, 6180–6181, 6186–6188
of nature, in Confucianism, 2632
negative effects of religion on, 6178
Nietzsche on, 6616
norms of
logical independence of, 6179, 6181–6183
superiority of, 6179, 6181–6183
universality of, 6179–6181, 6183–6186
of Pap (God) in Cuna religion (Panama), 2096
in Pindar's poems, 7174
in popular literature, 3062
in proofs for existence of God, 7422, 9106
in Puritanism, 7520
redemption in, 6188
reform of, 7651–7652
relativism and, 7685
retribution in, 6186–6187
revenge and, 7779
rules of, 6180
exceptions to, 6179
sainthood, path to, 8037
sanctions enforcing, religion as, 6178
secularization of, 8492
in Sikhism, popular, 8397–8398
Socrates on, 8503, 8504
soteriological function of, 8528
Spencer (Herbert) on, 8492
static and dynamic, 838
in Stoicism, 8743
universal, 7651, 7652
Vices, Cassian on, 1447
in Western religions and societies, 7652
in Yurupary myth, 9920
Morality plays, 2437, 2470
of Middle Ages, dance in, 2153
Moral Majority, 2892
Moral Man and Immoral Society (Niebuhr), 6466, 6611, 6612
Moral monotheism, 2302
Moral philosophy
casuistry *vs.*, 1456
Confucian (*See* Confucianism)
of Hume (David), 4192–4193
of Thomas Aquinas, 9163
Moral reform, religious concern for, 7651–7652
Moral self, in Chinese medicine, 3859, 3860
Moral (practical) theology, 9139. *See also* Ethics
Biblical, 1650
casuistry and, 1455
Eastern Orthodox, 1652–1653
Judaism and, 4902–4904
Roman Catholic, 1653–1654
Moravec, Hans, 512
Moravia, Christian missions in, 1683
Cyril and Methodius, role of, 2116–2117
Moravian Church in America, full communion agreement with Lutherans (ELCA), 1769
Moravian denomination (Unity of Brethren), **6190–6192,** 6873
clerical orders of, 6190, 6191
establishment of, 6190
Herrnhutian community at Gnadenfrei and, 8159
Hus (Jan), influence of, 4234
missions, 6191
in Nicaragua, 1700
in Saint Thomas (Caribbean), 1706, 1707, 6191
persecution of, 6190–6191
provinces of, 6191
Schleiermacher (Friedrich) and, 8159–8160
settlement congregations of, 6191
Wesley (John) influenced by, 9716
worship in, 6190, 6191
Zinzendorf (Nikolaus) in, 9975–9976
Morayā Gosāvī, in Gāṇapatyas, 3271
Mordecai (biblical figure), in *Esther,* 2848
Mordecai of Chernobyl, Maid of Ludmir and, 5611
Mordvin religion. *See* Mari and Mordvin religion
More, Gertrude, 822
More, Henry, Neoplatonism and, 6475
More, Thomas, 9491
humanism and, 4176
on utopia, 7720
Moreau de Saint-Méry, Mérédec Louis-Elie, 10024, 10026
Moreh nevukhei ha-zeman (Krochmal), 4902, 7107
Moreno, Jiménez, 5942–5943, 9223
Morenu ha-Rav (rabbinic title), 7580
Morenz, Siegfried
on book religion *vs.* cult religion, 8198
on Egyptian religion, 7757
on oral tradition, 8198
Morey, Charles Rufus, 500
Morgan, David, 502
Morgan, Lewis Henry, 730, 731, 732, 6670
on North American Indian ballgames, 754
Morgan, Ruth, 5414
Morgan, Sally, 3391
Morgan, Thomas Jay, 10054
Morgan, William, 3197
Morgannwg, Iolo, 2493
Morgenstuden (Mendelssohn), 5854
Morgenthaler, Walter, 9625
Morgenthau, Hans, 6613
Moriah, Mount. *See* Temple Mount
Morin, Stephen, 3196
Moriscos (baptized Muslims)
expulsion of, 4596
as slaves, 4684
Spanish Inquisition directed against, 4500, 4596
Moritz, Karl Philip, on dreams, 8909
Morley, Sylvanus G., 452
Mormo (female spirit), 2277
Mormonism, **6192–6195**
attacks on, 6548, 6558
Book of Mormon in, 6192–6193
catastrophic millennialism of, 6545
controversial doctrines of, 8447
dancing in, 2137
denominations and sects of, 6192
internal conflicts in, 6193
in Latin America, 6579
and Maori religion, 5683
marriage in, 6193, 6194
migration in, 6023, 6193, 6194
missions, 6195
modern, 6194–6195
as new religious movement, 1714, 6513
origins of, 6192–6194
in Pacific islands, 1739, 9321
pantheism in, 7449
persecution of, 6193
polygamy in, 6534, 6558
scriptures of, 6516, 6529
sexuality and, 8243
Smith (Joseph) in, 6192–6194, **8446–8448,** vol. 4 color insert, vol. 14 color insert
after Smith's murder, 6564–6565
temples in, 6193, 6195
tensions with society, 6548
theocracy in, 9109
violence in, 6551
women in, 6195, 6534
Young (Brigham) in, 6193–6194, 9913–9914

"Morning: The World in the Lake" (Hogan), 7225
Morning glory, 9218
Morning star. *See* Venus (planet)
Morocco and Moroccan religions
Hamadsha brotherhood in, 8691
handshaking in, 9259
hinna' rite in, 7803
immigrants from, 4675, 4676, 4678, 4679
Islam
conference, 4574–4575
ghosts in, 3476
mawlids in, 5789
'ulamā' in, 4590
Judaism
Maimuna feast, 3160
population of, 5000
Sephardic, 4996
literature of, 3088
mountains in, 6212, 6214
mūsims in, 7824–7825
polygamy in, 4707
rites of passage in, 7824–7825
birth, 7825
circumcision, 7826
death, 7827
marriage, 7826–7827
namic ceremonies, 7825–7826
spirit possession in, 8688, 8691, 8692
Sufism, dances of, 2139
textiles in, 9088
Tombouctou invaded by, 4603
Moro movement, 6796
on Guadalcanal, 8516–8517
Morone, Giovanni Cardinal, 9344–9345
Morozko (deity), 727
Morphology
of religion, 2755, 2761
Tiele (C. P.) on, 9192
Morphy, Howard, 2478, 4306
on academic study of Aboriginal religion, 686, 3490
on the Dreaming, 638, 640, 668
on Yolngu communities, 647, 648, 668
Morreale, Don, 1190
Morríghan (deity), 1490, 2984, 3056, 9390
Morris, Arline Maxine, 9729
Morris, C. W., symbol theory and, 8912
Morris, Christine, on goddess worship, 3617
Morris, Desmond, 6740
Morris, Herbert, 9423
Morris, Ivan I., on *seppuku* (ritual suicide), 8832
Morris, John, 2910
Morris, Paul, in New Zealand, 8770
Morris, Robert, 3198
Morris, William, calligraphy and, 1369
Morrison, John Robert, 6196
Morrison, Kenneth, 6422
Morrison, Robert, **6196**
in China, 1608, 1632, 6196
Morrison, Toni, 3059
Morse, Jedidiah, attack on liberal Congregationalists, 1530
Mortality. *See also* Immortality
human (*See also* Death)
in African religions, 84, 85–86, 92–93
in Greek religion, 3669
mythic ancestors in, 326
in North American Indian religions, 6661
in Kamba religion, 2575
natality *vs.*, in feminist theology, 4166
in Semitic myths, 1875
sexuality associated with, 4165
Mortal sins, 1888, 1889
Morte e pianto rituale nel mondo antico (de Martino), 2267
Morteira, Sha'ul Levi, Spinoza (Baruch) and, 8681
Mortification, **6196–6199**. *See also* Spiritual discipline
ascetic, 6197
in Christianity, of flesh, vol. 13 color insert
goals of, 6197
initiatory, 6197–6198
of kings, 6198
in New Testament, 6196–6197
seasonal rites of, 8208–8209
in Sun Dance, 8848
Morton, Alice, on spirit possession, 8691
Morton, John, 668–669
Morton, Nelle, 3654
Morton, Thomas, 6557
Mortuary houses, megalithic, 5823
Mortuary liturgy, Egyptian, 2718
Mortuary masks, Melanesian, vol. 9 color insert, vol. 10 color insert
Mortuary rituals. *See also* Funeral rites
in African religions
and afterlife, views of, 140–141
in East African religions, 2569
in Australian Indigenous religions, history of study of, 682–683
in Buddhism, Korean, 5231–5232
definition of, 3242
in Kushite religion, 5269, 5270
in Melanesian religions, 5837–5838, vol. 9 color insert, vol. 10 color insert
in Oceanic religions, 147, 6784–6785
gender roles in, 3396
Mortuary temples, 2714–2715, 2725
Mortuary texts, of Egyptian religion, 2703, 2704, 2718–2720
Morumachi period (Japan), Buddhism in, 1181–1182, 1245
Moryō. *See* Kamo no Mabuchi
Mosaic physics, nature in, 6434
Mosaic prophecy, 7107, 7434, 7440
Mosaics, 794
color in Byzantine mosaics, 1861
Moscow (Russia)
as religious center, 1684
Russian Orthodox church based in, 2588, 7280, 7941–7942
Moscow Patriarchate. *See* Russian Orthodox Church
Moscow Psychological Society, 9367
Moscow University, 836
Moses (biblical figure), **6199–6204**
Aaron and, 1–2, 5423
Adonis compared with, 34
Aristotle and, 4893–4894
and blood, 987
charisma of, 1545
days spent in wilderness, 6750
as deliverer from Egypt, 6200
in *Deuteronomy*, 9232–9233
encounter with God, humor of, in Midrash, 4196
in *Exodus*, 9232
fasting by, 2996
as founder of Israelite religion, 6201–6202
Freemasons on, 3195
God's covenant with
monotheism in, 3540
in rabbinic Judaism, 7584
as revelation, 7777
as hero figure, 6202, 7552, 7553
historicity of, 6199
horns associated with, 4131
in Islam, 6204, 6736
in *mi'rāj*, 6060
Jesus compared to, 6203–6204
Joshua and, 4958
as judge, 4739
and knowability of God, 182
as lawgiver, 6201
laws of, 6201
Abraham and, 15, 16
in rabbinic tradition, 3747–3748
leadership of, 6200–6201
as Levite, 5423
in literary tradition, 6199–6201
midrash and, 6014
miracles of, 6051
Miriam and, 6062
on Mount Sinai, 6213
in mystical union, 6338, 6339
name of, 6199
name of God *(Yahveh)*
revealed to, 3539, 6201–6202, 6406–6407
in New Testament, 6203–6204
in *Numbers*, 9232
perfection attained by, 7440
Philo Judaeus on, 9234–9235
in postbiblical Judaism, 6202–6203
as rabbi, 7584
Rastafarian reincarnations of, 1438
in Samaritan belief, 8070
Shakpana identified with in Trinidad, 1434
shekhinah concept and, 8313
Spinoza (Baruch) on, 8683
in Ten Commandments, 6201
on throne in heaven, 3508–3509
Torah of, 882, 883, 9233, 9234–9235
Moses, Apocalypse of, 3126–3127
Moses, Wilson Jeremiah, 75, 79
Moses ben Maimon. *See* Maimonides, Moses
Moses ben Nahman. *See* Maimonides, Moses
Moses David. *See* Berg, David Brandt
Moses de León, 9330
Mosese Dukumoi. *See* Navosavakadua
Mosha, Sambuli, on African worldview, 139
Moshav Me'or Modiim, 4869
Moshe ben Asher, Cairo Codex of the Prophets and, 1371
Mosheh. *See* Moses
Mosheh al-Ashqar, 9247
Mosheh ben Maimon. *See* Maimonides, Moses
Mosheh Hayyim Efrayim of Sedlikov, Hasidic sermons of, 3788
Mosheim, Johann Lorenz von, on Gnosticism, 3514, 3531
Moshinskai, Vanda, 3114
Moshnin, Prokhor. *See* Serafim of Sarov
Moskovskii ezhenedel'nik (journal), 9367
Moslem World, The (periodical), 4686
Moso (Na-hsi) religion (China), shamanism in, 8273
Mosques, **6204–6210**
architecture of, **6207–6210**
and church architecture, 794
classification of, 461, 467, 6208–6210
in first Medina mosque, 6205–6206
sacred space and negation of it, 7979–7980
built by Muḥammad, 6205–6206, 6208, 6223
calligraphy in, 6207, 6208
in Canada, 4685

in China, 4631, 4634, 4638–4639
destruction of, 4636–4637, 4638
reopening, 4637, 4638
contemporary, 6210
in Cuba, 4684
in Europe, 4676
history and tradition of, **6204–6207**
imams leading prayers in, 4396–4397
in Qur'ān, 6205, 6207–6208
in Jerusalem, 4836–4837
jumʿah masjid (great mosques), *ṣalāt* (prayer) in, 8058
learning and training at, 6206, 6210
meaning of term, 6204
North African, 4584
roles of, 6204, 6207–6208
in Russia
closure of, 4624
destruction of, 4617
sacredness of, 7698
in sub-Saharan Africa, 4608
in United States, 4688, 4690
urban sacred space and, in India, 1806
Verses of Light in, 6206–6207
women in, 3369, 6210
for *Ṣalāt* (prayer), 8055–8056
Mosquitoes, 4508
Mossi religion (Burkina Faso)
ancestors in, 9718
funeral rites of, 3234, 3235
Most Bitter Cry (myth), 5958
Mot (deity)
Anat's attack on, 319–320
Baal's conflict with, 723, 724, 1383, 1384, 2431, 2536, 7767
El and, 2742
in *Jeremiah,* 1393
Mota people
calendar, 1353
knot symbolism of, 5198
Mote (F. W.), on continuity of being, 8554
Motecuhzoma Ilhuicamina. *See* Moctezuma I
Motecuhzoma Xocoyotzin. *See* Moctezuma II
Moth and candle parable, 4508
introduction of, 3757
Mother. *See* Mothers and motherhood
Mother deities
Edo, 2697
Laima as, 5286
prehistoric, 7377
Rainbow Snake as, 7607
Mother Divine, 3007
Mother Earth, 2557–2559. *See also* Earth mothers
chaos and, 1538
death and, 2559
in Etruscan pantheon, 2871
mines in, 5987
in North American Indian religions
cave as symbol of, 1469
iconography of, 4310
prehistoric, 7377–7378
in Slavic religion, 8437
in South American Indian religions (*See* Pachamama)
temple at Delphi of, 5282
Mother Gita. See Bhagavadgītā
Mother goddesses. *See also* Goddess worship; Great goddess
in Arctic religions, 470
in Baltic religion, Saule (sun) as, 8133
castrated priests and, 1451
in Celtic religion, 1484, 1486, 1490
in Chinese religion
Eternal Venerable Mother, 1607
Unborn Venerable Mother, 1638
father god and, 2985
in goddess worship, 3588
in Greek religion, 5282
in Hinduism, in Trika Śáivism, 8046
Lady of the Animals, 5282
in Mesopotamian religion, 3594, 6624–6625
and sexuality, sacredness of, 7972
as sole generative principle, 1993
son-consorts of, 2983, 2984
Sophia as All-Mother, 8523
in South America
in Chamacoco religion (Gran Chaco), 8633–8634
in Mundurucú religion, 8580–8581
in White Lotus movement, 3155
worship of, 2983–2984
Mothering, 953
Mother of Life, in Manichaeism, 5666
Mother right, 731
Mothers, The (Briffault), 3611
Mothers and motherhood, 2983–2984
in Christianity, medieval, 3360
earth symbolism and, 3014–3015
figures
in agricultural myths, 191
in agricultural rituals, 189, 190
French feminists on, 3028, 3029
Freud (Sigmund) on, 2239
in Germanic religion, 3450–3451
God as, 2695
in goddess worship, 3588, 9602
Jesus as, 5029
in Orthodox Christianity, 2593–2594
in psychoanalysis, 7483
Śārāda Devi deified as Holy Mother, 8111
in Trobriand Islanders religion, 5184
virginity associated with, 2984, 3588
Mothers-in-law, conflicts with, masquerade dances to resolve, 2141
Mother Tantras. *See* Yoginī ("Mother") Tantras
Mother Worship (Preston), 3612
Mọ̄ thēvadā (shaman), 5313
Motif research, 6466
Motion, substantive, Mullā Ṣadrā on, 6232
Motoda Eifu, Confucianism and, 1928
Motolinía, Toribio de, 5915
Motoori Norinaga, **6211**
Hirata Atsutane and, 4022
historiography and, 4032
in Shintō revival, 4789
on *kami,* 5073, 6211
Kamo no Mabuchi and, 6211
Kojiki translated by, 4812
Kokugaku movement and, 5214–5215, 6211, 8365
literalism of, 4807
National Learning movement of, 5073, 9311
Mott, Lucretia, Stanton (Elizabeth Cady) and, 8730
Motu Koita people, 1001
Mo-tzu. *See* Mozi
Mounds, 9226. *See also* Stupas; Tombs
feminine sacrality of, 3017
Sídh and, 8393
Mountain deities, 3620, 6214
Adad as, 27, 28
in Andean religions, *Achachilas* (mountain spirits), 8615–8616
examples of, 3620
functions of, 3620
in nature worship, 6439
Pērkons as, 7053
Mountain lions, Inca calendar and, 1364
Mountain Peaks of Prophecy, The, vol. 1 color insert
Mountains, **6212–6215**. *See also specific mountains*
Avalokiteśvara associated with, 705
as *axis mundi,* 712, 6212
in Aztec religion, Mount Tlaloc, 5293–5294
in Buddhism, 6212–6214
bodhisattvas associated with, 5675, 6213–6214
Zen monasteries in, 3642
caves and, in geomancy, 1468
in Chinese religion, 1625
as divine dwelling, 6213–6214
Mount Buzhou as cosmic pillar, 1625
Mount Tai, 1590, 1591, 1592
sacred geography of, 3435
Taishan, 1619
as cosmic centers, 1501–1502, 6212–6213, 6886
in Daoism, 2178, 2197, 2199, 2207, 2208, 2637, 6214, 9056
deities of (*See* Mountain deities)
as divine dwelling, 462, 6213–6214
divine power of, 6214
as dwelling of supreme beings, 8871
in Egyptian symbolism, *vs.* Minoan horns, 40
feminine sacrality of, 3017
in gardens, Eastern cosmic, 3277–3278
in Greek religion, Zeus and, 9952
in Hinduism, 4439, 6212, 9039
of India, 6213
divinity of, 2621
in Shintō, 2640, 6214
as objects of devotion, 2317
in Islam, 6213
in Japanese religions, 4796
as cosmic centers, 6212
divine power of, 6214
Fuji-kō associations and, 8364
Shugendō movement and, 8379, 8380
women excluded from, 3348
life and death in, 6214
masculine sacrality in, 5759–5760
in Maya religion, 5796
sacred geography of, 3434
in Mesoamerica
contemporary beliefs about, 5927–5928
in Teotihuacán, 5899, 6213
in North American Indian religions, 6213, 6214
iconography of, 4310
in Navajo religion, 573–574
in poetry, 7226
paradise as, 6985
persistence of, 6214

Mountains ***continued***
revelations and visions on, 6213
of Rome, 7896
in Tibetan religion, sacred, 9185
towers imitating, 9265, 9266
worship of, 6439
as *yoni,* 9907
Mountain Spirits dance, 2462
Mountford, Charles P., 668, 686, 2480
on Rainbow Snake, 7605
Mount Hagener religion (New Guinea), body decoration in, 4160–4161
Mourides (disciples of Aḥmad Bamba), pilgrimage to Touba and, 1808–1809
Mourides (Senegalese Ṣūfī ethnic group), vol. 7 color insert, vol. 10 color insert
Mourners for Zion, as core of Karaite sect, 5083
Mourning, 3234–3235
ashes in, 541
in Australian Indigenous religions, 5051
in California Indian religions, 6717, 6719
Chinese clothing for, 1827
communication with dead in, 2241
in Garifuna religion, 3284
hair, cutting or tearing in, 3740–3741
in Hinduism, Sati (widow burning) and, 8831
images and, vol. 9 color insert
in Islam, 7827
in Judaism, 7822–7823
in Lakota religion, 5296–5297
media coverage in, 5809
in Melanesian religions, 5838
pain in, 6945
restrictions of, 8948–8949
in Selk'nam religion (Tierra del Fuego), 8225
tears in, 9025, 9026
Mourning Dove, *Co-ge-wea,* 3090
Moussey people (Cameroon), vengeance and, 7780
Moussinac, Léon, 3100
Mousso Koroni Koundyé (mythic figure), 98, 776
Mouth
devouring mouth image, 4165–4166
in gestures, 7343
healing by sucking, 3812
Mouth of Heaven, The (Goldman), 7345
Mouvement Croix-Koma (Nailed to the Cross), 105
Mouyu (Uighur leader), 4492
Mou Zongsan, on Confucianism and Buddhism, 1901
Movable type, invention of
and Karaite writings, 5086
and Rabbanite writings, 5086
Movement for Progressive Judaism, 7672
Movement for the Restoration of the Ten Commandments of God (MRTCG), 105–106, **6215–6217**
development of, 105, 6215
as fragile movement, 6517, 6549
mass suicide/homicide in, 6215, 6216–6217
revelations in, 105–106
violence in, 105, 106, 6216–6217
Movement of Spiritual Awareness (MSIA), 2603
Movements, new religious. *See* New religious movements
Mowinckel, Sigmund
on *Epic of Gilgamesh,* 3487
on Israelite religion, 6380, 6381–6382
in Myth and Ritual school, 6380, 6381–6382
on *Thronbesteigungsfest,* 5147
on Yahveh, 7464
Moxibustion, in Japanese *kampō* healing, 3868
Moyers, Bill
Campbell (Joseph) and, 1378
midrash and, 6021
Moynihan, Elizabeth, on paradise, 6984–6985
Mozak (priest), 5669
Mozambique
Apostolic Church of John Maranke in, 5695
masquerade dances in, 2140
Thonga people of, history of study of, 113
Mozarabs (Christians in Andalusia), 4593, 4596–4597, 7282
Mozart, Wolfgang Amadeus
as Freemason, 3195
music of, 6312
Mozi (Chinese philosopher), **6217–6218**
atheism and, 578
ethic of, 1894, 6218
philosophy, overview of, 1571, 1586–1587
on *tian,* 6217–6218
on *yi,* 7751
Mozley, J. B., on free will and predestination, 3208
Mpadism, Kimbangu's (Simon) influence on, 5144
Mpemba (otherworld), in Kongo religion, 5221–5222
Mpungu. *See* Nzambi
Mr. Butterfly and His Flowers (Japanese myth), 3135
Mrdanga (drum), 7036
Mrs. Dalloway (Woolf), 3056
MRTCG. *See* Movement for the Restoration of the Ten Commandments of God
Mṛtyu, sacrificial contest between Prajāpati and, 1025, 9567
Mrzḥ(symposium), in Ugaritic legend, 1396
MSA. *See* Muslim Student's Association
MSIA (Movement of Spiritual Awareness), 2603
Mt. Carmel: The Unseen Reality (Fagan), 1038
Mu (king), 1593
Muʿādh ibn Jabal, in modernism, 6096–6097
Muʿamalāt (conduct of interpersonal relationships), 4693, 4700, 4760
Muʿammar (Muslim scholar), soul, doctrine of, 8568
Muʿāwiya, ʿAlī challenged by, 258–259, 7285
Muʿawiyah
and origin of Khārijīs, 5126
and Umayyad caliphate, 4582
Muʿāwiya ibn Abī Sufyān, al-Ḥusayn ibn ʿAlī and, 4235
Muʾayyad al-Dawla, 3
Muʾayyad billāh Aḥmad ibn al-Ḥusayn al-Āmilī, al-, ʿAbd al-Jabbār and, 4
Muʾayyad fī al-Dīn, al-, Ismāʿīlīyah and, 8331
Mubaraʾah (divorce), 4708
Mubaraki, Majid Fandi al-, 5638
Mucalinda (serpent), vol. 8 color insert
Much, Rudolf, 3459
Muchapi movement (Malawi and Zambia), 1511
Muchay (reverence), in Andean religions, 8603
Mucilinda (*nāga* king), 6395
Mucius Scaevola, on theologies of poets, philosophers, and statesmen, 4038
Mudangs (shamans), 5228, 5231
Buddhism and, 5231
Communism and, 5235
consecration in, 4105
during Chosŏn dynasty, 5232
as preservers of Korean culture, 5235
types of, 5234–5235
Mudawwanah (Saḥnūn), 4584
Mudéjares (Muslims in Andalusia), 4596
Mud Hen (mythic figure), 6011
Mudimbe, V. Y., *Entre les Eaux,* 3088
Mudimbe, Valentin, 111
Muditā (sympathetic joy), 1555
in Buddhist meditation, 5105
Mudiyettu (dance drama), 2448
Mudrās (seals or gestures), 1217, 1218, 1219, 1243, 1287, **6219–6220,** 7343. *See also* Mahāmudrā; *specific gestures*
in Balinese dance drama, 2451
of *bodhisattvas,* 4329
of Buddha, 4328, 9257
in Buddha images, 3769
of celestial buddhas, 4329
in Hindu and Buddhist rituals, 3769–3770
ideas communicated by, 4171
mantras and, 6219
in meditation, 5820
of defeat of Māra, 9257
in Shingon Buddhism, 8351
Mudrooroo (Colin Johnson), 3079
Mudyi (shrub), 6446
Mudyi tree, 4484–4485, 9336
Mueller, Max, in religious studies, 2608
Muesse, Mark W., 3314
Muezzin (prayer caller), 9266
Mufawwiḍah (Delegationist) movements, as *ghulāt* (extremist), 8323
Mufīd, Shaykh al-, 4262
Muftī (teachers)
casuistry of, 1454
in Central Asia, 4627, 4629
kalām of, 5068
shaykh al-Islam and, 8306
status of, 4697
Muga (shaman songs), 5233
Mugawar (magic ritual), in Hittite religion, 4069, 4072
Mughal dynasty (India)
administrative structures of, 217
Akbar in, **216–217,** 8414
autobiographies from, 700
and Bengali conversion to Islam, 825
gardens in, 3282
music in, 6283
personality cults in, 4649–4650
Shiism in, 4646–4647
Sufism in, 4647, 4648–4649
syncretism in, 4007
Mughni fi abwab al-tawhid wa l-ʾadl, al- (ʿAbd al-Jabbār), 4
Mughni fi usul al-din, al- (ʿAbd al-Jabbār), 3, 4
Mughshin, *ḥawṭah* of, prohibitions in, 3776
Mugwe, in Meru priesthood, 2569
Muhajiroun, al- (Islamic group), 6568
Muḥammad (the Prophet), **6220–6228**
ʿAbd al-Rāziq (ʿAlī) on, 5
on ablutions, 10
on Abraham, 16, 6224
Abū Bakr's relationship with, 19–20
on afterlife, 159
in Agami Jawa, 4816
on alchemy, 248
ʿAlī ibn Abī Ṭālib and, 256–257
Andrae (Tor) on, 333
angels visiting, 346
on animals, 361
animal sacrifice by, 445
as apocalyptic prophet, 6545, 6546
as apostle, 436
ascension of (*See Miʿrāj*)
authority of, 695–696
biographies of, 945–946, 4716–4717, 6220
birthday of, 4713

birth of, 6220
calendar and, 1353–1354
caliphate as successor to, 1365–1366
cats, fondness for, 1463
charisma *(baraka)* of, 1546
  transmission of, 696
Christian polemics on, 7242, 7243–7244
circumambulation of, in the Ka'bah, 5049
continued existence of, 9819
converts gained by, first, 6221, 6222
daughters of, **3008–3009,** 6220, 6224
death of, 20, 6227
descendants of, 6227–6228
  Ḥusayn (grandson), 5088
  respect for, 199
devotional allegiance to, 9818–9819
devotion to, 6227–6228
on disease and illness, 3831
divine instructions received by, 8700
Dome of the Rock shrine and, 8377
election of, 2748
eschatology of, 2835
as ethical prophet, 5384
as example, 4565
as exemplar, 8852 (*See also* Sunnah)
on faith, 5062
family of *(ahl al-bayt),* **198– 199,** 3008
on fasting, 8140, 8141
foods preferred by, 2401
Gabriel transmitting Qur'ān to, 4510, 9271
on gambling, 3262
granddaughter of, 9937–9938
greeting used by, 7021
ḥājj pilgrimage by last, 6226–6227
  peace established during, 6226
historiography and, 4029
humanity of, 8014
humor and, 4197, 4215
Iblīs and, 'Ayn al-Quḍāt on, 8814
idolatry condemned by, 4287, 4350, 4362
imitation of, Muslim, 6227
in Ash'arīyah, 531–532
in 'Aṭṭār's (Farīd al-Dīn) poetry, 602
infidels, recovery of, 3885
in Ḥanafī creed, 2064
in Qurayẓah massacre, 6225– 6226
in Shahādah, 8014, 8266
inspiration of, 4510–4511
insulting, 974–975
intercession by, 129
  on Last Day, 2064

isra' of, 6058–6059, 6222– 6223
  in Jerusalem, 4836–4837, 4840
Jewish polemics on, 7241
on judgment of the dead, 5027
leadership of, emulation of, 6737–6738
life of, 6220–6227
light of *(nūr Muḥammad),* **6766–6768**
on lunar year, 6171
mawlid (birth) of, **5788– 5790**
in Mecca, 19, 20, 4561, 6220–6223
  early life of, 6220
  opposition to, 6222
  victory of (630), 5050, 6226
in Medina, 19, 20, 4561, 6205–6206, 6223–6227
  migration to, 6223, 6594
  mosque built by, 6205– 6206, 6208, 6223
  war against, 6225–6226
memorization of words of, 5852–5853
message of, 6221
as messenger of God, 6734– 6735
on messiah, 5979–5980
  false, 5979, 5980
military leadership of, 6225
on miracles, 6054
Mi'rāj of (*See* Mi'rāj)
in modernism, 6097
monotheism enforced by, 6222
Moses and, 6204
names of, 6410
narrative of, soteriology and, 8528
nature and, 2651
on nature of Islam, 5061– 5062
and Noah, comparison with, 6643
Nuwaubians on, 6769
on *ḥājj,* 7155–7156
on *īmān* and *islām,* 4398
on *jihād,* 6225
on memorization of Qur'ān, 7572
on *walāyah,* 9656
peace offensive by, 6226
poems dedicated to, 6738, 6766, 6767
poetry in honor of, 7222, 7223–7224
prayers attributed to, 6766
prophetic dreams of, 2489
on purity, 8057
Qur'ān as miracle of, 4370, 4564
Qur'ān delivered by, 7204
and Qur'anic exegesis, 7562
relics of, 7687

religious experience of, 7700
revelation of Qur'ān to, 5060, 6221, 7561, 7571, 7778, 9200
saliva of, 8722
sayings of (*See* Ḥadīth)
in Shiism, 6227
as social critic, 7425
social reforms by, 4561
successor to
  'Alī ibn Abī Ṭālib as, 257
  conflict over, 20, 257
  Ṣūfī and, relationship of, 9661
  in Sufism, 6227, 6736
touch of
  healing, 9256
  of power, 9257
visions of, 9612
vocation of, 9633
on vows, 9641
wars of, 6225–6226
wives of, 6223–6224
  'Ā'ishah bint Abī Bakr, **211,** 6224
  Khadījah bint Khuwaylid, 6220, 6223
  and women's rights, 6224
Muḥammad, Abul Qaim, vol. 1 color insert
Muḥammad, Elijah. *See* Elijah Muhammad
Muhammad, John, 4689
Muhammad, Silas, 4689
Muhammad, Wallace, 4689, 6563
Muhammad, Warithuddin (Wallace Deen), in Nation of Islam, 72, 6419–6420
Muḥammad Aḥmad, 2570–2572, **6228–6229**
  body marks of, 1004
  hijrah (migration) of, 6228– 6229
  as Mahdi, 5982, 6228–6229
  mission of, 6229
Muḥammad Ahmed Ibn Abdullāh. *See* Madhi, al-
Muhammad 'Alī, al-Azhar university under, 230–231
Muḥammad 'Alī Lāhorī. *See* Lāhorī, Muḥammad 'Alī
Muḥammad al-Madhī, *ghaybah* (concealment) of, 3468–3469
Muhammadan poverty, 2220
Muḥammad Askiya Ture, 4602– 4603
Muḥammad ibn 'Abdullāh. *See* Muḥammad (the Prophet)
Muḥammad ibn al-Ḥanafīyah and *mahdī,* 5982
  ghaybah (concealment) of, 3468
  Kaysānīyah movement and, 8321
Muḥammad ibn 'Alī, Abbasid revolution and, 8321
Muḥammad ibn Ismā'īl (imam), 4395

Muḥammad ibn Sa'ūd (prince of Najd), 4255
Muḥammad ibn 'Umar. *See* Rāzī, Fakhr al-Dīn al-
Muḥammad ibn 'Umayil, on alchemy, 249
Muḥammadīyah movement, 4667
  in Bengal, 829
  ideology of, 4651
  in Java, 4667, 4818, 8653
Muḥammad Qāsim Nanawtawī, 4652
Muḥammad Shāh, Sir Sulṭān. *See* Aga Khan III
Muḥammad-shāh, Qāsim-shāh *vs.,* 8333
Muhammad Speaks (newspaper), 5626
Muhammed: Hans liv och hans tro (Andre), 333
Muhammedan Anglo-Oriental College, 201
Muhammedanische Studien (Goldziher), 945
Muḥarram (month in Islamic year), 4712–4713
Muḥāsibī, al-Ḥārith al-, 5029– 5031
Muḥkam (clear verses), 8951
Mühlenberg, Henry Melchior, 5539, 7143
Muhpattī (mouth shield), 4766
Muḥsin (person of perfection), 4399
Mu'īn ad-Dīn Chishtī, 4648, 4649, 9009
Muir, John
  on exploration, 8724
  nature writing of, as spiritual autobiography, 703
Muir, William, 202, 945
Muirchú (biographer), 2493
Muisca religion (South America), **6229–6231**
  Bochica in, **993**
  creation myth in, 8587
  deities of, 6229–6230
  light in, 6229–6230
  myths of, 6229–6230
Mu'izz, al-, esoteric doctrine and, 8330
Mujaddids (reformers), 4605, 4650
  in Islamic eschatology, Mahdi *vs.,* 2838
  in messianism, 5981
  in modernism, 6097
  Sirhindī (Aḥmad) on, 8413
  Walī Allāh (Shāh) as, 9666
Mujāhidīn reform movement, 4650–4651, 4654
Mujawwad (recitation style), 9201, 9202
Mujer Enredadora. *See* Matlacihuatl
Mujerista theology, 3035, 5442, 9791

Vol. 1: 1–610, Vol. 2: 611–1340, Vol. 3: 1341–2120, Vol. 4: 2121–2850, Vol. 5: 2851–3580, Vol. 6: 3581–4292, Vol. 7: 4293–5046, Vol. 8: 5047–5748, Vol. 9: 5749–6448, Vol. 10: 6449–7176, Vol. 11: 7177–7864, Vol. 12: 7865–8572, Vol. 13: 8573–9286, Vol. 14: 9287–10018, Appendix: 10019–10091

ENCYCLOPEDIA OF RELIGION, SECOND EDITION

Mujtaba min al-Sunan, al-, in *ḥadīth* literature, 3730
Mujtahid muṭlaq (unrestricted *mujtahid*), 4375
Mujtahids (scholars), 4697
definition of, 5547
engaging in *ijtihād,* 4374–4375
hawzah and, 3801
legal rules carried on by, 4372
origin of term, 4373
ranks of, 4375
Shaykh Aḥmad on, 8308
Mukantabana, Specioza, 6215
Mukasa (deity), dances devoted to, 2137
Mukenge, Ida, 74
Mukerji, Radhakamal, 9284–9285
Mukhammisah (Pentadist) movement, as *ghulāt* (extremist), 8323
Mukharrimī, Abū Saʿd al-
Ḥanābilah and, 3766
al-Jīlānī and, 3767
Mukhtār, al-
and *mahdī,* 5982
ghulūw of, 225
Mukhyaprāṇa (principal breath), 7362
Mukti. See Mokṣa
Muktupāvela, Rūta, 328
Mukulumpe (Luba king), 817
Mukuṇḍarājā (philosopher), and Marathi religions, 5696
Mukundarāma Cakrabartī, 825
Mukyōkai (nonchurch), 9432
Mūlādhāra cakra
in *Haṭhayoga,* 3795
location of, 1348
Mūlamadhyamakakāriki (Nāgārjuna), 5100
as source of Mādhyamika school, 1299
and Chinese Buddhist philosophy, 1301
commentaries on, 1075
emptiness *(śūnyatā)* in, 8857
Mūlaprakṛti (original materiality), 7360
Mūlasarvāstivāda school of Buddhism
in Central Asia, 1146
expansion of, 1201
literature of, 1198
Maitreya in, 5619
origin of, 1194
Sarvāstivāda and, 8117, 8120
in Southeast Asia, 1132
in Tibet, 1223
Vinaya, 6760
Mūla Sūtras, in Jain scriptures, 4767
Mūlatantra (root text), 1275
Mulenga Lenshina, Alice. *See* Lenshina, Alice
Mulian (narrative figure), 3343
Mulian cycle, 1620
Mulien (disciple of Buddha), 5231
Mulieris, Adam Pulchrae, on nature, 6432
Mulk (offering), 4744, 7132, 7134
Mullahs (Muslim religious leaders)
as charismatic leaders, 1546
exorcisms performed by, 830
Mullā Ṣadrā, 728, **6231–6234**
and Ṭabāṭabāʾī, 8946
doctrine of *al-ishrāq* and, 2977
doctrines of, 6231–6233
Ibn Sīnā's influence on, 4276, 6233
on knowledge, 5204
life of, 6231
philosophy of, 4556
writings of, 6233
Mullen, Patrick B., 3144, 3145
Müller, Adam, 6435
Müller, Adelheide, 6234
Müller, F. Max, **6234–6237**
on animism, 363
on Buddhism, 1313, 1314, 1334
Chinese religious texts and, 1632, 1633
classification of religion by, 1818
comparative mythology of, 1873, 6234
comparative philology of, 1872, 6235
comparative study of religion, 6236
comparative theology of, 9125
critics of, 6234, 6235
critiques of, 4460
on Darwin's evolutionary theory, 6235–6236
education of, 6234
as "father of comparative religion," 1878
on Henotheism, 3913
on henotheism, 6158
imperialist bias of, 1856–1857
on Indo-European religions, 4446, 4459–4460
Lang (Andrew) on, 5299, 6234
on language, 5330
methodology of, 6235
on myth as "disease" of language, 6234, 6367
Nanjō Bunyū and, 6414
nature religions studied by, 2662
on nature worship, 6440
on religious experience, 10076
and science of religion, birth of, 8763
on scripture, 8197
on solar heroes, 8134
solar mythology of, 2518, 4459–4460
on South African religion, 1857
Starbuck (E. D.), influence on, 8732
on supreme beings, 8875
Tylor (E. B.) influenced by, 2914
on Vedas, 3913, 4446
Müller, G. F., 5709
Müller, Johann, 564
Müller, Karl Otfried, 730, 4458, **6237–6238**
on Greek religion and myth, 6237
methodology of, 6237
Müller, Klaus E., 4718
Müller, Max, 3458
Müller, Werner, 4307, 6671, 9413, 9418
Müller, Wilhelm, 6003, 6234
Müller-Karpe, Hermann, on Paleolithic sacrifice, 8005
Muller-Ortega, Paul, 8988
Müller-Wille, Michael, 990
Mullin, Robert Bruce, 75
Multan temple, Saura Hinduism and, 8136
Multazim (place of blessing), 7159
Multicultural theories of conversion, 1970–1971
Multiverse approach, anthropic principle and, 2033
Mulunga cult, 671
Mulungu (deity)
ancestor intercession with, 3817
as creator, 1507, 3572–3573
as supreme being, 3572–3573
variations of name, 3572
Mulvin, Jerry, 2603
Mumbai (India), Jews in, 5006–5007
Mumford, Catherine, 1020
Muʾmin (person of faith), 4399
Muʾminūn (persons of faith), 4398
Mummers, goats and, 8312
Mummification
in Andean religions, 8603
in Arabian religions, 445
in Egyptian religion, 3240
of animals, 2250
and deification, 2249
of pharoah, 5164
iconography of, 4319
in Inca religion, 3240
of kings, 5176–5177
resurrection of body after, 131
self-mummification, of Shugendō priests, 2241
textiles in, 9089
Mummu, 1450
Mumonkan, enlightenment in, 2795
Mumtāz ʿAlī, 4652
Mumtāz Mahal (Mughal empress), 4646
Mumuna (mythic figure), Gadjeri as, 3249, 3250
Mumunga (mythic figure), Gadjeri as, 3249
Munaggimīn (spiritist healers), in Egypt, as class of healer, 3836
Munajat (ʿAbd Allāh Anṣari), epigrams in, 8816–8817
Muṇḍaka Upaniṣad, gurūs in, 3713, 3714
Mundang people (Chad)
bride-price in, 7780
kingship of
death of king in, 5170
looting and, 5171
vengeance and, 7781–7782
Mundu mugu (diviner), in Kikuyu religion, 2576–2577
in Mundurucú religion (Amazon)
ancestor worship in, 8584
deities of, 8577
marriage among, 5726
mother spirit in, 8580–8581
secret societies of, 9920
Mundus imaginalis. See Imaginal world
Munetada, Kurozumi, 5267
Munga-munga (mythic figures), 3249, 3250
Mungiki movement, 109
Mungu (deity), in Swahili religion, 2567, 3572
Munich Book of Necromancy, 6452
Munio of Zamora (Dominican monk), 2414
Munīr, al- (journal), 4666
Muni-yati cult, 9498
Munkácsi, Bernát, 3112
Munkácsi, Bernhardt, 474
Munkar (angel), 346
Munmu (Silla king), 1171
Munn, Nancy, 3390, 4305, 9705–9706
Muṇoz Camargo, Diego, 5940
Munqidh min al-ḍalāl, al- (Ghazālī), 700, 3469–3470, 3471
Munsee Prophetess movement, 6667
Mun sel skor gsum (Longchenpa), 5193
Munshidah, in *zār* exorcism ceremony, 2148, 2149
Münster, Sebastian, 768
Müntzer, Thomas, 782, **6238–6239**
and Anabaptism, 304, 305, 6239, 7660
disagreement with Luther (Martin), 7659
education of, 6238
Prague Manifesto of, 6238
and Zwickau Prophets, 6238
Munyarryun, Djakapurra, 635, 637, 640, 641, 642, 646, 651
Munz, Peter, on myth, 8768
Mupashi (spirits), 817
Muqadassi, al- (geographer), 4594
Muqaddimah (Ibn Khaldūn), 4269, 4587
and *kalām,* 5059, 5064
Muqālāt al-Islāmīyīn (Ashʿarī), 530
Muqarnas (stalactite form), 6208
Muqātil (theologian), 6766

Muqātil ibn Sulaymān
on God's unity, 6322
tafsīr of, 8944, 8950, 8952
Muqniʿ fī al-fiqh, al- (Ibn
Bābawayhi), 4262
Muqriʾ (reciter), 9200
Murabitun, 6568
Murabitun (Islamic group), 6568
Murals
Mesoamerican
in Cholula, 5902
in Teotihuacán, 5899–
5900, 5901
Protestant, in Ethiopia, vol. 6
color insert
Murāqabah, 604
Murasaki Shikibu, 3057
Murata Shukō (Buddhist monk),
1181
Muratorian canon, 920–921
Murattal (recitation style), 9201,
9202
Murder, 986. *See also* Human
sacrifice; Martyrdom
of African religious leaders,
1722
in Australian Indigenous
religions, by sorcerers,
3871–3872
of Buddha, attempted, 8015
in Buddhism, in Vinaya
literature, 1259
Cain and Abel, 986, 1344–
1345
cults and, 2085
in culture hero myths, 2091–
2092
fratricide, theme of, 2985–
2986
in Germanic religion, 744
in Greek myth
of Argos by Hermes,
3936–3937
as original sin, 2965
in *haram* or *hawṭah,* 3777
in Islam, laws on, 4566
in Israelite religion, laws on,
4738
Jewish law on, 1843–1844
moral norms on, differences
among, 6184
and pollution, 7506, 7513
purification after, 1459
as redemptive sacrifice, 4955
in Temple Solaire, 9068
vengeance for, 7780, 7781
walāyah and, 9657
in warfare, 9681
Murder in the Cathedral (Eliot),
2472, 2476
Murdoch, Iris, on beauty, 812
Müri, Walter, on symbols, 8906
Murīd (seeker), 107, 9005
shaykhs and, 8710
Murīdīyah (Ṣūfī order), 9012
Murīd movement (Ṣūfī), 9011
Murie, James, 6670, 6672
Murillo, Esteban, 377
Muring people (Australia), 2310

Murjiʾah sect (Islam)
Abū Ḥanīfah in, 21
on afterlife, 161
on free will, 4568
īmān and *islām* in, 4399
origin of term, 4562, 4568
Umayyad caliphate
supporting, 4568
Murnane, Gerald, 3084
Murngin society (Australia), 5444
Muromachi period. *See* Ashikaga
period
Murphy, Francis, 3073
Murphy, Joseph, 80, 10023
Murphy, Tim, 5332, 5375
Murray, Charles, 2882
Murray, Gilbert
on Greek drama, 2436, 2443
on theater, 7050
Murray, John, 9470
Murray, John Hubert, 687
Murray, Margaret
on witchcraft, 6871, 9729,
9770, 9774
on witches' Sabbath, 8249
Murray, Stephen, 5414
Murray River (Australia), and
Ngarrindjeri people, 649
Murrinh-pata religion (Australia),
Stanner (W. E. H.) on, 8729–
8730
Mursal ("sent free"), *ḥadīths* and,
3729
Murshid (spiritual guide), 9005
Murshid Quli Khan, 827
Murshilish (Hittite king), illness
of, linked to epidemic, 3825
Murtaḍá, Sharif al-, 4726
Mūrti, **6239–6240,** 7501, 9040
Murton, John, 783
Murugan. *See* Murukan
Murukan (deity), **6240–6241**
as Śiva's son, 7196
devotional poetry of, 857,
6240
forms of, 6240
in Tamil religion, 6240,
8973, 8979
temple to, 8977
Murūwah (manliness), 4561
Mus, Paul, 1312, 3177
on cadastral cults, 8642
colonialist agenda of, 8638
Mūsā. *See* Moses
Mūsā al-Kāẓim, Imami succession
and, 8322
Musaf (additional service), 9807
Muṣāharah (affinity), 4706
Musamo Christo Disco Church,
104
Musang (Buddhist monk), 1172
Musannaf (classified) collections,
in *ḥadīth* literature, 3728
Musar movement (Judaism), 868,
5019, **6241–6242,** 6902
Kagan (Yisraʾel Meʾir)
influenced by, 5053
Salanter (Yisraʾel) in, 6241,
8053

Musaylamah, 20
Muscular Christianity, 5862
*Muséon, le: Revue d'études des
Morgenlandes* (journal), 10056
Museo Nacional (Mexico), 5940
Muses, **6242–6243**
inspiration of, 4509–4510
springs associated with, 3178
Museum of Biblical Art (New
York), 6244
Museum of Contemporary
Religious Art (St. Louis), 6244
Museum of Fine Arts (Boston),
spiritual art at, 500
Museums, **6243–6248.** *See also
specific museums*
art, 6244
audiences of, 6246
faith community, 6245
human history, 6244–6245
Mesoamerican exhibitions in,
5944
religious change and, 6246–
6247
sacred objects in, 6243–6244
temples as, 6245
world religion, 6246
Mushati, Simon, 5695
Mushkenum (poorer class), 4730
Mushrikūn (polytheism), 4362
Mushrooms
as psychedelic drug, 9613
used with *soma,* 849
Mushtabihāt al-Qurʾān (al-Kisāʾī),
8952
Music, **6248–6314.** *See also*
Chanting; Drums; Hymns
in affliction, healing of, 60,
61–62
in African American religions,
6313
history of study of, 77
women in, 10039
in African religions
African Independent
Churches, 103, 6259
organization of, 6256–
6258
in religious drama, 2456
sub-Saharan, **6256–6260**
Armenian notation, 1535
as art, 6249
in Australian Indigenous
religions, **6260–6263**
myths as songs, 655–656,
660–661
sequence of songs, 5705–
5706, 5707
tjurungas accompanied
with, 9212, 9213
in Balinese dance drama,
2450, 2451
Baltic folk songs, Saule (sun)
worship in, 8131–8132,
8133–8134
for blessing, 980
in Buddhism
Chinese, 6294–6295
Indian, 6282–6283

Japanese, 6300–6302
Korean, 6296, 6297–6298
of Mi la ras pa, 6027–
6028
Tibetan, 6283, 6298–
6299, 8052
Byzantine, 1534, **6302–6306,**
6309
at Carnival, 1442, 1444
cats and, 1463
center symbolism and, 1503–
1504
chanting (*See* Chanting)
cheironomy (hand
movements), 1533
in Chinese religion, **6292–
6299**
Classic of Odes as
collection of songs,
1905–1906
in Christianity, **6307–6314**
in Africa, 6258–6259
in Asia, 6264, 6285,
6292, 6296
Augustine on, 46, 6305,
6308, 6309, 7204
contemporary, 5808
early, 6305
Hildegard of Bingen,
compositions of, 3980
hymns, 1668–1669
in Protestant worship,
7456, 7459
classical, 6312, 6313
communicating with spirits
through, 2453–2455
creation of, divine role in,
6252
dainas, in Baltic cultures,
2127–2128
definitions of, 6249–6250
devotion expressed in, 2319
diversity of, 6249
Djanʾkawu, 2379
the Family and, 2988
of Finland, in *Kalevala,* 5511,
5512
in Garifuna religion, 3285
geometry of, 3441–3442
gospel music, 2477, 6313
in Greek religion, **6302–6306**
of Muses, 6242
in sacrifice, 3682, 6303
in healing dances, 3815
in Hinduism, **6278–6282**
of Mirabai, 6048–6049
saint-singer tradition in,
4005–4006
in Indian religions, **6278–
6287**
bhajan (singing) groups,
3985
dance drama, 2448, 2449
rural traditions of, 4434–
4435
intercultural, 6249
in Inuit religion, 4527
in Islam, 6276–6277
African, 6258

Vol. 1: 1–610, Vol. 2: 611–1340, Vol. 3: 1341–2120, Vol. 4: 2121–2850, Vol. 5: 2851–3580, Vol. 6: 3581–4292, Vol. 7: 4293–5046, Vol. 8:
5047–5748, Vol. 9: 5749–6448, Vol. 10: 6449–7176, Vol. 11: 7177–7864, Vol. 12: 7865–8572, Vol. 13: 8573–9286, Vol. 14: 9287–10018,
Appendix: 10019–10091

ENCYCLOPEDIA OF RELIGION, SECOND EDITION

in Islam *continued*
definitions of, 6250
Indian, 6283–6284
samā' (listening parties), **8064–8066,** 8822
in South Asia, 4642
in Sufism, 9004–9005
in Israelite religion, 927–928, 935 (*See also* Psalms)
in Jamaican ancestral cults, 1435
in Japanese religions, **6299–6302**
jazz, 6313
in Judaism, **6307–6314**
early, 6276–6278
on Passover, 7003, 7004
in Korean religions, **6292–6299**
magic power of, 6303
in Mardu religion, sequence of songs, 5705–5706, 5707
melodies of, 6250–6251
in Mesoamerican religions, **6266–6271**
colonial period of, 5918
in dance drama, 2465
in Middle Eastern religions, **6275–6278**
myths and, 6252, 6253
in Neopaganism, in seidr ritual, 8295
in North American Indian religions, 6702
in drama, 2459–2460
in Sun Dance, 8847
in Oceanic religions, **6263–6266**
and afterlife, 146
in Okinawan ritual, 6812–6813
origin of term, 6302
origins of, 6251–6252
Judaism and Islam on, 6277
poetry and, 7204, 7207
in Rastafari, 1438, 7625, 7628
Reformation and, 1691, 6310
ritual and, Bellah (Robert) on, 8470
in rituals, 7860
in Roman religion, **6302–6306**
in Sai Baba movement, *bhajan* (devotional songs), 8028, 8029
in Sami religion, bear-hunting songs, 8087
Satanic messages alleged in, 8127, 8128
Schweitzer (Albert) and, 8178
scripture, influence of, 8204
secular *vs.* religious, concepts of, 6250
in shamanism, 8278, 8283
drums in, 8282, 8284–8285
gourd rattle, in South America, 8291
Korean, 5233
sound in, 6249–6250
in South American religions, **6271–6275**
in Araweté religion (Amazon), 8628
sacred wind instruments in, 8582–8583
in Southeast Asian religions, **6287–6292**
space in, 6253–6255
in Sufism, Khusraw (Amīr), 5138
swan song and, 8894
symbolism of, 6252–6253
technical features of, 6250–6251
in Tehuelche religion, 9029
in Tibetan religions, **6292–6299**
time in, 6253–6255
in Western religions, **6307–6314**
winter solstice, **9740–9746**
words in, 6250–6251
of Yurupary, 9918–9919
Musical instruments. *See also specific instruments*
in African religions, 6257
in burials, Mesoamerican, 6267, 6268
classes of, 6251
in Greek religion, 6304
names of, 6251
origins of, 6252
in Aztec myths, 6270
in Middle Eastern accounts, 6277
in New Guinea myths, 6266
in Roman religion, 6304–6305
Mūsims (annual festivals), 7824–7825
Muskogean language, 6696–6697
Muskogee tribe (North America)
ballgame played by, 753, 754, 755
cosmogony of, water in, 9699
forced migration of, 6690
poetry of, 7225
region populated by, 6655
Muslim(s). *See also* Ummah
African religions studied by, 111–112
cultures, clothing and gender in, 1827
in Dogon creation myth, 100
election of, 2748–2749
groups of, 7564–7565
Kabīr as saint of, 5052
meaning of word, 2318, 4399, 6221
names of, 6409–6410
origin of word, 4560, 4561
religious communities of, 7700
second generation of, 7562
supreme leader of (*See* Imamate)
true, definition of, 4567, 4568
world population of, 4563
Muslim Brotherhood, **6314–6316**
doctrines of, 6315–6316
in Egypt, 6314–6315
establishment of, 6314
in Europe, 4681
goals of, 6314, 6315
Ḥasan al-Bannā' in, 6314–6315
impact of, 6316
Mawdūdī (Abū'l A'la) influencing, 108
Qutb (Sayyid) in, 7257, 7289, 7575
spread of, 6314, 6315
structure of, 6315
tafsīr of, 8955
Muslim communism, in Middle Volga, 4619
Muslim Council of Britain, 4680
Muslim feminism, 3366–3367, 3368, 7568. *See also* Feminism, in Islam
Muslim League (political group)
and foundation of Pakistan, 4654
Jamā'at-i Islāmī and, 4773
Mawdūdī and, 5788
Muslim Mosque, Inc., 72, 5626
Muslim socialism, in Middle Volga, 4619
Muslim Student's Association (MSA), 4690
Muslim Summit Conference, 4574
Muslim World League, 4574, 4575
Musnad (supported) collections
in *ḥadīth* literature, 3728
of Aḥmad ibn Ḥanbal, 3763
Musok (Korean shamanism), 5228–5236, 5593
ancestors in, 5233, 5235
cosmology of, 5232
Kut ritual of, 5232
in modern era, 5234–5236
mortuary rituals of, 5231
as native religion, 5228
politics and, 5235–5236
spirit possession in, 2140
state formation and, 5229
in Three Kingdoms period, 5230
women in, 5235
Musō Sōseki (Buddhist monk), **6316–6317,** 9947
Muspell (fire land), in Germanic creation myth, 3446
Mussolini, Benito, Evola (Julius) and, 2905–2906
Mustai, in Demeter Eleusinia cult, 2751–2752
Musta'lī Ismā'īlīyah, 4572
imams in, *ghaybah* (concealment) of, 3469
in South Asia, 4646
Mustanṣir, al- (imam), successor to, dispute over, 557
Mustapää, P. *See* Haavio, Martti
Muste, A. J., 6648
Muster, Nori, 6541
mustēria, 4482. *See also* Sacraments
Cabasilas (Nicholas) on, 1343
definition of, 6326–6327
as sacraments, 7954–7955
Mustes (deity), 2358. *See also* Dionysos
Mustēs (initiand), 4477
Must God Remain Greek? (Hood), 80
Muşu, Gheorghe, 3467
on Sabazios, 7953
Mut (deity), 5269
Muta (deity), 5321
Mut'ah (temporary marriage), 4707
Mutakalimūn (dialectical theologicians)
occasionalism of, 6779
soul, doctrine of, 8568
use of *kalām* by, 5059
"Mu'tammim-i Bayān" (Ṣubḥ-i Azal), 729
Muṭarrifīyah movement, Ḥusayniyah *vs.,* 8325
Mutashābihāt (unclear verses), 8951, 8954
Mutation
creationism and, 2910–2911
in neo-Darwinism, 2909
Mutawakkil, al- (caliph)
Dhū al-Nūn al-Miṣrī and, 8811
and Mu'tazilah, 6319, 6320
Mu'tazilah (school of Islamic theology), 3212, 4567–4568, **6317–6325**
'Abd al-Jabbār in, 3–4, 6320
Abū al-Hudhayl al-'Allāf in, 18–19, 6319, 6321–6324
on afterlife, 161, 162
on *Al'adam* (nonexistence), 8568
and *kalām,* 5063
apologetics of, 428
al-Ash'arī in, 530, 531, 619
on atomism, 6323
Baghdad school of, 6320–6321
Basran school of, 6320–6321
definition of Muslim by, 4567
Dhū al-Nūn al-Miṣrī *vs.,* 8811
doctrines of, 6321–6325
emergence of, 4562
epistemology of, 6324
five affirmations of, 5063–5064, 6321–6322
commanding the good, 5063–5064, 6321
intermediate position between faith and disbelief, 5063, 6321
justice of God, 5063, 6321–6322
the promise and the threat, 5063, 6321
tawḥīd, 5063, 6322
on free will, 2064, 8816
and predestination, 3204, 3212

God in, 3562–3563, 4567–4568
attributes of, 618–619, 3563, 6322–6323
exceptionalism of, 3562–3563
justice of, 3563, 6321–6322
power of, 3563
Greek philosophy and, 5061
ḥadīth rejected by, 4567
Ḥanafī *madhhab* and, 3761–3762
as heresy, 6317
Imami Shiism and, 8323
influence of, 6324–6325
in *ʿilm uṣūl al-fiqh,* 9490
ʿiṣmah in, 4725, 4726
Judaism influenced by, 4992
Karaites influenced by, 5086
al-Māturidī and, 5781
meaning of name, 6318
missionary work of, 6318
Murji'ah sect opposing, 4568
al-Naẓẓām in, 6319, 6444–6445
Nyberg (H. S.) and, 6774
on *miʿrāj,* 6060
on Qur'ān, 4567, 4568
created character of, 618, 3563, 6319
originality of, 6324–6325
origins of, 6317–6318
on personhood, 6323–6324
phases of history of, 6317
Qādarī movement and, 3210, 3212
Rabbanites influenced by, 5086
rationalist movement of Ḥanābilah *vs.,* 3760–3762
Inquisition and, 3760
Rāzī (Fakhr al-Dīn al-) opposed to, 7633
repentance in, 7758
scholastic phase of, 6320–6321
soul doctrine in, 8568
spread of, 6319–6320
success of, period of, 6318–6320
tafsīr in, 7565, 7566, 8954
theodicy in, 9118
worldview of, 6323–6324
al-Zamakhsharī and, 9929
Muʿtazilī school. *See* Muʿtazilah
Mutendi, Samuel, prophetic movement, 1720
Mutesa I (king of Buganda), Islam supported by, 2578
Mutilation. *See* Bodily marks
Mutimir (prince), Orthodox Christianity and, 1684
Mutiny of 1857. *See* Indian Revolution
Mutjingga (mythic figure), Gadjeri as, 3249, 3250, 3251
Muṭma'innah souls, in Islam, 8567
Mutter Erde (Dieterich), 2348, 2349
Mutterrecht (Bachofen), 730, 731, 3611, 3616, 7008–7009, 7079
Muttu Mīnākṣī (Māravaiyā), 10036
Mutual Broadcasting Network, religious broadcasting on, 7711
Muumbi (mythological figure), 2575
Muwaffaq, al-, 6640
Muwashashat (poetry), 4597
Mūwaththaq (reliable) *ḥadīths,* in Shīʿī collections, 3733
Muwatta' (Mālik ibn Anas), 5627
Muwlā, ʿAlī ibn Abī Ṭālib as, 257
Muwwaḥhidūn. See Druze
Muyingwu (deity), 6723, 6724
Muyu (musical instrument), 6294–6295
Muzaffar, Chandra, 6099
Muzdalifah (Saudi Arabia), as station of *ḥājj,* 7157, 7159
Mvskoke tribe (North America)
in Alabama, 6690–6691
Corn Woman narrative of, 6692
cosmology of, 6691
creation story of, 6692
Green Corn Ceremony of, 6694
shamanism practiced by, 6693
supernatural being of, 6691
Mwalule (sacred burial place), 818
Mwanga II (king of Buganda), 2578
Mwari (deity), 2313
regional cult of, 8373
Mwerinde, Credonia, in Movement for the Restoration of the Ten Commandments of God, 105, 6215, 6217
Mwindo (hero), 3086
gambling by, 3264
Myalism, 7623
as native Baptist movement, 1436–1437
Myanmar. *See* Burma
Mycenaean religion, 41–43, 3678
art depicting, 41, *42*
charity in, 1553
deities of, 41–43 (*See also specific deities*)
Greek religion and, 41–42, 3665, 3678
hieros as holy in, 7967
iconography of, 4320–4321
kingship in, 5166
language of, 37, 41
libations in, 5433
Semitic influence, 1388–1389
tablets of, 41–42, 43
temples in, 9062
Myerhoff, Barbara G., 1513, 1517, **6325–6326**
on ritual, 7849
Myers, F. W. H.
on states of consciousness, 1949
on subconscious, 7474
Myers, Fred, 640, 668, 2481, 3392, 4307
Myers, Frederick, on religious experience, 7738, 7742
My Faith as An African (Ela), 143
My Life in Christ (Ioann of Kronstadt), 4532
Mylitta (deity), 1002
Myōe (Buddhist scholar), 1179
Myoe Shonin. *See* Kōben
Myohi (Buddhist nun), 6761
Myōkō, Naganuma, 6574
Myŏngsŏng (Buddhist nun), 6761
Myō-ō, 2802
Myōryū (Buddhist monk), 9076
Myōzen (Buddhist monk), 1244, 2385
Myrddin (mythic figure), 5878
Myrtle, 9337–9338
Myrtle Beach (South Carolina), Meher Baba and, 5829
My Side of the Bridge (Brodie), 648–649, 650
Myss, Caroline, healing philosophy of, 3851
Mystagogue, 5384
Mystagogy of the Holy Spirit (Photios), 7135, 7136
Mystai, 6893–6894
Mysteries. *See also* Sacraments
of the Buddha, in Shingon Buddhism, 8351
in esotericism, 2842
God as, as Holocaust response, 4094
orgies as, 6863
of supreme beings, 8868
Mysteries (Mani), 5649, 5651
Mysteriosophy, 6332–6333
Mysterium Coniunctionis (Jung), 341
Mysterium cosmographicum (Kepler), 5112
Mysterium fascinans, 7349
Mysterium tremendum, 7349
Mysterium tremendum et fascinans, 6930
Mystery of Elche, The (play), 2467–2468
Mystery plays, 2469–2470, 2474
of Middle Ages, dance in, 2153
Mystery religions, **6326–6334**. *See also* Eleusinian Mysteries; Orphism; *specific cults*
agriculture and, 193, 6328–6329
alchemy in, 247
Attis in, 2110
Buddhism as, 6327
Creuzer (G. F.) on, 2070
Cumont (Franz) on, 2093
Cybele cult as, 1452
Dacian Riders as, 2123–2124
defilement and purification in, 1459
definition of, 6326–6327
deification in, 2249
Greek, 6329–6330
civic religion and, 3670–3675
Eleusinian, **2751–2753**
eschatology in, 3684–3685
healing in, 3840
mysticism and, 3670–3675
origins of, 6329
as preparation for afterlife, 165–166
reincarnation in, 7679
impact of, 6332
key symbolism in, 5116–5117
light and darkness symbolism in, 5451–5452
Meter (Mother) in, 2109
mustērion, and initiates *vs.* noninitiates in, 7954–7955
and novels, early, 3056
orgy in, 6866–6867
Oriental, 6330–6332
origins of, 6328
phenomenology of, 6327–6329
purification rites in, 7756
Roman
healing and, 3841–3842
of Mithra, 6087, 6090
music in, 6305
secret symbolic language in, 8907
structure of ceremonies, 6327
syncretism in, 8932
tarot cards and, 1414
universal religions and, 4067
use of term, 6327
Mystery societies/communities, 7719
Mystical communion, in mystical ecstasy, 2680
Mystical ecstasy, 2678–2679, 2680–2681
Mystical Element of Religions as Studied in St. Catherine of Genoa and Her Friends, The (von Hügel), elements of religion in, 4150
Mystical experience, in eternity, 2853
Mystical idealism, of Merezhkovskii (Dmitrii), 5869
Mystical monotheism, emanational, 6160
Mystical Theology (Dionysius), 2355, 2356, 6337, 6347, 6990
Mystical union, **6334–6341**. *See also* Devequt; See also Nirvāṇa
annihilation in, 6335, 6338, 6339, 6340
asceticism for, 527, 528
Cabasilas on, 1343–1344
Calvin on, 1375–1376
celibacy and, 1476

Mystical union ***continued***
child as symbol of, 1567
comparative study of, 6335
with cosmos, 6342
ecstasy and, 2680, 2681–2682
al-Ḥallāj on, 3755–3757, 6338, 6339
hearts, divine and human, in, 3882–3883
in Hinduism, 1349
identity in, 6335–6340
images and symbolism of, 6335
language used regarding, 6334–6335, 6337, 6338
monism and, 6334–6335
mysticism and, relationship between, 6334
origins of, 6336
pantheism and, 6334
by possession, in Caribbean, 1436
Smith (W. Robertson) on, 8451
Sorskii (Nil) on, 8525
in Sufism (*See also* Sufism)
annihilation and persistence in union, 8812
Qur'an exegesis and, 8810
Suhrawardī on, 8827
Swedenborg (Emanuel) on, 8899
Symeon the New Theologian on the Trinity and, 8919, 8920
Mystici corporis encyclical, 1550
Mysticism, **6341–6359**. *See also* Consciousness; Religious experience; *specific mystics*
in Acehnese religion, 25, 27
in African religions, women in, 3401–3402
ahistorical approaches to, 7741–7742
alchemy associated with, 235
Almond (Philip) on, 8769
of alphabets, 270–274
androgynes in, 339–340
anthropomorphism and, 390–391
in Armenian church, Gregory of Narek and, 3694
atheism and, convergence of, 391
attention and, 604
Buddhist, 6244–6245
in Caribbean religions, in Santería, 8108
chaos and, 1539–1540
characteristics of, 6341–6342, 6356
Christian, 3003, 6346–6350
autobiographies in, 698
definitions of, 6355
development of concept, 6341
early, 6346–6348
ecstasy of, 2680–2681
Eriugena and, 2831
gold symbolism in, 1861
heart of God or Jesus in, 3882–3883
history, mystic understanding of, 4055
Hügel (Friedrich von) on, 4150
Hugh of Saint-Victor on, 4151
language of fire, 3120
learned ignorance in, 6990
love in, 8706
modern, 6348–6350
Origen in, 6889
paradox in, 6989
prophets in, 7427
of Quakers, 7549
sexual symbolism in, 7081–7082
Suzuki (D. T.) and, 8886
Symeon the New Theologian on, 8919–8920
of Underhill (Evelyn), 9450
"unground" or abyss, 1540
constructivist theory of, 6356–6357
constructivist *vs.* perennialist models of, 7746
contextualist approach to, 6357
criticisms of, 7744–7745
Daoist, 1588
Japan, influences on, 8379
women in, 3342
definitions of, 2680, 6334, 6341, 6355–6356, 9277
deity in, 2259
desire in, 2309
devotional aspect of, 2320
doctrines in, 6357
of Eckhart (Johannes), 2603
enthusiasm in, 2808
epistemology and, 2819
experimentalist approach to, 6357
fate and, 3003
gender in, 6358
Greek, 3670–3675
Hindu, 6342–6344
in *Haṭhayoga,* 3794
in Krama Śaivism, 8045–8046
in Trika Sáivism, interiorization in, 8046–8047
and poetry, 7208
sacramental mysticism in, 7955
history of study of, 6358
in Indian religion, sacred emptiness and, 1539–1540
intuition in, 4525
Islamic, 2977, 3003, 6350–6352 (*See also* Sufism)
calendar of, 4714
dualism in, 2514
in Javanese Islam, 4816
origins of, 5204
poetry in, 7222
prophets in, 7427
religious experience and, 7739–7740
samā' (listening parties), **8064–8066**
Schimmel (Annemarie) on love in, 8149
studies on, 4718
ṣuḥbah ("companionship") in, **8825–8826**
Suhrawardī on, 8827
Ṭabāṭabā'ī's contribution to, 8946
travel and *ṣuḥbah* ("companionship") in, 8826
Jain, 4770
James (William) on, 4777, 7741–7742
Jewish, 3003, 6352–6354 (*See also* Heikhalot mysticism; *Merkavah* mysticism; Qabbalah)
'Aqiva' ben Yosef in, 442
ascension in, 522–523
in Ashkenazic Hasidism, 544–545
Baḥye on, 741
Buber (Martin) on, 1056
devotion in, 2320
diversity in forms of, 6352
Dov Ber of Mezhirich and, 2429–2430
of Eliyyahu ben Shelomoh Zalman, 2773–2774
eschatological, 6352–6354
God in, 3550–3551
Hasidic, 3791, 3792, 6352–6353, 6354, 7641, 8371
hierarchy in, 8709
iconography of, 4340–4341
intuition in, 4526
in Jewish Renewal, 4869, 4872
and *kashrut* laws, 5108
letter, 271–273, 6353
Löw (Yehudah ben Betsal'el of Prague) on, 5520
Lurianic, 5532–5533, 7534–7535
medieval, 4980–4981
messianism and, 5977
Philo Judaeus in, 7107
prophets in, 7427
religious experience and, 7739
in Safed, 4998–4999
Shim'on bar Yoh'ai and, 8347
spirit possession in, 2533
and Tosafists, 9250
of Joachim of Fiore, 4928–4929
of Joan of Arc, 4929
of John of the Cross, 4941–4942
light and darkness symbolism in, 5454
mirrors in, 6063–6064
in monasticism, 6125
monism and, 6143
mystical state, James (William) on, 1948
mystical union and, relationship between, 6334
nature mysticism, 6342
nature of, debates over, 7745–7746
nonreligious, 6342
obedience in, 6778
of Kabīr, 5051–5053
of Kook (Avraham Yitsḥaq), 5226
orgy and, 6860
origin of term, 6334, 6341, 6355
Otto (Rudolf) on, 7738
in poetry, 7207–7208
practices of, 6357–6358
in Protestant theology, liberal, 7738–7739
purist view of, 6357
Quietist, 7557–7559
redemption in, 7641
vs. religious experience, 7744–7745
religious experience in, 7695
as revelation, 7774
Schimmel (Annemarie) on, 8150
similarities across religions, 1869–1870
social dimension of, 6358
states of consciousness in, 1951, 6355, 6356
in study of religion, 6358
Ṣūfī (*See* Sufism)
tears in, 9025
and tradition, 9277–9278
Transcendentalism and, 2775
Troeltsch (Ernst) on, 7738–7739
union with deity through (*See* Mystical union)
unitive, 6334–6336, 6339–6340
use of term, 6334, 6355–6356
visionary journeys in, 9616
women and, 6358
French feminists on, 3029, 6358
Mysticism (Underhill), 9450
Mysticism (Zaehner), 6342
Mysticism and Kingship in China (Ching), 10031
Mysticism and Modernity (Cupitt), 7082
Mysticism and Philosophical Analysis (Katz), 7745
Myth. *See* Myths and mythology
Myth, Ritual, and Kingship (Hooke), 6380–6381
Myth, Ritual, and Religion (Lang), 2915, 5300
Myth and Ritual (Hooke), 6380

Myth and Ritual school, **6380–6383**
British, 6380–6381
critics of, 6381, 6382
influence of, 6382
James (E. O.) in, 4774
origins of, 6380
Scandinavian, 6380, 6381–6382
"Myth as History?" (Clarke), 2481
Mythengeschichte der asiatischen Welt (Görres), 3639
Mythe vécu (lived myth), 5390
Mythic ancestors, **325–327**
Mythic Image, The (Campbell), dreams in, 1378
Myth in Primitive Psychology (Malinowski), 5629
Myth of Kessi, in Hurrian religion, 4232
Myth of the Destruction of Mankind, 2715
Myth of the Eternal Return, The (Eliade), cosmic religion in, 1821
Myth of the Negro Past, The (Herskovits), 115
Mythologia Fennica (Ganander), 3104, 3105, 3111
Mythologiques (Lévi-Strauss), 3293, 3294
Mythology of All Races, The (Holmberg), 5709
Mythology of the Aryan Nations, The (Cox), 4459
Mythopoeic thinking. *See* Imaginal thinking
Mythopoetics, 5862
Mythos und Kult bei Naturvölkern (Myth and Cult among Primitive Peoples) (Jensen), 4825
Myths, Dreams and Mysteries (Eliade), 7374
Myths and Mythmakers (Fiske), 4460
Myths and mythology, **6359–6380**. *See also specific mythic subjects, themes, and religions*
ages of world in, serial periodization system of, 175–177
allegorical interpretation of, 6365
authority of, 692, 6359–6360, 6362
in ballet, 2162
Bianchi (Ugo) on, 863
binary periodization based on, 173
Campbell on, **1377–1380**
cannibalism in, 1403
Cassirer on, 1448
changes to, 6365
characters in, 6362
children in, **1566–1569**
classifying, 2898
colonialism in Africa interpreted through, 1854–1855
communing with transcendence through, 4814–4815
comparative study of (*See* Comparative mythology)
content of, 6362
about creation (*See* Creation)
creativity and, 8471
of Dacian Riders, 2124
definition of, 6359, 7696
dema myth complex, 4824, 4825–4826
descent into the underworld (*See* Descent into the Underworld)
disappearance of, 6365
dreams and, 2489–2490
dreams as, 5114
economic basis of, 2671
Ehrenreich (Paul), natural mythology theory of, 2090
eternity and, 2856–2857
in ethnoastronomy, 2865–2866
etiological, 6362–6363, 6378
euhemerism on, 6365–6366
euhemerization, Chinese mythology and, 1623
evil and
classifying, 2898
framework for, 2897–2903
expression of truth through, 9370–9372
family in, 2982
Finno-Ugric, 1453
Fraser on, 1878
Freud on, 3216
functions of, 6359, 6362, 6372
Harva (Uno), systematization of, 3783–3784
history and, **6371–6380**
Eliade on, 1821
among traditional peoples, 6658
history of study of, 6365–6368
Christianity in, 6365–6366
classical, 6365
modern, 6367–6368
Romanicism in, 6366–6367
of human origins (*See* Anthropogony)
humor in, 4194–4195, 6363–6365
independent origin *vs.* diffusion of motifs, 1994
justice and, 6361
Kerényi (Károly) on, 5113–5115
keys in, 5116
lamentation and, as response to, 2897–2898
language used for, 6363
laws and, 5328
Leenhardt (Maurice) on, 5389–5390
legend *vs.,* heroes in, 3957
Lévi-Strauss (Claude) on, 8753
Lewis (C. S.) on, 5430
as literature *vs.* religion, scholarly debate over, 3660–3663
in modern world, 6368–6369
neurotheology on, 6493
orgy and, 6861–6862
origin of terms, 6359
origins as primary concern of, 6361–6362, 6372
Otto (Walter F.) on, 6932–6933
overview of, **6359–6371**
Pettazzoni (Raffaele) on, 7075–7076
in political power, 6361
power of, 7350
psychology of
Jung on, 5034
Kérenyi (Károly) on, 5114
of quests (*See* Quests)
rational explanations of, 6365
raw *vs.* cooked in, 6821–6822
recitation of, for healing, 3813
reflexivity and, 7649
of rejuvenation (*See* Rejuvenation)
in religious life, 7696–7697
and ritual (*See also* Myth and Ritual school)
Frazer (James G.) on, 3288–3289, 3460
Gaster (Theodor H.) on, 3288–3289
in Germanic religion, studies of, 3460
interrelation between, 2957
manism influencing, 5673
the sacred in
in definitions, 6359–6360
in studies, 6368
Scholem (Gershom) on, 8178
science affected by, 6361
science and mythological images, 1996
secular, 5034–5035
Smith (W. Robertson) on, 8451, 8452
solar, 2518
soteriology and mythic narratives, 8527–8528
structuralist view of, 8752–8755
structure of, 6362–6365
style of, 6362–6365
symbols as language of, 7696
symbol *vs.,* Creuzer (G. F.) on, 2070
themes of, 6362
time and, 1352–1353, 1759–1760, 6362, 6371, 6372
in typology of narratives, 6375–6377
unity of
history of search for, 6368
vs. variability of culture, 6360–6362
universality of, 1379
variety of, methodological implications of, 6360–6361
vocabulary of, 6361
words of, authority of, 6359–6360
Myths and Symbols in Indian Art and Civilization (Zimmer), Campbell (Joseph) and, 1378
Myths of the New World, The (Brinton), 4460
Myths to Live By (Campbell), need for myths in, 1378
My Way of Faith (Petre), 7070

N

NAACP. *See* National Association for the Advancement of Colored People
Na'amah (demon), 5459
Naaman. *See* Adonis
Na Areau the Elder (deity), 5760, 6009–6010
Na Areau the Younger (deity), 5760, 5761, 6009–6010
Naaseene Gnostics, 1452, 3518–3519
NAASR. *See* North American Association for the Study of Religion
Naassene Sermon, Attis myth in, 2536
Nabatean kingdom, 6385–6386
archaeological sites of, 6386–6388, *6387*
inscriptions from, 6385, 6386
languages in, 6385
rulers of, 6386
sources on, 6385–6386
Nabatean religion (Middle East), **6385–6390**
afterlife in, 6388
aniconism in, 6389–6390
deities of, 6388–6389 (*See also specific deities*)
as *betyls,* 6388, 6389
female, 6386, 6389
temples dedicated to, 6386
Nabetans, rock city of, 1472
Nābhāga (mythic figure), 5679
Nābhānediṣṭha (mythic figure), 5679
Nabhānī, al-, 198
Nabi (prophet), 7426
Nabia (deity), 4253
Nabī-vaṃśa (Sultan), 829
Nābi Vaṃśa (Syed), 10035
Nabokov, Vladimir, 3061
Nabonedo (king), power usurped by, 5163

Nabonidus (king of Babylon), 222, 223
Babylon and, 5948
moon and, 6172
Nanna under, 6415
Sin (deity) under, 447–448
Nabopolassar (Aramean ruler), 5948
Naboth (Ahab's wife), 969
Nabu (deity), **6390**
in Akitu festival, 222, 223, 6390
as angel, 345
Marduk associated with, 6390
origins of, 6390
writing invented by, 269, 6390
Nabu (prophecy), 7431
NAC. *See* Native American Church
Nachtigall, Horst, 475
Nacirikaumoli (deity), cargo cults and, 1422, 1425
Nade 'kleshn (female sponsor), 10071
Naḍīr tribe, Muḥammad and, 6225
Nāḍis (arteries)
and breath, 1044, 7363
cakras and, 1348
in *Haṭhayoga,* 3794–3795
in Tantrism, 8993
Nadler, Steven, on Spinoza (Baruch), 8681–8682
NAE. *See* National Association of Evangelicals
Naess, Arne, 2561–2562
anthropocentrism criticized by, 2608
Spinoza and, 2664
Naewa, Ten, as prophet, 2007
Naf (self)
in Qur'ān, 8567
in Sufism, as lower soul, control over, 8815
Nafana people (Ivory Coast), masquerade dances of, 2141
Nafrah (stampede), 7159
Nafs (breath), 1042
NAFTA. *See* North American Free Trade Agreement
Nāga (breath), 1043, 7363
Nagano, Yasuhiko, 9190
Naganuma Myōkō, 7794
Naga Padoha (serpent), 800
Nāga Pañcamī (festival), 9824
Nagar, Richa, 5414
Nāgaraka (prosperous citizen), *Kāma Sūtra,* instructions in, 8122–8123
Naga religion (Madagascar), butterflies in, 4507
Nāgārjuna (Buddhist thinker), 1208–1210, **6390–6394**. *See also* Mādhyamika Buddhism
and Bhāvaviveka, 860, 1212–1213, 1299, 5552, 5553
and *māyā,* 5794
Buddhapālita on, 1299, 5552
Candrakīrti's commentaries on, 1213, 1401, 5552
on criminal law, 5350
in curriculum of colleges, 1156
on *dharmas,* 6752
dilemmas and tetralemmas of, 5552
"eight commentators" on, 1075, 5552–5553
esoteric writings of, 6391, 6393–6394
on Four Noble Truths, 3180
on human personality, 7365–7366
on *karman,* 5100, 7365
mysticism and, 6344, 6345
on *avidyā* (ignorance), 6391, 6392
on *Guhyasamāja Tantra,* 3708
on *nirvāṇa,* 1207, 1208–1210, 6392, 6393, 6629
on *prajñā,* 7358–7359
on *saṃsāra,* 1207, 1209, 1210, 6393
on *śūnyatā* (emptiness), 1119, 1209, 1211, 1299, 5551–5552, 6391–6393, 7365, 8857–8858, 9017
monism and, 6145
on *svabhāva* (essence), 1208, 1209, 5552, 6391–6392
on *tathāgata-garbha,* 9017
philosophy of, 1119, 1299
prasaṅga arguments of, 5552–5553
on realities, 6145, 6391–6392
māyā and, 5794
and recitative *nianfo,* 6602
Tantric writings of, 6393–6394
on women, 4164
writing style of, 6393–6394
and Zhiyi, 1237
Nāgārjuna (Tantric Buddhist thinker), 6393–6394
Nāgārjunakoṇḍa (Buddhist center), 9043
Nāgas (deities), **6394–6395**
dwellings of, 6394
as fertility deities, 6394
in Khmer origin story, 4010
kingship symbolism of, 6394–6395
myths of, 4438
Nāga Pañcamī celebration and, 4016
Nāgārjuna and, 6391
worship of, 778
Naga Sadhus (nude ascetics), militant Śaivism and, 8418
Nagasaki (Japan), port of, given to missionaries, 4788
Nāgā saṃnyāsīs ("naked" ascetics), in *akhāḍā* military units, 8021
Nāgasena (Buddhist monk), 1186, 1298
Nagayon (Buddhist temple), 9053–9054, 9055
Nag dban rgya mtsho (Dalai Lama), 2131–2132
Nägelsbach, Karl Friedrich, 2958
Nag Hammadi codices, **6395–6399**
aiones in, 209
apocalypses in, 6396
archaeology and, 455
asceticism in, 3530–3531
burial of, 6396
and Christian heresy, 3530–3531
content of, 6396–6397
Coptic manuscripts, 5202
in Coptic Museum, 6395
Corpus Hermeticum in, 6397
dialects used in, 6396
discovery of, 3535, 6395
Gnostic, 3508, 3517, 6396
Gnosticism in, 3941
Gospel of Thomas in, 6395, 6396
in Hermetic corpus, 3939, 3940, 3941–3942
hypostasis in, 4241, 4242
Jesus in, 6396, 6398
Jung Codex (Codex I), 3512–3513, 6395
library of, 919–920
Mary Magdalene in, 5757
vs. New Testament Gospels, 6396, 6398
origins of, 6396
publication of, 6395–6396
Sethian Gnostic, 3517, 6396
significance of, 6397–6398
Sophia (wisdom) in, 8523
in studies of Gnosticism, 3515, 3535, 6397–6398
translations of, 3508, 3535, 6395–6396
Valentinian, 3512–3513, 6396–6397
wisdom in, 9751
Nagid (head of Jewish community), 4990, 4994
Maimonides (Abraham) as, 5612, 5613, 5614
Nāgīs (deities), 6394
in Dakota religion, 8534
Nagiya (shadow), in Dakota religion, 8534
Naglowska, Maria de, sexual magic and, 8251–8252
Nago spirits, 9636
Nāg Pañcamī festival, in Marathi religions, 5698
NAGPRA. *See* Native American Graves Protection and Repatriation Act
Nagugur (mythic figures), 658
Nagy, Gregory, 5468
Nahalot avot (Abravanel), 17
Nahḍa movement, 1674–1675
Nahdatul Ulama (union of Muslim teachers), 3367, 4667–4668, 4669, 9012
in Indonesia, 8653
Naḥḥās, Muṣṭafā al-, 6315
Nahj al-balāghah, 259–260
'Alī as author of, 259
commentaries on, 259–260
influence of, 259
themes of, 259
Nahmanides, Moses, **6399–6401**
Adret (Shelomoh ben Avraham) studying with, 36
on afterlife, 154
biblical exegesis of, 866, 867, 6399–6400
and Christiani (Pablo), 7233
education of, 6399
on Ibn 'Ezra,' 4265, 6399
on Maimonides (Moses), 24, 6399, 6400
methodology of, 6399
polemics of, 5976, 6400
on rabbinic law, 3748–3749
on Sabbath, 8257
on Torah, 9237
on tosafists, 9243
on war, 7231
on Zion, 9978
Naḥman of Bratslav, **6401–6402**
as *tsaddiq ha-emet* ("true *tsaddiq*"), 3790, 6401, 9379
death of, 6402
disciples of, 6401
on faith, 6401–6402
teachings of, 6401–6402
Naḥottei, 2743
Na-hsi religion. *See* Moso religion
Nahualli (shaman), 5908–5909
Nahuatl religion (Mexico), **6402–6403**
Christian missions and, 5915
costumbre of, 5925
deities in, 5934
dogs in, 2393, 2394
drama in, 2465
evil beings in, 6403
fiestas in, 6402
gender roles of, 3412
Holy Family in, 6402–6403
marriage of, 7812–7813
in Postclassical period, 5907–5909
Roman Catholicism and, 6402–6403
Nahum, 879
pesher of, 7064
Nahum (prophet), 7436
Nahuṣa (demon), 4467
Nai-ho Bridge, 1051
Nā'ilah (deity), 444
Nailed to the Cross. *See* Mouvement Croix-Koma
Naiman tribe (Mongolia), 4493
Naimittika pralaya (dissolution), in Purāṇic cosmology, 2018
Na'īnī, Muḥammad, 4702
Nainuema (supreme being), 2311
Nairobi, urban nature of, 2566
Naī talīm (new education), 861
Najaf (Iraq)
'Alī's shrine in, 260
hawzah of, 3800–3801, 3802
Najāt (Ibn Sīnā), 4274
Najiahu Mosque (China), 4638
Najm al-Dīn Kubrā, 9006
Naj Tunich cavern, 1473
Nakae Tōju, **6403–6404**
education of, 6403–6404
Neo-Confucianism of, 6404
in Wang Yangming school, 6404

Nakagami Kenji, 3074
Nakankwien, Theresia, 7809–7810
Nakatomi clan. *See* Fujiwara clan
Nakatsu Hime Zo (deity), vol. 6 color insert
Nakausabaria (deity), cargo cults and, 1422, 1425
Nakayama, Zenbei, 6404
Nakayama-dera Temple, Japan, healing in, 3869
Nakayama Miki, 4799, **6404–6406,** 9082, 9083, 9256
 in Tenrikyō, 6404–6406
 Shintō and, 8367
Nakazawa Shinichi, postmodernism and, 8778
Nakedness. *See* Nudity
Nak-Ho debate, 1932
Nakir (angel), 346
Nakl (anecdotal literature), 10035
Nakṣatra (lunar constellation), in Hindu calendar, 4015
Nakṣatras (asterisms), 9040
Nakṣatras (lunar mansions), system of stars in, 8733
Naksh-i-Rustam, 1472
Naksibendiyye brotherhood (Turkey), 1518
Nālandā (Buddhist monastery), 1115, 1119, 1121, 1125, 1164, 2337
 Śāntideva at, 8109
 Śīlabhadra at, 8398–8399
Nālāyira-divya-prabandham, 279, 8974
Nalimov, Vasilij Petrovich, on Komi religion and society, 5216
Nama (Bambara society), 777
Naʿmān. *See* Adonis
Namangani, Juma, 4630
Nama people, mythology of, 5136
Nāma-rūpa (psychophysical personality), 7364, 7366
Namaskāra salutation, secularization of, 8062
Namāz (prayer). *See also* Ṣalāt
 in devotional life, 9816
Nambi (mythological figure), 2575
Nambikwára religion (South America), impersonal power in, 8580
Nāmdev (saint)
 in *bhakti* poetry tradition, 3985
 in *Ādi Granth,* 32
 poetry of, 7210
 Vārakarīs and, 9504
Names and naming, **6406–6412**
 in African religions, reincarnation and, 7677
 ancestor worship and, 5185
 of animals, in Bible, 6406
 in Buddhism, recitation of, 5310
 Canaanite, 1387
 of children, in North American Indian religions, 6683
 didactic, of Akhenaton's god, 218, *218,* 219, *220*
 in genealogical systems, 3424–3425
 of Germanic tribes, origins of, 3447
 of God and other sacred beings, 6406–6409
  in African religions, 3568, 6409
  Akhenaton's, 218, *218,* 219, *220*
  in Chinese religion, 6408
  in Christianity, 6407
  in Greek religion, 3678
  in Hebrew scriptures, 3537–3539
  in Hinduism, 6406, 6408
  in Islam, 619–620, 621, 3562, 6407
  in Judaism, 3537–3539, 3547–3548, 6406–6407, 8347
  as sacred word, 5304
  in Sikhism, 6407
  in Sufism, recitation of *(dhikr),* 8822
 Guo Xiang on, 3710
 in Islam, 7825–7826
 of Levites, 5421
 of Mesoamerican religions, 7811, 7812
 in Oceanic religions, 7807
 of people, 6409–6411
  as amulets and talismans, 298
  Arab, 19, 3562, 6410
  Chinese, 6409, 6410–6411
  Christian, 6409
  Hindu, 6410
  Jewish, 6409, 7819
  Muslim, 6409–6410
  power of, 6406, 6410
  secret, 6411
  Sikh, 3337, 3716
 in Sikh Dharma, 3879
 in Sikhism, 8397
 spells and, 8675
 visualization of, vol. 14 color insert
Names and the statues, the, Muʿtazilah on, 5063
Namgyal dynasty (Sikkim), 7262
Namibia
 Khoi religion in, 5135
 !Kung San of, spirit possession of, 2140
 San religion in, 5135
Nami budi (underworld), in Kulina cosmography, 2012
Namma (deity), as Enki's mother, 5953, 5954
Nammāḻvār (Hindu teacher)
 comments on, 7172
 inspiration of, 4509
 in Śrī Vaiṣṇavas Sampradāya, 8728
 poetry of, 7210, 8974
Nam mkha' 'jigs med, Lha btsun, 1232
Namoluk Island (Micronesia), 5198
Namphamo of Numidia, martyrdom of, 1678
Nampi Āntār Nampi (poet), 7210
Nampijinpa (Aboriginal woman), 2479–2480
Nampiḷḷai (guru), 7172
Namucī (demon), killed by Indra, 9685
Namunu, Simeon, 6508
Nana Buluku (deity), 3166
Nana Burukû (spirit), 122
Nanabush (mythical figure)
 in Anishinaabe religion, 369
 in Ojibwa religion, 6659, 6660, 6661, 6663
Ñāṉacampantar (Saiva saint), as Nāyāṉār, 8044
Nanahuatzin (deity), 5888, 9255
 self-sacrifice of, 4187
Nānak (Sikh gurū), **6412–6414**
 aesthetics of, 6413
 and *Ādi Granth,* 32, 6413
 birth of, 6413
 on consciousness, 8549
 disciples of, 6412
 ethics of, 6413
 family of, 6412
 hymns of, 6413
 idolatry opposed by, 4431
 image of, 9623, vol. 14 color insert
 in *janamsākhīs,* 6413
 Islamic Sufism and Hindu *bhakti* combined by, 4007
 legacy of, 6413–6414
 life of, 6412, 6413
 metaphysics of, 6413
 and monotheism, 6158
 poetry of, 7211
 religious education and, 7734
 sevā (voluntary service) in, 8393
 and Sikhism, origins of, 8393–8394
 teachings of, 3878
 women and, 3335
Nānaki (Nānak's sister), 3335, 6412
Nananhuatzin (deity), 5935
Nanay religion (Siberia), 9395
 shamanism in
  categories of, 8282
  spirits in, 8284
Nanchon (spirit nations), 9636
Nandādevī (deity), 3608
Nandaka (sword), 967
Nanderuvuçu (deity), as supreme being, 8578
Nanderuvusú (mythic figure), 5985–5986
Nandeva religion, 6886–6887
Nandin (zebu bull), 4324
Nandi religion (East Africa)
 calendar, 1353
 initiation rites of, 2569
Nandīśvara (island-continent), in Jain cosmology, 2024
Nandy, Ashis, 3319
Nanē (deity), 491
Na-ngawulu (spirit), 144
Nāng thiam (female mediums), 5313
Nanguan Mosque (China), 4639
Nānhaithya (deity), as archdemon, 2128
Nanicoke religion (North America), funerary rites in, 6684
Nanjing (China)
 captured by God Worshipers Society, 1609–1610, 6041
 Islam in, 4632
Nanjō Bunyū, 1314, **6414**
Nan Madol site (Micronesia), grand rituals at, 6006–6007
Nanna (deity), 4316, 5955–5956, **6414–6415**
 as city god of Ur, 5949, 5955
 after death of Baldr, 3456
 Enheduanna as human wife of, 3377
 Enlil and, 6172, 6414
 functions of, 6415
 iconography of, 5955–5956
 in *Journeys of the Gods,* 2799–2800
 as moon god, 6172, 6414–6415
 as Norse mythical figure, 744
 Sin (deity) identified with, 6414
 Suen identified with, 447
Nanquan Puyuan, 1522
Nansapwe (deity), 6010
Nanshe (deity), 5958–5959
 as city god of Nina, 5949, 5958
 functions of, 3594, 5959
Nantara, in Jivaroan agragrian rites, 2558
Nantes, Edict of (1598), 7662
Nantosvelta (deity), 1485
Nanyue Huairang, Huineng as teacher of, 4155
Nanyue zongsheng ji (Daoist text), 2208
Nao Deguchi, 4790, 6573, 6824
 on gender transformations, 8695
Naomi (biblical figure), **7947–7948**
Naoroji, Dadabhai, 6998, 6999
Napoleon Bonaparte (French emperor)
 Papal States annexed by, 6973
 Pius VI imprisoned by, 6973
Napoli (ballet), 2156
Napurrula (Aboriginal woman), 2479–2480

Naqada II culture, 6465
Naqd al-ḥadīth (*ḥadīth* criticism), development of, 3730
Naqshbandīyah (Ṣūfī order), 9009
'Alī Shīr Navā'ī in, 263
in Central Asia, 4621, 4629, 9007, 9010
characteristics of, 8824
in China, 4635, 9010
development of, 4571, 9010
dhikr of, 4616, 4621, 9010
establishment of, 4571, 9009–9010
in Europe, 4681
jihād of, 4614–4615
khānagāhs of, 5118
Sirhindī (Aḥmad), role in, 8413
in South Asia, 4647, 4651, 9010
vs. Chishtīyah, 9010
vs. Shādhilīyah, 9010
Nara Buddhism, Kōben and, 5213
Nāradasmṛti (Hindu text), *dharma* in, 2329
Naraka (demon), 2368
Naram-Sin (Akkadian ruler), 5948, 5960
Nara-Nārāyana cult, 9499–9500
Nara period (Japan)
Buddhism in
Chinese Buddhism and, 1237
impact of ruling family on, 1175
monasteries in, 1175, 1179, 1180
Pure Land Buddhism, 1179
scriptures copied in, 1181
sects in, 1241–1242
Shingon school, 1176–1177
temples of, 9048
Tendai school, 1176
calligraphy in, 1371
Gyōgi in, 3721
Izum fudōki in, 4811
pilgrimage in, 7165
popular religion during, 4795
religion during, 4783–4784
Ritsuryō staate during, 5073
Narasiṁha (man-lion), 7501
Narasiṃ hagupta, 8
Narayan, Jaya Prakash, in Sarvodaya movement, Gandhi (Mohandas) and, 3273
Narayan, Kirin, 3145
Narayan, R. K., 10036
Nārāyaṇa, 9499–9500, 9506, 9507, 9508. *See also* Viṣṇu
Narbutas, Teodoras, 762
Narcissism
development of, 7484
vs. reflexivity, 7648
and religion, Freud on, 3217
Narcissus
and Christ, association between, 3064
mirrors and, 6063, 6064
Narcotics. *See also* Psychedelic drugs
in Amazonian Quechua religions, 282
mysticism induced by, 6342
Narek. See Book of Lamentation
Narlikar, Jayant Viṣṇu, on steady-state cosmology and Hinduism, 2020
Narmadā (river), 7861
divinity of, 2621, 7861
Narmada Valley Development Project, BAPS movement and, 8890
Narmer (Egyptian king), slate palette of, 2703
Narokobi, Bernard, 6508
Nāropa (Buddhist monk), on chain of instruction, 8713
Nā ro pa (Nāropa) (Buddhist scholar), **6415–6416**
life of, 6415–6416
and Mar pa, 1215, 3966, 5715, 6415, 6416
teachings of, 1225, 1287, 6416
Ti lo pa and, 6415, 6416
wife of, 1226, 6416
on women, 1219
Narrative(s), 6375–6379
complexity of genre, 6375
Egyptian, 2724
historical understanding through, 6377–6378
in Purāṇas, 7498–7499
of myth *vs.* history, 6371, 6372, 6376
place and, in indigenous traditions, 2618
in poetry, 7204
in rituals, 7858–7859
tafsīr on, 8952
time in, 6378–6379
typology of forms of, 6375–6377
violence and, 9599
visual, vol. 2 color insert
Narrative of a Residence in New Zealand (Earle), 7306
Narrative theory, on conversion, 1971
Narseh (king of Persia), 5660
Narsī Mehtā (poet), 5254, 5457
Narunde (deity), 3594, 3595
Nasadīya hymn
cosmology in, 2014–2015
creation in, 8545
Nasafī, al-, 4399, 8957
Nasā'ī, Ḥāfiz Abū 'Abd al-Raḥmān Aḥmad ibn Shy'ayb al-, *sunan* collection of, 3730
Nasatyas (twin deities), 9416
Nash, June, 3411, 5926
Nash, Roderick, Earth First! influenced by, 2562
Nasi' (prince), 928, 929, 9880–9881
Nasi, Gracia, 4997–4998
Nasi, Yosef, 4998
Nāsik (India), Kumbha Melā at, 5265
Nāṣir, al- (Abbasid caliph), 9006, 9008
Nāṣir al-Dīn (Berber scholar), 4604
Nāṣir al-Dīn al-Ṭūsī. *See* Ṭūsī, Nāṣir al-Dīn al-
Nāṣir al-Din Chirāgh, 6639
Nāṣir al-Dīn Shāh, 728, 737
Nāṣir-i Khusraw, **6417**
Ismāīlīyah and, 8331
Naṣirīyah movement, Qāsimīyah *vs.*, 8325
Naso, Publius Ovidius, 2994
on Prometheus, 7420
on reincarnation, 9330
Nasr (deity), 444
Nasr, Seyyed Hossein
comparative theology of, 9130
on environment, sacred nature of, 2613
environmental crisis addressed by, 2610–2611
on Islamic environmental ethic, 2653
on Mullā Ṣadrā, 6233
Nasreen, Tasleema, 10035
Nasrid kingdom, 4592
Nasruddin Hodja (Mullah Nasruddin), as trickster, 4214
Nasser, Eugene Paul, on humor and religion, 4210
Nasser, Gamel Abdul
in Free Officers movement, 6315
and Greek Orthodox Church, 3658
Muslim Brotherhood and, 108, 6315
Nasta, Mihai, 3467
Nāstika (unorthodox interpretation), sacrilege and, 8015
Nástin religionistiky (Hellre and Mrázek), religious studies and, 8774
Nāstitva (nonexistence), 7364
Nasu (deity), 2128
Nasus (spirits), 2393
Natalicium (baptism of blood), 780
Natalis Solis Invicti festival, 1743
Natalist, 7008
Naṭamaṇḍapa (architectural structure), 2448
Natan ben Yeḥi'el, 9246
Natan of Gaza, Shabbetai Tsevi and, 8258–8259, 8261
Natan of Nemirov, 6402
Natanson, Maurice, on reflexivity, 7648
Nataraja. *See* Śiva Nataraja
Natchez Indians, 6654
Nat cultus (Burma)
baṇḍāra cult, similarities to, 8410
political idiom in, 8411
Nath, Chuon, 5131
Nāthamuni (poet), 7210, 8974
Nathan (prophet), **6417–6418**
Nathan the Wise (Lessing), 5854
Nātha sect, Ŀakulīśa Pāśupata system, influence of, 4019
Nātha Siddhas (Śaivite sect), 8990
Nath order (India), *sant* tradition and, 3987
Nāth Paṇthis (yogins), 7211
Nāths sect, 5697
Nation, meaning of, 4862
National Anti-Slavery Standard, 1569
National Association for the Advancement of Colored People (NAACP), Garvey (Marcus) criticized by, 3287
National Association of Colored Women, 10038
National Association of Evangelicals (NAE), 2890, 7032
religious broadcasting and, 7711
National Baptist Convention of the U.S.A., 69, 10038, 10039
National Baptist Publishing House, 69
National Camp Meeting Association for the Promotion of Holiness, creation of, 4083
National Catholic Laymen's Retreat Conference, 7772
National Child Labor Committee, 33
National churches, secularization and, 8217
National Church of Nigeria, 109
National Commission for Protection of Human Subjects of Biomedical and Behavioral Research, 1455–1456
National Council of Churches, on genetic engineering, 8187
National Council of Churches of Christ (NCC), 2684
religious broadcasting and, 7711, 7712
National Endowment for the Arts, 2439, 4282
National epics, 2816
National Federation of Temple Brotherhoods, 7671
National Federation of Temple Youth, 7672
National Holiness Association
Methodism and, 4084
Smith (Hannah Whitall) and, 8445
Nationalism. *See also* Civil religion
and antipapal bias, 6973
anti-Semitism and, 402
Arab, 7287 (*See also* Fundamentalism, Islamic)
Nahḍa movement in, 1674–1675
black, 78–79, 9435
Garvey (Marcus) and, 3287
of King (Martin Luther), 5398
in Nation of Islam, 2767
Rastafari and, 7622

caliphate and, 1367
cargo cults and, 1418–1419
civil religion and, 5398
Donatism and, 1679
in Egypt, 1982, 6314–6315
of Eliade, 2758
in Europe, Christianity and, 1693–1694
in expansionism, 6904
feminine sacrality associated with, 3021
and folklore, collection of, 8763
German, Strauss (David Friedrich) and, 8748
gurūs in, 3714
Hindu
sectarian movements and, 4007
Shiv Sena (army of Śiva) party and, 8418
Hirata Shintō and, 8365
Indian (*See* India, nationalism in)
Japanese, 7271, 7272, 7273–7274
historiography and, 4022, 4032
Shintō and, 8357, 8366–8367, 8368–8369
Sōka Gakkai and, 8509
Jewish (*See* Zionism)
in Latin America, 1699
legitimation and, 5398
militant religious, 7791
millenarianism and, 6032
in Orthodox Judaism, Hungarian, 6899
in Philippines, Philippine Independent Church and, 8654
religious, 7255–7256, 8472–8473
in India, 7255–7256
in Israel, 7255
Shintō used for, 2639
in Southeast Asia, new religious movements and, 8654
and terrorism, 7257–7258
Turkish
heritage politics and religion and, 1810
of Gökalp (Ziya), 3624–3625
ummah and, 9447–9448
in Zionism, 4984, 9978, 9979
National Laywomen's Retreat Movement, 7772
National Learning, in Japan, 5073, 9311. *See also* Kokugaku
National Legionary State (Romania), 2760
National Missionary Society, in ashram movement, 546
National Muhammadan Association, 289
National Museum of the American Indian (Washington), 6244
National religions, 9800–9801, 9802
history of religions approach on, 4066
National Religious Broadcasters (NRB), 7711
National Religious Partnership for the Environment (NRPE), 2613
National Religious Party (Mafdal), 788, 7681
National Religious Party (NRP), 9980–9981
National Secular Society, 844
National security state, criticized by Latin American bishops, 1704
National Socialism, German. *See* Nazism
National Spiritualist Association of Churches, 8718
National Woman Suffrage Association (NWSA), Gage (Matilda Joslyn) in, 3251–3252
National Women's League of the United Synagogue of America, Conservative Judaism and, 1959
Nation Dance. *See* Big Drum Dance
Nation of Gods and Earths (Islamic movement), 4689
Nation of Islam, 4688–4689, **6418–6421**
beliefs of, 4688
civil rights movement opposed by, 4688–4689
conversion to, 6418
doctrines of, 72, 6418–6419
under Elijah Muhammad, 70, 6418–6419
establishment of, 70, 72, 4563, 4688, 6418
in Europe, 6568
under Farrakhan (Louis), 72, 6420
gender roles in, 6516
history of study of, 77
leadership of, 72, 4688, 6418–6420, 6563
Malcolm X in, 72, 4688, 5626
Nuwaubians compared with, 6768, 6769
origins of, 6563
schism in, 6420
social work by, 4688
violence by, 6551, 6564
Nation-state movement, and religion
Arabs and, 1674–1675
cargo cults and, 1424–1425
in Eastern Europe, 1685–1686
Jewish law *(halakhah)* and, 3744
social differentiation and, 8472
universality of the church and, 1690
Nation Without Art, The: Examining Modern Discourses on Jewish Art (Olin), 4342–4343
Native American Christianities, **6421–6425**
belief and practice of, 6422–6423
Black Elk and, 957, 958
contemporary, 6424
conversion to, 6422
diversity of, 6421–6422
roots of, 6422
scholarly interpretations of, 6423–6424
Native American Church (NAC), 6667, 6701–6702, 6719, **10053–10055**
ceremonies of, 10053–10054
Christian elements in, 10053
conferences of, 10055
creation of, 7302, 10054
laws on practices of, 7304, 10054–10055
leadership of, 10055
number of groups in, 10054
peyote in, 406, 7470–7471, 10053–10055
Pueblo religions and, 6729
rituals in, 10054
self-definition of, 7304
shamanism and, 8289
study of, 6671
Native American Church of North America, 10054
Native American Church of Oklahoma, 10054
Native American Graves Protection and Repatriation Act (NAGPRA) (U.S., 1990), 6244, 6711, 7303
desecration issues and, 8011
Native American religions. *See* North American Indian religions
Native American Religious Action (Gill), 7857
Native American science, **6425–6427**
Native American Theology, A (Kidwell et al.), 6424
Native Baptist Church (Nigeria), 104
Native Church of Winnebago, 10054
Native Hawaiian Recognition Act, 5342
Native Learning. *See* Kokugaku
Native Title Act of 1993 (Australia), 640–641, 690, 2479
Native Tribes of Central Australia (Spencer and Gillen), 683, 3489, 3491
Native Tribes of South-East Asia (Howitt), 265
Native Tribes of Western Australia (White), 688
Nativism
in Australian Indigenous religions, 670
Catholicism and, 1445
in China, New Confucianism and, 1923–1924
Japanese (*See* Kokugaku)
in Latin America, 6576–6577
messianism of, 5973
in Micronesia, 6005
millennial, 6547
in North American Indian religions, Handsome Lake *vs.*, 3771
revival and renewal activities in, 7784
Nativist School. *See* Kokugaku
Nativity, Feast of the. *See also* Christmas
as winter solstice feast, 8841
Nativity scene, 2400
Nat kado (wives), 1331
Nat kana:, 1331
Nat pwe:, 1331
Natronai ben Ḥavivai, memorization of Talmud by, 5852
Nats (spirits), 1328–1331, 2315, **6427–6428**
festivals for, 6427–6428
functions of, 6427
official list of, 6427
structured system of, 6427
Nat sin, 1331
Natsume Sōseki, 3071, 3072
N'atthitā (nonexistence), 7364
Nattier, Jan, 1085, 1267
Nattier, Janice J., on Pāṭaliputra council, 2036–2037
Natufian culture, 6460–6461
archaeological evidence of, 5111
Naṭukkals (hero stones), 8973
Natura, Arabic term for, 2652
Natural and Supernatural Jew, The (Cohen), 1848
Natural disasters, Hittite myths and, 4069, 4070
Natural evil, 9114
Natural History (Pliny), magic in, 5575
Natural History of Religion (Hume), 365, 577, 7125
Naturalism, **6428–6431**
ancient, 6428
atheism and, 581, 585
Blavatsky's (H. P.), 977
in Chinese religion
of Dong, 1591
mysticism and, 1588
of Old Text school, 1575
of Wang Chong, 9671–9672
Conservative Judaism and, 1960
contemporary views of, 6428–6430

Naturalism *continued*
critical, 6429
and cultural-historical method, 5261
debates over, 6429–6430
definitions of, 6428, 6429
evolutionary psychology and, 8479
fangshi and, 2989–2990
French, 6434–6435
Japanese, 3072
justification of, 6429
materialism and, 5775, 5777, 6429
Otto (Rudolf) on, 6929
religious utterances in, 6430
restricted *vs.* unrestricted, 6428–6429, 6430
scientific, Wilson (Edward O.) on, 8478
in study of Celtic religion, 1498
supernaturalism *vs.*, 8861
Vatican I and, 9528
in Vedic mythology interpretation, 9559
Natural joy. *See Sahajānanda*
Natural law, 5366–5367
American civil religion and, 1814
attacks on, the Enlightenment and, 8491, 8492
Blackstone (William) on, 5368
divine *vs.*, 5326
ethics and, 1651, 1652, 1653, 1654, 1655
Finnis (John) on, 5370
Grotius's (Hugo) theory of, 3703
Hobbes (Thomas) on, 4074
in Islam, harmony *vs.* illness in, 3831
Leo XIII and, 5411
Lewis (C. S.) on, 5430
morality and, 5366–5367
in Spiritualism, 8716
Natural magic. *See* White magic
Natural mythology theory, culture heroes and, 2090
Natural philosophy
definitions of, 6431
development of, 6431
Gnosticism and, 3524–3525
Kepler (Johannes) on, 5112
of Thomas Aquinas, 9162–9163
"Natural Philosophy" (Edwards), 2699
Natural Questions (Seneca), 7336–7337
Natural religion. *See also* Nature religions
Herbert of Cherbury on, 8762
Hocking (William Ernest) on, 4076
Kant's (Immanuel) religion as, 5078, 5079
Reimarus (Hermann Samuel) on, 7675
Rousseau's (Jean-Jacques) as, 7931
Schleiermacher (Friedrich) on, 7702
Natural Religion (Müller), 2661, 6236
Natural (undifferentiated) religious groups, 1865–1866
Natural revelations, 7774–7776
Aristotle on, 7775
the Bible as, 7774–7775
Plato on, 7775
Thomas Aquinas on, 7775–7776
Natural selection
in evolution, 2908
evolutionary psychology and, 8477
religion and, 8479
in sociobiology, 2916
Natural Selection and Tropical Nature (Wallace), 379
Natural Theology (Paley), 2909, 4517
Natural wisdom, 9755
Nature, **6431–6441**. *See also* Nature religions
in African religions
relation of king to, 5155, 5169
supreme being and, 3568
alchemy as completion of, 236
in Andean religion, 5291
anthropocentric view of, 2608
Aristotle on, 480, 484
in Aztec religion, 5293
benevolence of God and, 2908
in Buddhism, *Sangha* and, 2629–2630
chaos and, 1538
children and, 1567
in Chinese religion
Heaven as order of, 1587–1588
society, relationship with, 1591
in Christianity
absent from creation, 2649
early theology and, 2647
in Eucharist, 2648
Newman (John Henry) on, 6510
Roman Catholicism, 7883
classification of religions and, 1818, 1819
in Confucianism, 2631–2632
protection of, 2632–2633
as religious symbolism, 2633–2634
self-realization and, 2633
culture and, 7796, 7803
dainas (folk songs) dealing with, 2128
in Daoism, 2631, 2636
in art, vol. 11 color insert
in *Neijing tu*, 2635
as sacred space, 2637, 9056
dao of, 2173
definition of
in naturalism, 6428
within religion, 2605
deities of (*See* Nature deities)
divinity in, Hindu, 2621
Eliade on sacrality expressed in symbolism of, 1879
in the Enlightenment, 2797
Eriugena's theology of, 2830
in esotericism, Faivre paradigm of, 2844
exploitation of, 2608–2609
female embodiment in, 3037
feminine sacrality in, 3014–3018
in feminist spirituality, 9788
gender associated with, 3421–3422
genetics and, 3430
in Germanic myths, 3458
goddess as, 9601–9602
in Hinduism, definition of, 2620
human interaction with (*See* Ecology)
human relationship with, 6438
in idealism, 4354–4355
intelligent design of, 4516, 4517–4518
in Jainism, 2624
in Judaism
ambivalence about, 2607
vs. revelation, 2642–2643
revelation and, 2641
sacred texts on, 2642–2643
scientific interest in, 2642
Kant on, 2649
kinship extended to, 5185
in Korean religion, worship of, 5229
laws of (*See* Natural law)
vs. magic, as causality, 5570
in Mari and Mordvin religion, 5710
masculine sacrality in, 5758–5763
mathematical basis for, Kepler (Johannes) on, 5112
in Mesoamerican religions, 1358
modern divinization of, "playing God" problem and, 8187
in Mongol religion, 6826–6827
motherhood associated with, 2984
in Neopaganism, 6471, 6472
in New Caledonia religion, 6500
North American Indian views of, 5444, 6691
oral tradition and, 6425–6426
science and, 6425–6427
objectification of, 2608–2609
in Oceanic religions, 2006, 6788–6789
ordering of, sky mythology and, 8428
personification of, worship of, 2662
in Rastafarianism, 1438
rejuvenating power of, 7682–7683
relation of kings to, 5155, 5157
religious communities focused on, 1864
as sacred, 2604, 6438–6440, vol. 5 color insert
contemporary, 2663–2664
in science, 2665–2666
Schleiermacher (Friedrich) on, 8164, 8166
in shamanism, Korean, 5229
Shintō and, canonical view on, 2639
speculations on, religious and philosophical, **6431–6437**
Spinoza (Barukh) on, 6148, 6435
spirits (*See* Nature spirits)
Steiner (Rudolf) on perception of, 8738
symmetry in, 6361
time and, 1759–1760
in Transcendentalism, Emerson's (Ralph Waldo) concept of, 2775
value of, among religions, 2665
virginity and, 9606
Western views of, 2606–2608
in Wicca, 9730, 9731
worship of, **6438–6441**
in Baltic religion, Latvian Saule (sun) cult, **8131–8135**
in Berber religion, 834
in Caribbean religions, 1427
by environmentalists, 2564
forms of, 6438–6440
the Grail myth as, 3651
studies on, 6440
writing on, as spiritual autobiography, 703
in Zulu religions, 10008
Nature Conservancy, founding of, 2608
Nature deities
in Chinese religion
Qin dynasty, 1590
Shang dynasty, 1582
Zhou dynasty, 1583
in Khanty religion, 5120–5122
in Mansi religion, 5120–5122
Nature mysticism, 6342
Nature of Christ. *See Physis*
Nature Religion in America (Albanese), 2661–2662
Nature religions
anthropology and, 2664–2665
diversity within, 2666
dominance in, 2663
ecology and, **2661–2668**
future of, 2666
history of idea of, 2661–2662

negative perspectives on, 2662–2663
political ideologies and, 2663
positive perspectives on, 2663–2664
religious studies and, 2664–2665
in Romanticism, 2664
science and, 2665–2666
"Nature Religion Today" (conference series), 2665
Nature's Economy: A History of Ecological Ideas (Worster), 2663–2664
Nature spirits
in African religions, in Kongo religion, 2001
in Haitian Vodou, 1433
in Micronesian religions, 6003
Nature writing, as spiritual autobiography, 703
Naturistic school of comparative mythology, 4459–4460
Naturopathy, in India, politics of, 3856
Naturphilosophie, Romanic, 6434–6437
essentials of, 6435–6436
influence of, 6436–6437
roots of, 6434–6435
Natya Ha 'Atse (deity), 2984
Nāṭya Śāstra (Sanskrit drama), 2136, 2436, 2447–2448, 7044
Naufian culture (Palestine and Syria), 6460–6461
Nau Fiora (deity), 9195
Naunet (deity), in Egyptian pantheon, 2705
Nauplian spring, 3177
Nauru people (Gilbert Islands), knotted ropes of, 5197
Nauvoo (Illinois), Mormons in, 6193
Navadvip, India, Vaiṣṇavas of, 1345
Navā'ī, 'Alī Shīr. *See* 'Alī Shīr Navā'ī
Navajo religious traditions (North America), **6441–6443,** 6657
androgynes in, 338
Apache traditions compared with, 6443
as Athapaskan nation, 573–574
bears in, 809
ceremonies of, 6442, 6443
Changing Woman in, 573, 3408, 6441–6442
chants in, 6442
cosmology of, 6441–6442, 6443
creation myth, 3015, 6441–6442, 6659–6660
castration in, 1450
and disease, source of, 3809
in *Diné Bahane',* 573–574, 8426
sky in, 8426
curing ceremony in, 6653
deities of, 573
Diné as proper term for, 6441
drama in, 2461, 2462–2463
dreams in, 2483, 2489
economic patterns and, 6720
gender in, 3408, 5762
classifications of, 3410
Gill's (Sam) study of, 7857
hózhó (beauty or harmony) and body in, 4160
iconography of, 4308, 4309, 4310
illness in, 6442
initiation rituals in, 4485–4486
Kinaaldá ceremony, 3019
life in, 5444
masculine sacrality in, 5759, 5762
medicine men in, 6652
pastoral mode of life and, 2302
poetry in, 7226
power in, concept of, 575–576
prayer in, 6652, 7369
Pueblo traditions compared with, 6441, 6443
quaternity in, 6442, 7550
rejuvenation myths in, 7682, 7684
rock painting and sacred places, 1471
sacred stories of, 573–574
sand paintings, vol. 3 color insert, vol. 11 color insert
shamanism in, 8289
sorcery, terms for, 2100
spiders in, 4507–4508
study of, 6672
taboo in, 8949
tricksters in, 9355
wind in, 575–576, 6442
witchcraft in, 9769
women in, 3408
Navajo tribe
as Bahā'īs, 739
in Native American Church, 7302
Navanābha Maṇḍala, 5641
Navapadma Maṇḍala, 5641
Navarātri (Hindu festival), 2526, **6443–6444**
in Hindu religious year, 4017
in Marathi religions, 5698
Navarro, Marysa, 3411
Navayana. See Engaged Buddhism
Naven (Bateson), 6801
Navi' (prophet), 7424, 7431, 7432, 9377
Navigation of Saint Brendan, 991
Navigium Isidis festival, 3384
Navosavakadua (Mosese Dukumoi), 6796
cargo cults and, 1422–1423, 1425
Nāwabs (Mughal representatives), 825, 827
Nawawi, al-, on Golden Rule, 3631
Nawawi al-Jawi, Muḥammad, 4665
Nawbakhtī, Abū Sahl Ismā'īl al-, and Mu'tazilah, 6320
Nawrūz (Persian New Year), 4714
Naxagoras, Ehrd de, on Hermetism, 3951
Nayaka people (South India), kinship in, 5185
Nāyakkas (supralocal rulers), 8976
Nä Yakku (kinsmen deities), in Vädda religion, 8409–8410
Nāyaṉārs, **8044–8045**
poetry of, 7210, 8974
saint-singer tradition and, 4005–4006
vs. Āḻvārs, 279
Nāyāyaṉ Deo (deity), 4434
Naykhiṃ (drum), 2497
Nayler, James, 973
Fox (George) and, 3181
Ñaymlap (deity), iconography of, 8602
Nayya Malachizodoq-El, 6769
Nazarenes. *See also* Church of the Nazarene; Ebionites
hair symbolism and, 3740
Nazareth Baptist Church. *See* AmaNazaretha
Nazarites, Samson as, 8099
Nāẓir (votive offerings), 3163
Nazirite Baptist Church. *See* AmaNazaretha
Nazism. *See also* Holocaust
anti-Semitism of, 402, 4085, 4984
astrology as instrument of, 2372
Baeck (Leo) fighting, 736–737
Baltic religious movements during, 764
Barmen Declaration adopted to address, 2061
Barth (Karl) fighting, 789, 791
Bonhoeffer (Dietrich) fighting, 1016–1017
Christianity in, 2663
attempt to blend, 6468
Eliade and, denunciation of, 2759
eugenics in, 2880
Evola (Julius) and, 2906
Fackenheim (Emil) imperative of resistance to, 2950
gay men in, 5864
Heidegger (Martin) and, 6637
Jewish resistance to, 6647
Jewish studies under, 4883
Jonas (Hans) and, 4948
Lutheranism in, 5540
Magen David in, 5559
national religion in, 1693–1694
as new religious movement, 6517
occult in, 2663
officers prepared for killing, 5743
Otto (Walter F.) and, 6932
paganism in, 2663
as portrayed in modern dance/ballet, 2163
as religion, 4088
renewal, promise of, 4085
as revolutionary millennial movement, 6546, 6549
in Romania, 2754
study of religion and, 10079
Vries (Jan de) and, 9644
women and, 3352
Naẓm (choice of words), 4371
Naẓm al-sulūk (Ibn al-Fāriḍ), 4261
Naẓẓām, al-, 4371, **6444–6446**
apologetics of, 428, 429
on God, 6445
in Mu'tazilah, 6319, 6444–6445
ontology of, 6445
originality of, 6324
soul, doctrine of, 8568
worldview of, 6324
NCC. *See* National Council of Churches of Christ
Ncwala ceremonies, in Swazi religion, 5169–5170, 8897
as rebellion, 5169
to strengthen king, 5170, 5171
Ndebele birth ritual (Zimbabwe), 7804–7805
Ndem (deity), dances devoted to, 2137
Ndembu Divination (Turner), 117, 9405
Ndembu religion (Zambia), **6446–6448**. *See also* Central Bantu religions; Southern African religions
Chihamba cult in, iniation rite in, 4197–4198
Christianity and, 6447
cicatrization in, 1003
circumcision in, 7505
color symbolism in, 1860
cults of affliction in, 62, 6446
divination in, 9405
God in (Nzambi), 6447
healing touch in, 9256
history of study of, 117, 118
initiation in, 7838, 9405–9406
life-crisis rituals in, 6446–6447
Lupinda in, 1004
marriage in, 5726, 6446
purification in, 7510
rites of passage in, 5460, 7799
spirits in, 6446, 6447

Ndembu religion (Zambia) ***continued***
taboo in, 8949
trees in, 9336, 9339
women's initiation in, 4484–4485
Ndi dibia ogwu (herbalist), 4366
Ndjambi (supreme being), 3574
Ndomadyiri (mythic figure), 776
N'domo (Bambara society), 777
Neander, August
on Gnosticism, 3514, 3531
Möhler (Johann Adam) and, 6113
Neanderthals
community of, 6950
flowers used by, 3136
funeral rites of, 6950–6951
Near-death experiences
afterlife revealed in, 135
of Judge (William Q.), 5023
Near East and Near Eastern religions, ancient. *See also* Mesopotamia and Mesopotamian religions; *specific countries and religions*
alphabet as calendrical, 1353
anti-Semitism in, 397–398
archaeology in, 455
Frankfort (Henri) and, 3188
attribution deities (planetary) in, 8427
comparative mythology, 1874–1875
contract, treaty, and loyalty oaths in, 2047
deities of (*See also specific deities*)
city, 3376
female, 3376–3377
warrior, 37
drama of, **2440–2446**
evil in mythology of, 2898–2901
fertility in, 3376, 3377–3378
gender in, **3375–3381**
and goddess worship, 3376–3377, 3592
goddess worship in, **3592–3599**
and development of civilizations, 3585–3587
evidence regarding, 3592–3593
figurines in, 3584–3585, 3592–3593
gender and, 3376–3377, 3592
Greek religion influenced by, 3678, 3679
haruspices in, 7336
healing and medicine in, **3824–3827**
Egyptian, 3826–3827
Hittite, 3825
Mesopotamian, 3824–3825
Hebrew scriptures and, 884–885
hierodouleia (sacred prostitution) in, 3966–3969
ḥokhmah in, 4079
Homeric poems and, 4108
homosexuality in, 4113
incense offering in, 4419
Jewish persecution in, 7055
judgment of the dead in, 5025–5026
kingship in, **5161–5169**
languages of, 3375
merit in, 5871
monolatry in, 3540
Neolithic religion of, 6460–6462
ocean in, 6806
repentance in, 7756–7758
Smith (Morton) on, 8448
soul in, **8535–8540**
temples in, **9061–9065**
theocracy in, 9109–9110
wisdom of
in *Ecclesiastes,* 2600
Israelite wisdom influenced by, 9764
studies of, 9764
women in, **3375–3381**
Near East studies, ancient, gender in, 3375
Nebesky-Wojkowitz, René de, 9191
Nebridius, 624, 627
Nebuchadrezzer
gold and silver of, 3626
Jewish persecution by, 7055
siege of Tyre by, 7128
Nebuchadrezzer I, Babylonian religion under, 5948
Nebuchadrezzer II, 221–222
Jewish exile under, 4830
Necessitarianism, chance and, 1527
Nechepsos, 563
Necho (pharaoh), 4959
Neckam, Alexander, on nature, 6433
Neckel, Gustav, on Baldr, 744
Necromancy, **6451–6454**
in Chinese religion, 6835
condemned in Torah, 2373
as demonic magic, 6452
demons conjured in, 5579, 5585
and exorcism, 2279
magic in, 5579, 5585
in New Caledonia religion, 6500–6501
Necrophilia, Kāpālika Śaivism accused of, 8049
Necropolis, 1472
Necropompa death rites, in Andean religions, pre-Incan, 8603
Nectanebo (pharaoh), Olympias and, 3903
Nectar of immortality, *khecarī* technique and, 3795
Nederlands Dans theater, 2163
Nedo, Tsering Yudron, 355
Needham, Joseph, 237–238, 240, 241, 1637, 5629
on *taiji,* 8959
on *wuwei,* 7022
Needleman, Jacob, 6522
on linear *vs.* cyclical time, 7992
on Socrates, 8709
Neevel, Walter, on Ramakrishna, 7613
Neferirkare I, 2725
Nefertem (deity)
in Egyptian pantheon, 2705
lotus associated with, 5518
Nefertiti (Egyptian queen)
Akhenaton as husband of, 217, 4285
as intermediary of the Aton, 2707
portrait of, vol. 10 color insert
Nefesh (soul), 1042, 9378, 9379
Maimonides (Moses) on, 8559
meaning of, 8556
psuchē and, 8561–8562
in Qabbalah, 8560
Negative confession (Egyptian), 2708
Negative eugenics, 2879
Negative theology, 2355, 9139
Derrida (Jacques) on, 2247
Negative way. *See Via negativa*
Negelein, Julius von, on bird, image of, 3127
Negi (senior priest), 7410–7411, 7412
Negrito religions, **6454–6457**
of Andaman Islands, 6455–6456
of Malay peninsula, 6456–6457
of Philippine Islands, 6454–6455
Negritos people (Philippines), vegeance of the dead and, 7781
Negro Church. *See also* African American religions
history of study of, 74
Negro Church, The (Du Bois), 73–74
Negro Church in America, The (Frazier), 74
Negro Family in the United States, The (Frazier), 74
Negro in the United States, The (Frazier), 74
Negro's Church, The (Mays and Nicholson), 74
Negro Spirituals (Shawn), 2159
Negro Spirituals (Tamiris), 2159
Negro World (weekly), 3287
Nehalennia (deity), 3450
Nehanda (spirit), possession by, 8696
Nehardea, *yeshivah* of, 9883
Nehemiah, 882, 6457
Asaph in, 7461
David in, 7461
Ezra and, 2946
Koraḥ in, 7461
miqra' in, 878
priests in, 5422, 5423
purity in, 7514
rewriting of, 898
Ro'sh ha-Shanah in, 7927
Temple procedures in, 925, 928, 930, 933
Torah in, 9231
Torah reading in, 883
Nehemiah (governor of Judah), **6457**
Neher, Andrew, on drumming, 2500, *2501*
Nehru, Jawaharlal, 556
Neidan (internal alchemy), 1603
creation of Laozi and, 5318
Neihardt, John, 361, 957, 958, 2484, 9609
role in *Black Elk Speaks,* 702
Neijing tu (Chart of inner passageways), nature and, 2635
Ne'ilah (closing), in Yom Kippur services, 7929
Neit (deity), 1002
Neith (deity), 3597
Neither Cargo nor Cult (Kaplan), 1421, 1422–1423
Nekhbet (deity), 2712
Nekhen (city), importance to Egyptian pharaohs, 5164
Nekliudov, Sergei Iu., 6142
Nekuia (descent into Hades), 5274. *See also* Hades
Nekyia (Dieterich), 2348
Nekyia (Homer), 2295
Neles (Cuna shamans), clairvoyance of, 2095
Nelson, Benjamin, on confession, 1941
Nelson, Geoffrey, 6523
Nelson, Hart, 74
Nelson, James, 5864
Nelson, Richard, 2618
Nelson, Robert, 3091, 3092
Nem ankh, relationship to keys, 5116
Nembutsu (Buddhist invocation), 3155–3156, 6602–6603. *See also* Nianfo
Buddha's name in, 6408
Genshin's role in, 3433, 6602
Hōnen and, 4119, 4120, 6602–6603
in Jōdo Shinshū, 4934–4935
in Jōdoshū, 4937
Nembutsu zammai (meditational trance), 4119
of Kūya, 5270
in popular religion, 4796
as sacred word, 5311
Shinran on, 8354, 8355
in Tendai school, 9079, 9080
Nembutsu-hijiri (ascetics), rites of, 3979
Nembutsu sect (Buddhist)
Benchō's role in, 818–819
Ennin's role in, 1242
suppression of, 1245
Nembutsu zammai (meditational trance), 4119
Nemean games, 8723
Nemequ (wisdom), translation of, 9764
Nemesis (deity), 7783
Nemesius (bishop), on souls, 8564
Nemeton (sacred place), 1491

Nemhain (deity), 1490
Nemi (lake), 7898
Nenbutsu (chanting), 1177, 1179
Nenets Samoyed. *See also* Samoyed religion
dream journey of, 1470
Nennius, on Arthur, 508, 509
Nentsy people (Arctic), 468
Nentsy Samoyed. *See* Samoyed religion; Southern Siberian religions
Neo-African cults, Caribbean, 1433–1435
Neo-Alexandrian Hermetism. *See* Hermetism
Neo-Buddhism, 1126, 1127. *See also* Engaged Buddhism
Hinduism challenged by, 6072
Neocatechumenate, 6568
Neo-comparative religious studies, 4461
Neo-Confucianism, 1589
Buddhism and, in Ming dynasty, 1607
Cheng-Zhu school
designation of, 1901
development of, 1603
metaphysics in, 1577
promoted by Qing emperors, 1579
Ching (Julia) on, 10031
in Japan, 1927, 2189
under Ashikaga regime, 4787
Hayashi Razan, role of, **3802–3803,** 8363
Shintō and, 8363
in Tokugawa period, 1245, 9310, 9311
under Tokugawa regime, 4789
Kaibara Ekken on, 5054–5055
kaozheng scholars on, 2129
in Korea, 1930–1933
Sŏ Kyŏngdŏk, role of, **8510**
Yi T'oegye in, 9891–9892
Yi Yulgok in, 9892–9893
Kumazawa Banyan and, 5264
li in, 9311
Lu Xiangshan in, 5540–5542
Mengzi in, 5858–5859
of Nakae Tōju, 6404
Ōgyu Sorai and, 6811
qi in, 7544, 7545, 9311
reassertion of, 1922–1923
as revival, 1603–1604
sagehood in, 8037
constructive discipline and, 8704
in Song dynasty, 2129
temples in, 9059
tian in, 9173
Wang Yangming school of (*See* Wang Yangming)
Zhang Zai in, 9957–9958
Zhou Dunyi in, 9967–9968
Zhu Xi in, 9972–9974
Neo-Darwinian synthesis, 2908–2909
Neoevangelicalism, 2890
Neofiti 1, 888
Neo-Frazerians, on ritual regicide, 5159
Neo-Gnosticism, 3527–3528
Neo-Hasidism, *vs.* Jewish Renewal, 4873
Neo-Hinduism
in Africa, 108
ashram revival in, 545–546
religious experience in, 7740
Vivekananda in, 9629–9631
Neo-Kantian philosophy
Cohen (Hermann), role of, **1850–1852**
Heschel (Abraham Joshua) and, 3961, 3962
Soloveitchik (Joseph Baer) and, 8518
Neolin (prophet), **6458–6459,** 6666, 6686, 9027
and Ghost Dance, 3474
Neolithic age, 6948
agricultural transition (Neolithic Revolution), 1464
Çatal Hüyük site (Turkey), 1801–1802
Lady of the Animals in, 5281
Natulfian culture in, archaeological evidence of, 5111
women in, 5281
Neolithic religion, **6459–6466**
agriculture and, 186
art of, geometry in, 3438, *3438*
birth in, 950
cave art, 1471
caves as sacred space in, 7974
circle in, 1791
doubleness in, 2423
funeral rites in, 7375, 7377
geometry in, 3438–3439
goddess worship in, 950, 3584–3585, 3593, 6462, 7377, 7378
limitations on knowledge of, 186
of Near East, 6460–6462
Çatal Hüyük site (Turkey), 6461–6462
Hacilar site (Turkey), 6462
Natufian culture, 6460–6461
percussion in, 7035
serpents in, 8457
sheep and goats in, 8309–8310
Southeast Asian
insular, 8647
mainland, 8641–8642
of Southeastern Europe, 6462–6464
syncretism and, 8928
in Tamil, 8973
textiles in, 9088
Neolithic revolution, 185–186, 9578
Neo-Lutherans, 5539
Neo-Manichaeanism, election in, 2747
Neo-Marxism, on liturgy, 5491
Neoorthodoxy, **6466–6470**
Edwards' (Jonathan) influence on, 2701
German, Hirsch (Samson Raphael) and, 5214
Jewish, Hirsch (Samson Raphael), role of, 4023–4024
theology of, 7118
Neopaganism, **6470–6474,** 6513
Baltic, 764
circles in, 7829
Crowley (Aleister) and, 2071, 2072
deities in, 6472–6473
druids, emphasis on, 1497
in Earth First!, 2563
feminism and, 7830
Gaia hypothesis and, 3022
gender in, 6516
initiation in, 7829
leadership in, 6560–6561
literature of, 6471
magic in, 6471, 6472
marriage in, 7829
nature in, 6471, 6472
neoshamanism (*See* Neoshamanism)
racial forms of, 1659
racist, 6549
rites of passage in, **7828–7831**
birth rituals, 7829–7830
for life changes, 7829–7830
marriage, 7829, 7830
of men, 7830–7831
seasonal, 7829
of women, 7830
rituals in, 6471
scholarly influence on, 2664
seidr ritual in, 8295
sexuality in, 7830
in United States, 6560–6561
witchcraft in, 9774–9775
Neo-Pentecostalism, 1550, 7030
in Africa, 106–107, 1724
Neoplatonism, **6474–6476,** 7191–7193
aesthetics in, 45
in alchemy, 252
Alexandrian school of, 6474, 6475
ascension in, 522
Athenian school of, 6474
of Augustine of Hippo, 7192
Boethius and, 1007, 6475, 7192
Bruno (Giordano) and, 1055, 6475
Cambridge Neoplatonists, Hermetism and, 3950
catharsis in, 1460
chief concerns of, 7113
Christian, eternity in, 2856
and Christianity, 6475, 6476
comparative theology of, 9128
on deification, 2249, 2250
on Demiurge, 2274
on demons, 2277
development of, 6474
eternity and time in, 2854
on evil, 7190
Ficino (Marsilio) and, 3049, 6475, 7193
Ghazālī (Abū Ḥāmid al-) on, 3470, 3472
on God, knowledge of, 9587
and grace, 3645
on *Henads,* 7191–7192
hypostasis in, 4240
Ibn Rushd opposing, 7192
Ibn Sīnā adopting, 4274
on images, 4352–4353
influence on *falsafah,* 2972
on intellect, 7191, 7199
intuition in, 4525
in Islam, 6475, 7192–7193
in Qarāmiṭah, 8328
soul in, 8569
in Italian Renaissance humanism, 4175
Jewish, 4889–4890, 4993
afterlife in, 154
Ibn Gabirol influenced by, 4266
souls in, 8558, 8559
knowability of God in, 182, 183
light and darkness symbolism in, 5452
Logos in, 5501
metaphysics of, 5990
in Middle Ages, 6475
mirrors in, 6063
in modern thought, 6475–6476
monism and, 6146
and mysticism, 6346
nature in, 6432, 6433
pantheism in, 6963
Plotinus as founder of, 7191, 7198, 7199
and Qabbalah, 6475, 7537
Rāzī (Fakhr al-Dīn al-) on, 7632
on reality, 7191
secret symbolic language in, 8907–8908
al-Shahrastānī and, 8267
ship symbolism in, 992
soul in, 2094, 7191, 7199
sun worship and, 8841
syncretism in, 8933
of Synesius of Cyrene, 1678
theurgy in, 9156, 9157
transmigration in, 9329
triadism in, 9348

Neoplatonism ***continued***
on Trinity, 7192
Neo-primal religious movements, in Africa, 102
Neoptolemos (mythic figure), Pindar on, 7174
Neopythagoreans
Numenius and, 7189
on transmigration of soul, 7186
Neoronke (mythical figure), 2312
Neoscholasticism, 9536–9537
Neoscholastic philosophy, Roman Catholic, Mercier (Désiré Joseph) in, 5868
Neoshamanism, 6470, **8294–8298**
aims, ideological premises, and worldview in, 8295–8296
compared to traditional shamanism, 8296–8297
democratic spirituality in, 8296
descent into the underworld in, 2297
drum journey in, 8294–8295, 8296
Native American practices in, 8297
seidr ritual in, 8295, 8296
Neo-Tantrism, 8993–8994
Neo-Templar movement, 9067
Neoteny, 10043
Neo-Thomism
in Latin America, 1701
Leo XIII and, 5411
of Maritain (Jacques), 5712–5713
Neotraditionalism
of American Orthodox Judaism, 6905
of Hungarian Orthodox Judaism, 6899
Nepal
affliction in, 57
Buddhism in (*See* Himalayan Buddhism)
dance in, 2138
Sherpas of, sacred offerings by, 3136
stupas in, 7837
trees in marriage ceremony, 9339
virgin goddess of, 9605
Nephrite. *See* Jade
Nephthys (deity), 3384
in Egyptian pantheon, 2704
in Kushite religion, 5269
worship of, 3596
Neptunus (deity)
priest of, 3126
trees as symbols of, 9337
Nergal (deity), 2963, 5959–5960, **6476–6478**
in Armenian religion, 492
functions of, 5959
iconography of, 4317
in Mesopotamian religions, 5950
Rasap identified with, 2596
Rashap identified with, 1384
Reshef and, 7761
in underworld, 9452
Nero (Roman emperor)
as Antichrist, 394
Christian persecution by, 7058
and Diana cult, 2347
Plutarch criticizing, 7200
in *Sibylline Oracles,* 8385
Nersēs I (Armenian catholicos), 488
Nersēs of Cla (Armenian catholicos), **6478**
on Council of Chalcedon, 490
Nersēs the Great, **6479**
Nerthus (deity), 3450
relation to Njǫrðr as, 6642
Nescience. *See Avidyā*
Neshamah (breath or soul), 1042, 9378, 9379
meaning of, 8556
in Qabbalah, 8560
Nesi'ut. See Patriarchate
Nespelen Indians. *See* Salish tribes
Nesti, Arnaldo, 4401
Nestor (monk), on Mari and Mordvins, 5709
Nestorian (Assyrian) Church, 2583–2584, **6479–6482**
in China, 1598–1599, 1725, 6480
debate with Buddhists and Muslims, 8197
Manichaeism and, 5669, 5670
development of, 3656
Eastern Orthodox distinguished from, 1765
vs. Greek Orthodox Church, 3656
in India, 6480
in Iraq, 1675, 6480, 6481
and *falsafah* movement, 2971
Mongol religions influenced by, 6140
Oriental Orthodox family and, 1673
and translation movement, 2971
Nestorianism, **6482–6483**
Athanasian Creed against, 2057
Cassian's refutation of, 1447
Council at Ephesus and, 2040, 2117
Council of Chalcedon and, 6483
Council of Ephesus and, 6483
Cyril of Alexandria and, 2117, 6483
doctrine of, 7876
Eutyches and, 2885–2886
Muslim polemics on, 7242, 7243
Theodoret of Cyrrhus and, 9123
Nestorian monument, 1725
Nestorius, 6480, 6482, **6483–6484**
Christology of, 4242
Cyril of Alexandria *vs.,* 2117, 6483
Ethiopian Church and, 2859
on Jesus, 6483
on Mary, 5753, 6482–6483
terminology used for, 2583
writings of, 6483
Neṣṭr (priest), 7405
Netherlands
in Aceh (Indonesia), 26
Anabaptism in, 7660–7661
Simons (Menno), role in, 8400–8401
colonialism
in Brazil, 1698
in Dutch Guiana, 1698
in Southeast Asia, 4660, 4661, 4666
comparative religion in, Otto (Rudolf) and, 4100
Grail movement in, 3653–3654
historiography in, 4041, 4047–4048
Islam in, 4675, 4676, 4679
Jews in, 5016
Mennonites in, 5860
missions from, to Indonesia, 1729
museums in, 6245
new religious movements originating from, 6568
Protestantism in, ethical theology movement, 1530
Renaissance humanism in, 4176–4177
study of religion in, 10081
Surinam under, 126
Netherworld. *See* Underworld
in Finnish religion (*See* Tuonela)
Netjeru (gods), 2711
Neto (deity), 4253
Nets. *See* Webs and nets
Netsilik people (North America), names of, 6406, 6411
Nettippakaraṇa (Buddhist text), 1270, 1272
Nettleford, Rex, 10026–10027
Nettles, Bonnie Lu (Ti), Heaven's Gate and, 3889–3891, 6555, 6561
Neturei Karta (guardians of the city), anti-Zionism of, 9982
Neues Organon (Lambert), 7087
Neugebauer, Otto, 3439, 3440
Neuland, Liene, 9421
Neumann, Erich, **6484–6485**
on Bachofen (J. J.), 3612
on feminine sacrality, 3018
on goddess worship, 3612, 3616
historiography of, 4043
on psychology of religion, 7476
on Sekhmet, 5464
Neumeier, John, 2162–2163
Neumer-Pfau, Wiltrud, 4298
Neumes, 1533, 1534–1535
Neuroepistemology, **6488–6492**
Neurophilosophy, consciousness and, 1952
Neuropsychology
aesthetics and, 50
of glossolalia, 3505, 3506
Neuroscience, **6485–6495**
anthropology and, 385, 386
current character of, 6485–6486
history of, 6485
on left *vs.* right hemisphere dominance, 5393
on mind-body relation, 6486–6487
on religious experience, 6487, 6492–6493
religious experience and, 2917
science and religion issues raised by, 8191
on shamanism, 8276–8279
states of consciousness, research on, 1952–1953
Neurosis, sacrifice explained by, 8004
Neurotheology, **6492–6495**
consciousness and, 1952
rituals and, 7850, 7857
Neusner, Jacob, 294
on 'Aqiva' ben Yosef, 441
on Hillel (Jewish sage), 3982
on midrash, 6020
on purity, 7513–7514
on Shim'on ben Gamli'el II, 8347
translations of midrash by, 6019
on unity in Judaism, 2287
Neutra, Richard, 796
Nevār Buddhism, *maṇḍalas* in, 5643–5644
Nevermann, Hans, on masks, 5769
Nevi'im (Prophets section of Hebrew scriptures)
author of, 889
dating of, 889
literal dramatization in, 4137
parts of, 879
as scripture, 1406
New Age movement, **6495–6500**. *See also* Metaphysical movements; Neopaganism
of 1950s–1970s, 6495
of 1980s–1990s, 6496–6497
alternative medicine in, **3848–3852**
energy healing systems, 3849–3850
holistic health and human potential movement, 3851–3852
metaphysics of health and healing in, 3849–3850
spiritual energies and, 3852
angels in, 348
Association for Research and Enlightenment in, 559–561
Besant (Annie) as source for, 844

Cao Dai movement, **1411–1412**
Cayce (Edgar), **1473–1474**
chakras (*See* Cakras)
Church Universal and Triumphant, **1781–1784**
cultic milieu and, 6495–6496
the Dreaming in, 666
in Earth First!, 2563
equinoxes and solstice pilgrimages in, 8429
Esotericism and, 6497–6498
firewalking in, 3120
folklorist studies of, 3148
future of, 6499
Holy Order of MANS in, **4101–4104**
individualism in, 6496, 6498–6499
in Japan, 4793
Worldmate movement, 8369–8370
Mesmerism in, 3849–3850
Native American traditions in, 8720
neoshamanism (*See* Neoshamanism)
as new religious movement, 6513
reincarnation in, 9330–9331
science and religion integrated in, 8186
Spiritualism and, 8718
spirituality and, cultural niche of, 3852
as spiritual supermarket, 6496, 6498
subtle energy in, healing and, 3850
Tantrism in, 8993–8994
texts claiming scriptural authority, 6531
Transcendental Meditation in, 9291
UFO religions in, 9433
vision quest in, 9610
women in, 6536
New Age Religion and Western Culture (Hanegraaff), 6781
New Apostolic Church movement (Pentecostal), 7031
Newark Museum, 6244
New Atlantis (Bacon), 253, 733, 734
"New Believers," in Russian Orthodox church, 2588
Newberg, Andrew
on meditation, 6487, 6490
and neurotheology, 6492
neurotheology and, 1952, 7857
on psychedelic drugs, 7467
New Britain religions
calendar, 1353
Christianity, Methodism, 9323
funeral rites in, 9227
Newbrough, John Ballou, 6531
New Buddhism, 7740
New Caledonia, missions to, 6791
New Caledonia religion, **6500–6502**. *See also* Oceania and Oceanic religions
Catholicism, 1738
deities of, 6500–6501
initiation, male, confession of sexual behavior in, 1884
Leenhardt (Maurice) on, 6801
origin myths of, 6501
New Christians. *See* Marranos
New Church. *See* Swedenborgianism
New Church of Southern Africa, 8902
New Collection Zhou Gong's Dream Interpretation, The, 2484
New Confucianism, 1923–1924
New Consensus, 7732, 7736
New Covenant, in New Testament, 2049
New Criticism, 5474, 5487
New Critics, 7206
New Dance (Humphrey), 2158
New Delhi (India), Jews in, 5007
New Dispensation (of Sen), 828
Sen (Keshab Chandra) on, 8227
New Earth rite, in Andean religion, 8617–8618
New England
Congregationalism in, 1938
funeral rites in, 9228
Praying Towns in, 7301
preparationist theology in, 4125
Puritanism in, 7519, 7520
Quakers in, 7547
search for paradise in, 6985
Twelve Tribes in (*See* Twelve Tribes)
New England Institute of Religious Research, 9411
New England Primer (Protestant text), vol. 14 color insert
"New England Way," Mather family and, 5778
New Fire Ceremony (Aztec), human sacrifice in, 4190
Newfoundland colony
Calvert (Lord Baltimore) and, 1373
Church of England in, 9300
under French rule, 9299
New France, Roman Catholicism in, 1711
Newgrange. *See also* Bruigh na Bóinne
Mac ind Óg and, 1484
Sídh and, 8392
New Guinea and New Guinea religions, **6502–6509**. *See also* Arapesh people; Kaluli people; Melanesia and Melanesian religions; Oceania and Oceanic religions
afterlife in, 145–147, 2006
ancestors in, 6266, vol. 6 color insert, vol. 10 color insert
ancestor worship in, 6504
birth rites in, 7807
boats in, 991
body decoration in, among Mount Hageners, 4160–4161
bull-roarers used in, 1321, 6265
cannibalism in, 1404, 3169
cargo cults, **1414–1425,** 1740, 6506, 6509, 7788
messianism of, 5973
celibacy in, 1475
Christianity, 1738–1739, 1741, 6507, 6508–6509, 7297
Catholicism, 9321, 9322
Protestantism, 9323
cosmology in, 6503, 6507
deities and ancestors in, 2005, 2007
deities in, 6503
Dobu Islanders, kinship of, 5185
Duna people, female spirits of, 3396–3397
Elema people, masks of, 5768
functions of, 6503–6506
funeral rites in, 3236, 7808, 9226
drumming in, vol. 13 color insert
gardens in, 3280–3281
gender in, 3396–3398, 6505, 6508
generation names in, 7809
genital operations in, 7808
homosexuality in, 4114, 4115
hypereridic rage reactions (amok) in, 3214
initiation rites in, 4477, vol. 9 color insert
Islam, introduction of, 5832
Kiwai people, agricultural myths of, 191
male cult in, 6505
Manus people
ghosts and, 5833, 5834
healing herbs and origin myths of, 3811
masks in, vol. 9 color insert
missionaries and, 5832
moon in, 6174
music in, 6265–6266
myths in, 6504
kukukuku myth, hair symbolism in, 3739
necromancy in, 6453
pig sacrifice in, 7145
political independence and, 9324
politics of, 5380
ritual calendar of, agriculture and, 187
rituals in, 6504
séances in, illness in, 3810
sorcery in, 6505
spirits in, 5833–5834
taboo in, 8948, 8949
tattooing in, 1001
transculturation in, 9296, 9321
Umeda people in, dances of, 2136
women in, 3396–3398
New Haggadah, The (Kaplan), 7636
New Hampshire Confession (1833), on free will and predestination, 3208
New Historicism, Jewish studies and, 4884
Ne Win, 9479
New Ireland (Melanesia), vol. 9 color insert, vol. 10 color insert
New Israel, 4859
New Jerusalem
the Family on, 2988
origins of, 6568
in Reformation, 7660
New Kalevala. See Kalevala
New Laws (1542), 5322
New Leadership movement, 1545
Newman, Barnett, 55
Newman, John Henry, **6510–6512**
autobiography of, 699
on conscience, 6510
epistemology of, 6510–6511
on faith, 2426, 6511
influence of, 6511
on liberalism, 6102
life and works of, 6510–6511
on Pusey (Edward Bouverie), 7523
on sacramentality, 6510
Tyrrell (George) influenced by, 9427
Newman, Richard, 75
New Pearl of Great Price, The (Bonus), 252
New religious movements (NRMs), **6512–6582**. *See also* Branch Davidians; Cults and sects; New Age movement; Syncretism
in Africa, **102–111**
Asian-derived, 108–109
among central Bantu, 1511
Christian, 102–107
classification systems for, 102–103
and disease and cure, interpretations of, 3815
Islam-derived, 107–108
neotraditionalist, 109–110
Zionist and prophetic movements, 1719–1721
African American membership in, 6563
aging of, 6571
anticult movements against, 395–397, 5375

New religious movements (NRMs) ***continued***
in Australia, among Indigenous people, **670–675**
history of study of, 670–671, 681–683
brainwashing in, 1031–1034, 5376–5377
allegations regarding, 6561–6562
debate on, 6515–6516, 6522–6523, 6525
characteristics of, 6513, 6518
charismatic leadership in, 6515, 6523, 6546, 6562
and development stages, 6564–6565
and violence, 6552, 6553
children in, 6516–6517, 6526, **6538–6544,** 6564
child abuse charges, 6516, 6526, 6539–6541
legal concerns and, 5377
in China (*See also* Falun Gong)
suppression of, 7270
civil suits against, 1033, 1034
classification schemes for, 6521
conservatorships and, 5375–5376
contexts conductive to producing, 6514–6515
on creation, 6530–6531
definitions of, 6523, 6557, 6572
diversity of, 6513–6514
economic differences and, 8152
education in, 6542
ethnic makeup of, 6563
in Europe, **6566–6572**
International Society for Krishna Consciousness, 4522, 4523
Temple Solaire, 9067–9069
experimentation in, 6513, 6514
and families, impact on, 6562–6563
financial resources of, 6562
founding of, divine encounters and, 6529–6530
functions of, 6533
government opposition to, 6518
human rights and, 5362
in Hungary, 4226, 4227
in India, Swaminarayan movement, **8889–8893**
indigenous, 5375
interpretation of disease and cure, and, 3815
in Japan, 3156, 6513, 6514, 6521, **6572–6575,** 7274–7275 (*See also* Shinkō shūkyō)
ancestor worship in, 324
Aum Shinrikyō, **631–633**
characteristics of, 6573
definition of, 6572
early, 6573–6574
globalization of, 6574
historical background for, 6572–6573
new, 6574–6575
periods of development of, 632
Risshō Kōseikai, 7794–7795
women in, 3346–3347
in Latin America, **6575–6582**
laws concerning, **5375–5379**
leadership in, controversy over, 6562
legal defenses of, 5378
legal perspectives on, 6525–6526
mainstream religions compared with, 6562
maturation and development of, 6564–6565
media's effect on, 5809
and millennialism, 6513, 6517, **6544–6551,** 6563–6564
Branch Davidians, 1036, 1037, 1039
in North America, 1714
Healthy, Happy, Holy Organization (3HO), **3877–3880**
Heaven's Gate, **3889–3892**
Holy Order of MANS, **4101–4104**
International Society for Krishna Consciousness, 4521, 4522, 4523
North American Indian, **6664–6668,** 6718–6719
contemporary social movements, 6667–6668
European colonization and, 6664–6666
fundamentalist movements, 6666–6667
reform movements, 6667
study of, 6671
in Oceania, 6794–6799, 9324
cargo cults, **1414–1425,** 1739–1740, 2007, 8516
prophets, role of, 2007
in Solomon Islands, 8516–8517
in Okinawa, 6813
opposition to, 1032, 1033, 1034, 1038, 6551, 6561–6562 (*See also* Anticult movements)
orgy and, 6874–6875
origin of term, 2085, 6522
pilgrimage and cities in, 1809
recruits of, 1031–1032, 1033
religious freedom and, 1714, 5362, 6518, 6541–6542
reversing programming by, 1032, 1033, 2291–2293
in Russia, 5377, 5378
scriptures of, 6516, **6528–6532**
secularization and, 8217–8218
sexual abuse in, 5377
solicitation laws and, 5378
in Southeast Asia
Cao Dai, **1411–1412**
Christian movements, 8653–8654
contemporary, 8654
Hindu-Buddhist movement, 8652–8653
in insular cultures, **8652–8655**
Muslim movements, 8653
studies on, 1032–1033, 1034, 6514, 6518, **6520–6528,** 6565–6566
syncretism in, 8933, 8936
in United States, 5376, 6514, **6556–6566**
Spiritualism, **8715–8718**
universalistic, religious experience in, 7738
use of term, 6513, 6557
violence in, 1034–1035, 1037–1038, 6217, 6517, **6551–6556,** 6564
case studies of, 6553–6556
explanations of, 6552–6553
study of, 6525
women in, 6516, 6526–6527, **6533–6538,** 6563
as founders, 9787
in Japan, 6573
in women's studies, 9788–9789
New Religious Right, The (Capps), analysis in, 1413
News, creation of, 4960–4961
New School Calvinism, Holiness movement and, 4083
New Science (Vico), 9589
New Spain. *See* Mexico
New Stone Age. *See* Neolithic age
New Temple Association, 7668
New Testament, **905–923**. *See also* Gospels, the Four; *specific books*
afterlife in, 156–157
aiōn in, 2855
allusions to humanity's fall in, 2968
Antichrist in, 394
apocalypse in, 410
apocatastasis in, 422
apocrypha to, 919
apologetics in, 427
apostasy in, 432
apostles in, 435–436, 920
atonement in, 594, 595–596
authority of (*See* Biblical literature, authority of)
baptism in, 1669
Bauer (Bruno) on, 804
Baur (F. C.) on, 805
on birth, 953
blasphemy in, 972
on breath and breathing, 1042
Canaanite parallels, 1394
canonization, 1406, 1408
ecclesiology and, 1771
canon of, 920–921
gospels, 920, 921
Muratorian canon, 920–921
Paul's letters, 920, 921
casuistry in, 1455
Cathari view of, 1456
charis and *charismata* in, 1545, 1549–1550
charity in, 1554
chastity in, 1558
church structure in, 1768
confession in, 1888
confession of faith in, 2056
conscience in, 1940
covenant in, 2049
cursing in, 2104–2105
David in, 2223
deity in, 2253
demons in, 2278, 3158
dreams in, 2489
early church and, 1660
ecclesiology in, 1770–1771
Elijah in, 2765–2766
excommunication in, 2921
exegesis of (*See* Biblical exegesis, Christian views)
exorcism in, 2928–2929
eye in, 2942
faith in, 2425, 2426
fasting in, 2996
fire in, 3119
Garden of Eden in, 6984
gender in, 3357, 3358–3359
ghosts in, 3475
glossolalia in, 3504
God in, **3543–3547**
attributes of, 615–616
names of, 6407
perfection of, 7039
Golden Rule in, 3630, 3632
"gospel" used in, 3640–3642
healing in, 3843
healing touch in, 9255–9256
heart symbolism in, 3882
heaven and hell in, 3884
hell in, Gehenna *vs.* Hades in, 8564
heresy, scripture as tool against, 3926–3927
heresy *(hairesis)* in, 3920
meaning of, 3926
Religionsgeschichtliche Schule on, 3920–3921
historical research on, Schweitzer (Albert) on, 8179
historiography in, 4028
and history, Christian views of, 4052–4053, 4055
hospitality in, 4139
humor in, 4196–4197
hupostasis in, 4241
idolatry in, 4357, 4358, 4359, 4385
Jesus in
family of, 5752
as God, 3546
God's relation to, 3543–3546

Jewish polemics on, 7233–7234
Jews in, 4855
justification in, 5039
kingdom of God in, 5149–5150
on law, 1670
leaven in, 5388
life in, 5445–5446
literary form of, 5470
Marcion on, 5701
Mark the Evangelist in, 5714
on martyrdom, 7057
Mary in, 5751–5753
Mary Magdalene in, 5756–5757
Matthew the Evangelist in, 5780
membership in the church in, 1777
merit in, 5871, 5875–5876
messianism in, 5972–5973
ministry in, 6044
miracles in, 6053–6054, 6056
Mishnah compared with, 6065–6066
mortification in, 6196–6197
Moses in, 6203–6204
music in, 6307
mustērion as disclosure of God's intention in, 7955
Myth and Ritual school on, 6381
number of books of, 905
oaths in, 9642–9643
origins of term, 1406
pain in, 6946
peace in, 7021–7022
Philistine religion in, 7103
pilgrimage in, 7152–7153
poetry in, 7218
possession by figures of, in Revival Zion (Jamaica), 1437
priesthood in, 7401–7402
in Protestantism, 7450–7451
proverbs and parables in, 6979
rain in, 7602
redemption in, 7640
resurrection in, 7766
sacramental theology in, 7959
sacrifice in, 8006
salt in, 8059
Sanhedrin in, 8101, 8103
Sarah in, 8112
Satan in, 2278, 2314, 8123, 8124, 8125
schism in, 8154
Schopenhauer (Arthur) on, 4447
as scripture, 8196, 8197
scripture, terms for, in, 8196, 8197
sheep in, 8310
sin and guilt in, 8404–8405
Solomon in, 8513
soul and spirit in, 8561, 8562–8564, 8565
sports metaphors in, 8724
Strauss (David Friedrich) on, 8747–8748
suffering in, 8806–8808
temptation in, 9070
text of, 921–922
theodicy in, 9116–9117
title of, Christian identity and, 871
translations of (*See* Biblical literature, translations of)
Trinity in, 3546, 9360
on tripartite canon of Hebrew scriptures, 879
Twelve Tribes on, 9410
"two books" metaphor originating from, 9421
variants of, 921
Vivekananda on, 828
vows in, 9641
wealth in, 9709
as wisdom literature, 9760
women in, 3357, 3358–3359
New Text school, 1574–1575, 1579, 1592
New Thought movement, 3095, 3096, **6582–6588**. *See also* Unity
Christian Science and, 2695, 6582, 6583, 6584
founders of, 6563, 6582
God in, Hopkins (Emma Curtis) on Divine Mind, 4128
growth of, 6582, 6584
healing in, 6584
mesmerism and, 3850
historical roots of, 6583
impact on American culture, 6582
leaders of, 6584, 6585
major communities of, 6585–6587
and New Age movement, 6497, 6498
in North America, as new religious movement, 1714
origins of, 6584
principles of, 6583–6584
prosperity teachings of, 6585
religious experience in, 7738
rituals in, 6583
studies on, 6582–6583
success of, factors responsible for, 6584–6585
Summit Lighthouse and, 1781–1782
women in, 6536, 6563, 6585
New Tidings religion, 6667
Newton, Isaac, 3005, **6588–6589**
antitrinitarian sentiment of, 6589
and attacks on theism, 582
chaos theory and, 1541
cosmology, effect on, 2031
Freemasons and, 3195
on Hermetism, 3949
mechanics of, 7136–7137
mechanistic model of, 8183
personality of, 6588
on space and time, 2878–2879
on "two books," 9423
worldview of, 3556, 3557
New Tribes Mission, Baniwa Indians and, 8625
New Win Myint, 3077
New World
dance in, 2149–2150
Islam in, 4682–4683
Neolithic religions in, 6460
Roman Catholicism in, pilgrimage in, **7149–7152**
search for paradise in, 6985
New World Translation of the Holy Scriptures, 4821
New Year festivals, **6589–6595**
in archaic cultures, 6590–6592
Babylonian
Akitu (*See* Akitu festival)
music in, 6275
Berber, 835
Buddhist, 1304, 1308, 9387
Chinese, 1641–1642, 2408, 2433
Egyptian, 2441
Greek, Panathenaia, **6958–6959**
hieros gamos (sacred marriage) and, 3976
in Inca religion, 8843
Japanese, 2410, 2411
purification of automobiles at, 3869–3870
Myth and Ritual school on, 6380, 6381
Nawrūz (Persian New Year), 4714
in North American Indian religions
Creek, 6656
Plains, 6656
as origin of ritual drama, 2440
in Portugal, 1442
Roman, 1353, 1354
Ro'sh ha-Shanah (*See* Ro'sh ha-Shanah)
time transformed as sacred in, 3973
in Tunguz religion, 9394
New York City
Hasidism in, Lubavitcher community in Brooklyn, 3793, 8171–8172, 8173
Vodou in
creolization and, 2068
urban space and, 1809
New York Library for the Performing Arts, Dance Collection of, 2151
New York Society for Ethical Culture, 2857–2858
Adler (Felix) in, 33
establishment of, 33
New Zealand. *See also* Maori religion
Christianity in, **1731–1737**
in 1960s, 1735–1736
Anglicanism, 1732, 1735–1736
church development in, 1732–1733
church-state relations in, 1733–1734, 1737
Maori culture, contact with, 1731–1732, 1735
Pentecostalism in, 1735
Presbyterianism, 7391
Roman Catholicism, 1732–1733
traditional culture merged with, 7297
women in, 1735–1736
World War II and Depression and, 1734–1735
church and state in, 1733–1734, 1737
colonialism in, and Maori religion, 5679, 5682, 5683
creation stories from, 3015, 7305–7306
education in, 1733, 1735
external influences, 1736
fiction of, 3084–3085
films from, 3097
incantations in, 7311
Māui in, 5782–5783
paepae in, vol. 13 color insert
protective images in, vol. 9 color insert
role of Tangaroa in, 8980
settlement of, 3083
soul in, 7311
study of religion in, 8768, 8770–8771
tapu in, 7310–7311
Treaty of Waitangi, 1731
witchcraft in, 7308
women in, 1734, 1735–1736
in World War II, 1734
New Zealand Baptist Union, formation of, 1733
Next Level, in Heaven's Gate movement, 3890, 3891
Neyārtha (implicit meaning), 1274
Neyiči Toyin, 6142
Nezahualcoyotl (king of Tetzcoco), 2465
Nez Perce (Niimíipuu) religious traditions, **6595–6597**
guardian spirits of, 6713
initiation of young girls in, 6715
'ipnúucililpt ritual in, 6596–6597
tuulíim cult in, 6596
wéeyekin system in, 6595–6596
Nga (deity), 6745
in Samoyed religion, 8095

Ngaanyatjarra, Pitjantjatjara, and Yunkunyatjara (NPY) Women's Council, 642
Ngag dbang bstan 'dzin nor bu, 1234
Ngai (deity), 3574
  ambivalence of, 5993
  in Kikuyu religion, 2567, 2568, 2575, 3574
  in Maasai religion, 3574, 5993
  on Mount Kenya, 3574
  prayers to, 3574
Ngaju Dayak religion (Borneo)
  afterlife in, 138
  cosmic center and, 6886
  creation myth of, language used for, 6363
  sexuality in, 8239
Ngaju people (Borneo), 1021, 7144
Ngakola (mythic figure), 93–94
Ngala. *See* Bemba
Ngal gso skor gsum (Longchenpa), 5193
Ngalki (essence), 6261–6262
Ngalmangii (mythic figure), 656
Ngalyod (Rainbow Snake), 7606
Nganasani people (Arctic), 468
Nganasani Samoyed. *See* Samoyed religion
Nganga (healer), 9370
  in Kongo religion, 5221
  witchcraft *vs.* Christianity and, 1721
Ngangkere (healer), counter-sorcery of, 3873
Ngang pa'i dris lan sprin gyi snying po (Longchenpa), 5193
Ngan wat (festival), 9831–9832
Ngarambe (city), Kinjikitile in, 5181
Ngarnmarra mats, 2379, 2380
Nga:rra ceremony, 2380
Ngarrangkarni (Time Long Past), in Australian Indigenous religions, 5050–5051
Ngarrindjeri people (Australia), 648–651
  and the Dreaming, 2479, 2481
  knowledge of, 650, 3392
  land of
    colonization of, 649
    struggle for, 649–651, 667, 3392
  Ngurunderi myth of, 649
  Seven Sisters story of, 648–651, 3392
  totemism of, 2481
Ngarunggani. See Dreaming, the
Ngathunggali (deity), 671
Ngatji (totem), 2479, 2481
Ngawang Namgyal (Buddhist monk), 7262
Ngejkurrewén rite, 5689
Ngenechen (deity), in Araucanian religion, 8580
Ngewo (deity), 3570–3571
  animals and, 3570–3571
  creation by, 3570–3571
  etymology of name, 3570
Nggd (to report or communicate), 7777
Ngillatún ritual complex, 5689
Ngo Dihn Diem, 7264
  Cao Dao movement and, 1412
Ngolobanzo (mythic figure), 7523
Ngoma (song-dance), 60
  divination identified with, 61
  as healing therapy, 3818
  history of study of, 118
  Lemba cult version of, 84
  role in society, 62
Ngonde people (Africa). *See also* Nyakyusa religion
  kingship of, 5170
Ngoni people (Africa), salve trade and, 1510
Ngor chen Kun dga' bzang po (Ngorchen Kunga Zangpo), 1225
Ngor pa order (Buddhist), 1225, 1230
Ngo Van Chieu, Cao Dao movement and, 1411
Ngubane, Harriet
  on illnesses, Zulu view of, 3817
  on solstice ritual, 8656–8657
Ngukurr religion, **6597–6601**
Ngundeng (prophet), 1547, 2570, 6745, 7443
Nguni religion (Southern Africa). *See also* Bantu religions; Zulu religion
  diviners in, diagnosis by, 3818
  gardens in, 3281
  rainbow princess cult in, 8663
Ngun Ki (deity), sickness attributed to, 3808
Ngurunderi (mythic figure), 649, 653, 2481
Nguyen Dong Chi, 3077
Nguyen Huy Tiep, 3078
Ngwa (magic), 9778
Nhat Hahn, Thich, 1142, 1283, 2785, 3078, 7264
  on wisdom and compassion, 2788
Nhialic (deity), 2567, 3573, 6744
  creation by, 3573
  name of, 6409
Nhok Them, 3077
Ni (deity), Huli territory and, 2006
Niagruisar, 2951
Nianfo (mindfulness of Buddha), 1239, 1293–1294, **6601–6603**. *See also* Nembutsu recitation
  in Pure Land devotion, 4923
  Shandao and, 8298–8299
Nias (Indonesia)
  Christianity in, 5827
  megalithic religion in, 5827
Nibandhas (digests), 2329
Nibbāna. See Nirvāṇa
Nibelungenlied (epic), journey of the soul in, 2814
Nicaea, Council of (325). *See also* Nicene Creed
  on Arianism
    Athanasius and, 571
    Constantius II rejecting, 572
  Arianism condemned by, 1966–1967, 3927, 7279
  Church of Cyprus at, 3658
  Constantine and, 1966, 7279
  and Easter, date of, 1741, 2579
  on incarnation, 3553, 4417
  on *Logos,* 5504
  overview of, 2039–2040
  Theodosius and, 9124
  on Trinity, 9361
Nicaea, Council of (787)
  idolatry condemned by, 4290, 4352, 4386
  Nikephoros at, 6619
  on relics, 7688
  Tarasios and, 9003
Nicaea, creed of, Nicene Creed *vs.,* 2056–2057
Nicaea Synod III (787), iconoclasm and, 2041
Nicaragua, Miskito Indians, conversion of, 1700
Nice, France, Feast of Fools in, 1441, 1442
Nicene-Constantinople Creed, 2583, 2585
Nicene-Constantinopolitan Creed, 490
Nicene Creed, 972, 2958. *See also* Nicaea, Council of
  Ambrose's contributions to, 287
  Arianism opposed in, 478, 1967
  in Armenian church, 490
  creed of Nicaea *vs.,* 2056–2057
  as ecumenical symbol, 2057
  filioque ("and the Son") clause, 1681 (*See also* Filioque)
  "holy catholic church" added to, 1771
  "I believe" used in, 2427
  Khomiakov (Aleksei) on, 5138
  as Niceno-Constantinopolitan Creed, 2056
    Council of Chalcedon and, 2040
  origins of, 2056
  Trinity doctrine and, 1666
Niceno-Constantinopolitan Creed. *See* Nicene Creed
Nicephoros. *See* Nikephoros
Nicephoros Callistus. *See* Nikephoros Kallistos
Nicetas of Byzantium, 7243
Nicetus Stethatos, on Symeon the New Theologian, 8919
Nichiji, Renge Ajari, 6606, 6620
Nichijō (monk), 6606
Nichiō, Busshōin, 6607
Nichiren (monk), 6574, **6603–6605,** 6605–6606
  disciples of, 6606, 6620
  influence in modern Japan, 6608
  Kubo Kakutarō influenced by, 7861
  life of, 6603–6604
  thought and works of, 6604–6605
Nichirenshū (Nichiren school of Buddhism), 1244, 6574, **6605–6610**
  and Nichirenshū, 1244
  and Risshō Kōseikai, 5400–5401
  and Sōka Gakkai, 1184, 4799, 5400, 6608
  Anesaki Masaharu as follower of, 342
  development of, 1180, 6606–6607
  drums in, 2497
  ethics of, 1282
  founder of, 6603–6606
  fuju fuse faction of, 6607–6608
  Jōdo Shinshū school and, 4935
  Kubo Kakutarō influenced by, 7861
  language in, 5310
  lay movements under, 6608
  modern, 7264
  and national identity, 7262
  nationalism and, Sōka Gakkai and, 8509
  and new religious movements, 6574, 6608
  observances of, 6608–6609
  organization of, 6608
  political power of, 7272
  Pure Lands in, 7503
  religious sources for, 6572
  in rural areas, 1182
  Shōshū sect of, Sōka Gakkai and, 8508, 8509
  tensions and controversies involving, 6606–6607
Nichirō, Diakoku Ajari, 6606, 6620
Nichizō (monk), 6606
Nicholas (pope), Photios opposed by, 2585
Nicholas (saint), in Finno-Ugric religions, 3108
Nicholas I (pope), 3690
  and Leo VI, fourth marriage controversy of, 8155–8156
  Photios (patriarch) and, 2041, 6967, 7135, 7136, 8155
  on supremacy of pope, 2585–2586, 6967
Nicholas I (Russian tsar), anti-Muslim campaigns of, 4617
Nicholas II (pope)
  Gregory VII under, 3690
  reform of, 6970
Nicholas V (pope), 6972
Nicholas, Feast of Saint, 2400
Nicholas, Gregor, 3097

Nicholas of Cusa, **6610–6611**
Bruno (Giordano) influenced by, 1055, 6610
Eckhart's (Johannes) influence on, 2603
on Hermetism, 3945
Italian Renaissance humanism, role in, 4175
on knowledge, 5206
on learned ignorance, 6989, 7193
on mathematics, 2878
on nature, 6433
Neoplatonism and, 6475
polemics of, 7244
Nicholas of Lyra
on hermeneutics, 5486
Rashi's influence on, 7620
Nicholas of Myra, anchor and, 332
Nicholson, H. B.
on Aztec religion, 716, 717
in *Handbook of Middle American Indians,* 5942
on Quetzalcoatl, 5936–5937, 5945
Nicholson, Henry B., on Quetzalcoatl, 5889–5890
Nicholson, Joseph, 74
Nicholson, Reynold, on Quietist Sufism, 8826
Nicholson, Reynold A., 4718, 7937
Nickerson, Peter, 7267
Nicklin, Keith, 5769
Nicomachean Ethics (Aristotle), 485
aesthetics in, 45
charity in, 1554
ethics and politics in, 7109
fine and just actions in, 1454
Ibn Rushd's commentary on, 4272
wit in, 4219
Nicomachus, on geometry, 3442, *3443*
Nicopeia (icon), 4390
Nicostratus, ethics of, 7189
Nicotiana rustica, 9216, 9217, 9218
Nicotiana tabacum, 9216, 9217
Nicotine, 9216, 9217, 9218
NI.DA.KUL (deity), 2597, 2598
Nidāna (setting), 1271
Nidānakathā (Buddhist text), 1064
Niddah (menstrual impurity), 7514–7515, 10052
Niðhǫggr, cosmic tree and, 1502
Nidra (deity), as sleeping god, 8440
Niebuhr, Barthold, 730
model for dialogue of, 3560
Niebuhr, H. Richard
on children in sectarian groups, 6538
on denominationalism, 2289–2290
on history as foundation of religion, 7117
on monotheism, 6161
and neoorthodoxy, 6466, 6469
on new religions, 6565
on Protestantism, 7449, 7450, 7457
on schism, 8152
on social action, 5397
Niebuhr, Reinhold, **6611–6614**
activism of, 6611
Detroit ministry of, 6611
development of thought of, 6612
on history, 4032
on human perfectibility, 7040
influence of, 6613
on film, 3100
Maritain (Jacques) compared with, 5713
and neoorthodoxy, 6466, 6469
on pastoral psychology, 7477
principal ideas of, 6612–6613
Nien-fo. *See Nianfo*
Niepan school, 1576
Nietzsche, Friedrich, **6614–6617**
on Antichrist, 395
on Apollo and Dionysos, 426
atheism and, 583
The Birth of Tragedy, 3053, 6614, 6615
on conscience, 1943
on dance, 2157, 2158
on Dionysos, 6865
Eastern philosophy influencing, 7112
in existentialism, 2925–2927
French feminists on, 3028
fundamentalism and, 2889–2890
Gnosticism and, 3527
on God, 3558, 6615
on heroism, 3956
influence of, 6616
on inspiration, 4511
on Jesus, 4845
life of, 6614–6615
metaphysics of, 5991
modernism criticized by, 7245
nihilism of, 2427, 6615
Otto (Walter F.) influenced by, 6932–6933
Ouspensky (P. D.) influenced by, 6935
on punishment, 5371
and religion, 6616–6617
schizoanalysis influenced by, 7490
on Spinoza (Baruch), 8685
Stoicism and, 8741
on Strauss (David Friedrich), 8748
thought of, 6615–6616
writings of, 6614–6615
Niezen, Ronald, 6678
on indigenous identity, 5340–5341
Niffari, 3123
Niflheimer (dark world), in Germanic creation myth, 3446
Nifoloa (deity), 6264
Nī-gan, 6812
Nigeria and Nigerian religions. *See also* Benin religion; Edo religion; Igbo religion; Ijaw religion; Jukun people; Yoruba religion
Aladura movement in, 103, 104–105
art of, 83–84
Christianity
Anglican church in, 1723
Pentecostalism, 7030
prophetic movements, 1720
and sociopolitical issues, 1723
dance in, 2137, 2141, 2142
Eckankar in, 2602
economics and Muslim identity in, 1810
films from, 3098
Islam, fundamentalist movements in, 7295
Islamic law in, 1724
literature of, 3087, 3088
Maitatsine movement in, 107
neotraditionalist movements in, 109–110
Nsukka Igbo people of, masquerade dances of, 2141
religious studies in, departments of, 8793
Rukuba people of, kingship of, 5170
Tiv people of, dances of, 2137
Nigerian Yoruba Assemblies of God, and dance, 2135
Niger River, 7862
Night
feminine sacrality of, 3017
in gardens, Eastern *vs.* Western, 3278
in Otomí religion, 6927
mythic origins of, in South American Indian religions, 8588
in Orphism, 6894–6895
Night Chant (ritual), 2462–2463
Nighthawk Keetoowahs, 1565
Nightingale, Florence, 3198, **6617–6619**
life of, 6617
theological ideas and activities of, 6617–6618
theological ideas influencing, 3297, 3361
and women's issues, 6618
Nightmares, 2484
Nigidius Figulus, Varro and, 4038
Niguma (Buddhist scholar), 1226
Nihāyat al-ḥikma (Ṭabāṭabā'ī), 8946
Nihilism, 2427–2428
in Mādhyamika philosophy, 860, 1209
Jonas (Hans) and, 4948–4949
Nietzsche on, 6615
Nihongi. See Nihonshoki
Nihongi kōsho (chronicle commentaries), 4802, 4804–4805, 4812
Nihonjinron (discourse on Japaneseness), 1248
Nihon ryōiki (Buddhist text), 2299, 4798
mappō in, 5686
women in, 3346
Nihonshoki (Nihongi) (Chronicle of Japan), 4804–4805, 4806, 7214
Age of the Gods in, *Kokugaku* interpretation of, 8365
age of the *kami* in, 7978–7979
alterations of, 4803–4804
Amaterasu Ōmikami in, 280
compilation of, 4783, 4809–4811
creation myths in, androgyny in, 2555
Daosim in, 2188
in early modern period, 4812
Emperor Yomei in, 8374
as history, 4801
interpretations of, 4805
on introduction of Buddhism to Japan, 1241
Izanagi and Izanami in, 4755
Jingō in, 4795
kami in, 8359
in medieval period, 4812
in modern period, 4813
mythology in, 4800
as national memory, 4806–4808
Ninigi stories in, 5180
Shotoku Taishi in, 8375
theater in, 2454
time in, 4807
Yamasaki Ansai on, 8363
Yamato Takeru in, 9868–9869
Niitsitapii religion. *See* Blackfeet religious traditions
Nijinsky, Vaslav, 2161
Nikāya (sect), 1193, 1290
Nikayabhedavibhangavyakhyana (Bhāvaviveka), 861
Nikāyas (schools)
division of Buddhism into, 8073–8074
in Theravāda Buddhism, 8074
in *saṃgha* and, 8079–8080
Nikāyas (writings)
dharma in, 2333
emptiness *(śūnyatā)* in, 8856
mediation in, 1111

Nikephoros (Byzantine patriarch), 4290, **6619–6620**
icon veneration defended by, 2585
on images, 4353
on prayer, 1046
Nikephoros Kallistos, **6620**
Nikkal (deity), marriage of, 1384, 1395
Nikkō, Byakuren Ajari, 6606, **6620–6621**
Nikkō shrine (Japan), Tokugawa shogunate and, 8363
Nikō, Sadokō, 6606, 6620
Nikodim of Leningrad, 7944
Nikodimos of the Holy Mountain, **6621**
Nikolais, Alwin, 2160
Nikomachos of Gerasa, on numbers, 6746
Nikon (patriarch of Moscow), 2588, **6621–6622,** 7942
Avvakum and, 712
Nikova, Rina, 2164
Nikowupwuupw (deity), 6009, 6011
Nilākaṇtha (deity), 4436
Nīlakēśi (Tamil text), on Ājīvikas, 212–213
Nile River, 7861
divine personifications of, 4319, 7862
in Shilluk cosmogony, 2567
water of, used for baptism, 779
Nile Valley, languages of, 2566
Nilo-Saharan languages, in East Africa, 2566
Ethiopia, 2572
Nilotic languages, in East Africa, 2566
Nilotic society, ritual regicide in, 5159
Nilsson, Martin P., **6622–6623**
on immortality of soul, 7871
on knots, 5197
on Minoan religion, 38, 40
on Mithraism, 6088
on myth, 6367
on Nock (Arthur Darby), 6643
on popular religion, 7327
Nilus of Sora. *See* Sorskii, Nil
Nilus the Ascetic, on spiritual guidance, 8710
Niʿmat Allāh Walī, 9010
Niʿmatullāhīyah (Ṣūfī order), 9010–9011
Gulshan-i raz (al-Shabistarī) and, 8263
Qāsim-shāh imāms and, 8333
Nimbārka (brahman), **6623–6624,** 9504–9505, 9548
and Kṛṣṇaism, 5253
on *mokṣa,* 6116
worship of Rādhā by, 7594
Nimbus, **6624**
Nimi (mythic figure), 5679
Nimngākān (myth), 9393
Nimrod, Freemasons on, 3194, 3195
Nimuendajú, Curt, 5985
South American ethnography of, 8595
Nina (Iraq), Nanshe as deity of, 5949, 5958
Ninana. *See* Inanna
Ninatta (deity), in Hittite religion, 4071
Ninazimua (deity), 5949
Ninazu (deity), 5959
Nine (number), interpretations of, 6748–6749
Nineiagara (deity), 5949
Nine Mountains school of Sŏn, 1646
Nine Saints, in Ethiopia, 2859–2860
Nineteen (number), interpretations of, 6750
Nineteen Letters on Judaism (Hirsch), 6900
Ninety-Five Theses (Luther)
controversy surrounding, 5535–5536
Eck's (Johann) response to, 2601
indulgences in, 5535, 7657
Ninety-nine (number), interpretations of, 6750
Nineveh (Assyria), destruction of, 5948
Ningal (deity), 5955
Ningirda (deity), 5959
Ningirsu (deity), 5958
anthropomorphism of, 5950–5951
as city god, 5950, 5958
Enki and, 5953
family of, 5951
household of, 5951
myths about, 5952–5953
Ningishzida (deity), 5949, 5950, 5959
Ningizzida (deity), 2521, 2522. *See also* Dumuzi
Ningublaga (deity), 5949
Ningxia (China), Hui Muslims in, 4638–4639
Ningxia Islamic Academy (China), 4634
Ningyo (mythic figure), 7683
Ninhursaga (deity), 5953, **6624–6626,** 7382
anthropomorphism of, 5950
Enki and, 5954–5955
Enlil and, 5952
names for, 5953
Ninib (deity), as keeper of keys, 5116
Ninigi (deity)
Buddhist use of, 4805
emperors descended from, 4801, 4810
as king, heavenly descent of, 5180
Nininsina (deity), 5959
Ninkū (Buddhist monk), 9079
Ninkurra (deity), 5956
Ninlil (deity)
Ashur and, 548
Enlil and, 2799, 5952
identification with Ninhursaga, 6624–6625
origins of, 3593
Ninmah. *See* Ninhursaga
Ninmar (deity), 5959
Ninnōkyō (Buddhist text), 1306
Ninomiya Sontoku, 6572
Ninshebargunu (deity), 5949
family of, 5952
Ninshō (Buddhist figure), 1180
Ninshubur (deity), 2521, 4403, 4404, 4405
Ninsuna (deity), 5949, 5950, 5958
Nin-ti (deity), 2896
Nintu (deity), 6625
Ninurta (deity), 5952–5953, **6626–6628**
anthropomorphism of, 5951
as city god, 5950, 5952
family of, 5951
mother of, 6624
Nabu and, 6390
Ningirsu identified with, 5958
Nio-zazen technique, Suzuki Shōsan on, 8887
Niphalios (monk), Severus of Antioch and, 8238
Nippon buppō chūkō ganbun (Eisai), 2741
Nippur (Sumerian city)
Enki and, 2791
Enlil in, 2799, 5949–5950, 5952
Ninurta in, 5952
Niqmaddu III (king), in tablets, 1390–1391
Niqmad II, Canaanite religion and, 1382
Nīrangdīn ritual, 9998
nirguṇa bhakti tradition
Saguṇa bhakti vs., 3984–3985, 10088–10089
Śaṅkara on, 4004
Sikhism and, 3986
Vallabha orders and, 3986
Nirguṇa brahman, 857, 9481
Śaṅkara on, 6144
Nirjarā (wearing away), 4768
Nirmala Sundari. *See* Ānandamayī Mā
Nirmāṇakāya (physical body), 1069, 1077, 1117, 4416, 9347, 9511
of Buddha, 9962
Nirodha (cessation of suffering)
in Four Noble Truths, 1296, 3178, 3179
nirvāṇa as, 6628
Nirṛti (deity)
and binding, 937
Rudra associated with, 7934
Nirvāṇa, **6628–6635**
in Buddhism, 996, 1206, 2628 (*See also* Enlightenment)
in Abhidharma tradition, 6628–6629, 6630
arhat and, 476
bodhisattvas refusal to enter, 1083, 1116
Buddhadāsa on, 1072
in Burmese Buddhism, 1331, 1332
in Chan (Zen) school, 6631–6632
in Chinese Buddhism, 1161
Dhammakāya movement on, 2325–2326
doctrine of, 2383
early, 6628
in East Asian traditions, 6630–6632
ecstasy and, 2682
emptiness and, 1117
as empty, 8856, 8857
eschatology of, 2834
in Esoteric traditions, 6632
as highest goal, 1204
in Hinayana cosmology, 2029, 2030
in *cakravāla* cosmology, 2027
in Mahāyāna Buddhism, 1116, 1207, 1208–1210, 1211, 1299, 2217, 6393, 6629–6630
karman and, 5099
Kṣitigarbha delaying entry into, 7408
liberation from desire and, 2306
merit making and, 5874
mysticism and, 6344–6345
Nāgārjuna on, 6392, 6393
neuroscience on, 6490
philosophy of, 1297
prajñā identified with, 7359
principles of, 1106
in Pure Land Buddhism, 6632, 8982
samādhi and, 4429
saṃsāra and, 8098
schools disputing over, 1195–1196, 1197, 1207
Stcherbatsky (Theodore) on, 8737
stupa representing, 1107–1108
Theravāda Buddhism, 7697
in Tibetan Buddhism, 1155
definition of, 6633
vs. eternity, 2854
in Hinduism, communion of soul with God in, 3886
in Jainism, 9207
as otherworld, 6924
Pure Land equivalent to, 1600
use of term, 6628
Nirvāṇa/Niepan school in China, 1576
Nirvāṇa Sūtra, in Buddhism, True Self in, 2217
Nirvikalpajñāna (unconstrued knowledge), 7359

Nis, 2951
Nisaba (deity), 4404
Nisbas (tribal affiliations), 4592
Nishapur (Iran), *madrasahs* in, 5556–5557
Nishida Kitarō, 1302, **6635–6638,** 7740, 9950
political life of, 6637
thought of, 6636–6637
Nishitani Keiji, 1302, 9315, 9950
Nisibis (Mesopotamia)
Ephraem of Syria in, 2812
hermits of, 2826
Niške-pas (deity), 5710
Niṣpannayogāvalī (Buddhist text), 1215, 4330
maṇḍalas in, 5643
Nisshō, Ben Ajari, 6606, 6620
Nisshō, Honda, 6608
Nissim, 4990
Nissim of Gerona, 867
Nisu'in (marriage), 7821–7822
Nītārtha (explicit meaning), 1274, 1300
in Mahāsāṃghika Buddhism, 5602
Nitchō, Iyokō, 6606, 6620
Nītiśāstra (science of right conduct), 6959
Nitobe Inazō, 3073
Nitschmann, David, 6191
Nityānanda, 5244
Vaiṣṇavism and, 1347
Nitya pralaya, in Purāṇic cosmology, 2018
Nitya pūjā (daily worship), 7494
Nityatva (infinitude), 7005
Nitze, William A., 3650, 3651
Niu cult, 5683
Niutou Farong (Chan master), 995
Nīvaraṇa (hindrances), 7357
Nivṛtti (renunciation)
Brahmā opposed to, 1024
mythic themes of, 4440
Niwabiuta (songs), 6300
Niwano Nikkyō, 5400–5401, 6574, 7794
Niya (vital breath), in Dakota religion, 8534
Nīyah (prayer), 7157–7158, 7343
Niyama (spiritual practices), 9894
aṣṭāṅgayoga (eight-limbed discipline), 8704
Niyati (fate), in Ājīvikas doctrine, 213
Niyyah (intention), *ṣalāt* (prayer) and, 8057
Niẓām al-Dīn Awliyā', **6638–6639**
and Khusraw (Amīr), 5139
khānagāh of, 5117, 5139, 9009
Niẓām al-Mulk, **6639–6641**
Ghazālī (Abū Ḥāmid al-) and, 3469
in Ash'arīyah, 533
madrasahs of, 5557
Nizami (Persian poet), sports metaphors of, 8724
Nizār (imam), 557
Nizārī Ismā'īlīyah, 4572. *See also* Ta'līmīyah movement
concealment, return to, 8333
development of, 557–558
doctrine of, 558
followers of (Assassins), **557–559**
ginēns of, 3494
Ḥasan-i Ṣabbāḥ leading, 558
imams in, 557, 558
ghaybah (concealment) of, 3469
in India, 8334
madrasahs of, 5557
opposition to, 558
origin of, 8324, 8331, 8332
origins of, 557
post-Alamūt developments, 8333–8334
qiyāmah doctrine in, 8332–8333
in South Asia, 4646
Njals saga, priestess in, 8024
Njǫrðr (deity), **6641–6642**
daughter of, 3218
in war with Æsir, 3449–3450
marriage to Skaði, 6641–6642
relation to Nerthus, 6642
and saga of Hadingus, 8142
son of, 3219
Tacitus on, 6942
Nkai (deity), in Maasai cosmology, 2000
N'Kamba (Democratic Republic of Congo), Kimbangu (Simon) on, 5143
Nkang'a ritual (Ndembu religion), 4484–4485
Nketia, J. H. Kwabena, 2496
Nkita (cult of affliction), 61, 5220
Nkongolo (mythic figure), 97
Nkore religion (Uganda)
creator god of, 2574–2575
hero gods of, 2575–2576
rituals of, 2577
Nkosi (sickness), 2457
Nkumbi (Pygmy ritual), 7525
Nkundo people, myths of, 93, 97
Nkwa Ese dance, of Ubakala people, 2138
Nkwa Uko dance, of Ubakala people, 2138
Noa (common/profane), 7310, 7311, 8947
Noah, **6642–6643**
Adam linked to, 6642
Atrahasis compared to, 598
Babylonian, 2982
biblical story of, 2968
Freemasons on, 3194
God's covenant with
animals in, 360
rainbow in, 7604
in Qur'ān, 2969, 6643
in Islam, 6736
moral laws received by, 3132
Muḥammad compared to, 198, 6643
nudity of, shame surrounding, 6741
qualities of, 3131
righteousness of, 6642–6643
Noahic laws
halakhah and, 3753
humanity bound by, 4859
Noah's ark, Hugh of Saint-Victor on, 4151
Noaiddi (shaman), and souls, protection of, 8088
Nōami (tea master), 847
Nobel prizes
for literature
to Agnon (Shemu'el Yosef), 179
to Bergson (Henri), 838
to Tagore (Rabindranath), 8957, 8958, 9319
for peace
to Aung San Suu Kyi, 1283
to Dalai Lama, 1283, 9186
to Ebadi (Shirin), 3365
for engaged Buddhists, 2786
to King (Martin Luther, Jr.), 5146
for physics, for Einstein, 2740
Nobili, Roberto de
as brahman, 6084
missions in India, 1729
missions in Tamil, 8978
writings of, 4445
Nobilior, Marcus Fulvius, 2994
Nobility, Cluniac monasticism linked to, 6132
Noble, Margaret, 9631
Noble Eightfold Path. *See* Eightfold Path
Noble ideal. *See Junzi*
Noble savage
idealization of, 2605
Rousseau on, 8594
Nobunaga, Oda (Japanese ruler), 6607, 7273
Catholicism under, 4787–4788
Nociception, 6944
Nock, Arthur Darby, 4416, **6643–6644**
approach of, 4044
on Apuleius' *Isis Book,* 3651
Cumont, challenges to, 2094
on suicide, 8830
Nocturnal teaching, Smith (Morton) on, 8449
Nodon (deity), 3123
Nō drama, 4798
Noel, James Anthony, 74
Noetic state, James (William) on, 1948, 6341
No Exit (Sartre), 2475
No Free Lunch (Dembski), 4517
Nogai Horde (Turkic tribe), 4613
Nogaret, Guillaume de, 1019
Noise, **7034–7038**
definition of, 7034–7035
examples of, 7034–7035
in rituals, 7037–7038
Noita (shaman or sage), 3109
Nokomis (deity), as Lady of the Animals, 5280
Nok sculpture, 84
Nolde, Emil, 4348
Nöldeke, Theodor, 4717, 5637
Noleby Stone, 7939, 7940
Noley, Homer, 6424
Noll, Heinrich, on Hermetism, 3949
Noll, Richard, on shamanistic visions, 8277
NOMA. *See* "Non-Overlapping Magisteria"
Nomadic cultures, New Year festivals in, 6591
Nomadism
and Finno-Ugric religions, 3108
in Inner Asia, 4488
in rural India, 4432, 4434
Nomads
development of monotheism among, 2301–2302
Dolgans as, 2394, 2395, 2396
Mesopotamian, kingship of, 5162
raids on agricultural societies, sexual images, destruction of, 3975–3976
visions of, 9615–9616
yogis as, 5192
Nomads of the Australian Desert (Mountford), 668
Nominalism, **6644–6645**
in Christianity, 3556
definition of, 3556
in epistemology, 2819
of Hobbes (Thomas), 4074
vs. realism, and nature, 6433
Nomlaki religion (North America)
bears in, 809
sweat houses in, 6715
Nommensen, Ingwer, missions in Sumatra, 1729
Nommo (primal spirits)
in creation myth, 95, 97, 100, 2390, 3569
cults dedicated to, 99
as culture heroes, 2091
iconography of, 4301
possession by, 2391
twin of, 9414–9415, 9416
Nonadorantism, Sozzini (Fausto Pavolo) on, 8673, 8674
Nonae (festival days), 7906
Nonassertion, in Buddhism, mysticism and, 6344, 6345
Nonattachment. *See* Detachment and nonattachment

Nonattainment, in Buddhism, mysticism and, 6344
Non-Chalcedonian (Oriental) Orthodox churches, 2584. *See also* Armenian church; Chalcedon, Council of; Coptic Church; Syriac Orthodox Church of Antioch
development of, 2584–2585, 3656
ecumenical agreement with Anglicans, 8940
ecumenical councils rejected by, 1765
in ecumenical movement, with Eastern Orthodox Church, 2589
vs. Greek Orthodox Church, 3656
Malankara Syrian Orthodox Church
formation of, 1729
relations with Syriac Orthodox Church of Antioch, 8941
in Middle East, 1673
Nubia, missions to, 1980
Nonconformist movement
Bunyan (John) in, 1322–1323
liberal Protestantism and, 6105
Nondenomenational schools, religious education in, 7732–7733
Nondualism. *See* Monism
in Hinduism (*See Advaita*)
Nonexistence, in Islam. *See Al'adam*
Nongqause (medium), in Xhosa religion, 8659, 8660
Nongqawuse (prophet), 7444
Non-harming, in engaged Buddhism, 2788
Noⁿhoⁿzhiⁿga (Little Old Ones), 6918
Nōnin (Buddhist monk), 9944
Noninjury. *See Ahiṃsā*
Noninterventionist strategy, 7137
Nonliterate ethnic traditions, as category of religion, 4065
Nonnus of Panopolis
on *aion,* 207
on cosmic waters, 3132–3133
on Lykorgos, 9170
Nonoalca Indians (Mexico), 9223
Non-ordinary reality, in neoshamanism, 8294
ontological issues regarding, 8295–8296
"Non-Overlapping Magisteria" (NOMA), 2658
Nonpossession, in Jainism, 2624
Non-self, in Buddhism, 5097–5098
Non-Separatist Independents, 2287–2288
Non-stealing, in engaged Buddhism, 2788
Nontheism, of Buddhism, 7316, 7318–7319
Nontheistic ecstasy, 2680
Nonu-Ma (deity), in Island Carib religion, 1427
Nonviolence, **6645–6649**. *See also* Ahiṃsā
Bernard on, 839
Bhagavadgītā on, 854
Bhave (Vinoba) on, 861, 862
in Buddhism, 6645
Nichiren, 6608
in Christianity, 6647–6648
in Earth Charter, 2657
in engaged Buddhism, 2785
Gaia hypothesis and, 3254
Gandhi (Mohandas) and, 6645, 6646, 6648
in Hinduism, 6646
in Indian religions, 6645–6646
in Islam, 6648
in Jainism, 4764, 6646
kingdom of God concept and, 5153
King (Martin Luther, Jr.) on, 5146, 5402, 6648, 7257
against political power, 7256–7257
in progressive Islam, 6100
in sermon on the mount, 4845
Noogenesis, 9033
Nootka people (North America)
knot symbolism of, 5198
masks of, vol. 4 color insert
whale feasts of, 6655
Wolf society of, 6656
Nō plays, 2454, 2455–2456, 7042, 7048
Norberg, Matthias, 5637
Norbertines, 7724
Norbert of Xanten, 6133
Norbu, Khyentse, 3098
Ṅor collection of *maṇḍalas,* 5643
Norden, Eduard
on Gnosticism, 3532
on *agnōstos theos,* 181, 182
Nordenskiöld, Erland, 474
Nordic Folklore Institute (NIF), Honko (Lauri) as director of, 4123
Nordic religions, rainbow symbolism in, 7604
Nordische Reisen und Forschungen (Schiefner), 1453
Norinaga, Motoori. *See* Motoori Norinaga
Norito, **6649–6650**
Norman, Ernest, 9448–9449
Norman, K. R., 996, 1313, 6956
Norman, Ruth, 9448–9449
Normative classification of religions, 1818–1819
Normative Judaism. *See* Rabbinic Judaism
Normativeness
canonization and, 1406, 1407–1409
Otto (Rudolf) on universality *vs.,* 4097
Norns (deities), 2984
moon associated with, 3018
number symbolism and, 6747
Norodom (king), 5131
Noroji (sorcerer), 2455
Norris, Kathleen, 703
Norse religion and mythology. *See* Germanic religion
North, Christopher R., on idolatry, 4357
North Africa and North African religions. *See also specific countries and religions*
academic study of religion in, **8780–8784**
Arab emigration to, 1680, 4581–4582
Berber (*See* Berbers and Berber religions)
Christianity, **1677–1680,** 4580
in Carthage, 1678–1679
Coptic, 1980
in Cyrenaica (Pentapolis), 1677–1678
Donatism (*See* Donatism)
and Islam, advent of, 1679–1680
persecution of, 2112
theologians in, 1679
theology developed in, 2581
Fatimid caliphate in, 1366
Heddawa cult of cats, 1463
hierodouleia (sacred prostitution) in, 3969–3970
inhabitants of, 4579
Islam, **4579–4591**
advent of, 1679–1680, 1981
Khārijīs, 835, 4583, 5126–5127
literature of, 4583–4584, 4586–4587, 4589
Mālikī school of law, 4579, 4584, 4585, 4601, 4698
marabout movement, 4588, 4589
mosques, 4584
origins of, 4579–4581
Ottoman Turks and, 4588
political, 4590–4591
rites of passage in, 7824–7825
Shiism, 4583, 4584
spread of, 4582–4583, 4600
zāwiyahs, 4586, 4588, 4589–4590
Judaism, 4579
to 1492, **4988–4995**
Northeast Africa, **5002–5004**
Sephardic Jews, 4996
since 1492, **4995–5002**
yeshivot of, 9884
l-'âr (compulsory relationship), implied curse in, 2101
monasticism in, 7724
Phoenician religion in, 4580
Roman religion in, 4580
Sanūsi Sufism in, 8824
zāwiyahs in, 5117
North America. *See also* Canada; Mexico; United States
academic study of religion in, **8784–8789**
anticult movements in, 395–397
archaeology in, 452, 456–457
Christianity in, **1708–1717**
churches, denominations, and sects in, 1711–1714
missions and conversions in, 1708–1711
national and regional churches in, 1714–1716
nuns and sisters, 6765
colonialism in
Anglicanism in, 350–352
impact on indigenous religions, 6664–6666, 6689–6690
engaged Buddhism in, 2786
Greek Orthodox Church in, 3659
Indian religions in (*See* North American Indian religions)
Islam, **4682–4691**
number of converts, 4563
as slave religion, 4682
spread of, 4683
ṭarīqah in, 9007
Jainism in, 4770
Jesuits in, 4842
Jewish studies in, 4884–4885
Judaism in
denominationalism in, 4985
environmentalism of, 2643
modern Jewish thought in, 4907–4909
ritual in, 4984
Mennonites in, 5860–5861
Nestorian Church in, 2584
Oriental Orthodox churches in, 2585
Orthodox, 2589
Protestantism, 7447
growth of, 7459
Puritanism, 7519, 7520
racism in, and nature religions, 2663
religion and ecology in, study of, 2608–2609
Sikh women in, 3337–3338
Spanish missions in, Serra (Junipero) and, 8231
Swedenborgian Church of, 8903–8904
North American Association for the Study of Religion (NAASR)
journal of, 10057
role of, 8788
North American Christian Convention, 2365
North American Conference on Christianity and Ecology, Eleventh Commandment Fellowship and, 4103
North American Free Trade Agreement (NAFTA)
Zapatismo and, 9930, 9933
Zapatista uprising and, 5931

North American Indian religions and societies, **6650–6730**. *See also specific tribes*
agricultural societies, religious themes in, 6654–6655
agriculture in, myths of, 191–192
ancestors in
mythic, 325
worship of, 2982
androgynes in, 338, 339
animals in
iconography of, 4309
in poetry, 7225–7226
prohibition against killing, 7299–7300
storm, 5995
of Anishinaabe, **368–371**
anti-colonial movements by, 9027–9029
appropriations of traditions of
New Age, 8720
Sun Dance and, 8848
Arctic influence on, 6653
astronomy in, 8734
Pleiades in, 8735
autobiography in, 702
Bahā'ī faith, 739
ballgames of, **752–756**
ball racing, 752–753
ball throwing, 752
racket games, 753–755
shinny, 752
and war, 754–755
baths of, 801
bears in, 806, 807–809, 4309
berdache gender reversal in, 4116
birds in, 948, 5995
Boas (Franz) studying, 988
boat burials in, 991
body in, symbolism and decoration of, 4160
body marks in, 1004
bones in, 1014
bull-roarers in, 7035
burial in, protection of burial sites, 8011
calendars, 1353
of California and Intermountain region, 6656–6657, **6712–6719**
creation stories of, 6713
first-fruit rites in, 6714–6715
postcontact religious change in, 6718–6719
puberty rites in, 6715
shamanism in, 6714
spirits of, 6713–6714
sweat baths in, 6715
tobacco use of, 9218
cannibalism in, 1403
ceremonial center at Mississippian sites, 1805
ceremony, role of, 1515–1516
charisma in, 1547
chiefs in, 7300
children in myths, 1568
Christianity, **6421–6425**
adaptations of, 2605
belief and practice of, 6422–6423
contemporary, 6424
diversity of, 6421–6422
Episcopal, 2264
missions, 1708–1709
and poetry, 7225, 7226
Protestantism, 7302
Roman Catholicism, 7301, 7302, 9035–9036
roots of, 6422
scholarly interpretations of, 6423–6424
Christian missions to, 6421–6424
in colonization efforts, 6422
and Ghost Dance movement, 3474
circle symbolism in, 1794
circumambulation in, 1795, 1796
clowns in, 1839, 6686
colonial influences on, and Ghost Dance movement, 3473–3474
color symbolism in, 1862
confession in, 7759
cosmologies in, **2008–2010**
creation stories in, 6659–6661
earth diver's role in, 6653, 6660, 6661, 6692
gambling in, 3260
games in, 3266
Mother Earth in, 2984, 3015
supreme beings in, 8869
trickster's role in, 6651
water in, 3016
cultural renaissance, in Haida culture, 3736–3737
dance in, 2136, 2139, 6651, 6653
Ghost (*See* Ghost Dance)
purpose of, 7343
deities in, 6650–6652 (*See also specific deities*)
supreme beings, 6650–6651, 8869
descent from ancient Israel argued for, 1856
descent into the underworld in, 2298
divine child as divine hero in, 2983
dogs in, 2394
dreams in (*See* Dreams, in North American Indian religions)
drums in, 2499–2500, 7035
dualism in, 2508
eagles in, 6698–6699
earth in, 2554
education of, 2264
elders in, 7300
encampments, as sacred hoops, 1794
of Far North, 6655, **6673–6679**
adaptations to climate, 6673–6674
iconography of, 4309
mythology of, 6675–6677
shamanism of, 6677–6678
supreme being of, 6677
fasting in, 2996, 2997
fiction of, 3089–3094
fishing cultures, New Year ceremonies of, 6591
food taboos in, 7299–7300
fox in, 3181–3182
frog in, 3223
funeral rites in, 3237, 6683–6684, 6697
games of, 3266
gambling on, 3260
gender in, **3406–3411**
diversity of, 3409–3410
multiple, 3409, 3410, 3422
recognition of, 3409–3410
sacredness and, 3406–3407
goddess worship in, 3588
graves of, law on, 7303
of Great Plains, 6656, **6696–6705**
ceremonialism of, 6698
cultural diversity of, 6697
iconography of, 4308
language diversity of, 6696–6697
religious diversity of, 6698
spiritual leaders of, 6699
tobacco use of, 9217
trickster stories of, 6699
vision quest of, 6700
guardian spirits and vision quests in, 6651–6652
as "historical artifact," 9609–9610
historical survey of, 6653–6655
home in, 4104
hunting societies, religions themes in, 6653–6654
iconography in (*See* Iconography, North American Indian)
incarnation in, 4415
inheritance in (*See* Potlatch)
initiation rituals in (*See* Initiation, in North American Indian religions)
in Limón's (José) works, 2160
insects in, 4507, 4508
land of, laws on, 7301–7302, 7303
languages of, diversity of, 6653, 6696–6697
life in, 5444
lord of the animals in, 5515
manitou in, 5673–5674
masculine sacrality in, 5759, 5760, 5762
masks in, 5767, vol. 4 color insert
medicine men and societies in, 6652
medicine wheels in, 1794
memorization in, 5850
messianism in, 5973
miracles in, 6049–6050
mountains in
divine power of, 6214
vision and, 6213
mythic themes in, **6658–6664**
Asian influence on, 6653–6654
Corn Mother, 3017
Corn Woman, 6692
earth diver, 1875–1876, 1988, 6653, 6660, 6661, 6692
nature, 6661–6662
sacred history, 6662–6663
names of, 6411
Neopagan borrowings from, 6470
new religious movements in, **6664–6668,** 6718–6719
contemporary social movements, 6667–6668
European colonization and, 6664–6666
fundamentalist movements, 6666–6667
reform movements, 6667
study of, 6671
of Northeast Woodlands, 6655, **6679–6688**
ceremonial practices of, 6682–6685
cosmological beliefs of, 6680–6682
shamanism of, 6685–6686
spirit-forces of, 6681
supreme being of, 6680–6681
of Northwest Coast, 6656, **6705–6712** (*See also* Potlatch)
ablutions among, 11
belief and ritual of, 6706–6710
guardian spirits in, 6707–6708
iconography of, 4308, 4309, 4310
material culture of, 6706
origin myths of, 6709
repatriation claims of, 6711–6712
shamanism in, 6708
transmigration belief of, 9326
winter ceremonials of, 6709–6710

of Northwest Coast *continued*
witchcraft in, 6708
ocean in, 6807
oral tradition of, 3090, 6658–6659
autobiography in, 702
natural world in, 6425–6426
validity of, 6425
owls in, 6937
pain in, 6945, 6947
Paleolithic ancestors of, 6653
performance and ritual in, 7043
pipe ceremony in, 6650, 6652, 6698
poetry of (*See* Poetry, Native American)
politics and (*See* Politics, and Native American religions)
portrayed as "savages," 1708
postcolonial indigeneity and, 1858
potlatch (*See* Potlatch)
potlatch of, 6656, 6706
powwow, 1515
prophets
Handsome Lake, role of, **3771–3772**
Neolin, 6458
proverbs in, 6977
Quaker friendships with, 7548
quaternity in, 7550
quests (*See* Vision quests)
rainbow symbolism in, 7604
rain dances of, 7603
rainmakers in, 7300
regional survey of, 6655–6657
religious communities in, 7699, 7700
religious freedom of, laws on, 7302
repentance in, 7759
rites of passage in, **10068–10072**
appropriation by modern society, 7802–7803
rituals in, 6650, 6652–6653
rivers in, 7862
sacred fires in, 4106
scalping in, 3805
science of, **6425–6427**
shamanism in, 6652, **8287–8290**
and Ghost Dance, 3474
neoshamanism and, 8297
origins of, 6653
prenatal memories of, 2557
shrines in, center as sacred space and, 1502
Smith (Joseph) on, 8447
smoking in, 8454
of Southeast Woodlands, 6655–6656, **6688–6696**
contemporary landscape of, 6690–6691
Corn Woman narrative of, 6692
creation stories of, 6692
current scholarship on religious traditions of, 6694–6695
green corn ceremonialism of, 6694
history of, 6689–6690
narrative traditions and cosmology of, 6691–6692
rituals of, 6693–6694
shamanism of, 6692–6693
supernatural beings of, 6691
of Southwest, 6657, **6720–6730**
cosmology of, 6722–6723
deities of, 6723–6724
economic patterns of, 6720–6721
iconography of, 4309, 4310
life, death, and beyond in, 6728–6729
organization and ritual practice of, 6724–6728
religious patterns of, 6721
syncretism and change in, 6721–6722, 6729
spiders in, 4507–4508, 9355
spirituality *vs.* religion, 10083–10084
stones in, 8747
study of, **6668–6673,** 6694–6695
Boas (Franz) and, 6671
by Walker (James), 9667–9668
Sun Dance in, **8844–8849**
sun in, 8841–8842
suppression of, 7248, 7255, 7257, 7282, 7302
textiles in, 9089
tobacco in, 8454, 9216–9219
totemism in, 9250–9251, 9252
transmigration in, 9326
trees in (*See* Trees, in North American Indian religions)
tribal governments of, law on, 7302
tricksters in (*See* Tricksters)
turtles in, 9407
twins in, 9413–9414, 9415, 9418
in United States, development of American religions and, 10083
U.S. government, relations with, Sun Dance, attempts to ban, 8846
visions in, 7299, 9613
wolf symbols in, 9785
women in, **3406–3411,** 6654, 6659–6660, 6682, 6692, 6713, 6714
as healers, 7300
Northampton (Massachusetts) Revival, 2698
North Christian Church (Columbia City, Indiana), 796
Northeast Africa, Judaism in, **5002–5004**
Northeast Bantu religions, **2574–2579**
creator gods of, 2574–2575
divination in, 2576–2577
hero gods of, 2575–2576
rituals of, 2576–2577
colonial opposition to, 2578
ritual states in, 2576
sacrifices in, 2576
spirits in, 2576
witchcraft and sorcery in, 2577–2578
Northeast Kingdom Community Church. *See* Twelve Tribes
Northern Baptist Convention, 784
Northern Europe, Judaism in, **5011–5014**
since 1500, **5014–5023**
yeshivot of, 9884
Northern Ireland, militant Protestantism in, 2892
Northern Rhodesia, Lumpa church movement in, 5408–5409
Northern school Buddhism, 1521–1522
origin of, 1601
Northern Song dynasty. *See* Song dynasty
Northern Territory Act. *See* Aboriginal Land Rights Act
Northern Tribes of Central Australia (Spencer and Gillen), 3489
Northern Wei kingdom, 1598
Buddhism in, Maitreya in, 5620, 5621
North Korea, Christianity in, 1727
Northrop, F. S. C., 502
Northrup, F. S. C., 9131
North Star, 2295
as center of heaven, 6886
in Finno-Ugric cosmology, 3109
in Purāṇic Hindu cosmology, 2018
in technomorphic cosmologies, 8423–8424
Northumberland, duke of, English reformation and, 2051
Northwest coast Indians. *See* North American Indian religions
Northwest Indian Cemetery Protective Association, Lyng v., 7303
North-West Rebellion of 1885 (Canada), 9302–9303
Northwest Semitic religion. *See* Canaanite religion
Norton, Bryan, 2657
Norton, Thomas, alchemy of, 251, 252
Norway. *See also* Germanic religion
Christianity in, 6814–6815
women's monasteries, 6763
Islam in, 4679, 4680
runic inscriptions in, 7941
Norwich (England), anti-Semitism in, 399–400
Nosta-Nōpantu (deity), 4508
Notes from the House of the Dead (Dostoevsky), 2422
Notes from the Underground (Dostoevsky), 2422
Notes on the Islands of the Unalaska District (Innokentii), 4497
Noth, Martin
on covenant theology, 2048
on Myth and Ritual school, 6381, 6382
Nō theater, 9946–9947
Nothingness
chaos and, 1539
creation from, 1986
in Islam, 2063
Nôtre-Dame-de-Toute-Grâce, Church of (Assy, France), 54–55
Nou Kan, 3077
Noumena, Kant (Immanuel) on, 5077, 5080
Nourishing Terrains (Rose), 638
Nous (baptismal crater), 780
Nous (Mind), 7182, 7184, 7190
in *Corpus Hermeticum,* 3944
death and, 8542
Plato on, 5201
soul and, 8541
submission to, 8405
Nouvelle théologie, 9130
Novalis (Friedrich von Hardenberg), 6435
on symbol theory, 8908
Nova Scotia
Catholicism in, 9301
Church of England in, 9300
Micmac calendar, 1353
Novatian schism, ecclesiastical discipline and, 8155
Novellas, in typology of narratives, 6376–6377
Novels. *See also* Fiction
development of term, 3051
the supernatural in, 8861
Noverre, Jean-Georges, 2155
Novgorod (city-republic), Christianity in, 7941
Novgorod-Moscow heresy, Sorskii (Nil) on, 8525
Novik, Elena S., 3114
Novum organum (Bacon), 733, 7340
Now. *See* Present
Nowét (supernatural being), in Tosa religion, 8636
Nowo (female spirit), 4303
Nowrūz (Iranian festival), **6730–6732**
Noy, Dov, 6020
Noyers de l'Altenburg, les (Malraux), 5480

Noyes, John Humphrey, 6534, 6535, **6732–6733,** 6874
modernity and, 6110
Swedenborgianism and, 8903
Nozick, Robert, on reflexivity, 7649
NPY. *See* Ngaanyatjarra, Pitjantjatjara, and Yunkunyatjara
NRB. *See* National Religious Broadcasters
NRMs. *See* New religious movements
NRP. *See* National Religious Party
NRPE. *See* National Religious Partnership for the Environment
Nsukka Igbo (Nigeria), masquerade dances of, 2141
Nu, U (Burmese prime minister), 5401
Buddhist government of, 1140–1141, 7264
sixth Theravādin council and, 2038
Nuadhu (mythic figure), 1488, 9390
Nubadig (deity), 7760
Nubia, Christianity, 1717
Chalcedonian *vs.* anti-Chalcedonian missionaries to, 1980
Nubian Islaamic Mission, 6768
Nubūwah (belief in prophets), **6733–6739,** 9818
worship and, 9816
Nuclear war, in Jones's (Jim) theology, 4953
Nuclein. *See* DNA
Nucleosynthesis, discoveries in, 2033
Nucleus of Mystery Tantra (Buddhist text), Klong chen Rab 'byams pa (Longchenpa) on, 5193
Nudimmud (deity). *See* Enki
Nudity, **6739–6743**
in art, 4171
in Christian baptism, 781, 782, 6740
in goddess images, significance of, 3976
and holy shame, 6741–6743
and holy shamelessness, 6740–6741
in Jain monasticism, 6123
in Mesopotamian art, 3379
in rites of passage, 6740
ritual
in Chinese religion, 7603
for rainmaking, 7603
and sexuality, 6740
Nuer, The (Evans-Pritchard), 115
Nuer and Dinka religion (East Africa), **6743–6745**
cattle-eating taboo, 1466
cattle raiding and, 1465
confession of adultery in, 1884
creation story of, 85, 92, 140, 3019, 3573
deities of, lesser, 2568
divinities and spirits of, 6743–6744
Evans-Pritchard (E. E.) and, 2895–2896
high deity in, 2567
history of study of, 113, 117
life in, 5445
marriage in
ghost, 5724–5725
woman-woman, 3420, 5724–5725
powers or spirits in, 8689
priesthood in, 2569
priests of, 6744
prophets of, 1547, 2570, 6744–6745, 7443
repentance in, 7758–7759
rites of passage in, 88
rituals in, 7842
sacred language in, 5304, 5305
sacrifices in, 2366, 2367, 5305, 7844, 7845
salutations in, 8061–8062
shrines in, 90
spear masters in myths of, 96
supreme beings in, 3573–3574
trees in, 9336
Nuer Prophets (Johnson), 117
Nuer Religion (Evans-Pritchard), 115, 2895
Nueva Jerusalén (Mexico), 6514, 6577–6578
Nügua (deity)
creation and, 1625, 1626
Fu Xi and, 1624
in Mesolithic, 1627
Nujugo Zammai-e, 3433
Nukat fī iʿjāz al-Qurʾān, al- (al-Rummānī), 4371
Nü-kua (deity), 2433
Nukunu Dictionary (Hercus), 643–644
Num (deity), **6745**
in Samoyed religion, 469, 6438, 8095
n/um (healing power), activation of, 2140
Numa (king of Rome), 3094, 7895
music and, 6304
Numana people (West Africa), sky and, 6438
Nuʿmānī, al-, on *miʿrāj,* 6061
Numa Pompilius (Roman royal law), 7901
Number Our Days (Myerhoff), 6326
Numbers, **6745–6753**. *See also specific numbers*
in alphabets, mystical speculation on, 270, 271–272
in astrology, 564
binary symbolism, **6751–6753**
cards and sacred mathematics, 1413
catharsis and, 1458
in Celtic religion, 1481
in Chinese correlation, 9888
in Sāṃkhya school of Hinduism, 8089–8090
interpretation of, 6746–6750
Maya calendar and, 1356–1357
odd *vs.* even, 6746
Plato on, 7530
Pythagoras on, 7530
role in religion, 6493–6494
transcendence of, in Islam, 3566
Numbers (biblical book), 878
Aaron in, 1, 5423, 6062
Aramaic translation of, 888
blasphemy in, 970
blessing in, 4742
content of, 9232
cursing in, 2103
laws in, 9232
criminal law, 4738
property law, 4735, 4736
Levites in, 5427
al-Maghribī (Samuel) on, 7239
midrashim on, 6018
miqveh in, 6046, 6047
Miriam in, 6062
Moabite religion in, 6094, 6095
Moses in, 9232
secular reading of, 10062
Temple procedures in, 926, 927, 930, 933
tithes in, 9209
in Torah, 9231, 9232
Numen (review), 979, 7074
Numen: International Review for the History of Religions (journal), 10057, 10059
Numenius, 182, 6475
Demiurge of, 2274, 5506, 7189
on matter, 7189
Plotinus influenced by, 7189, 7198
on theurgy, 9157
Numen/numina, **6753–6754**
in Roman religion, healing and, 3841
Numereji (Rainbow Snake), 7606
Numerology, 272–273
in Sāṃkhya school of Hinduism, 8089–8090
Pythagorean thought and, 6746
in Qabbalah, 8676
Shao's cosmology and, 1578
Numidia, Donatism and Nationalism in, 1679
Numinous, concept of, 6929–6930. *See also* Holy, idea of the; *Numen;* Sacred and the profane, the
Otto (Rudolf) on, 4096, 4097, 7976
typology of religions and, 4064
Numinous experience, 5948–5949
Numinous moment, 7126
Nŭm Kŭres (folklore figure), 5120
Nŭm Sĭwes (folklore figure), 5120
Num Torem Aś (deity), 5119
Num-Tūrem (deity), 469, 3107, **6754–6755**
Nŭm Turem Aśi (deity), 5119
Nun (deity)
in Egyptian pantheon, 2705
as water deity, 9699, 9703
Nunavut, territory of (Canada), 9304
Nunc fluens (flowing now), time as, 2854
Nunc stans (standing now), eternity as, 2854
Núņez, Corona, 5942
Nungarrayi (Aboriginal woman), 2479–2480
Nungui, in agrarian rites, 2558
Nunkwi (earth mother), in Jivaroan religion (Ecuador), 8583
Nunkwi (spirit master), 281–282
Nuns, **6756–6765**. *See also* Monasticism
Benedictine, 822, 1018
Buddhist, 6130, 6757, **6759–6763**
Buddhist women's movement and, 3033
Chinese, 6760–6761
Foguangshan and ordination of, 3141
and gender in Buddhism, 3330–3331, 3332, 3334
in *saṃghas,* 8073
international outreach of, 6762
ordination in, 6854–6855
ordination lineages of, 6130
Theravāda, 6760
Tibetan, 354–355, 6130, 6760, 6761–6762
Zhengyan, 1787–1790
calligraphy by, 1369
Christian, 6134–6135, 6758, **6763–6765**
clothing of, 1831, 1832, 1837
Dominican, 6135
in France, sexual frenzy among, 8250
in Oceanic missions, 6792
Poor Clares, 3182, 3183, 3184

Christian ***continued***
in South America, 3417
Syriac Orthodox, 8940
Vatican II and, 6765
Daoist, 6758
fasting by, 3171–3172
gender of, as third sex, 3422
Hindu, 6758
Jain, 3327–3328, 4768, 6757
ordination in, 6854
meaning of term, 6756
missionary, 6073, 6083
motivation, goals, and shared characteristics of, 6756–6757
possession of, 2930
restrictions on, prevalence of, 6123
Nupe people (Nigeria), Ifa divination by, 87
Nuqrāshī, Maḥūmud Fahmī al-, assassination of, 6315
Nūr al-anwār (light of lights), 4554
Nūr al-Dīn, in Aḥmadīyyah movement, 5284
Nūr al-Dīn al-Rānīrī, 25
Crusades and, 2078
Nūr aqrab (nearest light), 4554
Nurbakhsh, Javad
on attention, 604
on levels of consciousness, 1951
Nuremberg, Peace of (1532), 7659
Nuremberg Code (1947), 5810
Nūri, Abū al-Ḥasan ibn Muḥammad al-, on *ṣuḥbah* ("companionship"), 8826
Nūr Jahān (Mughal empress), 4646
Nūr Muḥammad (light of Muḥammad), **6766–6768**
Nūr qāhir (dominating light), 4554–4555
Nus'ayrīyah. *See* 'Alawīyūn
Nusku (deity), 5953
Nussbaum, Martha, 5375
Nuṣūṣ, 9488
Nut (deity), 2984
in Egyptian cosmogony, 2710
in Egyptian pantheon, 2704
rainbow associated with, 7604
worship of, 3596
Nutaqā' (spokesman), 2504
Nutcracker, The (Ivanov), 2156
Nutt, Alfred, 1498
Nü Wa (deity), gender studies on, 3339
Nuwaubian Nation of Moors, 6516, 6768
Nuwaubians, **6768–6770,** 9435
Nux (deity), daughters of, 7783
NWSA. *See* National Woman Suffrage Association
Nwyia, Paul, 5774
Nxele (prophet), 7444
Nyabingi movement (Uganda), 2571
Nya cult (Mali), 107
Nyahbinghi, Order of, 7623, 7624
Nyahbingi, House of, 7623, 7626
Nyakata-gara (medium), 4520
Nyakyusa religion (East Africa), **6770–6772**. *See also* Southern African religions
dances of, 2137, 2138
funeral riles in, dances in, 2138
high deity in, 2567
initiation rites of, 2569
kingship in, 5170, 5171
lineage sacrifice in, 2568–2569
prophecy in, 8659
witchcraft in, 9778
Nyale. *See* Mousso Koroni Koundyé
Nyama (life force), 2392, 4301
in sacred language, 5303
Nyame (deity), 214, 3570
attributes of, 3570
contact with, 9717
creation by, 3570, 5445
etymology of name, 3570
myth about, 214
temples of, 3576
variations of name, 3570
Nyanga people (Congo), gambling and, 3264
Nyang ral Nyi ma 'od zer (Nyangrel Nyima Özer), 1153, 2548, 6941, 9331
Nyanhehwe (mythic figure), 97
Nyankopon. *See* Nyame
Nyan Kupon (deity), 2984
Nyau cult, 1507
masquerade dances of, 2140
Nyawa souls, in Sudanese religion, 8849
Nyāya (Indian school of logic), **6772–6774**
atheism in, 578
and classical Hinduism, development of, 3997
cognitive elements in, 5200
īśvara in, 4752
jñāna in, 4927
unity and plurality in, 4421
Nyāyabindu (Dharmakīrti), 2336
Nyberg, H. S., **6774–6775,** 9735
and Myth and Ritual school, 6381
on study of religion, 10079
Nyctosophers (sorcerers), Zahan (Dominique) on, 2100
Nyenchen Lishu Takring (snyen chen li bshu stag rings), 2549
Nyes Pa (humors). *See also* Doṣas
in Tibetan medicine, 3865
Nygren, Anders
on agape, 2308
Capps (Walter) and, 1412
on dynamic of religion, 7038–7039
and neoorthodoxy, 6466, 6469
on *a priori* concept, 7976
Nyikang (hero), 95–96
deeds of, 2091
king as descendant of, 5158
in Shilluk cosmogony, 2567
Nyingmapa school of Buddhism. *See* Rnying ma pa school of Buddhism
Nymphaea ampla (water lily), 7470
Nymphaea caerulea (water lily), 7470
Nymphs
of Artemis, 506, 507
in Slavic religion, 8437–8438
Nyombi, Richard, 5445
Nyonin kekkai, 3348
Nyonin kinsei, 3348
Nyorai model of meditation, Suzuki Shōsan on, 8887
Nyoro religion (East Africa). *See also* Southern African religions
creator god of, 2574–2575
deities of, lesser, 2568
hero gods of, 2575–2576
mediums in, 4520
myths of, 93
Nyôwau (deity), 6500
Nyström, Samuel, 2302
Nzambe (deity), 1507
Nzambi (deity), 2984
as Bakongo supreme being, 113, 3573
as Ndembu supreme being, 6447
Nzambi-a-mpungu (supreme being), 112
Nzambi Kalunga (deity), in Kongo religion, 5220
Nzambi Mpungu (spirit/deity), selected by missionaries as Christian "God," 2001
Nzambi Mpungu Tulendo (deity), in Kongo religion, 5220
Nzema people (Ghana), history of study of, 117
Nzima people (Ghana), agriculture in myths of, 191
Nzondo (spirit), 2960

O

Oahspe: A New Bible in the Words of Jehovih and His Angel Embassadors (Newbrough), 6531
Oak, Synod of the, 1762
Oak of Zeus, 9577
Oak tree, 9337
Oasis belt (Central Asia), Islam in, 4620–4621
Oates, Wayne E., 7486, 7487
Oaths. *See* Vows and oaths
Oaxaca (Mexico)
in Classic period, 5902–5904
in Postclassic period, 5912
Oba (king of Benin), 2697, 4301–4302
funeral rituals for, 7805–7806
Obá (spirit), 122
Obadiah, 879
Ōbaku school of Zen, 9948–9949
size of, 9943
Obaluaiye. *See* Omolû
Obasi. *See* Chukwu
Ọbatala (spirit/deity)
annual ceremony for, 84
in Caribbean religions, 1433, 1434
and Lisa, 5790
myths regarding, 94, 95, 2310
role in creation, 3571
in Yoruba religion, 9910
Obeah (conjuration), in Caribbean religions, 1435, 1436
Obed (biblical figure), 7947, 7948
Obedience, **6777–6779**. *See also* Spiritual discipline
of Abraham, 15
in Christianity, 1670
Origen on, 8406
Simons (Menno) on, 8401
faith as, 2955
illness caused by disobedience, 3809
in monasticism, 6122
Christian, 6131
religion and
Bellah (Robert) on, 8489
Berger (Peter L.) on, 8488
Obedience of a Christian Man, The (Tyndale), 9426
Obelisk
Egyptian, 9264
Washington Monument, 9266–9267
Oberammergau Passion (play), 2468
Obermiller, Eugene, 1315
Obeyesekere, Gananath, 382, 383, 1313, 7480
on Cook (James), 3797–3798
on liminality, 5461
on spirit possession, 8690
Obiemwen (deity), in Edo religion, 2697
Objective idealism, 4355–4356
Objective values, 5397, 5403
Objectivity
comparative-historical method and, 1869
comparative religion and, 1879
Dilthey (Wilhelm) on, 3933
existentialism and, 2925
the objectively rational, Hegel on, 3894
in science, 6425
Weber (Max) on, 3933
in women's studies of religion, 9790
Object language, sacred *vs.* profane and, 7965
Object-relations theory, 7478, 7482
Objects
sacred, vol. 4 color insert
in Australian Indigenous religions, transgression of, 3873
healing in, 3811–3812
in visual culture, 9622
Oblate Sisters of Providence, 6765
Oblations. *See* Offerings

Obligations. *See also* Vows and oaths
almsgiving as, 266–268
in Judaism
of collective, 4857
of elect, 2744
in Roman religion, 7894
'Obodat (deity), in Nabatean religion, 6389
Obon festival (Japan), 2411, 3155. *See also* Ghost Festival
Oboo (bloodless rituals), 1327
Oboo (cairns), cult of, 1149–1150
Obosom spirits, 118
Obry, Nicole, 2930–2931
Observation, in empirical research, Honko (Lauri) on, 4123
Observations on the Feeling of the Beautiful and the Sublime (Kant), 811
Obsession, Xunzi on, 1573
Obshchina (Russian peasant commune), 5138
Obsolescence of Oracles, The (Plutarch), 2266, 7200
Obu, Olumba Olumba, in Brotherhood of the Cross and Star, 106
Ob-Ugrian religion, 3105, 6754. *See also* Khanty and Mansi religion; Southern Siberian religions
Hungarian religion compared to, 4224–4225
Reguly's (Antal) study of, 7674
Ocaña, Diego de, Virgin of Guadalupe de Extremadura of, 8610–8611
Ó Canchubhar kings of Connacht, 1493
Ó Cathasaigh, Tomás, 1498
Occasionalism, **6779–6780**
in Islam, in Ash'arīyah, 3564
scientific history and, 8181
Occidentalism, 6884
Occult, The (Wilson), 6780
Occultism, **6780–6783**
cannibalism and, 1404
of Cayce, 1473–1474
characteristics of, 6781–6782
in Chinese religion, *vs.* magic, 5592
Crowley (Aleister) and, **2071–2072**
current context of, 6782–6783
definitions of, 6780–6781
depiction in novels, 3062
Hermetism and (*See also* Hermetism)
Hermetism in occultist texts, 3951–3953
occultism in Hermetic texts, 3938–3940
historical survey of, 6781–6782
in Hungary, 4226
magic as element of, 5568–5569
moon in, 6175
in Nazism, 2663
sexual magic and, 8251–8252
in Western esotericism, 2843
witchcraft and, 9774
Occupations
deities of, 3623
in *jāti,* 9523
of Jain laity, 4770
Oceania (journal)
the Dreaming in, 668
Elkin (A. P.) as editor of, 687
first decade of, 683
Oceania and Oceanic religions, **6783–6805**. *See also* Melanesia; Micronesia; Polynesia
academic study of religion in, **8767–8771**
academic programs in, 8768–8771
biblical scholarship in, 8771
early intellectuals in, 8768
pioneer missionaries, reports of, 8767–8768
afterlife in, **145–148**
cannibalism in, 1403–1404
cargo cults in, **1414–1425**
women in, 3398
change in, 6803–6804
charisma in, 1547
chiefs in, 7295–7296, 7297
Christianity, **1737–1741**
conversion to, 9320, 9322
folk Christianity in, 1739
indigenous missionaries in, 1739
indigenous theologies in, 1741
interchurch relations in, 1739
introduction and distribution of, 1737–1739, 1740–1741
missionary movements of, 6790–6794
missions, 7297, 9321–9324
new religious movements in, 1739–1740
Pentecostalism in, 1741
Protestantism, 7297, 7447, 9321, 9323
religious movements influenced by, 6795–6796
rites of passage and, 7809–7810
Roman Catholicism, 1738, 1739, 7297, 9321, 9323, 9324
spread of, 7297
study of, 6804
traditional culture merged with, 7297, 9323–9324
women, 7298
women in, 3398
circumcision in, 7809
colonialism in
missionary resistance to, 6793
religious movements influenced by, 6796–6797
cosmologies, **2004–2007,** 6788–6789
creation myths in, supreme beings in, 8869
cult of the dead in, 6784–6785
deities of, 2006, 6785 (*See also specific deities*)
gender of, 3396–3397
supreme beings as creators, 8869
drums in, 2500
egg symbolism in, 2701
fertility in, 3396
fiction of, 3083–3085
funeral rites in, 7808
gardens in, 3280–3281
gender in, **3395–3400,** 7808–7809
gift giving in, women in, 3480–3481
history of study, **6799–6805**
independent churches in, 6797–6798
initiation in, 4478, 7296, 7807
kinship in, 7295–7296
language diversity in, 6794
languages of, Schmidt (Wilhelm) on, 8168
masks in, vol. 4 color insert
megalithic religion, 5826–5828
modernization in, 9324
music in, **6263–6266**
afterlife and, 146
mythology in, 6787–6788, 6802
naming ceremonies in, 7807
new religious movements in, 6794–6799
oral tradition in, memorization of, 5850
overview of, **6784–6790**
politics and (*See* Politics, and Oceanic religions)
power in, 6785–6787
regions of, 3395
rites of passage in, **7806–7810**
adulthood, 7807–7808
birth, 7807
cosmic significance of, 7809
death, 7808
genital operations, 7808, 7809
in modern society, 7809–7810
parenthood, 7807
personal significance of, 7808–7809
social significance of, 7809
tattooing, 7807–7808
rituals in
gender and, 3397–3398
jade in, 4760
secret societies in, 8212–8213
social structure and, 2004–2006
spirits of, gender of, 3396–3397
tattooing in, 7807–7808
textiles in, 9088
theology in, 6804
trade in, 9321
transculturation of, **9320–9325**
transmigration in, 9327
warfare in, 7296
women in, **3395–3400**
in Christian churches, 7298
gift giving by, 3480–3481
initiation of, 7807
male domination over, 7296
Ocean of Theosophy, The (Judge), 5023
Oceans, **6805–6808**. *See also* Water
African myths of, colonialism interpreted through, 1854–1855
in Australian Indigenous religions, 2003
Baal's battle with, 1392
as barriers to cultural transmission, 1426
as chaos, 1538
deities of
in Celtic religion, 1489–1490
Sedna as, in Inuit religion, 8220–8221
in Egyptian cosmogony, 2720
in Hinduism
in Purāṇic cosmology, 2017
narrative of churning of the ocean of milk, 4013
horses, mythical, in, 4133–4134
in Oceanic religions, sky *vs.* undersea realm, 2005
spirits of, in Haitian Vodou, 1433
universal, in Germanic cosmos, 3447–3448
Ocean seal diagram, 9437
Ocelots, in Aztec religion, 5891
Oc Eo area (Mekong Delta), archaeology in, 4011
Ochshorn, Judith, 3613
Ockeghem, Johannes, 6309
Ockham, William. *See* William of Ockham
O'Connor, Bonnie Blair, 3143–3144
O'Connor, Jerome M., 7016

O'Connor, June, 3024–3025, 3299, 3311
Octavian (Roman emperor), 7896
Octavianus (Roman emperor), 7896
Octavius, Gaius. *See* Augustus
October 1917 Revolution, and Finland's independence, 5092
Octoechos, 6306
Octopus
 in Micronesian religions, 6004, 6010
 in Polynesian religions, 7313
 religious symbolism of, 3123
Oda Nobunaga, 9075–9076
Odantapurī (Buddhist university), 1119
Odes, Classic of/Scripture of (*Shijing*), 7213
 commoners in, 1584
 contents of, 1905–1906
 in Five Scriptures, 1585
 human origins in, 1625, 5178
 li in, 5430
Odes of Solomon, 904
'Od gsal (yoga of radiant light), 1287–1288
Odilo (Benedictine monk), 821
Óðinn (deity), **6808–6810**
 in afterlife, 167, 3448
 in apocalypse, 3456–3457
 and Baldr, 744, 4461
 berserkers and, 842–843
 cosmic tree and, 1502, 3449
 in creation
  of earth, 3446–3447
  of man, 3454
 cult of, 6809–6810
 death of, 3456
 as deified hero, 3956–3957
 as eagle, 8522, 8722
 in Eddas, 2692–2693
 etymology of name, 3454
 eye of, 2941
 and Freyja, 3218
 functions of, 3452, 5995
 and *fylgjur*, parallels between, 3246
 giants and, 4960
 as god of poetry, 3455
 hall of, 9516
 hawk's plumage of, 2554
 Lóðurr and, 3455
 Loki and, 5508, 5509
 mead of, 8722
 and necromancy, 6452
 in origin of mead myth, 849, 3455
 in origin of writing, 270
 role in Germanic pantheon, 3452–3453
 in sagas, 8024
 and shamanism, 3219
 shape shifting of, 8440–8441
 shapes taken on by, 3452
 Snorri Sturlson on, 8460
 social structure reflected in, 4462
 sovereignty of, 5995
 and Thor, 9165, 9166
 Ullr and, 3453
 Valkyries of, 9517
 visionary journey of, 9615
 in war with Vanir, 3449
Odomankama. *See* Nyame
Odoric (Franciscan monk), on Buddhism, 1311
Odori nembutsu (dance), 4533
Odosha (evil being), in Makiritare religion (Amazon), 8626
Óðr (deity), and Freyja, 3218
Óðr (mind), 3454
Odrysi tribe (Thracian), 9168
Odua. *See* Oduduwa
Oduduwa (deity)
 myths regarding, 2310
 role in creation, 3571
 in Yoruba religion, 9910
Ọdun Egungun (ancestor festival), 9910
Odunlami, Sophia Adefobe, in Aladura movement, 104
Odysseus
 cattle and, 1466
 purification by, 1459
 quest of, 7552, 7553
 refusing immortality, 2298
 in underworld, 164–165
 visit to Hades, 6452
Odyssey (Homer)
 afterlife in, 164–165
 authorship of, 4107
 charity in, 1553
 chastity in, 1558
 deities in, 5468
 Demeter in, 2268
 dēmiourgos in, 2272
 descent into the underworld in, 2295
 divination in, 2376
 eagles in, 2554
 Epic of Gilgamesh and, 3487
 Hades in, 3725, 6452
 healing in, 3839
 Hermes in, 3937
 hospitality in, 4139
 human-divine relations in, 4108
 kingship in, 5166
 letter mysticism on, 271, 272
 magic in, 5574
 Mahābhārata cognate to, 4465
 paradise in, 6984
 purification in, 1459
 as quest story, 7552
 ritual practice in, 4108
 souls of the dead in, 8542
 sun in, 8839
 the supernatural in, 8862
 underworld in, 9452–9453
Oedipal complex, 2239, 7799
 Freud (Sigmund) on, 7474, 7478
 in heroes
  Girard (René) on, 3960
  Rank (Otto) on, 3958
 Malinowski (Bronislaw) rejecting, 5628
 Marxist criticism of, 7489
Oedipus, 986
 childhood of, 1568
 Girard (René) on, 3960
 quest of, 7552
 structuralist interpretation of, 1876
Oedipus and Job in West African Religions (Fortes), 321
Oedipus Rex, barrenness in, 2560
Oenghus (deity), 1484
 Maponos identified with, 5685
Ōe no Masafusa, 1178
Oersted, Hans Christian, 6435
Oesterley, W. O. E., 899, 900
Oesterreich, Traugott K., on spirit possession, 8687, 8688, 8689
Oeta, Mount, sanctuary of Herakles on, 3917
Oetinger, Friedrich C., 340, 3525, 6434
Oeuvre des Retraites de Perseverance, 7772
Of Being and Unity (Pico), 7141
Offenbarung nach dem Lehrbegriff der Synagoge (Steinheim), 4904
Offering-lists, 2718, 2724
Offering *maṇḍalas,* 5644
Offerings. *See also specific types*
 in African religions
  central Bantu, 1508
  Lugbara, 5527
  in southern African religions, to shades, 8657, 8658
 in Agami Jawi, 4817
 in agricultural rituals, 186–190
 alcoholic beverages as, 849
 in Andean religions, 8603
 in Arabian religions, 445
 in Arctic religions, 470–471
 Baal (Jan van) on, 725
 in Buddhism
  to *arhat,* 477
  to Buddha image, 4330
  incense, 4419
 in Bugis religion, 1317
 Cain and Abel, 1344
 Canaanite, 1386
 cannibalistic, 1403
 Caribbean religions, 1431, 1435
 in Chinese religion, 2408–2409, 4419
  Cheng Hao on, 1561
  Cheng Yi on, 1562–1563
  of food, vol. 7 color insert
  grave offerings (Shang dynasty), 1582
  of paper money, 6137–6138
 in Christianity, 4420
  on All Souls Day, 2229
 in Daoism, 4419
  system for, 2198
 of Ebliate religion, 2597
 in funeral rites, 3242, 3244
 at gravesites, 2241
 in Greek religion
  animal bones, 1014
  images, 4381
 in Hinduism, 4419, 7845
  bhakti synthesis and, 4001
  in Upaniṣadic cosmology, 2015
  in sacrifices, 9821
 in Hurrian religion, 4232
 in Igbo religion, 4366
 in Inca religion, 4412–4413
 in Vajrayāna (Tantric) Buddhism, 1220
 in Iranian religion, 4535
 in Islam, 4420
 in Israelite religion, 4972–4973
  burnt offering, 925, 926, 927, 931–932, 4746–4747
  domestic, 4744
  grain offering, 926
  guilt offering, 4741
  incense offering, 927, 931–932
  peace offering, 926
  presentation offering, 926–927
  sin offering, 4747, 7514
  in Temple, 928
  well-being offering, 4746–4747
 in Jainism, 4382
 in Japanese religion, 2410
 in Judaism, 4429–4420
  collective nature of, 4857
 language of, sacred, 5307
 Mauss (Marcel) on, 725
 in Muisca religion, 6230
 in Negrito religions, 6455
 in North American Indian religions, 6652
 in Oceanic religions, 6785–6786
 in Olmec religion, 6819
 in Phoenician religion, 7132, 7133, 7134
 sacrifice *vs.,* 7997
 in Sami religion, 8746
 in Sri Lankan religions, 8410
 textile, 9089–9090
 in Vodou, 9637
Office of Betrothal, Orthodox rite of, 7960
Office of Crowning, Orthodox rite of, 7960
Ofili, Chris, 4282, 4287
O'Flaherty, Wendy Doniger, 383, 2901, 5469
 on Campbell (Joseph), 1379
 on desire, 2305
 on Śiva, 7083, 7195
 structuralism and, 8752, 8755
 on suffering, 9112
Of the Contemplative Life (Philo Judaeus), 4359–4360
Of the Laws of Ecclesiastical Polity (Hooker), 350, 7663
 Church of England defended in, 4124
Ofudesaki (Deguchi Nao), 6824
Ofudesaki (Nakayama), 9082, 9083
Ōgai, Mori, 3072, 9315
Ōgami-sama. *See* Kitamura Sayo
Ogās, 123
Ogbanje (spirits), 4365–4366

Ògbóni society, 4303–4304
Ögedei (son of Chinggis Khan), 4493
Oghma (deity), 1485, 9390
Oghuz Kaghan (hero), 9402
Oghuz tribes (Turkic), 4493
Ogiuwu (deity), in Edo religion, 2697
Oglala religion (North America). *See also* Black Elk
color symbolism in, 1862
creation story of, 3015
fourfold structure of world of, 7550
iconography of, 4309
Moon and Sun myth of, 3017
rain symbolism in, 7603
study of, 6672
tricksters in, 9355
White Buffalo Calf Woman of, 3017
Ogmios (deity), 1485
Ogo (deity)
in creation myth, 2390
as trickster, 86, 95, 100, 9352, 9353
twin of, 9415, 9416
O'Gorman, Edmundo, 3063, 5939
on Virgin of Guadalupe, 5922
Ogotemmêli (sage)
on gardening, 3281
revelations to Griaule (Marcel), 100, 116, 3701, 7329
on tobacco, 9217
Ogres, in Oceanic religions, 6788
Ogun (Ogou) (deity), 95, 4301
in Caribbean religions, 1433, 1434–1435
in Edo religion, 2697
in Candomblé, 122, 123
in Vodou, 9635, 9638, vol. 8 color insert
Yemọja as, 7862
in Yoruba religion, 9911
Ogyū Sorai, **6810–6811**
Kobunjigaku methodology, 1928
O'Hanlon, Rosalind, 3322
on British colonialism, 1858
on subaltern studies, 8800–8801
Ohgiwe Society, 4542
Ohlmarks, Åke, 473
Oho-harahi (confession) ceremony, 1886
Ōhrmazd (deity), 203–204, 2985. *See also* Ahura Mazdā
Ahriman as co-creator with, and evil and sickness, source of, 3809
in Manichaeism, 5652
opposition to Ahriman, 5165
twin of, 9412, 9416
wisdom of, 9752
world-periods based on, 174
Zurvan and, 10014
Oi Aidei (deity), 2960
OIC. *See* Organization of Islamic Conferences
Oidheadh Chloinne Tuireann (Irish tale), 5529
Oikoumenē (community of inhabited world), 2606, 2683
Oil
healing functions of, 2840, 2841
libations of
in Greek religion, 5433
in Israelite religion, 5434
Oĭun (shamans), 2395
Ojibwa Dance Drum, The (Vennum), 2499
Ojibwa religion (North America), **368–371**
ballgame played in, 753, 754, 755
bears in, 807
Christian missions and, 6423
circle symbolism in, 1794
creation story in, 6660–6661
drama in, 2460–2461
Drummer movement in, 6667
drums in, 2499
fiction of, 3092
funerary rites in, 6697
iconography of, 4308, 4309, 4310
Medicine rite in, 6652, 6681
naming ceremony of, 6683
Nanabush in, 6659, 6660
poetry in, 7224, 7226
postcontact changes in, 6659
rock art, 1471
shamanism in, 6685
study of, 6670, 6672
Thunderers in, 6663
totemism in, 9250, 9252
vision quests in, 7551, 8703
Ōjin (emperor), *Analects* of Confucius sent to, 1926
Ōjōyōshū (Genshin), 1243, 3432–3433, 7503, 9079
Okada Mokichi, Seikai kyūsei-kyō movement and, 8369
Okagura dramas, 4798–4799
Okagura music, 6300
Okakura Tenshin, 9313
Oka Masao, on prehistoric Japanese culture, 4780
Okane (mythic figure), 3570
Okeanos (deity), 6805, 9699
Oken, Lorenz, 6435
Okiek people (Kenya), hunting/gathering system of, 2566
Ōkina (play), 2455
Okinawan religion (Japan), **6811–6814**
women in, 3347–3348
Okladnikov, Aleksandr P., 3114
Ōkuninushi no Mikoto, 4801, 4811, **6814**
Ōkuni Takamasa, on Hirata Atsutane, 8365
Okunoin cemetery (Japan), Shingon Buddhism and, 8352
Olaf Haraldsson, saga about, 8024
Olaf the Holy, **6814–6815**
Olaf Tryggvason, saga about, 8024, 8025
ʿOlah (offering), 926, 932, 4746
ʿOlam ha-ba,ʾ Maimonides' (Moses) interpretation of, *vs.* Abulafia (Me'ir), 24
ʿOlat tamid (Einhorn), Reform Judaism and, 8388
Olbers, Wilhelm, on uniform brightness of night sky, 2031
Olcott, Henry Steel, **6815–6816**
and Blavatsky (H. P.), 977
Buddhist revival by, 1126, 1187
eclectic worldview of, 6535
in engaged Buddhism, 2787–2788
Judge (William Q.) and, 5023–5024
and modern Buddhist philosophy, 1302
on religious experience, 7738
as Theosophical Society president, 845, 6815–6816, 7228, 9142, 9205
Olcott, Sidney, 3097
Old Babylonian period
Dagan in, 2126
kingship in, 5162
Nabu in, 6390
Old Believers
Avvakum in, 712
Karelians as, 5093
mass suicide of, 8830
migration of, 6023, 6024
persecution of, 6621
in Russian Orthodox church, 2588
Old Catholic churches, Anglicanism and, 352–353
Old Charges, 3195
Old Curiosity Shop, The (Dickens), 3062
Oldenbarneveldt, Johan van, Arminius (Jacobus) and, 493
Oldenberg, Hermann, 1312, **6816–6817**
history of Buddha by, 3177
on Vedic mythology, 9559
Oldenburg, Henry, Spinoza (Baruch), 8682–8683
Old English Rune Poem, The, 6943
Old European religion
goblins in, 8438
goddess of death in, 8437
life-giving and life-taking goddesses in, 8436–8437
Moist Mother Earth in, 8437
nymphs in, 8437–8438
Slavic religion and, 8432, 8436–8438
"Old Europe" civilization
definition of, 7376
Gimbutas (Marija) on, 3493, 5281
Lady of the Animals in, 5281
prehistoric religions in (*See* Prehistoric religions, in Old Europe)
Old Fashioned Revival Hour (radio program), 7711
Oldfield, Roger, 681
Old Hag. *See* Gráinne (mythic figure)
Old Kalevala. See Kalevala
Old Kingdom Pyramid Texts (Egypt), Hathor in, 3795
Old Man and the Sea, The (Hemingway), 5481
Old Muslim Opposition against Interpretation of the Koran (Birkeland), 8951
Old New Zealand (Maning), 7372
Old Roman Creed, Apostles' Creed and, 2056
Old Stone Age. *See* Paleolithic Period
Old Testament. *See* Hebrew scriptures
Old Testament Pseudepigrapha, The (Charlesworth), 901
Old Text school, 1575, 1592
Old Tibetan Documents Online, 9188
Olearius, Adam, 3110
on Mari religion, 5709
Olger the Dane (mythic figure), 7684
Olin, Margaret, 4342–4343
Olivelle, Patrick
on *dharma,* 2330
on *ānanda,* 7083
Olive tree, 9334, 9337–9338
Öljeitü (Mongol ruler), 956, 4372
Öljeitü Khudā-Banda (sultan of Persia), conversion to Twelver Shiism of, 3982
Ollama. See Hipball
Olmec Bird Monster, 6818
Olmec culture, 5880–5882
Olmec Dragon, 6818
in Maya religion, 5883
Olmec religion (Mexico), **6817–6820**
ballgames played in, 749
calendar in, 5881–5882
celts (axe heads) in, images on, vol. 3 color insert
deities of, 5881
supreme, 5881
in Formative (Preclassic) period, 5895
iconography of, 4311, 5881
jade in, 4759
jaguar in, 4762
pre-Columbian, 5880–5882
pyramids in, 7526

Olmec religion (Mexico)
 continued
  sculptures of infants in, vol. 13 color insert
  study of, 6817–6818
  temples in, 9065
Olmedo, Bartolomé de, 5915
Olo (Danish king), 9685
Olodumare (Idowu), 117
Olódùmarè. *See* Ọlọrun
Olofat (mythic figure), 6010, 6011, 6012
Olokun (deity), 4301
  in Edo religion, 2697
Olo Nyadju religion (Borneo), funeral rites in, 3235
Ọlọrun (deity), 3571–3572
  creation by, 3571, 5445
   divinities in, 94, 3571–3572
   gender in, 3401
  as *deus otiosus,* 2310–2311
  Eṣu and, 9353
  etymology of name, 3571, 6409
  imposed pantheon and, 1999
  judgment by, 140
  in reincarnation, 9719
Olrik, Axel, 474, 3459
Olschki, Leonardo, 3650
Olsen, Gary, 2603
Olsen, Magnus, 3459, 3460
Olsen, Regine, Kierkegaard's engagement to, 5140
Olson, Carl, 3612
Olson, Oliver K., 3124
Olupe, Edīte, 328
Olupona, Jacob, 80, 117, 10032–10033
Olympia, 4322
  Zeus temple in, 9063
Olympians, in Greek religion
  chthonic goddesses related to, 7783
  Harrison (Jane E.) on, 3781
  origins of, 5282
  religion and, 8723
Olympias (queen), Nectanebo and, 3903
Olympia the Deacon, charity taught by, 2582
Olympic Games
  in ancient Greece, 3265–3266
  in Sydney (2000), opening ceremony of, 634–647, 651
  Theodosius's suppression of, 3267
Olympus, Mount
  Hestia as fire at center of, 3964
  Hestia replaced by Dionysos on, 3964–3965
  as Zeus's palace, 9952
Ōm, in music, 6278, 6282
Oṃ, 980, **6820–6821**
  cosmic vibration in, 8676
  devotion to *īśvara* through, 4752
  Hindu texts opening with, 7022
  as sacred word, 5304
  as supreme *mantra,* 5677
Omacatl (deity), 9093
Omaha tribe (North America)
  ballgame played by, 752
  proverbs of, 6977
  rain dances of, 7603
  tattoos of, 1002
Omamori (amulets), 2410
Oman
  Khārijīs in, 5126, 5127
  marriage in, 7825
Omani Sultanate (Zanzibar), Islam spread by, 2571, 2578
Ó Maoil Chonaire (mythic figure), 1493
Omdurman (Sudan), Muḥammad Aḥmad in, 6229
Omechihuatl (deity), duality of, 5933–5934
Omecihuatl (deity), childbirth and, 7811, 7812
Omega point, in cybernetics, 2112
Omen accipere (to accept the omen), 7335
Omenali (values), 4366
Omen exsecrari, abominari (omen execrated, abominated), 7335
Omens. *See also* Portents; Prodigies
  accepting, 7335
  cats in, 1463
  definition of, 7335
  denouncing, 7335
  dreams and, 2485
  in East African divination, 2569
  in Greek religion, Homer on, 4108
  in Hurrian religion, 4232
  in Polynesian religions, 7306–7307
  in Roman religion, 7335
  in Sami religion, 8746
  transforming, 7335
Omen texts, Egyptian, 2724
'Omer period, in Jewish calendar, 4867
Omesurech rite (Palau, Micronesia), 7807
Ometecuhtli (deity), 5906
  duality of, 5933–5934
Ometecutli (deity), childbirth and, 7811, 7812
Ometeotl (deity)
  as creator god, 718
  duality of, 5933–5934
  in Toltec religion, 5889
Ometochtzin, Carlos, 4504
Ōmī (soul), 9394
Ōmine, Mount, women excluded from, 3348
Ōmīruk (small box), 9395
Oṃkāreśvara *(liṅga),* 779
Oṃ maṇi padme hūṃ (Tibetan prayer), 2131
  power of, 8676
Omnipartiality, 6185–6186
Omnipotence, 7124
  defense of, in view of evil (*See* Theodicy)
  definition of, 9113
  denials of, 9112
  in Islam
   free will and, 'Abd Allāh Anṣari on, 8816
   suffering and, 8809
  in Judaism, 614, 3549–3550
  miracles and, 481
  Schleiermacher (Friedrich) on, 8166
  of supreme beings, 8867
  in theism, 9104–9105
Omnipresence
  in Judaism, 614
   paradox of localization and, 7981
  of supreme beings, 8867, 8868
Omniscience
  in Judaism, 614, 3549
  Pettazzoni (Raffaele) on, 8878
  Spinoza (Baruch) on, 8683
Omnitemporality, 6379
Omol' (deity), in Komi religion, 5217
Omolû (spirit), 122, 123
Omophagia, **6821–6824**
  Dionysian, 2357, 6865–6866
Ōmotokagura (dance), 6300
Omotokyō (Ōmoto), 4790, 6573, **6824–6826**
  in Brazil, 6574
  Maitreya in, 5622
  new religions stemming from, 6573–6574
  religious sources for, 6572
Omphalos. *See* Center of the world
Omphalos (navel) at Delphi, as sacred stone, 8745
Omucwezi w'eka (medium), 4520
Ona, Francis, 6797
Onabasulu people, cannibalism among, 1404
On Aboriginal Religion (Stanner), 5707
On Aggression (Lorenz), 6947
Ona religion. *See* Selk'nam religion
Onari-gami, 6812
On Beauty and Harmony (Augustine), 3513
On Being and Essence (Aquinas), 9161
"On Being Woken Up: The Dreamtime in Anthropology and in Australian Settler Culture" (Wolfe), 2478
On Christian Doctrine (Augustine), 46, 871, 874, 1051, 2382, 2384, 4361, 5470, 5471, 5486
On Clemency (Seneca), Calvin's commentary on, 1374
On Conversion (Bernard), 839
Ondeto, Simon, in Legio Maria movement, 105
On Divination in Sleep (Aristotle), 2376
Ondo Yoruba religion (Nigeria), kingship and cosmological shifts in, 1999–2000
On Duties (Cicero), 287, 288, 1454–1455
One (number)
  interpretations of, 6746
  Neoplatonic, 6474
  sacrality of, 6752
One Hundred and Eighty Precepts of Lord Lao, ecology and, 2636
One Hundred Years of Solitude (García Márquez), 3063, 5438
Oneida community, 6534–6535
  founder of, 6732
  North American religious culture and, 1714
  response to modernity by, 6110
  sexuality and, 8243
  sexual relations at, 6535, 6558, 6563, 6732
  women at, 6535, 6563, 6732
Oneida tribe (North America). *See also* Iroquois religion
  ballgame played by, 754
O'Neill, Eugene, 2475
Oneiromancies, Egyptian, 2724
Oneiromanteis (diviner), 2376
One Man (deity), 1502
Oneness
  Nānak on, 6413
  of reality (*See* Monism)
Oneness (Jesus Only) Pentecostalism, 7029, 7030
Onesimus (Philemon's slave), 915
On Exhortation to Chastity (Tertullian), 9086
On Faith (Ambrose), 287
On Fasting (Tertullian), 9086
On First Principles (Origen), 873, 6888, 9135
On Flight in Persecution (Tertullian), 9086
Ong, Aihwa, on spirit possession, 8696
Ong Ndu (deity), 2960
Ongons, 1325, **6826–6827**
  in Mongol shamanism, 6141, 6142
On Human Nature (Wilson), 2919
On Idolatry (Tertullian), 4360, 4361, 9085
Onigbagbo, Aladura movement and, 104
Onílè (owner of earth), 4303–4304
  Eṣu and, 9353
Ōnin War (Japan), 4787
Onisaburō Deguchi, 6573, 6824–6825
Onkelos, 887–888
Onkoboykwe (spirits), 6456
On Learned Ignorance (Nicholas of Cusa), 7193
On Life (Tolstoy), 9220
On Loving God (Bernard of Clairvaux), 6349
On Lying (Augustine), 1455
On Magic (Bruno), 5580
On Modesty (Tertullian), 9086
On Monogamy (Tertullian), 9086
On Morality (Cyprian), evil in, 2113
Onmyōdō (way of *yinyang*), **6827–6830**

On Nature (Parmenides), 5989–5990, 6995–6996
Onniscienza di Dio, l' (Pettazzoni), 115
Onomastic legend
Irish, 1480, 1486
Phoenician, Eshmun in, 2842
Onomastikon (Hebrew names) (Jerome), 4834
Onondaga tribe (North America). *See also* Iroquois religion
ballgame played by, 754, 755
Midwinter festival of, 4543
turtles in, 9407
Ono Sōkyō, on Shintō, 8357
On Patience (Tertullian), 9086
On Philosophy (Aristotle), theology in, 483–484
On Prayer (Origen), 6888
On Precept and Dispensation (Bernard), 839
On Predestination (Eriugena), 2830
On Priesthood (Chrysostom), 7402
On Providence (Philo Judaeus), 7105
On Religion: Speeches to Its Cultured Despisers (Schleiermacher), 48
On Rewards and Punishments (Philo Judaeus), 7106
Onryo (vengeful spirits), in Buddhism, 5073
On Sacred Disease, epilepsy in, 3839–3840
On Socrates' Daemon (Plutarch), 521
Ontario (Canada), Church of England in, 9300
On Temporal Authority (Luther), 5150
On the Consolation of Philosophy (Boethius), 1007
On the Decalogue (Philo Judaeus), 4359
On the Dress of Women (Tertullian), 9085
On the Duties of the Clergy (Ambrose), 287
On the Eating of Flesh (Plutarch), 7200
On the Faith (Basil of Caesarea), 798
On the Flesh of Christ (Tertullian), 9086
On the Greatest Good (Isidore). *See Sentences* (Isidore)
On the Holy Spirit (Ambrose), 287
On the Holy Spirit (Basil of Caesarea), 798
On the Holy Supper against Lanfranc (Berengar), 837
"On the Idea of a Theology of Culture" (Tillich), 9203
On the Incarnation (Theodore of Mopsuestia), 9121
On the Incarnation against Nestorius (Cassian), 1447
On the Incarnation of the Word (Athanasius), 572
On the Judgment of God (Basil of Caesarea), 798
On the Lapsed (Cyprian), backsliders in, 2113
On the Life of Christ (Cabilas), spiritual life in, 1343–1344
On the Lord's Body and Blood (Lanfranc of Bec), 837
On the Lord's Prayer (Cyprian), allegorical interpretation in, 2113
On the Making of Man (Gregory of Nyssa), 3696, 3697
On the Morning of Christ's Nativity (Milton), 7220
On the Mysteries (Iamblichus), 7191, 9157
On the Obsolescence of Oracles (Plutarch), 3905–3906
On the Origin of the Species (Darwin)
Müller (F. Max) on, 6235
nature religions influenced by, 2662
writing of, 2908
On the Origins of Nuns (Abelard), 7
On the Ornaments of Virgins (Cyprian), modesty in, 2113
On the Perils of the Last Day (William of Saint-Amour), 9161
On the Resurrection (Athenagoras?), 589
On the Resurrection of the Flesh (Tertullian), 9086
On the Revolution of the Heavenly Spheres (Galileo), 3257
On the Right of Magistrates (Beza), 851
On the Sacred Disease, rationalism in, 4021
On the Song of Songs (Bernard), 839
On the Soul (Aristotle), 485
On the Soul (Tertullian), 9086
On the Spirit (Basil of Caesarea), 798
On the Testimony of the Soul (Tertullian), 9085
On the Three Principles of Divine Being (Boehme), 1006
On the Trinity (Augustine), 627–628
mysticism in, 6347
On the Trinity (Boethius), 1007
On the Unity of the Catholic Church (Cyprian)
schism in, 2113
unity of bishops in, 2113–2114
On the Usefulness of the Parts of the Human Body (Galen), 3255
On the Veiling of Virgins (Tertullian), 9086
On the Wearing of the Laurel Wreath (Tertullian), 9086
Ontology, **6830–6831**
Buddhist (See also Śūnyam and *śūnyatā*)
Tibetan Buddhist, Rang byung rdo rje on, 5102
of Buddhist ecology, 2628–2629
chaos theory and ontological openness, 1542
definition of, 7110
of evil, Basil of Caesarea on, 8406
Hypostasis (Greek concept), **4239–4243**
in Ashʿarīyah, 535, 536–537
in Indian philosophy, Śāntarakṣita on, 8106–8107
of *karman,* 5096
of Leibniz (Gottfried), 5406
liberation and, 5437–5438
of Vaiśeṣika, 9497–9498
original formula of, 7123
in proofs for existence of God, 7421–7422, 9103
of sacred and profane, 7976
Sartre (Jean-Paul) on, 8116
sexuality and, 8246
Tiele (C. P.) on, 9192
Upaniṣadic, 9482
On True Christianity (Tikhon), 9194
On True Religion (Augustine), 4361
On Virginity (Gregory of Nyssa), 3696
On Works and Charity (Cyprian), 5876
Onyame. *See* Nyame
Onyankopon. *See* Nyame
OOBE. *See* Out-of-body experiences
Opae (mythic figure), 191
Opa Osun (iron stick), 10033
Opele (divining chain), 10032
Open confessionalism
antidogmatism and, 2060
definition of, 2056
Opening of the Mouth ritual (Egypt), 2710, 2713, 6920
Open Theatre, 2438
Opera
and ballet, 2154
baroque, music of, 6311
Chinese, 1620
Samba schools in Brazil, 1444
Operating Thetan (OT) levels, in Scientology, 4149, 8193
Operational anthropology, Stanner (W. E. H.) on, 8729
"Operation Exodus," 4953
Ophite Gnostics, 3518
history of study of, 3532
Opias (spirits), in Caribbean religions, 1428
Opiconsiva (festival), 7899
Opigielguoviran (deity), in Island Arawak religion, 1427
Opioid-mediated attachment processes, in shamanism, 8278
Opium War (1839–1842) (China), 4633
Oplatek (bread), 2400
Opler, Morris, 404, 576
OPM. *See* Papuan Liberation Army
Opon Ifá (divining tray), 10032, 10033
Opossum, in Mesoamerican religions, myths about, 5938
Oppenheim, A. Leo, on *Epic of Gilgamesh,* 3488
Oppenheim, Leo, 4380
Oppidum (fortified village), 4251
Opposites, in humor, 6364
Oppositions. *See* Binary oppositions; Duality
Oppression
of animals, 358
Buddhism and, 2630
of indigenous cultures, 2616
Ops (deity), 3094, 7899
Optics, Spinoza (Baruch) and, 8682
Optina hermitage, in Russian Orthodox Church, 7943
Optina monastery (Russia), Serafim of Sarov and, 8229
Optino community, Kireevskii (Ivan) in, 5187
Optino Hermitage (Russia), Velichkovskii (Paisii) and, 8526
Optisthodomos (porch), 9063
Opus Dei, 6568
Opus majus (Bacon), 734, 7340
Opus minus (Bacon), 734
Opus tertrium (Bacon), 734
Opus tripartitum (Eckhart), 2603
Oracles, **6831–6838**. *See also* Divination
Canaanite, 1381, 1387
characteristics of, 6836
collections of, 6836
in divination, 2370, 2371, 2375, 2376
divination and, 6831–6832
in East African divination, 2569
Egyptian, Nag Hammadi and, 3941
enthusiasm and, 2807
function of, 6836
Greek, 3004
Delphic (*See* Delphi, oracle of)
heads, oracular, 3806
in Hittite religion, 4069, 4071, 4072, 4073
in Igbo religion, 4366
inspired, 4510
Israelite
Levites and, 5424
priests as, 7400
in Lugbara religion, 5527–5528
vs. magic, 5570, 5571
Mesoamerican, 1468

Oracles ***continued***
Mesopotamian, Shamas as god of, 8838
prophecy and, 6831
Sibylline Oracles, **8382–8386**
in Tibetan Buddhism, oracle ceremony, 9841
types of, 6832–6836
Oracles of Delphi No Longer Given in Verse, The (Plutarch), 2266
Oracle texts, Egyptian, 2724–2725
Or Adonai (Light of the Lord) (Crescas), 4895–4896
Orage, A. R., 3711
O'Rahilly, Thomas F., 1482, 1483, 1498
on Ferghus mac Roich's sword, 3040
Oral Lineage sect. *See* Bka' brgyud pa (Kagyu) order
Oral Roberts and You (television ministry program), 7712
Oral Torah, 4976, 4986, **6838–6842**
Oral tradition, **6842–6846**. *See also* Chanting; Lineage
African
religious studies based on, 117–118
studies of African scholars on, 8794
in African religions, Yoruba, 10032
in Ainu religion, 206–207
in Apache religion, 404, 405
in Australian Indigenous religions, 652
authority of, 692, 693–694
Blackfoot, 959–960
in Buddhism, Bka' Brgyud (Kagyu) school of, 5101, 5103
Canaanite literature and, 1391
in Caribbean religions, 10028
codification and, 1842
in Finland, Harva (Uno) on, 3782–3783
folk, 8199
forms of, 9269
Gesar epic in, 3464
in Greek religion, 3660
Hebrew accentuation and, 1533
images used in, 6425–6426
importance of, 9269–9270
in Candomblé, 123
in Judaism
oral Torah and, 6838–6839
rabbinic Judaism, 7584
in Mandaean religion, 5637–5638
in Maori religion, 5682–5683
memorization of, by specialists, 5850–5851
North American Indian, 6658–6659
autobiography in, 702
natural world in, 6425–6426
physiology of, 6425–6426
tricksters in, 9354, 9355
validity of, 6425
in performance, 9269
in popular religion, 7325, 7326
and sacred biography, 944
scripture and, 8198–8199
in Selk'nam and Haush religion, 8224
shamanistic accounts, similarity to, 8274
in Zoroastrianism, 708, 5561
Avesta transmitted through, 708
Orang Asli (Malaysia), 2616
Orange, Council of, 1448
on free will and predestination, 3207
Oration on the Dignity of Man (Pico), 7141
Oratorios, 6311, 6312
Orbis pictus (Comenius), 1863
Ordeal by Labyrinth (Eliade), 460
Ordeals, **6846–6851**
confession and, 1885
in East African divination, 2569
in Hindu legal system, 5346
in initiation rituals, 4477–4478, 4481–4482
in legal system, as process for truth-finding, 5371
in North American Indian religions, 8846
in Sun Dance, 8848
in Selk'nam shamanism (Tierra del Fuego), 8226
underworld journey as, 9451
witchcraft revealed through, 9777
Orden Mentalischer Bauherren, sexual magic and, 8252
Order and disorder. *See also* Chaos
accessibility of, in *Ecclesiastes,* 2600
in African religions
in central Bantu religion, 1506
in myths, 91, 93–96
southern African rituals and, 8660
Berger (Peter L.) on, 8488
in body symbolism, 4162
ceremony and, 1513
chaos, **1537–1541**
charisma and, 1544
in Chinese religion, 1588
cities as celestial order recreated on earth, 7984
combat myth, 1626
natural/moral order in Neo-Confucianism, 1603
in Egyptian religion, afterlife of, 129
evil and, 2899
geometry and, 3438
human sacrifice and, 4184
in nature, Confucianism and, 2633
rituals of, in Carnival, 1440
in sacred space, 7981–7982
sacred *vs.* profane and, 8010
and sky patterns and mythology, 8428
through violence, 9598
water in, 9701
in wisdom, 9756
in Zoroastrianism, 9989
gender and, 3372
Ordericus Vitalis, on secular *vs.* ecclesiastical history, 4038
Order of Amaranth, 3198
Order of DeMolay, 3198
Order of Friars Preachers. *See* Dominicans
Order of Hermits of Grandmont, 2827
Order of Lesser Brothers, 3182
Order of Nyahbinghi, 7623, 7624
Order of Penance, 3182, 3183
Order of Saint Benedict (OSB). *See* Benedictines
Order of the Eastern Star, 3198
Krishnamurti (Jiddu) in, 9143
Order of the Golden Dawn. *See* Hermetic Order of the Golden Dawn
Order of the Livonian Knights, 767
Order of the Solar Temple (OTS). *See* Temple Solaire
Order of the Star, Krishnamurti's dissolution of, 5244
Orders, religious. *See* Religious communities; *specific orders*
Ordinall of Alkimy (Norton), 251, 252
Ordinary, the, in Greek religion, Hestia and, 3965
Ordinatio (Duns Scotus), 2524
Ordination, **6851–6860**. *See also* Priesthood
authority of, 7397
in Buddhism, 7397
and charism, routinization of, 8080
in Theravāda, 8074
Saichō on, 8030
saṃgha laws on, 8072–8073
in Zen Buddhism, posthumous, 9946
ceremony of, 7397
in Christianity, 7397
as consecration, 1956
in Daoism, 7414, 7415
posthumous, 9846
in Eastern Orthodox Church, 7960
of exorcists, 2929
initiation rituals of, 4483
in Orthodox Church, 2593
process of, 7397
in Protestantism, 7963
of rabbis, 6857, 7578–7579
in Ashkenazic communities, 7579–7580
kings and, 7580
Maimonides (Moses) on, 7578
in medieval Spain, 7579
origins of, 7578
qualified *vs.* unqualified, 3749
in United States, 7582
women as, 7582, 7637
as sacrament, cognates of, in comparative studies, 7956
temporary, 6879
of women, 6852
androcentrism and, 336
in Anglicanism, 353, 1735–1736
and body, notions of, 4165
Christ the Saviour Brotherhood, influence of, 4103
in Daoism, 7413
in Episcopalianism, 68, 353, 7404
gender studies on, 3312
Shintō, 7411
in Judaism, 1963–1964, 3354–3355, 7582, 7637
orders of ministry and, 6045
rise of, 3361
in Unity, 9472
Ordine Osirideo Egizio, sexual magic and, 8252
Ordo Praedicatorum (O.P.). *See* Dominicans
Ordo Templi Orientis (OTO), 6471
Crowley (Aleister) and, 2072
sexual magic and, 8251–8252
Ordo Virtutum (Hildegard), 2471
Oré, Luis Jeronimo de, on Virgin images, 8612
Oreibasia (mountain dancing), 6865
Orelli, C. von, on supreme beings, 8876
Orenda (power), 7348, 7373, 8947
Ores. *See* Metals
Oresme, Nicole d', on astronomy, 1978
Oresteia (Aeschylus), 5469
Orestes (Greek mythical figure), 986
in Anthesteria, 374, 375
myth of guilt and, 7783
Organic rights, 2655
Organization for Afro-American Unity, 5626
Organization for Security and Co-Operation in Europe (OSCE), 5363
Organization of Islamic Conferences (OIC), 4574–4575
Organs (musical instruments), 6311, 6312
Organ transplantation, 5810
Orgasm, 6875
"Orgasmic Rapture and Divine Ecstasy: The Semantic History of Ānanda" (Olivelle), 7083

Orgeones (cultic association), 7719
Orgy, **6860–6881**
in agrarian ritual, 2559
agriculture and, 187–188
in Asia, **6877–6881**
definition of, 6877–6878
in diabolical witchcraft, 9771
Dionysian, catharsis through, 1459
in Europe, medieval and modern, **6869–6877**
failure of, 6880
in French nunneries, 8250
in Mediterranean religion, ancient, **6863–6869**
in New Year festivals, 6590, 6591, 6592
overview of, **6860–6863**
sacred character of, 8239
sacredness absent from, 6880
social control *vs.*, 8242
O rgyan dbang phyug, 1232
O rgyan gling pa (Orgyen Lingpa), 6941
O rgyan pa Rin chen dpal (Orgyenpa Rinchenpal), 1227
O rgyan 'phrin las rdo rje (Karma pa), 5103
Or ha-ḥayyim (Ibn Attar), 867
Oriental cults, in Roman religion, 2093
Orientalism, **6881–6885**
Āyurveda and, 3856–3857
British, 9316–9317
and China, study of, 1631–1632
Islam and, humor and, 4213
Islamic studies in, 4716, 4721–4722, 4723
Said (Edward) on, 8031, 8032
subaltern studies and, 8801
Orientalism (Said)
criticism of, 8032
influence of, 8031
postcolonialism started by, 3321
Oriental mystery religions, 6330–6332
Oriental Orthodox Church. *See also* Non-Chalcedonian Orthodox churches
development of, 2584–2585
in ecumenical movement, with Eastern Orthodox Church, 2589
Orientation, **6885–6887**
circumambulation, **1795–1798**
in sacred space, 7982
ultimate, 1581
Origen (theologian), **6887–6890**
on Adonis, 35, 2536
Alexandria school and, 1979
and Ambrose, 287
on Andrew in Scythia, 1682
on anthropological dualism, 2507
on apocatastasis, 421, 422
Arianism and, 478
on asceticism, 7723
biblical exegesis of, 873, 874, 5486
on comets, 8735
on contemplation, 5817
cosmology and, 2606
ethics of, 7191
Eusebius influenced by, 2884
Evagrios of Pontus influenced by, 2886
on free will, 3207
on God, 3554, 9281
on *Gospel of Thomas,* 920
Greek Bible revised by, 892, 893, 894
Gregory of Nyssa's critique of, 3697
on heart, 3882
on *Hebrews,* 916
on hell, 3884
on heretics, 3926
on *James,* 916
Jerome influenced by, 4833–4834
Jerome's translations of, 4832
on Jesus
as moral model, 4844
as savior, 4843
as scapegoat, 8144, 8145
on John the Baptist, 2301
on *Logos,* 5502, 5503
on magic, 5577
on medicine, 3843
and mystical union, 6336
on mysticism, 6346–6347
on nonviolence, 6647
Pelagius influenced by, 7026, 7027
on *2 Peter,* 917
on phallus of Jesus, 7081
and religion and philosophy, 7113
response to anti-Christian treaty by Celsus, 6474
on retreat, 7771
on *Romans,* 911, 912
on Satan, 2314
self-castration of, 1452, 8248
on *Song of Songs,* 6336, 6346–6347, 9763
on soul and body, 8564
on temptation, 9072
theology of, 9134, 9135
on transmigration, 9329
on Trinity, 628, 4241, 9361
Valentinians compared to, 3513
writings of, 798
Origenists, 6890
in Egypt, 1447
Leontius of Byzantium as, 5412–5413
Origin
myths of (*See* Anthropogony; Cosmogony; Creation)
of religion (*See* Religion, origins of)
Original sin. *See also* Fall, the
Augustine on, 3645, 8406
confession and, 1888–1889
Edwards (Jonathan) on, 2699
grace and, 3645–3646
in Orthodox theology (ancestral sin), 2590
in Roman Catholic theology, 7883
Thomas Aquinas on, 3645–3646
virginity and, 4164
Origines (Isidore). *See Etymologies* (Isidore)
Origin of Civilization and the Primitive Condition of Man, The (Lubbock), 2662
Origins of Evil in Hindu Mythology, The (O'Flaherty), 9112
Origins of History of Consciousness, The (Neumann), 6484
Ori inun (personal deity), 9911
Orion (constellation), in ethnoastronomy, 2865, 2866
Orion (Tilak), 9199
Oriṣa (deities). *See also* Yoruba religion
Catholic elements of, 10026, 10028
gender of, 10027
list of, 10028
in Trinidadian religion, 10027, 10028–10029
Òrìṣà (divinities), 3571–3572
and Lisa, 5790
Oriṣa-nla. *See* Ọbatala
Orishas (spirits), 94
in Cuba, 9306
in Cuban Santeria, 1434, 8107–8108
in Santería, petitions to, vol. 9 color insert
in Shango Cult of Trinidad, 1435
in Yoruba religion, Ondo king as, 2000
Orissa (India), migration to Southeast Asia from, 4011
Orit (Bēta Esra'ēl scripture), 5003
Orixás (spirits), 9308
in Candomblé, 122, 123, 6274
in Umbanda, 124
Orléans (France), 4929–4930
Ornithomanteis (diviner), 2376
Oro (deity), 7309
Orochi people (Siberia), 9394, 9395
Orokaiva religion (New Guinea), funeral rites in, 3236
Oromo people (Ethiopia), 2573. *See also* Galla religion
migration of, 2860
Oronmila (deity), in Edo religion, 2697
Oropa, hermitages of, 2826
Orozco y Berra, Manuel, 5940
Orpah (biblical figure), 7947, 7948
Orphanages
in Byzantine Empire, 2582
religious founding of, 1750
Orpheotelestai (Orphic initiators), 6893–6894
Orpheus, **6891–6897**
contrast with Olympian gods, 2965
cosmogony composed by, 2832
on Demeter and Persephone, 2271
descent into the underworld by, 2297–2298
on Dionysos, 2357
etymology of name, 3123
identity of, 6892
images of, vol. 2 color insert
mystery religion of (*See* Orphism)
scholarship on, 6891
writings of, 6892–6893
Orpheus theme, 2297–2298
Orphic Bacchants, and deification, 2249
Orphic Gold Tablets, 6891, **6897–6898**
Orphism, 3685, 6893
Apollo as sun in, 8839–8840
boundaries of, 6891–6892
catharsis in, 1459, 1460
civic religion and, 3671, 3673–3674
confession in, 1887
cosmic egg in, 3903
Dionysian omophagia and, 6823
dualism in, 2508, 2509, 2511
ecstasy in, 2678
eschatology of, 7679
fate and chance in, 1527
fish symbolism in, 3123
human condition explained by, 2965
judgment of the dead in, 5026
as mystery *vs.* missionary religion, 6330
Night in, 3017
Pythagoreanism and, 7529
reincarnation in, 7679
rise of, 6302
sin and evil in, 8405
transmigration of soul in, 7186, 9329
ORT. *See* Renewed Order of the Temple
Ort (soul shadow), in Komi religion, 5218–5219
Ortega y Gasset, José, on games, 3266
Orthodox Bishops of America, 941
Orthodox Christianity. *See* Eastern Orthodox Christianity

Orthodox Church. *See* Eastern Orthodox Christianity; *specific Orthodox churches*
Orthodox Church in America, 2589
Christ the Saviour Brotherhood in, 4103
polity, 1765–1766
recognition of, 7942
Orthodox Church of Finland, 3103
Orthodox Church of Japan, 7943
Orthodox Confession of Faith, The (Petr Moghila), 7072
Orthodox Hildesheimer Seminary (Berlin), 7581
Orthodox Judaism, **6898–6909**. *See also* Hasidism; Musar movement
afterlife in, 155
Agudat Yisra'el representing, 194–196
antimodernism of, 4901
anti-Zionism of, 9982
bat mitzvah in, 7821
circumcision in, 7819
clothing in, 1831
conflicts with Reconstructionist Judaism, 5081–5082
conversion to, 7824
development of, 7730
domestic rituals in, 2397–2398
emergence of, 5020
feminism in, 3350, 3353
God in, 3552
Habad messianism, debate over, 3793
haredi movement in, 6907
Hildesheimer (Esriel), role of, **3980–3981**
historiography in, 4059–4060
Hoffmann (David), defense of, 4077
in Hungary, Sofer (Mosheh) and, 8507
Jewish Renewal and, 4872–4873
Jewish Theological Seminary of America and, 1958
kashrut laws of, 5107, 7504–7505
marriage in, 7822
medical ethics in, 5812
messianism in, 5978
miqveh in, 6047
modern, 6906, 6907
Modern Orthodoxy movement, Soloveitchik (Joseph Baer) and, 8518
naming of girls in, 7819
nature and, 2645
Neo-Orthodoxy, Hirsch (Samson Raphael), role of, 4023–4024
"Old Orthodox" opposition to Reform Judaism, Sofer (Mosheh) and, 8507
oral Torah in, 6841
prayer books in, 8388
Reform opposed by, 4983
Return to Judaism movement, Schneerson (Menachem) and, 8172
Revel (Bernard) and, 7773
revelation in, 7666
in Russia, Spektor (Yitshaq Elhanan), role of, 8674
seminary of, in Germany, 7581
sexual segregation in worship, 3353
Shabbat laws in, 8256–8257
Soloveitchik (Joseph Baer) in, 4908
suburbanization of, 1964
Suffering Servant doctrine in, 4089
Talmudic law and, Sherira' Gaon and, 8320
torah 'im derkh erets philosophy, Hildesheimer (Esriel) as proponent of, 3980
Torah study in, 9239
in United States, Soloveitchik (Joseph Baer), role of, 8517, 8518
women in
feminism and, 3350, 3353
obligations of, 3352, 3353
role and status of, 3350, 3352, 3353–3354
Zionism and, 7681
Orthodox Missionary Society, 4497
Orthodox Presbyterian Church, 7391
Orthodox Rabbinical Seminary (Berlin), Hildesheimer (Esriel) and, 3980–3981
Orthodox Unity Daoism, 2192, 2193, 2200
Orthodoxy, **6909–6913**. *See also* Doctrine; Heresy
Bauer (Walter) on, 3921, 3922, 3928
in Christianity, 7730 (*See also* Councils, Christian)
confrontation with Gnosticism as critical factor in, 3924
early, 1661
reconstructions of early Church and, 3928–3929
in Roman Catholicism, Council of Trent and, 1978
Shenoute on, 8319
church, and establishment of, 3922
in confessional religions, 3921, 3922
creeds and, 2053
in Egyptian religion, curses and, 2102
in Hinduism
Muslim rule and, 4007
Pāṭaliputra council and, 2037
and Vedas, misinterpretation of, 8015
Indian, atheism in, 578, 580–581
inside *vs.* outside and meaning of, 3925–3926
in Islam
development of, 7730
heretical elements, incorporation of, 3924
madhhab membership as measurement of, 3761
Sufism and, 8814, 8824
in Korean Confucianism, 1932–1933
meaning of term, 2958
in medical science, 3848–3849
in Mennonites, 5861
sacrilege and, 8010
Orthopraxy, **6913–6916**
in Christianity, Shenoute on, 8319
in Judaism, sacrilege and, 8012
Ortiz, Alfonso, 383, 6672
Ortiz, Fernando, 3065
on transculturation, 9292, 9305
Ortiz, Simon, 7225, 7226
Ortiz, Tomás, 5915
Ortiz Echaniz, Silvia, 5945
Ortner, Sherry, 382
on gender
nature *vs.* culture in, 3421, 7079
in Polynesian religions, 3395
on ritual, 7800, 7842
Ọrunmila (deity), 94, 4304. *See also* Ifa (god of divination)
in Cuban Santeria, 1434
role in creation, 3571
in Yoruba religion, 9911–9912
Osage religious traditions (North America), **6916–6919**
ballgame played in, 752
poetry of, 7225
totemism of, 9252
Osanobua. *See* Osanobwa
Osanobwa (Osanobua) (deity), 3572, 4301
creation by, 3572
Osanoha (deity), 3572
Osanowa (deity), 3572
Ọsanyin (deity), in Cuban Santeria, 1434
Osashizu (Iburi), 9082, 9083
OSB. *See* Benedictines
Osborn, Fairfield, 2609
OSCE. *See* Organization for Security and Co-Operation in Europe
Osgood, Cornelius, 575, 576
Oshadage, eagle as, 2553
Oshitelu, Josiah, political message of, 104
Osho. *See* Rajneesh, Bhgwan Shree; Rajneesh movement
Osho Commune International (India), 7608
Oshōgatsu (New Year), 2411, 6594
Osho Meditation Resort (India), 7608
Oshun, in Caribbean religions, 1434
Osiander, Andreas
Copernicus, publishing agreement with, 8182
preface added to Copernicus's book by, 1977, 8182
Ōsīkta (bear's eyes), 9394, 9395
Osiris (deity), **6919–6922**
Adonis assimilated with, 34, 35
in afterlife, 2705, 7763, 7767
and ancient novels, 3054
Antinous identified with, 440
Anubis and, 403
Atum and, 623
castration of, 1451, 4557
cult of, 2711, 6920–6921
Dionysos identified with, 3908, 6866
as dying and rising god, 1875
in Egyptian pantheon, 2704
in fertility mythology, 2720
fish symbolism and, 3123
funerary boats and, 989
and gender roles, 3384
Horus and, 2704
iconography of, 4318
Isis as wife of, 3604, 3605, 4557, 5727
judgment by, 128, 129, 138, 139, 5026, 7763
merit and, 5871
kings assimilated with, 693, 2704, 2720
in Kushite religion, 5269
marriage of, 5727
murder of, 2538, 2985, 4557
mystery religion of
ecstasy in, 2678
origins of, 6328
Nile River and, 7861, 7862
parallels to, 1398
patrimony of, 2704
phallus of, 7080
Plutarch on, 2514–2515, 2538, 7201, 7202
resurrection of, 7767
in ritual drama, 2435, 2441
salvation and, 7640–7641
Seth and, 8233
struggle between, 5163
in triad, 9349
twin of, 9414
in underworld, 9452
in underworld literature, 2719
Oskep 'orik (Gregory of Datev), 3693
Ōsō ("going to the Pure Land"), Shinran on, 8354
Ossâin (spirit), 122, 1497
Ossianic Cycle, 1494–1495
Ostendorfer, Michael, vol. 12 color insert
Ostia Antica synagogue, 8924

Ostiaks. *See* Khanty
OSTS (Order of the Solar Temple). *See* Temple Solaire
Ostwalt, Conrad E., 3100
Osuculum infame (kiss of infamy), sacrilege and, 8013
Ọ̀ṣùgbó society, 4303–4304, 9912
O'Sullivan, Vincent, 3085
Ọṣun (deity), 4301
  in Cuban Santeria, 1434
  in Edo religion, 2697
  gender of, 3401, 3402
  as Lady of the Animals, 5280
  in Yoruba religion, 9911
Otabil, Mensa, political theology, 1723
O-tä-dä-jish'-quä-äge (ballgame), 754
Otago Museum, 840
Otfiti (deity), 7313
"Other Minds" (Austin), 2427
Otherness
  difference associated with, 3303–3304
  exposure to, through media, 5808–5809
  of music, 6252
  in warfare, 9681
  Zolla (Elémire) on, 9985
"Other-power" schools of Buddhism, meditation in, 5821
Otherworld, **6923–6926**
  Celtic (*See* Annwn)
  Jewish, in apocalypses, 410, 416, 418
  nonexistence of, 6924–6925
  owl associated with, 6936
  in shamanism, topography of, 8284
Othinus (Norse mythical figure), 744
OT levels. *See* Operating Thetan levels
Ot Marksizma k idealizmu (Bulgakov), 1319
OTO. *See* Ordo Templi Orientis
Ō-Tō-Kan school of Zen, Hakuin and, 3742
Otomí religion, **6926–6928**
  deities of, 5909–5910, 5935
  human sacrifice in, 5909
  myths of, 5935
  in Postclassic period, 5909–5910
  rituals in, 5910
Ôtomo, Katsuhiro, 3097
Otontecuhtli (deity), 5909
Ōtori Sessō (Buddhist monk), 9949–9950
OTS. *See* Temple Solaire
Ott, Heinrich, on Heidegger (Martin), 3896
Ottama, U, 1140
Óttarr, 2693
Ottawa tribe (North America), **368–371**
  ballgame played by, 755
  naming ceremony of, 6683
Ottchigin (prince of fire), 9399
Otterbein, Philip W., 7143
Ottilie of Gersen, 6238
Otto I (Holy Roman emperor), 6967
Otto, Rudolf, **6928–6931**. *See also* Idea of the Holy
  aesthetics of, 48
  on anthropomorphism, 388–389
  on art and religion, 499–500
  Baeck (Leo) influenced by, 7670
  de Martino (Ernesto) influenced by, 2266
  descriptive and interpretive trend and, 4064
  Durkheim (Émile) contrasted with, 4095–4096
  Eliade (Mircea) on, 7349
  on emotion, religious, 7978
  on faith as experience, 2957
  on God, 3557
  hermeneutics and, 3932, 4061
  on holy, idea of the, **4095–4101,** 8493
  on idea of God, 2779, 7975–7976
  on ideograms, 1989
  James (William) and, 7742
  on knowledge, 5208
  legacy of, 4100–4101
  Mensching (Gustav), influence on, 4043
  modern social theory, contributions to, 8493
  in modern studies, 6369
  morality and, 6178
  museum designed by, 6246
  on mysticism, 7738
  on numinous, concept of, 4096, 4097, 4100, 5948, 5969, 7126, 7976
  paradoxical statements by, 6989
  on phenomenology of religion, 7087, 7090–7091, 7094, 10078
  on power, 7348–7349
  preanimism criticized by, 7374
  on predestination, 3205
  on *a priori* and the idea of God, 7975–7976
  reductionism, opposition to, 4095
  on religion, 7126
  religion defined by, 7694
  Religiöser Menschheitsbund of, 2343
  on religious experience, 7694, 7738, 7745, 7835
  on religious feeling, 4096–4097, 4100–4101
  on Russian chanting of *sviaty* ("holy"), 4099
  on the sacred, 7842
  successor to, 3221
  symbol theory and, 8913
  sympathetic treatment of religion as pre-phenomenological, 4100
  on transcendent, problem of knowledge of the, 4096–4097
  Wach (Joachim) and, 9650, 9652
  on Wundt (William), 4096
Otto, Walter F., **6932–6935**
  on Athena, 588
  Kérenyi, Károly influenced by, 5113
  on myth, 6367
  Nilsson (Martin P.) on, 6622
  on soul, 7871
Ottoman Empire. *See also* Turkey
  ʿAlawīyūn in, 226
  al-Azhar university in, 230
  Armenians in, 488
  attack on Karbala by, 5088
  Bābīs in, 728, 737
  Bahāʾīs in, 737
  caliphate in, 1367
  Caucasus invaded by, 4614
  Christian missions and, 6083
  Constantinople, fall of, Western humanism and, 4175
  dissolution of, 1685
    and Islam as religion and state, 7286
  Egypt, conquest of, 1981–1982
  Greek Orthodox Church in, 3657
  Ḥanafī school of law in, 23, 4698
  humor, suppression of, 4216
  Janissary corps in, and Bektāshi Sufism and, 8823
  Jews in, 4995–5000, 5104
    legal jurisdiction of, 9981
    population of, 4995–4996
    presses of, 4997
  Judaism in, 3186
    dybbuk possession in, 2533
  Kosmas Aitolos in, 5239
  medicine in, 3833
  millet (nation) system, 1674, 1684
  mosques in, 6209
  narrative traditions of, 2447
  Orthodox Christianity under, 2587
    Scholarios (Gennadios) and, 8174
  shaykh al-Islam in, 8306
  spread of, 1684
    Crusades and, 2077
    in Europe, 4674
  Syriac Orthodox Church and, 8940
  ṭarīqah in, 9006, 9008
  Turkish nationalism in, 3624
  waqf in, 9678
  westernization of Islamic law in, 4701, 4702, 4703
  zāwiyahs in, 4588
Ottoman Family Rights Law (1917), 4701, 4704
Otto of Bamberg, on Slavic religion and, 8433
Oudjat eye, 2940
Ouija board, 2370
Ouktazaun (spirit), 4408
Ouranopolis, utopianism and, 3906
Ouranos (deity)
  castration of, 986, 1450, 1451, 4231
  in creation, parthenogenesis of, 2555
  as *deus otiosus*, 2311
  Kumarbi cycle and, 1450–1451, 4231
  phallus of, 7080
Our Corner (magazine), 844
Our Criminal Society (Shur), 9073
Our Lady of Guadalupe, 9622–9623
Our Lady of Guadalupe (Poole), 5922
Our Lady of Mercy, Obatala identified with in Santería, 1434
Our Lady of Mount Carmel (Ezili Danto), in Vodou, 9638
Our Mother Young Eagle Girl (deity), Virgin of Guadalupe as, 4152
Ouroboros
  cosmic power and, 8458
  as magic circle, 1792–1794
Our Plundered Planet (Osborn), 2609
Oury, Guy-Marie, and Marie de l'Incarnation, 5712
Ousia (being or substance). *See also* Homoousios ("of the same substance") doctrine
  hypostasis and, 4240
  in Neoplatonism, 4240
  trinitarian theology and, 4241
  in Trinity, 2583
Ouspensky, P. D., **6935–6936**
  and Bennett (John G.), 832–833
  Gurdjieff (G. I.) and, 3711
Outlaw figure, in popular religion, 7330
Outlaws of the Marsh (Chinese novel), 3056, 3068
Outline of the Religious Literature of India (Farquhar), 4447
Out-of-body experiences (OOBE), 6057
  ecstatic discipline and, 8703
  scientific study of, 6057
  in shamanism, soul's flight in, 8272
Out of the Depth (Boisen), 7486

Out of This World: Other-Worldly Journeys from Gilgamesh to Albert Einstein (Culianu), 2080
Outsider art, **9624–9627**
Outsiders. *See* Insiders and outsiders
Ouyang Xiu, 1577
Ovambo people (southwest Africa), supreme being of, 3574
Ovando, Nicolás de, 9305
Oved, Margalit, 2164
Overbergh, Cyrille van, 115
Overconsumption, in environmental degradation, 2653
Overmeyer, Daniel L., 7330
Overpopulation, Qur'ān on, 2653
Ovid
on Adonis, 2536
on apotheosis, 439
on Asklepios, 551
on chaos, 1537
on Daphne, vol. 13 color insert
on the Flood, 2965–2966
on golden age, 2964, 3627
on *lares,* 5320
on metamorphoses, 3903
on omens, 7335
on *Parentalia,* 6994, 6995
on *pontifex maximus,* 1051
on Priapus, 7393
on urban festivals, 2994
Owen, Robert
Campbell (Alexander), debates with, 1377
Spiritualism and, 8716
Owen, Wilfred, 7205
Owens, Joseph, on Rastafari, 7628
Owens, Louis, 3092, 3093
Owl goddess (prehistoric), 7377, 7378
Owls, 949, **6936–6937**
Athena and, 586
in megalithic religion, 5824
Owner of Heaven, in Ganda religion, 2575
Ownership, Rāmānuja on, 7615–7616
Oxalá (spirit), 122, 123
Oxen. *See also* Cattle
in Indus Valley religion, 4473
sacrifice of, 1466–1467
in Dinka religion, 2366
on Madagascar, 8746
in Swazi religion, 5169, 5170
as symbol of king, in Swazi religion, 5170
as symbol of Luke the Evangelist, 5530
Oxfam, 1555, 3174
Oxford, school of, nature in, 6432
Oxford Group Movement, 2343, 9138
Oxford movement (Anglicanism), 352, 6510, 6765, 7523
liturgy in, 5490
music in, 6313
Oxford University
'Abd al-Rāzīq ('Alī) at, 5
Goodenough (Erwin R.) at, 3637
Jewish studies at, 4883, 4884
liberalism at, 6105
Marett (R. R.) at, 5708
Müller (F. Max) at, 6234–6235
University Museum at, 6243
Oxhead school of Buddhism, Platform Sūtra and, 1522
Oxomoco (mythic figure), 5935
Oxôssi (spirit), 122
Oxtoby, Willard G., **10055–10056**
Oxum (spirit), 122, 123
Oxumarê (spirit), 122
Oxyrhynchus hymnus (song), 6305
Ọya (deity), 122, 123
in Caribbean religions, 1434
foods favored by, 3171
as Niger river, 7862
Oyomeigaku. *See* Yōmeigaku teachings
Oyono, Ferdinand, 3087–3088
Òyó religion (Caribbean), 10027
Ozal, Turgut, 1517–1518
Ozick, Cynthia, eleventh commandment suggested by, 3350
Oztoteotl (deity), names of, 1469
Ozu, Yasujiro, 3097, 3100, 3101
Ozu Yoshisada. *See* Motoori Norinaga

P

P (source). *See* Priestly source
Pa'ao (high priest), in Hawaiian religion, role in, 3796
Paasonen, Heikki, 2421, 3112
on Mari and Mordvin religion, 5709, 5710
Pabil of Udm, Canaanite religion and, 1398–1399
Pabilsag (deity), 5950
Pabonka (Buddhist teacher), Dge lugs Buddhism and, 8382
Pābujī (folk hero), 4434
Pacal (Maya lord), tomb of, 149, 7813
Pacchāgaṇa (late school), 1136
Pacem in terris (Peace on earth) (John XXIII), 4946
Pachacámac (deity), 4384, 4411, 4412
creation and, 8600
as high god, 8590
Spanish perceptions of, 8606–8607
Pachacuti (Inca king), 5983
calendar and, 1362, 1363–1364
consolidation of power by, 5176
Viracocha introduced as high god by, 8843
Pachakamaite (mythic figure), 5984–5985
Pachamama (deity), 2984, 4411
in agrarian rites, 2558, 8583
in Andean religions, in modern era, 8615
animals associated with, 5515
Atahuallpa regenerated by, 567
Blessed Mother associated with, 8615
daughters of, 3416–3417
gender parallelism and complementarity in, 3416
healing powers of, 3811
as Quilla (moon), 8601
sacredness of the earth and, 3971
Pachatira (deity), gender parallelism and complementarity in, 3416
Pachayachachic (deity), 4412
Pacheco Pereira, Duarte, 112
Pachisi (game), 3260–3261
Pachomius (ascetic), **6939–6940**
cenobitic monasticism and, 1980, 6131, 6939–6940, 7723
influence of, 6940
monasteries established by, 2582, 2710, 6939, 6940
social orientation of, 2829
writings of, 6940
Pacification, of dead, 2241
Pacific Conference of Churches, 1739
Pacific Islands. *See* Oceania
Pacific Islands Monthly, cargo cults and, 1423
Pacific Northwest, U.S.
Athapaskan religious traditions in, 572, 574–575
mountains in, 6214
Pacific School of Religion, Swedenborgianism and, 8904
Pacifism. *See also* Nonviolence
Christian movements, 6648
Day (Dorothy) and, 2226
of Mennonites, 5860
Pact of Omar, 4859
Pacts, in witchcraft, 9771–9772
Paddengngeng (hunters), 1317
Paddock, John, 5902
Padinattavadu atchakodu (Ashokamittiran), 10036
Padma gling pa, Klong che pa Rab 'byams pa reborn as, 7869
Padma gling pa, Rig 'dzin, 1232
Pad ma las 'brel rtsal. *See* Tsultrim Dorjé
Padmapāda, 9547
Padmapāṇi *(bodhisattva),* 1076, 9512
Padma Purāṇa (Hindu text), 854
Padmasambhava (Buddhist monk), **6940–6942**
and Bodnath stupa, 7167
and Bsam yas, 1152, 6940–6941
as buddha, 1068
ceremonies of, 1308
deification of, 1223
followers of, 1231, 6941
Gesar as emanation of, 3463
iconography of, 4330
influence of, 6941–6942
legend of, 6940–6941
and propagation of *dharma* in Tibet, 3156, 6941
reincarnation of, 5192
and shamanism, 3155
teachings of, 7868
texts concealed by, 1153
in Tibetan legend, 8106
translations by, 1256
and Treasure tradition, 6940, 6941, 9331–9332, 9333
Padmavat (Malik Muḥammad Ja'isi), 7223
Padmāvatī, 4819
Padma yang rtse (Buddhist monastery), 1232
Padminī (ideal woman), 5519
Padoux, Andre, 8987, 8989
Padwick, Constance, 4718
Pādyāb (protection water), 9997, 10000
Pad yātrā (journey on foot), 861
Paekche kingdom (Korea)
Buddhism in, 5231
Maitreya in, 5621
shamanism in, 5230
Paek Ijŏng, Confucianism and, 1930
Paepae (carved wooden bar), for waste excretion, vol. 13 color insert
Paganalia (festival), 5321
Pagan and Christian in an Age of Anxiety (Dodds), 7107
Paganism
abandonment of, as apostasy, 431–432
Anglo-Saxon, **6942–6944**
deities of, 6943
funeral rites, 6943
Germanic religion and, 6942, 6943
rituals in, 6943
sources on, 6942–6943
Baltic
construction of, 762–763, 769–770
sanctuaries of, 773–775
Campbell and, 1380
cargo cults and, 1415
Celtic (*See* Celtic religion)
Christian conquest and continuities with, 1689
Christianity and
analogies in, 5043
conversion to, 4859
festivals and, 9814
Christianity compared with
Frazer on, 3192
Merezhkovskii (Dmitrii) on, 5869
Christianity *vs.,* Shenoute's efforts in, 8319
Christian revisionism in Ireland, 1499
comparative theology of, 9127–9128
Constantine's denunciations of, 1966
contemporary movements (*See* Neopaganism)

creeds as defense against, 2054–2055
and dance, 2145
deities of, Christian perspectives on, 2883
in Earth First!, 2563
in Earth Liberation Front, 2562
in Eastern Europe, magic and, 5580
Eusebius and, 2885
in feminist spirituality movement, 9788
folklore as legacy of, 2144–2145
Gnosticism as, 3923–3924
vs. great religions, 7725–7726
Greco-Roman, Emperor's Cult in, 2777
inside *vs.* outside religious perspective and, 3926
Irish, Lugh in (*See* Lugh)
mundane *vs.* transmundane worlds in, 7726
nature religions connected to, 2663
in Nazism, 2663
Neoplatonism and, 6474
omophagia and, 6822
Renaissance views of, 4039
revival of, Frazer's (James G.) influence on, 2664
Roman (*See* Roman religion)
Rubenstein (Richard) on Judaism and, 4094
salvation in, 7726
scholarship within, 2665
secularization and, 8216
Sibylline Oracles and, 8385
superstition and, 8864–8865
survival of, witchcraft and, 9771
Vatican II on, 9537–9538
"Paganism Today" (conference series), 2665
Pagan religions. *See* Paganism
Page, David, 643
Page, Kirby, 6648
Page, Ruth, 2163
Page, Stephen, 639, 642–643, 646, 647, 651
Pagel, Walter, 6981
Pagels, Elaine
on Gnosticism, 3534
on Satan, 8125
Pagine di religione mediterranea (Pestalozza), 2555
Pagis, Dan, 6021
Pagodas
architecture of, 9045–9046, 9047
classification of, 461
basic form of, 9264–9265
in Korea, 9048
meanings of, 9264–9265
reverencing Buddha in, 1955
Paha Sapa (Black Hills), 5295
Pähkinaänsaari Treaty (1323), 5092
Pahlavi, Riḍa Shāh (shah of Iran), Imāmīyah and, 8340
Pahlavi books, 9993–9994
angels in, 344
apocalyptic tradition in, 411
ascension in, 519–520
magi in, 5560
world-periods in, 174
Zoroastrian traditions in, 9990
Pahlavi dynasty, Zoroastrians in, 10004
Pahlavi language
astrological books translated into, 563
Avesta translated into, 709
Pañcatantra translated into, 6959
Pahnke, Walter, 7471
Pahu (drum), 6263, 6264
Pahu hula (drum), 2500
Pai (Candomblé priest), 122
Paia shamans, creation as mythic struggle and, 2013
Paiawon (deity), 424
Paides e Parthenoi (Brelich), 1048
Paik, Nam June, vol. 11 color insert
Pai Marire movement (New Zealand), 6547
Pain, **6944–6948**. *See also* Suffering
in Christianity, 6946
and death, 6944–6945
definitions of, 6944–6945
in discursive contexts, 6945–6947
function of, 6947
in Hinduism, 6946
in Islam, 6946
juridical, 6945–6946
as medicine, 6946
models of, 6946–6947
in mortification, 6197, 6198
in North American Indian religions, 6945, 6947
praise of, 6945
psychoanalysis of, 6947
as purifier, 6946
rituals of, 6945, 6947
self-inflicted
as asceticism, 528
brain processes of, 6946
in mourning rites, 6945
and suffering, 6944
use of, 6945
and violence, 6944–6945
Painchaud, Louis, 6395
Paine, Thomas
blasphemy prosecutions against, 974
religious rhetoric used by, 7257
on "two books," 9423
Painting. *See* Art
Pais aph'hestias (boy from the hearth), in Demeter Eleusinia cults, 2751
Paisley, Ian, 2892
Paiute religion (North America)
Big Times in, 6715–6716
calendar of, 1353
dances of, 2139
Ghost Dance of, 3473, 6718
shamanism of, 6714
tricksters of, 9355
Wovoka in, 9846–9847
Paixiao (musical instrument), 6293
Pajelanĉa, African, 120
Pak, Chung Hwa, 9468
Pakalns, Guntis, 328
Pak Chi-wŏn, Practical Learning movement and, 1933
Pakistan and Pakistani religions
Aḥmadiyah in, 200, 4654, 6738
Buddhism, 1145
Christianity, 1730
creation of, 4773
diversity of practice in, folk stories reflecting tension resulting from, 3162
foundation of, 4641, 4654
immigrants from, 4675, 4678, 4679
Iqbāl (Muḥammad) as spiritual founder of, 4652, 4654
Islam
Imāmī (Twelvers) Shiism, 4698
law, 4645, 4703
literature, 4644
music in, 6283
Muslim majority, 4641
in organization of state, 4654
personality cults in, 4650
polygamy in, 4707
Jamā'at-i Islāmī in, 4772–4773
neofundamentalist government in, 4574
religious studies in, 8791
Zoroastrianism, fire in, 570
Pakits (spirits), in Kromanti dance, 1436
Pakpak people (Indonesia), 799
Pak Sedang, Zhu Xi, opposition to, 1932
Pakudha Kaccāyana, atomism of, in Ājīvikas, 213
Pak Yon, in Korean music, 6296
Pak Yŏng, Neo-Confucianism and, 1930
Pal, Bipincandra, 827
Palaces
in *maṇḍalas,* 5644
Japanese, music and dance in, 6300
Minoan, 38, 39, 40–41
Mycenaean, 41, 42
Pāla dynasty (India), 824, 1115, 1125, 1253
Buddhist monasticism in, 6129
Palaeologus dynasty (Byzantium), 4353
Palamas, Gregory. *See* Gregory Palamas
Palamite hesychasm. *See* Hesychasm
Palatua (deity), priest of, 3126
Palau (Micronesia)
birth rites in, 7807
divination in, 6004–6005
funeral rituals in, 6005
temporary prostitution in, 3970
yoni in, 9908
Palden Thondup Namgyal (Sikkim king), 7262
Palemon (ascetic), 6939
Palenque (Mexico), Maya inscriptions from
creation myth in, 5797
kings and ancestors in, 5798
Palenque Triad (deities), 5797
Paleolithic art, 1048
animals in, 7375
cave art, 1470–1471, 5280–5281, 6952–6953, 8279
goddess worship in, 3583–3584, 3593, 3613, 7375, 7377
ornaments, 6951–6952
Venus figures, 6953, 7079
Paleolithic Period
Lower, 6948, 6951
meaning of term, 6948
Middle, 6948, 6950–6951, 6953
Upper, 6948, 6949, 6951–6953, 6954
Paleolithic religion, **6948–6955**
ancestor skulls in, 3806
animals in, 6952–6953, 7375
archaeology of, 454–455
art in (*See* Paleolithic art)
birds in, 947, 6953
birth in, 950
bones in, 1014, 6953
Breuil (Henri) on, 1048
caves as sacred space in, 7974
doubleness in, 2423
evidence of, 6949
female-male polarity and sacred union in, 3974–3975
funeral rites in, 6952, 7375, 7377
goddess worship in, 2983, 2985, 7375, 7377, 7378
gods in, 7378
incarnation in, 4414
Lady of the Animals in, 5280–5281
percussion in, 7035
ritual performances in, 7042
sacrifice in, 7375, 8005, 8008–8009
shamanism in, 8279
sources of, 6949–6950
Southeast Asian, 8641–8642
survey and assessment of, 6950–6953

Paleolithic religion *continued*
theories of, 6953–6955
Paleosiberian language family, 468
Paleostrovskii monastery, mass suicide at, 8830
Pales (deity), 3118, 7900
Palestine
agriculture in
Kalischer (Tsevi Hirsch) on, 5069
origins of, 185
Agudat Yisra'el in, 195
archaeology in
biblical, 455
Kenyon's (Kathleen) work in, 5111
Bahā'īs in, 737
British administration of, Anglo-Israelites and, 1658
Byzantine, *piyyuṭim* (liturgical poems) in, 8390
as Christian Holy Land, 4836
cult of Reshef in, 7761
curses, Palestinian, 2097, 2098
Ebionite sect in, 2596
economy of, *Ecclesiastes* and, 2599
eremitism in, 2826
Essenes in, 2846
films from, 3098
Islamic conquest of, 20
Israeli conflict with
Buber (Martin) on, 1058
Christian emigration and, 1676
Ginzberg (Asher) predicting, 3496
Ḥamās and, 7257
Jewish studies in, 4882–4883
Judaism in
amoraim of, 294, 8318
Gaonate of, 4989, 4990–4991
Karaite sect, 5083
marriage law in, 3746
midrash in, 6014
Orthodox emigration to, 9979
prayers of, 8387
Qabbalah, 7534, 7537
Smith (Morton) on, 8449
synagogues in, 8922, 8923
yeshivot of, 9882–9883, 9885
kingship in, 5164–5165
Naufian culture in, 6460–6461
under Roman rule, anti-Semitism in, 398
Said (Edward) on, 8032
Samaritans in, 8067–8069
scapegoat rite practiced in, 2598
sects of, 2847
utopian communities in, 7720–7721
Zionism and, 4863
Palestinian Knights, in Crusades, 2075
Palestinian Talmud. *See* Talmud, Jerusalem
Palestrina, Giovanni Pierluigi da, 6311
Palette, Narmer, 4298
Paley, William, 3558, 4517, 6435
Darwin influenced by, 2909
P'algwanhoe (Buddhist festival), 5231–5232
Pali-English Dictionary, 6956
Paliku order of priests, rituals of, 3796
Palikur people (Amazon), 8627–8628. *See also* Arawak Indians
Pali language
as language of Therāvada, 1131, 1135, 1136, 1252–1253, 9145
Buddhist scriptures in (*See* Pali scriptures/texts)
Khmer use of, 5130
Mongkut's study of, 6139
music in, in Southeast Asia, 6290
as probable language of Buddha, 1108
as sacred Buddhist language, 1093, 9145
Pali scriptures/texts, 1110, 1198–1200, 1265–1267
Buddhaghosa's commentaries on, 1074
canon, 1253, 1254, 1265
arhat in, 476
eightfold path in, 2737–2738
formation of, 1407
in Khmer Buddhism, 5128
Maitreya in, 5618–5619
sexual relations in, 6877
in Southeast Asian Buddhism, 9826
upāya in, 9484–9485
contents of, 9146–9147
cosmology in, 2026, 2027
English translations of, 6955–6956
by Horner (I. B.), 4129
hells in, 3887
Mongkut's study of, 6139
Pāṭaliputra council in, 2037
Theravādin councils and, 2037, 2038
Western emphasis on, in Sinology, 1632
Western study of, by Horner (I. B.), 4129–4130
Pali Text Society (PTS), **6955–6957**
expansion of, 6956
financial support of, 6955
founder of, 1312, 6955–6956
goal of, 1253, 6955, 6956
Horner (I. B.), role of, 4129, 4130
publications of, 1126–1127, 1256, 6956
Palladio, Andrea, 795
Palladius (bishop of Helenopolis), on Chrysostom, 1761, 1762
Pallas (deity), 587
Pallas, P. S., 5709
Pallava period (Tamil), 8975
Paḻḻis (shrines), 8974
Palmas (carved stone), 750
Palmer, Daniel David, chiropractic and, vital energy and, 3850
Palmer, E. H., 616
Palmer, Phoebe, Holiness movement and, 4082–4083
Palmer, Susan J., 6526–6527
Palmo, Tenzin, 6761
Palm Sunday, 9815
music in, 6305
Palm tree, 9337, 9338
Palm Week (Byzantine rite), 1743
Palm wine, in West African libations, 9719
Palmyra (Syria), Aramean religion in, 449
Palnāḍu, Epic of, 2814–2815, 2816
Palpung (Buddhist monastery), 5223
Palulop (mythic figure), 6012
Pamiri tribes (Central Asia)
converting to Islam, 4621
sheep and goats of, 8311, 8312
Pampā (deity), Vijayanagara as sacred space and, 1806
Pampaikkarar, 2934
Pamphilus, Eusebius and, 2884
Paṃsukūlikas, 9148
Pan (deity), **6957–6958**
Artemis and, 506
birth of, 6957
cult of, 6957
death of, 6958
destiny of, 6957
as fertility god, 7079–7080
iconography of, 6957
in Neopaganism, 6472
origins of, 6957
Pindar on, 7173
as shepherd, 6957
Pān, Samtec Braḥ Sugandhādhipatī, 5131
Panacas (Inca lineages), Inca calendar and, 1363
Panaetius
Stoicism and, 8740, 8741
on world citizenship, 3906
Pan-Africanism
Ethiopian World Federation and, 7625
Garvey (Marcus) in, 3287, 7624
Rastafari repatriation of Africa and, 7627
Pan African Theology, A (Young), 78–79
Panahi, Jafar, 3098
Panajachel Maya, funeral rites of, 7813
Panama, Cuna religion in, **2095–2097**
Panama Conference (1916), Latin American missions and, 1702
Panamu I (king), 447, 450
Panamu II (king), 447
Panamuwa II, 28
Panathenaia (festival), **6958–6959**
Pan-Baltism, 764
Pañcābja Maṇḍala, 5641
Pañcabuddha (Five Buddhas), 1078
Pañcamākarapūjā (five m's), in Hindu Tantrism, 4003
Pañcāṅga (sacred calendar), 9824–9825
Pāñcarātra, 8989–8990, **9506–9509**
Bhāgavata and, 9502–9503
epic, 9507
maṇḍalas in, 5640–5641
Vaiṣṇavism and, 9499–9500, 9501, 10088
Pañcarātras (yogin)
doctrine of emanations of Viṣṇu elaborated by, 4005
influence on other Vaiṣṇava sects, 4020
Vaiṣṇava Tantras of, 4020
Pañcaskañdhaprakarana (Candrakīrti), commentary in, 1401
Pañcatantra, **6959–6960**
books of, 6959
characters of, 6959
frame story of, 6959
language of, 6959
popularity of, 6959
translations of, 6959–6960
Pañcatattvas (five M's), 8991
Pancathāgata (Five Tathāgatas), 1078
Pañcaviṃśatisāhasrikā-prajñāpāramitā Sūtra (Buddhist text), 1271
Pañcāyatanapūjā (five-shrine worship), Śaṅkara on, 4004
Panchāyat (Parsi council), 6998
Paṇchen bla ma Blo bzang chos rgyan (Lozang Chögyen), 1155
Panchen Lama, 1155, 2132
Chinese government on, 1158–1159, 7269
Panda, 808
Pāṇḍavas (Hindu figures). *See also* Arjuna
Balarāma and, 743
in *Mahābhārata,* 5595
in literature, 5467
in puppet theater, 2452
tapas exercised by, 8998
war between Kauravas and, 852
Pandemos, 408
Pandey, Gyan, subaltern studies and, 8800
Pāṇḍey, Kedārnāth, 10034–10035
Paṇḍharpur (India), 2320, 5253
Pandian, Jacob, on spirits, 8277
Pandora, myth of, 2965, 7419, 7420
Pandrosos (deity), 6958
Pāṇḍu, sons of. *See* Pāṇḍavas
Pane (deity), 2298
Pané, Fray Ramón, on high gods, 8589
Pane, Raymond, 10024

Panentheism, **6960–6965**
coining of term, 6963
definition of, 6960
monism and pluralism avoided by, 6961
necessity and contingency in God in, *6961,* 6962
Pangaeus, Mount, 6895
Pangratios Vrionis, Christ the Saviour Brotherhood and, 4103
Pangu (primal being)
center of the world annd, 1501
as chaos giant, 1624
as creator, 8428
Pangu Pati, cargo cults and, 1419
Panhuman comparison, 1880
Pani (deity), 192
Paṇidhāna (wish), 9833
Panikkar, Raimundo, 6086, 9130
Pāṇini, 5467, 7754
on chanting, 1535
grammar of, 7005
on *śaiva* ascestics, 8021
Pan Jingruo, 3069
Panj piyāre (five beloved), in Sikhism, 8408
Pan-Malayan Islamic Party (PMIP), 4668
Pan-Mayanism, 5932
Pan-Mongolism, Solov'ev (Vladimir) on, 8520
Pannenberg, Wolfhart
comparative theology of, 9130
on death of God, 8721
on free will and predestination, 3208
on God, 3559, 7423
on history as foundation of religion, 7117
on kingdom of God, 5152–5153
Pannomion (legal code), 5374
Panofsky, Erwin, 500, 501, 4297–4298
Panopticon (prison), 5374
Panpsychism, in Chinese religion, *qi* and, 8554–8555
Pansophia, Comenius on, 1863
Pansophy, 3524–3525, 6433
Pan'sori (narrative singing), 2454
P'ansori (storytelling), in Korean religion, 5233
Panspermia, 7190
Pantel, Pauline, structuralism and, 8758
Panthak (devotional cluster), 6997
Pantheism, **6960–6965**. *See also* Panentheism
in Buddhism, 6965
coining of term, 6963
definition of, 6960
al-Ḥallāj and, 3756
in Hinduism, 6964–6965
monistic, 2664, 6961
in Mormonism, 7449
mystical union and, 6334
necessity and contingency in God in, *6961,* 6961–6962
neoplatonic, 6963
pluralism in, 6961
post-Kantians' on, 5080
Schlegel (Friedrich) on, 8159
in Stoicism, 6961, 6962
syncretism and, 3909
Vatican I on, 9531
Pantheon (building)
circle symbolism in, 1792
Sol symbolism in, 8511
Pantheons, 9064, 9065
bureaucratic, of Daoism, 2178
definition of, 3618
development of, 3618
"king of the gods" in, 5146
structure of, 3618, 9064
supreme beings in, 8872–8873
Panyassis of Halicarnassus, on Adonis, 34, 2536
Paolo, Giovanni di, vol. 13 color insert
Pap (king of Armenia), 6479
Papa ("earth")
in Maori creation myth, 1450
hierogamy of, 2555
in Polynesian creation myths, 7312–7313, 8980
sacredness of the earth and, 3971
Papacy, **6965–6976**. *See also* Pope; *specific popes*
apostolic succession, 1763–1764
authority of, 694–695
Counter-Reformation strengthening, 6972–6973
Gregory I on, 3688
Gregory VII and, 3690–3691, 7876
height of, 6971
Marsilius of Padua on, 5729–5730
reform movement and, 3690–3691
vs. secular authority, 696–697, 3690–3691
Vatican I on, 2044, 6974
in Avignon, 6971, 7280
abuses during, 7877
Catherine of Sienna and, 1461
and centralization of authority, 2042, 6971
duration of, 6971
factors of, 6971
Babylonian Captivity of, 6971
canonization of saints and, 2082–2083
in church polity, 1763–1764, 7886
civil power and
conflicts with, 1690
ecclesiology and, 1772
colonial jurisdictions granted to Spain and Portugal, 1695
conciliar theory and, 2042–2043
convocation of ecumenical councils and, 2041
coronation by, 696
Counter-Reformation by, 6972–6973 (*See also* Counter-Reformation)
Crusades and, 2076
decline of, 6971
division of (*See also* Great Western Schism)
Catherine of Sienna and, 1461
Council of Pisa and, 4233
as proof of inadequacy of reforms, 1691
doctrinal disputes of 5th century and, 1763
early, 6966–6967
ecclesiology and, 1772
in ecumenism, 2689, 6974
emergence of, 1662, 6966–6967
during Enlightenment, 6973
feudalism in, 6970
fiscal system of, Boniface VIII and, 1019
Franciscans and, 3182, 3184, 3185
infallibility of
Döllinger (Johann) on, 2396
Vatican I on, 2044, 2396, 6974, 7180
kingship and
Gallicanism on, 3258–3259
tension between, 696–697, 3691
Luther on, 1773
medieval, 6967–6971
modern, 6973–6975
nationalism and bias against, 6973
origin of term, 6965, 7279
origins of, 1772, 6965–6966
political influences on, in Middle Ages, 2586, 7254, 7280
Protestantism rejecting, 7448
Reformation as against, 1663, 6972
Reformation underestimated by, 6972
reforms of, 6967–6971
by Avignon popes, 6971
during Counter-Reformation, 6972–6973
Gregory IX, 821
Gregory VII, 839, 6970
Innocent III, 821, 4496
John Paul II, 6975
Leo IX, 6967
Nicholas II, 6970
Vatican I, 6974
Vatican II, 6975, 7011–7012
in Renaissance, 6972
ultramontanism of, 9442
on women's apostolic congregations, 6764
during World War I, 6974
Papaeus (deity), in Scythian cosmology, 8205
Papago people (North America), 6721
Papal elections
Alexander III's reform of, 6971
law of conclave, 6971
Nicholas II's reform of, 6970
Ottonian privilege of, 6967, 6970
Papal legates, in Roman Catholic polity, 1764
Papal States
annexed by Napoleon, 6973
establishment of, 6967
loss of, 6974
under Pius IX, 7179, 7180
Sixtus IV expanding, 6972
theocracy in, 9109
Pa Pangisi (Melanesian missionary), 9197
Papatea (deity), 7313
Papa Wata (divinity), 5630
Pápay, József, 3112
Paper money, in Chinese religion, offerings of, 6137–6138
Papias (bishop)
on angels, 4540
on *John,* 4943–4944
on *Mark,* 907, 920
on Mark the Evangelist, 5714
on *Matthew,* 907, 920, 5780
on Matthew the Evangelist, 5780
on *1 Peter,* 917
Pap Ikar ("god's way"), chanting from, 2095
Paproth, Hans-Joachim, 474
Papsukkal (deity), 4404
Papua New Guinea. *See* New Guinea
Papuan Liberation Army (OPM), 9325
Papus (Gérard Encausse), 6782
Papyri Vindobonenses Graecae, Hermetic texts in, 3939, 3940
Papyrus, law codes and, 1842
Papyrus Harris I, 2709
Papyrus Jumilac, 2715
Papyrus Oslo, syncretism in, 3909
Pâques, Viviana, on myths, 99
Parā (deity), in Trika Śáivism, 8046
Parabalani (medical corps), in Alexandria, 3844
Parable of the Wicked Mammon, The (Tyndale), 9426
Parables, **6976–6980**. *See also* Proverbs
definition of, 6976, 7119

Parables ***continued***
in Hebrew scriptures, 6978
in *Rasā'il Ikhwān al-Ṣafā'*, 4376
of Jesus, 6979
language of, 7119
as literary form, 5470
midrash as, 6020–6021
modern, 6979–6980
rabbinic, 6978–6979
structuralist analysis of, 8755
in world religions, 6977–6978
Parables of the Kingdom (Dodd), 6979
Parabrahman (puruṣottama), as concept in Swaminarayan movement, 8891
Paracelsianism
criticism of, 3949
Hermetism blended with, 3949
in Western esotericism, 2843
Paracelsus, 2952, **6980–6981**
on alchemy, 252–253, 6980–6981
on angels, 348
and Boehme (Jakob), 1006
on free will, 6981
Gnosticism and, 3524
on knowledge, 5206
Luther compared to, 6981
on medicine, 6980
on nature, 6433–6434
reputation of, 6980, 6981
theory of knowledge by, 6981
on "two books," 9422
Paraclete (religious community), 7, 8
Parades
at Carnival, 1441, 1442, 1443, 1444
vs. procession, 7417
Paradigm Shift, in Jewish Renewal, 4872
Paradise, **6981–6986**. *See also* Heaven
in African myths
loss of, 139–140
primordial, 6983
in Buddhism
in Pure Land school, 3887–3888, 6984
recurring, 6983–6984
Western Paradise of the Buddha Amitābha, 1600–1601
in Celtic religion, 6985
in Christianity
as abode of righteous, 6984
as Garden of Eden (*See* Eden, Garden of)
eschatological, 6985–6986
flowers associated with, 3136
as garden, 3277, 3282, 6984–6985 (*See also* Eden, Garden of)
in Greek religion, 6984, 6985
in Hinduism, 6983, 6985
in Islam, 9455
food in, 3171
as garden, 3282, 6984
in Ḥanafī creed, 2064
in Qur'ān, 160, 3885, 6984
judgment of the dead and, 5027
in Sufism, 2839
as island, 6985
in Judaism, 3884, 6981, 6984
She'ol *vs.*, 8564
in Melanesian religions, 6985–6986
in Micronesian religions, 6985–6986
as mountain, 6985
mountains and, 1501
in New World
search for, 6985
and search for paradise, 6985
original human condition as, 2961, 2967
origin of word, 6981
primordial, 6982–6983
African myths of, 6983
characteristics of, 6983
as garden, 6985
nostalgia for, 6983
recurring, 6983–6984
in Roman religion, 6984
secular, 6986
in Sumerian religion, 6981
in Zoroastrianism, 9996
Chinvat Bridge and, 1647
Paradise as a Garden: In Persia and Mughal India (Moynihan), 6984–6985
Paradise Lost (Milton), 30, 3525
images used in, 6985
influence of, 5478
poetic style of, 7204
Shelley (Mary) references to, 3059
subject of, 7220–7221
Paradise of the Ceiba, 151
Paradox, **6986–6992**
in Buddhism, 6988, 6989, 6990
in Christian mysticism, 6989
death as
in African religions, 141
in Oceanic religions, 146
definitions of, 6988
of faith, 6990–6991
of free will and predestination, in Islam, 8816
functions of, 6988
in hierophany (manifestation of the sacred), 3972
of knowledge, 6989–6990
of life, 6991
logical, 6988, 6989
original meaning of, 6988
of redemption, 6990
in religious discourse, 6988–6989
rhetorical, 6988
in rites of passage, 7796–7797, 7803
of sin, 6990
and *via negativa,* 6990
visual, 6988
Paraguay. *See also* Gran Chaco region
Angaité people of, 8634
Ayoré and Chamacoco people of, 8633–8634
Jesuit missions in, 1697
Kaskihá people of, 8635
Lengua people of, 8634–8635
Sanapaná people of, 8635
Tapuí and Guasurangwe people of, 8634
Parākramabāhu I (king of Sri Lanka), 1200, 9149
Parakṛta (external causation), 7363
Parallelism
comparative-historical study and, 4063
in Southeast Asian ritual language, 8649
Parallelization, syncretism and, 8931–8932
Parallel Lives of the Greeks and Romans (Plutarch), 7200
Paramādibuddah Tantra (Buddhist text), 5056
Paramahamsa, Ramakrishna, 3323
Paramārtha (Buddhist monk), **6992–6993**
influence of, 6992
on *ālaya-vijñāna,* 229
on Asaṅga, 516–517
translations by, 1202, 1250, 1576, 6992
Yogacara Buddhism transmitted by, 9901
Paramārtha (ultimate reality), 1206, 1274, 7359
Paramārthataḥ, 860
Paramātman (divine soul), in Caitanya's theology, 1346
Paramatthapāramī (superior perfection), 6993
Pāramī (ordinary perfection), 6993
Paramilitary groups, Christian Identity movement and, 1658
Pāramitās (perfection), **6993–6994**
bodhisattvas developing, 6993–6994
degrees of, 6993
lists of, 6993
Para-Nilotic languages, in East Africa, 2566
Paranoia, in millenarian-type activities, 7788
Paranormal experience, scientific study of, 6057–6058
Parāparā (deity), in Trika Śáivism, 8046
Parapsychological Association, 6057
Parapsychological phenomena
as hermeneutical tool, by Benz (Ernst), 4043
Jung on collective unconscious and, 1950
otherworld in, 6925
Spiritualism and, 8718
Para-religion, 4401
Parā śakti (deity), in Tantras, 4020
Paraskeva-Piatnitsa, Mokosh and, 6115
Paraskeviia (saint), Mokosh and, 6115
Parasurama ("Rama with the axe"), celebration of, 4017–4018
Paratantra-lakṣaṇa (dependent character), 2338
Paratrantrasvabhāva (dependent nature), 1211, 1300
Parātriṃśikāvivaraṇa (Abhinavagupta), 9
Parchment, law codes and, 1842
Pardah-dārī (storytelling), 2446
PaRDeS (biblical interpretation), 867
Pardhans (musicians), 4434
Pardon, Robert, 9411
Pardulus of Laon, 2830
Parentalia (ceremony), **6994–6995**
Parents
cosmological (*See* Primordial parents)
curses of, 2100
defining, 5184
heaven and Earth as, in Confucianism, 2633
rites of passage of, in Oceanic religions, 7807
Paret, Rudi, 4717
Paretsky, Sara, 3062
Pargiter, F. E., 7499
Parham, Charles F., 70, 7029
Seymour (William J.) and, 8254
Paribhogakandhātu (objects used by Buddha), 7163
Parikalpita-lakṣaṇa (imaginary character), 2338
Parikalpitasvabhāva (constructed nature), 1211, 1300
Parīkṣāguru (Lāl Śrīnivās Dās), 10034
Parilia (festival), 3118, 7897, 7900
Parīndāna (transmission), 1271
Parinirvāṇa. See Buddha, death of
Parinispanna-lakṣaṇa (perfected character), 2338
Parinispannasvabhāva (perfect nature), 1211, 1300
Paris (France)
Eckhart (Johannes) in, 2603
Eliade in, 2755
Paris, Peter, 80
Paris (mythic figure), as child, 1568
Parischerá religion (South America), animal dances in, 8581
Parishes
in church polity
Episcopal, 1767
Roman Catholic, 1764, 7887, 7889

in early Christian structure, 2581
Parisian Society for Spiritist Studies, 5090
Paris Opéra, 2154, 2155
Paris Polyglot, 889, 894–895
Paris School of Theology, on foolishness, 4218
Paritta (verse), 1122, 1263, 1264, 4331, 7408, 9827–9828
Parjanya (deity), specialization of, 5993
Park, G. K., 2374
Park, Mungo, 4603
Parker, Joe, on Mesoamerican ballgames, 751
Parker, Joy, 5943
Parker, Matthew, as archbishop of Canterbury, 349, 7518
Parker, Quanah, 406, 6701, 7302
Parker, Robert, on Greek religion, 7506
Parker, Theodore, in Unitarianism, 9469–9470
Parks, Douglas, 6672
Parks, Rosa, 10039
Parliament (British), in Anglicanism, 349, 350
Parliament of World Religions, on global ethics, 2613
Parmenian (cleric), 2416
Parmenides, **6995–6996**
and Ājīvikas' doctrine of *niyati,* 213
astronomy of, 6996
followers of, 6995
geometry of, 3441
on light and darkness, 5452
metaphysics of, 5989–5990
monistic doctrine of, 2507, 6146, 6995
On Nature, 5989–5990, 6995–6996
on nature, 6431
physics of, 2776
Parmenides (Plato), 7182
Parmentier, Richard, on semiotics, 8759
Parochet (curtain), 9091
Parody. *See also* Carnival; Humor
in Feast of Fools, 4198
Parousia (presence), of Dionysos, 2358, 2359
Parousia (second coming of Christ)
immortality and, 8563–8564
questioning of, 7766
revelation at, 7778
soul and, 8565
Parpola, Simo, 549
Par pro toto (part for the whole), and human body in art, 4172
Parrinder, Geoffrey, on West African supreme being, 3816–3817
Parrish, Essie, 2488
Parry, Jonathan, 1015
Parry, Milman, 3145, 6843
Pārsā, Khwājah Muḥammad, 2340
Parsangs (Persian miles), 10052
Parshvanatha (Jain teacher), vol. 8 color insert
Parsiism. *See* Zoroastrianism
Parsis, **6997–7001**
clothing of, 6997
community founding legend of, 6997
converting to Islam, 6997
division of, 6998
doctrinal unity among, 6999–7000
in England, 6999
festival celebrated by, 6732
fire precincts of, 570, 6997
funeral rites of, 6998, 7506
as Hindu caste, 6998, 7000
international dispersal of, 6999
jizya (poll tax) paid by, 6997, 6998
marriage of, 6998–6999, 7000
origins of, 6997
priests in, 5560
secular education of, 6998
settlement patterns of, 6997
socioreligious transformation of, 6997–6998
westernization of, 6998–6999
women, 3373, 3374, 6998–6999
Parsons, Elsie Clews, 6671, 6723
Parsons, Nicholas, 3097
Parsons, Susan, 3036
Parsons, Talcott, 2675, 3232
on Durkheim and Weber, 8467
modern social theory, contributions to, 8495
on religious values, 8472, 8495
on society and religion, 8467
Parsons, William B., 7479
Pārśva (scholar)
in Jainism, 4764
Kaniṣka council and, 2037
Mahāvīra and, 5609
Pärt, Arvo, 6313
Partai Islam Se-Malaysia (PAS), 4668
Parthenogenesis, in creation myths, 2555
Parthenon (Athens), 4322, 9063, 9090
Parthey, Gustav, on Hermetism, 3951
Parthian empire, Saura Hinduism and, 8136
Parthian language, Manichaeism and, 5668, 5669
Participation, law of, 5429
Particular, in Buddhism, 2628
Particular Baptists, on humor, 4219
Particularism, in United States, 5261
Particularity, comparative-historical method and, 1870, 5261
Parti Québecois, 9303
Partridge, Christopher, 6524
Pārvatī (deity)
as androgyne, 339
and Śiva, 4324, 4326
in Ellora cave art, 1472
on equal status with male, 3608
gambling by, 3263
in Purāṇas, 7500
as Lady of the Animals, 5280
in mountains, 6213
Śiva, marriage to, 8415
Śiva choosing city for, 779
son of (*See* Gaṇeśa)
Śrīdhara cursed by, 4434
tapas of, 8998
temple to, 9039
in virgin-mother-crone triad, 2984
Parwa (dance drama), 2450
Parzifal (Eschenbach), 2772
Parzival (Wolfram), 3652
PAS. *See* Partai Islam Se-Malaysia
Pasai, sultanate of (Sumatra), 4659, 4661
Pasaule (world), 758–759
Pasaulīgs (not sacred), 758
Pascal, Blaise, **7001–7003**
on gambling, 3264
on God, 3548, 7002, 7421
on heart, 3883
on human nature, 7002–7003
as Jansenist, 7001
Jesuit casuistry, attack on, 1455, 7001
on Jesus, suffering of, 4845
on knowledge, 5205
on learned ignorance, 6990
on predestination, 3204
on reason, 7002
Stoicism and, 8741
Pascal triangle, 3442, *3444*
Pascha. *See* Easter
Paschal II (pope), Anselm and, 372
Paschal vigil
in Christian liturgical calendar, 1742
fast in, 1742
Paschasius, Peter, 7243
Pascola (clowns), 7045
Pa-shesh ND (Eblaite priest), 2598
Pasi, Marco, on esotericism and occultism, 6780–6781
Pasiphae (mythic figure), 6173
Pasitas (steps), 2464
Paskaal (Dolgan calendar), 2394–2395
Pasolini, Pier Paolo, 3097
Paso y Troncoso, Francisco del, 5940
Passacaglia and Fugue in C Minor (Humphrey), 2158
Passage, Janus as god of, 4778
Passage graves, 5823, 5824, 5825
Passage rites. *See* Rites of passage
Passamaquody tribe (North America), ballgame played by, 753
Passi, Dave, 679
Passion according to G. H., The (Lispector), 3064
Passion music, 6311–6312
Passion of Christ. *See* Crucifixion of Jesus
Passion of the Christ, The (film), 4348, 5808, 7323
Passion plays. *See Ta'ziyah*
Passions
in Ashkenazic Hasidism, 542
Cassian on, 1448
Passions of the Soul, The (Descartes), 2293
Passive emotion, Spinoza (Baruch) on, 8684
Passive iconoclasm, 4282, 4283, 4284, 4285, 4392
Passivity
of *deus otiosus,* 2311
of Dumuzi, 2522–2523
in mystical states, James (William) on, 1948, 6341
of supreme beings, 8870–8871
Passolini, Pier Paolo, 3100
Passover, **7003–7005**
in Apostolic Church of John Maranke, 5694–5695
Christian Paschal vigil and, 1742, 9809
contemporary celebration of, 4986
domestic observances of, 2397, 2400, 7003–7004
Easter as equivalent of, 2579
Easter celebrated at, 9814
Eucharist and, 2877
fasting and, 4867–4868
foods consumed on, 7003, 7004
food taboo during, 3167, 7003
in Jehovah's Witnesses, 4823
in Jewish calendar, 4866, 4867
maḥzor liturgy for, 8390
moon in, 6171
Myth and Ritual school on, 6381
names of, 7003
prohibition on leavening on, 7003
sacred time and, vol. 1 color insert
in Samaritan practice, 8070
Shavu'ot and, 8305
synagogue service on, 7003
unleavened bread for, 5388
Past, eternity and, 2853
Past lives. *See* Reincarnation
Pastor aeternus constitution, approved in Vatican I, 2044

Pastoral Constitution on the Church in the World. *See* Constitution on the Church in the Modern World
Pastoral Counseling (Hiltner), 7487
Pastoral counseling/psychology, 939, 7477, 7479, 7486–7487
Pastoralism, of Mongol religion, 6826–6827
Pastorals. *See 1 Timothy; 2 Timothy; Titus*
Pastoral societies
cattle, role of, 1464–1465
deities in, morphology of, 3617
sacrifice in, 7997, 8002
Schmidt (Wilhelm) on, 8168, 8877
sexual images, destruction of, 3975–3976
Paśubandha (animal sacrifice), 9562
place for, 9564–9565
Pāśupata Śaivism, **8049,** 8990
influence of, 4019
Pāśupata Sūtras
Pratyabhijñā Saivism and, 8049
prescriptions for ascetic life in, 4019
Pāśupata texts, as higher path *(atimārga)* literature, 4019
Paśupati (Lord of the Animals), 4324
on Idus Valley seals, 8039
Rudra as, 7934, 8414
Pasztory, Esther, 5900
Patai, Raphael, 3586
Pataki (divining system), 3065
Pātalas (netherworlds), in Purāṇic cosmology, 2018
Pāṭaliputra councils I and II
Mahāsāṃghika Buddhism in, 5601
overview of, 2036–2037
Sarvāstivāda and, 8119
Patañjali
on breathing, 9895
on meditation, 5819
on Kṛṣṇa and Śiva, 8041
on *samādhi,* 9896
rājayoga of, 3998, 8704–8705
in Yoga, 9893–9894
Yoga Sūtra of, 5095, 5819
Patañjali the Grammarian, **7005–7006**
prāṇāyāma recommended by, 1044
Pater, 2984
Pater, Walter, 7206
Paternity, in Islam, laws on, 4710–4711
Patet (expiation), 1889
Path (magazine), 7228
Path, *vs.* place, architecture of, 466–467
Pathans, pacifism of, 6648
Path of the Sages, in Pure Land Buddhism, 4922, 4934, 4938
Pathogenic-melogenic cantillation style, 1534
Paṭhommamagga (beginning of the path), 2325
Path on the Rainbow, The (Cronyn), 7224
Path under the Earth, 1469
Paṭicca samuppāda (law of interdependent co-arising), 2628
Patients and Healers in the Context of Culture (Kleinman), 2611
Paṭisambhidā (Buddhist text), 1062
Patkanov, Serafim, 3112
Patolli (game), 3260
Paton, Alan, 6613
Paton, E. Forrester, in ashram movement, 546–547
Paton, John G., 6791
Patriarchate, **7006–7007**. *See also specific patriarchs*
of Alexandria (Coptic Orthodox Church), 2585, 2589
of Antioch (Syrian Orthodox Church), 2585, 2589
of Bulgaria (*See* Bulgarian Orthodox church)
in church polity, 1765, 7887
of Constantinople (*See also* Constantinople)
Armenian, 489
in Eastern Orthodox structure, 2588, 2589
as ecumenical and universal patriarch, 1765
Greek Orthodox, 3657–3659
Jeremias II in, 4831–4832
demise of, 7007
development of, 1763
in Egypt, 1980–1981
emergence of, 7006
of Jerusalem, 2589
Jewish *nasi'* (patriarchs), Hillel ("the Elder") in, 3981
of Moscow and All Russia, in Russian Orthodox Church, 7946
prestige and authority of, 7006–7007
and Rabbinate, 7006
of Romania (*See* Romanian Orthodox church)
of Serbia (*See* Serbian Orthodox church)
sources on, 7006
Patriarchs
in early Christian structure, 2581
Jewish
historical setting for, 4758
Jacob, 4757–4758
Patriarchy, **7007–7009**
in American ethno-religious groups, 1834
Bachofen (J. J.) on, 731
in Chan Buddhism, 1163, 1239, 1520, 1577, 1601
clitoridectomy and, 1825
definition of, 3298, 7007
female body and, 4164
feminist critique of, 3298, 3311, 3312, 7007–7008
of Greece, ancient, 9602–9603
male creator gods and, 1993
in Mormonism, 8447
in Near Eastern religions, gender and, 3378–3379
in Rastafari, 7628
in religion, critique of, 3022, 3036, 9787
retribution rights and, 7783
terminology of, 7008
in Yurupary cult, 9919
Patricians, in Roman society, 7902–7903
Patricide
Freud (Sigmund) on, 2238–2239
purification and, 1459
Patrick (saint), **7009–7010**
Caoilte mac Rónáin and, 1495
enslavement of, 7009–7010
Legba identified with in Vodou, 1433
and pagan druids, 2493, 7010
Tara, travel to, 1491
in Vodou, 9636
writings of, 7009, 7010
Patrick, Theodore "Ted," 2987, 9410
deprogramming by, 1033, 2291–2292
Patrilineal descent
in Amazonian religion, 9919
ancestor identification and, 5185
Jewish identity and, 3751–3752
in Reconstructionist Judaism, 7639
in Reform Judaism, 7666, 7673
in Kongo society, 5220
Schmidt (Wilhelm) on, 8877
Patriotism
American, Church Universal and Triumphant and, 1782, 1783
in poems, 7218
Patristic teachings
in Eastern Christianity, development of, 2581–2582
ethics and morality, 1651, 1652, 1653
hypostasis in, 4241
Italian Renaissance humanism and, 4175
merit in, 5876
sacramental theology in, 7959–7960, 7962
Patrizi, Francesco, Hermetism and, 3948
Patron deities, in Micronesian religions, 6003
Pattācāra (Buddhist role model), 1087
Pattern
in ethology, 2868
vs. spontaneity, Heschel (Abraham Joshua) on, 3962
Patterns in Comparative Religion (Eliade), 2661, 2664, 7374, 7743, 7745
celestiality of divine beings in, 5759
sacrality expressed through natural symbolism in, 1879
Patterns of Culture (Benedict), 820
Patterson, Daniel, 2694
Patterson, Daniel W., 3144
Patterson, Orlando, 77
on haircutting, 3739
Patteson, John Coleridge, in Melanesia, 1847
Pátzcuaro (underworld), 151
Pauck, Wilhelm, **7010–7011,** 7452
Paul (apostle). *See* Paul the Apostle
Paul (bishop of Sidon), 7242
Paul (bishop of Tella), 894
Paul II (pope), election of, 6972
Paul III (pope)
Alexander VI as mentor of, 9341, 9342
and Charles V, 9342
and Council of Trent, 6972, 9342–9343
Counter Reformation and, 7877
election of, 9341
on Ignatius Loyola, 4368
Jesuits established by, 6972
and Mantua Council (1537), 9342
pontificate of, 9341–9342
on retreats, 7772
Roman Inquisition created by, 4501, 6972
Paul IV (pope)
on Benedict of Nursia, 823
statues castrated by, 7082
Paul V (pope)
and Bellarmino (Roberto), 816
on loyalty oath, 6973
on Suárez (Francisco), 8799
Paul VI (pope), **7011–7013**
administrative affairs of, 7012
on birth control, 6975, 7012–7013
on celibacy, 7013
and Dalai Lama, 2133
ecumenism of, 7011–7012
image of, 7012
on marriage, 3362
on Mary, 5754
on priesthood, 7012, 7013
sacrament defined by, 7881
and social doctrine, 7878
travels of, 7012
Vatican II and, 6975, 7011–7012, 7879, 9535, 9540
Paul, Apocalypse of, 919
Paul, Diana Y., on women in Buddhism, 3330, 3343
Paul, Jean, on humor, 4201
Paul, Robert A., 382
Paul, Vincent de, 6764

Paula (nun), 6763
Paul among Jews and Gentiles (Stendahl), 7014, 7020
Paul and Power (Holmberg), 7013
Pauli, Wolfgang, 6057
Paulician movement, 2747
  emergence of, 3523
  Manichaeism and, 5657, 5668
  persecution of, 3523
Paulinus, Ambrose's biography by, 287
Pauli Sententiae, 5333
Paul of Tarsus. *See* Paul the Apostle
Paul of Thebes, 2824
Paulos, Abune, 2861
Paulsen, Friedrich, 9230
Paulson, Graham, 676, 678
Paulson, Ivar, 3113
  on animals, 356
  on Arctic religions, 475
Paul the Apostle, **7013–7021**. *See also specific writings*
  on Abraham, 16, 7017, 7019
  in *Acts,* 911, 7014, 7020, 9274
  on afterlife, 156
  on altars, 277
  and anti-Semitism, 398
  apocalypse and, 412, 7013, 7014
  apostasy and, 431, 432
  apostleship of, 435–436
  Artemis and, 508
  ascension of, 523
  on ascension of Jesus, 523
  on asceticism, 7722
  assassination attempt on, 7019–7020
  on atonement, 595–596
  Augustine influenced by, 625, 698
  on baptism, 781, 1777
  celibacy of, 7018
  on circumcision, 7016–7017, 7081
  on conscience, 1940, 1945, 7018–7019
  conversion of, 7014
  on death, 156
  as devotee, 2320
  on divine righteousness, 7019
  Ebionite repudiation of, 2596
  ecclesiology and, 1771
  education of, 7014
  on enthusiasm, 2808
  Europe and, 1688
  execution of, 7020
  exorcism by, 2928–2929
  on "fools for Christ's sake," 4202
  on Gamli'el the Elder, 3270
  on Gentiles, 7014, 7016
  gifts of the Spirit, 1549–1550
  on glossolalia, 7019
  Gnosticism and, 3511, 3512, 7018
  on God, 3545
    Jesus as, 3546
    knowability of, 181, 182, 183, 6063
  on "gospel," 3640–3641
  on grace, 3644–3645, 6188
  healing touch of, 9256
  Hebrews formerly attributed to, 916
  on heretics, 7014
  and history, Christian views of, 4052
  on human beings, equality of, 3357
  on human body, 2135, 2153, 7018
  on idolatry, 4385, 7014
  on illness caused by poor ritual, 3810
  on immorality, 8563–8564
  imprisonment of, 914, 915, 7017, 7019, 7020
  influence of, 7020
  on interconnectedness of all things, 2650
  interest in the Fall, 2968
  Irenaeus influenced by, 4539, 4540
  on Isaac, 4544
  on Ishmael, 4552
  on Israel, election of, 2746
  James against teachings of, 917
  at Jerusalem apostolic conference, 7016
  on Jesus, 7014
    as God, 3546
    second coming of Christ, 7766
  on Jewish law, 7016, 7019
  on justification, 5039–5040
  on kingdom of God, 5149, 5153
  Kitagawa (Joseph M.) on, 5188
  on knowledge, 5202
  letters of
    Baur (F. C.) on, 805
    canonization and, 920, 921, 1410
    church factions addressed by, 2683
    creativity in, 7015
    hostile reactions to, 7013, 7014, 7019–7020
    literary form of, 5470
    Luther (Martin) on, 874
    Peter Lombard on, 7067
    poetry in, 7218
    purpose of, 7015
    revelation in, 7774–7775
    women in, 3359
  on life, 5446
  life of, 7014
  Luke as companion of, 908, 5529–5530, 7015
  on magic, 5576
  Mani influenced by, 5648, 5666
  Marcion on, 5701
  Mark the Evangelist and, 5714
  on marriage, 7018
  on membership in the church, 1777
  miracles of, 6054
  on mirror, 6063
  missionary travels, 6082, 7014–7016
    Corinth, 7015–7016, 7018, 7019
    Eastern Europe, 1682
    Ephesus, 7017, 7018–7019
    Jerusalem, 7019–7020
    Philippi, 7015
    Rome, 7019
    Thessalonica, 7015
  modern studies on, 7013–7014
  on mortification, 6196–6197
  on Moses, 6203
  and mystical union, 6336, 6337
  on mysticism, 6346
  on myth, 6368
  on new and old covenants, 2049
  on pagan gods as demons, 7923
  on Peter the Apostle, 7068
  on predestination, 3203, 3207
  on priesthood, 7401
  on redemption, 7640
  on relational discipline, 8706
  on resurrection, 7766, 8302
  on revelation, 7774–7775, 7777–7778
  on rituals, 7698–7699
  role in early Christianity, 1660, 7014
  on salvation, 7017
  on second coming of Christ, 7766
  on sin, 8404–8405
  on spirit and soul, 8562
  sports metaphors of, 8724
  on suffering, 8807, 8808, 9116, 9117
  on temptation, 9070, 9073
  as tent maker, 7014, 7015
  Thecla as disciple of, 9101
  on virginity, 9607
  vocation of, 9633
  on wisdom, 9751, 9760
  on women, 7018
Paulus Orosius, historiography of, 4028, 4054
Puamacariya (Vimalasūri), 7609
Pausanias, 35
  on Aphrodite, 408
  on Artemis, 507
  on Demeter, 2269
  on mirrors, 6063
  on *agnōstos theos,* 181
  on oracles, 3906, 8839
  on sun shrines, 8839
Pausanias's Description of Greece (Frazer), 3191
Pauthier, Jean-Pierre Guillaume, 1632
Pauttalikatā (idolatry), 828
Pava (mythic figure), 2312
Pavamāna hymns, Soma in, 8521
Pavāraṇa ("invitation") observance, confession and, 1886–1887
Pavese, Cesare, 2267
Pavia, Council of (1423-1424), 6972
Pavilion mosques, Chinese, 6209–6210
Pavu (spirit of darkness), in Cinta Larga creation myth, 2013
Pawahtuun (deity), 5791
Pawnee religion (North America)
  creation stories of, 6703–6704
  deities in, 6651
  Hako ceremony of, 6704
  sacrifice to Morning Star, 6653
  study of, 6672
P'awstos Buzand, 6479
Pax (deity), 7021
Pax deorum (peace of the gods), 2874
Pax vobis (peace be with you), 983
Payák (nonhuman nature), in Pilagá religion, 8636
Payame Ima (spirit), gender and, 3396–3397
Payām-i mashriq (Iqbāl), 4534
Payne, Daniel, 67, 68, 75, 10038
Payutto, P. A., 1283
P'Bitek, Okot, 117
PCE. *See* Pure Consciousness Event
Pe (city), importance to Egyptian pharaohs, 5164
Pe'a (tattoo), 7807
Peace, **7021–7023**. *See also* Nonviolence
  in Buddhism, 7023
  in Christianity, 7021–7022
  in Daoism, 7022
  deities of
    in Greek religion, 7021
    in Hawaiian religion, 3797–3798
    in Roman religion, 7021
  in Earth Charter, 2657
  in Hinduism, 7022–7022
  in Islam, 7021
  in Jainism, 7023
  in Judaism, 7021
  in kingdom of God, 5152–5153
  kiss of, 9259
  offerings
    Canaanite, 1385
    Israelite, 926
  in primordial paradise, 6983
  as salutation
    Arabic, 7021

as salutation ***continued***
Christian, 7022
Hebrew, 7021
Smart (Ninian) on, 8444
Peaceable Kingdom, The (Hicks), 5152
Peace Mission movement, 3006, 3007, 6563
Daddy Grace and, 2125
Peace studies. *See* Conflict and peace studies
Peacher, Eliza, 9404
Peacock, 949, 4438
Peacock, James L., 379, 3144
Peak-experiences, 7477
Peale, Norman Vincent, 6582
Peanut cultivation, Alinesitoue on, 262
Pear Garden school (Confucian), 2455
Pearl, **7023–7024**
in healing, 7024
nūr Muḥammad compared with, 6766–6767
as symbol of rebirth, 7023–7024
as symbol of soul, 7024
as symbol of spiritual striving, 7024
Pearl (English poem), 7218
Pearl, The (English tale), 7024
Pearl fishers, 7024
Pearl shells, associated with Rainbow Snake, 7605
Pearson, Birger A., 3533
Pearson, John, 4369
Peasant consciousness, in subaltern studies, 8800–8801
Peasant culture, common elements in, 2753–2754
Peasant of the Garonne, The (Maritain), 5712
Peasants, religion of. *See* Folk religion; Popular religion
Peasants' Crusade, 5012
Peasant Society and Culture (Redfield), 9276
Pecci, Giaocchino. *See* Leo XIII
Pecham, John, **7024–7025**
Pecherskaia Laura, 2826–2827
Peck, John Mason, 785
Pecked crosses, Mesoamerican, 1794, 5898
Pedammā (deity), 4432
Pedanda (high priest), 748, 2451
Pedanda bodha (high priest), 748
Pedersen, Johannes, and Myth and Ritual school, 6380, 6381
Pedi religion. *See* Sotho religion
Pedro III of Aragon (king), 7580
Peek, Philip, 117, 10032
Peet, Richard, 2611
Pege gnoseos (Fount of Knowledge) (John of Damascus), 4940
Peggs, James, 3320
Péguy, Charles, Maritain (Jacques) and, 5712
Peirasmos (temptation), 9070
Peirce, Carl Sanders (C. S.)
on chance, 1527
on God, 6962, 6963–6964
on miracles, 1528
on phenomenology, 7087
on reflexivity, 7649
on signs, 8227
symbol theory and, 8912
Peisistratus (tyrant of Athens), 2437
Peitho (deity), 408
Pekols (deity), 767
Pe'kwin (sun priests), Zuni cosmology and, 2008–2009
Péladan, 341
Peladan, Joséphin, 7930
Pelagianism, **7025–7026**
Augustine opposing, 627, 7025, 7026, 7027
Cassian and, 1447, 1448
criticism of, 7026
in early Christian theological issues, 2581
Jerome on, 4834
justification and, 5040
Roman Catholic opposition to, 7876, 7883
Pelagius, **7026–7027**
Augustine's polemics against, 8406
on baptism, 7025
followers of, 7026
on free will, 3201, 3207
on grace, 7025
on human nature, Augustine's conflict with, 626–627, 7025, 7026, 7027, 7353
on human perfectibility, 7039
Innocent I condemning, 7026, 7027
Irenaeus as forerunner of, 4540
Jerome's critique of, 7026
on merit, 5876
Origen influencing, 7026, 7027
on sin, 7025–7026
writings of, 7027
Pelagius II (pope), Gregory I and, 3687
Pele (deity), 3017, 7314
Pelekus (deity), 2359. *See also* Dionysos
Peli Association, 6797
Pelikan, Jaroslav, on afterlife, 157
Pelliot, Paul, 1634
Pelota of Auxerre (dance), 2153
Pema Gyatso, Ani Lochen as student of, 354
Pema Ledreltsel. *See* Tsultrim Dorjé
Pémaulk. *See* Témaukel
Pemba (deity), 98, 776
Pembélé (mythic figure), 776
Pemberton, John, 10033
Peṇa, Lorenzo de la, 406
Penance. *See also* Confession of sins
asceticism as, 528
in Ashkenazic Hasidism, 543, 544
in Christianity
cognates of, in comparative studies, 7956
confession and, 1888, 1889
penitential books, 1652
as punishment, 5372
as sacrament, 1670
in Hinduism
as punishment, 5345
Śiva, *mahavrata* (Great Vow) of, 8040, 8050
in Ājīvikas sect, 212
Penates (spirit), 2277, **7027**
Pencak-silat (martial art), 5732–5733
Pensée chinoise, la (Granet), 3655
Penelhum, Terence, on knowledge, 5211
Penfield, Wilder, 6486
Peng (mythic bird), 948
Peng Dingqiu, nonsectarian approach of, 1903
Peng Shaosheng, 3343
Penis. *See* Phallus
Penitence. *See also* Conscience; Repentance
in Christianity
Eastern Orthodox rite of, 7960
Lent, 1743, 9814–9815
at Pentecost, 1742
readmission to Eucharist and, 7959
in Hittite religion, 4072
kneeling and, 5196
prayer of, 7369
in repentance, 7755
Penitential books, 1455
Penitentiaries, sanctuaries *vs.*, 8101
Penn, William, 973, **7027–7028**
education of, 7027
as founder of Pennsylvania, 7027, 7028
Fox (George) and, 3181, 7028
pacifism of, 6648
as Quaker, 7027–7028, 7547
writings of, 7027–7028
Penner, Hans H.
historiography of, 4049
on Lévi-Strauss (Claude), 8758
on semiotics, 8759
on structuralism, 8758
Pennington, J. W. C., 68
Pennsylvania
Anglicanism in, 352
Penn (William) as founder of, 7027, 7028
Pensée chinoise, la (Granet), 3655
Pensées (Pascal), 3264, 7001–7003
critics of, 7002–7003
heart in, 3883
importance of, 7001–7002
writing of, 7001–7002
Pentagon, terrorist attack on. *See* September 11th, 2001, terrorist attack
Pentalagion (Theodoret), 9123
Pentapolis (Libya), Christianity in, 1677–1678
Pentateuch, 878, 9231. *See also* Torah
Aaron in, 1–2
Abraham in, 15
Arabic translation of, 894, 8950
Aramaic translations of, 887–889
authorship of, 883
canonization and, 1406
Christian polemics on, 7232
christological references *(Glaphura)* in, Cyril of Alexandria on, 2117
cultic praxis in, 926
English translation of, by Hertz (Joseph), 869
Enlightenment and interpretation of, 874–875
German translation of, 5854
God in, monotheistic worship of, 3539, 3540
Greek translation of, 890
Hirsch (Samson Raphael) on, 4024
Israel in, collective existence of, 4856–4857
kashrut laws in, 5107
Moses in, 6199
Nahmanides' (Moses) commentary on, 6399
Near Eastern legal culture and, 884
premonarchical prophets in, 7435
purity in, 7514
qabbalistic commentaries on, 7538
of Qirqisānī (Ya'qūb) on, 5085
Rashi's commentary to, 865, 7620
Ro'sh ha-Shanah in, 7927
Samaritan use of, 8069–8070
Shavu'ot in, 8305
variants from Masoretic text in, 885
in *Wissenschaft des Judentums,* analysis of, 4877
Pentecost. *See also* Shavu'ot
in *Acts of the Apostles,* 7028–7029
in Christian liturgical calendar, 1742–1743
enthusiasm at, 2807
in New testament, Holy Spirit and, 8562
Pentecostal Assemblies of the World, 7029
Pentecostal Fellowship of North America, 7033
Pentecostal Holiness Church, 7029
Pentecostalism, **7028–7034**. *See also* Charismatic Christianity
in Africa, 7030, 7031, 7032
new movements of, 106–107, 109, 1724
African Americans in, 69, 70, 7029, 10038
altered states of consciousness in, 2237

apocalypse in, 413
in Asia, 7030, 7031, 7032
in Australia, 1735
new movements of, 671
belief and practice in, 7031–7032
in Britain, 7029
cargoism, alternative to, 1414
in Caribbean, 1437, 1707
creolization and, 2067
charismatic revival of, 7030
condemnation of, 7029
deliverance or healing revival of, 7030
in Eastern Europe, 7029
enthusiasm in, 2808
evangelicalism of, 2888
exorcism in, 2931
faith healing in, 3847
Finished Work (Baptistic), 7029, 7033
in Germany, 7029
global expansion of, 7029–7030, 7033
glossolalia in, 70, 3504–3505, 7029, 7031
gospel of health and wealth in, 7030–7031
and history, view of, 4055
in Italy, 7029
in Latin America, 1702, 1704, 6579–6580
conversion and, 1973
Neo-Pentecostal movement, 7030
emergence and spread of, 1550
in New Zealand, 1735
in North America
perfectionism and, 1714
revivalism and, 1710
in Oceania, 6795, 6798
Oneness (Jesus Only), 7029, 7030
origin of term, 7028
origins of, 70, 7028–7029
in Holiness movement, 4084
in Pacific islands, 1741
percussive breathing in, 7037
and political activism, 6580
possession in, 6844
prohibitions in, 7032
public activism and, 1755
relations with other churches, 7032–7033
religious broadcasting and, 7714
radio, 7711
television, 7711, 7712, 7713
religious experience in, 7700
in Scandinavia, 7029
Second Work (Wesleyan), 7029, 7033
Seymour (William J.) as founder of, **8254**
signs of the Holy Spirit and, 1714
social character of, 7032
social ethics of, 7032
in South America, 7029, 7031, 7032
theatrical worship in, 2473
Third Wave, 7031, 7033
United House of Prayer and, 2124–2125
in United States
evangelicalism influenced by, 2893
glossolalia in, 7031
gospel of, 7030–7031
origins of, 7029
political orientation of, 7032
revival of, 7030
women in, 70
women preachers in, folklorist study of, 3147
worship in, 7031
Pentecostal World Conference, 7033
Pentheus (mythic figure), 2357, 3383, 3384, 6822
Pentikäinen, Juha, 3104, 3109, 3114
historiography of, 4047
Peony, 3137
People from Other Worlds (Olcott), 5023
"People from the Stars" (Revard), 7225
People of the Book. *See Scriptural religions; See Ahl al-kitāb (people of scripture)*
Peoples Liberation Army (PLA) (China), 4636–4637
Peoples of Southern Nigeria, The (Talbot), 97
Peoples Temple. *See* Jonestown and Peoples Temple
Pépin (king of Franks), 6967
Pepper, in Caribbean religions, 1430
Perception
and knowledge, in Cārvāka, 1446
Hocking (William Ernest) on, 4076
imaginative seeing, Steiner (Rudolf) on, 8738
Nyāya's theory of, 6773
Sa'adyah Gaon on, as source of truth, 7952
Sundén (Hjalmar) on, 8851
tacit, sacred *vs.* profane and, 7964–7965
Perceval (mythic figure), 3650, 3651, 3652
Percival, Thomas, on medical ethics, 5810
Percussion, **7034–7038**. *See also* Drums; Rhythm
affliction and, 60
definition of, 7034
examples of, 7035
origins of, 7030
religious evaluation of, 7035–7036
rituals of, 7030
Percussive breathing, 7037–7038
Peregrin, Jaroslav, on semantics, 8759
Peregrinus (play), 2471
Pereira, Nunes, 121
Pereira dos Santos, Nelson, 3099
Perennialism, esotericism in, 2843
Perets of Corbeil, *tosafot* of, 9244
Perfect
in Catharism, 1457
etymology of word, 7038
Perfected one. *See Zhenren*
Perfect Human Beings, in Islam. *See Insān al-kāmil*
Perfectibility, **7038–7041**
of human beings, 7038–7041
absence of concept in African religions, 84
in alchemy, 236–238
Aristotle on, 7038
in Christianity, 7039–7040
in Indian religions, 7040–7041
in Judaism, 7039
of matter, in alchemy, 242
Perfection
of Buddha's path, 2739
Cassian on free will and, 1448
Christian, Wesley (John) on, 5997
in Confucianism, through self-effort, 9674
diamond as symbol of, 2345
of God, 7039
in Christianity, 615, 3560, 7039
in Judaism, 7039
Greek cult of physical perfection, 4171
in Islam, Sirhindī (Aḥmad) on progess toward, 8413
in primordial paradise, 6983
Perfectionism. *See also* Holiness movement
Holiness-Pentecostal movement and, 1714, 4082
of Shakers, 8268
of Wesleyans, 4082, 4083
Perfection of Wisdom. *See* Sanlun school; *See* Prajñāpāramitā school of Buddhism
Perfection of Wisdom texts. *See Prajñāpāramitā Sūtras*
Perfection Stage yoga, *Hevajra Tantra* and, 3965, 3966
Perfect Lord, in Daoism, 2184
Performance. *See also* Dance; Drama
African rituals as, 118
in Australian Indigenous religions
history of study of, 682
of music, 6260–6263
in Warlpiri ritual, 9694, 9695–9697
clowns and, 1840
of Ge myths, 3293
gestures in, 7043
in healing, 3814–3815
humor in, in East Asia, 4209
in Indian religion, of *bhakti* poetry, 3985
liturgy as, 5492
oral tradition in, 9269
poetry as, 7203–7204
prayer as, 7368–7370
in rites of passage, 7800
and ritual, **7041–7053**
African, 7043, 7048
ancient Near Eastern, 2440–2441
biogenetic foundation of, 7049
carnivals as, 7045–7046
economic aspect of, 7042
efficacy-entertainment dyad of, 7042–7043
frames of, 7047–7048, 7051
Hindu, 7043, 7044, 7046–7047
invention of, 7050–7051
Islamic, 7044
Japanese, 7042, 7048
Jewish, 7043, 7516–7518
Native American, 7043
Paleolithic, 7042
process of, 7049–7050
shamanic and trance, 7048–7049
Turner (Victor) on, 7042, 9406–9407
varieties of, 7043–7045
Yaqui *waehma* as, 7045
Yoruba, 2435, 7048
of rituals (*See* Ritual)
Schechner (Richard) on, 7857
spirit possession as, 8696–8697
Performance theater, 2476
Performance theory, and folk religion, study of, 3145–3146
Perfume, 3137
Peri archon. See On First Principles
Periegesis (Pausanias), Demeter in, 2269
Periodical literature, **10056–10060**
languages of, 10059–10060
price of, 10060
Periodicity, 9920
calendars and, 1352
Periodization, of world
binary, 173–174
in Buddhism, 5685
serial, 174–177
Periphyseon (Eriugena), 2830
Periplus of the Erythraean Sea, Arabia in, 443
Perjury, in Germanic law, 9642

Perkins, William, on predestination, 3204, 7519
Pērkons (Perkun) (deity), **7053–7054**
as bridegroom, 760
in chronicles, 757, 767
and cosmic tree, 9419
cult of, 7053–7054
as fertility god, 7054
as god of mountains, 7053
as god of trees, 7053
in Latvian folklore texts, 769
origin of name of, 7053
and Saule, 758
Perlesvaus (Grail text), 3649
Perlitt, Lothar, on covenant theology, 2048
Permians. *See* Komi religion and society
Pernety, Dom, on alchemy, 251
Perpetua (martyr), 6742
Perrin, Norman, on kingdom of God, 5152
Perry, Richard, 575
Perry, W. J., and study of North American Indian religions, 6671
Persaeus, on ruler cults, 4036
Persecution, **7054–7062**. *See also* Martyrdom
in Antichrist concepts, 394
of Buddhists
in China, 7213, 7255, 7268
in Japan, 9075–9076
in Tibet, 9186
of Christians, **7057–7062**
at Carthage, 1678–1679
of Cathari sect, 4498, 6971
Christian missions and, 6082
of Coptic Church, 1979
Cyprian and, 2112
of Donatists, 2416–2417, 7060, 7061
in Gaul, 1688
of heretics and dissenters, 972, 973, 7060–7061
of Hutterian Brethren, 4239
in Japan, 1726, 9310
by Jews, 7058
of Mennonites, 5860
of Mormons, 6193
in Rome, 1688, 7058–7060, 7279, 7922
of Waldensians, 6971
encouragement in face of, in *Daniel*, 2169
of Jews, **7054–7057** (*See also* Anti-Semitism)
in ancient Greece, 7055
by Antiochus IV Epiphanes, 925, 7055, 7144
apocalypses based on, 410, 415, 417
in Germany, 5830 (*See also* Holocaust)
by medieval Christians, 7055–7056
by Muslims, 7055
in Roman Empire, 7055, 7056
in Spain, 5717
of Manichaeans, 5655–5656, 5660
in Central Asia and China, 5656, 5669, 5670
in Iran, 5660–5661
under Justinian I, 2513
in Roman Empire, 5664, 5667
of Mongol shamans, by Buddhists, 6142
of Moravians, 6190–6191
of Muslims
in China, 4636–4637, 4640
in Mecca, 6222–6223
in Russia, 4617, 4619, 4624, 4625, 4677
in United States, 4690–4691
of mystics, 6336
of Bābīs, 728, 737, 4573
in Russia, of all religions, 7943–7944
Persephone (deity), **2268–2272,** 2984
abduction of, 2269, 2270, 3724
Adonis and, 34, 7767
and agriculture, origins of, 191
as bride of Hades, 2269, 2271, 3382
cult of, 2271
as daughter of Zeus, 2268–2269
dema and, 4825
Demeter as mother of, 2268, 2269, 3382
in Demeter Eleusinia cult, 2751–2752
in Eleusinian mysteries, 3382–3383, 3671
French feminists on, 3028
functions of, 3680
and gender roles, 3382–3383
as goddess of underworld, 2268, 2269
Hekate and, 3899
Hermes and, 3937
in Orphic Gold Tablets, 6897–6898
Parmenides on, 6995–6996
virginity of, 9607
Perseus, birth of, 1568
Persia. *See also* Indo-Iranian religion; Iran; Manichaeism; Parsis
Achaemenid calendar, 1354
apocalyptic tradition in, 411
Aramaic as official language of, 887
Armenians under, 488, 491
astrology in, 564
cats in poetry of, 1463
Christensen's history of, 1649–1650
Christianity in, 2583 (*See also* Nestorian Church)
Constitutional Revolution in, 8339–8340
Egypt conquered by, 2709
gardens in, 3282
Israelite religion under, 4973
Jews in, 4999
forced conversion of, 5722–5723
laws of, 4727
magi in, 5559–5562
Mosaic Torah sanctioned by, 1409
mystical philosophy of illumination *(al-ishrāq),* 2977
Nestorians in, 6480
and novel, origins of, 3050
periods in history of (*See* Safavid dynasty; Sasanid period)
rock tombs, 1472
sports in, 8724
Türk alliance with, 4491
Persian language
biblical translations into, 922
al-Majlisī writing in, 5623
Nāṣir-i Khusraw writing in, 6417
poetry in, 7222–7223
Persians, The (Aeschylus), 5469
Persian Wars
divination in, 2375, 2376
Herodotus on, 6374, 6375
Persinger, Robert, 6487
Person
kinship and, 5183–5184
power and, in indigenous traditions, 2618
Person, Yves, 112
Personal consciousness, Jung on, 1949–1950
Personal experience, as authority, in Protestantism, 7453–7454
Personal hygiene, Buddhist practices for, 9837
Personalism, communitarian, 1653
"Personalist Controversy" (Buddhist philosophy), 1297
Personalistic theories of conversion, 1970
Personality
Eckhart (Johannes) on, 2603
in media coverage, 4963
neuroscience on, 6487
psuchē as, 8541
Socrates on, 8503
states of consciousness and, 1949
tests, 7476, 7477
Personality belief. *See Satkāyadṛṣṭi*
"Personal Narrative" (Edwards), 2699
Personal possession, dance as vehicle for, 2139–2140
Personal prayer, 7368
Personal status laws, Israelite, **4730–4733**
Personennamen der Texte aus Ugarit (Gröndahl), Canaanite religion in, 1387
Personhood. *See also* Human beings
neuroscience on, 6487
Person Muhammeds in lehre und glauben seiner gemeinde, Die (Andrae), 333, 945
Perspectiva communis (Pecham), 7025
Perspectivism, in South American cosmologies, 2012
Pertold, Otakar, Czech religious studies and, 8772, 8774
Peru and Peruvian religions. *See also* Inca religion; South American Indian religions
archaeology in, 452, 457
calendar, ancient, 1353
chronicle of, vol. 2 color insert
indigenous religions of, fish symbolism in, 3123
Inquisition in, 4504, 4505, 4506
Islam, 4685
Israelitas (Israelites of the New Universal Covenant), 6547
knotted ropes in, 5197
mesa divination and correspondence system in, 3810
messianism in, 5984–5985, 5986
moon in, 6173
music in, 6272
origins of, Huascar in, 568
Roman Catholicism, pilgrimage in, 7151
shamanism in, vol. 1 color insert
textiles in, 9089
Perugia, Leo XIII in, 5411
Perun (deity), **7062–7063**
in Slavic religion, 8435–8436
Perush ha-ṭtur ha-arokh (Asher), 867
Peruvian Quechua religions
cosmic mountain in, 6886
ethnoastronomy of
animals in, 2864
milky way in, 2863
moon in, 2863
Pervasiveness, masculine sacrality in, 5760–5761
Pesaḥ ritual, 6593
Easter derived from, 2579
Pesch, Alexandra, 3459
Peseyemu (deity), 6724
Pesharim. See Pesher/Pesharim
Peshaṭ (literal interpretation), 866, 867, 868, 7620, 9249
of Kimḥat (David), 5145
Pesher/Pesharim (commentary), 880, **7063–7066**
continuous, 7063–7064
in Dead Sea Scrolls, 2234
as exegetical method, 7065–7066
as genre, 7063

as introductory formula, 7065
in non-*pesher* works, 7065
sobriquets as allusions to, 7065
thematic, 7064–7065
Peshi (trance), in Indian exorcism, 2934
Peshitta (Syriac version of Bible), 893–894, 922
Pesiqta' de-Rav Kahana' (midrash), 6018
Peskowitz, Miriam, 6021
Pessinus, 1452
Pessoa, Fernando, 3528
Pestalozza, Uberto, 2555
Pestalozzi, Henri, Kardec (Allan) as student of, 5089
Pestles, in African myths, about personal encounters with God, 92
Pesuqei de-Zimra' (Verses of Song) recitation, in service liturgy, 8389
Peta (ancestors), 3477
Petach Tikva (agricultural colony), 9979
Petahyah of Regensburg, on Karaites, 5084
Peṭakopadesa (Buddhist text), 1270
Petén rain forest, Maya sites, 1359
1 Peter, 917
author of, 917
canon of, 920
date of, 917
Mark in, 5714
prediction of Jesus in, 873
purpose of, 917
2 Peter, 917
author of, 917
canon of, 920, 921
content of, 917
purpose of, 7020
Peter (apostle). *See* Peter the Apostle
Peter, Apocalypse of, 917, 919, 7068–7069
laughter of Jesus in, 4197
Peter, Gospel of, 7068
Peter (patriarch), Maximos the Confessor and, 5792
Peter Damian (saint), Gregory VII and, 3689
Peter Lombard, **7066–7067**
Abelard (Peter) influencing, 8
biblical exegesis of, 7066–7067
on demons, 2278
education of, 7066
on free will and predestination, 3207
influence of, 7067
on merit, 5876
theology of, 9136
Thomas Aquinas on, 9160–9161
writings of, 7066–7067
Petermann, Heinrich, 889
Ginza translated by, 3495
on Mandaean religion, 5637
Peter of Abano
Marsilius of Padua and, 5729
on nature, 6433
Peter of Alcántara, eremitism of, 2827–2828
Peter of Candia, 6645
Peter of Pisa, 1556
Peter of Poitiers, 7067
Peter of Prussia, on Albertus Magnus, 232
Peter Olivi, 395
Peters, Larry, 57–58
Peters, Ted, 3430
on cloning, 5814
Petersen, Johann Wilhelm, 9470
Peterson, Erik
on Gnosticism, 3514, 3533
on monotheism, 6161
Peterson, Indira V., poetry of Appar, translation of, 8417
Peter the Apostle (saint), 917, **7067–7069**
and Maximón, 5790–5791
apostolic succession, in Roman Catholicism, 1763–1764
as bishop of Rome, 7875
Caribbean spirits identified with, 1433, 1434
chair of, *vs.* see of Rome, Cyprian on, 2113
in Christian tradition, 7068–7069
Eastern Orthodox Christianity on, 7069
exorcism by, 2928
in Finno-Ugric religions, 3108
as first pope, 1772, 7067, 7069
images of, 7069
Jesus bestowing power upon, 6966, 6974, 7068
Jesus' naming as the Rock, 7875
keys of the kingdom of, 5117
Mam (deity) and, 5926
Mark the Evangelist and, 5714
martyrdom of, 7068
Mary Magdalene and, 5757
New Testament descriptions of, 7067, 7068
origin of name of, 7067–7068
Paul the Apostle on, 7068
as possible author of *Mark,* 907–908
relics of, 7689
in Roman Catholicism, 7069, 7874–7875
in South American cult of saints, in colonial Andes, 8609–8610
touch of
healing, 9255–9256
of power, 9257
as trickster, 4197
writings ascribed to, 7068–7069
Peter the Great (Russian czar), 6622
anti-Muslim campaigns of, 4617
church reforms of, 1685, 7418
Ecclesiastical Regulation of, 7942
on icon painting, 4354
patriarchal offices abolished by, 2588
Southern Siberian religions and, 8672
Peter the Venerable (abbot)
Abelard (Peter) and, 7
Qur'ān translations commissioned by, 4715, 7243
on scripture, 8197
Petihah (form of midrash), 6020
Petipa, Marius, 2156
Petition
as act of worship, sacred language of, 5307
in Buddhism, vol. 9 color insert
in Christianity, vol. 7 color insert
Roman Catholicism, vol. 9 color insert
in Heavenly Master Daoism, 9844
images directing, vol. 9 color insert
Petitionary prayers, 7368
Petitot, Émile, 575
on Algonquian and Athapaskan myths, 6675
Petosiris, 563
Petra (Jordan), 1472
archaeological sites in, 6386–6388
Dushara in, 6388–6389
as Nabatean capital, 6385, 6386
plan of, *6388*
Petrarch, autobiography of, 698
Petrarch, Francesco, as "father of humanism," 4174–4175
Petre, Maude Dominica, **7069–7071**
as biographer of Tyrrell (George), 7069, 7070
in Catholic modern movement, 7070, 7071
life of, 7070
writings of, 7070, 7071
Pétrement, Simone, 2509
on Gnosticism, 3534
Petri, Helmut, 671, 672, 673
Petrie, Flinders, 3188
Petrine ministry, in Roman Catholicism, 7874–7875
Petri-Oderman, Gisela, 673
Petr Moghila (Metropolitan of Kiev), 1653, **7071–7072,** 7942
life of, 7071
and Russian Orthodox revival, 7071–7072
theology of, Roman Catholic perspectives in, 2588, 7072
Petro, Nawezi, in Apostolic Church of John Maranke, 5695
Petroglyphs, Finno-Ugric, 3114
Petronius (Christian monk), 3051, 3052–3053, 6939
on sibyls, 8383
Petrukhin, V. Ia., 3113
Petrus de Dusburg
on Baltic religion, 767, 774
on Pērkons, 7053
Petrus Hispanus, 5497
Pettazzoni, Raffaele, **7072–7077**
on African religions, 115
and Ashur, 549
as Bianchi's (Ugo) mentor, 862, 863
collection of myths, 6361
on confession, 1884, 1886, 1887, 1889, 5197, 7075
criticism of, 7075
education of, 7072
and Eliade (Mircea), 7073–7074, 7075
on epics, 6362
and (de Martino) Ernesto, 2267
historiography of, 4045
journal founded by, 10056
on knots, 5197
life of, 7072–7074
on lord of the animals, 5513
on monotheism, 7074–7075, 8170
on myth, 7075–7076
on North American Indian religions, 6671
on phenomenology of religion, 7089
on polytheism, 7074–7075
prestige of, 10080
Roman School of, 4050
on sin, 8402
on supreme beings, 7074–7075, 8874, 8878–8879
teaching positions of, 7073
on Vedic motif of binding, 938
writings of, 7073, 7074–7076
Pettersson, Olof, 474
Pettinato, Giovanni
on *Epic of Gilgamesh,* 3486, 3487
on the Flood, 600
on Sumerians *vs.* Akkadians, 5963, 5964
Petwo spirits, 9636
Peul religion. *See* Fulbe religion
Peutinger, Conrad, German humanism and, 4176
Pewutún rite, 5689
Pey (possessing spirit), 2934

Peyote
in Apache religion, 404, 406
ban on, 7248, 7255, 7302, 10054
ecstasy from, 2679
in Huichol religion, 3136, 4153, 7471
iconography of, 4309
laws on, 7303–7304, 7471, 10054–10055
mysticism and, 6342
in myths, 10054
in Native American Church, 406, 7470–7471, 10053–10055
origins of, 7302, 10054
in purification, 7508
spread of, 7302, 7470
tobacco combined with, 9216, 9218
Peyote Church of Christ, 10054
Peyote religion. *See* Native American Church
Peyrère, Isaac La, 5722
Pfaiffer, Henry, 6239
Pfander, Carl, 7244
Pfemba cult, 5220
Pfister, Oskar, 7477
Pfleiderer, Otto
classification of religions by, 1819–1820
on supreme beings, 8875
Pgr sacrifices, in Canaanite religion, 1382
Pha Dam pa Sangs rgyas (Phadampa Sangye), 1227
Ma gcig Lab sgron studying with, 5558
Phädon (Mendelssohn), 5854
Phaedo (Plato)
analytic philosophy in, 306
Bacchants in, 2358
deification in, 2248
dēmiourgos in, 2273
forms in, 7182
inspiration in, 4510
intuition in, 4525
metaphysics in, 5990
recollection in, 309–311, 5990
transmigration in, 9329
Phaedrus (Plato)
God in, 7182
soul in, 7185
writing in, 9269
Phaethon (mythic figure), Apollo as sun and, 8839
Phag mo gru pa Rdo rje rgyal po (Phakmotrupa), 1226
'Phags pa (Buddhist monk), 1154, 1606, 7269
Phakmodrupas clan, under Jangchup Gyaltsen (Tai Situ), 5194
Phallocentrism, 3298, 7008
Phallogocentrism, 3298
Phallus, **7077–7086**. *See also* Castration; Circumcision; Sexuality
in Buddhism, 7083, 7084
Campbell's mythology and, 1379
in Christianity, 7081–7082
demonization of, 7080
of Jesus, 7081, 7082
crossroads and, 2071
cut off in myths, 1450–1451
in Daoism, 7084–7085
in Egyptian religion, 1451, 7080
explicit and implicit focus on, 7077–7078
feminist critique of, 3298
Freud (Sigmund) on, 7085
in Germanic religion, 9167
in Greek myth, 7079–7080
of Dionysos, 7079, 7082
Herms *(hermae)* as, 2071, 3936, 3937, 7079
of Priapus, 7392, 7393
in Hawaiian religion, stone of Kāne, 3797
in Hinduism, 7082–7083
horn as symbol of, 4131
in Indus Valley religion, 3989–3990
in Islam, 7082
in Judaism, 7080–7081, 7085
of Legba, 9352
in Melanesian religions, 4114
modern thought on, 7085
in Neolithic religions, 6465
of Śiva (*See Liṅga*)
in prehistoric religions, 7079
as procreative symbol, 7078
in Roman religion, 7080
in Scandinavian religion, 3220
as signal, 2867–2868
Skoptsy excision of, 1452
in South American religions, 1502
Stone of Fál (Celtic), 1492
studies on, 7077
as symbol of aggression, 7078
in Tantrism, 7083, 7084
in Western thought, 3028
Phanes-Metis (deity), 2357. *See also* Dionysos
Phänomenologie der Religion (Leeuw). *See Religion in Essence and Manifestation* (Leeuw)
Phantasiastai, 5028
Phantasms, definition of, 3475
Phantoms, definition of, 3475
Pharaohs. *See also* Akhenaton; Kings, in Egyptian religion
ablution of, 10
coronation of, 5164
as divine, 3902
divinity of, 2703, 5163
funeral rites for, 5164
ka of, 5163–5164
and *maat,* 5163
necropolis of, 1472
Osiris identified with, 6920
as son of the Sun, 8837
women in lives of, 3381
Pharisees
calendar of, 8018–8019
in canonization of Mishnah and Talmud, 9275
Hillel's role in transformation of, 3981, 3982
historical views of, 4974
history, view of, 4058
Josephus Flavius on, 3203
Judaism in, 8449
oral Torah and, 6838
rabbinic Judaism and, 4858
on resurrection, 7765, 8557
Sadducees *vs.,* on Jewish law, 8018
on Shavu'ot, 8305
Smith (Morton) on, 8448
Spinoza (Baruch) on, 8683
in *Wissenschaft des Judentums,* 4877
Pharmacology
of ecstasy, 2679–2680
of Egyptian religion, 2725
Phases, in Chinese philosophy. *See Wuxing; Yinyang wuxing* philosophy
Pheidias (sculptor), 9063
Phek'umo rites, dances of, 2137
Phelan, Helen, 7860
Phelan, John Leddy, on Franciscans, 5915–5916
Phenomena
entelecheia of, 7092
Kant (Immanuel) on, 5077, 5080, 7087
Logos of, 7092
theoria of, 7092
Phenomenalism, Buddhist, Sautrāntikas and, 8119
Phénomène humain, Le (Teilhard de Chardin). *See Human Phenomenon, The* (Teilhard de Chardin)
Phenomenological method, for understanding deity, 2257–2258
Phenomenological Movement, The: A Historical Introduction (Spiegelberg), 7087
Phenomenological philosophy, reflexivity in, 7648
Phenomenological psychology, 7476–7477
Phenomenology. *See also* Phenomenology of religion
definition of, 7111
etymology of term, 7087
Hamilton (William) on, 7087
Hegel (G. W. F.) on, 7087
meanings of term, 7087
nonphilosophical, 7087
philosophical, 7087–7089
characteristics of, 7088–7089
in France, 7088
in Germany, 7088
objective of, 7087
of religion, 7099–7100
in science, 7087
uses of term, 7086–7087
Phenomenology of religion, **7086–7101**. *See also* International Association for the History of Religions
African American, 66–67
African studies in, 8794
antireductionism in, 7091, 7092, 7094, 7097
autonomy in, 7094
Berger (Peter L.) and, 8495
Bertholet (Alfred) as founder of, 843
Bianchi (Ugo) opposing, 863
Bleeker (C. Jouco) on, 978–979, 7092
Cassirer on myth and, 1448
Chantepie de la Saussaye on, 1531–1532
characteristics of, 7093–7096
classification of religions in, 1820, 4065
comparative and systemic approach to, 7093
comparative-historical method and, 1868, 1870
confession as element of religion in, 1883
controversial issues in, 7096–7098
criticisms of
as ahistorical, 1820
as too theological, 1879–1880
definitions of, 4100, 10078
descriptive approach to, 7094, 7096
of ecstasy, 2678, 2681
Eliade (Mircea), historical phenomenology of, 7976
Eliade (Mircea) on, 7087, 7092, 7094, 10078
empirical approach to, 7093, 7097
Heiler (Friedrich) on, 3897, 7091–7092
Heschel (Abraham Joshua) on, 3961
historical approach to, 7094, 7097
historiography and, 4042, 4043
in history of religions, 7089
history of religions approach *vs.,* 4061, 4063, 4065
Husserl (Edmund), role of, **4236–4238**
intentionality in, 7094–7095
Klimkeit (Hans-Joachim) on, 5190
Kristensen (W. Brede) on, 5246, 7086–7087, 7090
Leeuw (Gerardus van der) on, 48, 1531, 2755, 5391–5392, 7086–7087, 7091, 7094
meaning of term, 1820
origins of, 7089
Otto (Rudolf), influence of, 4100, 4101
Otto (Rudolf) on, 7087, 7090–7091, 7094, 10078
perennial phenomenologies (recurring patterns), 1870
philosophical, 7099–7100
recent developments in, 7098–7099
religious studies preceded by, 2608
revival in, 4237

ritual defined in, 7833–7834, 7835, 7850
and sacraments, definition of, 7955, 7957–7958
sacred and profane as problem for, 7976
sacred time in, 7990
sacrifice in, 8002, 8003
Scheler (Max) as forerunner of, 8147
Scheler (Max) on, 7087, 7089–7090
Schimmel (Annemarie) on, 8150
Schleiermacher (Friedrich) and, 8162
Sharpe (Eric) on, 8305
Smart (Ninian) and, 7093, 8443, 8444
sociology and, 8495
symbol theory and, 8913
tears in, 9023–9026
unity in, 2757
Phenomenology of Religion (Smart), 8466
Phenomenology of Religious Life (Heidegger), 7099
Phenomenology of Spirit (Hegel), 7087
absolute knowing in, 3894
comedy in, 4219–4220
evolutionism influenced by, 2913
systematic thinking in, 3893
Phenomenon of Life, The (Jonas), 4949
Phenomenon of Man, The (Teilhard de Chardin). *See Human Phenomenon, The* (Teilhard de Chardin)
Phenotype, in neo-Darwinism, 2909
Phi (spirits)
exorcism of, 3814
vs. nats, 6427
parallels in Sri Lanka, 8410
in Thai Buddhism, 9094
Phī cult, 5313, 5314
Phidias (Greek sculptor), 971, 2273, 4322
Phi figurines, 4321
Philadelphia (Pennsylvania), Allen (Richard) in, 264
Philadelphian Society, 1006
Philae (Egypt), temple of Isis at, 2709
Philanthropia (kindness or love towards others), in Eastern Orthodox Church, medicine and, 3844–3845
Philanthropos, God as, 2590
Philanthropy. *See also* Charity
legitimation through, 5397
Philaret of Moscow, 2588
Philebus (Plato), 2273, 7182
Philemon, 914, 915–916, 920
author of, 915
Philip II (king of Spain), 4501, 4504
Escorial palace-monastery of, 6120
Philip IV (king of France)
in conflict with Boniface VIII, 2524, 7280
Council of Vienne and, 2042
Great Western Schism and, 8157
taxation of clergy by, 1019
Philip IV (king of Spain), 4505
Philip, Gospel of
Mary Magdalene in, 5757
sexuality in, 8247
Philip Arrhidaeus, Egyptian religion under, 2709
Philip of Flanders, Count, 3649, 3650, 3651–3652
Philippe, L. N. A., 6782
Philippi (Greece), Paul's missionary journey to, 7015
Philippians, 914, 920
content of, 914, 7017–7018
date of, 914, 7017
hymn cited in, 7017
Jesus' body in, 2381
Paul's life in, 7014
suffering in, 8808
Philippine Independent Catholic Church, 353
Philippine Independent Church. *See* Iglesia Filipina Independiente
Philippines. *See also* Southeast Asia and Southeast Asian religions
Christianity in, 1727–1728
new movements in, 8654
Roman Catholicism, 1727, 1728
schism in, 8151, 8152
demographics, religious, 8647
flood in mythology of, 3131
Islam in, 4671
in colonial era, 4660
reform movements in, 4672
spread of, 4658
languages in, 4658
liberation theology in, 5442
literature of, 3078–3079
millenarianism in, 8648
nationalism in, 8654
Negrito religions of, **6454–6455**
traditional religion in, 8648
Philippists, *vs.* Gnesio-Lutherans, 5539
Philips, Dirk, 305
Philips, Obbe, Simons (Menno) and, 8401
Philistine religion, **7086–7105**
Assyrian texts on, 7102
biblical texts on, 7102, 7103, 7104–7105
Canaanite religion and, 7104
deities of, 7102–7103 (*See also specific deities*)
Greek texts on, 7102
inscription from Eqron on, 7103–7104
temples in, 7102, 7103, 7104–7105
Philistines, invading Egypt, 7101–7102
Phillpotts, Bertha, 3460
Philo
cosmology and, 2606
on Therapeutae, 7722
Philo Byblius (Philo of Byblos)
on Astarte, 562
on castration of Ouranos, 1451
on Melqart, 5847
on Phoenician religion, 7129, 7131
on theocrasies, 8931
Philodemus of Gadara, musical theory of, 6304
Philo Judaeus (Philo of Alexandria), **7105–7108**
on Abraham, 16, 7107
on afterlife, 152
on *aion,* 207
and Ambrose, 287
on animals, 360
on apocatastasis, 421
apologetics of, 427, 428, 429
on archetypes, 458
on biblical canon, 879
biblical exegesis of, 872–873, 874–875, 7106, 7191
on Canaanite religion, 1380–1381
and contemplation, 5817
on conversion, 7757
on creation, 7107
on Demiurge, 7188–7189
on demons, 2277
on deserts, 2301
on dualism, 2507
on Enoch, 2803
Essenes described by, 2846
on *euaggelion,* 3640
on fasting, 2996
on free will, 3203
on God's existence, 7106, 7422
Goodenough (Erwin R.) on, 3637
Hermes Trismegistos and, 3940
on *hypostasis,* 4240–4241
on idolatry, 4359–4360
influence of, 7107
on Jewish election, 2745
in Jewish thought and philosophy, 4887
on knowability of God, 182
on knowledge, 5201
on leaven, 5388
life of, 7105–7106
on *Logos,* 5502, 5504, 5505
as Middle Platonist, 7188
on *mitsvot,* 3201
on monasticism, 7652–7653
on Moses, 6202–6203, 9234–9235
miracles of, 6051
mysticism of, 7107
on numbers, 6746, 6748
Platonism influencing, 7106, 7107, 7113, 7188
Plotinus influenced by, 7106, 7198
on prophecy, 7107
Pythagoras influencing, 7106, 7113
on repentance, 7757
on Sabbath liturgy, 8921
on scripture, 8197
on soul, 7106, 7107
on souls, 8558
Stoicism influencing, 7106, 7113, 7188
on wisdom, 5502
wisdom literature of, 9759–9760
Philokalia (anthology of monastic texts), 798
spiritual guidance in, 8710
Philokalia of Origen, 6888, 6889
Philolaus (Greek philosopher), 3441
Philology. *See also* Language
comparative-historical method and, 1871
Sanskrit, Renou (Louis) and, 7754–7755
and study of religion, emergence of, 8763
Philomena (saint), spirits identified with in Trinidad, 1434
Philo of Alexandria. *See* Philo Judaeus
Philo of Byblos. *See* Philo Byblius
Philo of Inawai'a
cargo cults and, 1415
prophecy of, 3398
Philo of Larissa, 7188
Philoponus, John, on Aristotle, 479
Philosopher's stone. *See also* Elixir
alchemy's search for, 251, 252, 5987
Philosophes, 2796
Philosophia perennis, 1324, 2343
Philosophical Investigations (Wittgenstein), 4297, 7375
Philosophical method, for understanding deity, 2258
Philosophical reductionism, in science and religion, 2658
Philosophical Theology (Tennant), 9105–9106
Philosophie bantoue, la (Tempels), 116
Philosophie bantu comparée, la (Kagame), 117
Philosophie comparée, La (Masson-Oursel), 4447–4448
Philosophie der symbolischen Formen (Cassirer), 1448

Philosophy, **7108–7128**. *See also specific movements, philosophers, and schools*
aesthetics (*See* Aesthetics)
at Alexandria, 2710
analytic, **306–309**
of Abū al-Hudhayl al-ʿAllāf, 18–19
applied, 940
areas of, 7110
and bioethics, 940
in Brahmanism, 5200
Cārvāka, 1446–1447
of Cassirer, **1448–1449**
Chinese, **1570–1580**
Buddhism, era of development of, 1575–1577
classical era of, 1571–1574
Confucian revival, 1577–1578
first imperial era of, 1574–1575
later empire era, 1578–1579
pre-classical era of, 1570–1571
in Qing dynasty, 2129–2130
in twentieth century, 1579
classical
and alchemy, 247
of eternity, 2853–2854
Confucian (*See* Confucianism; Neo-Confucianism)
current trends of, 7112
of devotion, 2321
diverse positions in, 7111
dualism in, 2505
Durkheim (Émile) on, 2527
dynamism in, 2540
empiricism (*See* Empiricism)
environmental
agenda for, 2654–2655
of Hippocrates, 2606
epistemology (*See* Epistemology)
ethics (*See* Ethics)
etymology of term, 7109
factors of, 7109
German (*See* German philosophy)
Gnosticism in, 3526–3527
Greek (*See* Greek philosophy)
ha-Levi on, 4891–4892
hermeneutics, **3930–3936**
Hermetic, 3939–3941
on divine essence, 3944
influence of, 3953–3954
in Renaissance, 3946
in Hermetic texts, 3939, 3942
Hindu (*See also* Sāṃkhya school of Hinduism)
in Śaivism, 8417–8418
smārta and *haituka* schools in, 3997–3998
of history (*See also* Historiography)
in evolutionism, 2913
Herder (Johann Gottfried) on, 3919
history of, 7109–7110
of Hugh of Saint-Victor, 4151
idealism (*See* Idealism)
Indian (*See* Indian philosophies)
intuition in, 4525
Islamic (*See Falsafah*)
in Japan
Kyoto school of, 6635
under Tokugawa regime, 4788
Jaspers (Karl) on, 4814
Jewish (*See* Jewish thought and philosophy)
Judaism influenced by, 4979–4980, 4984
of language, 7112, 7115–7116, 7119, 7127
linguistic, liturgy in, 5492
logic (*See* Logic)
metaphysics (*See* Metaphysics)
moral, 1456
of nature, 6431–6437
ontology (*See* Ontology)
orgy interpreted in, 6875
phenomenology in (*See* Phenomenology, philosophical)
on prophecy, 7428
questions in, 7109
reality in, 7114
reflexivity in, 7648
of religion, **7122–7128**
analysis of religious language, practice, and belief in, 7125–7127
Capps and Nygren, 1412–1413
classification of religions in, 1819–1820
cosmological argument in, 7123–7124
in Eastern Europe, 8773
of ecstasy, 2681
in Hegel and Chantepie de la Saussaye, 1531
and history, separated or integrated, 4035, 4041
vs. history of religion, 9650
history of religions and, 7126–7127
James (William) in, 4775–4777
justification of religious beliefs in, 7122–7125
ontological argument in, 7123
Schweitzer (Albert) on, 8179
Smart (Ninian) and, 8443, 8444
Soloveitchik (Joseph Baer) on, 8519
teleological argument in, 7124–7125
Wittgenstein in, 9781–9782
religion, relation to, 7110–7111, **7113–7122**
Barth (Karl) and, 7117–7118
chief concerns in, 7113–7114
Clement and, 7113
Descartes (René) and, 7110, 7111
dialogue of, 7119–7121
Eastern perspectives, 7111–7112, 7114–7115
expressed in revelation, 7118
expressed in social science, 7118
Hegel (G. W. F.) on, 3894
Kant (Immanuel) and, 7115–7119
Origen and, 7113
Roman, of Cicero, 1786
schools of, new schools as apostasy or heresy, 3921–3922
soteriological function of, 8529
symbolic theory and, 8912
of theism, 7122–7125
theology *vs.*
Heidegger (Martin) on, 3896
Mercier (Désiré Joseph) on, 5868
of Trinity, 1666–1667
Western, reflexivity in, 7648
wisdom and, 9747
women's studies and, 9792
on worldview or *Weltanschauung,* 1992
Philosophy as Scientia Scientiarum (Flint), 7340
Philosophy in a New Key (Langer), 4295
Philosophy of Fine Art (Hegel), 47
Philosophy of Freedom, The (Steiner), 392
Philosophy of History, The (Hegel), 113, 9109
heroes in, 3956
Philostratus, 2995
on Apollonius of Tyana, 3905, 4038
on dragons, 2346
Philoxenian Bible, 894
Philoxenus (bishop), 894
Phlegm. *See* Humors of the body
Phlegon of Tralles, sibylline oracles and, 8384
'Pho ba (transference of consciousness), 1288
death and, in Tibet, 3866
Phoenician History (Philo Byblius), 7129, 7131
Canaanite religion in, 1380–1381
Phoenician religion and society, **7128–7136**
Assyrian rule of, 7128, 7129
beliefs and practices of, 7131–7133
Canaanites and, 1385, 1388, 7129, 7130–7131
Carthage and, 1678
colonies of, 7128
creation myth in, 7131
curse-threats in, 2101–2102
deities of, 1383, 7129–7131 (*See also specific deities*)
festivals in, 7131–7132
funeral rites in, 7132, 7134
and Iberian religion, 4249–4250
influence in North Africa, 4580
kingship in, 5164, 7132
offerings in, 7132, 7133, 7134
origin of term, 7128
Ouranos and Krosnos myth in, 1451
Persian rule of, 7129
political power of, 7128
priesthood in, 7132–7133
sacrifice in, 4580, 7131–7133, 7134
sources on, 7129, 7131
territory of, 7128
Phoenix (bird), 6164
Phoenix Hall (Buddhist temple), 9049
Phoenix Halls *(luantan),* 1608
Phoinikika (Phoenician Histories), 6867
Pho lha (male god), 9185
Phonikika (Lollianos), 3053
Photian councils, 2041
Photinus, on *Logos,* 5504
Photios (patriarch of Constantinople)
abdication and reinstatement of, 7135
Bibliotheke, 3053
dual control theory of, 7135
Eastern Christianity influenced by, 2582
in *filioque* controversy, 7135
Gregory of Cyprus and, 3692
on Holy Spirit, 7135
on iconoclasm, 4289
influence of, 7135
missionary work of, 2585, 7135–7136
Nicholas I and, 2041, 6967, 7135, 7136
Pope opposed by, 2585
schism and, 8155
writings of, 7135, 7136
Photizomenoi (those awaiting baptism), catecheses to, 2118
Photoelectric effect, 2739–2740
Photogenie, idea of, 3100
Photographs
of the dead, 2241, vol. 9 color insert
as religious art, 500
Phra Mu'ang Kaew (king of Chiangmai), 1137
Phra Phimonlatham (Buddhist monk), 9096
Phra Phutthabat (pilgrimage site), 9832

Phra Rātchawaramunī, 9096
Phra Sat (mountain), 6213
Phra Sri Ratana Chedi (Buddhist stupa), vol. 4 color insert
Phrenology, 2373
Phrul 'khor (magical devices), 1288
Phrygia. *See also* Sabazios
shrines to Cybele in, 2108–2109
Phule, Jotibā, 5699
Phuntsok Namgyal (Sikkim king), 7262
Phusis (nature), in Christology, 4241–4242
Phutthatham (Buddhist text), 9096
Phutthathāt Phikkhu (Buddhist thinker), 9096
Phyogs las rnam rgyal (Chokle Namgyal), 1228
Phyrrho of Elis, skepticism and, 8420
Physical dualism, 2509
Physical evil, 2897
Physical work, 9798
Physical world
Orthodox Christian view of, 2591
in Orthodox sacraments, 2592
Physicians. *See* Healing and medicine
Physico-theology, 6434
Physics, **7136–7141**. *See also* Science
in 20th century, 7137–7138
anthropic principle in, 2033, 8189
Aristotle's, 481, 484, 582
Crescas (Ḥasdai), critique of, 2069
causation in, 2659
chaos theory and, 1541, 7139
Copernican revolution and, 1978, 7136
definition of, 7136
deism as response to, 7137
of Empedocles, 2776
historical roots of, 7136
immaterial in, 2659
interventionism as response to, 7137
liberalism as response to, 7137
Newtonian mechanism in, 7136–7137
Newton's, 582, 7136–7137
phenomenology in, 7087
Plutarch's, 7189
power in, 7346
relativity and, 2032, 7138
religion and, 2659–2660
science and religion, questions relating to, 8184, 8188
Physics (Aristotle), 7110
causes in, 484
chance in, 1526
motion in, 484
Sa'adyah Gaon influenced by, 4888
substance in, concept of, 484
Physics of Immortality, The (Tipler), 513
Physiology, Upaniṣadic, 9482
Physis (nature)
Arabic term for, 2652
in Christology, 2583, 2584
Pi, approximation of, 3439, *3439*, 3440
Pia desideria (Spener), 7142
Piaget, Jean, on psychology of religion, 7474
Piagnonism, Savonarola (Girolamo) and, 8140
Piankhy (Divine Adoratress of Amun), 2709
Piaroa religion (South America), creation myth in, 8587
Picasso, Pablo, 56, 4348
Picatrix (book of magical instructions), 5578–5579
Piciétl (tobacco), 9218
Pickel, Conrad, German humanism and, 4176
Pickwick Papers, The (Dickens), 3059
Pico della Mirandola, Giovanni, **7141**
on angels, 348
on astrology, 564
and Christian Qabbalah, 7535
on Gersonides' astronomy, 3462
on Hermetism, 3946
humanism of, 7141
Italian Renaissance humanism, role of, 4175–4176
life of, 7141
on magic, 5579
writings of, 7141
Pictographs, Chinese, 1370
Picumata-brahma Yāmala, rites in, 4020
Piddington, Ralph, 684
Pidr (deity), in Canaanite religion, 1387
Pidray (deity)
as daughter of Baal, 1384
Hirhib and, 1395
kings in sacred marriage with, 3377
Piekarz, Mendel, 9379
Pierbolte, Lietaert, on Hermetism, 3954
Piercing, 1003
Piercing the Ground (Watson), 643
Pier Damiani. *See* Damian, Peter
Pierre, Musumbu, in Apostolic Church of John Maranke, 5695
Pièrres tonneres (thunder stones), in Caribbean religions, 1436
Piersen, William, 77
Pierson, Donald, 121
Piers Plowman (English poem), 7218
Pietà, 813
Pietism
in Denmark, Kierkegaard's exposure to, 5140
evangelicalism and, 2887
Fellowship Movements, revival of, Smith (Hannah Whitall) and, 8446
in Germany, Kant's (Immanuel) family as members of, 5076
on Grace, 5079
Herder (Johann Gottfried) and, 3919
homo religiosus and, 4109
in Islam, Ḥasan al-Baṣrī and, 3785
in Jewish Renewal, 4869–4870, 4872
in Judaism, 4993–4994 (*See also* Hasidism)
Lutheran, 5539
and Mennonites, 5861
Moravian, 6191
Schleiermacher (Friedrich), effect on, 8159
in Protestantism, **7141–7144**
in 18th century, 7143
Baptist churches and, 785
characteristics of, 7142
goal of, 7141
heritage of, 7143
Lutheran, 7142
origins of, 7141–7142
Precisianism, 7142
radical wing of, 7142–7143
Spener-Halle type, 7142
Swabian, 7142
scripture and "back to the book" movements, 8200
Sophia in, 8523
Spener (Philipp Jakob), role of, 8679, 8680
and theology, 9137, 9139
in United States, 6558
Universalism influenced by, 9470
Wolff's (Christian) clash with, 9782–9783
Piety
in Christianity
early Eastern, 2582
Marian, 5753–5754
Thomas á Kempis on, 9159
in Egyptian religion, 2714
in Greek religion, 3677
in Islam, 9818–9819
Muḥammad in, 6227–6228
in Israelite wisdom, 9759
in Japanese folk tales, 4798
in Judaism
Baḥye on, 4890–4891
as ethical piety, 4902–4903
in Second Temple Judaism, 4974
Torah study as, 9238–9239
in Roman religion, 7278
Socrates on, 8503
in Sufism, 9004
visual, vol. 11 color insert, vol. 12 color insert
Pietz, William, 67
on fetishism, 3043, 9296
Pigafetta, Antonio, 6799
Pigafetta, Filippo, 112
Pig dragons, 4758
Pigeaud, Theodore, colonial agenda of, 8638
Piggott, Joan, 3346
Piggott, Stuart, 1499
Pigs, **7144–7145**
in Celtic religion, 1487
in Egyptian religion
sacrifice of, 7144
Seth as, 7144
in Greek religion, sacrifice of, 3682, 3683, 7144, 9156
in Hawaiian religion, sacrifice of, 3798
in Hinduism, as *avatar* of Viṣṇu, 4438, 7144, 7501
in megalithic religion, 5827–5828
in Melanesian religion
in ancestor worship, 322, 7144–7145
mortuary rituals of, 5838
Tsembaga pig festival, 7840
in Mesopotamian religion, sacrifice of, 7144
in New Guinea religion, 6507
sacrifice of, 7145
in Polynesian religion, 9598
taboos on eating of, 3167, 3172, 7144
in Central Asian Islam, 4625
in Chinese Islam, 2401
in Islam, 4683, 7144
in Judaism, 3167, 3172, 7144
in Vanuatu religions, 9519–9520
Pigs, Festival of (Melanesia), 6591–6592
Pigs for the Ancestors (Rappaport), 322, 2611, 2618, 7618
Piho, Apii, 1740
Pike, Albert, 3196
Pike, Nelson, 9113
Pilagá people (South America), religion of, 8636
Pilate, Pontius (Roman prefect), ordering Jesus' execution, 7058
Pilco-Kayma structure, on Titicaca Island, 5291, 5292
Piler (mythic figure), in Cuna creation myth, 2095

Pilet, Camille, 9068
Pilgrimage, **7145–7172**. *See also* Relics; Sacred space; Saint(s); Shrines
as act of devotion, 2319–2320, 7147
archaic, 7146–7147
Aztec, to water sources, 5293
Buddhist, 1111, 1157–1158
in China, 1097, 7164–7165
circumambulation in, 7167
crossroads and, 2071
in early Buddhism, 1063, 1091, 1107, 7163
in East Asia, 3010–3011, **7164–7166,** 9835
of Faxian, 7163–7164
goal of, 7163
in Himalayan Buddhism, 1234, 7166–7167
of Ippen, 4532
in Japan, 1097, 1183, 1184, 7165–7166
to Kapilavastu, 1064
modern, 7168
as ritual, 1097
in South and Southeast Asia, 1097, **7163–7164**
in Southeast Asia, 9832
to stupas, 8797, vol. 4 color insert
temples along routes of, 9043
in Thailand, 7164, 7982, 9832
in Tibet, 1151, **7166–7168,** 9185, 9840–9841
of Zhiyi, 9174, 9175
centers of
as sources of blessings, 980
spiritual magnetism of, 7146
Chinese, 1616
Aśoka and, 555
Buddhist, 1097, 7164–7165
modern, 7165
Christian
of Basil of Caesarea, 7153
in biblical literature, 7152–7153
circumambulation and, 1797
Crusades and, 2074
cult of saints and, 2082
early, 7153
Eastern Christian, **7152–7154**
of Hungarians, 4225, 4227
to Jerusalem, 4837, 7152–7153, 8377, 9293
of Kempe (Margery), 5110
to El Santuario de Chimayó, 8377
to martyria, 7153
New Age, at equinoxes and solstices, 8429
origins of, 7152
as precursor to retreats, 7771
Roman Catholic, **7148–7152**
sacred geography of, 3435–3436
to shrine of Saint Menas (Egypt), 1980, 1981
in cities, 1808–1809
communitas in, 7146, 7147
Islamic, 7158
Daoist, 7165
Eastern Christian, **7152–7154**
customs and traditions of, 7153–7154
and healing, 7154
Holy Fire ceremony in, 7154
vows and oaths during, 7154
experience of, 7145–7146
in fiction, Chinese, 3057
figurative, in Christian view of history, 4053
freedom from social structure during, 7146
general features of, 7145
in goddess worship
contemporary, 3588
for healing, 3590
healing and (*See* Saint(s), healing associated with)
high-period, 7147
Hindu, **7168–7172**
ancestor worship and, 7169, 7170
to Banaras, 778, 779, 3274, 7169
in devotional life, 9823–9824
"four dhāms" of, 7170
on Ganges River, 3274, 7170, vol. 5 color insert
in Mhānubhāv sect, 7978
Kumbha Melā, 5264–5266, **5264–5266**
"liṅgas of light" of, 7170
literature on, 7169, 7171
modern, 7171
motivation for, 7171
to Pandharpur, 2320
political and economic history of, 7169–7170
practices of, 7168–7169, 7171
Śaktipīṭhas system of, 7170
"seven cities" of, 7170
to Kurukṣetra, 5268
to Vṛndāvana, 9644–9645
water and bathing in, 7168–7169
in Indian religion, in North India, 3987
Israelite, 934, 935, 936, 4972–4973, 7152, 7161
Japanese, 4798
Buddhist, 1097, 1183, 1184, 7165–7166
in Shintō, 7165, 8360, 8362, 8364, 8369
in Shugendō, 8380
for utopian *kami,* 5072
Jewish, **7161–7163**
origins of, 7161
prayer during, 7162
sacrifice during, 7162
Temple wall in Jerusalem and, 8377
to tombs of saints, 7161–7162
in Kushite religion, 5269
in literature, 7554
to Lourdes, 1470
in Marathi religions, 5697
for Meher Baba's followers, 5829
in Mesoamerican religions
in Huichol peyote cult, 4153
myths of, 5937–5938
migration through, 6023
modern, 7147
Chinese, 7165
Hindu, 7171
Roman Catholic, 7148–7149
Tibetan, 7168
Muslim, **7154–7161**
to Dome of the Rock (Jerusalem), 8377
iconography of, 4351
in Imāmīyah, 8345
to Kaʿbah (*See* Kaʿbah)
to Karbala, 5088
to Mecca, 2319–2320, 4562 (*See also* Ḥājj; *ʿUmrah*)
of Ibn al-ʿArabī, 4257
of Ibn Khaldūn, 4269
of Ibn Taymīyah, 4277
of Muḥammad, 6226
in sub-Saharan Africa, 4605
textiles in, 9091
to ʿAlī's shrine, 260
to shrine of al-Ḥusayn in, 4236
ziyārah, 3834–3835, 7160
New Age, at equinoxes and solstices, 8429
pain in, 6945
portals in, 7333
vs. procession, 7417, 7418
prototypical, 7147
purification in, 7157, 7169, 7507, 7509
refraining from sexual activity during, 7158
Roman Catholic
in Europe, 775, **7148–7149**
modern, 7148–7149
in the New World, **7149–7152**
in Samaritan religion, 8070
South Asian, music in, 6280
tattoos as symbols of, 1002
to Meccan *ḥaram* (pre-Islamic), 3777–3778
and tourism, 7168, 7171, 9261, 9262
and transculturation, 9293–9294
Turner (Victor) on, 7163, 9293, 9406
in Vodou, 9637–9638
in Zoroastrianism, 9999
"Pilgrimage for Religion's Sake" (Erasmus), 9262
Pilgrimage of Buddhism and a Buddhist Pilgrimage, The (Pratt), 7367
Pilgrimage to the New Church of Regensburg (Ostendorfer), vol. 12 color insert
Pilgrim Holiness Church. *See* Holiness movement
Pilgrims (separatists). *See also* Plymouth Colony
American denominationalism and, 1712
Congregationalism and, 1938
covenant notion, and social reform, 1750–1751
Pilgrim's Progress (Bunyan), 1322–1323, 2952, 7521
novels inspired by, 3085, 3086
Pilgrim's Regress, The (Lewis), 5430
Pili (lizard), 7305
Piḷḷai, Vaṭakku Tiruvīti, 7172
Piḷḷai Lokācārya, **7172–7173**
on grace, 8728
Piḷḷaitamil (poetry form), 8977
Pillán (deity)
ambivalence of, 5994
role of, 8580
Piḷḷān (Hindu teacher), Śrī Vaiṣṇavas Sampradāya and, 8728
Pillar of Fire Church, founder of, 6536
Pillars. *See also* Five Pillars of Islam
axis mundi as, 713
in Chinese myth, breaking of cosmic pillars, 1625
in Chuvash cosmology, 1785
cosmic, supreme beings associated with, 8873
in Greek religion, 8745
in Hebrew scripture, 8744
in North American Indian religion, in Kwakiutl religion, 8873
as sacred center, 1502, 1503, 1504
in Siberian shamanism, 8283–8284
Pilling, Arnold, 3391
Pilpul (logic, literally "pepper"), 1454, 5015
development of, 9884
as method of Talmudic hermeneutics, 5533
Pima Indian religion, shamanism in, 8289
Pimander. See Corpus Hermeticum

Pima religion (North America), 6721
butterflies in, 4507
Pimiko (Japanese queen), 4780
Piña Chan, Román, on Olmec iconography, 5881
Pinamonti, Giovanni P., 6621
Pinard de la Boullaye, Henri, **7173**
on Ignatius Loyola, 7173
on Müller (Karl Otfried), 6237
writings of, 7173
Pinchas of Koretz, 9379
Pindar, **7173–7175**
on *aion,* 207
on Apollo, 7174
on ascension, 520
on Asklepios, 551
on Athena, 586
biographies of, 7173
on Delphi, 8745
on Demeter, 7173
on divine incarnation, 3902
on fortune, 1526
on games, 3265
on Golden Age, 3626
on Herakles, 7174
on heroes, 3681
on law, 4727
on memory, 5852
morality in poems of, 7174
on Neoptolemos, 7174
on Pan, 7173
riddles of, 6986
on transmigration, 9328, 9329
victory odes of, 7173–7174
on Zeus, 7174
Piṇḍola Bhāradvāja, 477
Pinengir (deity), 3594–3595
Pinga (supreme being), 4415
Pingala, on Pascal triangle, 3442
Ping River Valley (Thailand), pilgrimage shrines in, 7982
Pinkama ("act of merit"), as hospitality, 4140
Pink Angels, in Raëlian religion, 7598–7599
Pinn, Anthony, 74, 79, 80, 81
Pinnacle (Rastafari community), 7624
Pinnai (deity), 5252, 7593
Pintubi religion (Australia), iconography of, 4305, 4307
Pio of Pietrelcina (Saint) (Padre Pio), as stigmatic, 1004
Pipe, in peyote ceremonies, 10053
Pipe ceremony, in North American Indian religions, 6650, 6652
Lakota, 6662
Plains nations, 6698
Pipes, 9217, 9218
in Lakota religion, 5295, 5296, 5297
Piratāpa Mutaliyār Carittiram (Veetanāyakam), 10035
Pirckhiemer, Willibald, German humanism and, 4176
Pirlirrpa (life force), 9693, 9696
Pirqei de-Rabbi Eli'ezer, 2764
Pīrs (spiritual masters). *See also* Shaykhs
*ginān*s composed by, 3494
as spiritual guides, 8710–8711
Pirts māte (sauna mother), 760
Pisa, council of (1409)
conciliarism at, 2042, 6971
divided papacy and, 4233, 8157
*Pisaca*s (demon-like beings), 2276, 2315, 3477
Pisarev, Dmitrii, nihilism of, 2427–2428
Pishon (river), 7862
Piss Christ (Serrano), 4282
Pistis Sophia, 521
ouroboros serpent in, 1793
Pistoia, synod at (1786), overview of, 2044
Pitao Cozaana (deity), 5912
Pitao Cozaana-Pitao Cochaana (deity), 5887
Pitao Cozobi (deity), 5887, 5903, 5912
Pitao Huichana (deity), 5912
Pitao Pecelao (deity), 151
Pitao Pezelao (deity), 5912
Pitao Xicala (deity), 5912
Pitaraḥ (spirits)
fravashis compared with, 3190
in Vedism, 9559
Pitchpot (game), 3260
Pithanon (persuasive), 7188
Pitjantjatjara people (Australia)
the Dreaming and, 6260
myths of, history of study of, 668
Pīt pî (opening the mouth), 4389
Pitṛpakṣa ceremony, in Hindu religious year, 4016
Pitṛs (ancestral spirits), 2276
Pitṛ yajña (rituals), 748
Pitta (bile), in Āyurveda, 3854–3855
Pitt-Rivers, Julian, 2543
Pitts, Walter F., 75
Pittsburgh Platform (1885)
afterlife in, 155
declarations of, 7670–7671
messianism in, 5976
Pituri (hallucinogen), 7468–7469
Pius (Latin term), 2955
Pius II (pope)
Crusades and, 2076
humanism of, 6972
Pius IV (pope)
Borromeo (Carlo) as nephew of, 1023
and Council of Trent, 6972, 9344–9345
Pius V (pope)
declaring Thomas Aquinas as doctor of the church, 9164
election of, 1023
Pius VI (pope)
ballet about, 2155
on French Revolution, 6973
imprisonment of, by Napoleon, 6973
Pius VII (pope)
Jesuits restored by, 4842
relations with Napoleon, 6973
Pius VIII (pope), Nestorians and, 6480
Pius IX (pope), **7179–7181**
on animals, 361
as bishop, 7179
and devotional movement, 7181
Döllinger (Johann) condemned by, 2396
economic difficulties under, 7179
on French Revolution, 7180
on immaculate conception, 5754
Leo XIII and, 5411
against liberalism, 7179, 7180
missionary expansion under, 7180
in papal delegate in Chile, 7179
Papal States under, 7179, 7180
Romanticism and, 7878
temperament of, 7179
ultramontanism of, 6974, 7180, 9442, 9531–9532
Vatican I and, 2044, 6974, 7180, 9528
Pius X (pope)
and Catholic Modernism, 6102, 6106
Mercier (Désiré Joseph) under, 5868
modernism condemned by, 6974, 7878
modernist controversy and, 5507
on religious experience, 7739
on retreats, 7772–7773
and Vulgate Bible, 893
Pius XI (pope)
on Albertus Magnus, 233
Catholic Action established by, 5930
and Ignatius Loyola, 4368
on marriage, 6974
on missions, 7879
and social doctrine, 7878
Thérèse of Lisieux canonized by, 9155
Pius XII (pope)
on Albertus Magnus, 233
on Anthony of Padua, 377
on Barth (Karl), 789
on Big Bang, 7138
on charisma, 1550
Divino afflante Spiritu, 7879
on Jesuits, 6973
and *Lex Proprio,* 822
on Mary, 5754
on membership in the church, 1778
on missions, 7879
Möhler (Johann Adam) and, 6114
and social doctrine, 7878
theology of, 6974
Pixies, 2952
Pi Xirui, on Konzi (Confucius), 1904
Piye (Divine Adoratress of Amun), 2709
Piyyuṭim (liturgical poems), 6020, 6021, 6308, 7207
in *maḥzor,* 8389–8390
in *merkavah,* 10051
Pizarro, Francisco
Inca conquest by, 567, 5175
in Peru, 1695
Pizarro, Hernando, indigenous religion, perceptions of, 8606
Pizexi (fleeing-from-debt plays), 1642
PK. *See* Psychokinesis
PLA. *See* Peoples Liberation Army
Placard affair (1534), 7662
Place
in Australian Indigenous music, 6262
kami of, in Japanese religion, 5072
narrative and, in indigenous traditions, 2618
vs. path, architecture of, 466–467
sacred (*See* Sacred space)
Place for Strangers, A (Swain), 685
Placenta
representative of pharaoh's *ka,* 5163–5164
in Sudanese religion, 8849
Plagiarism, in Eckankar texts, 2602
Plagues
Christian care of the sick in, 3844
in Egypt, Moses and, 6200
Reshef causing, 7761
Plain dress, 1836
Plains peoples (North America), 6656, **6696–6705**. *See also* *specific tribes*
creation stories of, 6703–6704
cultural diversity of, 6697
funeral rites of, 6697, 6703
Ghost Dance of (*See* Ghost Dance)
Hako ceremony of, 6704
language diversity of, 6696–6697
and Native American Church, 6701–6702
rain dance of, 7603
religious complex of, 6656
sacred and profane for, 6702–6703

Plains peoples (North America) ***continued***
Sacred Arrow Renewal ceremony of, 6704–6705
shamanism among, 8289
smoking among, 8454
study of, 6670, 6672
Sun Dance of, 2138, 6656, 6698, 6699–6700, **8844–8849**
supreme being of, 6703
sweat lodge of, 6700
tipis of, 4104
vision quest of, 6700, 9610
Planck, Max
logical positivism and, 5498
quantum theory, 1543, 7138
Planck era, attempts to understand, 2034
Plan de Ayala, 9930
Planetary Dance (Halprin), 7047
Planets
in astrology, 565–566
deities of, 3619
in Confucianism, 1911
in Hinduism, in Purāṇic cosmology, 2017–2018
spirits of, evocation of, 5585
Planisphaerium (Ptolemy), 7492
Plantinga, Alvin, 7123, 7125, 9113
Plants. *See* Psychedelic drugs and psychoactive substances; Vegetation; *specific plants*
Plaskow, Judith, 3312–3313, 5459
on female divine, 4166
Platform Sutra of the Sixth Patriarch, 6631
Chinul on, 1646
Huineng and, 1601, 4154–4155
influence of, 1577
Oxhead school and, 1522
Plath, David W., 2411
Plato, **7181–7187**. *See also* Platonism
Academy of, 7181, 7187–7188
Antiochus of Ascalon proposing return to, 7188
Aristotle at, 483, 7187
and Neoplatonism, 6474
New Academy, 7188
on Adonis, 35
aesthetics of, 44–45, 810
on afterlife, 8543
on *aion,* 207
analytic philosophy of, 306
on anamnesis (recollection), 309–311, 315–316, 5990
on androgynes, 338
on anthropomorphism, 390
on Aphrodite, 408
on apocatastasis, 421
on ascension, 520
on asceticism, 6946
on Asklepios, 551
Augustine's study of, 625
on Bacchants, 2358
on Bendideia, 819
bridge image used by, 1050
cave allegory of, states of consciousness and, 1952
on chance, 1526
on change, 3056
on chastity, 1558
on classes of divine beings, 3667
on conversion, 7756
on cosmic day and year, 6750
on cosmic seeds, 7190
cosmology of, *ouroboros* mythology in, 1793
on cybernetics, 2111
on dance, 2143, 2154
on deification, 2248, 2249
on demons, 2283
on descent in the underworld, 2299
on divination, 2369
on divine knowledge, 6960, 6961
on divine madness, 2807
and divine man, 3509
on doctrine, 2384
dualism of, 2507, 2508, 2510, 2511, 2515, 7190
Er myth of, 7680
on Eros, 2833
eternal *vs.* everlasting in, 2855
ethics of, 7110
on fate, 3004
forms of, 44–45, 7110, 7181–7182, 7184
Aristotle's rejection of, 484, 7187
in Middle Platonism, 7189
Plotinus on, 7198
Speusippus's rejection of, 7187
Xenocrates accepting, 7187
on free will, 3200
on frenzy, types of, 3213
Galen influenced by, 3255
on geometry, *3440,* 3441, 3442
on God, 3685, 7182
on gods, 4321, 7183–7184, 7185, 7186, 7190
on God's compassion, 9283
on golden age, 2964, 3627
on Golden Rule, 3632
on the good, 3635
Greek religion rejected by, 3685
Gregory of Datev criticizing, 3693
on Hippocrates, 4021
homosexuality and, 4113
Ibn Rushd's commentary on, 4272
idealism of, 7111
ideas, theory of, 7110
circles and, 1791
on images, 4283
on imitation, 5486
on immortality, 7182, 7184
influence on *falsafah,* 2971, 2972, 2973
on inspiration, 4509–4510
on intellect, 7182
on intuition, 4525
on judgment of the dead, 5026
on knowability of God, 181, 182, 183
on knowledge, 5201
"knowledge" defined by, 2818–2819
on laughter, 4199, 4218
on Lethe (river), 3016
on light and darkness symbolism, 5452
on magic, 5573, 5575
on matter, 4355, 7119–7120
on memory, 5852
metaphysics of, 5990
on mirrors, 6063
and monism, 6146
on monotheism, 427, 6156
on moon, 6173
on morality, reason and, 6179
on mortal living beings, 7182, 7184–7185
on music theory, 6303–6304
mystery religions and, 6332
myth and, 6374
on nihilism, 2427
on numbers, 7530
on *dēmiourgos,* 2273–2274, 6963, 7183–7184, 7190
on *psuchē,* 7679–7680, 8542
ontology of, 6830
on Orphism, 3674
on Pan, 6957
on play, 3265
on poetry, 7205
on power, 5397
on prayer, 7370
on private *vs.* public spheres, 4107
on Prometheus, 7420
on prophecy, 7439
on purification, 1460
Pythagoreans and, 7181
realism of, 9282
on reality, 4355, 7110, 7181–7182
on recurring paradise, 6984
on reflexivity, 7648
on reincarnation, 7679–7680
on religious holidays, 7989
on resurrection, 4456
on revelation, 7775
riddles of, 6987
Schleiermacher (Friedrich) on, 8161
on shape shifting, 8302
ship symbolism of, 992
on sin, 8405
social philosophy of, 8464
on Socrates, 8501
on Socratic dialogue, 2342
on Sophists, 3052
on soul, 4415, 7181, 7182
of animals, 7185
of God, 7182
of gods, 7183–7184, 7185
of human beings, 7184, 7185
immortality of, 7182, 7184
likened to two-horse chariot, 4135
of men, 7185
of plants, 7185
transmigration of, 7185, 7186, 9328, 9329
tripartite soul theory, 7184
of women, 7185
words for, 1042
World Soul, 6960, 6963
on suicide, 8828–8829
on sun symbolism and worship, 8835, 8839, 8840
on theater, 7044
on theology, 2383, 9134
on *thiasoi,* 9159
on Thracian religion, 9169
on three elements in man, 9348
on tradition, 9272
on traditional religion, 7186
tripartite soul theory, 3882
on truth, 9374
on underworld, 9453
on vegetarianism, 7185
on wisdom, 7109
on writing, 9269
origin of, 269, 270
on Zalmoxis, 3466
Platon (Byzantine monk), 9122
Platonic Theology (Proclus), 2277
Platonism, **7187–7193**. *See also* Neoplatonism
Bible, attempts to reconcile with, 8181
catharsis in, 1460
in Christianity
chief concerns of, 7113
and God, 3555
Christian reincarnationism and, 8563
Cosmic Soul in, Hekate identified with, 3900
definition of, 7110
dualism of, 2506, 2507, 2508, 2511, 7189
eclecticism in, 3912
and Gnosticism, 7190
on gods, 7184
the good in, 3635
heart symbolism in, 3882
and Hermetism, 7190–7191
hypostasis in, 4240, 4242
in Italian Renaissance, 4897
in Jewish philosophy, soul and, 8558
of Justin Martyr, 5043, 5044
Logos in, 5504–5505
Middle, 7188–7190
Aristotle interpreted by, 7189
Christian, 7190–7191
on Demiurge, 7188–7189
eclecticism of, 7188
gnosis (knowledge) in, 3508
and Hermetism, 7190
on Platonic forms, 7189

on *Timaeus* (Plato), 7188, 7189
on World Soul, 7189
nature in, 6432
of Origen, 6890
Philo Judaeus influenced by, 7106, 7107, 7113, 7188
of Plutarch, 7200–7201
vs. Pythagoreanism, 7529–7530
Pythagorizing, 7189
in Renaissance, 7193
ship symbolism in, 992
and Stoicism, 7188
theology in, 9135
Valentinus influenced by, 7190
witchcraft and, 9772
Plautus, 35
on *penates,* 7027
on superstition, 8864
Play, **7193–7198**. *See also* Carnival; Ceremonies; Festivals; Games; Sports
attributes of, 7194
and cosmology, 7194–7196
creativity and, 7194
deep, in gambling, 3260, 3261
form of reference for, 7194
framing behavior as, semantics of, 3265
in Hinduism (*See Līlā*)
Huizinga (Johan) on, 4201–4202, 8725
meaning altered by, 7194
representations in, 3265
in rituals, 7196–7197
time and, 1761
untruth of, 3265, 7194
"Playing God," in science and religion debates, 8186–8188, 8190
Play of Daniel, 2471
Plays. *See* Drama; Performance
Pleasure
Epicurus on, 3910
in Judaism, as God's gift, 3548
in primordial paradise, 6983
Spinoza (Baruch) on, 8684
Stoic perspective on, 3912
Plebeians, in Roman society, 7902–7903
Pleck, Elizabeth H., 7859
Pledge. *See* Vows and oaths
Pleiades
in Australian Indigenous religions, Seven Sisters story of, 643, 655
in Aztec religion, 8735
in Caribbean religions, 1429
in ethnoastronomy, 2865–2866
in Greek religion, 8735
in Inca religion, 1362, 8735
myths of, 8734–8735
overview of, 8734–8735
Taqui Onqoy ("the dance of the Pleiades"), 3815
Pleistocene. *See* Paleolithic Period
Pleistoros (deity), 3466–3467
Plenitudo fontalis (God concept), 1011, 1012
Pleroma, Gnostic concept of, 2966
Plessy v. Ferguson, 69
Plethon, George, 6475
Pliny the Elder
on Arimaspeans, 6165
on Christian persecution, 7058
on colossus of Rhodes, 8839
on comets, 8735
on dragons, 2346
on druids, 2492
Essenes described by, 2846
on folk remedies and magic, 3841
on Fortuna, 1527
on magic, 5573, 5575, 7914
on shooting stars, 8736
on Vestal Virgins, 3385
Ploix, Charles, on supreme beings, 8875
Plotinianism. *See* Neoplatonism
Plotinus, **7198–7199**
aesthetics of, 45
Ammonius as teacher of, 7198
on archetypes, 458
Aristotle and, 480, 7198
on ascent to divine knowledge, 5817
Augustine's study of, 625, 7199
on Demiurge, 2274
on dualism, 2510
on ecstasy and union, 2681
on eternity, 2854–2855
as founder of Neoplatonism, 7191, 7198, 7199
against Gnosticism, 7199
on the good, 3635, 7191, 7198
on heart, 3882
hypostases (first principles), doctrine of, 4240, 4242, 4243
influence of, 3005, 6475
on *falsafah,* 2971
on intellect, 7184, 7191, 7199
on intuition, 4525
on knowledge, 5203
life of, 7198
on *Logos,* 5501
metaphysics of, 5990
on mirrors, 6063
monistic philosophy of, 6144, 6146–6147
on mystical union, 6336
on mysticism, 6346
Nag Hammadi codices and, 6398
and Neoplatonism, 6474
Numenius influencing, 7189, 7198
on the One, 6146–6147, 6346
on Ibn Bājjah, 4263
Philo Judaeus influencing, 7106, 7198
Porphyry as pupil of, 7191, 7198
on reality, 7191
on soul, 7191, 7199
symbolism and, 8907
on transmigration, 9329
on triads, 9348
on unity, 6474
on World Soul, 6963, 7199
Plouton (deity), Hades identified with, 3725
Ploutos (Eleusinian cult figure), Plouton and, 3725
Plowmen, in winter carols, 9744
Pluralism, legal, Buddhism in, 5349
Pluralism, religious
anticult movements opposing, 395
and art, 502
in Buddhism, Stcherbatsky (Theodore) on, 8737
education and, 8765
globalization and, 3497
heresy and, 3929
Hocking (William Ernest) on, 4076
in Islam
modernist, 6097, 6099
progressive, 6099
in Jainism, 4768
legitimation and, 5397, 5398
in North American Christianity, 1714–1715
social reform and, 1751
in pantheism, 6961
rational-choice theory and, 8472
in Roman Catholicism, 7889, 7890
in Roman religion, 7918–7919
secularization and, 8218
Smart (Ninian) on, 8444
Smith (Wilfred Cantwell) on, 8451
in United States, paradox of, 4044
Plurality, in Indian philosophies, 4420–4421, 4422–4423
Plural marriage, in Mormonism, 6193, 6194
Plutarch, **7199–7202**
on afterlife, 7200, 8543
on *aion,* 207
Ammonius as teacher of, 7189
on animals, 7200
and apocalypse, 411
on ascension, 521
on Astarte, 34
on Buddhism, 1186
on Cato the Elder, 3841
on Celtic religion, women in, 3387
on Christianity, 7201
comparative theology of, 9128
on confession, 1887, 7566
on cosmopolitanism, 3906, 3907
on cruelty in mythology, 3909
on deity, 2253
on Delphi, 2266
on Demiurge, 7188–7189, 7200–7201
on demons, 2277, 7189, 7200
on Dionysos, women and, 3384
on dualism, 2514–2515, 7200
on Egyptian religion, 7201, 7202, 9576
on Eleusinian mysteries, 3671
eschatological myths of, 7200
ethics of, 7189
on fasting, 2996
on festivals, 7200
on geometry, 3442
on God, 7200–7201
on Greek religion, 7201
on Hera, 3914
on Hesiod, 3667
on homosexuality, 4113
on incense offering, 4419
influence of, 7201–7202
on intellect, 7200
on intelligence, 4363
on Isis, 3384, 3605
Isis and Osiris, 2514–2515, 2538, 3907, 4557, 7201, 7202
on Judaism, 7201
on knowledge, 5202
on leaven, 5388
life of, 7199–7200
on Lupercalia, 5531
on Mithra, 6089, 6331
on moon, 6174
on musical theory, 6304
on oracles, 3905–3906, 8383
on orgiastic feasts, 8247
on Pan, 6958
physics of, 7189
Platonism of, 7200–7201
on *pontifex,* 1051
Pythagoreanism influencing, 7189
on relics, 7687
Roman imperial cult criticized by, 7200
on Roman religion, 7201
on Rome, founding of, 1791
on sacrifice, 7200
ship symbolism of, 991, 992
on soul, 7200
on Stoicism, 3912
on superstition, 8864
on syncretism, 8926

Plutarch *continued*
on Thoth, 1761
on *Timaeus* (Plato), 7189, 7200
on transmigration, 9329
writings of, 7200–7201
Plymouth Colony. *See also* Pilgrims
Congregationalism and, 1938
Williams (Roger) in, 9739
PMIP. *See* Pan-Malayan Islamic Party
Pnei ʿOr (Faces of Light), 4869
Pneuma (breath or soul), 1042
Anaximenes on, 8542
in New Testament, 8562, 8563
sarx and, 9070, 9073
Pneumatocracy, Sohm (Rudolf) on, 8507
Pneumatomachians (Christian heretics), 798
Pō (darkness), 7313, 7314
Po (earthly aspect of soul), 1043
death and, 1589
ghosts and, 1605
yinyang and, 8554, 8555
Poʿalei Agudah, 196
Pobedonostsev, Konstantin, **7202–7203**
Skobtsova (Mother Maria) and, 8422
Pocomania
compared to related religions, 1437
history of study of, 75–76
Podolia, Jewish movements in, 5017
Poe, Edgar Allen, Swedenborgianism and, 8903
Poʿel Mizraḥi (Mizraḥi workers), 9981
Poemandres, 7190
Poemata (Beza), 851
Poem of Dawn and Sunset (Ras Shamra), 2442
Poem on the Dove King (Russian poem), 4453
Poenaru, Emil, 3467
Poetic Edda, 167, 3446
Poetic justice, in drama, appropriate use of, 5356
Poetics (Aristotle), 45, 5469, 5486
music in, 6304
Poetry, **7203–7227**. *See also* Epics; *specific poets*
African, in Ifa divination, 87
Aristotle on, 5160
in Bible, 7204
Herder (Johann Gottfried) on, 3919
Job, 4930–4931
Buddhist, 1111, 1199, 2629, 7207, 7211–7212, 7215–7216
of Klong chen Rab ʾbyams pa (Longchenpa), 5193
of Nāgārjuna, 6393
in Zen monasteries, 9947
calligraphy and, 1369, 1371, 1373
Canaanite, 1384, 1386
cats in, 1463
chanting of, 1536, 7204
characteristics of, 7204
Chinese, **7212–7214**
Buddhist, 7207, 7212–7214
Confucian, 7212–7214
contemporary, 7214
Daoist, 7207, 7212–7214
Japanese poetry influenced by, 7215, 7216
shamanistic, 7213
Christian, 5471, **7218–7221**
in 17th century, 7220–7221
hymns, 7207, 7218
medieval, 7218–7219
metaphysical, 7220–7221
origins of, 7208, 7218
Renaissance, 7219–7220
of Symeon the New Theologian, 8920
vernacular, 7218
Confucian, 7212–7214
and creative dissonance, 7204
Daoist, 7207, 7212–7214
devotion in, 2319
eddic (*See* Eddas)
erotic, Bengali, 829
Finnish, Haavio (Martti) and, 3723
folk, 3162
genres of, 7204
Germanic (*See also* Sturm und Drang movement)
in funeral rites, 168
mead of inspiration for, 3455, 5509
sources of, 3446
Greek
historiography and, 4035–4036
Muses and, 6242
transmission of religion through, 3660, 3678
Herder (Johann Gottfried) and, **3918–3920**
heroic, 9679–9680
Hindu, 7205, 7209–7211
bhakti poetry to Śiva, 8417
erotic devotional poetry to Kṛṣṇa, 4005
Kṛṣṇa in, 5250, 5252, 5253
māyā in, 5795
of Māṇikkavācakar, 5670–5671
of Sūrdās, 8881–8882
Rādhā in, 7593
Indian, **7209–7212**
bhakti, 7207, 7208, 7209, 7210, 7211
bhakti genre of, 3984–3987
Buddhist, 1111, 7211–7212
in *Ādi Granth,* 32–33
Islamic, 7223
Jain, 7212
mystical, 7208
of Āḻvārs, **279–280**
rural traditions of, 4434
saint-singer traditions and, 4005
Sakya Paṇḍita on, 8052
Sanskrit, 7209
Sikh, 7211
Tamil, 857, 7207, 7210, 8974–8975, 8976, 8977
vernacular, 7209–7211
inspiration and, 4509–4510
Islamic, **7221–7224**
Andalusian, 4597, 7222
Arabic, 7221–7222
Egyptian, 7222
gardens in, 3283
gināns, **3494**
in honor of Muḥammad, 7222, 7223–7224
Persian, 7222–7223
Qurʾān as inspiration for, 7205
Qurʾān on, 6735
Shīʿī, 4712, 7207, 7222
Ṣūfī, 4261, 4570, 4644, 7207–7208, 7222–7223, 9012
vernacular, 7223
Jain, 7212
Japanese, 1371, 7207, **7214–7217** (*See also* Manʾyōshū)
Buddhist, 7215–7216
haiku, 8702
influences on, 7215, 7216
of Kamo no Mabuchi, 5074–5075
magico-religious power of, 7214–7215
prestige of, 7214
recitative, 7215
ritual functions of, 7215
Shintō, 7215, 7216
Jewish, 5471, 7207, 7208
of ha-Levi, 4891, 9877–9878
in *Hosea,* 4138
of ibn Gabirol, 4890
midrash and, 6020, 6021
in rabbinic liturgy, 4978
Zion in, 9977–9978
Kakawin, in Southeast Asia, 4010
kings in, 5160
in Latvian folk songs, 8134
in laws, 5328
medium of, 7204
modernist, 7206
and music, 7204, 7207
mystic, of Yunus Emre, 9917
Native American, **7224–7227**
in 19th century, 7224–7225
Christianity and, 7225, 7226
contemporary, 7225
Greek mythological elements in, 7225
oral tradition in, 7224, 7225
remembering traditions in, 7225–7226
translation of, 7224
Óðinn and, 6809
oral tradition of, 6843
of Orpheus, 6892–6893
as performance, 7203–7204
Persian
Ḥāfiẓ Shīrāzī, role of, **3733–3735**
of ʿAṭṭār, Farīd al-Dīn, **600–603**
of Nāṣir-i Khusraw, 6417
of Saʿdi, **8022–8023**
Plato on, 45, 7205
postmodern, 5483–5484
of protest, 7205
and religion, **7203–7209**
chanting, 7204
devotion, 7207–7208
mysticism, 7207–7208
prophecy, 7204–7207
revelation, 7204–7207
and society, 7208
religion and, Wach (Joachim) on, 9652
Roman, music and, 6304
Roman Catholic, of Gregory of Nazianzus, 3695–3696
Russian, of Skobtsova (Mother Maria), 8423
shamanistic euphoria as source of, 8274
Sikh, of Gobind Singh, 8395
Southeast Asian, in song form, 6288
Ṣūfī
mystical union in, 6338, 6352
by ʿAṭṭār, Farīd al-Dīn, **600–603**
of Khusraw (Amīr), 5138–5139
of Rābiʿah al-ʿAdawīyah, 7591
Tamil, 6240, 10088
Vālmīki as inventor of, 9518
vernacular
Christian, 7218
Indian, 7209–7211
Islamic, 4663–4664, 7223
Welsh, 1480
Arthur in, 508–509
Merlin in, 5878
Poetry of Baruch, The: A Reconstruction and Analysis of the Original Hebrew Text of Baruch 3:9-5:9 (Burke), 899
Pogroms, 4984–4985
Pohlenz, Max, on Stoicism, 8742
Pohnpei (Micronesia)
grand rituals in, 6006–6007
myths of, 6009
charter, 6002–6003
creation, 6004
Poiesis (aesthetic making), 44–45
Poimandres. See Corpus Hermeticum
Poimen (The Shepherd of Hermas), 3052
Poincaré, Jules-Henri, 1541
Pointing Southward Palace (Taiwan), 9058

Point Loma Theosophical Community, 6546, **7227–7230**
dedication ceremony at, 7229
education at, 7229, 9206
location of, 7227, 7228–7229, 9206
origins of, 7228, 9205–9206
Point of View for My Work as an Author, The (Kierkegaard), 5141
Poirier, Sylvie, 2487
Poison
in Afro-Caribbean religion, 3823
ordeal by, 6848–6849
from plants, 9575
witchcraft revealed by, 9777
Pokaiṇi phenomenon, 766
Poladi, Hassan, 3162
Polā festival, in Marathi religions, 5698
Poland and Polish religions. *See also* Slavic religion
Agudat Yisra'el in, 195
Christianity
history of, 1684, 1685, 1686
Orthodox–Catholic union in, 2114–2115
Protestantism, 1685
Uniatism and conquest of Moscow, 1685
Unitarianism in, 9468–9469
concentration camps in, 4086
films from, 3099
Islam, 4679
Judaism, 5015
communal autonomy of, 5015
Frankist movement in, 3786
Isserles (Mosheh) and, 4750–4751
in middle ages, 5014
Orthodox Judaism in, 6902
post-World War I, 5021–5022
Shabbateanism in, 3186–3187
Tamudic study in, 5015–5016
tsaddiq in, 9380, 9381
yeshivot of, 9884
Kagan (Yisra'el Me'ir) in, 5053
Karaite sect in, 5084
Kotler (Aharon) in, 5239
new religious movements in, 6568
oplatek (bread) in, 2400
partition of, 1686
study of religion in, 8772–8773, 8774–8775
Polanyi, Michael
hierarchical epistemology of, science and religion and, 2658
on knowledge, 5210
Polar bear, 808, 4527
Polarities. *See* Binary oppositions; Duality
Polarvölker, Die (Byhan), 473
Polelesi of Igurue village, cargo cults and, 1415
Polemics, **7230–7244**
vs. apologetics, 429
Christian-Muslim, **7242–7244**
on Bible, 7242
medieval, 7242–7243
modern, 7244
on Muḥammad, 7242, 7243–7244
on Qur'ān, 7242, 7243–7244
on Trinity, 7242
deity in, 2253
of Jerome, 4833
Jewish-Christian, **7230–7236**
in early Christianity, 7230–7231
economic aspects of, 7234
on Hebrew scriptures, 7231–7233
Jesus in, 4846
on Jewish exile, 7234
major works of, 7231, 7234
medieval, 7234
on New Testament, 7233–7234
on Reformation, 7234–7235
on Talmud, 7233
misconceptions of image in, 9624
Muslim-Jewish, **7236–7242**
decline of, 7241
on Hebrew scriptures, 7237–7240
on Jewish law, 7238, 7239
on Muḥammad, 7241
Poles. *See* Pillars
Polgar, Yitshaq, 7234
Poli'ahu (deity), 7314
Polis (city-state), 3665–3667
consecration of, *hieros gamos* (sacred marriage) and, 3976
historiography and, 4027
kingship in, 5166–5167
Plato on, as public sphere, 4107
Polish Brethren, Sozzini (Fausto Pavolo) and, 8673, 8674
Polish Laboratory Theater, 2476
Polish Orthodox Church, in Orthodox structure, 2589
Political activism, in engaged Buddhism, 2785
Political economy. *See also* Economics
of colonialism, 1854
Political Evensong, Sölle (Dorothee) and, 8512
Political ideologies
of Eliade, 2758–2760
nature religions and, 2663
Political legitimacy, in Confucianism. *See also* Mandate of Heaven
imperial cults and, 1914
Political movements
Christian social movements and, 1753–1755
heresy, and religio-political movements, 3923
in Islam, imitation of Muḥammad and, 6227
prophets inspiring, 87
Political philosophy. *See also* Kingship
Cārvāka, 1446
in China (*See also* Confucianism)
of Confucius, 1571
Han dynasty, 1590
Qin dynasty, 1574, 1590
in Christianity, of Hooker (Richard), 4124
in Korea, Confucianism and, 1930
might, rule of, Han Fei Zi on, 3773
Political theology. *See also* Liberation theology
Christian, **7244–7247,** 9140
African, 1723
American, 7246
Canadian, 7246
conscience and, 1941
European, 7245, 7246
Latin American, 7246
European, liberation theology and, 5440
Hobbes (Thomas) on, 4075
Islamic, al-Fārābī's, 2973, 2975
Kublai Khan and concept of Buddhist world state, 1645
of Savonarola (Girolamo), 8139–8140
Political theory, *ummah* in, 9447–9448
Politics, **7248–7304**. *See also* Church and state; Civil religion; Kings and kingship; Liberation theology
and African religions, **7290–7295**
in colonial era, 7291–7292
democratization in, 7293
modernization and, 7292–7295
new movements in, 105–106
social dynamics in, 7291
Aristotle on, 486, 7109
in Australia and New Zealand, 1734
awareness of link between religion and, 3230
in Axial Age, 7727
and Buddhism, 1140–1142, 7253, **7260–7266**
Burmese Buddhism, 9479
colonial, 7263
defining, 7260–7261
historical development of, 7261–7263
in Mahāyāna Buddhism, 7260, 7262
in *saṃgha,* 8077–8079
in Theravāda Buddhism, 9152–9153
in Vajrayāna Buddhism, 7254
modern, 7264–7265
in monasticism, 6128–6129
postcolonial, 7263–7264
in Burma, Buddhism in, 9479
Capps's study of religion and, 1413
cargo cults and, 1419
ceremony and political power, 1513–1516
charismatic leadership, 1544–1545
in China, **7266–7270** (*See also* Confucianism)
bureaucracy in, 7267–7268
court attire, religious symbolism on, 1830
immortality quests in, 7267
imperial cults, 7266–7267
modern, 7268–7269
portents and political power, 1592
rebellions in, 7267–7268
religious advisors in, 7268
religious suppression in, 7255, 7267–7268
state sponsorship of religion, 7268
and Christianity, **7279–7284**
in colonial era, 7282
in early Christianity, 7279–7280
in Enlightenment, 7282–7283
medieval, 7254, 7280
modern, 7283
in Pentecostalism, 6580
in Protestantism, 7453
in Reformation, 7280–7281
colonial (*See* Colonialism; Postcolonialism)
cosmopolitanism, in Hellenism and Stoicism, 3906–3907
Eblaite, religion and, 2597, 2598
the Enlightenment and, 2795
faith and, Niebuhr (Reinhold) on, 6613
fundamentalism and political ideology, 1517

- Politics ***continued***
  - Gandhi on, 5399
  - globalization of, 3498
  - Haitian Vodou and, 1434
  - human rights and, 4178–4179
  - in India
    - Āyurveda and, 3856
    - "Hinduness" *(Hindutva),* 1858
    - untouchables in, 9477
  - and Islam, **7284–7290** (*See also* Caliphate; Fundamentalism, Islamic; Imamate)
    - ʿAbd al-Rāzīq (ʿAlī) on, 5
    - as source of *kalām,* 5061
    - in colonial era, 7286
    - democracy debate, 7290
    - in early Islam, 7284–7285
    - in Europe, 4680
    - Ibn Rushd and, 4272
    - North African, 4590–4591
    - Rashīd Riḍā (Muḥammad) on, 7621
    - religio-political synthesis, 7253–7254, 7287
    - *sharīʿah* and, 4692, 4703
    - in Southeast Asia, 4668–4670
    - studies on, 4720, 4723
    - *ʿulamāʾ* in, 9440
  - in Israelite religion
    - Levites and, 5426
    - sacralization of, 4973
  - in Japan, **7270–7275**
    - Confucianism and, 1927, 4782, 4789, 4797
    - formative period of, 7271–7272
    - Jōdo Shinshū in, 4936
    - Kang Yuwei in, 5075–5076
    - middle period of, 7272–7273
    - modern period of, 7273–7275
    - religious groups in, 4792
    - Sōka Gakkai and, 8509
    - under Tokugawa regime, 4788
  - and Judaism, **10060–10064**
    - Abravanel (Isaac) on, 18
    - in Jewish Renewal, 4871–4872
    - in Orthodox Judaism, 6902
    - secularizing conceptions of, 10061–10063
    - theocratic conceptions of, 10061–10063
  - of martyrdom, 5738–5739
  - and Mediterranean religions, **7275–7279**
    - in Egypt, 7277
    - functions of, 7276
    - in Greece, 7275, 7277–7278
    - in Mesopotamia, 7276–7277
    - priests in, 7275, 7276
    - in Rome, 7255, 7278–7279
    - scholars on, 7276
  - in Micronesian myths, 6012
  - in mysticism, 6358
  - and Native American religions, **7299–7304**
    - in colonial era, 7301–7302
    - contemporary, 7303–7304
    - in protest era, 7302–7303
    - in reform era, 7302
    - in reservation era, 7302
    - tribal traditions of, 7299–7301
  - "natural" religious communities and, 1865
  - and Oceanic religions, **7295–7299**
    - in colonial era, 7296–7297
    - contemporary, 7297–7298, 9324–9325
    - missionary impact on, 6792
    - political functions of indigenous religions, 7295–7296
  - papacy, conflicts with, 1690
  - power in, myth and, 6361
  - priesthood in, 7397–7398
  - progressive, Spiritualism associated with, 8715
  - Rastafari, 7623, 7624, 7625
  - Reformation and, 7656–7657, 7664
  - Reiyūkai Kyōdan involvement in, 7862
  - and religion, **7248–7260,** 7790, 7791
    - authority in, 7249
    - colonialism and, 7248, 7282, 7286, 7291–7292, 7296–7297, 7301–7302
    - Durkheim (Émile) on, 7251
    - Eliade (Mircea) on, 7251–7252
    - Enlightenment and, 7248, 7249–7250, 7282–7283
    - feminist critique of, 7252
    - Foucault (Michel) on, 7252–7253
    - Marx (Karl) on, 7250–7251
    - patterns of relations between, 7253–7258
    - Reformation and, 7248, 7280–7281
    - secularism and, 7283–7284
    - Taubes (Jakob) on, 9021
    - Weber (Max) on, 7251
  - religious broadcasting's influence on, 7714–7715
  - rituals and, 7839–7840
  - schism and political differences, 8152–8153
  - secret societies and, 8211–8212
  - secularization and, 8217
  - in South Asia, religious studies, impact on, 8791–8792
  - in Southeast Asia, scholarly agendas and, 8638–8639
  - study of religion and, 10079
  - in United States
    - evangelicals in, 2891
    - fundamentalists in, 2892
    - Pentecostals in, 7032
    - public Christianity and, 1715
  - and violence, 7249, 7251, 7257
  - *vs. maṇḍalas,* structures of, 5645
  - in *Wissenschaft des Judentums,* 4877–4878
- *Politics* (Aristotle), 486
  - chance in, 1526
  - Hobbes (Thomas) and, 4074
  - Ibn Rushd's commentary on, 4272
- *Politics of God, The* (Washington), 964
- *Politics of Ritual in an Aboriginal Settlement, The* (Dussart), 644
- *Politics of the Secret* (Anderson), 689
- *Politicus* (Plato), 4456, 6984
- *Politische Theologie des Paulus, Die* (Taubes), 9021
- Polity (church government form)
  - in Buddhism, *saṃgha* and, 8077–8079
  - in Christianity (*See* Church polity)
- Polka, at *veglia,* 2148
- Pollard, Alton, 80
- Pollen, in Apache religion, 405, 10070, 10071
- Pollera, Alberto, 115
- Pollock, Frederick, on retribution, 5373
- Pollock, Jackson, 500
- Pollock, Sheldon, on Sanskrit use in Cambodia, 5128
- Pollution. *See also* Purification; Purity
  - ablutions for, 10–12
  - bodily functions and, 7504–7505
  - in Buddhism
    - sexual activity and, 7084
    - in Tibetan Buddhism, 7503
  - childbirth and, 2405, 2407, 4732, 7504, 7505, 7511
  - cultural diversity of, 7504
  - death and, 2405, 2408, 7505, 7506, 7511, 7513
  - definition of, 11
  - drums and, 2494
  - food and, 7504–7505 (*See also* Dietary laws)
  - in Greek religion, 3677–3678, 7506
  - in Hinduism, 2404, 2405
    - castes and, 7506
  - of homes, 4105
  - idolatry and, 7513
  - and illness, 7505
  - incest and, 7506
  - of Indian rivers, 2622
  - in Israelite religion, 7511–7513
  - Jainism and, call for action against, 2626
  - Japanese measures against, 2638
  - in Japanese religions, and women, 3348
  - loss of virginity and, 7506
  - in Melanesian religions, women and, 5836
  - menstruation and, 5866, 7504, 7505, 7511
    - contamination from, 7505
    - in Hinduism, 2405
    - in Israelite religion, 4732
    - in Judaism, 7511, 7512, 7514–7515, 10052
  - murder and, 7506, 7513
  - semen and, 7397, 7504
  - sexual activity and, 7505–7506, 7512
    - in African religions, 4486
    - in Buddhism, 7084
    - and celibacy, 7397
    - in Hinduism, 2405
    - in Israelite religion, 4732
  - spiritual, 7506–7507
  - tears and, 9024
  - in Zoroastrianism, 9997–9998
- Pollux (deity), 7902
- Polo, Marco
  - on Buddhism, 1311
  - in China, 1166
  - Manichaeism and, 5670
  - on Mari and Mordvins, 5709
  - on monsters, 6165
  - on Pasai sultanate, 4659
- Polo de Ondegardo, Juan de
  - chronicle of, 1361–1362
  - on temples, 8608
- Poltergeists, definition of, 3475
- Polyaenos (historian), 9170
- Polyandry
  - definition of, 5725
  - in Tibet, 5725
- Polybius, cyclical philosophy of history of, 4027
- Polycarp
  - anti-docetic views of, 2381
  - epistle of, 920
  - on "gospel," 3641
  - Irenaeus studying under, 4538
  - martyrdom of, 7059
  - on *1 Peter,* 917
- *Polycratius* (John of Salisbury), magic in, 5577
- Polydaemonism, 7316
- Polygamy
  - definition of, 5725
  - in Islam
    - ʿAbduh (Muḥammad) on, 4700, 7567
    - acceptance of, 7082
    - in Central Asia, 4625
    - *faqīh* supporting, 4700
    - Qurʾān on, 4564, 4573, 4707

slave traditions of, 4683
in Mormonism, 6193, 6194, 6534, 6558
Polygyny
conflict between wives in, 5725
Darwinism and, 8478
definition of, 5725
in Israelite religion, 4733
in Judaism
ban on, 3749–3750
Gershom ben Yehudah against, 3352, 3461
in Karaite Judaism, 5087
in rabbinic Judaism, 1559, 3352
in new religious movements, 6514, 6516
in Zoroastrianism, 3374, 10000
Polymorphic deities, in Celtic religion, 1482
Polynesia and Polynesian religions, **7304–7315**. *See also* Oceania and Oceanic religions; Solomon Islands religions; Tikopia religion
ancestors in, 7306, 8980
animals in, 7307
atuas in, **622–623,** 7306, 9195
birds in, 948
birth in, 7311
boat burials in, 991
cannibalism in, 1403–1404
chiefs in, 7296, 7307, 7309
Christianity
conversion to, 7305, 9195
effects of, 8980–8981
and politics, 7297
traditional culture merged with, 9324
Christian missions in, and music, 6264
colonization of, 6784
cosmogonies in, 6786
cosmologies in, 2004–2007, 7305–7306
dance in, 6264
death in, 7311
association with food, 3169
deities of, 7306–7307 (*See also specific deities*)
in creation myths, 7312–7314
dismissing, 7309–7311
gaining favor of, 7309
human contact with, 6263–6264
inviting, 7308–7309
parentage of, 8980
in physical world, 7305, 7306, 7307, 7308–7309
process of creation of, 8980
descent into the underworld in, 2298
diversity in, 2004
dreams in, 7306
drums in, 2500
Firth (Raymond) and, 3121–3122
food in, 7308, 7310
gender in, **3395–3400**
genealogy in, 3425
Hawaiian religion and, 3796
iconography in, 7309
incantation in, 7309, 7311
incarnation in, 4414
knot symbolism in, 5198
magic in, 5566–5567
mahu gender reversal in, 4116
mana in, **5631–5633,** 7307–7308, 8947
Māui in, 3018, **5782–5783**
megalithic religion, 5828
vs. Melanesia, 5832
millenarianism in, 6034
music in, 6263–6264
mythic themes, **7312–7315**
creation myths, 7305–7306, 7312–7314
origin of islands and people, 7314–7415
New Year ceremonies in, 6592
noa in, 7310, 7311
as Oceanic cultural area, 6784
ocean in, 6807
omens in, 7306–7307
pō in, 7313, 7314
priesthood in, 6263, 7305, 7306–7307, 7309
rainbow symbolism in, 7604
rituals in, 7308–7311
sacrifice in, 7309
soul in, 7311, 9195
spirit possession in, 7307
tapu in (*See Tapu*)
tattooing in, 7808
transculturation of, 9320–9325
transmigration in, 9327
trees in, 9335
trickster in (*See* Maui)
witchcraft in, 7308
women in, **3395–3400**
menstrual blood of, 7311
and release from *tapu,* 7310–7311
Polyonomous deities, history of religions approach on, 4065
Polyphony
in Christianity, 6309–6311
in Judaism, 6310
origins of, 6309
Polyrhythms, 2496
Polytheism, **7315–7319**
of African religions, 85, 86
analytical psychology of, 7485
as atheism, 577
Brelich (Angelo) on, 1047
characteristics of, 7316–7319
of Chinese religion, 7317–7318
in Christianity, saints and, 2228
decline of, 7318
deity in, 2258
and diffusion *vs.* parallelism, 4063
dualism in, 2505, 2507
etymology of term, 7315–7316
gods in
accessibility of, 7317
good and bad, 7318
history of, 7317
human becoming, 7318
immortality of, 7317
personality of, 7317, 7318
power of, 7318
specialization among, 7317
in Greek religion, 7317
in Hellenistic religions, equation of gods in, 3907–3909
henotheism and, 3913
historiography of, medieval, 4038
history of religions approach on, 4065–4066
in Indian religions, Vedic pantheon, 3990–3991
Islamic view of (*See Shirk*)
in Israelite religion, 3539–3541
in Japanese religions, *kami* as misinterpretation of, 5072
vs. monotheism, 6158
nature of divine in, 128–129
origins of, 7316, 7318
of Orphism, 6894
Pettazzoni (Raffaele) on, 7074–7075
vs. positivism, 7339
in Roman religion, 7317, 7318
in Tlaxcalan religion, 9214–9215
universalism in, 1482–1483
in Zoroastrianism, rejection of, 2128
Polythetic model of religion, cultural analysis and, 8471
Polyvalent deities, in Celtic religion, 1482–1483
Polzin, Robert, 742
Poma, Huaman, 3240
Pomaks (Muslims), 4674, 4677, 4678
Pomapoma (trickster), 664
Pomare II (Tahitian chief), 9322
Pomerium (demarcation line), in Rome, 7897
Pomeroy, Sarah B., methodology of, 3381
Pŏmnang (Buddhist monk), 1172
Pomo de Ayala, Felipe, on Inca calendar, 1361
Pomo Indians
calendar, 1353
fiction about, 3092–3093
knot symbolism of, 5198
Pomona (deity), priest of, 3126
Pomo religion (North America)
bears in, 808–809
dreams in, 2488
weaving in, 939
Pŏmp'ae (chant), 6297–6298
Pompa imaginum (funerary procession), 7903
Pompallier, Jean Baptiste, missions to New Zealand, 1732
Pompeii (Italy), religion in, 7894
Pomponazzi, Pietro
on Aristotle, 4273
on demons, 2280
Ponca tribe (North America)
ballgame played by, 752
healing in, 7300
Ponce, Pedro, 5940
Ponder, Catherine, 6585
Pong Banggai di Rante (deity), 9241
Pong Lalondong (deity), 9241, 9242
Pong Tulak Padang (deity), 9241
Poniatowski, Zgymunt, and study of religion in Poland, 8774
Ponikan (evil ones), in Cuna creation myth, 2095–2096
Poṅkal (rite), 2405
Pontiac (Ottawa chief), 6665
and Neolin, 6458, 6666
Pontian (pope), in exile, 7059
Pontifex, 1051, **7319–7320**
authority of, 7319
etymology of term, 1051, 7319
importance of, 7319
responsibilities of, 7319
Pontifex maximus, 1051, 7907
Augustus as, 7319, 7913
Caesar as, 7278, 7319, 7912
Gratian and, 7922
as head of Roman religion, 7319
Po'okanaka (type of *heiau*), function of, 3797
Poole, Elijah. *See* Elijah Muhammad
Poole, Fitz John Porter, on restrained comparison, 1880
Poole, Stafford, 5922
Poor Clares, 3182, 3183, 3184
Poor Folk (Dostoevsky), 2421
Poor people
almsgiving to, **266–269**
Baltic ancestors' food given to, 331
Jeremiah and, 4827
John the Baptist and, 4942
liberation theology and, 5439
tombs of, 9226, 9227
Poor tax. *See Zakāt*
Pope (bishop of Rome). *See also* Papacy; *specific popes*
as Antichrist, 395, 9772
authority of, 694–695
in Byzantine church, 2585–2586, 2587
in church polity, 7886, 7887

authority of *continued*
vs. secular authority, 696–697
becoming pope, 1662, 1763, 6966
changing first names, 6967
Damasus I on, 6966
in early Christian structure, 2581
increasing power of, 6965–6966
infallibility of
Döllinger (Johann) on, 2396
Vatican I on, 2396, 6974, 7180, 9528–9532
Jesuits under, 4842
list of, *6968–6970*
monepiscopacy of, 6966
most popular names of, 6967
Peter as, 7875
in ultramontanism, 9442
Popé (Indian medicine man), 3474, 6729
Pueblo Revolt led by, 6422
Pope, Alexander
as Freemason, 3195
on Golden Age, 3627
on Newton, 6588
on *Pilgrim's Progress* (Bunyan), 1323
Pope, G. U., 8978
Popenoe, Paul, 2881
Popol Vuh, The (Maya community book), 5797
afterlife in, 150
ballgames in, 751
ceremonial use of, 5933
creation myth in, 3130, 5797, 5933, 5935
divine duality in, 5883
iconography of, 4312
Maya calendar and, 1358
monkeys in, 6150
rediscovery of, 5797
second humanity in, 3132
sky in, 8428
sun in, 5935
tribal deities in, 9224
Popov, A. A., 475
on shaman initiation, 8271
Pŏpsŏng-chong school of Buddhism (Korea), 1171
Pŏpsŏng school of Buddhism (Korea), 9796–9797
Popular culture, **7320–7324**. *See also* Film
in 19th century, 7320–7321, 7322
art of, 7321, 7322, 7323
Brazilian, Afro-Brazilian religions and, 124–125
criticism of, 7321
in Europe, 7321, 7322
in Latin America, 7321, 7322
in United States, 7321, 7322
elements of, 7320
vs. folk culture, 7320
fundamentalism and, 2887, 2889
of joking, in Carnival, 1440
vs. mass culture, 7320
motivation of, 7321–7322
Rastafari connections to, 7622–7623, 7625
and religion, 7322–7324
rituals and, 7858–7859
use of term, 7320
in visual culture, 9620
as working-class culture, 7320–7321
Popular Culture in Early Modern Europe (Burke), 2144
Popular dance, **2143–2152**
definitions of, 2144–2146
Popular (folk) religion, **7324–7333**. *See also* Folk religion
anthropologists on, 7325, 7326
Canaanite, 1387–1388
Chinese, 1605–1606, **1613–1621**
concept of "religion" and, 1580–1581, 1614
Daoism's connection to, 3342
gender in, 3339–3340
historical constructions, 1614–1615
imperial ancestor cult and, 1912–1913
liturgy and ritual, 1619–1620
music in, 6292
in postimperial era, 1610, 1611
in Qing dynasty, 1609
religious specialists, 1617–1618
scholarship and historiography, 1620–1621
social structures, 1615–1617
soul in, 8556
state, relations with, 1618
temples, 1617
theology, 1618–1619
trickster fox in, 8303
Christianity and
campaign against superstition and, 8865–8866
humor in popular theology, 4203
as civil religion, 7327
created by elite level of society, 7328
Egyptian, healers, spiritist, 3836
esoteric beliefs in, 7327
in Europe, magical practices in, 8865–8866
forms of, 7325–7326
global structures of, 7330
Hindu, 4006–4007
in Islam
Shiism, popular practices in, 8345
in Sufism, 8822, 8824–8825
in Japan, **4794–4800**
institutionalization of, 4799–4800
Shotoku Taishi (prince), veneration of, 8375–8376
as mass religion, 7328
meanings and dimensions of, 7326–7328
Middle Eastern, hand of Faṭimah amulet in, 3837
as minority religion, 7327–7328
nature of culture and, 7328–7329
in Oceania, folk Christianity in, 1739
oral tradition in, 7325, 7326
outlaw figure in, 7330
prophetic figure in, 7330
social change and, 7329–7330
studies of, 7324–7326
the supernatural in, 8861
in Tibet, 9184–9186, 9191
Turkic religions as, 9400–9401, 9402
in Vietnam, 9591, 9593
in women's studies, 9790
Populorum progressio (Paul VI), 7012
Pordage, John, on androgyny, 8523
Pore (deity), in Yanoama religion, 8577
Porete, Marguerite, 3359
on mystical union, 6337
Pork. *See* Pigs
Poro society (Sierra Leone), 88, 4302, 4303
as secret society, 8213
Porphyry
on apostasy, 432
Iamblichus as pupil of, 7191
on images, 4352
metaphysics of, 5990
on Mithraism, 6091, 6092
as Plotinus's pupil, 7191, 7198
and problem of universals, 6644
on Pythagoras, 6050
and theurgy, 9157
on Thracian religion, 9169
on transmigration, 9329
on unity, 6474
writings of, 7191
on Zalmoxis, 9926, 9928
Portals, **7333–7335**
famous examples of, 7333
functions of, 7333–7334
motifs of, 7334
in pilgrimage, 7333
rites of, 7334
rudimentary forms of, 7333
symbolism of, 7333, 7334
Portents, **7335–7338**. *See also* Auspices; Divination; Haruspices; Omens
celestial, 7336–7337
in Chinese religion
political, 1592
qi and, 1575
comets and meteorites as, 8735–8736
in Etruscan religion, 7336–7337
etymology of term, 7335
in Greek religion, 7335–7336
vs. prodigies, 7337
in Roman religion, 2377, 7335–7336
Porter, Hal, 3084
Porterfield, Kay, 6426
Porthan, Henrik Gabriel, 3111
Portraiture, vol. 10 color insert
human body and, 4171
Portugal and Portuguese religion, study of religion in, 10081
Portugal and Portuguese religions
colonialism
in Africa, 1510, 1717–1718, 4607
and Inquisition, 4503–4506
in Latin America, 1695
in Southeast Asia, 4660, 4661, 4662, 4664
Entrudo (Carnival), 1442–1443
Ethiopia aided by, 2860
explorers from
on African religions, 112, 5220
in Japan, 9310
feitiços in, 3043
Iberian religion in (*See* Iberian religion)
Inquisition in (*See* Portuguese Inquisition)
Islam, 4679
Marranos in, 5716–5722
missionaries from
in Africa, 1717–1718
on African religions, 112
in Japan, 4787–4788
in Latin America, 1695
monopoly of, 6083–6084
Neolithic religion in, 6465
poetry in, 7219
saints in, healing and, 3812
Portuguese Inquisition
influence of, 4502
Marranos in, 5717, 5720–5722
in the New World, 4503–4506
origins of, 4501
purpose of, 4498
victims of, 4498, 4501, 4502
Portunus (deity), priest of, 3126
Posadha (confessional ceremony), in *saṃghas,* 8072
Poseidon (deity), **7338–7339**
Athena and, 587
functions of, 3680, 7338–7339, 9952
iconography of, 4321, 4322
Minos and, 5273–5274
in Mycenaean religion, 42
as ocean deity, 6805, 9701–9702
as stallion, 4133, 8301
Posey, Alexander, 7224, 7225

Pośhayank'ya, in Zuni creation myth, 2556
Posidonius (Stoic philosopher)
anti-Semitism of, 8743
Celtic ethnography, 1479, 1481
on Celtic religion
head cult, 3807
women in, 3387–3388
on contemplation of heavenly bodies, 8742
on druids, 2492
on evil, 8742
on fate, 8742
on Geto-Dacian religion, 3466
on *hypostasis,* 4240
on Iberian religion, 4253
on reality, 8741
Stoicism and, 8740–8741
Position of Women in Hindu Civilisation, The (Altekar), 3321
Positive eugenics, 2879
Positive-historical approach, historiography and, 4059
Positive-historical Judaism, 1957–1958. *See also* Conservative Judaism
Positive law, 5367, 5368, 5369
Positive philosophy, 47
Positive theology, 9139
Positivism, 2780, **7339–7341**
Brelich (Angelo) and, 4046
Comte as founder of, 1882, 7339–7341
consciousness, view of, 1946
definition of, 7339
impulse of, 7341
Leach (Edmund) on, 5382
legal, 5326, 5330
logical positivism and, 5498
materialism and, 5775
predecessors of, 7340
on religion, 7115–7116
religion and, 7341
Renan (Ernest) and, 7750–7751
as response to Kant (Immanuel), 7115
science and sociology and, 7340
scientific progress and, 7340
sociology and, 8480
and three-state law of human knowledge, 7339–7340
Posner, Richard, on law and literature, 5356, 5357
Posse, Abel, 3063
Possessed, The (Dostoevsky), 2422, 7943
Possession. *See* Spirit possession
Possession at Loudon (Certeau), 2930
Possession divination, 2370–2371
Possessions (ownership)
in Jainism, 2624
in Russian monasticism, 4957
Possidius, Augustine's biography by, 628–629
Post, R. R., 9159
Postaža, Lilita, 766
Postcolonialism, **1853–1860**. *See also* Colonialism
conversion, postcolonial theory of, 1971
feminist theory paralleling, 3303–3304
in gender studies, 3314–3315
Hinduism and, 3321–3322
historiography in age of, 4047–4051
and history of religions, 10042–10043
indigeneity and hybridity in, 1858–1859
in Japanese study of religion, 8778
Kenyan school ceremonies and national identity, 1515
prospects for academic study of religion, 1857–1859
Southeast Asia and, political agendas of scholarship on, 8638–8639
subaltern studies and, 8801
in women's studies, 9792
Postfeminism, 3024, 3298
Post-halakhic Judaism, 4871
Postman, Neil, 7321
Postmodern Bible, 5488–5489
Postmodern dance, 2161
Postmodernism
French influence on, 4049
Geertz (Clifford) and, 8501
Gnosticism and, 3526–3527
in Japan, 8778
Jewish, 9238
in Jewish studies, 4885
Jung and, 5032
literature of, 5482–5484
characteristics of, 5482–5483
critical theory of, 5487–5489
fragmentary in, 5482
God in, 5483–5484
objectivity challenged by, 1879
in progressive Islam, 6098
rejection of tradition in, 9273–9274
religion and modernity and, 5032
subaltern studies and, 8801
time in, 7993
and tradition, 9279–9280
women's studies and, 9792
Poststructuralism
cargo cults, analysis of, 1421, 1423–1424
on politics and religion, 7252–7253
postcolonial studies and, 1858
Reformation violence and, 1808
society-religion relations in, 8470–8471
in South American Indian religions research, 8596–8597
structuralism and, 8752, 8754
Post-Tantra meditation, 1288–1289
Postures and gestures, **7341–7345**. *See also* Dance; Hands; See also Mudrās; Touching
of animals, 7341
in art, 4170, 4171
Benedictio Latina (votive gesture), in cult of Sabazios, 7954
body symbolism and, 4161
of Buddha, 4171
cheironomy (melodic movement), 1533
in Christianity, 7342, 7343, 7344
in Eastern Orthodox Christianity, 7342, 7343
in Theravāda Buddhism, prostration in, 8061
in Islam, 7341–7342, 7343
during *ḥājj,* 7158, 7343, 7344
folk practices, 7343–7344
during funeral, 7343
in *ṣalāt* (prayer), 7342, 7343, 8057–8058
uniformity of, 7342
in Judaism, 7343, 7344
in Orthodox sacraments, 2592
in performances, 7043
in Shingon Buddhism, 8351
social, 7344
social functions of, 7342
symbolic range of, 7342–7344
in yoga, 1043–1046, 7343
aṣṭāṅgayoga (eight-limbed discipline), 8704
Potala (palace of Dalai Lama), 2131, 9051–9052, 9184
Potalaka Mountain, Avalokiteśvara and, 705, 7503
Potawatomi tribe (North America), **368–371**
ballgame played by, 753, 754
Medicine rite of, 6681
naming ceremonies of, 6683
puberty rites of, 6683
shamanism in, 6685
Potertan puping. See Mediator spirits
Pothinus (bishop of Lyons), 4538
Pothisarath (king), 5313
Potlatch, 6656, 6706, **7345–7346**
anthropologists on, 7345
as ceremonial distribution of property, 7345–7346
chiefs in, 7345
decline of, 7346
in Haida tradition, 3736
Hindu caste system compared with, 3480
as hospitality, 4141
as model for gift giving, 3479–3480
origins of, 3479
parody of, 4198
revival of, 6672
social protocols and moral prescriptions of, 7345
textiles in, 9089
Potnia Theron (deity), 9604
Potok, Chaim, 3060
Potṛ (priest), 7405
Potrimps (deity), 769
Potter, Karl, 4420, 6773
Potters, master, in Amazonian Quechua religions, 281, 282, 283
Pottery. *See also* Greek vases
feminine sacrality and, 3019
geometry in, 3438
invention by women, 5281
Mesoamerican, in Formative (Preclassic) period, 5895
Mesopotamian, 4315
Neolithic, 6465
Philistine, 7104
prehistoric, 7382, 7383
Pouillon, Jean, 381
Poulenc, Francis, 6313
Pounourville, Albert de, 3706
Pourushaspa, 9989
Poussin, Nicolas, 4347
Pouwer, Jan, 5770
Poverty. *See also* Poor people
in Buddhist monasticism, 8077
in Christianity, 9709
feminism and, 9791
Franciscans and, 3183, 3184, 6133
in Greek religion, charity and, 1553, 1554
in Tenrikyō, 6405
in *walāyah,* 9660
in monasticism, 6122–6123
Muhammadan, 2220
Powell, John Wesley, 6670
Powell, Peter J., 6672
Power, **7346–7354**
animals of, in neoshamanism, 8294
in Athapaskan religious traditions, **575–576**
in Australian Indigenous religions, 7346
authority and, 5397
authority *vs.,* in sociology, 8481
in Buddhism, 7350, 7353–7354
cargo cults, and conflict over, 1425
celibacy and spiritual power, 1475
central Bantu professional guilds and, 1509
ceremony and political power, 1513–1516
and charisma, 7352–7353

Power ***continued***
- charismatic (*See* Charisma)
- Dumézil (Georges) on, 7351–7352
- elephant as symbol of, 2750
- Eliade (Mircea) on, 2543, 7349–7350
- exorcism as, 2936
- expulsion and, 2938
- flight and, 3127
- Gennep (Arnold van) on, 7348, 7349
- of God (*See also* Omnipotence)
  - in Islam, 3562
  - ordained *vs.* absolute, 9738
  - in postbiblical Christianity, 3558–3559
- of gods, 7318
- head or skull as source of, 3804
- in Hinduism, 7347, 7350
- human body in art and, 4170–4171, 4172
- human sacrifices and, 2242
- in Shintō, 7346
- in *walāyah,* 9657–9658
- in Judaism, 7346–7347
- Jung (C. G.) on, 7350
- of kings, Homer on, 5166
- and magic, 7352
- magical notions of, written word and, 8201
- *mana* (*See Mana*)
- manifestation of (*See* Kratophany)
- in Micronesian myths, 6012
- of myths, 7350
- in North American Indian religions, 6680, 6713, 6714
  - of manitous, 5673–5674
- in Oceanic religions, 6785–6787, 6788
- ordeal and, 6847–6848
- through ordination, 6852, 6858–6859
- and origins of religion, 7347–7348
- Otto (Rudolf) on, 7348–7349
- person and, in indigenous traditions, 2618
- in physics, 7346
- political
  - Buddhism and, 2787
  - myth in, 6361
- purposive Daoism as basis for philosophy of, 1574
- in religious psychology, 7348–7349
- in rites of passage, 7803
- sacred space and, 7981
- and salvation, 7353–7354
- schism and, 8153
- of scripture, 8200–8201
- secret societies and, 8212
- of serpents, 8457–8458
- sexual intercourse and, in Cheyenne religion, 8239
- and social structure, 7351–7352
- of souls, 8531
- in Southeast Asian music, 6287–6288
- spirit possession and, 8696–8697
- of spirits of the dead, in manism, 5672
- in study of religion, 2541, 2542, 2543–2544
- of supreme beings, 8867
- of symbols, 7350
- of tears, 9026
- of time, 7991
- in totemism, 7351
- and tradition, 9272–9273
- of trees, 9334–9337
- in untouchables religions, 9475–9476
- van der Leeuw (Gerardus) on, 7350–7351
- in Vedism, 7351–7352

Power, William, 6672
Power animals, in neoshamanism, 8294
Power of Images: Studies in the History and Theory of Response, The (Freedberg), 4280, 4380
Power of Images, The (Freedberg), 500
Power of Myth, The (Campbell), impact of, 1378
Power of Positive Thinking (Peale), 6582
"Power of Prayer, The" (Schleiermacher), 7370
Powers, William K., on Lakota religion, 5296
Powhatan (Pamunkey chief), 6665
Powwow, 1515
Prabandham, 279
Prābhākara school of Indian philosophy, 6042–6043
Prabhāsvara (yoga of radiant light), 1287–1288
Prabhupada, A. C. Bhaktivedanta, 6529–6530, 6536, 6560, **7354–7355**
- as *sannyāsa,* 7355
- clothing of, 7354
- disciples of, 7355
- as founder of ISKCON, 826, 4521, 7354, 7355
- in India, 4522
- life of, 7354–7355
- in United States, 4521, 4523, 7354, 7355
- writings of, 7355

Practical Learning school. *See* Sirhak movement
Practical theology, 7479, 9139. *See also* Moral theology
Practical Vedānta, 7612, 7613, 9630, 10090
Practice
- in rituals, 7852–7854
- *vs.* study, of art and religion, 494–495

Pradakṣiṇā (circling), 1010, 1796
Pradhāna (main principle), 7360
Pradīpoddyotana (Candrakīrti), 1275
- Tantrism in, 1401

Pradkṣiṇa (circling), 1795
Praeparatio evangelica (Eusebius), 7131
- Canaanite religion in, 1381

Praetextatus, Vettius Agorius, 7919
Pragmatism
- in American study of religion, 8785
- definition of, 7111
- in environmental philosophy, 2657
- Hocking (William Ernest) on, 4076
- in Jewish Renewal, 4870–4871
- Kaplan (Mordecai) on, 5081
- Pratt's (James) critique of, 7366

Prague Manifesto (1521), 6238
Prāhlada (demon), 4442, 7501
Prairie Indians. *See* Plains peoples
Praise
- for God
  - Jewish limitations on, 3549
  - sacred language of, 5307
- prayer of, 7369
- psalms of, 7465
- as sacrificial intention, 8001

Praise of Folly, The (Erasmus), 6988
Praise the Lord (television program), 7713
Prajadhipok (Siamese king), 9096
Prajāpati (deity), **7356**
- Agni identified with, 7356
- and altars, 276
- as androgyne, 338
- as both victim and sacrificer, 1027, 7356
- breath of, 1043
- cosmic sacrifice of, 3992
- in creation story, 1023, 2963, 4439, 5302, 5447, 7356, 7640
  - lotus and, 5518
- on *dharma,* 2327
- as "fiery seed," 7356
- Indra and, 4467
- in sacrificial contest with Mṛtyu, 1025, 9567
- offsprings of, 9345
- Puruṣa associated with, 7356
- redeath of, 3992
- *tapas* resulting in, 7356, 8998
- Viṣṇu identified with, 9618
- water and, 9699
- zoomorphic expressions of, 7356

Prajñā (wisdom), 1296, 3201, 6629, **7356–7360**
- Asanga on, 5200
- attainment of, 7357, 7358
- *bodhisattvas* and, 8712
- in East Asian Buddhist meditation, 1290, 1291
- in *Abhidharmakośa,* 7357–7358
- in Mahāsāṃghika Buddhism, 5602
- in *Prajñāparamitā Sūtras,* 7358
- *karunā* and, 5105
- Nāgārjuna on, 7358–7359
- *nirvāṇa* identified with, 7359
- perfection of, 7358, 7359
- personified, 9764
- in religious training, 7357
- in Tantras, 7359
- threefold knowledge in, 7357
- in *Visuddhimagga,* 7357
- *vs. jñāna,* 7359
- *yoginīs* identified with, 7359

Prajṇākaramati, 3179
Prajñāpāramitā (deity), 1079, 1332
- gender of, 3333
- lotus associated with, 5519
- Sophia compared to, 9748
- temple to, 9051
- as wisdom, 9752–9753, 9764

Prajñāpāramitā (perfection of wisdom literature), 7358, 7359
- as sacred words, 5309

Prajñāpāramitā-piṇḍārtha-saṃgraha (Dignāga), 2351
Prajñāpāramitā (Perfection of Wisdom) school of Buddhism. *See also* Sanlun school
- Sengzhao and, 8228

Prajñāpāramitā Sūtras (Buddhist texts), 2171
- abhidharma criticized by, 1270
- attributed to Pūrvaśaila sect, 1114
- *bodhisattvas* in, 1298
- *dharma* in, 5100
- in Mahāyāna Buddhism, 6391
- Mañjuśrī and, 5675
- paradox in, 6989
- *prajñā* in, 7358
- and Pure Land Buddhism, 2176
- *śūnyatā* in, 1092, 1298
- *Sunyavadins* (teachers of emptiness) in, 8856–8857
- translation of, 1291
- *upāya* in, 9485–9486
- wisdom goddesses in, 4330

Prajñpati (conventional designation), 5308
Prajñaptivāda school of Buddhism
- *dharma* in, 2335
- doctrines of, 1196, 5602
- geographic distribution of, 5602
- origin of, 1194, 5602
- split from Mahāsāṃghika Buddhism, 5602

Prajñā woman, 1218–1219
Prākṛta pralaya (dissolution), in Purāṇic cosmology, 2018
Prakṛti (matter/nature), 2620, **7360–7361,** 9562
- development of concept of, 7360
- gender of, 3319
- *guṇas* of, 3709, 7361

in Sāṃkhya Hinduism, 3997, 3998, 8089, 8091
mysticism and, 6343
puruṣa caught up in, 853, 4422–4423, 7522
soul extricated from, in Yoga, 2016
in Swaminarayan movement, 8891
in Tantric Hinduism, 4003
and time, 4415
in Yoga, 9896
Praktikē (active way), 1447–1448
Praktikos (Evagrios of Pontus), 2886
Pralaya (doomsday), 4440, **7361–7362**
time and, 2018
Pramā (knowledge), *vs. jñāna,* 4927
Pramāṇas (valid sources of knowledge)
in Mīmāṃsā school, 6042
Jayarāśi's critique of, 1446
Sakya Paṇḍita on, 8051
Pramāṇasamuccaya (Dignāga), 1301, 2351–2352
Pramāṇavārttika (Dharmakīrti), 1120, 2323, 2336, 2352
Pramāṇaviniścaya (Dharmakīrti), 2336
Prambanan temple complex (Java), architecture of, 4012
Prāṇa (breath), 1043, **7362–7363**
binding symbolism of, 5198
therapeutic touch healing and, 3850–3851
Prānāmi cult, and Gandhi (Mohandas), 3272
Prānaṇāth, and Gandhi (Mohandas), 3272
Prāṇāpānau (breathin), 1043
Prāṇāyāma (breath control), 1043, 1044, 1045, 1046, 9895
aṣṭāṅgayoga (eight-limbed discipline), 8704
Prāng (tower), 9055
Praṇidhāna (vow). *See* Vows and oaths, Buddhist
Prapatti (surrender), 8976, 9505
Rāmānuja on, 7616
Prapti (appropriation or acquisition) doctrine
in Sautrāntika, 8137
karma and, 8118–8119
Prasād, Jayśankar, 10034
Prasāda (filled with grace), 858, 4384, 4391
Prāsāda (palace), 9040
Prasaṅga (unacceptable consequences), 1213
Buddhapālita on, 5552–5553
Prasaṅgavākya (philosophical approach), 1075
Prāsaṅgika school of Buddhism, 860, 1119, 1299, 1300, 5070
Candrakīrti and, 1401
emergence of, 5552
on language and logic, 8858
name of, 5552
Śāntideva and, 8109
Prasannapadā (Candrakīrti), 860
commentary in, 1401
Prasanthi Hilayam hermitage, Satha Sai Baba at, 8028
Praśastapāda (Indian philosopher), 2352
Praśāstṛ (priest), 7405
Prasenajit (king), 5348
Pratibhā (inspiration), 4509
Pratibhāṇa (inspired speech), 1269
Pratibimba (creation of divine regions), 9265
Pratikramana (repentance), 4769
Pratiloma marriages, in Indian caste system, 3996
Pratimā (image), 4323
Prātimokṣa (Buddhist rules), 1105–1106, 1107, 1258, 1259, 1306, 1886–1887
offenses in, 5348
of Mahāsāṃghika Buddhism, 5601
procedures for resolution in, 5348
recitation of, 5348
Prātimokṣasūtra (Buddhist text), 1146
Pratipad (way), 1296
Pratisaṃharaṇīya-karma (form of punishment), Vaiśālī council and, 2035
Pratisarana (points of reliance), 1274
Pratisaraṇa Sūtra (Buddhist text), 1269, 1274
Pratītya-samutpāda (dependent origination), **7363–7366,** 7678. *See also* Contingency
in Buddhist ethics, 1279–1280
doctrine of, 1297, 2332
emptiness *(śūnyatā)* and, 8857
in Huayan Buddhism, 4147
meaning of term, 7364
Nāgārjuna on, 6392–6393, 7365–7366
process philosophy compared to, 8859
as radical contingency, 1527
saṃsāra and, 8098
Stcherbatsky (Theodore) on, 8737
as theory of causality, 7363
Prätorius, Matthäus, 331, 768
Pratt, James B., **7366–7367**
on psychology of religion, 7475
on Suzuki (D. T.), 8887
Pratt, Mary Louise, 5928, 9292
Pratyabhijñā Śaivism, **8048–8049**
Abhinavagupta on, 9
Pratyahara (withdrawal of senses), 9895
aṣṭāṅgayoga (eight-limbed discipline), 8704
Pratyākhyāna (abandonment), 4769
Pratyakṣa (perception), 1301
Pratyekabuddhas (enlightened ones), 996, 1068, 1088
path of, 2029
Pratyutpanna samādhi sūtra (Buddhist text), 1291, 9331
in Jōdoshū, 4937
nianfo in, 6601
Pravargya, in Āraṇyakas, 1028
Pravrajyā (going out), 4483
Pravṛtti (active creation), 1024
Prawet Wasi (Thai social activist), 1072
Praxis
legitimation and, 5398–5404
liberation and, 5440
Praxiteles, Eros sculpture of, 2832
Prayāg (India)
Kumbha Melā at, 3987, 5265
rivers at, 7861–7862
Prayer, **7367–7372**
as act, 7368–7370
in African American religions, women leading, 10037
in Aladura movement, 104
attention in, 603, 604, 606
to Baal, 1385
of benediction, 7369
blessing as, 981
in Buddhism, 7369–7370
Tibetan, 9840, vol. 9 color insert
in Chinese religion, 1619–1620
in Christianity
breath and breathing and, 1046
of Catherine of Sienna, 1462
to Christ, Sozzini (Fausto Pavolo) on, 8673, 8674
to the dead, 2229
domestic rituals of, 2399
eagle associated with, 2554
at Easter, 2579
Eucharistic, of Syriac Orthodox Church, 8941
Heiler (Friedrich) on, 3897
Liturgy of the Hours for, 9812
mystical (*See* Hesychasm)
prayer of the heart in Eastern tradition, 3883
Sorskii (Nil) on, 8525
for souls of the dead, 8565
in Chuvash religion, 1785
of confession, 7369
creeds as, 2053
as devotion, 2319
in Diola religion, 2354
Epicurus on, 3911
as flow experience, 3138
formulaic character of, 7369
for gardens, 3280, 3281
in Greek religion, 3683–3684
hands and, 3769
healing through, 3812
Hermetic, 3939–3940, 3942
in Hinduism
Gandhi on, 4425
Great prayer *(mahā-mantra),* 1347
Rūmī (Jalāl al-Dīn) on, 7937
in Hittite religion, 4068
in Igbo religion, 4366
in Bēta Esra'ēl, 5002
vs. incantation, 4406
in Inca religion, 4412
in Ch'ŏndogyo, 1648
in Vaiṣṇavism, 9501
in Islam (*See also* Dhikr; See also Ṣalāt)
breath and breathing and, 1046
for dead and dying, 162, 8568
in devotion, 9816–9817
direction of (*See Qiblah*)
du'ā', 7342
during *ḥājj,* 7157–7158
in Five Pillars, 4565
for healing, 3831–3832
humor and, 4213, 4215
in *ṭarīqah,* 9005
at Karbala, 5088
Muḥammad's, 6766
nīyah, 7157–7158, 7343
for peace, 7021
Ramaḍān and, 8141
as sacramental, 7957
in Sunnism *vs.* Twelver Shiism, 8345
ummah and, 9446
in Israelite religion, 927–928, 935
in Japanese religions, 4785
to *kami,* 5071, 5072
in Okinawan ritual, 6812–6813
in Judaism
as devotion, 2319
domestic rituals of, 2397–2398
Dov Ber of Mezhirich on, 2430
Gamli'el of Yavneh and, 3269
for healing, 3828
kavvanot (intentions) in, 3789, 8314–8315
Marrano, 5718
on Passover, 7003
during pilgrimage, 7162
in Pseudepigrapha, 904
in rabbinic Judaism, 4977, 4978, 9806–9808
rabbinic public prayer, 8922

in Judaism ***continued***
in Reconstructionist Judaism, 5082
on Ro'sh ha-Shanah, 7928
shekhinah concept and, 8313, 8315
Shemu'el the Amoram on, 8318
siddur and *maḥzor* (prayer books), **8386–8392**
in worship, 9805–9806
kneeling during, 5195, 5196
language of, 7369
magic and, 9768
magic of, 7838
in Maya religion, 5884
in monasticism, 6123–6124
Christian, 6131
in Mongol religions, 6142–6143
motivation for, 7369
in North American Indian religions, 6652
in Navajo religion, 7369
in vision quest, 9609
in Oceanic religions, 6785–6786
in Orthodox Christianity
at home, 2593
Ioann of Kronstadt and, 4532
personal encounter with God through, 2587
in sacraments, 2592
in worship, 2591
of penitence, 7369
personal, 7368
as petition, 5307
petitionary, 7368
of praise, 7369
psychological and spiritual character of, 7368
reflexive character of, 7649–7650
ritual, 7368
ritual uses of, 7841–7842
sacred language of, 5303, 5304
as sources of purification, 7509
spells *vs.*, 8675
studies of, 7367, 7368, 7369
as subject, 7370–7371
as text, 7367–7368
of thanksgiving, 7369
in Trinidadian Shango, 1435
typology of, 7367–7368
use of term, 7371
work as, 9798–9799
in Zoroastrianism
in cosmogony, 9995
in initiation, 9999
Prayer: A Study in the History and Psychology of Religion (Heiler), 7368
Prayer of Azariah, 898–899
Prayer of Jacob, 904
Prayer of Joseph, 904
Prayer of Manasseh, 904
Prayer of Nabonidus, 899
Prayer tablets, Shintō, vol. 7 color insert
Prayer wheels, Tibetan Buddhist, vol. 9 color insert
Praying churches ("Aladura"), African, 1719–1720
Praying Towns (New England), 7301
Preachers. *See also* Priesthood
performance approach to, 3145
women, folklorist study of, 3147–3148
Preaching
in Christian worship, 9812
of Crusades, 2075, 2076
Protestant view of, 1668
Preaching of Peter, on attributes of God, 3553
Preaching Service, 9812
Preah Kan, temple at, 5129
Preanimism (animatism), **362–368, 7372–7374**
Codrington (R. H.) and, 2540, 7372
critique of, 2543, 7373–7374
dynamism and, 2540–2541
mana and, 7372–7374
Marett's theory of, 362–363, 5708, 7372, 7373
power and, 7347–7348
problems with, 364–365
Marett's (R. R.) theory of, 10077
of Preuss (Konrad), 7372, 7392
soul and, 8531
of Wundt (Wilhelm), 7372
"Preanimistic Religion" (Marett), 5708, 7372
Prebish, Charles S., on Pāṭaliputra council, 2036–2037
Precedent anthologies *(gongan ji)*, 1524
Precept (Buddhist lineage), 1181–1182
Precept and Practice (Gombrich), 6993
Precepts of Jesus, The: The Guide to Peace and Happiness (Roy), 828, 7932
Prechtel, Martin, 5796, 5945
Precious Stone-Faith Tabernacle prayer association, 104
Precisianism, 7142
Precognition, 6057
Predestination
in African religions, 89
Augustine's doctrine of double predestination, 8406
Beza (Theodore) on, 851
in Calvinism, 3002
Calvin on, 1375
Arminius (Jacobus) criticizing, 492, 493
vs. determinism, 3202
double, 3207
Eck (Johann) on, 2601
election and, 2748
free will and, **3202–3213**
Christianity on, 3203–3204, 3206–3209
Hinduism on, 3204–3205
Islam on, 3204, 3209–3213
Judaism on, 3203
Hincmar on, 3983
in Hinduism
free will and, 3204–3205
Madhva and, 8547
in Islam
ʿAbd Allāh Anṣari on, 8816
free will and, 3204, 3209–3213
Ḥasan al-Baṣrī on, 3785
Murji'ah sect on, 4568
Muʿtazilah *vs.* Ashʿariyāh on, 8816
Waṣīyah on, 5062
in Madhva's dualism, 8529
membership in the church and, 1777
in Puritanism, 7519
softened by concrete assurance of election, 4238
in Stoicism, 8742
Sufism and, 2749
Synod of Dort affirmation of, 2044
worldly success and, 2673
Predictive prophecy, 7107
Preexistence. *See* Reincarnation
Preface to Chaucer (Robertson), 7218
Pregadio, Fabrizio, 1638
Pregnancy
in Australian Indigenous religions, taboos in, 3873
calendar and gestation cycle, 1353
in Canaanite literature, 1395
Chinese rituals of, 2407
couvade and, **2046–2047**
divine, origin myths based on, 5179
figurines of pregnant women, Neolithic, 6461, 6463
in Japanese religion, Nakayama-dera Temple and, 3869
in Mesoamerican religions, 7811–7812
in Micronesian religions, 6005–6006
moon linked to, 3017
mother earth and, 2557
and number symbolism, 6750
pain of, 2896
sacred power of, 3020
sexual intercourse and celibacy during, 1475
Spiritualism and, 8717
Pregnant Goddess (prehistoric), 7377–7378, 7378, 7382–7383
Pre-Ha-rakhty (deity), 7634. *See also* Re
Prehension theory, 9282
Prehistoric religions, **7374–7388**. *See also* Neolithic religion; Paleolithic religion
agriculture and, 7376
animals in, 7376–7378, 7382–7385, 7387
archaeological study of, 452–453, 456, 7375, 7376, 7384
Gimbutas (Marija) in, 3492–3494
birds in, 947, 7376, 7377, 7378, 7387
birth in, 950–951, 7383
death in, 7377
in Eurasian steppes and Inner Asia, **7382–7388** (*See also* Saka religion)
cult centers in, 7383
funeral rites in, 7383–7384, 7386, 7387
goddess worship in, 7382–7383, 7386
sanctuaries in, 7382, 7383
female-male polarity and sacred union in, 3974–3975
funeral rites in, 7375, 7377, 7381, 7383–7384, 7386, 7387
iconography of, 7376, 7380–7381
in Japan, mountains in, 8379
kingship in, 7385, 7386–7387
masks in, 5767
in Old Europe, **7376–7382**
deities of, 7376–7378
funeral rites in, 7377, 7381
goddess worship in, 7376–7378
shrines and sanctuaries in, 7379–7381
psychedelic drugs in, 7468
sacrifice in, 7375, 7377, 7384, 7386
shamanism in, 7375
use of term, 7374
women in, 7381
Preideu Annwn (The spoils of Annwn), *Sídh* in, 8392
Preller, Victor, 7125
Premananda (Swami), 2602
Premcand (South Asian writer), 10034
Premier Radio (radio ministry), 7714
Premillennialism, in evangelicalism, 2888
Premonstratensian Order, Simons (Menno) and, 8400–8401
Prenatal screening, social consequences of, 2882
Preparationist theology, Hooker (Richard) and, 4125
Prepatriarchal societies, 3298
Pre-Romantic period, dance in, 2154–2155
Pre-Sanctified Gifts, Liturgy of, 2592
Presbyterial form of government, 1767–1768
Presbyterian Church (USA), 7391
Book of Confessions in, 2058

full communion agreement with other denominations, 1769
Presbyterian Church, ecumenical body of, 2684
Presbyterian Church in Canada, 7391
Presbyterian Church in the Confederate States, 7391
Presbyterian Church of America, 7391
Presbyterian Church of Australia, 7391
Presbyterian Church of New Zealand, 7391
Presbyterian denominations, **7388–7391**
on abortion, 941
in Africa, 1722
in Australia and New Zealand, 1732, 1733, 7391
Book of Confessions in, 2058, 2061
in Canada, 1713, 7391
Congregationalism and, 1937
on embryonic stem cell research, 941
in England, 7389, 7390, 7519
historical origins of, 7388–7390
in Ireland, 7390
in Latin America, 6579
liturgy of, 7389
meaning of term, 7388
missions
in Caribbean, 1707
in Pacific islands, 1738
on Taiwan, 1726
Plan of Union with Congregationalists (1801), 1938
polity of, 1767–1768, 1774, 7389–7390, 7453
Puritanism and, 1712, 7390
Reformation and, 7388–7389
in Scotland (*See also* Church of Scotland)
ecclesiology, 1774
origins of, 7389, 7390, 7391
Westminster Confession and, 2044
suppression of, by Act of Uniformity (1662), 1937
in Taiwan, 8963–8964
in United Reformed Church (England), 1938
in United States, 7389, 7390–7391
denominationalism and, 1712
divisions of, 7390–7391
missions among Nestorians, 6481
origins of, 7389, 7390–7391
in Wales, 7390
Westminster Confession as creed of, 2055
Presbyteries, responsibilities of, 1767
Presbyters (elders)
in church polity
in early church, 1763
in Methodist churches, 1767
in Presbyterian churches, 1767
in ministry, orders of, 6044
Prescriptions, Egyptian, 2724
Presence of God. *See also* Grace
in Judaism, 614, 3542 (*See also* Shekhinah)
Present, in eternity, 2853
Presentation offering, in Israelite religion, 926–927
Presented scholar *(jinshi)* degree, 1560, 1562
"Preserving and Cherishing the Earth: An Appeal for Joint Commitment in Science and Religion," 2612
Presidential Bioethics Commission (U.S.), 940
Pre-Socratics, on nature, 6431
Press. *See* Journalism; Media
Pressel, Esther, on spirit possession, 8688
Prestige, for warriors, 9679–9680
Presupposition of India's Philosophies (Potter), 4420
Pretas (ghosts), 2276, 2315, 3477
in Sinhala religion, 8412
Pretos velhos (slave spirits), 124
Prêtsavan (bush priest), 9635
Preuss, Konrad T., **7391–7392**
critique of, 2543, 7392
expeditions of, 7392
on Mesoamerican religions, 5941
preanimism of, 7372, 7392
on supernatural, 2541
on supreme beings, 7392, 8576, 8877
Preussische Chronik (Grunau), 767
Preyre, E.-Alexis, on doubt, 2428
Priapism, 7393
Priapus (deity), 6867, **7392–7394**
as fertility god, 7079–7080, 7393
phallus of, 7392, 7393
as son of Dionysos, 7392
Priber, Christian, 1566
Price, Daniel, 6985
Price, Richard, 10025
Price, Simon, 7278
Prichakon, Krom Luang Prichit, 3077
Pride
and decline of human race
in Greek mythology, 2965
in Iranian mythology, 2964
depiction in novels, 3059
in Islam, sin and, 8406–8407
Niebuhr (Reinhold) on, 6612–6613
"playing God" problem and, 8187
Priesand, Sally (rabbi), 7582, 7672
Priestesses
in Israelite religion, 5420
keys as symbols of, 5116
in Okinawan ritual, 6812–6813
in Sarmatian religion, 8115
Priesthood, **7394–7416**. *See also* Monasticism; Seminaries
in African religions
Mami Wata and, 5630
role of, 85
in Armenian church, 490
in Aztec religion, 5908
in Babylonian religion, 7398
in Balinese religion, 747, 748
in Buddhism, **7407–7410**
in Burma, 7408, 7409
in China, 7407–7408
criticism of, 7407–7408
functions of, 7407, 7409
in Theravāda Buddhism, 7408
in Japan, 7408, 7409
laity in, 7408–7409
ministerial aspects of, 7407
restricted to men, 7395
in Sri Lanka, 7407, 7408, 7409
in Thailand, 7408, 7409
in Tibet, 7407
use of term, 7394–7395, 7407
Vinaya Piṭaka and, 3275–3276
Canaanite, 1386
castrated priests, 1451–1452
celibacy in, 1477
in Christianity, **7400–7405**
celibacy in, 7395
Constantine I and, 7402
contemporary, 7404
in early Christianity, 7401–7402
marriage in, 7395
medieval, 7396, 7402–7403
Protestants on, 7394
Reformation and, 7403–7404
restricted to men, 7395
use of term, 7394, 7400–7401
clothing for (*See* Vestments)
consecration for, 1956
cross-cultural characteristics of, 7394–7395
in Daoism, **7413–7416**
code for, 7413–7414
criticism of, 7413
healing by, 3863
hierarchy in, 7413, 7414
lay-based, 7415–7416
origins of, 7413
in Quanzhen, 7415
reform movement in, 7413
restricted to men, 7395
vestments of, 1828–1829
women in, 7413
in East African religion, 2569
in Eblaite religion, 2598
in Edo religion, 2697
in Egyptian religion, 2714, 7277
iconography of, 4318–4320
study of, 2731–2732
eligibility for, 7395–7396
Episcopal, women in, 68, 7404
etymology of, 7394
future of, 7398–7399
in Germanic religion, priestesses in sagas, 8024
in Geto-Dacian religion, 3466, 3467
in Greek religion, 7277
in Hawaiian religion (*See Kahuna*)
hereditary, 7395
in Hinduism, **7405–7407** (*See also* Brahmans)
Brahmanic system of four classes of priest, 3991
classical, 7406
functions of, 7405
hereditary, 7395
modern, 7406
origins of, 7405–7406
restricted to men, 7395
rural traditions, 4435
training for, 7396
in Iberian religion, 4252, 4253
in Bēta Esra'ēl, 5002
in Candomblé, 122, 123
in Inca religion, 4412
in Indo-European religions, 4453, 4454, 4455
intellectuals in, 4513–4514
in Islam
in Iran, 4574
restricted to men, 7395
training for, 7396 (*See also* Madrasahs)
'ulamā' as, 7395
in Israelite religion, **7399–7400** (*See also* Levites)
appointment of, 7399
code of, 4729
financial support of, 7400
functions of, 7400
gifts to, 931
hereditary, 7395, 7399
as judges, 932
laws on, 4739
purification offering performed by, 934, 4747
status of, 7399

in Israelite religion
continued
support of, 929
training of, 7399
in Judaism (*See also* Sadducees)
Aaron in, 1–2
ablutions in, 10
election and, 2744
history of, 5424
Levites *vs.* priests, 5422–5423 (*See also* Levites)
restricted to men, 7395
Second Temple Judaism, 5426–5427
use of term, 7394
Zadokite *vs.* Hasmonean, Sadducees and, 8018
kingship and, 7398
leadership of, 5383–5385
Mandaean, 5635, 5636–5637
marriage in, 7395
in Maya religion, 5799, 5884, 5886
men in, 7395–7396
in Micronesian religions, 6006, 6007–6008
in ministry, orders of, 6044
in Mixtec religion, 5912
in Moabite religion, 6095
in Nuer and Dinka religions, 6744
Olmec, 6818
ordination into (*See* Ordination)
in Orthodox Christianity
in confession, 2592–2593
at Eucharist, 2592
ordination of, 2593
in Phoenician religion, 7132–7133
pollution rules in, 7506–7507
in Polynesian religions, 6263, 7305, 7306–7307, 7309
in Qemant religion, 2573
Roman Catholic
Augustine on role of, 626
authority of, Marsilius of Padua on, 5729–5730
clothing in, 1831
mediation and, 7881–7882
medieval, 7402–7403
ordination into, 4483
Paul VI on, 7012, 7013
Reformation and, 7403–7404
in Roman religion, **3124–3126,** 7279
Arval Brothers in, 513–514
early period, 7897–7898
imperial period, 7914
middle republic, 7907–7908
rule by, 9109
Russian Orthodox, Avvakum in, 712
sacrifice by, 7997–7998
Samaritan, 8068, 8070
Shintō, **7410–7413**
appointment of, 7412
clerical titles of, 7410–7411
under government control, 7411–7412
qualifications of, 7412
responsibilities of, 7412
women in, 7411
after World War II, 7412
in Sinhala religion, 8411
and state, 7397–7398
in Tamil religions, 8973
in Tarascan religion, 5909, 9002
in Tikopia religion, 9196
in Tlaxcalan religion, 9215
in Toraja religion, 9241, 9242
in Totonac religion, 5911, 9254, 9255
training for, 7396–7397
use of term, 7394
in Vedism, 7405–7406
vocational, 7395–7396
in Vodou, 9634
warrior subordinate to, 9684
Weber (Max) on, 8488
women's exclusion from, 7395–7396
androcentrism of, 336
in Zapotec religion, 5912
in Zoroastrianism, 5559–5561, 9989–9992
functions of, 5559–5561
hereditary, 7395
purity in, 7397
restricted to men, 7395
royal patronage of, 7398
training for, 7396
Zuni sun priests as mediators, 2008–2009
Priesthood of all believers, in ecumenism, 2689
Priestley, Joseph
Martineau (James) and, 5736–5737
in Unitarianism, 9469
Priestly, Joseph, in British Enlightenment, 2797
Priestly Code, covenant in, 2048
Priestly (P) source
and Aaron, 1
on Abraham, 14, 15
dating of, 6199
on God, names of, 3539
on Moses, 6199–6201
Priestly text, sacrifice in, 5434
Priests of Egypt, The (Lefebvre), 2732
Primal peoples, knowledge of, 5199
Primary cultures, Schmidt (Wilhelm) on, 5260, 8168
Primates, 6151
Prime mover, Aristotle's, 485
Primeval Ocean
in Egyptian cosmogony, 2720
Väinämöinen as creator of, 9496–9497
Primian (bishop), 2416
Primiano, Leonard Norman, 3143
Primitive Culture (Tylor), 114, 363, 2237–2238, 2661, 2914, 4460, 7347, 7368, 7372, 9424
hero myths in, 3958
Primitive Methodists, 5998
Primitive monotheism (*Urmonotheismus*) doctrine, 6156, 10065, 10077
Heilbringer and, 2090
Primitive Mysteries (Graham), 2158
Primitive Religion (Lowie), 5522
Primitive Religion (Radin), 7596
Primitive religions and societies. *See also* Paleolithic religion; Popular (folk) religion
anthropological studies of
methodological critiques of, 379–380
Radin's (Paul), 7596
asceticism in, 526–527
atheism in, 577
authority in, 692
birth in, 950–951
blood in, 985
bones in, 1014
as classification, 1818–1819, 1821
imperialist bias in, 1856–1857
replaced by "nonliterate ethnic traditions," 4065
definition of, 7693
deserts in, 2300
in evolutionary theory (*See also* Animism)
African religion as, 113–114
in evolutionism, 2914
games in, 3266
God in, Lang (Andrew) on, 5300
gods in, high, Söderblom (Nathan) on, 8878
Henotheism in, 3913
humor and, 4195, 4201
incarnation in, 4414–4415
initiation rituals in, 4480, 4481, 4482, 4483
Lévi-Strauss (Claude) on, 8751
Lévy-Bruhl (Lucien) on, 8464
the supernatural in, 8862
literacy and, 2896
Lowie (Robert H.) on, 5522
magic in, 2267, 5562–5565, 7695
masks in, 5764, 5765
mentality of, Lévy-Bruhl (Lucien) on, 5429
miracles in, 6049–6050
money in, 6137
monotheism in, 2915
Nilsson (Martin P.) on, 6622
organization of, kinship and, 5182, 7717
polytheism in, 7316
rationality in, 2895
religious communities in, 7699, 7716–7717
religious experience in, 7694, 7695
revenge in, 7780–7781, 7781
sacrifice in, Lanternari (Vittorio) on, 8004
salvation in, 7697
Schmidt (Wilhelm) on, 5260, 8168–8169
sin and guilt, cosmological perception of, 8402–8403
Smith (W. Robertson) on, 8452–8453
soul in, **8531–8534**
destiny of, 8533–8534
origin of, 8533
theoretical elaborations on, 8531–8532
varieties of, 8532–8533
Spencer (Herbert) on, 8678–8679
taboo in, 8948
totemism in, 9250, 9251, 9253
underworld in, 9451–9452
Primitivism, **10064–10066**
of Campbell and Church of Christ, 1377
in Chinese philosophy, 1572, 9969–9970
in Christianity, 10064
definitions of, 10064
fictive status of, 10066
leadership in, 10065–10066
in outsider art, 9625
ritual clothing and, 1828
totemism and, 10065
in *Zhuangzi,* 9969–9970
Primitivism (dance style), 2158
Primordiality. *See also* Chaos
as creation theme, 1989
of *deus otiosus,* 2311–2312
Eliade on, 1989
forms of, 325–326
masculine sacrality in, 5759
of ocean, 6805–6807
of paradise (*See* Paradise, primordial)
Schmidt (Wilhelm) on, 8169–8170
of supreme beings, 8869
of water, 3132, 9697–9700
Primordial parents
as cosmological theme, 1993–1994
in creation myths, 1450–1451, 1987–1988
Primordial religions
decline of, 4513
intellectuals in, 4512
religious beliefs of, 4512
Primus, Pearl, 2164
Prince, The (Machiavelli), 5367
Prince Edward Island, Church of England in, 9300
Prince Moonlight (legendary figure), 6039
Prince of Darkness, in Manichaeism, 5654, 5666
Principia (Newton), 6588
Principia Ethica (Moore), 2918–2919
Principia Mathematica (Russell and Whitehead), 49

Principi di scienza nuova di Giambattista Vico d'intorno alla comune natura delle nazioni (Vico), 9589
Principle, in Chinese thought. *See Li*
Principle, Neo-Confucian School of
philosophy of, 1932
sages and, 8037
Principle and material force, in Korean Neo-Confucianism, 1931–1932
Principles of Nature (Aquinas), 9161
Principles of Philosophy (Descartes), 2293
Principles of Psychology (James), 4775
Principles of Sociology (Spencer), 321, 2238, 5672
sociology of religion in, 2914
Prinzhorn, Hans, 9625
Prinzipalstück (liturgical focus), 795
Prip-Møller, Johannes, 1314
Prisca philosophia and *prisca theologica,* Hermetism and, 3946–3947
Prisca sapienta (priest-scientists), Newton's belief in, 6589
Priscilla (prophet), in Montanism, 6167
Priscillanism, Manichaeism and, 5656–5657, 5668
Priscillian of Ávila
asceticism of, 2826
Gnosticism of, 3522, 3523
Priscus (Greek historian), 4490, 4491
on Hun religion, 4228–4229
Prisons
Christian Identity movement in, 1659
in Mexico, tattooing in, vol. 6 color insert
Panopticon, 5374
as punishment, 5374
religious programs in, 5374
Privacy, media and, 5808
Private associations, Roman laws concerning, 5333–5334
Privatization of religion, social differentiation and, 8472
Privy Council, Calvert (George) and, 1373, 1374
Probabilism
skepticism and, 8421
Suárez (Francisco) on, 8799
"Problem for Theology: The Concept of Nature, A" (Kaufman), 2610
Problemi di storia delle religioni (Bianchi), 863
Problem of Pain, The (Lewis), 6944
Probus (emperor), Sol worship and, 8511
Process, the (movement), 6568
Procession, **7416–7418**
vs. circumambulation, 7416–7417
vs. dance, 7417
definition of, 7416
destination of, 7417
examples of, 7416
individual, 7417
linearity of, 7416
meditative tone of, 7417
vs. parades, 7417
participation in, 7417
vs. pilgrimage, 7417, 7418
textiles in, 9092
Process theology
attributes of God in, 616
ecology and, 2650
Holocaust responses and, 4093
logic in, 5497
monotheism in, 6161
Process theory, conversion, stages of, 1972
Proclus
on apocatastasis, 421
on demons, 2277
Dionysian writings relying on, 2356
on *Henads,* 7191–7192
on hypostases, 4240
influence of, 6475
on knowability of God, 182
metaphysics of, 5990
in Plato's Academy, 6474
on races of humans, 2965
Sahak Parthev, correspondence with, 8026
on symbol theory, 8907–8908
theology of, 9134
on unity, 6474
writings of, 7191
Procopius
on Perun, 7062
on Slavic religion, 8432
Procopius of Gaza, on Adonis festivals, 2536
Procosmic (cosmic) dualism, 2508–2509, 2509–2510, 2512
Procreation, Trobriand Islanders model of, 5184
Proctor, H. H., 69
Procuratio prodigiorum (prodigy management), 7338
Prodicus of Ceos
atheism and, 581
Greek religion critiqued by, 3685
Prodigal Son (Balanchine), 2162
Prodigal Son (Jooss), 2163
Prodigies, **7335–7338**. *See also* Divination
in Etruscan religion, 7337–7338
etymology of term, 7335, 7337
in Greek religion, 7337
vs. portents, 7337
in Roman religion, 2377, 7337, 7338, 7914–7915
Profane. *See* Sacred and the profane, the
Profanum/profanus (Roman concept). *See also* Sacred and the profane, the
sacrum vs., 7964, 7966
Professional cults, in central Bantu religion, 1509
Professions of faith. *See* Confessions of faith
Profound Inner Meaning (Rang byung rdo rje), 5102–5103
Progeny, in Abraham stories, 14
Prognostication. *See* Divination; Portents
Program to Combat Racism (WCC), 2686
Progress, historiography and notion of, 4031, 4040
"Progress: Its Law and Cause" (Spencer), 2913
Progressive Islam, 6098–6100
afterlife in, 162
gender equality in, 6099
jihād in, 6099–6100
social justice in, 6098–6099
women in, 6098, 6099
Progressive Judaism. *See* Reform Judaism
Progressive Muslims (Safi), 6098, 6099
Progressivism
in Jewish Renewal, 4871
modernism as type of, 6102
Progress of Religious Ideas (Child), 1569
Progrès successifs de l'esprit humain, Les (Turgot), 7340
Prohylic dualism, 2509
Projection, archetype in, 459–460
Projection theories of religion, 1870
Prokheiroi kanones (Ptolemy), 7492
Prokofeva, E. D., 475
Prokopovich, Feofan, **7418–7419**
and church reforms, 7418–7419
ethics of, 1653
Russian theology influenced by, 2588
writings of, 7419
"Prolegomena to a Discussion of Aretalogies, Divine Men, the Gospels, and Jesus" (Smith), 946
Prolegomena to the History of Greek Religion (Harrison), goal of, 3781
Prometeo, Orfeo e Adamo (Bianchi), 864
Prometheus (deity), **7419–7421**
agriculture and, 191, 9579
as bringer of fire, 7419, 7420
and Deukalion, 3132
Greek sacrifice as repetition of acts of, 1014
Hesiod on, 3118, 7419, 7420
iconography of, 7421
Indian variant of, 4439
legacy of, 7420–7421
origins of myth of, 7419–7420
"playing God" problem and, 8187
rebelliousness of, 7420–7421
sacrifice originated by, 2366, 3669–3670, 3683, 7419
as solar metaphor, 4460
as trickster, 7419, 7420
Zeus and, 1014, 7419–7420
Prometheus Bound (Aeschylus), 5469
Prometheus Unbound (Shelley), 3526
Promethia (procession), 7420
Promise. *See also* Vows and oaths
to Abraham, 15
Promise and the threat, the, Muʿtazilah on, 5063
Promise Keepers, 3362, 5863
Pronaos (porch), 9063, 9064
Prone, 9812
"Pro Nessia" incantation, 4407
Proof of Islam. *See Hujjatul-Islām*
Proof of the Apostolic Preaching (Irenaeus), 4538, 4539
Proofs for the existence of God, **7421–7423**. *See also* Theism
Albo (Yosef) on, 233
Anselm on, 373, 582, 7123, 7421, 7422, 9103
archetypes and, 460
Aristotle on, 480
attacks on, 582–583, 7422
responses to, 583–585, 7422–7423
Augustine on, 7421
Bonaventure on, 7421
Buber (Martin) on, 7422
in Christianity, 7421–7423
Cleanthes on, 7124
cosmological argument in, 7422, 9103–9105
Crescas on, 2069, 4896–4897
Descartes on, 2294, 7421
Duns Scotus (John) on, 7421
early arguments for, 582
empirically proving, 2780
epistemology and, 2819
Hume (David) on, 7124–7125
Ibn Rushd on, 7422
Ibn Sīnā on, 2974, 7422
in Islam, 7422
in Judaism, 7422
Kant on, 583, 5077, 5078, 7123, 7125, 7422
al-Kindī on, 2972
Leibniz on, 5406, 7421
logical positivism and, 2780, 5498–5499
Maimonides on, 7422
moral argument in, 7422, 9106
in Muʿtazilah, 6324
ontological argument in, 7421–7422, 9103

Proofs for the existence of God *continued*
Philo Judaeus on, 7106, 7422
in physics, 2659–2660
Rosenzweig (Franz) on, 7422
Saʿadyah Gaon on, 4888, 7952
science and, 2912
in Stoicism, 3912
teleological argument in, 7422, 9105–9106
Thomas Aquinas on, 582, 3555, 7123–7124, 7422, 7423, 9163
Maritain (Jacques) on, 5713
William of Ockham on, 7422
Propaganda
Egyptian
of dynasties, 2706
in temple inscriptions, 2725
of Mao Zedong, vol. 6 color insert
Proper of Saints *(sanctorale),* 1741
Proper of Seasons *(temporale),* 1741
Property
and Chinese ancestor worship, 323
common (*See* Common property)
endowment of, in Islam (*See Waqf*)
of Essenes, 2846–2847
Jewish law on, 3752
Prophecy and prophets, **7423–7445**. *See also* Oracles; Revelation; Sagehood; Visions; *specific movements and prophets*
in African religions, 87, **7442–7445**
Aladura movement of, 104
colonialism and, 7443–7444
vs. divination, 7443
in East African traditions, 7443–7445
as ecstatics, 7443
history of study of, 117–118
independent Christian movements, 1719–1721
Lugbara religion, 5528
Lumpa church movement, 5409
vs. mediums, 7442–7443
mediums and, 8659
Nuer and Dinka, 6744–6745
sickness, role of, in Cameroon, 3815
in Xhosa religion, 7444
ancient, 7424
astrology in, 564
biblical, **7429–7438**
apocalypse and, 415–416
end of, 7438
Heschel (Abraham Joshua) on, 3962
in *Isaiah,* 4546, 4547–4548, 4549, 4550
in Buddhism, Tibetan, 5192
in Canaanite religion, 1381
canon influencing, 7426–7427
canon resulting from, 7425
common features of, 7425–7426
in comparative religion, 7428
definition of, 6546, 7439
in Diola religion, 7444–7445
Alinesitoue, 261–262, 2355, 7444
women as, 261, 262
as divination, 2370
in Eblaite religion, 2599
in Egyptian religion, 2714, 2721
eschatological, 7426
Essene, 2846
ethical prophet, 5384
in Etruscan religion, 2872
etymology of term, 7424, 7431
exemplary prophet, 5384
the Family and, 2988
as founders of religious tradition, 7424–7426
in Greek religion, 7424
Hebrew, Rastafarians as reincarnations of, 1438
hermeneutical (divine-voice), 7107
in Hittite religion, 4072
images of, 9623
imaginative aspect of, 7439, 7440
in Bahāʾī faith, 739
in Raëlian religion, 7597
inspired, 4510
intellectual aspect of, 7439, 7440–7441
as intellectuals, 4514
in Islam
ʿAbduh (Muḥammad) on, 5067
in Druze movement, 8330
falsafah ideas on, 2972–2973, 2992
Ibn Khaldūn on, 4270
in Ismāʿīlīyah, 8326
nūr Muḥammad in, 6768
al-Shahrastānī and, 8267
Sirhindī (Aḥmad) on, 8414
"Stories of the Prophets" in Muslim histories, 8781
Ṣūfī saints *vs.,* 8814–8815
in Sufism, 7427, 7443
terms for, 7426
in Israelite religion, 7424–7425, **7429–7438**
authority of, 7433–7434
behavior of, 7432–7433
central prophets, 7434–7435
as ecstatics, 7432
evidence for, 7429–7430
in exile and postexile period, 7437
experience of, 7430–7433
in monarchical period, 7436
peripheral prophets, 7435, 7436, 7437
in premonarchical period, 7435–7436
speeches of, 7432–7433
titles of, 7431–7432
women, 7435
Jesus as, 4850, 7425
in Ebionism, 2596
eschatological, 7426
in Islam, 5979
in Judaism, **7438–7442**
Abravanel (Isaac) on, 17, 18
collective addressed by, 4857
ha-Levi on, 4892
in Jewish law, 7440
justice and, 10063
Maimonides on, 4893–4894, 7439–7440
modern, 7441–7442
qabbalistic, 6353, 7441
on repentance, 7757
Saʿadyah Gaon on, 7438–7439
Spinoza (Barukh) on, 7440–7441
women, 3541
as leaders, 5383–5385
meaning of term, 7423–7424
in Mesopotamian religions, 7424
vs. messiah, 5973
in Millenarianism, 6034, 6546, 7786
as healers, 6031
in Moabite religion, 6095
modern, 7427–7428
in Montanism, 6167–6168
moral reformation and, 7652
Mosaic, 7107, 7434, 7440
in North American Indian religions
and Ghost Dance, 3473–3474
shamanism and, 8289
in Oceanic religions, new religions and, 2007
oracles and, 6831
ordeal (*See* Ordeal)
Philo Judaeus on, 7107
philosophers on, 7428
Plato on, 7439
in poetry, 7204–7207
in political movements, 87
in popular religion, 7330
predictive, 7107
role of, 4510
diminished, 7427
in Roman religion, 7424
in Selk'nam religion, 8226
Smith (W. Robertson) on, 8453
as social critics, 7425–7426
Söderblom (Nathan) on, 8878
Spinoza (Baruch) on, 8683
subjectivity and, 8695
in Tibetan Buddhism, 5192
and tradition, 9270–9272
in Treasure tradition, 9332
vs. nubūwah, 6735
Weber (Max) on, 4512
Prophet, the. *See* Muḥammad
Prophet, Elizabeth Clare, 4247, **7445–7446**
avertive apocalypticism of, 6548
Church Universal and Triumphant and, 1781–1784
inner circle around, 6547
The Lost Teachings of Jesus, 6529
Prophet, Mark, 4247, **7445–7446**
Church Universal and Triumphant and, 1781–1784
Prophetae Chaldaice (Lagarde), 889
Prophet Dance
Ghost Dance and, 3474
spread of, 6718
today, 6719
Prophētēs (prophecy), 7424, 7431
Prophet Fard. *See* Fard, Wallace D.
Prophetic (visionary) dreams, 2483, 2488, 2489
Prophetic ecstasy, 2678–2679
Prophetic legends, 6376
Prophetic (Islamic) medicine *(tibb al-nabawi)*
history of, 3834
overview of, 3833
Prophetic movements
in East African religions, 2570–2572
vs. messianism, 5973
in Oceania, 6793–6794
Prophetic texts
Canaanite, 1381
in Confucianism, 1908
Prophet movements, revival and renewal activities in, 7785
Prophets (section of Hebrew scriptures). *See Nevi'im*
Prophets, The (Heschel), 7442
Propitiation, suffering of Christ and, 8808
Propp, Vladimir, 3114
on Russian fairy tales, 3958
Propriety, ritual *(li). See Li*
Propulaia (portal), 7333
Prose Edda (Snorri), 167, 1451, 2342, 2691–2692, 3446
apocalypse in, 3457
creation of man in, 3454
death of Baldr in, 3455–3456
euhemerism in, 5672
Indian narrative compared to, 8522
part of, 8460
Valhǫll in, 9516
Proselytism
human rights and, 5364
in Reiyūkai Kyōdan, 7862

of Reform Judaism, 7666
Proseprina (deity), 4253
Prose Refutations (Ephraem of Syria), 786
Proseuchē (prayer places, Jewish), in Egypt and Delos, 8920, 8921
Proslogion (Anselm), 373, 7123
Barth (Karl) studying, 791
Prosperity
deities of, 3622
in New Thought teachings, 6585
of wicked people, Sa'adyah Gaon on, 7952–7953
Prosperity (Fillmore), 6585
Prosperity gospel
affirmations and, 1782
African Pentecostalism and, 1724
Roberts (Oral) and, 7712
televangelism and, 7712, 7714
Prosper of Acquitaine, Cassian, attack on, 1447, 1448
Prosser, Gabriel, 66
Prostitution
in ancient Greece, 7079
Hosea's marriage to a harlot, 4136–4137
in Japan, homosexuality and, 4114
Mary Magdalene and, 5757
in Phoenician religion, 7131
sacred
in Aphrodite's cults, 407–408
hierodouleia, **3966–3970**
in Near Eastern religions, 3378
Prostration, 5195
in Theravāda, 8061
in Muslim worship, 7342
symbolism of, 7343
Protagoras, 971
atheism and, 581
Greek religion critiqued by, 3685
relativism and agnosticism of, 3909–3910, 7685
skeptical views of, 8420
Protagoras (Plato), 2273
Protection
in African religions, rituals and charms for, 3820, 9777
by Viṣṇu, 9619
deities of, 3621
female, 3589
Herakles as, 3917
spitting and, 8722
through violence, 9598
Protective curses, 2101–2104, 2105–2106
Proterius, lynching of, 6153
Protest, poetry of, 7205
Protestant Buddhism, 6816
Protestant Episcopal Church. *See* Episcopalianism
Protestant Ethic (Weber), translation of, 8467
Protestant Ethic and the Spirit of Capitalism, The (Weber), 2671, 9711
Protestantism, **7446–7459**. *See also specific countries, denominations, doctrines, and movements*
abortion in, 5812
afterlife in, 158–159
androcentrism in, 336
anthropocentrism in, 2649
antiritualism of, 7699
apocalypse in, 412–413
artistic expression in, 2141
ashram movement in, 546–547
atheism in, 584, 7449
atonement in, 596, 4844
Augsburg Interim, 7659
authority in, 694, 695
autobiography in, 698–699
baptism in, 7455, 9810
and biblical canonicity, 881, 896
biblical exegesis in, 874, 876
on blasphemy, 973
calendar of, 7456–7457
in capitalism
development of, 2669
Weber (Max) on, 8464, 8494
charismatic movement and, 1550, 7030
children in, humor and, 4199
church
architecture of, 795, 7456
authority of, 7451–7452
polity of, 7452–7453
sacredness of, 7698
views of, 1668
classification of religions in, 1818
clergy in, 7452
distinction from laity, 5287–5288
on cloning, 5814
on communion, 7882
confession in, 1889, 7452
confessions of faith in, 2053
confirmation in, 7455
creeds in, 7452
and dance, 2154
definition of, 7446–7447
deism in, 7449
denominationalism in (*See* Denominationalism)
denominations in
clusters of, 7447
common elements of, 7448–7449
diversity and coherence of, 7447–7448
lineage of, 7448–7449
number of, 7448
dogma in, 2387, 2388
Harnack (Adolf von) on, 3778–3779
Easter celebrated in, sunrise service for, 2580
ecclesiology and, 1773–1775
as economic catalyst, 2676
Elizabeth I and, 7663
ethics, 1651, 1654–1656, 7457–7458
Eucharist in, 7455–7456, 9811
evangelical (*See* Evangelical Christianity)
evangelical used in, 2887
excommunication equivalents in, 2105
exorcism in, 2930–2931
and fasting, 2997
food customs in, 3170
free will and predestination in, 3204
funeral rites in, 7455
future of, 7459
gender in, 3360–3362
God in, 7449–7450, 7454–7456
grace in, 158, 3646, 7454
healing and medicine in, 3846–3847
heaven and hell in, 3885
heresy and, 3928, 7449, 7450
heterodoxy in, 6912
historiography in, 4030, 4032–4033, 4042
human beings in, 7454
iconoclasm in, 7449, 7459
iconography of, 4346–4347, 7456, 7459
imagery in, words incorporated into, vol. 14 color insert
individualism in, 7453, 7457
initiation in, 7454–7456
Irenaeus as leading mentor of, 4540
Jesus in, 7450
justification in, 5041
doctrine of, 1667–1668
kingdom of God in, 5153
kneeling in, 5196
knowledge in, 5205, 5206–5207
Knox (John) and, 5212
laity in, 5287–5288, 5288
liberal (*See* Liberal Protestantism)
liberation theology in, 5438
Lord's Supper or communion in, 1669 (*See also* Eucharist)
and magic, decline of, 5568
marriage in, 7455
Mary in, 5753–5754
mediation and, 7881
media used by, vol. 7 color insert
medical ethics in, 5810–5814
membership in the church in, 1778
menstruation in, 5867
merit in, 5877
ministry in, 6044–6045
miracles in, 6056
missionaries (*See* Christian missions)
monasticism in, 6134
music in, 7456, 7459
modern, 6313
Renaissance, 6310–6311
nature in, fear of, 2607
Neoorthodoxy within, **6466–6470**
and Nestorian communities, interest in, 6480–6481
new, location of, 7447
in Oceania, 6790–6791
old, location of, 7447
origins of (*See* Reformation)
orthodoxy in, 6912
pacifist movements in, 6648
papacy rejected by, 7448
personal ethics in, 7457
personal experience as authority in, 7453–7454
pietism in (*See* Pietism, in Protestantism)
poetry of, 7206, 7220
political theology of, 7244–7247
politics in, 7453
predestination in, 3201
priesthood in, 7394
publishing and, vol. 7 color insert
recognition of
Peace of Augsburg and, 7659
Peace of Nuremberg and, 7659
relics in, opposition to, 7686–7687
as religion of word, 7456, 7458
religious experience in, 7737–7738
Ritschl (Albrecht) on, 7832
Roman Catholicism and, 7873, 7881
Inquisition directed against, 4498, 4500, 4501, 4504, 4505, 4506
and theological development, 7458
violence during Reformation, 1807, 1808
sacraments in, 7455–7456, 7881
rites and practices, 7962–7963
theology of, 7963
sacred space in, vol. 5 color insert
sacrifice in, 8007
as Satanism, 9772
schism patterns in, 8151
scripture, primacy of, 7450–7451, 7456
ethics and, 1651
medicine and, 3846
and theology, 7458

Protestantism ***continued***
sexuality in, 7457
social ethics in, 7457–7458
social reform in, 7653
social transformation in, 1671
social work in, 7487
stem cell research in, 5813–5814
substance in, 7454
theater forbidden in, 2467–2468, 2474
theocracy in, 9110
theology of, 7458, 9136–9138
traditionalism in, 7696
on Trinity, 7450
Vatican I and, 9528
at Vatican II, 4946
voluntarism in, 7453
wealth in, 9709
Weber and, 1544
witchcraft beliefs of, 9772–9773
women in, 6765
work ethic in, 7251, 7458
Marxist critique of, 7489
in World Council of Churches, 2685, 7448
worship in, 7456–7457
hymns, 1668–1669
preaching, emphasis on, 1668
Zoroastrianism influenced by, 9995
Protestant liberalism
definition of, 6103
vs. liberal Protestantism, 6103, 6105
Protestant Methodists, 5999
Protestant Principle, Tillich (Paul) on, 7453, 7459
Protestant Reformation. *See* Reformation
Proteus (deity), 9698–9699
shape shifting of, 8303
Protevangelium of James, Mary in, 5753
Protoasikritis (chief secretary), 9003
Proto-Austronesian language, 745
Protocols of the Elders of Zion, anti-Semitism based on, 402
Proto-Daoism, 9843
Protomonotheism, 2302
Protrepticus (Aristotle), 484
Protrepticus (Clement of Alexandria), 4360
Proudfoot, Wayne, 7745, 7746
Proust, Marcel, 3059
Proverbs, **6976–6980**. *See also* Parables
African, 6977
of East Africa, 2567
vs. myths, teachings of, 91
animals in, 6977
Confucian, 6978
definition of, 6976
in Hebrew scriptures, 6978
of Jesus, 6979
key features of, 6976–6977
modern, 6979–6980
North American Indian, 6977
in United States, 6976–6977
as wisdom, 9748
in world religions, 6977–6978
Proverbs (biblical book)
adultery in, 4738
Aramaic translation of, 889
authors of, 9757, 9763
dating of, 9755, 9757–9758
Egyptian wisdom collection influencing, 6978
Eliyyahu ben Shelomoh Zalman on, 868
female imagery in, 4078, 4079
"good wife" in, 1559
health wisdom in, 3828, 3831
ḥokhmah in, 4077, 4078
Solomon as author of, 8513
theodicy in, 9116
wisdom in, 8522–8523
as wisdom literature, 9750, 9757–9758
on women, 4732
Providence
Calvin on, 1375
chance and, 1529
in Christianity, Schleiermacher (Friedrich) on, 8166
in Greek thought, 8405
in Judaism
medieval, 3549
Saʿadyah Gaon on, 7953
Newman (John Henry) on, 6510
Spinoza (Baruch) on, 8681
in Stoicism, 8741, 8742
Provinces, in church government
in Anglicanism, 1764
in Roman Catholicism, 1764
Provincial Letters (Pascal), 1455
Pṛśni (deity), 7934
Pṛthivī (deity), 2984
Pruden, Leo, 1246
Prudentius (poet), 6946, 7218
Pruning the Bodhi Tree: The Storm over Critical Buddhism (Noriaki and Shirō), 1247
Prussia
anti-Semitism in, 5020
Bauer's (Bruno) critique of, 804
Prussian Learned Society, 843
Pruyser, Paul W., 7486
Pryderi (deity), 1490
in *Mabinogion,* 5545, 5546
Przyluski, Jean, 1313, **7459**
Psalmody
in Christianity, 6308
in Judaism, 6307
Psalms, **7459–7466**
Aaron in, 1
alternative titles of, 7460
Aramaic translation of, 887, 889
attribution of, 7461–7462
Augustine influenced by, 698
baptism in, 781
Canaanite parallels, 1392, 1400, 7462–7463
chanting of, 1534, 7463–7464
in Christian canon, 7460
cursing in, 2104
dance in, 2319
dating and provenance of, 7462
David and, 2223
assignation to, 1410, 7461–7462
in Pseudepigrapha, 904
David as author of, 2223
in Dead Sea Scrolls, 880, 7461, 7463–7464, 7465
divine kingship in, 5147
divine scrutiny in, 1939
doxology in, 7461
Elohim in, 7461
Ethiopianism based on, 75, 1437
gambling in, 3262
ghosts in, 3475
Hirsch (Samson Raphael) on, 868
humor of mockery and derision in, 4196
Jerome chanting, 7464
Jerome's translation of, 892–893
Jesus citing, 887, 7464
in Jewish canon, 7460
Levites as singers of, 927–928
Levites in, 5427
liturgical use of
in Christianity, 7464–7465
in Israelite religion, 7463, 7464
in Judaism, 7464
music in, 6276, 6307
nature described in, 2642
Near Eastern psalms and, 885
pesharim of, 7063, 7064, 7065
pessimism of, 4549
Pesuqei de-Zimra' (Verses of Song) recitation, 8389
Peter Lombard on, 7066
poetry of, 7204, 7205–7206, 7218, 7466
as revelation, 7465
Sa'adyah Gaon on, 865
as sacred drama, 2442
sections of, 7461
settings of, 7463–7464
suffering in, 8805
Sundén (Hjalmar) on, 8851
Temple in, 4746
themes in, 7462, 7464
theology of, 7465–7466
types of psalms in, 7461, 7462–7463
in worship, 9807
Yahveh in, 4296, 7461, 7464
Psalms of Solomon, 904, 7461
messianism in, 5972
Psalms of Thomas, Mandaean religion in, 5639
Psalter. *See Psalms*
Psellus, Michael, 6475, **7466–7467,** 9135–9136
on *lucerna extincta* rite, 8249
Pseudepigrapha, **878–896**. *See also* Biblical literature
apocalyptic literature in, 901, 902–903
demons in, 2277–2278
expansions of biblical stories in, 902, 903–904
ḥokhmah in, 4079
importance of, 896
number of books of, 896
prayers, psalms, and odes in, 902, 904, 7461
testaments in, 902, 903
wisdom and philosophical literature in, 902, 904
Pseudo-Aristeas, Philo Judaeus influenced by, 7106
Pseudo-Callisthenes, romance of Alexander by, 3177
Pseudo-Democritus, 246, 247
Pseudo-Dionysius. *See* Dionysius the Areopagite
Pseudo-Meliton, on Adonis, 34, 35
Pseudonymity, in wisdom literature, 9755
Pseudo-Phocylides, 904
Pseudo-Plutarch
on Epona, 4133
on music, 6305
Psi figurines, 4321
Psilocybin (hallucinogen), 7471
Pskov (city-republic), Christianity in, 7941
P source. *See* Priestly source
Psuchē (soul), 1042
meaning and tradition of, 8540–8542
in New Testament, 8561
Plato on, 7679–7680
Socrates on, 8503
Psyche (mythic figure), 811, 812, 813, 2298, 2833
Psyche (soul), 7182
Psyche: The Cult of Souls and Beliefs in Immortality among the Greeks (Rohde), 7871–7872
Psychedelic drugs and psychoactive substances, **7467–7473**. *See also* Peyote; *Soma*
in 1960s, 7471–7472, 7477
in African religions
Fang people, 7469–7470
in healing, 3821
in Australian Indigenous religions, 7468–7469
consciousness research and, 1951–1952, 7471–7472, 7477
in drug tourism, 7472
experience of, 7467–7468
haoma, **3775–3776**
in hunter-gatherer communities, 7468–7469
irregular relationships associated with, 6489
in Maya religion, 7470
in North American Indian religions, 6654, 6667, 6701–6702
toloache, 6716–6717
in prehistoric religions, 7468

and reality, 7467–7468
in shamanism, 7468
South American, 8292–8293
smoking and, **8453–8456**
Solandra, in Huichol religion, 4153
in South American Indian religions, 8292–8293
tobacco combined with, 9216, 9217
in Uniao do Vegetal (Brazil), 7470
unity with the divine and, 7957
in vision inducement, 9613–9614
yagé, 848
Psychiatry
African ethno-psychiatry, 3818, 3820–3821
materialist, 7488–7491
Psychic Observer (journal), Twitchell (Paul) in, 2601
Psychics
Cayce (Edgar), 559, **1473–1474**
Krishnamurti (Jiddu), 5245
Norman (Ernest), 9448
Psychoanalysis, 7481–7484. *See also* Freud, Sigmund
vs. analytical psychology, 7475, 7484
bridge symbolism in, 1051–1052
demons in, 2285
dreams in, 2483
of ecstasy, 2679
ego psychology in, 7476, 7482
evolutionism in, 2916
games in, 3268
God-image in, 7483
of illusion, 7481, 7482, 7483
Jung in, 5031–5036
Marxist criticism of, 7489–7490
mothering in, 7483
object-relations theory in, 7478, 7482
of pain, 6947
rational, 7484
ritual in, 7833
self psychology in, 7484
temptation in, 9072–9073
transitional phenomena in, 7483–7484
women's studies and, 9792
Psychoanalytic anthropology, Róheim (Géza) and, 7872
Psychoanalytic theory of conversion, 1970
Psychobiology, 7482
Psychohistory, 7476, 7482–7483
Psychokinesis (PK), 6057
Psychologia rationalis (Wolff), 2505
Psychological atheism, 7422
Psychological certainty, 2428
Psychological development, stages of, 5033
Psychological fact, 7484
Psychological-historical approach, to poetry, by Herder (Johann Gottfried), 3918
Psychological philosophy of religion, Chantepie de la Saussaye on, 1531
Psychologie und Erkenntnistheorie in der Religionswissenschaft (Troeltsch), 9365
Psychology, **7473–7491**. *See also* Psychotherapy; Schizoanalysis
of affliction, 59
of alchemy, 247
analytical (*See* Analytical psychology)
Aristotle on, 481
of asceticism, 529
association in, Harva (Uno) and, 3784
of attention, 603, 605
Capps's system of study and, 1413
of childhood and adolescence, Hall (G. Stanley), role of, 3755
child motif, interpretation of, 1568–1569
cognitive dissonance theory, 7798–7799
collective, 7349
in comparative religion, 7479
of consciousness, 1946, 1947–1949
of couvade, 2046
depth psychology, symbolic theory and, 8911–8912
dualism in, 2509
Eastern philosophy and, 1950, 7475, 7476, 7477, 7479, 7485
Eckhart (Johannes) and, 2603–2604
ego, 7476, 7482
of enthusiasm, 2807
and esotericism, 6498
existential, 7476–7477
exorcism studied in, 2935–2936
experimental, 7473–7474, 9847
folklore and, Hartland (E. Sidney) on, 3782
of games, 3268
of glossolalia, 3504, 3505
of goddess worship, 3611–3612
in Graham's (Martha) works, 2159
hermeneutics and, 3930, 3933
humanistic, 7476–7477, 7485
of initiation rituals, 4480, 4481
James (William) in, 4775–4777
Jung in, 5031–5032
Kierkegaard's influence on, 5142–5143
of magic, 5565
mental health, religiousness, relationship with, 3875–3876
of millenarian-type activities, 7788
of myths, Kérenyi (Károly) on, 5114
Neumann (Erich) and, 6484
pastoral, 939, 7477, 7479, 7486–7487
phenomenological, 7476–7477
as religion, 7480
of religion, **7473–7481**
Andrae (Tor) on, 333
Anesaki Masaharu on, 342
Beth (Karl) on, 846–847
comparative-historical method *vs.,* 1868
contemporary, 7477–7480
and culture studies, 7479–7480
decline of interest in, 7475
of ecstasy, 2679–2681
European contributions to, 7473–7475
feminist critique of, 7479
Flournoy (Théodore) on, 7474
formative period of, 7473–7476
Freud (Sigmund) on, 7474, 7482
Gestalt, 8878
Hall (G. Stanley), role in creation of, 3755
Hall (G. Stanley) on, 7475
James (William) on, 7475
journals devoted to, 10058
Jung (C. G.) on, 7474–7475, 7484–7485
Leeuw (Gerardus van der) on, 5391
Leuba (James H.) on, 5418
North American contributions to, 7475–7476
Piaget (Jean) on, 7474
in postwar era, 7476–7477
power in, 7348–7349
Pratt (James) on, 7366–7367, 7475
in Scandinavia, Sundén (Hjalmar), role of, 8850–8851
Starbuck (E. D.) on, 8732
therianthropism in, 9155
religion interpreted by, 7693–7694
of rites of passage, 7798–7799
in ritual studies, 7858
self, 7484
social, on conversion, 1971
Spinoza (Baruch), influence of, 8685
spirit possession and, 8689, 8690, 8696
Ṣūfī, *nafs* (lower souls), control over, 8815
Swedenborgianism and, 8903–8904
temptation in, 9072–9073
transcendental, Kant (Immanuel) on, 5077
transpersonal, 7478
Upaniṣadic, 9482
visions treated in, 9611
witchcraft studied in, 9779
Psychology of Religion: Classic and Contemporary (Wulff), 7474
Psychology of Religion, The (Starbuck), 7475
Psychology of Religious Belief, The (Pratt), 7366
Psychology of Religious Mysticism (Leuba), 5418, 7475
Psychopathology
sacrifice explained as, 8004
shamanism and, 8270
Psychophysics, Fechner and, 1947
Psychopomps, shamans as, 8272–8273
Psychotherapy, **7481–7488**. *See also* Analytical psychology; Psychoanalysis
client-centered, 7485
rebirthing analysis in, 7680
rituals analogous to, anthropological study of, 381–382
social workers providing, 7487–7488
spirituality in, 7485–7486
subconscious and, 1948
temptation in, 9072–9073
transcendental meditation in, 7485
Psychotherapy and Buddhism (Rubin), 7479
Psychotic art, in outsider art, 9625
Psychotria viridis (hallucinogen), 7470
Psychotropic drugs, in South American religions, 6274
Ptah (deity), **7491**
Atum and, 623, 7491
in creation story, 2720, 2961, 7491
in Egyptian pantheon, 2704–2705, 7491
heart of, 3881, 7491
Memphis temple of, 2704, 7491
Ptahil (demiurge), 2274, 5635–5636
Ptehincalaskawin (deity), 5296

Ptolemaeus (theologian)
on aeons, 7190
Irenaeus on, 4539
Ptolemy, **7491–7493**
astrology of, 563, 564, 565, 7492
astronomy of, 1976–1977, 7491–7493
on comets, 8735
Copernicus *vs.,* 8182
on the divine, 5501, 5503
Egyptian religion under, 2709
Galileo *vs.,* 8183
geometry of, 7492
Gersonides' modifications to, 3462
on Huns, 4490
on *hypostasis,* 4241
influence on *falsafah,* 2971
Maimonides (Moses) criticizing, 7492
mathematics of, 7491, 7492
on Mecca, 5049–5050
on meteors, 8736
translations of works of, 7491, 7492
Ptolemy II Philadelphus, 890, 7392
Ptolemy of Lucca, on comets, 8735
Ptolemy XIII (king of Egypt), 4416
PTS. *See* Pali Text Society
Puang Allataala (Bugis name of Allāh), 1317
Puang Matua (deity), 9241
Puberty rites, 4476
ablution in, 10
in African religions, 818, 4478, 4484–4485, 7796
Agikuyu, 7805
Ndembu, 6446–6447
Zulu, 10009
in Australian religions, 4476, 4477, 4480, 4481
psychedelic drugs in, 7468–7469
Freud (Sigmund) on, 7799
gender and, 7798
vs. initiation rites, 7807
in Judaism, 4482
in Melanesian religions, 5837
in modern society, 7802
nature and purpose of, 4480
in Neopaganism, 7830
in North American Indian religions
Algonquian, 6683
Apache, 574, 10069–10071
California, 6715
Lakota, 5297
Navajo, 4485–4486
Potawatomi, 6683
Shawnee, 6683
ordeals of, 4477–4478
pain in, 6945
patterns and issues of, 4480–4482
in primitive religions, 4480
psychological analysis of, 7798–7799
Public schools, religious education in, 7732–7733
Publishing. *See also* Media
by African Americans, 68, 69
by Protestants, vol. 7 color insert
Russian, Kireevskii (Ivan) and, 5187
Tibetan Buddhist, 5224
Puckett, Newbell Niles, 3142, 3143
Pudgala (person), 1297
Pudgalavādins (Personalists), on *saṃsāra,* 8098
Pudu ritual, 1643
Puebla CELAM conference, 1703–1704
Pueblo religions and societies (North America), 6657, 6720. *See also specific tribes*
caves and emergence myths, 1469
ceremonies of, 6721, 6725–6726
Christian missions and, 6423
clowns in, 1838, 1839
cosmology of, 6722–6723
council of, 7301
creation story of, 3015, 6660, 6722
moon in, 6174
dance in, 7302
deities of, 6723–6724
drama in, 2460, 2461
economic patterns of, 6720
fiction of, 3091–3092
iconography of, 4309, 4310
kachina concept in, 6723
Kachina dances of, 6653, 6725
land of, 7303
life, death, and beyond in, 6728–6729
maize symbolism and ritual of, 6726
medicine men of, 6652
medicine societies of, 6721
Mesoamerican influences on, 6654
in Native American Church, 7302
Navajo traditions compared with, 6441, 6443
oral storytelling of, 3090
persistence of religious patterns in, 6721
poetry in, 7225
pottery making by, 3019
religious societies of, 6724–6725
revolt against Spanish domination, 6666, 6667, 6729
secrecy in, 6721–6722
shamanism in, 8289
study of, 6672
syncretism and change in, 6729
tricksters in, 9355
underworld in mythology of, 2984
Pueblo Revolt (1680), 6422, 6441
Puech, Henri-Charles, 3535
Puerto Rico
Espiritistas in, 8691
hypereridic rage reactions (amok) in, 3214
Islam in, 4684
Roman Catholicism in, pilgrimage in, 7151
Pufendorf, Samuel, on natural law, 8491
Pughat (deity), in Canaanite religion, 1388, 1397–1398
Pugio Fidei (Martini), 7233
Puhr ilim (assembly of the gods), in Canaanite religion, 1384
Puhvel, Jaan, 4464
on horses in Indo-European religion, 4132
Pūjā (worship), **7493–7497**
in Brahmanism, 9571–9572
Buddhist, **7495–7497**
development of, 7496–7497
and liturgical order, 1118
origins and evidence for, 7495
practicing, 7495–7496
rituals of, 1124
Hindu, **7493–7495,** 9823
bhakti and, 858, 4002
brahmans performing, 9265
as domestic ritual, 4105
drums and, 2499
at home, 4429, 7493–7494
of International Society for Krishna Consciousness, 4522
mūrti in, 6239
origins and etymology of, 7493
rituals of, 2319
in Swaminarayan and BAPS movements, 8892
Tantric, 4430
types of, 7493–7495
vs. yajña, 7493
Jain, 4382
Pūjāri (priest), 7495
Pūjāśālā (worship), 7493
Puka-tala (sacred tree), 9335
Pūkis (dragon), 769
Pukulan (martial arts), 5732–5733
Pulaaku (code of honor), 3229
Pulcinella (Dieterich), 2348
Pulguksa Buddhist temple compound (Korea), 9048
Pullman, Philip, 3528
Puluga (deity), 2310, 2984
Schmidt (Wilhelm) *vs.* Radcliffe-Brown (A. R.) on, 8169–8170
Puma (mountain lion). *See also* Jaguars
Inca calendar and, 1364
Pumbedita (Babylonia)
Abbaye in, 2–3
Sherira' Gaon in academy at, 8320
Pumpurs, Andrejs, 762
Puṃsavana (pregnancy rite), 7814
Punarjanman (rebirth), Upaniṣadic concept of, Brahmanic precursor to, 3992
Pundol, Minocher, 6999
Pundolism, 9991
Punishment, **5371–5375**. *See also* Law
in Adamic myth, 2900
in afterlife, 5371 (*See also* Hell; Judgment)
differentiation of destinies and, 137–138
geography of death and, 136
in Islam, 7767
soteriology and, 8530
structure of universe and, 134
amputation, 3770–3771
Bentham (Jeremy) on, 5371, 5373, 5374
in Buddhism, Vaiśālī council and, 2035
of children, controversy over, 6540
in Chinese religion
Confucius on, 1894
Han Fei Zi on, 3773, 5395
in Legalism, 5395
in Christianity, 5372
Roman Catholicism, 7886
suffering as, 8806
communication function of, 5373–5374
corporal, of children, 5377
deterrent effect of, 5373
expulsion as, 2938
the Fall as, 2960
Foucault (Michel) on, 5374
guilt and, 2897
in Hinduism
karman as, 5327
penance and, 5345
incarceration as, 5374
in Islam
in afterlife, 7767
in eschatology, 2838
suffering as, 8808
in Judaism
Albo (Yosef) on, 233
capital and corporal, 3752
election and, 2744
Sa'adyah Gaon on, 7952–7953
suffering as, 8805
in Judeo-Christian tradition, sin, death as punishment for, 8404
law of talion, 7782–7783
mandatory sentences, 5374
in modern law, 5374
Nietzsche (Friedrich) on, 5371
in Orphism, body as, 8405
pain as, 6945–6946

in religious law, 5327, 5371–5372
purification as, 5371, 5372
restitution *vs.*, 1843
retribution as, 5372–5374, 7782–7784
vs. revenge, 7779–7780
as rhetoric, 5373
in Rome, ancient, mirror punishments, 7782
in secular law, 5327
shape shifting as, 8301–8302
suffering as, 9115
torture as, 5374
Pūniu (drum), 2500
Punjabi language, Eckankar use of, 2602
Punta dance, 3284
Puntan (deity), 6009
Puṇya (merit), 5872–5875
development of concept, 5870
Puṇyakṣetra (merit-fields), 5105
in Buddhism, 5873
in Jainism, 5870
Puppet kings, 5158
Puppet theater
Balinese, 2450, 2451
Indonesian, 7044
Japanese, 2455
Javanese, 2452–2453
Korean, 2454
music in, 6288, 6289–6290
Pura (deity), in Warikyana religion (South America), 8577
Pūraka (breathing), 1044
Purāṇa (monk), Rājagṛha council and, 2035
Pūraṇan̲, 213
Purāṇas (Hindu texts), **7497–7502**
Agni in, 179
Banaras in, 778
Bhagavadgītā and, 854
Brahmā in, 7500
brahman in, 7501
in Brahmanism, 9568–9569
canon status, 1407
characteristics of, 7497–7498
cosmology in, 2017–2019, 2019, 7500
sāhasra cosmology, parallels with, 2028
sectarian elaboration of, 4004
and time, conception of, 4015
creation story in, 1023–1024, 1986, 2963, 4439, 4440
Devī in, 7500
dharma in, 2621, 5343
Dīvālī in, 2368
diversity of, 7497
future of, 7501
Gaṇeśa in, 3271, 3273
Gaṅgā in, 7861
genealogies in, 4025
hell in, 9456
history of, 7499
in Vaiṣṇavism, 9501
Kuṇḍalinī in, 5266
list of, 7498
magic in, 5591
meaning of word, 7497
mokṣa through, for *śūdra* caste, 4004
mudrās in, 6219
narrative in, 7498–7499
narrative of churning of the ocean of milk in, 4013
pilgrimage sites in, 7169
Pratyabhijñā Saivism and, 8049
Rāmā in, 7609
Rudra-Śiva in, 8039, 8415
Sarasvatī in, 8113
significance of, 7499
Śiva in, 7500
Śiva-Kapālin myth in, 8050
sleeping gods in, 8440
in Southeast Asia, in bas reliefs, 4013
studies of, 4446
Tantric practice *vs.*, 4003
tapas in, 8998
time and space in, 7499–7500
Viṣṇu in, 7500
Pūravavideha (mythic island), in Buddhist *cakravāla* cosmology, 2026, 2027
Purcell, John B., Campbell (Alexander) and, 1377
Purdah (seclusion of women), 1559
Pure and Impure Lands, in *asaṃkhyeya* cosmology, 2026
Pure Consciousness Event (PCE), 7745
Pure Conversation *(qingtan),* 1595
Pure Land Buddhism. *See also* Jōdo Shinshū school of Buddhism; *See also* Jōdoshū school of Buddhism
Amitābha in, 291–292, 1238–1239, 8981, 8982
antiritualism of, 7699
bodhisattvas in, 1114, 8982
saving power of, 3887
Chan combined with, 1524, 4923–4924
in China, 1096, 1162, 1166, 1236, 1238–1239, 2175–2176, 4921–4925, 5310
consolidation of, 4922–4923
Daochuo and, 2175–2176
drama in, 2455
early masters, 1577
in East Asia, 9836–9837
eternity in, 2856
ethics of, 1281–1282
gender in, 3343
goddess worship in, 3587
Huiyuan, role of, 1576, 4156
human perfectibility in, 7041
iconography of, 4329
in Japan, 5310
Benchō's role in, 818, 819
Ennin and, 2801
Genshin in, 3432–3433
Hōnen's role in, 4119
in Kamakura period, 1096, 1243–1244
language in, 5310
in Nara period, 1179
popularity of, 4786, 4796
practices of, 1177–1178
Rennyo as leader of, 1182
Shandao and, 8299
Suzuki Shōsan, role of, 8887
Western Paradise in, 3887–3888
Land of the Western Paradise in, 3887–3888
language in, 5310
light and darkness symbolism in, 5453
lotus symbolism in, 5520
Maitreya in, 5620
mappō in, 5685, 5686
married monks in, 1183
meditation in, 1293–1294, 5821
as devotion, 2320
merit in, 5872
monotheism in, 6157
and Nembutsu, 3155–3156
nianfo in, 6601, 6602
nianfo recitation in, 8298–8299
Nichiren's criticism of, 6604
nirvāṇa in, 6632, 8982
opposition to, 4923
origins of, 291–292, 1239
overview of, 1600–1601
paradise in, 6984
paradox in, 6990
path to salvation in, Hinayana parallels, 2029
personification of compassion in, 3019
philosophy of, 1302
political power of, 7272–7273
power in, 7353–7354
recitation societies in, 9836–9837
scripture of (*See Sukhāvativyūha Sūtra*)
Shandao and, 2176, **8298–8299**
Shingon school and, 8350
Shin school of, Suzuki (D. T.) and, 8886
spread of, 4923
stupas and, 8798
Tanluan in, 291, 292, 1239, 1600–1601, 4922, 8981, 8982
temples of, 9049
and Tendai school, 9079–9080
White Lotus sect and, 1606
Xingyuan's interpretations of, 3139–3140
Zhuhong in, 9971–9972
Pure Lands (Buddhist concept), 1077, **7502–7503**
Pure Land sūtras, 7502, 7503
Pure Water observance, 1648
Purgation, 7508–7509
season rites of, 8209
Purgatory
in Chinese religion, 1606
in Christianity
and All Souls Day, 2229
development of doctrine of, 8565
origins of, 158
Protestant rejection of, 158
Roman Catholicism, 7886
and salvation as process, 3885
in *Commedia* (Dante Alighieri), 2170
in Mandaean religion, 5636
in Oceanic religions, 2007
Puri, Harbhajan Singh. *See* Bhajan, Yogi
Purification, **7503–7516.** *See also* Catharsis; Confession of sins; Pollution; Purity
ablution as, 10–11, 12
in Hinduism, 2621
in African religions
central Bantu, 1511
detergents in, 7508
in initiation rituals, 4486
Nuer, 7509
Nyakyusa, 6770, 6771
in southern African religions, 8656–8657
in Swazi religion, 8897
water in, 7510
in Akkadian religion, 2791
in animal sacrifice, 7509
in African religions, 88
by ashes, 540–541, 7508
in Buddhism, 7509
catharsis, **1458–1461,** 7509
celibacy as, 7509
in Cherokee rituals, 1564
in Chinese religion
cleaning graves as, 7509
Confucian ritual purity, 1914
Shangdi sacrifice, preparation for, 1915
in Christianity, 7510
baptism as, 7507
fasting as, 7508
circumcision as, 7505, 7508
clitoridectomy as, 1826
cow dung in, 7508
cultural diversity of, 7504
detergents in, 7507–7508
dietary laws as (*See* Dietary laws)
in East African religions
Qemant, 2573
sacrifice in, 2568

Purification ***continued***
emetics in, 7508
expiation sacrifices and, 8001
expulsion as, 2939–2940
fasting as, 2996–2997, 7508
fire in, 7507
in Greek religion, 7144, 7507, 7509, 7756
hands and, 3770
healing through, 3812
in Hinduism
cow dung in, 7508
Dumont (Louis) on, 7504
fire in, 7507
mantras and, 7509
for pilgrimage, 7169
rivers for, 7862
of sacred space, 7507
sadhus/sadhvis (renunciates) and, 8020
water in, 7507
yoga after, 7510
of homes, 4105
human sacrifice in, 7509
incense offering in, 4418–4419, 7507
in Shintō, 5197, 7504, 8369
in Iranian religion, 4535
in Islam (*See also* ṭahārah)
fasting during Ramaḍān as, 7508
for *ḥājj*, 7157
Ibn ʿAbd al-Wahhāb on, 4255
of Kaʿbah, 7160
for marriage, 7827
water in, 7507
in Israelite religion, 4732–4733, 4747, 4973, 7511–7513
in Jainism, *sallekhanā* (austere penance) and, 8831
in Japanese religion
of automobiles, 3869–3870
death and, 4797
for entry into shrines, 7981
in Shintō, 5197, 7504, 8369
in Judaism, **7516–7516**
laws on, 7511–7513
in *miqveh*, 6046–6048
in Mishnah, 6066
in rabbinic Judaism, 7514–7515
for Yom Kippur, 7928
libations and, 5433
in Manichaeism, salvation and, 4158–4159
in monasticism, relationships as, 2829
pain in, 6946
in pilgrimage, 7157, 7169, 7507, 7509
prayer and, 7509
as punishment, in religious law, 5371, 5372
Pure Water observance in Ch'ŏndogyo, 1648
purgation in, 7508–7509
seasonal, 8209
rain as symbol of, 7604
relics and, 7509
in rites of passage, 7504, 7505
rivers and, 7862
in Roman religion, lustratio and, 5534
sacraments and, 7509
of sacred space, 7507, 7981
scapegoat ritual as, 8143
secular forms of, 7510
substitution and, 7509
symbolism of, 7504
of Temple, 927, 934, 2945, 7511, 7512, 7515
by time, 7511
torture in, 7508–7509
in Vedism, *dīkṣā* for, 7816
water in, 7507, 7510, 7511, 9703
Puril Pojo, National Master, 1646
Purim (festival), **7516**
domestic observances of, 2397, 2400
Esther celebrated at, 7516, 7517
gift giving in, 3484
Holocaust destroying, 7517–7518
importance of, 7517
in Jewish calendar, 4867
maḥzor liturgy for, 8390
in Marrano Judaism, 5718
message of, 7517
origin of, 2848
origins of, 7516
of Shushan, in Jewish calendar, 4867
Purim plays, 7043, **7516–7518**
Purimshpiln. See Purim plays
Puritanism, **7518–7521**
American civil religion and, 1813–1815
in American colonies, 1709–1710, 7519, 7520
denominationalism and, 1712
evangelicalism and, 2887
American Protestantism and, 1715
Anglicanism opposition to, as Arminianism, 493
apocalypse in, 412
autobiography in, 699
Calvinism and, 7519
Christian Science, link to, 1746
Christmas and, 1757
concrete assurance of election doctrine, 4238
Congregationalism, shift to, 1712
on conversion, 7519–7520
covenant theology, 7519
social reform and, 1750–1751
in Westminster Confession, 2044
and dance, 2154
ecclesiology of, 1774
Edwards (Jonathan) influenced by, 2698
election in, 2748
in England, 1709, 7518–7519, 7520–7521
concrete assurance of election doctrine, 4238
Hooker (Richard), defense against, 4124
during Reformation, 7663
as flow activity, 3138
fragmentation of, 2287
funeral rites in, 9228
gambling in, 3262
God in, 7519, 7520
Hermetism and, 3948
homo religiosus and, 4109
Hooker (Thomas), role of, **4125**
humor, suppression of, 4219
iconoclasm in, 4347
individualism and, 5399
kingdom of God in, 5152
literature of, 7521
migration in, 6023, 6024
morality in, 7520
music in, 6310
and Native Americans, Praying Towns, 7301
origins of, 7518–7519
and persecution of other religions, 6557
persecution of Quakers by, 7547
Pilgrim's Progress (Bunyan) on, 1323
predestination in, 7519
preparation theology in, 4125
and Presbyterianism, 7390
religious experience in, 7737
sexuality in, 7520
theology of, 9138
Westminster Confession in, 7521
witchcraft and, 9774
Purity. *See also* Chastity; Pollution; Purification
in agrarian values, 193
Buddhism and, in post-Buddha period, 2035
in Confucianism, 7510
egg as symbol of, 2702
in enlightenment, 2795
of Essenes, 2847
hands and, 3770
in Hinduism, 1559, 9820
caste system and, 3996, 7843
pure *vs.* impure gods in, 4006, 4007
sacrilege and, 8015
holiness tied to, 4100
impurity, illness caused by, 3810
in Bēta Esraʾēl, 5003, 5004
in Islam
for *ṣalāt* (prayer), 8057
of knowledge, 6097
Muḥammad on, 8057
ritual *(ṭahārah)*, 1559, 2401
in Japanese religion, purity/impurity opposition, health and, 3867–3868
of knowledge, in Islam, 6097
lotus as symbol of, 5519
of priesthood, 7397
in primordial paradise, 6983
sacred space ad, 7981
sacred *vs.* profane and, 7974
trauma theory and, 8245
in Zoroastrianism, 9997–9998, 10004
Purity and Danger (Douglas), 7504, 7513, 7797
Purlapa (public performances), 9696–9697
Pūrnaprajñā. *See* Madhva
Pūrṇimā (full moon), in Hindu calendar, 4015
Purohita (priest), 7406
Purple (color), symbolism of, 1861, 1862
Purpose. *See* Teleology
Purposive Daoism, 1574
Pursel, Jach, 6532
Pursuit of the Millenium, The (Cohn), 6985
Purūravas (mythic figure), 5679
Puruṣa, **7521–7523**
Agnicayana (Vedic fire sacrifice) and, 4184
as transcendent Puruṣa-Nārāyaṇa
in Brāhmaṇas, 3992
in Upaniṣads, 3993
breath of, 1043, 7362
Buddhist denial of, 8551
as consciousness, 7521, 7522
development of concept of, 7521
gender of, 3319
in *Ṛgveda*, 7521–7522
in Sāṃkhya Hinduism, 3997, 3998, 8089, 8091
in Upaniṣads, 3993, 7521, 7522
mysticism and, 6343
Prajāpati associated with, 7356
sacrifice by, 1027, 2367, 7254
samādhi and, 8067
Sāṃkhya school on, 7522
as self, 4415, 7521, 7522
as spirit
liberation of, 4422–4423
plurality of, 4422
and *prakṛti*, 853, 4422–4423, 7522
in Tantric Hinduism, 4003
in Vedic cosmology, 2014, 7521–7522
Viṣṇu as, 9619
in Yoga, 9896
Puruṣamedha (human sacrifice), 9564
Puruṣārthas (four goals of humankind)
avātara theory and, 4001
in classical Hinduism, 3996–3997
Purusha, self sacrifice of, 2243

Puruṣottama (Highest Spirit), 853
Pūrva (Prior), 4766
Pūrvadevas (devils), 2314
Pūrva Mīmāṃsā. *See also* Mīmāṃsā school
on *karman,* 5094
as philosophy of ritual, 7835
Pūrvaśaila sect
doctrines of, 1197
origin of, 1194
texts attributed to, 1114
Pūṣan (deity), 9557
Pusey, Edward Bouverie, 6510, **7523**
Pushkin, Alexander, *Evgeny Onegin,* 3053
Puskaītis (deity), 767
Puṣkara (island-continent), in Jain cosmology, 2023–2024
Pusŏk monastery (Korea), 9437
Pu Songling, 3067
Pussars, Romāns, 765
Puṣṭimārgīya Sampradāyas, Kṛṣṇa worshipped by, 5250
Putnam, Hilary, 2951
Putney Community, 6732
Puttick, Elizabeth, 6541
Putumaipittan (South Asian writer), 10036
Putuo Shan, 6213
Puya (deity), 9241, 9242
Puyŏ, origin myth of, 5179
Pwyll (mythic figure), 1490
in Annwn, 371
in *Mabinogion,* 5546
Pye, Michael, historiography of, 4049
Pygmalion (mythic figure), shape shifting and, 8302
Pygmy religions (Central Africa), **7523–7526**
circumcision in, 7525
dance in, 7524
the Fall in, 2961
forest in, 7523–7524, 7525
history of study of, 114
hunting in, 7524, 7525
lord of the animals in, 5514–5515
moon symbolism in, 3018, 3971
rainbow symbolism in, 7604
rituals in, 7524, 7525
Schmidt (Wilhelm) on, 8168, 8170, 8876–8877
spirits in, 7523–7524
women in, 7524, 7525
Pylon (gateway), 9061
Pylos (Greece)
palace of, 41
tablets of, Poseidon in, 7338
Pyramids, **7526**. *See also* Ziggurats
architecture of
classification of, 461
origins of, 7526
Aztec, 1468, 5293, 5898
Egyptian, **7526–7528**
complexes of, 7527
early theories on, 2729
of government officials, 2705
Great Pyramid, 7527
iconography of, 4318
Jehovah's Witnesses and, 4820
in Old Kingdom, 2704
origins of, 7527
as royal tombs, 9225
Step Pyramid, 7527
as towers, 9264
Maya, 5799, 5886
Mesoamerican, 7526, 7527, 9065–9066, 9266
Mesopotamian, 7527
Moon Pyramid, 5898
sky hierophany and, 8428
Yopico (Aztec), 1469
Pyramid Texts, 2704, 2715, 2718, 7527
illustrations in, 4318
Isis in, 4557
of noble coffins, 2705
Osiris in, 6919–6920
publication of, 2728
redemption in, 7640–7641
Re in, 7634
Thoth in, 9167
translations of, 2728–2729
underworld in, 9452
Pyroscapulimancy, 6834
Pyrovasia (fertility rite), 7654
Pyrrha and Deukalion, myth of, 2965–2966
Pyrrho of Elis, 2823
Pyrrhus (patriarch), Maximos the Confessor and, 5792
Pythagoras, **7528–7531**
on alphabet, 270
and Apollo, 7528, 7529
ascension by, 520
asceticism of, 7722
astral thesis of, 8425
on charity, 1554
as charlatan, 7528
in decline of Greek religion, 3685
on deification, 2248
as god, 7528
on image veneration, 4381
instructions of, 7529
on judgment of the dead, 5026
life of, 7528
magic and, 5575
as mathematician, 7529, 7530
metempsychosis doctrine of, 8541
miracles of, 6050–6051
on numbers, 6752, 7530
Philo Judaeus influenced by, 7106, 7113
as philosopher, 7529–7530
and physics, 7136
as reformer, 7529
on reincarnation, 166, 7528, 9328–9329
on sacrifice, 1467, 7529
as shaman, 7528
on souls, 4415, 7528, 9328
sources on, 7528, 7529
as spiritual guide, 8708–8709
travels of, 7528
wisdom of, 9747
writings of, 7528
Zalmoxis and, 3466, 9926, 9928
Pythagoreanism
apotheosis and, 438
and deification, 2248–2249
on dualism, 2511
geometry of, *3440,* 3440–3443, *3443*
infinite breath, belief in, 8542
on knowledge, 5201
legacy of, 6752
on numbers, 6746, 6749
Orphism and, 6891, 7529
Plato in contact with, 7181
vs. Platonism, 7529–7530
Plutarch influenced by, 7189
revival of, 7530
secret symbolic language of, 8907
on souls becoming stars, 8733
on spiritual guides, 8709
spread of, 7530
taboos on food, 2997
transmigration of soul in, 7186
vegetarianism in, 7529, 9579
way of life in, 7529, 7530
Pythagorean theorem, 3440
Pythagorean triplets, *3440,* 3440–3441
Pythagorizing Platonism, 7189
Pythia (priestess of Apollo), 2265–2266, 6833–6834, 9607
Pythian Dialogues (Plutarch), 7200
Pythian games, 8723
Pythias (mythic figures), as oracles, 8383
Pythons. *See also* Yulunggul snake
in African religions
in myths, 96, 8664
Southern Bantu python cult, 8663–8664
Dangbi as python god, 3969
Pyvsyansa (bathhouse spirit), in Komi religion, 5218
Pyysiäinen, Ilkka, 7747

Q

Q (source of synoptic gospels), 906–907
Mary in, 5752
wisdom tradition and, 9760
Qabbalah, **7533–7539**
Abulafia (Me'ir) and, 24
Adam in, 29
Adret (Shelomoh ben Avraham) and, 36
afterlife in, 154–155
anamnesis (recollection) in, 313–314
androgyny of God in, 8315
angels in, 345
attention in, 604
Avraham ben David and, 711–712
and belief in demons, 3159
Boehme's (Jakob) interest in, 1006
and ceremonial magicians, 6471
Christian, 7535–7536
development of, 6527
in Western esotericism, 2843
circle of BeSHT and, 3786
contemplation in, 5817
Cordoverian system of, 7534, 7535
Cordovero's role in history of, 1984–1985
cosmogony in, 7536
language in, 5302
demons in, 2278, 5459
dualism in, 2512
ecstatic, 4981, 7534
Ashkenazic Qabbalah and, 7538
Ein Sof (the infinite), 1985
eschatological mysticism of, 6353–6354
eschatology of, 7538
ethical works of, 4912–4913, 4914
etymology of word, 7533
exorcism in, 2932
external influences on, 7538–7539
feminist analysis of, 8243
fire in, 3119
Frankist sexual rituals in, 8250
Gnostic concepts in, 3524, 6353
Scholem (Gershom) on, 8178
goddess worship in, 3586
God in, 1985, 3550–3551, 4981
attributes of, 615, 3550
halakhah and, 3751
Hasidism and, 3788, 3791
hermeneutics in, 7538
Hermetism and, 3949
historiography in, 4059
history of, 7533–7535
ḥokhmah in, 4079–4080
images of, vol. 3 color insert
intuition in, 4526
Israel in, 4862
in Jewish ecology, 2646
in Jewish ethics, 4913
Jewish poetry influenced by, 7208
in Jewish Renewal, 4872
Karo's (Yosef) interest in, 5104–5105
on *kashrut,* 5108
kavvanot (intentions), 3789
Kook (Avraham Yitsḥaq) and, 5226

Qabbalah ***continued***
literature of, 7538
Lurianic (*See* Lurianic Qabbalah)
magical interpretation of, 7535–7536
magic in, 5579
medieval, 4980–4981
meditation in, 5817
messianism in, 5977–5978
music in, 6277–6278
in Renaissance, 6309–6310
mystical techniques in, 7537
mystical union in, 6339–6340
Nahmanides (Moses) legitimizing, 6399–6400
nature in, 2643, 6433
Neoplatonism and, 6475
numerical allegory in, 6746, 6749, 6750
numerology in, 8676
oral Torah in, 6840
orgy and, 6872
origins of, 6353
parables in, 6978
phallic patterns in, 7080, 7085
philosophical interpretation of, 7539
prophecy in, 6353, 7441
Purim in, 7517
reincarnation in, 8806
religious experience in, 7739
revelation in, 7777
Sabbath, welcoming of, in, 8389
in Safad, 4998, 5104, 7534
Scholem (Gershom), role of, **8177–8178**
Scholem (Gershom) on, 7739
secret tradition in, 9278
Sefer yetsirah (Book of Creation) in, **8221–8222**
sefirot (divine radiances)
Ein Sof and, 1985
tsassiqim as intermediary with, 3789
Shabbateanism and, 8261
Shekhinah in, 8315
siddur and *maḥzor* (prayer books) in, 8387, 8388
soul in, 8560
sounds and words in, power of, 8675, 8676
Spanish, 7534
speculation in, 6353
on supernatural uniqueness of Jews, 2746
symbolism of, 4340–4341
tears in, 9025
theosophy of, 7533, 7534–7535, 7536, 8315
theurgy of, 7536–7537
Torah as law in, 9237
as tradition, 9268
transmigration in, 9330
tsaddiq in, 9378
tsimtsum concept in, 3524, 3551
chaos and, 1540
Luria (Isaac) on, 7534–7535
Tu B'Shevat of, 2645
unio mystica in, 7537–7538
Vital (Ḥayyim) in, 9628
Zohar in, 9983–9984
Qabbalat Shabbat (welcoming of the Sabbath), in *siddur* liturgy, 8389
Qādā' (restitution), for infractions against *ṣawm* (fasting), 8140
Qadar (free will), Ḥasan's doctrine of, 3785
Qādarī creed, traditionalism in, 3761
Qadarīyah (Qadarī heresy), 3210–3211
in China, 4635
God in, power of, 3562
move away from, 3211–3212
Qadar principle, in Ismāīlīyah, 8326
Qaddish (prayer)
kingdom of God in, 5149
in *siddur* liturgy, 8389
Szold (Henrietta) on, 8466
Qadesh (priest), 5420
Qadhdhāfī, Muʿammar al-, 4574
Nation of Islam and, 6420
Qāḍī, 4641, 4645, **7540–7541**
delegation of legal powers to, 7540–7541
jurisdiction of, 7540
qualifications of, 7540
responsibilities of, 7541
in *waqf,* 9677–9678
Qāḍī al-Nuʿmān, al-, **7541–7542**
and al-Azhar university, 230
Ismāʿīlī law and, 8329–8330
writings of, 4584
Qādir, al- (caliph), al-Māwardī and, 5787
Qādirī (Sufi poet), 2219
Qādirīyah (Ṣūfī order)
in Caucasus, 4615, 9007
in Central Asia, 4621, 4629, 9007
establishment of, 9007
founder of, 8824, 9008
Fulbe scholars and, 3229
as global order, 4571
initiation into, 9006
khānagāhs of, 5118
in South Asia, 4647, 4648
in sub-Saharan Africa, 4606
women in, 4610
Qādiriyya Ṣūfī *silsila,* Dārā Shikōh in, 2219
Qādiyānī branch, of Aḥmadiyah, 200. *See also* Lāhōrī branch
Qādiyānī Mas'alah, 4773
Qadosh
English translation of, in Bibles, 4098
Hebrew concept of, 7967
in Hebrew scriptures, 7967–7968
Yahveh as, 3542
Qā'id (representative of central powers), 4588
Qāʿidah, al- (Islamic movement), 7258, 7288–7289
as new religious movement, 6517, 6525
as revolutionary millennial movement, 6549
in Southeast Asia, 4671–4672
Qā'im, al-, as Mahdi, 2838
Qajar period, Zoroastrianism in, 10003
Qalandarī Ṣūfī order, 9006
Qalandār La'l Shahbāz, 4648
Qalandārs (wandering mendicants), 4648
Qalonimos family, 542–545, 5011
Qānūn al-Masʿūdi (al-Bīrūnī), 954
Qānūn fī al-ṭibb, al- (Ibn Sīnā), 4274
Qara', Yosef, 866
Qaradāwī, Yūsuf al-, on reliability of *ḥadīths,* 3732
Qarāfī, al-, 7240, 7242
Qarāmiṭah (Qarmatī), 4375, **7542–7544**
of Bahrein, 7542–7544
decline of, 8329
Epistles of Brethren of Purity and, 8329
Kaʿbah and, 5050
proclamation of the mahdī in, 8328–8329
schism from Ismāīlīyah, 8327, 8328–8329
teachings of, 7543
Qāri' (reciter), 9200
Qarigi (big men's houses), 4527
Qāshānī, ʿAbd al-Razzāq al-, 8955
Qasida (poetic form), 7222, 7223
Qasidah moderen (poetic form), 7223
Qāsim ibn Ibrāhīm, al-, 7242
and Muʿtazilah, 6320
Qāsimīyah movement, Naṣirīyah *vs.,* 8325
Qāsim-shāh, Muḥammad-shāh *vs.,* 8333
Qasiq (big men's houses), 4527
Qaṣr al-Bint (temple), 6386, *6389*
Qāṣṣ (story-teller), 2446
Qatabānians, in Arabia, 443
Qawa'id al-ahkam fī masāliḥ al-anām (Rules for Judgment in the Cases of Living Beings), 2652
Qawwālī (devotional music), 4642, 6283, 6284
Qaynuqāʿ tribe, Muḥammad and, 6225
Qayyūm al-asmaʿ (the Bāb), 728
Qazim, Safinaz, 3368
Qazwīnī, al-, on gold and silver, 3626
Qbb (curse or revile), in Balak/Balaam story, 2103
Qebatoch, 2861
Qedeshah (piestess), 5420
Qedushah (holiness), 9239–9240, 10051
Qedushat ha-Yom (Sanctification of the Day), in Sabbath prayers, 8389
Qedushat Levi (Levi Yitsḥaq of Berdichev), 5428
Qemant religion (Ethiopia), 2573
Qenē (poetic hymns), in Ethiopian liturgy, 2859
Qērelos, in Ethiopia, 2859–2860
Qeren ha-Torah, 195
Qeri, 868
Qessa-e Sanjān (Parsi legend), 6997, 9994
Qi (vital spirit), **7544–7545**
and afterlife, 172
basic concepts, 1597
as bodies of The Perfected, 2182
Cheng Hao on, 1561
in Chinese healing system, 3859–3860
in Confucianism
Kaibara Ekken on, 5055
nature as, 2631, 2632, 2633
cultivation of, 3862
in Daoism, 2177, 2635, 7544
nourishment of, 9843
definitions of, 2177, 7544
Dia Zhen on, 2129
grave location and, 1594
human nature and, 8555
humans composed of, 1589
Hwadam on, 8510
merging of, in Celestial Masters marriage ritual, 2181, 2182, 2193
monistic theory of, 5055
in Neo-Confucianism, 9311
soul and, 8554–8555
Wang Fuzhi on, 9673
Wang on portents and, 1575
yinyang wuxing and, 9888–9889
Zhang on cosmology and, 1578
Zhu Xi on, 7544, 9973
Zou Yan on, 2129
Qian (heaven), 1583, 1584
Qianlong, 1609
Qiblah (central point)
declaration of, 4562
imam facing, 4396
in Bahā'ī faith, 739–740
Kaʿbah as, 5049, 9816–9817, vol. 5 color insert
Kaʿbah determining, 7155
in mosques, 6205, 6208
Muḥammad's revision of, from Jerusalem to Mecca, 6224
new, 729
Qiblah-compass, vol. 14 color insert
Qiddush (benediction), 7004. *See also* Qedushat ha-Yom
Qiddush ha-shem (sanctification of divine name), 7056–7057
Qifṭī, al-, 4375

Qigong movement (China), 2978–2979, 6518
Communist government and, 1615
origin of, 2188
religious revival and, 1611
Qiguan (wife of Confucius), 9059
Qi kingdom, 1572
Qillel (curse), 971–972
in Hebrew scriptures, 2103
Qin (musical instrument), 6293
Qināqis (eunuch), 2859
Qin dynasty (China), 1614
Buddhism in, 1170
immortality quests in, 7267
kingship in, 5179
Legalism in, 5396
magic in, 5592
sacrifice in, 7267
Qingcheng, Mount, Daoist monastery on, 2637
Qing dynasty (China)
Buddhism in, 1166–1167
and canon, 1166, 1255
Chan Buddhism in, 1524
laws concerning, 5353
monasticism in, 6129
pilgrimage, 7165
temples, 9048
and Tibetan Buddhism, 1155, 1240
Confucianism in, 1578–1579, 1903–1904, 2187, 4338
temples in, 9059, 9060
Daoism in, 2187, 2188, 2197, 2201
Islam in, 4632–4633
kaozheng school of evidential research in, 2129–2130
martial arts in, 5735
missionaries and, 1631
music in, 6293
overview of religion in, 1609–1610
philology movement, 1579
philosophy in, 1574, 1578–1579, 1590
political and social context, 1589–1590
rebellions in, 7268–7269
Taiwan in, 8962
women in, 3339
Qingming Jie, 1642
Qingtan debates, 1595
Qingyuan (Buddhist monk), 6987–6988
Qingyuan Xingshi, Huineng as teacher of, 4155
Qingzhenjiao (Chinese term for Islam), 4631
Qingzhensi (Chinese term for mosque), 4631
Qi Niangma (deity), 1643
Qin Shihuangdi (Chinese emperor), 2990
Qirā' āt (readings/recitations of the Qur'ān), 7563, 8950, 9200
Qirqisānī, Ya'qūb al-, 4992
on Sadducees, 4058–4059
writings of, 5085
Qiṣṣat al-ghurbah al-gharbīyah (Suhrawardī), 4554
Qi state, Confucius in, 1934
Qiu Changchun (Qiu Chuji), 2186, 2199, 2207
disciples of, 7415
writings of, 2210
Qiuji (autumn sacrifice), 1643
Qiyāmah (resurrection), 558
in Nizārīyah, 8332–8333
worship and, 9816
Qiyās (analogy), 4271, **7545–7546**
Abū Ḥanīfah and, 5547
elements of, 4566
in *fiqh,* 9488–9489
ijtihād identified with, 4374, 4566
in Sunnī Islam, 4696
al-Shāfi'ī on, 8265
as source of *sharī'ah,* 4372, 4696–4697
in Twelver Shiism, 4696–4697
Qi zhen (Seven Perfected Ones), 2186
Qoa (deity), portrayal of, 8602
Qodashim (Sacred Things), 927, 6066
Qohelet. *See Ecclesiastes*
Qolla-huaya people (Bolivia)
ayllu of, 8617
herbal healers, 3811
Qom (Iran)
hawzah of, 3801, 3802
Shiism in, 8323
Qorban (offering), 926, 4746
Q'tub-ud-din (Asiatic conqueror), 9266
Quadratus, apologetics of, 427
Quadrille, at a *veglia,* 2148
Quadruplex reprobatio (Martī), 7243
Quakers, **7546–7550**
authority in, 695
autobiography in, 699
blasphemy prosecution of, 973
Bunyan (John) debating, 1323
church architecture of, 795
classification of, 461
denominationalism and, 1712
enthusiasm of, 2805
evangelical, 7548
government of, 7547–7548
on kingdom of God, 5152
leaders of
Fox (George), **3180–3181**
Penn (William), 7027–7028
meetings, 7547, 7548
membership of, 7548–7549
moral and social aspects of, 7651
mysticism of, 7549
as new religious movement, 6533
pacifism of, 6648
persecution of, by Puritans, 6557, 7547
in Rhode Island, 784
schools of, 7549
Smith (Hannah Whitall) and, 8445
theocracy in, 9111
theological writings of, 7547
universalism of, 7549
violence against, 6551
women in, 6533–6534
Qualitative methods, Haavio (Martti) and, 3724
Quang-Duc, Thich (Vietnamese monk), self-sacrifice of, 7257, 7264
Quan styles, 5734–5736
Quantum indeterminism, 7139
Quantum mechanics, 2659–2660
chance and, 1527
chaos theory and, 1541–1542
contingency and, 8188
Planck era and, 2034
sense of mystery in, 8184
Quantum physics
concepts of, 2739–2740
development of, 7138
physicists in, 7138–7139
Quanzhen Daoism, 1602–1603, 1608, 2185, 2186, 2199–2200
hagiographic works of, 2206–2207
literature of, 2210
Longmen branch of, 2188
Luü Dongpin and, 2200
monasticism in, 2186
ordination in, 6855–6856
priesthood in, 7415
in Qing Dynasty, 2188
Wang Zhe and, 2186, 2199, 7415, 9057, 9676
women in, 2186
Quanzhou (China), Islam in, 4631
Quartier, Thomas, 7860
Quasi-religion, 4401
Quasten, on Apollinaris of Laodicea, 423
Quaternity, **7550–7551**
in Aztec religion, 715–716, 717–718, 5907
interpretations of, 6747
in Islam, gardens of, 3277, 3282
in Maya religion, 5796
of nature, 6435–6436
in Navajo religious traditions, 6442
Qubilai Khan, 1148, 1149
Qudāmah family, Ḥanābilah and, 3768
Qudshu (deity)
in Canaanite religion, 1383
Reshef and, 7762
Quebec
Catholicism in, 1711, 9299, 9301
Church of England in, 9300
under English rule, 9300
under French rule, 9299–9300
movements to secure independence of, 9303
Quebec Act (1774), 9300
Quechua language, 281
Catholic priests, use by, 8612
Quechua religions
Amazonian, **281–285**
dreams in, 2484
myths in, 3130, 3131, 3132
Andean
deluge myth in, 8588–8589
fertility rites in, 8583
demographics of, 8614–8615
messianism of, 5986
Pachamama and, 5515
Peruvian
cosmic mountain in, 6886
ethnoastronomy of, 2863, 2864
Spanish rule resisted by, 567
Tello (Julio C.) on, 8595
Queen Mother of the West, 3342. *See also* Xi Wang Mu
in Daoism, 2179
Queen of Heaven
in Hurrian religion, Hebat as, 4230
Mary as, Sistine Chapel and, 8755
popular worship in Israel, 3157
Queens. *See also* Kings; Royalty
of Ebla, 5164
Queensland, Rainbow Snake in, 7607
Queensland Aborigines Act, 676, 677, 678
Queer, definitions of, 5413
Queer studies, 5864
differentiation from lesbian studies, 5413
in gender studies, 3300, 3314
sexuality in, 3300, 3314
Queer theory, 5864, 9792
Quem Queritis (troupe), 2437
Querétaro (Mexico), dances in, 2139
Querino, Manuel, 121
Quesnell, Quentin, on Smith (Morton), 8449
Quest for Paradise, The (Sanford), 6985
Quest for Therapy in Lower Zaire, The (Janzen), 58
Quests, **7551–7556**. *See also* Vision quests; *specific heroes and quests*
for immortality, 7684
as individual procession, 7417
in literature, 7554

Quests ***continued***
personal enactments of, 7553–7556
as stage in conversion, 1972
structure of, 7551–7553
symbolism of, 7553–7554
Quest Scale, 7478
Quetzalcoatl (deity), **7556–7557**. *See also* Kukulcan
in art, 1471
as Ehécatl, 7557
association with Apostle Thomas, 3063
in Aztec religion, 5906
banishment from Tollan, 5174
cosmogony of, 716–717, 5907, 6269
legitimacy of kings and, 5173, 5174
birth of, 1568, 5936
in creation myths, 5935, 6269
as culture hero, 5936–5937
in drama, 2464
family of, 5936
iconography of, 4313, 5906
life created by, 148
maguey and, 5936
maize and, 5936
music and, 6269–6270
piercing rays of, 1360
self-sacrifice of, 4187
studies of, 5889–5890, 5941, 5942
temples of, 5899, 7526
and Tezcatlipoca, 5936, 9093, 9357
in Toltec religion, 5889–5890, 5906, 9223–9224, 9224
twin brother of, 2393, 5937
Venus as, 8427
Qufu (China), Confucian temple complex in, 9058–9060
Quiché Maya
birth rites of, 7812
calendar and, 1358
cosmic rites of, 7813
creation story of, sky in, 8428
iconography of, 4312
ruling elite in, 9224
Quick Bear v. Leupp, 7302
Quicunque Vult. *See* Athanasian Creed
Quiercy, Council of, on free will and predestination, 3207
Quietism, **7557–7559**
Catholic condemnation of, 7876
enthusiasm of, 2805
Fénelon (François) and, 3039
Innocent XII disapproving, 6973
mysticism and, 6350
of Quakers, 7548
in Sufism, of Ibrāhīm ibn Adham, 8811
Quiet Revolution (Canada), 9301
Quiet sitting. *See Jing zuo*
Quilla (moon deity), 4411–4412, 5292
Pachamama as, 8601
worship of, 6439
Quilombos (slave settlements), 120
Quimby, Phineas P., 2694
on mind and healing, 3850
and New Thought Movement, 6582, 6584
Quinceañera (coming of age celebration), 7859
Quincunx (architectural structure), 794
Quine, W. V. O., 6988
metaphysics of, 5991
on naturalism, 6429
Quinisext Council (691/692)
and iconoclasm, 4289
on theology, 9135
Quinisext (Trullan) Synod
on eremitism, 2826
Orthodox canon law and, 2041
Quinlan, Karen, 5810
Quinquatrus festival, Minerva in, 6043
Quintana, Juan de, Servetus (Michael) and, 8232
Quintscher, Wilhelm, Orden Mentalischer Bauherren and, 8252
Quintus (Cicero's brother), 2378
Quipus (knotted strings), 4410, 5197
calendar and, 1360–1361
Quirinus (deity), **7559–7561**
identity and origin of, 7559–7560
in Jupiter, Mars, Quirinus triad, 7900–7901
Mars and, 5727, 5728
Romulus as, 5167
Quirite people, Rome's power over, 5167
Quispel, Gilles, on Gnosticism, 3528, 3533–3534
Qūmisī, Daniel al-
in Karaism, 4992
writings of, 5084–5085
Zionist teachings of, 5083
Qummī, ʿAlī ibn Ibrāhīm al-, 8954
Qummī, Sayyid Murtaḍā al-, 6641
Qumran documents. *See* Dead Sea Scrolls
Qumran sect. *See also* Essenes
asceticism of, 7722
beliefs of, 2234
connection to Karaites, 5087
"curses of the covenant" in, 2104
on divine kingship, 5147
as elect of God, 2745
eschatology of, 2835, 4974–4975
Essenes as, 2846, 2847
history of, 2234
and history of religions, 2234–2235
identification of, 2234
John the Baptist and, 4943
Judaism of, 4974–4975
light and darkness symbolism in, 5453
liturgical week of, 9813
revelation in, 7777
Sadducees and, 4974, 8018
scripture in, 4974–4975
Quodvultdeus (bishop of Carthage), on Hermetism, 3944
Qurʾān, **7561–7570**
ablutions in, 10, 8057
Abraham in, 16
Adam in, 2968, 2969
Afghānī's interpretation of, 64
in African American Islamic movements, 4687, 4688
afterlife in, 159–162
ahl al-bayt (family of the Prophet) in, 198–199, 3008
Ahmad Khan's commentary on, 201
analyzed for Muḥammad's biography, 945
angels in, vol. 8 color insert
animals in, 361
apocalypse in, 159–160, 413
apologetics in, 428
apostasy in, 433
Arabian deities in, 444, 445
as source of *kalām,* 5060
authoritative character of, 8201
authority of, 695–696
autobiography inspired by, 700
al-Bayḍāwī's commentary on, 806
bees in, 4508
blasphemy in, 975
as blessing, 981
breath in, 1042
bridge in, 1049
burial alive in, 445
caliphate and, 1366
calligraphy and, 1369, 1372
as canon, 1407, 1409
tilāwah and, 9200–9201
chanting of, 1535
charity in, 1555
and childbirth, verses used in, 3819
Chinese translation of, 4632
collection of, Abū Bakr in, 20
comfort offered by, 7572
covenant of Moses in, 2050
as created or uncreated word of God, 2063–2064
debate over, 695
hands of God in, 3769
Inquisition *(miḥnah)* and, 3760
Muʿtazilah on, 618, 3563, 6319
Sunnī view on, 3563
David in, 2223
daʿwah in, 2225
desert in, 2301
as devotional object, 9818
dhikr in, 2339–2340
djinn in, 2279
as doctrine, 2382
drums in, 2499
election in, 2748
elixir in, 2771–2772
Enoch in, 2803–2804
eschatology of, 2835
interpretations of, 2839
exegesis of (*See also* Tafsīr)
in Sufism, 8810
tafsīr (exoteric) *vs. taʾwīl* (esoteric), 8810
falsafah positions on, 2972
on fasting, 2996, 2997
fasting in, 8140
on fate, 3003
feminist interpretations of, Muslim, 3366–3367, 3368
in *fiqh,* 9488–9489
fire in, 3120
food taboos in, 7144
as form of divine expression, 5303, 7571
gambling in, 3262
gardens in, 3282–3283
gender in, 3368
ʿAbduh (Muḥammad) on, 3365
distinctions based on, 3368, 3369
Genesis compared with, 2969
ghaybah (concealment) in, 3468
ghosts in, 3476
God in, **3560–3567**
attributes of, 616, 618, 2063, 6322, 8809–8810
names of, 2063, 6407
power of, 3562
transcendence and immanence of, 8809–8810
unity of, 3561–3562
ḥadīth and, 3726
ḥājj in, 7155
health and healing in, 3831
prophetic medicine drawn from, 3833
Heaven and Hell in, 3885
hermeneutics of, 5485
as historical work, 7571
historiography and, 4029
Ḥudaybiyah treaty in, 6226
humanity in, 2651, 2968, 4564
humor in, 4197, 4211, 4212, 4215
Ibāḍis on, 4249
Ibn al-ʿArabī inspired by, 4256, 4259
Ibn Ḥazm's commentary on, 4268, 7238, 8781
Ibn Taymīyah's commentary on, 4276
idolatry condemned in, 4361, 4362, 4561
īmān and *islām* in, 4397–4398, 4400
in Ashʿarīyah, 531–532, 535
incomplete view of, *qiyās* and, 7545
influence of, 7573–7574
on inheritance, 4709–4710
inheritance in, 4564

in Imāmī (Twelvers) Shiism, 4696
in Sunnī Islam, 4696
Islamic studies on, 4717, 4719
Ja'far al-Ṣādiq's exegesis of, 4761
Jerusalem in, 4840
Jesus in, as messiah, 5979
Jewish people in, 6226
Jews in, 4855, 7237
jihād in, 4562, 4917–4918, 7289–7290
judgment of the dead in, 5027
Ka'bah in, 6205
language of, sacred, 5303
Last Day in, 6222
law in, al-Shāfi'ī on, 8264
left and right symbolism in, 5393–5394
letter mysticism in, 274
life in, 5447
light symbolism in, 5454
as literature, 7571
madhhabs (schools of law) disagreeing on, 5549
magic in, 5583
marriage in, 4564, 4573, 4707
memorization of, 5852–5853, 7572
menstruation and, 5866
messenger figures in, 6733–6735
messianism in, 5979
miracle of, 6738
miracles in, 6054
mi'rāj in, 6058–6059
modernist interpretations of, 6096–6097
modesty in, 1559
monasticism banned in, 6024
monotheism in, 6222
morality in, 4564
Moses in, 6204
mosques in, 6205, 6207–6208
Muḥammad in
family of, 198–199
light of, 6766
music in, 6283
of Muslim slaves, 4683
Mu'tazilah on, 4567, 4568, 5063
"mystery letters" in, 6733
and mysticism, 6350
narratives in, 7563–7564
nature in, 2604, 2651
new religious movements and reinterpretation of, 6529
oral tradition of, 6843–6844
origin, divine, 8014
paradigmatic nature of, 7570–7571
paradise in, 6984
peace in, 7021
poetry of, 6735, 7204, 7222
as inspiration of Islamic poetry, 7205
poet *vs.* prophet in, 7221
polygamy in, 4564, 4573, 4707
poor people in, 4564
powers of, 7571–7572
and practice of *istikharah,* 7572
prayers of need in, 7572
predestination in, 3204, 3209–3210, 3213
protection offered by, 7571–7572
recitation of, 5485, 7572
in *ṭarīqah* initiation, 9006
qirā' āt, 8950, 9200
rules for, 9201
speed of, 9202
styles of, 9201, 9202
relevance of, in today's world, 7568–7569
resurrection in, 7766–7767
revelations in, earlier, 6204–6205
revelation to Muḥammad, 5060, 6221, 7561, 7571, 7778, 9200
role in Muslim practice and life, **7570–7574**
rūḥ (spirit) and *naf* (self) in, 8566–8567
sacred character of, 7571
ṣalāt (prayer) in, 8054, 8056
salutation in, 8061
scholarship of, 7561–7570
scientific miraculous nature of, 7567
as scripture, 8197
Seven Sleepers of Ephesus legend in, 8440
shahādah and, 8266
Shaytan (Satan) in, 8124, 8125
Shiism on, 4572
sin in, 4725, 8406–8407
slaves in, 4564
Smith (Wilfred Cantwell) on, 8450
social doctrine and legislation in, 4564
Solomon in, 8513
as source of Islam, 4563
as source of *sharī'ah,* 4372, 4566, 4692, 4693, 4695, 4696
spiritual discipline and, 8700
on state functions, 7285
suffering in, 8808
suicide proscribed in, 8809
in Sunnism *vs.* Twelver Shiism, 8342
tafsīr (Qur'anic exegesis) of (*See Tafsīr*)
tax in, 4564
teaching of, 7572–7573
ten levels of understanding of, 7573
theodicy in, 5060, 9118
as theological statement, 7571
translations of, 8203
bilingualism in Spain and, 7965
in Islamic studies, 4717
of Lāhōrī (Muḥammad 'Alī), 5284, 5285
by Paret (Rudi), 4717
Peter the Venerable commissioning, 4715, 7243
by Sale (George), 4717
Trinity in, 5979
'ulamā' in, 9438
ummah in, 9446
underworld in, 9455
on unity of religion, 4575
Verses of Light in, 6206–6207
vows in, 9641
walāyah in, 9656–9657
walī/awaliyā (saints) in, 8034–8035
warfare in, 6225
women in, 3368, 4564
'Abduh (Muḥammad) on, 3365
as earth mother, 2558
rights of, 6224
writing in, origin of, 270
Qur'anic exegesis. *See Tafsīr*
Qur'ānic healing, 2933
Quranic Studies: Sources and Methods of Scriptural Interpretation (Wansbrough), 8952
Quraysh Allāh sanctuary, *ḥaram* and, 3777
Quraysh tribe
caliph selected from, 1365
massacre of, 6225–6226
Muḥammad and, 6220–6223
ḥājj pilgrimage, 6226
in Mecca, 6220–6223
migration to Medina, 6223
Muslim raids, 6225
treaty between, 6226
pre-Islamic, deities of, 444
Qurbah (purpose of endowment), 9677
Qurrat al-'Ayn Ṭāhirah, **7574–7575**
Qu Rukui, 7793
Qushayrī, al-, 6640
on mystical union, 6338
on *mi'rāj,* 6061
on soul, 8570
Quṣṣas (wandering preachers), 8951
Qusṭā ibn Lūqā, 2971
Qutaybah ibn Muslim, 4620
Quṭb (cosmic axis)
cosmic hierarchy and, 8821
Perfect Human Being as, 8819
Quṭb, Sayyid, **7575–7576**
bin Lādin influenced by, 6227
education of, 7289
execution of, 7257
fundamentalism of, Muḥammad in, 6227
on gender roles, 3367
Ikhwān al Muslimūn under, 108
intellectual influences on, 108
jihād of, 7257, 7289
sociopolitical exegesis of, 7567–7568, 7576
tafsīr of, 8955
writings of, 7575–7576
Quṭb al-Dīn Munawwar, 6639
Quṭb al-Dīn Shīrāzī, 4555
Quṭb al-Mulk, 4646
Qu Yuan, 1642
on afterlife, 169–170
poetry of, 7213

R

Ra (deity). *See* Re
Ra'ABaD. *See* Avraham ben David of Posquières
Ra-Atum. *See* Re-Atum
RABaD I. *See* Ibn Daud, Avraham
RABaD III. *See* Avraham ben David of Posquières
Rabbah bar Nahmani, **7577–7578**
Abbaye and, 2
death of, 7577
on salvation, 7586
Rabbanites
Karaites and, 5083, 5084, 5086
on postbiblical writings, 5086
in World War II, German treatment of, 5084
writings of, invention of printing press and, 5086
Rabbenu Tam. *See* Tam, Ya'aqov ben Me'ir
Rabbi (title). *See also* Rabbinate
changes in definition of, 7584
meaning of, 4976
Rabbi Isaac Elchanan Theological Seminary (New York), 7582
Rabbinate, **7578–7590**
all Jewish men as, in rabbinate Judaism, 7587
American, 6906
in Ashkenazic communities, 7579–7580
contracts of, 7580–7581
definition of, 7584
duties of
in Israel, 7582
in Mishnah, 7584
in pre-modern Judaism, 7578, 7580, 7581
in rabbinic Judaism, 7588–7589
in United States, 7582
in Geonic period, 7579

Rabbinate *continued*
in Hasidim, 7583
healers, rabbis as, 3829
hierarchy of
in Israel, 7582
in pre-modern Judaism, 7580
in Israel, 7582–7583
official role of, 9981–9982
Jesus as, 7578, 7584
as judges, 7578, 7579
in rabbinic Judaism, 7588–7589
in medieval Spain, 7579
in modern Judaism, **7581–7583**
monetary compensation of, 7578, 7579, 7580
Moses as, 7584
ordination of, 6857, 7578–7579
in Ashkenazic communities, 7579–7580
in Italy, 7580
kings and, 7580
Maimonides (Moses) on, 7578
in medieval Spain, 7579
origins of, 7578
in United States, 7582
women as, 7582, 7637
Orthodox, modern, 6908
orthodoxy and heterodoxy and, 6911–6912
and Patriarchate, 7006
in pre-modern Judaism, **7578–7581**
privileges of, 7578
in rabbinic Judaism, 7586–7588
in Reform Judaism, 7668, 7669, 7673
relationship with community, 7578
in rabbinic Judaism, 7587–7588
on Samaritans, 8070
seminaries of, in Europe, 7581
in Talmudic period, 7578
as teachers, 7578
and text of Hebrew scripture, 885
in United States, 7582
women as, in United States, 7582
Rabbinical Assembly
Committees on Jewish Law, 1960–1961
ordination of women and, 1963–1964
origins of, 1958
Rabbinic Judaism
afterlife in, 152–153, 3548, 4975
amoraim in, 294–295
atonement in, 593
cosmology in, 2641–2642
covenant in, 2050
David in, 2223
definition of, 4970, 7584
divine kingship in, 5148
divine order of creation in, 2606
dualism in, 2512
election in, 2745
Elisha' ben Avuyah in, 2769
Enoch in, 2803
Essenes' influence on, 2847–2848
extrabiblical sources in, 4977
God in, 3547–3548
on *halakhah,* 3747
on *hester panim* (hiding the face of God), 4090
hierarchy in, 8709
history, view of, 4058
history in, 7585–7586
hospitality in, 4139
institutions of, 7586–7587
Jerusalem in, sanctity of, 4840–4841
Jews defined in, 4859–4860
justice in, 7589
Karaism and, 4991
kashrut laws in, 4978, 5106–5107
in late antiquity, **7583–7590**
legislation and legal procedures, 3749–3750, 4978
in Islamic Empire, 4979
life in, 5445
magic in, 5575–5576
marriage in, 3352
masculinity in, 5864
merit in, 5870, 5871
merkavah in, 10050
messianism of, 7586
miqveh in, 6046–6047
Mishnah in, 7583, 7585–7586, 7589
Moses in, 6203
music in, 6307
myths of, 7584–7585
nonviolence in, 6647
oral Torah in, 6838–6839
oral tradition in, 1842
ordinary folk in, 7587–7588
ordination, qualified *vs.* unqualified, 3749
in Orthodox Judaism, Hungarian, 6899
Pharisaic movement in, 4858
polygyny in, ban on, 3352
prayer in, 8922, 9806–9808
proverbs and parables in, 6978–6979
public prayer in, 8922
purity in, 7514
rabbis in, 7586–7587
as judges, 7588–7589
relationship with common man, 7587–7588
as spiritual guides, 8709
Rav and, 7630
redemption of firstborn son in, 7820
repentance in, 7757
resurrection in, 152
rise of, 4976–4979
sainthood and, 8035
salvation in, 4976, 7584–7585
Sanhedrin in, 8102
Sarah in, 8112
Satan in, 8124
Schechter (Solomon) on, 8146
schooling in, 7587
scriptural *vs.* rabbinic law in, 3748–3750
scripture in, 7585–7586
Shabbat rules and, 8256
shekhinah in, 8313–8315
Shemu'el the Amora, role of, 8318
She'ol in, 8564
soul in, 8557–8558
Spinoza (Baruch) on, 8681
suffering in, 8805–8806
suicide, attitude toward, 8829
synagogues under, 9807
theodicy in, 9116
Torah in, 7584–7585, 7587
as law, 9235–9236
as revelation, 9235
study of, 9235
traits of, 7584
wisdom in, Torah as, 9763
Wissenschaft des Judentums and, 4877
women in, 3352–3353
worship and devotional life in, 5307, **9806–9809**
yetser ha-ra' (inclination toward evil) in, 8404
zekhut avot in, 9941
Rabbinic prayer, 9806–9807
Rabbinites, Karaites and, 865, 4861
Rabbits and hares, **7590**
in Buddhism, gift giving and, 3483
as Easter symbol, 2580
moon and, 6175, 7590
trickster myths about, 86, 94, 4308, 9355
Rabbi von Bacharach, Die (Heine), 4875
Rabe, David, 2477
Rabelais, François, 3051
Bakhtin (M. M.) on, 742
Crowley (Aleister), influence on, 2072
French humanism and, 4176
Rabelais and His World (Bakhtin), Carnival in, 1440
Rabel II (Nabatean king), 6386
Rābi'ah al-'Adawīyah, **7591**
and Ḥasan al-Baṣrī, in fables, 8811
on asceticism as a means to mystical love, 8811
on *dhikr,* 2341
eschatology of, 2839
on gardens, 3277
and language of fire, 3120
love mysticism of, 6350, 6351
love of God expressed in erotic terms, 8037
on mystical union, 6338
prayers of, 2309
Rabī' al-Awwal (month in Islamic year), 4713
Rabī' al-Thānī (month in Islamic year), 4713
Rabinal Achi (dance drama), 2435–2436
Rabindrānatha Thakūr. *See* Tagore, Rabindranath
Rabinovitch, Celia, 502
Rabinowicz, Harry M., 9381
Rābiṭah (hermitage), 2828
Rābiṭat al-'Ālam al-Islāmī. *See* Muslim World League
Raboteau, Albert, 76, 79
Race. *See also* Racism
and beauty, 812
in Caribbean, diversity, 1706
in Christianity, in United States, 964–965
in contact zones, 9296
culture and, 2088
debates over category of, 3304
in eugenics, 2882
gender studies and, 3304
in Golden Age, 3627
Greek myths of, 2964, 2965
in Bahā'ī faith, 739
in Nation of Islam, 6419
in visual culture, 9620
Race relations
cargo cults and, 1417
Rastafarianism and, 1438
Rachel (biblical figure), 4757, **7591–7592**
Rachmaninov, Sergei, 6312
Racial justice, social movements and, 1753
Racine, Jean, 2474
Racing
chariot races, in *Ṛgveda,* 8724
by Native Americans, 8723
New Testament imagery of, 8724
Racing Demon (Hare), 2477
Racism
Aboriginal Christianity against, 678
African theology on, 1722
anti-Semitism as, 402
Christian Identity movement and, **1657–1660,** 6564
of Christianity, scholarship on, 77
environmental, theology and, 2610
Evola (Julius) on, 2906
Father Divine's trial and, 3007
in feminism, 3311
feminism and, 9791
Gnosticism and, 3526
King's (Martin Luther, Jr.) work against, 5145–5146
in law, 5361
liberation theology and, 5440–5441
Malcolm X on, 72
monkeys and, 6151
nature religions connected to, 2663

Peoples Temple cult and, 4954
in South Africa, Dutch Reformed evangelical movement and, 1724
World Council of Churches program on, 2686
Racket games, 753–754
Rad, Gerhard von, 2649, 9764
on narrative forms, 6376, 6377–6378
Raḍā' (fosterage), 4706
RaDaK. *See* Kimḥi, David
Rada spirits, 9636
Radbertus, Paschasius, 821
Radcliffe-Brown, A. R., 2543, **7592–7593**
on Andaman Islanders, 7592
education of, 7592
on food customs, 3173
and functionalism, 3232
functionalist approach of, 4043, 8749
in history of study of Australian religions, 683, 686
Lévi-Strauss (Claude) *vs.*, 8749
on magic, 5566–5567
Marett (R. R.) and, 5708
on Rainbow Snake, 7605, 7607
Schmidt (Wilhelm), debate with, 8169–8170
on society and religion, 8467
Stanner (W. E. H.) and, 8729
symbol theory and, 8910
on tears, 9025
on totemism, 7592–7593
Radd (principle of reversion), 4710
Radd 'alā al-dahrīyīn, al- (Afghānī), 64
Rader, Paul, religious broadcasting and, 7710
Rādhā (deity), **7593–7595**
Bengali devotion to, 826
in Braj, 3986
Caitanya as, 826, 1345
dances devoted to, 2136
on equal status with male, 3608
erotic liaison with Kṛṣṇa, 4444
history of, 7593
humanism and domestication of, 827
in *Gītagovinda,* 4819–4820
Kṛṣṇa and, love of, 5250, 5252, 5253–5254, 7593, 7594
origins of, 7593
poetry on, 7211
Sūrdās on, 8881
Vaiṣṇava *bhakti* cult and, 9500
worship of, 7593–7594
Radha (St. Denis), 2157
Radhakrishnan, Sarvepalli, **7595–7596**
on *brahman,* 6145, 6149
on comparative religion, 8790
and dialogue of religions, 2343, 7595
interweaving Hinduism with Western ideas, 8978
on Jesus, 4845
monism of, 6144–6145, 6149
on religious experience, 7740, 7741, 7742
writings of, 7595
Rādhākṛṣṇa bhāgavatas, 9504
Radhasoami Satsang, *bhakti* heritage in, 3986–3987
Radhasoami Satsang Beas, plagiarism from, by Twitchell (Paul), 2602
Rādhikā. *See* Rādhā
Radiant light, yoga of, 1287–1288
Radiation. *See* Cosmic background radiation
Radical contingency, 1527
Radical dualism, 1457, 2507–2508, 2509, 2513, 7189
Radical environmentalism. *See* Earth First!
Radicalism
black, and African American religions, 78–79
Islamic, Qutb (Sayyid) as inspiration for, 7576
Radin, Paul, 6671, 6672, **7596**
autobiography recorded by, 702
on fear as root of religion, 8467
on *mana,* 2542
on North American Indian languages, 6653
preanimism criticized by, 7373
on primitive religions, 7596
secret societies in, 7719
on the supernatural, 8862
on supreme beings, 8877–8878
on trickster symbolism, 2092, 7596
on twins, 9414
Radio, religious broadcasting on. *See also* Media
in Asia, 7713
Christian, fundamentalist *vs.* modernist, 7710–7711
in Europe, 7713–7714, 7714
Fuller (Charles E.) and, 7711
in fundamentalist ministries, 2890
McPherson (Aimee Semple) and, 7710
Qur'ān recitation in, 9202
Rader (Paul) and, 7710
in South America, 7713
sustaining-time monopoly, 7710–7711
in United States, 7709–7711
Radio Maryja (Poland), 6568
Radio Revival Hour (radio program), 7711
Radlov, V. V., 474
on shamanistic śeances, 8272
Raël, 7597
Raëlians, 6513, **7596–7600,** 9434–9435
cloning efforts of, 7599
creation story of, 6530
embassy of, 7599
founder of, 7597
founding of, 6529
gender roles in, 6516
organizational structure of, 7597–7598
origins of, 6568
political projects of, 7597
practices and beliefs of, 7598–7599
swastika as symbol of, 7597, 7599
Raffles, Stamford, colonial agenda of, 8638
Rāfi'ī, Muṣṭafā Ṣādiq, 4371
Ragaz, Leonhard, 6468
Raghunāthadāsa, Gōsvamins and, 1346
Ragidup fabric, 1828
Raglan, Lord
Girard (René) on, 3960
on her myths, 3958–3959
Ragnarǫk (aftermath)
and Baldr, 744
Baldr's death as cause of, 5509
in Eddas, 2692
in Germanic eschatology, 2835–2836
Rahab, in Canaanite religion, 1392
Rahabi, David, 5006
Raheja, Gloria G., 3322
Raḥel. *See* Rachel
Rāhi Masūm Razā, 10035
Rahit Maryada. See Sikh Rahit Maryada
Rahman, al- (deity), 4561
Rahman, Fazlur, 3213
in exile, 6098, 6101
Islamic studies by, 4577–4579, 4719
modernism of, 6098, 6101
Qur'anic exegesis of, 7568, 7569
on *sunnah,* 9275
Rahman, Ziaur, 830
Rahner, Karl, **7600–7602**
on charisms, 1550
on free will and predestination, 3208
on God, 3558, 7423
on grace, 3646, 7600
Maritain's (Jacques) critique of, 5713
methods of, 7600
Metz (J.-B.) as disciple of, 7245
on poetry, 7206
on Trinity, 9362
Rāhula (Buddha's son), 7084
Rāhulabhadra (Buddhist thinker), 5552
Raiateans religion (Tahiti), afterlife in, 2006–2007
Raids
of cattle, 1465
and kingship, in Celtic tradition, 1493
Muḥammad's use of, 6225
Railton, George S., in Salvation Army, 8063
Rain, **7602–7605**. *See also* Storm deities; Water
accompanied by lightning, 7603
accompanied by thunderbolt, symbolism of, 7603
in African religions
in myths, 96, 97
in southern African rituals, 8657
in Australian Indigenous myths, 661
Rainbow Snake and, 7605
deities of (*See* Rain deities and spirits)
in Diola religion, 261–262
dragons associated with, 2433
elephant associated with, 2750
frogs associated with, 3223
for gardens, 3280, 3281
in Hinduism, Rudra associated with, 7934
makers of (*See* Rainmaking)
in North American Indian religions, 6651
iconography of, 4309
as purification symbol, 7604
as redemption symbol, 7604
sacrifices for, 7602
Rainbow Girls, 3198
Rainbow princess cult, in Nguni religion (Africa), 8663
Rainbows, 7604
in African myths, 92, 95, 96, 97
serpent spirit identified with in Vodou, 1433
Rainbow Snake (Rainbow Serpent), 4309, **7605–7608**
in African myths, 97
in Australian Indigenous myths, 656–657
of Gadjeri, 3250
as catalyst, 7606–7607
power of, human contact with, 7605–7606
as symbol, 7606–7607
in Ungarinyin religion, 9458
Yulunggul as, 9916
Rain charms, in Judaism, 7602–7603
Rain clouds, 7604
Rain dances, 7603

Rain deities and spirits, 5992–5996, 9701
 Adad as, 28–29
 in African religions, 6771
 Allāh as, 2301
 in Hawaiian religion, 3797
 Illapa as, 4411
 Indra as, 4466
 in Maya religion, 5884
 Mbona as, 5802
 in New Caledonia religion, 6501
 in North American Indian religions, 3280
 supremacy of, 7602
 supreme beings as, 8870
 Tlaloc/Chac (Aztec/Maya), 1469, 9213
 wandjina, 9669
 Zeus as, 9952
Rainey, Anson F., on Canaanite religion, 1386–1387
Rainier, Mount, 6212–6213, 6214
Rainmaking
 in African religions, 7602
  Berber, 835
  Lugbara religion, 5528
  Zimbabwe, 7602
 in Chinese religion, 7603
  women as, 3338
 in Finno-Ugric religions, 3108
 in Islam, white magic of, 5587
 in Judaism, 7602–7603
 in Lugbara priesthood, 2569
 in Mesoamerican religions, 7603
 in North American Indian religions, 7300
Rains retreat (Buddhist celebration), 1307
Ra'īs al-yahūd (office of the head of the Jews), 4990
Rajab (month in Islamic year), 4713
Rājadhammas (virtues), 1134
Rāja dharma, 2328, 2329
Rājagirika sect, origin of, 1194
Rajagopal, D., 5245
Rājagṛha, 1108, 1269, 4483
Rājagṛha, council of, overview of, 2035
Raja Haji Ali, 4664
Rājā Kṛṣṇacandra Rāy, 826
Rājam Aiyar, P. R., 10035, 10036
Rājarāja (Cōḻa king), 9265
Rājās (caste), 826, 4434
Rājas (kings), 1134
Rājās (passion, force), 853, 2305, 3709
 in Sāṃkhya cosmology, 2016
Rajasthan (India)
 sati (widow burning) in, 8129–8130
 spirit possession in, 8694, 8697
Rājasūya (sacrifice), 9563–9564
 in devotional life, 9821
Rājavārttika (commentary), Sāṃkhya teachings in, 8092
Rājayoga, 9822
 body discipline in, 8704–8705
 Īśvara (God) in, 3998
Rajneesh, Bhgwan Shree, 5378, 6536–6537, **7608–7609,** 8993–8994
Rajneesh movement (Osho), 6536–6537
 child socialization and education in, 6542, 6543
 in Europe, 6568
 master-disciple relationship in, 6541
 women in, 6537
Rajneeshpuram (Oregon), 7608
Rajputs
 Akbar's defeat of, 216
 ritual suicide *(jauhar)* among, 8129
Rak'ahs (bowing cycles), 7342
 in *ṣalāt* (prayer), 8057
Rakoczi. *See* Saint-Germaine, Comte de
Rakṣā Bandhana (festival), 9824
Rakshasas (demon-like beings), 2276, 2315, 4442
Ralbag. *See* Gersonides
Raleigh, A. D., on Hermetism, 3952
Raleigh, Walter, Hermetism and, 3950
Raluvhumba (mythic figure), in Bantu cosmogonies, 8663
Ram, N. Sri, 9143
Rām (deity), in Marathi religions, 5698
RaMa. *See* Isserles, Mosheh
Rāma (deity), **7609–7610**. *See also* Rāmāyaṇa
 as *avatāra* of Viṣñu, 3886, 7609, 7617
 Avadhi poetry devoted to, 3984
 ax of, 967
 in *bhakti,* 9572, 10089
 as *bodhisattva,* 7609
 in Buddhism, 7609
 in dance drama, 2449, 7046–7047
 Daśahrā festival to, performance at, 3985
 devotion to
  in Vaiṣṇavism, 4428
  Tulsīdās and, 9393
 humanism and domestication of, 827
 in *Śivagītā,* 854
 in Jainism, 7609
 monkeys and, 6152
 pilgrimage to places visited by, 7169
 in puppet theater, 2452
 reincarnated as monkey, 359
 return to northern kingdom, celebration of, 6594
 Vaiṣṇava *bhakti* cult and, 9500
 Vijayanagara as sacred space and, 1806
 Viṣṇu in form of, 708, 7501
Rama I (king of Siam)
 and Buddhist canon, 1253
 Buddhist temples built under, 9054
 reforms by, 9095, 9151
 Thai monarchy reestablished by, 1139
Rama II (king of Siam), death of, 6139
Rama III (king of Siam), 1253, 6139, 9054
Rama IV. *See* Mongkut
V (king of Siam)
Rāma V (king of Siam). *See* Chulalongkorn
Ramabai, Pandita, **7610–7611**
 conversion to Christianity, 5700
 feminism of, 3320, 7610–7611
 on Hinduism, 7610
Rāmacandracarita Purāṇa (Nagacandra), 7609
Rāmacaritamānas (Tulsīdās), 2449, 7609, 7618
Ramachandran, V. S., 6487
Ramaḍān, 2996, 4712, 4713–4714
 decorations for, vol. 7 color insert
 in devotional life, 9816, 9817
 domestic observances of, 2401, 2402
 fasting during, 3171, 8140–8141
  in Five Pillars, 4565
  as purification, 7508
 folklorist perspective on, 3144
 in Ismā'īlī Shiism, 4714
 meals during, 3170
 in Nation of Islam, 4688
 in northern countries, 4713
 prayers during, 8141
 recitation of Qur'ān in, 9202
 seclusion in, 4714
 slave practices of, 4682
RaMaH. *See* Abulafia, Me'ir
Rāmakerti, 5128
Rāma Khamhaeng (king of Sukhōthai), 1135, 1136–1137, 7262
Ramakrishna (Hindu mystic), **7611–7614, 10066–10068**
 absolute being of, 7611, 7612
 eclecticism of, 10067
 on ecstasy, 2680
 interpretations of, 7613–7614, 10067
 Ishwara Yoyāpurī as teacher of, 7612, 7613
 life of, 7611–7612
 on Mother Goddess, 826
 on *Bhagavadgītā,* 852
 as Tantric practitioner, 8988
 teachings of, 4431, 7612–7613
 Vajrayāna (Tantric) Buddhism and, 7612, 7613, 10067–10068
 Vivekananda and, 9629, 10067
 on wealth, 10067
 on women, 10067
 yoga practiced by, 1044
 Yogeśvarī as teaher of, 7612, 7613
Ramakrishna, Vivekananda and, 10089
Ramakrishna Math, 7612
Ramakrishna Mission, 546, 4431, 7612, 7613, 9629, 9630
 sadhvis (renunciates) in, 8020
 traditional Hindu values in, 4008
Ramakrishna Order, 546
Ramakrishna Paramahamsa, Sri and Śārāda Devi (wife of), **8111–8112**
 on cakras, 1348–1349
Rāma-līlā (performance), 2449, 7043, 7046–7047
 at Daśahrā festival, 3985
Rāmānanda sect
 akhāḍā military units in, 8021
 sadhus/sadhvis (renunciates) in, 8020
Ramananda Swami, Sahajanand Swami and, 8889
Rāmānuja, **7614–7616**
 and Nimbārka, 6623
 and Śrī Vaiṣṇavas, 4430
 bhakti of, 859, 8976
 on *brahman,* 4422, 6145
 epistemology of, 7615
 on God's will, 8529
 in Śrī Vaiṣṇavas Sampradāya, 8727, 8728
 monism of, 6144, 6344
 and mysticism, 6344
 on *ātman,* 8546–8547
 on *avidyā,* 710–711, 5200–5201
 on *Bhagavadgītā,* 852, 853, 854
 on *īśvara,* 4752
 on *līlā,* 5455, 5457
 on *māyā,* 5795
 on *mokṣa,* 6116
 on predestination, 3204
 qualified nondualism of, 6144
  bhakti sectarian repudiation of Advaita through, 4005
  and nature of divine, 128, 7615
  Swaminarayan movement and, 8891
 Rāmā cult of, 7609
 on reality, 7616
 theism of, 9104
 Vedānta of, 9548
 wife of, 7615
 writings of, 7615
 Yāmuna and, 4430, 7614
Rāmānujan, A. K., on Indian poetry, 7209, 7210
Rāma ṛjya (ideal harmony), 5399
Ramat (soul), 9334
Ramava (sanctuary), 774

Rāmāyaṇa (Indian epic), 5467, **7616–7618,** 9518. *See also* Rāma
as *kāvya* (great poem), 7205
Bengali version of, 825, 827
bhakti synthesis in, 3998–4002
in Brahmanism, 9568–9569
cosmology in, 2016–2017
dance drama based on, 2448, 2449, 7046
dating of, 7617
dharma in, 2329, 2621, 5343
folk versions of, 7618
Hanumān in, 3775, 4438, 4439
hell in, 9456
Iliad cognate to, 4465
Jain versions of, 7609
Khmer version of, 5128
magic in, 5591
monkeys in, 6151–6152
Murukaṉ in, 6240
organization of, 7616–7617
pilgrimage in, 7169
puppet theater based on, 2450, 2452, 7044
quest in, 7553
recensions of, 7616
in Southeast Asia, 4012
in bas reliefs, 4013
versions of, 3076
storyline of, 7617
studies of, 4446
Tulsīdās' commentary on, 9393
vernacular Hindi adaptations of, 3984
Rambam. *See* Maimonides, Moses
Ramban. *See* Nahmanides, Moses
Rambhā (deity), 4326
Rambo, Lewis R., process theory of, stages of conversion in, 1972
Rambu Solo' (ritual), 9241–9242
Rambu Tuka (ritual), 9241–9242
Rāmcaritmānas (epic), 7209, 7211, 9393
Avadhi dialect in, 3984
performances of, 3985
Ram Das, women and, 3336
Ramesseum Coronation Drama, 2441
Rāmeśvaram (India), pilgrimage to, 7170
Ramkhamhaeng (Thai king), 9094
Rāmkumār (brother of Ramakrishna), 7611
Ram'l (Arab geomancy), 3437
Ramlila epic, cosmic time in, 7988
Ramman. *See* Adad
Ram Mohan Roy. *See* Roy, Ram Mohan
Ramos, Arthur, 121
Rāmprasād Sen, 826, 7211
Rām rāj (kingdom of God), 862
Rams. *See* Sheep and goats
Ramsay, Chevalier Michael, 3195–3196
Ramses I (Egyptian king), religion under, 2707
Ramses II (Egyptian king)
as rainmaker, 7602
religion under, 2708
temple of, dedicated to Re, 7634
Ramses III (Egyptian king)
assassination of, 2713
religion under, 2708–2709
temple of, 2709
Ramses IV (Egyptian king), 2709
Ramsey, Frederick, Jr., 77
Ramsey, Paul, 5811
Ramtha, teachings of, 6532
Ramuva. *See* Romuva
Ranchos carnavalescos, in Carnival, 1443–1444
Ranchos de reis, in Carnival, 1443
Rand, Howard, British Israelism and, 1658, 1659
Rand, W. C., 9199
Randles, William G., on ritual regicide, 5157–5158
Randolph, Paschal Beverly
Affectional Alchemy of, 6874
Hermetism and, 3952
sexual magic and, 8251
Randomness. *See* Chance
Ranfaing, Elizabeth de, sexual frenzy and, 8250
Rangaku (Japan). *See* Dutch Learning (Japan)
Ranganātha, 859
Rang byung rdo rje (Rangjung Dorje), 1226, 5102, 5103
on *mahāmudrā,* 5598
Rang byung Rig pa'i rdo rje (Rangchung Rigpe Dorje), Ani Lochen and, 354
Rangda (deity), violence of, 3590
Ranger, Terence, 117, 9273
Rangga (sacred object), 4305
Rang grol skor gsum (Longchenpa), 5193
Rangi (deity)
in Maori creation myth, 1450
hierogamy of, 2555
in Polynesian creation myths, 7312–7313
Rangoon (Burma), 1253
Rānī Ketakī kī Kahānī (Inshā'allāh Khān), 10034
Rānīrī, Nūr al-Dīn al-, 4664
Ranjit Singh, women and, 3336
Rănk, Gustav, 474, 475
Rank, Otto, on hero myths, 3958
Campbell (Joseph) compared to, 3958–3959
Raglan (Lord) compared to, 3960
Ranke, Leopold von, 730
on China, 1631
on history, 4031, 4032
Ranke-Graves, Robert von, 9601
Ran nhialic (men of divinity), 7443
Ransom, in atonement, 595, 596
Ransom, Reverdy, 80
Ranterism, 973
Raouf, Heba, 3368
Rapaport, David, 7476
Rape
abortion after, 5812
of Australian Indigenous women, 3393
in Greek religion, 7079
in Israelite religion, laws on, 4733, 4737
Raphael (biblical figure), 897
Raphael (painter), 4346
Raphael, Ray, on rites of passage, 7802, 7803
Raphael (saint), Osanyin identified with in Santeria, 1434
Raphael House, Holy Order of MANS and, 4102, 4103
Rapine, Paschal, Hermetism and, 3950
Rapithwan (deity), 6731
Rapiu (deity), in Canaanite religion, 1386, 1387
Rapp, George, 6558
Rappaport, Roy A., 2611, 2618, **7618–7619**
on ancestor worship, 322
ecological theory of religion, 6507, 10043
on nature religions, 2664–2665, 7840
on ritual, 7849–7850
on ritual and language, 2868
Rāqilī, al-, polemics against Judaism, 7240
Rarámuri Indians, wrestling matches of, 8723
Rarotonga (Cook Islands), cosmology in, 2005
Rasa (aesthetic concept), 51, 857, 2771, 7208
Abhinavagupta on, 4006
in alchemy, 242
art and, 494
bhakti as state of, 4006
in Hindi and Bengali poetry, 4005
Kṛṣṇa and, 5252–5253
music and, 6282
Rasā'il, on study of nature, 2652
Rasā'il al-Ḥikmah (Druze text), 2504
Rasā'il Ikhwān al-Ṣafā', 4375–4377
authorship and dating of, 4375
contents of, 4375–4376
in Ṭayyibīyah, 8335
parables and animal stories in, 4376
philosophical system of, 4376–4377, 4572
Qarāmiṭah movement and, 8329
sources of, 4376
Rāsa-līlā (Hindi drama), 5456
Rasap (deity), Nergal identified with, 2596
Rasavāhinī (Buddhist text), 1199
Ras Boanerges, 7624, 7627
Ras chong pa Rdo rje grags (Rechungpa Dorje Drak), 1225
Rasef (deity), Nergal identified with, 2596
Rases (male Rastafarians), 7624
Rash (rabbi), *tosafot* of, 9243–9244
Rashap (deity), 7130, 7760. *See also* Reshef
in Canaanite religion, 1384, 1386, 1387
RaSHBa'. *See* Adret, Shelomoh ben Avraham
Rashbam. *See* Meir, Shemu'el ben
Rashdall, Hastings, 6105
Rashei yeshivah (heads of academies), 9248
Rashi (Rabbi Shelomoh ben Yitsḥaq), **7619–7621**
on Beruryah, 844
biblical exegesis of, 865–866, 4981
on enactments, legal, 3750
Gershom ben Yehudah and, 3461
oral Torah and, 6840
Schneerson (Menachem M.) on, 866
on suffering, 8805
Talmudic commentary by, 3745, 9243
teaching of, 5012
Rashīd al-Dīn Faḍl Allāh, 4372
Rashīd Riḍā, Muḥammad, 4400, 4574, 4589, **7621–7622**
modernism of, 6098
on *ijmā'* doctrine, 8265
Rāshidūn caliphs, 4693
'Alī ibn Abī Ṭalib as last of, 1366
considered only true caliphs, 1367
Rashnu (deity), Chinvat Bridge and, 1647
Rashtī, Sayyid Qā'im, Shaykhīyah and, 8308
Rashtriya Svayamsevak Sangh (RSS) (India), 7256
Ras Ibn Hani (city)
archaeology at, 1390
Canaanite religion and, 1381, 1382
Rask, Rasmus, 4458
Raskol'niki. *See* Old Believers
Rasmussen, Knud, 475
on miracles, 6050
Rasos (midsummer solstice), 763, 764
Rasps, wooden, in Mesoamerican music, 6267
Rasputin, 6873–6874
Rasputin, Grigorij, Khlysty rites and, 8248
Rassenhygiene, 2880

Ras Shamra (Syria), 2442
  archaeology at, 1390
  Canaanite religion and, 1381–1382
  Dagan in, 2126
  divine kingship in, 5146
Rastafari (Rastafarianism), **7622–7629**
  in Africa, 109
    repatriation efforts, 7622, 7627
  as Afro-Caribbean cult, 1437–1438, 7622
  attacks on, 6548–6549
  Bible in, 7627
  and black nationalism, 7622
  controversies within, 7627–7628
  development of, 10026
  doctrine of, 7623
  dreadlocks and, 7623, 7624, 7626–7627
  in Europe, 6568
  Garvey (Marcus) and, 7623–7624, 7626
  Haile Selassie and, 7622, 7623, 7624, 7625, 7626
  history of, 7623–7626
  history of study of, 75–76, 10026–10027
    controversies in, 7628
  idiosyncratic speech in, 9307
  inspirational text for, 6531
  marijuana and, 7623, 7624, 7626
  music in, 7625, 7628
  organizational patterns of, 7623
  politics in, 7623, 7624, 7625
  popular culture connections of, 7622–7623, 7625
  relocation to Africa as goal of, 7622
  repatriation of Africa in, 7622, 7627
  ritual practice in, 7623
  as spiritual *vs.* religious movement, 7622–7623, 7624
  spread of, 10026
  symbols of, 7625, 7626–7627
  transculturation of, 9306–9307
  as way of life, 7623
  women in, 7627–7628
Rastafari Centralization Organization (Jamaica), 7623
Rastī, Sayyid Kāẓim, 728
Rastislav (duke of Greater Moravia), Cyril and Methodius and, 2116–2117
Raṣṭrapālaparipṛcchā (Buddhist text), 1114
Rāṣṭrīya Svayaṃsevak Saṅgh (RSS), 5699
Rasū (prophet), 7426
Rasūl (messenger of God), Muḥammad as, in shahādah, 8266
Rasuli, Abdurrahman, 4619
Rat (mythic being), 6012
Ratana, Tahupotiki Wiremu, 5682, 5683
Ratana Church (Christian sect), 5682, 5683, 6797–6798
Ratatoskr (squirrel), 3448–3449
Ratha yātrā (car festival), 7494
Rathbun, Valentine, 6557–6558
Rational-bureaucratic authority, Weber (Max) on, 8483
Rational-choice theory, pluralism and, 8472
Rationalism. *See also* Reason
  alternative medicine and, 3849
  in Buddhism, of Kamalaśīla, 5070
  chance in, 1527
  in Chinese thought
    of Confucius, 1936
    Han dynasty, 1592
    in Neo-Confucianism, 1603
  Christianity and
    Christian movements against, 1664
    incarnation theology and, 8181
  continental, Kant's (Immanuel) reaction to, 5076
  definition of, 7111
  in Euhemerism, 2883
  Hegel (G. W. F.) on, 3894
  Herder (Johann Gottfried), criticism by, 3918
  in Hippocratic treatises, 4021
  in Islam (*See Ahl al-kalām; See* Uṣūlīyah movement)
  in Judaism, 4992
    Sa'adyah Gaon's use of, 4887
  of Jung, 5032, 5035
  of Muslim theology, 5060, 5067–5068
  in Neo-Kantian philosophy, Cohen (Hermann) and, 1850–1852
  and new religions, creation of, 6530
  Otto (Rudolf) on, 4096
  quantum theory and, 8188
  Reinach (Salomon) on, 7675
  relationship with empiricism, 5076
  religion and modernity and, 5032
  ritualistic behavior *vs.*, 7833, 7839
  Romanticism *vs.*, Creuzer (G. F.) and, 2070
  Schleiermacher (Friedrich) on, 8161, 8162
  secularization and, 8218
  Soloveitchik (Joseph Baer) on, 8518, 8519
  Spiritualism and, 8716
  supernatural, of Adams (Hannah), 30
  Vatican I and, 9528, 9529, 9531
  of Wolff (Christian), 9783
Rationalist Association, Harrison (Jane E.) as member of, 3781
Rationalization, syncretism *vs.*, 8935
Rational psychoanalysis, 7484
Rational religion, Weber (Max) on, 8488
Ratisbon (Germany), Protestant disputation at, Eck (Johann) in, 2601
Ratnagotravibhāga (Buddhist text), 1120, 9018
Ratnaguṇa (Buddhist text), 1114
Ratnaguṇasaṃcayagāthā (Buddhist text), 1114
Ratnakosin dynasty (Thailand), 7262
Ratnakūṭa (Buddhist text), 1114
Ratnapāṇi *(bodhisattva),* 1079
Ratnasambhava (buddha), 1068, 1078, 1217, 4329
Ratramnus (Benedictine monk), 821
  Hincmar, criticism by, 3983
Rattle-belts, 7035
Rattles
  Mesoamerican, 6268, 6269
  in South American shamanism, 8291
Rattray, Robert S., on African religions, 98, 115
Ratzel, Friedrich, 3222, 3648
  cultural studies of, 5259–5260, 5261
Rauchlin, Johann, 6527
Rauschenbusch, Walter, **7629–7630**
  and Christian socialism, 6468
  on kingdom of God, 5152, 7630
  King (Martin Luther, Jr.) influenced by, 5145
  Social Gospel Movement and, 1656
Rav (Abba' bar Ayyvu), **7630–7631**
  on afterlife, 153, 3548
  ordination of, 3749
  yeshivah under, 9883
Rava' (Babylonian amora), **7631**
  Abbaye and, 3, 7631
  on legislative power of rabbis, 3748
  on Mishnah, 3
Ravaisse (French scholar), on Southeast Asian Islam, 4659
Rāvaṇa (deity)
  in dance drama, 7047
  humanism and domestication of, 827
  in *Rāmāyaṇa,* 7617
  in *Śivagītā,* 854
  in puppet theater, 2452
  Sītā abducted by, 7609
Rave culture, spirituality of, 3099
Ravelstein (Bellow), 2758
Ravens
  in Haida myth, 3735
  in Japanese myths, 948
  in Muisca religion, 6230
  of Óðinn, 6808
  as tricksters, 4308, 6661, 6662
    in Arctic religions, 472, 4528, 9354–9355
    in Athapaskan religious traditions, 573
    in Tlingit religion, 6709
Ravidās (saint)
  in *bhakti* poetry tradition, 3985
  on caste, 3986
  in *Ādi Granth,* 32
Raw and the Cooked, The (Lévi-Strauss), 6821–6822
Rawḍat al-shuhadā' (Kāshifī), 7632, 9022
Rawda-yi taslīm (Ṭūsī), 9408
Raw-eating, 6821–6822. *See also* Omophagia
Rāwīs (secondary transmitters), 9200
Rawson, Beryl, 3381
Rawson, Jessica, 1637
Rāwẓah-khvānī (public lamentation), 2446, **7631–7632,** 9022
Ray, Charles, 68
Ray, John, on nature, inherent design of, 2607
Ra'y (personal opinion), in schools of law, 5547
Rāya, Rāmānanda, Caitanya and, 1345
Raychaudhuri, Tapan, 827
Raymond, Janice, 5413
Raymond of Capua, 1461
Raymond of Sabunde, on "two books," 9422
Rayo. *See* Illapa
Rayy (Iran), 'Abd al-Jabbār in, 3–4
Rāzī, Abū Bakr al-, on knowledge, 5203
Rāzī, Abū Bakr Zakariyā' al-, 2971, 2972–2973
Rāzī, Abū Muḥammad al-, on medicine, 3832
Rāzī, Abū Zur'a, *Sahīh Muslim* and, 3729
Rāzī, al-
  kalām of, 5067
  on soul, 8569
  tafsīr of, 8953
Rāzī, Fakhr al-Dīn al-, **7632–7634**
  as al-Bayḍāwī's source, 806
  as Shī'ī theologian, 4571
  on attributes of God, 618–619
  in Ash'arīyah, 537, 538, 7633
  life of, 7632–7633
  on magic, 5584
  Nawawi al-Jawi influenced by, 4665
  on *īmān* and *islām,* 4400
  Qur'anic exegesis of, 7633
  writings of, 538, 7633
Rāzī, Muḥammad ibn Zakariyā' al-, alchemy of, 249
Rāzī, Najm Dāyā
  and language of fire, 3120

on light of Muḥammad *(nūr Muḥammad),* 6766–6767
Ṛddhipur (pilgrimage site), as sacred space, 7978
Rdo bis Shes rab rgya mtsho (Dobi Sherab Gyatso), 1158
Rdo rje gsum gyi bsnyen sgrub order (Buddhism), 1227–1228
Rdo rje'i rnal 'byor order (Buddhism), 1227
Rdo rje phag mo, 1233
Rdo rje shugs ldan (Dorje Shugden). *See* Shugs ldan
Rdzogs chen. *See* Dzogchen
Rdzogs rim (perfection phase), 1286, 1287–1288
Rdzong gsar (Buddhist school), religious education at, 5224
Re (deity), **7634**
in afterlife, 2705
Amun assimilated with, 301, 7277, 7634
Atum assimilated with, 623, 7634
calendar and, 1354
in Egyptian pantheon, 2704
as eye, 2940
Horus as son of, 4136
Isis and, 4557
lotus associated with, 5518
magic from, 2706, 2712
in myth of the celestial cow, 2961–2962
obelisk as monument to, 9264
Osiris and, 6921
preeminence of, 2705
pyramids and, 2704
as Re-Atum, 8837
serpents and, 8456
son of, in title of kings, 7277
Thoth and, 9167
in Underworld literature, 2719
Reader in Comparative Religion (Lessa and Vogt), 379
Reader in the Anthropology of Religion (Lambek), 379
Readers (pietest movement), 5283
Reading circles, Swedenborgian, 8901
Readings in Ritual Studies (Grimes), 7857
Reagan, Ronald
Earth First! and, 2562
on redemptive sacrifice, 4955
Reagon, Bernice Johnson, 77
Real, in Hinduism, aesthetics and, 50–51
Real-Encyklopädie der classischen Altertumswissenschaften, 2784–2785
Real-Encyklopädie für protestantische Theologie und Kirche, 2784
Realism. *See also* Social realism
chaos theory and, 1542, 1543
Christian, social justice and, 1753
drama in, 2474–2475
in epistemology, 2819
vs. nominalism, and nature, 6433
of Plato, 9282
symbolic, Bellah (Robert) on, 8496, 8498
of Weber (Max), 9711
Realistic idealism, 9282
Realistic theology. *See* Christian Realism
Reality. *See also* Existence; Metaphysics; Ontology
in African religions, systems for teaching about, 91
art and, 53–54, 55
Descartes (René) on, 7137
in enlightenment, 2793
expression of truth through, 9374
in Mahāyāna Buddhism, 1208–1212
Nāgārjuna on, 6145, 6391–6392
in Upaniṣads, 9480, 9543–9544
in Vajrayāna (Tantric) Buddhism, Kālacakra tradition, 5056
in Yogācāra Buddhism, 9897, 9898
in Jainism, 4768
in Kevala Advaita, 9546
in Maori religion, 5679
māyā and, 5794–5795
mythology contrasted to, 5113
non-ordinary, in neoshamanism, 8294, 8295–8296
oneness or unity of (*See* Monism)
in otherworld, 6923–6924, 6925
Pauck (Wilhelm) on, 7011
as perception, 4355
philosophical views of, 5492, 7114
Plato on, 4355, 7110, 7181–7182
Plotinus on, 7191
psychedelic drugs and, 7467–7468
Rāmānuja on, 7616
in religion, 7114
Speusippus on, 7187
in Stoicism, 8741, 8742
structure of, and afterlife, 133–135
in theosophy, 9143
Whitehead (Alfred North) on, 49
Reason. *See also* Logos; Rationalism
Ahmad Khan on, 202
in apologetics, 428
as source of *kalām,* 5060–5061
body *vs.,* 4163
in Christianity
Byzantine, 2587
early Western, 2582
Cohen's three interests of, 1851
by contingency, in ancient Israel, 8181
ethics and, 1651, 1653
vs. faith, Locke on, 2798
al-Ghazālī on revelation and, 8815
Hegel (G. W. F.) on, 3893
Heschel (Abraham Joshua) on religion of, 3962
Hume (David) on, 8492
in Islam
knowledge of God through, 3563, 3565
mystical experience equivalent to, 3565
in Judaism
Mendelsson on, 4900–4901
revelation and, 4904
Kant (Immanuel) on
in *Critique of Practical Reason,* 5077–5078
in *Critique of Pure Reason,* 5076–5077
in Karaism, 4993
Lessing (G. E.) on, 5417
Locke (John) on, 5468
Maimonides on, 4893, 8559–8560
in Mesopotamian myth, 8536
nature religions and, 2662
Pascal on, 7002
progress in historiography and, 4031–4032
Reimarus (Hermann Samuel) on, 7675
Saʿadyah Gaon on, 7952, 7953
Saʿadyah Gaon's use of, 4887
Schleiermacher (Friedrich) on unity of nature and, 8164
in Stoicism *(logos),* 3911, 5501–5502, 8405, 8741, 8742
Suhrawardī on, 8827
in Unitarianism, 1530
Waardenburg (Jacques) on, 4048
Reasonableness of Christianity, The (Locke), 5496–5497
Reason and Revelation in the Middle Ages (Gilson), 4272
Reasoning (Rastafari practice), 7623
Re-Atum (deity), 2961, 5451, 7634
kings descended from, 5163
Reay, Marie, 3281
Rebaptism, 782, 783
Rebbe (leader), 9377. *See also* Rabbinate; *Tsaddiq*
in Hasidim, 7583
women as, 3351, 5611–5612
Rebbe's Daughter, The: Memoir of a Hasidic Childhood (Shapira), 9381
Rebecca (biblical figure), **7634–7635**
matchmaking for, 15, 4544, 7634
Rebellion in the Backlands (Cunha), 3063
Rebelliousness, of Prometheus, 7420–7421
Rebirth. *See also* Reincarnation; Resurrection; See also Saṃsāra; Transmigration
in African rites of passage, 88
of animals, rituals with bones and, 1014
in Australian Indigenous religions, 314–316, 951
healers and, 3873
myths of, 3250, 3251
baptism as, 953
bears as symbol of, 807, 809
in Buddhism, 952, 998, 1067, 2627–2628, 2737
Buddhadāsa on, 1072
in Chinese Buddhism, 1161, 1162
emptiness and, 1117
gender and, 3330–3331
in Japanese Buddhism, 1175–1176
Pure Land, 4923
in caste, 9524
in Daoism, 2183
in Delaware religion, 6681
egg as symbol of, 2702
in Germanic religion, 168
in *Bhagavadgītā,* 5096–5097
in initiation rituals, 951, 4476, 4477–4478, 4480–4481, 4482–4483
in Upaniṣads, *karman* and, 5095
in Jainism, 4764
freedom from, 2025
hells and, 2024
karman and, 5096
in Judaism, conversion as, 4859
karman and, 5095, 5096
lion symbolism of, 5465
in monotheism, 953
moon and, 6174
motif of, 950
pearl as symbol of, 7023–7024
rivers and, 7862
in shamanism
in initiation, 8270–8271
self-transformation through, 8277
soteriology and, 8529
Steiner (Rudolf) on, 8738
time and, conceptions of, 132–133
trees as symbols of, 9339
in Vedism, 952

Rebirth *continued*
in Yoga, classical, *karman* and, 5095
in Yurupary myth, 9920
Rebirthing analysis, 7680
Rebirth of the Goddess (Christ), 9100
Recaka (breathing), 1044
Recasting Women (Sangari and Vaid), 3321–3322
Reccared (Visigothic king), 4556
Recemundo (bishop), 4593
Receptivity, spirit possession and, 8695
Recherches sur le symbolisme funéraire des Romains (Cumont), funerary art in, 2094
Reciprocal generation, 944
Reciprocity. *See also* Hospitality; Potlatch
in Kodi religion (Indonesia), communal healing and, 3815
in oath-taking, 9639–9640
in Scientology, 8194
in Shang China sacrifice, 1582
Recitation. *See also* Chanting; Mantras
in Buddhism
of Dharma and Vinaya, 2035, 2036
nianfo recitation, 8298–8299
practices of, 9837
Prātimokṣa (recitation of transgressions), 1886–1887
in Pure Land devotion, 4922, 4923
of sacred words, for exorcism in Thailand, 3814
Tibetan, 9840
in Christianity
of Christ-*kerygma* (deeds of God in Jesus Christ), 2054, 2056
of scripture, 8198
in Daoism, 9844
in healing, of myths, 3813
in Islam
of Qurʾān, 5485, 7572
in Sufism, of names of God, in *dhikr* practice, 8822
in Judaism, 8198
power of the spoken word, 2099, 8200
of scriptures, 8198–8199
Recluses. *See also* Eremitism
Christian, 2825
rules for, 2827
in eremitism, 2823
Recognitiones (Clement), 3052
Recollection. *See* Anamnesis
Recompense, as doctrine in Judaism, 3884
Reconciliation. *See also* Confession of sins
Anselm on, 1667

in black theology, 78
in early church, 7959
in Eastern Orthodox Church, 7960
in Protestantism, 7963
in Roman Catholicism post-Vatican II, 7962
Reconstruction
in ecology and religion studies, 2609–2610
hope in transformation as, 4126–4127
Reconstructionist (periodical), 7636
Reconstructionist Federation of Congregations, 7637
Reconstructionist Foundation, 7637
Reconstructionist Judaism, **7635–7640**. *See also* Conservative Judaism
civilizational approach to, 7635–7636
community in, 7639
current status of, 7639
Durkheim's (Emile) influence on, 5081
on election of Israel, 2746
halakh reforms and, 1961
Ḥavurah Judaism and, 7637, 7638
Jewish peoplehood in, 4864
in Jewish Renewal, 4871
Jewish Renewal and, 4870–4871
Kaplan and, 1958, 1960, 5081–5082
leadership of, 7638–7639
in modern Jewish thought, 4908
"past has a vote, not a veto" in, 7636
patrilineal descent in, 4864, 7639
prayer books in, 7636, 7638–7639
rabbinical college of, 7637–7638
split from Conservative Judaism, 1962, 7636
spread of, 7636–7637
theology of, 7636
women in, 7637
Reconstructionist Rabbinical Association (RRA), 7638
Reconstructionist Rabbinical College
curriculum of, 7637
establishment of, 1962, 7582, 7637
Jewish Renewal movement at, 4871
leadership of, 7638, 7639
Reconstructionist theology. *See also* Neoorthodoxy
proponents of, 6466
Reconstruction of Religious Thought in Islam, The (Iqbāl), 4534
Reconstruction of the Spiritual Ideal, The (Adler), 33
"Recorded sayings" (*yulu*), 1524, 1604

Recorded Sayings of Layman P'ang, time-bound logic in, 7988
Records of Ritual
canonization of, 1900
as collection, 1893
contents of, 1907–1908
rites based on cosmology in, 1895
sacrifice methods in, 1891
Records of the Historian (Sima Qian), 1893
Records of the Ritual and Music of the Holy Temple of Chinese Confucianism, 10
Recovered memory, 9449
Rectifying Rites of Tianxin (Daoist rituals), 2185
Recurrence, myths of, in serial periodization, 175–176
Red (color), symbolism of, 1860, 1861, 1862
Red Book of Hergest, 1480, 5545
Redemption, **7640–7641**. *See also* Messianism; Salvation; Soteriology
Abelard (Peter) on, 8
in African religions, 7641
West African, 9717
androcentrism of, 336
in Catharism, 1457
in Christianity, 7640
flesh and, 2648
life and, 5446
nature opposed to, 2647
soul and, 8565
definition of, 7113
in Hinduism, mysticism and, 6342–6343
and history, Christian views of, 4053
history of doctrine, 1667
in Judaism, 7640
in eschatology, 2835
of firstborn male, 7819–7820
in Hasidism, 3788, 3790, 8173
Nahmanides (Moses) on, 6400
Naḥman of Bratslav on, 6402
shekhinah concept and, 8312
Shimʿon bar Yoḥʾai on, 8346
in Lutheran theology, ethics and, 1655
martyrdom and, 4183
in Mexican religions, 7641
in morality, 6188
in mysticism, 7641
paradox of, 6990
in Pyramid Texts, 7640–7641
rain as symbol of, 7604
ransom theory *vs.* reconciliation theory, 1667
as religious chief concern, 7113–7114
salvation and, 7640
Schleiermacher (Friedrich) on, 8165

through suicide, 4955
vegetation gods and, 7641
in Zoroastrianism, 7641
Saoshyants ("redeemers"), **8110–8111**
Redfield, James, 5469, 6496
Redfield, Robert, 116, 3151
on popular religion, 7325, 7326, 7327–7328
on religious communities, 7717
on tradition, 4448, 4722, 9276
Red Hat Karma pa, of Tibetan Buddhism, 2131
Redkey, Edwin, 75, 79
Red mda' ba Gzhon nu blo gros, 1228, 9386
Red Path, 1564–1565
Red Power movement, 6667, 6668, 6697
Red Sea, Moses parting, 6200
Red Stick War, 6666
Red Temples (Aztec), music and, 6269
Reductionism
Bellah (Robert) on, 8498–8499
in historicism, 4061
of Hobbes (Thomas), 4075
materialism and, 5775
neuroscience and, 8191
Newtonian physics and, 7137
Otto (Rudolf) on, 4095
in science and religion, 2658, 7745, 7851
Reductions (Jesuit missions), 1697, 4842
Reductive analysis, by Nāgārjuna, 6391–6392
Reductive materialism, 5776–5777
Redwood Valley, Peoples Temple at, 4951
Reed, Edward S., on James (William), 4776
Reed, Ishmael, 76
Reed, Samson, Swedenborgianism and, 8903
Reʾem (beast), 6164
"Re-Enchantment" (conference series), 2665
Rees, Alwyn, 1499
Rees, Brinley, 1499
on *Mabinogion*, 5545
Reese, Thomas, 7891
Reeves, J. C., on Gnosticism, 3534
Refectory, in monastery architecture, 6118, 6119
Reference groups, sociological theory of, 8483
Reference works, **7642–7647**. *See also* Encyclopedias
by Adams (Hannah), 30–31
Mesoamerican religions in, 5944
Refinement, hope in transformation as, 4126
Reflection
mirrors and, 6063–6065
vs. reflexivity, 7648

in Vanuatu religion, 8532
Reflexivity, **7647–7651**
in anthropology, 385–386
definition of, 7647–7648
in Mahāyāna Buddhism, *svasaṃvedanā* (reflexive self-consciousness), 8552
media and, 5807
myths and, 7649
negative connotations of, 7648
paradoxical nature of, 7647
in phenomenological philosophy, 7648
vs. reflection, 7648
in religion, 7649
in rites of passage, 7797
vs. self-consciousness, 7648
in study of religion, 10079
in Western philosophy, 7648
Reform, **7651–7656**. *See also* Reform movements
conservative *vs.* liberal, 7651, 7653
as hope, 4125
moral, 7651–7652
religious, 7651, 7653–7654
in founded religious communities, 7718
traditional practice and, 7654–7655
schism and, 8151
secularization and, 8217
social, 7652–7653
and traditional practice, 7654–7655
women and, 7655
Reformation, **7656–7665**
as act of state, 349
ages of history in, 4053
and All Saints Day, 2230
and All Souls Day, 2230
almsgiving in, 267
Anabaptism and, 782, 1663, 7660–7661
Antichrist in, 395
anti-Semitism in, 400–401
Antitrinitarianism in, 7661
atonement in, theories of, 596–597
authority and, 1663, 8483
authority in, 695
beginning of, 7657–7659, 7877
and biblical canonicity, 881
and biblical exegesis, 874
Bucer (Martin) in, 1059
Calvinist (*See* Calvin, John; Calvinism)
casuistry stimulated by, 1455
causes of, 7877
as challenge to Rome's authority, 1663, 6972
Christmas and, 1757
and church architecture, 794, 795
classification of religions and, 1818
conscience, defense of, 1941–1942
Contarini (Gasparo) at Regensburg colloquy, 1968
controversy within, 7658
covenant theology in, 2049–2051
creeds in, 2054, 2057–2060
differentiation of views in, 7659–7661
divination condemned by, 2373
doctrine following, 2958
Eastern Christians, perspective of, 8158
in Eastern Europe, 1685
ecclesiologies, 1773–1774, 1778
Eck's (Johann) battle against, 2601
ecumenical councils and, 2043–2044
in England, 7662–7663
Elizabethan settlement and, 7663
Puritanism and, 7663
Erasmus overshadowed by, 2821
ethics and, 1655
Eucharist during, 2877, 9811
European dimension of, 7661–7663
Calvin (John) and, 7661
exorcism during, 2930–2931
on faith *vs.* belief, 2425, 2426
Farel (Guillaume) in, 2992–2993
and Faust legend, 3009
in France, 7662
gender in, 3360
grace in, 3646
Harnack (Adolf von) on, as unfinished, 3778–3779
heresy and, 3920, 3928
historiography in, 4029, 7664
and history, view of, 4055
humanism and, 4177
on human perfectibility, 7040
humor and, 4219
in Hungary, 4226
iconoclasm in, 4281, 4286, 4346, 4361, 4386, 4392
indulgences contributing to, 158, 7657
Islamic, 6100–6101
Jewish reaction to, 7234–7235
justification in, 5041
kingdom of God concept in, 5150, 5152
liturgical year and, 1744
Marxist views of, 7664
mediatory role of saints, rejection of, 2083
medieval reform movements and, 1690–1691
membership in the church and, 1777
merit in, 5877
ministry in, 6044–6045
modern secularism and, 7656
monasteries destroyed by, 822, 6134
monasticism in, 6134
suppression of, 6764
music in, 6310
in North America, 1712
orgy and, 6870–6874
Orthodox Church involvement in, 2587
outside England, 350
Pauck (Wilhelm) on, 7011
peasant protests in, 7659
persecution of heretics in, 7061
political aspects, 8153
political climate of, 7656–7657, 7664
and politics and religion, 7248, 7280–7281
and Presbyterianism, 7388–7389
and priesthood, 7403–7404
Puritan wing of, Knox's (John) involvement in, 5212
radical wing of, 1663
ecclesiology, 1774
reconciliation with Roman Catholics in, 7658–7659
Ritschl (Albrecht) on, 7832
Roman Catholic Reformation (*See* Counter-Reformation)
Roman Catholic response to, 7656, 7657, 7663–7664
Canisus, role of, 1402
Rosicrucianism in, 7929–7930
sacrifice and, 8007
as schism, 8158
scientific history, role in, 8182–8183
and separation of church and state, 1968
significance of, 7664–7665
sola gratia, sola fide, sola Scriptura (only grace, only faith, only Scripture) principles, 1691
spectrum of structures and teachings, 1663
and superstition, views of, 8866
and "two books," 9422
use of vernacular in, 7658
violence in, urban, 1807, 1808
Whitehead (Alfred North) on, 7447
Zwingli in, 7660, 10015–10016
Reformed Church Council of Amsterdam, Spinoza (Baruch) condemned by, 8682
Reformed Churches, Protestant. *See also* Presbyterian denominations
chastity and, 1558
confessions of faith, 2058–2059
authority of, 2055
covenant theology and, 2050
in Eastern Europe, 1685
ecclesiology of, 1773–1774
in Germany, Barmen Declaration (1934) and, 2061
in Middle East, 1673
polity of, 7452–7453
of Scotland, 1692, 5212
at Synod of Dort, 2044
Reformed Church of America, full communion agreement with other denominations, 1769
Reformed movement. *See* Calvinism
Reformed Presbyterian Church of North America, 7391
Reformed theology
doctrine of God in, 7389
Edwards (Jonathan) in, 2698, 2699
glory of God in, 7389
humanism and, 7388–7389
Reformers (religious group), 2364. *See also* Disciples of Christ
Reform Judaism, **7665–7673**
Adler (Felix) in, 33
afterlife in, 155
Americanization of, 7670–7671
anti-Zionism of, 9982
bar/bat mitzvah in, 7672, 7821
beliefs and practices of, 7665–7666
after World War II, 7672
"A Centenary Perspective" and, 7672–7673
circumcision in, 7819
Classical, 7671
Columbus Platform and, 7671
conversion to, 7824
divorce in, 3754
education in, 7672
emergence of, 5019–5020
ethics in, 7666
in Europe, 7666–7670
collective activity and diffusion of, 7669–7670
ideologists of, 7668–7669
origins of, 7667–7668
feminism in, 3350
Frankel (Zacharias) in, 7669
Freehof (Solomon) and, 7672
Geiger (Abraham) in, 3291–3292, 7668–7669, 9238
gender in, 3350, 3354–3355
God in, 3552
halakhah and, 3744, 7666
Hebrew spoken in services, 7666
Hirsch (Samson Raphael), opposition of, 4023

Reform Judaism ***continued***
historiography in, 4059
Holdheim (Samuel) in, 4080–4081, 7669
interfaith marriages in, 7666
in Israel, 7672, 9982
Jacobson (Israel) in, 7668
Jewish integration and, 5019
Jewish law, abrogation of, 1960
Jewish peoplehood in, 4862–4863, 4864
Jewish Renewal and, 4872–4873
Jewish Theological Seminary of America and, 1958
in Jewish thought, 4902
Karaites and, 4877
kashrut laws of, 5107
Kohler (Kaufmann) in, 5214, 7671
vs. liberal Protestants, 7235
liturgy in, 7666
messianism in, 5976
modernity and, 4983
morality in, 7651
music in, 6312
origin of, 7667–7668
Orthodox Judaism and, 6898–6899, 6900
orthodoxy and heterodoxy and, 6912
patrilineal descent and, 4864
Pittsburgh Platform and, 7670–7671
prayer books in, 8388
proselytism in, 7666
rabbinate in, 7668, 7669, 7673
relationship with Reconstructionist Judaism, 5082
revelation in, progressive, 7666
Sadducees and, 4877
Schechter (Solomon) on, 8146
scope of, 7665
seminary of, in Germany, 7581
Shabbat laws in, 8256
as sin causing Holocaust, 4091
Sofer (Mosheh), opposition by, 8507
synagogues in, 7668, 7669–7670
as temples, 8925
Torah reading on Sabbath, 8257
theology of, 7665–7666, 7671–7672
in twentieth century, 7673
Wise (Isaac) in, 9766
women in, 3350, 3354–3355, 7666
as *mohels,* 7819
after World War II, 7671–7673
worship in, 7666, 9808
Zionism in, 7671, 7672
Reform movements
in Acehnese religion, 26–27
in Africa, 102
in Buddhist monasticism, in Thailand, 6139–6140
Hindu
Ārya Samāj, **515–516**
and ashram revival, 545–546
Brāhmo Samāj, 7932–7933
Islamic
in Africa, 107–108
modernism and, 6095–6096
Japanese Buddhist, women in, 3348
Jewish (*See* Reform Judaism)
social (*See* Social reform)
Refuge, sanctuary as place of, 8101
Refutation and Overthrow of Knowledge Falsely So-Called (Irenaeus). *See Against Heresies* (Irenaeus)
Refutation of All Heresies (Epiphanius), Mary in, 5753
Refutation of the Dogmas of the Christians (Crescas), overview of, 2069
Refutation of Twelve Chapters of Cyril, A (Theodoret), 9123
Regalado, Iñigo Ed., 3079
Regan, Tom, 2655, 2656
Regeneration
in Aztec religion, 718–719
baptismal, Spurgeon (Charles Haddon) on, 8727
Cyprian on, 2113
earth and, 2559–2560
in epics, 2816–2817
in gnostic deification, 2249–2250
of indigenous cultures, 2617
pearl as symbol of, 7023–7024
prehistoric goddess of, 7377
rituals of, orgy as, 6864, 6877–6878
Regensburg, Berthold von, 278
Reggae, 9307
Rastafari connection with, 1438, 7625
Regia, of Forum Romanum, 7897, 7900
Regicide, 5157–5159
in Africa, 5169, 5171
Regillus, Lake, battle of, 7902
Reginald of Piperno, 9161, 9162, 9163
Regiomontanus, Johannes, humanism and, 4226
Reglamento Echeveste, Serra (Junipero) and, 8231
Regula fidei (canon of truth), 2387
Regula pastoralis (Gregory I), 3688
Regularis Concordia (Ethelwold), 2437
Reguly, Antal, 3112, **7673–7674**
Re-Horus (deity). *See* Re
Reichard, Gladys, 575, 6671
Reichel-Dolmatoff, Gerardo, 383
on *yagé,* 848
Reichenbach, Charles von, crystal healing and, 3851
Reid, Graeme, 5414
Reikai Monagatari (Tale of the spirit world), 6825
Reiki healing, nonphysical touch in, 3813
Reikū (Buddhist monk), 9076
Reilly, Harold J., 561
Reimarus, Hermann Samuel, 875, **7674–7675**
on Gospels, 4846
influence of, 7675
on kingdom of God, 5151
on knowledge, 5206
Reimchronik (Baltic text), 767
Reinach, Salomon, **7675–7676**
Reincarnation, **7676–7680**. *See also* Saṃsāra; Transmigration
in African religions, 106, 7677, 9326
central Bantu, 1508
West African religions, 9326, 9327
Yoruba, 9326
for animals, 1014
in anthroposophy, 9330
in archaic cultures, 7676–7677
in Australian religions, 7677
in Balinese religion, 748
in Bambara religion, 777
in Buddhism, 2131, 7676, 7678–7679, 9327, 9328
in enlightenment, 2793–2794
karman and, 7678–7679
Śākyamuni Buddha on, 7678
in Catharism, 1457
Cayce and, 1473
Druze belief in, 2504
early Christian opposition to, 9329
in Egyptian religions, 7676, 7679
Empedocles on, 2776
evil identified with, 2899
geography of death with, 136
in Greek religion, 166, 7528, 7676, 7679–7680, 9328–9329
in Hinduism, animals and, 359
in Inca religion, 3240
in Islam
ʿAlawīyūn, 227, 9330
rejection of, 9330
in Jainism, 7676, 7679, 9327, 9328
ritual time and, 7987
in Manichaeism, 7676
in miracles, classification of, 6057
in Neopaganism, 6473
in New Age movement, 9330–9331
in North American Indian religions, 6707, 6708
in Oceanic religions, 147
in Orphism, 7679
otherworld in, 6924
Plato on, 7679–7680
Pythagoras on, 7528, 9328–9329
as shape shifting, 8301–8302
in Sikhism, 7676
sin and, 8405
in Sufism, 7676
in theosophy, 7228, 9143, 9330
in Tibetan Buddhism, 9328
of Klong chen Rab ʾbyams pa (Longchenpa), 5192, 5194–5195
and nongenealogical succession, 3426
of saints, 5192
time and, conceptions of, 132–133
in Tukanoan Amazonian religion, 8622
in Unarius, 9449
in West African religions, 9718–9719
Reincarnationism, Christian, soul theory of, 8563
Reindeer
in Arctic religions, 470, 471, 472
in Dolgan religion, 2394, 2395
in Paleolithic religion, 6953
in Sami religion, 8087, 8088
in Samoyed religion, 8095, 8096
in Tunguz religion, 9394
Reines, Yitsḥaq Yaʿaqov, 6901–6902, **7681,** 9980
Reintegration, hope in transformation as, 4126
Reiss, Beryl, vol. 14 color insert
Reiss, Jon, 3099
Reiter-Soffer, Domy, 2164
Reitzenstein, Richard, 2505
on Gnosticism, 3508, 3514, 3532
on mystery religions, 6327
in Myth and Ritual school, 6381
in Religionsgeschichtliche Schule, 7707
Reiyūkai (spiritual friends association), 6574
Nichirenshū and, 6608
Reiyūkai Kyōdan, **7861–7862**
ancestor worship in, 324, 7861–7862
Maitreya in, 5622
Niwano Nikkyō in, 7794
Rejuvenation, **7862–7865**
animal sacrifice and, 7684
desire for, implications of, 7684
elixirs for, 7683
imitation of nature and, 7682–7683
and immortality, 7684
in realm of the divine, 7684

reversal of time for, 7683–7684
Reland, Adrian, 4716
Relational Concepts in Psychoanalysis (Mitchell), 7484
Relationships
in Australian Indigenous religions, centrality of, 2002–2003
discipline of, 8706–8707
in East African cosmogony, 2567
in *walāyah,* 9656
in Orthodox theology, 2591
with God, 2592
icons and, 2594
in sacrificial gifts, 8002
Relatives. *See* Kinship
Relativism, **7685–7686**
in Benedict's (Ruth) anthropology, 820
in Buddhism, Stcherbatsky (Theodore) on, 8737
in Christianity, 7685
cultural, 7685–7686
anthropology, effect on, 2087
critics of, 7686
vs. ethical relativism, 6179
ethnocentrism *vs.,* 2086
Montaigne on, 7685
during Renaissance, 7685
in Daoism, 1588
ethical, criticism of, 6179
in Greek religion
Protagoras on, 7685
Sextus Empiricus on, 3910, 7685
of Sophists, 3909–3910
historicity and, in Catholicism, 9539
in Religionsgeschichtliche Schule, 7708
in Renaissance, 7685
structural, 4463
Relativity theory, 2739–2740, 2879
cosmology, relativistic, 2031–2032
Einstein's, 7138
Planck era and, 2034
Relatos de El Viejo Antonio (Marcos), 9932
Relazione del Reame di Congo (Pigafetta), 112
Release, eightfold path and, 2739
Releasement *(Gelassenheit),* Heidegger (Martin) on, 3896
Relics, **7686–7692**. *See also* Pilgrimage
of African kings, 5170–5171
of Buddha, 1107
commemoration of, 1305
as objects of devotion, 2317, 4383
pilgrimages to, 9832
in Southeast Asia, 8644
in Tibetan Buddhism, 9840
in Buddhism, 7690–7691
in Christianity
Calvin (John) on, 7686–7687
early Christianity, 7687–7688
enshrinement of, 7689
in exorcism, 2929
of Jesus, 7689–7690
in Middle Ages, 7689–7690
as objects of devotion, 2317
opposition to, 7686–7687, 7688
Roman Catholicism, vol. 4 color insert
consecration of space and, 1955
definition of, 7686
fraudulent, 7689
in Greek religion, 7687
in Hinduism, opposition to, 7687
housing, 793
as images, power of, 9623
impurity of, 7687, 7691
in Islam, 7687
objects associated with people as
in Buddhism, 7691
in Christianity, 7689–7690
in Greek religion, 7687
as objects of devotion, 2317, vol. 4 color insert
origins of, 7686
paradoxical nature of, 7691
places made sacred by, 7979
in Protestantism, opposition to, 7686–7687
revenue from, 7689
of saints, 2081–2082
healing and, 3811–3812
in Islam, 7687
pilgrimage to, 7148, 7150
in Sufism, 8035
as sources of purification, 7509
translation of, 7688
Relief, humor and, 4222
Relief sculptures, of Dacian Riders, 2123, 2124
Religio (Roman concept), 7894
Religio-historial method, Clemen on, 1822
Religio Laici (Dryden), 2251
Religion, **7692–7706**
classification of, **1817–1822,** 7703, 7704
concept of, 7702–7705
de Martino (Ernesto) on, 2266
in Religionsgeschichtliche Schule, 7707–7708
definitions of
in African scholarship, 8794
Alston's (William), 7703–7704
alternative terms for, 7705
anthropology and, 7693
Asad's (Talal), 7702
in Asian religions, 7693
Bianchi (Ugo) on, 863–864
comparative-historical method and, 1869
discursive purposes of, 7704–7705
within ecology, 2605
economic/technological, 6502
Eliade (Mircea) on, 864, 7251
during the Enlightenment, 7702
etymology and, 1812
Feil's (Ernst), 7702
Frazer's (James George), 7702
functional *vs.* substantive, 7703
future of, 7705
Geertz (Clifford) on, 7328, 8468
history of, 7702–7703
in history of religions approach, 4061–4063
the holy and sacred in, 7694
intellectualist, 6502
James (William) on, 4775–4776, 7693, 7741
in Japan, 8776, 8777
Lawrence's (Peter), 5379–5380
lexical, 7704
local variants of, 7705
polythetic *vs.* monothetic, 7703–7704
problem of, 8762
psychology and, 7693–7694
Reinach's (Salomon), 7676
Saler (Benson), 7704
Schleiermacher's (Friedrich), 7693, 7694, 7702
secularization and, 8215
Smith's (Jonathan Z.), 7704
social, 6502–6503
sociology and, 7693
Spiro's (Melford E.), 7703
stipulative, 7704
strategies of, 7703–7704
Tylor's (Edward Burnett), 7702
as ultimate transformation, in work of Streng (Frederick), 1581
within visual culture, 9622
in Western societies, 7692–7695
emergence of notion of, in Western scholarship, 4063
etymology of word, 7111, 7702
functions of
fundamental, 4530
integrative, 7790
James (William) on, 4776
genuine, distinguishing, 2700
historicism and, 2761
history as foundation of, 7117
history of (*See* History of religions)
locative *vs.* utopian, 10084
origins of
19th-century obsession with, 366–367
Africa in, 114, 115
animatism in, 7347–7348
animism in, 365–367, 7347, 7372
death and, 2236, 2237–2240
goddess worship in, 3611
manism on, **5671–5673**
power in, 7347–7348
preanimism in, 7372–7374
in primitive religions, 7696
sacred *vs.* profane and, 7973–7975
Schmidt (Wilhelm) on, 8168–8169
Spencer (Herbert) on, 8678–8679
supreme beings and, 8875–8876
Tiele (C. P.) on, 9192
in Western European studies of religion, 10077
as problematic category
for China, 1580–1581, 1614
Smith (Wilfred Cantwell) on, 8450
structure of, 7696–7700
ubiquity of, 2761
use of term, 7111
Religion (journal), 10057
Religion: A Journal of Religion and Religions, Smart (Ninian) as founder of, 8443
"Religion, Totemism, and Symbolism" (Stanner), 2478
Religion and Art in Ashanti (Rattray), 115
Religion and Ecology Group (American Academy of Religion), 2665
Religion and Gender (King), 3314
Religion and National Identity in the Japanese Context (Antoni), 7273

Religion and Nothingness (Nishitani), 1302
Religion and Reductionism (Idinopulos and Yonan), 7745
Religion and Resistance (Berger), 118
Religion and Society among the Coorgs of South India (Srinivas), 4448
Religion and the Decline of Magic (Thomas), 5568
Religio naturalis (natural religion), 9128
Religion Bambara, la (Tauxier), 116
Religion der Ägypter, Die (Erman), 2730
Religion der Vernunft (Cohen), 1851, 4903
Religionen och rollerna (Sundén), role theory in, 8851
La Religione primitiva in Sardegna (Pettazzoni), 7073
Religiongeschichtliche Methode in der Theologie, Die (Clemen), 1822
Religion in China (Groot), 3703
Religion in Context (Lewis), 2935
Religion in Essence and Manifestation (Leeuw), 48, 5391, 5392, 7091, 7350, 7351
Religion in the Making (Whitehead), 49
Religion of Ancestral Spirits. *See* Dini Ya Msambwa
Religion of Babylonia and Assyria (Jastrow), 5968
Religion of China, The (Weber), 1921–1922
Religion of Heavenly Wisdom. *See* Tenrikyō
Religion of Holy Water, 746
Religion of Mystery. *See* Daoism
"Religion of Savages, The" (Tylor), 9424
Religion of the Ancestors (Dini ya Msambwa), 2578
Religion of the Three Teachings, 3069
Religion of the Yellow Emperor (Taiwan), 8965
Religion on Trial (Dudley), 7097
Religions, Values, and Peak-Experiences (Maslow), 7477
Religionsgeschichtliche Schule, **7706–7709**
characteristics of, 7707–7708
concept of religion in, 7707–7708
development of, 7706–7707
on dualism, 2505, 2506
end of, 7707
on Gnosticism, 3532–3533, 3534–3535
on heresy and orthodoxy, 3920–3921
on knowledge, 5208
liberal Protestantism of, 6104
members of, 7706
on origins of Christianity, 7707, 10077
public activity of, 7706–7707
relativism in, 7708
on religious practice, 7708
on tradition history, 7708
Wikander (Stig) and, 9736
Religions in Practice (Bowen), 379
Religions of Ancient Egypt and Babylonia (Sayce), 5968
Religions of the Oppressed (Lanternari), 10027
"Religions of the World and Ecology" (conference series), 2613–2614, 2638, 2665, 8719
Religions orientales dans le paganisme romain, les (Cumont), 2093
Religionstheorie und Politische Theologie (Taubes), 9021
Religionswissenschaft. See also History of religions
in China, 10074
Kitagawa (Joseph M.) and, 5188, 5189
Klimkeit (Hans-Joachim) and, 5190
of Müller (F. Max), 7089
women's studies and, 9789
Religionswissenschaft: Prolegomena zu ihrer wissenschaftstheoretischen Grundlegung (Wach), 9649–9652
Religion und Magie bei den Naturvölkern (Beth), 846
Religion within the Limits of Reason Alone (Kant), 4901, 5078–5079, 5151, 6102–6103, 7125, 7370
Religio-Philosophical Society of Vladimir Solov'ev, 9367
Religio-political cults, Afro-Caribbean, 1437–1438
Religiöse Poesie der Juden in Spaniem, Die (Sachs), 4875, 4877
Religiöser Menschheitsbund (Interreligious League), 2343
Religiöse Wltbild einer frahen Kultur, Das (Jensen), 4824
Religious Action Center, of Union of American Hebrew Congregations, 7671
Religious and Social Ritual (Aune and DeMarinis), 7858
Religious broadcasting, **7709–7716**
in Africa, 7714
in Asia, 7714
in Australia, 7714
criticisms of, 7714–7715
anti-intellectualist bias of, 7715
dualistic worldview in, 7714
exploitative nature of, 7714
formats of, 7714
fundraising, 7714
goals of, 7715
Pentecostal dominance of, 7714
political influence of, 7714–7715
global, 7713–7714
in India, 7714
in Middle East, 7714
origins of, 7709–7711
Pentecostalism and, 7714
in United States, 7709–7713
World Wide Web, 7715
Religious communities, 7699–7700, **7715–7725**. *See also* Community; Utopianism
almsgiving to, **266–269**
in Asian religions, 7700
in Buddhism, 7699, 7700, 7716
in Christianity, 7700, 7716
religious orders, **7721–7725**
Schleiermacher (Friedrich) on, 8165
cult-based communities, 7719
definition of, 7715
ecological participation of, 2612–2613
founded, 7717–7718
in Hindi tradition, 3985–3987
in Hinduism, 7699, 7700
Holy Order of MANS, **4101–4104**
initiation into
dīkṣā for, 7816
retreats for, 7770
in Islam, 7700, 7716
in Judaism, 7700
mendicancy in, 5855–5856
mystery societies/communities, 7719
national, sacred, 7717
in primitive religions, 7699, 7716–7717
religious orders/monastic communities/service societies, 7719–7720
religious societies-turned-communities, 7718–7721
rituals of, 7699–7700
sacred national, 7717
secret societies, 7718–7719
and society, **7715–7721**
in Sufism, 7700
tribal, 7716–7717
utopian communities, 7720–7721
in Western societies, 7692–7693
women's
in Australia and New Zealand, 1734
in Catholicism, 3361
gender struggles over, 3302–3303
in Jainism, 3327–3328
in Mesoamerica, 3412
in South America, 3416, 3417
Religious Consciousness, The (Pratt), 7366, 7367
Religious Dances (Backman), 2144
Religious diversity, **7725–7731**. *See also* Dialogue of religions
monotheism *vs.* existentialism, 7728
mundane *vs.* transmundane worlds and, 7726, 7727, 7728
pagan *vs.* great religions, 7725–7726
salvation and, 7728
types of, 2605
among women, 9786–9787
Religious ecology. *See also* Ecology
definition of, 2606
Religious education, **7731–7736**. *See also* Education; Seminaries
"about" religion *vs.* "from" religion, 7732–7733
in Acehnese religion, 26
in Buddhism, 7734
in Dge lugs pa order, 2322–2323
Dharmapāla and, 1126
Foguangshan and, 3140
in Tendai school, 9075
Tibetan, 5224
at universities, 1118–1121, 1125, 1156, 2322–2323
Calvinist, 1376
Catecheses, of Cyril of Jerusalem, 2118
catechesis (confessional) approach to, 7731
in Christianity, 7735
nuns and, 6763, 6764
in Christian Science, 1747
Confucian, 1586
criticisms of, 7731–7732
in faith schools, 7733–7734
future of, 7735–7736
in Hinduism, 7734
"in" religion *vs.* "about" religion, 7731–7732
Islamic, 7734–7735 (*See also* Madrasahs)
in China, 4633–4634
in Europe, 4675–4676, 4680–4681
in *madhhabs* of law, 3760
modernity in, 6097
in mosques, 6206, 6210
Qur'ān recitation in, 9201
in Southeast Asia, 4666–4667, 4671
traditionalism and, 3761, 3763
in Jesuit order, 4842
Jewish, 7735 (*See also* Yeshivah)
Agudat Yisra'el in, 195
Conservative Judaism and, 1961–1962
in France, 5000
gender and, 3354
in Jewish Renewal, 4874
Kotler (Aharon) and, 5239
of Marranos, 5719, 5720
Musar movement in, 6241–6242
Orthodox, 6908
Reform Judaism, 7672
rituals of, 7820–7821

Schneerson (Menachem) and, 8171–8172
siyyum celebration in, 7821
Torah study in, 9238–9239
tosafot in, 9247
Mormon, 6195
of *'ulamā',* 9439
opposition to, 7732
patterns of provision in, 7732–7734
pluralism and, 8765
in public schools, 7732–7733
Roman Catholic, 7734, 7735
Thomism in, 8176
sainthood, path to, 8037
in Sikhism, 7734
Spener (Philipp Jakob) on, 8680
in supplementary schooling, 7733
types of, 7731–7732
in Western society, 7731
Religious Education Association of the United States and Canada, 7736
Religious ethnology, de Martino (Ernesto) and, 2266–2267
Religious Evolution (Bellah), classification of religions in, 1821
Religious experience, 7700, **7736–7750**. *See also* Mysticism; Ritual
aesthetics and, 48–50, 56
of Anglo-Americans, 7737–7738
in Asian religions, 7694, 7695
in Buddhism, 7694, 7695, 7700, 7737, 7740–7741
Capps's system of study and, 1413
Cardeña (Etzel) on, 7747
characteristics of, 7695–7696
in Christianity, 7700
Lonergan (Bernard) on, 5510–5511
pre-Reformation, 7737–7738
consciousness in, 7695
in Daoism, 7700
debates over nature of, 7745–7746
definitions of, 7694–7695, 7736
deserts and, 2300–2301
Dewey (John) on, 49
Dilthey (Wilhelm) on, 3932–3933
Eliade (Mircea) on, 7694
in empiricism, 2778
in epistemology, 2819
expression of truth through, 9374–9376
faith as, 2956–2957
gender studies on, 3302–3303
genuine *vs.* pseudo-religious experience, 7743
and health, 6493
in Hinduism, 7694, 7695, 7700, 7737, 7740, 7742, 9630–9631
Hollenbeck (Jess Byron) on, 7747
human body as vehicle for, 7834
interactive discipline and, 8702
of Isaiah, 7694, 7700
in Islam, 7700, 7739–7740
James (William) on, 7741–7742
in Judaism, 7700, 7737, 7739–7740
Krippner (Stanley) on, 7747
Laski (Marghanita) on, 7695
Lynn (Steven Jay) on, 7747
Maslow (Abraham) on, 7695
metaphysical, in Zolla's (Elémire) philosophy, 9985
in Methodism, 7737
mystical (*See* Mysticism)
vs. mysticism, 7744–7745
neuroscience on, 6487, 6492–6493
in New Guinea, 6508
of Muḥammad, 7700
of otherworld, 6925–6926
Otto (Rudolf) on, 4096, 7694, 7835
in Pentecostalism, 7700
poststructuralist approach *vs.,* 8471
in primitive religions, 7694, 7695
in Protestantism, 7737–7738
in Puritanism, 7737
Pyysiäinen (Ilkka) on, 7747
Radhakrishnan (Sarvepalli) on, 7741, 7742
in rites of passage, 7798–7799
in Roman Catholicism, 7737
after Council of Trent, 7739
the sacred in, 7694
discovery of, 7976
Schleiermacher (Friedrich) on, 8161, 8162, 8165
seeing as form of, vol. 11 color insert
Soloveitchik (Joseph Baer) on, 8519
soteriology and, 8527, 8528
Stanner (W. E. H.) on, 8729
study of
future of, 7746–7747
methods of, 7746
in Sufism, 4761
sui generis nature of, 7744, 7746
Sundén (Hjalmar) on, 8851
in universalistic new religious movements, 7738
Wach (Joachim) on, 7741, 7743–7744
in Western European religions, 10076
in women's studies in religion, 9790–9791
in Zen Buddhism, 7740
Religious Experience of Mankind, The (Smart), 7093
organic coordination in, 8466
Religious freedom. *See* Freedom, religious
Religious Human Rights, 5362
Religious instruction, 7731. *See also* Religious education
Religious leadership. *See* Leaders
"Religious Man," Soloveitchik (Joseph Baer) on, 8518
Religious movements, new. *See* New religious movements
Religious nationalism, militant, 7791
Religious orders. *See also specific orders*
Christian, **7721–7725**
asceticism of, 7722
definition of, 7721
historical development of, 7723–7725
origins of, 5287, 7722–7723
qualifications of, 7721
as religious communities, 7719–7720
in Roman Catholicism, 7722
Religious Organizations Law (Japan), 4792
Religious Orientation Scale, 7476, 7477
Religious persecution. *See* Persecution
Religious Philosophical Society of Saint Petersburg, 5869
Religious pluralism. *See* Pluralism
Religious practice
devotion and, 2318, 2319–2321
Religionsgeschichtliche Schule on, 7708
religious reform and, 7654–7655
technology and, 2142
Religious Psychologism, Macintosh (Douglas Clyde) on, 5207
Religious reform. *See* Counter-Reformation; Reform; Reformation
Religious Right. *See also* Evangelical Christianity; Fundamentalism, Christian
Capps on politics and, 1413
religious broadcasting and, 7714–7715
Robertson (Pat) and, 7713
Religious Science (denomination), 6586
founder of, 6584
Hopkins (Emma Curtis) and, 4128–4129
Religious sciences (Islamic), hawzahs as centers for, 3800–3801
Religious societies, 7716. *See also* Religious communities
cult-based communities, 7719
mystery societies/communities, 7719
religious orders/monastic communities/service societies, 7719–7720
secret societies, 7718–7719
societies-turned-communities, 7718–7721
utopian communities, 7720–7721
Religious Society of Friends. *See* Quakers
Religious stage of existence, Kierkegaard on, 5142
Religious studies. *See* Study of religion
Religious Studies (journal), 10057
Religious Systems of China, The (Groot), 3703
Religious Technology Center, in Church of Scientology structure, 8193
Religious Thought and the Modern Psychologies (Browning), 7479
Religious Viewpoints Scale, 7478
Reliogione e Società (journal), 4531
Reliquaries, 7689, 9227, vol. 4 color insert, vol. 5 color insert
Relly, James, 9470
Rembe (prophet), 2570–2571, 5528
Rembrandt (painter), 4347, 7459
Remembrance. *See Dhikr*
Remez (hint), 867
Remonstrant Brotherhood, 493
Remus
as child, 1568
Cicero on, 7895
killed by Romulus, 2393
Puhvel (Jaan) on, 4464
as twin, 9417
wolf and, 9785
woodpecker and, 5996
Rémusat, Abel, 1311, 1632
Ren (benevolence or humaneness), **7751–7752**
Cheng Hao on, 1561, 7752
Cheng Yi on, 7752
in Confucianism, 5075–5076
Confucius on, 1586, 1894, 1909, 1936
definitions of, 7751
Dong Zhongshu on, 7752
Han Yu on, 7752
Kanq Yuwei on, 5075–5076
in *Liji,* 7752
Mengzi on, 7751
yi and, 7751–7752
in *Yijing,* 7752
Zhang Zai on, 7752
Zhi Xi on, 7752

Renaissance
alchemy in, **250–254**
angels in, 348
art in
Mother and Child paintings, vol. 12 color insert
phallus in, 7082
study of, 499
Warburg's (Aby) study of, 9690
astrology in, 564
Barlaam of Calabria as forerunner of, 788, 789
Carnival in, 1440, 1442
church architecture during, 794
comparative theology in, 9128
dance in, 2136, 2153–2154
divination in, 2373
doubt in, 2424
drama in, 2438, 2470, 2472, 2473–2474
Eliade's interest in, 2753
erotic magic in, 8248
faith in, 2427
Golden Age in, 3627–3628
Hermetism in, 3945–3948
historiography in, 4038–4039
humanism in (*See* Humanism, of Renaissance)
iconography of, 4346
Jewish thought and philosophy in, 4897–4898
law in, 5358–5359
magic in, **5577–5580**
materialism in, 5776
music in, 6309–6312
mythology in, study of, 6366
nature in, 6433–6434
and novel, development of, 3058
occultism in, 6780
paganism, views of, 4039
papacy in, 6972
perception of artists in, 4283
Platonism in, 7193
poetry of, 7219–7220
Reformation and, 1691
relativism in, 7685
search for origins of religion in, 367
and tourism, 9261, 9262
views of desire in, 2308
Renaissance, Bengal, 828, 9316, 9319, 10035
Renan, Ernest, 3177, **7750–7751**
Celtic religion and, 1497
on desert as source of monotheism, 2301
Lévi (Sylvain) influenced by, 5418
Loisy (Afred) influenced by, 5506–5507
modernism of, 4035
on monotheism, 3913
Renard pâle, le (Griaule and Dieterlen), 100, 2350, 3701
Renatus in aeternum (baptism of blood), 780
Renel, Charles, on Madagascar religion, 8745
Renewal. *See also* Revival and renewal activities
as hope, 4125
Spener (Philipp Jakob) on, 8680
spiritual, retreats of, 7770–7773
in Christianity, 7770–7773
in Islam, 7770
in Roman Catholicism, 7772
in Sufism, 7770
Renewal Judaism, 7638
Renewal movements. *See* Holiness movement; Revival and renewal
Renewed Moravian Church, 7142
Renewed Order of the Temple (ORT), 9067
Renfrew, Colin, 456
Renga (verse form), 7216–7217
Rennyo (Buddhist leader), 1182, 4935, **7752–7753**
Shingonshū Buddhism and, 8355
writings of, 7752
Renou, Louis, 1024, 1025, **7753–7755,** 9270
on Rudra-Śiva, 8039
Renouvier, Charles, Durkheim (Émile) influenced by, 2527
Renovation. *See* Frashōkereti
Renunciant tradition
Brahmanic, 9569–9570
Jain, 4768–4770
karman in, 5094–5095
Renunciation. *See also* Asceticism
forest dwellers in Buddhism and, 8080–8081
hope in transformation as, 4126
in Indian religion (*See also* Saṃnyāsa)
Sadhus/Sadhvis, **8019–8022**
sainthood, path to, 8037
Renunciation life stage. *See Saṃnyāsa*
Ren-yi (morality), 5431, 7751
Reorganized Church of Jesus Christ of Latter Day Saints (Community of Christ), 6192, 6193–6194, 6195
Repatriation, to Africa, by Rastas, 7622, 7627
Repayment. *See* Retribution; Revenge
Repentance, **7755–7760**. *See also* Confession of sins; Purification
accusation in, 7755
in Buddhism
in meditation, 1291
rites for, 9838
in cargo cults, 7756
in Christianity, 7756, 7758
confession of sins and, 7755
conversion and, 7756
definition of, 7755
Eastern Orthodox rite of, 7960
in Greek religion and mythology, 7756
guilt and, 7755–7756
in Islam, 7757–7758
atonement not required with, 8407
in Muʿtazilah, 7758
in *Jonah,* 4947
in Judaism, 7757
and atonement, 593–594
of Judah, 4829
manifestations of, 7757
Kook (Avraham Yitsḥaq) on, 5226
morphology of, 7755–7756
in Near Eastern traditions, 7756–7758
in North American Indian religions, 7759
in Nuer religion, 7758–7759
penitential rites in, 7755
Philo Judaeus on, 7757
sacrament of confession and, 1889
Shenoute on, 8319
in Sufism, 7758
Repetition, in music, 6254–6255
Rephaim texts, Canaanite religion and, 1398
Replica (Eck), 2601
Replication cult, 4390–4391
"Report and Program of the Eugenics Society of the United States of America," 2881
Representation, nature of, 9620
Reprobation, predestination as, 3202
Reproduction. *See* Abortion; Pregnancy; Sexuality
Reproductive technology, and kinship relations, 5184
Republic (Plato), 390
ascension in, 520
Bendideia in, 819
bridge in, 1050
charity in, 1554
dēmiourgos in, 2273, 7183
descent in the underworld in, 2299
Er myth in, 7680
ethics in, 7110
God in, 7182
humans in, 7184
Ibn Rushd's commentary on, 4272
imitation in, 5486
immortality of soul in, 7184, 7185
music theory in, 6303–6304
in Nag Hammadi codices, 6396
sin in, 8405
theater in, 7044
theology in, 9134
three elements in man in, 9348
traditional religion in, 7186
Zarathushtra as character in, 491, 520
República eclesiástica (ecclesiastic republic), 9215
Republicanism, Marsilius of Padua on, 5730
Republican Party, U.S.
and African Americans, 69
fundamentalism and, 2892–2893
religious right and, 7713, 7714–7715
Republika (newspaper), 4670
Requiem for a Nun (Faulkner), 5480
Requiem Masses, 6312
Re religion
kings in, 2704
metaphysics and ethics of, 2705
theology of, 2705
Rerum novarum (Leo XIII), 5411
Rescue, distinction from liberation, 5436
Research. *See* Study of religion
Researchers into the Early History of Mankind (Tylor), 9424
Research Institute for Psychology of Religion, 846
Reseph (deity), 4742
Reservedness, subjective, in humor, 6364
Reserve heads, in Egyptian magic, 2713
Res gestae, 7912
ReSH. *See* Shimʿon ben Laqish
Reshef (deity), **7760–7762**
of Atanni, 7760
consorts of, 7761–7762
cult of, 7760
extension of, 7760
in Egyptian religion, 7760
etymology of name, 7760–7761
figurative connotations of name, 7762
of Gunu, 7760
Horus and, 7761
indefiniteness of action of, 7761
local associations of, 7760–7761
Min and, 7762
Nergal and, 7761
Qudshu and, 7762
Rashap as equivalent to, 1384
relations to other deities, 7761–7762
Resh Laqish. *See* Shimʿon ben Laqish
Resistance
images in, 9622–9623
of indigenous cultures, 2617
in Mesoamerica, 5920–5921
religion in conflict with politics and, 7256–7257
"Resolutions" (Edwards), 2699
Resolve, in eightfold path, 2738
Resonant causality, 1572
Resonating self, in Chinese medicine, 3859
Responsa. See Halakhah
Response theory, aesthetics and, 50

Responsibility model of ethics, 1650–1651, 1656, 4949
Respuesta, La (Sor Juana), 4967
Restitutio in integrum (restoration to original state), 4735
Restitution
in penitential rites, 7755
punishment *vs.*, 1843
Restitution (Servetus), 7661
Restitutionism, of Smith (Hannah Whitall), 8445
Restoration
Calvin on, 1376
hope in transformation as, 4126
Restoration comedy, 2438
Restorationism
Disciples of Christ and, 1712
in Universalism, 9470–9471
Restoration of Latvian Religion, The (manifesto), 763
Restorative rituals, 7843
Restraint, in yoga. *See Yama*
Resurgence (journal), 2626
Resurrection, **7762–7768**. *See also* Rebirth
afterlife and, views of, 131–132
as anthropogonic repetition, 4159–4160
of Atahuallpa (Inca ruler), 567–568
by Ahura Mazdā, 7764
in Canaanite religion, 724, 7764
in Christianity, 7765–7766
Athenagoras on, 589
biblical, 156
gender and, 3358
ghosts and, 3475
immortality and, 8563–8564
Jonah and, 4947
Lessing (G. E.) on, 5417
physical, 2803
shape shifting and, 8302
Sozzini (Fausto Pavolo) on, 8674
in worship, 9809
in Daoism, 7762–7763
definition of, 7762
dying and rising gods (*See* Dying and rising gods)
egg as symbol of, 2702
in Egyptian religion, 2237, 7763, 7767
the Family on, 2988
in Germanic religion, 744
hope in transformation as, 4126
in Indian religions, 7763
in Indo-European religions, 4456
in initiation rituals, 4476, 4477–4478, 4480–4481, 4482–4483
in Islam, 131, 133, 162, 7766–7767
barzakh and, 2837
falsafah ideas on, 2971, 2977
al-Ghazālī on, 8568–8569
al-Kindī on, 8569
Nizārīyah doctrine of, 8332
of Jesus (*See* Jesus, resurrection of)
in Judaism, 152, 153, 154, 7764–7765
in Apocrypha, 900
vs. Christianity, 156
in eschatology, 2835
in Hebrew scriptures, 8557
judgment and, 3884
Maimonides (Moses) on, 8560
messianism and, 3884
in rabbinic thought, 8558
Saʿadyah Gaon on, 7953
suffering and, 8806
lion symbolism of, 5464
in Orthodox Christianity, 2590
participation in, soteriological, 8527
in Persian religion, macrocosm-microcosm and, 4159–4160
reincarnationism and, 8563
retribution and, 7765
in Samaritan belief, 8070
by Saoshyant, 7764
soteriology and, 8528
in South American Indian religions, and death, myth of origins of, 8591
time and, conceptions of, 132–133
in Vedism, 7763
in Zoroastrianism, 7763–7764
Resurrection (Tolstoy), 9221
Resurrection play, 2468–2471
Re-Thinking Missions (Hocking), 2343
Rethinking Religion: Connecting Cognition and Culture (Lawson and McCauley), 7851, 7858
Reting Rinpoche. *See* Rva sgreng rin po che
Retractiones (Augustine), 629
Retreat houses, 7772
Retreats, **7768–7773**
at ashrams, 545–547
in Buddhism
Tibetan, 9840
Vassa, 9831
in Christianity, 7770
Devotio Moderna and, 7771–7772
for monastic initiation, 7770
for spiritual renewal, 7770–7773
definition of, 7768
forms of, 7768–7769
in Hinduism, 7769–7770
of initiation, 7768, 7769
monastic, 7769–7770
shamanistic, 7769
tribal, 7769
in Islam, for spiritual renewal, 7770
isolation in, 7768, 7769
of search for revelatory dream, 7769
of spiritual renewal, 7770–7773
in Christianity, 7770–7773
in Islam, 7770
in Sufism, of spiritual renewal, 7770
Retreat Sisters of the Sacred Heart, 7772
Retribution, **7779–7784**. *See also* Revenge
in the Bible, 7784
in Christianity, 5373, 7783
dead as agents of, 7780
as deterrent, 5373
in Golden Rule, 3632–3633
in Greek religion and mythology, 7783
in Islam, 7782–7783
in Judaism, 7782
in wisdom, 9758
in morality, 6186–6187
nature of, 7779
as punishment, 5372–5374, 7782–7784
in religious *vs.* secular law, 5372–5374
resurrection and, 7765
revenge as archaic form of, 7780–7782
in Roman religion, 7782
Retrieval, in ecology and religion studies, 2609
Retrocognition, 6057
Retrospection and Introspection (Eddy), 2694
Return, Law of. *See* Ḥoq ha-Shevut (Israeli Law of Return)
Return, theme of
in Chinese myth, 1628
in al-Junayd, 5030
Return to Judaism movement, Schneerson (Menachem) and, 8172
Reubeni, David, 5719
Reuchlin, Johannes, German humanism and, 4176
Reuchlin, John, 5831
Reunion, of Catholics and Protestants, Leibniz's work toward, 5405, 5406
Reuss, Theodor, sexual magic and, 8251
Reuter, John, 5831
Reuther, Johann Georg, 686, 690–691
Reva (deity), 4253
Revard, Carter, 7225
Revata (monk), Yaṣas and, 2035–2036
Revati (wife of Balarāma), 743
Revealing Prophets (Johnson and Anderson), 118
Revel, Bernard, **7773**
Revelation(s), **7773–7779**. *See also* Prophecy
in anthroposophy, 392
apocalyptic (*See* Apocalypse)
Aristotle on, 7775–7776
in Australian Indigenous religions, 639, 689–690
Barth (Karl) on, 7118
in the Bible, 7774–7775
in Buddhism, Nyingma school of, 5191, 5194
in Christianity, 7777–7778
Byzantine, 2587
early Western, 2582
ethics and, 1653
Irenaeus on, 4539
John and, 7778
neoorthodoxy on, 6467
Paul and, 7774–7775, 7777–7778
Psalms as, 7465
in *Revelation to John,* 7778
Roman Catholicism, 7882–7883
in synoptic gospels, 7778
content or object of, 7774
criteria for, 7773–7774
in Daoism, in literature, 2204–2206
definition of, 7773
and deism, 2251
effects and consequences of, 7774
in Egyptian religion, under Akhenaton, 220–221
of Enoch, 2803
in Etruscan religion, 2872
fasting and, 2996
Fichte (Johann Gottlieb) on, 3049
gnosis as, 7774
Hegel (G. W. F.) on, 3894
Herder (Johann Gottfried) on, 3918
Heschel (Abraham Joshua) on, 3962
in Hinduism, 7778–7779
Hirsch (Samson Raphael) on, 7441
images and, 9623
of incubation oracles, 6833
instrument or means of, 7774
in Iroquois religion, 4543
in Islam, 7778
al-Ghazālī on reason and, 8815
Ibn al-ʿArabī on, 8820
in Ismāʿīlīyah, 8326
in Qurʾān, 5060, 7561, 7571
in Shaykhīyah movement, 8308
reason and, 3565

Revelation(s) ***continued***
in Judaism, 7776–7777
Albo (Yosef) on, 233
Buber (Martin) on, 4905
in existential theology, 4904
Fackenheim (Emil) on Holocaust as new revelation, 4092
modern philosophy on, 7441–7442
at Mount Sinai, 7584
nature and, 2641, 2642–2643
oral Torah and, 6840–6841
Orthodox Judaism, 7666
progressive, 7666
Psalms as, 7465
purpose of, 7777
rabbinic Judaism, 4977
reason and, 4904
Reform Judaism, 7666
Rosenzweig (Franz) on, 4904–4905
Sa'adyah Gaon on, 7952, 7953
Steinheim (Solomon) on, 4904
verbs describing, 7776–7777
Kant (Immanuel) on, 3049, 5079, 7441, 7776
vs. magic, 7774
Mani's experience of, 5648, 5655, 5665
on mountains, 6213
mysticism as, 7774
natural, 7774–7776
origin or author of, 7773
Paul the Apostle on, 7774–7775
philosophy and religion expressed in, 7118
Plato on, 7775
in poetry, 7204–7207
recipients of addresses of, 7774
retreats for, 7769
of scripture, 8201–8202
shape shifting and, 8303
of Smith (Joseph), 8447
Söderblom (Nathan) on, 8506
Spinoza (Baruch) on, 8683
Steinheim (Salomon) on, 7441
Thomas Aquinas on, 7775–7776
in understanding God, in Orthodox theology, 2589–2590
Vatican I on, 9531
violence and, 9598
in vocation, 9632
wisdom as, 9748
of Wovoka, 9846
of Zarathushtra, 9934
in Zoroastrianism, 7778
Revelation, Book of, 919
afterlife in, 156
Antichrist in, 394
as apocalypse, 409, 412
author of, 919, 4944
canon of, 920, 921
Christian persecution in, 7058
condemnation of idolatry in, 4359
date of, 919
dualism in, 2512
ecstasy in, 2678
Eddy's (Mary Baker) exegesis on, 2695
Herder (Johann Gottfried) on, 3918
Houteff (Victor) on, 1036
interpreting, 919
Irving (Edward) on, 4544
Koresh (David) on, 1037
letter mysticism in, 272
Mary in, 5751, 5753
and millenarianism, origins of, 6544
new religions' interpretations of, 6531
paradise in, 6984, 6985
poetry of, 7218
resurrection in, 7766
Satan in, 2278, 2314
Shōkō (Asahara) on, 6531
sickle in, 968
Swedenborg (Emanuel) on, 8899
theodicy in, 9116
underworld in, 9454
Revelations (Ailey), 2159, 2164
Revelations of Divine Love (Julian of Norwich), 5028–5029
Revelation to John, 7778
in Montanism, 6167
Revenants
definition of, 3475
in Germanic religions, 167, 168
Revenge, **7779–7784**. *See also* Retribution
as archaic form of retribution, 7780–7782
in Australian Indigenous religions
blood vengeance, 7780
justifications for, 3872
blood-price *vs.* bride-price, 7780, 7782
collective *vs.* individual liability in, 7781
cycles of, prevention of, 7781
duty to carry out, kinship and, 7781
exogamy principle and, 7779, 7781
guilt and, 7781
of heroes, 3958
nature of, 7779
vs. punishment, 7779–7780
representation principle and, 7781
Reverence, in Confucianism, 2634
"Reverence for life," Schweitzer (Albert) on, 8179
Reveries of a Solitary Walker (Rousseau), 2607, 2664
Reversal rituals, orgy and, 6864–6865
Réville, Albert, 114, 10056
Réville, Jean
on liberal Protestantism, 6103, 6105
Maritain (Jacques) and, 5712
Revisionist Zionist Party, 9980
Revitalization, revival and renewal activities described by, 7784
Revival and Rebellion in Colonial Central Africa (Fields), 9297
Revival and renewal activities, **7784–7790**. *See also* Millenarianism
biological interpretations of, 7788
in Christianity, 7787
definitions of, 7784–7785
epilogue of, 7786
interpretive theories on, 7787–7789
morphology of, 7785–7787
prologue of, 7785–7786
psychological interpretations of, 7788
Smith (Hannah Whitall) and, 8445–8446
Revivalism. *See also* Holiness movement
Afro-Caribbean, 1436–1437
in Caribbean and South America, creolization and, 2066
Christian
civil religion and, 1814
and history, view of, 4055
in North America, 1710
Pentecostalism, 1741, 7030
postdenominationalism and, 1775
conversion and, 7756
Hindu, sectarian movements and *bhakti* revivalism, 4004–4005
Islamic, in Africa, 107–108
Jewish, Hasidism and, 3789
Maya, 5799
migration and, 6025
North American Indian (*See* Ghost Dance)
Quaker, 7548
repentance and, 7756
secularization and, 8217
Revival Zion, Carribean cult of, 1436–1437
Revolt in the Temple, The (Wijewardena), 1100
Revolution, **7790–7792**. *See also specific revolutions*
in Chinese religion, 7790
in Christianity, 7791
earth as symbol of, 2560
in Europe, Christianity and, 1692–1693
Geertz (Clifford) on, 8500
hope and, 4126
in Latin America, 1698–1699
leadership in, 7791, 7792
in Mexico, 1700
Millenarianism and, 7791, 7792
religion as agent of, 7790–7792
religion in conflict with politics and, 7256–7257
religion-society relations and, 8468
social action and, 1750
Sorokin (Pitirim Aleksandrovich) on, 8524
Revolutionist movements
in Africa, 102
in Latin America, 6576
millennial, 6546, 6549
new religious movements as, 6517
Revue de l'histoire des religions (journal), 10056
Revue des études juives (journal), 4879
Revue d'Etudes Tibétaines (journal), 9188
Reward
in afterlife
differentiation of destinies and, 137–138
geography of death and, 136
structure of universe and, 134
in Chinese religion, Han Fei Zi on, 3773
in Judaism
Albo (Yosef) on, 233
Sa'adyah Gaon on, 7952–7953, 7953
in wisdom, 9758
Rex sacrorum, 7907
Rey, Abel, 7341
Reynaud, Georges, 2436
Reynolds, Dwight, 700
Reynolds, Frank E., 944, 947, 1247–1248
Reynolds, Henry, Hermetism and, 3950
"Rez Litany" (Erdrich), 7226
Rgod ldem, Rig 'dzin, 1231, 1232
Ṛgveda (Vedic text), 9550–9551. *See also* Vedas
Brāhmaṇas of, 1026
Bṛhaspati in, 4326
bridge in, 1049
Burnouf (Eugène) on, 1334
ceremonial use of, 4426
chanting of, 1535
chariot races in, 8724
classes in, 9522
cognitive elements of, 5199
corporate symbolism in, 4161
cosmology in, 2014–2015, 5447
cows in, 1466, 1467
creation stories in, 4439, 4440, 7254
demons in, 4442
egg symbolism in, 2701
eye in, 2941
fire god in, 3116
funeral rite in, 2559, 4456
gambling in, 3260

goddess Vāc (Speech) as queen of the land in, 3975
goddess worship in, 2525
heaven in, 3886
hell in, 9456
hotṛ priests and, 3991
human flight in, 3126
in Indo-European language study, 4458
Indra in, 4466, 4467
as ram, 8311
inspiration in, 4509
īśvara in, 4751
magic in, 5590
mantras in, 5676
Manu in, 5678
māyā in, 5794
Meru (mythic mountain) in, 4439
Müller's edition of, 6234
multiple deities in, and atheism, 577
mythology in, 9555–9561
ocean in, 6806
Prajāpati in, 7356
priesthood in, 7405, 7406
puruṣa in, 7521–7522
redemption in, 7641
rejuvenation myth in, 7683
Renou (Louis) on, 7754
resurrection in, 7763
revelation in, 7779
riddles in, 6987
ritual in, 3990
ṛta in, 7934
Rudra in, 7934, 8039, 8414–8415
sacrifice in, transformation and, 8545
Sarasvatī in, 8112–8113
Soma/*soma* in, **8521–8522**
moon and, 6172–6173
praise of, 849, 4439
spiritual guides in, 8711
studies of, 4446
sun in, 7384, 8838–8839
tapas in, 8997–8998
translations of, 7753
triads in, 9345
twins in, 9420
Vedic religion reconstructed from, 3989–3991
in Vedic texts, 9553, 9554–9555
Viṣṇu in, 9617
Zoroastrianism compared with, 9935–9936
Rgyal po (kings), 9185
Rgyud bzhi (Four medical Tantras), in Tibetan *a mchi* medicine, 3865–3866
Rhabanus Maurus, on curses and blessings, 2105
Rhadamanthys (mythological figure), 9453
Rhapsodomancy, 1528
Rhazes. *See* Rāzī, Abū Bakr Zakariyā' al-
Rhea (deity), 2984
Rheticus, Georg Joachim, as disciple of Copernicus, 1977
Rhetoric, 2776
Jerome's use of, 4832
Rhetoric (Aristotle), chance in, 1526
Rhetorical paradox, 6988
Rhiannon (deity), 1487, 1490, 2820
in *Mabinogion,* 5546
Rhine, Joseph Banks, 6057
Rhineland, Jews in, 5011
Rhode Island, foundation of, 784, 7520, 9739
Rhodes (Greek island)
colossus of, 8839
sun cult on, 8839
Rhodes, Alexandre de, 3077
Rhodesia, Northern, Lumpa church movement in, 5408–5409
"Rhymed Chronicles," 757
Rhŷs, Sir John, 1498
Rhys Davids, C. A. F., 3330
Rhys Davids, Caroline, 6956
Rhys Davids, Thomas William
on Buddha biographies, 945
and English translation of Buddhist texts, 1313
Pali Text Society founded by, 1312, 6955–6956
Rhythm. *See also* Percussion
drums and, 2496
in music, 6251
in mystical states, 6342
of time, 7991
in vision inducement, 9613
Ri (rabbi), 9248
Ribā (usury), 4574
Ribāṭ (retreat), 9005, 9008. *See also* Khānagāh
Ribeiro, Rene, 121
Ribera, José, 377
Ricard, Matthieu, 9190
Ricard, Richard, 5915
Ricci, Matteo, **7792–7793**
in China, 1167, 1608, 1609, 1630–1631, 1725, 6084, 7792–7793
comparative theology of, 9128
Tasan influenced by, 1648
writings of, 7793
Rice
in Chinese religion, in Qingming Jie festival, 1648
in Diola religion, 261–262
Japanese reverence for, 3169
deity of, 4795
origins of, myths on, 192
in ritual meals, 3163
Sincerity Rice in Ch'ŏndogyo, 1648
in Southeast Asian religions, 8641
cadastral cults and, 8642
in Vedic rituals, 9566
Rice, Abraham (rabbi), 7582
Rice, Anne, 3062
Rice, Julian, 957
Rice, Luther, 785
Rice, Timothy, 2470
Rice Bandits. *See* Celestial Masters
Rice v. Cayentano, 5342
Rich, Adrienne
gynocentrism of, 3719
on lesbian studies, 5413, 5414
Richard (earl of Cornwall), 2952
Richard, Mira, 1549
in ashram revival, 545
Richard of Saint-Victor
Anthony of Padua influenced by, 377
Hugh of Saint-Victor and, 4151
on loving God, 8706
on meditation *vs.* contemplation, 5816
on mystical union, 6337
on Trinity, 9361
Richards, Audrey I., 4486
on Bemba maturity rituals, 8659
on kingship, in Africa, 5171
Richardson, Cyril C., **7793–7794**
Richardson, Henry Handel, 3084
Richardson, James T., 6515, 6522, 6524, 6525–6526
on children in new religions, 6539, 6541, 6542
Richardson, Samuel, 3051, 3059
Richerson, Peter J., on dual inheritance system, 8475
Richey, Russell, 75
Richman, Paula, 3314
Richmond, Farley, 2436
Richter, Johann Paul Friedrich. *See* Jean Paul
Rickaby, Joseph, 9427
Ricketts, Mac Linscott, on trickster-transformer-hero motif, 1989
Ricoeur, Paul, 383
on Augustine, 8406
biblical exegesis of, 876
comparative theology of, 9131
on evil, 8403
on Freud's hermeneutics, 3933
Geertz (Clifford), influence on, 8499
hermeneutics of, 5487
on liturgy, 5492
metaphysics of, 5991
on *atē,* 5469
on pastoral psychology, 7477
on phenomenology of religion, 7087, 7099
on "regional hermeneutics," 3932
on Satan as serpent, 8125
on symbol and thought, 1990, 7744, 8912, 8913–8914
on temptation, 9071
on truth, 7206
Riddah rebellion and wars, 20
Riddell, Peter G., 4662, 4670, 4671
Riddles, **6986–6992**
in Babylonian religion, 6986
brahman as, 1025–1026, 6987
in Christianity, 6987
of East Africa, 2567
features of, 6987
in Greek religion, 6986–6987
in Hinduism, 6987
in Judaism, 6987
in North American Indian religions, 6677
in Vedism, 6987
in Zen Buddhism, 6987–6988
"Riders of the Chariot," 3550
Ridge, John Rollin, 7224
Ridgeway, William, 2436–2437, 2443
Ridicule. *See also* Humor
in *adab* literature, 4214–4215
in Chinese Confucian tradition, 4206
of and by religion, 4200–4201
Ridington, Robin, 6677
Rieder, David, 888
Riedman, Peter, Hutterian Brethren and, 4239
Rieff, Philip, 3217, 7476, 7480
Riegl, Alois, 4298
Riek (shrine), 9336
Riel, Louis, 9302–9303, 9304
Ries, Julien, historiography of, 4049
Riesebrodt, Martin
on classification of religion, 8762
on history of religion, 7703
RIF. *See* Alfasi, Yitsḥaq ben Ya'aqov
Rifā'īyah (Ṣūfī order), 9008
characteristics of, 8823
Riffard, Pierre, 2844
Rift Valley
languages of, 2566
Ngai located in, 2567
Riga District Council Statutes, 329
Rigby, Thomas, 9427
Rigdon, Sidney
Mormonism of, 6193
Smith (Joseph) and, 8447
Riggs, Marcia, 79, 80
Right, religious. *See* Religious Right
Right and left. *See* Left and right
Righteousness
dharma as (*See Dharma*)
in kingdom of God, 5152–5153
Paul the Apostle on, 7019
Utu as god of, 9494

Rights. *See also* Civil rights movement; Human rights
animal, as environmental ethic, 2655
of church members, 1778–1779
Jewish law and, 3749–3750
Rigopoulos, Antonio, on Sai Baba movement, 8026–8027
Rig pa (purity of awareness), 2546
Rígr (deity), 2693
as Heimdallr, 3898
Rígsþula, 2693
Rig-Veda Samhitâ (Müller), 6234
Rijckenborgh, Jan van
on Hermetism, 3953
Lectorium Rosicrucianum, founding of, 3953
Rikyū (tea master), 847, 848
films about, 3097
on tea ceremony, 4141
Riley, Patricia, 3092
Rilke, Ranier Maria, 56
on angels, 348
Rime movement, in Tibetan Buddhism, 5222–5224
Rim Kin, 3077
Rin, Taro, 3097
Rin chen bzang po (Rinchen Zangpo), 1152, 1224, 1230
Guhyasamāja Tantra translated by, 3708
Rin chen gter mdzod (Buddhist text), 9333
Rinda (princess), 744
Ringatu (Christian sect), 5682, 5683
Ringelheim, Joan, 3352
Ringgren, Helmer, 5501
Rings
as amulets, 3770
as magical objects, 1793
Minoan, 37, 38, *38, 39,* 40
Ringwallbilder (labyrinth), 5276
Rini, Roseanne, 3148
Rink, H., 475
Rinka monasteries, 9947–9948
Rinkhart, Martin, 7450
Rinpoche (guru), 7262, 9190
Rinpoche, Patrul, 9191
Rinpoche, Sogyal, 9191
Rinzai school of Zen. *See also* Linji
in Ashikaga period, 4787
development of, 1180, 1181, 1244, 9944–9945
Eisai in, 847, 1244, 2741
enlightenment in, 4786
Gozan Zen and, 3644
Hakuin, role of, **3741–3742**
Ikkyū Sōjun and, 4377
meditation in, 1293, 2306
monasticism in, 9949
Musō Sōseki and, 6316–6317
size of, 9943
Rio, Alexis-François, 499
Rio de Janeiro, Carnival and samba schools, 1444
Ríos Montt, Efraín, 5924, 5931
Riots. *See* Violence
Ripley, George, on alchemy, 251
Rip Van Winkle motif, 8440
Risālah (al-Shāfiʿī)
ijmāʿ doctrine in, 8265
sources of law in, 8264
Risālah ilā ahl al-thaghr bi-Bāb al-Abwāb (Ashʿarī), 530
Risāla-i Ḥaqq numā (Dārā), 2219
Risālat al-iʿ tiqādāt (Ibn Bābawayhi), 4262
Risālat al-shirk wa-maẓāhirih (al-Mīlī), 4589
Risālat al-tafsīr (al-Ṭabarī), 8944
Risālat al-tawḥīd (ʿAbduh), 6
on existence of God, 5068
Risālat al-wāridāt (ʿAbduh), 6
Risāla-yi muʿīniyya (Ṭūsī), 9408
Risālo (ʿAbdul Laṭīf), 4644
"Rise" (Alexie), 7226
Rise and Progress of the New Jerusalem Church (Hindmarsh), Swedenborgianism and, 8901, 8902
Rise of Islam and the Bengal Frontier, The (Eaton), 4642
Riʿshonim ("first ones"), halakhic development and, 3743
Rising gods. *See* Dying and rising gods
Ris med (Rime) movement, 9333
Risshō Kōseikai (Society for Establishing Righteousness and Harmony), 5400–5401, **7794–7795**
in Europe, 6568
in Japan, 6574
Nichirenshū and, 6608
Risshun, eve of, 2411–2412
Risshu school. *See* Vinaya school of Buddhism
Ritchings, Edna Rose, 3007
Rite, *vs.* ritual, 7860
Rite of Spring (ballet), 2161
Rite of the House of Life (Egypt), 2719
Rites de passage, les (Gennep), 3432, 7348
Turner's (Victor) commentary on, 9405–9405
Rites of passage, **7795–7831**. *See also* Circumcision; Funeral rites; Initiation; Marriage; Puberty rites; Ritual
ablutions in, 9, 10, 11
in Acehnese religion, 25–26
in African religions, 87–89, **7804–7806**
Agikuyu initiation rites, 7805
bodily marking in, 88–89
circumcision in, 1799
functions of, 85, 88
iconography in, 4303
Limba funeral rituals, 7806
Ndebele birth ritual, 7804–7805
pattern of, 88
in southern African religions, 8658–8659, 8662–8663
thermodynamic conception in, 8662–8663
transition phase of, 88
Tswana marriage rituals, 7805
types of, 7804
in Australian Indigenous religions
circumcision in, 1799
Mardu, 5705
Ngukurr, 6600
Warlpiri, 9695–9696
in Bali, 7796
biological roots of, 2868
caves and, 1470
cicatrization as, 1003
circumcision in, 1798–1799
classification of, 7859
Combs-Schilling (Elaine) on, 7803
Durkheim (Émile) on, 7800
Eliade (Mircea) on, 7797–7798, 7801, 7802
experience in, 7798–7799
flowers used in, 3136
Frank (Jerome) on, 7798
Fried (Martha and Morton) on, 7798
Gennep (Arnold van) on, 3432, 5460, 7797, 7801, 7802, 7804, 7806–7807, 7811
Gluckman (Max) on, 7800
in Greek religions, Hera and, 3915
Grimes (Ronald) on, 7801, 7802
in Hawaiian religion, 3798
in Hinduism, **7813–7818**
āśrama, 7816–7817
dīkṣā, 7816
Saṃskāras, 7814–7816 (*See also* Saṃskāras)
śūdras, 7817
of women, 7817
history of study of, 7797–7798
imagery in, vol. 9 color insert
in Inuit religion, 4527–4528
in Islam, **7824–7828**
birth, 7825–7826
circumcision, 7826, 7828
death, 7827
hajj (*See Ḥājj*)
local variations in, 7827–7828
marriage, 7824, 7825, 7826–7827
naming, 7825–7826
in Judaism, **7818–7824**
bar and bat mitzvah, 7820–7821
circumcision, 7818–7819
conversion, 7823–7824
death, 7822–7823
of girls, 7819
Marrano, 5719
marriage, 7821–7822
memory books, 7823
mourning, 7822–7823
redemption of firstborn male, 7819–7820
learning in, 7798–7799
liminality in, **5460–5463,** 7797, 7801–7802
Lincoln (Bruce) on, 7801, 7802
liturgy of, 5492
in Marathi religions, 5698
marriage as, 5726
in Mediterranean religions, for women, 3382–3383
in Melanesian religions, 5837–5838
of men
in Agikuyu society, 7805
in modern society, 7802–7803
Neopagan, 7830
in tribal societies, 7796, 7799, 7801
in Mesoamerican religions, **7810–7813**
birth rites, 7811–7812
childhood development, 7812
cosmic, 7813
funeral rites, 7813
historical documentation of, 7810–7811
marriage, 7812–7813
in modern society, 5461–5462, 7799–7800, 7802
mystery religions and, 6328
Neopagan, **7828–7831**
birth rituals, 7829–7830
for life changes, 7829–7830
of men, 7830–7831
seasonal, 7829
of women, 7830
in New Year ceremonies, 6590
in North American Indian religions, 6682–6683, **10068–10072**
appropriation by modern society, 7802–7803
Salish, 1470
vision quest as, 9610
nudity in, 6740
in Oceanic religions, **7806–7810**
adulthood, 7807–7808
birth, 7807
cosmic significance of, 7809
death, 7808
genital operations, 7808
in modern society, 7809–7810
parenthood, 7807
personal significance of, 7808–7809
social significance of, 7809
paradigms of, 7801
paradox in, 7796–7797, 7803
personal significance of, Yakasere (Celine) on, 7808
power in, 7803

psychological interpretations of, 7798–7799
purification in, 7504, 7505
religious communities and, 1864, 1865
as sacraments, 7955, 7956
in Samoyed religion, 8095–8096
secret societies and, 8212–8213
sexual symbolism in, 7797–7798
in Sikhism, 8396, 8397
gender and, 3337
sleep location and, 8441
in South American Indian religions
in Kayapó religion (Amazon), 8630
in Pilagá religion (Gran Chaco), 8636
in upper Xingu religion, 2011
structuralist interpretation of, 7797
tattooing as, 1001, 1002, 1003, 7807–7808
in tribal societies, 7795–7799, 7801
of men, 7796, 7799, 7801
of women, 7796, 7799, 7801
Turner (Victor) on, 5460, 7796, 7797, 7799, 7801
of untouchables, 9476
in Vanuatu religions, 9520
Wallace (Anthony) on, 7798
of women
in Agikuyu society, 7805
feminist theory on, 7859
in Hinduism, 7817
in Middle Ages, 7802
Neopagan, 7830
in Oceanic religions, 7807
in tribal societies, 7796, 7799, 7801
Young (Frank) on, 7799
in Zoroastrianism, 9999–10001
Rites of Passage (Gennep), 4480
Rites of Passage, The (Gennep), 7049
Rites of the Jade Hall (Daoist rituals), 2185
Rites of Youthful Incipience (Daoist rituals), 2186
Rites of Zhou. See Zhou Rituals
Ritjuruki (totem), 2481
Ritman, Joost R., Bibliotheca Philosophica Hermetica library and, 3953
Ritschl, Albrecht, **7831–7833**
on atonement, 597
on Christianity, 7116
on God, ethics and, 3557
on Jesus, 7116
on knowledge, 5208
liberal theology of, 6103–6104
Söderblom (Nathan) and, 8506
on theology, 7137
and Troeltsch (Ernst), 9364
writings of, 7831–7832
Ritschlianism, German, 6104
Ritsuryō system of law, 4783
erosion of, 4784–4786
kami in, 5073
Kiki texts compiled in, 4800, 4801–4802
religious texts in, 4809–4810
Shintō and, 8358–8359, 8360
Ritsu sect (Buddhism), 1242
Ritter, Helmut, 4716
Ritter, J. W., on androgynes, 340
Ritter, Johann Wilhelm, 6435
Ritter, Karl, 730
Ritual(s), 7698–7699, **7833–7856**. *See also* Ceremonies; Rites of passage; Sacraments; *specific religious traditions and rituals*
agricultural, 186–190, 192–193
origins of, 7835
almsgiving in, 268
anxiety and, 3143
archetypes in, 7834
art making as, 498
as behavioral events, 2867
Bellah (Robert) on, 8470, 8471
Bell (Catherine) on, 7852–7853, 7859
biogenetic foundation of, 7049
for burials (*See* Funeral rites)
calendar-based (*See* Calendars)
ceremony distinguished from, 1512–1513, 1516, 1517
changes in, 7859–7860
Cheng Hao on, 1561
circle as ritual pattern, 1790
circumambulation in, 1795–1798
classification of, 7840–7841
confessional, 7858
ethical, 7858
of Freud (Sigmund), 7841
functional-enumerative, 7840–7841
of Durkheim (Émile), 7841
structural-analytical, 7840–7841
of Toy (Crawford Howell), 7840
of Wallace (Anthony F. C.), 7840–7841
clowns in, 1838–1841
cognitive theories of, 7839, 7851, 7854
communicative functions of, 7849–7851
components of, 2440
confession (*See* Confession of sins)
confirmatory, 7841–7843
consciousness in, 7841–7842
constructive discipline and, 8703
cosmic elements of, 7837
criticisms of, 7859–7860
cross-cultural variations in, 7845–7846
as cultural practice, 7852–7854
cultural theories of, 7849, 7852–7854
death confronted in, 7836–7837
decorations for, vol. 7 color insert
definitions of, 2436, 7833–7834, 7848–7849, 7860
Durkheim (Émile) on, 3231, 7043, 7840, 7841, 7850
ecological function of, 7840
economic basis of, 2671
eggs used in, 2702
Eliade (Mircea) on, 7800, 7802, 7834, 7835, 7837
for exorcism, 7836
expression of truth through, 9370–9372
failure of, 7803
features of, 7698–7699
film and, 3101
flowers and, 3136
as flow experience, 3138
food in, 7838
form of, 7851
as frame of awareness, 7841–7842
Fraser on, 1878
frequency of, 7851
Freud (Sigmund) on, 7838–7839, 7858
funeral (*See* Funeral rites)
gardening, 3280, 3281
Geertz (Clifford) on, 7833, 7842, 7850, 7852
gold and silver in, 3626
Grimes (Ronald) on, 7803, 7857, 7858, 7859
and heresy, development of, 3923
historical variations in, 7845–7846
hospitality and, 4141
human body in, 7834, 7853
human-nature connection in, 2619
humor and, 4197–4199
in East Asia, 4208
images in, 9623
in images veneration, 4380
of incantation, 4407
initiatory (*See* Initiation)
invention of, 7050–7051
journals devoted to, 10058
in kingship, 5155, 5156
in Africa, 5169
language and, coevolution of, 2868
language of, 5304, 5305, 5306, 5328, 7851, 7858
law and, 5327–5328
left and right symbolism in, 7837
libation as (*See* Libation)
liminality in, 1513, 7844
liturgy as, 5490–5491
magic and, 7858
meaninglessness in, 7850
microcosm-macrocosm and, 4159
in modern society, 7846
monsters in, 6163
music in, 6253–6255, 7860
Myerhoff (Barbara G.) on, 6326
and myth (*See also* Myth and Ritual school)
Frazer (James G.) on, 3288–3289, 3460
Gaster (Theodor H.) on, 3288–3289
in Germanic religion, studies of, 3460
interrelation between, 2957
manism influencing, 5673
vs. myth, 3662
myth as script for, 6363
Raglan (Lord) on, 3959
narrative in, 7858–7859
naturalistic theories of, 7849, 7852
neurotheology on, 6493
noise in, 7037–7038
for oath-taking, 9641–9642
order maintained through, between society and environment, 2611
orgy in, 6860–6861
of pain, 6945, 6947
of percussion, 7030
performance elements of, 7800, 7852–7854, 7857 (*See also* Performance, and ritual)
play in, 7196–7197
political value of, 7839–7840
poor performance of, illness caused by, 3810
popular culture and, 7858–7859
practice aspect of, 7852–7854
process of, 7049–7050
Radcliffe-Brown (A.R.) on, 7592–7593
Rappaport (Roy A.) on, 7618–7619
vs. rational behavior, 7833, 7839
as recentering events, 7835
of re-creation, in quest stories, 7552
reflexivity of, 7649
religious communities and, 1864, 7699–7700

Ritual(s) ***continued***
religious meaning of, 7834–7838
religious reform and, 7654–7655
restorative, 7843
of reversal, orgy and, 6864–6865
rites of passage (*See* Rites of passage)
sacraments *vs.*, 7957
sacred and profane in, 7970–7972
sacred language in, 5304, 5305, 5306
sacred time and, 7987
sacrificial (*See* Sacrifice)
salt in, 8058–8059
scripture as public ritual, 8199
self in, 7834–7835
sexual, in Europe (*See* Sexuality, European rites of)
sexual symbolism in, 7838
shame in, 7836–7837
similarity and contiguity in, 5373
Smith (W. Robertson) on, 8451, 8452
social value of, 7839–7840
soteriological function of, 8527
space in, 7837–7838
structuralist view of, 8753–8754
structural *vs.* personal approach to, 7835–7836
study of (*See* Ritual studies)
symbolic time and, 8917
symbolism in, 7838–7840, 7849
Freud (Sigmund) on, 7838–7839
integrations of, 7838
syncretism in, 8931
taboos of, 8949
time and, 1760–1761
sacred, 7987
time in, 7837–7838
timing of, agriculture and, 186–188
transformatory, 7843–7845
transitional, 7843
Turner (Victor) on, 7852
types of, 7840–7845
in United States, 7836
violence in, 7858, 9598
visions in, 9613
winter caroling as, 9741, 9745
Ritual, Records of (Confucian). *See Records of Ritual*
Ritual and Belief in Morocco (Westermarck), 3476
Ritual behavior, 2868
adaptive values of, 2868
Ritual Criticism (Grimes), 7859
Ritualism, in Vedic mythology interpretation, 9559
Ritualization, definition of, 7848
Ritual Process, The (Turner), 9406, 9407
Ritual process theory, 3144
Ritual sacrifice. *See* Sacrifice
Ritual studies, 7838–7840, **7856–7861**
biogenetic structuralism in, 7857
books on, 7857
cognitive science in, 7858
cognitive theories, 7839, 7851, 7854
cultural theories, 7849, 7852–7854
definition of, 7856–7857
ethnology in, 7858
future directions of, 7854–7855
international involvement in, 7859–7860
naturalistic theories, 7849, 7852
performance studies in, 7858
in popular culture, 7858–7859
psychology in, 7858
theoretical analysis in, 7859–7860
Ritual Theory, Ritual Practice (Bell), 7857
Rius-Camps, J., 4369
Riva' (rabbi), *tosafot* of, 9243
Rivail, Hyppolyte Léon Denizard. *See* Kardec, Allan
Riva Palacio, D. V., 5940
River civilizations, 7861
"River Murray Histories" (Hemming), 2481
River of Heaven (Milky Way), and stars as land of the dead, 8733
River of the Dead
in Southern Siberian religions, 8671
in Tukanoan Amazonian religion, 8622–8623
Rivers, **7861–7863**. *See also* Water
in African religions, 7862
in Akkadian religion, 2791
in Baltic religion, 774–775
in Buddhism, 7863
in Christianity, 7863
damming, environmental activism against, 2622
of death, 7862–7863
deities of, 3620, 7862
in Celtic religion, 1486
in Eden, 7862
in Egyptian civilizations, 7861
female sacrality of, 3016
in funeral rites, 3240
in Greek religion and mythology, 7862, 7863
healing waters of, 7862
in Hinduism, 7861
in Cambodia, 4012
Ganges River, 3274–3275, 7861, 7862
as objects of devotion, 2317
Sarasvatī associated with, 8113
shrines and, in India, 8377
Vaitaraṇī, 7863
of India, 7861–7862
divinity of, 2621
in Indus Valley civilizations, 7861
in Shintō, 7863
as living waters, 7862
in Mesopotamian civilizations, 7861
Milky Way as, 2863
in North American Indian religions, 7862
purification and, 7862
rebirth and, 7862
in Sumerian religion, 7862
in Syrian religions, 7862
in Vedism, 7861, 9558–9559
Rivers, W. H. R., 2420, 2421
Rivet, Paul, 5785
Rivière, Jean, on atonement, 597
Rivière, Peter, on transformation, 2011
Rivkin, Ellis, 5423
Rivqah. *See* Rebecca
Riy (rabbi), *tosafot* of, 9243, 9244, 9246
Riyawarra tree, 2380
Rizal, José, 3079
canonization of, 8654
Rizzuto, Ana-Maria, 7478, 7483
Rnam thar (biographies), 9189–9190
Rnga (drum), 2497
Rnying ma bka' ma (Buddhist text), 7869
Rnying ma pa (Nyingmapa) school of Buddhism, **7867–7871**. *See also* Dzogchen
Anuyoga in, 7870
Buddha Samantabhadra in, 7868
celebrations of, 1158, 1308
Dalai Lama and, 8382
doctrines of, 7869–7870
emergence of, 8083
formation of, 1223
gter chos (treasure-doctrines) in, 7868
historical development of, 7868–7869
Klong chen Rab 'byams pa (Longchenpa) and, 5191–5195
Kong sprul Blo gros mtha' yas and, 5223
lineages of, 7868
mahāmudrā in, 5598
Mahāyoga in, 7868, 7870
meditation in, 7868
monasteries in, 8084–8085
origins of, 7867–7868
Padmasambhava's role in, 6941–6942
revelations in, 5191
and revival of Buddhism, 1153
ritual in, 7868
study of, 9189
Tantric canon of, 7868
teachings of, 1157, 1223–1224
treasure-discoverers of, 1231, 1232, 7262
Vajrasattva in, 9515
visionaries in, 1009
women in, 1233
Rnying ma rgyud 'bum (Buddhist text), 7869
Roadmap for Rebel (Havice), 7486
Roads
crossroads, **2070–2071**
Hekate shrines or statuettes as, 3899–3900
in Greek religion, offerings at junctions of, 3899–3900
Mercurius as god of, 3937
shrines at side of, vol. 1 color insert
Road shows, by Earth First!, 2562–2563
Robbers Synod. *See* Ephesus, Council of
Robbins, Jerome, 2164
Robbins, Joel, 6508–6509
Robbins, Thomas, 6515, 6522
Robelo, Cecilio A., 5940
Roberson, Lizzie Woods, 10038
Robert de Borron, on Grail, 3649–3653
Robert le diable (ballet), 2155
Robert of Arbrissel, 6763
Robert of Chester, 250
Robert of Molesme, Benedict's rule and, 1800
Roberts, Ainslie, 2480
Roberts, B. T., Free Methodists, founding of, 4083
Roberts, David, 671
Roberts, Deotis, 5441
Roberts, Helene E., 4300
Roberts, J. Deotis, 77–78, 965
Roberts, Oral, 7030
television ministry of, 7711, 7712
Roberts, Rhoda, 646–647
Robertson, D. W., Jr., 7218
Robertson, George, 6540
Robertson, Noel, 7131
Robertson, Pat, 2892, 7714
religious broadcasting and, 7712–7713
Ríos Montt (Efraín) and, 5931
Robertson, Roland, 110, 383
on leadership, 5386
Robertson Smith, William. *See* Smith, W. Robertson
Robigalia (Roman procession), 7417, 7897
Robinet, Isabelle, 4333
Robin George v. ISKCON, 1033
Robins, Gay, 2732
Robinson, Francis, 3161
Robinson, Ida, 10039
Robinson, James M., in Nag Hammadi translation, 3508, 3535, 6395
Robinson, John, 3196
Robinson, John A. T., 584
Robinson, Richard, 1315
Roca, Alfred, time and, 7993

Rocher, Ludo, 7498
Rochford, Burke, 6541
Rock art, 1471
 in Africa
  in Khoi and San religion, 5137
  shamanism depicted in, 83
 in Arctic religions, 474
 in Australian Indigenous religions, the Dreaming in, vol. 1 color insert
 in Germanic religion, 3445
Rock Cave of Heaven, 280
Rockefeller, John D., Jr., 2289
Rock gardens
 Eastern cosmic, 3277–3278
 Zen, 9947, vol. 5 color insert
Rock of the Temple of Jerusalem, 1502
Rock piles. *See* Cairns
Rocks. *See also* Stones
 in Eastern cosmic gardens, 3277–3278
 feminine sacrality of, 3017
 in Shintō, 2640
 left at labyrinths, vol. 4 color insert
Rock tombs, 1472–1473
Rococo iconography, 4347
Rocquet, Claude-Henri, 460
Roden, Amo Paul Bishop, 1038
Roden, Ben, 1036–1037, 5237, 5238
Roden, Benjamin, 6561
Roden, George, 1037, 5238
Roden, Lois, 1036, 1037, 5237, 5238
Rödiger, Emil, Goldziher (Ignácz) and, 3634
Rodinson, Maxime, 4717, 4720
Rodney, Walter, 7625
Rodrigues, Raimundo Nina, 121
Ro'eh (seer), 7431
Roe v. Wade, 941
 and medical ethics, 5810
Rogacki, Sarah, 3099
Rogation Days, 2996
 procession in, 7417
Roger, Abraham, 4445–4446
Rogers, Carl, 7485
Roghair, Gene, on Palnāḍu, 2816
Rohde, Erwin, 3052, 6865, **7871–7872**
 on immortality, origins of belief in, 6622
Róheim, Géza, 3114, **7872–7873**
 on Australian Indigenous religions, 7872
  academic approaches to, 3490–3491
  women in, 3389
 on dreams, 2483
 Freud's (Sigmund) influence on, 7872–7873
Rök inscription, 7939, 7940
Rokuharamitsuji temple, 5270
Roku religion (Oceania), spirits of the dead in, 2006
Rokycan, Jan z, 6190
Roland, Alan, self theory of, 1970
Rolando, Gloria, 3099
Role playing
 in games, 3268
 in rites of passage, 7797–7798
Role theory
 in sociology, 8483–8484
 Sundén (Hjalmar) on, 8851
Rolle de Hampole, Richard, 3116
 and language of fire, 3120
Rol mo'i bstan bcos (Sakya Paṇḍita), musicology in, 8052
Rolston, Holmes III, 2655
Roma (deity), 7915, 7916
Roman arches, 794
 religious associations in, in middle republic, 7909
Roman Catholicism, **7873–7892.** *See also* Papacy; *specific countries, doctrines, and regions*
 abortion in, 941, 942, 5812
 action in, emphasis on, 7888–7889
 affections in, 7891
 African Americans in, 68
 in Afro-Brazilian religions, 120–121, 124
 afterlife in, 157–158, 7885–7886
 All Saints Day in, 2229, 2230
 All Souls Day in, 2229, 2230
 altars in, 278
 Anglicanism's dialogue with, 353
 animals in, 356
 anointing of the sick in, 3236, 3241
 anthropomorphism in, 391
 on Apocrypha, 896
 apologetics in, 429
 Aristotelianism in, 482
 asceticism in, 528
 ashram movement in, 547
 atheism in, 583
 atonement in, 596, 597
 attention in, 604
 authority in, 694–695
  exorcism as reaffirmation of, 2936
  hierarchical, 1668, 1681
 autobiography in, 699
 in Baltic religion, ancestors and, 328
 baptism in, 782
 barbarian invasions and, 7876
 biblical exegesis in, 877
 biblical movement in, 7879, 9533
 on bioethics, 939
  on beneficence *vs.* nonmalificence, 8191
  on genetic research and, 8190–8191
 bishops (*See* Bishops, Roman Catholic)
 blessing in, 982
 body marking forbidden in, 1001
 Byzantine Christianity, differences with, 1689–1690 (*See also* Schism)
 "cafeteria Catholics" in, 7890
 calligraphy and, 1368
 canon law in, 7876, 7886
 capitalism and, 2670
 cardinals (*See* Cardinals)
 Caribbean ancestral cults and, 1436
 Carnival, efforts to control, 1441
 "catholic" *vs.* "Catholic," 1771–1772
 celibacy in, 1475, 1477
 and censorship, 4282
 charismatic gifts and, 1550
 charismatic movement and, 1550, 6793, 7030
 charismatic sainthood, 1546
 chastity and, 1558
 child abuse scandal in, 6516, 6539, 7889–7890
 as church
  mission of, 7885
  organization of, 7874
 churches of
  architecture of, 794–795, 796–797
  consecration of, 1955
  sacredness of, 7698
 church of Constantinople and, 7877
 clergy in, distinction from laity, 5287
 on cloning, 5814
 color symbolism in, 1861
 communion in, 7882
  forbidden with Orthodox, 2588
 confession in (*See* Confession of sins)
 Confession of Faith (Dositheos) influenced by, 2588
 consecration in, 1956
 conservative-liberal continuum in, 7889, 7890
 contemplation in, 5818
 conversion to
  Nestorian, 6480
  of Newman (John Henry), 6510
 Counter-Reformation (*See* Counter-Reformation)
 creation story in, 7883
 creolization and, 2067
 Curia Romana and, in church polity, 7886–7887
 dance and, for worship and honor, 2137
 Day (Dorothy) and, 2226
 decline in membership, 7891
 definition of, 7874
 as denomination, 7873
 devotional movement in, Pius IX and, 7181
 discrimination against, 1753
  in Australia and New Zealand, 1733–1734
 divisions within, 7877
 doctrinal controversies in, 7876
 doctrine of, 7882–7886
 dogma in
  definition of, 2387
  development of, 2387–2389
 domestic observances in, 2399, 2400
 Eastern Orthodox Church and
  division between, 2585–2588
  Paul VI and, 7012
 ecclesiology, 1771–1772, 1775
 ecumenism in, 2686–2687, 7879
  in Pacific Conference of Churches, 1739
 on embryonic stem cell research, 941, 942
 the Enlightenment and, 7878
 environmental crisis and, responses of, 2613, 2650
 eremitism in, 2828
 ethics, 1651, 1653–1654, 7457
 Eucharist rites in, 2580, 2877–2878
 exorcism liturgy of, 2929–2930
 faith in, 7882–7883
 fasting in, 2997, 3171
  as purification, 7508
 fiesta system in, 5925
 in film, 3099
 Focolare (fireplace) movement, 5399
 fools in, 4202
 Franks as protectors of, 1689
 Freemasonry prohibited by, 3197
 on free will and predestination, 3204, 3208
 French Revolution and, 7878
 Gallicanism and, 3258–3259, 7877–7878
 in Garifuna religion, 3284
 gender in, 3358, 3362
 goddess worship in, 3587–3588
 God in, 7874, 7880, 7881
 grace in, 158, 3645–3646, 7876, 7880, 7881, 7883
 Grail movement in, **3653–3654**
 Greek Orthodox Church and
  Barlaam of Calabria's attempt at reconciliation, 788
  roots of schism between, 3657
 group activity in, 7889

Roman Catholicism
continued
healing in, 3845–3846, 3847
giving thanks for, vol. 7 color insert
heaven, hell, and purgatory in, 3885
Heiler (Friedrich) on, 3897
against heliocentrism, 7136
heresy and blasphemy in, 972, 973, 6971
heterodoxy in, 6912
historiography in, 4030, 4034
history of, 7874–7880
study of, 2396
against history of religions, 7073
Holy Spirit in, 7884
on homosexuality, 7404
human achievement in, 7454
iconoclasm opposed by, 2585
iconography of, 4345–4346, 4347
idolatry in, 4361, 4386, 4389, 4390, 4392
in Otomí religion, 6926–6927
Inquisition (*See* Inquisition)
Irenaeus as leading mentor of, 4540
Jansenism and, 7877–7878
Jesus Christ in, 7876, 7880, 7881, 7883–7884
Judaism and, 7234–7235
Paul VI and, 7012
justification in, 5040
Khomiavok (Aleksei) on, 5138
kingdom of God in, 5153, 7885
kneeling in, 5196
knowledge in, 5205, 5209–5210
labor unionism in, 2670
laity in, 5287, 7889, 7890
in ministry, 9533, 9540–9541
Latin used in, Vatican II on, 9536
Latin *vs.* Greek tradition, 1681
levitation in, 3128
liberal, Döllinger (Johann) and, 2396
life in, sanctity of, 5811
light symbolism in, 5453
liturgical dramas developed by, 2437
liturgical movement, 796–797, 7879, 9533
liturgy in, 5490
at local level, 7874
Lutheranism and, 5540, vol. 14 color insert
Luther's (Martin) effect on, 7663
Māra in, 5693–5694
Marcionism rivaling, 5701, 5702
marriage in, 3362
Mary in, 5754, 5755, 7882, 7884
in Maya religion, women in, 3413
mediation in, 7881–7882
medical ethics in, 5810–5814
meditation in, 5818
membership in the church in, 1777
decline in, 7891
mendicancy in, 5856
merit in, 5875, 5877
in Mesoamerican religions, gender and, 3412–3413
ministry of, 6044–6045
laity in, 9533, 9540–9541
miracles in, 6056
missions (*See* Christian missions)
modernism and, 7878–7879
Modernism of, 6102, 6106
modernist controversy in, 5506, 5507
modern movement in
Petre (Maude) in, 7070, 7071
Tyrrell (George) in, 7069, 7070, 9427–9428
monasticism in (*See* Monasticism, Christian; Nuns)
morality in, 7885
in Movement for the Restoration of the Ten Commandments of God, 6215–6216
music in
Enlightenment, 6312
modern, 6312–6313
Renaissance, 6311
in Nahuatl religion, 6402–6403
names in, 6409
Native American perspective on, 3092
nature in, 7883
control over, 2607
objections to term, by Catholics, 7873
opposition to, in Reformation (*See* Reformation)
oral tradition and, 6845
orthodoxy in, 6912
papacy (*See* Papacy; Pope)
parish level, 7887, 7889
Peter in, 7069, 7874–7875
petitions in, vol. 9 color insert
Petrine ministry in, 7874–7875
pilgrimage in (*See* Pilgrimage, Roman Catholic)
pluralism in, 5398, 7889, 7890
political theology of, 7244–7247
polity of, 1763–1765, 7886–7887
popular *vs.* official sanctions, healing and, 3847
postures and gestures in, 7342, 7344
preparation for death in, 2241
priesthood in
mediation and, 7881–7882
ordination into, 4483
Paul VI on, 7012, 7013
Protestantism and, 7873–7894
Inquisition directed against, 4498, 4500, 4501, 4504, 4505, 4506
and theological development, 7458
violence during Reformation, 1807, 1808
purgatory in, 158
in Reformation (*See* Reformation)
reforms in
Council of Trent and, 9340, 9343, 9344
Maximum Illud encyclical (1919), Schmidt (Wilhelm), role of, 8169
in Middle Ages, 1662–1663
in relation to other religions, 9537
relics in, veneration of, vol. 4 color insert
religious broadcasting and, 7712
religious education in, 7734, 7735, 8176
religious experience in, 7737
religious orders in, 7722, 7724
retreats in, for spiritual renewal, 7772
revelation in, 7775, 7882–7883
Romanticism and, 7878
sacraments in (*See* Sacraments, Christian)
salvation in, as process, 3885
schools and, 7734, 7889
sectarian movements within, 6568
seven (number) in, 6748
sexuality in, 8244–8245
sin in, 7883
social action movement, 7879
social doctrine of, 7878
socialism and, 2670
social movements, 1752–1753
social transformation in, 1671
Social Gospel movement and moralism, 1710–1711
social work in, 7487
Sohm (Rudolf) on, 8507
spirituality of, 7887
stem cell research in, 5813
stigmata in, 1004–1005
structure of, 2586
syncretic nature of, 2228–2229
Syriac Orthodox Church, relations with, 8940–8941
taxation of clergy in, 1019
term, origins of, 1774
theater forbidden in, 2437, 2467–2468
theocracy in, 9109, 9110
theology of, 7882–7886
culture and, 7888–7889
as tradition, 7874
traditionalism in, 7696
tradition in, 9268, 9270
Trinity in, 7884
ultramontanism in, 9442
Uniate churches in, 9462–9466
Uniatism (Eastern Rite), 1685
union with Eastern Orthodoxy
Gregory of Cyprus against, 3692
Gregory of Datev against, 3693
Mark of Ephesus against, 5713–5714
unity of, Vatican II and, 4945–4946
unity within diversity, 1691
universal church of, 7874, 7886
values of, 7880–7882
Vatican Councils (*See* Vatican Council)
before Vatican II, 9533–9534
vestments in (*See* Vestments)
violence and, 9598
Virgin of Guadalupe in, 5922
Vodou and, 1433, 1434, 9635–9636
Vulgate Bible as authoritative Bible of, 893
women in
loyalty of, 7891
religious orders of, 7889
world and, relation to, 9536
Romance (term), 3051
Romance languages
in Andalusia, 4593, 4596, 4597
"holy" and "sacred" in, 4099
Romance of the Three Kingdoms (Chinese novel), 3069–3070
Roman College, Bellarmino (Roberto) at, 816
Roman Empire. *See* Roman Republic and Empire
Romanesque church architecture, 793, 794, 9265
Romanesque iconography, 4346
Romania and Romanian religions
Căluş ritual in, 2147
Christianity
history of, 1684
Pentecostalism, 7029
Protestantism, 1685
creation myth in
bees in, 4508
hedgehog in, 3892, 4508
Eliade and, 2753–2754, 2758–2760
Evola (Julius) in, 2905
historiography in, 4046–4047, 4050–4051
icon painting in, 4353
Islam, 4679
magic in, 5580–5582

mortification rites in, 8209
Neolithic religion, 6464
new religious movement originating from, 6568
peasant cultures of, 2753–2754
politics of, Eliade in, 2758–2760
prehistoric culture in, 7379, 7381
study of religion in, 8775
winter solstice songs in, 9741–9746
Romanian Orthodox Church, 9464–9465
autocephalous status of, 2588
communism and, restrictions imposed on, 2588
in Orthodox structure, 2589
property rights of, disputed by Catholics, 2588
Roman Inquisition
Bruno (Giordano) burned by, 1055, 4501
influence of, 4502
origins of, 4501, 6972
procedures of, 4501
public knowledge of, 4501
purpose of, 4501
victims of, 4501
Roman law, 730
oaths in, 9642
revived in Christian Inquisition, 8013, 8014
Roman Mother, The (Dixon), 3381
Romanos the Melodist, 7205
Roman Questions (Plutarch), 7201
Roman religion and mythology, **7892–7925**. *See also* Hellenistic religions; Roman Republic and Empire; Rome
afterlife in, **163–166,** 3725
ages of world in, 176
Aion in, 208
altars in, 275
ancestors in, 326
honoring, 6994–6995
worship of, 321, 2982, vol. 10 color insert
animals in, 358
apologetics against, 427, 10076
apostasy in, 431–432
apotheosis in, 438–440
archaeological records of, 7893
Arval Brothers in, **513–514**
asceticism in, 7722
Asiatic cults in, 2093
astronomy in, 3901
Attis cult in, 2110
Augustus and, 630, 2232, 7279, 7912
auspices in, 7335–7336
birds in, 948, 949
blades in, 967
blood in, 985, 987
body symbolism for society in, 4161
calendar of, 1353, 1354, 7893
holidays in, 7906
moon and, 6170–6171
profane and sacred days in, 7906
ritual, agriculture and, 186
solar calendar, 7894
castitas as chastity, 1558
cats in, 1462, 1463
chance and fate in, 1527
charity in, 1554
Christianity in, polemics with pagans, 4038–4038
Christmas origins in, 7654
Cicero and, **1786–1787**
circle symbolism in, 6885
cocks in, 1841–1842
confession in, 1887
crossroads in, 2071
Cumont (Franz) on, 2093–2094
curses in, 2097–2098
Cybele cult in, 1452, 2110
death in, earth in, 2560
decadence in, ancient historians on, 4027
definition of, 7893
deification in, 2250
deities of (*See also specific deities*)
Celtic parallels, 1481–1486
changes in hierarchy, 7900–7901
Cicero on, 1786–1787
as divinized abstractions, 7899–7900, 7918, 7919
in Etruscan pantheon, 2870–2871
foreign, 7904, 7911
gender of, 7900
goddess worship, 3587
household deities, 4106
iconography of, 4322–4323
lack of personality of, 7899
in middle republic, 7904
minor (specialized) deities, 7899–7900
names applied to other cultures, 1873
names of, 6409
numen/numina as precursors to, 3841
syncretism by comparison and equation of, 3908
weapon bearer of, 2554
demons in, 2277
diamond in, 2345
divination in (*See* Divination, in Roman religion)
divine in, early period, 7899–7900
divine kingship in, 1517, 3902
dogs in, 2393
dragons in, 2432
dreams in, 2378
drums in, 2498
Dumézil (Georges) on, 4462
early period, **7892–7911**
middle republic, 7903–7909
Roman and Italian religion, 7893–7903
emperor worship in, 2776–2777
Etruscan influence on, 7896
family cults in, 7908–7909
fasting in, 2995
fate in, 3004
Feriae Latinae, 1466
festivals in, **6994–6995,** 7897–7898, 7906 (*See also specific festivals*)
fire cults in, 3118–3119
flowers in, 3137
funeral rites in (*See* Funeral rites)
gender in, **3375–3381**
gnosticism in, 7921
goddess worship in, 3587
hares in, 7590
haruspices in, 7336
head symbolism in, 3805
healing in, **3839–3842**
Hellenic impact on, 7893, 7902
in imperial period, 7911
in middle republic, 7904–7905, 7905
historiography, 4026–4027, 4030, 4036–4037
history of, 9767–9768
homosexuality in, 4113
horses in, 4132
iconography of (*See* Iconography, Roman)
imperial cults in, 7915–7916
imperial period, **7911–7925** (*See also* Roman Republic and Empire)
in Iron Age, 7894–7895
Italian religion and, 7893–7903
journals devoted to, 10059
judgment of the dead in, 5026–5027
kings in
divine, 1517, 3902
legendary, 1874
kissing holy objects in, 9258
kneeling in, 5195, 5196
laws of (*See* Law, Roman)
ludi saeculares in, 5525–5526
ludus (play) and time, 1761
magic in, **5572–5577**
in imperial period, 7914
sources on, 5573–5575
Megalesia festival of the Magna Mater in, 2110
meteorites in, 8736
middle republic, 7903–7909
deities of, 7904
divination in, 7903–7904
Hellenic influences on, 7904–7905
priesthood in, 7907–7908
private worship in, 7908–7909
public worship in, 7906–7907
religious associations in, 7909
rituals in, 7905
milk and honey in, 847
Mithraism (*See* Mithraism)
monkeys in, 6151
monotheism and, 7919
moon in, 6170–6171
music in, **6302–6306**
mystery cults (*See* Mystery religions)
mystery societies/communities in, 7719
necromantic practices in, 6452
North Africa influenced by, 4580
omens in, 7335
orgiastic feasts in, 8247
Oriental cults *vs.* Imperial cults in, 7913–7914
Oriental influences on, 7916–7918
paradise in, 6984
phallus in, 7080
piety in, 7278
Plutarch on, 7201
and politics, 7255, 7278–7279
polytheism in, 7317, 7318
polytheism *vs.* monotheism in, 4038, 4066
pompa imaginum in, 7903
postures and gestures in, 7343
priesthood in, 7279, 7897–7898
in middle republic, 7907–7908
private worship in, in middle republic, 7908–7909
procession in, 7417
prodigies in, 7337, 7338
prophecy in, 7424
public worship in, in middle republic, 7906–7907
purification in, lustratio and, 5534
regional context of, 7898–7899
religious pluralism and, 7918–7919
retribution in, 7782
rituals in
laws concerning, 5333
in middle republic, 7905
topography and, 7896
ruler worship in, 2776–2777
sacred and profane in, 7964
sacred space in, sky and, 8428

Roman religion and mythology ***continued***
sacrifice in
bridge and, 1051
for *Feriae Latinae,* 2366, 7898
of horses, 4132, 4133
for *lectisternia* ritual, 7905
of locks of hair, 3740
for lustratio, 5534
overview of, 8006
redemption and, 7641
of sheep, 8310–8311
salt used in, 8059
salvation in, 7697
Saturnalia, 1440
serpents in, 8457
sheep in, 8310–8311
ship symbolism in, 991–992
Sibylline Oracles, **8382–8386**
social structure of, 7895
solar calendar of, 7894
Sol Invictus (sun worship) in, **8510–8511**
soul in
celestial immortality and, 2094
eagle as, 2553
springs in, 3178
state repression and persecution of, in Roman Empire, 7921–7923
statuary in, 7895–7896
study of
history of, 7892–7893
Nilsson (Martin P.) and, 6622
by Otto (Walter F.), 6932–6933
sources for, 7893
suicide, attitudes toward, 8829
sun in, 8840–8841
syncretism in, 7918–7919, 8931
taboos in, 7351
temples in (*See* Temples, Roman)
theologies of poets, philosophers, and statesmen distinguished, 4038
transmigration in, 9330
triads in, 9349
twins in, 9417, 9420
underworld in, 9452–9453
Venus in, 9581–9582
Vestal Virgins, 1475–1476
virginity in, 9606
warfare in, rituals in preparation for, 7896, 7897
women in, **3375–3381**
in Diana cult, 2346
in imperial period, 7919–7920
Roman Republic and Empire. *See also* Roman religion; Rome
African religions studied in, 111
anti-Semitism in, 398–399
apologetics in
Christian, 427–428, 10076
Jewish, 427
apotheosis in, 439–440
Armenians under, 488
army of, 7912
astrology in, 2373, 2378
Augustine on, 1661
authority in, religious *vs.* secular, 696
Bacchanalia repressed by, 6866
barbarian attacks on, 1682
baths in, 801
calendars of *(fasti),* **2993–2995**
Carthage and, 1678–1679
Christianity in
Catholic Church in, 5334, 5335
church organization and, 1763
conversion to, 7922
Council of Chalcedon and, 2584
Donatism, **2416–2418**
early church, relations with, 1660–1661
evidence of, 7920, 7921
gender and, 3359
iconography of, 4344–4345, 4352
legal system and, 5333, 5334
medical philanthropy and, 3844
as official religion, 7060
persecution of, 7058–7060, 7279, 7922
private associations and, 5334
spread of, 2580
as state religion, 792–793
Theodosius and, 9124–9125
theological issues in, 2582
toleration of, 7059, 7060
cities of, cosmology reflected in, 7983
coins of, 7914
coloniae of, 7912
Demeter Eleusinia cults in, 2751
divination in, 7914–7915
emperors in
imperial cults and, 7915–7916
responsibilities of, 7913
encyclopedic works of, 2782
Etruscan religion under, 2874–2875
expulsion of Jews and Isis worshipers from, 4558
fall of, Augustine and, 628
flamines in, **3124–3126**
and Germanic religion, 3450–3451
Gnosticism in, 3524
golden age in, 2964–2965, 3627
Huns in, 4490–4491
imperial cults in, 7915–7916
Israelite religion in, destruction of Second Temple, 923, 933, 4747
Jerusalem under, 4836
Judaism in
evidence of, 7920, 7921
laws concerning, 5334
patriarchiate in, 7006–7007
persecution of, 7055, 7056
Judea under, 4973, 4975–4976
law in (*See* Law, Roman)
literature of, 3051–3052
magic in, 5574–5575
magic in, 7914
Manichaeism in, **5662–5665**
ban on, 5664
opposition to, 5663–5664
persecution of, 5656, 5664, 5667
sources on, 5662–5663
martyrs in, 5739
medals of, 7914
municipia of, 7912
Neoplatonism in, 6474
Oriental influences on, 7916
paganism banned in, 7922
paganism in (*See* Roman religion and mythology)
paternal power in, 2984
Plutarch criticizing, 7200
political reform in, under Augustus, 630
politics and religion in, 7278–7279
private associations in, 5333–5334
religion in, 9583
attitudes towards, 7912–7914
evidence of, 7920–7921
state repression and persecution of, 7921–7923
religious pluralism in, 7918–7919
revolt against, Essenes in, 2846
rulership of, changes in, 5167
sacrilege in, 8013
Shim'on ben Laqish on, 8348
suicide in, 8829
winter solstice in, 9740, 9741, 9743
women in, 7919–7920
lives of, 3382
Romans, 911–912, 920
Abraham in, 16
Barth's study of, 789, 790, 6467
content of, 912, 7019
criticism of, 7013
on divine righteousness, 7019
on ethics, 7019
Galatians compared to, 912
God in, 3545
"gospel" in, 3641
grace in, 3645
and history, Christian views of, 4052
Isaac in, 4544
justification in, 5039
original form of, 911–912
purpose of, 911, 7019
revelation in, 7774, 7775
suffering in, 8808
Taubes (Jakob) on, 9021
theodicy in, 9117
Romanticism
art in, studies of, 499
Carnival, effect on, 1442
Catholicism and, 7878
Coleridge, role of, **1853**
comparative theology in, 9128, 9129
conscience in, 1943
dance in, 2155–2156
drama in, 2474
Enlightenment, interaction with, 4040–4041
Enlightenment viewed by, 2798
German
Creuzer (G. F.), role of, **2070**
philosophy of nature in, 6434–6437
Schlegel (Friedrich), role of, **8159**
Schleiermacher (Friedrich) and, 8160
Scholem (Gershom), influence on, 8178
study of myth in, 6366–6367
Gnosticism and, 3525–3526
Hermetism and, 3950–3951
historiography and, 4040
Indo-European religion in, study of, 4458
Indological studies in, 4446
of Jung, 5032–5033, 5035–5036
literature of, 5477
Campbell on, 1379
Japanese, 3072
poetry, 7206
nature in
philosophy of, 6434–6437
as sacred, 2607
neopaganism and, 9774
racism and, 3526
Rationalism *vs.,* Creuzer (G. F.) and, 2070
religion and modernity and, 5032
Rousseau in, 2664
self, surrender of, 8715
sociology and, 8492
symbolic theory and, 8908–8909
Romantic movement, study of Indo-European religion in, 10076
Romanus
Kontakion and, 1534
on pain, 6946
Roman vault, 793–794
Rome (city)
ancient (*See* Roman religion; Roman Republic and Empire)

archaeology of, 7893, 7895
bishop of (*See* Pope)
Carnival at, 1442
catacombs in, 1472, 3637, vol. 4 color insert
Christianity in
apostolic See, Rome as, 1661
Christmas masses in, 1756–1757
exorcism by, 2929
founding of Christian church at, 1688
Paul's missionary journey to, 7019
persecution in, 1688
Peter and, 7068
in Christian structure, early, 2581
circle symbolism in, 1791
as cosmic city, 1503
under Etruscans, 2870
founding of, 1791, 1814–1815, 2873–2874
Cicero on, 7895
mythology of, 5167
wolf in, 9785
as goddess, 7913
hermits of, 2826, 2828
historiography of, 4027
imperial period (*See* Roman Republic and Empire)
kingship in, 5167–5168, 7901
mountains of, 7896
patricians and plebeians in, 7902–7903
pomerium (demarcation line) in, 7897
sacked by Celts, 1478
sacked by Gauls, 7894
senators of, 5167
state cult of, 2777
topography of, rituals and, 7896
urbanization of, 7895
Rome, Council of (382), 6966
Romera, Ricardo Olmos, 4252
Romero, Gabina, 6577
Romero, Joan A., 3313
Rome University, Bianchi (Ugo) at, 862
Römische Grablampen (Bachofen), 731
Romow (sanctuary), 767, 774
Romuald (ascetic), Damian (Peter) and, 2133
Romuald of Ravenna (hermit), 6133
Romulus
Acca Larentia and, 5321
apotheosis of, 438, 439, 7915
Arval Brothers and, 514
as child, 1568
Cicero on, 7895
as founder of Rome, 5167
lituus of, 7336
murder of, 5167
Puhvel (Jaan) on, 4464
as Quirinus, 5167, 7560
Remus killed by, 2393
ritual of, 2873–2874
Rome as cosmic city and, 1503
as twin, 9417
wolf and, 9785
woodpecker and, 5996
Romuva, 774
cult of ancestors in, 328–329
revival of, 764–765
writings on, 763
Ronan, Colin A., 7022
Roncalli, Angelo Giuseppe. *See* John XXIII
Rongerik (mythic figure), 6012
Rongo (deity), 7313, 7314, 8980
Rongorongo (oralists), 5850
Roosevelt, Franklin D., Native American policy of, 7302
Roosters, in Garifuna religion, 3285, 3286
Rooth, Anna Burgitta, 6671
Rooy, Felix de, 3098
Ropes
in African myths, 92, 140
knotted, 5197
Rorty, Richard, 2951
metaphysics of, 5991
Rosaldo, Renato, on sacrifice, 8009
Rosarium philosophorum, 235
Rosary
in art, vol. 3 color insert
in Pure Land Buddhism, 4922
Rosary of Philosophers, 252
Roscelin, on problem of universals, 6644
Roscoe, John, 115
Roscoe, Will, 3422
on lesbianism, 5414
Rose
in Christianity, 3136
in Islam, 3135
Rose, Deborah Bird, 638
on Australian Indigenous religions
land in, 689
myths of, 668
Rose, H. J.
critics of, 2543
on divination, 2369
dynamism of, 2542
Rose, Helvy Tiana, 3078
Rose, Herbert Jenkins, on Mars, 5728
Rose, Leo, 7262
Rose, Wendy, 7226
Rosen, Norma, 6021
Rosenberg, Bernard, 7321
Rosenberg, Bruce, 3145
Rosencreutz, Christian, 7929, 7930
Rosenstock-Huessy, Eugen, 7925–7926
Rosenthal, Franz, on humor in Islam, 4197, 4214–4215
Rosenthal, Judy, 386
Rosenzweig, Franz, **7925–7927**
Agnon (Shemu'el Yosef) and, 179
biblical exegesis of, 869
Buber (Martin) and, 1056, 7926
on Christianity, 7236
Cohen (Hermann) and, 1851, 1852, 7926
comparative theology of, 9130
Fackenheim (Emil) study of, 2949
on God, 3551
existence of, 7422
on *halakhah,* 7927
Hebrew Bible translated into German by, 7926
Heidegger (Martin) and, 7927
in modern Jewish thought, 4904–4905
Reform Judaism and, 7671–7672
on Torah, 9238
R'oSH. *See* Asher ben Yeḥi'el
Ro'sh amanah (Abravanel), 17
Ro'sh ha-Shanah, 4866, 6593, **7927–7928**
dating of, 4865, 4866
domestic observances of, 2397
food in, 7928
in Jewish calendar, 4866, 4867
maḥzor liturgy for, 8390
prayers in, 7928
ram's horn sounding on
Abbahu and, 2
symbolism of, 7757, 7928
Tashlikh rite on, 3159, vol. 1 color insert
Ro'sh ha-Shanah le-Ilanot (New Year for Trees), in Jewish calendar, 4867
Ro'sh Ḥodesh, 4865, 4867
Rosicrucians, **7929–7931**. *See also* Lectorium Rosicrucianum
alchemy and, 7930
ancient origins, claims of, 8213
Bacon (Francis) and, 253, 734
doctrines of, 7930
Fludd (Robert) and, 3950
and Freemasons, 3196
Hermetism and, 3949, 3951, 3952
history of, 7929–7930
manifestos on alchemy, 253
on nature, 6434
religious broadcasting by, 7710
and Solar Temple, 6554
Steiner (Rudolf) and, 8738
symbols used by, 7930
in Western esotericism, 2843
Roskoff, Gustave, 114
Rosmerta (deity), 1483
Ross, Anne, 1483, 1498
Ross, Clunies
on marriage among deities, 3460
on Týr, 9427
Ross, John, in Korea, 5234
Ross, Margaret Clunies, on Baldr, 744
Ross, Rick, 2292, 6541
Ross, Rosetta, 79
Ross, Scott v., 2292
Rossel, Hannibal, Hermetism and, 3948
Rossi, Andrew, Holy Order of MANS and, 4102–4103
Rossi, 'Azaryah dei, 7107
historiography, role in, 4059
science of Judaism and, 4041
Rossi, Giovanni, 9084
Rossi, Pellegrino, 730
Rossi, Salomone, 6310
Rossignol, Le (Magritte), vol. 11 color insert
Roşu, Arion, on *trivarga* and medical theory, 3854
Roth, Cecil, 4342
Roth, Rudolf, 4446
Roth, Walter, 671
Rothenberg, Jerome, 7224
Rothenbuhler, Eric, 3101
Rothko, Mark, 500, 6244
Rothko Chapel (Houston), 6244
Rothmann, Bernd, 7660
Rothschild, Edmond de, Mohilever's (Shemu'el) influence on, 6113
Rothschild family, 9979
Rothwell, Nicolas, on *Maparnjarra* healer, encounter with, 3873
Rotorua Museum (New Zealand), 6244
Rotse. *See* Lozi
Rotundas, circle symbolism and, 1792
Rouault, George, 4348
Rouch, Jean, 2350
Rouget, Gilbert, 2500
Rougier, L., on astral theology, 8425
Roumeguère-Eberhardt, Jacqueline, 97
Round dance. *See also* Ghost Dance
in Melanesia, 6265
religious meaning of, 3474
Round Dance of the Cross, 2153
Round Table conferences (1930, 1931), Ambedkar (B. R.) at, 286
Rouse, Carolyn, 10039
Rouse, Irving, on Arawak Indians, 1426
Rousseau, Jean-Jacques, **7931–7932**
autobiography of, 699, 7931
on civil religion, 1812–1813, 3230, 7256, 7931
on consciousness, 1943
criticisms of, 7931–7932

Rousseau, Jean-Jacques
continued
Émile, 811
religious thought in, 7931
work foreshadowing, 3039
"illumination of Vincennes" and, 7931
on knowledge, 5206
on moral education of men and women, 811
natural religion of, 7931
"noble savage" concept of, 363, 8594
on origins of religion, 2236
Romantics influenced by, 2607, 2664
symbol theory and, 8908
Routinization, 1544
Roux's L'Église Chrétienne Universelle, 6568
Ro Vilgale (archetypal woman), creation of, 5198
Rowcraft, Charles, 3083
Rowe, John Howland, on Inca calendar, 1362
Rowlands, Henry, 2493
Rowley, H. H., on Myth and Ritual school, 6380–6381
Rowling, J. K., 3062
Roy, M. N., 827
Roy, Manisha, on Hindu women, 3321
Roy, Ram Mohan, **7932–7933**
as founder of Brāhmo Samāj, 828, 1028, 1029, 4430, 7932, 9317
Bengali and English translation of Upaniṣads by, 4446
as father of modern India, 828, 9316–9317
monotheism of, 7932, 7933
Muslim and Christian influences on, 4007
opponents of, 2331
Orientalist studies used by, 9317
reforms initiated by, 4450, 9317
on religious experience, 7740
against sati, 3320, 7933
Royal Asiatic Society of Bengal, 4446, 4452, 4458
Royal Commentaries of the Inca (Garcilaso), 567
Royal Crown, The (Ibn Gabirol). *See Keter malkhut* (Ibn Gabirol)
Royal drums, 2494, 2496, 2499, 2500
Royal Institute for Interfaith Studies (RIIFS), comparative study at, 8783
Royal Music Academy of Paris, Carnival balls, 1443
Royalty. *See also* Kings and kingship
apotheosis of, 437–438
Buddhist monasticism supported by, 6128–6129
crown as symbol of, 5155
in Eblaite religion, 2598
in England, genealogy of, 3426
lineage and, 3424
lions associated with, 5464
in Minoan religion, 39
in Mycenaean religion, 41
ordeal and, 6848
in Vietnamese religion, 9592–9593
Royce, Josiah
on Bunyan (John), 1323
on Hegel, 4356
monistic philosophy of, 6146
pantheism of, 6962–6963
Rozanov, Vasilii, 3134
Rozīte, Rasma, 766
Rozvi dynasty (Zimbabwe), 2313
RRA. *See* Reconstructionist Rabbinical Association
RRC. *See* Reconstructionist Rabbinical College
Ṛṣabha *(tīrthaṃkara),* 9207, 9208
Ṛṣhis (poets), 7205
Ṛṣi yajña (ceremonies), 748
RSS. *See* Rāṣṭrīya Svayaṃsevak Saṅgh
Ṛṣyśṛṅga (mythic figure), courtesans and, 3967–3968, 3969
Ṛta (cosmic order), 2620, 3001, **7933–7934**
as antecedent of *dharma,* 2327, 7933
etymology of word, 7933
possessing, 4537
Ṛta chants, 1535–1536
Ṛtvij (priest), 7405
Ru (deity), 7313
Ru (scholarship), study of, 1916–1918. *See also* Confucianism
Confucius on, 1936
radical repudiation of, 1922
Third Wave of, 1923
Rua (deity), 7313
Rua (Hun leader), 4490
Ruaḥ (spirit or breath), 1042, 9378, 9379
meaning of, 8556–8557
as *pneuma,* 8562
psuchē and, 8561
in Qabbalah, 8560
Ruaḥ ha-qodesh (holy spirit), 4510
Ruan Ji (poet), 7213
Ruanruan people (Inner Asia), 4491
Rubens, Peter Paul, 4347, 4844
Rubenstein, Jeffrey, 6021
Rubenstein, Richard, on death of God, 3552
in response to Holocaust, 4094
Rubin, Gayle, 3420, 3422
Rubin, Jeffrey, 7479
Rubin, William S., 54–55
Rublev, Andrei, 7942
Ruch, Barbara, 3346
Rudolph, Kurt
Ginza translated by, 3495
on Gnosticism, 3514, 3535
historiography of, 4048
on Mandaean religion, 5635
Rudolph I, Jewish persecution under, 5830
Rudra (deity), **7934–7935**. *See also* Śiva
animals associated with, 7934
as precursor to Śiva, 3990–3991, 3992, 7934, 7935, 8038–8040
birth of, 8415
crossroads and, 2071
deities associated with, 7934–7935
in *Śatarudriya* hymn, 8415
lightning bolt of, 7603
portrayal of, 8039
Śiva as, 4428
in Vedas, 8039–8040, 8414–8415
in Vedism, 9557
Rudrāṇī (deity), 7934
Rudrasampradāya, 9505
Rudravarman (son of Jayavarman), 1133
Rue, Loyal, 2666
Ruegg, David Seyfort, 1315
Ruether, Rosemary Radford, 3035, 3037
on androcentrism, 3313
on female body, 4164
feminist ecotheology of, 2610
feminist theology of, 3356
on Gentile election, 2747
on God, 3559
on methodology in religious studies, 3313
and reform of Christianity, 3312
Rufeisen, Oswald, 4864
Ruffin, C. Bernard, 1005
Rufiji River, shrine to Bokero on, 5181
Rufinus
on bishop of Ethiopia, 2859
Jerome and, 4834
Rufus, Mutianus, German humanism and, 4176
Ruggerius, Michael, 1608
Rugs, in mosques, 6208
Rūh (breath), 1042
Rūḥ (spirit or soul)
in Qur'ān, 8566–8567
medical practice and, 3832
Ruha (spirit), 5636, 5638
Rūḥ al-quds fī munāsahāt al-nafs (Ibn al-ʿArabi), 4256
Ruhanga (deity), 4519
in northeast Bantu religions, 2574–2575
Ruhani Satsang, 2602
Rūhīyah Khānum, 738
Ruiz, Samuel, 5930, 5931, 5932, 6580
Ruiz de Alarcón, Hernando, on tobacco, 8455
Ruizong (emperor), Sima Chengzhen and, 8399
Rujing (Buddhist monk), 2385
Rukhmabai (Indian women), feminism of, 3320
Rukmiṇī (wife of Kṛṣṇa)
in Kṛṣṇa Bhagavatism, 9504
Vaiṣṇava *bhakti* cult and, 9500
Rukn al-Dawlah, 4262
Rukuba people (Nigeria), kingship of, 5170
Rule of Benedictions (Dead Sea Scroll), 2234
Rule of Life (Abelard), 7
Rule of Pachomius, in Ethiopia, 2859–2860
Rule of Saint Benedict, 7720, 7724. *See also* Benedict of Nursia
body discipline in, 8704
celibacy and, 1477
eremitism and, 2827
Francis of Assisi, modifications by, 8704
Rule of the Community (Dead Sea Scroll), 2234, 7063, 7065
Rule of the Master, Lent in, 7771
Rulership. *See* Kingship
Rules of Sociological Method, The (Durkheim), 2527
Rum, in Garifuna religion, 3285, 3286
Rumfa (king of Kano), 4605
Rūmī, Jalāl al-Dīn, **7935–7938**. *See also* Mevlevi order of Sufism
awareness of world, 7937–7938
on creation, 2653
dances of followers of, 2140, 5819
disciples of, 7936
friends of, 7936
Ḥusām al-Dīn and, 7936
Ibn al-ʿArabī's influence on, 4259, 7937
on laughter, 4202
legacy of, 7938
life of, 8818
on love, 7937, 8705
love mysticism of, 6352
Mathnavī, 6750
Mawlawi Sufism and, 8822–8823
on music, 6277
on mystical union, 6339
on al-Bisṭāmī, 956
al-Ḥallāj, 3757
on *miʿrāj,* 6061
on *ṭarīqah,* 9004, 9008
on pain, 6946
poetry of, 313, 4570, 7207, 7222, 7935–7938, 8818
on prayer, 7937
Ṣalāḥ al-Dīn and, 7936
Shams al-Dīn and, 7935–7936, 8818
on spiritual guides, 8699
successors of, 7936
on unity, 7937
Rummānī, al-, 4371
Rumtek Monastery, 5103
Rumūz-i bīkhudī (Iqbāl), 4534
Runcie, Robert Alexander Kennedy, 353
Runes, 7938–7941
origins of, 7939
uses of, 7939
Runge, Philipp Otto, 6435

Running script, calligraphy and, 1370
Runt (deity), Reshef and, 7761
Ruoff, LaVonne, 3090
Rūpa Gosvāmin, 826
works of, 1346
Rūpakāya (physical body), 1064, 1217, 1293, 9015
Rūpaloka (world of form), heavens in, 3887
Rūpārūpavibhāga (Buddhadatta), 10022
Rupertsberg (Germany), monastery at, Hildegard of Bingen and, 3979
Ruppert, James, 1515–1516
Ruppin, Arthur, 4881
Ruptures, as cosmogonic theme, 1989
Rural folk art, 9626
Rural Negro, The (Woodson), 74
Rusalii period, 2147
Rusalkas (nymphs), in Slavic religion, 8438
Rusalki, 2951
Ruse, Michael, on biology and culture, 8474–8475
Rush, Christopher, 68
Rushdie, Salman, 10036
as apostate, 433–434
condemnation of, 8014
Gnosticism and, 3528
Rushpan. *See* Reshef
Ruskin, John
on gold, 3625
and spiritualizing of art, 499
Russell, Bertrand
analytic philosophy of, 306
on knowledge, 2427, 5210
on mathematics, 49
metaphysics of, 5991
Smith (Hannah Whitall) and, 8446
Russell, Charles Taze, 4820–4821, 6559
Russell, Jeffrey, on Satan, 8124
Russell, Letty, on God, 3559
Russell, Maria Russell, 4820
Russell, Robert John, on quantum theory, 8188
Russia and Russian religions. *See also* Mari and Mordvin religion; Samoyed religion; Slavic religion; Soviet Union
academic study of religion in, **8771–8775**
Aum Shinrikyō in, 631
ballet in, 2156, 2161–2162
Buddhism, 1189
Tibetan Buddhism, 9182
calendar, 1355
Christianity (*See also* Russian Orthodox Church)
Baptist churches in, 785
history of, 1683, 1684, 1685
mass suicide at Paleostrovskii monastery, 8830
Merezhkovskii (Dmitrii) on, 5869
Pentecostalism, 7029
Roman Catholicism, 2588–2589
Skobtsova (Mother Maria) on, 8422
Chuvash religion, **1784–1786**
Dazhbog in, 2231
domestic spirits in, 4106
education in, Pobedonostsev (Konstantin) and, 7203
Filippov (Daniil), followers of, 8249
folklore of
Baba Yaga, **727**
domovois, 2951
goats in, 8312
rusalki, 2951
goddess worship in, 3587
icon painting in, 4354, 4392
International Society for Krishna Consciousness in, 4522
Inuit religious traditions in, 4526
Islam
in Caucasus, 4614–4615
in Central Asia, 4622–4630
in Middle Volga, 4616–4618
and persecution, 4617, 4619, 4624, 4625, 4677
Jewish studies in, 4879
Judaism, 5018–5019
communal authority, 5018
Karaite sect, 5084
pogroms against, 9979
Reform Judaism, 7669
response to anti-Semitism in, 5020–5021
Karelian religion in, 5091–5093
migration in, 6023
Mokosh in, 6115
museums in, 6246
new religious movements in, 5377, 5378
government policies on, 6518, 6571
native, 6568
Polish control of, 1685
religious renaissance in, early 20th-century, 5869
Revolution in (1905) (*See* Russian Revolution)
study of religion in, 8773
Uniate church in, 9463–9464
Russian Academy of Sciences, Stcherbatsky (Theodore) and, 8737
Russian Haskalah, 5019
Russian Jewish Historical Ethnographic Society, 4880
Russian language
sviaty as "holy" or "sacred" in, 4099
Talmud, translation into, Spektor (Yitshaq Elhanan) on, 8674
Russian Orthodox Archdiocese (United States), 2589
Russian Orthodox Church, **7941–7947**
Avvakum in, 712
biblical canonicity in, 881
Bishops' Council of, 7945
under Brezhnev (Leonid), 7944
Bulgakov (Sergei) in, 1320, 7943
in Canada, 1713
Catholics under, 9464
church and state relations, 7945
Chuvash religion and, 1784
in diaspora, 1652
dioceses of, 7946
Dolgans in, 2394–2395
Dostoevsky (Fyodor) in, 2422, 7943
eremitism of, 2826–2827
ethics, 1652–1653
after fall of Constantinople, 1664, 7942
fall of Soviet Union and, 1686, 7944–7945
governance of, 7945–7946
Holy Synod of, 7945–7946
Pobedonostsev (Konstantin) in, 7202–7203
in Imperial Period, 7942
Innokentii Veniaminov in, 4497
internal organization of, 7946
Ioann of Kronstadt in, 4532
Kiev school, 1652–1653, 7941, 7942
Kireevskii (Ivan) in, 5187
under Kruschev (Nikita), 7944
in Latin America, 1703
leaders of
Filaret of Moscow, **3094–3095**
Nikon, **6621–6622**
Local Councils of, 7945
missions of, 7942–7943
to Alaska, 4497, 9193
to North American Indians, 6422, 6423
Mokosh in, 6115
monasticism in, 4957
Sergii of Radonezh and, 8230–8231
Moscow as seat of, 7941–7942
music in, 6310, 6312
Nikonian reforms in, 6621
Old Believers in, 6621
Optina hermitage in, 7943
in Orthodox Christian development, 2588
in Orthodox structure, 2589
patriarchate created for, 4832
patriarch of Moscow and All Russia in, 7946
persecution of, 7943–7944
Peter the Great and, 7942
pilgrimage in, 7154
Prokopovich (Feofan) and reforms in, 7418–7419
Protestant missions challenged by, 2588–2589
reform of
Nikon and, 7942
Trubetskoi (Evgenii) and, 9367
revival of
in 18th and 19th centuries, 7943
Petr Moghila and, 7071–7072
Roman Catholic Church and, attempts to reunite, 8520
Roman Catholic dioceses disputed by, 2588–2589
Skobtsova (Mother Maria) and, 8422
Southern Siberian religions and, 8672
in Soviet era, 9193–9194
Soviet Union and
persecution under, 8229–8230
Sergii and, 8229–83200
spirituality in, Serafim of Sarov, role of, **8229**
under Stalin (Joseph), 7943–7944
Tatars in, 4616–4617
theocracy in, 9110
theology in
Khomiakov (Aleksei) on, 5137–5138
Roman Catholic perspectives in, 2588
Tolstoy's (Leo) attack on, 9220, 9221
in United States, 1713
Vladimir I in, 9631–9632
women in, restrictions on, 6115
in World Council of Churches, 2688
in World War II, 7944
Russian Orthodox Church in America. *See* Orthodox Church in America
Russian Orthodox Church Outside of Russia, 7946
Russian Orthodox Confession (1643), on free will and predestination, 3208
Russian Orthodox Theological Institute of Saint Serge (Paris), 7943
Russian Revolution (1905)
and Islam in Caucasus, 4615
Merezhkovskii (Dmitrii) after, 5869
Russian Orthodox Church in, 2588

Russian Revolution (1905)
continued
Samoyed religion, impact on, 8097
Skobtsova (Mother Maria) and, 8422–8423
Sorokin (Pitirim Aleksandrovich) on, 8524
Russo, Barukhya, 3186
Ruth, **7947–7948**
feminist interpretations of, 7948
genealogy in, 7947
laws in, 4739
in Shavu'ot liturgy, 8306
Ruth, Babe, 8725–8726
Ruthenians, 9463–9464
Rutherford, Joseph Franklin, 4821
Ruthwell Cross, runic inscriptions of, 7940
Rutibel, possession by, in Revival Zion (Jamaica), 1437
Rutilius Namatianus, on *Sibylline Oracles,* 8384
Rutter, John, 6313
Ruusbroec, Jan van, **7948–7949**
on mystical union, 6337
mysticism of, 6348, 6349
Ruwẓat al-shuhadā (Kāshifī), 2446
Ruysbroek, Willem von, 1311
Rva sgreng rin po che (Reting Rinpoche), Ani Lochen and, 354
Rwanda
Movement for the Restoration of the Ten Commandments of God in, 105, 6215
Tutsi people of, paradise lost in myths of, 139–140
Ubwiiru people of, memorization by, 5850
writers' project, 3088
Ryan, Leo, 7255
Ryan, Leo A., 4952, 4954
Ryangombe (mythic figure), 4519
Ryckmans, Gonzague, 443
Rydberg, A. V., 2964
Ryerson, Kevin, 560
Ryle, Gilbert
on mind-body dualism, 4163
on winks *vs.* twitches, 8499
Ryobu (two aspects) Shintō, 4783–4784
development of, 8361
Ryōchū (Buddhist monk), 818
Ryōge matsudai nembutsu jushuin shō (Ryōchū), 818
Ryōgen (Buddhist monk)
Genshin as disciple of, 3432, 9077
in Tendai school, 1178, 9075, 9077
Ryōnin (Buddhist monk), 9080
music of, 6301
Ryōun (Buddhist monk), 4551
Rytshkov, N., 5709
Ryūkan (Buddhist monk), 4938
Ryuku kingdom. *See* Okinawan religion

S

Sa'adia ben Joseph (rabbi), 9236
Sa'adyah Gaon, **7951–7953,** 8234
on afterlife, 154
biblical exegesis of, 865, 866, 867, 7438, 8950
biblical translation into Arabic by, 894, 895
condemnation of Karaites by, 5083
ethics of, 4911
on exile, 2922
on free will and predestination, 3203
on God
anthropomorphism of, 544
on nature and attributes of, 7952
omnipotence of, 3549–3550
proof of existence of, 4888, 7952
H'ai Gaon and, 3738
in Jewish thought and philosophy, 4886–4889
Karaism and, 4992
on prophecy, 7438–7439
religious philosophy of, 4992–4993
Sefer yetsirah and, 8221
on souls and judgment, 7953, 8559
writings of, 740
Yehudah ben Shemu'el influenced by, 544
Saami. *See* Sami
Sabaeans, in Arabia, 443
Sabaoth (demiurge), 2274
Sabazios identified with, 7954
Sabatier, Auguste, liberal theology of, 6103
Sabazios (deity), 6866, **7953–7954,** 9169
cult of, in Rome, 7917
Sabb (insult), 974
Sabbaba (deity), 5950
Sabbat (witch gatherings), 6871, 9730–9731
in African witchcraft, 9776–9777
in diabolical witchcraft, 9771
sexual rites alleged in, 8249–8250
wild hunt and, 9771
Sabbatai Sevi, 6872–6873
Sabbatarianism. *See also* Seventh-day Adventism
in Adventist theology, 8235, 8236
Sabbateanism. *See* Shabbetai Tsevi
Sabbath. *See* Shabbat
Sabbath and Festival Prayer Book, The, Conservative Judaism and, 1961
Sabbath Prayer Book (Kaplan), 5082, 7636
Sabbath-week system, in periodization systems, 174, 175
Sabbatical year (Jubilee)
debt practices in, Hillel's *prozbul* enactment on, 3981
male slaves freed in, 4731
redistribution of wealth in, 4731
Sabbatucci, Dario
historiography of, 4050
on Jensen (Adolf E.), 4826
Sabbioneta text (1557), 888
Śabda (correct speech), 7005, 9371
Rāmānuja on, 7615
Śabdādvaita, 9547
Sabellianism
Cyril of Jerusalem's fear of, 2118
origins of, 1678
Sabi, 51
Sabian sect, 2971
al-Shahrastānī and, 8267
Sabina, Flavia Vibia, 7920
Sabines
deities of, Quirinus, 7559–7560
incorporated into Rome, 9686
Sabotage tactics, of Earth First!, 2562, 2563–2564
Šābuhr (king), Mani and, 5649
Sabzawārī, doctrine of *al-ishrāq* and, 2977
Sacca (truth), 3179
Sacerdos (priest), 4559
Sacerdotalis caelibatus (Paul VI), 7013
Sachchidānanda, 634
Sachedina, Abdul Aziz, 3428
Sa chen Kun dga' snying po (Sachen Kunga Nyingpo), 1225
Sachkritik (interpretation), 875
Sachs, Michael, 4875, 4877–4878
Sachs, Nelly, Nobel prize for literature for, 179
Śacī (Indra's wife), 4467
Sack, Daniel, 3173
Sacrality. *See* Feminine sacrality; Masculine sacrality
Sacramentality, Newman (John Henry) on, 6510
Sacramentarian Controversy, 1059
Sacrament of the Last Supper (Dali), 4348
Sacraments, **7954–7964**
Buddhist
consecration and authority, 1956
zazen as, 7957
Christian (*See* Sacraments, Christian)
comparative religion perspective on
repeatable sacraments, 7956–7957
transition, sacraments of, 7955–7956
definitions of, 7955, 7957–7958
Hellenistic *mustērion* as, 7954–7955
Hindu
bodily action and, 7955
transition and, 7956
meal, sacrificial, as, 8000
meaning of term, 7954
overview of, **7954–7958**
prayer as, 7957
semantics and, 8227
in Sikhism, *karahprashad* in, 8396
as sources of purification, 7509
Sacraments, Christian, **7958–7964**
in Armenian church, 489
Augustine on, 626, 627
Cabilas on, 1343
classical perspective, emergence of, 7955
clothing for, 1832
consecration and authority, 1956
early history of, 7959–7960
ecumenical issues and, 7963
eremtism and, 2825, 2828–2829
excommunication and, 2921
as forms of gospel proclamation, in Augsburg Confession, 2058
and history, view of, 4053
Jewish roots of, 7958–7959
Lutheran, 5538
membership in the church and, 1778
in Middle Ages, 7960–7961
number of, 7958
Orthodox, 2592, 7960
overview, 1669–1670
penance, 1652
Protestant, 7455–7456, 7962–7963
Roman Catholic, 7881
controversy over, 7881, 7885
Mary in, 7884
post-Vatican II, 7961–7962
Salvation Army, abandonment by, 8063–8064
soteriology and, 8527
theology of
early history of, 7959–7960
Eastern Orthodox, 7960
medieval, 7961
Protestant, 7963
Roman Catholic, post-Vatican II, 7962
Sacred, the, 2261
in definition of religion, 7694
definitions of, 7692, 7964–7965
destruction of, *vs.* destruction of religion, 7975
Durkheim (Émile) on, 7971
Eliade (Mircea) on, 1624, 2761, 5436, 7743, 7975
Freud (Sigmund) on, 7974
Girard (René) on, 7974
Heidegger (Martin) on, 3896, 3897
hierophany (manifestation of the sacred), **3970–3974**

"holy" *vs.*, in semantics and translations, 4097–4100
human interaction with, through nature, 2604, 6438
in Judaism, maintenance of, 8012
language as manifestation of, 5302–5304
Latin roots of concept, 7964, 7965–7966
Marx on, 7974
in Maya religion, 5797–5799
in myth, 2898
in neoshamanism, 8296
in orgy, 6877–6878
origins of, 7973–7975
power of, 7350
in religious experience, 7694
in religious life, 7698
restoration of, 7975
sacrilege and, 8010–8011
scripture and, 8195, 8196, 8201
Smart (Ninian) on dimensions of, 8444, 8466
Smith (Jonathan Z.) on, 5436
symbol theory and, 8913
Weber (Max) on, 7975
Sacred actions. *See* Ritual(s)
Sacred and its Scholars, The (Idinopulos and Yonan), 7745
Sacred and Profane Beauty (van der Leeuw), 496, 500
Sacred and the profane, the, **7964–7978**
African scholars on, 8794
archetypes of, Eliade (Mircea) on, 458–459
art and, 4168
blood, 9705–9706
in body and soul/mind dualism, 4158, 4163
ceremonial *vs.* religious rituals and, 1516, 1517
curses and, in Islam, 4213
definition and means of identification, 7964–7973
anthropological methods, 7972–7973
philological methods, 7965–7970
sociological methods, 7970–7972
definition of, 7692
distinction between
taboos and, 7842–7843
as types of existence, 5444
of divine dwelling, in architectural classification, 462–463
Durkheim (Émile) on, 3231, 6359, 7970–7971, 8010
Stanner (W. E. H.), criticism by, 8729
Eliade (Mircea) on, 458–459, 7976, 8010
Gennep (Arnold van) on, 3432
in Greek religion, 3668, 3677
hierophany (manifestation of the sacred) and, 3971
historical approach to, 7973–7975
in history, Christian view of, 4056
ideogrammatics and hermeneutics, 7976–7977
in Judaism
in Sabbath service, 8257
sacrilege and, 8012
sin and, 8403
Latin terminology of, 7964
media and, 5805
in Melanesian religions, 5839–5840
homosexuality and, 4115
in Micronesian religions, 6008
in museums, 6243–6244
in mythic studies, 6368
in myth's definition, 6359–6360
in North American Indian religions, 6681, 6702–6703
gender in concepts of, 3406–3407
Otto (Rudolf) on, 7975–7976
relationships between, 7975–7976
sacrilege and, 8010, 8011
in Judaism, 8012
sanctuaries and, 8100
society and, 8462
sociology and, 8482
time and, 1758, 5197
Sacred and the Profane, The (Eliade), 7349, 7694
in Neopaganism, 2664
sacred time and space in, 5898
Sacred and the secular, the, in Australian Indigenous religions, boundaries between, 6260–6261
Sacred biography. *See* Biography, sacred
Sacred bonds, 938
Sacred Books of the East (Müller), 1633, 1832, 6236
Sacred Buffalo Calf Pipe, 5296
Sacred Congregation for Doctrine and Faith, 5439, 9537
Sacred cow. *See* Cattle and cows
Sacred dance, in Western religions, 2136, 2164–2165. *See also* Liturgical dance
Sacred Dance Guild, 2165
Sacred Dances (Gurdjieff), 3711
Sacred Depths of Nature, The (Goodenough, U.), 2666
Sacred experience. *See* Religious experience
Sacred gaze, vol. 11 color insert
Sacred Grove on Mount Tamalpais (Arpin), 2162
Sacred groves, in Ethiopian religion, 2573
Sacred Heart of Jesus, Pascal on, 3883
Sacred Heart orders, in Mesoamerica, 5930, 5931
Sacred History (Euhemeris), atheism in, 3910
Sacred Hoop, Plains Indians encampments as, 1794
Sacred Hoop, The (Allen), 3406–3407
Sacred languages, 5303. *See also* Language, sacred
Sacred lineage, in Confucianism. *See Zong*
Sacred matter, vol. 4 color insert
Sacred Mosque (Mecca), 7158, 7159, 7160
Sacred national community, 7717
Egypt as, 7717
Judaism as, 7717
Mesopotamia as, 7717
Sacred Pain: Hurting the Body for the Sake of the Soul (Glucklich), 6947
Sacred Pipe, The (Brown), 957
Sacred Serpent (magazine), 765
Sacred space, **7978–7986,** 9260, vol. 5 color insert. *See also* Land; Space; *specific spaces and kinds of places*
in Australian Indigenous religions, dreamtime and, 2002–2004
caves, **1468–1473**
prehistoric, 7974
in Celtic religion, 1480, 1486, 1491
cemeteries as, 2082
center of the world, **1501–1505**
in Christianity, architectural symbolism, 7980
circumambulation of, 1792
cities as, 1502–1503, 1803–1807
conflict over, desecration and, 8011
consecration of, 1954–1955
cosmogony and, 7983
cosmology and, 7981–7982, 7983
crossroads, **2070–2071**
definitions of, 7978
divine dwelling as, in architectural classification, 462–463
Eliade (Mircea) on, 7694
encoding of, 7982–7984
environmental dimension of, 2564
establishment of, 7978–7980
functions of, 7980–7982
geography of, **3433–3437**
gold and silver in, 3626
ḥaram and *ḥawṭah,* **3776–3778** (*See also* Haram)
in Hawaiian religion, *heiau,* 3796–3797
hierophany (manifestation of the sacred) and, 3972
in Hinduism, in Vedic cosmology, 2014
in Huichol religion, 4152–4153
human body and, 7982–7983
in Islam
Jerusalem as, 7979
mosques as, 7979–7980
sacrilege and, 8014
in Japanese religion
creation myth and, 7978–7979
Shintō shrines and, 7980
Jerusalem as, 4838
in Judaism, *shekhinah* (presence of God) and, 8313
as *locus consecratus,* 1491
in Maori religion, 5682
latrine as, 7978
in Micronesian religions, 6004
mountains as, 1502
naming, significance of, 2611
narratives in, 7984
nature as, in Daoism, 2636, 2637
negation of, 7979–7980
New Age pilgrims and, 8429
nude images in, 6739–6740
in Oceanic religions, 6788
in Okinawan religion, 6812
oracles and, 6832–6834
purification of, 7507
in Greek religion, 1459
rock art marking, 1471
in Roman religion, *sacer* and *profanus* concepts in, 7964
in Sami religion, *seite* (sacred landscape), 8087
sanctuary as, **8100–8101**
as set apart, 1504
and sky, hierophany of, 8428–8429
social organization in, 7984
textiles creating, 9090
time and, 7984
ultimate orientation and, 1581
in United States, 10084
in urban origins, 9723
variety in, 7978
Sacred texts, 7699. *See also* Bible; Scripture; *See also* Qur'ān; *specific texts*
archaeological search for, 451–452
in architectural design, 465
authority of, 692–697
of Buddhism, interpretation of, 7699
conversion, and translatability of, 1972
of Hinduism
focus on, 2620
interpretation of, 7699
nature in, 2620–2621

Sacred texts ***continued***
interpretations of, 7699
of Judaism
Agnon's (Shemu'el Yosef) anthologies of, 180
on nature, 2642–2643
as objects of devotion, 2317
study of, 5472–5475
of Yoruba religion, studies of, 80
of Zoroastrianism (*See* Avesta)
Sacred time, **7986–7997,** vol. 1 color insert. *See also* Time
Aristotle *vs.* Augustine on, 7989
calculation of, 5197
definitions and senses of, 7987–7989
Eliade (Mircea) on, 944, 945, 7694
gold and silver in, 3626
methodological problems with, 7991–7993
nature, origin, spectrum, power, and rhythm in, 7990–7991
notions and experience of the sacred and, 7989–7990
postmodern reformulation of, 7993
vs. profane time, 1758
reenactment of creation myths and, 7694
Sacre du printemps, le (ballet), 2161
Sacré sauvage, 5159
Sacrificati, Decian persecution and, 2112
Sacrifice, **7997–8010**. *See also* Offerings
in African religions
Bēta Esra'ēl, 5002
Dinka, 2366, 2367, 6744
East African, 2568
interlacustrine Bantu, 4519
Lugbara, 5527
myths of, 95
northeast Bantu, 2575, 2576
Nuer, 6744, 7844
West African, 9719
Yoruba, 3571, 9911
Zulu, 10009–10010
alcoholic beverages as, 849
altars in, 275–278
animal (*See* Animal sacrifice)
in Arabian religions, 8006
in Arctic religions, 470
and atonement, 594–595
autosacrifice, 1403
in Aztec religion, 717, 5891–5893
by Aztec gods, 717, 1358
Baal (Jan van) on, 725, 7997, 8000
in Batal religion, 799
in Blackfoot religion, 958–959
blood, 986, 7998 (*See also* Animal sacrifice)
bloodless, 7998
in Bugis religion, 1317
in Buriat religion, 1326, 1327
Burkert (Walter) on, 8008–8009
Canaanite, 1382, 1385
in Caribbean ancestral cults, 1436
in Chinese religion
Confucian imperial cult, **1910–1916**
divination and, 1582
emperor offerings, 8005
Han rituals, 1591, 7267
official state rituals, 1644
Qin rituals, 1590, 7267
at seasonal festivals, 1641, 1642
temple festival and, 1620
to Tian, 5178, 5179
Zhou rituals, 1584, 1891–1892, 5178
in Christianity, 986–987, 8007
beloved son in, 8009
Eucharist as, 1669, 8006–8007
classification of, 7845
communal meals associated with, 7957
in construction, 1504
of cosmic man, 2283–2284
in creation myths, 2556
criticism of, 8007
in Dacian Riders, 2124
in Daoism (*See Jiao*)
destruction and, 7997, 7999, 8000
dismemberment in (*See* Dismemberment)
in divination, 2373–2374
divine
rites commemorating, 7957, 8004
sacrificial objects, divinization of, 7999
in East African religions, 2366, 2367
in Egyptian religion, 8005
of pigs, 7144
Epicurus on, 3911
epic warfare as, 2816–2817
ethical and nonethical conceptions of, 8001
Eucharist as, 2877–2878
in exorcism, 2934
fertility and, Frazer (James G.) on, 4183
figura and, 8918
food and, 3171
in foundation rites, 4105
Frazer (James) on, 4183, 8001
Freud on, 8003, 8004
in Germanic religion, dismemberment in, 2366–2367
Girard (René) on, 8004–8005, 8009
in goddess worship, 3590
in Greek religion, 3667–3670, 3682–3683
altars of, 4381
animal bones, 1014
to Artemis, 506–507
bridge and, 1051
in Demeter cults, 2270
Detienne (Marcel) and Vernant (Jean-Pierre) on, 8009
in Dionysos cult, 2357–2358
goals of, 6302
Homer on, 4108
libations in, 5433
music in, 3682, 6303
origin of, 3669–3670, 3683
overview of, 8006
at Panathenaia, 6958
of pigs, 7144
Pythagoras on, 7529
hair used in, 3740
in Hinduism
abolition of, 986
and blessing, 983
brahman control o, 8006
bridge and, 1049
cosmology and, 2014–2015, 2016
in devotional life, 9821–9822
in Āraṇyakas, 3993
in Kurukṣetra, 5268
in *Śrauta* (solemn) rites, 3992
mysticism and, 6343
ritual patterns of, 7699
temple worship and, 4002
history of, 8005–8007
honorific *vs.* expiatory, Smith (W. Robertson) on, 4183
Hubert (Henri) and Mauss (Marcel) on, 8003
human (*See* Human sacrifice)
hunting theory of, 8008–8009
in Iberian religion, 4249–4250, 4252–4253
in Igbo religion, 4366
in Inca religion, 1364, 4411, 4412–4413
in Indo-European religions, 4454–4455, 4456
Shintō, 8005
intentions of, 8001
in Iranian religions, 4535, 8006
in Islam, 8006
blood sacrifice, 986
during *ḥājj,* 4714, 7159, 7160
in naming ceremonies, 7826
in Israelite religion, 4972–4973
animal, 925, 926, 927, 986, 4746
criticism of, 4747, 4748
Levites's functions in, 5424–5425
libations in, 5434
priestly system of, 4747, 7400
for purification, 4747
reason for, 927
in Temple, 925, 927–928, 931–932
types of, 926–927
voluntary, 4746–4747
Jay (Nancy) on, 8009
Jensen (Adolf) on, 8004
in Judaism
beloved son in, 8009
blood in, 7845
collective nature of, 4857
criticism of, 8007
in Hebrew scriptures, 8006
Hubert (Henri) and Mauss (Marcel) on, 8003
Kalischer (Tsevi Hirsch) on, 5069
for life of Israel, 5445
Marrano, 5718
during pilgrimage, 7162
in rabbinic Judaism, 4977
worship centered on, 9806
in Khanty religion, 5124–5125
in Komi religion, 5217, 5218
Lanternari (Vittorio) on, 8004
Leeuw (Gerardus van der) on, 8003
libations in, 5433, 5434
as magic, 8003–8004
in Mansi religion, 5124–5125
Mauss (Marcel) on, 725
in Maya religion, 5884
meal accompanying, 7999–8000
meaning of term, 7997
in Mesoamerican religions, myths of, 5935–5936
in Mesopotamian religion, 8005
of pigs, 7144
microcosm-macrocosm in, 4159
military, to Eros, 2832
in Moabite religion, 6094–6095
in Neolithic religion, 6463–6464, 6465
in New Year festivals, 6591
in North American Indian religions, 6652
Sun Dance and, 8845
offering *vs.,* 7997
in orientation, 6886
origin of
theories on, 8001–8005
totemism as, 4183
as origin of the sacred, 7974
in Paleolithic religion, 7375
in Phoenician religion, 4580, 7131–7133, 7134
place and time of, 8000
Plutarch on, 7200
in Polynesian religions, 7309
prehistoric, 7375, 7377, 7384, 7386
Promethean model of, 2366

purification by, lustratio and, 5534
for rain, 7602, 7603
recipient of, 7845, 8000–8001
location of, 7999
magic and, 8003
rite (manner and method) of, 7999–8000
ritual, 7835, 7844–7845
in Roman religion, 8006
ban on, 7923
bridge and, 1051
to Dia, 514
Feriae Latinae, 2366
during *ludi saeculares,* 5525–5526
during Lupercalia, 5531
to Mars, 5728
redemption and, 7641
sacrificer in, 7997–7998
in Samoyed religion, 8095
scapegoat theory of, 8004–8005
Schmidt (Wilhelm) on, 8002, 8004
in Scythian religion, 4489, 8205
in Semitic religions, 8005–8006
in Siberian religions, Khanty and Mansi, 6755
Smith (Jonathan Z.) on, 8009
Smith (W. Robertson) on, 8002–8003, 8452–8453
in Southeast Asian religions, prehistoric, 8643
substitutes in, 7998–7999
suicide as, 4955
Tylor (E. B.) on, 8002
in Vedism, 1504, 8006, 9563–9565
conflict and, 9561
dīkṣā in preparation for, 7816
dismemberment in, 2367
horse sacrifice, 1025, 4132–4133, 9563–9564
Hubert (Henri) and Mauss (Marcel) on, 8003
in Brāhmaṇas, 1026–1027, 7356
interpretations of, 9566–9568
place of, 9564–9565
redemption and, 7641
ritual for, 9561–9563
Rudra excluded from, 8415
system of, 9561–9563
transformation and, 8545
types of, 9562
in *Yajurveda,* 9551
in Vietnamese religion, 9592
Sacrificial expiation, in Judaism, 7757
Sacrificial love, Christian concept of, 6645
Sacrilege, **8010–8017**
Christian view of, 8010, 8013–8014
definition and overview, 8010–8011
desecration as, 8011–8012
Hindu view of, 8014–8015
interreligious *vs.* intrareligious, 8010
Islamic view of, 8014
Jewish view of, 8012–8013
Sacrosancta decree, 9340–9341
Sacrum (Roman concept). *See also* Sacred and the profane, the
profanum vs., 7964
Ṣaḍabhijñā (superknowings), 7357
Ṣaḍaṅgayogas (yogic exercises), 9894
Sadanira River, sacred space near, 7979
Sa'dan Toraja people. *See* Toraja religion
Sadāprarudita *(bodhisattva),* 1079
Ṣadāq (marriage payment), 7826
Ṣadaqa (truth), 9372
Ṣadaqah, gift giving in, 3485
Sadar Jahan, 4662
Sādāt, Ansar al-
assassination of, 6315
in Free Officers movement, 6315
Muslim Brotherhood and, 6315
Saddhammaghosa (Buddhist monk), 1199
Saddharmapuṇḍarīka Sūtra (Lotus Sūtra) (Buddhist text), 1146
arhat in, 1114
Avalokiteśvara in, 705, 706, 4329
Bhaisajyaguru in, 1084
Buddha preaching, 9177
buddhas in, 1067, 1077
celebrating, 1306
Chinese commentaries on, *honjisuijaku* theory in, 4121
devotion to, 1282
dharmakāya in, 1069, 4416
ekayana (single path to salvation) in, 2029
Ennin's translation of, 2801
French translation of, 1312, 1333–1334
gift giving in, 3483
Guanding lecturing on, 9179
illustrations in, 1262
images in, vol. 14 color insert
in Reiyūkai Kyōdan, 7681, 7862
in Risshō Kōseikai, 5400, 5401, 7794–7795
in Sōka Gakkai, 5400
Kumārajīva's translation of, 5263
Maitreya in, 5619
mountains in, 6439
name of, 6408
Nichiren doctrine and, 6603, 6605–6606, 6608
Nichiren on, 1244, 5310, 7262, 7272
nirvāṇa in, 1271, 2030
"perfect teachings" of, 8031
politics in, 7260
Pure Lands in, 7503
Saichō on, 1242, 8030
Shōtoku and, 1241, 4809
studies on, 1313
in Tendai school, 9076, 9078, 9079, 9080
Tiantai and, 1577
upāya in, 9485
women in, 3331–3332
Zhiyi's commentary on, 1237, 9175–9176
Sadducees, **8017–8019**
connection with Karaites, 4058–4059, 5087
historical views of, 4974
Josephus Flavius on, 3203
refusing to believe in spirits, 2280
on resurrection, 7765, 8557
on Shavu'ot, 8305
Sade Nāhn (ritual bath), 9997, 9999
Sādhaka (practitioner of Tantra), 8987
Sādhana (spiritual practice)
in Buddhist Tantrism, 1124, 1215, 1220
in Healthy, Happy, Holy Organization (3HO), 3879
in Hindu Tantrism, 4003, 8987
in Purāṇas, 7500
maṇḍalas in, visualization of, 5642–5643, 5644
Sādhanamālā (Buddhist text), 1215, 4330
Sādhana texts, *maṇḍalas* in, 5642, 5644
Sādhāraṇa dharma, 2330
Sādhukkaṛī bhāṣā dialect, literary tradition of, 3984
Sadhus/Sadhvis (renunciates), **8019–8022**
asceticism of, vol. 13 color insert
Naga Sadhus (nude ascetics), militant Śaivism and, 8418
as pilgrims, 7171
in Swaminarayan movement, 8889, 8890
vs. gurūs, 3713
Sa'di (poet), **8022–8023**
on *dhikr,* 2341
on gardens, 3283
Ṣādiq, Ja'far al-. *See* Ja'far al-Ṣādiq
Ṣādiq, Sayyid al-, 6229
Ṣadr, Mūsā al-, 'Alawīyūn and, 227
Ṣadr al-Dīn, on *ahl al-bayt,* 199
Ṣadr al-Dīn Qūnawī, 4258, 4259
Ṣadr al-Dīn Shīrāzī. *See* Mullā Ṣadrā
Ṣadyk, Muḥammad, 4626, 4627
Saecula (time period), in Estruscan destiny, 2873
Safad (Safed) (Israel)
Judaism in, 5104
mysticism in, 4998–4999
possession in, 2931, 2932
Qabbalah in, 4914, 5104, 5532, 7534
Sephardic Jews in, 4998–4999
Ṣafar (month in Islamic year), 4713
Safavid dynasty (Persia)
'Āshūrā' under, 550
founding of, 5982
Imāmīyah and, 8339
Islamic arts and sciences in, 3801
Islamic philosophy in, 4555–4556
al-Majlisī in, 5623
narrative storytelling in, 2446–2447
Ṣafawīyah, 9659
Safed. *See* Safad
Safīnat al-Awliyā' (Dārā), 2219
Ṣafwān ibn al-Mu'aṭṭal, 211
Safwa religion, witchcraft beliefs in, 9778–9779
Sagan, Carl, 4516
Sāgaropama years, in Jain cosmology, 2025
Sagas
Norse, **8023–8026**
in typology of narratives, 6376–6377
Sagbata (deity), 3166
Sagehood. *See also* Prophecy and prophets
in Ashkenazic Hasidism, 543, 544
in Confucianism
chaotic forces and, 1540
charisma of, 1549, 7353
Cheng Yi on, 1562
constructive discipline and, 8704
in Japan, 1928
as sainthood, 8037
self-transformation and, 1895–1897
ultimate transformation and, 1581
sage-kings (San Huang) in Chinese myth, 1627, 1642
in Stoicism, 8741
Sage Mother Hall (Taiyuan), 9057
Sages, The: Their Concepts and Beliefs (Urbach), 900
Sage von Tanaquil, Die (Bachofen), 731
Ṣaggoch, 2861
Sagnani, Arjun, 3098
Saguṇa bhakti tradition
Gauḍīya orders and, 3985–3986

Saguṇa bhakti tradition **continued**
nirguṇa bhakti vs., 3984–3985, 10088–10089
Śaṅkara on, 4004
Saguṇa brahman, Śaṅkara on, 6144
Sahā (mythic land), as Impure Land, 2026
Sahagún, Bernardino de, 150
on Aztec kings, 5174
on birth rituals, 7811
on caves, 1468
on Coatlicue, 1841
on creation myths and human sacrifice, 4187
Florentine Codex of, 5917, 5939
on Huitzilopochtli, 4155
importance of work of, 5939
on paganism, 4039
on purification rituals, 7862
on Templo Mayor, 4188
on tobacco, 8455
on Toltec religion, 9223
on Tonantzin, 5922
sahajānanda (natural joy), in *Hevajra Tantra,* 3965
Sahajanand Swami
divinization of, 8891
Swaminarayan movement, role in, 8889–8890
writings and philosophy of, 8890–8891
Sahajayāna, 1122, 1123
Sahaja Yoga
child socialization and education in, 6542, 6543
in Europe, 6568
Sahajiyās
Caitanya's influence on, 1347
Tantric elements in, 8990
Sahak (Armenian catholicos), 488
and Armenian alphabet, 5763
Sahak Parthev (bishop of Armenia), **8026**
Sahara
ethnic groups in, 83
Islam in, 4600–4601
Sāhasra cosmology
overview of, 2027–2030
variations on, 2026
Sahasrāra cakra
nature of, 1348
Śiva in, 1349
Sahelian savanna region
Islam in, 4600–4601
myths in, 92
Sahib Devan, 3336
Ṣāḥib ibn al-'Abbād, al-, 'Abd al-Jabbār and, 3–4
Sahīfas (booklets), collections of *ḥadīths* in, 3727, 3728
Sahīh al-Bukhārī, in *ḥadīth* literature, 3728, 3729–3730
Sahīh (sound) collections
in Shī'ī collections, 3733
Musnad of Ibn Ḥanbal *vs.*, 3763
in Sunni collections, 3728
Ṣaḥīh marriage (valid marriage), 4706
Sahīh Muslim, in *ḥadīth* literature, 3729–3730
Sahi snying po. *See* Kṣitigarbha
Sahlins, Marshall
on Cook (James), 3797–3798
on evolutionary psychology, 8475
Saḥnūn, 'Abd al-Salām ibn Sa'īd, 4584
Ṣaḥw (path of sobriety), in Sufism, 8812
Ṣaḥw (sobriety), 4569
Sai Baba movement, **8026–8029**
ethnic identities and, 1809
Saibaraburi (songs), 6300
Saichō (Buddhist monk), **8029–8031**
Buddhist texts obtained by, 9075
Chinese Buddhism studied by, 1176
disciples of, 995, 9075
and Ennin, 2801
Ganjin and, 3276
imperial favor for, 4784–4785
Kūkai and, 8350
monks ordained by, 9076
on Hīnayāna practices, 9079
on *mappō,* 5687
on realization of buddhahood, 9078
in Tendai school, 1242, 1294
texts collected by, 4809
writings of, 9076, 9077, 9079
in Zen development, 9943
Said, Edward W., **8031–8033**
American study of religion, role in, 8787
on colonialist agendas, 8638
on missionaries, 6073
in Orientalism, 6881–6884
Orientalism criticized by, 4721–4722, 4723
and postcolonial theory, 10042
secular humanism of, in progressive Islam, 6098, 6099
subaltern studies and, 8801
women in works of, 3321
Sa'īd al-Su'adā' (Ṣūfī monastery), 9005
Saifawa dynasty (Africa), 4604, 4605
Saignes, Thierry, on sacred images in Andean Christianity, 8610
saigū (shrine virgins), 7411
at Ise Shrine (Japan), 1528
Saigyō
death of, 2244
poetry of, 7216
Saihui (temple festival), 1620
Saiin (high priestess), 7411
Saikōji temple, 5270
Śailendra dynasty (Java), 1134
Sainokawara (river), 7863
Saint(s), **8033–8038**. *See also specific saints*
in Agami Jawi, 4816
authentication and canonization of, 2082–2083
in Buddhism
iconography of, 4330
lives of, 5192
overview of, 8036–8037
in Byzantine art, 4345
in Caribbean religions, spirits identified with
Santeria *orishas,* 1434, 8107–8108
Vodou *lwa,* 1433
charismatic, 1546
in Christianity (*See* Saint(s), in Christianity)
in Confucianism, 8037
corpses of, 2244
cult of, **2081–2084,** vol. 12 color insert
definition of category of, 8033–8034
exorcisms performed by, 2929
headless (cephalophoric), 3806
healing associated with
contagious magic and, 3811–3812
illnesses connected to specific saints, 3812
in Islamic *ziyārāt* pilgrimages, 3834–3835
in medieval Catholicism, 3845
in modern Catholicism, 3847
in Hinduism
Nāyaṉārs as, 8044
overview of, 8036
saint-singer tradition, 4005–4006
in Indian religion, *bhakti* poetry by, 3985
intercession of, 2083
in Islam (*See* Saint(s), in Islam)
in Judaism
overview of, 8035–8036
pilgrimages to tombs of, 7161–7162
in Komi religion, 5217
in Latin American folk religions, 6577–6578
in Mesoamerican religions, 2228, 5926
in Mexican Indian religions, 2228
in North African Arab religion, cairns as coercive claims on, 2101
as objects of devotion, 2317
paths to sainthood, 8037–8038
as posthumous phenomenon, 8033
as rainmakers, 7602
relics of, 2081–2082
in Christianity, 7687–7688
in Islam, 7687
pilgrimage to, 7148, 7150
as sacred matter, vol. 4 color insert
shrines and, 8376
ritual humiliation of, 2105
Sanctoral cycle in liturgical calendar, 1744
sleeplessnes and, 8441
in South America
colonial convergence of *huacas* with, 8605–8606, 8609–8612
in modern Andes, 8619
translation (moving the remains) of, 2082
in winter carols, 9745
women as, 8037–8038
worship of, 2228
Saint(s), in Christianity. *See also* All Saints Day; *specific saints*
African ancestors compared with, 2067
in Armenian church, 489
Catholic
African ancestors compared with, 142
healing associated with, 3845, 3847
in Mesoamerica, 5926
miracles of, 6056
veneration of images of, 4386
in Vodou, 9636
Eastern Orthodox, 8034
icons of, 2594
Greek Orthodox, 5239
in Hungary, 4225
images of, 4352, 9623
Eastern Orthodox, 2594
in Latin America, 8610
martyrdom and, 2228, 8034
miracles and, 7973
overview of, 8034
in Protestantism, 8034
relics of, 7687–7688
Sanctoral cycle in liturgical calendar, 1744
women as, 8037–8038
Saint(s), in Islam
in Central Asia, 4622
mawlids of, 5788–5789
overview of, 8034–8035
relics of, 7687
in Shiism, 8035
Sirhindī (Aḥmad) on, 8414
in Sufism, 4569
devotional allegiance to, 9819–9820
election of, 2749
prophets *vs.*, 8814–8815
veneration of, 8821
women as, 3369, 7591
ziyārāt pilgrimages to, 3834–3835
Saint Andrews (Scotland), castle at, 5212
Saint Anthony's Fire, 2138
Saint Barbara's Day, domestic observances of, 2400
"Saint Claire" (Erdrich), 7226
Saint Cyril monastery (Russia), Sorskii (Nil) and, 8525
Saint-Denis, Abbey of, Abelard (Peter) at, 7
Sainte Face, La (Champaigne), vol. 12 color insert

Saint Ephem Syriac Orthodox Seminary, 8940
Saint Gall, Plan of, 6117–6119
Saint George's Day, in Balto-Finnic areas, 3108
Saint George's Methodist Church (Philadelphia), 264
Saint Germain (ascended master), Ballard and, 1782
Saint-Germaine, Comte de, 2772
Saint Germain Foundation, 4246
  Summit Lighthouse and, 1781–1782
Saint Joseph's Day Feast, folklorist study of, 3147
Saint Joseph's Oratory (Montreal), 5196
Saint Lucia
  Feast of, 2400
  Kele ceremony in, 1436
Saint Luke Painting the Virgin (Gossaert), vol. 12 color insert
Saint Mamas monastery, Symeon the New Theologian at, 8919
Saint-Marcq, Chevalier Clément de, Kymris lodge and, 8252
Saint Mark's-in-the-Bowrie Church (New York), 2164
Saint-Martin, Louis-Claude de, 6435
Saint Mary's Seminary, Carroll (John) and, 1445
Saint Matthew's Passion (ballet), 2162–2163
Saint Médard (cemetery), convulsionaries at, 2805
Saint Peter Martyr (Guercino), vol. 13 color insert
Saint Peter's Basilica (Rome), 793. *See also* Sistine Chapel
  Christmas mass in, 1756–1757
Saint Sergius Trinity Monastery, 7942
Saint-Simon, 2669
Saint-Simon, Claude-Henri de Rouvroy
  Comte (Auguste) and, 1882
  on society and religion, 8465
Saint-Simon, Comte de, and functionalism, 3230, 3231
Saint Sophia's Church (Novgorod), 794
Saint Thomas (Danish West Indies), Christianity in, Lutherans and Moravians, 1706, 1707, 6191
Saint Thomas's African Episcopal Church, 4951
Saint Thomas's Protestant Episcopal Church, 68
Saint-Victor, Abbey of. *See also* Victorine tradition in Christianity
  Hugh of Saint-Victor and, 4150–4151
Saint Vincent (Caribbean island), Garifuna people on, 3283
Saiō (supreme priestess), 7411
Sai Santhan trust, Sai Baba movement and, 8027
Saisei-itchi (unity of ritual and government), 7271, 7411
Saishu (supreme priest/priestess), 7410, 7411
Saītaan (supreme beings), 2395
Śaiva Siddhānta, **8042–8043**
  in Kashmir, 8047
  metaphysics in, 8547
  in Tamil, 8042–8043, 8418, 9443
Śaiva Upaniṣads, 9484
Saiving, Valerie, 3035, 9789
Śaivism, 4430, **8038–8050**
  Bhagavadgītā in, 851, 854
  bhakti in, 857, 858
  Cakrasamvara Tantra and, 1349–1350
  in Cambodia, 1135
  canon of, *Civaṇāṉapōtam* (Meykaṇṭār) in, 5999
  Daśanāmī sect in
    akhāḍā military units in, 8021
    network of, 8105
    sadhus/sadhvis (renunciates) in, 8020
  deities of, Gaṇeśa, 3273
  devotees of, 8041–8042
  dualistic *vs.* nondualistic, 8047–8048
  guru in, 4430
  image veneration in, 4383, 4384, 4391
  Kālāmukha sect in, 8041
    Lakulīśa Pāśupata system, influence of, 4019, 8049
    location of, 8049
  Kāpālika sect in, 8041, **8049–8050,** 8990
    Cakrasamvara and, 1349–1350
    Kaula system and, 4020
    Krama Śaivism and, 8045
    Lakulīśa Pāśupata system, influence of, 4019
  in Kashmir, **8047–8048**
  Krama sect in, **8045–8046**
    in Kashmir, 8047
    kaula style of worship of Kālī in, 4020, 8047–8048
  līlā in, 5457
  Mahāśivarātri (Great Night of Síva) in, 8417
  maṇḍalas in, 5640–5641
  māyā in, 5795
  meditation in, 5819–5820
  Nāth (Siddha) sect, 8041
  Nāyaṉār sect in, 8041, **8044–8045**
    poetry of, 7210, 8974
    saint-singer tradition and, 4005–4006
    vs. Āḻvārs, 279
  orthodox *vs.* heterodox, 8047
  overview, **8038–8042**
  Pāśupata sect in, 8041, **8049,** 8990
    influence of, 4019
  philosophical dimensions of, 8417–8418
  poetry of, 5671, 7210, 8974, 8975
  political and militant dimensions of, 8418
  Pratyabhijñā sect in, **8048–8049**
    Abhinavagupta on, 9
  pūjā in, 7494
  Purāṇas in, 7500
  Rāmā in, 7609
  rituals in, of priests *vs.* laypeople, 8416–8417
  saint-singer traditions and, 4005–4006
  Śaiva Siddhānta sect, 8041, **8042–8043**
    Meykaṇṭār on, 5999–6000
    Nāyaṉmār poems in canon of, 4005
  samhāra (reabsorption) in, 8416–8417
  schools of, 4430
  sectarian movements and, 4004–4005
  Śiva, historical development of, 8038–8041 (*See also* Śiva)
  Śiva-*bhakti,* 8417
    in Siddhānta school, 8418
  Śiva worship in, 4428
  skull symbolism and cannibalism in, 3805
  in Southeast Asia, 4009
  Sṛṣṭi (emission) in, 8416–8417
  studies of, 4449
  in Tamil, 8975–8976
  Tantras (literature) of
    called Āgamas, 4019
    higher path and *mantra* path in, 4019–4020
  Tantric influences in, 8041
  temples in, 8042, 8416–8417
  temples of, 8975, 8977
  Trika (Kashmiri) sect, **8046–8047** (*See also* Trika Śaivism)
  Vīraśaivism (Liṅgāyat), 4430, 8041, **8043–8044**
    āvarṇas of, 4424–4425
    founder of, 4424
    origins of, 4421
    system of thought of, 4424
  in Western countries, 8418–8419
SAJ. *See* Society for the Advancement of Judaism
Sajda (gesture), 7342
Sajen (offerings), in Agami Jawi, 4817
Sajnovics, Janos, 3111
Saka religion (prehistoric), 7384–7387. *See also* Scythian religion
  birds in, 7387
  divine gifts in, 7384
  fire cult in, 7385–7386
  funeral rites in, 7387
  gold cult in, 7386
  horse cult in, 7385, 7387
  myths in, 7386
  sun cult in, 7384–7385
Sakau offerings, 6006–6007
Sakha people, shamanism of, 379
Śākhās (branches), 1026
Sakhībhāva cult
  dances of, 2137
  identification wih Rādhā, 5254
Śākhlā (branch), of Vedic texts, 9554
Sakhrah, al- (rock), 924
Sakīnah (presence of God)
  and construction of the Kaʿbah, 5050
  in form of cat, 1463
Sakīnat al-Awliyāʾ (Dārā), 2219
Sākṣin (passive witness), 7522
Śākta (Hindu concept), salvation through, in Trika Śáivism, 8047
Śākta Tantrism, Goddess as path to liberation in, 8547
Śakti (deity)
  Bengali worship of, 826, 4430
  cakras and, 1348, 1349
  Devī as, 4325, 4326
  Ganges as, 7862
  the Goddess as, 857
  Hindu worship of, 2526
  images of, 4435
  in Purāṇas, 7500
  in Śaiva Tantras, 4020
  lion associated with, 5464
  meditation on, 5819–5820
  Śiva, union with, 1349
  in Tantrism, 9822–9823
  three levels of, in Tantras, 4020
  yoni of, 9907
Śakti (power). *See also* Kuṇḍalinī; Tantrism
  cakras and, 1348
  Durgā as, 2525, 4435
  in kuṇḍalinī, 5266
  Kṛṣṇa and, 5254
  as *mana,* 2542
  masculine and feminine aspects of, 2305
  Rādhā and, 7594
  Ramakrishna and, 7611–7613
  symbols of, 4435
  women identified with, 1559, 3319
Śāktism
  māyā in, 5795
  meditation in, 5819–5820
Sakuma Shōzan, as Meiji Restoration leader, Confucianism and, 1928

Śākyabuddhi (Buddhist scholar), 1212
Sakyadhita (Buddhist organization), 6762
Śākyamuni Buddha. *See* Buddha, the
Sakya Paṇḍita (Sa skya Paṇḍita), **8050–8053**
intellectual legacy of, 8052
life of, 8050–8051
writings of, 8051–8052
Śākyasrībhadrda (Kashmiri master), Sakya Paṇḍita and, 8051
Sālā (public hall), in Buddhist monasteries, 5314
Salaf (ancestors), *fiqh* founded on, 4587
Salafīyah, 4589–4590
Ḥanābilah and, 3768
Islamic modernism and, 6095–6096, 6100
origins of, 4589, 4700
Rashīd Riḍā (Muḥammad) and, 7621
in sub-Saharan Africa, 4609, 4611
ṭarīqah criticized by, 4589–4590
urbanization and, 4590
victory of, 4590
Śālagrāma (stone), 4326, 7494
Ṣalāḥ al-Dīn (Saladin)
monastery established by, 9005
on *jihād*, 2078
Rūmī's (Jalāl al-Dīn) friendship with, 7936
Śalākapuruṣas (men with the staff), 9207
Rāmā as, 7609
Salām (peace), 6645, 6648, 7021
"Salām ʿalaykum, al-" ("Peace be upon you"), 7021
Hindu *vs.* Muslim use of, 8062
tradition of, 8061
Salant, Yosef Zundel, Salanter (Yisraʾel) and, 8053
Salanter, Yisraʾel, 4915, 5019, 6902, **8053**
in Musar movement, 6241
Zundel (Yosef) and, 6241
Ṣalāt (prayer), **8054–8058**. *See also* Prayer, in Islam; *Qiblah*
ablutions before, 10, 8057
as act of devotion, 2319
adhān and *iqāmah* (calls to prayer), 8056–8057
in Agami Islam Santri, 4818
communal prayer on Friday and at festivals, 8058
conditions for, 8055
in devotional life, 9816–9817
for *ḥājj*, 7158
etymology and evolution of term, 8054
five daily, 8056
heteronomous discipline and, 8700
imam as leader of, 4393, 4396–4397
in *Ḥadīth, Fiqh,* and the Pillars of Islam, 8054–8055
in Qurʾān, 8054, 8056
interpretations, diversity of, 8054
mental preparations and intention, 8057
minar reminder of, 9266
obligatory and voluntary forms of, 8055
as performance, 7369, 8057–8058
place for, 8055–8056
postures and gestures during, 7342, 7343
significance of, 8058
slave practices of, 4682
times for, 8056
Salathiel. *See* Ezra
Salazar Mendicuchia, Pablo, 6580
Sale, George, 4717, 7244
on scripture, 8197
Salem (Massachusetts), witchcraft trials in, 2930, 5372, 7755, 9774
Sale of Indulgences (Breu), vol. 7 color insert
Saler, Benson, 2869
religion defined by, 7704
Salesians, missions of, in Amazon, 8623
Saliba, John, 6523, 6527
Ṣāliḥ (prophet), 835, 4588
Salii (priesthood), 5728, 7897, 7908
music and, 6304
Salina people (California), cosmogonic myths of, 5198
Salisbury, Edward Eldridge, 1315
Salish language, 6697
Salish tribes (North America)
ablutions among, 11
area populated by, 6656
boat burials of, 991
confession among, 1884
puberty rites, 1470
and trees, 9334–9335, 9338
vision quests of, 6716
Saliva. *See* Spittle and spitting
Sallekhanā (death fast), 4769
Sallman, W. H., 4348
Sallman, Warner, vol. 12 color insert
Salma bint Sakhr, 19
Sālokya (communion), 858
Salome, dance of, 2135, 2153
Salome Alexandra (queen), 930
Pharisees, support for, 8018
Salomonsen, Jone, 7859
Salonika (Greece), Judaism in, 4997
Salons de la Rose + Croix, 7930
Ṣalota bēt (prayer house), 5002
Salt, **8058–8059**
in alchemy, 249, 8059
Salter, Richard, 6546
Salt Lake City (Utah), Mormons in, 6194
Saltu (deity), 4405
Salutations, **8060–8062**
ceremonial greetings, 8060
law, greetings prescribed by, 8060–8061
secularization of, 8062
spiritual achievement and, 8061–8062
Salutism, Kimbangu's (Simon) influence on, 5144
Salvation, 7697–7698. *See also* Afterlife; Enlightenment; Eschatology; Justification; Redemption; Saviors; Soteriology
Abraham's role in, 16
in African religions
absence of concept, 84
in new movements, 102
asceticism and, 527–528
as awakening (*See* Awakening)
in Bambara religion, 777
in Buddhism, 7112, 7641 (*See also* Nirvāṇa)
bodhisattva path, 996, 1088, 1090
cosmology and, 2026, 2027, 2028–2030
vs. Hinduism, 6344
in Japanese Jōdo Shinshu, 8354, 8355
jñāna in, 4928
of women, 7084
in Zen Buddhism, 527
in cargo cults, 1416
in Catharism, 1457
celibacy and, 1477
in Chinese religion
by becoming ancestors or gods, 1619
messianic hope, 1594, 1597
in myth, 1628
in Pure Land Buddhism, 1600
three ages theory of history and, 1576
in Way of the Celestial Masters, 1593
in Christianity (*See also* Justification; Predestination; Redemption)
in Adventism, 8235, 8236
androcentrism of, 335
Arminius (Jacobus) on, 492
Barth (Karl) on, 790
Basil of Caesarea on, 798
Bible as absolute authority on, 2888
Bonaventure on, 1012
Bultmann (Rudolf) on, 8807–8808
Calvin (John) on, 7661
Cassian on, 1448
in Christian Science, 1746
covenant theology and, 2050
cross labyrinth symbolizing, 5278
Cyprian on, 2114
depicted in churches, 7984
grace in, 3645
by grace through faith, in Calvin and Luther, 1375
history, 2608, 4055, 6378, 7984
Holy Spirit and, in Calvin, 1376
Hus (Jan) on, 4234
Jewish law and, 2746
Jews in, 4855
Justin Martyr on, 5044–5045
Luther (Martin) on, 158–159, 695, 1667
merit in, 5876–5877
Micah on, 6000–6001
in New Testament, 3544
Origen on, 8406
in Orthodox theology, 2590–2591
Paul on, 7017
prosperity as sign of, 2673
purgatory and, 3885
in Puritanism, preparationist theology of, 4125
Roman Catholic, 3885, 9538
sacraments, necessity of, 7961
suffering of Christ and, 8807–8808
Swedenborg (Emanuel) on, 8899
Symeon the New Theologian on, 8920
Vatican II concept of, 9538
Weber (Max) on, 5436–5437
Welsey (John) on, 9716
in Daoism, 2204, 9845
in Egyptian religion, 7640–7641
as form of beauty, 812
free will *vs.* predestination in, **3202–3213**
"from" and "to" aspects of, 7697
in Gnosticism, 3520, 3924
in Hinduism, 527, 7112
bestowed by Śiva at *Śivarātri* celebration, 4017
vs. Buddhism, 6344
in Pratyabhijñā Saivism, 8049
in Śaiva Siddhanta, 8043
in Śrī Vaiṣṇavas Sampradāya, 8728
in Trika Śáivism, 8047
in Vīraśaivism, 8044
jñāna in, 4928
through knowledge, 5199–5200
līlā in, 5457–5458
pralayas (destructions) and, 2018
reincarnation and, 7678
in Tantrism, 8050
three paths to, in *Bhagadvadgītā*, 4001

in Aum Shinrikyō, 632
in Jōdoshū, 4937–4938
in Reiyūkai Kyōdan, 7861
in Sāṃkhya, 527
in Islam
falsafah ideas on, 2972
Jews in, 4855
in Jainism
of women, 7084
women and, 3326
in Judaism
of non-Jews, 4859
in rabbinic Judaism, 4976
in Torah myth, 7584–7585
Kippenberg (Hans Georg) on, 4048
in Manichaeism, 1889, 5653
bodily purification and, 4158–4159
mediators of, 8529
millennialism as expectation of, 6544, 6545
in missionary message, 6070
in mystery religions, initiation into *musteria* as, 7955
mythic narrative and, 8527–8528
in paganism, 7726
power and, 7353–7354
in primitive religions, 7697
redemption and, 7640
religious *vs.* nonreligious, 7697–7698
ritual and, 8527
in Roman religion, 7697
sacred space and, 7981
Shinran on, 4934
social, 5398–5399
Sozzini (Fausto Pavolo) on, 8673
Teilhard de Chardin (Pierre) on, 4032
in universal founded religions, 4067
virginity in, 9605
in Zionism, 4984
Salvation Army, 3173, **8063–8064**. *See also* Holiness movement
Booth (William) as founder of, **1020–1021**
doctrines and practices of, 8063–8064
emergence of, 6567
history and aims of, 8063
social work provided by, 7487
Salvation history, 2608, 6378
depicted in churches, 7984
views of, 4055
Salzmann, Alexandre de, Gurdjieff (G. I.) and, 3711
Salzmann, Jeanne de, Gurdjieff (G. I.) and, 3711
Samāʿ (listening parties), **8064–8066**
in Mawlawi Sufism, Whirling Dervishes in, 8823
as music, 4420, 9004–9005, 9006
debate over, 6277
as mystical dance, 7936
Ṣūfī orders and, 8822
Samādhi (meditative absorption), 1290, **8066–8067**
and *nirvāṇa,* 4429
in enlightenment, 2793
aṣṭāṅgayoga (eight-limbed discipline), 8705
in Kālacakra tradition yoga, 5058
Kuṇḍalinī and, 1349
power in, 7350
in religious training, 7357
states of consciousness and, 1950–1951
in Tantric literature, 1216, 1218, 1219
self-apotheosis as preparation for, 4019
visualization of, 1294
in Yoga, 9895–9896
Zhiyi on, 1291
Sama'el (demon), 5459
Samāna (breath), 1043, 7362
Samantabhadra *(bodhisattva),* 9174, 9510–9511
in Rnying ma pa school of Buddhism, 7868
Samāpatti (coincidence), *samādhi* and, 8066–8067
Samarin, William J., on glossolalia, 3505
Samaritans, **8067–8071**
beliefs and practices, 8069–8070
biblical canon of, 879
cantillation of, 1534
Gnosticism and, 3510, 3515
history of, 8068–8069
in Jewish and Christian ideology, 8071
Jewish separation from, 4858
legal status of, Abbahu and, 2
literature of, 8070
origin, theories of, 8068
as priests, 7394
Sophia (wisdom) of, 3510
Samaritan Targum, 888–889
Samarkand (Uzbekistan), Jews in, 5009
Samarqandī, al-, Abū Ḥanīfah and, 22
Samatā (absolute sameness), 9019
Śamatha (calm abiding meditation), 603, 1284, 1290, 5820–5821
Samāvartana (rite of passage), 7815
Sāmaveda (Vedic text), 9551–9552, 9554
Brāhmaṇas of, 1026
chanting of, 1535
priesthood in, 7405
ritual use of, meaningless sounds in, 5677
udgātṛ priests and, 3991
Samayamudrā (Symbolic Seal), 1217, 1218, 1219
Sāmāyika (equanimity), 4769
Samba-enredo (Carnival Samba song), 1444
Sambandhaparīkṣā (Dharmakīrti), 2336
Sāmba Purāṇa, Saura Hinduism in, 8136
Samba schools, in Carnival, 1444
Sámbhala, in Kālacakra tradition, 5056, 5057
Śaṁbhava (self-realization), salvation through, in Trika Śaivism, 8047
Saṃbhogakāya (enjoyment body), 1063, 1069, 1077, 1117, 9347, 9510–9511, 9962
Śambhu Mahādev (deity), in Marathi religions, 5697
Sambia people (Papua New Guinea), birth rituals of, 7807
Samburu religion (East Africa), initiation rites of, 2569
Saṃdhinirmocana Sūtra (Buddhist text), 1275, 1276
in Yogācāra Buddhism, 9897–9898, 9900
Same-sex marriage, dispute on, in United States, 7283
Saṃgha (Buddhist monastic community), 945, 1104–1105, **8071–8086**
admission to, 8072
in Africa, 108
Aśoka's impact on, 1091, 6112
Buddha as part of, 1196
the Buddha on, 5347, 8073
buildings of, 9042–9043, 9045–9049
celebrating foundation of, 1306
celibacy in, 1477
Chan masters in, 1523
in China, 1162, 1163, 1164, 1165
in colonial era, 7263
council of Rājagṛha establishing, 1108
democratic character of, 7261
division of *(saṃgha bheda),* 8073
engaged Buddhism and, 2786
expulsion from, 8015
forest dwellers and millennial Buddhism in, 8080–8081
and formation of schools, 1193
hierarchy and socio-political structure in, 8073, 8078, 8085
historical and philosophical background of, 8076
history of, 8073–8074
in Mahāyāna Buddhism, 8075
International Buddhist movement and, 8075
in Khmer religion, 5131, 5132
lands and properties held by, 8077, 8084
life of monks in, 8073
Mahīśasaka school on, 1110
mappō and, 5686, 5687
merit in
making of, 5873
transference of, 5874
as model of Buddhist state, 7261
Moggaliputtatissa's influence on, 6112
moral development in, 1279
nature and, 2629–2630
nuns in, 8073
overview, **8071–8076**
priest role in, 8081–8082
procedures in laws of, 8072–8073
purges of, 8079
as refuge, 7409
ruins of, 1106
rules of, 1106, 1258, 1260
in laws, 8072–8073
Prātimokṣa, 1105–1106, 1107, 1258, 1259, 1306
source of, 8071–8072
and self, Buddhist notion of, 8076
in Sikhism, 4425
social classes represented in, 1105
societal influence of, 8463
in South and Southeast Asia, **8076–8081**
economic life of, 8076–8077
in Theravāda Buddhism, 8074–8075
political authority and, 8077–8079
sectarianism and, 8079–8080
in Southeast Asia, 1133–1142
on spirits, 1329
status levels in, 1864
stupas erected by, 8797, 9041–9042
suppression of, 7268
in Taiwan, 8962
in Tendai school, 9078–9079
term, meaning of, 8071, 8076
in Tibet, 1151, 1153, 6940, **8081–8086**
history of, 8082–8083
institutional structures and economic life, 8084–8085
monastic institution, 8083–8084
sectarian developments in, 8083
Saṃghabhadra (Buddhist scholar), 1201, 9526
Saṃghabheda (schism), 1193

Saṃghamittā (Buddhist nun), 2313–2314
Moggaliputtatissa and, 6112
Saṃgītiparyāya (Buddhist text), 10021
Saṃgīti Sūtra (Buddhist text), 10021
Samguk sagi (Historical record of the Three Kingdoms), Confucianism and, 1929–1930
Samguk yusa (Korean book of folklore), 5229–5230
Samhain
Aillén mac Midgna at, 1492
celebration of, 2230
in Celtic calendar, 1491
Halloween, **3758–3759**
Neopagan rituals for, 7829
in Wicca, 9731
Saṃhāra (reabsorption), in Śaivism, 8416–8417
Saṃhitās, 1026, 7405
in Vaiṣṇavism, 9501
Pāñcarātra thought in, 9507–9508
sacrality of, 8201
Vaikhānasa, 9496
Vaiṣṇava Tantras as, 4019
in Vedic canon, 3989
in Vedic texts, 9553
Sami Folklore Project, founding of, 4123
Sāmīpya (communion), 858
Sami (Lapp) religion and society, 3103, 3106, **8086–8089**
animal-human relations in, 8087
annual cycle and, 3107
Christianity, 8086
culture of, 468, 472
deities of, 8088
development of, 472
drum and singing among, 3110
epic poetry of, 3104
in Icelandic sagas, 8025
idols and holy sites in, 8087
Laestadian Lutheran revivalist movement of, 5283
language and culture of, 8086–8087
mythology of, 5284
sanctuaries of, 3109
soul conceptions and shamanism in, 8087–8088
stone cult in, 470
stones and *seite* cult in, 8746
studies of, 474, 3112
totemic ancestor of, 3107
Samitier, Manuel Llaras, 9030
Saṃkara. *See* Śaṅkara
Saṃkarṣaṇa cult, 9499, 9502
Sāṃkhyakārikā (Iśavarakṛṣṇa), enumeration teachings in, 8092
Sāṃkhyakārikā (Īśvarakṛṣṇa), 7361
Sāṃkhyapravacanabhāṣya (Vijñānabhikṣu), Sāṃkhya teachings in, 8092
Sāṃkhya school of Hinduism, **8089–8093**. *See also* Yoga
Advaita Vedānta *vs.*, 8105
afterlife in, human constitution in, 130
alchemy in, 242
atheism in, 578, 580
avidyā in, 710
bhakti, rejection of, 3997
and classical Hinduism, development of, 3997–3998
cosmology in, 2016, 3997
dualism in, 2508, 4427
guṇas in, 3709, 7361
history of, 8090–8092
in *Bhagavadgītā,* 852, 853
īśvara in, 4752
jīvanmukta and, 4925–4926
jñāna in, 4927–4928
knowledge in, 5200
literature of, 8092
masculine sacrality in, 5762
mysticism in, 6342, 6343, 6344
prakṛti in, 7360
puruṣa in, 7522
salvation in, 527
states of consciousness in, 1950–1951
syncretism in, 8091
teachings of, 8089–8090
unity and plurality in, 4421, 4422
Vijñānabhikṣu in, 9595
vs. Yoga, 9893–9894
Sāṃkhyatattvakaumudī (Vacaspati Misra I), Sāṃkhya teachings in, 8092
Saṃkrānti (transit of the sun), in Hindu calendar, 4015
Sammā ārahang (fullness of spiritual attainment), 2325
Sammānīyah Ṣūfī order, Muḥammad Aḥmad in, 6228
Sammas (statue), 4379
Sammatīya-nikāya-śāstra (Buddhist text), 1200
Sammatīya sect, 1132, 1196
doctrines of, 1196, 1197
expansion of, 1201
geographical distribution of, 1195
origin of, 1194
in "Personalist Controversy," 1297
Samnak Pū Sawan (Center of the Heavenly Ancients), 9097
Saṃnyāsa (renunciation), 4421, 4441–4442, 7195, **8093–8095,** 9630. *See also* Āśramas
Brahmanism and renunciation, 8093
celibacy and, 1476–1477
in *Bhagavadgītā,* 851
initiation in, 8093–8094
in International Society for Krishna Consciousness, 4523
lifestyle and goal of, 2330, 8093
meaning of term, 8093
qualification for, 8094
retired Brahmans in, 8020–8021
ritual and legal effects of, 8094
sadhus/sadhvis and, 8019
Śaṅkara on ten orders of, 4004
suicide and, 8831
Saṃnyāsa Upaniṣads, 9483
Samoa and Samoan religions. *See also* Oceania and Oceanic religions
Christianity, traditional culture merged with, 7297
comets in, 8736
cosmology in, 7305
marriage in, 5727
music in, 6263–6264
origin myths of, 7314
rituals in, 7310
Siovili movement in, 6795
Siovili of Eva as prophet in, 2007
Tangaroa in, 8980
tattooing in, 7807–7808
Samoilă, Cornel, 3467
Samojedische Sprachmaterialien (Lehtisalo), 1453
Samos (island)
Hera cult on, 3915
Melqart in, 5848
Samothrace, mystery religions of, 7756
Samoury Toure, 4606
Samoyed languages, 3105, 6745
Samoyed religion, **8095–8097**. *See also* Shamanism; Siberia and Siberian religions
animals in, 8096
birds, 948
reindeer, 8095
Castrén (Matthias) on, 1453
Christianity in, 8097
deities in, supreme, 469, **6745,** 8095
domestic spirits *(haha)* in, 4106
Donner's (Kai) study of, 2421
outside influences, 8097
rituals in, 8095–8096
sacrifices in, 470
shamanism in, 470
categories of, 8282
headdress in, 8285
initiation in, 1470, 8271
shamanhood in, 8096–8097
small-group shamans in, 8281
spirit world in, 8095
Sampley, Paul J., 7015
Sampo (support of the world), 4379
Sampradāya, 5251, 5252
as cult-based community, 7719
Samprajñāta samādhi (enstasis with support), 9896
Sampratti (Saṃpradāna) (rite of transmission), 7815–7816
Saṃsāra (cycle of rebirth), **8097–8099**. *See also* Punarjanman; Reincarnation; Transmigration
animals in, 359
Buddhist, 2627–2628, 4428
Buddhadāsa on, 1072
cause and effect in, 5448
healing and, 3866
heavens and hells and, 3886–3887
in Mahāyāna Buddhism, 1207, 1209, 1210, 1299
King's (Winston L.) definition of, 5401
morality and release from, 1280, 5448
Nāgārjuna on, 6393
nirvāṇa as release from, 6628
philosophy of, 1297
self-consciousness or soul and, 8551–8553
in Tantric Buddhism, practices to overcome, 8016
tathatā and, 9019
theories of, 8098
in Tibetan Buddhism, 1155, 3866
transition to *nirvāṇa,* 6629
fires in, 3116–3117
Hindu, 7676, 7677–7678
Brahmanic concept of redeath as precursor to, 3992
and ethics, 4428
in *Bhagavadgītā,* 853, 7677–7678
introduced in Upaniṣads, 3993
in Upaniṣads, 3886, 7677, 9327–9328
Jñānayoga and, 5200
mythic themes of, 4440
overview of, 8098
and play, 7195
Saṃnyāsa and, 8094
snake as symbol of, 4437
termination of, 5447
Jain theories of, 8098
karman linked to, 2963
liberation from
jīvanmukti and, 4925
karman and, 5099
karuṇā and, 5105
origins of theory, 8098
Pure Land as beyond, 1600, 8982
release from (*See Mokṣa*)
soul and, 8544
suffering in, 9119
taṅhā and, 7678
Saṃskāras (life-cycle rites), 3117, 7814–7816, 9822
of adolescence, 7814–7815
childhood, 7814
definition of, 7814
in devotional life, 9822
for *śūdras,* 7817
funeral, 7815–7816
in Gṛhyasūtras, 3991, 8884
marriage, 7814
prenatal, 7814
as sacraments of transition, 7956

Saṃskṛta (conditioned *dharma*), 2333–2335, 7357
Saṃśleṣa (union), 859
Samson (biblical figure), **8099**
Samsuiluna (Babylonian ruler), 5948
Samudaya (uprising), in Four Noble Truths, 1296, 3178, 3179
Samuel, 879, 882
Temple procedures in, 928, 929
1 Samuel
Astarte in, 7103
authorship of, 8099
Dagon in, 7103
David in, 2221–2222, 7461
exorcism in, 2931
ghosts in, 3475
kingship in, 4732
on pilgrimage, 934
politics in, 10062
prayer of Hannah in, 7460, 7464
priests in, 5420–5421
Samuel as *ro'eh* (seer) in, 7431
Saul in, 8131
2 Samuel
criminal law in, 4738
David in, 2222, 7461
kingship in, 1399, 1400
pesher of, 7064
sanctity of Jerusalem in, 933
tears in, 9026
Temple in David's honor in, 932
temptation in, 9070
thanksgiving song in, 7461
Samuel (Hebrew prophet), **8099–8100**
Levites and, 5420–5421
on obedience, 2955
prophetic activities of, 7436
Samuel, Geoffrey, 9191, 9837
Samuel, Moses ben, writings of, 5085
Samuel the Amora. *See* Shemu'el the Amora
Samurai
homosexuality among, 4114
preparation for death by, 2244
in Zen Buddhism, 7272–7273
Saṃvara (warding off), in Jainism, 4768
Saṃvartānis (destructions), in Hinayana Buddhist cosmology, 2028
Saṃvṛtti (conventional reality), 1206, 1210, 1274, 5309
Saṃyama (yogic practice), 9895–9896
miracles in, 6052
Samya Shakti (journal), 3322
Samyé. *See* Bsam yas monastery (Tibet)
Saṃyukta Piṭaka (Buddhist text), in Mahāsāṃghika Buddhism, 5601
Saṃyutta Nikāya (Buddhist text)
great commission in, 6077
on hearing word *buddha,* 1062
Lokāyata view described in, 1446
Māra in, 5690
natural law in, 2332
previous buddhas in, 1066
on spiritual guides, 8712
Śān (deity). *See* Kalteś
San (religion). *See* Khoi and San religion
San, Saya, 1141
Sanā'ī
on ascension, 523–524
mathnavī poetry of, 8817
Ṣanam (idol), 4361–4362
Ṣan'āni, 'Abd al-Razzāq al-, on afterlife, 160
Sanapaná people (Paraguay), religion of, 8635
Sanātana, theological works by, 1346
Sanātana dharma (eternal *dharma),* 2328, 2331
Sanbat (sabbath), of Bēta Esra'ēl, 5003
Sánchez, Miguel, 5921
Sanchuniathon, 1451
on Phoenician religion, 7131
Sancti (holy persons). *See also* Saint(s)
emergence of, 2081
Sanctification. *See also* Blessing; Grace; Justification
in Orthodox theology, 2590–2591
Sanctorale (Proper of Saints), 1741
"Sanctorum Communio" (Bonhoeffer), 1017
Sanctuaries, **8100–8101**. *See also* Shrines; Temples
architecture of, classification of, 461
Baltic (*See* Baltic sanctuaries)
of Demeter Eleusinia cults, 2751
as *domus dei* (house of god), 8100
as *domus ecclesiae* (house of the gathered assembly), 8101
Finno-Ugric, 3109
Greek, functions of, 3683
in Iberian religion, 4250–4251, 4253
in Amhara-Tigriña services, 2573
in Judaism *(miqdash), shekhinah* concept and, 8313
meaning of term, 8100
in Mesoamerican religions, in Huichol religion, 4152
Moabite, 6094
Nabatean, 6387–6388
Neopagan, 6472
prehistoric, 7379–7381, 7382, 7383
as refuge or asylum, 8101
rituals in, 4251–4252
Sanctuary doctrine (Adventist)
Edson (Hiram) on, 8235
Ford (Desmond) on, 8237
Sanctus, meanings of, 7966, 7970
Sandae (play), 2454, 2455
humor in, 4209
Sandawe people (Tanzania), dances of, 2137
Sanday, Peggy Reeves, 3313
on gender, nature and, 3421–3422
on ritual cannibalism, 8009
Sand County Almanac, A (Leopold), 2609
Sandella, Domenico, 7327
Sanders, Alex, 9729
Sanders, Cheryl, 75
Sanders, E. P., 431
Sanders, Jānis, 763
Sande society, 4303
Sandhinirmocana Sūtra (Buddhist text), 1300
Sandhyā-bhāṣā (coded language), 1216, 8992
in *Hevajra Tantra,* 3965
Sand maṇḍala, vol. 11 color insert
Sandmel, Samuel, 3637, 7014
Sandon. *See* Santas/Sandon
Sandong. See Three Caverns
Sandong zhunang (Wang Xuanhe), 5319
Sandpaintings
Australian Indigenous, 640
North American Indian, 4308, vol. 3 color insert
Sandstrom, Alan, 5925, 5927, 5929
Sandys, Edwin, Hooker (Richard) and, 4123, 4124
Sanenaga, Nambu, 6620
Sanford, Charles L., 6985
Sangari, Kumkum, 3321–3322
Sangat (sacred gathering), in Sikhism, 8393
Sangdong jingshu mulu (Daoist text), 2202
Sangdong qionggang (Daoist text), 2202
Sangdong zhunang (Daoist text), 2210
Sangh, Rashtriya Swayamsevak, on Hinduness, 1858
Sangha. See Saṃgha
Sanghamittā (daughter of Aśoka), 9146
Sangharāja (monastic head), 9149
Sangiang Serri (deity), 1317
Saṅgīti Suttanta (Buddhist text)
dharma in, 2333
mātṛkā in, 1270
Ṣango (deity), 4303
dances devoted to, 2137
in Edo religion, 2697
gender of worshipers of, 3403, 10027
as Shango, in Caribbean religions, 1434–1435
studies on, 10028–10029
wives of, 7862
in Yoruba pantheon, 9911
Sangoku buppō denzū engi (Gyōnen), 1246
Sang phu ne'u thog (Sangphu Neutok) monastic college, Klong chen Rab 'byams pa (Longchenpa) at, 5192
Sangs rgyas Rgya mtsho (Tibetan regent), medicine and, 3865
San Guan (three controllers), 1642
Sangul-san lineage, 1646
Sanhedrin, 7666, **8101–8104**
after 70 CE, 8103
condemning Jesus, 972
historical evidence on, 8101–8103
Me'ir in, 5830
proposed reconstitution of, 3754
in Second Temple, 925, 933
Sanhedrin (Mishnah tractate), resurrection in, 7765
San Huang (three sage-kings), 1627, 1642
Sanhuang scriptures (Daoist), 2195, 2203
Sanin, Ivan. *See* Joseph of Volokolamsk
Sanjaya (Mataram) kingdom, Hinduism in, 4011
Sanjie Jiao (Sect of the Three Stages), 1576, 5255, 9859
San José de la Paz, María Antonia, 7772
San Juan River, 7862
Śaṅkara (Hindu philosopher), **8104–8106**. *See also* Advaita Vedānta
on asceticism, 527
on atheism, 580–581
on *brahman,* 4422, 6144
on caste and life stages theory, 4004
on *dharma,* 9373
Gauḍapāda and, 3289–3290
idealism of, 4430
on images veneration, 4380, 4384
life of, 8104–8105
on magic, 5590
monism of, 6144, 6149, 6964
and mysticism, 6343
on *avidyā,* 710
on *Bhagavadgītā,* 852, 853, 854
on *gurūs,* 3714
on *māyā,* 5794, 5795
on *mokṣa,* 6116
on Upaniṣads, 6144

Śaṅkara (Hindu philosopher) *continued*
philosophy of, 8105–8106
pilgrimage of, 7170
poetry of, 7209
Ramakrishna on, 7613
rope and snake analogy of, 8105–8106
as saint, 8036
Śiva, devotion to, 8042
smārta orthodoxy revived in Advaita Vedānta by, 4003–4004
Smārtas and, 9503, 9572–9573
Vedānta of, 9545–9547
vs. Nimbārka, 6623
works attributed to, 8105
Śaṅkaracārya. *See* Śaṅkara
Ṣaṅkaradeva (poet), 7211
Sanlun (Three Treatises) school. *See also* Mādhyamika Buddhism
emptiness *(śūnyatā)* in, 8859
Kumārajīvi as founder of, 5262
level of truth in, 1576
Sengzhao and, 8228
Sanmon branch, 2781–2782, 2801
Ṣaṇṇagarika school of Buddhism, origin of, 1194
Sannazaro, Jacopo, 3627–3628
Sannō (mountain king), 9078
Sannō Shintō, 4784
Hiei Tendai and, 8361–8362
and Tokugawa Ieyasu, burial of, 8363
Sannyāsa (renouncer), 4421
Prabhupada as, 7355
Sannyasins (disciples of Osho), 7608
San Pedro, Fray Juan de, on Catequil, 8608
San Pedro cactus, mescaline hallucinogen in, shamanism and, 8292
San people (Kalahari Desert), New Year ceremonies of, 6590
Sanpoli Indians. *See* Salish tribes
San Qing (Three Pure Ones), 4916
San religion. *See* Khoi and San religion
Sanro (sacred places), 1316, 1317
Sanron sect (Buddhist), 1242
Sanskritization, 4448
spread of Hinduism through, 6070
Sanskrit language
Balinese use of, 746
Bengali use of, 824
Buddhist chanting in, 6301
Buddhist writings in, 1265–1267
adaptation of, 1199
by Nāgārjuna, 6393
Chinese translations of, 1110, 1147
hybrid, 1198, 1200
Mahāyāna Buddhism, 1205, 1253
used by Sarvāstivāda school, 1110, 1146
Caitanya stanzas, 1346
grammar of, 7005
and "holy," concept of, 7968
in Śrī Vaiṣṇavas Sampradāya, 8727, 8728
Khmer use of, 5128
mantras in, 5677
oṃ, 6820–6821
power of words in, 2099
as sacred Buddhist language, 1093, 5303
Schlegel (Friedrich) on, 8159
Southeast Asia, Sanskrit inscriptions in, 4010
study of, 4458
Renou (Louis) and, 7753–7754
in Tantras, "intentional language" in, 8240
terms referring to pain in, 6944
translation of, 8203, 10076
word for devotion/love (*See Bhakti*)
word for peace, 7022
Sanskrit literature, 5467
in Cambodia, 5128
drama, 2436, 2447–2448
fate in, 3001
in Japan, Nanjō Bunyū's studies of, 6414
poetry, 7209
vernacular Hindi adaptations of, 3984
Sansom, Basil, 668
Sansovino, Jacopo, 377
Santa Clara Catholic Convent (Cuzco), 3417
Santa Claus, 1757
Santa Cruz, Juan de, on Inca calendar, 1361
Santa Fe, New Mexico, 1517
Santa Maria della Vittoria, Church of (Rome), Cornaro Chapel of, vol. 11 color insert
Santa Maria Maggiora, Church of, Christmas mass in, 1757
Santāna ācāryas (hereditary teachers), 9443
Santānāntarasiddhi (Dharmakīrti), 2336
Santa Prisca Mithraeum (Rome), 6091
Śāntarakṣita (Buddhist monk), **8106–8107**
Bsam yas monastery established by, 1152, 8082
and debate at Bsam yas, 5069–5070, 6940
Kamalaśīla as disciple of, 1300, 5069
on Mādhyamika Buddhism, 1213, 1223, 5555
and Tibetan canon, 1256
writings of, 5070
Santarasa, 51
Santas/Sandon (deity), Herakles identified with, 3917
Santayana, George
aesthetics of, 48–49
on humor, 4219
on knowledge, 5207
Sant bhāṣā (saint language), in *Ādi Granth,* 32
Santee Dakota tribe (North America), ballgame played by, 753
Santería, **8107–8109**
Catholic saints and Yoruba spirits in, 8107–8108
creolization and, 2066–2067
in Cuba, 9305–9306
devotion in, 8108
food symbolism and ritual in, 3171
Ifa divination in, 8108
life in, 5449
meaning of term, 8108
media coverage of, 4964–4965
orishas (spirit-saints) in, 8107–8108, vol. 9 color insert
overview of, 1434
petitions in, vol. 9 color insert
sacred objects in, vol. 4 color insert
Santiago Atitlán (Guatemala), Maximón in, 5790–5792, 5926–5927
Śāntideva (Buddhist monk), 2630, **8109–8110**
on *bodhisattvas,* 999, 1084, 1119, 1281
on Four Noble Truths, 3179
and mysticism, 6344
on *pūjā,* 7497
on rituals, 1118
on wisdom, 1300
writings of, 999, 1084, 1119, 2322, 5554, 7211–7212
Śāntiḥ (peace), 7022
Santillán, Hernando de
on *huacas,* 8607–8608
on Topa Inca Yupanqui, 8607
Śāntiniketan Ashram, 546
Śantirakṣita (Buddhist scholar), 1120, 7167
in Mādhyamaka Buddhism, 5554
Lhasa council, views defended at, 2038
writings of, 5554
Śānti senā (peace brigade), 861
Sant Mat, Twitchell (Paul) influenced by, 2602
Santo Daime (South America), 6274
Santos (Portuguese author), 112
Santos, Boaventura De Sousa, 5364
Santoṣī Mā (deity), 3609
Sant tradition (Hindi)
bhakti poetry in, 3984, 3985
Nāth order and, 3987
Sanūsi, al-, 9011
kalām of, 5067
Sanusi of Cyrenaica, The (Evans-Pritchard), 2896
Sanūsīyah (Ṣūfī order), 2896, 9011
colonial politics and, 8824
founder of, 9011
initiation into, 9011
zāwiyahs of, 5118
Sanvitores, Diego Luis de, 6009
Sanzunokawa (river), 7863
Saoshyants ("redeemers"), **8110–8111**
days of *Gāthās* and, 1355
Maitreya compared to, 5619
in resurrection of bodies, 131, 7764
Sapan (Tsafon, Zaphon), Mount
Baal of, 1383, 1394
Il of, 1382
Sapay Inca (king)
as center of Inca society, 5176
death of, 5176–5177
Sapientia sinica ("wisdom of the Chinese"), 1918
Sapiṇḍīkaraṇa (funeral rite), 7815
Sapir, Edward, 6671
Sappho
on Adonis, 35
on Eros, 2833
Saptaalaṃkāra (preparations), 1275
Saptāṅgapūjā (Seven-Part Worship), 7496–7497
Saptapadi ceremony, 5726
Śarabha (beast), 4438
Saraca. *See* Big Drum Dance
Sāradā (wife of Ramakrishna), 7611, 7612
Śārāda Devi, **8111–8112**
Sarah (biblical figure), 897, **8112**
burial of, 15
doublets regarding, 14
laughter of, 4196
Sarah (solitary), 2825
Saraha, on *mahāmudrā,* 5597
Sarah Lawrence College, Campbell (Joseph) at, 1378
Sarai, name changed to Sarah, 15
Sarakhsī, al-, 2972
Sāramati, 1120
Sārameya (twin dogs), 2393
Śaraṇātigadya (Rāmānuja), 7615
Saraṇyū (deity), Vivasvant and, 4133
Sarapis (deity). *See also* Serapis cult
Dieterich (Albrecht) on, 2348
identified with Zeus and Helios, 3908
Isis and, 4559
miracles of, 6051, 6052
Osiris as, 6921–6922
Sarason, Richard, 6020
Sarasvanti, Bhaktisiddhanta. *See* Datta, Bimalprasad
Sarasvatī (deity), 1079, 3019, **8112–8113**
Anāhitā compared with, 305
as Brahmā's consort, 4326
Bengali worship of, 826
books on, 746
in Buddhism, 8113

as consort, 8113
cult of, 8113
in Navarātri festival, 6444
in Jainism, 3327, 8113
Mañjuśrī linked with, 1077
music and, 6280
mythic associations, 8113
nature and, 2620
as nurturing goddess, 3607
portrayal of, 8113
Sarasvatī (river), 7861, 7862
Saratcandra Chatterjee, 829
Sarawak Kaya people, 1003
Sarcophagus, Etruscan, vol. 4 color insert
Sardar Sarovar dam project (India), BAPS movement and, 8890
Sardinia, deities of, Eshmun, 2842
Sardis synagogue, 8924
Ṣarfah (turning away), 4371
Sargeson, Frank, 3085
Sargonic period, Dagan in, 2126
Sargonid dynasty
Ashur in, 548–549
religious obligations of kings in, 7276
Sargon II (king of Assyria), 28
Ashur and, 548
Sargon of Akkad (Mesopotamian ruler), 34, 2597
daughter of, 3377
reign of, 5948
urbanization and power of, 1803
women under, 3376, 3377
Sar ha-Ḥokhmah, 10050, 10052
Ṣarīḥ al-sunnah (al-Ṭabarī), 8944
Sarin gas attacks, by Aum Shinrikyō, 632
Śariputra (Buddha's disciple)
in Buddha biography, 1063
Buddhist texts by, 1270
on *dharma,* 1298
as master of wisdom, 1104–1105
on women, 3331–3332
Śāriputra-abhidharma (Buddhist text), 1198
Sāriputta (Buddhist monk), 1200, 9149
Śarīra (relics), 4383
Śarīra-śarīri-bhāva doctrine, of Rāmānuja, 7615
Sarita (sacred textile), 9090
Sarit Thanarat (Thai prime minister), 9096
Sárközi, Alice, 6142
Sarmatian religion, **8114–8115**
Sarmizegetusa Regia, calendar temple at, in Geto-Dacian religion, 3467
Sarnath (India), 778
Śārṅgadhara, on Āyurveda, 3853
Sarov monastery (Russia), Serafim of Sarov and, 8229
Sarrāj, al-, on mystical union, 6338
Sarris, Greg, 3090
Grand Avenue: A Novel in Stories, 3092–3093
Sar-Torah, 10050, 10051–10052
Sartre, Jean Paul, 2475, **8116–8117**
atheism of, 7422
on colonialism, 1857
in existentialism, 2925–2927
on human beings, 7117
Sarug, Yisra'el, and Qabbalah, 7535
Sārūpya (communion), 858
Saruta Biko (deity), 6152
Sarvadarśanasamuccaya (Mādhava), 1295
Sarva Dharma Stupa, universalism and, 8028
Sarvagāmin (monk), Vaiśālī council and, 2036
Sarvam asti ("everything exists") doctrine, Sarvāstivādin theory of time and, 8118
Sarva Seva Sangha, 861, 862
Sarvāstivāda school of Buddhism, 1092, 1298, **8117–8122**
Abhidharma Piṭaka in, 8118, 10020, 10021, 10022
and Mahāyāna Buddhism, 1113, 8120
arhat vs. nirvāṇa in, 2029
as Hīnayāna, 8120
bodhisattvas in, 999, 8119
canon of, 1110, 8117–8118
in Central Asia, 1146
dharmakāya in, 1069
dharma theory of, 2333–2335, 8118
doctrines of, 1196, 1197, 5554
eightfold path of, 2739
expansion of, 1201
historical development of, 8117
Kaniṣka council and, 2037
karman in, 5099–5100, 8118–8119
knowledge in, 5554
literature of, 1198, 1199, 1200
meaning of term, 8117
monasteries, distribution of, 8119
notable personalities of, 1201
ordination lineage established, 2038
origin of, 1108, 1194
Pāṭaliputra council and, 2037
Sanskrit language used by, 1110, 1146
sectarian outgrowths of, 8119–8120
in Southeast Asia, 1132
time and *sarvam asti* ("everything exists") in, 8118
Vasubandhu and, 9526
Sarvatathāgata-Tattvasamgraha Sūtra, 9961
in Shingon Buddhism, 8348, 8349, 8351
Sarvatobhadra Maṇḍala, 5641
Sarvodaya movement, 861–862
as Gandhi's (Mohandas) legacy, 3273
Sarvodaya Shramadana, 2686, 2689
Sarx (body), 9070, 9073
spirit *vs.,* 8562, 8563
Śaryāti (mythic figure), 5679
Sasak tribe (Indonesia), 9088
Sasana, 1134, 1140
Sasanid period (Iran)
Airyana Vaējah in, 210
Anāhitā in, 305
angels in, 344
Christensen on, 1649
festivals during, 6731
fire in, 569
kingship in, 5165
magi in, 5560
Mandaean religion in, 5639
Mani in, 5649, 5651, 5655, 5659–5660
Mazdakism in, 5800–5801
Nestorian Church in, 6479
rams in art of, 8311
Sahak Parthev removed in, 8026
world-period system in, 174
Zoroastrianism in, 10002
redemption in, 7641
Śaśīṅka (Bengali king), 1125
Sa skya Paṇḍita (Sakya Paṇḍita), 1154, 1225, 1230
on *mahāmudrā,* 5599
Sa skya pa order (Buddhist), 1224–1225, 1228, 1230
Hevajra Tantra in, 3966
inception as monastic order, 8051
monasticism and, 8082
Sakya Paṇḍita, role of, 8051
Tantrism in, 8083
Sasquatch (Bigfoot), 6166
Sassanid dynasty. *See* Sasanid period
Sassataditthiyo (eternalist views), 1446
Sassetti, Filippo, 4458
Sasso, Sandy Eisenberg (rabbi), 7582, 7637
Sassoon, Elias, 5008
Ṣaṣṭī (deity)
Bengali worship of, 826
cats and, 1462
Ṣaṣṭitantra (Hindu text), Sāṃkhya Hinduism and, 8091
Śāstṛ (teacher), 1060
Śāstra literature, 1204, 1271, **8122–8123,** 9527
animals in, 6959–6960
lesbianism in, 5415
meaning of term, 8122
Śiva in, 8043
Stcherbatsky (Theodore) on, 8737
Sastri, Hariprasad, 825
Śāstrīyabhāṣya (sacred speech), 7005
SAT-7 (Middle Eastern television station), 7713
Satan, **8123–8126**
and atonement, classical theories of, 596
in Catharism, 1456–1457
characteristics of, 8124
as chief of demons, 2277, 2314
in Christianity, 8124, 8125
defeat of, 9454
Hell presided over by, 3884
Servetus (Michael) on, 8232
in witchcraft, 9770
diabolical pact theory, Inquisition and, 8865
dogs associated with, 2393
dragon as, 2432
in emergence myths, 1988
as fallen angel, 2314
as father of Cain, in two-seed theory, 1658
in Gnosticism, 3525, 8125
Greek concept of, 8124
Heaven's Gate view of, 3890, 3891
in Islam, 2280, 2314–2315, 4564, 8124, 8125–8126 (*See also* Iblīs)
in Jehovah's Witnesses theology, 4822
as Jesus' brother, 9415
as Jesus' personal adversary, 2278
in Judeo-Christian tradition, 8123–8125
Luther (Martin) on, 5150
music invented by, 6277
in New Testament, 2278, 2314
origin of name, 8123
pacts with, 9771–9772
possession by, in Revival Zion (Jamaica), 1437
as serpent or snake, 8125
shape shifting and, 8301
in Sufism
al-Ḥallāj on, 3757, 8813
worship of, 8125
temptation by, 2278, 8125, 9071–9072
vs. Ha-śātān, 4931
in witchcraft, 9770–9771
witches seeking encounters with, 2279
worship of (*See* Satanism)
in Zoroastrianism, 9995
Śātān, ha- (the Adversary), in *Job,* 4931
Satanael (angel), 3523, 3524

Satanic Bible, The (LaVey), 6530, 6531
iconoclastic philosophy in, 8127
influence of, 8128
Satanic panics, 9775
Satanic Verses, The (Rushdie), 433–434, 3528, 10036
Satanism, **8126–8129**. *See also* Diabolical witchcraft
accusations of, 9598, 9775
Black Masses and, 8250
Christian accusations of, *osculum infame* (kiss of infamy) and, 8013
Church of Satan, 8126–8127
cults of, 1034, 2280
and the Satanism scare, 8127–8128
depiction in novels, 3062
divination viewed as, 2373
medieval fear of, 8126
modern expressions of, 9775
scriptural text of, 6530
sexual magic in, 8250–8252
study of, 6524
Temple of Set and, 8127
and violence, accusations of, 6564
Śatapatha Brāhmaṇa
ascension to upper world in, 1504
Kurukṣetra in, 5268
Mani in, 5678, 5679
money in, 6137
ritual system in, 3991
sacred space in, 7979
story of the Flood in, 2963–2964
suicide in, 8831
utterances in, 5677
women in, as earth mother, 2558
Śatapatha Brāhmana ritual, 9506
Śatarudriya hymn, Rudra-Śiva in, 8415
Śātavāhana dynasty (India), 1092
Ṣaṭ-cakra-nirūpaṇa, list of cakras in, 1348
Sathya Sai Baba
children in, 6543
in Europe, 6568
Sai Baba movement and, 8026, 8027–8029
Satī (deity), 9906
self-immolation of, 7170
Sati (immolation of widows), Vivekananda on, 10091
Sati (widow burning), 2242–2243, **8129–8131**
abolition of, 2330, 7933
colonialism and, 3320, 3321
as heroic suicide, 8827
in Hinduism, 8129–8130
chastity and, 1559
reform of, 3320, 7654–7655
resistance against, 8130
sahamaraṇa and *anumaraṇa* forms of, 8831
Satire. *See also* Humor
by and of religions, 4200
in Vodou, 9637
Satkāyadṛṣṭi (personality belief), rebirth and, 8552
Satmar Hasidism, **3793–3794**
Satō Norio
Konkōkyō and, 5225
Shintō and, 8367
Satori (enlightenment)
in Buddhism, 7696
Suzuki (D. T.) on, 7741
interactive discipline and, 8702
Sat Panth literature, Nizārīyah movement and, 8334
Saṭ-sandarbha, Gōsvamins and, 1346
Satsaṅg (community), in Swaminarayan movement, 8890, 8891
Satter, Beryl, 6582
Sättler, Franz, Hekate lodge and, 8252
Sattler, Michael, at Anabaptism conference, 305
Sattra (session), 9562–9563
Sattva (dynamic equilibrium), 853, 2305, 3709
Sattva (truth, light), in Sāṃkhya cosmology, 2016
Saturday, as sabbath, 2860
Saturn (deity)
in Berber religion, 834
sickle of, 967
Saturn (planet), deities of, 8428
Saturnalia (festival), 6864–6865, 7909
Carnival and, 1440
Saturninus
on asceticism, 8247
myth of, 3509, 3515–3516
Sātvatas (Vṛṣṇi), 9507
Satya (truth), Gandhi (Mohandas) on, 3272
Satyāgrahā (truth insistence), 861, 4425, 7023, 7257, 9072
Satyāgraha Ashram, 546
Satya Pīr (Hindu-Muslim figure), 829
Muslim/Hindu veneration of, 3162
Satyasiddhi Śāstra (Buddhist text), 1200, 1201, 1202
Kumārajīva's translation of, 5263
Satyricon (Petronius), 3051
Saudi Arabia. *See also* Arabia and Arabian religions
Ḥanābilah in, 4698, 4703
Muslim Brotherhood in, 6316
Wahhābīyah in, 6100
Sauk religion (North America)
bears in, 809
hunting rituals of, 6682
Medicine rite of, 6681
totemism in, 9252
Saul. *See* Paul the Apostle
Saul (biblical figure), **8131**
David and, 2222, 7436
as king, selection of, 6847
al-Maghribī (Samuel) on, 7239
possession of, 2931
priests and, 5421
Samuel and, 8099–8100
Saule (deity), **8131–8135**
and Pērkons, 758
as bride, 760
cult of, 759
descriptions of, 758
gender of, 758
in Latvian folklore texts, 769
twin daughters of, 9419
vs. Sūrya, 758, 760
Saules dainas (Latvian folk-song collection), sun worship in, 8132–8133
Saules koks (tree of sun), 759, 1502
Saules māte (mother sun), 758
Saules meita (daughter of sun), 758, 760
Saul of Tarsus. *See* Paul the Apostle
Saulteaux. *See* Anishinaabe religious traditions
Saumaise, Claude de (Claudius Salmasius), 3050
Sauna(s), 800–803
in Baltic religion, 760
building, 802
childbirth in, 802
core of, 801
in Finland, 800–803
in funeral rites, 803
as sacred place, 801–802
spirit of, 802, 803
in United States, 801
Saunahaltija (spirit of sauna), 802
Saunatonttu (spirit of sauna), 802
Saundaryalaharī (Śaṅkara), 7209
Saunders, Kay, 3392
Saura Hinduism, **8135–8136**
shamanism in, 8273
Sauromatians, Sarmatians and, 8114, 8115
Saurva (deity), as archdemon, 2128
Saussure, Ferdinand de, 741
critical analysis of work of, 8758
on film as religion, 3101
and French feminists, 3028
metaphysics of, 5991
structuralist thesis of language of, 2245
structural linguistics of, 8750, 8751
symbol theory and, 8913
Sautrāmaṇī (sacrifice), 9564
Sautrāntika school of Buddhism, **8136–8139**
dharma in, 2335, 8137
doctrines of, 1196, 1197, 5554–5555, 8137–8138
language in, 5308
notable personalities of, 1201
origin of, 1194, 8136
Sarvāstivāda and, 8119–8120
subtle thought *(sūkṣmacitta)* in, 8138
Vaibhāṣika school criticized by, 1206
Vasubandhu and, 9526, 9899–9900
Savage Mind, The (Lévi-Strauss), 9252
Savanna (Africa), Islam in, 4603–4604
Savanna Deer ceremony, 3294
Saverskii, Fedor, 5710
Säve-Söderbergh, Torgny, 5635, 5638
Savigny, Friedrich C., 3188
Savigny, Friedrich Karl von, 730
Saviors. *See also* Soteriology
afterlife and, 133
in Zoroastrianism, Saoshyants as, **8110–8111**
Savism, *vāmācāra* (left-handed conduct) in, 8015
Savitṛ (deity), 4509
as sun, 8839
in Vedic pantheon, 3990
Savonarola, Girolamo, **8139–8140**
against materialism, 4286
Pico della Mirandola influenced by, 7141
Savoy Declaration (Congregationalist, 1658), authority of, 2055
Saw, 967
Sawara (Japanese prince), as ghost, 3477–3478
Sawérigading (Bugis hero), 1317
Ṣawm (fasting), 4682, **8140–8141**
at Ramaḍān, 8140–8141
in devotional life, 9816
Sawyerr, Harry, on Ngewo, 3570
Sax, William S., 3323
Saxian (musical instrument), 6295
Saxl, Fritz, 9690–9691
Saxnote (deity), 3451
Saxo Grammaticus, **8141–8142**
on afterlife, 167
on Baldr, 744
on Finns, two types of, 3103
myths transcribed by, 4462
on Perun, 7062
on Sventovit cult, 8888–8889
Saxon Wica, 9730
Saya San, 6547
Sayce, A. H., 5968
Sayed, Daoud Abdel, 3098
Sayers, Dorothy, **8142–8143**
Sayings of Light and Love (John of the Cross), 2309
Sayings of the Fathers, Cassian in, 1447
"Sayings of the Lord," canon and, 1406
Sayles, John, 3099
Sayri Tupac (Inca ruler), 567
Sayr wa sulūk (Ṭūsī), 9408
Sāyujya (communion), 858
Sayyid (lord), 4588, 4643
Sbas don (Tsong kha pa), 1218–1219
Scaevola, Mucius, 3094, 7913
on *pontifex,* 7319
Scale disease, and pollution, 7511, 7513

Scales
in Greek music, 6303
in Japanese Buddhist music, 6302
Scandella, Domenico, 4501
Scandinavia and Scandinavian religions. *See also* Eddas; Eddic religion; Germanic religion; Sami (Lapp) religion; *specific countries*
Christianity in, 6814–6815
historiography in, 4041, 4047
Islam in, 4675
Jewish studies in, 4884
jöntar in, 4959–4960
libations in, 5343
Loki in, 5507–5510
Myth and Ritual school in, 6380, 6381–6382
open-air folklife museum in, 2145
Pentecostalism in, 7029
Protestantism in, Pietism in, 7143
rejuvenation myths in, 7684
royalty in, Óðinn and, 6808
runic inscriptions in, 7941
study of religion in, 10078, 10081
Transcendental Meditation in, 9290
Scapegoat, **8143–8146**
Christian understanding of, 8145
confession and, 1888
in Eblaite royal succession, 2598
expulsion as, 2939
Girard (René) on, 8145
Greek understanding of, 8143–8144
in Hebrew scriptures, 8311
in hero myths, 3960
Jesus as, 8005
Jewish understanding of, 8144–8145
king as, 5158, 5159
in North American Indian religions, Zuni priests as, 2009
in purification, 7509
sacrifice explained by, 8004–8005
as social phenomenon, 8145
witches as, 9773
Scapulimancy, 1015, 2372
Scarabs, 4508
as amulets and talismans, 299, 4508
in Egyptian popular religion, 2713
spells in preparation of, 8676
Scarberry-Garcia, Susan, 3091
Scarification, 1001, 1003. *See also* Bodily marks
in Mesoamerican religions, rites of passage and, 7812
in North American Indian religions, 6652, 6694
Scarlet Letter, The (Hawthorne), 3061
Scarry, Elaine, 6741, 6742, 6947
Scáthach (deity), 1490, 8960
Schacht, Joseph
Islamic studies of, 4717
on Shāfiʿī *madhhab,* 3760
Schachter-Shalomi, Zalman. *See* Eliyyahu ben Shelomoh Zalman
Schaeder, Hans H., 3532
Schaeffer, Claude F.-A., 455
Schafer, E. H., on Chinese women rainmakers, 3338
Schäfer, Peter, 6019, 10050, 10052
Schaff, Philip, on Augustine, 624
Schall, James V., 7246
Schalow, Paul, 5415
Schapiro, Meyer
on art and religion, 500
on Chagall (Marc), 53
Schärer, Hans, 1021
Schebesta, Paul, 114
on Pygmy religions, 7524–7525
Schechner, Richard, 2436, 2439, 7857, 9406
Schechter, Mathilde, National Women's League of the United Synagogue of America and, 1959
Schechter, Solomon, **8146–8147**
Jewish Theological Seminary of America and, 1958–1959, 8146
Scheeben, M. J., 6114
Schefferus, Johannes (Ioannus), 3110, 3112
Scheffler, Harold, on gods in Solomon Islands religions, 8514
Scheftelowitz, Isidor, 937
on binding, 5196
on knots, 5196
Schein, Edgar, 1031
Schele, Linda
on Maya religion, 5886, 5943
on Mesoamerican ballgames, 751
on Mesoamerican funeral rites, 7813
Scheler, Max, **8147–8148,** 9650
on *homo religiosus,* 4109
phenomenology, role in, 4237, 7087, 7089–7090
writings of, 7090
Schelle, Linda, 5943
Schellhas, Paul, 150
Schelling, Friedrich, **8148–8149**
aesthetics of, 47
in art history, 499
on Creuzer (G. F.), 2070
Eckhart (Johannes) and, 2603
Görres (Joseph von) and, 3639
on Henotheism, 3913
Kant (Immanuel) and, 47
in modern Jewish thought, 4901–4902
Müller (F. Max) and, 6234, 6235
on myth, 6366
on nature, 4355, 6435, 6436
Neoplatonism and, 6475
panentheism of, 6963
on Spinoza (Baruch), 8685
symbol theory and, 8908
on theology, 9136
Tillich's (Paul) theological method influenced by, 7120
Schenirer, Sarah, **8149**
Schenke, Hans-Martin, 6395
Schepelern, Wilhelm E., 6168
Schieffelin, Edward L., 5835
Schieffelin, Eric, on ritual failure, 7803
Schiefner, Anton, 1453, 9189
Schiller, Friedrich von
on anthropomorphism, 389
on gendering beauty, 811
on literary history, 3053
Schimmel, Annemarie, 4718, 7223, **8149–8152**
on Islamic mysticism, 7739–7740
on Satan, 8125
on spiritual guides, 8711
Schipper, Kristofer, 1638, 2636
Schism, **8151–8159**
in Buddhism, leading to Mahāsāṃghika Buddhism, 5601
in Christianity, **8154–8159**
in Apostolic Church of John Maranke, 5695
Donatism, **2416–2418**
early schisms, 8155
Eastern, 2586–2587, 2683
Great East-West (11th century) (*See* Great East-West Schism)
Great Western Schism (14th century) (*See* Great Western Schism)
in Methodist denominations, 5998
in New Testament, 8154
of papacy (*See* Great Western Schism)
in Protestantism, patterns in, 8151
Reformation as, 8158
confessional religions and, 3921
defined, 8151
in founded religious communities, 7718
ideological factors in, 8151–8152
inside *vs.* outside the church, and schismatics, 3926
in Judaism, Karaite sect as product of, 5083
in Manichaeism, 5668
meaning of term, 8154
in Nation of Islam, 6420
organizational dynamics of, 8153–8154
overview of, **8151–8154**
social factors in, 8152–8153
types of, 8151
Schism and Continuity in an African Society (Turner), 9405
Schizoanalysis, of religion, **7488–7491**
Schizophrenia, irregular relationships associated with, 6489
Schlagintweit, Emil, 9189
Schlatter, Adolf, 789
Schlatter, Michael, 7143
Schlegel, Alice, on rites of passage, 7798
Schlegel, August Wilhelm, 499, 4446
Schlegel, Friedrich, **8159**
on androgynes, 340
on classical ideal, 8159
on nature, 6436
Schleiermacher (Friedrich) and, 8160
studying Indo-European religions, 4446, 4458
Schlegel, Gustave, Groot (J. J. M. de) and, 3702, 3703
Schleiermacher, Friedrich, **8159–8167**. *See also* Liberal Protestantism
aesthetics of, 48
on apologetics *vs.* polemics, 429
against atheism, 7422
Barth (Karl) studying, 789
Baur (F. C.) and, 805
Christianity defined by, 1660
on creeds, 2060
criticism of, 8166
Dilthey (Wilhelm) on, 2352, 2353, 8160, 8163
dogma, reinterpretation of, 8165–8166
on emotion, religious, 7978
on essence of Christianity, 1665
on feeling, 4100, 8493
on feeling of religion, 6103
Fichte's influence on, 3049
Geiger (Abraham) and, 3292
hermeneutics of, 3930, 3931–3932, 5473–5474, 8163–8164
Augustine's influence on, 5486
Gadamer (Hans-Georg) on, 3934
organization of, 5486
Herrnhutian community and, 8159–8160, 8166
and Jewish thinking about Torah, 9237
on knowledge, 5208
legacy of, 8166
liberal theology of, 1656, 6103
life and works of, 8159–8161

Schleiermacher, Friedrich ***continued***
Möhler (Johann Adam) and, 6113, 6114
morality and, 6178
on myth, 6366
on natural religion, 7702
pantheism of, 2664, 6962
on phenomenology of religion, 7087
philosophical system of, 8164–8165
on prayer, 7370
on predestination, 3205
on religion, 7137
beliefs and practice, 7125–7126, 7127
definition of, 7693, 7694, 7702
interpretation of, 8161–8163
on religious consciousness, 4109
anthropomorphism and, 391
on religious experience, 7738, 10076
Romantic circle and, 8160
and spiritualizing of art, 499
theodicy of, 9117
theology of, 9129, 9130, 9131, 9137
on Trinity, 9362
Schleiermacher, Gottlieb, Herrnhutian community and, 8159
Schleitheim Confession of Faith. *See* "Brotherly Union" statement
Schlick, Moritz, logical positivism and, 5498
Schliemann, Heinrich, 5275
Schlier, Heinrich, on heresy, 3920
Schlözer, August Ludwig von, 3110–3111
Schmaus, Michael, 9139
Schmekel, August, on Stoicism, 8740
Schmid, Hans H., 6376
Schmidt, Isaak Jakob, 1311
Schmidt, K. D., 1018
Schmidt, Wilhelm, **8167–8171**
on African religions, 114
on Arctic religions, 473–474, 475
and Australian Indigenous religions, 686
critical debate concerning, 8169–8170
on deity, 2255
Freud on, 8169
on goddess worship, 3611
Graebner (Fritz) and, 3648
and King's (John H.) work, 2541
and *kulturkreiselehre,* 5260–5261
on lord of the animals, 5513
on monotheism among nomads, 2302
on mystery religions, 6328
and Pinard de la Boullaye, 7173
primitive monotheism *(Urmonotheismus)* doctrine of, 2090, 6156, 10065, 10077
on Pygmy religions, 7523
Roman Catholicism, role in, 8169, 8170
on sacrificial gifts, 8002, 8004
and study of North American Indian religions, 6671
on supreme beings, 7074, 8874, 8876–8877
works of, 8168–8169
Schmiedeleut Hutterites, division of, 4239
Schmithals, Walter, 7018
Schmitt, Carl, 9021
on nationalism, 5398
Schmitt, Richard, 7087
Schmitz, Carl A., on Jensen (Adolf E.), 4825
Schmucker, Samuel S., 5539
Schneerson, Joseph, 4869, 6902
Schneerson, Joseph Isaac, Menachem Schneerson and, 8171
Schneerson, Menachem M., **8171–8173**
in American Orthodoxy, 6905
Chabad House concept and, 8173
and contemporary Hasidism, 9382
Habad Hasidism and, 3792
on Jewish assimilation and education, 8171–8172
as messiah, 3793, 8173
on messianism, 8173
outreach of, 7583, 8172–8173
on Rashi, 866
scholarly work of, 8172
Schneerson, Yosef Yitsḥaq, as Lubavticher *rebbe,* 3793
Schneider, David, on kinship, 5183
Schneider, Heinrich, 3487
Schniewind, Julius, structuralism and, 8755
Schoenberg, Arnold, 6312
Schoenfeld, Rina, 2164
Schoeps, Hans Joachim, 3533
Schofeleers, Matthew, 117
Scholarios, Gennadios, **8173–8174**
on Cabilas, 1343
Mark of Ephesus and, 5714
on schism, 8174
on Thomas Aquinas, 8173–8174
Scholars, deities of, in Chinese religion, 1608, 1619
Scholarship. *See also* Study of religion
of Jesuits, 4842
of Sor Juana, 4967–4968
Scholasticism, **8174–8177**. *See also* Thomism
Aristotelianism in, 8175
in Buddhism, 5099–5100
Zen, 9949
on conscience, 1941
Dante Alighieri and, 2170
diabolical pact theory of, 8865
doctrinal teachings and history of, 8175–8177
humanism *vs.,* 4176
Ibn Rushd and, 4272
Kiev school of Russian Orthodoxy and, 1652–1653
knowledge in, 5204–5205
Leonine Thomism and, 8176–8177
logic in, 5497
meaning of term, 8174
medieval, 8175
methodology in, 8174–8175
sacramental theology and, 7961
Second scholasticism, 8175–8176
Suárez (Francisco) and, 8799
the supernatural in, 8860
on superstition, 8865
theology in, 9136, 9137
on truth, 8174
witchcraft and, 9771–9772
Scholem, Gershom, **8177–8178**
on Adret (Shelomoh ben Avraham), 36
Agnon (Shemu'el Yosef) and, 179
on angels, 348
Buber (Martin) criticized by, 1056, 8177
and Festschriften, 3041
Ginzberg (Asher) influencing, 3496
on Gnosticism, 3533, 8178
on Hasidism, 726, 3786
on messianism in, 3788, 5978
on Lilith, 5458
on *merkavah* mysticism, 10050, 10052
in modern Jewish thought, 4906
on mysticism, 6339, 6342
diversity of, 6352
on Qabbalah, 7739
on religious experience, 7739
on Shabbetai Tsevi, 8259, 8260, 8261
Smith (Morton) and, 8449
on souls, 8560
and Taubes (Jakob), 9021
Zionism of, 8177, 8178
Scholer, David, 6396
Scholia (comments), 930
Schön Erhard, vol. 3 color insert
School(s). *See also* Education; Religious education
home schooling, 5377
Kosmas Aitolos and, 5239
of Krishnamurti (Jiddu), 5245
monastic, in Eastern Christianity, 2582
Protestant, in Korea, 5234
public, religious education in, 7732–7733
Quaker, 7549
in rabbinic Judaism, 7587
Roman Catholic, 7734, 7889
as storehouse of wisdom, 9748, 9755–9756, 9761
Schoolcraft, Henry Rowe, 6670
School of Economic Science, 6543, 6568
School of Isfahan. *See* Isfahan, School of
School of Lost Borders and Rites of Passage, Inc., 7802
School of names, 1595
School of Principle tradition, in Yuan Confucianism, 1902–1903
School of Spiritual Science, 393
Schopen, Gregory, 1247, 1261, 10079
Schopenhauer, Arthur
Buddhism influencing, 1187
Eastern philosophy influencing, 7112
Glasenapp (Helmuth von) influenced by, 3496
Gnosticism and, 3526
on humor, 4221
on Indian religions, 4447
influence on Nietzsche, 6614, 6615
on nature, 6437
Tolstoy (Leo) influenced by, 9220
Upaniṣads influencing, 4446
Schorsch, Ishmar, on state of environment, 2613
Schott, Erdmann, on merit, 5875
Schrader, Eberhard, 5968
Schrader, Paul, 3101
Schreiber, Moses. *See* Sofer, Mosheh
Schrenk, Leopold Von, 474
Schriften zur Theologie (Rahner), 7600–7601
Schröder, E. E. W. G., 5827
Schröder, Franz Rolf, 3459
Schrödinger, Erwin, 7138
Schroeder, Leopold von, on supreme beings, 8874, 8875
Schubert, Franz, 6234
Schubert, Gotthilf Heinrich von, 6435, 6437
on dreams, 8909
Schuchard, Marsha Keith, 7085
Schuller, Robert, 7712, 7714
Schultes, Richard
on indigenous nature religions, 2665
on plant hallucinogens, 8292
Schultze, Quentin, 7714
Schumacher, E. M., Gandhi (Mohandas) influencing, 3273
Schumacher, Peter, 114
Schuon, Fritjhof, 1324
Guénon (René) and, 3706, 3707
Schurtz, Heinrich, 3222
Schutz, Alfred, 3265, 4530
Schütz, Heinrich, 6311

Schutz red (Eck), 2601
Schutzstaffel (SS)
Evola (Julius) and, 2906
policy against Jews, 4085–4086
Schuyler, Eugene, 4623
Schuyler, Philip D., 6525, 6553
Schwantes, Milton, 5440
Schwärmer, 2805
Schwartz, Christian, 8978
Schwartz, Regina M., on monotheism, 6161
Schwartz, Wilhelm, 3458
Schwartzerd, Philipp. *See* Melanchthon, Philipp
Schwarzschild, Steven, 2950
Schweitzer, Albert, **8178–8180**
animals as concern of, 358
autobiography of, 699
on Jesus, 4846–4847
on kingdom of God, 5151, 5152
on quest for historical Jesus, 944, 8179
Reimarus's (Hermann Samuel) influence on, 7675
Schwezigon Pagoda (stupa), 1135
SCI. *See* Science of Creative Intelligence
Science, **8180–8192**. *See also specific fields, scientists, and theories*
17th-century, 6752
Abraham's knowledge of, 16
aesthetics and, 49
African traditional thought compared to, 118
afterlife and, 135
alchemy's transition into, 250, 252–253
Aristotle on, 480
in Asia, ancient, 8180
Bacon (Roger) as harbinger of modern, 734–735
Bacon's (Francis) writings on, 253, 733–734
Big Bang cosmology and the anthropic principle, 8184, 8189
Buddhism and, 8180
chaos theory, **1541–1543**
Chinese, 8180
Christianity and
confrontation with, 1665, 1995, 1996
God and, 3556–3559
incarnation and history of science, 8181
Comte's (Auguste) concept of, 7340
Copernican revolution and Protestant Reformation and, 8182–8183
cosmology in, 1991, **2031–2034**
critical theory *vs.*, in study of religion, 8766
cultural *vs.* natural, Dilthey (Wilhelm) on, 3932
Darwinian evolution, battle over, 8185–8186
ecclesiastical authoritarianism and, 8185
ecology and, **2657–2661**
Einsteinian worldview, 8183–8184
empiricism in, 2780
ethical overlap model, 8186
ethology as, 2869
Etruscan religion as, 2872
eugenics and, 2879–2882
evolutionary biology and, 8189–8190
evolving from divination, 2369
Gaia hypothesis in, 2666
Galileo and
condemnation of, 8183
as first martyr, 3257
genetics and, 8190–8191
Gnosticism in, 3528
God and, in Christianity, 3556–3559
in Greece, ancient, 8180–8181
Hermetism and, 2843
Hinduism and
cosmology and, 2019–2020
parallels between, 2020
historiography and, 4033
history of (overview), 8180–8184
humanities *vs.*, 1991
hypothetical consonance model, 8186
interdisciplinary field of, 8180, 8184–8185
in Islam, 2651
and *tafsīr*, 8955–8956
cultivation of, 4574
overview of, 8181
Jonas (Hans) on, 4949
Judaism and
Eliyyahu ben Shelomoh Zalman and, 2773
reason by contingency in ancient Israel, 8181
response to, 2642
Schneerson (Menachem) on, 8172
Leuba (James H.) on, 5418
in logical positivism, 5498–5500
magic and, 5567
in indigenous societies, 5570–5571
materialism and, 5775–5777
medical (*See* Healing and medicine, modern biomedical)
medical orthodoxy in, 3848–3849
in medieval Europe, overview of, 8181–8182
methods of (*See* Scientific method)
miracles and, 6057–6058
modernity and religion and, 5032
mythology and
causality in, 6363
links between, 6361
Native American, **6425–6427**
vs. Western, 6425
in naturalism, 6428–6430
Wilson (Edward O.) on, 8478
naturalism *vs.* supernaturalism and, 8861
as natural philosophy, 7114
nature as sacred in, 2665–2666
neuroscience and, 8191
New Age spirituality and, 8186
Newtonian worldview, 8183
objectivity in, 6425
opposition as rare and unnecessary, 1995–1996
orthodoxy in, medical, 3848–3849
phenomenology in, 7087
philosophy of, 2911–2912
physics, questions in, 8184, 8188
"playing God," problem of, 8186–8188, 8190
positivist, 7340
Renan (Ernest) and, 7750–7751
quantum theory, sense of mystery in, 8184
reconciliation of, 5033–5034
as religion, 2740
of religion
birth of, 8763
Chantepie de la Saussaye's defense of, 1530–1531
Clemen's role in, 1822
evolution of conscience in, 1944
"heresy" in, 3920
Schleiermacher (Friedrich) and, 3931
as religious resource, in environmentalism, 2564
Rosicrucianism's influence on, 7930
Schleiermacher (Friedrich) on, 8164
scientific imperialism and, 8185
scientism and, 8185
in China, 8180
secularization and, 8218
Spiritualism and, 8716, 8718
as superstition, 8866
theology and, Newman (John Henry) on, 6511
theology as, 9138–9139
three-state law of human knowledge classifying, 7340
transcendence and, Jaspers (Karl) on, 4814–4815
in Transcendental Meditation, 9289
Two Language model, 8184, 8186
warfare and nonwarfare models of, 8185–8186
witchcraft and, 9769, 9773
worldview and, 1992
Science, Religion and Reality (Needham), 5629
Science and Being and Art of Living: Transcendental Meditation (Maharishi), 9290
Science and Health with Key to the Scriptures (Eddy), 1745, 2694–2695
Science et religion dans la philosophie contemporaine (Boutroux), 7341
Science fiction, 3062
artificial intelligence in, 512
Science of Creative Intelligence (SCI), 9289
Science of Judaism. *See Wissenschaft des Judentums*
Science of Logic (Hegel), dynamic methodology in, 3893
Science of Mythology, The (Jung and Kerényi), 5113, 5114
Science of opposites. *See Coincidentia oppositorum*
Scientia (Pettazzoni), 7075
Scientia experimentalis (experimental science), 7340
Scientia scientiarum (science of sciences), positivism as, 7340
Scientific atheism, Soviet ideology of, 8772, 8773
Scientific creationism. *See* Creationism
Scientific ecology, 2605–2606
Scientific imperialism, reductionism in, 8185
Scientific method
and North American Indians, 6425, 6426
objectivity in, 6425
origins of, 253
philosophy behind, 2911–2912
Scientific progress, and positivism, 7340
Scientific Revolution, North American Indians and, 6426
Scientific Society, Ahmad Khan in, 201
Scientific *tafsīr* (Qur'anic exegesis), 7567–7568
Scientism
Chinese, 8180
Thomism and, 8182
Western meaning of, 8185
Scientology (Church of Scientology), 6559–6560, **8192–8194**
in Africa, 109
beliefs in, 8192–8193
brainwashing civil suit against, 1033, 5376
child socialization and education in, 6542

Scientology (Church of Scientology) ***continued***
church organization, 8193
controversy over, 8193–8194
criticism of, 6559
Dianetics and, 4149
in Europe, 6569
founding of Church of Scientology, 8192
Hubbard (L. Ron), role of, **4149–4150**
origins of, 6559
as religion, 7705
scriptural text of, 6530
tax exemptions of, 5378
Twitchell (Paul) in, 2602
wealth of, 6562
Sciorra, Joseph, 3146
Scipio Africanus, 7901
Scissors, 968
Scivias (Hildegard), 2471
SCLC. *See* Southern Christian Leadership Conference
SCOBA (Standing Conference of Canonical Orthodox Churches), 2589
Scopes, John, 2890
Scopes Monkey Trial, ridicule and, 4200–4201
Scorpions
in Caribbean religions, 1429
in Egyptian mythology, 4557
in Mesopotamian iconography, 4316
Scorpius (constellation), in ethnoastronomy, 2865
Scorsese, Martin, 3097, 3098, 3100
Scot, Michael, on Hermetism, 3945
Scot, Reginald, 9773
Scotism, founder of, 2523
Scotland. *See also* Church of Scotland
Anglicanism in, 350
animal symbolism and beliefs, cats, 1463
Congregationalism in, 1938
Enlightenment in, *Encyclopaedia Britannica* in, 2784
Findhorn community in, 6495
Free Church of, Smith (W. Robertson) and, 8451
Freemasonry in, 3194, 3196
hermits of, 2826
museums in, 6245, 6246
philosophy in, Channing (William Ellery), influence on, 1530
Presbyterianism in (*See* Presbyterian denominations, in Scotland)
Reformed Protestantism and John Knox in, 1692, 5211–5212
Taigheirm ceremony, 1463
Scots Confession (1560), on free will and predestination, 3208
Scott, Jason, 2292
Scott, Joan, 3024
Scott, Joan Wallach, on gender, 3296
Scott, June, 68
Scott, Kim, 3080, 3084
Scott, Nathan A., Jr., 5482–5483
Scott, Orange, Wesleyan Methodist Connection of America and, 4083
Scott, Walter, 2365
as Freemason, 3198
Grimm brothers and, 3702
legends recorded by, 2953
posthumous works attributed to, the Family and, 2988
Scottish Episcopal Church, 350
Scottish Missionary Society, in Jamaica, 1706
Scottish Reformation, 5212
Scottish Rite, 3196
Scott v. Ross, 2292
Screening the Sacred (Martin and Ostwalt), 3100
Scribes
Canaanite, 1387
as class, 1843
Egyptian
comprehension of, 2703, 2716
duties of, 2714
importance of, 2717–2718, 2723
as teachers of wisdom, 9748
Script. *See also* Alphabets
Dogon, 101
Scriptural religions
history of religions approach on, 4066
idea of sacred book in, 8196
al-Shahrastānī's expansion of concept of, 8267
Söderblom (Nathan) on, 8878
Spinoza (Baruch) on, 8683
Scripture, **8194–8205**. *See also specific religions and texts*
anthologies or collections of, 8199
authority and sacrality of, 8201
canon, relation to, 1406, 1410, 8201, 8202 (*See also* Canon)
Child's compilation of, 1570
conversion and translatability of, 1972
cultural consequences of, 8203–8204
definition of, 6528, 9270
in devotional and spiritual life, 8199–8200
form and content, variation in, 8194–8195
generalization of the concept, 8197
as heavenly book, 8195–8196
in Hinduism, discrepancies in, 7615
as holy writ, 8197–8198
inspiration and eternality/antiquity of, 8201–8202
interpretation, traditions of, 8202–8203
subaltern studies and, 8802
Israelite, in Second Temple Judaism, 4974–4975
in liberation theology, 5402–5403
magic and superstitious use of, 8200, 8201
meaning of term, 8194–8195, 8196–8197
Smith (Wilfred Cantwell) on, 8450
new religious movements and, 6516, **6528–6532**
oral transmission of, 8194
origins and development of concept of, 8195–8197
in Orthodox Christianity, 2593
in sacraments, 2592
power in, 8200–8201
in public ritual, 8199
quasi-scriptural texts, 8201
as relational concept, 8195
and religion, definition of, African scholarship and, 8794
in Roman Catholicism
authority of, 2686, 2689
historicity of, 9539–9540
sacred book, idea of, 8196
sacred language of, 5304, 5309
as spoken word, 8198–8199
study of, 5472–5475
vs. tradition, 9270
translation of, 8203
unicity of, 8201
in vernacular language, schism and, 8152
Zoroastrian, 9992–9994
Scripture of Documents. *See Shujing*
Scripture of Great Peace (Daoist text), 2180, 2204
Scripture of Music. *See Yuejing*
Scripture of Odes. *See* Odes, Classic of/Scripture of
Scripture of Salvation. *See Duren jing*
Scripture of the Sacred Jewel. *See Lingbaojing*
Scripture of the Teachings of the Heavenly Master (Daoist text), 2193–2194
Scripture of the Yellow Court (Daoist text), 2181, 2205
Scripture on the Merits and Original Vows of the Master of Healing, the Lapis Lazuli Radiance Tathāgata, 855
Scrofula (king's evil), 9257
Scroll of the War of the Sons of Light against the Sons of Darkness (Dead Sea Scroll), 2234
Sculpture. *See also* Stele
African, 89, 90, 4302–4303
in Arctic religions, 471
Australian Aboriginal, 4305
Buddhist, 4327, 4328
Confucian, 4338
Daoist, 4333–4334
Egyptian, 4318
erotic, at Konarak (India), 7042
Greek, 4322, 4382
human body in, 4172
in Ajanatā caves, 1471–1472
Inca, 4413
Maya, 5799
Melanesian, 5838–5839
Mesoamerican, 4313
in Teotihuaćan, 5900
Mesopotamian, 4315, 4316, 4381
Mycenaean, 4321
Toltec, 9222
in Totonac religion, 9254
veneration of, 4380
Scylas (Scythian king), 2357
Scythian religion, **8205–8208**
Ares worship in, 9686
blood in, 986
burial rituals in, 8206
ceremonies in, 4489
Christianity, Andrew's missions to, 1682
cultic centers in, 8206
cult leaders in, 8206
deities of, 8205–8206
Dumézil (Georges) on, 4462
festivals in, 8206
iconography and art in, 8206–8207
sacrifice in, 4489, 8206
Sarmatians and, 8114
Saura Hinduism and, 8136
serpents in, 8457
sources on, 4489
Sdom gsum rnam dbye (Sakya Paṇḍita), doctrinal criticism in, 8052
Se (musical instrument), 6293
Sea. *See also* Oceans; Water; Yamm
defeat of, by god, 2812
in Neolithic religions, 6465
Sea bear, 808
Seabury, Samuel, 350, 352
Seal, Brajendranath, 4450
Seal of Solomon. *See* Magen David (Star of David)
Seals
Elamite, 4469–4470, 4472, 4473
Indus Valley, 4472–4474
Mesopotamian, 4315, 4316, 4317
Minoan-Mycenaean, 4320, 4321
mudrās as, 6219
Sedna (Sea Woman) and, 8220–8221
Seals (mammals), 4527
Sea monster. *See* Leviathan
Séances
in African religions, 87
in Cao Dai movement, 1411, 1412
in Dolgan religion, 2395

in Inuit religion, Sedna (Sea Woman) and, 8220–8221
in Israel, 6831
in Khanty religion, 5124
in Mansi religion, 5124
in New Guinea religions, illness and, 3810
in shamanism, 8285–8286
dramatic structure of, 8274
Samoyed, 8096
soul escorted in, 8272–8273
spirit links in, 8284
in Spiritualism, 8715, 8717, 8718
Sea Organization, Hubbard (L. Ron) and, 4149, 8193
Sea Peoples, Canaanite religion and, 1381
Search for extraterrestrial intelligence (SETI), 4516
Search for Security (Field), 118
Searle, John, 510, 5492
on news, 4962
Sears, Djanet, 2477
Seashells, Maya zero and, 1357
Seasonal ceremonies, **8208–8210**. *See also* New Year festivals
in Celtic religion, 1491 (*See also specific festivals*)
in Chinese religion, 1641–1644
in Christianity, liturgical year (*See* Liturgical year, Christian)
confession and, 1885
Halloween, **3758–3759** (*See also* Samhain)
Hindu religious year, **4014–4019**
invigoration rites, 8209–8210
jubilation rites, 8210
in Judaism, Shavu'ot, **8305–8306**
in Mediterranean religion, orgy in, 6863–6864
mortification rites, 8208–8209
purgation rites, 8209
sky hierophany and, 8429
symbolic time and, 8917
Seated meditation. *See Zazen*
Seated position. *See* Sitting
Seawater, in West African religions, 9720
Sea Woman. *See* Sedna
Sebastian, Mihail, Eliade and, 2758, 2759
Sebayt (teaching), 2722
Sebeok, Thomas A., 5709
Sebiumeker (deity), in Kushite religion, 5269
Secondary burial, 1014–1015, 2239, 2241
Secondary cultures, Schmidt (Wilhelm) on, 5260
Second Battle of Mag Tuired, The (Irish text), 5528
Second-Coming Movement (Japan), 9432
Second Coming of Christ, Swedenborg (Emanuel) on, 8899
Second Helvetic Confession (1566), on free will and predestination, 3208
Second scholasticism, doctrinal teachings of, 8175–8176
Second Sex, The (Beauvoir), 4484
Second Shepherds' Play, 2469
Second Temple (Jerusalem). *See also* Biblical Temple
biblical literature on, 926
building of, 4835
date of building of, 923
design of, 924–925, 933–934
destruction of, 4976
elect status and, 2745
exile and, 2922
hester panim (hiding the face of God) and, 4090
Jewish worship and, 9806, 9903
Ezekiel on, 2945
funding in, 928–929
history of, 924–925
Jesus' pilgrimage to, 7152–7153
Maccabean liberation of, 925
and messianism, 5974–5975
miqveh in, 6046
Mishnah and, 6067
music in, 6276
renovations of, 925, 4959
Roman destruction of, 923, 933, 4747
anti-Semitism in, 398
Gamli'el of Yavneh after, 3269
worship after, 6307
Sadducees of, **8017–8019**
Karaites, connection to, 4058–4059
sanctity of, 933
Sanhedrin in, 8102
worship at, 9806
Second Temple Judaism, 4973–4976
charisma and, 1545
in Dead Sea Scrolls, 2235
definition of, 4970
Enoch in, 2803
miqveh in, 6046
oral Torah and, 6838–6839
ordination of rabbis in, 7578
priesthood in, 5426–5427
Smith (Morton) on, 8448
sources for, 4974
and synagogue, history of, 8921
Second Treatise of the Great Seth, The (Gnostic text), 5202
Second Treatise on Government (Locke), 5367
Second Vatican Council. *See* Vatican Council II
Second Work (Wesleyan) Pentecostalism, 7029, 7033
Secrecy
in alchemy, 235, 246
in esotericism, 2842
in mysticism, 6341
as persecution protection, 8212
in Pueblo religion, 6721–6722
of Tarot cards, vol. 14 color insert
Secret Cycle. *See Gsang skor*
Secret Doctrine, The (Blavatsky), 844, 977, 5023, 7228, 9142
Secret Gospel of Mark, Smith (Morton) and, 8448–8449
Secret History of the Mongols, The (Mongolian text), 4493
Secret Rapture, The (Hare), 2477
Secret societies, **8210–8214**
in African religions
cannibalism among Sherbro, 1404
funeral rites and, 7806
of women, vol. 6 color insert
in China, 8213
defined, 8210–8211
distinguishing features of, 8211
initiation into, 4476–4477
Christian, 4479, 4482–4483
female, 4476, 4478
male, 4476, 4478, 4482–4483
in Kenya, 8213
Ku Klux Klan as, 8213
masks and, 5770–5771
Masonic orders as, 8213
among men, in tribal communities, 7717
as mystery societies, 7719
myths of origin in, 8211
in North America, 8213
origin and function, theories on, 8211–8212
as religious communities, 7718–7719
in South Pacific, 8212–8213
in Vanuatu religions, 9520
in Vodou, 9638
in West Africa, 8213
Yurupary cult, 9920
Secretum (Petrarch), 698
Sectarianism
in Baptist churches, 785–786, 1713
in Buddhism
engaged Buddhism and, 2787
in *saṃgha* and, 8079–8080
in Chinese religion, 1607
in Ming and Qing dynasty, 2187–2188
vs. denominationalism, 2286
enthusiasm as, 2804
and heresy, development of, 3923
in Hinduism, 4004–4006
under Islamic rule, 4007
in Judaism, in *Wissenschaft des Judentums,* 4876–4877
moral and social aspects of, 7651
opposed to Catholicism, 7874
social doctrine of, 7874
social movements and, 1749
in United States, 1713–1714
dress codes in ethno-religious groups, **1834–1837**
social control in, 1835–1836
Sect of the Three Stages, 5255
Sects. *See* Cults and sects; New religious movements; Sectarianism; *specific sects*
Sect Shintō, 4792
Secular, definition of, 7692
Secular dialogue of religions, 2344
Secular ecumenism, 7012
Secular feminism, in Muslim countries, 3366
Secular humanism
the Enlightenment and, 8491
in progressive Islam, 6098
Said (Edward) on, 8032
Secularism
anthropocentrism and, 2649
in anticult movements, 395–397
in Arab society, Said (Edward) on, 8032
Christianity and, relation to, 2688–2689
Copernicus and, 1978
and decline of priesthood, 7398
of education, in Australia and New Zealand, 1733
the Enlightenment and, 1693
and history, Christian views of, 4055–4056
homo modernus and, 4110
and iconoclasm, 4286–4287, 4347
and image veneration, 4386–4387
impact of, on church life, 2684
and invisible religion, 4529–4530
Marxism in Eastern Europe, 1686
in North America, 1716
and politics and religion, 7283–7284
Reformation and, 7656
ritual and, 7846
sacred *vs.* secular, in sociology, 8482
secularization *vs.,* 8214
and study of implicit religion, 4400, 4401

Secularization, **8214–8220**. *See also* Church and state
in Canada, 9301–9302
causes of, 8218
contemporary manifestations of, 8217–8218
definitions of, 8214–8215
epics as signs of, 6362
as historical process, 8216–8217
of historiography, 4032–4034
of homes, 4107
human rights and, 4178
implicit meaning of, 9931
indices of, 8215–8216
Kant's (Immanuel) influence on, 5080
of law, 5325–5326
of literature, 5477–5478
modernization and, 6109
monasticism and, 6134
naturalization of economy in, 2669
in non-Western contexts, 8218–8219
Orthodox Jews and, Schneerson (Menachem) and, 8172
privatization of religion and, 8472
and revivals of religion, 8217
of salutations, 8062
secularism and, 8214–8215
sociological views on, 8487, 8492–8493
of sports, 8724–8725
study of, 8468–8469
transcendence in, 2679
Weber (Max) and, 9711
Secular myths, 5034–5035
Secular paradise, 6986
Sedberg, Jesper, Swedenborg (Emanuel) and, 8898
Seder (Passover eve feast), 2397, 2400, 7003–7004
contemporary celebration of, 4986
egg symbolism of, 2701–2702
Elijah at, 2766
Eucharist based on, 2877, 7958
maḥzor liturgy for, 8390
sacred time and, vol. 1 color insert
Seder Eliyyahu Rabbah, 2765–2766
Seder Rav Amram (prayer book), circulation of, 8387
Sedhekah sacrifices, in Agami Islam Santri, 4818
Sedna (deity), 3017, **8220–8221**
as birth goddess, 470
ceremonies of, 4528
confession of sins and, 7759
as culture hero, 2092
forgiving sins, 7505, 7509
as lady of the animals, 5280, 5515
as mistress of animals, 470, 4528, 8220–8221
origin myths of, 8220
in shamanic rites, 6655
Seduction, shape shifting and, 8301
Seecho (deity), 9030
Seed, John, 2563
Seed and soil metaphor, 7078
in Christianity, 7081
in Islam, 7082
in Judaism, 7080
Seeing the Inside (Taylor), 4305
Seeker-oriented churches, 2893
See of Rome. *See also* Papacy
chair of Peter *vs.,* 2113
origins of, 1772
Seers, in Greek religion, 3683, 9927–9928
Seer stone, of Smith (Joseph), vol. 4 color insert
Sefardic Judaism. *See* Sephardic Judaism
Sefer emunot ve-de'ot (Sa'adyah Gaon), tenets of Judaism in, 7951–7953
Sefer ha-'arukh (Natan ben Yeḥi'el), 9246
Sefer ha-bahir, 9378
Scholem (Gershom) on, 8177–8178
theosophy in, 8315
Sefer ha-halakhot (Alfasi), 255
Sefer ha-'iqqarim (Albo), 233–234, 866
Sefer ha-Kuzari (ha-Levi), on election of Israel, 2746
Sefer hama'asim (Agnon), 180
Sefer ha-miqqah ve-ha-mimkar (H'ai), Talmudic law reorganized in, 3745
Sefer ha-mitsvot ('Anan), 317, 4991
Sefer ha-peliah (qabbalistic text), 4872, 9378
Sefer ha-qabbalah (Ibn Daud), 4264, 4265
Sefer ha-roqeaḥ (El'azar), 544
Sefer Ḥasidim (Book of the Pietists), 4913
Sefer ḥasidim (Yehudah), 543–544, 5012
mysticism in, 6352–6353
Sefer ha-temunah (qabbalistic text), 4872, 9378
Sefer ha-yashar (Tam), 8973
Sefer ha-yir'ah (Shemu'el), 543
Sefer ha-zohar. See Zohar
Sefer Heikhalot, 10051
Sefer Nestor ha-komer (Jewish text), 7231
Sefer nitstsaḥon yashan, 866
Sefer Torah. *See* Torah
Sefer yetsirah (Book of Creation), **8221–8222**
Gnosticism in, 3523
Sefer Zerubbavel, 419
Sefirot, 868
attributes of God among, 615, 3550
Ein Sof and, 1985
gender and, 8315
Ḥokhmah as, 4079–4080
in origin of evil, 6354
in Qabbalah, 4981, 7536, *7537*
commentaries on, 7538
in *Sefer yetsirah,* 8221
souls and, 8560
tsassiqim as intermediary with, 3789
in *Zohar* doctrine, 6362
Segal, Judah B., on New Year ceremonies, 6592–6593
Segal, M. H.
on Jewish Bible study, 867
rejecting Documentary Hypothesis, 869
Segal, Robert
on Campbell (Joseph), 1380
on nature of religion, 7745
on phenomenology, 7098
Ségalen, Victor, 5850
Segregation, racial, 69
in churches, 4950–4951
King's (Martin Luther, Jr.) work against, 5145–5146
and spread of Islam, 4687
Séguin, Pierre, 3125
Seicho no Ie, 6573–6574
in Brazil, 6574
in New Thought movement, 6587
Seidel, Anna Katherina, **8222–8223**
Seidenstücker, Karl, 1187, 1188
Seiðr divination, in sagas, 8024–8025
Seidr ritual, in neoshamanism, 8295, 8296
Seikai kyūsei-kyō movement, founding of, 8369
Seilangi (mythic figure), 6012
Sein und Seit. See Being and Time (Heidegger)
Seite (sacred landscape)
holy sites in, 8087
sacred stones and, 8746
Seiwa (Japanese emperor), music under, 6300
Seizan-ha school of Buddhism, 4938
Sejarah (family line), 4664
Sejarah Melayu (Malay chronicle), 4664
Sejo (Chosŏn ruler), 5232
Sejong (Chosŏn ruler), 1173, 5232
music under, 6296, 6297
Séjourné, Laurette, 5942
Sekai Kyusei Kyō (SKK), in Africa, 108–109
Şeker Bayrami (sugar feast), 4714
Sekhar butalah (monetary compensation for rabbis), 7578
Sekhmet (deity)
in Egyptian pantheon, 2704
iconography of, 5464
priests of, as healers, 3826
Seki, Eikakau, and Shingon Buddhism in Hawaii, 8353
Sekkyōbushi (parable), 6301
Sekos (open-air court), 9063
Selbständigkeit der Religion, Die (Troeltsch), 9364
Selden, Raman, 5486
Selections of Zatspram (Zoroastrian text), 7764
Selene (mythic figure), 6173
Seler, Eduard, 452, 5941
on music, 6266
Seleucia-Ctesiphon, bishop of, 2583
Seleucids, Nabateans in conflict with, 6386
Self
annihilation of, in mystical union, 6335
in Buddhism (*See also* Ātman)
asmimāna (ego conceit) and, 8552–8553
and autobiography, 701
reincarnation and, 7678
Śākyamuni Buddha on, 7678
Sthiramati on, 8739, 8740
in Chinese religion
cosmic relationality of, 8555
four modes of, healing and, 3859, 3860
qi cultivation and, 3862
in Confucianism
connectedness of, 2633
Wang Yangming on, 9674
Cooley (Charles H.) on, 8482
experience of, by Evola (Julius), 2904–2905
Heschel (Abraham Joshua) on, 3962
in Hinduism (*See Ātman*)
in Indian religions, *saṃsāra* and, 8098
in Upaniṣads, 9544
in Islam, *naf* as, 8567
in Mesopotamian anthropogeny, 8536
in New Age movement, 6498
orientation of, 6886–6887
out-of-body experience and, ecstasy and, 7972
recentering of, 7835
in rituals, 7834–7835
Schleiermacher (Friedrich) on, 8165
Socrates on, 8503
surrender of, Spiritualism and, 8715
Self-actualization, states of consciousness and, 1950
Self-consciousness
conscience and, 1943, 1944
Hegel (G. W. F.) on comedy and, 4220
in Mahāyāna Buddhism, *svasaṃvedanā* (reflexivity), 8552
vs. reflexivity, 7648
rituals and, 7841–7842
Schleiermacher (Friedrich) on, 8163, 8164, 8165
Smith (Wilfred Cantwell) on, 8451
Self-contemplation, in Trika Śáivism, 8046
Self-control, celibacy and, 1475

Self-criticism
in inner alchemy, 2187
in rituals, 7836–7837
Self-cultivation, in Chinese philosophy. *See also* Sagehood
in Confucianism, 2634
Mengzi on, 5858
Confucius on, 1586, 1894–1897
constructive discipline and, 8704
in contemporary spirituality, 8720
in Daoism, 2635
in Neo-Confucianism, 1578, 1604
Qigong and, 1611
sainthood, path to, 8037
School of Principle, 1901–1902
Study of Inner Mind, 1902–1903
Yang Zhu on, 1572
in *Zhuangzi,* 1573
Zhu Xi and, 1901, 9973–9974
Self-deception, 9369
Self-denial
asceticism as, 527–528
in monasticism, 6123
Self-destruction, of warrior heroes, 2815
Self-detachment, dance as means to, 2140
Self-directedness, 1030
Self-discipline, in Jainism, 8548
Self-exploration, in Neopaganism, 6472
Self-flagellation
of Khlysts, 6873
as mortification, 6197
objectives of, 528
Self-help, dance for, 2141
Selfhood, Kierkegaard on, 5141, 5142
Self-immolation, in Hinduism, 2242–2243. *See also* Sati
Self-interest
in Chinese tradition, Han Fei Zi on, 3772, 3773
in morality, 6179
Self in Transformation, The (Fingarette), 7476
Selfish Gene (Dawkins), sociobiology and, 8474
Self-knowledge
in Judaism, suffering and, 8805
mirrors and, 6064–6065
Selflessness, in Buddhism, Sthiramati on, 8740
Self-love, and religion, Freud on, 3217
Self-mutilation, in North American Indian religions, 6652
"Self-Portrait in a Convex Mirror" (Ashbery), 5483
"Self-power" schools of Buddhism, meditation in, 5821
Self psychology, 7484
Self-realization
in Confucianism, in harmony with nature, 2633
Hegel's classification of religions and, 1819
in Holy Order of MANS, 4102
Self-Realization Fellowship, 6559
Self Religion (Heelas), 6498
Self-representation
indigeneity and, 1858
and narrative theory on conversion, 1971
Self-Revelation Church of Absolute Monism, 2602
Self-rule, Gandhi (Mohandas) on, 3272
Self-taught art. *See* Outsider art
Self theory (Roland), on conversion, 1970
Self-transcendence, Luckmann (Thomas) on, 8468
Self-transformation
Confucian (*See* Self-cultivation, in Chinese philosophy)
hope and, 4126
in rituals, 7836 (*See also* Ritual(s))
shape shifting and, 8303
in South American creation myths, 2011–2012
Self-understanding, narratives and, 6377
Selim, Yavuz Sultan, Abbasid caliph and, 1367
Selim I (Ottoman sultan), flag of, 4351
Seljuk Turks
Abū Jaʿfar and, 3765
caliphate and, 1367
madrasahs under, 5556–5557
Sufism, impact on, 8820
Selk'nam religion (Tierra del Fuego), **8223–8226**
death, myth of origins of, 8591
deus otiosus in, 2310
geography of, 8576
hunting rituals in, 8582
initiation rites in, 8585
Moon in, 8224
mythology in, 8224
New Year ceremony in, 6590
rejuvenation in, 7683
ritual in, 8224–8225
shamanism in, 8225–8226
last woman shaman in, 8224
Moon and, 8224
sleep as death in, 8441
supreme being in, 8224, 8579
Selkup religion. *See* Southern Siberian religions
Sellin, Ernest, archaeological work of, 5111
Sellon, Edward, on Tantrism, 8251
Sells, Michael, 7222
Selu (deity), 1564
Selwyn, George Augustus, as bishop of New Zealand, 1732
Semaḥot (rejoicings), 7822–7823
Semangat (soul or universal spirit)
in Malay religion, 3810
in Sudanese religion, 8849
Semang religion (Malaysia), 6456–6457
disease attributed to supreme being in, 3808
Semantics, **8226–8227**
of *aion/aiones,* 207–209
structuralism and, 8759
Semar (clown), 2453, 4817
Sembène, Ousmane, 3087, 3098
Sēmeion (prodigy), 7335, 7337
Semele (deity), 3383
Semen
as elixir of immortality, 2771
Milky Way as, 8871
and pollution, 7397, 7504
retention of, 8240, 8248 (*See also* Tantrism)
vital force in, 8240, 8532
Semenkhkare (Egyptian king), 2707
Semikhah. See Ordination, of rabbis
Seminal Essence of the Great Expanse, 7869
Seminal Heart. *See Snying thig*
Seminal Heart in Four Parts, The (Longchenpa), 5193
Seminal logos, 5503
doctrine of, 3119
Seminaries
Islamic
Hawzah, **3800–3802**
uṣūl al-dīn departments and *sharīʿah* colleges, 8782–8783
Jewish
Jewish Theological Seminary of America, 1958–1959
Orthodox Rabbinical Seminary (Berlin), 3980–3981
vs. yeshivah, 9882
Orthodox, Saint Ephrem Syriac Orthodox Seminary, 8940
Protestant
in Latin America, 1704
Swedenborgian, 8903, 8904
in Scientology, 8193
training in counseling at, 7486–7487
Zoroastrian, 9991
Seminary by Extension movement, 1704
Seminole tribe (North America)
ballgame played by, 753, 755
creation story of, 6692
Green Corn Dance of, 6694
origins of, 6690
today, 6691
Semiotics. *See also* Structuralism
in African religious studies, 118
Barthes (Roland) and, 8751
Greimas (A. J.) and, 8749–8750
Lévi-Strauss (Claude) and, 8468
reflexivity and, 7649
in ritual studies, 7858
semantics, **8226–8227,** 8759
structuralism and, 8759
Semiramis and Nisus, 3053
Semitextualists, *Tafsīr* (Qurʾanic exegesis) of, 7569
Semitic culture and religion. *See also* Canaanite religion; Judaism; Mesopotamia and Mesopotamian religions
castration and, 1450
Christianity as, 9801
comparative mythology, 1874–1875
mythic themes in, dying and reviving god in, 1874–1875
pantheon of, in Eblaite religion, 2596–2597
sacrifice in, Smith (W. Robertson) on, 8002
sky gods in, 8424, 8837
Smith (W. Robertson) on, 8451, 8452, 8466
syncretism and, 8930
Semitic languages
"canon," relation to, 1406
in East Africa, 2566
Ethiopia, 2572
etymology of Dagan in, 2126
Sumerian *vs.* Akkadian, 8537–8538
Semitics, Northwest. *See* Canaanite religion
Semler, Johann, 5539
Semnones (Germanic people), 2366–2367
Semnos, as Greek concept, 7967
Semple, Robert James, 5803
Sen, Hun, 5133
Sen, Keshab Chandra, **8227–8228,** 9629
and Brāhmo Samāj, 1029, 4431, 9318
New Dispensation founded by, 828
Ramakrishna as teacher of, 7612
Sena dynasty (Bengal), 824
Senart, Émile, 945, 1312
and Foucher (Alfred), 3177
Senasis Žynys, 766
Senators, of Rome, 5167
Senchaku hongan nembutsushu (Hōnen), 1243, 4937–4938
Pure Land in, 4120
Seneca
on almsgiving, 267

Seneca *continued*
Calvin's commentary on, 1374
on Etruscan portents, 7336–7337
on Golden Rule, 3632
on meteors, 8736
on posthumous purification, 1460
religiosity of, 8742
Stoicism and, 8741
on *substantia,* 4240
on suicide, 8829
on superstition, 8864
Seneca religious traditions (North America). *See also* Iroquois religion
ballgame in, 753, 754
creation story of, 6680
gender in, 3409
Handsome Lake movement in, 6667
nature tales in, 6661
oral tradition in, 6845
tobacco in, 9218, 9219
trees in, 9336
Seneca the Younger, on comets, 8735
Senegal and Senegalese religions. *See also* Fulbe religion
Alinesitoue in, 261–262
childbirth practices in, 3819
commerce of images in, vol. 7 color insert
films from, 3098
funeral rites in, 3236, 3237
Islam-derived movements in, new, 107
Islam in, 4609
in Umarian *jihād,* 9445
Sufism in, vol. 5 color insert
literature of, 3087
pilgrimage to Touba, 1808–1809
Sengaku, Mayeda, on Śaṅkara, 8105
Sengcan (third patriarch in Chan), 1522
Seng-Chao. *See* Sengzhao
Sengchou (Buddhist scholar), 994
Sengguhu (high priest), 2451
Senghor, Léopold, 3222
Sengzhao (Buddhist monk), 1301, **8228**
on emptiness *(śūnyatā),* 1164, 8859
Senlatviešu religija (Adamoviçs), 770
Sennacherib (Assyrian king)
Ashur and, 548–549
Babylonia under, 5948
Beth-Dagon captured by, 7102
gambling by, 3262
successor of, 5163
Sens, Council of (1140), Abelard (Peter) condemned by, 7
Sensate materialism, Sorokin (Pitirim Aleksandrovich) on, 8523, 8524
Senses
in Hinduism, likened to horses, 4135
ideas derived from, 2778
in Qur'ān, 2837
life forms categorized by, in Jainism, 2624–2625
in parapsychology, 6925
Sa'adyah Gaon on, as source of truth, 7952
during visions, 9612
in Yoga, 9895
Sensory deprivation, in vision inducement, 9613
Sensual Meditation (Raël), 7597
Sentences (Capreolus), 9164
Sentences (Isidore), 4557
Sentences (Porphyry), 7191
Sentences of Sextus (Gnostic text), 7026
wisdom in, 9760
Senufo religion
funeral rites in, 3236
iconography of, 4302
masks in, 5767
rites of passage in, 88
Senusret I (Egyptian king), 2706
Senusret III (Egyptian king), 2706
Seow, C.L., on *Ecclesiasties,* 2600
Separation
in initiation rituals, 4478, 4480–4481, 4483, 4485
in ordination symbolism, 6858
in science and religion typology, 2658
Separatism
Jewish, Hirsch (Samson Raphael) on, 4023, 4024
schism and, 8151
Separatist groups. *See also* Pilgrims
Congregationalism and, 1937
ecclesiology and, 1774
fundamentalists as, 2890, 2892
Separatists, 1054
persecution in Europe, 6567
Sephardic Judaism
bar mitzvah in, 7820
in colonial America, 7582
expulsion of, 4996
halakhah and, 3743
in Hungary, 4224
in Jewish studies, 4877–4878
kashrut laws in, 5107
liturgy of, 9808
in Maghreb, 4996
marriage in, 7821–7822
messianism in, 4998
music in, 6308, 6312
naming rituals in, 7819
in Ottoman Empire, 4996–4997
philosophy in, 4889–4892, 4993
in Safed, 4998–4999
siddur and *maḥzor* (prayer books) in, 8387–8388
in *Wissenschaft des Judentums,* 4877–4878
Seppuku (ritual suicide), 8832
as human sacrifice, 4183–4184
September 11th, 2001, terrorist attack
and American Muslims, 4690–4691
as attack on U.S. financial dominance, 9267
and Canadian Muslims, 4686
impact on Central Asian Islam, 4630
media coverage of, 5807
memorials to, vol. 6 color insert
as religious power against political power, 7258
signaling threat of al-Qā'idah, 7288
Septimontium (festival), 7896
Septuagint (Greek Bible). *See also* Hebrew scriptures (Old Testament)
in Alexandrian canon, 880
Aramaic words in, 890
Augustine of Hippo on, 881
Baal Zebub in, 7103
blasphemy in, 969, 971, 972
Christian canon based on, 880–881
Codex Vaticanus, 891
covenant as testament in, 2049
demons in, 2277, 2314
eidōlon (image) in, 4357
Enoch in, 2803
"gospel" in, 3640
Hades in, 3725
hypostasis in, 4240
impact of, 890
as inspired text, 8203
Jeremiah in, 4827
Jerome and, 4832–4833
legend of, 890
liturgy in, 5490
multiple text traditions of, 890–891
nefesh as *psuchē* in, 8562, 8563
origin of, 886
paradise in, 6981
Philo Judaeus using, 7106
psalms in, 7461
Reshef in, 7760
revisions to, 891–892
Satan in, 2314
temptation in, 9070
translation of, 5484
variants from Masoretic text in, 886
Sequana (deity), 3388
Séquin, Pierre, 3125, 3126
Serafim of Sarov (saint), 2588, 7943, **8229**
Serapeum (Alexandria), 6921
Seraphic Dialogue (Graham), 2159
Séraphita (Balzac), 340–341
Serapion of Antioch, letter of, 2381
Serapis cult, 2710, 6921–6922. *See also* Sarapis
Serbia
Christianity in, history of, 1684
Islam in, 4674
Serbian Orthodox Church
autocephalous status of, 2588
in Orthodox structure, 2589
political involvement of, 2588
Serbian religions, Dabog in, 2231
Serdi tribe (Thracian), 9168
Sered, Susan Starr, 3147
on spirit possession, 8694, 8695
**Seren* (Philistine ruler), 7102
Serendipity, chance as, 1527
Sergent, Bernard, 4464
Sergii (patriarch of Moscow), **8229–8230**
Sergii of Radonezh, **8230–8231**
Sergius III (pope), and Leo VI, fourth marriage controversy of, 8156
Sergius IV (pope), 6967
filioque doctrine and, 8156
Sergius Tychikos, Paulician movement under, 3523
Sergiy (Russian saint), 7942
Serial periodization, 174–177
Seriff, Suzanne, 3146–3147
Serigne Bassirou Mbacke (Dione), vol. 10 color insert
Serigne Mouhadou Fadel Mbacke (Dione), vol. 10 color insert
Seri people (North America), 6720
Seriti (human personality), 9388–9389
Serl (Yiddish author), 9037
Sermon on the mount, 4845
"Sermon on the Plain" (Luke), 5149
Sermons. *See also* Preaching
in Christian worship, 9812
of Edwards (Jonathan), 2699
eugenic, 2881
of John of Damascus, 4941
Sermons on the Song of Songs (Bernard of Clairvaux), love in, 8706
Sernett, Milton, 74, 79
Serno, Jacinto de la, spell recorded by, 8677
Serpent, The: A Ceremony (play), 2438
Serpent and the Rainbow (Davis), 10023, 10025
Serpentarian Gnostics, 3518
Serpentine linear labyrinth, 5276
Serpents. *See* Snakes and serpents
Serra, Junipero, **8231**
millenarianism and, 5916
Serrano, Andre, 4282
Serrarius, Petrus, Shabbateanism and, 8261
Serrato-Combe, Antonio, 5893
Servants, 2986. *See also* Suffering Servant doctrine
Serveto y Conesa, Miguel. *See* Servetus, Michael
Servetus, Michael, **8231–8233**
and Antitrinitarianism, 7661
Christology of, 8232

convicted of blasphemy, 973
execution of, Calvin and, 3928, 7061, 7282, 7661
Service
as ecumenical concern, 2684, 2685, 2690
of Jews, as elect people, 2744
Service Day *(siil),* 1648
Service societies, as religious communities, 7719–7720
Servite order, origin of, 2827
Servius Tullius (Etruscan king), 5320, 7337, 7896
Śeṣa (serpent), 4325
Sesonchosis, 3053
Session, in Presbyterian polity, 1767
Sessions, George, 2608
Spinoza and, 2664
Sesŭmmu (Korean shaman), 5234–5235
Sesuto language, 3085
Set. *See* Seth
Setälä, Emil N., on poetry, 8134
Seth (biblical figure)
Freemasons on, 3194
in Nag Hammadi codices, 3517, 6396
Seth (deity), **8233–8234**
Adad assimilated with, 27
Atum and, 623
dragon defeated by, 2431
in Egyptian pantheon, 2704
emasculation of, 8233
fratricide by, 2985
in Gnosticism, 3517
Horus and, 4136
as incarnation of evil, 2962
kingship and, 2720, 5163
Osiris and, 2704, 4557, 5163, 6919–6920, 8233
pharaohs and, 8234
as pig, 7144
Plutarch on, 2514–2515
in Ramessid period, 2707–2708, 2709
representation of, 8233
Temple of Set (Satanist church) and, 8127
twin of, 9414
Sethe, Kurt, 2728, 2730
SETI. *See* Search for extraterrestrial intelligence
Seti I (Egyptian king), 1002
Setiloane, Gabriel M., 9388, 9389
on Tswana concept of God, 8656
Seton, Elizabeth, **8234**
Setsubun (eve of Risshun), 2411–2412
Seufert, Gunter, 1517–1518
Sevā (voluntary service) in
in Sikhism, 8393
in Swaminarayan movement, 8892
Sevādadan (Premcand), 10034
Sevāgrām Ashram, 546
Sevek (reindeer), 9394
Seven (number)
in alphabets, mystical speculation on, 270, 271
and ascension, 522–523
atomic substances, in Ājīvikas, 213
in Buddhist healing cults, 856
interpretations of, 6748
years of famine *vs.* plenty, 28
Seven (shaman's helper), 9394
"Seven commandments of the sons of Noah," in *halakhah,* 3753
Seven Emotions, Korean Neo-Confucianism and, 1931, 1932
Seveners Shiism. *See* Ismāʿīlī (Seveners) Shiism
700 Club, The (television program), 7712–7713
Seven Macaw (deity), 5797, 5798
Seven Real Persons (disciples of Wang Zhe), 2199
Seven Sacraments, The (Rubens), 4347
Seven Sacred Rites, Lakota, 5296–5297
Hanbleceyapi (vision quest), 5296
Hunkapi (making relatives), 5297
Inikagapi/Inipi (sweat lodge), 5296
Isnati Awicalowanpi (puberty ceremony), 5297
Tapa Wankayeyapi (throwing the ball), 5297
Wanagi Wicagluha (spirit keeping), 5296–5297
Wiwanyang Wacipi (Sun Dance), 5297
Seven Sisters story, 642–644
of Ngarrindjeri people, 648–651, 3392
regional versions of, 655
Seven Sleepers of Ephesus legend, 8440
Seven Story Mountain (Merton), 5879
Seventeen (number), interpretations of, 6749–6750
Seventh-day Adventism, **8235–8238**
apocalypse in, 413
and Branch Davidians, 6551
contemporary movement, 8237
and food taboos, 3168
"great disappointment" in, 8235
history of, 6558
institutionalization of, 8236
Koresh (David) on, 5237
and millennialism, 6552, 6558
in New Guinea, 9321
origins of, 1036, 8235–8236
on second coming of Jesus, 1036
transition period of, 8236–8237
and vegetarianism, 3173
White (Ellen Gould) in, 9724–9725
Seventh Seal, The (Bergman), 2472
Seven Treasures, The (Longchenpa), 5192–5193
Seventy (number), interpretations of, 6750
Seventy-two (number), interpretations of, 6750
Seven Valleys (Bahāʾ Allāh), 737
Seven Years' War (1756-1763), 9300
Severan dynasty (Roman Empire), 7006, 7059
Severus, Flavius Valerius (emperor), Constantine and, 1966
Severus, Septimius (Roman emperor)
Christian persecution by, 7059
Galen and, 3255
Severus of Antioch (patriarch), 5028, **8238**
on Monophysitism, 6154, 6155
on music, 6306
Syro-Egyptian revolt and, 8939
Severus Synagogue, 885
Seville, Council of (619), 4556
Sewamono (play), 2455
Sewell, William H., on practice, 8470
Sex, *vs.* gender, 3296–3297, 3299, 3420–3421
Sex and Repression in Savage Society (Malinowski), 5628
Sex and Temperament in Three Primitive Societies (Mead), 3420
Sex and the Empire that Is No More (Matory), 10027
Sexism
definition of, 3298–3299
feminism and, 9791
in Judaism, 3355
Sexism and God-Talk (Ruether), 3356
Sexton, Lorraine, 3398
Sextus Empiricus
on relativism, 3910, 7685
skepticism and, 8420
Sexual abuse. *See also* Incest
of children
in new religious movements, 5377
in Roman Catholicism, scandal, 7889–7890
Sexual assault. *See also* Rape
against Australian Indigenous women, 3393
gender hierarchy and, 3420
Tantrism, abuse in, 8244
trauma theory, on abuse, 8245–8246
in Turkey, legal assistance for, 3366
Sexuality, **8238–8254**. *See also* Androgyny; Castration; Celibacy; Chastity; Fertility; Homosexuality; Human body; Orgy; Phallus; Vagina
ablutions after, 12
accusations of, 8248–8250
in African religions
central Bantu, 1509
house symbolism and, in Dogon religion, 4104
Luba, 5523
in agricultural societies, 8239
alchemy and, 242
with animals, in horse sacrifices, Indo-European, 4133
Aphrodite as goddess of, 407–408
asceticism and, 7973
Augustine on, 3513–3514
in Australian Indigenous religion, 8239
in Buddhism, 2138, 5415
and pollution, 7084
cakras and, 1348–1349
in cargo cults, 1415
catharsis demanded by, 1460
in Celestial Masters, 2181, 2182, 2193
in Celtic religion, 1492–1493
Irish kingship and, 1490, 8239
in children, Fredu (Sigmund) on, 2239
in Chinese religion
myths of Huangdi and, 4144
self-control in, 8240
in Christianity, 2135, 3061
demonization of, 7080
gender and, 3357–3358
obscuration of, 2649
in Protestantism, 7457
in Puritanism, 7520
repression of, 8247–8248
in Roman Catholicism, 8244–8245
spirituality threatened by, 2647
clitoridectomy and, 1825
clothing and modesty and, 1833, 1835
coitus reservatus as self-control in, 8240
confession of, 1884
control of
by patriarchy, 9603
techniques, 8239–8240
in creation myths, 1987, 8239
critical thought on, 8241–8242
dance and, 2135
in Daoism, 2196, 9843
Darwinism and, 8478

Sexuality ***continued***
and death, Freud (Sigmund) on, 2238
between demons and humans, 2276, 2278
"deviant" forms of, 8242–8243
in Egyptian religions, 8239
Eliade (Mircea) on, 8239–8241
ethical issues in, 8245–8246
European rites of, **8247–8254**
in Black Mass, 8250
in Fedeli d'Amore, 8248
Frankist, 8250
in Khlysty sect, 8248
lucerna extincta rite, 8248–8249
magia sexualis, 8250–8252
Renaissance magic and, 8248
Skoptsy mutilations, 8248
witches' Sabbath, 8249–8250
female
feminist theologians on, 3037
as male possession, 7078
transformative power of, 9907–9908
feminist analysis of, 8243–8244
Foucault (Michel) on, 4163, 8241–8242, 8244
Freudian theory on (*See* Freudian psychology)
Freud (Sigmund) on, 2238
in gardens, 3280
gender and, 8244–8245
in Gnosticism, 3512, 8240–8241, 8247
of God, absence of, humor and, 4196
gods, intercourse with, 8239
in Graham's (Martha) works, 2159
in Greek and Roman religion, Dionysian feasts and, 8247
in Heaven's Gate, 3890–3891
hierodouleia (sacred prostitution), **3966–3970**
hieros gamos (sacred union), **3974–3978**
in Hinduism, 2135–2136, 5415
gender studies on, 3323
Kṛṣṇa and, 5457
in Hindu Tantrism, semen withheld in *maithuna* intercourse in, 4003
in Horton's (Lester) works, 2159
humor associated with, 4199, 4200
in East Asia, 4208
in Islam, 4212
incest (*See* Incest)
in Indian religions
horse sacrifice and, 8239
Kāma as god of, 4195
initiation rituals and, 4484, 4485, 4486
in Raëlian religion, 7597, 7598–7599
in Vajrayāna (Tantric) Buddhism
gender and, 3332, 3333
Guhyasamāja Tantra, 3708
Ramakrishna and, 7613–7614, 10067–10068
invigoration, sexual license as, 8208–8209
in Vinaya Piṭaka, 1258–1259
in Islam, 1559
sacred-sexual convergence and, 4212
in Jainism, among Vaimānika deities, 2025
in Japanese religion, women's role in, 3347
in Judaism, 2397, 2398
as commandment, 7586
Lilith and, 5458–5459
in Orthodox Judaism, 3353
Kāma Sūtra on, 2305
kuṇḍalinī and, 5266
in labyrinthine patterns, 5274
in Lao religion, 5314
Lawrence (D. H.) on, 5481
lotus symbolism and, 5519
magic, sexual, Crowley (Aleister) on, 2072
in Manichaeism, 5664
in men's studies, 5863
in Mesoamerican drama, 2463–2464
and metallurgy, 5988
of Minoan deities, 39
monsters and, 6164
moral norms in, differences among, 6184
mortality connected with, 4165
in Near Eastern religions, gender and, 3377–3378
in Neopaganism, 7830
in New Caledonia religion, between gods and humans, 6501
in new religious movements
the Family, 2987–2988, 6548, 6560
Oneida Community, 6535, 6558, 6563, 6732
in New Year festivals, 6590, 6591, 6592
in Ngaju Dayak religion, 8239
in nightmares, 4134
in North American Indian religions, 8239
nudity and, 6740
ontological questions on, 8246
orientations in, 8242, 8244–8245
in Orphism, 6895
of Osho, 7608
overview of, **8238–8247**
and pollution (*See* Pollution, sexual activity and)
positive *vs.* negative attitudes toward, 8239
in queer studies, 3300, 3314
in Quietism, 7558
ram symbolism and, 8310
religion and, in women's studies, 9792
renunciation of, nuns and, 6757
restraint in
in Jainism, 2624
during pilgrimage, 7158
in rites of passage, 7797–7798
in Roman Catholicism
abortion and, 5812
restrictions on, 5812
sacrality of, 8239–8241
sacred *vs.* profane and, 7972
semen, vital force in, 8240
in Shaker religion, 2138
Solov'ev (Vladimir) on, 8520
in spirit possession, 2934
in Tantrism, 8240, 8991, 8992
asceticism of, 529, 9822–9823
cakras and, 1045
caturānanda (four joys) in, 3965–3966
desire in, 2305
five *ma* sounds practice, 8050
in Trika Śáivism, 8046–8047
semen in, 1218, 2771
symbolism of, 1122–1123
transcendence in, 8015–8016
women in, 1218, 1221
yoni and, 9907
in Tikopia religion, 9197
transgressive practices, 1349–1350, 8242–8243
trauma and transcendence in, 8245
in Trobriand Islanders religion, 5184
utopianism and, 8242, 8243
during visions, 9612
water associated with, 9702
witch hunts and, 8249–8250
Devil and demons, alleged intercourse with, 8013, 8250
Sexuality of Christ in Renaissance Art and Modern Oblivion, The (Steinberg), 7082
Sexual misconduct
engaged Buddhism and, 2788
in Jehovah's Witnesses, 4821
Sexual organs. *See also* Phallus; Vagina
of animals, human consumption/transplantation of, for rejuvenation, 7684
Sexual Politics (Millet), 3311, 7007–7008
Sexual union, in agrarian ritual, 2559
Seyder Tkhines (ben Meir), 9037
Seyder tkhines u-vakoshes (tekhine collection), 9037
Seymour, William J., **8254**
Azusa Street Apostolic Faith Mission of, 7029
on speaking in tongues, 70
Sezgin, Fuat, 4717
Sforno, ʿOvadyah, biblical exegesis of, 867
Sgam po pa (Gampopa), 1153, 1225–1226, 1286, **8254–8256**
on *mahāmudrā,* 5598
Sgrub brgyud (Buddhist lineage), 1222
Sgrun pa (medium), 9185
Shaʿbān (month in Islamic year), 4713
Shabbat (Sabbath), **8256–8258**
in Christian week, 9812–9813
day and night in, 4866
domestic observances of, 2397
in Ethiopian Church, 2860
fasting on, 9813
feminine imagery for, 3019
Heschel (Abraham Joshua) on, 3963
Holdheim (Samuel) on, 4080
in Israel, 9982
Israelite laws on, 4740
in Israelite religion, 4548, 4550
Jesus on, 4849
law of, 8256–8257
Lent and, 1743
Maccabean revolt and, 3751
Marrano, 5718
meaning of term, 8256
nature in, 2645
number symbolism of, 6748
of Bēta Esraʾēl, 5003
in qabbalistic theology, 8389
return of Messiah and, 7586
in Samaritan religion, 8070
Shimʿon bar Yohʾai on, 8346
siddur prayers for, 8389
special Shabbats, 8257–8258
Torah readings at, 8257–8258
Shabbateanism. *See also* Shabbetai Tsevi
good and evil in, 3789
Hasidism and, 3786, 3790, 8173
historiography in, 4059
messianism in, 3786, 3790, 5978
Polish, 3186–3187
Qabbalah and, 8261
Scholem (Gershom) on, 8178
sexual rites and, 8250
underground cells of, 8262
women in, 8261
Shabbetai Sofer, liturgy by, 8387
Shabbetai Tsevi, **8255–8262**
aftermath from, 8259–8260, 8261–8262
apocalypses of, 420

Ba'al Shem Tov (BeSHT) on, 3786
background, 8258, 8260–8261
conversion of, 5017
ex-Marranos in, 5722
followers of, 2419, 2420
Magen David adopted by, 5558
influence of, 4999
Islam, conversion to, 3786, 8259, 8261
Jewish Renewal and, 4872
life and movement of, 8258–8259, 8261
messianism of, 1546, 3786, 3790, 5977, 5978, 7427
mysticism and, 6354
sexual rites and, 8250
as *tsaddiq,* 2768, 4983
Shabd Yoga, Twitchell (Paul) initiated into, 2602
Shabibiyya, 3211
Shabistarī, al-, **8262–8263**
on Perfect Human Beings, 8711
Shadare, Joseph, in Aladura movement, 104
Shades
in African religion
diviners and, 8659
healers called by, 3818, 3819
as intercessors and intermediaries, 3816, 3817
offerings to, 8657, 8658
in southern Africa, 8656, 8657, 8658, 8659
in Solomon Islands religions, 8514–8515
Shādhilī, Abū al-Ḥasan al-, Shādhilīyah and, 8823
Shādhilīyah (Ṣūfī order), 9009, 9010
characteristics of, 8823–8824
Ibn 'Aṭā' Allāh in, 4261–4262
Shadian incident (China), 4636–4637
Shādī Muqrī, 6638
Shād-Ohrmezd, 5660
Shadow puppet theater. *See* Puppet theater
Shadows
in Sotho religion (Africa), 8533
in Vanuatu religion, 8532
Shadow spirits
in Khanty religion, 5122–5123
in Mansi religion, 5122–5123
Shadow theater. *See Wayang*
Shafā'ī-Kadkanī, Muhammad Riḍā, on *Book of Khusraw,* 601
Shāfi'ī, al-, **8263–8266**
on *ahl al-bayt,* 198–199
Aḥmad ibn Ḥanbal and, 3762, 3763
at al-Azhar, 230
as "four source" theory architect, 9488–9489
Ibn Taymīyah and, 4277–4278
on *ijtihad,* 8264–8265
on imamate, 4393, 4394, 4396
on inheritance, 9657
jurisprudence theory of, 5548
on law, sources of, 8264–8265, 8854
al-Naẓẓām and, 6445
on *ḥadīth,* 3211, 3726, 4566
on *ijmā'* doctrine, 8265
on Qur'an, 3726
on *sunnah,* 3726, 8264, 8265
traditionalism and, 3760–3761
Shāfi'īyah (school of Islamic law), 9489
in Andalusia, 4594–4595
in Caucasus, 4614
development of, 4695, 5548
divorce in, 4708
doctrine of, 5548
founding of, 8265
Ḥanbālī *madhhab* constrasted with, 3761–3762
igmā' in, 4697, 5548
in Ash'arīyah, 533
inheritance in, 4709
marriage in, 4706, 4707
al-Māwardī on, 5787
paternity in, 4710
prevalence of, 4567
in South Asia, 4644, 4645, 4698
on *sunnah,* 4695, 4696
al-Taftāzānī on, 8957
and traditionalism *vs.* rationalism, 3761–3762
Shaft Tomb Complex, 5896
Shah, Raju, 2626
Shahādah (confession of faith), **8266–8267**
and adherence to Islam, question of, 8266–8267
for conversion to Islam, 5062
as creed, 2062
and *dhikr,* 2339
formulation of, 8267
in the Ka'bah, 5049
meaning of term, 8266
as pillar of Islam, 8266
in *ṣalāt* (prayer), 8058
in Sufism, 8267
transgression of, 8014
wording of, 8266
'Ayn al-Quḍāt on, 8813–8814
Ibn al-'Arabī on, 8819
in worship, 9816
Shahādah (messenger), 4398
Shahaptin tribes (North America), 6656
Shahar (deity), in Canaanite religion, 1395
Shaḥḥām, Abū Ya'qūb al-, as disciple of Abū al-Hudhayl al-'Allāf, 19
Shahīd, Ismā'īl, 4650–4651
Shāh-nāmah (epic), 2814
Shahnon Ahmad, 3078
Shahr (deity), in Canaanite religion, 1384, 1386
Shahrastānī, al-, **8267**
on Arabian deities, 444
in Ash'arīyah, 537–538
on Mazdakism, 5800, 5801
al-Milal wa al-Nihal work of, 8781
Shahrazūrī, Shams al-Dīn, 4555
Shahrour, Mohamad, on afterlife, 162
Shāh Walī Allāh. *See* Walī Allāh, Shāh
Shairp, John Campbell, 3695
Sha'irs (poet), 7221
Shaivism. *See* Śaivism
Shakan (deity), 5949
in divine bureaucracy, 5951
Shakarian, Demos, 7030
Shaked, Shaul, 203, 204
Shakers, **8268**
American
celibacy among, 5389
history of, 6557–6558
Lee (Ann) as founder of, 5389
and Athapaskan religious traditions, 574
celibacy among, 1475, 1477, 6516
dances of, 2138, 2149
dress code and social control among, 1835–1836
and family relations, 6562
female leadership of, 6563
founder of, 6516, 6534
Indian (*See* Indian Shakers)
Millerites and, 8268
monastic life of, 6122
sexuality and, 8243
tensions with society, 6548
Shakers, The (Humphrey), 2158
Shakers of Saint Vincent, 1437
Shakespeare, William
angels and, 348
on comets, 8735
ghosts in works of, 3475
Herder (Johann Gottfried) on, 3918
mana and, 5631, 5633
on necromancy, 6453
plays of, 2474
characteristics of, 2470
origins of, 2472
posthumous works attributed to, the Family and, 2988
on roles, 8483
tomb of, protective curse on, 2105
Yates's (Frances Amelia) study of, 9873–9874
Shake the Pumpkin. *See* Society of Medicine Men
Shaki, Mansour, 5801
Shaking Tent ceremonies, 471
in North American Indian religions, 6653
of Far North, 6655
of Northeast Woodlands, 6685
Shaking the Pumpkin (Rothenberg), 7224
Shakpana (deity), in Caribbean religions, 1434
Shaktis, women as, in Sikh Dharma, 3879
Shaku Sōen (Buddhist monk), 1188, 7740, 9805, 9950
Shakyō (copying of sutras), calligraphy and, 1371
Shala (deity)
as Adad's consort, 28
iconography of, 4317
Shalako ceremony (Zuni), 2461–2462
as sacrament, 7957
Shalash (consort of Dagan), 2126
Shalim (deity), in Canaanite religion, 1384, 1386, 1395
Shallum (king), Hosea and, 4137
Shālōm (peace), 6645, 6647, 7021
Shalshāla (Chain of High Priests), in Samaritan religion, 8070
Shaltiut, Mahmud, on *jihād,* 5742
Shaltūt, Maḥmūd, on *ḥadīths,* 3732
Shalu (Buddhist temple), 9051
Shalu Ribug Losal Tenkyong, 5224
Shamanism, **8269–8298**. *See also* Medicine men; Spirit(s); Witchcraft
in Africa
origins of, 83
in Sudanese religion, 8849–8850
in Ainu religion, 205, 206
animism in, 8277
anthropological studies of, problems with, 379
in Arctic religions
carved figures and, 471
history of study of, 474, 475
Inuit, 4528, 7505, 7509, 8220–8221, 8288–8289
prevalence of, 469
in sacrificial ceremonies, 470
soul beliefs in, 471
spirits' relationships with, 469
trances and, 471
ascension in, 519
asceticism and, 527
bears in, 808, 809
and binding, 938
birds in, 947–948
in Bon, 1007
in Bornean religion, 1022

Shamanism *continued*
Buddhist monks and, 3155, 3156
in Caribbean religions, 1430–1431
celestial ascents and underworld descents in, 8272
charisma and, 1548
in Chinese religion
healing in, 3862–3863, 8273
initiation rites of, 5179
magic of, 5592, 5593
Mongols and, 6141–6142
poetry of, 7213
spirit mediums and, 1589, 3862–3863
suppression of, 1589
women in, 3338, 3340
community rituals and psychosocial dynamics, 8278
and crisis of "presence," 2267
cross-cultural characteristics of shamans, 8275
cross-cultural differences in practices, 8275–8276
cross-gender dressing and, 1827
in Cuna religion (Panama), 2095
death and rebirth in, 8277–8278
in initiation, 8269–8270
debate over term, 5928
definitions and distinctions of, 8269–8270, 8280, 8281, 8287
demons and spirits in, 2284
descent into the underworld in, 2296–2297
divination in, 2370–2371
dreams in, 2488, 2490
drums in, 2494, 2497–2498, 2500, 7035, 7036
East Asian
ancestor worship associated with, 323
and dance and theater, 2453–2455
ecstasy or altered states of consciousness in, 2678–2679, 7349
induction of, 8285
integrative mode of, 8276–8277
South American, 8290–8291
techniques of, 8269, 8272
Eliade (Mircea) on, 946, 5528, 6983, 7349, 7387, 7769, 8269–8280, 8275, 8290
elixirs used in, 2770
emetics used in, 7508
enthusiasm in, 2807
in epics, 2814–2815, 8274
evolutionary roots of, 8279
in Finnish religion, Väinämöinen in, 9497
Finno-Ugric, 1453, 3109–3110, 3114
fire tricks in, 8274
in Garifuna religion, 3283–3284, 3286
Germanic, in myth, 8273
glossolalia in, 3507
healing in, 8273
hypnosis in, 8278
psychosocial therapies in, 8278–8279
soul loss in, 8279
healing touch in, 9256
hereditary, 8270, 8283, 8671
Hindu, exorcism by, 9825–9826
homosexuality and, 4116, 4117
Hungarian, 2415
importance of, religious and cultural, 8273–8274
initiation rites in, 4476, 4477
in Amazon, 8625, 8631
Australian Indigenous, 4477
caves and, 1470
in Central Asia, 5179
ecstatic discipline and, 8703
in Gran Chaco region, 8634, 8635
initiatory illness and selection of shamans, 8270, 8282–8283
as instruction, 8269
ordeals in, 8270–8271
public rites, 8271–8272
retreats for, 7769
Siberian, 4477, 8270–8271, 8282–8283
inspiration *vs.* ecstatic experience in, 4509
in Inuit religions, 4528, 7505, 7509, 8288–8289
Sedna (Sea Woman) and, 8220–8221
in Japan
female shamans in, 8273
health care and, 3867
in royalty, 4780
women in, 4795, 4921
in Khanty religion, 5123–5124
in Khoi religion, 5136
in Korea, 1548, 4105, 4208, 5228–5229, 5235
land and life in, 2618–2619
in Lao religion, 5313
magic *vs.*, 8269
in Mansi religion, 5123–5124
in Mapuche religion, 5689
medicine men distinguished from, 1785
in Mesoamerican religions
in Aztec religion, 5908–5909
in colonial period, 5920
contemporary, 5928
in Huichol religion, 4152, 4153
in Mixtec religion, 5912
in Tarascan religion, 5909
metamorphosis of shaman in, totemic figures portraying, vol. 1 color insert
meteorological beings in, 5992
miracles in, 6049–6050
modern, descent into the underworld in, 2297
in Mongol religions, 6140–6143, 6826–6827
development of, 6140–6141
in Negrito religions, 6455, 6457
neoshamanism, 2297, 6470, **8294–8298**
in nomadic-pastoralist societies, visions of, 9615
in Norse communities, 3219
North American, 6652, **8287–8290** (*See also* Vision quests)
of California, 6714
culture areas in, 8288–8290
drama in, 2462
of Far North, 6655, 6677–6678
and Ghost Dance, 3474
of Great Plains, 6699
Iroquois, 4542
of Northeast Woodlands, 6685–6686
of Northwest Coast, 6708
origins of, 6653
powers and functions, 8287–8288
of Southeast Woodlands, 6692–6693
of Southwest, 6721
Sun Dance and, 8844
symbolic death and resurrection in, 8703
and tricksters, 9354
vision quest in, 9610–9611
in Okinawan religion, 6813
in Olmec religion, 6818
ordination in, 6852
otherworld and, 6923, 6925
overview of, **8269–8280**
owl and, 6937
paradisial images in, 6983
performance and ritual in, 7048–7049
as polydaemonism, 7316
prehistoric, 7375
priests distinguished from Shamans, 1430
in primitive societies, 10065
psychedelic drugs in, 7468
psychobiological and neurological features of, 8276–8279
psychological aspects of, 7349
psychopathology and, 8270
psychopomp, shaman as, 8272–8273
research, cross-cultural, 8274–8276
in Sami religion, 8025, 8088
in San religion, 5136
séances in, 8285–8286
darkness in, 8285
dramatic structure of, 8274
soul escorted in, 8272–8273
spirit helpers in, 8285–8286
spirit links in, 8284
Siberian and Inner Asian (*See* Shamanism, Siberian and Inner Asian)
societal role
in North America, 8288
in Siberia, 8281–8283
songs in, 8283
sorcery in, 9769
soul flight in
and death, knowledge of, 8273
ecstasy and, 8272
séances and, 8286
as self-objectification, 8278
as source of religion, 2869
South American (*See* Shamanism, South American)
Southeast Asian, ascent to Heaven in, 8273
spirit possession and mediumship *vs.*, 8688
spirit possession in, 9370
spirits and
in neoshamanism *vs.* shamanism, 8297
relation between, 8269
self-representation and human consciousness in, 8277–8278
spiritual powers in, 8288
in Tibetan religion, 9191
healing and, 3864
tobacco in, 9216–9219
totemism in, 8277, vol. 1 color insert
traditions, survival and metamorphosis of, 8273
trees in, 9338
in Turkic religions, 2831, 9398, 9400, 9401
types of, 5123
clan shamans, 8281
core shamanism, 8275–8276
healers, 8276
institutional shamans, 8282
mediums, 8276
professional shamans, 8281–8282
shaman/healers, 8276
Siberian categories of, 8282
small-group shamans, 8281
underworld journey and, 9451
visionary experience as presentational symbolism, 8277
visions in, 9613

vocation in, 9633–9634
in Warao religion, 9575, 9688–9689
white *vs.* black shamans, 8272, 8273, 8282
women as
as mediums, 8276
in North America, 8288
in Yakut religions, 9866
Shamanism (Eliade), 7349
Shamanism, Siberian and Inner Asian, 5123, 6653, **8280–8287**
belief tradition in, 8283–8284
bridge symbolism of, 1052
in Buriat religion, 1325–1327, 4477
categories of shamans, 8282
in Chukchi religion
homosexuality and, 4116, 4117
occupational rites in, 8281
séances in, 8286
community status in, 8281–8283
cosmology in, 8283–8284
descent into the underworld in, 2296–2297
in Dolgan religion, 2395–2396
dress of shamans in, 8097, 8272, 8285
drums in, 2498, 7035
incarnation in, 4414
initiation in, 4477, 8270–8271, 8282–8283
Korean shamanism and, 5228–5229
vs. Mongol shamanism, 6140
mystical death and resurrection, in healing, 3813
origin of, 8280–8281
revival of, 8297
ritual objects in, 8284–8285
in Samoyed religion, 8096–8097
séances in, 8285–8286
in Southern Siberian religions, 8671, 8672
transmigration in, 9327
in Tunguz religion, 9394–9396
Shamanism, South American, **8290–8294**
alter ego in, 8584
in Amazonian religions
Araweté, 8628
Baniwa, 8624–8625
caboclo, 8632
Ge-Timbira, 8629–8630, 8631
Juruna, 8629
Quechua, 281–284
Tukanoan, 8623
Yanomami, 8625–8626
Yurupary and, 9918
in Andean religions, pre-Inca, 8603–8604
archaic patterns in, 8290
bird symbolism in, 8291–8292
common traits in, 8290
ecstasy trance in, 8290–8291
and forces of darkness *vs.* light, 2013
gender in, 3418
gourd rattle in, 8291
of Gran Chaco
Angaité, 8634
Caduveo, 8636–8637
Chamacoco, 8633–8634
Chiriguano, 8634
in Ayoré religion, 8633
Lengua, 8635
Makká, 8636
Mataco, 8635
hallucinogen plants in, 8292–8293
in Mundurucú religion, 8581
jaguars and, 4763, 8291, 8292, 8582
in Kulina religion, 2012
music in, 6272–6273
political *vs.* religious authority in, 1430
rattles in, 8291
in Selk'nam religion, 8224, 8225–8226
vision quest in, 8293
Shamanistic ecstasy, 2678–2679
Shamanistic illness, 9613
Shamanwa (supreme being), 5524
Shamar pa, 5103
lineage of, 5103–5104
Shamash (deity), 4316, 4317. *See also* Utu
crossing the sea, 989
eye of, 2940–2941
as god of justice, 4727
Mithra identified with, 8838
saw of, 967
as sun god, 8837–8838
in triad, 9349
Worm of Sickness and, 3811
Shamayim hadashim (Abravanel), 17
Shamayin (heavens), in Hebrew Scriptures, 3884
Shame. *See also* Guilt; Sin(s)
in rituals, 7836–7837
Shame cultures, *vs.* guilt cultures, 7755–7756
Shamen tong (office of superintendent), 8995
Shāmil (*imām* of Dagestan), 4615
Shammai
house of, on afterlife, 153
school of (Beit Shammai), **815–816**
Shams al-Dīn (Muslim writer), 4663
Shams al-Dīn al-Samatrā'
mysticism of, 25
Rūmī and, 7935–7936, 8818
Shamshi-Adad I (king), 5163
Shanak pas. *See* Karma pas
Shandao (Buddhist master), 1239, 1272, **8298–8299**
Hōnen, influence on, 4119
on *nianfo* recitation, 8298–8299
and Pure Land Buddhism, 1601, 2176, 4922
and recitative *nianfo,* 6602
vows of, 8298
Shangbo (Ṣangbo), in Caribbean religions, 1433
Shangdi (deity), **8299–8300**
and atheism, 577
Bible translation debate over, 1633
Daoism and, 8300
defined, 8300
displeasure over disruption of earth, 1625
Huangdi and, 8299
as Judeo-Christian God, 8300
king's relationship to, 5178
monotheism issue and, 1631
sacrifices to, 1911, 1914–1915
tomb offerings and heavenly realm, 1582
in Zhou dynasty, 1584
Shang dynasty (China)
atheism in, 577
bone oracles in, 1891, 6834
cities in, 1803
dao in, 2172
de in, 2173
divination in, 2372, 2374, 5352
entertainment of the dead in, 4206
human sacrifice in, 1570–1571, 4105, 4183
inscriptions from, afterlife in, 169
kingship in, 5178
law in, 5352
magic in, 5592
Mandate of Heaven and, 5178
origin myth of, 5178
overthrow of, 5352, 7790
religious beliefs and practices, 1582
shamanism in, 3340
Shangdi in, 8300
tao-t'ai pattern used in, 9273
tian in, 9172
women in, 3338, 3340
writing in, 1370
wu healers in, 3862
Shanghai (China), Judaism in, 5008
Shang Huang, 1584
Shangjunshu (Shang Yang), 5395
Shango (spirit/deity). *See also* Ṣango
in Caribbean religions, 1433, 1434
cult of, in Trinidad, 1434–1435
foods favored by, 3171
in Kele ceremony, 1436
in Latin American fiction, 3065
Shang pa Bka' brgyud school of Buddhism, 5223
Shangqing dao (Way of Highest Clarity), 2637
Sima Chengzhen and, 2174, 8399, 8400
visionaries in, 2205
Shangqing daolei shixiang (Daoist text), 2210
Shangqing scriptures (Daoist), 2182, 2194–2195, 2205
messianism in, 2195
organization of, 2203
Shang Shen, 1584
Shangs pa bka' brgyud order (Buddhist), 1226–1227
Shang-Ti. *See* Shangdi
Shang Yang, 1589
Han Fei Zi, influence on, 3772
legalism and, 5395
Shangyuan Jie festival, 1642
Shanhai jing (book), 1624
Shanhua Monastery (Buddhist temple), 9047
Shanindar Cave (Iraq), Neanderthal burial in, 3136
Shankara. *See* Śaṅkara
Shan sacrifices, 1590, 1591, 7267
Shanshu (Morality books), 2187
Shansi Pure Land movement, 4922
Shan-Tao. *See* Shandao
Shantiniketan (pedagogy), 8958
"Shanti Path" (Veda), nature in, 2620
Shāntivānam Ashram, 547
Shanwuwei. *See* Śubhākarasiṃha
Shaolin boxing, 5731, 5736
Shaolin Monastery, 994
martial arts at, 5735, 5736
Shao Yong, 1560
cosmology of, 1578
Neo-Confucianism and, 1603
on *taiji,* 8959
Shapash (deity)
Athirat (Asherah) and, 590
in Canaanite religion, 1384, 1387
Shape of Time, The (Kubler), 4297
Shaper (creator being), 5797
Shape shifting, **8300–8304**. *See also* Therianthropism
borderline and confused identities in, 8302–8303
in Celtic religion, 1487
escape by, 8301
immortalization and, 8302
liberation and, 8302
as punishment, 8301–8302
reincarnation as, 8301–8302
revelation function of, 8303
in sleep, 8440–8441
strategic deception by, 8301
Shapira, Malka, 9381

Shapshu (deity), 3376
Shāpūr I (king of Persia)
Mani and, 5649, 5651, 5655, 5659, 5662, 5665
Shemu'el the Amora and, 8318
Shāpūr II (king of Persia), 6479
Manichaeism under, 5660
Sharaga Sadan (Home of Learning), 7610
Sharar, 'Abdul Halīm, 10035
Sharashtānī, al-, 9128
Sha'rawi, Huda, 3365
Sharf, Robert, 7740, 9262–9263
Sharḥ (interpretation), 8950
Sharḥ al-'aqā'id (al-Nasafī), 4399, 8957
Sharḥ al-'aqā'id al-Nasafīyah (al-Taftāzānī), 8957
Sharh-i Ta'arruf (al-Mustamli), 5056
Sharḥ Tajrīd al-I'tiqād (al-Ḥillī), importance of, 3982
Sharī'ah. *See* Islamic law
Shariden (Zen temple compounds), 9049
Sharīf, Abū 'Alī al-Hāshimī, al-, Ḥanābilah and, 3764
Sharīf al-Murtaḍā, al-, 'Abd al-Jabbār and, 4
Sharīfs (descendants of Muḥammad), in *mawlids,* 5789–5790
Shark Ancestor (ancestral being), journey of, 2003
Sharks, in Australian Indigenous myths, 661
Sharma, Arvind, Sharpe (Erice) and, 8769
Sharma, Pandit Shav, Āyurveda and, 3857
Sharp, Henry, 5443
Sharpe, Eric J., 7091, **8304–8305**
historiography of, 4049
at University of Sydney, 8769
Sharpe Symposium, theology and scholarship at, 8305
Sharruma (deity), in Hurrian and Hittite religions, 4230
Shashamane (Ethiopia), Rastafari community at, 7627
Shasō (priest), 7411, 7412
Shas Party, 9982–9983
Shastri, Dharmendra Nath, 6773
Shaṭaḥāt (intoxicated utterance), 4570
Shaṭḥ (ecstatic utterance), 4511
Shaṭṭārī Ṣūfī order, in South Asia, 4647, 4648
Shattuck, Gardiner, 75
Sha'ul. *See* Saul
Shaushka (deity), 3595
in Hurrian and Hittite religions, 4230
Shaving, ritual
for *ḥājj*, 7157
for Hindu pilgrimage, 7169
in purification, 7508
Shavu'ot (Pentecost), 1040, **8305–8306**
in calendar of Boethusians *vs.* Pharisees, 8019
domestic observances of, 2397
in Jewish calendar, 4866, 4867
leavened bread for, 5388
maḥzor liturgy for, 8390
Shaw, George Bernard, 2475
Shaw, Gregory, 3005
Shaw, Rosalind, 3025–3026
on syncretism, 2089
Shawabtis (mummiform figures), 4319, vol. 9 color insert
Shawkani, Muḥammad al-, 6738
Shawn, Ted (Edward), 2157–2158
Shawnee religion (North America)
Prophet movement in, 6666
puberty rites of, 6683
rain dance in, 7603
study of, 6672
on witchcraft, myths of origin of, 6684–6685
women in, 6692
Shawwāl (month in Islamic year), 4714
Shayatin
exorcism of, 2933
vs. zār masters, 2933
Shaybānī, Muhammad ibn Hasan al-
Abū Yūsuf and, 22, 24, 25
in Ḥanafī school of law, 22, 24, 4695, 5547
al-Shāfi'ī and, 8263
Shaykhah, in *zār* exorcism ceremony, 2148, 2149
Shaykh al-Islam (title), **8306–8307**
Shaykh al-Islam, al-Majlisī as, 5623
Shaykhīyah movement, **8307–8309**
as *ghulāt* (extremist), 8324
Bābism and, 8307, 8308–8309
Shaykh Aḥmad, life and thought of, 8307–8308
succession of leadership in, 8308
Shaykhs (spiritual masters)
appointment of, 9005
charisma of, 1547
in Ṣūfī orders, 8820, 8821–8823
Rastī (Sayyid Kāẓim) as leader of, 728
residence of, 9005
as saints, 8821
spiritual authority of, 9005
as spiritual guides, 8710–8711
teaching recitation of Qur'ān, 9201
treatment of guests by, 9007
Shaykh Yusuf (saint), 4608
Shayṭān (Satan). *See* Satan, in Islam
Shcherbatskii, Fedor. *See* Stcherbatsky, Theodore
She (sacred earth mound or earth god), 1584, 1615–1616
cult of, 1913
Shearjashub (son of Isaiah), 4546, 4548
Sheba, Ethiopia influenced by, 224
Shedim (demon), 2533
Sheen, Fulton J., television ministry of, 7712
Sheen, Juliet, on human rights, 5363
Sheep and goats, **8309–8312**. *See also* Scapegoat
chthonic symbolism and, 8310–8311
in prehistoric art, 8309–8310
in prehistoric religions, 7378, 7383, 8310
qualities of, 8310
sacrifice of, 8310
in African religions, at childbirth, 3819
in Arabian religions, 445
in Bible, 8310
in Caribbean Kele cult, 1436
in Greek religion, 3682, 8310
in Islam, 8310
in Israelite religion, 926, 927
in prehistoric religions, 7384
in Roman religion, 8310–8311
of Thor, 9166
touching, to transfer evil to, 9256
weddings and fertility associated with, 8310
"She Had Some Horses" (Harjo), 7225
(Sheḥiṭah), 5106
Shehu. *See* Dan Fodio, Usuman
Shehu Ahmadu Lobbo, 4606
Sheik (Sufi elder), exorcisms by, 2933
Sheikhs. *See Shaykhs*
She'iltot (Aha), 9236
Shekhinah (presence of God), **8312–8316**
androgny and, 8243
gender of, 953, 3350, 3550, 3586, 8315–8316
hiddenness of, Esther and, 2848
meaning of term, 8312–8313
personifications of, 4080
as phallic vision, 7080
prayer and, 8313
in Qabbalah, 4981, 8315
qabbalist meaning of, 3550
rabbinic meaning of, 3550, 8313–8315
sacred space and, 8313–8314
seeing face of, by rabbis, 7587
Torah study and, 8314–8315
SHEkinah (magazine), 1037
Shelamim (offering), 4746
Sheldon, C. M., 4844
Sheldon, Wilmon, 6962
Shellagh-na-gig, 9908
Shelley, Mary, 811
Frankenstein, as rebellion against God, 3059
Shelley, Percy Bysshe
Gnosticism and, 3526
on Jesus, 4844
Shells
as money, 6137
as musical instruments, Mesoamerican, 6267, 6268, 6269
Shelomah. *See* Solomon
Shelomoh ben Yehudah, 4988–4989
Shelomoh ben Yitsḥaq. *See* Rashi
Shelomoh de Modena, 7234
Shelomoh ibn Gabirol
ethics of, 4912
in Jewish thought and philosophy, 4890
Shelters for homeless and victims of abuse, Raphael House as, 4102
Shelun school of Yogācāra Buddhism, 6992, 9901
textual basis of, 1576
Zhiyan and, 4146
Shema' (Hear O Israel)
as creed, 2052
in *siddur* and *maḥzor,* 8388, 8389
in rabbinic Judaism, 4976–4977
Torah study not interrupted by, 8346
Shema (High Egypt), 5163
Shemaryah ben Elḥanan, 4990
Shembe, Isaiah, **8316–8317**
AmaNazaretha founded by, 103
Jesus Christ, relation to, 8317
as messenger figure, 6733
prophetic movement, 1720, 7443
Shemini 'Atseret. *See* Sukkot
Shemittah (sabbatical year)
in Jewish ecology, 2644
Zionist agricultural settlements and, 9981
Shemot. See Exodus
Shemu'el, Yitsḥaq ben. *See* Riy
Shemu'el ben Ḥofni, monograph on benedictions by, 3745
Shemu'el ben Qalonimos the Elder
in Ashkenazic Hasidism, 542–545
eschatology of, 542
on passions, 542
writings of, 543
Shemu'el ibn Tibbon, *Guide of the Perplexed* translated by, 5616, 5617
Shemu'el of Nehardea
juridicial sovereignty principle, 3753
yeshivah under, 9883
Shemu'el the Amora, **8318**
Shen (lightning), 7604

Shen, Master, Confucianism and, 1898
Shen (positive spirits), soul and, 8555
Shen Buhai, Han Fei Zi, influence on, 3772
Shenchen Luga (Gshen chen klu dga), 2549, 9331
Shen Dao, 1572
Sheng (musical instrument), 6293
Sheng (sage). *See* Sagehood
Shengmin (Chinese poem), 7213
Sheng sheng (life life), in Confucianism, 2632, 2634
Shengyan (Buddhist monk), 1168
Shengzhao, 1576
Shenhui (Buddhist monk), 1292
  Huineng as teacher of, 4154
  on sixth patriarch, 1577
  Southern school and, 1522, 1601
Shen Nong (deity), as sage-king, 1627
Shennong bencao jing (Tao), 8996
Shenoute the Archimandrite (or "the Great"), **8318–8320**
Shenrab Miwoche (Gshen rab mi bo che), 2549
Shenshaī (Parsi community), 6998
Shentong Monastery (Buddhist temple), 9045
Shenxiao Fa order, 1602
Shenxiu (Buddhist teacher)
  on enlightenment, 6631
  Huineng and, 4154
  lineage of, 1601
  as sixth patriarch, 1577
  at Yuquansi, 1521
Shenxiu (Chan master), 995, 1292
Shen Yanbing, 3070
She'ol (underworld), 9453–9454
  in Bible, 152
  deliverance from, 8564
  Hades and, 3725
  in Hebrew scriptures, 3884
  merit and, 5871
  New Testament interpretation of, 8564
  Persephone identified with, 34
  in rabbinic Judaism, 8564
  soul and, 8557
Shepard, Paul, Earth First! influenced by, 2562
Shepenwepet I (Divine Adoratress of Amun), 2709
Shepherd
  deities of
    Hermes as, 3936
    Pan as, 6957
  in winter carols, 9743–9744, 9745
Shepherd, Gary, 6539
Shepherd of Hermas (Christian text), 7758
Shepherd of Hermas (Tertullian), 9086
Sheppard, H. J., 237
Sherbro people, cannibalism among, 1404
Sherira' Gaon, 4989, **8320**
  rabbinic authority, defense of, 4059
Sherpas (Nepal)
  dances of, 2138
  rituals of, 7842
  sacred offerings by, 3136
Sher Shah (emperor of India), Akbar and, 216
Shevah (praise), 983
She Who Changes (Christ), 9100
Shi (deity), 2312
Shibata Hamamori, Jikkyō-kyō Shintō and, 8364
Shi class, Confucius on, 1936
Shi Dao'an. *See* Dao'an
Shidian (festival), 5434
Shidian rites, 6293
Shidi jinglun (book), 1576
Shidoso (private monks), 4784
Shield of David. *See* Magen David
Shields, in warfare, 9682–9683
Shifā' ('Iyād), 4585
Shifā', al- (Ibn Sīnā), 4274, 4275, 4276
Shih-King (Book of Odes), 808
Shihuangdi (Chinese emperor), 7267
Shi Huiyuan. *See* Huiyuan
Shī'ī *madhhab,* 9490
Shiio Benkyō, 4939
Shiism, **8320–8346**. *See also specific countries and doctrines*
  Abbasid revolution and, 8321
  afterlife in, 161
  ahl al-bayt in, 198–199, 257
  'Alawīyūn's relation to, 225–227
  'Alī ibn Abī Ṭālib in, 257, 259, 8320
  allegiance to family of the Prophet, 3008
  and Howrūz festival, 6731
  'Āshūrā' in, 549–550, 1517
  authority in, 695–696
  Bābīs and, 728, 729
  in Bengal, 825
  bequests in, 4710
  blood in, 987
  caliphate in, 1365–1366, 1367
  charismatic leadership in, 1546–1547
  in Chile, 4684
  in China, 4634–4635
  Corbin (Henry) on, 1984
  creeds in, al-Ḥillī and, 3982
  cult of Fāṭimah, 3008–3009
  da'wah (missionary) aspect of, 2225
  definition of, 8320
  development of, 4571, 4693, 8320–8322
  devotional allegiance to, 9819–9820
  divorce in, 4708
  doctrine in, 2064–2065
  domestic observances in, 2402
  dominance of, 4583
  eschatology of, 2838, 2839
  esotericism of, 4572
  in Europe, 4678, 4681
  family law in, 3368
  fasting in, 2996
  Fourth Support doctrine of Shaykh Aḥmad, 8308
  free will and predestination in, 3212–3213
  gender in, 3368–3369
  ghaybah (concealment) in, 3468–3469
  ghulāt (extremists) in, 8323–8324
  Gnosticism in, 3523
  God in, unity of, 3561
  groups within, 7565
  ḥadīths in, 3732–3733, 4565
    al-Ḥillī, methodology of, 3982
  Hawzah (seminaries) in, **3800–3802**
  heterodoxy in, 6912
  hierarchy in, 5290
  al-Ḥusayn ibn 'Alī, role of, 4234, 4235
  Ḥusayn's (Ṣaddām) restrictions on, 5088–5089
  iconography of, 4297, vol. 1 color insert
  ijmā' in, 4374
  ijtihād in, 4375
  imamate in, 7285–7286
    development of, 4693
    doctrine of, 259, 4695, 8324–8325
    functions of, 259
    Husaynid, 8321
    Ismā'īlī Shiism, 4395, 4572
    Twelver Shiism, 4394–4395
    Zaydī Shiism, 4395–4396, 8324
  Imāmī (*See* Imāmī Shiism)
  incarnation in, 4416
  inheritance in, 4709
  'iṣmah in, 4724, 4725, 4726
  Ismā'īlīyah (*See* Ismā'īlī Shiism)
  Ithna Ashariyah (*See* Imāmī Shiism)
  Ja'far al-Ṣādiq in, 4760
  jihād in, 4918–4919
  kalām of, 5068
  Karbala as center of, 5088
  Kufan revolts and, 8320–8321
  leadership model of, 6737
  life in, 5446–5447
  literature of, 4584
  mahdī in, 5981–5982
  and Malayan Islam, influences on, 3076
  marriage in, 4705, 4706, 4707
  martyrs in
    Ḥusayn as, 5088
    public lamentation for, 7631–7632
  millenarianism in, 6030
  missionaries in, 4583
  mosques in, architecture of, 6208
  Muḥammad in, 6227
  Mu'tazilah in, acceptance of, 6320–6321
  narrative traditions of, 2446–2447, 4572
  in North Africa, 4583, 4584
  on Qur'ān, 4572
  orgy and, 6879
  origins of, 4571, 8320–8322
  orthodoxy in, 6912
  overview of, **8320–8325**
  paternity in, 4710
  pilgrimages of, 5088, 7155
  poetry of, 4712, 7207, 7222
  popular practices in, 8345
  prayer in, 4397, 9816 (*See also* Ṣalāt)
    authority on, 8054–8055
    for healing, 3831–3832
    number prayers in, 8056
    performance of, 8057–8058
    Seljuk Turks and, 1367
  Rāwzah-khvānī in, 7631–7632
  saints in, 8035
  schools of law in, 4567, 5547, 5549
    establishment of, 4695
    geographical distribution of, 4698–4699
    principal figures in, 4700
  self-sacrifice in, 8830–8831
  in South Asia, 4641, 4643, 4645–4647, 4649, 4654
  in Southeast Asia, 4664
  split from Sunnīs, schools of law after, 5547
  spread of Sufism and, 4562–4563
  subsects of, 4572
  sunnah in, 8853–8854
  of Ṭabāṭabā'ī's impact on, 8945–8946
  tafsīr (Qur'anic exegesis) in, 2225, 8954–8955
  taqīyah in, 8999
  ta'ziyah in, 4572, 9022–9023
  Twelver (*See* Imāmī Shiism)
  in United States, 4690
  vs. Ibāḍiyya sect, 4248, 4249
  walāyah in, 9658–9660
  women in, 3368–3369
  zakāt in, 9925
  Zaydī (*See* Zaydī Shiiism)
  Zoroastrians and, 10003
Shiji (Grand Scribe's Records)
  as historiography, 4026
  Huangdi in, 4144

Shiji (Grand Scribe's Records) ***continued***
study of *ru* in, 1917
Shi ji (Sima Qian), 5316
Li Shaojun in, 5465
Shijie zongjiao (Chinese periodical), 2214
Shijing. See Odes, Classic of/ Scripture of
Shikaku (realized enlightenment), 9077
Shikan (insight), 7216
Shikantaza, attention in, 605–606
Shikoku (Japan), pilgrimage to, 7165, 7166
Shikshapatri (Sahajanand), code of behavior in, 8890–8891
Shikwah (Iqbāl), 4534
Shilluk religion (East Africa)
cosmogony of, 2567
culture hero in, 2091
funeral rites in, 9226
high deity in, 2567
myths of, 93, 95–96, 97
regicide in, 5157, 5158, 5169
Shiloach, ha- (journal), Ginzberg (Asher) in, 3495
Shiloh (religious organization), in Jesus Movement, 4852, 4853
Shils, Edward, 1544
Shimao Toshio, 3073
Shimazaki Tōson, 3072
Shimazono Susumu, 6405
Shimenawa (straw rope), 2410
Shimen chengtong (Zhongqian), 9179
Shimon Bār Māma, 6480
Shim'on bar Yoḥ'ai (rabbi), 4867, **8346–8347**
as saint, 8035
tomb of, 7161–7162
Shimon Baṣīdi (catholicos), 6480
Shim'on ben Gamli'el, Me'ir against, 5830
Shim'on ben Gamli'el II, 3269, **8347**
on capital punishment, 3752
Shim'on ben Laqish, **8347–8348**
Abbahu and, 2
Shim'on ben Sheṭaḥ, 3158
Shimon Dinbah, 6480
Shim'on of Basra, 4989
Shimsang (Buddhist monk), Huayan Buddhism in Japan, role of, 4146
Shimshon. *See* Samson
Shimshon ben Avraham. *See* Rash
Shinakarani (shaman's wife), 3418
Shinan, Avigdor, 6020
Shin Arahan (Buddhist monk), 1132, 1136
Shinboku (sacred trees), in Shintō, 2640
Shin Buddhism, *karman* in, 5101
Shinchi (Buddhist monk), 9944
Shindai no maki (Scroll of the divine age), *Nihonshoki* interpreted with, 4805
Shinde, Tarabai
feminism of, 3320
translation and analysis of, 3322
Shingaku (religious and ethical movement), 4551, 9311
founder of, 6572
Shingi rules, in Zen Buddhism, 9945–9946
Shingon-Shugendo, 4785
Shingonshū school of Buddhism, 1221, 1243, **8348–8354**
Ajikan visualization in, 8351
Chinese transmission of, 8348–8349
doctrines of, 1178, 1179, 1217, 1243
drums in, 2497
esoteric elements in, 8348, 9075
formation of, 1176–1177, 1243
hand-copying works in, 1181
imperial favor for, 4784–4785
incarnation in, 4417
Indian origins of, 8348
Kōmyō Shingon (Clear Light Mantra) in, 8351
Kōyosan (Mount Kōya) in, 8352
Kūkai as founder of, 8349–8350
Mahāvairocana Buddha in, 5454
Mahāvairocana in, 5608
maṇḍalas in, 1217, 5644
maṇḍala training rituals, four-part, 8351–8352
medieval developments in, 8350
meditation in, 9834
music in, 6300
nirvāṇa in, 6632
patriarchs, traditional lineage of, 8349
poetry of, 7215
Pure Land school and, 8350
Pure Lands in, 7503
related terms and concepts, 8348
ritual practice and path to awakening in, 8350–8351
Ryobu Shinto and, 8361
Saichō and Kūkai in, 8350
Shugendō and new religions, relation with, 8352
Śubhākarasiṃha and, 8804
tantric elements of, 8985
temple of, 1180
vs. Tendai school, 8350, 9075, 9077, 9078
Vajrasattva in, 9515
Western form of, 8352–8353
Shinjō. *See* Shimsang
Shinkan (divine official), 7411
Shinkishinron (Hirata Atsutane), soul in, 4022
Shinkoku (divine nation), 7271
Shinkō shūkyō (new religions in Japan), 3156, 6513, 6514, 6521, **6572–6575,** 7274–7275
Agonshū movement, 8352
ancestor worship in, 324
Aum Shinrikyō, **631–633,** 6515
religious studies and, 8778
brainwashing in, 6515
characteristics of, 6573
definition of, 6572
and deprogramming, 6523
early, 6573–6574
globalization of, 6574
health care and, 3867
historical background for, 6572–6573
laity in, 5289–5290
legitimation and, 5400–5401
Maitreya in, 5622
Nakayama Miki in, 6404
new, 6574–6575
periods of development of, 632
Risshō Kōseikai, 5400–5401, 7794–7795
Seikai kyūsei-kyō, 8369
Shingon as basis of, 8352
Shintō and, 8358, 8367, 8369–8370
Sōka Gakkai, 5400, **8508–8510**
study of, 6523
Tenshō kōtai jingū kyō, 8369
women in, 3346–3347, 8695
Worldmate, 8369–8370
Shinny, 752
Shin'nyoen, 6574
Shinnyokan (Buddhist text), 9077
Shin Pure Land Buddhism, Suzuki (D. T.) and, 8886
Shinran (Buddhist monk), 1179, 4939, 6632, **8354–8356**
as founder of Jōdo Shinshū, 8981, 9080
ethical teachings of, 1086–1087
in Jōdo Shinshū school of Buddhism, 1244, 4934
on *karman,* 5101
and married monks, 1183
on meditation, 1294
on merit, 5872
on morality, 1281–1282
on Amitābha, 292
on *mappō,* 5687
on paradox of redemption, 6990
in popular religion, 4796
on power, 7353–7354
and recitative *nianfo,* 6602, 6603
relics of, 1087
in rural areas, 1182
Shotoku, veneration of, 8375
Tanluan as source for, 8981, 8982
Shinryū (Buddhist monk), 9076
Shinsen shojiroku (New compilation of the register of families), 4785
Shinshū. *See* Jōdo Shinshū school of Buddhism
Shintai (divine body), hills as, in Shintō, 2640
Shintō, **8356–8371**
aesthetics in, 51
amulets in, 2410
ancestor worship in, 324
and food offerings, 3171
Hirata Atsutane on, 5215
anthropomorphism in, 389
Buddhism, relationship with, 3154, 4796–4797, 4939, 9836
in combinatory cults, 8361
Hirata Atsutane's combination of, 8365
honjisuijaku theory and, 4121–4122
kami and buddhas, amalgamation of, 8359–8361
Kuroda on, 8357
and literature, 1180
in Meiji period, 8356, 8366
Shotoku Taishi and, 8375
Zen, 9948
clergy in, vestments of, 1828
Confucianism and, 3802, 8363, 9870
court offerings in, 8358–8359
creation in, 4754
deities of
Amaterasu as sun goddess in, 8841
Buddhist deities linked to, 4121–4122
doctrine in, 2382
domestic observances of, 2409, 2410
drama in, 2454
ecology and, **2638–2641**
enthronement ceremony, 1514–1515
eschatology and, 2834
etymology of term, 4782
festivals in, 8364, 8369
and fiction, 3074
Fuji-kō mountain cults in, 8364
goddess worship in, 3587
Great Teaching *(taikyō)* and, 8366–8367
healing in, 3868–3870
giving thanks for, vol. 7 color insert
Hirata school and Hirata Atsutane on, 4022, 8365
historical development of, 2639–2640
in history of Japan
contemporary, 8368–8370
early history, 8358–8359
Edo period, 8362–8365
medieval period, 8359–8362
Meiji period, 8365–8368
World War II and, 8368
Hokke, 6607
Jikkyō-kyō sect of, 8364
in Kamakura period, 4786
kami in, 5073, 7274
Kogaku (Ancient Learning), 5215

kō (religious confraternities)
in, 8362, 8364
Kokugaku (national learning)
movement and, 8364–8365
Konkōkyō and, 5225
laity in, 5289
laws on, 8356
libations in, 5434
lineages in
in early period, 8359
esoteric elements and, 8350
local rites in, in early period, 8359
magic in, 5594
in Meiji restoration, 4790, 4791
monkeys in, 6152
mountains in, 4796
divine power of, 6214
as objects of devotion, 2317
music in, 6300
nationalism and, 8357, 8366–8367, 8368–8369
Nihonshoki interpreted in, 4805
Oho-harahi (confession) ceremony, 1886
Omotokyō and, 6825
ordination in, 6856
pilgrimage in, 7165, 8360, 8364, 8369
poetry of, 7215, 7216
in popular religion, 4794–4795
postures and gestures in, 7343
power in, 7346
purification in, 5197, 7504
regulation of, 9310, 9311, 9313
as religion, 2640, 7692
and "religion," meaning of, 8762
religious texts of, 4813
revival of, 4789–4790
rituals in
ma principle and, 7989
norito in, 6649–6650
rivers in, 7863
Ryobu sect of, 8361
sacred and profane in, 7970
sacred language in, 5303
sacred objects in, 7698
sacrifice in, 8005
Sannō sect of, 8361–8362
scriptures of, 4783
sect movements and new religions *vs.* shrines, 8367
shrines in
civic shrines and shrine-temple complexes, 8360–8361
development of, 8359
as dwelling places for the *kami,* 7980, 7981
in Edo period, 8363–8364
healing and, 3868–3870
Ishikiri Shrine, 3869
registration of, 8358–8359, 8366
"twenty-two shrines" group of, 8360, 8361–8362
Yoshida (Kyoto), 8364
society, relations with, 8462–8463
State Shintō *(kokka shintō),* 8368, 9313, 9314
abolishment of (1945), 8777
and study of religion, 8776, 8777
study of, 8356–8358
Suika sect of, 8363
in syncretic religions, 5073–5074
as term
early references to, 8359
meaning of, 8356
in Tokugawa period, 4789
trees in, 9338
triads in, 9348
Watarai sect of, 8361
debunking of ancient texts of, 8364–8365
Yamazaki Ansai in, 9869–9870
Yūitsu (Yoshida) sect of, 4122, 8362
Shintō and the State, 1868-1988 (Hardacre), 7274
Shinva, Vandana, 2623
Shinwalule (burial ground), 818
Shipibo (trickster), 9358
Ships. *See* Boats
Shiqu imperial conference, 1575
Shi'r (poetry), 7205
Shirakawa, Go, music and, 6301
Shirakawa clan, licensing of priests by, 8363
Shīrāzī, Abū al-Faraj al-, Ḥanābilah and, 3765
Shīrāzī, Ḥasan Mahdī, on 'Alawīyūn, 227
Shīrāzī, Muḥammad ibn Ibrāhīm al-. *See* Mullā Ṣadrā
Shīrāzī, Muḥammad Ṣadrā. *See* Mullā Ṣadrā
Shirāzī, Shāh Faṭhullāh, 4647
Shīrāzī, Shaykh Abū Isḥāq al-, 6641
Shirdi Sai Baba
life of, 8027
Sai Baba movement and, 8026–8027
Shirk (polytheism or idolatry), 3562
meaning of, 8014
popular healing as, 3835
rejection of, 4362, 4564
relic veneration as, 7687
ṭarīqah in, 4589
Shiromani Gurwara Prabandhak Committee, Sikhism and, 8396
Shirun, H., 894
Shisen o koete (Kagawa Toyohiko), 5054
Shishikagura (dance), 6300
Shite (doer), 7048
Shitou Xiqian, 1522, 1523
Shi'ur Qomah, 10050, 10052
Shiv'ah (mourning), 7822
Shivaism. *See* Śaivism
Shivapuri Baba, 833
Shivḥei ha-Besht, 726
BeSHT as central hero in, 3791
Shiv Sena (army of Śiva) party, Śaivism and, 8418
Shi'wano'kia (Priestess of fecundity), in Zuni religion, 2008, 2009
Shixian (Buddhist monk), 8995
Shlain, Leonard, 4300
Shlmm sacrifice, in Canaanite religion, 1385
Shlomo. *See* Carlebach, Shlomo
Shloyshe sheorim (Tovim), 9037
Sh'ma' (prayer), 983, 9807
Sh'moneh 'esreh (prayer), 983, 9806
Shne'ur Zalman of Lyady, **8371**
on God, 3551
on mystical union, 6340
as *tsaddiq,* 3790, 9379
Shoah/Sho'ah. *See* Holocaust, the
Shoan Oromo religion (Ethiopia), 2573
Shōbō (True Dharma), 5685–5687
Shōbōgenzō (Dōgen), 2385, 2386, 9945, 9949
Shōbu no Sekku (Boys' Day), 2411
S'hodieonskon (trickster), 9355
Shodō ("way of writing"), in Japanese culture, 1371
Shoemaking, Welsh deity associated with, 1483
Shofar, blowing of, on Ro'sh ha-Shanah, 7757, 7928
Shoghi Effendi Rabbani, 738–739
Shōgūji (chief priest), 7410
Shoguns, homosexuality among, 4114
Shohat, Ella, on hybridity and syncretism, 1859
Shōheikō (School of Prosperous Peace), endowment of, 1927
Shoḥet (ritual slaughterer), 2398, 5106
Shōjyō. *See* Kamo no Mabuchi
Shōkō, Asahara. *See* Asahara Shōkō
Shōkōbō. *See* Benchō
Shōkū (Buddhist monk), 4938
Shōmangyō-gisho (Buddhist text), 1249–1250
Shōmonji (conjurers), 6829
Shōmono (Buddhist texts), 9947
Shomrei Adamah (Keepers of the Earth), 2646
Shomrim (Hebrew community), 879
Shōmu (Japanese emperor), 1175, 1306
Buddhism under, 7271–7272
Gyōgi and, 3721
Huayan Buddhism and, 4146
Shōmyō (chanting), 6300–6301
introduction of, 2801
Shona religion and society (Zimbabwe), **8371–8374**. *See also* Southern African religions
ancestral cult in, 8372
possession and, 8696
Apostolic Church of John Maranke, 5695
Christianity, 8373–8374
deus otiosus cult of, 2313
dialect groups in, 8372
divination in, 2370, 8372
drums of, 2495
high god in, 8372, 8373
kingship in, Great Zimbabwe in, 84
mediums in, 8372, 8373
mortuary rituals in, 141
peripheral cults in, 8373
regional cults in, 8373
social structure in, 8372
spirit possession in, 8696
spirits in
Christianity and, 8374
hierarchy of, 8372
mhondoro (chiefly or territorial spirits), 8372–8373
Shong religion. *See* Central Bantu religions
Shōnyō (Buddhist leader), 4935–4936
Shooting stars, 8736
Shor ha-bar (wild ox), 4340
Shor religion. *See* Southern Siberian religions
Short History of Buddhism, A (Conze), 1098
Shortland, Edward, 5679
Short stories, Jewish, by Agnon (Shemu'el Yosef), 180
Short Treatise on God, Man, and His Well-Being (Spinoza), 8682
Shoshalot (Hasidic houses), development of, 3787
Shoshan Yesod ha-'Olam, 2932
Shoshoni people (North America)
area populated by, 6656
cultural studies of, 2611
round dances of, 6716
Sun Dance of, 6667, 8846–8847
trickster stories of, 6713, 9355
Shōshū. *See* Nichirenshū
Shosinge-chu (Rennyo), 7753
Shosinge tai'i (Rennyo), 7753
Shotoku Taishi (prince of Japan), **8374–8376**
Anesaki Masaharu as admirer of, 342
Confucianism and, 1927
as *hijiri,* 3978

Shotoku Taishi (prince of Japan) ***continued***
image of, 1249
lectures by, 1249–1250
legend of, 995
Lotus Sūtra commentary of, 4809
monasteries founded by, Maitreya in, 5621
names of, 8374
as patron of Buddhism, 1094, 1175, 1241, 1248, 5349
popular veneration of, 8375–8376
priest-warriors under, 7262
as regent, 8375
religion, attitude toward, 8375
religion under, 4782–4783
ritual text of, 4810
youth of, 8374–8375
Shoubo combat, 5734
Shousui ritual, 1641
Shouters (Spiritual Baptists)
Shango cult and, 1435
of Trinidad, 1437
Shouts, 7037
Showalter, Elaine, gynocentrism of, 3719
Shōwa Shinseikai, 6825
Showings of Divine Love. See Revelations of Divine Love
Shramanic religions, in India, 1102–1103
Shree Rajneesh Ashram, 7608
Shrine dances, Carnival and, 1441
Shrine of the Virgin of Guadalupe (Mexico City), 5196, 7698
Shrine of Wisdom, on Hermetism, 3952–3953
Shriners, 3198
Shrines, **8376–8378**. *See also* Pilgrimage
African, 90
in Akan religion, 214, 215
to ancestors, 85, 89, 215
carved figures as, 90
central Bantu, 1508, 1509
in Diola religion, 261–262
in Edo religion, 2697
in Igbo religion, 3572
for kings, 5171
in Lugbara religion, 5527
to Mami Wata, 5629, 5630
role of, 85, 90
architecture of, classification of, 461, 462
Armenian, 491
Buddhist
portable, vol. 4 color insert
sacredness of, 7698
Chinese, to earth-god, 1584
Christian
Church of the Holy Sepulcher (Jerusalem), 8377
in exorcism, 2929
as destinations, 8378
as divine dwelling (*See* Temples)
East African, 2568
for ancestors, 2569
for spirits, 2576
Greek
to Asklepios, 552
to Meter, 2109
to Sun, 8839
Hindu
cave, 9039
home, 7493–7494
pilgrimages to, 9823–9824
to Gaṇeśa, 3271
trees, vol. 5 color insert
as historical markers, 8377
household, 4106
in India, sacred rivers and, 8377
in Japanese Shintō, 7411–7412
Buddhist temples and, 4783–4784
civic shrines and shrine-temple complexes, 8360–8361
development of, 8359
as dwelling places for the *kami,* 7980, 7981
in Edo period, 8363–8364
healing and, 3868–3870
Ishikiri Shrine, 3869
Kiki and, 4806
registration of, 8358–8359, 8366
"twenty-two shrines" group of, 8360, 8361–8362
Yoshida (Kyoto), 8364
Islamic (*See also* Kaʿbah)
Dome of the Rock (Jerusalem), 8377
in Karbala, 5088
Israelite, 934
in *Genesis,* 4746
in Temple, 924, 925
Japanese
to *kami,* 2639, 2640, 2641
music and dance in, 6300
Jewish (*See also* Synagogues)
pilgrimages to, 7162
Temple wall in Jerusalem as, 8377
meaning of term, 8376
in Mesoamerican religions, in Huichol religion, 4152–4153
Micronesian, in households, 6004
Minoan, 39–41
Mycenaean, 41
as nature-culture thresholds, 8377
Neolithic, at Çatal Hüyük (neolithic site), 1801–1802
in Oceanic religions, caves as, 2006
oracular, 6832–6834
Phrygian, to Cybele, 2109–2110
prehistoric, 7379–7381
roadside, vol. 1 color insert
and saints or holy persons, 8376–8377
as service and commerce centers, 8378
in Sikhism *(gurdwaras),* 8394–8395, 8396
sky hierophany and, 8428
in South American Indian religions, Andean (*See Huacas*)
Ṣūfī, of Bābā Farīd, 1806
in Tamil, 8974
textiles as, 9091
trees as, 9336, 9338
and urbanization, 7156
Shrine Shintō, 4793
Shrines of the Slave Trade (Baum), 118
shrine virgins *(saigū)* of Japan, 1528
Shri Sai Satcharita, Shirdi Sai Baba in, 8027
Shri Venkateswara Vanabhivriddhi scheme, 2622
Shroud of Turin, as holy relic, 2317, 7690, vol. 12 color insert
Shrove Tuesday, 1440. *See also* Carnival
Shu (deity)
communication between worlds by, 5163
in Egyptian pantheon, 2704
Shū (school), 1246
Shūbun no Hi (autumnal equinox), 2411
Shucman, Helen, 6531
Shugendō movement, 2802, **8378–8381**
Asian continental influences on, 8379–8380
cult of, 3226–3227
Konkō Daijin influenced by, 5224
dynamics and significance of, 8380–8381
formation of, 8379–8380
institutionalization of, 4787, 8378
meaning of term, 8378
origin of, 4785
priests of, self-mummification of, 2241
sacred mountains and, 8379, 8380
Mount Fuji and, 8364
Shingon Buddhism and, 8352
yamabushi practitioners of, 2188–2189
Shugenja (mountain ascetics), 4785, 4796. *See also* Yamabushi
Shug gseb (nunnery), established by Ani Lochen, 354
Shugs ldan (Shugden, deity), **8381–8382**
Shuhmaker, Wayne, 246
Shuhūdī school (Islam), 4665
Shujing (Classic of/Scripture of Documents)
carpets in, 9091
contents of, 1585, 1906
dragons in, 2433
Maspero on, 1634
Shukaku (Buddhist monk), 1178
Shukalletuda (mythic figure), 4404–4405
Shukū (tea master), 847
Shūkyō (sectarian teachings), 1580, 7271
Shulgi (Ur ruler), 3629
Shulḥan ʿarukh, 5104, 9236
halakhah and, 3743–3744
health and healing in, 3829
visiting the sick in, 3829
references to folk religion in, 3159
types of law in, 3751, 3752
writing of, 4751
Shulman, David D., on cosmology in temples, 7983
Shulshagana (deity), family of, 5951
Shumer. *See* Sumer
Shumma izbu (text), Canaanite parallel to, 1387
Shun. *See* Yao and Shun
Shundao (Buddhist monk), 1170
Shunjō (Buddhist monk), 9079
Shunning. *See also* Excommunication; Expulsion
as excommunication or curse, 2105
Shupe, Anson, 6527, 6539
Shur, Edwin M., 9073
Shūrā (electoral council), 4394, 4573
Shurdra caste, 4465
Shurṭah (Islamic legal body), jurisdiction of, 7540
Shurūḥ (commentaries), 4587
Shushan Purim, in Jewish calendar, 4867
Shushi Confucianism (Japan), 4789
Shushōgi (Buddhist text), 9950
Shut-door doctrine, in Seventh-day Adventism, 8235
Shute, Nevil, 3084
Shuten (priest), 7412
Shutruk-Nahunte of Elam, 5948
Shutsujō kōgo (Tominaga Nakamoto), 1277
Shwe Dagon shrine, Burma, sacred space and, 7982
Shweder, Richard, 5331
Si (monastery), 9056
Siam. *See also* Thailand; Thailand and Thai religions
and Khmer Buddhism, 5130
Siamese twins, 2423
Siarnaq (mythical figure), 2394
Sibbes, Richard, preparationism and, 4125

Siberia and Siberian religions. *See also* Arctic religions; Dolgan religion; Khanty and Mansi religion; Samoyed religion; Tunguz religion
cattle breeding in, vertical worldview associated with, 8672
cosmological ideas in, 2999, 6754
creation stories in, 3016
Donner's (Kai) anthropological studies in, 2420, 2421
Hungarian religions and, 4224–4225
hunting in, alliance and worldview associated with, 8669–8672
masks and garments, shamanic, 1827
New Year ceremonies in, 6591
ordination in, 6852
prehistoric (*See* Saka religion)
sacrifice in, 8004
shamanism in (*See* Shamanism, Siberian and Inner Asian)
Southern Siberian religions, **8668–8673**
Siberian mythology
bridge symbolism of, 1052
cosmological ideas in, water in, 9698
descent into the underworld in, 2296–2297
Siblings, 2985–2986. *See also* Twins
birth *vs.* adopted, in Langkawi culture, 5184
marriage of, 2985
in Melanesian myths, 5844
in Oceanic religions, gift giving and, 3481
in Okinawan religion, 6812
rivalry of, 2985
Sun and moon as, 2862
Sibulla. See Sibylline Oracles
Sibylline Oracles, 2377–2378, 6834–6835, **8382–8386**
Augustus and, 7913
content of, 8384–8385
history of the oracular texts, 8383–8384
Jewish apocalypses and, 417
and *lectisternia* ritual, 7905
meteorite showers and, 8736
nature of inspiration in, 8383
in Roman religion, 7903–7904
sibyls as inspired women, 8383
Sibyls (mythic figures)
Christianity and, 8384
in Greek tradition, 8382–8383
Sicarii (daggers), 9939, 9940
Sicarii sect, Smith (Morton) on, 8448
Sic et non (Abelard), 7, 8
Sicily
Byzantine territories of, Norman conquest of, 2586
Demeter cults in, 2269–2270
Melqart in, 5848–5849
Sickle, 967, 968
Sickness. *See* Disease and illness
Sickness Lord (deity), 5120
Sickness unto Death, The (Kierkegaard), 5142
Sicun (guardian spirit), in Dakota religion, 8534
Si Dao Ruang, 3077
Siddha alchemy, 244
Siddhadāta. *See* Gaṇeśa
Siddha medical system, Indian Medicine Central Council Act (IMCCA) and, 3856
Siddha movement
in *Hevajra Tantra,* 3965
sahajānanda (natural joy) in, 3966
Siddhānta (literary style), 861, 1204
Siddhanta sect of Śaivism, **8042–8043**
Śiva-*bhakti* in, 8418
Siddhartha Gautama. *See* Buddha
Siddhārthika sect, origin of, 1194
Siddhas (accomplished ones or liberation), 1121, 1122. *See also* Mahāsiddhas
biographies of, 5604–5606
Cakrasamvara Tantra and, 1349
caste status of, 5604
education of, 5604
eighty-four greatest, 5603
enlightenment of, 5604–5605
historical existence of, 5605
historical role of, 5605–5606
in Vajrayāna (Tantric) Buddhism, 5603–5606
in Jainism
in cosmology, 2025
karman and, 7679
temples of, 4429
Lakulīśa Pāśupata system, influence of, 4019
magic and, 5605
poetry of, 7210
seven lineages of, 5603
Śubhākarasiṃha as, 8804
as teachers, 5604–5605
writings of, 5606
Siddhasiddhānta-paddhati (Hindu text), 3638
Siddhis (powers), 6053, 9962
attainment of, 8987, 8993
in Hindu Tantrism, 4003
pursuit of, 8990
in Yoga, 9896
Siddīqī, Muḥammad Zubayr, on forged *ḥadīths,* 3732
Siddur and *Maḥzor* (prayer books), **8386–8392**
daily service in, 8388–8389
Hirsch (Samson Raphael) on the *Siddur,* 4024
history of, 8386–8388
holy day liturgies in, 8389–8391
meaning of terms, 8386
messianic expectations in, 7586
Reform and Conservative, 8388
Sabbath prayers in, 8389
Sefardic and Ashkenazic, 8387–8388
structure of, 8388
Siddur Sa'adyah (prayer book), contents of, 8387
Sidgwick, Henry, evolutionary ethics opposed by, 2918
Sídheóga, 1489
Sídh/Sídhe (underworld or supernatural beings), **8392–8393**. *See also* Celtic religion, deities of
in fairy mounds, 1489
Sidi Aḥmad, reverence for, 8035
Sidi Khadir, as trickster, 4214
Sīdīna ʿAlī. *See* ʿAlī ibn Abī Ṭālib
Šidlauskas-Visuomis, Domas, 763
Sidney, Philip, 3051
Hermetism and, 3948
on poetry of *Psalms,* 7205–7206
Sidon (Lebanon), 7129, 7131
Eshmun cult at, 2841
Sidorov, Alexei Semenovich, on Komi religion and society, 5216
Sidrah (section of Torah), Sabbath readings of, 8257–8258
Siebert, Otto, 671
Siedi. See Seite
Siegel, Bernard, 7599
Raëlian cloning and, 7599
on theophysics and holistic healing, 3851
Siegel, Lee, 5590
Siegmann, William, on masks, 5766
Siena, Council of (1423-1424), 6972
Sieroszewski, W. L., 474
Sierra Leone. *See also* Mende religion
Anglicanism in, 1718
cannibalism in Sherbro secret societies, 1404
Christianity in, 1718
clitoridectomy in, 1826
Limba people of, funeral rituals of, 7806
Sif (deity), 3453–3454, 5508
Sifat (qualities of God), in Ḥanafī creed, 2063
Sifen lü (Buddhist text), 1202
Saichō on, 8030, 8031
Ṣiffīn, Battle of (657), 258
Imāmīyah and, 8338
Sifraʾ (Jewish text), 7586
Sifrut ha-musar. See Jewish thought and philosophy, ethical literature in
Sigālovāda Sutta, religious education and, 7734
Sigd (pilgrimage festival), of Bēta Esra'ēl, 5003
Siger of Brabant, on Albertus Magnus, 233
"Sighting stones," 5828
Sigi (ceremony), 2391
Sigismund, John (Transylvanian king), 9469
Sigismund (Holy Roman Emperor), Great Western Schism and, 8157
Sigismund (king), Hus (Jan) tried for heresy by, 4233–4234
Signal functions, study of, 2867–2868
Signatures, calligraphy and, 1373
Signes graphiques soudanais (Dieterlen and Griaule), 2350
"Significance of History of Religion for Systemic Theology, The" (Tillich), 9130, 9203
Significations (Long), 67, 78, 965
Sign of Socrates, The (Plutarch), 7200
Signorelli, Luca, 377
Signs (journal), goddess worship in, 3612
Signs and signifiers. *See also* Semiotics
Cassirer on, 1448
in semantics, 8226–8227
Sigüenza y Góngora, Carlos de, 5922
Sīhaḷa order, 1136, 1137, 1138
Siḥr (magic), **5583–5587**. *See also* Magic, in Islam
Siikala, Anna-Leena, 3114
on shamanism, 8275
Siil (service day), 1648
Sikhara (tower), 9265
Sikh Dharma Brotherhood
Healthy, Happy, Holy Organization (3HO) and, 3878–3880
identity and gender roles in, 3879
tensions with older Sikh organizations, 3879
Sikhism, **8393–8398**. *See also* Gurū Granth Sāhib
Ādi Granth in, **32–33,** 2220, **3715–3718**
gender in, 3336
in Africa, 108
akhāḍā military units in, 8021
bhog ceremony in, 8396, 8397
celebrations in, 8396–8397
creed in, 2053

Sikhism ***continued***
Dasam Granth in, 32, 2220–2221
five *ks* (emblems) in, 8395, 8408
gender in, **3335–3338**
God in
Ādi Granth on, 33, 3336
gender of, 3336
names of, 6407
gurdwaras (shrines) in, 8394–8395, 8396
Gurū Arjan and crystallization of, 8394–8395
Gurū Gobind Singh, role of, 8395, **8407–8409**
Gurū Nānak and origins of, 8393–8394
gurūs in, 32, 3714, 3878
Ādi Granth as, 3716–3717
portraits of, vol. 10 color insert
women and, 3335–3336
iconoclasm in, 4284
idolatry condemned in, 4431
images in, 9623
words and, vol. 14 color insert
initiation into, Gurū Gobind Singh and, 3878
langar (community meal) in, 8393
love in, Singh (Gobind) and, 2221
Māharājā Ranjit Singh and the Sikh kingdom, 8395
mantras in, 5677
marriage in, 3337, 3716
mercantile castes and, 3986
monotheism in, 6158, 6160
Nānak's work as foundation for, 4007
in North America, Healthy, Happy, Holy Organization (3HO) and, **3877–3880**
origins of, 4421
panj piyāre (five beloved) in, 8408
poetry of, 7211
popular morality in, 8397–8398
rebellion of, 7257
reincarnation in, 7676
religious education in, 7733, 7734
rites of passage in, 8396, 8397
gender and, 3337
sacred time in, 7990
saṃgha in, 4425
sangat (sacred gathering) in, 8393
Sikh Rabit Maryada (code of conduct) in, 8396
Singh Sabha movement in, 8395–8396
soul in, 8548–8549
symbols of, 4424
and violence, 6647
women in, **3335–3338,** 3879–3880
worship in, 3986, 8396
Sikh Rahit Maryada (code of conduct), 8396
Amrit initiation in, 8397
gender in, 3337
Sikkim (India), Buddhism in, kingship in, 7262
Sikkimese religion. *See* Himalayan Buddhism
Śikṣāsamuccaya (Śāntideva), 1119
Mahāyāna philosophy in, 8109
Śikṣāvrata (Vows of Instruction), 4770
Siku Quanshu (Imperial Manuscript Library), 2129
Sila (deity), 469, 4528
Śīla (morality), 5873, 7357
Śīlabhadra (monk), **8398–8399**
as follower of Dharmapāla, 2337
Vijñānavāda theory of Dharmapāla of, 8399
Xuanzang and, 9861
Silas (prophet), 914
Si'lat (demonic figure), 2280
Silber, Ilana Friedrich, 6136
Silele religion. *See* Central Bantu religions
Silence
in Athapaskan culture, 6675
in Buddhism, 5308–5309
Zen Buddhism, 5310–5311
of God, as Holocaust response, 4094
in monasteries, 823
in mysticism, 6341
sacred, 5305, 5308
Sorskii (Nil) on, 8525
vows of, Meher Baba's, 5829
Silent iconoclasm, 4282, 4283, 4284, 4285, 4392
"Silent illumination" *(mozhao),* 1524
Silent Spring (Carson), 2609
Silhara dynasty (India), 6997
Silíceo, Juan Martínez, 5717
Silius Italicus, on Iberian religion, 4252, 4254
Silk, 9089
Silko, Leslie Marmon, 1515–1516, 3090, 7226
autobiographical writings of, 702
Ceremony, 3091–3092
poetry of, 7225
Silk Road
Buddhism introduced into China via, 1594, 5349
Buddhist temples along, 9046
expeditions along, 1313–1314
Judaism introduced to China via, 5005
Klimkeit (Hans-Joachim) on, 5190
and spread of Buddhism, 1145, 1146, 1148, 1151, 1160, 1163, 1170
and spread of Manichaeism, 5668
Silla kingdom (Korea)
Buddhism in, 1170–1172, 5231, 5232, 9437
Maitreya in, 5621
temples of, 9048
Confucianism and, 1929
hwarang (flower boys) and homosexuality in, 4117
kingship of, 5179
musok in, 5228, 5232
origin myths of, 5179
during Three Kingdoms period, 5230
Silone, Ignazio, 5480
Silsilahs (lineages), 4648, 4664, 8820–8821, 9005, 9006
Silumans (ghosts), in Sudanese religion, 8850
Silvanus (deity)
Celtic parallels, 1485
in Roman religion, 7918
Silver, **3625–3626**
as money, 6138
symbolism of, 3625, 3626
Silver, Lee, 3428
Silver (color), symbolism of, 1861, 1862
Silverblatt, Irene, 3416
Silver Bluff congregation, 5443
Silverman, Eric, 3396
Silverman, Ira, 7638, 7639
Silverstein, Theodore, 1049
Silvester, Bernard, 3650
Silwa (Egypt), marriage in, 7825
Sīmā (boundary)
Theravāda Buddhism, as consecration, 1954–1955
in Sinhala religion, 8411–8412
in temples, 9054
Sima Chengzhen, **8399–8400**
on *dao* and *de,* 2174–2175
Sīmantonnayana (ceremonial parting of hair), 7814
Sima Qian
on Confucius, 1893
on immortality quests, 7267
on Laozi, 5316
and *ru* as object of study, 1917
Simbang mudang (Korean shamans), 5234–5235
Simchŏng (Korean folk figure), 5233
Simelungun Batak people (Indonesia), 799
Simeon (Essene prophet), 2846
Simeon (rabbi), 7006
Simeon, eremitism of, 2826
Simeon bar Giora, 9940
Simeon bar Yohai. *See* Shim'on bar Yoh'ai
Simeon ben Gamaliel II. *See* Shim'on ben Gamli'el II
Simeon ben Lakish. *See* Shim'on ben Laqish
Simeon of Pious, on *shekhinah,* 8315
Simeon Stylites (saint), Syriac asceticism and, 8939
Simgo (meditative prayer), 1648
Simḥat Torah
dancing on, 2149
in India, 5005
Sukkot and, 8834
Simias (Greek poet), calligrams of, 1369
Simic, Charles, 5484
Simmel, Georg
on autonomous religious values, 8481
on games, 3265
on knowledge, 5207
on social groups, 8482–8483
Simmons, John K., 6582
Simon. *See* Peter the Apostle
Simon, Arthur, 3174
Simon, Linda, on James (William), 4777
Simon, Uriel, 869
Simonetti, Manlio, on Gnosticism, 3534
Simonides (poet), on memory, 5852
Simon Magus
as Antichrist, 394
as heretic, 3926
as magi, 5561
mythic theology of, 3515
on Sophia (wisdom), 3510
Simons, Menno, **8400–8402**
in Anabaptism, 304, 305, 7661
on kingdom of God, 5152
pacifist teachings of, 6648
Simonse, Simon, on ritual regicide, 5159
Simon the New Theologian. *See* Symeon the New Theologian
Simon the Stylite, on pain, 6946
Simonton, O. Carl, 6057
Simonton, Stephanie, 6057
Simony
definition of, 3690
in Roman Catholicism, criticism of, 3690
Simple vow, *vs.* solemn vow, 7721
Simplicity, in monasticism, 6122–6123
Simplicius
on Aristotle, 479
influence on *falsafah,* 2971
Simpson, George Eaton, 75–76, 10025, 10028
SIMS. *See* Students International Meditation Society
Simson, Otto Von, 501
Sims-Williams, Patrick, 1499
Simulacrum (idol), 4358, 4360–4361, 4361
Si Murg, ascension in, 523
Sin(s), **8402–8407**. *See also* Atonement; Redemption
in Buddhism, as violation of the five moral precepts, 8015
in Christianity, 8406
Abelard (Peter) on, 8
androcentrism of, 335
Calvin on, 1376
grace and, 3645–3646
history of doctrine, 1667

Holiness movement and, 4082
Hopkins (Emma Curtis) on, 4128
human body and, 4164, 4168
indulgences for, 158, 7657
Kant (Immanuel) on, 5078–5079
in Lord's Prayer, 5517
Mary's lack of, 5753, 5754
merit and, 5876
neoorthodoxy on, 6467
Pelagius on, 7025–7026
Protestant views of, 158
redemption from, 7640
suffering as punishment for, 8808
Tertullian on, 9086
types of sin, 1888–1889
confession of (*See* Confession of sins)
cosmological order and, 8402–8403
defilement of, 8403
depiction in novels, 3059
disease caused by, 3809
in East African religions, 2569
Edwards (Jonathan) on, 2699–2700
expulsion of, 2939
feminist perspectives on, 3029–3030, 3035
in Greek religion, 8405
in Hittite religion, 4072
in Inuit religion, 7505, 7509
in Islam, 8406–8407
Abū Ḥanīfah on, 21–22
in Ḥanafī creed, 2064
in *kalām,* 5060
Khārijīs on, 5126, 5127
Muʿtazilah on, 5063, 6321
suffering as punishment for, 8808
in Israelite religion, 8403–8405
sin offering, 4747, 7514
Jews rejecting Jesus as, 399
in Judaism, 8403–8405
body *vs.* soul and, 8557
casting off, in Jewish New Year, 6593
in Hasidic *tsaddiq* doctrine, 3789–3790
of Israel, and salvation, 7584–7585
mippenei hata'einu Holocaust paradigm, 4090–4091
overview of, 1888
Schneerson (Menachem) on, 8172
suffering as punishment for, 8805
latent, purgation rites and, 8209
magical conception of, 8402
in Manichaeism, 1889
Marx (Karl) on, 7246
in Mesopotamian religion, 8403
Niebuhr (Reinhold) on, 6612–6613
as offenses against God, 1843
original (*See* Original sin)
in Orphism, 8405
paradox of, 6990
Pettazzoni (Raffaele) on, 8402
previous *vs.* original, 2507
in primitive religion, 8402–8403
cosmological order and, 8402–8403
in Quietism, 7558, 7559
in religious law, 5327
serpents and, 8458
suffering produced by, 9116
taboo *vs.,* 8402
theistic *vs.* magical conceptions of, 1884
in Vedism, 1886
Sin (deity), 4316, 4404. *See also* Nanna
in Aramean religion, 447–448
moon and, 4316, 4404, 6172
Nanna identified with, 6414
in nature worship, 6439
in triad, 9349
Sinaati (spirits), 2354
Sinai, Mount
covenant of, 2049
vs. Abrahamic covenant, 15
in rabbinic Judaism, 7584
revelation on, 6213
transferring origin of law to, 4729
Sinaitic school, eremtism of, 2826
"Sin and Death" (Urbach), 900
Sincerity Rice, 1648
Sinchis (war leaders), in Inca society, 5176
Sinderesis (as conscience), 1941
Sindi, Muḥammad Ḥāyat al-, 4254, 4255
Singa (Batak monster), 799–800
Singapore
Daoism in, 2190
Islam in, 4671
Judaism in, 5010
Kaum Muda (new faction) movement, 8653
Singer, Kurt, on Zoroastrianism, 8768
Singer, Margaret
anticult theory of, 1032
on cults and brainwashing, 2085, 6522
Singer, Milton, 4448
Singer, Peter, 2655
Singh, Bhāī Manī, 32
and *Daran Granth,* 2220–2221
Singh, Gobind, **8407–8409**
and *Ādi Granth,* 32, 3716, 8407–8408
and *Dasam Granth,* 2220–2221, 8408
initiatory rites established by, 3878, 8408
Khālsā established by, 8408
Sikhism, role in, 8395
sons, death of, 8408–8409
women in life of, 3336
women under, 3336, 3337
Singh, Kirpal, 2602
Singh, Nikky-Guninder Kaur, 3717
Singh, Pashaura, 3717
Singh, Piar, 3717
Singh, Ranjit (Māharājā), Sikh kingdom and, 8395
Singh, Sudar, Eckankar and, 2602
Singh Sabha movement, in Sikhism, 8395–8396
Singina, Yali, cargo cults and, 1417, 1419
Singkelevun (ritual), 9395
Singken (helpers of hunters), 2395, 9395
Sinhala Buddha, vol. 12 color insert
Sinhala language
Buddhism *vs.* Christianity and, 1728
Buddhist writings in, 1074, 1096–1097, 1110
Sinhala religion, **8409–8413**. *See also* Sri Lanka
baṇḍāra cult in, 8410–8412
Buddha in, 8412
Buddhism and, 8409, 8411, 8412
changes in pantheon of, 8412–8413
demons and evil spirits in, 8412
deva worship in, 8410–8412
Dolaha Deviyo (twelve gods) in, 8410
h*Hatara varan dēviyō* (gods of four warrants) in, 8411–8412
healing rites in, spirit possession and, 2140
Hinduism and, 8412
karman theory in, 8409, 8411
priests in, 8411
sīmā (boundary) in, 8411–8412
Sinhala Theravāda Buddhism, 1131, 1133
dominance of, 1135–1138
exorcism in, 7197
literature, 9146
and nationalism, 1282
priesthood in, 7409
Upatissa in, 1200
Sinha Senāpati (Pāṇḍey), 10034
Siniga religion, Haitian Vodou, influence on, 1433
Sinjārī, Ḥasan al-Makzūn al-, 226
Sin-leqi-unnini, *Epic of Gilgamesh* of, 3486, 3487, 3488
"Sinners in the Hands of an Angry God" (Edwards), 2698
Sin offering, in Israelite religion, 4747, 7514
Sinology. *See* China and Chinese religions
Sino-Tibetan Buddhist Institute (Chongqing), 8967–8968
Siouan-speaking peoples (North America)
fasting by, 2997
geographic distribution of, 6655, 6656
in Northeast Woodlands region, 6679
in Plains region, 6697
Siouffi, Nicolas, on Mandaean religion, 5637
Sioux. *See also* Lakota religion
Canadian, New Tidings religion of, 6667
council of, 7301
drums of, 7035
funeral rites of, 3237
tricksters of, 9355
at Wounded Knee, 7303
Siovili Cult (Samoa), 3398, 6795
Siovili of Eva, as prophet, 2007
Siperian samojedien keskuudessa vuosina 1911-1913 ja 1914 (Donner), 2421
Sipirok Batak people (Indonesia), 799
Siponto, Synod of, *filioque* doctrine and, 8156
Sīq (Petra), 6386
Sīrah (biography of the Prophet), historiography in, 4029
Si Raja Batak, 799
Sīrat Muḥammad (Ibn Isḥāq), *miʿrāj* in, 6059–6060
Sīrat Rasūl Allāh (Ibn Isḥāq), 8952
Sirhak (Practical Learning) movement, 1932–1933
Chŏng Yagyong and, 1648, 1649
Sirhindī, Aḥmad, 4570, 4650, 6738, **8413–8414,** 9010
Siricius (pope), 6966
Sirige (mask), 5768
Siriono people (Bolivia), Yasi (moon) and, 6439
Sirius
in Dogon religion, 2391
as dog star, 2393
Isis and, 4557
Sirona (deity), 1483
Sirr-i Akbar, 2219
Sirr-i Akbar (Dārā Shikōh), 4421
Šīsaule (world), 758–759
Sishu. See Four Books

Sisinnius (patriarch), 6483
Sister. *See* Siblings
Sisterhood of Our Lady of the Good Death, 120–121
Sisters of Charity, 2321
medical philanthropy and, 3847
Seton (Elizabeth) and, 8234
Sisters of Mercy, 6764
Sisters of Penance, 6763
Sisters of the Love of God, 7724
Sistine Chapel, 4346
Adam in, 30
reality in, 53
Sixtus IV building, 6972
structuralism and, 8755
Sistrum (musical instrument), 6275
Śiśupāla (warrior figure), 4463
Sisyphus, 165
as modern hero, 3957
Sītā (deity). *See also* Rāmāyaṇa
as Śrī, 7609
in dance drama, 7046–7047
fertility and, 9908
humanism and domestication of, 827
in *Rāmāyaṇa,* 7617
in *Śivagītā,* 854
as nurturing goddess, 3607
in puppet theater, 2452
Rāmā and, 7609, 7617
Vālmīki and, 9518
Śītalā (deity)
Bengali worship of, 826
as dangerous goddess, 3607–3608
festival of, 9824
purification rituals for, 7505
regional differences in, 3608
Śītalāmaṅgals (Bengali text), 825
Sitar, Khusraw (Amīr) as creator of, 5138, 6284
Sitney, P. Adams, 3099, 3102
Sitting (posture)
in Buddhist meditation, 7343 (*See also* Zazen)
in Jewish worship, 7343
in Muslim worship, 7342
in yoga, 7343
Sitting Bull, assassination of, 3473
Sittler, Joseph, ecotheology of, 2610
Si tu chos kyi rgya mtsho (Situ Chokyi Gyatso), Ani Lochen and, 354
Siū (sun), 9395
Śiva (deity), **8414–8420**. *See also* Śaivism
in alchemy, 242
and Ādi Śakti, 4433
as androgyne, 339, 8417
antisocial nature of, 7500
Arjuna and, 487
asceticism and, 2305, 9822
ashes used by, 540
as Nāṭarāja (lord of the dance), multiple hands of, 3769
as Paśupati (Lord of the Animals), 8039
avatāras of, 708
Banaras as city of, 778–779, 7170
in Bhairava Tantras, 4020
bhakti synthesis and, 3998, 3999, 4000, 4001–4002
cakras and, 1348, 1349
cave temple of, 5242
choosing city for Pārvatī, 779
as cosmos, 8415
cults of, 7719
and dance, 2134, 2135–2136
dance of, 4324, 4428, 4444, 7043, 7170
death destroyed by, 8415
and demons, 4324
derivation of name, 2252
desire and asceticism of, 2305
devotion to, 857, 4428, 4436, 8417
dice game of, 8417–8418
divine forms of, 4324
Divodāsa evicted by, 779
drum symbol of, 3442, *3443*
Durgā as wife of, 2525, 2526, 4444
eightfold domain of, 8415
Fudō compared with, 3227
gambling by, 3263, 3266
gaṇas of, 2315
Gaṇeśa as son of, 4436
Gaṇeśa beheaded by, 8041
Ganges River and, 3275
Gorākhnāth and, 3638
Hanumān and, 6152
heads of, 7550–7551
historical development of, 8038–8041
as hunter, 8415
hymns to, 7209, 7210
iconography of, 4323–4324, 4383, 4384
in Aum Shinrikyō, 631, 632
in conflict with Brahmā, 1024
in conflict with Kāma, 2305
Indra's aspects transformed to, 4467
Indus Valley religion, suggested precursors in, 3989
in *Īśvaragītā,* 854
in Kāma festival, 4081–4082
in *Mahābhārata,* 8415–8416
in Purāṇas, 7500
in Śaivism (*See also* Śaivism)
in Kāpālika Śaivism, 8049–8050
in Pratyabhijñā Saivism, 8048
in Śaiva Siddhanta, 8042–8043
in Vīraśaivism, 8044
in myth cycle, 8040–8041
in *Śāstras,* 8043
in *Śivagītā,* 854
inspiration given by, 4509
in *Śvetāśvatara Upaniṣad,* 8415
in *trimūrti,* 4000
Kailash temple at Ellora caves, 1472
in Khmer religion, 5128, 5129
Kramrisch (Stella) on, 5242
left-handed Savism and, 8015
līlā and, 5455
liṅga of (*See Liṅga*)
as Lord of Dancers, 8415–8416
mahavrata (Great Vow) of, 8040, 8050
Māṇikkavācakar devoted to, 5670–5671
in *mantras,* 5677–5678
in Marathi religions, 5697
masculine sacrality in, 5760, 5762
moon and, 6173
mountain shrines of, 6213
Murukaṉ as son of, 6240
Pārvatī, marriage to, 8415
Pārvatī and, equal status of, 3608
Pārvatī as consort of, 4324, 4326
phallus of, 7083
poetry to, 5671, 8417
portrayal of, classical, 8038
pūjā to, 7494
as Rudra, 4428
Rudra as precursor of, 3990–3991, 3992, 7934, 7935, 8038–8040 (*See also* Rudra)
birth of, 8415
creation and, 8414
sacred number of, 4324
Śakti, union with, 1349
sanctuaries of, 778–779
sects, emergence 0f, 8041–8042
self-manifestations of, sacred space and, 7979
as self-transforming figure, 7195–7196
Śiva-Kapālin myth, 8050
Skanda as son of, 4444
and snakes, 4438
in Southeast Asia, 4012
Tamil poetry of, 857, 7207
in Tantrism, 9822–9823
tapas of, 8998
temples to, 8416–8417, 8977
in Southeast Asia, 4012
in United States, 8418–8419
third eye of, 4324
tree as symbol of, 9338
in Trinity, 4422, 4423, 4443, 9346
vajra of, 2345
Vighneśvara beheaded by, 4326
Vijayanagara as sacred space and, 1806
Viṣṇu, complementarity with, 3999, 8416
wives of, 2525, 2526, 4444
worship of (*See* Śaivism)
Yama and, 9867
yoga, relation to, 8415
yoni icons of, 9905, 9906
Śivadāsa (South Asian writer), 10034
Śivagītā (Hindu text), 854
Śivajñānabodham (Meykaṇṭār), 8976
Śivajñānasiddhiyār (Aruṇanti), 8976
Śivānanda, in ashram revival, 545, 546
Śivānanda Ashram, 546
Śiva Nataraja (deity)
in art, 498–499
creation by, 5455
as dancer, 4428
Śiva-nature, Abhinavagupta on, 8418
Sivaraksa, Sulak, on modern Buddhism, as state instrument, 2787
Śivarātri celebration, in Hindu religious year, 4017
Sivin, Nathan, 235
Sīwichai, Khrūbā, 1141, 9097
Six (number), interpretations of, 6748
Six Articles (1539), 7662
Six Dynasties period (China), 1576
Confucian texts in, 1908
Daoism in, 2192–2195
Tantric teachings in, 9960–9961
three teachings in, 1898–1899
Six National Histories (Japan), as historical canon, 4802–4803
Six Nations of the Iroquois, 4541, 7300–7301
Sixteen (number), interpretations of, 6749
Sixteen Cowries: Yorùbá Divination from Africa to the New World (Bascom), 10032
Sixth Ecumenical Council, 2584
Sixth Patriarch. *See* Huineng
Sixtine Bible, 893
Sixtus IV (pope)
and Torquemada (Tomás de), 9242
Bonaventure canonized by, 1011
expanding Papal States, 6972
Sistine Chapel built by, 6972
Sixtus V (pope)
and Bellarmino (Roberto), 816
Bonaventure declared doctor of church by, 1011
College of Saint Bonaventure founded by, 1013
reform of, 6972
and Sixtine Bible, 893
Sixty (number), interpretations of, 6750
Siyyum (celebration of conclusion), 7821
Size, hierarchy of, in science, 2659
Sjoestedt, Marie-Louise
on Celtic corpus, 1495
comparative study of, 1498
on local and tribal cults, 1482
Sidh, 8392

scholarship based on work of, 1499
Sjöö, Monica, on Goddess feminism, 4166
Skaði (giant)
Loki and, 5508
marriage to Njǫrðr, 6641–6642
Skáldskaparmál, 2692
Skan (deity), souls given by, 8534
Skanda (deity)
as Śiva's son, 4444
birth of, 8040
Buddhist/Muslim veneration of, 3162
peacock of, 4438
as slayer of the *asura,* 4017
in Tamil religions, as Murukaṉ, 6240
Skanda Purāṇa (Hindu text), 778, 8977
Skandha Gupta I, 1351
Skandhaka (Buddhist text), 1063, 1258, 1259–1260
Skandhas. See Soul, Buddhist concepts of
Skansen (Stockholm), 6245
Ska rhythm, Rastafarianism and, 1438
Skeggjason, Hjalti, 3219
Skeleton, in shamanistic initiations, 8271
Skeleton Key to Finnegans Wake (Campbell and Robinson), publication of, 1378
Skeptics and Skepticism (philosophical school), **8420–8422**. *See also* Atheism; Doubt
18th-century rise of, 3557
academic skepticism, 8420
Cārvāka and, 1446–1447
in Chinese religion
of Old Text school, 1575
Wang Chong and, 1592
Xunzi and, 1588
criticism of religion in, 3910
of Daddy Grace, 2124, 2125
in *Ecclesiastes,* 9759
in Israelite wisdom, 9756
in modern philosophy, 8421–8422
in Muslim and Jewish philosophy, 8420–8421
Phyrrhonism, 8420
relativism and, 7685
in Renaissance and Reformation thought, 8421
roots of, 8420
secularization and, 8218
sociology and, 8490–8492
in sociology of religion, 8490–8492
Sketches of Residence and Travel in Brazil (Kidder), Carnival in, 1443
Skin
flayed, in Aztec religion, 1469, 1548, 4190
shedding of, in rejuvenation myths, 7683
Skinner, Alanson, 6672
Skinner, B. F., materialism of, 6056
Skinner, Clarence, 9471
Skinner, H. D., 840
Skinwalkers (witches), 9769
Skírnir, 2692
Skírnismál, 2692
SKK. *See* Sekai Kyusei Kyō
Sklare, Marshall, on women in Conservative Judaism, 1963
Skobtsova, Mother Maria, **8422–8423**
Skoptsy community, castration among, 1452, 8248
Skulls. *See also* Head(s)
in animal sacrifice, 3804
detached, in Neolithic burials, 6460–6461
head hunting and, 3805, 3807
from Lower Paleolithic Period, 6951
as masks, 5769
in Micronesian religions, 6004
Neanderthal use of, 6950, 6951
from Upper Paleolithic Period, 6952
Skutch, Judy, 560
Skuyūkh bil-baraka (blessed *shaikhs*), in Egypt, as class of healer, 3836
Sky. *See also* Cosmology; Heaven; Moon; Stars; Sun
in African religions, supreme being and, 3567, 3574–3576
An's relationship to, 301, 302, 5952
in Australian Indigenous myths, 655
brightness of, as sign of omniscient supreme beings, 8869
deities and spirits of (*See* Sky deities and spirits)
Egyptian concepts of, 2710
in Germanic religion, 3448
hierophany, heavens as, **8423–8425**
anthropomorphic representations, 8424–8425
technomorphic representations, 8423–8424
as image of transcendence, 1994
in Iroquois religion, 4541
masculine sacrality in, 5759–5762
in Maya religion, 5796
in Micronesian religions, 6002
myths and symbolism of, **8425–8432**
astrology and, 8426
attribution deities (planetary), 8426–8428
celestial patterns and ordering, 8428–8429
in creation narratives, 8429–8430
cycles and, 8425–8426
sacred space and, 8430–8431
upper world, cosmological structure of, 8426
in nature worship, 6438
in Neolithic religions, 6464, 6465
in Oceanic religions, 2005, 6785, 6789
in Osage religion, 6917, 6918–6919
as portent, 7336–7337
in religion of farmers, 3108
sacred space and hierophany of, 8428–8429
in South American Indian religions, 8587–8588
in Tukanoan myth (Amazon), 8622
supreme beings, celestiality of, 8868–8869, 8870
Sky deities and spirits, 3618, 5992–5995. *See also* Sun
as anthropomorphic representations, 8424
in Australian Indigenous religions, 5993
Howitt (A. W.) on, 4142
in Baltic religion, 757–760
in Buriat religion, 1326–1327
in Caribbean religions, 1427, 1435
castration of, 1450
in Chinese religion, Shangdi as, 8300
in Chuvash religion, 1784
creation out of nothing by, 1986
as *dei otiosus,* 2309–2310, 2311, 2312
in Egyptian religion, Atum as, 623
examples of, 3618
in Finnish religion, 4378–4379
in Finno-Ugric religions, 3108
functions of, 3618, 5992–5993
in Greek myth, 1450
in Gurage religion, 2574
in Huichol religion, 4152
in Hun religion, 4228
in Igbo religion, 4365
in Inca religion, 5176
in Indo-European religions, linguistic evidence of, 8875
in Enawenê Nawê religion, 2012–2013
in Khanty and Mansi religion, 3107, 6754–6755
in Maori religion, 1450
masculine sacrality in, 5759, 5760
in Micronesian religions, 6003, 6004
in nature worship, 6438
in North American Indian religions, 6651
Skan, in Dakota tradition, 8534
in Nuer and Dinka religion, 2568, 6744
Pettazzoni (Raffaele) on, 8878
pictorial representation of, 4296
in Polynesian religions, 7312–7313, 7314
in primitive religions, 10065
in primordial couple, 1993–1994
in Samoyed religion, 469
vs. storm deities, 5994
in Turco-Mongol religions, 9080–9082
Vedic, 9524–9525
Sky Father (deity), 3015, 5119, 5125
Skyhorse, Paul, 10054
Sky Mother (folklore figure), 5120
Skyob pa 'Jig rten mgon po, 1230
Skyscrapers, 9267
Sky-Woman, 3407
SLA. *See* Symbionese Liberation Army
Slametan (communal meal), in Agami Jawi, 4817
Slametan feast, 5726
Slaughter, animal. *See also* Animal sacrifice
in Islam, 2651
in Judaism, 2644
in Vanuatu religions, 9519–9520
Slava, Modris, 766
Slavery and slave religion
abolition of slavery (*See* Abolitionism)
in Africa, religious transformation and, 1510
African American
African influences on, 65–66
Christian conversion, 1709
history of study of, 66–67, 76–77
institutionalization of, 68–69
Islam, 4682
women in, 10037
Afro-Brazilian, 120
Afro-Caribbean, 1433 (*See also* Caribbean religions)
creolization and, 2066–2067

Afro-Caribbean *continued*
poisoning in, 3823
study of, 10024, 10025–10026
Afro-Surinamese, 126, 127
in Caribbean, 1706–1707, 9305, 9306
Carnival and, 1443
Channing (William Ellery) on, 1530
Christianity
in Caribbean, 1706–1707
Photios's mission work and, 7135–7136
culture history and, 8476
dance in, 2135
debt slavery, law codes on, 1844–1845
in Egypt, Moses and, 6199, 6200
evangelicalism and, 2888
family hierarchy and, 2986
Fulbe religion on, 3229
gender roles and, 7627–7628
in Greece, ancient, slaves as sexual possessions, 7079
hair symbolism and, 3739
in Haiti, Vodou and, 9634, 9635
healing and, 3822
Hebrew laws on, 1845
Islam, 4608, 4682–4683
Israelite laws on, 4731
Jewish law and, 3753
liberation theology and, 5440, 5441
in Methodism, 5998
among Muslims, 71
in novels, ancient, 3055
Quakers and, 7548
in South Africa, 4608
in South America
Amazon slave commerce, 8621
in Brazil, 1696
and transculturation, 9296–9297, 9305, 9306
in United States, civil religion and, 1815, 1816
Zinzendorf on, 1706
Slave trade, 65–66
in Congo
attributed to witchcraft, 2002
Kongo religion and, 5220
Slavic language
Cyrillic alphabet, 2116
liturgy in, 2116
Slavic religion, **8432–8439**
Baltic and Indo-Iranian influences, 8432
Charlemagne and, 1556
Christianity in, 1682
arrival of, 8432
Church Slavic language in, 7943
Cyril and Methodius, role of, 2116–2117
pagan pantheon and, 8435–8436
pilgrimage in, 7148
Christian missions and from Church of Constantinople, 2585
East *vs.* West and, 1690
in Moravia, 1683
corporate (body) symbolism in, 4161
dawn cult in, 8435
Dazhbog in, 2231
deities of, 8434–8436 (*See also specific deities*)
domovoi (family founder spirits) in, 4106
formation of, 8432
goats in, 8312
household guardians in, 8436
migrations and cultural history, 8432
mythic images from Old European religion, 8436–8438
Baba Yaga and Ved'ma in, 8437
Fates in, 8436–8437
goblins in, 8438
Moist Mother Earth and Corn Mother in, 8437
nymphs in, 8437–8438
sources on, 8432–8433
temples and idols in, 8433–8434
Slavophiles
Aksakov (Ivan) as, 224
Khomiakov (Aleksei) and, 5137, 5138
Kireevskii (Ivan) as, 5187
Sleep, **8439–8442**. *See also* Dreams
as Adam's first fall, 339, 340
in African myths, 93
in Asklepios, cult of, 551, 552
in Christian eschatology, 8565
as death, 8441
as enlightenment, 8441–8442
gods, sleeping, 8440
in heroic tales and folklore, 8440
as ignorance, 8441
in Upaniṣads, 9482
Mesmer on, 1947
personifications of, 8439–8440
rejuvenating, 7683
rituals of, 8441
shape shifting in, 8440–8441
soul ascension in
in Islam, 8567
in Judaism, 8558
soul loss in, 8440
Sleeping Beauty, 8440
Sleeping sickness, 60
Sleep paralysis, witchcraft blamed for, 9770
Sleep yogas, 1288
Slepnir (mythic horse), 5508
"Slim Man Canyon" (Silko), 7226
Slit-drums, 2494, 2495, 7030, 7036
Mesoamerican, 6268, 6269, 6270
Slit-gongs, 9520
Sloane, Sir Hans, 6243
Slocum, Joe, 574
Slocum, John, 6718
on confession of sins, 7759
Slocum, Mary, 574
Śloka (verse form), 2329
Slonimsky, Henry, 2746
on suffering, 8805
Sloth bear, 808
Slotkin, J. S., 6671
Slovakia, Uniate church in, 9464
Slovenia, independence of, 1686
Smalcald League, 5536, 5539, 7659
Small, Alethea Brooks, 3096
Small, Charles, 3096
Small Alphabet for a Monk in the School of God (Thomas á Kempis), 9159
Smaller Sukhāvatīvyūha Sūtra, Kumārajīva's translation of, 5263
Smallpox
in Australia, 685
and Baiame *waganna,* 671
in Ugandan religion, 2568
in West African religions, 9717
Small seal writing, calligraphy and, 1370
Smaragdus (Benedictine writer), 821
Smart, Ninian, 6989, **8442–8445**
approaches to study of religions by, 8443–8444
dimensional approach of, 8444, 8466
historiography of, 4048–4049
life and achievements of, 8442–8443
on mysticism, 7744
on participatory study, 8786
on phenomenology of religion, 7093
on relevance of religion, 4179
Sharpe (Eric) and, 8304
significance and legacy of, 8444
on society and religion, 8466
Smārtas brahmans, 9502–9503, 9572–9573
Smārta schools of Hinduism
bhakti synthesis and, 3998–4002
and classical Hinduism, development of, 3997
Śaṅkara's revival of, in Advaita Vedānta, 4003–4004
Śiva temples and, 8042
Smārtasūtras (*smṛti* summaries), 9553–9554
Sma-tawy (symbol), 4319
Smelting
discovery of, 5987
rites associated with, 5988
Smenkhkare, 217, 219
Smin grol gling (Buddhist monastery), 7869
Smirnov, Ivan Nikolaevich, 3112
Smith. *See* Blacksmiths; Metals and metallurgy
Smith, Adam, 5399, 9294
on social systems, 8491
on sociology, 8491
Smith, Alfred, 7303–7304
Smith, Amanda Berry, 80
Smith, Bardwell, on goal of Buddhism, 2786–2787
Smith, David M., 576
Smith, E. Gene, 1315
Smith, Edwin W. *See also* Edwin Smith Papyrus
on African religions, 115–116
uNkulunkulu in, 96
Smith, Employment Division, Department of Human Resources of the State of Oregon v., 7303–7304
Smith, Erminnie, 6670
Smith, Gene E., 9188, 9189
Smith, George, 3487
Smith, Gerald L. K., anti-Semitism of, 1658
Smith, Grafton Elliot, Egyptocentric Diffusionist school and, 8768
Smith, Hannah Whitall, **8445–8446**
and Holiness movement in Europe, 4083
Smith, Houston, 7467
Smith, Howard, Sharpe (Eric) and, 8304
Smith, Huston, American study of religion, role in, 8786
Smith, Hyrum, 6193
Smith, John, 6985
Smith, John Maynard, 2908
Smith, Jonathan Z., 946, 3100
American study of religion, role in, 8786–8787
comparativism, criticism of, 1879
on cultural analysis of religion, 8470, 8471
on *dema* myth complex, 4825–4826
on facts, revisions of, 4962
historiography of, 4049
on humor, 4198
on linear *vs.* cyclical time, 7992
religion defined by, 7704
on religious experience, 7743–7744, 7745
on sacred, 5436
on sacred and profane, 8010
on sacred space, 7978
on sacrifice, 8009
on study of religion, methods of, 7746
on "world axis" and "center," 1879
Smith, Joseph, Jr., **8446–8448,** 9913
and *Book of Mormon,* 6516
as messenger figure, 6733

Mormonism after death of, 6564–6565
Mormonism founded by, 1714, 6192–6194, 6558, vol. 4 color insert, vol. 14 color insert
murder of, 6193, 6548, 8447
political ambitions of, 8447
on polygamy, 6534
polygamy practiced by, 6558
as presidential candidate, 6193
as prophet, 6546, 7428
seer stone of, vol. 4 color insert
visions and revelations of, 6192, 6193, 8447
Smith, Joseph, Sr., 6192
Smith, Joseph F., 6194
Smith, Kiki, vol. 13 color insert
Smith, Lucy Mack, 6192
Smith, M. G., 10026–10027
Smith, Margaret, 3369
Smith, Mark M., on clocks, 7986
Smith, Mohlan, 5388
Smith, Morton, 929, 935, 946, 7081, **8448–8450**
and midrash, 6020
on Moore (George Foot), 6176
Smith, Philip, on culture, 2087
Smith, Pierre, 5850
Smith, Pig, 1565
Smith, R. Drew, 74
Smith, Redbird, 1565
Smith, Robert
on ancestor worship, 324
and Holiness movement in Europe, 4083
Smith, Robertson
on purification, 7504
symbol theory and, 8910, 8911
Smith, Theophus, 80
Smith, Vincent, 555
Smith, W. Robertson, 3191, **8451–8453**
Durkheim influenced by, 2528, 3231
heresy charges against, 8451–8452
on left and right symbolism, 5394
on myth-ritualism, 3288
on sacrifice, 4183, 8002–8003
on Semitic religions, 8452
on society and religion, 8466
theories of, 8451
Smith, W. (William) Robertson, on Israelite religion, 10077
Smith, Wilfred Cantwell, **8450–8451**
Bangalore Consultation presentation, 8790, 8791
on comparative study of religion, 1877
comparative theology of, 9130
Islamic studies of, 4718, 4720
religion, view of, 4044
on sacred books, 8196
on tradition, 9279
Smither, Elizabeth, 3084
Smithsonian Institution
Native American skeletons at, 7303
study of Caribbean religions by, 10025
Šmits, Pēteris, 327, 770
on Māra, 5691, 5692
Smohalla (Native American prophet), 3015, 6597, 6718
Smoke, sacrifice and, 7999
Smoke cabins, 801
Smoking, **8453–8456**. *See also* Tobacco
in Mesoamerican religions, 8454–8456
in North American Indian religions, 8454
in South American Indian religions, 8454
Smon lam chen mo (Tibetan New Year festival), 9387
Smṛti (Hindu texts), 4423–4424. *See also* Dharmaśāstras; *See also* Dharmasūtras; See also Mahābhārata; *See also* Purāṇas; See also Rāmāyaṇa; *See also* Upaniṣads
authority of Veda in, 3995
Bhagavadgītā as, 852
in Brahmanism, 9568
canon formation and, 8202
definition of, 4423
dethroning of kings in, 5345
etymology of term, 4423
interpretation of, 5345
meaning of, 1407
popularity of, 8201
reformers of, 2330
religion governed by, 4423
revelations remembered in, 7205
Śāstra literature, place in, 8122
as source of *dharma,* 5343, 5344
śruti texts *vs.,* 2327, 3994–3995
varṇa and *jāti* in, 9570
Smyrna, 34
Smysl zhizni (Trubetskoi), 9367
Smyth, John, 783
Snakebites
diamond as remedy for, 2346
Māra and, 5693
protection from, vol. 8 color insert
Snake-bridge, 1503–1504
Snake goddess (prehistoric), 7377
Snake movements, North American Indian, 6666, 6667
Snakes and serpents, **8456–8460**. *See also* Dragons; Rainbow Snake; See also Kuṇḍalinī; Snakebites
in African religions
in cults of affliction, 62
Fulbe, 3228, 3229
Hyakyusa, 6771
moon and, in Pygmy religion, 3971
in myths, 95, 96–97
West African, Dangbi as python god, 3969
ancestor veneration and, 8457
of Asklepios, 551, 552
Athena and, 586
in Australian Indigenous myths, 655, 656–658, 9704–9706
in Baltic religion, in Latvian Saule (sun) cult, 8133
in Buddhism, vol. 8 color insert
chaos and, 1538
cosmic power and, 8458
in creation myths, 1986, 8456–8457
death and underworld associated with, 8458
in Dogon religion, 2391
eagles and hawks and, 2554
Eve and, 2896
in Garden of Eden, 6982
in Germanic religion, Niðhǫggr as cosmic serpent, 1502
in Gnosticism, 3518–3519
in Greek religion
guilt and punishment symbolized by, 7783
Hydra killed by Herakles, 3916
in Haitian Vodou, spirits of, 1433, 9636
in Hebrew scripture, evil and, 8404
in Hinduism, 4437–4438, 4439, 7500, 9824
Mucalinda, vol. 8 color insert
Nāga Pañcamī celebration and, 4016
in Hittite religion, Illuyanka as, 4068–4070
in Haṭha Yoga, 5266
labyrinths symbolizing, 5277
life and immortality associated with, 8458–8459
in Maya religion, 5883–5884
in megalithic religion, 5825
in Mesoamerican religions
at Chichén Itzá, 8429
Coatlicue and, 1841, 4155
myths about, 5938
in Olmec iconography, 5881
Quetzalcoatl, 1471
Milky Way as, 2863
in Minoan-Mycenaean iconography, 4320, 4321
in Minoan religion, deities of, *37, 37*
in North American Indian religions
California, 6714
Cherokee, 6692
Pueblo, 6724, 6725
ouroboros, as magic circle, 1792–1794
pearl and, 7024
in prehistoric religions, 7377, 7382–7383
as protector and bestower of happiness, 8457
in rejuvenation myths, 7683, 7684
Ricoeur (Paul) on, 8125
rope and snake analogy of Śaṅkara, 8105–8106
Satan as, 8125
in Semang cosmology, 6456
in Sistine Chapel, 8755
soul associated with, 8457
in South American religions
amaru, 1364, 4411
Amazonian Quechua, 282, 284
in Southeast Asian religions, *Nāga* figures, in Cambodian origin stories, 4010
and temptation, 9071
wisdom and power of, 8457–8458
Snefru (Egyptian king), 7527
Sneha (love), 854
Snellgrove, David, 1315, 9189, 9190
Sngags rim chen mo (Tsong kha pa), 1218, 9387
Snga 'gyur rnying ma pa order (Buddhist), 1223–1224
Snodgrass, Anthony, 3665
Snoek, Jan A. M., 7860
Snoldelev inscription, 7940
Snorri Sturluson, **8460**. *See also* Prose Edda
on afterlife, 167, 168, 3448
on Baldr, 744
death of, 3455–3456
on berserkers, 842
on boat burials, 990
on burial practices, 3457
on cosmic tree, 3448
on creation, 3446
of man, 3454, 3455
dialogue of religions by, 2342
euhemerism of, 366, 3458, 5672
on Freyja, 3218
on Freyr, 3219, 3220
on Heimdallr, 3898
historiography of, 4038
on Loki, 5508, 5509
on minor deities, 3454
myths transcribed by, 4462
on Æsir, 3449
on *álfar,* 254

Snorri Sturluson ***continued***
on Njǫrðr, 6641
on Óðinn, 6808–6809
on Týr, 9426
on pagan-Christian associations, 8025
on shape shifting, 8440–8441
on Thor, 9165–9166
on Vanir, 3449
work corroborated by Saxo Grammaticus, 8142
on world of the dead, 3448
Snouck Hurgronje, Christiaan, 25, 26, 4717, 4718, **8461**
colonial agenda and, 8638
Snowshoes, Athapaskan, 6675
Snoy, Peter, 9613
Snyder, Gary, 2563, 2628
Snying rje (compassion), meditation on, 1284, 1285
Snying thig (Seminal Heart), 2547
contemplative system of, 2547–2548
doctrine of, 2547
dominance of, 2548
Klong chen Rab 'byams pa (Longchenpa) on, 5191, 5193
literature of, 2547, 2548, 5193
philosophical character of, 2547
in Rnying ma pa (nyingmapa) school of Buddhism, 7868–7869
Treasure tradition in, 9331
Sōan bungaku (grass hut literature), 7216
Sobek (deity), Haroeris and, Kom Ombo temple of, 2709
Sobel, Mechal, 67, 75, 76
Sobornost', 5138
Kireevskii (Ivan) on, 5187
Soccer, in Oceania, 6787
Social action
definition of, 5397
for legitimation, 5396–5404
Social activism
Christian movements of, 1750
in progressive Islam, 6099
Social authority, sociological concept of, 8483
Social behavior, analyzing in Vodou, 9637
Social class. *See* Class, socioeconomic
Social Compass: Revue Internationale de Sociologie de la Religion (journal), 10057
Social Context of Paul's Ministry, The (Hock), 7014
Social contract
Hobbes (Thomas) on, 5367
Locke (John) on, 5367–5368
Social Contract, The (Rousseau), civil religion in, 1812–1813, 7931
Social control
by ethno-religious groups, dress and, 1835–1836
haircutting and, 3739–3740
sexuality and, 8242
Social dance, definition of, 2146
Social Darwinism
anti-Semitism, 4085
and history of religions, 10043
religious morality and, 2660
of Weber (Max), 9711
Social drama, 7050
Social evolutionism, Spencer (Herbert) on, 8678
Social functionalism, in African studies, 115, 116
Social Gospel movement, 964, 2670
Christianity way of life and, 1671
decline of, 1752
ethics and, 1656
evangelicalism and moral crusades, 1710
historiography and, 4032
kingdom of God in, 5152
as multiple movements, 1752
progressive millennialism of, 6546
Rauschenbusch's (Walter) influence on, 7629–7630
Smith (Wilfred Cantwell) and, 8450
sociologists and, 8495–8496
wealth and, 9709
Social groups, sociological theory of, 8482–8483
Social history, of art, 9620
Social interaction, sociological concept of, 8482
Socialism. *See also* Christian socialism
American religious opposition to, 2670
Besant's (Annie), 844
Buddhist, 1140–1141, 1283, 9152, 9153
community-oriented, 9230
Engels (Friedrich) on, 8480
Islamic conduciveness to, 2677
Jewish, 4863
anti-Semitism and, 5021
of Jones (Jim), 4953
legitimation and, 5399
of Mauss (Marcel), 5785, 5786
Muslim, in Middle Volga, 4619
Niebuhr (Reinhold) and, 6611
Roman Catholic Church on, 2670
Tillich's (Paul) analysis of, 9203
as utopianism, 9492
Socialist Decision (Tillich), 9230
Sociality
of Buddhist practice, in East Asia, 9836–9837
orgy and, 6860, 6861
in Zulu religion, 10009–10010
Social justice
in Australia, Stanner (W. E. H.) on, 8730
in Baltic religion, Latvian Saule (sun) cult and, 8133
charity and, 1553
Christian social movements and, 1753–1755
curses and, 2100–2101
Day (Dorothy) and, 2226
in Earth Charter, 2657
as ecumenical concern, 2685
food and, 3173–3174
in Islam
as cardinal virtue, 6222
environmentalism and, 2653
progressive, 6098–6099
Jones (Jim) and, 4951, 4952
in Judaism
environmental ethics of, 2644
Reform Judaism, 7666
in liberation theology, 9540
sacramental theology and, 7962
Social justice movement
environmental concerns and, 2610
religious leaders in, 2614
Social life, objects and images in, 9622
Socially engaged Buddhism. *See* Engaged Buddhism
Social movements
Christian, **1748–1756** (*See also* Healing and medicine, in Christianity)
Catholic developments in, 1752–1753
historical background of, 1748–1749
missionary movements, 1751–1752
modernizing movements, 1749–1751
political activism in, 1753–1755
Salvation Army programs, 8064
and heresy, development of, 3923
historiography and, 4032
as religion, 8473
shelters for homeless and victims of domestic violence, 4102
Social order
Calvinism and, 1692
cosmology and, 1993
in East African religion, witchcraft and, 2570, 2577–2578
in ethnoastronomy, 2863, 2865
Hasidism and, 3785–3786
in Hinduism, in Vedic cosmology, 2014
in Japan, under Tokugawa regime, 4788
in North American and Mesoamerican religions, cosmology linked to, 2009, 2010
sacred space and, 7984
scapegoat concept and, 8145
secularization and, 8215, 8218
Social philosophy, in Confucianism, 2632
Social protest, Religo-political cults in Caribbean and, 1437
Social realism
drama in, 2474–2475
Durkheim's (Émile), 2527
idealism turned into, 4356
Social reform
in Australia
Aboriginal Christianity in, 676
Catholics *vs.* Protestants and, 1733
Christian social movements, **1748–1756**
cultural interactions and, 7653
by Ethical Culture societies, 2857, 2858
in evangelicalism, 2888
in India
Ambedkar (B. R.) in, 285–286
Ārya Samāj in, 516
BAPS movement and, 8890
Gandhi (Mohandas) in, 3272–3273
Sen (Keshab Chandra) on, 8227
women-related, 3320
monasticism and, 7652–7653
in Protestantism, 7653
religious concern for, 7652–7653
in United States
Adler (Felix) in, 33
evangelicalism and moral crusades, 1710–1711, 1715
Social relations, illness and, 3810
Social roles
creating and re-creating, dance used for, 2136–2137, 2140–2141
sociological concept of, 8483–8484
Social role theory, 7478
Social salvation, 5398–5399
Social science
in American study of religion, 8786
conversion, theories of, 1970–1971
in ecology and religion studies, 2609
four-stage theory of development in, 9294
Haydon (A. Eustace), theory of religion based on, 3803
hermeneutics and, 3930
philosophy and religion expressed in, 7118

realism in, 9711
study of religion in, 2761
Weber (Max) in, 9711–9712
Social Science and the Ignoble Savage (Meek), 9294
Social service
in engaged Buddhism, 2785
in Vedānta, 9630
Social Setting of Pauline Christianity, The (Theissen), 7018
Social Sources of Denominationalism, The (Niebuhr), 2289–2290
Social Statics (Spencer), 2918
Social structure
in Buddhism, in *saṃghas,* 8077
ceremony and, 1512, 1513
in Chinese religion, 1615–1617
Christianity and, in West Indies, 1706
in Chumash religion, 9228
in Egypt, in afterlife, 2705
of Essene sect, 2846–2847
inverted in Carnival, 1440, 1444, 7196
inverted in play, 7196–7197
Israelite
Hellenization of, 4973–4974
sacralization of, 4973
Jesus and, 4850
in Khanty religion, 5121
kingship and, 5158
kinship and, 5182
in Mansi religion, 5121
in Oceanic religions, 6787, 6802
cosmology and, 2004–2006
in Solomon Islands religions, 8516
Osage, 6918–6919
power and, 7351–7352
prestige in, war and, 9679
Reformation and, 7664
religion and, mutual reinforcement of, 2674
reversing, in orgy, 6864
sacrificial context, signified in, 1466
in secret societies, 8211
Social systems, the Enlightenment and, 8491
Social welfare programs
in Buddhism, 2786
in Catholicism, 9709
Ethical Culture and, 2858
religion's influence on, 2670
Social workers, psychotherapy provided by, 7487–7488
Societas Rosicruciana, 7930. *See also* Rosicrucians
Societas Verbi Divini. *See* Society of the Divine Word
Société des Études, 4879
Society. *See also* Secularization
ablutions and, 11, 12
African
cults of affliction in, 58, 60, 62–63
witchcraft and sorcery accusations in, 90
zaar cult and, 107
agricultural, values of, 192–193
anthropological focus on, 2915
body symbolism for, 4161, 4169
vs. community, 7716, 8481
Durkheim (Émile) on, 7716
Marx, Karl on, 7716
Tönnies (Ferdinand Julius) on, 7716
control over, expulsion as, 2938
creation of, in East African cosmogony, 2567
duties in, conflicts among, 2656–2657
economy and
change achieved in, 2676
religion in, 2669
separation of, 2668–2669
ethics in, emergence of, 2656
evolution and, in eugenics, 2879, 2881
games and, 3267–3268
identical with God, 2528
Indo-European tripartite model, 1499
in Islam, *ummah* and, 9447
marginality of, social change stemming from, 5397
marriage for continuation of, 5724–5725
martyrdom's relation to, 5737–5743
modern, structure of, 5369
origins of, death and, 2238–2239
orthopraxy in, 6915
reintegration with, in exorcism, 2935
and religion (*See* Society and religion, relations between)
ritual importance in, 7839–7840
sacred and profane in, Durkheim (Émile) on, 7971
self and, in Confucianism, 2633
Steiner (Rudolf) on realms of, 8738
transcendence of, 4530
virginity in, 9606–9607
in warfare, preconditions in, 9680–9681
witchcraft and, 9769, 9773–9774
Society and religion, relations between, **8461–8473**. *See also* Church and state; Sociology
in Buddhism, 8463
in Christianity, 8464
in Confucianism, 8462
contemporary discussion of, 8469
in Daoism, 8463
in Hinduism, 8463
in Shintō, 8462–8463
institutional differentiation and, 8472–8473
in Islam, 8462
in Judaism, 8463–8464
poststructuralism and, 8468
sacred *vs.* secular in, 8462
secularization and, 8468–8469
study of, 8464–8469
Berger (Peter L.) in, 8468, 8488
Comte (Auguste) in, 8465, 8480
contemporary research on, 8467–8469
cultural analysis approach, 8470–8472
Durkheim (Émile) in, 8465, 8480–8481, 8487–8488
Geertz (Clifford) in, 8467–8468
Lévy-Bruhl (Lucien) in, 8465
Luckmann (Thomas) in, 8468
other contributions, 8466–8467
Parsons (Talcott) in, 8467
Saint-Simon (Claude-Henri de Rouvroy) in, 8465
Smart (Ninian) in, 8466
Wach (Joachim) in, 8466
Weber (Max) in, 8465–8466, 8488
Society for Establishing Righteousness and Harmony (Risshō Kōseikai), **7794–7795**
Society for Psychical Research (SPR), 977, 6057, 7738, 7742, 7747, 9142
Society for Spiritual Acts, 2157
Society for the Advancement of Judaism (SAJ), 5082, 7636
Society for the Buddhist Mission in Germany, 1187
Society for the Propagation of the Gospel in Foreign Part (SPG), 350–352
Caribbean missions and, 1706
Society for the Scientific Study of Religion (SSSR), role of, 8788
Society for the Study of Chinese Religions, 1636, 1637
Society Islands religion (Polynesia)
comets in, 8736
cosmology of, 7305
incantations in, 7311
octopus in, 7313
rituals in, 7309, 7310
Tangaroa in, 8980
Society of Friends. *See* Quakers
Society of Jesus. *See* Jesuits
Society of Medicine Men (Iroquois), 4542
Society of Muslim Brothers. *See* Muslim Brotherhood
Society of Rosicrucians, 7930. *See also* Rosicrucians
Society of Saint John the Evangelist, 7724
Society of Saint Joseph, 957
Society of Shangdi (Chinese secret society), 7719
Society of Silent Help, 3096, 9472
Society of the Daughters of the Heart of Mary, Petre (Maude) in, 7070
Society of the Divine Word (Societas Verbi Divini), Schmidt (Wilhelm) and, 8167–8168
Society of the Muslim Brothers. *See* Muslim Brotherhood
Society of the Rose Cross, 7929. *See also* Rosicrucians
Society of the Sacred Heart, 6764
Socinians
blasphemy prosecution of, 973
on eternity of God, 6963
Socinus. *See* Sozzini, Fausto Pavolo
Sociobiology (Wilson), 2916, 2919
Sociobiology and evolutionary psychology, 7478–7479, **8473–8480**. *See also* Evolution
Darwinism and religion, **8477–8480**
biological explanations in human affairs, scope of, 8477–8478
in evolutionary ethics, 2919–2920
evolutionary psychology
criticism of, 8479
overview of, 8475–8476
of religion, 8478–8479
evolutionism and, 2916–2917
and history of religions, 10043
overview of, **8473–8477**
sociobiology, 8473–8475
Socioeconomic atheism, 7422
Socioeconomic class. *See* Class, socioeconomic
"Sociological Theory of Totemism, The" (Radcliffe-Brown), 7592

Sociology, **8480–8501**. *See also* Culture; Society and religion, relations between; *specific scholars*
in anthropological studies, 382
charisma, concept of, 1544–1545
dualism in, 2505–2506
of ecstasy, 2679
of enthusiasm, 2807
of games, 3267–3268
history of religion and, 9650
identity theory, on conversion, 1971
on initiation, 4480, 4481
in Jewish studies, 4881
on liturgy, 5491
of magic, 5565–5566
on membership, 1779
orgy interpreted in, 6875
phenomenology and, 8495
and positivism, 7340
and religion, **8480–8490**
antinomies in, 8481–8482
classical *vs.* contemporary approach, 8487–8489
contemporary interest in, 8487
development of the discipline, 8480–8481
deviance and change concept in, 8484–8485
religious studies and, 8489
social aggregates concept in, 8482–8483
social authority concept in, 8483
social interaction concept, 8482
social roles concept in, 8483–8484
of religion, 944, **8490–8501**
African American, 73–76
in Australasia, 8771
birth of, 8491–8492
of civil religion, 1813
conservative and romantic reaction in, 8492
on cults and sects, 2084
Fustel de Coulanges as founding father of, 3245
hermeneutical approach to, 8499–8500
in history of religion, 9650
implicit religion in, 4401
impoverishment of, 8496
invisible religion in, 4530–4531
journals on, 10057
modern social theory scholarship, 8492–8496
on propriety of religion, 8497–8498
religious studies preceded by, 2608
skepticism and speculation in, 8490–8492
Spencer (Herbert) on, 8678
traditional social thought, 8490
on truth of religion, 8498–8499
Weber (Max) in, 9711
in women's studies, 9790
religion defined by, 7693
sacredness defined by, 7693
temptation in, 9073
in Vedic mythology interpretation, 9559
Vierkandt (Alfred) in, 9590
witchcraft studied in, 9779
Sociology of Religion (journal), 10057
Sociology of Religion (Wach), 7743, 9650
SOCOG. *See* Sydney Organising Committee of the Olympic Games
Socrates, **8501–8505**. *See also* Plato
analytic philosophy of, 306
as apologist, 427
Asklepios and, 551
casuistry of, 1454
charges against, 8504
on demons, 2277
divine, conception of, 8503
elenchus (questioning method) of, 8503
on free will, 3200
geometry of, 3441
homosexuality and, 4113
on *hypostasis* and *ousia,* 4240, 4241
Kierkegaard on, 5141
on knowledge, 5201
on learned ignorance, 6989
life of, 8502, 8504
philosophy and religion of, 8502–8504
on recollection, 309–311
on reflexivity, 7648
on shape shifting, 8302
on sin, 8405
against Sophists, 7109–7110
sources on, 8501–8502
as spiritual guide, 8708–8709
on suicide, 8828–8829
theodicy of, 8503
on tradition, 9272
trial of, 971
on truth, 9374
wisdom of, 9747
Socrates Scholasticus of Constantinople, on Chrysostom, 1761, 1762
Socratic dialogue, 2342
Sod (esoterica), 867
Sodales Titii, 7908
Soden, Wolfram von, 222, 4404
on the Flood, 600
Söderblom, Nathan, **8505–8506**
Andrae (Tor) influenced by, 333
dynamism of, 2542
on the Flood in Iranian mythology, 2964
on God, 3557
existence of, 8762
Heiler (Friedrich) and, 3897
holiness, comparative approach to, 4098–4099
Junod (Henri A.) and, 113
on nature of religion, 8506
and Nyberg (H. S.), 6774
on phenomenology of religion, 7090
preanimism criticized by, 7373
Sharpe (Eric), biography by, 4049
on supreme beings, 8878
Tylor (E. B.) compared to, 363
Sodipe, J. O., 10032
Sodom and Gomorrah, 14, 15
Sōen Shaku, Suzuki (D. T.) and, 8884, 8885
Sofer, Mosheh (Ḥatam Sofer), 5020, 6899, **8506–8507**
on Mendelssohn, 4901
yeshivot and, 9884–9885
Soferim (official scribes), 886, 891
Sofres (ritual), 9998–9999
Soga, Tiya, 1718
Soga clan (Japan), Mononobe clan *vs.,* 8374
Soga dynasty (Japan), 1174–1175, 1241
Sogaku, Harada, on humor, 4207
Soga no Umako, Emperor Sushun and, 8374–8375
Soga religion (Uganda), hero gods of, 2575–2576
Soga *uji* (Japan), Buddhism in, 4782
Sogbo (spirit), 3166
in Haitian Vodou, 1433
Sogdiana, Manichaeism in, 5668, 5669
Sogdian language, 9398
Sogyŏk sŏ (Daoist temple), 2189
Sohak (Western Learning), 1647
Sōhei (priest soldiers), 2781–2782, 7273
Sohm, Rudolf, 5385, **8507–8508**
Soil. *See* Earth
Soil Conservation Service, 2609
Sōjiji Zen monastery, 5109
Sōka Gakkai, **8508–8510**
in Africa, 108, 109
engaged Buddhism of, 2786, 2787
in Europe, 6568
expansion of, 1184, 8509
in Japan, 6574
legitimation and, 5400
Nichirenshū and, 6608
urbanization and, 1809
origin of, 1099, 8508
political involvement of, 4792
popularity of, 4799
Sokar (deity), 2708
cult of, 2711
Sŏkkuram Buddhist temple compound (Korea), 9048
Sokolov, Timofei Savelich. *See* Tikhon of Zadonsk
Sokolow, Anna, 2163
Sokushin jōbutsu (realization of buddhahood), 9077, 9078
in Shingon Buddhism, 8350–8351
Sŏ Kyŏngdŏk (Hwadam), **8510**
Solal (deity), 6009, 6012
Solandra (plant), in Huichol religion, 4153
Solar eclipses, Mesoamerican calendar and, 1356
Solarization, in Indo-European religions, 8838
Solar Light Retreat, 9434
Solar mythology, 2518, 4459–4460
Solar Temple. *See* Temple Solaire
Solás, Humberto, 3099
Sola scriptura, 2387
Solemn vow, *vs.* simple vow, 7721
Soliarskii, P. F., moral theology, 1653
Solicitation laws, new religious movements and, 5378
Solidarity
Durkheim (Émile) on, 8488, 8495
Stoics on, 8742
"Soliloquies" (Isidore). *See* *Synonyms* (Isidore)
Sol Invictus, **8510–8511,** 8840–8841
Solipsism
Hocking (William Ernest) on, 4076
vs. reflexivity, 7648
Sölle, Dorothee, **8511–8512**
on atonement, 597
Solmsen, Friedrich, on psyche, 8542
Solomon (biblical figure), **8512–8514**
Adonis and, 34–35
alliance between King Hiram and, 7128
court history of, 2222
as healer, 3829
judicial decisions by, 4739, 4740
Nathan and, 6417
reign of, 8512–8513
on *shekhinah,* 8313
in succession story, 6417
temple of, 8513 (*See also* Solomon's Temple)
altars in, 276
shekhinah concept and, 8313
wisdom of, 8513, 9750, 9763–9764
writings of, 8513
Solomon, Paul, 560
Solomon, Psalms of, 904, 7461
messianism in, 5972
Solomonid dynasty (Ethiopia), 2860, 4606
Solomon Islands religions, **8514–8517**. *See also* Oceania and Oceanic religions; Tikopia religion
cargo cults, 1414

Christianity
Anglican missions, 1738
arrival of, 8514
indigenous missions, 1739
nominal, 8517
traditional culture merged with, 7297
cults and indigenous churches in colonial period, 8516–8517
ghosts, gods, and spirits in, 8514
mana and taboo in, 8515–8516
Melanesian Brotherhood in, 1739, 8517
people groups in, 8514
political independence and, 9324
shades, souls, and abodes of the dead in, 8514–8515
social structure and, 8516
Solomon's Temple (Jerusalem)
Antiochus IV defiling, 7144
Babylonian destruction of, 923, 935, 4549, 4746
in Jewish exile, 2922
sleep legends and, 8440
cantillation in, 1532–1533
date of building of, 923
design of, 923–924, 931, 932, 933–934, 4835
Ezekiel on, 2945
Freemasons on, 3195
funding in, 929
history of, 923–924
holy center and, 7983
Jeremiah on, 4829
in *2 Maccabees,* 900–901
presence of Yahveh, paradox of, 7981
in *Psalms,* 4746
renovations of, 924, 929
Rock of, as sacred center, 1502
sanctity of, 933
shekhinah (presence of God) in, 8313, 8314
Solomon as builder of, 8513
Solon, laws of, 1846
Soloveitchik, Haym, on Jewish law, 3746
Soloveitchik, Joseph Baer, 6905, **8517–8520**
life and era of, 8518
in modern Jewish thought, 4908
on prophecy, 7442
on Torah, 9238
writings of, 8518–8519
Soloveitchik, Yosef Dov, on nature, human responsibility for, 2645
Solov'ev, Vladimir, **8520–8521**
and Florenskii (Pavel), 3133, 3134
Gnosticism and, 3527
Trubetskoi (Sergei) as confidant of, 9368
Trubetskoi's (Evgenii) study of, 9367
Solstices. *See also* Summer solstice; Winter solstice
Chinese religion and, 1591, 1643
Healthy, Happy, Holy Organization (3HO), gatherings in, 3879
in Hindu religious year, 4016
Inca calendar and, 1361–1362
Interfaith Peace Prayer Day at, 3879
in Japanese religion, 8841
megaliths and, 5825
circle symbolism and, 1791
New Age pilgrimages on, 8429
sky hierophany and, 8428
Stonehenge and, 8835–8836
and worship of sun, 6438
Soluna (Asturias), 2439
Solzhenitsyn, Aleksandr, 3059
banishment of, 2938
Russian Orthodoxy and, 3060
Soma (deity), **8521–8522**. *See also* Haoma
in Cambodian origin stories, 4010
moon and, 6172–6173
Rudra associated with, 7934
in Vedism, 3990
Soma (substance), 4455, **8521–8522**. *See also* Haoma
in creation, 4439
ecstasy from, 2679
as elixir, 2770
identity of, 9558
and immortality, 849, 4439
Indra receiving, 3455, 4439, 4466, 4467
in *Ṛgveda,* 849, 4439
in *Sāmaveda,* 9551
and inspiration, 4509
as libation, 5434
moon and, 6172–6173
and poetic inspiration, 3455
preparation of, 849
purified vision yielded by, 3990
as sacrifice, 849, 3992, 9562–9564
fire in, 3116, 9558, 9563
variations in, 9563–9564
studies on, 4449
sun associated with, 8521
symbolic importance of, 849
tapas producing, 8997
in Vedism, 9557–9558, 9562–9564
as water, 9577
Somadeva (South Asian writer), 10033–10034
Somalia
Islam in, 2571, 4611
languages of, 2566
literature of, 3088
Somali religion (East Africa), cosmogony of, written accounts of, 2567
Somāskanda (deity), 4324
Somatic yogas, 1287–1288
Somba religion (Benin), funeral rites in, 3236
Somer, Yossi, 3098
"Some Reflections on the Method and Theory of the *Kulturkreiselehre*" (Kluckhohn), 5261
Some Thoughts (Edwards), 2699
Sommaire appréciation de l'ensemble du passé moderne (Comte), 1882
Sommer, Manfred, 3528
Sommerville, Raymond, Jr., 75
Somnambulistic possession, defined, 8687
Somnium Scipionis (Cicero), 1787
Somnus (deity), as sleep personified, 8439
Sōmoku jōbutsu (realization of buddhahood), 9077
Son (Christian Trinity)
Edwards (Jonathan) on, 2700
in Orthodox theology, 2589–2590
Sonatorrek (Egill), 168
Sŏn Buddhism, 1172, 1173. *See also* Chan Buddhism
Chinul's role in, **1646**
Chogye school, 1646
Ch'ŏnt'ae school and, 9436
Soncino, Gershom, 9244
Song. *See* Hymns; Music
Song dynasty (China)
Buddhism in, 1604–1605
Chan Buddhism, 1239, 1520, 1523–1524, 1604, 9944
Gozan Zen monasteries in, 3642–3643
laws concerning, 5353
Maitreya in, 5620
patrons of, 1165, 1237
schools developing in, 1240
temples of, 9047
Zhenyan Buddhism, 9961
Buddhist texts translated in, 7269
Cheng Hao and Cheng Yi, philosophy of, 1560
Confucianism in, 4336, 4337–4338
Gu Yanwu on, 3718
Neo-Confucianism, 2129, 2632
revival of, 1577–1578, 1589, 1900–1901, 1909
temples in, 9059
tian in, 9173
Daoism in, 1602–1603, 2185–2186, 2197, 2198, 7267
iconography of, 4333
literature of, 2205–2206, 7269
pilgrimage, 7165
priesthood in, 7415
temples in, 9057
gender in, 3339
law in, 5353
lay societies in, 1604–1605
medicine in, 3859–3860, 3862
and meditation, 1179, 1294
as modern, 1602
music in, 6296
poetry in, 7214
popular religion in, 1605–1606
Zhu Xi and, 9972
Song Guangyu, 1638
Songhai empire (Africa), Islam in, 4602–4603
Sŏng Hon, on principle and material force, 1932
Song Huizong, and Daoist literature, 2202–2203, 2205–2206
Sŏngmi (sincerity rice), 1648
Song of Hedammu
comparisons to, 4232
Kumarbi in, 4231
Song of Kumarby. See Kumarbi
Song of Release, in Hurrian religion, 4232
Song of Songs
author of, 9763–9764
gardens in, 3277, 3279
gender in, 3359
Gersonides on, 866
incense offering in, 4420
love imagery in, 8706
mystical union in, 6336
mysticism in, 6346–6347, 6349
Origen on, 6889, 9763
phallus in, 7081
reading of, on Passover, 7003
as sacred drama, 2442–2443, 2445
Solomon as author of, 8513
wisdom of, 9763–9764
Song of the Harper (Egypt), 2712
Song of the Hoe, 302
Enlil in, 2800
Song of the Three Young Men, 898–899
Song of Ullikummi (Hittite myth), 9087
comparisons to, 4232
in Hittite religion, 4070
Kumarbi in, 4231
Songs. *See* Hymns; Music
Song Shan (mountain), 6214
Song Siyŏl, Confucian orthodoxy and, 1932
Songs of Dzitbalche (Maya text), divine duality in, 5883
Songs of the Sabbath Sacrifice, 10050

Songye religion. *See also* Central Bantu religions
iconography of, 4303
Songye Luba, 5522, 5523, 5524
Songyue Monastery (Buddhist temple), 9045
Songyun (Buddhist scholar), 995
Song Zixian, as Maitreya, 5620
Sonic Spectrum, 2603
Sonni Ali (West African monarch), 4602
Sono Ayako, 3072, 3073–3074
Sonoda, Minoru, 2638, **2638–2641**
Son of Heaven, Chinese concept of, 5178, 5179, 5352
"Son of man," 2835
"Son of Re" (title of Egyptian kings), 7277
Son on di kou, 405–406
Sons of God (Israelite deities), 4742
Sons of the prophets, Elisha in, 2768
Sonu, Chang, 3097
Sōō (Buddhist monk), 9078
Sootukw-nangw (deity), 6723
Soper, David, 2611
Sophia (wisdom), 3019, **8522–8523**
in Gnosticism, 3509–3511, 3517, 3518, 9751
in gnostic writings, 2966, 7190
as great goddess, 8523
as hypostasis, 4243
Mary as, 5754
Prajñāpāramitā compared to, 9748
Solov'ev (Vladimir) on, 8520
souls delivered from She'ol by, 8564
as virgin, 9604–9605
Sophia of Jesus Christ (Gnostic text), Mary Magdalene in, 5757
Sophiology, development of, 5754
Sophist (Plato), 2273
Sophists, 3052
atheism and, 581
Greek religion criticized by, 3685
magic, interest in, 3905
religion questioned by, 3909–3910
skeptical views of, 8420
Socrates against, 7109–7110
Sophocles, 375
dēmiourgos used by, 2272
on Hades, 3725
on physicians, 3842
ship symbolism of, 992
on sin, 8405
Sophós (inspired artist), 7174
Sophronios (patriarch of Jerusalem), 5792
Sōphrosunē (chastity), 1558
Ṣọ-pọna, in Santería, 1434
Sorabji, Cornelia, feminism of, 3320
Sorabji, Richard, 358
Soranus, on Hippocrates, 4021
Sora people, shamanism of, 379
Sorbonne, Maritain (Jacques) at, 5712
Sorcery. *See also* Magic; Necromancy; Witchcraft
in African religions, 9776–9781
accusations of, 90
in African Independent Churches, 104
concept of, 90
in East African religions, 2569–2570
healing and, 3820
Luba religion, 5524
Lugbara religion, 5528
misfortunes caused by, 90
northeast Bantu, 2577–2578
in Sudan, spells in, 8677
in West African religions, 9720
in Zulu religion, 10008
in Andean religions, modern, 8616–8617
anthropological concepts of, 9768–9770
in Australian Indigenous religions
counter-sorcery of healers, 3873–3874
death and illness from, 3871–3872, 7606–7607
Rainbow Snake and, 7606–7607
cannibalism and, 1404
in Chiriguano religion, 8634
in Chuvash religion, 1785
and crisis of "presence," 2267
death by, 2099
evil eye, 3809–3810
hair and, 3740
in Hawaiian religion, suspected in highborn deaths, 3799
magic's relation to, 5570
in Melanesian religions, 5835
in Middle Eastern popular tradition, amulets to nullify, 3836
and morality, 6186–6187
in New Guinea religions, 6505
in North American Indian religions
Navajo terms for, 2100
Zuni cosmology and, 2008
public *vs.* private, 9769
soul projection and, 8533
in Tswana religion, 9389
in Vanuatu religions, 9521
vs. witchcraft, 57, 9768, 9778
Soreg (balustrade), 925
Sorel, George, on revolution, 7790
Sørensen, Per, on Neolithic burial sites, 8642
Sor Juana. *See* Juana Inés de la Cruz de Asbaje y Ramirez
Sorjuanistas, 4967
Sorokin, Pitirim Aleksandrovich, **8523–8525,** 9034
on creative altruism, 8524
on Komi religion and society, 5216
legacy of, 8524–8525
Sororate, 5724
Soroush, 'Abd al-Karim, on truths, 6097
Sorrow, penitential, 7755
Sorrowful Ancient (prehistoric god), 7378
Sorskii, Nil, **8525–8526**
Sortition, 2375–2376
Sŏsan Hyujŏng (Buddhist scholar), 1173
Sōseki, Natsume, 3071, 3072, 9315
Sōshō (Buddhist scholar), 1179
Soskice, Janet Martin, 3036
Soṭah (adulteress), 4740
Soteira Tyche (Fortune the Savior), 1526
Soteriological dualism, 2509
Soteriology (doctrines of salvation), **8526–8530**. *See also* Atonement; Enlightenment; Millenarianism; Redemption; Salvation; See also Mokṣa; See also Saṃsāra
alternatives, systems of, 8526–8527
Calvin on, 1376
collective, 8528
doctrinal dimension of, 8529
ethical dimension of, 8528–8529
experience and, 8528
God's will and, 8529
healing and, 8527
human condition and, 8526
institutional dimension of, 8528
liberation and, 5437
in Lingbao Daoism, 2183
living liberation concept, 8527
meaning of term, 8526
means of salvation, 8527–8529
mythic narrative and, 8527–8528
places of salvation and damnation in, 8529–8530
rebirth and, 8529
religions without notion of, 8530
ritual and, 8527
in secular ideologies, 8527
spiritual leaders and, 8529
of UFO religions, 9434
ultimate value or being in, 8526
universalism *vs.* exclusivism, 8528, 8530
Sothis. *See* Sirius
Sotho religion (South Africa). *See also* Southern African religions
circumcision in, 8665–8666
myths of, 94
shadow in, 8533
Sot Jandasarō, Luang Phō (Čhanthasarō), 2324
Sōtō lineage
Keizan on, 5109
transmission to Japan, 1523
Sōtō school of Zen, 1293
assimilation of, 9948
attention in, 605–606
development of, 9945
Dōgen as founder of, 1244–1245, 2385, 2386, 5109, 6632
enlightenment in, 4786
Keizan as founder of, 5109
meditation in, 2306
scholasticism of, 9949
size of, 9943
Soul(s), **8530–8571**. *See also* Afterlife; Reincarnation; Transmigration
in African religions
in Fang religion, 8532
in Luba religion, 5523
in Lugbara religion, 5527
in Sudanese religion, 8849
in Ainu religion, 205
in Akan religion, 214
anamnesis (recollection) by, 309–313
Plato on, 309–311
and ancestor worship, 323
angels and, 344, 347
in Arctic religions, shamanism and, 471
Aristotle on, 484, 485
ascension of (*See* Ascension)
and asceticism, 528–529
in Athapaskan religious traditions, 576
in Australian Indigenous religions, 8532
in Batak religion, 799
birds as symbol of, 948–949, 3127
as breath, 1041–1043
bridge as symbol of, 1050–1051
Buddhist concepts of, 8547–8548, **8550–8554**
folk, 3155
in Caribbean religions, 1428, 1434
in Catharism, 1457
of child, 9443
Chinese concepts of, **8554–8556**
two souls *(po* and *hun),* 1589, 1605
yin and yang souls, 3860
Christian concepts of, **8561–8566**
bioethics and, 8190–8191
Cabilas on, 1343
destiny of, 8563–8565
Greek influence on, 7766
as image of God, mysticism and, 6347
Origen on, 873, 6889
origin of, 8563
in Orthodox deification, 2591

spirit *vs.,* 8562–8563
Swedenborg (Emanuel) on, 8898
terminology in, 8561–8562
Tertullian on, 1042, 8564, 9086
in Chuvash religion, 1785
definitions of
in Indian religions, 8544
in indigenous religions, 8532
Demiurge placing intellect in, 2273–2274
Descartes (René) on, 2294, 6486
destiny of
in Christianity, 8563–8565
in indigenous religions, 8533–8534
and dichotomy with body, 130, 140, 168–169
divine self, in New Thought teachings, 1782
in Egyptian religion, 2711, 7763
Empedocles on, 2776
in eternity, 2854
in eugenics, 2881
exiled, in paradigm of evil, 2899, 2900
external
in indigenous religions, 8532–8533
in Mesopotamian religion, 8536–8537
eye and, 2940, 2943
Finno-Ugric words for, 802
and geography of death, 136
in Gnosticism, 2966, 4415
ascension of, 521
Greek and Hellenistic concepts of, 3725, 4415, 7871–7872, **8540–8544**
Aristotle on, 8182
body-souls and afterlife in, 8542–8543
catasterism (becoming stars) in, 8733
free soul *(psuchē)* in, 8540–8542
in Hellenism, 8543–8544
Plato on, 4135
Socrates on, 8503
in Hawaiian religion, transfiguration of, 3799
Hindu concepts of, 8546–8547 (*See also* Ātman)
Caitanya on, 1346
in Pratyabhijñā Saivism, 8049
in Śaiva Siddhanta, 8043, 8418
pralayas and movement of the, 2018
Rāmānuja and, 5201
immortality of
in Essene theology, 2847
Kant (Immanuel) on, 5077
Plato on, 7182, 7184
in Ājīvikas, 213
in Inca religion, 4412
incarnation of, 4414, 4415
in Cārvāka, 4421
Indian concepts of, **8544–8550**
indigenous religions, concepts in, **8531–8534**
animatism and, 8531
destiny of soul in, 8533–8534
internal *vs.* external soul in, 8532–8533
origin of soul in, 8533
power in, 8531
theoretical elaborations of, 8531–8532
in Indo-European religions, 4456
intercession for, 130
internal, in indigenous religions, 8532
in Inuit religion, 4527
in Upaniṣads (*See Ātman*)
in Vaiśeṣika, 9498
in Iranian religions, 4537
in Iroquois religion, 4543
Islamic concepts of, **8566–8571** (*See also* Rūḥ)
alchemy and, 248
falsafah ideas on, 2972, 2974, 2977
Ibn Bājjah on, 4263
in *Rasā'il Ikhwān al-Ṣafā',* 4376–4377
Mu'tazilah on, 6323–6324
philosophical, 8569–8570
rūḥ (spirit) and *naf* (self) in Qur'ān, 8566–8567
in Sufism, 4569, 8570
theological *(kalām)* concepts, 8568–8569
traditional concepts, 8567–8568
Jain concepts of, 8548
in Japanese religion, Hirata Atsutane on, 4022
Jewish concepts of, **8556–8561**
body and soul in, 3831
in Hasidism, 3788
in Hebrew scriptures, 8556–8557
Ibn Gabirol on, 4266, 4890
medieval understanding of, 154
Mendelssohn (Moses) on, 5854
Philo Judaeus on, 7106, 7107
philosophical views of, 8558–8560
qabbalistic views of, 8560
rabbinic view of, 8557–8558
Sa'adyah Gaon on, 4889, 7953
supernatural uniqueness of, 2746
journey of, in epics, 2814–2815
in Kardecism, 5090
in Khanty religion, 5122–5123
in Komi religion, 5218–5219
in Korean religion, 5228
in Lakota religion, 5297
loss of
and disease, 2297
in sleep, 8440
in Mandaean religion, 5635–5636
in Manichaeism, 1889, 2966, 2967
in Mansi religion, 5122–5123
in Mari and Mordvin religion, 5709
materialist rejection of, 5775
in Maya religion, 5798
in Melanesian religions, 5833, 5836
Mesoamerican concepts of, 149–150
Mesopotamian concepts of, 8535–8538
external souls in, 8536–8537
ghosts and, 8535–8536
melammu (divine splendor) and, 8537
reason and, 8536
Sumerian, 8537–8538
in Micronesian religions, 6007
Middle Platonists on, 7189
mirrors and, 6064
multiple, afterlife of, 136, 149–150
Near Eastern concepts, ancient, **8535–8540**
Neoplatonism and, 7191, 7199
Cumont (Franz) on, 2094
in New Age teachings, Summit Lighthouse, 1782
in North American Indian religions, 6708
orientation of, 6886–6887
Origen on fall of, 8406
origin of
in Christianity, 8563
in indigenous religions, 8533
in Orphism, body as punishment to, 8405
out-of-body experience and, ecstasy and, 7972
pearl as symbol of, 7024
Plato on (*See* Plato, on soul)
Plotinus on, 7191, 7199
Plutarch on, 7200
in Polynesian religions, 7311, 9195
power of, 8531
in Chinese religion, 8555
Pythagoras on, 4415, 7528, 9328
reincarnation of (*See* Rebirth; Reincarnation)
release for service of the dead, in human sacrifice, 4183
retrieval of, in healing, 3813–3814
in Roman religion
Cumont (Franz) on, 2094
lares, 5320–5322
in Sami religion, 8087–8088
in Scientology as *thetan,* 4149, 8192
serpents associated with, 8457
in shamanism
escorted in séances, 8272–8273
flight of, 8272, 8278, 8286
loss of, 8279
search for, in illness, 8273
Sikh concepts of, 8548–8549
Ādi Granth on, 33
in South American Indian religions
cannibalism and, 1403
in Jivaroan religion, 8533
in Mbua religion, 8532
overview of, 8583–8584
in Selk'nam religion, 8225
in Stoicism, 8742
Syria-Palestinian and Anatolian Semitic concepts of, 8538–8540
in Tibetan religion, *bla* (vitality or soul) in, 3865
in Trobriand Islanders religion, 5184
in Tunguz religion, 9394, 9395
Tylor, (E. B.) on, 2237–2238
Universal
in Druze movement, 8330
in Qarāmiṭah Shiism, 8328
Vedic concepts of, 7763, 8545–8546
in Vietnamese religion, 9591–9592
in Vodou, 9636
in West African religions, 1434
in Zoroastrianism, 9996
journey to Paradise, 1647
Soul Clinic, Berg (David Brandt) and, 2987
Soul-ghosts, Tylor (E. B.) on, 4183
Soul-sleep doctrine, in Adventist theology, 8235
Souls of Black Folks, The (Du Bois), 66–67, 73–74

Soul Theology (Mitchell and Cooper-Lewter), 6977
Sound. *See also* Drums; Music; Noise; Percussion
in Buddhist exorcism in Thailand, 3814
in Buddhist meditation, 6282–6283
flexible qualities of, 5305
in Indian religions, 6278–6279
meaningless, as *mantras,* 5677
in music, definition of, 6249–6250
onomatopoeic value of, 8675
power of, 8675–8676 (*See also* Spells)
sacred, 5304–5305
in Hinduism, 6820
Sound and the Fury, The (Faulkner), 5480
Sourvinou-Inwood, Christiane, 7275
Sousa, Lisa, 5922
Sou Seth, 3077
Soushen ji (Daoist text), 2206
Soussloff, Catherine, 4342
South Africa. *See also* Venda religion; Zulu religion
Buddhism in, 108
engaged Buddhism, 2786
Christianity in
among Blacks, 1718
black theology, 1722
charismatic, 106
evangelicals and racial politics, 1724
Pentecostalism, 7030
drama in, 2477
International Society for Krishna Consciousness in, 4522
Islam in, 4607–4608
literature of, 3088
Lovedu people of, kingship of, 5170
religious studies in, 8794, 8795
Xhosa Cattle-Killing movement in, 6547
South America and South American religions. *See also* Latin America; South American Indian religions; *specific countries and religions*
African diaspora religion in (*See* Caribbean religions; Slavery)
archaeology in, 452, 454, 456–457
Buddhism, 1188, 1190
Christianity
and drama, 2438
iconoclasm in, 4286
and Inquisition, 4502–4507
colonialism in
and Afro-Surinamese religions, 126
and Catholic pilgrimage, 7149
and gender, 3415–3417
and Inca religion, 4410, 4411
indigenous religion, early chronicles of, 8593–8594
and Inquisition, 4501, 4502–4507
and music, 6272
Spanish and Portuguese conquest and missions, 1694–1698
films from, 3099
gender in, **3415–3420**
Greek Orthodox Church, 3659
Indian rebellion under Tupac Amarú, 1697–1698
Islam in, **4682–4691,** 4683–4685
as slave religion, 4682, 4683
spread of, 4683
kingship in, **5172–5178**
messianism in, **5983–5986**
mountains in, 6439
music in, **6271–6275**
nature in, worship of, 6439
Orthodox Christianity, 2589
Pentecostalism, 7029, 7031, 7032
Protestantism, women in, 3418
Roman Catholicism
music in, 6273
pilgrimage in, 7149, 7150, 7151
women in, 3417, 3418
tree of life in, 9335
women in, **3415–3420**
South American Indian religions, **8575–8637**. *See also specific religions*
Afro-Brazilian religions influenced by, 120
alcohol *(yagé)* in, 848
in Amazon (*See* Amazonian religions)
in Andes (*See* Andean religions; Inca religion)
animal rites in, 8581–8582
Arawak and Island Arawak, distinction between, 1426
Atahuallpa in, 567–568
bears in, 808
birth in, 950
body painting in, 1004
bull-roarers used in, 1320
cannibalism in, 1403
center of the world symbolism, 1502, 1504
Christianity adapted by, 2605
chronicles of, 1361
cosmologies in (*See* Cosmology)
creation myths in (*See* Creation)
dead, cults of, 8584–8585
drums in, 2499, 7036
ethnoastronomy in, 2862–2866
fertility rites in, 8582, 8583
flood myth in, 3131
gender in, **3415–3420**
parallelism and complementarity of, 3415, 3416, 3417
Golden Age in, 3629
of Gran Chaco region, **8632–8637**
history of study of, **8592–8599**
early- mid- twentieth century, 8594–8595
functionalism in, 8595
historical and poststructuralist views in, 8596–8597
Spanish chroniclers, 8593–8594
structuralism in, 8596
travel and expeditionary literature (19th century), 8594
initiation rituals in, into secret cults, 4478
insects in, 4507
masks in, 5767
matriarchy in, 7008
missions in (*See* Missions)
music in, 6271–6274
sacred wind instruments in, 8582–8583
mythic themes in, **8586–8592**
ancestors, mythic, 8589
death, origins of, 8590–8591
destruction myths, 8588–8589
fire, origins of, 8590
high gods in, 8589–8590
modern myths, 8591
origin and cosmological myths, 8586–8588
plants and culture, origins of, 8590
ritual and myths, relation, 8591
nature spirits in, 8580–8581
overview of, **8575–8586**
deities, culture heroes, and ancestors in, 8576–8580
initiation rites, 8585
nature spirits, hunting rituals, and vegetation rites, 8580–8583
regions in, 8575–8576
soul, the dead, and ancestors, 8583–8585
Selk'nam religion (Tierra del Fuego), **8223–8226**
shamanism in (*See* Shamanism)
smoking in, 8454
soul in, 8583–8584
stones in, 8747
supreme beings in, 8576–8580
as creators, 8870
syncretism in, 3143
time in, 2011
tobacco in, 9216–9219
transmigration in, 9326
tricksters in (*See* Tricksters)
twins in, 9413, 9418
women in, **3415–3420**
South Arabia. *See* Arabia
South Asia and South Asian religions. *See also specific countries and religions*
Aḥmadiyah movement in, 6738
Buddhism, temples of, **9041–9045**
Christian missionaries in, 4650
fiction in (*See* Fiction, South Asian)
Islam, **4641–4656**
under British rule, 4641, 4645, 4651–4653
conversion to, 4642
diversity of traditions in, 4642–4643
Hindu influence on, 4641, 4643–4644
indigenous nature of, debate on, 3161
literature, 4641, 4642, 4644, 4649, 10035
modern, 4654–4655
Muslim identity in, 4653–4654
number of devotees, 4641
personality cults in, 4649–4650
reform movements in, 4650–4651
role of culture in, 4643–4644
sharīʿah, 4643, 4698
Shiism, 4641, 4643, 4645–4647, 4649, 4654
spread of, 4641–4642
Sufism, 4642, 4643, 4644, 4647–4649, 4651
Sunnī Islam, 4641, 4643, 4644–4645, 4649, 4650, 4654
women in, 4652
Jainism, 4765
lesbianism in, 5414
magic in, **5587–5592**
intellectual foundations of, 5589–5590
practices of, 5588–5589
sources on, 5590–5591
studies of, 5588
techniques of, 5589
terminology of, 5588
tools of, 5589
music in, **6278–6287**
textiles in, 9088
turtles in, 9407
Southeast Asia and Southeast Asian religions, **8637–8655**. *See also specific countries and religions*
ancestor worship in, 323
Buddhism, **1131–1144**
capitalism and, 1098
celebrations in, 1304, 1306
Christian missionaries and, 1098

classical period of, 1131, 1133–1138
in colonial era, 7263
communism and, 1098
decline of, 1095
early development of, 1131–1133
future of, 1131
Hīnayāna Buddhism, 1132, 1133, 1202
Hinduism and, 1133, 1135, 1138
and Islam, 4657
kingship in, 1133–1135, 1139, 7261, 9150
of lay people, 1142
literature of, 1134, 1136, 1137
Mahāyāna Buddhism, 1132, 1133, 1137–1138, 1202
male initiation rites in, 1098
meditation in, 1142
misrepresentation of, 8638
modern, 1138–1143, 9833
monasteries, 1095, 1096, 1133–1142
music in, 6282–6283, 6288–6289
new religious movements in, 8653–8654
pilgrimage in, 1097, **7163–7164**
pūjā in, 7496
temples of, **9052–9056**
Vajrayāna (Tantric) Buddhism, 1132, 1133
worship and devotional life in, **9826–9834**
burial practices in, 2239
Chinese influences, 8643–8644
Christianity, 1727–1729
academic neglect of, 8639
new religious movements in, 8653–8654
Roman Catholicism, 1727–1728
diversity in, 4656–4657, 8641
fiction of, 3075–3079
geography and demographics of, 8647–8648
Hinduism, **4009–4014**
archaeological and textual evidence, 4010
Buddhism and, 1133, 1135, 1138
decline of, 4013–4014
deities of, 4012
early history of, 4011–4012, 8647
founding stories and, 4010
"Indianization," 4010
lineage in, 4013
migration from India and, 4010
new religious movements in, 8652–8653
temple architecture and, 4012–4013
historical geography of, 4656–4673
history of study of, **8637–8640**
cultural anthropology and, 8639–8640
on nature of religious traditions, 8639
political agendas in, 8638–8639
region, politics, and culture in, 8639
Indian influences, 8644–8645
importation of Indian ideas, 5128, 5346
insular cultures, **8647–8652**
new religious movements in, **8652–8655**
Islam, **4656–4673**
architecture in, 4672, 6209
of Batak people, 799, 800
Buddhism and, 4657
in colonial era, 4660–4661
conversion to, 4661–4662
education in, 4666–4667, 4671
evidence for, 4659
literature, 4662–4665
misrepresentation of, 8638
music in, 6289, 6290–6291
new religious movements in, 8653
revival of, 4670
scholarship in, 4660, 4662–4663
Shiism, 4664
spiritual and cultural dimensions of, 4661–4670
spread of, 4658–4661
Sufism, 4660, 4662, 4663
sultanates in, 4659–4660
women in, 4666–4667, 4670
Japanese occupation of, 4668–4669
Judaism, 5010
languages in, 4657–4658
mainland cultures, **8641–8646**
megalithic religion, 5826–5828
monuments in, Indian influence in, 8644
music in, **6287–6292**
national policies, effect of, 8647–8648
Negrito religions, **6454–6457**
organized religions, arrival of, 8647
prehistoric foundations of, 8641–8643
reform movements in, 4665–4669
traditional religions in
adherents to, 8648
dualism in, 8648–8649
of highlands, 8645
immanence of life (animism) in, 8649–8650
religious pressure on, 8648, 8651–8652
rituals of life and death, 8650–8651
spiritual differentiation, celebration of, 8651–8652
in world trade, 4658
Southeastern Europe
films from, 3098
magic in, 5580–5582
Neolithic religions in, 6459, 6460, 6462–6464
Southern, Eileen, 77
Southern African religions, **8655–8668**. *See also* Bantu religions; Khoi and San religion; Swazi religion; Tswana religion; Zulu religion; *specific countries and religions*
African Independent Churches and, 103
Buddhism in, 1190
communal ritual life in, 8656–8657
cults of affliction, spirit possession, and divination in, 8659
drums in, 7037
God, concepts of, 8655–8656
kinship rituals in, 8657–8659
New Church of Southern Africa (Swedenborgian), 8902
overview of, **8655–8662**
percussion in, 7035
ritual, order, and religious experience in, 8660
rituals in, 8660
shades in, 8656
witchcraft in, 8659–8660
Southern Bantu religions, **8662–8668**. *See also* Bantu religions
circumcision in, 8665–8668
cosmology and sacred kingship in, 8664–8665
python cult in, 8663–8664
thermodynamic conception in, 8662–8663
Southern Baptist Convention, 784
fundamentalist control of, 2893
Southern Christian Leadership Conference (SCLC), 5145–5146
racial justice and, 1753
Southern Cross (constellation), in ethnoastronomy, 2866
Southern school Buddhism, 1522
origin of, 1601
Southern Siberian religions, **8668–8673**. *See also* Buriat religion
cattle breeding and vertical worldview, 8672
Christianity and empire, interaction with, 8672
hunting, alliance, and horizontal worldview, 8669–8672
people groups in, 8669
Southern Song dynasty. *See* Song dynasty
Southey, Robert, 2952
South India, Church of, 353
South Korea
Buddhism in, capitalism and, 1098
films from, 3097
South Pacific. *See* Oceania and Oceanic religions
South Pacific Commission, cargo cults and, 1423
South Pacific religions. *See* Oceania and Oceanic religions
South Sea Evangelical Church
origins, 1738
revivalism and, 1741
South Woman (deity), 5120
Sovereign deities, 3621
examples of, 3621
functions of, 3621
in Greek religion, Zeus as, 3663–3664, 3679, 5994–5995
Jupiter, 5037
meteorological, 5992, 5994–5995
Sovereign Order of the Solar Temple (OSTS), 9067
Sovereignty. *See also* Kingship
cargo cults and, 1425
female power over, 9908
of God, in Islam, 2064
Hobbes (Thomas) on, 5367
in Judaism, juridicial sovereignty principle, 3753
Locke (John) on, 5367–5368
warriors and, 9684, 9686
Soviet Union. *See also* Russia
Arctic religious studies in, 475
Baltic religious movements in, 764
Baltic religious studies in, 770–771
Catholics in, 9464
Church Universal and Triumphant fear of, 1783

Soviet Union *continued*
communism and religion in,
in Baltic states, 764, 770–771, 775
dissolution of, 1686
fall of, religious freedom following, 7944
Holocaust and, 5022
Islamic studies in, 4723
Islam in
in Central Asia, 4623–4626
persecution of, 4619, 4624, 4625
Jews in
emigration of, 9982
Lubavitch outreach to, 8173
Judaism in, 5009
anti-Semitism and, 5021
Karaite sect, 5084
matriarchy in, studies of, 3613
May Day and, 1515
new religious movements in, 6567
Orthodox Church and
Sergii and, 8229–8230
Skobtsova (Mother Maria) and, 8422–8423
religion, restrictions on, 1686
religio-scientific research in, 3113–3114
Russian Orthodox Church in (*See* Russian Orthodox Church)
Samoyed religion, impact on, 8097
scientific atheism ideology in, 8772, 8773
Spinoza's materialism and, 8685
study of religion in, 8773
Soyinka, Wole, 2439, 3086
Sozialistische Entscheidung, Die (Tillich), 9203
Sozomenos, on miracles, 6056
Sozzini, Fausto Pavolo, **8673–8674,** 9469
Space. *See also* Sacred space
in Buddhism, in Mahāyāna *asaṃkhyeya* cosmology, 2030
in Celtic religion, 1491
in Daoism, 2178
Einstein (Albert) on, 7138
hierophany (manifestation of the sacred) and, 3972
in Hinduism
in Purāṇas, 2017, 7499–7500
in Upaniṣadic cosmology, 2015
in Vedic cosmology, 2014
Maasai view of, 2000
in mathematics, 2878–2879
in music, 6253–6255
public *vs.* private, Plato on, 4107
reestablishing, through epic, 2816
in rituals, 7837–7838
scientific view of, relativity and, 2032
and time
in calendars, 1353, 1356
in Chinese myth, 1625
Heschel (Abraham Joshua) on, 3962–3963
Hindu notion of auspiciousness and, 4016
Space (outer space). *See also* UFO religions
in physics, 2659
Space Brothers, 9448–9449
Space model of creation from chaos, 1986–1987
Spaceships. *See* UFO religions
Spaegel, Charles, 9449
Spain and Spanish religions. *See also* Iberian Peninsula
adoptionist heresy in (794), Alcuin's statement on, 254
Arab conquest of, 4581, 4591, 4592
calligraphy in, 1372
Carnival in, 1443
cave art in, 1471
colonies of (*See also specific colonies*)
Aztec in, 716, 719, 5174
in Caribbean, 9305
Cuna resistance in Panama, 2096
Hispaniola, 5322
Inca in, 567, 5175, 5177
and Inquisition, 4501, 4502–4506
in Latin America, 1694–1698, 1854
in Philippines, 1727
in Southeast Asia, 4660
drama in, 2474
England, alliance with, 1373
films from, 3099
folklore of, *duende* in, 2951
Franciscans in, and dance, 2136
funeral rites in, 3237
hermits of, 2826
Iberian religion in (*See* Iberian religion)
Inquisition in (*See* Spanish Inquisition)
Islamic, 4673
falsafah in, 2975–2976
Jews in, 6648
Judaism in (*See* Sephardic Judaism)
Karaite sect in, 5084
Ẓāhirī school in, 4699
Islam in, 4679, 4680
Charlemagne's campaign against, 1556
Christianization of Arabs in, 4596, 4597, 7282
Judaism (*See also* Sephardic Judaism)
Christianization of Jews in, 7282
Crescas (Ḥasdai) on massacres, 2069
expulsion of, 2922, 2939, 4996
forced conversion from, 4860
iconography of, 4340
Karaite sect, 5084
medieval, 4980
persecution of Jews, 5717
Qabbalah, 7534, 7537
synagogues in, 8925
yeshivot of, 9883–9884
Marranos in, 5716–5722
medieval, rabbis in, 7579
megalithic religion in, 5825
Melqart in, 5848
missions
in Latin America, 1694–1698
in North America, 1708, 6422
in Pacific islands, 1738
music in, 6308–6309
Neolithic religion in, 6465
new religious movements originating from, 6568
poetry in, 7218–7219, 7220
Renaissance humanism in, 4176
Roman Catholicism
All Saints Day, 2230
All Souls Day, 2230
of colonial period, 5915–5916
Roman conquests in, 7911
study of religion in, 10081
Todos Santos (Day of the Dead) in, 2230
Visigoth rule of, 4556
justice system under, 8013
Spalding, Martin, Gibbons (James) as secretary to, 3478
Spandaramet (deity), 491
Spangenberg, Augustus Gottlieb, 6191
Spangler, David, 6495
Spanish Conquest (1521), 7810
Spanish Inquisition
influence of, 4502
Jews during, 6647
Marranos in, 5717, 5720–5722
in the New World, 4502–4506
origins of, 4500, 4502
power of, 4501
procedures of, 4500–4501
purpose of, 4498, 4500, 4502
tears in, 9025
Torquemada (Tomás de) as grand inquisitor of, 9242–9243
victims of, 4498, 4500, 4501, 4502, 4596, 9242
Spanish Jews. *See* Sephardic Judaism
Spanish language, glossolalia and, 3505
Sparagmos. *See* Dismemberment
Sparlösa Stone, 7939
Sparta
agōgē in, 183–184
Artemis in, 507
homosexuality in, 4112, 4113
initiation in, 4478
kingship in, 5166–5167
Spataru, Nicolaie, 3110
Spatial dualism, 2509
Spaulding, Baird, 4246
Speaking in tongues. *See* Glossolalia
Speaking Land, The (Berndt and Berndt), 666
Speaking of Indians (Deloria), 2265
Speak to Me Words (Gould), 7226
Spear masters, in Dinka myths, 96
Speartus, on divine kingship, 5148
Special insight, for achievement of *bodhi,* 5070
Special relativity, theory of, 2739, 2879
Speciation, creationism and, 2911
Species spirit, 5513
Specification, 4516–4517
Specific (differentiated, voluntary) religious groups, 1865, 1866–1867
Specified complexity, 4516–4517
Speck, Frank G., 6671
on masks, 5767
Spectacled bear, 808
Speculation, in sociology of religion, 8490–8492
Speculative theology, 9139
Islamic (*See Kalām*)
Speculative wisdom literature, 9755
Speculum historiale (Vincent of Beauvais), 7243
Speculum principum genre, 1492
Speech. *See also* Language; Logos
in eightfold path, 2738
in engaged Buddhism, 2788
Speech act, 5301–5302
liturgy as, 5492
Speeches
in *Isaiah,* 4546–4548, 4549
melody of, 1532
prophetic, biblical, 7432–7433
Speech *maṇḍala,* 5642
Speiser, Felix, on masks, 5770
Spektor, Yitshaq Elhanan, **8674–8675**
on Magen David, 5559
Spells, **8675–8678.** *See also* Cursing and curses; Incantation; Names and naming; Postures and gestures
in Chinese religion, 8677
conditions of, 8675
in Egyptian religion
in *Book of Going Forth by Day,* 2708, 2712–2713, 2719, 8676
in Coffin Texts, 2705
in judgment of the dead, 5026
purposes of, 2722, 8676
in Pyramid Texts, 2718
for transformation, 2716

in Greek religion, 8676–8677
in Indian religion, 8677
in magic
East Asian, 5593
Greco-Roman, 5574
Islamic, 5583–5584
Melanesian, 5835
in Mesoamerican religions, 8677–8678
in Mesopotamian religions, 8676
modern-day, 8677–8678
and power of sounds and words, 8675–8676
in Roman religion, laws concerning, 5333
in Sudanese religion, 8677
Spence, Lewis T., 5941
Spencer, Baldwin, 671, **3489–3491**. *See also* Gillen, Francis James
on Australian Indigenous religions, 3489–3491
burial rituals of, 688
in history of study, 683
Kunapipi in, 3249–3250
totemism, 9251
transmigration, 9326–9327
Gillen's (Francis James) work with, 3489–3491
Spencer, Herbert, 2909–2910, **8678–8679**
on African religions, 114
on agnoticism, 8678
on ancestor worship, 321, 2982
animism and, 362, 366, 2540
Bergson (Henri) as disciple of, 838
on death, 2238
ethics of, 8679
on evolution, 8678, 8679
in evolutionary ethics, 2918
evolutionism influenced by, 2913–2914
and functionalism, 3231
on heroes, 3956
on humor, 4222
influence of, 8679
on knowledge, 5208
on manism, 5671–5673
on morality, 8492
as positivist, 7341
on primitive religions and origin of religion, 8678–8679
on society and religion, 8466, 8678–8679
structuralism and, 8748–8749
on the supernatural, 8861
on supreme beings, 8875
"survival of the fittest" coined by, 2908
Tylor (E. B.) arguing with, 5672
Spencer, Jon Michael, 77
Spencer, Paul, on Maasai religion, 2000, 2001
Spener, Philipp Jakob, **8679–8680**
Francke (August Hermann) and, 3185
and Pietism, 7142
pietism and, 8679, 8680
Spengler, Oswald, 3009
on Gnosticism, 3532
influence on Frye (Northrop), 3223, 3224
Jonas (Hans) influenced by, 4948
Spenser, Edmund, 7220
on Golden Age, 3628
Hermetism and, 3950
literary accomplishments of, 5471–5472
Neoplatonism and, 6475
Spenta Ārmaiti (spirit), 290
in Armenian religion, 491
gender of, 3372
Spenta Mainyu (spirit), 203–204, 9412
gender of, 3372
Spepherding/Discipleship movement (Pentecostal), 7031
Spepherd of Hermas, 920
Sperber, Alexander, 888, 889
Sperber, Dan
on cultural processes, 2088
on memorization, 5851
Sperm. *See* Semen
Speusippus
on the good, 3635
Philo Judaeus influenced by, 7106
Platonic forms rejected by, 7187
at Plato's Academy, 7187
on reality, 7187
Speyer (Germany), Jews in, 5011
SPG. *See* Society for the Propagation of the Gospel in Foreign Part
Sphinx, 4318
riddle of, 6986, 6987
"Spice merchant" scene in drama, 2469
Spider Man (mythic figure), 4507
Spiders
in African myths, 92, 94, 100, 9352
in North American Indian religions, 4507–4508, 9355
in Pueblo religion, 6724
Spider Woman (mythic figure), 939, 4507–4508
in Hopi religion, 6660
as Lady of the Animals, 5280
in Navajo religion, 6659
Spiegelberg, Herbert, 7087
Spier, Leslie, 3474, 6671
on Sun Dance, 8844
Spies, Johann, *Spies Faustbuch,* 3009–3010
Spillius, James, 9197
Spilsbury, John, 783
Spinning, 938–939
Athena and, 588
Spinoza, Baruch (Barukh), 2561, **8680–8687**
biblical exegesis of, 865, 883, 8683
on chance, 1527
on classical theism, 6962
deep ecology influenced by, 2608
Delmedigo (Yosef Shelomoh) and, 4898
on desire, 2308–2309
on evil, 9112
excommunication of, 8681, 8683
as ex-Marrano, 5722
on free will, 3200
on God, 3551, 6148
Herder (Johann Gottfried) and, 3919
Ibn ʿEzra' quoted by, 4265–4266
influence of, 8684–8686
on intuition, 4525
in Jewish thought and philosophy, 4898, 4900
on knowledge, 5205, 5207
life and works of, 8681–8683
Mendelssohn (Moses) on, 5854
metaphysics of, 5990–5991
monistic pantheism of, 2664, 6961
monistic system of, 6144, 6146, 6147–6148
naturalism of, 6429
on nature, 6148, 6435
inherent design of, 2607
Neoplatonism and, 6475
on political theology, 10062
on prophecy, 7440–7441
on *Psalms,* 7462
refutation of Lucretius' reflections on chance, 3002
Schleiermacher (Friedrich) and, 8160
skepticism and, 8421
Stoicism and, 8741
on theocracy, 10061
thought of, 8683–8684
Tönnies (Ferdinand) on, 9230
Spinoza Institute (Jerusalem), establishment of, 8685
Spiral, in Oceanic religions, 6788–6789
Spiral Dance, The (Starhawk), 3613, 3614, 6471, 9730
Spiral labyrinth, 5276–5277
Spirit(s). *See also* Angels; Animism; Demons; Devils; Exorcism; Fairies; Ghosts; Holy Spirit; Shamanism; Soul(s)
in Acehnese religion, 26, 1429
affliction by, 57
in African American religions, 67
in African religions, 86
Congolese, vol. 9 color insert
Swazi *emadloti* (world of spirits), 8896
water spirits, 7862
in Afro-Caribbean religions, 1433–1437, 3822
in Agami Jawi, 4817
in Akan religion, 214
in Amazonian Quechua religions, 281–282
in animism, 363–364
in Arabian religions, 444
in Arctic religions, 469–470, 4528
in Australian Indigenous religions, 5051
health and, 3872–3873
terms for, 6260
wandjina, 9668–9670
in Burmese religion, 1328–1331
nats, **6427–6428**
capturing of, 5198
in Caribbean religions, pre-Columbian, 1427, 1428, 1430
in central Bantu religions, 1506, 1508, 1509–1510
in Chinese religion *(shen)*
Cheng Hao on, 1561
Cheng Yi on, 1563
Confucius on, 1571
grave location and, 1594
law and, 5351–5353
sacrifice and, 1891–1892
in Christianity
soul and, 8562–8563
soul *vs.,* 8562–8563
in Chuvash religion, 1785
communicating with, 6925
through dance, 2453–2455
contact with, psychedelic drugs as facilitators of, 7467
in cosmogony, 9698
in Daoism, 2178
in Diola religion, 2354
domestic, 2951–2952
dualism between matter and, and asceticism, 528–529
in East African religions, 2568
Eckhart (Johannes) on, 2603
in Edo religion, 2697
in Egyptian religion, 2711
game, 5513
in gardens, 3277
guardian (*See* Guardian beings)
in Haitian Vodou, *Lwa,* 1433–1434
Hegel (G. W. F.) on, 47, 2913, 3894, 3895, 4219–4220, 6148–6149
house spirits, 4106
human spirit, in Scientology, 8192

Spirit(s) ***continued***
in Igbo religion, 4365–4366
incantations addressed to, 4407, 4408
incarnation of, 4414
in indigenous cultures, 2617
Enawenê Nawê religion, 2012–2013
in initiation rituals, 4486
in interlacustrine Bantu religions, 4519–4520
in Vädda religion, 8409–8410
in Iroquois religion, 4541, 4542–4543
in Japanese religion, 7272
of *kami,* 5071–5072
in Judaism (*See Ruaḥ*)
in Kardecism, 5090
in Khanty religion, 5119–5122
in Khoi religion, 5135
in Komi religion, 5217–5218
in Kongo religion, 2001
in Korean religion, 5229
in Kulina religion, 2012
in Luba religion, 5523, 5524
in Lugbara religion, 5527
in Mandaean religion, 5636
in manism, 5671–5673
in Mansi religion, 5119–5122
in Melanesian religions, 2006, 5833–5834
in Mesoamerican religions, stealing of spirits, 1470
in Micronesian religions, 6002–6004, 6007
nature and, identity of, 6436
in Ndembu religion, 6446, 6447
in Negrito religions, 6455, 6456
in New Age religion, "spirit" added to body, mind, and emotions by, 3851
in North American Indian religions, 6651, 6703, 6707, 6713–6714
manitous, 5673–5674
in vision quest, 9609
in Nuer and Dinka religion, 6744
in Oceanic religions, gender of, 3396–3397
and origins of religion, 2238
philosophical views of, Hegel (G. W. F.) on, 3893
in Polynesian religions, *atuas* as, 622
possession by (*See* Spirit possession)
pure, in Muslim traditions, 2148
in Pygmy religions, 7523–7524
in Roman religion, 2277, 7027
in sacred objects, vol. 4 color insert
in Sami religion, zoomorphic forms of, 8087
in San religion, 5135
in Scandinavian religions, 3246
Scheler (Max) on, 8147
in Selk'nam religion, 8224, 8225
in shamanism, 5229
initiation and, 8284
in neoshamanism *vs.* shamanism, 8297
relation between, 8269
in Shona religion, 8372–8373, 8374
in Sinhala religion, 8412
in Solomon Islands religions, 8514
in sorcery, 9768
species, 5513
in Stoicism, 8743
in Sumerian religion, 5968
in Tibetan religion, disease caused by, 3864–3865
in Tikopia religion, 9195, 9196
in Tiv religion, 9210
in Vanuatu religions, 9519
in Vietnamese religion, 9592
in Vodou, 9635, 9636
in Walpiri religion, 9693
water as abode of, 9701, 9702
in Winti religion, 126–127
in witchcraft, 9770
in Yakkut religion, 9865–9866
in Zoroastrianism, *fravashis,* 3190
Spirit and the Forms of Love, The (Williams), 2308
Spirit Baptism
Charismatics on, 7031–7032
doctrine of, 7031
in Finished Work Pentecostalism, 7029
glossolalia as evidence of, 7029, 7031
and healing, 7030
Pentecostals on, 7031
Protestant charismatics on, 7030
Roman Catholic charismatics on, 7030
Spirit bear, 807
Spirit cults, in East African religions, 2568
Spirit Dance, revival of, 6672
Spiritism. *See also* Necromancy; *See also* Séances; Spiritualism
in Britain, 5090
in Egyptian popular tradition, healers, spiritist, 3836
in France, 5090
in Kardecism, 5090–5091, 6578
Kardec's (Allan) introduction to, 5089–5090
vs. necromancy, 6451
Spiritualism *vs.,* 8716
in Umbanda, 124, 5091, 6578, 9308–9309
in Venezuela, 6578–6579
Spirit journey, in hunter-gatherer visions, 9614
Spirit keeping, in Lakota religion, 5296–5297
Spirit mediums. *See* Mediums
Spirit of Islam, The (Ameer Ali), 289, 429, 4652
Spirit possession, 2276, 2315, **8687–8699**. *See also* Exorcism; Mediums
affliction and, 59
in African American religions, 67
in African religions
charisma and, 1547
dance and, 2139–2140
for healing, 3813
increase of, 84
personality and, 89
vs. prophecy, 7442–7443
role of, 86
social impact of, 107
of women, 3402
zaar cult based on, 107, 3813
altered states of consciousness and, 8687, 8688–8689
by animals, 9155
in Buddhism, 2315, 9837–9838
in Caribbean religions, 1433–1438, 10027
in central Bantu religion, 1509
in Chinese religion, 1614, 6834
Christian view of, 2373
classifications of, 8687–8688
dance as vehicle for, 2139–2140, 2150
definitions of, 86, 8687, 8688, 8694
in Dogon religion, 2391
drums and, 2496, 2500–2501, *2501,* 7036
in East African religions, 2568
in ecstasy, 2678
ethnographies on, 8694–8695
exorcism and, 8691–8693
expression of truth through, 9369–9370
frenzy associated with, 3214
glossolalia in, 3506–3507
in Hinduism, 9825
host-spirit relationship in, 8689, 8692, 8695
incidence of, 8687
in India and Indian religions, 2140
initial possession experience, 8690–8691
in interlacustrine Bantu religions, 4519, 4520
in Islam, 2148, 2402
in Judaism, 2533–2534
in Kalabari religion, dance and, 2139
in Korean religion, 2140
in Kwakiutl religion, 2460
in Luba religion, 5524
materialist perspective on, 8696
mediumship *vs.,* 8688
mentality of, 2282–2283
in Micronesian religions, 6003, 6004, 6005
in Middle Eastern popular tradition, *zār* cult and, 3837
oracular, 6833–6835
overview of, **8687–8694**
as performance, 8696–8697
in Polynesian religions, 7307
psychological idiom and, 8689, 8690, 8692–8693, 8696
in Selk'nam religion, 8225
in shamanism, 9370
at séances, 8286
shamanism *vs.,* 8688
in Southern Africa, 8659
speech, possessed, 8695–8696
spirit idiom, cultural, 8689–8690
in Tamil religion, 8973
tears in, 9025
in Thai Buddhism, 2315
transcendence and sacred time in, 7987
types of
consecration, 2140
essence possession, 2140
invasion, 2140
invited, 2139–2140
in Vodou, 9635, 9636
dance and, 2139, 2150
women and, **8694–8699**
receptivity to gendered ability in, 8695
subjectivity and, 8694, 8695–8697
thematics of possession and power, 8696–8697
transhistorical and cross-cultural context of, 8694–8695
in Zulu religion, 10010–10011
Spirit quest. *See* Vision quests
Spiritual art, Coomaraswamy (Ananda) and, 500
Spiritual autobiography, 702–703
Spiritual Baptists (Shouters)
Shango cult and, 1435
of Trinidad, 1437
Spiritual bathing, 800–803
Spiritual Canticle, The (John of the Cross), 2309, 4942
mystical union in, 6338
Spiritual Counterfeits Project. *See* Anticult movements
"Spiritual" dancing, revivalism and, 1437
Spiritual dialogue of religions, 2344
Spiritual discipline, **8699–8708**. *See also* Asceticism; Contemplation; Eremitism; Martial arts; Meditation; Monasticism; Mortification; Obedience; Yoga
connotations of, 8699
modes of, 8702–8707
of body, 8704–8705
constructive, 8703–8704

ecstatic, 8703
of heart, 8705–8706
of mind, 8705
of personal relationships, 8706–8707
in monasticism, 6122
Christian, 6131
teachers or masters and, 8699, 8700
types of, 8699–8702
autonomous (inner), 8700–8701
heteronomous, 8700
interactive, 8701–8702
Spiritual Exercises (Ignatius Loyola), 4367, 4368, 4842, 5818, 7173, 7207, 7772
Spiritual experience. *See* Religious experience
Spiritual Guide (Molinos), 7558
Spiritual guides, **8708–8715**
in Buddhism, 8712–8714
in Christianity, 8709–8710
in Greece, ancient, 8708–8709
heteronomous, 8700
in Hinduism, 8711–8712
inner, 8700–8701
in Islam, 8710–8711
in Judaism, 8709
Rūmī on, 8699
spiritual discipline and, 8699, 8700
in Sufism
manuals as, 8814
obedience to, 8822
quṭb (axis) and cosmic hierarchy and, 8821
Spiritual Homilies (Symeon of Mesopotamia?), 5624, 6336
Spiritualism, 6559, **8715–8718**. *See also* Mediums; *See also* Séances; Spiritism
associations in, 8717
Cao Dai movement, **1411–1412**
doctrinal controversies within, 8716–8717
forms and practices of, 8717
founders of, 6535, 6559, 6563
in industrial revolution, 6782
and New Age movements, 6497
North American religious culture and, 1714
progress through 19th century and beyond, 8717–8718
religious experience in, 7738
spiritism *vs.*, 8716
theory and cultural background on, 8715–8717
transcendence and sacred time in, 7987
women's role in, 6535
Spiritualities of connection, 2666. *See also* Nature religions
Spirituality, **8718–8721**. *See also* Mysticism
as alternative to religion, 8719, 8720–8721
Australian Indigenous, native terms for, 6260
Christian, 8319
in Christian Science, 1745–1746
New Age, alternative healing and, 3852
Orthodox ethics and, 1652
Roman Catholicism, 7887
Russian Orthodox, Serafim of Sarov, role of, **8229**
sexuality as threat to, 2647
women in, 3359
classic forms of, 8719
contemporary forms of, 8719–8720
democratic, in neoshamanism, 8296
and freedom, 3199
"green," 8719
inspiration and, 4509
Jewish, in Hasidism, 3789
Neopagan, 6473
in North American Indian religions, 10083–10084
pearl as symbol of, 7024
in poetry, 7207–7208
postmodern, 6498–6499
psychotherapy in, 7485–7486
Rastafari, 7622–7623, 7624
religion *vs.*, 7622, 7623
in notions of health, 3875
Spirituality and Patient Care (Koenig), 7487
Spiritual pollution, 7506–7507. *See also* Pollution
Spiritual Regeneration Movement, 9290, 9291
Spiritual renewal, retreats of, 7770–7773
in Christianity, 7770–7773
in Islam, 7770
in Roman Catholicism, 7772
in Sufism, 7770
Spiritual Science, School of, 393
Spiritual shopping, New Age movement and, 6496, 6498
Spiritual Treasure Collected from the World, A (Tikhon), 9194
Spiritual work, 9799
Spiritus Vivens (demiurge), 2274
Spirit Worshippers' Association for the Victory over Communism, 5235
Spirit-writing cults, Chinese, 1608, 1615, 1616, 6835
Spiro, Melford E.
on Burmese political idiom, 8411
on religion, 7701–7702, 7703
religion defined by, 378
Spittle and spitting, 7343, **8721–8722**
in magic, 5593
in miracles, 6053
and pollution, 7504
Spivak, Gayatri, on subaltern theology, 8802
Spoila opima, 7901
Spoils of Annwm, The (Taliesin), 8969
Spoken logos, 5503–5504
Spoleto, hermitages of, 2826
Sponsus (play), 2471
Spontaneous naturalism school, 1595
Sports, **8722–8727**. *See also* Ballgames; Martial arts
ancient Greek religion and, 8723
Christianity and, 8723–8724
Hinduism and, 8724
modern sports and secularization, 8724–8726
Native American religions and, 8723
Persian religion and, 8724
Zen Buddhism and, 8724
Spotted Tail (Oglala Sioux man), 10053
SPR. *See* Society for Psychical Research
Sprachfamilien und Sprachendreise der Erde, Die (Schmidt), ethnological-linguistic synthesis in, 8168
Spretnak, Charlene
ancient Mediterranean religions and, 3386
on Mary, 5755
Spriggs, Elbert Eugene, 6547, 6560, 9409–9410
Spring and Autumn (Chunqiu)
historiography and, 4026
New Text school and, 1574–1575
as one of the Five Scriptures, 1585
overview of, 1907
Springs
in Celtic religion, 1483–1484, 1486
in Germanic religion, 1502
magic, in rejuvenation myths, 7683–7684
Spring scrolls, 1641–1642
Springs of Mende Belief and Conduct, The (Harris and Sawyerr), 3570
Spurgeon, Charles Haddon, **8727**
Spurinna (haruspex), 2874
Spyi ti (Crown Pith), 2548
Square
maṇḍalas as
Buddhist, 5644
Hindu, 5640–5641
in Native American religions, 7550
Śrāddha feast, 322–323
in devotional life, 9821
for ghost prevention, 3477
gift giving in, 3482
Mani and, 5679
Śraddhākaravarman, *Guhyasamāja Tantra* translated by, 3708
Śramaṇas (ascetics), 857, 1102–1103, 1105
Śramaṇa tradition, 4421
Sraosha (deity), Chinvat Bridge and, 1647
Śrauta rites, 1026, 1027, 4426, 4427, 7356, 9561, 9567–9568
in Brahmanism, 3991–3992
in devotional life, 9821
Śrautasūtras (Brahmanic manual), 9553–9554
ritual system in, 3991, 8883–8884
Śrāvaka (follower), 1280–1281, 7357
path toward *arhat,* 2028
Śravaṇa tradition, 4421
Sre religion (Indochina), on original humanity, 2960
Śrī (deity). *See also* Lakṣmī
as consort, 9618
Śrī Vaiṣṇavas Sampradāya and, 8727, 8728
Śrī Aurobindo. *See* Aurobindo Ghose
Śrīcaitanyacaritāmṛta, 826
Śrīdhara (mythic figure), 4434
Srid pa ho (Divination Chart), vol. 3 color insert
Śrīheruka (Buddhist figure), in Cakrasamvara tradition, 1350
Śrīheruka-abhidhāna (Buddhist text), divine couple in, 1349
Śrīkṛṣṇakīrtana (Baḍu Caṇḍīdāsa), 827
Sri Lanka. *See also* Sinhala religion
affliction in, 58
Buddhism in
Buddhaghosa and, 1073–1074
capitalism and, 1098
celebrations in, 1304, 1305, 1307, 1308
Christian missionaries and, 1098, 1099
chronicles on Buddha's life, 1061
in colonial era, 7263
decline of, 1095
drums in, 2496–2497
ethics of, 1280
exorcism in, 7197
gender and, 3331
Hīnayāna Buddhism, 1093
images in, 4390
introduction of, 5348
kingship in, 2530–2531, 7261
literature of, 1096–1097, 1199, 1260, 9146–9147
Mahīśasaka school, 1195
meditation in, 9152

Buddhism in *continued*
missions and, 1090, 1093, 1137, 1138
monasteries, 1095–1096
music in, 6282, 6283
nikayas (schools), division into, 8074
nuns in, 6760
Olcott (Henry Steel) and, 6815
origins of, 2037
orthodoxy and heterodoxy in, 6910–6911
pilgrimage centers of, 1097, 7164
politics and, 7260, 9152–9153
in postcolonial era, 7264
prevalence of, 1728
priesthood in, 7407, 7408, 7409
pūjā in, 7496
relics in, 7690, 7691
revival of, 1126
ritual calendar of, 1097
schools of, 1195
scriptural tradition of, 1110
sectarian schisms, 8077
Sinhala religion, relation to, 8409, 8411, 8412
spread of, 1091–1092, 1093, 1201, 4429, 9147
as state religion, *saṃgha* endowments and, 8077
studies on, 1311, 1312
synthesis of indigenous religions and, 3154, 3155
touch of reverence in, 9257
women in, 2313–2314
Christianity in, 1728
Roman Catholicism, 1728
drums in, 7036
exorcism rituals in, 7836
Islamic law in, 4644
religious studies in, 8791
Sinhala healing rites in, 2140
spirit possession and exorcism in, 8690, 8696, 8697
Vädda religion in, 8409–8410
violence, religious, 1808
Zoroastrianism in, fire in, 570
Śrima (Holy Mother), Śārāda Devi as, 8111
Śrīmad Bhāgavatam (Kṛṣṇa scripture), 4521, 7355
Śrīmāladevī Sūtra (Buddhist text), 9018
Śrīnathjī (deity), images of
in Nāthdwāra temple, 1955
Vallabha's discovery of, 9517
Srinivas, M. N., 4448
Śrīnivāsa, Nimbārka's teachings and, 6623
Śrī Pada (mountain), 6213
Śrīraṅgam temple, heavenly origination of shrine, 7979
Śrī Śāradā Maṭha, 6758
Sri Sathya Sai Baba movement, 108
Śrī Śrī Rāmakṛṣṇa Kathāmṛta, 7613, 7614
Śrīsūkta, 5518–5519
Śrī Vaiṣṇavas, **8727–8729,** 10088
Āḻvārs and, 279–280, 4430
Kṛṣṇa and, 5252
Pāñcarātra and, 10088
Piḷḷai Lokācārya formulating theology of, 7172
Rāmānuja and, 7614–7615
studies on, 4449
Yāmuna and, 9870–9871
Srivijaya kingdom, Buddhism in, 4011
Srong btsan sgam po (Tibetan emperor)
brides of, 9000
Buddhist temples under, 9050
legend of, 1231
teachings ascribed to, 1232–1233
Tibetan alphabet created by, 1256
Tibetan empire created by, 1151, 9184
Ṣṛṣṭi (emission) philosophy, in Śaivism, 8416–8417
Śruti (Hindu texts). *See also* Upaniṣads; Vedas
āśramas (life stages) and, 3995
Brāhmaṇas and, 1026
in Brahmanism, 9569
canon formation and, 8202
definition of, 4423
eternal and impersonal, 4423
etymology of term, 4423
meaning of, in Hindu canon, 1407
name of, and primacy of sound, 6278
revelatory utterances in, 7205
sacrality of, 8201
smārta schools and, 3997
smṛti texts *vs.*, 2327, 3994–3995
thirteen Upaniṣads considered as, 3993
in Vedas, 9553–9554
SS. *See Schutzstaffel*
SSSR. *See* Society for the Scientific Study of Religion
Ssu-ma Ch'eng-chen. *See* Sima Chengzhen
Ssu-ma Qian (historian), 4489, 4490
St. Brigid of Kildare Methodist Monastery of Minnesota, 6765
St. Denis, Ruth, 2157, 2158, 2164
St. Irinaeus of Lyon Information-Consultation Center, 6569
St. James-Bond United Church (Ontario), vol. 5 color insert
St. John, Ambrose, 6510
Staal, Frits, 2868–2869, 7849, 10043
Stace, W. T.
monistic philosophy of, 6146, 6148
on mysticism, 6356, 6357
Stace, Walter T., on mysticism, 7744
Stackhouse, Max, 7253
Staden, Hans von, on Tupi religion, 8593
Staerk, Willy, 3650
Stafford, J. Francis, 5754
Stages of Faith (Fowler), 7479
Stag lung Ma sprul Rin po che (Taklung Matrul Rinpoche), Ani Lochen and, 355
Stag tshang ras pa (Buddhist teacher), 1230
Staines, Graham, 828
Staka (deity), 5710
Stalin, Joseph, Sergii (patriarch of Moscow) and, 8230
Stalinism
Bakhtin (M. M.) criticizing, 742
on Muslims, 4624
persecution of Islam in, 4619
Russian Orthodox Church under, 7943–7944
Stallions. *See* Horses
Standard candle measure, star brightness and, 2031
Standards, accompanying Egyptian pharaohs, 5164
Standing (posture)
in Christianity, 7343
in Eastern Orthodox Christianity, 7343
in Islam, 7159, 7343
Standing Bear, Luther, 702, 7300
Standing Conference of Canonical Orthodox Churches (SCOBA), 2589
Standing Conference of Orthodox Bishops in the Americas (SCOBA), Christ the Saviour Brotherhood and, 4103
Standpoint theory, 9790
Stanislavsky, Konstantin, 7048
Stanley, A. P., 6105
Stanley, Henry M., on African religions, supreme beings of, 3576
Stanner, W. E. H., **8729–8730**
on Australian Indigenous religions, 315, 8729–8730
academic study of, 686, 8729–8730
the Dreaming in, 638, 2478–2479, 2481, 2482, 8730
Gadjeri in, 3250
initiation rites, 7845
innovations in, 5707
new movements in, 681, 682
religiosity of, 681
social justice and, 8730
studies influenced by, 684
study of, 685
totemism in, 2479
Stanton, Elizabeth Cady, **8730–8732**
Child (Lydia Maria) and, 1570
feminist biblical criticism of, 3361, 8731
Gage (Matilda Joslyn) and, 3251–3252, 3310
The Woman's Bible, 3035
Stanzione, Vincent, 5945
Staomi ritual, 9998
Starbuck, E. D., **8732**
American study of religion, role in, 8785
on psychology of religion, 7475
Starbuck, William, Anesaki Masaharu influenced by, 342
Starcevo culture (prehistoric), 7379
Starčevo-Körös-Cris culture, 6463
Starets (Orthodox elder), Serafim of Sarov as, 8229
Star Festival (Japan), 2411
Starhawk (feminist)
ancient Mediterranean religions and, 3386
on Goddess feminism, 4166
on matriarchy and goddess worship, 3613, 3614
on relationship between divine and human, 6472
on rites of passage, 7829, 7830
The Spiral Dance, 6471
as thealogian, 9100
Wicca of, 9730, 9731
Starina (bylina) (epic song), 2814
Stark, Rodney
American study of religion, role in, 8787
on children in sectarian groups, 6538
on churches, sects, and cults, 2084–2085
on European receptiveness to new religions, 6568
Starkaðr (Norse warrior), 9685
Starkaðr the Old, in *Gautreks saga,* 8024
Starobinski, Jean, 268
Star of David. *See* Magen David
Star of Redemption (Rosenzweig), 7926
Stars, **8733–8737**. *See also* Astrology; Ethnoastronomy; Sky
in Australian Indigenous myths, 655, 661
brightness of, 2031
catasterism (transfer of humans to the heavens), 8424–8425, 8733
Chinese deity of, 1591
comets, meteors, and shooting and falling stars, 8735–8736
constellations and zodiac as ordering of, 8733
deities of, 3619
in Arabian religions, 443–445

geometry of, 3442, *3443, 3444*
in Hinduism, in Purāṇic cosmology, 2017–2018
in Mesoamerican religions, 5935
in Micronesian religions, 6002
myths of, 5198
in North American Indian religions
iconography of, 4309
Pueblo, 6723
ordering of, 8428
Pleiades, 8734–8735
in Caribbean religions, 1429
Inca and, 1362
Taqui Onqoy ("the dance of the Pleiades"), 3815
polestar (North Star), 8734
in Hindu cosmology, 2018
in technomorphic cosmologies, 8433–8434
of Pythagoreans, 3442, *3443*
scientific view of, formation, stellar, 2033
sky in myth and, 8733 (*See also* Sky)
in South American religions, origin of, 8588
in technomorphic cosmologies, 8423–8424
temples and, 8733–8734
Startsy (elders), as spiritual guides, 8709–8710
Star Wars (film), Campbell (Joseph) and, 1378
State, the. *See also* Church and state; Nation-state movement, and religion
Buddhism in, 9836
China, Jesuit construction and defense of, 1920
distinction from kingship, 5156
Jewish autonomy and, 4983
nation as religious community, 1865
orthopraxy and, 6915–6916
priesthood and, 7397–7398
relationship with Church, 5150
State Bureau of Religious Affairs (SBRA) (China), 7266
State religions, religious nationalism and, 8472–8473
State Shintō, 4790, 4791, 4792, 4813
Kiki under, 4806
Statesman (Plato), 2273, 7182, 7184
States of consciousness. *See* Consciousness, states of
Stations of the Cross (Newman), 55
Statis, eternity and, 2855
Statistics, Nightingale on, 6618
Statius, 365
on Mithraism, 6091
music and, 6304
Status
class *vs.,* in sociology, 8481–8482
secret societies and, 8212
social roles and, 8484
Stcherbatsky, Theodore (Fedor), 1089, **8737**
Steady-state cosmology
Hinduism and, 2020
theory proposed, 2032
Stealing, prohibited
in engaged Buddhism, 2788
in Jainism, 2624
Stearn, Jess, 560
Steel drums, 2494
Steffens, Henrik, 6435
Steigmann-Gall, Richard, 2663
Stein, Sir Aurel, 5317
Stein, Ludwig, 2505
Stein, Marc Aurel, 1152, 1314
Stein, Rolf A.
on Bon religion, 1008, 1151
Tibetan studies by, 9188, 9189, 9191
Steinbach, Udo, 4718
Steinbeck, John, 5479–5480
Steinberg, Leo, 7082, 7085
Steinberg, Milton, Cohen (Arthur A.) and, 1848
Steiner, George, 5484
Steiner, Rudolf, **8738–8739**
anthroposophy of, 392–393, 2160
Eurythmy (dance system) of, 2160
on nature, 6437
and New Age movement, 6495, 6496
on reincarnation, 9330
Rosicrucianism and, 7930
Steinhardt, Menachem Mendel, 7668
Steinheim, Salomon, on revelation, 7441
Steinheim, Solomon Ludwig, in modern Jewish thought, 4904
Steinkeller, Piotr, on Enlil, 2799
Steinschneider, Moritz, 3462
Goldziher (Ignácz) studying under, 3634
in *Wissenschaft des Judentums,* 4878–4879
Stela D monument, Maya calendar and, 1358
Stelae of the Dancers (Olmec), 5881
Stele C at Tres Zapotes, 5882
Stele/stelae
Aramean, 448
definition of, 5799
Egyptian, 2714, 2725–2726
law codes and, 1842, 1843, 1844
Maya, 5799, 5882
astronomical placement of, 2009–2010
Mesoamerican, 149
calendar in, 5881
Olmec, 5881
Stella Marris (starfish), religious symbolism of, 3123
Stellatus (Christoph Hirsch), on Hermetism, 3949
Stellung der Israeliten und Juden zu den Fremden, Die (Bertholet), 843
Stemberger, Günter, 6020
Stem cell research
embryonic, 941–942, 5813–5814
Vatican on, 8190–8191
medical ethics on, 5813–5814
Stendahl, Krister, 7014, 7020
Stender, Gotthard Friedrich, 768–769
Steng po che (Buddhist monastery), 1234
Stenton, Frank, 1018
Stephan, Michael, aesthetics of, 50
Stephan of Tournai, 5337
Stephen, D. J., Horner (I. B.) and, 4129
Stephen, Michele, 6508
Stephen, on elect status of Israel, 2747
Stephen (archbishop of Nicomedia), Symeon the New Theologian and, 8919
Stephen (pope), on returning heretics, 2113, 6966
Stephen (saint), martyrdom of, 7058
Stephen I (pope), on bishops, 6966
Stephen II (pope), 6967
Stephens, Walter, on witch hunts, 8250
Step Pyramid (Saqqara), 7527
Stereotypes
of Muslims, as humorless, 4211
Weber (Max) on, 7972
Sterilization, in eugenics, 2880
Stern, David, 6020
Stern, Sacha, on linear *vs.* cyclical time, 7992
Stern, Theodore, on Mesoamerican ballgames, 750
Sternberg, Leo, 475
Sterne, Laurence, 3051
Sternhold, Thomas, 6310
Stesichorus of Himera, 4250
Steuco, Agostino, on Hermetism, 3946
Steude, E. G., on supreme beings, 8875
Stevens, Evelyn, on gender in Mesoamerica, 3411
Stevens, George, 3097
Stevens, Iris, 650
Stevens, Wallace, 5477, 5478, 5483
Stevenson, David, 3196
Stevenson, James, 6670
Stevenson, Matilda, 6670
on trial of Zuni priest, 2008
Steward, Julian, cultural ecology proposed by, 2611
Steward, Julian H.
archaeology and, 452, 453
on South American Indian religions, 8595
Steward, Theophilus G., 80
Stewardship, Judeo-Christian concept of, as environmental ethic, 2654
Stewart, Carlyle, 80
Stewart, Charles, on syncretism, 2089
Stewart, Dianne, 79, 81
Stewart, Pamela, 6508
Stewart, Tony K., 3161
on Caitanya, 1346
on Muslim poetry, 4644
Sthalapurāṇas (sacred texts), 7498
Sthānakvāsī sect of Jainism, 4766
Sthavira Buddhism, schism leading to, 6128
Sthaviras ("Elders" party), Pāṭaliputra council and, 2036–2037
Sthaviravāda Buddhism
arhat in, 1195–1196
geographical distribution of, 1195
nirvāṇa in, 1195–1196
origins of, 1090, 1193–1194
Sanskrit canon of, 1110
Sarvāstivāda as outgrowth of, 8117, 8119
schools developed from, 1194
vs. Mahāsāṃghika Buddhism, 9145
Sthiramati (Buddhist monk), 1301, **8739–8740**
extant works of, 8739
on Nāgārjuna, 5552
on Yogācāra philosophy, 8739–8740
sources on, 8739
Stickball, 749, 750, 751
Stieglitz, Alfred, 500
Stietencron, Heinrich von, 1548
Stigmata, 1004–1005
Still Thoughts Abode *(jinsi jinshe)* monastery, 1789
Stimulants, *haoma* as, 3775
Stirling hypothesis, 6818
Stobaei Hermetica, in Hermetic corpus, 3939, 3940
Egyptian traditions in, 3941
Stockholm syndrome, 1034
Stocking, George W., on biblical paradigm, 8169
Stoddard, Solomon, 2698
Stöhr, Waldemar, 1021
Stoicism, **8740–8744**
allegorical interpretation of gods, association of, 3912
historiography and, 4036
rhapsodic interpretation of Homeric scenes, 4108
apotheosis in, 438

Stoicism *continued*
of Cicero, Ambrose influenced by, 288
comparative theology of, 9128
cosmology and ethics in, 2606
desire in, 2307
discipleship in, 2360
divination and, 1528
doctrines of, 8741–8742
Epicureanism contrasted with, 3911
God in, 8742
Golden Rule in, 3632
Hellenism and, 3901, 3910, 3911–3912
Herakles myth, interpretation of, 3917
historical survey of, 8740–8741
hypostasis in, 4240
kingship in, 5147, 5148
knowability of God in, 181, 182
knowledge in, 5201
Logos in, 5501–5502
inner *vs.* spoken, 5503
seminal logos, 5503
moral precepts, 1454
naturalism in, 6428
nature in, 6432
pantheism in, 6961, 6962
Philo Judaeus influenced by, 7106, 7113, 7188
and Platonism, 7188
purification in, 1460
reason in, 8405
religion and theology in, 8742
semitic roots, alleged, 8742–8743
ship symbolism in, 992
on suicide, 8829
and Tertullian, 9086
on Trinity, 9360, 9361
virtue in, 3911
world citizenship in, 3906–3907
on Zeus, 3203
"Stoic Readings of Homer" (Long), 7106
Stoker, Bram, 3062
Stolcius, Daniel, on alchemy, 251
Stoller, Paul, 118
Stolz, Fritz, historiography of, 4048, 10080
Stomp dance, 1565–1566, 2461
Stone, Barton, 2364
Campbell (Alexander) and, 1377
Stone, Jacqueline, 6549
Stone Age. *See* Prehistoric religions
Stone-Campbell movement, 1779–1780, 1781
Stonehenge (England), 2493, 6465, vol. 3 color insert
astronomy and, 8734, 8835–8836
circle symbolism in, 1791
Merlin and, 5878
moon and, 6170
Stone Knife Carrier, in Australian Indigenous myths, 657
Stone of Fál, 1488
Stone of Kāne, as phallic symbol, 3797
Stone of Nordhuglo, 7939
Stones, **8744–8747**. *See also* Megalithic religion; Rocks
in amulets and talismans, 300
in ancient Western traditions, 8744–8745
in Arctic religions, 470
heaps of (*See* Cairns)
in Hinduism, 4326, 7494
in Madagascar religion, 8745–8746
maṇḍalas made of, 5643
in Native American religions, 8747
in Neolithic religions, 6465
in New Caledonia religion, 6501
runic inscriptions of, 7939–7940
sacred, vol. 4 color insert
in Arabian religions, 444
in Australian Indigenous religions, vol. 4 color insert
Eros as, 2832
in Hinduism, vol. 4 color insert
in Santeṛia, 1434
in Mardu religion, 5707
in Mormonism, vol. 4 color insert
in Sami religion, 8746
Stonewall riots (1969), 5864
Stoning, in Israelite religion, 4742
Ston pa Gshen rab, 1008, 1010
Stools
black, in Akan religion, 215
in Luba religion, vol. 13 color insert
Storå, Nils, 474
Storch, Nicholas, 6238
Storefront churches, vol. 5 color insert
Storm animals, 5995–5996
Storm deities, 3618, 5992–5996, 9701. *See also* Meteorological beings; Rain deities; Thunder deities
Adad as, **27–29**
in Andean religions, Illapa as, 8601–8602
animals associated with, 5995–5996
Baal as, **723–725**
creativity and chaos of, 5993–5994
diversity of, 5992
examples of, 3618, 5993
functions of, 3618, 3621, 5992–5993
in Hawaiian religion, 3797–3798
in Hittite religion, 4068–4070, 4071
in Hurrian religion, Kumarbi as, 4230
in Mesoamerican religions, smoking by, 8455
mountains associated with, 6214
in Phoenician religion, 7129
vs. sky deities, 5994
sovereignty of, 5992, 5994–5995
Teshub as, 9087
Zeus as, 9952
"Story of How a Wall Stands, A" (Ortiz), 7226
Story of My Experiments with Truth (Gandhi), 700–701
Story of My Misfortunes, The (Abelard), 7
Story of Nilus, The (Christian novel), 6823
Story of Sinuhe (Egypt), 2706
"Story of Sound, The" (Kim Nam Ha), 5441
Story of Taliesin (Welsh text), 8968, 8969
Story of the Apocrypha, The (Goodspeed), 897
Storytelling
images and, vol. 2 color insert
in journalism, 4961–4962
in Korean religion, 5233
in religion, 2882–2883, 2884
in Warlpiri religion, 9693–9694
Storytracking (Gill), contextual research in, 8786
Stotras (hymns), 7209, 7211, 7212, 9562, 9563
Stove gods, in Chinese and Japanese religion, 4106–4107
Stow, Randolph, 3082, 3083–3084
Stowe, Harriet Beecher, on Edwards (Jonathan), 2532
Strabo, 407–408
on Arabian history, 443
on Armenian religion, 491
on Celtic religion
head cult, 3807
women in, 3387
comparative theology of, 9128
on Council of the Galatians, 1491
on Diana cult, 2347
on divination, 2374
on druids, 2492
on Hermetic texts, 3939
on Iberian religion, 4252–4253
on Inner Asian religions, 4488
on Nabatean kingdom, 6386
on North Star, 8734
on Thracian religion, 9168, 9169, 9170
on Zalmoxis, 3466, 9926
Strack, Hermann, 6020
Strahlenberg, P. J., 3110
on Mari and Mordvin religion, 5709, 5710
Strang, James T., 6192
Strange attractors, 1542
Strangers. *See also* Hospitality
curses of, 2100
in Greek thought, *xenox* (welcomed stranger), 4138
greeting of, 8060
Strassburg, Eckhart (Johannes) in, 2603
Strategic essentialism, 1858
Strathern, Andrew, 6508
on Mount Hagener body decoration, 4160–4161
Strathern, Marilyn, 3395–3396, 5633
on kinship
in Melanesia, 5183–5184
reproductive technology and, 5184
on Mount Hagener body decoration, 4160–4161
on rites of passage, 7808–7809
Stratification, social. *See* Castes; Class, socioeconomic
Straubergs, Kārlis, 327, 770, 771
Strauss, Carl Theodor, 1187
Strauss, David Friedrich, **8747–8748**
as Baur's (F.C.) student, 805
on Gospels, 4846–4847
hermeneutics of, 5486
Marx (Karl) and, 5745
Reimarus's (Hermann Samuel) influence on, 7675
on Schleiermacher (Friedrich), 8166
Strauss, Heinrich, 4342
Strauss, Leo, 7246
Stravinsky, Igor
Le sacre du printemps of, 2161
music of, 6313
Strawson, P. F., 482
Strehlow, Carl
biblical translation by, 686
missionary work of, 683, 686
phenomenological work of, 3490
vs. Spencer and Gillen, 3490, 9326
Strehlow, T. G. H., 315, 3080
on Australian Indigenous religions, myths of, 653, 655–656, 662, 663, 664
Strelan, John, on cargo cults, 1416
Streng, Frederick, 1581, 6914
Strength
hair as symbol of, 3738–3739
Hanumān as god of, 3775
Strenski, Ivan, 7745
Striae (witches), 9770
Stribing, Johannes, 768
Stribins, Janis, on Baltic religion, 757
Stribof (deity), 2231
Strickmann, Michel, 241
Strict Observance, Cistercians of. *See* Trappists
Stri Dharma Niti (Ramabai), 7610
Strindberg, August, 2472, 2474

Strip of Land, Two Yards Long, A (Abdussamad), 10035
Stripping, in gambling, 3261, 3263
Strī-puruṣa maryādā (separation of sexes), in Swaminarayan movement, 8890, 8892
Strī śakti (woman power), 861
Strong, John, 555
Stroumsa, Guy, 2514
Stroumsa, Guy Gedaliahu, 3534
Structural anthropology, 2506
Structuralism, **8748–8760**. *See also* Semiotics
  in anthropology, 2506, 5262
    definition of, 5381
    Leach (Edmund) influenced by, 5381, 5382
  in Baltic studies, 771
  Celtic religious studies and, 1498–1499
  clitoridectomy, interpretation of, 1826
  in comparative mythology, 1876
  and continuity *vs.* discontinuity, 8752
  empirical and implicit forms of, 8758–8759
  in French historiography, 4045
  history of term, 8748–8752
  implications in study of myth and ritual, 8752–8755
    examples of analysis, 8754–8755
    myths and rituals as related sets, 8753–8754
    prerequisites for analysis, 8754
    universal *vs.* local applicability, 8752–8753
  Lévi-Strauss (Claude) and
    conservatism of, 8751
    formulation of, 8749–8750
    history of religion, influence on, 4045
    successors of, 8751–8752
  meanings, minds, and symbolic worlds in, 8759–8760
  as method and theory in study of religion, 8758
  poststructuralism and, 8752, 8754
  revisions and criticisms of, 8757–8758
  rites of passage interpreted in, 7797
  in semiotics and semantics, 8759
  Sistine Chapel and, 8755
  in South American Indian religions research, 8596
  structural functionalism, 8749
    Stanner (W. E. H.) and, 8730
  structural linguistics of Saussure (Ferdinand de), 8750
  in study of North American Indian religions, 6672
  validity, question of, 8750–8751, 8757
Structural relativism, 4463
Structural violence, 9596
Structure and Creativity in Religion (Allen), 7097
Structure and Dynamics of the Psyche, The (Jung), 6057–6058
Structure of Scientific Revolutions, The (Kuhn), 4459, 4723
Structure of Social Action (Parsons), Durkheim and Weber in, 8467
Strutynski, Udo, 4464
Struys, Jean, 6165
Stryjkowsky, Maciej, 768
Stryx (demon), 2277
Stuart, David, 5943
Stuart, Elizabeth, on body theology, 4167
Stuckey, Sterling, 76
Stuckrad, Kocku von, on esotericism and Faivre (Antoine), 2844–2845
Students International Meditation Society (SIMS), 9290
Student Volunteer Movement, 1709
Studi e materiali di storia delle religioni (journal), 10056
Studies in Arabic Literary Papyri II (Abbott), 8951
Studies in Religion (journal), 10057
Studies in the History of Religions (journal), 7074, 10057
Study of Inner Mind, 1902–1903
Study of Man, The (Haddon), 2421
Study of religion, **8760–8796**. *See also* Comparative religion; Historiography; History of religions approach; Religionsgeschichtliche Schule; *specific religions, schools of thought, and topics*
  in Africa
    biases and stereotypes in, 1998
    pantheon imposed on Yoruba cosmology, 1999
    in sub-Saharan Africa, **8792–8796**
  Afro-Brazilian, 76, 121
  androcentrism of, 3313
  art in, 494–496, 499–502
  in Australian and Oceania, **8767–8771**
    academic programs in, 8768–8771
    biblical scholarship in, 8771
    early intellectuals in, 8768
    pioneer missionaries, reports of, 8767–8768
  Bleeker (C. Jouco) on, 979
  in Britain, 1872
  Buddhist (*See* Buddhist studies)
  Capps's system of theory, practice, and aesthetics, 1412–1413
  of cargo cults, 1416, 1421–1425
  in China, **10072–10076**
  Christian bias in
    in classification of religions, 1818, 1819, 1820–1821
    in comparative religion, 1877
  classification of religion, **1817–1822**
  colonialist and imperialist bias in, 1855–1857
  comparative-historical method, **1868–1873**
  comparative religion, **1877–1881**
  critical theory *vs.* science in, 8766
  cultural perspective and, 2089
  data selection in, 7746
  development of, 8763–8765
  as discipline, in North America, 2608
  disciplines of, Goblet d'Alviella (Eugène) on, 3537
  doctrinal-based religions, bias toward, 1999
  dynamism in, 2540, 2541
  in Eastern Europe and Russia, **8771–8775**
    contributions of, 8773–8774
    emergence of, 8772–8773
    organizations and publications, scholarly, 8774–8775
    perspectives on, 8775
  Eliade in, 2756
    accuracy in, 2760
  emergence of, 8761–8763
  encyclopedic works in, 2784–2785
  environmental studies linked with, 2609, 2613
  ethical considerations in, 7628
  Eurocentrism in, 8761, 8762
  feminist (*See* Women's studies, in religion)
  feminist critique of, 3313
  folklorist approaches to, 3143–3148
    in Eastern Europe, 8772
  in Germany, 1872
  global character of, 8766–8767
  hermeneutics in, 3931, 3932 (*See also* Hermeneutics)
  Herodotus on, 4036
  homo religiosus in, 4111
  in humanities, 2761
  and increased mutual respect among religions, 2343
  intrareligious *vs.* extrareligious explanations, 1870
  James (William) in, 4777
  in Japan, **8775–8780**
    Anesaki Masaharu and, 342–343, 8777
    early developments in (1905-1945), 8776–8777
    prehistory of, 8762, 8775–8776
    recent developments in (since 1945), 8777–8779
  Jewish, 4878–4880
  kind of knowledge about religion, 8761
  leizistic, in Poland, 8772–8773
  literature in, 5472–5475
  methodological questions for, 7746
  methods and issues in, 8765–8767
  nature religions in, 2661–2662, 2664–2665
  new religious movements, 6514, 6518, **6520–6528,** 6565–6566
  in North Africa and Middle East, **8780–8784**
    by al-Bīrūnī, 8780
    challenges and trends in, 8783–8784
    history of religions in, 8781
    Jewish and Christian studies of Islam, 8782
    al-Milal wa al-Nihal studies ("Sects and Heresies") in, 8780–8781
    modern and contemporary studies, 8782–8783
    travel accounts and geographies, 8781–8782
  in North America, **8784–8789**
    contemporary trends in, 8786–8787
    early roots of, 8784–8785
    institutional trends in, 8787–8788
    professional organizations, projects, and publications in, 8788
    religious studies and related disciplines in, 8785–8786

Study of religion ***continued***
North American Indian, **6668–6673,** 6694–6695
Otto (Rudolf) in, 6928
overview of, **8761–8767**
participatory form of, 8785–8786
periodical literature in, 10056–10060
philosophical *vs.* historical approach to, 4035
power in, 2541, 2542, 2543–2544
problems in, Leeuw (Gerardus van der) exposing, 5392
Rastafari, 7628
reflexivity in, 10079
relativism in, 2867
religio-historical method of Clemens, 1822
self-awareness in, 2758
Smart (Ninian) on, 8444
social dimension of, 2528
in social science, 2761
in South Asia, **8789–8792**
Bangalore Consultation (1967), 8789–8790
comparative religion, shift to, 8790–8791
hindrances to, 8791
IAHR Congress (1960), 8789
IAHR Regional Conference (2003), 8791
recent trends, 8791–8792
specialization in, 8766
subaltern studies in, 8801–8802
and supernatural, notion of, 8861–8863
symbolic theory and, 8912
translations, impact of, in early modern Europe, 4039–4040
vocabulary in, 8765
in Japan, 8776
Waldman (Marilyn) in, 9663–9665
Wensinck (A. J.) in, 9715
in Western Europe, **10076–10082**
on evolution of religion, 10077
institutions for, 10077–10078, 10080
on national traditions, 10080–10081
on nonofficial religions, 10079–10080
on origins of religion, 10077
philology in, 10076–10077
politics and, 10079
reflexivity in, 10079
religious experience in, 10076–10077
resources for, 10080
words *vs.* images in, primacy of, 494
Zarathushtra in, 9935–9936
"Study of the Mystery." *See Xuanxue* movement
Stukeley, William, 2493
Stupas and stupa worship, 1111, 4383, **8796–8799**
architecture of, 2448
classification of, 461, 462
maṇḍalas and, 5645
mountain symbolism in, 6212
in Nepal, 7837
number symbolism in, 6753
basic form of, 9264
bodhisattvas and, 8797–8798
Buddha's relics in, 7690
Buddha's remains in, 7163, 9041, 9227
Buddhist orders, formation around, 8797–8798
Buddhist schools disputing over, 1110
caityas vs., 8796–8797
in Central Asia, 1145
circumambulation in, 1107, 1796
development of, 1107–1108, 7495
devotional aspects of, 9042
dome *(aṇḍa),* as dome of heaven, 1796
drums in, 2496
of Aśoka, 1066, 1107, 4383, 7163, 7495, 7690, 9041
erected by Kaniṣka, 1145
erected by laity, 9041
erected by *saṃgha,* 9041–9042
in Himalayan Buddhism, 1234
in India, 9264
temple urbanism and, 1708
in Japan, five-element stupas in Okunoin cemetery, 8352
large, 9042
Mahāyāna Buddhism and, 8798–8799
management of, 7496
meaning of term, 8796
monumental architecture, emergence of in India, 1805
mountain symbolism of, 6214
in Nepal, 7166–7167, 9264, vol. 4 color insert
nirvāṇa represented by, 1107–1108
origins of, 8796
Pure Land and, 8798
reverencing Buddha in, 1955
role of, 9042
sacred center and, 1502
as sacred objects, vol. 4 color insert
as sacred spaces, vol. 5 color insert
Sarva Dharma Stupa, Sai Baba universalism and, 8028
shrines on top of, 9043
small, 9041–9042, 9265
in South Asia, 9041–9042
in Southeast Asia, 1134–1135, 9052–9053
merit and, 8644
in Tibet, 9049, 9052
as visual representation of Buddha, 1065–1066, 1107, 1305
Stūpīka (small stupa), 9265
Sturluson, Snorri. *See* Snorri Sturluson
Sturm, Johannes, humanism and, 4177
Sturmer, John von, 666
Šturms, Eduards, 327
Sturm und Drang movement, 3010
Herder (Johann Gottfried) and, 3918
Stürzenhofecker, Gabriella, 3397
Stutterheim, William F., 5828
Style, in art history, 9621
Stylitism, Syriac asceticism and, 8939
Styx (river), 3016, 7863
Suan Mokhabalārāma (Garden of Empowering Liberation), 2629–2630
Suan Mokkh (monastery), 1071, 1072
Suárez, Francisco, **8799**
on membership in the church, 1778
theology of, 9137
on Thomism and Scotism, 8176
Subaltern studies, **8800–8803**
cultural studies, postmodernism, and postcolonialism and, 8801
emergence of, 3322
feminism and, 3322
Marxist/Gramscian view in, 8800–8801
in study of religion, 8801–8802
women in, 3322
Subartu region. *See* Hurrian religion
Subconscious. *See also* Consciousness
Catholic thinkers on, 7474
Janet (Pierre) on, 1948–1949
religion and, James (William) on, 4776
Sübetei (Mongolian general), 4493
Śubhākarasiṃha (monk and missionary), 1240, **8803–8804**
and Mahāvairocana, 5607
in Chinese Buddhism, 9510
Zhenyan, 9961
on Fudō, 3226
Subhāṣita (well spoken), 1274
Ṣubḥ-i Azal, 728–729, 737
Subincision, 4481. *See also* Circumcision
in Australian religions, androgyny and, 8239
Subjective idealism, 4355
Subjective values, 5397
Subjectivity
of art, 494
of author, in hermeneutics, 3931, 3932
cargo-cult theory and, 1425
comparative-historical method and, 1869
in existentialism, 2926
French feminists on, 3029
Heidegger (Martin) on, 3934
of knowledge, Native American Indian understanding of, 6425
in mythology, 6361, 6369
sacred *vs.* profane and, 7964
spirit possession and, 8694, 8695–8697
Subkī, al-, 6640
Subkī, Tāj al-Dīn al-, 5781
Sublimation, sexuality and, 8244–8245
Sublime
beauty and, 811
deus otiosus as, 2311
Kant (Immanuel) on, 47, 48
Subordination
images in, 9622–9623
virginity and, 9603
Subordinationism. *See* Sabellianism
Subramuniyaswami, Sivaya, Iraivan/Kadavul temple (Kauai) and, 8419
Sub-Saharan Africa. *See also specific countries and religions*
gardens in, 3281
Islam in, **4600–4612**
art and architecture, 4608
during colonialism, 4608–4609
cultural dynamics of, 4608
future of, 4611
jihād, 4604, 4606
kingship in, 4602–4603
languages of, 4611
literature, 4600, 4603, 4611
Mālikī school of law, 4603
pilgrimage in, 4605
revolution and reform in, 4605–4606, 4611
in savanna, 4603–4604
scholars and, 4602–4603, 4604, 4605, 4606
sharīʿah, 4605, 4610–4611
sources on, 4600
spread of, 4600–4601, 4603, 4604, 4607, 4608–4609
studies of, 4600
Sufism, 4605–4606, 4609
traditional cults and, 4609
women in, 4609–4610
kingship in, **5169–5172**
music in, **6256–6260**
Protestantism in, 7447, 7459
Subsidiarity, principle of, Suárez (Francisco) on, 8799
Subsistence gardens, 3278, 3279–3281

Substance, Spinoza on, 6148, 8683–8684
Substantia
Seneca on, 4241
Tertullian on, 4241
Substantive movement, Mullā Ṣadrā on, 6232
Substanzbegriff und Funktionsbegriff (Cassirer), 1448
Substitution. *See* Scapegoat
Substratum theory in Indus Valley religion, 3989
Subtle body
cakras and, 1348
Hindu Tantric analysis of, 4003
in *Haṭhayoga,* 3795
in Sāṃkhya Hinduism, 8090
saṃsāra and, 8098
Subtle energy, in New Age spirituality, healing and, 3850–3851
Subtle thought *(sūkṣmacitta),* in Sautrāntika Buddhism, 8138
Subūʿ (naming ceremony), 7825–7826
Suburbanization
Conservative Judaism and, 1961
Orthodox Judaism and, 1964
Sucancas (political division), Inca calendar and, 1363
Success, as sign of elect status, 2673
Successors
of kings, 5155
of leaders, legitimacy of, 5385
of spiritual teachers, difficulties of, 5245
Such-Gutierrez, Marcos, 6625
Suchindram, temple of, temple urbanism and, 1805–1806
Suchten, Alexander von, 6434
Sucking. *See also* Cupping
as healing technique, 3812
Sud (deity), Enlil and, 2799
Sudan and Sudanese religions, **8849–8850**. *See also* Azande religion; Hausa people; Mondari people; Nuer and Dinka religion; Shilluk religion
ceremonies in, 8850
civil war in, prophets as peacemakers in, 7443
clitoridectomy and infibulation in, 1825
Islam, 2571
fundamentalist movements in, 7295
law, 4703
spread of, 3229
Muslim Brotherhood in, 6316
prophetic movements in, 2570
soul in, 8849
spells in, 8677
supernatural world in, 8849–8850
women in, 3365–3366
zār cult in, 3837
Sudanic languages, in East Africa, 2566
Śuddha (pure) Āyurveda, politics and, 3857
Śuddhādvaita (nondualism), 858, 9518, 9548–9549
Sud e magia (de Martino), 2267
Sudhana (Buddhist figure), Maitreya and, 5620
Sudharman, 4765
Śūdras (caste), 9522–9523
in Bengal, 825
dharma of, 5346
mokṣa, available paths for, Śaṅkara on, 4004
restrictions on, 5289
rites of passage of, 7817
social duties of, 2329–2330, 5289
Sudre (undershirt)
in funeral rites, 10001
in initiation, 9999–10000
Sue, Eugène Marie-Joseph, 3062
Suen (deity), 447. *See also* Nanna
family of, 5952
Suetonius
on Christian persecution, 7058
on druids, 2492
Suffering, **8804–8809**
in Buddhism, 2627 (*See also* Duhkha)
engaged Buddhism, 2788, 2789
in enlightenment, 2794
responsibility for, 2689
Campbell on, 1379
in Christianity, 8806–8808
as communion with God, 9115
cults of (*See* Affliction, African cults of)
Cyprian on, 2113
defense of God's omnipotence in view of (*See* Theodicy)
educative value of, 9114
free will and, 9113–9114
genetics and, 3428–3429
in Hinduism, 9112, 9113, 9119
human sensitivity to, 2634
Vedānta tradition, 9113
in Islam, 8808–8809
in Israelite religion, 4748–4749
of Jesus, 4845, 9116–9117
in *Job,* 4930–4933
in Judaism, 8804–8806
God's concern for, 3548
as mark of election, 2744
Saʿadyah Gaon on, 7952–7953
Soloveitchik (Joseph Baer) on, 8519
of just man, in wisdom, 9749
in Manichaeism, 9112
meanings of physical suffering, variety in, 3808
in mortification, 6197
mystery of, 9114–9115
in North American Indian religion, Sun Dance and, 8845
and pain, 6944
as punishment, 5372, 9115
punishment as, 2897
reality of, denials of, 9112–9113
sin producing, 9116
in Tswana religion, 9389
in Vedism, 9119
in Yoga, 9894
in Zoroastrianism, 9112
Suffering Servant doctrine
as Holocaust paradigm, 4089–4090
Jesus and, 8807
vicarious suffering and, 8806
Suffrage movement, 7283
Gage (Matilda Joslyn) in, 3251–3252, 3310
Sufism, **8809–8825**
ʿAbd Allāh Anṣari in, 8816–8817
in Africa, 7295
afterlife in, 161–162
ʿAlī ibn Abī Ṭālib in, 260
anamnesis (recollection) in, 312–313
in Andalusia, 4596
and *nubūwah,* 6736
antinomianism in, 4214
asceticism in, 527, 6351
development of Sufism and, 8810–8812
authority in, modernism and, 6097
autobiography in, 700
ʿAyn al-Quḍāt in, 8813–8814
baqāʾ in, 4569
Bektashī order of (*See* Bektashī Sufism)
al-Bisṭāmī in, 955–956, 8812
blasphemy in, 975, 4569, 7427
breath and breathing in, 1046
cats as companions, 1463
in Caucasus, 4613, 4614–4615
in Central Asia, 4621–4622, 4625, 4629
charismatic leadership in, 1547
in Chile, 4684
in China, 1599, 4633, 4635–4636, 4640
Chishtī order (*See* Chishtīyah)
commerce of images in, vol. 7 color insert
Corbin (Henry) on, 1984
dance in, 2139, 2164, 2319
darwīsh in, 2220
Day of *Alast* (primordial covenant) in, 8810
desire in, 2309
devotion in (*See* Devotion, in Sufism)
dhikr in (*See Dhikr,* in Sufism)
Dhū al-Nūn al-Miṣrī in, 8811–8812
discipleship in, 2360, 2361, 9005–9006
doctrines of, 4569–4570
drums in, 2495, 2499, 7036
ecology in, 2653
ecstasy in
development of Sufism and, 8812–8814
meditation and, 5818–5819
and separation from Islam, 2679
election in, 2748–2749
of Eliyyahu ben Shelomoh Zalman, 4870
eremitism of, 2822, 2828
eroticism in, al-Hujwīrī on, 4157
eschatology of, 2838–2839
etymology of term, 4569
in Europe, 4681
fanāʾ in, 4569
fasting in, 2996
fire in, 3120
gender in, 3369
geographical patterns, 1547
ghaybah (concealment) in, 3469
al-Ghazālī in, 3470, 3472, 8815–8816
God in, 3565–3566
consciousness of otherness from, 4569
as immanent and transcendent, 8809–8810
knowledge of, 3565
unity of, 3566
al-Ḥallāj in, 8812–8813
Ḥanābilah and, 3762, 3767
Ḥanābili opposition to, 3759
Ḥasan al-Baṣrī, role in, 8810–8811
Hindu *bhakti* combined with, 4007
homosexuality in, 4113
al-Hujwīrī, role of, **4157**
humor in, 4202, 4211
Ibn al-ʿArabī in, 4259, 8818–8820
Ibn Gabirol influenced by, 4266
Ibn Khaldūn on, 4269
Ibn Sīnā's influence on, 4275–4276
Ibn Taymīyah against, 4277, 4570
Ibrāhīm ibn Adham in, 8811
iconography of, 4350
incense offering in, 4420
and increase in converts to Islam, 4563

Sufism ***continued***
inspiration in, 4511
intuition in, 4526
Islamic law, transcendence of, 8817
Ismāīlīyah and, 8333
Jaʿfar al-Ṣādiq in, 4761
Jamāʿī Sunni legalism and, 8855
in Java, 4818
Jewish (*See* Hasidism)
jihād in, 4563, 6648
Judaism and, Maimonides (Abraham) on, 5613
al-Junayd in, 5029–5031
khānagāh in, 5117–5118
Kubrawīyah order, 5256
Kufic calligraphy and, 1373
levels of consciousness in, 1951
on levitation, 3128
life in, 5446
literature, mystical, in, 8814–8818
epigrams in, 8816–8817
manual tradition in, 8814–8816
mathnavī (poetic genre) in, 8817–8818
Rūmi's poetry in, 8818
literature of, 4261
Burckhardt (Titus) translating, 1324
fiction, 10035
poetry, 4261, 4570, 4644, 7207–7208, 7222–7223, 9012
love in, 8705
love mysticism of, 6350–6352
mahdī in, 5982
Manichaeism and, 5661
maqāmāt in, 4569
masters of
disciples and, 8700
as saints, 8035
as spiritual guides, 8710–8711
mawlids in, 5788, 5789
meditation in, 5818–5819
mendicancy in, 5856
in Middle Volga, 4616, 4618–4619
militancy combined with, 4563
miracles in, 6054
miʿrāj in, 6061
mirrors in, 6063
modern, 9012–9013
monism in, 4570, 6146
moth and candle parable in, 3757
Muḥammad in, 6227, 6736
music in, 6277, 6284, 6285
mystical experience in, 7739–7740
in development of Sufism, 8812–8814
Mahāyāna Buddhism, similarities in, 1869–1870
mystical union in, 6338–6339
Niʿmatullāhī school of
Gulshan-i raz (al-Shabistarī) and, 8263
Qāsim-shāh imāms and, 8333
number symbolism in, 6748
on light of Muḥammad *(nūr Muḥammad)*, 6766–6767
orders of, 4570–4571, 8820–8825 (*See also* Ṭarīqahs; *specific orders*)
orgy and, 6879
origin of name, 6227, 7739, 9004
origins of, 8809–8814
ascetic movement and, 8810–8812
mystical ecstasy and, 8812–8814
Qur'anic exegesis and, 8809–8810
orthodoxy and, 5818, 8814
pain in, 6946
path of
ʿAṭṭār's fable of the birds on, 8817–8818
Ibn al-ʿArabī on gnosis as goal of, 8819–8820
stages analyzed in manuals, 8815
path of intoxication *(sukr) vs.* path of sobriety *(ṣaḥw)* in, 8812
Perfect Human Beings in, 8711, 8819–8820
piety in, 9004
pilgrimage in, sacred cities and, 1808–1809
popular, 8822, 8824–8825
prayer in, for healing, 3831
prophets in, 7427, 7443
psychology, spiritual, in, 8815
Qabbalah combined with, 7536, 7537
Qādiriyya Ṣūfī *silsila*, Dārā Shikōh in, 2219
Qur'anic exegesis in, 8809–8810
Rābiʿah al-ʿAdawīyah in, 7591, 8811
reincarnation in, 7676
religious communities in, 7700
repentance in, 7758
retreats in, of spiritual renewal, 7770
Rūmī in, 8818
sacred language in, 5304
ṣaḥw in, 4569
saints in
devotional allegiance to, 9819–9820
prophets *vs.*, 8814–8815
samāʿ (listening) in, 8822
samāʿ khānahs (music halls) in, 8065
Satan in, 8125
shahādah in, 8267
shrines *(dargāh)*, of Bābā Farīd, 1806
skepticism about, among Muslims, 6097
social and political aspects of, 8822
social ethics in, 9006–9007
soul in, 4569, 8570
in South Asia, 4642, 4643, 4644, 4647–4649, 4651
in Southeast Asia, 4660, 4662, 4663
spread of, 4562–4563, 4568
storytellers opposed by, 2446
in sub-Saharan Africa, 4605–4606, 4609
ṣuḥbah ("companionship") in, 8826
sukr in, 4569
Sunnah ("beaten track") and, 8855
tafsīr (Qur'anic exegesis) in, 7566–7567, 8953, 8954–8955
tears in, 9025
truth in, 9373
ʿulamāʾ and, 9440
in United States, 4690, 6563
visionary journeys in, 9616
waḥdat al-wujūd (unity of being) in
al-Ḥallāj on, 3756
Ibn al-ʿArabī on, 8819, 8820
walāyah in, 9660–9661
wisdom of, as anti-intellectualism, 9764–9765
women in, 3369
in Africa, 4610
in *ṭarīqah*, 9007
zakāt in, 9925
Sufis of Bijapur (Eaton), 4642
Sufrahs (ritual dinners), 2402
Ṣufrīyah sect, 5126–5127
Suga Atsuko, 3074
Sugawara Michizane, 7272
Suger (abbot), 7
on art, 4286
on relics, 7690
Sughushchan Allahsyzlar (Tatar group), 4619
Sugi (Buddhist monk), 1255
Sugmad (deity), in Eckankar, 2601
Sugrīva (monkey king), in *Rāmāyaṇa*, 7617
Sugriwa, I. G., 2451
Sugrue, Thomas, 1473
Cayce's (Edgar) biography by, 559
Suguṇa brahmna, 9481
Sugyah (Talmudic discussion), 9243, 9244, 9246
Suharto (Indonesian president), 4669–4670
Suhayl ibn ʿAmr, in opposition to Muḥammad, 6222
Ṣuḥbah ("companionship"), **8825–8826**
in Ṣūfī orders, 8820, 8826
Suhrawardī, Shihāb al-Dīn Yaḥyā, Suhrawardīyah and, 8823
Suhrawardī, al-Dīn Abū Ḥafṣ ʿUmar al-, 9008
Suhrawardī, Shihāb al-Dīn Yaḥyā, 4555, **8826–8828**
and *miʿrāj*, 6061
and Mullā Ṣadrā, 6231–6232
on angels, 4554–4555
as founder of *ishrāq, al-*, 2977
as founder of ishrāqīyah, 4553–4555
Corbin (Henry) on, 1983–1984
essentialism of, 6231–6232
on exile, 2923–2924
Ibn Sīnā's influence on, 4275–4276, 4553
imaginal thinking of, 4552, 4553–4554
influence of, 4555
on lights, 4554–4555
martyrdom of, 8826–8827
murder of, 4555
on *samāʿ* (listening parties), 8065
on *ṭarīqah*, 9006, 9008
philosophy and writings of, 8827
Suhrawardīyah and, 8823
writings of, 4552, 4554
Suhrawardīyah (Ṣūfī order)
characteristics of, 8823
founder of, 9008
influence of, 9008
khānagāhs of, 5118
as regional order, 4571
in South Asia, 4647, 4648
Suibhne Geilt (mythic figure), 5878
Suicidal attacks
fatalism and, 2998, 2999
martyrdom from, 9599
Suicide, **8828–8833**. *See also* Martyrdom
in Ashanti religion, and ghosts, 3476
assisted (*See* Euthanasia)
in Buddhism, 8831–8832
in Christianity, 8830
in Confucianism, 8831–8832
cults and, 2085
Heaven's Gate, 3889, 3891
Jonestown, 4952, 4954
Peoples Temple, 7255
Temple Solaire, 9067, 9068
Durkheim (Émile) on, 8828
in Greek and Roman thought, 8828–8829
in Hinduism, 8831 (*See also* Sati)
in Islam, 8830–8831
proscription against, 8809
in Jainism, 8831
in Japanese religion, *seppuku* (ritual suicide), 4183–4184
by Jews
Ashkenazic Hasidism on, 542–543
during Crusades, 542–543
mass suicide, 8828, 8829
in Judaism, 8829–8830

vs. martyrdom, 5737
mass
of Jews, 8828, 8829
in Jonestown Peoples' Temple, 8828
in Movement for the Restoration of the Ten Commandments of God, 6215, 6216–6217
in new religious movements, 6517, 6545, 6549, 6555–6556
at Paleostrovskii monastery, 8830
as sacrifice, 4955
types of, 8828, 8832
Weber (Max) on, 8484–8485
Suicide (Durkheim), 2527, 2528, 7800
Sui dynasty (China), 1576, 1596
Buddhism in, 1164–1165
Buddhist texts in, 1237, 1254
Paramārtha and, 6992
temples of, 9047
Tiantai school, 9175
Zhiyi and, 1238
Buddhist/Daoist conflict in, 2184
Daoist temples in, 9056
Suijin (deity), 2410
Suika Shintō, Yamazaki Ansai and, 8363
Suiko (empress)
relationship with China, 5180
Shotoku Taishi as regent for, 8375
Suiren (deity), as sage-king, 1627
Suits, in cards, history of, 1414
Sukarno (Indonesian president)
on five principles, 4669
on *wayang kulit,* 2453
Sukarno Putri, Megawati, 4670
Sukha (bliss), *duḥkha (suffering) vs.,* 2029
Sukhanvarī (storytelling), 2447
Sukhasiddhi, 1226
Sukhāvatī (Land of Bliss), 1114
description of, 7502
ekayāna path and, 2029
in Jōdo Shinshū, 4934
in Jōdoshū, 4937
jingtu as, 4921
rebirth in, 8981
Sukhāvativyūha Sūtra (Buddhist text)
Amitābha cult in, 1083
Avalokiteśvara in, 705
in Jōdoshū, 4937
nianfo in, 6601
paradise in, 6984
Sukhāvatī in, 7502
Sukhāvatīvyuopadeśa (Buddhist hymns), 4937
Sū khwan (calling back the souls), 5313
Sukkah (hut), in Sukkot (Festival of Tabernacles), 8834
Sukkot (Festival of Booths or Tabernacles), **8833–8834**
domestic observances of, 2397
Ecclesiastes read during, 2600
fasting after, 4868
four species in, 8834
in Jewish calendar, 4866, 4867
maḥzor liturgy for, 8390
nature in, 2645
piyyuṭim (liturgical poems) for, 8390
in Samaritan practice, 8070
Simḥat Torah (last day of), 8834
sukkah hut in, 8834
Yom Kippur preceding, 7929
Śukla Yajurveda (Sanskrit text), 1026, 9551–9552, 9554
Sukr (intoxication with God), 4569
in Sufism, 8812
Sukṣma śarīra, cakras and, 1348
Sukuma people, cults of affliction among, 62
Suku religion (Zaire). *See also* Central Bantu religions
ancestor worship in, 322
Sūkyō Mahikari, 6574
Sulakhni (Nānak's wife), 3335
Sulak Sivarksa, 1072, 1283, 9097
Sulamī, Abū ʿAbd al-Raḥmān al-, 8954, 9007
Sūlāqa, Yūḥanna (John), 6480
Sulawesi Islands (Indonesia), 5444
Sulaymạn ibn Ḥasan, Ṭayyibīyah and, 8335–8336
Suleiman, Elia, 3098
Sulfur, in alchemy, 249
Sulis (deity), 1484
Sulka people, calendar, 1353
Sulla (Roman leader), 7912
Sulla, Lucius Cornelius
and Diana cult, 2347
religious activities of, 7278
Sullivan, Lawrence, 5985
Sullivan, Winnifred Fallers, 5332
Sultan, Saiyid, 829
Sultan Galiev, Mīr Said, 4619
Sultan of Zanzibar, 5181
Sultansky, Mordecai, writings of, 5086
Suluk (books of songs), 4816
Sulzberg, Mayer, on Leeser (Isaac), 5390
Sulzer, Salomon, 6312
Sumana (Buddhist monk), 1137
Sumatra
Buddhism in, 4657
cats in, 1463
childbirth in, 7825, 7827–7828
Islam in
in colonial era, 4660
conversion to, 4661
evidence for, 4659
reform movements in, 4665, 4666
spread of, 4563, 4658
sultanates in, 4659, 4661
marriage in, 7825
music in, 6289
Snouck Hurgronje (Christiaan) in, 8460
Sumba (Indonesia), megalithic religion in, 5827–5828
Sumbanese people (Indonesia), 5445
Sumbur/Sumur/Semeru (mountain), 1501
Sumedha (ascetic), 997, 998, 1067
Sumer (Mesopotamia), 5946–5947
cities of, 5947
creation of, 2810
economic activity in, 5947
Sumerian King List
the Flood in, 599
organization of, 5162
Sumerian language
vs. Akkadian language, 5963
Akkadian language replacing, 3375
earliest writings in, 3375
gender in, 3375
geographic distribution of, 5946
problems with translation of, 5967, 5971
Sumerian religion, 5963–5967. *See also* Mesopotamia and Mesopotamian religions
Akkadian *vs.,* 8537–8538
archaeology of, 455
Atrahasis in, 598
Babylonian religion influenced by, 5964–5965
cities in, 1802–1803
cosmogony of, 2791
creation myths in, 5964
language in, 5302
deities of, 5964 (*See also specific deities*)
attribution deities (planetary) in, 8427, 8428
Babylonian influence on, 5965–5966
in Eblaite texts, 2596
supreme triad of, 5964, 5965
divine triad in, 6746
dragons in, 2431
drums in, 2498
gidim (ghost) in, 8537
Gilgamesh in (*See Gilgamesh, Epic of*)
hierodouleia (sacred prostitution) in, 3967
hieros gamos (sacred marriage) in, 3976
human nature in, 5964
and kingship, 598, 5965
Lady of the Animals in, 5280
laws of king Urnammu, 1844
lion symbolism in, 5464
moon in, 6172
myths of, *vs.* Akkadian myths, 5963–5964
number seven in, 6748
paradise in, 6981
postures and gestures in, 7343
repentance in, 7756–7757
rivers in, 7862
sacred and profane in, 7969
sacrifice in, 8005
spirits in, 5968
sun in, 8837
syncretism and, 8930
triads in, 9349
twins in, 9417
wisdom in, 9748–9749
Sumerians
chanting and gestures, 1533
ethnic relation to Akkadians, 5963–5964
geometry of, 3442–3443, *3444*
Sumeru, Mount. *See* Meru, Mount
Summa Angelica, 1455
Summa contra gentiles (Aquinas), 2607, 9161, 9422
Summary of Divine Dogmas (Theodoret), 9123
Summary of Heretical Slander (Theodoret), 9123
Summa sententiarum, Peter Lombard influenced by, 7066, 7067
Summa theologiae (Aquinas), 7123, 9161, 9162, 9163, 9375
Aristotelianism and, 8182
Dionysius the Areopagite in, 8908
Scholasticism and, 8175, 8176, 8177
Suárez (Francisco) on, 8799
Summer solstice
Baltic celebration of, 759, 763, 768
Berber celebration of, 835
in Hindu religious year, 4016
in Inca religion, 8843
and North American Indian drama, 2461
in Northern Europe, 8836
in southern African religions, 8656–8657
in Wicca, 9731
in Zuni calendar, 2009
Summit Lighthouse, 1781–1783, 4247, 6568, 7445–7446
Summit University, 1783
Summum bonum (complete good), Kant (Immanuel) on, 5077–5078
Sumptuary laws, clothing and, 1833
Sun, **8834–8843**. *See also* Solar mythology
in African religions
in Bantu rites of passage, 8666, 8667
Dogon, 3570

Sun *continued*
Apollo identified with, 426
in Aztec religion
cosmogony of, 716–717, 5907, 6269, 7813
human sacrifices to, 1403
in myths, human sacrifice and, 4187
periodization system of, 177
power of kings and, 5174
in Baltic religion, 758–759, 760, 769
Latvian Saule (sun) cult, **8131–8135**
binding of, myths of, 5198
in Buddhism, Mahāvairocana as, 5608
in Canaanite religion, 1384
in Caribbean religions, 1427, 1429
in Chinese myth, 1625, 1627
cock as symbol of, 1841
in comparative mythology, Müller on, 6234
deities of (*See* Sun deities)
eclipses of, 1356
in Egyptian religion, 8836–8837
in ethnoastronomy, 2862–2863
eye as, 2940–2941
female divinities associated with, 3018
in Ge-Timbira religions, 8629
gold symbolism and, 1861
in Greek religion and mythology, 8839–8840
hierophanies (sacred manifestations) of, 3971
in Hinduism
in Purāṇic cosmology, 2018
in Saura Hinduism, **8135–8136**
soma associated with, 8521
in Inca religion (*See also* Inti)
gender of, 3416
kings and, 5176
Manco Capac and, 5633
origins of, 5292
priests of, 1363–1364
temple of, 4384, 4411, 4524
in Indo-European religions, 8134, 8838–8839
in Japanese religion, 6173, 8841
in Komi religion, 5217
lions associated with, 5464
lotus as symbol of, 5518
marriage with moon, myths of, 3017
in Mesoamerican religions, 8842
birth of, 7813
contemporary worship of, 5927
creation of, 1468, 5901, 5935
in Teotihuacán, 5888–5889, 5901
Pyramid of the Sun, 1468, 5898
sacrifice demanded by, 5935–5936
in Totonac religion, 9254
in Mesopotamian religions, 8837–8838
iconography of, 4316, 4317
in Micronesian religions, 6002, 6010
mirrors and, 6063
moon paired with, 6170
in Muisca religion, 6230
in nature worship, 6438–6439
in Negrito religions, 6456
in Neolithic religions, 6464, 6465
in North American Indian religions, 6651, 8841–8842
iconography of, 4309
in initiation rituals, 4485–4486
Pueblo, 6722, 6723
overview of, 8834–8836
in Roman religion, 7913, 8840–8841
Sol Invictus, **8510–8511**
in Saka religion, 7384–7385
in Sami religion, 8088
in Slavic religion, 8435
as source of light, 5451
in South American religions, 8842–8843
origin of, 8588
swan as symbol of, 8894
technomorphic representations of, 8424
twins as sons of, 9414, 9415
worship of, 6438–6439
Akhenaton and, 218
in ancient religions, 2662
in Berber religion, 834
in Egyptian religion, 5451
under Josiah, 2662
in Toltec religion, 9223
at winter solstice, 9740, 9741, 9744
Sun Also Rises, The (Hemingway), 5481
Sunan Abū Dāwūd, in *ḥadīth* literature, 3730
Sunan al-Kubrā, al-, in *ḥadīth* literature, 3730
Sunan al-Nasā'ī, in *ḥadīth* literature, 3730
Sunan al-Tirmidhī, in *ḥadīth* literature, 3730
Sunan ibn Majāh, in *ḥadīth* literature, 3730
Sun bear, 808
Sun boats, in Egyptian religion, 989
Sun Chou (Chinese writer), 1062
Sun Dance, 2460, **8844–8849**
attempts to ban, 8846
ban on, 7248, 7255, 7257, 7302
contemporary practice of, 8848–8849
description of, 8845
drums in, 2499
government suppression of, 6698
of Great Plains, 2138, 6699–6700
iconography of, 4310
imitation of creation in, 6653
in Lakota religion, 5297
lodge construction for, 8845–8846
as New Year ceremony, 6656
pain in, 6945
performances, 8846–8847
revival of, 6672
self-mutilation in, 6652
spread of, 6718
study of, 9667–9668
today, 6719
translation of native language text on, 2264
women in, 3408
world pole/tree in, 6651
Sundance Film Festival, 3099
Sundanese language, 4657
Sundara. *See* Hanumān
Sundaramūrti (deity), 4324
Sundari (Sikh woman), 3336
Sunday, William A. (Billy)
in fundamentalism, 2889
men's movement led by, 5862
portraits of, vol. 10 color insert
revivalism and, 1710
Sunday (day), Easter falling on, 6171
Sunday schools, 7733
Sun deities, 3618–3619
as anthropomorphic representation, 8424
in Arabian religion, 443
in Aramean religion, 449
in Arctic religions, 469
in Armenian religion, 491
Athirat (Asherah) as, 589
blades of, 967
Bochica as, **993**
in Celtic religion, 8836
Dazhbog as, 2231
in Egyptian religion, 218, 219, *219*, 7634, 8836–8837
examples of, 3618–3619
functions of, 3618–3619
in Ge religion, 8578
in Greco-Roman religion, 3937, 8839–8841 (*See also* Sol Invictus)
in Hittite religion, 4069
in Inca religion, 8842–8843 (*See also* Inti)
in Indian religion, 4133
in Vedism, 3990, 8838–8839
Inti, 5176
Japanese, 4781
Amaterasu as, 1514–1515, 5157, 5180, 8841
in Maya religion, 5883
in Mesoamerican religions, 8842
in Huichol religion, 4152
in Mesopotamian religion, 8837–8838
in nature worship, 6438–6439
in North American Indian religions, 8841–8842
in Persian religions, 8838
in Slavic religion, 8434
Sol as, 8510–8511
in South American Indian religions, Inti as, 8600–8601
with thunderbolts, 7603
Utu, Sumerian, 9494–9495
Sundén, Hjalmar, **8850–8852**
on role theory, 4047
Sundiata (Mali epic)
Islamic influences on, 3086
Islam in, 2814
Sundkler, Bengt, 103
Sung, John, 8963
Śuṅga dynasty, Buddhist community under, 1091, 1105, 1108, 6128
Sun King. *See* Louis XIV
Sunnah (traditions of the Prophet), **8852–8855**. *See also* Ḥadīth
circumcision as, 1825
codification of, 4565
early evolution of concept, 8852
early meanings of, 9275
evolution of, 9274
in *fiqh*, 9488–9489
ḥadīth and, 3726, 3729–3730, 8853
in Sunnī Islam, 9268
madhāhib (schools) of, emergence of, 8854–8855
qiyās and, 7545
ṣalāt (prayer) based on, 8054
Shāfiʿī *madhhab* on, 4695, 4696
al-Shāfiʿī on, 8264, 8265
as source of Islam, 4565–4566
as source of *sharīʿah*, 4372, 4694, 4696
Sufism and, 8855
sunnat al-nabī (inspired prophetic example), 8852–8853
Sunnī *vs.* Shīʿī, 8853–8854
Sunnaoi theoi (temple-sharing gods), as syncretism, 3908
Sunnat al-nabī (inspired prophetic example), 4565. *See also* Ḥadīth
body of, 8852–8853
Sunnī Islam. *See also specific countries and doctrines*
in Africa, 7295
afterlife in, 161
against *taqīyah*, 8999
ahl al-bayt in, 198, 257
Aḥmadiyah opposed by, 200
ʿAlī ibn Abī Ṭālib in, 257

allegiance to family of the Prophet, 3008
authority in, 695–696
in Bengal, 825
bequests in, 4710
caliphate in, 1365, 1367, 4393–4394
in Caucasus, 4614
in Central Asia, 4620, 4621, 4627
charismatic leadership in, 1546
in Chile, 4684
in China, 4633, 4639
definition of Muslim by, 4568
development of, 4693, 7565
devotional allegiance in, 9819
eschatology of, 2837–2838
in Europe, 4678, 4681
on expansion of Islam, 7285
family law in, 3368
free will and predestination in, 3212
gender in, 3368–3369
ḥadīths in, 4565, 4696
in Ḥanafī creed in, 2062–2064
Ḥasan al-Baṣrī counted as predecessor to, 3785
heterodoxy in, 6912
hierarchy in, 5290
ijmāʿ in, 4373–4374, 4697
ijtihād in, 4374, 4697
imamate in, 4393–4394
incarnation in, 4416
inheritance in, 9657
ʿiṣmah in, 4724, 4725, 4726
law in (*See also* Islamic law, Sunni)
maṣlaḥah (public interest) in, 5772
schools of, 5547, 5549
leadership model of, 6737
life in, 5446–5447
mahdī in, 5981–5982
marriage in, 4706, 4707
mosques in, architecture of, 6208
Muʿtazilah in, 6321
name, origin of, 8854
narrative traditions of, 2447
on Qurʾān, 4696
created character of, 3563
orthodoxy in, 6912
paternity in, 4710
prayer in, 4397, 9816
for healing, 3831–3832
ṣalāt, 8054, 8055, 8057
Seljuk Turks and, 1367
Qarāmiṭah influence on, 7543
qiyās in, 4696
schools of law in, 4567
establishment of, 4694–4695
geographical distribution of, 4698
principal figures in, 4699–4700
Shīʿī doctrines compared to, 8342–8345
sunnah and, 8853–8854
Shīʿī split from, schools of law after, 5547
in South Asia, 4641, 4643, 4644–4645, 4649, 4650, 4654
tafsīr (Qurʾanic exegesis) in, 7564, 7565
tradition in, 9268
in United States, 4687–4688, 4690
vs. Ibāḍiyya sect, 4248, 4249
women in, 3368–3369
zāwiyahs criticized by, 4589
Sunrise (magazine), 7230
Sunrise service, at Easter, 2580
Sun Sheng, on Study of the Mystery, 1899
Suns of Jaguar, Wind, Fire-rain, and Water, in Aztec calendar, 1357
Sunsum (spirit), in Akan religion, 214
Sunü (deity), Huangdi (Yellow Emperor deity) and, 4144
Sun Woman (deity), 5119
Sun Wukong (monkey king), 6152
Śūnyam and *śūnyatā* (empty and emptiness), 1117, 1119, 1156, 2606, 5105, **8855–8860**
anātman as, 7365
bodhisattva path and, 8856–8857
in Chinese Buddhism, 1595, 8858–8860
Huayan perspective on, 4148
Huineng on, 4154
Sengzhao on, 8228
definitions of, 8855–8856
ecological ethic in, 2630
in Four Noble Truths, 3179, 3180
as freedom, 3201
Mādhyamika school, 8857–8858
in Mahāyāna Buddhism, 5200
in Vajrayāna (Tantric) Buddhism, 1216
Yogācāra school, 1211, 8858, 8859
in Japanese Buddhism, 8858–8860
meditation on, 1284–1285
mysticism of, 6344–6345
Nāgārjuna on, 1119, 1209, 1211, 1299, 5551–5552, 6145, 6391–6393, 7365, 9017
and practice of *nianfo,* 6601
Śāntideva on, 8109
Stcherbatsky (Theodore) on, 8737
tathatā equated with, 9019
Tsong kha pa on, 9387
Western philosophy, parallels in, 8859
in Zhenyan Buddhism, 9961
Śūnyatā-saptativṛtti (Candrakīrti), commentary in, 1401
Sunyavadins (teachers of emptiness), in Prajñāpāramitā Sūtras, 8856–8857
Sun Yirang, on cosmology and ritual, 1908
Sun Youyue, 8996
Suona (musical instrument), 6295
Suparṇā (deity), 4438
Supaya (ghosts), in Andean religion, 8616–8617, 8618–8619
Superego, Freud (Sigmund) on, 7474
Superhuman agency, in rituals, 7851
Superhuman immediacy, in rituals, 7851
Superincision, in Oceanic religions, 7808, 7809
Superior Court, Katz v., 1033
Superiority, humor and, 4221–4222
Supernatural, the, **8860–8864**
and Abbaye, 3
in Aramean religion, 450
in art, 53
body marks of, 1004–1005
and Chinese literature, 3066–3067
communicating with, 2459, 6733–6739
dramatic impersonations of, 2458
flowers and, 3136–3137
historical development of notion, 8860–8861
incorporation in Buddhism, 3154
in Japanese folk tales, 4798
Marett (R. R.) on, 2541
in North American Indian religions, 6703
secularization and, 8214, 8215, 8216
in study of religions and cultural systems, 8861–8863
systematic considerations on, 8863
in Tarascan religion, 9001–9002
universality of, 2089
Supernatural, The (King), 2541
Supernatural beneficence, dance as means to ask for, 2137–2138
Supernaturalism, ideational, Sorokin (Pitirim Aleksandrovich) on, 8523
Supernatural rationalism, of Adams (Hannah), 30
Supernatural revelation, Kant (Immanuel) on, 5079
Supernovae, Big Bang and, 2033
Superposition, syncretism and, 8928
Superstition, **8864–8867**
bibliolatry as, 8200
cats, 1462–1463
Chinese medicine criticized as, 3863
Christian views of
in early Christianity, 8864–8865
in Middle Ages, 8865–8866
Protestant *vs.* Catholic, 8866
colonialist opposition of religion *vs.,* 1855–1856
in Haiti, 3823
Enlightenment and post-Enlightenment views of, 8866
folklorists on, 3141, 3142
origin and classical usage of, 8864
in Roman Empire
laws concerning, 5333
persecution of, 7921
term, as judgmental and pejorative, 8864
in United States, 10084
Suppliant Women, The (Euripides), 4456
Supplicatio, 7906
Supplication
in Judaism, Taḥanun liturgy, 8389
sacrifices of, 8001
Suppression of the African Slave Trade, The (Du Bois), 67
Supreme beings, **8867–8880**. *See also* High gods; *specific gods*
in African religions (*See* Africa, supreme being in)
androgyny of, 3975
in Arctic religions, 469
in Bambara religion, 776
blessings from, 980
as creators, 8867, 8869–8870, 8872
definition of, 8867
in Diola religion, 2354, 2355
in Dolgan religion, 2395
general features of, 8867–8868
Henninger (Joseph) on, 8170
historical forms of, 8868–8874
activities in, 8871–8872
attributes in, 8868–8871
cults of, 8873–8874
relationship to other divinities, 8872–8873
Jupiter, 5037–5038
at leisure (*See Deus otiosus*)
masculine sacrality of, 5759, 5760
meteorological beings as, 5993

Supreme beings *continued*
North American Indian, iconography of, 4307
origin of religion and, Schmidt (Wilhelm) on, 8168–8169
Pettazzoni (Raffaele) on, 7074–7075
Preuss (Konrad T.) on, 7392
in primitive religions, and atheism, 577
scholarly theories on, 8874–8879
culture history approach, 8876–8878
early studies, 8875
of Eliade (Mircea), 8874, 8879
evolutionary theories of, 8875–8876
of Lang (Andrew), 8874, 8876
of Pettazzoni (Raffaele), 8874, 8878–8879
in South American Indian religions
culture heroes as, 8576–8577
Ge solar and lunar gods in, 8578
in Mundurucú religion, 8577
in Tupi-Guaraní religion, 8577–8578
in Waríkyana religion, 8577
mother goddesses in, 8578–8579
of Pampas, Patagonia, and southern Andes, 8579–8580
prevalence of, 8576
in Selk'nam religion, 8224
in Tierra del Fuego, 8579
in Yanoama religion, 8577
Tylor (E. B.) on, 8170
Ukko, 9438
Ülgen, 9441
in West African religions, 9717–9718
Supreme Court, U.S.
on abortion, 5810
on African Americans, 69
on involuntary sterilization, 2880
Supreme Emperor of Jadelike Augustness, 1641, 1642
Supreme Sūtra of the Golden Brilliance, gold symbolism in, 1861
Supreme Wisdom (Fard), 4688
Surā (drink), 849, 9564
Sura, *yeshivah* of, 9883
Śūra (monk), Māra and, 5690
Sūrahs (Qur'anic verses)
healing, 7572
on *tafsīr,* 8951, 8952
on paradise, 6984
on polygamy, 4700
protective, 7571–7572
theodicy in, 9118
Śūraṃgamasamādhi Sūtra (Buddhist text), 1077, 1078
Surāt al-Amr (Bahā' Allāh), 737
Sūrdās (saint), 5250, 7211, **8881–8882**
in *bhakti* poetry tradition, 3985
Sureśvara, 9547
Surgery
in Africa, 3819–3820
in Australian Indigenous religions, by sorcerers, 3871
Japanese view of, as violence to the body, 3868
Surinam
Afro-Surinamese religions in, **125–127**
Christianity in, 126
colonialism in, 126
ethnic populations of, 125–126, 1698
geography of, 125
slaves in, 126, 127
Suris (deity), 2871
Surjaningrat, Suwardi. *See* Dewantara, Ki Hadjar
Suro (founder of Karak), heavenly descent of, 5179
Śurpaṇakhā (demoness), in *Rāmāyaṇa,* 7617
Surrender, in Hinduism, in Śrī Vaiṣṇavas Sampradāya, 8728
Surrogate religion, 4401
Surrounded, The (McNickle), 3091
Sūrsāgar (Sūrdās), devotional poetry in, 8881
Ṣurūf al Ṣayy, 728
Survivalism, Christian Identity movement and, 1658
Survival theory, masks in, 5764, 5765
Sūrya (deity). *See also* Saura Hinduism
eye of, 2941
in *Mahābhārata,* 5595
lotus associated with, 5518
vs. Saule, 758, 760
in Saura Hinduism, 8135, 8136
as sun deity, 8838–8839
tapas of, 8997
in Vedic pantheon, 3990, 8135
Sūryavarman (king), 1133, 1135
Sūryavarman II (king), 4013, 5129
Suṣamā (happy period), in Jain cosmology, 2025
Suṣamā-duḥṣamā (happy period), in Jain cosmology, 2025
Suṣamā-suṣamā (extremely happy period), in Jain cosmology, 2025
Susanna, 898, 899
Susano-o no Mikoto (deity), **8882–8883**
Amaterasu (sister) and, 8841, 8882–8883
and Amaterasu Ōmikami, 280
in Ōmotokyō, 6824–6825
Izanagi creating, 4755
local beliefs in, 8883
Ōkuni and, 6814
relationship with sister, 2985
tears of, 9026
S üse, Heinrich, under Eckhart (Johannes), 2603
Suseneyos (Ethiopian emperor), 2860
Suseri (deity), 6814
Su Shi (poet), 7214
Sushumna (central channel), 8993
Sushun (emperor), ascension and assassination of, 8374–8375
Susiddhikāra Sūtra (Buddhist text), 9077, 9078, 9961, 9962
Śubhākarasiṃha on, 8804
Suso, Henry, on mystical union, 6337
Suśruta Saṃhitā
as Āyurvedic text, 3853
Āyurvedic principles in, 714, 3854–3855
magic in, 5591
Sustenance dances, 2135
Susurpuquio (legendary Inca place), Inca calendar and, 1362
Sūtrakṛtāṅga Sūtra, hells in, 2022–2023
Sūtra literature, **8883–8884**. *See also specific sūtras*
vs. Abhidharma, 10021
Buddhist, 1253
Buddha's biographies, 1063
calligraphy and, 1370
canonization, 1407
exegsis of, 4927
and meditation, 1284–1286
recitation of, 3979, 9837
Sautrāntika view of, 8119, 8136
Vasubandhu commentaries on, 9527
Kalpasūtras, 3994, 8883–8884
meaning and negation in, 5308–5309
proclamation of sinfulness in, 1886
pūjā in, 7493
Pure Land sūtras, 7502, 7503
Stcherbatsky (Theodore) on, 8737
Sūtra Piṭaka (Buddhist text), 1198
Buddhaghosa's commentary on, 1074
content of, 9146
in Mahāsāṃghika Buddhism, 5601
kingship in, 5348
personality structure in, 8548
politics in, 7260
Sūtrasamuccaya (Buddhist text), 1119
Sūtravibhaṅga (Buddhist text), 1258, 1259, 1269
Suttanipāta (Buddhist text), 1117, 1270
Sutton, Thomas, 9164
Suun, Ch'oe, 1647
Suvarnabhasottama Sūtra (Buddhist text), 7260
Suwā' (deity), 444
Suyá people (South America), myths of, fire in, 3293–3294
Suyuti, al- (Egyptian scholar), 4605
Suyūṭī, Jalāl al-Dīn al-
on *mi'rāj,* 6061
prophetic medical text of, 3833
Suzuki, D. T., **8884–8887**
on art and religion, 499–500
Carus and, 1635
early years of, 8884–8885
haiku of, 8702
on humor in Zen, 4207
impact of, 8886–8887
influences on, 8885–8886
on Japanese culture, 8886
on monism in Zen Buddhism, 6145
on *bushidō,* 1247
on *kōans,* 1292
on paradox, 6989
and popular Zen Buddhism, 1188, 1189, 1313, 9950
on religious experience, 7740
and theosophy and Swedenborgianism, 8885–8886
translations by, 1183
Zen philosophy of, 8886
Suzuki Masataka, 3348
Suzuki Shōsan (Buddhist monk), 4939, **8887–8888,** 9949
Švābe, Arveds, 770
Svabhāva (essence), 1206, 1208, 1300
Nāgārjuna on, 5552, 6391–6392
Svābhāvika. *See* Dvaitādvaita
Svābhāvikakāya (self-existent), 1077
Svadharma (personal obligation), 853, 2305, 2330, 4442
Svādhiṣṭhānā cakra, location of, 1348
Svārāj (self-rule), 3201
Svarog (creator of the sun), 2231
Svarozhich (deity), 2231
Svarūpa Dāmodara, Caitanya and, 1346
Svasaṃvedanā (reflexive self-consciousness), rebirth and, 8552
Svātantrika school of Buddhism, 860, 1119, 1299
emergence of, 5552
language and logic in, 8858
name of, 5552
Svayambhū liṅga (stone), 4326
Svayambhūnāth Stupa (Nepal), vol. 4 color insert
Svayaṃbhu Purāṇa (Buddhist text), 1126
Svayaṃ kṛta (self-causation), 7363
Šventas (sacred), 774, 775
Sventovit (deity), **8888–8889,** 9359

Śvetāmbara sect of Jainism, 4765–4766
enlightenment in, 5610
food of, 4769
gender in, 3326–3327, 4765
heavens in, 2024
Mahāvīra in, 5609–5610
nuns in, 6757
on *tīrthaṃkaras*, 9207, 9208
scriptures of, 4766–4767
Śvetāśvatara Upaniṣad
deification of *gurus* in, 8712
puruṣa in (*See Brahman*)
Rudra-Śiva in, 8415
monotheism and, 8040
Svet nevecherni (Bulgakov), 1320
Svēts (sacred), 774, 775
Swabian Pietism, 7142
Spener (Philipp Jakob) on, 8680
Swahili language
in East Africa, 2566
Islamization of, 4611
literature in, 3086
postcolonialism and, 1515
Swahili people, Islam among, 2571, 4607
mawlids in, 5789
Swahili Proverbs (Knappert), 6977
Swahili religion (East Africa)
cosmogony of, written accounts of, 2567
healing in, herbal doctors, 3819
high deity in, 2567
possession in, 2568
proverbs in, 6977
supreme being (Mungu) in, 3572
Swāikstiks (deity), 767
Swain, Tony, 671, 673, 685
on Australian aboriginal religion, 8770
Swaminarayan movement, **8889–8893**
contemporary issues in, 8892
devotional practices, 8891–8892
Hinduism, relation to, 8892
original movement, 8890
origin narrative in, 8889–8890
Sahajanand Swami, role of, 8889–8890
schisms and new sects in, 8890
texts and interpretation, 8890–8891
Swami Vivekananda. *See* Vivekananda
Swan Maiden, The (Hagoromo), 4798
Swan-maiden myth, mares in, 4134–4135
Swann, Brian, 7224
Swann, Valetta, 5629
Swans, 4438, **8893–8894**
swan-maiden myth, 4134–4135
Swanson, Guy E.
on guardian spirit quest, 8277
on monotheism, 8170
Swan's Questions and Answers, The (Longchenpa), 5193
Swantko, Jean, 9411
Swanton, John R., 6670, 6671, 6688, 6694
Haida spirit theory of, 3735
Swaraj (self-rule), Gandhi (Mohandas) on, 3272
Swarr, Amanda, 5414
Swartz, Michael, 10052, 10053
Swastika, as Raëlian symbol, 7597, 7599
Swazi religion (Southern Africa), **8894–8898**
ancestral cult in, 8896
Christianity in, 8897
cosmology and symbolic system of, 8895
diviners in, shades, calling by, 3818
emadloti (world of spirits) in, 8896
funeral rites in, 140
lion king in, 8666
Ncwala ceremonies in, 5169–5170
politics and geography of, 8894–8895
python spirit in, 8663
rituals in, 8895, 8896–8897
rituals of reversal in, 7844
sacred kingship in, 8664, 8665, 8895–8896, 8897
solstice celebration in, 8656
tangoma (diviners) in, 8896
Swear. *See* Vows and oaths
Sweat bath/lodge, 801, 7300
Mesoamerican, 1472, 7811
in North American Indian religions, 6653, 6655
California, 6715
Cherokee, 6694
Lakota, 5296
Plains, 6700
Sweden. *See also* Germanic religion
"age of freedom" in, 8898
álfar in, 254–255
folk dance in, 2145
historiography in, 4042, 4047
Islam in, 4679, 4680
museums in, 6245
new religious movements in government policy on, 6541, 6570
native, 6568
Paganism in, 6567
runic inscriptions in, 7940, 7941
Sweden, Church of
Andrae (Tor) in, 333
Söderblom (Nathan) as archbishop of, 8506
Swedenborg, Emanuel, **8898–8900**. *See also* Swedenborgianism
on angels, 348
correspondences system of, 8899, 8900
early life, 8898
natural philosophy and, 8898–8899
on phallus, 7085
religious crisis and spiritual call of, 8899
and secularization of Western Esotericism, 6497
spiritism of, 8715
and Strindberg (August), 2474
teachings, controversy, and impact of, 8899–8900
on visionary descent into the underworld, 2299
writings of, 8898–8899, 8900–8901
Swedenborgianism, **8900–8906**
art, influence on, 8899–8900
British Conference of, 8902–8903
Child (Lydia Maria) on, 1569
church governance in, 8902, 8903, 8904
establishment of the New Church, 8901–8902
General Church of the New Jerusalem, 8904–8905
in Japan, Suzuki (D. T.) and, 8885–8886
Swedenborgian Church of North America, 8903–8904
worldwide movement of, 8905
Swedenborgian School of Religion, 8904
Sweet Daddy. *See* McCollough, "Sweet Daddy" Walter
Sweet potatoes. *See* Yams and sweet potatoes
Swem (symbol), 9211
Swidler, Ann, on culture, 8470
Swift, Jonathan, 1323
as Freemason, 3195
Swift, Wesley, Christian Identity movement and, 1658, 1659
Swimme, Brian, 2666
Swints (sacred), 774
Swiss Brethren, 304
Switzerland
Anabaptism in, 304–305
Islam in, 4676, 4679
Mennonites in, 5860
new religious movements in government policy on, 6526, 6570
Temple Solaire, 9067–9068
Protestantism in, Pietism in, 7143
Roman Catholicism in, Inquisition in, 4498, 4500
study of religion in, 10081
Theban Legion, martyrdom of, 1980
Sword, George, 2264, 5296
Sword cults, 9686
Swords, 967–968. *See also* Blades
capital punishment by, 4742
of Ferghus mac Roich, 3040
in Hun religion, 4228, 4229
in Japanese martial arts, 5732
Sy, Serigne Omar, vol. 5 color insert
Syair (poetic form), 4663, 7223
Syddick, Linda, 4307
Sydney, University of, scholarship at, 8769
Sydney (Australia), Olympic Games in (2000), opening ceremony of, 634–647, 651
Sydney Organising Committee of the Olympic Games (SOCOG), 646
Syed Sultan, 10035
Syllables, mystical speculation on, 271
Syllabus of Errors (Pius IX), 7878
Syllaeus (Nabatean), 6386
Syllogisms, in Mādhyamika Buddhism, 5553
Sylphide, la (Bournonville), 2156
Sylphide, la (ballet), 2155
Sylvanus (Christian writer), 917
Sylvester, Joshua, 6746
Symbionese Liberation Army (SLA), 1034, 6522
Symbiosis, syncretism and, 8928
Symbol and symbolism, 7696–7697, **8906–8915**. *See also* Iconography; *specific symbols*
in African religions
gender in, 3402
rites of passage in, 88
in alchemy, 246, 252
of animals, 357 (*See also* Animals)
in anthropology, 6802–6803
in architecture, classification of, 466
Baal (Jan van) on, 725
Bachofen (J. J.) on, 731
of blessing, 980
of boats, 991–992
of body painting, 1004
of bread, 1041
of bridges, 1051–1052
cards and sacred mathematics, 1413
in cargo cults, 7789
Cassirer on, 1448, 4298
ceremony as, 1512
Child (Lydia Maria) on, 1569
children as, **1566–1569**
in Chinese alchemy, 240
of Christian baptism, 781
in Christianity, androcentric, 334–336
cosmogonic myths, symbolic structure of, 1985–1986
definition of, 4530
of diamonds, 2345

Symbol and symbolism
continued
of dragons, 2430, 2432
of drums, 2494–2495
of eggs, 2423
in Egyptian religion, 40
Eliade (Mircea) on, 781, 1878–1879
endurance of symbols, 8914
environment in shaping, 2611
in ethology, 2868
feminism and, 9792
gender studies on, 3302
Goblet d'Alviella (Eugène) on, 3537
of gold, 3625–3626
hair, **3738–3741**
hierophany (manifestation of the sacred) and, 3973–3974
history and theory of
anthropology and, 8910–8911
general symbolic theory, 8912–8913
in late antiquity, 8907–8908
origin of notion, 8906–8907
and philosophy and religious studies, 8912
Romantic movement and, 8908–8909
Symbolist movement, 8909–8910
of hope, 4127
in iconography, 4298
in Vajrayāna Buddhism, gender and, 3333
in Judaism, rabbinic Judaism, 7584–7585
of keys, 5116–5117
in Khanty religion
anthropomorphic, 5122
zoomorphic, 5122
of knots, 5197
Langer (Susanne) on, 5300–5301
as language of myth, 7696
of left and right (*See* Left and right)
Lévi-Strauss (Claude) on, 4298
of light and darkness (*See* Darkness; Light)
of Magen David (Star of David), **5558–5559**
in magic, 5563, 5567–5569
Greco-Roman, 5574
in Mansi religion
anthropomorphic, 5122
zoomorphic, 5122
of martyrdom, 5738
meaning, symbolic, 8913–8914
in Minoan religion, 40
of music, 6252–6253
in Mycenaean religion, 41
of mystical union, 6335
myth and
Campbell on, 1378–1379
Creuzer (G. F.) on distinction between, 2070
numerical, quaternity, **7550–7551**
in ordination, 6858–6859
of orientation, 6885–6887
of owls, 6936–6937
of portals, 7333, 7334
of postures and gestures, 7342–7344
power of, 7350
of purification, 7504
of quests, 7553–7554
in Rastafari, 7625, 7626–7627
in religious life, 7696–7697
Ricoeur (Paul) on thought and, 1990
ritual patterns and, 7699
in rituals, 7838–7840, 7849
sacred space, encoding of, 7982–7984
sexual
in Freudian psychoanalysis, 7838
in rites of passage, 7797–7798
in shamanism, Korean, 5229
of silver, 3625, 3626
Smart (Ninian) on, 8443
social interaction and, 8482
of tattoos, 1002
terminology and concepts in, 8906
of textiles, 9088
therianthropism in, 9155
Tillich (Paul) on, 9204
trees as, 9337–9338, 9339
Turner (Victor) on, 2303
on vestments, in Daoism, 1828–1829
Symbolic artificial intelligence, 510
Symbolic realism, Bellah (Robert) on, 8496, 8498
Symbolic time, **8915–8919**
development of symbolic structures, 8916–8917
intentional character of, 8915–8916
periodicity in, 8917–8919
ritual performance in, 8917
Symbolik (Möhler), 6114
Symbolique du mal, La (Ricoeur), 9071
Symbolism, the Sacred, and the Arts (Eliade), 500
Symbolism of Evil, The (Ricoeur), 2898–2901
Symbolist movement, history of, 8909–8910
Symeon. *See* Peter the Apostle
Symeon of Mesopotamia, 5624
Symeon the New Theologian, 2587, **8919–8920**
on God, 3554
hesychaism of, 2826
Symmachians. *See* Ebionites
Symmachus (biblical scholar), 892
on Baal Zebub, 7103
Symmetry
geometric, 3438, *3438*
in nature and myth, 6361
Sympathetic magic
healing and, 3811–3812
types of, 5571
Symphonia (Hildegard of Bingen), 7207
Symposium (Plato), 45, 408, 2277, 2283, 9283
revelation in, 7775
Synagogue-centers, emergence of, 1959
Synagogues, **8920–8926**
at archaeological sites, 8923–8924
architecture of
basilica-type, 8923
in earliest buildings, 8921
Galilean-type, 8923
location and alignment of, 8922
medieval, 8925
modern, 8925–8926
Chrysostom on, 8924
in colonial America, 7582
in Conservative Judaism, 1959
gender separation in
as custom *(minhag)*, 3750
in Middle Ages, 8922
history of, Zunz's (Leopold) study of, 4876
in Israel, 7582–7583
modern, 6905
joking in, 4203–4204
in late Roman and Byzantine periods, 8921–8924
medieval and modern, 8924–8926
music in
early, 6307
medieval, 6308
Renaissance, 6310
origin of, 935, 6307, 8920–8921
in Poland, built by Isserles (Mosheh), 4750
in rabbinic Judaism, 4978
in Reconstructionist Judaism, 5082
in Reform Judaism, 7668, 7669–7670
Sabbath services in, 8257
sacredness of, 7698
in Samaritan religion, 8070
term, origin of, 1770, 8920
in United States, 6905–6906
in Worms, Germany, 8925
Syncellus, George, on Hermes Trismegistos, 3938
Synchronicity
chance and, 1528
in the Grail myth, 3650
in import of myth, 5035
Jung on, 6057–6058
miracles and, 6057–6058
Syncletica, 2825, 6763
Syncretic diversity, 2605
Syncretism, **8926–8938**
Afro-Caribbean religions, **1432–1440**, 10025–10026, 10027
Berner (Ulrich) on, 8935–8936
in Burmese religion, 1328
in cargo cults, 1415–1416, 1422
in central Bantu religion, 1511
in Chinese religion, 1578, 1614
in Huayan Buddhism, 4145
Liu Deren and, 5495
in Christianity, 2228–2229
combination of particular elements, 8930–8932
complex unities, connections between, 8930
critical approaches to, 8935–8936
criticism of concept, 3161
cross-cultural studies and, 2089
in cults, history of study of, 75, 76
definition of, 217, 10025–10026
and divine personalities, formation of, 8936–8937
in East Africa, 2572
in Egyptian religion, 217, 2716
in Germanic religion, 3460
in Gnosticism, 8932–8933
in goddess worship, 3588
Hellenistic religions, 3907–3909
Hermetic-Christian, in Renaissance, 3946
in Hinduism, in Sāṃkhya Yoga, 8091
in history, 8927–8930
history and usefulness of concept, 8926–8927, 8934–8935
in ʿAlawīyūn, 227
in Indian religions
Āyurveda and, 3857
under emperor Akbar, 4007
in Zolla's (Elémire) philosophy, 9985
in Iranian religion, 10002
in Islam, in Bektāshi Sufism, 8823
in Japanese religion, 3868–3869
in Shugendō, 8352
kami and, 5073–5074
Jewish Renewal and, 4870
in Manichaeism, 8932
meaning of term, 3907, 8926, 8934, 8935–8936
in Mesoamerican religions, 5893, 5920, 5928
in Middle Ages, 8933
modern acculturation and, 8933
in mystery religions, 8932

and new religions, invention of, 8936
portals as object of, 7333
postcolonial hybridity and, 1859
postcolonial theories of conversion and, 1971
religions, syncretist, 8932–8933
revival and renewal activities described by, 7784
in Roman religion, 1787, 7918–7919
scholarship, late-twentieth-century, 8927
in Solomon Islands Christianity, 8517
in South American Indian religions, 3143
huacas and cult of saints, convergence of, 8605–8606, 8609–8612
studies moving away from notion of, 8597
in Tlaxcalan religion, 9215
typology of phenomena in, 8927
in Vietnamese religion, 9594
in Vodou, 3143
in *Zhuangzi*, 9970–9971
Synedoche, in visual narratives, vol. 2 color insert
Synesius of Cyrene, 1677–1678
on knowability of God, 183
Synge, John M., 1490
Synodical months, in Inca calendar, 1361
Synod of Bishops
establishment of, 6975, 7012
institution of, 1764
Synods. *See also specific locations*
episcopal synods in second and third centuries, 2039
in Lutheran polity, 1769
in United States, 5539
meaning of term, 2039
medieval, 2041
in Presbyterian polity, 1767
in Reform Judaism, 7669
in Roman Catholicism, 7886
Synonyms (Isidore), 4557
Synonyms, in Hebrew scriptures, Malbim on, 5626
Synoptic gospels, 906–907, 910, 911. *See also* Luke; *Mark; Matthew*
Jesus' pilgrimage in, 7152–7153
revelation in, 7778
Syntax, semantics and, 8226
Synthesis
in science and religion typology, 2658
syncretism and, 8928–8929
Synthetist movements, in Africa, 102
Syria and Syrian religions. *See also* Aramean religion
ʿAlawīyūn in, 226, 227
Baath Party in, 1675
Canaanite sites in, 1381
Christianity, 1675
Chalcedon statement rejected by, 2584
Council of Ephesus rejected by, 2583
Nestorian Church, 2584
Dagan in, 2125–2126
deities of (*See also specific deities*)
female, 3376–3377
Druze in, 2502
Ebionite sect in, 2596
Eblaite religion, 2596–2599
gender in, **3375–3381**
hare myths in, 7590
Islam, Nizārī Ismāʿīlīyah, 558
Islamic conquest of, 20
Jewish community in, Karaite sect, 5083, 5084
kingship in, 5164–5165
Muslim Brotherhood in, 6316
Nabatean religion, 6387, 6389
Naufian culture, 6460–6461
polygamy in, 4707
rivers in, 7862
scapegoat rite practiced in, 2598
women in, **3375–3381**
Syriac language
Aramaic language as cognate of, 447
Aristotle's works translated into, 479
Galen's works translated into, 3256
Hebrew scriptures in, 893–894
New Testament in, 922
Syriac Menander, 904
Syriac Orthodox Church of Antioch, 2585, **8938–8941**
and All Souls Day, 2230
ashrams of, 547
ecumenical activity of, 8940–8941
history of, 8938–8940
in India, 1729
liturgy of, 8941
in Middle East, 1673
in modern times, 8940
Severus of Antioch and, 8238
in South America, 1703
Syriac-speaking scholars, 2970–2971
Syrian Catholic Church, 1673
Syrian Goddess, The, 7129
Canaanite religion in, 1381
Syrian Orthodox Church. *See* Syriac Orthodox Church of Antioch
Syria-Palestine (region)
Christianity in, Bardesanites, **786–787**
soul, concepts of, 8538–8540
tattooing in, 1002
Syro-Ephraimite war (734/3-733/2 BCE), 4545, 4547, 4548
Syro-Hexapla, 894
Syro-Palestinian Bible, 894
Systematic Theology (Tillich), 6964, 9204
Système de politique positive (Comte), 1882
System of Transcendental Idealism (Schelling), 47
Systems
cybernetics, **2111–2112**
social, the Enlightenment and, 8491
Szold, Henrietta, **8941**

T

Ṭaʿ amei ha-miqraʾ, 1533
Taʿanit Ester (Fast of Esther), in Jewish calendar, 4867
Taanot. See Taqqanot
Ta'aroa (deity), 7305
Taʿarruf (al-Kalābādhī), 5055
commentaries of, 5055–5056
Taawa (Sun), 4309
Tabachnik, Michel, 9068
Tabakea (mythic figure), 6010
Ṭabaqāt ʿulamāʾ Ifrīqiyā wa-Tūnus (Ibn Tamīm), 4584
Ṭabarī, Abū Jaʿfar Muḥammad ibn Jarīr al-, **8943–8945**
and Sunnī *tafsīr,* 7565
ḥadīth collection by, 8944
historical writings of, 8944, 8945
in Ashʿarīyah, 534
on Islamic history, 4029
legal writings of, 8944
life of, 8943
on Mazdakism, 5801
on ʿAlī ibn Abī Ṭālib, 259
on *īmān* and *islām,* 4400
on *miʿrāj,* 6060
school of law established by, 8944
tafsīr of, 8943–8944, 8945, 8950, 8953
Ṭabarī, ʿAlī ibn Sahl al-, 7242
Tabarsī, Abū ʿAlī al-, 8954
Ṭabāṭabāʾī, ʿAllāma, **8945–8946**
education of, 8945
in sociocultural debates, 8946
tafsīr of, 8945–8946
writings of, 8945–8946
Ṭabāṭabāʾī, Sayyid Muḥammad Mahdī, 7241
Tabegasi (shinny), 752
Tabellae defixiones (Greco-Roman tablets), curses in, 2097–2098
Tabennis (monastery), 6939
Tabernacle, 795, 4745
shekhinah concept and, 8313
Tabernacles, Feast of, rainmaking at, 7603
Tabernaculo de Fe, Iglesia de Dios en Cristo (Los Angeles), vol. 5 color insert
Tabernanthe iboga (hallucinogen), 7469–7470
Tabiʿ a, 2652
Tabiti (deity), 4489, 7386
Tabl (drum), 7036
Tableaux vivants, 2156, 2162–2163
Table Talk (Plutarch), 7201
Tablets
cuneiform, 3375
goddess worship in, 3586
curse, in Greco-Roman magic, 5573–5574
Mycenaean, 41–42, 43
Tablets of Maklu, 779
Tablighi-jamāʿat (reform movement), 4653, 4681
Tabnit (king of Sidon), 7132
Tabo (Buddhist temple), 9050–9051
Taboo(s), **8947–8949**
in African religions
Ndembu, 8949
protection rituals and, 3820
anthropologists on, 8948
in Apache religion, 10071
in Australian Indigenous religions, 7842–7843, 8948
evangelistic discourse on, 8767
health and, 3872–3873
Aztec supernumerary days, 1355
in Caribbean religions, after childbirth, for father, 1430
Cassirer on, 1448
cattle, killing or eating of, 1465–1466
Cazeneuve (Jean) on, 7842
Celtic kings and, 1492
confession of sins and, 1884–1885
as confirmatory rituals, 7841–7843
couvade and, 2046, 2047
definition of, 8947
Durkheim (Émile) on, 7841, 7971, 8948
dynamistic theories on, 2541
etymology of term, 8947
food, 3167–3169 (*See also* Dietary laws)
in Chinese traditions, 3169
in Christianity, 3168
in Hinduism, 3167–3168, 8948
in Islam, 3168–3169
in Judaism, 3167, 8948
in Ndembu religion, 8949
theoretical perspectives on, 3172–3173
Frazer (James G.) on, 2540
Freud (Sigmund) on, 2239, 7974
Gennep (Arnold van) on, 3432

Taboo(s) ***continued***
in Greek religion, blood taboo, 1459
Hawaiian *kapu* system (*See Kapu* system)
in Hinduism, caste system and, 7843
incest as, 8949
in *ḥaram/ḥawṭah* enclaves, 3776
in Inuit religion, 4527
in Judaism, 7842
kings not bound by, 5155, 5170
in Korean religion, 5232
vs. mana, 5632
Marrett (R. R.) on, 2541
meanings of term, 5835
in Melanesian religions, 5835–5836
menstrual, **5866–5868** (*See also* Menstruation)
in Micronesian religions, 6008
on mirrors, 6064
modern concept of, 8948
mourning restrictions as, 8948–8949
on name use, 8948
as negative attitude toward power, 7346, 7351
in Oceanic religions, 6800
origins of, 5835, 7840
in Polynesian religions (*See Tabu; Tapu*)
in primitive religions, 8948
Reinach (Salomon) on, 7676
in rituals, 8949
in Roman religion, 7351
sacred and profane distinguished by, 7842–7843, 7974
in Samoyed religion, 8096
vs. sin, 8402
in Solomon Islands religions, 8516
totem and, 8948, 9251
in Warlpiri religion, 9696
Taboo rocks, in Australian Indigenous religions, 7606
Tabor, Mount, 1501
Tabora (Tanganyika), Islam in, 2571
Taborite movement, 6648, 6870–6871
Tabrīzī Shaykhīyah, Shaykhīyah movement and, 8308
Tabṣīr fī ma'ālim al-dīn (al-Ṭabarī), 8944
Tabu (ritual prohibition), 7296, 8947
Tabula praedestinationis (Beza), 851
Tabula Smaragdina (T.S.)
commentaries on, 3945, 3949, 3951
full text of, 3948
occultist texts on, 3951
Rijckenborgh (Jan van) on, 3953
spiritual growth in, 3954
Tacana religion (Andes), supreme beings in, 8576
Tachard, Guy, 112
Taché, A. A., 9303
Tacita (deity), 5321
Tacitus
on Anglo-Saxon paganism, 6942
on Baltic religion, 757, 767, 3103
on Celtic religion, women in, 3387
on Christian persecution, 7058
comparative theology of, 9128
on fasting, 2996
on Germanic religion, 6942
creation myth of, 3447
deities of, 3450
initiation in, 4478
on Judaism, 398, 7201
on Manu, 5678
on miracles of Vespasian, 6051
on *penates,* 7027
on religious persecution, 7921
on Semnones, 2366
Tadaharu, Akagi, 5267
Taddampali (Bugis mythical figure), 1317
Tadhkirat al-awliyā ('Aṭṭār), al-Ḥallāj in, 3757
Tadjo, Véronique, 3088
T'aebaek, Mount, in myth of Tan'gun, 5229
T'aego-chong school of Buddhism (Korea), 1173
T'aego Pou (Buddhist scholar), 1172
T'aejo (Chosŏn king), 5232
T'aejong (Chosŏn king), 1173
Tafhīm al-Qur'ān (Mawdūdī), 8955
Tafhimat al-ilāhiyya (Walī Allāh), 4643
Tafsīr (Qur'anic exegesis), 7561–7570, 7572–7573, **8949–8957**
allegorical, 8952–8953
categories of, 7564
tafsīr al-nabī, 8951
'afsīr bi-al-ma' thūr, 7564, 7565, 8953
'afsīr bi-al-ra' y, 7564, 7565, 8953
classical
consolidation of, 8953
specializations within, 8953–8954
of contextualists, 7569
development of, 7563, 8951–8953
discouragement of, 7561, 7564
early, 7563–7564
early development of, 7561–7563
feminist, 7568
ḥadīth as material of, 8950
Jewish and Christian traditions in, 7563, 7564
kalām-based, 7566
Khārijī, 7566
legal, 8952
on legal matters, 7563
legitimation of, in Qur'ān, 8951
literary-historical, 7568
modernist, 7567, 8955–8956
on narratives, 7563–7564, 8952
of 'Abduh (Muḥammad), 8955
of Aḥmad Khān, 8955
of al-Ash'arī, 5064
of Bahā'īs, 8954
of al-Bayḍāwī, 8953
of al-Ghazāli, 8955
of Jawharī (Ṭanṭāwī), 8956
of Kubrā (Najm al-Dīn), 5257
of al-Māturidī, 8950
of Muḥammad, 7562
of Muqātil ibn Sulaymān, 8944, 8950, 8952
of Quṭb (Sayyid), 8955
of al-Rāzī, 7633, 8953
of al-Ṭabarī, 8943–8944, 8945, 8950, 8953
of Ṭabāṭabā'ī, 8945–8946
of the Bāb, 8954
of al-Zamakhsharī, 8953, 8954, 9929
origins of, 8950–8951
practical, 7562
purpose of, 8950
rhetorical, 8952
scientific, 7563
of semitextualists, 7569
Shī'ī, 7565–7566, 8954
sociopolitical, 7567–7568
sources for, 7562
Southeast Asian, 4662, 4663
studies on, 8951
Ṣūfī, 7566–7567, 8953, 8954–8955
Sunnī, 7565
terms related to, 8949–8950
of textualists, 7569, 8952
thematic, 7568
vs. ta'wīl, 7561, 8810, 8950
writings of, 7563
Tafsīr al-manār ('Abduh), 6, 8955
Tafsīr al-Qur'ān (Ahmad Khan), 8955
Tafsīr al-Qur'ān (Muqātil), 8952
Tafsīr basīt naṣṣ al-Tūrāh (Sa'adyah Gaon), 8950
Tafsīr khams mī'ah āyah min al-Qur'ān (Muqātil), 8952
Taftāzānī, al-, 4399–4400, **8957**
on *mi'rāj,* 6060
Tafwīḍ (delegation), Shaykh Aḥmad on, 8307
Tagaroa (deity), 6264
Tages (divine child), 2872, 2875
Taglioni, Marie, 2155
Tagore, Debendranath
in ashram revival, 546
on *dharma,* 9318
in Hindu reform movement, 9317–9318
in Brāhmo Samāj, 1029
on religious experience, 7740
Sen (Keshab Chandra) *vs.,* 8227
son of, 8957, 9319
Tagore, Dwarkanath, 9319
Tagore, Rabindranath, **8957–8958**
in ashram revival, 545, 546
and Bengali religion, 827, 829, 8957–8958
ecstatic experiences of, 2681
on education, 8958
Gandhi (Mohandas) and, 3272, 5400
influence of, 8958
life of, 8957
on nationalism, 8958, 9319
Nobel Prize to, 8957, 8958, 9319
on *līlā,* 5457
poetry of, 7207, 8957, 8958
religion depicted in fiction of, 10035
spiritual vision of, 8958
Vaiṣṇavism and, 1347
Tahāfut al-Falāsifah (al-Ghazālī)
Ibn Rushd's rebuttal of, 4271–4272
Ibn Sīnā's influence on, 4569
Tahāfut al-Tahāfut (Ibn Rushd), 4271–4272
Ṭāhā Ḥusayn
autobiography of, 700
writings of, banned by al-Azhar, 231
Tahajjud (vigils), in Qur'ān, 8056
Taḥallul (deconsecration), 7157, 7159–7160
Taḥanun (supplications), in *siddur* liturgy, 8389
ṭahārah (ritual purity), 2401, 7511, 7515
for *ṣalāt* (prayer), 8057
sexual activity and, 1559
Taharat ha-mishpahah (laws of family purity), 7515
miqveh in, 6047
Tāhart (Algeria), imamate of, 5127
Ṭaḥawī, al-, Abū Ḥanīfah and, 22
Tahdhīb al-āthār (al-Ṭabarī), 8944
Ṭāhir Dakanī, Shāh, as Muḥammad-shāh, 8333
Tahiti and Tahitian religions. *See also* Oceania and Oceanic religions
afterlife in, 2006–2007
chiefs in, 7307
Christianity
Catholic charismatic movement, 6793
conversion to, 7305
missions, 1738, 6791–6792, 9322
colonization of, 6784
creation myths, 7305
funeral rites, 3136
genital operations in, 7808
human sacrifice in, 7309
mahu gender reversal in, 4116

Mamaia movement in, 6795
music in, 6263, 6264
naming of children in, 7807
oral tradition in, memorization of, 5850
origin myth of, 7315
rituals in, 7308, 7310
tapu in, 7307, 8948
Ṭahmāsp I (shāh of Iran), 4646
Taḥrīf (corruption), 7242
Tahuantinsuyu. *See* Inca religion and society
Tahzīb al-niswān (journal), 4652
Tai, Mount, 1590, 1591, 1619, 6214
afterlife at, 171
as realm of the dead, 1592
sacred geography of, 3435
Taidi (deity), Shangdi and, 8300
Ṭā'ifah (Sufi society), 9006
Taigheirm ceremony, black cats in, 1463
Taigiroku (Kaibara Ekken), 5055
Taigong Wang (deified general), military cult and, 1913
Taigu school, 3069
Taiji (great ultimate), **8959–8960,** 9973
in martial arts, 5736
Taiji tu (diagram of the supreme ultimate), 1578
Taijitu shuo (Zhou Dunyi), 8959
Taiko (drum), 7036
Taikyō (Great Teaching), Shintō and, 8366–8367
Taikyo Sempu movement, 4790
Tai language, 9094
Tailao (Great Sacrifice), 6293
Tailghan (sacrifice), 1326, 1327
Taimitsu, 2801, 4784
Táin Bó Cuailnge (saga), 3040, 5529, **8960**
brown bull of Cualinge in, 1485, 1487, 8960
Connall Cernach in, **1883**
Cú Chulainn in (*See* Cú Chulainn)
horse goddess in, 4133
Lincoln (Bruce) on, 8960
Taino Indian religion (Haiti)
deluge myth in, 8588
high god in, 8589
history of study of, 10024
wooden objects in, 10024
Taiping (component of Daoist canon), 2203
Taiping (great peace), **8961–8962**
etymology of term, 8961
in Han dynasty, 8961
Taiping dao (Way of the Great Peace), 1593
millenarianism of, 6039
Taiping jing (Scripture of great peace), 1593, 2192, 2204
on central harmony, ecology and, 2636
millenarianism in, 6039
on peace, 7022
Taiping movement, 1609–1610
Huangdi and, 4144
as revolutionary millennial movement, 6549
as utopian vision, 1628
Taiping Rebellion (184 CE), 8961
Taiping Rebellion (1850–1864)
Christian elements in, 7257, 7268, 8961
leader of, 7022, 7268, 8961
millenarianism of, 6041
Qing authority challenged by, 4633
Taiping tianguo (heavenly kingdom of highest peace), 6041
Taiqing (component of Daoist canon), 2203, 2205
Tai Shan (mountain). *See* Tai, Mount
Taishang ganying pian, 1632
Taishang Laojun (Lord Lao the Most High), 1593, 2204, 2209, 5319. *See also* Laozi
Taishang zhuguo jiumin zongzhen biyao (Daoist text), 2206
Taishen (fetus spirit), 2407
Taishitsu (inborn constitution), health and, 3867
Taishō period (Japan)
intellectual climate of, 9315
Kojiki commentaries during, 4807
Tait, Peter Guthrie, 937
Taittirīya Brāhmaṇa, lotus in, 5518
Taiwan and Taiwanese religions, **8962–8967**
affliction in, 59
Buddhism, 1168, 8962–8963
Chinese Buddhism and, 8963
Compassion Relief (Ciji) movement, **1787–1790**
Foguangshan, **3139–3141**
Japanese Buddhism and, 8962
laity in, 8963, 8964–8965
nuns, 6757, 6761
Tibetan Buddhism and, 8962
Buddhist organizations in, 8962–8963
Chinese religion in, 1610
Christianity, 1726, 8962, 8963–8964
missions, 8963–8964
Presbyterianism, 8963–8964
Protestantism, 8963–8964
Roman Catholicism, 8963, 8964
in colonial era, 8962, 8963
Confucianism, 8965
temples in, 9060
Daoism, 2189, 8963
jiao in, 4916
Jingming Daoism, 2207
music in, 6295
temples in, 9058
economic growth in, 8962
education in, 8963
freedom of religion in, 8962
history of, 8962
Islam, 8964
money in, 6138
as province of Republic of China, 8962
religious year in, 1641–1643
study of religion in, 1620, 1637, 8962
temple cults in, 8965–8966
travel to China from, 1610
vegetarianism in, 8964
Taiwan Association of Religious Studies, 8962
Taiwan Church News (journal), 8963
Taiwan Daoist Society, 2189
Taiwu (emperor)
as deity incarnate, 5317
as "Perfect Lord of Great Peace," 8961
and persecution of Buddhists, 2194
Taiwudi (Chinese emperor), 8994
Taixu (Buddhist monk), 1167, **8967–8968**
Taixuan (component of Daoist canon), 2203
Taiyi (deity), 1591
Taiyi sect, 1602, 9858, 9963
Ta'iyya (Ibn al-Fāriḍ), 7222
Tai-zhen ke (Daoist text), 2193
Taizhou school, 1578
Taizi (Buddhist monk), 4416
Taizōkai ritual, in Shingon training, 8351–8352
Taizong, 1599, 9861
Laozi and, 1602
Taizu (Ming dynasty ruler), 8995
and Daoism, 2187
Tāj al-Mulk, 6640
Tajāni Sufism, militant revivalism of, 8824
Tajdīd (renewal of Islam), in messianism, 5980–5981
Tajikistan, 4620. *See also* Central Asia and Central Asian religions
Islam in, 4621
in post-Soviet era, 4627, 4628
revival of, 4626
in Soviet era, 4624
sheep in, 8311
Tajin (deity), 9213
Taj Mahal, 4646
Tajrīd al-'aqā'id (Ṭūsī), 4571
Tajwīd (rules for Qur'ān recitation), 9201, 9202
Takachiho, Mount, 5180
Takaki (deity), Ninigi and, 5180
Takakusu Junjirō, 1314
Takao, Mount, 5213
Takemikazuchi no Mikoto (deity), 289
Takhts (seats of authority), in Sikhism, 8396
Takitumu canoe, 5682, 7309
Takīyah. See Khānagāh
Taklung Matrul Rinpoche. *See* Stag lung Ma sprul Rin po che
Takuan (tea master), 847–848
Takuan Sōhō (Buddhist monk), 9949
Tāla (rhythmic cycle), 2496
in Indian music, 6279
Ta'lab (deity), Meccan pilgrimage to, 3778
Talaba (body of scholars), 4595
Talabah (religious student), hawzah and, 3801
Talaing people. *See* Mon people
Talamantez, Inés, 575
Tālapurāṇas (mythological stories), 8975, 8976, 8977
Ṭalāq (unilateral repudiation), 4708
Talas, Battle of, 1599
Talbot, Percy Amaury, 97
on Chukwu, 3572
on hierodouleia (sacred prostitution) in Ibo religion, 3969
Taleju (deity), 9605
Tale of Genji, The (Murasaki Shikibu), 3057
Tales. *See also* Fairy tales; Folklore
in typology of narratives, 6376–6377
Ṭalḥa ibn 'Ubayd Allāh, 'Alī opposed by, 258
Taliban (Afghanistan)
destruction of art by, vol. 11 color insert
globalization and, 3501, 3502
and law, 4703
Taliesin (Welsh poet), **8968–8969**
poetry ascribed to, 1480
as vaticinatory poet, 8968–8969
Taliesin, Book of, Annwn in, 371
Ta'līmīyah movement. *See also* Nizārī Ismā'īlīyah
"new preaching" doctrine in, 8333
Talion, law of, 4738, 4742, 5372–5374, 7779, 7782–7783
Talismans. *See* Amulets and talismans
Talking drums, 2495–2496, 7037
Tallensi religion, ancestor worship in, 321
Tallis, Thomas, 6311
Tallith (garment), 9088
TallMountain, Mary, 7225–7226
Talmud, **8969–8972**. *See also* Halakhah; Mishnah
Abbaye in, Rava' and, 3
amoraim and, 294–295, 8970
'Aqiva' ben Yosef in, 441
authority of *Zohar vs.,* 3751

Talmud ***continued***
Babylonian, 868
Alfasi's preference for, 255
Aramaic citations in, 889
authors of, 8970
Beruryah in, 843, 844
biblical books listed in, 882
as center of Judaism, 4988
demons in, 2278, 3158, 5458
kashrut laws in, 5106
on *merkavah,* 10050
nonviolence in, 6647
Onkelos in, 887
primacy of, 8970–8971
in rabbinic Judaism, 4976
Rashi's commentaries on, 7619–7620
study of, 8970–8971
tannaitic texts in, 8983
technical terminology in, 8970
Torah commandments in, 9235
tsaddiq in, 9377
Beit Hillel *vs.* Beit Shammai disputes in, 815
blasphemy in, 969
canonization of, 9275
casuistry and, 1454
chanting of, 1532
Christian censorship of, 968
Christian polemics on, 7233
circumcision in, 7818–7819
commentary on (*See also* Tosafot)
geonic, 3745–3746, 4989
from Kairouan, 4990
dance in, 2137
demons in, 2277–2278
derashah (scholarly discourse) on, 4482
destruction of manuscripts of, 8971
developments of, 8970–8971
divination banned in, 2373
as doctrine, 2382
on *Ecclesiastes,* 2600
on Elisha' ben Avuyah, apostasy of, 2769
Eliyyahu ben Shelomoh Zalman and, 2773
God in, 3547–3548
names for, 3547–3548
H'ai Gaon on, 3737
healing and medicine in, 3829
Hillel (Jewish sage) in, 3981
Holdheim (Samuel) on, 4080
humor in, 4196
Jerusalem (Palestinian), 868
body and soul in, 8557
characteristics of, 8970
dating of, 8970
demons in, 2278, 3158
Eliyyahu ben Shelomoh Zalman and, 2773
Onkelos in, 887
tannaitic texts in, 8983
Jesus in, 7231
Kagan's (Yisra'el Me'ir) study of, 5053
Karaism and, 4991
kashrut laws in, 5106, 5107
martyrdom in, 5742
matrilineal Jewish identity in, 3751
meaning of term, 8970
memorization of, 5852
Messiah in, 7233
Mishnah in, 6068
mitsvot in, 3201
necromancy mentioned in, 6452
as oral law, not scripture, 1406
origins of, 8969–8970
purity in, 7514, 7515
in rabbinic Judaism, 4976
in Reform Judaism, 4983, 7665
rejection of, by Karaites, 5082
role of law in, 8971
role of study and intellect in, 8971
Satan in, 8124
service prayer liturgy in, 8389
Shavu'ot in, 8305
Sherira' Gaon on, 8320
Shim'on bar Yoh'ai in, 8346–8347
Shim'on ben Gamli'el II in, 8347
Shim'on ben Laqish in, 8347–8348
Soloveitchik (Joseph Baer) on, 8518–8519
soul in, 8557–8558
study of
in Geonic period, 3744–3745
Hoffmann (David) on, 4077
Luria (Shelomoh) on, 5533
medieval, 5012
Orthodoxy and, 6901
pilpul method of, 5533
and religious authority, 8971–8972
as religious experience, 8971, 8972
Soloveitchik (Joseph Baer) and, 8518
Tam's (Ya'aqov ben Me'ir) commentary on, 8972
teaching of, in rabbinical seminaries, 7581
Temple procedures in, 927
title of rabbi in, 7578
Torah personified in, 4079
translation of
Salanter (Yisra'el) on, 8053
Spektor (Yitshaq Elhanan) on, 8674
visiting the sick in, 3828
vows in, 9641
women in, 3352
Talmudic Judaism. *See* Rabbinic Judaism
Talus panel, 9066
Tam, Ya'aqov ben Me'ir, **8972–8973,** 9941
biblical exegesis of, 4982
Tama (animating spirits), 4781
Tamadad (diviner), 6005
Tamahori, Lee, 3097
Tamam Siswa movement, Hindu-Buddhist-Javanist revival and, 8652–8653
Tamaniu (double), in Mota religion (Melanesia), 8533
Tama no mahashira (Hirata Atsutane), creation myth interpreted in, 4022
Tamar (biblical figure), 34, 7948
Tamas (darkness/dullness), 853, 2305, 3709
in Sāṃkhya cosmology, 2016
Tamaš, Andželika, 766
Tambiah, Stanley J., 1313
on Buddhist polity, 8079
on canon, 1262
on forest dwellers, 8080
on Leach (Edmund), 8757
on magic, 5567, 5572
on *maṇḍalas,* 5645
on rituals, 7836
Tambor de Mata. *See* Terecô
Tambor de Mina (Brazil), 120
Tambor de Nagô (Brazil), 120
Tambourine, 2494
Tambu (relative by marriage), 8948
Tamfana (deity), 3450
Tamhīd (al-Bāqillānī), 5064–5066
Tamid (offering), 928
Tamil language, fiction in, 10035–10036
Tamil religions, **8973–8979**. *See also* Nāyaṉārs
Bhāgavatism, 9503
bhakti in, 857, 858, 859, 8974–8975, 8976, 8977
Buddhism, 8974, 8975
Christianity, 8977–8978
contemporary, 8978–8979
deities of, 4434 (*See also* Murukaṉ)
drums in, 2499
early, 8973–8974
festivals in, 8977
funeral rites in, 8973
gambling in, 3263
Hinduism
medieval, 8975–8977
spread of, 8974
Islam, 4644, 8976
literature, 4649
Jainism, 8974, 8975
Judaism, 8977
Kāma festival in, 4081
labyrinth patterns in, 5275
medieval, 8975–8977
Neolithic, 8973
poetry of, 857, 7207, 7210, 8974–8975, 8976, 8977, 10088
priesthood in, 8973
Rāmānuja and, 7614
saint-singer poetry and, 4005
in Śaiva Siddhanta in, 8042–8043, 8418, 9443
Śaivism
canon of, 5999
poetry of, 5671
spirit possession in, 8973
Śrī Vaiṣṇavas Sampradāya, **8727–8728**
temples in, 8975, 8977, 8979
texts of, Ājīvikas in, 212–213, 3639
Vaiṣṇavism, 4430
women in, 3020–3021
Tamīmī, 'Ubaydah Muslim al-, 5127
Tamīm ibn Baḥr, 4492
Tamiris, Helen, 2159, 2163
Tammaa (otherworld), 9396
Tammätamma (kettledrum), 2497
Tammuz (deity/mythic figure). *See also* Dumuzi
Adonis assimilated with, 34, 35
in Babylonian hymn, 3968
Christ, parallels with, 8303
as fecundator, 2985
iconography of, 4317
resurrection of, 2521, 2538–2539
rivers and, 7861
Tammuz, Fast of, in Jewish calendar, 4866
Tamoanchan (heaven), myths about, 5934
Tamoi (deity), as creator, 8578
Tam-tam gong, 7036
Tamure Encho, on Shotoku Taishi, 8375
Tam Wai-lun, 1638
Tanabata (Star Festival), 2411
Tanabe Hajime, 1302
Tanaka Chigaku, 6608
Tanaka Takako, 3347
Tanakh (scripture), 878. *See also* Hebrew scriptures
as canon, 1406, 1410
Tan Chundan, 2210
Tanco, Luis Becerra, 5922
Tandava (dance), 7043
Tane (deity), 6788, 7306, 7313, 7314. *See also* Kāne
Tanen (many-calling), 819
Tangaloa (deity), 5727, 7305, 7313, 7314, 8980. *See also* Tangaroa
Tanganyika
Christian missions to, colonial government established by, 2578
Islam in, 2571
Kinjikitile in, 5181
Maji Maji Wars in, 5181
water cults in, 2571
Tangaroa (deity), **8980–8981**. *See also* Kanaloa
Christianity's impact on, 8980–8981
cult of, 8980
fagu (sacred chant) of, 8980, 8981
mythology of, 7305, 7313, 7314, 8980

role of, 8980
Tang Code (Chinese code of law), 5353
Tang dynasty (China), 1576–1577, 1596, 2801
alchemy in, 2184–2185
Buddhism in, 1164–1165, 1250
Buddhist schools, 1240
Chinese canon, 1254, 1257, 7269
festivals, 1305, 1308
laws concerning, 5349, 5353
Maitreya in, 5620
meditation, 1294
monasticism of, 6129
Paramārtha and, 6992
persecution of, 7213, 7255, 7268
philosophy, 1302
pilgrimage, 7165
temples of, 9045, 9047
Tiantai school, 1237
Xuanzang and, 9860–9861
Zhenyan, 9963
Confucianism in, 1899–1900, 1909
and drama, 2455
iconography of, 4337
Mengzi and, 5858
temples of, 9059
tian in, 9173
Daoism in, 1602, 2184–2185, 2189, 2194–2197, 7267
Du Guangting and, 2517
iconography in, 4333–4334
literature of, 2205
priesthood in, 7414–7415
temples of, 9056–9057
Islam in, 4631
law in, 5353
Manichaeism in, 5669
poetry in, 7207, 7213–7214
taiping in, 8961
Tang Gaozu, 2196
Tan'gol mudang (Korean shamans), 5234–5235
Tangoma (diviners), in Swazi religion, 8896
Tango no Sekku (Boys' Day), 2411
Tängri (deity). *See* Tengri
Tang school, 1576–1577
Tangshangyue (ensemble), 6293
Tan'gun (Korean mythical figure), 5229–5230
Tangu religion, 6802
Tang Yongtong, **8981**
Taṅhā, reincarnation and, 7678
Tanḥuma' (midrash), 6018
Taniguchi, Masaharu, 6573–6574, 6587
Tanimbar Islands, 991
Tanit (deity), 7911
Latin name of, 4252
and North African Islam, 4580
in Phoenican religion, 7130, 7134
tattoo as symbol of, 1002
Tanjong (Chosŏn king), 5232
Tanka (New Year's verse), 7217
Tanlin (Buddhist monk), 994
Tanluan, 1577, **8981–8983**
Daochuo and, 2176
Daoism and, 292
life of, 8981–8982
in Pure Land Buddhism, 291, 292, 1239, 1600–1601, 4922, 8981, 8982
and recitative *nianfo,* 6602
and Shinran, 8981, 8982
Tao Hongjing and, 8982
writings of, 8981, 8982
Tanna (island). *See* Vanuatu
Tanna de-vei Eliyyahu, 2765–2766
Tanna/tannaim (Jewish scholars), **8983–8984**
amoraim and, 294
ʿAqiva' ben Yosef as, 441–442
Elʿazar ben ʿAzaryah as, 2743
Eliʿezer ben Hyrcanus as, 2763–2764
Elishaʿ ben Avuyah as, 2769
etymology of term, 8983
and exegesis, direct *vs.* indirect, 3748
Gamli'el of Yavneh as, 3269–3270
Me'ir as, 5830
memorization by, 5852
on resurrection, 8557
Yehoshuʿa ben Levi and, 9876
Yehudah bar Ilʿai, 9876–9877
Yehudah ha-Nasi', 9880–9881
Yishmaʿe'l ben Elishaʿ, 9890–9891
Yose ben Ḥalafta', 9912–9913
Tanner, Adrian, 6671
Tanngnjóstr (goat), 9166
Tanngrisnir (goat), 9166
Tannin. *See* Tunnan
Tannishō (Shinran), 5101
Tanqīḥ al-abḥāth fī al-milal al-thalāth (Ibn Kammūnah), 7240–7241
Tanshihuai (Xianbei leader), 4491
Tantalos, 165, 9453
Ṭanṭāwī, Muḥammad Sayyid, at al-Azhar university, 231
Tantiaishan zhi (Daoist text), 2208
Tantrāloka (Abhinavagupta), 8–9, 8990
mantras in, 5678
Tantras
arrangement of, 1215–1215
Cakrasamvara, **1349–1350**
definition of, 1214
Guhyasamāja, 1401, **3708–3709**
Hindu, **4019–4020**
"intentional language" in, 8240
in Vaiṣṇavism, 9501–9502
called Saṃhitās, 4019
of Pāñcarātra sect, 4020
language of, 1216
mahāmudrā in, 5596–5597
meaning of term, 4019
Mother or Yoginī, 1349
prajñā in, 7359
sexuality in, 8240
in Shingon tradition, 8348, 8349
Yoga, Vajrasattva in, 9514
Tāntrika (practitioner of Tantra), 8987, 8989
Tantrism, **8984–8994**. *See also* Zhenyan
asceticism in, 529
in Balinese religion, 748
body as interior *maṇḍala,* 1503
Buddhist (*See* Vajrayāna (Tantric) Buddhism)
cakras, **1348–1349**
in China, Mongols and, 1606
creation myths in, language in, 5302
of Crowley (Aleister), 6874–6875
Daoist, 8985
desire in, 2305
Evola (Julius) influenced by, 2905
French feminists and, 3029, 3030
fundamentals of, 8985–8986
geographical spread of, 8984–8985
Hindu, 4430, **8987–8994**
anti-ascetic attitude in, 8991–8992
as anti-Brahmanic, 4002–4003
asceticism of, 9822–9823
Āyurveda and, 714
in Bengal, 825, 827, 4430
Caitanya's influence on, 1347
controversial practices of, 8991
creation in, 5302
definitional traits of, 8990–8993
development of, 4002
as extension of Vedism and *bhakti* Hinduism, 4002
goddess worship in, 3609
Haṭhayoga in, 3794
invocations in, 5307
jīvanmuka and, 4926
language in, 5302
left-handed Savism, 8015
"left hand" *vs.* "right hand" practice in, 4003
maṇḍalas in, 5640–5641
mantras in, 4430, 5677–5678
meditation in, 5820
mystical physiology in, 8992–8993
non-Vedic practices of, 8990–8991
orgiastic practices in, 8050
origins of, 8985, 8989
pañcamākarapūjā (five m's) practice in, 4003
pūjā in, 4430
puruṣa and *prakṛti,* experience of unity of, 4003
Śākta tradition in, liberation in, 8547
Śakti worship in, 2526
secrecy in, 8992
sexuality in, 8991, 8992
siddhīs (magical powers) in, 4003
traditions of, 8989–8990
Western appropriations of, 8993–8994
yoga in, 1045, 9822
human body in, 8991–8993
iconoclasm in, 4284
institutionalization and domestication of, 8986
Jain, 8985
literature of (*See* Tantras)
lotus symbolism in, 5518
magic in, 5589
maithuna (ritualized sexual union) in, 8240
meaning of term, 8987
orgy in, 6878–6879
origin of term, 8984, 8987
origins of, 8985, 8987–8988
phallus in, 7083, 7084
practitioners of, 8987
primitive, 8986
representation of, 8988–8989
right-hand *vs.* left-hand, sexual practices in, 8240
sacred language in, 5304
Śaiva (*See* Śaivism)
sectarian, 8989–8990
semen as elixir in, 2771
sexual activity in (*See* Sexuality, in Tantrism)
Siddha practitioners and, 1349–1350
Sikh, White Tantric Yoga of Yogi Bhajan, 3878
silence in, 5305
stereotypes of, 8987
studies on, 8987, 8988–8989
use of term, 8987
vagina in, 7083, 7084
of Vajrabodhi, 9510
Vajradhara in, 9510–9511
violence of, 9599
virginity in, 9605
in West, sexual magic and, 8251

Tantrism *continued*
yoni in, 9905–9909
Tanu (Vedic concept), death and, 8545
Tanusi (deity), 9415
Tan Yang Zi, 3342
Tanyao (Buddhist monk), 1164, **8994–8995**
Tanzania
Chagga people of
African Independent Churches among, 2571
mortuary rituals of, 140
charismatic Christianity in, 106
cults of affliction in, 62
Gogo people of (*See* Gogo religion)
Islam in, 2571, 4608, 4609
masquerade dances in, 2140
Nyakyusa people of (*See* Nyakyusa religion)
prophetic movements in, 2570
Sandawe people of, dances of, 2137
Yao people of (*See* Yao religion and society)
Tanzhausen, and dance, 2154
Tan Zixiao, 2185
Tao Hongjing, 1597, **8996–8997**
alchemy and, 241, 8996
and Buddhism, 8997
Ge Hong and, 3291, 8996
and medicine, 8997
study of Daoism, 2182–2183, 2209, 8996
Tanluan and, 8982
writings of, 8996
Taoism. *See* Daoism
Tao Qian (poet), 7213
Tao-quân (deity), 9593
Tao-t'ai pattern (Chinese), 9273
Tapā Gaccha sect of Jainism, 4766
Tapahonso, Luci, 7226
Tapas (heat), **8997–8999**. *See also* Asceticism, Hindu
in devotional life, 9822
generated by ascetic, 4443
in Hinduism, 8998
power of, 7350, 8998
Prajāpati as result of, 7356, 8998
in Vedism, 8997, 8998
Tapasya (renunciation), Gandhi (Mohandas) on, 3272
Tapat (ritual expert), in Majangir religion, 2574
Tapa wankayeyapi (ball throwing), 752
Tapa Wankayeyapi (Lakota sacred rite), 5297
Tapirape religion (Brazil)
healers in, 3812
Sun and moon in, 2863
tricksters in, 9358
Ta Prohm, temple at, 5129
Tapu (forbidden/sacred), 3397, 6786, 7307–7308, 8947
consecrational, 8947
Cook (James) on, 8947
definition of, 5679, 5683
duration of, 7308
establishing, 7308, 7309, 8947
function of, 8947
and *mana*, 8947
in Maori religion, 5679–5682, 5683, 5684
termination of, 7309–7311
in Tikopia religion, 9195
Tapuí and Guasurangwe people (Paraguay), 8634
Taqāmus (reincarnation), 2504
taqīyah (self-protection), 729, **8999–9000**
Taqlīd (religious duty)
and *ijtihād*, 4374
Ash'arīyah opposing, 536
Baḥye ibn Paquda on, 741
doctrine of, 4697
and gender in Islam, 3365
Ibn Taymīyah on, 4699
modernist interpretation of, 6096
Uṣūlīyah and, 8307
Taqqanot (or *taanot*, enactments of Jewish law)
of Babylonian Gaonate, 4989
in *halakhah* system, 3746, 3749–3750
power of repeal, 3750
Taqui Onqoy ("the dance of the Pleiades")
messianism of, 5984
as resistance movement, 3815
Taqwā (protect or save), origin of word, 4560
Taqwiyat al-imān (Shahīd), 4651
Tārā (deity), **9000–9001**
as feminine counterpart of Avalokiteśvara, 1079, 1082, 9000
Atīśa and, 592
cult of, 1224, 9000
diamond as symbol of, 2345
gender of, 3333
iconography of, 4330, 9000
as Lady of the Animals, 5280
maṇḍala of, 9000
as mother of all buddhas, 1080
origins of, 9000
popularity of, 3977
Tara (sacred Celtic place)
sacral kingship and, 1492
as sacred space, 1491
Tarahumara Indians. *See* Rarámuri Indians
Tarai (deity), 6454
Tāraka (demon), Śiva and, 8040
Taraknatha, temple of, orientation of, 7982
Taranga (mythic figure), 5782
Taranis (deity), 1483
Tarascan religion, **9001–9002**
afterlife in, 151
deities of, 5909
fiestas in, 9001, 9002
in Postclassic period, 5909
priesthood in, 5909, 9002
rituals in, 9001, 9002
supernatural in, 9001–9002
Tarasios (Byzantine patriarch), 4290, 6619, **9003**
Tarde, Gabriel, 5785
Tardieu, Michel, 3535
Tardi-Gravettian culture, 6462
Tarekat (religious movements), 4818
Ṭarfon (Jewish scholar), **9003**
Justin Martyr and, 5044
Targhib wa'l-tarhīb, al-, authenticity of *ḥadīths* and, 3732
Targitaus (deity), mythological birth of, 8205
Targum Jonathan, 888
Targum Onkelos, 887–888
on *shekhinah*, 8313
Targum/targumin, 887–889
to *Deuteronomy*, 888
to *Ketuvim*, 889
to *Nevi'im*, 889
to *Numbers*, 888
to *Proverbs*, 889
Samaritan, 888–889
Targum Yerushalmi. *See Targum Jonathan*
Tarhunza (deity), Adad and, 28
Ta'rikh al-Fattash (West-African chronicle), 4603
Ta'rīkh al-rusul wa-al-mulūk (al-Tabari), 8943, 8944
Ta'rikh al-Sudan (West African chronicle), 4603
Ta'rīkh Ifrīqiyā wa-al-Maghrib (Ibn al-Raqīq), 4584
Tari Pennu, in Khond ritual sacrifice, 2556
Ṭarīqah (brotherhood), **9003–9015**
alternative terms for, 9005
in Anatolia, 9007
Mawlawīyah *vs.* Bektāshīyah, 8822–8823
in Caucasus, 4615, 9007
in Central Asia, 4621, 9007, 9010
communal life in, 9005–9006
decline of, 8824–8825
as established institution, 9006
influence of, 9004, 9012
initiation rituals in, 9006, 9011
in Iraq, Suhrawardīyah *vs.* Rifā'īyah, 8823
and Islamic reform movements, 9011, 9012
Jamā'ī Sunni legalism and, 8855
masters and disciples in, 8820
in Middle Volga, 4616
in North Africa, 9011
criticism of, 4588, 4589–4590
establishment of, 4588
popularity of, 4589
principle of, 4588
Shādhilīyah, 8823
in North America, 9007
opponents of, 9012
origin of term, 9004
origins and early development of, 9004
in Ottoman Empire, 9006, 9008
overview of, 8820–8825
ritual practice in, 8821–8822
dhikr (remembrance) and *samā'* (audition) in, 8822
role of women in, 9007
Schuon (Fritjhof) and, 1324
silsilahs (lineages) in, 8820–8821
social aspects of, 8822
social ethics and etiquette in, 9006–9007
spiritual authority of, 9005
spiritual exercises in, 9004–9005
in sub-Saharan Africa, 4609
in Turkey, 9007, 9012
variety of, 8824
veneration of saints in, 8821
Ṭarīqah (path), 9003
shaykhs and, 8710
Sirhindī (Aḥmad) on, 8414
Tarjumān al-ashwāq (Ibn al-'Arabī), 4257, 7222
Tarjumān al-Qur'ān (Azād), 8955
Tarjumān al-Qur'ān (journal), 4772
Tarkajvālā (Bhāvaviveka), 861, 1300
Tarn, Nathaniel, 5945
Tarn, William, on Alexander the Great, 3901
Tarot cards
history of, 1414
symbolic images on, vol. 14 color insert
Tarquinius Priscus (Etruscan king), 5167, 7337
Tarruku (ceremonial event), 9695
Tart, Charles, 607
on paranormal phenomena, 7478
on states of consciousness, 1952
Tartaros (underworld), Hesiod on, 8426
Tartessos. *See* Iberian Peninsula
Tarvos Trigaranus (The Bull of the Three Cranes), 1487
Taryō, Ōbayashi, 4464
Tarzs, Rebazar, Eckankar and, 2602
Tasan. *See* Chŏng Yagyong
Taṣdīq (affirmation), 4399
Tashahhud (witnessing), in *ṣalāt* (prayer), 8058
Taṣḥīh al-i' tiqād (al-Mufīd), 4262
Tashkent (Uzbekistan), Jews in, 5009
Tashlikh rite, 3159, vol. 1 color insert
Tasman, Abel, 5679
Tassel (garment), 9088
Tasso, Torquato, 3627–3628, 7219–7220
Tata, Jamshedji N., 6998

Tatariki *(atua),* 5680
Tatar republic, 5708, 5709
Tatars
in Caucasus, 4614
in Central Asia, 4622
in Europe, 4673–4674, 4678
in Middle Volga
converting to Christianity, 4616–4617
economic threat to, 4617–4618
jadid renaissance of, 4617, 4618–4619
language and literature of, 4618
persecution of, 4617, 4619
poetry of, 4616
politics of, 4618–4619
under Soviet rule, 4619
Tate, Nahum, 5356
Tatewarí (deity), 9357
in Huichol religion, 4152, 4153
Tath, Huot, 5131
Tathāgata, **9015–9017**
arising of, 7364
Buddha as, 1063, 1106, 9015
etymology of term, 9015
in Mahāsāṃghika Buddhism, 9015
in Mahāyāna Buddhism, 9015, 9016
in Theravāda Buddhism, 9015
as intuition, 4525
worship of, 1117, 7496
Tathāgata-garbha (buddha nature), 2628–2629, **9017–9019**. *See also* Buddha mind; Buddha nature
doctrine of, 1250, 9017, 9018
in East Asian Buddhism, 9018
elements of, 1123
Huayan school on truth in, 4148
in Mahāyāna Buddhism, 1070, 1120, 9017
rebirth and, 8552
innate potential for, 9016
in Vajrayāna Buddhism, 1070, 9018
Nāgārjuna on, 9017
in Tibetan Buddhism, 9018
Yogācāra school on emptiness and, 8858
Tathāgatagarbha Sūtra (Bu ston), 9017–9018
Tathāgataguhya Sūtra (Buddhist text), 1270
Tathatā (suchness), 9016, **9019–9020**
aspects of, 9019
sources on, 9020
true nature of, 9020
Tatian
on apocatastasis, 422
on *hypostasis,* 4241
on immortality, 157
writings of, 906, 922
Tatius, Achilles, 3050, 3052
Tattaro-Robuga (deity), 4508
Tattooing, 1001–1003, 9170
of hands, 3770
in Maori religion, vol. 13 color insert
masks and, 5765, 5766
in Oceanic religion, 7807–7808
in prison, in Mexico, vol. 6 color insert
religious iconography in, vol. 13 color insert
in Southeast Asian religions, traditional, 8650
of Zalmoxis, 9928
Tattvārtha Sūtra, 2624, 4768
Tattvasaṃgraha (Buddhist text)
arguments in, 8106–8107
influence of, 1214
mahāmudrā in, 5596
Mahāvairocana in, 5607
Shingon school based on, 1217–1218
Yoga Tantras in, 1215
Tattvavaiśāradī (Miśra), meditation in, 8704
Tattvopaplavasiṃha, 1446–1447
Taube, Karl, 750, 5943, 5944
Taubes, Jakob, **9020–9021**
Täubler, Eugen, 4881
Taufa'ahau (Tonga chief), 9322
Tauhid (exclusive divinity of Allāh), 4385
Tauler, Johannes, 3003, **9021**
asceticism of, 527
under Eckhart (Johannes), 2603, 9022
on mystical union, 6337
Neoplatonism and, 6475
sermons of, 9022
on spiritual life, 9022
Taulipáng religion (South America)
hunting dances of, 8581
World Fire myth in, 8589
Taurians, Artemis and, 507
Taurobolium (ritual)
as baptism of blood, 780
in cult of Cybele, 1452, 2110, 2249
in cult of Magna Mater, 3385, 7917, 7922
Tauros, Calvenus (Calvenos)
on Demiurge, 7189
on *Timaeus* (Plato), 7189
Taussig, Michael, 6440, 9297
on spirit possession, 8696
Tausun Tara (mythical dog), 2393
Tau-tau (effigy), use in funeral rites, 3234, 3237
Tauxier, Louis, 115, 116
Tavener, John, 6313
Tavernier, Jean-Baptiste, 4446
Tavgi Samoyed. *See* Samoyed religion
Tävibo (Indian), 3473
ṭawāf (circumambulation), in *ḥājj,* 1797, 7158, 7160
Tawahedo (Unionite) Orthodox Church. *See* Ethiopian Church
Tawajjuh (face-to-face concentration), 9005
Tawallā, 9656
Tawbah (repentance). *See* Repentance, in Islam
Taweret (deity), 3597
Tawḥīd (God's unity). *See also* Kalām
'Abd al-Jabbār on, 4
as attribute of God, 617, 618, 3562
in confession of faith, 8014
definition of, 3562
Druze on, 2502–2503, 2504
Ḥasan al-Bannā' on, 108
Ibn 'Abd al-Wahhāb on, 4255, 4258
Ibn al-'Arabī on, 3566
Ibn Tūmart on, 4586
in Qur'ān, 3562
in Wahhābīyah, 9654
Mu'tazilah on, 5063, 6322
mystical union and, 6338, 6339
nature in, 2604
in Sufism, 3566
worship and, 9816
Tawhiri (deity), 7313, 7314
Ta'wīl
comparison with *tafsīr,* 7561, 8810, 8950
in Qur'anic exegesis, 4761, 7561
Sufism and, 8810
Ta'wīlāt al-Qur'ān (al-Māturīdī), 8950
Ta'wīl mushkil al-Qur'ān (Ibn Qutaybah), 8952
Tawiskara (deity), 2985
Tawiskaron (deity), 6680, 9413, 9414
Tawney, R. H., 9709
Ṭawq al-ḥamāmah (Ibn Ḥazm), 4268
Tawwābīn, al-, 550
Taxation. *See also* Tithes
Charavilh tax on remarriage, 1441
of clergy, in Roman Catholicism, 1019
Crusade taxes, 2076
in Hawaiian religion, 3798
Islamic, 4582 (*See also* Zakāt)
jizyal/jizyah (poll tax), 4562, 6997, 6998
khums (religious tax) and the hawzah, 3801
Israelite, 928–931
Tayama Katai, 3072
Ṭayfūriyya, 956
Ta'yīd al-millah (al-Rāqilī), 7240
Taylor, Apriana, 3085
Taylor, Bron, 2612
Taylor, Caroline, 3095–3096
Taylor, Charles, 2951
Taylor, Clarence, 74
Taylor, Eugene, on James (William), 4776
Taylor, Hudson, 6084
Taylor, John (English farmer), 973
Taylor, John V., on African concept of God, 8656
Taylor, Joshua, on Swedenborg (Emanuel), 8899–8900
Taylor, Luke, 668, 4305
Taylor, Mark, 3297
Taylor, Mark C., 2247, 5487, 5489
Taylor, Nathaniel W., 2532
and Noyes (John Humphrey), 6732
Taylor, Paul, 2161, 2163, 2655
Taylor, Richard, on Maori religion, 5680
Taylor, Thomas, Shrine of Wisdom, influence on, 3953
Taylor, Walter, 452
Taylor, William B., on devotional landscapes, 8610
Taymīyah family, Ḥanābilah and, 3768
Tay Ninh, Vietnam, Cao Dao movement and, 1412
Tayū (priest), 7411
Ṭayyibīyah movement, 4395
doctrines of, 8335
imams in, 8334–8335
Indian communities of, 8335–8336
origin of, 8324
Ta'ziyah (passion play), 4572, **9022–9023**
al-Ḥusayn ibn 'Alī and, 4236
Taz religion. *See* Southern Siberian religions
TBN. *See* Trinity Broadcasting Network
Tchaikovsky, Pieter Ilyich, 6312
Te (deity), 6264
Tea, 847–848
in Japan, 2741
psychedelic, 7470
Tea ceremony, Japanese. *See Chanoyu*
Teachings of Silvanus (Nag Hammadi text)
hypostasis in, 4241
wisdom in, 9760
Tears, **9023–9027**
absence of, 9025
characteristics of, 9024
liminal nature of, 9024
phenomenological nature of, 9023–9026
physiological function of, 9023
and pollution, 9024
power of, 9026
as signs and symbols, 9026–9027

Tears ***continued***
sociopolitical function of, 9024–9025
Tebo Deves (deity), 757
Tech nDuinn (deity), 1485
Technical theosophy, 7230
Technology
and art, study of, 502
Buddhist, missions and, 6079
and dance, 2142
deities of, 3623
knotted ropes as, 5197
in Micronesian myths, 6012
and pilgrimage, 7147
and religious practice, 2142
Technomorphic cosmologies, sky and stars in, 8423–8424
Tecpillatolli (language of court), 2465
Tecuciztecatl (deity), 5888, 5935
self-sacrifice of, 4187
Tecuhtli (titled lord), in Aztec Mexico, 5172
Tecumseh (Shawnee leader), **9027–9029**
Cherokee and, 1565, 9027
as head of Iroquois Confederacy, 6665
influence of, 9027
in intertribal movements, 9027–9028
Tedlock, Barbara, 2485, 2488
Teellinck, Willem, 7142
Teens for Christ, 2987
Teê Pijopac (deity), 6500
Teeth
Assyrian chant-remedy for toothache, 3811
of the Buddha, as relic, 7690, 7691
filing of, in Balinese religion, 748
Tefillah (prayer), 983
in *siddur* and *maḥzor,* 8388, 8389
Tefillin (phylacteries), 4482, 7820
Tefnut (deity), in Egyptian pantheon, 2704
Tegh Bahadur, and *Ādi Granth,* 32
Tehbaek, Mount, 5179
Tehillim. See Psalms
Teḥinnot (supplications), 9036
Tehuelche Indians
annihilation of, 9029
language of, 9029
Tehuelche religion (Argentina), **9029–9032**
cosmology in, 9029
creation in, 9030
deities in, 9030
dualism in, 9030
high gods in, 8589
mythology in, 9030–9031
rituals in, 9029–9030
Selk'nam, relation to, 8224
supreme being in, 8579
Teichtal, Yissachar Shelomoh, 9382
Teichthal, Issachar, on Holocaust, 4091
Te-ika (mythic figure), 6012
Teilhard de Chardin, Pierre, 838, **9032–9035**
cosmology and, 2610
Eliade (Mircea) on, 9034
on evolution, 3558, 9032, 9033
evolution mysticism of, 2658
expeditions to China, 9033
on grace, 3646–3647
historiography of, 4032
on human beings, 9033–9034
on knowledge, 5209
life of, 9032–9033
Sorokin (Pitirim Aleksandrovich) compared to, 8525
theistic evolution and, 8190
Teima, Aramean religion in, 448
Teit, James A., 6671
Teitelbaum, Yo'el
on Holocaust, cause of, 4091
as *rebbe,* 9382
Satmar Hasidism and ultraorthodoxy of, 3793
Tekakwitha, Kateri, **9035–9036**
Tekhines, 3828, **9036–9038**
collections of, 9036–9037
modern developments of, 9037–9038
origins of, 9036–9037
significance of, 9037
Tekke (retreat), 9005. *See also* Khānagāh
Te Kooti, 5682, 5683
Tel Dan inscription, interpretations of, 2224
Teleios (perfect), 7038
Telemachus (Odysseus's son), power of, 5166
Teleological ethics, desire in, 2303
Teleology
of common good, 8492
Crescas (Ḥasdai) on, 2069
ethics, teleological approach to, 1650, 1656
of Herder (Johann Gottfried), 3919
Hobbes (Thomas) on, 4074
in proofs for existence of God, 7422, 9105–9106
Schleiermacher (Friedrich) on, 8165
scientific method and, 2911
Socrates on, 8504
Telepathy, 6057
in UFO religions, 9434
Telepinu (deity), 38
as vanishing deity, in Hittite myth, 4069
Telete (Orphic rite), 6893–6894
Televangelism, 5806
Television. *See also* Media
entertainment, 5806
evangelism on, 5806
popular culture rituals and, 7859
Qur'ān recitation on, 9202
religious broadcasting on, 7323, 7711–7712
in Communist countries, 7713–7714
in Europe, 7713–7714
fundamentalist Christian *vs.* modernist, 7711–7712
Graham (Billy) and, 7712
Humbard (Rex) and, 7711–7712
independent religious networks, 7712–7713
in Middle East, 7713
Roberts (Oral) and, 7712
Robertson (Pat) and, 7712–7713
Roman Catholic, 7712
Sheen (Fulton J.) and, 7712
in United States, 7711–7712
Tell al-'Amarna, 2707
Canaanite religion and, 1381
Tell Beydar(Syria), 2126
*Tell Bia (Syria), 2126
Tellem people, cave burial, 1472
*Tell Hariri (Syria), 1381, 2126
*Tell Mardih (Syria), 2125
Tell Meskene (Syria), Dagan in, 2126
Tell My Horse (Hurston), 76
Tello, Julio C., on Quechua religion, 8595
Tell Qasile (Philistine city), 7104
Tel Miqne inscription, 7103–7104
Telos (universal and ideal end), God as, Husserl (Edmund) on, 4237
Telpochcalli (people's houses), 9215
Te Makawe *(atua),* 5680
Témaukel (deity), 2310
in Selk'nam religion, 8224, 8579
Temazcal (sweat bath), 1472
Temenos (enclosed space), labyrinth as, 5275
Temmu (Japanese emperor), 6828
Tempels, Placide, 116, 117
Temperance movement, Social Gospel and, 1710
Tempier, Stephen, Aristotle and, 481
Templars. *See* Knights Templar
Temple, William, on free will and predestination, 3208
Temple festival *(Miaohui* or *saihui),* 1620
Temple Mount (Jerusalem)
Masjid al-aqsa as, 6205
in multiple religious traditions, 6214
Temple of Former Dynasts, 1913
Temple of Set, Satanism and, 8127
Temple of the Eastern Peak, 2200
Temple of the Sun, in Muisca religion, 6230
Temple of the Tooth (Sri Lanka), relic of the Buddha in, 7690
Temple of Vesta, circle symbolism in, 1792
Temple Propaganda: The Purpose and Character of 2 Maccabees (Doran), 901
Temple prostitution. *See* Hierodouleia
Temples, **9038–9067**. *See also* Sanctuaries; Shrines
African, 90
in Kushite religion, 5269
role of, 85, 90
for supreme beings, 3576
Aksumite, 224–225
altars in, 275
Arabian, 444
architecture of
classification of, 461, 464, 465
mountain symbolism in, 6212
for Ark of the Covenant
David and, 2222, 2223
music of, 2223
Armenian, 491
Balinese, 747, 748, 5828
Brahmanic, 9571–9572
Bronze Age, 9062
Buddhist, **9041–9056** (*See also* Stupas; Stupas and stupa worship)
along pilgrimage routes, 9043
anthropomorphism in, 389
based on *maṇḍalas,* 5643, 9047, 9050, 9051, 9052
in Brazil, 1188, 4789
Buddha images in, 9039
building materials of, 9049–9050
caves as, 9042, 9046, 9048
in China, 9045–9048
and Daoist temples, 9047
in East Asia, **9045–9049**
and Hindu temples, 9038, 9039
history of, 9054–9055
in Japan (*See* Japanese Buddhism, temples in)
in Korea, 9048
Shinto shrines and, 4784
in South Asia, **9041–9045**
in Southeast Asia, **9052–9056**
in Tibet, 9047–9048, **9049–9052,** 9184
in United States, 1188
Zen, 9948
as center of the world, 1502, 6886
Chinese, 1605, 1616, 1620
Christian (*See* Basilica; Cathedrals; Church architecture)
circular, 1792
Confucian, **9058–9060**
and Daoist temples, 9056
in Ming dynasty, 9060
in Qing dynasty, 9059, 9060
in Song dynasty, 9059

in Tang dynasty, 9059
Daoist, 2187, 2196–2197, 2200, **9056–9058**
Buddhist temples and, 9047
and Confucian temples, 9056
early, 9056
in Han dynasty, 9056
in Jin dynasty, 9057
in Liao dynasty, 9057
in Song dynasty, 9057
in Sui dynasty, 9056
in Tang dynasty, 9056–9057
terms for, 9056
in Zhou dynasty, 9057
Egyptian, 2714–2715, 9061–9062 (*See also* Pyramids, Egyptian)
at Abu Simel, 1472
administration of, 2725
of Amun, 301
daily rituals of, 2715
in Early Dynastic period, 9061
iconography of, 4318–4320
inscriptions on, 2725–2726, 2728
libraries of, 2715, 2723–2725
in Middle Kingdom, 9061
in New Kingdom, 9061–9062
in Old Kingdom, 9061
rituals performed at, 9061–9062
stellar alignment of, 8733, 8734
structure of, 9061
study of, 2731
of Eshmun, 2841, 2842
Etruscan, 2870, 9064
Geto-Dacian, 3467
of god, creation of, 2812
gold and silver in, 3626
Greek, 9062–9063
in Archaic period, 9063
circular, 1792
emergence of, 3665
in Geometric period, 9063
in Hellenistic period, 9063
to Hera, 3915
in Late Classical period, 9063
in Orientalizing period, 9063
in Protogeometric period, 9062
role of, 3665
to Zeus, 9953
Hindu, **9038–9041**
as access to aspirants and worshipers, 9040–9041
altars in, 9038, 9039–9040
architecture of, 7837
based on *maṇḍalas,* 5640, 9040, 9041
bhakti synthesis and, 4001–4002
body correlated with, 7983
Buddhist temples and, 9038, 9039
caves as, 9039
circumambulation of, 1796
construction of, 4429, 9265
cosmological meaning of, 2019
creation symbolism in, 7983
diagram of construction of, 9038, *9039*
eco-activism encouraged at, 2622
as enclosures, 9038
as fortress, 9040
in human image, 9041
as hut, 9040
iconicity of architectural form in, 9039–9040
in Śaivism, 8402, 8416–8417
Kramrisch (Stella) on, 5242
orientation of, 7982
outside India, 3609–3610
as palace, 9040
pūjā in, 7494, 9265
sacredness of, 7698
as shelter, 9039, 9040
sikhara as, 9265
sounds in, 6278
to Śiva, 8042
Vaikhānasas in, 9496
Vedic sacrifice and, 4002
visual narratives decorating, vol. 2 color insert
water in, 9265
yantras in, 9871–9872
Hittite, 4070–4072
Inca, 4384, 4410, 4411, 4413
Indian
heaven and earth connected in, 7980
Kramrisch (Stella) on, 5242
Marathi, 5697
temple urbanism, 1805–1806
in Śaivism, 8975, 8977
of International Society for Krishna Consciousness, 4522, 7355
in Vaiṣṇavism, 8975, 8977
Israelite (*See* Biblical Temple)
Jain, 4429, 4770
Jewish/Hebrew
as divine dwelling, 461–462
in Mishnah, 6066
Reform and Conservative synagogues as, 8925
Manichaean, in China, 5669, 5670
megalithic, 5822–5823
Mesoamerican, **9065–9067** (*See also* Pyramids, Mesoamerican)
Christian churches built on, 5916
in Huastec religion, 5910
in Huichol religion, 4152
in Teotihuaćan, 5898–5899
interpretations of, 9066
in Mixtec religion, 5911–5912
music in, 6269
in Preclassic period, 9065–9066
structures of, 9065–9066
in Tarascan religion, 5909
Temple 22 at Copán, 1359
Templo Mayor, 718, 719, 1359, 5892–5893
of Tlaloc, 9214, 9266
in Toltec religion, 5906–5907
Mesopotamian, 5960–5961, 9062
rituals performed at, 9062
role in society, 3375
structure of, 9062
on top of ziggurats, 9062
Moabite, 6094
Mormon, 6193, 6195
mountains as, 6214
as museums, 6245
Mycenaean, 9062
myths in, functions of, 6362
Nabatean, 6386–6387, *6389*
Near Eastern and Mediterranean, **9061–9065**
political role of, 3375
Olmec, 6819
Philistine, 7102, 7103, 7104–7105
prehistoric, 7379–7381
Roman, 9064–9065
circular, 1792
Samaritan, on Mount Gerizim, destruction of, 8068
Sikh, 8394–8395
women's *seva* (service) at, 3879–3880
sky and, 8428
in Slavic religion, 8433–8434
South American
Coriancha (Temple of the Sun), 1362, 1363
in Muisca religion, 6230
in Southeast Asia
architecture, Hindu aspects of, 4012–4013
astronomical and calendrical functions of, 4013
consecration of deities in, 4012
stupas included in, 4012
stars and, 8733–8734
Sumerian, urbanization and economy in, 1802–1803
in Taiwan, 8965–8966
Tamil, 8975, 8977, 8979
Zoroastrian, fire in, 569–570
Temple Scroll (Dead Sea Scroll), 886, 925, 2234, 9234
Temple Solaire, 1034, 6554–6555, **9067–9069**
anticult movement in Europe and, 2085
apocalypticism of, 6554
"cosmic marriages" of, 6554, 6555
as fragile movement, 6517, 6549
group murders and suicides by, 6545, 6555
Movement for the Restoration of the Ten Commandments of God compared with, 6216–6217
and violence, conditions leading to, 6553
Temple texts, of Egyptian religion, 2703, 2715
Templeton Foundation, and International Society for Science and Religion, 8185
Templeton prize, and field of science and religion, 8185
Temple to the Earth God (Wanrong), 9057
Temple to the Northern Peak (Quyang), 9057
Temple to the Water God, 9057
Templo Mayor (Aztec temple), 5892–5893
construction of, 718
excavation and study of, 5944
human sacrifices at, 4188, 5892
musical instruments in, 6269
myth reflected in, 4188
rituals performed in, 5892–5893
shrines in, 4155, 4188
Spanish destruction of, 718, 719
sun, alignment with, 1359
symbols used in, 5892
testimonies on, 5892
Templum (divination practice), 2377
Temporale (Proper of Seasons), 1741
Temporality, in Australian Indigenous religions, 314

Temptation, **9069–9074**. *See also* Fall, the; Sin(s)
in African religions, 9069
in Ashkenazic Hasidism, 542, 543
Cain and, 1344
in Christianity, 9069–9073
defeat of, in enlightenment, 2793
definition of, 9070
Fox (George) on, 3180
in Israelite religion, 9070–9071
of Jesus, 4848, 7771
in Judaism, 9069, 9070–9071
Kant (Immanuel) on, 9070
in Lord's Prayer, 5517
psychological perspectives of, 9072–9073
in quests, 7553
by Satan, 2278, 9071–9072
sociological perspectives of, 9073
Sorskii (Nil) on, 8525
and tempter, 9070–9072
theological perspectives of, 9073
Temrük (Kabardian prince), 4614
Temüjin. *See* Chinggis Khan
Temurah, 273–274
Ten (number), interpretations of, 6749
Tench, Watkin, 685
Tenchi Kane no Kami (deity), 5225, 6573
Ten Commandments, **9074**. *See also* Mitsvot
in Christianity, 9074
in Adventist theology, 8235, 8236
obedience and, 1670
in Israelite religion, 4745, 9074
in Judaism, 4971–4972
relational discipline and, 8706
Shabbat in, 8256
as laws, 5327
Maimonides (Moses) on, 866, 5615
Moses' role in, 6201
Movement for the Restoration of the Ten Commandments of God on, 6216
origin of, 9074
as positive guidance, 9074
prologue to, 9074
in Qabbalah, 7536
as universal morality, 7651
Ten Commandments, The (movie), vol. 7 color insert
Tendai school of Buddhism (Japan), 1242, **9074–9080**
and Hīnayāna Buddhism, 9078
Bodhidharma's legend in, 995
doctrines of, 1178, 1179, 9076–9080
education in, 9075
Enchin in, 2781
Ennin in, 2801
Esoteric practices in, 8985, 9077–9078
formation of, 1176, 9075
Genshin in, 3432
hand-copying works in, 1181
Hōnen and, 4118–4119
imperial favor for, 4784–4785
incarnation in, 4417
institutional history of, 9075–9076
Jien in, 4917
Jimon branch of, 2781–2782
Jōdo Shinshū school and, 4935
conflicts between, 7752
Kūya in, 5270
literature of, 1181
maṇḍalas in, 5644
meditation in, 1291–1292, 9076
mikkyō (esoteric form of), 8348
modern, 9076
monastic disciplines in, 9078–9079
music in, 6300
nembutsu zammai (meditational trance) in, 4119
Nichiren and, 6604, 6605
origin of name, 9074–9075
philosophy of, 1302
poetry of, 7216
priest soldiers in, 7273
Pure Land Buddhism and, 4119, 9079–9080
reform of, 1180, 2741, 9076
Ryōgen in, 1178, 9075, 9077
Saichō, role of, **8029–8031,** 8350
Sanmon branch of, 2781
Sannō Shintō and, 8361–8362
vs. Shingon school, 8350, 9075, 9077, 9078
Śubhākarasiṃha and, 8804
Tiantai school and, 9074, 9075
vs. Hossō school, 1242, 9075, 9076, 9077
women in, 9076
Tendaishōmyō (chanting), 6300–6301
Tendai-Shugendo, 4785
Ten Days of Penitence, in Jewish calendar, 4867
Tenes, labyrinth of, 2558
Tengere Kaira Khan (deity), 9081
Tengger people (Java), Neo-Buddhism and, 8653
Ten Great Religions: An Essay in Comparative Theology (Clarke), 9125
Tengri (deity), **9080–9082**
alternative names of, 9081
in Buriat religion, 1326–1327
in Chuvash religion, 1784
cult of, 9082
in Hun religion, 4228
in Turkic religions, 9398, 9400, 9402
Tengri (heaven), 4491, 9080
Tengri (lake), 9081
Tengri (mountain), 9081
Ten Gurus, The (painting), vol. 10 color insert
Tenino people (North America), guardian spirits of, 6713
Tenji (Japanese emperor), poetry under, 7215
Tenkai (Buddhist monk), 9076
Teṅkalai sect
inŚrī Vaiṣṇavas Sampradāya, 8728
Piḷḷai Lokācārya formulating, 7172
on predestination, 3204
Tenkei Denson (Buddhist monk), 9949
Tenkswatawa (prophet), 6686
Tenma, Toshihiro, 3097
Tenmu (Japanese emperor), 4783, 4810, 7271
Tennant, Frederick R., 9105–9106, 9117
Tennant, Kylie, 3084
Tennent, William, 66
Tennyo (deities), 3135
Tennyson, Alfred, on belief, 2427
Tenochtitlán
architecture of, 5893
astronomical alignment in, 8734
Aztec religion in, 715–716, 717, 5893
Chalchiuhtlicue ritual in, 5293–5294
in colonial period, 5916
comets and, 8736
Great Temple at, 718
Huitzilopochtli as patron deity of, 4155
human sacrifice at, 1469, 4188
installation of kings in, 5174
jaguar imagery at, 4763
musical instruments at, 6269
Pleiades and, 8735
pyramids of, 5293
rise in power of, 5292
as sacred city, 715–716, 1503, 5888–5889
Spanish conquest of, 5174
Tenrikyō, 3005, 4799, 6513, **9082–9083**
in Africa, 109
doctrine of, 9083
in Europe, 6568
founder of, 9082
government persecution of, 6405
healing touch in, 9256
history of, 9082–9083, 9312
in Japan, 6573
in Korea, 6574
Nakayama Miki in, 6404–6406
number of followers of, 9083
origins of, 6405
poverty in, 6405
rituals in, 9082
scriptures of, 6405, 9083
Shintō and, 8367
teachings of, 9082, 9083
women in, 6405–6406
Tenri Ō no Mikoto (lord of heavenly reason), 9083
Tenri religion, in Japan, founding of, 5073–5074
Tenshōdaijin. *See* Amaterasu
Tenshō kōtai jingū kyō movement, founding of, 8369
Tenskwatawa (Shawnee prophet), 1565, 3474, 6733, 9028
Tent of the Living God. *See* Mungiki movement
Tentori, Tullio, 7075
Tenufah (offering), 927
Teodorescu, D. M., 3467
Teostoria delle religioni (Bianchi), 863
Teotihuaćan (Mexico), 5898–5902
architecture of, 149, 5888, 5900
art of, 5899–5900
Avenue of the Dead in, 5898–5899
Aztec religion in, 715–716, 5888–5889
ballgames played in, 749
boys born near, 1470
caves and monuments in, 1468, 5898–5899
ceremonial center of, 1804
circle symbolism and pecked crosses in, 1794–1795, 5898
in Classic period, 5898–5902
collapse of, 5889, 5901–5902
deities of, 4313, 5888, 5900–5901, 9213
in Formative (Preclassic) period, 5896
founding of, 5898
funeral rites in, 149, 3242, 5900
iconography of, 4312–4313, 5888, 5900–5901
Monte Albán and, 5902
mountain symbolism in, 5899, 6213
musical instruments in, 6268
orientation of, 5898
pre-Columbian, 5888–5889
pyramids in, 5293, 5898
rise of, 5898
rituals in, 5901
sacrifices at, 1358, 4187, 5888–5889, 5891, 5935
structure of city, 5896, 5898–5899
quarters in, 715–716
sun in, 5888–5889
creation of, 5901, 5935
temples in, 5898–5899
tower in, 9266
as trade center, 5292
Venus as patron star, 1356
Tepanec empire
Aztec conquest of, 4186
collapse of, 5173
Tepanec people (Mexico)
Otomí religion and, 5909
Toltec religion and, 5907
Tepantitla complex, 149

Tepeyolotl (deity), 718, 9093
Teponaztles (drums), 7036
Tepozteco (mythic figure)
as culture hero, 5937
as trickster, 5937
Terafim skulls, divination and, 3806
Terāpanthī sect of Jainism, 4766
gender in, 3328
Teratoskopoi (diviner), 2376
Tere (mythic figure), 93–94
Terecô
influences on, 120
origins of, 120
Terence (Publius Terentius)
Hrotsvit and, 4143
on humanity as universal, 8761
Teresa, Mother, 828, 2321, vol. 12 color insert
Teresa of Ávila (saint), **9083–9085**
convents founded by, 9084
on desert meditation, 8724
and Discalced Carmelites, 6764
on ecstasy and union, 2682
eremitism of, 2827
human solidarity of, 2829
John of the Cross and, 4942
life of, 9084
male authority challenged by, 3357–3358
on meditation, 5818
on mirror, 6063
mysticism of, 6338, 6350
attention in, 604
religious experience of, 7696
on sleep as enlightenment, 8441
Sundén (Hjalmar) on, 8851
writings of, 9084
Teresa of Ávila, Bernini's (Gian Lorenzo) statue of, vol. 11 color insert
Teresita (saint), Oya identified with in Santería, 1434
Terjüman (magazine), 4618
Terminalia, 6171
in Roman calendar, 1354
Terminus, time and, 1353
Termites, in Dogon religion, 3570
Terqa, King of. *See* Dagan
Terraciano, Kevin, 5920
Terra del rimorso (de Martino), 2267
Terreiros (ritual communities)
in Candomblé, 121, 122–123
in Umbanda, 124
Terrell, JoAnne, 79
Territorial churches, in Lutheran and Calvinist ecclesiology, 1773
Territorial cults
in central Bantu religion, 1508–1509
Chinese, 1615–1616
Terrorism, 7257–7258. *See also* Violence
by Aum Shinrikyō, 631–632, 6531, 7274–7275
in *jihād,* 7257–7258, 7288–7290
nationalism and, 7257–7258
revolutionary millennial movements and, 6549
in Southeast Asia, 4672
urban religious violence, 1807–1808
Tersteegen, Gerhard, 7143
Tertiart cultures, Schmidt (Wilhelm) on, 5260
Tertullian, **9085–9087**
on aeons, 7190
antiheretical writings of, 9086
apologetics of, 428, 9085
on baptism, 1669
on bishops, 7401
on Carthage, 1677
on Christian associations, 5334
on Christian persecution, 7058
conversion of, 9085
on fasting on Sabbath, 9813
Galileo Galilei on, 3257
on Greek knowledge, 8181
on images, 4285, 4358, 4360–4361, 4385, 9085
influence of, 9085
on isolation, 2824
Jerome on, 9085
on knowledge, 5203
life of, 9085
on *Logos,* 5501
on *lucerna extincta* rite, 8249
on Luke, 908
on magic, 5577
against Marcionism, 9086
on martyrdom, 6946, 9085
on medicine, 3843
on merit, 5875, 5876
Montanism of, 6167, 6168, 9085, 9086, 9087
on moral teachings, 1651
on music, 6308
on nonviolence, 6647
overview of life and work, 1679
against philosophy, 7114
on repentance, 7758
on sin, 9086
on soul, 1042, 8564, 9086
on suicide, 8830
against theater, 2437, 2467, 7044
on Thecla, 9101
theology of, 2581, 9086–9087
on Trinity, 628, 4241, 9086
on "two books," 9421
writings of, 9085–9086
Tertullianists (Christian sect), 9085
Terumat ha-lishkah (tax), 930
Teshigahara, Hiroshi, 3097
Teshub (deity), **9087–9088**
Adad identified with, 28
in Hurrian religion, 4230
iconography of, 9087
Iupiter Dolichenus derived from, 4753
Kumarbi and, 4230, 4231
mythology of, 9087
prayer to, 9087
in *Song of Ullikummi,* 4231–4232
Teshuvah (repentance), 593, 4988, 7757. *See also* Repentance
Tesla Speaks, 9448
Tessmann, Günter, 115
Testament, covenant as, 2049
Testament of Abraham, 903
Testament of Adam, 903
Testament of Isaac, 903
Testament of Jacob, 903
Testament of Job, 903, 4932
Testament of Levi, messianism in, 5972
Testament of Moses, 903
Testament of Solomon, 903
Testament of the Twelve Patriarchs, 903
Testimonia (Cyprian), training of new Christians in, 2113
Testimony of Our Inexhaustible Treasure (Ramabai), 7610
Testimony of Truth (Gnostic text), 5202, 5203
Testing, of Abraham, 15
Tethys (deity), 9699
Teton Mountains, 6214
Tetrabiblios (Ptolemy), 7492, 7493
Tetrachords, 6303
Tetraktys (sacred numbers), 7530
Tetzauhteotl (deity), Huitzilopochtli and, 5937
Tetzel, Johann, sale of indulgences by, 7657
Te Ua, 6795–6796
Teustch, David, 7638–7639
Teutates (deity)
Hermes and, 3937
Lucan on, 1482, 1483
Teutonic Knights, 773
Teutonic Order, 773, 774
Tewaarathon (ballgame), 754
Tewa religion (North America), 6728
clowns in, 1838, 1839
cosmology in, 6722–6723
dualism in, 6728
Winter and Summer people in, 6724
Te Whiti-o-Rongomai (Maori prophet), 6795
Texas, Caddo calendar, 1353
Texcoco, Lake, 5292–5294
Texcoco religion (Mexico), astrology in, 8426
Textes et monuments figurés relatifs aux mystères de Mithra (Cumont), importance of, 2093
Textes sacrés d'Afrique noire (Dieterlen), 116
Textiles, **9088–9093**. *See also* Clothing
archaeological records of, 9088
Batak *ragidup* fabrics in Sumatra, 1828
for creating sacred place, 9090–9091
decorative, 9092
economic meaning of, 9091–9092
as icons, 9090
as offerings, 9089–9090
ritual uses for, 9088–9091
as symbols, 9088
in Turkic religions, 9091, 9403
Text pictures, calligraphy and, 1369
Texts. *See also* Sacred texts; *specific texts*
hermeneutics and (*See also* Hermeneutics)
authorial intention and, 3931–3932
Gadamer (Hans-Georg) on, 3934
vs. images, primacy of, 494, 495
Textual criticism, 5472–5475, 5484–5489
Textual interpretation, 5472, 5484–5489
translation and, 5485
Textualists, *Tafsīr* (Qur'anic exegesis) of, 7569
Teyrnon (deity), 1490
in *Mabinogion,* 5546
Teyyam (dance drama), 2448
Tezcatlipoca (deity), 718, **9093–9094**
Aztec people liberated by, 5890
confession to, 1885
creation by, 5907, 5934
duality of, 5891
feast of, 5173–5174
forms of, 9093
human sacrifice to, 4190, 7957
iconography of, 9093
omnipotence of, 5174, 9093
power of Aztec kings and, 5173–5174
and Quetzalcoatl, 5936, 9093, 9357
as sky deity, 8428
as sun of the underworld, 8842
Xochiquetzal and, 5934
Tezozomoc (Tepanec ruler), 5907
Tezozomoc, Alvarado, 5293
T'fillah, ha- (Jewish prayer), 9806
Thābit, Ḥāssan ibn, 6766
Thābit ibn Qurrah, 2971
Thab lha (fireplace), 9185

Thaddeus, 6479
in Armenia, 487
Thailand and Thai religions, **9094–9098**. *See also* Southeast Asia and Southeast Asian religions
Buddhism, 9094–9098 (*See also* Theravāda Buddhism)
amulets in, 8080
Buddhadāsa and, 1071–1073, 1142–1143
calendar of, 9831
celebrations in, 1304, 1306, 1307, 1308
colonial influences and, 1098, 1139
contemporary, 9095–9097
cremation, circumambulation before, 1797
devils in, 2315
divine images in, vol. 12 color insert
exorcism in, 3814
future of, 1131
ghosts in, 3477
iconography of, 4331
images in, 9829, vol. 12 color insert
imperial, 1134
Khmer religion influenced by, 5130, 5131
kingship in, 7262, 9095
literature of, 1253, 1262
liturgy in, 9828
Mahāyāna Buddhism, 9094
meditation in, 9096–9097, 9152
messianic groups in, 3155
millenarian movements in, 1100
modern, 1139–1140, 1142, 6139–6140
monasteries, 1096, 1137, 1139–1140, 1141, 7720, 9094, 9095, 9097, 9151
Mon Buddhism, 1136–1137
nikayas (schools), division into, 8074
nuns in, 6760
petitions in, vol. 9 color insert
pilgrimage in, 7164, 7982, 9832
politics and, 1141, 7260, 9153
in postcolonial era, 7264
prevalence of, 1728
priesthood in, 7408, 7409
pūjā in, 7496
reform movements in, 6139–6140, 9095–9096, 9151
revival of, 9149–9150
spirit possession in, 2315
spread of, 9147
studies on, 1311, 1313
stupa *(chedi),* circling of, 1796
synthesis of indigenous religions and, 3154, 3155, 3156
temples of, 9054, 9055
Vassa in, 9831
women in, 9095
Zen Buddhism, 9096
Christianity, 1728, 9097
Confucianism, 9094
cult of monk-saints in, 3155
fiction of, 3076, 3077
funeral rites in, 3240
Islam, 4671, 9097
music in, 6287, 6288, 6289, 6290
Neolithic burial sites in, 8641–8642
Neolithic culture in (Hoa Binh culture), 6459
orgy in, 6879
phī cult in
exorcism in, 3814
parallels in Sri Lanka, 8410
soul-calling rites in, 3155
spirit cults in, 7836
uprisings in, 9097
Thakur, Bhaktivinode. *See* Datta, Kedardnath
Thakur Dev (deity), 4435
Tha'labī, al-, on light of Muḥammad *(nūr Muḥammad),* 6766
Thalamos nymphon (Bridal chamber rite), in Gnosticism, 8247
Thalbitzer, William, 475
Thales of Miletus
on North Star, 8734
on water as primal substance, 1996
Thames, Battle of (1813), 9028
Thammayut (Dhammayuttika) Nikāya, Mongkut and, 6139–6140
Thanatology, 2236. *See also* Death
Thanatos, Freud (Sigmund) on, 2238
Thanh-hoang (tutelary deity), in Vietnamese religion, 9593
Thanksgiving
prayer of, 7369
psalms of, 7465
in *Isaiah,* 7461
in *2 Samuel,* 7461
public displays of, vol. 7 color insert
sacrifices of, 8001
Thanksgiving Scroll (Dead Sea Scroll), 2234
Thaṅs dbyaṅs rgya mtsho (Dalai Lama), 2132
Thanwī, Ashrāf 'Alī, 4652
Thappananon, Wanna, 3077
Thaqif tribe, deities of, 444
Thar pa gling monastery, 5194
Tharrawiirgal (deity), 671
Tharu, Susie, 3322
Thascius Caecilius Cyprianus. *See* Cyprian
Thasos (island)
Melqart in, 5848
sanctuary of Herakles on, 3917
That Which Is in the Netherworld (Egypt), 2708
That Ye May Know (Kapp), vol. 2 color insert
Thaumaturgical movements, in Africa, 102
Thawāb al-a' māl (Ibn Bābawayhi), 4262
Thayer, Ernest Lawrence, on baseball, 8725
Thayer, James, on Amma, 3569
Theaetetus (Plato), 7189
Theagenes of Rhegium
on Greek religion, 3660
on knowledge, 5201
Philo Judaeus influenced by, 7106
Thealogy, **9098–9101**, 9788
concepts of Goddess in, 9099–9100
vs. feminist theology, 9099
history and ethics in, 9100
origins of, 9098–9099
Theater. *See* Dance; Drama; Performance
"Theater of Cruelty" (Artaud), 2438, 2475
Theatetus (Plato), 7109, 7182
Theatrical dance, 2141–2142, **2152–2167**
Theban kings (Egypt), 2706–2707
tombs of, looted, 2709
Theban Legion, martyrdom of, 1980
Thebans, homosexuality in military corps of, 4112–4113
Thecla (saint), 760, **9101–9102**
devotion to, 9101, 9102
iconography of, 9102
legend of, 9101
Theft. *See also* Thief
Islamic laws on, 4566
Israelite laws on, 4738
Theias (Assyrian king), 34
Thein (masonry foundation), 9055
Thein Pe Myint, 3077
Theion (divine), 7182
Their Way (Jordan), 645–646
Theism, 2780, **9102–9108**. *See also* Monotheism; Proofs for the existence of God
in Brahmanism, 9571
as classification, 1818
in Confucianism, 6965
Tasan on, 1648, 1649
conversion in, 1973
devotion in, 2318–2319
in existentialism, 2927, 7111
finitistic, 9107
immanence in, 9281
in Islam, 6964
materialist rejection of, 5775
and monism, 9103–9104
vs. monotheism, use of terms, 6156
necessity and contingency in God in, 6961, *6961*
vs. pantheism and panentheism, 6960
philosophy of, 7122–7125
Spinoza on, 6962
structure of, 7692
subjective, henotheism and, 3913
theoretical problems with, 9106–9107
transcendence and immanence of God in, 9282–9283
Theissen, Gerd
on kingdom of heaven, 5149
on Paul, 7016, 7018
Theistic ecstasy, 2680
Theistic evolution, 2912, 8190
Theitmar, on Slavic religion, 8433
Thekla (nun), 822
Thelema, Abbey of, founding of, 2072
Thelema, law of, Crowley (Aleister) on, 2072
Themis (deity), 3001
justice and, 7783
Zeus and, 3663
Themis (Harrison), Greek religion in, 3781
Themistius
on Aristotle, 479
influence on *falsafah,* 2971
Themistocles (Athenian politician), interpreting oracle, 2375, 2376, 7278
Theocentrism
of Christianity, anthropocentrism and, 2649
of humanity, in Orthodox theology, 2590, 2591
Theocracy, **9108–9111**. *See also* Theokrasia
Buddhist, Tibetan, 9109
Christian
Catholic, 9109, 9110
eschatological, 9111
general, 9110
priestly, 9109
Protestant, 9110
royal, 9110
coining of term, 9108
definition of, 9108
Eastern Christian, 9110
Egyptian, 9109, 9110
eschatological, 9111
general, 9110–9111
Islamic
eschatological, 9111
general, 9110, 9111
priestly, 9109
Israelite
eschatological, 9111
general, 9110
priestly, 9109
royal, 9110
sources on, 9108–9109
Japanese, 9109
Josephus on, 10061
Mesopotamian, 9109
Minoan, 37, 38, 41

Mycenaean, 41
priestly, 9109
royal, 9109–9110 (*See also* Kings and kingship)
Theocritus
on Adonis, festival of, 35
on Pan, 6957
Theodicy, **9111–9121**
in *Ben Sira,* 9759
Bianchi (Ugo) on, 864
Boehme (Jakob) on, 1006
in Buddhism, 9112, 9119–9120
Calvin (John) on, 3556
in Christianity, 9116–9118
classical, 9113–9115
communion, 9115
deferring, 9114–9115, 9115–9116, 9117
definition of, 9112
dissolutions of, 9112–9113
educative, 9114, 9117
eschatological, 9114, 9116, 9118
etymology of term, 9112
free-will, 9113–9114
in Christianity, 9117
in Hinduism, 9119
Holocaust and, 4091–4092
in Islam, 9118
in Judaism, 9115
in Hinduism, 2901, 9112, 9113, 9119–9120
in Qur'ān, 5060, 9118
in Islam, 9118–9119
in Judaism, 9115–9116
Mu'tazilah on, 3212
myth and history in, 2903, 6378
punishment and, 5372
Socrates on, 8503
Stoicism and, 8741
theoretical positions of, 9112–9115
Weber's (Max), 2672, 9112, 9119
Theodicy, The (Leibniz), 5406–5407
Theodora (Byzantine empress)
and Monophysitism, 6154
Paulician movement under, 3523
Theodora (solitary), 2825
Theodore bar Koni, 5638
Theodore of Mopsuestia, 2583, 6480, **9121–9122**
biblical exegesis of, 9121–9122
on biblical interpretation, 5486
and Chrysostom, 9121
Cyril of Alexandria, opposition from, 2117
and Nestorianism, 6482
Sahak Parthev and, 8026
Theodore of Studios, **9122–9123**
icon veneration defended by, 2585
on images, 4290, 4353, 6619, 9122
monastery reorganized by, 9122
writings of, 9122
Theodoret of Cyrrhus (bishop), **9123**
Theodoric (Ostrogothic king), 1007, 7192
Theodoric II (Visigoth king), 4491
Theodoros, and Anthesteria, 375
Theodorus (rabbi), 7580
Theodorus of Cyrene, atheism and, 582
Theodosian Code of 438, 432, 972, 1846
Theodosius (patriarch of Alexandria)
Ambrose and, 288
ecclesiology and, 1771
Kievan Monastery of the Caves founded by, 7941
Mashtots' (Mesrop) and, 5764
Monophysitism and, 6154
Olympic Games suppressed by, 3267
Theodosius (Roman emperor), **9123–9125**
Ambrose and, 9124
baptism of, 9124
Catholicism and, 5338
Christianity as official faith under, 2580
condemning idolatry, 4361
and Donatists, 2417
legacy of, 9125
Manichaeism under, 5664
Nestorius condemned by, 6483
and Nicaea, Council of (325), 9124
paganism banned by, 7922, 7923
persecution of heretics by, 7060, 9124
and priesthood, 7402, 9124–9125
on relics, 7688
Theodosius II (Roman emperor), *Codex Theodosianus* of, 5333, 5334
Theodotion, 889, 891
Theodotus of Byzantium, Galen's influence on, 3256
Theodulf, 1556–1557
Theogenes, sports and, 8723
Theognis, on fate, 8405
Theogonie (Feuerbach), 3048
Theogony
in Hinduism, 4439–4440
in Orphism, 6894–6895
Theogony (Hesiod), 1014, 5468
and An, 302
birth of gods in, 4321
castration in, 1450
chaos in, 1537
comparisons to, 4231, 4232
Demeter in, 2268
divine kingship in, 5146
Eros in, 2832–2833
five ages in, 6984
genealogy in, 3679, 3963
hell in, 8426
history in, 4035–4036
Hypnos in, 8439
Okeanos in, 6805
Prometheus in, 3118
sacrifice in, 3683
tradition in, 9267
Theokrasia (mingling of gods)
Hellenistic, 3907–3909
syncretism and, 8930–8932
Theologia kataphaatika, vs. via negativa, 9587
Theologia Naturalis (Raymond of Sabunde), 9422
Theological dualism, 2509
Theological Essays (Maurice), 5784
Theological incompatibilism, 7137
Theological method, for understanding deity, 2257
Theological Orations (Gregory of Nazianzus), 3695
Theological-Political Treatise (Spinoza), 4265–4266
Theological schools, women's admission to, 3310
in Middle Ages, 3359
Theological wisdom, 9755
Theology, **9125–9142**
affirmative, 2355
at Alexandria, 2710
of analogy, 391
apophatic, 9139
black (*See* Black theology)
Buddhist, 9130
Christian, **9134–9142**
in Africa, 1722
Anglican, 9138
as anthropology, 3047–3048
of beauty, 812–813
of Calvin, 1375–1376, 9137
Catholic, 9130, 9136, 9137, 9138, 9139, 9140
Christian Science, 2695
comparative, 9127–9128, 9129–9130
contemplative mysticism in, 2856
contemporary, 9139–9140
convergences in, 2689
in Eastern Christianity, 2582–2585, 4940–4941
ecological, neglect of, 2647
empiricism and, 2780
environmental problems addressed by, 2610
epistemology in, 2819
of Eriugena, 2830
evangelical theology and China, 1632
first use of term, 1007
historical development of, 9134–9138
humor in, 4203
inculturation/contextualization, 1730
indigenous, in Pacific islands, 1741
indigenous approaches to, 2689–2690
of John of Damascus, 4940
justification in, 5040, 5041–5042
Latin American Protestant, 1704
liberal, 1656
of liberation (*See* Liberation theology)
of Luther (Martin), 9136–9137
in Oceania, 6804
of Origen, 6889–6890
Orthodox, 2587, 2589–2594, 9135–9136
parts and forms of, 9139
pietism and, 9137, 9139
practice of, 9138–9140
Protestant, 7458, 9130, 9136–9138, 9139
Puritan, 9138
Schleiermacher (Friedrich) on, 8165–8166
scholastic, 8175, 9136
as science, 9138–9139
Sharpe (Eric) on, 8305
of Tertullian, 1679, 9086–9087
of Thomas Aquinas, 9134, 9135, 9136, 9163–9164
of Vatican II, 9534, 9536–9537
comparative, **9125–9134**
Buddhist, 9130
Christian, 9127–9128, 9129–9130
clarification of, 9131
colonialism and, 9128–9129
contemporary, 9127
definition of, 9125
environmental, agenda for, 2654–2655
Greek, 9128
Hindu, 9130
Islamic, 9127–9128, 9130
Jewish, 9127, 9129–9130
methods of, 9131–9133
modern, 9129–9131
origins of, 9126
premodern, 9127–9131
questions addressed by, 9126–9127
Roman, 9128
use of term, 9125, 9126
vs. comparative-historical method, 1868–1869, 1871
of conversion, 1971–1972
doctrine and, 2383–2384

Theology ***continued***
dogmatic, 9139, 9140
ecumenical, 9140
of Erasmus, 2821–2822
Essenek, 2847
evolution and, 2909–2910
feminist (*See* Feminist theology)
fundamental, 9139–9140
future-oriented, 5152–5153
global (world), 9126
Greek, 9128, 9134
Hindu, 9130
in *Encyclopédie,* 2783–2784
Islamic, 4567–4569, 9134
comparative, 9127–9128, 9130
īmān and *islām* in, 4398–4400
sharī'ah and, 4692
speculative (*See Kalām*)
James (E. O.) in, 4774–4775
Jewish, 9134–9135
comparative, 9127, 9129–9130
Ethical Culture and, 2857
political nature of, 10061
of Jones (Jim), 4953
liberation (*See* Liberation theology)
moral (practical), 9139
Muslim, contemplative mysticism in, 2856
natural
Ockham and, 9738
Wolff (Christian) and, 9783
negative, 2355, 7774, 9139
Derrida (Jacques) on, 2247
vs. philosophy
ha-Levi on, 4891–4892
Heidegger (Martin) on, 3896
Maimonides on, 4892
Mercier (Désiré Joseph) on, 5868
political (*See* Political theology)
positive, 9139
vs. positivism, 7339
practical, 7479
in religion and ecology
feminism and, 2650
Jewish, 2645–2646
study of, 2604
Ritschl (Albrecht) on, 7137
Roman, 9128
as science, Duns Scotus (John) on, 2524
and sciences, Newman (John Henry) on, 6511
speculative, 9139
Stoic, 8742
subaltern, 8802
systematic, 6928
theoretic, 9125
transcendental, Kant (Immanuel) on, 5077
Unification, 9467
use of term, 3031, 7111, 9126
via negativa of, 9586–9588
visual, in art, 497
Theology and Pastoral Counseling, a New Interdisciplinary Approach (Hunsinger), 7487
Theology of Aristotle, 6475
Theology of Liberation, A (Gutiérrez), 5438, 5931
"Theology of Life," 2612
Theology of the Laity, The (Kraemer), 7452
Theology School of Paris, Carnival attacked by, 1441
Théon, Max, Hermetic Brotherhood of Luxor and, 8251
Theopantistic deities, history of religions approach on, 4065–4066
Theophaneia, 2818
Theophany (appearance of a god)
in Christianity, in time, 3973
as form of hierophany, 3972
in Judaism
in *1 Kings,* 8513
shekhinah concept and, 8315
sacred space and, 1504
at Sinai (*See* Sinai)
time and, 3973
Theophany, Feast of, 2400, 2593
Theophilus (legendary figure), 9771
Theophilus (Roman official), 909
Theophilus of Antioch
on Logos, 7191
on wisdom and *logos,* 5502–5503
Theophrastus
Aristotle's Lyceum under, 479
Orphism and, 3674
on stone worship, 8745
on superstition, 8864
Theophysics, holistic healing and, 3851
Theoretic theology, 9125
Theoretikē (contemplative way), 1447–1448
Theoria of phenomena, 7092
Theorie (series), 9021
Theories of Primitive Religion (Evans-Pritchard), 116–117, 379, 2896
Theories of relativity, 2739–2740, 2879
Theos (God), 7182
Theōsis (deification)
of humanity, Gregory Palamas on, 3698, 3699
in Orthodox theology, 2590–2591
prayer as means to, Sorskii (Nil) on, 8525
Theosophical Society, **9142–9144**
anthroposophy and, 392
in Australia, study of religions, influence on, 8768
Besant (Annie) in, 844–845, 9142–9143
Blavatsky (H. P.) in, 977, 978, 1187, 6516, 6535, 6559, 6563, 7228, 9142, 9205
Buddhist Lodge of, 1188
Buddhist revival by, 1126, 1187
in Cuba, 7228
democratic structure of, 6515
Eckankar influenced by, 2603
in engaged Buddhism, 2787–2788
in England, 9142
extensions of, 9144
Fathers of, on Hermetism, 3952
foundation of, 9142
Hermetism and, 3952, 3953
and I Am movement, 4245
in India, 7228, 9142
influence of, 9144
Judge (William Q.) in, 5023–5024
Krishnamurti (Jiddu) in, 5244
Mead (George) and, 3952
and modern Buddhist philosophy, 1302
and New Age movement, 6497
in occultism, 6783
Olcott (Henry Steel) in, 845, 6815–6816, 7228, 9142, 9205
Order of the Star of the East in, Suzuki (D. T.) and, 8885
origins of, 6513
Ouspensky (P. D.) in, 6935
social work of, 7228
Steiner (Rudolf) in, 392, 8738
Sunday schools of, 7228
UFO religions and, 9433
in United States, 7227–7230, 9142, 9143, 9205–9206 (*See also* Point Loma Theosophical Community)
women in, 6535
Theosophy, 6559, 9143–9144
Besant's (Annie), 844–845
Cayce and, 1474
Christian, nature in, 6434–6436
conversion to, 7228
doctrine of the sacred, 6535
evolution in, 9143
Hermetism and, 3947, 3951, 3952, 3953
Judge (William Q.) in, 5023–5024
karma in, 9143
in Latin America, 6578
Luria's (Isaac), 7534–7535
and Neopaganism, 6470
Ouspensky (P. D.) and, 6935
qabbalistic, 7533, 7534–7535, 7536, 8315
philosophical interpretation of, 7539
reality in, 9143
reincarnation in, 7228, 9143, 9330
religious experience in, 7738
Saint-Germaine and, 2772
Suzuki (D. T.) and, 8885
technical, 7230
therapeutic touch healing and, 3850–3851
in Western esotericism, 2843
women's rights in, 9144
Theotokos (Mother of God or "god-bearer"), 2583, 5753, 9605
Council of Ephesus and, 2040, 4345, 5753, 7884
Cyril of Alexandria and, 1979, 2117, 5753
Nestorius *vs.* Arian and Apollinaristic factions on, 2117, 5753
The Path of the Masters (Johnson), plagiarism of, by Twitchell (Paul), 2602
Thera (Cyclades), religious art in, 39
Therapeutae (Egyptian Jewish group)
asceticism of, 7722
eremitism of, 2823
fasting among, 2996
Therapeutic touch healing, development of, 3850–3851
Theravāda Buddhism, **9144–9154**. *See also* Burma/Myanmar and Burmese religions, Buddhism; Southeast Asia and Southeast Asian religions, Buddhism
Abhidharma in, 10020, 10021, 10022
antarābhava in, 1197
areas influenced by, 3075, 3076
arhat/arahant in, 476–477, 8036, 9146, 9152
asceticism in, 527
dualism and, 529
Aśoka in, 1091
attention in, 603
authority in, 694
bodhisattvas in, 997, 1085, 1329
Buddhadāsa's interpretation of, 1072
Buddhaghosa on, 1073–1074
buddhahood in, 1069
Buddha in, 1062, 1064–1065, 1067
miraculous powers of, 3155
in Cambodia, 5127, 5129, 5130, 5132, 9149–9150
celebrations in, 1304, 1306, 1307, 1308
celibacy in, 1475, 1477
civilizational character of, 9152
cosmology in, 1134
councils, Theravādin, 2037–2038
desire in, 2306
Devānaṃpiyatissa and, 2313

development of, 9145–9147
drums in, 2496–2497
Eightfold Path in, 2739, 3179
enlightenment in, 2794
ethics of, 1280
in Europe, 1189
expansion of, 1201, 1202
flight in, 3128
Four Noble Truths in, 1197, 3179
geographical distribution of, 1195
Hinduism and, 9148, 9150
history of study of
Horner (I. B.) in, 4129–4130
Pali Text Society and Thomas Rhys Davids in, 4129
images as divine presence in, 4390
in India, 9147–9148
individual realization in, 1549
karman in, 5098, 5099
laity in, 5288
in Laos, 5313, 9149–9150
of lay people, 9152
literature of, 1199, 1252–1253, 1262, 1263, 1265, 1266
Mahāyāna Buddhism and, 9150
Maitreya in, 1067, 5619
meaning of term, 9144–9145
meditation in, 9152, 9373
merit making in, 5874
missions of, 6071, 6079
modern, 9150–9153
monasticism in, 9148, 9149, 9150, 9151, 9153
Catholic compared to, 1549
gender and, 3331
morality in, 7651
music in, 6282, 6283
nāgas and *yakṣas* in, 6394–6395
New Year celebrations in, 6594
nirvāṇa in, 1197, 7697
notable personalities of, 1200–1201
nuns in, 6760
ordination in, 6855
origins of, 1108, 1132–1133, 1194, 9145–9146
orthodoxy, establishment of, in Southeast Asia, 8644–8645
Pali as language of, 1131, 1135, 1136, 1198, 1252–1253, 9145
pantheism in, 6965
pāramitās in, 6993, 6994
paritta in, 3156
pinkama ("act of merit") in, as hospitality, 4140
and politics, 9152–9153
prayer in, 7369
priesthood in, 7408
prostration in, 8061
pūjā in, 7496
Pure Lands in, 7502
rebirth in, 1067, 1197
reforms in, 9149, 9151
revival of, 9148–9150
saṃgha in, 8074–8075
saṃsāra in, 8098
schools *(nikāyas)* of, emergence of, 8074
scriptures of, Tipiṭaka canon established, 2037
sīmā (boundary) concept in, as consecration, 1954–1955
Sinhala (*See* Sinhala Theravāda Buddhism)
social awareness in, 5401
social impact of, 8463
in Sri Lanka
Burmese Buddhism and, 1135–1136, 1138
as civilizational religion, 9147
Devānaṃpiyatissa and, 2313, 9146–9147
dominance of, 1195, 1202
lay movements in, 9152
literature, 1200, 1201, 9146–9147
origins of, 9145–9146
and politics, 9152–9153
reforms in, 9151
revival of, 9148–9149
saṃgha, 9148, 9149
studies on, 1313, 6955–6956
tathāgata in, 9015
in Thailand
dominance of, 9094
refiguration of, 9096
revival of, 9149–9150
spread of, 1135, 1136–1137, 1195, 1202
three (number) in, 9347
Vietnamese religion influenced by, 9591
Vinaya, 6760
virtues of kings in, 1134
women in, 9146, 9147, 9152
There is a River (Sugrue), 1473
Theresa (Saint), cooking spell addressed to, 8678
Thérèse of Lisieux (saint), **9154–9155**
Therianthropism, **9155–9156**
vs. anthropomorphism, 388
in art, 4171–4172
contemporary interpretations of, 9155–9156
etymology of term, 9155
historical interpretations of, 9155
in rock paintings, in Africa, 5137
Therīgīthā (Buddhist text), 1087
Theriomorphism
vs. anthropomorphism, 388–389
of culture heroes, 2092
in rock paintings, in Africa, 5137
symbolism of, in Egypt, 5157
Thermodynamics, 7138
in Southern Bantu religions, 8662–8663
Theses (Pico della Mirandola), 7535
Theseus (Greek hero)
games dedicated to, 8723
Minotaur defeated by, 5274
relics of, 7687
ship of, 991
Thesmophora (goddess), 2270
Thesmophoria (Greek festival), 2269, 3684, **9156**
Athenian form of, 9156
Orpheus on, 2271
pig sacrifice in, 7144, 9156
Thespiae, Eros worshipped at, 2832
Thespis (Gaster), 2444
1 Thessalonians, 914–915, 920
asceticism in, 7722
content of, 914–915, 7015
God in, 3545
legal holiness in, 7014
relational discipline in, 8706
second coming of Christ in, 7766
2 Thessalonians, 915, 920
Antichrist in, 394
author of, 911, 915
circumcision in, 7016
content of, 7015
negative view of lawlessness in, 7014
Thessalonian school, on ethics, 1653
Thessalonica (Greece), Paul's missionary journey to, 7015
Thetan (soul), in Scientology, 4149, 8192
Theurgic deification, 2250
Theurgy, **9156–9158**
in Christianity, 9157–9158
definition of, 9156
deities of, Hekate as savior goddess, 3900
in Greek religion, 9156–9157
Iamblichus on, 6474
in Islam, 5585–5586
vs. magic, 9156
origins of, 9156–9157
practice of, 9157
qabbalistic, 7536–7537
philosophical interpretation of, 7539
Thiasoi (followers of deity), **9158–9159**
of Dionysos, 9158
etymology of term, 9158
origin of, 9158
Plato on, 9159
Thibault, Paul J., on Saussure, 8758
Thick description, Geertz (Clifford) on, 8499, 8500
Thief. *See also* Theft
Kṛṣṇa as, 5250
Thieme, Paul
on *brahman,* 1024, 1025
on death, 4456
on Indo-European pantheon, 4463
on *pūjā,* 7493
Thiên Buddhism. *See* Chan Buddhism
Think and Grow Rich (Hill), 6582, 6585
Thinking, in existentialism, 2926
Thiong'o, Ngugi wa, 3088
Thior, Amadou, 3098
Thiphakorawong, Chao Phraya, 1139
Third eye, 2942–2943
and intuition, 4526
of Maitreya, 5620
of Devī, 4326
of Gaṇeśa, 4327
of Śiva, 4324
Third Wave Pentecostalism, 7031, 7033
Thirst, of the dead, 9703
Thirst Lodge. *See* Sun Dance
Thirteen (number), interpretations of, 6749
Thirteen Classics *(shisanjing)*
as canon, 1909
modern use of, 1910
Thirteen Methods of Rabbi Yishma'e'l, rabbinic hermeneutics and, 3748
"Thirty Letters of the Alphabet, The" (Longchenpa), 5193
Thirty-nine Articles (England)
as creed, 2059
under Elizabeth I, 349
Parliamentary approval of, 349
Thirty-six (number), interpretations of, 6750
Thirty-three (number), interpretations of, 6750
Thirty Years War (1618-1648)
Jews in, 5016
papacy in, 6973
"This Is How They Were Placed for Us" (Tapahonso), 7226
"This Preparation" (Ortiz), 7225
Thitmanit (mythic figure), in Canaanite religion, 1399
Þjálfi (mythic figure), 9166
Þjazi (giant), Loki and, 5508
Tholoi (round buildings), 1792
Tholuck, Friedrich A. G., on al-Ḥallāj, 3756
Thom, A., on megaliths, 5825
Thom, Alexander, 453
Thomas, Acts of
ouroboros serpent in, 1793
virginity in, 9608
Thomas, Dylan
creative dissonance in works of, 7204
curse in work of, 2106

Thomas, Edward J., 945, 1312
on religious communities, 7718
Thomas, Gospel of. See Gospel of Thomas
Thomas, Keith
on animals, 358
on magic, 5563, 5568
Thomas, Linda, 79
Thomas, Martha Carey, Smith (Hannah Whitall) and, 8446
Thomas, Nicolas, on ethnocentrism, 7992
Thomas, Psalms of, Mandaean religion in, 5639
Thomas, Wesley, on gender classifications, 3410
Thomas à Kempis, **9159–9160**
Imitation of Christ, 9159–9160
on imitation of Jesus and Mary, 1670, 8704
influence of, 9159
on Jesus as moral model, 4844
Thomas Aquinas, **9160–9164**
aesthetics of, 46
Albertus Magnus as teacher of, 232, 9160
on angels, 347
on Aristotle, 46, 480, 481–482, 4273, 9162–9163
metaphysics of, 5990
against Averroists, 481–482
on baptism, 9163
biblical exegesis of, 9161
on blasphemy, 972–973
and Bucer (Martin), 1059
canonization of, 9164
on chance, 1527
on charisma, 1550
on chastity, 1558
classification of religions by, 1818
on conscience, 1941
on curses, 2105
on deity, 2257
on demons, 2278, 2280, 2281
on desire, 2308
on Dionysius the Areopagite, 9160
as doctor of the church, 8176, 9164
on doctrine, 2382
on Dominicans, 7724
early Western Christianity influenced by, 2582
Eastern theologians compared to, 2587
epistemology of, 2819
on eternity of world, 9362
on ethics, 1653, 1654, 9163
on faith, 2425, 9163
on female body, 4166
on free will, 3200
Gilson (Étienne) on, 3492
on God, 3555–3556
existence of, 582, 3555, 5713, 7123–7124, 7422, 7423, 9163
knowledge of, 157, 7775–7776
on goodness, 3636
on grace, 158, 3645–3646, 9163
Gregory X and, 9162
on Hell, 9454–9455
on hope, 4127
on human perfectibility, 7039–7040
on humor, 4218–4219
Ibn Rushd opposed by, 4272, 4273
on idea of God, 2779
influence of, 9164
on intuition, 4525
on Jesus' body, 3170
on Jesus' maleness, 335
on knowledge, 5204–5205
Leo XIII on, 8176
life and works of, 9160–9162
literary achievements of, 5471
on magic, 5577–5578
Maritain (Jacques) on, 5712–5713
on membership in the church, 1777
on merit, 5876
metaphysics of, 5990, 9163
on miracles, 1528
mysticism of, 390
on nature, 6432, 9162–9163
divine order of, 2607
Neoplatonism and, 6475
"occasional" used by, 6779
ontological argument criticized by, 7421–7422
ontology of, 6830
on Peter Lombard, 9160–9161
philosophy of, 9162–9163
against polemics, 7244
on polytheism, 4038
on predestination, 3203, 3207
on redemption, 7640
relics of, 7689
religious experience of, 7737
religious reform brought about by, 7654
on revelation, 7775–7776
Scholarios (Gennadios) on, 8173–8174
soul, doctrine of, 8564
on suicide, 8830
on the supernatural, 8860
on superstition, 8865
theology of, 9134, 9135, 9136, 9163–9164
on Trinity, 9361
on truth, 9375
on "two books," 9422
Tyrrell (George) influenced by, 9427
Urban IV and, 9161
via negativa used by, 6990
on virtues, 9163
on visions, 9611
Vulgate Bible as source for, 9163
on war, 6648
on William of Saint-Armour, 9161
Thomas Christianity. *See also* Malabar Church
in India, 1729
Nag Hammadi codices as evidence of, 6397
Syriac Orthodox Church and, 8939
Thomas Cranmer of Canterbury (Williams), 2472
Thomas Gallus, Hugh of Saint-Victor and, 4151
Thomas of Cantimpré
on heart, 3883
on nature, 6433
Thomas of Monmouth, 400
Thomas the Rhymer (Thomas of Erceldoune), 2953
Thomism. *See also* Neo-Thomism; Scholasticism
Council of Trent and, 8175–8176
Dominicans and, 2414
Leonine, 8176–8177
Leo XIII and, 5411
of Maritain (Jacques), 5712–5713
Mercier (Désiré Joseph) and, 5868
revival of, 6974, 9164
Roman Catholicism and, 7882
schism and, 8157
scientism and, 8182
spread of, 9164
Suárez (Francisco) and, 8799
Thompson, Bard, 2993
Thompson, Campbell, 5987
Thompson, David, 677
Thompson, Donald, 686
Thompson, E. J., 8957
Thompson, E. P., subaltern studies and, 8800
Thompson, Gertrude Caton, 445
Thompson, J. Eric S., 5886, 5941
Thompson, Randall, 6313
Thompson, Robert F., 117
Thompson River Indian religion
ablutions in, 11
bears in, 809
vision quest in, 8703
Thomsen, Harry, 6521
Thomson, Donald F., 684
Thomson, James, Latin American missions, 1699–1700
Thonga people (Mozambique), history of study of, 113
Thor (Þórr) (deity), **9164–9167**
and Óðinn, 9165, 9166
cult of, 9165
in Eddas, 2692–2693
functions of, 5995
hammer of, 9166, 9167
Loki and, 5508, 5509
myths of, 9165–9167
oak of, Boniface's destruction of, 6083
personality and function of, 9166
phallic symbols of, 9167
role in Germanic pantheon, 3452, 4462
in sagas, 8024, 8025
shape-shifting opponent of, 8303
sovereignty of, 5995
Thursday named after, 1689
Thoreau, Henry David
King (Martin Luther, Jr.) influenced by, 5145
on morality, 7652
nature writing of, as spiritual autobiography, 703
Thorn Birds, The (McCullough), 3061
Thornton, John K., 10027
Þórólfr (mythic figure), in sagas, 8025
Thorowgood, Thomas, on American Indians as Hebrew, 1856
Thoth (deity), **9167–9168**
in afterlife, 2705
baboon associated with, 6151
in creation story, 2961
in Egyptian pantheon, 2705
Hermes identified with, 3938, 9168
Hermes Trismegistos and, 3938
iconography of, 9167–9168
and Isis, 4557
in Kushite religion, 5268
magic of, 2712
moon and, 6175
playing chess, and chronological space, 1761
Re and, 9167
in story of the Fall, 2962
tarot cards and, 1414
temple to, 9168
Theban kings and, 2706
in writing, origin of, 269, 270
Thought
action and, in environmental ethics, 2654
open *vs.* closed systems of, 5567
and belief in magic, 5567
Thought reform. *See* Brainwashing
Thought Reform and the Psychology of Totalism (Lifton), 1031
Thought Woman, 3407
in Pueblo religion, 6724
Thousand and One Nights
ghosts in, 3476
Malay version of, 4665
Thracian religion and society, **9168–9171**. *See also* Geto-Dacian religion
Christianity, 1682
and Dacian Riders, 2123
deities of, 9169 (*See also* Bendis; Sabazios)
funeral rites in, 9170
history of, 9168–9169
and immortalization, 2248
language of, 9168–9169
sacrifice in, 9169
sources on, 9168, 9169

tattooing in, 9170
tribes of, 9168
Thracian Rider, **9171–9172**
Þræll (mythological figure), 2693
Thraetaona (monster), 2432
Thread
sacred, in Vedism, 5278, 7815
symbolism of, 5274, 5278
Three (number). *See also* Triads; Trinity
days, revivals after, 35
gods with three heads, 3804
Hekate and, 3900
interpretations of, 6746–6747
Three Books of Testimonies against the Jews (Cyprian), 2747
Three Books on Life (Ficino), 5579
Three Books on Occult Philosophy (Agrippa), 5579
Three Caverns
of Daoist texts, 2183, 2195, 2203, 7414
establishment of, 7414
Three Deaths (Tolstoy), 9220
Three Doctrines (painting), humor in, 4209
Three Dogmatic Answers to the Theologians of Tübingen (Jeremias II), 4832
Three Epitaphs (Taylor), 2161
Three-headed drum, 2497
3HO Foundation. *See* Healthy, Happy, Holy Organization
"Three in One Teaching," 2187
Three Jewels (Buddhism), 1103–1105, 2332, 7496, 7497
Three Kingdoms period (China), 1574, 1594, 5621
Three Kingdoms period (Korea), 1170–1171, 5230
Three Kings. *See also* Magi
carnivalization of, in Brazil, 1443–1444
feast of, 2818
as Zoroastrian magi, 9990
Three Miracles, Feast of, 2818
Three Mysteries, in Zhenyan Buddhism, 9961–9962
Three Pillars of Zen, The (Kapleau), 1189
Three Pure Ones, in Daoism, 4916
"Three Ritual Compendia" *(sanli),* 1907–1908
Three Stages school of Buddhism, 5686
Three Steps (Buddhist teaching), Śīlabhadra *vs.* Jñānaprabha on, 8399
Three Treatises school, 1576
Three Truths, 9966
Three Turnings (Buddhist teaching), 1275–1276
Three Wheeled maṇḍala, in Cakrasamvara tradition, 1350
Threlkeld, Lancelot Edward, 681, 686
Threshold of Religion, The (Marett), 7347, 7372
Thronbesteigungsfest, 5147
Thrones
Aztec, 5173
Maya, 1469
Minoan, 39, 5282
Mycenaean, 41
Þrymr, 2692–2693
Þrymskviða (Eddic poem), 2692–2693, 5508–5509, 9166–9167
Thubbstan rgya mtsho (Dalai Lama), 2132
Thucydides
dēmiourgos used by, 2272
time in works of, 6375
Thukapi (turtle), 2481
Thumāmah ibn Ashras, 6319
Thumos (body-soul)
death and, 8542
in Greek tradition, 8541
Plato on, 7184
Thunder, 7603–7604. *See also* Thunder deities and spirits
eagle equated with, 2554
in Etruscan divination, 2873
in North American Indian religions, iconography of, 4309
as portent, 7336
swords as symbol of, 967
Thunder, Whole Mind, The (Nag Hammadi writing), Sophia in, 8523
Thunderbird
in cave art, 1471
distribution of belief in, 5995
iconography of, 4309
masculine sacrality in, 5760
in Mesopotamian religions, anthropomorphism of, 5950
as monster, 6163
in North American Indian religions, 948, 6651
Thunderbolt Realm *Maṇḍala,* 5644
Thunder deities and spirits, 5992–5996
Amaru as, 4411
in Andean religions, 8601–8602
in Anishinaabe religion, 368
in Arctic religions, 469–470
in Caribbean religions, from Yoruba, 1433, 1434
in Chuvash religion, 1784
Illapa as, 4411
masculine sacrality in, 5760
in Negrito religions, 6454, 6457
in Ojibwa religion, 6663
Perun as, **7062–7063**
in Sami religion, 8088
in Slavic religion, 8435–8436
Ukko, 9438
Thunderstones, in Kele, 1436
Thunderstorms, 7604
Thung Yang (pilgrimage center), 9832
Thunor (deity), 6943
Thunr (Þun[a]r[az]) (deity), 3450, 3451
Thūpavaṃsa (Buddhist text), 1199
Thureau-Dangin, F., 2537
Thurii, golden tablets of, 2248–2249
Thurman, Howard, 67, 80, 963
Thurman, Robert, 9190
Thurneysen, Eduard, 790
and neoorthodoxy, 6467
Thurneysen, Rudolf, 8960
Thurston, Herbert, 1005
Thusia (burnt offering), 3667–3669
Thus Spoke Zarathustra (Nietzsche), 6615
Übermensch (overman) in, 3956
Thutmose I (Egyptian king), 2706
Thutmose II (Egyptian king), 2706
Thutmose III (Egyptian king), 2707
Thu'u bkwan Chos kyi nyi ma (Buddhist author), 1223
Þyrmr (giant), 9166
Ti (Bonnie Lu Nettles), Heaven's Gate and, 3889–3891
Tiahuanaco culture, 5291, 5292
llama sacrifices in, 1364
Tiamat (deity)
and Apsu as pair, 1994, 7861
Canaanite parallels, 1392, 1393
chaos and, 1539
in creation myth, 2962
in *Enuma elish,* 2809, 3377
in form of cow, 1466
iconography of, 4316
Marduk defeating, 2431, 2442, 3377
tensions between offspring and, 325, 952–953
as water, 9699, 9700
Tian (Heaven), 3888, **9172–9173**. *See also* Shangdi
ancestors in court of, 1583
and atheism, 577, 578
Bible translation debate over, 1633
in Buddhism, 9172
in Confucianism, 9172–9173
Confucius on, 1571, 1936
in Daoism, 9172
as deity, 1575, 1586–1587, 9172
earth, ruptured linkage with, 1625–1626
as impersonal nature, 9172–9173
king as Son of Heaven *(tianzi),* 1583, 1625, 1645, 1891, 7266
mandate of (*See* Mandate of Heaven)
Mengzi on, 1587
monotheism issue and, 1631
morality and, 1584, 1585
and moral teachings and quest for harmony, 3888
Mozi on, 1586–1587, 6217–6218
as natural entity in Old Text school, 1575
in Neo-Confucianism, 9173
as order of nature in Xunzi, 1587–1588
rituals of, 9172
sacred geography of, 3435
sacrifices to, 5178
Wang Chong on, 9671
will of, 1571, 1573, 1584, 1587
Xunzi on, 1573
Tianchang Guan (Tianchang Abbey), 2208
Tiandao (Way of the Cosmos), Confucian ethics and, 1896
Tiangong (deity), 9172
Tianhsin/Tianxin Zhengfa (orthodox rites of the heart of heaven), 2198, 2206
Tianli (heavenly principle), 5431, 9173
Tianshi Dao. *See* Celestial Masters/Heavenly Masters
Tianshi dong (Grotto of the Celestial Master), 2637
Tiantai, Mount, pilgrimage to, 9835
Tiantai school of Buddhism, 1237–1238, **9173–9181**
Bodhidharma's legend in, 995
classification systems in, 8031
cosmology of 1000 *dharmas* (realms) in, 2029
doctrines of, 1163, 1237, 1576–1577, 1596, 9175–9176
emptiness *(śūnyatā)* in, 8859
enlightenment in, 9174
exegesis in, 1272, 1274
factions of, 1240
Four Noble Truths in, 9177–9178
in Japan (*See* Tendai school of Buddhism)
in Korea, 9436
literature, 9175–9176, 9177–9178
masters in, 9179–9181
meditation in, 1291–1292, 1601, 9178
nature viewed by, 2629
nirvāṇa in, 6630–6631
origins of, 9174–9175
philosophy of, 1302, 9177–9179
Pure Land practices of, 4924
and Tendai school, 9074, 9075
Zhiyi in, 9965–9966
Tianxin movement, 1602
Tian zi (Son of Heaven). *See* Son of Heaven

Tiao huopen (jumping over the fire), 1641
Ti bananj (little guardian angel), 9636
Tibb al-nabawi (Islamic prophetic medicine)
history of, 3834
overview of, 3833
Tiberias (Israel), rabbinic academy at, 2743
Tiber Island, Asklepios in, cult of, 552
Tiberius (Roman emperor), and expulsion of Jews and Isis worshipers from Rome, 4558
Tiberius Julius Alexander (nephew of Philo Judaeus), 7105
apostasy by, 430–431
Tibetan and Himalayan Digital Library, 9188
Tibetan *Book of the Dead*. *See Book of the Dead* (Tibet)
Tibetan Buddhism, **1150–1159,** 9183–9186. *See also* Sa skya school
ālaya-vijñāna in, 229
Āryadeva in, 514–515
Atīśa in, 592
Avalokiteśvara in, 705, 706
beliefs and doctrines of, 1155–1156
Bhāvaviveka's contribution to, 861
in Bhutan (*See* Bhutan)
Bka' brgyud (Kagyu) school of (*See* Bka' brgyud pa order)
Bka' gdams pa order of (*See* Bka' gdams pa order)
Black Hat Karma pa of, 2131, 5101–5104
bodhisattvas in, 1082, 1152, 1156, 1224
and Bon religion, 1007–1010, 5222, 5223, 9182, 9186
in Brazil, 1190
breath and breathing in, 1045
canon, 1256, 1338
celebrations in, 1304, 1308
central buddha in, 1068
Cham dance in, 1827
chants in, 1535–1536
Chinese Buddhism and, 1151, 1152, 1154, 1155, 1158–1159, 1166, 9184
clothing in, 1827–1828, 1829
communism and, 1098, 1100, 1158–1159
consecration of images in, 4389
contemporary, 9186
Dalai Lama in (*See* Dalai Lama)
dances in, 2140
and debate at Bsam yas, 5069–5070, 6940–6941
decline of, 1095, 1152
deities, dilemma of, 8381
developments of, 1153–1155
Dge lugs pa order of (*See* Dge lugs pa order of Buddhism)
dreams in, 2488
eclectic movement in, 1155
Eight Systems of, 5223–5224
engaged Buddhism, 2786
Esoteric Buddhism, 1096, 1097
ethics of, 1282
exile in, 2924
feminist analysis of, 8243–8244
Guhyasamāja Tantra in, 3708–3709
healing in, 3864, 3866
Hevajra Tantra in, 3966
horrific buddhas in, 1081
iconography of, 4330
Indian Buddhism and, 1153, 1154, 9184
Kālacakra tradition in, 5057
Karma pas lineage in, 5101–5104
kingship in, 1230, 1232, 7262, 8985, 9183–9184
Klong chen Rab 'byams pa and, 5191–5195
Kong sprul Blo gros mtha' yas and, 5222–5224
and Korean Buddhism, 1171
Kṣitigarbha in, 5255
lamas in (*See* Dalai Lama; Lamas)
of lay people, 9184–9186
Lhasa council and, 2038
lineages of, 5223
literature of, 1152, 1155, 1198, 1199, 1266, 7167, 10021, 10022
Mādhyamika Buddhism, 5555
mahāmudrā in, 5596, 5597–5599
Mahāvairocana in, 5607
Maitreya in, 9898–9899
Manchu veneration of, 1609
maṇḍalas in, 5643–5644
mass monasticism in, 8083
meditation in (*See* Buddhist meditation, in Tibetan Buddhism)
Middle Way in, 5070–5071
monasteries
Chinese monasteries and, 1095, 1151
Chinese persecution of, 1158, 1159
and education, 1156
establishment of, 1152, 1153, 6940
royal function of, 1096
succession by incarnation in, 9184
in Mongolia, 1148, 1149, 1150, 1154, 1155, 3966, 9182
Mūlasarvāstivāda school, 1223
music in, 6283, 6298–6299
nongenealogical succession in, 3426
nuns in, 6760, 6761–6762
"Oṃ maṇi padme hūṃ" in, 8676
origins of, 1151–1152
Padmasambhava's role in, 6940–6942
past lives in, 5192
persecution of, 9186
philosophy of, 1301
pilgrimage in, 1151, **7166–7168,** 9185
pollution in, 7503
precepts for monks and nuns, 6760
priesthood in, 7407
prophecies in, 5192
pūjā in, 7496
Red Hat Karma pa of, 2131
religious education in, 5224
revival of, 1152–1153, 1158, 1224
Rime approach to, 5222–5224
ritual calendar of, 1097–1098
Rnying ma pa school of (*See* Rnying ma pa school of Buddhism)
in Russia, 9182
in *saṃgha* in, **8081–8086**
Śāntarakṣita's role in transmission of, 8106
schools of, 1204, **1222–1229,** 9182
sectarian development of, 1100
Shamar pa lineage in, 5103–5104
skull symbolism in, 3805
spread of, 1093, 1126, 1230, 1231, 9182
as state religion, 1095
studies on, 1223, 1311, 1312, 1314, 1315
Svātantrika logic in, 8858
synthesis of indigenous religions and, 3154, 3156
and Taiwanese Buddhism, 8962
tathāgata-garbha in, 9018
temples of, 9047–9048, **9049–9052,** 9184
textiles in, 9089, 9090
theocracy in, 9109
transmigration in, 9328
Treasure tradition in, 9331, 9332–9333
in United States, 1189–1190
Vajradhara in, 9510–9511
Vajrasattva in, 9515
Vajrayāna (Tantric) Buddhism, 8083
Atīśa establishing, 1096
dominance of, 1152, 1221
Indian Buddhism and, 1153
literature, 1214–1215
medicine and divination in, 3866
monastic morality in, 1218
Padmasambhava's role in, 6940–6942
rituals in, 1097
spread of, 1093–1094
women in, 3332–3333
women in, 1156, 3332–3333, 5557–5558, 7168
worship and devotional life in, **9839–9842**
Yellow Hat Dge lugs pa of, 2131
Yeshe Tsogyal in, 9881–9882
yoga in, 1153, 1157, 1286–1288
Tibetan Buddhist Resource Center, 9188
Tibet and Tibetan religions, **9181–9192**
autobiography in, 701
Bon religion (*See* Bon religion)
'Bro tradition, *Kālacakra Tantra* in, 5057
Buddhism
astrology in, vol. 3 color insert
prayer in, vol. 9 color insert
sacred time in, vol. 1 color insert
Wheel of Existence in, vol. 3 color insert
Candrakīrti in, 1401
'cham dance of, 2140
Chinese invasion of, 1100, 1158–1159, 1168, 1315, 2132, 7269, 9188
Christianity, missions and, 1186
civil administrator of, 2131, 2132
dance in
'cham dance, 2140
as means to enlightenment, 2140
death in, 3866
deities of
local and regional gods, 3866
Shugs ldan (Shugden) in, **8381–8382**
divination *(mo)* in, healing and, 3866
funeral rites in, 3236, 3238
tombless, 9225
gambling in, 3263, 3264
geomancy in, 3437
Gesar in, 3463–3464
government structure of, 2131, 2132
healing in (*See* Healing and medicine, in Tibet)
history of study of, **9187–9192**
in 19th century, 9188–9189
fascination with Tibetan Buddhism and, 9187
feminist, 9190
on Internet, 9188
organizations in, 9188
by Tibetan exiles, 9187, 9188
Tibetan texts in, 9187, 9188, 9189

Indian thought in, Sakya
Paṇḍita (Sa skya Paṇḍita)
and, 8052
invasion of (1950), 2132
kingship in, heavenly origin
of, 5179–5180
maṇḍala mapped onto, 1350
marriage in, 5725
mdos rituals in, 3156
Mongol attack on, 1154–
1155, 1228, 8051
music in, **6292–6299**
nonsectarian movement, Rang
byung rdo rje in, 5102
obedience in, 6778
orgy in, 6879
political and social upheaval
in, mid-14th century, 5193
popular religion, 9184–9186,
9191
prayers in, 2131
pre-Buddhist religions, 9182–
9183
cosmology in, 9183
demons in, 9183
kingship in, 9182–9183
sources on, 9182–9183
shamanism in, 9191
soul (*bla*) in, 3865
tourism in, 7269
Tsami tradition, *Kālacakra
Tantra* in, 5057
visualization in
attention in, 603
in Gcod rite, 5558
Tibetan language
Buddhist scriptures translated
into, 1266–1267
Mongolian Buddhist services
in, 1149
Tantric texts translated into,
1214–1215, 1223–1224
Tibetology. *See* Tibet and
Tibetan religions, history of
study of
Tibet Visual History Online,
9188
Ti bonanj (soul), in Caribbean
neo-African cults, 1434
Ticciviracocha. *See* Viracocha
Ti-chi-chu (lord of the
foundation), 2406
Tickling Dance, 2464
Tie chunlian (pasting up spring
scrolls), 1641–1642
Tiedemann, Dietrich, on *Corpus
Hermeticum*, 3951
Tiele, C. P., **9192**
Anesaki Masaharu influenced
by, 342
classification of religions by,
1818
on the Flood in Iranian
mythology, 2964
Kristensen's (W. Brede)
rejection of, 5246
on phenomenology, 7089
in Remonstrant Brotherhood,
493

"world religions" used by,
9802
T'ien (heaven). *See also* Tian
meaning of name, 6408
T'ien-t'ai. *See* Tiantai school of
Buddhism
Tiermes (deity), in Sami religion,
8088
Tiermes/Diermes (deity), 6755
Tierra del Fuego. *See also* Haush
religion; Selk'nam religion
deus otiosus in, 2310
feminine sacrality of women
in, 3021
high gods in, 8589
initiation rites in, 8585
lord of the animals in, 5516
rejuvenation myth in, 7683
supreme beings of, 8579
Tif'eret (beauty), 3550
Tigers
in Indus Valley religion,
4473–4474
in Korean religion, 5229
humor and, 4208
Tiglath-pileser III (Assyrian
ruler), 5948
Tigriña people. *See*
Amhara-Tigriña religion
Tigris River, 7861
Tiikuywuuti (deity), 6724
Tijānī, Abū al-'Abbās Aḥmad al-,
9011
Tijānīyah (Ṣūfī order), 9011
dhikr of, 9011
founder of, 9011
Fulbe scholars and, 3229
'Umar Tāl and, 9444–9445
Ṭīkā (commentary), 1271
Tikal (Maya city), ceremonial
complex of, 1804
Tikhon (patriarch), **9193–9194**
Tikhon of Zadonsk (saint), 7943,
9194
Tiki (Ti'i) (first man), 7314
Tikopia Island (Polynesia)
isolation of, 9195, 9197
location of, 9194–9195
population growth in, 9197,
9198
Tikopia language, 9198
Tikopia religion (Polynesia),
9194–9198
chiefs in, 9195, 9196, 9197
Christianity, 9197
concepts and rituals in, 9195–
9196
deities in, 9195
genital operations in, 7808,
7809
priesthood in, 9196
spirit mediumship in, 8690
spirits in, 9195, 9196
studies of, Firth (Raymond)
and, 3121–3122, 7808,
9195, 9197
women in, 9198
"Work of the Gods" ritual in,
9195, 9196–9197, 9198

Tiktin, Solomon, 3291
Tikúna people, secret societies of,
9920
Tilak, Bal Gangadhar, **9198–
9200**
imprisonment of, 9199
in Indian nationalism, 9198–
9199, 9319
on *Bhagavadgītā*, 854, 9199
writings of, 9199
Tilak, Narayan Vaman, 5700
Tilāwah (recitation of Qur'ān),
9200–9203
and canon, 9200–9201
contexts of, 9201–9202
rules for, 9201, 9202
speed of, 9202
styles of, 9201, 9202
on television and radio, 9202
Tilley, Maureen A., 6947
Tillich, Paul Johannes, **9203–
9205**
aesthetics of, 47
reality and, 55
apologetics of, 428, 429
on art and religion, 495,
499–500
Brunner's (Emil) critique of,
1054
on capitalism, 9203
on culture, 9203, 9204
on drama, 2475
Eliade on, 2757
on faith, 584
Freud's theories and, 3217
on God, 3557, 6964, 7423,
7454
on grace, 3646
on historiography, 4030,
4043
human being defined by,
7111
idea of God, 3003
influence of, 9204
influence on film, 3100
on Kant, 6103
on knowledge, 5210
and liberal Protestantism,
6104
and neoorthodoxy, 6466,
6468, 6469
Otto's (Rudolf) influence on,
4101, 6930–6931
on pastoral psychology, 7477
on phenomenology of
religion, 7087
postmodern literature and,
5482
on "Protestant Principle,"
3847, 7453, 7459
on racism, 1380
recovery of dialogue between
religion and philosophy by,
7120
response to attacks on theism,
584
on socialism, 9203
on symbols, 9204
symbol theory and, 8912

theology of, 9130, 9131,
9137, 9203, 9204
Tönnies (Ferdinand)
influencing, 9230
on transcendence, secular
need for, 2679
on truth, 7206
World War I influencing,
9203
Tillotson, John, 6103
Tilokarāja (king of Chiangmai),
1137
Tilopa (Buddhist scholar), 1225
Nā ro pa and, 6415, 6416
Tilton, Robert, 7714
Timaeus (Plato), 421
Demiurge in, 2273, 2274,
2507, 7183, 7190
dualism in, 2515
eternity in, 2854, 2855
Galen influenced by, 3255
geometry in, *3440*, 3442
God in, 3685
gods in, 7183, 7190
Gurdjieff (G. I.) and, 3711
intellect in, 7182
Middle Platonist
interpretation of, 7188,
7189
Plutarch interpreting, 7189,
7200
prayer in, 7370
Proclus's commentary on,
7191
soul in, 7182, 7184, 7185,
7186
sun in, 8835
triadism in, 9348
World Soul in, 6963
Timbira religion. *See* Ge-Timbira
religion
Timbuktu. *See* Tombouctou
Time. *See also* Calendars
in African religions
and kingship, 5170
in Maasai cosmology,
2000
in afterlife, views of, 132–133
in ages of world,
periodization systems of,
173–177
in Ainu religion, 7990
aiōn as, 2855, 7992
alchemy's mastery of, 236–
237, 7683
in Arabic culture, 3209
in art, 3005
Augustine on, 3555
Aztec notion of, 3064
in Buddhism
in Sautrāntika, 8137
sāhasra cosmology and,
2028
Sarvāstivādin theory of,
8118
in Celtic religion, 1491
in Christianity, in
historiography, 4028–4029
chronology, **1757–1761**

Vol. 1: 1–610, Vol. 2: 611–1340, Vol. 3: 1341–2120, Vol. 4: 2121–2850, Vol. 5: 2851–3580, Vol. 6: 3581–4292, Vol. 7: 4293–5046, Vol. 8:
5047–5748, Vol. 9: 5749–6448, Vol. 10: 6449–7176, Vol. 11: 7177–7864, Vol. 12: 7865–8572, Vol. 13: 8573–9286, Vol. 14: 9287–10018,
Appendix: 10019–10091

ENCYCLOPEDIA OF RELIGION, SECOND EDITION

Time *continued*
chronos as, 7992
concretization of, 1352–1353
in cultural-historical method, 5260
cyclical *vs.* linear concepts of, 6373, 6374
in Daoism, 2178
definitions and senses of, 7986–7989
Einstein (Albert) on, 7138
in eternity, 2853, 2854
experience of the sacred and, 7989–7990
in fiction, 3057
hierophany (manifestation of the sacred) and, 3973
in Hinduism
in Epic cosmology, 2016–2017, 3999
in Purāṇas, 2018, 4015, 7499–7500
in Upaniṣadic cosmology, 2015–2016
historicization of, 1355, 1357
in historiography, 6373, 6374–6375, 6378–6379
Hügel (Friedrich von) on, 4150
ideal, 132
in Vedānta, 9547
in Islam, *ḥājj*, space and time collapsed in, 7984
in Israelite religion, 6378–6379
in Jainism, 2025
in Judaism, and history, view of, 4058
kairos as, 7992
Manu's role in, 5679
in Maya religion, 5796–5797, 5882
Mesoamerican concept of, 177, 1357, 1359
in metaphysics, 2854
in millenarianism, 6029
modernity and, 6110
moon and, 6170–6171
in music, 6253–6255
in myth, 6362, 6371, 6372
nature, origin, spectrum, power, and rhythm in, 7990–7991
in North American Indian religions, sacred time, 6681–6682
periodicity and calendars, 1352–1353
periodicized in three, 6747
personification of, 1354
in physics, 2659
purification by, 7511
reestablishing, through epic, 2816
reversal of, in rejuvenation myths, 7683–7684
in rituals, 7837–7838
sacred (*See* Sacred time)
sacred space and, 7984
of sacrifices, 8000
scientific view of, relativity and, 2032
in South American Indian religions
cosmic time, 2011
and messianism, 5983
space and (*See* Space, and time)
stopped, at death, 7986
symbolic time and the figura, **8915–8919**
development of symbolic structures, 8916–8917
intentional character of, 8915–8916
periodicity in, 8917–8919
ritual performance in, 8917
in talismanry, 5585–5586
thealogical, 9100
in Vedism, 2014, 7984
Western conception of, and transculturation, 9294–9295
in Zurvanism, 10011–10015
Time and Mankind (Brandon), 1040
Timelessness, of eternity, 2853
Timely Message from Heaven, A (MRTCG handbook), 105–106, 6216
Time model of creation from chaos, 1986–1987
Timofeevich, Ivan, Filippov (Daniil) and, 8249
1 Timothy, 915
author of, 911, 915, 7013
content of, 915
2 Timothy, 915
author of, 911, 915, 7013
content of, 915
on Luke, 908
Timothy (bishop of Ephesus), 914, 915
Timothy, Saint, martyred in Anthesteria, 375
Timothy Ailuros, **9205**
Monophysitism and, 6153
Timothy I (catholicos), 6479
Tim people, mythology of, elephant in, 2750
Timurid dynasty. *See also* Mughal dynasty
in Dagestan, 4614
Timur Shah (Mongol emperor), Judaism under, 5009
Tinbergen, Nikolaas, instinctive behavior investigated by, 2867
Tin can rattles, 7035
Tindale, Norman
on Ngarrindjeri people, 649
research base of, 686
Tingley, Katherine, 845, 7228–7229, **9205–9207**
and Point Loma Theosophical community, 6546
in Theosophical Society, 6535
Tingley, Philo, 9205
Tinirau (mythic figure), 3397
Tinker, George, 6422, 6424
Tin/Tinia (deity), 2870–2871, 2873
Tintoretto, reality in art of, 54
Tinya (drum), 7036
Tipiṭaka ("three baskets") canon. *See also* Pali scriptures/texts
establishment of, 2037
Tipler, Frank, 510, 513
on cybernetics, 2111, 2112
Tippecanoe, Battle of (1811), 9028
Tipton, Steven, 6522
Tiqqun (mending/restitution of life), Luria (Isaac) on, 5533
Tiqqunei soferim, 865
Tiqqun middot ha-nefesh (Ibn Gabirol), 4266
Tir (deity), in Armenian religion, 491
Tirakuna (Fathers), Pachamama and, 3416
Tirawa (deity), 6651, 6703
Tirelo (service), 9388
Tiridates III (king of Armenia), conversion to Christianity, 488, 492, 3700
Tír inna mBan (Land of Women), 1491
Tirmidhī, Abū ʿIsā Muḥammad al-
on medical treatment, 3831
on *walāyah,* 9661
sunan collection of, 3730
Tirmūlar (Śaiva saint), on Śiva, 8042
Tīrtha (pilgrimage site), 778, 7168, 7169, 7170, 7863. *See also* Pilgrimage, Hindu
Kurukṣetra as, 5268
Tirtha (purifying water), 2451
Tīrthaṃkaras (Ford-makers), **9207–9209**
as *arhat,* 476, 9207
career of, 9207
concept of, 9207
cosmology of, 2023, 2024
cultic life of, 9208
gender of, 3326–3327
iconography of, 4382, 9207–9208
lineage of, 9207
mothers of, 3327
mythic importance of, 9208
number of, 1066–1067
phallus of, 7084
and religious experience, 9208
soul of, 9207
time of appearance, 2025
universality of, 1350
Tīrthayātrāparvan (Hindu text), 7169
Tirukkōvaiyār (Māṇikkavācakar), 5671
Tirumala Tirupati (Hindu temple), eco-activism encouraged at, 2622
Tirumūlar (poet), 8974
Tirumuṟai (poems), 5671, 7210
in Śaiva Siddhanta, 8042
Tiruvāymoli (Nammāḻvār), 7172
Tiryakian, Edward A., 6781
Tishʿah be-Av (Ninth of Av)
fasting on, 3171
in Jewish calendar, 4866, 4867
Tishby, Isaiah, on messianism in Hasidism, 3788
Tislātin (bride), 835
Tisza culture (prehistoric), 7378, 7379
Titans (mythic figures), 165. *See also* Prometheus
Dionysos torn apart by, 2965, 2983
in Greek creation myth, 1460
moon and, 6174
in Orphic Gold Tablets, 6898
Tithes, **9209–9210**
in Christianity, 9209, 9210
in Egyptian religion, 9209
in Greek religion, 9209–9210
in Israelite religion, 9209, 9210
in Judaism, 9210
Tithing
in Amhara-Tigriña religion, 2573
in Islam (*See Zakāt*)
Titicaca, Lake, 5291–5292
Titicaca Island, 5291–5292
Titicaca Rock, 5291–5292
Tito, Josip Broz, 4677
Tito Cusi Yupanqui, 567
Titon, Jeff Todd, 3144
Le titre d'honneur des Arou (Dieterlen), 2350
Titus, 915
author of, 911, 915, 7013
baptism in, 781
content of, 915
Titus (Roman emperor), and Isis cult, 4558
Titus Mercus, Hermes as, 3937
Titus of Bostra, on Manichaeism, 5664
Tiun (restoration of divine pattern), Luria (Isaac) on, 8560
Tiv religion (Nigeria), **9210–9211**
ancestors in, 9210
dances in, 2138
health in, 9210, 9211
rituals in, 9211
spirits in, 9210
yoni in, 9909
Tiw (deity), 6943
*Tiw[az] (deity), 3450–3451
Tiwi people (Australia)
gender relations among, 3391
marriage among, 5725
taboos of, 8948
Tixuan zhenren xianyi lu (Daoist text), 2207
Tizoc (king of Tenochtitlan), 2465, 2466–2467
Tjakamarra, Michael Nelson, 639
Tjurunga, 1320–1321, **9211–9213,** vol. 4 color insert
Tkhine imohes (Horowitz), 9037
Tkhine imohes fun rosh khoydesh elul (Serl), 9037
Tlacaellel (Aztec ruler), restructuring of Aztec government by, 5173
Tlacaxipeualiztli festival, human sacrifice in, 4190

Tlacolteótl (deity), 719
  confession and, 1885
Tlahuizcalpantecuhtli (deity), 5906
Tláloc (deity), 1469, **9213–9214**
  in afterlife, 149, 150
  ambivalence of, 5993–5994
  etymology of word, 9213
  as fertility-rain god, 718–719, 9213, 9214
  human sacrifice to, 9214
  iconography of, 4313, 5900, 9213–9214
  in Teotihuaćan, 5900
  in Olmec religion, 5881
  origins of, 5881
  quadrapartition and, 718
  temple to, 9214, 9266
  in Templo Mayor, 5892
  in Toltec religion, 5906
  worship of, 9213
Tlaloc, Mount, shrine at, 5293
Tlalocan, 150
Tlaloques (deities)
  quadrapartition of, 718
  sacrifice demanded by, 5936
Tlamatecuhtli (deity), 2984
Tlapanec religion, dogs in, 2394
Tlatelolco (Mexico), student massacre at, 9930
Tlatilco (Mexico)
  figurines at, 5895, 6268
  musical instruments at, 6267–6268
Tlatoani (speaker), 2465
  legitimacy of, 5173
  responsibilities of, 5172–5173
Tlatocayotl (Mesoamerican city-state), 5173
Tlaxcalan religion (Mexico), **9214–9216**
  All Souls Day in, 2230
  Aztecs, war with, 4186–4187
  characteristics of, 9215
  contemporary, 9215–9216
  deities in, 9215
  polytheism in, 9214–9215
  pre-Hispanic background of, 9214–9215
  Roman Catholicism, 9215–9216
  syncretic development of, 9215
Tlazolteotl-Ixcuina (deity), 5906, 5910
Tlingit people (North America)
  area populated by, 6656
  on bears, 807
  body marks of, 1004
  calendar, 1353
  Christian missions and, 6423
  concept of soul, 6708
  on mosquitoes, 4508
  Raven cycle of, 6709
  repatriation of sacred objects by, 6711
  Russian Orthodox missions to, 4497
  shamanic rituals of, 6708
TLV mirrors, *maṇḍalas* and, 5645
TM. *See* Transcendental Meditation
To Acquire Wisdom: The Way of Wang Yang-ming (Ching), 10030
Toads. *See* Frogs and toads
To Autolycus (Theophilus), 5503
Toba Batak people, 799, 800
  origin myths of, 5198
Tobacco, **9216–9219**
  in Caribbean religions, 1430, 9217
  combined with psychedelic drugs, 9216, 9217
  cultivated species of, 9216, 9217–9218
  growing, 3280, 9216
  iconography of, 4309
  in indigenous socioreligious life, 2616
  in Mesoamerican religions, 8454–8456
  in Mexico, 9216, 9217
  mythology of, 9217–9218
  in North American Indian religions, 6652, 8454, 9216–9219
    Cherokee, 1564
    Huron, 6684
    Iroquois, 3280
    Plains nations, 6698
    Pueblo, 6726
  religious associations of, 8453
  sacrifice of, in Arctic religions, 470
  in shamanism, 9216–9219
  smoking of, 8454
  in South American Indian religions, 8454, 9216–9219
    fertility rites and, 8583
    shamanism and, 8292–8293
  spread of, 9216–9217
  therapeutic applications of, 9218–9219
  wild species of, 9217–9218
Tobacco and Shamanism in South America (Wilbert), 9216
Toba people (South America), religion of, 8636
Tobey, Mark, calligraphy and, 1369
Tobias (biblical figure), 897
Tobin, Thomas H., 7106
Tobit, 897
  Ahiqar and, 904
  author of, 897
  Charles (R. H.) on, 900
  demons in, 2277, 2278
  magic in, 3158
  on pilgrimage, 935
  tithes in, 9209, 9210
Tocapu (deity), 4412
Tocharian language, 1147
Toci (deity)
  in Aztec sacrifice, 2556
  tobacco and, 8455
Tocqueville, Alexis de
  on religion, 8480
  on religion and democracy, 3230, 7328
  on religion and journalism, 4960
  on religion and law, 5368
Tōdai Temple, Huayan Buddhism and, 4146
Toda Jōsei, 6574
  Sōka Gakkai and, 8508
To Demetrianus (Cyprian), suffering in, 2113
To Donatus (Cyprian), regeneration in, 2113
Todorov, Tzvetan, structuralism and, 8749
Todorova, Henrieta, 7380–7381
Todos Santos
  in Mexico, 2230
  in Spain, 2230
Todros (rabbi), 7580
T'oegye. *See* Yi T'oegye
"Toe'osh: A Laguna Coyote Story" (Silko), 7225
Tofa religion. *See* Southern Siberian religions
Tofet (sacrificial precinct), 7132
Togano-o monastic complex, 5213
Togato Barbarini, vol. 10 color insert
Toga virilis, 7908
Togawa Shūkotsu, 3072
Togo, Ewe of, 3165. *See also* Fon and Ewe religion
Tohi ritual (Maori religion), 7807
To His Wife (Tertullian), 9086
Tohu (deity), 7313
Tōjō Kagenobu, 6604
Toj-Tuva religion. *See* Southern Siberian religions
Tokahe (first man), 5296
To'Kenali (Muslim scholar), 4666
Tokhuah (trickster), and death, origins of, 8591
Tokhwáh (supernatural being)
  in Mataco religion, 8635
  as trickster, 9358
Tōkoku-san Yōkōji monastery, 5109
Tokoyo-gami (*kami* of eternal paradise), 5072
Tokugawa Ieyasu, 3228
  Buddhism of, 4939
  Buddhist sects suppressed by, 6607
  Confucianism and, 1927
    Hayashi Razan and, 3802
  military tactics of, 9310
  Suzuki Shōsan and, 8887
  tomb of, 8363
Tokugawa Mitsukuni, Confucianism and, 1927, 4789
Tokugawa (Edo) period (Japan)
  arts in, 9311
  Bellah (Robert) on, 8489
  Buddhism in, 5073
    control of, 3741
    Jōdoshū Buddhism in, 4939
    Maitreya in, 5622
    pilgrimage in, 1183
    regulation of, 1182–1183, 1245, 9310, 9311
    Sōtō school, 2386
    Tendai school, 9077, 9079
    women in, 1183
    Zen, 9948–9949
  bushidō (warrior code) in, 1335–1336
  Christianity in, suppression of, 9310
  Confucianism in, 1927–1928
    Hayashi Razan, role of, 3802–3803
    Neo-Confucianism in, 1245, 9310, 9311
    Shintō and, 8363
  economics in, 9311
  humor, suppression of, 4206
  kami in, 5073
  Kamo no Mabuchi on, 5075
  Kokugaku in, 5215–5216
  kōshin day in, 2188
  martial arts in, 5732
  and new religions, rise of, 6572
  pilgrimage in, 7166
  poetry in, 7217
  political power of, 7273–7274
  religion in, 4788–4790
  Shintō in, 8362–8365
    control of shrines, 8363
    regulation of, 9310, 9311
  Tenrikyō in, 9082
Tokway (wood sprite), 9337
Tokyo (Japan), Aum Shinrikyō in, 631–632, 4800
Toland, John, 1497
  pantheism coined by, 6963
Toldot ha-emunah ha-Yisre'elit (Kaufmann), 5108
Tole (mythic figure), 7523
Toledan Tables (al-Zarḳālla), 7492
Toledo, Council of (633), 4556
Toledot Yeshu (Jewish folk tales), 7231
Tolerance
  in ancient Greece and Rome, 9128
  in Buddhism, 2786
  Calvert (Lord Baltimore) on, 1373
  Chateillon, Sébastien on, 8232
  in Constitution of United States, 7283
  denominationalism and, 2286–2287
  doubt and, 2428
  in Enlightenment, 2798
  Freemasons and, 3194
  Jainism on, 4429
  Locke (John) on, 5368, 5496, 7282–7283
  Quakers on, 7547–7548

Tolerance ***continued***
for religious reform, 7654
Servetus (Michael) on, 8231–8232
Toleranzpatent (Joseph II), 5019
Toleration Act (1689), 973
Tolkien, J. R. R.
Gnosticism and, 3528
Lewis (C. S.) and, 5430
Neopagan retreat inspired by, 6472
riddles by, 6987
Tollan. *See* Tula
Tollan (city)
collapse of, 5174
Quetzalcoatl as patron deity of, 7557
Quetzalcoatl banished from, 5174
royal lineage of, 5173
Toller, Ernst, 2475
Tolowa tribe (North America), ballgame played by, 752
Tolstoi Farm, 3272
Tolstoy, Leo, **9219–9221**
Bakhtin (M. M.) on, 741–742
Christianity of, 9220, 9221
disciples of, 9221
estate of, 9219, 9220, 9221
obsession with death, 9220, 9221
pacifism of, 6648
school operated by, 9219, 9220
sermon on the mount interpreted by, 4845
temperament of, 3060, 9219
tension in novels of, 3062
Toltec religion (Mexico), **9221–9225**
architecture in, 5906–5907
calendar in, 5906
ceremonies in, 5906, 9222
of Chichimeca, 9224
collapse of, 5907
Aztec religion after, 716
deities of, 5906
Quatzalcoatl, 5889–5890, 5906, 7557, 9223–9224
human sacrifice in, 9222, 9223
iconography of, 4313, 9222
kingship lineage of, acquisition by Aztecs, 5173
meaning of term, 9221–9222
origins of, 716
pre-Columbian, 5889–5890
in Postclassic period, 5906–5907
sun god in, 8842
of Tollan Xicocotitlan, 9223–9224
Toltec-Maya religion, 9222–9223
of Tula, 5889, 5906, 9222
water in, 9223
Tolui (son of Chinggis Khan), 4493
Tomasa (shaman), 2484
Tomasetti, Friedegard, 6804
Tombouctou (Mali)
as Islamic learning center, 4602–4603
Moroccan invasion of, 4603
Tombs, **9225–9228**. *See also* Burial; Funeral rites; Relics
Aksumite, 225
Arabian, 445
architecture of, classification of, 461, 463–464
of Attila the Hun, 4228–4229
Bornean, 9227
changing styles of, 9227–9228
Chinese, 170–171
location of, 9227
royal, 9225
Christian
catacombs, 1472, 3637
earth burials, 9226
of saints, veneration of, 2082
circular, 1792
Egyptian
communications in, 2719–2720
curse-threats on, 2101–2102
iconography of, 4318, 4319–4320
locations of, 2703
looting of, 2709
of rock, 1472
royal, 9225 (*See also* Pyramids)
grave goods in, 9225–9226
gravestones, on Madagascar, 8745
Greek
cocks on tombstones, 1842
earth burials, 9227
of heroes, 3665, 3667
secondary, 9226
as homes for the dead, 4105–4106
Indonesian, 9227
as Jewish pilgrimage sites, 7161–7162
location of, 9227
mausoleums, 9227
megalithic, 1791, 5822–5826
Mesoamerican, 1472–1473, 3242–3243
at Monte Albán, 5903
in Formative (Preclassic) period, 5896
Zapotec, 5887
Muslim, 162
in China, 4635–4636
earth burials, 9226
pilgrimages to, 7160
Nabatean, 6386, 6388
New Guinea, 9226
Persian, 1472
Phoenician, 7132
curse-threats on, 2101
prehistoric, 7381
for primary and secondary storage, 9226
of rock, 1472–1473
Roman, earth burials, 9227
royal, 9225
as sacred space, 7979
Scythian, 8205
in shape of doorway, 7334
social status and elaboration of, 9226
in Southeast Asian religions, traditional, 8650
Tombstones, 9226, 9227
Tome (Leo I), 5410
To Mend the World (Fackenheim), 2950
To minaa (priest), 9241
Tominaga Nakamoto, 1277, 1310
methodology of, 8776
Tomol (canoe), **9228–9230**
Tom-tom (drum), 2494
Tomyris (Massagetae queen), 7384
Tonacayohua (deity), 9254
Tonaia festival, statue of Hera in, 3915
Tonalamatls (books of destiny), 5939
Tonalco ritual, 5892
Tonal geometry, 3441–3442
Tonalpohualli (ritual calendar), in Maya religion, 1356
Tonanhueyatl (Lake Texcoc), 5293
Tonantsi (deity), worship of, 3588
Tonantzin (deity), 3064
Sahagún (Bernardino de) on, 5922
Tonatiuh (deity)
in creation-destruction cycles, 1357
as sun god, 8842
Tones, in Greek music, 6303
Tonga people (Africa). *See* Central Bantu religions
Tonga people and religion (Pacific). *See also* Oceania and Oceanic religions
burials in, 2005
Christianity
London Missionary Society, 9322
Methodist missionaries, 1738
creation in, 7313
democratic movement of, 7298
human sacrifice in, 7309
origin myth of, 7314, 7315
piracy of, 9321
Tongbo Guan (Tongbo Abbey), 2208
Tongdao Guan (Observatory for Comprehending the Dao), 2184, 2194, 2210
Tonghak (Eastern Learning), 1647
Tonghak Scripture, 1647
Tong Il. *See* Unification Church
Tongtai Si (Buddhist temple), 5432
Tongues, speaking in. *See* Glossolalia
Tongxin Arabic Language School (China), 4634
Tongxin Mosque (China), 4638–4639
Tonkawan language, 6697
Tonkō Dōkyō, 2214–2215
Tönnies, Ferdinand, 7325, **9230**
on community, 8481
on community *vs.* society, 7716
on Gemeinschaft and Gesellschaft, 8481, 8482
on society and religion, 8466–8467
Tons (darkness), 9030
Tonzanga (mythic figure), 7523
Tooby, John, on evolutionary psychology, 8475
Toohey, John, on Aboriginal women's ceremonies, 3391
Too Jewish: Challenging Traditional Identities (Kleebatt), 4342
Tooker, Elisabeth, 6672
Tools
magical
Greco-Roman, 5574
South Asian, 5589
metal, 5986–5987, 5988
in metallurgy, 5988
Tooth-filing ceremony, in Bali, 7796
"Tooth" goddesses, 3607–3608
Topa Inca Yupanqui, oral tradition about, 8607
To Papunna (deity), 1316–1317
Topeng (dance drama), 2450
Topiltzin Quetzalcoatl (Nicholson), 5890
Topiltzin Quetzalcoatl (priest-king), 5906. *See also* Quetzalcoatl
abdication of, 5174
drunkenness of, 9093
miracles performed by, 9223–9224
Topographia Hiberniae, 1493
Topography
in Daoist literature, 2207–2209
of Rome, rituals and, 7896
Topophilia, 2611
Toporov, Vladimir, 771
on Māra, 5691
Topos (place), eternity and time in, 2854
TOPY, 6568
To Quirinius (Cyprian), training of new Christians in, 2113
Torah, 878–879, **9230–9241**. *See also* Pentateuch; *specific biblical books*
acceptance of, coercion in, 4860
in Alexandrian canon, 880
Aramaic translation of, 887–888
atonement in, 593
authoritative character of, 8201
authority of, 694
Berlin (Naftali) on, 868

body marking forbidden in, 1001
Breuer (Mordecai) on, 869
canonizing process of, 882, 1406, 1409
celebrations of, Simḥat Torah, 2149
chanting from, 1532
commandments in, 9074, 9235, 9237
in contemporary Judaism, 4986, 9234
contents of, 878–879, 9232–9233
in creation myth, 7584
Dead Sea Scrolls, 9234
definition of, of Crescas (Ḥasdai), 2069
derivation of term, 5424
divination banned in, 2373
as doctrine, 2382
Documentary Hypothesis on, 9233–9234
election and, 2745
Eliyyahu ben Shelomoh Zalman on, 868
etymology of word, 9231
food taboos in, 3167, 7144
formation of, 9233–9234
German translation of, by Mendelssohn (Moses), 869
hermeneutics of, 5485
Hillel ("the Elder") on, 3981
Hirsch (Samson Raphael) on, 868, 4023, 4024
Hoffmann (David) on, 869
identity and, 8013
interpretation of (*See* Midrash)
Jerusalem and, 4839
in Jesus's ministry, 4849–4850
as law, 9231, 9232, 9235–9237
Levites in, 5423
as link between law and historical narrative, 4729, 9237–9238
Löw (Yehudah ben Betsal'el of Prague) on, 5520–5521
Luzzatto (Shemu'el David) on, 869
Maimonides (Moses) on, 5614
meanings of word, 879, 6017, 6065, 9231
messianic expectations in, 7586
micrography and, 1369, 1372
of Moses, 882, 883, 9233, 9234–9235
myth of, in rabbinic Judaism, 7584–7585
Nahmanides (Moses) on, 867
nation-statehood and, 4862
nature and, 2641, 2642–2643
ontological principle of, 9236–9237
oral, 4976, 4986, **6838–6842**
halakhah and, 3747, 9235
memorization of, 5852
Mishnah in, 6065–6066
in Orthodox Judaism, 6898
particularism of, 4855–4856
Paul's critique of, in *Romans,* 912
personification of, *Ḥokhmah* and, 4079
in Pharisaic-rabbinic view of history, 4058
as preexistent and created, *vs.* Qur'ān, 3563
public reading of, 882–883, 4482
in Qabbalah, 4080
rabbinate study of, 7578, 7584
in rabbinic Judaism, 4977, 7584–7585, 7587
Rashi's commentary to, 865
reading, 9239–9240, 9807
in Reform Judaism, 7665, 7672
as revelation, 9234–9235
Sabbath readings of, 8257–8258
Sadducees' view of, 8018
salvation and, 7584–7585
in Samaritan belief, 8070
Schneerson (Menachem) on science *vs.,* 8172
scrolls of, 879, 9231, 9239–9240, 9258
as sacred objects, vol. 4 color insert
from Severus Synagogue, 885
Sforno ('Ovadyah) on, 867
in Shavu'ot liturgy, 8305–8306
sin as abandonment of, 8404
Sofer (Mosheh) on, 8507
Spinoza (Baruch) on, 865, 8681
study of
Abbaye on, 3
amoraim and, 294–295
at Ḥanukkah, 3774
as form of Judaic piety, 9238–9239
gender and, 3354
in Habad Hasidism, 3792
rabbinic, 9235, 9238–9239
as religious experience, 8972, 9375
shekhinah concept and, 8314–8315
Shemu'el the Amora's blessing prior to, 8318
Shim'on bar Yoh'ai on, 8346
Shim'on ben Laqish on, 8348
as theme of midrash, 6017
Sukkot and, 8834
supernatural powers of, 7587
superseded by Jesus, 4858–4859
as symbol of Judaism, 9230
synagogues and, 8922
Temple procedures in, 926, 928, 929, 930, 931
Ten Commandments in, 9074
universalism of, 4855–4856
violation of, as sacrilege, 8012–8013
Wellhausen (Julius) on, 9714
as wisdom, 9762–9763
women and, 3354
in worship, 9807
written (*See* Hebrew scriptures)
Torah shelemah (Kasher), 868
Torah temimah (Epstein), 868
Toraja religion (Indonesia), **9241–9242**
ancestor cult in, 9241
Christianity, 9241
cosmology in, 9241
deities in, 9241
funeral rites of, 3234, 3236, 3237
myths of
agriculture in, 192
cosmology, 5445
priesthood in, 9241, 9242
ritualsi n, 9241–9242
textiles in, 9090
Toraṇa (portal), 7333
Torat ha-'olah (Isserles), 4751
Tore (mythic figure), 94
as bringer of fire, 2091, 7525
as trickster, 9352
Toré rituals, 6274
Torgbi-nyigbla (deity), 3166
Torii (portal), 7333, 7334
Torimonouta (songs), 6300
Toririhnan (deity), 6501
Tork' (deity), 490, 491–492
Torquemada, Juan de, 5940
Torquemada, Tomás de, 2939, **9242–9243**
Torques, in Celtic religion, 1481
Þórr (deity). *See* Thor (Þórr)
Torral, Francisco de, 4504
Torrance, Thomas F., 6466
Torres, Camilo, 3063
Torres, González, on human sacrifice, 4187
Torres Strait Islanders
population of, 635–636
societies of, 636
use of term, 635
Tortoises. *See* Turtles and tortoises
Torts, 4737
Torture. *See also* Violence
in Inquisition, 6971, 8014
and pain, 6945
as punishment, 5374
in purification, 7508–7509
Tosafists
authority of, 9244
halakhic works of, 9248
Jewish mysticism and, 9250
method of study of, 9246
peshaṭ favored by, 9249
sources of, 9246
Talmudic commentary of, 3745
Tosafot, 866, **9243–9250**
in deciding *halakhah,* 9246
editing, 9244
education of, 9247
emergence of, 9243, 9248
French, 9243, 9244, 9247–9250
genre of, 9248
German, 9243, 9244, 9247–9250
vs. glossarists, 9246–9247
influence of, 9247
meaning of term, 9243
method of interpretation in, 9244–9246
origins of, 9244, *9245*
Polish, 9244
printing, 9244
Spanish, 9244
types of, 9243–9244
Tosefta (supplements to Mishnah), **6065–6068**
Beruryah in, 843
composition and compilation of, 6065
contents of, 6065
synagogue in, 8922
Total Overcomers Anonymous, Heaven's Gate and, 3891
"To-ta Ti-om" (Blue Cloud), 7226
Totem and Taboo (Freud), 321, 3389, 7474, 9251
classification of rituals in, 7841
death in, 2238–2239
Malinowski (Bronislaw) on, 5628
primal horde theory in, 7872
Totemism, **9250–9253**
in African religions, 9252
Nuer and Dinka, 6744
as antecedent of Egyptian religion, 9252
in Australian Indigenous religions, 3490, 7872
Eliade (Mircea) on, 7251
Gillen and Spencer on, 3490, 9251
Mardu, 5704–5705
Ngarrindjeri, 2481
Ngukurr, 6598
reincarnation and, 7677
Róheim (Géza) on, 7872
Stanner (W. E. H.) on, 2479
Walbiri religion, 9252
wandjina, 9668–9670
controversy over, 9251
definition of, 9250
Durkheim (Émile) on, 7971, 9250
and dynamism, 2542

Totemism ***continued***
economic basis of, 9251
evolutionary, 9250, 9251–9252
Frazer (James G.) on, 9250, 9251
Freud (Sigmund) on, 7872, 9251
genealogy in, 3423
Gennep (Arnold van) on, 3432, 9251
Goldenweiser (Alexander A.) on, 3634, 9251
and Hindu mythic themes, 4437
in Khoi religion, 5137
in Korean religion, 5229
Lévi-Strauss on, 1422, 9250, 9251–9252
and *mana,* 9251
in Melanesian religions, 5835–5836
in Micronesian religions, 6010
in neoshamanism, 8294
in New Caledonia religion, 6500, 6501
in New Guinea religions, 6504, vol. 6 color insert
in North American Indian religions, 9250–9251, 9252
first use of concept, 6670
guardian spirits and, 6652
in Oceanic religions
evangelistic discourse on, 8767
in Solomon Islands religions, 8514
as origin of sacrifice, 4183
origin of term, 9250
origins of, 9250–9252
power in, 7351
in primitive religions, 10065
Radcliffe-Brown (A.R.) on, 7592–7593
Reinach (Salomon) on, 7676
religious communities and, 1864
Róheim (Géza) on, 7872
sacrificial meal and, 8002–8003
in San religion, 5137
in shamanism, 8277, vol. 1 color insert
sheep in, 8310
social units symbolized in, 9252, 9253
solidarity function of, 9251
souls in, 8532, 8533
and taboo, 8948, 9251
trees used in, 9576
in Turkic religion, 9400–9401, 9402
Totemism (Lévi-Strauss), 9250, 9251–9252
"Totemism: An Analytical Study" (Goldenweiser), 9251
Totemism and Exogamy (Frazer), 9251
Totem poles, in Haida tradition, 3736
Totenrita (invisible beings), 1317
Tóth, István, 4559
To the Nations (Tertullian), 4361, 9085
To the Young, on How They Might Derive Benefit from Greek Literature (Basil of Caesarea), 798
Totman, Conrad, on Japanese environmental history, 2638–2639, 2640
Totonac people (Mexico)
vs. Aztecs, 9254
colonialization of, 9253–9254
language of, 9254
Totonac religion (Mexico), **9253–9255**
in Classic period, 5904–5905
confession of sins in, 9254
deities in, 5910–5911, 9213, 9254, 9255
El Tajín ceremonial center in, 9254–9255
festivals in, 9254, 9255
myths of, maize in, 5936
in Postclassic period, 5910–5911
priesthood in, 5911, 9254, 9255
rituals in, 5911
Roman Catholicism, 9255
Spanish sources on, 5910, 5911
Zempoala ceremonial center in, 9253, 9254
Touba, Senegal, pilgrimage to, 1808–1809
Touching, **9255–9260**. *See also* Postures and gestures
ban on, 9259
healing with, 3813, 9255–9256
of power, 9257–9258
of reverence, 9256–9257
royal, 9257–9258
Toulouse (France), 1458
Catharism in, 3524
T'oung pao (journal), 2272
Toure, Drissa, 3098
Tourism
at Daoist monasteries, 2637–2638
drug, 7472
modern, 9262–9263
origin of term, 9261
and pilgrimage, 7168, 7171, 9261, 9262
and religion, **9260–9264**
cultural relations between, 9262–9263
historical relations between, 9261–9262
spatial relations between, 9260–9261
in Tibet, 7269
Toussaint, Gustave Charles, 9188
Tovim, Sarah bas, 9037
Tower Abbey (Lou Guan), 2196, 2199
Tower of Babel
and divine separated from human, 3957
Freemasons on, 3194
"Tower of Salvation, The" (Abravanel), 17
Tower of silence. *See Dakhma*
Towers, **9264–9267**. *See also* Pyramids; Temples
in African myths, 92
as *axis mundi,* 9266
in Buddhism, 9264–9265 (*See also* Pagodas; Stupas)
in Christianity, 9265–9266 (*See also* Basilica; Cathedrals)
definition of, 9264
in Hinduism *(sikhara),* 9265
in Islam *(minar),* 9266
Mesoamerican, 9266 (*See also* Pyramids, Mesoamerican)
modern, 9266–9267
mountains imitated by, 9265, 9266
Towii'sas Society (Iroquois), 4542
Towne, Elizabeth, 6584
Townes, Emilie, 79
Toxcatl festival, 9093
human sacrifice in, 4190
Toy, Crawford Howell, classification of rituals by, 7840
Tōya (lay member of local parish), 7411
Toynbee, Arnold, 5701, 9131
Smith (Wilfred Cantwell) and, 8450
Toyotomimi. *See* Shotoku Taishi
Toyouke shrine (Japan), Watarai Shintō at, 8361
Toys, dreidel (spinning top), 3774–3775
Tozzer, Alfred, 5941
Trabalhos (spiritual healing works), 122
Trabelin' On (Sobel), 67, 75, 76
Trace Foundation, 9188
Traces on the Rhodian Shores: Nature and Culture in Western Thought from Ancient Times to the End of the Eighteenth Century (Glacken), 2663–2664
Tractarian movement. *See* Oxford movement
Tractatus logico-philosophicus (Wittgenstein), 306, 307
Tractus Politicus (Spinoza), 8683
Tractus Theologico-Politicus (Spinoza), 7440, 8682, 8684–8685
Tracy, David, 5482
Trade
African religions impacted by, 66
Kongo religion, 5219–5220
spread of Islam, 4601, 4603, 4604, 4607
Arabian, 443
Australian Indigenous, 637
of Chumash Indians, 9228, 9229
missionaries and, 6073
in Oceania, 9321
mission involvement in, 6792
slave, 65–66
in Southeast Asia, 4658
and transculturation, 9292
Tradition, **9267–9281**
androcentrism and, 336
in Buddhism, 9277
canonization as regimentation of, 9274–9275
and change, 9278–9180
characteristics of, 9268
in China, 9273
classic, multiformity of, 9275–9276
concept of, 9267–9269
in Confucianism, 2633
definition of, 9270
descriptive concept of, 9268
in Eastern Christianity, 9268
esotericism and, 9278
ethics and, 1651, 1652
etymology of term, 9267
faith and, 2958
folklorist perspective on, 3161–3162
formation of, 9272–9274
globalization and, 9280
"great" *vs.* "little," 9276
in Hinduism, 9270, 9276–9277
idealization of, 9274
in Islam, 9268, 9270, 9274–9275 (*See also* Sunnah)
in Japan, 9277
in Judaism, 9268
Kaplan (Mordecai) on, 7635, 7636
legitimation via, 9273
memory in, 9268
and modernity, 9279
mysticism and, 9277–9278
nonverbal, 9269
as normative, 9268
oral (*See* Oral tradition)
Plato on, 9272
postmodernism and, 9279–9280
and power, 9272–9273
progress and, in historiography, 4031–4032
Redfield (Robert) on, 4448, 4722, 9276
rejection of, 9273–9274
religious originators and, 9270–9271
religious reform and, 7654–7655
in Roman Catholicism, 9268, 9270
vs. scripture, 9270
secret, 9278
Socrates on, 9272
as source of knowledge, 9267, 9268
verbal, 9269–9270 (*See also* Oral tradition; Writing)
wisdom as, 9757
Traditional environmental knowledge (TEK)
of indigenous cultures, 2616
nature religions and, 2664
Traditionalism
of Eliade, 2760
in Hinduism, 7696

in Islam, 7696 (*See also* Ahl al-hadīth)
in Judaism, 4985
in Protestantism, 7696
in religious life, 7696
in Roman Catholicism, 7696
in Maya religion, 3413, 5799
women in, 3413
in Zen Buddhism, 7696
Tradition history, Religionsgeschichtliche Schule on, 7708
Tradition of instrument, ordination and, 1956
Traditions of Divine Transcendents (Ge Hong), 2181
Traducianism, soul theory of, 8563
Tragedie of Abraham's Sacrifice, A (Beza), 851
Tragedy. *See also* Drama
Aristotle on, 45, 6304
failure in, 5469
Greek
music in, 6304
origins of, 6304
time in, 6375
Hegel (G. W. F.) on, 4219–4220
Tragedy of the Six Marys, The (Pak), 9468
Tragicall History of Doctor Faustus, The (Marlowe), 2438, 3010, 5580
Tragicus, Ezekiel, 3508–3509
Traherne, Thomas, 7220
Trai Bhūm, 5130
Traibhūmikathā (Buddhist text), 1137, 1139
Traikālya-pa-rīkṣā (Dignāga), 2351
Trail of Tears, 1564
Trailokya (Triple World), in Cakrasamvara tradition, 1350
Trailokyavijaya, 9513
Traité (Eliade), 2755
Trajan (Roman emperor)
Christian persecution by, 7058–7059
Ignatius executed by, 4369
Trajan's column, calligraphy rooted in, 1368
Trance. *See also* Consciousness, states of
in affliction, 57, 58, 59
in Africa
early history of, 83
in Khoi religion, 5136–5137
in San religion, 5136–5137
in Arctic religions, in shamans, 471
in Balinese religion, 5804, 7048–7049
Cayce and, 1473, 1474
in dance drama, 2450
in divination, 2370, 2371
in East African divination, 2569
experience of, 7048–7049
glossolalia associated with, 3505, 3506
in Greek narrative, 8541
in healing, 3813
history of study of, 76
hypnotic, 7048
in Micronesian religions, 6005
oracular, 6834–6836
possession-trances, 7048
in Haitian Vodou, 1433
in Polynesian religions, 7307
in Selk'nam religion (Tierra del Fuego), 8225
psychiatric explanations for, 59
sacred *vs.* profane and, 7972
in seidr ritual (Neopagan), 8295
in shamanism
in Sami religion, 8088
Siberian, 8285
in spirit possession, 8688–8689
tobacco and, 9216, 9217
Tränker, Heinrich, Fraternitas Saturni and, 8252
Transactional religiosity, merit in, 5872
Transcendence and immanence, **9281–9286**. *See also* Ecstasy
Baal, immanence of, 1383
cakras and, 1349
of consciousness, expression of truth through, 9372–9374
of creation, in Islam, 2652
crown as symbol of, 2072
of the Dao, 2636
definition of, 9281
of *deus otiosus,* 2312
dual, 9282–9283, 9284
existence and, 4814–4815
in existentialism, 2926
Fedeli d'Amore and, 8248
of God
in anthropomorphism, 9283
in Christianity, 616, 1655, 1656
in doctrine of Trinity, 9283
in Islam, 3566, 8307
in Judaism, 3542, 3543, 3548
in realistic idealism, 9282
in Sufism, 8809–8810
in theism, 9282–9283
via negativa and, 9283–9284
of great goddess, 3975
in Hinduism, swan as symbol of, 8894
historiography and, 4031
Husserl (Edmund) on, 4237
Ibn al-'Arabī on, 8819
inspiration and, 4509
kingship and, 5159–5160
knowledge of
of God, 8394
Otto (Rudolf) on, 4096–4097
liberation and, 5437–5438
Logos and, in Jewish philosophy, 8558
Luckmann (Thomas) on, 4530
masculine sacrality in, 5760–5761
in mysticism, 6342
nature and, 2637
Neopagan belief in, 6472
of number, in Islam, 3566
a priori concept and, 7976
psychologies of, 1949, 1950
religious intellectuals and, 4511–4512, 4513
sacred places as link between, 7980
sacred time and, 7987
through the secular, 5478
shekhinah concept and, **8312–8316**
simple (nondual), 9284
sky as first image of, 1994
Smith (Wilfred Cantwell) on justice and, 8450
of society, 4530
stars and, 8733
of supreme beings, 8867, 8868
Pettazzoni (Raffaele) on, 8878
in theism, 9281
in theologies of conversion, 1971–1972
in Zen Buddhism, 9950
"Transcendence of Nature and Society, The: Symbols" (Schutz), 4530
Transcendental dialectic, Kant (Immanuel) on, 5077
Transcendental ground, Schleiermacher (Friedrich) on, 8164
Transcendentalism
Buddhism and, 1187
Channing (William Ellery) and, 1530
Emerson (Ralph Waldo) in, 2774–2775
God in, Emerson's (Ralph Waldo) concept of, 2775
Hermetism and, 3951
nature in, 2607
religious experience in, 7738
Schelling (Friedrich) and, 8148
Spinoza (Baruch), influence of, 8685–8686
Stanton (Elizabeth Cady) and, 8730
Transcendental Meditation (TM), **9289–9292**
brainwashing civil suit against, 5376
breath in, 9290
children in, 6542, 6543
consciousness in, 9291
in Europe, 6568
of Maharishi Mahesh, 9289, 9290–9291
millenannialism in, 9291–9292
in psychotherapy, 7485
states of consciousness and, 1951
techniques and message of, 9290–9291
Western missions of, 9290
Transcendental phenomenology, Husserl (Edmund) on, 4236
Transcendental Wordplay (West), 380
Transcendents *(Xian),* in Daoism, 2178, 2179, 2182
Transculturation, **9292–9325**
in Canada, **9299–9304**
and cargo cults, 9296, 9321–9322, 9323, 9324
in Caribbean, **9304–9309**
in Brazil, 9308–9309
in Cuba, 9292, 9305–9306
Garifuna religion, 3283–3284, 9307–9308
in Jamaica, 9306–9307
Rastafarianism, 9306–9307
colonialism and, 9292, 9294, 9295–9297
Crusades and, 9293
exchanges in, 9295–9297
in India, **9316–9320**
in Japan, **9309–9316**
in Mesoamerica, 5928
normative modes of Western time and, 9294–9295
in Oceania, **9320–9325**
origin of term, 9292, 9305
pilgrimage and, 9293–9294
trade and, 9292
travel and, 9292–9294
in United States, **10082–10087**
Transference of consciousness (yogic practice), 1288
Transfiguration
of Jesus, as shape shifting, 8303
of souls, in Hawaiian religion, 3799
Transfiguration, Mount of the, Origen on, 6889
Transformation. *See also* Self-transformation
in Chinese tradition, *dahua* (great transformation or becoming), 8554
of culture heroes, 2091–2092
in Daoism, 2636

Transformation ***continued***
in Ge mythology, 3293–3294
hope and, 4125–4126
in Jewish thought, suffering and, 8806
orgy and, 6862
in rites of passage (*See* Rites of passage)
sacred language as means of, 5305–5306
in Sikhism, in *sangat* (gathering), 8393
in South American cosmologies, 2011–2012
in spirit possession, 8692
syncretism and, 8929
ultimate, 1581
Transformational Theory of Aesthetics, A (Stephan), 50
Transformative knowledge, 2361–2362, 2363
Transformatory rituals, 7843–7845
Transformer (culture hero), 325. *See also* Culture heroes
Transgression
in Baltic religion, Latvian Saule (sun) cult and, 8133
Cakrasamvara and, 1349–1350
in Judaism
sacrilege and, 8012–8013
Shabbetai Tsevi, ritualized transgression of, 8259
in North American Indian religions, in Zuni religion, 8016
sacrilege and, 8010–8011
in Islam, 8014
in Judaism, 8012
sexuality and, 1349–1350, 8242–8243
in Tantric Buddhism, exploration of boundaries of, 8015–8016
Transhuman rites, in secret societies, 8212
Transience, in mystical states, James (William) on, 1948, 6341–6342
Transition(s)
in African rites of passage, 88
clowns and, 1838
death as, 7956
deities of, Hekate as, 3900
in New Year ceremonies, 6590
sacraments of, 7955–7956
"Transitional Objects and Transitional Phenomena" (Winnicott), 7483
Transitional phenomena, in psychoanalysis, 7483–7484
Transition rituals, 7843
of birth, 950, 952
Translated Chants (Buddhist text), 9828
Translation
conversion and, 1972
of relics, 7688
scriptures, translation and untranslatability of, 8203
Translation and Harmony of the Four Gospels (Tolstoy), 9220
Translation of the Works of Saint Dionysius the Areopagite, 2830
Transmigration, **9325–9331**. *See also* Rebirth; Reincarnation; See also Saṃsāra
in African religions, 9326
anthropologists on, 9326
in Australian Indigenous religions, 9326–9327
in Buddhism, 9327, 9328
in Catharism, 9330
in Celtic religion, 9329
definition of, 9325
in Gnosticism, 9329
in Hasidism, 2644
in Hinduism, in Upaniṣads, 3886, 9327–9328
in Islam, Mullā Ṣadrā on, 6233
in Jainism, 9327, 9328
in Judaism
in Hasidism, 9330
in Qabbalah, 9330
rejection of, 9330
in Luba religion, 5523
in Manichaeism, 9325, 9329–9330
in Neoplatonism, 9329
in North American Indian religions, 9326
in Oceanic religions, 9327
origin of concept, 9326
in Orphism, 7186, 9329
Plato on, 7185, 7186, 9328, 9329
in Pythagoreanism, 7186
in Qabbalah, 9330
and anamnesis, 313–314
in Roman religion, 9330
in South American Indian religions, 9326
in Sufism, and anamnesis, 313
in Tibetan Buddhism, 9328
Transmission, in esotericism, Faivre paradigm of, 2844
"Transmission of the lamp" texts, 1522, 1523, 1524
"Transmission of the Way" *(daotong)*, 1899–1900
Transmutation. *See* Alchemy
Transnationalism, religion as institution of, 3499–3500
Transoxiana
Islam in
spread of, 4620–4621
under tsarist rule, 4623
Sufism in, 5055–5056
Transpersonal psychology, 7478
states of consciousness and, 1950
Transposition, binding and, 5197
Transtheistic ecstasy, 2680
Transubstantiation
consecration and, 1956
in Eucharist, 2877
Petr Moghila on, 7072
as real presence and sacrifice, 1669
Transvestism
in African religions, 3402, 3403
Zulu, 10009
in Bugis religion, 1316, 1317
gender-reversed homosexuality as, 4115–4116
in Greek religion, initiation rites of, 184
in Hebrew scriptures, interdiction against, 3968
hierodouleia (sacred prostitution) and, 3967, 3968–3969
in North American Indian religions, 6686
Trans-Volgan elders, Sorskii (Nil) and, 8526
Trans World Radio (TWR), 7713
Transylvania
Judaism in, Satmar Hasidism in, 3793
Lutheran and Reformed Protestantism in, 1685
Orthodox Church in, 9464–9465
in communion with Rome, 2588
Unitarianism in, 9469
Dávid (Ferenc) convicted of blasphemy, 973
vampires in, 4226
Trappists (Cistercians of Strict Observance), 1801
eremitism in, 2828
Trauma theory, sexuality and, 8245
Travel. *See also* Pilgrimage; Tourism
in Judaism, to supplement education, 7821
social reform and, 7653
and transculturation, 9292–9294
Travelers. *See also* Hospitality
accounts of
of Muslim travelers, 8781–8782
in South America, 8594
in Australian Indigenous myths, 657
Travels of Sir John Mandeville, 1630
Travel stories, 2882–2883
Travers, Walter, Hooker (Richard) and, 4123–4124
Treason
apostasy as, 431
judgment on, 6848
Treasure of Life (Mani), 5649, 5651
Treasures of Darkness, The (Jacobsen), 2522
Treasure tradition, **9331–9333**
in Bon religion, 9331, 9333
criticism of, 9332
Padmasambhava and, 6940, 6941, 9331–9332, 9333
prophecies in, 9332
in Tibetan Buddhism, 9331, 9332–9333
Treasury of Abiding Reality, The (Longchenpa), 5194
Treaties
Assyrian, Melqart in, 5847
Near Eastern, curses in, 2102–2104
Phoenician, Eshmun named in, 2841
Treatise Concerning Religious Affections (Edwards), 2698, 2699
Treatise of Human Nature, A (Hume), reception of, 4191, 4192
Treatise of Reformation without Tarrying for Any, A (Browne), 7663
Treatise on Atonement, A (Ballou), 9470–9471
Treatise on Buddha Nature (Rang byung rdo rje), 5102
Treatise on Resurrection (Maimonides), 154
Treatise on Sufism (al-Qushayrī), 6338
Treatise on the Essentials of Cultivating the Mind, 1521–1522
Treatise on the Transcendence of Cognition, 1522
Treatise on the Two Entrances and Four Practices, 1521
Treatise on the World (Descartes), 2293
Treatise on the Worship of Priapus and Its Connexion with the Mystic Theology of the Ancients (Knight), 7085
Treaty of New Echota (1836), 1564
Treaty of Waitangi, 1731
Tree of knowledge, 9335, 9577
Tree of life, 9335, 9577–9578
dragon as custodian of, 2432
in Mesopotamian religion, 2967
rejuvenation and, 7684
in Semitic myths, 1875
in Sistine Chapel, 8755
in Warao religion, 9335
water and, 7602
in Zoroastrianism, 9335
Trees, **9333–9340**. *See also* Forest
Ācārāṅga Sūtra on, 2625
as African shrines, 90
in Ainu religion, 9334, 9336, 9337
in Arabian religions, 444
and ascension, 519
Athirat (Asherah) and, 590, 591
in Australian Indigenous religions, 9336, 9337
axis mundi as, 712, 3449
in Baltic religion, 759, 768, 773, 774, 1502
Sun Tree in, 8132
in Brazilian religions, 9337
in Buddhism, 2629, 9335, 9337
in Buriat religion, 1326
in Celtic religion, 1486–1487

in Chinese religion, 1584, 9334
in Christianity, 9337–9338, 9339
cosmic, 9334–9335, 9576–9577
access to supreme beings by, 8871
as ancestor, 9336–9337
in Babylonian religion, 3449, 9335
in creation, 9336
dragon as custodian of, 2432
in Germanic religion, 3448–3449 (*See also* Yggdrasill)
levels of cosmos connected by, 2295
in Siberian shamanism, 3813
in South American Indian religions, 8587–8588
as tree of knowledge, 9577
as cosmic center, 1502, 6886
in Daoism, 9334
in death symbolism, 9339
deities as, 9337
deities symbolized by, 9337–9338
divine intoxicants from, 9338 (*See also* Soma)
in Egyptian religion, 9335, 9338
as food, 9335–9336
in Garden of Eden, 29–30, 6982, 9335
in gardens, 3277, 3282
in Greek religion, 9337, 9338
Artemis and, 507
in Hinduism, 4439, 9334, 9335, 9337, 9338, vol. 5 color insert
in Indian religions, 3449
innate power of, 9334–9337
in Shintō, 2640, 9338
in Japanese religion, 9334, 9337, 9338
in Javanese religion, 9339
in Judaism, 2644
of knowledge, 9335, 9577
in Komi religion, 5218
of life (*See* Tree of life)
in Mesoamerican religions, 9335, 9338, 9339
in Micronesian myths, 6011–6012
in Minoan religion, 39–40
mudyi, 4484–4485, 9336, 9339
in Ndembu religion, 7799, 9336, 9339
in Nepali marriage ceremony, 9339
in North American Indian religions
cottonwood tree in Sun Dance, 8845–8846
Haida, 9334
Karuk, 9336
Lakota, 9336
Mandan, 9337
Salish, 9334–9335, 9338
Seneca, 9336
in Nuer religion, 9336
Pērkons as god of, 7053
planting of
in Hinduism, 2621, 2622
in Islam, 2651
protection of, in Chipko movement, 2622
ritual use of, 9338–9339
sacred, of Yahveh, 4743
in shamanism, 9338
birch tree in Buriat initiation, 8271–8272
as shrines, 9336, 9338
with souls or spirits, 9337
in South American Indian religions, jaguars associated with, 8292
symbolic, 9576–9578
as symbol of hope, 4127
in Turkic religions, 9399–9400
as vehicles of communication with deities, 9338
in Vietnamese religion, 9594
in West African religions, worship sites and, 9720
worship of, 6440
in Zuni religion, 9336
Tremendum, The (Cohen)
Holocaust in, 1849, 4091, 4093–4094
Otto (Rudolf) on, 7349
Trench, Battle of the (627), 6225, 6226
Trend (Jooss), 2160
Trent, Council of (1545–1563), 7663–7664, 7877–7878, **9340–9345**. *See also* Counter-Reformation
on Apocrypha, 896
astronomy, effect on, 1978
Borromeo's (Carlo) role in, 1023
Canisus, role of, 1402
canons and decrees of, 2059–2060
on confession, 1455
on episcopal residence, 9344
on Eucharist, 9343
events leading to, 9340–9341
on free will and predestination, 3208
function of, 7663
on iconography, 4346, 4392
on indulgences, sale of, 158
Julius III and, 9343–9344
on justification by faith, 1667–1668, 9343
on Luther's doctrines, 5539, 9343
on marriage, 4505
on Mass, 795, 9344
on merit, 5877
on monasticism, 822, 7724
nuns after, 6764
organization of, 9342
orthodoxy and heterodoxy at, 6912
and orthodoxy *vs.* superstition, 8866
overview of, 2043, 6972
Paul III and, 6972, 9342–9343
Pius IV and, 6972, 9344–9345
on priesthood, 7404
problems at, 9343
Protestant theologians at, 9343
reforms of, 1692, 9340, 9343, 9344
on religious experience, 7739
and revival of pilgrimage, 7148
on sacraments, 7885
schedule of, 9342–9343
Scholasticism and, 8175–8176
Vatican II and, 9533
on Vulgate Bible, 893
Tres Zapotes (Mexico), Stele C at, 5882
Tretayuga (period of time), in Purāṇic cosmology, 2018, 2019
Tretyakov Gallery (Moscow), 6244
Tre variazioni romane sul tema delle origini (Brelich), 1047
Trevelyan, George, 6495
Trevisarus, Gottfried Reinhold, 6435
Trhi Songdetsen. *See* Khri Srong Ide btsan
Triads, **9345–9350**. *See also* Trinity
in Buddhism, 9346–9347
in Chinese religions, humans in, 2631
in Daoism, 9347–9348
divine, 6746–6747
in Egyptian religion, 9349
in Etruscan religion, 9349
temples dedicated to, 2870
in Greek religion, 9348–9349
in Hinduism, 9345–9346
in Shintō, 9348
in Mesopotamian religions, 9349
origins of, 9348
in Roman religion, 9349
Triads in Defense of the Holy Hesychasts (Gregory Palamas), 3698, 3699
Triakontaeterikos (book), 5168
Trial, life as, in Ashkenazic Hasidism, 542–543
Trial of Jesus of Nazareth, The (Brandon), 1040
Triangles, in *maṇḍalas,* 5642, 5643
Tribal communities, 7716–7717. *See also* Primitive religions
initiation in, retreats of, 7769
migration of, 7716–7717
rites of passage in, 7795–7799
secret societies in, 7719
Tribes of the Ashanti Hinterland (Rattray), 98
Trible, Phyllis, 3036
on *Genesis,* 3358
Tribulation. *See also* Millenarianism
Christian Identity movement beliefs on, 1658
Tribulations of Marduk, 5703
Tribunal of conscience (confession)
Reformation rejection of, 1942
as spiritual guidance, 1941
Tribute Money, The (Masaccio), vol. 2 color insert
Tricakra maṇḍala, in Cakrasamvara tradition, 1350
Tricephalus, slaying of, 9685
Tricksters, **9350–9359**. *See also* Clowns; Culture heroes; Fools
in African religions, 86, 93–94, **9352–9354**
Ashanti, 9352
Azande, 9352
Dogon, 9352
Fon, 9352–9353
Luba, 5524
study of, 9352
Yoruba, 9353
in Arctic religions, 472, 4528
in Australian aboriginal religions
myths of, 664
trickster-souls in, 8532
in Caribbean religions, 1429, 1435
chaos and, 1538
characteristics of, 9350–9351
in Chinese religion, fox as, 8303
contemporary, 9356–9357
in creation stories, sickness caused by, 3809
definition of, 9350
fox as, 3181–3182
gender of, 9351, 9357–9358
in Germanic myths, Loki as, 5508
in Greek religion, Prometheus as, 7419, 7420
human *vs.* animal forms of, 4214
humor and, 4194–4195
in Indian religions, 4195
insects as, 4507, 4508
in Islam, 4210–4211, 4213–4214
in Korean religion, tigers as, 4208
Mercury as, 8428

Tricksters ***continued***
in Mesoamerican and South American religions, **9357–9359**
Aztec, 9357
cross-dressing, 9357, 9358
Desana, 9358
female, 9357–9358
Huichol, 9357
Makiritare, 8626
myths of, 5937
Tapirape, 9358
in Micronesian religions, 6003, 6011
monkeys as, 6152
in North American Indian religions, 6651, 6661–6662, **9354–9357**
Algonquian, 9355
as androgynes, 339
of Anishinaabe, 369
of Athapaskans, 573
of California, 6713
characteristics of, 9354
of Great Plains, 6699
iconography of, 4307
Iroquois, 9355
Lakota, 5296, 5297, 9355
Navajo, 9355
of Northwest Coast, 6709
in oral tradition, 9354, 9355
Paiute, 9355
in poems, 7225
powers of, 9350–9351
Pueblo, 9355
scholarly accounts of, 9356
and shamanism, 9354
Shoshone, 9355
in Polynesian religion (*See* Maui)
Radin (Paul) on, 7596
shape shifting and, 8301
trickster-transformer-hero, in earth diver myths, 1988–1989
in West African religions, 1435
Trier, Lars von, 3099
Triglav (deity), **9359–9360**
Trika (Kashmiri) Śaivism, **8046–8047**
Abhinavagupta on, 8–9
emergence of, 8041
in Krama Śaivism and, 8046
sectarianism in, 4005–4006
Trikāya (three bodies), 1063, 1069, 9346–9347
Trilles, O. Henri, 114
Trilogy of Dispelling Darkness, The (Longchenpa), 5193
Trilogy of Natural Freedom, The (Longchenpa), 5193
Trilogy of Quintessences, The (Longchenpa), 5193
Trilogy of Resting-at-Ease, The (Longchenpa), 5193
Triṃśikā (Buddhist text), 1300, 9527, 9899
Triṃśikābhāṣya (Sthiramati), Yogācāra philosophy in, 8739–8740
Trimūrti (three forms), 1025, 4421–4422, 4423, 4443, 9346
bhakti and, 4000
head symbolism in, 3804
Trinh, Sylvaine, 6525, 6553
Trinidad and Tobago
carnivals in, 7045, 7046
oriṣa movement in, 10027, 10028–10029
Roman Catholicism in, 1707
Sai Baba movement in, ethnic identities and, 1809
Shango cult, 1434–1435
Spiritual Baptists (Shouters), 1435, 1437
websites on, 10028
women in, 10027, 10028
Trinity, **9360–9364**
Antitrinitarians and (*See* Antitrinitarianism)
in Athanasian Creed, 2057
Augustine on, 627–628, 9361
Barth (Karl) on, 791
Basil of Caesarea on, 798
blasphemy against, 972, 973
Bonaventure on, 1011, 1012
Council of Constantinople and, 2040, 9361
Council of Nicaea and, 2040, 9361
current directions in, 9362–9363
Cyril of Alexandria on, 2117
Cyril of Jerusalem on, 2118
in *Divine Comedy* (Dante), 5373
in early Christian theological issues, 2582, 2583
Eckhart (Johannes) on, 2603
in Ethiopian Churhc, 2860
female, 9601
feminist theology on, 3036
filioque addition and, 2585
Harnack (Adolf von) on dogma of, 3778
historiography of ages and, 4028
history of doctrine, 1666–1667, 9349–9350, 9360–9361
Huiopatoria doctrine, Cyril of Jerusalem on, 2118
hypostasis and *ousia* concepts and, 4241
Islamic rejection of, 5979
Jewish polemics on, 7232, 7233
Joachim of Fiore on, 4928
Kant (Immanuel) on, 5079
Logos in, 5503
masculine imagery of, 9363
Maximos the Confessor on, 5793
Meister Eckhart on laughter and, 4202
modalistic trinitarianism, Servetus (Michael) and, 8232
mystery of, 3553
in mysticism, 6347
Neoplatonism on, 7192
in New Testament, 3546, 9360
Newton on, 6589
number symbolism and, 6747
Oneness Pentecostals rejecting, 7029
in Orthodox theology, 2589–2590, 9350
philosophical version of, 1666–1667
in postbiblical Christianity, 3553
principles of doctrine of, 9361–9362
in Protestantism, 7450
in Roman Catholicism, 7884
Sayers (Dorothy) on, 8142
Schelling (Friedrich) on, 8148
Stoicism on, 9360, 9361
Symeon the New Theologian on, 8919–8920
term first used by Tertullian, 1679
Tertullian on, 9086
Theodosius on, 5338
Thomas Aquinas on, 9163, 9361
three divine persons loving each other in, 9283
Trinity (Arpin), 2162
Trinity Broadcasting Network (TBN), 7713
Trinkūnas, Jonas, 765
Trioedd Ynys Prydein, 1480
Tripartite cognitive model, 2519
Tripartite Treatise (Gnostic text), 3513, 3530
Tripiṭaka (Buddhist text), 1108, 1252
Buddhist historiography and, 4025
Chinese translation of, 1265
cult of, 5309
in Mahāsāṃghika Buddhism, 5601
parts of, 1110, 1198–1199, 1269
Sarvāstivādin, 8117
three (number) in, 9347
Triple Alliance (Mesoamerica), 5907, 5909, 5910, 5912
in Aztec Mexico, 5173
Triple Goddess, 7830, 9099
Triple Refuge (teaching of Buddha)
music settings for, 6255
as profession of faith, 2053
Triple unreality, in Yogācāra Buddhism, 9898
Triple World, maṇḍalas and, 1350
Tripolitania, Khārijīs in, 5127
Tripolye-Cucuteni religion (prehistoric), 7382–7383
Tripta (Nānak's mother), 3335
Tri Ralpacen (emperor), monasticism and, 8082
Trisāhasramahasāhasralokadhatu in Hinayana Buddhist cosmology, 2027–2028
in Tiantai Buddhism, 2029
Triśalā (Mahāvīra's mother), 5609
Triśaraṇa (Three Refuges), 9347
Triśaraṇa[gamana]saptati, authorship of, 1401
Triśiras (mythic figure), three heads of, 3804
Triskandhaka (threefold service), 1118
Trismegistos. *See* Hermes Trismegistos
Trismosin, Salomon, on alchemy, 251
Tristan and Isolde
Campbell (Joseph) on, 1379
Irish analogues of, 1495
Tristes Tropiques (Lévi-Strauss), 6368
Triṣṭhalīsetu (Hindu text), 7169
Trisvabhāva (three natures), 1211, 1212, 1300, 2338, 9900
Trisvabhāvanirdeśa (exposition on the three natures), 9527
Trita (deity), in Vedism, 9556
Triumph of the Therapeutic, The (Rieff), 7476, 7480
Triumphus, in Roman religion, 5167
Trivarga (three goals)
in *Puruṣārthas* (four goals of humankind) in, 3996
medical theory and, 3854
Śāstra literature and, 8122
Trivia. *See* Hekate
Trobriand Islanders
calendar of, 1352
creation stories of, 3015
culture hero myth of, 2091
ethnography of, 6800–6801
gardens of, 3280
incantation of, 4406, 4408
kinship of, 5184
magic of, 5566, 5567, 5571
Malinowski (Bronislaw) studying, 5566, 5567, 5571, 5628–5629
marriage among, 5726
Milamala festival of, 6591
money and, 6137
music of, 6266
sexuality of, 5628
transmigration belief of, 9327
trees of, 9337
Troeltsch, Ernst, **9364–9367**
on churches, sects, and mysticism, 2084, 8467, 8481, 8493, 9365–9366
comparative theology of, 9129–9130, 9364, 9365
criticism of, 9366
on denominationalism, 2289, 2290
on economics and religion, 2671
education of, 9364
on God, 9364, 9366
on heresy, rise of, 3922–3923
on history as foundation of religion, 7117, 9364, 9365
on James (William), 7741–7742

on Jesus, 9364, 9366
Kant (Immanuel) and, 9365
and liberal Protestantism, 6104
on Luther (Martin), 9364
modern social theory, contributions to, 8493–8494
on mysticism, 7738–7739
on new religions, 6565
on orthodoxy, 3928
Pauck (Wilhelm) studying under, 7010
political activities of, 9366
on predestination, 3205
in Religionsgeschichtliche Schule, 7708
on religious experience, 7738–7739
Ritschl (Albrecht) and, 9364
on social action, 5397
on social groups, 8482
on social organization, 8467
on Sohm (Rudolf), 8508
systematic theology of, 9364–9365
Weber (Max) on, 2672, 9365
Trogus, Pompeius, 4250
Trojan War, 6374
images from, vol. 2 color insert
Venus in, 9581, 9582
as war of foundation, 9686
Troki, Isaac ben Abraham, writings of, 5085
Trollope, Anthony, 3060
Trolls, 2952, 4960
Trompf, Garry, 6508
at University of Sydney, 8769
Trophonios
vs. Asklepios, 551
oracle of, 3906, 6833
sanctuary of, 780
Tropology, Hugh of Saint-Victor on, 4151
Tropos Spondeiakos, 6305
Trotman, David, 10026
Trout, myths of, 5198
Trows, 2952
Troxler, Ignaz, 6435
Trubetskoi, Evgenii, **9367–9368**
liberalism of, 9367
philosophy of, 9367
Trubetskoi, Sergei, **9368**
on consciousness, 9368
and Florenskii (Pavel), 3133
idealism of, 9368
Truchsess of Augsburg, Canisus, appointment of, 1402
True Cross, from crucifixion of Jesus, relics from, 7688
True Discourse (Celcus), 6888
Trueno Viejo (deity), 9255
True Parents, 9467
True Pure Land school of Buddhism. *See* Jōdo Shinshū school of Buddhism
True Virtue (Edwards), 2699
Truhujo, John, Sun Dance and, 8847
Trullan Synod. *See* Quinisext Synod
Trulshig Rinpoche. *See* 'Khrul zhig rin po che
Trumpets
Mesoamerican, 6268, 6269
Middle Eastern, 6276
Trumpp, Ernst, 3717
Trust, faith as, 2956
Truth, **9368–9377**. *See also* Knowledge; Orthodoxy
absolute, 9369
aesthetics and, 54
Kierkegaard (Søren) on, 47
Anselm on, 373
apologetics *vs.* polemics on, 429
aspects of, 9369
in Bantu religions, 9370
in Buddhism, Mādhyamika
multiple truth in, 1576
two modes of, 8857–8858
in Chinese religion, 1576, 9372
in Christianity
of faith, 9375
God and, 3555
John of the Cross on, 9373–9374
classification of religions as true or false, 1818
in Confucianism, 9372
as Confucian Way, in Xunzi, 1573
as corrective to deception, 9369
definition of, 9369
evolution of, 2888
expression of
through cognition of realities, 9374
through experience, 9374–9376
through moral wisdom, 9372
through myth and ritual, 9370–9372
through spiritual presence, 9369–9370
through transcendent consciousness, 9372–9374
of faith, 9375
fire as test of, 178
Gandhi (Mohandas) on, 3272, 5399–5400
Greek philosophy on, 9374
Hegel (G. W. F.) on, 3894
heresy and, 3920, 3926
highest, 9369, 9373
in Hinduism, 9372
in Huichol religion, 9370
in Mīmāṃsā school, 9371
in Islam, 9371, 9372
modernism and, 6097
in Sufism, 9373
in Judaism, 9372, 9375
and poetic imagination, 7206
prophetic *vs.* philosophical, Islamic philosophy on, 6736
relative, 9369
Ruler's Truth, in Celtic religion, 1492
Sa'adyah Gaon on sources of, 7952
in Scholasticism, 8174
in Sikhism, in *Ādi Granth,* 32–33
Smart (Ninian) on, 8443
Spinoza (Baruch) on, 8680, 8681
Suhrawardī on, 8827
understanding of, 9369
validity of, 9370, 9371–9372
in Zoroastrianism, 9371, 9372
journey of souls and, 1647
Truth, Gospel of. See Gospel of Truth
Truth, Sojourner, 10037
Truth and Excellence of the Christian Religion Exhibited, The (Adams), 30
Truth and Method (Gadamer), 7245
Truth Centers, in New Thought movement, 4128
Truthfulness, in Jainism, 2624
Truzzi, Marcello, 6781
Trypho, 873
T.S. See Tabula Smaragdina
Tsaddiq/Tsaddiqim (righteous man/men), 2767–2768, **9377–9386**
as angels, 9378
Ba'al Shem Tov as, 9378, 9379, 9381
biblical and rabbinic doctrines of, 9377–9378
as charismatic leaders, 1546
David as, 9378
function of, 727
in Hasidism, 3789–3791, 4983, 5017, 6401, 8035–8036, 9377–9386
women as, 3351, 5611–5612
insights by, 2370
levels of, 9378–9379
practical, 9380
in Qabbalah, 9378
as saints, 8035–8036
teachings of, 9377
Tsadra Foundation, 9188
Tsamit (beyond reclaim), 4735
Tsantsa (shrunken heads), in Jivaroan religion, 8583
Tsav (talent), 9210–9211
Tsembaga people (Melanesia)
ancestor worship among, 322
balance in rituals of, 2618
pig festival of, 7840
Tsemitut (beyond reclaim), 4735
Tsetse fly, 60
Tsevi, Shabbetai, 3186
Tshahorpata (Egyptian figure), vol. 9 color insert
Tshangs dbyangs rgya mtsho (Tshangyang Gyatso), 1155
Tshar pa order (Buddhist), 1225
Tshis, father god of, 2984
Tshoghu (national assembly), 7263
Tshogs shing (assembly tree), 1286
Tsidqaniyot (female *tsaddiq*), 9377–9378
Tsimshian people (North America), 6656
on mosquitoes, 4508
Tsimtsum (divine self-contraction), 3524, 3551
in Hasidism *vs.* Luranic mysticism, 3788
Luria (Isaac) on, 5532, 6353, 7534–7535
Tsízhu (sky), 6917, 6918–6919
Tso chuan (Confucian text), 946
Tsofeh, ha- (daily), 788
Tsom Gedalyah (Fast of Gedaliah), in Jewish calendar, 4866
Tsomo, Lekshe, 6536
Tsonga religion (Southern Africa). *See also* Southern African religions
hot and cold in, 8662–8663
myth of the Fall in, 2960
rites of passage in, 8666–8667
Tsong kha pa (Tibetan lama), 1228, **9386–9388**
as emanation of Mañjuśrī, 9387
cult of, 9387–9388
disciples of, 1154, 1230, 9386
as founder of Dge lugs pa order, 2322, 9386, 9387
in Mādhyamika Buddhism, 5555
life of, 9386–9387
on meditation, 1279, 1286
monasticism, role in, 8083
on *mahāmudrā,* 5598
on *samādhi,* 1218
on *śūnyatā,* 9387
ordination of, 9386
philosophy of, 1301, 9387
teachers of, 9386
writings of, 1218–1219, 1276, 2322, 2323, 9386–9387
Tsuchiya, Kiyoshi, 5485
Tsui //goab (deity), 5136
Tsukamoto Zenryū, 5620
Tsukiyomi (deity), 4755
Tsukiyomi no Mikoto (deity), in cosmogony, 4801
Tsukushisō (chant), 6301–6302
Tsultrim Dorjé, reincarnation of, 5192

Tsunesaburō, Makiguchi, 6574, 6608
Tsungremmung feast, 187
Tsunki (spirit master), 281–282, 284
Tsurot ha-yesodot (Abravanel), 17
Tsurphu (Tibetan Buddhist monastery), 5102
Tswana religion (Africa), **9388–9390**
 ancestors in, 9388–9389
 circumcision in, 8665–8666
 contemporary, 9389
 cults of affliction in, 62
 God, concept of, 8656
 healing in, 9389
 initiation in, 9389
 marriage in, 7805
 sorcery in, 9389
Tu (deity), 7313. *See also* Kū
Tuan, Yi-Fu, 2611
Tuanyuanfan yu weilu (family reunion meal), 1641
Tuareg religion, visions in, 9615–9616
Tuarere (winged maiden), 6785
Tuath (tribal kingdom), 1482
Tuatha Dé Danann, 2951, **9390–9391**
 in battles of Magh Tuiredh, 9390
 characteristics of, 9390–9391
 and Fomhoire, 3164–3165
 in Irish mytho-history, 1488–1489, 5528–5529
 Sídh and, 8392
 sovereignty of, 9391
 in war of foundation, 9686
Tubalcain (biblical figure), as Cain's descendant, 1344
Tubers, cultivation of, mythology from, 9578–9579
Tübingen school, 805, 875
 Luthern theologians of, Orthodox correspondence with, 2587–2588, 4832
 on orthodoxy, 3928
Tübingen university
 Glasenapp (Helmuth von) at, 3496, 3497
 Mannhardt (Wilhelm) at, 5676
 Möhler (Johann Adam) at, 6113
Tubman, Harriet, 3361, 10037
Tu B'Shevat (New Year for Trees), 2645
Tucano religion and society (Colombia)
 mythic ancestors of, 326
 plant fertility rites in, 8582
 ritual and myth in, 8591
 source of illness in, 3809
Tucci, Giuseppe, **9391–9392**
 awards of, 9392
 expeditions of, 9391
 historiography of, 4045–4046
 honorary doctorates of, 9391–9392
 on Avalokiteśvara, 704
 on *maṇḍalas,* 5644
 as president of Instituto Italiano per il Medio ed Estremo Oriente, 9391
 on sexual magic, 8252
 Tibetan studies by, 1315, 9189, 9190, 9392
 writings of, 9392
Tuchē (fortune), 1526–1527
Tucker, James, 3083
Tucker, Joseph, 7487
Tucker, Mary Evelyn, 2613, 2665
Tudava (culture hero), Trobrian Islanders myth of, 2091
Tudigong (deity)
 sacrifices to, 1641
 territorial communities and, 1615–1616
Tudor, Anthony, 2162
Tudor, Dumitru, 2123
Tu Fu (poet), 7213–7214
Tughluq, Muḥammad, 6638
Tughrā'i, Ḥusayn 'Ali al-, 249
Ṭughril Beg, *madrasah* sponsored by, 5556
Tuḥfat al-mujāhidīn (al-Ma'barī), 4644
Tuḥfat al-muwāḥḥidīn (Roy), 7932
Tuhfat al-nafis (Raja Haji Ali), 4664
Ṭuhr (period between menstruations), 4708
Tuisto (mythic figure), 3447
Tui Tokelau (deity), 6264
Tujue people (Central Asia), kingship of, 5179
Tuka movement, 6796, 7298
 cargo cults and, 1421–1423, 1425
Tukanoan peoples (Amazon), 8622–8624
Tukārām (poet), 7210
Tu Kū Khong Kū (Buddhadāsa), 1072
Tukulti-Ninurta I (king), 5163
Tula (Tollan) (Mexico), Toltec religion in, 5889, 5906, 9222
Tulasi plant, 2403
Ṭūlī (angels), 4554–4555
Tulku, Ganteng, 9189
Tulkus (reincarnated lamas)
 establishment of leadership of, 8083
 Karma pas lineage of, 5101–5104
 and women, exclusion of, 8244
Tulsi, Ācārya, 2626
Tulsīdās (poet), 2449, 7209, 7210–7211, **9393**. *See also* Rāmcaritmānas (epic)
 in *bhakti* poetry tradition, 3985
Tum'ah (impurity), 7511, 7513
Tumbuka people, *vimbusa* healing dance of, 2140
Tummim, in casting of lots, 5425
Tumpanon (drum), 2498
Tumpkin, May Ann, 6586
Tumulus culture, 1479
Tumur (mythic figure), 6002
Tuna (mythic figure), 3397
Tunbridge, Dorothy, 667
Tŭngga (orchestra), 6296, 6297
Tungus people, and Korean shamanism, 5228
Tunguz language family, 468
Tunguz religion (Siberia), **9393–9396**. *See also* Shamanism; Southern Siberian religions
 animal ceremonialism in, 474, 9394
 bear myths in, 9394–9395
 cosmology in, 9394
 creation myths in, 9394
 deities of, mother-goddess, 470
 development of, 472
 funeral rites in, 9395–9396
 Japanese religion influenced by, 4780
 New Year festival in, 9394
 North American Sun Dance and, 8844
 shamanism in, 470, 9394–9396
  miracles and, 6050
 shamanistic initiation account, 8271
 soul in, 9394, 9395
 underworld in, 472, 9394
Tunisia and Tunisian religions
 family law in, 3368, 4703, 4707, 4709
 films from, 3098
 humorous stories from, 4212, 4213
 immigrants from, 4675, 4678, 4679
 Islam in, as state religion, 4590
 Judaism in, 4996
 trickster tale in, 4210–4211
Tunkashila (deity), 5295–5296
Tunnan (mythic figure), in Canaanite religion, 1384
Tuns (division of time), in Maya calendar, 1358
Tunstall, Cuthbert, 9425
Tuoba Empire (Central Asia)
 Cui Hao in, 5240
 kingship of, 5179
Tuonela ("the abode"), **9396–9397**
Tupac Amarú, 567, 1697–1698
Tupac Amarú II, 5986, 6576
Tupian religions (Brazil)
 Araweté, 8628
 cults of the dead in, 8584
 early accounts of, 8593
 jaguar god in, 8581–8582
 Juruna religion, 8628–8629
 master of the animals in, 8580
 in Mundurucú
  deities of, 8577
  mother spirit in, 8580–8581
 music in, 6272
 myth of Korupira, 2091
 plant fertility rites in, 8582
 World Fire myth in, 8589
Tupí-Guaraní religion (Amazon)
 dancing and soul movement in, 8533
 nativistic movements in, 6576
 overview of, 8634
 supreme beings of, 8577–8578
Tupinamba religion (South America)
 cannibalism in, 1403
 early accounts of, 8593
 Golden Age in, 3629
 jaguar in, 8581
 as model for "noble savage," 8594
 supreme being in, 8578
Tură (deity), in Chuvash religion, 1784
Turan (deity), 35
Turbina (morning glory), 9218
Turco-Mongol people (Inner Asia), rabbit symbols of, 7590
Turgot, Anne-Robert-Jacques, 7340
Turificati (burners of incense), 4420
Turing, Alan, 510, 511
Turing Test, 511
Turjumān, 'Abd Allāh, al-, 7242–7243
Turjumān, Murād Bay, 7243
Turk Allah. *See* Khusraw, Amīr
Turkestan. *See also* Xinjiang
 Buddhism in, 1145, 1147
 Islam in, 4624
Turkey and Turkish religions. *See also* Anatolia and Anatolian religions; Ottoman Empire
 Armenian Christians in, 1675
 baths in, 801
 calligraphy by women, 1369
 Çatal Hüyük (neolithic site), 1801–1802
 cats in, 1463
 dance in, 2140
 deportation of Dönmeh to, 2420
 Greek Orthodox Church in, patriarchate of Constantinople, 3658
 heritage politics and religion in Istanbul, 1810
 immigrants from, 4675, 4676, 4677, 4678, 4679
 Islam
  calendar in, 4713, 4714
  and Central Asian Islam, 4629
  creationism in, 8186
  narrative traditions of, 2447
  public life and, 1518
  Sufism, suppression of, 4571, 8824
  ṭarīqah in, 9007, 9012
 Jews in, during Ottoman Empire, 5104
 John XXIII (pope) in, 4945
 nationalism of, Gökalp (Ziya) in, 3624–3625
 Seljuk Turks and the caliphate, 1367

state funeral of Ozal, significance of, 1517–1518
women's organizations in, 3366
after World War I, Bennett (John G.) involved in politics of, 832
Turkhan religion. *See* Southern Siberian religions
Turkic language family, 468, 4491
Turkic religions, **9397–9404**. *See also* Southern Siberian religions
ancestors in, 9402
animism in, 9398
astrology in, 9399
birds in, 9400, 9402
Chuvash religion, **1784–1786**
common heritage of, 9398–9400
cosmology in, 9398–9399
deities of
Erlik, 2831–2832
Tengri, 9398, 9400, 9402
development of, 9398–9399
dualism in, 9398
fire in, 9399
funeral rites in, 9399, 9403
as imperial religion, 9401–9403
initiation in, 9400
mystic poetry of, 9917
as popular religion, 9400–9401, 9402
shamanism in, 9398, 9400, 9401
sources on, 9398
textiles in, 9091, 9403
totemism in, 9400–9401, 9402
trees in, 9399–9400
water in, 9399
Turkmenistan, 4620. *See also* Central Asia
archaeological research in, 4468
goddess worship in, 4469, 4470–4471
Islam in
ʿAlawī movement in, 8324
in Soviet era, 4624
Türks (Inner Asia), 4491
Turmair, Johannes, German humanism and, 4176
Turmeric, 9198
Turms (deity), Hermes as, 3937
Turnbull, Colin, 2495, 7525
Turnèbe, Adrien, Hermetism and, 3946
Turner, David, on Australian Indigenous myths, 668
Turner, Edith
on African initiation rituals, 4484, 9405–9406
on goddess worship, 3615
on pilgrimage, 7163, 9406
on rites of passage, 5460, 7799
on women's cicatrization, 1003
Turner, Harold, 102
on *domus dei* (house of god), 8100
Turner, Henry McNeal, **9404–9405**
Turner, Kay, 3147
Turner, Lorenzo, 76
Turner, Michael, 2603
Turner, Nat, 66, 70
Turner, Richard Brent, 81
Turner, Terence S., 1004
on Ge mythology, 3295
Turner, Victor, **9405–9407**
on African divination, 117, 9405
on African initiation rituals, 4484–4485, 9405–9406
on African rituals, 118
on biogenetic foundation of rituals, 7049
on ceremony, 1512
on Chihamba initiation rite, 4197–4198
on cults of affliction, 1509
on Diola religion, 262
on games, 3268
and Gennep (Arnold van), 7049, 9405–9405
and Germanic religion, studies of, 3460
on goddess worship, 3615
historiography and, 4048
on liminality, 4481, 5461, 7330, 7797, 7801, 9406, 9407
on liturgy, 5492
Marett (R. R.) and, 381
on naked body, 6740
on pilgrimage, 7163, 9293, 9406
on purification, 7510
on reflexivity, 7649
on religious symbols, 9405
on rites of passage, 5460, 7796, 7797, 7799, 7801
on ritual, 2436, 7833, 7844, 7852
on ritual liminality, 8242
on ritual performances, 7042, 9406–9407
on ritual process, 3144, 7049–7050
on ritual symbols, 7838
on sacred symbols, 2303
on social change, 9406
on social drama, 7050
symbol theory and, 8911
on witchcraft and sorcery, 9778, 9779
Turning the Wheel (Boucher), 3330
Turnour, George, 1311
Turo (deity), 9420
Turretinus, Franciscus, on predestination, 3204
Turtles and tortoises, **9407–9408**
in African myths, 98–99
bones of, 1015
in Chinese religion, 9407–9408
in Egyptian religion, 9408
in Greek religion, 9408
in Indian religions, 9407
in Inner Asian religions, 9407
in *Pañcatantra,* 6959
in Micronesian religions, 6006
in North American Indian religions, 6680, 9407
in South Asian religions, 9407
as trickster, 9358
Viṣṇu in form of, 707, 4325, 7500, 9407
Turul (falcon), 948
Tuscanic columns, 9064
Tuscany (Italy), *veglia* (social event) in, 2147–2148
Tushka (Nubia), rock shrine of, 7760
Ṭūsī, Nāṣir al-Dīn al-, **9408–9409**
as Shīʿī theologian, 4571
autobiography of, 9408
doctrine of *al-ishrāq* and, 2977
education of, 9408
in Ismāʿīlīyah, 558, 8333, 9408
writings of, 9408, 9409
Ṭūsī, Shaykh Muḥammad ibn al-Ḥasan al-
ḥadīth collections of, 3732
hawzah of, 3800–3801
Tuṣita Heaven, 1067, 1092, 1162, 1164, 7503
popularization of, 3155
Tusko (deity), 9420
Tustarī, Sahl al-
al-Ḥallāj and, 3755–3756
on light of Muḥammad, 6766
tafsīr of, 8953
Tutankhamen (Egyptian king), 217, 219
gold in tomb of, 3625
religion under, 2707
tomb of, 4320, 9225
Tutī-yi Hind. *See* Khusraw, Amīr
Tutsi people (Rwanda), myths of, paradise lost in, 139–140
Tuttul, Lord of. *See* Dagan
tuuliim cult (Nez Perce), 6596
Tuuruu (World Tree), 9394
Tuva religion. *See* Southern Siberian religions
Tuvin religion, deities of, Erlik, 2831
Tu Weiming, 2632
New Confucianism and, 1923
Tuxatmăš (sorcerer), 1785
Tu Yu, 2783
Tuzin, Donald, on rites of passage, 7807
Tuzuk-i Jahāngīrī (Jahāngīr), 4650
TV Buddha (Paik), vol. 11 color insert
Twain, Mark, 7370–7371
on Halley's comet, 8735
satire by, 4200
Twalen (Balinese epic character), 746
Twana tribe, boat burials of, 991
Twelve (number), interpretations of, 6749
Twelve Articles (peasant Reformation program), 7659
Twelve Classics *(shi'erjing),* as canon, 1909
Twelver Shiism. *See* Imāmī (Twelvers) Shiism)
Twelve-step programs, community involvement in healing in, 3814
Twelve Tables, law of the, 1846, 5332
codification of, 7902–7903
law of talion in, 7782
on private associations, 5333–5334
on private rituals, 5333
Twelve Tribes, 6560, **9409–9411**
children in, 6540, 9410–9411
gender roles in, 6516
leadership of, 6547
men in, 9410
origins of, 9409–9410
practices of, 9410
women in, 9410
Twelve Tribes of Israel (Rastafari organization), 7625, 7627
Twenty-eight (number), interpretations of, 6750
Twenty-five (number), interpretations of, 6750
Twenty-four (number), interpretations of, 6750
Twenty-two (number), interpretations of, 6750
Twenty-two shrines system (Japan)
cults of, 8361–8362
teachings of, 8360
Tokugawa restrictions on, 8363
Twi language, 214
Twins, 2985, **9411–9421**. *See also* Dualism
in African myths, 98–99, 100, 325
Dogon, 1987, 3569, 9414–9416
Nyakyusa, 6770, 6772
in Australian Indigenous religions, 9414
Baltic twin deities, **9419–9421**
in Caribbean religions, 1433, 1434, 9415, 9418
culture heroes as, 2092
disparity in value of, 9416
in Egyptian religion, 9414, 9415

Twins ***continued***
Eliade (Mircea) on, 9413, 9414
as first humans, 2985
in Germanic religion, 3450, 3451
in Greek religion, 9416–9417
historical examples of, 9412–9416
in Indo-European cultures, 9416–9417, 9420
of Mani, 3513, 5648, 5655
in Manichaeism, 3513, 9413
in Maya creation myth, 5797, 5935
in Mesoamerican myths, 5937
in Mesopotamian myths, 6477
in North American Indian religions, 9413–9414, 9415, 9418
Iroquois, 4541, 6680, 9413–9414, 9418
Lakota, 5297
Navajo, 1450
Pueblo, 6722, 6724
Zuni, 6660
in origin myths, 9417–9418
in Roman religion, 9417, 9420
Siamese, 2423
in Slavic religion, 8435
as sons of Sun, 9414, 9415
in South American Indian religions, 9413, 9418
in Sumerian religion, 9417
symmetry of, 9416, 9417
weddings of, 9419
in Zoroastrianism, 9412–9413, 9416
Twitchell, Paul, Eckankar founded by, 2601
Two (number), interpretations of, 6746
Two Books, The, **9421–9424**
decline and survival of, 9423–9424
establishment of metaphor of, 9422
origins of metaphor of, 9421–9422
variations on theme of, 9422–9423
Two Books model
scientific history and, 8181
Two Language model *vs.*, 8186
Two Language model
and science and religion, 8184
on science and religion, 8186
Two-realm theory (creation and redemption), ethics and, 1655
"Two Rivers and a White Path" parable (Shandao), enlightenment in, 8299
Two-seed theory, 1658
Two Sources of Morality and Religion, The (Bergson), 838
Two-spirit people, 3409, 3422
2001: A Space Odyssey (film), 512
Two Treatises on Government (Locke), 7282
Two-truths doctrine (Buddhist), 860, 1206
Two-world dualism, 2509
TWR. *See* Trans World Radio
Tyberg, Judith, 7229
Tyche (deity), 1526–1527, 3002
and Fortuna, 3175
Tychism, 1527
Tyconius
on Antichrist, 394
biblical exegesis of, 874, 2417
Tyiwara (Bambara society), 777
Tykwer, Thomas, 3099
Tylor (Marett), 5708
Tylor, Edward Burnett (E. B.), 2883, **9424–9425**
animism of, 114, 362–365, 367, 2237–2238, 2914–2915, 6440, 9424, 10077
African religions in, 114
as classification of religion, 1818–1819
criticism of, 8168
dynamism and, 2540
influence of, 363–365, 7372
motivation for, 363, 367
nature worship and, 6440
power and, 7347
problems with, 364–365, 367
supreme beings and, 8876
Codrington and, 1847, 1848
on culture, 2087, 2088
on death, 2237–2238
on degenerationism, 5260
on deity, 2255
on European folk culture, 2144
on evolutionary theory, 9424–9425
Müller (F. Max) and, 6235–6236
evolutionism of, 2914–2915
Graebner (Fritz) on, 3648
hero myths, study of, 3958
imperialist bias of, 1857
Indo-European religious studies of, 4460
Lang's (Andrew) critique of, 5300
on liturgy, 5491
on magic, 5564, 5588
Marett (R. R.) and, 5708
and masks, 5764
on origin of religion, 4183
on prayer, 7368
religion defined by, 7702
on religion *vs.* magic, 6502
on rituals, 7839
sacrifice, gift theory of, 8002
rejection of, 8002, 8003
on soul, 8531
on soul loss in sleep, 8440
Spencer (Herbert) arguing with, 5672
and study of North American Indian religions, 6671
on supreme beings, 8170, 8874, 8876
symbol theory and, 8910
on totemism, 9251
on transmigration, 9326
Tympanum (drum), 2498
Tyndale, William, **9425–9426**
Typhon (monster), 2431
Typhon (mythic figure), 3384. *See also* Seth
"Typographic Revolution: Antecedents and Legacy of Dada Graphic Design" (Cohen), 1849–1850
Typological Imaginary, The (Biddick), 9295
Typology. *See also* Classification of religions
of evil, 2898–2903
of science and religion, 2658
of wisdom, 9747–9748
Týr (deity), **9426–9427**
Garmr killing, 9426
Óðinn and, 6809
role in Germanic pantheon, 3452
sacrifice of, 9426
sources on, 9426
worship of, 9427
Tyrannius Rufinus, on Apostles' Creed, 2054
Tyrant, definition of, 5156
Tyre (Phoenician city), 7128, 7129
Melqart as god of, 5846–5847
Tyre, Synod of (335), on Athanasius, 571
Tyrrell, George, **9427–9428**
in Catholic modern movement, 7069, 7070, 9427–9428
Hügel (Friedrich von) and, 4150
Mercier (Désiré Joseph) against, 5868
Modernism of, 6106
Petre (Maude) as biographer of, 7069, 7070
Tyson, Ruel W., Jr., 3144
Tza'ar ba'alei hayyim ("distress of living creatures"), 2644
Tzahui (deity), 9213
Tz'aqol (creator being), 5797
Tzeltal Maya religion, tobacco in, 8455
Tzeltal Revolt (1712), 5920–5921
Tzetzes (Byzantine poet and scholar), on Hippocrates, 4021
Tzitzit (garment), 9088–9089
Tzolkin (ritual calendar)
Maya almanac and, 1359
in Maya religion, 1356
Tzompantlis (skull racks), 751
Tzu Chi. *See* Ciji
Tzu Chi Compassionate Relief Foundation, 1168, 2786, 2787

U

UAHC. *See* Union of American Hebrew Congregations
UAICC. *See* Uniting Aboriginal and Islander Christian Congress
UAM. *See* United Aborigines Mission
Uarichao (underworld), 151
Uayeb' (month), 5791
Ubaid period (Mesopotamia), 5947
Ubakala, dances of, 2137, 2138
Ubasoku (unordained monks), 4784
'Ubayd Allāh ibn Ziyād, 550
Kūfah revolt and, 4235
Ubayyid culture, al-, 6462
Ubelluri (deity), in Hurrian religion, 4231
Über den Ursprung der Sprache (Herder), language in, 3919
Über die neuere deutsche Literature, Fragmente (Herder), language in, 3918
Über die Religion (Schleiermacher), anthropological theory of religion in, 8161
Übermensch (Neitzsche's concept of overman), as hero, 3956
Uberoi, J. P. S., 4424
Ubertino da Casale, on heart of God, 3883
Übged (ancestors), 1325
Ubhaya Vedānta (dual theology), in Śrī Vaiṣṇavas Sampradāya, 8728
Ubu roi (Jarry), 2475
Ubwiiru people (Rwanda), memorization by, 5850
UCA. *See* Uniting Church in Australia
Uccheda-ditthiyo (annihilationist views), 1446
Uchimura Kanzō, 6608, **9431–9432**
and Nitobe Inazō, 3073
religious protest by, 4813
Udaba' (masters of *adab*), humor and, 4214–4215
Udaghans (female shamans), 1326, 2395
Udäkki (drum), 2497
Udāna (breath), 1043, 7362
Udānavarga (Buddhist text), 1146
Udayana (Hindu logician), 1301, 6774
Uddesikadhātu (marks of Buddha), 7163
Udgātṛ priests, *Sāmaveda* as province of, 3991
Udjat (Eye of Horus), 2713
Udkha (shaman essence), 1326
Udmurts (Votiaks), 3105
cult priests of, 3110
rural ritual feasts of, 3108
sanctuaries of, 3109
studies of mythology of, 3112
UDV. *See* Uniao do Vegetal
Udyoktara, 6774
Ueber die Autonomie der Rabbinen und das Prinzip der jüdischen Ehe (Holdheim), Reform Judaism in, 4080
UFBL. *See* Universal Foundation for Better Living

UFO religions, **9432–9436**
  Heaven's Gate movement, 3890, 3891
  in new religious movements, 6545
  and origins of New Age movement, 6495
  Raëlians, 6513, **7596–7600**
  Unarius Academy of Science, 9448–9449
Ufufunyane (spirit possession), 10010–10011
Uganda and Ugandan religions (East Africa)
  apocalyptic movements in, 6216–6217
  Bunyoro people of, kingship of, 5170
  charismatic Christianity, 106
  Chiga myth, 2961
  Christian missions to, colonial government established by, 2578
  funeral rites in, 3237
  Ganda people of
    creation story of, 85
    dances of, 2137
  kings in, 84
  Lango people of, spirit possession in, 2140
  Lord's Resistance Army in, 106
  new religious movements in (*See* Movement for the Restoration of the Ten Commandments of God)
  Nyoro people of, myths of, 93
  smallpox as deity in, 2568
Ugar (mythic figure), in Canaanite religion, 1384, 1394
Ugarit (Syria). *See also* Canaanite religion
  Anat in texts from, 319
  archaeology at, 455, 1381–1382
  Astarte in, 561–562
  Athirat in texts from, 589, 590
  Baal as protector of, 723
  cult of Reshef in, 7760, 7761, 7762
  cuneiform script found at, 1390, 3375
  Dagan in, 2126
  El in texts from, 2742
  gender in art of, 3379
  goddess worship in, 3595–3596
  kingship in, 5164
    divine, 5146
  Ouranos and Kronos myth, 1451
  women in, 3375, 3376
  written records from, 5161
Ughu bugha (upper world), 9394
Ugradattaparipṛcchā (Buddhist text), 1114
Ugric peoples (Arctic), 468
Uhlhorn, Gerhard, on Gnosticism, 3532
ʿUhud, Battle of (625), 6225
  Abd al-Raḥmān in, 19
Ŭiam, Sohn, 1647
Ŭich'ŏn (Buddhist scholar), 1172, **9436**
U'i dum btsan (Tibetan emperor), 1152
Uighur language, 1148, 4640
Uighur religion (Mongolia), 4492. *See also* Inner Asia
  Buddhism, 1148, 1149, 4492
  Christianity, 1725
  Islam, 4640
  Manichaeism, 1598, 4492, 5656, 5668
    as official religion, 5669
Ui Hakuju, on Sthiramati, 8739
Uinigumasuittuq (mythical figure), 2394
Ŭisang (Buddhist scholar), 1171, 4146, **9437**
Uisnech, 1491
Uji (clan)
  in early Japanese society, 4781
  family records of
    function of, 4802
    Nihonshoki in, 4802
    popular propagation of, 4806
    Six National Histories and, 4802–4803
  in Kamakura period, 4786
  Kiki texts separate from, 4801
Ujigami (ancestral deities), 4795
Ujiji (Tanganyika), Islam in, 2571
Ujjain (India), Kumbha Melā at, 5265
Ujjvalanīlamaṇi (Rūpa Gosvāmin), 826
Uka no Mitama (deity), 3182
ʿUkbarī, Abū ʿAlī al-. *See* Ibn Shihāb
Ukhedu (bodily substance), in Egyptian healing, 3826
Ukine (spirits), 2354, 7444
Ukiyo, 51–52
Ukko, **9437–9438**
Ukraine
  colonization of, Jews in, 5015
  Cossack uprising in, 5016
  Karaite sect in, 5084
  Mennonites in, 5860
  new religious movement originating from, 6568
  prehistoric culture in, 7379, 7380
  Uniate church in, 9464
  winter solstice songs in, 9741–9746
Ukrainian Catholic Church, 9464
Ukrainian Orthodox Church, 7946
  in Canada, 1713
  in communion with Rome, 2588
  latinization in, 7942
  property rights of, 2588
Uk'u'xkaj (creator being), 5797
Ulaidh people, 1493
Ulakan oĭun (shamans), 2395
ʿUlamāʾ (Muslim scholars), **9438–9441**
  ʿAbd al-Rāziq, (ʿAlī) opposed by, 5
  in Acehnese religion, 26
  in Africa, 7295
  Almohad opposition to, 4585
  in Andalusia, 4594
  authority of, 6097
  caliphate and, 1366, 1367
  in Central Asia, 4623, 4625, 4627
  on character of caliph, 7285
  consensus of, 4566
  ijmāʿ (consensus) of, 8854
  in Imami Shiism, 8323
  in Iran, 4702
  in Marinid dynasty, 4587
  modernism and, 6097
  in Morocco, 4590
  power of, 4587
  as priests, 7395
  prophetic medicine *(tibb al-nabawi)* and, 3833
  samāʿ (listening parties), opposition to, 8065, 9004
  in South Asia, 4641, 4644–4645, 4647, 4648, 4651, 4652, 4654
  in Southeast Asia, 4659, 4665, 4667–4668, 4672
  in sub-Saharan Africa, 4602
  Sufism complementary to, 4563
  Tatar, 4617–4618
  waqf and, 9677
  on women, 3365
Ulanov, Belford, 7483
Ulfa, Maria, 3369
Ulfheðnar (warriors), 842
Ulfilas (missionary), 922
  as missionary and bishop to the Goths, 1682, 1689
Úlfr Uggason
  on Baldr, 743–744
  on Loki, 5509
Ülgen (deity), 2831, 3223, **9441–9442**
Uli figure (Melanesian portrait), vol. 10 color insert
Ullama. See Hipball
Ullikummi (stone monster), in Hurrian religion, 9087
Ullikumu (deity), in Hurrian religion, 4231
Ullr (deity), 3452–3453
Ulpian (Roman jurist)
  on divination, 7915
  on physicians, 3842
Ulrich of Strassburg, Albertus Magnus and, 232, 233
Ulster Cycle, 1493–1494, 1499–1500, 2820
Ultimate transformation and ultimate orientation, 1581
Ultraism, in United States, 1715
Ultramontanism, **9442–9443**
  Gallicanism replaced by, 3259
  Gregory XVI and, 6973
  Leo XIII and, 6974
  Pius IX and, 6974, 7180
  Vatican I and, 9528–9532
Ultra-Orthodox Judaism, 4901
Ultra Pitch. *See Yang tig*
Ulug-Khorum *kurgan,* 7385
Uluru (Australia), 9260
Ulutún rite, 5689
Ulysses' Sail (Helms), 9292
Umā (deity)
  as wife of Śiva, 2526
  Bengali worship of, 826
  in virgin-mother-crone triad, 2984
Umai, **9443**
Uma pacha (mountain head), in Andean religion, 8619
Umāpati Śivācārya, **9443–9444**
ʿUmar I (caliph)
  in Jerusalem, 4841
  on *tafsīr,* 7561, 7563, 8951
ʿUmar II (caliph), 3211
  collection of *ḥadīths* commissioned by, 3728
ʿUmar ibn al-Khaṭṭāb, **9444**
  Abū Bakr supported by, 20
  as Abū Bakr's successor, 20
  conversion of, 6221
  daughter of, as Muḥammad's wife, 6224
  electoral council set up by, 4394
  interest in Fāṭimah bint Muḥammad, 3008
ʿUmar Tāl, 3229, **9444–9446**
Umaru Pulavar, 4644
Umāsvāti, 2624, 4768
Umay, 9443
Umayado no Miko. *See* Shotoku Taishi
Umayyad caliphate
  and Abbasid caliphate, 4591, 4594, 4695, 8321
  Abū Ḥanīfah and, 21
  in Andalusia, 4591–4593, 4594
  and Muʿawiyah, 4582
  authority, 1366
  Berber revolt against, 4583, 4592
  divine power and, 3562
  dynasty of, 9658
  Fatimids and, 1366
  gardens in, 3282
  Ḥasan al-Baṣrī and, 3784
  Kaʿbah under, 5050
  kalām under, 2970
  legal developments under, 4693
  Manichaeism under, 5656
  Murjiʾah sect supported by, 4568
  Muʿtazilah in, 6317, 6318

Umayyad caliphate ***continued***
origins of, 1366, 4582
Qādāri heresy during, 3210–3211
qāḍī under, 7540–7541
Samaritans and, 8069
Shī'ī opposition to, 8320–8321
status of Iranians in, 4562
and Sufism, development of, 8810
Syriac Orthodox Church and, 8939
Umayyad Mosque (Damascus), architecture of, 6206, 6208
Umbanda (Brazil), 124, 6578
Catholicism in, 124
creolization and, 2066–2067
distribution of, 120
influences on, 120, 124
origins of, 120, 124, 9308
Spiritism in, 124, 5091
spirit possession in, glossolalia and, 3506–3507
transculturation of, 9308–9309
Umbilical cord
in Maori birth rituals, 7807
in Mesoamerican birth rituals, 7812
in Ndebele birth rituals, 7804
Umeda people, gender status in, 2136
Ummah (Muslim community), **9446–9448**
in afterlife, 131–132
caliphate and, 1365, 1366
creation of, as first duty, 6222
divine mandate of, 7285
early development of, 4561–4562
Khārijīs declaring war on, 4562
Muḥammad's creation of, 6223
organization of, 4575
responsibility in, 7284
in sub-Saharan Africa, 4602, 4609
unity of, 7286
Ummah party (Sudan), 6229
Umm Kulthūm bint Muḥammad, 3008
Umm Salāmah, 6224
UMNO. *See* United Malay National Organisation
Umnyama (weakened state), 10009
Umozrenie v kraskakh (Trubetskoi), 9367
'Umrah (lesser pilgrimage), 4565
prayer during, 7157
stations of, 7158–7159
'Umrān badawī (rural civilization), 4588
'Umrān madanī (urban civilization), 4588
uMvelinqangi (deity), 10008
Unai, 283–284
Unaipon, David, 3079–3080
Unamuno, Miguel de, on knowledge, 5208
Ūnānī, Indian Medicine Central Council Act (IMCCA) and, 3856
Unarius Academy of Science, 9434–9435, **9448–9450**
Unas (Egyptian king), 7527
Una Sancta movement, 2686
Una società guineana (Grottanelli), 117
Unborn Venerable Mother, 1638
Uncanny Australia (Gelder and Jacobs), 690
Uncertainty
chance and, 1528–1529
Heisenberg's uncertainty principle, 1542, 1543
Unclean Spirits (Walker), 2930
Unconscious
and archaic mentality, 2282–2283
as atheist, 7489–7490
collective
Eliade (Mircea) on, 7476
Jung on, 7475, 7485
Freud (Sigmund) on, 3216, 7474
in Jungian psychology
collective unconscious, 1950
hero myths and, 3959
philosophy of nature and, 6437
projection of, 2285
in psychology, 1946
Ricoeur (Paul) on, 3933
Unction. *See also* Sacraments, Christian
in Ethiopian Church, 2860–2861
Underhill, Evelyn, **9450–9451**
Hügel (Friedrich von) and, 4150
Underhill, Ruth M., 6671
Understanding
German notion of *Verstehen*, 2353
Dilthey (Wilhelm) on, 3932, 3933
Heidegger on, 3933–3934
Wach (Joachim) on, 3933, 9649–9651
hermeneutics and, 3932–3935
historical, through narratives, 6377–6378
Wittgenstein (Ludwig) on, 3935
Underworld, 2871, **9451–9458**. *See also* Cosmology; Hades; Hell
in *Aeneid*, 9583
afterlife located in, 137–138
in Arctic religions, 469, 472
Canaanite offerings to gods of, 1386
caves associated with, 3015–3016
center of the world and communication with, 1503
chaos and, 1538
in Chinese religion
bureaucratic metaphor, 1614
Yellow Springs and Mount Tai, 1592
deities of, 2984, 3016, 3020, 3620
in Altaic religion, Erlik Khan as, 8272
blades of, 968
examples of, 3620
functions of, 3620
in Hurrian and Hittite religions, 4230
in Mesoamerican religions, Mictlantecuhtli as, 8677–8678
in Mesopotamian religions, 3900, 6476–6478
in Selk'nam religion, 8225
Sumerian, 9494–9495
descent into (*See* Descent into the Underworld)
in Egyptian religion
iconography of, 4319
literature on, 2719 (*See also* Book of Going Forth by Day)
in Etruscan religion, 2871
in Finnish mythology, 3104
fox in, 3182
in Germanic religion, 3448
in Greek religion (*See also* Hades; Persephone)
cock symbol and, 1841–1842
Hermes as messenger to, 3937
in Homer, 8542–8543
in Hawaiian religion, *'aumakua* (guardian gods) and, 3799
in Hinduism, Pātalas in Purāṇic cosmology, 2018
in Celtic religion *(Sidh)*, **8392–8393**
in Japanese religion, Yomi as, 3888
in Judaism (*See* She'ol)
keys to, 5116
in Komi religion, 5219
layers of, 2295–2296
in Luba religion, 5523–5524
in Mesoamerican religions, 150–151
Aztec, 3243
in Cuna religion (Panama), 2095, 2096
Mictlantecuhtli as god of, 8677–8678
Xibalba, caves connecting to, 1473
in Mesopotamian religions, 3900, 6476–6478
in New Caledonia religion, 6500–6501
in North American Indian religions, 6651
Cherokee, 6692
Iroquois, 4541
Pueblo, 2984
sun's motion tied to, 2008
in Oceanic religions, 2005
otherworld and, 6923
in Samoyed religion, 8096
secular concepts of, 9457
serpents associated with, 8458
shamanic descents to, 8272
in initiation, 8270–8271
sheep, rams, and goats in, 8310–8311, 8312
sky as polar opposite of, 8426
in Slavic religion, 8435
in South American Indian religions
in Andean religion, 8618–8619
nami budi, in Kulina cosmography, 2012
overview, 2010, 8587
in Tukanoan religion, 8622–8623
in Toraja religion, 9241
in Tunguz religion, 9394
visions of, 2299
water in, 9703
Unetanneh toqef (liturgical poem), Ro'sh ha-Shanah and, 8390
Unfinished War, The (Capps), influence of, 1413
Ungarinyin religion, **9458–9462**
Unger, John, 5831
Ungnad, Arthur, on *Epic of Gilgamesh*, 3487
Ungud (Australian mythic figure), 7605
Unguentarius ("spice merchant") scene in drama, 2469
Uni (deity), 5036
UNIA. *See* Universal Negro Improvement Association
União do Vegetal (UDV) (South America), 6274
psychedelic drugs in, 7470
Uniate Churches, **9462–9466**
Council of Brest and, 1685
establishment of, 2587
objection to term "Roman Catholic," 7873
in South America, 1703
UNICEF, 1555
Unicorns, 6164
in Indus Valley religion, 4473
Unidentified Flying Objects. *See* UFO religions
Unification Church, **9466–9468**
in Africa, 109
brainwashing civil suit against, 1033
child socialization and education in, 6542
conferences on new religious movements, 6524
deprogramming members of, 2292
in Europe, 6568, 6569, 6570
on the Fall, 6530
gender roles in, 6516
in Japan, 5376–5377, 6574

membership in, decline of, 6538
as religion, 7705
scriptural text of, 6529
solicitation laws and, 5378
teachings of, 6560
theological seminary of, 6565
in United States, 6560
women in, 6536
Unification theology, God in, 9467
Unified field theory, 2740
Unified Silla period (Korea), 9437
Uninitiated Druze, 2502
Unio mystica
in Qabbalah, 7537–7538
use of term, 6334, 6336
Union, with God. *See* Mystical union
Union for Traditional Judaism, split from Conservative Judaism, 1964
Union Hymnal, 6312
Union Libérale Israélite, 7670
Union of American Hebrew Congregations (UAHC), 7665, 7670, 7671
Religious Action Center of, 7671
Torah commentary of, 7672
Union of Brest-Litovsk, 9462, 9464
Union of Concerned Scientists, 2612
Union of Israel. *See* Agudat Yisra'el
Union of the Religion of Ancient Balts, 765
Union of Welsh Independents, Congregationalism and, 1938
Union Prayer Book, 7671
Reform Judaism and, 8388
Unions. *See* Labor movement
Union Theological Seminary (New York)
Black Theology at, 963
Bonhoeffer (Dietrich) at, 1016
liberal Protestantism and, 6105–6106
Niebuhr (Reinhold) at, 6611, 6612
Unitarianism, 9468–9470. *See also* Antitrinitarianism
blasphemy prosecution of, 974
Brāhmo Samāj influenced by, 828, 1029, 7932, 9317
Channing (William Ellery), role of, **1529–1530**
church architecture of, 796
Congregationalism and, 1938
Free Religious Association, 1570
human achievements in, 7454
India, influence in, 4007
liberal Protestantism of, 6105
morality in, 7651
Stanton (Elizabeth Cady) and, 8730
theology and Christology in, 1530
in Transylvania, Dávid (Ferenc) convicted of blasphemy, 973
in United States, emergence of, 1712
Unitarian Universalist Association, **9468–9472**
Unitary reality status, of art, 53–54
Unitary states
vs. baseline reality, 6491–6492
experience of, neuroscience on, 6490
Unitas Fratrum. *See* Moravian denomination
United Aborigines Mission (UAM), 671, 677
United Brethren. *See* Moravian denomination
United Buddhist Association, 1141
United Christian Broadcasters Europe, 7714
United Church of Canada
formation of, 1713, 7391, 9301
at Methodist Conferences, 5999
United Church of Christ
congregational form of Polity, 1768
formation of, 1938
full communion agreement with other denominations, 1769
United Church of Germany, Barmen Declaration (1934) and, 2061
United Church of Japan. *See* Kyōdan
United Church of Zambia, 1722
United House of Prayer for All People of the Church on the Rock of the Apostolic Faith, 2124–2125, 6563
United Keetoowah Band, 1563–1564
United Kingdom. *See* Britain
United Lutheran Synod of the South, 5539–5540
United Malay National Organisation (UMNO), 4668
United Methodist Church. *See also* Methodist denominations
establishment of, 5998, 5999
polity of, 1767
size of membership in, 5999
United Methodist Free Churches, establishment of, 5998
United National Independence Party, of Zambia, 5408
United Nations
Earth Charter and, 2657
human rights and, 4178, 4179, 4181
and women's studies, 3321
United Nations Assembly Hall (New York), abstract art in, 55
United Nations Conference on Environment and Development (1992), 3254
United Nations Convention on the Elimination of All Forms of Discrimination against Women, 4181
United Nations Convention on the Rights of the Child, 6540, 6541–6542
United Native African Church, 1719
United Nuwaubian Nation of Moors, 6769
United Pentecostal Church, 7029
United Presbyterian Church in the United states, 7391
Book of Confessions (1967) in, 2058, 2061
United Reformed Church (England)
formation of, 1938
proposed covenant with Anglicans and Methodists (1980–1982), 1939
United Society of Believers in Christ's Second Appearing. *See* Shakers
United Society of Brethren. *See* Shakers
United States. *See also* North America
African Americans in (*See* African American religions)
Agudat Yisra'el in, 195, 196
Anglicanism in, 350–352
anticult movement in, 2086
birth of, 2987
apostasy in, 433
Bahā'īs in, 738, 739
Baltic religion in, 764, 765
Baptist churches in, 783, 784–785
bioethics in, 940–942
blasphemy cases in, 973–974
British Israelism in, 1657–1658
Buddhism in
Foguangshan, 3140–3141
immigrants bringing, 1187–1188, 1189, 1190
Japanese Buddhism, 1187–1188, 1189
as new religious movement, 6559
Shingon school of, 8352–8353
Tibetan Buddhism, 1189–1190
transcendentalists and, 1187
women in, 6536
Zen Buddhism, 1188, 1189
Buddhist studies in, 1315–1316
Bureau of Ethnology, and study of North American Indian cultures, 6670–6671
censorship in, 4282
China, study of, 1635
Christianity in, **1708–1717** (*See also specific denominations and movements*)
of African Americans (*See* African American religions)
conversions to, 1709–1710
denominational union in, 2687
diet and righteousness for, 3173
Edwards' (Jonathan) influence on, 2701
evangelicalism in, 1710, 2887–2888, 2890–2891
fundamentalism in, 2889–2890, 2891–2893
Hutterian Brethren in, 4239
missions in, 1708–1709
moral crusades in, 1710
nature of, 1715–1716
pacifist ideas in, 6648
in politics, 2891, 2892
race in, 964–965
regionalism in, 1715
retreats and, 7772
revivalism in, 1710
sectarian movements, 1713–1714
spread of, 7283
vestements and clothing in, 1831
church attendance in, 2473
cities, religion in, 1809–1810
civil religion in, **1812–1817,** 7256, 7327
Bellah (Robert) on, 8468
symbols of, 9266–9267
Vietnam Veterans Memorial as shrine, 8376–8377
civil rights movement in (*See* Civil rights movement)
Civil War in (*See* American Civil War)
colonial
Anglicanism in, 350–352
Whitefield (George) evangelizing in, 9726–9727
communist brainwashing allegations in, 1030–1031
communitarian movements in, 5398
Confucian studies in, 1922
Congregationalism in, 1938
Constitution of, First Amendment of, 5330

United States *continued*
counterculture movement in, neoshamanism and, 8294
culture of
Orthodox Judaism and, 6907–6908
Sikh Dharma criticism of, 3879
transcultural contact and, 10084–10085
definitions of religion in, 10082
demons in, belief in, 2280
denominational ecclesiology, rise of, 1774–1775
denominationalism in, 2288–2290
drama in, 2475, 2476–2477
Earth First! in, 2561, 2562
Eastern Orthodoxy in, 1713
economy of, government in, 2671
Eliade in, 2756–2757
the Enlightenment in, 2797
eremitism in, 2828
eugenics in, 2879–2880
films from, 3099
foreign policy of, 5331, 5362
formation of, religion in, **10082–10087**
founding myths of, 10083
freedom of religion in, 5330, 5362
First Amendment on, 6556
in practice, 6557
Freemasonry in, 3196, 3197
Garifuna religion in, 3286
Golden Age in, 3628
Grail movement in, 3653
in Hawaii, sovereignty issues and, 5341–5342
Hinduism in
Bengali, 830–831
as new religious movement, 6559
Śaivism in, 8418–8419
Swaminarayan movement in, 8892
temple culture in, 8418
Vedanta Society in, 4008
Yogananda in, 9902–9903
historiography in, 4043–4044, 4049
Holiness movement in, 7029
human rights and, 5362
iconoclasm in, 4282, 4347
iconography in, 4348, 4349
immigration in
formation of U.S. and, 10082–10087
policy on, 830
inaugural address as ceremony, 1515
indigenous religious practices in, 10083–10084
International Society for Krishna Consciousness in, 4521, 4522, 4523, 7354, 7355
Islamic studies in, 4723
Islam in, 4686–4691
African Americans in, 6418 (*See also* Nation of Islam)
as American/Western Islam, 6100
Bengali, 830–831
of European-Americans, 4690
of immigrants, 4690–4691
of Latino Americans, 4690
and persecution, 4690–4691
progressive, 6100–6101
social work in, 4688, 4689, 4690
spread of, 4687, 4689
Sufism, 6563
Sunnī Islam, 4687–4688
women in, 4687, 4688
Jesuits in, 4842, 4843
Jewish studies in, 4878, 4883
in Jones's (Jim) theology, 4953, 4955
Judaism in (*See also* Habad Hasidism)
Conservative Judaism, **1957–1966**
denominational, 4868–4869
environmental focus of, 2613
exile of, 2923
folk elements in, 3160
Hasidism, 9382, 9383
messianism in, 5976
modern Jewish thought, 4907–4909
Orthodox Judaism, 6904, 6905–6906, 6907–6908, 8517, 8518
rabbinate in, 7582
Reconstructionist Judaism, 7635–7637
Reform Judaism, 5976, 7665, 7666, 7670–7673
Soloveitchik (Joseph Baer), role of, 8517, 8518
synagogues in, 8925–8926
women in, 3354–3355, 7582
after World War II, 7671–7673
yeshivot of, 9885
Zionism in, Szold (Henrietta) and, 8941
kinship in, 5183
landscapes of, 10085
Latin America, economic and cultural penetration into, 1702
laws in
debates over, 5356
on immigration, 4686–4687
on Native American graves, 7303
on Native American lands, 7301–7302, 7303
on Native American religious freedom, 7302
on Native American tribal governments, 7302
on peyote use, 7303, 7471, 10054–10055
punishment and, 5374
liberation theology in, 5442
literature of, 5478–5480
Lutheranism in, 5539–5540, vol. 1 color insert
Marranos in, 5723
media in, religion and, 4960–4967
Mennonites in, 5860
Methodist denominations in
development and growth, 5997–5998
divisions in, 5998–5999
missions
to African American slaves, 1709
to European Americans, 1709–1710
in Latin America, 1702–1703
to Native Americas, 1708–1709
in Philippines, 1727–1728
to post-emancipation Southern blacks, 1751
monasticism in, 6125
money, importance of, 10086
Moravians in, 6191
museums in, 6244, 6246
Native Americans in (*See* North American Indian religions)
nature religions in, dominance in, 2663
necromancy in, 6453
Neopaganism in, 6471, 6472
neoshamanism in (*See* Neoshamanism)
Nestorians in, 6481
New Age movement in, 6496
new religious movements in, 1714, 5375–5376, 6514, **6556–6566** (*See also specific movements*)
legal cases against, 1033, 1034
opposition to, 1032, 1033, 1034, 1038
obsession with religion in, 4043–4044
Orthodox Church in, 2589
outsider art in, 9626
particularism in, 5261
political theology in, 7246
popular culture criticism in, 7321, 7322
power shift toward, in 20th century, 1700
Protestantism in, 1712, 1715
civil religion and, 1813
colleges in, 8787
denominationalism, 1711, 1712
faith healing in, 3847
liberal, 6105–6106
nature of, 1715
Pentecostalism (*See* Pentecostalism, in United States)
Pietism influencing, 7143
Presbyterianism (*See* Presbyterian denominations, in United States)
schism patterns in, 8151, 8153
women in, 6765
proverbs in, 6976–6977
psychology of religion in, 7475–7476
psychotherapy in, rebirthing analysis in, 7680
Puritanism in, 1709–1710
Quakers in, 7547–7549
religious broadcasting in, 7709–7713
religious education in, 7734, 7735
Religious Right and politics, 1413
revolutionary spirit, civil religion and, 1815
rituals in, 7836
Roman Catholicism in, 1711–1712, 7889–7890
Benedictines, 822
Carroll's role in, 1445–1446
colleges in, 8787
environmental responses by, 2613
history of, 1711–1712
nature of, 1715
pilgrimage in, 7149, 7150, 7151
sacred space in, 10084
same-sex marriage dispute in, 7283
Santeria in, 1434
saunas in, 801
sectarian movements (*See* Sectarianism, in United States)
social reform in
Adler (Felix) in, 33
Christian movements, 1750–1752
social work in, 7487–7488
sociology in, 8495–8496
Sōka Gakkai in, 8509
Southern, missionaries to, 1451
Spiritualism in, **8715–8718**
study of religion in, **8784–8789**
contemporary trends in, 8786–8787
early roots of, 8784–8785
institutional trends in, 8787–8788
Mesoamerican religions in, 5941
professional organizations, projects, and publications in, 8788

religious studies and related disciplines in, 8785–8786
suffrage movement in, Gage (Matilda Joslyn) in, 3251–3252, 3310
Summit Lighthouse beliefs on, 1782, 1783
superstitions in, 10084
Swedenborgianism in, 8901, 8903–8904
tattooing in, 1003
Theosophical Society in, 7227–7230, 9142, 9143, 9205–9206 (*See also* Point Loma Theosophical Community)
tombs in, 9227–9228
tourism in, shrine-like natural sites and, 8377
Transcendental Meditation in, 9290
transculturation in, **10082–10087**
Unitarianism in, 9469
urbanization in, 10085
wars of (*See also specific wars*)
civil religion and, 1814
water in, 10086
women's liberation movement in, 3310
Yoruba religion in, 10032–10033
Zoroastrianism in, fire in, 570
United Stateschi Lokasthiti ani Pravasaritta (Ramabai), 7610
United States v. Fishman, on cults and brainwashing, 2085, 6523
United Synagogue of America, Schechter (Solomon) and, 8146–8147
United Synagogue of Conservative Judaism (formerly United Synagogue of America)
formation of, 1959
membership trends, 1961, 1964
United Synagogue Youth
future rabbis and, 1962
havurah movement and, 1963
United Torah Judaism, 196
Uniting Aboriginal and Islander Christian Congress (UAICC), 678–679
Uniting Church in Australia (UCA), 679–680
at Methodist Conferences, 5999
Unitive mysticism
characteristics of, 6334–6336
in Judaism, 6339–6340
Unity
Comte on religion as unity, 1882
Cyprian on, 2113–2114
of the divine, syncretism and pantheism, 3909
in ecumenical movement, 2683
and human unity, 2689
of God
in Ethiopian Church, 2860
in Greek religion, 6156
in Islam, 3561–3563 (*See also* Tawḥīd)
in Judaism, 4992–4993
in Indian philosophies, 4420–4421, 4422–4423
in Kevala Advaita, 9546
mission in, 2684
number one as, 6746
Plotinus on, 6474
of primeval religion, magic, and science, 7974–7975
soi, 3913
waḥdat al-shuhūd (unity of witness), 3756–3757
waḥdat al-wujūd (unity of being), 7937
al-Ḥallāj on, 3756
Ibn al-ʿArabī on, 8819, 8820
Iqbal (Muhammad) on, 8824
of world religions (*See also* Ecumenism)
Heiler (Friedrich) on, 3898
Qurʾān on, 4575
syncretism and, 8929
Unity (Unity School of Christianity) (denomination), 6585, 6586, **9472–9474**. *See also* Universalism
founders of, 3095–3096, 6563, 6584
Hopkins (Emma Curtis) and, 4128
publications of, 6585
religious broadcasting by, 7710
women in, 6536
Unity of Brethren. *See* Moravian denomination
Unity of Wiliam James's Though, The (Cooper), 4776–4777
Unity School of Christianity. *See* Unity
Unity Temple (Oak Park, Illinois), 796
Universal(s). *See also* Universalism
in aesthetics, 54
in ethology, 2869
of gestures *vs.* sounds, 8675
in human behavior, 2867
logical problem of, 6644
meaning, need for, conversion and, 1970
panhuman comparison and, 1880
in Scholasticism, 5204, 8175
sexuality as, 8242
supernaturalism, debate on universality of, 2089
Universal Awakening through Cooperative Work. *See* Sarvodaya Shramadana
Universal Brotherhood and Theosophical Society, 7228. *See also* Theosophical Society
Universal church
as category, 1867, 2084
Cyprian on, 2113
Universal Church of the Kingdom of God (Brazil), 107
Universal consciousness, Fechner on, 1947
Universal Declaration of Human Rights (1948) (UN)
ethics of, 2656
overview of, 4178
purpose of, 5362
religious freedom in, 5363, 7704
Universal Foundation for Better Living (UFBL), 6586
Universal House of Prayer, 3173
Universal Intellect
in Druze movement, 8330
in Qarāmiṭah Shiism, 8328
Universal Islamic Declaration of Human Rights, 7704
Universal Islamic Society, 4687
Universalism, 9470–9471
of churches, *vs.* sects, 2084
in comparative religion, 1877–1878
doctrine of salvation, as soteriology, 8530
Groot (J. J. M. de) on, 7692
in Hellenism and Stoicism, world citizenship in, 3906–3907
humanism and, 4177
of Quakers, 7549
in Sai Baba movement, 8028
in salvation-oriented religions, in founded religions, 4067
Schimmel (Annemarie) on, 8150
in structuralism, 8752–8753, 8754
translation of scriptures and, 8203
violence and, 9598
in Zoroastrianism, 3907
Universalist Church of America. *See* Unitarian Universalist Association
Universality
of homosexuality, 4112
human rights and, 4181
in Indian religions, *Cakravartin* (universal king ideal), **1350–1352**
of missionary visions, 6069–6071
of moral norms, 6179–6181, 6183–6186
myth and, 1379
Otto (Rudolf) on normality of religion *vs.*, 4097
Universal morality, 7651, 7652
Universal Negro Improvement Association (UNIA)
Garvey (Marcus) as founder of, 3287
Rastafarianism and, 1438
Universal religions. *See* World religions
Universal religious groups, 1865, 1866–1867
Universal Soul
in Druze movement, 8330
in Qarāmiṭah Shiism, 8328
Universe. *See also* Cosmology
as *māyā* (illusion), 4422
axis of (*See Axis mundi*)
cooling of, 2032–2033
expansion of, 2031
inflation (boiling) of, 2033–2034
in orientation, 6885–6886
as polis, 3906
recreation of, Viṣṇu in, 9618–9619
self and, in Confucianism, 2633
structure of, and afterlife, 133–134
Universe Story, The (Teilhard de Chardin), 2610
Universism, in Chinese religion, 3703
Universities. *See* Colleges and universities; *specific schools*
University Museum at Oxford, 6243
University of Basel, Nietzsche at, 6614
University of Berlin, 4883
Bertholet (Alfred) at, 843
Beth (Karl) at, 846
Bonhoeffer (Dietrich) at, 1016
Mannhardt (Wilhelm) at, 5676
Marx (Karl) at, 5744
Tillich (Paul) at, 9203
University of Bonn, Marx (Karl) at, 5744
University of Bordeaux, 2527
University of California, Los Angeles, Gimbutas (Marija) at, 3492
University of California, Santa Barbara, Walter H. Capps Center at, 1412
University of Chicago
Eliade (Mircea) at, 2756–2757, 7743
Kitagawa (Joseph M.) at, 5188
Rahman (Fazlur) at, 6098
Wach (Joachim) at, 7743
University of Constantinople, 2582
University of Göttingen, Religionsgeschichtliche Schule and, 7706–7709
University of Halle, and Lutheran Pietism, 3185

University of Heidelberg,
Troeltsch (Ernst) at, 9364, 9365
University of Leiden
Bleeker (C. Jouco) at, 978
Groot (J. J. M. de) at, 3702, 3703
Grotius (Hugo) at, 3703
University of London
Gaster (Theodor H.) at, 3288
Institute of Archaeology of, 5110
Malinowski (Bronislaw) at, 5628
Myth and Ritual school at, 6380
University of Otago, 840
University of Padua, Galileo Galilei at, 3256
University of Paris, Thomas Aquinas at, 9160, 9161
University of South Australia, program development at, 8770
University of Stockholm, Andrae (Tor) at, 333
University of Sydney, 841
University of the West Indies, Rastafari study of, 7624–7625
University of Toronto
Ching (Julia) at, 10030
Fackenheim at, 2949
Oxtoby (Willard G.) at, 10055
University of Western Australia, 840, 841
uNkulunkulu (deity), **9474**
as hero *vs.* supreme being, 96, 3574
in Zulu religion, 10008
Unleavened Bread, Feast of. *See* Ḥag ha-Matsot
uNomkhubulwana (deity), 96, 10008–10009
Unspoken Words (Falk and Gross), 3300
Untouchables. *See also* Dalits; *See also* Caṇḍālas
Ambedkar (B. R.) as, 285–286, 5400
engaged Buddhism of, 2785–2786, 2789
Gandhi's (Mohandas) work with, 3273, 5400
Olcott (Henry Steel) and, 6816
religions of, **9474–9478**
rituals in, 9475, 9476
U Nu, **9478–9479**
Unveiled Mysteries (Ballard), 4246
Unwerth, Wolf von, 474
Upacāras (attendances), 7494
Upādāya-prajñapti-prakaraṇa (Dignāga), 2351
Upagupta (monk), 477, 6395
in Māra's conversion, 5691
Upāli (disciple of Buddha), 1062, 1105
Rājagṛha council and, 2035
Upāliparipṛcchā (Buddhist text), 1118
Upanayana (Vedic ritual), 7815
caste system and, 3995
Upāṅga, in Jain scriptures, 4767
Upaniṣads, **9480–9484**. *See also* Vedānta; *specific texts*
ahiṃsā and, 197
ānanda in, 7083
ashrams and, 545
atheism and, 577–579
bhakti and, 857
in Brahmanism, 9568–9569
Brahmodya in, 1025, 1026
breath in, 1043
bridge in, 1049
canon status of, 1407
classification of, 9482–9484
cognitive elements of, 5199
connotations of term, 9480–9481
cosmic tree of, 9576
cosmology in, 2015–2016, 5447
Dārā's translation of, 2219
death in, 4440
deity in, 2259, 2260
desire in, 2305
development of, 1026
in development of Hinduism, 3992–3994
enlightenment in, sleep and, 8442
eremitism of, 2823
eternity in, 2856
eyes in, 2941
funeral rites in, 7815–7816
Gnosticism of, 4925–4926
guṇas in, 9346
Sāṃkhya school and, 8090–8091
gurūs in, 3712, 3713, 8036
heart symbolism in, 3881–3882
Hellenistic culture influenced by, 3119
hell in, 9456
historiography in, 4025
human perfectibility in, 7040
in Vaiṣṇavism, 9501
in Vedānta, 9543–9544
īśvara in, 4751
karman in, 3993, 5095, 5096
light and darkness symbolism in, 5452
līlā in, 5455
magic in, 5589
māyā in, 5794
meaning of term, 3993, 8546
metaphysics in, 8545–8546
mokṣa in, 3993, 6115, 6116
monism in, 6144
mysticism in, 6343
objective of, 4427
oṃ in, 6820–6821
personal ethics in, 1555
prakṛti in, 7360
purpose of, 9543–9544
puruṣa in, 7521, 7522
quaternity in, 7550
reincarnation in, 7763
revelation in, 7779
ritual in, 9553
saṃsāra in, 3116–3117, 3993, 7677, 9327–9328
Śaṅkara on, 8105
on senses, likened to horses, 4135
spiritual guides in, 8711–8712
sports metaphors in, 8724
suicide in, 8831
tapas in, 8998
teachings of, 9481–9482
translations of, 4446
transmigration and reincarnation in, heaven *vs.*, 3886
trees in, 9335
triads in, 9345–9346
Vedism, relation to, 3989
via negativa used in, 6990
yogic practices in, 3794–3795
Upapāramī (inferior perfection), 6993
Upapāti nat (spirit), 1329
Upaprāṇa (breath), 7363
Upapurāṇas (Bengali text), 826, 7498
Upasad days, 9563
Upāsakaśīla (Buddhist text), 1114
Upasaṃpadā (ordination), 4483
Upatissa (Buddhist writer), 1200
Upāya/Upāyakauśalya (skillful means), 1207, 1213, 1274–1275, 5309, **9484–9486**
bodhisattvas and, 8712
development of, 1271
goals of, 1123
perfection of, 1281
Tanluan on, 8982
Updike, John, on the novel, 3058
Upekṣā (equanimity), in Buddhist meditation, 5105
Uposatha hall, 9054, 9055
Uposatha observance, confession and, 1886
Upper Sky Father (deity), 5119
Upper Volta. *See* Burkina Faso
Upper World. *See also* Heaven
in Jainism (*See Ūrdhvaloka*)
shamanistic ascent to, 8272
Upper Xingu peoples (Brazil). *See also* Tupian religions
music of, 6273
myths of, 2011
Uppsala University (Sweden), Andrae (Tor) at, 333
Upriver Man. *See* World-Overseeing Man
'Uqba ibn Na'fi', 3229, 4581
'Uqqāl (initiated Druze), 2502
Ur (Mesopotamia)
dynasties of, 5948
establishment of, 5947
fall of, 5948
moon in, 6172
musical instruments in, 6275
Nanna as god of, 5949, 5955, 6172
Woolley's (C. Leonard) excavation at, 6172
'Urābī revolt (1881–1882), 'Abduh (Muḥammad) in, 5
Uralchylar (Tatar group), 4619
Uralic language family, 468, 4488
Uralic religions. *See* Finno-Ugric religions; Siberia and Siberian religions
Uralo-Altaic cosmology, 1501
Uramot Baining people (Melanesia), vol. 6 color insert
Urania, 408
Urantia Book, The, 6531, 6559
Urartu kingdom and Urartean religion. *See* Hurrian religion
Urasa (mobile dwellings), 2395, 2396
Urbach, Ephraim, 900
on sin and the body, 8557
Urban II (pope)
Anselm and, 372
Crusades and, 2075, 2076, 9293
East-West harmony and, 8157
Gregory VII and, 3692
reform of, 3692
Urban IV (pope)
Albertus Magnus and, 232
death portended by comet, 8735–8736
Feast of Corpus Christi established by, 2437
Thomas Aquinas and, 9161
Urban VI (pope)
denunciation of, 1461, 6971
Great Western Schism and, 8157
Urban, Hugh, 8989
on androgyny, 8243
Urban VIII (pope), Galileo Galilei and, 3257
Urbanization. *See also* Cities
and African religions, 87
among central Bantu, 1511
and changing styles of tombs, 9227
development of, 5161
of Jerusalem, 4973
in Latin America, 1700
Mesopotamian, 1802–1803
shrines and, 7156
in United States, 10085
visions and, 9616
Urbano, Henrique, on Inca calendar and, 1364
Urban planning. *See also* Cities
sacred space and, 1810, 7982
Urban shamanism. *See* Neoshamanism
Ūrdhvaloka (Upper World), in Jain cosmology, 2024–2025
Urðr (Urd), 3001
spring of, 1502
Urdu language
fiction in, 10035
Hindi and, 3983–3984
Urdummheit (primal stupidity), 2541
Urendecuaucara (deity), 5909
Urgeschichte und älteste Religion der Ägypter (Sethe), 2730
Urheimat theory, 1453
Ur-hero, 7552
Uri. *See* Akkad
Uriel the Archangel, 9448
Ur III period, Dagan in, 2126

Urim, in casting of lots, 5425
Urine, and pollution, 7504
Urkultur (oldest culture)
Bornemann (Fritz) on, 8170
Schmidt (Wilhelm) on, 8168, 8876
Urmonotheismus. See Primitive monotheism doctrine; Schmidt, Wilhelm; Supreme beings
Ur-myth, 7552
Urnammu (king), laws of, 1844
Urnfield culture, 1479
Urns, at Monte Albán, 5903
Uroboros. *See Ouroboros*
Urrea, Teresa (Saint of Cabora), 6578
ʿUrs (spiritual wedding), 4714
Urshanabi (Babylonian figure), 989
Ursinus, Johann Heinrich, on Hermetism, 3949
Urso (Roman *colonia*), 7912
Der Ursprung der Gottesidee (Schmidt), 114, 7074
monotheism in, 8168–8169
"Der Ursprung der Religion und Kungst" (Preuss), 2541
Ursuline order, 6764
Marie de l'Incarnation in, 5711–5712
Uruguay, music in, 6274
Uruk (Mesopotamia), 5947
Akitu festival in, 223
Amaushumgalana in, 5949
An (deity) in, 5952
development of, 5161
establishment of, 5947
Gilgamesh in (*See Gilgamesh, Epic of*)
government of, 5161
image veneration at, 4380, 4381
Inanna as deity of, 3586, 3594, 5949, 5956
Inanna cult at, 4402
sacred marriage in, 5961
Urukagina (king), 1553
Urukáme (medicine bundle), as protector, 4152
Uru religion (South America), human origin myth in, 8589
Urvan (soul), 4537
Urvaśī (mythic figure), 5679
ʿUrwah al-wuthqā, al- (association), establishment of, 5
ʿUrwah al-wuthqaā, al- (journal)
ʿAbduh (Muḥammad) in, 5, 6098
Afghānī (Jamāl al-Dīn al-) in, 64, 6098
'Uryānī, al-, 4257
U.S. v. Fishman, 1033
Usai Atsuko, 3346
Usāmah ibn Zaid, army under, 20
Uṣas (deity), 9559, 9560
in Vedic pantheon, 3990
Usen (deity), 574
Usener, Hermann, **9486–9487**
Dieterich (Albrecht) studying under, 2348
on names of Roman deities, 6409
on Roman religion, 7893
on spirits, 8690
Usha (deity), nature and, 2620
Ushabtis (mummiform figures), 4319
Usharaya (deity), 3376
Ushharay (deity), in Canaanite religion, 1384
Ushiyama Yoshiyuki, 3348
Ushu (Silver, deity), in Hurrian religion, 4232
Ūsiṇš (deity), 769, 9419, 9420
Uṣṇīśasitātapatrā (Buddhist figure), 1079
Ussher, James, on predestination, 3208
USSR. *See* Soviet Union
Uṣūl (sources of law)
hawzah and, 3801
al-Shāfiʿī on, 8264–8265, 8854
Uṣūl al-dīn (principles of religion)
al-Ṭabarī on, 8944
in university curricula, religious studies and, 8782
Uṣūl al-fiqh (principles of jurisprudence), 4695–4697, **9487–9491**
basic principles of, 4696–4697
ijtihād in, 4373, 4374, 4375
study of, 4696
Uṣūl al-thalāthah wa-adillatuha, al- (Ibn ʿAbd al-Wahhāb), 4255
Uṣūlīyah, 4697
ijtihād in, 8343
in Iran, 4700
Shaykh Aḥmad and, 8307
Usury
and anti-Semitism, 400
in Islam, prohibition of, 4564, 4574
in middle ages, 5013
Uswah ḥasanah (example), 4565
Utah, Mormons in, 6194
Utaki (sacred place), 6812
Utanapishtim. *See* Atrahasis
Ute people (North America), round dances of, 6716
Útgarðr (outer abode), 3447, 3448
Uthht (deity), in Canaanite religion, 1384
Uthmān al-Tawīl, Abū al-Hudhayl al-ʿAllāf under, 18
ʿUthmān ibn ʿAffān (caliph)
ʿĀʾishah bint Abī Bakr opposing, 211
ʿAlī opposing, 257
as *kāfir,* 4567
assassination of, 257, 258, 1366
disagreement on caliphate under, 257
revolt against, 257
Utilitarianism
animal liberation based on, 2655
the good in, 3636
Utksepaniya-karma (banishment), of Yaṣas, by Vaiśālī council, 2035
Utley, Francis Lee, 474
Uto-Aztecan language, 6697
Utopia, **9491–9493**
in Chinese tradition
in myths of Datong and Taiping, 1628
in Xiu's Confucianism, 1577–1578
Hellenistic images of, 3906
in Japanese religion, *kami* of, 5072
in millenarianism, 6030–6031, 6036, 6038
paradise in, 6986
Utopianism, 9491–9493. *See also* Communitarianism, Christian; Religious communities
Abbey of Thelema and Crowley (Aleister), 2072
in Africa, 102
alchemy and, 253
in Axial Age, 7728
communities, 7720–7721
in Hellenistic period, 3906
Jonestown mass suicide and, 4184
Mannheim (Karl) on, 8467
and New Age movement, origins of, 6495
Niebuhr's (Reinhold) criticism of, 6613
in revival and renewal activities, 7785
sexuality and, 8242, 8243
soteriology and, 8527
of Summit Lighthouse movement, 1782
time and, 7993
Utpaladeva, Abhinavagupta on, 9
Utraquists, 6190
Hus (Jan), influence of, 4234
Utsava (festival), *vrata vs.,* 4016
Uttamchand, Karamchand, 3272
Uttamchand, Putalibai, 3272
Uttar (rituals), 2445
Uttarādhyayana Sūtra
hells in, 2022–2023
liberation in, 8548
Uttarakuru (mythic island), in Buddhist *cakravāla* cosmology, 2026, 2027
Uttarasanga (shawl), 1829
Uttu (deity), 4316
in divine bureaucracy, 5951
Enki and, 5954–5955
Utu (deity), 4316, 4317, 4403, 4404, 5956, **9494–9495**
as city god, 5949, 5956
in divine bureaucracy, 5951
Dumuzi and, 5957, 5958
Utug (deity), in Sumerian religion, 8538
Utuhegal of Uruk, 5948
U-Vikashtem Mi-Sham (Soloveitchik), Man of God in, 8519
Úvod do religionsistiky (Hornya), 8774
Uwaysīs Ṣūfī order, 9006
ʿUyūn akhbār al-Riḍā (Ibn Bābawayhi), 4262
Uzbekistan, 4620. *See also* Central Asia and Central Asian religions
Islam in
in post-Soviet era, 4626–4630
in Soviet era, 4624
Jews in, 5009–5010
Uzbek Khan, 4613, 4616
ʿUzzā, al- (deity), 444, 445
as epithet *vs.* deity, 6389
in Nabatean religion, 6386, 6389, 6390
ʿUzzāh, al- (deity), Muḥammad's ban on, 6222

V

Vāc (speech), 1024, 2525, 5302
Vacanas (poetic form), 7210
Vācaspati, 9547
Vachanamritam (Sahajanand)
devotional actions in, 8892
discourses in, 8890–8891
Vādanyāya (Dharmakīrti), 2336
Vädda religion (Sri Lanka), Sinhala religion and, 8409–8410
Vadkovskii, Antonii, 7203
Vafþrúðnir (giant), 2692, 3446
Vafþrúðnismál, 2692
Vāgbhaṭa
on balance and imbalance, 3855
on Āyurveda, 3853
Vagina, **7077–7086**. *See also* Clitoridectomy; Sexuality; *Yoni*
in Buddhism, 7084
in Christianity, 7081–7082
in Daoism, 7084–7085
explicit and implicit focus on, 7077–7078
in Greek religion, 7079
in Judaism, 7080
lack of studies on, 7077
modern thought on, 7085
in prehistoric religions, 7079
as procreative symbol, 7078
as symbol of submission, 7078
in Tantrism, 7083, 7084
Vagina dentata (vagina with teeth)
in goddess worship, 3590
as portal variant, 7334
Vahagn (deity), 491
Vahanian, Gabriel, on death of God, 584–585

VaHosanna of Masowe, 1720–1721. *See also* Masowe, John
Vaibhāṣika school of Buddhism, 1199, 1298. *See also* Sarvāstivāda school of Buddhism
critique of, 1206, 1207–1208, 1210
doctrines of, 1206, 1207
origin of name, 10022
realities in, 1208–1210
Vaicekauskas, Arūnas, 328
Vaid, Sudesh, 3321–3322
Vaidilų Ratas (elders), 765
Vaidyas (caste), in Bengal, 825, 826
Vaikhanāsas, **9495–9496,** 9501, 9503, 10088
Vailala Madness, 6796–6797, 6801
cargo cults and, 1414, 1416
repentance in, 7756
Vaimanika gods, in Jain cosmology, 2024–2025
Väinämöinen (hero), 801, 2298, 4379, 7838, **9496–9497**
Vaipulya repentance, 1291
Vairocana (buddha), 1600, 4922, 9515. *See also* Mahāvairocana
as *tathāgata,* 9016
as central buddha, 1068, 1078
Dṛḍimati and, 1077
iconography of, 4329
in literature, 5607
in Tantric rituals, 1217, 1221
temple to, 9050
vajra of, 7604
Vairocanābhisaṃbodhi Tantra (Buddhist text), 1214, 1215, 1217
Vais' (water spirit), in Komi religion, 5218
Vaiśālī, council of
dispute provoking, 5601
Mahāsāṃghika Buddhism in, 5601
overview of, 2035–2036
split in Buddhist community after, 1090, 1109, 1193
Vaiśeṣika school of Indian philosophy, 6752, **9497–9498**
and Nyāya school, 6772
atheism of, 578
and classical Hinduism, development of, 3997
cosmology of, 3997
guṇas in, 3709
īśvara in, 4752
unity and plurality in, 4421
Vaiṣṇava Upaniṣads, 9484
Vaiṣṇavism, 4430, **9498–9509, 10087–10089**. *See also* International Society for Krishna Consciousness; *See also* Pāñcarātra; Swaminarayan movement
in Bengal, 4430
Bhagavadgītā in, 851, 854, 4428
Bhāgavata Purāṇa in, 4430
bhāgavatas and, **9501–9506**
bhakti in, 857, 858, 859, 4430, 8976, 9500, 10088–10089
Caitanya, 826, 854, **1345–1348**
Dvaita Vedānta influencing, 5551
Ganges River in myths of, 3275
Kabīr and, 5052
Kṛṣṇa in, 5248, 5251, 5252
Lakṣmī, accessibility of, 3977
līlā in, 5455, 5456
Mahābhārata in, 4428
maṇḍalas in, 5640–5641
mantras in, 5678
meditation in, 5819
Nimbārka and, 6623
overview of, **9498–9501**
performance and ritual in, 7043, 7046–7047
poetry of, 7210, 8974, 8975, 10088
pūjā in, 7494
Purāṇas in, 7500
Rādhā in, 7593–7594
Rāmā in, 7609, 10089
Rāmānanda sect in, *sadhus/sadhvis* (renunciates) in, 8020
ritual uses of images in, 4391
saint-singer traditions and, 4005–4006
schools of, 4430
sectarian movements and, 4004–4005
in Southeast Asia, 4009
Śrī Vaiṣṇavas, **8727–8729,** 10088
studies of, 4449
Tagore influenced by, 1347
in Tamil, 8976, 10088
Tantras (literature) of, 9501–9502
called Saṃhitās, 4019
of Pāñcarātra sect, 4020
temples of, 8975, 8977
Vaikhanāsas tradition of, 10088
Viṣṇu in, 4428, 9618, 10088
Vṛndāvana and, 9645
Vaiṣṇodevī (deity), 3608
Vaiśvānara, Agni as, 178, 179
Vaiśya (merchant class), 9522–9523
initiation of, 7815
social duties of, 2329–2330, 5289
Vaitāḍhya mountains, in Jain cosmology, 2023
Vaitaṇḍika (nihilist), 860
Vaitaraṇī (river), 7863
Vaitkevičienė, Daiva, 328, 329, 330
Vaitkevičius, Vykintas, 328
Vājapeya (sacrifice), 7356, 9563–9564
Vajiravudh (king of Siam), 1141
Vajjipattaka sect, 1132
Vajra (lightning/thunderbolt), 1122, 2345, 7603–7604
Vajrabodhi (Buddhist monk), **9509–9510**
Amoghavajra as disciple of, 293
and Mahāvairocana, 5607
and Chinese Tantrism, 1214, 1240
in Indonesia, 1133
Vajrācaryās (Buddhist priests), 1126
Vajracchedikā (Buddhist text), Kumārajīva's translation of, 5263
Vajracchedikā-prajñāpāramitā (Buddhist text), 1270
Vajradhātu Mahāmaṇḍala, 9963
Vajradhaātvīśvarī (deity), 1080
Vajradhara (buddha), 1068, 1080, **9510–9511**
Vajrasattva identified with, 9514, 9515
Vajradhātu (Diamond World) *maṇḍala*
in Shingon Buddhism, 8351
Shugendō movement and, 8380
Vajrapāṇi *(bodhisattva),* 1076, 1081–1082, **9511–9514**
Avalokiteśvara under command of, 1077
handmaidens of, 1080
Indra's development into, 1645, 9511–9512
in Vajrayāna (Tantric) Buddhism, 1080
and martial arts, 5736
multiple, 9513
Vajradhara and, 9510, 9511
Vajrasattva and, 9514–9515
Vajrasattva *(bodhisattva),* 1080, 1286, **9514–9516**
Vajraśekhara Sūtra (Buddhist text), 9077
Vajrāvalī (Buddhist text), *maṇḍalas* in, 5643
Vajravārāhī (deity)
in Cakrasamvara tradition, 1350
maṇḍalas of, 5642
Vajra Verses (Buddhist text), 5223
Vajrayāna (Tantric) Buddhism, 1122–1124, 1214. *See also* Esoteric Buddhism
Amoghavajra studying, 293
in Bengal, 827
bodhisattvas in, 1000, 1123, 1125, 1221
buddhahood in, 1069
buddhas in, 1080, 1214
Candrakīrti, works by, 1401
cave art reflecting, 1472
charisma in, 1549
in China, 1121, 1214, 1215, 1221, 8985 (*See also* Zhenyan Buddhism)
consecration of images in, 4389–4390
definition of, 1221
development of, 1093–1094
dhāraṇīs in, 1121–1122
dharmakāya in, 1069–1070, 1217
diamond symbolism in, 1122, 2345
doctrines of, 1124–1125
documented history of, 1121
drums in, 2496–2497
ethics of, 1282
exorcism in, Gcod rite for, 8273
female imagery in, 3033
gender in, 3332–3333
goddesses in, 1080
worship of, 3587
gurūs in, 1216, 3714
hermeneutics, 1123, 1275
Hevajra Tantra in, 3965–3966
iconography of, 4327–4328, 4329–4330
in India, 1121–1125, 1153, 1214, 1221
in Japan, 1096, 1214, 1215, 1217, 1243, 8985 (*See also* Shingonshū school of Buddhism)
Kālacakra in, 5056–5058
in Khmer Buddhism, 5130
kingship in, 1221
Klong chen Rab 'byams pa (Longchenpa) on, 5191
Kōben and, 5213
Kuṇḍalinī in, 5266
language of, 1216, 5310, 5311
life-empowerment rituals, 3866
light and darkness symbolism in, 5453
lightning symbolism in, 7604
lion symbolism in, 5465
literature of, 1124, 1214, 1215–1216
magic in, 5593
mahāmudrā in, 5596–5597
mahāsiddhas in, **5603–5606**
Mahāvairocana in, 5607, 5608
maithuna (ritualized sexual union) in, 8240
Maitreya in, 5619–5620
maṇḍalas in, 5641, 5642, 5643, 5645
kapaladharin ("skull cup–bearing") *maṇḍala,* 3965
mantras in, 5677–5678
in *Hevajra Tantra,* 3965
masculine sacrality in, 5759
meditation in (*See* Buddhist meditation)
monasticism, 1121
in Mongolia, 1097
monotheism in, 6157
Nāgārjuna and, 6393–6394
nirvāṇa in, 6632
offering in, 1220
origins of, 1214–1215
politics and, 7254
practices of, 1216–1219
pūjā in, 7496, 7497
quaternity in, 7550
renunciant yogins, role of, 3965

rituals of, 1123, 1124, 1219–1220
salvation in, 1088
Sarasvatī in, 8113
schools of, **1214–1222,** 8985
sexual abuse in, 8244, 8245–8246
sexuality in
in *Guhyasamāja Tantra,* 3708
Ramakrishna and, 7613–7614, 10067–10068
sexual union in
caturānanda (four joys) in, 3965–3966
transcendence in, 8015–8016
siddhas in, 5603–5606
in Southeast Asia, 1132, 1133
studies of, 1221
Śubhākarasiṃha as missionary of, 8803
śūnyatā in, 1216
in Taiwan, 8963
tathāgata-garbha in, 1070, 9018
in Tibet
medicine and divination in, 3866
in *saṃgha* and, 8083–8084
transgression as tool in, 8015–8016
of Vajrabodhi, 9510
Vajrapāṇi in, 9513
varieties of, 1122–1124
wisdom in, 9753
women in, 1221, 3332–3333
yoga in, 1157, 1217, 1221, 1286–1288
Zhenyan identified with, 9963
Vajra yoga, 5224
Vajrayoginī (deity), in Gcod rite, 5558
Vakarelski, Christo, 5581
Vakhtangov, Evgeny, 2534
Vaku atua (spirit vessels), 9196
Valabhī (Buddhist university), 1119, 1120
Valdès, Pierre, 2083, 6648
Valencia, Martín de, 4504, 5915
Valens (Roman emperor)
Arianism and, 479
astrology and, 2249
against paganism, 7061
Valens, Vettius, astrology of, 563
Valenti, Cardinal, 757
Valentinian Exposition, A, hypostasis in, 4242
Valentinian II (Roman emperor), 9124, 9125
Valentinians
cosmogony of, archetype in, 458
on *hypostasis,* 4242
on knowability of God, 182, 183
on matter, 7190
in Nag Hammadi codices, 6396–6397
Jung Codex of, 3512–3513, 6396–6397
on Sophia, 3518
Valentinius, Basilius, 3014
Valentinus (philosopher)
on aeons, 7190
on duality, 3512
Gnosticism of, 3511, 3512, 3518
Irenaeus on, 4539
on *hypostasis,* 4241
metaphysics of, 7190
and Nag Hammadi codices, 6397
Platonism influencing, 7190
on Sophia, 8523
Valentius, 2966
Valenzuela, Romana, 6579
Valeri, Valerio, on sacrifice, 8009
Valerian (Roman emperor), Christian persecution under, 5743, 7059
Valeriano, Antonio, 5917, 5922
Valerius, Augustine and, 625–626
Valesian mystery sect, castration among, 1452
Valhalla. *See* Valhǫll
Valhǫll (hall of Óðinn), 167, 168, 3448, **9516–9517**
Valiant Venture (Raëlian cloning company), 7599
Validity
in sacramental theology, 7961, 7963
structuralism and, 8750–8751, 8757
Valiente, Doreen, 9729
Valikhanov, Shokan, 4622
Valkyries, 3001, **9517**
fravashis compared with, 3190
Valla, Lorenzo
Italian Renaissance humanism and, 4175
on predestination, 3203, 3207
Vallabha (Vallabhācārya) (philosopher), 9505, **9517–9518**
on dualism and nondualism, 6623
Kṛṣṇaism and, 5253, 5254
on *mokṣa,* 6116
Sūrdās and, 8881
Vedānta of, 9548–9549
worship of divine child by, 2983
worship of Rādhā by, 7594
Vallabha Sampradāya (order), 9517
bhakti movement and, 3986
initiation in, 3986
Sūrdās and, 8881
Swaminarayan movement and, 8892
Vallely, Anne, on contemporary Jainas, 2626
Valley of Mexico, 5292–5294
Valley of the Kings, 1472
burial texts of, 2708
Valmiera (Latvia), 775
Vālmīki, 7609, 7616, 7617, **9518–9519**
Valois, Ninette de, 2162
Value(s)
agriculture associated with, 192–193
Christian, in autobiography, 699
in Germanic religion, 3457–3458
legitimation and, 5396
masculine sacrality in, 5758–5763
Parsons (Talcott) on, 8472, 8495
in religion, *vs.* science, 2658
subjective *vs.* objective, 5397, 5403
Troeltsch (Ernst) on, 5397
ultimate, soteriology and, 8526
Value Creation Society. *See* Sōka Gakkai
Value wisdom, 9749
Valverde, Vicente de, 567
Vāmācāra (left-handed conduct), in Savism, 8015
Vāmamarga (left-handed path), 8991
Vāmana (incarnation of Viṣṇu), 2368, 7501
Vāmana Purāṇa (Hindu text), *dharma* in, 2330
Vámbéry, Arminius, 3634
Vampires, in Transylvania, 4226
Vaṃśapurāṇas (sacred texts), 7498
Vānaprasthin (forest-dweller), 2330, 4421. *See also* Āśramas
celibacy and, 1476–1477
retreat of, 7769
Vanaratna (Buddhist scholar), 1230–1231
Vanavāsin (Buddhist monks), 9149
Van Baal, Jan. *See* Baal, Jan van
Van Baalen, Jan Karel, 6521
Van Beek, Walter, 3701
van Binsbergen, Wim, 118
on millenarianism, 6033
Van Buitenen, J. A. B., 9506–9507
Van Buren, Paul M., 585
on Barth (Karl), 3558
Vandals
and Arianism, in Carthage, 1679
and Huns, 4490
van der Leeuw, Gerardus. *See* Leeuw, Gerardus van der
van der Linden, Wim, 50
van Dijk, Jan, 302
on Barton cylinder, 6624
Van Doren, Mark, Merton (Thomas) and, 5879
Van Dyck, Anthony, 377
Van Gennep, Arnold. *See* Gennep, Arnold van
Vanggaard, Jens H., 3125
Van Gogh, Vincent, 4347
on creative discipline, 8702
Vanir (Germanic deities), 3449–3450
as hostages of Æsir, 3218, 3219, 3220
in war with Æsir, 3449–3450, 9685, 9686
marriage among, 3218, 3460
in mead myth, 849
origin of, 3449
Vanishing god myths, in Hittite religion, 4068, 4069
Vanita, Ruth, 3321, 5415
van Leyden, Jan, 7660
van Oss, Adriaan, 5924
van Renselaar, H. C., on masks, 5769
Van Ruusbroec, Jan. *See* Ruusbroec, Jan van
Van Seters, John, 6376
Vansina, Jan, 117
Vanth (demon), 2871
Vanuatu and Vanuatu religions, **9519–9522**. *See also* Oceania and Oceanic religions
cargo cults, 1414
Christianity
missionaries, 1738
traditional culture merged with, 7297
homosexuality in, 4115
Malekula mythology, 5278
missions to, 6791
mythology of, 9519
phallic worship in, 4114
reflections and shadows in, 8532
Vao Ðam (feast), 9593–9594
Vaque (deity), in Island Arawak religion, 1427
Vara (blessing), 983
Varadamudrā (blessing), 980
Varāha (boar), 7501
Varāhamihira, 564
Varāha Purāṇa, on planting trees, 2621
Vārakarī, 9504
Vārāṇasī. *See* Banaras
Vardhamāna. *See* Mahāvīra
Varela, José, 3146–3147
Varese, Stéfano, 5985
Vargas Llosa, Mario, 3063, 3064
Varick, James, 68
Varieties of Religious Experience, The (James), 378, 386, 4775, 4776–4777, 7741, 7742
consciousness in, 1948
mysticism in, 6341, 6356
philosophy of religion in, 7126
positivism in, 7341
prayer in, 7370
psychology of religion in, 7475
redemption in, 7113

Varisco, Bernardino, 6963
Vārkarī sect, 5696
Varṇa and *jāti,* **9522–9524**. *See also* Castes; *specific castes*
in Brahmanism, 9570–9571
in Indian caste system, 3996
karman and, 5289
in Vedic cosmology, 2014
Varṇāśramadharma theory of caste, 2329–2330. *See also* Castes
avātara theory and, 4001
Dayananda Sarasvati on, 4008
in epics, 4001
in Dharmasūtras and Dharmaśāstras, 3995–3996
relational discipline and, 8706–8707
Sahajanand Swami on, 8889
Śaṅkara on, 4004
Varro, Marcus Terentius, 1051, 2994
on Diana, 2346
as feast of Argei, 7897
on *numen,* 6753
as research source, 7893
on Roman religion, 7912, 7918
as Roman statuary, 7895–7896
on Sabine divinities, 3175
on theology, 4038, 9128, 9134
Varsas (mythic regions)
in Purāṇic Hindu cosmology, 2017
in Jain cosmology, 2023
Varsissima (deity), 834
Vārttika (Kātyāyana), commentary on, 7005
Varuṇa (deity), **9524–9525**
Ahura Mazdā originating from, 4536
Apąm Napāt compared to, 205
as Āditya, 9556
as guardian of *ṛta,* 3001, 7352, 7934
and binding, 938
dharma of, 2327
Dumézil (Georges) on, 7352
inspiration given by, 4509
knots of, 5275, 5278
lasso of, 5197
nature and, 2620
Óðinn and, 6810
power of, 8873
purification of sins and, 1886
as sun deity, 8838
and tree of life, 9335, 9338
water and, 9701
Varuṇapraghāsa, feast of, confession at, 1886
Vasa (water spirit), in Komi religion, 5218
Vases, Greek. *See* Greek vases
Vasilevich, G. M., 475
Vassa (rains-retreat), 9831
Vassal treaties. *See also* Covenant and covenant theology
curse formulae in, 2102–2103
Vāstoṣpati (lord of the residue), Rudra as, 8414
Vastumaṇḍala (square), 5640
Vāstupuruṣa Maṇḍala (square diagram), *9039*
as blueprint of the temple, 7983, 9038
myth of, 9038
Vastuśātras, *maṇḍalas* in, 5640
Vasubandhu (Buddhist teacher), **9525–9528**
on abhidharma, 1297
and Dignāga, 2351
Asaṅga as brother of, 516–517
as founder of Yogācāra, 1119–1120, 1210–1212, 1300
in Yogācāra Buddhism, 9899–9900
life of, 1201
on *nirvāṇa,* 6629
on *prajñā,* 7357–7358
on *śūnyatā,* 1211
on *trisvabhāva,* 1211
on "Personalist Controversy," 1297
on realities, 1210–1211
and recitative *nianfo,* 6602
Sautrāntika school and, 8119, 8136–8137
translation of works of, 1202, 1313
writings of, 1093, 1199, 2322
Vāsudeva (deity), in Vaiṣṇava Tantras, 4020
Vāsudeva Kṛṣṇa, 5248–5249
as supreme divinity, 5249
Vāsudeva-Viṣṇu, 9502
Vāsudevism, 9498–9499
Vasuki (snake), 4439, 7500
Vasumitra (scholar), on Abhidharma doctrine, 2037
Vat (monastery). *See* Monasteries, Buddhist
Vāta (wind), in Āyurveda, 3854
Vaṭakalai sect
inŚrī Vaiṣṇavas Sampradāya, 8728
on predestination, 3204–3205
Vaṭasāvitrī festival, in Marathi religions, 5698
Vates (poet), 7205
Vatican
interreligious gatherings sponsored by, on environment, 2613
on nonviolence, 6648
as sacred space, 9261
sovereignty of, 6974
Vatican Council I (1869–1870), 6974, **9528–9533**
on authority of pope, 6974
on centrality of revelation, 6974
constitutions of, 9531–9532
on dogma, 2387
on faith, 7882
on Gallicanism, 6974, 7877–7878
overview of, 2044
on papal infallibility, 2396, 6974, 7180
Pius IX and, 6974, 7180
on religious experience, 7739
on revelation, 7775, 7776
on social doctrine, 7878
Vatican Council II (1962–1965), 6974–6975, 7879–7880, **9533–9542**
on abortion, 5812
on anti-Semitism, 2688
and ashram movement, 547
on atonement, 597
Australia and New Zealand and, 1735
and biblical exegesis, 877
on chastity, 1558
and church architecture, 796
comparativist elements of, 9130
on dialogue of religions, 2344
and Dominicans, 2414
ecclesiology in "Dogmatic Constitution of the Church," 1775
on ecumenical consciousness, 1665, 2044, 2045
ecumenism at, 2686–2687, 7011–7012
episcopal collegiality in, 1668, 6975, 7011
on exorcism, 2280
and feminist theology, 3035
Franciscans after, 3183
and gender, 3361
Grail movement after, 3654
historiography and, 4034
history of, 9534–9538
impact of, 2687
Jesuits and, 4843
under John XXIII, 4945–4946, 6975, 7011, 7879–7880, 9534–9535
justification doctrine in, 5041–5042
on kingdom of God, 5153
Latin America and, 1701, 1703
and legitimation, 5398, 5404
liberation theology and, 5438
on liturgy, 5490
on Mary, 5754, 5755
medicine and, 3847
on membership in the church, 1778
and Mesoamerican religions, 3413
modernism and, 7878–7879
and moral theology, 1654
on music, 6313
nuns and sisters after, 6765
orthodoxy and heterodoxy at, 6912
overview of, 2044–2045
on papal leadership, 6975
Paul VI and, 6975, 7011–7012, 7879
peace and social justice addresses at, 2061
pluralism and, 5398
principles of, 7879–7880
progressive millennialism after, 6546
rejection of, 2931
on religious experience, 7739
on religious orders, 7724
on retreats, 7773
sacraments and, 7961–7962
science, openness to, 8184
Synod of Bishops instituted by, 1764
themes of, 9534–9538
Vatican Radio, 7713
Vātsalya (calf love), 5249
Vātsāyana, 6773
Vātsīputrīya school of Buddhism
doctrines of, 1196, 1197
literature of, 1199–1200
origin of, 1132, 1194
in "Personalist Controversy," 1297
vs. Sautrāntika, 8137
Vaṭṭagāmaṇī (king of Sri Lanka), 1110, 1252, 1269, 2037
Vauchez, André, on saints, 2083
Vaughan, Henry, 7220
Vault, Roman, 793–794
Vaybruma (deity), in Island Arawak religion, 1427
Va-yiqra'. See Leviticus
Vaysī Ṣūfī order, 4618–4619
Vāyu (deity)
in cosmogonic myths, 4536
Hanumān and, 3775
in Vedism, 9556
Vayū: Texte und Untersuchungen (Wikander), 9735
Vāyu Purāṇa, on golden age and origin of castes, 2963
Vāyūs (wind), 1043, 7362
Vé (deity), in creation
of earth, 3446–3447
of man, 3454
Vecsey, Christopher, 6672
Vedāṅgas, **9542–9543,** 9554
Vedānta Deśika (Hindu teacher), on grace, 8728
Vedāntagrantha (Roy), 7932–7933
Vedāntasāra (Roy), 7932–7933
Vedānta school of Indian philosophy, **9543–9549**
Advaita school of (*See* Advaita Vedānta)
avidyā in, 710–711
and classical Hinduism, development of, 3997
Dvaita school of
Madhva in, 5550–5551
metaphysics in, 8547
eternity in, 2856
hell in, 9456
in *Bhagavadgītā,* 852, 853
īśvara in, 4752
knowledge in, 5200–5201
Madhva's dualistic form of, 4005
māyā in, 5795
monism in, 6144
mysticism in, 6342
Radhakrishnan (Sarvepalli) on, 7595, 7742

Rāmānuja on, 4005, 7614–7616 (*See also* Viśiṣṭādvaita school)
reality in, 7616
religious experience in, 7742
scriptural foundation of, 8105
societies in U.S., 6559
states of consciousness in, 1950, 7616
suffering in, 9113
unity and plurality in, 4421, 4422
Vijñānabhikṣu in, 9595
Vivekananda in, 9630–9631, 10090
Vedanta Society, 9630
New York founding of, 4008
Vedānta Sūtra, 9483
author of, 735–736
concept of deity in, 2254
in Śrī Vaiṣṇavas Sampradāya, 8727–8728
in Vedānta, 9543, 9544–9545
līlā in, 5455
Rāmānuja's commentaries on, 7615
Vedas (Indian texts), **9549–9552**. *See also* Ṛgveda; *See also* Upaniṣads
Agnicayana (fire ritual) in, 3127
apauruṣeya of, 3994, 3995, 9549–9550
atheism and, 577–581
authority of, 4420, 4423
in Brahmanism, 9553, 9568–9569
chanting of, 1535
cognitive elements of, 5199
cosmology in, 2014–2015
dating of, 9553
death and soul in, 8545–8546
deities in
great goddess, 3975
Müller (F. Max) on henotheism in, 3913
desire in, 2305
dharma in, 2327, 2328–2329, 5343, 5344
divinity of, 5467
division of, 1026
fire god in, 3116
glossolalia in, 3504
heaven in, 3885–3886
heresy and, 3922
historiography in, 4025
human flight in, 3126
in Ārya Samāj, 515–516
Indian religions, relationship with, 8545
initiation to, 9566
karman in, 3001
life in, 5447
māyā in, 5794
memorizing texts of, 5852, 7396
Mīmāṃsā school on, 6042
music of, 6281–6282
Naess (Arne) influenced by, 2561
nāstika (unorthodox interpretation) of, 8015
nature in, 2620
Nyāya on, 6773
oral *vs.* written, 1535, 8194
organization of, 9553–9555
as revelation, 7778–7779
ṛta in, 3001
Rudra in, 8039
Sarasvatī in, 8113
studies of, 4446, 4449
sun worship in, 8135
in Transcendental Meditation, 9289
tree of life in, 9335
as uncreated, 5677
Vajapeya rite in, 3127
Viṣṇu in, 4428
women in, 3318–3319
words of, as *mantras,* 5677
Veddas. *See* Vädda religion
Vedder, Heinrich, 115
Vedi (altars), 275–276
Vedic language, comparative study of, 756
Vedic studies, Oldenberg (Hermann) in, 6817
Vedism, 4426–4427, **9552–9568**
Ahiṃsā in, 197
altars in, 276
Amesha Spentas in, 290
archaeology and, 456
arhat in, 476
āśrama in, 7817
Āyurveda and, 3853
Baghavatism and, 9501
in Bengal, 824–825
blades in, 967
blessing in, 981, 983
and Brahmanism, **9568–9574** (*See also* Brahmanism)
castes in, 3990
cattle in, 1465
ceremonies in, 4426
charity and, 1555
cosmology in, 2014–2015
language in, 5302
creation and cosmogonic myths in, 9559–9560 (*See also* Ṛgveda)
corporate symbolism in, 4161
water in, 9698
dance drama in, 2447
Dayananda Sarasvati and, 2227
defined, 9552–9553
deities of, 9555–9559 (*See also specific deities*)
and binding, 937, 938
creation of, 4440
crossroads and, 2071
devas vs. asuras, 3990
Dharma as name of, 2327
in *Mahābhārata,* 9736
īśvara, 4751–4752
pantheon of, 3990–3991
demons in, Indra fighting, 4467
dragons in, 2431
drums in, 2499
eschatology of, Yama in, 9867
fire and heat in, 178–179, 9557, 9564–9565
domestic, 9565–9566
in funeral rites, 9566
installation of, 9565
funeral rites in, 9566
in Āraṇyakas, 1028
goddess worship in, 2525–2526
and Hinduism, 4427
Hinduism as reaction against, 1407
in Ārya Samāj, 515–516
incantation in, 4408
initiation in, 7815, 7816
inspiration in, 4509
karman in, 4442, 5094, 5098
king, ritual coronation of, 1350
knot symbolism in, 5197, 5198
Kṛṣṇaism and, 9499
literature of, 4426–4427, 9553–9555
theory and interpretation of, 5484–5485
types of, 3989
magic in, 5589, 5590
maṇḍalas in, 5645
mantras in, 4426, 4433
marriage in, 7814
memorization in, 5852
mysticism in, 6343
mythology of, 9555–9561
interpretations of, 9559–9561
number symbolism in, 6747
oṃ in, 6820
orgy in, 6878
origins of, 4426
power in, 7351–7352
priesthood in, 7405–7406
quaternity in, 7550
rainmaking in, 7602
rebirth in, 952
resurrection in, 7763
riddles in, 6987
rituals in, 3990, 4426–4427, 7835, 9561–9568
constructive discipline and, 8703
fire in, 178, 4427
interpretations of, 9566–9568
performance by priests, 7835
temporal symbolism in, 7984
Veda organization around, 9553–9555
rivers in, 7861
Ṛta in, 7933–7934
rural traditions of, 4433–4434
sacred language in, 5303, 5304
sacrifice in, 1504, 8006, 9563–9565
conflict and, 9561
as cosmic journey, 1504
dīkṣā in preparation for, 7816
dismemberment in, 2367
horse sacrifice, 1025, 4132–4133, 9563–9564
Hubert (Henri) and Mauss (Marcel) on, 8003
in Brāhmaṇas, 1026–1027, 7356
interpretations of, 9566–9568
place of, 9564–9565
redemption and, 7641
ritual for, 9561–9563
Rudra excluded from, 8415
system of, 9561–9563
transformation and, 8545
types of, 9562
in *Yajurveda,* 9551
saints in, 8036
Saṃnyāsa as separation from, 8093
saṃsāra and, 8098
sin and purification in, 1886
soma in, 849, 5434, **8521–8522** (*See also* Soma)
soul in, 8545–8546
speculative-philosophical literature on, 3991
suffering in, 9119
tapas in, 8997, 8998
Upaniṣads of, 9483
Vaiṣṇavism and, 9498
violence in, 6645
Viṣṇu in, devotion to, 857
Yama in, 9867
Zoroastrianism compared to, 9936
Ved'ma (demonized goddess), in Slavic religion, 8437
Veetanāyakam Piḷḷai, 10034, 10035
Vega, Lope de, 2474
Vegetables
in gardens, 3278, 3280–3281
offering of, in African rituals, 88
Vegetarianism
of Adam, 29, 6982
in animal liberation, 2655
animal rights and, 3174
in Brahmanism, 9571
in Buddhism, 360, 3483
in Catharism, 3524
of Cistercians, 5879
in Elcasaite sect, 9329
of Gandhi (Mohandas), 3272
in Geto-Dacian religion, 3466
in Golden Age, 3627

Vegetarianism ***continued***
in Greek religion
of Orphic Bacchants, and deification, 2249
Orphism, 3671, 6893, 6894
Plato on, 7185
Pythagoras and Pythagoreans, 7529, 9579
as rejection of blood sacrifice, 3670
in Hinduism, *Laws of Manu,* 5327, 5373
human sacrifice and, 9598
in *ahiṃsā,* 197, 7505
in Jainism, 2625, 4770, 5610, 6646
in Manichaeism, 5669, 5670, 6040
in recent history of religion, 3173
reincarnation and, 2776
in Seventh-day Adventism, 3173
in Taiwan, 8964
of Zhuhong, 9972
Vegetation, **9574–9580**. *See also* Gardens; Trees
in Australian Indigenous myths, 653
in Caribbean religions, cult of, 1427
deities of (*See* Vegetation deities)
dying and rising gods and, 1875
feminine sacrality of, 3017
in hero myths, 3959
in indigenous traditions, in balance of life, 2618
in Islam, talismanry of, 5586
in Judaism, rite of the four plants, at Sukkot, 8834
in Micronesian myths, 6011–6012
in North American Indian religions, creation stories, 6661, 6692
power of, in agricultural rituals, 188–189
in primitive religions, 10065
protection of, in Jewish environmental ethics, 2644
psychedelic drugs derived from, 7467–7473, 9613
psychotropic, in South American religions, 6274
rights of, 2655
in South American Indian religions, plant fertility rites in, 8582
in Sudanese religion, 8850
as teleological centers of life, 2655
at Tirumala Tirupati temple, 2622
worship of, 6440
as *yoni,* 9907
Yurupary and, 9918, 9919–9920
Vegetation deities, 3620
Adad as, 28–29
Adonis as, 34, 35
in Andean religions, Pachamama as, 8601
in Aztec religion, 1469
as dying and rising, 6328
examples of, 3620
functions of, 3620
in mystery religions, 6328
in nature worship, 6440
as redeemer-gods, 7641
supreme beings as, 8870
Veglia (Italian social event), 2147–2148
Vei (deity), 2871
Veiling
in Islam, Muslims opposing, 3365
in Zoroastrianism, 3374
Veil of Veronica (portrait), 4286, 9090
Veil of Veronica (Zurbarán), vol. 12 color insert
Vekhi (journal), 1319
Vēlans (priests), 8973
Velasco, Francisco Diez de, 5944
Velázquez, Diego, 54
Velázquez de Cuéllar, Juan, 4367
Veles-Volos, **9580–9581**
in Slavic religion, 8435
Velichkovskii, Paisii, 2588, 7943
Sorskii (Nil) and, 8526
Vėlinės, 328, 329
Vėlius, Norbertas, 328, 771
Venancio Christo movement (Brazil), 6577
Venda religion (South Africa)
drums of, 7037
myths of, 94, 97, 8663, 8664, 8665
rites of passage in, 8666–8667
ritual calendar of, agriculture and, 187
sacred kingship in, 8664
Vendetta killing, 986
Vendidad, 709, 9998
funeral rites in, 2130
Vendryes, Joseph, 1482, 1483, 1495, 1498
Venerable Bede. *See* Bede, the Venerable
Venerable Company of Pastors, 851
Veneration, "sacred" and, 4098
Venezuela. *See also* Warao religion
funeral rites in, 3235, 3240
Islam in, 4684–4685
spirit possession cult in, 6578–6579
Vengeance. *See also* Retribution; Revenge
of the dead, 7781
in Greek religion, Sun and, 8839
land as price for, 7781–7782
for murder, 7780
regulation of, in archaic societies, 7780–7781
religious basis of, 7781–7782
Venial sins, 1889
Veniaminov, Innokentii. *See* Innokentii Veniaminov
Veniaminov, John Popov. *See* Innokentii Veniaminov
Venice (Italy)
Carnival at, 1442
Contarini (Gasparo) on, 1968
John XXIII (pope) in, 4945
Savonarola (Girolamo) and, 8139–8140
Venn, Henry, 1718
Vennum, Thomas, 2499
Vēntaṉ (deity), 8973
Ventriloquism
in Chukchi séances, 8286
use in necromancy, 6453
Ventris, Michael, 41
Venus (deity), **9581–9582**
Adonis and, 35
concern with chance or fate, 3002
and fish symbolism, 3122
Friday named after, in France, 1689
Inanna (Mesopotamian), 4402–4406
Jupiter and, 5037
as Kukulcan (Maya), 1359
in Lavinium, 7899
in Paleolithic Age, 5280
as Shalim (Canaanite), 1384
trees as symbols of, 9337
Venus (planet)
in African religions, in Southern Bantu myths, 8665
deities of, 8424, 8427–8428
Eckankar from, 2601
Maya and, 1356, 1357, 1358–1360, 5935
names of, 8427
Venus Erycina (deity), 7905, 7906
Venuses (goddess figures), 4380
Neolithic, 3584
Paleolithic, 2983, 2985, 3583–3584, 6953, 7079
Venus of Willendorf, 3584, vol. 9 color insert
Venzago, Alberto, 3099
Vera Christiana Religio (Swedenborg), New Church movement and, 8901
Veracruz religion, iconography of, 4313
Veralltäglichung, 1544
Verbermacher, Hannah Rachel. *See* Maid of Ludmir
Verdi, Giuseppe, 6312
Verdon, Timothy, 495
Verein Ernst Mach, 5498
Verein für Kultur, in *Wissenschaft des Judentums,* 4874
Ver et brevis divinarum rerum expositio, 1918
Verethraghna (deity), 4536, 7387
Verger, Pierre, 76, 121, 10025
Vergerio, Pietro Paolo, on humanist education, 4175
Vergerius, Angelos, Hermetism and, 3946
Vergil, **9582–9584**
on afterlife, 137, 166
on Charon's boat, 989
on descent into the underworld, 2297–2298
on fate, 3000–3001
on Golden Age, 3627
on golden age, 2964
on innocence, 7973
on magic, 5575
on mistletoe, 774
on music, 6304
on *numen,* 6754
on *pius,* 2955
on serpents, 8457
on *Sibylline Oracles,* 8384
souls purified in hell, 1460
Stoicism and, 8741
on underworld, 9453
Verification, of facts, and knowability, 2780
Verification principle, in logical positivism, 5498–5500
Verlaine, Paul, symbol theory and, 8910
Vermeil, Edmond, on Möhler (Johann Adam), 6113
Vermès, Géza, 2745
Vermigli, Peter Martyr, on predestination, 3204
Vermont, Island Pond community in, 6540
Vernacular art. *See* Outsider art
Vernacular dance, 2146–2148, 2151
Vernacular drama, 2471–2472
Vernacular poetry
Christian, 7218
Indian, 7209–7211
Islamic, 4663–4664, 7223
Vernacular religion, definition of, 3143
Vernal equinox
in Hindu religious year, 4016, 4017
in Japan, 2411
Vernant, Jean-Pierre, 1014
on dismemberment, 2366
on Prometheus, 7419
on sacrifice, 1466, 8009
structuralism of, 4045
Veronica's Veil, vol. 12 color insert
Verrellen, Franciscus, 1638
Ver sacrum rites, sacred *vs.* profane and, 7966
Verses of Light, 6206–6207
Verses of Song. *See* Pesuqei de-Zimra' recitation
Verstehen (understanding), 2353
Dilthey (Wilhelm) on, 3932, 3933
Heidegger on, 3933–3934
Wach (Joachim) on, 3933, 9649–9651
Vertical dualism, 2509
Vesak (Buddha's Day), 1304–1305
Vespasian (Roman emperor)
and Diana cult, 2347
and Isis cult, 4558–4559
Josephus Flavius and, 4957

miracles performed by, 6051, 7915
Vessantara *(bodhisattva),* 1084, 1306
Vessantara Jātaka (Buddhist text), 1305–1306
Vessey, Denmark, 66
Vesta (deity), 3018, **9584–9586**
cult of
penates associated with, 7027
women in, 3385
eternal flame of, 3118
Hestia as, 3964
place in Roman pantheon, 7899
in *pomerium* of Rome, 7897
Tabiti as, 4489
Vestal Virgins, 1475–1476, 7907, 9585
functions of, 7897–7898
gender ambiguity of, 9607
and gender roles, 3385
Vestments. *See also* Clothing
in Daoism, 1828–1829
in Shintō, 1828
in Israelite religion, of Levites, 5424
in Protestant Christianity, 1831
in Roman Catholicism, 1831, 1837
Vestries, in Episcopal Church, 1767
Vetālapañcaviṃsatikā (Śivadāsa), 10034
Vetalas (demon-like beings), 2276, 2315
Veyne, Paul, Cumont, challenges to, 2094
Via (soul), 9591
Via negativa (negative way), 4895, 9283–9284, **9586–9588**
as apophatic meditation, 5816
paradox and, 6990
Vibhajyavāda school of Buddhism
Dharmaguptaka school and, 8120
geographical distribution of, 1195
origin of, 1194
Pāṭaliputra council and, 2037
Vibhaṅga (Buddhist text), 10021, 10022
Vibhāṣā (commentary), 10022
Vibhavas (manifestions), in Pāñcarātra, 9508
Vicar, ruler of Assyria known as, 5163
Vicarious Sacrifice (Bushnell), 597
Vices
Cassian on, 1447
Spinoza (Baruch) on, 8684
Vico, Giovanni Battista, 5259, 7325, **9588–9590**
historiography of, 4031, 4040
Vicomagistri, 7908
Victimae paschali laudes (Praise to the Paschal Victim), 2580
Victims
of abuse, shelters for, 4102
of affliction, 56, 57, 58
of *dybbuk* possession, 2534
martyrs as, 5740–5741
of New World Inquisition, 4504, 4505
of Portuguese Inquisition, 4498, 4501, 4502
of Roman Inquisition, 4501
of Spanish Inquisition, 4498, 4500, 4501, 4502, 4596, 9242
Victor I (pope), 4538, 6966
Victor III (pope), 823
Victor, Jeffrey S., 6524
Victoria (deity), 7911, 7918
Victoria, Brian, 1247
Victoria, Tomas Luis de, 6311
Victorian scholars, on homosexuality, 4112
Victoria University, 840
Victorine tradition in Christianity (Abbey of Saint-Victor), Hugh of Saint-Victor and, **4150–4152**
Victorinus, Marius, 6475
Neoplatonism of, 7192
Victory, deities of, 7911, 7912
Victory of Jewry over Christendom, The (Marr), 402
Victricius (bishop), 4495
Vidal, Mary, 3084
Vidal-Naquet, Pierre, on linear *vs.* cyclical time, 7992
Víðarr (deity), 3457
Videha (mythic region), in Jain cosmology, 2024
Vidēvdād (Avesta text), 9993
Vidler, William, 9470
Vidman, Ladislav, 4558
Vidyāpati (poet), 826, 5253, 7211
Vidyā pīṭa (seat of vidyā), Śakti in, 4020
Vidyasagar, Isvaracandra, 828
on women, 3320
Vie de Jésus (Renan), 7750
Vieira, Antonio, 4967
Vienna, Congress of (1814–1815), 6973
Vienna Circle
analytic philosophy and, 306
logical positivism and, 5498–5500
symbol theory and, 8913
Vienne, Council of (1311–1312), 6971
Philip IV ("the Fair") of France and, 2042
Viennese cultural-historical school
on confession, 1884
Schmidt's (Wilmelm) contributions to, 5260–5261
Vierkandt, Alfred, 2542, **9590**
Vietnam and Vietnamese religions, **9590–9595**. *See also* Southeast Asia and Southeast Asian religions
Buddhism, 9591, 9592
in Australia, 1190
colonial influences and, 1139
communism and, 1100
Hinduism and, 1138
law and, 5349
Mahāyāna Buddhism, 1138
millenarian movements in, 1100
monasteries, 1095, 1141
origins of, 1133
political role of, 1141, 1142
in postcolonial era, 7264
Sammatīya sect, 1201
temples of, 9055
Cao Dai movement, **1411–1412**
Chinese influence in, 8643
Christianity, 1728, 9591, 9594
Roman Catholicism, 1728, 7264, 9594
communism in, 7264
Confucianism, 9592
Daoism, 9592, 9593
deities of, 9593
fiction of, 3076, 3077–3078
funeral rites in, 3235
Hinduism, Buddhism and, 1138
metallurgy in, 5987
music in, 6287, 6290
Neolithic burial sites in, 8642
new religious movements with origins in, 6568
religious resistance in, 7257, 7264
Vietnamese language, 9591
Vietnam Veterans Memorial (Washington, D. C.), as shrine, 8376–8377, vol. 14 color insert
Vietnam War
Capps (Walter) on, 1413
engaged Buddhism during, 2785
social movements and, 1754
View, in eightfold path, 2738
Viganó, Salvatore, 2155
Vighnarāja. *See* Gaṇeśa
Vighneśvara, 4326
Vigilantius, on relics, 7688
Vigilius I (Roman bishop)
at Council of Constantinople II, 2040
Justinian I and, 5042–5043
Vigil of Easter. *See* Paschal vigil
Vigils, sleeplessness and, 8441
Vihāras (monasteries)
at Ajanta caves, 1471–1472
Chinese versions of, 9046
evolution of, 9042
as retreat, 9043
Thai versions of, 9054, 9055
Tibetan versions of, 9050, 9051
Vihārayātrās (excursions for enjoyment), 7163
Vijayabāhu I (king of Pagan), 1135–1136, 9148
Vijayādaśamī rites, in Navarātri festival, 6444
Vijayanagara (city), sacred space and, 1806
Vijayanagar period (Tamil), 8976–8977
Vijñāna (conceptual thought), 1274, 4928, 7364
Vijñānabhikṣu (Hindu teacher), 7522, **9595**
on Sāṃkhya teachings, 8092
Vijñānakāya (body of consciousness), 1298
Vijnana-parinama (modification of consciousness), 9900
Vijñānavāda school of Buddhism. *See* Yogācāra school of Buddhism
Vijñaptimātra (representation), 8739, 8740, 9900
Vijñaptimātratā, Kuiji on, 5258
Vijñāptimātratāsiddhi (Dharmapāla), 2338
Vīķe-Freiberga, Vaira, 771
Vikings, libations of, 5343
Vikramabāhu I (king of Sri Lanka), 9149
Vikramaśīla (Buddhist university), 1119, 1120, 1125, 1230
Vīks, Ivars, 766
Vikukṣi (mythic figure), 5678–5679
Vilas (nymphs), in Slavic religion, 8437–8438
Vili (deity), in creation
of earth, 3446–3447
of man, 3454
Village
in Okinawan religion, 6812
orientation of, 6886
Village India (Marriott), 4448
Villagómez, Pedro de, 4506
Villa of the Mysteries, vol. 2 color insert
Villa Rojas, Alfonso, 5941, 5942
Vilna Gaon. *See* Eliyyahu ben Shelomoh Zalman
Vilnius University, 764
Vimalā, 8
Vimalakīrti *(bodhisattva),* 1079
Vimalakīrtinirdeśa Sūtra (Buddhist text)
bodhisattva ideal in, 1298
Chinese translation of, 1164
laity in, 1114–1115
language in, 5308–5309
Maitreya in, 5619–5620
Pure Lands in, 1077, 7503
Sengzhao on, 8228
upāya in, 9486
women in, 3332

Vimalamitra (Buddhist scholar), 1223
Vimbusa healing dance
of Chewa people, 2140
of Tumbuka people, 2140
Viṃśatikā (Buddhist text), 1300, 9527, 9899
Vimuktisena, writings of, 5555
Vimuttimagga (Buddhist text), 1199, 1200
Vīṇā (musical instrument), 6280
Vinalia (festival), 7897
Vinamalakirtinirdesa (Buddhist text), Kumārajīva's translation of, 5263
Vinatā (deity), 4438
Vināyaka. *See* Gaṇeśa
Vinayamātṛkā (Buddhist text), 1199
Vinaya Piṭaka (Buddhist text), 1200, **1258–1261,** 1259, 1269. *See also* Buddhist books and texts
arahant in, 476
authoritative character of, 8201
Buddhaghosa's commentary on, 1074
Buddha's biographies in, 1063, 1064
Chinese translation of, 1202, 5601, 8072, 8118
content of, 9146
decision making of Buddha in, 5347–5348
Dharmaguptaka school and, 8120
ethical codes in, 1258
Ganjin and, 3275–3276
great commission in, 6077
in Mahāsāṃghika Buddhism, 5601
in Sautrāntika, 8136
Mahāvibhāṣā commentary added to, 2037
monasticism in, 6126, 6127
monastic rules in, 1108, 1198–1199, 1258, 1259, 1260, 5347
Mūlasarvāstivādin, 8120
for nuns, 6760
in ordination, 3275–3276
parts of, 1198, 1258
recitation of *(vinayasaṃgīti)*
Rājagṛha council and, 2035
Vaiśālī council and, 2036
revisions of, 1110, 1260–1261
saṃgha and, 8072, 8075
in Tibet, 8084
sexual implications, 1258–1259, 1477
Vinaya (humble petition) poetry, as *bhakti* poetry genre, 3985
Vinayasaṃgraha (Buddhist text), 1199
Vinaya school of Buddhism
Ganjin in, 3275–3276
lesbianism in, 5415
Vinay-patrika (Tulsīdās), 9393
Vinca culture, 6464, 7379
Vincent, Kasanda, in Apostolic Church of John Maranke, 5695
Vincent of Beauvais, 7243
on nature, 6433
Vincent of Lerins, 7026
Vindhyavāsin (Hindu teacher), 9526
Sāṃkhya school and, 8091
Vindication of the Rights of Woman (Wollstonecraft), 811
Vindonnus (deity), 1494
Vine Community Church, 9410
Vinet, Jean-Pierre, 9067–9068
Vinoba Bhave. *See* Bhave, Vinoba
Vinterberg, Thomas, 3099
Violence, **9595–9600**. *See also* Conflict; Nonviolence
in African religious movements, 105–106, 107
aftermath of, 9599
charismatic leadership and, 6552, 6553
Christian Identity movement and, 1659
cultural, 9596
death through
and afterlife, in Ocean religions, 145–146
and ghosts, 3477–3478
direct, 9596
in Earth First! movement, 2562, 2563
end of, 9599
gender studies and, 3304
in goddess worship, 3590
in hero myths, 3958, 3960
and iconoclasm, 4281–4282, 4284
in Aum Shinrikyō, 631–633
of initiation rituals, 4477–4478, 4481–4482
King (Martin Luther, Jr.) on, 5146
millennialism and, 6545, 6546, 6548–6549, 6552
in mortification, 6198
nature religions connected to, 2663
in new religious movements, 6217, 6517, **6551–6556,** 6564
in orgy, 6878–6879
and pain, 6944–6945
passive, 9599
political power and, 7249, 7251, 7257
and pollution, 7506
Quakers on, 7547, 7548, 7549
Reformation and, 1807, 1808
in ritual, 7858
structural, 9596
study of, 9596
urban violence, religious, 1807–1808
in Vedism, 6645
against women (*See also* Domestic violence)
Australian Indigenous, 3393
Mesoamerican, 3412
Oceanic, 3396
Violence and the Sacred (Girard), 6944
Violet (color), symbolism of, 1861
Vipassanā (vipaśyanā) meditation, 603, 1284, 1290, 5820, 9096
Vipaśyin (buddha), 1066, 1105
Vira (heroic path), 8991
Viracocha (deity), 5292, **9600–9601**
association with Apostle Thomas, 3063
deification of, 8576
in flood myth, 3130, 3131, 3132
as high god, 8590
Inti, relationship with, 1364, 4524
introduced by Pachacuti Inca, 8843
legitimacy of Inca kings and, 5176
prayers to, 4412
as rain god, 7603
as supreme god, 4412
as sustenance god, 8600
temples of, 4413
tiara of, 6624
veneration of image of, 4384
Viracocha Inca (king)
calendar and, 1363, 1364
flight from Cuzco of, 5176
Viraha (separation), 859, 3985, 4644
Virāj, as epithet of Viṣṇu, 9617
Viraṇs (hero-warriors), 8978
Virās (heroes), 4435–4436
Vīraśaivism, 4430, 8041, **8043–8044**
āvarṇas of, 4424–4425
founder of, 4424
origins of, 4421
system of thought of, 4424
Virāṭaparvan (Hindu text), Durgā in, 2526
Viret, Pierre, 851
on deism, 2251
Virgil. *See* Vergil
Virgin birth
controversy over, 7884
doctrine of, development of, 7081
Jewish polemics on, 7232–7233
ordinary women relating to, 953
Virgin goddess, **9601–9606**
Virginia
Anglicanism in, 350, 352
as paradise, 6985
Virginia Beach (Virginia), Association for Research and Enlightenment in, 559–561
Virgin Islands, Lutheran missions in, 1706
Virginity, **9606–9609**. *See also* Virgins
androcentrism in, 335
Artemis and, 507
of Athena, 588
castration and, 1452
celibacy and, 1476
chastity and, 1558
in Christianity, 7081
asceticism and, 7723
notion of, 4164
clitoridectomy and, 1825
Cyprian on, 2113
definitions of, 9602
of goddesses, 3588
as beyond male power, 4164
Hera as goddess of, 3914
in Israelite religion, laws on, 4733–4734
loss of, and pollution, 7506
of Mary, 3588
vs. Eve, 5755
in New Testament, 5752
in postbiblical Christianity, 5753
meanings of, 4164
motherhood and, 2984, 3588
myrtle as symbol of, 9337–9338
permanent, 9607
sacred power of, 3020
Vatican II on, 1558
Virgin Mary. *See* Mary
Virgin of Cobre, Osun identified with in Santeria, 1434
Virgin of Copacabana
Andean iconography and, 8610
Pachamama associated with, 8615
Virgin of Guadalupe, 3064, 5921–5922
Andean localization of, 8610–8611
controversy over historicity of, 5922
in Huichol religion, 4152
iconography of, 5927, vol. 12 color insert
Oré (Luis Jeronimo de) and, 8612
origins of tradition, 5921–5922
pilgrimage to, 7149
protective role of, 3589
as sacred space, 9260
Shrine of, 5196, 7698
studies of, 5922
syncretism in worship of, 3588
Virgin of Regla, Yemaja identified with in Santeria, 1434
Virgin of Remedies, 5921
Virgin of Urkupiña, Pachamama associated with, 8615
Virgins. *See also* Virginity
in Africa, sacrifice of, 99
in agricultural rites, sacrifice of, 5277
Hekate and, 3899
in Inca religion, 3417
in Islamic afterlife, 160
shrine virgins *(saigū)* of Japan, 1528
Vestal (*See* Vestal Virgins)
Virgins of Saint Jacob Baradeus, Syriac Orthodox Church and, 8940

Viriditas (greenness) of God, Hildegard of Bingen on, 3980
Virtue(s)
acquiring, 812
in Buddhism, social impact of, 8463
chastity, **1557–1560**
in Chinese thought (*See De*)
in Christianity
Augustine on, 1670
Thomas Aquinas on, 9163
cultivation of, 810
in Daoism, 2179
in eightfold path, 2738
environmental, in Judaism, 2644
hope as, 4127
in Judaism, suffering and, 8805
knowledge as, Plato on, 310
in Roman religion, Marcus Terentius Varro on, 4027
Socrates on, 8503
Spinoza (Baruch) on, 8684
in Stoicism, 3911, 8741
subjective *vs.* objective, 5397, 5403
Virūpākṣa (deity), Vijayanagara as sacred space and, 1806
Visākhā Pūjā (Buddha's Day), 1304–1305
in Lao religion, 5314
Viśeṣādvaita (qualified dualism), in Vīraśaivism, 8044
Visible and Invisible Realms: Power, Magic, and Colonial Conquest in Bali (Wiener), 9297
Visigoths
Clovis and, 1689
converting to Christianity, 4556
and Huns, 4490–4491
Muslim victory over, 4593
in Spain, 4556
Vision (eyesight), in visual culture, 9622
Visionary (prophetic) dreams, 2483, 2488, 2489
Visionary experience. *See* Ecstasy; Trance; Visions
Visionary journeys
in Chinese religion, 2182, 2205
of horticulturalists, 9615
of hunter-gatherers, 9614
of nomadic pastoralists, 9615
Vision quests, **9609–9611**. *See also* Quests
in Anishinaabe religion, 369–370
caves and, 1470
ecstatic discipline in, 8703
incubation in, 8441
in North American Indian religions, 6651–6652, 9609–9611
of California and Intermountain region, 6713, 6716
of Great Lakes, 6683
of Great Plains, 6700
Lakota, 5296
Salish, 1470
in shamanism
guardian spirit quests, 8277
hallucinogens and, 8293
South American, 8293
techniques for, 8293
Visions, **9611–9617**. *See also* Dreams; Ecstasy; Vision quests
of Alinesitoue, 261–262
of Amos, 297
of descent into the underworld, 2299–2300
in Diola religion, 2354
of Hildegard of Bingen, 3979, 3980
of Joan of Arc, 4929–4930
of Longchenpa, 5195
of Maranke (John), 5694
as messages, 9615–9616
of missionaries, universality of, 6069–6071
on mountains, 6213
in Movement for the Restoration of the Ten Commandments of God, 105, 6215–6216
new religions in Africa and, 1511
in North American Indian religions, 6650, 7299
Blackfoot, 960
of Ibn al-ʿArabī, 4256, 4257, 8819
oracular, 6835–6836
physical changes during, 9611–9612
at pilgrimage centers, 7146
prophetic
Maimonides (Moses) on, 7439
Saʿadyah Gaon on, 7438–7439
of Sergii of Radonezh, 8230
in shamanism
initiation and, 8270–8271, 8283
as presentational symbolism, 8277
of Smith (Joseph), 6192, 8447
Viśiṣṭādvaita (qualified nondualism), 828, 8976, 9548
mysticism and, 6343
of Rāmānuja, 4005
in Swaminarayan movement, 8891
Viśiṣṭādvaita school of Vedānta
Pāñcarātra and, 10088
self in, 8546–8547
Visitation order, Carroll's sponsorship of, 1446
Visitatio sepulchri (Visit to the Tomb), 2580
Visiting the sick, in Judaism, 3828–3829
Viśleṣa (separation), 859
Viṣṇu (deity), **9616–9619**. *See also* Vaiṣṇavism
and Ādi Śakti, 4433
and Prāhlada, 4442, 7501
associations of, 9618
as Vyāsa, 4415
avatāras of, 707–708, 4415–4416
animal themes of, 4438, 7500–7501
Balarāma as, 743
bhakti synthesis and, 4000–4001
iconography of, 4325
in Purāṇas, 7500–7501
Jesus as, 4845
number of, 707
Parasurama, holiday to, 4017–4018
pigs as, 4438, 7144, 7501
purpose of, 707
Rāma as, 3886, 7501, 7609, 7617
turtles as, 4325, 7500, 9407
Vāsudeva as, 4020
worship of, 4428, 4443
bhāgadvata and, 9501
as Bhagavat, 9572
bhakti synthesis and, 3998, 3999, 4000–4002
bird of, 4438
Buddha as, 708, 824, 1312, 4442
as Cakravartin, 4415
in creation story, lotus and, 5518
emanations *(vyūhas)* of, Pañcarātras on, 4005
and fish symbolism, 3123
Ganges River and, 3275
holidays to, 4016
hymns to, 7209, 7210
iconography of, 4324–4325, 4383, 4384, vol. 8 color insert
in Brạhmaṇas, 3992
in Dvaita Vedānta, 5551
in Purāṇas, 7500–7501
in *Rāmāyaṇa,* 7617
inspiration given by, 4509
in *trimūrti,* 4000
in Vaiṣṇavism, 4428, 9618, 10088
devotion to, 4428
as Kalki, 4416
as Kapila, 4415
in Khmer religion, 5129
Kṛṣṇa as, 4415, 5248, 5251, 7501
lion associated with, 5464–5465
lotus associated with, 5518
meditation on, 5819
pervasiveness of, 9617
priests of, Vaikhānasas, 9495
pūjā to, 7494
rain and drought myth associated with, 7604
serpent of, 4438, 4439, 7500
shape shifting of, 8301
Śiva, complementarity with, 3999, 8416
Śiva revealing himself to, 4324
sleeping, myth of, 4017
as sleeping god, 8440
in Southeast Asia, 4012
as sun, 8839
sword of, 967
Tamil poetry of, 857, 7207
temples to, 8977
in Southeast Asia, 4012, 4013
in United States, 8418
in Trinity, 4422, 4423, 4443, 9346
and tulasi plant, 2403
Vāmana as incarnation of, 2368, 7501
in Vedas, 4428
in Vedism, 3990, 9557
devotion to, 857
Viṣṇudharmottara Purāṇa
mudrās in, 6219
on planting trees, 2621
Viṣṇumāyā (deity), 2526
Viṣṇu Purana
cosmology in, 2017
creation story in, 1986
English translation of, 4446
Kṛṣṇa in, 5456, 7501
Śrī in, 5519
Viṣṇuśarman (brahman), 6959
Viṣṇusvāmin, 9505
Visotzky, Burton L., on midrash, 6019, 6020
Vīsperad (Avesta text), 9992
Vīsperad ritual, 9998
Vissarion's Church of the Last Testament, 6568
Visser 't Hooft, W. A., 2685
Visual aesthetics. *See* Aesthetics; Art
Visual culture and religion, **9619–9627**
defining, 9620, 9621–9622
history of study of, 502
interpretation of, 9622–9623
outsider art, **9624–9627**
overview of, **9620–9624**
self-taught art, 9626–9627
study of, challenges to, 9623–9624
Visualization
in Buddhism, 9834, 9836
Shingon Ajikan practice, 8351
in Daoism, 9845
in Neopaganism, 6472

Visualization ***continued***
of *maṇḍalas*
in *sādhana,* 5642–5643, 5644
in meditation, vol. 11 color insert
and scientific knowledge, 6426–6427
Tibetan practice of
attention in, 603
in Gcod rite, 5558
Visual narratives, vol. 2 color insert
Visual paradox, 6988
Visual piety, vol. 11 color insert, vol. 12 color insert
Visual theology, 497
Viśuddha cakra, location of, 1348
Visuddhimagga (Buddhaghosa)
anecdotes in, 9148
arahant in, 477
as Theravāda teaching, 1074, 1093, 1199, 1200
pāramitās in, 6993
prajñā in, 7357
sensual desire in, 1475
Viśvakarman, eyes of, 2941
Viśvapāṇi *(bodhisattva),* 1079
Viśvarupa (monster), killed by Indra, 9684–9685
Viśveśvara *(liṅga),* 779
Visweswaran, Kamala, on women, 3322
Vital, Ḥayyim, 4998, 7535, **9628**
Vital energy, chiropractic and, 3850
Vitalistic revival and renewal activities, 7784
Vitality, hair as symbol of, 3738–3739
Vita Merlini (Geoffrey of Monmouth), 5878
Vita nuova (Dante), 7219
Vita Romualdi (Damian), 2133
Vitebsky, Piers, 379
Viṭhobā (deity), in Marathi religions, 5697
Vitruvius (Roman author), 7914
Viṭṭuciṭṭaṉ (poet), 8974
Vivādārṇavasetu (Hindu code of law), 5346
Vivante, Paolo, 5468
Vivasvant (sun deity), Saraṇyū and, 4133
Vivekananda, **9628–9631, 10089–10091**
in ashram revival, 545, 546
autobiography of, 700
on caste system, 10090
comparative theology of, 9130
as disciple of Ramakrishna, 7611, 7612, 10089
on equal value of all religions, 2343
in Hindu reform movement, 9318–9319
on image worship, 828–829
on New Testament, 828
on *māyā,* 5795
Practical Vedanta of, 7612, 7613, 10090
Ramakrishna Mission, role in, 4008
on religious experience, 7740
as religious nationalist, 7255–7256, 9319
Śārāda Devi and, 8111
self-assessment of, 10091
on social service, 10090
Tantrism opposed by, 8988
Western missions of, 9290, 10089–10090
on women, 10090–10091
at World's Parliament of Religions, 6559, 9805, 10090
Vivekananda (swami), as disciple of Ramakrishna, 10067
Vivier-van Etveldt, L. M., 3505
Vizenor, Gerald, 3092, 3093
on trickster, 6662
Vladimir I (prince of Kiev), **9631–9632**
Christianization of Russia and, 1683, 7941
conversion of, to Eastern Christianity, 2585
Kievan pantheon of, Mokosh in, 6115
Slavic religion and, 8432–8433
Vocation, **9632–9634**
in Catholicism, of laity, 9541
initiation into, 4476, 4477, 4483
in Jainism, 2625
Vodou (voodoo), **9634–9639**
Catholic iconography appropriated by, vol. 8 color insert
commerce of images in, vol. 7 color insert
creolization and, 2066–2067, 2068
deities in, 9636
divination in, healing through, 3822
in film, 3099
flags in, vol. 8 color insert
food symbolism and ritual in, 3171
head, ritual importance of, 3806
history of study of, 73, 76, 10026
initiates in
initiation ceremony of, vol. 6 color insert
postfunerary rites of, 6453
lwa (spirits) in, 1433–1434
characteristics of, 8690
as Neo-African cult in Haiti, 1433–1435
in New York, 1809, 2068
possession and transcendence in, 7987
rituals in, 9634–9635
sacred objects in, vol. 4 color insert
spirit possession in, 8690, 8692
dance and, 2139, 2150
glossolalia and, 3506
syncretism in, 3143
urban *vs.* rural, 9635
"Vodou death" (by sorcery), 2099
Voegelin, Eric
Gnosticism and, 3527
and political theology, 7246
Voelva (wise woman), in Scandinavian mythology, seidr ritual and, 8295
Vofiono (deity), 7894
Vogt, Evon Z., 379, 453, 5798, 5943
Vogul religion. *See* Finno-Ugric religions; Khanty and Mansi religion; Southern Siberian religions
Voguls. *See* Mansi
Vohu Manah (good thought), 290
Chinvat Bridge and, 1647
Voice of Africa, The (Frobenius), 3576
Voice of My Beloved Knocks (Soloveitchik), Zionism in, 8519
Voice of the Andes (radio ministry), 7713
Voice of the I Am, The (periodical), 4246
Voice of the Silence, The (Blavatsky), 977
Voices
of God, Heschel (Abraham Joshua) on, 3962
in visions, 9612
Void. *See* Nothingness
Voipel (deity), in Komi religion, 5217
Volador ceremony
in Mixtec religion, 5911
in Totonac religion, 5911
Volcanoes, 2296
masculine sacrality in, 5760
Volcanus (deity)
priest of, 3126
temple of, 3118
Volga, Middle. *See* Middle Volga
Volga Bulgar empire, Chuvash religion and, 1784
Volga Finnic protolanguage, 5709
Volga language group, 5708
Volition, in Sautrāntika Buddhism, 8137
Volk, Herder (Johann Gottfried) on, 4031
Völkerpsychologie theory, Otto (Rudolf), criticism from, 4096
Völkisch movement, anti-Semitism, 4085
Volkmar, Gustav, on Gnosticism, 3532
Vollers, Caroli, 889
Volmar (monk), Hildegard of Bingen and, 3979
Volos. *See* Veles-Volos
Volsuspa (Eddic poem), Heimdallr in, 3898
Voltaire
anti-Semitism of, 401
Encyclopédie and, collaboration on, 2783
as Freemason, 3195
in French Enlightenment, 2796
on gardens, 3279
Reinach (Salomon) influenced by, 7675
on religion, 7790
skepticism and, 8421
on superstition, 8866
Volturnus (deity), priest of, 3126
Völundarvkiða, 2693
Völundr, 2693
Voluntarism, 1030
Baptist, 783, 785
in Islam, 3563–3565
in Protestantism, 7453
Tönnies (Ferdinand) on, 9230
Voluntary associations
African Americans in, 68
as natural religious communities, 1866–1867
Voluntary exile, 2938
Voluntary simplicity, in engaged Buddhism, 2788
Volusian (Roman emperor), Christian persecution by, 7059
Vǫluspá (Germanic text)
afterlife in, 167
apocalypse in, 3456–3457
Baldr in, 744
creation in, 3446
of man, 3454
Golden Age in, 3628
in *Hyndluljóð,* 2693
in *Poetic Edda,* 2692
war between deities in, 3450
Yggdrasill as cosmic tree in, 1502, 3448, 3449
Vom Ewigen im Menschen (Scheler), absolute in, 8147
Vom Geist der Ebräischen Poesie (Herder), Old Testament poetry in, 3919
Vomit
and pollution, 7504
in purification, 7508
Von Glasenapp, Helmuth. *See* Glasenapp, Helmuth von
Von Görres, Joseph. *See* Görres, Joseph von
Von Harnack, Adolf. *See* Harnack, Adolf von
Von Hügel, Friedrich. *See* Hügel, Friedrich von
Voodoo. *See* Vodou
Vorbichler, Anton, on firstling sacrifices, 8002
Vorhilon, Claude (Raël), 6529
on *Elohim,* 6530
Vorilhon, Claude. *See* Raël
Voris' (foreṣt spirit), in Komi religion, 5218
Vorlesungen über das Wesen des Judentums (Baeck), 737
Vorsa (forest spirit), in Komi religion, 5217
Vorstius, Conrad, Calvert (George) and, 1373
Vos, G. J., on paganism and Judaism, 4039

Voss, Johann Heinrich, on symbols, 8909
"Vote with Your Pocket" (Shah), 2626
Votiaks. *See* Udmurts
Votive offerings
Cheng Yi on, 1562–1563
Egyptian, 2714
in Greek religion, 4381
in Roman religion, 7898
in south and southwest Asia, 3163
Vowels, mystical speculation on, 271
Vows and oaths, **9639–9643**
Buddhist (*See* Vows and oaths, Buddhist)
in Chinese religion, 5352
distinction between, 9639
in East African divination, 2569
during Eastern Christian pilgrimage, 7154
false, as blasphemy, 970
formulated by Humbert of Silva Candida, 837
in Greek religion, Sun and, 8839
hand gestures with, 3770
Hindu, in devotional life, 9824
Hippocratic Oath, 4021, 5810
in Indo-European religions, 4455
Jaina, 2624
laws and, 5327–5328
meteorological deities in, 5995
ordeal and, 6848
solemn *vs.* simple vows, 7721
supreme beings as witnesses to, 8871–8872
taken before images, 4391
Vows and oaths, Buddhist
of *bodhisattvas,* 5309
faith in, 1114
individualized, 1086
in Mahāyāna Buddhism, 5105
Kamalaśīla on, 999
and lay people, 1162
power of, 1084
reasons for taking, 998, 1116
role of, 1113, 1118
success of, 997
of celestial buddhas, 1086
of child monks, 1156
of Master of Healing, 855
Voyage de Théo, Le (Clément), 3061
Voyage of Bran, 991
Voyage of Maeldúin, 991
Vraja region, Caitanya and, 1345, 1346
Vrata (vow), 858, 4435
Hindu, in devotional life, 9824
Jaina, 2624
utsava festivals *vs.,* 4016
Vrātyastomas, 9567
Vremia (journal), 2422
Vries, Jan de, 1499, **9643–9644**
on Baldr, 744
on end of world, 3456
on Euhemerus, 2883
on Njǫrðr, 6642
review of literature by, 3458, 3459
Vrijānanda, and Dayananda Sarasvati, 2227
Vṛjiputraka *bhikṣus* (monks), Vaiśālī council and, 2035, 2036
Vṛndāvana, 5253, **9644–9645**
temple at, 7593–7594
Vṛndāvanadāsa, Caitanya in, 1346
Vṛndāvana Kṛṣṇalīlā (ritual dance), 2449, 2450
Vṛtra, **9645–9646**
and binding, 937
killed by Indra, 2431, 4439, 4467, 9556
water held back by, 9699
Vṛtrahan (deity), 4536
Vṛtti (Buddhist text), 1120, 1271
Vucub Hunahpu (mythic figure), 5935
Vulcan, Celtic parallels to, 1484–1485
Vulgate Bible, 892–893, 4833
Alcuin in, 254
Apocrypha in, 896
authority of, 881
Baal Zebub in, 7103
Damasus I and, 892, 922, 6966
idolatry in, 4357
as inspired text, 8203
opposition to, 893
Satan in, 2314
as source for Thomas Aquinas, 9163
Vulgate Cycle (Grail story), 3649
Vulture goddess (prehistoric), 7377, 7378
Vultures, 9225
Vulva. *See also* Yoni
as signal, 2868
Vyākaraṇa, 1085, 7005
Vyākhyā (commentary), 1271
Vyākhyāprajñapti Sūtra, *loka* cosmology in, 2022
Vyākhyayukti (Buddhist text), 1271
Vyāna (breath), 1043, 7362
Vyāsa
Bādarāyaṇa identified with, 735
Mahāpurāṇas attributed to, 7498
on meditation, 8704
Viṣṇu as, 4415
Vyas Committee, Āyurveda and, 3857
Vyavahāra (legal transaction), 2328
Vydūnas, Wilhelm Storosta-, 763
Vyūhas, in Pāñcarātra cosmology, 9508

W

Waardenburg, Jacques
historiography of, 4047–4048
on phenomenology of religion, 7087, 7091
Wáátawa (possessed one), 6004, 6005
Wabokieshiek (prophet), 6686
Wabu (pure ones), 2714
Wach, Joachim, **9649–9653**
on death of founders of religions, 1062
on faith and community, 2957
on hermeneutics, 3933
historiography of, 4043
on *homo religiosus,* 4109–4110
Kitagawa (Joseph M.) and, 5188, 5189
on leadership, 5385–5386, 5387
on master-disciple relationship, 946
on phenomenology of religion, 7086–7087
on religious experience, 7741, 7743–7744
on saints, 8033
on society and religion, 8466
on sociology of religion, 944
Wachirayān (Siamese prince), 9095–9096
Wachtel, Nathan, on Andean messianism, 8604
Waco (Texas). *See* Branch Davidians
Wadd (deity), 444
Athirat and, 589
Waddell, L. Austine, 9189
Waddington, C. H., 2919
Wade, Roe v., 941
Wadley, Susan S., 3321
Wadud, Amina, on afterlife, 162
Wadud-Mushin, Amina, Qur'anic exegesis of, 7568
Waehma (ritual performance), 7045
Waelhens, Alphonse de, 6369
Waen-Re. *See* Akhenaton
Wafd party (Egypt), 6314, 6315
Wagap mission, 6791
Wagenvoort, Hendrik, 6754
on *gurus,* 8711
Waggoner, Ellet J., Seventh-day Adventism and, 8236
Wagner, C. Peter, 7031
Wagner, Johann Jakob, 6435
Wagner, Peter, 6305
Wagner, Richard
horse symbolism used by, 4134
music of, 6253, 6312
and Nietzsche, 6614
Wagner, Roy, 6507, 6802
on kinship, 5185
Wagner-Hatfield Amendment (1934), 7710
Waḥdat al-shuhūd (unity of witness), al-Ḥallāj on, 3756–3757
Waḥdat al-wujūd (unity of being)
al-Ḥallāj on, 3756
Ibn ʿArabī on, 4255, 4258–4259, 4570, 8819, 8820
Iqbal (Muhammad) on, 8824
Rūmī (Jalāl al-Dīn) on, 7937
al-Suhrawardī on, 6232
Wahgi religion (Papua New Guinea), ancestors in, 2005
Wahhābīyah, **9653–9655**
in Central Asia, 4626, 4627, 4628
definition of, 6100
founder of, 4254, 4255, 4573
God in, 3565
Ḥanābilah and, 3768, 5548
ʿiṣmah in, 4726
on *ijtihād,* 4699
on Sanūsīyah, 5118
political power of, 7254
samāʿ (listening parties), opposition to, 8065
in South Asia, 4645
in Southeast Asia, 4665
spread of, 6100
Wahiawa Temple (Oahu), Śaivism and, 8419
Wahid, Abdurrahman, 3367, 4670, 4671
Wahl, Jean, 5478
Wahrām I (king), Mani condemned by, 5648, 5659–5660
Waḥy (revelation), 7778
Waʿi, al- (journal), 4630
Waidan (external alchemy), 1603
Wailaki tribe (North America), weaving in, 939
Waimariwi (mythological figure), 9704–9705
Waitangi, Treaty of (1840), 5683, 5684
Waiting for Godot (Beckett), 2475
Waito (hero), 7524
Waitz-Gerland, Theodor, 114
on supreme beings, 8876
Wáiuwen spirits, in Selk'nam religion, 8224
Waiwai religion (Guyana)
human origin myth in, 8589
origin of agriculture in, 8590
Wak (deity), in Gurage religion, 2574
Waka (deity), in Macha Oromo religion, 2573
Waka (poetic form), 7215
Wakan (power), 6650, 7348, 7373, 8947

Wakantanka (deity), 2996, 5295–5296, 5297
and sweat lodge as center of universe, 7981–7982
Wakashan people (North America), 6656
Wakdjunkaga (trickster), 9351
Wākea (deity), *kapu* (taboo) system and, 3796, 3799
Wakefield Cycle (drama), 2469
Wakeman, Mary, space and time models of chaos myths, 1986–1987
Wako (primordial man), in Cuna creation myth, 2095
Wako^{n}da (Osage spirit), 6917–6918
Walanganda (Milky Way), 9460
Walāyah (spiritual authority), **9656–9662**
imamate as, 4395
of ʿAlī ibn Abī Ṭālib, 257
Walbiri Iconography (Munn), 3390, 4305
Walbiri religion (Australia)
Gadjeri in myths of, 3250–3251
totemism in, 9252
Walburga (nun), 822
Waldensians, 6648, **9662–9663**
Cartharis compared to, 1456, 1457
enthusiasm of, 2805
and mendicancy, 6133
monastic traditions rejected by, 6133
and Moravian denomination, 6190
persecution of, 6971
spread of, 6869
Waldman, Marilyn Robinson, **9663–9665**
on subjectivity in prophets, 8695
Waldorf School movement, 393
Steiner (Rudolf) and, 8738
Walens, Stanley
on animal symbols, 357
on Kwakiutl religion, 6672
Wales. *See also* Britain
Congregationalism in, 1938
hermits of, 2826
literature of
Arthur in, 508–509
horses in, 4133
Mabinogion, **5545–5547**
Merlin in, 5878
mythology and folklore, 1483, 1489–1490, 4133
oral tradition, 1480
women in, 3388
Presbyterianism in, 7390
religion of (*See* Celtic religion)
religious education in, 7732, 7735
Union of Welsh Independents, 1938
Waley, Arthur, 1635
Walī Allāh, Shāh, 6736, **9665–9667**
on fasting, 8141
on modernism, 4573
reform movement of, 4643, 4650, 9010
tafsīr of, 8955
Walī/awaliyā (saints), 4588, 9656
in Java, Islam spread by, 4816
meaning of, 8034–8035, 8821
shaykhs as, 8821
Walid ibn Yazīd, Caliph, 1599
Walī-Tarāsh. *See* Kubrā, Najm al-Dīn
Waliullah, Shah, 829
Walker, Alice, 966, 5441
Walker, Christopher, 4381
Walker, Daniel Pickering, 2930
Walker, David, 73, 963
Walker, James R., 6672, **9667–9668**
and Athapaskan religious traditions, 576
on Lakota religious traditions, 5296
Walker, Kath, 3080
Walker, Sheila, 76
Walker's Appeal in Four Articles (Walker), 963
Wall, Patrick D., 6947
Wallā, 9656
Wallace, Alfred Russell
evolutionary ethics opposed by, 2918
methodological critique of, 379
Wallace, Anthony
on religious revitalization, 6575
on rites of passage, 7798
Wallace, Anthony F. C., 3409
classification of rituals by, 7840–7841
on dreams, 2483
on Handsome Lake religion, 6671
on psychedelic drugs, 7467
Wallace Line, 745
Wall-contemplation *(biguan),* 1521
Wallerstein, Immanuel, world-system theory of, 2675–2676
Walleser, Max von, 3289
Wallin, Georg, Andre's (Tor) monograph on, 333
Wallis, Roy, 102–103, 6521, 6542, 6543
Walliullah, Syed, 10035
Walls, Neal, 319
Walmajarri people, in new religious movements, 673
Walpola Rahula, 7264
Walsh, Dennis, 3092
Walsh, Roger, on death-and-rebirth, 8277
Walter H. Capps Center, establishment of, 1412
Walter of Saint-Victor, in Victorine tradition, 4151
Walters, Anna Lee, 3093
Waltz, at *veglia,* 2148
Walumbe (mythological figure), 2575
Walzer, Richard, 4718
Wambar, in Qemant religion, 2573
Wampanoags, in King Philip's War, 6665
Wampum, 10086
Wampun, colors of, 1862
Wanadi (deity), in Makiritare religion (Amazon), 2312, 8626
Wanagi Wicagluha (Lakota sacred rite), 5296–5297
Wa-na-ka (king), 41, 42
Wanalirri, 9459–9460
Wanambi (Rainbow Snake), 7605
Wanax (Mycenaean king), 5166
Wandjina (life-spirit), 7605, 9458–9462, **9668–9670**
Wang, C. K., 1638
Wanga charms, healing and, 3823
Wang Anshi, 1560, 1578, 7214
Wang Bi, **9670–9671**
commentaries by, 1575
on *li,* 5431
Wang Changyue, and Longmen branch of Quanzhen Daoism, 2188
Wang Chong, 3004, **9671–9672**
on afterlife, 172
on human nature, 1575
rationalism, 1592
Wang Chongyang. *See* Wang Zhe
Wang Chuyi, 2207, 2210
Wang Daiyu, 4632, 4639
Wang Fou, 5317
Wang Fuzhi, 1579, **9672–9673**
Han Studies *(Hanxue)* movement and, 1903
Wang Gen, 1578
Wang Hansheng, Huangdi, vision of, 4145
Wang Ji, 1578, 1608
Wang Jian (Chinese emperor), 2517
Wang Kŏng, "Ten Injunctions" of, 1929
Wang Mang, 1592, 2990
magic used by, 5592
Wangsheng lunzhu, 4934
Wan'gurri clan, 641
Wang Wei (Buddhist poet), 1165, 7207, 7213
Wang Xizhi
calligraphy and, 1368
running script of, 1370
Wang Xuanhe, 5319
Wang Yangming, **9673–9676**
Ching (Julia) studying, 10030, 10031
on Golden Rule, 3633
Japan, influence in, 1927–1928
Korean Confucianism and, 1931
Kumazawa Banzan and, 5264
on *li,* 5431
Lu Xiangshan's influence on, 5542
Nakae Tōju in, 6404
on natural/moral order, 1603
on nature, 2632
Neo-Confucianism and, 1607, 1924, 5264, 5542, 9311
philosophy of, 1167, 1578, 1579
on Study of Inner Mind, 1902–1903
unity of knowledge theory, 1931
Wang Zhe, 1602, **9676**
disciples of, 2199
and Quanzhen Daoism, 2186, 2199, 7415
teachings and writings of, 2209–2210
temple dedicated to, 9057
Wani (Korean scribe), calligraphy and, 1370
Wanjad (Rock Python), 9458
Wan people (Ivory Coast), dances of, 2138
Wansbrough, John, 4719, 8952
Waqāʾiʿ al-misrīyah, al- (gazette), ʿAbduh (Muḥammad) in, 6
Waqf (endowment), **9676–9679**
for Mansuri Hospital (Cairo), 3832
nationalization of
in China, 4636
in Soviet Union, 4624
traditionalism and, 1555, 3761
Wāqifah Shiism, schism from Imāmīyah, 8322
Warai Matsuri festival, laughter at, 4208
Waramurungundji (mythic figure), 657
War and Peace (Tolstoy), 9220
War and warriors, **9679–9687**. *See also* Martial arts; Violence; *specific figures and wars*
in African religions
Sotho circumcision and, 8666
West African, 1434
ambivalence about, 9684
American civil religion and, 1814
in Aztec religion, 5891
Xochiyaoyotl (Flowery Wars), 4186–4187
in Brahmanism, vegetarianism of, 9571
in Buddhism, 2787
cannibalism and, 1403, 1404
in Caribbean religions, 1429, 1430, 1431, 1434
cattle raiding, 1465
in Chinese religion, Confucian military cult, 1913
in Christianity, just war notion, 1694
combat myth and chaos, 1539
deities of (*See* War deities)
eagle and hawk identified with, 2554
enemies incorporated after, 9685–9686
in epics, 2815–2816
and fatalism, 2998–2999
foundation, wars of, 9685–9686

Germanic, afterlife for, 167
in Geto-Dacian religion, 3466, 3467
in Greek religion, homosexuality and, 4112–4113
in Hawaiian religion, war temples in, 3797
in Hinduism, *Bhagavadgītā* on, 852
homosexuality and, 4112–4113, 4114
in Indo-European religions, 1874, 4453–4454, 4455, **9683–9687**
inherent ferocity of, 9684
in Islam
in Qur'ān, 4918, 6225
Muḥammad and, 6225–6226
just war, Christian doctrine of, 6648
Kagawa Toyohiko on, 5054
Mesoamerican, in Teotihuaćan, 5900
in Middle East, and Christian emigration, 1676
as monster, 9682–9683
natural law in, Grotius (Hugo) on, 3703
North American Indian
ballgames and, 754–755
Cherokee Red Path, 1564–1565
European colonization and, 6664–6665
gender and, 3409
in Osage religion, 6918
in Oceanic religions, 6786, 7296
ordeal and, 6849–6850
overview of, **9679–9683**
prestige for, 9679–9680
religion as cause of, al-Rāzī on, 2973
religious *vs.* optional, 6647
in Roman religion
Iupiter Dolichenus as deity of, 4753–4754
rituals of, 7896, 7897
shields in, 9681–9683
sins of, 9684–9685
social boundaries in, 9680–9682
subordination of, to priest, 9684
in Vedism, 9560–9561, 9567–9568
Wikander (Stig) on, 9735
Warao religion (South America), **9687–9689**
basket weaving in, 9575
death, myths of origin of, 8590–8591
shamanism in, gender and, 3418
snake-bridge as cosmic transition, 1503–1504
tobacco in, 9217
tree of life in, 9335
Waraqa ibn Nawfal, and Muḥammad's revelation, 6221
War band, 4462, 9683–9684
Warburg, Aby, **9689–9691**
on iconography, 4297, 10043
Warburg Institute. *See* Kulturwissenschaftliche Bibliothek Warburg
Warburton, William, 9109
War Cry, Salvation Army and, 8063, 8064
Ward, Donald, 9421
Ward, Lester F., on androcentrism, 3298
Ward, Mary, 6764, **9691–9693**
Ward, Nancy, 1565
Ward, Samuel Ringgold, 68
War dances, 2466, 2499
War deities, 3621
Adad as, 28
Artemis as, 506–507
Athena as, 586
in Celtic religions, 1490
epic heroes and, 2815
examples of, 3621
as fertility figure, 9686–9687
functions of, 3621
in Hittite religion, 4069
Indo-European, 9683
Indra as, 4466, 4467
Iupiter Dolichenus as, 4753–4754
Mars as, 5727–5728
Mēness as, 759
Mithra as, 6087
in Near Eastern religions, 37
Óðinn, 6809
in Phoenician religion, 7130
violence of, 9597
virginity and, 9604
wolf symbolism of, 9783–9784
Yahveh as, 3542
Warden, The (Trollope), 3060
Wardley, James, Shakers and, 8268
Wardley, Jane, Shakers and, 8268
Warfield, B. B.
theistic evolution and, 8190
on Wesleyanism, 4083
Warikyana religion (South America), Pura as supreme being in, 8577
Wari' people, cannibalism among, 1403
Warlord guardian spirits, in Khanty and Mansi religion, 5120
during bear festival, 5121
function of, 5121
hierarchy of, 5122
Warlpiri religion (Australia), 644–646, **9693–9697**
art in, 666, 2480, 4305
Christianity in, 645–646
dance in, 640
the Dreaming in, 666
gender roles in, 645, 3390, 3392
new movements in, 673–674
rituals in, 9694, 9695–9697
women as healers, 3874
Warmi-qhari (woman-man), 3416, 3417
Warne, Randi R., 3025
on gender, 3304–3305
vs. sex, 3297
on women's studies in religious studies, 3313
Warneke, Sara, 9261
Warner, J. C., on Xhosa religion, 1856
Warner, Marina, 3360
on Mary, 5755
Warner, William Lloyd, 659, 683, 684, 3390, 9705
on ritual, 7836, 7846
Warnock, G. J., 6179
War of Saint Rose. *See* Cuscat's War
War of the End of the World, The (Vargas Llosa), 3063
Warrabri Aboriginal community, 644
Warraja (ceremonial event), 9695
Warrāq, Abū ʿĪsā al-, 7242
Warren, Henry Clarke, 1315
Warring States period (China)
afterlife in, 169, 170, 171
Confucian essays in, 1894
law in, 5352
Legalism in, 5395
magic in, 5592
manuscripts of, 1637
Yao and Shun and, 9873
yinyang wuxing in, 9888
Warrior bands, 9683–9684, 9735
Wars of Religion (1563), 851
French Reformation and, 7662
urban violence in, 1807
Wars of the Lord, The (Gersonides), 3462, 4895
War Twins, in Pueblo religion, 6722, 6724
Wasan (chanting), 6300, 6301
Washat Dreamers religion, 6667
Washburn, Michael, 7478
Washings. *See* Ablutions
Washington, Booker T., Garvey (Marcus) inspired by, 3287
Washington, George, symbolism and rituals surrounding, 1814–1815
Washington, James, 80
Washington, James Melvin, 75
Washington, Joseph, 77
Washington, Joseph R., 964
Washington Monument, 9266–9267
Washo people (North America)
Big Times of, 6715
trickster story of, 6713
Wāṣil ibn ʿAṭā', in Muʿtazilah, 6318, 6321
Wāṣilīyah. *See* Khārijīs
Waṣīyah (Islamic creed), of Abū Ḥanīfah, 5062
Waskow, Arthur
in Jewish environmentalism, 2646
at Reconstructionist Rabbinical College, 7638
Wasserstein, David, 4593
Wasserstrom, Steven M., 3528
American study of religion, role in, 8786
Wasson, R. Gordon
augmenting work of, 385
on *soma,* 4449
Waste Land, The (Eliot), 5482
Watarai Shintō
debunking of ancient texts of, 8364–8365
Toyouke shrine and, 8361
Watauineiwa (deity), 5516
in Yahgan religion, 8579
Watchmaker theory, 2909
Watchman, Heimdallr as, 3898, 3899
Watchtower (Jehovah's Witnesses publication), 4823
Watchtower Society, 4820
Water, **9697–9704**. *See also* Flood, the; Lakes; Rain; Rivers
in Aztec religion, 5891, 9213–9214
in Babylonian religion, 779
in cosmogony, 2809
in Buddhism
cold water austerities, 3226, 3227
destruction by, 2028
New Year celebrations, 6594
ceremonial washings with (*See* Ablutions)
children as messengers to gods of, 1469
in Christianity (*See also* Baptism)
blessing of, at Epiphany, 1744, 2818
cosmogonic, 3177
in creation stories, 2811
Dao as, 9842–9843
deities of (*See* Water deities)
dragons associated with, 2433
in East Africa, cults of, 2570–2571
feminine sacrality and, 3016
frogs associated with, 3223
in funeral rites, 3240
in Garden of Eden, 6982
in Haudenosaunee religion, 10086
healing and, Adventist water cures, 8236
in Hinduism
during pilgrimage, 7168–7169
in temples, 9265
immersion in (*See also* Baptism)
for healing, 3812

Water *continued*
in Iranian religions, 4535
irrigation systems, at Cambodian temples, 4013
in Islam
distribution of, 2652
in gardens, 6208
in mosques, 6208
Qur'ān on, 2651
in Komi religion, 5217, 5218
libations of, 5433
in magic, East Asian, 5593
monsters of, 6439–6440
motherhood associated with, 2984
mountain-cave-water energy tradition, 1468
in Neolithic religions, 6465
in North American Indian religions, 6707
passive, 9700
as portent, 7337
powers of, 9702–9703
primordial, flood as, 3132
Pure Water observance in Ch'ŏndogyo, 1648
in purification, 7507, 7510, 7511
qualities of, 9702–9703
in rejuvenation myths, 7683–7684
in Southern Siberian religions, 8671
in Toltec religion, 9223
tree of life and, 9577
in Turkic religions, 9399
in Ungarinyin religion, 9459–9460
in United States, 10086
watersheds, Islamic law on protection of, 2652
in West African religions
in libations, 9719
worship sites at, 9720
worship of, 6439–6440
in Zoroastrianism, 4535
Water, Sun of, in Aztec calendar, 1357
Water-bird goddess (prehistoric), 7376–7377
Water buffalo, sacrifice of, in Southeast Asian religions, traditional, 8650
Water deities, 3619–3620, 9701–9702
in African religions, 7862
Mami Wata as, 5629–5631
in Baltic religions, Māra as, 5693
in Celtic religion, 1486
in Edo religion, 2697
examples of, 3619–3620
functions of, 3619–3620
in Hawaiian religion, 3797
in Mesoamerican religion, 1468, 1472–1473
in nature worship, 6439–6440
Water drum, 2499
Water King (deity), 5121
Waterland, Daniel, on Trinity doctrine, 2057
Water lily. *See also* Lotus
as psychedelic drug, 7470
Waterlily (Deloria), 2265
Water monsters, 6439–6440
Water of life, 2770
Water of Life, The (Grimm brothers), 7554–7556
Water People gods, of Kalabari people, 2139
Waters, Clara Erskine Clement, 499
Watersheds, protection of, Islamic law on, 2652
Wat Haripuñjaya (sacred complex)
cosmology reflected in, 7983
sacred narratives in, 7984
Watkins, Calvert, 1500
Watkins, Greg, 3099
Wat Luang Pho Sodh Dhammakāyaram (monastery), 2324
Wat Mahāthāt (monastery), Mongkut at, 6139
Wat Paknam (monastery), 2324
Wat Phra Chettuphon (monastery), 9054, 9055
Wat Phra Dhammakāya (monastery), 2324–2325, 2326
Watra Mamma (divinity), 5630
Wats (temple-monasteries), 9094
Wat Samorai (monastery), Mongkut at, 6139
Watson, Christine, 643, 687
Watson, James, 1014–1015
Watt, Ian, 3051
Watt, James, Earth First! and, 2562
Watt, W. Montgomery, 4717
Watts, Alan
on androgynes, 339
on Easter eggs, 2702
LSD experiments of, 2680
on Suzuki (D. T.), 8887
Watts, Isaac, hymns of, 5152, 6310
Watts, Michael, 2611
Watzinger, Carl, archaeological work of, 5111
Waugh, Earle H., 946
Waugh, Evelyn, 3061
conversion of, 3170
Wawalag myths, **9704–9707,** 9915–9916
Djanggawul myths interconnected with, 659–662
everyday life in, 653, 654
fertility in, 659
fire in, 653, 654
gender in, 663
Waxaklahun-Ubah-K'awil, Maya calendar and, 1358
Way. *See Dao*
Wayang (puppet theater)
complementary dualism in, 8649
in rituals, 2451
sources of, 2450, 2452
variants of, 2450, 2452–2453
Wayang golek (puppet theater), 2452
Wayang kulit (puppet theater), 2450, 2452, 7044
Wayang purwa (puppet theater), 2450, 2452
Wayang wong (puppet theater), 2450, 2451, 2452
Way International, 6568
Wayman, Alex, 9189
Way of Filial Piety (Xiaodao), 2197–2198
Way of Great Peace *(Taiping Dao),* 2180, 2192, 2636, 5240, 7022
Way of Highest Clarity *(Shangqing dao),* 2637
Way of Jesus, The (Finster), vol. 14 color insert
Way of Orthodox Unity (Zhengyi Mengwei Dao), 2192, 2193, 2200
Way of Perfection (Teresa of Ávila), 9084
Way of Purity and Perspicacity (Jingming Dao), 2207
Way of Tea. *See Chadō*
Way of the Celestial Masters (Tianshi dao). *See* Celestial Masters/Heavenly Masters
Way of the Cosmos. *See Tiandao*
Way of the Five Pecks of Rice *(Wudoumi dao),* 1593
Way of the Great Peace *(Taiping dao),* 1593
millenarianism of, 6039
Way of the Heavenly Masters (Tianshi Dao). *See* Celestial Masters/Heavenly Masters
Way of the Kami. *See* Shintō
Way of Unity movement, 8965
Ways and Power of Love, The (Sorokin), measure of love in, 8524
Way to Happiness, The (Currier), vol. 11 color insert
Wayward Servants (Turnbull), 2495
WCC. *See* World Council of Churches
WCER. *See* World Congress of Ethnic Religions
Wealth, **9707–9710**
cargo cults and, 1417, 1424
of Caribbean shamans, 1431
cattle as, 1464
ceremonial display of, 1513–1514
deities of, Indo-European, comparative, 1874
in monasticism, 6122–6123
Buddhist, 6129
yoni association with, 9909
Weapons
Gaia hypothesis and, 3254
in Japan, 9310
new religious movements and, 6564
Wearing the Morning Star (Swann), 7224
Weather
deities associated with (*See also* Storm deities; Thunder deities)
in Negrito religions, 6454, 6456
shamanistic control of, in Selk'nam religion (Tierra del Fuego), 8225–8226
Weaver, Jace, 3092
Weaver, John, 2155
Weaver, Mary Jo, 3654
Weaving, 938–939
feminine sacrality and, 3019
geometry in, 3438–3439
invention by women, 5281
moon/sun and, 3018
symbolic center and, 1503
symbolism of, 3001, 9088
in cosmogonic myths, 5198
Weaving maid and cowherd legend (China), 1643
Weaving the Past (Kellogg), 3412
Webb, Catherine Helen. *See* Berndt, Catherine H.
Webb, Muhammad Alexander, 4686, 4690
Webb, Stephen, on animal sacrifice, 360
Webber, Andrew Lloyd, 2470
Webber, Sabra, 3144
Weber, Albrecht, 4446, 4447
Weber, Max, **9710–9713**
on asceticism, 529
on authority, 8483
on capitalism and Protestantism, 8464, 8494
Celtic religious studies and, 1498
on charisma, 944, 1543, 1544, 5385, 6515, 7352–7353, 9271
on China, 1635, 1921–1922
on covenant, 2048
on disenchantment of the world, 8483
Durkheim (Émile) and, 8494
on economics and religions, 2671–2674
on emergence of religions of salvation, 9328
English-speaking world and, 8467
evolutionism and, 8494–8495
and games, 3266, 3268
on Gandhi (Mohandas), 3272
"great man" approach to history, 1544
on hermeneutics and cultural sciences, 3933
on implicit religion, 4401
on Indian castes, 4448
influence on archaeology, 454
influence on contemporary anthropology, 378
influence on Indian religious studies, 4450
on law, 5330, 5369
on leadership, 5383–5387
and liberal Protestantism, 6104

on magic, 5565–5566, 5568, 5588
on martyrdom, 5738
on meaning context and communal action, 7971–7972
modern social theory, contributions to, 8494
on monasticism, 6135
on needs served by religion, 8488
on new religions, 6565
on Hinayānā-Mahāyāna division, 8152
on orthodoxy, 3928
on politics and religion, 7251
on predestination, 3205, 3208
on prophets, 4512
Protestant work ethic of, 107, 2671–2674, 8481, 8494, 9707
Marxist critique of, 7489
on rationality, 8472
on religious sense, 9649–9652
on sacred and profane, 7970–7972
on salvation, 5436–5437
on secularization, 8216
on social class, 8484
on society and religion, 8465–8466
sociological approach of, 382
Sohm (Rudolf), influence of, 8508
on status *vs.* class, 8481–8482
on stereotypes, 7972
and study of religion, emergence of, 8763
theodicy of, 9112, 9119
and Troeltsch (Ernst), 9365
on violence, 7249
on world religions, 9802
Weber, Otto, 3487
Webs and nets, 939, **9713**
Websites. *See also* Internet
as reference tools, 7642, 7644–7645
Webster, Nikki, in opening ceremony of Olympic Games (2000), 635, 637, 640, 641, 642, 646
Wedding Feast of Tara (Feis Temhra), 1492
Weddings, 5726. *See also* Marriage
in agricultural rituals, 189–190
Burmese, 5726
Christian, 5726
circumambulation in, 1797
Hera as goddess of, 3914
Javanese, 5726
Jewish, 5726
breaking of glass in, 7822
dancing at, 2137
domestic rituals of, 2397
phases of, 7821
seven blessings in, 7822
mirrors in, 6064
Muslim, 7827
Near Eastern, gender roles in, 3378
sheep symbolism and, 8310
Sikh Anand Karaj, 8397
Tarascan, 9001
tears in, 9026
trees in, 9339
of twins, 9419
in Unification, 9467
women's initiation as, 4486
of Zeus and Hera, 3914
Zoroastrian, 10000–10001
Weeks, Apocalypse of, 174–175, 431
Weeks, E. B., 3096
Weeks, Feast of. *See* Shavu'ot
Weeks, John H., 113
Weems, Renita, 79, 80
Weeping. *See* Tears
Weeramunda, A. J., 3588
wéeyekin system (Nez Perce), 6595–6596
Wegner, Judith Romney, 3352
Wegscheider, Julius, 9137
Weidman, Charles, 2158, 2159
Wei dynasty (China)
Buddhism in, 7165, 8994
temples of, 9046, 9047
Daoism in, 7267
Weigel, Gustave, 2686
Weigel, Valentin, 1006
Hermetism and, 3947
Weihnachtsfeier, Die (Schleiermacher), Christian beliefs in, 8160–8161
Weil, Simone, **9713–9714**
Gnosticism and, 3527, 3534
on knowledge, 5211
on warfare, 9682
on work, 9798–9799
Weiler, Gershon, 10061
Weiler, Ingomar, 3266
Weill, R., on synagogues, 8921
Weilu (deity), 2962
Weinberg, Stephen, 2658
Weiner, Annette B., 3480–3481
Weinreich, Otto, 181
Weinstein, Stanley, 1236, 1237, 1246–1247
Weintraub, Karl, 698
Weisberg, Richard, 5328–5329
Weisenfeld, Judith, 81
Wei Shao, Lady, on calligraphy, 1368
Weishi ("mere ideation" or "consciousness only") school, 1576, 1577, 1599–1600. *See also* Yogācāra school
Weiss, Johannes
on Jesus, 4846
on Jesus' preaching, 9364
on kingdom of God, 5151
in Religionsgeschichtliche Schule, 7707
Weiss, Leopold, on hospitality, 4140
Weiss, Me'ir, 869
Weiss, Paul, 6964
Weisse, Christian, 6234
Weissler, Chava, 3352
Wei state (China), Confucius in, 1934, 1935
Wei wu wei (nonintentional doing), in magical idealism, 2905
Wei zhi (History of the Wei Kingdom), Japan in, 4809
Weizmann, Chaim, Ginzberg (Asher) and, 3495, 3496
Welch, Holmes, 1314
Seidel (Anna) and, 8223
Welch, James, 3092, 7226
Welfare. *See also* Social welfare programs
in Baltic religion, deities of, 760–761, 769
in Catholicism, 9709
Han Fei Zi on, 3773
Well-being offering, in Israelite religion, 4746–4747
Wellesz, Egon, 6306
Wellhausen, Julius, **9714–9715**
on Abraham, 14
and Documentary Hypothesis, 883, 9233–9234
on head tax, 930
Islamic studies of, 4716
on Israelite polytheism, 3539
on priests, 5423
Wellman, Carl, on human solidarity, 4179–4180
Wells, H. G., on Aśoka, 556
Wells, in Celtic religion, 1486
severed heads associated with, 3807
Welsh myth. *See* Wales, literature of
Weltanschauung (worldview)
Catholic, 5261
cosmology and, 1992
Weltbild der Primitiven, Das (Graebner), 3648
Weltgeist (world spirit), 4447
Wen (Chinese emperor), 1583
Buddhist monks under, 1237
and Shelun school of Buddhism, 6992
Shōtoku influenced by, 4782
Wenceslas (king), Hus (Jan) and, 4233
Wenchang (patron saint), 1608, 1619
Wencheng (emperor), 5241
Wenders, Wim, 348
Wendes (pagan), 839
Wendland, Paul, 3532
Wends, Helmold of Bosau on, 8433–8434
Wensinck, A. J., 4717, **9715**
Wenwu dance, 6293
Wen Yido, 3339
Weor, Samael Aun, 3527
Werbmacher, Hannah Rachel, 9381
Werden des Gottesglaubens, Das (Söderblom), 113
Were (deity), in Gisu religion, 2575
Were-jaguar (image), 4311
Werewolves, 9784–9785
Wergild, 1464
Werner, Alice, 115
Werner, Karel, on Buddhist personality structure, 8548
Werner Zeitschrift für die Kunde des Morgenlandes (journal), 10056
Wesen des Christentums, Das (Harnack), historical criticism in, 3779
Wesensschau (intuition of essences), 7089
Wesler Colony (Venezuela), 1698
Wesley, Charles, **9715–9717**
Arminianism of, 493
hymns of, 5152, 5998
Methodism of, 5996–5997
Wesley, John, **9715–9717**
in American Methodism, 5997–5998
Arminianism of, 493
Asbury (Francis) and, 518
Augustine's influence on, 629
as clerical physician, 3846
Coke (Thomas) and, 1852
death of, 5998
deed poll of, 5998
on denomination, 2287
enthusiasm of, 2805–2806
on free will and predestination, 3204, 3208
Holiness movement and, 4082
on human perfectibility, 7040
Methodism of, 5996–5998
on ministry, orders of, 6045
and Moravians, 2887, 6191
preaching by, 5997
on religious experience, 7737
Salvation Army and, 8063
Wesleyan Church. *See* Holiness movement
Wesleyan Methodist Church. *See* Holiness movement
Wesleyan Methodist Connection, 5998
Wesleyan Methodist Connection of America, 4083
Wesleyan (Second Work) Pentecostalism, 7029, 7033
Wesley brothers, **9715–9717**
Wessinger, Catherine, 6525, 6526, 6533
West, Cornel, 79
on black theology, 78, 5441
West, Louis J., 6522
West, Michael, 380
West, Morris, 3080, 3084
West, Myrtice, 9626
West, Traci, 79

West Africa and West African religions, **9717–9722**. *See also* Akan religion; Diola religion; Fulbe religion; Yoruba religion; *specific countries and religions*
and African American religions, 65–66
African Independent Churches in, 103–105
ancestors in, 9718–9719
"well-disposed ones" (ancestral spirits) in, 4106
blood-pact rite in Benin, 3806
cannibalism in, 1404
Christianity
among Blacks, 1718
Crummell (Alexander), role of, 2073–2074
correspondence systems in, 3810
Danhom religion, possession and sacred time in, 7987
French occupation of, and Alinesitoue's prophecy, 261–262
hierodouleia (sacred prostitution) in, 3969
household spirits and gods in, 4106
illness and healing in
healer *vs.* witch in, 2100
health, conception of, 3817
herbal medicine, 3819
insects in, 4508
Islam, 4601–4603
architecture, 4608
cultural dynamics of, 4608
Fulbe and, 3228, 3229
jihād, 4604
scholars and, 4602–4603
secret societies and, 8213
spread of, 4601, 4607
Tajāni Sufism in, 8824
traditional cults and, 4609
women in, 4610
mediums (priests) in
medical diagnosis by, 3818
possession and sacred time for, 7987
myths in, 92, 97–98
predestination in, 89
religious studies in, departments of, 8793
Schweitzer (Albert) in, 8178–8179
secret societies in, 8213
soul, concept of, 1434
supreme beings in, pantheon of intermediaries and, 3816–3817
tobacco in, 9216–9217
transmigration in, 9326, 9327
twins in, 9414–9416
uniqueness of, 3816
Westcott, Catharine Augusta. *See* Tingley, Katherine
Westcott, William Wynn, on Hermetism, 3952
Westermann, Diedrich, 115, 116
Westermarck, Edward, 3476
on Berber religion, 2100
cultural evolutionism of, 2098
on cursing, 2098, 2101
Donner (Kai) and, 2421
Harva (Uno) and, 3782
Islamic studies of, 4718
on matriarchy, 3611
on relativism, 7686
Western Buddhism, **1186–1192**
children in, 6543
early, 1186–1188
gender in, 3333–3334
Horner (I. B.) as teacher in, 4130
immigrants and, 1187–1188, 1189, 1190
internationalization of, 1187, 1190–1191
literature of, 1187, 1189
meditation in, 1189
Shingon forms of, 8352–8353
spread of, 1189–1190
Western Desert language, of Mardu people, 5704
Western Esotericism, 2843, 6514
and New Age movement, 6497–6498
and Solar Temple, 6554
study of, 6527
Western Europe. *See also* Europe; *specific countries and religions*
Christianity in, **1687–1694**
beginnings of, 1688–1689
Eastern Christians in, 2589
medieval, 1689–1690
in modern period, 1692–1694
Nestorian Church in, 2584
Oriental Orthodox churches in, 2585
in Reformation, 1690–1692
study of religion in, **10076–10082**
institutions for, 10077–10078, 10080
on national traditions, 10080–10081
on nonofficial religions, 10079–10080
on origins and evolution of religion, 10077
politics and, 10079
reflexivity in, 10079
resources for, 10080
Westernization, and Islamic modernism, 6096–6097
Western religions and societies
congregations in, 7693
dance in, 2136, 2152
definitions of religion in, 7692–7695
kinship in, 5183
literature of, **5477–5484**
morality in, 7652
reflexivity in philosophy of, 7648
reincarnation in, 7680
religious communities in, 7692–7693
religious education in, 7731
rites of passage in, 7800, 7802
Western Samoa. *See* Oceania and Oceanic religions
Western Sioux. *See* Lakota religion
Western Wall (Jerusalem)
pilgrimage to, 7161
as sacred space, 9261, vol. 5 color insert
Western Zhou dynasty (China), 1583, 1624
law in, 5352
West Indies. *See* Caribbean region
West London Synagogue, 7669
Westman, Robert S., on Hermetism and Yates (Frances), 3954
Westminster Confession
on Apocrypha, 881
authority of, 2055
on free will and predestination, 3208
in Puritanism, 7521
Synod of Dort and, 2044
Weston, Jessie L., 3651
Westphalen, Ludwig von, 5744
Westphalia, Judaism in, 7668
Westphalia, Peace of (1648), 6973
Lutheranism accepted in, 5539
West Syrian Church. *See* Syriac Orthodox Church of Antioch
Weyer, Johann, 9773
Weyland, Petra, 1517–1518
Whakanoa rituals, 5680–5681
Whakapapa (oral genealogies), 5682–5683
Whale, John Seldon, 5479
Whales
in Arctic religions
ceremonies for, 471
Inuit, 4527
in Australian Indigenous myths, 3392
Wharton, Annabelle, 4342
Whatcoat, Richard, 264
What Congress and Gandhi Have Done to the Untouchables (Ambedkar), 286
Whately, Richard, 6105, 6510
Whatever Became of Sin? (Menninger), 7487
What I Believe (Tolstoy), 9220
What is Christianity? (Harnack), 6104, 6106
"What Is Happening to Our Beautiful Land," 2613
What Is Pragmatism? (Pratt), 7366
Wheat. *See also* Bread
in ritual meals, 3163
Wheatley, Paul, **9722–9724**
on ceremonial centers, 7984
on Chinese urbanization, 1803
on Mesopotamian ceremonial centers, 453–454
on sacred space, 8428
on shrines and urbanization, 7156
Wheeler, Mortimer, archaeological work of, 5111
Wheeler, Tessa, archaeological work of, 5111
Wheeler-Howard Act (1934) (United States), 7302
Wheel of doctrine, in Yogācāra Buddhism, 9897
Wheel of Existence
as cosmic vision, vol. 3 color insert
maṇḍalas and, 5645
Wheel of the Year, 7829, 9730–9731
Wheels. *See also* Cakras; Circle
as Viṣṇu symbol, 4325
in Buddhism, wheel of life, 5448
in Celto-Roman art, 1481
in Indian religions, as symbol of universality, 1350, 1351
in Jainism, time and, 2025
When a Great Tradition Modernizes (Singer), 4448
When Religion Gets Sick (Oates), 7486
Whinfield, E. H., on al-Shabistarī, 8262
Whipping, in Yurupary cult, 9919
Whirligigs, 1840
Whirling Dervishes, 2140, 7935, 7936
in Bektashī Sufism, 8823
Whirlpool, monsters and, 6163
Whirlwind, in North American Indian religions, 6651
Whistles, Mesoamerican, 6268
White (color)
supreme beings as, 5760
symbolism of, 1860, 1861, 1862
in visionary experiences, 9612
in winter carols, 9745
White, Alma B., 6536
White, David Gordon, 5589, 7083, 8987, 8990, 8992
White, David Manning, 7321
White, Deborah Gray, 10037
White, Ellen Gould, 6558, **9724–9725**
Koresh (David) on, 5237
prophecy of, 1036
Seventh-day Adventism and, 8235–8237
White, Hayden, 10044
White, Isobel M., 664, 688, 3391
White, James
prophecy of, 1036
Seventh-day Adventism and, 8235–8236+
White, James Boyd, on law and literature, 5356–5357
White, Leslie, 453

White, Lynn
anthropocentrism criticized by, 2608
on Christian environmental impact, 2627, 2649
Earth First! influenced by, 2562
on religion in ecology, 2614
White, Patrick, 3081, 3082, 3083, 3084
White, William, 352
White Americans
exclusion from African American religion, 67
Nation of Islam on, 6419
White Angels, in Raëlian religion, 7598–7599
White bear, 807
White Book of Rhydderch, 1480, 5545
White Buffalo Calf Woman, **9725–9726**
White Buffalo Woman, Lakota myth of, 6662
White Cloud, 3155
White Cloud Abbey (Daoist), 2201
White Crucifixion (Chagall), 4348
White Deer Hollow academy, 1901
White Drink, 1564
White Elephant (Xiangshan) Academy, 5541
Whitefeminism, 3304
Whitefield, George, 2698, **9726–9727**
Great Awakening and, 1710
and Wilkinson (Jemima), 6534
White Goddess (Graves), 9774
Whitehead, Alfred North, **9727–9728**
aesthetics of, 49–50
atheism and, 584
on Buddhist metaphysics, 51, 6965
"cosmic epochs" hypothesis of, 9281
dependent co-origination doctrine and, 8859
on God, 3448, 3559–3560, 7423, 9284
on God's compassion, 9283
on individual religion, 3901
influence on Frye (Northrop), 3224
on knowledge, 5210–5211
on logic, 5497
metaphysics of, 5991, 7121
on monotheism, 6161
Newman's (John Henry) influence on, 6511
pantheism of, 2664, 6962, 6963, 6964
on paradox, 6988
on Plato, 7110
prehension theory of, 9282
in process theology, 2650
science and religion and, 2658
recovery of dialogue between religion and philosophy by, 7120
on Reformation, 7447
Whitehead, Henry, 8978
Whitehouse, O. C., 899
White Huns. *See* Ephthalites
White Jade (St. Denis), 2157
White Lady (prehistoric goddess), 7377
White lily, in Greek mythology, 3135
White Lotus movement, 3155
Huiyuan and, 4156
millenarianism of, 6040
aesthetic of, 6030
teachings of, 1606–1607
White Lotus Sectarianism, 2188
White Lotus Society, 4922, 4924
White magic
in Agta religion, 6455
in Islam, 5586–5587
White Monkey (epic figure), 6152
White Painted Woman (divine mother), 2462
White Path
in Cherokee religion, 1564–1565
in Pure Land Buddhism, 8299
White Path's Rebellion, 1565, 6666
White Sea Karelians, 5092, 5093
White Shrine of Jerusalem, 3198
White Supremacism, Christian Identity movement, **1657–1660**
White Tantric Yoga, Yogi Bhajan and, 3878
Whitfield, George, 66
Whitman, Walt, Swedenborgianism and, 8903
Whitney, William Dwight, 4449
Whittemore, Robert, 6964
Whittington, Dick, 1464
"Why Women Need the Goddess" (Christ), 9100
Wibert of Ravenna. *See* Clement III
Wicasa wakan (holy men), 5297
Wicca, 6471, 6560, **9728–9732**
beliefs of, 6471
in Earth First!, 2563
and feminine sacrality, 3021–3022
in feminist spirituality movement, 9788
literature of, 6471
rites of passage in, transformation in, 7859
ritual magic in, 9729
rituals in, 9730–9731
seasonal, 7829
sexual magic in, 8251
in thealogy, 9099
witchcraft and, 9774–9775
Wiccan Rede, 9731
Wicca Study Group, 9730
Wichmann, Yrjö, 3112
Wichtigsten Instanzen gegen die Graf-Wellhausensche Hypothese, Die (Hoffmann), 869
Wicoh'an Wakan Sakowin (Seven Sacred Rites), 5296
Wicomb, Zoë, 3088
Widdershins, circling in, 1796
Widengren, Geo, **9732–9734,** 10081
on apostles, 436
and Bleeker (C. Jouco), 979
on flight, human fascination with, 3127
on the Flood in Iranian mythology, 2964
on Gnosticism, 3508, 3514, 3535
on heavenly book concept, 8195
historiography of, 4042
on Mandaean religion, 5639
and Mithraism, 6088
in Myth and Ritual school, 6382
Nilsson (Martin P.) on, 6622
on phenomenology of religion, 7086, 7089
preanimism criticized by, 7373
Widows and widowers
ablutions for, 11
Christian, asceticism of, 7722–7723
Israelite laws on, 4736
living, cremation of, 9170
in Melanesian religions, 5838
Muslim, 7827
provisions for, in rabbinic Judaism, 7589
widow burning (*See* Sati)
Wiebe, Donald, 7745
Wiederlegung der Abgotterey und nichtigen Aberglaubens (Einhorn), 768
Wieger, Léon, 1633
Wieman, Henry Nelson
atheism and, 584
liberalism of, 6106
Wiener, Margaret J., 9297
Wiener, Norbert, on cybernetics, 2111
Wieschhoff, H. A., on left and right symbolism, 5394
Wiesel, Elie, 2950, 3059, 4985
Wiesner, Merry, 3360
Wigand, Johann, Canisius's opposition to, 1402
Wigglesworth, Michael, 7520
Wigman, Mary, 2160
Wigs, Hasidic Jewish women and, 1832
Wijewardena, D., 1100
Wikander, Stig, **9734–9737**
on *Mahābhārata,* 4463, 5595
on war bands, 4462, 10079
Wiko Makishi masquerade dances, 2141
Wilāyah. See Walāyah
Wilber, Ken, 7478
Wilberforce, Samuel, 6243
Wilbert, Johannes, on tobacco, 9216, 9217, 9218, 9219
Wilbour Papyrus, 2709
Wilcox, Ella Wheeler, 6584
Wild, Stephen, 674
Wilde, Oscar, 5864
Wilder, Amos, 5477
Wilderness
in African myths, 98–99
encounter with divine in, 2606
vs. gardens, in Islam, 3282
in Oceanic religions, ghosts in, 2006
Wilderness gatherings, of Earth First!, 2563
Wilderness Society, 2562
Wild Honey (ancestor), 4306
Wild hunt, 9771
Wildness, virginity and, 9603
Wild Tigers Corps (Thailand), 1141
Wile, Douglas, on androgyny, 8243
Wilfrid (bishop), 6943
Wilhelm II (emperor of Germany), 790, 2263
Wilhelm, Richard, 1635
Wili, W., 3041
Wilkins, Charles, 4446
Wilkinson, Jemima, 6534
Will
in Calvinism, ethics and, 1655
free (*See* Free will)
of God
in Ashkenazic Hasidism, 542
in Islam, 2064, 3563, 6233
and morality, 6183
salvation and, 8529
in Sikhism, 32, 8394
Thomas Aquinas on, 3556
of Jesus, in monothelitism, 5792, 5793
Mullā Ṣadrā on, 6233
in Ordo Templi Orientis (OTO), 8251
Will, Édouard, 6138
Willard, Frances, Smith (Hannah Whitall) and, 8446
Willard, Samuel, 2287
Willey, Gordon, 452
William, Michael A., 947
William II (William Rufus) (king of England), Anselm and, 372
William de la Mare, 9164
William Durandus of Mede, conciliarist theory of, 2042
William of Aquitaine, 821
William of Auvergne
on Hermetism, 3945

William of Auvergne
continued
Ibn Sīnā criticized by, 4275
on magic, 5578
William of Champeaux
Abelard (Peter) studying under, 7
realism of, 6644
William of Conches, on nature, 6432
William of Moerbeke, 6475
Aristotle translated by, 5990
William of Ockham, 3183, **9737–9738**
on existence of God, 7422
on free will and predestination, 3203, 3207
on knowledge, 5205
metaphysics of, 5990
on problem of universals, 6644–6645
theology of, 9136
William of Rubrouck
historiography of, 4038
on scripture, 8197
William of Saint-Armour
Albertus Magnus and, 232
Thomas Aquinas and, 9161
William of Saint-Thierry
Abelard (Peter) opposed by, 7
on mystical union, 6337
mysticism of, 6349
on wounded heart, 3883
Williams, Charles, 2472
Sayers (Dorothy) and, 8142–8143
Williams, Daniel D., 2308
Williams, Delores, 79
on story of Hagar, 3036–3037
Williams, Demetrius, 80
Williams, Eric, 67
Williams, Francis E., 6801
on cargo cults, 1416
on masks, 5768
Williams, George Hunston, on Anabaptist shunning, 2105
Williams, Peter, 68
Williams, Ralph Vaughan, 6313
Williams, Roger, **9738–9740**
in Baptist church, 784
exiled from Massachusetts Bay Colony, 784, 7520
Williams, Terry Tempest, nature writing of, as spiritual autobiography, 703
Williams-Hogan, Jane, on Swedenborgianism, 8905
Williamson, Robert W., 991
William the Jew of Pisaro. *See* Ebreo, Guglielmo
Willibrord (bishop), 1018, **9740**
Willis, Darlene, 676
Willis, Jan, 6536
Willis, Janice, 9190
Will-o'-the-wisp, 2952
Willow Creek church (Chicago), 2893
Willow tree, 9337
Wills, David, 75
Wilmans, Helen, 6584
Wilmore, Gayraud
anthology by, 79
on black churches after Civil War, 69
on black nationalism, 79
on black theology, 77, 78, 79, 965, 5441
Wilson, Bryan, 3233
on charisma, 1544–1545
on open *vs.* closed systems of thought, 5567
on religious values, 8472
on sects, 2084, 3923
classification system for, 6521
Wilson, Bryan R., 102
on revival and renewal activities, 7789
Wilson, Colin, 6780
Wilson, David, 7850
Wilson, Edward O., 2916, 2919–2920
sociobiology of, 7850, 8474, 10043
Wilson, Godfrey, 5568
Wilson, H. H., 4446, 8988
Wilson, Jack. *See* Wovoka
Wilson, John, 9995, 10053
Wilson, Monica, 5568
Wilson, Richard, 5928
Wilson, Robert McLachalan, 3533
Wimber, John, 7031
Wimbush, Vincent, 80
Wimmer, Boniface, 822
Winch, Peter, 5568
Geertz (Clifford) and, 8499–8500
Winchester, Elhanan, 9470
Winchester Profession, 9470
Winckelmann, Johann Jakob, 424
Winckler, Hugo, 3487
Wind
in Buddhism, destruction by, 2028
in Haitian Vodou, spirits of, 1433
Āyurveda *(vāta)*, 3854–3855
in North American Indian religions, 6651
Athapaskan, **575–576**
iconography of, 4309
Navajo, 575–576, 6442
Wind, Sun of, in Aztec calendar, 1357
Windelband, Wilhelm
on "holy" as noun, 4096
on knowledge, 5207
Windigo, in Anishinaabe religion, 368–369
Windigo monster, cannibalism and, 1403
Wind Old Men (deities), 5119
Windsor, Gerard, 3084
Wine. *See also* Alcoholic beverages
in Anthesteria festival, 374–375
in Christianity, in Eucharist, 848, 987, 1040, 1041, 3171
in Greek religion
Dionysian rites, 1459
Dionysos as god of, 2356
as libation, 5433
in Indo-European religions, 4455
Iranian story on origin of, 848
in Judaism
kashrut laws on, 5107
on Passover, 7004
in orgy, 6865
in West African libations, 9719
Winfrith. *See* Boniface
Winged disk, migration of symbol of, 3537
Winged Lions, Temple of the (Petra), 6386
Winged Serpent, The: An Anthology of American Indian Prose and Poetry (Astrov), 7224
Wings
in angel iconography, 346, vol. 8 color insert
images of, vol. 8 color insert
Wings of Desire (film), 348
Winkelman, Michael, on shamanism, 8275
Winkte, 3410
Winnebago tribe (North America)
ballgame played by, 753
cosmology of, 6680
Earthmaker (deity) in, 8870
Medicine rite of, 6681, 6684
narratives of, types of, 6681
in Native American Church, 10054
Prophet movement of, 6666, 6667, 6686
religious societies of, 6685
sacred clowns of, 6686
secret societies in, 7719
tricksters of, 9351
Winnicott, D. W.
on games, 3265
object-relations theory of, 7478
transitional phenomena of, 7483–7484
Winograd, Terry, 510
Winroth, Anders, on Roman law, 5336–5337
Winston, David, 900
Winter counts, Native American, vol. 2 color insert
Winter solstice
in Chinese religion
Dongjie festival, 1643
emperor offerings at, 8005
jiao sacrifice, 1591
in Christianity, Christmas associated with, 1743, 9814
in Hindu religious year, 4016
in Northern Europe, 8836
songs of, **9740–9746**
in Totonac religion, 9254
Winthrop, John
civil religion and, 1814
as governor of Massachusetts, 7520
Winti religion, 126–127
Christianity distinct from, 126
gods of, 126
Winton, Tim, 3082
Wintun religion (California)
bears in, 809
cosmogonic myths of, 5198
Wipf, Karl, 5926
Wiradthuri people, All-Father of, 265
Wired (Joy), 512
Wiri (ceremonial event), 9695
Wirikúta (sacred site), pilgrimage to
healing rites in, 2559
in Huichol religion, 4153
Wirtschaft und Gesellschaft (Weber), 1544, 5383
meaning context and communal action in, 7971–7972
Wirtz, Paul, 725
Wisara, U, 1140
Wisdom, **9746–9754**. *See also* Wisdom literature
Blavatsky (H. P.) on, 977
in Buddhism
compassion and, 2630
engaged Buddhism, 2788
goddesses of, 4330
Mañjuśrī associated with, 5675
Bulgakov (Sergei) on, 1320
in Christianity, 5502
of God, 3545–3546
Jesus identified with, 3545
Servetus (Michael) on, 8232
in *Ecclesiastes,* 2600
evil and, question of, 2903–2904
factors of, 7109
al-Fārābī on, 7193
feminine symbolism of, 335–336
fountains and, 3178
in Gnosticism, 3509–3510, 3517, 9751
in Greek thought (*See* Sophia)
in Hebrew thought (*See Ḥokhmah*)
inner eye of, 2942–2943
in Judaism, 5502
Logos and, 5502–5503
in North American Indian traditions, oral tradition and, 6425–6426
of Oðinn, 6808–6809
owl as symbol of, 6936
personified, 9757, 9764 (*See also* Sophia)
Plato on, 7109
rejection of, 9750
sacred *vs.* profane and, 7973
Saturn and, 8428
of serpents, 8457–8458
of Socrates, 8503
of Solomon, 8513
in Sufism, gnosis *(mar'rifah)* in, 8819–8820

Suhrawardī on, 8827
systematic (*See* Philosophy)
terminology, 9746–9747
theology of, 5502–5503
of water, 9702
Wisdom, John, 307, 5499
Wisdom divination, 2371–2372, 2374
Wisdom literature, **9754–9766**
in Apocrypha, 899–900
biblical, 884–885, **9754–9762**
Job, 4930–4933
characteristics of, 9754–9755
Egyptian, 2722–2723
in Pseudepigrapha, 902, 904
temptation in, 9070–9071
theodicy in, 9115
theoretical perspectives on, **9762–9766**
Wisdom of Amenemope, 2723
Wisdom of Solomon, 899
afterlife in, 152
audience of, 900
content of, 900
Enoch in, 2803
ghosts in, 3475
idolatry in, 4359
language of, 896
revelation in, 7775
Sophia in, 4079, 8522
tradition in, 9757
wisdom in, 9750, 9759
personified, 9757, 9759
Wisdom Site in Places (Basso), 2611
Wise, Carroll, 7487
Wise, Isaac M., 7582, **9766**
and Reform Judaism, 7670
Wise, John, **9766–9767**
Wise, Stephen S., 7671, **9767**
Wiseman, Eddie, 9411
Wise Women
in Canaanite religion (Kotharatu), 1395, 1396
in Germanic religion (Voelva), 8295
Wishart, George, 5212
Wissenschaft der Juden, in Jewish studies, 4875
Wissenschaft des Judentums (scholarly study of Judaica), 4863, 4875–4879. *See also* Jewish studies
concept of development in, 4876
Hirsch (Samson Raphael), opposition of, 4023
and history, modern awareness of, 4059
institutional standing of, 4878–4879
Judaism defined in, 4969–4970
in modern Jewish thought, 4902, 4905–4906
Rossi (ʿAzaryah dei), influence of, 4041
Wissler, Clark, 6655, 6671
Wissowa, Georg, 2993, **9767–9768**
on *flamines maiores* and *flamines minores,* 3125
on Isis cult, 4558
on Roman religion, 7893, 7896
Wištāsp (king), 9934
Witch cleansing, Kinjikitile on, 5181
Witchcraft, Oracles, and Magic among the Azande (Evans-Pritchard), 2895, 5567, 5571
"Witchcraft and Sorcery: Taxonomy versus Dynamics" (Turner), 9405
Witchcraft Today (Gardner), 9728–9729
Witch craze, 9772–9773
Witch Dance (Wigman), 2160
Witch doctors. *See* Shamanism
Witches and witchcraft, **9768–9781**. *See also* Necromancy
accusations of, 9773
affliction in, 56–57
in African religions, **9776–9781**
accusations of, 90, 3402, 7755
in Akan religion, 215
in Ashanti religion, 7755
in Bete religion, 7755
in central Bantu religion, 1506, 1509, 1511
Christianity and, 1721
concepts of, 90
in East African religions, 2569–2570
in Edo religion, 2697
healer *vs.* witch, 2100
holistic healing and, 3820
Hyakyusa, 6771–6772
illness and, 3817
in Kongo religion, 5221
in Luba religion, 5524
in Lugbara religion, 5528
in Lumpa church movement, 5409
misfortunes caused by, 90
ndoki in Kongo religion, 2001
in northeast Bantu religion, 2577–2578
in Southern Africa, 8659–8660
Turner (Victor) in, 9405
witch-finding movements in, 1511, 8660
anthropological concepts of, 9768–9770
in Baltic religion, 775
cannibalism and, 1404
cats as familiars of, 1463
concepts of, **9768–9776**
African, 90
definition of, 9768
detecting, 9777, 9779
diabolical, 9770–9774
neopaganism and, 9775
disease attributed to, 9769
in Eastern European magic, 5582
in Europe, 9770–9773
spells in, 8677
and fetishism, 3043
foxes associated with, 3181
in Germanic sagas, 8025
Hekate associated with, 3899
as heretics, 2279, 2280
involuntary, as magic, 5570
in Israelite religion, laws on, 4737
vs. magic, 5570
in Mapuche religion, 5689
mares associated with, 4134
meetings in (*See* Sabbat)
in Mesopotamian religion
counter-curse formulae, 2098, 2102
incantations in, 2100
modern, 9774–9775
and morality, 6186–6187
Neopagan (*See also* Wicca)
Crowley (Aleister) and, 2071, 2072
initiation in, 7829
rites of passage in, 7830
in North American Indian religions
of California and Intermountain region, 6714
of Northwest Coast, 6708
Shawnee myths of origin of, 6684–6685
in Oceanic religions, 3397, 6787
orgy and, 6871–6872
persecution of (*See also* Witch hunts and trials)
in Middle Ages, 6452
in Polynesian religions, 7308
possession used in, 2930
in Russian folklore, 727
schools of interpretation of, 9770
seeking encounters with Satan, 2279
in Slavic religion, 8437
society and, 9773–9774
vs. sorcery, 57, 9768, 9778
soul projection by, 8533
in South American Indian religions, forces of light *vs.*, 2013
in Sumerian religion, 9494
Talmudic references to, 3158–3159
Witches' Sabbath, sexuality and, 8249–8250
Witches' Way, The (Farrar and Farrar), 9730
Witch hunts and trials
in Africa
by British, 8696
in southern Africa, 8660
in Christianity, 3360
diabolical pact theory and, 8865
in Hungary, 4226
Inquisition in, 4499–4500
sacrilege and, 8013
in Salem, Massachusetts, 2930, 5372, 7755, 9774
Satanism scare and, 8126
scapegoat mechanism in, 8145
witches' Sabbath and, sexuality and, 8249–8250
With a Great Master in India (Johnson), plagiarism of, by Twitchell (Paul), 2602
Witherspoon, Gary, 5762, 6442, 6672
Witness (Bennett), 832
Witnesses
to marriage rituals, 5726
martyrs as, 5737
Witóto religion (Amazon), 2311
deities of, 8576–8577, 8583, 8870
knot symbolism of, 5198
origin of agriculture in, 8590
Witsen, Nicolaes, 3110
Witte, Sergei, 7203
Witte, Vilija, 765
Wittgenstein, Ludwig, **9781–9782**
analytic philosophy of, 306–307, 308
Bakhtin (M. M.) and, 741
epistemology and, 2819
on family resemblance, 6633
on Frazer (James G.), 381, 2916
Heidegger, affinities with, 3935
hermeneutics and, 3930, 3935, 8499
on iconography, 4297
on knowledge, 5210
on language, 7112, 7115–7116, 7119, 7127, 7375
on liturgy, 5492
logical positivism and, 5498, 5500
metaphysics of, 5991
on mind-body dualism, 4163
on Śaṅkara, 6144
structuralism and, 8759
Wittig, Monique, 3027, 3029, 3030
Wit Xōn (deity). *See* Water King
Witzen, N., 5709
Wives, in goddess worship, 3588–3589
Wiwanyang Wacipi (Sun Dance), 5297
Wiyot (deity), 6713
WJBB radio station (Tampa), religious broadcasting on, 7710
WJBT radio station (Chicago), religious broadcasting on, 7710
Woagaia cults, 672
Woagaia-Jinimin movement, 672–673

Wobbermin, Georg, on knowledge, 5207, 5208
Wodan (*Woðan[az]) (deity), 3450, 3451
Woden (deity), 2393, 6943. *See also* Óðinn
Wodoy (Spotted Nightjar), 9460
Wodziwob (Indian prophet), 6718
  Ghost Dance introduced by, 3473, 5973
Wok Meri movement, 3398
Wolf. *See* Wolves
Wolf, Arthur, on ancestor worship, 322
Wolf, Eric, 3152
Wolf, Immanuel, in *Wissenschaft des Judentums,* 4874
Wolf, Lucien, 4879
"Wolf 'Aunt" (Kenny), 7226
Wolfe, Peter, 2478
Wolfenden Report (1957), 5369
Wolff, Christian, **9782–9783**
  on dualism, 2505
  in German Enlightenment, 2797
  metaphysics of, 7110
  ontology of, 6830, 7110
  Reimarus (Hermann Samuel) influenced by, 7675
  Spinoza (Baruch) and, 8685
Wolfram, Stephen, 510
  on cybernetics, 2111
Wolfram von Eschenbach, 3652–3653
  poetry of, 7219
Wolfson, Elliot, 3350
  on phallic patterns, 7080
  on Qabbalah and the feminine, 8243
Wolfson, Harry A., 5617
  Smith (Morton) and, 8448
Wollo Oromo religion (Ethiopia), 2573
Wollstonecraft, Mary, 811
  theological ideas influencing, 3297, 3360
Wolof language, literature in, 3086
Wolters, O. W., on "men of prowess," 8643
Wolterstorff, Nicholas, 501
Wolves, **9783–9785**
  in Arctic religions, 471
  in Geto-Dacian religion, 3466
  in Greek mythology, 7783
  in Indo-European religions, 4455–4456
  in North American Indian religions, 9355
    Koyukon, 6676
    Ojibwa, 6660, 6661
  in Scandinavian religions, 3246
Womack, Craig, 3090
Womack, Mari, on sports and religion, 8725–8726
Woman, Church, and State (Gage), 3252, 3310
"Woman Hanging from a Thirteenth Floor Window" (Harjo), 7225
Womanist theology, 966, 3035, 5441
  body in, 4167
Womanist thought, 9791
  and African American religions, 79, 10040
Woman's Bible, The (Stanton), 1570, 3035, 8731
  Gage (Matilda Joslyn) as contributor to, 3252, 3310
Woman's Christian Temperance Union, Smith (Hannah Whitall) and, 8446
Woman Shaman, 2863
Woman's National Liberal Union, Gage (Matilda Joslyn) in, 3252
Womanspirit Rising (Christ and Plaskow), female divine in, 4166
Woman Warrior, The (Kingston), 701
"Woman with the Horn," 9906
Womb. *See also* Yoni
  death and damnation associated with, 4165–4166
  earth as, 2557
  memories from, 2557–2558
Womb Maṇḍala, 5608, 5644, 9962–9963
Womb World Mandala. See Garbhakośadhātu (Womb World) *maṇḍala*
Women. *See also* Feminine sacrality; Feminism; Gender
  abducted by dragons, 2431–2432
  in Acehnese religion, 26
  affliction among, 56, 57, 58
  in African American religions
    in abolitionism, 10037–10038
    Christian, 10037–10039
    churches established by, 10037, 10039
    in civil rights movement, 10039–10040
    as educators, 10038
    as leaders, 10036, 10037–10040
    as missionaries, 10037–10038
    in music, 10039
    Muslim, 10037, 10039–10040
    roles of, 67, 70, 10036, 10037
    and slave religion, 10037
    studies by, 76, 80–81, 10040
    studies on, 10036–10037
  in African religions, **3400–3406**
    creation myths of, 85
    Dogon, 2391
    exclusion in central Bantu religion, 1510
    Luba, vol. 13 color insert
    and moon, 3971
    possession of, 2568
    in Pygmy religions, 3971, 7524, 7525
    ritual state rectified by, 2576
    secret societies of, vol. 6 color insert
    as subordinate, 1799
    West African, 9721
    zaar cult, 107
    Zulu, 10009, 10010
  in Afro-Brazilian religions, 10027
    Candomblé, 122–123
  in afterlife, 136
  in agriculture
    myths of, 191–192
    rites of, as earth mother, 2558–2559
    rituals of, 189–190
    women as inventors of, 5281
  in Amazonian Quechua religions, 283
  in Andean religion, Pachamama and, 8601
  ascetics, 6757 (*See also* Nuns)
    nudity of, 6740–6741
  as *gurūs,* 3715
  in ashrams, 546
  astrology favored by, 2372
  attitudes toward, nature devalued by, 2620
  in Australian Indigenous religions, 638–639, 840–841, **3389–3395**
    as healers, 3874
    history of study of, 682, 686–687, 690
    Kaberry (Phyllis M.) on, 5050–5051
    Mardu, 5705
    Ngukurr, 6598, 6599–6600
    secrecy among, 649–651
    as subordinate, 1799
  base communities and reinventing the church, 1776
  beauty of, 810, 811, 812–813
  in Bemba religion, 817, 818
  blood of, in Wawalag myth, 9705–9706
  body symbolism and, 4163–4167
  in Bornean religion, 1022
  in Buddhism, 3033, **3330–3335,** 6536
    advances for, 6757
    Chinese, 3343–3344
    Himalayan, 1233
    Horner (I. B.) on, 4129
    in *saṃghas,* 8073
    international association of, 6762
    Japanese, 1180, 1183, 2410, 2411, 3346, 3348, 4785
    monasticism of, 6130
    pilgrimage of, 7168
    salvation of, 7084
    sanctuary access of, 9830
    Sri Lankan, 2313–2314
    in Tendai school, 9076
    in Thailand, 9095
    Theravāda Buddhism, 9146, 9147, 9152
    Tibetan, 1156, 3332–3333, 5557–5558, 7168
    Vajrayāna (Tantric) Buddhism, 1219–1220, 1221
    Zen, 9948
  in Burmese religion, 1331
  calligraphy by, 1369, 1371
  in Caribbean religions, 10027–10028
  in Catharism, equality of, 2748
  in Celtic religion, **3387–3389**
  changing standards for, 8485
  in Chinese religion, **3338–3345**
    Buddhism, 1595
    Confucian "woman's Way," 1591
    in domestic observances, 2407
    qi cultivation and, 3862
  Chisungu, dances of, 2138
  in Christianity, **3356–3364**
    African American, 966
    androcentrism and, 334–336
    Anglicanism, ordination of, 353
    asceticism of, 7722–7723
    in Australia and New Zealand, 1734, 1735–1736
    Benedictine, 822, 1018
    Christian Science, 1747, 2695, 6535
    Congregationalism, 1939
    discrimination against, 2687–2688
    Dominican, 2412, 2414, 6135
    Episcopalianism, ordination of, 68, 353, 7404
    evangelical Christianity, 1755
    Franciscan, 3183
    fundamentalism, 6844–6845
    in Jesus Movement, 4853
    justified domination of, 2647
    Latin American Protestant churches, 6579
    in monasticism, 6134–6135 (*See also* Nuns)
    music of, 6308
    in Orthodox Church, as deacons, 2593
    Pentecostalism, 70
    Protestant, 6765
    Protestant Fundamentalism, clothing and modesty, 1832
    public ministry of, Holiness movement and, 4083
    Quaker, 6533–6534, 7547

Ramabai (Pandita) on, 7610
Roman Catholicism, 7889, 7891
Russian Orthodox Church, restrictions on, 6115
subordination of, 3252
in Unity, 9472
virginity, notions of, 4164
in Christ the Saviour Brotherhood, 4103
cicatrization of, 1003
circumcision of, in Islam, 7828
conception dreams of, 2489
confession of adultery, 1884
in Confucianism, 3340–3341, 3346
conversion, experience of, 1972
corpse preparation by, 2242
creativity of, 10039
curses and, 2100
dancing by
in Chisungu society, 2138
in Hamadsha society, 2138
in Gẹlẹdẹ society, 2141
recreational, 2141–2142
in Yemenite Jewish communities, 2149
in Daoism, 3341–3342
Celestial Masters, 2180, 2192
nuns, 6758
Quanzhen, 2186
death associated with, 4165
in Diola religion, as prophets, 261, 262
domestic sphere and, 4107
dress codes and, 1831, 1832, 1834–1835
Druze, 2502
in ecstatic cults, 2679
ecumenical focus on, 2686, 2687–2688
education for (*See* Education, for women)
in Egyptian religion, 2715, **3375–3381**
in Ramessid burial texts, 2708
study of, 2732
in enthusiastic movements, 2805
eremitism of, 2825, 2827–2828
Etruscan, 2871–2872
exclusion of (*See* Androcentrism)
feminine sacrality of, 3020–3021
and feminist spirituality movement, 3022
Finnish, 802–803
foxes associated with, 3182
in funerary rites, involvement of, 2242
vs. gender, 3296, 3330
in Gnosticism, 6867
goddess cults and, 8243
in Grail movement, 3653–3654
in Greek novels, 3055–3056
in Greek religion, **3375–3381**
Artemis and, 506, 507–508
in Dionysos cult, 2358
inferior position of, 3677
as priestesses in Demeter cult, 2270–2271
as sexual possessions, 7079
in Greek society, 9602–9603
position of, 4298–4299
Hamadsha, dances of, 2138
in Hawaiian religion, taboos and exclusion in, 3799
in Hellenistic religions, **3375–3381**
in Hinduism, **3318–3326**
ascetics, 6758
duties of, 2403, 2404
environmental activism of, 2623
goddess worship and, 3609, 3613
Ramabai (Pandita) on, 7610
Ramakrishna on, 10067
as renunciates, 8020, 8094
rites of passage of, 7817
rural traditions, 4435
in Swaminarayan and BAPS movements, 8890, 8892
Vivekananda on, 10090–10091
widow burning (*See* Sati)
homosexuality of (*See* Lesbianism)
humor and, 4198–4199, 4212
in Inca religion, 4411–4412
infertility of, 7078, 7080
in Gẹlẹdẹ society, dances of, 2141
initiation rituals of (*See* Initiation, women's)
in Omotokyō, 4790
in Raëlian religion, 7598–7599
in Reiyūkai Kyōdan, 7862
in International Society for Krishna Consciousness, 4523, 6536
in *zār* cults, 2933
in Islam, **3364–3371**
in Africa, 4609–4610
in Canada, 4686
clothing and, 1831, 1833, 1835
an concept of *fitnah* (disorder), 8055
in domestic observances, 2401–2402
duties of, 2401, 2402
folk, 3163
ḥājj of, 7156, 7158
humor and, 4212
in Qur'ān, 6224
in *ṭarīqah,* 9007
laws on, 4564, 4573
majority age for, 4705
in mosques, 3369, 6210
progressive Islam, 6098, 6099
Rābi'ah al-'Adawīyah as example for, 7591
ṣalāt (prayer) and, 8055
socializing, 2402
in South Asia, 4652
in Southeast Asia, 4666–4667, 4670
in United States, 4687, 4688
zayārāt pilgrimages by, 3834–3835
in Israelite religion, 5420
excluded from Temple, 934–935
laws on, 4731, 4732–4734, 4736
as prophets, 7435
in Jainism, **3326–3330,** 4765, 4768
salvation of, 7084
in Japanese religions, **3345–3350**
Buddhism, 1180, 1183, 2410, 2411, 3346, 3348
in Shintō, 8361
in new religious movements, 8695
as shamans, 4795
in Jehovah's Witnesses, 4820–4821, 4823
Jesus accompanied by, 4849
in Judaism, **3350–3356**
bat mitzvah and, 1962, 7820–7821
clothing in, 1831–1832
Conservative Judaism, 1959, 1962, 1963–1964
in domestic observances, 2397
Gamli'el the Elder on, 3270
Haddasah (women's Zionist organization), 8941
Hasidism, 5611–5612
Kochi Judaism, 5005
limitations on, 3541
Marrano, 5719, 5720
miqveh used by, 6047
in Mishnah, 6066
naming of, 7819
ordination of, 1963–1964, 3354–3355, 7582, 7637
as prophets, 3541
as rabbis, 7582
reciting tekhines, 9036–9038
Reconstructionist Judaism, 5082, 7637
Reform Judaism, 7666
rites of passage of, 7819
Schenirer (Sarah), schools founded by, 8149
Schneerson (Menachem) on empowerment of, 8173
in Shabbateanism, 8261
Szold (Henrietta) on, 8941
as victims of *dybbuk* possession, 2534
in worship, 9808
in Khanty religion, 5124
in Khoi religion, 5136
in Korean religion, 5233
as shamans, 5235
as Lady of the Animals, 5279–5283
as lamenters, in Finno-Ugric religions, 3110
as majority adherents, 9786–9787
in Mansi religion, 5124
in Maori religion, 7311
ritual roles of, 5681
in Marathi religions, 5699
as martyrs, 3341, 5741, 6742
masks and, 5770–5771
in Masonic organizations, 3196, 3198
in Mazdakism, 5800, 5801
in Mediterranean religions, **3381–3387**
in Melanesian religions, **3395–3400,** 5836–5837
goddesses and, 5834
menstruating (*See* Menstruation)
in Mesoamerican religions, **3411–3415**
in Mesopotamian religions, **3375–3381**
in Micronesian religions, **3395–3400**
in millenarianism, 6034
in Minoan religion, 38–39
monastics (*See* Nuns)
moon and, 6170
in Mormonism, 6195, 6534
as mothers (*See* Mothers and motherhood)
and mysticism, 6358
French feminists on, 3029, 6358
in Near Eastern religions, ancient, **3375–3381**
in Neolithic age, 5281
in Neopagan movements, 6560–6561
in New Age movement, 6536
in new religious movements, 6516, 6526–6527, **6533–6538,** 6563
in Japan, 6573
Oneida community, 6535, 6563, 6732

Women *continued*
in New Thought movement, 6536, 6563, 6585
in North American Indian religions, **3406–3411**
Apache, 10069–10071
of California, 6713, 6714
as healers, 7300
introduction of corn and, 6654
Iroquois, 4541, 4542, 6682
Navajo, 6659–6660
as shamans, 8288
of Southeast Woodlands, 6692
vision quest of, 9610
in Oceanic religions, **3395–3400,** 6792
in Christian churches, 7298
gift giving by, 3480–3481
initiation of, 7807
male domination over, 7296
in Solomon Islands religions, *mana* and, 8516
tattooing of, 7807–7808
in Okinawan religion, 6812
old, in goddess worship, 9602
ordination of (*See* Ordination, of women)
origin of, 2896
Orpheus killed by, 6895
in Polynesian religions, **3395–3400**
menstrual blood of, 7311
and release from *tapu,* 7310–7311
pottery invented by, 5281
preachers
in 18th century, 6534
folklorist study of, 3147–3148
in prehistoric religions, 7381
in priesthood, 7395–7396 (*See also* Ordination)
androcentrism and, 336
Christ the Saviour Brotherhood, influence of, 4103
in Daoism, 7413
debate in Australia and New Zealand, 1735–1736
in Episcopal Church, 68, 7404
Shintō, 7411
women's exclusion from, 7395–7396
purdah seclusion of, 1559
in Rajneesh movement (Osho), 6537
in Rastafari, 7627–7628
religious lives of, study of (*See* Women's studies, in religion)
religious reform and, 7655
rights of, 5364–5365
rites of passage of
in Agikuyu religion, 7805
feminist theory on, 7859
in Hinduism, 7817
in Judaism, 7819
in Middle Ages, 7802
Neopagan, 7830
in Oceanic religions, 7807–7808
in tribal societies, 7796, 7799, 7801
in Roman religion, **3375–3381**
in Diana cult, 2346
in imperial period, 7919–7920
sainthood, path to, 8037–8038
in Samoyed religion, 8096
in San religion, 5136
secret societies and, 8211
sexual mores of, in Hinduism, 2136
in shamanism
as mediums, 8276
in North America, 8288
as shamans
in Buriat religion, 1326
in Dolgan religion, 2395
drums of, 2497–2498
in Japan, 4795, 4921
shelters for victims of domestic violence for, 4102
in Sikh Dharma and 3HO, 3879
in Sikhism, **3335–3338,** 3879–3880
social movements, 1752
in South American religions, **3415–3420**
in Southeast Asian religions
consecration by, 4012
as rulers, 4011
spirit possession of, 2928, 2933, 2934
speech in, 2936
status gained through, 2935
in Spiritualism, 8717
in Syrian religions, **3375–3381**
as temptresses, 4165
in Theosophical Society, 6535
in Tikopia religion, 9198
trinity of, 9601–9602
in Twelve Tribes, 9410
in Unification Church, 6536
untouchable, 9476
in Vanuatu religions, 9520–9521
in Vietnamese religion, 9593
Vivekananda and, 9631
in Warlpiri religion, 9694–9695
weaving invented by, 5281
wise (*See* Wise Women)
witchcraft and, 9773, 9777
as witches (*See* Witches)
World Conference on, 4180
in Yurupary cult, 9919
in Zoroastrianism, **3371–3375**
funeral rites for, 2130
Parsis, 6998–6999
Women and History (Lerner), 3360
Women in Between (Strathern), 3395–3396
Women in Buddhism (Paul), 3330
Women in India (Jacobson and Wadley), 3321
Women of Spirit (Ruether and McLaughlin), 3312
"Women's Changing Ceremonies in Northern Australia" (Berndt), 840
Women's Day (African American), 10039
Women's history, field of, 3024
Women's Indian Association, 845
Women's League for Conservative Judaism. *See* National Women's League of the United Synagogue of America
Women's liberation movement. *See* Feminism, second wave of
Women's movement. *See* Feminism
Women's rights movement. *See* Feminism
Women's Role in Aboriginal Society (Gale), 3391
Women's studies
development of field, 3311, 9785
feminism in, second wave of, 9785
gender studies and, 9792–9793
difference between, 3296
in Hinduism, 3321, 3322–3324
homogeneity in, 9791
institutionalization of, 3313
paradigm shifts in, 3299
in religion, **9785–9796**
in visual culture, 9620
Women's Studies in Religion (Harvard Divinity School), 9786
Women under Primitive Buddhism (Horner), prominence of, 4129
Women Who Run with the Wolves (Estes), 7485
Wonambi (Rainbow Snake), 7605
Wŏn Buddhism, 1173
Wonderful Wizard of Oz, The (Baum), 7323
Wondijna (Australian mythic figures), 7605
Wongthet, Sujit, 3077
Wŏnhyo (Buddhist scholar), 1171, **9796–9797**
Wŏnyung-chong school of Buddhism (Korea), 1171
Wood. *See also* Trees
Ācārāṅga Sūtra on, 2625
in Taino Indian religion, 10024
Wood, Annie. *See* Besant, Annie
Wood, Peter, 77
Woodbridge, Frederick, 6429
Wooden figures, in Arctic religions, 471
Woodhead, Linda, 3036
Woodland tribes (North America), rain dance of, 7603
Woodpeckers, as storm animals, 5996
Woodrofe, John George, 4446, 8988
Woodroffe, John, Evola (Julius) and, 2905
Woodruff, Wilford, 6194
Woodson, A. E., 10054
Woodson, Carter G., 74
Woodville, Anthony, Hermetic texts and, 3946, 3950
Woodward, John, on nature, inherent design of, 2607
Woolf, Virginia, *Mrs. Dalloway,* 3056
Woolley, C. Leonard, 455
Ur excavation by, 6172
Worcester v. Georgia, 7301–7302
"Word of Ešnuwérta" (mythic narrative), in Chamacoco religion (South America), 8633
Word of Faith teaching (Pentecostal), 7030–7031
Word of God
in Christianity (*See also* Hebrew scriptures; Logos; New Testament)
Barth (Karl) on, 790, 791
Calvin on, 1375
creation and, 1344
neoorthodoxy on, 6467
Preaching and, 1668
Servetus (Michael) on, 8232
shape shifting and, 8303
in Islam
in devotion, 9818
Ibn Ḥazm on, 4268
in Judaism, Heschel (Abraham Joshua) on, 3962
Justin Martyr on, 5043, 5044
water linked to, 9702
Words
vs. images, primacy of, 494, 495
images incorporated with, 9623, vol. 14 color insert
implicit meanings of, 9931–9932
in media coverage, 4964–4965
recovery of, in Zapatismo, 9932–9933
Words (Sartre), religion in, 8116
Words and Speeches (Prokopovich), 7419
Wordsworth, William, 7206
Work(s), **9797–9800**
faith and, 2955–2956
superstition, charges of, 8866
Humanistic Buddhism and, 3139
Hus (Jan) on, 4234
justification and, 5039–5041
merit and, 5876, 5877
in monasteries, 824, 6124
Christian, 6132, 6135
as ritual, 9578
Shabbat and, 8256–8257

time and, 1760
Work ethic
of Bamba (Ahmadu), 107
Japanese, Bellah (Robert) on, 8489
Protestant, 7251, 7458
Marxist critique of, 7489
of Weber (Max), 107, 2671–2674, 8481, 8494, 9707
Working class
in Afro-Brazilian religions, 121
culture of, 7320–7321
Working Group on Women and Religion, 9786
Working Party on World Religions in Education, Smart (Ninian) and, 8443
Work of Culture, The (Obeyesekere), 7480
"Work of the Gods" (Tikopia ritual), 9195, 9196–9197, 9198
Works and Days (Hesiod), 3626–3627
advice in, 3963
World
ages of (*See* Ages of the world)
Catholic relation to, 9534, 9536
engagement with, as religious devotion, 2673
eternity of, 2855
in Kevala Advaita, 9546
origin of word, 173
recreation of, Viṣṇu in, 9618–9619
renunciation of, Brahmanic, 9569–9570
as text, 2782
World Alliance of Reformed and Presbyterian Churches, 2684
World Alliance of Reformed Churches, Congregationalism in, 2055
World and God, The (Farmer), 7118
World as Will and Idea, The (Schopenhauer), humor in, 4221
World Christian Encyclopedia (Barrett), 6085, 7447
on Pentecostals, 7033
World Christian Soldiers Church (Kenya), 105
World Christian Temperance Movement, Smith (Hannah Whitall) and, 8446
World chronicles, in Christian historiography, 4029
World Community of Islam in the West, 72, 6419
World Conference on Faith and Order, at Lausanne (1927), 352
on free will and predestination, 3208–3209
World Conference on Human Rights, universality *vs.* inequality and, 4181
World Conference on Women, human rights and, 4180
World Congress of Ethnic Religions (WCER), 765
World Council of Churches (WCC)
assemblies of, 2686
East Asia Secretariat and, 1730
ecclesiology and, 1775
in ecumenical movement, 2685–2686
environmental and social challenges addressed by, 2612, 2650
Faith and Order Commission
on ecclesiology, 1776
Lima Document on Baptism, Eucharist, and Ministry of, 2061
on ministry, 1769
Faith-Man-Nature group founded by, 2610
formation of, 2044
Greek and Russian Orthodox churches in, 1652
International Missionary Council merging with, 2684
Justice, Peace and Integrity of Creation program of, 3502
Mead (Margaret) in, 5804
membership of, 1775
Methodist denominations at, 5999
on ministry, orders of, 6045
on nonviolence, 6648
Orthodox Churches in, 2589
orthodoxy and heterodoxy and, 6912
Pentecostal denominations in, 7033
Protestant denominations in, 7448
purpose of, 2685
Roman Catholicism and, 2687
Sixth Assembly of, on kingdom of God, 5153
social ethics and, 1656
structure of, 2685–2686, 2690
World egg, 2701. *See also* Cosmic eggs
World Faiths Development Dialogue, 2613
World Fellowship of Buddhists, 9152
establishment of, 2038, 6080, 6911
Malalasekera (G. P.) in, 5624, 5625
World Fellowship of Faiths, 2343
World History of the Jewish People (Dubnov), 4882
Worldliness, Ḥasan al-Baṣrī on, 3784–3785
World maintenance rituals (African), iconography in, 4303–4304
Worldmate movement, 6574
founding of, 8369–8370
World Messianity, 6574
World Methodist Council, 5999
World Missionary Conference (1910), 6085
ecumenical movement and, 2044
World music, South Asian music as, 6286
World of the First Australians, The (Berndt and Berndt), 841–842
World order, Sumerian, 2791
World Outlook of the Ancient Balts, The (Vėlius), 771
World-Overseeing Man (deity), 5119, 5120, 5125
World parents. *See* Primordial parents
World-periods
systems of, 174–175
in Zoroastrianism, 174, 203–204
World-rejection, in asceticism, 528–529
World religions, **9800–9804**
Christianity and, 9800–9803
relationship to, 2684, 2688
definition of, 9800
as doctrinal religions, 4512
ecology and, **2654–2657**
elixirs used in, 2770
expansion of, 4513
intellectuals in, 4512
proverbs and parables in, 6977–6978
Roman Catholicism and, relation to, 2686–2687
as term, 9800–9803
World Religions: Eastern Traditions (Oxtoby), 10056
World Religions: Western Traditions (Oxtoby), 10056
World Renewal cult (North America), 6717–6718, 6719
World Renewal System, in Athapaskan religious traditions, 574
"World Scientists' Warning to Humanity," 2612
World Services, 2988
World Soul (Plato), 6960, 6963
Middle Platonists on, 7189
Plotinus on, 7199
World's Parliament of Religions, 2342–2343, **9804–9805**
Vivekananda at, 9629–9630
Zen Buddhism at, 9950
World Spirituality: An Encyclopedic History of the Religious Quest (book series), 8719
World-system theory, 2675–2677
World-Teacher. *See also* Maitreya
Krishnamurti (Jiddu) as, 844, 845, 5244, 5245
World theology, 9126
World Trade Center, terrorist attack on. *See* September 11th, 2001, terrorist attack
World Union for Progressive Judaism, 736, 7665, 7670, 7672
Worldview
Catholic, 5261
cosmology and, 1992
human rights and, 4181
in neoshamanism, 8295–8296
Smart (Ninian) on, 8443
Stolz (Fritz) on, 4048
World War I
Australia and New Zealand in, 1734
fundamentalism and, 2889
German Protestant support for, 790
Hook (Sidney) on, 3956
Japan affected by, 4792
John XXIII (pope) in, 4944
Judaism and, 5021–5022
Neoorthodoxy following, 6466, 6467
Nestorians during, 6481
papacy during, 6974
Quakers as conscientious objectors to, 7549
quest for religious values following, 4100
Tillich (Paul) influenced by, 9203
World War II. *See also* Holocaust
Agudat Yisra'el during, 195
cargo cults and, 1417
Conservative Judaism and, 1960, 1961
and dialogue of religions, 2343–2344
Eliade during, 2754
fatalism during, 2998–2999
German treatment of Jews in
Karaite sect, 5084
Rabbanite sect, 5084
Grail movement during, 3653
impact on church order in Eastern Europe, 1686
Japanese kamikaze pilots in, 7270–7271
Japanese Shintō and, 8368
Japan's surrender in, Kagawa Toyohiko's involvement in, 5054
John XXIII (pope) in, 4945
Quakers as conscientious objectors to, 7549
Reform Judaism after, 7671–7673
Russian Orthodox church during, 2588, 7944
Worldwide Church of God, 6571
World Wide Fund for Nature, 2623

World Wildlife Fund (WWF), 2613
World Zionist Organization, 7681, 9980
Mohilever (Shemu'el) in, 6113
Worm of Sickness (Assyrian), healing myths and, 3811
Worms (Germany)
Jews of, 5012
synagogue in, 8925
Worms, Colloquy of (1539), 7659
Worms, Edict of (1521), 7657, 7658
Worship and devotional life, 2319, **9805–9846**. *See also* Devotion
in African religions
Aladura movement of, 104–105
music in, 6257
in West African religions, 9719–9721
Yoruba, 9911–9912
in Buddhism
East Asia, **9834–9839**
Southeast Asia, **9826–9834**
Tibet, **9839–9842**
in Christianity, **9809–9815**
church as context of, 1668
early, 6307
emphasis on preaching in, 1668
hymns, 1668
Orthodox, 2591, 2593
Pentecostal and Charismatic, 7031
Protestant, 1668, 7456–7457
sacraments and, 1669–1670
Spener (Philipp Jakob) on, 8680
as system of hope, 1668
congregational, and architecture, 466
in Daoism, **9842–9846**
faith and, 2957–2958
heroes, worship of, 3956–3957
in Hinduism, **9820–9826**
in Hurrian religion, 4232
in Islam, 2318, **9815–9820**
ṣalāt (prayer) in, 8054
of Jehovah's Witnesses, 4823
in Judaism, **9805–9809**
in rabbinic Judaism, synagogue in, 4978
after Second Temple destruction, 6307
Smith (W. Robertson) on, 8466
orthodoxy in, 3921
poetry of, 7207–7208
postures and gestures in (*See* Postures and gestures)
sacred language as means of, 5305, 5306–5307, 5309
sanctuary as place of, 8100
scripture in, 8199–8200
in Sikhism
Ādi Granth in, 3716
gender roles in, 3337
syncretism in, 8931
taboos of, 8949
in Zoroastrianism, 9998
Worship of Nature, The (Frazer), 2661
Worsley, Peter, on cargo cults, 1416, 1422, 7789
Worster, Donald, 2663–2664
Wot (chief), 9228
Wotjobaluk people (Australia), Seven Sisters story of, 655
Wound, *yoni* associated with, 9906–9907
Wounded Knee
massacre at, 5295
protest at (1973), 7303
Wovoka (Indian prophet), **9846–9847**
Ghost Dance of, 3473, 3474, 6701, 6718
visions of, 9612
vocation of, 9633
Wraiths (apparitions), 3475
Wreaths, meaning of, 2073
Wrede, William, in Religionsgeschichtliche Schule, 7707
Wren, Christopher, 795, 3193
Wrestling
by Rarámuri Indians, 8723
in India, 5730
Wright, Arthur, 1250
Wright, Charles, 5483
Wright, Frank Lloyd, 796
Wright, Lucy, Shakers and, 8268
Wright, Theodore, 68
Wrightson, Patricia, 3080
Writing. *See also* Alphabets; Calligraphy
on amulets and talismans, 298–300
"beautiful," 1369
calendars and, 1353
of Canaanite texts, 1390
Chinese, history of, 1370
constellations as, 8424
cuneiform, 1382, 3375
deciphering of ancient forms of, and study of religion, emergence of, 8763
in Egypt
development of, 5161
importance of, 2717
hieroglyphic (*See* Hieroglyphic writing)
independence of, 9269
in magic, 6844
materials written on, 1842
in memory and memorization, 5850
oral tradition turned into, 9269
origin of, 269–270
myths of, 269–270
Nabu in, 269, 6390
in Orphism, 6892–6893
Plato on, 9269
runic (*See* Runes)
sacred (*See* Sacred texts; Scripture; *specific texts*)
scripture as holy writ, 8197–8198
in Southeast Asia, 8643
spirit writing, 6835
as tool for managing society, 3375–3376
Writings in Time of War (Teilhard de Chardin), 9033
Writings section of Hebrew scriptures. *See Ketuvim*
Wsjr. *See* Osiris
Wstęp do religioznawstwa (Poniatowski), religious theory in, 8774
Wu (king), 1583
Wu (military official), 9060
Wu (shamans or spirit mediums, in China). *See* Mediums, in Chinese religion; Shamanism, in Chinese religion
Wu, Emperor. *See* Liang Wudi
Wu, Empress
Buddhism *vs.* Daoism, 1602
Chan Buddhism and, 1238, 1239, 1521
on Daoist sculptures, 4333–4334
Manichaeism and, 5669
as manifestation of Maitreya, 5620
Shandao and, 8298
Wu, Pei-Yi, 701
Wu (nonbeing), Guo Xiang on, 3710
Wuchang Buddhist Institute, 8967
Wu Cheng'en, 3069
Wudal (mythic figure), 653, 660–662
Wu Daozi (Wu Daoxuan) (Buddhist artist), 1165, 4334, 4337
gardens of, 3278
Wudi (emperor), 1591, 4490, 7267, 8996
Wu Di (five model emperors), 1627
Wuding (king), 1582
Wudoumi dao (Way of the Five Pecks of Rice), 1593. *See also* Celestial Masters/Heavenly Masters
Wuḍū (ablution), *ṣalāt* (prayer) and, 8057
Wujing (Five Scriptures/Classics), 1585. *See also* individual books
canon status, 1905–1909
in *Huainanzi,* 5494
modern use of, 1910
Nakae Tōju studying, 6404
ru as scholars of, 1917
Wu Jingzi, 3068
Wujūdī school (Islam), 4665
Wu kingdom (China), Ge Hong in, 3290
Wulf, Elizabeth Clare. *See* Prophet, Elizabeth Clare
Wulff, David, 7474
Wulfstan (Anglo-Saxon traveler), 767, 6943
Wuliang duren jing (Daoist text), 2194
Wuliangshou jing (Buddhist text), 2176
Wumen (Chan master), 6989
Wumen Huikai, 1524
Wundt, Wilhelm, **9847–9848**
as founder of experimental psychology, 7473–7474
on internal soul, 8532
on magic, 5565
on origin of the sacred, 7974
Otto (Rudolf), criticism from, 4096
on preanimism, 7372
Wunggurr (life force), 9458–9460
Wunzh (Ojibwa boy), vision quest of, 7551
Wūquf (standing), 7159, 7343, 9818
Wuragag (mythic figure), 657
Wurunshemu (deity), 3595
Würzburg (Germany), anti-Semitism in, 399
Wushang biyao (Daoist text), 2184, 2195, 2210
Wushang huanglu dazhai licheng yi (Daoist text), 2205
Wushu (martial arts), 5733–5734
Wutai, Mount (China)
as divine dwelling, 6213
Mañjuśrī cult at, 5675
pilgrimage to, 7164–7165, 9835
Pure Land Buddhism of, 2801
Wu-tang, Mount, importance in Daoism, 2200
Wuthnow, Robert, 6522
Wutnyang Gatakek (prophet), 7443
Wuvoka. *See* Wovoka
Wuvulu religion (Micronesia), *puala*-spirits in, 2007
Wuwarr (spirit), 144
Wuwei (nonaction), in Daoism
ahiṃsā compared with, 6646
Buber (Martin) on, 1057
nature and, 2636
peace and, 7022
in politics, 9671
taiping and, 8961
Wuwei (Lo) sect, 3155
Wuwu dance, 6293
Wuxing (book). *See* "Five Kinds of Action"
Wuxing (five elements or phases). *See also* Yinyang wuxing philosophy
in martial arts, 5736
Wu-xue (Zen master), 1180
Wuyouzi. *See* Liu Deren
Wuyue zhenxing (Daoist text), 2207
Wu Yun
Sima Chengzhen and, 8400
writings of, 2209
Wu Zetian (Chinese empress), 3012, 7267
Wu Zhao (Chinese empress), 1164, 1600
and Daoism, 2184

Wuzhen pian (Daoist text), 2211
Wuzhong Mosque (China), 4638
Wuzhun (Buddhist master), portrait of, vol. 10 color insert
Wuzong (Chinese emperor)
Buddhist persecution under, 7213, 7255, 7268
campaign against Buddhism, 1602
WWF. *See* World Wildlife Fund
Wyclif, John, **9848–9850**
on Antichrist, 395
apocalypse and, 412
Bible translation by, 881, 9425
condemnation of teachings of
by council at Constance, 2043
heresy charges, 4233
on free will and predestination, 3207
Hus (Jan) and, 4233
and iconoclasm, 4286
literacy and, 8152
pacifist teachings of, 6648
Wyman, Leland C., 6442, 6672
Wynema: A Child of the Forest (Callahan), 3090–3091
Wyschogrod, Michael, on election of Israel, 2746

X

X, Malcolm. *See* Malcolm X
Xálpen (deity), in Selk'nam religion, 8225
Xangô (spirit), 122, 123
Xangô religion, origins of, 120
Xapiripë (shamanic spirits), in Yanomami religion, 8625
Xaratanga (deity), 5909
Xărpan (deity), 1785
Xastvanift (book), confession in, 1889
Xavante religion (South America), primordial beings in, transformation of, 2012
Xavier, Francis, **9853–9854**
in Japan, 1726, 4787–4788, 9310
Xbalanque (mythic figure), 5797, 5935, 5937
Xeno (welcomed stranger), hospitality and, 4138
Xenocrates of Chalcedon
demonology of, 7187, 7189
on gods, 7187
Platonic forms accepted by, 7187
at Plato's Academy, 7187
Xenophanes of Colophon, **9854–9856**
on anthropomorphism, 390, 3685, 4108, 5201
atheism and, 581
criticism of religion by, 390, 3685
on deities, 4321
on gods *vs.* humans, 2883
on image veneration, 4380, 4382
on knowledge, 5201
monotheism and, 6156
on myths, rational explanations of, 6365
Parmenides as pupil of, 6995
on Pythagoras, 9328
on transmigration of soul, 7186
Xenophon
homosexuality and, 4113
interpreting oracles, 2375
on knowability of God, 181
Xenophon of Ephesus, *Ephesiaka,* 3052
Xenoteia, 2825
Xerente religion (Brazil)
origin of agriculture in, 8590
sun and moon in, 2862, 8578
Xevioso (deity). *See* Sogbo
Xhosa language, 3085
Xhosa religion (Southern Africa). *See also* Southern African religions
Cattle-Killing Movement, 6547
colonialism and, 1855–1856
Nongqause (medium) in, 8659, 8660
prophets of, 7444
shades in, 8656
Xia dynasty (China), 1166
as dynasty, 1581
founding of, in myth, 1626
rulers of, 1570
Xian (Transcendents or Immortals), **9856–9857**
in Daoism, 2178, 2179, 2182
Xianbei people (Inner Asia), 4491
Xiang (image), 4336
Xiang'er commentary, to *Dao de jing,* 2180–2181, 2193, 2204
Xiang Kai, 5317
Xiangshan Academy, 5541
Xiang Tuo (child prodigy), iconography of, 4337
Xiang Xiu, 1575
Xiangyang (China), Dao'an in, 2171
Xianshou. *See* Fazang
Xianyi lu (Daoist text), 2210
Xianyuan Jiao movement, Huangdi in, 4145
Xianzong (Chinese emperor), 1165
Xiao, **9857–9858**
Xiao Baozhen, **9858–9859**
Xiaodao (Way of Filial Piety), 2197–2198
Xiaojing (Classic of Filial Piety) (Confucian text), 1908
authority in, vol. 6 color insert
iconography in, 4336
in Japan, popularity of, 4813
Xiao Yan. *See* Liang Wudi
Xiao zhuan calligraphy, development of, 1370
Xiayuan Jie festival, 1643
Xibalbá (underworld), 1473
journey to, 150
life associated with, 150
Xi Daozang (Daoist text), 2203
Xie Liangzuo, 1560
Xie Lingyun, 2217, 7213
on mountains, 6212
Xie Shouhao, 2209, 5318
Xi He (deity), gender studies on, 3339
Xijouji. *See* Drama
Xikrin religion (Amazon), 8630–8631. *See also* Ge religions
Xilai An Incident (1915), 8964
Xilonen, in Aztec sacrifice, 2556
Ximénez, Francisco, 4503
Xin (heart-and-mind), cultivation of, Mengzi on, 5857, 5858
Xin dynasty, 1592
Xing (musical instrument), 6293
Xing shu writing, calligraphy and, 1370
Xingu peoples. *See* Upper Xingu peoples
Xingwikáon (big house), 4307
Xingyun (Buddhist monk), 1168
Xingyun, Master, 3139–3140
Xingzheng, 1642
Xinjiang (East Turkestan), Islam in, 4631, 4639–4640
ḥājj in, 4637
language of, 4640
persecution of, 4640
Ṣūfī, 4635, 4640
Xǐn Wirt (deity). *See* Sickness Lord
Xinxing, **9859**
on *mofa,* 5686
Sanjie Jiao sect and, 1576, 5255
Xiong, Victor, 7266
Xiongnu people (Inner Asia), 1595, 4489–4490
Chinese defeat of, 4491
language of, 4489–4490
military power of, 4490
rituals of, 4490
sources on, 4489
Xiong Yaohua, 3070
Xipe Totec (deity), 5890
agriculture and, 719
in Aztec religion, 1469
in Mixtec religion, 5911
in Toltec religion, 5906
in Zapotec religion, 5912
Xisheng jing, dao and *de* in, 2174
Xiuhtecuhtli (deity), 718
tobacco and, 8455
Xiuhtecuhtli-Huehueteotl (deity), 5906, 5909
Xiuzhen shishu (Daoist text), 2211
Xi Wang Mu, **9859–9860**
as Eternal Venerable Mother, 1607
as personified saving deity, 1593
and Pure Land Buddhism, 292
Xiyouji (Chinese pilgrimage tale), 7554
humor in, 4209
monkey in, 6152
Xiyue Huashan zhi (Daoist text), 2208
Xiyu ji (Xuanzang), 9526
Xizong (Chinese emperor), 2517
!xo (deity), 5135–5136, *5136,* 5137
Xochicalco religion (Mesoamerica), iconography of, 4313
Xochipilli (deity)
drums and, 6269, 6270
identified with music, 2464, 2465
Xochipilli Cinteotl (deity), 3135
Xochipilli Macuilxochitl (deity), 5911
Xochiquetzal (deity), 719, 3135, 5934
identified with music, 2464
smoking and, 8455
Xochiyaoyotl (Flowery Wars), human sacrifice and, 4186–4187
Xolas (deity), in Alacaluf religion, 8579
Xolotl (deity), 717
in creation cycle, 2394
as Quetzalcoatl's twin, 2393, 5937
temple to, 9254
Xóno (deep sea), 9030
Xo'on shamans, in Selk'nam religion, 8225–8226
Xot łungx. *See* Family guardian spirits
Xu, Paul, on Confucianism and Christianity, 1920
Xuandang (Buddhist philosopher), 1301
Xuanfeng qinghui lu (Daoist text), 2210
Xuan Huaichang, 2741
Xuan Jiao. *See* Daoism
Xuannü (deity), Huangdi (Yellow Emperor deity) and, 4144
Xuanpin lu (Daoist text), 2206
Xuanren, Empress Dowager, 1562
Xuanwu (deity), 2207
Xuanxue movement
Guo Xiang in, 3710
Tang Yongtong in, 8981
three teachings and, 1899
Wang Bi in, 9670
Xuanzang (Buddhist monk), 1266, **9860–9862**
as follower of Dharmapāla, 2337
on *bodhisattva* cults, 1080
on Buddhist monasteries, 1118
on Buddhist schools, 1194, 1195, 1201, 1301, 1310

Xuanzang (Buddhist monk) *continued*
and Faxiang school, 1238
French study of, 1632
iconography of, 4330
Kuiji as student of, 5258
on Kushan empire, 4490
on *ālaya-vijñāna,* 229
on Asaṅga, 517
on Avalokiteśvara, 705, 706
on Sautrāntika, 8136
pilgrimage undertaken by, 5265
novel built on, 3069
on Potalaka Mountain, 705
Shelun school modified by, 6992
Śīlabhadra and, 8399
on Sthiramati, 8739
translations by, 855, 1164, 1202, 1250
travels and translations of, 1577, 1600
Yogacara Buddhism transmitted by, 9901
Xuanzong (Chinese emperor)
and Mahāvairocana, 5607
and Daoism, 2184, 2196–2197, 2202, 7267
drama under, 2455
and iconography, 4334
Sima Chengzhen and, 8399–8400
Śubhākarasiṃha and, 8804
temple established by, 9056–9057
Xu Dishan, 3070
Xue Xuan, Study of Principle and, 1902
Xu gaoseng zhuan (Buddhist text), 994, 2210, 2530
Xu Guangqi, 7793
Xu Heng, 1578
Xul Öter (deity). *See* Sickness Lord
Xu Mi, 1597
and Heavenly Masters, 2195
Xun (musical instrument), 6293
Xunzi (Xun Qing), **9862–9863**
atheism and, 578
Han Fei Zi and, 3772, 5395
on Legalism, 5395
on *li,* 5431
noble ideal and sagehood in, 1896–1897
philosophy of, overview, 1573, 1587–1588
on *tian,* 9172
on *yi,* 7751
Xu Sun, hagiographies of, 2207
Xu Xing, 1572
Xuyun, 1524
Xylophones, 2495
in African religions, 6257

Y

Ya'āq (deity), 444
Ya'aqov. *See* Jacob
Ya'aqov bar Nissim ibn Shahin, 4989–4990
Ya'aqov ben Asher, **9863–9864**
biblical exegesis of, 867
and *halakhah,* development of, 3743
Karo (Yosef) on, 5104
tosafot of, 9244
Ya'aqov ben Me'ir, 7619
Ya'aqov ben Nissim, Sherira' Gaon, epistle requested from, 8320
Ya'aqov ben Yaqar, Rashi influenced by, 7619
Ya'aqov Polak, 5014
Ya'aqov Yitsḥaq, 2768
Ya'aqov Yosef of Polonnoye
as Ba'al Shem Tov's disciple, 726
on Noah, 6643
as *tsaddiq,* 9379, 9380, 9381
works of, 3787
Yabuduruwa cult (Australia), 6598–6600
history of study of, 683
Yácatas (pyramids), 7526
Yachaj (diviners). *See also* Divination, in South American Indian religions
in Andean religion, 8616, 8619
Yadaadji (rainmaker), 9400
Yafet ben Eli, 894
Yagé (intoxicant), 848
South American shamanism and, 8292
Yagé Woman, 848
Yaghūth (deity), 444
Yagnapurushdas, Swami, BAPS movement and, 8890, 8891
Yahalom, Yosef, 6020
Yahgan religion (South America)
geography of, 8576
initiation rites in, 8585, 8874
supreme being in, 8579
Yahrīyah (Ṣūfī order)
in China, 4635
dhikr of, 4635
origins of, 4635
practices of, 4635
Yahrzeit (anniversary of parent's death), 5013
Yahuna religion (South America), sun hero in, 8582
Yahval Balamil (deity), sacred geography and, 3434
Yahveh (Yahweh). *See also* Judaism, God in
vs. Abraham's God, 14, 15
absence of wife of, 4742–4743
Anat as consort of, 320
angel of, 345
anger of, toward Judah, 4828–4829
vs. Baal, 2765
as Bes, 4296
Canaanite influence on, 724
covenant with, 4971–4972
demons sent by, 2277
derivation of name, 2252
divine court of, 4078–4079
divine kingship of, 5147
El identified with, 2742, 4742
Elohim as synonym for, 3538, 4742
emotions of, 3542–3543
enthronement festival for, 5147
eye of, 2942
flashing sword of judgment of, 967
in Hebrew scriptures, **3537–3543**
in *Psalms,* 7461, 7464
and history, Jewish view of, 4058
"holy" attributed to, 7968
horns associated with, 4131
on human propensity toward evil, 4744
idolatrous worship of, 4358
imagery of, 3542–3543
in Israelite religion, 4742
in Israel's collective existence, 4856–4857
justice of, 129
kavod of, 3542
as king, of gods *vs.* Israel, 3542
laws attributed to, 4728
in magical texts, syncretism and, 3909
as meteorological god, 5995
monotheistic worship of, 3539–3542, 6157–6158
monsters defeated by, 2431
Moses and, 6201–6202
name of, as magical, 5575
obligations of cult of, 4829
as only God, 4857
origins of, 2985
origins of worship of, 3539
other gods blended into, 3541
pictorial representation of, 4296
polytheistic worship of, 3539, 3541
presence in Temple, paradox of, 7981
prophets transmitting will of, 7424
sacred poles or trees of, 4743
sacrifice commanded by, 4746–4747
sovereignty of, 5995
as storm and sun god, 7603
transcendence of, 3542
Yahveh Elohim, in Hebrew scriptures, 3538
"Yahveh is king," 5147
Yahvist (J) source
on Abraham, 14, 15
dating of, 6199
E source and, 6199
on Moses, 6199–6201
Yahweh. *See* Yahveh
Yaḥyā ibn 'Adī, 2971, 2991, 7242
Yaḥyā ibn al-Biṭrīq, 2971
Yaḥyā ibn Mu'ādh al-Rāzī, eschatology of, 2839
Yahya ibn Yahya al-Laythi, 4594
Yahyā ibn Zakarīyā'. *See* John the Baptist
Yai (jaguar shaman), in Tukanoan religion, 8623
Yajamana (sponsor of sacrifice), 983, 2447, 7406
Yajña (sacrifice)
in Balinese religion, 747–748
in devotional life, 9821
rituals of, 2447, 4535
vs. pūjā, 7493
Yājñavalkya (sage)
on deities and the mind, 2016
on oblations, 2015
smṛti of, 5344
Yājñavalkyasmṛti (Hindu text)
commentaries on, 2329
dharma in, 2329
Yajurveda (Vedic text), 9551–9552, 9554
adhvaryu priests and, 3991
Brāhmaṇas of, 1026
chanting of, 1535
priesthood in, 7405
ritual formulas of, 4426
Rudra in, 7934, 7935, 8039–8040
Śatapatha Brāhmaṇa and, 3991
Śatarudriya hymn in, 8415
tapas in, 8998
Yakairiti spirits, in Enawenê Nawê cosmology, 2012–2013
Yakan (spirit), 2570
Yakan cult (Africa), 5528
Yakasere, Celine, on rites of passage, 7808
Yakhin (column), 924
Yakipong (deity), in Kromanti dance, 1436
Yakkakhiṃ (drum), 2497
Yakkha cult (Buddhist), 2497
Yakṣas (deities), **6394–6395**. *See also* Nāgas
and Buddha statues, 1066
cult of, 1111
depiction of, 856
dwellings of, 6394
as fertility deities, 6394
ghosts as, 3477
in Kurukṣetra, 5268
kingship symbolism of, 6394–6395
riddles by, 6987
rural traditions of, 4436
worship of, 778
Yakṣīs (deities), 778, 1111, 6394. *See also* Nāgas; See also Yakṣas
Yākush (deity), 835
Yakut people (Arctic), culture of, 468, 472
Yakut religion, **9864–9866**. *See also* Siberia and Siberian religions
Animal Mother in, 8284
birds in, 948
Christianity and, 9864–9865
development of, 472
Erlik in, 2831
shamanism in
miracles and, 6050
vs. Mongol shamanism, 6140

prestige of shamans, 8282
sky god in, 9081
Yākwa ritual, Yakairiti spirits and, 2012–2013
Yalafath (deity), 6010, 6011, 6012
Yale University
Dwight (Timothy) as president of, 2532
Goodenough (Erwin R.) at, 3637
Malinowski (Bronislaw) at, 5629
Yali (prophet), 7788
Yaliwan, Matias, 6797
cargo cults and, 1419
Yalquṭ Shim'oni (midrash), 6018
Yam (sea), 924, 932
Yama (deity), **9867**
and binding, 937
blades of, 968
demon in battle with, 4329
dogs associated with, 2392, 2393
as judge of the dead, 4440, 5026
Māra and, 5690
rewards from, 134
Rudra associated with, 7934
twin of, 2369, 9416, 9420
in Vedism, 9559
vision of God and, 128
worship of, 2369
Yama (yogic practices), 9894
aṣṭāṅgayoga (eight-limbed discipline), 8704
Yamabushi (mountain ascetics), 2640, 3156. *See also* Shugenja
Konkōkyō and, 5225
miracles of, 6052–6053
in popular religion, 4785, 4796
practitioners of Shugendō and, 2188–2189
Yamaga Sokō (Confucian scholar), **9868**
Ancient Learning and, 1928
on *bushi,* 1335
on Shintō, 8363
Yamamoto Tsunetomo, 1335
Yámana religion. *See* Yahgan religion
Yama no kami (mountain divinities), 6214
Yāmantaka (demon), 4329
Yamashima (Japan), Rennyo in, 7752
Yamassee Native American Tribe, 6769
Yamatai (Japanese state), 4809
location of, 4780
Yamatodamashi (soul of Japan), 7274
Yamato dynasty (Japan)
Buddhism in, 1174, 1175
Jimmu in, 4920
religion in, 4780–4782
Shintō and, 8358
Yamato Takeru, **9868–9869**
Yamazaki Ansai, **9869–9870**
Confucianism and, 1927
Suika Shintō and, 8363
Yamazaki Bennei, 4939
Yami (twin sister of Yama), 9416, 9420, 9559
worship of, 2369
Yamim nora'im (Agnon), 180
Yamm (deity), Baal's conflict with, 723, 724, 1383, 1384, 1387, 1391–1392, 1393, 2431, 2442
Yams and sweet potatoes
in Australian Indigenous myths, 653
in Maori religion, 5680, 5681
in Melanesian religion
ancestor worship and, 322
magic and, 5563
myths on origins of, 192
in Trobriand Islander marriage, 5726
Yāmuna (philosopher), **9870–9871**
Rāmānuja and, 4430, 7614
on relationship between deity and devotee, 8976
Yamunā (river), 743, 7861, 7862
Yamunotri shrine (India), nature-culture threshold in, 8377
Yāna (vehicle), 996, 1088, 1094, 1122
Yanagida Seizan, 1638, 9950
Yanagita Kunio, 3347
Yanbu' al-hayat (Ibn Gabirol), 4266–4267, 4980
Yanderú Túmpa (mythic figure), in Chiriguano religion (South America), 8634
Yang (nurture), 2634
Yang, C. K., 1637
Yangchi sublineage, 1523
Yangge dances, humor and, 4208
Yang Hu, Confucius and, 1934
Yangming. *See* Wang Yangming
Yangsai, Dui, cargo cults and, 1419
Yang-shao culture (China), 6465
Yang Shi, 1560
Yang tig (Ultra Pith), 2547
Yang ti gsum (Longchenpa), 5193
Yang Xi, 1597
and Celestial Masters religion, 2182
hagiographies of, 2206
Yang Xiong, 1575
Yang Xizhen, 2186
Yang Xuanzhi, 994
Yang Zhu, 1571–1572
Yan Hui, 1562
as disciple of Confucius, 1935
Yanna'i (rabbi)
on God's favoritism, 3548
on merit, 5871
on suffering, 8806
Yanoama religion. *See* Yanomamö religion
Yanoma Indians (Venezuela), funeral rites of, 3240
Yanomamö religion (South America)
humanity and subhumanity in, 9681
overview of, 8625–8626
plant hallucinogens in, 8292
Pore as supreme being in, 8577
soul in, 8584
Yanshou, 1604
Yantras (mystical diagrams), **9871–9872**. *See also* Maṇḍalas
image serving as, 4323, vol. 3 color insert
aṣṭāṅgayoga (eight-limbed discipline), 8705
in *Haṭhayoga,* 3795
as magical tool, 1288, 5589
in meditation, 5820
Yan Yuan, 1579
Han Studies *(Hanxue)* movement and, 1903
on Mengzi, 5858–5859
Yanyuwa religion (Australia)
afterlife in, 144–145
cosmology of, 6260
relational, 2003
music in, 6260–6262
categories of, 6261
the Dreaming and, 6260
essence of, 6261–6262
sacred and secular in, 6260–6261
Yao and Shun (legendary rulers), **9872–9873**
flood and, 1626
as model emperors, 1627
at New Year, 1642
Yao religion and society (Tanzania)
anthropogony of, elephant in, 2750
Daoism practiced by, 2189
initiation dances of, 2136
Islam conversion among, 2571
masquerade dances of, 2140
ocean and, 6807
supreme being (Mulungu) in, 3572–3573
Yap (Micronesia)
burial rituals in, 6005
dance in, 6007
kinship in, 5183
Roman Catholicism in, 6007
spirits in, 6003
uncreated deity in, 6003
Yaperikuli (trickster), 9358
Yaqui millenarian movement (North America), 6576, 6667, 6721
Yaqui people (Mexico), *waehma* (ritual performance) of, 7045
Yarḥei kallah (months of assembly), 9883
Yarhibol (deity), 449
Yārhīñ (month in Islamic year), 4713
Yarih (Yarikh) (deity), marriage of, 1384, 1395
Yarjon (Buddhist abbot), vol. 10 color insert
Yarker, John, on Hermetism, 3952
Yarlung dynasty (Tibet), 1231
Yarmulke *(kippah),* in Reform Judaism, 7666
Yarthkins, 2952
Yaruro religion (Venezuela)
moon goddess in, 8579
mother earth in, 2558
Yasa (Buddha's disciple), 1104, 1105
Yasa (rules), 948
Yaṣas (monk), Vaiśālī council and, 2035–2036
Yasawī Ṣūfī order, 4616, 4621
Yashikigami (house deity), 2410
Yashts (section of Avesta), 709, 9992–9993
asha in, 4537
comparison of deities in, 4535–4536
translation of, 9994
Yasi (moon), worship of, 6439
Yasna (Avesta text), 709, 9992
author of, 9935
confessions of faith in, 2052
Yasna (ritual), 4535, 9998
Yasnaia Poliana (Tolstoy's estate), 9219, 9220, 9221
Yaśodạ (Hindu figure), 743
Yasovarman (king), 5129
Yasuiqian (money of the passing year), 1641
Yasutoki, Hōjō, 5213
Yates, Frances, **9873–9874**
on alchemy, 252
on Freemasonry, 3196
on Hermetism, 2843, 3954
Yates paradigm of esotericism, 2843, 2844–2845
Yathrib. *See* Medina
Yātra (pilgrimage), in devotional life, 9823
Yatsi'a (stone chamber), 924
Yavneh academy, Gamli'el of Yavneh at, 3269
Yawakayi. *See* Dreaming, the
Yawalngura (mythic figure), 661
Yawm al-dīn (day of judgment), 9118
Yawney, Carole, 10027
Yawulyu (public rituals), 9696
Yaxche (first tree), 1502
Yayoi culture (Japan), 4779–4780
kami in, 5072–5073
Yayue (elegant music), 6292–6293, 6296
Yazatas (beings worthy of worship), 4535, **9874–9875**
Haoma, **3775–3776**
Yazdegerd I (Sasanian king), 5661
Yazīd (caliph)
and 'Āshūrā', 550
al-Ḥusayn ibn 'Alī and, 4235

Yazīd (caliph) ***continued***
rebellion against, 7285
Yazīdī sect (Islamic), dualism in, 2514
Yāzijt, Ibrāhīm al-, 895
Yazkert II of Persia, 488
Yazza, Zelda, 406
YBF. *See* Youth Black Faith
yd ʿ (to proclaim), 7776–7777
Year. *See also* Calendars; Seasonal ceremonies
concepts of, diversity in, 6589
Year Bearer (deity), 5791
Yeats, William Butler, 348
Celtic religion and, 1497
on fairies, 2951
Neoplatonism and, 6475
in Order of the Golden Dawn, 6471, 7930
plays of, 2475
on Tagore (Rabindranath), 8958
Yeha, before Christianity, 224–225
Yehan Numata Foundation, 1256
Yehida (transcendent unity), 9378
Yeḥi'el ben Yequti'el, 4913
Yeḥi'el ben Yosef, 7233
Yehi'el of Pais (rabbi), 9248
Yehimilk (king of Byblos), 7129
Yehoshuʿa ben Ḥananyah, **9875–9876**
Eliʿezer ben Hyrcanus and, 2763
Gamli'el of Yavneh and, 3269
Yehoshuʿa ben Levi, **9876**
Yehoshuʿa ben Sira. *See Ben Sira*
Yehoshuʿa Shelomoh, 9244
Yehuda ha-Levi, soul, theory of, 8559
Yehudah bar Il'ai, 9003, **9876–9877**
Yehudah bar Yeḥezqe'l, **9877**
Yehudah ben Bava', Me'ir ordained by, 5830
Yehudah ben Natan, 7619, 9243
Yehudah ben Shemu'el (Yehudah the Pietist)
on anthropomorphism of God, 544
asceticism of, 542, 543
in Ashkenazic Hasidism, 542–545
eschatology of, 542
on mysticism, 6353
pietism of, 5012
as saint, 8035
socioreligious program of, 543–544
writings of, 543, 544
Yehudah ben Yaqar, Nahmanides (Moses) studying under, 6399
Yehudah ha-Kohen ben Yosef, 4990
Yehudah ha-Levi, **9877–9880**
on election of Israel, 2746
on God's providence, 3549
history, approach to, 4038, 4059
Ibn ʿEzra' and, 4265
in Jewish thought and philosophy, 4891–4892
on nature of Israel, 4862
poetry of, 9977–9978
Yehudah ha-Nasi', **9880–9881**
ʿAqiva' ben Yosef influencing, 441
Mishnah compiled under, 6065
Mishnah of, 8969
poetry of, Rosenzweig's (Franz) translations of, 7926
Rav as student of, 7630
tanna' consulted by, 8983
Yehudah ibn Alfakhar, Maimonides (Moses) criticized by, 24
Yehudah ibn Tibbon, 740, 4266
Yehudah Löw ben Betsal'el. *See* Löw, Yehudah ben Betsal'el of Prague
Yehud'ai Gaon, 4989
Yei (deities), rock paintings of, 1471
Yeibichai (ritual), 2462–2463
Yellow (color)
Klee (Paul) on, 1860
in Native American tradition, 1862
Yellow Emperor tradition. *See* Huangdi
Yellow Hat sect. *See* Dge lugs pa order of Buddhism
Yellow Heaven, 2180
Yellow Scarves, 1593, 1594, 1597
Yellow Spring, 169, 1592
Yellowtail, Thomas, Sun Dance and, 8847
Yellow Turban Rebellion
in Han dynasty, 2180, 2192, 7257, 7268
Huangdi (Yellow Emperor deity) and, 4144
millenarianism and, 6039
Yellow Turban sect, 9954–9955
Yeloguy religion. *See* Southern Siberian religions
Yemaja (deity), in Cuban Santeria, 1434
Yemen
circumcision, 7828
family law in, 4703
Hijrah/hijar (protected enclave) in, 3776
Judaism in, 4991, 4999
cantillation and accents in, 1533–1534
dancing, 2149
under Ottoman Empire, 4998
as state religion, 4860
Mu'tazilah in, ʿAbd al-Jabbār and, 4
Shādhilīyah in, 9009
Ṭayyibīyah in, 8334–8335
Zaydī Shiism in, 4572, 4699, 8325
Yemọja/Yemaja (deity), 7862
in Santería, 1434
Yen Hui, 5434
Yenisei Samoyed. *See* Samoyed religion; Southern Siberian religions
Yen-lo (deity), merit and, 5870
Yenshou, Yungming, 4923–4924
Yerushalmi, Elijah, writings of, 5085
Yeshaʿyahu. *See* Isaiah
Ye shes de (Tibetan scholar), 5555
Ye shes Mtsho rgyal (Yeshe Tsogyal), **9881–9882**
as disciple of Padmasambhava, 6941, 9332
and gender in Buddhism, 3333
Ye shes 'od (Tibetan emperor), 1152
Yeshivah University, 7773, 9885
founding of, 7773
rabbinical school of, 7582
Yeshivah/yeshivot (Jewish academies), 4982, **9882–9886**
of Babylonian Judaism, 4988, 9883
Kagan's (Yisra'el Me'ir), 5053
Kotler's (Aharon), 5239
Musar movement in, 6241–6242, 8053
in Orthodox Judaism, 6901–6902
American, 6905–6906
Eastern European, 6902
Hildesheimer (Esriel), and secular component of study in, 3980
Hungarian, 6899
Israeli, 6903
Lubavitch, outreach and, 8171
Reines's (Yitsḥaq Yaʿaqov), 7681
Revel's (Bernard), 7773
vs. seminary, 9882
in United States, 7582
Yeshkun shaman, shamanistic illness of, 9613
Yeshuʿot ot meshiho (Abravanel), 17
Yesod Mora' (Ibn ʿEzra'), 4265
Yetanti moiety, in Qemant religion, 2573
Yeti (monster), 6166
Yetser (inclinations), 9070
*Yetser ha-ra*ʿ (inclination toward evil), in Apocrypha and rabbinism, 8404
Yetsirah, Sefer. *See* Sefer Yetsirah
Yevtushenko, Yevgeny, 7205
Yeyaguliba (deity), 6505
Yggdrasill (tree), 1502, 3448–3449, 9335, 9576
in apocalypse, 3456
Heimdallr and, 3899
as tree of knowledge, 9577
Valhǫll and, 9516
worship of, 6440
YHVH (God). *See also* Yahveh
in Hebrew scriptures
occurrences of name, 3538
original meaning of, 3539
YHVH (House of Yahveh), 931
Yi (propriety or rightness), **7751–7752**
Confucius on, 1571
definitions of, 7751
Dong Zhongshu on, 7752
Han Yu on, 7752
Mengzi on, 7751
Mozi on, 7751
ren and, 7751–7752
Xunzi on, 1573, 7751
Yang Zhu on, 1572
in *Zhuangzi,* 1573
Yibaibashi jie (One hundred and eighty precepts), 2637
Yiddish culture and religion. *See also* Judaism; Purim plays; Tekhines
Agnon's (Shemu'el Yosef) works in, 179–180
decline of, 9037–9038
naming rituals in, 7819
Yiddish language, in Jewish studies, 4882
Yi dynasty (Korea)
Confucianism and, 1930
music in, 6296
Yi Hwang. *See* Yi T'oegye
Yi I. *See* Yi Yulgok
Yi Ik, Practical Learning movement and, 1933
Yijing (Book of Changes)
and alchemy, 2185
Cheng brother on, 1560, 1562–1563
classical philosophy and, 1572
description of, 1906–1907
divination with, 1583–1584, 1906
in Japan, 6828
nature in, 2631
Neo-Confucianism and, 2634
randomness and divination, 1528
ren in, 7752
taiji in, 8959–8960
tian in, 9172, 9173
transformation delineated in, 2637
translations of, 1633, 1635
zhen in, 7604
Yijing (Buddhist monk), 1577, **9886–9887**
on Buddhist schools, 1132, 1133, 1194, 1195, 1201
translations by, 1164
Yi Kan, in Nak-Ho debate, 1932
Yi li (Confucian text), 5431
Yima (mythic figure)
Golden Age of, 3629–3630
world of shadows ruled by, 4537
Yimak (deity), 9416
Yin and yang, 3021. *See also* Yinyang wuxing philosophy
in art, vol. 3 color insert
in Confucianism, 1591
nature as, 2632
dao and, 2173
as dialectical dualism, 2508
Dong Zhongshu on, 1898
duty of king to regulate and harmonize, 5179

in flower arrangement, 3135
in food customs, 3170
games and, 3266
in gardens, 3277
gender and, 3859–3860
in *Huainanzi,* 5494
hun and *po* corresponding to, 1043
iconography of, 4333
Itō Jinsai on, 4752
in Japan, 4782
left and right symbolism in, 5394
light and darkness symbolism of, 5453
in martial arts, 5736
in music, 6295
qian-kun polarity and, 1584
rainfall and, 7604
soul conceived as, and ancestor worship, 323
souls and, 1589, 3862, 8554, 8555
as spiral labyrinth, 5276
taiji producing, 8959
in trees, 9334
Ying (dragon), 2433
Yinger, J. Milton, on sects and cults, 2084, 6523, 6565
Yinguang (Buddhist monk), Pure Land and, 4924–4925
Yin Kesheng, 4639
Yin Niangniang (deity), 1643
Yinqing (musical instrument), 6294
Yinshun (scholar-monk)
Pure Land and, 4924–4925
Zhengyan and, 1788
Yin Xi, as Laozi's disciple, 5316
Yinyang wuxing (five phases) philosophy, **9887–9890**. *See also* Yin and yang
in classical Chinese philosophy, 1572
feng-shui and, 1594
healing system and, 3859–3861
in *Huainanzi,* 5494
in *onmyōdō,* 6827
New Text school on, 1575
physiology in, 3860, 3861
in religious form of Daoism, 1575
in Song dynasty Confucianism, 1578
taiji and, 8959
Yinyuan Longqi, 1524
Yi Ŏnjŏk, Neo-Confucianism and, 1931
Yirawadbad (mythic figure), 664
Yiridja clans, myths of, 660–661
Yirritja people (Australia), 2379, 2380
Yishan Yining, Musō Sōseki and, 6316
Yishma'e'l. *See* Ishmael
Yishma'e'l ben Elisha' (rabbi), **9890–9891**
on atonement, 593
biblical exegesis of, *vs.* 'Aqiva' ben Yosef, 442
Gersonides' commentary on, 3462
Me'ir studying with, 5830
Yisilanjiao (Chinese term for Islam), 4631
Yisra'el. *See* Israel; Jewish people
Yisra'el ben Eli'ezer. *See* Ba'al Shem Tov
Yisra'eli, Yitsḥaq, on souls, 8558–8559
Yi Sŭnghun, 1648
Yi T'aejo, Confucianism and, 1930
Yi the archer (deity), 1626, 1627
Yi T'oegye, **9891–9892**
on Four Beginnings and Seven Emotions, 1931
on principle and material force, 1931, 1932
Yi Yulgok and, 9893
Yitsḥaq. *See* Isaac
Yitsḥaq ben Shemu'el, 4990
Yitsḥaq of Troki, 7235
Yitshaq Tsarfati, 4996
Yitsḥaq Yisra'eli, 4993
Yitsḥaq ben Yehudah, Rashi influenced by, 7619
Yitsḥaq ha-Levi, Rashi influenced by, 7619
YIVO Institute for Jewish Research, 4882–4883
Yixing (Buddhist monk), 1240
commentary by, 9078
Śubhākarasiṃha and, 8804
Yixuan. *See* Linji
Yi Yulgok, **9892–9893**
school of Material Force and, 1931–1932
Yizkor (memorial rubric), in Yom Kippur liturgy, 8391
YMBA. *See* Young Men's Buddhist Association
YMCA. *See* Young Men's Christian Association
Ymir (deity)
birth by, 2985
in creation myth, 3446–3447
Ynglingar (royal Norse line), 842
Ynglinga Saga (Norse saga), 842
war among deities in, 3449
Yobanua-Borna (deity), in Island Arawak religion, 1427
Yocahu (deity), in Island Arawak religion, 1427
Yocippa (deity), 5909
Yoder, Don, 3142, 3143
Yoga, **9893–9897**. *See also specific types*
alchemical function of, 7641
asceticism of
vs. normal behavior, 529
objectives of, 527, 528
atheism and, 578–579, 580
attention in, 603, 605
of Aurobindo Ghose, 633–634
breath and breathing in, 1043–1046, 5819, 7038
cakras and, **1348–1349**
classical, *karman* in, 5095
in Daoism, 1045–1046
definitions of, 5819
desire in, 2305
in devotional life, 9822
ecstatic trances in, 2679
Eliade (Mircea) on, 7350
elixir in, 2771
fasting in, objectives of, 528
French feminists on, 3029, 3030
G tumo (Tibetan), altered states of consciousness and, 1952–1953
Hatha (*See Haṭhayoga*)
and immortality, 2237
in Aum Shinrikyō, 631, 633
in *Bhagavadgītā,* 853, 857
in Indian Medical Systems politics, 3856
in Vajrayāna (Tantric) Buddhism, 1157, 1217, 1221, 1286–1288
Kālacakra tradition of, 5056, 5058
Perfection Stage meditation, 3965, 3966
in Yogācāra Buddhism, 9897
īśvara in, 4752
Kabīr on, 5052
Kuṇḍalinī, 5266–5267
Campbell and, 1380
liṅga as object of meditation in, 4423
lotus symbolism in, 5518
martial arts and, *kaḷarippayaṯṯu,* 5731
meditation in, 5819
miracles in, 6052
mysticism and, 6344
objectives of, 528, 3128, 5266, 5819
origins of, 9905
post-Tantra, 1288–1289
postures and gestures in, 1043–1046, 7343
purification before, 7510
rājayoga
body discipline in, 8704–8705
Īsvara (God) in, 3998
in Rnying ma pa (Nyingmapa) school of Buddhism, 5223, 7870
samādhi in, 8066–8067
Sāṃkhya as basis of, 2016
Sāṃkhya school and (*See* Sāṃkhya school)
as school of philosophy and classical Hinduism, development of, 3997–3998
eight limbs of Yoga in, 3998
semen as elixir in, 2771
Siddha practitioners, 1349
in Sikhism
controversy over, 3879
Kuṇḍalinī in 3HO organization, 3877, 3878
White Tantric Yoga, 3878
sitting position in, 7343
Śiva and, 8415
in Tantric Hinduism, 1045, 1347
in Tibetan Buddhism, 1045, 1153, 1157, 1286–1288
and time, transcendence of, 7989
unity and plurality in, 4421
vital energy, harnessing of, 1475
yoni and, 9905
Yoga (disciplined concentration), 9507
Yogabhāṣya (Vyāsa)
meditation in, 8704
samādhi in, 8067
Yogācārabhūmī (Buddhist text), 1119–1120
in Yogācāra Buddhism, 9898
Yogācāra school of Buddhism, 1119–1120, **9897–9902**
ālaya-vijñāna in, 228–229, 1211–1212, 2338
Bhāvaviveka's critique of, 861
buddhahood in, 1069
in China, 1202, 1238, 1599–1600, 6992
consciousness in, 8858
dharma in, 2335
Dignāga and, 2351
divisions within, 1120
doctrines of, 1119–1120, 5554
Faixang version of, 5258
founders of, 516–517, 1119, 1210–1212, 1300, 2337
Huayan Buddhism compared with, 3012
karman in, 5100
knowledge in, 5200
Mādhyamika Buddhism and, 5554
mysticism in, 6345
nirvāṇa in, 1211, 6629–6630
origins of, 1093, 1210–1212
Paramārtha and, 6992
philosophers of, 1120, 1212, 2351
philosophy of, 1300–1301
prajñā in, 7359
Pure Land devotion opposed by, 4923
realities in, 1210–1212, 5554
Sautrāntika and, 8137
Stcherbatsky (Theodore) on, 8737
Sthiramati and, 8739–8740
śūnyatā (emptiness) in, 1211, 8858, 8859
three (number) in, 9347
trisvabhāva in, 1211, 1212, 1300, 2338

Yogācāra school of Buddhism *continued*
Vijñānavāda theory of Dharmapāla in, 8399
Xuanzang and, 9861
Yogācāra-Vijñānavāda school
Candrakīrti and, 1401
Śīlabhadra, role of, **8398–8399**
Yogācāra-Svātantrika-Madhyamaka Buddhism, 5554
Kamalaśīla as member of, 5070–5071
Śāntarakṣita and Kamalaśīla in, 8107
Yogananda, Paramahansa, **9902–9903**
activities in U.S., 6559
autobiography of, 700
Yoganidrā (deity), 2526
iconography of, 4325, 4326
Yogaśāstra, 4766
Yoga Sūtra (Patañjali), 9822, 9893–9894
body discipline in, 8704–8705
breathing in, 9895
ecstasy in, 2680
karman in, 5095
meditation in, 5819
nonviolence in, 6645
samādhi in, 8066, 8067, 9896
Yoga Tantras, 1215–1218
bodhisattvas in, 1080–1082
sections of, 1215, 1217
Vajrasattva in, 9514
Yogatattva Upaniṣad, levitation in, 3128
Yoga Upaniṣads, 9482, 9483
Yoga Vāsiṣṭha, relativity of time in, 7989
Yogavāsiṣṭha, 7362
Yogeśvarī, Ramakrishna as student of, 7612, 7613
Yogi, The (St. Denis), 2157
Yogi Divine Society, Swaminarayan movement and, 8890
Yoginīs (goddesses), 779
prajñā identified with, 7359
rituals of, 7083
Three Wheeled maṇḍala and, 1350
Yoginī ("Mother") Tantras, 1215, 1218
Cakrasamvara Tantra as, 1349
Hevajra Tantra as, 3965
images in, 2546–2547
mahāmudrā in, 5596, 5597
Yogins
Abhinavagupta on Śiva-nature and, 8418
Hevajra as idealized image of, 3965
aṣṭāṅgayoga (eight-limbed discipline), 8704
in Pratyabhijñā Saivism, 8048
visualization of body by, 7837
Yoḥanan bar Nappaḥa', **9903–9904**
Abbahu and, 2
on afterlife, 153
El'azar ben Pedat under, 2743
Shim'on ben Laqish and, 8347, 8348
Yoḥanan ben Zakk'ai, **9904–9905**
Eli'ezer ben Hyrcanus and, 2763
Gamli'el of Yavneh succeeding, 3269
on sacrifice, 4977
son of, miracle of healing in, 6051
on Torah, importance of, 2745
Yehoshu'a ben Ḥananyah and, 9875
Yoḥanan of Treves (rabbi), 7579–7580
Yoido Full Gospel Church (Seoul), 1727
Yōkigurashi (joyous and blissful life), 9082
Yokuts religion (North America)
bears in, 808
trickster tales of, 6661
turtles in, 9407
Yŏlban-chong school of Buddhism (Korea), 1171
Yoldashev, Ṭāhir, 4628
Yolngu Matha language, 637
Yolngu people (Australia), 647–648
ancestors of, 647, 648
clans of, 641–642, 647
cosmology of, relational, 2003
Djan'kawu mythology of, 2379, 2380
the Dreaming of, 647
history of study of, 647, 648, 668
iconography of, 4306
knowledge of, 648
inside and outside, 6261
land of, 647, 648
Macassans's annual visits with, 647–648
settlements of, 647
stories of, 2481
Yolokantamulu (deity), 9415
Yombe people (Africa), cosmogony of, 2960
Yōmei (Japanese emperor), Buddhism and, 1241, 8374
Yōmeigaku teachings, 4789. *See also* Wang Yangming
propagation of, 1928
Yom ha-Atsma'ut (Independence Day), 4868
Yom ha-Sho'ah (Holocaust Day), 4868
Yom ha-Zikkaron (Day of Remembrance), 6593
Yomi (realm of darkness), in Japanese religion, 3888, 4755
Yom Kippur (Day of Atonement), 4866, 6593, 7927, **7928–7929**. *See also* Ro'sh ha-Shanah
angel in, 345
'Āshūrā' and, 549
casting of lots on, 5425
confession on, 7757, 8390
domestic observances of, 2397
fasting on, 2996, 3171, 7928
in Jewish calendar, 4866
Kapparah on the eve of, 3159, 7928
maḥzor liturgy for, 8390–8391
in Marrano Judaism, 5718
pain as redemption on, 6946
purification of Temple on, 927, 934, 4747
in Samaritan practice, 8070
services on, 7928–7929
white clothing on, 7929
Yom Kippur Qatan (Minor Yom Kippur), 4867
Yom Teruah (Day of Sounding the Shofar), 6593
Yon (deity), in Komi religion, 5217
Yonan, Edward, 7745
Yonatan, Rabbi, on suffering, 8805
Yong-gyun, Bae, 3097
Yongle Emperor, and Daoism, 2187
Yongle Gong (Palace of Eternal Joy), 2187, 2200, 9056
Yongning Monastery (Buddhist temple), 9046, 9048, 9264
Yongxin, on martial arts, 5736
Yongzheng emperor, 1609
Yoni, **9905–9909**
Yon tan rgya mtsho (Dalai Lama), 2131
Yonthu Yindi, 639
Yopico pyramid, 1469
Yoritsuna, Nagasaki, 6620
York, Malachi, 6769, 9435
York, Michael, 6768
arrest of, 6769–6770
teachings of, 6769
York Rite, 3196
Yorkshire High Commission, Calvert (George) and, 1373
Yorta Yorta people (Australia), land claims of, 690
Yoruba language, 3085, 10028
Yoruba religion (Nigeria), **9909–9912**. *See also* Santería
afterlife in, judgment in, 140
Aladura movement in, 104
ancestors in, 4302
art of, 84, 90
body–soul relationship in, 140
Caribbean religions, spirits adopted in, 1433, 1434, 1435
changes in Ondo cosmology, 1999–2000
cosmology, 1998–2000
creation in, 3571
gender in, 3401
dance in, 2137, 2435, 7048
deities of, 9910–9911
deus otiosus in, 2310–2311
Edo influenced by, 2697
Egungun ritual in, 2435, 2439
food symbolism and ritual in, 3171
Gẹlẹdẹ society of (*See* Gẹlẹdẹ society)
gender in, 3401, 3404
ghosts in, 3476
healing in
divination, and correspondence system, 3810
mediums, diagnosis of illness by, 3818
protective charms and, 3820
psychiatric, 3821
iconography of, 4302, 4303–4304
Ifa divination in, 87, 94, 117, 3437, 10032–10033
impersonal power in, concept of, 86
in Candomblé, 120, 121–122
kingship in, relics and, 5170
Maasai, similarities with, 2001
masks in, 2458
Mawu-Lisa and, 5790
mountains in, 6212
myths of, 9910–9911
blacksmith, 95
trickster, 86
oral tradition in, 10032
percussion in, 7037
proverbs in, 6977
reincarnation in, 106, 7677, 9326, 9719
rivers in, 7862
Roman Catholic elements in, 10026
sacred texts of, studies of, 80
sacrifices in, 3571
soul in, 8533
spread of, in African diaspora, 3404
study of, 117
hierarchical pantheon model, as imposed, 1999
Olupona's reinterpretation of, 1999–2000
supreme being of (*See* Ọlọrun)
tricksters in, 9353
in United States, 10032–10033
women in, 4610
Yōsai. *See* Eisai
Yose ben Halafta', **9912–9913**
on *shekhinah,* 8314
Yosef bar Ḥiyya', Abbaye and, 2
Yosef ben Ḥiyya' (amora), 889
Yosef ben Shalom Ashkenazi, on *Sefer yetsirah,* 8221
Yosef ben Yehudah Sham'um, 5616
Yose the Galilean, 844
Yoshida, Atsuhiko, 4464
Yoshida clan, licensing of priests by, 8363
Yoshida Kanetomo, Yūitsu Shintō and, 4122, 8362
Yoshida Shintō. *See* Yūitsu Shintō

Yoshida Shōin, as Meiji Restoration leader, Confucianism and, 1928
Yoshida shrine (Kyoto), Amaterasu at, 8364
Yoshie Akiko, 3347
Yoshikawa Koretari, Yoshida Shintō and, 8363
Yoshimi Yoshikazu, research of, 4801
Yoshioka Yoshitoyo, 2213
Yoshizaki (Japan), Rennyo in, 7752–7753
Yōsō Sōi (Buddhist monk), 4378
Youlong zhuan (Daoist text), 2209
Young, Arthur, 3528
Young, Brigham, **9913–9914**
 on dance, 2137
 Mormonism under, 6193–6194, 6565
 polygamy practiced by, 6558
Young, Frank, on rites of passage, 7799
Young, Iris Marion, on gynocentrism, 3719
Young, Josiah, 75, 78–79
Young, Karl, 2468
Young, M. J., 3146
Young, Michael W., on kingship, 5159
Young, Serenity, 7084
Young Bear, Ray, 3093, 7225
Young earth creationism, 2910–2911, 8189
Young Hebrew movement, 9980
Young Hegelians, 3047
 Marx (Karl) in, 5744–5745
Young India (James), 7370
Young Man Luther (Erikson), 7482
Young Men's Buddhist Association (YMBA), 1140, 1142, 6074, 6080
Young Men's Christian Association (YMCA), 6074
 Moody (Dwight L.) in, 6169
 social work provided by, 7487
Young Women's Christian Association (YWCA), 6074
"Your Money, Our Money, the Government's Money" (Foster), 1421, 1424
Your Word Is Fire, attention in, 606
Youth. *See also* Children
 in Conservative Judaism, 1962
 ecumenical focus on, 2686
 fountains of, 7683–7684 (*See also* Rejuvenation)
 in Jesus Movement, 4852–4853
Youth Aliyah movement, Szold (Henrietta) and, 8941
Youth Black Faith (YBF), 7624
You Zuo, 1560
Yu (Chinese emperor and hero), **9914–9915**
 and dragons, 2433
Yu (deity)
 flood and, 1626–1627
 at New Year, 1642
Yu (musical instrument), 6293–6294
Yü, Chün-fang, 3343
Yuan Code (1291), 5353
Yuan dynasty (China)
 Buddhism in
  Chan Buddhism, 1523
  Chogye-chong school, 1172
  pilgrimage, 7165
  rebellion of, 7257, 7268
  religious advisors in, 7269
  Tibetan Buddhism, 1240, 1256
 Confucianism in, 1166, 1901–1902, 1917
 Daoism in, 2185–2186, 2197, 2199
  ban on, 1166
 establishment of, 1606
 Korea under, 5230
 law in, 5353
 Muslims in, 1599
 shamanism in, 6141–6142
 Tibetan-Mongol interactions in, 3966
Yuan qi, 2177
Yuanwu Keqin, 1524
Yuanxiao Jie (festival), 1642
Yuan Ye (treatise), 3278
Yubu ritual, 9914–9915
Yuca, discovery legend, 1427
Yucatec Maya. *See also* Maya religion
 rites of passage of, 7812
Yucatec Mayan Caste War movement of the Talking Cross, 6576
Yuchi (Euchee) language, 6697
Yuchi tribe (North America), ballgame played by, 753
Yu Dafu, 3070
Yudhiṣṭhira
 in *Mahābhārata,* 852, 4438, 7362
 solving riddles, 6987
Yue, Pang, 2614
Yüeh-chih people, 1109
Yuejing (Scripture of Music), 1585
Yuendumu Aboriginal community, 644
Yuezang zhijin (Zhixu), 9180, 9181
Yuezhi people (Inner Asia), 4490
Yugas (ages)
 bhakti synthesis and, 4000
 cycle of, 4000
 deterioration of *dharma* in, 2327, 6983
 in dice game, 3263
 duration of, 7499
 in Purāṇas, 2018–2019, 7499–7500
 in millenarianism, 6030
 myth of, 176–177
Yugen, 51
Yugoslavia
 disintegration of, 1686
 Islam in, 4677
 pluralism in, 1686
 prehistoric culture in, 7381
 Reformed and Lutheran
  Protestantism in, 1685
Yugoslavian Orthodox church, communism and, restrictions imposed on, 2588
Yugra (Mansi) religion. *See* Khanty and Mansi religion
Yugyō Shōnin (wandering sage), 4939
Yuḥannā ibn Haylān, 2973, 2991
Yuhuang (deity), 1619, **9915**
Yuhuang dadi/Yuhuang Shangdi (deity), 1606, 1641, 9172
Yu Hyŏng-wŏn, Practical Learning movement and, 1932–1933
Yūitsu Shintō, 4806
 Yoshida Kanetomo and, 4122, 8362
 Yoshikawa Koretari and, 8363
Yukagir religion (Siberia), 468. *See also* Shamanism; Siberia and Siberian religions
 clan shamanism in, 8282
Yuki people (California), cosmogonic myths of, 5198
Yuktidīpikā (commentary), Sāṃkhya teachings in, 8092
Yuktiṣaṣṭikāvṛtti (Candrakīrti), commentary in, 1401
Yule feast, 9741
Yule logs, 1757
Yulgok. *See* Yi Yulgok
Yulinggul (Rainbow Snake), 7606
Yulong Abbey, 2207
Yulu (recorded sayings), 1524, 1604
Yulunggul snake, **9915–9917**
 in Wawalag myth, 9704–9705
Yuman tribe (North America), dreams of, 2489
Yum Kimil (deity), 5883
Yum Kippur. *See* Yom Kippur
Yunāni medical system, superceded by prophetic medicine, 3834
Yungang caves (China), Maitreya in, 5620
Yunga religion (Andes), *huacas* in, 8607
Yunguang ji (Daoist), 2210
Yun Hyu, Confucian orthodoxy and, 1932
Yunjian (cloud collar), 9090
Yunji qiqian (Daoist text), 2185, 2210
Yunmen lineage, 1523
Yunnan rebellion, 1599
Yunqi Zhuhong (Buddhist monk), 1167, 1607
Yunupingu, Djoki, 841
Yunus Emre, 2839, **9917**
Yunzhong yinsong (Daoist text), 5240
Yūpa (stake), as center of the world, 1504
Yup'ik Eskimo (Alaska), hunting among, in balance of life, 2618
Yupik language, 4526
Yurak Samoyed. *See also* Samoyed religion; Shamanism
 dream journey initiation, 1470
 holy triad of, 2982
Yuro Ima (spirit), gender and, 3397
Yurok religion (North America)
 ballgame played in, 752
 bears in, 809
 river in, 7861
Yurugu (mythic figure), 95, 100, 3569
 ability to speak, 2390
 in divination rites, 2391
 as trickster, 9352, 9353
 twin of, 9415, 9416
Yurupary, **9917–9921**
 in Macuna myth, 8591
 plant fertility rites and, 8582
Yusa Michiko, 3348
Yūsuf, Muḥyī al-Dīn, Ḥanābilah and, 3768
Yūsuf ibn Tāshfīn, 4585
Yuta (shaman), 6813
Yuwipi (ceremony), 957, 5297, 5444
Yu Yingshi, on Dai Zhen, 2129
Yvon, Claude, in French Enlightenment, 2796
YWCA. *See* Young Women's Christian Association

Z

Zaar cult. *See Zār* cult
Zababa (deity), in Hittite religion, 4069, 4071
Zablocki, Benjamin, 1032
Zacher, Christian, 9293
Zadok (biblical figure), 5421, 5422
Zadokite Fragments (Hebrew text), 2233
Zadokite priesthood, 7399
 Sadducees and, 8018
Zadonsk Monastery (Russian Orthodox), 9194
Zaehner, R. C., **9923–9924**
 on ecstasy, 2680
 historiography and, 4043
 on mysticism, 6342, 6356, 7744
 on Ibn al-ʿArabī, 6146
Zaghlūl, Saʿd, in revolt against British (1919), 6314
Zāghūnī, Abū al-Ḥasan al-, Ḥanābilah and, 3766

Zāgwē kings (Ethiopia)
Ethiopian Church under, 2860
Islam under, 4606
Zahan, Dominique, 109, 117
on healers *vs.* sorcerers, 2100
on knowledge, 5199
on women's curses, 2100
Zāhid, Kamāl al-Dīn, 6638
Ẓāhir (literal meaning of words)
as aspect of religion, Qarmaṭī on, 7543
Ibn Ḥazm on, 4268
al-Ṭabarī on, 8944
Ẓāhir, al- (Fāṭimid caliph), 2503
Ẓāhirī school of Islamic law, 9490
establishment of, 4695
Ibn Ḥazm in, 4268, 4593, 4595, 4699, 7238–7239, 9490
in Muslim Spain, 4699
prevalence of, 4567
Zaidman, Louise Bruit, structuralism and, 8758
Zaire
ancestor worship in, 322
Apostolic Church of John Maranke in, 5695
cults of affliction in, 62
ghosts in, 3476
Zajíc, Zbyněk, Hus (Jan) and, 4233
Zaka (spirit), in Caribbean neo-African cults, 1433
Zakāt (tax), **9924–9926**
in Acehnese religion, 25
almsgiving and, 268
in devotional life, 9817
establishment of, 4562
in Five Pillars, 4565
as gift giving, 3485
levied on the wealthy, 4564
reinstitution of, 4574
as sign of repentance, 7758
Zakī, Salīm, 6315
Zakīyya, Hagga, 3369
Zakkur (king), 28, 448
Základy všeobecné vědy náboženské (Pertold), classification of religion in, 8774
Zālīte, Māra, on Māra, 5691
Zallaqa, battle of (1086), 4592
Zalman. *See* Eliyyahu ben Shelomoh Zalman
Zalmoxis (deity), **9926–9929**
deification of, 3466
dualism of, 2511
and immortalization, 2248
kingship associated with, 3466
psychosomatic medicine of, 3466
Pythagoras and, 3466
in Thracian religion, 9169
Zamakhsharī, al-, **9929–9930**
as al-Bayḍāwī's source, 806
tafsīr of, 8953, 8954
Zaman (newspaper), 4629
Zaman i Ohrmazd (Bianchi), 863
Zambia. *See also* Bemba religion; Central Bantu religions; Ndembu religion
Apostolic Church of John Maranke in, 5695
Christianity in
charismatic, 106
politics and, 1723–1724
cults of affliction in, 62
Ila people of
ghosts of, 3476
myths of, 97
Khoi religion in, 5135
Lumpa church in, 105, 5408–5409
San religion in, 5135
United Church of Zambia in, 1722
Wiko Makishi masquerade dances in, 2141
Zamuco peoples, religion of, 8633–8634
Zamzam, well of, 5050
Zâna (moon), 6927
Zanabazar (incarnate lama), 1149
Zand (Zoroastrian texts), 5560–5561, 9993
authorship of, 9935
Zandbergs, Uldis, 766
Zanj. See Lwa
Zanjānī, Muḥammad Najmī, on *ḥadīths,* 3732
Ẓann (opinion), 4374
Zanzibar
Islamic influence of, 2571, 2578
Sultan of, 5181
urban nature of, 2566
Zaojun (deity), 1641, 2407
Zaothra (libations), 4535
Zao-wang (deity), as stove god, 4106
Zaowuzhu (creator), 9172
Záparo religion, moon in, 2863
Zapata, Emiliano, 9930
Zapata Olivella, Manuel, 3065
Zapatismo and indigenous resistance, **9930–9933**
Zapatista Army of National Liberation (EZLN), 3414, 9930, 9933
uprising of, 2617, 5931–5932
Virgin of Guadalupe in, 3064
Zaphon, Mount, 6213
Zapiteri religion (Amazon), World Fire myth in, 8589
Zapotec religion (Mexico)
birth rites of, 7812
deities of, 5887, 5903, 5912
fertility god of, 9213
funerary practices of, 3243, 5887
in Monte Albán, 5902–5904
knot rituals of, 5197
natural forces in, 5903
pre-Columbian, 5887
in Classic period, 5902–5904
in Postclassic period, 5912
priesthood in, 5912
rituals in, 5912
Zapotec writing, 5887
Zaqqum (underworld tree), 9455, 9577
Zār (ceremony), 2148–2149, 2402, 2933
Zarādusht (priest), and Mazdakism, 5800
Zarathushtra (Zoroaster), **9933–9937**. *See also* Zoroastrianism
on afterlife
community in, 132
divine justice in, 129, 133
on Amesha Spentas, 290
on angels, 344
and Armenian religion, 491
cattle sacrifice condemned by, 1466
Christensen on, 1650
condemnation of *daivas* by, 2128
on cult of *haoma,* 3776, 5434
dates for, 9988–9989
as ethical prophet, 5384
European scholars on, 6999
Golden Age of, 3630
Greek works issued under authority of, 2094
historical, 9988–9989
in Airyana Vaējah, 210
monotheism of, 6157
Nyberg (H. S.) on, 6774
on Ahura Mazdā, 4536
on passing of bridge, 1049
in Plato's *Republic,* 491, 520
polytheism rejected by, 2128
post-Islamic biographies of, 6738
as prophet, 7425
on revelation, 7778
on sacrifice, 8006
Saoshyants as born from seed of, 8110
sons of, 9934
theology of, orthodoxy *vs.* heresy and, 3924
vocation of, 9632
in Western traditions, 9935, 9990
in world-periods, 174, 203–204
in Zoroastrianism, 9988–9989
Zarathushtrian Assembly, 9991–9992
Zarathustra: En Bog om Persernes gammle Tro (Lehmann), 5405
Zār (zaar) cult, 107
in East Africa
glossolalia in, 3507
healing in, 3813
rattles used in, 7035
in Middle East
suppression of, 3837
women and healing in, 3837
possession in, 2568
Zarḳālla, al-, 7492
Zasu (leader of Buddhist school), 9075
Zaw-gyi, 3077
Zāwiyahs (monastery), 9005. *See also* Khānagāh
critique of, 4589–4590
origins of, 4586, 4588
in Ottoman Empire, 4588
responsibilities of, 4588
Zaya Paṇḍita, 6142
Zayde (Segrais), 3051
Zayd ibn ʿAlī. *See also* Zaydī Shiism
revolt of, 8321
Zaydī Shiism
development of, 8321–8322
distribution of, 8325
doctrine of, 2064–2065, 5549
on free will and predestination, 3213
Hijrah/hijar (protected enclave) in, 3776
imamate, doctrine of, 4395–4396, 8324
Muʿtazilah in, 6320–6321
tafsīr (Qurʾanic exegesis) in, 7565
in Yemen, 4572, 4699, 8325
Zayn, al-Qurashī wad al-, 6228
Zaynab bint ʿAlī, **9937–9939**
Zaynab bint Muḥammad, 3008
Zayn al-ʿĀbidin, Imāmīyah and, 8338
Zayyanid dynasty, 4587
Zazen (seated meditation), 1292, 9946
Caodong school and, 4154
Dōgen advocating, 2386
kōan and, 1293, 2306, 6987
Nio-zazen technique, Suzuki Shōsan on, 8887
redefined by Huineng, 4154
as sacrament, 7957
Zealots, **9939–9940**
Smith (Morton) on, 8448
Zeami Motokiyo, 2455, 2456
Zebaḥ (slaughter), 4746
Zebunnisa (princess), calligraphy and, 1369
Zechariah, 879
Adad in, 28
Temple procedures in, 929, 932
Zechariah (king), Hosea and, 4137
Zedekiah (king of Judah), 4827
Zeitschrift der Deutschen Morgenländischen Gesellschaft (journal), 10056
Zeitschrift für Religionspsychologie (journal), 847
Zekher ṣaddiqim (Sultansky), 5086
Zekhut Avot, **9940–9942**
Zelenin, Dimitri K., 475, 3114
Zell, Morning Glory, 6472–6473
Zeller, Eduard, 7191
Zeme (deity), 760–761, **9942–9943**
Zemes māte (earth mother), 760
Zemi spirits
in Caribbean religions, 1429, 1430
in Island Arawak religion, 1427

in Island Carib religion, 1428
Zempléni, Andras, on exorcism, 8692
Zempoala (Mexico), Totonac religion in, 5910, 9253, 9254
Žemýna. *See also* Zeme
in Lithuanian birth beliefs, 2557
Zen and Japanese Culture (Suzuki), 500
Zen at War (Victoria), 1247
Zen Buddhism, **9943–9951**. *See also* Chan Buddhism
and abstract art, 500
aesthetics and, 51
asceticism in, 527
under Ashikaga regime, 4787
attention in, 603, 605–606
authority in, 694
Bodhidharma and, 995
buddha-nature in, 1183
Chan lineages from China, 1523
and culture of learning, 1181
in Cunningham's (Merce) works, 2161
desire in, 2306
Dōgen and, 5109
drama in, 2455
drums in, 2497
early modern, 9948–9949
Eisai in, 2741–2742
emptiness *(śūnyatā)* in, 8859
enlightenment in, 2794–2795
ethics of, 1281
of Evola (Julius), 2906
and film, 3097
formative period of, 9943–9945
gardens in, 3278
Gozan Zen, **3642–3644,** 4377, 4787
hermeneutics, 1276–1277
humor in, 4202, 4207
iconoclasm in, 4284
intuition in, 4525
under Kamakura regime, 4786
Keizan and, 5109–5110
Kōan (*See Kōan* Zen)
language of, 5310–5311
martial arts and, 5732
medieval, 9946–9948
meditation in (*See* Buddhist meditation, in Zen Buddhism)
Merton (Thomas) and, 5879
modern, 9949–9950
monism in, 6145
mysticism in, 6345
Neo-Confucianism and, 1927
Nichiren's criticism of, 6604
Nio-zazen technique, Suzuki Shōsan on, 8887
nirvāṇa in, 6631–6632
Nishida Kitarō's practice of, 6636
Nyorai model of meditation in, Suzuki Shōsan on, 8887
oral tradition of instruction in, 8713–8714
Ō-Tō-Kan (*See* Ō-Tō-Kan school of Zen)
paradox in, 6988, 6989
patriarchs and masters as spiritual guides in, 8713–8714
philosophy of, 1302
political power of, 7272–7273
procession in, 7417
pūjā in, 7496
Pure Lands in, 1524, 7503
redemption in, 7641
religious experience in, 7740–7741
revelation and sacred time in, 7988
riddles in, 6987–6988
Rinzai (*See* Rinzai school of Zen)
sacred space in, vol. 5 color insert
salvation in, 527, 7679
satori experience in, 7696
schools of, 1244–1245
seppuku (ritual suicide) honored in, 8832
silence in, 5310–5311
social discrimination in, 1184
Soto sect of (*See* Sōtō school)
sports and, 8724
Suzuki (D. T.), role of, **8884–8887**
Suzuki Shōsan, role of, 8887
temples in, 9049
in Thailand, 9096
traditionalism in, 7696
in United States, 1188, 1189
Victoria (Brian) on, 1247
at World's Parliament of Religions, 9805
Xingyuan's interpretations of, 3139–3140
Zen Buddhism and Psychoanalysis (Fromm), 7476
Zeng Cao, 2211
Zenkovskii, Vasilii, 3134
Zeno (Roman emperor), 6153, 6154, 7923
schism and, 8155
Virgin Mary, church to, 8069
Zenon (philosopher)
national background of, 8742
Stoicism, role in, 8740
Zeno of Citium. *See also* Stoicism
cosmopolitanism of, 3906
integrity of, 3912
Zeno of Elea, on paradox, 6988
Zen Sickness, 9949
Zephaniah, 879
pesher of, 7064
Zephaniah (prophet), 7436
Zero
in Babylonian number system, 6752
as emptiness, religious symbolism of, 6752–6753
in Indian number system, 6752
in Maya philosophy, 1357
Zerries, Otto, on bird in shamanism, 8291
Zerubbabel (biblical figure), 419, 898, 924, 929
Zeus (deity), **9951–9954**
Adad identified with, 28
on Adonis' split life, 34–35, 7767
Aphrodite and, 407
Apollo and, 424
Artemis as daughter of, 506
Asklepios and, 551
Athena and, 586–587
ax of, 967, 5275
Baal identified with, 7129
birth by, 2985
Cleanthes (Stoic) on, 3912
complexity of relationships of, 3663–3664
cults of, 9952–9954
Demeter as bride of, 2268
Diana as female counterpart of, 2346
divine kingship of, 5146–5147
Dushara identified with, 6386, 6389
Epimenides and, 9927–9928
epithets of, 3663, 3664, 5994
Euhemerus on, 4036
family of, 2982, 3663, 3679
as father, 3663
and the Flood, 2965–2966
in form of swan, 4135
functions of, 3663–3664, 9952
games dedicated to, 8723
Hera and, 3914
Herakles and, 3916
Hesiod on, 3963
Hestia and, 3964
Homer on, 4108
hypostasis and, 4240
iconography of, 4321, 4322
in *Iliad* (Homer), 3000, 3663, 3679
in *Hiera Anagraphē,* 2883
justice of, 3663
kingship linked with, 3663
Lucian on, 3910
in magical texts, 3909
as meteorological deity, 5994–5995
in Minoan religion, 2895
miracles of, 3903
in Mycenaean religion, 42
in oaths, 5995
Olympian games and, 8723
oracle of, 6832–6833
origins of, 3663
in Orphic Gold Tablets, 6898
in Orphism, 6891, 6894–6895
Persephone as daughter of, 2268–2269
Pindar on, 7174
and Prometheus, 1014, 7419–7420
in origin of sacrifice, 3669–3670, 3683
Prometheus and, 8187
and races of humans, 2965
Sabazios identified with, 7953, 7954
shape shifting of, 8301
as solar metaphor, 4459
sovereignty of, 3663–3664, 3679, 5994–5995
Stoics on, 3203
in Stoic theology, 8742
syncretism and, 8937
temple of, 9063
in *Theogony* (Hesiod), 5468
as theopantistic, 4066
thunderbolt of, 7603
Tin identified with, 2870–2871
trees as symbols of, 9337
Typhon killed by, 2431
virgin goddesses and, 9604
Zeus-Amun, 834
Zeus Hypsistos, 7129
Zeus Meilichios, 7129
Zeutas (Getae priest), 3466
Zevah (offering), 927
Zevah pesah (Abravanel), 17
Zevah shelamin (offering), 926
Zhabs drung Ngag dband rnam rgyal, 1232
Zhai. See Jiao
Zhaijiao (vegetarian religions), 8964
Zha Liangyong, 3070
Zhamtsarano, Tsyben, 1150
Zhang, K. C., 456
Zhang Boduan, 1603, 2211
Zhang Daoling, 1593, 2635, 2637, **9954**
and Celestial Masters/ Heavenly Masters, 2180, 2192, 9843
millenarianism of, 6038
mystery society of, 7719
and Rectifying Rites of Tianxin, 2180
Zhang Enpu, 8963
Zhang family, lineage of, 2198–2199
Zhang Jizong, 1608
Zhang Jue, 1593, **9954–9955**
millenarianism of, 6039
Taiping Dao established by, 7022
and Yellow Turban rebellion, 2180, 6039
Zhang Junfang, 2210–2211
Zhang Ling. *See* Zhang Daoling
Zhang Lu, 1593, 5317, **9955–9956**
and Celestial Masters/ Heavenly Masters, 2181, 2192, 2193
millenarianism of, 6038
Zhang Sanfeng (legendary Daoist figure), 2187

Zhang Shengyan, 1524
Zhang Shouzhen, 2198
Zhang ston Chos 'bar (Zhangdön Chöbar), 1225
Zhang tshal pa Brtson du grags (Zhangtselpa Tsondudrak), on *mahāmudrā,* 5598
Zhang Xuecheng, 1579, **9956–9957**
Zhang Yimou, 3097
Zhang Yuchu, and inner alchemy, 2187
Zhang Yue, on Sima Chengzhen, 8400
Zhang Zai, **9957–9958**
Cheng Hao and, 1560
cosmology of, 1578, 1931
on cultivation of sagehood, 8704
on nature, 2632
Neo-Confucianism and, 1603
on *ren,* 7752
on supreme ultimate, 1900
Zhang Zhung empire, 2545, 2549
Zhang Zhung language, 2545–2546, 2549
Zhang Zongyan, 2199
Zhanran (Buddhist monk), 1577, 6631
scriptures interpreted by, 1276
and Tendai school, 9075, 9077
and Tiantai school, 1237, 9179–9180
writings of, 9180
Zhan Ruoshui
on Study of Inner Mind, 1902
Wang Yangming and, 9674
Zhao Daoyi, hagiographic works of, 2206
Zhao lun (Sengzhao), Mádhyamika teachings in, 8228
Zhao Qi, *Mengzi* edited by, 5857
Zhaoxuan si (office to illumine mysteries), 8995
Zhao Yizhen, and inner alchemy, 2187
"Zhaozhou and the dog" (riddle), 6987
Zhaozhou Congshen, 1522
Zhenda school of Daoism, 5495–5496
Zhen Dexiu, 1578
Zhengao, the (Declarations of the Perfected) (Daoist text), 1597, 2182–2183, 2205, 8996
Zheng Chenggong (Manchu commander), 9060
Zhenghe wanshou Daozang (Daoist text), 2203
Zhengjiao zhenquan (Wang Daiyu), 4632
Zhengtong Daozang (Daoist text), 2203
Zheng Xuan, 1898
Zhengyan (Buddhist nun), 1168
Compassion Relief (Ciji) movement of, **1787–1790,** 6761
Tzu Chi Foundation founded by, 2786, 2787
Zhengyi (component of Daoist canon), 2203
Zheng Yi, on *li,* 5431
Zhengyi Daoism, 1608, 2187
consolidation of, 1602
ordination in, 6855–6856
in Qing Dynasty, 2187, 2188
Zhengyi Mengwei Dao (Way of Orthodox Unity), in Wei dynasty, 2192, 2200
Zheng-Zhu school of Confucianism, in Korea, 1930–1932
Zhen Luan, 2183–2184
Zhenren (perfected person), **9958–9960**
in Daoism, 2178, 2182
revelations to Yang Xi by, 1597
Tao Hongjing on, 8996
Zhuangzi on, 1588
Zhen shu calligraphy, development of, 1370
Zhenwu (deity), 1619, 2187, 2207, 9057–9058, vol. 3 color insert
Zhenyan Buddhism, **9960–9964**. *See also* Tantrism
Amoghavajra propagating, 293
dualistic monism in, 1577
Mongols and, 1606
Śubhākarasiṃha, roel of, **8803–8804**
Vajrabodhi in, 9510
Zhenyi, Master. *See* Sima Chengzhen
Zhenzong, 1606, 9057
Zhezong, Emperor, 1562
Zhi (musical instrument), 6293
Zhi (temple), 9056
Zhi byed order (Buddhist), 1227, 1228, 5223–5224
Zhi Dun (Zhi Daolin) (Buddhist monk), 1576, 1600
on *li,* 5431
on perfection of wisdom, 1163
Zhi gnas (calming meditation), 1284
Zhig po gling pa, 1232
Zhili (Buddhist monk), 9180
Zhi li (ultimate *li*), 5431
Zhili, Siming, Pure Land practices of, 4924
Zhipan (Buddhist monk), 9179
Zhixiang monastery, Huayan Buddhism and, 4146
Zhixu (Buddhist monk), 9178–9179, 9180–9181
Zhiyan (Buddhist monk), **9964–9965**
and Ŭisang, 9437
as Dushun's disciple, 2530
and Fazang, 3012
Huayan Buddhism and, 4146
Zhiyi (Buddhist monk), 3180, **9965–9967**
celebration of, 1308
lectures by, 9174–9175
on meditation, 1290, 1291, 1601, 9178
on Amitābha, 1239
on emptiness *(śūnyatā),* 8859
philosophy of, 1271, 1272, 1302
pilgrimage of, 9174, 9175
Pure Land practices of, 4924
studying under Huisi, 9174
and Tendai school, 9077, 9079
and Tiantai school, 1237–1238, 1576–1577, 1596, 6630, 9075, 9174–9175
writings of, 1237, 1291, 9174–9176
Zhizheng (Buddhist monk), Huayan Buddhism and, 4146
Zhong (bells), 6293
Zhongguo Musilin (magazine), 4637, 4639
Zhongguo Qingzhen zonglan (Survey of mosques in China), 4634
Zhonghe (central harmony), ecology and, 2636
Zhongli (deity), 1625
Zhongli Quan, 2200
portraits of, vol. 10 color insert
Zhong Lü chuangao ji (Daoist text), 2211
Zhongnanshan shuojing tai lidai zhenxian beiji (Daoist text), 2208
Zhongqian (Buddhist monk), 9179
Zhongyangzi. *See* Wang Zhe
Zhongyong (Doctrine of the Mean), 2634
as canon, 1909
harmony in, 8462
Jesuits and, 1918
Mencian school and, 1587
nature in, 2632
Zhongyuan Jie festival, 1643
Zhötön Ngödrub (G/bzhod ston dngos grub grags), 2549
Zhou Dunyi, **9967–9968**
Cheng brothers and, 1560
cosmology of, 1578
on nature, 2632
Neo-Confucianism and, 1603
on supreme ultimate, 1900
on *taiji,* 8959
on *Yinyang wuxing,* 8959
Zhou dynasty (China)
afterlife during, 169–170
Buddhist/Daoist conflict during, 2183–2184
cities in, 1803
Confucianism in, 1891–1892
evolution of, 3341
Confucius and, 1934, 1936
Daoism in, 3341
temples in, 9057
disintegration of, 1589
divination in, 2372
dream interpretation in, 2484
Empress Wu Zhao and, 1600
funerary practices in, 1570–1571
kingship in, 5178
Korean religion and, 5229
law in, 5352
magic in, 5592
myth in, 1623–1624
overview, 1582–1585
political structure of, 1570, 7266–7267
rituals of
jade in, 4759
sacrifices in, 1911
ritual taken from, 1894–1895
Shangdi and, 8300
spirit mediums in, 1589
tian in, 9172
writing in, 1370
Zhou Rituals (Zhouli), 1907, 5431
imperial sacrifices and, 1912
Zhoushi mingtongji (Tao), 8997
Zhouyi cantong qi, 240
and alchemy, 2185
Zhou Ziliang, 8996–8997
Zhu (musical instrument), 6293–6294
Zhuang Lin xu Daozang (Daoist text), 2211–2212
Zhuang Zhou, 1573, 1588
Zhuangzi (Daoist philosopher), **9968–9971**
on dragons, 2433
monism of, 6146
on pearl, 7024
on shape shifting, 8302
on *taiping,* 8961
on visions, 9613
Zhuangzi (Daoist text), 2174, 2176, **9968–9971**
afterlife in, 172
birds in, 948
chaos and time in, 7987
Dao de jing and, 1574
dao in, 2177
de in, 2174
early Daoist thought and, 1588
fully realized person in, 4332
German translation of, 1057
Guo Xiang's commentary on, 3710
humor in, 4206–4207
Lao Dan/Laozi in, 5315–5316
meditation in, 5821
miracles in, 6052
mythic image of emperor in, 1624
overview of, 1572–1573
philosophical Daoism in, 1575
self-transformation in, 1896
syncretic Daoism in, 1574
on transformation, in nature, 2636
translations of, 1633
zhenren in, 9958–9960
Zhuanxu (deity), as model emperor, 1627
Zhuchi (temple managers), 1617
Zhu Daosheng. *See* Daosheng
Zhuhong (Buddhist monk), 1578, 9180, **9971–9972**

Zhurong (deity). *See* Suiren
Zhu Shixing, 1146
Zhushuang suibi (Zhuhong), 9180
Zhu Xi, **9972–9975**. *See also* Cheng-Zhu school of Confucianism
on ancestor worship, 323
canon formulation and, 1909
Ching (Julia) studying, 10031
commentary of the Four Books, 1909
on Confucian education, 9674
as founder of *daoxue* (learning of the path), 1917, 1923
on images of Confucius, 4338
Japan, influence in, 1927, 3802, 8363
Kaibara Ekken as follower of, 5055
Korean Confucianism and, 1931, 1932
Hwadam and, 8510
Kumazawa Banzan influenced by, 5264
Lu Xiangshan and, 5541, 5542
on *Mengzi,* 5857
metaphysics of, 1578
Nakae Tōju and, 6403, 6404
on nature, 2632
Neo-Confucianism and, 1603
on *qi,* 7544
reformism of, 1578
on *ren* and *yi,* 7752
revival of Confucianism and, 1900–1901
on *taiji,* 8959–8960
Wang Yangming and, 9674–9675
Yamazaki Ansai influenced by, 9869–9870
Yi T'oegye influenced by, 9892
Zhu Xiangxian, 2208
Zhu Yuanzhang (Chinese emperor), 1607, 1608
capital chosen by, 4632
military success of, 1166
Zhwa lu Ri sbug Blo gsal bstan skyong, 5224
Zhwa lu (Zhalu) school of Buddhism, 5224
Ziakpokpo (spirit), 7523
Zicāns, Eduard, on solar weddings, 8134
Ziegenbalg, Bartholomaus, 8978
Ziggurats
architecture of
classification of, 461, 462
origins of, 7526
Neolithic temples resembling, 6462
temples on top of, 9062
as tower, 9264
of Ur, moon in, 6172
urbanization and, 1803
Zigong, as disciple of Confucius, 1935
Zilie kalnia (blue hills), 775
Zilu, as disciple of Confucius, 1935
Zimbabwe. *See also* Central Bantu religions; Shona religion
Apostolic Church of John Maranke in, 5695
charismatic Christianity in, 106
civil wars of, aftermath of, 9599
Great Zimbabwe ruins in, 84
Khoi religion in, 5135
Korekore people of, myths of, 97
Ndebele birth ritual in, 7804–7805
San religion in, 5135
stone birds in, 8665
Zimermann, Günter, 5886
Zimmer, Heinrich, **9975**
Campbell, influence on, 1378
on lion symbolism, 5465
on Ramakrishna, 7613
on Tantrism, 8988
Zimmerman, Francis, on health as well-being, 3854
Zimmern, Heinrich
on Babylonian religion, 5968
on *Epic of Gilgamesh,* 3487
on Marduk, 222, 2522
Zimón, Henryk, on Schmidt (Wilhelm), 8170
Zimri-Lim, 27
Zinacantan, Maya people of
concept of souls, 5798
sacred geography of, 3434–3435
Zinacantecos, marriage among, 5724
Zindīq (heretic), 5657
Zingg, Robert M., 5942
Zinzendorf, Ludwig, 6873
Zinzendorf, Nikolaus, **9975–9976**
in Moravian church, 6191
Pietism of, 7142, 7143
on slavery, 1706
Zion (journal), 4882
Zion, Mount, as divine dwelling, 6213
Zionism, **9976–9983**
African church movements, 1719–1720
afterlife in
community in, 132
time in, 132
Agudat Yisra'el on, 194, 195, 196
Alkalai (Yehudah ben Shelomoh) as forerunner of, 263
Anglo-Israelites hostility toward, 1658
anti-Semitism and, 402–403, 5021
Bar-Ilan (Me'ir) in, 788
Buber (Martin) in, 1055
Cohen's rejection of, 1851
expulsion and, 2939
Ginzberg (Asher) in, 3495–3496
Hasidic opposition to, 3790, 3793
Herzl (Theodor) in, 3496
in Israel, 6903–6904
in Jehovah's Witnesses theology, 4820
Jerusalem in, 4841
Jewish identity in, 4863–4864
in Jewish Renewal, 4871
Jewish Theological Seminary of America and, 1958
Kalischer (Tsevi Hirsch) described as follower of, 5069
Kaplan (Mordecai) in, 7636
Karaite sect and, 5083
Kook (Avraham Yitsḥaq) in, 5226, 5227
Löw (Yehudah ben Betsal'el of Prague) in, 5520–5521
Magen David in, 5559
messianism in, 5978
in modern Jewish thought, 4906–4907, 4984–4985
Mohilever's (Shemu'el) influence on, 6113
nationalism in, 4984
nature in, 2643
politics and, 10062–10063
in Reform Judaism, 7671, 7672
Reines (Yitsḥaq Ya'aqov) in, 7681
religious, 9980–9981
Rubenstein (Richard) on, 4094
Schechter (Solomon) on, 8146
of Scholem (Gershom), 4906
Scholem (Gershom) and, 8177, 8178
secular, 9979–9980
sociology and, 4881
Sofer (Mosheh) on, 8507
Soloveitchik (Joseph Baer) on, 8519
Szold (Henrietta), role of, 8941
Teichthal (Issachar) on messianism and, 4091
Teitelbaum (Yo'el) on Holocaust and, 4091
of Wise (Stephen), 9767
Zionist African Independent Churches, 103
worship style in, 8316
Zionist Congress, Tenth (1911), Agudat Yisra'el responding to, 194
Zion Watch Tower and Tract Society, 4820
Zirid dynasty, 4582
Zis, Bartolo, 2435, 2436
Zisi (Confucius' grandson), 5857
Zitkala-Sa, *American Indian Stories,* 3090
Ziusudra (Sumerian king). *See also* Atrahasis
Enoch identified with, 2803
in Flood, 2791
Ziya, Mehmed. *See* Gökalp, Ziya
Ẓiyā' al-Dīn Barānī, 6639
Ziyārah (visitation of holy places), 7160
Ziyārāt pilgrimages
in devotional life, 9819–9820
women and healing associated with, 3834–3835
Ziyuan, Mao, 4924
Zizhilu (Zhuhong), 9180
Zmeja Marina (snake Marina), 770
Zōbō (Counterfeit Dharma), 5685–5687
Zodiac. *See also* Astrology
animals of, 8835
invention of, 563
ordering of sky in, 8428, 8733
signs of, 565
Zoega, Georg, on Mithraism, 208, 6088
Zohak (monster), 2431–2432
Zohar (qabbalistic text), 7534, **9983–9984**
afterlife in, 154–155
authority of, *vs.* Talmud, 3751
author of, 6353
demons in, 2278, 5459
eschatological mysticism in, 6353
fire in, 3119
Gnostic concepts in, 3524
halakhah and, 3751
Hasidism and, 3788
historiography in, 4059
ḥokhmah in, 4080
in medieval Judaism, 4980–4981
menstruation in, 7515
mystical union in, 6340
number symbolism in, 6747
Scholem (Gershom) on, 8178
sefirot in, 6362, 7536
Shim'on bar Yoh'ai and, 8347
soul in, 8560
Torah in, 9237
transmigration in, 9330
tsaddiq in, 9378–9379
Zokā (songs), 6300
Zolla, Elémire, **9984–9987**
Gnosticism and, 3534
historiography of, 4050
Zolla, Émile, 3059
Zolotarev, A., 2506
Zolotarev, A. M., 475
Zolotarev, Aleksandr, 3114
Zoloth, Laurie, 3428, 3430
Zōmatsu (Period of Counterfeit Dharma), Saichō on, 8030
Zombies
ghosts as, 3476–3477
in Kumina, 1435
in Vodou, 9638

Zong (sacred lineage), in Confucianism, gender and, 3341
Zong (school), 1246
Zong (to honor, revere, and obey), 10072–10073
Zongjiao (sectarian teachings), 1580, 10073
Zongli zhongjing mulu (Chinese Buddhist texts), 2171
Zongmi (Buddhist monk), 6631, **9987–9988**
Huayan Buddhism and, 1577, 4147
Zongxuan xiansheng wenji (Daoist text), 2209
Zorba the Buddha, 7608
Zoroaster. *See* Zarathushtra
Zoroastrian Association, 6999
Zoroastrianism, **9988–10008**. *See also* Avesta; Parsis; Zarathushtra
afterlife in, 130–131, 9996
Chinvat Bridge, **1647**
heaven and hell in, 3884
resurrection of body in, 131
women in, 3373
Airyana Vaējah in, 210
Amesha Spentas in, **290–291**
origins of, 4537
angels in, 344–345
apocalypse in, 9996–9997
apostasy in, 433
in Arabia, 442
and Armenian religion, 491–492
ascension in, 519–520, 3129
ateshgah in, 568–570
Bianchi (Ugo) on, 863
calendar, 1355
of Parsis, 6998
cattle in, 1466, 6997–6998
in China, 1598, 1599
confession in, 1889
confession of faith in, 2052
conversion to, 7000
cosmogony of, 9995, 10014
creation in
evil and sickness, source of, 3809
multiple versions of, 5561
origins of, 4536
daivas (demonic powers) in, 2128
death in, 7763
deities of, 9994–9995 (*See also* Ahura Mazda; Angra Mainyu; Haoma; Mithra)
gender of, 3372
origins of, 4535–4536
twin, 2985
Devil in, 8124
devils in, 2314, 2315
divine kingship in, 5147
doctrines of, 9994–9997
dogs in, 2393
dokhma (tower of silence) in, 9264
dominance of, in Persia, 2583
drugs and substances in
Ephedra, 3775
haoma in, **3775–3776**
dualism in (*See* Dualism, in Zoroastrianism)
eschatology in, 2834, 9996–9997
fate in, 3004
festivals in, 6730–6731
final judgment in, 3118
fire in, 568–570, 3118, 4535, 6997
flight in, 3128
flowers associated with deities in, 3135
Frashōkereti in, **3189–3190**
fravashis in, **3190**
funeral rites in, 3136, 3238
dakhma in, 2130
of Parsis, 6998, 7506
gender in, **3371–3375**
gender studies in, 3371–3372
globalization of, 10004–10005
goats in, 8312
God in, 9995
Golden Age in, 3629–3630
good and evil in, 203–204, 7778
haoma in, 519, 850
history in, 9995–9996
Ibn Sīnā's thoughts in, 4274–4275
Ibn Taymīyah on, 4569
influence on other religions, 3119
Ishrāqīyah influenced by, 4554
and Islam, 4575
Islamic eschatology and, 2836
and Judaism, 2277
khvarenah in, 5139–5140
kingship in, 5165
laity of, 9991–9992
libations in, 4535
light and darkness symbolism in, 5451
literature of, transmission of, 5560–5561
magi in, 5559–5561, 9989–9992, vol. 8 color insert
Manichaeism opposed by, 5655, 5660–5661
Mani influenced by, 5646, 5648, 5659
marriage in, of Parsis, 6998–6999, 7000
Mazdakism and, 5800
Mongol religions influenced by, 6140
monotheism in, 6157, 6160
mountains in, 6212
mythology of, 9994–9997
oral tradition in, 708, 5561
ordination in, 6853
origins of, 4535–4537
orthodoxy and heresy in, 3924
perfume ceremony in (Dhup-sarvi), 3137
priesthood in (*See* Priesthood, in Zoroastrianism)
redemption in, 7641
rejection of polytheism in, 2128
resurrection in, 7763–7764
revelation in, 7778
rituals in, 9935, 9997–9999
magi in, 9991
sacred book of (*See* Avesta)
sacred history of, 9995
sacrifice in, 8006
saviors in (*See* Saoshyants)
Singer (Kurt) on, 8768
suffering in, 9112
sun in, 8838
syncretism and, 8929
texts of, 9992–9994
theology of, priests in development of, 5561
tree of life in, 9335
truth in, 9371, 9372
twins in, 9412–9413, 9416
universalism in, 3907
universal morality in, 7651
water in, 4535
wisdom in, 9751–9752, 9764–9765
women in, **3371–3375**
Parsis, 6998–6999
world-periods in, 174, 203–204
yasatas in, 9874–9875
Zarathushtra in, 9934–9935, 9988–9989
Zurvanism and, 10011, 10012
Zorzi. *See* Giorgio, Francesco
Zosimos of Panopolis, 245, 246, 247
Zou Yan, 1572, 1591, 2989
on *qi,* 7544
yingyang wuxing and, 9889
Zubayr ibn al-ʿAwwām, al-, ʿAlī opposed by, 258
Zuhayr (poet), 7221
Zuhayr, Kaʿb ibn, 6738
Žulhotilde;asi people, 5135–5136
Zuhrī, al-, *ḥadīth* collection of, 3728
Zuhuri, al-, 4601
Zukru festival, 2126
Zulu language, 3085
Zulu religion (South Africa), **10008–10011**. *See also* AmaNazaretha; Nguni religion; Southern African religions
ancestors in, 3817
creation myth of, 96
disease and illness in, 3817
diviners in, shades, calling by, 3818
emergence myth, colonialism interpreted through, 1854
hot and cold in, 8662
imperialist interpretation of, 1857
marriage in, 5724–5725
proverbs in, 6977
python cult in, 8663
reincarnation in, 7677
shades in, 8656
solstice celebration in, 8656–8657
taboo in, 8948
uNkulunkulu in, 9474
as hero *vs.* supreme being, 96, 3574
warfare in, 9682
Zumárraga, Juan de, 4504, 5917, 5921–5922
Žumi (dwelling), 9394
Zundel, Yosef, and Musar movement, 6241
Zungsheng Guan (Abbey of the Holy Ancestor), 2196
Zuni religion (North America)
androgynes in, 338
astronomy and calendar in, 2008–2009
ballgame played in, 752
Benedict (Ruth) on, 820
clowns in, 1838, 1839, 8016–8017
cosmology in, 2008–2009, 6660, 6722–6723, 9697
cave myth and, 1469
creation myth of, 1469, 3015, 6660
emergence in, 2556–2557
hierogamy in, 2555–2556
cult system of, 6726–6727
deities of, mediation of priests with, 2009
drama in, 2461–2462
dreams in, 2484, 2485
earth divinity of, 2554
economic patterns and, 6720
gambling in, 3260
geographical distribution of, 6720
masks in, 5767
pe'kwin (sun priests) in, 2008–2009
rain dance in, 7603
sacred language in, 5305
seasonal divisions and, 6724
Shalako ceremony in, as sacrament, 7957
totemism in, 9252
transgression in, 8016–8017
trees in, 9336
Zuntz, Gunther, 2269, 6897
Zunz, Leopold
prayer books and, 8388
in *Wissenschaft des Judentums,* 4876
Zuo (guilds), 1616
Zuochan (seated meditation), 1292. *See also* Zazen
Zuo Chi, miracles of, 6052
Zuo Qiuming, commentary of, 1907
Zuo zhuan (book), Confucius in, 1934
Zurbarán, Francisco de, vol. 12 color insert
Zürcher, Erik, 1314
Zuri, Jacob, on ʿAqivaʾ ben Yosef, 441
Zur Logik der Kulturwissenschaften (Cassirer), 1448
Zurvanism, 3004, 9991, **10011–10015**. *See also* Zurwān
Ibn Sīnā and, 4275
priests' role in, 5561
world-periods in, 174

Zurwān. *See also* Zurvanism
aiōn as, 2855–2856
"heresy" of, 3004, 3005
origins of, 4536
twins created by, 9412, 9416
Zusya, Rabbi, on suffering, 8805–8806
Zuṭa', 2765–2766
Źwa lu (Buddhist monastery), 1338
Zwickau Prophets, 6238
Zwilling, Leonard, 5415
Zwingli, Huldrych (Ulrich), **10015–10017**
and Anabaptism, 304
on Lent, 7659
on Lord's Supper, 7660
Luther (Martin) and, 5536, 7658, 7659–7670
at Marburg colloquy, 7660
on music, 6310
on predestination, 3204
on priesthood, 7403
Reformation views of, 7659–7660
on religious art, 4286, 7659–7660
Zwischen den Zeiten (journal), 6467, 6468
Zygon Center for Science and Religion, 2661
Zyrians/Zyryans. *See* Komi religion and society
Zysk, Kenneth G., on Vedic *vs.* Āyurvedic medicine, 3853

ISBN 0-02-865984-8
9 780028 659848 90000